Caribbean Sea
75°W
60°W
15°N
CENTRAL AMERICA
Maracaibo
Santa Marta
Barranquilla
Cartagena
Barquisimeto
Coro
Caracas
Barcelona
Cumaná
Maturín
Valencia
Maracay
Mérida
Barinas
Cúcuta
San Cristóbal
Orinoco R.
Ciudad Guayana
Ciudad Bolívar
Bucaramanga
Gulf of Panama
Medellín
Tunja
Manizales
Pereira
Bogotá
Villavicencio
VENEZUELA
GUYANA
Georgetown
Paramaribo
SURINAME
FRENCH GUIANA (France)
ATLANTIC OCEAN
Galápagos Islands (Ecuador)
Cali
COLOMBIA
Neiva
Florencia
Boa Vista
Pasto
Esmeraldas
ECUADOR
Quito
Ibarra
Negro R.
Macapá
0°
Portoviejo
Ambato
Riobamba
Guayaquil
Cuenca
Machala
Loja
Amazon R.
Manaus
Santarém
Belém
São Luís
Iquitos
Piura
Chiclayo
Cajamarca
Trujillo
Chimbote
PERU
Pucallpa
Huánuco
Cerro de Pasco
Lima
Huancayo
Ayacucho
Ica
Cusco
Madeira R.
Rio Branco
Porto Velho
Tapajós R.
Xingu R.
Tocantins R.
Teresina
Fortaleza
Natal
João Pessoa
Recife
Maceió
Aracaju
Salvador
São Francisco R.
BRAZIL
Trinidad
BOLIVIA
Juliaca
La Paz
Arequipa
Santa Cruz
Cochabamba
Tacna
Oruro
Arica
Sucre
Potosí
Iquique
Tarija
15°S
PACIFIC OCEAN
Cuiabá
Brasília
Goiânia
Uberlândia
Campo Grande
Belo Horizonte
Vitória
Paraguay R.
Pedro Juan Caballero
PARAGUAY
Antofagasta
San Salvador de Jujuy
Salta
Asunción
Ciudad del Este
Campinas
São Paulo
Rio de Janeiro
Niterói
Santos
Curitiba
San Miguel de Tucumán
Copiapó
Resistencia
Posadas
Encarnación
Corrientes
Florianópolis
CHILE
Catamarca
Santiago del Estero
La Rioja
La Serena
Paraná R.
Porto Alegre
30°S
Córdoba
Santa Fe
Rivera
Salto
Paysandú
San Juan
Mendoza
Valparaíso
Santiago
San Luis
Rosario
URUGUAY
Rancagua
Buenos Aires
Montevideo
Talca
Río de la Plata
45°W
Concepción
Chillán
ARGENTINA
Bahía Blanca
Mar del Plata
Temuco
Neuquén
Puerto Montt
ATLANTIC OCEAN
45°S
Comodoro Rivadavia
Falkland Islands (Islas Malvinas) (U.K.)
Strait of Magellan
Punta Arenas
Ushuaia
75°W
60°W
South America
Elevation in Feet
15,000
10,000
5,000
2,000
1,000
0
Below sea level
Major Cities
Capital city
Over 5,000,000
1,000,000–5,000,000
500,000–999,999
250,000–499,999
100,000–249,999
Less than 100,000
0 250 500 mi.
0 250 500 km

ENCYCLOPEDIA OF

# LATIN AMERICAN HISTORY AND CULTURE

# EDITORIAL BOARD

ENCYCLOPEDIA OF

# LATIN AMERICAN HISTORY AND CULTURE

SECOND EDITION

## Volume 3

E–I

*Jay Kinsbruner*

EDITOR IN CHIEF

*Erick D. Langer*

SENIOR EDITOR

**CHARLES SCRIBNER'S SONS**

*A part of Gale, Cengage Learning*

Detroit • New York • San Francisco • New Haven, Conn • Waterville, Maine • London

**Encyclopedia of Latin American History and Culture**

Jay Kinsbruner, Editor in Chief
Erick D. Langer, Senior Editor



For product information and technology assistance, contact us at
**Gale Customer Support, 1-800-877-4253.**
For permission to use material from this text or product,
submit all requests online at **www.cengage.com/permissions.**
Further permissions questions can be emailed to
**permissionrequest@cengage.com**

While every effort has been made to ensure the reliability of the information presented in this publication, Gale, a part of Cengage Learning, does not guarantee the accuracy of the data contained herein. Gale accepts no payment for listing; and inclusion in the publication of any organization, agency, institution, publication, service, or individual does not imply endorsement of the editors or publisher. Errors brought to the attention of the publisher and verified to the satisfaction of the publisher will be corrected in future editions.

**Library of Congress Cataloging-in-Publication Data**

Encyclopedia of Latin American history and culture / Jay Kinsbruner, editor in chief; Erick D. Langer, senior editor. -- 2nd ed.
p. cm. --
Includes bibliographical references and index.
ISBN 978-0-684-31270-5 (set) -- ISBN 978-0-684-31441-9 (vol. 1) -- ISBN 978-0-684-31442-6 (vol. 2) -- ISBN 978-0-684-31443-3 (vol. 3) -- ISBN 978-0-684-31444-0 (vol. 4) -- ISBN 978-0-684-31445-7 (vol. 5) -- ISBN 978-0-684-31598-0 (vol. 6)
1. Latin America--Encyclopedias. I. Kinsbruner, Jay.

F1406.E53 2008
980.003--dc22 2008003461

Gale
27500 Drake Rd.
Farmington Hills, MI, 48331-3535

978-0-684-31270-5 (set) 0-684-31270-0 (set)
978-0-684-31441-9 (vol. 1) 0-684-31441-X (vol. 1)
978-0-684-31442-6 (vol. 2) 0-684-31442-8 (vol. 2)
978-0-684-31443-3 (vol. 3) 0-684-31443-6 (vol. 3)
978-0-684-31444-0 (vol. 4) 0-684-31444-4 (vol. 4)
978-0-684-31445-7 (vol. 5) 0-684-31445-2 (vol. 5)
978-0-684-31598-0 (vol. 6) 0-684-31598-X (vol. 6)

This title is also available as an e-book.
ISBN-13: 978-0-684-31590-4 ISBN-10: 0-684-31590-4
Contact your Gale, a part of Cengage Learning, sales representative for ordering information.



Printed in the United States of America
1 2 3 4 5 6 7 12 11 10 09 08

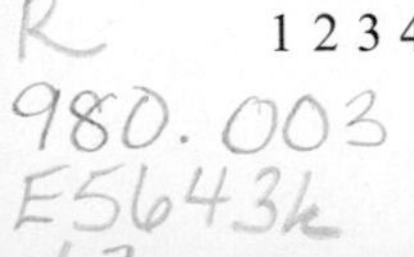

# CONTENTS

**EARTHQUAKES.** Much of Latin America is an active seismic zone, and devastating earthquakes are a common occurrence. Some of these have had profound long-term social and political consequences. For example, in 1773 massive destruction led colonial Guatemalans to move their capital from Antigua to its present site. The 1812 earthquake in Caracas not only severely damaged the city and its environs, but also the nascent independence movement under Simón Bolívar. The 1944 earthquake in San Juan, Argentina, led to the acquaintance of future populist leaders Juan and Evita Perón. In Peru a 1970 earthquake-landslide eliminated the elite of Yungay more thoroughly and quickly than any social revolution could have done. Dissatisfaction with Anastasio Somoza's management of relief and reconstruction following the 1972 Managua quake turned many Nicaraguans against his government and may have enabled the Sandinista revolution of 1979. Finally, the devastating Mexico City earthquake of 1985 exposed the inefficiency and corruption of the government and ultimately contributed to the crisis and decline of the ruling party that had governed Mexico since 1929. More generally, earthquakes—like other natural disasters such as hurricanes—have led to official responses that have caused inhabitants to question their leaders' competence or interest, with political consequences.

Most South American countries—and particularly those located along the Pacific Rim—have been affected by earthquakes. Andean Argentina sustained considerable loss of life in 1861 (Mendoza) and 1944 (San Juan). In present-day Chile, earthquakes and tsunamis with catastrophic impact occurred in 1730 (Concepción), 1822 (Valparaíso), 1835 and 1837 (Concepción), 1868 (Arica and off the northern coast), 1877 (Iquique and Tarapacá), and in 1965 (without a tsunami) in central Chile. More than 1,000 people died in each of the following: 1906 (Santiago and Valparaíso), 1922 (Copiapó), 1939 (28,000 in Chillán), and 1960 (Concepción). Within the boundaries of modern Colombia, there were earthquakes in 1644, 1785, and 1804. The May 1875 earthquakes in Cúcuta took thousands of lives. Severe damage resulted from the Colombian quakes of 1851, 1923, 1935, 1938, 1950, 1955, 1958, 1961, 1966, 1967 (especially), 1979, and 1983. The Ecuadorian cities of Quito, Ambato, and Riobamba are situated in an earthquake-prone area. The quakes of 1575, 1640, 1645, 1698, 1755, 1797, 1859, 1868, 1949, and 1979 are regarded as especially devastating, most notably that of 1868, which also struck Guayaquil and Ibarra, and that of 1797.

Peru was shaken by strong earthquakes in 1746 (Callao and Lima, with tsunami) and in 1868 (Chala, Arequipa, Moquegua, and Tacna). In colonial times, there were other significant quakes in 1604 (Arequipa), 1619 (Trujillo, Piura, Santa), 1658 (Trujillo), 1664 (Ica, Pisco), 1687 (Lima, Arequipa), 1699 (Lima), 1724 (Callao), and 1821 (Camaná, Ocoña, Caravelá). Five severe earthquakes occurred in the 1940–1950 period; three between 1970 and 1974. In Venezuela, there are reports of severe quakes in Cumaná in 1530, Bailadores in 1599, and Caracas in 1641. The 1812 Caracas quake was the deadliest and most destructive of the colonial era. In the national

**Ambata, Ecuador, August 10, 1949.** Sitting in a highly active seismic zone, much of Latin America is at risk for damaging earthquakes, as evidenced in this 1949 picture of Ambata, Ecuador. © BETTMANN/CORBIS

period, heavy damage resulted from quakes in 1929, 1966, 1967 (especially), and 1981.

Mexico, Central America, and the Caribbean have also experienced frequent earthquakes; indeed, anthropologist Eric Wolf labeled the inhabitants of Mexico and Guatemala the "sons of the shaking earth." Colonial documents indicate more than a dozen earthquakes in the vicinity of Antigua, Guatemala, before the relocation of the city; those of 1717 and 1765 caused considerable damage. Colonial San Salvador experienced quakes in 1671, 1715, 1719, 1776, and 1798. Among the more significant twentieth-century Central American earthquakes were those in 1902 (Guatemala), 1910 (Costa Rica), 1917 (El Salvador), 1917–1918 (Guatemala), 1931 (Nicaragua), 1951 (Honduras), 1965 (El Salvador), 1972 (Nicaragua), 1973 (Costa Rica), 1976 (Guatemala), 1982 (El Salvador), 1983 (Costa Rica), 1986 (El Salvador), and 1991 (Costa Rica). Mexico City and Jalisco endured earthquakes in 1611; Oaxaca, in 1701. The state of Guerrero had notable quakes in 1845, 1874, 1882, 1887, 1907, 1956, 1964, and 1979; Michoacán, in 1858, 1911, and 1981; southern Mexico, in 1962, 1973, and 1980. As one of the largest metropolitan population concentrations in the world, Mexico City suffered extreme casualties in the earthquake of 1985.

In 1692 Jamaica's capital, Port Royal, sank beneath the ocean during an earthquake; an earthquake damaged Kingston in 1907. Other significant quakes in the Greater Antilles were in 1766, 1775, and 1932 (Cuba); 1918 (Puerto Rico); 1751, 1770, 1842, and 1953 (Haiti); and 1691, 1751, 1842, and 1946 (Dominican Republic).

Social scientists began systematic studies of natural hazards only in the 1950s. Researchers consider such indicators as the impact of earthquakes on physical and mental health, disrupted infrastructures, new social relationships, exacerbation of inequities or inefficiencies, and retarded economic growth. Scholarly interest in earthquakes continues to increase as the field of Latin American history considers more seriously the effect of the environment on human and social relationships.

*See also* **Environment and Climate.**

BIBLIOGRAPHY

Bates, Frederick L., ed. *Recovery, Change, and Development: A Longitudinal Study of the 1976 Guatemalan Earthquake; Final Report.* Athens: University of Georgia, Department of Sociology, 1982.

Bode, Barbara. *No Bells to Toll: Destruction and Creation in the Andes.* New York: Scribner, 1990.

Buchenau, Jurgen, and Lyman Johnson, eds. *When the Earth Moves: Earthquakes in Latin American History.* Albuquerque: University of New Mexico Press, forthcoming.

Feldman, Lawrence. *Mountains of Fire, Lands That Shake: Earthquakes and Volcanic Eruptions in the Historic Past of Central America (1505–1899).* Culver City, CA: Labyrinthos, 1993.

Ganse, Robert A., and John B. Nelson, eds. *Catalog of Significant Earthquakes 1900–1979.* Boulder, CO: National Geophysical and Solar-Terrestrial Data Center, 1981.

Oliver-Smith, Anthony. *Martyred City: Death and Rebirth in the Andes.* Albuquerque: University of New Mexico Press, 1986.

Silgado Ferro, Enrique. *Programa para la Mitigación de los Efectos de los Terremotos en la Región Andina (Proyecto SISRA).* Vol. 10: *Terremotos destructivos en América del Sur, 1530–1894.* Lima: CERESIS, 1985.

Tomblin, John. "Earthquakes, Volcanoes, and Hurricanes: A Review of Natural Hazards and Vulnerability in the West Indies." *Ambio* 10:6 (1981), 340–345.

Wolf, Eric R. *Sons of the Shaking Earth: The People of Mexico and Guatemala, Their Land, History and Culture.* Chicago: University of Chicago Press, 1964.

JURGEN BUCHENAU

---

**EARTH SUMMIT, RIO DE JANEIRO (1992).** The United Nations Conference on Environment and Development, known as the Earth Summit, was the second major international conference on the environment sponsored by the United Nations. Its legacy is defined by the action plan known as Agenda 21, by bringing the term *sustainable development* into common usage, and by encouraging the environmental dialogue to include stakeholders as well as shareholders.

In 2002 the United Nations hosted a follow-up conference in Johannesburg, South Africa, called the World Summit on Sustainable Development. Critics of the 1992 summit complained it focused too much on specific environmental issues. Critics of the 2002 conference argued it overemphasized poverty issues. The UN definition of sustainability comprises three pillars: a prosperous economy, protection of the Earth, and social development. But the original concept of sustainable development itself, some scholars argue, has become distorted to fit the needs of special interest groups.

The Earth Summit's impact is regarded as uneven. On the positive side, Agenda 21 continues to be the blueprint for environmental action in the twenty-first century. Major industry sectors have adopted environmental management systems and developed global sustainability reports that measure reductions in their global environmental footprints. Multinational corporations and nongovernmental organizations engage in dialogues needed to advance Agenda 21. New institutions have been established, including the UN's Commission on Sustainable Development (CSD) and, in the host country of Brazil, a ministry of environment.

On the negative side, economic growth is outpacing the modest post-1992 environmental gains. The developed North continues to consume the planet's resources at high levels while a global shift in manufacturing production toward poorer countries is fueling a correspondingly higher demand for those same resources. Poverty is on the rise. Environmentally, planetary conditions have worsened in terms of biodiversity, air pollution, land degradation, chemical emissions and wastes, and water quality. Regulatory regimes remain inadequate to achieve Agenda 21's desired outcomes. Realizing major environmental change will require more sophisticated integration of effort across multiple sectors of diverse societies and cultures.

In Brazil itself, the Earth Summit institutionalized environmental awareness, especially in the urban periphery, which in turn has increased participation in environmentalism by civil society.

*See also* **Environmental Movements.**

BIBLIOGRAPHY

Crespo, Samyra, and José Augusto Drummond. *O que o Brasileiro pensa do meio ambiente e do desenvolvimento sustentável: Pesquisa com lideranças /What Brazilians Think about Environment and Sustainable Development: Survey with Leaders.* Rio de Janeiro: Instituto de Estudos da Religião; and Brasília, D. F.: Secretaria de Qualidade Ambiental no Assentamentos Humanos, Ministério do Meio Ambiente, 2002.

Esty, Daniel C., and Maria H. Ivanova. *Globalization and Environmental Protection: A Global Governance Perspective.* New Haven, CT: Yale School of Forestry and Environmental Studies, 2004.

Garcia Guadilla, María-Pilar. *Environmental Movements, Politics, and Agenda 21 in Latin America.* Geneva: United Nations Research Institute for Social Development, 2005.

Inter-Parliamentary Union. *Towards Sustainability.* Geneva: Author, 2003.

Oels, Angela. *Evaluating Stakeholder Participation in the Transition to Sustainable Development: Methodology, Case Studies, Policy Implications.* Münster: Lit Verlag; distributed in North America by Transaction Publishers, 2003.

Programa Chile Sustentable, Instituto de la Mujer (Chile). *Rio + 10: Hacia una plataforma de géneno y sustentabilidad: Bases para una revisíon de los acuerdos de la Cumbre de la Tierra: Rio de Janeiro 1992, Johannesburgo 2002.* Chile: Isis Internacional, Instituto de la Mujer, MEMCH, IEP, Chile Sustentable, Heinrich Böll Foundation, 2002.

Robinson, Nicholas A. *Strategies toward Sustainable Development: Implementing Agenda 21.* Dobbs Ferry, NY: Oceana Publications, 2004.

Sachs, Wolfgang, ed. *The Jo'burg Memo: Fairness in a Fragile World: Memorandum for the World Summit on Sustainable Development*, 2nd ed. Berlin: Heinrich Böll Foundation, 2002.

United Nations Environment Programme, Division of Technology, Industry and Economics. *Industry as a Partner for Sustainable Development: 10 Years after Rio: The UNEP Assessment.* Paris: Author, 2002.

LAURA JARNAGIN

**EASTER ISLAND.** Easter Island, a Chilean possession in the South Pacific approximately 2,000 miles west of South America. This territory became part of Chile in 1888. This small isle, known for its monumental statues, was originally inhabited by a Polynesian people who were decimated by European diseases and forced work on Peru's Chincha Islands, remained largely isolated. It attracted the attention of Chile, which coveted a Pacific enclave and saw Easter Island as both economically valuable and strategically important. After Chilean occupation, the land's economy remained primitive, from a lack of resources to support agriculture and an unwillingness by the Chilean government to provide assistance. Easter Island's economy remained essentially pastoral until the development of jet aviation made the island a tourist attraction, thus diversifying its economic base.

*See also* **Chile, Geography; Tourism.**

BIBLIOGRAPHY

John Dos Passos, *Easter Island: Island of Enigmas* (1971).

J. Douglas Porteous, *The Modernization of Easter Island* (1981).

*Additional Bibliography*

Flenley, John, and Paul G. Bahn. *The Enigmas of Easter Island: Island on the Edge.* New York: Oxford University Press, 2003.

WILLIAM F. SATER

**EASTERN COAST OF CENTRAL AMERICA COMMERCIAL AND AGRICULTURAL COMPANY.** The Eastern Coast Company metamorphosed from a speculative venture calculated to restore value to worthless Mosquito Coast securities (1833) into a legitimate colonizer. Its agent, Thomas Gould, fortuitously obtained (1834), as one of several grants the state government of Mariano Gálvez made for colonization under his development program (and to confine Belize within Anglo-Spanish treaty limits), all the public lands in the vast department of Verapaz. Critics immediately voiced sharp protests against sacrifice of Guatemalan interests by cession to foreigners of virtually all remaining public lands and natural resources within the state, by concession to alien colonists of privileges denied nationals, and by risk of state territory through affording aggressively expanding Belize an opportunity to incorporate adjacent English settlements.

Deterred from occupying coastal areas by the British government's stated intent to prevent any activity that might transgress Belize boundaries (which it refused to define), the company in 1836 established New Liverpool, an inland settlement on the Cajabón River near its confluence with the Polochic that failed miserably. Two years later a reorganized company negotiated revalidation of its Verapaz charter and cession of the port and district of Santo Tomás on the Bay of Honduras. Projecting a deepwater port at Santo Tomás and an inland center on the Polochic River, it planned a huge agricultural development in Verapaz and a commercial empire embracing Central America and adjacent parts of Mexico. It introduced steamer service between Izabal and Belize and briefly on the Polochic, and provided an iron bridge for the Motagua River crossing on the road between the Polochic and the capital.

A victim of underestimated difficulties, undercapitalization, mismanagement, and perhaps sabotage by employees, the company sought to avert forfeiture of its charter by selling to Belgian speculators 1 million acres of land to be selected from its Verapaz and Santo Tomás concessions. On arrival in Guatemala, the Belgian agents found the British company in disrepute and its land sale effectively invalidated by pending abrogation of its charters. They seized the opportunity to negotiate for themselves an independent cession of the port and district of Santo Tomás. Its concessions voided (1842), the British company ceased operation.

The episode is representative of the postindependence Latin American pursuit of foreign colonization as the most viable route to rapid population growth and development; the speculative, often fraudulent, Latin American enterprises that fueled British investment "bubbles"; the early appearance in Latin America of issues that have since accompanied "development" by international corporations; and the persistence after independence of colonial boundary and sovereignty disputes.

*See also* **Colonialism.**

BIBLIOGRAPHY

William J. Griffith, *Empires in the Wilderness: Foreign Colonization and Development in Guatemala, 1834–1844* (1965), gives fully documented coverage of the company's activity. Jorge Luis Arriola, *Gálvez en la encrucijada: Ensayo crítico en torno al humanismo político de un gobernante* (1961), criticizes the colonization grants and the company's operation as a threat to the integrity of Guatemala that, fortunately, failed. Pedro Pérez Valenzuela, *Santo Tomás de Castilla: Apuntes para la historia de las colonizaciones en la costa atlántica* (1956), includes the English and Belgian company projects but lacks essential documentation.

*Additional Bibliography*

Pompejano, Daniele. *La crisis del antiguo régimen en Guatemala (1839–1871)*. Guatemala: Editorial Universitaria, Universidad de San Carlos de Guatemala, 1997.

Woodward, Ralph Lee. *Rafael Carrera and the Emergence of the Republic of Guatemala, 1821–1871*. Athens: University of Georgia Press, 1993.

WILLIAM J. GRIFFITH

## ECHANDI JIMÉNEZ, MARIO (1915–).

Mario Echandi Jiménez (*b.* 1915), president of Costa Rica (1958–1962). Echandi, who received his law degree from the University of Costa Rica, first came to prominence in national affairs as the general secretary of the National Union Party (PUN), which backed Otilio Ulate Blanco's successful presidential campaign (1948). Under Ulate, he served as ambassador to the United States (1950–1951) and as foreign minister (1951–1953).

While in the national legislature (1953–1958), he was a recognized leader of the opposition to President José Figueres Ferrer's social democratic programs. His leadership in Congress served as a springboard for his political ascension.

With the support of the followers of Ulate and Rafael Angel Calderón Guardia, Echandi led the PLN opposition to victory in the 1958 election. His administration emphasized fiscal restraint, the expansion of the highway network, and a program to foster industrial development. True to his conservative credentials, he opposed the proposed Central American Common Market. After his presidency Echandi remained a conservative leader. He ran unsuccessfully for president on two other occasions, first in 1970 against his old adversary José Figueres Ferrer and again in 1982 against Luis Alberto Monge.

*See also* **Central American Common Market (CACM); Costa Rica.**

BIBLIOGRAPHY

Parker, Franklin D. *The Central American Republics*. London: Oxford University Press, 1964.

Ameringer, Charles D. *Democracy in Costa Rica.* New York: Hoover Institution Press, 1978.

Harold D. Nelson, ed. *Costa Rica: A Country Study.* Washington, DC: Headquarters, Dept. of the Army, 1983.

JOHN PATRICK BELL

## ECHAVE ORIO, BALTASAR DE

(c. 1558–c. 1623). Baltasar de Echave Orio (*b.* ca. 1558; *d.* ca. 1623), painter. Echave was in New Spain by around 1573 and is considered one of the most important of the second generation of mannerist painters in colonial Mexico. It is not clear how much of his training was European, since he does not seem to have been famous when he arrived in the New World. In 1582 he married Isabel de Ibía, the daughter of the painter Francisco de Zumaya, reportedly an artist in her own right. Two sons, Baltasar and Manuel, were both painters. Among the surviving works by Echave is the earliest known copy of the Virgin of Guadalupe, signed and dated 1606, as well as some of the panels from the retablo of Tlatelolco. Also attributed to Echave are the paintings of the retablo of Xochimilco. Beyond artistic pursuits, Echave wrote a treatise on the Basque language which was published in 1607.

*See also* **Art: The Colonial Era.**

BIBLIOGRAPHY

Burke, Marcus B. *Mexican Art Masterpieces.* New York: Hugh Lauter Levin Associates, 1998.

Guadalupe Victoria, José *Un pintor en su tiempo, Baltasar de Echave Orio.* Mongrafías de Arte, 23. Ciudad de México: Universidad Autónoma de México-IIE, 1994.

CLARA BARGELLINI

## ECHEANDÍA, JOSÉ MARÍA DE

(?–1833). José María de Echeandía (*d.* after 1833), governor of Alta California (1825–1831), in control of the southern part of the territory from 1832 to 1833. His most important policies concerned the Franciscan missions. He refused orders to expel the Spanish-born Franciscans in 1828, because most of the missionaries were from Spain and the missions would thus have been left without priests. Echeandía also initiated a partial emancipation of more acculturated Indian converts living primarily in the southern missions, most of whom left the missions.

Internally, Echeandía faced several revolts, which he successfully repressed, but he took power in the south following a military uprising against then-governor Manuel Victoria. In foreign relations, Echeandía allowed the Russians at Fort Ross to hunt for otters in Mexican waters. Wounded in an 1833 uprising, Echeandía returned to Mexico.

*See also* **Franciscans.**

BIBLIOGRAPHY

David J. Weber, *The Mexican Frontier, 1821–1846: The American Southwest Under Mexico* (1982).

### *Additional Bibliography*

Miller, Robert Ryal. *Juan Alvarado, Governor of California, 1836-1842.* Norman: University of Oklahoma Press, 1998.

ROBERT H. JACKSON

## ECHENIQUE, JOSÉ RUFINO

(1808–1887). José Rufino Echenique (*b.* 1808; *d.* 16 June 1887), president of Peru (1851–1854). Chosen by the national congress, he had been a counselor to President Ramón Castilla. But he was politically naive and chose anti-Castilla ministers and counselors, some of them reputedly dishonest. He accepted fraudulent claims against the public treasury, leading to a tremendous increase in the internal debt. In 1853 he secretly converted nearly half of this debt into claims on Peru's foreign debt. Intended to strengthen domestic public bonds weakened by speculation and embezzlement, the debt consolidation was funded by huge foreign loans backed by guano. A great scandal ensued, which combined with the outrages of his ministers, encouraged a popular revolution. During the rebellion, Echenique decreed abolition of black slavery, apparently to generate an army. His opponent, former president Castilla, duplicated this decree. In 1855 Echenique was forced into exile, first in Panama and then the United States. His successors continued the policy of linking the national debt to foreign trade.

*See also* **Peru, Political Parties: Overview.**

BIBLIOGRAPHY

David Werlich, *Peru: A Short History* (1978), pp. 83–84.

Paul Gootenberg, *Between Silver and Guano: Commercial Policy and the State in Postindependence Peru* (1989), esp. pp. 126–127.

*Additional Bibliography*

Salinas Sánchez, Alejandro. *Caudillos, partidos políticos y nacionalismo en el Perú, 1850–1879*. Lima: Seminario de Historia Rural Andina, Universidad Nacional Mayor de San Marcos, 2003.

VINCENT PELOSO

## ECHEVERRÍA, ESTEBAN (1805–1851).

The Argentine poet and intellectual Esteban Echeverría (September 2, 1805–January 17, 1851) was born in Buenos Aires. He left for Paris at the age of twenty, following a somewhat unruly adolescence and interruptions in his course of study. He lived there for more than four years and studied a variety of subjects, but what finally captivated his spirit and eventually guided his intellectual career were the tendencies that dominated French intellectual life at the time: literary romanticism, philosophical eclecticism, and Saint-Simonian social beliefs.

Echeverría returned to his home in 1830 and began his career as a writer. His central work was *La cautiva* (1837; The Captive), a narrative poem based on a drama that takes place in the desert, the Argentine plains that are free of European civilization. Together with other young Argentines who saw him as their leader, he founded the Salón Literario, a society of ideas in which Echeverría and his circle articulated the precepts of Pan-American romanticism: to free themselves from the intellectual culture of Spain and create their own literature and schools of thought that reflected the nature, customs, and problems of the Americas. *La cautiva* represented such a school of thought. The hostility of the government of Juan Manuel de Rosas, who controlled the nation with an iron fist, led to the closing of the Salón Literario and radicalized the position of the youths, who regrouped in a secret lodge. In 1838 Echeverría wrote a declaration of principles for his lodge, the Joven Generación Argentina (Young Argentine Generation) and two years later went into exile in Uruguay. He lived there, in Montevideo, until his death in 1851, writing texts that cemented his reputation as an intellectual.

Echeverría brought literary romanticism to the River Plate region and was a mentor to the first generation of intellectuals born after national independence, the generation that led the reorganization of the nation as a liberal republic after 1853. His ideological writings gave rise to socially oriented intellectual thought in Argentina.

*See also* **Literature: Spanish America; Rosas, Juan Manuel de.**

BIBLIOGRAPHY

Halperin Donghi, Tulio. *El pensamiento de Echeverría*. Buenos Aires: Sudamericana, 1951.

Jitrik, Noé. *Esteban Echeverría*. Buenos Aires: Centro Editor de América Latina, 1967.

Palcos, Alberto. *Historia de Echeverría*. Buenos Aires: Emecé, 1960.

CARLOS ALTAMIRANO

## ECHEVERRÍA ÁLVAREZ, LUIS (1922–).

Luis Echeverría was president of Mexico from 1970 to 1976. To the surprise of most analysts, Echeverría, although a disciple of Gustavo Díaz Ordaz, was a president in the populist mold, reintroducing, in certain respects, a style similar to that of Lázaro Cárdenas.

Echeverría was born on January 17, 1922, in the Federal District, as were so many leading politicians of his and succeeding generations. He was the son of an army paymaster. Echeverría attended school in Mexico City and Ciudad Victoria, then, after graduating from the National Preparatory School, he enrolled in the National Law School in 1940, completing his degree in August 1945. He married the daughter of José Zuno Hernández, a former governor of Jalisco and a member of an important political family. A political disciple of division general Rodolfo Sánchez Taboada, the president of the Institutional Revolutionary Party (PRI), he first held positions in the party, including press secretary and *oficial mayor*, before following his mentor to the navy secretariat. In 1954 he became *oficial mayor* of public education, after which he attached himself to the career of another influential political mentor, Gustavo Díaz Ordaz, as undersecretary of the government secretariat (1958–1964). Upon his mentor's nomination as the PRI presidential candidate, Echeverría replaced Díaz Ordaz as secretary, a position that he held from 1963 to 1969, when he resigned to become himself a presidential candidate, designated by his mentor. He was the last official party presidential candidate to come from this influential cabinet agency and to have held important positions in the PRI. The new generation of top politicians he helped to spawn were career bureaucrats from economically oriented agencies.

Echeverría's regime was characterized by greater levels of economic and political uncertainty than were those of his immediate predecessors. He tried to placate opposition within and outside his party by recruiting an important generation of younger politicians in their thirties. Early in his administration he faced strong internal opposition within his own cabinet, led by Alfonso Martinez Domínguez, the head of the Federal District Department. Martínez Domínguez used a paramilitary force in 1971 to suppress student demonstrators, after which the president removed him from office. Echeverría also faced what had not happened for many years: the formation of well-organized guerrilla opposition groups. They emerged in both urban and rural settings, most notably the band of Lucio Cabañas in Guerrero, which the army eventually eliminated. Significant human rights violations were committed by the government and the armed forces against the guerrillas.

On the economic front, Echeverría was responsible for the rapid growth of state-owned enterprises and the alienation of many elements of the Mexico's private-sector leadership. He exacerbated divisions between the state and the private sector by nationalizing agrarian properties in northwest Mexico immediately before leaving office and by presiding over the first devaluation of the peso in many years. Given his anti-private sector posture and a more assertive nationalist posture in the United Nations, relations with the United States became more difficult. He left the presidency further delegitimized than when he took office, passing on to his successor, José López Portillo, a difficult set of economic and political problems, some of which were not addressed until the administration of Carlos Salinas (1988–1994).

After leaving the presidency in 1976, Echeverría served as ambassador to the United Nations Educational, Scientific and Cultural Organization (UNESCO) from 1976 to 1978, then briefly to Australia. He also directed a third world studies institute upon his return to Mexico in 1979. He subsequently retired from all public activities. During the presidency of Vincente Fox (2000–2006), a special prosecutor who explored human rights abuses committed during Echeverría's administration sought, without success, to bring legal charges against Echeverría personally. Only two high-ranking generals, both involved in the Guerrero campaign, have been convicted on these human rights charges.

*See also* **Mexico, Political Parties: Institutional Revolutionary Party (PRI); Mexico: Since 1910.**

BIBLIOGRAPHY

Cosío Villegas, Daniel. *El estilo personal de gobernar*, 4th edition. Mexico City: J. Mortiz, 1974.

Hellman, Judith Adler. *Mexico in Crisis.* 2nd edition. New York: Holmes & Meier, 1983.

Krauze, Enrique. *El sexenio de Luis Echeverría*. Mexico City: Clío, 1999.

Schmidt, Samuel. *El deterio del presidencialismo mexicano: Los años de Luis Echeverría*. Mexico City: EDAMEX, 1986.

RODERIC AI CAMP

---

**ECHEVERRÍA BIANCHI, JOSÉ ANTONIO** (1932–1957). José Antonio Echeverría Bianchi (*b.* 16 July 1932; *d.* 13 March 1957), Cuban revolutionary. Born in Cárdenas, Matanzas, Echeverría was educated in primary school at the Colegio Hermanos Maristas de Cárdenas and graduated from high school in the same city. He entered the University of Havana School of Architecture in 1953, where he was elected president of the Federation of University Students (1954, 1955, and 1956). Echeverría, along with Fauré Chomón, founded the Revolutionary Directorate in 1956. In the same year he attended the Congress of Latin American Students in Chile. He and Fidel Castro were signers of the "Letter from Mexico." He participated in the organization that attacked the presidential palace in March 1957, and he directed the takeover of a Havana radio station, where he was killed in a gun battle with police.

*See also* **Cuba: The Republic (1898–1959).**

BIBLIOGRAPHY

*Additional Bibliography*

García Oliveras, Julio A. *Los estudiantes cubanos.* La Habana: Casa Editora Abril, 2003.

Nuiry Sánchez, Juan. *Presente!: Apuntes para la historia del movimiento estudiantil cubano.* Ciudad de La Habana: Editora Política, 2001.

MARÍA DEL CARMEN ALMODOVAR

---

**ECKHOUT, ALBERT** (c. 1610–c. 1665). Albert Eckhout (*b.* ca. 1610; *d.* ca. 1665), Dutch painter, noted for his portraits of the flora, fauna, and inhabitants of Brazil. Eckhout was born in Groningen in the Netherlands, the son of Albert Eckhout and Marryen Roeleffs. Eckhout and Frans Post were the most famous of the artists in the entourage of Johan Maurits of Nassau while he was governor-general of Dutch Brazil from 1637 to 1644. Little is known of Eckhout's training, early career, and the reasons for his appointment, and it is not known exactly when he arrived in Brazil. Because some paintings attributed to Eckhout portrayed Araucano and African peoples as well as llamas, plants, and trees, some have suggested that Eckhout might have been part of Hendrick Brouwer's expedition to Chile in 1643 or might have visited West Africa with the forces of Colonel Hans Coen that captured Elmina in 1637 or with those of Admiral Cornelis Jol and Colonel James Henderson that occupied Angola in 1641. Finally, it is uncertain when Eckhout returned to Europe or how long he remained in the service of Maurits. In any case, by 1645 Eckhout was back in Groningen. From at least 1648 to 1652 he lived in Amersfoort before moving to Dresden, where he spent ten years (1653 to 1663) as a painter at the court of the elector of Saxony, Johann Georg II. Eckhout is thought to have died in Groningen in 1665.

Relatively few of Eckhout's paintings were signed or dated. Although most were probably painted in Brazil, others were completed after his return to Europe. He seems to have made a large number of preliminary sketches while in Brazil. Moreover, other artists based their works on Eckhout's paintings and drawings. At times, it is not entirely clear which paintings are copies, which were made under his supervision, and which are his own. In addition, Eckhout's artwork was the basis for many of the woodcut illustrations of Caspar Barlaeus's *Rerum per octennium in Brasilia* (1647) and Johannes de Laet's *Historia naturalis Brasiliae* (1648). The latter included 533 woodcuts and published notes by the German naturalist, geographer, and astronomer Georg Marcgraf on the fauna and flora of Brazil, and a section on medicine by the Dutch physician Dr. Willem Piso, both of whom had served Maurits in Brazil. The basis for these woodcuts was more than 800 paintings, most of them probably by Eckhout. These works later formed part of the collection sold by Maurits to his cousin Friedrich Wilhelm, elector of Brandenburg. They have survived as the *Handbooks* (two volumes of watercolors), the *Theatri rerum naturalium Brasiliae* (four volumes, mostly oil paintings), and the *Miscellanea Cleyeri.* Formerly housed in Berlin, these collections disappeared during World War II. In 1977 they were rediscovered in Kraków, Poland.

Probably the most famous and valuable of Eckhout's paintings are his ethnographic works. Many were done in Brazil in 1641 and 1643 for Maurits, who later gave them to another cousin, King Frederik III of Denmark. They include life-size portraits of a Tapuya (Tarairiu) man, a Tapuya woman, a Tupinambá man, a mestizo man, a mameluco woman, an African man, an African woman, and a Tapuya dance. Both Alexander von Humboldt and Emperor Dom Pedro II of Brazil enthusiastically praised these paintings when they visited Copenhagen in 1827 and 1876, respectively. Eckhout is credited by scholars with having created the best and most numerous portraits of Brazil's plants, birds, fish, reptiles, mammals, and peoples during the first three centuries of Europe's presence there.

*See also* **Art: The Colonial Era; Brazil: The Colonial Era, 1500–1808; Dutch in Colonial Brazil; Maurits, Johan.**

BIBLIOGRAPHY

The standard study on Eckhout is Thomas Thomsen, *Albert Eckhout, ein niederländischer Maler und sein Gönner Johan Maurits der Brasilianer: Ein Kulturbild aus dem 17.* Jahrhundert (1938).

Valuable for its reproductions is Clarival Do Prado Valladares and Luiz Emgydio De Mello Filho, *Albert Eckhout: Pintor de Maurício de Nassau no Brasil 1637–1644* (1981).

*Additional Bibliography*

Joppien, R. "The Dutch Vision of Brazil: Johan Maurits and his Artists." In *Dutch Brazil*, vol. 2, edited by E van den Boogart. Rio de Janeiro: Editora Index, 2001.

Whitehead, Peter J. P., and Marinus Boeseman. *A Portrait of Dutch Seventeenth-Century Brazil: Animals, Plants, and People by the Artists of Johan Maurits of Nassau.* Amersterdam: North Holland, 1989.

FRANCIS A. DUTRA

**ECONOMIC COMMISSION FOR LATIN AMERICA AND THE CARIBBEAN (ECLAC).** Economic Commission for Latin America and the Caribbean (ECLAC), one of five commissions created after World War II as part of resolution 106 adopted in 1948 by the Economic and Social Council (ECOSOC) of the United Nations. The original title was Economic Commission for Latin America; "and the Caribbean" was added in 1984. The body is also known by its Spanish acronym CEPAL (Comisión Económica para América Latina y el Caribe). ECLAC was created to study and find solutions to Latin American and Caribbean development problems, particularly those derived from the international economy, and to design common regional efforts that contribute to worldwide and economic progress. Latin American and Caribbean members include Antigua and Barbuda, Argentina, Bahamas, Barbados, Belize, Bolivia, Brazil, Chile, Colombia, Costa Rica, Cuba, Dominica, Dominican Republic, Ecuador, El Salvador, Grenada, Guatemala, Guyana, Haiti, Honduras, Jamaica, Mexico, Nicaragua, Panama, Paraguay, Peru, Saint Kitts and Nevis, Saint Vincent and the Grenadines, Saint Lucia, Suriname, Trinidad and Tobago, Uruguay, and Venezuela, with Aruba, British and U.S. Virgin Islands, Montserrat, Netherlands Antilles, and Puerto Rico as associate members. Canada, France, Italy (since 1990), the Netherlands, Portugal, Spain, the United Kingdom, and the United States are members from the industrialized world.

The executive secretariat of ECLAC is headquartered in Santiago, Chile, with subregional offices in Mexico and Port-of-Spain, Trinidad, as well as offices in Bogotá, Brasília, Buenos Aires, Montevideo, and Washington; it forms part of the Secretariat of the United Nations and includes the Latin American Institute for Economic and Social Planning (ILPES) and the Latin American Demographic Center (CELADE). The commission meets every two years.

Several prominent Latin American economists have served as executive secretary, including Gustavo Martínez Cabañas (Mexico) 1949–1950; Raúl Prebisch (Argentina) 1950–1963; José Antonio Mayobre (Venezuela) 1963–1967; Carlos Quintana (Mexico) 1967–1972; Enrique Iglesias (Uruguay) 1972–1985; Norberto González (Argentina) 1985–1987; and Gert Rosenthal (Guatemala) since 1986.

Since its founding, ECLAC has distinguished itself through its advocacy of specific economic remedies, which have evolved in response to the changing circumstances of both the regional and world economy. For example, under the leadership of Prebisch, it recommended import substitution, planning, and economic integration as components of a strategy to overcome underdevelopment. Today, however, it supports a more integrated approach, whereby technical progress, international competitiveness, and social equity—in terms of gender, race, class, and the environment—are all considered essential for the region's sustainable development.

*See also* **Economic Development; United Nations.**

BIBLIOGRAPHY

Gert Rosenthal, "ECLAC: Forty Years of Continuity with Change," in *CEPAL Review,* no. 35 (August 1988): 7–12.

Pedro Castro Suarez, *Teorías del desarrollo: Crítica a la teoría de la CEPAL* (1992).

Enrique Iglesias, ed., *The Legacy of Raúl Prebisch* (1994).

*Additional Bibliography*

Berthelot, Yves. *Unity and Diversity in Development Ideas: Perspectives from the UN Regional Commissions.* Bloomington: Indiana University Press, 2004.

Gutierrez, Martha. *Macro-economics: Making Gender Matter: Concepts, Policies and Institutional Change in Developing Countries.* New York: Zed Books, 2003.

Haffner, Jacqueline A Hernández. *A CEPAL e a industrialização brasileira, 1950-1961.* Porto Alegre: EDIPUCRS, 2002.

United Nations. *La CEPAL en sus 50 años: notas de un seminario conmemorativo.* Santiago de Chile: Naciones Unidas, Comisión Económica para América Latina y el Caribe, 2000.

ISAAC COHEN

**ECONOMIC DEVELOPMENT.** *Economic development* refers both to increases in human productivity and to improvements in physical and psychological well-being or welfare. The productivity of national and regional economies, and of the global economy, is usually measured by dividing an estimate of the total output of goods and services, such as gross domestic product (GDP), by the total population of the relevant area. The same GDP per capita, however, may be achieved in economies with vastly different characteristics. Some may be rich in natural resources, whereas others rely more on skills and technology. Some economies depend on external trade and capital flows, whereas others enjoy deep internal markets and high rates of domestic investment. In some countries the distribution of economic output is highly concentrated; others achieve greater equality. In some places productivity advance has depleted resources or damaged the environment; in others the use of renewable resources and ecology-friendly technologies has limited the impact. Thus, although GDP per capita may be convenient for measuring and comparing the *productivity* of economies, it does not capture many other important dimensions of economic activity.

Human well-being or welfare depends critically on productivity, but the relationship is not straightforward. Productivity advance has coincided with stagnation or even decline in welfare indicators for some populations over extended periods of time (e.g., during the Industrial Revolution in most countries). The measures commonly employed by economists to gauge human well-being refer only to physical welfare. Such measures include life expectancy, average height or body-mass (the ratio of height to weight), or poverty rates (that show the percentage of the population lacking one or more of the basic necessities of life). Poverty rates are usually higher in societies where wealth and income are concentrated in fewer hands. There is no simple and straightforward relationship between physical and psychological well-being; human populations have proved to be resilient even in the face of severe physical deprivation. Economists generally assume that people who are materially better off are likely to enjoy life more.

**GDP per capita, 2001 (in 1990 Geary-Khamis international dollars)**

| Country/Region | GDP per capita | Percent USA |
|---|---|---|
| Argentina | 8,137 | 29 |
| Bolivia | 2,559 | 9 |
| Brazil | 5,570 | 20 |
| Chile | 10,001 | 36 |
| Colombia | 5,087 | 18 |
| Costa Rica | 6,126 | 22 |
| Cuba | 2,477 | 9 |
| Dominican Republic | 3,651 | 13 |
| Ecuador | 3,849 | 14 |
| El Salvador | 2,713 | 10 |
| Guatemala | 3,363 | 12 |
| Haiti | 785 | 3 |
| Honduras | 1,958 | 7 |
| Mexico | 7,089 | 25 |
| Nicaragua | 1,571 | 6 |
| Panama | 5,715 | 20 |
| Paraguay | 2,959 | 11 |
| Peru | 3,630 | 13 |
| Uruguay | 7,557 | 27 |
| Venezuela | 8,507 | 30 |
| LATIN AMERICA | 5,811 | 21 |
| United States | 27,948 | 100 |
| WESTERN EUROPE | 19,256 | 69 |
| Japan | 20,683 | 74 |
| AFRICA | 1,489 | 5 |
| ASIA (excluding Japan) | 3,256 | 12 |
| EASTERN EUROPE | 6,027 | 22 |
| FORMER USSR | 4,626 | 17 |

SOURCE: Maddison (2003).

Table 1

At the beginning of the twenty-first century, most of the Latin American economies suffered from low levels of productivity and physical welfare relative to the advanced economies. Table 1 compares the GDP per capita of the twenty Latin American countries with those of the wealthier developed nations, including the United States, Western European countries, and Japan. It also compares Latin America to the even poorer nations of Africa and Asia. The figures in the table adjust the GDP estimates produced by each country to take into account differences in the purchasing power of each country's currency. Using the same unit of account (in this case international Geary-Khamis 1990 dollars), with roughly the same purchasing power in each country, makes comparison across countries more accurate. These estimates and others like them are usually referred to as having been adjusted for "purchasing power parity," or PPP estimates. Because less-developed countries often have weaker currencies and lower labor costs, their price levels tend to be lower than those of wealthier nations. PPP-adjusted estimates thus tend to increase local currency GDP estimates for the developing world and in turn show a narrower gap in GDP per capita between developed and developing nations.

Table 1 shows that the twenty Latin American countries (including Haiti) had an average per capita GDP in 2001 of $5811, or about one-fifth that of the United States, which had the world's most productive economy, but closer to one-fourth the levels of Western Europe and Japan. By contrast, Latin America's average stood at nearly four times that of Africa and nearly twice the Asian level (excluding Japan), and was higher in 2001 than the level to which the countries of the former USSR have fallen since 1990. Latin America's GDP per capita in 2001 was roughly comparable to that of Eastern Europe. In short, *on average*, Latin America is a "middle income" region.

The table also shows that there is great variation within Latin America. The GDP per capita of Chile, with the most productive economy in the region, was thirteen times higher than that of Haiti and over six times more than that of Nicaragua, the region's poorest economies. Latin America's most productive economies in 2001 were large, resource-rich countries with (except for Mexico) better-educated populations: Argentina (temperate agriculture), Chile (temperate agriculture, copper, timber, fish), Mexico (oil, temperate agriculture), Uruguay (temperate agriculture), and Venezuela (oil). Latin America's least productive economies were small exporters of tropical products, with less-educated populations, and with a history of political instability (Haiti, Honduras, Nicaragua), or landlocked (Bolivia, Paraguay). The gap between the richest and poorest Latin American countries, at 13:1, was large, but nonetheless much smaller than the gap between the world's richest and poorest nations, the United States and Chad, which was 238:1 in 2003.

**Global inequality in c. 2000 (Gini index for income distribution)**

| Region | Country | Gini Index |
|---|---|---|
| Latin America | Argentina | 0.493 |
| | Bolivia | 0.601 |
| | Brazil | 0.585 |
| | Chile | 0.559 |
| | Columbia | 0.562 |
| | Costa Rica | 0.461 |
| | Cuba | – |
| | Dominican Republic | 0.478 |
| | Ecuador | 0.562 |
| | El Salvador | 0.545 |
| | Guatemala | – |
| | Haiti | – |
| | Honduras | 0.584 |
| | Mexico | 0.538 |
| | Nicaragua | 0.602 |
| | Panama | 0.565 |
| | Paraguay | 0.569 |
| | Peru | 0.493 |
| | Uruguay | 0.439 |
| | Venezuela | 0.467 |
| North America | USA | 0.408 |
| | Canada | 0.326 |
| Eastern Europe | Czech Republic | 0.254 |
| | Poland | 0.345 |
| | Russia | 0.399 |
| | Ukraine | 0.281 |
| Western Europe | Denmark | 0.247 |
| | France | 0.327 |
| | Germany | 0.283 |
| | United Kingdom | 0.36 |
| Asia | China | 0.447 |
| | India | 0.325 |
| | Indonesia | 0.343 |
| | Japan | 0.249 |
| Africa | Botswana | 0.63 |
| | Egypt | 0.344 |
| | Nigeria | 0.437 |
| | South Africa | 0.578 |

SOURCE: For Latin America, Szekeley and Montes (2006), pp. 596–597; dates vary from 1996 to 2000. All others from World Bank, *World Development Indicators* (2006).

**Table 2**

In addition to low productivity in comparison to the developed countries, Latin America is the most unequal region in the world. Table 2 uses a standard measure of inequality, the Gini index, to compare the twenty Latin American countries to other countries and regions. This index has a value of zero, when there is perfect equality of income, and 100, when all of the income accrues to a single individual. As the table shows, the Gini index values for the developed countries vary from a low of 0.247 (Denmark) to a high of 0.408 (the United States). Every Latin American country is more unequal than even the most unequal developed county. Latin American inequality also stands out in comparison to poorer regions (Asia and highly variable Africa) and the regions closest to it in GDP per capita (Eastern Europe and the former USSR).

How and why did Latin America come to occupy its current position in the world economy? How and why did the productivity of the region's economies come to be so backward in comparison to the advanced nations, yet so far ahead of Asia and Africa? How and why did income distribution in Latin America come to be so unequal, and poverty rates so high? To address these questions, this entry first examines data on long-term trends in productivity and welfare in Latin America. It then offers a review of the geographic, institutional, and policy environment that shaped the Latin American economies in each major epoch since the Columbus voyages. It concludes with an analysis of the prospects for economic development in Latin America in the twenty-first century.

## LONG-TERM TRENDS

Measuring productivity and welfare in the distant past requires the use of imperfect data and much guesswork. The principal sources for guesswork about trends in GDP per capita in the colonial era are trade and fiscal data collected by Spanish colonial officials, and demographic data from pre-Columbian tax and tribute records and Church registries of births and deaths. Portuguese colonists and administrators arrived later in Brazil than in Spanish America and kept fewer records. A few rough estimates of colonial GDP exist for the larger colonies, beginning with Cuba in the late seventeenth century. In the unstable half-century or so after independence in the 1820s, record-keeping did not improve and in many cases deteriorated, though compilations of data by scientifically minded individuals and even government agencies became common after midcentury. Toward the end of the nineteenth century, Latin American governments began carrying out regular population censuses; in the 1920s and 1930s, central banks and census bureaus began collecting economic data on a regular basis. Retrospective GDP estimates for the nineteenth and early twentieth centuries based on such sources have been constructed by historians for Cuba and for several of the larger countries (Argentina, Chile, Mexico, Uruguay). In the post–World War II era, Latin American

**GDP per capita, 1500–2001 (in 1990 Geary-Khamis international dollars)**

| Year | USA | Spain | Latin America[a] | Argentina | Brazil | Chile | Colombia | Cuba | Mexico | Peru | United Kingdom | Eastern Europe[b] | Japan | China | Africa[c] |
|---|---|---|---|---|---|---|---|---|---|---|---|---|---|---|---|
| 1500 | 400 | 661 | 550 | | 400 | | | | 550 | | 714 | | | | 414 |
| 1600 | 400 | 853 | 703 | | | | | | 755 | | 974 | | | | 422 |
| 1700 | 527 | 853 | 675 | | | | | | 755 | | 1,250 | | | | 421 |
| 1800 | 1,171 | | 703 | 1,194 | 422 | 539 | 395 | 1,312 | 755 | 480 | | | | | |
| 1820 | 1,257 | 1,008 | 713 | | 646 | | | | 566 | | 1,706 | 683 | 669 | 600 | 420 |
| 1850 | 1,806 | 1,079 | | | 704 | | | 1,409 | 592 | | 2,330 | 869 | | 600 | |
| 1870 | 2,445 | 1,207 | 749 | 1,311 | 713 | | | | | | 3,190 | 937 | 737 | 530 | 500 |
| 1900 | 4,091 | 1,789 | 1,200 | 2,756 | 678 | 1,949 | 973 | | 1,157 | 817 | 4,492 | 1,438 | 1,180 | 545 | |
| 1930 | 6,213 | 2,620 | 1,914 | 4,080 | 1,048 | 3,143 | 1,474 | 1,505 | 1,618 | 1,417 | 5,441 | 1,942 | 1,850 | 567 | |
| 1950 | 9,561 | 2,189 | 2,700 | 4,987 | 1,672 | 3,821 | 2,153 | 2,046 | 2,365 | 2,263 | 6,939 | 2,111 | 1,921 | 439 | 894 |
| 1980 | 18,577 | 9,203 | 5,886 | 8,206 | 5,198 | 5,738 | 4,265 | 2,664 | 6,289 | 4,205 | 12,931 | 5,786 | 13,428 | 1,067 | 1,536 |
| 2001 | 27,948 | 15,659 | 6,327 | 8,137 | 5,570 | 10,001 | 5,087 | 2,477 | 7,089 | 3,630 | 20,127 | 6,027 | 20,683 | 3,583 | 1,489 |

[a] Includes Mexico only in 1500 and 1600; 1700 is the unweighted average of Cuba and Mexico; 1800 includes Argentina, Brazil, Chile, Columbia, Cuba, Mexico, and Peru; thereafter Argentina, Brazil, Chile, Colombia, Mexico, Peru, Uruguay, and Venezuela.

[b] Includes Albania, Bulgaria, Czechoslovakia, Hungary, Poland, Romania, Yugoslavia

[c] 57 countries

[d] 1929

SOURCES: Maddison (2003), except for Mexico from Coatsworth (2003); figures for 1800 Colombia from Kalmanovich (2006); and other 1800 data from Coatsworth (1998).

**Table 3**

governments began routinely issuing estimates of economic activity, many for the first time.

What is known about trends in productivity in Latin America over the long run from the Conquest to the twenty-first century is summarized in Table 3. The estimates indicate that, by the end of the seventeenth century, and possibly much earlier, average GDP per capita in the European-dominated regions of Latin America was comparable to that of Western Europe and the thirteen British North American colonies. By the end of the colonial era, the region had slipped behind, though slave (Cuba) and settler (Argentina) economies continued to outpace the newly independent United States. As economic growth accelerated in northern Europe and the United States in the nineteenth century, most Latin American countries found themselves challenged by foreign invasion and internal civil strife. In these conditions, most of the region experienced stagnating or even falling productivity, just as growth accelerated in the industrial economies. By the late nineteenth century, Latin America had become underdeveloped.

As postindependence turmoil subsided, international trade flourished and capital flows from the developed world, especially from Great Britain, accelerated after 1870. As a result, the Latin American countries experienced a burst of economic growth that carried them well beyond the levels achieved in the late colonial era. This growth spurt was fueled primarily by a spectacular rise in exports, which was briefly interrupted by World War I and then continued until the onset of the Great Depression in 1929. Growth resumed from the depths of the Depression and accelerated somewhat between 1950 and 1980, but never returned to the rates of Latin America's economic belle epoque (1870–1930). Moreover, the financial and economic crisis that struck the region in 1982 stalled economic growth for over a decade throughout Latin America. By the end of the twentieth century, the productivity of the major economies in Table 3 averaged over eight times the levels of the early nineteenth century. Most of these gains occurred in the twentieth century, which saw nearly sixfold increases in GDP per capita.

Impressive as these gains were, they did not match the growth achieved in the developed world. Less-developed economies might be expected to grow faster than mature industrial economies by leapfrogging over older technologies, as occurred in much of East Asia beginning in the late 1960s. Catching up, or what economists refer to as "convergence," did not occur in Latin America in the twentieth century. From 1900 to 2001, the region's GDP per capita fell from over one-fourth to barely one-fifth the U.S. level. Although the productivity gains of the past century were impressive in absolute terms, the Latin American economies nonetheless failed to keep pace with the growth of the developed world. Nor did any of the region's economies come close to matching the spectacular growth of the less developed Asian economies in the second half of the twentieth century.

**Life expectancy**

[in years at birth]

| Region | Country | Prior to 1960 | 1960 | 2000 |
|---|---|---|---|---|
| Latin America | Argentina | | 65 | 74 |
| | Bolivia | | 43 | 63 |
| | Brazil | 37 (1920) | 55 | 70 |
| | Chile | 37 (1930) | 57 | 77 |
| | Colombia | | 57 | 72 |
| | Costa Rica | | 62 | 78 |
| | Cuba | | 64 | 76 |
| | Dominican Republic | | 54 (1962) | 71 (2002) |
| | Ecuador | | 53 | 73 |
| | El Salvador | | 51 | 70 |
| | Guatemala | 37 (1939–1941) | 46 | 66 |
| | Haiti | | 42 | 51 |
| | Honduras | | 47 | 67 |
| | Mexico | 33 (1930) | 57 | 74 |
| | Nicaragua | | 47 | 69 |
| | Panama | 52 (1941–1943) | 61 | 74 |
| | Paraguay | | 64 | 70 |
| | Peru | | 48 | 69 |
| | Uruguay | | 68 | 75 |
| | Venezuela | | 60 | 73 |
| North America | USA | 60 (1929–1931) | 70 | 77 |
| | Canada | 61 (1930–1932) | 71 | 79 |
| Eastern Europe | Czech Republic | 54 (1929–1932) | 70 | 75 |
| | Poland | | 68 | 74 |
| | Russia | | | 65 |
| | Ukraine | | 69 | 68 |
| Western Europe | Denmark | 63 (1931–1935) | 72 | 77 |
| | France | 57 (1928–1933) | 70 | 79 |
| | Germany | 61 (1932–1934) | 70 | 78 |
| | United Kingdom | | 71 | 78 |
| Asia | China | | 36 | 70 |
| | India | | 44 | 63 |
| | Indonesia | | 41 | 66 |
| | Japan | | 68 | 81 |
| Africa | Botswana | | 51 | 43 |
| | Egypt | | 46 | 69 |
| | Nigeria | | 39 (1962) | 47 (2002) |
| | South Africa | | 49 | 48 |

SOURCE: For early years, *UN Demographic Yearbook 1951*; for 1980, *UN Common Database*; for 2000, *World Development Indicators*.

**Table 4**

Data on trends in welfare for the colonial era and the nineteenth century are much scarcer than for output, trade, and taxes. Precolonial and early post-Conquest living standards have been studied, based on a small number of sites where skeletal remains have made it possible to estimate average height and life expectancy. This information can be supplemented with data on the height of recruits into the colonial militias in the late eighteenth century and of soldiers in the new national armies after independence in the 1820s. The era of census taking in the late nineteenth century, which could not begin until Liberal governments wrested control of civil registries from the Catholic Church, inaugurated the era of modern data collection. Trends in the twentieth century are generally well-documented from censuses and, especially after World War II, by government statistical agencies and health ministries.

The data summarized in the next three tables make it clear that improvements in welfare in Latin America were inextricably linked to economic growth. As productivity (GDP per capita) rose in the twentieth century, living conditions and living standards improved. Table 4 provides comparative data on life expectancy for the twentieth century, which rises from 30 to 40 years (comparable to the Middle Ages) to over 70 in most countries. Life expectancy in Cuba and Costa Rica at the end of the twentieth century was equal to or above that of the United States. Similarly, infant mortality rates that hovered near 300 per 1,000 live births at the turn of the century in Mexico and the Andes fell to near 100 by 1940 (see Table 5), and then fell to less than 50 by 2000 in every country except for Bolivia and Haiti. Finally, as Table 6 shows, literacy rates in Latin America, which were below 50 percent, and in some cases below 20 percent, at the beginning of the twentieth century rose steadily to more than 90 percent in most countries by 2000. Nonetheless, as Table 7 shows, Latin America suffers from unusually high poverty rates due to its unequal income distribution.

## PRECOLONIAL AND COLONIAL ERAS

The current state of knowledge makes it impossible to compare the pre-Columbian economies of the Western Hemisphere. In 1492 most of the New World's population lived in nomadic or seminomadic societies organized into bands and chieftaincies. Division of labor was rudimentary and based mainly on gender. Productivity levels were well below those of Western Europe. In the Andes and Mesoamerica, however, complex societies and states emerged after the development of sedentary agriculture. The development of agriculture occurred later in the Western Hemisphere than in the Old World for three main reasons. First, human populations did not arrive until about 13,000 BCE, during the last Ice Age and prior to the agricultural revolution in the Fertile Crescent. Immigration slowed after the land link to northwest Asia fell beneath the sea; those that reached the New World had no knowledge of agriculture. Second, the food crops eventually adapted for cultivation (maize, beans, potatoes) were more difficult and time-consuming to breed for food consumption than the Eurasian grasses that became wheat, barley, rye, and other food grain staples in the Old World. Third, the abundance of wild life (game, fish, and wild plants) in a hemisphere with few humans made foraging more productive than in the Old World, just as the mass death of megafauna in Eurasia pushed people to seek new sources of food. It took more time, too, to discover that the mineral rich soils of the highland plateaus were better suited to cultivation than other regions. While some urban centers did develop along the north coast of Peru, by using the water of mountain-fed streams for irrigation, most of the agricultural societies of the New World developed inland at higher elevations, far from the ocean.

By the beginning of the first millennium CE, city states and even large territorial empires arose in the Andean highlands and from Central Mexico south into northern Central America. Some of these new societies, such as the Mayan city states, failed because of mismanagement of fragile ecosystems or in the face of natural disasters—catastrophes common in the Old World, too. Nonetheless, by the time the Spaniards invaded the mainland in the first half of the sixteenth century, as many as 30 million people were living in highly organized and productive societies centered on imperial cities with populations as high as that of Tenochtitlan (Mexico City), which numbered 100,000 to 200,000 inhabitants. Although no data exist on which to base direct estimates of productivity, urbanization rates can be used as an indirect

**Infant mortality (in first year, per 1000 live births)**

| Region | Country | 1940 | 1960 | 1980 | 2000 |
|---|---|---|---|---|---|
| Latin America | Argentina | 90 | 61 | 32.2 | 17 |
| | Bolivia | 79 | 152 | 109.2 | 63 |
| | Brazil | 163 | 115 | 64.4 | 35 |
| | Chile | 214 | 118 | 23.7 | 10 |
| | Colombia | 141 | 77 | 48.4 | 20 |
| | Costa Rica | 132 | 87 | 19.2 | 12 |
| | Cuba | 83 (1938) | 35 | 17 | 7 |
| | Dominican Republic | 61 | 102 | 62.5 | 33 |
| | Ecuador | 159 | 107 | 68.4 | 27 |
| | El Salvador | 121 | 129 | 77 | 29 |
| | Guatemala | 109 | 136 | 78.8 | 39 |
| | Haiti | 219 (1950) | 169 | 122.1 | 88 |
| | Honduras | 109 | 137 | 65 | 33 |
| | Mexico | 126 | 94 | 47 | 25 |
| | Nicaragua | 109 | 130 | 79.8 | 34 |
| | Panama | 93 (1950) | 58 | 30.4 | 20 |
| | Paraguay | 80 | 68 | 48.9 | 23 |
| | Peru | 128 | 160 | 81.6 | 33 |
| | Uruguay | 87 | 47 | 33.5 | 14 |
| | Venezuela | 122 | 59 | 33.6 | 21 |
| North America | USA | 47 | 26 | | 7 |
| | Canada | 57 | 27 | | 9 |
| Eastern Europe | Czech Republic | 99 | 20 | 18 | 4 |
| | Poland | 140 (1938) | 62 | 21 | 8 |
| | Russia | 182 | 48 | 27 | 19 |
| | Ukraine | | 41 | | 18 |
| Western Europe | Denmark | 50 | 22 | 8 | 5 |
| | France | 91 | 27 | 10 | 4 |
| | Germany | 64 | 35 | 25 | 4 |
| | United Kingdom | 61 | 22 | 12 | 6 |
| Asia | China | | 150 | | 33 |
| | India | 160 | 146 | | 68 |
| | Indonesia | | 128 | | 36 |
| | Japan | 90 | 30 | | 3 |
| Africa | Botswana | | 118 | | 74 |
| | Egypt | 162 | 186 | | 40 |
| | Nigeria | 143 (1945/50) | 165 | | 107 |
| | South Africa | | | 118 (1970) | 50 |

SOURCES: Data for 1940 infant mortality rate, *UN Demographic Yearbook 1949–50*; 1960 infant mortality rate, *World Development Indicators*; 1980 infant mortality rate, *Statistical Abstract of Latin America*, Vol. 38 and B. R. Mitchell, *International Historical Statistics: Europe 1750–2000,* 5th ed. (New York: Palgrave Macmillan, 2003); 2000 infant mortality rate, *World Development Indicators.*

**Table 5**

measure. See the comparative data in Table 9. City populations included many people who contributed little or nothing to food production. These groups—rulers, priests, war-riors, administrators, architects, construction workers, craftspeople, and traders—survived only because agricultural productivity was high enough to provide surpluses for their subsistence. In turn, some of these nonagriculturalists contributed in their own ways to increasing GDP: rulers made laws enforced by warriors; administrators, architects, and construction workers produced housing and fortifications; craftspeople produced a wide variety of products like clothing, weapons, and religious art; traders pioneered markets that promoted exchanges linking distant producers.

Conquest and colonization in the century after Columbus's voyages raised the productivity of pre-Columbian societies, but killed most of the New World's people. Disease compounded by mistreatment reduced the New World's population from tens of millions (estimates vary from 30 million to over 100 million on the eve of the Conquest) to less than 10 percent of the pre-Conquest level (estimated at between 3 and 8 million). Meanwhile, the opening of the Western Hemisphere to international trade, the introduction of Old World flora and fauna (sugar, wheat, hoofed animals), and the transfer of Eurasian technologies (ocean shipping and navigation, the wheel, deep shaft mining, metallurgy) and organization (money, credit, private property) yielded a substantial increase in the productivity of the surviving populations. In the mainland colonies, vast mining enterprises arose using native as well as imported African slave labor. Cattle and grain estates took over the lands of empty (or merely defenseless) villages. Tropical agriculture (sugar, cacao, tobacco) arose in the northeast of Brazil and the Caribbean islands, with slaves kidnapped and forcibly removed from Africa to replace the dead or dying indigenous populations. GDP per capita rose, both because the output of exportables rose dramatically and because the population in the export-producing territories fell. By the seventeenth century, the regions dominated by European enterprise (that is, excluding the vast unconquered interior) had reached levels of output comparable (or in the Caribbean sugar islands, well above) those of Spain and most of western Europe. (See Table 3 above.)

Latin America's economies tended to stagnate, however, at levels determined by their natural resource endowments and the technology and organization imported to exploit them. Like the Iberian peninsula and most of the rest of the world as well, colonial Latin America imported, but did not produce, technological innovations. Once Eurasian technologies had been assimilated, GDP per capita leveled off unless energized by the discovery and exploitation of some new natural resource or increased demand (and therefore prices) of export products already being produced. This helps to account both for the economic stagnation that gripped the mainland colonies in the seventeenth century and persisted into the eighteenth century, despite the revival of mining in Mexico (after 1690) and Peru (after 1730). Economic decline in the mainland colonies in the seventeenth century coincided with the introduction of sugar cultivation using masses of African slaves along the tropical coasts of South America and the Caribbean islands. Slave imports and sugar production rose even more rapidly in the eighteenth century, especially in the islands wrested from Spain by the Dutch Republic, Britain, France, and others, but there is little evidence that sugar production became more efficient in the Spanish islands or Brazil. In the mining industry, no major technological innovations occurred after the amalgamation process, which uses mercury to extract silver from low-grade ores, was introduced in the 1550s. In short, colonial Latin America gained from Smithian growth—that is, as described by the eighteenth-century economist Adam Smith, from applying world-class (for the age) technology and organization to the production of natural resource-based exports. Although this sufficed to make some of the colonies and the Iberian mother countries wealthy by contemporary standards, it did not produce sustained growth.

The distribution of income and wealth in colonial Latin America was unequal by modern standards but does not appear to have been more skewed than in other, more successful economies. Table 9 compares Gini indices of wealth distribution at various sites in colonial and nineteenth-century Latin America with estimates for Great Britain and the United States. This quantitative comparison does not, however, reflect the far more significant inequalities in civic and property rights that developed and persisted in Latin America. Latin America's slaves, like those of the United States, possessed few rights and were subject to special legal codes that defined their status as inferior in nearly every respect to that of free men and women. Iberian legal codes also defined indigenous peoples as inferior in rights and status, an inferiority that persisted long after independence. The unequal distribution of civic and property rights institutionalized by slave and caste systems, rather than greater economic inequality in wealth or income, helps to explain Latin America's persistent failure to invest in human resources, even in the modern era, in contrast to other developed and developing societies.

***Causes of Economic Stagnation.*** The principle causes of Latin America's economic stagnation from the colonial era to the late nineteenth century were an inhospitable geography, inadequate institutions,

**Literacy rates in Latin America, 1900–2000 (% literate over 15 years)**

| Country | Late 19th century or 1900 | 1940 | 1950 | 1970 | 2000 |
|---|---|---|---|---|---|
| Argentina | 52 | | 87 (1947) | 93 | 97 (2001) |
| Bolivia | 17 | | 32 | 73 (1976) | 87 (2001) |
| Brazil | 25.6 | 44 | 54 | 66 | 86 |
| Chile | 43 | 71 | | 89 | 96 (2002) |
| Colombia | 32 (1918) | 56 (1938) | | 81 (1973) | 93 (2004) |
| Costa Rica | 33 | | 79 | 88 (1973) | 95 |
| Cuba | 40.5 | 79 (1943) | | 95 (1979) | 100 (2002) |
| Dominican Republic | 43 | | 64 | 77 | 87 (2002) |
| Ecuador | N/A | | 56 | 74 (1974) | 91 (2001) |
| El Salvador | N/A | 29 (1930) | 38 | 57 (1971) | 81 (2004) |
| Guatemala | 11.3 | 35 | | 46 (1973) | 69 (2002) |
| Haiti | N/A | | 11 | 20 | |
| Honduras | 33 | 36 (1945) | | 57 (1974) | 80 (2001) |
| Mexico | 22.2 | 48 | | 74 | 91 |
| Nicaragua | N/A | | | 58 (1971) | 77 (2001) |
| Panama | N/A | 63 | 70 | 78 | 92 |
| Paraguay | N/A | | 66 | 80 (1972) | 93 (2004) |
| Peru | 38.0 (1925) | 42 | | 73 (1972) | 88 (2004) |
| Uruguay | 54 | | | 94 (1975) | 97 (1996) |
| Venezuela | 34.0 (1925) | 43 (1941) | 51 | 77 (1971) | 93 (2001) |

SOURCES: Data for late 19th century and 1900, Sokoloff and Engerman (2000), p. 229; 1940 literacy rates, *UN Demographic Yearbook 1949–50*; 1950 literacy rates, *UN Demographic Yearbook 1955*; literacy rates for c. 1970, *Statistical Abstract of Latin America,* Vol. 38; year 2000 literacy rates, UNESCO.

**Table 6**

and excessive political risk. The main geographic constraint on productivity in the colonial era was the lack of navigable rivers linking exploitable natural resources to external markets. Most navigable rivers, like the Amazon system, ran through tropical regions with thin soils unsuitable for export agriculture. Rich soils and plentiful supplies of indigenous labor could be found in the highlands, but only precious metals and gems, with high value to bulk ratios, could be exported profitably given exorbitant transport costs. Overland transport, whether by wagon or mule train, cost ten times or more per ton kilometer than water transport.

Institutional constraints included legal discrimination against populations of African or indigenous descent (slave and caste systems), poorly defined and enforced property rights (even for European and creole elites), colonial trade monopolies that tied the colonial economies to their stagnant Iberian mother countries, and primitive fiscal systems that relied on state monopolies, burdensome taxes and fees, forced loans and confiscatory measures in wartime, and intrusive regulatory schemes to extract revenues from the most productive regions.

Political risk, that is, the risk of expropriation, was reflected in persistently high interest rates in comparison to Britain and its colonies. After independence, when freer trade, lower taxes, and looser regulation should have stimulated productive advance, political instability and international warfare wiped out most of the potential gains.

Economic historians used to argue that external dependence and even exploitation contributed to Latin America's relative backwardness. But research has shown that GDP per capita has been positively correlated with greater dependence on trade for as far back as data can be found. Table 10, for example, compares trade as a percentage of GDP with GDP per capita in 1800. In every case but Brazil, the economies that traded more were more productive than those in which exports accounted for a smaller proportion of GDP. (And the GDP estimate for Brazil may be too low.) Similarly, sustained economic growth, delayed until the late nineteenth century, was highly correlated with export spurts fueled by capital and technology imported from Western Europe and the United States.

### INDEPENDENCE AND DELAYED GROWTH (1820 1870)

Most of the Latin American colonies of Spain and Portugal secured their independence in the 1820s. By this time, the cumulative effects of the Napoleonic Wars (1796–1815) and the wars for independence (1810–1824) had caused a region-wide economic decline. Unlike Europe and the United States, however, the Latin American colonies failed to recover rapidly. In most cases economic recovery took decades. Mexico, for example, did not return to the level of its 1800 per capita GDP until the 1870s. The main exceptions were the export-intensive settlement colonies of Argentina (hides, salted beef, wool, and then grain) and Chile (copper), though Peru experienced a growth spurt in the 1840s to 1870s based mainly on the export of guano from offshore islands. In most cases, however, economic stagnation or even decline lasted for decades, just as industrial revolutions accelerated growth in the north Atlantic economies. As shown in Table 3 above, GDP per capita in the Latin American countries for which there are estimates fell from an average level well above that of the thirteen British colonies in North America in 1700, to 60.4 of the U.S. level in 1800, and then to 30.6 percent of U.S. GDP per capita in 1870.

This relative decline occurred despite a favorable external economic environment. Terms of trade moved in Latin America's favor for most of this troubled era. The Industrial Revolution made manufactured goods cheaper to import and simultaneously raised demand and relative prices for Latin America's exports. In addition, a dramatic decline in ocean shipping rates favored exporters of most raw materials (heavy bulk commodities with low value to volume and weight). The end of the Spanish and Portuguese commercial monopolies also helped to make imports cheaper and raised the income of export producers by eliminating compulsory transshipment through ports in the Iberian mother countries. In the early 1820s, in anticipation of export booms that never materialized, capital began flowing from Britain to Latin America, mostly into the public debt of the newly independent countries; but substantial quantities of direct investment also flowed to revive mining production in Colombia and Mexico, and into tropical agriculture. Despite expectations, sustained economic growth did not occur in most of Latin America until after 1870.

The unexpected and prolonged stagnation after independence had two principal causes: institutional constraints and political risk. Transport costs that had impeded growth throughout the colonial era were less important, not only because of the fall in ocean shipping rates and other costs, but also because railroads, a revolutionary technological innovation that became widely available in the 1830s, lowered land transport costs throughout the world. The first contracts and concessions for railroad construction in Latin America were signed in that decade. Unfortunately, railroad building could take place on a large scale only where stable governments could provide reasonable security, give credible guarantees against expropriation, exert eminent domain to create rights of way, and grant construction subsidies to private developers. These conditions did not exist in most of Latin America. The most rapid adoption of the new technology occurred in Cuba, which avoided instability (until 1868) by remaining a colony of Spain. Railroad development, which eventually proved even more crucial for economic growth in Latin America than in Britain or the United States, could not begin until Latin America achieved stable government and began modernizing the antiquated economic institutions inherited from the colonial era.

***Institutional Modernization.*** Institutional modernization occurred in two phases. In the first, lasting as long as five decades, Latin America emancipated itself from the most debilitating institutional constraints inherited from the colonial era: caste systems and slavery, archaic property rights (entail, mortmain), internal taxes, state monopolies, centralized public regulation and controls, and separate court systems—taxes, and other rights for privileged groups. These constraints persisted longest where creole elites faced potentially hostile slave and indigenous populations and clung to inherited institutions for protection against liberal egalitarianism. Large slave or indigenous populations in Brazil, the Caribbean, Mexico, Guatemala, Peru, and Bolivia pushed elites toward conservatism and reaction. In these cases, institutional modernization did not begin in earnest until destructive civil wars had made it impossible to sustain major components of the colonial

**Poverty headcount ratios (percentage of population below $1/day and $2/day)**

| Region | Country | Year | $1/day | $2/day |
|---|---|---|---|---|
| Latin America | Argentina | 2004 | 7 | 17 |
| | Bolivia | 2002 | 23 | 42 |
| | Brazil | 2004 | 8 | 21 |
| | Chile | 2003 | 2 | 6 |
| | Colombia | 2003 | 7 | 18 |
| | Costa Rica | 2003 | 3 | 10 |
| | Cuba | – | – | – |
| | Dominican Republic | 2004 | 3 | 16 |
| | Ecuador | 1998 | 18 | – |
| | El Salvador | 2002 | 19 | 41 |
| | Guatemala | 2002 | 13 | 32 |
| | Haiti | 2001 | 54 | 78 |
| | Honduras | 2003 | 15 | 36 |
| | Mexico | 2004 | 3 | 12 |
| | Nicaragua | 2001 | 45 | 80 |
| | Panama | 2003 | 7 | 18 |
| | Paraguay | 2003 | 14 | 30 |
| | Peru | 2003 | 11 | 31 |
| | Uruguay | 2003 | 2 | 6 |
| | Venezuela | 2003 | 19 | 40 |
| North America | USA | – | – | – |
| | Canada | 2000 | 7 | |
| Eastern Europe | Czech Republic | 1996 | 2 | – |
| | Poland | 2002 | 2 | 2 |
| | Russia | 2002 | 2 | 12 |
| | Ukraine | 2003 | 2 | 5 |
| Western Europe | Denmark | 1997 | 8 | – |
| | France | 1995 | 7 | – |
| | Germany | 2000 | 9 | – |
| | United Kingdom | 1999 | 6 | – |
| Asia | China | 2004 | 10 | 35 |
| | India | 2004 | 34 | 80 |
| | Indonesia | 2002 | 8 | 52 |
| | Japan | 1993 | 11 | – |
| Africa | Botswana | 1993 | 28 | – |
| | Egypt | 2000 | 3 | 44 |
| | Nigeria | 2003 | 71 | 92 |
| | South Africa | 2000 | 11 | 34 |

SOURCES: Data from World Development Indicators and World Bank.

**Table 7**

legacy. Elsewhere, institutional changes occurred as a by-product of independence or took less time to achieve unless complicated (as is the case of Argentina) by political struggles between poorly integrated regional interests. By the 1870s most of Latin America had experienced liberal revolutions embodied in new constitutions and legal codes that clearly signaled a break with the colonial past.

Consolidation of the new order required political stability. Harbingers of the new era were the shift from reliance on internal direct taxes to indirect (mainly tariff) revenues, reforms of fiscal and tax systems, the adoption of new civil and commercial codes, judicial reforms that made courts more efficient protectors of elite property rights, the privatization of public lands and other assets, and the beginning of specialized legislation to encourage banking, insurance, mining, and other vital sectors of the economy. The defeat of conservative forces, or more often the recognition by new generations of creole elites that the colonial past had become

**Urban population as percentage of total, 1500**

[percentage living in towns of over 5,000]

| Country | Percentage urban |
|---|---|
| Argentina, Brazil, Chile, Paraguay, Uruguay, Venezuela | 0 |
| Bolivia | 10.6 |
| Colombia | 7.9 |
| Costa Rica | 9.2 |
| Dominican Republic | 3 |
| Ecuador | 10.6 |
| El Salvador | 9.2 |
| Guatemala | 7 |
| Honduras | 9.2 |
| Mexico | 14.8 |
| Nicaragua | 9.2 |
| Panama | 9.2 |
| Peru | 10.5 |

SOURCE: Paul Bairoch, *Cities and Economic Development: From the Dawn of History to the Present* (Chicago: University of Chicago Press, 1988); Daron Acemoglu, Simon Johnson, and James A. Robinson, "Reversal of Fortune: Geography and Institutions in the Making of the Modern World Income Distribution," *Quarterly Journal of Economics* 117, no. 4 (November 2002):1280–1289.

**Table 8**

irretrievable, facilitated the transition to stability. Consolidation of the new order would have taken much longer, however, without the incentives to peace, especially among contending elites, offered by the realistic prospect of attracting foreign capital and technology and profiting from export growth. In several countries, for example, new commercial codes and banking laws passed national legislatures only when leaders understood that interested foreign investors—especially railroad companies—insisted on them. In short, sustained growth began after 1870 in an unusually favorable conjuncture, when external incentives helped to consolidate political stability and encourage governments to press forward with institutional modernization.

**ORIGINS OF SUSTAINED ECONOMIC GROWTH: THE BELLE EPOQUE (1870–1930)**

With elite dominance consolidated by political stability and the exclusion of contentious underclasses, and wealth now concentrating in elite hands, belle epoque regimes focused on managing their remarkable successes. Between 1870 and 1930, Latin America's eight largest economies grew at roughly 1.6 percent per year, the same rate as the benchmark U.S. economy and faster than any other region in the world (see Table 11). Although the productivity gap between Latin America and the United States did not diminish, the gap between Latin America and Western Europe declined notably. Export-led economic growth with high rates of targeted protectionism enabled most of the larger economies (especially Argentina, Brazil, Chile, and Mexico) to expand and develop their light manufacturing industries, such as textiles, food processing, beverages, glassworks, paper, and the like. Banking, virtually absent from Latin America at midcentury, suddenly took off, encouraged by new legal codes and government fiscal operations. Investments in infrastructure, nonexistent for more than a half century (in some areas since the first century after Conquest) took off when governments recovered their credit rating, borrowed heavily in London, Paris, and Frankfurt, and used the proceeds to subsidize railroad building, rebuild ports, and modernize towns and cities.

Foreign capital, technology, and trade reached unprecedented levels during the belle epoque. Table 12 compares trade (exports and imports as a percentage of GDP) in 1928, 1938, and 2003–2005, and capital flows (as a percentage of net investment) in 1900, 1950, and 1989–1990 in the Latin American economies for which estimates have been constructed. The table shows that "globalization," that is, the degree of economic integration of the Latin American and world economies, was greater at the beginning of the twentieth century than at any time since. The post-1982 market-friendly reforms, often acclaimed (or denounced) for having opened a new era of globalization, have yet to lead to the levels of global economic integration that characterized the economies of the belle epoque.

The most enduring and positive results of the growth achieved in the belle epoque can be seen in the huge investments made by governments of this era to improve urban life. Parks, monuments, public buildings, and opera houses are not the only legacies of this era. Trolley and later bus and metro systems proliferated, as did gas lines, then electric wiring, and telephones. Most important of all, elites learned that their own health and that of their families could not be safeguarded without improving heath conditions for all, because infectious diseases could not be confined to poor neighborhoods. Initially, urban reforms were designed to beautify city centers through slum clearance, forcing the poor to move out toward the fringes. Eventually, the growth of investments in sanitation, sewage treatment, and other public health initiatives dramatically cut death rates, especially infant mortality rates, and raised life expectancy, fueling a population explosion that did not abate for nearly a century.

Globalization between 1870 and 1930 spurred economic growth and improved living standards but did not usher in an era of free trade, inclusive citizenship, and progress for all. Latin American exports grew rapidly, but after early experiments with low tariffs in the 1820s, nearly every country pushed rates up to unprecedented levels to raise revenues as state capacities to collect other kinds of taxes declined and chronic political instability set in. By midcentury Latin America had become the most protectionist region in the world. (The United States briefly imposed even higher tariff rates during the Civil War, but allowed them to decline sharply thereafter.) The high tariff regime persisted, even after political stability and economic growth eased fiscal constraints, because instead of lowering tariffs the Latin American countries began to target their already high tariff rates to protect new industries. Latin America continued to be the most protectionist region in the world until the rest of the world caught up by raising tariffs in the 1920s. Latin America experienced export-led growth, but nothing like free trade, in the belle epoque.

Similarly, the nominal equality enshrined in constitutions did not extend to suffrage or elective office. Property and literacy requirements limited the right to vote or hold office to tiny minorities of citizens until well into the twentieth century. As intra-elite conflicts subsided, opportunities for popular participation in political life (e.g., urban "mobs" and machines, informal militias, local and regional rebellions) diminished. Concessions to popular classes became less urgent. In Argentina and Uruguay, with highly successful export economies and largely populated by immigrants from Europe, suffrage and office holding (for men) became more democratic early in the twentieth century; elsewhere it took the Great Depression of the 1930s or World War II to extend the suffrage. Most countries did not permit women to vote in national elections until after World War II.

**Distribution of wealth, 18th–19th centuries**

| Year | Country or region | Gini coefficient |
|---|---|---|
| 1774 | 13 British colonies | 0.73[a] |
| 1774 | New England | 0.8[a] |
| 1820 | Massachusetts | 0.72[b] |
| 1820 | Buenos Aires (province) | 0.63[c] |
| 1830 | Buenos Aires (city) | 0.66[d] |
| 1830 | Rio de Janeiro | 0.87[d] |
| 1830 | Massachusetts | 0.775[b] |
| 1838 | Buenos Aires (city) | 0.78[e] |
| 1838 | Buenos Aires (province) | 0.86[e] |
| 1840 | Massachusetts | 0.771[b] |
| 1843–1846 | Costa Rica | 0.84[f] |

[a]data from Alice Hanson Jones, *Wealth of a Nation to Be: The American Colonies on the Eve of the Revolution* (New York: Columbia University Press, 1980).
[b]Richard H. Steckel and Carolyn Moehling, "Rising Inequality: Trends in the Distribution of Income in Industrializing New England," *Journal of Economic History* 61 (2001): 160–183; male household heads only
[c]Lyman L. Johnson, "The Frontier as an Arena of Social and Economic Change: Wealth Distribution in Nineteenth-Century Buenos Aires Province," (unpublished paper, n.d.).
[d]Lyman L. Johnson and Zephyr Frank, "Cities and Wealth in the South Atlantic: Buenos Aires and Rio de Janeiro before 1860," *Comparative Studies in Society and History* 48, no. 3 (May 2006): 634–668; upper bound estimate for Rio de Janeiro
[e]Jorge Gelman and Daniel Santilli, *Historia del capitalismo pampeano*, vol. 3 *De Rivadavia a Rosas: Desigualdad y crecimiento económico* (Buenos Aires: Siglo XXI: 2006), p. 97.
[f]Lowell Gudmundson, "Costa Rica before Coffee: Occupational Distribution, Wealth Inequality, and Elite Society in the Village Economy of the 1840s," *Journal of Latin American History* 15, no. 2 (November 1983): 442.

**Table 9**

As politics become more stable, and often less democratic, economic inequality increased. Everywhere, liberal reforms made land available for purchase by individuals and land companies by abolishing entail (*mayorazgo*) and mortmain (inalienable property rights of indigenous villages, the Catholic Church, and many town councils). Liberal governments also sold off public lands at low prices designed to encourage private development. The onset of economic growth, combined with railroad construction linking many formerly isolated areas to distant markets, stimulated the commercialization of agriculture throughout the hemisphere. Commercialization made Latin American agriculture more productive, but it often coincided with land and labor policies that initially encouraged usurpation and theft of peasant lands and the virtual enslavement of peasant laborers in labor-scarce regions, such as the *henequen* (sisal) growing region of Mexico's Yucatan peninsula. Many regions of thriving peasant agriculture and pastoralism, with widespread ownership and access to land in Mesoamerica and the Andes as well as the interior of Brazil, became simultaneously more productive and more unequal as commercialization accelerated. The onset of economic growth tended to concentrate the benefits from productivity advances in the hands of small minorities and away from unskilled labor. The concentration of income and wealth, already high in many urban areas, probably worsened in much of the region.

The notable economic growth of the belle epoque tended to obscure deeper institutional and policy failures that economic growth could not solve and may in fact have worsened. Elites learned early in the era that economic growth required conditions that facilitated capital flows and the transfer of technology. Institutional and policy changes that inspired confidence among both domestic and foreign investors were crucial. Less vital, perhaps even unnecessary, were institutional and policy changes that might have inspired greater confidence in ordinary citizens. Judicial systems and law enforcement authorities became more stable and professional but served mainly to protect the rights and properties of important investors and companies. Public education helped to promote order in the cities but hardly seemed necessary in rural areas. Whereas attempting to replicate the scientific and technical establishments of the developed countries would have been expensive, even in the early twentieth century, importing technology embodied in foreign direct investment was virtually cost-free. (Only Argentina, with a GDP per capita rapidly overtaking that of Western Europe and a substantial immigrant population that included a scattering of highly trained Europeans, moved toward such a goal in the early twentieth century.)

Had external capital and technology not become available in such abundance, economic growth would have proved more difficult to get started, required deeper reforms than liberal leaders envisioned, and perhaps exacted a more egalitarian consolidation than that achieved in the "oligarchic" republics of the belle epoque. Growth might have started later, as in most of Asia, but, other things being equal, might have proved to be more robust and rapid. Instead, Latin America opted for a trajectory in which tiny political and economic elites shaped institutional development in ways that initially facilitated economic growth but soon proved both politically fragile and economically vulnerable to external shocks.

**Trade as percentage of GDP, c. 1800**

| Colony | Total exports (current US dollars) | Exports per capita | Exports % of GDP | GDP per capita (current US dollars) |
|---|---|---|---|---|
| Cuba | 5,000,000 | 18.35 | 20.4 | 90 |
| Argentina | 3,300,000 | 10.03 | 12.2 | 82 |
| Mexico | 12,640,800 | 2.11 | 5.2 | 40 |
| Chile | 874,072 | 1.63 | 4.4 | 37 |
| Peru | 2,998,000 | 2.31 | 7 | 33 |
| Brazil | 15,526,750 | 4.78 | 16.4 | 29 |
| Columbia | 1,900,000 | 2.02 | 7.9 | 27 |

Note: In 1800, the US dollar and the Spanish peso were equal in value, as both were based on the Spanish silver peso.

SOURCE: John H. Coatsworth, "Economic and Institutional Trajectories in Nineteenth-Century Latin America" in Coatsworth and Taylor, 1998, p. 33; Salomon Kalmanovitz, "El PIB de la Nueva Granada en 1800: Auge colonial, estancamiento republicano," *Revista de Economía Institucional* 8, no. 15 (2006): 161–183.

**Table 10**

**PARTIAL DEGLOBALIZATION, ECONOMIC GROWTH, AND LAGGING WELFARE, 1930–1982**

From the onset of the Great Depression (1929–1930) to the financial and economic crisis of 1982, the eight largest Latin American economies grew at an average annual rate of 2.2 percent, faster than during the belle epoque but again roughly equal to the growth of the U.S. economy. (See Table 12.) As in the previous era, however, Latin American growth rates varied considerably from one country to the next and tended to be more volatile than the U.S. rate. With World War II providing a powerful stimulus, the U.S. economy grew more rapidly than that of Latin America between 1930 and 1950, whereas Latin America grew faster during the postwar boom from 1950 to 1980. Welfare indicators advanced incrementally throughout this period, despite rapid population growth and persistent inequality. The consolidation of a cold war alliance between Latin American elites and the U.S. government helped to restore or retain more conservative regimes than the region's voters generally preferred (see Tables 4, 5, and 6 above).

***Depression, War, and Recovery, 1930–1950.*** The political economy of the belle epoque collapsed with the worldwide economic crisis that began in 1929. Between 1929 and 1932, export prices and volumes plummeted dramatically. The purchasing power of

Latin America's exports fell to 43 percent of their former level. Capital flows ceased and most countries became net capital exporters to the developed world as profits, dividends, and interest continued to be due from prior investments. Mineral exporters like Bolivia (tin), Chile (copper, nitrates), and Mexico (oil, copper, lead, zinc) suffered the steepest declines. Cuba was hit by the collapse of sugar prices but suffered mainly from political manipulation of the U.S. sugar market on which it had become dependent. Export prices and volumes fell less sharply in the rest of the region. The economic collapse precipitated fiscal and monetary crises. As in the developed countries, policymakers initially sought to stimulate recovery through orthodox stabilization measures, that is, by reducing expenditures and raising taxes. As foreign exchange earnings from exports continued to fall, external investment dried up, and economic activity declined, governments found it impossible to raise enough revenue to make payments on their outstanding external debt. Only Argentina managed to continue servicing its debt. Most declared a moratorium on external debt payments or defaulted outright. Ending debt service payments tended to ease fiscal problems, but did so by driving a wedge between policies aimed at the external sector (default, reducing imports) and those developed to repair the domestic economy (fiscal deficits to stimulate recovery financed by internal debt).

Recovery was facilitated by a rapid fall in imports. Terms of trade (export versus import prices) fell sharply throughout the region, so imports fell even faster than exports. This increased the demand for import-competing sectors, especially light manufacturing, but did so only where governments acted to shore up internal demand through deficit spending. Because governments could not borrow abroad, deficits had to be financed by internal borrowing, which proved effective only where domestic manufacturing could increase output by reactivating idle capacity or making more intensive use of existing plant and equipment. Otherwise, as in Bolivia, deficit spending merely fueled inflation. Cut off from new foreign direct investment, and thus new technology, productivity tended to decline. Industrial production recovered and even surpassed pre-Depression levels by the mid- to late 1930s in the larger countries, but the productivity gap between Latin American manufacturing and that of the industrialized countries also grew. Import-substituting industrialization (ISI) along with import-substituting agriculture (largely neglected in the literature) played a major role in the recovery, but much of the growth in the major economies (e.g., Brazil, Chile, Cuba) that occurred between 1931–1932 and the end of the decade depended on renewed growth in the export sector. Moreover, in the smaller economies of the region (e.g., Bolivia, Central American countries), which lacked a manufacturing base, ISI played no role in recovery from the Depression.

The economic crisis of the 1930s exposed the political fragility of the regimes that had presided over the region's export-led growth spurt. In Mexico, where economic growth had been especially rapid, economic recession, a prolonged drought, and intra-elite conflicts had already precipitated a major political upheaval. The Mexican Revolution of 1910–1916 overturned the political elite that had managed the economic growth achieved during the dictatorship of Porfirio Díaz (1877–1911). Similar challenges had already rocked oligarchic governments in Argentina, Chile, Peru, and Uruguay. With the onset of the Great Depression, the challenges multiplied. Popular protests and demands for inclusion fueled new political parties, coalitions, and movements. Many found support in the countryside, where commercialization of agriculture had pushed peasants off their lands. Urban workers, themselves recent migrants from the countryside or immigrants (as in Argentina and Uruguay), played a significant role. In most countries, however, the main beneficiaries of belle epoque growth—urban professionals, skilled and white collar-workers, shopkeepers—contributed disproportionately to shattering the old regimes. The Depression also tended to weaken export lobbies and simultaneously empower manufacturing interests.

The international environment added fuel to the flames that heated this complex mix. The importance of foreign investment fell dramatically from the onset of the Great Depression until after World War II. In 1920 the value of all foreign investment in Latin America was greater than the region's GDP. By 1950 it had fallen to only 23 percent. As it became clear that capital from the developed countries could not be enticed to resume flowing to Latin America, the opportunity cost of social and political reform declined. Economic competition between the capitalist democracies and fascist regimes (mainly the

**Growth rates of GDP per capita, 1870–2001**

| Country/Region | 1870–1900 | 1900–1930 | 1930–1950 | 1950–1980 | 1980–2001 |
|---|---|---|---|---|---|
| United States | 1.7 | 1.4 | 2.2 | 2.2 | 2.1 |
| Spain | 1.3 | 1.3 | -0.7 | 4.9 | 2.6 |
| Latin America[a] | 1.6 | 1.6 | 1.7 | 2.6 | 0.3 |
| Latin America[b] | | | | 2.2 | 0.3 |
| Argentina | 2.5 | 1.3 | 1 | 1.7 | -0.1 |
| Brazil | -0.2 | 1.5 | 2.4 | 3.3 | 0.3 |
| Chile | N/A | 1.6 | 1 | 1.2 | 2.7 |
| Colombia | N/A | 1.4 | 1.9 | 2.4 | 0.8 |
| Cuba | 0.1 (1850–1930) | | 1.5 | 0.9 | -0.3 |
| Mexico | 2.6[e] | 1.1 | 1.9 | 3.4 | 0.6 |
| Peru | N/A | 1.9 | 2.4 | 2.1 | -0.8 |
| Uruguay | | | | | |
| Venezuela | | | | | |
| United Kingdom | 1.2 | 0.7 | 1.2 | 2.1 | 2.1 |
| Eastern Europe[c] | 1.4 | 1 | 0.4 | 3.4 | 0.2 |
| Japan | 1.6 | 1.5 | 0.2 | 6.7 | 2.1 |
| China | 0.1 | 0.1 | -1.3 | 3 | 5.9 |
| Africa[d] | | 0.7(1870–1950) | | 1.8 | -0.1 |

[a]Argentina, Brazil, Chile, Colombia, Mexico, Peru, Uruguay, and Venezuela.
[b]Bolivia, Costa Rica, Cuba, Dominican Republic, Ecuador, El Salvador, Guatemala, Haiti, Honduras, Jamaica, Nicaragua, Paraguay, Puerto Rico, Trinidad and Tobago
[c]Includes Albania, Bulgaria, Czechoslovakia, Hungary, Poland, Romania, and Yugoslavia
[d]57 countries
[e]1877–1900

SOURCE: Maddison (2003).

**Table 11**

United States versus Germany) escalated after 1933, reducing the likelihood of external intervention. These conditions made it easier for governments to tax, regulate, and even nationalize foreign assets, when popular demands escalated for government intervention to restore growth and reduce vulnerability to external shocks. In its initial phase, therefore, import-substituting industrialization coincided with a shift toward nationalist, populist, and even socialist political discourse along with redistributive social policies, which included substantial wage concessions, land distribution (especially in Mexico), and a rise in public expenditures in health and education.

***Import-Substituting Industrialization (ISI), 1950–1980.*** By the end of World War II, most of Latin America had rejected the political economy of the belle epoque and embraced ISI as a conscious strategy for promoting economic development. In the eight largest economies (Argentina, Brazil, Chile, Colombia, Mexico, Peru, Uruguay, and Venezuela), governments not only retained and even intensified the high tariffs that had protected new industries prior to the Depression, but also added an array of new measures to promote industrialization. These included import quotas and prohibitions, tax exemptions and subsidies to new industries, development banks to provide low-cost credit, infrastructure and energy policies designed to lower costs, subsidies to urban consumption to keep wages low, labor policies to weaken unions and re-duce wages, and a wide range of inducements and regulations to channel investment from export activities into industry. The mix of policies varied widely from country to country, but taken together they amounted to a deliberate strategy for fostering economic development through state-led industrialization. ISI achieved undeniable successes. The growth rate of GDP per capita in the eight countries that adopted ISI averaged 2.6 percent per year for the thirty years from 1950 to 1980. Brazil (3.3%) and Mexico (3.4%) were the top performers. Argentina (1.7) and Chile (2.1) were the least successful of the ISI countries.

In the postwar era, international trade and capital markets recovered rapidly. With dollar and sterling reserves accumulated during the war, the Latin American countries resumed importing manufactured goods they were not yet producing. A number of countries (most notably Argentina) used a portion of their reserves to nationalize foreign assets, such as railroads, trolleys, and utilities. As the import flood and buyouts drew down reserves, and governments turned to protecting and subsidizing new industries, balance of payment crises erupted, pushing policymakers to abandon the populist policies of the 1930s in order to balance budgets and control imports. Fortuitously, Latin America's new ISI strategy coincided with efforts by the U.S. government to forge an anticommunist alliance with the region's economic and political elites. Governments that had built popular credibility with progressive social legislation in the 1930s, such as Mexico, managed the transition to more orthodox stabilization programs with less turmoil. Elsewhere, however, elected governments that proved unable or unwilling to move rightward fell to military regimes.

The new ISI strategy received support from economists associated with the United Nations Economic Commission for Latin America (ECLA, now with the Caribbean added, ECLAC), established in 1948. ECLA's founding executive secretary, Argentine lawyer turned central banker Raúl Prebisch, argued that a strategy based on exporting raw materials, such as minerals and agricultural products, could not produce sustained economic growth. This was because over the long run the prices of manufactured imports tended to rise relative to those of raw materials. Because of deteriorating terms of trade, developing countries were trapped in an endless cycle, struggling to produce more and more raw materials to pay for a dwindling basket of imports. The solution, according to Prebisch, was to break the cycle of dependence on exports by actively promoting industrialization. Unfortunately, as ECLA-trained economists soon discovered, the new strategy had two flaws. First, the terms of trade argument turned out to be faulty. Better data showed either that there had been no long-term decline in terms of trade, or that the decline had been trivial—too small to impede growth. Second, the ISI countries soon discovered that fostering industry actually increased the need for imports, such as machinery, technology, petroleum for energy, and even raw materials. By ignoring or even discouraging export promotion, the Latin American ISI countries found themselves trapped in an endless cycle of balance-of-payments crises—too few exports to pay for the imports that their industries needed.

Meanwhile, however, the U.S. government for its own reasons endorsed ISI. Unable to secure congressional majorities for new trade agreements that would have lowered barriers to U.S. exports, the Eisenhower administration (1953–1961) shifted its strategy. Because tariff and other barriers made it difficult for large U.S. companies to export cars or refrigerators, they began to "leap over" the barriers

**Foreign trade and foreign capital as percent of GDP**

| Country | Total foreign capital invested as percent of GDP: 1900, 1950, 1989/90 | Exports plus imports as percent of GDP: 1928, 1938 and 2003/5 |
|---|---|---|
| Argentina | 415, 12, 64 | 59.7, 35.7, 43.2 |
| Brazil | 255, 18, 36 | 38.8, 33.3, 29.5 |
| Chile | 188, 49, 40 | 57.2, 44.9, 71.7 |
| Columbia | 74, 24, 21 | 62.8, 43.5, 40.4 |
| Costa Rica | | 109.6, 80.7, 45.8 |
| Cuba | 133, 47, N/A | |
| Guatemala | 136, 12[a], 8[d] | 51.2, 29.5, 45.8 |
| El Salvador | | 81.0, 62.4, 71.5 |
| Honduras | 158, 38[a], 69 | 69.8, 39.5, 99.8 |
| Mexico | 155, 17, 32 | 47.7, 25.5, 60.1 |
| Nicaragua | | 54.9, 52.3, 97.3 |
| Paraguay | 70, 18[b], 31 | |
| Peru | 178, 22, 48 | 53.2, 42.6, 44.0 |
| Uruguay | 314, 18, 31 | 38.0, 37.1, 56.9 |
| Venezuela | 252, 55, 47 | 120.4, 55.7, 56.9 |

[a]1970
[b]1980

SOURCE: For investment as a percentage of GDP, see Michael J. Twomey, "Patterns of Foreign Investment in Latin America in the Twentieth Century" in John H. Coatsworth and Alan J. Taylor, *Latin America and the World Economy since 1800* (Cambridge, MA: Harvard University, 1998), 182–185; for trade ratios, see Victor Bulmer-Thomas, *The Economic History of Latin America since Independence* 2nd ed.(Cambridge, UK: Cambridge University Press, 2003), p. 190.

**Table 12**

to invest in manufacturing plants within the larger Latin American countries. The U.S. government then moved to support ISI as a strategy and simultaneously to lobby to make sure that U.S. companies would not be excluded, overregulated, or taxed excessively. U.S. efforts focused on discouraging state ownership, regulations that required local investors in new projects and restrictions or taxes on profit remittances. U.S. support for ISI crystallized just as ECLA was discovering its limitations and urging Latin American governments to overcome them through regional and subregional trade agreements, export promotion, and other measures.

Some economists have argued that Latin America's ISI strategy prevented the region from achieving even faster growth. World trade increased dramatically in the three decades after World War II. Latin America's share of world trade fell from a high of 13.5 percent in 1946 to 4.4 percent in 1975. Although some part of this loss was due to the recovery of war-ravaged economies, Latin America's share continued to fall into the 1980s. With abundant labor and raw materials, Latin America might have been able to become an exporter of manufactured goods as well as raw materials by following the strategy later adopted by several rapidly growing East Asian economies, such as Japan, South Korea, and Taiwan. Such a strategy would have been difficult, however, because of U.S. and West European protectionism. The breakthrough in liberalizing trade did not occur until the successful completion of the Kennedy Round of negotiations for a new General Agreement on Trade and Tariffs (GATT) in 1967. As the markets of the industrial countries now opened to manufactured goods from the developing world, the East Asian "tigers" moved aggressively to take advantage of the new opportunities. By that time, however, the major Latin American economies were so committed to ISI that joining the GATT would have imposed huge economic costs (closed factories) and generated high unemployment among the most protected (and unionized) workers. In most of Latin America, political and social turmoil had produced authoritarian and military regimes unwilling to provoke even more unrest. In addition, many of the industries that would have suffered from freer trade were branches of multinational companies (many based in the United States) who could call on powerful ambassadors to defend them.

In the 1970s unsettled conditions in the global economy and instability in U.S. economic policymaking also contributed to Latin America's economic difficulties. With balance-of-payments problems of its own, the United States in 1971 abandoned the fixed-exchange-rate regime negotiated at the Bretton Woods Conference in 1944 and implemented in 1946. Then, in 1973, the Organization of Petroleum Exporting Countries (OPEC) quadrupled oil prices; at the end of the decade, in 1978–1979, oil prices again tripled. To pay for essential imports of petroleum, needed for generating electricity, running factories, and fueling transportation systems, the Latin American countries resorted to borrowing. Commercial banks in the United States and Western Europe, into which the oil-producing countries were depositing their windfall gains, had plenty to lend at reasonable interest rates. The ISI countries as well as the smaller non-ISI regimes borrowed heavily to keep their economies running. Latin America's main oil-producing economy, Venezuela, profited from high oil prices, but at the cost of becoming more dependent on oil exports to cover a rising import bill. Mexico also grew rapidly after the discovery of new oil reserves announced in 1976, but borrowed heavily, nonetheless, to pay for drilling, pipelines, and infrastructure. Latin America's accumulated external indebtedness rose from $28.2 billion in 1970 to $314.4 billion in 1982.

As Tables 4, 5, and 6 above suggested, indicators of human welfare improved during the ISI era. Economic growth fueled urbanization, making public services more accessible to an increasing proportion of Latin America's population. Nonetheless, income inequality remained high and poverty rates declined only slowly. The persistence of inequality was partly the result of the ISI strategy itself. Workers in protected industries received wages above what their low productivity would have earned them in open economies. Protection made it possible for employers to pass on higher labor costs to consumers, including the poor, in the form of higher prices and lower-quality goods. By the 1970s, at least, open economies could have provided more and better jobs for Latin America's abundant unskilled labor pool, though at the cost of closing inefficient ISI industries. Even without dismantling ISI, however, inequality could have been reduced by land reform, by taxes designed to shift income from the top percentiles, and, above all, by greater advances in education. Instead, the conservative drift in social policy put an end to most land reforms, left the wealthiest Latin Americans largely untaxed, and notably slowed educational progress. The children born between 1930 and 1950 increased their average level of schooling by 2.7 years. Between 1950 and 1970, as Asian countries accelerated, Latin Americans born in those years increased their average level of schooling by only 1.9 years. Moreover, the gap in educational levels between the richest and poorest Latin Americans remained exceptionally high—seven years or more in Argentina, Brazil, Chile, Ecuador, El Salvador, Mexico, and Panama.

## LOST DECADES AND RECOVERY, 1982–2007

A major financial and economic crisis struck Latin America in the summer of 1982. The crisis originated in the United States. To cope with inflationary pressures, the U.S. Federal Reserve raised interest rates to unprecedented levels in 1981 and 1982. The result was a rapid rise in global interest rates (already rising due to inflation) and a sharp contraction in the U.S. economy that soon spread throughout the globe. Commodity prices (especially oil prices) plummeted. In Latin America, Mexico fell first. With oil exports accounting for over 80 percent of Mexico's exports, Mexico's dollar earnings were no longer sufficient to cover its rising debt payments. Nor could Mexico's central bank continue to support the peso by buying dollars at the official rate. In August the Mexican government announced that it could not meet the payments due on its external debt. The peso was freed to float and quickly sank to less than a third of its former value against the dollar. When bankers and investors in the developed countries stopped investing anywhere in Latin America, the crisis spread. For most of the world, recovery from the U.S. recession began in 1983. In Latin America, with its huge debt overhang, governments quickly found it impossible to continue borrowing abroad to pay for the imports needed by their inefficient industries. The Latin American economies stagnated or declined for more than a decade. Only two Latin American countries had higher levels of GDP per capita in 1989 than in 1980: Colombia, because of rising exports of cocaine, and Cuba, because its socialist economy was closely aligned to the Soviet Union's rather than the United States'. In the two decades from 1980 to 2001, the eight largest Latin American countries averaged an annual rate of growth of only 0.3 percent—the lowest growth since the early nineteenth century. Only Chile's rebounded, beginning in 1985, producing a satisfactory 2.7 percent rate of growth over these twenty-one years.

***The Washington Consensus.*** The prolonged era of stagnation and decline after 1982 forced most Latin American countries to abandon the ISI strategy and to reexamine the state's role in their economies. It soon became evident that it would be impossible to stimulate economic recovery through government spending, because there were no external lenders willing to finance the deficits of Latin America's nearly bankrupt governments. Government spending in such conditions led to inflation, which taxed the poor, but did not stimulate recovery. Moreover, the crisis and ensuing recession forced deep spending cuts that not only savaged social spending, but made it impossible to continue subsidizing inefficient public and private enterprises as well as urban living standards. Most governments felt compelled to continue making payments on their external debt, scaled back through negotiations with creditors, in the hope that foreign investors (and their own citizens with capital and savings safely invested abroad) could be persuaded to begin investing again. Public investment in infrastructure and human capital virtually ceased, which gave added urgency to renewing private investment.

Unlike the 1930s, when the global economy faced a prolonged crisis and the United States recovered slowly, most of the world rebounded quickly. This made some form of reglobalization not only an option, but the only feasible option available to most Latin American economies. The Soviet Union and its allies, hit hard by declining oil prices and internal problems, offered little aid in contrast to the economic and political competition of Germany and its allies a half century earlier. Popular discontent with economic stagnation was contained by transitions to democratic regimes in most of the hemisphere.

Eventually, all of the Latin American governments were forced to adopt a package of economic policy reforms that amounted to a new economic strategy. Unable to rely on spending to stimulate economic recovery, governments began reducing the restrictions on trade and foreign investment that had been the centerpiece of the ISI strategy. Most joined the GATT, predecessor to the World Trade Organization (WTO), to gain access to world markets on better terms, but this move required them not only to lower their own tariffs, but also to abandon most nontariff barriers to imports, such as prohibitions, quotas, special permits, and the like. To stimulate both domestic and foreign investment, governments adopted market-friendly domestic reforms to reduce the burden of cumbersome regulations, price controls, licenses, and monopolies. These reforms, predicated on keeping budget deficits low and allowing market forces to play a major role in determining interest and exchange rates, eventually came to be known as the Washington Consensus because both the U.S. government and the Washington-based multilateral lending institutions (the International Monetary Fund, the World Bank, and the Inter-American Develop-ment Bank) endorsed them. Latin American governments seeking aid or loans from these sources found that help was now conditional on carrying out the Washington Consensus reforms.

Privatizing state-owned enterprises (SOEs) became a significant part of the Washington Consensus strategy by the late 1980s. Chile and Mexico moved first and by the 1990s, the trend had spread throughout the region. Mexico privatized hundreds of SOEs including commercial banks (reversing a 1982 nationalization decree), telecommunications, transportation, utilities, and hundreds of companies producing goods as diverse as fertilizers, steel, trucks, buses, minerals, and textiles. Privatization yielded three main benefits. First, it helped balance budgets by eliminating public subsidies to those SOEs that had been operating at a loss. Second, privatization attracted foreign investment at a time when it was badly needed. By 2001, 18 Latin American governments had realized the equivalent of six percent of their combined GDP from sales of SOEs. Third, the privatized companies benefited from new infusions of capital and better management and became more efficient. For example, the number of private phone lines in Argentina more than doubled, the wait time for a new line in Mexico fell from more than two years to a mere 30 days, and in Bolivia, long distance phone service reached scores of towns that had never been served.

Critics of privatization noted that Latin American governments could have cut subidies and instructed managers to operate SOEs more efficiently without privatizing, though without massive borrowing (which would have been impossible) they would not have been able to invest in new technology or service extension. Critics also pointed to some privatizations that lacked transparency, rewarded cronies, or involved corrupt payments to officials or their relatives. In many cases, increased efficiency meant eliminating jobs; in Argentina alone 150,000 workers lost their jobs due to privatizations between 1987 and 1997. Lack of strong regulatory bodies to enforce competition resulted in the creation of private monopolies that needlessly raised prices to consumers. While nearly all of the economists who studied Latin America's privatizations concluded that they contributed to economic growth and did not lead to greater unemployment, inequality, or proverty, public opinion in the region turned decidedly negative by the early 2000s. Governments in Bolivia, Peru, and Venezuela among others renationalized sensitive public utilities.

The impact of the Washington Consensus reforms should have become visible by the 1990s, but the results were disappointing. Capital did begin flowing to Latin America again from the developed countries beginning in 1990. Most of Latin America began growing again in the early 1990s, but a series of financial shocks, most unrelated to Latin America, interrupted capital flows again and induced recessions or sharply curtailed growth throughout the region. The turmoil began in Mexico again in December 1994 with another peso collapse and near default, triggered by intense conflicts within the ruling elite during an election year. By the time the U.S. government responded with a loan guarantee to help Mexico avoid default and stabilize its economy in early 1995, the "Tequila effect" had pushed cautious investors to pull funds out or abandon planned projects throughout Latin America. Succeeding crises touched off by exchange-rate and balance-of-payments crises in Asian countries (1997) and Russia (1998), and a new U.S. recession in 2000–2001, had similar effects. In the two decades after the 1982 crisis engulfed the region, and after more than a decade of market-friendly reforms, economic growth in the region (with few exceptions) remained anemic.

Most (though not all) indicators of human physical welfare in the era of the Washington Consensus deteriorated or failed to improve. The poor performance of most countries in both economic and social development led voters to reject incumbent conservative or centrist governments in favor of center-left or socialist alternatives. With the threat of U.S. intervention receding because of the end of the cold war, and the prestige of the region's military establishments still sinking, voters in the late 1990s and early 2000s turned to parties, movements, and personalities long excluded from power and thus not responsible for past failures. Rhetoric aside, however, most of the new left-leaning regimes adhered to the basic Washington Consensus reforms, such as fiscal stability, freer trade, and deregulation.

## THE FUTURE OF ECONOMIC DEVELOPMENT IN LATIN AMERICA

The Latin American economies began to grow at or above their twentieth-century (historic) rates in the first decade of the twenty-first century. Despite notable acceleration in growth after two decades of poor performance, Latin America still compares poorly with other world regions. Even in the boom period from 2003 to 2007, Latin America grew more slowly than any other world region, including Africa. The region's exceptional inequality continued to generate higher poverty rates than other regions at comparable levels of GDP per capita.

Latin America's persistent economic failure led to a revival of debates over economic strategy. Some economists argued that the Latin American countries failed to implement fully the Washington Consensus reforms. Many urged greater liberalization of domestic economies and new trade agreements—bilateral and regional, as well as global—to make it easier for Latin America's exports to compete in the global market. An important trend in economic thinking also focused on deeper institutional issues, notably the persistent failure of most Latin American countries to provide effective protection for the civic and property rights of ordinary citizens and the equally intractable failure to assure adequate education and health services for all.

Among critics of the Washington Consensus, two lines of argument predominated. Some argued that the reforms themselves were flawed, because they tended to undermine the effectiveness of governments in the region at a time when more effective public policies were needed. Though agreeing on the need for deep institutional reforms, proponents of this view were skeptical of free-trade agreements that tended to limit the ability of governments to eliminate bottlenecks, correct imbalances, and channel resources to promising new growth opportunities. A second body of opinion among those opposed to the Washington Consensus asserted that many of the economic policy reforms of the 1980s to 1990s should be reversed, including privatizations of state enterprises, some kinds of deregulation, and the end of subsidies to improve urban living standards. Both anti–Washington Consensus schools criticized the failure of proponents to take into account the social costs and increased inequality that often accompany the productivity gains from freer trade.

As the twenty-first century advances, a new political economy appears in prospect. The elitist regimes installed at the end of the nineteenth century, some with diminishing popular clienteles added in the 1930s and 1940s, persisted into the 1980s because they were backed by powerful military establishments and external allies. Many of the democratic regimes installed as military rule ended in the 1980s and 1990s proved to be more inclusive than in the past, in part because of popular mobilizations spurred on by economic failures. Restrictions on the franchise, both formal and informal, ended throughout the hemisphere. Public demands on democratic governments—for better economic performance as well as more effective efforts to reduce inequality and poverty, to improve public institutions, and to provide greater security of rights and property for all—have risen with each new election. Elected governments with failed economic policies or that were broadly viewed as elitist or exclusionary fell from power in the 1990s and 2000s as a result of popular protests in Argentina, Bolivia, Ecuador, Guatemala, Peru, and Venezuela.

By the first decade of the twenty-first century, Latin American economic strategies tended to converge toward the macroeconomic prescriptions of the Washington Consensus (especially fiscal stability and more market friendly policies), but with increasing experimentation in the microeconomics of social policy. For example, Mexico's conservative governments and Brazil's center-left governments pioneered efforts to link modest welfare benefits for poor families to school attendance and medical checkups. On the other hand, the Hugo Chavez government in Venezuela embraced a more radical design by importing Cuban teachers and doctors in exchange for oil sold to Cuba at below market prices. This made it possible for Venezuela to increase educational and health services to the poor more rapidly than would have been possible if the country had been forced to wait until Venezuelans could be trained to do so. Still more radical was the Venezuelan decision to abandon the Washington Consensus to embrace "Bolivarian socialism." While Chavez succeeded in displacing Venezuela's traditional political parties and taming the country's economic elite, the country's economy remains highly dependent on oil revenues and therefore vulnerable to external shocks. Moreover, even with high oil prices, the success of Bolivarian socialism may well depend on better management of the state-owned oil company, Petroleos de Venezuel, SA and of the government' fiscal balances. Declining oil production and rising inflation would threaten any economic model.

It is still an open question whether Latin America will be able to develop a new political economy to supersede the exhausted elitist model that proved so resilient over the past century. Governments that can mobilize popular support to deepen institutional modernization without sacrificing the notable gains in productivity and welfare achieved in the past one hundred years will still face daunting economic dilemmas, both internal and external.

*See also* **Agriculture; Foreign Investment; Foreign Trade; Industrialization; Privatization.**

BIBLIOGRAPHY

Contemporary data and analysis on world economic conditions is now widely available via the Web sites and annual reports of major multilateral lending institutions and international development organizations such as the World Bank, International Monetary Fund, the UN Development Programme, Inter-American Development Bank, and the UN Economic Commission for Latin America and the Caribbean. For historical and comparative purposes, the population and PPP GDP estimates of Angus Maddison are indispensable; see *The World Economy: A Millennial Perspective* (Paris: Organization for Economic Co-operation and Development, 2001) and the companion volume of data *The World Economy: Historical Statistics* (Paris: OECD, 2003).

Recent work on the history of the Latin American economies, from the pre-Columbian era to the twentieth century, is summarized in the two volumes of the *Cambridge Economic History of Latin America* edited by Victor Bulmer-Thomas, John H. Coatsworth, and Roberto Cortés Conde (Cambridge, U.K., and New York: Cambridge University Press, 2006). Four other collections of original essays have contributed to defining the field: Stephen Haber, ed., *How Latin America Fell Behind: Essays on the Economic Histories of Brazil and Mexico, 1800–1914* (Stanford, CA: Stanford University Press, 1997); John H. Coatsworth and Alan M. Taylor, eds., *Latin America and the World Economy Since 1800* (Cambridge, MA: Harvard University Press, 1998); Enrique Cárdenas, José Antonio Ocampo, and Rosemary Thorp, eds., *An Economic History of Twentieth-Century Latin America*, 3 vols. (New York: Palgrave, 2000); and Richard H. Steckel and Jerome C. Rose, eds., *The Backbone of History: Health and Nutrition in the Western Hemisphere* (Cambridge, U.K., and New York: Cambridge University Press, 2002).

For an excellent survey of the economic historiography, see Paul Gootenberg's review essay "Between a Rock and a Softer Place: Reflections on Some Recent Economic History of Latin America," *Latin American Research Review* 39, no. 2 (2004): 239–257.

An innovative approach to the pre-Columbian economies, which suggests a far greater sophistication in economic organization and resource management than is commonly assumed, can be found in Charles C. Mann's *1491: New Revelations of the Americas before Columbus* (New York: Knopf, 2005). On the demographic impact of the Conquest, see the review essay by Massimo Livi-Bacci, "The Depopulation of Hispanic America after the Conquest," *Population and Development Review*, 32, no. 2 (2006): 199–232. The rich economic historiography of the colonial era is well represented in the collections cited above and by studies of institutions, sectors, and entire regions. Outstanding examples are Elinor G. K. Melville, *A Plague of Sheep: Environmental Consequences of the Conquest of Mexico* (Cambridge, U.K., and New York: Cambridge University Press, 1995); Stanley Stein and Barbara H. Stein, *Silver, Trade, and War: Spain and America in the Making of Modern Europe* (Baltimore, MD: Johns Hopkins University Press, 2000); and Enrique Tandeter, *Coercion and Market: Silver Mining in Colonial Potosí, 1692–1826* (Albuquerque: University of New Mexico Press, 1993).

The search for deeper institutional causes that could explain Latin America's poor economic performance over the very long run has reawakened debates on the colonial heritage of inequality and inefficient economic organization. See, for example, Daron Acemoglu, Simon Johnson, and James A. Robinson, "The Colonial Origins of Comparative Development: An Empirical Investigation," *American Economic Review* 91, no. 5 (2001): 1369–1401; Kenneth L. Sokoloff and Stanley L. Engerman, "Institutions, Factor Endowments, and Paths of

Development in the New World," *Journal of Economic Perspectives* 14, no. 3 (2000): 217–232; John H. Coatsworth, "Structures, Endowments, and Institutions in the Economic History of Latin America," *Latin American Research Review* 40, no. 3 (2005): 126–144.

The economic impact of independence on nineteenth-century Latin America is well covered by the essays in Leandro Prados de la Escosura and Samuel Amaral, *La independencia americana: Consecuencias económicas* (Madrid: Alianza Editorial, 1993). On the modern (post-1870) economic history of Latin America, see Victor Bulmer-Thomas, *Economic History of Latin America since Independence*, 2nd edition (Cambridge, U.K., and New York: Cambridge University Press, 2003) and Enrique Cárdenas, José Antonio Ocampo, and Rosemary Thorp, *Progress, Poverty and Exclusion: An Economic History of Latin America in the Twentieth Century*. Washington, DC: Inter-American Development Bank, 1998. On the political economy of the belle epoque, see Stephen Haber, Armando Razo, and Noel Maurer, *The Politics of Property Rights: Political Instability, Credible Commitments, and Economic Growth in Mexico, 1876–1929* (Cambridge, U.K., and New York: Cambridge University Press, 2003); William R. Summerhill, *Order Against Progress: Government, Foreign Investment, and Railroads in Brazil, 1854–1913* (Stanford, CA: Stanford University Press, 2003); and Jeffrey G. Williamson, "Real Wages, Inequality, and Globalization in Latin America before 1940," *Revista de Historia Económica* 17 (1999): 101–142.

On the economic development of individual countries or subregions, the following are especially helpful: Gerardo Della Paolera and Alan M. Taylor, eds., *A New Economic History of Argentina* (Cambridge, U.K., and New York: Cambridge University Press, 2003); Renato Baumann, *Brazil in the 1990s: An Economy in Transition* (New York: Palgrave, 2002); Victor Bulmer-Thomas, *The Political Economy of Central America since 1920* (Cambridge, U.K., and New York: Cambridge University Press, 1987); World Bank, *Chile's High Growth Economy: Poverty and Income Distribution, 1987–1998* (Washington, DC: World Bank, 2002); Miguel Urrutia Montoya, ed., *El crecimiento económico de Colombia en el siglo xx* (Bogota: Banco de la República, 2002); Jorge I. Domínguez, Omar Everleny Pérez Villanueva, and Lorena Barberia, eds., *The Cuban Economy at the Start of the Twenty-First Century* (Cambridge, MA: David Rockefeller Center for Latin American Studies, Harvard University Press, 2004); Stephen Haber, et al., *Mexico since 1980* (New York: Cambridge University Press, 2008); and Carol Wise, *Reinventing the State: Economic Strategy and Institutional Change in Peru* (Ann Arbor: University of Michigan Press, 2002).

For helpful surveys of contemporary ideas on key institutional and policy issues, see Esteban Pérez Caldentey and Matias Vernengo, eds., *Ideas, Policies, and Economic Development in the Americas* (London and New York: Routledge, 2007), and Charles H. Wood and Bryan R. Roberts, eds., *Rethinking Development in Latin America* (University Park: Pennsylvania State University Press, 2005).

John H. Coatsworth

---

**ECONOMIC INTEGRATION.** The economic integration of Latin America—either of the entire region (as was agreed to in 1967 but never realized) or subregions—was advocated by the United Nations Economic Commission for Latin America in the late 1940s and thereafter. The United Nations body, under Raúl Prebisch and others, saw economic integration as a means of promoting development, especially industrialization.

The first concrete step toward economic integration came in 1958 when Costa Rica, El Salvador, Guatemala, Honduras, and Nicaragua signed the Multilateral Treaty on Central American Free Trade and Economic Integration, providing for a limited and gradual approach to the economic merger of the five countries. Costa Rica did not ratify the agreement. In early 1960 some signatories expressed dissatisfaction with integrative programs. El Salvador, Guatemala, and Honduras concluded a more ambitious agreement, the Treaty of Economic Association, which prompted another round of negotiation. The main result was the General Treaty of Central American Economic Integration (1960). It provided for an expanded and much accelerated approach to regional economic merger and established a modest institutional structure. Also in 1960, the Central American countries concluded the agreement establishing the Central America Bank for Economic Integration. (Costa Rica signed and ratified the agreements only in 1963.)

During the 1960s under the General Treaty, intra–Central American trade expanded several hundredfold, industrialization increased, capital flowed in, and the region experienced both economic development and growth; however, the all-important agrarian sector was all but ignored by the integration effort, a serious flaw. Functioning of the Central American Common Market was seriously interrupted by the 1969 war between El Salvador and Honduras and came to a virtual halt as political violence consumed the region in the 1970s and 1980s.

In 1960 Mexico plus most of the South American countries concluded the Treaty of Montevideo, creating the Latin American Free Trade Association (LAFTA). LAFTA's modest goals were to be achieved through annual negotiation, over an extended period of time. The overall objective was to realize free trade among the member countries for most, but not all, products; there was no provision for a common external tariff on imports into the free-trade area.

Despite these limited goals, LAFTA members experienced difficulty meeting treaty commitments from the outset. Eventually, they totally failed to do so. In 1980 the LAFTA countries signed a new agreement establishing the Latin America Integration Association, an even looser and less demanding arrangement than LAFTA. Bilateral, rather than regional, agreements were emphasized. The 1980 agreement achieved no more, perhaps less, than the Treaty of Montevideo.

The most ambitious and far-reaching effort at economic integration came in 1969 with the creation of the Andean Group, or Andean Common Market, by Bolivia, Chile, Colombia, Ecuador, Peru, and Venezuela. Their Andean Pact set the following objectives: a virtually free market among the member countries, a common external tariff, allocation of certain industries among the member countries, special provisions for the less-developed members (as did the LAFTA and Central American agreements), and restrictions on foreign investment. The agreement also established a significant institutional structure, including a quasi-supranational Junta. Restrictions on foreign investment were detailed in decision 24, which declared certain sectors of the economy off-limits to foreign owners and otherwise phased out foreign investment.

The Andean Common Market achieved some of its objectives; however, both economic and political factors prevented full implementation. Deadlines were repeatedly set back and requirements downgraded. Chile withdrew in 1976 when its military government adopted an economic approach at odds with that of the integration effort. By the early 1980s, forward momentum for the remaining members had all but halted.

Each of the Latin American economic integration efforts encountered problems. Among the commonest were a lack of political will, instability in some member countries, conflict among some members, complaints on the part of less-developed members, unwillingness on the part of the more-developed countries to make sacrifices to benefit the less-developed, and competition among member countries for developed resources.

Two important agreements emerged in the 1990s. Brazil, Argentina, Uruguay and Paraguay formed the Mercado Común del Sur (Mercosur) in 1994. While a severe economic crisis in Argentina in the early twenty-first century weakened the pact, trade continues to grow among these countries. A totally different sort of economic integration effort is the North American Free Trade Agreement (NAFTA), which joins Mexico, the United States, and Canada into a single market. Latin American countries and the United States have been working on a free trade pact for all the Americas called the Free Trade Area of the Americas (FTAA). However, protectionist politicians in both the United States and Brazil have slowed this ambitious endeavor. Nevertheless, free trade with the United States has expanded. The United States has concluded free trade agreements with Central America and Colombia and is trying to finish a treaty with Peru.

Attempting to limit U.S. influence in Latin America, leftist Venezuelan President Hugo Chávez in 2006 proposed an opposing trading pact called the Bolivarian Alternative for the Americas (ALBA). While ALBA reduces trade barriers, the agreement focuses more explicitly on social welfare and justice than FTAA. As of 2007, only Cuba, Bolivia and Nicaragua had signed the treaty. Chávez, whose government has benefited from high oil prices, has also proposed a regional development bank for Latin America and the Caribbean to be called the Banco del Sur. While some countries welcome these alternative projects, others, such as Brazil and Mexico, have been lukewarm towards Chávez's regional economic plans.

*See also* **Central American Common Market (CACM); Organization of Central American States (ODECA).**

BIBLIOGRAPHY

Atkins, G. Pope. *Latin America in the International Political System*, 4th edition. New York: Westview Press, 1997.

Avery, William P. "The Politics of Crisis and Cooperation in the Andean Group." *Journal of Developing Areas* 17 (January 1983): 155–183.

Estevadeordal, Antoni, et al., eds. *Integrating the Americas: The FTAA and Beyond.* Cambridge, MA: David Rockefeller Center for Latin American Studies, Harvard University Press, 2004.

Garza Toledo, Enrique de la, and Carlos Salas, eds. *NAFTA y MERCOSUR: Procesos de apertura económica y trabajo.* Buenos Aires: Consejo Latinoamericano de Ciencias Sociales (CLACSO), 2003.

Krause, Walter, and F. John Mathis. *Latin America and Economic Integration.* Iowa City: University of Iowa Press, 1970.

McClelland, Donald H. *The Central American Common Market.* New York: Praeger, 1972.

Milenky, Edward S. *The Politics of Regional Organization in Latin America: The Latin American Free Trade Association.* New York: Praeger, 1973.

Porrata-Doria, Rafael A., Jr. *MERCOSUR: The Common Market of the Southern Cone.* Durham, NC: Carolina Academic Press, 2005.

Wionczek, Miguel S., ed. *Latin American Economic Integration.* New York: Frederick A. Praeger, 1966.

JAMES D. COCHRANE

**ECOPETROL.** Empresa Colombiana de Petróleos, Colombia's national oil company, was created in accordance with Law 165 of 1948. It has supervised the country's oil industry since the reversion of the De Mares concession—controlled for thirty years by a former subsidiary of Exxon, the Tropical Oil Company—to the national government on 25 August 1951. From its original base in Barrancabermeja (department of Santander), in the area of the concession, Ecopetrol has expanded its operations into the Llanos and Magdalena Valley. In contrast to the more familiar Latin American pattern, it has pursued its goal of oil development through a policy of close cooperation with foreign oil companies and multinational corporations, as illustrated by its entering into "association" contracts with several of the latter in the 1980s. In 2003 the state reorganized Ecopetrol into a public stock company. Ecopetrol no longer administers national oil policy; instead, the Colombian government formed the National Hydrocarbons Agency to regulate energy production and distribution.

*See also* **Energy.**

BIBLIOGRAPHY

Harvey Kline, *Colombia: Portrait of Unity and Diversity* (1983).

René De La Pedraja, *Energy Politics in Colombia* (1989).

### *Additional Bibliography*

Avellaneda C., Alfonso. *Petróleo, colonización y medio ambiente en Colombia: De la Tora a Cusiana.* Santafé de Bogotá: Ecoe Ediciones, 1998.

Bendeck Olivella, Jorge. *Ecopetrol, historia de una gran empresa.* Bogotá: Ediciones Punto Llano, 1993.

PAMELA MURRAY

## ECUADOR

*This entry includes the following articles:*



### CONQUEST THROUGH INDEPENDENCE

When the Spanish armies of Sebastián de Belalcázar invaded the north Andes in 1533, the region had already undergone fifty years of turmoil. The Inca Empire (Tawantinsuyu) had not incorporated the region's six independent indigenous chiefdoms until 1495, and the subsequent succession struggle between Atahualpa and Huascar had only prolonged the period of disorder.

#### THE ERA OF CONQUEST

The Spanish overthrow of the Inca state brought additional problems, as the distribution of Native American towns as grants of *encomienda* precipitated squabbles among the conquistadores that developed into civil strife. In 1534 the Spanish leader Francisco Pizarro tried to consolidate political control by establishing for the region a governorship that extended from Popayán in the north to Loja in the south, and from the eastern cordillera of the Andes to the Pacific. Nevertheless, the persistent civil wars among the conquistadores prolonged the political turmoil in the region until 1563, when the crown formed in the city of Quito an *audiencia* (high court) that had jurisdiction over the old governorship, the northwestern province of Atacames, and the eastern provinces of Quijos, Macas, Mainas, and Jaén de Bracamoros. After consolidating their political power, the

**Ecuadorian from Quito,** detail from ***Warriors of the Esmeraldas,*** 1599 (oil on canvas) by Adrian Sanchez Galque (fl. 16th century), one of the earliest known surviving paintings from this region. MUSEO DE AMERICA, MADRID, SPAIN/ THE BRIDGEMAN ART LIBRARY

Spaniards began laying the foundations of a stable society and a colonial economy based on the production of woolen textiles.

By the late sixteenth century, the *audiencia* district of Quito was linked to a prosperous, integrated network of regional economies extending throughout the Viceroyalty of Peru. While silver mining formed the link between Spain's Andean colonies and the international economy, numerous smaller regional markets evolved to supply foodstuffs, textiles, labor, and alcoholic beverages for the burgeoning mining zones. Quito's textile economy occupied a central place in these emerging secondary regional markets. Local elites used the fertile lands in the narrow Andean valleys and the extensive stretches of *páramo* pasturelands to establish an extensive network of *obrajes* (textile mills) in the provinces from Otavalo in the north to Riobamba in the south. These mills supplied woolens to markets in Peru and New Granada (Colombia) in return for specie, which the Spanish elite used to purchase the luxury goods needed to maintain a comfortable European lifestyle.

### THE ERA OF PROSPERITY: 1570–1690

The inability of Spanish textile manufacturers to supply the growing demand for cloth in the mining and urban centers of South America led to the founding of numerous *obrajes* in the *audiencia* of Quito. The rich agricultural and grazing lands in the Ecuadorian Andes, stocked with Spanish merino sheep, and the dense Native American population supplied the raw materials, foodstuffs, and labor to support the growing *obraje* sector. By the mid-seventeenth century more than 10,000 workers annually were producing 230,000 yards of the region's famous *paño azul* (blue cloth) and an additional 470,000 yards of *bayetas* and *jergas* (coarser woolens), fetching over 3 million pesos in the marketplaces of Peru and New Granada. Throughout the seventeenth century the woolen textile industry served as the foundation of the *audiencia's* economic prosperity.

***The Textile Boom.*** The first Spaniards to establish cloth manufactures were the region's *encomenderos,* who sought viable sources of income from the indigenous communities. Placer mining deposits were quickly exhausted, so the original European settlers began to found textile mills, called *obrajes de comunidad,* on their grants as money-making enterprises. The profits from the mills were used to pay the Native American communal tax levies, the salaries of the local priest and *corregidor* (magistrate), and an annual pension for the *encomendero.* Although legally owned by the indigenous Amerindian community, the *obraje* was, in reality, treated by the local Spanish *encomendero* as his own personal property. The mills grew into extremely large operations, often employing more than 200 laborers from the local Andean villages. By the early seventeenth century, the *encomenderos* had founded fourteen *obrajes de comunidad* scattered throughout the Ecuadorian highlands, and there were two additional mills in Otavalo owned directly by the crown.

The crown and the Audiencia of Quito issued numerous laws regulating the operation of the *obrajes de comunidad*—laws that ultimately undermined their profitability. To curb the local power of the *encomenderos,* the crown first began appointing special administrators to run the mills. When these officials too often proved corrupt and inept, the audiencia leased to local elites the right to run the *obrajes,* but this change provided no improvement. In addition, deducting the salaries of the local priest, magistrates, and workers drained the profits. The crown also set abnormally high tribute rates for the Andean villagers to encourage them to work in the *obrajes,* but these rates were so exorbitant that the mills seldom met more than half the communal tax assessment. As a result, the crown had sold these large and increasingly unprofitable mills to private owners by 1728.

From the early seventeenth century on, the most lucrative and productive *obrajes* were privately owned. The crown demanded that all *obrajeros* (mill owners) purchase a license, which gave them the right to operate their enterprises, recruit wage laborers, and in some cases to employ slaves or receive allotments of *mitayos* (corvée workers). The largest and most profitable *obrajes* tended to be located on rural estates, with medium and small-scale mills found on modest rural holdings or on the outskirts of towns. Entrepreneurs founded most of the mills in the provinces of Quito, Latacunga, and Riobamba, which possessed the fertile land and Amerindian laborers needed for the industry's growth. Early in the century the crown had licensed only 41 private mills, but by 1690 the number of legal operations had grown to more than 100—an indication of the profitability of the private cloth industry.

***Colonial Society.*** With the prosperity of the textile industry a small, tightly knit network of peninsular (European-born) and creole (American-born) families made substantial fortunes based on ownership of *obrajes* and land. The greater profitability of larger, integrated estate complexes organized around *obrajes* only concentrated more economic and social power in these elites. Some wealthy and powerful families even acquired noble titles and entails. Regardless of whether they secured titles, however, most consolidated their social position through intermarriage and alliances with powerful peninsular bureaucrats and nouveau riche merchants. By the late seventeenth century, important families—the Villacis, Sánchez de Orellana, Guerrero, Pérez Ubillus, Larrea, Maldonado, Monteserín, Ramírez de Arrelano, Galarza, Londoño—were related through a complex nexus of business and family connections, which they used to dominate the audiencia district.

Despite the devastating effects of European epidemic diseases, the Amerindian population of the north-central highlands began to expand during the seventeenth century. Most of this increase was apparently the result of migrations from adjacent frontier zones in the north and south. Highland communities had long sent colonists to those regions to gain access to their resources, and refugees from the Inca and Spanish conquests had also found havens there. These colonists and refugees evidently returned later to the north-central highlands to repopulate the Andean communities hard hit by epidemic diseases. After returning, these migrants formed the core of the labor force for the *obrajes* in the late sixteenth century, and their integration into the Spanish textile economy was a major reason for its success.

Despite their importance to the *obrajes,* the Native Americans suffered ongoing abuses in the mills. Wages remained low, and owners often paid their workers in overvalued cloth rather than in specie. Likewise, *socorros* (supplies) of foodstuffs were often inedible, overpriced, and distributed at *haciendas* several miles away. Workers were also beaten, forced to work long hours, and often bound to the *obrajes* through debt peonage. *Obrajeros* even coerced the wives and children of laborers into service in the mills. Amerindian laborers tolerated these abysmal working conditions only because their wages helped defray the heavy taxes levied on their village communities. For the Native Americans the prosperity of these sweatshops brought heavy burdens and few tangible benefits.

**ECONOMIC CRISIS AND CHANGE: 1690–1809**

By the 1690s, the prosperity of the woolen textile industry had begun to erode. A gradual decline of the mining economy in Peru and Bolivia lessened the demand for cloth in Lima, the most lucrative market for the *quiteños.* In addition, the growth of textile mills in closer proximity to the mines provided more competition amid the mining decline. By the 1690s, a number of droughts, earthquakes, and epidemics, which accounted for the death of nearly one-third of the Amerindian labor force in the *audiencia* district, ended the period of relatively cheap labor for mill owners.

***Decline of the Textile Industry.*** According to contemporaries, the crucial blow to the local textile economy came with the influx of cheap, high-quality European cloth, first brought by French traders during the War of the Spanish Succession (1700–1716). As the Spanish crown began liberalizing trade regulations after ending the system of Galeones and *flotas* in 1740, the importation of foreign cloth increased, which further restricted the market share available to Quito's *obrajes.* As a result, the prices for *quiteño* cloth fell dramatically, and the net output of the region's *obrajes* dropped by some 50 to 75 percent during the eighteenth century.

The rigid organizational structure of the textile business frustrated efforts by the *obrajeros* to compete with foreign imports. By licensing elite-run enterprises and providing the legal mechanisms to recruit laborers, the crown had created an oligopoly in the *audiencia* that nurtured selected producers. Most of the successful mill owners flourished in this protected environment by establishing family run enterprises that linked the clothing mills to food-producing estates and sheep ranches. Such rural estate complexes integrated the key elements of production in one enterprise, thus reducing the problem of cash outlays needed to pay for labor and raw materials. These textile mills, however, used no sophisticated machinery capable of lowering the unit cost of production, a principal advantage associated with modern factory production. Instead, the *obraje* absorbed many of the functions of the market, supplying the capital, labor, and raw materials needed for production.

This organizational structure had served mill owners well in the protected colonial markets of the sixteenth and seventeenth centuries, but it made it impossible for them to increase the quality of their cloth or to lower prices to compete with European imports. In short, by liberalizing trade policies and allowing the importation of relatively cheap European cloth, the crown effectively ended the oligopolistic arrangement responsible for the prosperity of Quito's mills.

The influx of European cloth drove the *quiteños* from the lucrative Lima market. Large mill owners in Quito had traditionally transported their higher-quality cloth to the viceregal capital, where they exchanged it for specie, Peruvian products, and European wares. The earnings from these transactions could be substantial, since the *obrajeros* controlled the sale of their own woolens and the importation of much European merchandise into the district. Although the northern trade to New Granada maintained greater vigor during the eighteenth century than earlier, it offered more modest profits. New Granada's merchant houses purchased mostly cheap, lower-quality cloth while also taking charge of introducing European goods into the *audiencia.* As a result, the loss of the Lima market curtailed the long-term profits of Quito's textile producers.

***The Results of the Decline in Textiles.*** The diminishing demand for local textiles from the 1690s onward prompted a slow agrarian decline in much of the north central highlands. Most agrarian enterprises there had organized the abundant land and labor resources in the rural zones to export textiles, not food or livestock. Geographical barriers and high transport costs limited the ability of most *hacendados* to change over from exporting textiles to selling their bulk crops in distant colonial markets. Attempts to find a suitable cash crop usually proved impracticable, and only the largest estates of the religious orders or the wealthy elites could muster the political clout and economic resources needed to profit from textile production.

The decline of the *obrajes* had negative repercussions also on regional commerce and state revenues. The sale of woolens had financed the importation of European luxury goods and provided the specie for domestic enterprise, regional trade, and the fiscal needs of the colonial state. As cloth exports declined, however, so too did imports, commerce, and government tax receipts. As a result, the decline in the textile sector prompted an overall economic recession, which in turn led to a marked shift in the socioeconomic structure of the *audiencia* of Quito.

***The Rise of the Southern Highlands.*** As the *obraje* economy in Quito declined, there emerged a prosperous cotton and woolen textile industry centered in the province of Cuenca. This industry was concentrated in the Amerindian villages of the south, where merchants from Lima organized a cottage, or putting-out, system of manufacturing. The merchants usually supplied the raw cotton and wool, while the villagers—many of them women—used traditional Andean methods of spinning and weaving to produce cheap, light cloth. The Andean villagers could supplement their income from agriculture by participating in this vibrant cottage industry. The Lima merchants then used their commercial connections to market these *tocuyos* or *lienzos* (cottons) and *bayetas* (woolens) at considerable profit in the cities and mining centers of northern Peru.

The Spanish agricultural economy of the southern highlands also experienced steady growth during the eighteenth century. The prosperity of most Spanish estates depended on the demand for agricultural products in local highland markets, Guayaquil, and northern Peru. Some Spanish landowners also prospered by selling abundant supplies of a local tree bark called *cascarilla,* which was rich in quinine. The Spanish landlords seldom participated in the cottage textile industry, but the trade in coarse cloth undoubtedly stimulated the local agrarian economy and promoted the introduction of European luxury items.

In the early nineteenth century, the textile business in the southern highlands began to decline. The diminished productivity of the Peruvian mines and the disruptions of the independence era led to a falloff in demand for southern Ecuadorian cloth. As a result, Lima's merchants began abandoning the industry, and textile exports dropped rapidly. The cottage industry system was simply too limited in scale and lacking in capital to survive without its merchant backers. The Amerindian villages suffered most from this decline. The Spanish estates, which were less directly connected to the local textile trade, continued to experience modest prosperity.

***The Coastal Export Boom.*** The export economy of the coast did not begin to prosper until the crown allowed free trade within the empire between 1778 and 1789. Along the extensive river system of the coastal plain, Spanish elites established increasing numbers of plantations to produce cacao for export to markets in South America, Mexico, and Europe. From the 1780s to 1810, cacao production increased nearly 300 percent. The fertile coastal soils also yielded copious amounts of tobacco, sugar, and hardwoods, but the cultivation and export of cacao became the economic core of the coastal economy until cacao exports began to decline markedly by the 1840s.

Large and medium-size plantations growing cacao developed rapidly in the late eighteenth century, particularly in the parishes of Baba, Babahoyo, Palenque, and Machala. Abundant rainfall, a hot climate, and cheap transportation along the river system in these zones contributed to the expansion of cacao cultivation. These cacao zones produced the only major export crop in the Audiencia of Quito capable of generating large amounts of hard currency in the colonial and international markets. By the nineteenth century, this export crop had finally begun to ease the specie shortage accompanying the decline of Ecuador's textile trades.

Although it was the cacao plantations that linked the productivity of the coast to the international economy, the outside merchant houses were often the ones to reap the largest profits from the export trade. The coastal planters lacked access to credit and did not have the commercial connections of the large mercantile companies based in Lima, Mexico City, and Spain. These outside merchant companies also profited from introducing European wares. The concentration of land in the hands of a small elite also guaranteed that only a very few *costeños* (coastal residents) would benefit from the export bonanza.

***Colonial Society.*** Although the elites of the north-central highlands remained powerful during the eighteenth century, the long-term decline of the textile industry undermined their economic position. Estates became ever more heavily encumbered, which prompted the elite to petition (successfully) to have the interest rate on all *censos* (loans and liens held by the church) lowered from 5 to 3 percent by 1755. Rural landowners also tried marketing foodstuffs and commodities such as *aguardiente* (cane liquor) to compensate for declining textile sales, with only limited success. By the late eighteenth century, only the largest estate complexes (owned by the clergy and the wealthiest elite families) had the scale, access to credit, and marketing connections to prosper.

A network of landowners and merchants came to dominate the socioeconomic life of the southern

***Distinguished Woman with Her Negro Slave***, 1783 (panel) by Vicente Alban (18th century). MUSEO DE AMERICA, MADRID, SPAIN/ INDEX/ THE BRIDGEMAN ART LIBRARY

highlands. Powerful families such as the Valdivieso, Veintimilla, Otando, Bermeo, Crespo, and Ochoa owned large estates and maintained their wealth and status through skillful business and marriage connections. This elite was active in the economic life of the province, buying and selling luxury imports, land, and urban properties throughout the late colonial period. Business and family ties also linked the powerful families of Cuenca and Loja to their counterparts in northern Peru and the coast. In fact, land ownership became a powerful asset after the commercial and industrial downturn by the early nineteenth century.

The rapidly expanding coastal economy allowed greater social mobility than could occur in the more established social hierarchies of the highlands. Within a short time, however, a few powerful families began consolidating their control over the best cacao lands. In the 1780s, for example, just five plantation owners accounted for more than 40 percent of the new cacao trees along the coast; and one man, Silvestre Gorostiza Villamar, planted more than 90,000 trees in Machala. Indeed, by the independence era, five landowners—Martín de Icaza, Domingo Santísteban, Josefa Pareja, Francisco Vitores, and General Juan José Flores—controlled over 25 percent of the total cacao production. These wealthy planters and the leading mercantile families made considerable fortunes and formed the new political elite along the coast during the late colonial and independence periods.

The decline of the *obraje* economy and the rising importance of the southern highlands and the coast had a profound effect on the Amerindian population. Many Andeans had already left their traditional ethnic communities to participate in the regional market economies, working in Spanish *obrajes* and *haciendas* and in the chief cities. By the eighteenth century, large numbers of Indians had migrated from the depressed provinces of the north-central highlands to regions of greater economic opportunity.

The first of these movements promoted the development of the southern highlands until the cottage textile industry declined by the early nineteenth century. The pattern of migration began shifting to the coast in the late eighteenth century and continued to attract large numbers of migrants until the export market for cacao declined by the 1840s. In short, the regional economic realignments during the late colonial period encouraged major demographic movements that reflected the diminished economic opportunities for Amerindians in the highlands.

***The Bourbon Reforms and Political Unrest.*** By the seventeenth century, Ecuadorian elites had gained considerable influence over local government—even over the Audiencia of Quito. This trend gained momentum only when the crown began selling appointments to important bureaucratic offices: the royal treasury in 1633, *corregimientos* (magistracies) in 1678, and *audiencia* judgeships in 1687. By the early eighteenth century, the institutions of royal government had a well-deserved reputation for representing local over imperial concerns.

This pattern of local control began to shift during the eighteenth century. The crown enacted policies permitting the influx of European cloth without consulting the Audiencia of Quito, which proved powerless to resist them. In addition, the metropolis began to impose stricter control over the local royal government by ending the sale of offices after 1750 and enforcing the more efficient collection of local taxes. In 1765, for example, the viceroy of New Granada, Pedro de Messía De La Cerda, transferred control over the sales tax and the *aguardiente* monopoly from local tax farmers to the royal treasury. When the audiencia proved unable to convince the crown's agents in Bogotá to reverse this unpopular measure, a popular revolt—supported by all social classes in the capital city—overthrew the royal government. In fact, a popular coalition ruled the city until internal dissension and the arrival of royal troops a year later ended the affair. The failure of this revolt left the citizenry deeply divided and pessimistic about their ability to influence important crown policies.

A decade after this turbulence, the Madrid government dispatched a special inspector-general, José García de León y Pizarro, as president-regent (a newly created office of presiding officer) of the Audiencia of Quito. García Pizarro was an influential protégé of the minister of the Indies, José de Gálvez, who implemented a far-reaching set of reforms aimed at increasing state power and raising taxes. The keystone of these reforms was the creation of a militia system and a new fiscal bureaucracy, which the president-regent controlled by appointing kin, friends, and a few loyal allies among the creole elite. García Pizarro then used this regalist state bureaucracy to raise unprecedented amounts of tax revenue. In the depressed north-central highlands, for example, state income rose from more than 860,000 pesos in the period 1775–1779 to nearly 2.5 million pesos in the next five years.

Despite these successes, prominent citizens charged that García Pizarro and his group had ruled despotically in Quito, intimidating the local aristocracy and the church, extorting bribes, selling public offices, and using the militia to enforce his corrupt designs. A long, acrimonious investigation, which continued until 1790, uncovered startling abuses by the bureaucracy, but the crown imposed no punishments. Most of García Pizarro's clan and allies were transferred, but taxes remained high and government abuses continued. Throughout the remainder of the colonial period, many among the elite remained discontented and disillusioned with the colonial government and the crown.

Discontent also spread to the Indian and mestizo populations as high taxes and the economic depression of the north-central highlands led to hardship in many communities. Periodic uprisings against escalating taxes, poor working conditions on Spanish estates and *obrajes,* and dishonest government officials broke out during the eighteenth century. Revolts in Otavalo (1777), Guano (La Matriz, 1778), Ambato (1780), Alausí (1781), Chambo (1790), and even the larger insurrections in Guamote and Columbe (1803) caused considerable loss of life and property, but they never spread like the great rebellions of Upper Peru in the 1780s.

In Ecuador the Spanish authorities always managed to combine brutal repression with judicious concessions to restore order.

## THE MOVE TO INDEPENDENCE: 1809–1830

A serious challenge to Spanish power occurred in 1809, after the abdications of Charles IV and Ferdinand VII, when *quiteño* elites formed a *junta* (provisional government) under the leadership of the marqués de Selva Alegre. Dissension within the *junta* and its failure to gain widespread popular support, however, led to its downfall within three months. In 1810, when royalist troops feared a new uprising, most of the rebel leaders were summarily executed in their jail cells. Popular outrage at this massacre prompted the establishment of another popular *junta* in 1810, which ruled until a new president, Toribio Montes, and a royal army extinguished the popular government two years later.

The defeat of these *juntas* in Quito discouraged any new movements for independence, until discontent in Guayaquil in 1820 led the coastal elites to rise. Like the Quito revolts, however, this movement did not spread beyond the coast, and formal independence for the entire audiencia district did not come until the insurgent armies of Antonio José de Sucre won the Battle of Pichincha in 1822. For the next eight years Ecuador remained a province of the independent republic of Gran Colombia (Colombia, Venezuela, and Ecuador). Finally, in 1830 Ecuador withdrew from that union to become an independent republic.

*See also* **Cacao Industry; Pizarro, Francisco; Quito, Audiencia (Presidency) of; Quito Revolt of 1765; Textile Industry: The Colonial Era.**

### BIBLIOGRAPHY

Although the number of historical studies on the Andes during the colonial period has increased dramatically, few have dealt specifically with Ecuador. The best work on bureaucratic politics remains John Leddy Phelan, *The Kingdom of Quito in the Seventeenth Century* (1967). For Native American rebellions see Segundo E. Moreno Yáñez, *Sublevaciones indígenas en la Audiencia de Quito: Desde comienzos del siglo XVIII hasta finales de la colonia,* 3d ed. (1985). Landholding among the clergy is treated in Nicholas P. Cushner, *Farm and Factory: The Jesuits and the Development of Agrarian Capitalism in Colonial Quito, 1600–1767* (1982). Two influential works on the export boom along the Ecuadorian coast are Michael T. Hamerly, *Historia social y económica de la antigua provincia de Guayaquil, 1763–1842,* 2d ed. (1973; 1987), and María Luisa Laviana Cuetos, *Guayaquil durante el siglo XVIII: Recursos naturales y desarrollo económico* (1987). Disease and population patterns are the subject of Suzanne Austin Alchon (née Browne), *Native Society and Disease in Colonial Ecuador* (1992). Some major articles on landholding patterns, the transfer of land from Andeans to Spaniards, and the early *obrajes* include Christiana Borchart De Moreno, "Composiciones de tierras en la Audiencia de Quito: El valle de Tumbaco a finales del siglo XVII," *Jahrbuch für Geschichte von Staat, Wirtschaft und Gesellschaft Lateinamerikas* 17 (1980): 121–155, and "La transferencia de la propiedad agraria indígena en el corregimiento de Quito hasta finales de siglo XVII," *Caravelle* 34 (1980): 5–19; Segundo E. Moreno Yáñez, "Traspaso de la propiedad agrícola indígena a la hacienda colonial: El caso de Saquisilí," *Jahrbuch für Geschichte von Staat, Wirtschaft und Gesellschaft Lateinamerikas* 17 (1980): 97–119; Javier Ortiz De La Tabla Ducasse, "El obraje colonial ecuatoriano: Aproximación a su estudio," *Revista de Indias* 149–150 (1977): 471–541. The best survey of the *obraje* economy is Robson Brines Tyrer's "The Demographic and Economic History of the Audiencia of Quito: Indian Population and the Textile Industry, 1600–1800" (Ph.D. diss., Univ. of California, Berkeley, 1976). A significant study of Amerindian migration is Karen M. Powers, "Indian Migration and Sociopolitical Change in the Audiencia of Quito (Ecuador)" (Ph.D. diss., New York Univ., 1990). Other important dissertations are Martin Minchom's "Urban Popular Society in Colonial Quito, c. 1700–1800" (Ph.D. diss., Univ. of Liverpool, 1984) and Rosemary D. F. Bromley's demographic work "Urban Growth and Decline in the Central Sierra of Ecuador" (Ph.D. diss., Univ. of Wales, 1977). Two fine published master's theses for the Facultad Latinoamérica de Ciencias Sociales (FLACSO) in Quito are Silvia Palomeque, *Cuenca del siglo XIX: La articulación de una region* (1990), and Galo Ramón Valarezo, *La resistencia andina: Cayambe, 1500–1800* (1987).

### *Additional Bibliography*

Andrien, Kenneth J. *The Kingdom of Quito, 1690–1830: The State and Regional Development.* New York: Cambridge University Press, 1995.

Caillavet, Chantal. *Etnias del norte: Etnohistoria e historia de Ecuador.* Madrid: Casa de Velázquez; Lima: IFEA; Quito; Abya Yala, 2000.

Chaves, María Eugenia. "Honor y libertad: Discursos y recursos en la estrategia de libertad de una mujer esclava (Guayaquil a fines del período colonial)." Ph.D. diss., Universidad de Gotemburgo, 2001.

Gauderman, Kimberly. *Women's Lives in Colonial Quito: Gender, Law, and Economy in Spanish America.* Austin: University of Texas Press, 2003.

Jamieson, Ross W. *Domestic Architecture and Power: The Historical Archaeology of Colonial Ecuador.* New York: Kluwer Academic/Plenum Publishers, 2000.

Mena V., Claudio. *El Quito rebelde (1809–1812).* Quito: Abya-Ayala: LetraNueva, 1997.

Newson, Linda A. *Life and Death in Colonial Ecuador.* Norman: University of Oklahoma Press, 1995.

Powers, Karen Vieira. *Andean Journeys: Migration, Ethnogenesis, and the State in Colonial Quito.* Albuquerque: University of New Mexico Press, 1995.

Sevilla Larrea, Carmen. *Vida y muerte en Quito: Raíces del sujeto moderno en la colonia temprana.* Quito: Ediciones Abya-Yala, 2002.

KENNETH J. ANDRIEN

## SINCE 1830

Since independence, Ecuador has faced two fundamental obstacles to development: geographic fragmentation and limited natural resources. Geography, which has been a major barrier to national integration, fostered political, social, and economic division. Regionalism, the political expression of the division and isolation imposed by geography, has been a significant and enduring factor in Ecuadorian politics. The development of divergent economic and social systems on the coast and in the sierra (highlands) resulted in antagonistic political attitudes and interests.

The demise of Spanish authority and the creation of Ecuador in 1830 plunged the country into a crisis of legitimacy. The ruling elite failed to reach a consensus that would have allowed them to resolve their conflicts amicably. To curb the tendencies toward fragmentation, strong national leaders resorted to force to maintain power. From 1830 to 2007 only twenty-one presidents completed their constitutional terms of office. There have been only three periods (1921–1925, 1948–1961, and 1979–1997) when several presidents were elected, completed their terms, and transferred power to other elected chief executives. Ecuador is an extreme example of the crisis that engulfed most of Spanish America in the post-independence period.

### CHARACTERISTICS OF ECUADORIAN POLITICS

Historically, a small elite has dominated effective political participation in Ecuador. Large landowners, wealthy businessmen, professionals, and high-ranking military men were the principal power contenders in the nineteenth century. Despite the trend toward greater political participation that emerged in the twentieth century, the elite continue to dominate Ecuadorian politics. Literacy requirements denied the vote to large segments of the population until 1979. As the nineteenth century progressed, ideologies grew in importance in national and regional politics. Whereas the coast became the home of liberalism, the highlands were the stronghold of conservatism. However, the development of political parties dedicated to implementing these competing world views had little effect on the manner in which national leaders governed. Both liberals and conservatives responded in similar ways to the challenges of ruling a divided country. The characteristic features of Ecuadorian politics—regionalism, authoritarianism, militarism, and personalism—provide coherence and continuity to the nation's chaotic political history.

From the time of Ecuador's independence, regionalists struggled to receive adequate representation in national government, to obtain a significant share of national revenues for their areas, and to maintain local autonomy. During the nineteenth century Ecuador endured four civil wars that threatened to dismember the country. Although Ecuador was, in theory, a constitutional republic, force became the accepted method of transferring or retaining power. All eleven constitutions promulgated during the period provided for elected officials. Political reality, however, was quite different. Elections were generally held not to select a president but to ratify or legalize the power of a person who gained office through force. In such cases, elections were usually preceded by the writing of a new constitution. In other instances, the government controlled elections to ensure the victory of its official candidate. In either situation, disappointed presidential contenders often violently challenged the outcome.

The use of force was not limited to politicians: Generals Juan José Flores (1830–1834, 1839–1845), José María Urvina (1851–1856), Francisco Robles (1856–1859), and Ignacio Veintimilla (1876–1883) relied on armed might either to bring them to power or to help them retain it, as did the leading civilian politicians. The two great nineteenth-century statesmen Vicente Rocafuerte (1835–1839) and Gabriel García Moreno (1861–1865, 1869–1875) achieved power through armed conflict and then relied on force to remain in office.

A pattern of authoritarian politics developed in Ecuador. Liberals, conservatives, and opportunists relied on controlled elections, press censorship, and extralegal coercion to limit the opposition. A close relationship between authoritarianism and militarism emerged. The willingness of many groups to use force to attain political goals meant that national leaders, whether civil or military, had to rely on the army for support. The system favored strong and ruthless chief executives, whether civilian or military. The pressures of war, economic decline, and political instability led to the rise of powerful individuals who could circumvent legal structures. Individual leaders, rather than political parties or institutions, governed the country. The failure to develop strong political institutions meant that men, rather than ideas or abstract political principles, shaped political movements. Individuals with strong personalities and political ambition took control of existing political parties or formed their own organizations.

**Ecuador**

| | |
|---|---|
| **Population:** | 13,755,680 (2007 est.) |
| **Area:** | 109,483 sq mi |
| **Official language:** | Spanish |
| **Languages:** | Spanish, Quecha, other Amerindian languages |
| **National currency:** | Ecuador has no national currency; the U.S. dollar is used. |
| **Principal religions:** | Roman Catholic, 95% |
| **Ethnicity:** | mestizo (mixed Amerindian and white) 65%, Amerindian 25%, Spanish and others 7%, black 3% |
| **Capital:** | Quito (est. pop. 1,451,000 in 2005) |
| **Other urban centers:** | Cuenca, Guayaquil, Machala, Portoviejo |
| **Annual rainfall:** | 50 inches at Quito, 97 inches along the northern coast, 200 inches in the east, little rain in the south |
| **Principal geographical features:** | *Mountains:* The Andes Mts. run north to south through the center of the country, with two principal ranges, Cordillera Occidental and Cordillera Central. Between them is the Callejeón Interandino, a series of elevated basins and plateaus. Chimborazo (20,561 ft) is the highest peak, and Cotopaxi (19,344 ft) is one of the world's tallest active volcanoes.<br>*Rivers:* Daule, Esmeraldas, Guayas, Napo, Pastaza, Putumayo<br>*Islands:* Galápagos, Puná |
| **Economy:** | *GDP per capita:* $4,500 (2006 est.) |
| **Principal products and exports:** | *Agricultural:* balsa wood, bananas, cocoa, coffee, flowers, tuna, shrimp<br>*Manufacturing:* chemicals, food processing, refining, textiles<br>*Mining:* petroleum |
| **Government:** | Independence from Spain, 1822. Constitution, 1998. Republic. The president is elected by popular vote to a 4-year term and is both chief of state and head of government. The legislature is a unicameral National Congress, whose 100 members are elected through a party-list proportional representation system to 4-year terms. Cabinet appointed by the president. 22 provinces. |
| **Armed forces:** | *Army:* 50,000<br>*Navy:* 5,500<br>*Air force:* 4,000<br>*Paramilitary:* 270 Coast Guard<br>*Reserves:* 118,000 |
| **Transportation:** | *Rail:* 600 mi<br>*Ports:* Esmeraldas, Guayaquil, La Libertad, Manta, Puerto Bolivar<br>*Roads:* 4,018 mi paved; 22,823 unpaved<br>*National airline:* Ecuatoriana de Aviación<br>*Airports:* 104 paved runway and 302 unpaved runway airports, international airports in Quito and Guayaquil, 1 heliport |
| **Media:** | Leading newspapers include *El Comercio, El Extra, El Universo,* and *Hoy.* There are 392 AM and 35 FM radio stations, and 7 television station. Radio Nacional del Ecuador is a government-operated broadcaster. |
| **Literacy and education:** | *Total literacy rate:* 91% (2001)<br>Education for children ages 6 to 15 is compulsory and free. Major institutes of higher education include the Central University of Ecuador, National Polytechnical, and the Polytechnical School of the Littoral. |

During the twentieth century, groups such as the liberals, conservatives, socialists, and social democrats attempted to replace personalist politics by creating effective mechanisms for selecting candidates and developing programs. However, the traditional patterns of social and political relations retarded the formation of a modern political structure. The most enduring personalist movement in Ecuadorian politics, *velasquismo*, led by José María Velasco Ibarra, remained an important force into the 1970s. Although the movement's leader served as president on five different occasions (1934–1935, 1944–1947, 1952–1956, 1960–1961, 1968–1972), it failed to develop an institutional structure that could function in the absence of Velasco Ibarra.

## THE CACAO AGE

In the late nineteenth century expanding cacao exports provided Ecuador with its first period of sustained economic prosperity since the decline of sierra textile production in the colonial period. Cacao growers and exporters financed the successful liberal revolution of 1895, which shifted the balance of political power to the coast. The liberals, who retained power until 1925, used growing government revenues to form a secular, activist state. The liberal development program sought to remove obstacles to social and economic progress and to foster national development.

Although the liberals were successful in defeating the conservatives and fostering modernization

**Cacao plantation, Ecuador, c. 1900.** Increased demand for cacao on the world market at the turn of the twentieth century strengthened the Ecuadorian economy and introduced some stability to the country. By the late 1940s, bananas would replace cacao as Ecuador's primary source of revenue. © UNDERWOOD & UNDERWOOD/CORBIS

through an ambitious public works program, they were less successful in establishing a mechanism for the peaceful transfer of power. The liberal triumph did not herald a change in Ecuador's political culture. Personalism and regionalism remained crucial factors. The emergence of an activist state in Ecuador provided a new arena for regionalist struggles, while two men, Eloy Alfaro (1895–1901, 1906–1911) and Leonidas Plaza Gutiérrez (1901–1905, 1912–1916) dominated the first decades of liberal rule. Their rivalry was a major cause of the turbulence that lasted until 1916. The death of Alfaro in 1912 as the result of an abortive rebellion enabled Plaza to initiate the process of strengthening political institutions and to accomplish the peaceful transfer of power in the period between 1916 and 1924.

### THE 1920 TO THE 1940S

The combined effects of unsound liberal fiscal practices and the economic crisis resulting from a decline in the value and volume of cacao production ended the political stability established by Plaza. Because the government received the majority of its revenue from customs receipts, cacao exports were the primary determinant of government income. As the scope of government activity expanded after 1896 to meet the growing demands for material progress, liberal administrations relied on loans from Guayaquil banks to cover perennial budget deficits. The symbiotic relationship between successive liberal administrations and coastal banks angered sierra regionalists, who viewed the relationship as proof that coastal exporting interests controlled the country.

As the economy deteriorated, Quito journalists and politicians were increasingly vocal in their criticism of the "corrupt coastal banking oligarchy." A few of these critics courted young army officers, arguing that only the military could save the country from disaster by returning political control to the sierra. In July 1925 a group of these military officers overthrew the government. In the period 1925–1931, military-backed governments, acting on the advice of a team of foreign advisers led by Princeton economist Edwin W. Kemmerer, implemented a number of reforms that restructured the nation's banking and fiscal systems. A major objective of the reforms was to eliminate the budget deficits that had characterized liberal administration by centralizing tax collection and disbursement. Ecuadorians, however, found it easier to enact laws than to implement them. Many of the institutional and procedural changes proved incapable of maintaining fiscal integrity during a period of economic, social, and political stress.

The severe economic dislocations of the 1930s exacerbated Ecuador's perennial problems of insufficient government revenues and chronic political instability. President Isidro Ayora's ouster in 1931 ushered in the most turbulent period in the country's history. Between 1931 and 1948 nineteen men served as chief executive; none completed his term of office. The period witnessed the rise of populist politics and the loss of half of the national territory to Peru in 1941. Political stability would not be restored until the country entered a second period of economic expansion based on a new agricultural export, bananas.

**Protest, Quito, Ecuador, 1968.** Farmers protesting government actions in the late 1960s hold signs spelling out "revolution." Since declaring independence in 1809, Ecuador has been plagued by political instability, leading to frequent changes in government, often by force. © BETTMANN/CORBIS

### THE POSTWAR ERA

Banana exports underwrote a twelve-year period of political stability in which three presidents, Galo Plaza Lasso (1948–1952), José María Velasco Ibarra (1952–1956), and Camilo Ponce Enríquez (1956–1960), completed their constitutional terms. The export boom allowed expanded government investments in economic and social infrastructure and promoted population movement from the sierra to the coast. When the economy deteriorated in the 1960s, however, the weakness of the political system resurfaced; no president completed his term of office during the next decade, and for three years (1963–1966) the country was ruled by a military junta.

The 1970s were a period of rapid economic growth based on the export of petroleum, which fostered the emergence of a relatively autonomous state. From 1972 to 1979 Ecuador was governed by two moderate military juntas. Although these military governments, like their 1960s counterparts, sought to implement socioeconomic reforms, economic inequity and political underdevelopment continued to characterize Ecuador in the 1980s.

### RETURN TO CIVILIAN RULE

The return to civilian rule in 1979 with the inauguration of President Jaime Roldós Aguilera initiated a new state of Ecuadorian political development. Although Roldós was a member of Assad Bucaram's populist Concentration of Popular Forces (CFP), he and his running mate, Osvaldo Hurtado, represented a new generation of politicians who stressed programmatic rather than personalist concerns. They supported the modernization of the political system through the expansion of the electorate, issue-oriented campaigning, and the development of modern political parties.

Roldós and Hurtado proposed using petroleum revenues to promote national agricultural and industrial production through investment in economic and social infrastructure. Hydroelectric, transportation, and communication projects; agricultural credits; and rural education were priorities. In addition, the government proposed to improve tax collection, to promote national integration, and to expand the political and economic participation of the lower socioeconomic groups.

The ambitious reform program failed when Assad Bucaram withdrew his support and assumed leadership of the anti-Roldós congressional majority. Congress thwarted the efforts of the Roldós administration to contain deficit expenditures and to introduce a national development strategy, which included educational and agrarian reform. With the fall of petroleum prices in 1980 and a burgeoning public debt, the administration was forced to implement an austerity program and to abandon its efforts to introduce structural reforms. The worsening economic situation eroded public support for the government. Labor, the economic elite, and politicians on the right and left became increasingly strident in their criticism of the government.

In May 1981 Osvaldo Hurtado inherited a deteriorating economic and political situation when Jaime Roldós was killed in a plane crash. His administration faced a series of political and economic crises that threatened to provoke military intervention. Hurtado managed to preserve civilian rule by forming an unstable center-left coalition within Congress. With this uncertain support, the administration was unable to pass reform legislation, but did manage to restrain public spending. The energies of the executive branch were consumed in managing the country's finances, including renegotiating the foreign debt and maintaining fiscal austerity. The political costs of the austerity program were high, particularly in 1983, when the worsening economic crisis resulted in a sharp devaluation of the sucre (the national currency) and a burst of inflation. The economic decline had begun to moderate by the 1984 presidential campaign.

The campaign highlighted a central weakness of the Ecuadorian political system: highly factionalized politics that promoted unstable coalitions and personalism. Nine presidential candidates and seventeen political parties participated in the elections. In the first electoral round, Rodrigo Borja Cevallos, founder of the center-left Democratic Left Party (ID), barely beat the right-wing Social Christian León Febres-Cordero. However, in the runoff, populist appeals and regional rather than ideological factors determined the outcome: Febres-Cordero edged out Borja.

The election of Febres-Cordero was less a reflection of the general appeal of the coalition of right-wing parties that endorsed his candidacy than a protest vote against the economic problems that crippled the Roldós and Hurtado administrations. Febres-Cordero took office with a Congress controlled by the opposition. Of the thirteen parties represented in Congress, the four rightist parties elected sixteen of the seventy-one members of Congress. His free market, neoliberal economic program, which failed to control inflation or end the nation's economic recession, sparked an upsurge in political confrontation and violence, including abortive coup attempts and clashes between students, labor, and the government. The situation was exacerbated by declines in the price of petroleum and disruptions in exports when an earthquake in 1987 damaged the trans-Amazonian pipeline. A series of confrontations between Febres-Cordero and Congress led to the censoring of a number of administrative officials for corruption and abuse of civil rights. Economic uncertainty fueled capital flight and the depreciation of the sucre.

The 1988 presidential election was won by Rodrigo Borja, whose campaign called for a mixed economy, the rescheduling of the nation's foreign debt, and an end to the neoliberal economic program of Febres-Cordero. Borja's platform stressed reducing unemployment through public works projects and tax incentives to companies, increasing the minimum wage, promoting social welfare, and reforming public finances.

Unlike Roldós, Hurtado, and Febres-Cordero, Borja took office with significant congressional support: ID elected twenty-nine of the seventy-one deputies, and Borja had the support of other major parties. Despite this advantage, he faced a difficult economic situation, including a large public-sector deficit, high unemployment, unresolved foreign debt negotiations, and high inflation. During his first year in office he introduced mini-devaluations of the sucre; increased taxes, the minimum wage, and prices for electricity, gasoline, and basic foods; and imposed import restrictions. Although the program fell short of the requirements of the World Bank and International Monetary Fund, which included elimination of public subsidies, sharp cuts in public expenditures, the privatization of state enterprises, and the freezing of interest rates, the gradualist approach satisfied neither labor nor business. Borja's limited austerity policies had a high political cost, including strikes and the re-emergence of a highly fragmented political system.

In the 1990 congressional elections, the president's party lost sixteen of its thirty seats. None of the twelve parties represented in the legislature achieved a majority, returning Ecuador to government by unstable coalition. Labor unrest and confrontations between the legislature and the other branches of government, including impeachment proceedings against a number of Borja's ministers, increased in 1991.

Confrontations between Congress and the Borja administration continued in 1992 as politicians positioned themselves for the presidential elections. As in the 1980s, the 1992 campaign was dominated by bitter personal rivalries and a fragmented party system. Sixto

Durán-Ballén defeated Jaime Nebot Saadi in a runoff election. Durán-Ballén, a founder of the Social Christian Party (PSC) with Febres-Cordero, broke with the party when Jaime Nebot Saadi was selected to run for president in the 1992 elections. Nebot and his supporters formed the Republican Unity Party (PUR) as a vehicle to support his candidacy. Although Sixto Durán-Ballén won the election, his party secured only twelve seats in the seventy-seven- seat legislature.

The new government faced the difficult task of implementing tough austerity measures and structural economic reforms in a country with a highly inequitable distribution of income, where living standards had fallen steadily throughout the 1980s. Durán-Ballén's program, which included the privatization of state-owned industries, a sharp reduction in the public-sector payroll, and policies to stimulate foreign investment, threatened a number of important groups. Despite repeated efforts to establish and maintain coalitions with other parties, including the Social Christian Party, which held twenty legislative seats, the administration was unable to avoid the legislative gridlock and repeated votes of censure that have crippled Ecuadorian governments since 1979.

**THE CRISIS OF ECUADORIAN DEMOCRACY**

Former Guayaquil mayor Abdalá Bucaram (brother-in-law of Roldós and the nephew of Assad Bucaram) won the 1996 election, defeating Jaime Nebot, a Febres-Cordero protégé. Bucaram's election would open a new chapter in Ecuadorian politics, a time when widespread popular disaffection with government unwillingness or inability to retreat from neoliberal economic policies led to several serious blows to Ecuadorian democratization. During his campaign for the presidency, Abdalá Bucaram made a strong appeal to the Ecuadorian underclass by verbalizing a great contempt for the wealthy. In his speeches he sharply rejected neoliberalism, signing agreements with organized labor denouncing austerity measures and free market policies. Bucaram pledged to provide government subsidies for basic necessities, block further privatizations, and promote social programs. Nicknamed *el loco* (the crazy person), Bucaram's campaign appearances were noteworthy for their unconventional style.

Despite his campaign promises, in December 1996, four months after taking office, Abdalá Bucaram and his leading economic adviser, Domingo Cavallo, launched a neoliberal austerity program, radically reducing government subsidies and price controls. By January 1997 the cost of basic goods and services had risen dramatically, with the heaviest blows absorbed by the nearly two-thirds of the nation that lived in poverty. Angry protests followed, and by early 1997 Abdalá Bucaram's approval rating plummeted. Three former presidents, Febres-Cordero, Hurtado, and Borja, called for Abdalá Bucaram to resign. Massive anti-Abdalá Bucaram marches occurred daily, as protesters rallied in opposition to his neoliberal economic policies, his often outrageous personal conduct, and widespread allegations of government corruption. A nationwide general strike began on February 5, 1997, with two million people demanding Abdalá Bucaram's resignation. In response, Abdalá Bucaram announced a reduction in electricity and gas taxes and hinted at suspension of neoliberal austerity measures. Nevertheless, opposition forces in Congress voted February 6, 1997, to remove Abdalá Bucaram on the grounds of mental incapacity.

During the crisis, the Confederation of Indigenous Nationalities of Ecuador (CONAIE) emerged as a key political actor. The CONAIE had formed in 1986 when indigenous peoples came together in the first truly national Indian organization in Ecuador. In June 1990 CONAIE organized a mass *levantamiento* (uprising) calling for recognition of Indians rights and demanding social programs from government. In what became the CONAIE's signature protest tactic, Indians set up roadblocks on the Pan-American Highway, cutting down trees and setting tires on fire to block the nation's sole commercial artery. CONAIE roadblocks in February 1997 played a critical role in forcing Bucaram from office.

After Abdalá Bucaram's removal, Congress named legislative chief Fabián Alarcón as interim president, refusing to appoint then vice president Rosalía Arteaga. Arteaga objected, asserting that her power was being usurped because she was a woman. Later that year voters approved a plebiscite calling for a new constitution, Ecuador's eighteenth. Alarcón served as Ecuador's interim president until 1998 when elections were held under the new constitution. Former Quito mayor Jamil Mahuad took office (1998–2000), defeating right-wing candidate Álvaro Noboa.

Mahuad's administration was immediately beset by intractable problems. The economy floundered,

**President Rafael Correa in May Day parade, 2007.** An economist and outspoken critic of U.S. economic policy, Correa exemplified Latin America's shift toward the left since the late 1990s. RODRIGO BUENDIA/AFP/GETTY IMAGES

burdened by heavy foreign debt and the vast damage caused by the arrival of El Niño in 1998. In response Mahuad adopted deeply unpopular austerity measures. As the crises deepened, more than a third of Ecuadorian banks failed. In 1999 Mahuad froze all bank accounts for a year, and when they were finally reopened, rampaging inflation had dramatically reduced the value of deposits. Leading bankers fled the country with bank assets in tow, including significant funds from a $6 billion government bailout. When news broke of an illegal $3.1 million donation to Mahuad's 1998 election campaign by Banco del Progreso owner Fernando Aspiazu, citizens were enraged. Mahuad could give no accounting of the money. By January 2000 Mahuad's approval had fallen to single digits. In a hastily designed, last ditch effort to staunch inflation and save his rapidly collapsing presidency, Mahuad dollarized the Ecuadorian economy, adopting the United States dollar as Ecuador's national currency.

Mahuad was forced out of office on January 21, 2000, in a movement led by Colonel Lucio Gutiérrez; Carlos Solórzano, former chief of the high court; and CONAIE leader Antonio Vargas. The uprising brought together junior military officers who were outraged at Mahuad's apparent corruption, supported by mass protests organized by the CONAIE. Within hours of the overthrow, however, a counter-coup led by senior military officers turned the presidency over to Mahuad's vice president, Gustavo Noboa Bejarano (2000–2003).

In the 2003 elections, former coup leader Gutiérrez won the presidency, bolstered by the enthusiastic support of CONAIE's political party, Pachakutik. As a candidate Gutiérrez had angrily decried neoliberalism, but almost immediately upon assuming office he entered into a fresh agreement with the International Monetary Fund, launching a new round of austerity measures, raising gasoline prices and bus fares and freezing wages. Cabinet members from Pachakutik resigned in protest.

Like other Ecuadorian presidents, Gutiérrez enjoyed scant support in Congress, and by November 2004 the legislature had initiated impeachment proceedings against him, alleging misuse of campaign funds. In December Gutiérrez sought to neutralize political opposition in the Supreme Court, appointing all new judges. To gain support in Congress for this action, Gutiérrez reached a deal with the supporters of former president Abdalá Bucaram, dropping all charges against the former leader and permitting him to return to Ecuador. Following massive protests in early 2005, Congress voted on April 20 to remove Gutiérrez from office, naming vice president Alfredo Palacio (2005–2007) to complete the term.

Leftist university professor Rafael Correa won the 2006 presidential elections with a 57 percent to 43 percent victory over Álavaro Noboa, the richest man in Ecuador. Correa's victory was consistent with the broader trend in Latin American politics since the late 1990s, which has seen the emergence of leaders openly skeptical of the efficacy and fairness of neoliberal economic policies.

*See also* **Alfaro Delgado, José Eloy; Borja Cevallos, Rodrigo; Bucaram, Abdalá; Confederación de Nacionalidades Indígenas del Ecuador (CONAIE); Durán-Ballén, Sixto; Ecuador: Conquest Through Independence; Febres-Cordero Ribadeneyra, León; Flores, Juan José; García Moreno, Gabriel; Hurtado Larrea, Osvaldo; Plaza Gutiérrez, Leonidas; Plaza Lasso, Galo; Ponce Enríquez, Camilo; Robles, Francisco; Rocafuerte, Vicente; Roldós Aguilera, Jaime; Veintemilla, José Ignacio de; Velasco, José María; Velasco Ibarra, José María.**

BIBLIOGRAPHY

*Leading Overviews*

Corkill, David, and David Cubitt. *Ecuador: Fragile Democracy.* London: Latin America Bureau (Research and Action), 1988.

Hanratty, Dennis M., ed. *Ecuador: A Country Study*, 3rd edition. Washington, DC, Government Printing Office, 1991.

Hurtado, Osvaldo. *Political Power in Ecuador*, trans. Nick D. Mills, Jr. Albuquerque: University of New Mexico Press, 1980.

Quintero, Rafael, and Erika Silva. *Ecuador: Una nación en ciernes*, 3 vols. Quito: Abya-Yala, 1991.

Schodt, David W. *Ecuador: An Andean Enigma.* Boulder, CO: Westview Press, 1987.

*Focus Studies in Ecuadorian History*

Acosta, Alberto. *Breve historia económica del Ecuador.* Quito: Corporación Editora Nacional, 1995.

Conaghan, Catherine M. *Restructuring Domination: Industrialists and the State in Ecuador.* Pittsburgh, PA: University of Pittsburgh Press, 1988.

de la Torre, Carlos. *Populist Seduction in Latin America: The Ecuadorian Experience.* Athens: Ohio University Center for International Studies, 2000.

Gerlach, Allen. *Indians, Oil, and Politics: A Recent History of Ecuador.* Wilmington, DE: Scholarly Resources, 2003.

Hey, Jeanne A. K. *Theories of Dependent Foreign Policy and the Case of Ecuador in the 1980s.* Athens: Ohio University Center for International Studies, 1995.

Isaacs, Anita. *Military Rule and Transition in Ecuador, 1972–1992.* Pittsburgh, PA: University of Pittsburgh Press, 1993.

Martz, John D. *Politics and Petroleum in Ecuador.* New Brunswick, NJ: Transaction, 1987.

Pineo, Ronn. *Ecuador and the United States: Useful Strangers.* Athens: University of Georgia Press, 2007.

Pineo, Ronn. *Social and Economic Reform in Ecuador: Life and Work in Guayaquil.* Gainesville: University Press of Florida, 1996.

Roberts, Lois J. *El Ecuador en la época cacaotera: Respuestas locales al auge y colapso en el siglo monoexportador.* Quito: Universidad Central del Ecuador, Editorial Universitaria, 1980.

Roberts, Lois J. *The Lebanese Immigrants in Ecuador: A History of Emerging Leadership.* Boulder, CO: Westview Press, 2000.

Rodríguez, Linda Alexander. *The Search for Public Policy: Regional Politics and Government Finances in Ecuador, 1830–1940.* Berkeley: University of California Press, 1985.

Spindler, Frank MacDonald. *Nineteenth Century Ecuador: A Historical Introduction.* Fairfax, VA: George Mason University Press, 1987.

Van Aken, Mark J. *King of the Night: Juan José Flores and Ecuador, 1824–1864.* Berkeley: University of California Press, 1989.

LINDA ALEXANDER RODRÍGUEZ
RONN PINEO

**ECUADOR, CONSTITUTIONS.** Ecuador's constitution of the early twenty-first century was adopted by popular vote on 15 January 1978 (43 percent yes; 32 percent no; 23 percent spoiled ballots) and went into effect in August 1979. It is the nation's seventeenth since Ecuador became independent in 1830, but few have touched the lives of most of the population. The impact on the political process has been greater, however, as institutional rules and procedures have been altered through the years.

The 1830 charter, which brought together the departments of Quito, Guayaquil, and Cuenca in a confederation, was replaced five years later by a more centralized constitutional system. This, in turn, was supplanted in 1843 by the "Charter of Slavery" imposed by Juan José Flores, who, having begun his second term as president in 1839, sought to enshrine his personalist rule through a constitution that granted him dictatorial powers while stressing separation of church and state. It was replaced following his ouster from power in 1845, and in 1861 another constitution provided for direct popular suffrage and recognized Catholicism as the state religion. Eight years later Gabriel García Moreno decreed a new document, known as the "Black Charter," which further enhanced the role of the Roman Catholic Church by giving it unchallenged control over education. The secular authority of the Church was underlined by the requirement that citizenship be denied to non-Catholics.

The Constitution of 1897, adopted after Eloy Alfaro led the Liberals to power, reversed the position of Catholicism and broadened the recognition of individual rights; the death penalty was abolished and religious freedom was made explicit. In 1906 Alfaro convened a Constituent Assembly to draft a new document that explicitly called for separation of church and state while extending the constitutional commitment to the protection of basic civil rights and privileges.

Women acquired the right to vote in the Constitution of 1929—the first such action in Latin America. It was also a document that, in reaction against presidential excesses, provided Congress with powers that virtually crippled the central government. Any minister could be dismissed through a vote of no confidence, and presidential authority was severely restricted. Reorganization of Congress included the establishment of both regional and functional representation. Thus there were, among others, senators for industry and for agriculture from both the coast and the highlands. Representatives of labor and of the armed forces were also included. Overall, traditional elites benefited from the introduction of functional senators chosen by leaders of Ecuador's major interest associations.

Ecuador's fourteenth and fifteenth constitutions were promulgated in 1945 and 1946, at a time when José María Velasco Ibarra had returned to power and was seeking to legitimize and restructure the nature of executive rule. The second of these survived until the convening of a Constituent Assembly in 1966 following the resignation of a military junta. It resulted in the sixteenth constitution, promulgated on 25 May 1967, which took effect upon the inauguration of Velasco Ibarra to his fifth term on 1 September 1968. It created a large number of new autonomous state agencies outside the budgetary and administrative control of the chief executive; regional interests were also strengthened at the expense of the central government through a decentralized system of disbursing taxes. When Velasco was forced out of office in 1972, the 1967 constitution was set aside.

When the military junta decided in 1976 to move toward the reestablishment of elected government, it named a commission to study the question of constitutional forms. The commission eventually drew up two choices for submission to a plebiscite: a revision of the 1945 constitution and a new charter. The second was chosen by nearly 75 percent of the electorate and, with minor adjustments, has been in effect since the re-inauguration of civilian government in August 1979. Perhaps the most striking change was the extension of suffrage to illiterates for the first time. In addition, the bicameral legislature became a unicameral body from which functional representatives were excluded. Four economic sectors were specified: public, private, mixed public-private, and communitarian. There was controversy over the communitarian, which was viewed by traditional elites as a threat to private property. In practice this would prove to be a misplaced concern.

New electoral regulations accompanying the 1978 Constitution introduced a double round of presidential elections, so that the eventual victor would enter office with a clear majority. There were also efforts to regulate political parties in order to minimize the degree of fragmentation which had long been prevalent. Among other things, parties failing to poll 5 percent of the vote in two consecutive elections would lose official recognition by the Supreme Electoral Tribunal.

The new constitution was viewed as a reflection of the reformist mood which gripped Ecuador in the 1970s, underlined by the emergence of a new generation of political leaders to replace Velasco, Camilo Ponce Enríquez, Galo Plaza Lasso, Otto Arosemena Gómez, and Carlos Julio Arosemena Godoy. In practice it has encouraged popular electoral participation and some opening of the system, but not to such an extent that traditional elitist attitudes and interests have been threatened. While there have been three successive constitutional periods since the armed forces relinquished power, each has been plagued by instability, intransigent opposition, congressional obstructionism, and judicial timidity in the face of partisan attacks. Thus the constitutional structures, while more consistent with a modernizing nation, have not significantly encouraged a maturation of the political process in Ecuador. In 1997, when Congress voted Abdalá Bucaram, then president, out of office, the political leaders formed a new constitutional assembly. The new constitution became law in 1998. It generally strengthened the executive branch, reduced congressional power to remove cabinet-level officials, and abolished the congressional mid-term elections.

*See also* **Alfaro Delgado, José Eloy; Bucaram Elmhalin, Asaad; Ecuador: Since 1830; Flores, Juan José; García Moreno, Gabriel; Velasco Alvarado, Juan.**

BIBLIOGRAPHY

George I. Blanksten, *Ecuador: Constitutions and Caudillos* (1951).

Albert William Bork and Georg Maier, *Historical Dictionary of Ecuador* (1975).

Howard Handelman and Thomas G. Sanders, eds., *Military Government and the Movement Toward Democracy in South America* (1981).

Osvaldo Hurtado, *Political Power in Ecuador,* translated by Nick D. Mills, Jr. (1980).

John D. Martz, *The Politics of Petroleum in Ecuador* (1987).

David W. Schodt, *Ecuador, an Andean Enigma* (1987).

*Additional Bibliography*

Echeverría, Julio. *El desafío constitucional: Crisis institucional y proceso político en el Ecuador.* Quito, Ecuador: Ediciones AbyaYala, 2006.

JOHN D. MARTZ

**ECUADOR, GEOGRAPHY.** Ecuador's borders have been in doubt during most of the nation's existence. When it seceded from Gran Colombia in 1830, the new nation claimed 282,972 square miles. Two years later with the incorporation of the Galápagos Islands the figure increased to 285,944 square miles. Colombia and Peru disputed Ecuador's claim to much of this territory, however. Border incidents became a frequent source of friction among the three nations. Ecuador and Colombia finally settled their boundary conflict in 1916; an agreement with Peru has proved more difficult to achieve.

Most of the area claimed by both Ecuador and Peru was in the Oriente, the lands east of the Andes. Ecuador failed to occupy the region effectively. In contrast, Peru advanced steadily into the disputed territory. By 1892 the southern republic had occupied 46,772 square miles of the contested area and claimed another 154,600 square miles. After two wars and decades of conflict, Ecuador and Peru seemingly agreed to a firm border in 1942 by signing the Protocol of Rio de Janeiro. The agreement reduced Ecuador to approximately 105,800 square miles. President José Maria Velasco Ibarra repudiated the accord in 1960, claiming that it had been imposed by force of arms. The issues remain unsettled and border clashes continue in the region.

The twin cordilleras of the Andes, which traverse the country from north to south, divide mainland Ecuador into three distinct geographic zones. These great mountain ranges include among their high peaks Mount Chimborazo (20,561 feet above sea level), Cotopaxi (19,347 feet), Cayambe (18,996 feet), and Antisana (18,228 feet). They partition the country into the Oriente, or eastern region, the Sierra, or highland region, and the Costa, or coastal region.

The Oriente contains approximately 46 percent of the national territory. It extends from the foothills of the eastern cordillera to the lower regions of the Amazon basin. Most of the area is a single floodplain covered with tropical woodlands and rain forest. This hot and humid region has a heavy annual rainfall that ranges from 71.4 inches in the south to 166.6 inches in the north. Median temperatures range from 73F to 80F. The Oriente has an excellent system of navigable rivers, but they flow southeastward, away from the heavily settled parts of Ecuador into Brazil and the Atlantic.

The Oriente is sparsely populated and, until recently, produced nothing of sufficient value to attract large-scale settlement or investment. Only since the

1960s with the discovery of petroleum has the region begun to enter the mainstream of national political and economic life. Previously the area did not command national attention unless a border dispute became the subject of intense diplomatic activity or exploded into open conflict. Since most of the Oriente's tiny population consisted of Indians with no political power, the national government could avoid committing its scarce development capital to the area. Even if sufficient capital had existed, the contemporary level of technology could not develop the area efficiently. The cost of exploiting the Oriente remained prohibitive, even after World War II, when scientific advances removed many barriers. Circumstances changed in the late 1960s because of the growing world demand for energy, dwindling petroleum reserves, and the rise of OPEC. At that time significant petroleum deposits were confirmed in the Oriente's Aguarico basin. The increase in the world market price of oil made the cost of developing the area acceptable. The Oriente is an important focus of national concern and government development policy. Petroleum resources comprise a sizeable portion of Ecuador's exports and the government's budget revenues.

The highlands, sandwiched between the Cordillera Occidental and the Cordillera Oriental, comprise about a quarter of the nation's territory. This central zone is divided into a series of narrow basins formed when lava flows linked the Andean ranges. The eleven basins between 7,029 feet and 9,075 feet—Tulcán, Ibarra, Quito, Ambato, Riobamba, Alausí, Canar, Cuenca, Jubones, Loja, and Macará—are isolated from each other as the sierra is from the Oriente or from the coast. Each basin varies from mountainous to slightly rolling terrain and, in most, there are deep valleys cut by streams. The rivers that drain the region are not navigable in the highlands. All the basins are densely populated, with most of the land exploited either for subsistence agriculture or for livestock.

Temperatures range from below freezing above the permanent snow line (about 16,689 feet) to a pleasant 71F in the subtropical valley. Sierra agriculture varies with altitude. Most basins contain four climatic zones. The *páramos,* a barren windswept region above 10,065 feet, are used for pasture and to grow potatoes and other native tubers. The *altiplano,* which lies between 8,052 feet, and 10,065 feet, is suitable for grain cultivation and pasture. The growing season, however, is short and frequent frosts endanger even hearty crops. Annual rainfall in the *páramos* and the *altiplano* is about 40 inches. The temperate valley, at elevations from 6,039 feet to 8,052 feet, is devoted to a variety of temperature crops. The average yearly rainfall of 20 inches is supplemented by the runoff from higher altitudes. Located at elevations between 3,018 feet and 6,039 feet are tropical valleys that produce vegetables, cotton, sugarcane, citrus fruits, as well as the highland staples: potatoes and grains.

The productivity of the sierra varies. Centuries of continuous cultivation by primitive methods have eroded and depleted soils. The fertility of the Ambato and Riobamba basins suffers because the soil is of recent volcanic origin and does not retain moisture. In contrast, the Cuenca basin, with ample rainfall and one of the least porous soils in the highlands, enjoys much greater agricultural potential. Slightly less favorable conditions exist in Quito; the rolling hills in the southern part of the basin are the site of extensive grain cultivation and livestock raising.

The coastal, or littoral, region of Ecuador encompasses approximately 69,300 square miles of plain, hills, and Andean piedmont. It is bounded by the Pacific Ocean on the west and by the Andes on the east. About half of the region is a low alluvial plain known as the Guayas lowlands; it lies below 990 feet and varies in width from 19 to 111 miles. The littoral region also contains two hilly areas: the foothills of the Andes that rise to an altitude of 1,617 feet and the hilly region that extends west of Guayaquil to the coast and northward.

The natural vegetation of the coast reflects the decrease in rainfall from north to south. While there are two rainy seasons at the Colombian border, most of the littoral has a single rainy season that becomes shorter as it moves south. The rain forests of the north give way to semideciduous forest and tropical woodlands in the south. Along the Santa Elena peninsula and in the extreme south only xerophytic shrubs can survive without irrigation. In the east, however, the foothills of the Andes receive enough precipitation to support rain forest.

The littoral region is very productive. Coastal soils are generally fertile, well watered, with a temperature that averages between 73F and 77F. While a wide variety of fruits and vegetables are grown for local consumption, coastal agriculture is oriented primarily toward an export market. The Guayas lowlands, which extend north and southwest of Guayaquil, possess ideal conditions for tropical agriculture. Navigable rivers provide the region with access to the sea. As a result, the Guayas basin became the country's primary producer of agricultural exports including cacao, bananas, and coffee. Since these products constituted Ecuador's most important exports for most of the national period, the coast and its major port, Guayaquil, dominated the country's economy.

Across the country, Ecuador must contend with increasing deforestation, soil erosion, landslides, desertification, and the impact of prolonged droughts.

The Galápagos Islands, or the Archipiélago de Colón, are a group of volcanic islands about 600 miles due west of the mainland. The islands suffer from a scarcity of water, and consequently they are thinly populated and of little economic value. However, the wide variety of exotic fauna and flora that survives makes the Galápagos interesting to scientists and to tourists. The waters surrounding the archipelago are excellent fishing grounds, and in the 1980s fishing and related industries grew significantly.

*See also* **Agriculture; Altiplano; Andes; Galápagos Islands; Guayaquil; Oriente (Ecuador).**

BIBLIOGRAPHY

Lilo Linke, *Ecuador: Country of Contrasts,* 3d ed. (1960, reissued 1981).

### *Additional Bibliography*

Gerlach, Allen. *Indians, Oil, and Politics: A Recent History of Ecuador.* Wilmington, DE: Scholarly Resources, 2003.

Gómez E., Nelson. *Transformación del espacio nacional: Pasado y presente del Ecuador.* Quito: EDIGUIAS C., 1999.

Pearson, David, and Les Beletsky. *Ecuador and the Galápagos Islands.* Northampton, MA: Interlink Books, 2005.

Winckell, Alain. *Las condiciones del medio natural.* Quito: C.E.D.I.G., 1997.

Wunder, Sven. *The Economics of Deforestation: The Example of Ecuador.* New York: St. Martin's Press, 2000.

Linda A. Rodríguez

# ECUADOR, ORGANIZATIONS

*This entry includes the following articles:*

ECUADORIAN CONFEDERATION OF CLASS-BASED ORGANIZATIONS (CEDOC)
WORKERS CONFEDERATION OF ECUADOR (CTE)

## ECUADORIAN CONFEDERATION OF CLASS-BASED ORGANIZATIONS (CEDOC)

The Ecuadorian Confederation of Class-Based Organizations (Central Ecuadoriana de Organizaciones Clasistas—CEDOC) was founded in 1938 as a Catholic labor federation. It was originally called the Ecuadorian Confederation of Catholic Worker Organizations, It is the oldest labor federation in Ecuador. Conservative, sierra-based, and linked with the ruling elite, CEDOC favored employee-employer harmony under capitalism. CEDOC appealed to artisans who rejected the anticapitalist positions taken by the rival CTE (Confederation of Workers of Ecuador). CEDOC broke ties with the Catholic Church in 1955 and moved toward a philosophy of Christian humanism. By the 1970s CEDOC had evolved into a much less conservative organization. After 1971 CEDOC began to cooperate with the CTE in the United Workers Front (FUT).

BIBLIOGRAPHY

For a concise and highly perceptive summary, see Richard Lee Milk, "Ecuador," in *Latin American Labor Organizations,* edited by Gerald Michael Greenfield and Sheldon L. Maram (1987), pp. 289–305. See also Milk's 1977 Indiana University dissertation, "Growth and Development of Ecuador's Worker Organizations, 1895–1944," which provides an excellent general account of Ecuadorian labor. Patricio Ycaza, *Historia del movimiento obrero ecuatoriano,* 2d ed. (1984), also contains much worthwhile information.

### *Additional Bibliography*

Alexander, Robert Jackson, and Eldon M Parker. *A History of Organized Labor in Peru and Ecuador.* Westport, CT: Praeger, 2007.

Espinoza, Leonardo. *Historia del movimiento obrero ecuatoriano: proceso político y proceso sindical.* Cuenca: Instituto de Investigaciones Sociales de la Universidad de Cuenca, 1995.

Paz y Miño Cepeda, Juan J. *La C.E.D.O.C. en la historia del movimiento obrero ecuatoriano: 50 años de lucha, 1938-1988.* Quito: Editorial Voluntad, 1988.

Ronn F. Pineo

### WORKERS CONFEDERATION OF ECUADOR (CTE)

The Workers Confederation of Ecuador (Confederación de Trabajadores del Ecuador—CTE) is Ecuador's largest union federation. In 1944 elements of the radical labor movement reached an agreement with leading politician José María Velasco Ibarra: Labor supported Velasco's return to power and he permitted the legal founding of the CTE. The CTE organized principally coastal workers from the more advanced sectors of the economy. It frequently provided important support for populist and reform-oriented politicians. Led at different times by both socialists and communists, the CTE has historically been the most staunchly militant of Ecuador's labor federations. As a result, it has repeatedly been the target of vigorous government repression. The CTE has also often been harmed by bitter left-wing factional disputes. Prior to the 1970s, the CTE was usually openly hostile to its key rival labor federation, the generally more conservative Ecuadorian Confederation of Class-Based Organizations (CEDOC). Since 1971, however, the CTE and CEDOC have sometimes cooperated in the United Workers Front (FUT).

*See also* **Velasco Ibarra, José María.**

BIBLIOGRAPHY

For a concise and highly perceptive analytical summary, see Richard Lee Milk, "Ecuador," in *Latin American Labor Organizations*, edited by Gerald Michael Greenfield and Sheldon L. Maram (1987), pp. 289–305. See also Milk's 1977 Indiana University dissertation, "Growth and Development of Ecuador's Worker Organizations, 1895–1944," for an excellent general account of Ecuadorian labor. Patricio y Icaza, *Historia del movimiento obrero ecuatoriano*, 2d ed. (1984), also contains much worthwhile information. For the broader political economic context, see Osvaldo Hurtado, *Political Power in Ecuador*, translated by Nick D. Mills, Jr. (1985).

*Additional Bibliography*

Alexander, Robert Jackson, and Eldon M. Parker. *A History of Organized Labor in Peru and Ecuador.* Westport, CT: Praeger, 2007.

Espinoza, Leonardo. *Historia del movimiento obrero ecuatoriano: Proceso político y proceso sindical.* Cuenca: Instituto de Investigaciones Sociales de la Universidad de Cuenca, 1995.

Torre, Carlos de la. *Populist Seduction in Latin America: The Ecuadorian Experience.* Athens: Ohio University Center for International Studies, 2000.

RONN F. PINEO

**ECUADOR–PERU BOUNDARY DISPUTES.** From their foundation the nations of Ecuador and Peru have disputed the demarcation of their common border. The chief point of contention is control over 120,000 square miles of mostly uninhabited Amazon jungle between the Marañón–Amazon and the Putumayo rivers. The nations appeared to have settled the issue as early as December 1823 in the Mosquera–Galdiano Agreement, a document that reaffirmed the 1809 colonial boundary between the viceroyalties of Peru and New Granada. However, in 1827 Peru attacked Ecuador, then part of the nation of Gran Colombia. In 1829 Gran Colombia defeated Peru at the battle of Tarqui, and Peru signed the Treaty of Girón. In September 1829 the two nations agreed to the Treaty of Guayaquil, also known as the Larrea–Gual Treaty, which again designated the boundary as that of the former viceroyalties. The Pedemonte–Mosquera Protocol of August 1830, designed to implement the prior treaties, granted Ecuador access to the Amazon River.

In 1857 Ecuador attempted to retire its debt to Great Britain by issuing bonds for Amazonian territory still under dispute. Peru objected, and war followed. In the Treaty of Mapasingue (January 1860), victorious Peru secured considerable Ecuadorian concessions. However, the treaty was ratified by neither nation. In August 1887 the two nations signed the Espinoza–Bonifaz Arbitration Convention, calling for the intercession of the king of Spain; his decision was to be binding and without appeal. The García–Herrera Treaty of May 1890 divided the disputed zone in half. Again, however, neither nation ratified the treaty. Finally, in 1924 Peru and Ecuador signed a protocol naming the United States as arbiter, and in 1933 both nations formally requested that President Franklin D. Roosevelt intercede. In 1936 the two nations agreed to a protocol resolving the matter. However, the ensuing talks broke off in 1938.

It fell to military power, not diplomacy, to determine the boundary. Of the two nations, Ecuador's position has historically been weakened by its failure to establish a physical presence in the disputed area. Peru, on the other hand, has been more effective in settling the region. In 1935 Colombia ceded to Peru territory that Ecuador continued to claim. After Ecuadorian efforts to provoke an incident, in 1940 Peruvian troops massed along the southern border. Argentina,

Brazil, and the United States offered joint mediation, but border skirmishes flared in 1941 and rapidly escalated into a serious military engagement. Nevertheless, Ecuadorian president Carlos Alberto Arroyo Del Río maintained his troops in Quito, guarding his presidency against internal enemies. As a result, Ecuador was powerless to respond to Peru's July 1941 invasion of the rich, densely populated coastal province of El Oro. Ecuadorian forces lacked basic supplies; in all respects they were woefully unprepared for the conflict. Peru had an air force of 25 planes and troops numbering from 5,000 to 10,000; Ecuador had neither an air force nor anti-aircraft weapons, and its troops totaled only from 635 to 1,600.

Ecuador retreated headlong before the Peruvian advance. The civilian population of El Oro did almost nothing to oppose the invading army, and some 20,000 refugees streamed into Guayaquil. Ecuador suffered some 150 killed and wounded; Peru, about 400. Peru seized the province of El Oro and began to move on Guayaquil, Ecuador's most important port. As Peru bombed coastal towns and advanced, troops in Guayaquil designated as frontline reinforcements mutinied. Ecuador sought peace talks. Following negotiations, Ecuador and Peru agreed to a military pullback and in January 1942 signed the Rio Protocol. Both nations ratified the accord. During the discussions, the United States, Argentina, Brazil, and Chile—mediators and later guarantors of the agreement—were preoccupied with World War II. They made it plain to Ecuador that if it refused to sign, they would withdraw from the talks, leaving Ecuador to deal with the victorious and still menacing Peru. Ecuador surrendered two-thirds of the disputed Amazonian territory: some 80,000 square miles of uninhabited lands and an additional 5,000 square miles of settled territory. Ecuador also lost its outlet to the Amazon River. Still, if Ecuador had not signed, it stood to lose a great deal more. Following the agreement, Peru withdrew from El Oro.

In 1951 new problems arose when the discovery of the Cenepa River in the Amazon complicated the final demarcation of the border. In August 1960 populist Ecuadorian president José María Velasco Ibarra declared the Rio Protocol null and void and the Ecuadorian Supreme Court later followed suit. Ecuador has since continued to regard the settlement as invalid. Problems persisted along the frontier, with brief clashes in 1981 and 1995 leading to several deaths. In 1998 the United States, Brazil, Argentina, and Chile initiated an approach toward peaceful resolution of the conflict. On October 26, 1998, Peru and Ecuador signed an agreement that resolved their boundary disputes.

*See also* **Boundary Disputes: Overview; Gran Colombia; New Granada, Viceroyalty of; Peru: From the Conquest Through Independence; Zarumilla, Battle of.**

BIBLIOGRAPHY

For the most evenhanded treatment of this disputatious matter, see David Hartzler Zook, Jr., *Zarumilla–Marañón: The Ecuador–Peru Dispute* (1964). Brief overviews of the issues are in John D. Martz, *Ecuador: Conflicting Political Culture and the Quest for Progress* (1972); and George I. Blanksten, *Ecuador: Constitutions and Caudillos* (1964).

*Additional Bibliography*

Denegri Luna, Félix. *Perú y Ecuador: Apuntes para la historia de una frontera.* Lima: Bolsa de Valores de Lima, Instituto Riva-Agüero, Pontificia Universidad Católica del Perú, 1996.

Simmons, Beth A. *Territorial Disputes and Their Resolution: The Case of Ecuador and Peru.* Washington, DC: U.S. Institute of Peace, 1999.

Ronn F. Pineo

## ECUADOR, POLITICAL PARTIES

*This entry includes the following articles:*



### OVERVIEW

Political parties in Ecuador have been marginal actors in the democratic process. The first political parties, Conservative and Liberal (founded in 1885 and 1890, respectively), were formed around individual loyalties rather than ideological or programmatic affinities. For the first half of the twentieth century, the absence of strong political parties contributed to cycles of political instability in which an influential caudillo could be intermittently replaced by a military coup, a constitutional assembly, or a populist dictator.

A charismatic figure of this period, José María Velasco Ibarra, was elected president five times but completed only one of those terms. The idiosyncratic nature of his government alliances with the military, the business elites, the labor unions, and urban popular sectors, and his reluctance to organize a political party help explain his erratic trajectory, but his populist legacy profoundly shaped the political system. The formula of a charismatic caudillo appealing directly to the impoverished masses was repeated by parties such as Concentración de Fuerzas Populares (Concentration of Popular Forces, CFP) and its later counterpart, Roldosista Ecuatoriano (PRE). A new party following that same trajectory is Prian, institutional renewal party of national action. Other parties founded during the prosperous postwar era, such as Izquierda Democrática (Democratic Left, ID), Unión Demócrata Cristiana-Democracia Popular Christian Democratic Union-Popular Democracy (DP), and Partido Social Cristiano Social Christian Party (PSC), represented more ideological and programmatic policy options, but remained equally subject to strong individual leaders.

## THE DEMOCRATIC PERIOD

In the late 1970s and early 1980s, the strengthening of political parties became a key concern for the makers of a new constitution. With the goal of consolidating existing national parties and designing them to be less personality-based and more accountable to voters, political reformers established stricter criteria for party registration, required parties to nominate candidates nationwide, and established thresholds for eradicating parties with poor electoral performance. Other reforms were adopted to introduce midterm legislative elections and impose term limits.

In practice, these reforms did not produce the expected results, partly because of weaknesses in the institutional design itself, and partly because the reforms did not take into account the divisive influence of social, ethnic, and regional differences. For example, electoral rules encouraged the proliferation of political parties with loyal constituencies at the subnational level, while term limits and midterm elections promoted legislative amateurism and hindered accountability. Because of the inchoate nature of the party system—what Catherine Conaghan (1995) has called "floating politicians and floating voters"—the fate of political parties remained tightly linked to the whims of its charismatic leaders. Weak party institutionalization further hindered the prospects for democratic governance because minority presidents often relied on clienteles to assemble fickle legislative alliances.

By the late 1990s, the proliferation of government corruption scandals and a widespread economic crisis challenged the legitimacy and effectiveness of the party system. A constitutional assembly gathered in 1997 to explore new forms of participation, representation, and governance. Reforms adopted during this period included the abolition of term limits and midterm elections, the participation of independent candidates, and a personalized voting system that favored individual candidates over party organizations. The party system has also been shaped by the entry of the indigenous population into the formal political process. Since its first appearance in the 1996 general elections, Pachakutik has become one of the most successful ethnic parties in Latin America. Since 1996 its candidates have held several elected and appointed public posts, including cabinet positions and legislative seats in the National Congress and municipal governments; the party also supported the successful presidential bid of Lucio Gutierrez in 2002 and introduced important legislation on behalf of indigenous peoples in the 1998 constitution.

Another important change is the shift of party competition to the subnational arena. The introduction of legislation, such as the 1997 earmarking of 15 percent of government revenues for local governments, offered greater incentives for parties to become more accountable to their provincial constituencies. This shift also contributed to the consolidation of party competition along regional lines, with at least two parties (PRE and PSC) competing in the coastal region, and two (ID and Pachakutik) in the Andes and the Amazon. These parties remain influential players in the policy-making process, despite their lack of popularity and the rise of outsider candidates. Their success is partly explained by their ability to broker government alliances in exchange for targeted rewards for their constituents. But in the absence of payoffs for cooperation, parties have also contributed to the ousting of presidents in 1997, 2000, and 2005.

The 2006 election dramatically altered the party system in Ecuador. The legislative majority usually composed of traditional parties with strong regional representation was replaced by the presence of mass organizations led by charismatic outsiders. Such parties as the Sociedad Patriotica Party (PSP) and Prian effectively capitalized on voters' growing sentiment of frustration with poor government performance. Far from delivering on their promise of political renewal, this fragmentation of the party system was anticipated to extend the period of policy instability and democratic erosion in Ecuador.

*See also* **Ecuador-Peru Boundary Disputes; Velasco Ibarra, José María.**

BIBLIOGRAPHY

Conaghan, Catherine. "Politicians against Parties: Discord and Disconnection in Ecuador's Party System." In *Building Democratic Institutions: Party Systems in Latin America*, edited by Scott Mainwaring and Timothy R. Scully. Stanford, CA: Stanford University Press, 1995.

Hurtado, Osvaldo. *El poder político en el Ecuador*, 6th ed. Quito: Letraviva-Planeta, 1988. Translated by Nick D. Mills Jr. as *Political Power in Ecuador*. Boulder, CO: Westview, 1985.

Jones, Mark P., and Scott P. Mainwaring. "The Nationalization of Parties and Party Systems." *Party Politics* 9, no. 2 (2003): 139–166.

Mainwaring, Scott, and Timothy R. Scully. *Building Democratic Institutions: Party Systems in Latin America*. Stanford, CA: Stanford University Press, 1995.

Mejía Acosta, Andrés. *Gobernabilidad Democrática: Sistema electoral, partidos políticos y pugna de poderes en Ecuador (1978–1998)*. Quito: Fundación Konrad Adenauer, 2002.

Mejía Acosta, Andrés. "Ghost Coalitions: Informal Institutions and Economic Reform in Ecuador." In *Informal Institutions and Democracy: Lessons from Latin America*, edited by Gretchen Helmke and Steven Levitsky. Baltimore, MD: Johns Hopkins University Press, 2006.

Torre, Carlos de la. *Populist Seduction in Latin America: The Ecuadorian Experience*. Athens: Ohio University Center for International Studies, 2000.

Van Cott, Donna Lee. *Indigenous Peoples and Democracy in Latin America*. New York: St. Martin's Press, 1994.

Yashar, Deborah J. 2005. *Contesting Citizenship in Latin America: The Rise of Indigenous Movements and the Postliberal Challenge*. Cambridge, U.K., and New York: Cambridge University Press, 2005.

ANDRÉS MEJÍA ACOSTA

## CONCENTRATION OF POPULAR FORCES (CFP)

The Concentration of Popular Forces (Concentración de Fuerzas Populares—CFP) has been the leading populist political party of Ecuador since 1946. It generally favors an agenda of socioeconomic reform. Founder Carlos Guevara Moreno finished third in the presidential balloting in 1956. Asaad Bucaram Elmhalin (1921–1981), twice mayor of Guayaquil, followed as CFP leader. Bucaram was a leading presidential contender twice: in 1972, when the military canceled the elections; and in 1978, when the military disqualified him on the grounds that his parents were Lebanese. In 1978 Bucaram's nephew-in-law, Jaime Roldós Aguilera, took Bucaram's place, campaigning under the slogan,"Roldós to govern, Bucaram to power." Roldós led the CFP to victory over conservative Sixto Durán Ballén of the Social Christian Party (PSC) in the runoff election of 1979. Bucaram became leader of the National Chamber of Representatives, but soon broke with Roldós over the president's austerity program. Roldós left the CFP and formed a new party, the People, Change, and Democracy (PCD) in 1980. While not a member of the CFP, Bucaram's nephew, Abdalá Jaime Bucaram Ortiz, won the presidency in 1996. The congress accused him of corruption and in 1997 removed him from office.

*See also* **Bucaram Elmhalin, Asaad; Ecuador: Since 1830; Roldós Aguilera, Jaime.**

BIBLIOGRAPHY

For an excellent overview of modern Ecuadorian political economy, see David W. Schodt, *Ecuador: An Andean Enigma* (1987). For a focused treatment of the recent transition to elected government, see the analysis offered in Catherine M. Conaghan, *Restructuring Domination: Industrialists and the State in Ecuador* (1988). Amparo Menéndez-Carrión, *La conquista del voto en el Ecuador: De Velasco a Roldós* (1986), examines the party's popular basis of support. John D. Martz provides an insightful treatment of the Bucaram/Roldós feud in *Politics and Petroleum in Ecuador* (1987).

*Additional Bibliography*

Freidenberg, Flavia, and Manuel Alcántara Sáez. *Los dueños del poder: Los partidos políticos en Ecuador (1978–2000)*. Quito, Ecuador: Facultad Latinoamericana de Ciencias Sociales, 2001.

Mejía Acosta, Andrés. *Gobernabilidad democrática: Sistema electoral, partidos políticos y pugna de poderes en Ecuador (1978–1998)*. Quito, Ecuador: Fundación Konrad Adenauer, 2002.

O'Neill, Kathleen. *Decentralizing the State: Elections, Parties, and Local Power in the Andes*. Cambridge, UK: Cambridge University Press, 2005.

RONN F. PINEO

### CONSERVATIVE PARTY

One of Ecuador's two historic political parties, the Partido Conservador emerged informally in the 1860s during the dictatorship of Gabriel García Moreno and was officially founded in 1883. Consistent with the tenets of García Moreno, the party staked out a position as the unyielding champion of Catholic Church interests, as well as of public education and many other secular matters. Advocates of a strong central government, the Conservatives remained influential during the long period of Liberal hegemony (1895–1944).

Traditionally the vehicle for the political expression of conservative interests in general and of highland landowners' interests in particular, the party enjoyed renewed influence during the 1956–1960 presidency of Camilo Ponce Enríquez. It then began to decline, and was notably weakened by introduction of universal suffrage in 1978. Even before then, however, its progressive wing had split off in 1964 to form Democracia Popular (Popular Democracy—DP). In 1978 and 1984 the Conservatives joined rightist coalitions while running their own congressional slate. They placed ten members in Congress in 1978 but only two in 1984. By the 1990s they had lost these seats, the party was moribund, and former followers had gone over to the Social Christians. Perhaps the party's last political effort was a desperate stab at staying relevant by supporting the socialist candidate, León Roldos, in the 2002 elections.

*See also* **Ecuador: Since 1830; García Moreno, Gabriel; Ponce Enríquez, Camilo.**

BIBLIOGRAPHY

George I. Blanksten, *Ecuador: Constitutions and Caudillos* (1951).

John D. Martz, *Ecuador: Conflicting Political Culture and the Quest for Progress* (1972).

*Additional Bibliography*

Demélas, Marie-Danielle. *La invención política: Bolivia, Ecuador, Perú en el siglo XIX*. Lima, Peru: IFEA, Instituto Francés de Estudios Andinos, 2003.

Freidenberg, Flavia, and Manuel Alcántara Sáez. *Los dueños del poder: Los partidos políticos en Ecuador (1978–2000)*. Quito, Ecuador: Facultad Latinoamericana de Ciencias Sociales, 2001.

Mejía Acosta, Andrés. *Gobernabilidad democrática: Sistema electoral, partidos políticos y pugna de poderes en Ecuador (1978–1998)*. Quito, Ecuador: Fundación Konrad Adenauer, 2002.

JOHN D. MARTZ

### DEMOCRATIC ALLIANCE (ADE)

The Democratic Alliance (Alianza Democrática—ADE), an ad-hoc, wide-ranging political coalition, was formed in 1944 to support exiled populist José María Velasco Ibarra's bid to remove the government of Carlos Alberto Arroyo Del Río (1940–1944). The coalition, led by Francisco Arízaga Luque, brought together socialists, conservatives, independents, and communists, joined only by their shared dissatisfaction with Arroyo del Río. Arroyo had earned the enmity of Ecuadorians by presiding over the nation's disastrous defeat in a war with Peru. In January 1942 Arroyo del Río agreed to the Rio Protocol, whereby Ecuador surrendered 80,000 square miles of territory in Amazonia to Peru. The Democratic Alliance, assisted by elements within the military, overthrew Arroyo del Río in May 1944. Velasco Ibarra returned from exile and claimed the presidency. In May 1964 various conservative groups briefly revitalized the ADE as part of a failed effort to force out the military government of Ramón Castro Jijón (1963–1966).

*See also* **Ecuador-Peru Boundary Disputes.**

BIBLIOGRAPHY

David W. Schodt, *Ecuador: An Andean Enigma* (1987), provides a summary overview of political economy. John D. Martz, *Ecuador: Conflicting Political Culture and the Quest for Progress* (1972).

George I. Blanksten, *Ecuador: Constitutions and Caudillos* (1964), offer accounts of the return of Velasco Ibarra.

### *Additional Bibliography*

Bravo, César Augusto. *Historia del Ecuador de la década de 1950 a la década de los 70.* Cuenca: Editorial Gráficas Hernández, 1995.

Echeverría, Julio. *La democracia bloqueada: Teoría y crisis del sistema político ecuatoriano.* Quito: Letras, 1997.

RONN F. PINEO

## DEMOCRATIC LEFT (ID)

The Democratic Left (Izquierda Democrática—ID), the center-left political party of President Rodrigo Borja Cevallos and Vice President Luis Parodi Valverde (1988–1992), began as a splinter party in 1977, when young reformers broke away from the Radical Liberal Party (Partido Liberal Radical, PLR). In 1984 ID candidate Borja lost the presidential runoff election to conservative Guayaquil businessman León Febres-Cordero (1984–1988). However, in 1988 Borja defeated former Guayaquil mayor Abdalá Bucaram Ortiz, with Bucaram carrying the coast and Borja taking the sierra. Although Borja campaigned on a platform of progressive policies, in office he dealt with the deepening economic crisis caused by a drop in oil prices (Ecuador's leading export) by adopting an austerity program, devaluing the *sucre* (Ecuador's national currency), increasing taxes, and loosening price controls on basic necessities. The ID, unlike most Ecuadorian political parties that serve principally as vehicles to advance the electoral aspirations of single individuals, is an institutionalized political party built around a moderately progressive ideology. The ID continues to play a central role in Ecuadorian politics, maintaining a large presence in the Congress.

*See also* **Borja Cevallos, Rodrigo; Febres-Cordero Ribadeneyra, León.**

BIBLIOGRAPHY

*Izquierda Democrática.* Available from www.izquierdademocratica.org.

Gerlach, Allen. *Indians, Oil, and Politics: A Recent History of Ecuador.* Wilmington, DE: Scholarly Resources, 2003.

Schodt, David W. *Ecuador: An Andean Enigma.* Boulder, CO: Westview Press, 1987.

RONN PINEO

## RADICAL LIBERAL PARTY (PLR)

One of Ecuador's two historic political parties, known officially as the Radical Liberal Party (Partido Liberal Radical—PLR), the Liberal Party was officially organized by Ignacio de Veintimilla in 1878 and convened the first party assembly two years later. First seizing power through the 1895 revolution led by its renowned leader Eloy Alfaro, the PLR remained the dominant force in national politics until 1944, when its last president, Carlos Arroyo Del Río, was ousted. The PLR, originally firmly committed to church-state separation, to public education, and to promotion of external trade and commerce, gradually grew more conservative as these issues became less salient to the nation. During this time the PLR established strong ties with the military and the country's financial sector. Although the PLR's relationship with the military deteriorated in the 1940s, business and financial groups continued to support the party.

In the 1950s, despite their support for the administration of Galo Plaza Lasso, the Liberals progressively declined. The party's last serious bid for national power came in 1968 when its venerable leader, Andrés F. Córdova, ran for the presidency and was narrowly defeated by José María Velasco Ibarra. During the 1970s the PLR was weakened by internal schisms, most notably that of younger militants who founded the Izquierda Democrática (Democratic Left—ID). In 1978 the Liberal old guard made a final electoral effort but was rebuffed. After that time the PLR sought legislative and electoral coalitions with other parties and leaders. Its congressional representation had dropped to three by 1990, and the PLR became irrelevant to national politics as newer parties emerged to engage the electorate.

*See also* **Ecuador: Since 1830; Veintemilla, José Ignacio de.**

BIBLIOGRAPHY

George I. Blanksten, *Ecuador: Constitutions and Caudillos* (1951).

John D. Martz, *Ecuador: Conflicting Political Culture and the Quest for Progress* (1972).

### *Additional Bibliography*

Bravo, César Augusto. *Historia del Ecuador de la década de 1950 a la década de los 70.* Cuenca, Ecuador: Editorial Gráficas Hernández, 1995.

Echeverría, Julio. *La democracia bloqueada: teoría y crisis del sistema político ecuatoriano.* Quito: Letras, 1997.

JOHN D. MARTZ

# ECUADOR, REVOLUTIONS

*This entry includes the following articles:*
REVOLUTION OF 1895
REVOLUTION OF 1925

## REVOLUTION OF 1895

The liberals were brought to power in Ecuador by an uprising that followed the resignation of the progressive president Luis Cordero in the face of a conservative-inspired rebellion. The provisional government lost control as the country disintegrated into warring factions, with insurrections in Ambato, El Oro, Guayaquil, Latacunga, Los Ríos, Manabí Province, and Quito. Coastal liberals saw an opportunity to achieve national supremacy by inviting Eloy Alfaro to return from exile and assume command of their forces. With the support of other *guerrilleros,* including Leonidas Plaza, Alfaro's coastal *montoneras* decisively defeated government troops in August 1895. Alfaro first assumed power and then called an assembly that wrote a new liberal constitution and elected him interim president in October 1896. The triumphant liberals, who dominated national politics until 9 July 1925, stressed the necessity of establishing a secular state to promote social and economic development and modernization.

*See also* **Ecuador: Since 1830.**

BIBLIOGRAPHY

Luis Robalino Dávila, *Orígenes del Ecuador de hoy,* vol. 7 (1969).

Linda Alexander Rodríguez, *The Search for Public Policy: Government Finances in Ecuador, 1830–1940* (1985), esp. pp. 44–52, 88–92.

Frank MacDonald Spindler, *Nineteenth-Century Ecuador* (1987), esp. pp. 147–169.

### *Additional Bibliography*

Ayala Mora, Enrique. *Historia de la revolución liberal ecuatoriana.* Quito: Corporación Editora Nacional, 2002.

Cárdenas Reyes, María Cristina. *José Peralta y la trayectoría del liberalismo ecuatoriano.* Quito: Ediciones Banco Central del Ecuador, 2002.

Iglesias Mata, Dumar. *Eloy Alfaro, Cóndor de América.* Manabí, Ecuador: Casa de la Cultura Ecuatoriana, 2003.

Núñez, Jorge. *La revolución alfarista de 1895.* Quito: Centro para el Desarrollo Social, 1995.

LINDA ALEXANDER RODRÍGUEZ

## REVOLUTION OF 1925

The coup of 9 July 1925 was the first institutional intrusion of the military into politics. The young officers, who believed they represented national rather than regional interests, justified their actions in a twelve-point reform program. The coup followed an extensive campaign by sierra publicists and politicians who portrayed the professional military as the only body that could free the government from the domination of a corrupt coastal oligarchy. These critics argued that the government was the captive of Guayaquil bankers and that the professional military was being dishonored and compromised by corrupt political officers who supported liberal governments. The reforms advocated in the name of national unity and rehabilitation actually were used by sierra (conservative) politicians to return political control to Quito.

*See also* **Ecuador: Since 1830.**

BIBLIOGRAPHY

Luis Robalino Dávila, *El 9 de julio de 1925* (1973).

Linda Alexander Rodríguez, *The Search for Public Policy: Regional Politics and Government Finances in Ecuador, 1830–1940* (1985), esp. pp. 118–133.

### *Additional Bibliography*

Albornoz Peralta, Osvaldo. *Del crimen de El Ejido a la Revolución del 9 de Julio de 1925.* Quito: Subsecretária de Cultura, Sistem Nacional de Bibliotecas, 1996.

Paz y Miño Cepeda, Juan J. *La Revolución Juliana: Nación, ejército, y bancocracia.* Quito: Abya-Yala, 2000.

Pérez Ramírez, Gustavo. *Virgilio Guerrero: Protagonista de la Revolución Juliana, su praxis social.* Quito: Academia Nacional de Historia, 2003.

LINDA ALEXANDER RODRÍGUEZ

**EDER, SANTIAGO MARTÍN** (1838–1921). Santiago Martín Eder (*b.* 24 June 1838; *d.* 25 December 1921), Colombian agricultural entrepreneur. Born in Mitau, in present-day Latvia, Santiago emigrated in 1851 to the United States to join his brother Henry, who was engaged in various mercantile activities in California, Panama, and Chile. His Harvard law education sustained his later activities as U.S. consul in Buenaventura, but his family's commercial relations shaped his life.

In 1864 Eder purchased La Rita and La Manuelita plantations near Palmira to develop export agriculture. After spotty success with tobacco, indigo, coffee, and sugar, Eder devoted himself to the general economic development of the Cauca Valley. His investments in the Buenaventura-Cali railroad, the Cauca steamship company, and various banks in Cali placed him at the fore of regional developers. Eder's son Charles married the daughter of Italian entrepreneur Ernesto Cerruti and assumed control of the family's Cauca properties. Another son, Phanor, became active in international commerce and law. The Manuelita mill, completely modernized by 1903, became the country's leading producer of domestically consumed refined sugar.

*See also* **Agriculture; Sugar Industry.**

BIBLIOGRAPHY

Phanor J. Eder, *El fundador: Santiago M. Eder* (1959).

Carlos Davila L. De Guevara, *El empresariado colombiano: Una perspectiva histórica* (1986), pp. 52–67.

*Additional Bibliography*

Dávila L de Guevara, Carlos. *Empresas y empresarios en la historia de Colombia: Siglos XIX-XX: Una colección de estudios recientes.* Bogotá: Naciones Unidas, CEPAL: Norma: Universidad de los Andes, Facultad de Administración: Ediciones Uniandes, 2003.

DAVID SOWELL

# EDUCATION

*This entry includes the following articles:*

OVERVIEW
NONFORMAL EDUCATION
PRE-COLUMBIAN EDUCATION

## OVERVIEW

Education in Latin America today is largely a product of what the Spanish began in the colonial period. Yet, there were pre-Conquest institutions and organized modes of learning. Indigenous people learned from their parents and acquired skills through a system of apprenticeship. The Aztecs also required youth at age 15 to attend school. The majority attended the *telpochalli*, for military education and the elite went to the *calmecac*, for advanced study of writing, astronomy, and theology, among other topics. As part of the destruction of indigenous governments and institutions, the Spanish replaced these schools with European-style education systems.

The first schools established in the sixteenth century were aimed at Christianizing the local population. These were established by the Catholic Church, particularly the Dominican and Jesuit orders, who worked largely with children of privileged families. Jesuits opened and staffed numerous schools and colleges, wrote about historical matters and the various regions of the empire, and came to dominate the intellectual life of the times. The order administered ranches and forest rights, and used their considerable resources to train peasants in horticulture, weaving, reading, and writing. By the seventeenth century there were universities in Santiago de Chile, Córdoba, La Plata, Cuzco, and Quito, most of which trained clergy as well as some doctors and lawyers. By the eighteenth century chairs of classical and Indian languages were added to natural science and after the expulsion of the Jesuits for fear of their dominance in the New World, higher education exhibited a new secularism that reflected the philosophy and influence of the Enlightenment.

The dominance of scholasticism was being challenged by a new introduction of science and the empirical method. The effort to rationalize the doctrines of the church by wedding philosophy and theology yielded to the new ideas which rejected the notion of using reason to justify faith. When the Jesuits departed, they left a legacy of some twenty-five institutions of higher education in Latin America. The importance of some of these continued for at least two centuries. While most of the population during the colonial period could neither read nor write, the cultural life of the times produced a number of celebrated intellectuals. Among these notables may be included Fray Bartolomé de Las Casas (1474–1566), author of *History of the Indies,* and Bernal Díaz Del Castillo (1492–1584), known for his *True History of the Conquest of New Spain.*

After the Independence movement the Catholic Church remained a dominant influence in education but gradually this control was eroded by the demands of citizens for a more enlightened intellectual atmosphere and by the end of the century secularism dominated schooling in the area. Major advances in education were made particularly in Argentina, Chile, and Uruguay, where a combination of citizen demand and the need for more technical training eroded the rigidity of church doctrine. Under President Domingo Sarmiento, Argentina became the educational leader in Latin America. But the introduction of more scientific studies at the expense of humanism also brought an increase in state control of education. Idealism was replaced by positivism and the curriculum no longer required Latin. In Mexico President Benito Juárez's educational reform commission, influenced by Comte's philosophy, aimed at a new way to train elites. In Argentina the Escuela Normal de Panana, created in 1870, provided a training ground for the new leaders of society. By the end of the nineteenth century secularism had overtaken Catholic control in all of Latin America and was codified by the Argentine law of 1884, which settled the matter.

What appeared at the end of the nineteenth century was a varied system of education that reflected diverse European influences. Argentina was influenced by the British system, Chile by the German, and many other Latin American countries by the French. National governments established ministries of education to run the schools, and a system of hierarchical levels of administration created a pattern that is only now being seriously challenged. Though literacy grew, the rigid class divisions that characterized Latin American society remained. Both internal as well as external developments helped to influence change in early-twentieth-century schooling. In Córdoba in 1918 the new middle classes succeeded in making the university more democratic by including research and student participation in university affairs. Here, too, improved teaching and a new curriculum was influenced by radical ideas inspired by the Mexican and Russian revolutions. Militant student strikes led by the student union incited an examination reform, an end to nepotism, and social accountability.

This new radicalism was reflected in Mexico during the 1930s, when left-leaning teachers were

**Educational indicators in Latin America**

| | Primary school enrollment as a percentage of population age 6–11 | | | Secondary school enrollment as a percentage of population age 12–17 | | | University enrollment as a percentage of population age 20–24 | Illiteracy rate as a percentage of population age 15 and older |
|---|---|---|---|---|---|---|---|---|
| | 1965 | 1985 | 2004 | 1965 | 1985 | 2004 | | |
| Argentina | 101 | 108 | 112 | 28 | 70 | 86 | 65 (2005) | 2.8 (2004) |
| Bolivia | 73 | 91 | 113 | 18 | 37 | 86 | 40 (2005) | 13.3 (2004) |
| Brazil | 108 | 104 | 140 | 16 | 35 | 105 | 23.8 (2005) | 11.4 (2005) |
| Chile | 124 | 109 | 103 | 34 | 69 | 89 | 47.8 (2005) | 4.3 (2005) |
| Colombia | 84 | 117 | 111 | 17 | 50 | 74 | 29.3 (2005) | 7.2 (2005) |
| Ecuador | 91 | 114 | 117 | 17 | 55 | 61 | 29.0 (1987) | 9 (2004) |
| Paraguay | 102 | 101 | 104 | 13 | 31 | 63 | 24.5 (2005) | 6.5 (2005) |
| Peru | 99 | 122 | 113 | 25 | 65 | 91 | 33.5(2005) | 12.1 (2005) |
| Uruguay | 106 | 110 | 109 | 44 | 70 | 105 | 40.5 (2005) | 2.3 (2004) |
| Venezuela | 94 | 108 | 105 | 27 | 45 | 72 | 41.2 (2005) | 7 (2004) |
| Costa Rica | 106 | 101 | 111 | 24 | 41 | 77 | 25.3 (2005) | 5.9 (2004) |
| Cuba | 121 | 105 | 100 | 23 | 85 | 92 | 61.5 (2005) | .2 (2004) |
| Dominican Republic | 87 | 124 | 112 | 12 | 50 | 68 | 32.9 (2005) | 13 (2005) |
| El Salvador | 82 | 70 | 114 | 17 | 24 | 63 | 19 (2005) | 19.4 (2005) |
| Guatemala | 50 | 76 | 113 | 8 | 17 | 48 | 9.5 (2005) | 30.9 (2005) |
| Haiti | 50 | 78 | | 5 | 18 | | 1.2 (1985) | 4811 (2003) |
| Honduras | 80 | 102 | 113 | 10 | 36 | 65 | 16.4 (2005) | 20 (2005) |
| Mexico | 92 | 115 | 109 | 17 | 55 | 79 | 24 (2005) | 8.4 (2005) |
| Nicaragua | 69 | 101 | 112 | 14 | 39 | 63 | 17.8 (2005) | 23.3(2005) |
| Panama | 102 | 105 | 112 | 34 | 59 | 70 | 43.9 (2005) | 8.1 (2004) |

SOURCE: World Bank, *Development Data Book*, 2nd ed. (n.d.); UNESCO, *Statistical Yearbook* (1993); United Nations Development Programme, *Human Development Report* (1993). USAID, *Latin American and the Caribean: Selected Economic and Social Data* (2004); World Bank, EdStats, (2005).

**Table 1**

urged to become social reformers by playing a role in rural uplift. They were asked to help the peasants struggle for land and to help the workers struggle for wages. President Lázaro Cárdenas demanded a school in every village; while the program proved successful in Oaxaca, in other areas teachers often faced popular indifference and even hostility. Despite these changes all over Spanish America, a centralized and standardized form of primary education persisted and was promoted from the 1930s onward. Municipalities lost control of schools to the ministries of education, which assumed control of teacher recruitment, training, and placement and inspection. This policy was justified in the name of using education to develop the nation and establish national identity. Despite these national efforts, fully half the population of Latin America remained illiterate in 1964. In all countries after World War II the attraction of education was a force that increased enrollments substantially, and resources were poured into schools.

In Brazil there were 2.1 million students in 1932, with 2 million in primary schools, 103,000 in secondary, and 22,000 in higher education. By 1985 there were 30 million students, with 1.5 million in higher education. While questions of enrollment, resources, and national development are still important concerns of educators and politicians in Latin America, the more recent global competitive environment has added new dimensions to traditional views of education.

Global political and economic changes have altered traditional views of education in Latin America and throughout the world. The increasing interdependence of trade, commerce, and finance now challenges the conventional view of education as an exclusive function of sovereign states and leads to a reassessment of the broader objectives of education in an internationally competitive environment. Organizations such as the United Nations, the Organization of American States, and the Organization for Economic Cooperation and Development routinely play significant roles as advisors and consultants to national ministries. This development has brought about the inclusion of new educational concepts, such as gender issues, environmental problems, human rights, the cultural integrity of indigenous people, and the disparity between the technical and scientific work forces in poor versus developed economies. With these increased demands have come the recognition that government resources are inadequate. International lending institutions such as the International Monetary Fund and the World Bank insist that officials find ways to curtail expenditure, increase taxes, and consider user fees and more privatization of schooling. However, these policy reforms have met resistance. For instance, in 1999, the rector of the National Autonomous University of Mexico tried to raise fees, but a group of students launched a strike disrupting classes for several months. While many Mexicans found the strikers' demands unreasonable and the federal government arrested the protesters, the activities did limit privatization attempts.

The South Commission (1990), for example, pointed to the widening "knowledge gap" between developed countries and the third world. In their report, they found that "unless the South learns to harness the forces of modern science and technology, it has no chance of fulfilling its developmental aspirations or its yearning for an effective voice in the management of global interdependence." The information age, with its requirements for technical and scientific workers, demands a more competitive population six to fifteen years old than was ever required in the past. Latin American ministries of education are now called upon to emphasize basic science and mathematics preparation as never before.

This emphasis is not just for an elite, but rather for a much wider population of children. *The World Education Report* issued by UNESCO in 1993 calls for making education for all a universal reality, not just a universally recognized right. Many nations have moved forward in providing primary schooling for most of their eligible population. However, Bolivia, El Salvador, Guatemala, and others have not succeeded in providing even this minimal level of education for all children. At the secondary level, usually considered appropriate for ages twelve to seventeen, no country in Latin America reported very high enrollment ratios. Cuba led the list with 85 percent, followed by Argentina, Chile, and Uruguay, but many countries barely had a third of eligible students enrolled. Other statistics underline the severe diversity that characterizes educational attainment in Latin America. The illiterate population of persons over fifteen years of age rises from single-digit percentages in Argentina,

**A teacher leads a class in an outdoor school in the Amazon, Ecuador, 1995.** There is increased recognition throughout Latin America of the need to expand education beyond its traditional formal boundaries and to provide more instruction for its indigenous populations. © OWEN FRANKEN/CORBIS

Costa Rica, and Uruguay to very high rates in Guatemala and Nicaragua. Countries with the highest college and university enrollment ratios have the smallest number of illiterates, and those countries with the lowest ratios have the highest rates of illiteracy. These national figures do not reveal the kinds of disparities between rural and urban areas or among marginalized indigenous populations.

More important, perhaps, than the numbers of children receiving instruction is the changing philosophical outlook of government, from a traditional acceptance of exclusive governmental responsibility to a broader social mandate for meeting educational needs that includes the family, the workplace, the media, and other community organizations. The traditional role of schooling as an instrument for molding social personality and work-force training for human capital are being eroded by a new focus on alternate agencies of education.

The Chilean Ministry of Education enunciated a program in 1992 to improve the quality of primary schools by inviting the community to participate actively in the education of their children. Some educators see this development as an opportunity for greater democratization whereby citizens help establish their own priorities. The International Institute for Educational Planning sponsored a study of decentralization in Latin America in which the older view of exclusive governmental responsibility is altered by the need for broader citizen participation in education. This trend is also evident in the development of rural women's education in the Andean subregion, as reported by the International Bureau of Education. It is increasingly recognized that the rights of indigenous people have been neglected in many countries, and that they have legitimate cross-national concerns that need to be addressed by local and international agencies. In Peru, for example, the 1979 Constitution established that peasant and native communities are autonomous in their organization and community work, although these populations do not feel that they have equal rights to education, health, and other government services. Efforts are currently under way to institute bilingual schools, train teachers in their native language, and provide expanded instruction for the indigenous population.

By the 1960s and 1970s a new genre of educational criticism had emerged in North and South America, taking as its starting point the apparent inability of governments to make schools alter social injustice and poverty. Critics such as Everett Reimer, Paulo Freire, and Ivan Illich carefully detailed the ways that schools served to perpetuate privilege in general and specifically in Latin America. They concluded that the formal school system could not be saved and instead called for a whole new "informal" system that would educate children outside the regular classroom.

*See also* **Díaz del Castillo, Bernal; Dominicans; Freire, Paulo; International Monetary Fund (IMF); Jesuits; Las Casas, Bartolomé de; Literacy; United Nations; Universities: Colonial Spanish America; Universities: The Modern Era; World Bank.**

BIBLIOGRAPHY

John Johnson, *Political Change in Latin America* (1958).

Harold R. W. Benjamin, *Higher Education in the American Republics* (1965).

Paulo Freire, *Pedagogy of the Oppressed* (1968).

Everett Reimer, *School Is Dead: Alternatives in Education* (1970).

Joseph Maier and Richard W. Weatherhead, eds., *The Latin American University* (1979).

Mary Kay Vaughan, *The State, Education and Social Class in Mexico, 1880–1928* (1982).

United Nations, *Convention on the Rights of the Child* (1989).

South Commission, *The Challenge to the South* (1990), pp. 227–228.

*World Declaration on Education for All* (conference in Jomtien, Thailand, 1990).

Chilean Ministry Of Education, "Programme to Improve the Quality of Primary Schools in Poor Areas," in *Bulletin of the Major Project of Education in Latin America and the Caribbean,* no. 27 (1992): 30–31.

Beatrice Edwards, "Linking the Social and Natural Worlds: Environmental Education in the Hemisphere," in *La Educación,* no. 115 (1993).

International Bureau of Education, *Innovation and Information* (December 1993): 4.

Nelly Stromquist, "The Political Experience of Women: Linking Micro and Macro-Democracies," in *La Educación,* no. 116 (1993).

UNESCO, *Statistical Yearbook* (1993).

World Bank, *Development Data Book,* 2d ed., n.d.

United Nations Development Programme, *Human Development Report* (1993).

International Institute for Educational Planning, *IIEP Newsletter XII,* no. 1 (1994).

British Comparative Education Society, Conference on Education Beyond the State, September 1994.

## *Additional Bibliography*

Babb, Sarah L. *Managing Mexico: Economists from Nationalism to Neoliberalism.* Princeton, NJ: Princeton University Press, 2001.

Ball, Stephen J., Gustavo E. Fischman, and Silvina Gvirtz. *Crisis and Hope: The Educational Hopscotch of Latin America.* New York: Routledge Falmer, 2003.

Britton, John A., ed. *Molding the Hearts and Minds: Education, Communications, and Social Change in Latin America* Wilmington, DE: Scholarly Resources, 1994.

Castro, Cláudio de Moura, and Daniel C. Levy. *Myth, Reality, and Reform: Higher Education Policy in Latin America.* Washington, DC: Inter-American Development Bank, 2000.

Cortina, Regina, and Nelly P. Stromquist, eds. *Distant Alliances: Promoting Education for Girls and Women in Latin America.* New York: Falmer Press, 2000.

Di Gropello, Emanuela, Rossella Cominetti, and Roberto Bisang. *La descentralización de la educación y la salud: Un análisis comparativo de la experiencia latinoamericana.* Santiago: Naciones Unidas, 1998.

Puiggrós, Adriana. *Neoliberalism and Education in the Americas.* Boulder, CO: Westview Press, 1999.

Reimers, Fernando, ed. *Unequal Schools, Unequal Chances: The Challenges to Equal Opportunity in the Americas.* Cambridge, MA: David Rockefeller Center for Latin American Studies, Harvard University, 2000.

Reunión Regional sobre la Educación Superior de los Pueblos Indígenas de América Latina (Guatemala City, 2002). *La educación superior indígena en América Latina.* Caracas: UNESCO: Instituto Internacional de la Educación Superior en América Latina y el Caribe (IESALC), 2003.

Téllez, Magaldy, ed. *Educación, cultura y política: Ensayos para la comprensión de la historia de la educación en América Latina*. Caracas: Universidad Central de Venezuela, Facultad de Ciencias Económicas y Sociales, Facultad de Humanidades y Educación, 1997.

JOSEPH DI BONA

## NONFORMAL EDUCATION

Nonformal education includes a range of organized instructional activities that usually occur outside of the formal educational system. Popular, alternative, adult, experimental, and grass-roots education are terms that have been used to describe recent nonformal educational activities in Latin America.

While many examples can be found in early Latin American history, including the creative educational programs sponsored by religious institutions and the *Sociedad económica de amigos del país,* the term "nonformal education" more appropriately refers to twentieth-century educational activities. The activities were at times linked to traditional educational institutions, but they usually relied on different methods and served different populations.

Mexico, which initiated many educational innovations outside of the traditional school setting during the colonial period, was often at the forefront of educational experimentation in the twentieth century. It was one of the first countries to have a "popular university," established by intellectuals and educators in 1912, to educate workers. Popular universities followed in many countries, most notably the González Prada Popular Universities in Peru, which offered courses in culture, health, and vocational training. Mexico was also the initiator of another, more comprehensive program of grass-roots education in the 1920s. Under the leadership of José Vasconcelos, the famous cultural missions program sought to transform rural life in Mexico. Interdisciplinary teams of teachers, health professionals, and technical workers traveled to remote villages for short periods to teach and to promote social change. Variants of the Mexican cultural missions were adopted in other Latin American countries (the socio-pedagogical missions of Uruguay, for example) and in Spain during the early 1930s. In addition, rural schools, emphasizing technical and vocational training along with academic subjects, had appeared in many Latin American countries by the 1930s.

These activities set precedents for broadening the scope of nonformal educational activities during the 1940s. In response to development needs and the inadequacy of formal educational systems, individuals and groups created new methods of attacking the massive social problems of illiteracy, unemployment, and malnutrition. Experimental programs sought to improve the education, health, and welfare of the poor. At times these programs were comprehensive national efforts, designed to increase literacy and basic skills in the hopes of integrating marginal populations into a national polity and economy; at other times they were grass-roots movements, emerging from individuals, communities, and religious organizations.

Extension education, though a part of formal educational and governmental organizations, has long supported nonformal, alternative educational activities. Extension programs that emphasized social development rather than simple cultural diffusion became an avowed aim of Latin American universities, especially after the Córdoba Reforms of 1918 initiated efforts to make universities more socially responsible. During and after World War II international and national development agencies relied on extension to promote development. One of the earliest of these was the Inter-American Cooperative Food Production Service in Peru, started in 1942 by the Institute of Inter-American Affairs, and designed to increase food and fiber for domestic and international markets. Through agent contact with farmers, youth, and women's organizations, and diffusion of information, all essential to extension programs, most Latin American ministries of agriculture had tried to initiate some type of agricultural extension program by the late 1950s.

Population increases and social and economic needs led to the rapid increase of nonformal education in the 1960s. Brazil offers an example of the range and diversity of programs that were established for literacy (Fundação Movimento Brasileiro de Alfabetização), vocational training (Serviço Nacional de Aprendizagem Comercial and Serviço Nacional de Aprendizagem Industrial), using television for primary education (Fundação Centro Brasileiro de Televisão Educativa), university extension (Centro Rural Universitário de Treinamento e Ação Comunitaria), and for merging religious beliefs and social action (Comunidades Eclesiais de Base).

As popular education became recognized as an agent of social change, reform and revolutionary movements employed it as a method of achieving their objectives. The Cuban literacy crusade of 1961 set the standard and was imitated by other countries in Latin America and Africa. One well known example was the creation by the revolutionary Sandinista government of Nicaragua in the 1980s of a corps of ambulatory teachers who went from town to town in the rural countryside to teach. Important theoretical and practical work came from Paulo Freire and Ivan Illich. Freire developed a program for literacy and *conscientização* (critical consciousness) that influenced many grass-roots educational efforts around the world. Ivan Illich, recognizing the inability of Latin American nations to provide traditional education to all, stressed the need for flexible, alternative education. More recently, new methods and educational programs have been created in many Latin American countries to address the growing number of street children. New pedagogies, adapted to the complex cultural milieu of street life, are a part of programs that provide shelter, food, clothing, health care, and job training to street children. These programs, like those before them, are based on the conviction that traditional educational institutions are no longer capable of addressing the changing needs of Latin America.

From the 1950s to the 1980s, international institutions like the World Bank and the United Nations Educational, Scientific and Cultural Organization (UNESCO) actively supported nonformal education programs. Since the 1990s, multilateral agencies have shown less enthusiasm for these programs and have instead pushed 'market-based' solutions for education needs. Nevertheless, nonformal education continues to provide learning alternatives.

*See also* **Freire, Paulo; González Prada Popular Universities; Literacy; Universities: The Modern Era; Vasconcelos Calderón, José; World Bank.**

BIBLIOGRAPHY

Thomas J. La Belle, *Nonformal Education and Social Change in Latin America* (1976) and *Nonformal Education in Latin America and the Caribbean: Stability, Reform, or Revolution* (1986), provides a good introduction to the diversity of programs and philosophies.

Carlos Alberto Torres, *The Politics of Nonformal Education in Latin America* (1990) analyzes adult education.

Adriana Puiggrós, *La educación popular en América Latina: Orígenes, polémicas y perspectivas* (1984), gives a theoretical overview of the history of popular education.

Myles Horton and Paulo Freire, *We Make the Road by Walking* (1990), compare experiences in nonformal education.

### *Additional Bibliography*

Arnove, Robert F., and Carlos Alberto Torres. "Adult Education and State Policy in Latin America: The Contrasting Cases of Mexico and Nicaragua." *Comparative Education* 31:3 (1995), 311–325.

Arríen, Juan B. and Miguel de Castilla Urbina. *Educación y pobreza en Nicaragua: Las apuestas a la esperanza.* Managua: Universidad Centroamericana, Instituto de Educación de la UCA, 2001.

Belle, T. J. L. and Carlos Alberto Torres. "The Changing Nature of Non-formal Education in Latin America." *Comparative Education* 36:1 (2000), 21–36.

Jung, Ingrid and Linda King, eds. *Gender, Innovation and Education in Latin America.* Hamburg, Germany: Unesco Institute for Education; Bonn, Germany: German Foundation for International Development, 1999.

JOHN C. SUPER

## PRE-COLUMBIAN EDUCATION

The Aztec, Inca, and Maya of ancient America had formal educational systems. Although the Inca and Maya generally restricted formal training to the nobility, the Aztecs or Mexica educated the children of each *calpulli* in Tenochtitlán. The Aztecs established two schools, one for the nobility and the other for commoners. Noble Aztec boys received training to become political leaders or priests in the *calmecacs* that were attached to their temples. Since the Aztecs dedicated each *calmecac* to a different Aztec deity, training varied from school to school, but officials in all *calmecacs* dealt severely with their pupils. They ordered serious offenders, such as drunkards, to be shot with arrows or to be burned to death. Harsh punishments helped train future political and military leaders to endure pain in battle or in ritual bloodletting ceremonies.

By the age of fifteen, sons of Aztec commoners were given a military education in the *telpochcalli*, or "young men's house." School officials trained the boys to use weapons and to capture victims because, if needed, every young adult male went to war. These young men also performed manual labor, such as tending fields, which strengthened their bodies and helped them develop stamina and self-discipline.

The Aztecs insisted that all children, including girls, between the ages of twelve and fifteen train in the *cuicacalli,* or "house of song" for a few hours each evening. They memorized songs and poetry that told them of their past and helped them understand what their relationship with their various gods should be. Although some daughters of the nobility were sent to temples to train as priestesses, most mothers taught their daughters skills, such as spinning cotton or grinding maize on the *mano* and *metate,* that would enable them to be efficient housewives.

Much like the Aztecs, the Inca educated men and women of the nobility in Cuzco at the Coricancha. Garcilaso de la Vega wrote that Inca Roca, the sixth Inca and first "emperor," felt "it was proper that the sons of common people should not learn the sciences, and that these should be restricted to the nobility." The Inca expected children of commoners to begin serving the empire at an early age in order to help their families meet their quota for the Inca. Instruction would have interfered with service time.

Since the Spanish esteemed alphabetic languages, they assumed that Native Americans, who had not developed alphabetic writing, did not have active intellectuals. However, *Amautas,* philosophers held in high esteem, taught in schools for the Inca nobility and for the sons of rulers the Inca conquered. They focused on religious instruction, principles of government administration, Inca history, public speaking, the use of the quipu, and the official language, Quechua. The entire course of elite instruction culminated in a military-style examination (the *huarachicoy*). Inca officials collected a select number of girls—chosen for their beauty, pleasant dispositions, or good figures—as *acllas* (the chosen ones). For five years, *mamaconas* (cloistered women dedicated to the services of their gods) taught young girls between the ages of eight or nine and fourteen the arts of brewing *chica* (maize beer) and weaving fine textiles, after which a select few were sent to Cuzco, where the Inca assigned some to a cloistered religious life in the temples or redistributed others as wives to relatives of the Inca or neighboring lords.

The Maya, much like the Inca, educated their nobility. The sons of Maya lords and priests learned to read hieroglyphic texts or to study the movement of the stars and planets under the direction of priests. Much learning may also have occurred at the village warrior houses, where young men gathered to play ball and lived together until marriage. Sons of commoners spent most of the day with their fathers helping them in the cornfields or with other work, while daughters remained at home with their mothers, who taught them spinning, weaving, and other household tasks.

*See also* **Amauta; Aztecs; Calpulli; Incas, The; Maya, The; Quechua; Quipu.**

BIBLIOGRAPHY

Friar Diego De Landa, *Yucatán Before and After the Conquest* (1566; repr. 1978).

Father Bernabé Cobo, *History of the Inca Empire* (1657; repr. 1988).

Huaman Poma, *Letter to a King,* translated by Christopher Dilke (1978).

Frances F. Berdan, *The Aztecs of Central Mexico* (1982).

Fray Bernadino De Sahagún, *Florentine Codex,* vols. 2, 3, 4, 8, 9, 10 (1982).

Brian Fagan, *The Aztecs* (1984).

Nancy Farriss, *Maya Society Under Colonial Rule* (1984).

R. Tom Zuidema, *Inca Civilization in Cuzco* (1990).

### *Additional Bibliography*

Clendinnen, Inga. *Aztecs: An Interpretation.* Cambridge, U.K. and New York: Cambridge University Press, 1991.

Demarest, Arthur Andrew. *Ancient Maya: The Rise and Fall of a Rainforest Civilization.* Cambridge, U.K. and New York: Cambridge University Press, 2004.

García Márquez, Agustín. *Los aztecas en el centro de Veracruz.* Mexico City: Universidad Nacional Autónoma de México, Instituto de Investigaciones Antropológicas, Programa de Posgrado en Estudios Mesoamericanos, 2005.

Guamán Poma de Ayala, Felipe. *The First New Chronicle and Good Government.* Abridged. Translated by David Frye. Indianapolis, IN: Hackett, 2006.

Hassig, Ross. *Time, History, and Belief in Aztec and Colonial Mexico.* Austin: University of Texas Press, 2001.

Malpass, Michael A. *Daily Life in the Inca Empire.* Westport, CT: Greenwood Press, 1996.

Mignolo, Walter D. *The Darker Side of the Renaissance: Literacy, Territoriality, and Colonization.* Ann Arbor: University of Michigan Press, 2nd ed., 2003.

Niles, Susan A. *The Shape of Inca History: Narrative and Architecture in an Andean Empire.* Iowa City: University of Iowa Press, 1999.

Tovar, Juan de, José. *Historia y creencias de los indios de México.* Edited by Javier Fuente del Pilar. Transcribed into modern Castilian by Susana Urraca Uribe. Madrid: Miraguano Ediciones, 2001.

CAROLYN JOSTOCK

## EDWARDS, AGUSTÍN (1878–1941).

Agustín Edwards (*b.* 17 June 1878; *d.* 1941), Chilean politician, financier, and writer. At age twenty-two, Edwards became one of the youngest members in Chile's House of Representatives. At the same time he became active in the Edwards Bank of Valparaíso. Elected vice president of the House and president of the Ministry of Finance in 1902, he negotiated a peace treaty with Bolivia and initiated the construction of a railroad from Arica to La Paz. In 1906 he began his diplomatic career, serving successively in Italy, Spain, and Switzerland. Upon his return to Chile, he served as finance minister under President Pedro Montt. During World War I he was named envoy to Great Britain in charge of diplomatic and financial affairs and, in 1920, became special envoy to the Court of St. James. In 1921 he was named representative to the League of Nations. He received many honors in Chile and Europe.

While living abroad Edwards studied newspaper and magazine production, then utilized this knowledge in Chile, where he founded the newspaper *El Mercurio* and several magazines, including *Zig-Zag.* In the financial domain, he reorganized the Edwards Bank, founded several companies, and was involved in nitrate mining. In 1925 he resolved a conflict with Bolivia and reestablished peace. Among his writings are his *Memoria sobre el plebiscito tacneño* (1926), in which he opposes a plan to allow Tacna and Arica to determine their nationality; *My Native Land* (1928), a cultural history of Chile; *Peoples of Old* (1929), on the Araucanian Indians; *The Dawn* (1931), on Chilean history from Independence (1810) to the first elected president (1841); and *Cuatro presidentes de Chile* (1932), on the period from 1841 to 1932.

*See also* **League of Nations; World War I.**

BIBLIOGRAPHY

Virgilio Figueroa, *Diccionario histórico, biográfico y bibliográfico de Chile,* vol. 2 (1974), pp. 20–25.

*Additional Bibliography*

Uribe, Armando. *Carta abierta a Agustín Edwards.* Santiago: LOM Ediciones, 2002.

BARBARA MUJICA

## EDWARDS, JORGE (1931–).

Jorge Edwards was born in Santiago on July 29, 1931. He studied law at the University of Chile before venturing into a diplomatic career and later achieving literary fame. Having joined Chile's diplomatic corps in the late 1950s, Edwards worked for several years in Paris, where he forged important friendships with Gabriel García Márquez, Julio Cortázar, and Mario Vargas Llosa. While serving in Europe he also began his writing career, publishing *El Patio* (The Patio), *Gente de la ciudad* (People of the City), and *El peso de la noche* (The Weight of Night), among others.

In 1971 President Salvador Allende tasked Edwards with reopening the Chilean embassy in Havana. It was as a result of this assignment that Edwards wrote what is likely his most famous work, *Persona Non Grata*—the title bestowed on Edwards by Fidel Castro's government after three months. The book, which was unmistakable in its distaste for authoritarian governments, especially Cuba's, drew the rebuke of extremists on the left and right while launching Edwards into the international spotlight. General Augusto Pinochet's coup in 1973 truncated Edwards' diplomatic career, and exiled him to Spain where he became a journalist and literary figure. Upon returning to Chile in the late 1970s Edwards renewed his political activism. President Eduardo Frei appointed him as ambassador to UNESCO from 1994 to 1996. In 1999, Edwards was awarded the Cervantes Prize, the most prestigious award for Spanish-language literature. He is a regular contributor to the major international newspapers *Le Monde* (Paris), *El Pais* (Madrid), and *La Nacion* (Buenos Aires).

*See also* **Allende Gossens, Salvador; Cortázar, Julio; García Márquez, Gabriel; Literature: Spanish America; Pinochet Ugarte, Augusto; Vargas Llosa, Mario.**

BIBLIOGRAPHY

*Works by Jorge Edwards*

*El patio* [The Patio], 1952; 2nd edition, 1980.

*Gente de la ciudad: Cuentos* [People of the City: Stories], 1961.

*El peso de la noche* [The Weight of Night], 1967.

*Persona non grata* (1973; *Persona Non Grata*, 1976).

*Los convidades de piedra* [The Guests of Stone], 1978.

*El anfitrión* [The Host], 1987.

*Adios, poeta* [Goodbye, Poet], 1990.

*El origin del mundo* [The Origin of the World], 1996.

*El sueño de la historia* [The Dream of History], 2000.

*El inútil de la familia* [The Useless One of the Family], 2004.

### *Secondary Source*

Oviedo, José Miguel. *Historia de la literatura hispanoamericana*, 4 vols. Madrid: Alianza Editorial, 1995–2001.

SEAN H. GOFORTH

## EDWARDS BELLO, JOAQUÍN (1887–1968).

**EDWARDS BELLO, JOAQUÍN** (1887–1968). Joaquín Edwards Bello (*b.* 10 May 1887; *d.* 1968), Chilean journalist and novelist. A prolific writer and memorialist, Edwards Bello created an extensive commentary on Chilean life from a personal perspective. As a *criollista,* he was interested in creating an autochthonous literature, using South American subjects and a literary style free of European influences. He was a harsh critic of Chilean society and its decadence. In many newspaper columns and in novels such as *El inútil* (1910), *El roto* (1920), and *La chica del "Crillón"* (1935), he studied, from a naturalist perspective which underlined the grotesque in everyday life, the human and social weaknesses of the system.

*See also* **Journalism.**

### BIBLIOGRAPHY

Julio Orlandi Araya, *Joaquín Edwards Bello: Obras, estilo, técnica* (1958).

### *Additional Bibliography*

García-Huidobro, Cecilia. *Joaquín Edwards Bello: Un transatlántico varado en el Mapocho.* Providencia, Santiago de Chile: El Mercurio/Aguilar, 2005.

Martínez Gómez, Juana. "Chilenos en Madrid." *Anales de Literatura Chilena* 4 (December 2003): 73–91.

S. DAYDÍ-TOLSON

## EDZNÁ.

**EDZNÁ.** Edzná, site in northern Campeche, Mexico, first known for its complex Late Classic Maya architecture. Investigations at the site center and in the surrounding area by Mexican and American archaeologists have demonstrated that Edzná was a large urban center occupying an area of perhaps 6.8 square miles during some time periods. The first known occupation occurred during the Middle Preclassic period (ca. 400–300 BCE), when the site apparently was sparsely occupied, followed by a surge of development and population during the Late Preclassic period.

Edzná functioned as a major center from about 150 B.C. to A.D. 200, possibly the period of its greatest extent and population. An ancient, complex hydraulic system was constructed during that time. Thirty-one canals and twenty-five reservoirs made possible collection of rainwater and had a storage potential of more than 71 million cubic feet. They may have provided the Preclassic and later Classic city with water reserves for the dry season because there is little or no surface water available in the area. Edzná was occupied, at a lesser level, during the Protoclassic and Early Classic periods, until a second population and development surge in Late Classic times. Its final period of occupation, during the Terminal Classic period, ended by approximately 900.

In the 1980s investigations by Antonio Benavides Castillo, under the auspices of Mexico's Instituto Nacional de Antropología e Historia, focused on the site center. Excavations revealed new information about the Large Acropolis and the Small Acropolis. Of particular interest is a large modeled stucco mask associated with a structure buried inside a later building on the Small Acropolis. Its style and associated artifacts date the mask to the Protoclassic period or earlier. In a brief discussion of the known carved stelae from Edzná, Benavides Castillo notes that two date to Baktun (between CE 41 and 435).

*See also* **Archaeology; Maya, the.**

### BIBLIOGRAPHY

Ray T. Matheny, Deanne L. Gurr, Donald W. Forsyth, and F. Richard Hauck, *Investigations at Edzná, Campeche, Mexico,* vol. 1, pt. 1, *The Hydraulic System,* and pt. 2, *Maps* (1983).

George F. Andrews, *Edzná, Campeche, Mexico: Settlement Patterns and Monumental Architecture* (1984).

Antonio Benavides Castillo, "Edzná, Campeche, Mexico: Temporade de campo 1989," in *Mexicon* 12, no. 3 (May 1990): 49–52.

### Additional Bibliography

Benavides Castillo, Antonio. *Edzná: A Pre-Columbian City in Campeche/Edzná: Una ciudad prehispánica de Campeche.* México, D.F.: Instituto Nacional de Antropología e Historia; Pittsburgh: University of Pittsburgh, 1997.

Forsyth, Donald W., Deanne L. Gurr; F. R. Hauck, and Ray T. Matheny. Investigations at Edzná, Campeche, Mexico. vol. 2, *Ceramics.* Provo: New World Archaeological Foundation, Brigham Young University, 1983.

Mayer, Karl Herbert. *The Hieroglyphic Stairway 1 at Edzna, Campeche, Mexico.* Graz: Academic Publishers, 2004.

Suárez Aguilar, Vicente, coord. *Exploraciones arqueológicas en Edzná, Campeche.* Campeche: Universidad Autónoma de Campeche, 2001.

RAY T. MATHENY

**EFFECTIVE SUFFRAGE, NO REELECTION.** No Reelection Effective Suffrage, a slogan (*sufragio efectivo, no reelección* in Spanish) characterizing much of the philosophy of the political movement in Mexico that led to the overthrow of long-time president and dictator Porfirio Díaz (1876–1880, 1884–1911) and marked the beginning of the Mexican Revolution of 1910. The idea of a free vote with no possibility of reelection was most thoroughly explored in revolutionary leader Francisco I. Madero's (1873–1913) book, *La sucesión presidencial de 1910* (1908), written in reaction to Díaz's multiple reelections to the presidency through largely fraudulent means. Madero also named his anti-Díaz political party the Anti-Reelectionist Party. No reelection, as opposed to effective suffrage, became a principle of the postrevolutionary political system, enshrined in the Constitution of 1917. It was breached only once, in the 1920s, when Alvaro Obregón (1880–1928) maneuvered to have himself chosen president a second time.

*See also* **Madero, Francisco Indalecio; Mexico, Constitutions: Constitution of 1917; Mexico, Wars and Revolutions: Mexican Revolution.**

BIBLIOGRAPHY

Charles C. Cumberland, *Mexican Revolution: Genesis Under Madero* (1952), pp. 55–61.

Stanley R. Ross, *Francisco I. Madero: Apostle of Mexican Democracy* (1955), pp. 50–64.

### Additional Bibliography

Katz, Friedrich. *De Díaz a Madero.* México, D.F.: Ediciones Era, 2004.

DAVID G. LAFRANCE

**EGAÑA FABRES, MARIANO** (1793–1846). Mariano Egaña Fabres (*b.* 1 March 1793; *d.* 24 June 1846), Chilean lawyer, diplomat, and intellectual. The son of Juan Egaña, from whom he inherited his strong intellectual streak, Mariano Egaña qualified as a lawyer in 1811, and held office briefly in the patriot governments of 1813–1814. Like his father, he was confined to Juan Fernández (an island prison for exiled political prisoners) during the Spanish reconquest (1814–1817). In 1824 he was sent as Chilean envoy to London. His credentials were not accepted because Britain had not yet recognized Chile's independence, so Egaña settled in Paris. He returned to Chile in 1829. It was as a result of his initiative that Andrés Bello (1781–1865), a prominent Venezuelan intellectual, was offered government employment in Chile.

In the new Conservative regime of 1830, in which he was a key figure, Egaña served as minister of finance (1830), of the interior (1830), and of justice (1837–1841), as well as senator (1831–1846). He was a leading influence on the drafting of the Constitution of 1833, though his more reactionary proposals (such as indefinite re-eligibility of presidents and hereditary senators) were excluded. Egaña's death (he collapsed and died in the street) had a great impact on Santiago. His book collection, the best in Chile, was bought by the state for the National Library.

*See also* **Chile, Constitutions; Santiago, Chile.**

BIBLIOGRAPHY

Simon Collier, *Ideas and Politics of Chilean Independence, 1808–1833* (1967).

Mariano Egaña, *Documentos de la misión de Mariano Egaña en Londres, 1824–1829* (1984).

*Additional Bibliography*

Collier, Simon. *Chile: The Making of a Republic, 1830–1865: Politics and Ideas.* New York: Cambridge University Press, 2003.

Ivulic Gómez, Jorge. *Importancia del Partido Conservador en la evolución política chilena.* [Chile] : Universidad Bernardo O'Higgins, Area de Ciencia Política, 1998.

SIMON COLLIER

## EGAÑA RISCO, JUAN (1768–1836).

Egaña Risco Juan (*b.* 31 October 1768; *d.* 20 April 1836), Chilean patriot and intellectual. One of the most learned men of his time and place, Juan Egaña Risco was born in Lima, the son of a Chilean father. He studied at San Marcos University, Lima, from which he graduated in 1789, the year he moved to Chile. An active patriot after 1810, he was a member of the first national congress (1811), for which he was banished to Juan Fernández (an island prison for exile of political prisoners) during the Spanish reconquest (1814–1817). He served several times in the congresses of the 1820s, but his moment of greatest influence came in 1823, when he was the principal author of the idiosyncratically conservative constitution of that year. It proved unworkable and was swiftly abandoned. Egaña's cast of mind was conservative, moralistic, and steeped in admiration for classical antiquity, the Inca empire, and China. Several volumes of his writings were published in London in the 1820s, and another volume in Bordeaux in 1836.

*See also* **Chile: The Nineteenth Century; Chile: Constitutions; Incas, The.**

BIBLIOGRAPHY

Raúl Silva Castro, *Egaña en la Patria Vieja, 1810–1814* (1959).

Simon Collier, *Ideas and Politics of Chilean Independence, 1808–1833* (1967), chap. 7.

*Additional Bibliography*

Ivulic Gómez, Jorge. *Importancia del Partido Conservador en la evolución política chilena.* [Chile]: Universidad Bernardo O'Higgins, Area de Ciencia Política, 1998.

SIMON COLLIER

## EGAS, CAMILO ALEJANDRO (1895–1962).

Camilo Alejandro Egas (*b.* 1895; *d.* 1962), Ecuadorian artist. Egas was born in Quito and attended the Academy of Arts in that city. A disciple of Paul Bar and Víctor Puiz, he won first prize in a national competition in celebration of Ecuadorian independence (1909). With the aid of an Ecuadorian government grant he studied at the Academy of Rome (1918) and the following year continued his studies at the Academy of San Fernando in Madrid. On another trip to Europe, he met Picasso in Paris, where he studied at the Colorrossi Academy (1922). Egas exhibited at the Salon des Indépendents and Salon d'Automme (Paris, 1924–1925). His expressionist paintings of Ecuadorian Indians frequently depict women in mourning or tragic instances (*Desolation*). In 1929 he received an appointment to teach painting at the New School for Social Research and in 1935 became the director of the school's painting department, a position he held until his death. In 1938 he collaborated on a mural project for the Ecuadorian Pavilion at the New York World's Fair. Egas was influenced by the surrealist exiles in New York in the 1940s and by Mexican muralist José Clemente Orozco. He died in New York.

*See also* **Art: The Twentieth Century.**

BIBLIOGRAPHY

*Arte Ecuatoriano,* vol. 2 (1976), pp. 246–247.

Dawn Ades, *Art in Latin America: The Modern Era, 1820–1980* (1989).

*Additional Bibliography*

Landázuri Camacho, Carlos, and Adriana Grijalva de Dávila. *Museo Camilo Egas.* Quito: Banco Central del Ecuador, 2003.

MARTA GARSD

## EGERTON, DANIEL THOMAS (1800–1842).

Daniel Thomas Egerton (*b.* 1800; *d.* 1842), English painter. One of the first traveling painters to arrive after Mexican independence, when the borders were opened to non-Hispanics, Egerton remained in Mexico from 1829 to 1836. Europeans came to Mexico moved by curiosity about its natural wonders, exoticness, and legendary mineral wealth, which explains the predominance in their work of landscapes, both rural and urban, popular sites, folkloric scenes, and representations of pre-Columbian ruins.

Returning to London, Egerton published *Vistas de México* in 1840. The twelve plates that illustrate the book, stone lithographs retouched with watercolors, are accompanied by brief textual explanations in which scientific and folkloric information are mixed, indicating the fascination of Europeans with the exotic aspects of Mexico. In this publication, which focuses primarily on the images, Egerton depicts a series of cities: some characterized by their agricultural and commercial wealth, such as Puebla and Guadalajara; others as mining centers, such as Zacatecas; and still others as supply points, such as Aguascalientes. These works inspired Egerton to produce oil paintings on the same themes.

At the end of 1840, Egerton returned to Mexico and took up residence in Tacubaya (Mexico City), where both he and his wife were murdered in 1842. The murderers' cases were extensively publicized in 1844.

*See also* **Mexico City; Guadalajara.**

BIBLIOGRAPHY

Manuel Romero De Terreros, *Paisajes mexicanos de un pintor inglés* (1949).

Justino Fernández, *Artistas británicos en México* (1968).

*Additional Bibliography*

Mac Adam, Alfred J. "Daniel Thomas Egerton, The Unfortunate Traveler." *Review* 47 (Fall 2003): 9–13.

ESTHER ACEVEDO

**EGUREN, JOSÉ MARÍA** (1874–1942). José María Eguren (*b.* 7 July 1874; *d.* 29 April 1942), Peruvian poet. Eguren began writing poetry at the height of the Spanish American *modernismo* movement at the turn of the century. Ironically, he was one of the select Peruvian poets to break out of the mold and bring Peruvian poetry into the twentieth century. Both in personality and poetry, he was radically different from such contemporaries as José Santos Chocano. In fact, Eguren was something of a recluse, and in his poetry he created imaginary worlds in which to cocoon himself. Steeped in French symbolism, his poetry at first blush seems to imitate the *modernistas* because of certain typical motifs, among them, mystery, love and dreams, but his language is a storehouse of creativity that had tremendous influence on later Peruvian poets. His works also led Peruvian poetry into the modern age in their themes of alienation, skepticism, and imitation of earlier forms.

Eguren produced three books of poetry: *Simbólicas* (1911), *La canción de las figuras* (1916), and *Poesías* (1929). Lyrical, telluric, symbolic, and imaginative, his poetry enriches the Spanish language with regionalisms, archaic terms, neologisms, and even foreign and invented words. Inspiration, for instance, is allegorized in the form of a small girl with a blue lamp who leads the poet into the spheres of the imagination and the spiritual. In his later poetry, Eguren draws on the work of the European vanguard in his use of metaphor and dream imagery.

*See also* **Literature: Spanish America.**

BIBLIOGRAPHY

Badenes, José Ignacio. "Lo nocturno como espacio de la creación artística: Lectura paradigmática del 'Nocturno' de *La canción de las figuras* de José María Eguren. " *Revista de Estudios Hispánicos* (Río Piedras) 26.2 (1999): 97–106.

Higgins, James. "The Rupture Between Poet and Society in the Work of José María Eguren." *Kentucky Romance Quarterly* (1973): 59–74.

Higgins, James. *The Poet in Peru*. Liverpool: Liverpool Monographs in Hispanic Studies, 1982.

Rodríguez—Peralta, Phyllis W. *Tres poetas cumbres en la poesía peruana: Chocano, Eguren y Vallejo*. Madrid: Playor, 1983.

Renato Sandoval Bacigalupo, *El centinela de fuego: Agonía y muerte en Eguren*. Lima: IPLAC, 1988.

DICK GERDES

**EICHELBAUM, SAMUEL** (1894–1967). Samuel Eichelbaum (*b.* 14 November 1894; *d.* 4 May 1967), Argentine playwright and short-story writer. When he was only twelve years old, Samuel Eichelbaum left the town of his birth, Domínguez, Entre Ríos Province, to travel to Rosario, where he tried to interest theater companies in producing his *sainete Un lobo manso* (1906). Although this early attempt met with rejection, it exemplifies his lifelong dedication to the theater. Eichelbaum's work reflects characters who are archetypes within Argentine society, yet critics frequently recognize in his works the presence of Dostoyevsky, Ibsen, and Strindberg rather than any direct influence from other Argentine writers. His plays are rooted in introspection, as for example in *Dos brasas* (1952); through a seemingly psychoanalytic approach to drama he explores the self and the nature of conflicts between the conscious and unconscious. Other major themes include the importance for Argentina of both rural and urban areas, the strength of women, individual tragedy found at all socioeconomic levels, and the need to survive as an individual against all adversity. The theater of Eichelbaum is clearly distinguished by the intellectual capacity of the characters and their ability to think and reason, as expressed through dialogue.

Although few of his plays are political in nature, Eichelbaum does direct his attention to social problems. In *El dogma* (1922) he alludes to the role of Jewish activists in the labor movement, and in *Nadie la conoció nunca* (1926) there is a reference to attacks on Jewish neighborhoods after the workers' strikes of 1910 and 1919 (the latter known as *La Semana Trágica*). More than twenty years later, *Un patricio del 80* (1948), written in collaboration with Ulises Petit de Murat, was subject to official opposition because it was considered to imply criticism of Perón's interest in supporting foreign exploitation of Argentine natural resources.

*Un guapo del 900* (1940), Eichelbaum's best-known and most commercially successful play, explores the moral codes of the *guapo,* a bodyguard to a political boss. Individual freedom of choice and sacrifice are bound to machismo and self-destruction in the search for dignity among the lower classes of Argentine society. As in other plays, Eichelbaum concentrates on the internal turmoil of his characters and the psychological processes guided by honor and individuality that lead to sorrowful outcomes.

*See also* **Theater.**

BIBLIOGRAPHY

Jorge Cruz, *Samuel Eichelbaum* (1962).

Panos D. Karavellas, *La dramaturgia de Samuel Eichelbaum* (1976).

Marta Lía Godoy Froy, *Introducción al teatro de Samuel Eichelbaum* (1982).

Ulises Petit De Murat, *Samuel Eichelbaum* (1986).

*Additional Bibliography*

Heffes, Gisela. *Judíos, argentinos, escritores.* Buenos Aires: Ediciones Atril, 1999.

Izaguirre, Héctor César. *Samuel Eichelbaum, cuentista y dramaturgo.* Paraná, Argentina: Editorial de Entre Ríos, 1996.

Danusia L. Meson

**EINAUDI, LUIGI R.** (1936–). A U.S. diplomat, Luigi Einaudi retired from the Department of State in 1997 after a distinguished career that included eight years on the secretary of state's policy planning staff, twelve as director of policy planning in the Bureau of Inter-American Affairs, and four as U.S. ambassador to the Organization of American States (OAS). At the OAS he played an instrumental role in the 1991 passage of Resolution 1080, a historic regional agreement to protect democracy in the hemisphere. When war broke out between Ecuador and Peru in January 1995 over a border dispute (the longest continuing such dispute in the Western Hemisphere), he was named the U.S. special envoy for the extended negotiations that finally produced a definitive settlement and peace treaty in October 1998, and was decorated by both countries' presidents for his contribution. In 2000 he was elected to a five-year term as assistant secretary general of the OAS, and served as acting secretary general from October 2004 to May 2005.

*See also* **Ecuador-Peru Boundary Disputes; Organization of American States (OAS).**

BIBLIOGRAPHY

Einaudi, Luigi R. "The Ecuador-Peru Peace Process." In *Herding Cats: Multiparty Mediation in a Complex World,* edited by Chester A. Crocker, Fen Osler Hampson, and Pamela Aall. Washington, DC: United States Institute of Peace Press, 1999.

David Scott Palmer

## EISENHOWER-REMÓN TREATY (1955).

Eisenhower-Remón Treaty (1955), one of a series of accords (signed 25 January) redefining the status of the Panama Canal Zone. According to this agreement the United States gradually relinquished privileges gained in the Hay-Bunau-Varilla Treaty of 1903, an accord already revised, in particular through the Hull-Alfaro Treaty of 1936, in which the United States relinquished its protectorate over Panama.

The Eisenhower-Remón Treaty addressed the economic issues related to the status of U.S. citizens of the Canal Zone, a source of constant irritation to Panamanians, who considered the zone a colonial enclave. Although it did not alter U.S. sovereignty over the zone, the treaty increased the annual payment to Panama to $1,930,000, granted Panama the right to tax the income of Canal Zone employees who were not U.S. citizens, and modified the zone boundaries. Commissary and post exchange (PX) privileges of U.S. citizens in the zone were limited to those citizens who actually worked for the canal, and Panama gained the right to impose import duties on some goods entering the zone. These provisions increased the share of zonian business controlled by Panamanian firms. The United States also relinquished its control of sanitation in Panama City and Colón, and its exclusive rights to construct transisthmian railroads and highways. Panama granted the United States a fifteen-year lease on 19,000 acres of land outside the zone for military exercises.

The treaty was supplemented by a Memorandum of Understandings Reached, pledging the establishment of a single wage level for all Canal Zone employees and equal employment opportunities for Panamanian citizens in zone posts, thereby eliminating the privileged status of U.S. citizens in the zone.

*See also* **Panama Canal.**

BIBLIOGRAPHY

J. Lloyd Mecham, *A Survey of United States–Latin American Relations* (1965).

Walter La Feber, *The Panama Canal: The Crisis in Historical Perspective* (1978).

*Additional Bibliography*

Fitzgerald, Luis I. *Historia de las relaciones entre Panamá y los Estados Unidos.* Panamá: Editorial Universitaria "Carlos Manuel Gasteazoro," 2000.

Perigault Sánchez, Bolívar. *Historia de las relaciones entre Panamá y los Estados Unidos.* Panamá: Editorial Universitaria, 1998.

Kenneth J. Grieb

## EJIDOS.

In Mexico, an *ejido* is an area of corporative land of town shared by the people of the community in small lots. The land of the *ejido* could not be sold or given legally to third parties; it was only possible to inherit. *Ejidos* have their origins in the pre-Hispanic (*calpulli* and *altepetlalli*) and Hispanic (*exidos* and *propios*) land-ownership traditions. After the Conquista the Spanish laws gave to the "pueblos de indios" land for the communal use that were administered by the republic. These lands were apportioned for public uses (forests and area of grass for the cattle).

In the nineteenth century, liberal land reforms pushed to end communal privileges, and *ejidos* were officially abolished by law. The Ley de Desamortización of 1856 and the Constitution of 1857 transferred land-ownership from the civil and church corporations to citizens. "Los pueblos de indios" lost their right to own *ejidos* and other communal lands. The *ejido* reappeared after the Mexican Revolution with the Ley Agraria of 1915 and the Mexican Constitution of 1917. In the 1930s Lázaro Cárdenas's Reforma Agrarista made land *ejido* property; 53 percent of Mexican lands were *ejidos.*

After the 1940s, communal landholding decreased because of lack of investment in this sector. In 1970 more than 3 million farmers were *ejidatarios.* With the neoliberal project of the Mexican government of Carlos Salinas de Gortari, Article 27 of the Constitution of 1917 was altered in 1992 to authorize the private sale of parcels of *ejidos* by the farmers, with the character of individual property.

*See also* **Cárdenas del Río, Lázaro; Mexican Liberal Agrarian Policies, Nineteenth-Century; Mexico, Wars and Revolutions: Mexican Revolution.**

BIBLIOGRAPHY

Bartra, Roger. *Agrarian Structure and Political Power in Mexico*, trans. Stephen K. Ault. Baltimore: Johns Hopkins University Press, 1993.

De Janvry, Alain, Gustavo Gordillo, and Elisabeth Sadoulet. *Mexico's Second Agrarian Reform: Household and Community Responses, 1990–1994.* La Jolla: University of California at San Diego, Center for U.S.–Mexican Studies, 1997.

DIANA BIRRICHAGA

**EL BAÚL.** El Baúl, a Late Classic (A.D. 600–900) center of the Cotzumalhuapan culture in the department of Escuintla, on the Pacific coast of Guatemala. The site is one of six architectural centers clustered on the rich cacao lands. Located near mountain corridors, these centers were strategically situated for coastal, piedmont, and highland trade. El Baúl is famous for its carved stelae and boulders, and sculptures in the round executed in a Mexican-derived Cotzumalhuapan style. The site also has an Izapan-style monument, Stela 1, dated CE 36, and a decapitated potbelly sculpture from 500–200 BCE

The mapped portion of El Baúl has an acropolis, 83 feet high and 660 feet with four courts, a ball court, and twenty two platforms. Some of the earthern structures have ramps. Pavements, staircases and drains are of stone.

There are twenty-eight Cotzumalhuapan-style monuments on the site. The themes of the sculptures are ritual scenes involving humans. Some include cacao imagery, reinforcing the idea that the elite of El Baúl were involved in the production and distribution of the crop. Other scenes show ball players and confrontation scenes between older and younger individuals. The death theme is represented by death's heads and figures in the round with closed eyes and crossed arms. Tenoned heads of serpents were architectural decorations. There are individual boulder sculptures of gods, one of which, the "Dios del Mundo," is used in present-day Maya ritual. There also are portraits of rulers. Speech scrolls, elements of dress, and glyphs indicate the art is of Mexican derivation.

The ethnic group associated with the art of El Baúl is thought to derive from southern Mexico. The style is found for 90 miles along the Pacific coast and perhaps as much as 30 miles into the mountainous interior of Guatemala.

*See also* **Ball Game, Pre-Columbian; Mesoamerica.**

BIBLIOGRAPHY

John Eric Sidney Thompson, *An Archaeological Reconnaissance in the Cotzumalhuapan Region: Excuintla, Guatemala,* Carnegie Institution of Washington Publication 574, Contribution to American Anthropology and History no. 44 (1948).

Michael D. Coe, "Cycle 7 Monuments in Middle America: A Reconsideration," in *American Anthropologist,* 59, 4 (1957): 597–611.

Lee Parsons, *Bilbao, Guatemala: An Anthropological Study of the Pacific Coast Cotzumalhuapa Region,* Publications in Anthropology (Milwaukee Public Museum) 11 and 12 (1967–1969).

*Additional Bibliography*

Evans, Susan Toby. *Ancient Mexico & Central America: Archaeology and Culture History.* London: Thames & Hudson, 2004.

Orellana, Sandra L. *Ethnohistory of the Pacific Coast.* Lancaster: Labyrinthos, 1995.

Oswaldo Fernando Chinchilla Mazariegos, Oswaldo Fernando, and Bárbara Arroyo, eds. *Iconografía y escritura teotihuacana en la costa sur de Guatemala y Chiapas.* Guatemala: Asociación Tikal, 2005.

EUGENIA J. ROBINSON

**ELCANO, JUAN SEBASTIÁN DE** (c. 1476–1526). Juan Sebastián de Elcano (*b.* ca. 1476, *d.* 4 August 1526), Spanish navigator. Elcano was born in Guetaria, Vizcaya. He completed the first circumnavigation of the world by sea, at a time of intense rivalry between Spain and Portugal over the spice trade. In 1519 he joined the expedition of Ferdinand Magellan to the Orient via South America; it entered the Pacific in November 1520. When Magellan was killed in the Philippines in 1521, Elcano, one of his captains, assumed leadership of the expedition. The only remaining ship, *Victoria,* sailed for Spain via the Cape of Good Hope (May 1522). After a voyage fraught with deprivation and sickness, Elcano and the seventeen other surviving men reached Spain in September 1522. As chief navigator and guide of an expedition to claim the Molucca Islands for Spain in June 1525, Elcano died en route in the Pacific.

*See also* **Explorers and Exploration: Spanish America; Magellan, Ferdinand.**

BIBLIOGRAPHY

Carlos Martínez Shaw, ed., *El Pacífico Español: De Magallanes a Malaspina* (1988).

Mauricio Obregón, *La primera vuelta al mundo: Magallanes, Elcano y el libro de la nao Victoria* (1984).

*Additional Bibliography*

Cervera Pery, José, and Rafael Estrada Giménez. *Juan Sebastián de Elcano: Embajador y navegante.* Barcelona: Lunwerg Editores, 2002.

Lucena Salmoral, Manuel. *Juan Sebastián Elcano.* Barcelona: Ariel, 2003.

HILARY BURGER

**EL CERREJÓN.** El Cerrejón, area of Colombia's La Guajira peninsula, known for its rich coal deposits. Discovered in 1865 by an engineer named John May (probably of British origin), the Cerrejón deposits did not draw much attention until the outbreak of World War II, with its accelerating demand for fossil fuels. In 1941 demand for coal motivated the Colombian government to sponsor a geologic study of the deposits. Yet coal production began only in the late 1970s in response to the energy crisis produced by the rising oil prices of those years. From 1976, coal production has proceeded under the auspices of Carbocol, the state coal company, which expects to reap the benefits of the vast coal reserves concentrated in the North Cerrejón region, with the technical assistance of Intercor, a subsidiary of Exxon.

*See also* **Energy.**

BIBLIOGRAPHY

Harvey Kline, "The Coal of 'El Cerrejón': An Historical Analysis of Major Colombian Policy Decisions and MNC Activities," in *Inter-American Economic Affairs* 35, no. 3 (1981): 69–90.

René De La Pedraja, *Energy Politics in Colombia* (1989).

*Additional Bibliography*

Jonish, James. *Social and Economic Effects of El Cerrejon Coal Project in Colombia.* Geneva: International Labour Organisation, 1987.

Maya, Maureén. *Bajo el manto del carbon.* Colombia: Casa Editorial Pisando Callos, 2007.

PAMELA MURRAY

**EL DORADO.** El Dorado, the European legend of great South American wealth associated with the Muisca (Chibcha) traditions of a chieftain who covered himself in gold dust before immersing himself in the waters of Lake Guatavita, north of Bogotá.

The European legends of El Dorado, "Land of Cinnamon," became a central element in the lore of Spanish and English exploration and conquest in northern South America in the sixteenth century. The El Dorado fantasy had both Amerindian and Spanish origins. On one hand, New World informants repeated rumors of the pre–Columbian Muisca rite of accession to political leadership in which the chieftain of Guatavita, covered with gold dust, dipped himself in the sacred lake and shed his gold covering while attendants and spectators threw golden offerings into the water. The extensive artistry of indigenous Colombian goldsmiths and native practices of body painting have lent credence to this account. On the other hand, the conquistadors Gonzalo Jiménez De Quesada, Sebastián de Belalcázar, and Nicolás Federmann, all of whom met in Muisca territory in 1539, and their chroniclers (including Gonzalo Fernández Oviedo, Pedro de Cieza De León, Juan de Castellanos, and Fray Pedro Simón) embellished the myth to explain feats of conquest and to enliven their narratives.

Over the course of the sixteenth century and into the eighteenth, the legend was transformed from that of the golden man of Guatavita to a golden land in northeastern South America, which is what attracted Walter Raleigh in 1595 and 1617–1618. The persistent association of the legend with Guatavita, however, led to several attempts between 1562 and 1913 to drain the lake and expose its alleged hidden treasure.

*See also* **Goldwork, Pre-Columbian.**

BIBLIOGRAPHY

Walker Chapman, *The Golden Dream: Seekers of El Dorado* (1967).

John Hemming, *The Search for El Dorado* (1978).

Demetrio Ramos Pérez, *El mito del Dorado: Su génesis y proceso* (1973).

Victor W. Von Hagen, *The Golden Man: The Quest for El Dorado* (1974).

*Additional Bibliography*

Ainsa, Fernando. *De la edad de oro a El Dorado: Génesis del discurso utópico americano.* México: Fondo de Cultura Económica, 1992.

Nicholl, Charles. *The Creature in the Map: A Journey to El Dorado.* Chicago: University of Chicago Press, 1997.

Silverberg, Robert. *The Golden Dream: Seekers of El Dorado.* Athens: Ohio University Press, 1996.

LANCE R. GRAHN

---

**ELECTRIFICATION.** Electrification is regarded as the pacesetter for economic and social advancement in most developing countries. Electric utilities in Latin America are rapidly expanding their installed capacity and undergoing change, assisted by loans from the World Bank and Inter-American Development Bank.

Total net electricity consumption in Latin America grew throughout the 1980s, reaching 577.8 billion kilowatts in 1989. Brazil was responsible for most of this growth, doubling its electricity consumption from 1980 to 1989. As of 2005, Brazil consumed 415.9 billion kilowatts of electricity annually and produced 546 billion, some of which was exported.

Hydropower represents the largest single supply source for electricity in Latin America. In 1989, 61 percent of all electricity supplied came from hydropower. Brazil has always dominated hydroelectric generation in Latin America and accounted for 60 percent (211.2 billion kilowatt-hours) of the total hydro power generated in 1988. Brazil encouraged electricity-intensive industries such as aluminum smelters to use relatively cheap hydropower, and many industries substituted electricity for imported oil. By the early 1990s, hydro provided almost 90 percent of all electricity generated in Brazil.

In 1988, hydro provided 55 percent of the electricity generated in Venezuela. Ecuador also depends on hydropower from the Paute River for 80 percent of its electricity. Mexico, by contrast, received 20 percent of its electricity from hydro and 59 percent from oil. In 1988, petroleum, natural gas, and coal burned in thermal plants generated 36 percent of the electricity consumed in Latin America in 1988, while geothermal and other sources provided 3 percent. Geothermal development proceeded rapidly during the 1970s and 1980s in Mexico and El Salvador, but remains relatively insignificant.

Like most developing countries, those of Latin America have substantial potential to increase the efficiency of their power systems. Subsidized electricity prices reduce the incentive for energy conservation. Distribution and transformation losses have been increasing to 21.5 percent in 1987. The Inter-American Development Bank is financing electric system upgrades to reduce power outages and losses in Jamaica and Bolivia, among other countries.

Most electricity generation, transmission, and distribution in Latin America is the responsibility of government ministries and corporations, except for self-generation by industrial facilities. Bolivia, Costa Rica, Ecuador, El Salvador, Guyana, Honduras, Mexico, Nicaragua, Panama, Paraguay, Uruguay, and most Caribbean islands have centralized public utilities. Self-generation at aluminum factories, cement plants, sugar mills, and other industrial facilities assists the centralized power sector in Belize, the Dominican Republic, French Guiana, Haiti, Jamaica, and Suriname. Decentralized electric sectors exist in Argentina, Brazil, Colombia, Guatemala, Peru, and Venezuela.

The failure of most state-owned utilities in Latin America to generate sufficient revenues to cover normal expansion has combined with their nations' overall debt problems to place utilities in a precarious position with respect to meeting growing demands. Some countries permit private power generation for distribution by the central grid (Mexico, Argentina, and Costa Rica) and others discuss privatization as an option (El Salvador, Venezuela, and Brazil).

Chile has privatized its electricity sector, keeping only 10 percent of the previously public entity under public ownership. The process was scheduled for completion in 1992 at a cost of $27 million. The U.S. Agency for International Development has encouraged El Salvador to follow Chile's lead and return its distribution companies to the private sector.

In Bolivia in 2006, President Evo Morales signed a decree nationalizing the country's profitable natural gas reserves. Foreign companies with holdings were given six months to renegotiate contracts with the Bolivian government or to leave. Morales's actions echoed those of President Hugo Chavez in regards to the oil deposits in Venezuela. The central idea of these moves is that Latin American energy should be for Latin Americans.

Regional cooperation has developed despite political differences. Grid interconnections exist in Central America, between Mexico and the United States, and in parts of South America. Paraguay has been exchanging electricity with Brazil and Uruguay since 1971 and with Argentina since 1973. Mexico has been selling power from its geothermal plants in Baja California to San Diego (California) Gas and Electric. Further cooperation is likely in the future. In February 1990, Venezuela and Guyana signed an agreement to interconnect their electricity grids. Venezuela was to supply up to 70 percent of Guyana's electricity requirements by 1995, mostly from the Raúl Leoni hydroelectric complex at Guri. In March 1989, Venezuela and Colombia agreed to extend the Maracaibo grid into eastern Colombia.

Rural electrification continues to be an important issue in Latin America, despite the fact that 60 percent of the population live in urban areas. The availability of reliable electric power can substantially increase the ability of rural areas to produce for outside markets. Many countries have found it excessively expensive to extend the central power grid to small, dispersed load centers. As a result, many governments are working with international aid agencies to develop decentralized power, such as mini-and micro-hydroelectric facilities, photovoltaic, and wind.

*See also* **Chávez, Hugo; Energy; Morales, Evo.**

BIBLIOGRAPHY

Mohan Munasinghe, *Rural Electrification for Development: Policy Analysis and Applications* (1987). Lee Catalano, ed., *International Directory of Electric Utilities* (1988). Latin American Energy Organization, *Energy Balances for Latin America and the Caribbean* (1988). U.S. Department Of Energy, *1989 International Energy Annual* (1991).

*Additional Bibliography*

Millán, Jaime. *Entre el mercado y el Estado: Tres décadas dereformas en el sector eléctrico de América Latina.* Washington, DC: Banco Interamericano de Desarrollo, 2006.

Millán, Jaime, and Nils Fredrick M. von der Fehr. *Keeping the Lights On: Power Sector Reforms in Latin America.* Washington, DC: Inter-American Development Bank, 2003.

Rudnick, Hugh. *Second Generation Electricity Reforms in Latin America and the California Paradigm.* Santiago: Pontífica Universidad Católica de Chile, Instituto de Economía, 2002.

MINDI J. FARBER

---

**ELETROBRÁS.** Eletrobrás, the state-owned electric power holding company in Brazil. After World War II, Brazil's need for power expanded faster than the ability of its private power companies to produce it. By the 1960s, more than half the electricity consumed in Brazil was generated by Rio Light and São Paulo Light, two subsidiaries of Toronto-based Brazilian Traction, Light, and Power. In addition to this Canadian firm there were small local generating companies throughout the country. Each produced a different voltage of power, a legacy that continues to this day.

In 1962, Eletrobrás (Centrais Elétricas Brasileiras, S.A.) was set up to develop and enforce a national electric energy policy for Brazil. After 1964, the military gave Eletrobrás the authority to implement the objective of national electric energy self-sufficiency. The American Foreign Power Company, for instance, sold its Brazilian subsidiary to Eletrobrás. Rio Light and São Paulo Light agreed to turn over its operations to Eletrobrás in phases. By the early 1970s, Eletrobrás emerged as the unchallenged holding company of Brazil's electric generators and distributors, taking over small local state corporations and expanding their activities.

Eletrobrás built two of the world's largest hydroelectric power stations—Itaipú, on the Brazilian-Paraguayan border in the south, and Tucuruí, in the north. It also built the nuclear power stations Angra I and Angra II, in collaboration with Westinghouse and with KWU-Siemens of Germany. In 2000 Angra II officially began to deliver energy. Several years of drought led to an energy crisis in 2001, when Brazil had to deal with frequent blackouts, and this led some politicians to push for the completion of a third nuclear power plant.

*See also* **Electrification; Energy.**

BIBLIOGRAPHY

Judith Tendler, *Electric Power in Brazil: Entrepreneurship in the Public Sector* (1968); *A energia elétrica no Brasil: Da primeira lâmpada à Eletrobrás* (1977).

Luiz Pinguelli Rosa, ed., *Energia e crise* (1984).

*Additional Bibliography*

Centro da Memória da Eletricidade no Brasil. *Energia elétrica no Brasil: Breve histórico 1880–2001* (*Electric energy in Brazil: A Succinct History 1880–2001*). Rio de Janeiro: O Centro, 2001.

Sauer, Ildo Luis. *A reconstrução do setor elétrico brasileiro.* São Paulo: Paz e Terra., 2003.

EUL-SOO PANG

## ELHUYAR, JUAN JOSÉ DE (1754–1796).

Juan José de Elhuyar (*b.* 15 June 1754; *d.* 20 September 1796), Spanish chemist and mineralogist and director of mines in New Granada (1783–1796). Born in Logroño, Spain, to Juan D'Elhuyar and Ursula de Zubice, Juan José de Elhuyar studied medicine in Paris from 1772 to 1777. After he returned to Spain, the Ministry of the Navy sent him and his younger brother Fausto de Elhuyar in 1778 to study at the Mining Academy of Freiberg. Elhuyar's main objective was to learn better techniques for manufacturing cannon, but he also studied geology, metallurgy, and chemistry and visited many mining operations in Central Europe. Back in Spain the two brothers isolated tungsten and published *Análisis química del volfram y examen de un nuevo metal que entra en su composición* (1783).

In late 1783 Minister of the Indies José de Gálvez selected Elhuyar as director of mines for New Granada, a position he occupied for the remainder of his life. He adapted the baron von Born's barrel method for amalgamating silver ores to local conditions and worked to raise the technological level of the Mariquita silver district. Elhuyar also developed a means for isolating platinum and carried out geological explorations. His work met resistance from both colonial officials and the mine operators. He died in Bogotá.

*See also* **Granada; Mining: Colonial Spanish America.**

BIBLIOGRAPHY

Arthur P. Whitaker, "The Elhuyar Mining Missions and the Enlightenment," in *Hispanic American Historical Review* 31, no. 4 (1951):557–585.

Stig Rydén, *Don Juan José de Elhuyar en Suecia y el descubrimiento del tungsteno, 1781–1782* (1963).

Bernardo J. Caycedo, *D'Elhuyar y el siglo XVIII neogranadino* (1971).

*Additional Bibliography*

Pelayo, Francisco. "Las actividades mineras de J. C. Mutis y Juan José Elhuyar en Nueva Granada." *Revista de Indias* 50:189 (May-August 1990): 455–471.

KENDALL W. BROWN

## ELHUYAR Y ZÚBICE, FAUSTO DE (1757–1833).

Fausto de Elhuyar y Zúbice (*b.* 11 October 1757; *d.* 6 January 1833), Spanish scientist and director general of the Mining Tribunal of New Spain (1788–1821). A native of Logroño, Spain, Elhuyar was educated in Paris and at the famous Mining School of Freiberg, Germany (1778–1781, 1787), and taught mineralogy at the Patriotic Seminary of Vergara, Spain (1782–1786). He and his brother Juan José discovered tungsten in 1783 while experimenting with wolframite.

In July 1786, while Elhuyar was in Austria to recruit mining experts for service in Spanish America and to study the Baron Ignaz von Born's method of amalgamating silver ores, Secretary of the Indies José de Gálvez appointed him director general of the Mexican Mining Tribunal. According to Walter Howe, "the renaissance of the Tribunal may be said to have begun with Elhuyar's arrival" in 1788. As director general he was an influential and energetic advocate for the mining industry, but his bureaucratic service hindered the promise of his early scientific achievements. Elhuyar established a school of mines in 1792, the first secular academy in the Spanish colonies. With Mexican independence, Elhuyar returned to Spain in 1821 and served as director general of mining, until his accidental death in 1833.

*See also* **New Spain, Colonization of the Northern Frontier.**

BIBLIOGRAPHY

The most thorough treatment of Elhuyar's early years is Arthur P. Whitaker, "The Elhuyar Mining Missions and the Enlightenment," in *Hispanic American Historical Review* 31, no. 4 (1951): 557–585. Walter Howe,

*The Mining Guild of New Spain and Its Tribunal General, 1770–1821* (1949), details his labors in Mexico.

*Additional Bibliography*

Castillo Martos, Manuel. *Creadores de la ciencia moderna en España y América: Ulloa, los Delhuyar y del Río descubren el platino, el wolframio y el vanadio.* Brenes: Muñoz Moya Editores Extremeños, 2005.

Ibáñez Rodríguez, Santiago. *La proyección mundial de los hermanos Delhuyar en el campo de la cienica y la economía.* Logroño: Universidad de La Rioja, Servicio de Publicaciones, 2002.

KENDALL W. BROWN

---

**ELÍAS, DOMINGO** (1805–1867). Elías Domingo (*b.* 19 December 1805; *d.* 3 December 1867), Peruvian plantation owner and statesman. Born to aristocratic parents in the Ica Valley, the wine-growing center of the southern coast, he was educated in elite Peruvian schools and in Spain and France. On returning home he married Doña Ysabel de la Quintana y Pedemonte, sister of the new archbishop of Lima. Beginning as a merchant and lender, he later became one of the largest landowners in the coastal valleys of Peru. He owned more than 600 slaves by 1850 and cultivated wine, *pisco,* and cotton on his plantations. Elías soon became politically active. A convinced liberal, he strongly favored free trade, and by 1843 he had formed a partnership with Ramón Castilla. After Castilla became president in 1845, Elías joined his council of state, a three-member body of presidential advisers who by serving as liaisons with the national congress, held a great deal of power. A philanthropist, he donated large sums to found a high school, the Colegio de Nuestra Señora de Guadalupe, which became the source of liberal thought in Peru for decades. Elías also sought to preserve black slavery in Peru.

A major scandal erupted when he tried to bypass the prohibition against the African slave trade with a purchase in Colombia. The purchase included children, who under Peruvian law were free. In 1849 he designed a law to regulate the importation of indentured Asian labor. When José Rufino Echenique became president in 1851, Elías strenuously opposed his debt consolidation program because it would overburden the state, and he called the program a fraud. Echenique resorted to censorship and terrorism to stop his opponents, and Elías rebelled. Soon he joined forces with the popular uprising led by Castilla. Returning to the private sector, probably by 1859, he converted most of his remaining vineyards to cotton and focused completely on international cotton commerce. His efforts in this trade foundered on inadequate marketing techniques, and by the time of his death his cotton empire was in ruins.

*See also* **Castilla, Ramón; Cotton; Plantations; Slavery: Spanish America.**

BIBLIOGRAPHY

Fredrick B. Pike, *The Modern History of Peru* (1967), esp. pp. 101–102, 105.

Peter Blanchard, *Slavery and Abolition in Early Republican Peru* (1992).

Alfonso Quiroz, *Domestic and Foreign Finance in Modern Peru, 1850–1950* (1993).

*Additional Bibliography*

Blanchard, Peter. "The 'Transitional Man' in Nineteenth-Century Latin America: The Case of Domingo Elías of Peru." *Bulletin of Latin American Research* 15:2 (May 1996): 157–176.

Milla Batres, Carlos, and Luis Ponce Vega. *Historia económica y política republicana: Siglos XIX-XX.* Madrid: Editorial Milla Batres, 1998.

VINCENT PELOSO

---

**EL INCA.** *See* **Garcilaso de la Vega, El Inca.**

---

**ELÍO, FRANCISCO JAVIER** (1767–1822). Francisco Javier Elío (*b.* 4 March 1767; *d.* 4 September 1822), last viceroy of the Río de la Plata. Born in Navarre, Spain, he began his military career as a lieutenant in the defense of Oran and Ceuta in North Africa. Elío was sent to the Río de la Plata in 1805 with the rank of colonel, to command the Banda Oriental. Shortly after the first English invasion (1806), Viceroy Santiago de Liniers y Bremond named Elío interim governor of Montevideo. After the second English invasion (1807), he became one of Liniers's chief opponents and assumed the post of viceroy. After Liniers's successor, Cisneros, was relieved of his post by the Cabildo Abierto in May 1810, Elío returned to Spain and convinced the Regency Council to appoint him viceroy. The junta established in Buenos Aires refused to recognize his appointment, however, so he governed from Montevideo until he was forced from power by an antiroyalist uprising in the Banda Oriental. Elío returned to Spain in 1812 and became involved in Spanish political life. He was executed at Valencia.

*See also* **Banda Oriental.**

BIBLIOGRAPHY

Sociedad Rural Argentina, *El virreinato del Río de la Plata, 1776–1810* (1976).

Guillermo F. De Nevares, *Como se desintegró el virreinato del Río de la Plata y se consolidó Brasil* (1987).

*Additional Bibliography*

Acevedo, Edberto Oscar. *Controversias virreinales rioplatenses.* Buenos Aires: Ediciones Ciudad Argentina, 1997.

Szuchman, Mark D., and Jonathan C. Brown. *Revolution and Restoration: The Rearrangement of Power in Argentina, 1776-1860.* Lincoln: University of Nebraska Press, 1994.

Susan Socolow

**ÉLITE (HAITI).** Élite (Haiti), a social class of Haiti. The *élite* of Haiti find their cultural traditions in the *gens de couleur* (mulattoes) of colonial Haiti (Saint-Domingue). The *gens de couleur* established individual status on the basis of the number of slaves owned, European education, orthodox Catholicism, and especially skin tone. The lighter one's complexion, the higher one's social position. This class, which makes up about 2 percent of the Haitian population, survived the Haitian Revolution (1789–1804) and has generally controlled Haitian politics since independence.

Even though the *élite* promoted white French values through their political and social domination of Haiti, there are notable individual exceptions. Alexandre Pétion, who ruled the Republic of Haiti from 1807 to 1818, supported black culture and economic patterns. But in the twentieth century the *élite* has run afoul of rising black political control and cultural nationalism. Black Haitians have often resented *élite* attitudes toward their culture and the stain of collaboration the *élite* gained by supporting the U.S. occupation of Haiti (1915–1934).

In 1957 François "Papa Doc" Duvalier (1957–1971) launched a campaign of extermination against the *élite.* Claiming that they were whites with black skins, he had thousands of them murdered while he convinced the masses that he was the reincarnation of Jean-Jacques Dessalines. "Papa Doc" argued that he was completing the Haitian Revolution by destroying the *élite.* The *élite* survived because Duvalier abandoned his policy of mulatto extermination.

The elite enjoyed a resurgence of power after the death of Papa Doc. Under the rule of his son, Jean-Claude Duvalier (1971–1986), and under military rule, the government promoted its restoration. Jean-Bertrand Aristide (1991; 1994–1996; 2001–2004), on the other hand, publicly stated his opposition to the *élite.* Re-elected to a second term in 2006, President René Préval has sought elite support without alienating his largely poor political base.

*See also* **Aristide, Jean-Bertrand; Duvalier, François; Duvalier, Jean-Claude; Haiti.**

BIBLIOGRAPHY

Cyril L. R. James, *The Black Jacobins* (1938).

James Leyburn, *The Haitian People* (1941).

Thomas Ott, *The Haitian Revolution, 1789–1804* (1973), and "Haitian National Consciousness and the Revolution," in *Journal of Great Lakes History* 1 (1976): 71–78.

David Nicholls, *Haiti in Caribbean Context* (1985).

*Additional Bibliography*

Dubois, Laurent. *Avengers of the New World: The Story of the Haitian Revolution.* Cambridge: Belknap Press of Harvard University Press, 2004.

Geggus. David. *Haitian Revolutionary Studies.* Bloomington: Indiana University Press, 2002.

King, Stewart R. *Blue Coat or Powdered Wig: Free People of Color in Pre-Revolutionary Saint-Domingue.* Athens: University of Georgia Press, 2001.

Ridgeway,James. ed. *The Haiti Files: Decoding the Crisis.* Washington, D.C.: Essential Books, 1994.

Thomas O. Ott

## ELIZAGA, JOSÉ MARÍA (1786–1842).

José María Elizaga (*b.* 27 September 1786; *d.* 2 October 1842), Mexican pianist, organist, and composer. Piano study in his native Morelia and in Mexico City prepared Elizaga for a position as assistant organist in the Colegio de San Nicolás in Morelia (1799). Among his piano pupils was Doña Ana María Huarte, the future wife of emperor Agustín de Iturbide; he eventually became music director of Iturbide's imperial court (1822). Elizaga started his own music publishing business and in 1825 founded a conservatory that later formed the basis of the National Conservatory of Music. He served as *maestro de capilla* of the Guadalajara cathedral from 1827 to 1830 and retired to Morelia in 1842. His works include sacred music for orchestra and chorus, two didactic music treatises, and *Vals con variaciones* for piano.

*See also* **Music: Art Music.**

BIBLIOGRAPHY

Robert Stevenson, *Music in Mexico: A Historical Survey* (1952).

*Additional Bibliography*

Miranda, Ricardo. "Haydn en Morelia: José Mariano Elízaga." *Revista Musical Chilena* 52:190 (July–December 1998): 55–63.

ROBERT L. PARKER

## ELIZALDE, RUFINO DE (1822–1887).

The Argentine politician Rufino de Elizalde began his career as an attorney in 1846. In 1852 he conspired against the military leader Juan Manuel de Rosas, who at the time was governor of the province of Buenos Aires. After Rosas' defeat in the battle of Caseros, Buenos Aires held the status of an autonomous state within the Argentine Confederation. Elizalde established close ties with Bartolomé Mitre, who sought to form a national union dominated by Buenos Aires. Mitre was elected governor of the province in 1860, and Elizalde took over the post of minister of the treasury. The confederation and Buenos Aires armies clashed several times, and Buenos Aires finally prevailed in 1861 at the battle of Pavón. The country was reunified under the command of Mitre, who was named president in 1862. Elizalde occupied the post of minister of foreign affairs.

Mitre was forced to resolve substantial problems related to national organization, including the abolition of the provincial militias. Elizalde's foreign policy, anti-American and pro-European in nature, was forced to address border disputes with the Argentine state. He also tried to reaffirm the principle of national sovereignty with regard to foreign powers. The most important event in foreign affairs was the Paraguayan War (1865–1870) between the Triple Alliance (Argentina, Brazil, and Uruguay) and Paraguay. The origins of this bloody war lay in the conflicts among Paraguay, Brazil, and Argentina during the consolidation of their respective nation-states. The incident that set off the conflict was Paraguay's interference in the internal politics of Uruguay. The Triple Alliance was victorious, and Argentina and Brazil won territory from Paraguay. Elizalde was minister once again during the presidency of Nicolás Avellaneda (1874–1880).

*See also* **Argentina: The Nineteenth Century; Avellaneda, Nicolás; Mitre, Bartolomé; Rosas, Juan Manuel de; War of the Triple Alliance.**

BIBLIOGRAPHY

Doratioto, Francisco Fernando. *Maldita Guerra: Nova historia da Guerra do Paraguai.* Sao Paulo: Companhia das Letras, 2002.

Halperín Donghi, Tulio. *Una nación para el desierto argentino.* Buenos Aires: Centro Editor de América Latina, 1982.

Oszlak, Oscar. *La formación del estado argentino*, 3rd edition. Buenos Aires: AR Planeta, 1999.

VICENTE PALERMO

## ELIZONDO, SALVADOR (1932–2006).

Salvador Elizondo was a Mexican poet and author. A notable figure in Mexican letters, he had an eclectic interest in poetry, film, essays, and fiction that has given him a well-deserved reputation for experimental work.

Born on December 19, 1932, in Mexico City of wealthy parents, Elizondo resided for several years in Europe, where he studied in Paris and Cambridge. He was also a student at the University of Ottawa, in Canada, and Mexico's School of Philosophy and Letters of the National University (1952–1953, 1959), where he later taught. As a fellow at the Center for Mexican Writers, he wrote *Farabeuf* (1965), an innovative and intellectually challenging novel that represents the opposing literary current to magical realism in Latin America; it received the distinguished Villaurrutia Prize in 1965. He co-founded the magazine *S.NOB*, an exploration of eroticism in Mexican letters, and served as editor in chief of *Estaciones*, a literary magazine. Twice a Guggenheim fellow (1968–1969 and 1973–1974), he was considered a leader of the Nuevo Cine group. He conducted the *Contextos* radio program for the National University (1968–1978) and served on the board and contributed to Octavio Paz's journal *Vuelta* in the 1980s. He was both a member of the Mexican Academy of Letters (1976) and the prestigious Colegio Nacional (1981) and received the National Prize in Literature in 1990. He died on March 29, 2006.

*See also* **Literature: Spanish America.**

BIBLIOGRAPHY

*Work by Salvador Elizondo*

*Escritos mexicanos*. Mexico: ISTSE, 2000.

*Other Works*

Guerrero, Fernando. *Farabeuf a través del espejo: Análisis del erotismo y las voces narrativas de la novela*. Mexico: Juan Pablos, 2001.

*Salvador Elizondo*. Mexico: Conaculta, 1999. Video recording.

RODERIC AI CAMP

**EL MIRADOR.** El Mirador, a very large Late Formative Maya site in the northern part of Petén, Guatemala, near the Mexican border. Its inaccessibility has limited research, but evidence now shows that the site was occupied in the Middle Formative Period, grew to prominence and power during the Late Formative, and declined in the Protoclassic—ultimately relinquishing its power by A.D. 300 to Tikal, 40 miles south. The site was superficially reoccupied during the Late Classic Period. Like Tikal, El Mirador derived its importance from its domination of transpeninsular trade routes and control of portages between the Gulf drainage and the Caribbean drainage.

The architecture of El Mirador is of the grandest scale. In the central area of the site, to the east, the Danta complex includes a multitiered grouping of platforms and truncated pyramids on a basal platform nearly 1,000 feet square. The summit of the crowning pyramid rises 230 feet above the ground. Danta is both the tallest Maya structure and the Maya structure of greatest volume.

About one mile to the west, and linked to the Danta complex by a *sacbe* (causeway), are several additional large-scale architectural groupings. Next in size to the Danta complex is El Tigre, whose tallest pyramid stands 180 feet high. Some 400 yards south of El Tigre, the Monos group includes a pyramid 130 feet high.

Construction utilizes cut-stone facings on rubble cores, and there are substantial remains of extensive stucco decoration of the exterior surfaces. Excavation of Structure 34 uncovered large masks of modeled stucco adjacent to the plastered front steps. Groupings of pyramids on large basal platforms are frequently in triples, with two smaller pyramids flanking the front plaza of the largest structure. Structures are linked by walls and causeways, and the region around the site center is dotted with *bajos* (lowlands), which flood seasonally.

*See also* **Maya, The.**

BIBLIOGRAPHY

Ray T. Matheny, ed., *El Mirador, Petén, Guatemala: An Interim Report* (1980).

Sylvanus G. Morley and George W. Brainerd, *The Ancient Maya,* 4th ed. (1983), esp. pp. 296–300.

*Additional Bibliography*

Forsyth, Donald W. *The Ceramics of El Mirador, Petén, Guatemala*. Provo, UT: New World Archaeological Foundation, Brigham Young University, 1989.

Fowler, William R. *Analysis of the Chipped Stone Artifacts of El Mirador, Guatemala*. Provo, UT: New World Archaeological Foundation, Brigham Young University, 1987.

Hansen, Richard D. *Excavations in the Tigre Complex, El Mirador, Petén, Guatemala*. Provo, UT: New World Archaeological Foundation, Brigham Young University, 1990.

Masson, Marilyn A., and David A. Freidel, eds. *Ancient Maya Political Economies.* Walnut Creek, CA: Altamira Press, 2002.

Nelson, Fred W., and David S. Howard. *Trace Element Analysis of Obsidian Artifacts from El Mirador, Guatemala.* Provo, UT: New World Archaeological Foundation, Brigham Young University, 1986.

WALTER R. T. WITSCHEY

**EL MORRO (HAVANA).** El Morro Castle (Castillo de los Tres Reyes del Morro) is the monumental fortress that dominates the narrow entrance to Havana's vast harbor. Designed by the famed military engineer Bautista Antonelli, it was completed in 1590. The exterior walls blend with massive rocks on the elevations overlooking the port from the east and still stand as an impressive symbol of Hapsburg and Bourbon authority. Throughout the colonial period, El Morro functioned as a prison and as the key strong-point in Havana's defense complex. To close off Havana harbor to pirates and invaders, authorities on several occasions laid a huge iron chain or cable across the water from El Morro to the smaller western fort of Salvador de la Punta. When El Morro fell to a British land and sea attack on 31 July 1762, the city of Havana was doomed. For most of the next year, the Cuban capital remained in British hands. After the Treaty of Paris was signed in 1763, El Morro's defenses were again strengthened, financed by the *situados* (subsidies) from Mexico. Other Cuban fortresses, including the impressive one built in Santiago in 1633, also bear the name El Morro.

*See also* **Havana.**

BIBLIOGRAPHY

J. H. Parry and P. M. Sherlock, *A Short History of the West Indies,* 3d ed. (1971).

Vicente Báez, ed., *La enciclopedia de Cuba: Arquitectura, Artes Plásticas, Música,* vol. 7 (1974), pp. 5–9.

Leví Marrero, *Cuba: Economía y sociedad,* vol. 2 (1974), pp. 406–409 and vol. 6 (1978), pp. 112–119.

Allan J. Kuethe, *Cuba, 1753–1815: Crown, Military, and Society* (1986).

LINDA K. SALVUCCI

**EL MORRO (SAN JUAN).** The Castillo San Felipe del Morro (El Morro), located in San Juan, is one of the oldest military fortifications built by the Europeans in the Western Hemisphere. Defending Puerto Rico's strategic position as the gateway to the Spanish possessions in the Americas, El Morro played a key role in a highly structured system of fortresses and massive walls enclosing the old colonial district of San Juan. El Morrow was designed to protect the harbor from attacks by sea, and it withstood four major attacks—three by the British (1595, 1598, and 1797) and one by the Dutch (1625)—and saw action for the last time during the Spanish-Cuban-American War of 1898.

The original construction dates from 1539, when a modest round tower and battery at the base of the promontory (*morro*) overlooked the entrance to the harbor. Between 1589 and 1597 new hornwork walls, bastions, and batteries buttressed the original structure. Work continued through the 1600s, transforming El Morro into a multiple-level defense. In the 1760s the strengthening of San Juan's fortifications became central to the Bourbon reforms pursued by King Charles III of Spain. The town walls were expanded, a large new fort (Castillo San Cristóbal) was built, and El Morro gained a robust battery, huge new walls, and thicker parapets, becoming the colossal structure it is today. These improvements were funded by royal subsidies (*situado*) flowing from the viceroyalty of New Spain (Mexico). The workforce was drawn from day laborers, slaves, prisoners, off-duty soldiers, and civilians from neighboring areas, who also supplied the building materials. Following the U.S. occupation of Puerto Rico in 1898, El Morro and all of the other Spanish-era fortresses passed into the control of the U.S. Army. In 1961 the U.S. National Park Service took responsibility over the fortifications in Old San Juan, preserving them as a museum of military history. Due to their historical importance and enduring architectural value, the walls and fortifications of San Juan became a UNESCO World Heritage Site in 1983.

*See also* **Bourbon Reforms; Puerto Rico.**

BIBLIOGRAPHY

Manucy, Albert, and Ricardo Torres-Reyes. *Puerto Rico and the Forts of Old San Juan*. Old Greenwich, CT: Chatham Press, 1973.

LUIS A. GONZÁLEZ

**EL NIÑO.** El Niño, or El Niño–Southern Oscillation (ENSO), a warm current that temporarily raises the surface-water temperature off the Peruvian and Ecuadorian coasts around Christmas, hence the name ("the child"). Occasionally, especially warm waters disrupt the food chain significantly. Notably strong El Niño episodes have occurred in 1541, 1578, 1614, 1624, 1652, 1701, 1720, 1728, 1763, 1770, 1791, 1804, 1814, 1828, 1845, 1864, 1871, 1877–1878, 1884, 1891, 1899, 1911, 1918, 1925–1926, 1941, 1957–1958, 1972–1973, 1982–1983, 1991–1992, 1993, 1994, 1997–1998, 2002–2003, 2004–2005, and 2006–2007. Observers have noted "teleconnections," such as drought in central Chile and northeast Brazil and heavy rain in Peru and Ecuador. During strong El Niño years, eastern Africa gets more rain and Canadian winters are warmer. Moreover, global climate change further exacerbates the effects of El Niño. The research of Sir Gilbert Walker (1868–1958), Jakob Bjerknes (1897–1975), and the 1985–1995 Tropical Ocean and Global Atmosphere (TOGA) study have contributed to a comprehensive explanation for El Niño events and their global implications. In the twenty-first century, many countries employ numerical prediction models to better adapt to and prevent the climate variability effects El Niño produces. International bodies such as the Center on Research El Niño (CIIFEN) headquartered in Guayaquil, Ecuador, likewise generate scientific research to assist on a regional scale.

*See also* **Fishing Industry.**

BIBLIOGRAPHY

William H. Quinn et al., "Historical Trends and Statistics of the Southern Oscillation, El Niño, and Indonesian Droughts," in *Fishery Bulletin* 76, no. 3 (July 1978): 663–678.

Kevin Hamilton and Rolando R. García, "El Niño / Southern Oscillation Events and Their Associated Midlatitude Teleconnections, 1531–1841," in *Bulletin of the American Meteorological Society* 67 no. 11 (November 1986): 1354–1361.

M. H. Glantz et al., eds., *Teleconnections Linking Worldwide Climate Anomalies: Scientific Basis and Societal Impact* (1991).

*Additional Bibliography*

Caviedes, César. *El Niño in History: Storming through the Ages.* Gainesville: University Press of Florida, 2001.

Gasparri, Enrico; Carlo Tassara; and Margarita Velasco. *El fenómeno de El Niño en el Ecuador, 1997–1999: Del desastre a la prevención.* Quito, Ecuador: Ediciones Abya-Yala, 1999.

Lawas, Edward A. *El Niño and the Peruvian Anchovy Fishery.* Sausalito, CA: University Science Books, 1997.

Sandweiss, Daniel H.; Jeffrey Quilter; and Joanne Pillsbury. *El Niño, Catastrophism, and Culture Change in Ancient America: A Symposium at Dumbarton Oaks, 12th–13th October 2002.* Washington, DC: Dumbarton Oaks Research Library and Collection, 2008.

Sesé, José María, and Ruth Magali Rosas. *El fenómeno "El Niño" en la costa norte del Perú a través de la histoira; Perú-Ecuador: Un espacio compartido.* Piura, Peru: Universidad de Piura, 2001.

ROBERT H. CLAXTON

**EL PARAÍSO.** El Paraíso (Chuquitanta), a Late Preceramic-period monumental site on the central coast of Peru. Among the many archaeological treasures of the desert coast of Peru are massive stone and adobe architectural complexes, which served as ceremonial or administrative centers, dating to the Late Preceramic and Initial (early ceramic) periods (ca. 2000 BCE–1400 BCE). Among the most impressive of these is the El Paraíso site, a complex of eight or nine stone buildings covering about 125 acres in the Chillón River valley north of Lima. The site, which was occupied between 1800 and 1500 BCE, has been investigated by the archaeologists Frédéric Engel (mid-1960s) and Jeffrey Quilter (mid-1980s).

El Paraíso is the largest of the early monumental sites of the Peruvian coast. Complexes of rooms that make up the site are constructed of fieldstone laid in clay; walls were often covered by clay plaster, now disintegrated. The two largest architectural units are 1,320 feet long and parallel to each other, about 594 feet apart. The area between these units may have been a plaza. Other room complexes are smaller; the presence of architectural units and public spaces of different sizes suggests that a variety of ceremonial, administrative, and residential activities were carried out at the site.

Quilter and colleagues focused their research on recovering food remains from residential areas of the site. They found that fish was the most important animal consumed along with a variety of cultivated and wild plant foods. Cotton remains were abundant at the site—the Late Preceramic of the Peruvian coast is traditionally called the Cotton Preceramic—and researchers propose that El Paraíso controlled and developed cotton production in the Chillón-Rímac region.

*See also* **Archaeology.**

BIBLIOGRAPHY

Frédéric-André Engel, "Le complexe précéramique d'El Paraíso (Pérou)," in *Journal de la société des américanistes* 55 (1966):43–95.

Jeffrey Quilter, "Architecture and Chronology at El Paraíso, Peru," in *Journal of Field Archaeology* 12 (1985):279–297.

Jeffrey Quilter, Bernardino Ojeda E., Deborah M. Pearsall, Daniel H. Sandweiss, John G. Jones, and Elizabeth S. Wing, "Subsistence Economy of El Paraíso, an Early Peruvian Site," in *Science* 251 (1991):277–283.

*Additional Bibliography*

Moseley, Michael E. *The Incas and their Ancestors: The Archaeology of Peru.* New York: Thames and Hudson, 1992.

Quilter, Jeffrey, et al. "Subsistence Economy of El Paraíso, an Early Peruvian Site." *Science* Vol. 251, No. 4991 (Jan. 18, 1991): 271-283.

Silva, Jorge. "Prehistoric Settlement Patterns in the Chillón River Valley, Peru." Ph.D. diss., University of Michigan, 1996.

Stanish, Charles. "The Origin of State Societies in South America." *Annual Review of Anthropology* Vol. 30. (2001): 41-64.

DEBORAH M. PEARSALL

**EL SALVADOR.** The State of El Salvador developed around its capital, San Salvador. About fifty miles wide and less than two hundred miles in length along a volcanic chain paralleling the Pacific coast, it is the only state in Central America without a Caribbean shoreline. It is bounded on the south by the Pacific Ocean, on the west and northwest by Guatemala, on the north and east by Honduras, and on the southeast by the Gulf of Fonseca, which it shares with Honduras and Nicaragua. Much of the population lives in valleys at altitudes of between 2,000 and 3,000 feet above sea level. El Salvador's fertile valleys and coastal plain have determined much of its modern history, as agricultural exports have been responsible for both the enrichment of a small landed oligarchy and the impoverishment of the rural masses.

The smallest of the Central American states in area (8,124 square miles), its population of 6.82 million (2006 estimate) makes it the most densely populated country in Latin America (839.8 per square mile) and second only to neighboring Guatemala in total population among the states that formerly comprised the Kingdom of Guatemala. Its population grew especially during the twentieth century, when after rising at a rate of about 1.5 percent in the nineteenth century its annual growth rate increased to more than 3 percent in the twentieth century before moderating to 1.72 percent by 2006 (see Table 1).

## THE COLONIAL PERIOD

Although Mayans inhabited El Salvador before its conquest by Pedro de Alvarado in 1524, Nahuatl peoples from Mexico were also important, and the aggressive and industrious Pipil have, at least in the country's mythology, been given credit for Salvadorans' greater tendency toward those traits than other Central Americans.

Throughout most of the colonial period San Salvador was part of the province of Guatemala, within the Kingdom of Guatemala in the Viceroyalty of New Spain. It was subdivided into *alcaldías mayores* centered on the towns of San Salvador, San Miguel, San Vicente, Santa Ana, and Sonsonate.

In the eighteenth century the rise of indigo production under the impetus of Bourbon economic policy brought changes to El Salvador that would lead to its emergence as a separate political unit. The establishment of the intendancy of San Salvador in 1786, although it remained within the Kingdom of Guatemala, marked the beginning of Salvadoran nationalism, a sentiment encouraged by several of its intendants, who defended and promoted Salvadoran economic interests. Smaller

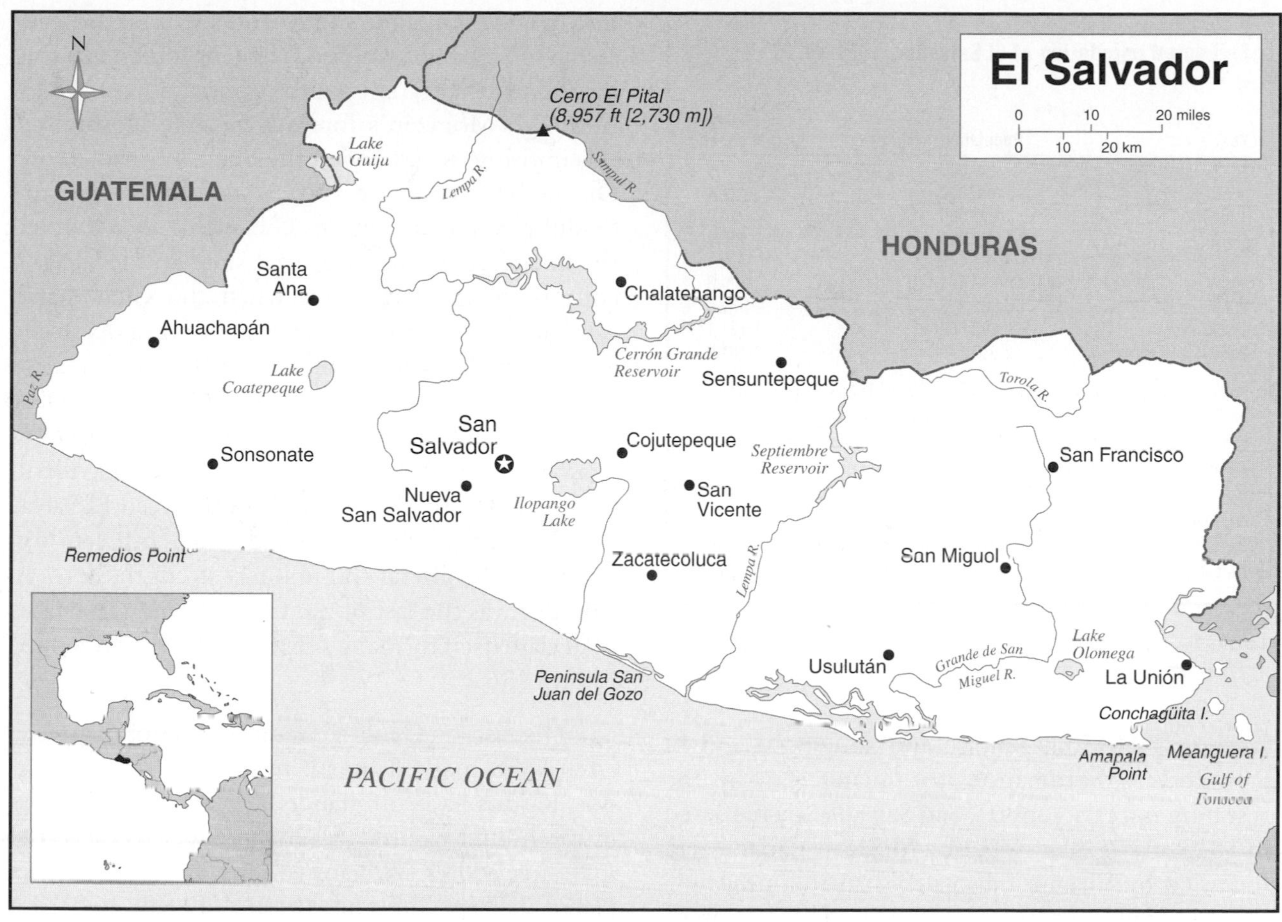


indigo planters chafed under the economic dominance of Guatemalan merchant capitalists, who financed the export trade, whereas the Salvadoran clergy objected both to the anticlericalism of the Bourbons and to the conservative ecclesiastical hierarchy in Guatemala City. They demanded a separate diocese for San Salvador, which remained under the jurisdiction of the bishop of Guatemala.

In Guatemala, earthquakes in 1773 had destroyed the capital city, Antigua Guatemala, resulting in a decision to move to a new site, present-day Guatemala City. Disruption of the kingdom's capital coincided with the rise of Salvadoran indigo as the leading agricultural export of the kingdom and caused many Salvadoran Creoles to favor, unsuccessfully, moving the capital to San Salvador, heightening their rivalry with Guatemala City.

These issues became more acute at the close of the colonial period when severe economic decline troubled the kingdom. Regional separatism and resentment toward conservative Guatemala made San Salvador a hotbed of liberalism in the nineteenth century. An abortive independence attempt in 1811, led by Father José Matías Delgado, reflected that sentiment but was crushed by military force from Guatemala under the command of a new intendant, José de Aycinena, scion of the most powerful Guatemalan merchant family. This defeat intensified Salvadoran resentment toward Guatemala.

### INDEPENDENCE TO 1900

Independence from Spain came fairly suddenly on September 15, 1821, when a meeting of notables in Guatemala City endorsed Mexican Agustín de Iturbide's Plan of Iguala. Officials in San Salvador accepted and proclaimed the act on September 21, and on September 29, Salvadoran Creoles met and issued their own declaration of independence from Spain, but they resisted incorporation into

**Estimated population of El Salvador, 1821–2050**

| Year | Population | Density (per sq. km) |
|---|---|---|
| 1821 | 248,000 | 11.8 |
| 1850 | 366,000 | 17.4 |
| 1900 | 800,000 | 38.0 |
| 1950 | 1,860,000 | 88.4 |
| 1980 | 4,525,000 | 215.1 |
| 2000 | 6,739,000 | 320.3 |
| 2006 | 6,822,378 | 839.8 |
| 2025 | 9,107,608 | 1,121.1 |
| 2050 | 12,039,149 | 1,481.9 |

SOURCE: Ralph Lee Woodward, Jr., "Crecimiento de población en Centroamérica durante la primera mitad del siglo de la independencia nacional," *Mesoamérica* (Antigua, Guatemala: El Centro de Investigaciones Regionales de Mesoamérica, 1980), pp. 219–231; James W. Wilkie, ed., *Statistical Abstract of Latin America*, vol. 28 (1990): 9, 114, 122; "El Salvador Facts and Figures," *MSN Encarta*, available from http://encarta.msn.com/fact_631504759/El_Salvador_Facts_and_Figures.html.

**Table 1**

Iturbide's Mexican Empire and sought to end El Salvador's subordination to Guatemala. In the resulting military conflict, San Salvador surrendered in 1823 after a long siege by a Mexican-Guatemalan force led by Vicente Filísola, but in the meantime the Mexican Empire itself collapsed. Salvadorans successfully led the movement to declare Central America independent of Mexico, and on July 1, 1823, El Salvador became an autonomous state in the United Provinces of the Center of America.

The deep animosities that developed during the independence process and the strong differences between the liberal and conservative approaches to national development plagued the administration of the new federal president, a Salvadoran military officer named Manuel José Arce, elected under the constitution of 1824. The takeover of the federal government by Guatemalan conservatives led to civil war from 1826 to 1829, principally between El Salvador and Guatemala, although Hondurans and Nicaraguans were also involved. Liberal victory, under the leadership of a Honduran general, Francisco Morazán, restored Salvadoran importance in the Central American federation, and San Salvador became its capital in 1835, after having first moved from Guatemala to Sonsonate in 1834.

The Pipil people of El Salvador, however, resisted development efforts, taxes, and reforms that threatened their lands and customs. Under the leadership of Anastasio Aquino, a violent Indian uprising threatened the stability of the government in 1833. Although Morazán's forces were able to suppress this uprising, it weakened the liberals considerably. On the heels of that revolt came a similar but successful peasant uprising in Guatemala that toppled the liberal government of that state and led to the collapse of the federation when the Guatemalan caudillo Rafael Carrera defeated Morazán decisively at Guatemala City in March 1840. Conservative strength in Nicaragua and Costa Rica sealed the fate of the federation as each of the individual states began to go its separate way. Carrera's iron rule in Guatemala from 1839 to 1865 influenced El Salvador through much of the mid-nineteenth century, curtailing the liberal and unionist strength there. El Salvador was the last of the Central American states to declare itself formally a separate, sovereign republic, in 1856.

The rise of General Gerardo Barrios Espinosa after 1858 marked liberal resurgence in El Salvador. Barrios had commanded the Salvadoran forces in the united Central American effort to drive the U.S. freebooter William Walker from Nicaragua (1856–1857). Upon his return to El Salvador from that campaign, Barrios failed in an 1857 attempt to unseat president Rafael Campo, but the following year he regained influence during the administration of Miguel Santín Castillo. He became acting chief of state in 1858 and again from 1859 to 1860 and president from 1861 to 1863. As president of El Salvador in 1861 he consolidated his political and military strength and began to initiate liberal economic and anticlerical reforms. The immediate result was an invasion by Rafael Carrera in 1863, which Barrios repulsed at Coatepeque on February 24 of that year, but Carrera returned later in the year to defeat Barrios and place the more conservative Francisco Dueñas in power (1863–1871). Nevertheless, many of the economic reforms begun by Barrios continued, and the process of liberalization once more accelerated under the rule of Santiago González (1871–1876) and Rafael Zaldívar (1876–1885).

Liberal Party dominance from 1871 to 1944 brought remarkable changes to El Salvador. Independence from Guatemalan intervention was achieved with the defeat of the invading army and the death of the Guatemalan liberal caudillo Justo Rufino Barrios at Chalchuapa in 1885. Barrios was trying to restore the Central American union under his military leadership, and although El Salvador had traditionally favored union, its antipathy toward Guatemala outweighed unionist sentiment.

The Salvadoran governments that followed concentrated on economic development as they facilitated the expansion of coffee exports by the planter elite at the expense of peasant land and labor. Indigo exports had continued to be important for El Salvador, but the development of aniline coal-tar dyes diminished their importance after 1860. The loose, volcanic soil in the tropical highlands of the country produced high-quality coffee and enabled a few planters to become dominant in economic and political affairs. Under their leadership, El Salvador became highly dependent on international markets for coffee. They modernized the transportation system and capital city, and gained control over more rural land for coffee production. In the early twentieth century this "coffee prosperity" gained El Salvador a reputation as the most progressive of the Central American states. It became the first nation in Central America to have paved highways. With new ports and railways, the city of San Salvador grew impressively in size and economic activity. A stronger military force maintained the liberal oligarchy, often referred to as the "fourteen families," although there were always more than that. Between 1913 and 1927 members of these families, notably the Meléndez and Quiñónez dynasty, presided over governments that were generally more stable than those in the neighboring states.

### THE EARLY TWENTIETH CENTURY

Spanish colonialism had left a heritage of a small elite ruling a servile mass, and feudal traditions persisted well into the twentieth century. The principal features of the Salvadoran social structure, however, are especially related to the rise of coffee cultivation and the emergence of a dominant oligarchy in the late nineteenth and early twentieth centuries. Expansion into other agricultural exports, the rise of manufacturing, and the growth of the military officer corps, especially since 1950, expanded and diversified this elite to more than 250 families. Moreover, the modernization of the economy contributed to the growth in San Salvador of a significant middle class, which played a growing role in the intellectual, political, and cultural development of the country. The vast majority of the population, however, remained poor, uneducated, and lacking in economic opportunity. The widening gulf between urban modernization and rural backwardness, and between rich and poor, is perhaps nowhere so obvious in Latin America as in El Salvador. These serious social and economic inequities worsened in the late twentieth century as rapid population growth exceeded economic growth. Modernization sometimes obscured the growing social inequities that were aggravated by rapid population growth. While San Salvador became a modern urban center, rural poverty and malnutrition soared.

Challenges to the liberal oligarchy began to appear in the 1920s, especially as articulated by the Salvadoran intellectual leader Alberto Masferrer, whose ideas influenced the founding of the Labor Party in 1930. The Communist Party of El Salvador, organized in 1925, reflected more radical opposition, whose most outspoken representative was Agustín Farabundo Martí. The economic hardships occasioned by the international depression following 1929 intensified the problems and encouraged labor organization and agitation. Yet the 1930 victory of the Labor Party candidate, Arturo Araujo, a progressive member of the planter elite, came as a surprise to the oligarchy, who were unprepared to make concessions to social democracy, land reform, and improved health and education along the lines Masferrer had advocated. Following nearly a year of chaotic government and massive labor demonstrations, the army intervened and ousted Araújo in favor of his vice president, General Maximiliano Hernández Martínez of the Liberal Party, on December 2, 1931. Martí and the Communists led a rural revolt in January 1932, but in a struggle that essentially pitted peasant machetes against army machine guns, the result was the massacre of between 10,000 to 30,000 peasants, followed by repression and establishment of a military dictatorship that would last until 1944.

The 1932 massacre, known as La Matanza, was a watershed in Salvadoran history, for it marked the end of a period of relatively tolerant civilian oligarchic rule and the growth of labor organizations. The elite, frightened by the 1932 peasant uprising,

**El Salvador**

| | |
|---|---|
| **Population:** | 6,948,073 (2007 est.) |
| **Area:** | 8,124 sq mi |
| **Official language:** | Spanish |
| **Languages:** | Spanish, Nahua |
| **National currency:** | El Salvador has no national currency; the U.S. dollar is used. |
| **Principal religions:** | Roman Catholic, 57.1%; Protestant, 21.2% |
| **Ethnicity:** | mestizo 90%, white 9%, Amerindian 1% |
| **Capital:** | San Salvador (est. pop. 1,424,000 in 2005) |
| **Other urban centers:** | San Miguel, Santa Ana |
| **Annual rainfall:** | 72 in |
| **Principal geographical features:** | *Mountains:* Sierra Madre range contains El Pital (8,957 ft); many volcanoes scattered throughout the country including Izalco (6,396 ft)<br>*Rivers:* Grande de San Miguel, Lempa<br>*Lakes:* Cerrón Grande, Coatepeque, Ilopango, Guija |
| **Economy:** | *GDP per capita:* $4,900 (2006 est.) |
| **Principal products and exports:** | *Agricultural:* coffee, sugar, shrimp<br>*Manufacturing:* food processing, textiles |
| **Government:** | Independence from Spain in 1821. Constitution, 1983. Republic. The president is popularly elected for a 5-year term and is both chief of state and head of government. The legislature is a unicameral Legislative Assembly with 84 seat; its members are elected by direct, popular vote for 3-year terms. 14 departments. |
| **Armed forces:** | *Army:* 13,850<br>*Navy:* 700<br>*Air force:* 950<br>*Paramilitary:* 12,000 National Civilian Police<br>*Reserves:* 9,900 |
| **Transportation:** | *Ports:* Acajutla, Puerto Cutuco<br>*Roads:* 1,757 mi paved; 5,008 mi unpaved<br>*Airports:* 4 paved runway and 61 unpaved runway airports, 1 heliport; international airport at San Salvador |
| **Media:** | San Salvador's major newspapers include: *El Diario de Hoy, El Mundo,* and *La Prensa Gráfica.* 150 radio and 11 television stations, including the government-run Radio Nacional. |
| **Literacy and education:** | *Total literacy rate:* 80.2% (2003 est.)<br>Primary education is free. Nine years are required but truancy is high. There are 15 institutes of higher learning. |

became reactionary and relied on a repressive military to defend it from the masses, whose economic situation steadily deteriorated. Even after the end of Hernández Martínez's fascist-style dictatorship in 1944, the military continued to rule the country. The 1932 revolt also marked the end of identifiable indigenous communities and culture in most of El Salvador, for the massacre had especially concentrated on indigenous people. Culturally, the remaining Indians quickly adopted mestizo dress and lifestyles.

Whereas coffee continued to be the primary export of the country, after World War II there was considerable expansion of other agricultural exports, especially cotton, sugar, rice, and beef, as the planter class expanded its holdings along the Pacific coastal plain. This expansion of agricultural exports enriched the elite, but in a period when the population was expanding rapidly it also caused poverty among rural peasants who were forced off their land and into unemployment or jobs paying very low wages. Production of corn, beans, and other staples, forced onto the poorest land, could not keep pace with the expanding population, and in the latter half of the twentieth century, El Salvador became one of the most poorly nourished countries in the world.

Profits from agricultural exports and a growing awareness of the limitations of El Salvador's small area combined with its rapid population growth encouraged investment in manufacturing and service industries in San Salvador from the 1950s forward. The establishment of the Central American Common Market (CACM) in 1960 contributed notably to industrial expansion as trade among the Central American states rose through the following two decades and was especially beneficial to Salvadoran industry. While much of this development came from the same families who had developed agricultural exports, foreign investment and multinational corporations also became important to the Salvadoran economy for the first time.

### THE MID-TWENTIETH CENTURY

Following the relatively peaceful overthrow of Hernández Martínez in 1944 by a combination of students, workers, and progressive military officers, a more open political climate returned to El Salvador. Although military men continued to head the government, there was greater tolerance for political parties and labor unions, and the urban middle class became politically active. New parties replaced the long monopoly of the Liberal Party, which now disappeared, having been discredited by its association with the Hernández Martínez dictatorship (1931–1944). The military-dominated Party of Democratic Revolutionary Unification (PRUD), with the support of the coffee elite, maintained power until 1961. Then the new but similar Party of National Conciliation (PCN), dominated by General Julio Rivera, replaced it and ruled until 1979.

Notable during this period, however, was the growth of broader-based popular parties, especially the Christian Democratic Party (PDC) and the National Revolutionary Movement (MNR). Under the dynamic leadership of a U.S.-trained civil engineer, José Napoleón Duarte, the PDC was effective in the 1960s in organizing students and workers and in gaining support from Catholic clergy and laypeople. Duarte won election as mayor of San Salvador in 1964, but the 1969 war with Honduras interrupted the Christian Democratic surge.

The Soccer War, so called because rioting between rival Honduran and Salvadoran fans at a June 1969 World Cup playoff match touched it off, had much more fundamental causes. Border disputes had occurred between the two states since colonial times, but more serious were the trade imbalances in their common market relations. Honduran imports exceeded exports and Salvadoran manufactured goods damaged Honduran infant industries. Most serious, however, was the basic social inequity and overpopulation in El Salvador, causing massive immigration into Honduras. The Salvadoran immigrants threatened Honduran jobs, wages, land, and businesses. Large Honduran landholders led a campaign against Salvadoran immigrants that gained widespread popular support among the Honduran working class, who felt threatened by the Salvadorans. A Honduran agrarian reform law of April 1968 displaced thousands of Salvadoran squatters and increased tensions that led up to the riots.

The war itself, which began on July 14, 1969, when Salvadoran troops invaded Honduras, was brief but costly. The Honduran air force inflicted serious damage to Salvadoran port installations at Acajutla and elsewhere. The Organization of American States (OAS) arranged a cease-fire on July 18 and Salvadoran troops withdrew on August 3, but a peace treaty was not finally agreed upon until 1980. The war was a setback to the Central American economic integration movement. In El Salvador it led to a resurgence of the military, which placed patriotism in support of the war effort ahead of the grim socioeconomic realities of the country.

Returning refugees from Honduras put an even greater strain on El Salvador's land-poor population, and there was widespread opposition to the government by 1972. An opposition coalition, the National Union of Opposition (UNO), with Duarte at the head of the ticket and Guillermo Ungo of the MNR as the vice presidential candidate, appeared to win a majority in the election of that year. Yet the government declared the PCN candidate, Arturo Molina, victorious and drove Duarte and Ungo into exile. Repressive, reactionary rule followed. El Salvador became notorious for human rights violations as the tide of civil disorder and dissent continued to rise.

### CIVIL WAR IN THE 1980S

The Sandinista success in ending the Somoza dynasty in neighboring Nicaragua in July 1979 and rising popular opposition to the PCN government of Carlos Humberto Romero (1977–1979) prompted a military coup in October 1979 that sought conciliation with the opposition but was primarily concerned with preserving the power and prestige of the military. Continued military repression led to the resignation of nearly all the civilians on the junta, including Guillermo Ungo, precipitating a new crisis in January 1980. The PDC collaborated with the military to form a new junta, and Duarte became its chief later in the year.

Under Duarte's leadership, and with strong U.S. backing, the government tried to restrain military repression and to begin socioeconomic reform, including an agrarian reform plan. But Duarte appeared to be ineffectual and the real power remained with the military chiefs. Political assassinations by the right, including those of outspoken Catholic archbishop Óscar Romero, several PDC leaders, and four U.S. Catholic churchwomen, were common in 1980 and 1981. On the left, guerrilla organizations, headed by the Farabundo Martí National Liberation Front (FMLN), launched a civil war against the government. A new political party, the National Republican Alliance (ARENA), consolidated right-wing opposition behind the leadership of the charismatic Major Roberto D'Aubuisson, who had been linked to death squad assassinations, including that of Archbishop Romero.

U.S. military aid to the government became an element of rising importance in the escalating civil war. With U.S. assistance, the junta held a free election for a constituent assembly in 1982. Leftist parties did not participate and the PDC won a plurality, but a coalition of the rightist ARENA and PCN held a commanding majority. The constituent assembly elected D'Aubuisson as its head, but U.S. pressure prevented his selection as provisional president of the country, and under the constitution that was drafted in 1983, Duarte won a decisive victory in the presidential election of 1984. During his five-year term, Duarte could not revive the sagging economy. As a signatory to the Central American Peace Accord of 1987 (the Arias Plan), he agreed to seek peace with the guerrilla forces but made little progress toward that end, and his country continued to be torn by violence and civil war. In June 1988 he entered a hospital in the United States for treatment of stomach cancer (he died in 1990).

The failure of the Christian Democrats to bring peace or economic recovery and widespread charges of corruption among Christian Democratic bureaucrats allowed the consolidated, neoliberal ARENA to win a decisive victory in 1989. An earthquake that destroyed much of San Salvador in 1986 had further eroded PDC strength. Under D'Aubuisson's leadership, ARENA skillfully organized rural and urban voters into a powerful political force, capitalizing on national exhaustion with the violence and fear of the extreme left. The inherent conservatism of a portion of the peasant class was successfully exploited, as D'Aubuisson's 1982 victory in congressional elections had reflected. Moreover, the close association of ARENA leaders with the military gave that party a significant advantage that helps to explain its success in rural areas. ARENA's 1989 presidential candidate—an affable sportsman named Alfredo Cristiani, who was much more acceptable to the U.S. Congress than the tainted D'Aubuisson—thus swept to victory. After tortuous negotiations, the government achieved a peace accord with the FMLN at the end of 1991, signed at Chapultepec, Mexico, on January 16, 1992. Demobilization of armed forces proceeded slowly and was marked by mutual distrust. Outside economic aid brought only limited recovery as the country gradually fell out of the limelight of international attention by the mid-1990s.

Christianity has long played an important role in El Salvador, the Land of the Savior. The strong anticlericalism that characterized the liberal period in nineteenth- and early-twentieth-century El Salvador, however greatly weakened the Roman Catholic Church, removing it from its close relationship with the government and reducing the number of clergy in the country, thereby reducing its influence, especially in rural areas. In the mid-to-late twentieth century, though, a rejuvenated Catholic clergy once more became important in mobilizing the Salvadoran people for political change. They were a force in the Christian Democratic Party, but El Salvador was also a place where the theology of liberation was important in the radicalizing of political opinion. From parish priests through the hierarchy, the Catholic Church has played an important part in the struggle to curb the terrible violations of human rights that have afflicted El Salvador, and as a result has often been a victim, as in the murder of six prominent Jesuits at the University of Central America (UCA) in San Salvador on November 16, 1989. At the same time, as in Guatemala, there has been an astonishing increase in converts to Pentecostal Protestant sects in the country, as these groups gained among those who sought religion outside the framework of political controversy. In fact, Protestants have been important in building the more conservative, or apolitical, constituency that is reflected in ARENA's rise to power.

### NEOLIBERALISM SINCE 1989

Since 1989 ARENA, committed to a strongly neoliberal agenda of free market reforms and expanded industry and agricultural exports, has dominated El Salvador. Under the Chapultepec Peace Accords of 1992, Cristiani reduced the Salvadoran army to half its former size, created a new civilian peace force, the National Civilian Police (PNC), and established an office to defend human rights in the country. The FMLN thereafter participated politically in elections as the leading opposition party to the ruling ARENA party. Peace came only slowly, however, as continued political violence characterized the decade of the 1990s.

A United Nations Truth Commission in 1993 reported that more than 96 percent of the human rights atrocities committed during the twelve-year civil war were carried out by the Salvadoran military or its paramilitary death squads. Especially notorious was the slaughter of more than a thousand peasants around the village of Mozote in 1981. The Truth Commission report recommended reforms in the military and judiciary and that those guilty of human rights violations be removed from office. The Salvadoran government resisted full implementation of these recommendations and the Assembly gave amnesty from criminal prosecution to most of those implicated in the report. The government did, however, remove many officials from office and in 1994 the Assembly completely replaced the Supreme Court of Justice with new justices. Officers implicated in the murder of six Jesuits at the University of Central America in 1989 went free, but they were discharged from active duty along with hundreds of others.

Armando Calderón Sol continued ARENA's rule of El Salvador from 1994 to 1999 as he presided over El Salvador's difficult recovery from the civil war. With considerable U.S. economic assistance the country had remarkable economic vitality by the end of the century, with substantial expansion of agricultural exports as well as light manufacturing, especially of clothing. By 1995 agriculture accounted for only 14 percent of El Salvador's gross domestic product (GDP), and it was down to 10.3 percent by 2005. Although coffee remained the country's largest export, it occupied a declining percentage of total exports in a more diversified economy. The government privatized banking and other government enterprises, including the pension system, as it pursued the neoliberal agenda. Yet despite considerable economic growth, the standard of living for most Salvadorans remained low as real wages declined amid serious inflation. Moreover, El Salvador continued to have a serious balance of payments deficit, which was only in part made up by remittances from the rising number of Salvadorans living in the United States to their relatives in El Salvador. Illicit drug traffic was another important source of revenue for the country, although its extent cannot be accurately calculated.

The unequal distribution of wealth and widespread poverty stimulated an alarming increase in violent crime in El Salvador. Gangs, such as Los Benedictos, and later Mara 18 and Mara Salvatrucha (also known as MS 13), were notorious for assassinations, kidnappings, and car thefts and were also involved in arms and drug trafficking with organized crime in Central America. Deportation of some of the gang members from the United States back to El Salvador contributed to the increased violence in the country. A United Nations report in 2001 ranked El Salvador 95th among 162 countries for human development on the basis of its poverty, low rate of tax collection, and meager spending on social programs. In the same year a series of devastating earthquakes added to the misery and dislocation in the country. Charges of corruption and misappropriation of funds clouded the massive international relief effort that followed.

In the early twenty-first century, ARENA presidents Francisco Flores Pérez (1999–2004) and Elías Antonio (Tony) Saca González (2004–) continued to promote diversification and pro-business, free market policies, although massive popular protests and strikes forced Flores to abandon plans to privatize the health-care system in 2000. Flores and Saca both cultivated close relations with the United States, where Salvadoran immigrants numbered more than 2.5 million. El Salvador was one of only four Latin American nations to join the U.S.-led coalition that invaded Iraq and by 2006 it was the only one of them that continued to maintain troops

**Members of the Mara 18 gang in prison.** The kidnappings, car thefts, and murders carried out by the Mara 18 gang have contributed to the sharp rise in violent crime that has plagued El Salvador since the 1990s. AP IMAGES

there. Saca took the lead in organizing the Central American Free Trade Agreement (CAFTA), together with the United States and the other Central American states and the Dominican Republic. Despite widespread popular protest against CAFTA, Saca and ARENA believed that it would significantly increase Salvadoran exports. El Salvador also signed separate free trade agreements with Chile, Mexico, and Panama, with negotiations underway for similar agreements with Canada and other American nations. El Salvador adopted the U.S. dollar as its national currency in 2001.

Crime remained a problem for El Salvador as Saca's government faced alarming increases in crime and gang violence, with the murder rate rising from 37 per 100,000 people in 2002 to 45 per 100,000 by 2005. The gangs Mara 18 and Mara Salvatrucha became especially deadly as unemployment and the U.S. deportation of Salvadoran gang members provided a steady increase in new recruits for these gangs. Saca's hard-line police methods, with U.S. assistance, brought criticism from human rights advocates, as the PNC reportedly ignored paramilitary death squads that targeted gang leaders.

*See also* **Alvarado y Mesía, Pedro de; Araujo, Arturo; Arce, Manuel José; Carrera, José Rafael; Central America; Central American Common Market (CACM); Coffee Industry; Cristiani, Alfredo; d'Aubuisson, Roberto; Delgado, José Matías; Duarte Fuentes, José Napoleón; Filísola, Vicente; Gangs; Hernández Martínez, Maximiliano; Income Distribution; Martí, Agustín Farabundo; Masferrer, Alberto; Maya, The; Morazán, Francisco; Nahuatl; North American Free Trade Agreement; Pipiles; Romero, Carlos Humberto; Truth Commissions; Ungo, Guillermo Manuel; United States-Latin American Relations.**

BIBLIOGRAPHY

Anderson, Thomas P. *Matanza: El Salvador's Communist Revolt of 1932.* Lincoln: University of Nebraska Press, 1971.

Baloyra, Enrique A. *El Salvador in Transition.* Chapel Hill: University of North Carolina Press, 1982.

Browning, David. *El Salvador: Landscape and Society.* Oxford: Clarendon Press, 1971.

Cardenal, Rodolfo, and Luis Armando González, eds. *El Salvador, la transición y sus problemas.* San Salvador: UCA Editores, 2002.

Dunkerley, James. *The Long War: Dictatorship and Revolution in El Salvador.* London: Junction Books, 1982.

Dunkerley, James. *Power in the Isthmus: A Political History of Modern Central America.* London: Verso, 1988.

Durham, William H. *Scarcity and Survival in Central America: Ecological Origins of the Soccer War.* Stanford, CA: Stanford University Press, 1979.

Gordon Rapoport, Sara. *Crisis política y guerra en El Salvador.* México: Siglo Veintiuno, 1989.

LADB in affiliation with the University of New Mexico. *Latin American Data Base.* Available from http://ladb.unm.edu/.

Leistenschneider, María, and Freddy Leistenschneider. *Gobernantes de El Salvador: Biografías.* San Salvador: Ministerio del Interior, 1980.

Lindo-Fuentes, Héctor. *Weak Foundations. The Economy of El Salvador in the Nineteenth Century.* Berkeley: University of California Press, 1990.

Miller, Andrew P. *Military Disengagement and Democratic Consolidation in Post-Military Regimes: The Case of El Salvador.* Lewiston, NY: Edwin Mellen, 2006.

Montgomery, Tommie Sue. *Revolution in El Salvador: From Civil Strife to Civil Peace*, 2nd edition. Boulder, CO: Westview Press, 2995.

Parkman, Patricia. *Nonviolent Insurrection in El Salvador: The Fall of Maximiliano Hernández Martínez.* Tucson: University of Arizona Press, 1988.

Roggenbuck, Stefan, ed. *Neoliberalismo versus economía social de mercado: Los desafíos de El Salvador ante la globalización.* San Salvador: Fundación Konrad Adenauer, 1996.

Russell, Philip L. *El Salvador in Crisis.* Austin, TX: Colorado River Press, 1984.

Solano Ramírez, Mario Antonio. *Derecho constitucional de El Salvador*, 4 vols. San Salvador: Universidad Tecnológica de El Salvador, 2005.

Webre, Stephen A. *José Napoleón Duarte and the Christian Democratic Party in Salvadoran Politics, 1960–1972.* Baton Rouge: Louisiana State University Press, 1979.

White, Alastair. *El Salvador.* New York: Praeger, 1973.

Woodward, Ralph Lee, Jr., comp. *El Salvador.* Oxford: Clio Press, 1988.

Woodward, Ralph Lee, Jr. *Central America: A Nation Divided*, 3rd edition. New York: Oxford University Press, 1999.

RALPH LEE WOODWARD JR.

## EL SALVADOR, CONSTITUTIONS.

Although it was part of the Kingdom of Guatemala during the colonial period, the region of modern-day El Salvador began to act with increasing independence in the late eighteenth century. Salvadorans came to resent the power and status of Guatemalans and were quick to adopt a liberal, progressive attitude as a counterweight to the latter's conservatism. In general, Salvadorans and their constitutions have been among the most consistently liberal in Central America and have been the most active advocates of isthmian attempts at unity and federation. However, the constitutions of El Salvador have followed a Napoleonic pattern in being documents designed and decreed from above with the intent of creating a smoothly functioning, just society. Accordingly, the documents often bear little resemblance to the society they are intended to govern and have been modified frequently, because they have no roots in tradition. The student of legal and constitutional history must therefore proceed with caution and skepticism, for the documents may say one thing but translate into action quite differently.

Since 1824, El Salvador has had twenty-three constitutions, some of them virtually identical except for a few key clauses.

### CONSTITUTION OF 1824

Central America achieved its independence from Spain without bloodshed and immediately consolidated its gains with a liberal constitution based on both the 1812 Cádiz Constitution of Spain and that of the United States. The 1824 Constitution provided the structure of the federation and its component parts. In it the newly named Federal Republic of El Salvador consisted of five states, each with its own assembly and head of state. The federation had a congress and a president, but both the states and the federation were granted the rights to raise armed forces and taxes, wherein lay the basis for much future disunity. The 1824 Constitution abolished slavery and recognized Catholicism as the official, exclusive religion. In general, it was a powerfully worded document that could not overcome the divisive forces arrayed against it. A Salvadoran-based attempt to revamp the constitution (1835) granted freedom of religion and introduced more parliamentary-style forms of government but proved insufficient to prevent the total breakdown of Central American unity in 1838.

Following this disruption, El Salvador and its politicians continued to hope for isthmian federation and provided a haven for other Central Americans of similar sympathies. Both in 1898 and 1921, representatives of the dream of federation met in San Salvador to draft constitutions for the United States of Central America and the Republic of Central America.

### CONSTITUTION OF 1886

After decades of struggle between liberals and conservatives (never as violent in El Salvador as elsewhere in Central America), a series of strong liberal presidents established a new governmental ethos epitomized in the Constitution of 1886. President Francisco Menéndez was the primary architect behind this liberal-idealist document, which guaranteed the free expression of ideas, regular elections with universal suffrage for literate males, and similar tenets of political liberalism. This constitution contained a clause precluding successive terms in office, a process of alternating presidencies that became a respected and honored tradition in El Salvador which was not challenged until the period of Maximiliano Hernández Martínez in the 1930s.

Despite its high ideals, the liberal Constitution of 1886 did not guarantee equality in practice. For instance, the titles to recently expropriated communal lands of the Indian communities were legally turned over to their new entrepreneurial owners. Also, there were no provisions for taxation and public works, and urban development was placed above the welfare of the rural areas. Furthermore, political participation and the control of the emerging state remained in the hands of a very few elite families with access to education and financial resources. With a few modifications, the Constitution of 1886 survived until 1939 and served as the inspiration for the democratic movement of 1944.

### CONSTITUTION OF 1939

The more authoritarian Constitution of 1939, initiated by General Maximiliano Hernández Martínez, was a thoroughly twentieth-century document that introduced the idea of state intervention to El Salvador. Under its provisions the state had the exclusive right to regulate money, mail, telegraph, telephone, and radio services. The government recognized an obligation to protect and promote small businesses and credit institutions and to offer some workers' protection. This constitution also gave the military courts jurisdiction over civilians charged with rebellion and extended the presidential term from four to six years, with no provision for reelection. The 1939 constitution and Hernández Martínez's dictatorship together spawned a military-civilian coup in 1944, but the trend toward government interventionism continued unchecked and actually extended its scope.

### CONSTITUTIONS OF 1950 AND 1962

The constitutions of 1950 and 1962 are virtually identical, except for a few changes in wording and the location of specific clauses. Their major social concerns, which were concentrated on urban areas, allowed for the existence of muted political opposition. Women were granted the vote, and the right of the people to insurrection was guaranteed in principle. The army, renamed the Armed Forces, was held to a limit of 3,000 men, a figure that did not include the security forces. The constitutions of 1950 and 1962 revealed lofty ideals but also laid bare the apprehensions of the ruling powers, who wanted to orchestrate and manage social change from above.

Salvadoran constitutional history reveals some striking consistencies throughout the nineteenth and twentieth centuries; indeed, much of the wording is retained from one version to another. The Constitution of 1983 drew much inspiration from its predecessors of 1962 and 1950, which in turn owed a debt to those that had gone before. The various constitutions all share a desire for improvements in the general welfare and for isthmian union, but they suffer from fear of the dislocations that such changes necessarily imply.

*See also* **Hernández Martínez, Maximiliano; Slavery: Abolition.**

BIBLIOGRAPHY

Government of El Salvador, *Independencia: Objetivos y constitución* (n.d.); *Constitución política de la República de*

*El Salvador* (1886); *Constitution of the Republic of El Salvador* (1950); *Constitution of the Republic of El Salvador* (1962); *Constitución política de la República de El Salvador* (1980), and *Proyecto político de la nueva constitución política de El Salvador* (1983).

Julio Alberto Domínguez Sosa, *Génesis y significado de la Constitución de 1886* (1958).

Ricardo Gallardo, ed., *Las constituciones de la República Federal de Centro-América* (1958), *Las constituciones de El Salvador* (1961).

Seminario De Historia Contemporánea Centroamérica, *El constitucionalismo y la vida institucional centroamericana* (1964).

Thomas Karnes, *The Failure of Union: Central America, 1824–1975* (1976).

Mario Rodríguez, *The Cádiz Experiment in Central America, 1808 to 1826* (1978).

Maria Leistenschneider and Freddy Leistenschneider, *Períodos presidenciales y constituciones federales y políticas de El Salvador* (1980).

Ralph Lee Woodward, Jr., *Central America: A Nation Divided*, 2d ed. (1985).

### *Additional Bibliography*

Anaya B, Salvador Enrique. *Teoría de la constitución salvadoreña*. San Salvador: Proyecto para el Fortalecimiento de la Justicia y la Cultura Constitucional en la República de El Salvador, Unión Europea: Corte Suprema de Justicia, 2000.

Castaneda, Ricardo Guillermo, and Cynthia Arnson. *El Salvador's Democratic Transition Ten Years after the Peace Accord*. Washington, DC: Woodrow Wilson International Center for Scholars, Latin American Program, 2003.

KAREN RACINE

## EL SALVADOR, NATIONALIST DEMOCRATIC ORGANIZATION (ORDEN).

ORDEN, Spanish for "order," was a paramilitary vigilance organization in El Salvador during the 1960s and 1970s. Founded in about 1964 by National Guard commander José Alberto Medrano, ORDEN sought to indoctrinate peasants in anticommunism, mobilize support for the governing National Conciliation Party, and police the countryside for suspected subversives. In return for protection and benefits, ORDEN members engaged in domestic espionage and the physical harassment of enemies of the regime, and they played a major role in the political violence of the 1970s. Most of ORDEN's estimated 100,000 members, however, probably joined only for self-protection. When a power struggle in 1970 led to Medrano's ouster, the Salvadoran army assumed control of ORDEN, and the president of the republic became its titular head. The provisional junta that replaced president Carlos Humberto Romero dissolved ORDEN in November 1979.

*See also* **Paramilitaries in Latin America.**

### BIBLIOGRAPHY

Good discussions of Salvadoran politics in the 1960s and 1970s are in James Dunkerley, *Power in the Isthmus: A Political History of Modern Central America* (1988), and Sara Gordon Rapoport, *Crisis política y guerra en El Salvador* (1989).

### *Additional Bibliography*

Brockett, Charles D. *Political Movements and Violence in Central America*. New York: Cambridge University Press, 2005.

Ellacuría, Ignacio. *Veinte años de historia en El Salvador (1969-1989): Escritos políticos*. San Salvador: UCA Editores, 1991.

STEPHEN WEBRE

## EL SALVADOR, POLITICAL PARTIES

*This entry includes the following articles:*



### FARABUNDO MARTÍ NATIONAL LIBERATION FRONT (FMLN)

The Farabundo Martí National Liberation Front (Frente Farabundo Martí para la Liberación Nacional—FMLN) was the insurgent alliance in El Salvador during the civil war of the 1980s. It took its name from Agustín Farabundo Martí (1893–1932), an early leader of the Salvadoran Communist Party.

The FMLN was a unified command structure created in October 1980 to coordinate the military and political activities of five separate leftist guerrilla organizations. Its leaders were Marxist-Leninists seeking to make the front a vanguard revolutionary party governed by the principle of democratic centralism. However, the armed groups that made up the FMLN continued to maintain ties with their own political parties and mass movements, and doctrinal disputes were common, especially over revolutionary strategy and tactics.

The oldest and largest of the FMLN member movements, the Farabundo Martí Popular Liberation Forces (Fuerzas Populares de Liberación Farabundo Martí—FPL), founded in 1970, advocated "prolonged popular warfare" inspired by the Vietnamese example, while the other groups favored insurrectionist tactics. The member groups also disagreed on the relative importance of political organizational activity. For example, the People's Revolutionary Army (Ejército Revolucionario del Pueblo—ERP), organized in 1972, emphasized the military struggle, while the National Resistance Armed Forces (Fuerzas Armadas de Resistencia Nacional—FARN), which had split from the ERP in 1975, stressed the cultivation of popular mass movements and attempts to penetrate the government's armed forces by appealing to disaffected offices. Such internal quarrels occasionally resulted in violence. In April 1983, for example, a debate within the FPL over strategy led to the brutal murder of Commander Mélida Anaya Montes (Ana María) and to the apparent suicide of the group's founder and leader, Salvador Cayetano Carpio (Marcial).

In spite of the failure of its final offensive, launched on 10 January 1981, the FMLN was able to survive as a fighting force, and in 1985 may have had some 8,000 combatants in the field, compared with the government's 50,000. Although never much larger than this and not always unified, the FMLN maintained a strong base of occupied territory in the northern provinces, especially Chalatenango and Morazán, from which it repeatedly struck at military and economic targets.

Although Cuban president Fidel Castro may have taken a personal role in bringing about the front's formation in 1980, Soviet and Cuban material support appears never to have been as significant as claimed by the United States. Support by the Sandinista regime in nearby Nicaragua was probably more important, but that government's electoral defeat in February 1990, along with the declining prestige of revolutionary socialist movements worldwide, left the FMLN increasingly isolated.

In May 1990, the FMLN entered into a series of United Nations–sponsored direct talks with the Salvadoran government aimed at achieving a ceasefire and reintegrating the insurgents into national political life. From the beginning, however, these discussions bogged down over guerrilla insistence on the reform of the government's armed forces. Demobilization began after the 1991 peace accord, and the FMLN began to move warily into the political arena.

Entry into electoral politics caused numerous splits and divisions within the FMLN. In 1995, five different offshoots came together under the FMLN banner. However, the party split between the Renovadores (Renovators) and the Coriente Revolucionario y Socialista (Revolutionary Socialist Current, CRS). The CRS, the more leftist faction, won the internal power struggle. Again in 2004, five FMLN representatives broke off and formed a new party called Frente Democratico Revolucionario (Democratic Revolutionary Front, FDR). Despite these divisions, the FMLN is one the largest political parties in El Salvador and won 39.7 percent of the popular vote in the 2006 legislative elections.

*See also* **Martí, Agustín Farabundo.**

BIBLIOGRAPHY

Tommie Sue Montgomery, *Revolution in El Salvador: Origins and Evolution* (1982).

James Dunkerley, *Power in the Isthmus: A Political History of Modern Central America* (1988).

### *Additional Bibliography*

Alegría, Claribel, and Darwin J. Flakoll. *No me agarran viva: La mujer salvadoreña en lucha.* México, D.F.: Ediciones Era, 1983.

Alegría, Claribel, and Darwin J. Flakoll. *On the Front Line: Guerrilla Poems of El Salvador.* Willimantic, CT: Curbstone Press, 1989.

McClintock, Cynthia. *Revolutionary Movements in Latin America: El Salvador's FMLN and Peru's Shining Path.* Washington, DC: United States Institute of Peace Press, 1998.

Wood, Elisabeth Jean. *Insurgent Collective Action and Civil War in El Salvador.* New York: Cambridge University Press, 2003.

Zamora, Rubén. *La izquierda partidaria salvadoreña: Entre la identidad y el poder*. San Salvador, El Salvador: Facultad Latinoamericana de Ciencias Sociales, 2003.

STEPHEN WEBRE

## NATIONAL CONCILIATION PARTY (PCN)

The National Conciliation Party (Partido de Conciliación Nacional—PCN) was the official party in El Salvador during the 1960s and 1970s. Founded in September 1961, it represented military and business interests and was also a vehicle for the personal ambitions of army officer Julio Adalberto Rivera, who had seized power in a coup d'état on 25 January. The party strongly opposed communism and Cuban influence in Central America and was an enthusiastic supporter of U.S. policy in the 1960s. Although its natural constituency was the conservative Salvadoran landowning class, early PCN leaders were pragmatists. Their modernizing agenda and occasional populist rhetoric led to defections on the right, which by the early 1970s forced the PCN to abandon reformist initiatives and to adopt a more openly repressive style. PCN elements controlled the armed forces and the electoral machinery for almost twenty years. Consecutive PCN presidents of El Salvador, all military officers, included Rivera (1962–1967), Fidel Sánchez Hernández (1967–1972), Arturo Armando Molina (1972–1977), and Carlos Humberto Romero (1977–1979). Following Romero's ouster in the coup d'état of 15 October 1979, the PCN survived as a minority opposition party. While the PCN only received 11 percent of the popular vote in the 2006 legislative elections, it is the third largest political party. Through strategic alliances with larger parties, the PCN can still significantly shape law and policy.

*See also* **Molina, Arturo Armando; Rivera Carballo, Julio Adalberto; Romero, Carlos Humberto; Sánchez Hernández, Fidel.**

### BIBLIOGRAPHY

Stephen Webre, *José Napoleón Duarte and the Christian Democratic Party in Salvadoran Politics, 1960–1972* (1979).

Sarah Gordon Rapoport, *Crisis política y guerra en El Salvador* (1989).

### *Additional Bibliography*

Brockett, Charles D. *Political Movements and Violence in Central America*. New York: Cambridge University Press, 2005.

Ellacuría, Ignacio. *Veinte anos de historia en El Salvador (1969–1989): Escritos políticos*. 3 vols. San Salvador, El Salvador: UCA Editores, 1991.

STEPHEN WEBRE

## NATIONAL REPUBLICAN ALLIANCE (ARENA)

National Republican Alliance (Alianza Republicana Nacional—ARENA) is a conservative political party in El Salvador. Founded in September 1981, chiefly by former army officer Major Roberto d'Aubuisson, who was reputed to have links to right-wing death squads, ARENA champions private property and opposes land reform. Although founded to preserve the power of the ruling obligarchy, it has proved popular with a wide spectrum of the Salvadoran people. The first test of ARENA's popular appeal was the March 1982 election of members of a constituent assembly. Although its chief opponent, the Christian Democratic Party, won more seats in the assembly, ARENA, which was second in the balloting, was able to create a majority by forming coalitions with other conservative parties. D'Aubuisson was elected speaker of the assembly and prevented from becoming provisional president only by pressure from the United States, which feared his extremist views.

D'Aubuisson resigned as speaker in December 1983 to become ARENA's candidate in the March 1984 presidential election. In the first round of the multiparty election, Christian Democrat José Napoleón Duarte and d'Aubuisson came in first and second; Duarte won the May runoff by 54 percent to 46 percent. In 1988 d'Aubuisson stepped down as party head and was replaced by Alfredo Cristiani, a wealthy coffee grower and industrialist. D'Aubuisson, however, continued to be regarded as the spiritual leader of ARENA until his death in 1992.

Profiting from public dissatisfaction with the handling of the civil war against leftist rebels and the country's economic collapse, ARENA gained exactly half the seats in the sixty-member national assembly elected in March 1988 and was able to dominate the assembly with the aid of its conservative allies. Cristiani ran as the party's candidate for president in March 1989 and won on the first ballot with 53.9 percent of the vote. The ARENA government appeared to have a close working relationship with the military.

The prestige of Cristiani was increased by the success of peace talks with the leftist rebels in December 1991 and the termination of the civil war. In the presidential elections of March 1994, ARENA ran San Salvador mayor Ernesto Calderón Sol, who won almost 50 percent on the first ballot and easily won election in the runoff. The party continued to dominate the national assembly. Despite competition from the FMLN, ARENA won the 1999 and 2004 presidential elections. In 2006, ARENA won 39.4 percent of the popular vote in the legislative elections.

*See also* **Cristiani, Alfredo; d'Aubuisson, Roberto.**

BIBLIOGRAPHY

Enrique Baloyra, *El Salvador in Transition* (1982).

Thomas P. Anderson, *Politics in Central America,* rev. ed. (1988), pp. 112–123.

*Additional Bibliography*

Lungo Uclés, Mario. *El Salvador in the Eighties: Counterinsurgency and Revolution.* Edited by Arthur Schmidt. Translated by Amelia F. Shogan. Philadelphia: Temple University Press, 1996.

Villalobos, Joaquín. *"Sin vencedores ni vencidos": Pacificación y reconciliación en El Salvador.* San Salvador, El Salvador: INELSA, 2000.

Wood, Elisabeth Jean. *Insurgent Collective Action and Civil War in El Salvador.* New York: Cambridge University Press, 2003.

THOMAS P. ANDERSON

## EL SEÑOR DE LOS MILAGROS.

El Señor de los Milagros (Lord of Miracles), the most popular religious procession in Peru. It is based on a painting of the crucified Christ done by an anonymous black slave in Lima around 1650. After the wall on which the image was painted remained intact following the earthquake of 1655, the painting was perceived to be miraculous and devotion to the "Holy Christ of Miracles" spread rapidly. A copy of the painting was first taken out in procession in October 1687, following another earthquake. By the eighteenth century it had become the most popular procession in Lima. It continues to be held in October. The original painting is on permanent display in the church of the order of Nazarenes, and the Confraternity of the Bearers of the Lord of Miracles is the largest and most important in Peru. Although the devotion has not lost its original popular character, by the late twentieth century Peruvians of all social classes have come to accept the devotion as part of their Peruvian identity.

*See also* **Catholic Church: The Colonial Period.**

BIBLIOGRAPHY

Rubén Vargas Ugarte, *Historia del Santo Cristo de los Milagros,* 3d ed. (1966).

*Additional Bibliography*

Boone, Elizabeth Hill, and Cummins, Tom, eds. *Native Traditions in the Postconquest World: A Symposium at Dumbarton Oaks, 2nd through 4th October 1992.* Washington, DC: Dumbarton Oaks, 1998.

Pini, Francesco. *El rostro de un pueblo: Estudios sobre el Señor de los Milagros.* Lima: Universidad Católica Sedes Sapientiae, Fondo Editorial UCS, 2005.

Rostworowski de Diez Canseco, María. *Pachacamac y el Señor de los Milagros: Una trayectoria milenaria; Señoríos indígenas de Lima y Canta.* Lima: Instituto de Estudios Peruanos, 2002.

JEFFREY KLAIBER

## EL SEÑOR DE LOS TEMBLORES.

El Señor de los Temblores, or Taytacha Temblores (Lord of Quakes), one of the principal objects of devotion in Cuzco. It is a carved image of the crucified Christ, popularly believed to have been sent as a gift by Charles V but most probably fashioned by local artists. Originally known as the Lord of a Good Death, after the earthquake of 1650 the figure became known as the Lord of Quakes. Since 1741, its procession has taken place on Monday of Holy Week. Over time the image of Christ has become so darkened by the smoke and heat of the candles that accompany it in procession that it now appears to be an Indian or a black Christ. Declared the patron of Cuzco, the image is housed in the cathedral. The procession, accompanied by city officials, is a major tourist attraction.

*See also* **Catholic Church: The Colonial Period.**

BIBLIOGRAPHY

Víctor Angeles Vargas, *Historia del Cusco* (1979), vol. 2, bk. 1, pp. 129–131.

Jesús Lámbarri, "Imágenes de mayor veneración en la ciudad del Cusco," in Banco de Crédito, *Escultura en el Perú* (1991), pp. 251–255.

*Additional Bibliography*

Valencia E., Abraham. *Taytacha Temblores: Patrón jurado del Cuzco.* Cuzco: Consejo Nacional de Ciencia y Tecnología CONCYTEC: Universidad Nacional de San Antonio Abad del Cuzco, 1991.

JEFFREY KLAIBER

**EL TAJÍN.** The El Tajín archaeological site is located in the municipality of Papantla, in the north-central region of the state of Veracruz, Mexico, in the foothills of the Sierra Madre Oriental. The name Tajín means "thunder" in the Totonac language. It was originally a great urban center that flourished from around 800 to 1150 CE. The region is currently inhabited by the Totonac people, although their ethnic relationship with the pre-Hispanic peoples who built El Tajín has not been fully established. The architectural features and ceramics found on the site are different from those that generally characterize the Totonac culture, which has been known since the arrival of the Spaniards and whose features are clearly identifiable in Cempoala and Quiahuiztlan. For this reason, archaeologists prefer to distinguish the two, and speak of an El Tajín culture.

The ruins of El Tajín were discovered in 1785, then excavated from 1938 to 1963 by José García Payón, who restored some of the buildings and set up the bas-reliefs of its South Ball Court. In addition, between 1984 and 1992, Juergen Brueggemann uncovered and reinforced fifty of the approximately two hundred structures that make up the site. Murals were found in both ceremonial and residential buildings. The city was laid out on a natural slope. Its central area was reserved for ceremonial activities, and is made up of pyramid-shaped buildings that served as a base for temples lined up in sets, forming plazas, along with seventeen ball courts. The higher ground was most likely used by the elite to live and work.

El Tajín inherited the traditions of Teotihuacan design, such as its use of slopes and panels, and added niches and cornices to create its own recognized style. Its most outstanding buildings are the Pyramid of the Niches, decorated with 365 niches, and the Great Xicalcoliuhqui, a wall that encloses a series of pyramidal platforms and whose layout resembles a squared spiral, a theme that is repeated throughout the entire site. Equally notable are the bas-reliefs that illustrate mythical scenes and rituals in panels and friezes, as well as the historical and epic tales sculpted in its columns. These scenes each name a relevant character, among them 13 *Conejo* (rabbits), who appear in the garb of a governor and as a ball player.

This archeological site is presently under the care of INAH (Mexico's National Institute of Anthropology and History), and the region has an infrastructure that is adequate for tourism.

*See also* **Cempoala; Tenochtitlán; Totonacs; Veracruz (State).**

BIBLIOGRAPHY

Brueggemann, Juergen, et al. *Tajín.* México: Gobierno del Estado de Veracruz, 1992.

Ladrón de Guevara, Sara. *Imagen y pensamiento en El Tajín.* México, D.F.: Instituto Nacional de Antropología e Historia, 1999.

SARA LADRÓN DE GUEVARA

**EMBOABA.** *Emboaba,* a term used in Minas Gerais during the early eighteenth century to refer to an outsider or to a non-Paulista. The origin of the word is disputed, with the most likely interpretation being that it derived from the Tupi-Guarani name of a bird whose feathered legs reminded some of the Portuguese style of wearing knee-high boots with the trousers tucked in.

The term is most commonly associated with the Guerra dos Emboabas (War of the Emboabas). The discovery of gold in the mining zone bounded by Ouro Prêto, São João del Rei, and Sabará during the last decade of the seventeenth century led to an immediate gold rush. Control of the mining zone was cause for a dispute that can best be seen as two distinct conflicts between Paulistas and non-Paulistas, the first in 1706–1707 and the second in 1708–1709. While the period of actual fighting was relatively short and produced few casualties, the Guerra dos Emboabas is important on two levels. The first was the displacement from the core gold-mining zone of the discoverers and initial settlers, the Paulistas, by those who later flooded into the zone from other areas. The other was the disagreement over the philosophy that was to govern the exploitation of gold. The Paulistas and allied royal authorities wanted controlled and gradual exploitation. The victory of the *emboabas* ensured a mass influx of settlers and a loss of royal control as well as the withdrawal of Paulistas to outlying areas of the mining zone.

The defeat of the Paulistas forced a reappraisal of Portuguese policy in the area. It was clear that the mining zone could not be closed for gradual development, so royal authorities turned to other measures to maintain control. Generally, this meant imposing royal authority on the mining camps. In 1709, São Paulo and Minas de Ouro were made into a separate captaincy that survived until 1720, when another uprising led to the separation of Minas Gerais as a distinct captaincy. That same year the first Ouvidores (royal judges) in the area were created and the governor authorized to establish the first towns and militia units.

*See also* **Gold Rushes, Brazil; Minas Gerais; Mining: Colonial Brazil; Paulistas, Paulistanos.**

BIBLIOGRAPHY

Manoel S. Cardozo, "The *Guerra dos Emboabos,* Civil War in Minas Gerais, 1708–1709," in *Hispanic American Historical Review* 22 (August 1942): 470–492.

Francisco De Assis Carvalho Franco, "Paulistas e emboabas," in *IV Congresso de historia nacional, Annais,* vol. 3 (1950), pp. 63–168.

Charles R. Boxer, *The Golden Age of Brazil: 1695–1750* (1964).

*Additional Bibliography*

Kiddy, Elizabeth W. *Blacks of the Rosary: Memory and History in Minas Gerais, Brazil.* University Park: Pennsylvania State University Press, 2005.

DONALD RAMOS

**EMERALDS.** *See* **Gems and Gemstones.**

**EMPARÁN, VICENTE** (1747–1820). Vicente Emparán (*b.* January 1747; *d.* 3 October 1820), the last Spanish general of Venezuela. With the rank of rear admiral, Emparán left the Spanish Royal Navy for his first major appointment in America as naval commander at Puerto Cabello, on the Venezuelan coast. In 1792 he was appointed governor of Cumaná, a post he held for twelve years. Emparán returned to Spain briefly in 1808 and was appointed captain-general of Venezuela. When he returned to Venezuela in May 1809, he was confronted with the conspiratorial movements of late 1809 and early 1810. News of French advances in Spain prompted the agitators to convoke a meeting with Emparán on 19 April 1810. By popular demand, Spanish authority was renounced and the Junta Suprema de Caracas was formed to take over the government, thereby effectively declaring Venezuela's independence. Emparán was taken prisoner and later exiled to Philadelphia. He returned to Spain in 1810.

*See also* **Venezuela: The Colonial Period.**

BIBLIOGRAPHY

Héctor García Chuecos, *La capitanía general de Venezuela* (1955).

Instituto Panamericano De Geografía E Historia, *El 19 de abril de 1810* (1957).

Angel Grisanti, *Emparán y el golpe de estado de 1810* (1960).

*Additional Bibliography*

Archer, Christon. *The Wars of Independence in Spanish America.* Wilmington, DE : Scholarly Resources, 2000.

Armas Chitty, José Antonio de. *La independencia de Venezuela.* Madrid: Editorial MAPFRE, 1992.

INÉS QUINTERO

**EMPHYTEUSIS, LAW OF.** Law of Emphyteusis, a measure granting long-term rights of access to and exploitation of land that was the state's property. The law of emphyteusis (enacted in 1826) was used in Argentina in the 1820s by Bernardino Rivadavia in an effort to populate the vast interior of the fledging republic. The government could lease land to private individuals or companies for a rent equal to 8 percent of the assessed value of pastureland and 4 percent of that of cropland. The system did not function well and did not produce the results Rivadavia had hoped for. In the first place, assessments of the land were made by the people who were going to rent it, and thus were undervalued. Second, the law did not specify how much land a person could rent out. Since it imposed no limitations, it contributed to a large extent to the formation of Latifundios. The law benefited only land speculators, who obtained large tracts for practically no cost at all.

*See also* **Argentina: The Nineteenth Century; Latifundia; Rivadavia, Bernardino.**

BIBLIOGRAPHY


Emilio Ángel Coni, *La verdad sobre la enfiteusis de Rivadavia* (1927).

Juan Carlos Rubinstein, *Filiación histórica y sociopolítica de la enfiteusis rivadaviana* (1984).

*Additional Bibliography*

Adelman, Jeremy. *Republic of Capital: Buenos Aires and the Legal Transformation of the Atlantic World.* Stanford: Stanford University Press, 1999.

Barsky, Osvaldo. *Historia del capitalismo agrario pampeano.* Buenos Aires, Argentina: Siglo Veintiuno Editores Argentina, 2003.

Gelman, Jorge, Juan Carlos Garavaglia, Blanca Zeberio. *Expansión capitalista y transformaciones regionales: Relaciones sociales y empresas agrarias en la Argentina del siglo XIX.* Buenos Aires: La Colmena y Universidad del Centro de la Provincia de Buenos Aires, 1999.


Juan Manuel Pé rez

## EMPRESA PETROLERA FISCAL.

*See* **Petroleos del Peru (Petroperu).**

## ENCARNACIÓN.

**ENCARNACIÓN.** Encarnación, port city of Paraguay on the Paraná River in the department of Itapúa (estimated 2005 population 69,770). Founded in 1615 by Jesuits from the Itapúa mission and a significant center of christianized Guaraní Indians, it is today the capital of the department of Itapúa. For a long time it was the outpost of Paraguayan resistance against expanding Argentine interests in the area of Misiones, but now it is an active center of trade with the nearby Argentine city of Posadas. Its surroundings are actively farmed by the descendants of German, Slavic, and Japanese settlers, who raise cotton, tobacco, yerba maté, and citrus fruit. A university and radio station maintain a high cultural level for the population.

*See also* **Guarani Indians.**

BIBLIOGRAPHY


Tomás L. Micó, *Antecedentes históricos de Encarnación de Itapúa* (Asunción, 1975).

*Additional Bibliography*

Schiavoni, Lidia. *Pesadas cargas, frágiles pasos: Transacciones comerciales en un mercado de frontera.* Asunción: CPES; Misiones: Editorial Universitaria, Universidad Nacional de Misiones, 1993.

Znacovski de Sánchez, Teresa. *Los Jesuitas: Investigación bibliográfica.* Encarnación: Facultad de Ciencias de la Educación, Universidad Católica, Sede Regional Itapuá, 2001.


César N. Caviedes

## ENCILHAMENTO.

**ENCILHAMENTO.** Encilhamento, a horse-racing term that refers to the stock-market boom in Brazil, especially in Rio de Janeiro, between 1889 and 1893. The abolition of slavery in Brazil in 1888 and the desire to attract immigrants and foreign investment demanded a greatly enhanced national banking system. To placate ex-slaveowners, ease the transition to wage labor, and take advantage of unusually abundant and interested European capital markets, the last imperial ministry began in July 1889 to lend funds and liberalize banking and currency issue laws. This ignited an explosion of national and foreign investments in banks, railways, and many other activities. The Rio stock market saw more activity in the second half of 1889 than it had in its previous history. Although much of the dealing was speculative and even fraudulent, as was depicted in the Viscount of Taunay's novel *O Encilhamento,* there were authentic efforts to create enormous corporations.

The demise of the empire on 15 November 1889 and the rise of the republic did not stop the dealing. The republican minister of finance, Rui Barbosa, relaxed corporation laws and awarded generous government concessions to buy friends for the new regime and promote a laissez-faire state. Although European interest in Brazil waned in 1890, Brazilian investors continued to speculate. Mammoth investment banks created vast corporations.

The investors in the Encilhamento were behind President Deodoro da Fonseca's closing of Congress in November 1891. Opponents of the investors backed Marshal Floriano Peixoto's overthrow of Fonseca twenty days later. Peixoto began attacking some of the key bankers, whom he considered enemies of the republic. The stock boom fizzled in early 1893 and ended with the defeat in 1893–1894 of the naval revolt the financiers had supported.

*See also* **Brazil: Since 1889.**

BIBLIOGRAPHY

Barbara Levy, "O Encilhamento," in *Economia brasileira: Uma visão histórica,* edited by Paulo Neuhaus (1980).

Luiz Antonio Tannuri, *O Encilhamento* (1981).

Gustavo Henrique Barroso Franco, *Reforma monetária e instabilidade durante a transiçao republicana* (1983).

Steven Topik, "Brasil's Bourgeois Revolution," in *The Americas* 48 (October 1991): 245–271.

*Additional Bibliography*

Schulz, John. *A crise financeira da abolição, 1875–1901.* São Paulo: Edusp: Instituto Fernand Braudel, 1996.

Triner, Gail D. *Banking and Economic Development: Brazil, 1889–1930.* New York: Palgrave, 2000.

STEVEN TOPIK

## ENCINA, FRANCISCO ANTONIO

**(1874–1965).** The Chilean historian and politician Francisco Antonio Encina was born on September 10, 1874, in the city of Talca. Encina studied law at the University of Chile but soon tired of the profession, devoting himself instead to agriculture and politics. He served two terms in Congress (1906–1912) and joined the Unión Nacionalista, a strongly nationalistic party that emphasized economic development. His first significant work was *Nuestra inferioridad económica* (1912), a polemical book that criticized the predominantly humanistic educational curriculum. Encina's historiographical work was also characterized by a polemical tone, and his idiosyncratic views on race and national character derived from the ideas of Gustave Le Bon and Nicolás Palacios. The author of *Portales* (1934), *La literatura histórica chilena y el concepto actual de la historia* (1935), and *La presidencia de Balmaceda* (1952), Encina also ventured into wider Latin American history with his eight-volume series *Bolívar y la independencia de la América española* (1954–1963). His most significant work, however, is *Historia de Chile desde la prehistoria hasta 1891* (20 vols., 1940–1952), a general history in the tradition of Diego Barros Arana's work but less research oriented and more favorable to Chilean authoritarian figures and institutions. The abridgement of this book by Leopoldo Castedo, *Resumen de la Historia de Chile* (3 vols., 1954), helped popularize Encina's unwieldy multivolume work. Encina died on August 23, 1965.

*See also* **Chile: The Twentieth Century.**

BIBLIOGRAPHY

Gazmuri, Cristián. *La historiografía chilena (1842–1970).* Santiago: Taurus Historia, 2006.

Donoso, Ricardo. *Francisco Antonio Encina, simulador,* 2 vols. Santiago: Ricardo Neupert, 1968.

IVÁN JAKSIĆ

## ENCINAS, JOSÉ ANTONIO

**(1886–1958).** José Antonio Encinas (*b.* 1886; *d.* 1958), a prominent leader of the *indigenista* movement of early-twentieth-century Peru. As a land commissioner, in 1918 he drew up a program to help native Peruvians regain lands that had been stolen by white aristocratic lawyers. After the revolutionary military government of Juan Velasco Alvarado issued the Agrarian Reform Law of 24 June 1969, Agrarian Reform officials turned to some of Encinas's findings to guide them in organizing the formation of agrarian reform zones. The section of the law creating peasant cooperatives reflected in part the writings of Encinas.

*See also* **Agrarian Reform.**

BIBLIOGRAPHY

Thomas M. Davies, Jr., *Indian Integration in Peru, 1900–1948* (1974).

José Tamayo Herrera, *Historia del indigenismo cuzqueño: Siglos xvi-xx* (1980).

*Additional Bibliography*

Encinas de Zegarra, Aurora. *El maestro José Antonio Encinas: Testimonio de su itinerario como hermano, maestro, escritor, político y humanista*. Lima: A. Encinas de Zegarra, 1999.

VINCENT PELOSO

## ENCISO, MARTÍN FERNÁNDEZ DE

(c. 1470–c. 1528). Martín Fernández de Enciso (*b.* ca. 1470; *d.* ca. 1528), a lawyer and central figure in an early sixteenth-century Vasco Núñez de Balboa venture. In 1508 Diego de Nicuesa and Alonso de Ojeda sealed a contract with the Spanish crown to divide the entire coast of South America into two governing areas. Explorer Francisco Pizarro was sent on expedition.

After it became clear that Pizarro's attempt at colonization in 1509 had failed, Ojeda contracted Martín Fernández de Enciso to travel to present-day Central America in relief of Pizarro. Meanwhile, Vasco Núñez de Balboa had secretly boarded Enciso's ship in Hispaniola. Balboa's popularity grew among the other passengers, who disliked the often petty and temperamental Enciso. In the end, Balboa emerged from this power struggle as the natural leader of the early settlements in northern South America. Although Enciso's group took Darién (probably in November 1510), Balboa and his supporters forced them to leave the colony, thus triggering a series of events which led to Balboa's later execution.

Enciso eventually returned to Spain, where he joined others who opposed Balboa and were finally successful in instigating Balboa's beheading in 1519.

Later, Enciso helped lead an ill-fated expedition to Cenu, in northwestern South America. This attempt to secure wealth, like the first, failed, and Enciso again returned to Spain. Enciso is remembered primarily for his role in the Balboa story.

*See also* **Explorers and Exploration: Spanish America.**

BIBLIOGRAPHY

Bancroft, Hubert Howe. *History of Central America, v. 6–8* San Francisco: A.L. Bancroft, 1883.

Gerbi, Antonello. *De Cristóbal Colón a Gonzalo Fernández de Oviedo*. México: Fondo de Cultura Económica, 1978.

Romoli, Kathleen. *Balboa of Darién: Discoverer of the Pacific*. Garden City, NJ: Doubleday, 1953.

Barlow, Roger, E.G.R. Taylor, ed. *A Brief Summe of Geographie*. London: Hakluyt Society, 1932.

BLAKE D. PATTRIDGE

## ENCOMIENDA.

*Encomienda,* the right to control the labor of and collect tribute from an Indian community, granted to subjects, especially the first conquerors and their descendants, as a reward for service to the Spanish crown. Unlike the Spanish peninsular version of the *encomienda,* the grant in the New World did not give the grantee, or *encomendero,* legal right to own land. It also did not give *encomenderos* legal jurisdiction over the natives, although many *encomenderos* assumed that right. In return the *encomendero* promised to settle down and found a family in the nearest Spanish town, or *villa;* to protect the Indians; and to arrange for their conversion to the Roman Catholic faith.

In the Antilles the institution was firmly established under Governor Nicolás de Ovbando. Hernán Cortés granted the first *encomiendas* in Mexico, and Francisco Pizarro did so in Peru. In the sixteenth century, *encomiendas* ranged in size from as many as 23,000 heads of households (Cortés's personal *encomienda*) to a few hundred in some areas of Central America and Peru.

Although there were never enough such grants to reward all those who felt they deserved one, the *encomienda* proved a useful institution, from the crown's point of view, in the first two or three decades after the discovery and conquest of the New World kingdoms of Mexico and Peru. It placed hundreds and sometimes thousands of Indians under the control of individual Spaniards at a time when a bureaucracy had not yet been established. The *encomenderos* put the Indians to work mining gold and silver; building houses, town halls, and churches; cultivating indigenous and imported crops; herding animals; and transporting goods.

Control of Indian labor became the basis of the fortunes of the *encomendero* elite, who became wealthy by selling provisions to arriving Spanish immigrants and by renting them stores and homes that had been built with the Indian labor they controlled. They invested revenues generated by their *encomienda* laborers in stock-raising enterprises. Some even became silent partners with merchants involved in lucrative import and export activities. Their wealth and their status as first- and second-generation conquerors gave them the leisure and respect that enabled them to exercise an early monopoly of the town councils. As councilmen they set prices for basic goods and services as well as the standards of morality and sanitation for the Spanish community. They screened applicants for formal citizen status in the town and gave out house lots and suburban lands for kitchen gardens and orchards. They also were empowered to grant lands further afield. Their wealth, political power, influence, and prestige as conquerors and first settlers (later transferred to their descendants) made them almost omnipotent and, as such, independent of the wishes of the crown.

To counter their power, the crown began to issue protective legislation, such as the Laws of Burgos (1512) and the New Laws (1542). One provision of the latter abolished *encomiendas* at the death of the current holder. The resulting widespread protest throughout Spanish America along with a rebellion and civil war in Peru forced the crown to back down in the short run, but they also strengthened its resolve to break the power of the *encomendero* elite. It eventually did so by regulating the amount of tribute that the Indian population had to deliver; by abolishing personal, unpaid service by the Indians to the *encomendero;* by creating a loyal royal bureaucracy; and by fostering the rise of an independent class of Spanish farmers that would counterbalance the *encomendero* class. It was the landowners (and the mine owners) who eventually displaced the *encomenderos* at the top of the colonial social pyramid.

The connection between the *encomienda* and the hacienda, or large landed estate, has been the subject of debate. Some have argued that the hacienda developed directly from the *encomienda.* This was the case when and where *encomenderos* used their positions of authority—on the town council, for example—to grant themselves land parcels (*mercedes*) from among the lands once used by their Indian charges. However, such cases were relatively few in number.

Far more often, other scholars contend, haciendas developed independently of *encomiendas.* Like the *encomenderos,* many individuals who received land grants were given parcels from among those that had been abandoned by Indians because of either death or flight. However, the owners of these parcels depended on the *repartimiento* or *mita* (rotating draft of forced Indian labor) system that had been instituted after the crown prohibited the use of free personal services by the *encomendero* around the middle of the sixteenth century. These small enterprises were expanded over the years by the obtaining of additional land grants, by usurpation of Indian lands, by *composición* (obtaining legal title to untitled land by paying a fee to the royal treasury), by purchase, and by long-term lease to become the nuclei of what someday would be large estates, or haciendas.

The task of collecting tribute and overseeing the Indian communities was given to the *corregidor de indios,* a district administrator or governor, who was part of the bureaucratic apparatus established by the crown to regain control of the New World kingdoms from the all-powerful *encomenderos.* Except in peripheral areas of the Spanish New World Empire, like Paraguay, the *encomienda* had become by the start of the seventeenth century little more than a prestigious claim to a government pension, divorced of any direct control over the Indians.

*See also* **Hacienda; Mita; Repartimiento; Slavery: Indian Slavery and Forced Labor; Spanish Empire.**

BIBLIOGRAPHY

C. H. Haring, *The Spanish Empire in America* (1947).

Charles Gibson, *Spain in America* (1966).

James Lockhart, "*Encomienda* and *Hacienda:* The Evolution of the Great Estate in the Spanish Indies," in *Hispanic American Historical Review* 49, no. 3 (1969): 411–429.

Robert G. Keith, "*Encomienda, Hacienda,* and *Corregimiento* in Spanish America: A Structural Analysis," in *Hispanic American Historical Review* 51, no. 3 (1971): 431–446.

### *Additional Bibliography*

Guamán Poma de Ayala, Felipe. *Nueva crónica y buen gobierno.* 3 vols. Ed. John Murra, Rolena Adorno &

Jorge L. Urioste. Madrid: Historia 16, 1987, folios 547[561]–559[573].

Mira Caballos, Esteban. *El indio antillano: Repartimiento, encomienda y esclavitud (1492–1542).* Sevilla: Múñoz Moya Editor, 1997.

Presta, Ana María. *Encomienda, familia y negocios en Charcas colonial (Bolivia): Los encomenderos de La Plata, 1550–1600.* Lima: IEP, Instituto de Estudios Peruanos, 2000.

Rodríguez Baquero, Luis Enrique. *Encomienda y vida diaria entre los indios de Muzo, 1550–1620.* Bogotá: Instituto Colombiano de Cultura Hispánica, 1995.

SUSAN E. RAMÍREZ

**ENDARA, GUILLERMO** (1936–). Guillermo Endara was born in Panama City, Panama, on May 12, 1936. Like many Panamanians of his generation, his parents were immigrants who fought to establish their position within the country's growing middle class. After attending primary school in Panama City, he completed his secondary education at a military institute in the United States. Now fully bilingual, he returned to his home country, where he studied law and political science at the University of Panama. Upon graduation, he began his career teaching at the university and working in a private law firm.

Endara is an important figure in the history of his country and in Panamanian politics for a number of reasons. First, he was one of the main political allies of Dr. Arnulfo Arias Madrid, a legendary populist who dominated the political arena (whether in or out of power) from the 1930s until his death in the late 1980s. Second, he played a critical role as a member of the political opposition during the 1970s and 1980s in the effort to remove the military government that ruled the country from 1968 until 1989. And finally, Endara is important because of his positive impact as civilian president following the U.S. armed invasion that ended the rule of military dictator Manuel Noriega in 1989.

As president of the Republic of Panama from 1989 to 1994, Endara had to weather several attempted coups by disgruntled former military officers. Once the survival of his government was assured, he set about restoring the economic health of the country. However, his role in Panamanian politics did not end there. He remained active following his presidential term, first as an important participant in the government of President Mireya Moscoso (1999–2004) by giving it more legitimacy and continuity, and later as a candidate in the 2004 presidential election. Over the years, he has also remained an influential member of Panama's academic and business communities.

*See also* **Arias Madrid, Arnulfo; Noriega Moreno, Manuel Antonio.**

BIBLIOGRAPHY

"Guillermo Endara Galimany." Fundacio CIDOB (Centro de investigacion, docencia, documentacion y divulgacion de Relaciones Internacionales y Desarrollo, Barcelona, España). Available from http://www.cidob.org/en/documentacion/biografias_lideres_politicos/america_central_y_caribe/panama/guillermo_endara_galimany.

Scranton, Margaret E. *The Noriega Years: U.S.-Panamanian Relations, 1981–1990.* Boulder, CO: Lynne Rienner Publishers, 1991.

STEVE C. ROPP

**ENDER, THOMAS** (1793–1875). An Austrian painter known for his landscapes of Brazil, Thomas Ender was born in St. Ulrich in the outskirts of Vienna, on November 3, 1793. After winning the Imperial Court Gold Medal for landscape painting from the Vienna Academy of Art, Ender joined the scientific expedition assembled to accompany the Hapsburg princess Leopoldina to Rio de Janeiro to join her husband, the future emperor Pedro I. The group, which also included the naturalists Johann Baptist von Spix and Karl Friedrich Philipp von Martius, was to explore the flora and fauna of Brazil. Setting sail in March 1817, Ender spent almost one year exploring the area between Rio de Janeiro and São Paulo, documenting not only the natural beauty of the country but its architecture and people as well. He intensively documented Rio de Janeiro and the Vale do Paraíba, where coffee was starting to be cultivated.

Upon his return to Vienna, Ender delivered a total of 782 works to the Imperial government. These watercolors and sketches, which constitute the majority of his work in Brazil, remain one of the most beautiful and evocative sources of information on Brazilian colonial life and society. Along with Jean-Baptiste Debret and Johann Moritz Rugendas, Ender stands as one of the greatest documentarians of Brazil's past.

*See also* **Art: The Nineteenth Century; Debret, Jean-Baptiste; Pedro I of Brazil; Rugendas, Johann Moritz.**

BIBLIOGRAPHY

Ferrez, Gilberto. *O Brasil de Thomas Ender*. Rio de Janeiro: Fundação João Moreira Salles, 1976.

GLORIA KAISER
ANA LUIZA NOBRE

**ENERGY.** Latin America is rich in energy resources, but these resources are unevenly distributed among the region's countries. Petroleum dominates commercial energy production and consumption at every level throughout Latin America. The region is also richly endowed with natural gas and hydroelectric power potential, and Colombia and Venezuela have begun to develop their coal reserves for export.

Development of Latin American energy resources has come at great expense. Brazil is a prime example, with over 40 percent of public investment in the early 1980s accounted for by domestic energy investment. Foreign debt mounted during the 1970s and 1980s as the World Bank, Inter-American Development Bank, and other lenders injected much-needed capital into grandiose petroleum, gasohol, nuclear, and hydroelectric projects. Oil price fluctuations eroded the ability to repay these debts, causing many to rethink the approach to development of Latin American energy resources.

## ENERGY CONSUMPTION

Latin America and the Caribbean are dependent on oil for a disproportionate share of their energy needs—almost 52 percent in 2004. The degree of dependence on oil among the smaller countries is more pronounced. For the Caribbean islands, oil represents 90 percent of the commercial energy requirements. From 2002 to 2006 Venezuelan oil exports to the United States slowed as relations between the two countries soured. However, Venezuela increased its oil exports to Latin America, with 36.7 percent going there in 2006.

Total primary energy consumption for Latin America and the Caribbean in 2004 equalled 28.45 quadrillion Btu, of which oil consumption represented 14.8 quadrillion Btu. Natural gas and hydropower contribute approximately 21 percent each, whereas coal represents 4 percent.

Most of the region's energy is consumed in Brazil (30 percent) and Mexico (22 percent). Mexico is the region's largest consumer of petroleum, using 29 percent of the petroleum available in 2004. Brazil also relies more on hydropower as a commercial source of energy than does any other major country in Latin America.

The primary determinants of increased energy consumption in developing countries are population growth, income growth, industrialization, and urbanization, each of which requires more energy services. Increases in energy prices tend to reduce the rate of growth in energy demand; this occurred

**Primary energy consumption in Latin America, 2004**

(quadrillion Btu)

| Country | Petroleum | Natural gas | Coal | Net hydro | Net nuclear | Total |
|---|---|---|---|---|---|---|
| Argentina | 0.94 | 1.39 | 0.024 | 0.303 | 0.086 | 2.742 |
| Brazil | 4.34 | 0.632 | 0.463 | 3.183 | 0.12 | 8.741 |
| Colombia | 0.53 | 0.203 | 0.081 | 0.398 | 0.00 | 1.3 |
| Mexico | 3.9 | 1.83 | 0.304 | 0.25 | 0.088 | 6.284 |
| Venezuela | 1.09 | 1.144 | 0.00 | 0.694 | 0.00 | 2.898 |
| Other | 4.0 | 1.001 | 0.27 | 1.267 | 0.00 | 6.52 |
| **Total** | **14.8** | **6.2** | **1.142** | **6.095** | **0.294** | **28.45** |

**Table 1**

during the early 1980s. Latin American energy demand surged in the late 1980s, increasing at an annual rate of 2.9 percent. Most of the growth was in hydroelectric, natural gas, and coal demand.

### COMMERCIAL ENERGY PRODUCTION

Latin America produced surplus energy throughout the twentieth century. The region will likely remain a net exporter into the twenty first century despite the fact that the rate of growth in energy production has fallen below that of energy consumption. Venezuela is a member of OPEC and must abide by its production quotas. (Ecuador withdrew from OPEC in 1992.)

Most Latin American countries exercise strong, monopolistic control over energy development. The lack of competition has negative effects on energy resource management. In Mexico and Venezuela, state control of oil and gas exploration and production sectors is absolute. In other countries, private sector participation is strictly controlled. Brazil in the 1990s began to let its oil company operate more independently and allowed foreign investors to buy shares.

***Oil and Gas.*** In 2004 Latin America produced 36.144 quadrillion Btu of primary energy (petroleum, natural gas, coal, hydropower, and nuclear) while consuming only 28.45 quadrillion Btu. Petroleum production of 21.4 quadrillion Btu represented 59 percent of total energy production.

Latin America had 116 million barrels of conventional crude oil reserves in 2006. Venezuela and Mexico together accounted for 79.25 percent of that total. Venezuelan reserves are the sixth-highest in the world, and in 2006 Venezuela was also the world's sixth-largest oil exporter; Mexico was the tenth-largest. Nine other countries (Bolivia, Brazil, Chile, Colombia, Argentina, Ecuador, Guatemala, Peru, and Trinidad and Tobago) have oil reserves of varying sizes that are not considered significant by world standards.

Natural gas reserves are also dominated by Venezuela, which in 2006 accounted for 60 percent of the 250.8 trillion cubic feet in Latin America. Nearly all current gas production is associated gas, and production levels have been restrained by oil production levels. Brazil has a huge natural gas resource that is being underutilized. In 2007, natural gas met only 2 percent of the country's energy requirements, mainly due to lack of infrastructure.

Intraregional oil and gas trade has become common in Latin America. Petroleum dominates intraregional trade in northern Latin America, whereas natural gas is more popular in the south. Argentina renewed a twenty-year agreement to import 2.19 billion cubic meters of natural gas annually from Bolivia. Brazil signed a deal with Bolivia whereby 1.28 billion cubic meters of gas will be burned annually in the thermal power plant to be built at the Bolivian border town of Puerto Suárez, and the electricity will be sent to the Brazilian state of Mato Grosso do Sul.

Bolivia and Argentina have turned to Chile, which also is in need of gas. Argentine-Chilean negotiations over routing, volume, price, and pipeline construction delayed bidding until November 1991. Bolivia entered the Chilean scene, offering alternative supply to mining complexes in northern Chile. However, any deal may founder due to the lack of diplomatic relations between Bolivia and Chile.

***Coal.*** Recoverable coal reserves in Latin America were estimated to be 23,263 million short tons in 2006. Brazil's reserves represent 62 percent of Latin American reserves, and the country produced 47.9 percent of the region's total. Colombia has the largest export coal mine in the world, the opencast El Cerrejón. The mine has been exporting one million tons of coal per month since the mid-1980s.

Brazil, Chile, Mexico, and Venezuela are investing to spur bituminous coal production. Coal use in Brazil is very low despite substantial resources, due to its poor quality. Mexico has offered to invest in the mining of Colombian coal, which would be used in Mexican power generation.

***Hydropower.*** Hydropower represents the largest single supply source for electricity in Latin America. In 2004, 55.7 percent of all electricity supplied came from hydropower. Several Latin American nations have pursued development of hydro resources as a means of reducing their dependence on oil imports. Brazil, Argentina, Colombia, Venezuela, and Paraguay all have large shares of hydropower in their electricity generation. Hydro incurs high capital costs long before electricity begins

**Primary energy production in Latin America, 2004**

(quadrillion Btu)

| Country | Crude | Natural gas | Coal | Net hydro | Net nuclear | Total |
|---|---|---|---|---|---|---|
| Argentina | 1.607 | 1.656 | 0.001 | 0.303 | 0.086 | 3.653 |
| Brazil | 3.196 | 0.355 | 0.070 | 3.183 | 0.120 | 6.924 |
| Colombia | 1.166 | 0.203 | 1.454 | 0.398 | 0.00 | 3.221 |
| Mexico | 7.44 | 1.565 | 0.191 | 0.25 | 0.088 | 9.534 |
| Venezuela | 5.741 | 1.144 | 0.205 | 0.694 | 0.00 | 7.784 |
| Other | 2.249 | 1.499 | 0.012 | 1.267 | 0.00 | 5.027 |
| **Total** | **21.4** | **6.421** | **1.934** | **6.095** | **0.294** | **36.144** |

**Table 2**

flowing, and these projects accounted for sizable proportions of these countries' foreign and domestic debts.

The Itaipú plant on the Paraná River along the Paraguay-Brazil border has the largest hydro capacity in the world, at 11.7 megawatts. Brazil underwrote all the construction costs and purchases all electricity generated. Despite supplying 24 percent of current primary energy needs and nearly 90 percent of its electricity, Brazil has exploited less than 20 percent of the country's estimated hydro potential. Another 12 percent is under construction or planned through 2000.

***Nuclear.*** Nuclear-generated electricity provides less than 1 percent of Latin America's primary energy. Argentina has the longest experience with nuclear power; its 344-megawatt Atucha 1 heavy-water reactor has been operational since 1974, but by 1984, Atucha 1 was operating at half capacity, unable to compete with cheaper hydroelectricity. Work on Atucha 2 was delayed. Brazil brought its 626-megawatt Angra dos Reis 1 plant into operation in 1981. Angra 2 came online in 2000.

Construction on Mexico's first reactor, the 650-megawatt Laguna Verde, began in 1970, but it never went into operation, and Uramex, the state-run mining company that had begun exploiting uranium reserves, closed in 1985. Mexico's nuclear program calling for twenty reactors by the year 2000 was canceled during the 1980s after it was estimated that the program accounted for more than half of the public-sector debt attributable to the energy sector. Nuclear power in Latin America was not anticipated to have much of a future.

***Traditional Fuels.*** Wood and agricultural-animal wastes are used in the rural sectors and account for an estimated 800,000 barrels per day of oil equivalent. Firewood provided as much as half of the region's energy in 1945. It continues to be used by rural populations in residential applications.

Sugarcane waste (bagasse) has become a significant source of energy for sugar mills producing their own electricity and steam. Bagasse is used in independent facilities, isolated from electricity grids, in Belize, Brazil, Mexico, Cuba, the Dominican Republic, Jamaica, and other Caribbean islands.

***Renewables.*** The island nations of the Caribbean face pronounced isolation problems. Regional solutions such as electricity interconnections or cross-border road networks are not viable. Caribbean islands are ideal candidates for smaller-scale renewable energy applications. Geothermal, wind, biomass, and photovoltaic technologies have been demonstrated with the assistance of international agencies.

The tectonic regions of Mexico, Central America, and the Caribbean offer ample geothermal resources. El Salvador has exploited geothermal resources since 1975. Mexico is operating geothermal wells in Baja California, exporting half the output to southern California utilities. Guatemala is planning to build a 15-megawatt geothermal plant.

In addition to funding geothermal development in Central America, the Inter-American Development Bank has financed wind power in Barbados, bagasse cogeneration studies in Guyana,

**Angra II nuclear plant, Angra dos Reis, Brazil, January 19, 2006.** Though rich in natural resources, much of Latin America relies on imported oil to satisfy energy needs, resulting in high levels of foreign debt. Retrieving energy from hydro and nuclear power offer alternatives, though few Latin American countries can afford the initial investment. VANDERLEI ALMEIDA/AFP/ GETTY IMAGES

biogas from chicken manure in Guatemala, microhydro in Brazil, and photovoltaic cell production in Mexico.

***Alcohol Fuels.*** The alcohol fuel program, seen at one time as the savior of Brazil, was moribund by August 1990. Heavy subsidies on alcohol cost Brazil $7 billion since the fuel was introduced fifteen years earlier in an effort to reduce the country's heavy dependence on imported oil. Removal of sub-sidies would mean that the 4.5 million owners of alcohol-fueled cars would be grounded. Production of alcohol fuel costs twice as much as gasoline. Excessive production costs are blamed on bureaucratic bungling, greedy sugarcane producers, corruption, and the vested interest of Petrobrás, the monopoly distributor of alcohol fuel.

Sales of alcohol-fueled vehicles in Brazil fell from 85 percent of total vehicle sales in 1985 to less than 5 percent in July 1990. Fuel production was not expected to meet demand, and imports will be required if rationing is to be avoided. In 1989, 29 distilleries closed down, and ten more closed during the first half of 1990. However, there was renewed interest in the ethanol program due to the high oil prices in the early twenty-first century. Guatemala also has a small alcohol fuel program.

## DEVELOPMENT AND COOPERATION

In order to develop an energy infrastructure that will sustain economic growth, the countries of Latin America will have to attract new investment. World Bank lending for energy projects in 1990 totaled $3 billion. Of that, $1 billion went to Latin America. Two-thirds of the bank's lending goes directly to utilities to reinforce internal electric transmission systems. The balance goes to coal and oil-gas projects.

The U.S. Trade and Development Program has been operating in the private and public sectors of Latin America since the 1980s. Energy funding has been almost exclusively for oil and gas. The U.S. Agency for International Development energy programs are limited and small, except for Central America. Their period of active involvement in large thermal and hydroelectric projects was in the 1960s and 1970s, particularly in Brazil. The Inter-American Development Bank allocated an average of 27.6 percent of its loans ($10.97 billion) to energy projects from 1961 through 1987. In 1988, $405 million was lent for energy, of which 88 percent was for electric projects. A small portion of the Caribbean Development Bank's loans are for energy.

Under President Hugo Chávez, the petroleum-rich nation of Venezuela has promoted alternatives for energy development. In 2005 Chávez's new energy policy focused on six new projects, including refining, infrastructure, and integration in the Magna Reserve, and the Orinoco and Delta-Caribbean regions. In 2007 he announced the nationalization of the oil industry, and the state took over holdings by foreign multinational companies such as ExxonMobil, which had failed to give majority control of hydrocarbons to Venezuela.

Regional cooperation was promoted as the best way to develop Latin American energy resources. In the past, the joint energy option was for costly, controversial, and time-consuming hydroelectric projects. Cross-border hydro projects account for 25 percent of Latin America's generating capacity and much of its crippling debt. Grandiose schemes financed by the World Bank, the Inter-American Development Bank, and the United Nations fell out of favor. For example, Argentine president Carlos Saúl Menem shelved the Yacireta Dam on the Paraná River between Paraguay and Argentina after receiving approval for an Inter-American Development Bank loan of $250 million.

Latin America was anticipated to look to its own regional organizations specifically established to assist in energy development: the Organization of Latin American States for Energy Cooperation, the Regional Electrical Intergration Commission, and the Latin American State Oil Company Assistance Organization.

*See also* **Chávez, Hugo; Electrification; Industrialization; Inter-American Development Bank (IDB); Mining: Modern; United Nations; World Bank.**

BIBLIOGRAPHY


Bamber, Derek. "Brazil: Coping with the Conflict." *Petroleum Economist* 57 (October 1990): 13–17.

Campodónico, Humberto. *Reformas e inversión en la industria de hidrocarburos de América Latina.* Santiago de Chile: Naciones Unidas, Comisión Económica para América Latina y el Caribe, División de Recursos Naturales e Infraestructura, 2004.

De la Pedraja, René. *Energy Politics in Colombia.* Boulder, CO: Westview Press, 1989.

García Dodero, Vicente, and Fernando Sánchez Albavera. *Fundamento y anteproyecto de la ley para promover la eficencia energética en Venezuela.* Santiago de Chile: Naciones Unidas, Comisión Económica para América Latina y el Caribe, División de Recursos Naturales Infraestructura, 2001.

González, Alejandro, and Lisa Pearl. *Venezuela's Natural Gas—Why the Lack of Interest?* Cambridge, MA: Cambridge Energy Research Associates, 2001.

Imran, Mudassar, and Phillip Barnes. "Energy Demand in the Developing Countries." World Bank Staff Commodity Working Paper. Washington, DC, 1990.

Imran, Mudassar, and Phillip Barnes. "Latin America: Governments Eyeing Gas and Oil Deals." *Petroleum Economist* 57 (May 1990): 142.

Latin American Energy Organization. *The Foreign Debt and the Energy Sector of Latin America.* Quito, Ecuador: Author, 1989.

Leonard, H. Jeffrey. *Natural Resources and Economic Development in Central America.* New Brunswick, NJ: Transaction Books, 1987.

Smith-Perera, Roberto. *Energy and the Economy in Venezuela.* Cambridge, MA: Harvard University Press, 1988.

U.S. Department of Energy. *Report on the Western Hemisphere Energy Cooperation Study.* Washington, DC: Author, 1990.

U.S. Department of Energy. *1989 International Energy Annual.* Washington, DC: Author, 1991.

U.S. Department of Energy. "South America: International Gas Deals as Far Away as Ever." *Petroleum Economist* 58 (March 1991): 18–50.


MINDI J. FARBER

**ENGENHO.** *Engenho,* an agricultural establishment with machinery for refining sugar from sugarcane; such a facility typically includes a mill for milling cane as well as cauldrons and distilleries for preparing sugar. Begun in São Vicente and in Pernambuco in the 1500s, sugar production later expanded to Bahia, Rio de Janeiro, and other coastal areas. Profitable sugar production attracted the Dutch, who dominated the Brazilian Northeast until their expulsion in 1654. In financial terms, ownership of a mill could be just as important as the ownership of land.

The *engenho* first used two and later three wheels in milling. The first *engenhos* were run by animal power, then water power, and eventually steam. The designation *engenho* initially referred to the production unit where the milling of cane and the preparation of sugar took place. This term was eventually extended to encompass the entire agrarian structure, including the cultivation of cane, manioc, corn, rice, and beans in addition to the preparation of food, the weaving of cotton and wool, and manufacturing, processing, and various other services not exclusively related to agriculture.

Seen by some as a self-sufficient establishment, the *engenho* was a complex hierarchical, social, and economic unit involving field and domestic slaves, qualified salaried workers, tenants, and resident farmers in a network of kinship and nonkinship dependencies, at the center of which was the patriarchal figure of the *senhor do engenho*. Considerable conflict existed between the engenho and independent cane producers over the milling schedule, because a long delay could destroy a farmer's crop. As the sugar economy expanded in colonial Brazil, the *engenho* absorbed increasing numbers of African slaves and free cane farmers. In the aftermath of slavery, cane growers working under a variety of labor arrangements became the principal suppliers of cane to the *engenhos*. In the late nineteenth century, modern steam mills led to the disappearance of the older *engenhos*.

*See also* **Plantations; Sugar Industry.**

BIBLIOGRAPHY

Caio Prado, Jr., *The Colonial Background of Modern Brazil* (1971).

Auguste De Saint-Hilaire, *Viagem pelas províncias do Rio de Janeiro e Minas Gerais* (1975).

Ruy Gama, *Engenho e tecnologia* (1983).

Stuart B. Schwartz, *Sugar Plantations in the Formation of Brazilian Society: Bahia, 1550–1835* (1985).

*Additional Bibliography*

Araújo, Tatiana Brito de. *Os engenhos centrais e a produção açucareira no Recôncavo Baiano, 1875–1909.* Salvador, Brazil: FIEB, 2002.

NANCY PRISCILLA SMITH NARO

---

**ENGINEERING.** Engineering is a discipline that puts scientific knowledge to practical use by utilizing natural resources for the benefit of society. Throughout history, engineering has enabled the building of structures, the manipulation of natural energy sources, and the creation of new technologies. There are at least thirty-five subfields of engineering, including civil, mechanical, electrical, chemical, metallurgical, and geologic. Scientific discoveries in the nineteenth and twentieth centuries opened up the new subfields of electronic, computer, genetic, nuclear, environmental, biomedical, and aerospace engineering. Most engineering projects, such as building a bridge or a pipeline, involve several of these fields.

## PRECOLONIAL AND COLONIAL ENGINEERING

Precolonial engineers contributed much to Latin American civilization. The Maya mastered the principles of stress to construct corbeled arches (vaults) in their palaces, and raised lofty pyramids that supported temple structures, such as those in Tikal, Guatemala, and Chichen Itza, Mexico, which is one of the seven New Wonders of the World. In South America, the Inca constructed the great sawtoothed fortress of Sacsayhuaman near Cuzco, Peru, and the 2,250-mile road system that stretched from Quito to Santiago. Perhaps most emblematic of the Inca engineering acumen is Machu Picchu, a ruined city situated almost 8,000-feet above sea level in the Peruvian Andes. Such engineering feats attest to the ingenuity of the pre-Columbian era.

In the colonial era the Spanish and Portuguese built massive public-works projects, including ports, roads, forts, mines, buildings, churches, and cities, to reflect the flavor of European metropolitan life. Engineering facilitated metropolitan civilization in town squares throughout the colonies.

### THE TWENTIETH CENTURY

The region's most impressive engineering achievement of the twentieth century was the Panama Canal, an artificial waterway that connects the Caribbean Sea and the Pacific Ocean. Opened in 1914, the canal is 50.72 miles long. The United States invested more than $352 million in its construction. Yellow fever and other diseases took an extraordinary toll on the construction workers.

The canal has six locks at three separate locations. The locks are flooded to lift ships, which are then pulled through the canal by trains on either side of its banks. At its widest point the canal is 163 square miles (Gatun Lake); the narrowest point is 300 feet wide. Approximately 5 percent of the world's seagoing traffic passes through the Panama Canal. In 2006 Panamanian voters passed a referendum with 78 percent support that provided for an enlargement of the canal to accommodate roughly twice as many ships.

In the nineteenth and twentieth centuries engineering underpinned the Latin American ethos of "order and progress." Railroads and telegraphic lines crisscrossing the Andes and connecting Rio to the mountains and the interior provinces to the great harbors of Buenos Aires, Santos, and Veracruz, sparked an era of global capitalism. The rail line between Rio and São Paulo, Brazil, that passed through the Pariacuteba Valley was essential for the growth of the coffee economy. One of the most technically difficult railway engineering achievements was the building of the Madeira-Mamoré railroad in the Amazon.

The Cananea copper mine in northern Mexico was Latin America's largest at the end of the nineteenth century. By 1915 Chuquicamata, Chile, located 8,860 feet above sea level, had replaced it as the world's largest open-pit copper mine. Carajás, in southern Pará, Brazil, is the world's largest iron-ore mine, with 18 billion metric tons of confirmed reserve. Seven times the size of Switzerland and five times that of Texas, Carajás is connected to the port of São Luís, Maranhão, via 540 miles of railroad through the tropics. The rail line was the first in Latin America designed with environmental protection as a primary goal.

The two hydroelectric power plants on the Parana River testify to the achievements of integrated civil engineering technologies. The Itaipu dam is a binational project built, owned, and operated by Brazil and Paraguay. Constructed between 1975 and 1982, the dam houses twenty turbines generating 14,000 megawatts. Some 100,000 workers were involved in building the dam, which is 5 miles wide and 643 feet high, and is the world's largest hollow-gravity dam. Brazil and Paraguay spent more than $15 billion to complete the power station. Downriver, Argentina also shares a hydroelectric dam with Paraguay. Although construction began on the Yacyreta dam in 1983, it was not operational until 1994 due to political instability and corruption in Argentina. Because of miscalculation, the dam generates only about 60 percent of its planned power.

The Rio-Niterói Bridge in Brazil is among the world's most notable bridges. Brazil's military junta, fashioning itself as a modernizing technocratic regime, dedicated itself to material progress. The urban congestion of Greater Rio required a rapid transportation system that would connect Rio de Janeiro and Niterói, across the Guanabara Bay. The Rio-Niterói Bridge spans 8.25 miles (5.5 miles over water) and opened for traffic in 1974.

Argentina, Brazil, and Chile possess the engineering capabilities required to build sophisticated defense industries. During the 1960s and 1970s all three countries were denied access to the world arms market and so became self-sufficient in small arms, munitions, and motor vehicles, as well as aircraft, ships, tanks, armed personnel carriers, and a line of rockets and missiles. By 1990 Brazil had emerged as the seventh-largest arms maker in the world.

It is the knowledge, talent, and vision of engineers that make such accomplishments possible. Until recently, however, the training of engineers in the region was left to the military academies. These institutions bred the notion that a better society could be constructed via technical and scientific education and by emphasizing material progress. This became the harbinger of Latin America's modernization drives.

With assistance, Latin America entered the nuclear age. In Brazil two nuclear power plants, Angra I and Angra II, were built by Westinghouse and Siemens AG, respectively. Siemens AG also built Argentina's first nuclear power plant in the late 1960s, Atucha I. Construction of Atucha II was started in 1980, but has never been completed. A third plant, built at Embalse, was contracted to

Canada and Italy in 1972 and was operational in 1984. In both Brazil and Argentina, the navy played a key role in nuclear technology and development. Given Latin America's wealth of natural resources, and the commodity demand that underpins the growth of emerging markets, the region was expected to continue to host some of the world's largest and most exciting engineering projects.

*See also* **Mining: Modern; Nuclear Industry; Railroads.**

BIBLIOGRAPHY

Diehl, Richard A. *The Olmecs: America's First Civilization.* London: Thames and Hudson, 2004.

Gibson, Charles. *The Aztecs under Spanish Rule.* Stanford, CA: Stanford University Press, 1961.

Lins Ribeiro, Gustavo. *Transnational Capitalism and Hydropolitics in Argentina: The Yacyreta High Dam.* Gainesville: University Press of Florida, 1994.

Maldifassi, Jose O., and Pier A. Abetti. *Defense Industries in Latin American Countries: Argentina, Brazil, and Chile.* Westport, CT: Praeger, 1994.

McCullough, David. *The Path between the Seas: The Creation of the Panama Canal, 1870–1914.* New York: Simon and Schuster, 1977.

"Panama Votes for a Bigger Canal." *Economist*, October 23, 2006.

Summerhill, William R. *Order against Progress: Government, Foreign Investment, and Railroads in Brazil, 1854–1913.* Stanford, CA: Stanford University Press, 2003.

Turolla, Pino. *Beyond the Andes: My Search for the Origins of Pre-Inca Civilization.* New York: Harper and Row, 1980.

EUL-SOO PANG
SEAN H. GOFORTH

**ENLIGHTENMENT, THE.** Historical opinion on the role of the Enlightenment in Ibero-America was for a long time paradoxically united in that two different groups, each proceeding from wholly different premises, saw little of the light of the eighteenth century in the Hispanic and Portuguese worlds.

Catholic traditionalists, vociferously captained by the Spanish polymath Marcelino Menéndez y Pelayo (1856–1912) and loudly heard in Spain till the demise of Franco, gloried in what they saw as scant Hispanic involvement in a movement that to them was both repugnant and dangerous. Viewing the same complex history from beyond the Pyrenees or from overseas, many of the self-styled "lights" of Paris and their heirs saw little of their own brand of enlightenment and ample justification for the famous jeer of the encyclopedist Nicolas Masson: Has any good thing ever come out of Spain?

It would be misleading to say that either of these two views was entirely wrong. Certainly enlightenment in the Iberian world did not flourish from the beginning. The ideas and attitudes clustered around scholasticism long remained powerful. They continued to be intellectually satisfying to most Hispanic people well into the nineteenth century, and they were closely identified with strong vested interests. Yet, in spite of all these reservations, it is clear that Hispanic and Portuguese intellectual life did change in the course of the eighteenth century. Moreover, this change was instigated by an active, articulate minority that perceived the possibility of a different world but that, with few exceptions, remained emphatically Hispanic and Portuguese in fundamental outlook. The key point seems to be that all but a few reformers retained some aspect or form of Catholicism.

The most clear-cut of the changes was the entry of modern science. Its presence in Ibero-America can first be seen in the work of a few lonely pioneers. One was Carlos de Sigüenza y Góngora in Mexico, who as early as 1681 criticized scholasticism, explained comets in Copernican terms, and showed familiarity with the works of René Descartes and Pierre Gassendi. Another pioneer was Pedro de Peralta Barnuevo y Rocha in Peru.

More appreciable change came a generation later, perhaps from about 1720 on. Over the next half century, the freely circulated works of such authors as the Spanish reformer Benito Jerónimo Feijóo y Montenegro, the Portuguese João Baptista da Silva Leitão de Almeida Garrett and Luis Antonio Verney, and the Italian Antonio Genovesi; the "Port Royale" logic of Antoine Arnauld; and the works of "Lugdenensis" (Antoine de Montazet, archbishop of Lyon) all advocated mathematical education and set forth new scientific ideas drawn from Descartes, Gassendi, Locke, Newton, and others.

In the eighteenth century, the Inquisition was no longer an effective block against new scientific ideas. Control of the book trade was ineffective; much seminal scientific work was never on the index of proscribed works; and popularized or adapted versions of new discoveries and ideas were found in numerous legally circulated books. Poverty and poor communications constituted far more significant obstacles.

Frequently, new works and ideas became known through the scientific and technical missions that came to America. Groups led by Charles-Marie de La Condamine; Aimé Jacques Bonplánd; Thaddeus, Baron von Nordenflycht; Helm; Anton Zaccarias; Thaddeus Haenkes; and Alexander, Baron von Humboldt as well as José Celestino Mutis, Hipólito Ruiz, José Pavón, José Longinos, and Alessandro Malaspina, to cite only the best known, traveled extensively and had free interchange with local scholars. The travelers had new books and scientific apparatus; they knew the latest scientific gossip; and they generated immense interest.

New ideas and innovative organizations received strong official backing after Charles III came to the Spanish throne in 1759. The king's ministers, many of the officials he appointed, and the policies they put into action had clear ties to the Enlightenment. The attempts to rationalize administration, centralize authority, update law codes, collect accurate demographic and economic information, and improve the economy—to somehow manage Spain and its empire into a prosperous, well-ordered, and unified state—paralleled similar attempts all over Europe.

All these factors came together in the last third of the eighteenth century. There were numerous changes in university and in some seminary and convent school curricula that provided more training in mathematics and modern physics. The hitherto dominant training in Aristotelian logic and scholastic metaphysics, though hotly defended, was gradually reduced and made available only to those preparing for the clergy. The gradualness of this process and the determination—based partly on prudence but also on conviction—to preserve fundamental Catholic values must be emphasized.

The crown demanded and won significant changes in the teaching of law and some aspects of theology. Spanish law replaced Roman law as the dominant subject of study, and canon law strongly emphasized the *regalias,* the rights of the crown over the church. The most dramatic manifestation of this matter was the repression of the Jesuits and the proscription of their doctrines. A more constructive approach sought to use the critical study of church councils and ecclesiastical history to strengthen the position of the crown and the bishops against the papacy. This new approach to ecclesiastical history went hand-in-hand with a shift in emphasis toward dogmatic theology at the expense of speculative scholasticism.

In many respects, more up-to-date education exemplified the Enlightenment's preoccupation with useful projects. There were numerous attempts to develop the economy by official action, including encouraging private enterprise. The inmates of asylums and orphanages were put to work, *cabildos* (town governments) and *intendants* (provincial governors) saw to it that land was paved and drained. Newly founded economic societies discussed schools and new crops.

Just as the presence of the Enlightenment is in dispute among historians, so too is its outcome. Many have discerned its most clear impact in the Wars of Independence, in which they clearly see the influence of the political writings of the Baron de Montesquieu, John Locke, Gaetano Filangieri, Emmerich von Vattel, Samuel von Pufendorf, Thomas Jefferson, and other theorists of natural law. But traditionalists do not see this. For them, the wars of independence are conservative movements based on the scholastic natural law of Francisco Suárez and Saint Thomas Aquinas. A third group of historians see home-grown revolutionary movements such as Tupac Amaru's having a significant impact in weakening the colonial state. Most likely all three elements had their role, the Enlightenment representing a major ideological force.

Resolution of this problem seems to depend on how one sees the wars of independence. If they were the culmination of a developmental era, then the question of sources is all-important. If, however, independence came more from the collapse of the Spanish throne than from any process of colonial maturation, then the effects of the Enlightenment are to be seen not so much in the wars of independence as in the tumultuous struggles of the nineteenth century.

*See also* **Bourbon Reforms; Catholic Church: The Colonial Period; Humboldt, Alexander von; Longinos Martínez, José; Malaspina, Alejandro; Sigüenza y Góngora, Carlos de; Spanish Empire; Universities: Colonial Spanish America; Wars of Independence, South America.**

BIBLIOGRAPHY

Indispensable for seeing the spectrum of views on the Enlightenment in Latin America are Arthur P. Whitaker et al., *Latin America and the Enlightenment* (1961), and A. Owen Aldridge, ed., *The Ibero-American Enlightenment* (1971). A useful bibliography on the Enlightenment as well as other aspects of the Bourbon period is Jacques A. Barbier and Mark A. Burkholder, "Colonial Spanish America: The Bourbon Period," in *The History Teacher* 20, no. 2 (1987): 221–250. On university curricula see John Tate Lanning, *The Eighteenth-Century Enlightenment in the University of San Carlos de Guatemala* (1956). For a model treatment of a scientific expedition see Arthur R. Steele, *Flowers for the King: The Expedition of Ruíz and Pavón and the Flora of Peru* (1964). For two representative and differing treatments of the Enlightenment in specific areas see José Carlos Chiaramonte, *La Ilustración en el Río de la Plata* (1989), and Juan Manuel Pacheco, S.J., *La Ilustración en el Nuevo Reino* (1975). O. Carlos Stoetzer, *The Scholastic Roots of the Spanish American Revolution* (1979), presents the case for the continued influence of scholasticism.

*Additional Bibliography*

Díaz Caballero, Jesús. "Nación y patria: Las lecturas de los Comentarios reales y el patriotismo criollo emancipador." *Revista de Crítica Literaria Latinoamericana* 59 (2004): 81–107. Available from http://www.dartmouth.edu/~rcll/rcll59/59pdf/59diaz2.pdf.

Maher, John, ed. *Francisco De Miranda: Exile and Enlightenment.* London: Institute for the Study of the Americas, 2006.

Rodríguez O., Jaime E. *The Independence of Spanish America.* Cambridge Latin American Studies 84. Cambridge, U.K.: Cambridge University Press, 1998.

Saladino García, Alberto. *Ciencia y prensa durante la ilustración latinoamericana.* Toluca: Universidad Autónoma del Estado de México, 1996.

Soto Arango, Diana, Miguel Angel Puig-Samper, and Luis Carlos Arboleda. *La ilustración en América colonial: Bibliografía crítica.* Madrid: Consejo Superior de Investigaciones Científicas, 1995.

Williams, Jerry M., and Pedro de Peralta Barnuevo. *Censorship and Art in Pre-Enlightenment Lima: Pedro De Peralta Barnuevo's "Diálogo de los muertos: La causa académica."* Potomac, MD: Scripta Humanistica, 1994.

GEORGE M. ADDY

## ENRÍQUEZ, CARLOS (1901–1957).

Carlos Enríquez (*b.* 3 August 1901, *d.* 2 May 1957), Cuban artist. Born in Santa Clara, Cuba, Enríquez was sent by his parents to the United States to study engineering, but upon his arrival he instead entered the Pennsylvania Academy of Fine Arts. He was expelled from the school because of his rebellious personality and returned to Cuba. During a 1930–1934 sojourn in Europe, he became particularly attracted to the art of El Greco, Zurbarán, Velázquez, and Goya. During the 1930s he incorporated political and historical themes in his paintings. He won a prize at the National Salon in Havana in 1938.

His paintings depict nature in a state of turmoil, an effect achieved by swirling forms, translucid planes, and overlapping figures (*The Rape of the Mulattas,* 1937). Sensualism and the female body, to which he alluded even in the shapes of animals and vegetation, are characteristic of his work (*Cuban Outlaw,* 1943).

*See also* **Art: The Twentieth Century.**

BIBLIOGRAPHY

José Gómez Sicre, *Pintura cubana de hoy,* English text by Harold T. Riddle (1944), pp. 79–87.

Adelaida De Juan, *Pinturas cubana: Temas y variaciones* (1980), pp. 71–74.

*Additional Bibliography*

Martínez, Juan A. *Cuban Art and National Identity: The Vanguardia Painters, 1927-1950.* Gainesville: University Press of Florida, 1994.

Sánchez, Juan. *Carlos Enríquez.* La Habana: Editorial Letras Cubanas, 1996.

MARTA GARSD

## ENRÍQUEZ, MANUEL (1926–1994).

Manuel Enríquez (*b.* 17 June 1926; *d.* 26 April 1994), Mexican violinist, composer, and music administrator. At age six Enríquez began violin study with his father in Ocotlán, Jalisco, and continued with Ignacio Camarena in Guadalajara. He directed the Guadalajara Symphony (1949–1955). A scholarship to the Juilliard School of Music (1955–1957) allowed him to study violin with Ivan Galamian and composition with Peter Mennin. With a Guggenheim Fellowship in 1971 he researched folk music in Spain and the same year enrolled in the Columbia-Princeton Research Center for Electronic Music. His music, written largely in nontraditional graphic notation, embraces, at times, serially recurring patterns of pitch, rhythm, and timbre, and free sections in which some elements of chance are left to the performers. He deliberately avoids nationalistic references. Enríquez taught composition at the National Conservatory of Mexico and has directed both the Carlos Chávez Center for Music Research and the music department of the National Institute of Fine Arts.

*See also* **Mexico: Since 1910.**

BIBLIOGRAPHY

Gérard Béhague, *Music in Latin America: An Introduction* (1979).

*Additional Bibliography*

Moreno Rivas, Yolanda. *La composición en México en el siglo XX.* México, D.F.: Consejo Nacional para la Cultura y las Artes, 1994.

ROBERT L. PARKER

## ENRÍQUEZ DE ALMANSA, MARTÍN

(c. 1508–1583). Martín Enríquez de Almansa (*b.* ca. 1508; *d.* 1583), viceroy of New Spain (1568–1580) and of Peru (1580–1583). Although from a noble family of Castile, Enríquez did not inherit a title and little is known of his early life. Appointed viceroy of New Spain at the age of sixty, he brought a strong rule to the colony in the aftermath of the Cortés– Ávila conspiracy. He was authoritarian and at times bad tempered, but he was also just and kindly toward the Indians. He refused to grant colonial demands for a total war against the wild Chichimecs of the north. That and his imposition of the detested *alcabala* (sales tax) made him unpopular. A wise administrator, he is generally credited with having raised the prestige of the viceroy's office. He reluctantly accepted the viceroyalty of Peru in 1580 and died in Lima three years later.

*See also* **Spanish Empire.**

BIBLIOGRAPHY

Antonio F. García-Abásolo González, *Martín Enríquez y la reforma de 1568 en Nueva España* (1983).

*Additional Bibliography*

Cañeque, Alejandro. *The King's Living Image: The Culture and Politics of Viceregal Power in Colonial Mexico.* New York: Routledge, 2004.

STAFFORD POOLE C.M.

## ENRÍQUEZ DE GUZMÁN, ALONSO

(c. 1501–c. 1549). Alonso Enríquez de Guzmán (*b.* ca. 1501; *d.* ca. 1549), author of a picaresque account of Peru's conquest and civil wars. Born in Seville, he was a courtier in the service of the emperor.

Guzmán sailed towards the Indies and in 1534 to South America's western coast in search of gold. He was in Lima in August 1535 and continued to Cuzco, eventually fighting during the great native uprising of Manco Inca.

When the Chilean expedition returned, Guzmán helped the Almagrists retake Cuzco from the Pizzarists; however, he was captured in 1539 by Pizzaro and sent to jail in Spain. Offered a military command by the duke of Alba, he fought in Germany against the Lutherans in the Battle of Mühlberg.

Guzmán left two important manuscripts: an autobiography, *Libro de la vida y costumbres de don Alonso Enriques, caballero*, and a poem on the death of Diego de Almagro. Originally believed to be more fictional than true, the work reveals upon careful reading that the Peruvian sections at least are largely accurate.

*See also* **Almagro, Diego de; Spanish Empire.**

BIBLIOGRAPHY

Lockhart, James. *Spanish Peru, 1532–1560: A Colonial Society.* Madison: University of Wisconsin Press, 1968.

Porras Barrenechea, Raul. *Los cronistas del Perú (1528–1650).* Lima: Banco de Crédito del Peru, 1986.

Stewart, Paul. "The Battle of Las Salinas, Peru, and Its Historians." *Sixteenth Century Journal* (Autumn, 1988): 407–434.

NOBLE DAVID COOK

## ENRÍQUEZ GALLO, ALBERTO

(1894–1962). Alberto Enríquez Gallo (*b.* 24 July 1894; *d.* 13 July 1962), military figure and president of Ecuador (nonelected 1937–1938). Born in Tanicuchi, León, Enríquez graduated from the Colegio Militar Eloy Alfaro in Quito (1912). He served as minister of defense from 1935 to 1937, using his position to reform and professionalize the military. Promoted to general in 1937, Enríquez took over the presidency in October, when the military ousted interim president Federico Páez (1936–1937).

Enríquez's administration undertook a broad-based reform of juridical, educational, administrative, and financial structures and legislation. His government also enacted a number of social reforms, including an advanced labor code and laws to protect children. Enríquez relinquished power to Manuel María Borrero after calling the Constituent Convention of 1938. Ten years later (1948) he was an unsuccessful presidential candidate of the liberal socialist coalition. He served as senator for the province of Pichincha from 1956 until 1960.

*See also* **Ecuador, Political Parties; Overview.**

BIBLIOGRAPHY


Enrique Ayala Mora, ed., *Nueva historia del Ecuador: Época republicana,* vol. 10 (1983), esp. pp. 103–104.

Luis Cristóbal Cabezas, *50 años de vida política y anecdótica del Ecuador* (1986), esp. pp. 32–34.


*Additional Bibliography*


Coral Patiño, Héctor. *Vida y obra del Señor General Alberto Enríquez Gallo.* Quito: Banco Central del Ecuador, 1988.

Martz, John D. *The Military Coup d'État as a Political Process: Ecuador, 1948–1966.* Baltimore, MD: Johns Hopkins University Press, 1977.


LINDA ALEXANDER RODRÍGUEZ

## ENSENADA, CENÓN DE SOMODEVILLA, MARQUÉS DE LA (1702–1781).

Marqués de la Ensenada, Cenón de Somodevilla (*b.* 2 June 1702; *d.* 2 December 1781), secretary of state of Spain (1743–1754). Termed the "secretary of everything" by a contemporary because he was secretary of state, finance, war, marine affairs, and the Indies, Ensenada was the most powerful minister in Spain during the early reign of Ferdinand VI. Early in his bureaucratic career he specialized in naval administration, and once in office he became firmly committed to increasing Spain's naval power. In an effort to increase the crown's revenues from the Indies trade, he encouraged the use of register ships rather than fleets and imposed strict trade regulations. However, Ensenada is best known for his domestic fiscal reform policies, which included a proposed single tax on income, based on ability to pay and applicable to all citizens. A ministerial power struggle in 1754 brought about his dismissal and exile.

*See also* **Ferdinand VI of Spain; Spanish Empire.**

BIBLIOGRAPHY


León, Felipe Abad. *El Marqués de la Ensenada: Su vida y su obra,* 2 vols. Rioja: Diputación, Unidad de Cultura, 1981.

Rodríguez Villa, Don Antonio. *Don Cenon de Somodevilla, Marques de la Ensenada.* Madrid, 1878.


SUZANNE HILES BURKHOLDER

## ENTRADA.

*Entrada,* an armed expedition, or literally "entry," into the Brazilian wilderness in search of indigenous slaves, gold, or trade. In the Northeast, *entradas* sought native slaves for sugar plantations and domestic service in the sixteenth century. In Amazonia they pursued slaves, nuts, spices, wood, and herbal drugs in the sixteenth, seventeenth, and eighteenth centuries. In southern Brazil, *entradas,* along with the larger Bandeiras, forcibly relocated thousands of indigenous people to Portuguese towns in the seventeenth century and searched for gold in the eighteenth century. These long expeditions charted much of the Brazilian west and led to the discoveries of gold, emeralds, and diamonds in the interior.

*See also* **Slavery: Brazil.**

BIBLIOGRAPHY


John Hemming, *Red Gold: The Conquest of the Brazilian Indians* (1978).

John M. Monteiro, "From Indian to Slave: Forced Native Labour and Colonial Society," *Slavery and Abolition* 9 (1988): 105–127.


*Additional Bibliography*


Carvalho, João Renôr Ferreira de. *Resistência indígena no Piauí colonial: 1718-1774.* Imperatriz: Ética, 2005.

Langfur, Hal. *The Forbidden Lands: Colonial Identity, Frontier Violence, and the Persistence of Brazil's Eastern Indians, 1750-1830.* Stanford: Stanford University Press, 2006.

Metcalf, Alida C. "The Entradas of Bahia of the Sixteenth Century." *The Americas.* 61:1 (2005): 373-400.

ALIDA C. METCALF

## ENTRE RÍOS.

**ENTRE RÍOS.** Entre Ríos is a province of northeastern Argentina (2001 population 1,158, 147) located between the Uruguay and Paraná rivers, whose capital city is Paraná (2001 population 250,000). Owing to its swamps, it was a neglected territory during colonial and early republican times, and most efforts toward colonization and settlement were directed at central Paraguay and the plains of Santa Fé, west of the Paraná River. The original inhabitants were Guaraní, Charrúa, and Chaná natives who occupied different areas of the region. By 1520 the region was settled by the Spanish. The drive to populate Entre Ríos began after the city of Paraná was safely established at its present site in 1883. A large number of the original settlers were immigrants who became agricultural workers and eventually took up residency in the territory. Secondary centers in the province, such as Diamante, Concórdia, Concepción del Uruguay, and Monte Caseros, grew as supporters of the mainly agrarian activities of Entre Ríos. The province's main commodities are flax (main national product, grown on 1,150,000 acres), corn (500,000 acres), rice (145,000 acres), and citrus. In the southern segment of Entre Ríos, sunflower and wheat are important crops, but the volume of production does not compare with that of other agricultural regions of the country. Husbandry comprises more than 3 million cattle, 4 million sheep, and 1.3 million hogs, most of them processed in the packing plants of Paraná, Concepción del Uruguay, and Gualeguaychú. Chicken and egg production also contribute to the region's economy.

*See also* **Agriculture; Argentina, Geography; Paraná, Argentina.**

BIBLIOGRAPHY

Manuel E. Macchi, *Entre Ríos: Síntesis histórica* (Concepción, 1977).

*Additional Bibliography*

Carriego, Evaristo. *Crónicas de Entre Ríos.* Buenos Aires: Editorial J. Alvarez, 1967.

Galafassi, Guido. *El campo diverso: Enfoques y perspectivas de la Argentina agrarian del siglo XX.* Buenos Aires: Universidad Nacional de Quilmas Editorial, 2004.

Rousseaux, Andrés René. *Historia del Puerto de Concepción del Uruguay Entre Rios.* Argentina: Junta de Estudios Históricos, 1995.

CÉSAR N. CAVIEDES

## ENVIRONMENTAL MOVEMENTS.

**ENVIRONMENTAL MOVEMENTS.** During the 1980s environmental matters gained strong currency in Latin America, especially with the proliferation of democracies throughout the region. By the 1990s nongovernmental environmental organizations numbered in the thousands. Some had their beginnings in the late 1960s or early 1970s, but most appeared in the 1980s.

Beginning in the 1980s, Latin American environmental issues were usually related to development, whether the subject be deforestation, industrial pollution, sanitation, transportation, indigenous populations, public education, or animal rights. Poverty itself was considered a major environmental concern, since the poor placed serious strains on natural resources for their livelihood in the absence of more environmentally sound alternatives. In short, environmental issues had strong political and economic implications and thus provoked much controversy.

The United Nations chose to hold its second major international conference on development and the environment in a Latin American setting (Rio de Janeiro) in 1992. (The first conference had taken place in Stockholm in 1972.) One objective of the 1992 conference was to establish a financial mechanism for industrialized nations to aid Third World environmental programs. It was suggested that developed countries should pay an "ecological debt" to Latin American nations and transfer pollution control technologies without charge. More than 178 governments adopted Agenda 21, the Rio Declaration on Environment and Development, and the Statement of Principles for the Sustainable Management of Forests at the 1992 UN conference. The commitment to Agenda 21 and the accompanying Rio documents was reasserted at the 2002 World Summit on Sustainable Development in Johannesburg, South Africa. However, in Latin America, support and implementation of Agenda 21 by national governments, NGOs, and social movements have been uneven due to priorities other than sustainable development, such as alleviating poverty and achieving political stability.

Most international attention to Latin America's environmental problems tended to focus on global warming as it related to the destruction of tropical forests, especially in the Amazon and Central America. Brazil received much adverse attention in late 1988 when Chico Mendes Filho, an Amazon rubber tapper and political activist, was murdered at the behest of a local rancher. Mendes's political success in the Brazilian Congress had resulted in legislation rendering the rancher's property worthless, so Mendes Filho was killed in revenge.

Tropical forests, however, had always been relatively underpopulated. A far greater number of Latin Americans were adversely affected by urban pollution problems, especially deficient sewage treatment (São Paulo and Rio de Janeiro, Brazil) and smog (Mexico City and Santiago, Chile).

While Latin America's environmental problems remained widespread and serious in the mid-1990s, progress was being made on some fronts. For instance, Cubatão, the Brazilian city once called the most polluted site on earth, reduced petrochemical and fertilizer pollutants to a fraction of their former levels with the assistance of a World Bank loan. The health indicators for the city's inhabitants improved dramatically, and lush vegetation reappeared in once-decimated areas.

***Green Politics.*** The importance of environmental issues in Latin American politics was undeniable by the late 1980s. In Mexico, for example, President Carlos Salinas De Gortari chose to seize the environmental initiative and pursue "preemptive reforms"

**Protesting illegal deforestation.** Greenpeace marks illegally harvested timber from the Amazonian rainforest, 2003. TOM STODDART/ HULTON ARCHIVE/ GETTY IMAGES

rather than wait for grassroots mobilization and pressures. Salinas declared the health of the Mexican people to be a greater priority of his administration than development. His words were followed with substantive actions: $2.5 billion was budgeted to improve Mexico City's air quality, a major petroleum refinery operated by Pemex (Mexico's state-owned oil company) was closed, unleaded gasoline was introduced, and 3,500 city buses were replaced. As a result, Salinas was awarded the United Nations–backed United Earth Association award in 1991, a move applauded by many of Mexico's environmental groups.

Meanwhile, the intensity of international attention to the Amazon provoked a political backlash. In 1990 the state of Amazonas readily elected a governor whose platform was blatantly anti-environment; he had declared that since there were no healthy trees in the Amazon, people should use them up before the termites did. Subsequently, some military officers and conservative civilian politicians accused international environmentalists of threatening Brazil's national sovereignty and security.

While some Latin American countries had "green" political parties by the 1990s, they were relatively small and their political impact limited. Most were not formally linked to the European-based international Green Party movement.

***The State and the Environment.*** Cabinet-level environment posts (either ministries or secretariats) were created in many but not all Latin American countries in the 1980s and early 1990s. They were notably lacking in Central America, except for Guatemala. Some of the agencies were exclusively environmental ministries (Brazil and Argentina) while others combined environmental matters with such development-related areas as natural resources (Venezuela and Colombia) or urban planning and development (Uruguay and Mexico). Often, these new entities represented an upgrading of earlier, less powerful government agencies with environmental mandates.

Environmental legislation varied markedly throughout the region in the early 1990s. Some countries had fairly comprehensive laws and policies, while others lacked them almost totally. Even where such measures existed on paper, implementation and enforcement were difficult or sometimes even impossible; frequently the measures were simply ignored.

***Debt-for-Nature Swaps.*** In the 1960s and 1970s, Latin American governments contracted foreign public and private loans for development projects. When the world's economy entered recession in the early 1980s, these loans quickly became unserviceable. Several contentious years of debt negotiations followed, but by the late 1980s more creative approaches to the problem had emerged. One such idea was the debt swap, whereby a country's debt paper could be purchased at a fraction of its original worth on secondary markets and then utilized in that country for approved projects, including those related to the environment. Projects for such swaps were further encouraged in the Enterprise for the Americas Initiative of 1990, promoted by U.S. President George Herbert Walker Bush. It was difficult, though, for environmental groups to raise substantial amounts of capital for such undertakings. Nevertheless, a few debt-for-nature swaps have occurred, most notably in Bolivia, Ecuador, and Costa Rica.

In the early 1990s, debt-for-nature initiatives included a project by Argentina's National Development Bank for natural grassland and forest preservation in the ecologically sensitive Patagonia region. There was also a swap proposal from the Central American Bank for Economic Integration to create a trust fund that could be tapped by Central American environmental organizations and university groups. In general, debt-for-nature initiatives have been looked upon favorably by conservation groups and debtor governments. In October of 2006, Conservation International and The Nature Conservancy arranged a landmark $24 million debt-for-nature swap between the governments of the United States and Guatemala. Earmarked for protecting threatened Guatemalan tropical forests and stimulating economic activity, this is the largest swap of its kind to date.

Debt swaps, however, can be politically sensitive issues. Mexico refused to participate in debt swaps instigated by third parties because it was unwilling to cede national territory and sovereignty to such ventures. Instead, it invented a variation on the debt swap theme by contracting a loan from the World Bank to purchase its own debt. This in turn created a $150 million fund for reforesting 173,000 acres of Mexico City with 200 million trees. In Brazil, the Collor administration reversed the policy of its predecessor and accepted debt-for-nature swaps in principle. This added to the criticism within Brazil that the country was losing control over the Amazon.

***Development Versus the Environment.*** At the root of many Latin American environmental issues in the early 1990s were government development policies and objectives. Past development strategies of the 1960s and 1970s were often identified as the source of many of the most serious environmental problems of the 1980s and 1990s. By the 1990s new development projects were more likely to be scrutinized and criticized, often under the concept of sustainable development. Ecuador and Guatemala, for example, faced serious choices between opening new areas to petroleum production or forgoing same in favor of conserving the biologically diverse and unique areas involved.

*See also* **Amazon River; Economic Development; Environment and Climate; Forests; Mendes Filho, Francisco "Chico" Alves; Salinas de Gortari, Carlos; United Nations.**

BIBLIOGRAPHY

The environmental movement in Latin America is just beginning to receive systematic scholarly attention, and sources remain scarce. Two of the few monographs covering the region as a whole are David A. Preston, ed., *Environment, Society, and Rural Change in Latin America: The Past, Present, and Future in the Countryside* (1980), and David Goodman and Michael Redclift, eds., *Environment and Development in Latin America: The Politics of Sustainability* (1991). Another recent scholarly effort to survey the Latin American environmental movement is the entire issue of *Latin American Perspectives* 19, no. 1, issue 72 (1992). Latin America often receives attention in works with broader, global themes, such as the UN World Commission on Environment and Development, *Our Common Future* (1987). Articles with regionwide foci include Eduardo Gudynas, "Environment and Sustainable Development in Latin America: The Challenge to Recover 'El Dorado,'" in *International Transnational Associations* 4 (1989): 197–199, and Scott Whiteford, David Wiley, and Kenneth Wylie, "In the Name of Development: Transforming the Environment in Africa and Latin America" in *Centennial Review* 35, no. 2 (1991): 205–219. Other articles often focus on a specific country or theme, such as Stephen P. Mumme, "System Maintenance and Environmental Reform in Mexico: Salinas's Preemptive Strategy," in *Latin American Perspectives* 19, no. 1, issue 72 (1992): 123–143. An indispensable source for updated information on environment-related developments throughout the world, usually organized on a country basis, is the Bureau of National Affairs's biweekly *International Environment Reporter: Current Reports.*

*Additional Bibliography*

Deere, Carolyn L., and Daniel C. Esty. *Greening the Americas: NAFTA's Lessons for Hemispheric Trade.* Cambridge, MA: MIT Press, 2002.

García-Guadilla, María Pilar. *Environmental Movements, Politics, and Agenda 21 in Latin America.* Geneva, Switzerland: United Nations Research Institute for Social Development, 2005.

Roberts, J. Timmons, and Nikki Demetria Thanos. *Trouble in Paradise: Globalization and Environmental Crises in Latin America.* New York: Routledge, 2003.

LAURA JARNAGIN

---

**ENVIRONMENT AND CLIMATE.** The physical environment of Latin America is varied, complex, and frequently spectacular. Extending more than 6,000 miles from north to south, Latin America encompasses environmental conditions from the northern subtropics to the sub-Antarctic. Within this size and diversity there are broad subdivisions.

## RELIEF

Mexico continues the surface forms and geology of North America southward to about 20 degrees N, and includes the Pacific and Gulf coastal plains, the upland Mexican plateau at around 8,000 feet, and its peripheral mountain chains. Beyond the Isthmus of Tehuantepec, the circum-Caribbean region consists of the limestone lowland of Yucatán, the rugged east-west mountain ranges of Central America and the Greater Antilles, and the volcanic axes of the Isthmus of Panama and the island arc of the Lesser Antilles.

South America, the largest of the structural elements, itself has three broad subdivisions. Half its area is occupied by the Guiana and Brazilian shields, north and south of the Amazon, and the Patagonian plateau. These geologically ancient and eroded uplands have limited surface relief, but in

Brazil substantial scarplike edges form barriers along the Atlantic coast.

On the western margins the Andes extend for more than 5,500 miles as a series of parallel mountain ranges of more than 10,000 feet, rising to 22,800 feet. They divide Pacific from Atlantic drainage, and their rugged topography is a major obstacle to east-west movement. Within the Andes small valleys and upland basins above 10,000 feet have provided important niches for human settlement.

The shields and Andes restrict coastal lowlands, and there are few good harbors. However, between these uplands stretch the broad plains of the Orinoco, Amazon, and Paraná-Paraguay-La Plata river basins. Despite their size, these major rivers have not created arteries of communication into the interior; elsewhere waterfalls, rapids, and shoals limit navigation.

### CLIMATE

Although three-quarters of the region are within the tropics, there is considerable climatic diversity, in response to the influence of latitude, altitude, and, on the Pacific coast, cold ocean currents. Humid tropical climates have average monthly temperatures above 64 degrees Fahrenheit and annual rainfall of more than 80 inches, with little seasonality; the savanna-type climate has less (30 to 60 inches) and more seasonal rain. The former occurs in Amazonia, the Guianas, the Colombian and Ecuadorian Pacific lowlands, and the circum-Caribbean, and the latter in southern Mexico and the region surrounding the Amazon Basin. Markedly contrasting dry conditions exist in northern Mexico, Patagonia, the Chaco, and the arid coastlands of Peru and north Chile, whereas in northeast Brazil, low, strongly seasonal rainfall may extend into periodic drought. In the mountains, altitude and latitude give a vertical zonation with tropical to cold conditions in Mexico and the central Andes and tundra conditions, with glaciers and permanent snow, in the far south. More restricted but distinctive climates occur in the mediterranean area of central Chile and the subtropical conditions of the pampas, with winter and summer average temperatures of 50 to 82 degrees Fahrenheit and relatively low (20 to 40 inches) but year-round rainfall.

### ALTITUDE

Altitude plays a critically important role in the control of temperature in Latin America, especially in tropical areas, and many different temperature regimes can express themselves over relatively short distances in highland areas. For the most part, highland locations near the equator manifest no real seasonal differences in temperature, although they do show considerable temperature change from day to night. As one moves away from the equator, however, there is an increasingly greater change in temperature from one season to the next. Also, the altitudinal zonations of temperature vary with latitudinal location as well as with their position on the east- or west-facing slope; therefore, altitudinal zonations are not given definite limits. The recognition of the importance of altitudinal zonation goes back at least to the colonial period as the basis for the growing of crops; indigenous peoples too incorporated such insights. It is known that the Incas traditionally moved peoples from one part of their empire to another, but they would always ensure that they stayed at approximately the same altitudinal position.

Many different zonation patterns have been used in the literature, but the traditional folk classification has been the most widely accepted. It divides the highlands into five zones or *tierras*, each one defined by prevailing temperature regimes, dominant vegetation (although the type of vegetation is also influenced by rainfall regimes), and typical crop complex. The *tierra caliente* is the region that lies between sea level and about 2,500 to 3,000 feet. Daytime temperatures usually reach 85 to 90 degrees Fahrenheit, and mild temperatures (70 to 75) prevail at night; rarely will temperatures drop below 50, and there is no threat of frost at any time. The *tierra templada*, considered the most ideal for human occupation and highly desired by the Spaniards, lies between 2,500 and about 6,000 feet. This area typically experiences mild, pleasant days of 75 to 80 degrees, although the mercury will rise to a hot 90 to 95 at higher altitudes during the warmer months. Nighttime temperatures fall to 60 to 70, with a rare frost, especially during the cooler months as one moves north or south from the equator. The *tierra fría* defines altitudes between 6,000 and 12,000 feet, and occurs throughout the Andes and in some higher elevations in Mexico and Central America.

It is known for its mild daytime temperatures (75 to 80) and cool nights (50 to 55), with frost very common in cooler months away from the equator and at higher elevations. The *tierra helada* lies above 12,000 feet in the Andes, between the daily frost line and the boundary of permanent snow (about 15,000 feet), and is typified by low-growing bunch grasses. The mountain peaks with year-round permanent snow are classified *tierra nevada* and are above the vegetation zone.

The *tierra helada*, located above the tree line and below the zone of permanent snow, is a bitterly inhospitable cold desert dominated by highland meadows that provide pasturage for a number of native species (e.g., deer, vicuña, and guanaco) and domesticated animals. These grasslands are referred to as the *páramo* in the damper highland areas between Costa Rica and northern Peru, but they are replaced by *puna* in the dry highland Altiplano region between Central Peru and northern Chile. The *páramo* is typified by a dense tussock grassland with concentrations of woody vegetation in sheltered areas, while the drier *puna* is dominated by a more xerophytic grassland that includes ichu, a type of poor-quality bunch grass, and tola, a resinous bush that thrives in areas of low temperature and rainfall. In both areas, the use of fire and the cutting of trees have tended to expand the grasslands into lower elevations.

### SOILS AND VEGETATION

Poor latosols and podzolic soils, which are strongly weathered and leached, cover almost half the continent. Though they may carry luxuriant vegetation, they have limited nutrients and do not long sustain cultivation. In mountain areas steep slopes and erosion inhibit soil formation. Within such zones tracts of better soils exist, but the most productive soils are the black earths of the pampas and the *terra roxa* formed on volcanic material in south Brazil.

Vegetation cover reflects the influence of relief, geology, and climate. The three major but internally varied forms are forest, savanna, and desert. Forest cover ranges from the evergreen rain forest of Central America and Amazonia, surrounded by tropical seasonal forest, to the temperate woodlands of southern Chile. The savannas and grasslands occupy almost one-fifth of the area, grading from the woodland-grass scrubland of the Brazilian *campos* and Venezuelan Llanos to the Pampas grassland. One-quarter of the vegetation is dryland, including the thorn scrub of north Mexico, Patagonia, Chaco, and the Brazilian Sertão and the barren Atacama Desert. In the mountains, altitude modifies cover from tropical forest to *puna-páramo* grassland and bare rocks.

In the early twenty-first century clear rises in global temperatures, the ongoing deforestation of the Amazon rain forest, and extreme weather conditions made environmental change and protection a major policy concern. Scientists have linked the production of carbon dioxide, mainly by cars and industrial plants, to global warming. The United States contributes the most to atmospheric carbon dioxide pollution whereas Latin America produces approximately 4 percent. Related to this debate has been the deforestation of the Amazon. The vast rain forest, which lies mainly in Brazil, absorbs a great deal of the world's carbon dioxide; in addition, the destruction of trees releases stored carbon dioxide, further contributing to global warming. Consequently, Brazilian and international environmental organizations have opposed the cutting down of the rain forest. Elsewhere, higher temperatures have created noticeable environmental changes: Hurricanes have become more intense and frequent, battering Central America, Mexico and the Caribbean. Ac-cording to the World Bank, global climate change has caused water sources in the Andes to dry up. International and Latin American policymakers are looking at ways of slowing this process and crafting solutions to changes that cannot be halted.

### ENVIRONMENT AND PEOPLE

Though the environment can be summarized in these broad terms, to do so would mask much local diversity, in that individual countries have conditions ranging from arid to humid or temperate to tropical. There are negative environments that have been inimical to settlement because of ruggedness, aridity, cold, or soil poverty, or because episodic hazards such as earthquakes, volcanoes, frost, drought, hurricanes, and El Niño put life and economic activity at risk. Conversely, the forest, fertile soils, ecological niches in the mountains, precious and base metals in the sierras and shields, and, more recently, lowland petroleum deposits have attracted people and development.

BIBLIOGRAPHY

Araya Dujisin, Rodrigo, ed. *Una mirada regional a la relación comercio internacional y medio ambiente.* Ñuñoa, Santiago: FLACSO-Chile, 2000.

Caviedes, César, and Gregory Knapp. *South America.* Englewood Cliffs, NJ: Prentice-Hall, 1995.

Fittkau, Ernst Josef, et al., eds. *Biogeography and Ecology in South America.* The Hague, Netherlands: Dr. W. Junk N.V., Publishers, 1969.

James, Preston, and Clarence Minkel, *Latin America,* 5th edition. New York: Wiley, 1986.

Kent, Robert B. *Latin America: Regions and People.* New York: Guilford Press, 2006.

Martinson, Tom L., and Gary S. Elbow, eds. *Geographic Research on Latin America: Benchmark 1980.* Muncie, IN: Conference of Latin Americanist Geographers, Ball State University, 1981. See esp. pp. 22–33 and 269–311.

Morris, Arthur.*South America,* 3rd edition. Totowa, NJ: Barnes and Noble, 1987.

Prance, Ghillean T., and Thomas E. Lovejoy, eds. *Amazonia.* Oxford, U.K., and New York: Pergamon Press, 1985.

Roberts, J. Timmons, and Nikki Demetria Thanos. *Trouble in Paradise: Globalization and Environmental Crises in Latin America.* New York: Routledge, 2003.

Schwerdtfeger, Werner ed. *Climates of Central and South America.* Amsterdam: Elsevier, 1976.

Veblen, Thomas T., Kenneth R. Young, and Antony R. Orme, eds. *The Physical Geography of South America.* Oxford and New York: Oxford University Press, 2007.

West, Robert, and John Augelli. *Middle America: Its Lands and Peoples,* 3rd edition. Englewood Cliffs, NJ: Prentice-Hall, 1989.

JOHN P. DICKENSON

**ERÁRIO RÉGIO.** Erário Régio, the Royal Treasury of Portugal. Its creation, on 22 December 1761, and the extinction of the Casa dos Contos were key measures of the reform program of the Marquês de Pombal to overhaul the fiscal bureaucracy. In the reorganized exchequer, four departments, staffed by trained accountants and reporting to the treasurer-general, supervised the income and expenditures of the crown with respect to the geographical divisions of Portugal and its empire: (1) the Court (the heartland) and Estremadura; (2) other provinces and Azores and Madeira; (3) Africa, Maranhão, and Bahia; and (4) Rio de Janeiro, East Africa, and Asia. Headed initially by Pombal himself, succeeding treasurers-general included other eminent statesmen: the Marquês de Angeja, the Marquês de Ponte de Lima, and Rodrigo de Sousa Coutinho. With the passage of the court to Rio in 1808, the treasury was recreated in the colony. Subsequently abolished in 1832 in Portugal, in Brazil after independence (1822) the colonial department was superseded by the Tesouro Publico in 1824.

*See also* **Pombal, Marquês de (Sebastião José de Carvalho e Melo); Portuguese Empire.**

BIBLIOGRAPHY

Ruy D'abreu Torres, "Erário Régio," in *Dicionario de Historia de Portugal,* edited by Joel Serrão, vol. 2 (1965), pp. 67–68.

*Additional Bibliography*

Maxwell, Kenneth. *Conflicts & Conspiracies: Brazil and Portugal, 1750-1808.* New York: Routledge, 2004.

CATHERINE LUGAR

**ERCILLA Y ZÚÑIGA, ALONSO DE** (1533–1594). Alonso de Ercilla y Zúñiga (*b.* 1533; *d.* 1594), Spanish poet. Although he was in Latin America for only a short period, Alonso de Ercilla can be considered one of the first writers of the New World. In *La Araucana* (1569, 1578, 1589), an exemplary Renaissance epic poem based on his brief experience as a soldier fighting the Araucanian Indians in southern Chile, he combines the imagination of the poet with the observations and commentaries of the historian. He began writing the poem during the campaign, but he completed it years later in Spain, adding several passages about other important Spanish triumphs in Europe. Dedicated to King Philip II, in whose court he served from an early age, *La Araucana* praises the glories of the empire while also offering a sympathetic and admiring view of the Araucanians. Lacking an individual hero, the poem stresses the valiant defense by the Indians against the Spanish invasion and even criticizes some aspects of the war.

*See also* **Araucana, La.**

BIBLIOGRAPHY

Alonso De Ercilla y Zúñiga, *La Araucana,* edited by Marcos A. Morínigo and Isaías Lerner (1979).

Isaías Lerner, "Don Alonso de Ercilla y Zúñiga," in *Latin American Writers,* edited by Carlos A. Solé and Maria Isabel Abreu, vol. 1 (1989), pp. 23–31.

*Additional Bibliography*

Mejías López, William. *Las Ideas de la guerra justa en Ercilla y en La Araucana.* Santiago de Chile: Editorial Universitaria, 1992.

Nicolopulos, James. *The Poetics of Empire in the Indies: Prophecy and Imitation in La Araucana and Os lusíadas.* University Park: Pennsylvania State University Press, 2000.

S. DAYDÍ- TOLSON

## ERRÁZURIZ ECHAURREN, FEDERICO

**ERRÁZURIZ ECHAURREN, FEDERICO** (1850–1901). Federico Errázuriz Echaurren (*b.* 16 November 1850; *d.* 12 July 1901), president of Chile (1896–1901). Son of former president Federico Errázuriz Zañartu, Errázuriz was a lawyer by education and a farmer by profession. He entered politics in 1876, serving three terms as a deputy. Although he served as a minister in José Manuel Balmaceda's government (1886–1891), he joined the Congressionalist forces in the 1891 Revolution. Reelected to the chamber of deputies, he later became a senator. Errázuriz apparently spent heavily—probably over a million pesos—to win the presidency in 1896. Despite this sum, he barely defeated his opponent, the highly principled Vicente Reyes, who possessed neither Errázuriz's funds nor his political connections.

Despite these inauspicious beginnings, Errázuriz did manage to resolve the nation's frontier problems with Argentina over the Puna de Atacama, preserve Chile's territorial gains from the War of the Pacific, and personally intervene to avoid war with Argentina. In 1899 he met with the president of Argentina at the Strait of Magellan, where they declared that their two nations would never fight each other.

Errázuriz's fellow countrymen seemed less pacific, however, attacking the partially paralyzed and increasingly ill president. Forced by poor health to turn over his government in 1900 to his vice president for four months, Errázuriz returned to rule, but in May 1901 he again transferred power to the vice president. Errázuriz died before completing his term of office.

*See also* **Balmaceda Fernández, José Manuel; Chile, Revolutions: Revolution of 1891.**

BIBLIOGRAPHY

Jaime Eyzaguirre, *Chile durante el gobierno de Errázuriz Echaurren, 1896–1901* (1957).

Luis Galdames, *A History of Chile* (1941), pp. 366, 406, 444.

*Additional Bibliography*

Collier, Simon, and William F. Sater. *A History of Chile, 1808-1994.* Cambridge: Cambridge University Press, 1996.

WILLIAM F. SATER

## ERRÁZURIZ VALDIVIESO, CRESCENTE

**ERRÁZURIZ VALDIVIESO, CRESCENTE** (1839–1931). Crescente Errázuriz Valdivieso (*b.* 1839; *d.* 1931), archbishop of Santiago, Chile (1918–1931), during a period when the Catholic Church distanced itself from its traditional alliance with the Conservative Party and accepted the separation of church and state.

Born in Santiago, Errázuriz was educated as a diocesan priest but subsequently joined the Dominican Order (1884–1911). Also trained in law, he worked as a journalist directing both *El Estandarte Católico* and *La Revista Católica,* and became one of Chile's best-known historians.

In 1918 the seventy-nine-year-old Errázuriz was named archbishop of Santiago after then President Juan Luis Sanfuentes, with the support of the Senate, convinced the Vatican that the appointment was essential for the maintenance of good relations with the new Liberal government. Throughout his term as archbishop, Errázuriz played a major role in the modernization of the Church, as well as the maintenance of its influence with Chilean society. He believed that unless the Church was adaptable, its power would be diminished. He was also concerned about the direct involvement of priests in politics, and in 1922 he issued a decree forbidding it. While Errázuriz did not himself support the separation of church and state, he pragmatically participated in the drafting of the relevant parts of the 1925 Constitution that mandated it. This document ended government involvement in the appointment of priests, as well as state subsidies for church purposes.

*See also* **Catholic Church: The Modern Period; Chile, Constitutions.**

BIBLIOGRAPHY

Brian H. Smith, *The Church and Politics in Chile: Challenges to Modern Catholicism* (1982).

Hannah W. Stewart-Gambino, *The Church and Politics in the Chilean Countryside* (1992).

### *Additional Bibliography*

Krebs, Ricardo. *La Iglesia de América Latina en el siglo XIX*. Santiago, Chile: Ediciones Universidad Católica de Chile, 2002.

Silva Cuevas, Luis Eugenio. *La elección del arzobispo Crescente Errázuriz Valdivieso.* Santiago: Pontificia Universidad Católica de Chile, 1989.

MARGARET E. CRAHAN

## ERRÁZURIZ ZAÑARTU, FEDERICO

**ERRÁZURIZ ZAÑARTU, FEDERICO** (1825–1877). Federico Errázuriz Zañartu (*b.* 25 April 1825; *d.* 20 July 1877), president of Chile (1871–1876). A lawyer, Errázuriz became president after serving numerous terms as a national deputy, provincial governor, and cabinet minister. Errázuriz broke with the Conservative Party when it opposed his attempts to secularize the cemeteries, permit non-Catholics to marry, and exempt non-Catholics from having to attend religious courses in public schools. After 1873, Errázuriz led a coalition known as the Liberal Alliance, which consisted of members of the Radical and Liberal parties.

Although Errázuriz was the first president to serve only one term, his administration nevertheless implemented numerous reforms, among which were those that limited the power of the state, altered voting procedures, and modernized the penal and mining codes. His term began during a period of prosperity, which allowed Errázuriz to finance railroad construction and purchase ironclads for the navy. However, a fall in metal prices as well as a decline in copper and silver production limited Chile's economic growth, devastated the national economy, and ushered in a period of budget deficits and trade imbalances.

*See also* **Chile, Political Parties: Conservative Party; Chile: The Nineteenth Century.**

BIBLIOGRAPHY

Alfonso Bulnes, *Federico Errázuriz Zañartu: Su vida* (1950).

Luis Galdames, *A History of Chile* (1941), pp. 314–319.

### *Additional Bibliography*

Collier, Simon, and William F. Sater. *A History of Chile, 1808–1994.* Cambridge, U.K.: Cambridge University Press, 1996.

Stuven, Ana María. *La seducción de un orden: Las elites y la construcción de Chile en las polémicas culturales y políticas del siglo XIX.* Santiago: Ediciones Universidad Católica de Chile, 2000.

WILLIAM F. SATER

## ERRO, ENRIQUE

**ERRO, ENRIQUE** (1912–1984). Enrique Erro (*b.* 14 September 1912; *d.* 10 October 1984), Uruguayan politician and trade unionist. A journalist employed by *La Tribuna,* Erro was a founding member of the Uruguayan Press Association. He was subsequently a member of the House of Representatives (1953–1966), minister of industry and labor (1959–1960), and a senator (1971–1973).

Ideologically Erro followed the principles of a Latin American "Patria Grande"—the name of his slate of candidates within the Frente Amplio (Broad Front) in the 1971 elections—and a popular, revolutionary nationalism. He served on the Anti-imperialist Committee and was a member of the Blanco Party. Erro was a founder of the Unión Popular in 1962, later formed a coalition with the Socialist party, then joined the newly founded Frente Amplio in 1971.

From 1973 to his death, Erro rejected all negotiations with the military regime and called for abstention from the 1980 constitutional referendum and the 1982 elections. He denounced Uruguayan human rights violations before European governments and the U.N. Commission on human rights.

*See also* **Labor Movements; Journalism; Uruguay, Political Parties: Broad Front.**

BIBLIOGRAPHY

Roberto Gilardoni and Luis Imas, *Biografía de Enrique Erro: Su vida, su lucha, su obra* (1988).

Nelson Caula, *Erro,* 3 vols. (1989–1990).

*Additional Bibliography*

Gatto, Herbert. *El cielo por asalto: el Movimiento de Liberación Nacional (Tupamaros) y la izquierda uruguaya (1963–1972).* Montevideo: Taurus, 2004.

Myers, Scott L. *Los años oscuros: Uruguay, 1967–1987.* Montevideo, Uruguay: Editorial Latina, 1997.

DIETER SCHONEBOHM

## ESCALADA, ASUNCIÓN (1850–1894).

Asunción Escalada (*b.* 1850; *d.* 1894), Paraguayan educator. At the time of Escalada's birth in the mid-nineteenth century, education in Paraguay was almost entirely limited to male students; women were rarely permitted to take part in education except occasionally at the primary level. Escalada dedicated her career to opening Paraguayan education to women at all levels.

The War of the Triple Alliance (1864–1870) provided Escalada and other women with an opportunity to teach when so many male teachers were called to the front. She herself worked at a small primary school in the interior hamlet of Atyra. During the final stages of the fighting, however, Escalada was forced to abandon the town and accompany her grandfather, the noted Argentine educator Juan Pedro Escalada (1777–1869), on the tragic retreat to Cerro Corá.

After the war, Escalada convinced the new provisional government to fund the Escuela Central de Niñas, which she directed until 1875. This institution served as the model for the Colegio Nacional de Niñas, the best-known school for young women in today's Paraguay.

Aside from her efforts in education, Escalada was also instrumental in fomenting culture and the arts in the country, donating time and money to advance the career of guitarist Agustín Barrios and many others. She died in Buenos Aires.

*See also* **Education: Overview; Cerro Corá, Battle of; Colegio Nacional de Buenos Aires; War of the Triple Alliance.**

BIBLIOGRAPHY

Carlos R. Centurión, *Historia de la cultura paraguaya,* 2d ed., 2 vols. (1961).

Charles J. Kolinski, *Historical Dictionary of Paraguay* (1973), p. 91.

*Additional Bibliography*

Stover, Richard D. *Six Silver Moonbeams: The Life and Times of Agustín Barrios Mangoré.* Clovis, CA: Querico Publications, 1992.

THOMAS L. WHIGHAM

## ESCALANTE, ANÍBAL (1909–1977).

Aníbal Escalante (*b.* 1909; *d.* 11 August 1977), secretary-general of the Partido Socialista Popular (Cuban Communist Party—PSP) and editor of the party's organ *Hoy.* Born in Oriente Province into an affluent family, Escalante graduated with a degree in law from the University of Havana in 1932, the same year he joined the Communist Party. During that year Escalante founded *Hoy,* the official organ of the Cuban Communist Party. He was the paper's editor from 1938 into the early 1960s as well as the party's elected representative in the lower house of the Cuban Congress from 1948 to 1952.

Escalante survived the Batista dictatorship and the Cuban Revolution of 1959 to play a key role in the reformed Communist Party under the leadership of Fidel Castro. In 1961 he was given the task of merging Castro's own Twenty-sixth of July Movement with the Revolutionary Student Directorate and the Cuban Communist Party. Escalante attempted to forge a single party, the Integrated Revolutionary Organizations, modeled after the Soviet Communist Party. Perceived as a threat to Castro's power, he was dismissed from the National Directory in 1962 and was forced out of Cuba that same year. After a brief exile, Escalante returned to Cuba in 1964, and once again became active in politics.

In 1968 Escalante, along with other members of the old PSP, was accused of forming a "microfaction" within the new, ruling Cuban Communist Party (PCP), and was sentenced to fifteen years in prison for "attempting to destroy the unity" of the Cuban Revolution. He died in Havana.

*See also* **Cuba, Political Parties: Communist Party.**

BIBLIOGRAPHY

Ralph Lee Woodward, Jr., "Urban Labor and Communism: Cuba," in *Caribbean Studies* 3, no. 3 (1963): 17–50.

Ramón Eduardo Ruiz, *Cuba: The Making of a Revolution* (1970).

Samuel Farber, *Revolution and Reaction in Cuba, 1933–1960* (1976).

*Additional Bibliography*

Sweig, Julie. *Inside the Cuban Revolution: Fidel Castro and the Urban Underground.* Cambridge, MA: Harvard University Press, 2002.

MICHAEL POWELSON

## ESCANDÓN, ANTONIO (1824–1877).

Antonio Escandón (*b.* 1824; *d.* 1877), Mexican entrepreneur. The younger brother of the notorious Mexican moneylender Manuel Escandón, he was born in Puebla. He married Catalina Barrón, daughter of Eustaquio Barrón, another influential moneylender of the period. Escandón spent the years of the French Empire in Europe trying to raise funds for building a railroad from Mexico City to Veracruz, a project that was completed in 1873.

Escandón is also noteworthy for his commitment to the beautification of Mexico City following the fall of the empire. He believed that the national government should make the newly renamed Paseo de la Reforma into a Mexican version of the Champs-élysées with streets intersecting to form traffic circles. In 1877, to celebrate the completion of the railroad, Escandón presented the city with a statue of Christopher Columbus that still stands in the second *glorieta* (traffic circle) on the Paseo. Ironically, he died in Europe, on a train en route from Seville to Córdoba.

*See also* **Mexico: 1810–1910; Railroads; Mexico City.**

BIBLIOGRAPHY

Luis García Pimentel, *El monumento elevado en la ciudad de México a Cristóbal Colón* (1872).

Barbara A. Tenenbaum, "Development or Sovereignty: Intellectuals and the Second Empire, 1861–1867," in *The Intellectuals and the State in Mexico,* edited by Charles Hale et al. (1991).

*Additional Bibliography*

Zavala, Silvio Arturo. *En defensa del Paseo de la Reforma.* México City: Universidad Iberoamericana, División de Arte, 1997.

BARBARA A. TENENBAUM

## ESCANDÓN, JOSÉ DE (1700–1770).

José de Escandón (*b.* 1700; *d.* 1770), founder of Nuevo Santander. Born in Soto la Marina, Santander, Escandón came to New Spain in 1715 and settled in Querétaro, where he participated in numerous campaigns against the northern Indian tribes, the most notable of which being the pacification of the Sierra Gorda. In response to Indian attacks around Nuevo León and the threat of English and French expansion from Florida and Louisiana into Texas, the viceroy, the first Count of Revillagigedo, selected Escandón to conquer and settle the region around Tamaulipas and both sides of the lower Rio Grande. In 1749, after extensive planning and exploring, Escandón led a colonizing force of over 3,000 people to Tamaulipas and established twenty-one Spanish and Tlaxcalan communities and fifty-seven Franciscan and three Dominican missions. To pacify rebellious tribes in the area, he granted land and agricultural supplies to them and assigned Tlaxcalan instructors to their communities. The new region, Nuevo Santander, became one of the most successful colonies on New Spain's northern frontier and the birthplace of the Texas cattle industry.

*See also* **Missions: Spanish America; Nuevo Santander; Rebelión Sierra Gorda.**

BIBLIOGRAPHY

Lawrence Francis Hill, *José de Escandón and the Founding of Nuevo Santander: A Study in Spanish Colonization* (1926).

John Francis Bannon, *The Spanish Borderlands Frontier,* 2d ed. (1974), pp. 139–140.

Oakah Jones, *Los Paisanos: Spanish Settlers on the Northern Frontier of New Spain* (1979), pp. 65–72.

*Additional Bibliography*

González Salas, Carlos. "La obra del Coronel Don José de Escandón en la evangelización del Nuevo Santander." *Humanitas* 23 (1990): 269-288.

Osante, Patricia. *Orígenes del Nuevo Santander (1748 1772).* Mexico City: Universidad Nacional Autónoma de México, Instituto de Investigaciones Históricas; Ciudad Victoria: Univ. Autónoma de Tamaulipas, 1997.

AARON PAINE MAHR

**ESCANDÓN, MANUEL** (1808–1862). Manuel Escandón (*b.* 1808; *d.* 7 June 1862), Mexican entrepreneur. Son of an Asturian merchant and a mother linked to the military and agricultural families of Jalapa, Veracruz, Escandón was born in Orizaba, Veracruz. Educated partly in Europe, he returned to Mexico in 1826 and moved to the capital in the early 1830s. By 1833, he was operating an important stagecoach line from Veracruz to Mexico City and had become involved in political wheeling and dealing through his relationships with prominent generals like Antonio López de Santa Anna, Mariano Arista, and others. Escandón quickly took advantage of the precarious financial situation of the Mexican treasury by lending money to the government and by agreeing to provide important services to it. In 1848 he purchased the French-owned Cocolapam textile mill in Orizaba and gained even greater wealth after he and a consortium purchased the British-owned Real del Monte silver mines just before it hit a bonanza. By 1853 he and other moneylenders offered to found Mexico's first bank, but were turned down by Treasury Minister Antonio de Haro y Tamariz.

During the last years of his life Escandón turned his attention to building a railroad from Mexico City to Veracruz, a project his younger brother Antonio completed in 1873.

*See also* **Escandón, Antonio; Mexico: 1810–1910; Railroads.**

BIBLIOGRAPHY

Margarita Urías Hermosillo, "Manuel Escandón: de las Diligencias al Ferrocarril, 1833–1862," in *Formación y desarrollo de la burguesía en México: Siglo XIX,* edited by Ciro F. S. Cardoso (1978).

Barbara A. Tenenbaum, *The Politics of Penury: Debts and Taxes in Mexico, 1821–1856* (1986).

*Additional Bibliography*

Bazant, Jan. "José María Tornel, Mariano Riva Palacio, Manuel Escandón y la compraventa de una hacienda." In *Cincuenta años de historia en México: En el cincuentenario del Centro de Estudios Históricos.* México: Colegio de México, Centro de Estudios Históricos, 1991.

Ludlow, Leonor, and Carlos Marichal, editors. *La Banca en México, 1820-1920.* Mexico: Instituto Mora, El Colegio de Michoacán, El Colegio de México, UNAM, 1998.

BARBARA A. TENENBAUM

**ESCOBAR, LUIS ANTONIO** (1925–1993). Luis Antonio Escobar (*b.* 14 July 1925; *d.* 11 September 1993), Colombian composer and diplomat. Born in Villapinzón, Escobar studied at the Bogotá Conservatory (1940–1947). In 1947 he received a scholarship to study with Nicholas Nabokov at the Peabody Conservatory in Baltimore. He attended composition courses at New York's Columbia University (1950–1951) and took classes with Boris Blacher at the Berlin Hochschule für Musik (1951–1953) and the Salzburg Mozarteum (1951). Upon his return to his native land he was named secretary of the National Conservatory, where he taught harmony, composition, and instrumentation. Escobar received several awards, including the National Prize (1955) for his *Sinfonía Cero* and two Guggenheim fellowships. In 1960 the New York City Ballet commissioned his *Preludios para percusión.* Escobar presented his *Pequeña sinfonía* at the Third Latin American Music Festival, held in Washington, D.C., in May 1965. He was appointed director of musical programs for television in Colombia and served on the national board of the Colombian National Orchestra. He was also chairman of the National Music Council and director of the cultural division of the Ministry of National Education. Escobar also served as consul (1964–1966) and second secretary (1967–1970) of the Colombian embassy in Bonn, West Germany. He died in Miami while serving as Colombia's cultural chargé d'affaires.

*See also* **Music: Art Music; Radio and Television.**

BIBLIOGRAPHY

*Composers of the Americas,* vol. 8 (1962), pp. 65–70.

John Vinton, ed., *Dictionary of Contemporary Music* (1974).

Gérard Béhague, *Music in Latin America* (1979); *New Grove Dictionary of Music and Musicians,* vol. 6 (1980).

SUSANA SALGADO

## ESCOBAR, PABLO.

*See* **Drugs and Drug Trade.**

## ESCOBAR, PATRICIO (1843–1912).

Patricio Escobar (*b.* 1843; *d.* 19 April 1912), president of Paraguay (1886–1890) and soldier. Born in San José, Escobar entered the army just before the outbreak of the War of the Triple Alliance and rose in rank from private to general during the course of the conflict. Like his mentor, the cavalry general Bernardino Caballero, Escobar remained loyal to the cause of President Francisco Solano López and doggedly resisted the Brazilians until he was captured at Cerro Corá, the war's last battle.

Returning to Paraguay after several years' captivity, Escobar attached himself to Caballero and to Conservative figures associated with President Cándido Bareiro. After Caballero's accession to the presidency in 1880, Escobar received the portfolio of war minister. Six years later, he himself succeeded to the highest office and generally continued the conservative, paternalistic policies of his friend and predecessor, though Escobar was perhaps more tolerant of opposition criticism. He opened the National University in 1889 and helped to expand the Paraguay Central Railway and other public works. In partisan politics, Escobar collaborated in the organization of the Asociación Nacional Republicana (or Partido Colorado), one of the country's two traditional parties. Unfortunately, his administration was also marked by corruption.

Stepping down from office in 1890, the by-now-wealthy Escobar continued to influence Paraguayan politics through various surrogates and intrigues. He died in Asunción less than two months after the death of Caballero.

*See also* **Cerro Córa, Battle of; Paraguay: The Nineteenth Century; War of the Triple Alliance.**

BIBLIOGRAPHY

Harris G. Warren, *Rebirth of the Paraguayan Republic: The First Colorado Era, 1878–1904* (1985).

Carlos Zubizarreta, *Cien vidas paraguayas,*2d ed. (1985), pp. 202–205; *The Cambridge History of Latin America,* vol. 5 (1986), pp. 475–496.

### *Additional Bibliography*

Gondra, César, and Victor I. Franco. *El General Patricio Escobar.* Asunción: Arte Nuevo Editores, 1990.

Lewis, Paul H. *Political Parties and Generations in Paraguay's Liberal Era, 1869-1940.* Chapel Hill: University of North Carolina Press, 1993.

THOMAS L. WHIGHAM

## ESCOBEDO, MARIANO (1826–1902).

Mariano Escobedo (*b.* January 1826; *d.* 1902), Mexican Liberal army commander. Born in Galeana, Nuevo León, Escobedo fought as an ensign in the national guard against U.S. forces in 1846–1847, becoming a lieutenant in 1852. He supported the Plan of Ayutla and fought under Santiago Vidaurri in 1854–1855. He became a lieutenant-colonel in the cavalry in 1856. During the Civil War of the Reform (1858–1861), he again fought alongside Vidaurri in the north central states. During the French Intervention, he fought at Puebla in 1862 and 1863, when he was captured.

Escobedo opposed Vidaurri's defection to the empire in 1864. He played the major role in the resurgence of Liberal forces in late 1865, capturing Maximilian, Miguel Miramón, and Tomás Mejía at Querétaro in 1867 and convening the summary military tribunal that sentenced them to death. A close friend of Sebastián Lerdo, he became a senator in September 1875 and minister of war in 1876. He fought against Porfirio Díaz in the rebellion of Tuxtepec (1876) and conspired to restore Lerdo in 1877–1878. He was a federal deputy at the time of his death.

*See also* **Díaz, Porfirio; Vidaurri, Santiago.**

BIBLIOGRAPHY

Cavasos Garza, Israel. *Mariano Escobedo: El glorioso soldado de la República.* Monterrey: Gobierno del Estado de Nuevo León, 1949.

López Gutiérrez, Gustavo. *Escobedo, republicano demócrata benemérito de Chiapas, 1826-1902.* Tuxtla Gutiérrez, Chiapas: 1968.

Taibo, Paco Ignacio. *El general orejón ese* Mexico City: Grupo Editorial Planeta, 1997.

BRIAN HAMNETT

**ESCOCESES.** *Escoceses,* Scottish rite Masonic lodges. Introduced into Mexico in 1817 or 1819 by Spanish officers, the *escoceses* had earlier been established by these officers in the peninsula during the war against Napoleon. In 1821 the last Spanish ruler of New Spain, Juan O'Donojú, provided great impetus for the expansion of the *escocés* lodges. His physician, Manuel Codorniu, founded the newspaper *El Sol,* which became the organ of the group. Some Mexican deputies to the Spanish Cortes also joined lodges in the Peninsula, emerging as the nucleus of the *escoceses* after 1822. The lodge rapidly became a clandestine political organization. In 1825 some members splintered, founding the "populist" Yorkinos (York rite Masons), while the *escoceses* became the "aristocratic" party. Vice President Nicolás Bravo, Grand Master of the *escoceses,* ultimately led a revolt against the government in January 1828. When the lodges were banned, the *escoceses* formed another secret group known as the *novenarios,* which continued to function as a political organization for some time.

*See also* **Bravo, Nicolás; Masonic Orders; O'Donojú, Juan; Yorkinos.**

BIBLIOGRAPHY

Luis J. Zalce y Rodríguez, *Apuntes para la historia de la masonería en México,* 2 vols. (1950).

Virginia Guedea, "Las sociedades secretas durante el movimiento de independencia," in *The Independence of Mexico and the Creation of the New Nation,* edited by Jaime E. Rodríguez O. (1989), esp. pp. 45–62.

*Additional Bibliography*

Bastian, Jean Pierre. *Protestantes, liberales y francmasones: Sociedades de ideas y modernidad en América Latina, siglo XIX.* Mexico: Comisión de Estudios de Historia de la Iglesia en América Latina: Fondo de Cultura Económica, 1990.

Rodríguez O, Jaime E. *The Origins of Mexican National Politics, 1808–1847.* Wilmington: SR Books, 1997.

JAIME E. RODRÍGUEZ O.

**ESLAVA Y LAZAGA, SEBASTIÁN DE** (1685–1759). Sebastián de Eslava y Lazaga (*b.* January 1685; *d.* 21 June 1759), military figure and viceroy of the New Kingdom of Granada (1740–1749). Born in Navarra, he studied at the Real Academia Militar in Barcelona and entered active military service. He reached the rank of lieutenant general of the royal armies.

Philip V named Eslava, brother of Rafael de Eslava, former president of the Audiencia of Santa Fe (1733–1737), the first viceroy of the reconstituted viceroyalty of New Granada in 1738. Unlike his predecessor, Jorge de Villalonga (1719–1724), Eslava put the colony on a firm footing. He disembarked at Cartagena de Indias in April 1740 and, because of the hostilities with England, stayed there throughout his tenure. English Admiral Edward Vernon's failed attempt to capture Cartagena (1741) made heroes of Eslava and the naval commander Blas de Lezo, a judgment widely supported by modern Colombian historiography. The pressures of wartime rule, however, took their toll; in 1742 the viceroy began to lobby the crown for reassignment. He subsequently declined the promotion to viceroy of Peru in favor of returning to Spain. Eslava served with distinction in New Granada until his appointment as captain-general of Andalusia and the arrival of his replacement, José Alonso Pizarro (1749–1753). He served as minister of war from 1754 to 1759.

*See also* **Granada, Spain; New Granada, Viceroyalty of.**

BIBLIOGRAPHY

Eslava apparently left no *relación de mando* (end-of-tenure report), but an important defense of his administration by Antonio de Verástegui can be found in Germán Colmenares, ed., *Relaciones e informes de los gobernantes de la Nueva Granada,* vol. 1 (1989). See also Sergio Elías Ortiz, *Nuevo Reino de Granada: El virreynato,* pt. 1, 1719–1753, in *Historia extensa de Colombia,* vol. 4, pt. 1 (1970).

*Additional Bibliography*

Gallup-Diaz, Ignacio. "The Spanish Attempt to Tribalize the Darien, 1739-50." *Ethnohistory* 49 (Spring 2002): 281–317.

Ramos Gómez, Luis J. "Los intentos del virrey Eslava y del presidente Araujo en 1740 para obtener préstamos del comercio del Perú desplazado a Quito y la requisa de 100,000 pesos en 1741." *Revista de Indias* 63 (September–December 2003): 649–673.

LANCE R. GRAHN

---

**ESMERALDAS.** Esmeraldas, one of Ecuador's most isolated and sparsely populated areas, visited by Francisco Pizarro during one of his early expeditions to South America. The province is located on the northwest coast of Ecuador and shares its northern border with Colombia. Lured by stories of gold and emeralds, a few hardy Spaniards returned to the area, administered by the Audiencia of Quito. They established the city of Atacames, originally a native settlement, as the capital of the Atacames government, as the province was then known.

Historians hypothesize that blacks arrived in Ecuador in 1553, when a slave ship ran aground along the southern coast of the province. Alonso de Illescas, a former slave, governed a territory of free black survivors of the shipwreck so effectively that the province was almost completely outside of Spanish domination for about sixty years. Many of the shipwrecked blacks intermarried with natives. Seventeenth- and eighteenth-century migrations of blacks brought to work the mines in the Barbacoas area of Colombia swelled the black population of Esmeraldas. Today, the majority of Ecuador's black population (500,000) resides in the province and maintains traditional customs such as the Marimba dance and a form of oral literature known as the *décima*.

Pedro Vicente Maldonado, perhaps the province's most renowned citizen, worked as a geographer and assisted the French Geographic Mission, headed by Charles-Marie de la Condamine, during its travels throughout the province in the mid-1730s. Appointed governor and captain-general of Atacames and Esmeraldas in 1738, Maldonado had ambitious plans to build roads and a shipyard, but died in 1748 of a tropical fever before he could carry them out.

Two years before Antonio José de Sucre Alcalá led his troops to victory in the battle of Pichincha in 1822, a group of stalwart Esmeraldas residents in Ríoverde declared independence from Spain. The movement quickly spread to neighboring towns, but this early revolutionary attempt was put down by government troops sent from Quito.

Following the murder of former president Eloy Alfaro and his supporters in 1912, Esmeraldas's black population again controlled much of the province, fending off well-armed government troops with machetes and sticks. The Concha War, essentially a skirmish protesting the second administration of President Leonidas Plazas Gutiérrez, lasted from 1913 to 1916 and resulted in great loss of life.

More recently, the province experienced a number of periods of growth and expansion, beginning with the export of cacao, the rubber and balsa wood boom during the two world wars, record exports of bananas from 1948 to 1968, and the opening of the country's largest oil refinery during the 1970s. Yet despite these intermittent booms, the province remains both geographically and politically isolated from the mainstream of Ecuadorian life; until the 1990s it was only accessible by boat. The 2000 census estimates that 140,300 people live in the city and metro areas.

*See also* **Ecuador, Geography; Pizarro, Francisco; Quito, Audiencia (Presidency) of.**

BIBLIOGRAPHY

Theodoro Wolf, *Geografía y geología del Ecuador* (1892).

Norman E. Whitten, Jr., *Class, Kinship, and Power in an Ecuadorian Town: The Negroes of San Lorenzo* (1965).

Alfredo Pareja y Diez Canseco, *Ecuador, la república de 1830 a nuestros días* (1979).

Sabine Speiser, *Tradiciones afro-esmeraldeñas* (1985).

Karen M. Greiner and José G. Cárdenas, *Walking the Beaches of Ecuador* (1988), esp. 31–120.

*Additional Bibliography*

DeBoer, Warren. *Traces behind the Esmeraldas Shore*. Tuscaloosa: University of Alabama Press, 1996.

Moschetto, Pedro. *El Diablo y el arco iris: Magia, sueños, tabúes en Esmeraldas*. Quito: Ediciones Abya Yala, 1995.

KAREN M. GREINER

## ESPAILLAT, ULISES FRANCISCO

**ESPAILLAT, ULISES FRANCISCO** (1823–1878). Ulises Francisco Espaillat (*b.* 1823; *d.* 25 April 1878), president of the Dominican Republic (29 May–5 October 1876). A white *criollo* (creole) whose Spanish parents belonged to an old, well-established family, Espaillat was born in Santiago de los Caballeros, the main city in the fertile Cibao Valley in the north. A pharmacist by profession, he was an intellectual and a patriot who became involved in politics in an effort to stabilize and unify the country after the *restauración* from Spain in 1863. He served as vice president in the provisional governments of General José Antonio Salcedo (1863–1864) and General Gaspar Polanco (1864–1865).

Espaillat was an honest and liberal nationalist (author of the liberal constitution of 1858). Elected president in the spring of 1876 with the strong support of General Gregorio Luperón, Espaillat appointed the best people to his cabinet (Luperón was minister of war) and stressed honesty, a balanced budget, and the end of foreign entanglements. His financial reforms were unpopular and the military, used to regular pay-offs, opposed his efforts to create a professional army. Two former presidents, Buenaventura Baez (1856–1857, 1865–1866, and 1868–1873), and Ignacio María González (1874–1876) organized uprisings against him. The capital, Santo Domingo, fell to supporters of González in October 1876; Espaillat took refuge in the French embassy and in December returned to his home in the Cibao.

*See also* **Dominican Republic; Santo Domingo.**

BIBLIOGRAPHY

José Gabriel García, *Compendio de la historia de Santo Domingo, 1865–1880,* vol. 4 (1906).

Sumner Welles, *Naboth's Vineyard: The Dominican Republic, 1844–1924,* vol. 1 (1966), chap. 6.

Frank Moya Pons, *Manual de historia dominicana* (1978), pp. 384–387.

### *Additional Bibliography*

Cassá, Roberto. *Ulises Francisco Espaillat.* Santo Domingo: Tobogan, 1999.

Sang, Mu-Kien Adriana. *Una utopía inconclusa: Espaillat y el liberalismo dominicano del siglo XIX.* Santo Domingo: Instituto Tecnológico de Santo Domingo, 1997.

LARMAN C. WILSON

## ESPEJO, ANTONIO DE

**ESPEJO, ANTONIO DE** (c. 1538–c. 1585). Antonio de Espejo (*b.* ca. 1538; *d.* ca. 1585), Spanish explorer. From Córdoba, Spain, Espejo was a lay officer of the Inquisition and a wealthy cattleman, with properties in Querétaro and Celaya, Mexico. In 1582–1583 he financed and led an expedition with the Franciscan friar Bernadino Beltrán to New Mexico and Arizona. The men hoped to rescue Fray Agustín Rodríguez, who had remained in New Mexico after having accompanied Francisco Sánchez Chamuscado from Mexico in 1581. The small force left Santa Bárbara in New Biscay in 1582 and traveled north, up the Rio Grande valley. After learning of Rodríguez's death, Espejo decided to prospect for mines and went west to Acoma, Zuni, and Hopi, and then southwest into Arizona, where he found evidence of mineral deposits. After a failed mutiny at Zuni in 1583, Beltrán and the rebels went back to Santa Bárbara. Espejo, however, turned north and east from the Rio Grande, and returned to New Biscay by way of the Pecos River valley. An account of his experiences, published in 1586, contributed to a knowledge of and interest in New Spain.

*See also* **Explorers and Exploration: Spanish America.**

BIBLIOGRAPHY

George P. Hammond and Agapito Rey. *The Rediscovery of New Mexico, 1580–1594.* Albuquerque: The University of New Mexico Press, 1966.

Mecham, J. Lloyd. "Antonio de Espejo and His Journey to New Mexico." *Southwestern Historical Quarterly 30* (October 1926).

RICK HENDRICKS

## ESPERANZA COLONY

**ESPERANZA COLONY.** Esperanza Colony is a frontier settlement in Santa Fe Province, Argentina. Its population is about 36,000 (2001), and it covers approximately 289 square kilometers. Santa Fe was among the first Argentine provinces to attract European settlers to cultivate marginal public lands in frontier areas during the early national period. In 1856 Aarón Castellanos brought 840 colonists to establish a colony at Esperanza, 20 miles from the city of Sante Fe, capital of the province. During the first four years, very little was produced due to the lack of agricultural experience of the Swiss and Northern Italian colonists, whose hardships were exacerbated by drought, the visitation of locusts, Indian attacks, and intermittent warfare between political factions over national unification. Esperanza, San Carlos, and other early colonies settled by European immigrants grew wheat, for the most part, which helped satisfy the demand for flour by the burgeoning number of immigrants arriving in Rosario and Buenos Aires. After 1862 Esperanza thrived, expanded, and became a prototype for many successful agricultural colonies which played an important role in the economic development of Argentina. The area of Santa Fe settled by agricultural colonists became known as the pampa gringa because of the large number of northern Italian settlers. It remained noted for its agricultural innovation, and in 1979 it was named a permanent part of the National Festival of Agriculture and National Agricultural Worker Day.

*See also* **Agriculture; Castellanos, Aarón González; Santa Fe, Argentina.**

BIBLIOGRAPHY

William Perkins, *Las colonias de Santa Fe: Su orígen, progreso, y actual situación* (1964).

James R. Scobie, *Revolution on the Pampas: A Social History of Argentine Wheat, 1860–1910* (1964).

*Additional Bibliography*

Canas Bottos, Lorenzo.*Christenvolk: Historia y etnografía de una colonia menonita.* Buenos Aires: Antropofagia, 2005.

Gori, Gastón. *Familias fundadoras de la colonia Esperanza.* Santa Fe, Argentina: Librería y Editorial Colmegna, 1974.

Georgette Magassy Dorn

## ESPÍN DE CASTRO, VILMA (1930–2007).

Vilma Espín de Castro (*b.* 1930, *d.* 2007), Cuban revolutionary and feminist. Vilma Espín was part of the underground resistance that fought to overthrow Fulgencio Batista and offered intelligence assistance to Fidel Castro's 26 July 1952 attack on the Moncada Barracks. She studied chemical engineering at the University of Oriente, graduating in 1954, and then attended the Massachusetts Institute of Technology. She left her studies to join Castro's movement in the Sierra Maestra mountains in 1956, where she married Raúl Castro. After the overthrow of Batista's government, Espín rode into Havana with the triumphant revolutionary army. She became president of the new Federation of Cuban Women in 1960. In 1969 she became director of industrial development in the Ministry of Food Industries, and in 1971 she was named president of the Institute of Child Care. Espín joined the Central Committee of the Cuban Communist Party in 1965. She became a member of the Council of State in 1976 and of the Politburo of the Communist Party in 1986. She was removed as a member of the Central Committee in 1989. Although it was never officially confirmed, most sources indicate that she and Raul divorced, but they still appeared together at formal functions, and Vilma Espín maintained an active public role in Cuba. She died on 18 June 2007, at age seventy-seven.

*See also* **Batista y Zaldívar, Fulgencio; Castro Ruz, Fidel; Castro Ruz, Raúl; Cuba, Organizations: Federation of Cuban Women (FMC); Cuba, Political Parties: Communist Party; Cuba, Revolutions: Cuban Revolution.**

BIBLIOGRAPHY

*Additional Bibliography*

Luciak, Ilja A. *Gender and Democracy in Cuba.* Gainesville: University Press of Florida, 2007.

K. Lynn Stoner

## ESPINOSA, JOSÉ MARÍA (1796–1883).

José María Espinosa (*b.* 1796; *d.* 1883), Colombian artist. Born to an aristocratic and distinguished creole family in Bogotá, Espinosa began studying painting with artist Pablo Antonio García, but the revolution of July 1810 against Spain interrupted his training. He served in the army until independence was achieved in 1819 and then published his account of his experiences fighting under General Antonio Nariño from 1813 to 1816 in *Memorias de un abandero.* While on the southern campaign, he was taken prisoner and drew caricatures of fellow prisoners as well as landscapes and battle scenes.

At the conclusion of the war, Espinosa returned to Bogotá and took his position in the social and political life of the new republic. He painted many portraits of the heroes of the independence struggle, and of Bolívar in particular, in a style that marked a transition from the colonial to the republican period.

*See also* **Art: The Nineteenth Century; Creole; Colombia: From the Conquest through Independence.**

BIBLIOGRAPHY

Gabriel Giraldo Jaramillo, *La miniatura, la pintura y el grabado en Colombia* (1980).

*Additional Bibliography*

González, Beatriz, and Marta Calderón. *Caricatura y costumbrismo: José María Espinosa y Ramón Torres Méndez, dos colombianos del Siglo XIX.* Museo Nacional de Colombia, 1999.

BÉLGICA RODRÍGUEZ

## ESPINOSA Y ESPINOSA, (JUAN) JAVIER

**ESPINOSA Y ESPINOSA, (JUAN) JAVIER** (1815–1870). (Juan) Javier Espinosa y Espinosa (*b.* 20 January 1815; *d.* 4 September 1870), president of Ecuador (1868–1869). During Gabriel García Moreno's domination of Ecuador (1861–1865, 1869–1975), Espinosa briefly served as figurehead president. The son of Quito notables, his prior government experience had been limited to a few relatively minor posts. Espinosa selected for his cabinet a group of moderate Liberals and Conservatives, a move that outraged García Moreno; he had fully expected to control Espinosa. In August 1868 a violent earthquake devastated the northern sierra, leveling the cities of Ibarra and Otavalo. Espinosa appointed García Moreno to oversee aid and reconstruction. These chores (and, critics allege, the theft of charity funds) kept the former president preoccupied for a time. However, in 1869, as Ecuador prepared to hold elections for a new presidential term, García Moreno staged a coup, removed Espinosa, and returned to office. Espinosa died in Quito.

*See also* **Carbo y Noboa, Pedro José.**

BIBLIOGRAPHY

Hurtado, Osvaldo. *Political Power in Ecuador.* Trans. Nick D. Mills, Jr. Albuquerque: University of New Mexico Press, 1980.

MacDonald Spindler, Frank. *Nineteenth Century Ecuador: A Historical Introduction.* Fairfax: George Mason University Press, 1987.

Schodt, David W. *Ecuador: An Andean Enigma.* Boulder: Westview Press, 1987.

RONN F. PINEO

## ESPÍRITO SANTO

**ESPÍRITO SANTO.** Espírito Santo, a small mountainous state (1993 metropolitan population 3,412,746) located on the coast of Brazil, northeast of Rio de Janeiro, whose capital is Vitória. The original Indian inhabitants were the Papanazes, who were forced out by the Goaytacazes and the Tupiniquins. The first Europeans to settle in the area were a band of Portuguese who accompanied the Donatário Vasco Fernandes Coutinho in 1535. The captaincy of the state had been granted to Coutinho by the Portuguese crown to honor his services in India. He founded Vila Velha, the first capital of the captaincy of Espírito Santo, from which the state gets its name.

The early history of Espírito Santo was marked by frequent warfare against the Indians, the English, and the French. Coutinho's successor, D. Simoni de Castello-Branco, was murdered by Tamayo Indians. In 1592 the state was attacked by the English pirate Thomas Cavendish, who was successfully defeated by the Portuguese and their Indian allies. Some sugar plantations flourished in the seventeenth century, when the Dutch also invaded the captaincy.

The first gold extracted from Minas Gerais was displayed in Espírito Santo in 1695. This gold arrived via the Rio Doce as a gift to the Capitão Mor from Antônio Rodriguez Arzam. Henceforth, Espírito Santo would be linked to Minas Gerais via trade, first to the goldfields of the eighteenth century and then to the iron ore deposits of the twentieth century. It is the country's second-largest exporter of ore.

The year 1830 marked the beginning of the national government's colonization efforts in the state. Immigrants who have settled in Espírito Santo include Germans, Italians, and Poles. These immigrants shaped the primarily agricultural nature of the state, whose people, nicknamed *capixabas,* cultivate coffee and rice. In 1991 Albuino Azeredo was the first black to become governor of the state. During the late 1990s and the early twenty-first century, Espirito Santo experienced a crime wave requiring federal intervention. Its numerous ports that export products to Europe have made it an attractive location for drug traffickers.

*See also* **Minas Gerais; Mining: Colonial Brazil.**

BIBLIOGRAPHY

Robert Southey, *History of Brazil,* 3 vols. (1819; repr. 1969); *Brazil A/Z: Enciclopédia alfabética em um único volume* (1988).

*Additional Bibliography*

Aguiar, Maciel di. *Brincantes & quilombolas.* São Mateus, Brazil: Memorial, 2005.

Bittencourt, Gabriel Augusto de Mello. *Café e modernização: O Espírito Santo no século XIX.* Rio de Janeiro: Livraria Editora Cátedra, 1987.

Novaes, Maria Stella de. *História do Espírito Santo.* Vitória, Brazil: Fundo Editorial do Espírito Santo, 1968.

Osório, Carloa; Adriana Bravin; and Leonor de Araujo Santanna. *Negros do Espírito Santo.* São Paulo: Escrituras, 1999.

Rocha, Haroldo Corrêa, and Angela Maria Morandi. *Cafeicultura e grande indústria: A transição no Espírito Santo, 1955–1985.* Vitória, Brazil: Fundação Ceciliano Abel de Almeida, 1999.

Souza Filho, Hildo M. de. *The Adoption of Sustainable Agricultural Technologies: A Case Study in the State of Espírito Santo, Brazil.* Brookfield, U.K.: Ashgate, 1997.

SHEILA L. HOOKER

**ESQUILACHES.** Esquilaches (Escuilaches), a secret, antigovernment group of students, primarily from the School of Law of the University of San Carlos in Guatemala, who mildly protested Jorge Ubico's anti-Communist massacre of 1934 and his repressive regime. From this group, led by Mario Méndez Montenegro, Hiram Ordóñez, and Manuel Galich, came many of those who in the 1940s organized the resistance to the Ubico regime that led to its downfall in 1944.

Galich says the group was named after Fausto Squillace (Squillach), the early-twentieth-century Italian sociologist, but others have suggested that the group took its name from the 1766 Esquilace Revolt in Spain, a popular uprising in opposition to Bourbon attempts to change local customs and dress habits, especially as proposed by a foreign adviser, the Italian Marquis de Squillace. The group was sometimes compared to earlier Freemason groups in its conspiratorial political role.

*See also* **Ubico y Castañeda, Jorge.**

BIBLIOGRAPHY

Manuel Galich, *Del pánico al ataque* (1949; 2d ed. 1977), pp. 41–49.

*Additional Bibliography*

Dosal, Paul J., and Oscar Guillermo Peláez Almengor. *Jorge Ubico (1931-1944): Dictadura, economía y "La tacita de plata".* Guatemala: Ediciones CEUR-USAC, 1996.

Holden, Robert H. *Armies without Nations: Public Violence and State Formation in Central America, 1821–1960.* New York: Oxford University Press, 2004.

RALPH LEE WOODWARD JR.

**ESQUIPULAS.** Esquipulas, city in Guatemala and the destination of religious pilgrims—Indian and Ladino— throughout Central America. Famous since the late sixteenth century as the site of the venerable Black Christ, the town is located in the department of Chiquimula in southeastern Guatemala. The Guatemalan sculptor Quirio Cataño (*d.* 1620) carved the dark brown statue from wood in 1594, and miracles were soon attributed to it. The beautiful church that houses the statue was founded in 1737 and declared a basilica in 1961 by Pope John XXIII. Those devoted to the cult of the Black Christ arrive every day of the year, but on 15 January, the day of the Christ of Esquipulas, the town is in full celebration. Pilgrims arrive to attend mass, to burn candles or incense in front of images of the saints, to obtain edible white clay tablets said to harbor curative powers, or to contemplate the Black Christ. The Black Christ of Esquipulas has long served as a religious symbol for Central America in much the same way as the Virgin of Guadalupe has served for Mexico. Esquipulas was also the site and name given to 1987 regional Central American peace accords.

*See also* **Esquipulas II.**

BIBLIOGRAPHY

Juan Paz Solórzano, *Historia del Señor Crucificado de Esquipulas,* 2 vols. (1914–1916).

José Luís García Acietuna, *Esquipulas: Reseña histórica del culto del Señor Crucificado que se venera en este santuario; origen de la imagen y las romerías; crónicas, leyendas y tradiciones: documentación histórica desde los tiempos de la colonia hasta nuestros días* (1940).

Vitalino Fernández Marroquín, *Remembranzas de Esquipulas* (1972).

### *Additional Bibliography*

Crumrine, N. Ross, and E. Alan Morinis. *Pilgrimage in Latin America*. New York: Greenwood Press, 1991.

FLASCO and Friedrich Ebert Stiftung. *Esquipulas, el camino de la paz*. Guatemala: FLACSO-Guatemala: Fundación Friedrich Ebert, 1990.

Horst, Oscar H., and Terry Bond. *Hace cuatro siglos: Las romerías y tradiciones de Esquipulas*. Guatemala: s.n., 1995.

MICHAEL F. FRY

## ESQUIPULAS II.

**ESQUIPULAS II.** Esquipulas II, the 1987 accord based on a peace plan of Oscar Arias Sánchez, president of Costa Rica, and a proposal for a Central American parliament by Marco Vinicio Cerezo Arévalo, president of Guatemala. It was signed by the five Central American presidents on 7 August 1987. The provisions were designed to promote national reconciliation, cessation of hostilities, democratization, free elections, cessations of assistance to irregular forces, nonuse of national territory by irregular forces attacking other states, and international and national verification. Five mechanisms were created to implement the plan: a national commission of reconciliation in each country, an executive commission of the five foreign ministers, a Central American parliament, an International Commission of Verification and Follow-up, and yearly presidential summit commissions.

The plan was met with worldwide acclaim and earned Oscar Arias the Nobel Peace Prize, but U.S. president Ronald Reagan strongly resisted and criticized it. The U.S. government even took a variety of steps that appeared designed to undermine the peace process. Esquipulas II was supported by the United Nations specifically through the creation of the United Nations Organization in Central America (ONUCA), with the support of Canada, Spain, and West Germany. The role of the United States, Cuba, and the Soviet Union in the region was reduced.

In the months immediately after the signing of the agreement, some initial advances were made. A meeting between the Guatemalan government and the URNG (a guerrilla group) was held, a meeting between Salvadoran president José Napoleón Duarte and the FMLN-FDR (an opposition party and guerrilla group coalition) took place, and contacts between the Sandinista government in Nicaragua and the Contras were made.

Esquipulas II contributed to the holding of democratic elections in El Salvador, Guatemala, Honduras, and Nicaragua and to ending the armed hostilities in Nicaragua (1990) and El Salvador (1992).

*See also* **Contadora; Esquipulas.**

BIBLIOGRAPHY

Marco Vinicio Cerezo Arévalo, "Esquipulas II, tres años después," in *Panorama centroamericano* (*Pensamiento y acción*) no. 19 (1990): 3–11.

Francisco Rojas Aravena, Ponencia presentada a seminario *Esquipulas: El camino de la paz* (Guatemala, 1990).

John A. Booth and Thomas W. Walker, *Understanding Central America,* 2nd ed. (1993).

Howard H. Lentner, *State Formation in Central America: The Struggle for Autonomy, Development, and Democracy* (1993).

### *Additional Bibliography*

Murillo Zamora, Carlos. *Paz en Centroamérica de Nassau a Esquipulas*. San José, Costa Rica: Fundación Arias para la Paz y el Progreso Humano: Editorial de la Universidad de Costa Rica, 2006.

Zamora R., Augusto. *La paz burlada: Los procesos de paz de Contadora y Esquipulas*. Madrid: SEPHA, 2006.

DAVID CAREY JR.

## ESQUIÚ, MAMERTO (1826–1883).

Mamerto Esquiú (*b.* 11 May 1826; *d.* 10 January 1883), Argentine Catholic spokesman and bishop of Córdoba. The son of a devout family of farmers in Callesita, Catamarca Province, at the age of ten he entered the Franciscan order. He taught at the Franciscan convent school in Catamarca and for much of his career was closely associated with Catholic educational institutions. Also a noted preacher, he first gained national renown for a sermon he delivered on the occasion of the swearing of allegiance to the 1853 Constitution. Esquiú criticized the liberalism that permeated many provisions of the Constitution, but he called on Argentines to obey it in a spirit of submission to the constituted authorities.

Esquiú at various times was a member of deliberative assemblies in his native province, even as he became increasingly disillusioned with the factional wrangling and civil warfare that afflicted the country as a whole. He spent the years 1862–1875 in Bolivia (except for one brief trip to Peru and Ecuador), where he again earned prominence as a Catholic educator and publicist. For the final years of his life he was mainly in Argentina, despite his dismay over political and cultural trends there. Nevertheless, in view of his prestige among Argentine Catholics and his reputation as "orator of the Constitution," Esquiú was nominated as archbishop of Buenos Aires (which he refused) and bishop of Córdoba (which he reluctantly accepted). From the time he took over the Córdoba diocese in January 1881 until his death, he set an example of apostolic simplicity and tireless energy in service to his flock. Though he was never formally canonized, his biography appears in a series of "Popular Lives of Saints" published in 1977. He died in Suncho, Catamarca province.

*See also* **Argentina: The Nineteenth Century; Education; Franciscans.**

BIBLIOGRAPHY

John J. Kennedy, *Catholicism, Nationalism, and Democracy in Argentina* (1958), pp. 91–97.

David Peña, *La materia religiosa en la política argentina* (1960), pp. 181–210.

Juan Alberto Cortés, *Fray Mamerto Esquiú* (1977).

*Additional Bibliography*

Bazán, Armando Raúl. *Esquiú: Apóstol y ciudadanos.* Buenos Aires: Emecé Editores, 1996.

Navarro Santa Ana, Luis Horacio. *El pensamiento americanista de Fray Mamerto Esquiú.* Catamarca: Editorial Sarquís, 2000.

Sánchez Parodi, Horacio M. *Las ideas político-jurídicas de Fray Mamerto Esquiú.* Buenos Aires: Editorial Quorum, EDUCA, 2002.

DAVID BUSHNELL

**ESQUIVEL, LAURA** (1950–). Mexican author Laura Esquivel was born in Mexico City on September 30, 1950, the third of four children born to a telegraph operator and his wife. She graduated from the National Teachers' College (Escuela Normal de Maestros) and taught kindergarten. Her writing career began with writing plays for children, followed by writing for children's public television.

Esquivel's first novel, *Como agua para Chocolate: Novela de entregas mensuales con recetas, amores, y remedios caseros* (1989), became a best seller in Mexico, rare for a novel written by a woman. The story, set on the Mexico-U.S. border from 1910 to 1933, is about love thwarted by imposed traditions and its expression in culinary traditions. It became an internationally acclaimed film, with the screenplay by Esquivel, directed by her then-husband Alfonso Arau. The book, translated into more than thirty languages, has sold more than three million copies worldwide and won awards including the American Booksellers Book of the Year (ABBY) in 1994. Esquivel's other works include *La ley del amor* (1995), claimed to be the first multimedia novel ever published, which included a CD to be listened to while reading. She is currently married to Javier Valdez, a dentist.

*See also* **Literature: Spanish America.**

BIBLIOGRAPHY

*Works by Laura Esquivel*

*Like Water for Chocolate: A Novel in Monthly Installments, with Recipes, Romances, and Home Remedies*, trans. Carol Christensen and Thomas Christensen. New York: Doubleday, 1992.

*The Law of Love*, trans. Margaret Sayers Peden. New York: Crown, 1996.

*Íntimas suculencias: Tratado filosófico de cocina* [Intimate Succulents: Philosophical Treaty of the Kitchen]. Madrid: Ollero & Ramos, 1998.

*Between Two Fires: Intimate Writings on Life, Love, Food, and Flavor*, trans. Stephen Lytle. New York: Crown, 2000.

*Estrellita marinera: Una fábula de nuestro tiempo* [Marine Estrellita: A Fable of Our Time]. Madrid: Ollero y Ramos, 1999.

*El libro de las emociones: Son de la razón sin corazón* [The Book of Emotions: They Are of the Reason Not the Heart]. Barcelona: Plaza & Janés, 2000.

*Swift as Desire: A Novel.* New York, Crown, 2001.

*Malinche.* México, D.F.: Alfaguara, 2006.

### *Critical Studies*

López González, Aralia. "Laura Esquivel: Ética y estética del fuego." In *Sin imágenes falsas, sin falsos espejos: Narradoras mexicanas del siglo XX*, ed. Aralia López. México, D.F.: Colegio de México, Programa Interdisciplinario de Estudios de la Mujer, 1995.

CLAIR JOYSMITH

---

**ESQUIVEL, MANUEL AMADEO** (1940–). Manuel Amadeo Esquivel (born May 2, 1940) was prime minister of Belize from 1984 to 1989 and again from 1993 to 1998. The youngest of four children, he was born in Belize City. His mother was a housewife and part-time music teacher; his father repaired office machines. He grew up in a modest, two-story frame house that the family still owns. After attending the Jesuit-run St. John's College, he enrolled in Loyola University of New Orleans, graduating with a bachelor of science degree in physics in 1962. He returned home and began a teaching career at St. John's that would last until 1984. In 1966 he won a scholarship to Bristol University in the United Kingdom. Here he met his future wife, Kathleen Levy, and received a postgraduate certificate in physics education in 1967. Returning to Belize, he resumed teaching at St. John's while developing an interest in politics.

In 1973 Esquivel was a founding member of the United Democratic Party (UDP), an alliance of three parties opposed to the People's United Party (PUP), led by George Price, which then dominated Belizean politics. From 1974 to 1980 he served two terms on the Belize City Council and was appointed to the Senate, the upper chamber of the national legislature, in 1979. Because the last pre-independence elections had been held on November 21, 1979, the first national elections following independence were not scheduled until December 14, 1984. Esquivel led the UDP to an upset victory, winning twenty-one seats to the PUP's seven, becoming Belize's second prime minister on December 17. The *New York Times* dubbed him the "Comet of Belize." In 1985 Queen Elizabeth II appointed him to her Privy Council.

During a five-year term in which he also held the finance and defense portfolios, Esquivel oversaw an International Monetary Fund economic stabilization plan. His sound fiscal management and encouragement of foreign investment in tourism, agriculture, and manufacturing helped invigorate the economy. His government achieved balance of payment surpluses for four consecutive years, with foreign exchange reserves at record levels. Despite these economic gains, his government was criticized for selling citizenship to Hong Kong Chinese. Overly optimistic, he called for an early election on 4 September 1989. A split in party ranks, allegations of ministerial corruption, and a series of contested party caucuses contributed to the UDP's narrow loss. The PUP, led by George Price, won fifteen of twenty-eight seats, while Esquivel's UDP won the other thirteen. The PUP margin increased from two to four when a UDP member switched parties. Esquivel became leader of the opposition.

Just four years later on June 30, 1993, Esquivel, in a stunning upset, led the UDP back to power as it captured sixteen of twenty-nine seats in the new parliament. He hosted Queen Elizabeth and Prince Philip during a royal visit in 1994. During his second term as prime minister, he faced a gauntlet of difficult problems, including high employment and a rising tide of urban violence brought on by the drug trade. In his budget speech of March 1997, he was able to report that the decline in Belize's economy had been arrested, major infrastructure improvements were underway, and pensions were raised. To accomplish this, however, his government approved a value-added tax (VAT) on April 1, 1996. Within a year it had generated almost $77 million.

On 29 July 1998 Esquivel won the largest libel suit in Belizean history against two officials of the opposition PUP. This did not prove to be a good omen. In the elections of 28 August 1998, the PUP, led by Said Musa, blasted the UDP for its "killa taxes," and the UDP was swept out of office, left with only three of twenty-nine seats. Esquivel lost his own seat by more than three hundred votes and resigned as party leader. Out of office, the former prime minister has overseen the education of his three children:

David, twenty-four; Laura, twenty-one; and Ruth, sixteen. He and his wife Kathleen, an author and playwright whom he married in 1971, own an office supply business and remain party activists. They were no doubt buoyed by the UDP's electoral success in the municipal elections of March 4, 2006, when it captured sixty-four of sixty-seven seats in nine municipalities. Daughter Laura became the youngest member of the Belize City Council.

*See also* **Belize; International Monetary Fund (IMF); Price, George.**

BIBLIOGRAPHY

*Primary Works*

Esquivel, Manuel. "Prime Minister's New Year's Message." *Belize Today*, January–February 1996.

Esquivel, Manuel. "Developing a Competitive Edge." *Belize Today*, May–June 1996.

*Secondary Works*

Fernandez, Julio A. *Belize: Case Study for Democracy in Central America.* Brookfield, VT: Gower Publishing Co., 1989.

Payne, Anthony J. "The Belize Triangle: Relations with Britain, Guatemala and The United States." *Journal of Interamerican Studies and World Affairs* 32, no. 1 (Spring 1990): 119–135).

Pitt, David. "The Comet of Belize: Manuel Amadeo Esquivel." *New York Times*, December 16, 1984.

BRIAN E. COUTTS

**ESTADO DA INDIA.** *See* **Portuguese Trade and International Relations.**

**ESTADO NOVO.** Estado Novo (New State), Brazil's fascist-inspired dictatorship. On 10 November 1937, President Getúlio Vargas overthrew the constitutional government that he had helped to establish in 1934, replacing it with a totalitarian regime that would continue in power until 1945. The coup d'état was justified as an emergency measure prompted by fear of class warfare and a Communist takeover in Brazil. This threat was trumped up, however, as was the document, the so-called Cohen Plan, that Vargas and his supporters brought forth as evidence for the Communist plot. Created by the Integralists, the Cohen Plan was crafted to play on anti-Semitism, xenophobia, and fear of communism, all of which flourished in Depression-era Brazil.

The Estado Novo constitution allowed for both executive and legislative branches, but Vargas actually ruled by decree. Political parties were banned, as were, by extension, elections, the Congress, and politics. Vargas and his advisers, many of them supporters of the Revolution of 1930 from Vargas's home state of Rio Grande do Sul, created a highly centralized state whose main goal was domestic industrialization. Vargas himself was a populist and successfully co-opted much of the working class by placing all labor unions under a single national umbrella. These antidemocratic moves were accepted by an urban industrial class that found its wages, and education, and health standards rising rapidly.

Although based on European fascist models, the Estado Novo did not have an absolute or clear ideology. After flirting economically and politically with the Axis Powers, Brazil linked itself to the United States in 1939, eventually joining the Allies in World War II and sending troops to Italy in 1942. The defeat of fascism, and the increasing inability of the regime to pay for the benefits it had granted to the urban working class, led the armed forces to overthrow Vargas and the Estado Novo in October 1945. On December 2, seven years after the establishment of the Estado Novo and fifteen years after Vargas first took national power, democratic rule returned to Brazil.

*See also* **Brazil: Since 1889; Cohen Plan; Vargas, Getúlio Dornelles.**

BIBLIOGRAPHY

Thomas Skidmore, *Politics in Brazil, 1930–1964: An Experiment in Democracy* (1967), esp. pp. 3–53.

Robert Levine, *The Vargas Regime: The Critical Years, 1934–1938* (1970).

Edgard Carone, *O Estado Novo* (*1937–1945*) (1988).

*Additional Bibliography*

Aggio, Alberto, Agnaldo de Sousa Barbosa, and Hercídia Mara Facuri Coelho Lambert. *Política e sociedade no Brasil, 1930–1964.* São Paulo, SP, Brasil: Annablume, 2002.

Levine, Robert M. *Father of the Poor?: Vargas and His Era*. Cambridge: Cambridge University Press, 1998.

Williams, Daryle. *Culture Wars in Brazil: The First Vargas Regime, 1930-1945*. Durham: Duke University Press, 2001.

JEFFREY LESSER

## ESTANCIA.

**ESTANCIA.** *Estancia* (livestock ranch), the most important socioeconomic institution on the pampa. Gauchos considered the pampa's resources to be in the public domain, available to all. But *estancias* developed during the eighteenth century, when large ranchers began to extend their control over land, water, and cattle. Larger ranches traditionally had a central ranch house, usually topped by a tower (*mirador*) from which to spot Indian raiders. A modest bunkhouse and kitchen served the workers. Ranchers divided their ranges into many units, each under the charge of a manager.

By the nineteenth century, large, extensive *estancias* dominated the countryside. Wealthy ranchers built veritable castles that dominated their rural estates. Small ranchers often had to rent their land. Because of the vast distances between towns on the plains, many ranches included a Pulpería, a combination general store and tavern.

The *estancia* and *pulpería* were the most important institutions in the rural Río de la Plata. In economic terms, the ranches provided employment for gauchos and generated great wealth from livestock and agriculture. The *estancia* had political importance because ranch owners and managers often served as justices of the peace and dominated local politics. In cultural terms, ranches served as important settings for movies, novels, and poetry in the gauchesque genre.

*See also* **Finca; Fundo; Hacienda; Latifundia.**

BIBLIOGRAPHY

Jonathan C. Brown, *A Socioeconomic History of Argentina* (1979), pp. 123–145.

Richard W. Slatta, *Gauchos and the Vanishing Frontier* (1983), pp. 69–72.

*Additional Bibliography*

Amaral, Samuel. *The Rise of Capitalism on the Pampas: The Estancias of Buenos Aires, 1785-1870*. Cambridge: Cambridge University Press, 2002.

Mayo, Carlos A. *Estancia y sociedad en la pampa, 1740-1820*. Buenos Aires: Biblos, 2004.

RICHARD W. SLATTA

## ESTANCO, ESTANQUERO.

**ESTANCO, ESTANQUERO.** The *estanco*, or *estanco de tabacos*, was the state tobacco monopoly introduced into Spanish America in the second half of the eighteenth century, starting with Peru in 1752. It was easily the most profitable of the imperial monopolies. After independence some countries established the estanco as a state monopoly. Perhaps the most famous was the Chilean tobacco monopoly, established in 1824. The Chilean government farmed out the estanco to the Valparaíso trading house of Portales, Cea, and Company, which agreed to assume responsibility for a £1 million loan secured in London in 1822 by the Bernardo O'Higgins government. When payments on the loan were not met, the government rescinded the contract in 1826, to the considerable resentment of Diego Portales, a partner in the trading house. Portales and several like-minded associates (some connected with the estanco contract) formed a political group that demanded a stronger government and an end to the liberal approach favored by the regimes of the 1820s. The *estanqueros*, as these politicians became known, took a leading role in the Conservative capture of power in 1829–1830, following which Portales became the most powerful figure in Chile.

*See also* **O'Higgins, Bernardo; Portales Palazuelos, Diego José Pedro Víctor; Tobacco Industry; Tobacco Monopoly.**

BIBLIOGRAPHY

Kinsbruner, Jay. *Diego Portales: Interpretative Essays on the Man and Times*.

Villalobos R., Sergio. *Los estancos en Chile*. Santiago, Chile: Fiscalía Nacional Económica: Centro de Investigaciones Diego Barros Aran, 2004.

SIMON COLLIER

**ESTEBAN** (?–1539). Esteban (Estevan; *d.* May 1539), guide and explorer of New Spain. Esteban, a black Arab from the Atlantic coast of Morocco, traveled across Florida, Texas, and northern Mexico from 1527 until 1536 with his owner and Andrés Dorantes, Alvar Núñez Cabeza De Vaca, and Castillo Maldonado, all fellow survivors of Pánfilo de Narváez's ill-fated expedition to Florida. He was then purchased by the viceroy of New Spain, Antonio de Mendoza, who was eager to take advantage of his knowledge of the largely uncharted north country. In 1539, Esteban guided Franciscan friar Marcos de Niza in his search for the Seven Cities of Cíbola. The travelers departed from San Miguel de Culiacán in Sinaloa, Mexico, where they had been accompanied by Francisco Vásquez de Coronado, governor of the province of New Galicia. On the journey north into Sonora, Arizona, and New Mexico, Esteban and a number of Indian allies ranged far ahead of Niza, sending back reports of their progress. Esteban apparently angered the Pueblo Indians by demanding women and turquoise. He was killed at Hawikuh, the southernmost of the six Zuni pueblos.

Niza's report of his travels with Esteban helped persuade Vásquez de Coronado to launch his 1540 expedition to find the great cities and untold riches implied in Niza's descriptions. Among the Zunis, Esteban is known as an *ogre kachina*, or evil spirit.

*See also* **Explorers and Exploration: Spanish America.**

BIBLIOGRAPHY

Cyclone Covey, *Cabeza de Vaca's Adventures in the Unknown Interior of America* (1983).

Cleve Hallenbeck, *The Journey of Fray Marcos de Niza* (1987).

*Additional Bibliography*

Montané Martí, Julio C. *Por los senderos de la quimera: el viaje de Fray Marcos de Niza.* Hermosillo: Instituto Sonorense de Cultura, 1995.

Rick Hendricks

**ESTEFAN, GLORIA** (1957–). The Cuban-born singer and songwriter Gloria Estefan, born September 1, 1957, has sold more than 70 million recordings during a career built on a Caribbean-influenced mix of dance tunes, ballads, and pop music. Born Gloria Fajardo in Havana, she immigrated to Miami with her family in 1959 following the Cuban revolution. In 1977 she joined the Miami Sound Machine (known at the time as the Miami Latin Boys), a group led by keyboardist Emilio Estefan, Jr., whom she married in 1978. With her, the group recorded a series of Spanish-language albums that earned them a following in Central and South America. Their first English-language album, 1984's *Eyes of Innocence*, earned them a gold record and subsequent English-language hits such as "Conga," "Bad Boy," "Words Get in the Way," "Rhythm Is Gonna Get You," and "1, 2, 3" all reached the Top 10 on the U.S. Billboard pop charts, transforming Estefan into an international star. A 1990 tour bus accident sidelined her for almost a year, but she returned in January 1991, performing at the televised American Music Awards. In 1993, she recorded *Mi Tierra*, an album of Cuban songs from her youth, and in succeeding years has released a series of records in both English and Spanish. As a collaborator, she has written and produced songs for Ricky Martin, Jennifer Lopez, and Shakira, among others. In addition to her musical activities, Estefan has appeared in the films *Music of the Heart* (1999) and *For Love or Country: The Arturo Sandoval Story* (2000). While she generally avoids overt political references in her music, as a Cuban exile, Estefan is an outspoken critic of the socialist government in Cuba.

*See also* **Music: Popular Music and Dance.**

BIBLIOGRAPHY

Niurka, Norma. "'Abriendo Puertas,' un canto a Latinoamérica." *El Nuevo Herald* (Miami), September 26, 1995.

Taylor, Chuck. "Gloria Estefan: A Return to the Spotlight." *Billboard*, October 11, 2003: 21, 26, 44.

Andrew Connell

**ESTIGARRIBIA, ANTONIO DE LA CRUZ** (?–?). Antonio de la Cruz Estigarribia, Paraguayan soldier. When the War of the Triple Alliance began in 1864, Estigarribia was one of the most highly respected officers in the Paraguayan army. He had been an adviser to war minister

Francisco Solano López during the 1859 mediation of a dispute between Buenos Aires and the Argentine Confederation, and, thanks to Solano López's sponsorship, was promoted to full colonel and given command of a major Paraguayan column.

In mid–1865, Estigarribia and his forces crossed the Alto Paraná into Brazil as part of a coordinated attack on Corrientes and Río Grande do Sul. As Estigarribia's troops moved south, they destroyed town after town in Brazil, but they also began to lose touch with their own supply bases. After taking the town of São Borja, Estigarribia split up his forces, sending Major Pedro Duarte and 2,500 men down the right bank of the Río Uruguay while he continued with the main body of 8,000 men down the left bank to the town of Uruguaiana. In early August, he occupied the town and awaited news from Duarte. The news was not good: on 17 August Duarte's entire command was obliterated in an Allied attack, leaving Uruguaiana surrounded and Estigarribia without much chance of resupply.

The Paraguayan colonel debated for some time what his next move might be. He was completely cut off and without clear instructions from López. Finally, on 18 September, he agreed to generous Allied terms for surrender, which stipulated that the rank and file would be treated as prisoners of war and that his officers would be allowed to take up residence in any of the Allied nations but not to return to Paraguay.

Estigarribia, whose action was bitterly denounced by López, chose to go to Rio de Janeiro. He then dropped from sight except for a brief, pathetic moment in March 1869, when he petitioned the Brazilian emperor to offer his services as a guide for the armies then advancing into the Cordillera of central Paraguay.

*See also* **War of the Triple Alliance.**

BIBLIOGRAPHY

González, Natalicio. *Procesco y formación de la cultura paraguaya.* Asunción–Buenos Aires: Editorial Guaranda, 1938.

Kilinski, Charles J. *Independence or Death! The Story of the Paraguayan War.* Gainesville: University of Florida Press, 1965.

THOMAS L. WHIGHAM

## ESTIGARRIBIA, JOSÉ FÉLIX (1888–1940).

José Félix Estigarribia (*b.* 21 February 1888; *d.* 5 September 1940), president of Paraguay (1940) and soldier. Born at Caraguatay, Estigarribia came from a poor but distinguished family of Basque extraction. His ancestors included Colonel Antonio de la Cruz Estigarribia, who had surrendered his army at Uruguaiana during the War of the Triple Alliance.

Young José Félix passed his early years in the countryside, and there was reason to think he might choose farming as a career. In 1903 he enrolled in the Agricultural School at Trinidad and then moved on to attend the Colegio Nacional at Asunción. The revolutions of the first decade of the new century, however, propelled Estigarribia into the ranks of the army. In 1911, he was sent to Chile for further military training, from which he returned two years later, becoming a first lieutenant in 1914. Estigarribia remained loyal to the government during the disturbances of 1921–1922, a fact that provisional president Eusebio Ayala never forgot. As a partial reward, the young captain was sent to France for further military study under Marshal Foch. When he returned to Paraguay in 1927, he became chief of the general staff.

During Estigarribia's absence, the dispute with Bolivia over the Chaco Region had provoked a series of ugly incidents. These, in turn, developed into a full scale war by 1932. In August of that year Estigarribia was given command of 15,000 men, with which he forged a powerful fighting force.

Estigarribia gained a legendary status in the Chaco. Though his troops were regularly outnumbered by the Bolivians, still they boasted certain advantages over their counterparts from the Altiplano: they were closer to home bases, they were more accustomed to the terrain and climate, and, in Estigarribia, they had a commander who had a clear goal, who was a master tactician, and who understood his men. Over the next three years, Colonel Estigarribia went from victory to victory fighting on some of the roughest land in South America. After his exhausted troops gained the foothills of the Andes in 1935, a truce was signed. It was affirmed three years later in a boundary treaty generally favorable to Paraguay.

Meanwhile, President Eusebio Ayala had been removed by restive army officers and young radicals. Ayala's ally Estigarribia went on an extended tour abroad, teaching for a time at the Montevideo War College. In 1938 he became ambassador to Washington, and in 1939, though still in the United States, he ran unopposed as the Liberal candidate for president. When he returned for his inauguration at Asunción, however, Estigarribia discovered that radicals were demanding more far-reaching action than the Liberal program called for. Compromising, the new president proposed a semi-authoritarian constitution that had socialist, democratic, and fascist elements. Despite some inner doubts as to the wisdom of this document, Estigarribia ruled under it as dictator. Two months after its ratification, he died in an airplane crash outside Asunción. By executive decree, the Chaco hero was posthumously promoted to field marshal.

*See also* **Ayala, Eusebio; Basques in Latin America; Chaco Region; Chaco War; War of Triple Alliance.**

BIBLIOGRAPHY

Harris G. Warren, "Political Aspects of the Paraguayan Revolution, 1936–1940," *Hispanic American Historical Review* 30 (February 1950): 2–25.

Pablo Max Ynsfrán, ed., *The Epic of the Chaco: Marshal Estigarribia's Memoirs of the Chaco War, 1932–1935* (1950).

Michael Grow, *The Good Neighbor Policy and Authoritarianism in Paraguay* (1981), esp. pp. 50–58.

### *Additional Bibliography*

Castillo, Jorge Celio. *Los dos últimos presidentes austeros del Paraguay.* Asunción, 2003.

Filártiga, Joel, and Luis Agüero Wagner. *Un Napoleón de hojalata.* Asunción: Fundación "Joel Filártiga" Ediciones, 2002.

Llano, Mariano. *Estigarribia: el león del desierto.* Asunción, 1999.

Seiferheld, Alfredo M. *Nazismo y fascismo en el Paraguay: los años de la guerra, 1939-1945.* Asunción: Editorial Histórica, 1986.

THOMAS L. WHIGHAM

## ESTIMÉ, DUMARSAIS (1900–1953).

Dumarsais Estimé (*b.* 1900; *d.* 20 July 1953), president of Haiti (1946–1950). A native of Verrettes and a former mathematics teacher at the Lycée Pétion, Estimé was a member of the National Assembly and secretary of education before becoming president. He came to power on 16 August 1946 with the support of elite blacks (members of the Noiriste Party) who had been excluded from government under the regime of Élie Lescot.

Lasting until 10 May 1950, Estimé's government also drew support initially from young radicals and Communists who looked forward to a social revolution that would benefit Haiti's black masses, both workers and peasants. Although it never went far enough to satisfy leftist desires, the government did make use of its popular mandate to carry out genuine reforms. In addition to granting greater liberty of speech and the press, Estimé established a populist and nationalist program that embraced inclusion of blacks in the state patronage system; support for unions; social legislation recognizing workers' rights; public education; attempts to curb U.S. economic control of the country, in part by breaking up the Standard Fruit Company's monopoly on banana production; and the agreement with the Export-Import Bank to finance the Artibonite Valley irrigation project. Estimé also encouraged development of Haiti's tourist industry by granting credits to the hotel business and investing millions of dollars in an international fair celebrating the founding of Port-au-Prince (1949). He was exiled to the United States and died in New York City.

*See also* **Banking: Overview; Haiti; Tourism.**

BIBLIOGRAPHY

Rayford W. Logan, *Haiti and the Dominican Republic* (1968).

David Nicholls, *From Dessalines to Duvalier: Race, Colour and National Independence in Haiti* (1979), and "Haiti Since 1930," in *The Cambridge History of Latin America,* vol. 7, edited by Leslie Bethell (1990), pp. 545–577.

### *Additional Bibliography*

Smith, Matthew Jordan. "Shades of Red in a Black Republic: Radicalism, Black Consciousness, and Social Conflict in Post-Occupation Haiti, 1934–1957." Ph.D. diss., University of Florida, 2002.

Voltaire, Frantz. *Pouvoir noir en Haïti: L'explosion de 1946.* Mont-Royal: V & R éditeurs; Montreal: Editions du CIDIHCA, 1988.

PAMELA MURRAY

## ESTÍPITE. *See* **Churrigueresque.**

## ESTRADA, CARLOS (1909–1970).

Carlos Estrada (*b.* 15 September 1909; *d.* 7 May 1970), Uruguayan composer, conductor, and teacher. Born in Montevideo, Estrada studied there with Adelina Pérez Montero (piano), Carlos Correa Luna (violin), Father Pedro Ochoa (Gregorian chant), and Manuel Fernández Espiro (harmony, counterpoint, and composition). In 1938 he traveled to Paris and attended classes at the National Conservatory given by Jean-Jules Aimable Roger-Ducasse and Henri Busser (composition), Noel Gallon (counterpoint and fugue), and Albert Wolff, Paul Paray, and Philippe Gaubert (conducting). Contrary to the prevailing Uruguayan nationalist style, Estrada utilized modal harmonic systems and neoclassical forms, with a strong influence, initially, from the French school. In 1936 he founded the Orquesta de Cámara de Montevideo.

In the early 1940s Estrada began to work in the major forms, composing the oratorio *Daniel* (1942) and incidental music for Paul Claudel's play *L'Annonce faite à Marie* (1943). He premiered and conducted his first symphony in Paris in 1951, and his string quartet no. 1, a SODRE Composition First Award, was premiered at the First Latin American Music Festival of Montevideo in 1957.

Estrada was director and professor of harmony and composition at the National Conservatory of Montevideo (1953–1968) and also taught at the Institute of Musicology (University of Montevideo School of Humanities). He founded the Municipal Symphony Orchestra in 1959 and conducted it until 1970; he also conducted several European orchestras. The French government honored Estrada by making him Officier de l'Académie and Chevalier des Arts et Lettres. He died in Montevideo.

*See also* **Music: Art Music; Uruguay: The Twentieth Century.**

BIBLIOGRAPHY

*Composers of the Americas,* vol. 16 (1970).

John Vinton, ed., *Dictionary of Contemporary Music* (1974); *New Grove Dictionary of Music and Musicians,* vol. 6 (1980).

Susana Salgado, *Breve historia de la música culta en el Uruguay,* 2d ed. (1980).

### *Additional Bibliography*

Ríos, Mary. *Guía de la música uruguaya, 1950-1990.* Montevideo: Arca, 1995.

Susana Salgado

## ESTRADA, JOSÉ DOLORES (1792–1869).

José Dolores Estrada (*b.* 16 March 1792; *d.* 12 August 1869), Nicaraguan general and hero of San Jacinto. Born in Nandaime to an agricultural family descended from the Gonzalo de Sandoval group of conquistadores, Estrada showed an affinity for the military at an early age. During the independence movement, Estrada accompanied Argüello but achieved real fame only decades later, when he led a dramatic victory against the filibuster forces of William Walker and Byron Cole. The battle of San Jacinto (14 September 1856) was fought on an old hacienda near Tipitapa. There 160 men led by Estrada barricaded themselves in the house and fought the North Americans bravely. Their successful effort convinced other Central Americans that Walker could indeed be beaten, and Estrada and his forces quickly became symbols of nationalism and patriotism.

*See also* **San Jacinto, Battle of; Walker, William.**

BIBLIOGRAPHY

Ildefonso Palma Martínez, *La guerra nacional* (1956).

Francisco Pérez Estrada, *José Dolores Estrada: Héroe nacional de Nicaragua* (1970).

Marco Antonio Soto V., *La guerra nacional de Centroamérica,* 2d ed. (1975).

Ernesto De La Torre Villar, ed., *La batalla de San Jacinto, Nicaragua, 1856* (1987).

### *Additional Bibliography*

Bolaños Geyer, Alejandro. *La Guerra Nacional de Centroamérica contra los Filibusteros en 1856-1857: Conversaciones con el Doctor Alejandro Bolaños Geyer.* Alajuela: Museo Histórico Cultural Juan Santamaría, 2000.

Molina Jiménez, Iván. *La campaña nacional, 1856-1857: Una visión desde el siglo XXI.* Alajuela: Museo Histórico Cultural Juan Santamaría, 2000.

Karen Racine

**ESTRADA, JOSÉ MANUEL** (1842–1894). Born in Buenos Aires on July 13, 1842 José Manuel Estrada was a writer, law professor, director of the Argentine Colegio Nacional, and congressman. As a member of the so-called Generation of 1880, Estrada typifies the multifaceted man of letters in Argentine public and intellectual life in Buenos Aires. In addition to serving as rector of the Colegio Nacional, an institution that has traditionally provided secondary-school training to the brightest of the nation's youth, Estrada played an energetic role in the burgeoning field of cultural journalism. He was the founding editor of the *Revista Argentina*, an excellent example of the comprehensive cultural publications of the period that contributed to a sense of sophisticated nationalism by serving as a forum for the exchange of ideas among privileged literati, most of whom had ties to the economic boom of the late nineteenth century. This exchange was abetted by the way in which such publications functioned as a channel for the intensive European and American intellectual production of the day.

Estrada is notable for his identification with a conservative Catholicism that was opposed to what he viewed as an immoral and tyrannical capitalist expansion at the expense of traditional values. Estrada's antiliberalism is typified by his early *El catolicismo y la democracia* (1862) and in his work as leader of the highly orthodox Unión Católica. His *Lecciones sobre la historia de la República Argentina* (1868), based on his lectures as a law professor, constitute a notable example of his unified conservative Catholic point of view and typify the sort of grandiloquent rhetoric customarily found in militant writings of those who sought to shape national consciousness. As a consequence of his ideas and the tenor of his rhetoric, Estrada was dismissed from the Colegio Nacional in 1983. He died of heart failure in Asuncion, Paraguay, on September 17, 1894, while serving as Argentine Minister Plenipotentiary.

*See also* **Colegio Nacional de Buenos Aires; Journalism.**

BIBLIOGRAPHY

Casal Castel, Alberto. "La actualidad de José Manuel Estrada." In his *Vidas ejemplares.* Buenos Aires: Librería Hachette, 1942.

Giusti, Roberto F. "Preliminary Study." In *Jose Manuel Estrada, Antología.* Buenos Aires: A. Estrada, 1941.

DAVID WILLIAM FOSTER

**ESTRADA, JOSÉ MARÍA** (?–1856). José María Estrada (*d.* 13 August 1856), acting president (1854) and president (1855-1856) of Nicaragua. President Fruto Chamorro turned over the presidency to José María Estrada on 27 May 1854 in order to give full attention to leading the Legitimist (Conservative) army against the Democratic (Liberal) insurgents headed by Máximo Jerez. Estrada had earlier served as foreign minister and as a member of the Assembly. After Chamorro died (12 March 1855), the Assembly authorized Estrada to continue in office. When Granada fell to William Walker, Estrada opposed the Walker-backed government of Patricio Rivas, repudiating the treaty of 23 October 1855. He established a government first at Masaya, then at Somotillo, and later at Matagalpa, allying himself with the conservative governments of the other Central American states against Walker in the National War. Democratic guerrillas attacked and killed Estrada at El Ocotal.

*See also* **National War; Rivas, Patricio; Walker, William.**

BIBLIOGRAPHY

Federico Hernández De León, *El libro de las efemérides: Capítulos de la historia de la América Central,* vol. 3 (1930), pp. 283-287.

Andrés Vega Bolaños, *Gobernantes de Nicaragua: Notas y documentos* (1944), pp. 194-222.

José Dolores Gámez, *Historia de Nicaragua desde los tiempos prehistóricos hasta 1860, en sus relaciones con España, México y Centro-América* (1975).

E. Bradford Burns, *Patriarch and Folk: The Emergence of Nicaragua, 1798-1858* (1991).

RALPH LEE WOODWARD, JR.

**ESTRADA, JOSÉ MARÍA** (c. 1810–c. 1862). José María Estrada (*b.* ca. 1810; *d.* ca. 1862), Mexican painter. Born in Guadalajara, Estrada signed his paintings sometimes as José

María Estrada and sometimes as José María Zepeda de Estrada, which has caused some confusion about his work. He studied under José María Uriarte, director of painting at the Academy of Guadalajara, who had received his education at the Academy of Mexico City. Estrada did not, however, follow the path of academic painters. Specializing in portraits, he painted in a style typical of his native state of Jalisco. His portraits are enchanting and are characterized by meticulous detail, with subjects in sober dress, their faces in three-quarter position, and their hands always holding a fruit, a kerchief, or a fan. Estrada used unadorned backgrounds to emphasize his subjects, and his colors tended toward the cool end of the spectrum. Unlike his adult subjects, he portrayed children full–bodied.

Estrada's compositional style was typical of popular painters who paint what they know, as opposed to painting what "should be seen" according to the rules of illusionist perspective imposed in the academies. He also painted dead children, a custom common in traditional painting. Estrada died in Guadalajara.

*See also* **Art: The Nineteenth Century.**

BIBLIOGRAPHY

Burke, Marcus. *Mexican Art Masterpieces.* New York: Hugh Lauter Levin Associates, 1998.

Montenegro, Roberto. *Mexican Painting 1800–1860.* New York: Appleton–Century Co., 1933.

ESTHER ACEVEDO

## ESTRADA, JUAN JOSÉ (1865–1947).

Juan José Estrada (*b.* 1865; *d.* 1947), provisional president of Nicaragua (29 August 1910–9 May 1911). Estrada, governor of the Caribbean department of Mosquitia, launched an uprising against President José Santos Zelaya, whose government fell in 1909. He continued the revolt against Zelaya's successor, José Madriz, and in 1910 established a provisional government at Bluefields, where he received assistance from U.S. marines. Madriz turned over power to Estrada's brother, José Dolores Estrada, on 20 August 1910, and Juan José Estrada formally became provisional president on 29 August. A new Constituent Assembly unanimously elected him for a two-year term on 31 December 1910, but the real power rested with General Luis Mena, who commanded the military. Under pressure, Estrada resigned on 9 May 1911, turning power over to his vice president, Adolfo Díaz.

*See also* **Diaz, Adolfo; Estrada, José Dolores; Nationalism.**

BIBLIOGRAPHY

José Joaquín Morales, *De la historia de Nicaragua de 1889–1913* (1963).

Charles E. Frazier, *The Dawn of Nationalism and Its Consequences in Nicaragua* (1972).

### *Additional Bibliography*

Arellano, Jorge Eduardo. *La Pax americana en Nicaragua: (1910-1932).* Managua: Academia de Geografía e Historia de Nicaragua: Fondo Editorial CIRA, 2004.

Selser, Gregorio. *La restauración conservadora y la gesta de Benjamín Zeledón: Nicaragua-USA, 1909-1916.* Managua: Aldilà Editor, 2001.

RALPH LEE WOODWARD JR.

## ESTRADA CABRERA, MANUEL (1857–1924).

Manuel Estrada Cabrera (*b.* 21 November 1857; *d.* 24 September 1924), president of Guatemala (1898–1920). In 1898 Estrada Cabrera secured the Guatemalan presidency following the assassination of his protector and predecessor, President José María Reyna Barrios. A Quetzaltenango lawyer of limited ability and humble parentage, Estrada Cabrera has been described as one of the strangest personalities who ever raised himself to great power. Even though he served the Reyna Barrios administration (1892–1898) as minister of the interior and justice and first designate (vice president), upon his ascendancy to the presidency as the constitutionally recognized presidential successor, Estrada Cabrera was largely regarded as an undistinguished rural politician. The violence of Reyna Barrios's assassination, however, proved to be a fitting introduction to Estrada Cabrera's twenty-two-year reign of terror, which still ranks as the longest uninterrupted rule in Central American history. The president's renowned tendencies toward cruelty and corruption, combined with his legendary resourcefulness and invulnerability undoubtedly contributed to the longevity of his administration.

Like the father of Guatemalan liberalism, the revered Justo Rufino Barrios (1873–1885), Estrada Cabrera was a typical Latin American *caudillo.* Careful to cultivate the support of the coffee elite and dedicated to the Positivist watchwords of "order" and "progress," the dictator guided Guatemala on a course common in Latin America in the latter half of the nineteenth century. Throughout his presidency, Estrada Cabrera fostered the creation of a society typified by large landed estates, forced labor, an export-oriented economy, and highly centralized political power. Latin American caudillos rarely delegated political authority to subordinates and Estrada Cabrera was no exception to this rule. According to Dana G. Munro, a U.S. State Department representative in the first quarter of the twentieth century, the dictator "had no friends or personal followers except the army officers and government officials who supported his regime" and these only "for the sake of the license and graft" that he permitted.

During the Estrada Cabrera presidency, the exploitative and exclusive nature of Guatemalan society became increasingly obvious. Instead of real development, what emerged was a landed oligarchy, engaged primarily in the production of coffee, that utilized its economic might to construct a state that protected its dominant social and political status. Although economic growth and modernization proceeded at a moderate pace during the first two decades of the twentieth century, political and social problems associated with increased economic activity, lack of development, and the altered fabric of Guatemalan society arose. Significant among these were the rapid growth of the capital's middle class, the emergence of a significant labor element, and a vocal and politically conscious student population, all of which were refused a forum for political expression, not to mention an equitable share in the profits of the republic's lucrative coffee industry. The cumulative effect of these forces, augmented by the extremely repressive nature of Estrada Cabrera's administration, presented the republic with a rare opportunity to implement real and significant reform.

In late 1917 and 1918 general disenchantment with the political and economic status quo of the Estrada Cabrera regime was accelerated by a series of devastating earthquakes that left much of Guatemala City in rubble. Estrada Cabrera's apathetic response to the earthquakes, coupled with the student protests of the same years, aroused a heretofore unknown reaction in the capital. Awakened by the students' commitment to reform, other sectors of society, notably the Roman Catholic church, an incipient urban middle class, organized labor, and eventually the military and the landed elite, pledged their support to a new unified political coalition, the Unionist Party, to oppose the dictator. By April 1920, the president's inability to adapt to the republic's changing political and social conditions and the coalition's commitment to the dictator's unconditional surrender, prompted the Guatemalan National Assembly to impeach a physically weakened and politically alienated Manuel Estrada Cabrera.

*See also* **Coffee Industry; Guatemala City; Reyna Barrios, José María.**

BIBLIOGRAPHY

Dana G. Munro, *Intervention and Dollar Diplomacy in the Caribbean, 1900–1921,* (1964).

Chester Lloyd Jones, *Guatemala: Past and Present* (1966).

Rafael Arévalo Martínez, *¡Ecce Pericles! La tiranía de Manuel Estrada Cabrera en Guatemala,* 3d ed. (1983).

David McCreery, "Debt Servitude in Rural Guatemala, 1876–1936," in *Hispanic American Historical Review* 63 (1983): 735–759.

Jim Handy, *Gift of the Devil: A History of Guatemala* (1984).

Ralph Lee Woodward, Jr., *Central America: A Nation Divided* (1985).

Mary Catherine Rendon, "Manuel Estrada Cabrera, Guatemalan President, 1898–1920" (Ph.D. diss., Oxford Univ., 1988).

Wade Kit, "Precursor of Change: Failed Reform and the Guatemalan Coffee Elite, 1918–1926" (Master's thesis, Univ. of Saskatchewan, 1989).

### *Additional Bibliography*

Buchenau, Jürgen. "Little Patience with a Little Neighbor: Understanding Mexico's Hostile Policies towards Guatemala's Manuel Estrada Cabrera, 1898–1920." *Jahrbuch für Geschichte von Staat, Wirtschaft und Gesellschaft Lateinamerikas* 33 (1996): 289–311.

Dosal, Paul J. *Power in Transition: The Rise of Guatemala's Industrial Elite, 1871–1994.* Westport, CT: Praeger, 1995.

Luján Muñoz, Jorge. *Las revoluciones de 1897, la muerte de J.M. Reina Barrios y la elección de M. Estrada Cabrera.* Guatemala: Artemis Edinter, 2003.

Rendón, Catherine. *Minerva y la palma: El enigma de don Manuel.* Guatemala: Artemis Edinter, 2000.

WADE A. KIT

## ESTRADA DOCTRINE.

**ESTRADA DOCTRINE.** Estrada Doctrine, precept formulated in a 27 September 1930 note sent by Mexican foreign minister Genaro Estrada to Mexican diplomatic representatives throughout the world. Recent revolutions in Argentina, Bolivia, Peru, and Central America had presented the Mexican government with the question of recognizing a number of de facto regimes. Given Mexico's problems in obtaining diplomatic recognition from the United States and other powers during its own revolutionary period, it was understandable that the Mexican government would be sympathetic to the plight of other revolutionary governments. Accordingly, Estrada asserted that Mexico would "not make any declarations regarding recognition because it considers that such a policy is an insulting practice which, in addition to offending the sovereignty of other nations, places them in a position of having their internal affairs judged by other governments."

The Estrada Doctrine was received enthusiastically by many Latin Americans who felt that the region had been unfairly discriminated against by the great powers through the selective application of de jure recognition. With the exception of the Franco regime in Spain, Mexico has been remarkably consistent over the years in adhering to the Estrada Doctrine.

*See also* **Mexico: Since 1910.**

BIBLIOGRAPHY

John W. F. Dulles, *Yesterday in Mexico: A Chronicle of the Revolution, 1919–1936* (1961), esp. pp. 497–498; *Enciclopedia de México,* edited by José Rogelio Álvarez (1987), esp. vol. 5, p. 2, 596.

*Additional Bibliography*

Buchenau, Jürgen. *In the Shadow of the Giant: The Making of Mexico's Central America Policy, 1876-1930.* Tuscaloosa: University of Alabama Press, 1996.

Gonzales, Michael J. *The Mexican Revolution, 1910-1940.* Albuquerque: University of New Mexico Press, 2002.

RICHARD V. SALISBURY

## ESTRADA PALMA, TOMÁS

**ESTRADA PALMA, TOMÁS** (1835–1908). Tomás Estrada Palma (*b.* 9 July 1835; *d.* 4 November 1908), Cuban patriot and politician, president of Cuba (1902–1906). Born in Bayamo, Tomás Estrada Palma grew up in Oriente, the center of Cuba's protracted struggle for independence. He was sent by his family to study in Havana and then pursued a law degree at the University of Seville in Spain. A family crisis required Estrada to return home and assume administration of the family estate before he had finished his studies; nevertheless, he retained his passionate belief in the value of education and tried to set up rural schools for the benefit of his community.

As a young and progressive man, Estrada Palma participated in the Ten Years' War (1868–1878), joining the rebels in 1868 and quickly rising to the rank of general. In 1876 Estrada was elected president of the Republic in Arms but fell prisoner to the Spanish the following year. He was transported to Spain and released in 1878, when the Pact of Zanjón ended the war. Estrada then moved to Paris, where he began a discussion group for political exiles and took an interest in the intellectual life of Europe.

Estrada Palma left Europe for America in the late 1880s, passing through New York, where he visited José Martí, and continuing on to Central America. He settled in Honduras, where he met and married Genoveva Guardiola, the daughter of the Honduran president. At the insistence of Martí, Estrada moved his family to New York, where the two expatriates formed the Cuban Revolutionary Party in 1892. Following Martí's death in battle in 1895, Estrada Palma reluctantly accepted the title of provisional president of Cuba after the defeat of Spain. He was elected president in his own right in Cuba's first independent election for the office, held in 1902.

A decent, honest, and hardworking man, Estrada Palma accomplished much as president: expansion of public education; a treaty of reciprocity with the United States; the completion of a national railroad; and the repayment of debts and reconstruction after a decade of war. His reputation, however, has suffered from his preference that the island remain a protectorate of the United States rather than a fully independent state. Estrada's decision to employ government resources to support his reelection efforts in 1905 prompted the opposition Liberal Party to boycott the proceedings. In the ensuing crisis, Estrada invited in a U.S. military force, which remained on the island from 1906 until 1909. Estrada resigned in 1906 and returned to his humble family plot.

*See also* **Cuba: The Republic (1898–1959); Ten Years' War.**

BIBLIOGRAPHY

Pánfilo D. Camacho, *Estrada Palma, el gobernante honrado* (1938).

Fermín Peraza Sarausa, *Diccionario biográfico cubano,* vol. 14 (1968).

Allan Reed Millett, *The Politics of Intervention: The Military Occupation of Cuba, 1906–1909* (1968).

Luis Aguilar, *Cuba 1933: Prologue to Revolution* (1972).

Louis A. Pérez, Jr., *Cuba Under the Platt Amendment, 1902–1934* (1986).

### *Additional Bibliography*

Cordoví Núñez, Yoel. *Liberalismo, crisis e independencia en Cuba, 1880–1904.* Havana: Editorial de Ciencias Sociales, 2003.

Hernández, José M. *Cuba and the United States: Intervention and Militarism, 1868–1933.* Austin: University of Texas Press, 1993.

Hidalgo Paz, Ibrahím. *Cuba, 1895–1898: Contradicciones y disoluciones.* Havana: Centro de Estudios Martianos; Centro de Investigación y Desarrollo de la Cultura Cubana Juan Marinello, 1999.

Núñez Vega, Jorge. *La república ambigua: Soberanía, caudillismo y ciudadanía en la construcción de la I República cubana.* Barcelona: Instituto de Ciències Polítiques i Socials, 2002.

Pérez-Stable, Marifeli. "Estrada Palma's Civic March: From Oriente to Havana, April 20–May 11, 1902." *Cuban Studies/Estudios Cubanos* 30 (2000): 113–121.

KAREN RACINE

**ETCHEPAREBORDA, ROBERTO** (1923–1985). Roberto Etchepareborda (*b.* 19 December 1923; *d.* 10 April 1985), Argentine historian, educator, and diplomat. Born in Milan, Italy, where his father was serving as an Argentine diplomat, Etchepareborda was educated in Europe and Argentina. As a prominent figure of the Radical Party, he was a member of the City Council of Buenos Aires (1958–1962), over which he later presided. In 1962 President Arturo Frondizi, a short time before he was deposed by a military coup, appointed Etchepareborda his foreign minister. From 1962 to 1964 Etchepareborda served as Argentina's ambassador to India. He was also director of the National Archives and a member of the Argentine Academy of History, as well as of similar academies in other American countries and in Spain. He was professor (1966–1971) and president (1971–1973) of the National University of the South in Bahía Blanca, Argentina, and in the 1970s and 1980s he taught at the University of North Carolina in Chapel Hill, and at the School of Advanced International Studies of Johns Hopkins University, and American University, both in Washington, D.C. In 1974 he held a Wilson Fellowship at the Woodrow Wilson International Center for Scholars, also in Washington. From 1979 to 1984 he was director of the Department of Cultural Affairs of the Organization of American States. An authority on Argentine political and diplomatic history, his most important works are: *Hipólito Yrigoyen: Pueblo y gobierno,* a twelve-volume compilation (1956); *Tres revoluciones: 1890, 1893, 1905* (1968), for which he received the National Book Award in 1970; *Rosas: Controvertida historiografía* (1972); and *Zeballos y la política exterior argentina* (1982). From 1981 until his death he was a contributing editor of the *Handbook of Latin American Studies.*

*See also* **Argentina, Political Parties: Radical Party; Education: Overview.**

CELSO RODRÍGUEZ

**ETHNIC STUDIES.** With the rise of powerful indigenous movements in the 1990s, ethnic studies have gained renewed interest in academic circles. This heightened attention was manifest in the creation of a new Ethnicity, Race, and Indigenous

Peoples (ERIP) section of the Latin American Studies Association (LASA) and an associated journal, *Latin American and Caribbean Ethnic Studies* (LACES). Directly or indirectly, subject populations have always set the agenda for ethnic studies.

An interest in ethnicity can be traced back to the beginnings of the European conquest of the Americas. Most notable was Bartolomé de Las Casas (1484–1566), a Dominican priest who accompanied early Spanish conquistadores. Along with other priests, he engaged in a sustained study of indigenous cultures and languages—often for the purposes of conversion to Christianity. Under colonial administration, European powers divided the Americas into two republics—one for Europeans and another for Indians. In the nineteenth century, liberal politicians emphasizing equality attempted to erase these racial differences. Rather than improving the lives of indigenous peoples, this led to increased poverty and oppression for them. In the 1920s educated urban elites engaged in an *indigenista* discourse that attempted to address indigenous poverty. Most notably, the Peruvian José Carlos Mariátegui argued for the necessity to study indigenous cultures in order to understand the social reality of Peru.

In the 1960s agrarian reform programs again attempted to de-ethnicize indigenous populations, believing that turning Indians into peasants would be a way to improve their lives. In a surprise to outsiders, indigenous peoples continued to cling to their ethnic identities. Out of this situation emerged powerful indigenous-led movements for liberation. With increased politicization of ethnic identities, academic interest in ethnic studies increased as well. It spread out from its roots in anthropology to become an interdisciplinary field of inquiry that incorporates sociology, political science, geography, history, and other disciplines.

Historically, studies of ethnically distinct populations have tended to debate whether their marginalization would best be solved through extermination or assimilation. It was rare to argue for maintenance of ethnic identity, and equally rare for members of a marginalized ethnic group to study their own heritage. In the twentieth century a long-running debate raged over whether oppression of subaltern populations was due to racial or class discrimination. Increasingly, scholars recognized this as a false debate, as these issues often merged, together with gender and other factors, into a singular system of domination. Many studies began to look at ethnicity as a cultural construct that served to advance a specific group's political, economic, and social interests.

The term *ethnicity* itself has come under scrutiny. Sometimes it has referred to culture, as distinct from race, which was seen as a biological category. Often it has been used as a gloss for *race,* particularly as scientists have proved that in biological terms distinct races do not exist. *Ethnicity* has also been commonly used to refer to indigenous populations, whereas *race* has been used for Afro-descendants. All of these categories imply a homogeneity that has never existed in the Americas. Not only is *Indian* a colonial term that grouped thousands of different groups together under one rubric, but it also ignored the presence of other ethnicities. Particularly since the nineteenth century there has been a significant and diverse Asian immigration to the Americas. Arguably, descendants of the European conquistadores also have their own ethnic heritages, though these are rarely considered within the framework of ethnic studies.

Ethnic studies have traditionally been the domain of elites studying other, marginalized, populations. One of the most noted developments is *ethnic* populations' studying their own history and culture. There has also been a strong move toward collaborative research between academics and indigenous intellectuals. Scholars of ethnic studies increasingly recognize their responsibilities to those they study, often reversing the power dynamics as ethnic peoples increasingly refuse to be subjugated or marginalized.

*See also* **Indigenous Peoples; Las Casas, Bartolomé de; Mariátegui, José Carlos.**

BIBLIOGRAPHY

Postero, Nancy Grey, and León Zamosc, eds. *The Struggle for Indigenous Rights in Latin America.* Brighton, U.K. and Portland, OR: Sussex Academic Press, 2004.

Rappaport, Joanne. *Intercultural Utopias: Public Intellectuals, Cultural Experimentation, and Ethnic Pluralism in Colombia.* Durham, NC: Duke University Press, 2005.

Van Cott, Donna Lee. *From Movements to Parties in Latin America: The Evolution of Ethnic Politics.* Cambridge, U.K.: Cambridge University Press, 2005.

Wade, Peter. *Race and Ethnicity in Latin America.* London and Chicago: Pluto Press, 1997.

MARC BECKER

**EUCEDA, MAXIMILIANO** (1891–1987). Maximiliano Euceda (*b.* 1891; *d.* 1987), Honduran portrait painter. Born in Caridad, Honduras, near Tegucigalpa, Euceda, like other members of Honduras's Generation of '20, studied art in Spain, where he was especially influenced by the naturalism and realism of Romero de Torres. Euceda returned to Honduras in 1927, and gave art lessons until 1940, when he joined the staff of the newly formed Escuela Nacional de Bellas Artes in Tegucigalpa, where he taught for several decades thereafter. He and Carlos Zúñiga Figueroa were especially important in training the generation of Honduran painters that emerged in the 1940s.

*See also* **Art: The Twentieth Century; Honduras.**

BIBLIOGRAPHY

J. Evaristo López R. and Longino Becerra, *Honduras: 40 pintores* (1989).

*Additional Bibliography*

Oyuela, Irma Leticia de. *La batalla pictórica: Síntesis de la historia de la pintura hondureña.* Tegucigalpa: Banco Atlántida, 1995.

RALPH LEE WOODWARD JR.

**EXALTADOS.** Exaltados, advocates of republicanism, federalism, and political egalitarianism in an important political movement in Brazil during the late 1820s and the 1830s. Inspired by the Jacobin ideas of the French Revolution, the *exaltados* ("enthusiasts") were strongly anti-Portuguese and generally xenophobic. Their program and the use of the popular press, open public meetings, and street action—all innovations in Brazilian politics—generated strong support from urban elements, including artisans and shopkeepers, many of them mulattoes and all having socioeconomic grievances. Various developments, including the death of Pedro I, the introduction of federalism in 1834, and increasing fears of social anarchy, deprived the *exaltados* of their political viability.

*See also* **Federalism.**

BIBLIOGRAPHY

Jancsó, István. *Brasil: Formação do estado e da nação.* São Paulo: Editora Hucitec, 2003.

Needell, Jeffrey D. *The Party of Order: The Conservatives, the State, and Slavery in the Brazilian Monarchy, 1831–1871.* Stanford, CA: Stanford University Press, 2006.

RODERICK BARMAN

**EXCÉLSIOR (MEXICO CITY).** For most of the twentieth century the Mexico City newspaper *Excélsior* maintained one of the largest readerships in the country, but political meddling in the 1970s led to a decline in popularity and an eventual sale in 2006. Rafael Alduncin founded the newspaper in 1917 but died six years later. Following his death, *Excélsior* declared bankruptcy, but the 248 workers there restarted the paper in 1924 as a workers' cooperative. Two figures, however, dominated the paper until the 1960s. Gilberto Figueroa successfully managed the business side of the paper, and Rodrigo de Llano directed the editorial page. During the mid-twentieth century, the opinion page of *Excélsior* endorsed moderate positions and generally supported the Institutional Revolutionary Party (PRI), which governed Mexico from 1929 to 2000. Nevertheless, the paper's high journalistic standards and solid news coverage made it one of the most respected and popular papers in the country.

The deaths of Figueroa and de Llano, in 1962 and 1963 respectively, marked a transition for the paper. In 1968, Julio Scherer García took over as editor and promoted independent journalism that took a more critical stance towards government administration, PRI politicians, and the overall absence of Democracy in post-revolutionary Mexico. The paper, for instance, covered in detail the 1968 government massacre of student protestors at Tlatelolco in Mexico City. During the 1970s, prominent Mexican intellectuals such as Elena Poniatowska, Carlos Monsiváis, and Enrique Krauze wrote for

*Excélsior*. Displeased with the paper's critique of his foreign policy and coverage of union repression, President Luis Echeverría Álvarez (1970–1976) in 1976 ousted Scherer García. Over 200 of the paper's writers left in protest. Former *Excélsior* journalists went on to found many of Mexico's most important independent media outlets. Scherer García, for instance, started *Proceso*, a respected leftist weekly magazine focused on investigative journalism. The new *Excélsior* editors supported the governing party, but this stance greatly weakened the reputation of the newspaper. Through the 1990s, the periodical barely survived on government advertising. Opposition candidate Vicente Fox, of the National Action Party (PAN), won the 2000 election and quickly cut off state support for *Excélsior*, causing the paper to experience severe financial stress. The owners ultimately sold the paper in 2006 to Olegario Vázquez Raña, a hotel owner, who then restarted the daily under the name *El Nuevo Excélsior*.

*See also* **Journalism; Mexico: Since 1910; Mexico, Political Parties: Institutional Revolutionary Party (PRI); Mexico, Political Parties: National Action Party (PAN).**

BIBLIOGRAPHY

Lawson, Chappell H. *Building the Fourth Estate: Democratization and the Rise of a Free Press in Mexico*. Berkeley: University of California Press, 2002.

Scherer García, Julio, and Carlos Monsiváis. *Tiempo de saber: Prensa y poder en México*. Mexico City: Aguilar, 2003.

BYRON CRITES

# EXPLORERS AND EXPLORATION

*This entry includes the following articles:*

BRAZIL
SPANISH AMERICA

## BRAZIL

Europeans, at the turn of the sixteenth century, began to explore territories now a part of modern Brazil. In mid–November 1499, Vicente Yáñez Pinzón, a former lieutenant of Christopher Columbus, sailed from Palos in southern Spain and proceeded southwest from the Cape Verde Islands. Late in January 1500 he made a landfall, presumed to be along the present state of Pernambuco, and sailed north and then northwestward along the littoral of South America until he returned to the Caribbean. A month later Diego de Lepe, a kinsman of Yáñez Pinzón, replicated his predecessor's voyage and is believed to have entered the Genipapo River (later called the Pará), which bounds the southern extremity of the island of Marajó at the mouth of the Amazon. Pinzón then traveled about sixty miles up the Amazon. Spain did not pursue the discovery claims of these two Andalusians because much of the coast they traversed belonged to Portugal by the terms of the Treaty of Tordesillas (1494).

### EARLY EXPLORATION

The first Portuguese encounter with the Brazilian littoral occurred on 22 April 1500, when Pedro Álvarez Cabral, commander of the squadron sent from Lisbon to Calicut, India, to follow up the achievements of Vasco da Gama, made contact with some Tupi people near the future harbor of Porto Seguro. There the first mass was said on Brazilian soil. Cabral took possession of the unexpected land, thought to be an island, and his lieutenants wrote King Manuel I concerning Brazil's promise as a haven for distressed ships engaged in sailing to and from India and as an opportunity for evangelization.

The Portuguese crown gained a broader undertanding of Brazil's importance, through an expedition led by Gonçalo Coelho. In 1501 Coelho was sent to Brazil by the king to determine the extent of Cabral's discovery. With three ships he not only examined the coast of the new land between the future states of Pernambuco and Rio Grande do Sul but also named outstanding landmarks in accordance with prominent church days when headlands, bays, river estuaries, and other features were first observed (for example, Cape São Roque, Cape São Agostinho, the São Francisco River, All Saints Bay, Rio de Janeiro, and São Vicente). Gonçalo Coelho returned to Lisbon two years later. The earliest map to include the Brazilian littoral incorporated the findings of the Coelho expedition. Prepared by an unknown cartographer, that planisphere was sent secretly by an Italian diplomat stationed in Lisbon, Alberto Cantino, to his patron, the duke of Ferrara, in 1502.

As the full extent of the seacoast of the new land gradually became known, the names attached to it evolved. Originally called the Island of Vera Cruz (because Cabral, like all navigators of his time, was convinced by medieval geographers that apart from Europe, Asia, and Africa, the land masses of the world consisted exclusively of islands), Brazil was successively termed the Land of the Holy Cross, the Land of Parrots, and, by about 1510, the Land of Brazilwood, after the red dyestuff that became Brazil's first significant export to Europe. That commodity, together with parrots, monkeys, and other exotica, remained Brazil's principal attraction during the first three decades of the sixteenth century while Portugal was establishing its empire in the East. Meantime, a series of navigators in Spain's service, including Juan Díaz de Solís, discoverer of the Río de la Plata; the circumnavigator Ferdinand Magellan; and Sebastian Cabot, seeker of the "city of the Caesars" in Paraguay, sailed along the Brazilian littoral but made no contribution to an understanding of Brazilian geography. It was the intrusions by French competitors, seeking brazilwood and Tupi alliances, that compelled the Portuguese crown to devise the captaincy system during the 1530s to promote the settlement and defense of Brazil.

### COLONIZATION

When this approach failed to secure Portugal's hold upon Brazil, Portuguese officials established a royal government after 1549. Nevertheless it was not until the first decades of the seventeenth century that Portugal's control over Brazil's north coast as far as the Amazon was assured. As the early captaincies were being established, the full extent of the world's greatest river was revealed by a Spanish contingent led by Francisco de Orellana in 1541–1542. Orellana was a lieutenant of Gonzalo Pizarro, governor of Quito (Ecuador), who led a large expedition eastward from the city of Quito in February 1541, seeking what Indian informants assured him was the "land of cinnamon." As the expedition encountered increasing difficulties, he sent Orellana ahead with fifty to sixty men in two brigantines to forage for food and to seek verification of the land's existence. Instead of returning to the Pizarro camp, Orellana sailed the length of the Amazon (February to August 1542), which he named after a serious encounter with the Omagua led by female warriors whose fighting ability seemed to confirm the substance of a widely believed medieval legend.

In 1616, Portuguese forces asserted their claim to one of the major estuaries of the Amazon when they founded the fortress of Santa Maria de Belém do Grão Pará. From this base, a series of patrols eliminated groups of forest-dwelling European competitors in the lower Amazon during the next decade and a half.

During the 1630s the human and natural resources of the Amazon were more closely scrutinized by Portuguese based at Belém and Spaniards from Quito. In 1636 Luís Figueira, a veteran north-coast Jesuit missionary, traveled throughout the lower reaches of the Amazon as far as the Rio Xingu. Figueira's reflections on the Amazon's material and spiritual promise were published in Lisbon in 1637, four years before the appearance of an even more impressive assessment of the river by another Jesuit, the Spaniard Cristóbal de Acuña, author of *Nuevo descubrimiento del gran río de las Amazonas* (1641).

Although Madrid acted promptly to suppress *Nuevo descubrimiento* because it revealed weaknesses concerning Spanish defenses in the interior of South America, it could not undo the damage caused by the action of a Portuguese captain, Pedro Teixeira. Teixeira was directed by the Portuguese governor of the Captaincy of Pará to return to Spanish territory two Franciscan missionaries who had descended the river in 1637. His massive party, some 2,000 people, was clearly intended to send a message to Spanish authorities in the Viceroyalty of Peru. After delivering his charges to Quito, Teixeira headed back to Belém. When he reached the confluence of the Napo and Aguarico rivers (16 August 1639), Teixeira, apparently pursuant to his superior's secret instructions, formally asserted Portugal's possession of the entire Amazon Valley. Although that act was in clear violation of the Treaty of Tordesillas, it served as a basis for Portugal's and later Brazil's claims to legal possession of the Amazon region.

### NATURAL HISTORY

While missionaries, traders, and Indian slavers were assessing the resources of the Amazon, other Portuguese, joined by *Mamelucos* and supported by indigeneous guides, bearers, foragers, and canoe paddlers, were exploiting the resources inland from the coastal captaincies of Pernambuco, Bahia, and especially São Vicente (the future state of São Paulo) and Spanish Paraguay. These roving teams, known as Bandeiras, began their quest in the 1590s and continued until the early decades of the eighteenth century to search the backlands for precious wealth, gems, and minerals, and to pay their expenses by the enslavement of indigenous peoples. Among their accomplishments were the destruction of two entire fields of missions planted by Paraguay–based Jesuits in what is today western São Paulo, Paraná, and Rio Grande do Sul, between 1628 and 1640, the discovery of labyrinthine river systems permitting passage between the seacoast and the remote interior, and the discovery of fluvial gold in a half dozen captaincies between the 1690s and the 1730s. The essential linkage between important southern rivers, such as the Tietê, Paraná, and Paraguay, and the northern rivers, including the Mamoré, Guaporé, Madeira, and Amazon, was demonstrated by the most famous of all of the *bandeiras*, that supposedly led by Antônio Rapôso Tavares, veteran *bandeirante* captain, between 1648 and 1651. His expedition traversed 8,000 miles between São Paulo, western Brazil (Mato Grosso), the Andes, and the length of the Amazon.

Three outstanding assessments of Brazil's human and natural resources were published between 1587 and 1711. Two were by Portuguese secular authors, the other by an Italian–born Jesuit. They include Gabriel Soares de Sousa's *Tratado descritivo do Brasil* (1587), Ambrósio Fernandes Brandão's *Diálogos das grandezas do Brasil* (1618), and Giovanni António Andreoni, S.J., *Cultura e opulencia do Brasil por suas drogas e minas* (1711). Although each is richly informative, none was composed by a scientist. The first scientists (and artists) to describe Brazil's physical and human resources appeared during the Dutch occupation of the Northeast (1630–1654). Most noteworthy was Georg Marcgraf, botanist, zoologist, mathematician, and astronomer, and coauthor with Willem Piso of the seminally important *Historia naturalis brasiliae* (1648), and two famous landscape painters, Frans Post and Albert Eckhout.

No significant advances were made toward the classification of Brazil's flora and fauna and the exploration and mapping of the seacoast and interior between the departure of the Dutch and the mid–eighteenth century. The signing of the Luso–Spanish boundary treaties of 1750 and 1778 led to the dispatch to Brazil of small groups of artists, architects, astronomers, cartographers, engineers, and naturalists. Among them were António Giuseppe Landi, architect and naturalist who labored in the Amazon, and Ricardo Franco de Almeida Serra, who with António Pires da Silva Pontes confirmed the connection between the Branco, Rupununi, and Essequibo rivers. They were followed by the so–called Portuguese Humboldt, Alexandre Rodrigues Ferreira, a Bahian–born naturalist who spent nearly a decade in the Amazon and in Mato Grosso (1782–1792) collecting flora and fauna specimens and recording observations that unfortunately never were published. More successful was Fr. José Mariano da Conceição Velloso, a Minas Gerais–born Franciscan friar who compiled the eleven–volume *Flora fluminense* and found a publisher in Paris (1790).

Oddly, when the French–born naturalist Auguste de Saint–Hilaire accompanied Marshal Andoche Junot, the commander of the French army of occupation, to Lisbon in 1808 and encountered the prints of Conceição Velloso's work, he resolved to proceed to Brazil to undertake his own botanical investigations. Between 1816 and 1821, Saint–Hilaire traveled extensively throughout central and southern Brazil. Beginning in 1830, he published nine volumes of his botanical observations.

Saint Hilaire was only one of a group of foreign scientists and travelers to examine the Brazilian landscape during the period when João VI resided in Brazil (1807–1821). Others included the mineralogist John Mawe, the first foreigner to see and write about the remains of the gold diggings in Minas Gerais. In 1817 a group of Austrian scientists arrived in honor of Brazil's new queen, Maria Leopoldina. Among them were Johann Emanuel Pohl, a botanist and mineralogist; and Johann Natterer, a zoologist at the Imperial Zoological Gardens and a horticulturist, specialist in flower painting, and taxidermist. Natterer spent nineteen years collecting specimens and returned to Vienna only in 1835 to found a special museum dedicated to Brasiliana. By then Pohl had already published his encyclopedic *Plantarum Brasiliae* (Vienna, 1827–1831). Two other scientists were sent by the queen's grandfather, the king of Bavaria, to identify Brazilian resources. They were Johann

Baptist von Spix and Karl Friedrich Philip von Martius. Spix was the curator of the Munich Museum, and the youthful Martius already had an enviable reputation as one of Europe's leading young botanists. Together they traveled overland from central Brazil to the Amazon gathering specimens and providing some of the best quality ethnographic observations on Brazil since the early seventeenth century. Apart from their popular travel account, their *Flora Brasiliensis* (37 folio vols. 1840–1906) was one of the towering descriptions of the uniqueness and richness of Brazil.

An avid naturalist, Georg Heinrich von Langsdorff originally went to Brazil as its first Russian consul general from 1813 to 1820. He returned to the country in 1822 as head of a scientific expedition that included artists Moritz Rugendas and Adrien Taunay. The group went to Minas Gerais in 1824, traveled from São Paulo down the Tietê River in 1825, and in 1827–1828 visited various Bororo peoples. Next, they descended the Arinos and Tapajós, but Langsdorff contracted malaria and purportedly went insane.

Englishman Henry W. Bates explored Brazil from 26 May 1848 to June 1859, collecting over 3,000 new species of insects and other specimens. He began on the lower Amazon and Tocantins rivers and then went up the Solimões. He returned to Belém and settled for three years at Santarém. Sailing up the Amazon again, he spent four and a half years based in Ega (present–day Tefé) before returning home, publishing *The Naturalist on the River Amazon* (1863), and becoming the first paid secretary of the Royal Geographical Society (1864). In 1865, Swiss–born Harvard University professor Jean Louis Rodolphe Agassiz headed an expedition up the Amazon, traveling from Manaus to the Solimões River. Members of the party measured indigeneous peoples on the Amazon, Tapajós, Içá, Jataí, and Branco rivers, while a team of geologists worked in Minas Gerais. In 1867, Sir Richard Burton, then serving as British consul in Santos, ventured to northern Minas Gerais and descended the São Francisco River, encountering Xavange, Xikriabá, and Karirí peoples at São João dos Indios.

Brazilian explorers too made important contributions to the exploration and description of their country. Antônio Gonçalves Dias, head of the ethnographic section of the Imperial Scientific Commission, went to Ceará in 1858–1859 and wrote a Tupi dictionary after studying the Potiguar branch of those peoples. The next year he spent six months on the Amazon visiting the Mawé, Mundurukú, and Mura peoples. His romantic poems inspired the Indianist literary movement. In 1862 José Vieira Couto de Magalhães visited the Xavante, Karajá, and Tupi–speaking Anambé, collecting Tupi legends. He founded Isabel College on the upper Araguaia River for Amerindian children and established forts and steamship navigation on the Araguaia and Tocantins. His journal, *Viagem ao Araguaya* (1863), and his *O selvagem* (1876), discussed methods of acculturation for the descendents of Brazil's pre–Iberian peoples.

In 1871 João Barbosa Rodrigues went to Pará and Amazonas on behalf of the imperial government to conduct scientific studies. He identified many new species of palms and orchids, and published accounts of the Tembé in Pará, the Mundurukú, and Mawé of the Tapajós River, and the Tukâno of the Solimões in Alexandre Jose de Mello Moraes, ed., *Revista da Exposição Anthropologica Brazileira,* published as part of the Anthropological Exhibition in Rio de Janeiro, organized by Ladislau Neto in 1882. In 1884 he founded the botanical gardens of Amazonas in Manaus, which also contained important ethnographic collections. In 1884 he and his wife Constança contacted the Crishana (present–day Waimiri) tribe of the Jauaperi tributary of the lower Rio Negro, described in *Io Jauapery: Pacificaçao dos Crichanás* (1885).

One of the greatest Brazilian explorers of the twentieth century, Cândido Mariano da Silva Rondon, began his career by setting up telegraph lines throughout Amazonia from 1890 to 1915. In 1910 he was made head of the newly created Indian Protection Service and embarked on an exploration of the rivers in present–day Rondônia. In 1913–1914 he traveled with former U.S. President Theodore Roosevelt down the Dúvida (now Roosevelt) River. From 1927 to 1930 he surveyed all of the frontiers and led a mixed boundary commission in 1934–1938 on the Brazilian–Colombian border.

According to John Hemming, the exploration of the Amazon and contact with the indigenous peoples there often brought diseases and devastation to those areas. Nevertheless, the exploration of the Amazon and other parts of Brazil has proceeded inexorably throughout the twentieth century, as its vast territory fascinates the adventurous and those looking for new sources of wealth.

*See also* **Dutch in Colonial Brazil; French Colonization in Brazil; Portuguese Empire.**

BIBLIOGRAPHY

Albuquerque, Luís de, Max Justo Guedes, and Gerald Lombardi. *Portugal–Brazil: The Age of Atlantic Discoveries.* New York: Brazilian Cultural Foundation, 1990.

Bueno, Eduardo. *Náufragos, traficantes e degredados: As primeiras expedições ao Brasil, 1500–1531.* Rio de Janeiro: Objetiva, 1998.

Diacon, Todd A. *Stringing Together a Nation: Candido Mariano da Silva Rondon and the Construction of a Modern Brazil, 1906–1930.* Durham: Duke University Press, 2004.

Espínola, Rodolfo. *Vicente Pinzón e a descoberta do Brasil.* Fortaleza: COELCE, 2001.

Galvani, Walter. *Nau Capitânia: Pedro Álvares Cabral: como e com quem começamos.* Rio de Janeiro: Record, 1999.

Perrone-Moisés, Leyla. *Vinte luas: Viagem de Paulmier de Gonneville ao Brasil, 1503–1505.* São Paulo: Companhia das Letras, 1992.

Voigt, Lisa. "'Por andarmos todos casy mesturados': The Politics of Intermingling in Caminha's Carta and Colonial American Anthologies." *Early American Literature* 40.3 (2005): 407–39.

Dauril Alden

## SPANISH AMERICA

The voyage of Christopher Columbus in 1492, sailing under the flag of Castile, is commonly seen as the beginning of the European exploration of Latin America, even though others, such as Saint Brendan and Leif Eriksson, Africans or Asians, may have arrived centuries before, and even though South and North Americans already had long-term and long-distance trading relationships. What is different between Ecuadorian or Nahua exploration and European exploration is that the latter left written records of their "discoveries." The European Age of Discovery began in 1433 when Portugal sent a succession of captains down the western and southern coasts of Africa in search of a maritime route to the East and access to its spices and silks. Columbus had unsuccessfully sought Portuguese patronage for his plan to reach the East by sailing west, but he found support in Castile, where Ferdinand II of Aragon and Isabella I of Castile agreed to finance his voyage.

### EARLY EXPLORATION

Columbus (Cristóbal Colón) sighted land on October 12, 1492. During his first voyage he explored the northeast corner of Cuba and the island of Bohio, which he rechristened La Isla Española, later to be known as Hispaniola. Following Columbus's discoveries, the Spanish and Portuguese crowns asked Pope Alexander VI to draw what became known as the Line of Demarcation dividing future discoveries between them. On June 7, 1494, both powers signed the Treaty of Tordesillas, which established a line 370 leagues west of the Azores (cutting through present-day Brazil), giving Portugal all lands to the east and Spain those to the west. Columbus completed three more voyages, from 1493 to 1504, in which he explored the Caribbean, established a settlement in Hispaniola at La Isabela (later moved to Santo Domingo, the oldest European city in the Western Hemisphere), and made the first formal landing on the land mass of South America. Following up on these voyages, Alonso de Ojeda sailed in May 1499 and, along with Juan de la Cosa and Amerigo Vespucci, explored along the Caribbean coast from Dragon's Mouth of modern-day Venezuela as far as the Guajira Peninsula of present-day Colombia. Pedro Alonso (Peralonso) Niño and Cristóbal Guerra sailed along the Venezuelan coast from Paria to Cape Codera, and Vicente Yáñez Pinzón, in his controversial voyage, traveled around the Bulge of Brazil, discovering the mouth of the Amazon. When Amerigo Vespucci participated in a year-long exploration of the Brazilian coast beginning in August 1501 he understood that this area was not the extreme shore of Asia, but a world unto itself—a New World.

The next phase of the European exploration of the Western Hemisphere began when Juan de la Cosa captured Darién, Panama, during his 1504 voyage. From that year until 1530, Darién (Panama), Hispaniola, and Cuba would become the launching sites of many expeditions to Mexico and Central and South America. In 1508 Pinzón and Juan Díaz de Solís presumably reconnoitered the coast of Yucatán while Sebastián de Ocampo circumnavigated Cuba, and Juan Ponce De León occupied present-day Puerto Rico. The following year Juan de Esquivel and Pánfilo de Narváez explored Jamaica, Ojeda explored the Caribbean coast of Colombia, and Diego de Nicuesa sailed around the Caribbean coast of neighboring Panama. In September 1513 Vasco Núñez de Balboa discovered the Pacific Ocean; that same year Ponce de León sailed up the Atlantic coast to the Gulf side of present-day Florida. On October 8, 1515, Solís sailed to Brazil, then south to the estuary of the Río de la Plata. Diego de Velázquez, governor of Cuba, dispatched first Francisco Hernández De Córdoba (1517) and then Juan de Grijalva (1518) to search for new discoveries. Hernán Cortés set sail on February 18, 1519, at the same time that Pedro Arias de Ávila (Pedrárias) was supervising the founding of Nombre de Dios and Panama City (August 15, 1519) as terminal points of an interoceanic road, the overland forerunner of the Panama Canal. On April 21, 1519, Cortés had arrived on the Mexican mainland and founded the city of Veracruz. In mid-May 1519 Cortés renounced his position as the agent of Velázquez; he arrived in the center of the Aztec confederacy, Tenochtitlán (modern Mexico City), on November 8, 1519, and conquered it for Spain on August 13, 1521.

Following the fall of the rich empire of Tenochtitlán, Europeans learned of the wealth available to those courageous enough to risk their lives in the New World. From 1521 to the 1550s, Spaniards could explore largely without fear of interference from other European powers. During these decades Cortés traversed Pánuco (north of Veracruz), Cristóbal de Olid traveled through Michoacán, Nuño de Guzmán pillaged Nueva Galicia, and Francisco de Montejo struggled for Yucatán. Meanwhile, Pedro de Alvarado went to Guatemala and Olid led an expedition to Honduras.

### MAGELLAN AND CABOT

At the same time, Spain never abandoned its hope of finding an easy way to Asia. While Cortés was conquering Mexico, Ferdinand Magellan left Spain on September 20, 1519, to search for the connecting strait between the seas and reach the East. He sailed to Brazil, entered the strait that now bears his name on October 21, 1520, and arrived in the present-day Philippines on March 16, 1521, where he got involved in a local power struggle and was killed in the Battle Mactan by Lapu-Lapu, the Muslim *datu* (king) of the Visayan people, Mactan Island, Cebu. The Basque Juan Sebastián El Cano (or del Cano) continued the voyage and arrived at the Spice Islands (Ternate and Tidore) on November 8, 1521. Sebastián Cabot, originally dispatched as a follow-up to Magellan, became diverted at the Río de Solis (Río de la Plata). He founded Sancti Spíritus on May 19, 1528, and explored the Paraná and the Paraguay rivers as far north as the junction with the Pilcomayo River, at present-day Asunción. In 1535 Simón de Alcazaba Sotomayor entered the Strait of Magellan and explored Patagonia, and the following year Pedro de Mendoza founded Puerto de Santa María del Buen Aire (present-day Buenos Aires), while Juan de Ayolas sailed up the Paraná and built the settlement and fort of Corpus Christi near modern-day Santa Fe on June 15, 1536. He continued beyond the junction of the Paraná and Pilcomayo to Corumbá on February 2, 1537, and was exploring the region near present-day Bolivia when he was killed by the people he encountered there. Juan de Salazar y Espinosa founded Nuestra Señora de la Asunción on August 15, 1537.

***The Northern Pacific.*** While these men searched the southern Atlantic and Pacific, Cortés began the exploration of the northern Pacific and on May 3, 1535, discovered the Bahia de La Paz (which he called the Santa Cruz). In 1542 Juan Rodríguez Cabrillo sailed from Acapulco and explored the western shore of Baja California as far north as the present California-Oregon border. He died at sea, leaving Bartolomé Ferrelo to pilot the ships home.

***Southward toward Peru.*** While Spain explored Mexico and the Pacific Ocean, it was also marching south from Panama toward the wealthy empire described by Balboa. In 1522 Pascual de Andagoya explored the coast of northwestern Colombia, and Pedro Arias de Ávila founded Natá on the western edge of the Bay of Panama on May 20, 1522. Gil González Dávila progressed farther up along the Pacific coast of Costa Rica around Lake Nicaragua, and in 1525 Francisco Hernández De Córdoba explored Nicaragua, initially as the agent of Árias.

The exploration of Tahuantinsuyo or the Inca Empire proceeded in several phases. Francisco Pizarro and Diego de Almagro participated in a voyage of exploration and reconnaissance from 1526 to 1528. Subsequently, Pizarro sailed to Spain to secure the rights to the conquest of this new territory from Charles V, which he received in

**Gonzalo de Pizarro (c. 1502–1548) Kills Diego de Almagro (1475–1538)** (woodcut) by Felipe Huaman Poma de Ayala (1526–1613). BIBLIOTECA DEL ICI, MADRID, SPAIN/ INDEX/ THE BRIDGEMAN ART LIBRARY

the Capitulation of Toledo in 1529. Upon his return to Panama, Pizarro launched the conquest of Peru in January 1531. He arrived by sea and marched overland to Tumbes, which he regarded as the gateway to the Inca Empire. On May 16, 1532, Pizarro marched inland and founded San Miguel in July. He arrived in Cajamarca on November 15, taking the Inca emperor Atahualpa prisoner the next day. Almagro arrived in mid-February 1533, and Atahualpa was summarily tried and executed on July 26, 1533. Pizarro and Almagro traveled along the Inca highway, arriving in Cuzco on November 14 or 15, 1533. On January 18, 1535, Pizarro founded a new capital, La Ciudad de los Reyes (present-day Lima), near the coast. In 1545 silver was discovered in Potosí, located in present-day Bolivia.

***Northern South America.*** Not all explorers went to Peru, however. Juan de Ampíes sailed from Santo Domingo and founded Coro, Venezuela, on July 26, 1527. On February 24, 1529, Ambrosio Alfinger, a factor of the Welser banking family, took over the colony in payment of debts owed by the Spanish crown. On September 1, 1530, he led an expedition west across Lake Maracaibo and founded the city of the same name. On September 12, 1530, Nicolás Féderman, Alfinger's deputy, explored south of Coro to the east of Maracaibo as far south as Acarigua and Barquisimeto. Diego de Ordás explored the Orinoco River Basin from its mouth as far as the cataracts of Atu in 1531–1532, the precursor of many searches for El Dorado. On August 5, 1532, Pedro de Heredia sailed from Spain, founding Cartagena, Colombia, the following year. Gonzalo Jiménez de Quesada led an expedition from Santa Marta on April 5, 1536. He followed the Magdalena River first to La Tora, then proceeded over the Andes and founded the city of Santa Fé de Bogotá on August 6, 1538.

***North America.*** The Spaniards also continued north from the Caribbean. Lucas Vásquez De Ayllón established San Miguel de Gualdape in the vicinity of Sapelo Sound in present day Georgia, the first European settlement in the lands that would later become the United States, in 1526. Two years later, Panfilo de Narváez led a disastrous expedition to Florida, from which only four members, including the African slave Esteban and Alvar Núñez Cabeza de Vaca, ultimately reappeared, surfacing in Mexico in July 1536 after years spent wandering across North America among various nations and peoples. Fray Marcos de Niza and Esteban went north in an unsuccessful search for the rumored Seven Cities of Cíbola; only Fray Marcos returned, telling tales of golden villages. In 1540 Francisco Vázquez de Coronado hunted for those cities, traveling as far as present-day Kansas. His lieutenant, García López de Cárdenas, discovered the Grand Canyon, but Coronado found no gold. Nor did Peruvian conquistador Hernando de Soto, who explored the southeast of the United States from 1539 to 1543, discovering the Mississippi River.

***Searching for New Treasure.*** Most explorers searched for territories such as Mexico and Peru that they could claim for the crown and themselves. Some went north, like Sebastián de Belalcázar, who left San Miguel in October 1533, arriving in Riobamba on his march toward present-day Quito. (The Incas, hearing of his approach, burned the city and fled with Atahualpa's treasure.) Belalcázar entered Quito at the end of 1533, but used Riobamba as his headquarters until Quito was rebuilt. As they searched for the treasure, Belalcázar and his assistant, Juan de Ampudia, then founded Guayaquil (1534), Portoviejo (1534), Popayán (1536), and Cali (1537). Following the conquest of Peru, Gonzalo Pizarro went to Quito as governor in December 1540. Two months later, joined by his kinsman Francisco de Orellana, Pizarro set out to explore lands to the east. When the expedition failed, Orellana sailed down the Napo River, entering the Amazon on February 11, 1542. He returned to the Paria Peninsula at Cubagua on September 9, 1542 after six months exploring the Amazon.

Almagro left Cuzco on July 3, 1535, to seek his fortune southward, toward present-day Chile. By March 1536 his party had marched through the Andes and arrived at the valley of Aconcagua. Almagro became dissatisfied and returned to Peru to contest Pizarro's possession of Cuzco. After the death of Almagro, the exploration of Chile was undertaken by one of Pizarro's lieutenants, Pedro de Valdivia. He arrived via the coastal route at the present-day valley of the Copiapó River, and marched farther south, founding present-day Santiago on February 12, 1541. In 1543 Diego de Rojas left Cuzco to search for a province between Chile and the Río de la Plata. He reached Tucumán but died en route, and Francisco de Mendoza then commanded soldiers on the march to the original settlement of Sebastián Cabot on the Paraná. Valdivia returned to Chile as governor in April 1549 and founded numerous cities, including Concepción (1550) and Valdivia (1552), before he died in December 1553. Juan Francisco de Aguirre crossed the Andes in 1552 and founded the Argentine city of Santiago del Estero in 1553.

### POST-1550 EXPLORATION

By the 1550s Spain was no longer alone in the New World, and its exploration would often come in response to foreign threats to its sizeable possessions, which included the entire Caribbean and the Western Hemispheric mainland from Zacatecas, Mexico, to Valdivia, Chile, and Patagonia, Argentina. During the centuries that followed, Spain went north through present-day Mexico into Texas, the Southwest, and California; took possession of the Philippines; explored the Amazon, Paraguay, and Argentina; but lost almost all of the Caribbean and the opportunity to claim much of present-day Brazil.

Once silver mines were discovered in Zacatecas, Mexico, in 1546, explorers were eager to march farther north, often accompanied by priests who established *reducciones* (missions) along the way. Francisco de Ibarra founded Durango in 1563. Two years later Pedro Menéndez De Avilés led an expedition to fight the French in Florida. In 1565 he founded present-day Saint Augustine, the oldest still-existing European city in the United States, and the following year members of his group founded Santa Elena in present-day South Carolina. Juan Pardo marched from that colony to present-day North Carolina, and in 1573, Pedro Menéndez Márquez explored the Chesapeake Bay area. But the Spanish soon lost the area north of Saint Augustine to British attack.

***Northern Mexico and the Amazon.*** The Spanish continued exploring northern Mexico. In 1581 Fray Augustine Rodríguez and Captain Francisco Sánchez Chamuscacho led an expedition into New Mexico, as did Antonio de Espejo the next year. In 1598 Juan de Oñate crossed the Rio Grande at El Paso and marched to San Gabriel, founding San Juan de los Caballeros. Later, as governor, Oñate descended the Colorado River to the Gulf of California (1604–1605). His successor, Pedro de Peralta, founded Santa Fe in 1610, two years after the French founded Quebec and three years after the British built Jamestown. Spaniards traversed the Pimeria Alta (present-day northern Sonora and southern Arizona), founding Sinaloa (1593) and settlements along the Mayo (1614), Yaqui (1617), and Sonora (1636) rivers.

In October 1560 Pedro de Ursúa and Lope de Aguirre began to sail down the Amazon. By July 1, 1561 Aguirre had entered the North Atlantic, the second successful transcontinental crossing of the river. The Portuguese quickly wrestled with the Spanish for control of the Amazon. In January 1616 the Portuguese entered the mouth of the Amazon and constructed Fort Presepio, the precursor of present-day Belém, in Pará state. In 1622 Luis Aranha de Vasconcelos explored the eastern third of the river, mapping the lower Amazon as it split into two branches. In 1638 Pedro Teixeira arrived in Quito from Belém with orders to establish a Portuguese settlement west of the Line of Demarcation.

In the march northward from Mexico, Fray García de San Francisco y Zúñiga founded the Misión de Nuestra Señora de Guadalupe in El Paso del Norte in 1659. Fray Damián Mazanet built Misión San Francisco de los Tejas near the banks of the Trinity River in 1690. In 1718 Misión San Antonio de Valero (the Alamo) was founded, followed by Misión San José y San Miguel de Aguayo; in the San José Valley in 1720.

The exploration of the Southwest continued under the leadership of the Jesuit father Eusebio Kino. In 1700 he founded the Misión San Xavier del Bac in Tucson, Arizona, and in March 1701, he discovered that present-day Baja California was a peninsula, not an island. In 1706 New Mexico governor Francisco Cuervo y Valdes founded Albuquerque and Juan de Ulibarri explored the area of the upper Arkansas River. Spanish explorers of the Midwest, however, now faced a conflict with the French, who had become established since the explorations of Jacques Marquette and Louis Joliet in 1673 and René-Robert Cavelier de LaSalle in 1685–1687.

In the eighteenth century, Spaniards explored and colonized present-day California in response to news of Russian threats to their control of the area. In 1769 Captain Gaspar de Portolá and Fray Junípero Serra led an expedition to Alta California and founded San Diego. By 1782 Serra had founded eight more missions, including Misión San Gabriel Arcángel in Los Angeles (1771). Juan Bautista de Anza commanded an expedition from Fort Tubac, Arizona, to San Francisco Bay and on March 28, 1776, selected the sites for the Presidio of San Francisco and Mission San Francisco de Asis, which although were established by others later on, represent the origins for present-day San Francisco, California. During those same years Fray Francisco Atanasio Domínquez and Fray Silvestre Vélez De Escalante explored Arizona, New Mexico, Colorado, and Utah. With the founding of Misión Santa Bárbara in 1786, the Spanish completed their exploration of the Western Hemisphere.

*See also* **Colonialism; Explorers and Exploration: Brazil; Spanish Empire.**

BIBLIOGRAPHY

*Primary Sources*

Cabeza de Vaca, Alvar Núñez. *Naufragios.* Ed. Roberto Ferrando. Madrid: Historia 16, 1984. There are many editions in Spanish and English.

Casas, Bartolomé de las. *Historia de las Indias*, 3 vols. Edited by André Saint-Lu. Caracas: Biblioteca Ayacucho, 1986.

Colón, Cristóbal. *Textos y documentos completos.* Edited by Consuelo Varela. Madrid: Alianza, 1984.

*Secondary Works*

Bedini, Silvio A., ed. *The Christopher Columbus Encyclopedia*, 2 vols. New York: Simon & Schuster, 1992.

Bethell, Leslie, ed. *Cambridge History of Latin America*, vols. 1–2. Cambridge, U.K.; New York: Cambridge University Press, 1984.

Boorstin, Daniel. *The Discoverers*, 2 vols. New York: H. N. Abrams, 1991.

Diffie, Bailey W. *A History of Colonial Brazil, 1500–1792.* Malabar, FL: R. E. Krieger Publishing, 1987.

Gerhard, Peter. *A Guide to the Historical Geography of New Spain.* Cambridge, U.K.: Cambridge University Press, 1972.

Goodman, Edward J. *The Explorers of South America.* New York: Macmillan, 1972.

Hemming, John. *Red Gold: The Conquest of the Brazilian Indians, 1500–1760.* Cambridge, MA: Harvard University Press, 1978.

Hemming, John. *Amazon Frontier: The Defeat of the Brazilian Indians.* Cambridge, MA: Harvard University Press, 1987.

Lucena Salmoral, Manuel, coord. *Historia de Iberoamérica*, tomo 1, *Prehistoria e historia Antigua.* Madrid: Cátedra, 1982

Mignolo, Walter. "The Movable Center: Ethnicity, Geometric Projections, and Coexisting Territorialities." In *The Darker Side of the Renaissance*, 2nd edition. Ann Arbor: University of Michigan Press, 2003.

Morales Francisco, Padrón. *Historia del descubrimiento y conquista de América*, 5th edition. Madrid: Gredos, 1990.

Morison, Samuel Eliot. *The European Discovery of America*, vol. 2. New York: Oxford University Press, 1974.

O'Gorman, Edumndo. *The Invention of America.* Westport, CT: Greenwood Press, 1961.

Parry, John H. *The Discovery of South America.* New York: Taplinger Publishing, 1979.

Van Sertima, Ivan. *They Came before Columbus: The African Presence in Ancient America.* New York: Random House, 1976.

*Maps*

Fernández-Armesto, Felipe, ed. *The Times Atlas of World Exploration: 3,000 Years of Exploring, Explorers, and Mapmaking.* New York: HarperCollins, 1991.

Wolff, Hans, ed. *America: Early Maps of the New World.* New York; Neues Publishing, 1992.

BRIAN LORDAN
THOMAS WARD

---

**EXTRACTIVE RESERVES.** Extractive reserves are tropical forest areas set aside as a public trust for sustainable development by local residents. They first appeared in Brazil in 1990 with the formation of the 1,250,000-acre Chico Mendes Extractive Reserve. The idea is said to have originated in 1985 at the first national conference of Brazilian rubber tappers in Brasilia. This meeting formally united the tappers with environmentalists who were interested in saving the Amazon rain forest from destruction by loggers and builders of roads and dams. Struggling to protect their livelihood against encroaching cattle ranchers, miners, and land-hungry settlers, the tappers had already formed cooperatives such as the Projeto Seringueiro (Rubber Gatherers Project) of Acre. United, they strengthened their bargaining power with rubber merchants and pooled resources for food production, education, and health care. Whereas the environmentalists envisioned the establishment of pristine national parks, the tappers sought support for their co-operatives.

The anthropologist Carlos Teixeira is said to have coined the term *extractive reserves*, which was presented as a positive alternative to capitalist development strategies and promised to save both the forest and the way of life of those who exploited its abundance in the least destructive manner. The details of the concept were elaborated in Brazil's 1987 agrarian reform law.

The idea helped consolidate support for rain forest protection in Brazil and abroad. Nongovernmental agencies, already enamored of sustainable development schemes in other contexts, embraced the idea, as did politicians, human and cultural rights groups, and ecologists. In other Latin American countries, where tropical forests formerly had been preserved as national parks and Indian reservations, new campaigns were inspired by the Brazilian model. As in Brazil, anthropologists and environmentalists joined with local peasants, such as resin tappers in Honduras and nut gatherers in Peru, to establish extractive reserves. In Costa Rica foreign pharmaceutical companies encouraged establishing reserves in order to protect potential medicinal resources from being destroyed. Extractive reserves have been debated in Belize, Bolivia, Colombia, Ecuador, Mexico, and Venezuela. Ironically, the movement became even stronger after the 1988 assassination of Francisco Chico Mendes Filho, a leader among Brazilian rubber tappers and a principal force behind the 1985 conference. In March 1990 Brazil created the first extractive reserve, the 1,250,000-acre Reserva Extrativista Chico Mendes. Others were created in Brazil in later years, including five in 2002 alone.

Critics charge that as a protective entitlement, the reserves interfere in the free flow of market forces and block economically depressed Latin American nations from fully exploiting their natural resource wealth. Even some supporters of the reserve concept believe they ultimately will fail, given capitalist pressure to exploit Latin American's resources, and they advocate more diversified strategies for the protection of the forest and its people. Lines on the map, they say, will not be able to stop the in-migration of masses of hungry settlers, exploitation by debt-ridden governments, and entrepreneurs anxious to capitalize on forest resources.

In fact, the reserves depend on government protection, and few Latin American states have been able to commit adequate funding to the task. In 2007 the Brazilian president Luis Inacio Lula da Silva asked rich countries to compensate poor countries such as his for setting aside forest in different forms of reserves. All the same, studies show that the reserves have been effective in reducing forest destruction, with Indian reservations being the most effective barrier and extractive reserves just a little more effective than uninhabited parks. Thus, whereas fires set by commercial agricultural interests have continued to destroy rain forests, the reserve system has saved millions of acres from destruction. Extractive reserves have the added benefit of raising *seringueiro* income and autonomy.

*See also* **Forests; Rubber Gatherers' Unions.**

BIBLIOGRAPHY

Allegretti, Mary Helena. "Chico Mendes: tempo de convicção e ideologia." *Revista Parabolicas* (São Paulo, Brazil) 44 (1998).

Nepstad, Daniel C., and Stephan Schwartzman. "Extractive Reserves Examined: Non-Timber Products from Tropical Forests, Evaluation of a Conservation and Development Strategy." *Bioscience* 43, no. 9 (October 1993): 644–646.

Nepstad, Daniel C., et al. "Inhibition of Amazon Deforestation and Fire by Parks and Indigenous Lands." *Conservation Biology* 20, no. 1 (2006): 65–73.

Place, Susan E., ed. *Tropical Rainforests: Latin American Nature and Society in Transition.* Wilmington, DE: Scholarly Resources, 1993.

Revkin, Andrew. *The Burning Season: The Murder of Chico Mendes and the Fight for the Amazon Rain Forest.* Boston: Houghton Mifflin, 1990.

CLIFF WELCH
BASTIAAN P. REYDON
RAIMUNDO CLÁUDIO GOMES MACIEL

## EZPELETA Y GALDEANO DICASTILLO Y DEL PRADO, JOSÉ MANUEL DE

**EZPELETA Y GALDEANO DICASTILLO Y DEL PRADO, JOSÉ MANUEL DE** (1742–1823). José Manuel de Ezpeleta y Galdeano Dicastillo y del Prado (*b.* June 1742; *d.* 23 November 1823), captain-general of Cuba (1785–1789), viceroy of New Granada (1789–1797).

Born in Barcelona of Basque parentage, Ezpeleta came to Havana in 1779 as colonel of the Regiment of Navarre. During the American Revolution, he commanded the advance on Pensacola from Mobile (1780–1781). Later, after serving with distinction as captain-general of Cuba, he was promoted to viceroy of New Granada. An enlightened, effective administrator, Ezpeleta ranked among the best of New Granada's viceroys. He faced the monumental tasks of soothing the political tensions that had lingered since the *Comunero Revolt* (1781) and reducing the colonial debt through curtailing the size of the army and eliminating unproductive programs.

He was acutely embarrassed when Antonio Nariño published the *Declaration of the Rights of Man and the Citizen*, obtained from his own personal library. Replaced by Pedro Mendinueta y Muzquiz at the end of his term, Ezpeleta returned to Spain, becoming governor of the Council of Castile and captain-general (1797–1798) and, later, councilor of state (1798), captain-general of Catalonia (1808), and viceroy of Navarre (1814–1820).

*See also* **Nariño, Antonio; New Granada, Viceroyalty of.**

BIBLIOGRAPHY

Beerman, Eric. "José de Espeleta." *Revista de historia militar* (1977): 97–118.

Kuethe, Allan J. *Military Reform and Society in New Granada, 1773–1808.* Gainesville: University Press of Florida, 1978.

F. De Borja Medina Rojas, *José de Ezpeleta, gobernador de La Mobila, 1780–1781.* Sevilla: Escuela de Estudios Hispano-Americanos de Sevilla, 1980.

ALLAN J. KUETHE

## FABELA ALFARO, ISIDRO (1882–1964).

Isidro Fabela Alfaro (*b.* 29 June 1882; *d.* 12 August 1964), Mexican public figure and international jurist who contributed numerous works on international politics and law and taught international law for many years at the National University. With expertise in international arbitration from his long career in foreign relations, he was appointed a judge of the International Court of Justice, the Hague (1946–1952).

Fabela was born in Atlacomulco, in the state of México, which subsequently produced many leading political figures. He was the son of Francisco Trinidad Fabela and Guadalupe Alfaro. In 1909, Fabela was one of the founders of the Ateneo de la Juventud, which included José Vasconcelos and Antonio Caso y Andrade. He began his public career in Chihuahua in 1911 and became a federal deputy under Francisco Madero in 1912–1913. Under Venustiano Carranza he served as secretary of foreign relations (1914–1915), after which he held a variety of diplomatic posts, eventually representing Mexico in 1937–1940 at the International Office of Labor. He governed his home state of Mexico from 1942 to 1945.

*See also* **Judicial System: Spanish America; Madero, Francisco Indalecio.**

BIBLIOGRAPHY


Fedro Guillén, *Isidro Fabela* (1970?).

Baldomero Segura García, *Antología del pensamiento universal de Isidro Fabela* (1959).

Michael C. Meyer, "A Venture in Documentary Publication: Isidro Fabela's *Documentos Históricos de la Revolución Mexicana*," in *Hispanic American Historical Review* 52 (1972): 123–129.


*Additional Bibliography*


Guillén, Fedro. *Fabela y su tiempo: España, Cárdenas, Roosevelt*. Mexico City, 1976.

Ordóñez, Andrés. *Devoradores de ciudades: Cuatro intelectuales en la diplomacia mexicana*. Mexico City: Cal y Arena, 2002.

Zea Prado, Irene. "Isidro Fabela y su causa: América Latina." *Cuadernos Americanos* 48, Nueva época (November–December 1994): 173–180.


RODERIC AI CAMP

## FABINI, [FÉLIX] EDUARDO (1882–1950).

[Félix] Eduardo Fabini (*b.* 18 May 1882; *d.* 17 May 1950), Uruguayan composer and violinist. Born in Solís de Mataojo, Lavalleja, Fabini studied violin with Romeo Masi at the Conservatorio La Lira in Montevideo; he also received instruction under Virgilio Scarabelli and Manuel Pérez Badía. At the age of eighteen Fabini entered the Royal Conservatory in Brussels and enrolled in the classes of César Thomson (violin) and Auguste de Boeck (composition). In 1904 he was awarded the first prize with distinction in violin. Upon his return to Uruguay he gave recitals and performed chamber music in Montevideo. During his years in Brussels Fabini began to compose works for piano and guitar based on tunes, rhythms, and dances from the folk traditions of his homeland. With Alfonso Broqua and Luis Cluzeau-mortet, he became a major exponent of musical nationalism in Uruguay. His best-known work is the symphonic poem *Campo.* Premiered by Vladimir Shavitch on 29 April 1922, it is considered Uruguay's major nationalist work of the period. Richard Strauss conducted it in Buenos Aires in 1923. *Campo* and *La isla de los ceibos* (1924–1926), another symphonic poem, were recorded by RCa Victor in the United States. *Mañana de Reyes* (1936–1937), *Melga sinfónica* (1931), and the ballet *Mburucuyá* (1933) completed Fabini's symphonic production. He also composed several *tristes* for piano and voice. He died in Montevideo.

*See also* **Music: Art Music; Music: Popular Music and Dance; Uruguay: The Twentieth Century.**

BIBLIOGRAPHY

Roberto E. Lagarmilla, *Eduardo Fabini: Músico nacional uruguayo* (1954); *New Grove Dictionary of Music and Musicians,* vol. 6 (1980).

Susana Salgado, *Breve historia de la música culta en el Uruguay,* 2d ed. (1980).

### *Additional Bibliography*

Barrios Pintos, Aníbal. *Eduardo Fabini* Montevideo: Arca, 1978.

Paraskevaídis, Graciela. *Eduardo Fabini: La obra sinfónica.* Montevideo: Ediciones Tacuabé; Ediciones Trilce, 1992.

SUSANA SALGADO

## FACIO BRENES, RODRIGO (1917–1961).

**FACIO BRENES, RODRIGO** (1917–1961). Rodrigo Facio Brenes (*b.* 23 March 1917; *d.* 7 June 1961), perhaps the most influential social and political thinker in twentieth-century Costa Rica. Facio, son of a Panamanian immigrant father, served as both national deputy (1948–1949) and rector of the University of Costa Rica (1952–1961), whose main campus today bears his name.

Facio earned his law degree in 1941, at the age of twenty-four, with the thesis *Estudio sobre economía costarricense* (1942), which was to have enormous influence on subsequent generations. He had already organized the Law Students Cultural Association in 1937 and was a key figure in the Center for the Study of National Problems (1940). This group became, after 1945, the Democratic Action and Social Democratic parties, which led eventually to the formation of the National Liberation Party after its victory in the 1948 civil war. He was an assembly deputy in 1949 and, subsequently, a director and vice president of the Central Bank. After many years of working with party leader José Figueres Ferrer, Facio broke with him out of anger at not being chosen to succeed Figueres as the presidential candidate for 1962. He left Costa Rica to work for the Inter-American Development Bank. He drowned soon afterward in El Salvador.

Facio's other major historical works are *La moneda y la banca central en Costa Rica* (1947) and *La federacíon de Centroamérica: Sus antecedentes, su vida y su disolucíon* (1957).

*See also* **Costa Rica; Judicial Systems: Spanish America.**

BIBLIOGRAPHY

Basic sources on Facio include Jorge Enrique Romero Pérez, *La social democracia en Costa Rica* (1982); Raúl Hess Estrada, *Rodrigo Facio, el economista* (1972); and Carlos Molina, *El pensamiento de Rodrigo Facio y sus aportes a la ideología de la modernización capitalista en Costa Rica* (1981).

### *Additional Bibliography*

Castro Vega, Oscar. *Rodrigo Facio en la constituyente de 1949.* San José: Editorial Universidad Estatal a Distancia, 2003.

Rodríguez Vega, Eugenio. *Ideas políticas de Rodrigo Facio.* San José: Editorial Universidad Estatal a Distancia, 1990.

LOWELL GUDMUNDSON

## FACIO SEGREDA, GONZALO (1918–).

**FACIO SEGREDA, GONZALO** (1918–). Gonzalo Facio Segreda (*b.* 28 March 1918), Costa Rican ambassador to the United States on three occasions, former president of congress, minister of justice, and foreign minister.

Facio was appointed ambassador to the United States in 1990 by the newly inaugurated president of Costa Rica, Rafael Angel Calderón Fournier (*b.* 1949). His credentials included nearly one half-century of prominence in political, cultural, and economic affairs. His most salient contributions have been in international affairs.

Born in San José, Facio entered the national scene while he was still in law school and was a founding member of the Center for the Study of National Problems (March 1940). He graduated from the University of Costa Rica in 1941. During the social reform–oriented government of Rafael Angel Calderón Guardia (1940–1944), the Center developed a social democratic alternative to the Calderón–led alliance between the National Republican Party and a communist party, the Bloque de Obreros y Campesinos (BOC), which was renamed the Popular Vanguard Party (PVP) in 1943.

He entered the direct action group under the leadership of José Figueres Ferrer, which paved the way for the armed uprising that overthrew the Teodoro Picado Michalski administration (1944–1948) after the disputed election in February 1948. After the successful revolt, Figueres appointed Facio minister of justice in the Founding Junta of the Second Republic (1948–1949), where he played an active role in suppressing communists and Calderónist leaders who had held high–level positions in the previous two administrations (1940–1948) through the establishment of special courts, such as the Court of Immediate Sanctions, which tried public officials who served between 1940 and 1948 for offenses committed, and the Court of Probity, which intervened the property of public officials who served during that same period. The decisions of these courts could not be appealed.

After the return to constitutional government in 1949, he worked actively with Figueres to form the National Liberation Party (PLN), which represented the ideological position of the junta and the revolutionary movement that brought it to power. With Figueres's election to the presidency in 1953, Facio served as president of congress (1953–1958). He served as foreign minister under Figueres in his third presidency (1970–1974) and also under Daniel Oduber Quirós (1974–1978). Facio later broke with the PLN and became active in the Unidad coalition that elected Rodrigo Carazo Odio (1978–1982) and Rafael Angel Calderón Fournier (1990–1994) to the presidency.

Facio has also been active in business, professional, and academic affairs and has served as an officer and board member for several organizations. He has published numerous articles on national and international politics. He holds a doctorate in law from New York University.

*See also* **Costa Rica, National Liberation Party.**

BIBLIOGRAPHY

Ameringer, Charles. *Don Pepe.* Albuquerque: University of New Mexico Press, 1978.

Araya Pochet, Carlos. *Liberación nacional en la historia política de Costa Rica, 1940–1980.* San José: Editorial Nacional de Textos, 1982.

Bell, John Patrick. *Crisis in Costa Rica.* Austin: Institute of Latin American Studies, University of Texas Press, 1971.

English, Burt H. *Liberación Nacional in Costa Rica.* Gainesville: University of Florida Press, 1971.

JOHN PATRICK BELL

**FACÓN.** Facón, a long, swordlike knife, the gaucho's favorite and most dangerous weapon. Worn thrust through the back of the gaucho's broad, leather belt (*tirador*), the *facón* could easily inflict death in a duel. When dueling, a gaucho wrapped his poncho around one arm as a shield. Knife fights became storied events in gauchesque literature, like José Hernández's *Martín Fierro* (1872–1879) and Eduardo Gutiérrez's *Juan Moreira* (1879). Government officials repeatedly outlawed the dangerous weapon, but gauchos rejected firearms in favor of the *facón* through the twentieth century. They generally used smaller *facones* for eating, skinning animals, and fashioning equipment out of leather.

*See also* **Gaucho.**

BIBLIOGRAPHY

Madaline Wallis Nichols, *The Gaucho* (1968), p. 13.

Ezequiel Martínez Estrada, *X-Ray of the Pampa* (1971).

Richard W. Slatta, *Gauchos and the Vanishing Frontier* (1983); *Cowboys of the Americas* (1990), p. 150.

### Additional Bibliography

Assunção, Fernando O. *Historia del gaucho: El gaucho, ser y quehacer.* Buenos Aires: Editorial Claridad, 1999.

De la Fuente, Ariel. *Children of Facundo: Caudillo and Gaucho Insurgency during the Argentine State-Formation Process (La Rioja, 1853-1870).* Durham: Duke University Press, 2000.

Domenech, Abel. *Dagas de Plata: Cuchillos criollos rioplatenses historia y coleccionismo.* Buenos Aires: Casano Gráfica S.A., 2005.

Slatta, Richard W. *Comparing Cowboys and Frontiers.* Norman: University of Oklahoma Press, 1997.


RICHARD W. SLATTA

**FACTOR.** In the late Middle Ages, merchants in foreign countries often grouped themselves into a community enjoying mutual protection and sometimes special privileges vis-à-vis local authorities. The head of such a foreign merchant group or colony was termed the "factor" and the community the "factory." Bruges, for example, in the fourteenth and fifteenth centuries, was the site of Portuguese and Castilian factories through which much of those nations' trade with northern Europe was channeled.

When the Portuguese began their expansion down the west coast of Africa, they adapted and made use of this system by establishing fortified warehouses and administrative offices through which they dealt with the native merchants. Such factories (*feitorias*) were established at Arguin in 1451 and at São Jorge de Mina in 1481.

Similarly, shortly after the discovery of Brazil in 1500, the merchant group that had leased the trade rights from the king established a factory there (1504) in order to have a place to store the dyewood awaiting shipment to Portugal. While claims have been made for the existence of Portuguese factories at various points along the coast in the period 1502–1534, according to the historian Rolando Laguardia Trías there was only one indisputable factory in Brazil before the arrival of Martim Afonso de Sousa, and until recently it was thought to have been located at Cabo Frio. Trías, however, gives good reasons for thinking that it was actually situated on an island in Guanabara Bay (Rio de Janeiro). In 1516, with expiration of the royal lease and the crown's resumption of direct control over Brazilian trade, this factory was moved north to Itamaracá near the present-day town of Igaraçu, both because better quality brazilwood was found there and because the site was closer by ship to Lisbon.

*See also* **Brazilwood; Portuguese Overseas Administration.**


BIBLIOGRAPHY

*História naval Brasileira,* vol. 1 (1975), pp. 254–256.

John Vogt, *Portuguese Rule on the Gold Coast, 1469–1682* (1979).

A. H. De Oliveira Marques, *Ensaios de história medieval Portuguesa,* 2d ed. (1980), pp. 164–166, 178–179.

### Additional Bibliography

Bueno, Eduardo. *Náufragos, traficantes e degredados: As primeiras expedições ao Brasil, 1500-1531.* Rio de Janeiro: Objetiva, 1998.

Machado, Paulo Pinheiro. *A política de colonização do Império.* Porto Alegre, RS: Editora da Universidade, Universidade Federal do Rio Grande do Sul, 1999.


HAROLD B. JOHNSON

**FACTORY COMMISSIONS, BRAZIL.** Brazil Factory Commissions, unofficial shopfloor committees of rank-and-file workers formed to bargain directly with employers. As early as the 1910s, industrial workers in São Paulo organized informal shop-floor committees, known as *comissões de fábrica.* Women textile workers pioneered this form of organizing in response to their exclusion from the male-dominated anarchist unions of their day. When the women's independent factory commissions initiated successful strike movements (e.g., São Paulo's General Strike of 1917), anarchist activists moved to incorporate the *comissões* in their union structures.

Male and female Brazilian workers were drawn to these shop-floor commissions because unions were often quite weak in the first half of the twentieth century. The local *comissões* offered workers not only an ongoing organization that they controlled, but also a form of local microunionization that survived government and industrialist repression of labor and leftist leadership cadres.

The factory commissions initially served as a tool that groups without access to power in anarchist and socialist unions (e.g., women) used to bargain with their employers. With the establishment of a corporatist industrial-relations system in the 1930s and early 1940s, male and female workers throughout Brazil were forced to rely on their own factory-level organizations because the state-sponsored *sindicatos* did not effectively support workers' demands.

Factory commissions took on the leadership of Brazil's labor movement at various times. In 1945–1947, workers who were organized in such commissions launched widespread strike movements throughout the country. In the early and mid-1950s, men and women who were organized in separate commissions took control of government-sponsored *sindicatos*. The commission structure became increasingly important during the 1964–1985 military dictatorship. Once again, by relying on nominally democratic, local organizations such as the *comissões*, industrial workers could maintain a de facto union structure even during a period of intense government repression.

The founders of the Brazilian Workers Party (Partido dos Trabalhadores—PT) relied on the factory-commission experience in the late 1970s and the 1980s. Metalworkers in São Paulo's industrial suburbs organized *comissões* within their factories as the bases for direct negotiations with their employers and eventually for establishing new, highly representative unions.

*See also* **Brazil, Political Parties: Workers Party (PT); Labor Movements.**

BIBLIOGRAPHY

For an analysis of the development of factory commissions in the 1910s and their continued importance to workers throughout the 1950s, see Joel Wolfe, *Working Women, Working Men: São Paulo and the Rise of Brazil's Industrial Working Class* (1993). On commissions in the 1945–1950 period, see Ricardo Maranhão, *Sindicato e democratização: Brasil, 1945–1950* (1979). A detailed study of the commission structure in the founding and ongoing operation of the Workers Party is presented in Margaret E. Keck, *The Workers Party and Democratization in Brazil* (1992).

*Additional Bibliography*

Renner, Cecília Ornellas. *Duas estratégias sindicais: O sindicato metalúrgico de S. Paulo e o de S. Bernardo do Campo, 1978-1988*. São Paulo: Letras à Margem, 2002.

Weinstein, Barbara. *For Social Peace in Brazil: Industrialists and the Remaking of the Working Class in São Paulo, 1920-1964*. Chapel Hill: University of North Carolina Press, 1996.

JOEL WOLFE

---

**FACUNDO.** *See* **Quiroga, Juan Facundo.**

---

**FADO.** Fado, the national song of Portugal. The fado is a folk music and dance form embodying the popular customs, poetic traditions, and cultural heritage of the Portuguese people. The fado, derived from the Latin *fatum* meaning fate, expresses the melancholic nature of destiny. Themes of the fado range from the travails of unrequited love to the matador's anxiety before a bullfight. Plaintive descriptions of lonely moonlit rivers and desolate cobblestone streets imbue this music with a sense of *saudade*, a Portuguese word referring to the yearning for the unattainable. Although some musicologists contend that the fado is entirely of Brazilian origin, research suggests that its roots include Provençal poetry, Moorish culture, and medieval troubadour songs.

Since achieving national popularity in the mid-nineteenth century, the fado has been associated with two principal styles: the fado of Lisbon, sung in cafés and taverns, and the University of Coimbra fado, performed by strolling student troubadours extolling their masculinity. Accompanied by the twelve-string Portuguese lute and the Spanish six-string guitar, singers of the fado, or *fadistas*, deliver their lyrics with a great sense of tragic drama. Whether sung in modern fado houses or on concert stages in Europe and America, the fado offers a chronicle of Portuguese history and culture. An influential *fadista* of the twentieth century was Amália Rodrigues (1920–1999). Recent stylistic changes in fado include the addition of electronic music, new instruments, and a return to nineteenth-century traditional song. Contemporary artists include Mariza, Mísia, and Tereza Salgueiro.

*See also* **Music: Art Music; Music: Popular Music and Dance; Portugal.**

BIBLIOGRAPHY

Rodney Gallop, "The Fado: The Portuguese Song of Fate," *Musical Quarterly* 19 (1933): 199–213.

Mascarenhas Barreto, *Fado: Origens liriicas e motivacao poetica* (1961).

Marvine Howe, "Fado in Portugal," *Saturday Review* (September 12, 1970): 49, 108.

David P. Appleby, *Music of Brazil* (1983).

### *Additional Bibliography*

Tinhorão, José Ramos. *Fado, dança do Brasil, cantar de Lisboa: O fim de um mito.* Lisboa: Editorial Caminho, 1994.

Velho, Gilberto. *Antropologia urbana: Cultura e sociedade no Brasil e em Portugal.* Rio de Janeiro: J. Zahar Editor, 1999.

Vernon, Paul. *A History of the Portuguese Fado.* Brookfield, U.K.: Ashgate, 1998.

JOHN COHASSEY

## FAGES, PEDRO

**FAGES, PEDRO** (1734–1794). Pedro Fages (*b.* 1734; *d.* 1794), Spanish soldier and explorer. Fages, a native of Guisona, Catalonia, joined the Barcelona-based Catalonian volunteers in 1767 and participated in the Sonora Expedition of 1767–1771 in Mexico. In 1769 Visitador General José de Gálvez ordered him and twenty-five Catalonian Volunteers to join Governor Gaspar de Portolá's California expedition. Between 1769 and 1774, Fages participated in the founding of San Diego, the march to Monterey that named many sites in California, and the discovery of San Francisco Bay. Nicknamed "The Bear" ("El Oso"), Fages was the European discoverer of the Central and San Joaquín Valleys. In 1774 he wrote *A Historical, Political, and Natural Description of California,* an important ethnographic account of the area featuring references to its flora and fauna. Between 1774 and 1778, Fages commanded the Second Company of Catalonian Volunteers in Guadalajara. In 1776 he married Eulalia Callis, daughter of Agustín Callis, captain of the First Company of Catalonian Volunteers. In 1778 Fages served in Sonora, where in 1781 he commanded troops in the Colorado River campaign against the Yuma Indians who had destroyed a Spanish outpost at the confluence of the Colorado and Gila Rivers. In 1782 he was the first European to reach San Diego by crossing the Colorado River. He served as governor of California from 1782 to 1791, a generally peaceful time of mission building. Fages died in Mexico City.

*See also* **California; Catalonia Volunteers; Colorado River; Sonora.**

BIBLIOGRAPHY

Donald A. Nuttall, "Pedro Fages and the Advance of the Northern Frontier of New Spain, 1767–1782" (Ph.D. diss. University of Southern California, 1964).

Joseph P. Sánchez, *Spanish Bluecoats: The Catalonian Volunteers in Northwestern New Spain, 1767–1810* (1990).

### *Additional Bibliography*

Rodríguez Sala de Gomezgil, María Luisa, and Pedro López González. *Exploraciones en Baja California y Alta California, 1769-1775: Escenarios y personajes.* Mexico City: UNAM, Instituto de Investigaciones Sociales: Amat, 2002.

Soler Vidal, Josep. *California, la aventura catalana del noroeste.* Mexico: Libros del Umbral, 2001.

JOSEPH P. SÁNCHEZ

## FAGOAGA Y LIZAUR, JOSÉ MARÍA

**FAGOAGA Y LIZAUR, JOSÉ MARÍA** (1764–1837). José María Fagoaga y Lizaur (*b.* 1764; *d.* 1837), Mexican politician. Fagoaga was born in Villa de Rentería, Guipúzcoa, Spain, of a distinguished family, and educated in Mexico City. A determined autonomist, he was in contact with like-minded individuals, among them the marqués de San Juan de Rayas and Jacobo de Villaurrutia. Fagoaga held several important posts, including magistrate of the criminal chamber (1808–1812) and member of the Ayuntamiento of Mexico (1812). As a member of the secret society of Los Guadalupes, he aided the insurgents and later took part in the electoral processes established by the Constitution of Cádiz. He was elected to the Provincial Deputation in 1813 and in 1820 and served as deputy to the Cortes in 1814 and in 1820. Well known for his dissatisfaction with the colonial regime, Fagoaga was imprisoned and prosecuted in 1815. He was deported to Spain, but returned in 1821, in time to sign the Declaration of Independence and to become a member of the Provisional Governing Junta. He was one of the founders of the Scottish rite Masonic lodges, the *escoceses,* and he distinguished himself as a parliamentarian. In 1822 Fagoaga was one of the deputies imprisoned by Agustín de Iturbide. When the Spanish were expelled in 1827, he was forced into exile. Although Fagoaga subsequently returned to Mexico, he no longer participated in politics. He died in Mexico City.

*See also* **Peimbert, Margarita; Sánchez de Tagle, Francisco Manuel.**

BIBLIOGRAPHY

*Diccionario Porrúa de historia, geografía y biografía de México,* 5th ed. (1986), vol. 1, pp. 1,049–1,050.

Virginia Guedea, *En busca de un gobierno alterno: Los Guadalupes de México* (1992).

*Additional Bibliography*

Gómez Alvarez, Cristina, and Miguel Soto, editors. *Transición y cultura política: De la colonia al México independiente.* Mexico City: Facultad de Filosofía y Letras, Dirección General de Asuntos del Personal Académico, Universidad Nacional Autónoma de México, 2004.

Luna Argudín, María. "De Guadalupes a borbonistas: Desarrollo y proyección política de Fagoaga, Sardaneta y Sánchez de Tagle, 1808–1824." *Secuencia: Revista de Historia y Ciencias Sociales* 38 (May–August 1997): 24–49.

Méndez Reyes, Salvador. "José María Fagoaga y el dictamen de la comisión de esclavos." *Cuadernos Americanos* 84 nueva época (November–December 2000): 171–179.

VIRGINIA GUEDEA

## FAJARDO, FRANCISCO (c. 1524–1564).

Francisco Fajardo (*b.* ca. 1524; *d.* 1564), conquistador in Venezuelan territory. Fajardo was the son of a Spanish male and a female Indian chieftain of the Guaquerí tribe. He undertook various expeditions from Margarita Island to the mainland beginning in 1555 and in 1557 obtained authorization from the governor of El Tocuyo to rule and settle the coast. During a 1559 expedition, Fajardo headed inland and reached as far as the Valley of La Guaire, site of present-day Caracas. He returned to the coast, where he founded the settlement of El Collado. On a second expedition to La Guaire Valley, Fajardo discovered gold in Teque Indian territory. When the governor learned of the discovery Fajardo was stripped of his authority and sent to El Collado as its chief justice. In his place, Pedro Miranda was sent to exploit the gold, but he quickly alienated the local *cacique,* Guacaipuro. There followed a series of clashes in which Fajardo aided the Spanish forces despite his dispute with the governor. By 1562 the Indians had driven the Spanish from the valley and forced Fajardo to abandon El Collado. As Fajardo was provisioning yet another expedition in the settlement of Cuma-ná in 1594, he was arrested by the local chief justice. Though the charges are unclear, he was tried and sentenced to death. In retaliation, his followers on Margarita Island went to Cumaná and seized the chief justice, Alonso Cobos, whom they tried before the Audiencia of Santo Domingo, where he too was sentenced to death.

*See also* **Conquistadores.**

BIBLIOGRAPHY

Jesús Antonio Cova, *El capitán poblador margariteño Francisco Fajardo* (1954).

Juan Ernesto Montenegro, *Francisco Fajardo: Origen y perfil del primer fundador de Caracas* (1974).

Graciela Schael Martínez, *Vida de Don Francisco Fajardo* (1975).

INÉS QUINTERO

## FALCÓN, JOSE (1810–1883).

Jose Falcón (*b.* 1810; *d.* 1883), Paraguayan archivist, historian, and government official. Born in Asunción in the year of Platine independence, Falcón was well placed to participate in many key events during his country's formative years. Educated in the capital, he lived in seclusion in the far south of the country with his wealthy *hacendado* uncle during the dictatorship of José Gaspar Francia. In 1844, President Carlos Antonio López chose Falcón as Paraguay's first foreign minister. In this capacity, he convinced foreign powers—especially Brazil, Britain, and the United States—to recognize Paraguay's independence. After stepping down from the foreign ministry, Falcón served successively as justice of the peace, criminal court justice, and, finally, director of the national archive (from 1854), which he organized along modern European lines.

When Francisco Solano López succeeded to the presidency in 1862, he named Falcón to the posts of interior minister and foreign minister. Falcón also remained director of the archive, which he had to move several times during the War of the Triple Alliance (1864–1870) as Brazilian forces advanced into Paraguay. He also witnessed some of the worst scenes of the war, notably the massacres at San Fernando, where many of his colleagues in government were executed on López's orders.

Falcón's fortunes improved after the war. He again occupied many official posts: senator, high court justice, president of the Asunción city council, and, once again, foreign minister. He helped to establish the Colegio Nacional in 1877. During the mid-1870s he went to Argentina to negotiate boundary agreements with that country.

During his thirty-six years of government service, Falcón kept copious notes, which he always meant to weave into a series of historical studies and memoirs. Although evidently these were never published, they are available in manuscript in the Manuel Gondra Collection in the Nettie Lee Benson Library at the University of Texas, Austin.

*See also* **López, Francisco Solano; Paraguay: The Twentieth Century; War of the Triple Alliance.**

BIBLIOGRAPHY

Justo Pastor Benítez, *Carlos Antonio López (Estructuración del estado paraguayo* (1949), pp. 245–246.

Harris Gaylord Warren, *Paraguay and the Triple Alliance: The Postwar Decade, 1869–1878* (1978).

Andrew R. Nickson, *Historical Dictionary of Paraguay* (1993).

*Additional Bibliography*

Benítez, Luis G. *Cancilleres y otros defensores de la República: Documentos.* Asuncíon: Talleres Reprográficos de S.R.L. Ind. & Com., 1994.

THOMAS L. WHIGHAM

## FALCÓN, JUAN CRISÓSTOMO

(1820–1870). Juan Crisóstomo Falcón (*b.* 1820; *d.* 29 April 1870), Venezuelan president (1863–1868). Born in Coro (now Falcón) Province to a wealthy landowning family, Falcón participated in the civil wars of the mid-nineteenth century and rose to the rank of general. He was the outstanding commander of the Federalist armies in Venezuela's bloody Federal War (1859–1863) and, as a reward for leading the victorious forces, he was named provisional president in 1863. Falcón's five years in office were marked by administrative ineptitude, corruption, civil turmoil, and rebellion. Uninterested in the day-to-day operations of government, he spent long periods of time in his home province of Coro. In 1868 a temporary coalition of liberals and conservatives raised the banner of the Blue Revolution and drove the largely discredited president into exile, from which he never returned.

*See also* **Federalism; Venezuela: Venezuela since 1830.**

BIBLIOGRAPHY

Robert L. Gilmore, *Caudillism and Militarism in Venezuela, 1819–1910* (1964).

Guillermo Morón, *A History of Venezuela,* edited and translated by John Street (1964).

José Luis Salcedo Bastardo, *Historia fundamental de Venezuela,* 3d rev. ed. (1972).

*Additional Bibliography*

Banko, Catalina. *Las luchas federalistas en Venezuela.* Caracas: Monte Avila Editores, 1996.

WINFIELD J. BURGGRAAFF

## FALKLAND ISLANDS (MALVINAS).

The Falkland Islands (Islas Malvinas) comprise an archipelago of approximately 200 islands located in the South Atlantic, 298 miles from the Patagonian coast. Its principal islands are West Falkland (Gran Malvina) and East Falkland (Soledad). Its current political status is as an overseas autonomous territory under British control. It has 3,000 inhabitants, 2,000 of which live in its capital, the city of Port Stanley (Puerto Argentino) located on East Falkland. The residents call themselves Falkland Islanders.

The climate is cold and humid, with strong, steady winds. The terrain is rocky, covered with grass, moss, and bushes. Marine fauna is plentiful, and includes native and migrating birds, cetaceans, crustaceans, fish, and mollusks. Squid fishing is the principal economy activity, followed by sheep farming, the export of high-quality wool, and tourism. Permits have been issued for petroleum exploration, the results of which are not yet decisive.

The archipelago was occupied by the French and the English around 1760, and then became part of the Spanish Empire in the late eighteenth century. The United Provinces of the River Plate considered themselves the heirs to the Spanish Crown, and in 1820 they claimed ownership of the islands. After conflicts with U.S. fishing vessels and a punitive expedition by the United States, the United Kingdom began a military occupation of the islands in 1833. Following almost 150 years of diplomatic demands, the Argentine military dictatorship took over the islands by force in April 1982, with widespread domestic support. The British government, with the support of a United Nations Security Council resolution, sent an expeditionary force to the islands. After a few short air and naval battles, the British forces landed at San Carlos Water on May 21 and obtained the surrender of the Argentine forces on June 14. The conditions of the Falkland Islanders improved noticeably from that point: They were declared British citizens with full rights, and a new phase of great prosperity was ushered in with the advent of British investment and the exploitation of marine resources. Argentina continues to demand its territorial rights over the islands.

*See also* **Falklands/Malvinas War; Vernet, Louis.**

BIBLIOGRAPHY

Goebel, Julius L. *The Struggle for the Falkland Islands.* New Haven, CT: Yale University Press, 1927.

Gustafson, Lowell S. *The Sovereignty Dispute over the Falkland (Malvinas) Islands.* New York: Oxford University Press, 1988.

Smith, Wayne S., ed. *Toward Resolution? The Falklands/Malvinas Dispute.* Boulder, CO: Lynne Rienner, 1991.

VICENTE PALERMO

**FALKLANDS/MALVINAS WAR.** The Falklands/Malvinas War, which broke out in 1982 after a long-standing dispute between Argentina and Great Britain, was the most serious outbreak of interstate conflict involving a Latin American nation since the Chaco War of the 1930s. The historic causes of the 1982 war go back to eighteenth-century disputes between Spain and Great Britain over settlement and possession of the islands. In 1833, shortly after Argentina gained independence from Spain, the British expelled the remaining Argentine settlers and began their period of continuous occupation of the islands. During his first administration (1946–1955) Argentine president Juan Domingo Perón focused on the Malvinas issue in an appeal to Argentine nationalism, linking it to the Argentine Antarctic claim and his plan to create a "greater Argentina." In 1965 a United Nations resolution called on both parties to resolve the issue peacefully, but meaningful negotiations were blocked by the islanders themselves, who strongly preferred to remain under British administration.

For many years the Argentine military had contingency plans for an invasion of the islands, and in early 1982 these plans were activated when a number of circumstances convinced the ruling military junta, headed by Army Commander General Leopoldo F. Galtieri, that the time was right. These circumstances included the fact that the junta was losing control over Argentina and was seeking some cause to unite the country under its leadership; the coming of the symbolic 150th anniversary of British possession; a diminishing British military and financial commitment to its South Atlantic possessions; geopolitical links to Argentina's Antarctic and Beagle Channel interests; and, finally, a jurisdictional incident involving the Argentine scrap metal dealer Constantino Davidoff on the island of South Georgia in March 1982.

Argentina "recovered" the islands on April 2, 1982, with an amphibious task force of 5,000 men that overwhelmed the small Royal Marine garrison after a short firefight. The British military and civilian authorities were expelled via Montevideo, and the approximately 2,000 islanders were placed under the authority of the Argentine military governor. International reaction reflected shock and surprise that possession of a few seemingly unimportant islands could have led to the invasion. The Argentine military government had hoped that the United States would support them, but President Ronald Reagan firmly backed the British and provided them with military supplies. Most of Latin America supported Argentina's position on the sovereignty issue, although not necessarily the use of force. The UN Security Council quickly passed a resolution favorable to Britain, which then promptly mounted a naval task force that set sail on April 5, 1982. In Argentina there was euphoria over the recovery of the islands, and for a while it seemed that the junta had achieved its objective of distracting most Argentines from the abuses and failures of their government.

The first military action after the invasion of the Falkland Islands took place on the island of South Georgia in late April as the ships of the British task force neared the operational area. On April 25 the British retook South Georgia, damaging and capturing an Argentine submarine in the process. For the next three weeks the war was fought in the air and sea around the Falkland Islands as the British prepared for their landing on the islands. In the principal air and naval actions, the Argentines lost a cruiser and numerous aircraft; the British lost two destroyers, two frigates, and a landing ship. After the sinking of the cruiser *Belgrano*, with a loss of over 300 lives, the Argentine ships stayed in port or close to shore, and most of the fighting was undertaken by the Argentine Air Force.

The ground war began with the British amphibious landing at San Carlos on May 21. The British crossed East Falkland and hit weak Argentine defensive positions around the capital of Port Stanley. Although some regular Argentine Army and Marine units fought effectively, the majority of the Argentine infantry were recruits with little training and poor leadership who resisted only briefly before falling back to Port Stanley and eventually surrendering on June 14, 1982.

The war cost the Argentines 746 killed, 1,336 wounded, and 11,400 imprisoned (the remaining force at the time of surrender). The British suffered 256 killed and 777 wounded. In addition, three Falkland Island civilians were killed in the final assault on Port Stanley. The political consequences of the war included the strengthening of British Prime Minister Margaret Thatcher's Tory Party and her subsequent reelection. In Argentina there was strong resentment of the military's misjudgment and deception; the junta was dismantled and Argentines inaugurated an elected civilian president, Raúl Alfonsín (1983–1989), in December 1983. Full diplomatic relations between Argentina and Great Britain remained broken for eight years. For the 2,000 Falkland islanders the war meant that their status as British subjects was secure, at least for the midterm, although their lives had been altered by both the war and the large and expensive garrison the British now felt obliged to keep on the islands. Postwar disputes over control of foreign fishing vessels and reports of possibly substantial oil fields in the waters surrounding the Falkland Islands have added resource issues to this longstanding dispute between Argentina and Great Britain. One final consequence of the war was that any hope for an amicable settlement of the Falklands/Malvinas sovereignty dispute was set back for many years to come. In 2007, the twenty-fifth anniversary of the conflict, Argentina's President Nestor Kirchner continued to press Argentina's claims to the islands.

*See also* **Alfonsín, Raúl Ricardo; British-Latin American Relations; Falkland Islands (Malvinas); Galtieri, Leopoldo Fortunato; Kirchner, Néstor; Perón, Juan Domingo.**

BIBLIOGRAPHY

Max Hastings and Simon Jenkins, *The Battle for the Falklands* (1983).

Oscar Raúl Cardoso et al., *Malvinas: La Trama Secreta* (1983).

Alberto R. Coll and Anthony C. Arend, eds., *The Falklands War: Lessons for Strategy, Diplomacy, and International Law* (1985).

Rubén O. Moro, *The History of the South Atlantic Conflict* (1989).

Lawrence Freedman and Virginia Gamba-Stonehouse, *Signals of War: The Falklands Conflict of 1982* (1990).

*Additional Bibliography*

Boyce, David George. *The Falklands War.* New York: Palgrave Macmillan, 2005.

Gúber, Rosana. *Por qué Malvinas? De la causa nacional a la guerra absurda.* Buenos Aires: Fondo de Cultura Económica, 2001.

JACK CHILD

**FALLAS SIBAJA, CARLOS LUIS** (1909–1966). Carlos Luis Fallas Sibaja (*b.* 21 January 1909; *d.* 6 May 1966), the best-known and most widely translated Costa Rican author, primarily through his classic work *Mamita Yunai* (1941). Fallas was an indefatigable labor organizer and politician who played a key role in the formation of the Communist Party in 1931 and in the Atlantic Coast banana workers' strike of 1934. Often writing from an autobiographical perspective in his novels, Fallas had worked as a youth of sixteen in the banana plantations of Límon province and on the docks of the port of Limón, loading the fruit. He knew firsthand the oppressive and absurd conditions suffered by local residents at the hands of the United Fruit Company and corrupt local politicians.

Fallas returned to his native Alajuela in the Central Highlands in 1931 and joined in the newly formed Communist Party as a leader of his fellow shoemakers in that city. The court system "exiled" him to Limón in 1933 for an incendiary speech; he then took up the task of organizing the banana workers, whose 1934 strike was by far the largest labor mobilization in Costa Rican history to that date. He was imprisoned briefly but later served as national deputy (1944–1948) before assuming a major military leadership role on the losing side of the 1948 civil war. He was again jailed and spent a year in prison, being the last prisoner released owing to his refusal to request a pardon from the Figueres-led junta. Over the next nearly twenty years Fallas led the fight to regain formal political rights for the defeated Communist Party, serving finally as *regidor* of the San José municipal government (1966).

Although he completed only eight years of formal schooling, Fallas could count on a rich store of life experiences. His *Mamita Yunai* emerged from a report on the manipulation of the 1940 presidential voting in the Talamanca region in far southeastern Costa Rica. Likewise, his other major novels (*Marcos Ramírez*, 1952; *Gente y gentecillas*, 1947) are based on working-class life in his home town. Fallas received recognition abroad for his literary achievements long before local cultural authorities would challenge political conventions at home. *Mamita Yunai* was widely read, and the novel *Marcos Ramírez* won a William Faulkner Foundation Prize in 1963. Fallas was officially declared Benemérito de la Patria on 14 November 1967, but his life and work still remain polemical subjects in Costa Rica.

*See also* **Communism; Costa Rica; Fruit Industry; Labor Movements; Literature: Spanish America.**

BIBLIOGRAPHY

Basic sources on Fallas include Marielos Aguilar, *Carlos Luis Fallas: Su época y sus luchas* (1983); and Victor Manuel Arroyo, *Carlos Luis Fallas* (1977).

*Additional Bibliography*

Molina Jiménez, Ivan. *Ensayos políticos.* San José: Editorial de la Universidad de Costa Rica, 2000.

Ortíz Ortíz, María Salavadora. "La novela de plantación bananera centroamericana: Espacio de reconstrucción de la memoria." *Casa de las Américas* 213 (October–December 1998): 24–36.

LOWELL GUDMUNDSON

---

**FAMILY.** It would be difficult to overemphasize the role of the elite family in the organization of the colonial economy (production and distribution) and in the development of political institutions in Latin America. One explanation is that both Spain and Portugal established the family as the appropriate institution for purposes of settlement, land distribution, and political power. For example, Spain preferred to award *encomiendas* (grants of Indian labor) to married men (who were, preferably, married to Spanish women). These *encomenderos* (who also received a seat on the city council) were required to establish a Casa Poblada, a house on the town square of the Spanish seat of government large enough to house thirty-five people and to supply horses and arms sufficient for seventeen men. One result of this policy was that many of the *encomendero*'s Spanish relatives or friends migrated and became a part of his effective extended family and business arrangements.

In Brazil the Donatario system that originally was intended to facilitate settlement and development also resulted in the dominance of the original grantee and his relatives. Land grants were based on the productive potential (capital, slaves) of the petitioner and led to a system of Latifundia, in which a small group of families had effective control over production. In the same way, the Brazilian city councils were made up of *homens boms* (good men). "Good men" were defined as married men of property, legitimate birth, and clean blood (i.e., no Jewish or Moorish background and no history of vile occupations, such as merchant). "Good men" were "elected" by the "good men" already serving on the council. Thus the hierarchy reproduced itself. The city councils had unusual importance in Brazil because there were so few crown administrators. Many villages were literally hundreds of miles from the residence of any official. The "royal judges" constantly traveled between towns and villages, attempting to provide some semblance of law. But much of this was completely ineffective, and only the power of the dominant families and their personal "armies" determined what could happen within a settlement.

In terms of economic development, the elite family was essential. Neither the Spanish nor the Portuguese crown provided much in terms of resources to build public buildings, roads, or port facilities. Nor did they provide armies separate from the colonial militias. Instead, it was the elite families who organized contributions of building materials, slave labor, and other materials for these projects. True, the Indians in Repartimiento labor in Spanish America also worked and often died working on public projects, but the labor of these Indians was directed through elite Spanish *encomenderos,* who organized the gathering of appropriate materials. For Brazil these tasks were always performed by the slaves of elite families who contributed their labor for the cause.

Elite families in Latin America intermarried with each other, creating within politically defined regions clusters of kin who controlled both politics and the local economy. In addition, the inherited Iberian trait of "patriarchalism," enforced through law and tradition, gave the male head of lineage authority over his kindred throughout the colonial period. By the nineteenth century, it was the domestic group, rather than the kindred, that was dominated by the patriarchal figure.

Inheritance was the major means of property distribution until the end of the nineteenth century, when limited partnerships and incorporation laws were passed. In the absence of limited liability, prudence dictated that business partners also be cousins or brothers-in-law. Furthermore, most elite men established their households and businesses with the help of their wife's dowry until the nineteenth century, when other factors such as education became more important and the dowry gradually disappeared.

Indigenous families in Latin America went through an exceedingly difficult period in the sixteenth century, when from 40 to 90 percent of them died, mostly of European diseases brought in by the conquistadores. The recovery of these populations involved substantial miscegenation with Europeans and Africans, as well as the forced coresidence of tribes (*congregación*) formerly hostile to each other. Indigenous families utilized the European institution of ritual kinship to reestablish ties of reciprocity and exchange in their shattered communities. This means of "family creation" was also adopted by African slaves brought in from diverse areas of Africa, who sometimes also viewed those who traveled in the same slave ship as members of their family.

In religious and legal terms the Latin American family system was based on European categories. Kinship was bilateral, with kin counted on both the maternal and the paternal side. It was also widely extended, with kinship recognized to the seventh or tenth degree. Ritual kinship (*compadrazgo* in Spanish) had substantial importance as both a means of recognizing reciprocal obligations and as a category that required church dispensation for marriage to take place. It could also be used to reinforce a kin relationship or to formalize a patron-client relationship, and was highly significant as a means of expanding kindred on an interclass basis. Divorce and remarriage had been common among the pre-Hispanic cultures of Latin America. While the Catholic Church sometimes allowed "separation of bed and board" in exceptional circumstances, remarriage was never permitted in colonial Latin America. Furthermore, spouses were legally required to cohabit.

The average household in eighteenth- and nineteenth-century Latin America was relatively small (between four and six free members), both in urban and rural areas, with more affluent households generally being larger. This picture is similar to that of Europe over three centuries. What was unexpected, however, was the evidence that household size in Latin America increased significantly in both the rural and urban areas during the nineteenth century as the domestic unit expanded its productive capacity and oriented itself toward the marketplace. Just as families played an important role in the development of roads and other infrastructures and were important sources of credit, so also the early stages of commercialization and industrialization were almost always organized through the household. The low levels of liquid capital, the precarious condition of markets, and poor communications all meant that factories developed very slowly and that, for a long time, households followed a mixed economy of subsistence and market production. At a later stage in industrialization, the participation of the household and family in the exchange economy ceased to be a matter of choice. Capitalism overpowered prior modes of production as the economy took on an export character.

From the late eighteenth century until at least 1870, commercialization and protoindustrialization in Latin America were characterized by urban communities with 25 to 45 percent female-headed households. In some cases they were more common than couple-headed or single-male–headed households. This is particularly startling, for the female-headed household has never been the modal type in published studies of European or American communities, nor have female-headed households typically been portrayed as exceeding 10 to 15 percent of total households in a comparable historical period elsewhere. The high frequency of the female-headed household in eighteenth- and nineteenth-century Latin America appears to have been related to the peculiar characteristics of the changes in modes of production in Latin America and to the development of protoindustrial households based on domestic industry.

The prevalence of this form of household in nineteenth-century Latin America suggests much greater autonomy for women of all classes than had been perceived previously. It indicates that the nineteenth-century domestic unit was determined more by the productive organization of the household than by consumption, sexual ties, or affective needs. The reproductive unit (a mother with her children) was generally retained, but stable couple units were notable by their absence, particularly among the urban lower classes.

Female-headed households in the early nineteenth century were predominantly lower-class and involved in such occupations as subsistence agriculture (in the rural areas), textile or cigarette manufacture, and services such as laundering, ironing clothes, or preparing food to sell in the street. Many female-headed households were created through the dissolution of consensual unions that had been organized around the domestic mode of production in agriculture. The commercialization of agriculture resulted in a change in productive patterns and the migration of many men to areas of agricultural employment, leaving women and children either to continue subsistence agriculture or to migrate in search of better opportunities in urban areas. In the nineteenth century, development efforts tended to victimize the lower-class family, as they still do today.

Another dimension of eighteenth- and nineteenth-century household organization was the presence of nonrelated members (*allegados, agregados*), particularly in lower-class or female-headed urban households, often comprising up to 30 percent of household members. Accepting *allegados* into a household appears to have been a major strategy to alleviate financial difficulties in periods of urbanization and economic change for both family and nonrelated members. In some cases the nonrelated members may simply have been boarding with a family, either paying money or providing services such as housework, child care, water carrying, and the like. Housing shortages also accounted for some of this development. Still another dimension of the presence of nonrelated members in the household was the expansion in this period of the workshop attributes of the household. It became common to include apprentices, clerks, cashiers, and other helpers involved in the productive side of the household in its residential arrangements. Elite families also commonly incorporated *agregados* (including orphans, relatives, Indian captives in Brazil, and others) into their households, where they generally functioned as domestic servants.

Today, families in urban working-class communities depend on wages for support, though these are often uncertain and frequently insufficient to cover the needs of the household. Consequently household members try to acquire access to auxiliary resources, including extra employment benefits, state services, nonmonetary inputs from home production, and benefits from wider exchanges among kin or neighbors. In addition, the household often has multiple earners as well as earners with multiple employment.

Positive mechanisms utilized by poor households to defend themselves against inadequate wages and poor access to social services have been characterized as "family survival strategies." In the case of female-headed families, the increase in poor households headed by women is directly related to processes of modernization, including internal and international migration, mechanization of agriculture, the development of agribusiness, urbanization, overpopulation, lower-class marginality, and the emergence of a class system of wage labor. Female-headed households are not only more likely to be poor than are other households, but they are also less likely to be employed in formal-sector jobs and, therefore, are frequently excluded from other benefits associated with employment.

In twentieth-century rural communities, household size, the organization of household labor, the use or sale of household production, and the overall mode of production continue to be closely related. Important strategies for survival and social mobility among peasant families include marriage, fertility, inheritance, and migration. Among Peruvian peasant families, it is common for the youngest son to inherit the parents' house, living with them in their declining years and taking over the farm after their deaths by purchasing the inheritance shares from his siblings. In some areas, the migration of adult children to new farmlands (in order to avoid extreme parcelization of properties) has been succeeded, as lands become unavailable, by migration to urban areas for employment, as well as by rural wage labor. Remittances from migrants in the United States to family members in their home countries have in fact become critical to the overall economic growth in Mexico and Central America. In Mexico, only oil and *maquiladora* profits surpass revenue from remittances. Diverse family survival strategies involving several workers and types of relations (wage laborer, sharecropper, unpaid family laborer, estate tenant) are commonly joined for mutual benefit. Thus, while proletarianization makes labor more of an individual enterprise, it may still be strongly oriented toward family goals.

Often scholars of the family have assumed an "ideology of solidarity and cooperation within the family." Recent studies, although acknowledging that such an ideology exists, have emphasized that it is important to know how economic changes affect power relations within the household and family. For example, the proletarianization of rural labor in Brazil may have resulted in a decline in the solidarity of the lower-class rural family. This occurs because the husband cannot fulfill his role as provider and because the redefinition of wage labor tasks by gender has forced women and young girls into the most intensive, seasonal, and the lowest-paying jobs. Women give their entire wage to the household, but the older sons resist, paying only room and board, and the husband keeps drinking money. Many women resent having to accept wage labor and prefer to care for their houses and their families themselves. In addition, women's labor is often used to facilitate the entrance of children into the labor force. People sometimes ask whether the contemporary family in Latin America has declined in importance as compared to the colonial period. While modernization has definitely changed the definitions and roles of the family, in the twenty-first century the family and kin network continue to be the primary units on which individuals depend for support, regardless of their class. In that regard, the Latin American family will always be critical.

*See also* **Agregado; Children; Class Structure in Modern Latin America; Donatários; Encomienda; Marriage and Divorce.**

BIBLIOGRAPHY

Gilberto Freyre, *The Masters and the Slaves,* translated by Samuel Putnam (1933); *Journal of Family History,* special issues on Latin America: 3, no. 4 (1978), 10, no. 3 (1985), and 16, no. 3 (1991).

Elizabeth Kuznesof, "Household and Family Studies," in K. Lynn Stoner, ed., *Latinas of the Americas: A Source Book* (1989), pp. 305–388.

Ramón A. Gutiérrez, *When Jesus Came, the Corn Mothers Went Away: Marriage, Sexuality and Power in New Mexico, 1500–1846* (1991).

### *Additional Bibliography*

Borges, Dain. *The Family in Bahia, Brazil, 1870–1945.* Stanford, CA: Stanford University Press, 1992.

Boyer, Richard E. *Lives of the Bigamists: Marriage, Family, and Community in Colonial Mexico.* Albuquerque: University of New Mexico Press, 1995.

Fomby, Paula. *Mexican Migrants and Their Parental Households in Mexico.* New York: LFB Scholarly Publishers, 2005.

Frank, Zephyr L. *Dutra's World: Wealth and Family in Nineteenth-Century Rio de Janiero.* Albuquerque: University of New Mexico Press, 2004.

Htun, Mala. *Sex and the State: Abortion, Divorce, and the Family under Latin American Dictatorships and Democracies.* New York: Cambridge University Press, 2003.

Hünefeldt, Christine. *Paying the Price of Freedom: Family and Labor among Lima's Slaves, 1800–1854.* Berkeley: University of California Press, 1994.

Martínez, Rubén. *Crossing Over: A Mexican Family on the Migrant Trail.* New York: Metropolitan Books, 2001.

Novais, Fernando A., ed. *História da vida privada no Brasil.* 4 vols. São Paulo: Companhia das Letras, 1997–1998.

Pino, Julio César. *Family and Favela: The Reproduction of Poverty in Rio de Janeiro.* Westport, CT: Greenwood Press, 1997.

Teixeira, Paulo Eduardo. *O outro lado da família brasileira: Mulheres chefes de famílias, 1765–1850.* Campinas, Brazil: Editora UNICAMP (State University of Campinas), 2004.

Torrado, Susana. *Historia de la familia en la Argentina moderna (1870–2000).* Buenos Aires: Ediciones de la Flor, 2003.

Twinam, Ann. *Public Lives, Private Secrets: Gender, Honor, Sexuality, and Illegitimacy in Colonial Spanish America.* Stanford, CA: Stanford University Press, 1999.

ELIZABETH KUZNESOF

## FANGIO, JUAN MANUEL (1911–1995).

Juan Manuel Fangio is one of the most important icons of Argentine history. He was born to Italian immigrants in a modest home in a village in the province of Buenos Aires, and he left school at the age of twelve to learn the trade of auto mechanics. In the course of his work he developed a passion for auto racing, and he entered in his first race in 1929. For years he competed in Argentina in the category of Touring Car Racing, winning two championships. Fangio left for Europe at the end of the 1940s with financial support from the government of Juan Domingo Perón. Between 1950 and his retirement in 1958, he won twenty-four of the fifty-one races he entered, including five world Formula One championships driving four different makes of vehicle (Mercedes Benz, Maserati, Ferrari, and Alfa Romeo). His racing feats made him one of the great popular idols of his time. Fangio's image was further enhanced by his unassuming and modest demeanor, and because the story of his rise to fame resonated with Argentines: He was a man who had been born in a humble home, became one of the greatest race-car drivers of all times, and finished his life as a prosperous businessman at the head of an automobile company.

*See also* **Sports.**

BIBLIOGRAPHY

Brudenell, Mike. "An Ode to Fangio, an Icon for All Time." *Detroit Free Press*, October 14, 2003.

"Prince of the Pampas." *Sports Illustrated* 83, no. 5 (July 31, 1995): 91. Obituary.

JUAN SURIANO

## FAORO, RAYMUNDO (1925–2003).

Brazilian jurist and essayist Raymundo Faoro was born April 27, 1925, in Rio Grande do Sul, of Italian forbears. Faoro received his law degree in 1948. He served as state prosecutor (*procurador do estado*) in Rio de Janeiro from 1951 until his retirement, and headed the Brazilian bar association (Ordem dos Advogados) as president from 1977 to 1979, during the military dictatorship. Faoro secured the reinstitution of habeas corpus and helped restore a constitutional regime through public advocacy and political journalism.

Faoro published his best-known book, *Os donos do poder* (The Masters of Power) in 1958; but it had a greater impact during the dictatorship, when it appeared in a revised and much-expanded edition in 1975. Faoro was the first to apply Weberian analysis to Brazilian history, and his book has joined a short list of celebrated essays on the nature of Brazilian society. *Donos* surveys the national experience, focusing especially on the political estate (*estamento*, Weber's *Stand*). For Faoro, this group controlled the state, which he saw as fundamentally unaltered from its Portuguese prototype.

Regarding civil society, Faoro broke with conventional historiography, which characterized nineteenth-century conservatives as owners of large estates. Faoro viewed them rather as controlling "mobile wealth": slaves and credit. It was not conservatives but liberals, he held, who predominated among latifundistas. Merchants and creditors allied with the political estate after independence in 1822. Excepting the early Empire (1831–1837) and the Old Republic (1889–1930), when relative decentralization strengthened landed elites, the political estate and its commercial allies succeeded in dominating civil society through a centralized state.

The political estate has shaped the stratified character of Brazilian society; it has been impervious to the needs of the people, but also inattentive to the demands of powerful economic interests. State dominates civil society, but the ruling estate has no clear national project. *Donos* is obviously influenced by Weber in its interpretation of bureaucracy, but departs from him in its ahistorical claim for the unchanging continuity of the patrimonial state. It offered an explanation of the enormous power of the contemporary Brazilian government, authoritarian and heavily engaged in parasitical enterprises when the second edition appeared. The work challenged dominant Marxist currents, among which political sociologist Nicos Poulantzas's (1936–1979) interpretation of the "exceptional capitalist state" and its "relative autonomy" was then popular in Brazil.

*Donos do poder* and other social and literary studies secured Faoro's election to the Brazilian Academy of Letters in 2000. Brazil's ministry of justice building was named for him in 2003.

*See also* **Judicial Systems: Brazil.**


BIBLIOGRAPHY

Faoro, Raymundo. *Machado de assis, a pirâmide r o trapézio.* São Paulo: Companhia Editora Nacional, 1974.

Faoro, Raymundo. *Os donos do poder: Formação do patronato político brasileiro*, 2nd edition. Porto Alegre, Brazil: Editora Globo, 1975.

Love, Joseph L. Review of *Machado de assisa, piramide e o trapezio* by Raymundo Faoro. *Hispanic American Historical Review* 58, no. 4 (November 1978): 753–755.

Schwartzman, Simon. "Atualidade de Raymundo Faoro." *Dados* 46, no. 2 (2003): 207–213.


JOSEPH L. LOVE

## FARIÑA NÚÑEZ, ELOY (1885–1929).

Eloy Fariña Núñez (*b.* 25 June 1885; *d.* 1929), Paraguayan writer. Probably the most respected author in Paraguay during the first quarter of the twentieth century, Fariña Núñez was born in the tiny hamlet of Humaitá, site of a major battle during the disastrous War of the Triple Alliance some seventeen years earlier. Perhaps owing to the isolated position of his hometown, Fariña Núñez chose to go to Argentina for his education. He graduated from the Colegio Nacional of Corrientes and later studied law at the University of Buenos Aires.

Fariña Núñez spent most of his adult life in Buenos Aires, where he worked as a clerk in the internal revenue administration. His true love, however, was literature and his prime subject Paraguay. In 1913, when the Buenos Aires daily *La Prensa* opened a literary competition, Fariña Núñez won it with a short story entitled "Bucles de oro" (Golden Curls). He later published volumes of poetry (*Canto secular; Poesias escojidas*), miscellaneous prose (*Las vértebras de Pan; La mirada de los muertos; Cuentos guaraníes*), philosophical treatises (*Conceptos estéticos; Asunción; Crítica*), an essay in economics (*El estanco del tabaco*), and even a novel on Graeco-Egyptian life and customs (*Rhódopis*). His death at age forty-four robbed Paraguayan letters of one of its chief practitioners.

*See also* **Education: Overview; Literature: Spanish America.**


BIBLIOGRAPHY

William Belmont Parker, *Paraguayans of To-Day* (1921), pp. 31–32.

Carlos Zubizarreta, *Cien vidas paraguayas,* 2d ed. (1985), pp. 273–275.

*Additional Bibliography*

Delgado, Susy. *25 nombres capitales de la literatura paraguaya.* Asunción: Servilibro, 2005.


THOMAS L. WHIGHAM

## FARQUHAR, PERCIVAL (1864–1953).

Percival Farquhar (*b.* 19 October 1864; *d.* 4 August 1953), American entrepreneur and railroad magnate. Born in York, Pennsylvania, Farquhar graduated from Yale University in 1884 with a degree in mechanical engineering. His Latin American business ventures began in Cuba shortly after the end of the Spanish-American War. There he profited from connections with U.S. occupation officials, purchased the Havana tram system, and electrically equipped it at the turn of the century. Beginning in 1900 he organized, along with Sir William Van Horne (of Canadian Pacific fame), the construction of the Cuba Railroad across the eastern half of the island.

In 1904 Farquhar purchased a Guatemalan concession to build a railroad connecting United Fruit Company lands and the Caribbean port of Puerto Barrios. With Indian draft labor, the line was completed in 1908. In the meantime, Farquhar had moved to

Brazil, where he resided for the rest of his life. He invested in public utility companies in Rio de Janeiro and Salvador, managed the construction of port facilities in the north of the country, and directed the construction of the Madeira-Mamoré Railroad through the Amazon jungle. He also created and presided over the Brazil Railway Company, a syndicate that in 1912 controlled one-half of all Brazilian railroad mileage.

Farquhar spent the last decades of his life building and managing the steel plant at Itabira, Minas Gerais. From the start, this project faced fierce opposition from Brazilian nationalists. President Getúlio Vargas nationalized Itabira in 1942, making it part of the Companhia Vale do Rio Doce. Farquhar died in Rio de Janeiro.

*See also* **Railroads.**

BIBLIOGRAPHY

Charles Gauld, *The Last Titan: Percival Farquhar: American Entrepreneur in Latin America* (1964).

Steven Topik, *The Political Economy of the Brazilian State, 1889–1930* (1987).

Todd A. Diacon, *Millenarian Vision, Capitalist Reality: Brazil's Contestado Rebellion, 1912–1916* (1991).

*Additional Bibliography*

Zanetti, Oscar, and Alejandro García. *Sugar and Railroads: A Cuban History, 1837–1959.* Chapel Hill: University of North Carolina Press, 1998. See especially chapters 13 and 14.

TODD DIACON

**FARRELL, EDELMIRO** (1887–1980). Edelmiro Farrell was an important figure in the emergence of Peronism in Argentina. Descended from Irish ancestors, Farrell had a notable military career, becoming a general in 1941. As a founder of Grupo de Oficiales Unidos (GOU), a military group that supported Argentina's neutrality in World War II, he participated in the military coup that overthrew the unpopular president Ramón Castillo on June 4, 1943.

After the 48-hour term of General Arturo Rawson (1885–1952) in June 1943, General Pedro Pablo Ramírez became president and appointed Farrell minister of war. On October 15, 1943, the military chose Farrell as Ramírez's vice president. Farrell had a protégé: his secretary, Colonel Juan Domingo Perón, who jumped to the Secretariat of Labor and Social Welfare, a base he used to recruit workers, mainly communists and socialists, to create a new movement.

Farrell became president on January 24, 1944, replacing Ramírez, who distrusted Perón's rising star. Perón obtained two new positions: minister of war and vice president. The team of Farrell and Perón used political pragmatism to face the new times. When Argentina declared war on Germany and Japan on March 27, 1945, the government looked for the support of the traditional political parties. This attempt failed, and civilian opposition matched military support. Farrell called for elections by July 1945, but the trade unions nominated Perón. Military officers forced Farrell to arrest Perón on October 13; four days later, masses of workers marched downtown, demanding Perón's liberation. Farrell freed his friend, who famously addressed the masses.

Farrell instituted several policies that had the effect of increasing support for Perón in the elections of February 1946, such as the grant of the annual thirteenth salary (a bonus of an extra month's salary at the end of the year). Perón won the election, and on June 4, 1946, Farrell transferred the presidential sash to his friend. In 1947 Farrell retired from all military and political activities, and he died on October 31, 1980.

*See also* **Argentina: The Twentieth Century; Perón, Juan Domingo.**

BIBLIOGRAPHY

Byrne, Jim, Philip Coleman, and Jason King, eds. *Ireland and the Americas: Culture, Politics, and History.* Santa Barbara, CA: ABC-CLIO, 2007.

Potash, Robert. *The Army and Politics in Argentina: Yrigoyen to Peron, 1928–1945.* Stanford, CA: Stanford University Press, 1969.

Rouquié, Alain. *Poder militar y sociedad política en la Argentina.* Buenos Aires: Emecé, 1981.

FERNANDO ROCCHI

**FARROUPILHA REVOLT.** Farroupilha Revolt, or Ragamuffin War (1835–1845), uprising in Brazil's southernmost province of Rio Grande do Sul, the longest and most dangerous of the five major regional revolts that shook Brazil during the regency (1831–1840). First ridiculed as *farrapos,* or "ragamuffins," for their characteristic fringed leather garb, the rebels adopted the name as a banner of pride and defiance. Political and economic grievances fueled the rebellion. Complaints that the distant central government neglected the province's needs, undervalued its military sacrifices, and pursued policies that discriminated against its pastoral products generated intense regionalism and pressure for decentralization and increased autonomy. Attempts by unpopular imperial officials to strengthen central control and extreme interparty rivalry brought matters to the breaking point, dividing coastal cities from cattle ranchers of the interior. The revolt was cast in the rhetoric of radical liberalism and republicanism and attracted the participation of Italian exiles Giuseppe Garibaldi and Luigi Rossetti.

The revolt began on 20 September 1835, under the capable leadership of rancher Bento Gonçalves da Silva. The rebels quickly captured the provincial capital of Pôrto Alegre but lost it in June 1836 to legalist forces, which controlled the coastal zone for the remainder of the conflict. When the Regency did not answer their demands, rebels met in the interior town of Piratini and declared an independent republic in September 1836, electing Bento Gonçalves provisional president. Imperial forces had little military success against the rebels in the interior, where most of the fighting occurred. Bento Gonçalves was captured in October 1836 but escaped the following year, lending the revolt renewed energy. The rebels received arms, supplies, and financial support from Uruguay's caudillo leader José Fructuoso Rivera, who, along with some Riograndenses, had designs of forming a new state uniting Uruguay, Rio Grande do Sul, and the Ar-gentine provinces of Entre Ríos and Corrientes. Rio Grande was a natural extension of the pastoral culture to its south, its ranchers had many ties across the border, and it had long been entangled in the political unrest of the Río de la Plata.

The Farrapos' successes influenced the outbreak of the Sabinada Revolt in Bahia in 1837, and rebels proclaimed a second independent republic in Santa Catarina in 1839, following an expedition across Rio Grande's northern border. That republic fell four months later and the tide of battle turned against the rebels, who were beset by factionalism and shortages of supplies. On the imperial side, bungling, troop shortages, and conflicts of authority hampered efforts to suppress the uprising.

In 1842 Brazil's most formidable nineteenth-century military commander, Luis Alves de Lima E Silva, barão de Caxias, took over command of the legalist forces and administration of the province. The following year the rebels drew up a moderate constitution for the republic, retaining slavery, Catholicism as the official religion, and providing for indirect elections. The political skill of the barão de Caxias and his military victories in Caçapava, Bagé, and Alegrete gradually brought the province back under imperial control. His generous peace, which included freedom for slave soldiers, brought the conflict to an end in February 1845.

Subsequent disruption of Brazil's trade with the Río de la Plata due to renewed instability there, together with new Brazilian duties on jerked beef imports, alleviated Rio Grande's economic grievances by easing competition, at least temporarily. The extent to which the rebellion was separatist or federalist is still a matter of debate. In subsequent years, Riograndenses stressed the revolt's federalist and republican strains, seeing in it antecedents of the federalist republic of 1889.

*See also* **Brazil, The Regency.**

BIBLIOGRAPHY

Dante De Laytano, *Historia da República Riograndense, 1835–1845* (1936).

Moacyr Flores, *Modelo político dos farrapos* (1978).

Spencer L. Leitman, *Raízes socio-econômicas da guerra dos Farrapos* (1979).

Walter Spalding, *A revolução farroupilha,* 2d ed. (1980).

### *Additional Bibliography*

Barman, Roderick. *Brazil: The Forging of a Nation.* Stanford, CA: Stanford University Press, 1988.

Costa, Emilia Viotti da. *The Brazilian Empire: Myths & Histories.* Chapel Hill: University of North Carolina Press, 2000.

Davies, Catherine, Claire Brewster, and Hilary Owen. *South American Independence: Gender, Politics, Text.* Liverpool: Liverpool University Press, 2006.

Dolhnikoff, Miriam. *O pacto imperial: Origens do federalismo no Brasil.* São Paulo: Editorial Globo, 2003.

Needelll, Jeffrey. *The Party of Order: The Conservatives, the State, and Slavery in the Brazilian Monarchy, 1831-1871.* Stanford, CA: Stanford University Press, 2006.

JOAN BAK

**FASCISM.** The fascist movement in Latin America is not easily equated with such movements in Europe or elsewhere. European fascism emerged before 1914 amid the alienation caused by rapid industrialization. At first an intellectual mood comprising rejection of positivism, liberalism, and (in the arts) bourgeois formalism, it grew mightily owing to the psychic and social mobilization, military experience, sacrifice, and disillusionment of World War I. Its salient characteristics were charismatic leadership; rituals, costumes, and symbols; an ethic of voluntarism, struggle, and instinct; nationalisms that sought to restore folk communities (often mythologized); and the belief that social justice could be achieved only through those folk communities. It comprised a youth revolt and the project of creating a moral, integral New Man. It rejected Marxism and class-based politics as well as bourgeois parliamentarism and democratic institutions generally. In power, fascists proved incompetent and corrupt; some movements (as in Italy) resorted to irredentism and foreign conquest to sustain revolutionary élan. Fascist leadership was middle class; however, mass followings were built among war veterans, uprooted and alienated individuals, and preexisting labor organizations disillusioned with or forcibly wrenched away from Marxism. In central and eastern Europe, fascism was markedly racist and anti-Semitic. In Hitler's Germany the genocidal "Final Solution" was the consequence.

Latin American movements called "fascist" lack many of these attributes; their closer affinities are with populism and authoritarian nationalism. Populist movements emerged before 1914 from the conjunction of increased rural-urban migration and the ambitions of reformist, upper-status politicians (such as Guillermo Billinghurst in Peru and José Batlle y Ordóñez in Uruguay); they arose in part from the "ruralization" of the cities, that is, transplantation of the personalistic patron-client relationships of the countryside. The context of these movements was municipal politics and the content pragmatic, not ideological, issues. Between the world wars the several strains of Latin American populism embraced nationalism, seeking to establish the idea of national identity ("Peruanidad," "Mexicanidad"), to create integrated modern nation-states, and to make the state—not low-level clientelism—the vehicle for social justice. This inclusive nationalism embraced, if only rhetorically, hitherto repressed or marginalized peoples; it denounced as "vendepatrias" (those who sold out their country) those elite groups that had collaborated in the annexation of Latin America's economies to the European- and U.S.-dominated world trade system.

When in the crisis-ridden 1930s the military seized power in several countries, some military politicians (such as Luis Miguel Sánchez Cerro in Peru) combined traditional repression with expedient labor alliances, trading public works projects, housing, and beneficial legislation for political support. Others (such as José Félix Uriburu in Argentina) envisioned the military corporation as the only competent, dedicated agent of national integration, a concept adumbrated by the Brazilian *tenentes* ("lieutenants"), restless, nationalistic young officers who staged the first of a series of minor revolts in July 1922. Although the utility of such projects in thwarting opposition Marxists or Apristas (in Peru) was obvious, they proved unpopular at the time, even among the military; but they would reappear in various guises after 1945.

In the early 1930s a number of fascist groups were founded in emulation of those in Antonio de Salazar's Portugal, Benito Mussolini's Italy, and José Antonio Primo de Rivera's Spain. "Mediterranean" fascisms, which evoked past imperial grandeur and drew strength from conservative Roman Catholicism, were preferable to German Nazism, which harbored strains of irreligion and "Aryan" racial exclusivism. Among rightist intellectuals, particularly in Colombia, corporatism became fashionable; it also figured in the theorizing of Catholic intellectuals who, reacting against the anticlericalism of the Spanish Republic (1931–1936) and the outrages of the Civil War (1936–1939), promoted clerical fascism in the style of Engelbert Dollfuss's Austria or the Spanish CEDA (Confederation of Autonomous Rightist Organizations) of J. M. Gil Robles. Following General Francisco Franco's triumph in 1939, Spain's Nationalist regime promoted the doctrine of "hispanidad" throughout Latin America; it, too, enjoyed a vogue.

The most important Latin American fascist movements of the 1930s were the Brazilian Integralistas and the Chilean Nacistas—both of which staged abortive putsches in 1938, then went into decline—the

**Integralistas with their arms raised in a fascist salute, Rio de Janeiro, Brazil, 1930s.** Inspired by fascist movement in Europe, Brazil's Integralistas attempted an unsuccessful revolt against President Getulio Vargas in 1938. © BETTMANN/CORBIS

Mexican Sinarquistas; factions among the Bolivian veterans of the disastrous Chaco War (1932–1935), some of whom later helped form the Movimiento Nacional Revolucionario (MNR); and a congeries of authoritarian nationalist groups in Argentina. The latter, unable to gain either a mass following or the unconditional backing of the traditional right, specialized in street fighting and anti-Semitic terrorism. They later attached themselves to Peronism; notwithstanding the vicissitudes of Peronism itself, anti-Semitic violence has remained the hallmark of the Argentine right.

The seeds—and charismatic leaders—were present, yet none of these movements developed into a full-fledged European-style fascism. This can be explained in part by the Axis defeat in 1945, in part by socioeconomic and political factors. The former include the inherent difficulties of creating national identities in societies still strongly rooted in primary local, or ethnic solidarities, much less of mobilizing those societies; and the fact that although European capitalists had sheltered within their respective fascisms and supported them, many Latin American capitalists chose to work within foreign systems. Political factors include the emphasis in populist regimes on redistributive—rather than ideological—politics; and the postwar success of Christian Democratic parties (as in Chile and Venezuela), which offered to conservative electorates nonviolent modernizing alternatives to Marxism. In regimes slow to modernize, the Right retained its privileges through traditional means, which did *not* include the mobilizations characteristic of fascism. In regimes fractured or paralyzed by modernization—as in Argentina, Brazil, Chile, and Uruguay in the 1970s, and in Central America in the 1980s—the new military relied on state terror to suppress dissent rather than on demagogy to mobilize and deflect it.

The fundamental structure of fascism is sometimes taken to be an authoritarian, centralized state apparatus sustained ideologically by nationalism, economically by state capitalism, and socially by a dependent syndically organized mass following. If so, five regimes since the 1930s—Getúlio Vargas's Brazil, especially after 1937; Juan Perón's Argentina; the Bolivia of the MNR after 1952; Fidel Castro's Cuba since 1959; and the Mexico of the PRI since 1928—merit possible inclusion under the fascist rubric. The first two—which were characterized also by charismatic leadership, ritual, and (in Argentina) anti-Semitism—most closely approximated European fascisms. In Brazil, regimes subsequent to Vargas's death in 1954—particularly the military regimes from 1964 to 1983—have dismantled the mass base of *varguismo;* Argentine Peronism, however, despite its vicissitudes during intervening years, retains some of its earlier dynamic. Bolivia's MNR leadership was uncharismatic; its social mobilization was incomplete and was soon reversed by the military. Cuba's Castro has proven an effective leader; the Cuban people have been mobilized for nationalistic or social justice purposes. However, the regime's affirmation of egalitarianism and rejection of irrationalisms and of capitalism place it outside the fascist category. Mexico's leadership is uncharismatic by design; in recent decades the practice of revolutionary nationalism and populism has drifted far apart from the rhetoric. Even the latter may disappear altogether as the North American Free Trade Agreement was implemented after 1 January 1994.

A revival of Latin American fascism is possible, perhaps in response to the swallowing up of national economies in globalization; violence will undoubtedly remain endemic. Elites appear, however, to have learned from the fascist experience that it is easier to create caudillos than to dismiss them, easier to mobilize masses than to demobilize them.

*See also* **Caudillismo, Caudillo; Military Dictatorships: 1821-1945; Military Dictatorships: Since 1945; Tenentismo.**

BIBLIOGRAPHY

John D. Wirth, *The Politics of Brazilian Development, 1930–1954* (1970).

Alistair Hennessy, "Fascism and Populism in Latin America," in *Fascism: A Reader's Guide, Analyses, Interpretation, Bibliography,* edited by Walter Z. Laqueur (1976).

James D. Cockcroft, *Mexico: Class Formation, Capital Accumulation, and the State* (1983).

Frederick C. Turner and Enrique Miguens, eds., *Juan Perón and the Reshaping of Argentina* (1983).

Carlos Waisman, *Reversal of Development in Argentina: Postwar Counterrevolutionary Policies and Their Structural Consequences* (1987).

Max Azicri, *Cuba: Politics, Economy, and Society* (1988).

T. Halperin Donghi, *La historia contemporánea de América Latina,* 2d ed. (1988).

*Additional Bibliography*

Deutsch, Sandra McGee. *Las Derechas: The Extreme Right in Argentina, Brazil, and Chile, 1890-1939.* Stanford, CA: Stanford University Press, 1999.

García Sebastiani, Marcela. *Fascismo y antifascismo, peronismo y antiperonismo: Conflictos políticos e ideológicos en la Argentina (1930-1955).* Madrid: Iberoamericana, 2006.

Ronald C. Newton

**FAVELA.** *Favela*, an urban shantytown in Brazil, often either perched precariously on a steep hillside or occupying low-lying, humid river lands, vulnerable to heavy rains and flooding. Individual houses are typically constructed from scrap wood, corrugated metal, or cement blocks. As squatter settlements without official recognition, *favelas* are deprived of city services such as water, sewage, and electricity, and they lack municipally sponsored schools and health clinics. One or two spigots located on the outside perimeter may supply residents with water, carried home in cans, for cooking or washing. Dwellers pay high prices for illegal electricity hookups. Although outsiders have frequently condemned *favelas* as lawless places, sociologists have demonstrated that *favelas* can become communities, displaying the range of solidarities and conflicts that the word "community" implies. Some *favelas* have persisted for decades, their residents even resisting attempts to forcibly remove them to more remote sites.

The first *favela* arose in the Morro da Providência, near the Ministry of War in Rio de Janeiro, when disabled soldiers returned home after the Canudos expedition in 1897. The soldiers doubtless named the settlement after Mount Favela, a point near Canudos that had figured prominently in battle strategies. As Rio de Janeiro expanded to the southern seaside suburbs in the early twentieth century, hillside *favelas* replaced the razed slums of the central city known as *cortiços,* or beehives.

To an extent, *favela* is a regional term most commonly used in the center-south of Brazil. In the Northeastern city of Recife, for example, similar neighborhoods are referred to as *mucambos,* a term that once referred to slave quarters or runaway-slave settlements.

In recent decades, high levels of largely drug-related violence between gangs, police, and militias has increased the precariousness in the lives of many *favela* residents.

*See also* **Brazil: Since 1889; Cities and Urbanization; Class Structure in Modern Latin America; Drugs and Drug Trade.**

BIBLIOGRAPHY

Janice E. Perlman, *The Myth of Marginality: Urban Poverty and Politics in Rio de Janeiro* (1976).

*Additional Bibliography*

Caldeira, Teresa Pires do Rio. *City of Walls: Crime, Segregation, and Citizenship in São Paulo.* Berkeley: University of California Press, 2000.

Campos, Andrelino. *Do quilombo à favela: A produção do "espaço criminalizado" no Rio de Janeiro.* Rio de Janeiro: Bertrand Brasil, 2005.

Castriota, Leonardo Barci, ed. *Urbanização brasileira: Redescobertas.* Belo Horizonte: Editora C/Arte, 2003.

Pandolfi, Dulce Chaves, and Mário Grynszpan, eds. *A favela fala: Depoimentos ao CPDOC.* Rio de Janeiro: FGV Editora, 2003.

Pino, Julio César. *Family and Favela: The Reproduction of Poverty in Rio de Janeiro.* Westport, CT: Greenwood Press, 1997.

Sheriff, Robin E. *Dreaming Equality: Color, Race, and Racism in Urban Brazil.* New Brunswick, NJ: Rutgers University Press, 2001.

Sandra Lauderdale Graham

**FAWCETT, PERCY** (1867–c. 1925). Born in Torquay, England, Percy Harrison Fawcett (August 31, 1867–1925?) served the British army and government in Asia and Africa. In 1906 he traveled to South America for the Royal Geographic Society to survey the border between Bolivia and Brazil. Between 1906 and 1921 Fawcett participated in seven expeditions to South America. His reports inspired Arthur Conan Doyle to write *The Lost World* (1912). In 1925 Fawcett entered the Brazilian Matto Grosso, accompanied by his son Jack Fawcett and Jack's friend, Raleigh Rimmell. He sought a lost city called "Z." The three never returned. A number of expeditions have sought to clarify Fawcett's disappearance but have failed.

*See also* **Explorers and Exploration: Brazil.**

BIBLIOGRAPHY

Fawcett, P. H. *Exploration Fawcett.* 1953. London: Phoenix Press, 2001.

Fleming, Peter. *Brazilian Adventure.* New York: Grossett & Dunlap, 1933.

Robert Smale

**FAZENDA, FAZENDEIRO.** Fazendeiro Fazenda, a plantation, large farm, or ranch; a planter, owner of a *fazenda,* great landholder, or, until slavery's abolition in 1888, a slave owner. *Fazendas* were large rural properties with a house and outbuildings as well as land divided into agricultural production units that could include coffee, cattle, food crops, and occasionally sugarcane. On some *fazendas* there were processing units for coffee, sugar, and manioc in addition to grazing areas and forested reserves. Although resident free farmers were part of a *fazenda's* labor force, these establishments largely operated with slave labor, which was utilized in all aspects of domestic and field production and, where available, in processing units for coffee, sugar, manioc, corn, and beans.

*See also* **Hacienda; Plantations.**

BIBLIOGRAPHY

Stanley J. Stein, *Vassouras, a Brazilian Coffee County, 1850–1900* (1970).

Robert G. Keith, ed., *Haciendas and Plantations in Latin American History* (1977).

*Additional Bibliography*

Araújo, Tatiana Brito de. *Os engenhos centrais e a produção açucareira no Recôncavo Baiano, 1875-1909.* Salvador: FIEB, 2002.

Barickman, B. J. *A Bahian Counterpoint: Sugar, Tobacco, Cassava, and Slavery in the Recôncavo, 1780-1860.* Stanford: Stanford University Press, 1998.

Geld, Ellen Bromfield. *View from the Fazenda: A Tale of the Brazilian Heartlands.* Athens: Ohio University Press, 2003.

NANCY PRISCILLA SMITH NARO

**FEBRES-CORDERO RIBADENEYRA, LEÓN** (1931–). León Febres-Cordero Ribadeneyra (*b.* 9 March 1931), president of Ecuador (1984–1988). Born in Guayaquil, Febres-Cordero began his education in his native city and completed his secondary education in the United States. He studied mechanical engineering at the Stevens Institute of Technology in New Jersey. Returning to Guayaquil in 1956, he developed a successful business career, working as a mechanical engineer, manager, and executive in a variety of public and private enterprises, including the Exportadora Bananera Noboa S.A. He was active in a variety of business and civic organizations, serving terms as president of the Guayaquil Chamber of Industries in the 1970s, the National Federation of Chambers of Industries of Ecuador, and the Association of Latin American Industries.

Febres-Cordero entered politics in the 1960s as deputy to the Constituent Assembly (1966–1967), and senator and president of the Economic and Financial Commission of the National Congress (1968–1970). He was principal spokesman for rightist critics of the military juntas that ruled Ecuador from 1972 to 1979 and led the opposition to the Constitution of 1979. Elected deputy to Congress in 1979 as a candidate of the Social Christian Party, he emerged as the leading critic of the governments of Jaime Roldós Aguilero (1979–1981) and Osvaldo Hurtado Larrea (1981–1983), and a staunch defender of coastal business interests.

Febres-Cordero won the 1984 presidential election as the candidate of the Frente de Reconstrucción Nacional, a coalition of rightist parties. His administration sought to restructure the Ecuadorian economy by reducing government regulations, freeing exchange rates, promoting the export of manufactured items, and encouraging foreign investment. His ability to implement his neoliberal reform program was undermined by an opposition congress and a deteriorating economy. Falling petroleum prices and the subsequent loss of oil revenues after the destruction of the trans-Amazonian oil pipeline forced the administration to adopt austerity measures that quickly alienated labor and opposition political parties. The administration's problems mounted when it failed to control burgeoning budget deficits or to shield the working classes from the impact of the austerity program. Although Febres-Cordero completed his presidential term, his dictatorial style provoked a series of constitutional crises and increased political violence. Despite his mixed presidential legacy, Febres-Cordero continued to be a major player in Ecuadorian politics. He served as mayor of Guayaquil from 1992 to 2000, and as leader of the Social Christian Party, he won a seat in the National Congress.

*See also* **Ecuador: Since 1830; Guayaquil.**

BIBLIOGRAPHY

Howard Handelman, "The Dilemma of Ecuadorian Democracy. Part III: The 1983–1984 Presidential Elections," in *UFSI Reports* 36 (1984).

Ramiro Rivera, *El pensamiento de León Febres-Cordero* (1986).

David W. Schodt, *Ecuador: An Andean Enigma* (1987), esp. pp. 157–168.

*Additional Bibliography*

Isaacs, Anita. *Military Rule and Transition in Ecuador, 1972–92.* Pittsburgh, PA: University of Pittsburgh Press, 1993.

Montúfar, César. *La reconstrucción neoliberal: Febres Cordero o la estatización del neoliberalismo en el Ecuador, 1984–1988.* Quito, Ecuador: AbyaYala, 2000.

LINDA ALEXANDER RODRÍGUEZ

**FEDERAL ELECTORAL INSTITUTE (IFE).** The Federal Electoral Institute (IFE; Insituto Federal Electoral) of Mexico is an independent agency responsible for the federal election process. The IFE is a publicly funded agency, independent of the government, responsible for organizing federal elections for president, the Chamber of Deputies, and the Senate. The IFE emerged from the Federal Code of Electoral Institutions and Procedures (COFIPE) legislation in 1990. Three major revisions of this code contributed to IFE's current responsibilities and structure. The 1993 reform gave the Institute the power to validate the elections and to establish campaign spending limits. The 1994 reform increased the importance of independent citizen members, giving them the majority of votes over partisan representatives. The 1996 reform, the most influential, separated the IFE from the executive branch and assigned all decisions to a body of independent citizen members.

IFE's most important functions, all designed to achieve a fair, honest, and democratic electoral process, include registering voters and certifying voting credentials, staffing voting booths with trained volunteers, establishing voting lists of eligible voters for each balloting precinct, printing and distributing ballots and other materials, counting the results, and regulating other aspects of the electoral process. There are also local and district councils.

The IFE has played a central role in making Mexican elections more competitive and honest since 1994. Its most controversial decisions were in response to the contested presidential election of 2006. Felipe Calderón, the winner, won by fewer than 250,000 votes, and the losing candidate, Andrés Manuel López Obrador, alleged fraud, calling for a recount. In the case of a legal appeal, the decision is passed on to the Federal Electoral Tribunal (TRIFE). Despite the controversy surrounding this election, IFE and the Federal Electoral Tribunal are viewed positively by most Mexicans.

*See also* **López Obrador, Manuel Andrés.**

BIBLIOGRAPHY

IFE. Available from www.ife.org.mx. Includes an option for English version.

Domínguez, Jorge I., and Chappell H. Lawson, eds. *Mexico's Pivotal Democratic Election: Candidates, Voters, and the Presidential Campaign of 2000.* Stanford, CA: Stanford University Press, 2004.

RODERIC AI CAMP

**FEDERALISM.** Federalism, a constitutional system in post-Independence Latin America and, often, still a hotly debated political issue. Formally, it denoted a type of government in which power was explicitly divided between central (national) and regional (state or provincial) authorities. As such it bore resemblance to the system incorporated in the United States Constitution and, to a lesser extent, certain ancient and modern European models. It was first adopted by several Latin American countries during the independence movement, for example, in Venezuela in 1811 in the constitution of the so-called First Republic.

Critics of federalism, of whom the most prominent was Simón Bolívar, condemned it as a dangerously weak system and as a foreign construct ill suited to the historical traditions and circumstances of Latin America. In its most common guise, it took provinces that in the colonial regime had enjoyed no administrative autonomy and suddenly equipped them with their own executive, legislative, and judicial branches that shared power with organs of the national government; sometimes these provinces, improvised as "sovereign" entities, did not even have enough qualified individuals to fill the offices created. However, federalism was a response to genuine regional loyalties and interests repressed or at least denied institutional expression during the colonial period. Moreover, federalism as a technique for dividing and thus curbing the power of government was compatible with the liberal ideology of individual rights that most Latin American leaders following independence professed to one degree or another.

The identification of federalism with political liberalism was perhaps clearest in Mexico, where it became a central dogma of the Liberal Party and of its twentieth-century revolutionary heirs. Thus the three constitutions under which Mexico has been governed for most of its national history—those of 1824, 1857, and 1917—all gave the country a federalist organization. This did not prevent the eventual emergence of a national presidency stronger than that in the U.S. model of federalism; yet the states have retained a distinct role in Mexican politics and government.

Federalism has been equally characteristic of the system of government in Argentina, where initially it was associated not with liberals but with traditionalist forces, especially in the interior provinces. These provincials distrusted the reforming tendencies of the liberal Unitarios, whose greatest strength was in the national capital, Buenos Aires. In the end, however, all factions came to accept the federalist Constitution of 1853. It was the country's first truly effective constitution and, though briefly replaced by the Peronista Constitution of 1949, is today the oldest Latin American constitution anywhere in force. Brazil, too, has been formally a federation most of the time since the adoption in 1891 of its first republican constitution, which closely followed the U.S. model even in the use of the name *Estados Unidos do Brasil* (United States of Brazil).

The countries mentioned, Latin America's three largest, are the only ones that still have a strictly federal constitution. The smaller countries, such as the individual Central American republics, Paraguay in South America, and the Dominican Republic in the West Indies, have never adopted anything other than a unitary organization. The other Latin American nations commonly experimented with federal or quasi-federal forms of government at different times in the nineteenth century. Colombia, under its Constitution of 1863, adopted the most extreme version of federalism ever known in Latin America, whereby the various states even had their own armies and postage stamps. Colombia turned to strict centralism with its Constitution of 1886, but in its current charter (that of 1991) included such measures of partial decentralization as the popular election of departmental governors. Still other countries that have opted for constitutional centralism have likewise retained particular features typical of federalism, and in the same way federalist charters (among them the Argentine constitution) commonly have included centrist provisions allowing the national president or congress to "intervene" in the government of the provinces or states when specified conditions arise.

*See also* **Argentina, Constitutions; Colombia, Constitutions: Constitution of 1863; Mexico, Constitutions: Constitutions Prior to 1917; Venezuela, Constitutions.**

BIBLIOGRAPHY

L. S. Rowe, *The Federal System of the Argentine Republic* (1921).

Miron Burgin, *Economic Aspects of Argentine Federalism, 1820–1852* (1946).

Charles A. Hale, *Mexican Liberalism in the Age of Mora, 1821–1853* (1968).

Jorge Carpizo, *Federalismo en Latinoamérica* (1973).

Helen Delpar, *Red Against Blue: The Liberal Party in Colombian Politics, 1863–1899* (1981), esp. chap. 5.

Frank Safford, "Politics, Ideology, and Society in Post-Independence Spanish America," in *Cambridge History of Latin America,* edited by Leslie Bethell, vol. 3 (1985).

Nettie Lee Benson, *The Provincial Deputation in Mexico: Harbinger of Provincial Autonomy, Independence, and Federalism* (1992).

*Additional Bibliography*

Gibson, Edward L. *Federalism and Democracy in Latin America.* Baltimore: Johns Hopkins University Press, 2004.

Koth, Karl B. *Waking the Dictator: Veracruz, the Struggle for Federalism and the Mexican Revolution, 1870-1927.* Calgary, Alta: University of Calgary Press, 2002.

Segreti, Carlos S. A. *Federalismo rioplatense y federalismo argentino: (El federalismo de Córdoba en los comienzos de la época independiente, 1810-1829).* Córdoba: Centro de Estudios Históricos, 1995.

DAVID BUSHNELL

## FEDERALIST WAR (1898–1899).

Federalist War (1898–1899), the conflict in Bolivia that marked the end of the hegemony of the Conservative (or Constitutionalist) Party run by the Sucre-based silver-mining oligarchy and the beginning of the predominance of tin mining interests based in La Paz. In 1898 a constitutional crisis developed when Sucre delegates to Congress forced through a bill that made their city the permanent site of the national government. The La Paz delegates stormed out and began a revolt, coordinated by the rival Liberal Party. The Liberals also were able to engineer an uprising of the Aymara Indians of the Altiplano under the leadership of Pablo Zárate Willka. The rebel army led by Liberal José Manuel Pando and composed of Liberals, La Paz Federalists, and, most importantly, the Aymaras, was able to defeat the federal army under Conservative president Séver Fernández Alonso near La Paz in 1899. After the rebel victory, however, the Indians turned against all whites in the largest nineteenth-century Indian rebellion in Bolivia. Only a combined effort of the creoles was able to contain the incipient caste war. In the aftermath, Zárate Willka and other Indian leaders were executed, La Paz became the de facto capital of Bolivia, and the Liberal Party began its twenty-year reign.

*See also* **Bolivia, Political Parties: Liberal Party.**

BIBLIOGRAPHY

The definitive work is Ramiro Condarco Morales, *Zárate, el "Temible" Willka: Historia de la rebelión indígena de 1899,* 2d ed. (1983).

*Additional Bibliography*

Irurozqui, Marta. *La armonía de las desigualdades: Elites y conflictos de poder en Bolivia, 1880-1920.* Madrid: Consejo Superior de Investigaciones Científicas; Cusco, Peru: Centro de Estudios Regionales Andinos Bartolomé de las Casas, 1994.

Erick D. Langer

---

**FEDERAL WAR (VENEZUELA, 1859-1863).** Federal War (Venezuela, 1859–1863) the most significant civil strife in Venezuela since the War of Independence. When the consensus among the political elite that had dominated the republic dissolved after 1830, a prolonged period of political instability ensued. Several factors led to war, including social problems inherited from the struggle for independence, tensions among the diverse economic and political groups, a succession of armed movements in rural areas, and hopes for change in the centralist-federalist model of government adopted in 1830. The Conservative Party, under the leadership of Jose Antonio Páez (until his defeat in August 1849), advocated a strong central government. Its supporters consisted of the commercial elite concentrated in Caracas. The Liberals, on the other hand, argued for greater regional autonomy. Their ranks consisted mostly of the remnants of the old landed aristocracy and new groups that arose as a result of the privileges and land grants bestowed upon them for their role in the wars of independence.

After José Tadeo Monagas was driven from power by the March Revolution of 1858—in which both Liberals and Conservatives participated—a new regime was set up under General Julián Castro. This government did not satisfy the aspirations to power of many Liberals, however, and the members of the Conservative Party fended off Liberal opposition until Castro issued a decree on 7 June 1858 expelling the most prestigious liberal leaders from the country.

The political conflict resulted in diverse armed uprisings, an atmosphere of profound political confusion, and the adoption on 31 December 1858 of a new fundamental charter produced by both Conservatives and Liberals (except for those in exile). Since this charter did not authorize the adoption of a federal system, federalists in exile began plotting a revolution to drive the Conservative majority from power.

On 20 February 1859 in the city of Coro, the federalists took over the military headquarters, proclaiming the creation of a federation, the abolition of the death penalty, universal suffrage, and political pluralism. This was the start of war. Fighting broke out in various parts of the country, and the war went on for four years until, in April 1863, the signing of the Treaty of Coche put an end to it.

After the war, there was no modification of Venezuela's economic or social structure. However, it did result in the establishment of a federal system that in the 1990s still underpinned the national Constitution. It also produced a *caudillo*-centered political system that was dominated by the Liberal Party, the political victor of the war.

*See also* **Venezuela, Political Parties: Conservative Party; Venezuela, Political Parties: Liberal Party; Venezuela: Venezuela since 1830.**

BIBLIOGRAPHY

Joaquín Gabaldón Márquez, *Documentos políticos y actos ejecutivos y legislativos de la Revolución Federal desde el 20 de febrero de 1859 hasta el 18 de marzo de 1864* (1959).

Lisandro Alvarado, *Historia de la Revolución Federal en Venezuela* (1975).

Adolfo Rodríguez, *Exequiel Zamora* (1977).

*Additional Bibliography*

Banko, Catalina. *Las luchas federalistas en Venezuela.* Caracas, Venezuela: Monte Avila Editores Latinoamericana: Centro de Estudios Latinoamericanos Rómulo Gallegos, 1996.

Inés Quintero

---

**FÉDERMAN, NICOLÁS** (1505–1542). Nicolás Féderman (*b.* 1505/09; *d.* 21/22 February 1542), German conquistador. Born Nikolaus

Federmann, probably in the free imperial city of Ulm, Féderman worked for the Welsers, a German commercial house. The Welsers had authorization for a trading depot in Santo Domingo by 1526, and in 1528 their agents in Seville signed an agreement with Spanish officials to conquer and settle Venezuela. Féderman was one of several Germans sent to explore, conquer, govern, and exploit the commercial possibilities of the Venezuelan concession.

In his *Historia indiana* Féderman recounts how he crossed the Atlantic to Santo Domingo in 1529 and reached Coro, Venezuela, the following January. In July the ailing governor, Ambrosio Alfinger (Ambrosius Dalfinger), retired to Santo Domingo, leaving Féderman in charge. He boldly organized a successful six-month expedition into the interior, returning to Coro on 17 March 1531. Alfinger, now recuperated, banished him for four years for this unapproved expedition.

In Augsburg in 1532, Féderman shrewdly composed his *Historia indiana,* touting his exploits and the richness of Venezuela, with an eye on his employers, the Welsers. The *Historia,* with its keen analysis of Indian life and warfare, had its desired effect. Féderman signed a contract with the Welsers, and the Council of the Indies made him governor and captain-general of Venezuela.

After his return to Coro, Féderman and Jorge Espira (Georg Hohermuth) organized a two-pronged conquest of the Chibcha (Muisca) Indians of highland Colombia, where some legends located El Dorado. Espira was to approach from the east by crossing the llanos, and Féderman was to enter from the west by moving up the Magdalena River, but the plan went awry. Espira left Coro in 1535 and spent three ruinous years before struggling back without having penetrated Chibcha territory.

In the meantime, Féderman secured the western boundary of the Welser concession, but then rival and vastly superior forces from Santa Marta blocked movement up the Magdalena. He returned to Coro, where, to avoid an unexpected *residencia* (impeachment), he suddenly resumed his expedition. Following the route taken by Espira, he traversed the Venezuelan and Colombian llanos, always keeping the Andes to the west in view. The two expeditions never met.

Upon finding gold, Féderman turned west and climbed the Andes, but discovered that Gonzalo Jiménez De Quesada and his expedition from Santa Marta had arrived two years earlier (1537) and had already conquered the Chibchas. Then a group from Popayán, led by Sebastián de Belalcázar, appeared. Each conquistador claimed the Chibcha territory, but they agreed to journey to Spain together to resolve the dispute there. Before departing, Féderman accepted seven shares of any future booty taken by the Jiménez group and the *encomienda* of Tinjacá. Most of his men joined Jiménez's forces and helped them establish new cities and colonize central Colombia. They sold their horses and armament at great profit to Jiménez's men, who were in desperate need of these resources.

Back in Flanders in 1540, Féderman disagreed with the powerful Welsers over his accomplishments and was jailed. Petitions to the Council of Flanders were to no avail. Desperate for a way out, Féderman denounced the Welsers before the Council of the Indies for defrauding the royal treasury. Since the council wanted to separate the Welsers from their Venezuelan concession, the case was transferred to the council's jurisdiction in Spain and Féderman was brought to Valladolid, where he died. The Welsers pursued their Venezuela claim before the council until 1557, when the bankruptcy of Philip II led them to abandon it.

*See also* **Council of the Indies; Indigenous Peoples; Mining: Colonial Spanish America; Welser, House of; Venezuela: The Colonial Period.**

BIBLIOGRAPHY

An excellent survey of the German effort to conquer Venezuela and Colombia is Juan Friede, *Los Welser en la conquista de Venezuela* (1961). See also José Ignacio Avellaneda Navas, *Los compañeros de Féderman. Cofundadores de Santa Fé de Bogotá* (1900). Féderman's own account of his accomplishments down to 1532 is found in his *Historia indiana* (1958). In English a lively read is John Hemming, *The Search for El Dorado* (1978).

### *Additional Bibliography*

Avellaneda Nava, José Ignacio. *Los compañeros de Féderman: Cofundadores de Santa Fe de Bogotá.* Bogotá: Academia de Historia de Bogotá: Tercer Mundo Editores, 1990.

Castillo, Gilberto. *Caminando en el tiempo: el encuentro de tres conquistadores en la Sabana de Bogotá.* Bogotá: Intermedio Editores, 2003.

MAURICE P. BRUNGARDT

**FEIJÓ, DIOGO ANTÔNIO** (1784?–1843). Diogo Antônio Feijó (baptized 17 August 1784; *d.* 10 November 1843), Brazilian statesman and regent. Feijó's upbringing, career, style of life, and outlook personified the nativist, anti-Portuguese current in Brazilian affairs in the years after independence. A foundling, born in São Paulo, Feijó was educated for the priesthood and ordained in 1808. A deputy from São Paulo province to the Lisbon Cortes in 1822, he made his mark in the Chamber of Deputies elected in 1826 and 1830 as a prominent opponent to Pedro I.

Absent from Rio de Janeiro, Feijó played no role in the crisis preceding Pedro I's abdication in April 1831. In July 1831, he accepted the key portfolio of justice. Defeating several armed risings and organizing the National Guard, Feijó served as bulwark of the new regime. Losing patience, he resigned in July 1832. He was a prime mover in the ensuing and abortive parliamentary coup, designed to turn Brazil into a federation of states. Despite this failure, Feijó remained the preeminent figure in liberal, nativist politics, becoming senator from Rio province in 1833. In the elections for a single regent, instituted by the constitutional amendment enacted in 1834 (the Ato Adicional), he was the Moderado party candidate and gained a plurality of votes cast. Worsening health and his own doubts about his suitability delayed his taking office until 12 October 1835.

Feijó's two years as regent proved as barren as he had feared, due in part to his foes' unrelenting hostility but also to his intransigence, belligerence, and, above all, failure to take drastic action against regional revolts. Reduced to impotence, he resigned on 18 September 1837. He stayed active in politics but no longer played a central role. Despite a paralytic stroke in 1840, Feijó actively supported the São Paulo revolt of 1842. Deportation to Espírito Santo and then a trial before the Senate probably hastened his death.

*See also* **Brazil, The Regency.**

BIBLIOGRAPHY

Octavio Tarquino De Sousa, *História dos fundadores do império,* vol. 1, *Diogo Antônio Feijó* (Rio de Janeiro, 1957).

Novelli Júnior, *Feijó: Um paulista velho* (Rio de Janeiro, 1966).

*Additional Bibliography*

Ricci, Magda. *Assombrações de um padre regente: Diogo Antônio Feijó, 1784–1843.* Campinas: Editora da UNICAMP: CECULT; São Paulo: FAPESP, 2001.

RODERICK J. BARMAN

**FEIJÓO, BENITO JERÓNIMO** (1676–1764). Benito Jerónimo Feijóo (*b.* 8 October 1676; *d.* 26 September 1764), Benedictine monk who popularized modern European ideas in Spain and the colonies. Feijóo studied in Galicia and Salamanca before becoming professor of theology at the University of Oviedo. Through reading foreign works, Feijóo became aware of his country's intellectual backwardness, which he attempted to correct with his nine-volume collection of essays, *Teatro crítico universal* (1726–1739) and five volumes of *Cartas eruditas y curiosas* (1742–1760). The wide range of subjects he covered included literature, art, philosophy, natural science, mathematics, geography, and history.

Feijóo questioned contemporary medicine, exaggerated devotion to the saints, and religious superstition. He tried to persuade his countrymen that scientific progress need not undermine religious belief. Although his enlightened skepticism aroused controversy, he remained devoted to the Catholic faith and found favor with Ferdinand VI, who silenced his critics with a royal order in 1750. While few of Feijóo's ideas were new, many were relatively unknown in eighteenth-century Spain and its colonies. His writings enjoyed enormous popularity at home and, in part because of his favorable view of creoles' abilities, in the Indies.

*See also* **Benedictines; Catholic Church: The Colonial Period; Creole.**

BIBLIOGRAPHY

University Of Oviedo, *P. Feijóo y su siglo,* 3 vols. (1966).

Ramón Otero Pedrayo, *El padre Feijóo: Su vida, doctrina e influencias* (1972).

*Additional Bibliography*

Ardao, Arturo. *Logica y metafísica en Feijóo.* Montevideo: Biblioteca de Marcha, Facultad de Humanidades-Centro de Estudios Gallegos, 1997.

González Feijoo, José Antonio. *El pensamiento ético-político de B.J. Feijoo.* Oviedo: Pentalfa Ediciones, 1991.

López Vázquez, Ramón. *O padre Feixoo, escolástico.* Santiago de Compostela: Xunta de Galicia: Centro de Investigacións Lingüísticas e Literarias "Ramón Piñeiro," 1995.

Xavier, Adro. *Feijóo: cátedras y críticas: vienen los Borbones.* Barcelona: Editorial Casals, 1994.

SUZANNE HILES BURKHOLDER

**FEITOR.** *See* **Factor.**

**FEITORIA.** *See* **Fleet System: Colonial Brazil.**

**FELGUÉREZ, MANUEL** (1928–). Manuel Felguérez (*b.* 12 December 1928), Mexican artist. Born in San Agustín Valparaíso, Zacatecas, Felguérez is one of the most important exponents of abstract art in Mexico. From 1947 to 1952 he lived in Paris, studying at the Academy of the Grande Chaumière; he also studied sculpture with Ossip Zadkine and Constantin Brancusi. Upon his return to Mexico City in 1953, he studied with Francisco Zúñiga. Felguérez's work includes a number of highly abstract sculptures, stained glass, and murals that he created with found objects. Most of his geometric paintings preserve figurative elements pointing to the dualism between order and disorder that characterizes his entire oeuvre. Felguérez has also worked as a set designer for such plays as *La lección* (1961) and *La ópera del orden* (1961), directed by Alexandro Jodorowsky. His work has been the subject of numerous individual and group exhibitions in Mexico and Europe. The Museo Arte Abstracto Manuel Felguérez in Zacatecas, named for the artist, honors his great contribution to abstract art.

*See also* **Art: The Twentieth Century.**

BIBLIOGRAPHY

Del Conde, Teresa. "Felguérez: Los bordes de una trayectoria." *Anales del Instituto de Investigaciones Estéticas* 22, no. 77 (December 2000): 251–263.

Manrique, Jorge Alberto. *El geometrismo mexicano.* México: Universidad Nacional Autónoma de México, 1977.

Rodríguez, Antonio. *History of Mexican Mural Painting.* Translated by Marina Corby. New York: Putnam's Sons, 1969.

Schneider, Luis Mario, and Teresa del Conde. *Manuel Felguérez: Muestra antológica.* México: Instituto Nacional de Bellas Artes, 1987.

ILONA KATZEW

**FELICIANO, JOSÉ** (1945–). The Puerto Rican singer, guitarist, and songwriter José Feliciano, born September 10, 1945, occupies a salient place in contemporary popular music. His early success in reaching both English- and Spanish-speaking audiences makes him a major crossover performer. Born to a working-class family, he was raised in New York City's Spanish Harlem. As a child he demonstrated his penchant for music by teaching himself to play several instruments, including the concertina, the accordion, and especially the guitar, which he plays as a virtuoso. This is indeed remarkable for a person who was born blind and received little formal musical training. Feliciano started playing as a teenager in Greenwich Village clubs and was performing professionally by 1963. RCA Records produced his first album, *The Voice and the Guitar of Jose Feliciano* (1964), a work that brought him international recognition. He captivated the North American market with his album *Feliciano!* (1968), featuring his version of the Door's famous piece "Light My Fire." This hit not only earned him two Grammy Awards, it also established his reputation as a gifted performer. In the 1970s, Feliciano scored two more hits with the theme song for the popular television show *Chico and the Man* and the highly popular seasonal favorite "Feliz Navidad (I Wanna Wish You a Merry Christmas)." Since then, Feliciano's growing fame throughout Latin America has made up for his dwindling popularity in North America. His international success brought him four more Grammys and more than forty gold and platinum albums. In 1996, *Billboard* magazine accorded José Feliciano a Lifetime Achievement Award for his contributions to Latin music. A formidable acoustic guitar sound and the skillful fusion of diverse musical styles—Latin, jazz, soul, and folk—characterize José Feliciano's distinctive music.

*See also* **Music: Popular Music and Dance.**

BIBLIOGRAPHY

*Detroit Free Press,* May 28, 1993.

Heredia, Juanita. "Feliciano, José." In *Encyclopedia of Latino Popular Culture*, edited by Cordelia Chávez Candelaria. Westport, CT: Greenwood Press, 2004.

*Newsday,* August 9, 1995, p. A8.

*New York Times,* October 8, 1968.

LUIS A. GONZÁLEZ

**FÉLIX, MARÍA** (1914–2002). María Félix (*b.* 8 April 1914; *d.* 8 April 2002), Mexican film actress. Born near Alamos, Sonora, as a young girl Félix moved to Guadalajara, where she completed her early schooling. She made her film debut in 1942 in the classic *El penon de las ánimas.* One year later, she starred in *Doña Bárbara,* a screen adaptation of the famous Venezuelan novel. The character Félix portrayed in that film epitomized the dominant, self-assured, strong-willed, and seductive heroine that became the actress's screen persona. Among her greatest and best-known films are *Enamorada* (1947), *La diosa arrodillada* (1947), *Maclovia* (1948), *Río escondido* (1949), *Doña Diabla* (1951), *El rapto* (1954), *Tizoc* (1957), *La cucaracha* (1959), and *Juana Gallo* (1961). The Mexican film academy awarded Félix the Ariel for best actress for the films *Enamorada, Río Escondido,* and *Doña Diabla.* Known as *La Doña,* Félix was a living legend and symbol of Mexican beauty, femininity, and strength, and was arguably the greatest screen presence of twentieth-century Mexican cinema. In 1985 she won a lifetime achievement award and the Mexico City Prize for her lifelong contribution to arts and culture. In 1996 the French government named her *commandeur de l'orde des arts et des lettres*, making her the first Latin American woman to win this honor. She died on 8 April 2002.

*See also* **Cinema: From the Silent Film to 1990.**

BIBLIOGRAPHY

Luis Reyes De La Maza, *El cine sonoro en México* (1973).

E. Bradford Burns, *Latin American Cinema: Film and History* (1975).

Carl J. Mora, *Mexican Cinema: Reflections of a Society: 1896–1980* (1982).

John King, *Magical Reels: A History of Cinema in Latin America* (1990).

*Additional Bibliography*

Cluzet, Enrique Mourigan. *María Félix a todo color: Los secretos mejor guardados de la Doña.* México: Debolsillo: Random House Mondadori, 2005.

Philippe, Pierre. *María Félix.* New York: Assouline, 2006.

Taibo, Paco Ignacio. *María Félix: 47 pasos por el cine.* México, DF: Ediciones B. México, 2004.

DAVID MACIEL

**FEMINISM AND FEMINIST ORGANIZATIONS.** The rise of a feminist consciousness in Latin America has often been obscured by assumptions about Latin American society, cultural Catholicism, and stereotypic ideas of "Latin" femininity as well as by ahistorical assertions that feminist thought in the "Third World" is derivative rather than sui generis. The historical record belies these assumptions.

### THE NINETEENTH CENTURY: CITIZENSHIP AND EDUCATION

The issues of full citizenship for women and access to education for girls were addressed in the immediate aftermath of the Wars of Independence. An 1824 petition presented to the government of Zacatecas, Mexico, states: "Women also wish to have the title of citizen ... to see themselves counted in the census as 'La ciudadana.'" In Argentina, the Society of Beneficience was created in 1823 to establish public elementary schools for girls.

Women who founded girls' schools were among the first voices calling for women's rights in Latin

America. Nisia Floresta Brasileira Augusta, who took a patriotic name (Nisia of the Majestic Brazilian Forest) to illustrate her claim to full citizenship, translated Mary Wollstonecraft's *A Vindication of the Rights of Women* into Portuguese in 1832 and sold out two printings. She wrote numerous articles on the education of women, published in *O Liberal,* and ran a girls' school from her home.

The periodical or political journal has a long history as a central forum for the public debate of women's issues in Latin America. Argentine writer Juana Manuela Gorriti founded *La Alborada del Plata* (1850), which engaged in the intense international debate surrounding women's role in the modern state. Juana Manso, while in exile from Argentina in Brazil, founded *O Jornal das Senhoras,* which dealt primarily with female education and politics. Similar journals appeared in Mexico (*La Semana de las Señoritas Mejicanas* [1851–1852]), Cuba (*Album Cubano de lo Bueno y lo Bello,* founded in 1860 by Gertrudis Goméz De Avellaneda), Peru and Bolivia (*El Album,* 1860s), and elsewhere. In the prestigious *El correo del Perú,* Carolina Freyre de Jaimes engaged in an ongoing debate on the role of women in society with the well known writer Francisco de Paula González Vigil. The linkage of the ideas of independence, the emancipation of slaves, and the drive for political and economic modernity with full citizenship for women permeates the writings of these early feminists, as in the 1869 speech by Cuban patriot Ana Betancourt de Mora to a constituent assembly of male patriots: "Citizens: ... you have emancipated men of servitude.... [Now] the Cuban male ... will also dedicate his generous soul to women's rights."

By the latter half of the nineteenth century, arguments for women's equality were cast in terms of progressivism and the hope of a better life in the New World. The first issue of *O Sexo Feminino,* edited by Francisca Motta Diniz and "dedicated to the emancipation of women," appeared in Campanha, Minas Gerais, Brazil, on 7 September 1873, Brazil's independence day, as a symbol of patriotism—one of the hallmarks of Latin American women's movements. *O Sexo Feminino* declared: "It will be seen that America will give the cry of independence for women, showing the Old World what it means to be civilized, that women are as apt for education as young men." *La Mujer,* published in Chile in the 1890s, was committed to the idea that "woman is the basis of universal progress."

The emergence of women novelists, poets, journalists, and political activists and the development of a shared feminist consciousness in Latin America are directly linked to trends that combined to produce a modernization process in certain nations. Feminists found their voice—and their audience—in Argentina, Uruguay, Chile, and Brazil, states that received thousands of European immigrants and that had significant social and political reform movements, as well as in Mexico and Cuba, countries that experienced major social upheavals.

It was female schoolteachers who formed the nucleus of the first women's groups to articulate what may be defined as a feminist critique of society, that is, to protest the pervasive inequality of the sexes in legal status, marriage, access to education, and political and economic power. The teachers represented a new group in Latin American society—the educated middle sector—that included skilled workers, clerks, and government employees as well as educators. These groups were in touch with one another through their institutions of learning and through professional associations, forums where they could share their common experiences.

In Mexico, poet and educator Rita Cetina Gutiérrez, Cristina Farfán de García Montero, and several primary schoolteachers formed in 1870 La Siempreviva, a female society dedicated to overcoming women's unequal status and to fighting social problems by improving hygiene and by educating mothers in nutrition and child care. By founding a publication to espouse their ideas and by opening schools to train a new generation, the members of La Siempreviva employed tactics used by earlier advocates of women's rights; the critical change was that their activities were collective, not individual.

In South America a collective female critique of discriminatory practices based on gender occurred at a series of scientific congresses held between 1898 and 1909. Men and women delegates presented papers on health care, hygiene, the welfare of mothers, and botanical research. The divisive issue proved to be female education: Should women have equal access or be educated only in "suitable" professions, such as primary teaching? The women delegates were indignant that the debate should be cast in these terms and broadened the discussion into a wide-ranging attack on the pervasive inequality of the sexes within their societies.

### THE EARLY TWENTIETH CENTURY: SUFFRAGE

In the following decades, women called numerous conferences to discuss these issues. In 1910, the date of the centennial celebration of Argentine independence, the first Congreso Femenino Internacional convened in Buenos Aires with more than 200 women from Argentina, Uruguay, Peru, Paraguay, and Chile in attendance. The congress was organized by the National Women's Council with Cecilia Grierson presiding. Sponsoring groups included the Association of University Women, the National Argentine Association against the White Slave Trade, the Socialist Women's Center, the Association of Normal School Teachers, the Women's Union and Labor Group, and the National League of Women Freethinkers.

The wide differences in political orientation among the women at the Congreso Femenino reflected the enormous political diversity of Buenos Aires, Montevideo, São Paulo, Santiago, and Lima at the time. Many of the reformist women belonged to the Argentine Socialist Party; others rejected the Socialist platform as too concerned with class and labor and aligned themselves with the anarchists, whose platform called for a complete reform of the bourgeois household. The loyalties of others lay with the Argentine Radical Party, a more traditional form of political opposition. Topics addressed ranged from international law, particularly as it related to the rights of married women to retain their citizenship, to health care and the problems of the married working woman, to equal pay for equal work. A resolution was passed commending the government of Uruguay for the enactment in 1907 of the first divorce law in Latin America.

Universal suffrage was part of the Socialist Party platform and women's suffrage was an issue of debate at women's congresses in Latin America in the first half of the twentieth century. In 1916 two feminist congresses were convened in Mexico to discuss the future role of women in post-Revolutionary Mexico and to attempt to influence the Mexican Constitutional Convention then meeting in Querétaro. On its promulgation in 1917, the Mexican Constitution was hailed as the most advanced social and political document of its day; political rights, including the right to vote, were granted "to all Mexican citizens." Women, however, were excluded from the category of citizen.

The history of feminism in Peru offers an example of a woman's movement in a country where a strong middle class had not developed by the early twentieth century and the secularization of schools had not occurred. María Jesús Alvarado Rivera, who studied at feminist thinker and author Elvira García y García's private secondary school for girls, founded Evolución Femenina in 1914 to discuss "the woman question." The core group of members had all attended the Congress Feminino Internacional in 1910. Also in 1914, Zoila Aurora Cáceres, a novelist and essayist, founded Feminismo Peruano, an organization dedicated to women's right to vote. The conservatism and class bias of the Peruvian political milieu is apparent in the women's nine-year campaign not for access to government positions but merely for the right of women to be appointed as directors of the powerful private charitable organization Sociedades de Beneficencia Pública.

In the 1920s and 1930s, a number of national and international women's conferences met to discuss civil, legal, and educational reform; suffrage; and the rights of working women. In 1922, with the example of U.S. women's successful drive for suffrage (1920) and in the wake of World War I, the war to "make the world safe for democracy," 2,000 women from throughout the hemisphere convened in Baltimore and formed the Pan-American Association for the Advancement of Women. Veterans of the scientific congresses, such as Amanda Labarca of Chile and Flora de Oliveira Lima of Brazil, were among the Latin American delegates, as was a rising generation of feminist leaders that included Elena Torres, who was at that time designing the radical rural education program in post-Revolutionary Mexico; Sara Casal de Quirós of Costa Rica; and Bertha Lutz, founder of the Liga para a Emancipação Intelectual Feminina in Rio de Janeiro in 1920. Lutz's vision contrasts with that of the Peruvian women: "In Brazil the true 'leaders' of feminism . . . are the innumerable young women who work in industry, in commerce, in teaching."

In the 1920s Cuban women were heavily involved in the effort to establish democratic practices and social equality in their newly independent nation. In 1923 the Club Feminino De Cuba (1917) formed the Federación Nacional de Asociaciones Femeninas, an umbrella group of thirty-one women's organizations, led by Pilar Morlon de Menéndez, to plan the First National Women's Congress, held in Havana on 1–7 April 1923. Government officials were invited to the event in an effort to influence national reform policy. A Second Congress met in Havana in 1925 to call for social equality between men and women, protection of children, equal pay for equal work, equality of the claims of illegitimate children, elimination of prostitution, and a prohibition against the unequal treatment of women.

In Mexico, Sofia Villa de Buentello organized a Congreso de Mujeres de la Raza in July 1925. The ideological splits that were to characterize the women's movement in the hemisphere in later decades were manifest at the congress. Irreconcilable differences emerged between the socialist left, led by Elvia Carrillo Puerto and Cuca García, who insisted on the economic basis of women's problems, and conservatives and moderates, led by Sofia Villa, who believed female inequality to be rooted in social and moral conditions.

In Argentina, feminists Alicia Moreau De Justo and Elvira Rawson joined with a broad umbrella of reformist groups, including the conservative Catholic women's trade union, to support passage of protective legislation for women industrial workers in 1924. Encouraged by this success, the National Feminist Union and the Women's Rights Association formed a coalition to push a comprehensive reform of the Civil Code through the legislature in 1926. The reform granted married women civil rights equal to those of adult men; mothers parental rights over their children; and married women the right to enter professions, make contracts, and dispose of their earnings without spousal permission. In order to maintain the coalition, the Argentine National Council of Women agreed not to connect the reform to the divisive issue of women's suffrage.

In 1928 Cuban women's associations, including the Alianza Femenina Cubana and the Club Femenino de Cuba, hosted women from all over the hemisphere who came to Havana as unofficial delegates to the Sixth International Conference of American States. By the end of the conference, the women had presented an equal rights treaty for the consideration of the governments of the hemisphere and successfully lobbied for the creation of an officially designated body, the Inter-American Commission of Women (IACW), charged with the investigation of the legal status of women in the twenty-one member states. The use of the transnational forum for the discussion of women's issues proved particularly efficacious for Latin American women, who often found it difficult to create sympathetic political space in their own communities. Bringing international attention to an issue was a political strategy that Latin American feminists helped to pioneer, and it was one that would serve them well over time.

The enactment of women's suffrage should not be viewed as a signpost that the women's program had triumphed: The meaning of the vote and the reasons women's suffrage was enacted in a particular nation at a particular time vary greatly. In Brazil, Uruguay, and Cuba, the enactment of women's suffrage was the result of years of hard work and carefully planned campaigns by groups of women who were prepared to act when a political opening occurred. When the Brazilian Revolution of 1930 brought a reformist government to power, the Federação Brasileira Pelo Progresso Feminino, led by Bertha Lutz and Carlota Pereira de Queiroz, presented the leaders with a platform of thirteen principles that included women's suffrage and equality before the law. In Cuba numerous women's organizations, including the Alianza Nacional Feminista, the Partido Nacional Sufragista, and the Partido Demócratica Sufragista were in the forefront of groups fighting for political reform and were poised to demand the extension of the franchise to women when the new provisional constitution was drafted in 1934.

The 1920s and 1930s saw the emergence of the first generation of educated, urban women. This was notably so in Cuba, Argentina, Uruguay, and Chile, where the number of women attending post–grade-school institutions was nearly equal to that of male students, if teacher preparation is included in the count. New associations of women seeking broad-based reform, inclusive of women's suffrage, appeared in the 1930s. One example is the *Movimiento Pro-Emancipación de la Mujer Chilena* (MEMCH, 1935–1953), established by Chilean university women under the leadership of lawyer Elena Caffarena. Journals such as Nelly Marino Carvallo's *Mujeres de América* (1930–

1935, Buenos Aires) appealed to an international audience and carried articles written by Bolivian, Paraguayan, Peruvian, and Uruguayan women as well as Argentines.

Women leaders also emerged within the political left, though their politics as spokeswomen on behalf of their own sex often put them in sharp conflict with their male comrades, as illustrated by the career of Patricia Galvão, known as Pagú, who joined the Partido Comunista Brasileira (PCB) in 1930. Pagú shared the scorn of most radical women for bourgeois feminists, but she had a feminist vision of her own. In her novel *Parque industrial* (1933), she described the sexual discrimination and duress experienced by female industrial workers. While her Marxist analysis of labor and call for revolution were orthodox enough, Pagú had the temerity to link the issue of sexual inequality with that of racism in the Brazilian work force. The leadership of the PCB was outraged by the sexually explicit descriptions in the book and even more so by Pagú's daring to address the taboo subject of race; the party demanded that the book be suppressed.

In Mexico, women loyal to the Revolutionary Party were deeply disappointed when reformist president Lázaro Cárdenas (1934–1940) failed to fulfill his campaign promise to "reform the constitution to grant equal rights." At the Eighth International Conference of American States at Lima in 1938, it was the Mexican delegation to the IACW, led by Amalia González Caballero de Castillo Ledón, which successfully lobbied for passage of the Declaration in Favor of Women's Rights. The resolution established the precedent for incorporation of the phrase "the equal rights of men and women" into the charter draft of the United Nations in San Francisco in October 1945.

## DEMOCRACY AND SOCIAL JUSTICE

During World War II and its immediate aftermath, many women's groups were incorporated into established political parties, often in "women's sections." Those who maintained their autonomy took on patriotic nomenclature and sought to draw on their wartime loyalty to demand full citizenship in the late 1940s. Incorporation, combined with the repression of women's associations involved in community action in many areas of the hemisphere, effectively muted a separatist woman's politics in the 1950s.

Taking their political cue from the Cuban revolutionary experience, women who joined the revolutionary left in the 1960s adopted a class analysis that repudiated "feminism" as bourgeois and divisive to the cause. Liberation theology, the other potent social critique to emerge in Latin America in the 1960s, retained a traditional view of women. But it was from this generation of women activists—the most highly educated generation of women in Latin American history—that the feminists of the 1970s emerged, giving up not a whit of their commitment to radical social change but adding to it a new brand of gender analysis. By 1985 these feminists had developed a stinging critique of the traditional left within their own communities, challenged the "First World" view of European and U.S. feminists, and contributed organizational models, political strategies, and a new understanding of grass-roots social movements to global feminism.

In 1975 the Conferencia Mundial del Año Internacional de la Mujer convened in Mexico City to draw up the World Plan of Action for the United Nations Decade for Women 1976–1985. It was at the sessions of the Tribune of Non-Governmental Organizations, where representatives of voluntary associations and individuals could speak, that Latin American women made their presence felt. The majority of the 6,000 women who attended the Tribune were from North, Central, and South America; 2,000 were from Mexico alone. The lines of debate that were to dominate the first half of the UN Decade emerged in the confrontation between Betty Friedan and Domitila Barrios de Chungara, who came to Mexico to represent the Housewives Committee of Siglo XX, an organization of Bolivian tin miners' wives.

By 1977 the incorporation of a feminist political critique was visible in the new women's movement in many areas of Latin America. Over the next decade newsletters, feminist journals, and women's movement periodicals appeared, indicating the presence of women's groups in every region of the continent. One of the earliest and most notable is *fem,* produced since 1976 by a collective editorship, Nueva Cultura Feminista, in Mexico City. The subjects addressed provide a microcosm of the concerns of Mexican feminists over the years: abortion, work, sexuality, feminism, language, family, education, mothers and children, women writers, the history of women in Mexico, and women in the struggle for social justice. *MUJER/* Fempress, published monthly in Santiago, Chile, carries articles by correspondents in every country in the hemisphere. In 1984 the independent women's studies group, Grupo de Estudios sobre la Condición de la Mujer en Uruguay, began publication of *La Cacerola* (referring primarily to the banging of casseroles with spoons as part of demonstrations against the military regime). In Peru the Centro de Flora Tristán publishes *VIVA;* Movimiento Manuela Ramos (Manuela Ramos signifying "everywoman") issues pamphlets on health and community resources; *Mujer y Sociedad* addresses the politics of violence in the nation and in the home. Brazilian women have been leaders in the innovative use of film and have succeeded in incorporating the concerns of the women's movement into popular telenovelas such as *Malu mujer.* Since the late 1980s new journals have continued to appear: *Feminaria* in Buenos Aires and *Enfogues de Mujer,* published by the Grupo de Estudios de la Mujer Paraguaya.

In July 1981, 250 women from Brazil, Chile, Colombia, Ecuador, Mexico, Panama, Peru, Puerto Rico, the Dominican Republic, and Venezuela met in Bogotá at the Primero Encuentro Feminista Latinoamericano y del Caribe. The *encuentros feministas* have since convened in Peru (1983), Brazil (1985 and 2005), Mexico (1987), Argentina (1990), El Salvador (1993), Chile (1996), the Dominican Republic (1999), and Costa Rica (2002), with upwards of 2,000 women in attendance.

Numerous organizations grew out of the Sandinista revolution in Nicaragua, among them Asociación de Mujeres Nicaraguenes Luisa Amanda Espinoza (AMNLAE), dedicated to making the FSLN more gender conscious. Since the mid-1980s a number of women's studies programs have been instituted in Latin America. Almost without exception, the programs grew out of independent feminist study groups and women's community action collectives that are only now finding an institutional home. These include the Programa Interdisciplinario Estudios de la Mujer (PIEM) at El Colegio de México, the Programa Interdisciplinario Estudios de la Mujer (PIEM) at La Universidad Autónoma de Costa Rica, the Núcleo de Estudos Interdisciplinares sobre a Mulher (NEIM) da Universidade Federal da Bahia, and Carreras de Posorado Interdisciplinaria de Especilización de Estudios de la Mujer (CIEM) at La Universidad de Buenos Aires.

Strategies developed by Latin American women activists over the past century have been widely adopted in other areas of the world. The Organizaciones de Trabajadores del Hogar de América Latina y el Caribe, founded in 1988 by women household workers, is a model for similar organizations in Africa and Asia. International Day Against Violence Against Women, observed on 25 November, was initiated by Latin American feminists at the IV Encuentro Feminista in Mexico to commemorate the deaths by torture of six Dominican peasant women at the hands of military troops; in 1992 the United Nations declared 25 November a global day of protest against violence directed at women.

In February 1993 the Programa Interdisciplinario de Estudios de Género (PRIEG), the women's studies program instituted at the Universidad de Costa Rica in 1987, hosted the V Congreso Interdisciplinario y Internacional de Mujeres. Although the 2,000 participants represented women's organizations from throughout the world, the organization and the content of the program were telling indicators of the breadth and depth of feminist thought in Latin America in the 1990s. The concerns included women and the environment, heterosexual AIDS, gender and sexuality, indigenous women and peoples, feminism and democratic practice. These matters of urgent concern in Central America and elsewhere in Latin America dominated the weeklong event, which culminated in a march from the university campus to the Plaza de la Democracia to celebrate "Women's Rights/Human Rights."

In the new millennium women, and society in general, are thinking in new ways about women's equality and emancipation. In the context of a transition to democracy in Latin American countries since the 1990s, the feminist movement has made great strides in terms of establishing women's studies programs at universities, nongovernmental organizations (NGOs) and governmental departments devoted to women's issues, and sponsorship of programs in support of women. A younger generation of feminists who have benefited from the earlier struggles has emerged. Yet some women closely attuned to feminist issues view these strides with skepticism. They raise concerns about the "institutionalization" of feminism and feminist organizations, arguing that receiving state or international agency support has resulted in the moderating or "mainstreaming" of feminist agendas. Likewise, some feminists question a divide between scholarship and activism.

New issues such as neoliberal reforms, technology, globalization, and the environment are on the feminist agenda, along with longstanding questions about race, ethnicity, and class.

*See also* **Education: Overview; Education: Nonformal Education; Gorriti, Juana Manuela; Labarca Hubertson, Amanda; Lutz, Bertha Maria Julia; Moreau de Justo, Alicia; Sociology; Women.**

BIBLIOGRAPHY

Asunción Lavrin, *The Ideology of Feminism in the Southern Cone, 1900–1940* (1986).

Marifran Carlson, *¡Feminismo! The Woman's Movement in Argentina from Its Beginnings to Eva Perón* (1988).

Jane S. Jaquette, ed., *The Women's Movement in Latin America: Feminism and the Transition to Democracy* (1989).

Sonia E. Álvarez, *Engendering Democracy in Brazil: Women's Movements in Transition Politics* (1990).

June E. Hahner, *Emancipating the Female Sex: The Struggle for Women's Rights in Brazil, 1850–1940* (1990).

Seminar on Feminism and Culture in Latin America, *Women, Culture, and Politics in Latin America* (1990).

Shirlene Ann Soto, *Emergence of the Modern Mexican Woman: Her Participation in Revolution and Struggle for Equality, 1910–1940* (1990).

Francesca Miller, *Latin American Women and the Search for Social Justice* (1991).

K. Lynn Stoner, *From the House to the Streets: The Cuban Woman's Movement for Legal Reform, 1898–1940* (1991).

*Additional Bibliography*

Caldwell, Kia Lilly. *Negras in Brazil: Re-envisioning Black Women, Citizenship, and the Politics of Identity.* New Brunswick, NJ: Rutgers University Press, 2007.

Femenías, María Luisa, ed. *Perfiles del feminismo iberoamericano.* 3 vols. Buenos Aires: Catálogos, 2002–2007.

French, John D., and Daniel James, eds. *The Gendered Worlds of Latin American Women Workers: From Household and Factory to the Union Hall and Ballot Box.* Durham, NC: Duke University Press, 1997.

Gargallo, Francesca. *Las ideas feministas latinoamericanas,* 2nd revised edition. Mexico: Universidad de la Ciudad de México, 2006.

González, Victoria, and Karen Kampwirth. *Radical Women in Latin America: Left and Right.* University Park: Pennsylvania State University Press, 2001.

Kampwirth, Karen. *Feminism and the Legacy of Revolution: Nicaragua, El Salvador, Chiapas.* Athens: Ohio University Press, 2004.

Lavrin, Asunción. *Women, Feminism, and Social Change in Argentina, Chile, and Uruguay, 1890–1940.* Lincoln: University of Nebraska Press, 1995.

Macías, Anna. *Against All Odds: The Feminist Movement in Mexico to 1940.* Westport, CT: Greenwood Press, 1982.

Molyneux, Maxine. *Women's Movements in International Perspective: Latin America and Beyond.* New York: Palgrave, 2001.

Montoya, Rosario, Lessie Jo Frazier, and Janise Hurtig, eds. *Gender's Place: Feminist Anthropologies of Latin America.* New York: Palgrave Macmillan, 2002.

Olea Mauleón, Cecilia, ed. *Encuentros, (des)encuentros y búsquedas: El movimiento feminista en América Latina.* Lima: Flora Tristan, 1998.

Pinto, Céli Regina J. *Uma história do feminismo no Brasil.* São Paulo: Editora Fundação Perseu Abramo, 2003.

Rodríguez, Victoria E., ed. *Women's Participation in Mexican Political Life.* Boulder, CO: Westview Press, 1998.

Rosemblatt, Karin Alejandra. *Gendered Compromises: Political Cultures and the State in Chile, 1920–1950.* Chapel Hill: University of North Carolina Press, 2000.

Shayne, Julie D. *The Revolution Question: Feminisms in El Salvador, Chile, and Cuba.* New Brunswick, NJ: Rutgers University Press, 2004.

Stephen, Lynn. *Women and Social Movements in Latin America: Power from Below.* Austin: University of Texas Press, 1997.

Stromquist, Nelly P. *Feminist Organizations and Social Transformation in Latin America.* Boulder, CO: Paradigm, 2007.

Valdés, Teresa. *De lo social a lo político: La acción de las mujeres latinoamericanas.* Santiago: LOM Ediciones, 2000.

FRANCESCA MILLER

**FEMINIST CONGRESSES, FIRST AND SECOND, 1916, YUCATAN.** Seven hundred women attended the First and Second Feminist Congresses at the Peon Contreras Theatre in Mérida, Yucatán, in January and December 1916. The congresses, held against the backdrop of the Mexican Revolution (1910–1920), were the first to address women's rights and participation in Mexico. They reflected the swell of feminist thought, liberalism, and radical ideas that had grown particularly since the late nineteenth century.

Scholars credit Salvador Alvarado, the Yucatán governor (1915–1918), with the idea to hold the congresses, though women carried out the logistics and organization. A proclaimed socialist, Alvarado implemented liberal reforms and supported greater roles for women in public life, particularly in education. President Venustiano Carranza, who appointed Alvarado, likewise raised awareness about women's contributions to the nation. His private secretary was Hermila Galindo de Topete (1896–1954), a vocal feminist and editor from 1915 to 1919 of the journal *Mujer Moderna* (Modern woman), which promoted Carranza and feminist ideas. Although Galindo did not attend the conferences, she sent a speech about the "woman of the future" to be read in her absence; its discussion of female sexuality generated great controversy.

Because literacy was required, the majority of conference attendees were middle-class schoolteachers. Education was an important theme: Though separated among radicals, moderates, and conservatives, in general the attendees agreed on the centrality of education in addressing the condition of women in society. Some women believed that education was more important for men than for women; others stressed the importance of women's roles as mothers and as educators within and outside the home. Although vague, conference resolutions demanded the same job opportunities for women and men. The Catholic Church was a subject of much debate and disagreement. Reflecting the government's anticlerical attitudes, some women decried the Church as the "yoke of tradition" and criticized its influence in education. Their opponents defended it as a critical educational and moral compass.

The moderate and radical factions of the Congress united in favor of reforming the 1884 Civil Code, which denied married women legal and property rights. Their critique had some influence on President Carranza's decision to enact the Law of Family Relations in 1917, expanding women's legal rights. Although the conferences' more ambitious goals, such as women's suffrage, were still far off, the discussions and debate that took place gave voice to the major concerns of middle-class women in early-twentieth-century Mexico.

*See also* **Alvarado, Salvador; Carranza, Venustiano; Feminism and Feminist Organizations; Women.**

BIBLIOGRAPHY

Blanco Figueroa, Francisco. *Mujeres mexicanas del siglo XX: La otra revolución*, 4 vols. Mexico: Editorial Edico, 2001–.

Macías, Anna. *Against All Odds: The Feminist Movement in Mexico to 1940.* Westport, CT: Greenwood Press, 1982.

Mitchell, Stephanie, and Patience A. Schell, eds. *The Women's Revolution in Mexico, 1910–1953.* Lanham, MD: Rowman and Littlefield, 2007.

MEREDITH GLUECK

## FERDINAND II OF ARAGON (1452–1516).

Son of John II of Aragon and Juana Enríquez, Ferdinand II, born March 10, 1452, was king of Aragon (1479–1516), Sicily (1468–1516), Naples (1504–1516), and—through his marriage in 1469 to Isabella I of Castile—Castile and León (1574–1516). In this last capacity he helped shape Spanish policy toward the New World, though he paid less attention to the New World and the welfare of its inhabitants than did his first wife. Even after her death in 1504, when the administration of these Castilian realms fell to him, he usually delegated responsibility to his advisers, especially Bishop Juan Rodríguez de Fonseca, head of the Casa de Contratación in Seville. Ferdinand's interest in the Indies stemmed primarily from the material wealth that they might provide to finance his Mediterranean ventures.

Ferdinand and Isabella met Christopher Columbus around 1486 and appointed a commission to consider the merits of his plan to reach Asia by a westward route. Although they believed, correctly, that Columbus had vastly underestimated the distance of such a journey, they finally decided, after conquering Granada in 1492, that his expedition was worth the modest investment of approximately two million maravedís.

Upon Columbus's return, Ferdinand and Isabella obtained a papal bull (*Inter caetera*) that granted them title to the newly discovered lands. Pope Alexander VI had received significant favors from Ferdinand and was eager to accommodate the sovereigns' wishes. Nevertheless, they, or Columbus, found this first bull insufficient. A second bull *Inter caetera*, dated May 4, 1493, more clearly distinguished Castilian territories from those of Portugal. It drew a line of demarcation 100 leagues west of the Azores or Cape Verde Islands and granted Castile title to those territories west of this line not already under Christian rule. In 1494, with the Treaty of Tordesillas, Castile and Portugal moved the line of demarcation 270 leagues farther to the west.

The Spanish monarchs had granted Columbus extraordinary privileges and titles (admiral, viceroy, and governor), but they quickly took steps to limit his power and prevent him from establishing a monopoly. With an arrangement that set a pattern for future conquests, they granted licenses to private adventurers, who had to finance their own expeditions and give the Crown one-fifth of their gross profits. In 1500 Ferdinand and Isabella sent Francisco de Bobadilla to Hispaniola to assume command and investigate charges of Columbus's mismanagement. He arrested Columbus and his brothers, confiscated their property, and sent them back to Spain in chains. The monarchs had Columbus's property returned to him, but not his authority. In 1501 they replaced Bobadilla with Nicolás de Ovando, whom Ferdinand replaced eight years later with Columbus's elder son, Diego.

The question of how to treat the inhabitants of these lands had troubled the monarchs, or at least the queen, from the outset, when Columbus started sending shipments of enslaved Tainos back to Spain. Isabella eventually made it clear that she wanted her new subjects to remain free, adopt Christianity and Spanish customs, and be compensated for their labor, to which Europeans would have access only with the Crown's approval. Neither monarch opposed the institution of slavery. Indeed, Ferdinand authorized the shipment of enslaved Africans to Hispaniola. But he and Isabella usually treated Indians differently, because they considered them to be their vassals, and therefore entitled to their protection.

It was under Ferdinand's rule, after the death of Queen Isabella in 1504 and archduke Philip in 1506, that the Crown first developed a comprehensive Indian policy. The Dominican Fray Antón Montesinos met Ferdinand in 1512 and informed him of the abuses that the natives were suffering at the hands of the Spanish colonists. In response, the king summoned a group of theologians and royal officials to consider the "Indian problem." After lengthy discussion, this group drew up the Laws of Burgos (1512 and 1513), which prohibited the enslavement of the Indians and sought to protect them from the worst abuses. At the same time these laws required them to abandon their homes and many of their customs, so that they might more easily be converted to Christianity and incorporated into the colonial economy as laborers. For the most part the Laws of Burgos were not enforced.

With no surviving son or son-in-law from his marriage to Isabella or his marriage to Germaine de Foix, and with his daughter Juana deemed unfit for rule, Ferdinand bequeathed the Spanish kingdoms to his grandson, Charles of Ghent. He died January 23, 1516.

*See also* **Columbus, Christopher; Isabella I of Castile; Spain; Spanish Empire; Tordesillas, Treaty of (1494).**

BIBLIOGRAPHY

Céspedes del Castillo, G. "Las Indias en el reinado de los Reyes Católicos." In *Historia de España y América*, vol. 2, ed. Jaime Vicens Vives, pp. 493–547. Barcelona: Vicens Vives, 1961.

Hernández Sánchez-Barba, Mario. *La corona y el descubrimiento de América.* Valencia: Asociación Francisco López de Gómara, 1989.

Prescott, William Hickling. *History of the Reign of Ferdinand and Isabella.* 1837. New York: Heritage Press, 1967.

Thomas, Hugh. *Rivers of Gold: The Rise of the Spanish Empire, from Columbus to Magellan.* New York: Random House, 2003.

GLEN CARMAN

---

**FERDINAND VI OF SPAIN** (1713–1759). Ferdinand VI of Spain (*b.* 17 September 1713; *d.* 10 August 1759), king of Spain (1746–1759). Ferdinand's ascent to the throne marked the end of the pro-Italian policy of his stepmother, Isabel (Elizabeth) Farnese, and the inauguration of policies determined by his Portuguese wife, Barbara of Braganza, and his three chief advisers, the marqués of Ensenada, José de Carvajal, and Francisco de Rávago (the king's confessor). Ferdinand was well intentioned but had little interest in politics and experienced lapses into insanity. Thus, during his reign the government of Spain was entrusted to his ministers.

In foreign policy, Ensenada and Carvajal advocated peace and neutrality and sought to keep Spain out of hostilities brewing between France and England, with Ensenada hoping to maintain peace by adopting a pro-French stance and Carvajal favoring England. Under their joint leadership the Spanish state became an instrument of reform and, to a degree, modernization, as it pursued tax reform and investment in public works.

A colonial conflict with Portugal over its Uruguayan capital of Colônia do Sacramento, the death of Carvajal (1754), and the machinations of an anti-Ensenada faction ended Ferdinand's first ministry. The second, no less marked by internal divisions, ended tax reform and replaced single register ships (an important commercial innovation of 1740) with the old fleet system. After the death of his wife (17 August 1758) Ferdinand went into a terminal state of mourning. His refusal even to sign documents brought the government to a halt until his death a year later.

*See also* **Spanish Empire.**

BIBLIOGRAPHY

Ciriaco Pérez Bustamante, "El reinado de Fernando VI en el reformismo español del siglo XVIII," in *Revista de la Universidad de Madrid* 12 (1954): 491–514.

Manuel Tuñón De Lara, ed. *Historia de España,* vol. 7, *Centralismo, ilustración, y agonía del Antiguo Régimen (1715–1833)* (1980), esp. pp. 199–213.

John Lynch, *Bourbon Spain, 1700–1808* (1989).

*Additional Bibliography*

Delgado Barrado, José Miguel. *El proyecto político de Carvajal: Pensamiento y reforma en tiempos de Fernando VI.* Madrid: Consejo Superior de Investigaciones Científicas, 2001.

Gómez Urdáñez, José Luis. *Fernando VI.* Madrid: Arlanza Ediciones, 2001.

Voltes Bou, Pedro. *La vida y la época de Fernando VI.* Barcelona: Planeta, 1998.

SUZANNE HILES BURKHOLDER

**FERDINAND VII OF SPAIN** (1784–1833). Ferdinand VII of Spain (*b.* 14 October 1784; *d.* 29 September 1833), king of Spain (1808–1833). The early years of Ferdinand's life were marked by fear and rebellion against his parents, Charles IV and Queen María Luisa, and their chief minister, Manuel de Godoy, who excluded the young prince from participation in government and even threatened him with disinheritance. Ferdinand's rebellion was manifested in intrigues with Napoleon I as early as 1807. During the peak of Godoy's unpopularity, the young prince of Asturias became a symbol for those disaffected with the regime of Charles IV. After the riots at Aranjuez by supporters of the prince (1808), Charles IV abdicated in his son's favor. Nevertheless, Ferdinand, like his father and Godoy, remained Napoleon's pawn and spent the first years of his reign a captive in France during the Peninsular War (1808–1814).

Restored to the throne after signing a treaty of alliance with Napoleon (1813), Ferdinand returned to Spain and repudiated the work of those who had governed in his absence, especially the liberal Cortes of Cádiz (1810) and the Constitution of 1812. Ferdinand treated the liberals, including Americans, as traitors, and revived royal absolutism. Equally shortsighted in his colonial policy, he tried to recover the colonies and restore their traditional obedience to the crown through military force. He restored the Council of the Indies but abolished the ministry of the Indies and reassigned its agenda to the ministries of war and finance.

Ferdinand's return to absolutism was supported by the church and wealthy landowners. Although he governed through ministers, his regime was unstable: during the first part of his reign (1814–1820) his ministers served an average of six months. In 1820 an army revolt forced Ferdinand to accept the constitution; thereafter, the revolutions at home and in the colonies were inextricably linked in his mind. In 1823, when Louis XVIII sent an army to restore Ferdinand's authority, the Spanish king once again revoked the constitution and embarked upon a policy of absolutism and repression.

Despite being unable to produce a male heir in four marriages, Ferdinand passed over his brother, Don Carlos, in favor of his daughter, the future Isabella II. His death thus provoked what became known as the Carlist wars, between the supporters of Isabella and those of Don Carlos. Ferdinand never abandoned the illusion that he could recover Spain's lost colonies—by 1824 only Cuba, Puerto

Rico, and the Philippines remained—and died without recognizing their independence.

See also **Napoleon I.**

BIBLIOGRAPHY

Miguel Artola, *La España de Fernando VII* (1968).

José Fontana, *La quiebra de la monarquía absoluta* (1971).

*Additional Bibliography*

Díaz-Plaja, Fernando. *Fernando VII: El más querido y el más odiado de los reyes españoles.* Barcelona: Planeta, 1991.

Landavazo Arias, Marco Antonio. *La máscara de Fernando VII: Discurso e imaginario monárquicos en una época de crisis: Nueva Espana, 1808-1822.* Mexico City: Colegio de México, Centro de Estudios Históricos; Morelia: Universidad Michoacana de San Nicolás de Hidalgo; Zamora: Colegio de Michoacán, 2001.

Moral Roncal, Antonio M. *El enemigo en Palacio!: Afrancesados, liberales y carlistas en la Real Casa y Patrimonio (1814–1843).* Alcalá de Henares: Universidad de Alcalá, 2005.

Puga, María Teresa. *Fernando VII.* Barcelona: Editorial Ariel, 2004.

SUZANNE HILES BURKHOLDER

**FERNANDES, FLORESTAN** (1920–1995). Florestan Fernandes (*b.* 22 July 1920, *d.* 10 August 1995), Brazilian sociologist and reformer who founded the São Paulo school of sociology, which studied capitalist modernization in Brazil. Fernandes began his career with theses on social organization and war among the Tupinambá Indians (1949, 1952). In the 1950s, after establishing himself at the University of São Paulo, he turned to topics in folklore and race relations. A UNESCO–sponsored project, conducted in collaboration with Roger Bastide and others, resulted in *Relações raciais entre negros e brancos em São Paulo* (1955; Race Relations Between Blacks and Whites in São Paulo), the first of his several revisionist studies of race relations in the context of São Paulo's twentieth–century transition to a competitive, class society, including *The Negro in Brazilian Society* (1964; English trans. 1969). Fernandes influenced a generation of sociologists, including Fernando Henrique Cardoso and Octávio Ianni, through his studies of slavery and race relations. Fernandes was purged from the University of São Paulo in 1969 and exiled. Upon his return to Brazil, he wrote an analysis of Brazil's transition to modern capitalism, *A revolução burguesa no Brasil: Ensaio de interpretação sociológica* (1975; The Bourgeois Revolution in Brazil). In the 1980s he published treatises on political redemocratization, and in 1986 was elected to the Constituent Congress by the socialist Partido dos Trabalhadores (Workers' Party).

See also **Sociology.**

BIBLIOGRAPHY

D'incao, Maria Angela ed., *O saber militante: Ensaios sobre Florestan Fernandes.* São Paulo: Editora UNESP, 1987.

Mota, Carlos Guilherme. *Ideologia da cultura brasileira, 1933–1974.* São Paulo: Editora Ática, 1977.

Sampaio, Plinhio de Arruda. *Entre a nação e a barbárie.* Petrópolis: Editora Vozes, 1999.

Soares, Eliane Veras. *Florestan Fernandes: O militante solitário.* São Paulo: Cortez Editora, 1997.

Tótora, Silvana. "A questão democrática em Florestan Fernandes." *Lua Nova* (1999): 109–126.

DAIN BORGES

**FERNANDES, MILLÔR** (c. 1924–). Millôr Fernandes (*b.* ca. 1924), Brazilian humorist, poet, playwright, and artist. Brazilian society and politics are favorite themes of Fernandes's highly original and satirical views, and most of his works underscore his keen ability to expose the incoherence of everyday life. He often highlights his writings with his own illustrations. His critical but extremely creative irreverence is also found in his "fables"—*Fábulas fabulosas* (1964) and *Novas fábulas fabulosas* (1978)—and in his protest theater—*Liberdade, liberdade* (1965). Fernandes has published frequently in newspapers and journals (such as *O Cruzeiro, Tribuna da Imprensa, Correio da Manhã, Pif-Paf*), is an important contributor to *Veja*, and has worked in radio and television. His works of art have been exhibited in the major cities of Brazil. Fernandes has also translated drama, of special note being his translations of works by Shakespeare, Molière, Brecht, and Synge. He is perhaps Brazil's most famous humorist. In addition, in early

2000, he expanded his repertoire to include online periodicals.

*See also* **Radio and Television; Theater.**

BIBLIOGRAPHY

Doria, Gustavo A. "Sobre Millôr Fernandes," *Revista de teatro* January–March 1985: 29–31.

Fiorin, José Luí. "Millôr e a destruição da fábula," *Alfa: Revista de lingüística* (1986–1987): 84–94.

Silverman, Malcolm. *Moderna Sãtira Brasileira*. Trans. Richard Goodwin. Rio de Janeiro: Nova Fronteira, 1987.

Witte, Ann. "Feminismo e anti–Feminismo em Leilah Assunção e Millôr Fernandes," *Dactylus* (1988–1989): 15–20.

GARY M. VESSELS

## FERNÁNDEZ, EMILIO "EL INDIO"

**FERNÁNDEZ, EMILIO "EL INDIO"** (1904–1986). Emilio "El Indio" Fernández (*b.* 26 March 1904; *d.* 6 August 1986), Mexican film director. Beginning his studies in the military academy, by the mid-1920s Fernández was in Hollywood, learning the craft of filmmaking. In the next decade, he returned to Mexico and worked as an actor in cinema. He debuted as a director with *La isla de la pasíon* in 1941. Among his most celebrated films are *María Candelaria* (1943), *Bugambilia* (1944), *Flor silvestre* (1944), *Pueblerina* (1946), *Enamorada* (1946), *Río escondido* (1946), *Salón México* (1954), and *La red* (1954). His films won numerous national and international awards and brought Mexican cinema to the attention of both Mexican and foreign audiences. Through a nationalistic and artistic treatment of subjects, Fernández extolled the beauties and virtues of Mexico and its people, particularly the *campesino* and the Indian. Fernández is one of Mexico's leading directors and a major figure of world cinema.

*See also* **Cinema: From the Silent Film to 1990; Mexico: Since 1910.**

BIBLIOGRAPHY

Luis Reyes De La Maza, *El cine sonoro en México* (1973).

E. Bradford Burns, *Latin American Cinema: Film and History* (1975).

Carl J. Mora, *Mexican Cinema: Reflections of a Society: 1896–1980* (1982).

John King, *Magical Reels: A History of Cinema in Latin America* (1990).

*Additional Bibliography*

Cuesta, Javier, and Helena R. Olmo. *Emilio El Indio Fernández.* Madrid: Dastín, 2003.

Rozado, Alejandro. *Cine y realidad social en México: Una lectura de la obra de Emilio Fernández.* Guadalajara: Universidad de Guadalajara, Centro de Investigación y Enseñanza Cinematográficas, 1991.

Tuñón, Julia. *Los rostros de un mito: Personajes femeninos en las películas de Emilio Indio Fernández.* Mexico City: Conaculta, 2000.

DAVID MACIEL

## FERNÁNDEZ, JUAN

**FERNÁNDEZ, JUAN** (c. 1530–1599). Juan Fernández (*b.* ca. 1530; *d.* 1599), Spanish navigator and discoverer of the Juan Fernández Islands. Actively engaged in navigation between Peru and Chile by 1550, Fernández theorized that Chile could be reached much more quickly by sailing further offshore, west of the Humboldt Current. Testing this theory, he discovered the islands that later bore his name, about 400 miles west of Valparaíso, Chile, on 22 November 1574. He reached Chile only thirty days after leaving Callao, Peru, a voyage that formerly took three months or more. Although Magellan may have seen these islands earlier, Fernández's sighting gave them navigational significance and greatly improved communications between Lima and Chile. His efforts to colonize the islands failed, but his leadership in the Peru-Chile trade earned him recognition in 1589 as "chief pilot of the South Sea." Minor difficulties with the Inquisition earned him the nickname "El Brujo" (the sorcerer). In 1592 he retired to his Chilean estate of Rautén, where he lived until his death seven years later.

*See also* **Explorers and Exploration: Spanish America.**

BIBLIOGRAPHY

Benjamín Vicuña Mackenna, *Juan Fernández, historia verdadera de la isla de Robinson Crusoe* (1883), esp. pp. 7–94.

José Toribio Medina, *El piloto Juan Fernández, descubridor de las islas que llevan su nombre, y Juan Jufré, armador de la expedición que hizo en busca de otras en el Mar del Sur* (1918; 2d ed. 1974).

Ralph Lee Woodward, Jr., *Robinson Crusoe's Island: A History of the Juan Fernández Islands* (1969), esp. pp. 3–14.

*Additional Bibliography*

Sánchez-Ostiz, Miguel. *La isla de Juan Fernández: Viaje a la isla de Robinson Crusoe.* Barcelona: Ediciones B, 2005.

RALPH LEE WOODWARD JR.

**FERNÁNDEZ, MAX** (1942–1995). A self-made millionaire from modest roots in Quillalloco, Bolivia, Max Fernández had a brief political career. He rose to prominence in the business world, becoming the president and largest shareholder of the Bolivian National Brewery, the country's largest brewery. As a means of expanding his commercial markets, he distributed gifts of beer and provided modest public works such as public lighting and potable water. This strategy resulted in his growing following and popular image as a benefactor, which he parlayed into politics. In 1989, after aborting a presidential campaign with another party, he created the Unión Cívica Solidaridad (UCS; Civic Solidarity Union). He ran as its candidate in 1993, earning 13 percent of the vote (compared to the winner's 35%). Along with Carlos Palenque of Conciencia de Patria (CONDEPA; conscience of the fatherland), he presented a clear challenge to the country's main political parties. Both were outsiders who campaigned against the political establishment, appealing to the largely indigenous urban lower class. Supporters appreciated the attention; Fernández's provision of socially minded public works distinguished him from the political class, which was increasingly perceived as aloof and unresponsive.

Although neither won office, their emergence started a trend of declining fortunes for the traditional parties that culminated in the presidency of Evo Morales in 2005. Nevertheless, Fernández diminished his own outsider credentials by joining with the Nationalist Revolutionary Movement (MNR) to form the governing coalition. His political career was cut short on November 26, 1995, when he and six others were killed in an airplane accident. His son Johnny took control of his party.

*See also* **Alcoholic Beverages; Bolivia, Political Parties: Overview; Palenque, Carlos.**

BIBLIOGRAPHY

Mayorga, Fernando. *Max Fernández, la política del silencio: Emergencia y consolidación de Unidad Cívica Solidaridad.* La Paz: ILDIS y la Facultad de Ciencias Económicas de la UMSS, 1991.

Mayorga, Fernando. "Neopopulismo y Democracia en Bolivia." *Revista de Ciencia Política* 23, no.1 (2003): 99–118.

ROBERT R. BARR

**FERNANDEZ, OSCAR LORENZO** (1897–1948). Oscar Lorenzo Fernandez (*b.* 4 November 1897; *d.* 27 August 1948), Brazilian composer, best known for his art songs. His first works, written between 1918 and 1922, were principally songs and piano compositions, but in the early 1920s he became interested in the nationalist movement and began to write works based on Brazilian subjects. In 1924 he was appointed professor of harmony at the National Music Institute and in 1936 established the Brazilian Conservatory, which he directed until his death in 1948.

In 1946, in recognition of the importance of the work of Heitor Villa-Lobos, Fernandez wrote an article, "A contribuição harmonica de Villa-Lobos," which stressed the innovative quality of the harmonic practices of Villa-Lobos. Fernandez shared with him an interest in the Indian melodies collected by explorer Roquette Pínto and in the use of native percussion instruments in orchestral composition. Fernandez's principal contribution to the emerging nationalist movement in music in Brazil was his ability to capture authentic elements of the Afro-Brazilian tradition in art songs and operas based on folk songs. He is best known as the composer of "Batuque," a movement from the suite "Malazarte," taken from an opera of the same title. This piece has been frequently arranged for various band and orchestral ensembles.

*See also* **Art: Folk Art; Education: Overview; Music: Art Music.**

BIBLIOGRAPHY

Oscar Lorenzo Fernandez, "A contribuição harmonica de Villa-Lobos," *Boletín latino-americano de música* 6 (April 1946).

Vasco Mariz, *A canção brasileira,* 5th ed. (1985).

*Additional Bibliography*

Igayara, Susana Cecília. "Oscar Lorenzo Fernandez." *Revista do Instituto de Estudos Brasileiros* 42 (1997): 59–73.

Wolff, Marcua Straubel. *Modernismo nacionalista na música brasileira: Camargo Guarnieri e Oscar Lorenzo Fernândez nos anos 30 e 40.* Rio de Janeiro: Pontificia Universidade Católica do Rio de Janeiro, Departamento de História, 1991.

DAVID P. APPLEBY

**FERNÁNDEZ ALONSO, SÉVERO** (1849–1925). Sévero Fernández Alonso (*b.* 15 August 1849; *d.* 12 August 1925), president of Bolivia (1896–1899). Born in Sucre, Fernández Alonso was a silver-mine owner, lawyer, and minister of war (1892–1896). He was the last president of the Conservative oligarchy that ruled Bolivia in the last two decades of the nineteenth century. Despite his efforts at conciliation with the rival Liberal and Federalist parties, the Federalist War (1898–1899) broke out during his presidency and effectively ended Conservative Party hegemony. Unable to fashion a compromise between the Sucre-based Conservatives and the northern Federalists, Fernández Alonso personally led the national army in an effort to crush the rebellion by the La Paz-based Federalists and Liberals. By remaining in Oruro with his army and vacillating in his attack on the city of La Paz, Fernández Alonso assured the military defeat of his government and the rise to power of the Liberal Party.

*See also* **Bolivia, Political Parties: Conservative Party; Bolivia, Political Parties: Liberal Party.**

BIBLIOGRAPHY

The best and most detailed summary of Fernández Alonso's term is in Ramiro Condarco Morales, *Zárate, el "Temible" Willka: Historia de la rebelión indígena de 1899,* 2d ed. (1983).

*Additional Bibliography*

Irurozqui, Marta. *La armonía de las desigualdades: Elites y conflictos de poder en Bolivia, 1880-1920.* Madrid: Consejo Superior de Investigaciones Científicas; Cusco: Centro de Estudios Regionales Andinos Bartolomé de las Casas, 1994.

ERICK D. LANGER

**FERNÁNDEZ ARTUCIO, HUGO** (1912–1974). Hugo Fernández Artucio (*b.* 1912; *d.* 1974), Uruguayan professor and publicist, was political editor of *El Día* from 1941 to 1966. In 1966 he supported the presidential campaign of Oscar Gestido and became director of the University of Uruguay's Vázquez Acevedo Institute. Fernández Artucio gained public recognition through a series of interviews on the "Espectador" radio station in 1940, in which he revealed a Nazi plot to overthrow the Uruguayan government. His findings helped a parliamentary investigation commission, established in 1940, to analyze NSDAP (Nationalsozialistische Deutsche Arbeiter-Partei) activities in Uruguay and to prepare legal action against its members.

BIBLIOGRAPHY

Hugo Fernández Artucio, *Nazis en el Uruguay* (1940) and *The Nazi Underground in South America* (1942). See also Roque Faraone, *El Uruguay en que vivimos, 1900–1968,* 2d ed. (1968).

Martin H. J. Finch, "Three Perspectives on the Crisis in Uruguay," in *Journal of Latin American Studies* 3 (November 1971): 173–190.

DIETER SCHONEBOHM

**FERNÁNDEZ CRESPO, DANIEL** (1901–1964). A Uruguayan educator and leader of the Blanco (National) Party, Daniel Fernández Crespo was born on April 28, 1901, in a rural area of the department of San José. He received his teaching degree and worked in education until 1932. His political career included his election to the town council of Montevideo in 1928, five terms as national representative (1931–1950), a senate seat in 1950, and the role of national adviser in 1954, in which he strove to unify distant sectors of the Blanco Party. Following the end of ninety-three years of government control by the Colorado Party, he presided over the departmental council of Montevideo (1959–1963) and in 1963–1964 served as president of the Consejo Nacional de Gobierno (National Council of Government), a nine-member committee established in 1952 to institutionalize co-participation in the exercise of executive power.

Fernández Crespo personified the popular forces of nationalism in an urban setting, where the Colorado Party, and particularly *Batllismo*, usually predominated, and was recognized for following *Herrerismo*, Luis Alberto de Herrera's brand of politics. He focused much of his attention on issues of social justice, especially education, social security, workers' rights, pension benefits, and unemployment aid. He was also an active sports director, associated with the Liverpool soccer club and the Aguada basketball club. He died on July 28, 1964.

*See also* **Batllismo; Herrera, Luis Alberto de; Uruguay, Political Parties: Blanco Party; Uruguay, Political Parties: Colorado Party.**

BIBLIOGRAPHY

Cocchi, Angel Mario. *Nuestros partidos.* Montevideo: CIEP, Departamento de Educación Permanente, 1984.

Pedemonte, Juan Carlos. *Los presidentes del Uruguay,* 4th edition. Montevideo: Ediciones de la Plaza, 1992.

Pérez, Wilfredo. *Grandes figuras blancas (Aportación a sus biografías).* Montevideo: Ediciones de la Plaza, 2001.

Scarone, Arturo. *Uruguayos contemporáneos: Nuevo diccionario de datos biográficos.* Montevideo: A. Barreiro y Ramos, 1937.

José de Torres Wilson
William G. Acree Jr.

## FERNÁNDEZ DE CABRERA BOBADILLA CERDA Y MENDOZA, LUIS GERÓNIMO

**FERNÁNDEZ DE CABRERA BOBADILLA CERDA Y MENDOZA, LUIS GERÓNIMO** (1590–1647). Luis Gerónimo Fernández de Cabrera Bobadilla Cerda y Mendoza (Conde de Chinchón; *b.* 1590; *d.* 28 October 1647), viceroy of Peru (1629–1639). The fourth conde de Chinchón and member of the Council of State (Aragon and Italy) and War assumed his viceregal duties on 14 January 1629. Reputed to be penurious, austere, and abstemious, Chinchón focused much of his attention on fiscal matters, especially new taxes imposed during his tenure, such as the Media Anata, Unión de Armas, Mesada Eclesiástica, and Composición *de pulperías* (bar taxes). He also vigorously pursued donations from individuals and communities throughout the viceroyalty to meet exigencies in Spain. In fact, during the eleven years he was in office, Chinchón remitted over 4 million ducats to Spain despite the fall in silver production at Potosí. Fortunately, silver strikes at Cailloma and Pasco in part made up for the drop in output in Upper Peru.

Militarily, the viceroy strengthened the fortifications at Callao, built two new vessels for the Pacific fleet, reinforced garrisons in Chile, and counteracted both the Dutch corsairs plying the Pacific coast and Portuguese encroachments on the eastern part of Peru. When the usefulness of quinine for treating malaria was discovered in the Loja province of Ecuador in 1630, the viceroy enthusiastically endorsed its effectiveness, but when word reached Rome, church officials there called it a "pact of the Peruvians with the devil." In Lima, Chinchón certified guilds for hatmakers, tailors, ironworkers, locksmiths, and potters. Known for his social conscience, Chinchón vigorously defended Indian rights and provided basic necessities for newly arrived slaves and for orphans and abandoned children. Evidently, too, he had a strong sense of religious and moral propriety: during Lent he ordered men and women separated in the churches of Lima. Relieved of his duties on 18 December 1639, he returned to Spain, where he died.

*See also* **Spanish Empire; Viceroyalty, Viceroy.**

BIBLIOGRAPHY

Mendiburu, Manuel De. ed., *Diccionario histórico–biográfico del Perú,* vol. 3. Lima: Imprenta Enrique Palacios 1932.

John Jay TePaske

## FERNÁNDEZ DE CASTRO ANDRADE Y PORTUGAL, PEDRO ANTONIO

**FERNÁNDEZ DE CASTRO ANDRADE Y PORTUGAL, PEDRO ANTONIO** (c. 1635–1672). Pedro Antonio Fernández de Castro Andrade y Portugal (Conde de Lemos; *b.* ca. 1635; *d.* 6 December 1672), viceroy of Peru (1667–1672). The tenth count of Lemos, Pedro Fernández de Castro was born in Spain and was only thirty-three when he assumed his post in Lima in November 1667. Upon arrival his most immediate task was quelling a civil war in the mining area of Laycacota in the province of Paucarolla, where armed bands led by the Salcedo brothers, Gaspar and José, who terrorized other miners. In 1668 Lemos personally led a force of soldiers and militia into the mountains to put down the revolt, ruthlessly executing forty–two rebels. Returning to Lima in 1669 after visiting Chucuito and Cuzco, Lemos attached himself to the Jesuits, supporting their missions in the interior at Mojos and on the Marañon River and the construction of a sumptuous new chapel for their church of Nuestra Señora de los Desamparados, dedicated in June 1672. At the same time the viceroy sponsored construction of a new convent for female penitents and the Betelmite Indian Hospital of Santa Ana. An outspoken critic of the forced labor system (*Mita*) that supplied workers for the silver mines at Potosí, Lemos advocated its elimination but was successful only in reducing the number of *mita* Indians by half to approximately 2,000 annually.

Devout, fervent, and somewhat pompous, Lemos loved the panoply surrounding rites and ceremonies, ordering thirty masses each for the forty–two rebels he executed and elegant celebrations whenever religious or state occasions called for them. After only five years in office, Lemos suddenly fell ill and died at the age of thirty–eight.

*See also* **Spanish Empire; Viceroyalty, Viceroy.**

BIBLIOGRAPHY

Basadre, Jorge. *El Conde de Lemos y su tiempo*. Lima: Editorial Huascaran, 1945.

Mendiburu, Manuel De ed., *Diccionario histórico–biográfico del Peru*, vol. 3. Lima: Imprenta Enrique Palacios, 1978.

Miller, Robert R. ed. *Chronicle of Colonial Lima: The Diary of Josephe and Francisco Mugaburu, 1640–1687*. Norman: University of Oklahoma Press, 1975.

JOHN JAY TEPASKE

## FERNÁNDEZ DE CÓRDOBA, DIEGO

**FERNÁNDEZ DE CÓRDOBA, DIEGO** (1578–1630). Diego Fernández de Córdoba (marqués de Guadalcázar; *b*. 1578; *d*. 1630), viceroy of Mexico and Peru. Born in Seville, Guadalcázar served as viceroy of New Spain from 1612 until 1621, when he moved to Peru, serving as viceroy there until 1629. During his reign in New Spain he was noted for the establishment of the *tribunal de tributos* (tribute court) and for two important public works projects: the continuing effort to drain the Valley of Mexico and the construction of the castle of San Diego in Acapulco.

In Peru, Guadalcázar put down a civil war in Potosí between the "Vicuñas" (Creoles) and "Vascongados" (Peninsulars). A Dutch fleet threatened the coast in 1624–1625, forcing the viceroy to fortify the coastal towns of the kingdom. Because the mercury mines at Huancavelica continued to pose health problems to the Indian miners, Guadalcázar eliminated nighttime mine activity and reduced the number of Indians assigned to the mines in the Mita. He sought to improve communications through the construction and maintenance of bridges. Rather than depend on a legal adviser, he took an active role in supervising lawsuits dealing with Indians. Although he, like his predecessor, attempted to deal with the issue of the Potosí *mita*, no concrete changes were implemented. He died in Córdoba, Spain.

*See also* **Mining: Colonial Spanish America; New Spain, Viceroyalty of.**

BIBLIOGRAPHY

Manuel De Mendiburu, *Diccionario histórico-biográfico del Perú*, 8 vols. (1874 1890).

*Additional Bibliography*

Téllez Lúgaro, Eduardo. "El informe del marqués de Guadalcázar al rey: un testimonio colonial acerca de la mita, las encomiendas y los indios atacameños." *Cuadernos de Historia* 6 (July 1986): 135–141.

JOHN F. SCHWALLER

## FERNÁNDEZ DE LIZARDI, JOSÉ JOAQUÍN

**FERNÁNDEZ DE LIZARDI, JOSÉ JOAQUÍN** (1776–1827). José Joaquín Fernández de Lizardi (*b*. 15 November 1776; *d*. 21 June 1827), Mexican writer. Born in Mexico City, Fernández de Lizardi began his education in Tepozotlán, where his father was a physician. He later went to Mexico City for further education and in 1793 entered the Colegio de San Ildefonso. After abandoning his studies in 1798 at his father's death, Fernández de Lizardi held various bureaucratic positions and initially opposed the independence movement, a stance that he soon reversed in support of Iturbide. As a journalist he is most remembered for the newspaper *El Pensador Mexicano* (*The Mexican Thinker* [1812–1814]), which he founded when the Spanish Constitution of 1812 established freedom of the press. His writings reflect the Mexican social milieu at the time of the country's struggle for independence. His special concern was the place of Spaniards born in the New World. Because of newspaper censorship, he resorted to fiction and wrote *El periquillo sarniento* (*The Itching Parrot* [published serially 1816; complete version published posthumously 1830–1831]). This picaresque tale is recognized as the "first" Spanish–American novel. It achieves compositional complexity and development, and it treats contemporary New World themes. Fernández de Lizardi wrote three other novels—*Noches tristes y día alegre* (*Sad Nights and Happy Day* [1818, 1819]), *La Quijotita y su prima* (*Quijotita and Her Cousin* [1818]), and *Don Catrín de la Fachenda* (written about 1819, published posthumously in 1832)—before he returned to journalism and pamphleteering in 1820. By 1822 Fernández de Lizardi became disenchanted with Iturbide and began to advocate liberal causes, and his modest social position became increasingly precarious. He died of tuberculosis in Mexico City.

*See also* **Literature: Spanish America.**

BIBLIOGRAPHY

Madrigal, Luis Íñigo. "José Joaquín Fernández de Lizardi," *Historia de la literatura hispanoamericana. Vol. 2, Del neoclasicismo al modernismo.* Madrid: Cátedra, 1982.

Spell, Jefferson Rea *Bridging the Gap: Articles on Mexican Literature.* México, D.F.: Editorial Libros de México, 1971.

Vogeley, Nancy. "José Joaquín Fernández de Lizardi," *Latin American Writers* vol. 1, eds. Carlos A. Solé and Maria Isabel Abreu. New York: Scribner, 1989.

DANNY J. ANDERSON

## FERNÁNDEZ DE PIEDRAHITA, LUCAS

**FERNÁNDEZ DE PIEDRAHITA, LUCAS** (1624–1688). Lucas Fernández de Piedrahita was a Jesuit historian. Born in Santa Fe de Bogotá, Colombia, he earned degrees from the Colegio de San Bartolomé and the Universidad de Santo Tomás. He held several ecclesiastical positions in the cathedral, including that of archiepiscopal governor, which he used to improve relations with the Real Audiencia. He also served as bishop of Santa Marta and Panamá. He traveled to Spain to defend himself of the accusations by a visitador and after six years obtained a favorable judgment of the Consejo de Indias. In Madrid he began to write his *Historia general de las conquistas del Nuevo Reino de Granada*, based on the chronicles of Gonzalo Jiménez de Quesada, Juan de Castellanos, Antonio Medrano, and Pedro de Aguado. With this work, he intended to demonstrate to Europeans the importance of the territory, "third in greatness and Majesty of all those that exist in this expanded monarchy."

In a writing style more modern than that of his predecessors, Piedrahita provided a chronological narration of events, tied to the geography, resources, and population of the region and giving historical identity to the society of New Granada. He was one of the first writers to describe the emergent, distinguishing characteristics of Colombianness. He also had a major influence on colonial historiography in its account of the diminution of the indigenous population through the mestization process. He died in 1688, without having seen the edition of his history published in Amberes that same year.

*See also* **Audiencia; Colombia: From the Conquest through Independence; Jesuits.**

BIBLIOGRAPHY

Fernández de Piedrahita, Lucas. *Historia general del Nuevo Reino de Granada.* [1688.] Bogotá: ABC, 1942.

Fernández de Piedrahita, Lucas. *Noticia historial de las conquistas del Nuevo Reino de Granada*, 2 vols. Bogotá: Kelly, 1973.

Vergara y Vergara, José María. *Historia de la literatura en Nueva Granada*, 2 vols. [1867.] Bogotá: Banco Popular, 1974.

RODRIGO DE J. GARCÍA ESTRADA

## FERNÁNDEZ GUARDIA, RICARDO

**FERNÁNDEZ GUARDIA, RICARDO** (1867–1950). Ricardo Fernández Guardia was born in Alajuela, Costa Rica, on January 4, 1867. He began his diplomatic career alongside his father, Leon Fernández, who was the Costa Rican ambassador to London, Paris, and Madrid. Fernández Guardia was named first secretary of the Special Mission in London and secretary of the Costa Rican legation in Germany, Belgium, France, and Spain; he was also ambassador to Rome.

He was elected member of the municipality of San José; vice secretary of foreign affairs, secretary of foreign affairs, and minister of public education.

Fernández Guardia was also a prolific author. His works of fiction include *Tapaligui* (1892), *Hojarasca* (1894), *Cuentos Ticos* (1901, translated into English by G. Casement as *Short Stories*), *Crónicas coloniales* (1921), and *Cosas y gentes de antaño* (1935). He also published the nonfiction works *Historia de Costa Rica* and *El Descubrimiento y la Conquista* (1905); *Cartilla histórica de Costa Rica* (1909); *Reseña histórica de Talamanca* (1918); *La independencia y otros episodios* (1928); *La guerra de la liga y la invasión de Quijano* (1934); and five volumes of the *Documentos para la Historia de Costa Rica* (1907).

In 1930 he was appointed director of the National Archives, a position he held until 1940. The Constitutional Congress of Costa Rica declared him *Benemérito de la Patria* (Meritorious of the Mother Country), the highest distinction the country bestows on its citizens, on March 7, 1944. In 1947 the University of Costa Rica granted him an *honoris causa* doctorate. He died on February 5, 1950.

*See also* **Costa Rica; Literature: Spanish America.**

BIBLIOGRAPHY

*Primary Works*

*Cuentos Ticos: Short Stories of Costa Rica* [1901], trans. G. Casement. Freeport, NY: Books for Libraries, 1970.

*History of the Discovery and Conquest of Costa Rica*, trans. Harry Weston Van Dyke, NY: T.Y. Crowell, 1913.

*La independencia y otros episodios.* San José, Costa Rica. Imprenta Trejos, 1928.

RODOLFO CERDAS CRUZ

## FERNÁNDEZ (HERNÁNDEZ) DE CÓRDOBA, FRANCISCO (c. 1475–1526).

Francisco Fernández (Hernández) de Córdoba (*b.* ca. 1475; *d.* June 1526), conqueror of Nicaragua. (not to be confused with Francisco Hernández De Córdoba [*d.* 1518], a conquistador of the Yucatán.) Fernández de Córdoba was a Spanish soldier of fortune who came to Panama sometime between 1514 and 1517. In the service of Pedro Arias de Ávila (Pedrarias Dávila), he was captain of the guard at Panama City in 1519. Pedrarias sent him to Nicaragua in 1523 to check the pretensions of Gil González Dávila. There Fernández founded the cities of Granada and León in 1524, as well as the village of Bruselas, the first European settlement in what is today Costa Rica. He also tried to take control of the territory of Honduras and to establish a kingdom independent of Pedrarias, perhaps in alliance with Hernán Cortés. Learning of this in 1525, Pedrarias came to Nicaragua and captured Fernández. After a speedy trial, in which Fernández was convicted of treason, he was beheaded in León in late June 1526. The Nicaraguan unit of currency, the córdoba, is named for him.

*See also* **Explorers and Exploration: Spanish America.**

BIBLIOGRAPHY

Carlos Meléndez Chaverri, *Hernández de Córdoba: Capitán de conquista en Nicaragua* (1976).

John H. Parry and Robert G. Keith, *New Iberian World: A Documentary History of the Discovery and Settlement of Latin America to the Early Seventeenth Century*, (1984), vol. 3, pp. 86–101; vol. 4, pp. 19, 27, 30.

RALPH LEE WOODWARD JR.

## FERNÁNDEZ HIDALGO, GUTIERRE (?–1620).

Gutierre Fernández Hidalgo (b. 1553; *d.* after 1620), Spanish composer. Born in Andalusia, Fernández Hidalgo arrived at New Granada (Colombia) in 1584 as the *maestro de capilla* of the Bogotá cathedral. He became sixteenth-century America's most eminent composer. As chapelmaster, Fernández Hidalgo asked the Bogotá bishop to require the seminarians of the newly founded Seminario Conciliar de San Luis to sing under his direction every day at cathedral services. In 1585 he was appointed rector of the seminary, but a dispute with his students over his demanding teaching style led him to leave Bogotá in 1586. He moved to Quito, where he was music director at the cathedral and seminary until 1589. Again, he proved too demanding for his subordinates. On 13 July 1591, he was appointed *maestro de capilla* of the Cuzco cathedral, where he conducted the cathedral choir and taught polyphony and counterpoint while composing in his free time. In 1597 he accepted a new assignment with a better salary, as *maestro de capilla* of the La Plata cathedral (present-day Sucre, Bolivia). He remained there, presumably, until his retirement in 1620. It is believed he died in Cuzco.

Fernández Hidalgo was technically and stylistically the best representative in America of the Spanish polyphony initiated by Tomás Luis de Victoria, Cristóbal de Morales, and Francisco Guerrero. Among his works are nine Magnificats for four and six voices, ten four-voice psalms, three Salve Reginas for four and five voices, and *villancicos,* motets, and hymns.

*See also* **Music: Art Music.**

BIBLIOGRAPHY

Robert Stevenson, *The Music of Peru* (1950), and *Renaissance and Baroque Musical Sources in the Americas* (1970).

José Ignacio Perdomo Escobar, *El archivo musical de la catedral de Bogotá* (1976); *New Grove Dictionary of Music and Musicians,* vol. 6 (1980).

SUSANA SALGADO

## FERNÁNDEZ MADRID, JOSÉ (1789–1830).

José Fernández Madrid (*b.* 19 February 1789; *d.* 28 June 1830), president of the United Provinces of New Granada. Born in Cartagena and trained in law and medicine, José Fernández Madrid was a prominent figure of New Granada's intellectual scene in the last years of colonial rule. A leading spokesman for the federalist cause in the independence movement, he was made president of the United Provinces in 1816, shortly before its final collapse. During the Spanish reconquest he was exiled from New Granada. He lived for a time in Havana, but at the time of his death in London was serving as envoy of Gran Colombia to England and France. Fernández Madrid is further remembered as a noted journalist and author of poetry and drama.

*See also* **New Granada, United Provinces; Gran Colombia; Journalism.**

BIBLIOGRAPHY

Carlos Martínez Silva, *Biografía de don José Fernández Madrid,* edited by Luis Martínez Delgado (1935).

Ignacio Arizmendi Posada, *Presidentes de Colombia 1810–1990* (1989), pp. 31–32.

*Additional Bibliography*

Triana y Antorveza, Humberto. "Dos colombianos en Cuba: José Fernández Madrid (1780–1830) y Félix Manuel Tanco y Bosmeniel (1796–1871)." *Boletín de Historia y Antigüedades* 92 (January–March 2005): 65–94.

DAVID BUSHNELL

## FERNÁNDEZ OREAMUNO, PRÓSPERO (1834–1885).

Próspero Fernández Oreamuno (*b.* 18 July 1834; *d.* 12 March 1885), president of Costa Rica (1882–1885). Born in San José, Fernández studied there and in Guatemala. His presidency marked a watershed in Costa Rican history, ending the political domination by the "coffee barons" and ushering in fifty years of steady progress toward democracy. Following Costa Rica's first brush with dictatorship under Tomás Guardia Gutiérrez (1870–1882), a new generation of Costa Ricans, constituting a fiercely democratic emerging middle class, undertook to extend the suffrage and eliminate the influence of the Catholic Church.

Identifying with this rising group, Fernández sponsored educational reform and tough anticlerical laws. He enacted the Liberal Laws of 1884, which established free, compulsory education, expelled the Jesuits, made marriage a civil contract, legalized divorce, and secularized cemeteries. Fernández died during a military campaign against the Guatemalan caudillo Justo Rufino Barrios, but he had set the course for the so-called generation of 1889 that dominated Costa Rican affairs until the mid-1930s. The Legislative Assembly awarded him the Benemérito de la Patria in 1883.

*See also* **Coffee Industry; Jesuits; Liberalism.**

BIBLIOGRAPHY

Carlos Monge Alfaro, *Historia de Costa Rica* (1948).

Samuel Stone, *La dinastía de los conquistadores* (1975).

Charles D. Ameringer, *Democracy in Costa Rica* (1982).

CHARLES D. AMERINGER

## FERNÁNDEZ RETAMAR, ROBERTO

**FERNÁNDEZ RETAMAR, ROBERTO** (1930–). Roberto Fernández Retamar (b. 1930), Cuban essayist and poet. Fernández Retamar was born in Havana and received a doctorate in philosophy and literature in 1954. In 1951 he was awarded the National Poetry Prize for his book *Patrias.* He studied linguistics in Paris (1955) and London (1956). After returning to Cuba in 1958, he wrote using the pseudonym David for the underground revolutionary publication *Resistencia.* After the Cuban Revolution of 1959, he continued his academic career until the following year, when he was named cultural adviser for the Cuban embassy in Paris. He was elected coordinating secretary of the Cuban Union of Writers and Artists (UNEAC).

During the 1970s and 1980s Fernández Retamar made a name for himself as an essayist. Noteworthy among his essays are "Para una teoría de la literatura hispanoamericana" (1975) and "Calibán." This latter essay was a socialist response to the Uruguayan José Enrique Rodó's canonical *Ariel,* a text that idealized and even Hellenized the Spanish-speaking Americas. "Caliban" first appeared in the journal *Casa de las Américas* in 1974; it appeared in book form in Mexico the same year, and in English translation in the *Massachusetts Review.*

As of the mid-1990s, Fernández Retamar was a frequent representative of Cuba in international cultural activities and was active also in his own country's cultural affairs. His essays are among the best examples of revolutionary aesthetics in literature that Cuba has produced. Among his best collections of poems is *Cuaderno paralelo* (1973). Other works include *Introducción a José Martí* (1978), *Juana y otros poemas personales* (1981), and *Entrevisto* (1982).

*See also* **Literature: Spanish America; Rodó, José Enrique.**

BIBLIOGRAPHY

Campuzano, Luisa. "La revista: *Casa de las Américas* 1960–1995." *Unión* (La Habana) 8, no. 24 (July–September 1996): 25–34.

Colombres, Adolfo. *América Latina: El desafío del tercer milenio.* Buenos Aires: Ediciones del Sol, 1993.

Fernandez Retamar, Roberto. *Caliban and Other Essays.* Translated by Edward Baker. Foreword by Frederic Jameson. Minneapolis: University of Minnesota Press, 1989.

González Echevarría, Roberto. "Roberto Fernández Retamar: An Introduction." *Diacritics* 8, no. 4 (Winter 1978): 70–75.

Ortiz, Ricardo. "Revolution's Other Histories: The Sexual, Cultural, and Critical Legacies of Roberto Fernández Retamar's 'Caliban'" *Social Text* 17, no. 1 (Spring 1999):33–58.

ROBERTO VALERO

## FERNÁNDEZ Y MEDINA, BENJAMÍN

**FERNÁNDEZ Y MEDINA, BENJAMÍN** (1873–1960). Born in Montevideo on March 31, 1873, Benjamín Fernández y Medina was a Uruguayan writer and diplomat who held numerous positions in public administration, especially in the diplomatic corps. He was secretary to the chief of police in Montevideo in 1897 and drafted the new police code. In the late 1890s he served on the departmental board of elementary education in the capital (one of the chief administrative bodies overseeing the new national public education system), and during the first two decades of the twentieth century he worked as the first official for the interior ministry and for the ministry of foreign relations. Fernández y Medina sympathized with the Colorado Party and supported two-time Colorado president José Batlle y Ordóñez. During Batlle's second term (1911–1915), Fernández y Medina was appointed undersecretary of foreign affairs. He later held diplomatic appointments in Germany, Holland, Spain, Portugal, Cuba, and Mexico, retiring from the foreign service in December 1935.

In addition to Fernández y Medina's career in public service, he was a member of literary and historical societies, including the Real Academia Española and the Real Academia de la Historia, and a founding member of the Instituto Histórico y Geográfico del Uruguay. He also established a reputation as a newspaper and magazine editor, and author of *criollista* short stories, anthologies of poetry, and literary and historical studies. He died in Madrid on July 16, 1960.

*See also* **Batlle y Ordóñez, José; Education: Overview.**

BIBLIOGRAPHY

Fernández y Medina, Benjamín. *Cuentos. Clásicos Uruguayos,* no. 74. Montevideo: Ministerio de Instrucción Pública y Previsión Social, 1965.

Scarone, Arturo. *Uruguayos contemporaneos: Nuevo diccionario de datos biográficos y bibliográficos.* Montevideo: A Barreiro y Ramos, 1937.

José de Torres Wilson
William G. Acree, Jr.

---

**FERNANDINI, EULOGIO E.** (1860–1947). Eulogio E. Fernandini (*b.* 13 September 1860; *d.* 24 December 1947), a pioneering Peruvian mine owner and cattleman who upgraded his mining operations during the copper boom of 1897–1898. Importing an entire mill in parts on muleback, he built a highly modern smelter. Like his peers, he relied on local capital and initiatives. When copper prices and technology attracted foreign investment, Fernandini fought to maintain his independence, but Cerro de Pasco Corporation drove out local business. Cerro spent massively on improvements and government contracts. By World War I, Fernandini was a minor shareholder in Cerro, to which he supplied food. In the 1920s and 1930s he turned to gold mining in the Andes.

*See also* **Mining: Modern.**

BIBLIOGRAPHY

Rosemary Thorp and Geoffrey Bertram, *Peru, 1890–1977: Growth and Policy in an Open Economy* (1978).

Florencia E. Mallon, *The Defense of Community in Peru's Central Highlands* (1983), esp. pp. 136–137, 172–173.

*Additional Bibliography*

Clayton, Lawrence. *Peru and the United States: The Condor and the Eagle.* Athens, GA: University of Georgia Press, 1999.

Mallon, Florencia. *Peasant and Nation: The Making of Postcolonial Mexico and Peru.* Berkeley: University of California Press, 1995.

O'Brien, Thomas F. *The Revolutionary Mission: American Enterprise in Latin America, 1900–1945.* Cambridge: Cambridge University Press, 1999.

Vincent Peloso

---

**FERNANDO DE NORONHA.** Fernando de Noronha, an island 200 miles northeast of Cape São Roque, Brazil. Covering 10 square miles and supporting a population of 2,051 (2000 est.), the island, of volcanic origin, is dominated by a 1,050-foot peak and is known for interesting wildlife. The archipelago consists of twenty-one islands, islets, and rocks of volcanic origin. The main island, from which the group gets its name, makes up 91 percent of the total area.

Discovered about 1503 by Fernando de Noronha, a Portuguese participant in the dyewood trade, the island later became a dependency of Pernambuco and in 1942, together with neighboring islets, a territory of Brazil. Strategically positioned off the bulge of Brazil, the island suffered several attacks, none of them successful, in the seventeenth and eighteenth centuries. It served as a penal colony in the 1700s and continued to receive a few political prisoners as late as the 1980s. During 1957–1962, the United States Air Force used the island as a tracking station for guided missiles based at Cape Canaveral, Florida. The Brazilian military controlled the territory, and the population consisted primarily of fishermen or civilian employees of the military. In 1989, surrounding waters were declared a Marine National Park. It is home to two endemic birds, the Noronha Elaenia and the Noronha Vireo. Though much of the natural vegetation has been lost, there are several sea animals that are a principal attraction of the island. Its economy is heavily dependent on tourism, although its delicate ecosystem makes it difficult to support heavy traffic. In 2001 UNESCO declared the island a World Heritage Site.

*See also* **Brazil, Geography; Noronha, Fernão de.**

BIBLIOGRAPHY

*Additional Bibliography*

Fernandes, Hélio. *Recordaçoes de um desterrado em Fernando de Noronha.* Rio de Janeiro: Editora Tribuna da Imprensa, 1967.

Teixera, Wilson. *Arquipélago Fernando de Noronha: O paraíso do vulcao.* São Paulo: Terra Virgem Editora, 2003.

Cara Shelly

---

**FERRÉ, ROSARIO** (1938–). Rosario Ferré is one of the most important authors in Puerto Rico and throughout Latin America. Born in Ponce, Puerto Rico, Ferré completed her undergraduate education in the United States at Manhattanville College (1960) and earned her master's degree in Spanish literature at the University of Puerto Rico, where she studied with the Peruvian novelist Mario Vargas Llosa. She holds a Ph.D. in Latin American literature from the University of Maryland and received an honorary doctorate from Brown University.

As a young woman in the 1970s she was part of a group of radical Puerto Rican intellectuals who created *Zona de carga y descarga* (Loading and unloading zone), a journal that published young local writers, many of whom became well known. From 1977 to 1980 she wrote a column called *Carga y descarga* for the Puerto Rican newspaper *El Mundo.*

In her book of feminist essays, *Sitio a Eros* (1982), Ferré criticized traditional Puerto Rican class and gender relationships. Her 1976 collection of short stories, *Papeles de Pandora* (published in English as *The Youngest Doll* in 1991), rejects the cultural characterization of women as dolls who exist only for the pleasure of men. In addition to her stories, written in a magical-realist style, she has published novels, books of poetry, literary essays, and children's stories. In 1992 she published *Memorias de Ponce*, a biography of her father, Luis A. Ferré, a businessman who became rich in the island's mid-twentieth-century industrialization boom and later served as governor (1969–1973).

In 1989 her collection of four related novellas, *Maldito Amor* (first published in 1985), was translated into English as *Sweet Diamond Dust.* Her English-language novel *The House on the Lagoon* was a finalist for the 1995 National Book Award. In 2004 Ferré was the recipient of a Guggenheim Fellowship. She is a professor at the University of Puerto Rico in San Juan.

*See also* **Literature: Spanish America.**

BIBLIOGRAPHY

Gutiérrez, Mariela. *Rosario Ferré en su edad de oro: Heroínas subversivas de Papeles de Pandora y Maldito Amor.* Madrid: Editorial Verbum, 2004.

Henao, Eda B. *The Colonial Subject's Search for Nation, Culture, and Identity in the Works of Julia Alvarez, Rosario Ferré, and Ana Lydia Vega.* Lewiston, NY: E. Mellen Press, 2003.

Lindsay, Claire. *Locating Latin American Women Writers: Cristina Peri Rossi, Rosario Ferré, Albalucía Angel, and Isabel Allende.* New York: Peter Lang, 2003.

EMILY BERQUIST

## FERRÉ AGUAYO, LUIS ANTONIO

**FERRÉ AGUAYO, LUIS ANTONIO** (1904–2003). Luis Antonio Ferré Aguayo (*b.* 1904 *d.* 2003) businessman, politician, and leading advocate of Puerto Rican statehood. Born into a wealthy Cuban family in 1904, Ferré spent his early years achieving commercial success. Through ventures such as the Puerto Rican Cement Company of Ponce, his hometown, Ferré added significantly to his family's fortune. His experience in business convinced him that Puerto Rico's future rested in North American–style capitalism. He became a leader of Puerto Rico's statehood movement and closely allied himself with the mainland Republican Party.

In 1951 Ferré was elected to Puerto Rico's constitutional convention. After 1952 Ferré and his brother-in-law, Miguel A. García Méndez, assumed leadership of the Republican Statehood Party (PER). Business successes such as the Puerto Rican Cement Company and philanthropic endeavors such as Ponce's art gallery brought Ferré widespread respect. While cultivating friendships among Eisenhower Republicans, Ferré appealed to the Puerto Rican working and middle classes by touting the economic benefits of statehood. Although badly losing the 1956 gubernatorial election to his rival, Luis Muñoz Marín, Ferré continued to develop a mass following. His defeat notwithstanding, PER demonstrated respectable electoral strength in urban centers such as San Juan, where a new middle class was taking shape. Ferré again ran for governor in 1964, but lost to Muñoz's handpicked successor, Roberto Sánchez Vilella.

In the 1967 plebiscite regarding Puerto Rico's status, Ferré led an alliance favoring statehood, the United Statehooders, and gained a respectable 38.9 percent of the vote. Again displaying urban electoral muscle in San Juan and Ponce, the Statehooders had high hopes for the 1968 elections. They were not disappointed. Ferré and the Statehooders organized a new party, the New Progressive Party (PNP), under whose banner Ferré won a narrow victory in the November 1968 gubernatorial race. Ferré served only one term as governor (1969–1973), but remained a leading PNP personality. He maintained close contacts with Republican presidents Nixon, Ford, and Reagan, and in November 1991 received the Medal of Freedom from President George Bush. His daughter, Rosario Ferré, is a well known novelist and short story writer.

*See also* **Ferré, Rosario; Puerto Rico.**

BIBLIOGRAPHY

Carrión, Arturo Morales. *Puerto Rico: A Political and Cultural History.* Nashville: American Association for State and Local History, 1983.

Nelson, Anne. *Murder Under Two Flags: The U.S., Puerto Rico, and the Cerro Maravilla Cover–up.* New York: Ticknor and Fields, 1986.

Knight, Franklin W. *The Caribbean: The Genesis of a Fragmented Nationalism,* 2d ed. New York: Oxford University Press, 1990.

JOHN J. CROCITTI

**FERREIRA, BENIGNO** (1840–1920). Benigno Ferreira (*b.* 18 February 1840; *d.* 24 November 1920), president of Paraguay (1906–1908) and soldier. Born in Limpio, Ferreira moved with his family to Argentina at an early age. He studied law at the University of Buenos Aires, where he affiliated with a group of radical Paraguayan emigrés opposed to the government of Carlos Antonio López and his son, Francisco Solano López. With the outbreak of the War of the Triple Alliance in 1864, Ferreira helped convert this group into the Legión Paraguaya, which fought alongside the Argentines in their invasion of Paraguay. With the defeat of Solano López in 1870, Ferreira's prospects should have dramatically improved, but the chaos of the postwar era meant that he had to limit himself to temporary alliances with various political patrons. He was interior minister under Salvador Jovellanos and later vice president of the Partido Liberal.

During most of the late nineteenth century Ferreira was back in exile in Buenos Aires, but after the successful Liberal revolt of 1904, he was recalled to Asunción. Though he was without major popular support, he nonetheless was appointed president two years later. New revolts that threatened to oust him from that position quickly coalesced into full-scale civil war. In July 1908, having had little chance to do anything with his presidency, Ferreira was forced from office, and from Paraguay, this time for good. He died in Buenos Aires.

*See also* **Paraguay: The Nineteenth Century; War of the Triple Alliance.**

BIBLIOGRAPHY

Carlos Zubizarreta, *Cien vidas paraguayas,* 2d ed. (1985), pp. 210–213; *The Cambridge History of Latin America,* vol. 5 (1986), pp. 475–496.

*Additional Bibliography*

Pesoa, Manuel. *General doctor Benigno Ferreira: su biografía, insertada en la historia del Paraguay.* Asunción: Intercontinental Editora, 1995.

THOMAS L. WHIGHAM

**FERREIRA ALDUNATE, WILSON** (1919–1988). Known by friend and foe alike simply as "Wilson," Wilson Ferreira Aldunate was a Blanco (National Party) senator and presidential candidate and an outspoken critic of the military dictatorship that controlled Uruguay from 1973 to 1984. He was a charismatic political leader and a modern caudillo within the Blanco Party, and his faction, Por la Patria, was the highest vote getter for the Blancos in the 1971 and 1984 elections. Born in Nico Pérez on January 28, 1919, Ferreira began his political career as a deputy and then as a senator (1967–1972) and served as minister of agriculture (1963). He was a presidential candidate in 1971 and received more votes than any other candidate, but his party lost the presidency to the Colorado Party, whose candidates received more total votes. After the military coup in 1973 Ferreira went into exile in Buenos Aires and later fled to London. He testified before the U.S. Congress in 1976 and was a valuable voice in achieving a cutoff of military aid to the Uruguayan dictatorship. By early 1984, with the military convinced it had to exit politics but unwilling to accept the possibility of a Ferreira presidency, the generals released from prison Liber Seregni, leader of the leftist political coalition known as the Frente Amplio. The strategy was to re-legalize the Left so that its followers would not support Ferreira in an upcoming election. When Ferreira returned to Montevideo in June 1984, he was promptly arrested and incarcerated in a remote military installation, where he remained until after the November elections. The military, the Colorado Party, and the Frente Amplio agreed to the elections in negotiations known as the Pact of the Naval Club. With Ferreira excluded from running, the Colorados won the presidential election. Ferreira backed the incoming Julio Maria Sanguinetti administration but favored some accounting for the military's human rights abuses. Yet with a constitutional crisis arising two years later, he reluctantly supported an amnesty law, some say in order to run in the 1989 presidential elections. However, he was diagnosed with cancer in 1987 and died on March 15, 1988. At his funeral there was a massive turnout as Uruguayans buried their last modern caudillo.

*See also* **Caudillismo, Caudillo; Naval Club, Pact of the; Sanguinetti, Julio María; Uruguay: The Twentieth Century; Uruguay, Political Parties: Blanco Party; Uruguay, Political Parties: Colorado Party.**

BIBLIOGRAPHY

*Primary Work*

Ferreira Aldunate, Wilson. *El exilio y la lucha*. Montevideo: Ediciones de la Banda Oriental, 1986.

*Secondary Works*

Pérez, Wilfredo. *Grandes figuras blancas: Aportación a sus biografías.* Montevideo: Ediciones de la Plaza, 2001.

Weinstein, Martin. *Uruguay: Democracy at the Crossroads.* Boulder, CO: Westview Press, 1988.

Martin Weinstein
William G. Acree Jr.

## FERREIRA DA SILVA, VIRGOLINO.

*See* **Lampião.**

**FERRER, JOSÉ** (1912–1992). Born in Puerto Rico on January 8, 1912, actor, director, and producer José Ferrer (José Vicente Ferrer de Otero y Cintrón) received numerous honors, including three Antoinette Perry Awards for Excellence in Theatre (Tony Awards) and an Academy Award (Oscar Award) for Best Actor, throughout his distinguished career. This feat places him among a select group of actors who have earned both the Tony (1947) and the Oscar (1950) for playing the same role—in his case, Cyrano de Bergerac—on both stage and film. Ferrer was the first Hispanic American actor to have garnered such prestigious awards. The son of a well-off family, Ferrer received a privileged education, attending one year of preparatory school in Switzerland before entering Princeton University, and graduating in 1933 with an architecture degree. In 1935 he debuted professionally on Broadway and by the early 1940s was poised to become a leading figure on the theatrical scene. He made his film debut in 1948 with *Joan of Arc*, and began screen directing in 1955, once again breaking new ground as Hollywood's first Hispanic American director with the film *The Shrike*. In the 1960s, he added television to his portfolio. Ferrer has been associated with some of Hollywood's most important films, including *Joan of Arc* (1948), *Moulin Rouge* (1952), *The Caine Mutiny* (1954), *Return to Peyton Place* (1961), and *Lawrence of Arabia* (1962). Ferrer supported various progressive causes—including opposition to segregation policies affecting African American artists and condemnation of the Francisco Franco dictatorship in Spain—that often put him at odds with the political establishment. In the McCarthy era, the celebrated actor came under the scrutiny of the United States Congress's House Committee on Un-American Activities that investigated the alleged influence of the Left in the entertainment industry. He was cleared of any political transgressions and never blacklisted. His induction in 1981 into the Theater Hall of Fame and the National Medal of Arts accorded to him in 1985—the highest recognition given to artists by the United States Government—confirmed Ferrer's lifetime achievements. José Ferrer remained active in the performing arts until the eve of his death on January 26, 1992.

*See also* **Cinema: From the Silent Film to 1990.**

BIBLIOGRAPHY

Bucklet, Michael. "Jose Ferrer (Part I)." *Films in Review* (February 1987): 66–75.

Bucklet, Michael.. "Jose Ferrer (Part II)." *Films in Review* (March 1987): 130–145.

Lambert, Bruce. "José Ferrer, Actor, Writer and Director, 80, Is Dead." *New York Times*, 27 January 1992, p. A1.

Luis A. González

**FERRER, RAFAEL** (1933–). Rafael Ferrer (*b.* 1933), Puerto Rican artist. Ferrer, a native of Santurce, studied literature and music at Syracuse

University. He received art training from Eugenio Fernández Granell at the University of Puerto Rico in 1953. A resident of the mainland United States since 1966, Ferrer has taught at the Philadelphia College of Art (1967–1977), the School of Visual Arts in New York (1978–1980), and the Skowhegan School of Painting and Sculpture in Skowhegan, Maine (1981). During the late 1960s and early 1970s, he created conceptual art pieces, installations, and mixed–media sculptures and contributed to the development of process art and body art. His more recent paintings and mixed–media sculptures evoke the Caribbean through expressionistic means. His work has been included in numerous solo and group exhibitions throughout the United States.

*See also* **Art: The Twentieth Century.**

BIBLIOGRAPHY

Contemporary Arts Center (Cincinnati, Ohio), *Deseo: An Adventure* (1973).

Laguna Gloria Art Museum (Austin, Texas), *Rafael Ferrer: Impassioned Rhythms* (1986).

Bronx Museum Of The Arts (Bronx, NY), *The Latin American Spirit: Art and Artists in the United States, 1920–1970* (1988).

MIRIAM BASILIO

## FERRERA, FRANCISCO (1800–1851).

Francisco Ferrera (*b.* 1794 or 1800; *d.* 1851), president of Honduras (1841–1845). Ferrera was born in Cantarranas (later renamed San Juan de Flores), Honduras. Orphaned at an early age, he was educated by the village priest, José León Garín.

Ferrera rose to prominence when he laid siege to the fortresses on Honduras's north coast that Honduran conservatives had seized with aid from Spanish Cuba in 1831. He served as vice chief of state under Governor Joaquín Rivera (1833–1836) and then rose to power as he led conservative Honduran and Nicaraguan forces against Francisco Morazán's Central American government in 1839, forming an alliance with José Rafael Carrera in Guatemala. Although he suffered reverses at Morazán's hand, notably at Espíritu Santo (5–6 May 1839) and at San Pedro Perulapán (25 September 1839), he became identified with the separation of Honduras from the Central American federation. Elected president by the National Assembly on 30 December 1840, he took office on 1 January 1841 as Honduras's first constitutional president. Ferrera served two two-year terms, until 1 January 1845, and was closely allied with Guatemala's Carrera and El Salvador's Francisco Malespín, who assisted him in resisting the liberal forces of José Trinidad Cabañas. Ferrera was elected to a third term in 1847, but declined to serve; however, he did continue to be the country's dominant caudillo as minister of war and as armed forces chief until 1848.

*See also* **Central America; Honduras.**

BIBLIOGRAPHY

Ramón Rosa, "Francisco Ferrera," in *Oro de Honduras, antología,* 2 vols. (1948), vol. 1, pp. 25–31.

Paulino Valladares, *Hondureños ilustres en la pluma* (1972), pp. 31–33.

Harvey K. Meyer, *Historical Dictionary of Honduras* (1976), p. 133.

Raúl A. Pagoaga, *Honduras y sus gobernantes* (1979).

Ralph Lee Woodward, Jr., *Rafael Carrera and the Emergence of the Republic of Guatemala, 1821–1871* (1992).

*Additional Bibliography*

Pérez Chávez, Porfirio. *Estructura económica de Honduras: Gobierno del general Francisco Ferreira, 1840–1844.* Tegulcigapa: Universidad Nacional Autónoma de Honduras, 2001.

RALPH LEE WOODWARD JR.

## FERREZ, MARC (1843–1923).

Marc Ferrez (*b.* 7 December 1843; *d.* 12 January 1923), Brazilian-born portrait and landscape photographer. The son of a French sculptor who arrived in Brazil with the 1816 French Artistic Mission, Ferrez studied in Paris before returning to Rio de Janeiro to apprentice as a photographer with Franz Keller at the German-owned Leuzinger Studio. After a fire destroyed his first studio, he returned to Paris to order new equipment manufactured to his design to allow him to produce panoramic views. His most lasting photographs have as their subjects what he considered the wonders of the Brazilian landscape: natural features, such as mountains, waterfalls, and jungles, and man-made feats of engineering, such as railroads, bridges, and urban buildings. Ferrez also photographed members of the indigenous Botocudo tribe while serving as a member of the American Charles Fredrick Hartt's 1875–1876 geolog-ical and geographic expedition to the interior of the province of Bahia. Following late-nineteenth-century custom, he posed his Indian subjects against artificial backdrops. Highly skilled at neutralizing the effects of ship movement, Ferrez was named "photographer of the Royal Navy" by Emperor Pedro II. Photographic historians consider him to be the equal of such late-nineteenth-century master photographers as William Henry Jackson (1843–1942) and Eadweard Muybridge (1830–1904). Ferrez's grandson, Gilberto Ferrez, a leading collector and scholar, has devoted his life to publishing and publicizing his grandfather's work.

*See also* **Brazil, Geography; French Artistic Mission; Photography: The Nineteenth Century.**

BIBLIOGRAPHY

Boris Kossoy, *Origens e expansão da fotografia no Brasil—Século XIX* (1980).

Rainer Fabian and Hans-Christian Adam, *Masters of Early Travel Photography* (1983).

Gilberto Ferrez, *A fotografia no Brasil, 1840–1900* (1985).

Pedro Vasquez, *Fotógrafos pioneiros no Rio de Janeiro* (1990).

*Additional Bibliography*

Billeter, Erika. *A Song to Reality: Latin American Photography, 1860–1993.* Barcelona; New York: D.A.P., 1998.

Lago, Bia Corrêa do, and Pedro Corrêa do Lago. *Brésil, les premiers photographes d'un empire sous les tropiques.* Paris: Gallimard, 2005.

*O Brasil de Marc Ferrez.* Sao Paulo: Instituto Moreira Salles, 2005.

ROBERT M. LEVINE

**FICHER, JACOBO** (1896–1978). An Argentine composer, violinist, and conductor, Jacobo Ficher was born in Odessa, Ukraine, on January 15, 1896. He began violin lessons when he was nine years old with Pyotr Solomonovich Stolyarsky and M. T. Hait, then entered the St. Petersburg Imperial Conservatory at sixteen and studied under Sergei Korguyev and Leopold Auer. In 1923 he immigrated to Argentina, where he became active in the musical life of Buenos Aires. In 1929 he was a founding member of the Grupo Renovación; he was also one of the founders of the Argentine Composers League (1947). Ficher taught composition at the University of La Plata as well as other important conservatories and institutions.

Ficher received numerous awards, including the Buenos Aires Municipal Prize three times (1929, 1931, and 1943) and the Coolidge Prize for his String Quartet no. 2 (1937). Ficher's Concerto for Violin and Orchestra received honorable mention from the Free Library of Philadelphia (1942), and the Indianapolis Symphony commissioned the Suite for Strings (1954). Ficher also composed two operas, *El oso* (1952) and *Pedido de mano* (1956). He died in Buenos Aires on September 9, 1978.

*See also* **Music: Art Music.**

BIBLIOGRAPHY

Ficher, Miguel, Martha Furman Schleifer, and John M. Furman, eds. *Latin American Classical Composers: A Biographical Dictionary*, 2nd edition. Lanham, MD: Scarecrow Press, 2002.

Zipman, B. "Jacobo Ficher." In *New Grove Dictionary of Music and Musicians*, edited by Stanley Sadie. London and Washington, DC: Grove's Dictionaries of Music, 1980.

SUSANA SALGADO
VICENTE PALERMO

**FICO.** *See* **Brazil, Independence Movements.**

**FIERRO RIMAC, FRANCISCO** (1803–1879). Francisco Fierro Rimac (*b.* 1803; *d.* 1879), Peru's foremost painter of everyday life and prevailing customs (*costumbrista* painter). A mulatto, Fierro Rimac was born into a humble Lima family. Most of what is known about "Pancho Fierro," as he was called, is contained in a letter by Peruvian author Ricardo Palma dated 1885. Fierro Rimac was self-taught and began his career as an artist drawing maps and painting coats of arms of Peruvian cities. Among his popular subjects were *Zambos* (natives of Indian and black origin), artisans, water carriers, street vendors, fishermen (*Stream Fishermen*, 1850), dances, and bullfights (*Juanita Breña Challenging a Bull* *with a Cloak*, 1821). He painted the mentally ill living in the streets of Lima and left some of the earliest images of the *tapadas* (Peruvian women wearing a unique costume consisting of a cloak that covers the bust and most of the head, leaving only one eye uncovered). He also designed street posters advertising bullfights and decorated walls with *costumbrista* scenes, allegories, and bucolic landscapes, which have not survived.

An intuitive and talented colorist, Fierro Rimac worked primarily in watercolor, favoring small formats. His drawing was rudimentary; he did not use perspective. His work has been compared to some of Goya's *The Caprices* because of his caricaturesque style and his penchant for writing comments on drawings.

*See also* **Art: The Nineteenth Century; Bullfighting; Indigenous Peoples.**

BIBLIOGRAPHY

Juan E. Ríos, *La pintura contemporánea en el Perú* (1946).

Dawn Ades, *Art in Latin America: The Modern Era, 1820–1980* (1989), pp. 84–85.

### *Additional Bibliography*

León y León Durán, Gustavo. *Apuntes histórico genealógicos de Francisco Fierro: Pancho Fierro.* Lima: Biblioteca Nacional de Perú, Fondo Editorial, 2004.

Cantuarias Acosta, Ricardo. *Pancho Fierro.* Lima: Editorial Brasa, 1995.

MARTA GARSD

---

**FIESTAS.** Fiestas, a Spanish term whose meaning ranges from private celebrations to nationwide fetes, from saint-day parties to the commemoration of national independence. Community holidays, especially civic and religious celebrations, serve as an occasion for social interaction, political negotiation, historical lessons, and turning-the-world-upside-down mimicry. Above all, fiestas serve as an occasion for the enjoyment of family, friends, compatriots, and coreligionists. The most dramatic Latin American celebrations contain a popular element—drawn from the indigenous peoples, blacks, mixed-ethnic groups, and European traditions—that often overwhelms official, sanctioned affairs. Carnival, for example, has become a Brazilian cultural expression that long ago surpassed in popularity and participants the Ash Wednesday initiation of Roman Catholicism's Lenten period.

One description of fiestas in Latin America classifies them as civic, religious, and commercial holidays. Commemoration of independence serves generally as the most significant holiday in each of the region's nations (see the following list), although it might be joined by an additional political anniversary. Two examples of the latter are the Cinco De Mayo holiday that celebrates the victory of the Mexican army over invading French troops (5 May 1867), and 26 July, which marks Fidel Castro's first (and unsuccessful) revolutionary effort in 1953 to seize power in Cuba, provided the name of his guerrilla movement, and commemorates his fellow rebels who died in the effort.

#### INDEPENDENCE FIESTAS

Haiti (1 January)
Dominican Republic (27 February)
Paraguay (14–15 May)
Cuba (17 May)
Venezuela (5 July)
Argentina (9 July)
Colombia (20 July)
Peru (28 July)
Bolivia (6 August)
Ecuador (10 August)
Uruguay (25 August)
Brazil (7 September)
Costa Rica (15 September)
El Salvador (15 September)
Guatemala (15 September)
Honduras (15 September)
Nicaragua (15 September)
Mexico (15–16 September)
Chile (18 September)
Panama (3 November)

Because Roman Catholicism served as one instrument of conquest and acculturation in Latin America, church holidays of this religion have the most general participation. Jewish, Protestant, and African-derived religious holidays are also celebrated throughout the region. The most impressive celebrations during the colonial years occurred on Corpus Christi and Holy Week, climaxing with Easter services. In the last century the Christmas holiday has emerged as more popular, with the suppression of many public aspects of the Corpus Christi and Holy Week festivals. In the Antilles, the circum-Caribbean region, and Brazil, Carnival has generally emerged as one of the most significant holidays. Of special importance throughout Latin America are the celebrations of the manifestations of virgins and saints. The best-known and most widely celebrated of these are the Virgin of Guadalupe, the patron of Mexico, on 12 December, and Santa Rosa De Lima, the first saint of South America, on 30 August. Other feasts mark the church's holy days of obligation. Such fiestas include the Feast of Christ of Esquipulas, called the Black Christ festival, in Guatemala (15 January) and the festival of Santiago (Saint James the Greater), the patron saint of Chile (25 July).

Commercial and special fiestas include those holidays created to honor special groups, such as Mother's Day and Teacher's Day. Others are attempts to revive, expand, and popularize celebrations to promote tourism. For example, Mexico's Day of the Dead fiestas in Pátzcuaro, Michoacán, resulted from the deliberate plans of the national tourism department. Carnival in several Caribbean nations today has taken on the character of a spectacle intended primarily for tourists. However commercial these events, they demonstrate what government officials want outsiders to recognize as typical of their culture.

Associated with most Latin American fiestas are special customs, artifacts, foods, band music, dancing, and fireworks. Gifts have become associated with special holidays—helmets at Corpus Christi, *matracas* (rattles) during Holy Week, and candy skulls at the Day of the Dead. Holiday cuisine ranges from special meals (for example, *chiles en nogada,* a green, stuffed chile pepper in a white cream sauce with red pomegranate seeds that displays the colors of the national flag for Mexican Independence Day), to preparations for religious feasts (for example, the Virgin's Tears, made from beet juice, for Holy Week; special egg-yolk bread made for the Day of the Dead; Three Kings Bread, a kind of sweet bread eaten on 6 January that has a ring baked in it to bring good luck to the person who finds it), to special beverages for holidays (Noche Buena beer brewed only during the Christmas holidays; *cuba libre,* a rum-and-cola drink, for national independence day; *chicha,* hard cider made from apples or grapes; and wine for Chile's major holidays).

The parades and processions often display visual lessons in social prominence and hierarchy through the order of march, the inclusion of different groups, and the nature of floats. Individuals find it necessary to participate as members of a residential, occupational, ethnic, or religious group. Fiesta organization in the past reflected these same groupings, with perhaps the religious confraternities (Cofradías) dominant in the colonial years, occupational and ethnic associations slightly superior in the nineteenth century, and residential groups emerging as more important in the twentieth century. Displaying these groups during fiestas, while portraying social hierarchy, demonstrates and reaffirms the solidarity of the society.

Fiestas also mark individual rites of passage, including birth, christening, saint day, *quinciñera* (fifteenth birthday for girls), marriage, and death. The nature of these fiestas varies from family to family and differs by religion. Nevertheless, the nature of the family holiday, its proper celebration, remains the province primarily of the leading (or centralizing) woman.

Finally, many festivals of Quechua origins have survived in South America, some depicting the conquest itself where the Inca must meet Pizarro, other festivals are of pre-Hispanic origin. Regarding the latter variety, the Inti Raimi festival is most notable since it is the second largest on the continent. This festival is the Incan festival of the sun. Despite being banned in 1572 by the Viceroy Toledo it has survived, making Cuzco once again the center (belly button) of the world. Throngs of revelers arrive in the old Incan capital from all over South America and the world. The most important day is June 24th, when the Sapa Inca calls on blessings from the sun.

*See also* **Carnival; Catholic Church: The Colonial Period; Cinco de Mayo; Cofradía; Cuzco; Guadalupe, Virgin of; Incas, The; Quechua; Rosa de Lima.**

BIBLIOGRAPHY

Lawrence Urdang and Christine N. Donohue, eds., *Holidays and Anniversaries of the World* (1985).

Patricia Quintana with Carol Haralson, *Mexico's Feasts of Life* (1989).

William H. Beezley, Cheryl E. Martin, and William E. French, eds., *Rituals of Rule, Rituals of Resistance: Public Celebrations and Popular Culture in Mexico* (1994).

### Additional Bibliography

Aranda, Antonio Garrido. *El mundo festivo en España y América*. Córdoba, Spain: Servicio de Publicaciones, Universidad de Córdoba, 2005.

Brading, David A. *Mexican Phoenix: Our Lady of Guadalupe: Image and Tradition across Five Centuries*. New York: Cambridge University Press, 2001.

Brugal, Yana Elsa, and Beatriz J. Rizk. *Rito y representación: Los sistemas mágico-religiosos en la cultura cubana contemporánea*. Madrid: Iberoamericana, and Frankfurt am Main: Vervuert, 2003.

Burga, Manuel. *Nacimiento de una utopía: Muerte y resurrección de los incas*. Lima: Universidad Nacional Mayor de San Marcos and Universidad de Guadalajara, 2005.

Calvo C., Rossano. *Qosqo sociedad e ideología, siglo XX: Estudios de antropología del Qosqo*. Qosqo, Peru: Municipalidad del Qosqo, 1995.

Carrasco, David. *Aztec Ceremonial Landscapes*. Niwot, CO: University Press of Colorado, 1999.

Dean, Carolyn. *Inka Bodies and the Body of Christ: Corpus Christi in Colonial Cuzco, Peru*. Durham, NC: Duke University Press, 1999.

Ferreira, César, and Eduardo Dargent-Chamot. *Culture and Customs of Peru*. Westport, CT: Greenwood Press, 2003.

Guss, David M. *The Festive State: Race, Ethnicity, and Nationalism as Cultural Performance*. Berkeley: University of California Press, 2000.

Matta, Roberto da. *Carnivals, Rogues, and Heroes: An Interpretation of the Brazilian Dilemma*. Notre Dame, IN: University of Notre Dame Press, 1991.

Mauldin, Barbara, ed. *Carnaval!*. Seattle: University of Washington Press, 2004.

Moreno Yáñez, Segundo, and José Figueroa. *El levantamiento indígena del Inti raymi de 1990*. Quito, Ecuador: Fundación Ecuatoriana de Estudios Sociales, 1992.

Norget, Kristin. *Days of Death, Days of Life: Ritual in the Popular Culture of Oaxaca*. New York: Columbia University Press, 2006.

Reis, João José. *Death Is a Festival: Funeral Rites and Rebellion in Nineteenth-Century Brazil*. Translated by H. Sabrina Gledhil. Chapel Hill: University of North Carolina Press, 2003.

Sahagún, Fray Bernardino de. "Que trata del Calendario, fiestas y ceremonias, sacrificios y solemnidades que estos naturales de esta Nueva España hacían a honra de sus dioses." In *Historia general de las cosas de Nueva España*, edited by Angel María Garibay. México, Porrúa, 1985.

Shaw, Lisa, and Stephanie Dennison. *Pop Culture Latin America!: Media, Arts, and Lifestyle*. Santa Barbara, CA: ABC-CLIO, 2005.


William H. Beezley

---

**FIGARI, PEDRO** (1861–1938). Pedro Figari (*b.* 29 June 1861; *d.* 24 July 1938), Uruguayan painter. Born in Montevideo, Figari had no formal art training in his youth but later studied drawing and painting with Godofredo Sommavilla in Montevideo and with Virgilio Ripari in Venice (1886). His astonishing artistic career did not begin until 1921, at age sixty, when he had his first exhibition in Buenos Aires at the Galería Müller. In 1925 he moved to Paris, where he remained for nine years. In the seventeen years following his first exhibition in Buenos Aires he turned out some 3,000 cardboard designs consisting of social topics, landscapes, colonial patios, folk dances, black country women, horses, and gauchos. His style displays an inner dynamism deriving from rapid strokes and a poetic vision of color. He received the grand prize at the Centennial of Uruguayan Independence Exhibition in Montevideo, and the gold medal at the Ibero-American Exhibition, Seville, Spain, both in 1930. He was one of the founders of Uruguay's school of arts (1898), as well as a founding member of the Sociedad Amigos del Arte in Buenos Aires (1924). Figari was the author of several books, including *Art, Aesthetics and the Ideal* (1912), in which he developed ideas taken from Herbert Spenser, and *La historia Kiria* (1930), the description of a Uruguayan utopia.

*See also* **Art: The Twentieth Century; Gaucho.**


BIBLIOGRAPHY

Vicente Gesualdo, Aldo Viglione, and Rodolfo Santos, *Diccionario de artistas plásticos en la Argentina* (1988).

### Additional Bibliography

Anastasía, Luis V., and Walter Rela. *Figari, lucha continua*. Montevideo: Academia Uruguaya de Letras, 1994.

Sanguinetti, Julio María. *El doctor Figari*. Montevideo: Aguilar: Fundación BankBoston, 2002.


Amalia Cortina Aravena

## FIGUEIREDO, AFONSO CELSO DE ASSIS (1860–1938).

Afonso Celso de Assis Figueiredo (*b.* 31 March 1860; *d.* 11 July 1938), Brazilian politician and man of letters. The son of a prominent Liberal politician and nobleman, the viscount of Ouro Prêto, Figueiredo left his native Minas Gerais to study in São Paulo. After earning a doctorate in law in 1881, he quickly embarked on his political career, winning election to the parliament four times. In contrast to his father, he showed himself to be reform-minded, most notably supporting proposals for the gradual abolition of slavery in Brazil.

Although he had embraced republican ideas as a student, Figueiredo had become a strident monarchist by the time his father headed the final cabinet of the Brazilian Empire in 1889. When the empire gave way to the new republic late in that year, Figueiredo chose to follow his father into European exile. Upon his return he practiced and taught law, and dedicated himself to political journalism and other writings. Although he also produced poetry and novels, his greatest literary fame came from his nonfiction works. Figueiredo's historical memoirs, *Oito anos de Parlamento* (1981; originally published in 1929), and biography *Visconde de Ouro Prêto* (1935), are important sources for the study of politics in the late nineteenth century. By far his most widely read literary work was *Porque me ufano do meu país* (1900, 1943), a celebration of all things Brazilian. Hailed by many as a model of civic pride, this book gave rise to the term *ufanismo* (facile, unthinking patriotism).

Honored by France with the Legion of Honor and by Pope Pius X with the title of count, Figueiredo became a central figure in Brazil's literary and intellectual organizations. One of the founding members of the Academia Brasileira de Letras, he served as president of the Instituto Histórico e Geográfico Brasileiro from 1912 until his death.

*See also* **Brazil: Since 1889; Brazil, The Empire (Second); Slavery: Brazil.**

BIBLIOGRAPHY

Robert E. Conrad, *The Destruction of Brazilian Slavery, 1850–1888* (1972).

Emília Viotti Da Costa, *The Brazilian Empire: Myths and Histories* (1985).

### Additional Bibliography

Rodrigues, João Paulo Coelho de Souza. *A dança das cadeiras: Literature e política na Academia Brasileira de Letras (1896–1913).* Campinas, São Paulo: Editora da UNICAMP, 2001.

ROGER A. KITTLESON

## FIGUEIREDO, JACKSON DE (1891–1928).

Jackson de Figueiredo (*b.* 9 October 1891; *d.* 4 November 1928), Brazilian writer and Catholic layman who founded the Centro Dom Vital, a major center for orthodox Catholic thought.

Born in Aracajú, Sergipe, Figueiredo was an atheist who converted to Catholicism in 1918 and thereafter dedicated his life to church affairs. Influenced by nineteenth-century and contemporary European conservatives, he saw in Catholicism "the most fundamental element of Brazilian heritage," which could serve as a bulwark against the forces of disorder.

In 1922 he founded the Centro Dom Vital in Rio de Janeiro. It became the Catholic hierarchy's vehicle to mobilize opinions among educated Brazilians and advocated liturgical piety, theological thought, personal austerity, and conservatism. Figueiredo used the Centro to spark a powerful Catholic political movement that sought to regenerate the country morally. His political passion and intolerance, however, contrasted with his private gentleness and bohemianism. He died in Barra la Tijuca.

*See also* **Brazil: Since 1889; Catholic Church: The Modern Period.**

BIBLIOGRAPHY

Robert M. Levine, *Historical Dictionary of Brazil* (1979); *Latin American Politics: A Historical Bibliography* (1984).

### Additional Bibliography

Azzi, Riolando. *Os pioneiros do centro dom vital.* Rio de Janeiro: Educan, 2003.

Fontes, José Silvério Leite. *Razão e fé em Jackson de Figueiredo.* Aracaju, Sergipe: Editora UFS, Universidad Federal de Sergipe, 1998.

ROSS WILKINSON

**FIGUEIREDO, JOÃO BAPTISTA DE OLIVEIRA** (1918–1999). João Baptista de Oliveira Figueiredo (*b.* 15 January 1918), president of Brazil (1979–1985). At the time of his inauguration, Figueiredo was largely unknown to the public, though he had been an early conspirator in the 1964 military coup that overthrew President João Goulart. After the coup, he rose to the rank of general and served as chief of the Military Cabinet, secretary-general of the National Security Council, and head of the National Intelligence Agency (SNI).

Born in Rio de Janeiro, Figueiredo grew up in the town of Alegrete in Rio Grande do Sul. His father, General Euclides Figueiredo, commanded anti-Getúlio Vargas troops during the 1932 São Paulo Rebellion. João Baptista chose a military career, graduating first in his class at the numerous military schools he attended, including the military academy at Realengo, where he graduated as a cavalry officer in 1937. One brother, General Euclides de Oliveira Figueiredo, also followed a military path. Another brother, Guilherme de Figueiredo, is a well-known playwright and essayist.

The last of the post-coup military presidents, Figueiredo supervised the transition to civilian rule. Bridging the gap between hard-liners and moderates, he continued the cautious relaxation (*distenção*) of military rule begun by Ernesto Geisel and completed the process of opening the political system (*abertura*). Under Figueiredo, prisoners who lost their political rights (*cassados*) were granted amnesty. His government abandoned the two-party system and promoted the creation of multiple parties. In 1982, Figueiredo allowed direct elections of state governors for the first time since 1965. Figueiredo tried to foster a populist image, but resorted to the hard line when necessary, as he did in the 1979 labor strikes.

Figueiredo left politics with the return to civilian rule in 1985. According to 1993 opinion polls, Brazilians rated Figueiredo's presidency high. Though mentioned as a possible candidate for the 1994 presidential elections, Figueiredo claimed little enthusiasm for the idea. He died on December 24, 1999.

*See also* **Brazil: Since 1889.**

BIBLIOGRAPHY

Although there is no biography of Figueiredo available in English, a number of works address his administration. Thomas E. Skidmore, *The Politics of Military Rule in Brazil, 1964–1985* (1988), devotes chap. 8 and part of chap. 9 to the subject. Ronald M. Schneider, *Order and Progress: A Political History of Brazil* (1991), also discusses the Figueiredo government.

*Additional Bibliography*

Bacchus, Wilfred A. *Mission in Mufti: Brazil's Military Regimes, 1964-1985.* New York: Greenwood Press, 1990.

Frota, Sylvio. *Ideais traídos.* Rio de Janeiro: Jorge Zahar Editor, 2006.

Gaspari, Elio. *A ditadura envergonhada.* São Paulo: Companhia da Letras, 2002.

SONNY B. DAVIS

**FIGUERES FERRER, JOSÉ** (1906–1990). José Figueres Ferrer (*b.* 25 September 1906; *d.* 8 June 1990), president of Costa Rica. José Figueres, "Don Pepe," presided over the Costa Rican nation on three separate occasions: once as head of a junta government (8 May 1948 to 8 November 1949) and twice as constitutional president (1953–1958 and 1970–1974). He was one of Costa Rica's most important political figures, setting the economic and social course of his country following the 1948 civil war and creating the National Liberation Party (PLN), Costa Rica's dominant political party after 1953. Moreover, during the 1950s and 1960s, he stood almost alone as the champion of democracy and economic and social reform in Central America and the Spanish-speaking Caribbean.

Born in rural San Ramón shortly after his parents had emigrated from Spain, Figueres had little formal education beyond the secondary level. He went to the United States in 1924 intending to study electrical engineering at the Massachusetts Institute of Technology, but he never matriculated. Instead, with the Boston Public Library as his classroom, he acquired the social democratic philosophy that guided his future political career. In 1928, he returned to Costa Rica to become a farmer-entrepreneur on a *finca* (ranch) he named La Lucha Sin Fin (The Endless Struggle), where he raised *cabuya* (a Central American agave) and built a factory to manufacture rope and bags from the homegrown fiber. La Lucha was the model for Figueres Ferrer's later national programs, wherein he developed the region, creating new jobs and skills and providing an array of benefits and social services. In 1942, Figueres Ferrer's life changed abruptly when he was expelled from the country in a dispute with President Rafael Ángel Calderón Guardia.

Figueres criticized Calderón publicly for failing to prevent a riot in San José after an Axis submarine had attacked Puerto Limón. Calderón Guardia, for his part, accused Figueres of revealing military secrets and of participating in a scheme to shelter the properties of German and Italian residents of Costa Rica. When Figueres returned from exile in Mexico two years later, he was greeted as a hero who had opposed the authoritarian Calderón.

During his exile, Figueres and other Caribbean exiles developed the Caribbean Legion, a plan to rid Costa Rica (and the entire region) of tyranny. Figueres put his plan into operation in March 1948, when Calderón tried to steal the presidential election from the clear winner, Otilio Ulate Blanco. Though most politicians hoped for a peaceful solution to the crisis, Figueres and Calderón were on a collision course. With a citizen-volunteer army and the help of his Caribbean allies, Figueres waged a successful six-week "war of national liberation," and took control of the nation as head of the Founding Junta of the Second Republic in May.

During the eighteen months that the junta governed, Figueres made fundamental changes in the life of the nation. He abolished the army, nationalized the banking system, imposed a 10 percent tax on wealth, and held elections for a constituent assembly to draft a constitution. The new constitution (1949) embraced Figueres's socialist tendencies, providing for government regulation of the private sector and creating "autonomous institutions" to perform the economic and social functions of the public sector. With the constitution in place, Figueres turned over the presidency to Ulate.

In 1953, Figueres became constitutional president himself and resumed where he left off four years earlier. Figueres expanded the role of government through the creation of additional autonomous institutions to provide such services as the production and distribution of electrical energy, banking, health care, insurance, and telephones. He established the National Council of Production to stimulate agriculture and business through credits, price supports, and marketing facilities.

Despite the economic growth and social progress that Costa Rica experienced under Figueres, his presidency was not tranquil. The Figueres era was particularly troubled by foreign policy. Costa Rica's safe democracy attracted political exiles from throughout the region, and Figueres openly opposed the dictatorships of Anastasio Somoza in Nicaragua, Rafael Trujillo in the Dominican Republic, Fulgencio Batista in Cuba, and Marcos Pérez Jiménez in Venezuela. Though he made promises of military support to his Caribbean allies that he could not keep, he collaborated closely with Venezuelan exile Rómulo Betancourt and sought to influence U.S. policy against the dictators.

In 1954, Costa Rica was the only country to boycott the inter-American conference in Caracas, and in the same year Figueres aided Nicaraguan exiles in an attempt to overthrow Somoza. Figueres supplied arms to Fidel Castro after 1956. On two occasions, the dictators retaliated. In 1948, while Figueres was heading the junta, and again in 1955, Somoza sponsored "exile" invasions of Costa Rica. Both times, Figueres, with no army, appealed to the Organization of American States for help. Though the OAS came to his rescue, it pressured him to expel the so-called Caribbean Legion from Costa Rica and to enter into agreements to reduce tensions in the region.

The U.S. State Department labeled Figueres a "troublemaker" in the 1950s, but during the 1960s, in the context of the Cuban Revolution, the attitude changed. The Central Intelligence Agency sought his assistance in covert action against Trujillo and secretly funded his efforts to strengthen the democratic Left. Figueres had criticized Castro in April 1959, advising him to remain on the side of the United States in the cold war, and he became an avid supporter of President John F. Kennedy and the Alliance for Progress. After Kennedy's assassination, Figueres's role in international affairs diminished. His decline was especially steep after 1967, when it became known that he had collaborated with the CIA.

With Figueres barred by the constitution from succeeding himself in 1959, and the party badly split in choosing a candidate, the PLN lost the presidential election. It did manage to reunite for victory in 1962, but lost again four years later, convincing Figueres to run in 1970.

Figueres's second presidency was no less controversial than his first, but had fewer accomplishments to claim. Needing to recharge the economy, Figueres established trade and diplomatic relations with the Soviet Union and proposed the creation of an international financial district in Costa Rica. Both measures bedeviled his presidency. There were street demonstrations against any sort of relations with the Soviet Union, and militant right-wing groups used the situation to agitate. The plan for the international financial district brought Robert Vesco to Costa Rica. Though Figueres argued that Costa Rica needed capital, Vesco's reputation as a swindler and his holdings in Figueres's La Lucha caused a crippling scandal. Figueres believed that he was acting in the best interests of his country, but the principal achievement of his second presidency was that its shortcomings paved the way for a new generation of PLN leaders to take charge.

During the remaining years of his life, Figueres permitted the institutions and party that he had created to take shape without him. Because of a near-even division in Costa Rica between pro-Liberation and anti-Liberation sentiment, an informal two-party system evolved through the process of coalition politics. Figueres himself enhanced his country's democratic traditions and formalized the nation's general commitment to economic and social well-being, which enabled Costa Rica to avoid the bloodshed of Central America in the 1980s.

*See also* **Calderón Guardia, Rafael Ángel; Caribbean Legion; Costa Rica, National Liberation Party; Organization of American States (OAS).**

BIBLIOGRAPHY

Arturo Castro Esquivel, *José Figueres Ferrer: El hombre y su obra* (1955).

Alberto Baeza Flores, *La lucha sin fin* (1969).

John Patrick Bell, *Crisis in Costa Rica: The 1948 Revolution* (1971).

Bert H. English, *Liberación Nacional in Costa Rica: The Development of a Political Party in a Transitional Society* (1971).

Charles D. Ameringer, *Don Pepe: A Political Biography of José Figueres of Costa Rica* (1978).

### *Additional Bibliography*

Gámez Solano, Uladislao. *José Figueres Ferrer: El hombre y su destino: semblanza.* San José, Costa Rica: EUNA, 2001.

Guerra, Tomás. *José Figueres y la justicia social.* San José, Costa Rica: EDUCA, 1997.

Longley, Kyle. *The Sparrow and the Hawk: Costa Rica and the United States during the Rise of José Figueres.* Tuscaloosa: University of Alabama Press, 1997.

CHARLES D. AMERINGER

---

**FIGUEROA, GABRIEL** (1908–1997). Gabriel Figueroa (*b.* 26 April 1908; *d.* 1997), Mexican film photographer. Figueroa learned his trade in Mexico and in Hollywood. He was the principal photographer of *Allá en el Rancho Grande* (1938). Since then, he has filmed over 200 features for Mexican, North American, and European directors. Noted particularly for his work with black and white film, Figueroa was called "the greatest muralist of Mexico" by Diego Rivera. His aesthetic style is characterized by contrasts of darkness and light and by the use of panoramic shots. He has worked for such acclaimed directors as Emilio Fernández, Luis Buñuel, John Ford, and John Huston. Figueroa has received more Ariels from the Mexican film academy than any other photographer in Mexican cinema. In addition, he has been awarded major international prizes in Venice, Cannes, Prague, Madrid, and San Francisco. In 1971 he received the National Award for the Arts in Mexico.

*See also* **Ariel; Cinema: From the Silent Film to 1990; Rivera, Diego.**

BIBLIOGRAPHY

Luis Reyes De La Maza, *El cine sonoro en México* (1973).

E. Bradford Burns, *Latin American Cinema: Film and History* (1975).

Carl J. Mora, *Mexican Cinema: Reflections of a Society: 1896–1980* (1982).

John King, *Magical Reels: A History of Cinema in Latin America* (1990).

*Additional Bibliography*

Figueroa, Gabriel. *Gabriel Figueroa: Memorias*. México, D.F.: Universidad Nacional Autónoma de México: DGE/Equilibrista, 2005.

Castro, Antonio. *Miradas sobre el mundo: Veinte conversaciones con cineastas*. Cáceres: Asociación Cinéfila Re Bross, 1999.

Rivera, Héctor J. *Tinta sangre del corazón*. San Ángel, D.F., México: Consejo Nacional para la Cultura y las Artes, 1996.

DAVID MACIEL

## FIGUEROA, JOSÉ (?–1835).

José Figueroa (*d.* 1835), governor of Alta California (1833–1835). General Figueroa was one of the most important Mexican governors of the territory. In 1833 he initiated a new emancipation of a limited number of Indian converts living in Franciscan-run missions. That same year he also established Indian towns at three sites in the southern part of the territory—the San Juan Capistrano mission, the Las Flores rancho, and the San Dieguito rancho—with the hope of creating stable Indian villages with formal municipal governments. This scheme, however, failed when the Spanish government secularized the missions.

Figueroa also cooperated in implementing the secularization of the missions ordered by the Valentín Gómez Farías government by way of a bill signed on 17 August 1833, working with local politicians to craft the secularization decree to benefit the elite of the territory. On 9 August 1834, Figueroa approved the secularization plan. Prominent Californios received appointment as *mayordomos* of the former missions, many using their positions to enrich themselves. Most of the converts still living in the missions were not legally emanicipated.

After Figueroa died in office in 1835, a period of political chaos followed, and in 1836 local politicians seized control of the government.

*See also* **Missions: Spanish America.**

BIBLIOGRAPHY

David J. Weber, *The Mexican Frontier, 1821–1846: The American Southwest Under Mexico* (1982).

*Additional Bibliography*

Jackson, Robert H. *New Views of Borderlands History*. Albuquerque: University of New Mexico Press, 1998.

Teja, José F. de la, and Ross Frank. *Choice, Persuasion, and Coercion: Social Control on Spain's North American Frontiers*. Albuquerque: University of New Mexico Press, 2005.

ROBERT H. JACKSON

## FIGUEROA, PEDRO JOSÉ (1780–1838).

Pedro José Figueroa (*b.* 1780; *d.* 1838), Colombian artist. Son of a wealthy Bogotá family and descendant of a notable group of seventeenth-century Colombian painters, Figueroa began his studies with Peruvian painter Pablo Antonio García (1744–1814). During the war for independence in Colombia, he painted scenes of some of the battles as well as at least ten portraits (1819–1822) of Simón Bolívar. He served as director of the construction of the Church of Las Nieves in Bogotá and painted the *Holy Trinity* mural for the Bogotá cathedral. He painted many portraits of influential Colombians including archbishops. Figueroa established a studio for his pupils, among whom were his sons José Celestino and José Miguel y Santos.

*See also* **Art: The Colonial Period; Colombia: From the Conquest through Independence.**

BIBLIOGRAPHY

Gabriel Giraldo Jaramillo, *La miniatura, la pintura y el grabado en Colombia* (1980).

Dawn Ades, *Art in Latin America* (1989).

BÉLGICA RODRÍGUEZ

## FIGUEROA ALCORTA, JOSÉ (1860–1931).

José Alcorta Figueroa served as president of Argentina from 1906 to 1910. He was born on November 20, 1860, to a traditional family in the province of Córdoba and was educated in its best establishments, the Montserrat School and the Faculty of Law. He began his political career as a Juarista, a faction within the dominant National Autonomist Party, and held positions in the provincial legislature and presidential cabinet between 1885 and 1892, when he was elected deputy to the National Congress. From 1895 to 1898 he served as governor of Córdoba, and when his administration ended he was elected senator in the National Congress.

In 1904 Figueroa successfully ran for vice president on a ticket with Manuel Quintana. When Quintana died in 1906, Figueroa became president. His presidential legacy is somewhat problematic; in the name of democracy he devoted himself to fighting the faction of Roque Sáenz Peña within his party. Sáenz Peña succeeded him, however, and implemented a decisive electoral reform in 1912. Figueroa's methods included excessive use of federal intervention for party purposes, for example, using the police to close the special sessions of Congress in 1908. Appointed a member of the Supreme Court of Justice in 1915, he held that position until his death on December 27, 1931.

*See also* **Quintana, Manuel.**

BIBLIOGRAPHY

Botana, Natalio R. *De la república posible a la república verdadera: 1880–1910.* Buenos Aires: Compañía Editora Espasa Calpe Argentina, 1997.

PAULA ALONSO

**FIGUEROA GAJARDO, ANA** (1907–1970). Ana Figueroa Gajardo (*b.* 19 June 1907; *d.* 8 April 1970), Chilean career diplomat, journalist, women's rights activist. After graduating from the Instituto Pedagógico, Universidad de Chile, in 1928, Figueroa was a high-school teacher and principal. In 1946 she attended Columbia University and a summer institute at Colorado State University. From 1947 to 1949, she was general supervisor of the Chilean high-school system. In 1948 she became president of the Federación Chilena de Instituciones Femeninas (FECHIF) and was appointed director of the Chilean Women's Bureau. In 1950 she served as Chilean delegate to the Inter-American Commission of Women; from 1950 to 1952 she was the Chilean minister plenipotentiary to the Third General Assembly of the United Nations; and from 1952 to 1959 she served on the Security Council, UNESCO, and the UN Commission on the Juridical and Social Condition of Women. From 1950 to 1967, Figueroa was the first woman to serve as director-general of the International Labor Organization. She was also on the board of directors of the international YWCA.

*See also* **Feminism and Feminist Organizations; United Nations.**

BIBLIOGRAPHY

Inter-American Commission of Women, *Libro de oro* (1980).

*Additional Bibliography*

Hutchison, Elizabeth Quay. *Labors Appropriate to Their Sex: Gender, Labor, and Politics in Urban Chile, 1900–1930.* Durham, NC: Duke University Press, 2001.

CORINNE ANTEZANA-PERNET
FRANCESCA MILLER

**FIGUEROA LARRAÍN, EMILIANO** (1866–1931). Emiliano Figueroa Larraín (*b.* 1866; *d.* 16 May 1931), lawyer, politician, diplomat, and president of Chile. A member of the Partido Democrático, he served as president twice. Following the death of President Pedro Montt, he occupied the Moneda as interim president from September through December 1910, until the election of Ramón Barros Luco. He was elected to the presidency in 1925, following President Arturo Alessandri Palma's second resignation. His naive attempts to govern, however, were frustrated by the maneuverings of the minister of war, Carlos Ibáñez Del Campo, and in April 1927 Ibáñez forced him to resign his office. Figueroa later represented Chile as ambassador to Peru.

*See also* **Alessandri Palma, Arturo; Chile, Political Parties: Democratic Party.**

BIBLIOGRAPHY

Luis Galdames, *A History of Chile,* translated and edited by Isaac J. Cox (1941; repr. 1961).

Frederick M. Nunn, *Chilean Politics, 1920–1931* (1970).

*Additional Bibliography*

Navarrete, Mariano. *Mi actuación en las revoluciones de 1920 y 1925.* Santiago de Chile: Ediciones Centro de Estudios Bicentenario, 2004.

WILLIAM F. SATER

**FILIBUSTERING.** Filibustering, the process by which groups of men left U.S. territory on private military expeditions intended to liberate, subjugate or annex foreign—often Latin—nations or colonies. Persons engaged in such enterprises were known as "filibusters." Filibustering violated international law and several statutes, most particularly the Neutrality Act of 1818. The term "filibuster" came into English-language currency during the second half of the nineteenth century. It is derived from the Dutch *vrijbuiter* (freebooter) and related to the Spanish *filibustero* and French *flibustier*.

During America's early national period, filibuster plots and invasions were directed primarily against Spanish territory in North America. Then, in the late 1830s and early 1840s and the Fenian excitement of the late 1860s, filibustering focused upon Canada. But filibustering had its greatest impact in the 1850s, when thousands of U.S. residents, including many immigrants, joined filibuster units that invaded Mexico, the independent states of Central America, several South American countries, and the Spanish possession of Cuba. Although filibustering was never an exclusively U.S. phenomenon, it came to be identified within the international community as a dangerous manifestation of U.S. imperialism to the degree that during the nineteenth century it seriously complicated U.S. diplomacy with Mexico, Central America, the major European powers, and other governments.

The most significant filibustering expeditions of the 1850s were the 1850 and 1851 expeditions of Narciso López against Cuba, and William Walker's 1853–1860 invasions of Mexico, Nicaragua, and Honduras. Walker succeeded in conquering Nicaragua and ruling it for parts of 1855–1857. Other significant expeditions of the decade included Californian Joseph Morehead's invasion of Mexican Sonora in 1851, Alexander Bell's expedition to Ecuador the same year, French adventurer Count Gaston Raoul de Raousset-Boulbon's expeditions to Mexico from California in 1852–1854, Henry L. Kinney's conquest of San Juan del Norte (Greytown), Nicaragua, in 1855, and Henry A. Crabb's thrust into Sonora in 1857. Some filibustering expeditions, such as former Mississippi governor John A. Quitman's conspiracy to invade Cuba in 1853–1855 and the plot of the Knights of the Golden Circle to attack Mexico in 1860, were aborted at the last moment.

The filibustering expeditions of the 1850s caused extensive destruction and many deaths in the countries victimized and contributed to a legacy of anti-Americanism throughout Mexico, Central America, and parts of South America. The Latins resented the inability—sometimes perceived as refusal—of the U.S. government to enforce its own neutrality laws effectually. None of the filibustering expeditions achieved permanent success, however, and many of the adventurers died during their campaigns. López, Raousset-Boulbon, Crabb, and Walker were all executed after being captured.

Filibustering continued to have an impact upon U.S. relations with Latin nations in the late nineteenth and early twentieth centuries. Several U.S.-based expeditions attacked Mexico in that period, and filibustering played a salient role in U.S. disputes with Spain over Cuba that triggered the Spanish-American War, such as the Virginius Affair of 1873. Filibustering diminished dramatically after World War I.

*See also* **United States–Latin American Relations.**

BIBLIOGRAPHY

Harris G. Warren, *The Sword Was Their Passport: A History of American Filibustering in the Mexican Revolution* (1943).

Robert E. May, *The Southern Dream of a Caribbean Empire, 1854–1861* (1973).

Joseph A. Stout, *The Liberators: Filibustering Expeditions into Mexico, 1848–1862 and the Last Thrust of Manifest Destiny* (1973).

Wilfried S. Neidhardt, *Fenianism in North America* (1975).

Charles H. Brown, *Agents of Manifest Destiny: The Lives and Times of the Filibusters* (1980).

### *Additional Bibliography*

Chacón M., Euclides. *Indice cronológico de la Campaña Nacional, 1856-1857.* Alajuela, Costa Rica: Museo Histórico Cultural Juan Santamaría, 2002.

Lazo, Rodrigo. *Writing to Cuba: Filibustering and Cuban Exiles in the United States.* Chapel Hill: University of North Carolina Press, 2005.

Stout, Joseph Allen. *Schemers & Dreamers: Filibustering in Mexico, 1848-1921.* Fort Worth: Texas Christian University Press, 2002.

Robert E. May

**FILÍSOLA, VICENTE** (c. 1789–1850). Vicente Filísola (*b.* ca. 1789; *d.* 23 July 1850), captain-general of Guatemala (12 June 1822–4 July 1823). Born in Rivoli, Italy, Filísola immigrated to Spain at a young age and began his military career. By 1810 he had attained the rank of second lieutenant and had received honors for his valiant fighting. He was sent to Mexico with royalist forces in 1811, but by 1815 he had become a close friend of Agustín de Iturbide. In 1821 he gave his support to Mexican independence, proclaimed in Iturbide's Plan of Iguala. At the head of four thousand men, he was the first insurgent leader to enter Mexico City on 24 September 1821, securing it for Iturbide's triumphal entry. Iturbide promoted him to brigadier general and gave him the title of Knight of the Imperial Order of Guadalupe, then sent him on a mission to Central America. There he was to keep order while the region decided on annexation to Mexico. On 4 November 1822, after most of Central America had voted in favor of union with the Mexican Empire, Filísola published a decree splitting the captaincy-general of Guatemala into the three commandancies-general of Chiapas, Sacatepéquez, and Costa Rica, with their capitals at Ciudad Real, Nueva Guatemala, and León respectively. Later that month, on Iturbide's orders, he led about two thousand men against San Salvador, the only major city to resist union with the Mexican Empire. After routing Manuel José Arce's troops, he entered the city on 9 February 1823. Upon learning of Iturbide's overthrow, he returned to Guatemala and convoked a congress of the provinces. Believing the basis for Mexican annexation to be gone, he accepted their declaration of independence.

After returning to Mexico, Filísola fought as a division general in the Texas Revolution in 1835 and ended his career as president of the Supreme Court of War. He also wrote extensively. He published his two-volume *Memorias para la historia de Tejas* in 1848–1849, and conducted a lively polemic with José Francisco Barrundia. Most of the documents ended up in Central America and were burned, but Filísola's biographer, Don Jenaro García, was able to obtain copies of Filísola's papers from one of his descendants and published them in two volumes as *La cooperación de México en la independencia de Centro America* (1911). Filísola died in Mexico during a cholera epidemic.

*See also* **Central America, United Provinces of.**

BIBLIOGRAPHY

Alejandro Marure, *Bosquejo histórico de las revoluciones de Centroamérica desde 1811 hasta 1834,* 2 vols. (1834–1837), pp. 92–110, 113.

Hubert Howe Bancroft, *History of Central America* Vol. 8, *The Works of Hubert Howe Bancroft* (1887), pp. 56–57, 62–64.

Pedro Zamora Castellanos, *Vida militar de Centro América,* 2 vols. (1966–1967), pp. 120–125.

Luis Beltranena Sinibaldi, *Fundación de la república de Guatemala* (1971), pp. 42–45.

*Additional Bibliography*

Pearcy, Thomas L. *The History of Central America.* Westport, CT: Greenwood Press, 2006.

Philippe L. Seiler

**FINCA.** Finca, Spanish term for farm or other rural estate. In Guatemala and other Central American states, it usually refers to a coffee plantation.

*See also* **Estancia; Fundo; Hacienda; Latifundia.**

BIBLIOGRAPHY

McCreery, David. *Rural Guatemala, 1760–1940.* Stanford, CA: Stanford University Press, 1994.

Ralph Lee Woodward Jr.

**FINLAY, CARLOS JUAN** (1833–1915). Carlos Juan Finlay (*b.* 3 December 1833; *d.* 20 August 1915), a Cuban physician and epidemiologist. After earning his medical degree at Jefferson Medical College in Philadelphia, Finlay pursued additional studies in Havana and Paris before beginning his medical practice in Cuba. He represented the Cuban government to a commission from the United States that arrived on the island in 1879 to study the transmission of yellow fever. In 1881, Finlay concluded that a mosquito, known as the

*Aëdes aegypti,* was the carrier of the disease, but his theory was largely ignored by the medical community until 1900, when U.S. General Leonard Wood ordered Walter Reed to test Finlay's theory. Reed's experiments in Havana confirmed Finlay's findings, a discovery that led to the eradication of yellow fever in much of the tropics. Unfortunately, Reed, rather than Finlay, has received most of the credit for the elimination of yellow fever.

*See also* **Diseases; Medicine: The Modern Era.**

BIBLIOGRAPHY

L. O. Howard, *The Yellow Fever Mosquito* (1913).

James H. Hitchman, *Leonard Wood and Cuban Independence, 1898–1902* (1971).

Hermio Portell-Vila, *Finlay: Vida de un sabia cubano* (1990).

*Additional Bibliography*

López Sánchez, José. *Carlos J. Finlay: His Life and His Work.* La Habana: Editorial José Martí, 1999.

THOMAS M. LEONARD

---

**FISHING INDUSTRY.** Fishing was an established part of preconquest subsistence and exchange in Latin America. Archaeological evidence from the Peruvian coastal plain, for example, suggests that the population around 2,500 to 2,000 BCE was heavily reliant on shellfish, seabirds, and marine mammals and fish caught using lines or beach nets. In the Classic Period (500–900 CE) hunting and fishing from boats using lines, nets, and harpoons was integral to coastal livelihoods. Fishing was also important to the Inca civilization, and fish supplemented the basic vegetarian diet of the Aztecs. Fishing was not merely a subsistence activity in precolonial times—the Mayans traded conserved fish, fairs (which proved integral to the development of north-south trade) were organized around the Orinoco turtle fisheries, and both dried and smoked fish products contributed to subsistence and exchange activities in the south Atlantic region.

### THE COLONIAL AND EARLY POSTCOLONIAL PERIODS

Regional colonial and early postcolonial histories make only infrequent references to fishing. However, there is evidence that Catalan fishermen were active in the sea bream and conger eel fisheries off Chile in the 1770s, drying and exporting their catches to Peru's mining towns. Nicholas de Arredondo (viceroy of Rio Plata, 1789–1795) promoted whaling and fishing off Patagonia through a royal monopoly. Fur and elephant seals were early targets of colonial seafarers and fishers; the trade in skins peaked in 1822 when more than 1.2 million animals were slaughtered on the island of South Georgia alone. In Brazil a state whaling monopoly coexisted alongside artisanal fishing by slaves until the turn of the twentieth century, though evidence shows that social elites preferred to import salted cod from Portugal. Efforts to introduce modern fishing practices in the late nineteenth century, including the recruitment of British fishermen to develop a Chilean trawl fishery, were largely unsuccessful.

Catches increased modestly through the early twentieth century, reaching some 255,850 tonnes in 1938. Brazil accounted for around 40 percent of the regional catch, as Portuguese and Spanish migrants employed ever larger boats to fish for sardines out of Brazil's southern states. Migrants—this time, Italian and Spanish migrants venturing out from Mar de Plata—also provided the bulk of Argentine catches (22% of the regional catch). By the outbreak of World War II, Latin America contributed a mere 1.2 percent of world production.

### THE EMERGENCE OF A MODERN FISHING INDUSTRY

The situation changed markedly in the second half of the twentieth century. Concerned at the growing incursion of foreign vessels into territorial waters, Mexico approved legislation in 1947 and 1949 that granted the cooperative sector exclusive access to the nine most important inshore marine and shellfish fisheries, and limited foreign fishing within the coastal zone. In Brazil the state-sponsored formation of fishermen's guilds in the early 1920s was an early harbinger of a statist development strategy that reached its apogee with the introduction of an extensive national fisheries development program in the 1960s.

The most notable postwar change occurred in Peru. Frustrated by the national government's failure to control the extensive operations of the Japanese tuna fleet off the Peruvian coast during the late

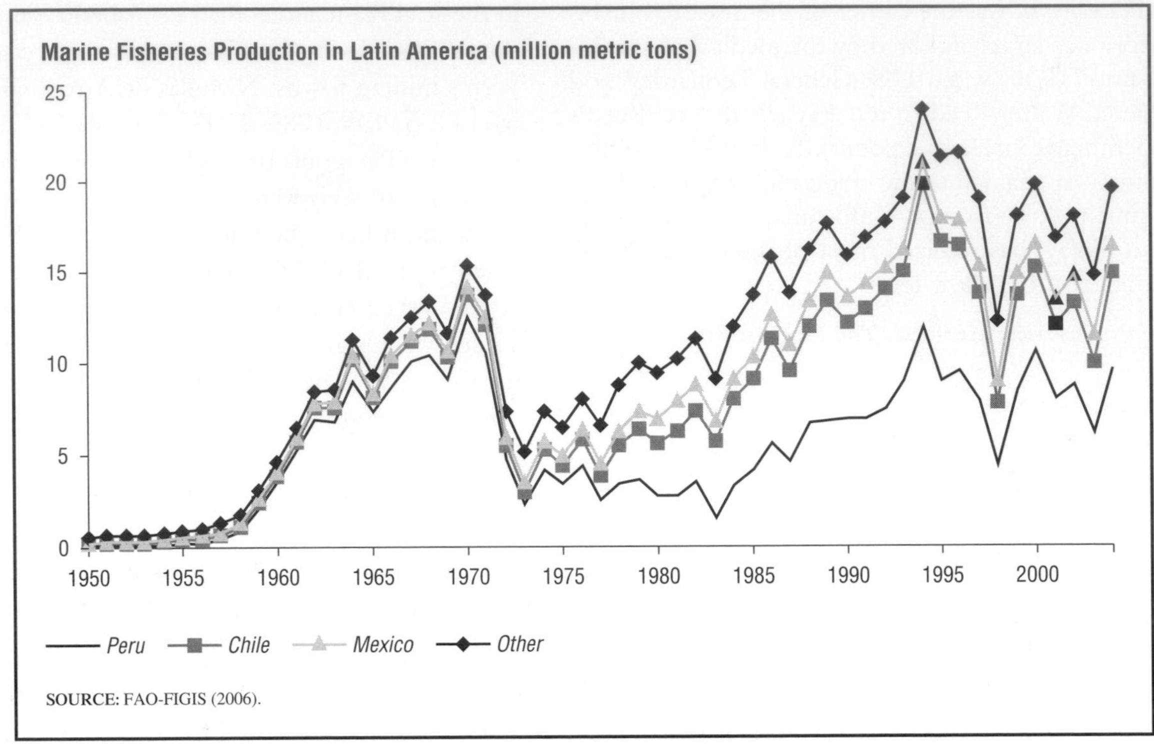


SOURCE: FAO-FIGIS (2006).

**Figure 1**

1940s and early 1950s and a growing inability to compete with Japanese exporters in the U.S. canned tuna market, Peruvian fishing entrepreneurs switched their attention to the anchovy instead.

Anchovy catches grew swiftly following the collapse of the Californian sardine fishery in 1949 to 1950 as redundant capital equipment and expertise migrated southwards, with Peru's first fishmeal plant established in 1953. The relaxation of domestic constraints (export taxes and restrictions on fishing activity) that had protected the Guano Administration Company, allied to the adoption of modern fishing techniques, saw an extraordinary escalation in production and exports (see Figure 1). At its peak in 1970 the industry employed more than 1,400 boats and 21,700 fishers to catch 12.3 million tonnes of anchovy, nearly one-quarter of world marine fisheries production and approximately five-sixths of the regional marine catch. This was converted by some 170 factories, employing more than 9,000 workers, into fishmeal, which supplied one-third of the country's export earnings. The bonanza proved short-lived, and the abrupt collapse in anchovy stocks—due to overfishing and the 1972 to 1973 El Niño event—led to the fishery's nationalization.

## NEOLIBERALISM AND CONTINUED FISHERIES EXPANSION

The emergence of neoliberal governments and their commitment to export-oriented growth provided a substantive boost to fisheries production across the region (see Figure 1). In Chile, the privatization after 1974 of the northern pelagic fleet (catching fish that shoal on the surface), the gradual exclusion of foreign vessels from national fishing grounds, and the removal of access restrictions to pelagic stocks were supplemented by aggressive exchange-rate and export-promotion strategies—and saw Chile displace Peru as the region's leading fish exporter in 1980. New investment swiftly entered the Peruvian fisheries sector after the neoliberal government of Alberto Fujimori (1990–2000) privatized anchovy fishing and processing, introduced a more competitive exchange rate, and established fiscal and monetary regimes favoring exporters. However, although investment encouraged a reduced dependency upon the anchovy fishery, the industry remains critically exposed to a repeat of the crisis it experienced in the early1970s, as was evidenced in 1997 to 1998.

In Argentina, the decisions by the administration of Carlos Menem (1989–1999) to exempt new

**Principal Latin American marine fisheries and present status of exploitation (as defined by FAO)**

| Status | Species (pelagic species in italics) | Participating Countries |
|---|---|---|
| Fully to overexploited | *Peruvian anchovy*<br>*Araucanian herring*<br>*South American pilchard*<br>*Chilean jack mackerel*<br>Argentine, South Pacific and Patagonian hake<br>Patagonian grenadier<br>Shortfin squid | Peru, Chile, Ecuador, Argentina and Uruguay |
| Fully exploited | Yellowfin tuna<br>Southern blue whiting | Mexico and Venezuela<br>Argentina |
| Moderately to fully exploited | *Californian pilchard*<br>*Pacific anchovy* | Panama, Chile, Peru, Ecuador, Mexico, Argentina |
| Moderately exploited | *Chub mackerel* | Chile, Ecuador, Peru |
| Status unknown | *Round sardinella* | Venezuela |

Note: Criterion for inclusion as a "principal" fishery: catches exceeding 50,000 metric tons in at least one country over the period 1980–1995.

SOURCE: Thorpe and Bennett (2000), p. 151 and FAO (2004).

Table 1

vessels from trade taxes, to allow Argentine firms to lease foreign vessels, and to simplify procedures for "naturalizing" foreign vessels saw the rapid incorporation of new factory and freezer vessels into the Argentine fleet. But as catches increased, so did the number and intensity of fishery conflicts. Mexico was an exception insofar as industrial expansion preceded neoliberalism: The gross registered tonnage of the Mexican fleet rose swiftly, from 8,000 to 289,000 tonnes, between 1970 and 1988. Tuna was the newly targeted resource, though U.S. embargoes on Mexican tuna exports in 1980 and 1986 and a worsening macroeconomic environment saw the sector become overly reliant on state support. Carlos Salinas de Gortari's neoliberal regime (1988–1994) sharply cut this support and also rescinded the cooperative's exclusive fishing rights, causing fishery conflicts to intensify while catches remained static. Other examples of neoliberal governments encouraging domestic and foreign investment into the sector include the reflagging of Spanish tuna boats in Costa Rica, Norwegian investment in Nicaragua's shellfish industries, Spanish and Venezuelan joint ventures, and Taiwanese and U.S. participation in Uruguayan fisheries. The intensification of fishing across the region has brought many of the major commercial fisheries to the point of collapse (see Table 1).

The response to this crisis has been two-fold. First, greater attention is being paid to stock management, with a number of countries (most notably Argentina, Mexico, Peru, and Chile) employing or moving toward the use of individual transferable quotas (ITQs) as a method of apportioning TACs (Total Allowable Catches) in regulating marine fishing activity. Second, recognition of the limited opportunities for future capture fisheries growth has led to ever greater emphasis on the development of regional aquacultural activities (see Figure 2).

### AQUACULTURE AS A SOLUTION TO THE CRISIS IN MARINE FISHERIES?

Commercial salmon and trout farming evolved in Chile during the early 1980s and, benefiting from the economic incentives offered to exporters by neoliberal governments, grew rapidly from 500 tonnes in 1985 to 25,000 tonnes in 1990. By 2000 342,000 tonnes were exported; this leaped to 563,000 tonnes, worth U.S.$2.3 billion, by 2004. In 2007 aquaculture was Chile's fourth largest export earner by value, and the country was likely to become the world's largest salmon producer in the next few years. Elsewhere, the emphasis has been on shrimp culture. Led by Ecuador, where shrimp farming began in the late 1970s, Latin America now harvests 287,000 tonnes of shrimp worth U.S.$1.3 billion, around one-quarter of the world's cultivated shrimp production. Shrimp production and exports are particularly important in Brazil, Belize, Colombia, Honduras, and Venezuela. However, scientists have raised concerns about the ecological problems caused by aquacultural activities—in particular the widespread destruction of coastal mangroves, in the case of shrimp farming, and the disposal of effluent waste, in the case of salmon and shrimp farming.

*See also* **El Niño; Menem, Carlos Saúl; Salinas de Gortari, Carlos.**

BIBLIOGRAPHY

Bushnell, Geoffrey H. S. *Peru.* London: Thames and Hudson, 1963.

Cole, John P. *Latin America: An Economic and Social Geography.* London: Butterworths, 1965.

Davidson, Alan. *The Oxford Companion to Food.* Oxford, U.K.: Oxford University Press, 1999.

Deligiannis, Tom. "Peru's Ingenuity Gap: Constraints on the Management of Natural Resources and the Crash of the Peruvian Anchovy Fishery." Ph.D. diss. University of

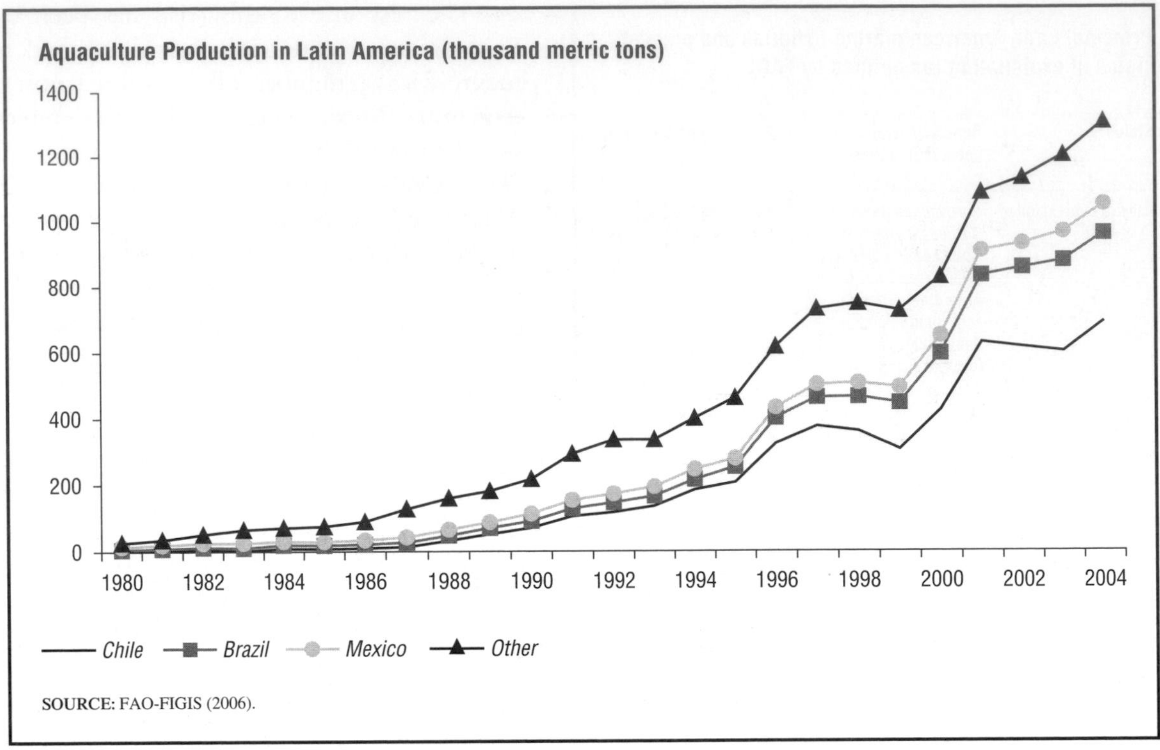


SOURCE: FAO-FIGIS (2006).

**Figure 2**

Toronto, 2000. Available from http://www.edc-news.se/Reviews/Deligiannis2000.rtf.

Diegues, Antonio Carlos. "Sea Tenure, Traditional Knowledge, and Management among Brazilian Artisanal Fishermen." São Paulo: Research Center on Human Population and Wetlands in Brazil (NUPAUB), 2002. Available from http://www.usp.br/nupaub/english/icsfoct.doc.

Elliott, G. F. S. *Chile: Its History and Development, Natural Features, Products, Commerce, and Present Conditions.* London: T. Fisher Unwin, 1911.

Food and Agriculture Organization of the United Nations (FAO). *The State of World Fisheries and Aquaculture 2004.* Rome: Author, 2004. Available from http://www.fao. org/DOCREP/007/y5600e/y5600e00.htm.

FAO-FIGIS. 2006. Fisheries Statistics, 2006. Food and Agriculture Organization of the United Nations, 2006.

Frank, Murray. "The Fishing Industry." In *Industrialization of Latin America*, ed. Lloyd J. Hughlett. New York: McGraw-Hill, 1946.

Gajardo, Gonzalo, and Linda Laikre. "Chilean Aquaculture Boom Is Based on Exotic Salmon Resources: A Conservation Paradox." *Conservation Biology* 17, no. 4 (2003): 1173–1174.

Helms, Mary W. "The Indians of the Caribbean and Circum-Caribbean at the End of the Fifteenth Century." In *The Cambridge History of Latin America* Vol. 1, ed. Leslie Bethell. Cambridge, U.K.: Cambridge University Press, 1984.

Hidalgo, Jorge. "The Indians of Southern South America in the Middle of the Sixteenth Century." In *The Cambridge History of Latin America*, Vol. 1, ed. by Leslie Bethell. Cambridge, U.K.: Cambridge University Press, 1984.

Ibarra, Alonso Aguilar, Andy Thorpe, and Chris Reid. "The Political Economy of Marine Fisheries Development in Peru, Chile, and Mexico." *Journal of Latin American Studies* 32, no. 2 (2000):503–528.

Madaria, Edgardo. "El Sector Pesquero Argentino: Informe General (Preliminar II)." Programa de Investigación Geográfico Político Patagónico. Buenos Aires: Pontificia Universidad Catolica Argentina, 1999. Available from http://www2.uca.edu.ar/esp/sec-pigpp/esp/docs-estudios/investigacion/pesca/pesquero.pdf.

Mason, J. Alden. *The Ancient Civilizations of Peru*, Revised edition. London: Pelican Books, 1971.

National Environmental Trust. "Destined for Extinction: The Fate of Chilean Sea Bass." Washington, DC: Author, 2001. Available from http://www.net.org/relatives/4300.pdf.

Parry, John Horace. 1966. *The Spanish Seaborne Empire.* London: Hutchinson, 1966.

Thorpe, Andy, and Elizabeth Bennett. "Globalisation and the Sustainability of World Fisheries: A View from Latin America." *Marine Resource Economics* 16 (2001): 143–164.

Thorpe, Andy, Alonso Aguilar Ibarra, and Chris Reid. "The New Economic Model and Marine Fisheries Development in Latin America." *World Development* 28, no. 9 (2000):1689–1702.

Townsend, Richard F. *The Aztecs.* London: Thames and Hudson, 1992.

Valiela, Ivan, Jennifer L. Bowen, and Joanna K. York. "Mangrove Forests: One of the World's Threatened Major Tropical Environments." *Bioscience* 51, no. 10 (2001): 807–815.

ANDY THORPE
CHRIS REID

## FLAG RIOTS.

*See* **Panama Canal, Flag Riots.**

## FLEET SYSTEM

*This entry includes the following articles:*

COLONIAL BRAZIL
COLONIAL SPANISH AMERICA

### COLONIAL BRAZIL

Unlike the *carrera de Indias* elaborated by Castile during the first half of the sixteenth century, which restricted all shipping between Spain and its colonies to a highly regulated system of fleets, voyages during the sixteenth century between Portugal and Brazil took place largely at will. Two factors contributed to this difference: the small size (60–160 tons) of most of the caravels used in the Brazil trade; and complications arising from the variety of departure points in Portugal, such that many ships left from small ports (for example, Viana and Aveiro), and the numerous ports of arrival in Brazil, especially after the establishment of the donatary captaincies in the period 1534–1536. Neither characteristic was conducive to organizing shipping in fleets.

Individual ships could put out at any time, the only requisite being that they have a proper license and pay the duties demanded by the crown. Throughout the sixteenth century these unprotected ships were often attacked by corsairs and pirates. Finally, in 1592, the crown levied a 3 percent ad valorem duty on merchandise to pay for an armada of twelve warships intended to ward off attacks, but the merchant vessels themselves were still not organized into fleets. The Consulado, as the tax was called, produced considerable revenue for the crown, but the escort system itself did little to protect shipping. In fact, 83 percent of the ships sailing in the years from 1647 to 1648 were lost to pirates, a situation that finally led the distraught king to prohibit the sailing of sugar ships as long as the Dutch remained strong at sea.

Ultimately it was Father Antônio Vieira, a Jesuit with long experience in Brazilian affairs, who came up with a solution to the piracy problem. In 1649 he proposed the establishment of a com-pany, the Companhia Geral do Comércio, modeled upon Dutch precedents. It would regulate shipping between Portugal and Brazil by organizing it into two fleets per year, each to be protected by an escort squadron of eighteen galleons. To defray the cost, the company was granted monopoly rights over four essential imports into Brazil—wine, flour, oil, and codfish—and one lucrative export, brazilwood. The resulting system proved reasonably satisfactory. In most years after 1650 escorted fleets of ships left Rio de Janeiro about the end of March, stopped in Bahia in April to pick up the ships waiting there, and arrived in Lisbon in July and August. Departure times from Lisbon were less regular: sometimes in the late fall, sometimes in the early spring. Though the company was dissolved in 1720, the fleet system it had created continued under the control of the Conselho Da Fazenda (Ministry of the Treasury) until it was abolished by the marquês of Pombal in 1765.

During the eighteenth century this fleet system, created largely to protect the sugar trade, was complemented by additional fleets that served other specialized companies: the Companhia Geral do Comércio do Grão Pará e Maranhão (1755–1778), created to develop the economy of the northern region; and the Companhia Geral do Comércio de Pernambuco and Paraíba (1759–1779), intended to revive the sugar industry of Pernambuco and Paraíba. While they lasted, these companies and their fleets monopolized shipping to and from the ports of Belem de Pará, São Luis de Maranhão, and Pernambuco, leaving the older fleet system created in 1649 to control the shipping from Rio and Bahia until its extinction in 1765.

*See also* **Commercial Policy: Colonial Brazil; Companies, Chartered.**

BIBLIOGRAPHY

C. R. Boxer, "Padre Antônio Vieira, S. J., and the Institution of the Brazil Company in 1649," in *Hispanic American Historical Review* 39 (1949): 474–497.

Joel Serrão, ed., *Dicionário de história de Portugal,* vol. 1 (1963), pp. 637–644.

Manuel Nunes Dias, *A Companhia Geral de comércio do Grão Pará e Maranhão* (1971).

Leslie Bethell, *The Cambridge History of Latin America* (1984) vol. 1, pp. 441–508.

### *Additional Bibliography*

Costa, Leonor Freire. *Império e grupos mercantis: Entre o Oriente e o Atlântico (século XVII).* Lisboa: Livros Horizonte, 2002.

Mauro, Frédéric. *Portugal, o Brasil e o Atlântico, 1570-1670.* Lisboa: Editorial Estampa, 1997.

Pedreira, Jorge Miguel Viana. *Estrutura industrial e mercado colonial: Portugal e Brasil (1780-1830).* Lisboa: DIFEL, 1994.

Schwartz, Stuart B. *Tropical Babylons: Sugar and the Making of the Atlantic World, 1450-1680.* Chapel Hill: University of North Carolina Press, 2004.

H. B. Johnson

## COLONIAL SPANISH AMERICA

The definitive organization of Spain's Indies trade into a structure characterized by the dispatch from Seville of regular merchant convoys, protected by warships, dates from 1564. Its origins lie, however, in the first half of the sixteenth century, when the Casa De Contratación arranged for armed patrols both along the coast of Cuba and in the maritime triangle between Andalusia, the Canaries, and the Azores to counter attacks on shipping from foreign navies and French and Barbary corsairs. From 1543 until 1554 a single annual fleet sailed from Seville to the Caribbean, dividing in the vicinity of Dominica into two groups destined for Cartagena–Nombre de Dios and Santo Domingo–Veracruz.

In 1554 the crown ordered that two fleets a year, protected by warships, should sail for America. Prolonged hostilities with France, however, followed by increasing Dutch and English attacks on shipping, delayed the practical introduction of the new system until 1564. From this date two annual fleets were to sail for America: the first, known as the *flota* would leave in April for Veracruz, the principal port of the viceroyalty of New Spain, accompanied by a few vessels destined for the Caribbean islands and Honduras; it would be followed in August by the Galeones, which traded indirectly with Peru via the Isthmus of Panama. The departure dates from Seville were designed to enable the respective fleets to winter in their Indies ports before meeting in Havana during March and April for repairs and revictualing, and leaving together for Spain in time to get out of the Gulf of Mexico before the onset of the hurricane season in August.

This idealized structure was vulnerable to many imponderables, including adverse weather, piracy, warfare, the availability of cargoes, ships, and capital, commercial confidence, and bureaucratic incompetence. The synchronization of the returning fleets was frequently not achieved. Moreover, from as early as 1580 there was a clear shift toward biennial departures from Seville, and in the seventeenth century the gaps were often of several years' duration, particularly in periods of international warfare. Other problems included widespread fiscal fraud to avoid payment of the Avería. Nevertheless, the system functioned effectively within its somewhat narrow terms of reference, the principal purpose of which was to protect the convoys from attack and thereby bring back to Spain the American silver destined for both the crown and merchants. The treasure of the *flota* was lost only once, in 1628, when the Dutch privateer, Piet Heyn, captured it at Matanzas, on the north coast of Cuba, provoking the bankruptcy of the crown and the onset of a prolonged period of commercial depression.

Although with this exception the fleet system functioned effectively in its prime task of protecting transatlantic trade, it also had the negative effect of constricting trade, both geographically and structurally, and failing to provide the commercial flexibility necessary to respond to the changing needs of American consumers and producers, particularly in the late-seventeenth and early eighteenth centuries. The Consulado (guild) of Mexico City, incorporated in 1592, whose merchants controlled the Veracruz trade fairs (and, in the eighteenth century, those held inland at Jalapa) had a powerful vested interest in preserving its monopoly control, and indeed, in tolerating scarcity of (and high prices for) imported goods, notwithstanding the consequential growth of contraband. Although the *galeones* were replaced by register ships in 1740, the New Spain *flotas* survived until 1776, and a further thirteen years were to pass before New Spain was finally incorporated into the free trade system introduced in 1778 in most other ports of Spanish America.

*See also* **Commercial Policy: Colonial Spanish America; Piracy.**

BIBLIOGRAPHY


D. A. Brading, *Miners and Merchants in Bourbon Mexico, 1763–1810* (1971).

Kenneth R. Andrews, *The Spanish Caribbean: Trade and Plunder, 1530–1630* (1978).

Geoffrey J. Walker, *Spanish Politics and Imperial Trade, 1700–1789* (1979).

Lutgardo García Fuentes, *El comercio español con América, 1650–1700* (1980).

Fernando Serrano Mangas, *Los galeones de la Carrera de Indias, 1650–1700* (1985)


*Additional Bibliography*


Arazola Corvera, Ma Jesús. *Hombres, barcos y comercio de la ruta Cádiz-Buenos Aires, 1737-1757.* Sevilla: Diputación de Sevilla, 1998.

Bustos Rodríguez, Manuel. *Los comerciantes de la carrera de Indias en el Cádiz del siglo XVIII (1713-1775).* Cádiz: Servicio de Publicaciones, Universidad de Cádiz, 1995.

Hill, Ruth. *Hierarchy, Commerce and Fraud in Bourbon Spanish America: A Postal Inspector's Exposé.* Nashville: Vanderbilt University Press, 2005.


John R. Fisher

**FLORENTINE CODEX.** *See* **Sahagún, Bernardino de.**

**FLORES.** Flores, department in southern Uruguay not far from Montevideo. It was founded in 1885 to commemorate General Venancio Flores, born in Trinidad, the capital of the department. The small territory of 1,982 square miles has 25,104 inhabitants (2001), most of whom live in the capital, Trinidad. Most of them are engaged in raising sheep and in garden agriculture. Although the region maintains some agricultural traditions, it is also completely digitized in terms of its communications system.

*See also* **Flores, Venancio; Uruguay, Geography.**

BIBLIOGRAPHY


Sosa, Sonia. *Paso de las Flores: Vida de seis familias en el Uruguay rural.* Montevideo: Editorial Signo, 1968.


César N. Caviedes

**FLORES, JUAN JOSÉ** (c. 1800–1864). Juan José Flores (*b.* ca. 1800; *d.* 1 October 1864), president of Ecuador (1830–1835, 1839–1845). Born in Puerto Cabello, Venezuela, Flores received little formal education before he was swept into the Wars of Independence, first in a royalist army and then in the patriot forces of Bolívar. He received rapid promotions: to colonel in 1821 and to general in 1826.

Assignment to the command of the difficult royalist region of Pasto (southern Colombia) prevented Flores from fighting in the campaigns to liberate Ecuador and Peru. In 1826 he assumed authority over the department of Ecuador and soon exercised authority over most of the territory later to comprise the Republic of Ecuador. Marriage to the aristocratic Mercedes Jijón y Vivanco facilitated his rise to regional prominence. Flores, who came to favor monarchism, urged Bolívar to convert Gran Colombia (Venezuela, New Granada, and Ecuador) into a monarchy.

In May 1830 an extraordinary assembly of officials and citizens in Quito decided to separate Ecuador from Gran Colombia and named General Flores supreme civil and military commander. He was elected president soon after the assassination of General Antonio José de Sucre, which removed his only serious competitor for leadership.

Though endowed with a lively intelligence, Flores was poorly prepared intellectually to provide wise leadership. He attempted to make up for his shortcomings by engaging tutors, such as the poet José Joaquín Olmedo, but his basic inclinations remained those of a military man. As president he tried unsuccessfully to incorporate the Cauca region into Ecuador, but he defended Ecuadorian independence from New Granada and helped establish the Carchi River as the northern border. In domestic matters Flores pursued liberal policies by restricting the privileges of the clergy, creating a public education system with special schools for Indians, and reforming tax laws.

These reforms, along with treasury deficits and other financial problems, aroused opposition to the foreign-born president. Publishers of the anti-administration newspaper *El Quiteño Libre* organized a violent uprising that Flores quelled only after agreeing to allow Vicente Rocafuerte, a rebel leader, to succeed him to the presidency in 1835.

During Rocafuerte's administration (1835–1839), Flores exerted much influence as commander-in-chief of the armed forces, and he arranged his own reelection to the presidency in 1839. When his policy of cordiality toward opponents failed, Flores secretly decided to convert Ecuador into a monarchy. In league with Andrés Santa Cruz of Peru, he sought to monarchize Peru and Bolivia, too. He had himself reelected president in 1843 under the new, authoritarian constitution. He secured the backing of Spain to erect a throne in Quito, but an uprising in 1845 sent him into exile.

In Spain, Flores received official but secret support for an armed expedition to seize power and, presumably, to erect a monarchy in Ecuador. Public reports of the expedition, however, forced its abandonment before it could depart Spanish shores.

General Flores returned to Spanish America in 1847 and spent the next thirteen years conspiring in various countries to regain power. His plots seriously undermined the Ecuadorian government but did not topple it. Finally, in 1860, with Ecuador in near anarchy, the struggling regime of Gabriel García Moreno invited Flores to return to the country, to take command of the army, and to put down the opposition to the government.

Playing the role of senior statesman thereafter, Flores was elected president of a constituent congress in 1860 and helped draft the conservative Constitution of 1861. He supported a fruitless effort by the president to secure French backing for yet another monarchical scheme. As general in chief of the armed forces, Flores was a mainstay of the administration and was expected by many to succeed to the presidency in 1865.

When New Granada threatened Ecuador's independence in 1863, General Flores, though in poor health, led a poorly equipped army to defend the northern border. Subsequently he helped crush a rebel invasion near Guayaquil but fell ill and died aboard a warship invoking the "Supreme God of Battles."

*See also* **Ecuador: Since 1830; Gran Colombia.**

BIBLIOGRAPHY


Pedro Fermín Ceballos, *Resumen de la historia del Ecuador desde su origen hasta 1845,* vols. 4–5 (1870).

Elías Laso, *Biografía del General Juan José Flores* (1924).

Luis Robalino Dávila, *Nacimiento y primeros años de la República* (1967).

Gustavo Vásconez Hurtado, *El General Juan José Flores: La República, 1830–1845* (1984).

Mark J. Van Aken, *King of the Night: Juan José Flores and Ecuador, 1824–1864* (1989). Revised and published in Spanish in 1995 as *El rey de la noche: Juan José Flores y el Ecuador, 1824-1864.* Quito: Banco Central del Ecuador, 1995.


### *Additional Bibliography*


Aristizábal, Armando. *Juan José Flores en Berruecos: Síntesis de una infamia.* Quito: Casa de la Cultura Ecuatoriana, 1995.

Romero Mendoza, Serápio Eduardo. *General Juan José Flores, fundador del Ecuador.* Caracas: s.n., 1994.

Villalba F., Jorge. *El general Juan José Flores: Fundador de la República del Ecuador.* Puerto Cabello, Venezuela: s.n., 1995. First edition, Ecuador: Centro de Estudios Históricos del Ejército, 1994.


MARK J. VAN AKEN

---

**FLORES, LUIS A.** (1899–1969). Luis A. Flores (*b.* 1899; *d.* 1969), Peruvian politician, lawyer, and diplomat. Born in Ayabaca, Piura, he is best known for his leadership of the Revolutionary Union, a radical nationalist party adopted by Colonel and President Luis Sánchez Cerro (1931–1933). Flores had been imprisoned during the Leguía regime but became deputy for Lima during the term of the Constituent Assembly (1931–1936). After the assassination of Sánchez Cerro in 1933, Flores assumed the leadership of the Revolutionary Union and espoused overt fascist principles, tactics, and organization, modeled after Benito Mussolini's party. Flores sought popular support and battled communism and populist *aprismo.* In the 1936 presidential elections, which were annulled by President Oscar Benavides, Flores finished second behind the candidate supported by the Aprista Party. Flores was subsequently exiled by Benavides but returned to become senator for Piura (1947–1948) and ambassador to Italy (1948–1950) and Nicaragua and Paraguay (1956–1962). He died in Lima.

*See also* **Fascism; Sanchez Cerro, Luis Manuel.**

BIBLIOGRAPHY

Steve Stein, *Populism in Peru: The Emergence of the Masses and the Politics of Social Control* (1980).

*Additional Bibliography*

Manrique, Nelson. *Historia de la república*. Lima: Fondo Editorial de COFIDE, 1995.

Villanueva, Armando, and Guillermo Thorndike. *La gran persecución, 1932–1956*. Lima: Empresa Periodística Nacional, 2004.

ALFONSO W. QUIROZ

**FLORES, VENANCIO** (1808–1868). Venancio Flores (*b.* 18 May 1808; *d.* 19 February 1868), Uruguayan military and political leader (Colorado Party). Flores was born in the town of Porongos, today called Trinidad. He took part in the campaign to free Uruguay from Brazil in 1825. He was political chief of the department of San José and military commander of that department at the outbreak of the Guerra Grande (1839–1852). A rising figure in the Colorado Party, he was appointed political chief of Montevideo and minister of war and the navy in 1852. Upon the resignation of President Juan Francisco Giró in 1853, Flores formed a triumvirate with General Juan Antonio Lavalleja and General Fructuoso Rivera in an attempt to avoid another outbreak of civil war. When these two men died, both of natural causes, Flores became a preeminent figure in his party.

Political hostilities and a popular disdain of the caudillo tradition that he represented led Flores to withdraw to the Entre Ríos province of Argentina (1857–1863). While there, he played an active role in the civil wars of that country, supporting the Liberal Party led by Bartolomé Mitre. When Mitre became president of Argentina in 1862, Flores gained his support and that of Emperor Pedro II of Brazil for his campaign to win back the government in Uruguay. The leaders of these two powerful, neighboring countries, who were already planning what would come to be called the War of the Triple Alliance against Paraguay, were motivated by their need for the port of Montevideo. This was especially true for Brazil.

Calling his revolution the "liberation crusade," in memory of the 1825 campaign of that name, Flores began his assault against National Party President Bernardo Prudencio Berro in 1863, and, with the help of an army of 5,000 Brazilian soldiers who entered Uruguayan territory, marched into Montevideo triumphantly in February 1865. Immediately, Argentina, Brazil, and Uruguay made public the treaty of the Triple Alliance, which committed them to fighting Paraguay to the end. Under the leadership of Francisco Solano López, Paraguay had become an important economic and military power, which made the War of the Triple Alliance (1865–1870) one of the bloodiest in the history of South America. Although scholars disagree on the total casualties, they agree that Paraguay suffered huge demographic losses.

Returning to Uruguay from the war in 1866, Flores resigned in 1868 and called for new elections. Flores was slain four days later by unknown assassins.

*See also* **Guerra Grande; Uruguay, Political Parties: Colorado Party.**

BIBLIOGRAPHY

Alfredo Lepro, *Años de forja* (1962).

José Pedro Barrán, *Apogeo y crisis del Uruguay pastorial y caudillesco* (1974).

Washington Lockhart, *Venancio Flores, un caudillo trágico* (1976).

*Additional Bibliography*

Leuchars, Chris. *To the Bitter End: Paraguay and the War of the Triple Alliance*. Westport, CT: Greenwood Press, 2002.

JOSÉ DE TORRES WILSON

**FLORES DA CUNHA, JOSÉ ANTÔNIO** (1880–1959). José Antônio Flores da Cunha (*b.* 5 March 1880; *d.* 4 November 1959), Brazilian politician. Born to an oligarchical family from Santana do Livramento, Rio Grande do Sul, Flores was an important political figure in the three decades following the Revolution of 1930. He was educated at the São Paulo Law School from 1898 to 1902, and completed his studies at the Rio de Janeiro Law School in 1903.

Flores was among the dissident oligarchs who supported the revolution against the dominant oligarchies of São Paulo and Minas Gerais. Indeed, his support of Getúlio Vargas was crucial to the overthrow of the First Republic and Vargas's seizure of power. However, as governor of Rio Grande do Sul and a senator in the 1930s, he staunchly defended federalism and worked to limit the centralization of political power under Getúlio Vargas's regime (1930–1945). His federalist stance, often backed by his threat to use the nation's largest state militia, made him too dangerous for Vargas to ignore. After a near outbreak of civil war in 1937, Flores was exiled to Uruguay until 1942. When he retur-ned to Brazil, he was imprisoned.

Flores saw reaction against centralization as the only means of assuring oligarchical elites political space in the post-1930 world. Despite his support for the Revolution of 1930, Flores gradually distanced himself from Vargas after 1935. As governor of Rio Grande do Sul from 1935 to 1938, he was a major force in the continuing influence of traditional politicians and regionalism after 1930. In 1945, Flores joined the National Democratic Union Party (UDN), which opposed Vargas, and he supported the military's successful ouster of the dictator. In 1950 he was elected to Congress on a UDN ticket. In 1955 he broke with the UDN because he opposed its *golpistas,* who had conspired to mount a coup against the government. He lost his final campaign for office in 1958, completing his term in Congress in January 1959. Flores died in Rio Grande do Sul.

*See also* **Brazil, Political Parties: National Democratic Union of Brazil (UDN); Brazil, Revolutions: Revolution of 1930; Vargas, Getúlio Dornelles.**

BIBLIOGRAPHY

John W. F. Dulles, *Vargas of Brazil* (1967).

Robert M. Levine, *The Vargas Regime: The Critical Years, 1934–1938* (1970).

Joseph L. Love, *Rio Grande do Sul and Brazilian Regionalism: 1882–1930* (1971).

Carlos E. Cortés, *Gaúcho Politics in Brazil: The Politics of Rio Grande do Sul, 1930–1964* (1974).

Thomas E. Skidmore, *Politics in Brazil, 1930–1964: An Experiment in Democracy* (1986).

*Additional Bibliography*

Bellintani, Adriana lop. *Conspiração contra o Estado Novo.* Porto Alegre, RGS: EDIPUCRS, 2002.

Caggiani, Ivo. *Flores da Cunha: Biografia.* Porto Alegre, RGS: Martins-Livreiro Editor, 1996.

Masina, Léa, Myrna Bier Appel, and Antônio Hohlfeldt, eds. *A geração de 30 no Rio Grande do Sul: Literature e artes plásticas.* Porto Alegre, RGS: Editora da Universidade, Universidade Federal do Rio Grande do Sul, PPG-Letras, 2000.

Brian Owensby

## FLORES GALINDO, ALBERTO C.

(1949–1990). Alberto Flores Galindo was born in Lima on May 28, 1949. He was trained as a historian at the Pontificia Universidad Católica del Perú in Lima and the École des Hautes Études en Sciences Sociales in Paris. His early works on social and political movements of the early twentieth century established him as the leader of a generation whose writings would transform Peruvian intellectual life. Inspired by Antonio Gramsci, Eric Hobsbawm and Pierre Vilar, Flores promoted a nondogmatic brand of Marxism that, combined with the contributions of the Annales school, would provide the basis for an innovative historical perspective.

During the 1980s Flores Galindo laid the basis of his exploration of the Andean utopia as a *longue durée* (long-term) conceptual key to interpret the history of the Andean peoples under colonial and republican domination. His findings were first published in 1986 under the title of *Buscando un Inca*, his most important book aside from his *La agonía de Mariátegui* (1980). In Flores Galindo's view, an unresolved messianic hope acted as a catalyst for movements that confronted successive establishments aimed at excluding the Quechua and Aymara peoples from the life of "official" Peru.

Written in the midst of a profound national crisis, his work stirred debate and controversy. His unique literary style and his gift for journalistic writing allowed him to reach a broad audience. Besides his work as a university professor, by the time of his untimely death on March 29, 1990, Flores Galindo was a respected public intellectual whose influence has been compared with that of José Carlos Mariátegui in the 1920s.

*See also* **Andes; Indigenous Peoples; Mariátequi, José Carlos.**

BIBLIOGRAPHY

Obituary, *Hispanic American Historical Review*, Vol. 71, No. 2 (May 1991), pp. 375–377.

José Luis Rénique

## FLORES JIJÓN, ANTONIO (1833–1915).

**FLORES JIJÓN, ANTONIO** (1833–1915). Antonio Flores Jijón (*b.* 23 October 1833; *d.* 30 August 1915), president of Ecuador (1888–1892). Born in Quito, Antonio was the son of Juan José Flores, Ecuador's first president. Antonio Flores Jijón completed his secondary education in Paris. In 1845, he entered the University of San Marcos in Lima, where he completed a law degree and joined the faculty.

Flores Jijón returned to Ecuador with Gabriel García Moreno (president, 1860–1865) in 1860. Thereafter, he represented Ecuador in various diplomatic posts in Colombia, France, England, the Vatican, Peru, Spain, and the United States.

An unsuccessful candidate for the presidency in 1875, he opposed the government of General Ignacio de Veintimilla (1876–1883), for which he was exiled. He lived in New York from 1878 to 1883, then returned to Ecuador in 1883 to participate in the ouster of Veintimilla and in the writing of a new constitution. During the José María Plácido Caamaño presidency (1883–1888), Flores Jijón represented Ecuador in Europe, and in fact was in Paris in 1888 when he was elected president.

During his term, Flores Jijón sought to implement a progressive program with the support of moderates within the conservative and liberal parties. His government emphasized improved and expanded public education and public works, respect for civil liberties, and administrative, financial, and tax reforms. His accomplishments in the area of public finances included the suppression of the tithe, a renegotiation of the internal and external debt, reform of the customs tariff, state monopolies, and taxes on real estate. Many of his initiatives met strong opposition from conservatives and the clergy. After completing his term in 1892, Flores returned to Europe. He died in Geneva.

*See also* **Ecuador: Since 1830; Garcia Moreno, Gabriel; Veintemilla, José Ignacio de.**

BIBLIOGRAPHY

Luis Robalino Dávila, *Orígines del Ecuador de hoy: Diez años de civilismo,* vol. 6 (1968).

Carlos Manuel Larrea, *Antonio Flores Jijón* (1974).

Frank MacDonald Spindler, *Nineteenth-Century Ecuador* (1987), esp. pp. 126–137.

*Additional Bibliography*

Guzmán Polanco, Manuel de. *Antonio Flores Jijón.* Quito: Casa de la Cultura Ecuatoriana "Benjamín Carrión," 2002.

Linda Alexander Rodríguez

## FLORES MAGÓN, RICARDO (1874–1922).

**FLORES MAGÓN, RICARDO** (1874–1922). Ricardo Flores Magón (*b.* 16 September 1874; *d.* 21 November 1922), Mexican journalist and revolutionary. Born in San Antonio Eloxochitlán, Oaxaca, Flores Magón was the second of three sons; his older brother, Jesús, was born in 1872, and his younger brother, Enrique, in 1877. In 1900 he founded the newspaper *Regeneración* to oppose the tyranny of the government of Porfirio Díaz. Flores Magón was arrested in May 1901 and *Regeneración* was suppressed soon after, closing in September 1901. He became a writer for Daniel Cabrera's *El Hijo del Ahuizote* until its demise early in 1903. Arrested again, Flores Magón was prohibited from publishing in Mexico. In January 1904 he and his brother Enrique entered the United States at Laredo, Texas, and went to San Antonio, where they renewed the publication of *Regeneración.* They settled in St. Louis, Missouri, between 1905 and 1906 to escape harassment from local legal authorities along the border and to join revolutionary and radical labor groups. Persecution—including activities of local spies, police seizure of the printing press, and imprisonment of local partisans of a revolutionary exile group Flores Magón had founded in St. Louis—eventually forced them to move to Los Angeles, where they established a new organ, *Revolución.* Arrested in August 1907, Flores Magón was tried in Arizona in 1909, sentenced to eighteen months in the Florence territorial prison, and released in August 1910.

When World War I began in 1914, Flores Magón, now an anarcho-Communist and pacifist, was a vociferous critic. Arrested on 22 March 1918 and charged with sedition, he was eventually found guilty of violating the Espionage Act of 1917.

Sentenced to twenty-one years at McNeil Island, he was transferred in November 1919 to Leavenworth penitentiary because of failing health. On the morning of 21 November 1922, Flores Magón was found dead in Cell House B at Leavenworth. Although several radical scholars claim that he was murdered, the most likely explanation is that he died of natural causes, probably a heart attack.

*See also* **Journalism; Revoltosos.**

BIBLIOGRAPHY

An excellent current biography of Flores Magón is Ward S. Albro, *Always a Rebel: Ricardo Flores Magón and the Mexican Revolution* (1992). For a general study of the *magonistas* see W. Dirk Raat, *Revoltosos: Mexico's Rebels in the United States, 1903–1923* (1981).

*Additional Bibliography*

Flores Magón, Ricardo, and Fernando Zertuche Muñoz. *Ricardo Flores Magón: El sueño alternativo.* México, D.F.: Fondo de Cultura Económica, 1995.

Maldonado Alvarado, Benjamín. *La utopia de Ricardo Flores Magón: Revolución, anarquía y comunalidad India.* Oaxaca: Universidad Autónoma "Benito Juarez" de Oaxaca, 1994.

W. DIRK RAAT

## FLORES MALDONADO MARTÍNEZ Y BODQUÍN, MANUEL ANTONIO

**(1723–1799).** Manuel Antonio Flores Maldonado Martínez y Bodquín (*b.* 27 May 1723; *d.* 20 March 1799), viceroy of New Granada (1776–1782) and of New Spain (1787–1789).

Born in Seville, Flores pursued a naval career, holding the rank of lieutenant general of the Royal Armada at the time of his assignment to New Granada in 1776. An enlightened man, strongly interested in science, he was an efficient, perceptive administrator. He urged Regent Visitor Gutiérrez De Piñeres to show restraint when imposing administrative and fiscal reforms, at least until the armed forces could be readied to discourage potential unrest, but his warnings went unheeded. While Flores was on the coast commanding the viceregal defenses during the War of the American Revolution, the *Comunero Revolt* (1781) swept the interior, compelling him to order nearly a battalion of coastal troops to Santa Fe to bolster royal authority.

Becoming severely ill with arthritis, he resigned and was replaced by Cartagena's governor, Juan Pimienta. Flores later brought enlightened rule to New Spain, but, his health again failing him, he was soon replaced by the Segundo Conde de Revillagigedo. He died in Madrid.

*See also* **Spanish Empire; Viceroyalty, Viceroy.**

BIBLIOGRAPHY

Calderón Quijano, José Antonio ed., *Los virreyes de Nueva España en el reinado de Carlos IV,* vol. I. Sevilla: Publicaciones de la Escuela de Estudios Hispano–Americanos de la Universidad de Sevilla, 1972.

Kuethe, Allan J. *Military Reform and Society in New Granada, 1773–1808.* Gainesville: University Presses of Florida, 1978.

Phelan, John Leddy *The People and the King: The Comunero Revolution in Colombia, 1781.* Madison: University of Wisconsin Press, 1978.

ALLAN J. KUETHE

## FLORES NANO, LOURDES

**(1959–).** Lourdes Flores Nano is the first woman to be a major contender for the presidency of Peru. A lawyer by profession and a member of the Popular Christian Party (Partido Popular Cristiano, PPC), Flores was elected to the Lima provincial council in 1986 and 1989 and then served in congress from 1990 to 2000. As the presidential candidate of the National Unity electoral alliance, Flores barely missed making runoff elections in 2001 and 2006 that she might well have won. Flores has tried to lead the PPC back to its social Christian roots.

*See also* **Peru, Political Parties: Overview.**

BIBLIOGRAPHY

Flores Nano, Lourdes. *El Evangelio y la Tierra.* Lima: JL Disegraphics, 2000.

Schmidt, Gregory D. "The Great Minority: Christian Democracy in Peru." In *Christian Democracy in Latin America: Electoral Competition and Regime Conflicts,* edited by Scott Mainwaring and Timothy R. Scully. Stanford, CA: Stanford University Press, 2003.

GREGORY D. SCHMIDT

**FLORIANÓPOLIS.** Florianópolis, coastal port and capital of the state of Santa Catarina, was founded in the late seventeenth century and became the provincial capital in 1823 under its original name, Destêrro. In 1893 Custódio José de Melo led a short-lived naval revolt against President Peixoto at Rio de Janeiro and ordered Captain Frederico de Lorena to set up the rebel government seat at Destêrro. That year the city was renamed after president Floriano Peixoto. From then on, the main thrust of the civil war moved from Rio Grande do Sul to Santa Catarina.

As of 2006 the population of Florianópolis was about 406,564. The city lies on Santa Catarina Island, between Baía Norte and Baía Sul. Pointe Hercílio Luz, one of the longest steel suspension bridges in Brazil, is one of two that connect the island and the mainland. Since 1983 it has been closed to traffic. Its natural beauty and forty-two beaches have made Florianópolis a popular tourist resort.

*See also* **Peixoto, Floriano Vieira.**

BIBLIOGRAPHY

José Maria Bello, *A History of Modern Brazil, 1889–1964,* translated by James L. Taylor (1966).

*Additional Bibliography*

Lisboa, Teresa Kleba. *Gênero, classe e etnia: Trajetórias de vida de mulheres migrantes.* Florianópolis: Editora da UFSC, 2003.

Pimenta, Margareth de Castro Afeche. *Florianópolis do outro lado do espelho.* Florianópolis: Editora da UFSC, 2005.

CAROLYN E. VIEIRA

**FLORIDA.** The name of Florida, which Juan Ponce De León gave to the land he discovered in 1513, was once applied by Spain to all of eastern North America from Tampico to the Gulf of Saint Lawrence. For half a century, hurricanes and Indian hostility defeated one expedition after another: those of Ponce de León (1521); Lucas Vásquez De Ayllón (1526); Pánfilo de Narváez, whose story was told by Álvar Núñez Cabeza De Vaca (1528); Hernando de Soto (1539); Luis Cáncer de Barbastro (1549); and Tristán de Luna y Arellano (1559). In 1565 Philip II responded to the appearance of French forts along the strategic Gulf Stream by naming a new *adelantado,* the Asturian admiral Pedro Menéndez De Avilés, who drove the French from Florida and established a number of fortified settlements. Most of these succumbed to Indian attacks, often provoked by the raids of hungry soldiers on native granaries. One of these, Saint Augustine, survived, thanks to a set of royal subsidies (the *situado*) that maintained the presidio, guaranteed the cooperation of chiefs, and supported a growing number of Franciscans.

The missionaries proved their value to the crown by adding an Indian hinterland, province by province: first the Timucuans of the east coast and the Saint Johns River, divided into saltwater and freshwater districts; then the Guales of the Georgia coast; then the Timucuans of central and western Florida; and finally the Apalaches, west of the peninsula and close to the Gulf. At their greatest extent the provinces included some 26,000 Christian Indians.

Spanish and Indian relations passed through several distinct stages: alliances for defense and exclusive trade aimed against foreign interlopers; conquest by the Christian Gospel; uprisings provoked by interference in their political, social, and economic affairs; conquest by the sword; and, finally, the institutionalization of demands on Indian commoners through the *sabana* system (the communal planting of maize fields for chiefs and other leaders), the *repartimiento* (a labor levy for public works), and the *servicio personal* (the diversion of the labor levy to private use). As a result of war, famine, and introduced diseases, each province experienced a decrease in population that increased the burden of supporting the area's chiefs, soldiers, missionaries, and settlers on the natives who were left.

During the first half of the seventeenth century, Spanish soldiers were busy combating Dutch and French enemies, salvaging wrecks, and putting down uprisings, while friars baptized thousands of plague victims and extended the mission frontier. Opportunities for a provisioning trade with Havana led to the opening of new ports on the Gulf and the expansion of ranching and agriculture. This economic development was interrupted by the onset of yellow fever, which attacked Spaniards and Indians alike, followed by epidemics of smallpox and measles. A 1656 rebellion in central Florida, harshly punished, led to the virtual desertion of the province of Timucua. By the 1660s, Florida was a hollow peninsula.

Exterior threats to the captaincy general then began to escalate. Pirates from English Jamaica sacked Saint Augustine in 1668. Traders from Carolina fomented wars among southeastern Indians by exchanging firearms for slaves. And buccaneers seconded La Salle's venture into the Gulf by raiding western ports. The crown reacted by strengthening the defenses of Saint Augustine. The price was high, for the construction of the stone Castillo de San Marcos, coupled with neglect of defenses in the provinces, led to wholesale flight—the commoner's form of resistance. Spain had just responded to French intrusion in the Gulf by establishing a new presidio at Pensacola in 1698, when the War of the Spanish Succession (1701–1714) forced the French and Spanish colonies into an alliance. Carolina seized the opportunity to attack Florida. From Charleston, Colonel James Moore led two invasions of Florida, destroying Saint Augustine and Guale in 1702 and depopulating Apalache in 1704. Indian raids finished off Timucua in 1706. Eighteenth-century Pensacola, Saint Augustine, and the trading post of San Marcos de Apalache were without a hinterland. The wild cattle of abandoned ranches attracted fugitive slaves and nonaligned Indians. By 1763, when the colony changed hands after the Seven Years' War, these frontiersmen and women were ready to confront the British as the Seminoles (from the Spanish *cimarrón,* for "runaway").

*See also* **Adelantado; Apalachee; Cabeza de Vaca, Alvar Núñez; Guale; Luna y Arellano, Tristán de; Menéndez de Avilés, Pedro; Missions: Spanish America; Narváez, Pánfilo de; Pensacola; Ponce de León, Juan; Repartimiento; Saint Augustine; Seven Years' War; Soto, Hernando de; Spanish Empire; Timucua; Vázquez de Ayllón, Lucas; War of the Spanish Succession.**

BIBLIOGRAPHY

Verne E. Chatelain, *The Defenses of Spanish Florida, 1565 to 1763* (1941).

John Jay Te Paske, *The Governorship of Spanish Florida, 1700–1763* (1964).

Michael V. Gannon, *The Cross in the Sand: The Early Catholic Church in Florida, 1530–1870* (1965).

Eugene Lyon, *The Enterprise of Florida: Pedro Menéndez de Avilés and the Spanish Conquest of 1565–1568* (1976).

John H. Hann, *Apalachee: The Land Between the Rivers* (1988).

David J. Weber, *The Spanish Frontier in North America* (1992).

Amy Turner Bushnell, *Situado and Sábana: Spain's Support System for the Presidio and Mission Provinces of Florida* (1994).

*Additional Bibliography*

Landers, Jane. *Colonial Plantations and Economy in Florida.* Gainseville: University Press of Florida, 2000.

Teja, Jesús. *Choice, Persuasion, and Coercion: Social Control on Spain's North American Frontiers.* Albuquerque: University of New Mexico Press, 2005.

Amy Turner Bushnell

---

**FLORIDA, EAST.** East Florida, remnant of the Spanish borderlands. In 1763, when Great Britain acquired the Florida peninsula from Spain and eastern Louisiana from France, the combined territory was divided at the Chattahoochee River into two colonies: East and West Florida. During the American Revolution, Bernardo de Gálvez captured West Florida, and by the Treaty of Paris of 1783, Spain recovered East Florida, to the chagrin of southern loyalists. Both colonies were military governorships, accountable politically to the captaincy general of Cuba and spiritually to the bishopric of New Orleans.

Outlawry was the immediate problem in East Florida. Havana used the presidio as a dumping ground for criminals, and armed bandits mounted slave and cattle raids across the Florida-Georgia border. Settlement was perceived as the solution. For lack of Spanish Catholics, Spain invited British Protestants to take an oath of loyalty and stay. Soon the gates were opened to American backwoodsmen, who avoided the plantations along the Saint Johns River and took the high road from Saint Marys, Georgia, to the Alachua prairie, where they could range their cattle.

Religion took a back seat to trade. The handful of Irish priests who came to convert Protestants reported little success. The Franciscans did not return to the friary, which the British had used for barracks, and the southeastern Indians wanted no more missions. To keep the Indians peaceful, Governor Vicente Manuel de Zéspedes renewed the exclusive franchise of the English firm of Panton, Leslie, and Company, a measure that ran counter to the rising sentiment for free trade in both the British and Spanish empires and was heartily disliked by the Americans. The grievances that prompted the East Florida settlers to rebel in 1795 centered on this issue, which grew worse as Spain declined in sea power. In 1806 only five of the forty-two ships entering the Saint Augustine harbor came from the closest Spanish port of Havana.

When Napoleon's efforts to enforce his continental blockade turned Spain into a battleground and its king into a puppet, the Spanish Empire in America began to dissolve. American settlers in West Florida twice declared sections of their colony republics and turned them over to the United States. East Florida's Patriot Rebellion, during the War of 1812, was a similar bid for annexation. The patriots took the plantations along the Saint Johns but did not attempt the formidable defenses of Saint Augustine. The rebellion fell apart, disowned by President James Madison. Then the Creek War of 1813–1814 conclusively ended dreams of an Indian buffer state under British sponsorship.

In 1817 Sir Gregor MacGregor, a Scot, made one final attempt at an independent republic in the name of the republics of Venezuela, New Granada, Mexico, and Buenos Aires, but with the backing of merchants in Savannah and other U.S. ports. Leading a force recruited chiefly in Georgia, he captured the Amelia Island port of Fernandina, sister city in smuggling to Saint Marys and home of 40 percent of East Florida's civilian population. When East Florida's Anglo settlers failed to flock to his Republic of the Floridas, MacGregor left. The French corsair Louis Aury, with a force of free black Haitians, opened the port to privateers and slave traders, triggering a peacekeeping intervention by U.S. forces. General Andrew Jackson sparked a series of international incidents in 1817 and 1818, when he crossed the border of West Florida to capture Pensacola, then entered East Florida to execute two British subjects trading with the Seminoles.

Having lost an empire, Spain lost the will and the means to maintain a lone military colony on the North American mainland. The Adams–Onís Treaty in 1819 transferred ownership of East and West Florida to the United States. Two years later, when the treaty was ratified, the flag of Spain came down from the Castillo de San Marcos.

*See also* **Adams-Onís Treaty (1819); Aury, Louis-Michel; Gálvez, Bernardo de; MacGregor, Gregor; New Orleans; Spanish Empire.**

BIBLIOGRAPHY

Rembert W. Patrick, *Florida Fiasco: Rampant Rebels on the Georgia-Florida Border, 1810–1815* (1954).

Helen Hornbeck Tanner, *Zéspedes in East Florida, 1784–1790* (1963).

Pablo Tornero Tinajero, *Relaciones de dependencia entre Florida y Estados Unidos (1783–1820)* (1979).

David Bushnell, *La República de las Floridas: Texts and Documents* (1986)

David J. Weber, *The Spanish Frontier in North America* (1992).

AMY TURNER BUSHNELL

**FLORIDA, SPANISH WEST.** Florida, Spanish West (1783–1821). From 1513 to 1763, Florida was merely La Florida and included both Saint Augustine and Pensacola. After acquiring La Florida in 1763, the British created East Florida and West Florida. West Florida extended from the Apalachicola and Chattahoochee rivers on the east to the Mississippi and from the Gulf of Mexico, Lakes Borgne, Pontchartrain, and Maurepas, and the Iberville River to 31 degrees north latitude. In 1764, the British moved the northern boundary to 32 degrees, 28 minutes north latitude. Except for Canada, West Florida was the largest British colony on the North American mainland.

By 1781, Bernardo de Gálvez's victories during the American Revolution had brought West Florida under Spanish control. This fact was formalized in the Treaty of Paris (1783). From 1783 until 1821 West Florida belonged to Spain. At its peak (1783–1798) West Florida included Pensacola (the capital) and Mobile, Baton Rouge, Natchez, Nogales (Vicksburg), and Chickasaw Bluffs (Memphis). Unfortunately for Spain, however, the United States gnawed at West Florida until by 1813 it was reduced to an area perhaps half its original size, if that. Of its major cities only Pensacola remained under Spanish control.

Spain appointed military officers to govern West Florida, including several Irishmen in the Spanish service, such as Col. Arturo O'Neill, who ruled from 1781 to 1793. Because of the need for English-speaking priests, another Irishman, Father James Coleman, served as Pensacola's parish priest from 1794, and then as vicar-general and ecclesiastical judge of West Florida (1806–1822). Economically, Spanish West Florida was not a glowing success. It depended upon lumber, naval stores, indigo, tobacco, and the fur trade, the latter largely controlled by Scotsmen, for its limited income. Thus it required the annual government subsidy, the *situado,* for its economic support.

Following the disasters of the Napoleonic era (1807–1815), Spain was unable effectively to control the Floridas and in 1819 negotiated their transfer to the United States by means of the Adams–Onís Treaty. In 1821, Andrew Jackson reached Pensacola and formally accepted what was left of Spanish West Florida from Col. José de Callava, the last Spanish governor.

*See also* **Adams-Onís Treaty (1819); Florida, East; Gálvez, Bernardo de; Pensacola; Spanish Empire.**

BIBLIOGRAPHY

James A. Servies, *A Bibliography of West Florida,* 3 vols. (1982).

Jack D. L. Holmes, "West Florida, 1779–1821," in *A Guide to the History of Florida,* edited by Paul S. George (1989), pp. 63–76.

William S. Coker and Jerrell H. Shofner, *Florida, 1492–1992* (1992).

### *Additional Bibliography*

Kennedy, Roger. *Mr. Jefferson's Lost Cause: Land, Farmers, Slavery, and the Louisiana Purchase.* New York: Oxford University Press, 2003.

Mancall, Peter. *American Encounters: Natives and Newcomers from European Contact to Indian Removal.* New York: Routledge, 2000.

WILLIAM S. COKER

## FLORIDABLANCA, CONDE DE (1728–1808).

Conde de Floridablanca (*b.* 21 October 1728; *d.* 30 December 1808), secretary of state in Spain (1776–1792). As secretary of state, Floridablanca was a conservative reformer and devoted servant of absolutism. After 1776, when he was appointed *fiscal* (crown attorney), his power and influence over the king, Charles III, were unparalleled, and he was accused of ministerial despotism by his opponents. The outbreak of the French Revolution (1789) horrified Floridablanca, and he tried to prevent revolutionary ideas from entering Spain.

Floridablanca found it impossible to sanction his monarch's approval of Louis XVI's acceptance of the French Constitution. His inability to compromise on this issue resulted in his dismissal from office on 28 February 1792. Retirement in Murcia was interrupted by arrest and confinement to a fortress in Pamplona while his enemies investigated him for abusing his former powerful position.

In 1794 Manuel de Godoy, Charles IV's minister, released Floridablanca and allowed him to return to Murcia. He was recalled to government service as president of the central junta meeting at Aranjuez (1808) but died shortly after the group fled to Seville in the wake of the Napoleonic invasion of Spain.

*See also* **Spain; Spanish Empire.**

BIBLIOGRAPHY

Cayetano Alcázar Molina, *El Conde de Floridablanca: Su vida y su obra* (1934).

A. Ferrer Del Río, ed., *Obras originales del conde de Floridablanca, y escritos referentes a su persona* (1952).

Richard Herr, *The Eighteenth-Century Revolution in Spain* (1958), esp. pp. 239–268.

Antonio Rumeu De Armas, *El testamento político del conde de Floridablanca* (1962).

### *Additional Bibliography*

Sánchez-Blanco, Francisco. *El absolutismo y las luces en el reinado de Carlos III.* Madrid: Marcial Pons, 2002.

Stein, Stanley J., and Barbara H. Stein. *The Apogee of Empire: Spain and New Spain in the Age of Charles III, 1759–1789.* Baltimore: Johns Hopkins University Press, 2003.

SUZANNE HILES BURKHOLDER

## FLORIT, EUGENIO (1903–1997).

Eugenio Florit (*b.* 15 October 1903; *d.* 1997), Cuban-Spanish poet. Florit was born in Madrid and lived in

Spain until 1918, when his family moved to Havana. He received a law degree from the University of Havana in 1926. In 1936 Florit befriended the Spanish poet Juan Ramón Jiménez. In 1940 he moved to New York to work for the Cuban consulate there. From 1945 to 1969 he taught at Barnard College, then part of Columbia University, and during summers, at Middlebury College, Vermont. He was the first codirector and later the director of the New York literary magazine *Revista Hispánica Moderna*. Florit edited and introduced such anthologies of poetry as *La poesía hispanoamericana desde el modernismo*, on which he collaborated with the eminent critic José Olivio Jiménez. In 1982 he moved to Miami, where he continues to reside.

As of the mid-1990s, Florit was one of the best-known living Cuban poets. His work is noted for its muted tones, religious—almost mystical—themes and its mastery of traditional poetic forms. *Asonante final* (1955) and *Doble acento* (1937) are two of the most important of his books. Florit has also been an excellent translator of American poets.

*See also* **Literature: Spanish America.**

BIBLIOGRAPHY

Luis González Del Valle and Roberto Esquenazi-Mayo, eds., *Obras completas*, 5 vols. (1991).

### *Additional Bibliography*

Florit, Eugenio, Ana Rosa Núñez, Rita Martín, and Lesbia Orta Varona. *Homenaje a Eugenio Florit*. Miami: Ediciones Universal, 2000.

Florit, Eugenio, Bertha Hernández, Jesús David Curbelo Rodríguez, and Virgilio López Lemus. *Orbita de Eugenio Florit*. El Vedado, Ciudad de la Habana: Ediciones Unión, 2003.

Roberto Valero

**FLOTA.** *See* **Fleet System: Colonial Spanish America.**

**FLOWERY WARS.** Flowery Wars, (*guerras floridas*) a term derived from the Nahuatl *xochiyaoyotl* (flower-war) referring to the semiritual battles between the Aztec and other states of ancient Mexico for purposes other than conquest. Contenders fought at a prearranged site and used tactics that demonstrated individual skills. Flowery wars provided military training and offered both sides an opportunity to capture prisoners for religious sacrifice. Such captures, once thought to have been the wars' primary purpose, are now seen as a minor one. More important were the strategic functions: to test the relative military strength of the contending forces, to keep one opponent occupied so that Aztec forces could concentrate on defeating another, and to intimidate potential enemies through a display of military strength. The earliest recorded flowery wars were between the Aztec and Chalco in the fourteenth century. Later and more deadly ones include many between the Aztec and the Valley of Puebla states in the late fifteenth and early sixteenth centuries.

*See also* **Aztecs; Nahuas.**

BIBLIOGRAPHY

The best treatment is in Ross Hassig, *Aztec Warfare* (1988), which deals with flowery war in the context of Aztec warfare in general. Other studies include Frederic Hicks, "'Flowery War' in Aztec History," in *American Ethnologist* 6 (1979): 87–92; and Barry Isaac, "The Aztec 'Flowery War': A Geopolitical Explanation," in *Journal of Anthropological Research* 39 (1983): 415–432.

### *Additional Bibliography*

Aguilar, Raúl Fuentes *De la guerra florida al combate de los flores* (1994).

Frederic Hicks

**FONSECA, GONZALO** (1922–1997). Gonzalo Fonseca (*b*. July 1922; *d*. June 1997), Uruguayan sculptor. Born in Montevideo, Fonseca traveled frequently and was carving in stone by the age of fifteen. He entered the school of architecture at the Universidad de la República Oriental del Uruguay, Montevideo, in 1939 but stayed only three years. Instead, he worked with the Taller Torres García studio (TTG) and began to study pre-Columbian art and architecture, and painted several constructivist murals in Montevideo. He settled in New York City in 1958 and began making reliefs in cement and wood that featured semi-abstract motifs and objects; in the aggregate, these function as symbols or, almost linguistically, as signs. In 1959 he completed a glass mosaic for the New School for Social Research.

In the mid-1960s, Fonseca began to carve quasi-architectural stone sculptures that simultaneously evoke ancient ruins, ritual fetishes, and mysterious games. He designed a cement *Tower* for the 1968 Olympic Games in Mexico City. In 1971 the Jewish Museum in New York City mounted an exhibition of his work; that same year he began to divide his time between New York and Italy, where he could create large-scale marble sculptures at his studio near Carrara. Fonseca represented Uruguay in the 1990 Venice Biennale. He died in Italy in 1997.

*See also* **Art: The Twentieth Century.**

BIBLIOGRAPHY

Bazzano Nelson, Florencia. "Joaquín Torres-García and the Tradition of Constructive Art." In *Latin American Artists of the Twentieth Century*, edited by Waldo Rasmussen et al. New York: Museum of Modern Art, 1993.

De Torres, Cecilia Buzio. "Gonzalo Fonseca." In *El Taller Torres-García: The School of the South and Its Legacy*, edited by Mari Carmen Ramírez. Austin, TX: Archer M. Huntington Art Gallery, 1992.

Fonseca, Gonzalo. *Gonzalo Fonseca*. Montevideo: Ministerio de Educación y Cultura, Museo Nacional de Artes Plásticas y Visuales, 1990.

Ramírez, Mari Carmen. "Re-Positioning the South: The Legacy of El Taller Torres-García in Contemporary Latin American Art." In *El Taller Torres-García: The School of the South and Its Legacy*, edited by Mari Carmen Ramírez. Austin, TX: Archer M. Huntington Art Gallery, 1992.

JOSEPH R. WOLIN

**FONSECA, GULF OF.** Gulf of Fonseca. This large bay on the Pacific coast, named after Queen Isabella of Spain's counselor, Juan Rodríguez De Fonseca, is partitioned among El Salvador, Honduras, and Nicaragua; the lion's share pertains to Honduras. In 1849, Ephraim George Squier, partly with an eye toward securing a Pacific terminus for the Honduras Interoceanic Railroad, persuaded Honduras to cede Tigre Island to the United States. British consul-general Frederick Chatfield sought to preempt this cession by occupying the island. The upshot was the signing of the Clayton–Bulwer Treaty in 1850. The insular security afforded by the port Amapala has made it a favorite launch site for Honduran insurrectionists since independence.

*See also* **Clayton–Bulwer Treaty (1850).**

BIBLIOGRAPHY

Bustillo Lacayo, Guillermo. *El Golfo de Fonseca: Región clave en Centroamérica*. Tegucigalpa, Honduras: Editorial Guaymuras, 2002.

Zamora R., Augusto. *Intereses territoriales de Nicaragua: San Andrés y Providencia, Cayos, Golfo de Fonseca, Río San Juan*. Managua: Fondo Editorial de lo Jurídico, 1995.

KENNETH V. FINNEY

**FONSECA, HERMES RODRIGUES DA** (1855–1923). Hermes Rodrigues da Fonseca (*b*. 12 May 1855; *d*. 9 September 1923), president of Brazil (1910–1914). The nephew of Manoel Deodoro da Fonseca, the republic's first president, Marshal Fonseca advanced his army and future political career by adroitly quelling a cadet rebellion during the 1904 Vaccine Revolt (an uprising by citizens opposed to forced vaccination against smallpox). Nominated as war minister in 1906, Fonseca championed efforts to modernize the army, outlining recruitment reforms, sending officers to study in Germany, and staging large-scale maneuvers. His victory as the conservative Republican Party's candidate marked the republic's first hotly contested presidential campaign.

The marshal's presidency was equally tumultuous. In his first week, the government was forced to negotiate an end to the Chibata Revolt, in which rebel sailors protesting barbarous corporal punishment commandeered newly purchased battleships and threatened to bombard Rio de Janeiro with impunity. This conflict was followed by Fonseca's "salvationist" campaigns, or his frequent use of federal troops to interfere in conflicts between political parties at the state level. After his presidential term Fonseca became a controversial military spokesman. President Artur Bernardes arrested Fonseca in 1922 after the marshal openly advised an army colonel not to obey government orders to intervene in Pernambucan politics. The marshal argued ironically that the army should not be politicized. His arrest precipitated the first *tenente* (lieutenant) revolt in 1922, a coup intended to reinstate Fonseca as president. Shaken by imprisonment and weakened by inveterate smoking, Fonseca soon died of a stroke.

*See also* **Brazil, Political Parties: Conservative Party; Chibata, Revolt of the; Pernambuco.**

BIBLIOGRAPHY

Sources in English on Hermes are piecemeal at best. The marshal's unique role in politics is touched on in Joseph L. Love, *Rio Grande do Sul and Brazilian Regionalism, 1882–1930* (1971). Frank D. McCann highlights Fonseca's role as a military reformer in "The Nation in Arms: Obligatory Military Service during the Old Republic," in *Essays Concerning the Socioeconomic History of Brazil and Portuguese India,* edited by Dauril Alden and Warren Dean (1977), pp. 211–243. The most complete account of Fonseca's life to date is a hagiography written by his son: Hermes Da Fonseca Filho, *Marechal Hermes: Dados para uma biografia* (1961).

*Additional Bibliography*

Arias Neto, José Miguel. "Em busca da cidadania: Praças da armada nacional 1867–1910." São Paulo: Ph.D. dissertation, 2001.

Beattie, Peter. *The Tribute of Blood: Army, Race, and Nation in Brazil, 1864–1945.* Durham, NC: Duke University Press, 2001.

Silva, Marcos A. de, and Emilio Damiani. *Contra a Chibata: Marinheiros brasileiros em 1910.* São Paulo: Brasiliense, 2002.

Peter M. Beattie

## FONSECA, JUAN RODRÍGUEZ DE

**FONSECA, JUAN RODRÍGUEZ DE** (1451–1524). Juan Rodríguez de Fonseca (*b.* 1451; *d.* 4 March 1524), head of the Casa de Contratación, the Spanish House of Trade. Born in Seville to a noble family, Fonseca came to Queen Isabella's court as a page, became a priest and royal chaplain, and in 1514 the bishop of Burgos. He was entrusted with diplomatic missions, administering the sale of indulgences and the outfitting of Christopher Columbus's second voyage in 1493. In 1503 he was instrumental in establishing the Casa de Contratación, which, merging into the Council of the Indies set up in 1524, was to retain exclusive control of the Indies trade for nearly 300 years. In 1518 Fonseca fitted out Ferdinand Magellan's fleet. Reputedly tight-fisted, arrogant, and impatient, he was at odds with Columbus and, later, Hernán Cortés. He presided over the 1512 Junta of Burgos, which was concerned with the theology of the rights of the Indies. He died in Burgos.

*See also* **Columbus, Christopher; Council of the Indies; Magellan, Ferdinand.**

BIBLIOGRAPHY

Quintin Aldea Vaquero et al., *Diccionario de Historia Eclesiástica de España* (Madrid, 1972).

Manuel Giménez Fernández, *Bartolomé de Las Casas,* 2 vols. (Madrid, 1984).

Helen Nader, "Fonseca," in *The Christopher Columbus Encyclopedia,* edited by Silvio A. Bedini (1992).

*Additional Bibliography*

Sagarra Gamazo, Adelaida. *Burgos y el gobierno indiana: La clientele del obispo Fonseca.* Burgos: Caja de Burgos, 1998.

Sagarra Gamazo, Adelaida. *Colón y Fonseca: La otra version de la historia indiana.* Valladolid: Universidad de Valladolid, 1997.

Peggy K. Liss

## FONSECA, MANOEL DEODORO DA

**FONSECA, MANOEL DEODORO DA** (1827–1892). Manoel Deodoro da Fonseca (*b.* 5 August 1827; *d.* 23 August 1892), a career army officer who became the first president of the Brazilian republic (1889–1891). Born in Alagoas, in Brazil's poor Northeast, Fonseca and his seven brothers all followed family tradition and entered the army. He helped subdue the liberal Praieira Revolt in Pernambuco in 1848, and served in the War of the Triple Alliance (1864–1870), achieving the ranks of brigadier general in 1874 and marshal in 1884. Through personal bravery and steadfastness, he became one of the most popular and respected army officers under the empire. Fonseca was a major figure in the so-called Military Question, a series of political conflicts during the 1880s between members of the armed forces and representatives of the imperial government that served gradually to weaken the imperial government.

Although not a republican by conviction, Fonseca was persuaded to join and lead the military movement that brought about the overthrow of the monarchy on 25 November 1889 and the proclamation of a republic that afternoon. A successful revolt toppling the monarchy would not have been possible without the support of influential senior career officers like Fonseca, who assumed the position of provisional president of the new republic. Elected to a four-year term as president of the republic by the Constituent Congress in February 1891, he continually clashed with this largely civilian body that often protested what it perceived as infringements on civil liberties by military men. Unable to adjust to the give-and-take of politics and lacking political sophistication and astuteness, Fonseca judged legislative opposition to his policies to be personal insults and unconstitutionally dissolved Congress early in November 1891. A few weeks later, he was forced out of office by dissatisfied military factions, notably members of the navy. His resignation as president late in November 1891 permitted the vice-president, Marshal Floriano Peixoto, to assume office and reconvene Congress. Fonseca died several months later.

*See also* **Pernambuco; War of the Tripple Alliance.**

BIBLIOGRAPHY

June E. Hahner, *Civilian–Military Relations in Brazil, 1889–1898* (1969).

*Additional Bibliography*

Beattie, Peter. *The Tribute of Blood: Army, Race, and Nation in Brazil, 1864–1945.* Durham, NC: Duke University Press, 2001.

Mosher, Jeffrey. "Challenging Authority: Political Violence and the Regency in Pernambuco, Brazil, 1831–1835." *Luso-Brazilian Review* 37:2 (Winter 2000): 33–57.

Mosher, Jeffrey. "Political Mobilization, Party Ideology, and Lusophobia in Nineteenth-Century Brazil: Pernambuco, 1822–1850." *Hispanic American Historical Review* 80:4 (Nov. 2000): 881–912.

JUNE E. HAHNER

**FONSECA AMADOR, CARLOS** (1936–1976). Carlos Fonseca Amador (*b.* 23 June 1936; *d.* 8 November 1976), Nicaraguan leader and cofounder of the Sandinista National Liberation Front. Born in the city of Matagalpa, Fonseca was an illegitimate son of Fausto Amador. His father was administrator of Anastasio Somoza García's rural properties in the department of Matagalpa. The family had a stable, middle-class lifestyle that enabled Fonseca to enter law school at the National Autonomous University in León in 1954. He immediately became involved in student politics and began studying the writings of Augusto César Sandino. He joined a Conservative Party youth organization but left after a few months, complaining that it was "too perfumed." He then became a member of the Nicaraguan Socialist Party. In 1957 Fonseca toured eastern Europe and the Soviet Union as a delegate of the General Union of Nicaraguan Workers. After his return in 1958, the Socialist Party published the pamphlet "A Nicaraguan in Moscow," a compendium of Fonseca's impressions of the Communist world. Fonseca increased his activities in the student opposition to the Somoza regime and participated in the unsuccessful attempt, launched from El Chaparral, Honduras, to oust the dictatorship in June 1959. He recognized the futility of agitating within the restrictive ideology of the Socialist Party, and in 1960 started the New Nicaragua Movement, the basis for the creation of the Sandinista National Liberation Front in July 1961.

Fonseca was the principal thinker behind the revolutionary organization, but he was not a Marxist-Leninist theorist. Rather, he carefully refined Sandino's eclectic ideology in order to build popular support for revolution. From the early years of the Sandinista guerrilla army in Río Coco, Fonseca accepted the necessity of cooperating with diverse urban and rural social groups. The strategy of armed struggle through the gradual accumulation of forces was borrowed directly from Sandino.

Fonseca was captured by the National Guard in 1964 and deported to Guatemala. He returned clandestinely and participated in the failed attack at Pancasán in 1967. Two years later he was arrested for bank robbery in Costa Rica and spent more than a year in jail. Freed after Sandinistas hijacked a jetliner, Fonseca spent the early 1970s shuttling between Nicaragua and the safety of Cuba. He was responsible for developing the main objectives of the Sandinista program that guided the revolutionary government in the 1980s.

In November 1976 Fonseca was killed by the National Guard near Matagalpa. He is still considered the most important historical figure of the Sandinista National Liberation Front. After the victory over Somoza in 1979, his body was exhumed and reburied in the Plaza of the Revolution in Managua, where a monument was erected in his memory.

*See also* **Nicaragua, Political Parties: Sandinista National Liberation Front (FSLN).**

BIBLIOGRAPHY

Victor Tirado López, Tomás Borge, and Humberto Ortega, *Carlos Fonseca siempre* (1982).

Carlos Fonseca, *Obras,* 2d ed., 2 vols. (1985).

Donald Hodges, *The Intellectual Foundations of the Nicaraguan Revolution* (1986).

Steven Palmer, "Carlos Fonseca and the Construction of Sandinismo in Nicaragua," in *Latin American Research Review* 23, no. 1 (1989): 91–109.

*Additional Bibliography*

Bolaños Geyer, Alejandro. *El iluminado.* Masaya, Nicaragua: A. Bolaños Geyer, 2001.

Sinclair, Minor, ed. *The New Politics of Survival: Grassroots Movements in Central America.* New York: Monthly Review Press, 1995.

Zimmerman, Matilde. *Sandinista: Carlos Fonseca and the Nicaraguan Revolution.* Durham, NC: Duke University Press, 2000.

MARK EVERINGHAM

## FONSECA E SILVA, VALENTIM DA

**FONSECA E SILVA, VALENTIM DA** (1750–1813). Valentim da Fonseca e Silva (Mestre Valentim; *b.* 1750; *d.* 1813), Brazilian sculptor, wood-carver, and architect. Although he was born in Minas Gerais, Mestre Valentim lived most of his life in Rio de Janeiro. The mulatto son of a Portuguese diamond contractor and black mother, he was orphaned at a young age. While studying wood carving under the Portuguese master craftsman Luis da Fonseca Rosa, he began to receive numerous commissions for candelabras, altarpieces, statuary, and other religious decorative work for churches throughout the city.

Mestre Valentim's best-known commissions include the carvings for the Church of Santa Cruz dos Militares, the carving and main altar in the Church of São Francisco de Paula, and the chapel of the novitiate in the Church of the Third Order of Carmo.

Beyond religious wood carvings, Mestre Valentim was the first in Brazil to apply enamel to metal. He also devoted himself to secular projects such as public fountains and architectural design. His masterpiece, the plans for the Passeio Público, was undertaken in collaboration with the painter Leandro Joaquim and the designers Francisco dos Santos Xavier and Francisco Xavier Cardoso Caldeira. Viceroy Luiz de Vasconcellos commissioned the public park as part of the government's attempt at the beautification of Rio de Janeiro.

*See also* **Art: The Colonial Period; Brazil: The Colonial Era: 1500–1808.**

BIBLIOGRAPHY

*Arte no Brasil,* vol. 1 (1979), esp. pp. 246–254.

*Additional Bibliography*

Andrade, Jorge. *Passeio Público: A paixão de um vice-rei.* Rio de Janeiro: Litteris Editora, 1999.

CAREN A. MEGHREBLIAN

## FONTAINEBLEAU, TREATY OF (1807).

Treaty of Fontainebleau (1807), a secret agreement between Spain and France regarding the partition of Portugal. In the Treaty of Fontainebleau, Charles IV and Napoleon I outlined a proposed conquest and partition of Portugal by Spain and France as part of Napoleon's ongoing attempt to isolate England. Consisting of twenty-one articles, seven of which were secret, the treaty divided Portugal into three parts. The north would go to the king of Etruria, the grandson of Charles IV; the central provinces to Napoleon, until a general peace could be concluded; and the south, the Algarve, to Manuel de Godoy, Charles's first minister. At the conclusion of the peace, Charles IV would be recognized as emperor in Spanish America. The treaty also allowed a French army of 25,000 men and 3,000 cavalry to cross Spain into Lisbon with a 40,000-troop reserve just north of the Spanish-French border at Bayonne, in case of English intervention. The treaty was signed 27 October 1807, nine days after a French army crossed into Spain and began its march on Lisbon.

Although this treaty permitted French soldiers on Spanish soil legally, it was never published, and the terms of the division of Portugal remained unfulfilled. The Treaty of Fontainebleau ultimately led to the Napoleonic occupation of Spain, the capture of Charles IV, and the designation of Napoleon's brother Joseph Bonaparte as ruler of Spain.

*See also* **Bonaparte, Joseph; Charles IV of Spain; Godoy, Manuel; Napoleon I.**

BIBLIOGRAPHY

Manuel De Godoy. *Memorias.* 2 vols. Madrid: Ediciones Atlas, 1956.

Carlos Seco Serrano. *Godoy: El hombre y el político.* Madrid: Espasa-Calpe, 1978.

Douglas Hilt. *The Troubled Trinity: Godoy and the Spanish Monarchs.* Tuscaloosa: University of Alabama Press, 1987.

SUZANNE HILES BURKHOLDER

## FONTANA, LUCIO

**FONTANA, LUCIO** (1899–1968). Lucio Fontana (*b.* 19 February 1899; *d.* 7 September 1968), Argentine sculptor. Born in Rosario, Sante Fe Province, the son of Italian parents, Fontana went to Italy when he was six. He studied at the Brera Royal Academy in Milan, graduating in 1922. The following year he returned to Argentina. In the mid 1920s he was back in Milan studying under Adolfo Widt. After that he lived several years in Paris. Fontana's repertory of forms includes figures that produce a sense of wonder and fascination in the viewer. His sculptures are in various museums and collections in Argentina and Europe. He wrote a series of manifestos on "spatialism," asserting the need to integrate all the physical elements (color, sound, movement, and space) in an ideal material unity. He died in Varese, Italy.

*See also* **Argentina: The Twentieth Century; Art: The Twentieth Century.**

BIBLIOGRAPHY

Vicente Gesualdo, Aldo Biglione, and Rodolfo Santos, *Diccionario de artistas plásticos en la Argentina* (1988).

*Additional Bibliography*

Fontana, Lucio, and Enrico Crispolti. *Fontana.* Milano: Charta, 1999.

Whitfield, Sarah, and Lucio Fontana. *Lucio Fontana.* Berkeley: University of California Press, 1999.

AMALIA CORTINA ARAVENA

## FOOD AND COOKERY

**FOOD AND COOKERY.** To speak of food in Latin America requires mention of its biodiversity and the multiplicity of geographies and histories that define its member nations and the regions within them. Inhabitants of Latin America were first the "corn people" of the pre-Columbian times, with dynamic interregional trade. Then came their transformation over five centuries as a result of intermixing with European immigrants, and then with African and Asian peoples. Latin America in the early twenty-first century is experiencing an intense process of transmigration and globalization. All of these eras have shaped a number of regional cuisines in a complex blend of traditions and histories.

The first notable cuisine comes from Mexico. There, from pre-Hispanic times, the great indigenous cultures, predominantly the Aztec confederation, had developed important culinary traditions. The chronicler Bernal Díaz del Castillo wrote about court life: "their cooks had thirty ways of preparing stews . . . and they would cook over three hundred dishes of whatever the great Moctezuma would eat. . . . And after [he] had eaten, then all his guards would eat, and a great many more of his house servants, and it seemed to me that over one thousand dishes of these foods were brought out." According to the conqueror Hernán Cortés, the Aztecs "had a great variety of substances for their cooking, chickens, cocks with jowls [turkeys], sugarcane birds [*chichicuilotes* or plovers], fine-tasting birds with beautiful plumage such as quails, doves, and pheasants, fish and shellfish, both sweetwater and saltwater, that were transported via relays from the coast to the emperor's kitchen, where they were seasoned with truly masterful techniques."

Despite repeated attempts by the colonizers and later by the Europeanized republican elites to subordinate it, the native culinary influence persisted. A notable example was the famous cultural struggle between wheat and corn, and between bread and tortillas, that paralleled attempts to preserve native traditions in the face of a modernizing tendency that favored the European way of living and, of course, eating. As a result of the Mexican revolution of the early twentieth century, the subsequent consolidation of a nationalist and pro-indigenous model, and the drive to preserve a rich culinary tradition, Mexico's cuisine is truly national, and indeed arguably exemplary in all of Latin America.

A second significant example can be found in the Andean realm of South America, particularly Peru. This important center of pre-Columbian cultures adapted to diverse climate layers, thereby taking advantage of the variety of available products to enrich the culinary traditions that continue to the present day.

On the Peruvian coast alone can be found more than two thousand kinds of soup. Cooking with fruits, potatoes, corn, peanuts, chili, fish, and shellfish goes back to the days of the Incas, and there is still also widespread use of *quinua*, or "Inca flour," a grain that is three thousand years old. Following colonization, African, Italian, Chinese, and Japanese immigrants helped create new combinations of foods, particularly *ceviche*, a combination of fish and shellfish marinated in lime juice. No survey would be complete without reference to the liquor known as *pisco* (a type of brandy made from grapes), which both Peru and Chile claim as their national beverage.

Another noteworthy culinary region is that of the Caribbean islands. There, as in the rest of the Americas, the arrival of formerly unknown animals, particularly cattle and pigs, radically transformed the countryside and added to the array of meats and fish available to the island peoples. As immigrants gradually mixed with the depleted indigenous population, a cuisine took shape that, as dependence on the tourist industry grew, would later bring about unique and sophisticated combinations of foods, which blended further with a variety of European, African, and Asian influences. The *run down* (stew), *rotis* (flatbread), the many varieties and mixtures of fruits such as coconut, curries of Asian origin, and particularly seafood, though also beef and pork, are all consumed together with rum, the classic Caribbean beverage.

A third cuisine, which one might call Euro-american, chiefly reflects the European influence. This is the example of Argentine cooking, which is greatly influenced by the cuisines of Spain and Italy, and somewhat less so by Japan. Once again, following the success of cattle-raising as a driver of the national economy, a strong *parrilla*, or "grilling" culture developed, using all possible varieties of beef, complemented with pasta and polenta, favorite dishes of the immigrant European workers particularly from the nineteenth century on.

An exceptional case is that of Brazil, where the immigrant population, primarily of European and African origin, with some Japanese influence, mixed with the native population to produce a vibrant racial blend that generated some highly regionalized cuisines. Particularly noteworthy is the *feijoada carioca* (a stew from Rio de Janeiro), which many consider the classic Brazilian dish. It is made of black beans in a thick stew, cooked with a variety of meats to which chopped cabbage, *farofa* (cassava flour fried in butter), and fresh orange slices are added. All this is preceded by a drink of the famous *caipirinha*, the national beverage, made of *cachaça* (cane liquor), lime, and sugar.

Two tendencies in Latin American cuisine have emerged as a result of unstoppable globalization. One of these is the penetration of U.S. fast-food ideas (the "McDonaldization" of food), which threatens the uniqueness of regional cuisines. The other is the adaptation of "fusion" cuisines (sometimes called *mestizas*, or mixed), involving free experimentation with culinary traditions from many parts of the world in combination with the flavors and preparation techniques characteristic of local cultures and natural Latin American products. Brazil and Colombia, as two of the world's most bio-diverse nations, have much to contribute to the wave of fusion cooking. At the same time, the region is home to millions of native peoples who have resisted the pressures colonialism for more than five hundred years, and whose cuisines preserve their own originality and uniqueness amid the mixture of cultures and foods of the world.

In the Americas another interesting case is the United States, which, in the words of the anthropologist Sidney Mintz, is a nation "without a cuisine," but one that instead has assimilated all the cuisines of the world. Those of Latin America—particularly Cuba, Puerto Rico, Central America, and Mexico—are highly influential, given that these groups make up the largest minority population in the country. Their presence has been one of the driving forces in U.S. culture, including its inhabitants' culinary tastes and habits.

*See also* **Aztecs; Incas, The; Nutrition.**

BIBLIOGRAPHY

Arciniegas, Germàn. *América en Europa.* Buenos Aires: Editorial Sudamericana, 1975. Also published as *America in Europe: A History of the New World in Reverse.* Translated by Gabriela Arciniegas and R. Victoria Arana. San Diego: Harcourt Brace Jovanovich, 1986.

Cortés, Hernán. *Cartas de Relación.* México: Editorial Porrúa, 1969.

Critser, Greg. *Fat Land: How Americans Became the Fattest People in the World.* Boston: Houghton Mifflin, 2003.

Crosby, Alfred W. *The Columbian Exchange: Biological and Cultural Consequences of 1492.* Westport, CT: Greenwood Press, 1972. Repr., Westport, CT: Praeger, 2003.

Díaz del Castillo, Bernal. *Historia Verdadera de la Conquista de la Nueva España.* México: Editorial Porrúa, 1983.

Domingo, Xavier. *De la olla al mole: Antropología de la cocina del descubrimiento.* Málaga: BmmC Editores, 2000.

Mintz, Sidney. *Tasting Food, Tasting Freedom: Excursions into Eating, Power, and the Past.* Boston: Beacon Press, 1996.

Pilcher, Jeffrey. *¡Que Vivan los Tamales! Food and the Making of Mexican Identity.* Albuquerque: University of New Mexico Press, 1998.

Ritzer, George. *The McDonaldization of Society,* rev. edition. Thousand Oaks, CA: Pine Forge Press, 2004.

Alberto G. Flórez-Malagón

**FOOTBALL WAR.** Football War, the name popularly given to the war between El Salvador and Honduras (14–18 July 1969), so called because the immediate provocation was violence surrounding soccer playoffs between the Salvadoran and Honduran national teams. The real causes lay much deeper, and although the war was brief, it had a lasting impact on Central America.

Domestic problems in both countries, as well as Honduras's dissatisfaction with its position in the Central American Common Market, led to growing tensions between the two neighbors, but the most serious issue was demographic. Since the 1920s, immigrants had left crowded El Salvador to settle in Honduras, which was much less densely inhabited. Many Salvadoran peasants squatted on public lands along the frontier between the two countries, sometimes remaining there for generations without formal title. During the 1960s, as relations worsened, Salvadorans living in Honduras were often the victims of harassment. In 1969, when Honduran president Oswaldo López Arellano attempted to distribute to Honduran peasants government-owned lands already occupied by Salvadorans, the result was a massive exodus back to El Salvador. Returning peasants carried tales of atrocities, which were widely believed.

Mob violence at the soccer games played in San Salvador and Tegucigalpa in June 1969 brought calls for action on both sides of the border. The pressure on Salvadoran president Fidel Sánchez Hernández was particularly intense, coming from military officers anxious for larger budgets and modern equipment and from conservative opponents of land reform, who feared that the repatriation of so many peasants in an already crowded country would lead to greater agitation from the Left. On 26 June, Sánchez Hernández severed diplomatic relations with Honduras, and on 14 July, Salvadoran troops marched into Honduran territory.

The fighting itself lasted only four days. Salvadoran ground troops advanced rapidly, seizing Nueva Ocotepeque and Santa Rosa de Copán along the western border and seeking to position themselves in the east for an assault on Tegucigalpa. But Honduras had air superiority and successfully bombed Salvadoran fuel storage facilities. Finally, on 18 July, under pressure from the United States and the Organization of American States, El Salvador agreed to a cease-fire. The two countries did not agree to final peace terms until 1980. The number of war-related deaths is frequently reported as 2,000, many of them Honduran civilians. Long-term effects included the crippling of the Central American Common Market and the aggravation of the impending social crisis in El Salvador. The return of thousands of landless peasants created demands that contributed to the failure of the political system in the 1970s and the onset of civil war in the 1980s.

*See also* **Central American Common Market (CACM); El Salvador; Honduras.**

BIBLIOGRAPHY

The standard work on the war itself is Thomas P. Anderson, *The War of the Dispossessed: Honduras and El Salvador, 1969* (1981). For its causes and consequences, see Marco Virgilio Carías and Daniel Slutzky, eds., *La guerra inútil: Análisis socioeconómico del conflicto entre Honduras y El Salvador* (1971), and William H. Durham, *Scarcity and Survival in Central America* (1979).

*Additional Bibliography*

Briscoe, Charles H. *Treinta años después.* Honduras: s.n., 2000.

Euraque, Darío A. *Reinterpreting the Banana Republic: Region and State in Honduras, 1870-1972.* Chapel Hill: University of North Carolina Press, 1996.

STEPHEN WEBRE

## FORAKER ACT.

Foraker Act, legislation that created a civilian government in Puerto Rico to replace the military regime that had governed the island since its conquest by U.S. military forces during the Spanish–American War (1898–1899). Introduced in 1900 by U.S. Senator Joseph B. Foraker of Ohio, the bill allowed only limited participation by Puerto Ricans. The governor, cabinet, and all judges of the Supreme Court were to be appointed by the president of the United States, a lower house of thirty-five delegates was to be elected by Puerto Ricans. In addition, the Foraker Act provided for Puerto Rico's commercial integration with the United States through the extension of U.S. currency for Puerto Rican coins. In sum, it formalized the colonial relationship that had emerged between the United States and the Puerto Rican people, among whom the act was highly unpopular. In 1917, largely due to skillful Puerto Rican diplomacy, the U.S. Congress passed the Jones Act, which granted Puerto Rico a bill of rights and full citizenship, thus mitigating the effects of the Foraker Act.

*See also* **Puerto Rico.**

BIBLIOGRAPHY

Raymond Carr, *Puerto Rico: A Colonial Experiment* (1984).

Franklin W. Knight, *The Caribbean: The Genesis of a Fragmented Nationalism,* 2d ed. (1990).

*Additional Bibliography*

Bernabe, Rafael. *Respuestas al colonialismo en la política puertorriqueña: 1899-1929.* Río Piedras, P.R.: Ediciones Huracán, 1996.

Cabán, Pedro A. *Constructing a Colonial People: Puerto Rico and the United States, 1898-1932.* Boulder, CO: Westview Press, 1999.

PAMELA MURRAY

## FORASTEROS.

Forasteros, indigenous peoples and their descendants who lived outside of the *reducciones* (settlements) to which they or their ancestors had been assigned by Viceroy Francisco de Toledo y Figueroa in his 1570s efforts to stabilize and exploit the indigenous labor force of the Andes. Under the *reducción* system, *originarios* (native-born members of those new communities) owed taxes and labor service to the state; because these levies were not assessed against *forasteros,* many individuals migrated, trading access to their community's resources for freedom from its tribute requirements. Regional demographic, migration, and labor patterns produced numerous types of *forasteros* with varying degrees of integration into rural society, mining and urban centers, and economic and political systems. *Forasteros* became a major force in the transformation of indigenous society under colonial rule. Numerous efforts to control indigenous migration and exploit the *forasteros* ended in failure, but in the early eighteenth century many *forasteros con tierra* (those with land) were redefined as taxpaying members of the communities in which they had access to land.

*See also* **Indigenous Peoples; Peru: From the Conquest Through Independence.**

BIBLIOGRAPHY

For a study of the *forasteros* and their impact on colonial society see Ann M. Wightman, *Indigenous Migration and Social Change: The Forasteros of Cuzco, 1570–1720* (1990). Various aspects of indigenous migration are presented in David J. Robinson, ed., *Migration in Colonial Spanish America* (1990), esp. the chapters by Noble David Cook, Brian Evans, Karen Powers, Edda O. Samudio A., and Ann Zulawski.

ANN M. WIGHTMAN

**FORBES, JOHN MURRAY** (1771–1831). John Murray Forbes (*b.* 13 August 1771; *d.* 14 June 1831), U.S. diplomatic and commercial agent. Originally assigned to commercial posts in Europe, in 1820 Forbes was appointed by the State Department to serve as commercial attaché in Buenos Aires, where he remained until his death. His public and private correspondence provides an eyewitness account of the turbulent period following Argentine independence. Forbes described the anarchy among the independent Río de la Plata republics, including rivalry among contending provincial rulers, the presidency of Bernardino Rivadavia, and the rise to power of Juan Manuel de Rosas, all part of the ongoing conflict between Buenos Aires and the provinces over the issue of national consolidation. Forbes also followed events in the rest of South America, and was particularly observant of the British presence in the Río de la Plata region.

*See also* **Rivadavia, Bernardino; Río de la Plata.**

BIBLIOGRAPHY

John Murray Forbes, *Once años en Buenos Aires, 1820–1831* (1956).

Harold F. Peterson, *Argentina and the United States, 1810–1960* (1964).

*Additional Bibliography*

Fernández Cistac, Roberto. *Caudillos e intelectuales de la Argentina tradicional.* Mar del Plata, Argentina: EH, Fondo Editorial: "Esto es Historia," 2001.

HILARY BURGER

**FORBES, WILLIAM CAMERON** (1870–1959). William Cameron Forbes (*b.* 21 May 1870; *d.* 24 December 1959), businessman and presidential adviser. Forbes, born in Milton, Massachusetts, graduated in 1892 from Harvard, where he later coached football. In 1894 he took a position at a Boston brokerage firm. He was named a life partner in the family investment house in 1899.

In 1904, President Theodore Roosevelt appointed Forbes to the Philippines Commission. He served there in various capacities, including governor-general, until 1913. The following year, he was appointed receiver of the Brazil Railway Company, which had operations in five South American countries.

Forbes was sent back to the Philippines in 1921, as part of a commission to study the future of U.S. relations there. The commission concluded that it would be a mistake to withdraw from the islands at that time. Later, Forbes wrote a history of the Philippines (1929).

In 1930, Herbert Hoover appointed Forbes to head a commission to advise him on U.S. policy regarding Haiti. There had been anti-American demonstrations in 1929 and expressions of discontent with the continued American military occupation of Haiti. Hoover wanted assistance in settling civil disturbances and in assessing the continued occupation.

Some of the commission members wanted the troops pulled out immediately. However, a majority, including Forbes, recommended a phased withdrawal to be completed no later than 1936, and they recommended that all services run by Americans be Haitianized.

*See also* **Philippines; Railroads.**

BIBLIOGRAPHY

Rayford W. Logan, *Haiti and the Dominican Republic* (1968), pp. 138–140.

Robert M. Spector, *W. Cameron Forbes and the Hoover Commissions to Haiti (1930)* (1985).

*Additional Bibliography*

Boot, Max. *The Savage Wars of Peace: Small Wars and the Rise of American Power.* New York: Basic Books, 2002.

CHARLES CARRERAS

**FOREIGN DEBT.** From the time of independence, Latin American nations have accumulated large foreign debts, most of them the result of loans to the respective governments. The size of these debts and repayment difficulties led to repeated debt crises during the nineteenth and twentieth centuries, generally coinciding with international economic recessions. What is referred to as the "great Latin American debt crisis," which began in 1982 and lasted most of the decade, was the largest and most devastating in its impact on the economies and societies of the region. But more recently, in the late 1990s, a new set of financial crises buffeted Mexico, Brazil, and Argentina. The nature of these crises can best be understood in the light of the long, complex history of foreign debt in Latin America. It is important to note, however, that the changing nature of financial instruments and markets over time has modified the character of foreign debt.

Foreign debt is the result of domestic agencies or residents (public or private) contracting abroad short- or long-term loans that are payable in a foreign currency. In Latin America during the nineteenth and early twentieth centuries, most such loans were taken by national, provincial, and municipal governments in the form of bonds payable in gold and issued on international capital markets, first in London and Paris, later in other European stock markets, and, after the turn of the century, in the United States, especially on the New York Stock Exchange. The bulk of Latin American foreign debt was in the form of long-term public external liabilities. The bonds usually paid between 4 and 7 percent annual interest and were amortized over ten to thirty years, depending on the loan contract. In the 1970s external bond issues declined in importance for Latin American governments, which took a larger number of direct loans from European, U.S., and Japanese commercial and investment banks. Since the 1990s most debt instruments have been equity finance, in which a large number of international mutual and pension funds invest. At the same time, private companies have gone abroad for short- and long-term loans. A brief review of the historical experience illustrates the changing nature of these loans over time, as well as changes in volume of the debt, interest rates, and impact of the debt service on the Latin American economies.

### DEBT CRISES OF THE NINETEENTH CENTURY

Latin America's first foreign loans were negotiated in 1822 to 1825 by the founding fathers of the newly independent nations. Simón Bolívar, José de San Martín, Bernardo O'Higgins, and Bernardino Rivadavia negotiated loans with British bankers for their respective governments of Gran Colombia, Peru, Chile, and Buenos Aires. Most of these loans were used to finance the acquisition of military equipment and warships for the new nations. In this sense the loans were not unproductive, because they contributed to the consolidation of the Latin American independence movements. However, as a result of an international trade crisis in 1825 to 1826, most of the debtor governments were obliged to suspend payments, giving rise to the first Latin American debt crisis.

From 1828 until mid-century, all the Latin American nations except Brazil remained in default on their external debts, a situation that provoked conflicts with European creditors and cut off the flow of foreign capital until the 1850s. The nation that suffered most as a result of the debt moratorium was Mexico. As a result of its war with the United States (1845–1847), the Mexican government was obliged to use the indemnity payments received in exchange for California and the other territories ceded to the United States to pay British bondholders. Subsequently, as a result of Benito Juárez's suspension of payments on the foreign debt in 1861, Britain, France, and Spain occupied the port of Veracruz. The French troops remained and conquered the nation, establishing the empire of Maximilian (1863–1867). International debt politics in nineteenth-century Latin America were thus enmeshed with imperialist adventures and wars.

After 1850 the economic situation of Latin America improved, largely because of rising exports in primary goods and minerals: coffee, sugar, leather, wool, silver, guano, and nitrates. As a result, Latin American governments once again became good credit risks and were able to negotiate approximately fifty foreign loans in the two decades preceding the international economic crisis of 1873. Although some of these loans were used for military purposes, as had been the case in the Latin American loan boom of the 1820s, now a greater portion was utilized for financing public works, including state railways in Peru, Chile, Brazil, and Argentina. As the second loan boom gathered strength, the smaller Latin American republics entered the fray and took numerous loans, many of

**Latin American government issues floated in England 1822–1825**

| Year and Borrower | Nominal Value (£) | Price to Public | Nominal Interest (%) | Real Interest (%) | Sums Realized (£) | Bankers |
|---|---|---|---|---|---|---|
| **1822** | | | | | | |
| Chile | 1,000,000 | 70 | 6 | 8.6 | 700,000 | Huelletts |
| Colombia | 2,000,000 | 84 | 6 | 7.1 | 1,680,000 | Herring, Powels & Graham |
| Peru | 450,000 | 88 | 6 | 6.8 | 396,000 | Thomas Kinder; Everett, Walker & Co. |
| **1824** | | | | | | |
| Brazil | 1,200,000 | 75 | 5 | 6.7 | 900,000 | Fletcher, Alexander & Co.; Thomas Wilson & Co. |
| Buenos Aires | 1,000,000 | 85 | 6 | 7.0 | 850,000 | Barings |
| Colombia | 4,750,000 | 88 | 6 | 6.8 | 4,203,750 | Goldschmidts |
| Mexico | 3,200,000 | 58 | 5 | 8.6 | 1,856,000 | Goldschmidts |
| Peru | 750,000 | 82 | 6 | 7.3 | 615,000 | Frys & Chapman |
| **1825** | | | | | | |
| Brazil | 2,000,000 | 85 | 5 | 5.9 | 1,700,000 | Rothschilds |
| Central America | 163,000 | 73 | 6 | 8.2 | 188,990 | Barclay, Herring, Richardson & Co |
| Mexico | 3,200,000 | 89 | 6 | 6.7 | 2,872,000 | Barclay, Herring, Richardson & Co |
| Peru | 616,000 | 78 | 6 | 8.2 | 480,480 | Frys & Chapman |

**Summary by state**

| State | Total Value of Bonds Issued in London, 1822–1825 (£) |
|---|---|
| Brazil | 3,200,000 |
| Buenos Aires | 1,000,000 |
| Central America | 163,300 |
| Chile | 1,000,000 |
| Colombia | 6,750,000 |
| Mexico | 6,400,000 |
| Peru | 1,816,000 |
| Total | 20,329,300 |

SOURCE: Carlos Marichal: *A Century of Debt Crises in Latin America*, 1820–1930 (Princeton, N.J.: Princeton University Press, 1989), Table 1, p. 28.

**Table 1**

which were highly speculative, in London and Paris. By 1873 the boom had run its course and the subsequent economic crisis caused a new debt crisis as Peru, Costa Rica, the Dominican Republic, Paraguay, and Bolivia suspended payments.

In the 1880s the larger Latin American nations participated in a new rush of foreign loans that was combined with the first major wave of direct foreign investment in mines, haciendas, railways, and urban infrastructure. In this regard it is worth pointing out that, according to the standard economic definition, government loans constitute a different type of foreign investment, one generally defined as portfolio investment. The largest debtor of the 1880s was Argentina, which took a grand total of fifty loans by national, provincial, and municipal government entities. The not unsurprising result was the financial crisis of 1890, known in England as the Baring Crisis because the banking house of Baring Brothers was the major creditor of the Argentine government.

### THE EARLY TWENTIETH CENTURY

In the years preceding World War I virtually all Latin American nations again approached the international capital markets for public loans; as a result, by 1914 the combined foreign debts of the Latin American governments approached $2 billion. During the war there was no suspension of payments; on the contrary, various Latin American countries were able to repatriate a portion of their foreign debts as a result of the extraordinary wartime export boom that provided them with substantial revenues. Nevertheless, after the war and the profound economic crisis of 1920 to 1921, most Latin American leaders began to turn to the United States for

**Foreign loans to Latin American governments, 1850–1875**

| Country | Total No. of Loans | Nominal Value (£ thousands) | Purpose: Military (%) | Public Works (%) | Refinance (%) |
|---|---|---|---|---|---|
| Argentina | 7 | 13,488 | 20 | 68 | 11 |
| Bolivia | 1 | 1,700 | – | 100 | – |
| Brazil | 8 | 23,467 | 30 | 13 | 57 |
| Chile | 7 | 8,502 | 37 | 51 | 12 |
| Colombia | 2 | 2,200 | – | 9 | 91 |
| Costa Rica | 3 | 3,400 | – | 100 | – |
| Ecuador | 1 | 1,824 | – | – | 100 |
| Guatemala | 2 | 650 | – | 77 | 23 |
| Haiti | 1 | 1,458 | – | – | 100 |
| Honduras | 4 | 5,590 | – | 98 | 2 |
| Mexico | 2 | 16,960 | 70 | – | 30 |
| Paraguay | 2 | 3,000 | – | 80 | 20 |
| Peru | 7 | 51,840 | 10 | 45 | 45 |
| Santo Domingo | 1 | 757 | – | 100 | – |
| Uruguay | 1 | 3,500 | – | – | 100 |
| Venezuela | 2 | 2,500 | | 30 | 70 |
| **Combined Subtotals by Subperiods** | | | | | |
| **Years** | | | | | |
| 1850–1859 | 9 | 10,862 | – | 32 | 68 |
| 1860–1869 | 20 | 56,705 | 41 | 12 | 47 |
| 1870–1875 | 22 | 73,270 | – | 60 | 40 |

SOURCE: Carlos Marichal, *A Century of Debt Crises in Latin America*, 1820–1930 (Princeton, N.J.: Princeton University Press, 1989), Table 3, p. 80.

**Table 2**

financial assistance. As a result, New York bankers agreed to provide a considerable number of loans to most of the governments of the region.

The loan expansion of the 1920s lost strength in 1928 and collapsed after the crash of 1929. During the first years of the Great Depression, most Latin American nations continued to pay a part of the interest on their foreign debts, but as the economic crisis deepened and international trade plummeted, one nation after another confronted rising fiscal deficits. As a result, several nations defaulted on their external debts—first Bolivia, Chile, and Peru in 1931 and 1932, soon followed by Brazil and most of the other nations of the region. Only Argentina, the Dominican Republic, and Haiti did not suspend payments during the 1930s.

This new and widespread debt crisis led to prolonged renegotiations with bankers and investors, beginning with several accords in the 1930s to maintain partial debt service, but it was not until the end of World War II that most foreign debts were restructured. In some cases, such as Mexico and Brazil, the creditors (under heavy pressure from the U.S. government) accepted steep reductions of the real value of the debts. In others, such as Argentina, all debts were paid off in gold.

During the 1950s and early 1960s most Latin American nations received little in the way of foreign loans, although they became associates of the International Monetary Fund (IMF) and the International Bank for Reconstruction and Development, or World Bank (WB), innovative multilateral institutions designed to stabilize and coordinate international capital flows. However, by the mid-1960s new economic development programs that required heavy injections of external capital led most Latin American governments to negotiate a rising level of loans from those multilateral agencies as well as from the recently created Inter-American Development Bank (IDB). Most of the loans from the IMF were used to cover deficits in the balance of payments, whereas the WB and IDB loans went basically to economic infrastructure closely linked to industrial and agricultural projects and to growing state enterprises in petroleum, electricity, steel, nuclear energy, and telecommunications.

Although loans from multilateral financial agencies were dominant until the early 1970s, after the oil crisis of 1973 the private banks of the United States, Europe, and Japan began to channel a much larger flow of loan capital to virtually all the Latin American nations, providing money for both public and private enterprises. There was a big jump in foreign indebtedness in this period, with the biggest debtors clearly being Brazil and Mexico, followed at some distance by Argentina, Peru, and Chile. No region in the world absorbed such large external debts as Latin America in the decade of the 1970s, a fact that merits more comparative reflection and discussion. The remarkable feature was that virtually all Latin America governments and public enterprises sought easy money abroad at what were argued to be low interest rates. The supply-side explanation of the lending boom was underlined by numerous economists who argued that the excess sums of petrodollars in Western banks stimulated a ferocious competition to obtain clients who would take loans. On the other

**Foreign loans to Latin American governments, 1920–1930 (in thousands of U.S. dollars)**

| Country | No. of Loans | Nominal Value | Purpose: Public Works | Purpose: Refinance | Purpose: Other |
|---|---|---|---|---|---|
| Argentina | 25 | 419,418 | 124,995 | 281,301 | 19,122 |
| Bolivia | 3 | 66,000 | 43,000 | 23,000 | – |
| Brazil | 36 | 641,318 | 247,514 | 246,821 | 145,983 |
| Chile | 18 | 342,538 | 200,446 | 52,092 | 90,000 |
| Colombia | 21 | 179,775 | 146,185 | 8,750 | 21,840 |
| Costa Rica | 3 | 10,990 | 9,800 | 1,190 | – |
| Cuba | 5 | 155,973 | 40,000 | 79,000 | 36,973 |
| Dominican Republic | 2 | 20,000 | 15,000 | 5,000 | – |
| El Salvador | 3 | 21,609 | – | 21,609 | – |
| Guatemala | 3 | 9,465 | 4,950 | 4,515 | – |
| Haiti | 2 | 18,634 | – | 18,634 | – |
| Panama | 2 | 20,500 | 4,500 | 12,000 | 4,000 |
| Peru | 7 | 110,314 | 60,366 | 49,948 | – |
| Uruguay | 5 | 70,388 | 70,388 | – | – |

SOURCE: Data from A. Kimber, *Record of Government Debts* (New York: Author, 1929, 1934); Council of the Corporation of Foreign Bondholders, *Annual Report* (London: Author, 1928–1935); Foreign Bondholders Protective Council. *Annual Report* (New York: Author, 1934, 1936).

**Table 3**

hand, the lemming-type behavior of all Latin American governments in seeking loans has yet to be adequately explained in theoretical terms, although both the supply and demand sides of the equation were clearly important. In any case, any such explanation requires a political economy component to be able to explain why different types of regimes in Latin America all became engulfed in the financial frenzy.

In the case of Argentina the expansion of the foreign debt took place mostly during the bloody military dictatorship of 1976 to 1983, although it had begun on a small scale before then. In 1975 the Argentine foreign debt stood at $7.9 billion, but it rose to $45 billion by 1983. A review of the bond issues of those years indicates that a large part was guaranteed by state companies such as Yacimientos Petrolíferos Fiscales, the state-owned water, electrical, and telephone companies. Great sums were expended in hydroelectric projects and highways, and an unknown amount in military expenditures. Private corporations also took debt abroad, although these debts were mostly absorbed by the state by means of exchange-rate insurance schemes in the years 1982 to 1983.

In the case of Mexico, in contrast, the reasons for increasing foreign indebtedness were linked to the need of the state political party, the Partido Revolucionario Institutcional (PRI), to reinforce populist strategies that could guarantee the immense party bureaucracy and its allies a continued political monopoly (not a democracy). One of the key instruments was the financing of state companies that provided jobs, bureaucratic plums, and thousands of contracts. In the 1970s two public enterprises, Petróleos Mexicanos (PEMEX), the profitable state petroleum monopoly, and Comisión Federal de Electricidad (CFE), the state electrical consortium, took the greatest number of loans. The foreign debt of PEMEX had stood at barely $367 million in 1970, but by 1981 had surpassed $11 billion, representing 27 percent of total long-term Mexican public debt. Promoting electrical expansion was also a major government priority under the administrations of presidents Luis Echeverría (1970–1976) and José López Portillo (1976–1982); this led the external obligations of the public electricity corporation, CFE, to rise from a mere $990 (i.e., less than one thousand dollars) in 1970 to more than $8.2 billion by end of 1981.

### THE GREAT LATIN AMERICAN DEBT CRISIS AND RESTRUCTURING

By the early 1980s the debt service had become a major problem. The abrupt rise of interest rates in the United States in 1980 and 1981 provoked severe, international monetary instability and a decline in world trade in 1980 to 1982. At the same time, a sharp drop in petroleum prices in early 1982 added fuel to the impending financial collapse. As sources of funds dried up in the foreign capital markets and hard-currency fiscal revenues dropped, many governments of the region were confronted by the fact that they could no longer meet their debt payments. The outbreak of the debt crisis was signaled most clearly in the announcement by Mexican Finance Secretary Jesús Silva Herzog in August 1982 in which he ratified temporary suspension of payments on external debt. The upheaval that this decision caused in international money markets led to the first renegotiating program between Mexico and the creditor banks, but at first there was much doubt about whether an agreement could be reached—

**Public external debt of Latin American nations, 1970–2000 (in millions of dollars)**

| Country | 1970 | 1980 | 1990 | 1995 | 2000 |
|---|---|---|---|---|---|
| **Argentina** | | | | | |
| Total external debt | 5.81 | 27.157 | 62.232 | 98.802 | 146.172 |
| Annual service | 1.11 | 4.182 | 6.158 | 8.889 | 27.345 |
| **Bolivia** | | | | | |
| Total external debt | 588 | 2.702 | 4.275 | 5.272 | 5.762 |
| Annual service | 26 | 366 | 385 | 372 | 662 |
| **Brazil** | | | | | |
| Total external debt | 5.735 | 71.52 | 119.877 | 159.073 | 237.953 |
| Annual service | 752 | 14.757 | 8.168 | 21.677 | 62.788 |
| **Colombia** | | | | | |
| Total external debt | 2.237 | 6.941 | 17.222 | 25.048 | 34.081 |
| Annual service | 287 | 951 | 3.889 | 4.345 | 5.171 |
| **Ecuador** | | | | | |
| Total external debt | 365 | 5.998 | 12.108 | 13.994 | 13.281 |
| Annual service | 43 | 1.008 | 1.084 | 1.417 | 1.276 |
| **Peru** | | | | | |
| Total external debt | 3.211 | 9.386 | 20.004 | 30.052 | 28.66 |
| Annual service | 522 | 2.151 | 476 | 1.24 | 4.305 |
| **Uruguay** | | | | | |
| Total external debt | 363 | 1.66 | 4.415 | 5.318 | 8.196 |
| Annual service | 97 | 299 | 987 | 862 | 1.313 |
| **Venezuela** | | | | | |
| Total external debt | 1.422 | 29.344 | 33.17 | 35.848 | 38.196 |
| Annual service | 120 | 6.037 | 4.99 | 4.867 | 5.846 |
| **Dominican Republic** | | | | | |
| Total external debt | 360 | 2.002 | 4.372 | 4.448 | 4.598 |
| Annual service | 45 | 379 | 232 | 409 | 521 |
| **Guatemala** | | | | | |
| Total external debt | 159 | 1.18 | 3.08 | 3.655 | 4.622 |
| Annual service | 38 | 145 | 214 | 350 | 438 |
| **Honduras** | | | | | |
| Total external debt | 91 | 1.47 | 3.718 | 4.571 | 5.487 |
| Annual service | 6 | 207 | 389 | 553 | 578 |
| **Mexico** | | | | | |
| Total external debt | 6.969 | 57.378 | 104.442 | 166.874 | 150.288 |
| Annual service | 1.301 | 10.962 | 11.313 | 26.887 | 58.259 |
| **Nicaragua** | | | | | |
| Total external debt | 203 | 2.19 | 10.707 | 10.359 | 7.019 |
| Annual service | 36 | 115 | 16 | 288 | 300 |

SOURCE: The World Bank, *Global Development Finance*, Washington D.C., several years.

**Table 4**

indeed, there was concern that a world financial crash might result from the Latin American debt crisis.

Virtually all Latin American nations suspended payments on their debts at different times during the 1980s, each time provoking a minor financial panic. Simultaneously, the IMF and the large international banks pressured Latin American financial authorities to impose drastic austerity programs. Government deficits were gradually cut, but at the expense of economic growth. As a result, the 1980s was a time of negative growth, resulting in the loss of an important part of the socioeconomic advances of the previous two decades. In particular, working sectors suffered a steep decline in real wages at the same time that educational and health services deteriorated in quantity and quality. As a result, the living standards of the vast majority of Latin Americans fell significantly, provoking social and political discontent.

By the late 1980s some countries began to experience a slight improvement that made possible more solid debt renegotiations. In 1988, with the establishment of the Brady Plan—beginning first with Mexico—it became evident that the U.S. Treasury was taking an increased role in the resolution of the debt crisis in order to stabilize world financial markets and assure the banks that they would recover most of their money. Following new restructuring agreements with the international commercial banks, a series of proposals made by successive secretaries of the United States Treasury, James Baker (1985–1988) and Nicholas Brady (1988–1993), served as the basis for a more long-term resolution of the Mexican debt crisis in 1988. The basic accord was based on the exchange of the old bonds for new so-called Brady bonds, which were long-term debt instruments with a U.S. Treasury guarantee. The net result was a limited discount of the total capital owed to banks and a drop in debt service payments.

The Mexican debt restructurings reflected the success of the alliance of the IMF, the U.S. Treasury, and the international private banks in guaranteeing continued debt service payments and at the same time impelling a dramatic restructuring of the Mexican public sector, including privatization of state enterprises and liberalization of foreign trade. This set of neoliberal policies—which were, in part, the offspring of the debt crisis and which were applied in many developing nations—came to be known as the Washington Consensus. Once neoliberalism was generally adopted by most Latin American political and financial elites, it became possible to carry out new programs of financial engineering such as the Brady Plan, which, it was expected, could help reconcile debtor countries and their numerous international creditors.

In the early 1990s other nations undertook the process of drafting similar far-reaching agreements.

As a result, there was a new boom in capital flows to the Latin American nations. According to the IMF, between 1990 and 1993 Mexico received $91 billion, or roughly one-fifth of all net inflows to developing countries. Mexico was followed by Brazil and Argentina, and throughout the region these years were a time of financial euphoria and renewed indebtedness. However, the boom was short-lived. The financial bankruptcy of the Mexican government in December 1995 not only led to a general economic crisis but also threatened international financial markets, particularly because of the large amount of Mexican debt that had been issued on the emerging markets. Bankers and investors everywhere were terrified by the prospect of capital flight from Latin America back to Europe, Japan, and the United States. As a result, the head of the U.S. Treasury, Robert Rubin (by profession a banker who had been heavily engaged in global finance), convinced the U.S. president, William Clinton, that a Mexican rescue program was urgently needed. It was the first of various rescue plans—most headed by the IMF—to confront a succession of financial crises; in fact, the IMF virtually exhausted its resources when it organized similar bailouts in the late 1990s for Indonesia, South Korea, Russia, Brazil, and Turkey, and then in 2001 for Argentina. These financial collapses demonstrate that as financial markets have become more complex in recent decades, the role of governments has been crucial in confronting crises, but also that there is a need for profound reform of the international financial architecture.

*See also* **Banking: Overview; Banking: Since 1990; Bolívar, Simón; Foreign Investment; Foreign Trade; Inter-American Development Bank (IDB); International Monetary Fund (IMF); Mexico, Political Parties: Institutional Revolutionary Party (PRI); O'Higgins, Bernardo; Petróleos Mexicanos (Pemex); San Martín, José Francisco de; World Bank.**

BIBLIOGRAPHY

Cline, William. *International Debt Reexamined.* Washington, DC: Institute for International Economics, 1995.

Marichal, Carlos. *A Century of Debt Crises in Latin America: From Independence to the Great Depression, 1820–1939.* Princeton, NJ: Princeton University Press, 1989.

Payer, Cheryl. *The Debt Trap: The IMF and the Third World.* New York: Monthly Review Press, 1974.

Sebastián, Luis de. *La crisis de América Latina y la deuda externa.* Madrid: Alianza, 1988.

Stallings, Barbara. *Banker to the Third World: U.S. Portfolio Investment in Latin America, 1900–1986.* Berkeley: University of California Press, 1987.

CARLOS MARICHAL

---

**FOREIGN INVESTMENT.** In the colonial period, foreign investment in Latin America was made as human capital in the form of the knowledge and skills of immigrants, as physical capital in the form of the animals, tools, and equipment that they brought with them, and in the form of financial investments. Funds transferred from the mother countries to Latin America for running the colonies provided resources which, after independence, were obtained from sales of bonds by the newly formed national governments.

### BRITISH INVESTMENT

In the early nineteenth century, Latin American nations obtained from Great Britain both recognition of their independence and funds in exchange for improved access to their markets. The increased trade provided information to the British on profitable investments, which consequently increased. The pattern of British investment, the most important in Latin America before World War I, was typical of the operation of all foreign investment in the region. Mexico, Central America, Colombia, Venezuela, Peru, Chile, Argentina, and Brazil had obtained loans in the British market before 1826. The loans often were guaranteed by customs receipts. High commissions were often paid to middlemen with political connections to place the loans. At various times, blockades of ports and armed intervention were used to obtain repayment of loans.

The Latin American nations were politically unstable during the first decade after their independence. Loans were limited until the 1850s, when new government issues were floated and railroad investment began. British loans were concentrated in transportation and public utilities, and particularly in enterprises whose obligations were guaranteed by a provincial or national government. Beginning in the 1890s, they also invested in

**Latin America and the Caribbean: Net FDI inflows by subregion, 1991–2005 (in millions of U.S. dollars)**

| | 1991–1995[a] | 1996–2000[a] | 2001–2005[a] | 2004 | 2005[b] |
|---|---|---|---|---|---|
| Mexico | 6,804.6 | 12,608.8 | 18,805.8 | 18,244.4 | 17,804.6 |
| Central America | 659.2 | 2,340.2 | 2,250.7 | 2,728.8 | 2,745.0 |
| Caribbean | 945.1 | 2,519.1 | 2,857.9 | 2,861.2 | 2,971.3 |
| Subtotal: Mexico and Caribbean Basin | 8,408.9 | 17,468.1 | 23,914.4 | 23,834.3 | 23,520.8 |
| MERCOSUR | 6,445.2 | 36,757.1 | 19.883.1 | 22,822.1 | 20,398.5 |
| Andean Community | 3,685.5 | 10,746.7 | 9,701.1 | 7,674.0 | 16,918.5 |
| Chile | 1,666.2 | 5,667.0 | 5,087.7 | 7,172.7 | 7,208.5 |
| Subtotal: South America | 11,797.0 | 53,170.7 | 34,671.9 | 37.668.8 | 44,525.4 |
| Total: Latin America and the Caribbean | 20,205.8 | 70,638.9 | 58,586.2 | 61,503.2 | 68,046.3 |

[a]Annual averages.
[b]Data available as of 24 April 2006.

Note: Excludes financial centers. Net FDI inflows are defined as FDI inflows to the reporting economy minus capital outflows generated by the same foreign companies. These FDI figures differ from those published by ECLAC in its preliminary overview of the economies of Latin America and the Caribbean because in that study, FDI was defined as the inflows to the reporting economy minus outflows from residents.

SOURCE: United Nations, *Foreign Investment in Latin America and the Caribbean*, p. 10. Based on data from Economic Commission for Latin America and the Caribbean (ECLAC) on the basis of statistics from the International Monetary Fund and official figures.

**Table 1**

financial, land, and investment companies. Investment was concentrated in Argentina, Brazil, and Mexico.

British investors accepted a lower rate on loans to Latin America than on funds invested in Europe because they invested in risky manufacturing ventures in Europe, whereas in Latin America the monopoly of railroads and public utilities promised safer returns. Foreign investment in railroads was especially important in Latin America: By promoting exports, the railroads contributed to increased foreign exchange earnings and export-oriented economic development. Foreign-owned railroads, however, were as extortionate in their rates abroad as they had been in their home countries, and Latin Americans demanded that they be regulated or nationalized. Increasingly harsh regulation led foreign investors to stop investing in railroads. Conflicts over the railroads and the competition from other nations for funds made Latin America a less important destination for European capital by 1913.

From 1825 to 1913, portfolio investment (in bonds) was larger than direct investment (in equities) because of the large share of government loans absorbed by the British market. However, the portfolio share fell from almost 80 percent in 1865 to less than 55 percent by 1913, when corporate securities accounted for 30 percent of portfolio investment. In 1865 almost all direct private investment (excluding government loans) was in ordinary shares, but by 1913 they constituted just over 40 percent, with preference shares rising from 1 to 15 percent and debentures and mortgages growing from 12 to 44 percent. British holdings in Latin America in 1913 comprised about one-fifth of its overseas capital and were roughly equal to the British investment in the United States.

### U.S. AND OTHER NON-LATIN INVESTMENT

Both the rise of the United States as a creditor nation and its proximity to Latin America led to the emergence of the United States as the dominant source of foreign capital in the twentieth century, accounting for more than 60 percent in the 1980s. Western European corporations provided 25 percent. Japanese investment in Latin America,

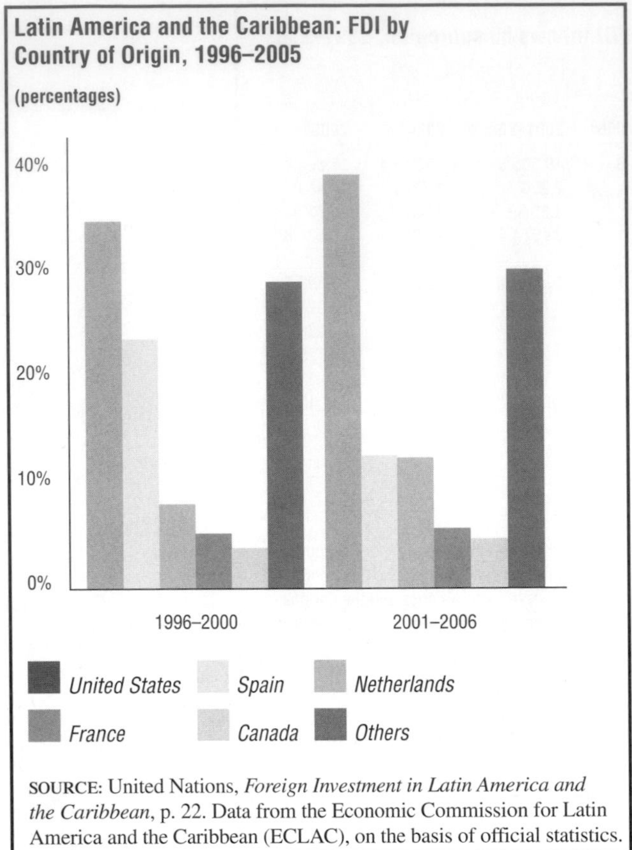


SOURCE: United Nations, *Foreign Investment in Latin America and the Caribbean*, p. 22. Data from the Economic Commission for Latin America and the Caribbean (ECLAC), on the basis of official statistics.

**Figure 1**

mostly in manufacturing, became noticeable in the 1950s and increased along with Japan's trade surpluses, but other nations became more prominent in subsequent years. In 2001–2005, the United States accounted for almost 40 percent of foreign direct investment, as shown in Figure 1. The apparent increase of foreign direct investment by the Netherlands may reflect the use of subsidiaries in the Netherlands by many companies to redirect their financial resources to Latin America, among other regions, to obtain tax benefits. In mid 2007 the weakening of the dollar made it likely that relative share of the United States in total foreign investment in Latin America would decline.

Figure 2 illustrates how the share of foreign direct investment in manufacturing increased from 1996–2000 to 2001–2005, while investment in natural resources fell, and services remained roughly constant. U.S. investments in Latin America in 1897 were concentrated in railroads (42 percent), mining and smelting (26 percent), and agriculture (19 percent). U.S. multinational corporations undertook investment to secure supplies and improve their competitive position in domestic and world markets. Latin America's changing economic structure led to a shift of foreign investment. By 1950 the share of U.S. funds in transport and communication and in mining and smelting had fallen to half the 1897 level, whereas investment in oil had risen to 28 percent and in manufacturing to 17 percent. The countries to which investment flowed reflected their governments' actions. Castro's expropriation of U.S. property was the largest in U.S. history. In the subsequent absence of U.S. investment, Cuba relied on subsidies from the Soviet Union. In 1982, 16 percent was in petroleum (reflecting the nationalization of the Venezuelan oil industry), 48 percent in manufacturing, 16 percent in finance, and 9 percent in trade. In 1992, 46 percent was in finance, insurance, and real estate, 9 percent in banking, 30 percent in manufacturing, and 5 percent in oil.

## FORMS OF FOREIGN INVESTMENT

Foreign investment took increasingly varied forms over the course of the twentieth century. Direct investment, which was 75 percent of the total in 1900–1913, rose to 92 percent in 1914–1920 but fell to 15 percent in 1954–1980. Portfolio investment fluctuated widely, providing 25 percent in 1900–1913 but rising to 58 percent in 1954–1980. Supplier credit, in which an exporter extends credit to a buyer, was not important until World War II; in the 1950s and 1960s, however, it rose to 6 percent of total private investment but fell to less than 1 percent of the total in 1976–1980, for an average of 1 percent for 1954–1980. Government loan holdings fell during the Great Depression, rose to 50 percent of the total for 1939–1953, and then fell to 26 percent for 1954–1980.

The debt crisis of the early 1980s led to a net transfer abroad of $221.3 billion. The consequent fall in economic capacity led to a decline of Latin America's share in world trade to under 4 percent, just one-third of its 1950 share. To reverse this trend, Latin American nations restructured their debt and opened their financial markets. Increasingly deep discounts in the secondary market for debt issues from 1987 to 1989 led, in some cases, to the swapping of government debt for equity (attractive because the debt was

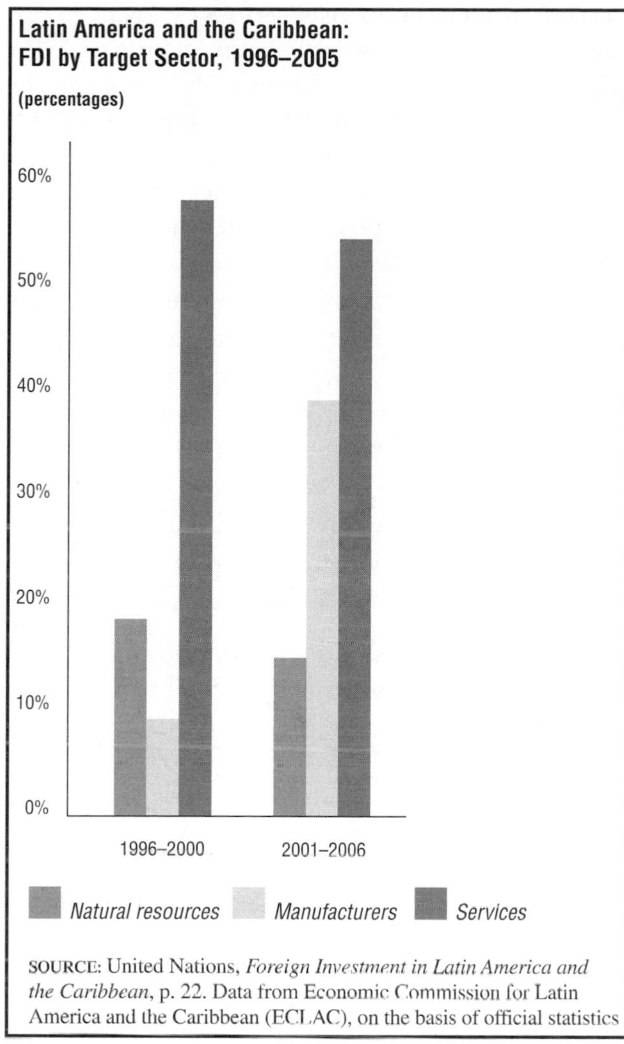


SOURCE: United Nations, *Foreign Investment in Latin America and the Caribbean*, p. 22. Data from Economic Commission for Latin America and the Caribbean (ECLAC), on the basis of official statistics

**Figure 2**

accepted at close to par for conversion purposes), whereas commercial debt was reduced under the Brady Plan. Initiated by the United States in March 1989, the plan facilitated private debt forgiveness in exchange for International Monetary Fund (IMF) and World Bank debt guarantees and greater Latin American fiscal, monetary, and international commercial reforms. Consequently, the private sector increased its share of total investments from 57 percent in 1983 to 62 percent in 1990, although this was still below the 1970s level of 64 percent.

The improved economic climate for investment in the late 1980s revived foreign interest in Latin American stocks; they were increasingly purchased through foreign investment funds. In some cases Latin American nations restricted the share of a domestic company that could be owned by foreign investors. In others, trusts were established to hold accounts receivable, mortgages, and export income to guarantee the servicing of securities. Other investment techniques made it possible to acquire nonvoting shares previously restricted to domestic owners. Perhaps the most important innovation was the use of American Depositary Receipts, which eased acquisition of foreign assets. ADRs are issued when foreign shares have been deposited with the bank's overseas branch or custodian. The bank obtains dividends on these stocks, pays foreign withholding taxes, and pays the net dividends in dollars to the receipt holders.

In 1991 Latin America obtained roughly $40 billion in new private capital flows. Private borrowing—private bonds, commercial paper, certificates of deposit, trade financing, and term bank lending—provided 39 percent; ADRs and other funds supplied 16 percent; and other direct foreign investment—in part resulting from privatization of government enterprise—accounted for 35 percent. The largest developing-nation corporations financed more of their growth from external sources during the 1980s than developed nations at similar stages of development. In the 1980s the controlling interest of privately owned firms held a higher proportion of the total voting shares than was the case with firms in the United States; the former are not expected to relinquish control by opening their capital to outsiders.

Foreign direct investment in Latin America and the Caribbean rose from an annual average of U.S. $20,205.8 million in 1991–1995 to $70,638.9 million in 1996–2000, reflecting one-time privatizations of state-owned property in South America, and settling at $68,046.3 million in 2005. Latin America was less able to attract foreign direct investment—especially investment that would generate high multiplier effects in the economy—from outside the region. Such investment was often in natural resources in South America and in processing, rather than integrated production, in Mexico. Mexico and the Caribbean received investment largely from the United States for establishing export platforms, primarily for manufactures of electronic, automotive, and apparel products, while South America received investment largely from Europe, directed to the national market for services and manufactures.

### TRANS-LATIN INVESTMENT

Many trans-Latins, emerging Latin American transnationals that have made direct investments outside their home countries, are concentrated in basic industries, including petroleum and natural gas, mining, steel, and cement, with the exception of América Móvil (telecommunications), founded in 2000. Soft-drink and food-product firms focused on regional versus international investments. They adjusted to competition from other transnational corporations by finding niche markets, making licensing arrangements, or selling equity in their firms to their competitors. Trans-Latin firms that obtained state assistance were more successful than other firms in moving into international markets outside the region. Recommendations by CEPAL (the United Nations Economic Commission for Latin America) to increase foreign investment by Latin American firms include both government assistance in improving and distributing technology to firms and cutting red tape and corruption affecting business.

Argentine foreign investment was concentrated in petroleum, steel, and food products, dominated by four firms, two of which have since been acquired by foreign companies. Brazilian foreign investment notably was made by Petróleo Brasileiro (Petrobras), the state-owned oil firm, which explored for oil with consortiums of foreign firms, diversifying its risk. High oil prices spurred transnational investment in biofuels and proposals for transfer of Brazil's technology. Brazilian president Luiz Inácio Lula da Silva (2003–) suggested that rich countries should finance bio-diesel projects in developing countries as a means of reducing global inequality.

Other government firms as well as private ones used their investment in other nations to become more competitive by increasing the scale of their operations, diversifying their assets, and lowering their capital costs. Chilean foreign investment, largely in Argentina and Peru, was concentrated in forestry, metals, air transportation, beverages, and retail trade. Some of the Chilean transnationals were taken over by other firms; some succeeded, and others incurred heavy losses. Mexican foreign investment was largely undertaken by private firms, in some cases affiliated with transnational corporations. Mexico's many free-trade agreements facilitated investment abroad.

### THE ROLE OF FOREIGN INVESTMENT

Foreign direct capital stock in Latin America has been estimated at almost 12 percent of GNP, or 4 percent of capital stock—close to $200 per capita for 1982. The largest per capita foreign invest-ments were in Trinidad and Tobago (oil refineries), Panama (the canal), Barbados, Venezuela, Jamaica, Uruguay, Argentina, and Guyana. Latin American nations that frequently excluded some areas of their economies from foreign capital investment had lower per capita foreign direct capital stock. The relatively small proportion of foreign direct capital overall stemmed from the large amount of domestic capital in rural areas and from limitations in some countries on foreign capital to investments in raw materials, production of goods previously sold by a foreign enterprise, and to areas where foreigners have proprietary technology.

Foreign investment often went into mining and other raw materials because the capital requirements of such ventures were too large for local financiers. In Latin America the government was often the only local entity with sufficient funds to risk investing in mining or oil. Foreign investors, with more funds available, could invest in capital-intensive ventures as one of many such investments that they made in several nations. Foreign investment in banks had the advantage of serving firms from the home country with branches or subsidiaries in Latin America, facilitating their investment and trade.

Investment was tied to the growth of multinational corporations, which raised the issue of whether those firms were run for the benefit of the nation in which the affiliates were located or for that of the parent firm or nation. An often-cited example was the practice of adjusting accounting records of intrafirm sales from affiliates in one nation to affiliates in another (transfer pricing) so as to minimize the overall tax burden. Favoritism for foreign employees of multinational corporations gave rise to successful demands after World War II that jobs be increasingly reserved for Latin American nationals and that they be trained for the more skilled jobs and for managerial positions.

Opponents of foreign investment objected to its use of capital-intensive production methods. They regretted the displacement of labor-intensive artisan production. An extension of this argument was that foreign techniques and foreign goods replaced local culture and products. Foreign firms were perceived as crowding out local borrowers, and when foreign investors bought out existing firms rather than investing in new ones they were criticized for weakening the domestic entrepreneurial class and for not increasing the capital assets of the economy. Many feared that foreign capital would come to dominate individual industries and sectors. This led to restrictions on the quantity of foreign investment and on the sectors in which it was invested. At the same time, remittances of profits and capital were limited in order to alleviate strains on the balance of payments.

Andean Community of Nations members forged stringent common policies for foreign capital, requiring foreign investors to reduce their ownership in local enterprises to a minority share over a fifteen-year period. Because there was strong world competition for investment funds, such restrictions in Latin America contributed to a sharp fall in the share of foreign capital going there. The exports from U.S. majority-owned affiliates in Latin America were one-quarter of those in other developing nations because sales within the highly protected Latin American markets were more profitable than exports. But the proportion of manufactured exports to total exports of the Latin American affiliates was above the proportion for the developing-nation average.

Those favoring foreign investment point out that some foreign corporations provide services such as housing and community health and social welfare programs, as well as promoting economic development. Traditional proponents of foreign capital argued that foreigners provided capital and technology unavailable within Latin American nations, without which some domestic investments would not be possible. Some of the resentment of foreign capital was eased by stipulations that unless oil and pharmaceuticals utilized concessions and produced patented items within a few years, the concession or patent would be void.

The cost of obtaining foreign investment was reduced as a result of the increasing number of suppliers of capital and technology, and of the growing sophistication of Latin American negotiators. This made it possible to unbundle technology. Instead of seeking a single supplier to provide the technology for all parts of a process, Latin Americans broke the process into its component parts. Several suppliers who could provide the technology for some, if not all of these process segments, were invited to bid for contracts, which greatly reduced cost.

Fears that foreign trade and investment would lead to domination by foreign nations were somewhat mitigated by the distinction made between the interests of a foreign corporation and that of its government. In the early twentieth century, the United States took measures to encourage and protect U.S. investment abroad. Multinational corporations sometimes were accused of meddling in Latin American politics and bribing governments, with their greater financial strength giving them an unfair advantage over Latin American firms attempting to use the same strategy. According to Albert O. Hirschman, "internal disputes over the appropriate treatment of the foreign investor gravely weakened, or helped to topple, some of the more progressive and democratic governments that held power in such countries as Brazil, Chile, and Peru" (1969, p. 8).

Paul E. Sigmund states that broader political interest in good foreign relations not only led to U.S. acceptance of Latin American nationalization of U.S. property but also to establishment of economic boycotts by the U.S. government that harmed U.S. firms (1980, p. 304). Further easing concern about the impact of foreign investment is the indication that in 1973–1986 foreign investment was most likely to go to nations with democratic political regimes, especially those with IMF support. It has also been pointed out that domestic firms faced with foreign competition either improve their competitive performance or fail. For all these reasons, restrictions on foreign investors were eased in the 1980s.

## INTERNATIONAL RELATIONS

The creation of the North American Free Trade Agreement (NAFTA) between Canada, Mexico, and the United States in 1994 provided for foreign investment, thus consolidating the opening of the Mexican economy in the 1980s by reducing barriers to trade, eliminating red tape, and extinguishing unprofitable government enterprises in nonstrategic sectors. Similar measures favoring investors were enacted in most Latin American nations, but more slowly in Brazil, which attracted less multinational investment than countries with stronger economic reforms or oil exports. Bilateral and regional free trade and common market agreements were made throughout Latin America in the 1990s and early 2000s, although progress was slow and it proved difficult to strengthen regional and international trade agreements.

Foreign economic diplomacy is an important part of Latin American nations' foreign policy, in the early twenty-first century, and in Brazil it has become the subject of university-level formal study. A proposal introduced to a conference held by the Organisation for Economic Co-operation and Development (OECD) in 2004 led to a regional emerging markets technology transfer network project that will implement a portal and a network for knowledge and technology transfer among emerging markets, initially including Turkey, Brazil, Austria, Spain, Greece, Italy, Pakistan, and Portugal. Governments, universities, and trade associations are to cooperate in this program. Similar programs emphasizing technology and development to meet economic competition have been proposed in other Latin American nations.

The United Nations' Economic Commission for Latin America—CEPAL—criticized Latin American policies to promote foreign investment in the region as inadequate compared to that of other regions. Richard M. Bird (2006) doubts that the nations have sufficient information to fine tune and implement tax incentives well. He suggests that incentives be few and simple. CEPAL recommends strengthening investment promotion agencies through greater emphasis on a professional staff and establishing offices abroad. It calls for integration of investment policies into national development policies, and emphasizes the need to create a better business environment by supporting qualified workers and suppliers of inputs to business. It recommends evaluation of the effect of incentives on investment and shifting from general to targeted incentives, paying particular attention to investment in research and development.

Instead of looking for ways to encourage foreign investments, some Latin American nations preferred to reduce foreign investment or modify the terms investors enjoyed in their nations. Venezuela, under president Hugo Chávez (1999–), signed an agreement to buy a controlling stake in Electricidad de Caracas from its U.S.-based owner, AES Corporation, for $739 million, and to purchase Verizon's share in the country's largest telecommunications company, CA Nacional Telefonos de Venezuela (CANTV). He planned to nationalize other smaller companies in the electrical sector.

In April 2006, Bolivia, Venezuela, and Cuba signed the People's Trade Agreement. It favored establishing joint companies that strengthen the capacity for social inclusion, resource industrialization, and food security in a framework of respect and preservation of the environment. An important feature was Venezuela's offer to buy Bolivian agricultural exports, including all the soybeans that could be excluded from sales to Colombia because of Colombia's trade agreement with the United States. In October, Bolivia and Brazil signed a framework agreement for Bolivia's nationalization of the natural gas industry, in which Petrobras is the largest investor. On February 9, 2007, Bolivia nationalized the nation's only tin smelter without compensation. The Swiss owners of the firm said that they would seek arbitration.

The Latin American nations began as recipients of foreign investment. The forms in which foreign investment was accepted shifted according to these nations' perception of their national interest. Attitudes shifted from welcoming, to placing restrictions on, to rejecting foreign investment, and later to welcoming it again. The technicalities governing trade and investment became more complex, and regional agreements were increasingly important in setting not only traditional requirements on trade and investment, but also requirements that trading partners conform to European union democracy and human rights provisions to obtain new investment. Similarly, the Central American Free Trade Agreement (CAFTA) requires enforcement of environmental and labor legislation, whereas NAFTA's impact on work conditions and the environment has led to strenuous debate over whether North American or Mexican conditions will dominate trade and investment in Canada, Mexico and the United States. Foreign investment has evolved from bilateral to multilateral relations, forming a strategic part of globalization.

*See also* **Economic Development; Foreign Debt; Foreign Trade; Industrialization.**

BIBLIOGRAPHY

Birch, Melissa, 1991. "Changing Patterns of Foreign Investment in Latin America," In Baer, et al. (eds.) *Latin America: The Crisis of the Eighties and the*

*Opportunities of the Nineties*, edited by Werner Baer, Joseph Petry, and Murray Simpson. Urbana, IL: Bureau of Economics and Business, Board of Trustees of the University of Illinois, 1991.

Bird, Richard M. "Tax Incentives for Foreign Investment in Latin America: Do They Need to Be Harmonized?," Working Papers no. 601 (January 2006): International Tax Program, Rotman School of Management, University of Toronto.

Dunning, John H., and John Cantwell. *IRM Directory of Statistics of International Investment and Production.* New York: New York University Press, 1987.

Hirschman, Albert O. *How to Divest in Latin America, and Why.* Princeton, NJ: International Finance Section, Princeton University, 1969.

Jenkins, Rhys. *Transnational Corporations and Industrial Transformation in Latin America.* New York: St. Martin's Press, 1984.

Lewis, Cleona. *America's Stake in International Investments.* Washington, DC, The Brookings Institution, 1938.

Officer, Dennis T., and J. Ronald Hoffmeister. "American Depositary Receipts: A Domestic Alternative for International Diversification," *The Handbook of International Investing*, ed. Carl Beidleman. Chicago: Probus, 1987.

Pastor, Jr., Manuel, and Eric Hilt. "Private Investment and Democracy in Latin America.," *World Development* 21, no. 4 (1993): 489–507.

Paus, Eva. "Direct Foreign Investment and Economic Development in Latin America: Perspectives for the Future," *Journal of Latin American Studies* 21, no. 2 (May 1989): 221–239.

Pfeffermann, Guy P., and Andrea Madarassy. "Trends in Private Investment in Developing Countries, 1992." International Finance Corporation, Discussion Paper 14, 1992.

Randall, Laura. *The Political Economy of Venezuelan Oil.* New York: Praeger, 1987.

Sigmund, Paul E. *Multinationals in Latin America: The Politics of Nationalization.* Madison: University of Wisconsin Press, 1980.

Singh, Ajit, and Javed Hamid. *Corporate Financial Structures in Developing Countries.* Washington, DC: World Bank, 1992.

Stallings, Barbara. *Banker to the Third World: U.S. Portfolio Investment in Latin America, 1900–1986.* Berkeley: University of California Press, 1987.

Stone, Irving. "British Long-Term Investment in Latin America, 1865–1913," *Business History Review* 42, no. 3 (Autumn 1968): 311–339.

Stone, Irving. "British Direct and Portfolio Investment in Latin America Before 1914," *Journal of Economic History* 37, no. 3 (September 1977): 690–722.

Suchlici, Jaime. *Historical Dictionary of Cuba*, 2nd edition. Lanham, MD: Scarecrow Press, 2001.

Thirión, Jordy Micheli, and Rubén Oliver Espinoza. "Changing Patterns in Mexican Science and Technology Policy: 1990–2003: Still Far from Economic Development," In *Changing Structure of Mexico: Political, Social, and Economic Prospects*, 2nd edition, edited by Laura Randall. Armonk, NY: M.E. Sharpe, 2006.

United Nations. *World Investment Report.* New York: United Nations, 1991–.

United Nations. *Foreign Investment in Latin America and the Caribbean.* Santiago, Chile: United Nations, Economic Commission for Latin America and the Caribbean, 2005.

Welch, John H. "The New Face of Latin America: Financial Flows, Markets, and Institutions in the 1990s," *Journal of Latin American Studies* 25, no. 1 (1993): 1–24.

West, Peter J. "Latin America's Return to the Private International Capital Market," *CEPAL Review* 44 (1991): 59–78.

LAURA RANDALL

**FOREIGN TRADE.** Countries trade with one another to obtain goods and services that are of better quality than, less expensive than, or simply different from, those produced at home. Since independence, Latin American foreign trade conditions have been characterized first by free trade and unprecedented prosperity (1820–1930), then by protectionism (1930–1973), and increasingly since 1973 by trade liberalization. For many observers, foreign trade and external factors have played a central role in shaping the region's development. For others, these factors have played, at best, a supplementary, secondary role to dominant internal forces.

### THE YEARS OF PROSPERITY (1820–1930)

The foreign trade of most Latin American countries increased gradually between 1820 and 1860 as colonial restrictions were abolished and political stability in the region increased. As the vital collective need for freedom of international exchange, global movement and flow of commodities, people and capital increasingly is both recognized and satisfied, Latin America becomes an integral, vibrant segment of the global production system. Exports and imports rose sharply during the so-called golden age from 1860 to 1910. The speed of trade expansion slowed down, however, between 1910 and 1930, as rich mineral deposits were exhausted and the best lands had been incorporated into agriculture. The period from 1820 to 1930, which is often described as one of free trade, laissez faire, or "outward orientation," also included instances of protectionism associated with import duties imposed because of low administrative collection costs. These occurred because the cost of collecting import duties/taxes is often low (less than 5%) in comparison to other taxes such as those on income (often as high as 30%) or on sales (ranging from 10% to 50%).

Most of the products exported from Latin America between 1820 and 1930 have been described as "primary," that is, originating in agriculture or mining. All were "composite" in that they embodied not only value from agriculture and mining but also value added by manufacturing and services, such as trade, transportation, finance, and insurance.

Latin American foreign trade expanded explosively after 1860 owing to a convergence of favorable supply-and-demand factors. As the industrial revolution transformed Britain, Germany, France, and the United States, there emerged a strong demand for raw materials. Furthermore, Britain abolished tariffs protecting its domestic agriculture. A simultaneous technological revolution, which brought the invention of the steam engine, propeller, and metal hull, precipitated an unprecedented reduction in maritime transportation costs. Consequently, agricultural or mineral products from distant Latin America could now compete with those from the Caribbean and the more industrialized countries. Furthermore, rapidly rising incomes pushed up the demand for food, other consumer products, and raw materials. Unable to meet rapidly rising demand internally, Europe and North America increasingly turned to Latin America for supplies of more, better, and less expensive agricultural products and raw materials.

As a consequence, by the middle of the nineteenth century Argentina had become a major exporter of meat and hides, Cuba of sugar, Brazil of coffee, Venezuela of cacao, Peru of guano, and Chile of copper and wheat, which went to California during the gold rush years. Supplies of agriculture- and mining-based exports increased as new land was incorporated into production in Argentina, Uruguay, Brazil, and Chile. Export growth was facilitated by successive waves of immigrants, especially from southern Europe, into these regions. In addition, recurrent export bonanzas attracted large investments, first by the British and subsequently by the Americans, in agriculture, mining, railroads, public utilities, and industry. They also made it easier for Latin American governments to borrow in the capital markets of Europe and the United States.

The impact of free and rapidly growing, foreign trade on Latin American incomes was considerable but uneven. According to estimates by Angus Maddison, by 1929 real per capita gross domestic product (GDP) in U.S. dollars at 1965 factor cost (that is, calculated at the value of the dollar in 1965) had reached $908 in Argentina. This was almost double the income level of Japan ($485), about half that of the United States ($1,767), and more than 80 percent of the income in the United Kingdom ($1,105). Per capita incomes were, however, lower in other countries: In Brazil it was $175, in Chile $580, in Colombia $236, in Mexico $252, and in Peru $177.

By 1913, according to Maddison, exports of Latin American countries had reached levels close to or even higher than those in the rest of the world. Average Latin American per capita exports, expressed in U.S. dollars at then-current prices and exchange rates, were $31.90 (in Argentina it was $66.70; Brazil, $13.30; Chile, $41.20; Colombia, $6.80; Cuba, $66.70; Mexico, $9.90; Peru, $9.70; Uruguay, $61.60; and Venezuela, $10.90) as compared to an average for developed countries of $37.30 (France, $33.40; Germany, $35.90; Japan, $6.90; Netherlands, $67.00; United Kingdom, $56.00; and the United States, $24.50), $0.70 for China, and $2.60 for India. For Latin America, agriculture- and mining-based exports provided both an engine and a facilitator. The outflow of exports raised welfare by bringing a corresponding inflow of imports, immigrants, capital, institutions (e.g., broad-based educational), government (decentralization), finance (improved capital markets), transportation (railroads), and ideas. Latin America, Europe, and North America achieved an unprecedented degree of economic interdependence. Latin America supplied the agricultural and mineral primary commodities; Europe and the United States the industrial ones.

**Value of Latin American exports, 1913–1985**

(US $ million)

| | Argentina | Brazil | Chile | Colombia | Cuba | Mexico | Peru | Uruguay | Venezuela | Total |
|---|---|---|---|---|---|---|---|---|---|---|
| 1913 | 510.3 | 315.7 | 142.8 | 33.2 | 164.6 | 148.0 | 43.6 | 71.8 | 28.3 | 1,458.3 |
| 1929 | 907.6 | 461.5 | 282.8 | 123.5 | 272.4 | 284.6 | 116.8 | 92.0 | 149.3 | 2,690.5 |
| 1930 | 517.0 | 317.8 | 37.1 | 163.8 | 167.4 | 216.3 | 83.8 | 87.8 | 139.0 | 1,730.0 |
| 1931 | 428.0 | 241.1 | 19.7 | 102.2 | 118.9 | 166.7 | 49.2 | 45.2 | 113.3 | 1,282.3 |
| 1932 | 331.4 | 178.1 | 34.3 | 66.3 | 79.9 | 97.3 | 37.1 | 27.4 | 93.2 | 945.0 |
| 1933 | 357.4 | 224.3 | 51.9 | 61.1 | 85.0 | 103.8 | 46.1 | 40.3 | 114.3 | 1,084.0 |
| 1934 | 426.0 | 287.5 | 93.7 | 94.2 | 107.5 | 178.4 | 71.2 | 49.6 | 166.0 | 1,474.1 |
| 1935 | 500.5 | 271.9 | 95.7 | 80.6 | 127.8 | 209.3 | 75.0 | 76.9 | 182.2 | 1,619.9 |
| 1936 | 537.4 | 321.9 | 113.1 | 90.1 | 155.1 | 215.9 | 83.5 | 72.3 | 193.2 | 1,782.5 |
| 1937 | 757.9 | 350.5 | 192.3 | 104.5 | 185.9 | 247.7 | 93.3 | 78.1 | 253.8 | 2,264.0 |
| 1938 | 437.9 | 296.3 | 138.8 | 91.4 | 144.6 | 186.3 | 77.2 | 58.9 | 267.5 | 1,698.8 |
| 1950 | 1,178.0 | 1,359.0 | 281.0 | 394.0 | 642.0 | 532.0 | 193.0 | 254.0 | 929.0 | 5,762.0 |
| 1973 | 3,266.0 | 6,199.0 | 1,231.0 | 1,177.0 | 1,410.0 | 2,261.0 | 1,112.0 | 322.0 | 4,680.0 | 21,658.0 |
| 1985 | 8,396.0 | 25,639.0 | 3,823.0 | 3,552.0 | 8,567.0 | 22,108.0 | 2,996.0 | 855.0 | 12,272.0 | 84,626.0 |

SOURCE: Angus Maddison, "Economic and Social Conditions in Latin America, 1913–1950," in *Long-Term Trends in Latin American Economic Development*, edited by Miguel Urrutia (1991), p. 3.

**Table 1**

Latin American economies remained, however, highly dependent on one, or a few, export products. The following figures show the percentage of each country's total exports represented by individual products in 1929: Argentina (wheat, 29.2; maize, 17.6; frozen, chilled, and tinned meat, 12.8; linseed oil, 12.6), Brazil (coffee, 71.0), Chile (nitrates, 42.1; copper, 40.4), Colombia (coffee, 60.6; petroleum, 21.3), Cuba (sugar, 79.5), Mexico (silver, 20.6; other minerals, 47.0), Peru (petroleum, 29.7; copper, 22.4; wool, 21.0; sugar, 11.5; lead, 5.1), Uruguay (wool, 30.7; frozen, chilled, and tinned meat, 30.2; hides and skins, 12.7), and Venezuela (petroleum, 74.2; coffee, 17.2).

Between 1900 and 1930 agriculture-based products dominated exports from Colombia (coffee), Paraguay (quebracho, other timber), El Salvador (coffee), Brazil (coffee), Argentina (wheat, maize), Guatemala (coffee, bananas), Costa Rica (coffee, bananas), Cuba (sugar), Nicaragua (coffee, bananas), Uruguay (meat, wool), Ecuador (cacao), and Panama (bananas). Mining-based products dominated exports from Venezuela (copper, petroleum), Mexico (petroleum, silver), Chile (nitrates, copper), and Bolivia (tin). Peru exported both mineral (petroleum) and agricultural (cotton) products.

In the eyes of many, however, foreign trade was by no means an unmitigated blessing for the region before 1930. Demand and prices for primary exports fluctuated wildly, unleashing large shocks that Latin America could not always master. Because cyclical booms were followed regularly by precipitous declines, export revenues, exchange rates, capital inflows, trade-based tax revenues, and domestic income experienced unprecedented instability. Exhaustion of rich mineral deposits and fertile agricultural lands exposed the region's excessive dependence on primary commodities and its uncertain growth potential. Finally, some perceived that the benefits from trade accrued primarily to the workers and (foreign) capitalists of isolated production areas, without a lasting and positive impact on the majority of the population. Not even the worst prognosis, however, anticipated the calamitous collapse of foreign trade between 1929 and 1932 (see Table 1).

## THE YEARS OF PROTECTIONISM (1930–1973)

The degree of recognition and satisfaction of the collective need for freedom of trade and movement of people and capital experiences a precipitous decline after 1930. The Great Depression of the 1930s reduced the demand for primary export products, caused a decline in the relative prices of primary exports with respect to industrial imports, and suddenly stopped capital flows from Europe and the United States to Latin America. According to figures compiled by Angus Maddison, between 1929 and

1932 the average export volume for Argentina, Brazil, Chile, Colombia, Cuba, Mexico, Peru, and Venezuela fell by 35.8 percent, the average purchasing power of exports by 55.1 percent, the average import volume by 65.9 percent, and GDP by 18.5 percent. Chile suffered the most, with export volume declining by 71.2 percent, purchasing power of exports by 84.5 percent, import volume by 83.0 percent, and GDP by 26.5 percent. After initial adherence to old policy weapons and gold-standard rules, Latin America responded to the collapse of foreign trade with new approaches such as exchange controls, quantitative and bilateral trade restrictions, debt delinquency, and debt renegotiation with much larger write-offs than in the past.

The role of foreign trade was further reduced as a consequence of the protectionist, inward-oriented policies advocated after 1950 by Raúl Prebisch, the United Nations Economic Commission for Latin America, and their structuralist theory of development. Import-substitution policies, which promoted domestic production of previously imported industrial commodities, frequently resulted in the neglect of exports. This exacerbated the isolation of Latin America from the rest of the world. According to Maddison, the average ratio of merchandise exports to GDP at current prices for Argentina, Brazil, Chile, Colombia, Mexico, and Peru declined from 22.1 percent in 1929 to 9.1 percent in 1973. In contrast, the average ratio of merchandise exports to GDP for France, Germany, the Netherlands, the United Kingdom, and the United States increased from 15.8 percent to 19.2 percent during the same period.

Latin America's share of the value of world exports experienced a sharp decline, from 10.9 percent in 1950 to a meager 3.9 percent in 1992. Between 1950 and 1990, Argentina's share declined from 1.92 to 0.37 percent, Brazil's from 2.22 to 0.95 percent, Cuba's from 1.10 to 0.20 percent (in 1980), and Venezuela's from 1.91 to 0.53 percent. The decline in the relative importance of Latin America in world exports coincided with the widespread implementation of protectionist policies of import substitution. In contrast, between 1950 and 1990 the share of West Germany in the value of world exports increased from 3.29 to 12.39 percent and that of Japan from 1.37 to 8.69 percent. Similarly, Latin American imports as a percentage of world imports declined from 8.10 in 1950 to 2.82 in 1990. The introduction of neoliberal policies of trade liberalization, privatization, and stabilization, beginning with Chile in 1973, has contributed to a slight increase in the relative importance of Latin America in world imports and exports since 1989.

At least in part, the post-1930 decline in the relative importance of Latin America in world trade can be explained by its continued dependence on primary exports and the decline in their prices relative to industrial imports. As the figures presented in Table 2 reveal, the principal export commodities of most Latin American countries in 1985 were of agricultural and mineral origin. According to Richard Lynn Ground, Latin America's merchandise, or net barter, terms of trade fell from 100.0 in 1928 to 51.8 in 1933, reaching a level of 63.6 percent in 1987. (The merchandise, or net barter, terms of trade measure the relative movement of export prices against that of import prices. The merchandise terms of trade index is calculated as the ratio of a country's index of average export prices to its average import price index. Numbers above 100.0 are favorable, and those below 100.0 are unfavorable, relative to the base year.) After a sharp deterioration during the Great Depression, the merchandise terms of trade of Latin America recovered by 1950 (93.6 percent), declined in the 1960s (49.2 percent in 1965), rose again in the 1970s (76.7 percent in 1980), only to retreat in the 1980s (62.1 percent in 1986).

As a consequence of the Great Depression and the popularity of protectionist ideologies, most Latin American countries increased nominal tariffs after 1930. By the 1960-to-1965 period, average nominal tariffs had risen to 148.8 percent in Argentina, 85.0 percent in Brazil, 89.0 percent in Chile, and 139.0 percent (1972–1977) in Uruguay. Nominal tariffs on consumer goods were even higher, reaching 235.0 percent in Argentina (1960–1965) and 204.0 percent in Chile (1960–1965). The 1930-to-1973 period of protectionism and import-substitution industrialization has been gradually replaced by a new era of neoliberal trade liberalization.

Even though the 1930-to-1973 period is generally described as the age of import-substitution industrialization and inward-oriented, protectionist development, it also contained the seeds of trade liberalization efforts. Initially, such efforts were

**Principal export commodities of nineteen Latin American countries, 1985**

| Country | Commodity | Value (US$) | Total export revenues (%) |
|---|---|---|---|
| Argentina | Wheat | 1,133.2 | 13.5 |
| | Corn | 766.1 | 9.1 |
| Bolivia | Natural gas | 372.6 | 59.8 |
| | Tin | 186.7 | 29.9 |
| Brazil | Soybeans and products | 2,540.0 | 9.9 |
| | Coffee | 2,369.0 | 9.2 |
| Chile | Copper | 1,761.0 | 46.1 |
| Colombia | Coffee | 1,784.0 | 50.2 |
| | Fuel oil | 408.8 | 11.5 |
| Costa Rica | Coffee | 15,644.0 | 32.2 |
| (M. Colones) | Bananas | 10,706.0 | 22.1 |
| Dominican Republic | Sugar | 190.1 | 25.9 |
| | Ferronickel | 120.7 | 16.4 |
| | Doré | 113.6 | 15.5 |
| | Cocoa beans and products | 64.8 | 8.8 |
| | Coffee | 57.6 | 7.8 |
| Ecuador | Crude petroleum | 1,824.7 | 62.8 |
| | Bananas | 220.0 | 7.6 |
| El Salvador (M. Colones) | Coffee | 1,131.4 | 66.9 |
| Guatemala | Coffee | 450.8 | 42.5 |
| (M. Quetzales) | Cotton | 71.6 | 6.8 |
| Haiti | Coffee | 226.4 | 26.0 |
| (M. Gourdes) | Bauxite (1982) | 74.6 | 8.6 |
| Honduras | Bananas (1984) | 464.5 | 31.1 |
| (M. Lempiras) | Coffee (1984) | 338.2 | 22.7 |
| Mexico (B. Pesos) | Petroleum | 3,799.0 | 66.6 |
| Nicaragua | Cotton | 1,344.8 | 34.1 |
| (M. Córdobas) | Coffee | [illegible] | [illegible] |
| Panama | Bananas | 78.1 | 23.3 |
| (M. Balboas) | Shrimp | 59.8 | 17.8 |
| Paraguay | Cotton | 47,281.0 | 48.9 |
| (M. Guaraníes) | Soybeans | 32,134.0 | 33.2 |
| Peru | Copper | 464.2 | 15.6 |
| | Petroleum products | 418.1 | 14.1 |
| | Zinc | 268.9 | 9.1 |
| | Crude petroleum | 227.3 | 7.7 |
| Uruguay | Wool | 163.8 | 19.2 |
| | Meat | 117.9 | 13.8 |
| Venezuela (M. Bolívares) | Petroleum | 77,599.0 | 84.3 |

SOURCE: James W. Wilkie et al., eds., *Statistical Abstract of Latin America,* vol. 30, pt. 2 (1993), Table 2402, p. 747.

**Table 2**

largely cornerstones of the region's integration schemes aimed at promoting import substitution by enlarging the size of the market. The Latin American Free Trade Association (LAFTA), which was launched in 1961, brought together Argentina, Brazil, Chile, Colombia, Ecuador, Mexico, Paraguay, Peru, and Uruguay, which were joined later by Bolivia and Venezuela. In 1980 LAFTA was transformed into the Latin American Integration Association (LAIA), as a result of the Treaty of Montevideo. Sub regional groupings gave rise to the Central American Common Market (CACM) in 1960, the Andean Pact (ANCOM) in 1969, and the Caribbean Community and Common Market (CARICOM) in 1973. For the most part, these schemes lacked a clear commitment to free trade and made little progress.

### THE YEARS OF LIBERALIZATION (1973–)

Beginning with Chile in 1973, the degree of recognition and satisfaction of the collective need for freedom of trade and movement of resources, which had collapsed following the Great Depression of the 1930s, increases to historically unprecedented levels in many countries of Latin America. As part of their far-reaching liberalization policies in this period, Argentina, Bolivia, Brazil, Guatemala, Jamaica, Mexico, Nicaragua, Paraguay, Peru, and Uruguay have reduced tariffs, simplified tariff structures, and dismantled nontariff measures. Import licenses, quantitative restrictions, import prohibitions, discretionary licensing, additional taxes, and surcharges have been abolished or significantly reduced in Argentina, Bolivia, Brazil, Chile (where quantitative restrictions were prohibited by law), Colombia, Costa Rica, Jamaica, and Peru. Substantial reductions in tariffs and simplification of the tariff structure have been introduced in Argentina, Bolivia, Brazil, Chile, Costa Rica, Honduras, Jamaica, Mexico, Nicaragua, Peru, and Venezuela. By the years 1978 to 1981, average nominal tariffs had been reduced to 34.4 percent in Argentina, 10.0 percent in Chile, 28.0 percent in Colombia, 16.8 percent in Costa Rica, and 11.5 percent in Mexico.

### TRADE AGREEMENTS

Latin America has participated in such multilateral trade agreements as the General Agreement on Tariffs and Trade (GATT), which was created by the Bretton Woods Conference after World War II to reduce barriers to international trade, and the World Trade Organization (WTO), which replaced GATT after its 1986-1994 Uruguay Round. Cuba and Venezuela have criticized the decision-making process of the WTO as being dominated by a few developed nations at the detriment of developing nations. Many complaints have been raised in the GATT and the WTO about unfair protectionist and environmental practices. Trade integration begun in the 1960s, and has accelerated since the first Summit of the Americas Conference in December 1994.

As mentioned previously, a regional trade integration association, the Asociacion Latinoamericana de Integracion, ALADI (Latin American Integration Association, LAIA), was created in 1980 with Argentina, Bolivia, Brazil, Cuba, Chile, Colombia, Ecuador, Mexico, Paraguay, Peru, Uruguay, and Venezuela as members. Its central objective was the advancement of regional economic and social development through the establishment of a common market.

In addition to the multilateral and regional trade agreements, four major custom unions were created. The first customs union trade bloc, called the Andean Pact until 1996, was founded in 1969 by Bolivia, Chile, Colombia, Ecuador, and Peru with the signing of the Cartagena Agreement. In 1996 it was renamed the Andean Community of Nations (Co-munidad Andina de Naciones, CAN). Venezuela joined in 1973 and announced its potential withdrawal in 1996.

The second Southern Common Market, Mercosur or Mercosul (Mercado Comun del Sur) customs union movement originated in July 1990, when Argentina and Brazil agreed to the elimination of tariff barriers between them by December 1994. This agreement, which was extended to Paraguay and Uruguay on March 26, 1991, called for free intra-Cone movement of products by December 1995. The collapse of the Argentine economy in 2001 and continued internal conflicts between Argentina and Uruguay, Brazil and Argentina, Paraguay and Brazil, and so forth, have slowed economic integration.

On December 13, 1960, in a conference in Managua, Guatemala, El Salvador, Honduras, and Nicaragua established the Central American Common Market (CACM). Costa Rica joined the CACM in 1963. A phenomenal increase in trade between member nations had materialized by 1970. The organization was, however, paralyzed after the 1969 Football War between Honduras and El Salvador, which led to the latter's effective withdrawal, and by the political and social unrest in Central America in the 1970s and 1980s. A significant revival of the organization occurred in the 1990s. The fourth customs union/common market trade agreement is that of the Caribbean Community (CARICOM) which was established in 1973 with Antigua and Barbuda, Bahamas, Barbados, Belize, Dominica, Grenada, Guyana, Jamaica, Montserrat, St. Kitts-Nevis-Anguilla, St. Lucia, St. Vincent, and the Grenadines, Trinidad, and Tobago as members.

Among the free trade agreements, the most prominent is the North American Free Trade Agreement (NAFTA), which came into effect in January 1994, with Canada, Mexico, and the United States as members. Intra-NAFTA trade increased significantly as the majority of tariffs were eliminated upon the signing of the treaty and other tariffs were gradually phased out over a fifteen-year period. However, the per capita income gap between Mexico and the United States/Canada was not reduced, i.e., there was no economic convergence, and Mexican poverty rates were not substantially reduced. Furthermore, on January 1, 1995, Colombia, Mexico, and Venezuela established the G3 Free Trade Agreement. A planned withdrawal from this agreement was announced by Venezuelan President Hugo Chavez in May 2006. In addition, the Dominican Republic–Central America Free Trade Agreement (called DR–CAFTA) between the United States, Costa Rica, El Salvador, Guatemala, Honduras, Nicaragua, and the Dominican Republic has been ratified by all member nations except Costa Rica, which will hold a referendum on it. An ongoing proposal for a Free Trade Area of the Americas (FTAA), which is opposed by Cuba, Venezuela, Bolivia, Ecuador, and Nicaragua, was discussed on November 16, 2003, by representatives of thirty-four nations at a meeting in Mexico. A large number of bilateral free trade agreements have been signed in recent years by Mexico (16), Costa Rica (9), Chile (at least 15), Bolivia, Colombia, Dominican Republic, El Salvador, Honduras, Nicaragua, Panama, Peru, Uruguay, Dominican Republic, Guatemala, Venezuela and so forth. A union of South American and/or Central American nations is always contemplated. The widespread adoption of neoliberal philosophies of trade liberalization, privatization, and stabilization since 1973 has strengthened efforts to form or revive sub-regional trade blocks.

The value of Latin American exports reached $123 billion in 1990. The share of nonfuel primary composite commodities (food, live animals, beverages, tobacco, crude materials, and vegetable oils) in total exports had declined from 65.8 percent in

**Growth of merchandise trade, Latin America, 1970–1992**

| | Merchandise trade (million US$) | | Average annual growth rate (%) | | | | Terms of trade (1987=100) | |
|---|---|---|---|---|---|---|---|---|
| | | | Exports | | Imports | | | |
| | Exports 1992 | Imports 1992 | 1970–1980 | 1980–1992 | 1970–1980 | 1980–1992 | 1985 | 1992 |
| Argentina | 12,235 | 14,864 | 7.1 | 2.2 | 2.3 | −1.7 | 110 | 110 |
| Bolivia | 763 | 1,102 | −0.8 | 6.1 | 7.3 | 0.1 | 167 | 53 |
| Brazil | 35,956 | 23,115 | 8.5 | 5.0 | 4.0 | 1.5 | 92 | 108 |
| Colombia | 6,916 | 6,684 | 1.9 | 12.9 | 6.0 | 0.2 | 140 | 79 |
| Costa Rica | 1,834 | 2,458 | 5.2 | 5.2 | 4.2 | 3.9 | 111 | 85 |
| Chile | 9,646 | 9,456 | 10.4 | 5.5 | 2.2 | 3.5 | 102 | 118 |
| Dominican Republic | 566 | 2,178 | −2.0 | −2.2 | 1.3 | 2.5 | 109 | 113 |
| Ecuador | 3,036 | 2,501 | 12.5 | 4.8 | 6.8 | −2.0 | 153 | 91 |
| El Salvador | 396 | 1,137 | 1.3 | −0.4 | 4.6 | −2.9 | 126 | 65 |
| Guatemala | 1,295 | 2,463 | 5.7 | 0.0 | 5.8 | −0.1 | 108 | 79 |
| Honduras | 736 | 1,057 | 3.8 | −0.8 | 2.1 | −0.8 | 111 | 79 |
| Jamaica | 1,102 | 1,758 | −1.7 | 1.1 | −6.8 | 2.0 | 95 | 96 |
| Mexico | 27,166 | 47,877 | 13.5 | 1.6 | 5.5 | 3.8 | 133 | 120 |
| Nicaragua | 228 | 907 | 0.8 | −4.8 | 0.1 | −4.1 | 108 | 75 |
| Panama | 500 | 2,009 | 7.0 | 0.0 | 6.1 | −3.0 | 130 | 93 |
| Paraguay | 657 | 1,420 | 8.3 | 11.4 | 5.3 | 5.4 | 108 | 88 |
| Peru | 3,573 | 3,629 | 3.3 | 2.5 | −1.7 | −1.6 | 111 | 86 |
| Trinidad and Tobago | 1,869 | 1,436 | −7.3 | −2.4 | −9.6 | −9.7 | 156 | 100 |
| Uruguay | 1,620 | 2,010 | 6.5 | 2.9 | 3.1 | 1.3 | 89 | 97 |
| Venezuela | 13,997 | 12,222 | −11.6 | 0.6 | 10.9 | 0.6 | 174 | 157 |
| World | 3,575,198 | 3,785,925 | 4.0[a] | 4.9[a] | 4.0[a] | 4.9[a] | — | — |
| Latin American & Caribbean | 127,605 | 149,330 | −0.1[a] | 2.9[a] | 3.6[a] | 0.6[a] | 114[b] | 95[b] |

[a]Weighted average.
[b]Median value.

SOURCE: World Bank, *World Development Report 1994: Infrastructure for Development* (1994), pp. 186–187.

**Table 3**

1970 to 41.2 percent in 1990. The growth of merchandise trade during the period 1970 to 1992 is presented in Table 3.

Exports of manufactures in 1990 were $40.6 billion, or 32.9 percent of total exports, up from 10.9 percent in 1970. Exports of machinery and transportation equipment, which were dominated by internal combustion piston engines and passenger motor vehicles, equaled $13.9 billion, or 11.2 percent of total exports, up from 2.3 percent in 1970. These originated mainly in Brazil and Mexico. Exports of basic manufactures were $14.6 billion, or 11.8 percent of total exports, up from 4.4 percent in 1970. The principal exports of basic manufactures consisted of iron and steel, which originated mainly in Brazil, Mexico, and Argentina. Other important exports were leather from Argentina, Uruguay, and Brazil; textile yarn from Brazil, Mexico, Peru, and Argentina; nonmetallic mineral manufactures from Brazil, Mexico, and Colombia; and paper and paperboard from Brazil, Chile, and Mexico. In 1990 exports of chemicals, principally from Brazil, Mexico, and Argentina, reached $7.0 billion, or 5.7 percent of total exports, up from 2.7 percent in 1970. Brazil and Mexico were the major exporters of plastics.

Brazil accounted for 90 percent of all Latin American exports of footwear in 1990. Brazil and Colombia accounted for more than 60 percent of the region's exports of textile clothing, although Argentina, Barbados, Colombia, Costa Rica, the Dominican Republic, El Salvador, Guatemala, Guyana, Haiti, Honduras, Jamaica, Mexico, Panama, Paraguay, Peru, and Uruguay also produced large volumes.

Brazil, Mexico, and Argentina accounted for more than 80 percent of the region's foreign exchange earnings from manufactured exports. Other countries have achieved in recent years a significant growth of their manufactured exports. Chemical elements and compounds have been

**Geographical composition of Latin America and Caribbean exports, 1995–2005**

(in millions of US dollars)

| LAC countries' exports to: | 1995 | 1996 | 1997 | 1998 | 1999 | 2000 | 2001 | 2002 | 2003 | 2004 | 2005 |
|---|---|---|---|---|---|---|---|---|---|---|---|
| World | 229,663 | 263,692 | 289,851 | 285,374 | 305,783 | 369,301 | 354,020 | 354,928 | 387,900 | 488,078 | 577,657 |
| Latin America and Caribbean | 45,610 | 51,875 | 57,661 | 55,891 | 47,523 | 64,747 | 62,247 | 55,951 | 58,804 | 81,275 | 96,719 |
| Percent of exports to world | 19.9 | 19.7 | 19.9 | 19.6 | 15.5 | 17.5 | 17.6 | 15.8 | 15.2 | 16.7 | 16.7 |
| Non-LAC countries | 184,053 | 211,817 | 232,189 | 229,484 | 258,260 | 304,584 | 291,773 | 298,977 | 329,095 | 406,803 | 480,938 |
| Percent of exports to world | 80.1 | 80.3 | 80.1 | 80.4 | 84.5 | 82.5 | 82.4 | 84.2 | 84.8 | 83.3 | 83.3 |
| United States | 101,499 | 121,197 | 140,131 | 145,659 | 171,398 | 210,807 | 198,654 | 200,199 | 208,375 | 254,232 | 272,107 |
| Percent of exports to world | 44.2 | 46.0 | 48.3 | 51.0 | 56.1 | 57.1 | 56.1 | 56.4 | 53.7 | 52.1 | 47.1 |
| European Union | 38,703 | 39,126 | 40,539 | 40,069 | 40,616 | 42,445 | 42,907 | 43,506 | 50,657 | 62,789 | 79,662 |
| Percent of exports to world | 16.9 | 14.8 | 14.0 | 14.0 | 13.3 | 11.5 | 12.1 | 12.3 | 13.1 | 12.9 | 13.8 |
| Japan | 9,074 | 8,939 | 9,231 | 7,003 | 7,298 | 7,720 | 6,443 | 6,721 | 7,185 | 9,569 | 13,070 |
| Percent of exports to world | 4.0 | 3.4 | 3.2 | 2.5 | 2.4 | 2.1 | 1.8 | 1.9 | 1.9 | 2.0 | 2.3 |
| China (P.R.C.) | 2,618 | 2,878 | 3,326 | 2,643 | 2,127 | 3,800 | 5,116 | 6,493 | 11,162 | 15,531 | 23,594 |
| Percent of exports to world | 1.1 | 1.1 | 1.1 | 0.9 | 0.7 | 1.0 | 1.4 | 1.8 | 2.9 | 3.2 | 4.1 |

SOURCE: USAID, *LAC Databook 2006*, table 9.1, p. 106.

**Table 4**

exported from Trinidad and Tobago; plastics from Colombia, Uruguay, and Venezuela; other types of chemicals from Chile, Peru, Trinidad and Tobago, and Uruguay; clothing and textile yarn from Peru; plumbing, heating, and lighting equipment from Chile and Venezuela; and iron and steel from Colombia, Trinidad and Tobago, and Venezuela.

High-technology products (i.e., products having high research-and-development costs relative to total production costs) have grown at the impressive long-term annual rate of 20 percent. By 1989, Latin America's exports of high-technology products (chemicals and pharmaceuticals; plastic materials; nonelectrical and electrical machinery; transport equipment; and professional, scientific, and controlling instruments) reached $17.6 billion, with Brazil and Mexico accounting for 90 percent of the total. By the late 1980s high-technology export products represented 50 percent of Latin America's manufacturing exports.

The post-1930 policies of protectionism and import-substitution industrialization drastically changed the relative income position of most Latin American countries. Whereas per capita income (real per capita GDP in dollars at 1965 factor cost) of the export-oriented Japanese economy increased nearly twelve fold between 1913 ($332) and 1985 ($3,952), and that of the United States more than tripled (from $1,358 to $4,569), that of Argentina less than doubled (from $790 to $1,417). Per capita income in Brazil (which increased almost tenfold between 1913 [$118] and 1985 [$1,114]), Chile ($1,137), and Venezuela ($1,199) has come close to that of Argentina. Trade liberalization schemes aim at accelerating the region's growth of income through closer integration into international trade.

As the statistics of Table 4 demonstrate, exports from Latin America and the Caribbean (LAC) to the world increased from $230 billion in 1995 to $578 billion in 2005. LAC exports to LAC countries as a percentage of exports to the world declined from 19.9 in 1995 to 16.7 in 2005. LAC exports to non-LAC countries increased from 80.1 in 1995 to 83.3 in 2005. The share of exports during the same years to the United States increased (from 80.1 to 83.3), to the European Union fell (from 16.9 to 13.8), to Japan fell (from 4.0 to 2.3), and to China increased

**Geographical composition of Latin America and Caribbean imports, 1995–2005**

(millions of US dollars)

| LAC countries' imports from: | 1995 | 1996 | 1997 | 1998 | 1999 | 2000 | 2001 | 2002 | 2003 | 2004 | 2005 |
|---|---|---|---|---|---|---|---|---|---|---|---|
| World | 255,899 | 296,787 | 340,706 | 361,833 | 354,658 | 411,247 | 405,583 | 381,957 | 390,264 | 480,115 | 532,820 |
| Latin America and Caribbean | 46,222 | 53,778 | 61,180 | 60,919 | 53,453 | 66,060 | 64,676 | 58,838 | 63,833 | 87,046 | 107,063 |
| Percent of imports from world | 18.1 | 18.1 | 18.0 | 16.8 | 15.1 | 16.1 | 15.9 | 15.4 | 16.4 | 18.1 | 20.1 |
| Non-LAC countries | 209,676 | 243,008 | 279,526 | 300,914 | 301,206 | 345,187 | 340,907 | 323,119 | 326,430 | 393,069 | 425,757 |
| Percent of imports from world | 81.9 | 81.9 | 82.0 | 83.2 | 84.9 | 83.9 | 84.1 | 84.6 | 83.6 | 81.9 | 79.9 |
| United States | 106,442 | 124,483 | 153,696 | 166,293 | 173,537 | 198,543 | 181,889 | 166,214 | 164,635 | 183,359 | 210,241 |
| Percent of imports from world | 41.6 | 41.9 | 45.1 | 46.0 | 48.9 | 48.3 | 44.8 | 43.5 | 42.2 | 38.2 | 39.5 |
| European Union | 48,983 | 54,999 | 57,157 | 62,738 | 58,896 | 58,046 | 60,928 | 56,434 | 58,643 | 69.335 | 79,930 |
| Percent of imports from world | 19.1 | 18.5 | 16.8 | 17.3 | 16.6 | 14.1 | 15.0 | 14.8 | 15.0 | 14.4 | 15.0 |
| Japan | 13,389 | 13,230 | 15,232 | 16,638 | 13,922 | 16,559 | 18,171 | 18,078 | 15,828 | 21,868 | 17,928 |
| Percent of imports from world | 5.2 | 4.5 | 4.5 | 4.6 | 3.9 | 4.0 | 4.5 | 4.7 | 4.1 | 4.6 | 3.4 |
| China (P.R.C.) | 3,275 | 3,910 | 5,303 | 6,251 | 6,105 | 8,604 | 11,014 | 13,049 | 18,365 | 28,799 | 22,887 |
| Percent of imports from world | 1.3 | 1.3 | 1.6 | 1.7 | 1.7 | 2.1 | 2.7 | 3.4 | 4.7 | 6.0 | 4.3 |

SOURCE: USAID, *LAC Databook 2006*, table 9.2, p. 107.

**Table 5**

(from 1.1 to 4.1). During the same years, as the statistics of Table 5 reveal, imports by LAC from the world increased from $260 billion to $533 billion. LAC imports from LAC countries as a percentage of imports from the world increased (from 18.1 to 20.1), and from non-LAC countries decreased (from 81.9 to 79.9; from the United States from 41.6 to 39.5, from the European Union from 19.1 to 15.0, and from Japan from 5.2 to 3.4; but imports from China increased from 1.3 to 4.3).

Tables 5 and 6 provide information with respect to the relative importance of primary (Table 5; agricultural, i.e., food and raw materials, and mining, i.e., ores and other minerals, fuels and nonferrous metals) and manufactured (Table 6; iron and steel, chemicals, other semi manufactures, machinery and transport equipment, i.e., automotive products, office and telecom equipment and other machinery and transport equipment, textiles, clothing and other consumer goods) products expressed as percentages of total exports from Latin America and the Caribbean for 1995 and 2000–2005. Primary products range between 49.9 (1995) and 58.8 percent and manufactured ones between 41.2 (2002) and 50.1 (1995) percent of total exports. Countries exporting mainly primary products include Barbados, Costa Rica, El Salvador, Haiti, Jamaica, Mexico, and the Dominican Republic. Countries exporting primarily manufactured products include Argentina, Belize, Bolivia, Chile, Colombia, Nicaragua, Panama, Paraguay, Peru, and Venezuela.

There is a strong ongoing debate in Latin America and the rest of the world about the costs and benefits of free trade and globalization. Satisfying the collective need for free internal and external trade can increase technological (producing output with the least expensive inputs) and allocative (producing the best combination of outputs with the least expensive inputs) efficiencies. In most countries, however, the benefits have accrued primarily to highly productive export sectors, their privately- or state-owned corporations, powerful trade unions, and skilled labor. Furthermore, both internal and external trade liberalization can carry, and have carried, high short- and medium-term transition costs in the form of increased unemployment, inequality, poverty and misery. The degree to which free trade (satisfaction of the collective

**Exports of primary products as percentage of total exports of Latin America and Caribbean, 1995–2005**

(percentages of the total value of f.o.b. exports of goods)

| Country | 1995 | 2000 | 2002 | 2003 | 2004 | 2005 |
|---|---|---|---|---|---|---|
| Argentina | 33.9 | 32.4 | 30.5 | 27.8 | 28.8 | 30.7 |
| Barbados | 58.8 | 51.7 | 49.6 | 41.9[a] | 55.6[a] | 40.1[a] |
| Belize | 10.9 | 11.3 | 0.7 | 17.2[a] | 15.0[a] | 14.9[a] |
| Bolivia | 16.5 | 27.7 | 15.8 | 16.1 | 13.4 | 10.9 |
| Brazil | 53.1 | 58.0 | 52.6 | 51.5 | 53.0 | 52.7 |
| Chile | 13.2 | 16.0 | 16.8 | 16.2 | 13.2 | 13.7 |
| Colombia | 34.2 | 34.1 | 37.8 | 34.3 | 37.0 | 34.7 |
| Costa Rica | 25.1 | 65.5 | 63.3 | 65.4 | 62.7 | 63.8 |
| Ecuador | 7.6 | 10.1 | 10.3 | 12.0 | 9.3 | 9.0 |
| El Salvador | 38.8 | 48.4 | 58.4 | 57.1 | 59.9 | 57.5 |
| Guatemala | 27.7 | 32.0 | 35.0 | 40.3 | 41.8 | 39.8 |
| Guyana | — | — | 21.7 | 26.4 | — | — |
| Haiti | 62.1 | — | — | — | — | — |
| Honduras | 22.8 | 22.1 | 24.6 | 33.5 | 36.4 | 35.8 |
| Jamaica | 71.2 | 72.8 | 64.0 | 67.3[a] | 67.1[a] | — |
| Mexico[b] | 77.5 | 83.5 | 84.3 | 81.4 | 79.8 | 77.0 |
| Nicaragua | 20.3 | 7.5 | 18.3 | 11.8 | 10.6 | 10.4 |
| Panama | 20.3 | 15.9 | 12.0 | 11.1 | 10.0 | 9.1 |
| Paraguay | 19.3 | 19.3 | 14.9 | 13.7 | 12.7 | 17.1 |
| Peru | 13.5 | 16.9 | 17.0 | 17.0 | 16.9 | 14.7 |
| Dominican Republic | 77.7 | 40.7 | — | — | — | — |
| Trinidad and Tobago | 42.1 | 28.8 | 33.1 | 35.9[a] | 36.0[a] | 26.2[a] |
| Uruguay | 38.7 | 41.5 | 36.3 | 33.7 | 31.6 | 31.5 |
| Venezuela | 14.2 | 9.1 | 13.8 | 12.7 | 13.1 | 9.4[c] |
| **Total** | **49.9** | **58.2** | **58.8** | **55.7** | **53.6** | **50.0** |
| **LAIA[d]** | **50.5** | **59.1** | **59.5** | **56.2** | **54.0** | **50.5** |
| **Andean community[e]** | **18.6** | **16.3** | **19.7** | **18.6** | **18.9** | **15.5** |
| **MERCOSUR[f]** | **46.5** | **49.2** | **45.5** | **44.0** | **45.9** | **46.5** |
| **MERCOSUR, Boliviaand Chile[g]** | **40.1** | **43.1** | **40.4** | **39.3** | **39.5** | **39.8** |
| **CACM[h]** | **26.9** | **47.5** | **49.8** | **52.4** | **51.2** | **50.7** |
| **Other countries[i]** | **58.3** | **36.4** | **35.6** | **38.0** | **38.3** | **25.2** |

[a]Includes re-exports.
[b]Includes goods processed under maquila arrangements.
[c]Preliminary figures.
[d]Argentina, Bolivarian Republic of Venezuela, Bolivia, Brazil, Chile, Colombia, Ecuador, Mexico.
[e]Bolivarian Republic of Venezuela, Bolivia, Colombia, Ecuador and Peru.
[f]Argentina, Brazil, Paraguay and Uruguay.
[g]Argentina, Bolivia, Brazil, Chile, Paraguay and Uruguay.
[h]Costa Rica, El Salvador, Guatemala, Honduras and Nicaragua.
[i]Barbados, Belize, Dominican Republic, Guyana, Haiti, Jamaica, Panama and Trinidad and Tobago.

SOURCE: ECLAC, *Statistical Yearbook for Latin America and the Caribbean, 2006*, table 2.2.2.1, p. 186.

**Table 6**

economic need for free exchange in all input and output markets) increases technological and allocative efficiency in each country, and also increases the welfare of all inhabitants, depends on the degree to which the other collective needs for safety, security and protection of life and private and public property, equitable treatment by government, political freedom, social harmony, and environmental protection—also are satisfied. In other words, it also depends, on the one hand, on the degree to which a nation has attained procedural democracy (through satisfaction of the collective need for political freedom); and on the other hand, civil society (through satisfaction of the other collective needs).

No Latin American nation has as yet successfully created the economic, social and political conditions which could turn free trade into a reliable instrument of attaining universal, sustainable prosperity. By itself, free trade has been unable to lead to universal prosperity in the Americas. And without it, universal prosperity has remained a mirage. Cuba, Venezuela, Bolivia, and Argentina are, to varying degrees, against free trade. They are also forming their own trade bloc and distancing

**Exports of manufactured products as percentage of total exports of Latin America and the Caribbean, 1995–2005**

(percentages of the total value of f.o.b. exports of goods)

| Country | 1995 | 2000 | 2002 | 2003 | 2004 | 2005 |
|---|---|---|---|---|---|---|
| Argentina | 66.1 | 67.6 | 69.5 | 72.2 | 71.2 | 69.3 |
| Barbados | 41.2 | 48.3 | 50.4 | 58.1[a] | 44.4[a] | 59.9[a] |
| Belize | 89.1 | 88.7 | 99.3 | 82.8[a] | 85.0[a] | 85.1[a] |
| Bolivia | 83.5 | 72.3 | 84.2 | 83.9 | 86.6 | 89.1 |
| Brazil | 46.9 | 42.0 | 47.4 | 48.5 | 47.0 | 47.3 |
| Chile | 86.8 | 84.0 | 83.2 | 83.8 | 86.8 | 86.3 |
| Colombia | 65.8 | 65.9 | 62.2 | 65.7 | 63.0 | 65.3 |
| Costa Rica | 74.9 | 34.5 | 36.7 | 34.6 | 37.3 | 36.2 |
| Ecuador | 92.4 | 89.9 | 89.7 | 88.0 | 90.7 | 91.0 |
| El Salvador | 61.2 | 51.6 | 41.6 | 42.9 | 40.1 | 42.5 |
| Guatemala | 72.3 | 68.0 | 65.0 | 59.7 | 58.2 | 60.2 |
| Guyana | — | — | 78.3 | 73.6 | — | — |
| Haiti | 37.9 | — | — | — | — | — |
| Honduras | 77.2 | 77.9 | 75.4 | 66.5 | 63.6 | 64.2 |
| Jamaica | 28.8 | 27.2 | 36.0 | 32.7[a] | 32.9[a] | — |
| Mexico[b] | 22.5 | 16.5 | 15.7 | 18.6 | 20.2 | 23.0 |
| Nicaragua | 79.7 | 92.5 | [illegible] | [illegible] | 89.4 | 89.6 |
| Panama | 79.7 | 84.1 | 88.0 | 88.9 | 90.0 | 90.9 |
| Paraguay | 80.7 | 80.7 | 85.1 | 86.3 | 87.3 | 82.9 |
| Peru | 86.5 | 83.1 | 83.0 | 83.0 | 83.1 | 85.3 |
| Dominican Republic | 22.3 | 59.3 | — | — | — | — |
| Trinidad and Tobago | 57.9 | 71.2 | 66.9 | 64.1[a] | 64.0[a] | 73.8[a] |
| Uruguay | 61.3 | 58.5 | 63.7 | 66.3 | 68.4 | 68.5 |
| Venezuela | 85.8 | 90.9 | 86.2 | 87.3 | 86.9 | 90.6[c] |
| **Total** | **50.1** | **41.8** | **41.2** | **44.3** | **46.4** | **50.0** |
| **LAIA[d]** | **49.5** | **40.9** | **40.5** | **43.8** | **46.0** | **40.6** |
| **Andean community[e]** | **81.4** | **83.7** | **80.3** | **81.4** | **81.1** | **84.5** |
| **MERCOSUR[f]** | **53.5** | **50.8** | **54.5** | **56.0** | **54.1** | **53.5** |
| **MERCOSUR, Bolivia and Chile[g]** | **59.9** | **56.9** | **59.6** | **60.7** | **60.5** | **60.2** |
| **CACM[h]** | **73.1** | **62.6** | **50.2** | **47.6** | **48.8** | **49.3** |
| **Other countries[i]** | **41.7** | **63.6** | **64.4** | **62.0** | **61.7** | **74.8** |

[a]Includes re-exports.
[b]Includes goods processed under maquila arrangements.
[c]Preliminary figures.
[d]Argentina, Bolivarian Republic of Venezuela, Bolivia, Brazil, Chile, Colombia, Ecuador, Mexico, Paraguay, Peru and Uruguay.
[e]Bolivarian Republic of Venezuela, Bolivia, Colombia, Ecuador and Peru.
[f]Argentina, Brazil, Paraguay and Uruguay.
[g]Argentina, Bolivia, Brazil, Chile, Paraguay and Uruguay.
[h]Costa Rica, El Salvador, Guatemala, Honduras and Nicaragua.
[i]Barbados, Belize, Dominican Republic, Guyana, Haiti, Jamaica, Panama and Trinidad and Tobago.

SOURCE: ECLAC, *Statistical Yearbook for Latin America and the Caribbean*, 2006, table 2.2.2.2, p. 187.

**Table 7**

themselves from the rest of pro-free trade Latin American nations. Unless these aforementioned complementary collective needs are satisfied to similar degrees, free trade by itself cannot lead, and has not led, to technological and allocative efficiency, and a reduction in the historically high levels of relative inequality in total and labor incomes, as well as in educational, health, and other forms of capital endowments. The failure of Latin American countries to attain sustainable development, or deal effectively with its multiple problems of poverty, inequality, and underemployment, both during periods of relative free trade (1830–1930 and 1973–present) and protectionism (1930–1973), may be best understood in terms of the inability of their collective markets to attain high degrees of satisfaction of all these fundamentally complementary collective needs.

*See also* **Agriculture; Andean Pact; Caribbean Common Market (CARIFTA and CARICOM); Central American Common Market (CACM); Chicago Boys; Economic Commission for Latin America and the Caribbean (ECLAC); Economic Development; Free Trade Area of the Americas (FTAA);**

**Industrialization; International Monetary Fund (IMF); Labor Movements; Latin American Free Trade Association (LAFTA); Mining: Modern; Neoliberalism; North American Free Trade Agreement; Plantations; Prebisch, Raúl; World Bank.**

BIBLIOGRAPHY


Balassa, Bela. "Outward Orientation." In *Handbook of Development Economics*, vol. 2, edited by Hollis Chenery and T. N. Srinivasan. Amsterdam and New York: North-Holland, 1989.

Bruton, Henry. "Import Substitution." In *Handbook of Development Economics*, vol. 2, edited by Hollis Chenery and T. N. Srinivasan. Amsterdam and New York: North-Holland, 1989.

*CEPAL Review*. Santiago: United Nations, Economic Commission for Latin America and the Caribbean (ECLAC), 1976–.

Cole, Harold L., Lee E. Ohanian, Alvaro Riascos, and James A Schmitz, Jr. "Latin America in the Rearview Mirror." *Journal of Monetary Economics* 52:1 (2005), 69–107.

Díaz Alejandro, Carlos F. *Essays on the Economic History of the Argentine Republic*. New Haven, CT: Yale University Press, 1970.

Ground, Richard Lynn. "The Genesis of Import Substitution in Latin America." *CEPAL Review* 36 (December 1988), 179–203.

*Latin America and the Caribbean: Selected Economic and Social Data*. Washington, DC: United States Agency for International Development (USAID), 2006.

Levin, Jonathan V. *The Export Economies: Their Pattern of Development in Historical Perspective*. Cambridge, MA: Harvard University Press, 1960.

Lewis, Stephen R., Jr. "Primary Exporting Countries." In *Handbook of Development Economics*, vol. 2, edited by Hollis Chenery and T. N. Srinivasan. Amsterdam and New York: North-Holland, 1989.

Lord, Montague J. "Latin America's Exports of Manufactured Goods." In *Economic and Social Progress in Latin America*. Washington, DC: Inter-American Development Bank, 1992.

Maddison, Angus. "Economic and Social Conditions in Latin America, 1913–1950." In *Long-Term Trends in Latin American Economic Development*, edited by Miguel Urrutia. Washington, DC: Inter-American Development Bank, 1991.

Mamalakis, Markos. "The Export Sector, Stages of Economic Development, and the Saving-Investment Process in Latin America." *Economia Internazionale* 23, no. 4 (1970), 283–307.

Mamalakis, Markos. "The Role of Government in the Resource Transfer and Resource Allocation Processes: The Chilean Nitrate Sector, 1880–1930." In *Government and Economic Development*, edited by Gustav Ranis. New Haven, CT: Yale University Press, 1971.

Mamalakis, Markos. *The Minerals Theory of Growth: The Latin American Evidence*. Göttingen, West Germany: Ibero-Amerika Institut für Wirtschaftsforschung, 1978.

Mamalakis, Markos J. "Social Justice in a Global Environment: A Theory of Natural Law and Social Justice." In *The Quest for Social Justice III: The Morris Fromkin Memorial Lectures 1992–2002*, edited by Peter G. Watson-Boone. Milwaukee: UWM Libraries, University of Wisconsin–Milwaukee, 2005.

Mamalakis, Markos J. "Sustainable Democracy and the Golden Rules." *Global Currents*, Center for International Education, University of Wisconsin–Milwaukee, 1:2 (Spring 2005), 18–19.

*Statistical Yearbook for Latin America and the Caribbean*. Santiago: United Nations Commission for Latin America and Caribbean (ECLAC), 2006.

Wilkie, James W., ed. *Statistical Abstract of Latin America*, vol. 30, part 2. Los Angeles: Latin American Institute, University of California, Los Angeles, 1993.


MARKOS J. MAMALAKIS

**FOREIGN TRAVELERS IN LATIN AMERICA.** European travelers began to write about their adventures in the New World in the seventeenth century. At first the writings were purely descriptive, although often colored by the specific interests of the writer. The genre provides a comprehensive introduction to every aspect of Latin America. There are literally thousands of books written by travelers who visited the region; the countries most frequently commented on are Mexico, Brazil, and Argentina. Some writers were experts on the area they describe; others digested their experiences in a day or two, just enough time to produce a generalized reaction to the little that they saw. Travelers who write books come from every walk of life: They are missionaries, soldiers, adventurers, artists, and scientists who reinforce their words with drawings and graphic material; others are businessmen, retired statesmen, venturesome women, novelists, photographers, and professional journalists dedicated to the area of travel.

One of the earliest chronicles of a European's sojourn in South America was written by an Austrian Jesuit missionary, Antonio Sepp, who traveled to Buenos Aires in the 1690s. He describes the arduous sea journey and the precariousness of the Spanish settlements he visited between Buenos Aires and Asunción, far up the Paraná River, in Paraguay. His text provides a colorful sketch of Jesuit entrepreneurship and effectiveness. In subsequent centuries botanists sketched plants, artists painted watercolors of local customs, and cartographers gradually adjusted the mythical boundaries of the New World to the reality that sailors needed for navigation.

At first, visitors concentrated on what they saw: the landscape, the vegetation, and the native population. As the Spanish occupation expanded, foreign writers began to concentrate on the ins and outs of Spanish occupation: the compounds of the different Catholic missionary groups, the search for mineral wealth, and the eventual competition between mainland Spaniards and their local offspring, often born of Indian or in some cases black mothers. Independence brought new viewpoints, and nineteenth-century economic expansion and population growth produced a wave of optimistic predictions from enthusiastic authors for a miraculous future, from Mexico to Argentina.

**President Theodore Roosevelt and Marshal Cândido Rondon, Mato Grosso, Brazil, 1913–1914.** Since the early 1700s, Westerners have been documenting their travels in Latin America. While some visitors focus on peoples and cultures, other adventurers have set off to explore less inhabited areas, looking for lost cities, uncharted rivers, and precious natural resources. © BETTMANN/CORBIS

Books range from light, highly readable panoramas, such as the U.S. novelist Richard Henry Dana's *To Cuba and Back: A Vacation Voyage* (1859) or the British novelist Christopher Isherwood's revealing chronicle *The Condor and the Cows* (1949), to the more technical studies of U.S. Naval researchers who investigated the Amazon valley in the 1850s or Alexander von Humboldt and Charles Darwin's scientific reflections on their trips through different parts of South America. Stretching the genre, one could also include Herman Melville's *Moby-Dick*, the novelized version of his travels on a whaling ship, and Joseph Conrad's *Nostromo* and *A Set of Six*.

Internationally recognized statesmen such as Lord Bryce and Georges Clemenceau provided insights into their fields of interest, especially in terms of the geopolitical future of the hemisphere. Theodore Roosevelt related his adventures in the Amazon basin and anticipated an animated genre dedicated to the legends of the Amazon and the search for elusive city of El Dorado. Julian Duguid's *Green Hell: Adventures in the Mysterious Jungles of East Bolivia* (1931) remains a classic in the field, as does Peter Fleming's *Brazilian Adventure*, written three years later.

Patagonia was another region that fascinated writers and their readers. The 1977 best-seller *In Patagonia*, by the English travel writer, novelist, and photographer Bruce Chatwin, described with passion and insight the intimate details of an overland tour through Southernmost Argentina.

Mexico has been the prerogative of renowned English novelists, such as D. H. Lawrence, Aldous Huxley, and Graham Greene, who visited that country in the 1920s and 1930s and wrote sensitive accounts of their experiences. Lawrence Durrell and V. S. Naipaul have touched on Argentina in rather critical overviews, and Evelyn Waugh wrote about his three-month adventure in the backlands of British Guiana and Brazil in the early 1930s.

Businessmen have provided another point of view, sometimes euphoric and sometimes disgruntled, according to the personal experiences of each. John Foster Fraser wrote *The Amazing Argentine* in 1910: He, like so many others, predicted a brilliant future for the up-and-coming country. The Englishman Thomas A. Turner, by contrast, a self-proclaimed dyspeptic, criticized the Argentine's business customs and predicted a less prosperous future.

Another group of writers, less frequently encountered, who provide a parallel version of life in Latin America are the women travel writers. The Bostonian Charlotte Cameron wrote *A Woman's Winter in South America* in 1910, and Annie Peck produced *The South American Tour* in 1913. The books were designed to prepare a woman of means for the adventures she would meet in her sojourn in Spanish America. The Swedish traveler Dr. Hanna Rydh described her experiences a generation later in *Argentine to Andes*, continuing the tradition of women preparing women for the Latin American experience.

Many of the interpretations that the peripatetic travelers made were based, at best, on hearsay, and time has proved their lack of validity. Also, much of the material has become outdated and only retains its value in its contribution to a generalized understanding of time and place. John Gunther's classic chronicles of his world travels, based on well-researched and carefully edited views, are examples of practical travel writing that survives. In other cases, the writing itself is good enough to outweigh the errors in facts and interpretation.

There are a number of anthologies that include fragments of texts from the writings of a selection of travelers. Examples are *Viajeros Extranjeros por Colombia*, edited in Bogotá; *La ruta argentina*, compiled by Christian Kupchik; and Frank MacShane's *Impressions of Latin America*, which covers five centuries of travel by English and North American travelers, from Sir Francis Drake to Waldo Frank. Reading these anthologies provides a varied and anecdotal introduction to what has intrigued visitors and voyagers as they discover the idiosyncrasies of a world that is new to them. Travel writing often provides the reader with an awareness of the peoples of the region, their aspirations and frustrations that is complementary to the information found in more formal academic texts.

*See also* **Amazon Region; Naipaul, V. S.; Patagonia; Travel Literature.**

BIBLIOGRAPHY

Cameron, Charlotte. *A Woman's Winter in South America.* Boston: Small, Mayward, c. 1910.

Dana, Richard Henry, Jr. *To Cuba and Back: A Vacation Voyage.* Boston: Ticknor & Fields, 1859.

Díaz Granados, José Luis. *Viajeros Extranjeros por Colombia.* Bogota: Presidencia de la República, 1997.

Duguid, Julian. *Green Hell: Adventures in the Mysterious Jungles of East Bolivia.* New York: Century, 1931.

Fleming, Peter. *Brazilian Adventure.* New York: Scribners, 1933.

Green, Graham. *The Lawless Roads: A Mexican Journey.* London: Longmans, 1939.

Herndon, William Lewis. *Exploration of the Valley of the Amazon.* Washington, DC: Taylor & Maury, 1854. New edition, edited and with a foreword by Gary Zinder, New York: Grove Press, 2000.

Huxley, Aldous. *Beyond the Mexique Bay: A Traveller's Journal.* London: Chatto & Windus, 1934.

Isherwood, Christopher. *The Condor and the Cows.* London: Methuen, 1949.

Kupchik, Christian, ed. *La ruta argentina.* Buenos Aires: Grupo Editorial Planeta, 1999.

Lawrence, D. H. *Mornings in Mexico.* London: Martin Secker, 1927.

McShane, Frank, ed. *Impressions of Latin America: Five Centuries of Travel and Adventure by English and North American Writers.* New York: William Morrow, 1963.

Merwin, Mrs. George B. *Three Years in Chile.* Columbus, Ohio, 1863. Edited by C. Harvey Gardiner. Carbondale, IL: Southern Illinois University Press, 1966.

Peck, Annie S. *The South American Tour.* New York: George H. Doran, 1913.

Roosevelt, Theodore. *Through the Brazilian Wilderness and Papers on Natural History.* New York: Scribners, 1914.

Rydh, Dr. Hanna. *Argentine to Andes.* London: Blackie & Sons, 1940.

Sepp, Anthony. *An Account of a Voyage from Spain to Paraquaria.* Nuremberg, 1697.

Waugh, Evelyn. *Ninety-Two Days: The Account of a Tropical Journey through British Guiana and Part of Brazil.* New York: Farrar & Rinehart, 1934.

EDWARD L. SHAW

**FORESTS.** The forests of the Neotropic plant realm, which corresponds roughly to modern Latin America, had been reduced in area by the last glacial epoch and were once again on the advance as the first humans entered the region. For them this was a strange biotic world. South America had evolved largely in isolation from the other continents, and its myriad species were mostly unique to it. Tropical and subtropical evergreen forest covered the Caribbean coast and highlands of Mesoamerica and northern South America, the Pacific coast of modern Colombia and Ecuador, the vast basin of the Amazon, and the coast of modern Brazil. On the rain-shadowed inland slopes of these regions, evergreens were replaced by deciduous trees. A broad swath of what is now Brazil's Northeast and Center-West and northern Argentina was covered with forests habituated to dry seasons, wildfire, and aluminum-toxified soils. In southern Brazil and along the southernmost Andes there are forests of araucaria, cyprus, and beech that display a close relationship to the forests of Australia and New Zealand.

The first human groups to arrive in the Western Hemisphere preferred open country, gallery forests, flood plains, and estuaries, where hunting and fishing were most productive. As they came to adopt agriculture, however, the forest necessarily became their principal resource. The technique of slash-and-burn farming offered extremely high yields for low labor input. It could be practiced even on poor soils and proved, at low levels of human population density, relatively stable. The continued burning of forest over a period of several thousand years, however, probably modified forest composition even where it did not eliminate it. In a few areas, notably highland Mesoamerica and northwestern South America, slash-and-burn farming had to be replaced by more laborious irrigation systems, representing a more permanent replacement of forest.

### SEVERE FOREST DEGRADATION

The European invasion of the Neotropic realm marked the beginning of extreme modification and degradation of its forests. Slash-and-burn could now be practiced with iron tools that made weeding easier, thereby encouraging the exploitation of cleared patches until soils were eroded and forests could not reestablish themselves. Most critically, the Spanish and Portuguese brought with them cattle, sheep, and horses and a social tradition that favored their maintenance in large numbers, unintegrated with farming. Cattle replaced farmers as soon as soils degraded, and their continued grazing prevented trees from returning. Fertile forest soils located near seaports were given over to plantation crops, especially sugarcane. The forests were mined for the large quantities of fuelwood needed by the sugar mills. Some of the smaller Caribbean islands lost nearly all of their forests to the plantations. Other colonial activities, especially gold and silver mining, deforested limited areas.

The eighteenth and nineteenth centuries witnessed the growth of forest extraction, as New World populations grew once again and as urban and industrial demand increased in Europe and the United States. Dyewoods had been exploited since the earliest days of colonization. Numerous exotic products were sought in the forest: sarsaparilla, supposedly a remedy for syphilis; quinine, decidedly a remedy for malaria; and medicinals, orchids, pelts, chicle, tannins, resins, feathers, balsams, and essences. Hardwoods suitable for fine cabinetry were logged in lowlands close to sizable streams and harbors. Most important of all was wild rubber, for which the market grew rapidly from the 1840s onward.

The installation of railroads made possible in some areas a fuller exploitation of highland timber resources. Brazilian araucaria forest, one of the few homogeneous and, therefore, easily exploitable forests in South America, was nearly eliminated. Railroads extended the range of plantation agriculture and encouraged the inflow of small farmers seeking subsistence or cash crops for the city market. The penetration of forests was greatly accelerated in the

**Slash and burn logging in the Brazilian rainforest, Rondonia, c. late twentieth century.** Deforestation continues at a steady rate in the Amazon, home to the world's largest rainforest. Industrial agriculture—cattle ranching—is the leading source of deforestation, though the subsistence activities of poor farmers also account for significant forest loss. © STEPHANIE MAZE/ CORBIS

1960s and 1970s, as heavy road vehicles became common and governments invested more and more in road and bridge building in the interior.

Government policy and foreign capital have been blamed for the heedless destruction of the forest. Frontier expansion was politically advantageous. It reduced the pressure for land reform, created grateful constituencies, and fortified sovereignty in border areas. Timber and cattle grazing have attracted foreign capital, and foreign markets have been a principal motive for government incentives. In Central America, for example, the forest has been largely replaced by pasture for cattle grazing. However, products such as timber and beef are also important inputs to the growing economies and populations of Latin America. Wood fuel and charcoal remain important sources of energy, not only in households, but even in modern sectors, such as Brazil's steel industry. Furthermore, long-term inflation has enhanced the speculative value of rural properties. Pressure on the forest, therefore, has continued regardless of government policies.

## CONSERVATION

Conservationism is practiced very little in forestry. The introduction of the chain saw greatly increased the speed of timber felling, but the industry is in most places undercapitalized. Fifty to one hundred trees of lesser value may be destroyed to obtain one specimen. This waste is partly the result of the extraordinary richness of species of the tropical forest. Unfortunately, this same complexity makes it unlikely that even rationally logged forests will grow back to resemble their original state. Reforestation has taken place on a scale insufficient to meet requirements for industrial raw materials such as

**Argentine forest in Los Alerces National Park, c. late twentieth century.** This Argentine national park, created in 1937, is representative of a forestry conservationist practice and gets its name from the large evergreens it was designed to protect. © ANTHONY JOHN WEST/CORBIS

plywood, chipboard, and paper pulp. Nearly all of the plantings are of fast-growing exotic species, especially eucalyptus and pines, not of species that would contribute to the restoration of native ecosystems. Large-scale reforestation has relied heavily on tax incentives, which are unpredictable.

A conservationist impulse has been present in at least a few Latin American countries since the turn of the twenty-first century and even before. Since the 1970s and 1980s, consciousness of the scientific, tourist, and economic values of the forests has grown and an environmental movement of considerable dimension has spread, favored by a renewed democratic political climate. Large areas of forest have been set aside as reserves and national parks, and conservationist laws have been strengthened. The conservationist practices of native peoples and forest dwellers have been given more attention, and many are beginning to understand and act upon the global implications of nature protection. It remains to be seen whether this new consciousness will be effective in protecting remaining forest resources.

*See also* **Agriculture; Cinchona; Colonialism; Environmental Movements; Lumber Industry; Mining: Modern.**

BIBLIOGRAPHY

Brailovsky, Antônio Elio. "Política ambiental de la generación del 80." In *Tres estudios Argentinos*, by Nora L. Siegrist de Gentile, Noemí Girbal de Blacha, and Antônio Elio Brailovsky. Buenos Aires: Editorial Sudamericana, 1982.

Contreras M., Rodolfo. *Más allá del bosque: La explotación forestal en Chile.*. Santiago, Chile: Editorial Amerinda, 1989.

Crosby, Alfred W. *Ecological Imperialism: The Biological Expansion of Europe, 900–1900.* New York; Cambridge, U.K.: Cambridge University Press, 1986.

Flick, Frances. *The Forests of Continental Latin America.* Washington, DC: U.S. Government Printing Office, 1952.

Fittkau, E. J., J. Illies, H. Klinge, G. H. Schwabe et al., eds., *Biogeography and Ecology of South America*. The Hague, Netherlands: W. Junk, 1969.

Parsons, James J. *Hispanic Lands and Peoples: Selected Writings of James J. Parsons*, edited by William M. Denevan. Boulder, CO: Westview Press, 1989.

Rodríguez C., Silvia, and Emilio Vargas M. *El recurso forestal en Costa Rica: Políticas públicas y sociedad, 1970–1984*. Heredia, Costa Rica: Editorial de la Universidad Nacional, 1988.

Vos, Jan de. *La paz de Dios y del Rey: La conquista de la Selva Lacandona, 1525–1821*. Chiapas, Mexico: Fonapas/Gobierno del Estado de Chiapas, 1980.

Vos, Jan de. *Oro verde: La conquista de la Selva Lacandona por los madereros tabasqueños, 1822–1949*. Villahermosa, Mexico: Gobierno del Estado de Tabasco, Instituto de Cultura de Tabasco, 1988.

WARREN DEAN

## FORNER, RAQUEL (1902–1988).

Raquel Forner (*b.* 22 April 1902; *d.* 10 June 1988), Argentine painter. Born in Buenos Aires, Forner studied at the National Academy of Fine Arts in Buenos Aires, graduating in 1923, and with Othon Friesz in Paris (1929–1930). In 1932 she helped found the first private school of fine arts in Buenos Aires. She became a member of the Royal Society of Arts (England) in 1951 and received the National Prize for painting (Buenos Aires, 1942) and the grand prize at the First American Biennial of Art (Córdoba, Argentina, 1962). Through her encounter with the surrealists in Paris, Forner discovered the cosmic character of experience and endeavored to give it structural expression. In later years her paintings focused on a science-fiction interpretation of the cosmos, as exemplified in *Black Astrobeings*. From the technical point of view her compositions are highly unusual in structure; color plays a secondary role, inclining toward the monochromatic. Forner's work reflects the image of the human soul amid the complexity of the world.

*See also* **Argentina: The Twentieth Century; Art: The Twentieth Century; Education: Overview.**

BIBLIOGRAPHY

*Museum of Modern Art of Latin America* (1985).

Vicente Gesualdo, Aldo Biglione, and Rodolfo Santos, *Diccionario de artistas plásticos en la Argentina* (1988).

*Additional Bibliography*

Forner, Raquel, and Fermín Fèvre. *Raquel Forner*. Buenos Aires: Editorial El Ateneo, 2000.

Lorenzo Alcalá, May. "Raquel Forner: Del apocalipsis a la utopia." *Cuadernos Hispanoamericános* 629 (Nov. 2002): 103–112.

AMALIA CORTINA ARAVENA

## FORRÓ.

Forró is the generic name given to music from the rural areas of northeastern Brazil. Although the word may be used in a more strict sense, it usually refers to a fairly wide variety of styles of dance music with roots in European couple dancing. The word itself is commonly though not uncontroversially attributed to the parties held either by English railroad companies in the late nineteenth century or on air bases in the northeast during World War II, when English speakers promoted celebrations "for all." Others, however, maintain that it derives from *forrobodó* or *forrobodança*, words used to refer to celebrations centered around dancing.

The migration of northeasterners to the central southern areas of Brazil beginning in the 1940s gave the music more national appeal, if not a national identity. The style is indelibly associated with the career of Pernambuco-born accordionist, singer, and composer Luiz Gonzaga, whose radio broadcasts in the 1940s and 1950s made many outside of the northeast aware of the music for the first time. After declining in popularity with the rise of bossa nova and rock music in the late 1950s and 1960s, it made a comeback in the 1970s. For many in Brazil, the music is primarily associated with the saints' day festivals celebrated most distinctively in the northeast, such as the São João (St. John's festival). Although musicians more recently have employed electric instruments to play the music, it is still the accordion, bass drum, and triangle combination that gives the music its distinctive sound and propulsion.

*See also* **Gonzaga, Luiz; Music: Popular Music and Dance.**

BIBLIOGRAPHY

Albuquerque Jr., Durval Muniz de. *A invenção do Nordeste e outras artes*, 2nd edition. Recife: Editora Massangana, 2001.

Bishop, Jack. "Vem Arrasta-pé: Commoditizing *Forró* Culture in Pernambuco, Brazil." In *Musical Cultures of Latin America: Global Effects, Past and Present,* edited by Steven Loza. Los Angeles: UCLA Department of Ethnomusicology and Systematic Musicology, 2003.

Feretti, Mundicarmo Maria Rocha. *Baião dos dois: A música de Zedantas e Luiz Gonzaga no seu contexto de produção e sua atualização na década de 70.* Recife: Editora Massanga, 1988.

McCann, Bryan. *Hello, Hello Brazil: Popular Music in the Making of Modern Brazil.* Durham, NC: Duke University Press, 2004.

Murphy, John P. *Music in Brazil: Experiencing Music, Expressing Culture.* New York: Oxford University Press, 2006.

Sá, Sinval. *O sanfoneiro do Riacho da Brígida: Vida e andanças de Luiz Gonzaga, rei do baião.* Fortaleza, Brasil: Edições a Fortaleza, 1966.

ANDREW J. KIRKENDALL

**FORTALEZA.** Fortaleza, capital of the state of Ceará in Brazil. On the northern coast of the Brazilian bulge, the city in 2006 has a population of 2.4 million in the city proper and 3,415,455 in the metropolitan area . Ceará's principal commercial center, Fortaleza is a port of call for European and North American lines and for coastal steamers. The harbor, previously an open roadstead (less sheltered harbor), is now protected by a breakwater with port facilities at the Ponta de Mucuripe, 3.6 miles to the east. Chief exports include sugar, cotton, hides, carnauba wax, and other agricultural products of the region.

Originating in the early seventeenth century as a village adjoining a Portuguese fort, hence its name, the settlement was occupied by the Dutch in the mid-1600s. Fortaleza became the capital of the captaincy of Ceará in 1810, receiving city status and designation as the provincial capital in 1823.

Fortaleza's population swelled during northeastern Brazil's periodic droughts as Sertanejos (inhabitants of the backlands) flocked to cities in search of work or relief. The capital was often ill equipped to meet such crises. During the drought of 1877–1879, the provincial administration in Fortaleza, overwhelmed by problems in the city, stopped sending aid to the interior.

*Sertanejos* sometimes manifested antagonism toward the government at Fortaleza. In 1914, followers of Padre Cícero Romão Batista, a priest in Joaseiro (now Juazeiro Do Norte) popular among the *sertanejos,* marched on Fortaleza. Governor Marcos Rabelo, striving to avert bloodshed, entrusted the state government to federal authorities.

*See also* **Batista, Cícero Romão; Brazil, Geography; Messianic Movements: Brazil.**

BIBLIOGRAPHY

Ralph Della Cava, *Miracle at Joaseiro* (1970).

*Additional Bibliography*

Jucá, Gisafran Nazareno Mota. *Verso e reverso do perfil urbano de Fortaleza, 1945–1960.* Fortaleza: Governo do Estado do Ceará, Secretaria da Cultura e Desporto; São Paulo: Annablume, 2000.

Nunes, Márcia Vidal. *Rádio e política: Do microfone ao palanque: Os radialistas políticos em Fortaleza, 1982-1996.* São Paulo: Annablume, 2000.

Pessar, Patricia R. *From Fanatics to Folk: Brazilian Millenarianism and Popular Culture.* Durham, NC: Duke University Press, 2004.

Silva Filho, Antonio Luiz Macêdo. *Paisagens do consumo: Fortaleza no tempo da Segunda Grande Guerra.* Fortaleza: Museu do Ceará, Secretaria da Cultura e Desporto do Ceará, 2002.

CARA SHELLY

**FORT ROSS.** Fort Ross, located in Spanish California, marked the southernmost point of Russian expansion in North America. Beginning in the first decade of the nineteenth century, representatives of the Russian-American Company in Alaska visited Spanish Alta California in search of both grain for the Alaskan colonies and sea otters and fur seals. In 1811 the company's directors approved a plan to establish an agricultural colony north of the Spanish territory in Alta California. Accordingly, in March 1812, Ivan Kuskov established Fort Ross on the coast some eighteen miles north of Bodega Bay. By 1820, Fort Ross had a population of 273, including Russians, Aleuts from Alaska, people of mixed Russian–Aleut ancestry, and local Kashaya Pomo and Coast Miwok tribes.

The agricultural operation at Fort Ross and at several farms established in the Bodega Bay area proved disappointing, never reaching expected production levels, but the hunt for fur-bearing marine mammals was somewhat more successful. Between 1824 and 1834 the company exported 1,822 pelts from mature otters, 94 from pups, and 2,669 fur-seal pelts. In 1841 the company sold Fort Ross to John Sutter, a Swiss entrepreneur who in the mid-1830s established a farming and ranching operation at the confluence of the San Joaquin and Sacramento rivers. Sutter went on to gain notoriety when the initial gold deposits that sparked the 1848 Gold Rush were discovered at his mill.

*See also* **California.**

BIBLIOGRAPHY

Petr A. Tikhmenev, *A History of the Russian-American Company*, edited and translated by Richard A. Pierce and Alton S. Donnelly (1977).

Glenn J. Farris, "The Russian Imprint on the Colonization of California," in David Hurst Thomas, ed., *Columbian Consequences*. Vol. 1, *Archaeological and Historical Perspectives on the Spanish Borderlands West* (1989), pp. 481–497.

*Additional Bibliography*

Bolkhovitinov, N. N. *Istoriia Russkoi Ameriki: 1732–1867*. Moskva: Mezhdunar, 1999.

Kalani, Lyn, and Sarah Sweedler. *Fort Ross and the Sonoma Coast*. Charleston: Arcadia Pub., 2004.

ROBERT H. JACKSON

## FORTS AND FORTIFICATIONS, BRAZIL.

*See* **Santa Cruz, Fortaleza de.**

**FORTS AND FORTIFICATIONS, SPANISH AMERICA.** Almost from the outset of the Spanish occupation of the Americas, raids by English, French, Dutch, North African, and other competitors made the construction of coastal and port defenses essential. By the 1540s, certain strategic ports had become fortified centers: Santo Domingo, Hispaniola, and San Juan, Puerto Rico—the centers of Spanish power in the islands; Cartagena—guardian of northern South America and the approaches to the Isthmus of Panama; Nombre de Dios and later Portobelo at the isthmus; San Juan De Ulúa at Veracruz—the key and entry to Mexico; and Havana—the strategic center and rendezvous point for the convoys returning to Spain. Additional secondary fortifications in Yucatán, Florida, Central America, and the islands were designed to deter raiders and foreign settlers. The early defenses were quite simple—keep and bailey forts armed with a few iron or bronze culverins and smaller cannon. But the capture of Havana by French raiders in 1555 underscored the need for stronger fortifications and garrisons. In the late sixteenth and the seventeenth centuries, beginning with Sir Francis Drake's circumnavigation (1577–1580), English, French, Dutch, and buccaneer raiders plundered Spanish commerce and ports along the Pacific coasts and forced Spain to fortify Callao, Panama City, Acapulco, and other towns.

In the Caribbean and Gulf of Mexico, the construction of massive fortifications designed by Spanish and Italian military engineers incorporated revolutionary architectural changes stemming from European advances. In 1563 the engineer Francisco Calona began the redesign of Havana's fortifications to incorporate modern bastions, gun platforms, thick vaults, and a dry moat. These improvements gave defenders the best possible field of fire against enemy attackers as well as protection against the intense cannonades of besieging forces. The capture of the fortress of San Juan de Ulúa and the town of Veracruz (1568) by John Hawkins, and Drake's Caribbean raid (1585–1586), during which he took Santo Domingo and Cartagena, caused Philip II to dispatch the well-known Italian engineer Juan Bautista Antoneli to design modern fortifications at San Juan de Ulúa and to survey the defenses of the Caribbean. Antoneli's proposals led to the construction of an expensive but fairly effective system of fortifications that in the case of Havana resisted capture for nearly 200 years until 1762. Indeed, renewed assaults by Drake and Hawkins in 1595 against improved fortifications failed at San Juan, Puerto Rico, and at Cartagena, where yellow fever, ma-laria, dysentery, and other tropical diseases forced the besieging force to desist. Drake went on to devastate Nombre de Dios at the isthmus, after which the town was abandoned permanently in favor of Portobelo.

After the Treaty of London in 1604, European competitors occupied vacant American territories that were excellent staging points for more serious attacks. Also, small forces of marauding buccaneers, often supported by European allies, plundered Spanish fortified ports. They massacred the garrison of Portobelo in 1668 and managed to capture many Spanish port towns and fortifications. On several occasions, buccaneer forces crossed the isthmus, captured Spanish shipping, and attacked the poorly fortified Pacific ports of Central America, Mexico, and Peru. Although the major Caribbean fortifications should have been impregnable against such raiders, problems with manpower in the garrisons and failures to maintain expensive works, artillery, and magazines presented opportunities for successful lightning attacks.

With the decline in revenues during the seventeenth century, hastily recruited Spanish American militiamen lacked the resolve to defend fortifications against the implacable buccaneers. Campeche fell in 1672, and in 1683 a buccaneer force assaulted the fortress of San Juan de Ulúa and captured Veracruz. They pillaged the town, killed 300 of the 6,000 inhabitants, and even threatened to massacre the entire populace if a ransom was not paid. With the arrival of the annual Spanish fleet, Mexican militia forces from Puebla, Orizaba, Jalapa, and Córdoba reoccupied the town to find buildings gutted and the corpses of people and animals rotting in the streets. In the aftermath of this disaster, the Mexican authorities convened special tribunals to investigate and punish military officers who had failed to defend the fortifications.

Although international treaties gradually brought the buccaneers under control, the Spaniards were slow to improve their defensive fortifications. In April 1697, a French force of seven warships escorted by frigates and bomb vessels—more than 4,000 soldiers and seamen—surprised Cartagena, which was considered to be impregnable. Spanish cannons mounted on weak cedar-wood carriages proved no match for the effective artillery fire of the attackers. The undermanned forts capitulated on 3 May, and the French sacked the city, holding wealthy residents for ransom. Fortunately for the defense of Spanish American possessions, the nadir had been reached. Compelled by the increasing ability of enemies to mount larger amphibious attacks against fortified ports, the eighteenth-century Spanish Bourbons invested heavily to upgrade and modernize the fortifications at Havana, Cartagena, Veracruz, Panama, and elsewhere. Critics argued that a defensive strategy centered upon a few major strongholds provoked enemies to direct their attacks against weaker secondary targets. But Spain improved its defenses to the point that would-be opponents no longer challenged fortifications without significant planning and much larger forces. Beyond looking after its own defensive works, the Viceroyalty of New Spain provided *situados* (financial subsidies) to improve and maintain Havana, Santo Domingo, and the Florida fortifications.

Spanish preoccupation with the upgrading of Caribbean defenses coincided with the possibility of large amphibious attacks by Britain during the succession of eighteenth-century wars. In the War of Jenkins's Ear (1739–1748), a major assault in 1741 by forces commanded by Admiral Edward Vernon and Brigadier-General Thomas Wentworth failed to capture Cartagena, which had been upgraded and modernized by the engineer Juan de Herrera y Sotomayor. Despite successful attacks upon outlying forts, the 14,000 British regulars, Anglo-American militiamen, and some companies of black troops succumbed to tropical diseases as the siege progressed. Finally, Vernon abandoned Cartagena to attack Santiago de Cuba and the isthmus, but the expedition found no easy targets. In the end British forces lost more than 10,000 troops and many seamen. Spain's best defensive use of fortifications was to hold besiegers in place until yellow fever, malaria, and dysentery took hold. While Vernon misjudged the strength of improved Spanish fortifications, it was also obvious that Britain now possessed the logistical and marine strength to assault coastal defenses and even to undertake invasions inland against Spanish American provinces.

In 1762, during the Seven Years' War, Britain used its marine ascendancy to dispatch a force of thirty-five ships and an army of 14,000 troops—regular infantry, American provincials, black companies, and slaves. Arriving at Havana in June, the British caught the Spaniards completely off guard. On this occasion, the formidable fortifications of El Morro and the almost impenetrable seaward and landward defenses of Havana were insufficient to deter invasion. Striking quickly against disorganized defenders, the British stormed El Morro, which had been weakened by heavy fire from siege batteries set up ashore and by cannonades from the warships. The Spaniards hoped to prolong the siege until tropical diseases and the advancing hurricane season forced the British to desist, but full cooperation between the besieging army and navy units corrected earlier weaknesses from Vernon's day. Havana surrendered and was occupied for ten months until the Peace of Paris.

The fall of Havana, the strategic key to the Spanish Caribbean, caused repercussions that altered all aspects of defense planning. Not only were fortifications strengthened, but Spain introduced a military reform program designed to overcome deficiencies in the garrisons. Aware that Britain might contemplate an invasion of Mexico, the Spaniards spent five years (1770–1775) constructing a new fortress at Perote, inland from Veracruz, to protect against a surprise coup de main. Situated in the healthy uplands, this fortress was designed to impede the march of an enemy army on unfortified Mexico City. An invader would require heavy siege artillery, munitions, supplies, and sufficient troops to besiege a fortress distant from the coast. While Perote was not tested in the colonial period, its existence permitted Mexican viceroys to remove un-acclimatized soldiers from garrison duty in the fortifications of Veracruz. According to most plans, potential invaders were to be bottled up on the coast until yellow fever destroyed their capacity to fight.

During the late-eighteenth-and early-nineteenth-century wars against Britain, Spanish forces and fortifications helped to defeat British attacks at San Juan, Puerto Rico (1797), and deterred invasion plans for Mexico in the period from 1805 to 1807. While the fortress of San Juan de Ulúa remained the last bastion of Spanish power in Mexico until 1825, it did not help Spain to reoccupy the viceroyalty. Through the nineteenth century, many of the fortifications became infamous prisons and penitentiaries rather than serving as sentinels to protect strategic ports against foreign intrusions.

*See also* **Armed Forces; Militias: Colonial Spanish America.**

BIBLIOGRAPHY

The best study on the early period in English is Paul E. Hoffman, *The Spanish Crown and the Defense of the Caribbean, 1535–1585: Precedent, Patrimonialism, and Royal Parsimony* (1980). John H. Parry, *The Spanish Seaborne Empire* (1966), presents a good general survey, as does Arthur P. Newton, *The European Nations in the West Indies, 1493–1688* (1933). For maritime attacks on Spanish possessions in the Pacific, see Peter T. Bradley, *The Lure of Peru: Maritime Intrusion into the South Sea, 1598–1701* (1989). Clarence H. Haring, *The Buccaneers in the West Indies in the Seventeenth Century* (1910), provides a good survey of their raids on Spanish fortifications, as does the more recent work by Juan Juárez Moreno, *Corsarios y piratas en Veracruz y Campeche* (1972). For the eighteenth century, British attacks on Spanish fortifications are examined in Richard Pares, *War and Trade in the West Indies, 1739–1763* (1936); David Syrett, comp., *The Siege and Capture of Havana, 1762* (1970); and Richard Harding, *Amphibious Warfare in the Eighteenth Century: The British Expedition to the West Indies, 1740–1742* (1991). For specific studies on the histories of fortifications see José Antonio Calderón Quijano, *Historia de las fortificaciones en Nueva España* (1953), and Guillermo Lohmann Villena, *Las defensas militares de Lima y Callao* (1964).

### *Additional Bibliography*

Blanes Martín, Tamara. *Fortificaciones del Caribe.* La Habana, Cuba: Letras cubanas, 2001.

Marchena Fernández, Juan. *Ejército y milicias en el mundo colonial americano.* Madrid: Editorial MAPFRE, 1992.

Serrano Alvarez, José Manuel. *Fortificaciones y tropas: El gasto militar en tierra firme, 1700-1788.* Sevilla: Diputación de Sevilla, 2004.

CHRISTON I. ARCHER

---

## FORTUNY, JOSÉ MANUEL (1916–).

José Manuel Fortuny (*b.* 22 March 1916), Guatemalan Communist leader. Fortuny was born in Cuilapa in the department of Santa Rosa to a middle–class family. He studied law at the University of San Carlos but never graduated. Beginning in 1938 he worked as a journalist, and the following year he began to write poetry and theatrical works for radio. In 1940 he won a national poetry prize. Until 1942 he was a journalist with the radio news program *Diario del Aire*, directed by the novelist Miguel Angel Asturias.

Fortuny began his political career in the student struggle against the dictator Jorge Ubico (1931–1944) and participated in the revolution of October 1944. From 1945 to 1949 he was a representative to the National Constituent Assembly and to the Guatemalan Congress. He founded the leftist Popular Liberation Front (FPL) in 1944 and served as secretary–general to both the FPL and the Revolutionary Action Party (PAR) in 1947. In that same year he formed a faction within the PAR called the Democratic Vanguard, which gave rise in 1949 to the Guatemalan Communist Party (PCG), renamed the Guatemalan Labor Party (PGT) in 1952. He was the secretary–general of this group until 1954.

Fortuny played a key role in the administration of President Jacobo Arbenz (1951–1954) as the president's friend, personal adviser, and member of the so–called "kitchen cabinet," writing many of his speeches. After the American intervention and subsequent fall of Arbenz, Fortuny went into exile. He continued as leader of his party, and between 1971 and 1974 lived clandestinely within Guatemala. He later moved to Mexico City and went to work for the newspaper *Uno Más Uno*. In the 1990s he remained a Marxist and followed the moderate evolution of the former Italian Communist Party.

*See also* **Guatemala, Political Parties: Guatemalan Labor Party (PGT); Guatemala, Political Parties: Revolutionary Action Party (PAR).**

BIBLIOGRAPHY

Flores, Marco Antonio. *Fortuny: Un comunista guatemalteco.* Guatemala: Universidad de San Carlos de Guatemala, 1994.

Gleijeses, Piero. *Shattered Hope: The Guatemalan Revolution and the United States, 1944–1954.* Princeton: Princeton University Press, 1991.

James, Daniel. *Red Design for the Americas: Guatemalan Prelude.* New York: John Day Co., Inc., 1954.

Schlesinger, Stephen and Stephen Kinzer. *Bitter Fruit: The Untold Story of the American Coup in Guatemala.* Garden City: Doubleday, 1982.

Schneider, Ronald M. *Communism in Guatemala, 1944–1954.* New York: Praeger, 1958.

VÍCTOR ACUÑA

**FOX QUESADA, VICENTE** (1942–). The businessman and right-wing politician Vicente Fox served as Mexico's seventy-second president from December 1, 2000, to November 30, 2006. He ran for president with the National Action Party (Partido de Acción Nacional, PAN) and was able to establish an electoral democracy after more than seventy years of the authoritarian administrations of the Institutional Revolutionary Party (Partido Revolucionario Institucional, PRI) that had arisen during the Mexican Revolution.

Although he had been born in Mexico City on July 2, 1942, Fox had spent much of his adolescence and youth on the San Cristóbal ranch in the town of San Francisco de Rincón, in Guanajuato. His father, José Luis Fox Pont, was of German descent, born in Irapuato, Guanajuato, and his mother, Mercedes Quesada Etxaide, was born in San Sebastián, Spain.

His early years were spent doing fieldwork and in the family business. He received his primary education in religious schools and later studied business administration at the Iberoamerican University starting in 1960. There the Jesuits gave him "an excellent technical and academic, but above all, moral education," but he did not complete his thesis until 1999, in the middle of his presidential campaign (Fox, 1999, p. 19). In the early 1970s he earned a degree in upper management from Harvard.

From 1965 to 1979 Fox worked for the Coca-Cola Company, where he rose in the ranks, beginning as a distributor with a soft-drink delivery truck and ultimately becoming the company's president for Latin America. There he became convinced of the need to bring a rational administrative and productive business approach to the government of Mexico. That is why some have accused him of "wanting to manage the country as if it were Coca-Cola" (Fox, 1999, p. 45). When he resigned from the company, he devoted himself to his farming business and the shoe business. Fox was married to Lilian de la Concha, an assistant at Coca-Cola, from 1971 to 1991 and adopted four children with her.

### "LET'S DO SOMETHING NOW"

Before joining the National Action Party, aside from the tension that Fox, as a businessman working for a transnational company, had experienced with the nationalist presidents of the PRI, his only experience with politics had been social projects in business and Roman Catholic NGOs. This changed following a telephone call on November 3, 1987. "In Mexico we complain about the system, the dishonesty and the corruption, but we don't do anything to change it. Let's do something now," he told the Sinaloan businessman Manuel J. Clouthier, then a presidential candidate for the National Action Party, who brought many businessmen into the party (Fox, p. 57). These Neo-National Action Party members, such as Fox—also called the "northern barbarians"—were characterized by their desire to do away with the PRI administrations, which they saw as politically irresponsible and inefficient, although they had shared the PRI's neoliberal approach to economics in the 1980s.

Fox joined the National Action Party on March 1, 1988. In the elections that year, he was elected federal deputy and participated with Clouthier in the 1988 civil resistance movement against electoral fraud. In 1991 Fox ran for governor of Guanajuato but officially lost. However, the leaders of the National Action Party reached an agreement with PRI president Carlos Salinas de Gortari outside the election results; in exchange for installing an interim governor from the National Action Party, the PAN would support the PRI's legislative initiatives. After this interim period (1991–1995), Fox was elected governor of Guanajuato with 52 percent of the vote. He was a successful governor (1995–1999) and in 1997 began to plan his campaign for the presidency.

### FROM THE "USEFUL VOTE" TO LESS-THAN-USEFUL PRESIDENTIAL TERM

Fox announced his candidacy for president in 1998 and kicked off an election campaign that many felt was a true, nonviolent war and ended in victory on July 2, 2000. Polls during the campaign revealed that the real fight would be between Francisco Labastida Ochoa of the PRI and Fox of the PAN. Like their personalities, Fox's and Labastida's platforms did not differ much. Fox capitalized on his persona as an open, sincere man from the countryside, who told each sector what it wanted to hear without getting caught in his own contradictions, running against a weak candidate and an old, corrupt party. Fox also used sophisticated marketing strategies to gain both the PAN vote and that of voters who did not sympathize with the PAN but believed he was the best choice and a "useful vote" and that the PRI had to be ousted in order to transition to democracy. Fox fed the nation's desire for change without defining precisely what he meant by change and won with 42.52 percent of the votes as compared to the PRI's 35.1 percent and the Left's 16.64 percent.

Fox's victory over the candidate of the party in power provoked great national and international enthusiasm and was even compared to the storming of the Bastille or the fall of the Berlin Wall, but expectations fell during his term in office. Fox was faced with a divided Congress in which no party had a majority. This prevented him from passing structural economic reforms. According to Fox himself, this was the reason why per capita gross domestic product grew a mere 0.7 percent and the unequal distribution of wealth held steady. In social policy, Fox continued the welfare programs of the PRI, reducing extreme poverty slightly. During his entire six-year administration, he demonstrated little ability to implement innovative programs to fight poverty or to lead social movements. This was made clear in the negotiations in 2001 with poor farmers of San Salvador Atenco to expropriate their lands in order to build a new airport for Mexico City. Popular uprisings ended the negotiations and the project was canceled. Another clear example was the repression, in 2006, of the People's Popular Assembly of Oaxaca, a coalition of professors and social movements in one of the nation's poorest states.

After a year in office, Fox married his former spokeswoman, Marta Sahagún Jiménez, on July 2, 2001. Within a few months, Sahagún's interference in public life and her interest in pursuing the presidency in 2006 added to continual scandals of corruption and tainted the political atmosphere. This was aggravated by instability within the cabinet and the PAN's loss of electoral strength in the by-elections of 2003. Fox then declared that he could "co-govern change" with the PRI.

His attempt to "co-govern" with Mexico's authoritarian party led to discretionary application of the law. While the corruption of individuals close to the president and of self-confessed PRI criminals was concealed, Fox used all resources at his command to try to strip Andrés Manuel López Obrador, the leftist head of the Federal District government, of his political rights so that he would not compete in the elections of 2006.

Fox's foreign policy was characterized by alienation from Latin America—especially from Cuba, with which he was on the point of breaking off relations—and his fruitless turn toward the United States in order to obtain an agreement on immigration. He failed to achieve his goal, in part due not only to his lack of sensitivity toward the United States but also his lack of solidarity with his northern neighbor following the terrorist attacks of September 11, 2001.

The elections for Fox's successor were especially turbulent. The president's office used resources and endorsed the intervention of the business class in the campaign to prevent the imminent victory of the leftist candidate. After a post-electoral period in which protests took place all over the nation, Fox handed over the presidency to Felipe Calderón Hinojosa, under suspicion of fraud among some of the electorate, on December 1, 2006. Afterward, in the style of former U.S. presidents, he announced that he would build, on land near his ranch, a study center, library, and museum devoted to assessing his term in office.

*See also* **Clouthier del Rincón, Manuel J; Mexico: Since 1910; Mexico, Political Parties: Institutional Revolutionary Party (PRI); Mexico, Political Parties: National Action Party (PAN).**

BIBLIOGRAPHY

Davidow, Jeffrey. *The Fox and the Porcupine: The U.S. and Mexico.* Princeton, NJ: Markus Wiener, 2007.

Fox, Vicente. *A Los Pinos: Recuento autobiográfico y político.* México, D.F.: Océano, 1999.

Human Rights Watch. *Lost in Transition: Bold Ambitions, Limited Results for Human Rights under Fox.* New York: Author, 2006.

FROYLÁN ENCISO

**FRANCIA, JOSÉ GASPAR RODRÍGUEZ DE** (1766–1840). José Gaspar Rodríguez de Francia (*b.* 6 January 1766; *d.* 20 September 1840), dictator of Paraguay (1814–1840). One of three major nineteenth-century rulers of Paraguay, Francia was viewed by his elite contemporaries and traditional historians as a ruthless dictator who isolated Paraguay from outside contact and whose iron rule destroyed all who opposed him—foreigners, intellectuals, and the Paraguayan elite. Revisionist historians perceive him as an honest, populist ruler who promoted an autonomous, social revolution within Paraguay and encouraged the economic development of the country.

Born in Asunción to a Brazilian military officer and his elite Paraguayan wife, Francia earned a doctorate in theology in 1785 at the University of Córdoba, Argentina. He then taught theology at Asunción's Real Colegio y Seminario de San Carlos. Upon his dismissal for his liberal ideas on religion and politics, he turned to law. He never married and did not use his political opportunities to amass wealth. He gained political experience by serving on the municipal council of Asunción from 1807 to 1809 and won enough respect for his legal and administrative knowledge to be given the responsibility of defining the qualifications for participation in the revolutionary junta. Eventually dominating the junta, he espoused Paraguayan independence from both Spanish and Argentine hegemony and wrote the first constitution of Paraguay, which the Congress adopted in October 1813. The dual consulship of Colonel Fulgencio Yegros and Francia soon failed. Francia's popularity, personality, and political ability led the National Congress of 1814 to elect him supreme dictator. Even though there were periods of shared power as well as self-imposed exile between 1811 and 5 June 1816, when the Popular Congress elected him perpetual dictator, Francia was the most powerful and popular politician for the first twenty-nine years of Paraguayan independence.

Francia destroyed the traditional power of the Spanish elite and the church, strengthened the military, and appealed to the peasants. He did not abolish the municipal councils in small towns but did terminate those in Asunción and Villa Rica that were controlled by the elite. He promoted state-operated cattle ranches and state commerce, which competed with the private *estancias* and mercantile houses and undermined the elite's ability to increase its wealth. Francia dominated the operations of the Roman Catholic Church by collecting tithes, paying the clergy's salaries, and constructing churches. Although he closed the seminary at which he had once taught, between 1815 and 1840 he had at least ten new churches constructed and increased the number of priests in the villages.

To promote the nation's self-sufficiency, Francia encouraged greater utilization of state lands through government enterprises and low rents for small farmers who produced food for local consumption. He promoted internal trade, controlled external commerce and immigration, increased industrial production in both the private and public sectors, improved communications and transportation, and reduced taxes. To limit government costs, he maintained only a small bureaucracy. His frugality and careful attention to detail resulted in governmental fiscal surpluses. A paternalistic ruler, Francia supported religious celebrations and paid for pauper burials and the care of orphans. The state helped pay soldiers' debts, provided food for indigent prisoners, and aided foreign exiles.

To maintain internal security, suppress banditry, protect against Indians, and define the nation's boundaries, Francia built border forts and established garrisons at the northern border with Brazil at the Apa River, in the south at Pilar on the Argentine border, and in the southeast, which expanded control over the Misiones region. To end Paraguayan political independence, Francia sought Argentine recognition and free trade on the border along the Paraná River. When Argentine caudillos disrupted trade between 1817 and 1822 and Buenos Aires refused to recognize Paraguayan independence, Francia closed Paraguay's borders in 1819 and again between 1823 and 1840, redirecting Paraguayan external trade through the department of Itapúa (Encarnación) to Brazil and Uruguay. The conduct of trade down the Paraná, although regulated by Francia, never entirely ceased, because small boats were able to get through Pilar to Corrientes. By maintaining neutrality in Río de la Plata affairs and using Brazilian commercial interests to balance Argentine political demands, Francia assured Paraguayan independence.

In contrast to other Spanish-American states after independence, Francia's government was stable, efficient, and honest. At his death Paraguay possessed a prosperous, independent national economy and a centralized political system. His economic and political power and willingness to use force created critics among the elite and laid the basis for autocratic rule in Paraguay. Even though military officers and civilians maneuvered for power after his death, the peaceful transfer of government that occurred testifies to the strength of his administration. A dedicated nationalist, popular with the masses, Francia was a dictator whose paternalistic policies benefited a large majority of Paraguayans.

*See also* **Paraguay, Constitutions; United Provinces of the Río de la Plata.**

BIBLIOGRAPHY

The two major monographs are Richard Alan White, *Paraguay's Autonomous Revolution, 1810–1840* (1978), which views Francia's rule as having fomented a social revolution, and John Hoyt Williams, *The Rise and Fall of the Paraguayan Republic, 1800–1870* (1979), a revisionist interpretation, which assesses Francia as one of the three major nineteenth-century dictators to rule Paraguay. Julio César Chaves, *El supremo dictador* 4th ed. (1964), is a well-researched, multi-archival political study examining Francia sympathetically within the context of Paraguayan history. Raul De Andrada E Silva, *Ensaio sobre a Ditadura do Paraguai, 1814–1840* (1978), analyzes the social and economic system of eighteenth- and nineteenth-century Paraguay under Francia. José Antonio Vázquez, *El Doctor Francia visto y oido por sus contemporáneos* (1975), is an excellent collection of 465 documentary excerpts on Francia, beginning with his youth and proceeding chronologically to his death.

*Additional Bibliography*

Canese, Gino. *Karai Guasu: Doctor José Gaspar Rodríguez de Francia: Artífice de la nación paraguaya*. Asunción: Servilibro, 2004.

Ribeiro, Ana. *El Caudillo y el Dictador*. Montevideo: Editorial Planeta, 2003.

Rivarola Paoli, Juan Bautista. *El regimen jurídico de la tierra: Época del Dr. Francia y de los López*. Asunción: J.B. Rivarola Paoli, 2004.

VERA BLINN REBER

---

**FRANCISCANS.** Franciscans, men and women affiliated with a far-reaching tradition within the Roman Catholic Church, who embrace a life that may involve a state of consecration, or the taking of vows, and that follows one of several interpretations of the thirteenth-century rule set down by Saint Francis of Assisi. The largest single branch of the Franciscans, the Order of Friars Minor (OFM), shares company with other members of the Franciscan family, such as the Capuchin Friars, the Conventual friars, numerous branches of religious sisters, the Third Order of Saint Francis, and an assortment of lay associations. The term "Franciscan," especially in the history of Latin America, is most popularly employed in reference to the Friars Minor, the primary focus of the present article.

Saint Francis received approval of a rule in 1209 from Pope Innocent III, officially founding the Friars Minor as an order of mendicants; its members voluntarily relinquish all rights to the ownership of property and live solely from alms. The Franciscan habit, a brown tunic with a hood and a rope belt ending in three knots to signify the three vows of poverty, chastity, and obedience, is universally recognized. Franciscan men and women have been at work in Latin America since the beginning of European contact; their legacy of evangelization is pervasive, and the Franciscan presence in Latin America remains strong. From the second voyage of Columbus on, Franciscans made their way to the Americas in the rush to spread the Christian message. They founded their first missions in the Antilles, from which expeditions to the mainland were undertaken.

In Mexico, a group of reformist, millenarian Franciscans dominated the first generation of missionaries, seeing the newly found territories as inviting the dawn of a radical new social order, the kingdom of God on earth. The responsibility for building this new order, they believed, sat squarely on their shoulders, and the extreme zeal with which they undertook its realization has been alternately lauded and criticized.

In 1522 Emperor Charles V responded to requests from Hernán Cortés to send Franciscans to Mexico to undertake the systematic conversion of the natives. Thus began a steady stream of missionaries from Spain and other countries, the most notable among the first arrivals being Fray Pedro de Gante, a Belgian who worked tirelessly among the poor and who established schools, chapels, and health facilities for the Indians. He was joined in 1524 by a group of friars known as "The Twelve," a name that symbolically connected the missionaries to the twelve Apostles. These friars firmly implanted Franciscanism, with its emphasis on poverty, communal living, and the passion of Christ, as the primary Christian force among the newly converted in Mexico. They battled, at times fiercely, with civil and church authorities over control of native populations. The first bishop of Mexico, Juan de Zumárraga, himself a Franciscan friar, defended with a great sense of urgency the idea that the friars had primacy in all matters. By learning the native language and by instilling confidence in the church as the organizing principle of society, the friars met with success in their catechetical efforts. Accounts of mass baptisms found their way into early Franciscan accounts; the friars often recalled their exhaustion at administering the sacraments in towns near and far. By the mid-sixteenth century, the friars were organized into administrative units, or provinces, extending south from the central valley of Mexico to the Yucatán and Central America, north to Guadalajara, and eventually into the south and west of what is now the United States. Missionary colleges to train friars for work in the farthest reaches of New Spain were established in the seventeenth century in Querétaro, Mexico City, and Zacatecas. Friars were trained to teach not only Catholic doctrine but also those arts, crafts, and agricultural techniques considered beneficial to Christian living.

Policies of the ruling Bourbon dynasty in the mid- to late-eighteenth century, aimed at centralizing the church under tighter royal regulation, had profound effects on the friars. The crown secularized, or turned over to clergy not affiliated with a religious order, most properties and parishes that had come under the friars' corporate control over the course of two and a half centuries. Though the friars maintained certain principal monasteries, the decree of secularization forced them to abandon much of their pastoral work. By the period of independence in the 1820s, their numbers had declined sharply.

Franciscan involvement in South America parallels that in New Spain, with missionaries taking part in the evangelization program from the early colonial period. Friars arrived in Peru in 1532, embarking on a program of conversion and beginning the construction of churches, hospitals, and schools throughout the region, including present-day Bolivia, northern Argentina, and Chile north of the Bío-Bío River. Their first foundation in Ecuador, in Quito, dates to 1534. The symbolism of sending twelve friars into a new region was repeated in 1542, lending the name "Twelve Apostles" to one Peruvian province. As at

**The Church and Monastery of San Francisco, late 19th century.** Built by the Spanish in the mid-sixteenth century, the Franciscan church is famous for its library and the catacombs that lie beneath it. © MICHAEL MASLAN HISTORIC PHOTOGRAPHS/CORBIS

New Spain, missionary colleges served to train friars for the more remote areas; only the Jesuits had as extensive a network of missions in South America, and once the Jesuits were expelled (Brazil, 1760; Spanish America, 1767), the friars took over these South American missions as well as the ones in New Spain. The annals of the Franciscans show that their missionary activities in South America met with varying degrees of success. The Friars Minor were much less active in what is now Colombia and Venezuela; those areas were dominated by their fellow Franciscans of the Capuchin branch.

Instability wrought by the Wars of Independence in the 1820s, combined with the already weakened state of the order resulting from eighteenth-century royal decrees aimed at curbing their power, made the Franciscans particularly vulnerable to attack from emerging social and political forces unfriendly to the clergy. The story of each individual country differs in the nineteenth century, but it is safe to conclude that the friars suffered persecutions of some type in nearly every locale. Over the course of the nineteenth century, the number of friars in Latin America declined, beginning with the flight of the Spanish Franciscans back to Europe after independence. The resuscitation of the order in the twentieth century likewise differs from one region to another. The most often cited catalyst for this rejuvenation, in any event, is the 1891 papal encyclical *Rerum Novarum* of Leo XIII, which brought to the fore the need for social action of a type reminiscent of the Franciscan spirit.

*See also* **Capuchin Friars; Gante, Pedro de; Sahagún, Bernardino de; Zumárraga, Juan de.**

BIBLIOGRAPHY

John Leddy Phelan, *The Millennial Kingdom of the Franciscans in the New World* (1956).

León Lopetegui and Félix Zubillaga, *Historia de la Iglesia en la América Española* (1965).

Robert Ricard, *The Spiritual Conquest of Mexico*, translated by Lesley Byrd Simpson (1966); *New Catholic Encyclopedia* (1967).

Francisco Morales, ed., *Franciscan Presence in the Americas* (1984); *The Americas: A Quarterly Journal of Inter-American Cultural History* (published by the Academy of American Franciscan History).

*Additional Bibliography*

Abad Pérez, Antolín. *Los Franciscanos en América*. Madrid: Editorial MAPFRE, 1992.

Jackson, Robert H., and Edward D. Castillo. *Indians, Franciscans, and Spanish Colonization: The Impact of the Mission System on California Indians.* Albuquerque: University of New Mexico Press, 1995.

Molina, Alonso de, Barry D. Sell, Larissa Taylor, and Asunción Lavrin. *Nahua Confraternities in Early Colonial Mexico: The 1552 Nahuatl Ordinances of Fray Alonso de Molina, OFM.* Berkeley: Academy of American Franciscan History, 2002.

Pellichi, Pedro María, and Ana A. Teruel. *Misioneros del Chaco Occidental: Escritos de franciscanos del Chaco Salteño, 1861 1914.* Jujuy: Centro de Estudios Indígenas y Coloniales, 1995.

Sahagún, Bernardino D., Thelma D. Sullivan, and H. B. Nicholson. *Primeros memoriales.* Norman: University of Oklahoma Press, 1997.

BRIAN C. BELANGER

**FRANCO, GUILLERMO** (?–?). Guillermo Franco (active mid-1800s), Ecuadorian military and political figure. Following the ousting of Juan José Flores in 1845, Ecuador entered a period of extreme political instability that culminated in the country's splintering into four regions in 1859. General Franco assumed leadership of Guayaquil on 6 September 1859 and signed a treaty with Peru conceding El Oriente to Peru in return for recognition of his presidency of Ecuador. As a result of this agreement, he lost popular support on the coast. The following year, in September 1860, Franco's forces were defeated by the army of the provisional government commanded by former president Juan José Flores. Franco fled into exile.

*See also* **Ecuador: Since 1830.**

BIBLIOGRAPHY

Dávila, Luis Robalino. *Orígenes del Ecuador de hoy,* vol. 6. Quito: Quito Casa de la Cultura Ecuatoriana, 1967

Spindler, Frank Macdonald. *Nineteenth–Century Ecuador.* Fairfax: George Mason University Press, 1987.

LINDA ALEXANDER RODRÍGUEZ

**FRANCO, HERNANDO** (1532–1585). Hernando Franco (*b.* 1532; *d.* 28 November 1585), Spanish-born composer who, after his training in the Segovia cathedral and brief service in Guatemala, was brought to Mexico by Spanish patron Arévalo Sedeño. Music flourished under his direction at the Mexico City cathedral from 1575 until financial problems prompted his resignation in 1582. He returned to the post as conditions improved, but died shortly thereafter. His sacred music style incorporates the alternation of simple unison and intricate polyphonic part singing in a manner typical of the cathedral practice that existed during his apprentice and journeyman years in Spain.

*See also* **Music: Art Music.**

BIBLIOGRAPHY

Robert Stevenson, *Music in Mexico: A Historical Survey* (1952)

*Additional Bibliography*

Franco, Hernando, and Juan Manuel Lara Cárdenas. *Obras.* México, D.F.: Instituto Nacional de Antropología e Historia: Centro Nacional de Investigación, Documentación e Información Musical Carlos Chávez, 1996.

ROBERT L. PARKER

**FRANCO, ITAMAR AUGUSTO CAUTIERO** (1931–). Itamar Augusto Cautiero Franco (*b.* 28 June 1931), president of Brazil (1992–1995). Franco was born on board the ship *Itamar*, along the coast of Bahia. His mother, Italia Cautiero, who had just lost her husband, a public-health doctor in the interior of that state, was returning with her children Augusto and Matilde to raise them in Juiz de Fora, Minas Gerais. Although his birth certificate gives Salvador, Bahia, as the birthplace, Franco has always considered himself a Mineiro, and many of his initial curricula vitae, once he was elevated to the presidency, erroneously gave Juiz de Fora as his birthplace. His cultural background and his accent are Mineiro, and he was influenced by such nationally known Mineiro politicians as Joś Maria Alkimin, Bias

Fortes, Carlos Luz, and former presidents Juscelino Kubitschek and Tancredo Neves.

Franco attended Colégio Granbery, a school established by American Methodist missionaries at the turn of the twentieth century. During a later visit to the school, then Vice President Franco declared that it was to his mother, to Granbery, and to the local engineering school that he owed his moral, intellectual, and professional training. As an engineering student from 1950 to 1955, he was twice elected president of the academic center and demonstrated great debating skills while advocating student concerns.

Two years after graduating, Franco ran for city councilman on the Brazilian Labor Party (PTB) slate and was defeated. Four years later he also lost an election for deputy mayor. He finally succeeded in becoming mayor as a candidate on the Brazilian Democratic Movement (MDB, later PMDB) slate. His administration was marked by public works and major improvements that changed the face of the city. While mayor, he married journalist Ana Elisa Surerus. The marriage lasted nine years and the couple had two daughters.

In 1975 he ran successfully for a seat in the federal Senate, where he served until he ran for vice president in 1990. When President Fernando Collor De Mello resigned from office because of malfeasance, Franco served as interim chief executive and then as president from 29 December 1992 on.

His cabinet reflected his nationalistic tendencies and his penchant to trust old and intimate friends. He postponed a number of initiatives that had been undertaken by his predecessor, notably in the area of privatization. When he took office, Brazil was in an extreme economic crisis. Franco helped improve the economy but was unsuccessful in his reelection campaign in 1994, losing to Fernando Henrique Cardoso. He was later elected governor of Minas Gerais (1999–2003). He then worked as the Brazilian ambassador in Italy and again tried to become a presidential candidate in 2006, but was not selected by the PMDB Party. His works include *O negro no Brasil atual* (The Blacks in Today's Brazil, 1980), an attempt at a sociological interpretation, and *Trabalho parlamentar* (Parliamentary Work, 1984), detailing his years in the senate.

*See also* **Brazil: Since 1889; Brazil, Political Parties: Brazilian Democratic Movement (MDB).**

BIBLIOGRAPHY

Ferreira, Jose de Castro. *Itamar: O homen que redescobriu o Brasil.* Rio de Janeiro: RJ Editora Record, 1995.

Flynn, Peter. "Collor, Corruption, and Crisis: Time for Reflection." *Journal of Latin American Studies* 25 (May 1993): 351–371.

Mendes, Antonio Manuel Teixeira. "Eleição presidencial: O Plano Real na sucessão de Itamar Franco" *Opinao Pública* (1994): 39–48.

ÍÊDA SIQUEIRA WIARDA

**FRANCO, RAFAEL** (1897–1973). Rafael Franco (*b.* 1897; *d.* 1973), Paraguayan president (1936–1937), Chaco War military figure, and founder of the Partido Revolucionario Febrerista, or Febrerista Party.

In December 1928 Paraguayan forces led by Major Rafael Franco, a relatively unknown army officer, launched an unprovoked attack against Bolivian-held Fortín Vanguardia in the disputed Chaco region. This incident, though successful in its immediate aim, was repudiated by the Asunción government, which was seeking a diplomatic solution to the conflict. Now regarded as an uncontrollable hothead, Franco lost his command, only to be recalled in 1932 when the border dispute gave way to open war. Franco's military exploits in the conflict were noteworthy, though hardly more so than his open political maneuvering against the Liberal regime of Eusebio Ayala. With the conclusion of the fighting, Franco, now a colonel, made his own position clear: on 17 February 1936, he led the armed forces in a mutiny that swept Ayala from office and installed the colonel as dictator.

Franco had no intention of ruling in the manner of previous dictators. He announced a reform program that focused on land redistribution, workers' rights, and statist politics. Before he could implement these plans, his regime was overthrown in August 1937 by military leaders loyal to the Liberal Party. Franco went into exile, though he remained influential in revolutionary circles within Paraguay.

From exile, the former colonel organized the Febrerista Party, a curious movement that drew support from students, workers, some military officers, and both left- and right-wing ideologues. The Febreristas burst onto the Paraguayan political scene in 1946, when dictator Higínio Morínigo invited Franco to return to the country to participate in a coalition government. This coalition failed to materialize, however, and one year later the situation degenerated into civil war with the Liberals, Communists, and Franco's Febreristas on one side and the Colorados (and the majority of the military) on the other. Franco commanded the rebel forces in the fighting but, after a short time, had to accept defeat and exile once again.

The Febreristas retained some of their influence in Paraguay, though, as the years went by, the movement abandoned its earlier radicalism and adopted a social democratic line. Franco returned several times from exile at the behest of Alfredo Stroessner (president 1954–1989); the Febrerista Party was permitted, in a limited way, to contest several elections after 1964, with the understanding that they would present little more than token opposition to the governing Colorados. Franco accepted this as a necessary compromise, but his own death in 1973 left the Febreristas without viable leadership.

*See also* **Chaco War; Paraguay, Political Parties: Febrerista Party.**

BIBLIOGRAPHY

Harris Gaylord Warren, "Political Aspects of the Paraguayan Revolution, 1936–1940," in *Hispanic American Historical Review* 30: 1 (1950), pp. 2–25.

Paul H. Lewis, *The Politics of Exile: Paraguay's Febrerista Party* (1968).

José Carlos Marcet, *Antecedentes, desarollo y resultado de la Guerra del Chaco* (1974).

*Additional Bibliography*

Amaral, Raúl. *Los presidentes del Paraguay (1844-1954): Crónica política.* Asunción: Centro Paraguayo de Estudios Sociológicos, 1994.

Farcau, Bruce W. *The Chaco War: Bolivia and Paraguay, 1932–1935.* Westport, CT: Praeger, 1996.

Rahi, Arturo. *Franco y la revolución de febrero.* Asunción: Augusto Gallegos, 2001.

MARTA FERNÁNDEZ WHIGHAM

## FRANCO, WELLINGTON MOREIRA

(1944–). Wellington Moreira Franco (*b.* 19 October 1944), Brazilian politician. Moreira Franco entered Brazilian politics in the early 1970s, just as the military regime, which had controlled the federal government since 1964, began to liberalize national political life in a process known as Abertura. While serving as a federal deputy for the state of Rio de Janeiro (1975–1977), mayor of the city of Niterói in the state of Rio de Janeiro (1977–1982), and governor of the state of Rio de Janeiro (1986–1990), he became well-known for his vocal advocacy of the return to and consolidation of democratic political processes. During his mayoral and gubernatorial tenures, Moreira Franco sought to build grassroots support through government sponsored projects in the areas of social welfare and political participation.

Born in the northern city of Teresina, Piauí, Franco moved to Rio de Janeiro in 1955, where he was trained in economics and public administration at the Universidade do Brasil (1966); the Pontífica Universidade Católica of Rio de Janeiro (1968); and the École Pratique des Hautes Études in Paris. A member of the opposition Brazilian Democratic Movement (MDB) during the 1970s, Franco joined the Social Democratic Party (PDS) in 1980. The PDS candidate for governor of the state of Rio de Janeiro in 1982, he was narrowly defeated. He later joined the Brazilian Democratic Movement Party (PMDB), which supported him during his successful 1986 gubernatorial bid. In 1994 he was elected federal deputy and was a great supporter of President Fernando Henrique Cardoso. In 2004 he was a precipitator in the scandal of Niterói when he abruptly attempted to change his running mate from Tania Rodrigues to Sérgio Zveiter. Rodrigues protested the illegality of the switch and was reinstated as his running mate. Zveiter was given the opportunity to run on his own, but instead chose to support Franco. Only days after this scandal was resolved, Franco announced that the election had been falsified and that the reelection of Godofredo Pinto had been fixed. In the end, Pinto was officially reelected.

*See also* **Abertura; Brazil, Political Parties: Brazilian Democratic Movement (MDB); Brazil, Political Parties: Brazilian Democratic Movement Party (PMDB); Rio de Janeiro (Province and State).**

BIBLIOGRAPHY

Franco, Wellington Moreira. *Rio, a nosso desafio.* Rio de Janeiro: Sedrega, 1982.

Franco, Wellington Moreira. *Em defesa do Rio.* Rio de Janeiro: Topbooks, 1991.

Franco, Wellington Moreira. *Antes que seja tarde.* Rio de Janeiro: Topbooks, 2002.

DARYLE WILLIAMS

## FRAY BENTOS.

**FRAY BENTOS.** Fray Bentos, capital city of the Department of Río Negro (2004 population 23,125) in western Uruguay, founded as Independencia on the banks of the Uruguay River in 1859. In 1861 the name was changed in honor of a hermit who had lived on that site during the eighteenth century. In 1859 Jorge Gilbert built a meat-packing plant, the first in Uruguay to can beef following the procedure invented by Julius Liebig in Germany. The plant does not operate any longer; today, hides and wool are the department's main exports. The international Puerto Urzué bridge, constructed in 1969, links Fray Bentos to Gualeguaychú, Argentina. Recent construction of a large cellulose factory on the Uruguay River, however, has generated conflict between the two countries.

*See also* **Meat Industry; Uruguay River.**

BIBLIOGRAPHY

Arbuet Vignali, Heber, Luis Barrios, and Héctor Babace. *Chimeneas en Fray Bentos: De un ámbito local a una proyección globalizada.* Montevideo: Arca, 2006.

Silva, Emilio. *Departamento de Río Negro.* Montevideo: Editorial Fin de Siglo, 1998.

CÉSAR N. CAVIEDES

## FREDONIA, REPUBLIC OF.

**FREDONIA, REPUBLIC OF.** Republic of Fredonia (a.k.a. Fredonian Rebellion), brief revolt by Anglo-American adventurers in East Texas that took place from December 1826 to January 1827. Land speculator Haden Edwards antagonized settlers when he claimed that those who could not prove ownership of their land had to pay him for it under terms of his 1825 contract with the Mexican government. Settler protests led the government to revoke the contract and order his expulsion. On 16 December 1826, during Edwards's absence from Texas, his brother Benjamin led about thirty armed men into Nacogdoches and proclaimed the Republic of Fredonia. Unable to muster support from local Cherokees and Anglo-Americans, the group fled to the United States on the approach of Mexican military forces. The incident heightened Mexican government unease with continued Anglo-American immigration.

*See also* **Texas.**

BIBLIOGRAPHY

Eugene C. Barker, *The Life of Stephen F. Austin: Founder of Texas, 1793–1836,* 2d ed. (1969), esp. pp. 148–177.

### *Additional Bibliography*

Anderson, Gary Clayton. *The Conquest of Texas: Ethnic Cleansing in the Promised Land, 1820-1875.* Norman: University of Oklahoma Press, 2005.

Cantrell, Gregg. *Stephen F. Austin, Empresario of Texas.* New Haven: Yale University Press, 1999.

Kessell, John L. *Spain in the Southwest: A Narrative History of Colonial New Mexico, Arizona, Texas, and California.* Norman: University of Oklahoma Press, 2002.

Reséndez, Andrés. *Changing National Identities at the Frontier: Texas and New Mexico, 1800-1850.* Cambridge: Cambridge University Press, 2005.

Winders, Richard Bruce. *Crisis in the Southwest: The United States, Mexico, and the Struggle over Texas.* Wilmington, DE: SR Books, 2002.

JESÚS F. DE LA TEJA

## FREDRICKS, CHARLES DEFOREST

**FREDRICKS, CHARLES DEFOREST** (1823–1894). Charles DeForest Fredricks (*b.* 1823; *d.* 1894), one of the New World's first successful commercial photographers. By 1843, when Fredricks traveled to Latin America, he was already a master of the daguerreotype process, which had been introduced in France just four years earlier. He spent nine years traveling on the Orinoco and Amazon rivers in Venezuela and Brazil, where he recorded the images of indigenous tribes and documented local scenes in coastal cities from Recife to Buenos Aires. He is said to have exchanged a daguerreotype portrait of a local caudillo for a live jaguar, which he kept as a pet. Familiar with Cuba—where as a boy he had been sent from

New York to learn Spanish—in 1855 he opened a photographic studio in Havana, C. D. Fredricks y Daries, on Havana Street. His scenes, very similar to the works of the French-born lithographer Pierre Toussans Fredorie Mialhe, seek to memorialize urban architectural monuments, not to capture everyday life. Fredricks visited Cuba occasionally but mostly left his studio in the hands of Cuban employees.

*See also* **Amazon Region; Photography: The Nineteenth Century.**

BIBLIOGRAPHY

Robert M. Levine, *Cuba in the 1850s: Through the Lens of Charles DeForest Fredricks* (1990).

*Additional Bibliography*

Vasquez, Pedro. *O Brasil na fotografia oitocentista.* São Paulo: Metalivros, 2003.

ROBERT M. LEVINE

## FREE BIRTH LAW.

**FREE BIRTH LAW.** Free Birth Law (known also as the Rio Branco Law, after its principal sponsor, Visconde de Rio Branco, and as the Law of the Free Womb), a decree passed by the Brazilian Parliament in September 1871 that declared free all children henceforth born to slave women. Enacted after five months of tempestuous and impassioned debate, the law marked a watershed in the history of Brazilian slavery. The freedom of these children was carefully circumscribed, however, for they remained under the custody of their mother's master, who could elect to release them at age eight and be indemnified by the state or retain their labor until they reached majority at age twenty-one. Emancipation of the newborn combined with the earlier suppression of the African slave trade by the Queirós Law in 1850 was intended to force the eventual end of slavery in Brazil by depriving future slaveowners of fresh supplies of slaves, either imported or native-born. The law carried further provisions: (1) an emancipation fund from which to sponsor a limited manumission of adult slaves, and (2) a slave's right to accumulate savings and purchase freedom at a fixed price or in exchange for labor (not to exceed seven years).

Although the standard view locates the law in a series of steps that inevitably led to the final abolition of slavery, other scholars have emphasized that planters and politicians responded out of fear of perceived slave restiveness and a complete collapse of slave-owning authority. The bill simultaneously sought to buttress the position of landowners and placate a restless rural labor force by making individual freedom more accessible. Conservatives and liberals who joined to pass the law refused to give it teeth, leaving the law's execution in the arbitrary hands of planters. The lawmakers had acted cautiously and out of fear; the controversial law satisfied no one.

*See also* **Children; Golden Law; Sexagenarian Law; Slavery: Brazil; Slavery: Abolition.**

BIBLIOGRAPHY

Robert Conrad, *The Destruction of Brazilian Slavery, 1850–1888* (1972), esp. pp. 90–117.

Warren Dean, *Rio Claro: A Brazilian Plantation System, 1820–1920* (1976), esp. pp. 125–129, 135.

Sandra Lauderdale Graham, "Slavery's Impasse: Slave Prostitutes, Small-Time Mistresses, and the Brazilian Law of 1871," in *Comparative Studies in Society and History* 33, no. 4 (1991): 669–694.

*Additional Bibliography*

Conrad, Robert Edgar. *Children of God's Fire: A Documentary History of Black Slavery in Brazil.* University Park: Pennsylvania State University Press, 1994.

Mattoso, Katia M. de Queiros. *To Be a Slave in Brazil, 1550–1888.* Trans. Arthur Goldhammer. New Brunswick: Rutgers University Press, 1986.

Rio-Branco, Miguel do. *Centenário da Lei do ventre livre.* Rio de Janeiro: Conselho Federal de Cultura: Departamento de Assuntos Culturais, 1976.

Vasconcelos, Sylvana Maria Brandão de. *Ventre livre, mae escrava: A reforma social de 1871 em Pernambuco.* Recife: Editora Universitária UFPE, 1996.

SANDRA LAUDERDALE GRAHAM

## FREEDPERSONS.

**FREEDPERSONS.** *See* **Manumission.**

## FREE TRADE ACT.

**FREE TRADE ACT.** Free Trade Act, measure signed on 12 October 1778 that crowned Charles III's work to modernize Spanish mercantilism through commercial deregulation. Preceded by piecemeal reforms for the Caribbean islands (1765), Yucatán (1770), Santa Marta and Riohacha (1776), and Buenos Aires, Chile, and Peru (2 February 1778), it extended imperial free trade to all of the American empire except Venezuela and Mexico and opened thirteen Spanish ports to the colonial trade. For Spanish exports, licensing procedures were simplified and ad valorem tariffs replaced levies based on weight and volume. Duties on imports into Spain varied, totaling 4 percent for most, and 5.5 percent for silver. Venezuela, where the Caracas Company commanded influence, and Mexico, whose commercial strength threatened to overwhelm the other colonies, were not brought under the act until 1788–1789, except for tax rates. Meanwhile, tonnage limits constricted Spanish exports to Veracruz. Imperial trade increased impressively following deregulation, although it waned during the wars of the French Revolution and Napoleon.

*See also* **Commercial Policy: Colonial Spanish America.**

BIBLIOGRAPHY

John R. Fisher, *Commercial Relations Between Spain and Spanish America in the Era of Free Trade, 1778–1796* (1985).

Josep Fontana and Antonio Miguel Bernal, eds., *El "comercio libre" entre España y América (1765–1824)* (1987).

*Additional Bibliography*

Booker, Jackie R. *Veracruz Merchants, 1770-1829: A Mercantile Elite in Late Bourbon and Early Independent Mexico.* Boulder, CO: Westview Press, 1993.

Fisher, John R. *Trade, War and Revolution: Exports from Spain to Spanish America, 1797-1820.* Liverpool: Institute of Latin American Studies, University of Liverpool, 1992.

Mazzeo, Cristina Ana. *El comercio libre en el Perú: Las estrategias de un comerciante criollo, José Antonio de Lavalle y Cortés, Conde de Premio Real, 1777-1815.* Lima: Pontificia Universidad Católica del Perú, Fondo Editorial, 1994.

Silva, Hernán A. *El comercio entre España y el Río de la Plata (1778-1810).* Madrid: Banco de España, Servicio de Estudios, 1993.

ALLAN J. KUETHE

**FREE TRADE AREA OF THE AMERICAS (FTAA).** In 1994 the United States hosted a Summit of the Americas in Miami, Florida, and proposed the negotiation of a Free Trade Area of the Americas (FTAA) that would include all thirty-four democratically elected countries in the Western Hemisphere. The FTAA negotiations were formally launched in 1998, a 2005 completion date was set, and nine negotiating groups were created for issues ranging from market access to services, investment, and competition policy. Despite outward efforts to complete the FTAA on time, the 2005 deadline has long passed and the negotiations remain stalled.

What went wrong? The United States had proposed the FTAA, but after the launching of the North American Free Trade Agreement (NAFTA) and the conclusion of the eight-year Uruguay Round negotiations in 1994, the Clinton administration faced mounting opposition to further trade liberalization within its own Democratic Party. The collapse of the World Trade Organization's (WTO) Seattle Trade Ministerial in November 1999 amid violent protests, and Clinton's continued failure to obtain the necessary trade negotiating authority from the U.S. Congress, are partial explanations of the limbo into which the FTAA fell.

For the South American countries of Argentina, Brazil, Paraguay, and Uruguay, the FTAA was eclipsed by internal conflicts specific to their own subregional integration project (Mercosur) and by the onset of various macroeconomic and political crises in the late 1990s. Mexico had quietly shunned the FTAA, as it had little incentive to share its newly won access to the U.S. market under NAFTA; countries such as Canada and Chile voiced a commitment to the FTAA while also compensating for the lapse of U.S. leadership under Clinton by signing bilateral free trade agreements with regional partners.

The FTAA process gained traction when the newly elected Bush administration took the helm of U.S. trade policy. In August 2002 President George W. Bush obtained the "fast track" negotiating authority (later called Trade Promotion Authority, or TPA), which allows the executive to send a trade bill to the U.S. Congress for an up or down vote with no amendments. The Bush team now had the credibility to proceed with the new multilateral round of trade negotiations that had been launched in Doha, Qatar, in 2001. It simultaneously pursued a "competitive negotiations" strategy based on the negotiation of bilateral free trade agreements with a broad geographical range of countries (including Singapore, Chile, Australia, and Bahrain).

Prior to the adoption of this new U.S. strategy, the Latin American countries had perceived the FTAA as the fastest way to secure greater access to the U.S. market. Yet the new U.S. policy of negotiating bilateral free trade agreements in tandem with the FTAA sent countries such as Colombia, Panama, and Peru scrambling to negotiate bilaterally with the United States. By the time of the 2003 FTAA ministerial meeting in Miami, the U.S. competitive negotiating strategy, along with severe conflicts between the United States and Brazil over the content and pace of the FTAA negotiating agenda, had basically taken the wind out of the FTAA's sails.

*See also* **Latin American Free Trade Association (LAFTA); Mercosur; North American Free Trade Agreement.**

BIBLIOGRAPHY

Destler, I. M. "The United States and a Free Trade Area of the Americas: A Political-Economic Analysis." In *Integrating the Americas: FTAA and Beyond*, edited by Antoni Estevadeordal et al. Cambridge, MA: Harvard University Press, 2004.

Fishlow, Albert. "Brazil: FTA or FTAA or WTO?" In *Free Trade Agreements: US Strategies and Priorities*, edited by Jeffrey J. Schott. Washington, DC: Institute for International Economics, 2004.

Masi, Fernando, and Carol Wise. "Negotiating the FTAA between the Main Players: The U.S. and MERCOSUR." In *MERCOSUR and the Creation of the Free Trade Area of the Americas*, edited by Marcel Vaillant and Fernando Lorenzo. Washington, DC: Woodrow Wilson Center for International Scholars, 2005.

Salazar, José Manuel, and Maryse Robert, eds. *Toward Free Trade in the Americas*. Washington, DC: Brookings Institution, 2001.

Zabludovsky, Jaime, and Sergio Gómez Lora. "Beyond the FTAA: Perspectives for Hemispheric Integration." In *Requiem or Revival? The Promise of North American Integration*, edited by Isabel Studer and Carol Wise. Washington, DC: Brookings Institution, 2007.

CAROL WISE

## FREI MONTALVA, EDUARDO

**FREI MONTALVA, EDUARDO** (1911–1982). Eduardo Frei Montalva (*b.* 16 January 1911; *d.* 22 January 1982), president of Chile (1964–1970). Frei was born in Santiago and entered politics as a law student, founding what later became the Christian Democratic Party. After graduation from the Catholic University of Chile (1933) he specialized in labor law, then turned to editing a newspaper in the nitrate region of Tarapacá, in Chile's extreme north. He entered the Chamber of Deputies in the late 1930s, eventually becoming minister of public works in the government of President Gabriel González Videla (1946–1952). For some years he represented the province of Santiago in the Chilean Senate, running unsuccessfully for president in 1958. In 1964, however, he ran again, this time in a two-way race, and defeated Socialist Salvador Allende, who was also supported by the Chilean Communists.

Frei's campaign came at a time when the prestige of the Cuban Revolution was at its height in Latin America, and Allende its chief beneficiary in Chile. The Christian Democrats neutralized the appeal of the Left by conceding profound changes were needed to address inequality and injustice, but proposed to implement them without tampering with the country's historic commitment to the rule of law and due process (Frei's successful slogan was "A Revolution in Liberty"). Frei defeated Allende by a decisive majority, but one that owed much to the tacit support of the Chilean Right, which chose not to run a candidate of its own.

During Frei's presidency serious efforts were made at agrarian reform, tax reform, and the nationalization of the copper industry. The Right managed to obstruct some of Frei's legislative projects in Congress, often joining hands with the Left, for whom they were too conservative. Meanwhile, the Christian Democratic youth movement was pulling Frei's own party to the left, even imposing a candidate of their own, Radomiro Tomic, for the 1970 presidential elections. The result was a three-headed race in which Socialist Salvador Allende emerged with a slight plurality.

At the time of Allende's election Frei predicted that the former's Socialist-Communist government (Popular Unity) would end in "blood and horror." At first these concerns were dismissed even by members of his own party. However, three years later, Chilean society was polarized to the point of civil war. The stalemate was broken by an exceptionally bloody military coup, which produced a sixteen-year political "recess," in which the country was ruled by the iron-handed Army commander General Augusto Pinochet Ugarte. Frei's remaining years were spent resisting Pinochet and helping to rebuild the Christian Democratic Party. He also served on the Brandt Commission and other international bodies.

*See also* **Allende Gossens, Salvador; Chile, Political Parties: Popular Unity; Chile: The Twentieth Century.**

BIBLIOGRAPHY

Eduardo Frei Montalva, *Aun es tiempo* (1942); *Chile desconocido* (1942); *La verdad tiene su hora* (1955); and *Pensamiento y acción* (1958).

Leonard Gross, *The Last, Best Hope: Eduardo Frei and Christian Democracy in Chile* (1967).

*Additional Bibliography*

Fontaine Aldunate, Arturo. *Apuntes políticos.* Santiago de Chile: Universidad Santo Tomás, 2003.

Gazmuri R., Cristián, Patricia Arancibia Clavel, and Alvaro Góngora Escobedo. *Eduardo Frei Montalva (1911–1982).* Santiago de Chile: Fonod de Cultura Económica, 1996.

Moulián, Luis, and Gloria Guerra. *Eduardo M. Frei (1911–1982): Biografía de un estadista utópico.* Santiago de Chile: Editorial Sudamericana, 2000.

Stern, Steve J. *Remembering Pinochet's Chile: On the Eve of London 1998.* Durham, NC: Duke University Press, 2004.

Vitale, Luis. *Para recuperar la memoria histórica: Frei, Allende, y Pinochet.* Santiago de Chile: ediciones ChileAmérica-CESOC, 1999.

MARK FALCOFF

**FREIRE, GILBERTO.** *See* **Freyre, Gilberto (de Mello).**

**FREIRE, PAULO** (1921–1997). Paulo Reglus Neves Freire was the major educational figure of the cold-war era in Latin America. His writings and activities linking literacy training and consciousness raising had an impact not only in Latin America but throughout the world. The son of an army sergeant and a seamstress, he was born September 19, 1921, in Recife, Pernambuco, in northeastern Brazil. He graduated from the law school there in 1946 and then spent more than a decade working in educational activities with the poor for the local branch of Servico Social da Industria (SESI [Social Service for Industry]). While working with the local Movimento de Cultura Popular (MCP [Popular Culture Movement]), he and his wife Elza began developing techniques to teach newly urban northeasterners how to read and write. His work with the municipal and state governments led by Miguel Arraes and with the federal university in Recife as extension director led him to develop literacy programs throughout the northeast, culminating in a program funded by the Alliance for Progress in Angicos, Rio Grande do Norte.

Convinced that Freire's techniques could bring in new voters to support reform, President João Goulart invited him to create a national campaign. This was still in its planning stages in April 1964 when the coup that ousted Goulart took place and Freire himself was imprisoned. Upon his release from prison and fearing that he would be sent back, he sought refuge in the embassy of Bolivia. On his arrival in the Andean nation, however, he discovered that the government that had promised him employment had been overthrown. He moved to Chile, where friends helped him gain employment planning literacy programs for campesinos with the recently installed Christian Democratic government of Eduardo Frei. The ideas he continued to work on in Chile spread throughout much of the Spanish-speaking world. He influenced, and was influenced by, the ongoing development of liberation theology. Toward the end of his time in Chile he wrote his most famous book, *Pedagogy of the Oppressed* (1986).

In 1969 he left Chile for a brief stint at Harvard. The following year he went to work for the education department of the World Council of Churches in Geneva, Switzerland. During his decade with the council he traveled all over the globe, working with activists and educators and influencing the development of critical pedagogy. His most significant activities with the council in Third World countries were in post-independence Portuguese Africa, particularly Guinea Bissau and São Tomé and

Príncipe, and with the Sandinista government in Nicaragua (although his time there was brief). When with the amnesty law of 1979 allowed Brazilian exiles to return, Freire relocated to São Paulo in 1980 to teach at the Universidade de Campinas and the Pontifica Universidade Católica de São Paulo. From 1989 to 1991 he was the secretary of education in the Partido dos Trabalhadores (PT [Workers Party]) government of mayor Luiza Erundina de Souza. His extensive writings were widely translated and he received many honorary degrees from universities around the world. In 1986 he was awarded UNESCO's Prize for Education for Peace. He died in São Paulo on May 2, 1997.

*See also* **Education: Overview; Liberation Theology.**

BIBLIOGRAPHY

Beiseigel, Celso de Rui. *Política e educação popular: A teoria e a prática de Paulo Freire no Brasil.* São Paulo: Editora Ática, 1982.

Freire, Paulo. *Pedagogy of the Oppressed.* Translated by Myra Bergman Ramos. New York: Continuum, 1986.

Freire, Paulo. *Pedagogy of Hope: Reliving Pedagogy of the Oppressed.* Translated by Robert R. Barr. New York: Continuum, 1994.

Freire, Paulo, and Sérgio Guimarães. *Aprendendo com a própria história.* Rio de Janeiro: Paz e Terra, 1987.

Gadotti, Moacir. *Reading Paulo Freire: His Life and Work.* Translated by John Milton. Albany: State University of New York Press, 1994.

Kirkendall, Andrew J. "Paulo Freire, Eduardo Frei, Literacy Training, and the Politics of Consciousness Raising in Chile, 1964–1970." *Journal of Latin American Studies* 36, no. 4 (November 2004): 687–717.

O'Cadiz, Maria del Pilar, Pia Lindquist Wong, and Carlos Alberto Torres. *Education and Democracy: Paulo Freire, Social Movements, and Educational Reform in São Paulo.* Boulder, CO: Westview Press, 1998.

Paiva, Vanilda P. *Paulo Freire e o nacionalismo-desenvolvimentista.* São Paulo: Graal, 2000.

JOHN ELIAS
ANDREW J. KIRKENDALL

**FREIRE SERRANO, RAMÓN** (1787–1851). Ramón Freire Serrano (*b.* 29 November 1787; *d.* 9 September 1851), Chilean patriot, supreme director of Chile (1823–1826, 1827). Freire enlisted in the patriot army in 1811 and fought with great valor in many actions of the Chilean Wars of Independence. (During the restored colonial regime of 1814–1817 he served in Admiral William Brown's corsair squadron.) In 1819 he was named intendant of Concepción. The desperate conditions in that war-ravaged southern province turned Freire against the Bernardo O'Higgins government. His *pronunciamiento* was the main cause of O'Higgins's downfall (January 1823). Freire was the inevitable successor. During his supreme directorship, he expelled the Spanish troops still holding out on the island of Chiloé (January 1826). In domestic affairs, Freire's liberalism allowed politicians a free rein; their failure to organize stable institutions made this a frustrating period. Freire soon had enough. In July 1826 he resigned, returning to power briefly in 1827 to restore order after a military mutiny.

Early in 1830 Freire once again took up arms, to oppose the Conservative seizure of power then well under way. His small army was defeated at the battle of Lircay (April 1830), after which he was arrested and exiled to Peru. From there, in mid-1836, he led an expedition to Chile in the vain hope of overthrowing the Conservatives. He was captured, put on trial, and exiled to Australia. (Diego Portales wished to have him shot, but did not get his way.) By the end of 1837 Freire was living in Tahiti (where he is said to have befriended Queen Pomaré). In 1839 he settled in the Bolivian port of Cobija. The amnesty of 1841 enabled the general to return at last to his native land: The remaining years formed a quiet coda to an adventurous life.

*See also* **Chile: The Nineteenth Century; O'Higgins, Bernardo.**

BIBLIOGRAPHY

Julio Alemparte, *Carrera y Freire, fundadores de la república* (1963).

*Additional Bibliography*

Ibáñez Vergara, Jorge. *O'Higgins, el Libertador.* Santiago, Chile: Instituto O'Higginiano de Chile, 2001.

SIMON COLLIER

**FREI RUIZ-TAGLE, EDUARDO** (1942–). The fourth of the seven children of the marriage of Eduardo Frei Montalva (president of Chile, 1964–1970) and María Ruiz-Tagle Jiménez, Eduardo Frei Ruiz-Tagle was born in Santiago on June 24, 1942. In 1960 he became a civil engineering student at the Universidad de Chile. He graduated in 1966, specializing in hydraulics. In 1969 he resided in Italy, where he studied business administration. In 1967 he married Marta Larraechea, a family counselor, with whom he has four daughters. Between 1970 and 1982 he worked in the private sector. In 1982 Frei joined the opposition to Augusto Pinochet's dictatorship and in 1989 was elected to the Chilean Senate. In December 1993 Frei—a Christian Democrat running as the candidate of the Concertación alliance—was elected president of Chile for the 1994–2000 term of office with 57 percent of the popular vote. His presidency was marked by political stability and a combination of pro business and social policies. Since leaving office in March 2000, he has served as a Senator and in March 2006 he became the Senate's president.

*See also* **Chile, Political Parties: Christian Democratic Party (PDC); Frei Montalva, Eduardo.**

BIBLIOGRAPHY

Angell, Alan. *Democracy after Pinochet: Politics, Parties, and Elections in Chile.* London: Institute for the Study of the Americas, 2006.

Collier, Simon, and William F. Sater. *History of Chile, 1804–1994.* Cambridge, UK: Cambridge University Press, 1996.

Correa, Sofía et. al. *Historia del siglo XX chileno.* Santiago, Chile: Editorial Sudamericana, 2001.

LUIS ORTEGA

**FRÉMONT, JOHN CHARLES** (1813–1890). John Charles Frémont (*b.* 21 January 1813; *d.* 13 July 1890), U.S. Army officer, explorer, and politician. A native of Savannah, Georgia, Frémont gained renown in part through the political influence of his father-in-law, Senator Thomas Hart Benton of Missouri, and the literary skills of his wife, Jessie Benton Frémont. He rose from an obscure position with the U.S. Army's Corps of Topographical Engineers to fame as a western explorer during two expeditions to the Rocky Mountains (1842) and Oregon and California (1843–1844).

In 1845–1846, at a critical point in U.S.-Mexican relations, Frémont returned to California with another military expedition. There he clashed with the Mexican authorities, took a leading part in the Bear Flag Revolt, and cooperated with Commodore Robert Stockton in the U.S. conquest of California. A dispute with Brigadier General Stephen W. Kearny ended with Frémont's court martial for mutiny and insubordination.

Though restored to duty by President James Polk, Frémont resigned his military commission and moved to California, where he supervised gold mining on his Mariposa estate. He served briefly as U.S. senator from California (1850–1851), became the first presidential candidate of the Republican Party in 1856, and was again the center of controversy during a short term as a major general in the Union Army during the Civil War. After losing the Mariposa estate in 1864, Frémont attempted to restore his fortune through land, mining, and railroad speculations in Arizona, where he was also territorial governor (1878–1881).

A heroic and popular figure during the 1840s, Frémont epitomized the U.S. expansionist spirit; but an impulsive, imprudent nature tarnished his early exploits and later thwarted his ambitions for wealth and high office.

*See also* **Mexico, Wars and Revolutions: Mexican-American War.**

BIBLIOGRAPHY

The basic biography is Allan Nevins, *Frémont, Pathmarker of the West,* new ed. (1955). His career as an explorer is documented in Donald Jackson and Mary Lee Spence, ed., *The Expeditions of John Charles Frémont,* 3 vols. (1970–1984). For his military role during the Mexican-American War, see Neal Harlow, *California Conquered: War and Peace on the Pacific, 1846–1850* (1982).

### *Additional Bibliography*

Chaffin, Tom. *Pathfinder: John Charles Frémont and the Course of American Empire.* New York: Hill and Wang, 2002.

KENNETH N. OWENS

**FRENCH ARTISTIC MISSION.** French Artistic Mission, the forerunner of the Brazilian Academy of Fine Arts in Rio de Janeiro. In 1808, fleeing the Napoleonic invasion of the Iberian Peninsula, Portuguese Emperor Dom João Vi (1767–1826) transferred the court from Lisbon to Rio de Janeiro. Upon the arrival of the Portuguese court in Brazil, the emperor contracted a group of French artists to organize an art academy in Rio de Janeiro along the lines of the French Academy. French painters, sculptors, architects, musicians, and engineers of the Missão Artística Francesa arrived in Rio de Janeiro in 1816. The original group included the painter Jacques Lebreton (1760–1819), the landscape painter Nicolas Antoine Taunay (1755–1830), the sculptor Auguste Marie Taunay (1768–1824), the history painter Jean-Baptiste Debret (1768–1848), the architect Auguste Henri Victor Grandjean De Montigny (1776–1850), the engraver Charles Simon Pradier (1786–1848), and the composer Sigismund Neukomm (1778–1858). Their goal was the establishment of what João VI called the Royal School of Sciences, Arts, and Crafts. The Royal School would elevate Brazil, then the seat of the Portuguese Empire, and imbue it with European, specifically French, culture.

Having received training in the French Academy, the artists implanted French-inspired artistic and pedagogic models. They replaced the isolated attempts by the Jesuit fathers in the colonial period to encourage artistic teaching. They replaced the colony's religious baroque styles with French secular neoclassicism, an aesthetic orientation that endured through much of the First and Second Empires. This cultural transformation corresponded to the political and social changes that accompanied the royal family's arrival in Brazil: the opening of ports to world trade, the lifting of limitations of manufacturing in the colony, the establishment of military academies, the creation of a national library, and the introduction of the printing press.

Financial and political disruptions, coinciding with the personal crises of some of the artists, delayed the formal inauguration of the Royal School until 1820. The school underwent a number of name changes until 1824, when it was changed to the Imperial Academy of Fine Arts, the name it held until the fall of the Second Empire in 1889.

The original artists of the mission served as mentors for the first generation of academically trained Brazilian artists. Jean-Baptiste Debret chronicled the events of the colony with his royal family portraits and coronation paintings. His students, Simplicio Rodrigues de Sá, Manoel de Araujo Pôrto Alegre, and José Correia de Lima, continued his aesthetic influences. The legacy cast a shadow long after De-bret returned to France in 1820. Dom Pedro I named Simplicio de Sá court painter, and Pôrto Alegre became the Academy's fifth director in 1854.

*See also* **Art: The Nineteenth Century.**

BIBLIOGRAPHY

Affonso De Escragnolle Taunay, *A missão artística de 1816* (1956).

Caren Ann Meghreblian, "Art, Politics, and Historical Perception in Imperial Brazil, 1854–1884" (Ph.D. diss., University of California at Los Angeles, 1990).

*Additional Bibliography*

Lima, Valéria. *Uma viagem com Debret.* Rio de Janeiro: Jorge Zahar Editor, 2004.

Schultz, Kirsten. *Tropical Versailles. Empire, Monarchy, and the Portuguese Royal Court in Rio De Janeiro, 1808-1821.* New York: Routledge, 2001.

CAREN A. MEGHREBLIAN

**FRENCH COLONIZATION IN BRAZIL.** Brazil was the first region in the Americas frequented by the French, who competed with the Portuguese from 1504 to 1615. Brazil was a port of call en route to the East Indies, and it abounded in profitable resources, including logwood (used to dye Rouen cloth).

French sailors visited the coast, establishing posts where they traded with the indigenous population. The sailors used their compatriots, who had been adopted by the Indians, as guides and interpreters. Normans and Bretons supported the Tupinambá peoples against their enemies and the encroaching colonization by the Portuguese. The Norman Binot Palmier de Gonneville made the first confirmed voyage to Brazil in 1504, reaching the coast at 26 degrees south latitude and proceeding to just north of the equator. On his return voyage, near the island of Jersey, he was attacked by Breton pirates. All his cargo was lost, but Essomericq, a native Brazilian whom Gonneville had brought with him, was baptized and was married to a cousin of the family. The descendants of that union took an interest in Brazil and appealed for missionaries from France. The two resulting French colonization efforts failed: La France Antarctique (1555–1560) founded by Nicolas Durand de Villegaignon, and La France Equinoxiale (1612–1615).

In the sixteenth century the French heavily fortified the "island" of Brazil, challenging the growing monopoly of the Portuguese. Francis I supplied the funding for the competition of empires. Between 1526 and 1529 the Verrazano brothers, discoverers of New York Harbor, made three voyages to Brazil. In 1550, Rouen honored Henry II with a Brazilian festival, including dozens of French sailors and Amerindians. Churches near Dieppe and houses in Rouen have stained glass windows and sculptures representing ships, the lumber trade, and the native peoples of America.

Shipwrecked on the Brazilian coast, the German Hans Staden later attested that the natives, who had been rumored to be cannibals, were actually friendly. The native peoples living at Cape Frio were on good terms with the French, those at Pôrto Seguro with the Portuguese. In 1551, Guillaume le Testu of Le Havre explored as far as the Río de la Plata. English and Norman merchants contracted to trade jointly with Brazil. The French, English, and Dutch all opposed the Catholic powers of the South. The French court took an interest in Brazil, as did businessmen, humanists, and Protestants. A manual compiled by Cordier, a Rouen merchant, set forth French and Brazilian words, but made no reference to any hostile terms.

The first French colony, La France Antarctique, has often been portrayed as Huguenot refuge, but other scholars have seen the settlement as a part of France's larger colonial ambitions. Villegaignon's project prospered despite internal problems. But in 1560, the Portuguese began an all-out conquest. The unsubjugated Indians fled to the north, accompanied by the French. Still, commerce between France and Brazil continued. In 1565, maritime insurance in Rouen had an 18 percent premium for Brazil and 17 percent for the Roman port of Civitavecchia. Between 1560 and 1610 an estimated 500 French ships sailed to Brazil.

Vaux de Claye opened the Amazon coast for trade in 1579. In 1612, La Ravardière and Rasilly established "Equinoxial France" at Maranhão with Saint Louis (São Luís) as capital. The French Capuchin friars made known the plight of the indigenous peoples, and when the Portuguese attacked Saint Louis in 1615, the French fled. Later, they would aid the Dutch in their attempts at colonization in Brazil.

Thereafter the French shifted their enterprises to the Guianas. France and Brazil contested the frontier until World War I, and in 1711 René Duguay-Trouin, corsair of Louis XIV, actually attacked Rio de Janeiro. In the nineteenth century, however, French visits to Brazil were strictly scientific and commercial.

BIBLIOGRAPHY

Charles André Julien, *Les français en Amérique* (1946) and *Les débuts de l'expansion et de la colonisation françaises* (1947).

Samuel Eliot Morison, *The European Discovery of America,* vol. 2 (1974).

Brasíl, Serviço De Documentação Gerál Da Marinha, *História naval brasileira,* vol. 1 (1975).

Michel Mollat and Jacques Habert, *Giovanni et Girolamo Verrazano, navigateurs de François ler* (1982).

Frank Lestringant, *Le Huguenot et le sauvage* (1990).

Philippe Bonnichon, *Los navegantes franceses y el descubrimiento de América* (1992).

*Additional Bibliography*

Elmalan, Serge. *Nicolas Durand de Villegagnon ou l'utopie tropicale.* Lausanne: Favre, 2002.

Lopez, Adriana. *Franceses e tupinambás na terra do Brasil.* São Paulo: Editora SENAC, 2001.

Mariz, Vasco, and Lucien Provençal. *Villegagnon e a França Antártica: Uma reavaliação.* Rio de Janeiro: Biblioteca do Exército Editora: Editora Nova Fronteira, 2000.

McGrath, John. "Polemic and History in French Brazil, 1555–1560." *Sixteenth Century Journal* 27:2 (Summer 1996): 385–397.

PHILIPPE BONNICHON

**FRENCH GUIANA.** French Guiana, country on the northeast coast of South America between Suriname and Brazil and the only French territory in

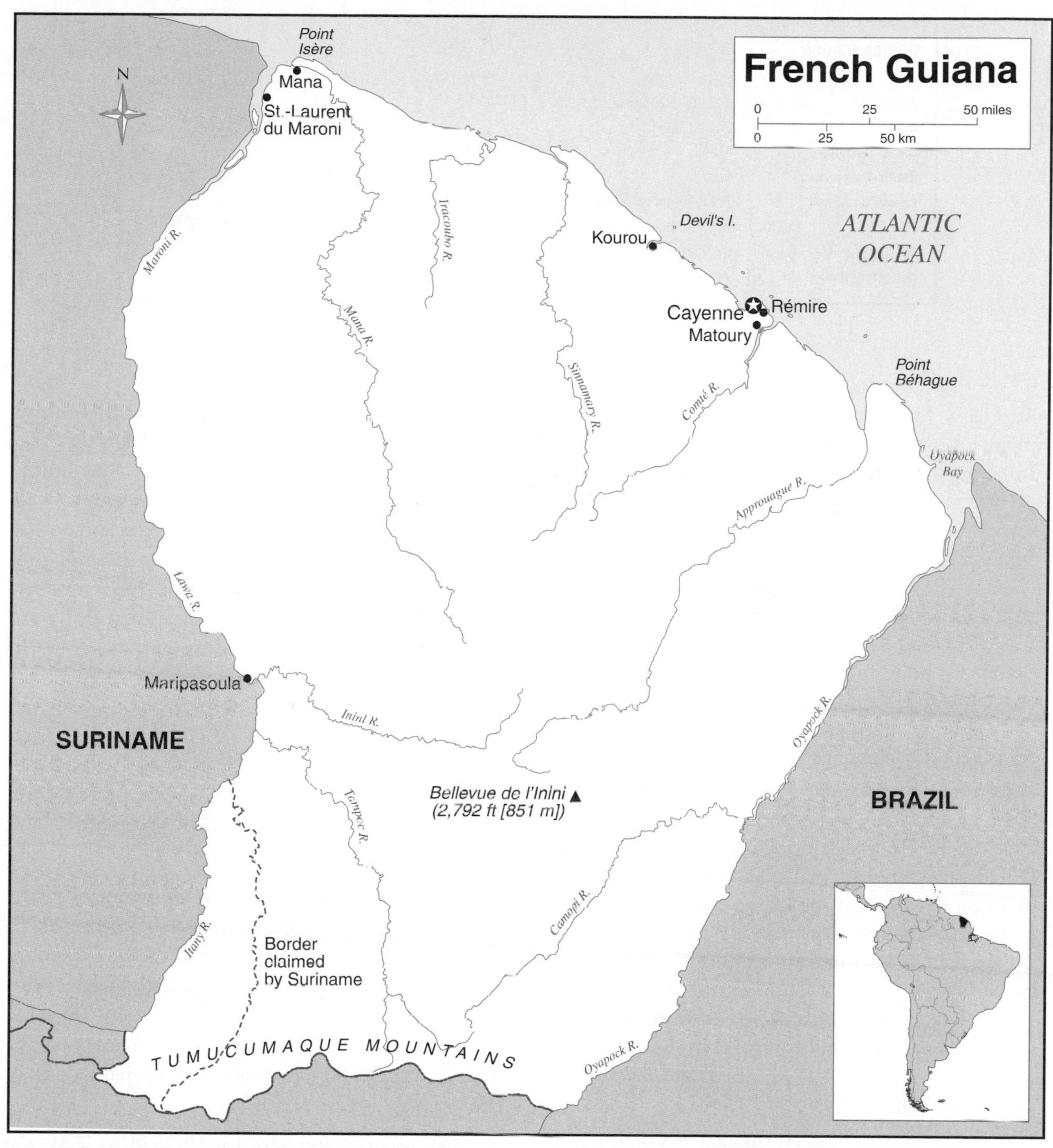


South America. A Département d'Outre-Mer (Overseas Department—DOM) of France since 1946, La Guyane, as it is officially called in French, encompasses some 35,600 square miles of a narrow coastal savanna (where most of the inhabitants live and work) and an extensive and largely unsettled wilderness interior. The extraordinarily diverse population of an estimated 199,509 (2006) is overwhelmingly black or racially mixed but not homogeneous culturally: Creoles are fragmented into locally born, Haitians, French Antilleans, Brazilians, Dominicans, Maroons, Colombians, Surinamers, and more. The remaining perhaps 20 percent is made up of whites, mostly metropolitan French, as well as of Chinese, Lebanese, Hmong

**French Guiana**

| | |
|---|---|
| **Population:** | 199,509 (2006 est.) |
| **Area:** | 35,600 sq. mi |
| **Offical language:** | French |
| **National currency:** | Euro |
| **Principal religion:** | Predominantly Roman Catholic |
| **Ethnicity:** | Black or mixed-race 66%; white 12%; East Indian, Chinese, or Amerindian origin 12%; other 10% |
| **Capital:** | Paris, France |
| **Annual rainfall:** | Averages 140–160 in |

(Laotians), Javanese, Vietnamese, and various Amerindian groups. Although it is potentially rich in gold, timber, bauxite, and fish, French Guiana has a standard of living that is the result of massive subsidies from France meant to extend metropolitan social and economic benefits to this distant but integral part of France. The official language is French, though a number of other languages are regularly used by various ethnic groups. The predominant religion is Roman Catholic, but various ethnic groups have their own faiths.

Although the French had been around the Guianas since the fifteenth century, it was not until 1664 that a permanent French colony was established at Cayenne, the present capital. Amerindian attacks and rivalries among the Spanish, French, Dutch, and English made successful colonization precarious at best. In the late seventeenth and again in the early nineteenth centuries Cayenne was briefly occupied by the Dutch and the Portuguese, respectively. During the eighteenth century the colony was under French control but never grew in population or wealth, as did neighboring Dutch Suriname and the French Antillean colonies of Haiti, Martinique, and Guadeloupe.

French Guiana was chronically short of capital investment (in labor, particularly African slaves), of settlers (who might have established plantations and farms), and of technology (to build the water control systems needed for agriculture to prosper). One result was that plantation agriculture barely established itself. A number of plans were made to overcome labor deficiencies in the eighteenth and nineteenth centuries; all were disappointments, especially those aimed at recruiting large numbers of French farmers. The plantation economy prospered briefly in the early nineteenth century, when slavery was reimposed in 1802 after a short period of emancipation during the Revolution. Cotton, sugar, and annatto were exported, as were some spices and hardwoods; both sugar and cotton lost out to international competition by mid-century. Slavery was finally abolished in 1848, and the former slaves moved from plantations and onto wilderness lands as private cultivators, further weakening the plantation sector. Some Asians were imported as contract laborers to replace slaves, but this failed to stop the steady decline of the plantation sector and the small white planter class. By the twentieth century there was no locally born, white planter elite left, in contrast with Martinique and Guadeloupe.

The postemancipation developments of greatest import were not related to plantation agriculture. First, a gold rush lasting from the 1870s until the Great Depression made gold the major export, pushed the center of economic activity into the interior and away from the coast, and enticed the immigration of fortune seekers from many parts of the world.

The wealth extracted was allowed to leave the colony, and never served as the basis for reinvestment, development, and local productivity, although it did encourage the survival of a myth of great wealth in the interior.

The second development involved immigration of inmates from overcrowded French prisons. Intended originally to populate the colony with prisoners who would be given land and a chance at a new life through small-scale farming, the scheme degenerated rapidly into the transformation of Guyane into a penal colony during the reign of Napoleon III. This innovation has given French Guiana its international reputation as Devil's Island. Devil's Island, one of the milder prison camps, achieved notoriety due to the incarceration in 1895 of Captain Alfred Dreyfus, whose plight was publicized in Emile Zola's famous open letter "J'accuse." The prison complex on the coastal islands and mainland was shut down in the late 1930s but did not officially close until 1947.

Agriculture continued to decline, and by 1942 was unable to produce enough food to feed the local population. In 1946, the colony's status was changed to that of DOM. The economic benefits of that change have raised the standard of living while, paradoxically, the local level of productivity has declined. As an integral part of France, Guyane is more dependent on public subsidies now than before. Unemployment runs at about 25 percent. Average per capita income is about U.S. $2,800, placing French Guiana in the middle income range of Caribbean countries.

Political parties in French Guiana tend generally to debate the degree of local autonomy that might be desirable within French nationality. The independence movement is minuscule, less than even that of Martinique and Guadeloupe, in part a result of having accepted settlers and refugees from throughout the former French empire who are particularly pro-French and loath to loosen their bonds to France. "Decolonization through integration" of former colonies into the French state continues to be French policy supported by most Guianese.

Today, French Guiana is particularly important to the French because of the huge space station and rocket-launching facilities at Kourou, begun in the 1960s, which services the European Community.

*See also* **Slavery: Abolition; Slave Trade.**

BIBLIOGRAPHY

Jean-Claude Michelot, *La Guillotine sèche: Histoire du bagne de Cayenne* (1981).

Pierre Pluchon, Louis Abenon, et al., eds., *Histoire des Antilles et de la Guyane* (1982).

Jean-Claude Giacottino, *Les Guyanes* (1984).

Neuville Doriac, *Esclavage, assimilation et guyanite* (1985).

Anne-Marie Bruleaux, Régine Calmont, and Serge Mam-Lam-Fouck, eds., *Deux siècles d'esclavage en Guyane Française, 1652–1848* (1986).

Kenneth Bilby, "The Remaking of Aluku: Culture, Politics, and Maroon Ethnicity in French South America" (Ph.D. diss., Johns Hopkins University, 1990).

*Additional Bibliography*

Cardoso, Ciro Flamarión. *La Guyane française: 1715-1817: Aspects économiques et sociaux: contribution à l'étude des sociétés esclavagistes d'Amérique.* Petit-Bourg: Ibis rouge, 1999.

Mam-Lam-Fouck, Serge. *La Guyane française au temps de l'esclavage, de l'or et de la francisation (1802-1946).* Petit-Bourg: Ibis Rouge, 1999.

Polderman, Marie. *La Guyane française, 1676-1763: Mise en place et évolution de la société coloniale, tensions et métissages.* Petit-Bourg: Ibis Rouge, 2004.

Redfield, Peter. *Space in the Tropics: from Convicts to Rockets in French Guiana.* Berkeley: University of California Press, 2000.

West, Alan. *African Caribbeans: A Reference Guide.* Westport: Greenwood Press, 2003.

ROSEMARY BRANA-SHUTE

**FRENCH INTERVENTION (MEXICO).** French Intervention (Mexico), the protracted attempt from 1862 until 1867 by the Second Empire under Napoleon III to establish military supremacy in Mexico in order to maintain the Mexican Empire as a counterbalance to U.S. expansion. Napoleon III resuscitated earlier Bourbon aspirations to hegemony over Hispanic dominions and thereby gain access to bullion supplies. The intervention was not motivated by the demands of French industry or commerce, in spite of significant growth in the 1850s. In fact, it was unpopular in business circles. The French were, however, interested in the construction of an interoceanic canal across the Isthmus of Tehuantepec. Prince Louis Napoleon Bonaparte had been interested in such schemes while a political prisoner at Ham in the early 1840s.

French diplomats and a handful of Mexican monarchists mooted the idea of a European monarchy as a solution to Mexico's post-Independence instability. Predominant mid-nineteenth-century racism encouraged the belief that Mexicans were incapable of governing themselves. Napoleon III adopted the idea already given some prominence in France that France as the senior "Latin" state should have a role in Latin American affairs. A "Latin" bloc in Europe and America could hold back the Slavs and Anglo-Saxons. Foreign monarchs had already ascended thrones in Belgium and Greece, and two American countries, Canada and Brazil, were constitutional monarchies. Napoleon III was not fully briefed on Mexican affairs and erroneously believed there to be significant support there for a monarchy. He was, however, careful not to alienate Great Britain, which had its own commercial interests in Latin America.

The intervention went far beyond the initial tripartite (Great Britain, France, Spain) debt-collecting mission of January 1862. The scheme had precise political objectives that corresponded to a specific phase in French foreign and colonial policy and should be viewed in the context of expansion in Algeria and Indochina. Marshal François Bazaine, a veteran of the Algerian campaigns, was the commander who led the French forces, which included Algerian and Egyptian soldiers.

The fortuitous occurrence of the American Civil War (1861–1865) enabled the intervention to take place without effective American challenge. Napoleon, however, mistakenly believed that the Confederate states would endure, thus allowing the extension of pro-French monarchies into Central and South America. But imperial Brazil showed little interest in Napoleon's plan, and the Juárez regime determined to resist the French to the end. Overconfidence caused the French disaster at Puebla on 5 May 1862, which delayed the capture of Mexico City until 10 June 1863.

In the meantime, Napoleon embarked upon the process of establishing a Mexican empire with the Hapsburg archduke Maximilian as emperor. The Fontainebleau Instructions of 3 July 1862 provided for both protection of the Catholic church and consolidation of Liberal disamortization policies (state policy of transferring ecclesiastical and Indian properties to private ownership, in accordance with the Ley Lerdo of 25 June 1856). Napoleon wanted a liberal empire legitimized by elections and supported by moderates. Conservatives and the Mexican hierarchy, however, had no sympathy for the liberalism of either French military commanders or Maximilian. General Élie-Frédéric Forey established the Assembly of Notables, which in July 1863 invited Maximilian to assume the throne.

When Bazaine replaced Forey as supreme commander in October 1863, there were 40,000 French troops in Mexico. Bazaine's coolness toward the Conservative regency established by Forey lasted until Maximilian's arrival in June 1864. Bazaine advised Napoleon of the difficulty of establishing a Mexican imperial army on European lines, but in the military campaign to hold down Mexico, Bazaine benefited from a unified command. The French formed a *contre-guérilla* unit to combat Juarista bands that were attacking supply lines in the Veracruz hinterland. Guanajuato fell on 8 December 1863, and Bazaine entered Guadalajara on 5 January 1864. The fall of Durango (4 July 1864), Saltillo (20 August), and Monterrey (26 August) were the high points of the campaign in the north. In October 1864 Juárez was forced into Chihuahua, where he remained until December without being forced out of the country. Liberal guerrilla bands operated behind French lines.

The growth of Prussian power on the European continent and the ending of the U.S. Civil War encouraged Napoleon to press for the evacuation of French forces, leaving only the Foreign Legion. This made the formation of a Mexican army urgent. The French army had always been relatively small as a result of domestic opposition to the Mexican "adventure." Maximilian refused to leave with the French. He had decided to commit himself to a last stand in order to try to save the empire. This decision threw him into the arms of the Mexican Conservatives, whom he had largely abandoned since June 1864. The urgent task of forming an imperial army was left to the Conservative generals Miguel Miramón, Tomás Mejía, and Leonardo Márquez. Bazaine departed with the last French troops. In eight weeks, 28,000 troops left Veracruz, one-tenth of the entire French army.

*See also* **Afrancesado; French-Latin American Relations.**


BIBLIOGRAPHY

Jack Autrey Dabbs, *The French Army in Mexico, 1861–1867* (1963).

Alfred J. and Kathryn A. Hanna, *Napoleon III and Mexico: American Triumph over Monarchy* (1971).

*Additional Bibliography*

Cunningham, Michele. *Mexico and the Foreign Policy of Napoleon III.* Houndmills; New York: Palgrave, 2001.

García Cantú, Gastón. *La intervención francesa en México.* México: Clío, 1998.

Meyer, Jean A. *Yo, el francés: La intervención en primera persona: biografías y crónicas.* México: Tusquets Editores, 2002.

BRIAN HAMNETT

**FRENCH-LATIN AMERICAN RELATIONS.** France became involved in the discovery, conquest, and colonization of Latin America as early as 1504, when its ships began to prowl the coasts of Brazil looking for dyewoods to trade. France did not view itself as bound by the Treaty of Tordesillas, for as King François I remarked, "I should very much like to see the passage in Adam's will that divides the New World between my brothers, the Emperor Charles V and the King of Portugal." Although from 1532 to 1550 the Portuguese drove the French from their outposts in northern Brazil, in 1555 a French expedition founded a Huguenot colony, France d'Antarctique, on an island in the harbor of Rio de Janeiro, that lasted until 1566–1567. In 1594 another French mission established a settlement, this time in the Bay of Maranhão (São Marcos Bay) that was destroyed in 1614–1615.

In 1624 merchants from Rouen established a trading post on the coasts of Tierra Firme known as Guiana. Other Frenchmen followed and in 1643 founded Cayenne, today the capital of French Guiana. Cayenne was occupied by the Dutch in 1664 but awarded to France by the Treaty of Breda (1667), which gave France a legal presence it had never obtained in Brazil. The Dutch were driven out in 1676, and the area around Cayenne has remained under French control ever since. From 1624 to the present, settlement in French Guiana has centered around Cayenne and adjacent coastlands. Agriculture and forest products have anchored the economy for 300 years. The inhabitants, mostly creoles of African and European descent, have been citizens of France since 1877, and French Guiana has been a *département* of France since 1946. From 1852 to 1939 it was a penal colony and received 70,000 convicts at Devil's Island and other points. Since 1968 French Guiana has hosted the rocket-launching program of the European Space Agency. The population of about 100,000 (1992) remains highly dependent on France.

Although the French pirate François Le Clerc destroyed Yaguana, the forerunner to Port-au-prince, in 1553, it was not until the seventeenth century that the French would become active in the Caribbean. In 1635 Pierre Belain d'Esnambuc conquered the island of Martinique for France, while Jean du Plessis did the same for Guadeloupe during that year. Martinique became a great sugar producer and France assumed sovereignty over the island in 1674. Many important contributors to French and international culture were born there, including the Empress Josephine and the revolutionary theoretician Frantz Fanon. In 1946 both Martinique and Guadeloupe became overseas *départements* of France. Jacques Jean David Nau, known as L'Ollonais from his French birthplace, grew up in the Caribbean and became a buccaneer on the island of Tortuga, terrorizing the Spaniards with his atrocities, including the sack of Maracaibo (1667), from 1653 until 1671.

In 1641 other buccaneers established themselves on the northwestern shores of Hispaniola. In 1664 Louis XIV claimed settlements there for France and gave control over them to the French West India Company, a title that was sustained by the Treaty of Ryswick in 1697. French settlers founded Port-au-Prince in 1749. The Treaty of Aranjuez (1777) determined the boundary between that territory, known as Saint Domingue, and the Spanish part known as Santo Domingo. On 14 August 1791, the slaves in Saint Domingue revolted, and three years later they murdered 800 white planters, prompting many to flee to other French islands. In 1800 the leader of the revolt, Toussaint Louverture, took control over Saint Domingue, which the following year promulgated its first constitution. Although the French tried to recapture their part of the island with twenty thousand troops in 1802, the nation of Haiti proclaimed itself independent in 1804 and was recognized as such by France in 1825.

French activity sparked Spanish exploration in many parts of the present-day continental United States. For example, Admiral Pedro Menéndez de Avilés defeated the French settlement at Fort Caroline prior to establishing Saint Augustine in 1565.

French explorations of the Midwest under Jacques Marquette and Louis Joliet in 1673 and Chevalier Robert La Salle in 1685–1687 halted Spanish incursions into the area. The French gave possession of Louisiana to Spain in late 1762, but in 1800 Napoleon I demanded that the territory be returned. In 1803 it was sold to the United States as the Louisiana Purchase.

French military technology and practice had a decided impact on the Spanish American officers who fought the wars of independence, including Simón Bolívar. The copying of French uniforms in the nineteenth century was such that when Argentine intellectual and politician Domingo Fausto Sarmiento joined Justo José de Urquiza's troops to oust Juan Manuel de Rosas from power, he was attired as a French officer. French immigrants came to northern Argentina after independence and by the 1830s had set up sugar refineries, known as *ingenios,* while others went to central Argentina, especially Buenos Aires province. French merchants were active in Mexico, Chile, and Peru during the nineteenth century. In Central America the French economic impact was weaker, but schools run by French nuns and priests influenced politicians. During that period the French occasionally meddled in Latin American affairs, usually in Mexico where a series of inept ministers only worsened relations. In 1838 they bombarded Veracruz in hostilities dubbed the Pastry War because France was demanding reparations for damage to the shop of a French baker. During the same year they sought to extend their trade and power in the Río de la Plata area and to show their displeasure at the Rosas regime by organizing an ineffective blockade on Buenos Aires in the 1830s. However, the worst example of French interference in Latin American affairs came with the ill-fated "French Empire" in Mexico.

In late 1861 France, Britain, and Spain agreed to force Mexico to pay outstanding debts by blockading the port of Veracruz in December. Britain and Spain bowed out once they learned that the French intended to invade Mexico and establish an empire there. French forces suffered a humiliating defeat at the battle of Puebla (5 May 1862) but took Mexico City in June 1863. Hapsburg prince Ferdinand Maximilian, younger brother of Emperor Franz Joseph, accompanied by his Belgian wife, Charlotte, arrived in Mexico in June 1864 and became Emperor and Empress Maximiliano and Carlota of Mexico. Maximilian was too liberal for his clerical supporters and became heavily dependent on French troops, which deserted him soon after the U.S. Civil War ended and French emperor Napoleon III faced a growing challenge across the Rhine from Otto von Bismarck's Prussia. Empress Carlota traveled to Europe in the summer of 1866, hoping to restore the commitment of Napoleon III and secure the intervention of the pope. These efforts failed (and cost Carlota her sanity), leaving Maximilian to be captured and executed on 19 June 1867. The invasion helped solidify the political dominance of the Liberals; consequently the Mexican government became generally stable until the 1910 Revolution.

The most enduring consequence of this French fiasco has been the term Latin America. French publicists coined the phrase in an effort to justify Napoleon's intervention by claiming a kinship among the peoples who spoke languages derived from Latin.

The Mexican adventure was the last major French enterprise in Latin America. Subsequently, French influence has been felt chiefly in the financial and cultural spheres. In the nineteenth and twentieth centuries, France has been among the major investors in Latin America. In 1900 France had $600 million invested in Latin America, twice as much as the United States but less than one-third of Britain's total. By 1970, French investment in Latin America totaled about $540 million, well below the U.S., British, and German figures. France continues to be economically important through the European Union. Trade doubled between the EU and Latin American countries between 1990 and 2002.

Even as the works of Latin American intellectuals and artists gave rise to national cultures, France played an important part in the evolution of Latin American culture. Enlightenment ideology and the example of the French Revolution helped spark the revolutions of 1808–1826; when King João VI wished to invite an artistic mission to visit Brazil in 1816, he sought a French one. Virtually every Latin American capital was remade in the late nineteenth century to look like Baron Georges-Eugène Haussmann's Paris, with its wide boulevards. In Argentina, French intellectual Paul Groussac was influential in improving education and enhancing the role of the National Library, of which he became the director. The impact of French socialist theories was felt in Latin America into the twentieth century, as were the works of Charles Maurras from the 1930s on fascism. Especially important is the respect accorded to existentialist works by Jean-Paul Sartre and Albert Camus along with French cinema in the post-World War II era. Although its cultural prestige in Latin America has declined somewhat in the twentieth century, those countries with large European immigrant populations still regard Paris as the source of cultural trends and fashion.

*See also* **Enlightenment, The; French Artistic Mission; French Guiana; Haiti; L'Olonnais, Francis; Louverture, Toussaint; Maracaibo; Martinique and Guadeloupe; Maximilian; Mexico: 1810-1910; Pastry War; Piracy; Puebla, Battle and Siege of; Santo Domingo; Tordesillas, Treaty of (1494); Veracruz (City).**

BIBLIOGRAPHY

For books from a French perspective, see Fernando Campos Harriet, *Veleros franceses en el Mar del Sur, 1700–1800* (1964); W. Adolphe Roberts, *The French in the West Indies* (1971); Carl Ludwig Lokke, *France and the Colonial Question: A Study of Contemporary French Opinion, 1763–1801* (1976). For a more Latin American focus, see Pierre Chaunu, *L'Amérique et les Amériques* (1964); Alfred Jackson Hanna and Kathryn Abbey Hanna, *Napoleon III and Mexico: American Triumph over Monarchy* (1971); Yuyu Guzmán, *Estancias de Azul y pobladores franceses en la zona rural de Azul* (1976); and Angel Sanz Tapia, *Los militares emigrados y los prisioneros franceses en Venezuela durante la guerra contra la revolución: Un aspecto fundamental de la época de la preemancipación* (1977); Nancy Nichols Barker, *The French Experience in Mexico, 1821–1861: A History of Constant Misunderstanding* (1979).

*Additional Bibliography*

Bohdziewicz, Jorge C. *Rosas y Lefebvre de Bécourt: Actuación del encargado de negocios de Francia en el Río de la Plata, 1840–1842.* Buenos Aires: Scholastica, 2003.

Cunningham, Michele. *Mexico and the Foreign Policy of Napoleon III.* Houndmills, Basingstoke, Hampshire, U.K., and New York: Palgrave, 2001.

Meyer, Jean A. *Yo, el francés: La intervención en primera persona: Biografías y crónicas.* Mexico: Tusquets Editores, 2002.

Pelosi, Hebe Carmen. *Vichy no fue Francia: Las relaciones franco-argentinas (1939–1946).* Buenos Aires: Nuevohacer Grupo Editor Latinoamericano, 2003.

Schoonover, Thomas David. *The French in Central America Culture and Commerce, 1820–1930.* Wilmington, DE: Scholarly Resources, 2000.

JOHN MCNEILL

**FRENCH WEST INDIES.** In 1625 French settlement began on Saint Christopher (Saint Kitts), which was shared with the British. In 1635 the first settlers appeared on Martinique and Guadeloupe, supported by the Company of the Islands of America, which had been chartered by the French crown to provide *engagés* (white indentured labor) and free settlers and missionaries in return for fees payable in tobacco and cotton. The company went bankrupt for lack of government and merchant support, and the colonies were sold to private investors. Under the new owners, Martinique, Guadeloupe, Marie Galante, Désirade, the Iles des Saintes, Grenada, and part of St. Kitts emerged as plantation colonies worked by African slaves. In the western Caribbean, the French planted sugar in the unoccupied western end of Hispaniola. On the mainland of South America, they sank roots at Cayenne.

By the 1660s, the colonies were prospering sufficiently to attract the attention of the French government. Jean-Baptiste Colbert, minister of trade, arranged to repurchase the colonies in 1664; set up the French West Indies Company to control and tax trade with the colonies; built slave trading forts in West Africa; forced the withdrawal of Dutch merchant competitors from the French West Indies by 1678; and forced Spain to accept French plantations on St. Domingue. Colbert also institutionalized the *exclusif,* which forbade colonial trade with non-French territories, as well as any trade or industry in the colonies that might compete with metropolitan merchants and manufacturers. The colonies were limited to producing the raw materials needed by French industry, and to consuming French products.

The colonies did not have local assemblies or councils empowered to make laws. The Council of State in France passed colonial laws and appointed all colonial officials. The intendants were French; the governors answered to the governor-general in Martinique.

In the eighteenth century, French losses to Britain included St. Kitts (1713) and Grenada (1763). Saint Barthélémy went to Sweden in 1784, returning to France in 1877. France acquired Saint Lucia in 1763 and Tobago in 1783, then lost them to the British in 1815.

The end of plantation slavery began in the French colonies in 1793 with the massive slave rebellion on

Saint Domingue, which succeeded in ending both slavery and French rule in what was renamed Haiti. In 1794, the French Revolutionary government declared the end of slavery in all French colonies. In 1802 Napoleon reimposed slavery on the remaining Caribbean possessions.

Martinique and Guadeloupe, important producers of sugarcane, used slave labor imported from Africa. However, French farmers began growing sugar beets, thereby lowering demand for cane sugar. Abolition came finally in 1848.

Planters received compensation for lost slaves and help in acquiring 70,000 indentured laborers from India. Former slaves received limited political rights (e.g., universal male suffrage in 1848). Sugar and its by-products continued to dominate the island economies through much of the twentieth century. French Guiana experienced a gold rush at the turn of the twentieth century, and today exports jungle hardwoods. From the 1850s until 1947, French Guiana also functioned as a penal colony.

French Guiana, with an area of 36,400 square miles, consists of low coastal plains and tropical rain forests. Guadeloupe and its dependencies cover 700 square miles of coastal plains and interior volcanic mountains. Martinique, with similar topography, covers 440 square miles. By 1990 the population of Guadeloupe was 342,000, that of Martinique was 340,000 and that of French Guiana was 98,000. French Guiana was the most ethnically heterogeneous.

The Caribbean Départements d'Outre-Mer (DOMs) were created in 1946. One consequence has been the significant decline of agriculture in all three; their economies are dominated by the administrative and service sectors. As integral parts of France, they are provided with all the government services available in mainland France. French Guiana provides the French, and through them the European Community, with the space and missile complex at Kourou. Tourism is increasingly important to the economies of the two island territories. Unemployment is significant, over 25 percent, in all three territories but is offset by welfare programs and subventions from France that yield living standards that are among the best in the Caribbean.

The dominant political issue facing the three territories today is their political relationship with France. Virtually all political parties support the present relationship with France, although they differ on how much local autonomy is desirable. The several small independence parties are electorally insignificant but add to the ongoing debate.

*See also* **French Guiana; French-Latin American Relations; Haiti; Martinique and Guadeloupe; Plantations; Saint Christopher (Saint Kitts); Santo Domingo; Slave Revolts: Spanish America; Slavery: Spanish America; Slavery: Abolition; Slave Trade; Sugar Industry.**

BIBLIOGRAPHY

Philip P. Boucher, *Les Nouvelles Frances: France in America, 1500–1815. An Imperial Perspective* (1989).

Robert Aldrich and John Connell, *France's Overseas Frontier; Départements et Territoires d'Outre-Mer* (1992). For recent developments, see the essays on the Western Indian DOMs in the annual *Latin American and Caribbean Contemporary Record* (1983–).

### *Additional Bibliography*

Dubois, Laurent. *A Colony of Citizens: Revolution and Slave Emancipation in the French Caribbean.* Williamsburg: University of North Carolina Press, 2004.

Farnsworth, Paul. *Island Lives: Historical Archaelogies of the Caribbean.* Tuscaloosa: University of Alabama Press, 2001.

Kadish, Doris. *Slavery in the Caribbean Francophone World: Distant Voices, Forgotten Acts, Forged Identities.* Athens: University of Georgia Press, 2000.

ROSEMARY BRANA-SHUTE

---

**FRESNO LARRAÍN, JUAN FRANCISCO** (1914–2004). Juan Francisco Fresno Larraín (*b.* 26 July 1914; *d.* 14 October 2004), archbishop of Santiago, Chile (1983–1990), during the last years of the military government of General Augusto Pinochet.

Born in Santiago, Fresno was educated in the diocesan seminary and at Gregorian University in Rome, where he received a bachelor's degree in canon law. Ordained on 18 December 1937, he served in the influential posts of vice rector of the minor seminary in Santiago and as an adviser to the reformist lay group Catholic Action, which was particularly active in Chile from the 1940s into the 1960s. In 1958 Pope Pius XII named him bishop of the recently created diocese of Copiapó, and in 1967 Pope Paul VI named him archbishop of the more important archdiocese of La Serena.

Fresno participated in the Second Vatican Council (1962–1965), supporting greater involvement of the Catholic Church in social justice activities. He also influenced the deliberations of the second Conference of Latin American Bishops (CELAM) in 1968, which translated into Latin American terms the general mandates of Vatican II to promote peace, justice, and human rights.

On 3 May 1983 he was named archbishop of Santiago and two years later was elevated to the rank of cardinal. While he had publicly justified the coup that brought Pinochet to power in 1973, ten years later he engaged in negotiations to speed the return of elected government. In addition, he traveled widely to generate pressure within and without Chile to encourage Pinochet to resign. While his efforts were not successful, they did contribute to the ultimate defeat of Pinochet in a 1988 plebiscite and to the return of democratic government in 1990. On 30 March 1990 Fresno resigned as cardinal archbishop of Santiago. He lost the right to participate in the papal conclave when he turned eighty years old in 2004. He died in his home in Santiago that same year.

*See also* **Catholic Action; Catholic Church: The Modern Period; Pinochet Ugarte, Augusto.**

BIBLIOGRAPHY

Escudero, Jaime Caiceo. *Cardenal Juan Francisco Fresno Larraín: Un Pastor para Chile.* Santiago de Chile: Universidad Católica Clas Cañas, 1996.

Smith, Brian H. *The Church and Politics in Chile: Challenges to Modern Catholicism.* Princeton, NJ: Princeton University Press, 1982.

MARGARET E. CRAHAN

---

**FREVO.** Frevo, frenetic carnival dance music of northeastern Brazil. The *frevo* first appeared around the turn of the twentieth century among newly formed carnival clubs of black and mestizo urban workers in Recife, Pernambuco. The acrobatic dance steps done to the *frevo* developed largely from the Capoeira (an Afro-Brazilian athletic dance), and the music itself grew out of the marches and polkas of military-style marching bands that accompanied Carnival parades. The *frevo* quickly became a mainstay of the Recife carnival, and several distinct substyles developed, including the *frevo de rua,* instrumental street music played by marching bands; *frevo de bloco,* played by small string and percussion ensembles with a female chorus; and *frevo canção,* middle-class sentimental songs involving a lead singer, a chorus, and a brass, woodwind, and percussion band. City-sponsored competitions take place each year in Recife, and numerous recordings have been released. Beginning in the 1950s, *frevo* was incorporated into the carnival of Salvador, Bahia, by *trios elétricos* (electric trios) using electric guitars and drums. This electric *frevo baiano* (Bahian *frevo*) entered mainstream Brazilian popular music in the 1970s and 1980s via such pop star luminaries as Caetano Veloso and Moraes Moreira. Alceu Valença and other northeastern popular musicians have added Recife-style *frevos* to their repertoires.

*See also* **Carnival; Music: Popular Music and Dance.**

BIBLIOGRAPHY

Valdemar De Oliveira, *Frevo, capoeira e passo* (1971); Fred De Góes, *O país do carnaval elétrico* (1982).

*Additional Bibliography*

Araújo, Rita de Cássia Barbosa de. *Festas: máscaras do tempo: Entrudo, mascarada e frevo no carnaval do Recife.* Recife, PE: Fundacão de Cultura Cidade do Recife, 1996.

Carvalho, Nelly, et al. *Dicionário do frevo.* Recife, PE: Editora Universitária, UFPE, 2000.

Teles, José. *Do frevo ao manguebeat.* São Paulo, SP, Brasil: Editora 34, 2000.

LARRY N. CROOK

---

**FREYRE, GILBERTO (DE MELLO)** (1900–1987). Gilberto (de Mello) Freyre (*b.* 15 March 1900; *d.* 18 July 1987), pivotal Brazilian cultural historian and essayist of the 1930s. His historical essay *Casa-grande & senzala* (*The Masters and the Slaves,* 1933) popularized Franz Boas's anthropological concept of culture as an antidote to pessimistic race science. Freyre argued that Brazil's "mixture" was psychic and cultural in addition to racial. Modern Brazilians were not doomed racial mongrels but rather the fortunate heirs of the colonial plantation's fusion of Portuguese, Indian, and African culture. This energetic and erotic essay became a best-seller. It eventually inspired Carnival samba pageants (1962) as well as nationalist political propaganda. For example, the claim that Brazil was a model of racial harmony became a theme of Brazilian diplomatic initiatives. Many of the ideas of *Casa-grande & senzala* and its two sequels, *Sobrados e mucambos* (*The Mansions and the Shanties,* 1936) and *Ordem e progresso* (*Order and Progress,* 1959), established themes for the next generation of social scientists in Brazil. These included the centrality of the patriarchal family as a social institution, Brazil's historical formation as a slave society, the sugar plantation as an institution, and the importance of folkways, especially those related to the house, food, and healing.

Outside of Brazil, Freyre's ideas had their greatest repercussion in the United States, where his studies at Baylor (1918–1920) and Columbia (1920–1922) universities, bohemian life in New York, and travels in the South had refined his sense of Brazil's uniqueness. In the 1940s scholars influenced by Freyre, such as Frank Tannenbaum, challenged Americans to measure themselves against the model of race relations presented in *Casa-grande & senzala.* Their debates developed into the contemporary fields of comparative race relations and comparative history of slavery. Freyre's impact was not limited to the United States. *Casa-grande & senzala* was translated into at least six languages. Freyre lectured, visited universities, and received honors throughout the world, including an honorary British knighthood in 1971.

Freyre's history of Brazil took a nostalgic and regional perspective, centering on the rise and decline of the sugar plantations of the Northeast. According to *Casa-grande & senzala,* Brazil was founded in a burst of energy by the "miscible" Portuguese, who were culturally suited to the task of building a multiracial tropical colony. During three centuries of near isolation from Portuguese government, Brazil's "patriarchal" society centered around the self-sufficient plantation big house. In its kitchens and bedrooms, a cultural and sexual fusion of peoples was accomplished. The result was a culturally "Oriental" society, in which the Jesuit religious order was the only disciplined, "European" counterweight to patriarchal whims. Plantation paternalism harmonized Brazilians and encouraged racial democracy; but plantation slavery, "like a great economic God," divided Brazilians into masters and slaves and encouraged authoritarianism.

*Sobrados e mucambos* chronicles the decline of this order. Upon the arrival of the exiled Portuguese king in 1808, Brazil centralized, urbanized, and "re-Europeanized." During the nineteenth century, plantation families moved from country big house to city mansion. Once there, urban social institutions—doctor, street, and school—destroyed patriarchalism. The woman and the child emerged as individuals, free from the father's tutelage. Ultimately, "white" planter fathers acceded to the marriage of their daughters to mulatto men of talent, forming a multiracial, "semipatriarchal" establishment. *Ordem e progresso* argues that the abolition of slavery in 1888 and the overthrow of the emperor in 1889 completed the dissolution of patriarchy. From 1890 forward, republican Brazil cast about for identity, having symbolically rejected its father. By 1914 the institutions of the republic had begun to forge a modern order that could accommodate the challenge of the "social question" of the working class while preserving the legacy of racial harmony.

A political interlude from 1946 to 1950 marked a watershed in Freyre's career. Previously, he had been secretary to the governor of Pernambuco (1926–1930) and had briefly gone into exile in 1930. During the dictatorship of Getúlio Vargas, his sponsorship of two Afro-Brazilian congresses in 1934 and 1937 and the audacious reputation of *Casa-grande & senzala* placed him under political suspicion. With the fall of Vargas, Freyre was elected to the 1946 Constituent Assembly and the Chamber of Deputies by a União Democrática Nacional (UDN) coalition. While in congress, Freyre championed cultural causes, including the chartering of the Instituto Joaquim Nabuco de Pesquisas Sociais in Recife, which eventually became his institutional base. In 1949 he was Brazilian delegate to the General Assembly of the United Nations. Freyre left political office in 1950, but he remained an active voice in Brazilian politics, now generally from the right. He contributed to the platforms of the pro-government Aliança Renovadora Nacional (ARENA) in the 1960s and 1970s.

After 1950 Freyre proposed the creation of a discipline of "Lusotropicology" that would study common aspects of the adaptations of Portuguese culture and rule to tropical colonies in Brazil, Africa, and Asia. Because Lusotropicalism appeared to embrace a defense of modern Portuguese colonialism in Africa, many other currents of social science in Brazil avoided it. Lusotropicalism never became a widespread intellectual movement. Furthermore, during the 1960s and 1970s, historians revised and criticized Freyre's descriptions of the supposedly benign components of slavery and race relations. Cultural anthropologists in the 1980s looked back to the insights of his early work but not to Lusotropicology.

Freyre's presence in Brazilian intellectual life was not confined to his roles as anthropologist, historian, or politician; he was also a distinctive literary voice. In the 1920s he urged the literary avant garde of his native Recife to explore regionalist themes in contrast to the futurist avant garde of São Paulo. Later, he published a sequence of two "semi novels," *Dona Sinhá e o filho padre: Seminovela* (*Mother and Son*, 1964) and *O outro amor do Dr. Paulo* (1977), that portray the traditional family relations and religiosity of the Brazilian Northeast. It was the style of his historical essays, however, that was his major contribution to Brazilian prose. He sometimes invoked Proust as his model for the autobiographical tone and nonlinear style of *Casa-grande & senzala;* other critics have detected a baroque aesthetic with Brazilian roots.

*See also* **Literature: Brazil; Race and Ethnicity.**

BIBLIOGRAPHY

Gilberto Amado et al., *Gilberto Freyre: Sua ciência, sua filosofia, sua arte* (1962), a collection of interpretive essays.

Thomas E. Skidmore, *Black into White: Race and Nationality in Brazilian Thought* (1974; rev. ed, 1993), on racial ideology in Brazil.

Edson Nery Da Fonseca, *Um livro completa meio século* (1983), a study and reference guide to *Casa-grande & senzala.* For criticism, see Thomas E. Skidmore, "Gilberto Freyre and the Early Brazilian Republic: Some Notes on Methodology," *Comparative Studies in Society and History* 6, no. 4 (1964): 490–505.

Carlos Guilherme Mota, *Ideologia da cultura brasileira* (*1933–1974*), 4th ed. (1978).

Luiz A. De Castro Santos, "A casa-Grande e o sobrado na obra de Gilberto Freyre," *Anuário Antropológico /83* (1985), pp. 73–102, a review of critiques. Recent evaluations of Freyre's legacy include Richard M. Morse, "Latin American Intellectuals and the City, 1860–1940," *Journal of Latin American Studies* 10, no. 2 (1978): 219–238.

Gilberto Felisberto Vasconcellos, *O xará de Apipucos* (1987).

Roberto Da Matta, "A originalidade de Gilberto Freyre," *BIB: Boletim Informativo e Bibliográfico de Ciências Sociais* 24 (1987): 3–10. There is self-analysis in Gilberto Freyre, *Como e porque sou e não sou sociólogo* (1968); and *Tempo morto e outros tempos: Trechos de um diário de adolescência e primeira mocidade, 1915–1930* (1975), memoirs in the form of an edited diary.

*Additional Bibliography*

Araújo, Ricardo Benzaquen de. *Guerra e paz: Casa Grande e Senzala e a obra de Gilberto Freyre nos anos 30.* Rio de Janeiro: Editora 34, 1994.

Bocayuva, Helena. *Erotismo à brasileira: Excesso sexual na obra de Gilberto Freyre.* Rio de Janeiro: Garamond, 2001.

Chacon, Vamireh. *A construção da brasilidade: Gilberto Freyre e a sua geração.* Sao Paulo: Marco Zero, 2001.

Isfahani-Hammond, Alexandra. *The Masters and the Slaves: Plantation Relations and Mestizaje in American Imaginaries.* New York: Palgrave Macmillan, 2005.

Pallares-Burke, Maria Lúcia G. *Gilberto Freyre: Um vitoriano dos trópicos.* Sao Paulo: Editore UNESP, 2005.

DAIN BORGES

---

**FRÍAS, ANTONIO** (1745–1824). Antonio Frías (*b.* 13 October 1745; *d.* 1824), Argentine-born astronomer. Frías was born in Santiago del Estero and entered the Society of Jesus in 1764, just three years before the Jesuits were expelled from the Río de la Plata. Exiled, he sailed on the *Venus* to the Papal States, where he was ordained to the priesthood. Frías became interested in astronomy as a seminarian and retained the interest throughout his life. He worked under the Jesuit astronomer and mathematician Roger Boscovich. Frías conducted research in the observatory of Brera, near Milan, and published his findings in the *Efemeridi astronomiche* of Milan. He left several unpublished manuscripts, which today are in the Jesuit archive of the Colegio Salvador in Buenos Aires. He died in Milan.

*See also* **Astronomy; Jesuits.**

BIBLIOGRAPHY

Francisco Talbot, "Otro astrónomo argentino. Antonio Frías, S.J., 1745–1824," in *Estudios* (Buenos Aires) 18 (1920): 346–349.

*Additional Bibliography*

Proverbio, Edoardo, and Letizia Buffoni. *Nuovo catalogo della corrispondenza di Ruggiero Giuseppe Boscovich.* Roma: Accademia nazionale delle scienze detta dei XL, 2004.

NICHOLAS P. CUSHNER

## FRIGERIO, ROGELIO (1914–2006).

Rogelio Frigerio (*b.* November 1914; *d.* September 2006), Argentine industrialist, journalist, and politician. Born in Buenos Aires, Frigerio achieved business success in textiles, mining, and agriculture. He served as editor and political director of the newsmagazine *Qué Sucedió en Siete Días,* director of the Center for National Research (1956–1988), and secretary for Economic-Social Relations of the Nation (1958). In 1959 he became economic counselor to the presidency. As Arturo Frondizi's closest advisor, Frigerio was responsible for the accord between Frondizi's Intransigent Radicals (Unión Cívica Radical Intransigente) and Juan D. Perón (then in exile), which had provided Peronist voting support for Frondizi's presidential victory in 1958. Frigerio influenced Frondizi's industrial strategy for national economic independence, which required large-scale involvement, on favorable terms, of foreign capital and technology. The strategy—particularly as it affected the petroleum industry, which Frondizi had until shortly before defended as the cornerstone of economic nationalism—outraged nationalists; moreover, it failed to achieve the intended results.

The president's attempt to bring the Peronist remnant into a permanent Radical-led coalition aroused increasing opposition among military anti-Peronists; in late March 1962 Frondizi was ousted by a military coup—the first of many as Argentina descended into chaos in the 1960s and 1970s. Once in power, the military charged Frigerio and his associates with "economic crimes." Thereafter, Frigerio remained close to Perón, but stayed out of public life until the 1980s. He became affiliated with the Movement for Integration and Development after 1975, and in 1983 he made an unsuccessful run for the presidency.

Frigerio published a score of books on politics and political economy, including *Los cuatro años (1958–1962)* (1962), *Petroleo y desarrollo* (1962), *Historia y política* (1963), *Crecimiento económico y democracia* (1963), *Estatuto del subdesarrollo: Las corrientes del pensamiento económico argentino* (1967), *Síntesis de la historia crítica de la economía Argentina* (1979), *Diez años de la crisis Argentina: Diagnóstico y programa del desarrollismo* (1983), and *Ciencia, tecnología y Futuro* (1995).

*See also* **Argentina, Political Parties: Intransigent Radicals; Frondizi, Arturo; Perón, Juan Domingo.**

BIBLIOGRAPHY

Amato, Alberto. *Cuando fuimos gobierno.* Buenos Aires: Editorial Paidós, 1983.

Merchensky, Marcos. *Las corrientes ideologicas en la historia argentina.* Buenos Aires: Editorial Concordia, 1961.

Szusterman, Celia. *Frondizi and the Politics of Developmentalism in Argentina, 1955–1962.* Pittsburgh, PA: University of Pittsburgh Press, 1993.

RONALD C. NEWTON

## FRIGORÍFICOS.

Frigoríficos (refrigerated meat-packing plants). On the traditional Estancia, workers killed cattle for their yield of hides, tallow, and dried meat. By the early nineteenth century, the processing of cattle moved from the plains to Saladeros, meat-salting plants. During the 1880s, *frigoríficos* began replacing *saladeros.* At the meat-packing plants, workers butchered animals and packed the meat for shipment in refrigerator ships to Europe. The *frigoríficos* required higher-quality meat, so ranchers introduced blooded bulls from Europe and planted alfalfa for feed to improve their stock. The British controlled the packinghouses of Buenos Aires until the early twentieth century, when the Chicago "beef trust" supplanted them. Meat packing remains an important industry in Argentina and Uruguay.

*See also* **Meat Industry.**

BIBLIOGRAPHY

David Rock, *Argentina, 1516–1987,* rev. and enl. ed. (1987).

*Additional Bibliography*

Valenzuela de Mari, Cristina Ofelia. *Ganaderia y estancias En Chaco y Formosa (1888-1998)*. Chaco: Instituto de Investigaciones Geohistóricas, 1998.

RICHARD W. SLATTA

**FRISCH, ALBERT** (c. 1840–1918). Albert Frisch (*b.* ca. 1840; *d.* 1918), German pioneer of anthropological photography. Frisch journeyed from Europe to the upper Brazilian Amazon region, especially on the Solimões River in the early 1860s to record the indigenous population. He posed them as noble savages, sometimes contriving or alternating backgrounds so that his subjects appeared as living sculptures. His works were displayed at the Paris Universal Exposition of 1867 before any other photographer recorded images of the indigenous populations of North America, the Far East, or Africa. Little is known about Frisch's life. He did not stay in Brazil, but contracted with the Leuzinger Studio in Rio de Janeiro to sell his prints.

*See also* **Photography: The Nineteenth Century.**

BIBLIOGRAPHY

Ferrez, Marc. *A fotografía no Brasil, 1840–1900.* Rio de Janeiro: Fundacao Nacional de Arte, 1985.

Lago, Bia Correa do. *Brésil, les premiers photographes d'un empire sous les tropiques.* Paris: Gallimard, 2005.

Vasquez, Pedro. *Fotógrafos alemães no Brasil do século XIX.* Sao Paulo: Metalivros, 2000.

Vasquez, Pedro. *A fotografia no Império.* Rio de Janeiro: Jorge Zahar, 2002.

ROBERT M. LEVINE

**FRONDIZI, ARTURO** (1908–1995). Arturo Frondizi was an Argentine politician who was president of the Republic from 1958 to 1962. He completed a law degree in 1930 and became an activist in the Radical Civic Union (Unión Cívica Radical, or UCR) following the coup d'état that overthrew Hipólito Irigoyen in 1930.

Frondizi quickly became a prominent party figure, and in 1946 was elected national deputy. He was the vice presidential running mate of Ricardo Balbín (1904–1981) in the presidential elections of 1951. The UCR lost the election to Juan Domingo Perón, but Frondizi became a well-known opponent of the Peronist regime. In 1954 he was elected president of the party's national committee. In 1955 he published *Petroleum and Politics*, which advocated the nationalization of the nation's fuel reserves and criticized Perón's petroleum policy.

Following the coup in 1955 the Liberating Revolution (Revolución Libertadora) group outlawed Peronism, an action that posed an impossible dilemma for the remaining political organizations. The UCR was incapable of coming up with a unified position on the restoration of Peronism to the political system, and therefore split into two factions: the Intransigent UCR (Intransigente), led by Frondizi, and the People's UCR (del Pueblo), led by Balbín. As the 1958 national elections approached, Frondizi signed a semisecret pact with Perón that gave him the support he needed to win the presidency.

Frondizi awarded amnesty to Peronist political prisoners and restored the legal status of the nation's trade unions. However, he was blocked by the military, which was deeply annoyed by his pact with Perón and refused to allow him to lift the ban on Peronism. Frondizi's economic policies were clearly developmentalist. In contrast to his previous nationalist positions, he signed contracts with foreign petroleum and automotive companies. He also took a loan from the International Monetary Fund that was conditioned upon the implementation of an orthodox adjustment strategy. These steps sparked strong opposition from trade unions and Peronists. In 1959, under pressure from the military, he removed Rogelio Frigerio, who had been his principal adviser, and replaced him with the liberal Álvaro Alsogaray as minister of the economy. He also set in motion a plan known as the Internal State Shakeup (Conmoción Interna del Estado) that gave the army the power to repress trade unions and Peronist activists. He managed to win the support of the church by allowing the creation of private universities, but this provoked strong opposition from mostly secular student organizations. Frondizi restored good relations with the United States while still maintaining an independent foreign policy. In 1961 he opposed the White House's move to expel Cuba from the Organization of American States, but the military soon forced him to break relations with Havana.

Frondizi never managed to come up with a strategy to rise above his highly vulnerable political situation. He allowed the Peronists to run in the 1962 elections, and they won ten of the fourteen provincial governorships. The military, alarmed at the Peronist victory, removed Frondizi from office. He returned to political life in the 1970s as the leader of the Movement for Integration and Development (Movimiento de Integración y Desarrollo). In 1988 he abandoned the party and his positions became more closely aligned with nationalism and the conservative right wing. He died in Buenos Aires in 1995 from cardiovascular problems.

*See also* **Alsogaray, Alvaro; Argentina, Political Parties: Justicialist Party; Argentina, Political Parties: Radical Party (UCR); Balbín, Ricardo; Irigoyen, Hipólito; Perón, Juan Domingo.**

BIBLIOGRAPHY

*Primary Works*

*Petroleum and Politics* (tract). 1955.

*Secondary Works*

Altamirano, Carlos. *Arturo Frondizi.* Buenos Aires: Facultad de Ciencias Económicas, 1998.

Cavarozzi, Marcelo. *Autoritarismo y democracia, 1955–1996. La transición del Estado al mercado en la Argentina.* Buenos Aires: Ariel, 1997.

Nosiglia, Julio E. *El desarrollismo.* Buenos Aires: Centro Editor de América Latina, 1983.

Smulovitz, Catalina. *Oposición y gobierno: Los años de Frondizi.* Buenos Aires: Centro Editor de América Latina, 1988.

VICENTE PALERMO

## FRONDIZI, RISIERI (1910–1985).

Risieri Frondizi (*b.* 20 November 1910; *d.* 1985), Argentine philosopher and author. Born in Posadas, Misiones Province, and brother of President Arturo Frondizi, Risieri Frondizi studied at the National Secondary Teaching Institute and then accepted a teaching position at the University of Tucumán (1938–1946). He continued his training abroad while writing and translating the works of George Berkeley, Alfred North Whitehead, and others. He received a master's degree in philosophy from the University of Michigan in 1943 and a doctorate from the National University of Mexico in 1950. For political and intellectual reasons, he accepted positions at universities in the United States and Puerto Rico.

Through his research and writing, he gained an international reputation as an expert in the study of individuals within society and of the nature of value and value judgments. His work includes *Substancia y fundación en el problema del yo* (1952), published in 1970 as *El yo como estructura dinámica.* After the 1955 overthrow of Juan Perón, Frondizi returned to Argentina and became rector of the University of Buenos Aires in 1957. After political events forced him from his university position, he returned to his research and writing. For an example of his works see *The Nature of the Self* (1953) and *Introducción a los problemas fundamentales del hombre* (1977).

*See also* **Philosophy: Overview.**

BIBLIOGRAPHY

Garcia, Jorge J.E. ed. *El hombre y su conducta: Ensayos filosóficos en honor de Risieri Frondizi.* Río Piedras: Universidad de Puerto Rico, 1980.

Hartman, Robert S. "Risieri Frondizi on the Nature of Value." *Philosophy and Phenomenological Research* (1961): 223–232.

DANIEL LEWIS

## FRONTIERS IN LATIN AMERICA.

Frontiers in Latin America can be defined in three ways. The more traditional definition is the line of demarcation between different nations. A second definition conceives of a frontier as contested space where European and indigenous influences pass back and forth, as through a membrane. In both cases, frontiers are often theaters of political, social, economic, and cultural clashes. In its third incarnation, the frontier takes on symbolic or mythological significance (Slatta 2001a, pp. 6, 27, 32–33, 53).

### FRONTIERS AS BOUNDARIES

The fuzziness of national boundaries in Latin America begins in 1494, with the line of Tordesillas, running 370 leagues west of the Cape Verde Islands. That bit of geographical intervention produced centuries of conflict first between Spain and Portugal and later between Brazil and Argentina over who controlled the territory between them. British intervention in 1826, which turned the Banda Oriental (aka Provincia Cisplatina) into Uruguay, finally resolved the issue.

Conflicting land claims, often over remote and lightly populated regions, have continued into the early twenty-first century. In some cases, even clear natural features, such as rivers, have failed to prevent conflict. War erupted between Mexico and the United States in the mid-1840s because each claimed a different river, the Rio Grande and Nueces respectively, as the boundary between Texas and Mexico. In the War of the Pacific (1879–1884), Chile defeated two neighbors and annexed the mineral-rich provinces of Tarapacá from Peru and Litoral from Bolivia. During the 1930s three boundary wars broke out: Bolivia and Paraguay over the Chaco region, Peru and Colombia over the Leticia region, and Peru and Ecuador over the Zarumilla region (Domínguez, p. 20).

The late twentieth century featured a number of conflicts over national boundaries. Wars erupted between El Salvador and Honduras (1969), Argentina and the United Kingdom over the Falklands/Malvinas (1982), and Ecuador and Peru (1995). Serious disputes not resulting in warfare included Argentina and Chile (1978), Chile versus Bolivia and Peru (late 1970s); and Colombia and Venezuela (1987). Tensions remain over longstanding disputes between Venezuela and Guyana and between Guatemala and Belize (Domínguez, pp. 18–19).

Many factors can exacerbate frontier boundary disputes. Natural resources, such as oil, can fan frontier conflicts, such as between Ecuador and Peru. Revolutionary groups and drug traffickers have fomented shootings near the long border between Colombia and Venezuela. Cross-border migration heightened the tension between El Salvador and Honduras, and illegal immigration across the Mexican–U.S. border remains a political hot issue.

## FRONTIERS AS CONTESTED AREAS

Throughout the Americas, frontier regions have served as membranes through which trade goods and intercultural exchanges passed in both directions. Vicente de Zaldívar noted in 1598 that the Apache of northern New Spain "sell meat, hides, tallow, suet, and salt in exchange for cotton, blankets, pottery, maize, and some small green stones" (quoted in Slatta 2001, p. 71). In Uruguay, Argentina, and southern Brazil, gauchos and *gaúchos* adapted many elements of native language, cuisine (maté), dress, and riding equipment. Similar borrowings occurred on the llanos of Venezuela and Colombia and in southern Chile (Slatta 1994, pp. 160–161). Indians likewise adopted elements of European culture. Navajos, for example, took up sheep raising. Firearms and metal knives also became important to many native groups.

However, the policy of domination by colonial powers quickly turned natives from cooperation toward resistance and conflict. Competition for resources, including livestock, water, land, and salt, precipitated Indian-white conflicts. Resistance became even more formidable after native groups acquired horses that turned Indians from the pampas of Argentina to the Great Plains of the United States into highly successful hunters and cavalrymen. J. Ignatius Molina observed of the Araucanians of the pampas: "perceiving the great advantage which their enemies derived from cavalry, they soon began to discipline themselves in the same manner. Their first care was to procure a good breed of horses" (quoted in Slatta 2001a, p. 41). Not surprisingly, equestrian Indians resisted longer than sedentary groups, and whites in Chile, Argentina, Mexico, and the United States did not subdue them until the waning decades of the nineteenth century (Slatta 1994, pp. 161–162, 170–171).

## FRONTIERS AS SYMBOLS AND MYTHS

As a symbolic or mythical place, the frontier in Latin America appears in a number of guises. One is the "Golden Frontier of Treasure, Abundance, and Opportunity." Beginning with the wanderings of Alvar Núñez Cabeza de Vaca (1528), there are tales of a land "abounding in gold and silver, with (seven) great cities whose houses were many stories high, whose streets were lined with silversmiths' shops, and whose doors were inlaid with turquoise." A decade later, Francisco Vasquez de Coronado, after traveling for months in the wilderness, reached the so-called Seven Cities of Gold in the land that he named Cibola. In South America, the wealth of the Chibchas or Muiscas of the Andes created a vision of El Dorado, "the gilded one" (Slatta 2001b, pp. 96–97).

A second incarnation is the polar opposite of the golden frontier, the "Desert Frontier of Barbarism and Emptiness," devoid of civilization. Dangerous frontiersmen, often horsemen, inhabited these distant reaches. Alexander von Humboldt accurately described life in llaneros, the cowboys of Colombia and Venezuela. "Men naked to the waist and armed with a lance, ride over the savannahs to inspect the animals.... Their food is meat dried in the air and a little salted; and of this even their horses sometimes eat" (quoted in Slatta 2001a, p. 91).

Argentina's Domingo F. Sarmiento provided one well-known paradigm of frontiersmen with his portraits of gauchos in his 1845 book *Civilization and Barbarism.* He described the pampas frontier in unflattering terms: "the evil from which the Argentine Republic suffers," "desert," "wastes containing no human dwelling," "savages ever on watch" (Sarmiento, p. 2). Also writing in the mid-nineteenth century, Ramón Páez, a European-educated Venezuelan, found many shortcomings in the "barbarous" life of the llaneros, the "mongrel breed" inhabiting the plains. In *Doña Bárbara* (1929), Rómulo Gallegos reprised Sarmiento's theme of civilization versus barbarism, this time set in the Venezuelan llanos. Gallegos has his protagonist describe the frontier: "Wild plains! Wild vastness! Illimitable deserted prairies—deep, silent, solitary streams!" (Gallegos, p. 17).

Yet a third symbolic incarnation posits the "Frontier as the Future." Brazilian politicians acted on this myth with their push to the West in the 1960s and the creation of the new national capital of Brasilia on the edge of the Amazonian wilderness. In the early twenty-first century, gold miners, or *garimpeiros,* in the Amazon, most working illegally, have created a new gold rush. Hoping to emulate Brasilia's success, Argentina briefly renamed its currency the "austral" to point national energy south toward its vast, still sparsely settled Patagonian frontier. In similar fashion, Venezuela pins its hopes on the remote inland Orinoco River basin. In each case, the frontier is visualized as the key to future national greatness (Slatta 2001a, p. 24).

Frontiers, real and imagined, have played a huge role in Latin American history, culture, and mythology. Expect future reincarnations to continue to influence the region's culture and politics. Given its allure and malleability, as metaphor, myth, historical category, place, and process, the frontier shows little real signs of passing. Nor should it.

*See also* **Araucanians; Cabeza de Vaca, Alvar Núñez; Gallegos, Rómulo; Humboldt, Alexander von; Sarmiento, Domingo Faustino; Tordesillas, Treaty of (1494); War of the Pacific.**

BIBLIOGRAPHY


Barran, José Pedro, and Benjamin Nahum. *Historia rural del Uruguay moderno,* 7 vols. Montevideo: Ediciones de la Banda Orienta, 1967–1978.

Domínguez, Jorge I., with David Mares, Manuel Orozco, David Scott Palmer, Francisco Rojas Aravena, and Andrés Serbin. *Boundary Disputes in Latin America.* Washington, DC: United States Institute of Peace, 2003. Available from http://www.usip.org/pubs/peaceworks/pwks50.pdf.

Gallegos, Rómulo. *Doña Bárbara,* 1929. Translated by Robert Malloy. Reprint, New York: Peter Smith, 1948.

Góngora, Mario. *Vagabundaje y sociedad fronteriza en Chile, siglos XVII a XIX.* Santiago: Universidad de Chile, 1966.

Guy, Donna J., and Thomas E. Sheridan, eds. *Contested Ground: Comparative Frontiers on the Northern and Southern Edges of the Spanish Empire.* Tucson: University of Arizona Press, 1998.

Hennessy, Alistair. *The Frontier in Latin American History.* Albuquerque: University of New Mexico Press, 1978.

Sarmiento, Domingo F. *Life in the Argentine Republic in the Days of the Tyrants; or, Civilization and Barbarism.* 1845. Translated by Mrs. Horace Mann, 1868. Reprint, New York: Hafner, 1971.

Slatta, Richard W. *Cowboys of the Americas.* New Haven, CT: Yale University Press, Western Americana Series, 1990, 1994.

Slatta, Richard W. *Comparing Cowboys and Frontiers: New Perspectives on the History of the Americas.* Norman: University of Oklahoma Press, 1997, 2001a.

Slatta, Richard W. *The Mythical West: An Encyclopedia of Legend, Lore, and Popular Culture.* Santa Barbara, CA: ABC-CLIO, 2001b.

Weber, David. *The Spanish Frontier in North America.* New Haven, CT: Yale University Press, 1992.

Weber, David J., and Jane M. Rausch, eds. *Where Cultures Meet: Frontiers in Latin American History.* Wilmington, DE: Scholarly Resources, 1994.


RICHARD W. SLATTA

**FRUGONI, EMILIO** (1880–1969). Emilio Frugoni (*b.* 30 March 1880; *d.* 28 August 1969), Uruguayan lawyer, professor, writer, and founder of the Uruguayan Socialist Party. Frugoni promoted Marxist and socialist ideas in highly regarded works such as *Socialismo, batllismo y nacionalismo* (1928), *La revolución del machete* (1935), *Ensayos sobre marxismo* (1936), and *Génesis, esencia y fundamentos del socialismo* (1947).

Frugoni was a supporter of Colorado Party president José Batlle y Ordóñez, whose first term from 1903 to 1907 marked an end to the country's long civil wars and the beginning of peace, prosperity, and undisputed Colorado control of government. Frugoni supported Batlle's important moral legislation (permitting divorce and ending the death penalty), state enterprises (strengthening of the state-owned Bank of the Republic and the Montevideo Electric Power System), support of labor (police neutrality in strikes and the promotion of an eight-hour work day), public works, and school construction. He also approved of Batlle's opposition to the church and to intransigent conservatism. In 1910 he supported the government against the threat of the "October Revolution" led by Nepomuceno Saravia, son of Aparicio Saravia, the famous Nationalist (Blanco) Party caudillo, and Basilio Muñoz, military commander of the Radicals.

Beginning in 1904 Frugoni promoted the formation of a Socialist Party that would constitute the country's workers as a political force. The Socialist manifesto that he authored in 1910 supported the constitutional order, in contrast to the Anarchists' destabilizing politics. As Socialist deputy to the national congress (1911–1914), he again collaborated with Batlle, who had been elected to a second presidential term, by authoring several important legislative projects aimed at socioeconomic reform on behalf of the working class. Frugoni's Socialist Party never came to rival the country's two traditional parties; it did not attract a significant working-class membership, perhaps due to the successes of Batlle's Colorado Party in implementing the greater part of its social program.

In subsequent years Frugoni was dean of the National University (1933). While serving as Uruguay's ambassador to the Soviet Union (1945–1948), he wrote *La esfinge roja* (1948), which praised the significant transformations of that nation but raised a voice of alarm about its denial of individual rights in favor of an omnipotent state. Between 1900 and 1959 he published twelve collections of lyrical poetry.

*See also* **Batlle y Ordóñez, José; Uruguay, Political Parties: Socialist Party.**

BIBLIOGRAPHY

Milton I. Vanger, *The Model Country: José Batlle y Ordóñez of Uruguay, 1907–1915* (1980).

*Additional Bibliography*

Giudice, Gerardo. *Frugoni.* Montevideo: Proyección, 1995.

WILLIAM H. KATRA

**FRUIT INDUSTRY.** Nineteenth-century improvements in transportation technology allowed tropical fruits to become a profitable Latin American export for the first time in the 1860s. Bananas were, and continue to be, the most profitable of the fruit exports; their commercial cultivation has been largely confined to the Caribbean Basin (including Central America and the northern coast of Colombia) and Ecuador. In addition to bananas, other tropical fruits are exported from the Caribbean Basin and Mexico, and grapes and other fruits are important to Chile's export economy.

Bananas were first exported to the Gulf coast of the United States in small quantities by shipping companies that occasionally bought the fruits from small independent producers in the Caribbean. In the 1870s the Costa Rican banana industry got off the ground as a subsidiary of the U.S.-based Tropical Trading and Transport Company. At the same time a Boston sea captain, Lorenzo Baker, began to import bananas to New England; this was to become the basis of the Boston Fruit Company. In 1899 the two companies merged to form the United Fruit Company. United Fruit was eventually organized as a vertical monopoly which included plantations, rail and sea transportation, and even a supermarket chain.

United Fruit and its major competitors, Standard Fruit and Cuyamel Fruit Company, were often deeply involved in the politics of the countries in which they operated, especially in Central America. The fruit companies operated on larger budgets than did any of the

**Workers sort citrus fruits in a processing plant in Belize, c. early twenty-first century.** Citrus is now Belize's leading export. © JIM WEST/THE IMAGE WORKS

Central American republics, and the companies were able to buy off both politicians and mercenary soldiers to influence politics in their favor. Their power challenged the sovereignty of the Central American republics.

Although the fruit companies were in many ways model employers, paying higher wages than other agricultural enterprises and providing benefits such as schools and health care for employees, their power came to be resented among Latin Americans.

During the 1960s disease and political problems decreased the profitability of Caribbean-grown bananas. However, bananas continued to provide important export earnings and employment. Throughout the 1990s the Caribbean banana industry fought challenges by the United States and Ecuador over European Union (EU) tariff preferences that favored former European colonies. In the twenty-first century, however, the World Trade Organization ruled against this arrangement. Though the EU in 2007 declared a commitment to Caribbean fruit, banana farmers in the Windward Islands remained concerned.

Ecuador is now Latin America's largest exporter of bananas. Although the United Fruit Company started operations in Ecuador in 1933, the fruit industry did not expand significantly until after World War II. Unlike the industry in the Caribbean Basin, the Ecuadorian banana industry has been dominated by small and medium- sized producers who sell their produce to the large corporations. They have accordingly avoided many of the political problems experienced in the Caribbean Basin.

Chile since the 1970s has become an increasingly important supplier of fresh fruit. Between 2006 and 2007 alone, fruit sales abroad increased 10 percent. In addition to more traditional exports such as grapes, Chilean farmers have successfully experimented with exports of citrus fruits, apples, pears, blueberries, stone-fruits, and kiwi.

Since the late 1960s exports of tropical fruits such as mangoes, papayas, passion fruit, and guava have been increasinly important in Spanish America. Globalization, economic liberalization, and technology have further increased Latin America's fruit production. Many countries now grow nontraditional varieties. For instance, the apple is Brazil's number-one fruit export, and Argentina also has expanded its apple and pear exports. Mexico specializes in strawberries. Still, they had yet to threaten the dominance of the banana.

*See also* **Agriculture.**

BIBLIOGRAPHY

Thomas Mc Cann, *An American Company: The Tragedy of United Fruit,* edited by Henry Scammell (1976).

Thomas L. Karnes, *The Standard Fruit and Steamship Company in Latin America* (1978).

José Roberto López, *La economía del banano en Centroamérica* (1986).

Carlos Larrea M., Malva Espinosa, and Paola Sylva Charvet, *El banano en Ecuador: Transnacionales, modernización y subdesarrollo* (1987).

Stephen Schlesinger and Stephen Kinzer, *Bitter Fruit: The Untold Story of the American Coup in Guatemala,* 3d ed. (1990).

*Additional Bibliography*

Barahona, Marvin, ed. *El silencio quedó atrás: Testimonios de la huelga bananera de 1954.* Tegucigalpa, Honduras: Editorial Guaymuras, 1994.

Barrientos, Stephanie. *Women and Agribusiness: Working Miracles in the Chilean Fruit Export Sector.* New York: St. Martin's Press, 1999.

Barros, Magdalena. *From Maize to Melons: Struggles and Strategies of Small Mexican Farmers.* Amsterdam: Centre for Latin American Research and Documentation in Amsterdam, 2000.

Bendini, Mónica, and Nélida Bonaccorsi V. *Con las puras manos: Mujer y trabajo en regiones frutícolas de exportación.* Buenos Aires: Editorial La Colmena, 1998.

Bucheli, Marcelo. *Bananas and Business: The United Fruit Company in Colombia, 1899–2000.* New York: New York University Press, 2005.

Casaburi, Gabriel G. *Dynamic Agroindustrial Clusters: The Political Economy of Competitive Sectors in Argentina and Chile.* New York: St. Martin's Press, 1999.

Chomsky, Aviva. *West Indian Workers and the United Fruit Company in Costa Rica, 1870–1940.* Baton Rouge: Louisiana State University Press, 1996.

McNeil, Cameron L. *Chocolate in Mesoamerica: A Cultural History of Cacao.* Gainesville: University Press of Florida, 2006.

Medel, Julia, and Verónica Riquelme. *La salud ignorada: Temporeras de la fruticultura.* Santiago: Ediciones CEM, 1994.

Paulillo, Luiz Fernando. *Redes de poder and territórios produtivos: Indústria, citricultura e políticas públicas no Brasil do século XX.* São Carlos, Brazil: RiMa Editora, 2000.

Striffler, Steve. *In the Shadows of State and Capital: The United Fruit Company, Popular Struggle, and Agrarian Restructuring in Ecuador, 1900–1995.* Durham, NC: Duke University Press, 2002.

Striffler, Steve, and Mark Moberg. *Banana Wars: Power, Production, and History in the Americas.* Durham, NC: Duke University Press, 2003.

Rachel A. May

**FUENTES, CARLOS** (1928–). Carlos Fuentes (*b.* 11 November 1928), Mexican writer, major literary figure, and spokesman not only for his country, but for all of Latin America. A prolific writer of novels, short stories, plays, and essays that possess intellectual brilliance and a powerful style, Fuentes is also a pioneer in narration and structure. A highly visible figure, he has been the subject of several television documentaries and interviews.

Son of Mexican diplomat Rafael Fuentes Boettiger and Berta Macías Rivas, Fuentes was born in Panama City and attended elementary school in Washington, D.C., and secondary schools in Buenos Aires and Santiago, Chile. He studied law at the Institut des Hautes Études Internationales (Geneva) and received a law degree from the National University of Mexico. He was named secretary to the Mexican delegation of the International Law Commission of the United Nations (Geneva) in 1950. He launched his literary career in 1954 with a collection of short stories, *Los días enmascarados* (Masked Days) and his first novel, *La región más transparente* (1958; *Where the Air Is Clear,* 1960) which brought him immediate recognition.

From 1956 to 1959 Fuentes served as director of international cultural relations at the Mexican Ministry of Foreign Affairs. In 1962 he published one of his major works, *La muerte de Artemio Cruz* (1962; *The Death of Artemio Cruz,* 1964), a novel that vividly depicts the corruption of the Mexican Revolution through the portrayal of a man in his last twelve hours of agony, during which he relives twelve crucial moments of his life. The main themes of his novella *Aura* (1962), found in most of Fuentes's works, are time, history, identity, desire, and civilization. *Cambio de piel* (1967; *A Change of Skin,* 1968) received the Biblioteca Breve prize in Barcelona the same year it was published. In an important book of literary criticism, *La nueva novela hispanoamericana* (1969; The New Latin American Novel) Fuentes analyzed the internationally acclaimed group of Latin American writers of the 1960s. While serving as ambassador to France (1974–1977), he published his essay *Don Quixote; or, the Critique of Reading* (1976), arguably the best guide to a full understanding of Fuentes's ideas.

Fuentes's most ambitious novel, *Terra nostra* (1975), published in English under the same title in 1976, is a powerful epic illustrating how the discovery of America provided a second opportunity for utopia that was defeated by human events. Among the many literary accolades Fuentes has received are Mexico's Javier Villaurrutia Prize (1975), the Rómulo Gallegos Prize of 1977 in Caracas for *Terra nostra,* and in 1987 Spain's prestigious Cervantes Prize. *Burnt Water* (1980) is a collection of Fuentes's best short stories written between 1954 and 1980. They depict the Spanish and indigenous past with force and nostalgia. In *Cristóbal Nonato* (1987; *Christopher Unborn,* 1989), the tone is similar to that of *Terra Nostra,* offering an apocalyptic vision of Mexico's future in which he uses humor, as well as his trademark remarkable play of words.

During the 1992 year of the quincentenary of the meeting of the Old World with the New, Fuentes narrated a popular television series, *The Buried Mirror,* on the epic of "encounter" of the European and the indigenous world of Hispanic America. *Todas las familias felices* (2006) is a collection of short stories that reflect his political stance and depict controversial situations in Mexican society. He continues writing, delving into Mexico's past, defining Mexico's national identity, and serving as Mexico's goodwill ambassador. He has also spent much time teaching at various universities in the United States.

*See also* **Literature: Spanish America.**

BIBLIOGRAPHY

Brody, Robert, and Charles Grossman, eds. *Carlos Fuentes: A Critical View.* Austin: University of Texas Press, 1982.

Faris, Wendy B. *Carlos Fuentes.* New York: Frederick Ungar, 1983.

Giacoman, Helmy F., ed. *Homenaje a Carlos Fuentes: Variaciones interpretivas en torno a su obra.* Long Island City, NY: Las Américas, 1971.

Grenier, Yvon. "Cambio de piel: Disposiciones y posiciones políticas de Carlos Fuentes." *Foro Hispánico: Revista Hispánica de los Países Bajos* 22 (2002): 121–135.

Penn, Sheldon. *Carlos Fuentes's Terra Nostra and the Kabbalah: The Creation of the Hispanic World.* Lewiston, NY: Edwin Mellen, 2003.

Van Delden, Maarten. *Carlos Fuentes, Mexico, and Modernity.* Nashville, TN: Vanderbilt University Press, 1998.

Williams, Raymond. *The Modern Latin American Novel.* New York: Twayne Publishers, 1998.

MARTHA PALEY FRANCESCATO

---

**FUENTES, MANUEL ATANASIO** (1820–1889). Manuel Atanasio Fuentes (*b.* 1820; *d.* 2 January 1889), Peru's foremost statistician of the era was also an acute observer of Lima in the mid-nineteenth century. A census taker, journalist, administrator, social commentator, satirist, historian, and folklorist, he also delivered expert opinion on legal and medical questions. Fuentes drew notice as a journalist in the 1840s, when he began writing on the everyday life and customs of Lima. A traditionalist who feared that guano excesses would destroy Peru's subsistence highland village economy and thus alter traditional highland culture, Fuentes sought to awaken intellectuals to thinking about the primacy of Andean culture. He also documented the size and variety of the artisan population of Lima in *Guía histórico-descriptiva administrativa, judicial y de domicilio de Lima* (1860), a study carried out after the artisan uprisings of 1858. Between 1858 and 1878 he produced a series of statistical studies based on painstaking research. His voluminous *Estadística general de Lima* (1858) listed data on every aspect of urban life: population, architecture, customs, and industry. He updated this survey four times and issued editions in French and English. He also wrote street guides and almanacs on Lima. As a public administrator, he directed the organization of a new faculty of political science and administration at the National University of San Marcos, a task undertaken at the behest of President Manuel Pardo, and he undertook the country's first scientific national census (1876).

*See also* **Journalism; Peru: Peru Since Independence.**

BIBLIOGRAPHY

Paul Gootenberg, *Imagining Development: Economic Ideas in Peru's "Fictitious Prosperity" of Guano, 1840–1880* (1993), esp. pp. 64–71.

Alfonso W. Quiroz, *Domestic and Foreign Finance in Modern Peru, 1850–1950: Financing Visions of Development* (1993).

*Additional Bibliography*

Coloma Porcari, César. *La ciudad de los reyes y la guía del viajero en Lima de Manuel Atanasio Fuentes.* Lima: Instituto Latinoámericano de Cultura y Desarrollo, 1997.

VINCENT PELOSO

## FUENTES Y GUZMÁN, FRANCISCO ANTONIO DE (1642–1699).

Francisco Antonio de Fuentes y Guzmán (*b.* 9 February 1642; *d.* 1 August 1699), Central American historian, poet, bureaucrat, and soldier. He was born in Santiago de los Caballeros (now Antigua), Guatemala; little is known about his early life. At age eighteen he was named *regidor* of his native city, and later first (and then second) *alcalde* of Santiago de Guatemala. He also held the post of *alcalde mayor* in the town of Totonicapán and the province of Sonsonate. In the army he attained the rank of captain. Among his poems are "El Milagro de América" and "La vida de Santa Teresa de Jesús."

The work for which Fuentes y Guzmán is remembered today is his monumental history of Guatemala, the full title of which is *Recordación florida: Discurso historial y demostración natural, material, militar, y política del reyno de Guatemala*. He embarked on the project with a number of aims in mind. First, he wanted to take advantage of the deteriorating documents still at his disposal, especially those pertaining to the Spanish conquest of Guatemala. Second, he hoped to fulfill a request of the crown to provide a detailed history of the region. Finally, Fuentes y Guzmán hoped to answer some of the criticisms directed at Bernal Díaz Del Castillo, a lieutenant under Cortés whose own *True History of the Conquest of New Spain* drew attacks from many Spaniards and creoles. Fuentes y Guzmán was a great-great-grandson of Díaz and thus may have hoped that writing the *Recordación florida* would clear his family's name.

The *Recordación florida* covers the history of Guatemala from antiquity to the end of the seventeenth century, and includes detailed studies of the topography, climate, population, minerals, and natural resources of the kingdom. In addition to published materials, Fuentes y Guzmán relied on documents stored, and long ignored, in the capital city, as well as on information he gathered as *alcalde* of Totonicapán.

Although by the standards of the day his work was a model of scholarship, Fuentes y Guzman reflected many of the biases held by his contemporaries. In his work Spaniards were invariably depicted as heroes; Indians, generally as slothful and immoral. Amid sound scholarship Fuentes y Guzmán included fantastic stories and doctored historical fact in order to portray the conquistadores in the most favorable light. Nevertheless, the *Recordación florida* continues to be a standard work for scholars of the pre-Columbian and colonial periods in Guatemala. Its contributions on the religion, geography, history, and natural sciences of the region are still significant today. The writing is first rate, reflecting the highly educated and erudite individual who wrote the first secular history of the kingdom of Guatemala. Fuentes y Guzmán died in Santiago de Guatemala.

*See also* **Díaz del Castillo, Bernal; Guatemala.**

BIBLIOGRAPHY

Francisco Antonio Fuentes y Guzmán, *Recordación florida: Discurso historial y demostración natural, material, militar, y política del reyno de Guatemala*, 2d ed., 3 vols. (1932–1933) and *Obras históricas de Francisco Antonio de Fuentes y Guzmán* (1969).

Murdo Mac Leod, *Spanish Central America: A Socioeconomic History, 1520–1720* (1973).

*Additional Bibliography*

Pastor, Rodolfo. "De moros en la costa a negros de Castilla: Representación y realidad en las crónicas del siglo XVII centroamericano." *Historia Mexicana* 44:2 (Oct.–Dec. 1994): 195–235.

MICHAEL POWELSON

**FUENZALIDA GRANDÓN, ALEJANDRO** (1865–1942). Born in the northern Chilean mining city of Copiapó, Alejandro Fuenzalida grew up in an environment of progressive liberal and positivist ideas, the region being one of the major strongholds of the Radical Party. Educated at the Instituto Nacional in Santiago, Fuenzalida also studied law at the University of Chile, where he obtained his degree in 1889. He taught law at his alma mater and history at the Instituto Nacional while devoting himself to research and writing. His most lasting contribution to Chilean intellectual and political history is his edition of the *Obras Completas* by José Victorino Lastarria (1908), a thinker and statesman to whom he also devoted a considerable biography, *Lastarria y su tiempo* (1902; 2nd rev. ed., 1911), a far from celebratory account. In addition to writing for the periodicals *La libertad electoral* and *La ley*, Fuenzalida also published *Historia del desarrollo intelectual en Chile, 1541–1810* (1903), a pioneering work of Chilean intellectual history, and *La evolución social de Chile, 1541–1810* (1906), an ambitious essay reflecting the secular views of his Radical contemporaries. In addition to writing, Fuenzalida collaborated with his mentor, the prominent historian Diego Barros Arana in the cataloging of the library of the Instituto Nacional.

*See also* **Chile, Political Parties: Radical Party, Chile: The Twentieth Century.**

BIBLIOGRAPHY

Donoso, Ricardo. "El Instituto Pedagógico: Tres generaciones de maestros." *Atenea* 401 (1963).

Feliú Cruz, Guillermo. *Alejandro Fuenzalida Grandón.* Santiago de Chile: Imprenta "Jeneral Díaz," 1938.

Gazmuri Riveros, Cristián. *Historia de la Historiografía chilena (1842–1970)*. Santiago de Chile: Taurus, 2006.

IVÁN JAKSIĆ

**FUEROS.** Fueros, local laws and privileges extended to towns, provinces, or particular groups such as the clergy or military. In Spain, the term *fueros* is commonly associated with the constitutional liberties of non-Castilian provinces and towns that each new king promised to maintain before he could be formally recognized as monarch. These local and provincial privileges limited the authority of the king in matters of taxation and military recruitment and protected the authority of local elites. In Aragon, for example, *fueros* ensured the perpetuation of aristocratic privilege in the guise of territorial autonomy. Not until the reign of Philip V were the *fueros* of Aragon and Valencia (1707) and Catalonia (1714) abolished.

Ecclesiastical and military *fueros* constituted corporate privileges that provided the protection of these two areas of law. In the New World, militia members granted the *fuero militar* were exempt, together with their families, from trial in civil courts and certain forms of taxation.

*See also* **Judicial Systems: Spanish America.**

BIBLIOGRAPHY

John H. Elliott, *Imperial Spain, 1469–1716* (1963).

Henry Kamen, *Spain, 1469–1714* (1983).

*Additional Bibliography*

Méndez Sereno, Herminia Cristina. *La iglesia católica en tiempos de Guzmán Blanco.* Caracas: Academia Nacional de la Historia, 1995.

Zimmermann, Eduardo A. *Judicial Institutions in Nineteenth-century Latin America.* London: University of London, Institute of Latin American Studies, 1999.

SUZANNE HILES BURKHOLDER

**FUJIMORI, ALBERTO KEINYA** (1938–). Alberto Fujimori, the son of Japanese immigrants who worked as farm laborers, was the president of Peru from 1990 to 2000. Raised in a working-class neighborhood and educated in public schools, Fujimori earned an agricultural engineering degree from Peru's National Agrarian University (La Molina) and a master's degree in mathematics from the University of Wisconsin (Milwaukee), taught at La Molina, and was elected the university's rector (president). Although he gained some recognition as host of a public issues television talk show, he was a political unknown when he launched his presidential campaign in 1989 as the candidate of Change 1990 (Cambio 90), newly formed by professionals, small businessmen, and evangelical Protestants.

**Former Peruvian president Alberto Fujimori's extradition from Chile to Peru, September 2007.** Controversial president Fujimori was extradited to face charges in Peru ranging from corruption to abuse of human rights. © IAN SALAS/EPA/CORBIS

To virtually everyone's surprise, he won the 1990 elections when the majority of the Peruvian electorate rejected the candidates of the political parties they deemed responsible for the country's worst economic and political crisis in more than a hundred years. Over the course of his administrations, Fujimori presided over the end of hyperinflation (from 7,650 percent in 1990 to 10 percent by 1995); the restoration of economic growth (from minus 10 percent in 1990 to more than 12 percent in 1994) through the application of neoliberal policies that included the reduction of government employees by some 400,000; and the demise of the Shining Path guerrillas (from more than 4,000 deaths attributed to Shining Path attacks in 1990 to less than 200 by 1995). The capture of guerrilla leader Abimael Guzmán Reynoso and the organization's master files in September 1992 was followed by a forgiveness decree encouraging more than five thousand guerrilla militants and sympathizers to return to society, and a major microdevelopment program that focused on Peru's poorest rural districts, which reduced extreme poverty from 31 percent to 15 percent between 1993 and 1998. In foreign affairs, the Fujimori government restored Peru's good standing in the international financial community and, in October 1998, following the Ecuador-Peru war that broke out along the frontier in January 1995, negotiated a definitive settlement of the countries' long-standing border dispute.

In spite of such successes, Fujimori progressively undermined Peru's democracy. In an April 1992 self-coup (*autogolpe*), he suspended congress, the judiciary, and constitutional guarantees. Although pressured by the Organization of American States (OAS) to restore democratic institutions, a new constitution allowed the president to seek a second successive term. After his 1995 reelection, Fujimori and his close adviser, Vladimiro Montesinos, increasingly engaged in manipulation of democratic institutions and the media to pursue an unconstitutional third term. Such blatant affronts to democracy, combined with an economic downturn beginning in 1998, contributed to growing popular disquiet and protest in the 2000 re-reelection campaign, tainted by what the OAS Election Observation Mission termed a fraudulent process. Within months, however, Montesinos and Fujimori fled Peru after revelations of a sale of Peruvian arms to Colombian guerrillas and of videotapes showing Montesinos buying off opposition members of congress to achieve a government majority; an interim administration took over in November 2000.

From exile in Japan, the discredited ex-president resisted Peru's extradition efforts by revealing that he had never renounced Japanese citizenship, and retained contact with supporters through a Web site. When he abandoned Japan for Chile in early 2006 so as to influence Peru's April elections, however, he was arrested and jailed. As of May 2007, a Chilean court continues to review Peru's request for Fujimori's extradition to stand trial for extrajudicial killings during his administration.

*See also* **Cambio 90, Cambio 90-Nueva Mayoría (C90-NM); Ecuador-Peru Boundary Disputes; Montesinos, Vladimiro; Peru: Peru Since Independence; Peru, Revolutionary Movements: Shining Path.**

BIBLIOGRAPHY

Carrión, Julio, ed. *The Fujimori Legacy: The Rise of Electoral Authoritarianism in Peru.* University Park: Pennsylvania State University Press, 2006.

Conaghan, Catherine M. *Fujimori's Peru: Deception in the Public Sphere.* Pittsburgh, PA: University of Pittsburgh Press, 2005.

DAVID SCOTT PALMER

**FUNAI.** *See* **Brazil, Organizations: National Indian Foundation (FUNAI).**

**FUNDO.** Fundo, a Chilean landed estate that often includes ranching and farming. A benign climate and good soils made the narrow, central valley of Chile a rich agricultural and grazing region. Since the colonial era, a small number of landowners has controlled most of the arable lands. During the seventeenth century, *fundos* produced mostly food for local markets and cattle for tallow exports to Peru. *Fundos* began growing wheat at the end of the century, but the small internal market limited production.

Authorities differ slightly on the definition and size of a *fundo,* but they agree that large estates dominated the Chilean countryside. During the latter half of the nineteenth century, some subdivision of agricultural lands took place. The resulting Chacras, or *minifundios* (tiny plots), seldom included enough land for profitable farming or grazing. The twentieth century witnessed a rise both in land concentration and in the gulf between Chile's landed oligarchy and the rural masses. Not until the frustrated attempts at land reform under Salvador Allende (1970–1973) was the position of large *fundo* owners challenged. His overthrow and death removed for a time threats to the Chilean rural elite.

*See also* **Estancia; Hacienda; Latifundia.**

BIBLIOGRAPHY

Benjamín Vicuña Mac Kenna, *A Sketch of Chili* (1866).

Arnold J. Bauer, *Chilean Rural Society from the Spanish Conquest to 1930* (1975).

Brian Loveman, *Struggle in the Countryside: Politics and Rural Labor in Chile, 1919–1973* (1976).

*Additional Bibliography*

Academia Chilena de la Historia. *Partners in Conflict: The Politics of Gender, Sexuality, and Labor in the Chilean Agrarian Reform, 1950-1973.* Santiago: Academia Chilena de la Historia, 2001.

Tinsman, Heidi. *Vida rural en Chile durante el siglo XIX.* Durham, NC: Duke University Press, 2002.

RICHARD W. SLATTA

**FUNDO LEGAL.** Fundo Legal, a minimum endowment of corporate lands for indigenous communities of Latin America from the sixteenth through the nineteenth centuries officially recognized to ensure their survival and viability as sources of agricultural goods and human labor. The sizes of central area pueblos were subject to legal guidelines. In 1567 the area of a *fundo* was 500 *varas* (1,375 feet) in each cardinal direction; in 1687, 600 *varas* from the last house in town; and in 1695, 600 *varas* from the parish church. Other factors in *fundo* size were the availability of resources and the density of population. The larger allotment seems to have overlapped with the concept of the Ejido (commons), better known today yet fairly rare in many colonial indigenous towns, at least in central New Spain.

*See also* **Ayllu; Encomienda; Hacienda; Repartimiento.**

BIBLIOGRAPHY

The legal endowment (not given the name *fundo legal* until the late eighteenth century) is best studied in Mexico. Stephanie Wood critiques old assumptions about the allotment in "The *Fundo Legal* or Lands *Por Razón de Pueblo:* New Evidence from Central New Spain," in *The Indian Community of Colonial Mexico,* edited by Arij Ouwensel and Simon Miller (1990).

*Additional Bibliography*

Maximilian, Emperor of Mexico, and Miguel León Portilla, *Ordenazas de tema indígena en castellano y náhuatl* (2003).

STEPHANIE WOOD

**FUNES, GREGORIO** (1749–1829). Gregorio Funes (*b.* 25 May 1749; *d.* 10 January 1829), Argentine priest and statesman. Funes was born in

Córdoba, educated at the College of Montserrat, and continued his studies at the University of San Carlos, where he received his doctorate in 1774. He studied in Spain at the University of Alcalá de Henares, where he received a law degree in 1778. After returning to Córdoba, he became dean of the cathedral in 1804 and was elected rector of the University of Córdoba (1808). Having become familiar with and sympathetic to the ideas of the Spanish Enlightenment while in Spain, he declared his support for the May Revolution in 1810.

The *cabildo* of Córdoba elected him representative to the Congress of the United Provinces of the Río de la Plata, where he became an ardent spokesman for the interior provinces, which felt alienated from Buenos Aires. In 1811, he supported a freedom of the press law, and in 1816, following the uprising of José Gervasio Artigas's supporters in Córdoba, Funes became governor of the province. A staunch supporter of public education, he was elected senator in General Juan Gregorio de Las Heras's national congress in 1820. In 1823 he edited the periodical *El Argos de Buenos Aires,* and in October of that year the minister of Colombia named him agent of that country in Buenos Aires, a post linking him to Simón Bolívar and Antonio José de Sucre, through whom he was offered the deanship of the cathedral of La Paz, Bolivia. Funes accepted Bernardino Rivadavia's reforms but protested what he thought were his anticlerical excesses. The best-known of his scholarly works is *Ensayo de la historia civil del Paraguay, Buenos Aires y Tucumán* (1816–1817). In 1825 he published *Examen crítico de la constitución religiosa para el clero.* He was elected deputy to the Constitutional Assembly in 1826, participating in the deliberations and in the formulation of a new constitution. Funes died in Buenos Aires.

*See also* **Education: Overview; United Provinces of the Rió de la Plata.**

BIBLIOGRAPHY

Guillermo Furlong Cardiff, *Bio-bibliografía del dean Funes* (Córdoba, 1939).

Ricardo Levene, *A History of Argentina* (1963).

*Additional Bibliography*

Acevedo, Edberto Oscar. "La ruptura en la historia: España entre el deán Funes y Echeverría." *Investigaciones y Ensayos* 43 (January–December 1993): 147–166.

Sábato, Hilda, and Alberto Rodolfo Lettieri. *La vida política en la Argentina del siglo XIX: Armas, votos y voces.* Buenos Aires: Fondo de Cultura Económica, 2003.

NICHOLAS P. CUSHNER

## FÚRLONG CÁRDIFF, GUILLERMO

(1889–1974). Guillermo Fúrlong Cárdiff (June 21, 1889–May 20, 1974) was a prolific Argentine Jesuit historian. His body of work is made up of more than eighty books and some 1,500 articles. He explored colonial religious history, with an emphasis on the work of the Society of Jesus, with the aim of demonstrating the civilizing influence of the Spanish Catholic colonization. Thus, he defended the position of Manuel Giménez Fernández related to the scholastic inspiration of the Latin American independence movements, underlining the influence of the theologian Francisco Suárez, in opposition to the argument that they were inspired by the enlightenment. His most widely published books include *Los Jesuitas y la cultura rioplatense* (1933; The Jesuits and the culture of the River Plate), *Cartografía jesuítica del Río de la Plata* (1936; Jesuit cartography of the River Plate), *Entre los mocobíes de Santa Fe* (1938; With the Mocoví in Santa Fe), *Médicos argentinos durante la dominación española* (1947; Argentine physicians during Spanish rule), *Naturalistas argentinos durante la dominación hispánica* (1948; Argentine naturalists during Spanish rule), *Historia y bibliografía de las primeras imprentas rioplatenses* (3 vols., 1953, 1955, 1960; History and bibliography of the first publishers of the River Plate region), *Nacimiento y desarrollo de la filosofía en el Río de la Plata* (1952; Origins and development of philosophy in the River Plate region, 1949), and *Los jesuitas y la escisión del reino de las Indias* (1960; The Jesuits and the secession of the Kingdom of the Indies).

Fúrlong Cárdiff studied in Spain and the United States, where he received his doctorate in philosophy in 1913 from Georgetown University in Washington, D.C. Upon his return to Argentina, he was a professor of history at the Colegio del Salvador (Academy of the Savior). Following a second period in Spain, during which he was ordained as a priest in 1924, he returned to Argentina to teach once again literature, history, and English at the same *colegios*. He was one of the founders of the Junta de Historia Eclesiástica Argentina (Society for the Study of Argentine Ecclesiastical History) in 1942 and of the Academia Nacional de Geografía (National Academy of Geography) in 1956. He was director of the Jesuit journal *Estudios* (Studies) from 1947 to 1952. Fúrlong Cárdiff's academic work received recognition when he was named a full member of the Academia Nacional de la Historia (National Academy of History) in 1939, and he was awarded various honorary doctorates.

*See also* **Catholic Church: The Modern Period; Jesuits.**

BIBLIOGRAPHY

*Boletín de la Academia Nacional de la Historia*, vol. 48 (1975). Includes articles related to Guillermo Fúrlong Cárdiff and a complete bibliography.

Chiaramonte, José Carlos. *La Ilustración en el Río de la Plata, Cultura eclesiástica y cultura laica durante el Virreinato*, 2nd edition. Buenos Aires: Sudamericana, 2007.

Di Stefano, Roberto. "De la teología a la historia: Un siglo de lecturas retrospectivas del catolicismo argentino." *Prohistoria* 6 (2003): 173–201.

ROBERTO DI STEFANO

---

**FURTADO, CELSO** (1920–2004). Celso Furtado (*b.* 26 July 1920; *d.* 20 November 2004), public administrator, economic development theorist, economic historian, and educator. Born in Pombal, Paraíba, Brazil, Celso Furtado received an M.A. from the University of Brazil (1944) and a Ph.D. from the University of Paris (1948). As director of the Economic Development Division of the United Nations Economic Commission for Latin America (ECLA) from 1949 through 1953 in Santiago, Furtado argued that developing Latin American economies required agrarian reform and import-substituting industrialization. In 1953 he was given the chance to advance these ideas when he became head of a Joint Study Group established by ECLA and the Brazilian National Bank for Economic Development. The group's seven-year plan for Brazil, reported in 1956 and 1957, became the structure of President Juscelino Kubitschek's economic development program.

After teaching at Cambridge (1958) and returning to Santiago, Furtado joined forces in Brazil with the Working Group for the Development of the Northeast. Furtado prepared a plan calling for colonizing frontier areas, boosting electricity supply, changing the agrarian structure, industrialization, and creating the Development Superintendency for the Northeast (Sudene). Sudene was established in 1959, with Furtado serving until 1964 as its superintendent. In 1961, at Furtado's prompting, President Jânio Quadros initiated a system of fiscal incentives to encourage Brazilian companies to invest in the Northeast. In July 1961, Furtado met with U.S. President John Kennedy and, by some accounts, persuaded him that the Northeast could be a showcase for the Alliance for Progress. In 1962, the U.S. Agency for International Development pledged $131 million to develop the region.

Late in 1962, President João Goulart named Furtado Brazil's first minister of planning. The Goulart administration's attempts to slow inflation through fiscal reform failed, and in June 1963 Furtado resigned. Ten days after seizing power in 1964, Brazil's generals included Furtado on the list of those deprived of their political rights, causing him to leave the country.

Furtado was a visiting professor at Harvard, Cambridge (1973–1974), and Columbia (1977), a professor at the Sorbonne (1965–1979), and in 1980 became director of research at the College for Advanced Studies in the Social Sciences at the University of Paris. He was later invited to participate in the Government Planning Commission, and was the minister of culture under José Sarney (1986–1988). He was a candidate for the Nobel Prize in Economics, and in 1997 was elected to the *Academia Brasileira de Letras.* His principal books include *Formação econômica do Brasil* (1959; *The Economic Growth of Brazil,* 1963), *Formação econômica da América Latina* (1969; *Economic Development of Latin America,* 1970), *Teoria e política do desenvolvimento econômico* (1967), *Um projeto para o Brasil* (1968), *O mito do desenvolvimente econômico* (1974), *Transformação e crise na economia mundial* (1987), and *O capitalismo global* (1998).

*See also* **Agrarian Reform; Brazil, Organizations: Development Superintendency of the Northeast (SUDENE); Brazil, Organizations: National Bank for Economic Development (BNDE); Economic Development.**

BIBLIOGRAPHY

Dell, Edmund. *Brazil: The Dilemma of Reform*. London: Fabian Society, 1964.

Mallorquín, Carlos. "El institutionalismo norteamericano y el estructuralismo latinoamericano: ¿Discursos compatibles?" *Revista Mexicana de Sociología* (January 2001): 71–108.

DAVID DENSLOW

## GABEIRA, FERNANDO NAGLE (1941–).

Fernando Nagle Gabeira (*b.* 1941), Brazilian political activist and a leading participant in covert, often violent opposition to military rule established in Brazil in April 1964. As a member of the 8 October Revolutionary Movement (Movimento Revolucionário 8 de outubro—MR-8) Gabeira participated in the September 1969 kidnapping of Charles Elbrick, U.S. ambassador to Brazil. The military response to the kidnapping included severe repression and counterintelligence, which led to the eventual capture, torture, and exile of many revolutionaries, including Gabeira. Following a general amnesty for all political exiles, Gabeira returned to Brazil in 1979 and reemerged politically as a cofounder and 1986 gubernatorial candidate of the Green Party (PV), a leftist political party dedicated to social justice, the expansion of citizenship rights, and ecological management and preservation. He was elected to the Chamber of Deputies in 1994 and reelected in 1998, 2002, and 2006. His writings include *O que é isso, companheiro?* (1978) and *Goiânia, Rua 57* (1987). The film version of *O que é isso, companheiro?*, released in the U.S. as *Four Days in September*, premiered in 1997 and was nominated for an Academy Award in 1998.

*See also* **Brazil, Amnesty Act (1979); Brazil, Revolutions: Revolution of 1964.**

BIBLIOGRAPHY

A. J. Langguth, *Hidden Terrors* (1978), pp. 166–200.

Andy Truskier, "The Politics of Violence: The Urban Guerrilla in Brazil," in *Urban Guerrilla Warfare in Latin America,* edited by James Kohl and John Litt (1974), pp. 136–148.

*Additional Bibliography*

Cunha, Derneval Ribeiro Rodrigues da. "Entre Gabeira e Guevara: Notas sobre os escritos da luta armada." M.A. thesis, Universidade de São Paulo, 2002.

Reis Filho, Daniel Aarão. *Versões e ficções: O seqüestro da história.* 2nd ed. São Paulo: Editora Fundação Perseu Abramo, 1997.

DARYLE WILLIAMS

## GABRIEL, JUAN (1950–).

A Mexican composer and singer, Juan Gabriel was born on January 7, 1950. His original name was Alberto Aguilera Valadez and his childhood was somber. He was raised in Parácuaro, Michoacán, but later moved to Ciudad Juárez, where he began as a composer and singer. He started by composing such songs as "La Muerte del Palomo" (The Death of Palomo; recorded by Rocío Dúrcal), "Ases y Tercia de Reyes" (Aces and a Trio of Kinas) and "Tres Claveles y un Rosal" (Three Carnations and a Rose). His earliest hits were released in 1973, including "En esta Primavera" (In the Springtime) and "Tú Sigues Siendo el Mismo" (You Continue Being the Same). More hit songs followed, including "El Noa Noa" (The Noa Noa), "Con Tu Amor" (With Your Love), "Siempre Estoy Pensando en Ti" (I'm Always Thinking of You), "Frente a Frente" (Face to Face), "Podria Volver" (I Could Return),

"Lo Pasado Pasado" (The Past Is Past), "Esta Rosa Roja" (This Red Rose), "Ya no me Vuelvo a Enamorar" (I Will Never Fall in Love) and "NoVale la Pena" (It Isn't Worth the Worry)—all produced over the span of a few years. In 1983 he received a Heraldo award for his Mexican songs and compositions—in particular, "No Vale la Pena," "Caray," and "La Farsante"—that gained international attention throughout South America and Spain as well as Mexico.Well-known for his longtime musical collaboration with Dúrcal, Gabriel is also hailed for his popular nightclub and music school in Ciudad Juárez. He has served as a musical mentor to numerous up-and-coming Mexican singers and musicians.

*See also* **Music: Popular Music and Dance.**

BIBLIOGRAPHY

Emerick, Laura. "Mexico's Juan Gabriel Celebrates Life." Chicago Sun. Times, April 10, 2006.

PETER J. GARCIA

## GACHUPÍN. *See* **Peninsular.**

**GADSDEN PURCHASE.** In 1853, Mexico agreed to sell to the United States nearly 30 million acres (45,535 square miles) in present-day southern Arizona and New Mexico. The United States sought land in northern Mexico for a proposed southern transcontinental railroad route that would include a port on the Gulf of California. It also wanted to resolve a boundary controversy that had arisen from errors in John Disturnell's map, which according to the Treaty of Guadalupe Hidalgo, was the basis for delineating the southern limits of New Mexico. Factional interests in both the United States and Mexico eventually limited the amount of land that changed hands. In the United States, sectional rivalries linked to the railroad and slavery led the Senate in 1854 to ratify an amended treaty that bought only the Mesilla Valley. James Gadsden, U.S. minister to Mexico, had been empowered to discuss, in addition, mutual claims, trade issues, and U.S. rights in Tehuantepec; yet only one of these issues figured in the final treaty. The United States wanted to be relieved of its obligation in Article XI of the Treaty of Guadalupe Hidalgo to protect Mexico from Indian incursions originating north of the border. Mexican President Antonio López de Santa Anna succumbed to the fiscal exigencies of his beleaguered government as well as to the fear that an expansionist United States, which had done little to discourage filibustering expeditions to northern Mexico since the war, would take what it wanted by force. Mexico ceded the Mesilla territory and abrogated Article XI of the 1848 treaty in return for ten million dollars.

*See also* **Guadalupe Hidalgo, Treaty of (1848).**

BIBLIOGRAPHY

Paul N. Garber, *The Gadsden Treaty* (1959).

Josefina Z. Vázquez and Lorenzo Meyer, *The United States and Mexico* (1985).

*Additional Bibliography*

Rebert, Paula. *La Gran Línea: Mapping the United States-Mexico Boundary, 1849–1857.* Austin: University of Texas Press, 2001.

Vázquez, Josefina Zoraida. *México al tiempo de su guerra con Estados Unidos, 1846–1848.* México: Secretaría de Exteriores: El Colegio de México: Fondo de Cultura Económica, 1997.

Winders, Richard Bruce. *Crisis in the Southwest: The United States, Mexico, and the Struggle over Texas.* Wilmington: SR Books, 2002.

SUSAN M. DEEDS

**GAGE, THOMAS** (c. 1602–1656). Thomas Gage (*b.* c. 1602; *d.* early 1656), British Dominican friar and author of the strongly anti-Spanish *The English-American his travail by sea and land; or a new survey of the West India's, containing a journall of three thousand and three hundred miles within the main Land of America* (1648). Gage came from a fiercely devout English Catholic family that suffered persecution by the English government. Educated by the Jesuits in France and Spain, Gage rebelled against Jesuit discipline and joined the Dominican Order at Jerez, Spain, in 1625, causing his ardently pro-Jesuit father to disinherit him. Gage's descriptive *English-American* begins soon thereafter, with his departure for the Americas as a missionary under the name Tomás de Santa María. Gage described his voyage through the Caribbean to Veracruz and on to Guatemala, where he spent nearly a decade before fleeing the Dominicans when his requests for transfer were denied.

After traversing the rest of Central America, Gage returned to England via Spain at the end of 1637. By then ardently anti-Catholic, he converted to the Anglican Church. The 1648 publication of his inflammatory journal was an instant success and became an important part of the Black Legend (of Spanish misrule in the Indies). Oliver Cromwell ordered the work reprinted in 1655, and many subsequent editions appeared. While it was strongly anti-Catholic and anti-Spanish, this work reflected Gage's keen observations on many aspects of life in Mexico and Central America, including comments on social and economic affairs as well as on crops, natural history, and flora and fauna. As such, it is one of the more important seventeenth-century descriptions of Central America. Oliver Cromwell consulted Gage regarding the 1655 British invasion of the West Indies, and Gage served as a chaplain to the British forces that captured Jamaica in that year. Gage died in Jamaica the following year.

*See also* **Anticlericalism; Dominicans.**

BIBLIOGRAPHY

A. P. Newton, ed., *Thomas Gage: The English-American* (1946).

J. Eric S. Thompson, [Thomas Gage's] *Travels in the New World* (1958).

Norman Newton, *Thomas Gage in Spanish America* (1969).

Frederic Rosengarten, Jr., *Thomas Gage: The English-American Traveler* (1988).

*Additional Bibliography*

Pastor, Rodolfo. "De moros en la costa a negros de Castilla: Representación y realidad en las crónicas del siglo XVII centroamericano." *Historia Mexicana* 44:2 (Oct.–Dec. 1994): 195–235.

SUE DAWN MCGRADY

**GAHONA, GABRIEL VICENTE** (1828–1899). Gabriel Vicente Gahona (Picheta; *b.* 1828; *d.* 1899), Mexican engraver. Gahona's early artistic calling took him from his birthplace of Mérida, Yucatán, to Italy for study. In Italy, probably through magazines and newspapers, he came to know the lithographic work of Doré, Daumier, Gavarni, and Guy, whose work mirrored Gahona's inclinations and temperament and provided the inspiration for his next project.

Gahona returned to Mérida in 1847 and, under the pseudonym of "Picheta," he began publishing *Don Bullebule,* a comical periodical "published for a society of noisy people." Its themes of satire and social criticism were illustrated with eighty-six xylographs. Although it ceased publication later that year, *Don Bullebule* stands out as one of the first examples of journalistic social criticism in Mexico. It is preserved in two volumes, the first consisting of fifteen issues and the second of seventeen, at the National Library of Newspapers and Periodicals in Mexico City.

In 1851, Gahona opened a lithography studio. In 1880 he served as city council president of Mérida, where he died.

*See also* **Art: The Nineteenth Century; Journalism.**

BIBLIOGRAPHY

Manuel Toussaint, *La litografía en México en el siglo XIX* (1934).

Raquel Tibol, *Historia general del arte mexicano,* vol. 3 (1964).

*Additional Bibliography*

Rodríguez Prampolini, Ida. *La crítica de arte en México en el siglo XIX.* México: Universidad Nacional Autónoma de México, Instituto de Investigaciones Estéticas, 1997.

ESTHER ACEVEDO

**GAÍNZA, GABINO** (1753–1824). Gabino Gaínza (*b.* 26 October 1753; *d.* 1824), acting captain-general of Guatemala (1821–1822). Born in Pamplona, Spain, Gaínza joined the military at the age of sixteen and served in various posts throughout South America for most of his adult life. He commanded the Spanish force that reconquered Chile in 1814.

Gaínza arrived in Central America from Chile in early 1821 amidst the political turmoil of impending independence from Spain to assume the post of army inspector general. That March, the very ill captain-general of Guatemala, Carlos Luis de Urrutia y Montoya (1750–1825), delegated his authority to Gaínza. After independence on 15 September 1821, Gaínza, who had tolerated creole rebellion, remained in office as chief executive. He played an active role in the decision to annex Central America to Agustín de Iturbide's Mexican empire, and he often mediated between the polemical political factions of the era. He was relieved of his command on 22 June 1822 by the new captain-general, Vicente Filísola. Afterward, he went to Mexico to become an aide-de-camp to Emperor Agustín I (Iturbide).

*See also* **Chile: Foundations Through Independence; Iturbide, Agustín de.**

BIBLIOGRAPHY

Enrique Del Cid Fernández, *Don Gabino de Gaínza y otros estudios* (1959).

*Additional Bibliography*

Jones, Oakah L. *Guatemala in the Spanish Colonial Period.* Norman: University of Oklahoma Press, 1994.

MICHAEL F. FRY

**GAINZA PAZ, ALBERTO** (1899–1977). Alberto Gainza Paz was an Argentine newspaperman and editor of the Buenos Aires newspaper *La Prensa.* He gained international attention in 1951 when his newspaper was expropriated by the government of Juan Domingo Perón.

Gainza Paz studied law, graduating in 1921. By 1943 he had succeeded his uncle, Ezequiel Paz, as editor of *La Prensa.* Founded in 1869 by the Paz family, *La Prensa* maintained an independent conservative editorial position dedicated to the expression of public opinion. In 1944 Perón, then minister of war in the military government of Edelmiro Farrell, closed the newspaper for five days for "distorting the truth." In 1945 Gainza Paz and the owner of *La Nación*, another important conservative newspaper that opposed to Perón's policies, both were imprisoned temporarily, charged with conspiring against the government. Between 1947 and 1951 Gainza Paz clashed with the Perón government. Juan Domingo Perón and his wife Eva thought of *La Prensa* as one of their worst enemies.

The paper and its publisher became international beacons of democracy, standing firmly against dictatorship. The Sindicato de Vendedores de Diarios (newspaper salesmen's union), controlled by Perón, forced the paper to suspend its publication. Ultimately, the paper was expropriated in April 1951 and transformed into a trade-union tabloid. Gainza Paz fled into exile, where he became a symbol of freedom of the press and received many honors. With the fall of Perón in 1955, *La Prensa* was returned to the Paz family, resumed publication under Gainza Paz's direction early in 1956, and regained its former stature.

*See also* **Journalism; Perón, Juan Domingo.**

BIBLIOGRAPHY

Page, Joseph. *Perón: A Biography.* New York: Random House, 1983.

Panella, Claudio, et al. *La prensa y el periodismo: Crítica, conflicto, expropiación.* La Plata, Argentina: Ediciones de Periodismo y Comunicación, Universidad Nacional de la Plata, 1999.

Potash, Robert A. *The Army and Politics in Argentina, 1945–1962: Perón to Frondizi.* Stanford, CA: Stanford University Press, 1980.

Sirvén, Pablo. *Perón y los medios de comunicación (1943–1955).* Buenos Aires: Conselho de Empresários da América Latina, 1984.

PAUL GOODWIN
VICENTE PALERMO

**GAIRY, ERIC** (1922–1997). Eric Gairy, a Grenadian politician, was born of peasant parents near Grenville, Grenada, on February 18, 1922. In the early 1940s he migrated to Trinidad and from there to Aruba to work in the ESSO refinery. It was on that Dutch island that he got involved in the trade union movement. Made unwelcome by the Dutch, Gairy returned to Grenada in December 1949 and began organizing the Grenada Manual and Mental Workers' Union. His immediate targets were the low wages paid on the cocoa and sugar estates. The successful strike of 1951 launched Gairy on a political career as head of the Grenada United Labour Party. In 1954 he was elected chief minister of the colonial government.

In 1957 he became a minister in the West Indies Federation until its collapse in 1962. Elected premier in 1967, he became Grenada's first prime minister when it became independent in 1974. Knighted by the Queen, he earned the title Sir Eric Gairy. At the same time his behavior became increasingly bizarre—he called on the United Nations to investigate a threat from UFOs—and his politics increasingly oppressive. The elections of 1974 were probably tampered with. In March 1979 a coup d'etat led by Maurice Bishop and the New Jewel Movement overthrew his regime. Upon the collapse of the Bishop regime in 1983, Gairy returned to Grenada in 1984 from exile in the United States. He was already semi-incapacitated and died of a stroke in 1997.

*See also* **Bishop, Maurice; Grenada; West Indies Federation.**

BIBLIOGRAPHY

Singham, A. W. *The Hero and the Crowd in a Colonial Polity.* New Haven, CT: Yale University Press, 1968.

Thorndike, Tony. *Grenada: Politics, Economics and Society.* Boulder, CO: L. Rienner, 1985.

ANTHONY P. MAINGOT

**GAITÁN, JORGE ELIÉCER** (1898–1948). Jorge Eliécer Gaitán (*b.* 23 January 1898; *d.* 9 April 1948), Colombian political leader. The man who was widely expected to accede to the presidency of Colombia in 1950 was walking out of his law office in downtown Bogotá with a group of friends at 1:05 P.M. on Friday, 9 April 1948, when he was fatally wounded by a lonely drifter. In life Jorge Eliécer Gaitán commanded the attention of his compatriots through fear-inspiring oratory and masterful political performances. In death he incited uprisings in Bogotá and other cities by passionate followers desperate to bring about quick political change.

In part because he died before rising formally to power, Gaitán's legacy is uncertain. Some are convinced that he was a careful man with a profound sense of equanimity who would have brought peace to Colombia. Others describe him as an inveterate rabble-rouser who would have turned La Violencia bloodier still had he lived. The scholar Richard Sharpless sees him as a left-leaning socialist, while others describe him as a rather conservative man of lower-middle-class values.

Gaitán was born in Bogotá to parents who struggled to keep a hold on the middle class. His father sold books and his mother was a well-known schoolteacher. Both were rank-and-file members of the Liberal Party, and Jorge Eliécer grew up hearing about the heroic exploits of "progressive" Liberals against the "reactionaries" of the Conservative Party. Although Gaitán would antagonize the leaders of his party throughout his life, confounding them and others at every turn, he would never seriously depart from the ideals of the Liberal Party. At the time of his death, many leaders of the party, and many Conservatives as well, felt a sense of relief, for they could never quite be certain of his allegiance, or how they might manage to control him and his many followers, whom he had formed into disciplined urban crowds that seemingly did only his bidding.

Although his parents were always seeking to ease his way by drawing on their meager political connections, Gaitán strove mightily to rise in society through his own merits. In 1924 he obtained his law degree from the Universidad Nacional with an unorthodox thesis titled *Las ideas socialistas en Colombia.* He then went to Italy to study with Enrico Ferri, and while there he became drawn to the closely knit crowds created by the fascists.

On his return to Colombia in 1928 Gaitán toured the nation, making inflammatory speeches with his trademark guttural voice on the massacre of the United Fruit Company banana workers. This massacre was the same one Gabriel García Márquez wrote about in the novel *One Hundred Years of Solitude.*

Regardless of what his ideology may have been, Gaitán was in a sense Colombia's first modern politician. Upon election to the House of Representatives, he worked assiduously to reach the masses and elicit their support. He developed basic programs and ideas that he believed even his most uneducated followers could and should understand. Beyond the lofty and abstract rhetoric of Colombia's traditional politicians, Gaitán referred incessantly to detailed aspects of the daily, personal lives of his followers. He traveled extensively throughout the country, moving electoral politics outside the narrow confines of the two traditional parties. He produced his own newspaper, and was the first to use the radio to reach his followers. When he appeared to be stymied by the Liberals in the 1930s, he briefly formed the Unión Nacional Izquierdista Revolucionaria (UNIR). When troubles continued to appear on the horizon, he could always fall back on his own Gaitanista movement. He went in and out of public office, serving briefly first as mayor of Bogotá in 1936 and 1937, then as minister of education and of labor in 1940 and 1943, until he ran unsuccessfully for the presidency in 1945 and 1946 as a Liberal against the official Liberal candidate. Upon his death he was poised to take over the Liberal Party and win the presidential election of 1950.

The huge riot following his death, in which Gaitán's followers destroyed much of downtown Bogotá and caused disturbances in many other cities as well, is known in Colombia as *el nueve de abril* (the ninth of April), and elsewhere as the Bogotazo. At the time, the eyes of the world were on Bogotá, for the Ninth Pan-American Conference was being held in the city. U.S. Secretary of State George Marshall was there, and so too was Fidel Castro, who had met with Gaitán days earlier and had another meeting scheduled with him for that very afternoon. For a few brief moments Gaitán became well known to the outside world. And during at least the next three decades in Colombia, Jorge Eliécer Gaitán remained a central and enigmatic force in politics, the source of countless passions, untold conversations, and sundry questions about whether his unfulfilled policies would have succeeded, the answers to which few Colombians have found satisfactory.

*See also* **Bogotazo; Colombia, Political Parties: Liberal Party; United Fruit Company.**

BIBLIOGRAPHY

Richard Sharpless, *Gaitán of Colombia: A Political Biography* (1978).

Herbert Braun, *The Assassination of Gaitán: Public Life and Urban Violence in Colombia* (1985).

*Additional Bibliography*

Green, W. John. *Gaitanismo, Left Liberalism, and Popular Mobilization in Colombia*. Gainesville: University Press of Florida, 2003.

Zalamea, Alberto. *Gaitán: Autobiografía de un pueblo.* Bogotá: Zalamea Fajardo Editores, 1999.

HERBERT BRAUN

## GAITÁN DURÁN, JORGE (1924–1962).

Jorge Gaitán Durán (*b.* 12 February 1924; *d.* 22 June 1962), Colombian poet and essayist. Despite his death at a young age, Gaitán Durán exerted a lasting influence on Colombian letters. A native of Pamplona Kúcuta, he is remembered primarily as a talented poet who published several books of profound metaphysical poetry. They include *Insistencia en la tristeza* (1946), *Presencia del hombre* (1947), and *Si mañana despierto* (1961). Much of this poetry deals with love and death in an existential void. Love emerges in many of the poems as an attempt to forget the flow of time. Poets and critics in Colombia considered him extraordinarily talented, and a mature writer for his age. His most accomplished book was *Si mañana despierto.*

Gaitán Durán is also remembered as the founding director of the prestigious journal *Mito,* which was published from 1955 until his death in an auto accident at Pointe-a-Pitre, Guadeloupe, in 1962. *Mito* was a cosmopolitan periodical that published the best of European, Latin American, and Colombian writing, thus serving as the voice of a generation of intellectuals in Colombia. Latin American writers who later became internationally recognized, such as Octavio Paz, Julio Cortázar, and Carlos Fuentes, all appeared in *Mito,* as did the Colombian Nobel laureate Gabriel García Márquez. *Mito*'s most important impact was its modernization of a provincial literary scene in Colombia.

*See also* **Colombia: Since Independence; Literature: Spanish America.**

BIBLIOGRAPHY

Giuseppe Bellini, *Historia de la literatura hispanoamericana* (1985).

George R. Mc Murray, *Spanish American Writing Since 1941* (1987).

Raymond Leslie Williams, *The Colombian Novel, 1844–1987* (1991).

*Additional Bibliography*

Galeano, Juan Carlos. "Jorge Gaitán Durán: Política y ser." *Revista de Estudios Colombianos* 17 (1997): 32–37.

Pulido, Flor Delia. *La palabra como expresión de la corporeidad en Jorge Gaitán Durán*. Pamplona, Colombia: Universidad de Pamplona, 1999.

RAYMOND LESLIE WILLIAMS

**GAITO, CONSTANTINO** (1878–1945). Constantino Gaito (*b.* 3 August 1878; *d.* 14 December 1945), Argentine composer and teacher. Born in Buenos Aires, Gaito began his musical studies with his father, a violinist. At age eleven he began to compose. He received a scholarship from the Argentine government and went to Italy, where he enrolled at San Pietro a Maiella in Naples, studying under Pietro Platania (composition) and Simonetti (piano). He traveled to Milan to meet Giuseppe Verdi, who helped the young Gaito in his career by conducting a concert of his music at the Milan Conservatory. Initially influenced by the Italians, Gaito returned toward the nationalist style upon his return to Argentina in 1900. He wrote eleven operas, among them *Flor de nieve* (1922), *Ollantay* (1926), and *Sangre de las guitarras* (1932), all of which premiered at the Teatro Colón in Buenos Aires. He also wrote two ballets, an oratorio, chamber music, and vocal and piano works.

Gaito was the most renowned music professor of his time, and taught a generation of eminent Argentine composers. He founded a conservatory and taught harmony at the National Conservatory in Buenos Aires. He was also director of the Teatro Argentino in La Plata. Gaito died in Buenos Aires.

*See also* **Music: Art Music.**

BIBLIOGRAPHY

*Composers of the Americas,* vol. 12 (1966), pp. 50–54.

Gérard Béhague, *Music in Latin America* (1979); *New Grove Dictionary of Music and Musicians,* vol. 7 (1980).

*Additional Bibliography*

Ficher, Martha, Martha Furman Schleifer, and John M. Furman. *Latin American Classical Composers: A Biographical Dictionary.* Lanham: Scarecrow Press, 2002.

SUSANA SALGADO

**GALÁN, JOSÉ ANTONIO.** *See* **Comunero Revolt (New Granada).**

**GALÁN, JULIO** (1959–2006). Julio Galán, a Mexican painter and native of Múzquiz, Coahuila, was born on December 5, 1959. He studied architecture at Monterrey University from 1978 to 1982. By 1980 he had begun exhibiting in Monterrey at the Galería Arte Actual Mexicano. After graduation he abandoned architecture and dedicated himself to painting. Influences on his work included Frida Kahlo, Andy Warhol, and David Hockney, as well as Mexican popular painting, comic books, and both Mexican and American kitsch. Kahlo was for many Mexican artists of the 1980s a symbol of freedom from the Mexican artistic status quo, giving young artists license to explore themselves and their *mexicanidad,* or Mexican national identity. The traditional *ex-voto*and *retablo* formats of the nineteenth and early twentieth centuries are echoed in Galán's work. His images are often autobiographical and surrealistic, manifested in narratives that are ambiguous—with individual elements appearing to be unrelated—and that make use of disjunctive perspectives.

Galán's pictures frequently contain both gay and religious references. In this context, the artist often included his own image in his works, suggesting personal ambiguities. After the mid-1980s Galán lived in Monterrey, New York, and Paris. He died on August 4, 2006. His work is widely collected and exhibited internationally.

*See also* **Art: The Twentieth Century.**

BIBLIOGRAPHY

Galan, Julio, Luis Mario Schneider, Luis Mario, Ida Prampolini, et al. *Julio Galán: Fotografías de Graciela Iturbide.* Mexico City: Grupo Financiero Serfin, S.A. de C.V., 1993.

Hilty, Greg. *Julio Galán.* London: Timothy Taylor Gallery, 1998.

*Julio Galán: Carne de Gallina.* Oaxaca, Mexico: Museo de Arte Contemporaneo de Oaxaca, 2002.

*Julio Galán: Exposición Retrospectiva.* Monterrey, Mexico: Monterrey: Museo de Arte Contemporáneo de Monterrey, 1993.

Rasmussen, Waldo, Fatima Bercht, and Elizabeth Ferrer, eds. *Latin American Artists of the Twentieth Century.* New York: Museum of Modern Art, 1993.

Sullivan, Edward J. *Aspects of Contemporary Mexican Painting.* New York: Americas Society, 1990.

CLAYTON C. KIRKING

## GALÁN, LUIS CARLOS (1943–1989).

Luis Carlos Galán (*b.* 29 September 1943; *d.* 18 August 1989), Colombian politician. Born into a middle-class family in Bucaramanga, Galán was educated in Bogotá. In 1971, at the age of twenty-seven, he was named minister of education in the bipartisan administration of Misael Pastrana Borrero. As editor of the magazine *Nueva Frontera* and later as a senator, Galán inherited from former president Carlos Lleras Restrepo the banner of reformist opposition to the "officialist" Liberal regimes of the 1974–1982 period. His attacks on human-rights abuses and the vices of clientelist politics won him much admiration but limited electoral success. His New Liberalism movement peaked at 11 percent in the 1982 presidential election; in late 1986 he returned to the official Liberal fold. In the late 1980s Galán spoke out against the growing power of Colombia's drug cartels; he was considered the likely successor to Virgilio Barco Vargas in the presidency. His assassination in August 1989, presumably the work of the Medellín cartel, was the most dramatic moment of the Colombian crisis of 1989–1990.

*See also* **Barco Vargas, Virgilio; Colombia, Political Parties: Liberal Party; Lleras Restrepo, Carlos.**

BIBLIOGRAPHY

Luis Carlos Galán, *Ni un pusa atraí, siempre adelante* (1991).

### *Additional Bibliography*

Richani, Nazih. *Systems of Violence: The Political Economy of War and Peace in Colombia.* Bogotá: Editorial Planeta Colombiana, 2003.

Salazar, Alonso. *Profeta en el desierto: Vida y muerte de Luis Carlos Galán.* Bogotá: Editorial Planeta Colombiana, 2003.

RICHARD J. STOLLER

## GALÁPAGOS ISLANDS.

Galápagos Islands, a group of nineteen volcanic islands and numerous islets in the eastern Pacific, lying astride the equator, 600 miles west of mainland Ecuador, of which the islands are a province. The island group, officially named the Archipiélago de Colón by Ecuador in 1892 to honor Christopher Columbus, encompasses a land area of 3,075 square miles and is spread out over 36,000 square miles of sea. The population of the Galapagos was listed as 9,785 in the 1990 census.

Each island was named by both Spanish and English explorers and renamed by Ecuador in 1892. The official Ecuadorian names are cited in this article; however, researchers will find the English names in most earlier descriptions of the islands. The largest island is Isabela, approximately 82 miles long, covering an area of 1,700 square miles, over half the land mass of the others combined. Isabela is typical of the islands in its lava composition; it also has the highest peak, Mount Azul, at 5,541 feet. The five other larger islands are Santa Cruz, Fernandina, San Cristóbal, San Salvador, and Santa María.

In 1535, Thomás de Berlanga, bishop of Panama, inadvertently discovered the Galápagos when his ship was blown off course en route to Peru. He named them Las Encantadas (The Enchanted) due to their mist-shrouded otherworldly appearance and the unusual wildlife typified by giant tortoises and iguanas. The islands were a haven for pirates in the seventeenth century and became a regular stop for whaling vessels in the eighteenth and nineteenth centuries. The islands were unclaimed until 1832, when Ecuador took official possession.

In 1835 the English naturalist Charles Darwin visited the islands and chronicled their flora and fauna. His experiences in the Galápagos contributed significantly to his ideas about evolution and natural selection and his account of the islands brought them international acclaim.

In the early twentieth century, Ecuador considered selling the islands to France, Chile, and the United States but decided to retain possession. In World War II, Ecuador permitted the United States to construct an air base on Baltra Island for the purpose of patrolling Pacific approaches to the Panama Canal. The base was turned over to Ecuador in 1946 and today serves as the principal airstrip.

The unique native animals and plants remain the main attraction of the islands. The archipelago's tortoise is thought to be the longest-lived animal on earth. While there are only nine mammals, two bats, and seven rodents, no amphibians, few reptiles, and approximately eighty species of birds indigenous to the islands, animal life is nevertheless of extreme scientific importance due to the islands' centuries of isolation from humans in an austere environment that has led to unique adaptive changes. Large parts of the islands are now preserved as national parks and wildlife refuges.

BIBLIOGRAPHY

Charles Darwin, *A Naturalist's Voyage Round the World in HMS Beagle* (1839).

William Beebe, *Galápagos, World's End* (1924).

Theodore Wolf, *Geography and Geology of Ecuador* (1933).

Herman Melville, *The Encantadoas or Enchanted Islands*, with an introduction, critical epilogue, and bibliographical notes by Victor Wolfgang von Hagen (1940).

Victor Wolfgang Von Hagen, *Ecuador and the Galápagos Islands* (1949).

Ian Thornton, *Darwin's Islands. A Natural History of the Galápagos* (1971).

John Hickham, *The Enchanted Islands* (1986).

*Additional Bibliography*

De Roy, Tui. *Galapagos, Islands Born of Fire*. Toronto: Warwick Pub., 1998.

Luna Tobar, Alfredo. *Historia política internacional de las islas Galápagos*. Quito, Ecuador: Ediciones Abya-Yala, 1997.

Ospina Peralta, Pablo. *Galápagos, naturaleza y sociedad: Actores sociales y conflictos ambientales en las islas Galápagos*. Quito, Ecuador: Corporación Editora Nacional, 2006.

Palmerlee, Danny, Michael Grosberg, and Carolyn McCarthy. *Ecuador and the Galápagos Islands*. Footscray, Vic.: Lonely Planet, 2006.

Rachowiecki, Rob, and Teresa Bladé. *Ecuador y las islas Galápagos*. Barcelona: GeoPlanet, 2001.

Stewart, Paul D. *Galápagos: The Islands that Changed the World*. New Haven, Conn.: Yale University Press, 2006.

Tagliaferro, Linda. *Galápagos Islands: Nature's Delicate Balance at Risk*. Minneapolis, MN: Lerner, 2001.

George M. Lauderbaugh

---

**GALARZA, ERNESTO** (1905–1980). Ernesto Galarza worked in the United States to organize Mexican farm laborers. He also taught there and worked for educational reform.

Born August 15, 1905, in Nayarit, Mexico, Galarza came to the United States with his family when he was eight years old. He lived in Sacramento and worked as a farm laborer while going to school. His academic abilities earned him a scholarship to Occidental College in Los Angeles and graduate degrees in history and economics from Stanford University in California in 1929 and Columbia University in New York City in 1944.

In the post–World War II period Galarza returned to California, where he dedicated his life to the plight of Mexican farm workers. He joined the National Farm Labor Union and helped organize migrant workers. His experience and research led him to write *Merchants of Labor* (1964), a book arguing for abolishing the Bracero Program. His *Spiders in the House and Workers in the Fields* (1970) and *Farm Workers and Agri-business in California, 1947–1960* (1977) also sought to reform the exploitative farm labor system.

Ernesto Galarza devoted the later years of his life to educational reform. He taught at San Jose State University, the University of California at San Diego and Santa Cruz, the University of Notre Dame in Indiana, and Stanford University and served on many commissions and committees that dealt with educational issues. He was an advocate of bilingual education and wrote a series of Mini Libros (little books) that were used in bilingual classrooms. His autobiography, *Barrio Boy* (1971), relates how he overcame obstacles to getting an education in the United States. Ernesto Galarza died on June 22, 1984, at his home in San José, California.

*See also* **Labor Movements; Hispanics in the United States.**

BIBLIOGRAPHY

Chabran, Richard. "Activism and Intellectual Struggle in the Life of Ernesto Galarza (1905–1984) with an Accompanying Bibliography." *Hispanic Journal of Behavioral Sciences* 7, no. 2 (June 1985): 135–152.

Pitti, Stephen. "Ernesto Galarza Remembered: A Reflection on Graduate Studies in Chicano History." In *Voices of a Chicana/o History*, edited by Refugio I. Rochin and Dennis N. Valdés. East Lansing: Michigan State University Press, 2000.

Richard Griswold del Castillo

---

**GALDAMES, LUIS GALDAMES** (1881–1941). A leading educator and historian of his generation, and one of the few whose work has been translated into English, Luis Galdames Galdames graduated from the Instituto Pedagógico at the University of Chile in 1900, and subsequently studied law at the same university, receiving his degree in 1903. He taught at several leading secular secondary schools, including the Instituto Nacional. In 1925, he was a member of the commission that drafted the constitution of that year.

An admirer of educator and jurist Valentín Letelier, Galdames authored the classic biography, still unsurpassed, *Valentín Letelier y su obra* (1937). His interests in history are well reflected in *El decenio de Montt* (1904), *Estudio de la historia de Chile* (1906), *Historia de Chile: La evolución constitucional* (1925), and *La juventud de Vicuña Mackenna* (1932). In education, his most important scholarly contributions are the editorship of the *Revista de Educación* (1912), and the brief but pioneering *La Universidad de Chile, 1843–1934* (1934). He served briefly as director of national secondary education under the first government of Carlos Ibáñez del Campo (1927), issuing the important general regulations for secondary education. In 1928 he returned to teaching and served as dean of the Faculty of Philosophy and Education at the University of Chile.

*See also* **Education: Overview; Letelier Madariaga, Valentín.**

BIBLIOGRAPHY

Gazmuri, Cristián. *La Historiografía Chilena, 1842-1970.* Santiago: Taurus, 2006.

Jobet, Julio César. *Doctrina y praxis de los educadores representativos chilenos.* Santiago: Editorial Andrés Bello, 1971.

IVÁN JAKSIĆ

## GALEANA, HERMENEGILDO

**GALEANA, HERMENEGILDO** (1762–1814). Hermenegildo Galeana (*b.* 13 April 1762; *d.* 27 June 1814), Mexican insurgent leader. Like other members of his family, Galeana, born in Tecpan, joined José María Morelos at La Sabana in January 1811. He proved valiant and able from the outset, and Morelos named him his lieutenant in May 1811. Galeana won victories in numerous important battles. He took Taxco in December 1811, and occupied Tenancingo the following January. From February to May 1812, he participated in the defense of Cuautla, where his aid proved to be of great importance. Morelos named him field marshal in September 1812, at Tehuacán. Galeana participated in the capture of Orizaba in October 1812 and in the taking of Oaxaca that November. He played a decisive role in the taking of Acapulco in April 1813, and in the capture of the fortress of San Diego four months later, when he convinced its commander to surrender. In December 1813 Galeana participated in the attack against Valladolid, where the insurgents were defeated. In January 1814, after the defeat at Puruarán, Galeana headed south, pursued by the royalists. After his death in combat at El Salitral, Galeana's head was exhibited in the plaza of Coyuca.

*See also* **Mexico: 1810–1910; Morelos y Pavón, José María.**

BIBLIOGRAPHY

Wilbert H. Timmons, *Morelos: Priest, Soldier, Statesman of Mexico* (1970).

Virginia Guedea, *José María Morelos y Pavón: Cronología* (1981); *Diccionario Porrúa de historia, geografía y biografía de Mexico,* 5th ed. (1986).

*Additional Bibliography*

Ríos Ruiz, Arturo. *El príncipe Hermenegildo Galeana: Lo desconocido del héroe de la independencia de México.* México: Instituto Politécnico Nacional, 2002.

VIRGINIA GUEDEA

## GALEANO, EDUARDO HUGHES

**GALEANO, EDUARDO HUGHES** (1940–). Born in Montevideo on September 3, 1940, Eduardo Galeano is one of the best-known Uruguayan authors internationally. His books and newspaper columns engage political debates in Uruguay and Latin America and often address U.S.–Latin American relations. He is also recognized as an important voice in the *Frente Amplio* coalition of leftist parties in Uruguay. Galeano began developing his writing talents at an early age, first with drawings and later with articles in periodical publications. From 1960 to 1964 he wrote for Montevideo's *Marcha*, where he also served as editor in chief. During Uruguay's military dictatorship (1973–1984) Galeano lived in exile in Argentina and later in Spain. He returned to

Uruguay in 1984 and assumed editorial responsibilities at the newly founded periodical *Brecha.*

Galeano's early fiction includes *Los días siguientes* (1963) and *Los fantasmas del día del león y otros relatos* (1967). Later fiction, which depicts a personal encounter with the despised military dictatorship, includes *La canción de nosotros* (1975) and *Días y noches de amor y de guerra* (1978). Galeano's most widely read work is *Las venas abiertas de América Latina*, with more than thirty editions since its first publication in 1971. Rooted in dependency theories popular during the 1960s, this essay presents a history of Latin America as an exploited continent from the time of the European encounter with indigenous inhabitants of America to the late twentieth century. Also noteworthy is the three-volume *Memoria del fuego*, which provides a comprehensive view of Latin American history and identity through vignettes. This set of books, as well as *Las venas abiertas* and later writings such as *Fútbol a sol y sombra* (1995) and *Bocas del tiempo* (2004), have been translated into English, French, and other languages. Galeano is an active contributor to national and international newspapers and is interviewed regularly on television and radio programs.

*See also* **Uruguay: The Twentieth Century; United States-Latin American Relations.**

BIBLIOGRAPHY

*Primary Works*

*Las venas abiertas de América Latina.* 36th ed., rev. and exp. Mexico, D. F.: Siglo Veintiuno, 1983. Translated by Cedric Belfrage as *Open Veins of Latin America: Five Centuries of the Pillage of a Continent*, 25th edition. New York: Monthly Review Press, 1997.

*Uselo y tírelo: El mundo del fin del milenio, visto desde una ecología latinoamericana.* Buenos Aires: Planeta, 1984.

*Memoria del fuego*, 4th edition. 3 vols. Mexico, D. F.: Siglo Veintiuno, 1983–1986. Translated by Cedric Belfrage as *Memory of Fire*, 3 vols. New York: Pantheon, 1985–1988.

*El libro de los abrazos.* 5th ed. México, D. F.: Siglo Veintiuno Editores, 1991. Translated by Cedric Belfrage with Mark Schafer as *The Book of Embraces: Images and Text.* New York: Norton, 1991.

*Nosotros decimos no: Crónicas, 1963–1988.* Madrid: Siglo Veintiuno de España, 1989 Translated by Mark Fried et. al as *We Say No: Chronicles 1963–1991.* New York: Norton, 1992.

*Fútbol a sol y sombra.* Madrid: Siglo Veintiuno de España Editores, 1995. Translated by Mark Fried as *Soccer in Sun and Shadow*, 2nd edition. London: Verso, 2003.

*Bocas del tiempo.* Montevideo: Ediciones del Chanchito, 2004. Translated by Mark Fried as *Voices of Time.* New York: Metropolitan, 2006.

*Secondary Works*

Campodónico, Miguel Angel. *Nuevo diccionario de la cultura uruguaya: Sepa quién es quién en artes visuales, música, cine y video, teatro, letras y periodismo.* Montevideo: Linardi y Risso, 2003.

Palaversich, Diana. "Eduardo Galeano's 'Memoria del Fuego' as Alternative History." *Antípodas: Journal of Hispanic Studies of the University of Auckland and La Trobe University* 3 (July 1991): 135–150.

Palaversich, Diana. *Silencio, voz y escritura en Eduardo Galeano.* Frankfurt: Vervuert; Madrid: Iberoamericana, 1995.

Saz, Sara M. "Breath, Liberty, and the Word: Eduardo Galeano's Interpretational History." *Secolas Annals: Journal of the Southeastern Council on Latin American Studies* 21 (March 1990): 59–70.

WILLIAM H. KATRA
WILLIAM G. ACREE JR.

**GALEONES.** Galeones, one of two fleets dispatched to convoy merchant vessels to the New World. The fleet system was set up in 1564. One fleet, known as the *flota,* went to New Spain; the other, the *galeones,* went to the mainland of South America, or Tierra Firme. This latter, which returned from the trade fair at Portobelo laden with Peruvian silver, was customarily convoyed by six or eight men-of-war (*galeones* in Spanish) and thus came by its name. After trading was finished, the two fleets would usually reunite at Havana for the return voyage to Seville. The crown defrayed the cost of supporting the convoys by levying an ad valorem tax, known as the Avería, in Seville and the Indies.

By the seventeenth century, foreign pirates, shipwrecks, the contraband trade, the diversification of the colonial economy, and Spain's economic decline had all contributed to the decay of this Atlantic trade. Although officials in Spain favored yearly voyages of the fleets, only twenty-nine sailings to Tierra Firme took place between 1600 and 1650. In the second half of the century that number declined to nineteen.

The War of the Spanish Succession (1700–1716) further disrupted the system as French traders entered the Pacific and flooded colonial markets with European wares.

The crown tried to revitalize the system of *flotas* and *galeones* in the eighteenth century but had only limited success. Subsequent trade fairs proved disappointing for the participants until in 1740 the crown reluctantly abandoned the convoy system, substituting individual sailings by licensed merchant vessels coming around Cape Horn.

*See also* **Fleet System: Colonial Spanish America; War of the Spanish Succession.**

BIBLIOGRAPHY

The classic study of the system of *flotas* and *galeones* is Clarence Haring, *Trade and Navigation Between Spain and the Indies in the Time of the Habsburgs* (1918). The most detailed quantitative studies remain Pierre Chaunu and Huguette Chaunu, *Séville et l'Atlantique, 1504–1650,* 8 vols. (1955–1959); Lutgardo García Fuentes, *El comercio español con América, 1650–1700* (1980); and Antonio García-Baquero González, *Cádiz y el Atlántico (1717–1778),* 2 vols. (1976). For the collapse of the convoy system see Geoffrey J. Walker, *Spanish Politics and Imperial Trade, 1700–1789* (1979).

*Additional Bibliography*

Arazola Corvera, Ma Jesús. *Hombres, barcos y comercio de la ruta Cádiz-Buenos Aires, 1737–1757.* Sevilla: Diputación de Sevilla, 1998.

Bustos Rodríguez, Manuel. *Los comerciantes de la carrera de Indias en el Cadiz del siglo XVIII (1713–1775).* Cádiz: Servico de Publicaciones, Universidad de Cádiz, 1995.

Hill, Ruth. *Hierarchy, Commerce and Fraud in Bourbon Spanish America: A Postal Inspector's Exposé.* Nashville: Vanderbilt University Press, 2005.

KENNETH J. ANDRIEN

---

## GALÍNDEZ, JESÚS DE (1915–1956).

Jesús de Galíndez (*b.* 12 October 1915; *d.* 13/15 March 1956), a critic of the Trujillo regime in the Dominican Republic. A native of Amurrio, Spain, Galíndez held a law degree from the University of Madrid. He had fought against Franco in the Spanish Civil War and in 1939 fled to the Dominican Republic, where he taught in the Diplomatic School and worked as a lawyer in the Department of Labor. When some labor disputes he arbitrated were too favorable to the workers, he got in trouble with the dictator Rafael Trujillo. He therefore moved to the United States in 1946 and became a political activist among anti-Trujillo exiles. He enrolled in Columbia University's doctoral program and became a leading critic of Trujillo. In addition to writing a number of articles, he produced a dissertation on Trujillo. He was also a part-time instructor. Galíndez defended his dissertation at the end of February 1956 and disappeared after finishing an evening class on 12 March 1956. There is general agreement that Trujillo had him kidnapped and flown, drugged, to the Dominican Republic, where he was killed after being tortured. His degree was awarded in absentia in June. He had left a Spanish draft of his dissertation with a Chilean friend, which was published as *La era de Trujillo: Un estudio casuístico de dictadura hispanoamericano* (1956). In 1973 an English edition appeared, edited by Russell H. Fitzgibbon: *The Era of Trujillo, Dominican Dictator.*

The disappearance of Galíndez became a cause célèbre. The young pilot Gerald Murphy, who had flown the chartered plane from Amityville, Long Island, on the night of 12 March, with a drugged man aboard, had disappeared in the Dominican Republic the previous December. Murphy was from the state of Oregon; his congressman, Charles Porter, and Senator Wayne Morse put great pressure on the U.S. Justice and State departments to investigate. The Justice Department turned the investigation over to a federal grand jury that indicted a man associated with the plane's rental on Long Island. He was tried and convicted for violation of the Foreign Agents Registration Act. The body of Galíndez was never found. That of Murphy was found months later hanged in a Dominican jail, reported to be a "suicide."

*See also* **Trujillo Molina, Rafael Leónidas.**

BIBLIOGRAPHY

Germán E. Ornes, *Trujillo: Little Caesar of the Caribbean* (1958), chap. 19.

Robert D. Crassweller, *Trujillo: The Life and Times of a Caribbean Dictator* (1966), chap. 21.

Howard J. Wiarda, *Dictatorship and Development: The Methods of Control in Trujillo's Dominican Republic* (1968), pp. 58–59, 149–153, 176–177.

*Additional Bibliography*

Vega, Bernardo. *Almoina, Galíndez y otros crímenes de Trujillo en el extranjero.* Santo Domingo, República Dominicana: Fundación Cultural Dominicana, 2001.

LARMAN C. WILSON

**GALINDO, ALEJANDRO** (1906–1999). Associated with the Golden Era of Mexican Cinema, Alejandro Galindo directed seventy-eight films during a varied career (1934–1985). Born on January 14, 1906, in Monterrey, Nuevo León, his family moved to Mexico City when he was still young. Rejecting his original plan to become a dentist, Galindo studied scriptwriting at the Hollywood Institute of Scriptwriting and Photoplay, gained practical experience as a laboratory technician/editor at MGM and worked alongside Gregory La Cava. His scriptwriting in *La isla maldita* (The Accursed Island, 1934), followed by his directorial debut in *Almas rebeldes* (Rebel Souls, 1937), established his career. *Una familia de tantas* (A Family Like So Many Others, 1948) used the common social denominator to draw in the public, and *Espaldas mojadas* (Wet Backs, 1953) offered an early snapshot of immigration to the United States. The swan song of Galindo's career, *Lázaro Cárdenas* (1985), a film about the onetime Mexican president (1934–1940), was not screened for political reasons. Galindo died on February 1, 1999. He is now remembered for films based on everyday life and believable dialogue.

*See also* **Cinema: Since 1990.**

BIBLIOGRAPHY

Mora, Carl J. *Mexican Cinema: Reflections of a Society, 1896 to 2004.* 3rd ed. Jefferson, NC: McFarland and Company, 2005.

Noble, Andrea. *Mexican National Cinema.* London: Routledge, 2005.

STEPHEN HART

**GALINDO, BLAS** (1910–1993). Blas Galindo (*b.* 3 February 1910; *d.* 19 April 1993), Mexican composer, teacher, and administrator. A Huichol Indian, Galindo came to Mexico City in 1931 from San Gabriel, Jalisco, and began composition study with Carlos Chávez at the National Conservatory. He was affiliated with three other Chávez students, labeled "Los cuatro," a group committed to the creation and performance of a genuine Mexican music, engendering pieces like his picturesque *Sones de mariachi,* which was premiered at a Mexican exhibit in New York's Museum of Modern Art in 1940. In 1941 he studied composition with Aaron Copland at the Berkshire Music Center and returned to Mexico to complete his conservatory training. He taught at the National Conservatory from 1944, and became its director in 1947, the year in which he was also appointed head of the music department of the National Institute of Fine Arts. His output—encompassing works for piano, small ensembles, orchestra, voice, and chorus—ranged from folkloric to neoclassic to boldly dissonant.

*See also* **Music: Art Music.**

BIBLIOGRAPHY

Gérard Béhague, *Music in Latin America: An Introduction* (1979).

*Additional Bibliography*

*Hacer música: Blas Galindo, compositor.* Guadalajara, Jalisco, México: Universidad de Guadalajara, Dirección de Publicaciones, 1994.

Ruiz Ortiz, Xochiquetzal, and Blas Galindo. *Blas Galindo: Biografía, antología de textos y catálogo.* México, D.F.: CENIDIM, 1994.

ROBERT L. PARKER

**GALINDO, JUAN** (1802–1840). Juan Galindo (christened John; *b.* spring or summer 1802; *d.* 30 January 1840), émigré Anglo-Irish activist in Central America. The eldest child of Philemon Galindo, an Anglo-Spanish actor–fencing master, and Catherine Gough, an Anglo-Irish actress, Galindo arrived in Guatemala in 1827 after service with Lord Thomas Cochrane in South American wars of independence. His varied activities brought him distinction as a scientist, Liberal propagandist, military and administrative officer, and amateur diplomat. Duty and travel provided him opportunity to survey topography, examine archaeological sites, and observe native populations and natural history phenomena that he described in articles published in European scholarly journals. Galindo decried encroachments on Central American territory and involved himself in several defensive countercolonization projects, the major one of which ignited the smoldering Belize boundary and sovereignty issue. His diplomatic mission (1835–1836) to secure British recognition of Central American sovereignty over Belize proved futile. He died while fleeing the site of the battle of El Potrero, near Tegucigalpa, Honduras.

*See also* **Cochrane, Lord Thomas Alexander; Tegucigalpa.**

BIBLIOGRAPHY

Ian Graham, "Juan Galindo, Enthusiast," in *Estudios de cultura Maya* (Mexico City) 3 (1963): 11–35, stresses Galindo's scientific activities and achievements.

William J. Griffith, "Juan Galindo, Central American Chauvinist," in *Hispanic American Historical Review* 40, no. 1 (1960): 25–52, emphasizes his role in the boundary disputes and territorial encroachment controversies of the region. William J. Griffith, *Empires in the Wilderness: Foreign Colonization and Development in Guatemala, 1834–1844* (1965), lays out Galindo's involvement in a number of colonization and development projects.

*Additional Bibliography*

Woodward, Ralph Lee. *Rafael Carrera and the Emergence of the Republic of Guatemala, 1821–1871.* Athens: University of Georgia Press, 1993.

WILLIAM J. GRIFFITH

**GALINDO, SERGIO** (1926–1993). Sergio Galindo (*b.* 2 September 1926; *d.* 3 January 1993), Mexican writer. Born in Xalapa, Veracruz, Galindo first published a collection of short stories in 1951, *La máquina vacía* (The Empty Machine), and in the following years produced a sizable corpus of narrative, mainly novels. They include *Polvos de arroz* (Rice Powder, 1958), *Justicia de enero* (Justice in January, 1959), *El bordo* (The Precipice, 1960), and *La comparsa* (Carnival, 1964). Galindo received the 1986 Premio Xavier Villaurrutía for his novel *Otilia Rauda* (1986). In his writing, Galindo explores the tensions in middle-class Mexican families and the dynamics of intimate relationships. In contrast to the predominant emphasis on national identity in Mexican literature, such psychological concerns emphasize widely shared human behaviors. In addition to his literary production, from 1957 to 1964 Galindo edited the journal *La Palabra y el Hombre* (Word and Man) and directed the publishing department of the University of Veracruz, where he inaugurated an influential fiction series. Between 1965 and 1976 Galindo served in a variety of positions for the National Institute of Fine Arts and the Secretariat of Public Education. Since 1975 he has been a member of the Mexican Academy of Language.

*See also* **Literature: Spanish America; Mexico: Since 1910.**

BIBLIOGRAPHY

John S. Brushwood, "The Novels of Sergio Galindo: Planes of Human Relationship," in *Hispania* 51 (1968): 812–816, and *The Spanish American Novel: A Twentieth-Century Survey* (1975), pp. 239–241, 275–277, 316; *La Palabra y el Hombre,* nueva época no. 59–60 (1986), a special issue in honor of Sergio Galindo.

*Additional Bibliography*

Anhalt, Nedda G de. *Allá donde ves la neblina: Un acercamiento a la obra de Sergio Galindo.* Xalapa: Universidad Veracruzana, 2003.

Martínez Morales, José Luis, and Sergio Pitol. *Miradas a la obra de Sergio Galindo.* Xalapa: Instituto de Investigaciones Lingüístico-Literarias, Universidad Veracruzana, 1996.

DANNY J. ANDERSON

**GALLEGO OTERO, LAURA** (1924–). Laura Gallego Otero (*b.* 9 February 1924), Puerto Rican poet, essayist, and educator. Closely identified with her native Bayamón, a suburb of San Juan, Laura Gallego taught high-school Spanish and was an education professor at the University of Puerto Rico. Her published books of poetry are *Presencia* (Presence, 1952), *Celajes* (Clouds, 1959), and *Que voy de vuelo* (Flying Away, 1980). A 1972 anthology of her work includes the prose poems of *Almejas de tu nombre* (Clams of Your Name, 1954) and the previously unpublished collections of verse *En carne viva* (In the flesh), *La red* (The Net), and *La del alba seria* (The Woman of Serious Dawn). Gallego often speaks of words and silence in her verses, and in poetic dialogue addresses nature, God, an unnamed presence, and love lost. In *Celajes* Gallego writes about the natural beauty of Puerto Rico and of its people. Wounding images of arrows, darts, daggers, knives, and spines yield in her later poetry to meditative contemplations of the world, mankind, life, God, and the past. In 2002 Gallego was named Humanist of the Year by the Puerto Rican Endowment for the Humanities.

*See also* **Puerto Rico.**

BIBLIOGRAPHY

Laura Gallego, *Obra poética,* edited by Luis de Arrigoita (1972), pp. 5–15.

Josefina Rivera De Alvarez, *Literatura puertorriqueña: Su proceso en el tiempo* (1983), pp. 577–578.

*Additional Bibliography*

Martínez Planell, Sahyly. *Los temas en la poesía de Laura Gallego.* M.A. thesis, Universidad de Puerto Rico, 1998.

Pagán Tirado, Lydia. *Mambiche: La historia de Vieques en poemas.* Rio Piedras, Puerto Rico: Fundación "Palabras y más," 2006.

ESTELLE IRIZARRY

**GALLEGOS, RÓMULO** (1884–1969). Rómulo Gallegos (*b.* 21 August 1884; *d.* 7 April 1969), president of Venezuela (1947–1948). Best known as author of *Doña Bárbara* (1929), Gallegos also made major contributions to Venezuela as a secondary teacher and a politician. As a teacher during the 1920s he influenced a significant number of important politicians, including Rómulo Betancourt and Raúl Leoni. As a politician he was elected senator from Apure in 1931, but went into voluntary exile until the death of Juan Vicente Gómez, (1935). On his return he served as minister of education under Eleázar López Contreras, won a seat in the House of Deputies in 1947, and in 1941 took part in the organization of the Democratic Action Party (Acción Democrática).

Among his literary accomplishments, in 1909 Gallegos founded a reformist magazine called *La Alborada* (Dawn of Day), which dealt with political as well as literary topics. His novels combined realism with a deep-seated conviction that civilization would overcome barbarism, that goodness would prevail over evil. Gallegos, never polemical or directly critical of the Gómez dictatorship, published his best work while in exile in Spain. *Doña Bárbara* reflected his positivist background, depicting in an optimistic manner the ultimate victory of the educated Santos Luzardo over the backward Doña Bárbara. Two other novels, both written in exile, also portrayed in beautiful language the reality of Venezuelan life. *Cantaclaro* (1931) was a fictional account of the *llaneros* (plainsmen). *Canaíma* (1935) described the life of Marcos Vargas in the jungle of the Orinoco River valley, where the forces of justice fought those of evil. Later novels, such as *Pobre negro* (1937), which treated a slave rebellion of the 1860s, *El forastero* (1942), and *Sobre la misma tierra* (1943), never reached the high quality of Gallegos's earlier work, probably because of his involvement in political activities.

Gallegos was elected president in 1947; after his overthrow in November 1948, he spent time in Cuba and Mexico. He returned to Venezuela in 1958 and received a hero's welcome. He was awarded many prizes for both his political activities in the past and his writing. Two late novels, *La brizna de paja en el viento* (1952) and *La tierra bajo los pies* (1971), dealt with Cuban and Mexican themes, respectively.

*See also* **Literature: Spanish America; Venezuela: Venezuela since 1830.**

BIBLIOGRAPHY

Harrison Howard, *Rómulo Gallegos y la revolución burguesa de Venezuela* (1976).

José Vicente Abreu, *Rómulo Gallegos: Ideas educativas en* La Alborada (1978).

Hugo Rodríguez-Alcala, ed., *Nine Essays on Rómulo Gallegos* (1979).

Rómulo Gallegos, *Cuentos completos* (1981).

José Agustín Catala, comp., *El golpe contra el presidente Gallegos: Documentos para la historia* ... (1983).

Guillermo Morón, *Homenaje a Rómulo Gallegos* (1984).

Rafael Fauquie Bescos, *Rómulo Gallegos: La realidad, la ficción, el símbolo* ... (1985).

*Additional Bibliography*

Bravo, Manuel J. *Militarismo y política en Venezuela, 1945-1958.* Caracas: Fondo Editorial de la Universidad Pedagógica Experimental Libertador, 1999.

Isea, Antonio. "La narración de lo racial-nacional en 'Pobre negro' de Rómulo Gallegos." *Afro-Hispanic Review* 20:2 (Fall 2001): 18–22.

Marinone de Borrás, Mónica. *Escribir novelas, fundar naciones: Rómulo Gallegos y la experiencia venezolana.* Mérida: Centro de Letras Hispanoamericanas, Facultad de Humanidades, 1999.

WINTHROP R. WRIGHT

---

**GALLET, LUCIANO** (1893–1931). Luciano Gallet (*b.* 28 June 1893; *d.* 29 October 1931), Brazilian composer and musicologist. In 1913 Gallet enrolled in the Instituto Nacional de Música, where he studied piano with Henrique Oswald and harmony with Agnelo França. His first compositions were in a romantic or impressionistic style, but contact with Mário de Andrade resulted in serious studies of Brazilian popular and folk music. Some of Gallet's earliest works consisted of harmonizations and arrangements of folk songs. It is significant that Mário de Andrade, the most important figure in the emerging nationalist movement in music, considered Gallet's research and studies sufficiently significant to arrange for the publication of Gallet's *Estudos de folclore.* Although Gallet has never been considered a major composer, except possibly in the area of the art song, his influence on Brazilian musical life has been significant in numerous areas, including concerts, teaching, composition, discography, radio, journalism, and folk music. In each endeavor he gave evidence of keen analytical thought and contributed to the development of the musical life of Brazil.

*See also* **Andrade, Mário de; Music: Art Music.**

BIBLIOGRAPHY

Luciano Gallet, *Estudos de Folclore* (1934).

Vasco Mariz, *A canção brasileira,* 5th ed. (1985).

*Additional Bibliography*

Fernandes, Juvenal. *História da música brasileira: Com tópicos da história do Brasil (1500–2000).* São Paulo: EDICON, 2004.

DAVID P. APPLEBY

---

**GALLINAZO.** Gallinazo, a culture that flourished on the north coast of Peru from *c.* 100 BCE to 200 CE. The center of the Gallinazo polity was located in the Virú Valley, about twenty-one miles south of the contemporary city of Trujillo. Gallinazo cultural remains are found from the Casma to the Lambayeque valleys, but the culture's contacts and sphere of influence can be seen as far south as the Rimac Valley to as far north as the Piura Valley.

Research suggests that the Gallinazo polity was the first multivalley state in the Andes, and that this state had an urban capital at the Gallinazo Group site in the Virú Valley. The possibility that this polity had a highly organized form of government was first recognized by Gordon Willey, who suggested that during the Gallinazo period the Virú Valley may have attained state-level political organization. This view has been disputed by David Wilson, whose work in the neighboring Santa Valley led him to believe that the succeeding Moche culture was the first state in the region.

Characteristic Gallinazo artifacts include negative, or resist, painted pottery, and handmade redware pots that were decorated with incision, triangular punctuations, appliqué, and notched strips of clay. The most characteristic Gallinazo architecture is large apartment-like complexes that consist of a honeycomb of rooms made of adobe bricks. The structures lack doorways and windows, and were entered through openings in the roof. The architecture that served public functions include adobe pyramids associated with a complex series of rooms including domestic and administrative structures. The administrative architecture has doorways opening onto long corridors. A number of these rooms are decorated with adobe brick mosaics in distinctive geometric designs and/or yellow paint.

During the Gallinazo occupation of Virú, the valley had a highly organized, integrated settlement system, which included a network of fortifications that protected access to the irrigation system and the capital city. The Gallinazo occupation of the Virú Valley marked the largest extension of the irrigation of the valley throughout the prehistory and history of the valley. At the peak of the Gallinazo polity it incorporated the neighboring Moche and Santa Valleys. The Gallinazo occupations of these valleys were also complex settlement systems, with a number of smaller administrative centers that were subordinate to the Gallinazo Group site.

*See also* **Archaeology.**

BIBLIOGRAPHY

Wendell C. Bennett, *The Gallinazo Group Virú Valley, Peru* (1950).

Gordon R. Willey, *Prehistoric Settlement Patterns in the Virú Valley, Peru* (1955), and *Archaeological Researches in Retrospect* (1974), pp. 149–178.

David J. Wilson, *Prehispanic Settlement Patterns in the Lower Santa Valley, Peru: A Regional Perspective on the Origins and Development of Complex North Coast Society* (1988).

Heidy P. Fogel, "Settlements in Time: A Study of Social and Political Development During the Gallinazo Occupation of the North Coast of Peru" (Ph.D. diss., Yale University, 1993).

HEIDY P. FOGEL

**GALLINAZO GROUP SITE.** Gallinazo Group Site, archaeological region located in the Virú Valley on the north coast of Peru. The Gallinazo Group was the largest and most complex site in this region during the Gallinazo period (*c.* 100 BCE–200 CE). Consisting of some thirty numbered mounds, the site measures five square miles and contains evidence of some 30,000 rooms on its surface. Covering this area is a large variety of architectural types, including pyramids, dwellings, cemeteries, and administrative structures. Between these is a combination of low-lying architecture not visible on the surface, public spaces, and some agricultural plots.

The dating of the standing architecture has revealed that most of these structures were occupied during the Middle and Late Gallinazo phases. It is clear that during these periods the Gallinazo Group site was a city, and thus it constitutes one of the first known cities in the Andes. The Gallinazo Group site was the location of a concentration of wealth and power during the Gallinazo period, and as such it very likely served as the capital of the Gallinazo multivalley polity.

The site was occupied during all three phases of the Gallinazo sequence and was abandoned at the end of the Late Gallinazo period. Evidence for subsequent occupation of the area is scarce, and is confined mostly to a few intrusive burials dating to the succeeding Moche culture. This may be due to the fact that the plain upon which the site is located is extremely arid, and its occupation is only possible when a dependable flow of water can be diverted from the upper valley. The sustained occupation of the Gallinazo Group site was made possible through its integration into a unified valley system with well-defended and extensive irrigation works.

*See also* **Archaeology.**

BIBLIOGRAPHY

Wendell C. Bennett, *The Gallinazo Group Virú Valley, Peru* (1959).

Gordon R. Willey, *Prehistoric Settlement Patterns in the Virú Valley, Peru* (1955); Heidy P. Fogel, "Settlements in Time: A Study of Social and Political Development During the Gallinazo Occupation of the North Coast of Peru" (Ph.D. diss., Yale University, 1993).

*Additional Bibliography*

Bonnier, Elisabeth, and Henning Bischof, eds. *Arquitectura y civilización en los Andes prehispánicos/Prehispanic Architecture and Civilization in the Andes.* Mannheim: Sociedad Arqueológica Peruano-Alemana: Reiss-Museum Mannheim, 1997.

HEIDY P. FOGEL

**GALLO GOYENECHEA, PEDRO LEÓN** (1830–1877). Pedro León Gallo Goyenechea (*b.* 12 February 1830; *d.* 16 December 1877), Chilean politician. Born into a prosperous mining family at Copiapó, Atacama Province, Gallo took a lifelong interest in politics, strongly supporting President Manuel Montt (to whom he was related by marriage) at the time of his election (1851) but later turning against his authoritarianism. In January 1859 he launched an armed rebellion against Montt (the Constituent Revolution), sinking much of his fortune into the cause. At his base, the mining town of Copiapó, he recruited an army and manufactured weapons, also issuing his own locally minted currency (constituent pesos). Although Gallo staged a brilliant march to capture La Serena (March 1859), his army was defeated at the battle of

Cerro Grande, just south of the city, two weeks later in April. Gallo fled into exile, returning to Chile in 1863, when, with his friend Manuel Antonio Matta, he founded the Radical Party, often nicknamed *la tienda de los Matta y los Gallo* (The Matta and Gallo store). In his later years he served as a member of the Chamber of Deputies, and in 1876 he was elected to the Senate.

*See also* **Chile, Political Parties: Radical Party; Chile: The Nineteenth Century; Montt Torres, Manuel.**

BIBLIOGRAPHY

Mario Bahamonde Silva, *El caudillo de Copiapó: Copiapó, 1859* (1977), and Simon Collier, "Chile from Independence to the War of the Pacific," in *Cambridge History of Latin America,* edited by Leslie Bethell, vol. 3 (1985), pp. 583–613.

*Additional Bibliography*

Collier, Simon. *Chile: The Making of a Republic, 1830–1865: Politics and Ideas.* New York: Cambridge University Press, 2003.

SIMON COLLIER

---

**GALTIERI, LEOPOLDO FORTUNATO** (1926–2003). Leopoldo Fortunato Galtieri, born July 15, 1926, was an Argentine military officer and politician who was de facto president of Argentina from 1981 to 1982.

As a young graduate of the Military Academy, Galtieri pursued further studies in the School of the Americas, where he received training in counterinsurgency methods. Following the coup d'état of March 24, 1976, he was in charge of the illegal repression in Rosario, in the province of Santa Fe. In 1981, during the de facto presidency of Roberto Viola, he became commander of the Army, and developed close ties with the conservative government of the United States. As a member of the Military Junta, an organization with executive and legislative powers over and above those of the president, he stood out as the leader of the most hardline sector of the army and conspired against Viola, accusing him of being soft on the political parties. He plotted with Admiral Anaya, commander of the Navy, to return the Falkland Islands to Argentine control, and in December 1981 the Military Junta appointed him president of the nation in the midst of a profound economic crisis and a prolonged wave of civil unrest against the dictatorship. On April 2, 1981, with the hope of bolstering the political capital of the "Process" and heading up a controlled institutionalization of military domination, the Armed Forces occupied the Falkland Islands, which were then under British control. On June 14, the Argentine forces surrendered in defeat. Galtieri was forced to resign.

With the return of democracy, he was tried for crimes committed during the "Process" and sentenced to prison by a military tribunal for negligence during the war. In 1990 he was pardoned by President Carlos Menem, but in 2002 he was convicted and sentenced for the kidnapping of infants during the dictatorship. He died January 12, 2003.

*See also* **Argentina: The Twentieth Century; Dirty War; Falkland Islands (Malvinas); Viola, Roberto Eduardo.**

BIBLIOGRAPHY

Cardoso, Oscar Raúl, Ricardo Kirschbaum, and Eduardo Van Der Kooy. *Malvinas, la trama secreta.* Buenos Aires: Planeta, 1992.

Freedman, Lawrence, and Virginia Gamba-Stonehouse. *Signals of War: The Falklands Conflict of 1982.* Princeton, NJ: Princeton University Press, 1991.

Novaro, Marcos, and Vicente Palermo. *La dictadura militar.* Buenos Aires: Paidós, 2003.

VICENTE PALERMO

---

**GALVÁN, MANUEL DE JESÚS** (1834–1910). Manuel de Jesús Galván (*b.* 1834; *d.* 1910), Dominican writer, politician, and jurist. Galván was considered the Dominican Republic's greatest writer for his book *Enriquillo,* which dealt with the confrontation between the indigenous Tainos and Spanish colonizers. Galván was also a member of the Dominican Congress and a justice of the Supreme Court. Considered a masterwork of Spanish literature, *Enriquillo* is a fictionalized account of the struggle of the last Taino cacique, Enrique, who fled his Spanish landlord into the Bahoruco Mountains and organized with his followers a thirteen-year resistance (1520–1533) to Spanish rule. While Enrique and his followers never surrendered, and while a peace agreement that moved the surviving Tainos to reservations was signed, by the 1550s the Taino population had been virtually wiped out. Galván's novel was not published until 1882 and contains considerable embellishment, including the oft-repeated nineteenth-century style of depicting the indigenous Americans as "noble savages." Despite its nostalgia for the vanquished, Galván's novel is considered one of the greatest novels produced by a Dominican.

*See also* **Dominican Republic; Literature: Spanish America.**

BIBLIOGRAPHY

Manuel De Jesús Galván, *Manuel de Jesús Galván's* Enriquillo: *The Cross and the Sword,* translated by Robert Graves (1975).

Louise L. Cripps, *The Spanish Caribbean: From Columbus to Castro* (1979).

*Additional Bibliography*

Durán-Cogan, Mercedes F., and Antonio Gomez-Moriana, eds. *National Identities and Sociopolitical Changes in Latin America.* New York: Routledge, 2001.

Summer, Doris. "Borrón y cuenta nueva: Comienzos tardíos y razas tempranas en Enriquillo, Cumandá y Tabaré." *Casa de las Américas,* 187 (Apr.–June 1992): 136–140.

MICHAEL POWELSON

## GALVÁN RIVERA, MARIANO (1791–1876).

Mariano Galván Rivera (*b.* 12 September 1791; *d.* 1876), Mexican publisher. After becoming established in Mexico City as a bookseller, Galván, a native of Tepotzotlán, opened a print shop, with Mariano Arévalo as manager, in 1826. That year he began publishing his *Calendario manual,* which continues to appear under the name *Calendario del más antiguo Galván.* From 1827 to 1830 he published *El observador de la República Mexicana,* and from 1833 to 1834, *El indicador de la Federación Mexicana,* edited by José María Luis Mora. From 1838 to 1843 he published the *Calendario de las señoritas mexicanas.* Other works that he published include *Sagrada Biblia* in twenty-five volumes; *El periquillo sarmiento; Colección eclesiástica mexicana; Don Quijote; Dicionario razonado de legislación;* Count de Segur's *Historia universal; Nueva colección de leyes y decretos mexicanos;* and *Concilio III provincial mexicano.* His bookstore became a gathering place for literary and political figures. In 1862 Galván was a member of the Assembly of Notables who decided to establish a monarchy in Mexico. Although imprisoned after Maximilian's fall, he was soon freed. He died in Mexico City.

*See also* **Assembly of Notables.**

BIBLIOGRAPHY

*Diccionario Porrúa de historia, geografía y biografía de México,* 5th ed. (1986).

*Additional Bibliography*

Suárez de la Torre, Laura. *Constructores de un cambio cultural: Impresores-editores y libreros en la ciudad de México, 1830–1855.* México, D.F.: Instituto de Investigaciones Dr. José María Luis Mora, 2003.

VIRGINIA GUEDEA

## GALVARINO (?–1557).

Galvarino (*d.* December 1557), Araucanian warrior and hero. Nothing is known about Galvarino's life before the events in which he figured during the Spanish invasion of Chile. At the battle of Lagunillas (or Bío-Bío) during Governor García Hurtado De Mendoza's (1535–1609) advance into Araucanian territory in 1557, he was captured and had both his hands cut off. The fiery speeches he delivered following his mutilation rallied his people to resist the Spaniards. Soon afterward, at the battle of Millarapue (November 1557), Galvarino was again captured and later hanged with other Araucanian prisoners.

The events of Galvarino's demise were witnessed by the poet-soldier Alonso de Ercilla y Zúñiga (1533–1594), who recounted them in memorable passages in his epic *La Araucana.* This more than anything else gave Galvarino the legendary status he enjoys in the pantheon of Araucanian heroism. While some of the speeches attributed to Galvarino in this poem must have been invented by Ercilla, the events themselves are confirmed by independent sources.

*See also* **Araucanians; Ercilla y Zúñiga, Alonso de.**

BIBLIOGRAPHY

Dillehay, Tom D. *Monuments, Empires, and Resistance in the Andes: The Araucanian Polity and Ritual Narratives.*

Cambridge; New York: Cambridge University Press, 2007.

Ferrando Keun, Ricardo. *Y así nació la frontera: Conquista, guerra, ocupación, pacificación, 1550–1900.* Santiago: Editorial Antártica, 2007.

SIMON COLLIER

## GÁLVEZ, BERNARDO DE (1746–1786).

**GÁLVEZ, BERNARDO DE** (1746–1786). Bernardo de Gálvez (*b.* 25 July 1746; *d.* 30 November 1786), Spanish military officer, governor of Louisiana (1777–1783), and viceroy of New Spain (1785–1786), Gálvez was born at Macharavialla, near Málaga, to a family that held many important posts under the Spanish Bourbons. He accompanied his uncle, José de Gálvez, to New Spain, where he gained valuable experience against the Apaches on the northern frontier in 1769. After a tour of training with the French Cantabrian Regiment, he served under General Alejandro O'Reilly in a campaign against Algeria (1774), after which King Charles III named him commander of the Louisiana Regiment in 1776.

Upon arriving in New Orleans, however, he received orders to relieve Luis de Unzaga as governor of Louisiana, which he did on 1 January 1777. His administration in Louisiana coincided with the American Revolution, in which he played a prominent role. He increased the population and military strength of the colony and promoted its economic growth in accordance with the instructions of his uncle José, who now served as president of the Council of the Indies. In collaboration with Oliver Pollock, he clandestinely channeled arms to American revolutionaries operating in the Mississippi Valley, significantly aiding George Rogers Clark. Once Spain declared war on England, he launched a successful military campaign, with major victories at Baton Rouge (21 September 1779), Mobile (March 1780), and Pensacola (8–10 May 1781). His forces were also instrumental in breaking British military power in the northern Mississippi Valley. Gálvez's victories enabled Spain to recover Florida under the Treaty of Paris (1783) and contributed significantly to the achievement of American independence. Promoted to captain-general, Gálvez governed Cuba from 4 February until 20 April 1785, after which he succeded his father, Matías de Gálvez, as viceroy of New Spain. He died in Mexico City.

*See also* **Louisiana; New Spain, Viceroyalty of.**

### BIBLIOGRAPHY

John W. Caughey, *Bernardo de Gálvez in Louisiana, 1776–1783* (1934).

Jack D. L. Holmes, *A Guide to Spanish Louisiana, 1762–1806* (1970).

José R. Boeta, *Bernardo de Gálvez* (1977).

Bernardo De Gálvez, *Yo solo: The Battle Journal of Bernardo de Gálvez During the American Revolution* (1978).

Ralph L. Woodward, Jr., *Tribute to Don Bernardo de Gálvez* (1979).

William S. Coker and Robert R. Rea, eds., *Anglo-Spanish Confrontation on the Gulf Coast During the American Revolution* (1982).

Carmen De Reparz, *Yo solo: Bernardo de Gálvez y la toma de Panzacola en 1781* (1986).

### *Additional Bibliography*

Chavez, Thomas E. *Spain and the Independence of the United States: An Intrinsic Gift.* Albuquerque: University of New Mexico Press, 2002.

RALPH LEE WOODWARD JR.

## GÁLVEZ, JOSÉ DE (1720–1787).

**GÁLVEZ, JOSÉ DE** (1720–1787). José de Gálvez (*b.* 2 January 1720; *d.* 17 June 1787), a leading Spanish bureaucrat and statesman instrumental in the reform of eighteenth-century colonial administration. Born a poor hidalgo in Macharaviaya, an Andalusian hill village, Gálvez earned a law degree at the University of Salamanca. Later, he conducted a successful practice in Madrid, in which he handled many cases involving parties in the Americas. He attracted the attention of Abbé Béliardi, a French agent, and through him, gained the patronage of the marqués de Esquilache and the marqués de Grimaldi, enlightened ministers of King Charles III of Spain. Their favor secured him the risky opportunity to conduct a *visita*, that is, a thorough inspection and overhaul of the administration of Mexico, where he arrived in July 1765.

Gálvez carried out a speedy and ruthless reorganization of tax collection and accounting procedures.

He jailed corrupt officials, changed the tax structure, instituted a highly profitable tobacco monopoly, and shifted the control of trade with Spain from Mexican to Spanish merchants. In so doing, he forced capital into mining, which he aided with tax reductions, cheap mercury, and technical assistance. In this way, he decisively redirected the Mexican economy.

The *visitador* proposed the introduction of the intendancy system (provincial governors) and the establishment of the Provincias Internas, which created a separate government for the northern region of the country. In addition, Gálvez dealt with the expulsion of the Jesuits, Indian revolts in Sonora, raids in Chihuahua, and orders to colonize Alta California all at the same time. He brutally suppressed the uprisings occasioned by the ban, reorganized government in the north, and got the colonization effort under way by 1769.

Then, the strain of work, the responsibility, and the exhausting and indecisive struggle with the Sonoran Indians broke Gálvez's health, and in late 1769 he suffered a physical and mental collapse. He recovered and returned to Spain in 1771, but the end of the *visita* was clouded.

In Spain Gálvez assumed his place on the Council of the Indies, to which he was appointed in 1767. He was gradually given more important assignments, and when Julián de Arriaga y Rivera died, Charles III made Gálvez minister of the Indies (February 1776).

As minister, Gálvez tried to institute the reforms he had instituted in Mexico throughout the whole Empire. *Visitadores* cast in Gálvez's mold were sent to Peru, New Granada, Venezuela, and Ecuador to increase revenue, establish intendancies, and invigorate government. The situation in Buenos Aires was complicated by the opportunity, offered by Great Britain's preoccupation with the American Revolution, to settle long-pending disputes with the Portuguese regarding boundaries and smuggling. Eventually Spain declared war and sent a military expedition to the area. The result was the establishment of a viceroyalty of Buenos Aires, organized according to Gálvez's program.

When Spain followed France into an alliance with the Americans against Britain in 1779, Gálvez's reforms were again shouldered aside. Moreover, the need for money and the errors and misfortunes of two *visitadores* produced the Túpac Amaru rebellion (1780–1781) in Peru and the Comunero Revolt (1781) in New Granada. Gálvez reacted to them with the same fierce repression he had unleashed in Mexico against those who questioned royal authority.

Nevertheless, when Gálvez became marqués de Sonora in 1785, he could claim an important role in winning back Florida and ejecting the British from the Mosquito Coast and Darién. Unfortunately, just as Gálvez sought to bring his full authority to bear on the completion of the internal reforms, he died.

The consequent reorganization of the ministry redirected the course of policy, but Sonora's reforms had been too extensive to be abandoned totally. Gálvez was a hard-working and hard-edged administrator, efficient but not noted for accommodation or suppleness. His legacy of a more rational administration and higher revenues was purchased with the political alienation of many Americans and not a few Spaniards, whom he pushed from their traditional places and powers.

*See also* **Council of the Indies; Intendancy System; Túpac Amaru; Visita, Visitador.**

BIBLIOGRAPHY

There is no comprehensive biography of Gálvez. However, the Mexican *visita* is well covered in Herbert Ingram Priestly, *José de Gálvez: Visitor-General of New Spain, 1765–1771* (1916, repr. 1980). The Provincias Internas scheme and the intendant system are thoroughly considered by Luis Navarro García in *Don José de Gálvez y la comandancia general de las provincias internas del norte de Nueva España* (1964), and *Intendencias en Indias* (1959). Mario Hernández Sánchez-barba provides an *Annales* approach in *La última expansión española en America* (1957). Gálvez's impact on trade and government is analyzed in D. A. Brading, *Miners and Merchants in Bourbon Mexico, 1762–1810* (1971). Brading's "Bourbon Spain and Its American Empire," in Vol. 1, *The Cambridge History of Latin America*, edited by Leslie Bethell, vol. 1 (1984), pp. 389–439, provides a comprehensive view of the whole period. In most works dealing with the so-called Bourbon reforms there is some treatment of Gálvez and his policies. For example see J. R. Fisher, *Government and Society in Colonial Peru: The Intendant System, 1784–1814* (1970), and John Leddy Phelan, *The People and the King: The Comunero Revolution in Colombia, 1781* (1978).

*Additional Bibliography*

Rodríguez O, Jaime E., ed. *Mexico in the Age of Democratic Revolutions, 1750–1850.* Boulder, CO: Lynne Rienner, 1994.

GEORGE M. ADDY

**GÁLVEZ, JUAN MANUEL** (1887–1972). Juan Manuel Gálvez (*b.* 1887; *d.* 19 August 1972), president of Honduras, 1949–1954. Gálvez succeeded the long-time dictator, Tiburcio Carías Andino, whom he had served as minister of defense. As Carías's handpicked successor, Gálvez perpetuated National Party dominance and many of his predecessor's policies. He launched a more vigorous program of public works, infrastructure development, economic diversification, and tax reform while also easing restrictions on civil liberties.

The United Fruit Company workers' strike in 1954 precipitated a political crisis at the end of Gálvez's administration. Gálvez, who had been a United Fruit attorney for many years, showed little sympathy for the strikers and was clearly annoyed by the encouragement that Guatemala's pro-labor government of Jacobo Arbenz gave the strikers. He actively collaborated with Guatemalan exiles and the U.S. Central Intelligence Agency in the overthrow of the Arbenz government in June 1954. In the November 1954 elections, Carías sought to return to office, but Liberal candidate Ramón Villeda Morales received a plurality of the votes, with no one receiving a majority. Before the Congress could decide the election, Gálvez's vice president, Julio Lozano Díaz, seized power, ending Gálvez's administration. Gálvez, now in ill health, did not contest Lozano's seizure of dictatorial power, and Lozano later appointed Gálvez president of the Supreme Court.

*See also* **Carías Andino, Tiburcio; Honduras; United Fruit Company.**

BIBLIOGRAPHY

James D. Rudolph, ed., *Honduras, a Country Study,* 2d ed. (1983).

James A. Morris, *Honduras: Caudillo Politics and Military Rulers* (1984).

Alison Acker, *Honduras: The Making of a Banana Republic* (1988).

James Dunkerley, *Power in the Isthmus: A Political History of Modern Central America* (1988).

Tom Barry and Kent Norsworthy, *Honduras: A Country Guide* (1990).

*Additional Bibliography*

Funes, Matías. *Los deliberantes: El poder militar en Honduras.* Tegucigalpa: Editorial Guaymuras, 2000.

Salomón, Leticia. *Política y militares en Honduras.* Tegucigalpa, Honduras: Editorial Millenium, 1992.

RALPH LEE WOODWARD JR.

**GÁLVEZ, MANUEL** (1882–1961). Manuel Gálvez (*b.* 18 July 1882; *d.* 14 November 1962), Argentine novelist and essayist. Gálvez was born in the provincial capital of Paraná. When he was three years old, his family moved to Santa Fe, where he studied at the Jesuit school La Inmaculada. In 1897, he completed his secondary studies in Buenos Aires at the Colegio del Salvador. He graduated from the University of Buenos Aires with a law degree in 1904, but never practiced his profession. His dissertation on the theme of white slavery, reveals an early interest in social problems that never abated in his long career as a novelist and essayist.

One of Argentina's foremost novelists from 1915 until 1950, Gálvez played an important role in his country's cultural life. He was conservative in his political ideology, although as a young man he espoused a form of anarchism and defended Tolstoy's Christian socialism. In Gálvez's concept of nationalism, certain ideas were dominant: the central role of the church in maintaining the spirit and traditions of Argentina; an adherence to law and order above individual freedom; a distrust of Anglo-Saxon civilizations; and doubts about the advisability of having a totally democratic government. Nowhere was this nationalism more evident than in Gálvez's biography of the dictator Juan Manuel de Rosas (1829–1852), whom Gálvez defended on the ground that he unified the country and prevented it from succumbing to the economic and political pressures of the French and English. In *El solar de la raza* (The Birthplace of Our Race, 1913), Gálvez underscored the cultural and spiritual affinity between Argentina and Spain. In works like *La sombra del convento* (The Shadow of the Convent, 1917), Gálvez preached a return to the traditional moral and religious values that could still be found in the provinces and opposed the utilitarian values he associated with life in Buenos Aires.

For twenty-five years, Gálvez served as national inspector of secondary and normal schools, an experience he drew on to write *La maestra normal* (The Normal School Teacher, 1914), which many critics interpreted as an attack on the normal schools and secular education. In novels of social protest such as *Nacha regules* (1919), Gálvez became a social reformer, defending the poor and downtrodden against society's indifference to human suffering.

During his career, Gálvez did much to promote Argentine letters and to make the country's writers known throughout Hispanic America. In 1917, he established the Cooperative Publishers of Buenos Aires and in 1919 founded Pax Publishers to introduce European works in translation to Argentine readers.

*See also* **Literature: Spanish America; Rosas, Juan Manuel de.**

BIBLIOGRAPHY

William Rex Crawford, "Manuel Gálvez," in *A Century of Latin American Thought* (1944), pp. 149–164.

Ignacio B. Anzoátegui, *Manuel Gálvez* (1961).

Norma Desinano, *La novelística de Manuel Gálvez* (1965).

Myron I. Lichtblau, *Manuel Gálvez* (1972).

David W. Foster, "Ideological Ruptures in Manuel Gálvez's *Historia de arrabal: Linguistic Conventions,*" *Hispanic Journal* 4, no. 2 (1983): 21–27.

John C. Walker, "Ideología y metafísica en Manuel Gálvez," *Revista Canadiense de Estudios Hispánicos* 10, no. 3 (1986): 475–490.

### *Additional Bibliography*

Delaney, Jean H. "Imagining 'El ser argentino': Cultural Nationalism and Romantic Concepts of Nationhood in Early Twentieth-Century Argentina." *Journal of Latin American Studies* 34:3 (Aug. 2002): 625–658.

Lvovich, Daniel. *Nacionalismo y antisemitismo en la Argentina.* Buenos Aires: Javier Vergara, Grupo Zeta, 2003.

Szmetan, Ricardo. *La situación del escritor en la obra de Manuel Gálvez (1916–1935).* New York: P. Lang, 1994.

MYRON I. LICHTBLAU

---

**GÁLVEZ, MARIANO** (1794–1862). Mariano Gálvez (*b.* 26 May 1794; *d.* 26 May 1862), chief of state of Guatemala (1831–1838). Gálvez was adopted as a foundling by an influential family in Guatemala City and eventually received a royal dispensation from the legal disadvantages of his suspicious birth. He was educated in the law, and his enthusiasm for the Enlightenment ideas of his day led him to a career in politics. He was much involved in the negotiations and turmoil that preceded independence from Spain. Indeed, he voted in favor of independence, but promoted, in fear of instability, political union with the new Mexican empire. After the fall of Agustín de Iturbide, emperor of Mexico, in 1823 and the separation of Central America from Mexico that same year, Gálvez held public offices at both the state and federal level, and in 1831, after a devastating civil war that destroyed conservative power, he was elected chief of state of Guatemala.

With the leading conservatives in exile and with the power to squash opposition, Gálvez fervently sought to set an example in Guatemala that would eventually turn all of Central America into a modern, progressive republic through enlightened social and economic legislation. His attack on the clergy reduced drastically the wealth and power of the church. He proclaimed religious toleration and destroyed the hegemony of the clergy in education by establishing a system of free, public, lay instruction. He began a series of projects for economic development designed to bring new life to sparsely populated and neglected areas of the country, often using foreign colonization to achieve his goals. He attempted to impose a new and alien system of common law, the Livingston Codes, on a society accustomed to the civil law of Spain. Most important, he sought to promote economic competitiveness and prosperity by reducing the communal lands of municipalities to private property. During his term of office, Gálvez instituted the most radical liberal program of reform of nineteenth-century Guatemala.

Gálvez's reforms alienated, offended, and often threatened the livelihood of large sectors of the population, especially the impoverished peasantry. Liberal trade policy damaged native industry. A head tax of two pesos per capita excessively burdened peasants who found themselves landless after the agrarian reforms. The liberal demand for forced labor on public works projects further increased resentment. Peasants also found burdensome the travel that jury duty required. Eventually, profound discontent became outright rebellion. Peasants formed an unlikely alliance with disgruntled conservatives and clergymen that relied on the leadership of a brilliant guerrilla fighter, José Rafael Carrera. Gálvez tried desperately to amend the errors of his reform program, but his stopgap measures were too late to impede a revolutionary movement that had gained tremendous momentum. When he tried unsuccessfully to stop the growth of a cholera epidemic in 1837 by implementing the most modern controls, his measures were misinterpreted by peasants as deliberate poisonings. For these reasons, Gálvez's liberal program was destined to die. He was overthrown in February 1838 and later forced into exile in Mexico.

*See also* **Guatemala; Guatemala City.**

BIBLIOGRAPHY

Antonio Batres Jáuregui, *El Dr. Mariano Gálvez y su época* (1957).

Jorge Luis Arriola, *Gálvez en la encrucijada: Ensayo crítico en torno al humanismo político de un gobernante* (1961).

Miriam Williford, "The Reform Program of Dr. Mariano Gálvez," Ph.D. diss., Tulane University, 1963.

William Joyce Griffith, *Empires in the Wilderness: Foreign Colonization and Development in Guatemala, 1834–1844* (1965).

Francis Polo Sifontes, *Mariano Gálvez, éxitos y fracaso de su gobierno* (1979).

*Additional Bibliography*

Argueta, Mario. *La primera generación liberal: Fallas y aciertos (1829–1842).* Tegucigalpa: Banco Central de Honduras, 1999.

Torres Moss, José Clodoveo. *El doctor Mariano Gálvez en el exilio.* Guatemala: Universidad Mariano Gálvez de Guatemala, 1999.

MICHAEL F. FRY

## GÁLVEZ, MATÍAS DE (1717–1784).

Matías de Gálvez (*b.* 2 July 1717; *d.* 3 November 1784), captain-general of Guatemala and forty-eighth viceroy of New Spain. He was born in Macharaviaya, Málaga, Spain, the eldest of at least five sons. His younger brother José de Gálvez, minister general of the Indies from 1776 to 1787, made possible Matías's success. Matías's son Bernardo Gálvez (1746–1786) succeeded his father as viceroy.

After a military career characterized by devotion to duty, Gálvez was ordered to Central America as inspector general of the Spanish forces. He arrived at San Fernando de Omoa, Honduras, in July 1778. Gálvez's immediate duty was to prepare the defense of Central America against possible British attack. On 15 January 1779, Gálvez was appointed to replace Martín de Mayorga, who was named viceroy of New Spain, as captain-general and governor of Guatemala. His principal responsibilities were to speed implementation of the Bourbon reforms, to drive the British from the Caribbean coast of Central America, and to finish the construction of a new capital city.

Gálvez reformed the militia and led successful attacks against the British in Honduras in 1779 and in Nicaragua in 1781. He also negotiated successful treaties with the Miskito Indians on the coast. His successes earned him the accolades of the Ayuntamiento of Guatemala as a "true father" of the region and a promotion to field marshal.

As a Bourbon reformer Gálvez attempted to encourage the economy of the region by offering economic incentives and by weakening the economic domination by a clique of merchants in Guatemala City. He established a *banco de rescate* in Tegucigalpa, and granted *repartimientos* of Indians to increase mining production in Honduras. To stimulate indigo production, Gálvez created a *monte pío* (fund for widows and orphans) for the growers so they would not have to rely on the credit extended by Guatemalan merchants. Also to weaken the Guatemalan oligopoly over the prices paid at the annual indigo fair, Gálvez instituted a pricing board and moved the fair. To assure an adequate supply of cattle and full collection of taxes, he moved the annual cattle fair deeper into El Salvador. During his tenure, tax collections increased over 20 percent, but control of the local economy was never wrested from Guatemala City. Despite short-term success, within two decades most of the changes wrought by Gálvez, both military and administrative, were completely undone.

As a result of his accomplishments in Central America and his family connections, Gálvez was named interim viceroy of New Spain on 14 August 1782 and assumed that post in April 1783. Four months later he earned a full viceregal appointment. His term in Mexico was marked by the reconstruction of Chapultepec Palace, improvement of the drainage system of Mexico City through the construction of dikes and drainage canals, installation of a lighting system, establishment of a branch of the Banco de San Carlos, and tighter administration of the *real hacienda*. During his tenure there was a tripling of royal receipts, due more to external factors than to administrative changes by Gálvez. He died in Mexico City.

*See also* **Indigenous Peoples; New Spain, Viceroyalty of.**

BIBLIOGRAPHY

Cayetano Alcázar Molina, *Los Virreinatos en el siglo XVIII,* (1945).

Troy S. Floyd, "Guatemalan Merchants, the Government, and the *Provincianos,* 1750–1800," in *Hispanic American Historical Review* 41, no. 1 (1961): 90–110, and *The Anglo-Spanish Struggle for Mosquitia* (1967), esp. pp. 133–162.

Mariana Rodríguez Del Valle and Angeles Conejo Díez De La Cortina, "Matías de Gálvez," in *Los virreyes de Nueva España en el reinado de Carlos III,* edited by José Antonio Calderón Quijano, vol. 2 (1968).

Wilbur E. Meneray, *The Kingdom of Guatemala During the Reign of Charles III, 1759–1788* (1975).

Agustín Mencos Franco, *Estudios históricos sobre Centro América* (1982).

### *Additional Bibliography*

García Granados, Sergio. *Libre crezca fecunda: Guatemala en el siglo de las luces, 1729–1821.* Guatemala: Magna Terra Editores, 2005.

Rodríguez O, Jaime E., ed. *Mexico in the Age of Democratic Revolutions, 1750–1850.* Boulder, Co: Lynne Rienner, 1994.

WILBUR E. MENERAY

## GAMA, JOSÉ BASILIO DA (1741–1795).

José Basilio da Gama (*b.* 1741; *d.* 31 July 1795), Brazilian poet. Born in Minas Gerais, Gama studied in Rio de Janeiro under the Jesuits and then in Rome after 1759, when the order was banished from Portuguese possessions. Later, while living in Portugal, he was arrested as a Jesuit sympathizer but escaped exile by gaining favor with the marquês of Pombal, the realm's chief minister. His most famous work, *O Uruguai,* was published in Lisbon in 1769.

A long poem in ten blank-verse cantos, *O Uruguai* is constructed around episodes from the War of the Seven Reductions (1752–1756), which the Portuguese and Spanish waged jointly against the Jesuits and their Tupi-guaraní Indian mission congregations in Uruguay. Sometimes regarded as an epic, it has also been considered a lyrical narrative and a poetic drama. The original version had been openly pro-Jesuit, but the published version criticizes the Jesuits scathingly, in consonance with Pombal's policies.

*O Uruguai* is considered the most important literary work of Brazil's colonial period. It presents sympathetically the inevitable demise of indigenous culture before the advance of white men. Its Indian heroes contributed to its popularity among the romantics, who also admired the freedom of its blank verse and who viewed its pictures of Indian life and the Brazilian landscape as a precursor of the autonomous national literature they sought to create.

*See also* **Brazil: The Colonial Era (1500–1808); Literature: Brazil.**

BIBLIOGRAPHY

Sir Richard F. Burton published a translation of *O Uruguai, the Uruguay,* in 1878; a modern scholarly edition of the Burton translation, with introduction and notes by Frederick C. H. García and Edward F. Stanton, was published in 1972. David M. Driver, *The Indian in Brazilian Literature* (1942), pp. 22–33, contains a discussion of the poem.

### *Additional Bibliography*

Brandão, Roberto de Oliveira. *Poética e poesia no Brasil (Colônia).* São Paulo: Editora UNESP, 2001.

Chaves, Vania Pinheiro. *O Uruguai e a fundação da literatura brasileira.* Campinas: Editora da Unicamp, 1997.

Teixeira, Ivan. *Mecenato pombalino e poesia neoclássica: Basílio da Gama e a poética do encômio.* São Paulo: FAPESP: Edusp, 1999.

NORWOOD ANDREWS JR.

## GAMA, LUÍS

**GAMA, LUÍS** (1830–1882). Luís Gama (*b.* 21 June 1830; *d.* 24 August 1882), Brazilian poet, lawyer, and abolitionist. The son of a profligate aristocrat and a rebellious free African woman, Gama was born free in Bahia. At the age of ten he was sold into slavery by his father and shipped to São Paulo. In 1847, while serving as a household slave, Gama was befriended by a student and taught to read and write. Soon afterward, having become aware of the illegality of his enslavement, Gama fled his master's house. He served in the militia for six years and later established himself as a journalist, poet, and self-educated lawyer. In 1859, literate for scarcely a dozen years, he published his first and most successful book of verse, *Primeiras trovas burlescas de Getulino.* Ten years later, by then a noted author, he coedited with Rui Barbosa, Joaquim Nabuco, and others the journal *Radical Paulistano,* which supported the reformist program of parliamentary liberals led by José Tomás Nabuco de Araújo. As a lawyer, Gama specialized in defending persons kept illegally in slavery, especially Africans held in violation of the anti-slave-trade law of 1831. According to his own count, he thereby freed more than five hundred persons. At the time of his death, Gama was the undisputed leader of the antislavery movement in the province of São Paulo.

*See also* **Bahia; Literature: Brazil; Slavery: Abolition; Slavery: Brazil.**

BIBLIOGRAPHY

Sud Menucci, *O precursor da abolicionismo no Brasil (Luíz Gama)* (1938).

Robert Brent Toplin, *The Abolition of Slavery in Brazil* (1972).

Robert Edgar Conrad, *Children of God's Fire: A Documentary History of Black Slavery in Brazil* (1983), and *The Destruction of Brazilian Slavery, 1850–1888,* 2d ed., rev. (1992).

*Additional Bibliography*

Azevedo, Elciene. *Orfeu de carapinha: A trajetória de Luiz Gama na imperial cidade de São Paulo.* Campinas: Editora da UNICAMP, 1999.

Barbosa, José Carlos. *Luiz Gama: O precursor abolicionista.* Ribeirão Preto: Barbosa, 2004.

ROBERT EDGAR CONRAD

## GAMA, VASCO DA

**GAMA, VASCO DA** (1524). Vasco da Gama (*b.* 1460s; *d.* 24 or 25 December 1524), Portuguese explorer, discoverer of the maritime route to India. Son of a member of the household of Prince Fernando, da Gama had been a *fidalgo* in the royal household of King João II and, at the time of his first voyage, a knight and commander in the Order of Santiago. About 1507 he transferred to the Order of Christ, and in 1519 he became first count of Vidigueira.

King Manuel I named da Gama leader of the armada that sailed from the Tagus River on 8 July 1497 in search of a maritime route to India. Two of the four ships, the *São Gabriel* and the *São Rafael,* were commanded, respectively, by Vasco and his brother, Paulo. After more than ninety days at sea—the longest known voyage out of sight of land by a European to date—da Gama dropped anchor in the Bay of Santa Helena, 100 miles north of the Cape of Good Hope. On 22 November 1497, da Gama rounded the cape and on Christmas Day reached what is now known as Natal. On 2 March 1498, he reached the island of Mozambique. After stopping at Mombasa and Malindi, da Gama—with the help of a Muslim pilot from Gujarat—departed across the Indian Ocean on 24 April, and on 20 May he anchored several miles north of Calicut.

Da Gama remained in India for over three months. Early in his stay, he met with Calicut's Hindu leader, whom the Portuguese called the samorim. But relations with him deteriorated, and da Gama sailed northward to Angediva Island, along India's west coast, south of Goa. Beginning the return voyage on 5 October, da Gama rounded the Cape of Good Hope on 20 March 1499. He arrived in Lisbon in very late August or during the first three weeks in September, though one of his ships, the *Berrio,* already had arrived on 10 July. Honored for his efforts, da Gama was made admiral of India, became a member of the king's council, and was given financial rewards.

Made leader of the fourth Portuguese expedition to India, da Gama set sail from Lisbon in February 1502. After exacting reprisals in Calicut from the natives for the massacre of the Portuguese stationed there, da Gama left India on 28 December 1502 and reached Lisbon on 1 September 1503.

In 1524 da Gama returned to India for a third and final time at the behest of King João III. Sent to clean up corruption and restore authority in Portuguese Asia, he was given the post of viceroy of India, the second to receive that title. Sailing from Lisbon on 9 April 1524, da Gama reached Chaul on 5 September. His administration was an energetic one, but it was also short, as he died in Cochin less than four months after his arrival.

*See also* **Explorers and Exploration: Brazil.**

BIBLIOGRAPHY

The definitive biography of Vasco da Gama as of 2008 remains to be written. To date, the best book-length account in English of the first voyage of da Gama is Elaine Sanceau, *Good Hope: The Voyage of Vasco da Gama* (1967). It is based largely on the sixteenth-century Portuguese chroniclers. The best short study in English is probably the chapter, "The Indian Ocean Crossing," in John H. Parry, *The Discovery of the Sea* (1974). The most important source for the first voyage is the diary of an anonymous eyewitness. It has been published in Portuguese in a number of editions and is included in José Pedro Machado and Viriato Campos, *Vasco da Gama e a sua viagem de descobrimento* (1969). The diary has been edited and translated into English by E. G. Ravenstein (with excellent notes, introduction, and accompanying materials) in *A Journal of the First Voyage of Vasco da Gama, 1497–1499* (1898). A judicious summary in English of da Gama's career is found in Bailey W. Diffie and George D. Winius, *Foundations of the Portuguese Empire, 1415–1580* (1977). Two other useful surveys are found in Damião Peres, *História dos descobrimentos portugueses,* 3d ed. (1983), and Luis De Albuquerque, *Os descobrimentos portugueses* (1983). Augusto C. Teixeira De Aragão published many documents dealing with Vasco da Gama in *Vasco da Gama e a Vidigueira, Estudo historico,* 3d ed. (1898).

*Additional Bibliography*

Disney, A. R., and Emily Booth. *Vasco da Gama and the Linking of Europe and Asia.* New Delhi: Oxford University Press, 2000.

Garcia, José Manuel. *A viagem de Vasco da Gama à India 1497–1499.* Lisboa: Academia de Marinha, 1999.

Subrahmanyam, Sanjay. *The Career and Legend of Vasco da Gama.* Cambridge, U.K.: Cambridge University Press, 1997.

Francis A. Dutra

## GAMARRA, AGUSTÍN (1785–1841).

Agustín Gamarra (*b.* 1785; *d.* 1841), quintessential military caudillo of nineteenth-century Peru, born in Cuzco, and twice president of Peru (1829–1833, 1839–1841) during an unstable period in which there were more than thirty presidents in twenty years (1826–1846). Like Andrés de Santa Cruz and Ramón Castilla, Gamarra was initially trained by the Spanish colonial army. Under creole Generals José Manuel Goyeneche and Pío Tristán, Gamarra fought against independence movements in the regions of Upper and Southern Peru between 1809 and 1820. In 1820, however, the entire royalist Numancia battalion in which Gamarra served passed over to General José de San Martín's independence forces, at the time active on the Peruvian coast. Consequently, Gamarra fought in the independence army in the battles of Junín and Ayacucho that finally removed Spanish colonial presence in Peru.

Soon after independence Gamarra became prefect of Cuzco and military commander of the southern Peruvian armies. Gamarra was a zealous creole-patriot, politically conservative and protectionist in trading matters. He achieved renown in early "national" military campaigns against Colombian influence in Bolivia (1828) and in the dispute over the port of Guayaquil with Colombia (1829). In the middle of the latter, unsuccessful campaign in Ecuador, Gamarra forcibly exiled President José de la Mar to become president of Peru. In his first presidency, Gamarra foiled at least seventeen rebellions with the aid of his belligerent wife Francisca Zubiaga de Gamarra, but was finally defeated in a civil war by General Luis José Orbegoso in 1833.

Gamarra continued to conspire but did not seize power until 1839, after he led the opposition against General Santa Cruz's Peru-Bolivia Confederation (1836–1839). The Chilean army, employing Peruvian dissenters such as Gamarra himself, defeated Santa Cruz in the battle of Yungay (1839). Finally, Gamarra's attempt to incorporate Bolivia into Peru was soundly defeated in the battle of Ingaví (1841), in which Gamarra lost his life.

*See also* **Peru: Peru Since Independence.**

BIBLIOGRAPHY

Jorge Basadre, *Historia de la República del Perú,* vols. 1–2 (1963).

Celia Wu, *Generals and Diplomats: Great Britain and Peru 1820–40* (1991).

*Additional Bibliography*

Manrique, Nelson. *Historia de la república.* Lima: Fondo Editorial de COFIDE, 1995.

Walker, Charles. *Smoldering Ashes: Cuzco and the Creation of Republican Peru, 1780–1840.* Durham, NC: Duke University Press, 1999.

ALFONSO W. QUIROZ

## GAMARRA, FRANCISCA ZUBIAGA BERNALES DE (LA MARISCALA)

(1803–1835). Francisca Zubiaga Bernales de (La Mariscala) Gamarra (*b.* 1803; *d.* 1835), Peruvian first lady and woman-at-arms. Gamarra was born in Cuzco, the daughter of a Basque merchant and a Cuzqueña. She abandoned a monastic career because of ill health and married the prefect of Cuzco, General Agustín Gamarra, in 1825. While the former commander of Peruvian forces under Simón Bolívar rose to the presidency of the country, the flamboyant Doña Francisca was making a reputation in her own right. Known as La Mariscala (the lady marshal) for her unusual martial skills, particularly precision shooting, use of the sword, and superb equestrianship, she was also known to lead troops into battle in the country's interminable civil wars. Her political acumen and daring were equally renowned, earning her the sobriquet "La Presidenta" while at her husband's side in the National Palace. Her picturesque career and life ended prematurely in exile and impoverishment in Valparaíso, where she died of tuberculosis at the age of thirty-two.

*See also* **Gamarra, Agustín.**

BIBLIOGRAPHY

Francisco Vegas Seminario, *Bajo el signo de la Mariscala* (1960).

*Additional Bibliography*

Takahashi, Mary. *La pintura de miniatura en Lima durante la primera mitad del s. XIX: El caso de doña Francisca Zubiaga de Gamarra, La Mariscala.* Lima: Seminario de Historia Rural Andina, Universidad Nacional Mayor de San Marcos, 2006.

Vega, Carlos B. *Conquistadoras: Mujeres heroicas de la conquista de América.* Jefferson, NC: McFarland & Co., 2003.

PETER F. KLARÉN

## GAMARRA, JOSÉ

(1934–). José Gamarra (*b.* 12 February 1934). Uruguayan artist. Gamarra was born in Tacuarembó, Uruguay, and studied at the School of Fine Arts in Montevideo as well as with Vicente Martin (1952–1959). He studied engraving with John Friedlaender and Iberé Camargo in Rio de Janeiro (1959). In 1963 he was selected for the Biennial of Young Artists in Paris, after which he settled in Arcueil, France.

Gamarra's early works were abstractions inspired by pre-Conquest art motifs and Uruguayan vernacular ironwork. After moving to Paris, he began to paint tropical landscapes modeled after nineteenth-century European and North American visions of Central and South America as a primeval and exotic territory. Historical, mythological, and contemporary figures (Indians, conquistadores, guerrillas, nuns, and pre-Conquest idols) coexist in Gamarra's painted rain forests. War vehicles and artifacts disturb his paradisiacal settings. Objects and human figures have been interpreted as suggesting narratives and critical comments about Latin American history, such as the Spanish Conquest or North American interventions (*Five Centuries Later,* 1986).

*See also* **Art: The Twentieth Century.**

BIBLIOGRAPHY

Dawn Ades, *Art in Latin America: The Modern Era, 1820–1980* (1989), pp. 293–296.

Oriana Baddeley and Valerie Fraser, *Drawing the Line: Art and Cultural Identity in Contemporary Latin America* (1989), pp. 24–30.

*Additional Bibliography*

Pérez-Barreiro, Gabriel, ed. *Blanton Museum of Art: Latin American Collection.* Austin: Blanton Museum of Art, University of Texas at Austin, 2006.

MARTA GARSD

## GAMBARO, GRISELDA (1928–).

Griselda Gambaro (*b.* 28 July 1928); Argentine playwright, short-story writer, and novelist. In *El campo* (1967; *The Camp,* 1971), *El desatino* (1965; *The Blunder*), *Los siameses* (1967; *The Siamese Twins,* 1967), and other works, Gambaro uses symbolic constructions to depict the real nature of human beings and of their relationships, to open "an imaginary space that, in turn, discovers, invents or anticipates new dimensions of reality." For her, valid literature must have an anticipatory quality and should question what constitutes reality and reveal what reality could be. Gambaro, in all her works, is preoccupied with the absurdity of the human condition, the schizophrenic nature of man, and the exercise of power by men and women alike. Her theater and, to some degree, her novels are absurdist constructions with elements of the theater of cruelty and black humor. Gambaro herself has related it to the *grotesco criollo,* a parodic genre rooted in the distortion of the traditional bourgeois drama: that of the love triangle. Her characters are isolated, defeated, and devastated in a brutal, hostile world. Her mostly nonverbal language and violent physical images underline a dramatic vision of life and bestow a nightmarish and Kafkaesque quality to her plays.

Although Gambaro's writings deal with universal problems, not limited to a specific place or time, they could be related to the Argentine reality of the recent past. She won the Drama Critics' Prize for best play of 1990 with *Penas sin importancia* (Unimportant Sorrows), and in 1999 was awarded the Argentine Academy of Letters Prize for her collection of stories *Lo major que se viene.*

*See also* **Literature: Spanish America; Theater.**


BIBLIOGRAPHY

Tamara Holzapfel, "Griselda Gambaro's Theatre of the Absurd," in *Latin American Theatre Review* 4, no. 1 (1970): 5–11.

Sandra M. Cypess, "Physical Imagery in the Plays of Griselda Gambaro," in *Modern Drama* 18, no. 4 (1975): 357–364, and "The Plays of Griselda Gambaro," in *Dramatists in Revolt: The New Latin American Theater,* edited by Leon F. Lyday and George W. Woodyard (1976), pp. 95–109.

David W. Foster, "The Texture of Dramatic Action in the Plays of Griselda Gambaro," in *Hispanic Journal* 1, no. 2 (1979): 57–66.

Marguerite Feitlowitz, "Crisis, Terror, Disappearance: The Theater of Griselda Gambaro," in *Theater* 21, no. 3 (1990): 34–38.

*Additional Bibliography*

Contreras, Marta. *Griselda Gambaro: Teatro de la descomposición.* Concepción, Chile: Ediciones Universidad de Concepción, 1994.

Tarantuviez, Susana. *La narrativa de Griselda Gambaro: Una poética del desamparo.* Mendoza, Argentina: Universidad Nacional de Cuyo, Facultad de Filosofía y Letras, 2001.

Zandstra, Dianne Marie. *Embodying Resistance: Griselda Gambaro and the Grotesque.* Lewisburg, PA: Bucknell University Press, 2007.


Angela B. Dellepiane

## GAMBOA IGLESIAS, FEDERICO

(1864–1930). Federico Gamboa Iglesias (*b.* 22 December 1864; *d.* 15 August 1930), Mexican public figure and intellectual, a major essayist for Mexican and international newspapers. A multifaceted intellectual whose contributions ranged from fiction to plays, he documented Mexican intellectual life in his major five-volume memoir *Mi diario.* He also supported intellectual activities by providing important leadership to the prestigious Mexican Academy of Language from 1923 to 1939.

Born in the capital, the son of General Manuel Gamboa, the governor of Jalisco, and Lugarda Iglesias, the sister of the leading Liberal politician José María Iglesias, he studied in New York City and then attended the National School of Law. After joining the Foreign Service in 1888, he served in numerous posts in Latin America and the United States. He was a federal deputy from Chihuahua before representing Mexico as minister to the Netherlands (1911–1912). He became undersecretary of foreign relations (1908–1910) and rose to secretary under Victoriano Huerta in 1913. Discredited as a public official for his service under Huerta, Gamboa was in exile from 1914 to 1919.

*See also* **Journalism; Mexico: Since 1910.**


BIBLIOGRAPHY

Alberto María Carreño, *La Academia Mexicana correspondiente de la Española, 1875–1945* (1946).

Federico Gamboa, *Diario de Federico Gamboa, 1892–1939* (1977).

### *Additional Bibliography*

Gutiérrez, Harim B. *En el país de la tristeza: Las misiones diplomáticas de Federico Gamboa en Guatemala*. México: Secretaría de Relaciones Exteriores, Dirección General del Acervo Histórico Diplomático, 2005.

Prendes, Manuel. "Cerca del mundanal ruido: Una interpretación romántica de Federico Gamboa." *Literatura Mexicana* 15:1 (2004): 37–52.

Sedycias, João. *The Naturalistic Novel of the New World: A Comparative Study of Stephen Crane, Aluísio Azevedo, and Federico Gamboa*. Lanham: University Press of America, 2005.

RODERIC AI CAMP

## GAMIO MARTÍNEZ, MANUEL (1883–1960).

Manuel Gamio Martínez (*b.* 2 March 1883; *d.* 16 July 1960), a Mexican anthropologist considered the initiator of modern *indigenismo* studies in Mexico and an activist in Latin American and European societies promoting the examination and preservation of indigenous cultures.

The son of Gabriel Gamio and Marina Martínez, wealthy landowners in the Dominican Republic and Mexico, Gamio was educated in private schools and the National Preparatory School before studying archaeology under Nicolás León and Jesús Galindo y Villa in the National Museum in Mexico City. A student of Franz Boas at Columbia University, he obtained his M.A. in 1911 and returned for a Ph.D. in anthropology in 1921.

Returning to Mexico, Gamio undertook the organization of and became director for the department of anthropology in the secretariat of agriculture (1917–1920). From 1917 to 1920 he also led the first comprehensive exploration of the Teotihuacán ruins in the center of Mexico City's commercial district, where he discovered the *templo mayor*. Before 1925 he led other explorations and restorations of archaeological sites, including ones in Yucatán and Guatemala. He was a leader of educational and government institutions devoted to archaeological research and served briefly as undersecretary of public education in 1925. Thereafter he gave up archaeology to devote himself to protecting contemporary Indian cultures.

While concentrating on his research and academic pursuits, Gamio also held positions in the secretariat of agriculture and at the Institute for Social Research of the National University during the 1930s. In 1942 he became director of the Inter-American Indigenous Institute, a position he held until his death. Francisco Goitia, a noted Mexican painter, was a close collaborator. Gamio left a prolific body of published works.

*See also* **Anthropology; Indigenous Peoples.**

BIBLIOGRAPHY

Manuel Gamio, *Forjando patria* (1916).

Manuel Gamio and José Vasconcelos, *Aspects of Mexican Civilization* (1926).

Universidad Nacional Autónomo De México, *Estudios antropológicos publicados en homenaje al Dr. Manuel Gamio* (1956).

Angeles González Gamio, *Manuel Gamio, una lucha sin final* (1987).

### *Additional Bibliography*

Alanís Enciso, Fernando Saúl. "Manuel Gamino: El inicio de las investigaciones sobre la inmigración mexicana a Estados Unidos." *Historia Mexicana* 52:4 (April–June 2003): 979–1020.

Tenorio Trillo, Mauricio. "Stereophonic Scientific Modernisms: Social Sciences between Mexico and the United States, 1880s–1930s." *The Journal of American History* 86:3 (December 1999): 1156–1187.

Walsh, Casey. "Región, raza y riego: El desarrollo del norte mexicano, 1910–1940." *Nueva Antropología* 19:64 (January–April 2005): 53–73.

RODERIC AI CAMP

## GAMONALISMO.

Gamonalismo, the phenomenon of local political bossism, in the figure of the *gamonal*. The term is Spanish-American rather than peninsular and probably dates from the early nineteenth century; but even the eminent Colombian philologist Rufino José Cuervo was unable to determine its precise origins. The word *gamonal* is largely synonymous with the older *cacique*, an Arawak term adopted by the Spanish in the sixteenth century to denote indigenous chieftains, but which in the republican period came to denote personalist local political power in rural and small-town settings. *Gamonal* achieved wider currency in Colombia and Peru, while *cacique* was apparently favored in Mexico; where both are found, *gamonal* seems to have implied a more self-made, less tradi-tional-bound mode of bossism than did *cacique*.

The origins and bases of *gamonalismo* remain largely unexplored; to many nineteenth-century commentators local bossism was the political expression of landowner power, but *gamonal* formation also occurred in regions of relatively democratic land tenure. Commerce was a frequent path to *gamonal* status, as was knowledge of the intricacies of the legal and administrative systems of the republican state. (The extreme version of this latter path is the Colombian *tinterillo*.) In highland Peru, *gamonalismo* often had an ethnic dimension as the multifaceted dominance of mestizos over indigenous communities. Apart from local social and economic conditions, an important variable in the historical assessment of *gamonalismo* is its role in national politics: the *gamonal* in firmly entrenched party systems (such as those of Chile or Colombia) was (and is) quite different from his role in more fluid, caudillo-driven polities. Some of the most sensitive depictions of *gamonalismo* are to be found in fiction, such as the novel *El último gamonal* by the Colombian Gustavo Álvarez Gardeazábal.

*See also* **Mestizo.**

BIBLIOGRAPHY

Robert H. Dix, *Colombia: The Political Dimensions of Change* (1967).

José Carlos Mariátegui, *Seven Interpretive Essays on Peruvian Reality*, translated by Marjory Urquidi (1971).

José María Samper, "El triunvirato parroquial," in *Museo de cuadros de costumbres*, vol. 1 (1973), pp. 237–249.

*Additional Bibliography*

Mariátegui, José Carlos. "Regionalismo y gamonalismo," in *Siete ensayos de interpretación de la realidad peruana*. México: Ediciones Era, 1979.

Poole, Deborah. *Unruly Order: Violence, Power, and Cultural Identity in the High Provinces of Southern Peru*. Boulder, CO: Westview Press, 1994.

Salinas Sánchez, Alejandro. *Parroco y señor: Gamonalismo en Macate (Ancash), 1853–1893*. Lima: Seminario de Historia Rural Andina, Universidad Nacional Mayor de San Marcos, 2005.

RICHARD J. STOLLER

## GÁNDARA ENRÍQUEZ, MARCOS

(1915–). Marcos Gándara Enríquez (*b.* 1915), ideological leader of the military junta that assumed power in Ecuador in 1963. Born in Latacunga, Colonel (later General) Gándara, former director of the war academy and functional representative of the armed forces in the Senate, justified the military's assumption of power not simply as the product of contemporary conditions, including the military's perception of a rising threat of Communist subversion, but as a product of a long series of mistaken policies. The military assumed the responsibility for establishing new socioeconomic structures that would permit the evolution of democratic structures dedicated to serving the interests of all citizens.

During its first year in office, the junta suppressed political dissent, announced a series of development projects financed by U.S. loans, adopted a ten-year development plan proposed by the National Planning Board, approved an income tax, and issued an agrarian reform program. Although public opinion toward the junta was generally favorable at the end of its first year in office, the junta refused to develop political alliances or mobilize popular sectors to support its moderate reform program. The junta's rejection of partisan politics was rooted in its image of the military as the only truly national institution whose nonpartisan decisions would naturally generate public support.

Mounting economic problems during the second year of military rule quickly translated into growing public opposition expressed as demonstrations, strikes, and antigovernment media campaigns. By early 1966 the government faced daily challenges to its authority, frequently from students. Civilian politicians forged multiparty alliances that pressed for a return to constitutional government. The government's vacillating response to challenges, particularly from coastal economic and political elites, eroded support for continued military rule within the higher officer corps. A national strike and violent confrontations between students and the military at the Central University in Quito resulted in the fall of the government on 29 March 1966. Gándara went to Bolivia but later returned to Ecuador.

*See also* **Ecuador: Since 1830.**

BIBLIOGRAPHY

República Del Ecuador, *Plan político de la Junta Militar de Gobierno* (1963); *La Junta Militar de Gobierno y la opinión pública* (1964).

Martin Needler, *Anatomy of a Coup d'état: Ecuador 1963* (1964).

John Samuel Fitch, *The Military Coup d'état as a Political Process: Ecuador, 1948–1966* (1977), esp. pp. 55–73.

*Additional Bibliography*

Blum, William, and William Blum. *Killing Hope: U.S. Military and CIA Interventions Since World War II.* Monroe, ME: Common Courage Press, 2004.

Velasco M., Lisímaco. *Civiles + militares = (El hábito no hace al monje): Intento de golpe militar, a un gobierno militar nacido de un golpe, dado a un autogolpista*. Ecuador: CCE Benjamin Carrión, 2004.

LINDA ALEXANDER RODRÍGUEZ

## GANDAVO, PERO DE MAGALHÃES

(?–1576). Pero de Magalhães Gandavo (*d.* 1576), Portuguese historian. In 1576 Gandavo wrote and published the *História da Província de Santa Cruz, a que vulgarmente chamamos Brasil.* His *Tratado da terra do Brasil,* written before 1573, was not published until 1824 by the Royal Academy of Sciences in Lisbon. Gandavo justifies his enterprise in the prologue to his History, on the basis of the fact that although Brazil had been discovered several decades previously, no Portuguese writer had written about its discovery, and on his intention to persuade people in Portugal to emigrate and settle in the rich and healthy new land. His conception of history made him select as relevant the following elements: the description of the captaincies, the form of government, the distribution of land under the traditional Portuguese *sesmarias* (conditional grants), and the need for slaves as a labor force. With descriptive and narrative elements, Gandavo adroitly mixes past and present in each chapter. As other sixteenth-century writers, he dedicates part of his History to the description of plants and their uses; he also describes animals, real and mythical. In the last chapter, Gandavo gives the colonists some hope of finding "much gold and precious stones."

*See also* **Portuguese Empire.**

BIBLIOGRAPHY

José Honório Rodrigues, *História da história do Brasil,* vol. 1, *Historiografia colonial* (1979).

Massaud Moisés, *História da literatura brasileira,* vol. 1, *Origens, barroco, arcadismo* (1983).

Maria Beatriz Nizza Da Silva, *Guia de história do Brasil colonial* (1992).

*Additional Bibliography*

Janiga-Perkins, Constance G. "Pero de Magalhaes Gandavo's 'Historia da Provincia Santa Cruz': Paradise, Providence, and How Best to Turn a Profit." *South Atlantic Review* 57:2 (May 1992): 29–44.

Moura, Vasco Graça. *Sobre Camões, Gândavo e outras personagens: Hipóteses de história da cultura.* Porto: Campo das Letras, 2000.

MARIA BEATRIZ NIZZA DA SILVA

## GANDINI, GERARDO

(1936–). Gerardo Gandini (*b.* 16 October 1936), Argentine composer, pianist, and conductor. He was born in Buenos Aires. His principal teachers on piano were Pía Sebastiani and Roberto Caamaño and in composition, Alberto Ginastera. In 1964 Gandini resided in New York City while on a fellowship from the Ford Foundation. In 1966 he obtained a fellowship from the Italian government that permitted him to study under Goffredo Petrassi at the Accadémia Santa Cecilia in Rome.

He was professor of composition at the Catholic University in Buenos Aires (1962–1970) and at the celebrated Latin American Center for Advanced Musical Studies at the Di Tella Institute in Buenos Aires (1963–1970). An eager participant of the avant-garde school as a composer, Gandini became an active organizer of contemporary music series. He became the director of the Experimental Center for Opera and Ballet (CEOB) sponsored by the Teatro Colón in Buenos Aires. At the CEOB, Gandini premiered many staged works and also commissioned a number of mini-operas, most of them by composers from Argentina. Gandini was a founding member of the Agrupación Música Viva (AMV), a Buenos Aires organization devoted to the promotion of new music. Other members included Antonio Tauriello, Armando Krieger, Hilda Dianda, and Alcides Lanza. Besides his career as a composer and promoter of new music, Gandini is a renowned conductor and pianist who performs frequently in Europe and North America.

His early compositions include Concertino for piano and orchestra (1960); *Variaciones* for orchestra (1962); *Per Mauricio Rinaldi* for chamber orchestra (1963); Concertino no. 3 for harpsichord and ensemble (1964); *Hecha sombra y altura* for ensemble (1965); *A Cow in a Mondrian Painting* for flute and instruments (1967); *Fantasía impromptu* for piano and orchestra (1970); *L'adieu* for piano, vibraphone, three percussionists, and conductor (1967); *Piange e sospira* for flute, violin, clarinet, and piano (1970).

In his more mature style Gandini has written a number of almost impressionistic compositions, always with a strong poetic vein, such as ... *e sará* for piano (1973); *7 Preludios* for piano (1977); *Concierto* for Viola and Orchestra (1979); *Eusebius* (1984–1985), five nocturnes for orchestra; *Paisaje imaginario* for piano and orchestra (1988), which was commissioned by the BBC for the Welsh Symphony Orchestra. In 1996, he won the National Prize for Music for his opera *La ciudad ausente*. As of 2007, he taught at Argentina's Academia Nacional de Bellas Artes, and was also resident composer of Buenos Aires' Teatro Colon.

*See also* **Buenos Aires; Music: Art Music.**

BIBLIOGRAPHY


Rodolfo Arizaga, *Enciclopedia de la música argentina* (1971), p. 151.

John Vinton, ed., *Dictionary of Contemporary Music* (1974), p. 261.

Gérard Béhague, *Music in Latin America: An Introduction* (1979), p. 339; *Octavo festival de música contemporánea de Alicante* (1992), pp. 26, 94–95.


### *Additional Bibliography*


Fessel, Pablo, ed. *De música*. Buenos Aires: Secretaría de Cultura de la Nación, 2006.

Gandini, Gerardo, and Griselda Gambaro. *La casa sin sosiego: Ópera de cámara sobre un libreto de Giselda Gambaro*. Italian and Spanish. Translated into Italian by Camila Nicolini. Buenos Aires: Ricordi, 1992.


ALCIDES LANZA

**GANGA ZUMBA** (?–1680). Ganga Zumba was a leader of the *quilombo* or Maroon state of Palmares. The little that historians know about him comes from accounts of the Luso-Brazilian campaigns against Palmares between 1675 and 1680. Ganga Zumba successfully resisted frequent colonial incursions with defensive strategies that included fortification, espionage, and relocation. Despite the continual threats, Palmares thrived through agriculture, manufacture, and trade. Ganga Zumba was probably a title rather than a proper name, derived from a religious official responsible for caring for ancestral spirits among the Imbangala of west central Africa. The Ganga Zumba known to history was possibly a native Palmarino of West African Allada descent.

During the 1670s Ganga Zumba governed a quilombo with at least nine *mocambos*, or settlements. Contemporary sources describe him as a king, with a palace, houses for his three wives and many children, and royal guards and officials. His fortified royal town of Macaco was on the Serra da Barriga, in present-day Alagoas. In 1677–1678 Palmares suffered devastating attacks by militia captain Fernão Carrilho. Two of Ganga Zumba's children were taken prisoner; another one was killed in battle. Ganga Zumba himself was wounded in one attack. In 1678 the beleaguered Maroon leader accepted terms of peace from the governor of Pernambuco that included relocating his people from Palmares to the Cucaú Valley, closer to the watchful eye of the colonial government. Ganga Zumba and several hundred followers soon moved to Cucaú, but the majority opposition faction, led by Palmares's war commander, Zumbi, preferred resistance to removal.

In 1680 Zumbi or his partisans poisoned Ganga Zumba and ignored an ultimatum to join Ganga Zumba's brother and successor, Ganga Zona, in Cucaú. The Cucaú settlement faded from history, and Palmares survived under Zumbi for fifteen more years. Ganga Zumba's concessions caused a rift in Palmares and failed to guarantee its survival. His image as a weak accommodationist contrasts with the elevation of Zumbi as the national hero of Black Brazilian resistance. Historians have argued, however, that Ganga Zumba's quest for peace was not out of line with the treaties by other maroon leaders in the Americas, as in Surinam and Jamaica. Under different circumstances, Ganga Zumba's choice might have secured the Maroon state's future.

*See also* **Palmares; Quilombo; Zumbi.**

BIBLIOGRAPHY

Alves Filho, Ivan. *Memorial dos Palmares.* Rio de Janeiro: Xenon, 1988.

Anderson, Robert Nelson. "The *Quilombo* of Palmares: A New Overview of a Maroon State in Seventeenth-Century Brazil." *Journal of Latin American Studies* 28, no. 3 (October 1996): 545–566.

Carneiro, Edison. *O quilombo dos Palmares, 1630–1695*, 1st Brazilian edition, São Paulo: Editora Brasiliense, 1946; 2nd edition, São Paulo, Brazil: Companhia Editora Nacional, 1958. The first and second Brazilian editions reprint valuable primary sources.

ROBERT NELSON ANDERSON

**GANGS.** The presence of youth gangs, drug warlords and their enforcers, criminal bands, and other violence brokers in Latin American cities is a phenomenon that emerged in the 1980s. The appearance of these urban-based armed gangs was accompanied by the fragmentation and deterioration of urban areas, a by-product of the economic crisis of the 1980s and its massive spin-off of transgenerational poverty, informality of economy and society (labor without formal labour rights and formal protection by the law), and increasing social exclusion. Geographically, this process surfaced in the expansion and consolidation of the huge metropolitan slums of Latin America.

Poverty and violence are facts of everyday life in cities fractured by inequality, exclusion, and inadequate municipal administration. Persistent social exclusion, linked to alternative (i.e., informal and/or illicit) sources of income and power, combined with absent or failing national and municipal authorities, provides the means and motives for violence and intergang mini-wars. The whole or partial withdrawal of the national and municipal security functions (e.g., the police, the judiciary) in poor urban areas such as favelas, barrios, and *comunas o barriadas* generates a system of territorial "governance voids," where civilians fill the gap left

**Brazilian police on patrol in the Vidigal slum, Rio de Janiero, Brazil, November 22, 2004.** Throughout Latin America, many large cities are plagued by well-organized gangs, particularly in impoverished slum areas. Social and economic unrest in the 1980s fostered the rampant growth of gang activity, particularly in the trade of illegal drugs. © BRUNO DOMINGOS/REUTERS/CORBIS

by the legitimate (local) authorities. Governance voids exist where the legal authorities and the representatives of law and order are absent or only symbolically present. In these local vacuums of "regular" law and order, a kind of osmotic symbiosis emerges between the state (the police, the law system) and "common" criminals and criminalized former members of the armed forces, the police, paramilitary units, and, sometimes, guerrilla combatants. In this situation, "law and order" is the result of a fluctuating order of parallel forces of local power players in shifting alliances. The political dimension of this phenomenon is that the national and municipal authorities oscillate between selective involvement and abandonment. In these governance voids—generally smaller enclaves of territorial violence—informal or parallel structures arise, seeking various forms of confrontation or accommodation with the legitimate authorities and with civil society.

In many cases, the police and the judiciary are ineffective in dealing with crime and violence. Sometimes they are the most active protagonists. At present, in many of the largest Latin American cities the police are highly distrusted and often seen as the most undesirable of all the armed groups in the slums and poor neighborhoods. Even the explicitly violent youth gang leaders and drug lords—who at least are residents of the poor neighborhoods—are less hated than the formal representatives of legitimate law, order, and public security, who are widely detested for their militarized approach and warlike tactics. This sentiment has been voiced time and again by leaders of slum associations and federations and confederations of poor neighborhood organizations across the Latin American and Caribbean region. The urban poor are disproportionally affected by violence and criminals: This has been demonstrated by anthropological and sociological research in the major cities of Argentina, Brazil, Colombia, the Dominican Republic, El Salvador, Honduras, Guatemala, Jamaica, Mexico, Nicaragua, and Peru during the 1990s and 2000s. This research often comes under the heading "divided" or "fragmented cities"—*cidades partidas* in Brazil and *ciudades divididas* in the Spanish-speaking Americas—and indicate an "uncivil society" in the larger cities of Latin America and the Caribbean. Scholarly attention to this relatively new problem of urban violence has been reinforced by moving and critically acclaimed films, such as *City of God* (*Cidade de Deus*, 2002), which depicts youth gangs and mini-narco-wars in a well-known favela of Rio de Janeiro, and *Carandiru* (2003), a film about Latin America's largest prison, in São Paulo, which culminates in the police's ruthless repression of an inmate rebellion that leaves 111 prisoners dead.

**BRAZIL**

In the metropolitan cities of Brazil a spatial segregation has taken place, resulting in the formation of hundreds of local favelas where children and adolescents gain prestige, income, identity, and respect through criminal activities associated with drugs and violence. The formal labor market is not easily accessible to slum dwellers, and informal and illegal work is the alternative. Most of the informal jobs involve low-paid, microentrepreneurial or self-employment activities. Drug-related opportunities of the illicit economy are more attractive to many, particularly the favela youth. In cities such as Rio de Janeiro, law and justice often is represented by the local drug traffickers (*traficantes*) and their drug gangs (*quadrilhas*). The *traficante* dominates significant aspects of the favela economy, and his political weight must be acknowledged on matters of codes of conduct, protection, and contact with rivals and with the municipal authorities, including the police and the judiciary. Infractions are severely sanctioned, often by expulsion or by death. Sometimes the *traficante* is also the local development benefactor, financing educational and recreational facilities, sports clubs, religious centers, and various community groups. Employers and enforcers in the drugs trade act as the local mediators, judges, and punishers. In 2007 these local drugs associations were loosely organized in several city-wide factions; even in the penal institutions the differences between the rival factions are strictly perceived. Conflicts between competing factions occur frequently; when mini-wars spill out of the favelas into public consciousness, the police enter the favelas with hundreds of special troops. Then the favela communities are caught between two competing armed groups on different sides of the law, and the effect typically is distrust, even hatred, toward the official representatives of law and order and the municipal authorities. Since the 1980s a continuous cycle of violence and repression has been one of the leading characteristics of everyday life in large segments of the Brazilian urban environment.

**CARIBBEAN COUNTRIES**

In the case of the Caribbean—and of Central America—migration flows and of previous deportation schemes from the United States influenced the origin of youth gangs and drug-related bands. Violence and drugs determine the ambience in which armed youth gangs operate in Kingston, Jamaica. The first territorial gangs operated in the city's ghettos and slums where the underprivileged and the poor received a hard-handed "suggestion" during electoral campaigns. Clientelist political entrenchment to a system of bipartisan political representation was accompanied, from the 1970s on,

**Gang member, Ciudad Juárez, Mexico, 1997.** In poor Mexican towns along the border with the United States, young people often cannot find gainful employment and look to gangs as a way to obtain money. © LICHTENSTEIN ANDREW/CORBIS SYGMA

by gunmen organized in gangs and affiliated to one of the two political parties. More than half of the constituencies of the poor Kingston districts are characterized by ingrained preferences for political candidates. Whereas politicians previously protected ganja trading and drugs bosses, the affluence of the drugs money started to reverse the relation between gangs, drugs and political support. In the 1980s a crack and cocaine trafficking network was consolidated in Kingston—in fact, across Jamaica—with linkages to the Colombian producer market and the U.S. and European consumer markets. In the early twenty-first century, drugs gangs finance politicians and even share part of the drugs surplus with the police to buy "protection." The Jamaican posse—a loose collection of Jamaican gangs—have established "posse colonies" on the U.S. West Coast and especially in New York City. The U.S. posses and their British affiliates—called "yardies"—are notorious for their use of violence in drugs-related activities.

**CENTRAL AMERICA**

Violence is also the characteristic of the Central American *maras*, youth gangs in El Salvador, Honduras, Guatemala, and—in lesser degree—Nicaragua. The *maras* emerged during the 1980s and were consolidated after the Central American Peace Agreements in the 1990s. The names of the oldest *maras* in San Salvador, Tegucigalpa, and San Pedro Sula are reminders of their U.S. origins: The Salvadoran *maras* Salvatruchas and Barrio 18, for example, are named after Salvadoran street gangs in Los Angeles, and were formed by gang leaders deported from the United States to El Salvador. *Maras* proliferated in the poor barrios in Central America's most important cities, recruiting the unemployed—and unemployable, because of their tattoos—young boys and girls in the slums. In 2007 the *maras* were considered a serious threat to national security in El Salvador, Honduras, and Guatemala. The estimates of their affiliates vary widely, from 10,000 to 35,000 in each country.

In the early twenty-first century the number of victims of *mara* violence had already surpassed the number of victims of the civil war in the 1980s. In 2003 deaths from *mara* confrontations accounted for 45 percent of all homicides in El Salvador and Honduras and for 20 percent of homicides in Guatemala.

The *mareros* (*mara* members) form a very loose collection of rival gangs engaged in disputes over small territories. Their subsistence is guaranteed by extortion of local smallholders, taxi drivers, and transporters, and by petty drugs trafficking. They have comparable repertoires of rituals, tattoos, codes of conduct, internal loyalty, and extreme violence in order to "be respected." The Central American authorities have specific anti-*mara* laws and special anti-*mara* units, formed from the armed forces and the national police. In Nicaragua and Costa Rica, where the national police have elaborate intelligence networks and rely strongly on community policing, there are considerably fewer local *maras.*

## COLOMBIA

Of all the Latin American countries, Colombia is the country most plagued by armed gangs of various kinds. Organized crime associated with the drug economy manifested itself openly in Colombia in the 1980s, and Medellín and Cali acquired a lugubrious reputation as the capital cities of the world's major drugs cartels—criminal rings that controlled the regional illicit economy. Bogotá was less affected, but the southern sectors of the city, where the poor neighborhoods are concentrated, is a territory of violence. In Medellín, the worst affected, after the destruction of the drug cartels by army and police in 1993 about 250 mini-cartels were established, each with its associated *sicarios* (young hired assassins) and *oficinas* (cartel-controlled outfits and enforcers). The possibility of controlling urban territories attracted other power players—urban-guerrilla units (*frentes*), criminal gangs (*bandas*, *combos*, and *parches*, a typology in descending order of violence and internal organization), and paramilitary units (*bloques*)—who disputed local territories and sometimes fought mini-wars over the control of a few street blocks. Between the early 1990s and the mid-2000s Medellín was the theater of continuously shifting territorial wars in shifting alliances, always accompanied by violence, extortion, and deaths. Sometimes the municipal administration succeeded in negotiating local pacts and cease-fires. But the variety of (state and nonstate) armed groups, and the fact that most gangs are fuelled by the illicit economy, was a certain guarantee that after a while a new succession of urban mini-wars would erupt. The national pact between the government and the paramilitary forces, and the subsequent disarmament and reintegration of most of the rank-and-file members, resulted in a substantial reduction of the urban violence. As of 2007, Cali was becoming a new focal point of urban violence, with a growing presence of criminal bands and guerrilla *frentes* moving from the Amazon regions of the country to the Pacific Coast to safeguard "their" drug trafficking corridors.

Colombia's cities are not the only areas affected by violence and criminality. The disputed drug regions, the (former) zones of paramilitary forces, and the territories of guerrilla influence are mostly in the country's periphery: in the mountains of the three *cordilleras* (mountain ranges), in the northeastern and northwestern Pacific and Atlantic Coast zones, in the Amazon regions, and in the frontier regions with Ecuador, Brazil, and Venezuela. These are also the regions of illicit coca cultivation protected by the drug gangs, the remaining paramilitary forces, and the criminalized segments of the guerrilla. Armed disputes over control of the regional economy by contesting gangs, bands, and other armed groups; interventions by the Colombian armed forces; and the effects of the Colombian and U.S. spraying programs account for most of the internally displaced persons. This refugee stream and the inhabitants of the large urban slums provide a continuous recruitment reservoir of new rank-and-file members for Colombia's manifold gangs and armed groups.

*See also* **Cities and Urbanization; Drugs and Drug Trade.**

BIBLIOGRAPHY

Chaves Pandolfi, Dulce, and Mario Grynszpan. *A favela fala: Depoimentos ao CPDOC.* Rio de Janeiro: Editora Fundação Getulio Vargas, 2003.

Clarke, Colin. "Politics, Violence, and Drugs in Kingston, Jamaica." *Bulletin of Latin American Research* 25, no. 3 (2006): 420–440.

Koonings, Kees, and Dirk Kruijt, eds. *Fractured Cities: Social Exclusion, Urban Violence, and Contested Spaces in Latin America.* London: Zed Books, 2007.

Moser, Caroline, and Cathy Mcllwaine. *Encounters with Violence in Latin America: Urban Poor Conceptions from Colombia and Guatemala.* London: Routledge, 2004.

Rotker, Suzana, Katherine Goldman, and Jorge Balán, eds. *Citizens of Fear: Urban Violence in Latin America.* New Brunswick, NJ: Rutgers University Press, 2002.

Ventura, Zuemir. *Cidade partida*, 1st edition. Rio de Janeiro: Editora Companhía das Letras, 2002.

Walton, John. "Guadalajara: Creating the Divided city." In *Metropolitan Problems and Governmental Responses in Latin America*, edited by Wayne Cornelius and R. U. Kemper. Beverly Hills, CA: Sage, 1976.

DIRK KRUIJT

## GANTE, PEDRO DE (c. 1480–1572).

Pedro de Gante (*b.* ca. 1480; *d.* 1572), Franciscan missionary and educational pioneer in Mexico. Gante was originally from Ghent, Belgium, where he absorbed the refined choral style of the Low Countries. One of the first three Franciscans (all Flemish-born) to arrive in Mexico in 1523, he brought this musical foundation with him, later training the Indian singers employed by the cathedral in Mexico City. Although Gante never took holy orders, remaining a lay brother, his accomplishments and example did much to shape the Franciscan missionary enterprise. Like other early friars, Gante combined Christian fervor with Renaissance humanism. He assumed the inferiority of the indigenous cultures but believed the Indians fully capable of mastering European learning, and he made native education his life's work.

In 1526, Gante founded San José de los Naturales to teach Indian boys reading, writing, music, and basic Catholic doctrine. In addition, the school instructed Indians in Spanish artisanal skills, producing a generation of painters and sculptors who embellished the rapidly proliferating Christian churches (many of them built under Gante's supervision), and trained Indian catechists to aid the Franciscans' Christianization efforts. This institution became a model for the Colegio de Santa Cruz de Tlatelolco, whose goal (later abandoned) was to create a native priesthood.

A superb linguist, Gante composed an early and influential Christian doctrine in Nahuatl (1528), the Aztec language. Gante also wrote regularly to the crown, condemning Spanish abuses and advocating reforms to benefit the Indians. Among other things, he successfully urged Charles V to found an Indian hospital in Mexico City.

### BIBLIOGRAPHY

Robert Ricard, *The Spiritual Conquest of Mexico: An Essay on the Apostolate and the Evangelizing Methods of the Mendicant Orders in New Spain: 1523–1572,* translated by Lesley Byrd Simpson (1966).

Peggy K. Liss, *Mexico Under Spain, 1521–1556: Society and the Origins of Nationality* (1975), esp. pp. 69–94.

Lino Gómez Canedo, *La educación de los marginados durante la época colonial: Escuelas y colegios para índios y mestizos en la Nueva España* (1982); *La música de México,* edited by Julio Estrada, vol. 1, pt. 1, *Período prehispánico* (Mexico City, 1984).

### *Additional Bibliography*

Edgerton, Samuel Y. *Theaters of Conversion: Religious Architecture and Indian Artisans in Colonial Mexico.* Albuquerque: University of New Mexico Press, 2001.

Ramírez Vázquez, Pedro. *Fray Pedro de Gante: El primero y más grande maestro de la Nueva España.* México: M.A. Porrúa Grupo Editorial, 1995.

R. DOUGLAS COPE

## GAOS, JOSÉ (1900–1969).

José Gaos (*b.* 26 December 1900; *d.* 10 June 1969), Spanish-Mexican philosopher. Gaos was born in Gijón, Spain. He lived in Oviedo with his maternal grandparents until he was fifteen, then moved to Valencia where his parents were residing. While reading the philosophy of James Balmes, Gaos discovered the topic that became the focus of his later thought: the radical historicity of philosophy (i.e., the extent to which any philosophy is grounded in the thinker's historical circumstances). Gaos began to study philosophy at the University of Valencia, then transferred to the University of Madrid in 1921, where he studied with Manuel García Morente, Xavier Zubiri, and, most important, José Ortega y Gasset. He earned his bachelor's degree in 1923 and his doctorate in 1928, both from the University of Madrid.

A firm supporter of the Republican cause, Gaos was named rector of the University of Madrid in 1936. Shortly thereafter, he fled the regime of

Francisco Franco, living briefly in Cuba before arriving in Mexico in 1938. He declared himself a *transterrado* (transplant) rather than an exile, and spent the rest of his career encouraging research on the history of ideas in Latin America. His teaching at the Colegio de México and the Universidad Nacional Autónoma de México decisively influenced a generation of major Mexican thinkers, including Leopoldo Zea. His philosophical work, a unique blend of metaphysics and historicism, was published in Mexico between 1940 and 1972. Gaos died in Mexico City.

*See also* **Latin America; Literature: Spanish America.**

BIBLIOGRAPHY

For Gaos's works, see José Gaos, *Obras completas, VI: Pensamiento de la lengua española,* prologue by José Luis Abellán, edited by Fernando Salmerón (1990); *Obras completas, VII: Filosofía de la historia e historia de la filosofía,* prologue by Raúl Cardiel Reyes, edited by Fernando Salmerón (1987); *Obras completas, XII: De la filosofía,* prologue by Luis Villoro, edited by Fernando Salmerón (1982); and *Obras completas, XVII: Confesiones profesionales,* prologue by Vera Yamuni, edited by Fernando Salmerón (1982). For discussion of his life and thought, see Vera Yamuni Tabush, *José Gaos: El hombre y su pensamiento* (1980), and *José Gaos: Su filosofía* (1989).

### *Additional Bibliography*

Salmerón, Fernando. *Escritos sobre José Gaos.* México: Colegio de México, 2000.

Zea, Leopoldo. *José Gaos: El transterrado.* México, D.F.: Universidad Nacional Autónoma de México, Centro Coordinador y Difusor de Estudios Latinoamericanos, 2004.

AMY A. OLIVER

**GARAGAY.** Garagay, an archaeological site in the lower Rimac valley. One of the largest centers of pre-Columbian culture on Peru's central coast during the second millennium BCE, Garagay is 5 miles inland from the Pacific shore. The site was constructed and utilized by agriculturists who grew cotton, sweet potato, and other crops using gravity canals. Although much of Garagay has been destroyed by the metropolitan expansion of Lima, some 39.5 acres survive intact. The surviving portion corresponds to monumental architecture that served as the focus of the site.

The most conspicuous remains are those of a U-shaped platform complex embracing a 22-acre open plaza area. In its final form the terraced central pyramid-platform rose some 75.5 feet above the plaza, and access to its atrium and level summit was provided by a broad inset stairway. Corrected radiocarbon measurements from the site range from 1643 BCE to 897 BCE, and it is evident that Garagay's massive public constructions are the product of a multitude of superimposed fills and buildings erected over many centuries. In its general ground plan and coarse masonry construction, Garagay resembles dozens of other public centers also dating from the same period that have been found from the Lurin valley to the Pativilca valley.

Garagay is best known for fine clay friezes that decorated the walls of its central and lateral mounds. Excavations of Garagay's central atrium in 1974 revealed a mural painted in yellow, white, red, pink, and grayish blue mineral-based pigments. The main theme was a fanged supernatural creature with spider attributes. Among the Incas, spiders were closely associated with predicting the onset of rainfall, so it is likely that the ceremonies conducted at Garagay and other similar centers on the central coast were intended to ensure the necessary conditions for irrigation agriculture in this arid zone. Elaborate votive offerings of figurines and exotic items such as Ecuadorian *Spondylus* shell were found associated with the atrium and a similar atrium that had been superimposed above it.

*See also* **Archaeology.**

BIBLIOGRAPHY

A summary in English of investigations at Garagay and related central coast sites can be found in Richard L. Burger, *Chavín and the Origins of Andean Civilization* (1992). The Garagay excavations and the analysis of the materials recovered there have been published in the following articles: Rogger Ravines and William Isbell, "Garagay: Sitio ceremonial temprano en el valle de Lima," in *Revista del Museo Nacional* 41 (1984): 253–275, and Rogger Ravines, "Sobre la formación de Chavín: Imágenes y símbolos," in *Boletín de Lima* 35 (1984): 27–45. A model for interpreting Garagay and other U-shaped complexes is presented by Carlos Williams, "A Scheme for the Early Monumental Architecture of the Central Coast of Peru," in *Early*

*Monumental Architecture in the Andes,* edited by Christopher Donnan (1985).

*Additional Bibliography*

Druc, Isabelle C., Richard L. Burger, Regina Zamojska, and Pierre Magny. "Ancón and Garagay Ceramic Production at the Time of Chavín de Huántar." *Journal of Archaeological Science* 28 (1): 29–43.

Tello, Julio C. *Arqueología del valle de Lima.* Lima: Museo de Arqueología y Antropología, Universidad Nacional Mayor de San Marcos, 1999.

Von Hagen, Adriana, and Craig Morris. *The Cities of the Ancient Andes.* New York: Thames and Hudson, 1998.

RICHARD L. BURGER

**GARAY, BLAS** (1873–1899). Blas Garay (*b.* 1873; *d.* 19 December 1899), Paraguayan historian. Born in Asunción, Garay was something of a prodigy, publishing scholarly articles in local newspapers while still a teenager. He was one of the first Paraguayan historians to make systematic use of archives and primary documents of all kinds. He was sent to Spain in 1897 to visit Seville's Archive of the Indies in order to fulfill a government commission to substantiate Paraguay's legal claim to the Chaco Boreal region. While in Europe, Garay held several minor diplomatic posts.

As a member of the governing Partido Colorado, there was little way that Garay could avoid the passionate politics of his day. His newspaper pieces in *La Prensa,* which he founded, freely attacked his opponents, one of whom challenged Garay to a duel at Villa Hayes on 19 December 1899. Garay was shot, dying at the age of twenty-six.

Among his works, all of which are still read today, are *Compendio elemental de historia del Paraguay* (1896), *El comunismo de las misiones* (1897), and *La revolución de la independencia del Paraguay* (1897).

*See also* **Paraguay: The Nineteenth Century.**

BIBLIOGRAPHY

Harris G. Warren, *Rebirth of the Paraguayan Republic: The First Colorado Era, 1878–1904* (1985).

Carlos Zubizarreta, *Cien vidas paraguayas,* 2d ed. (1985), pp. 222–224.

*Additional Bibliography*

Carrón, Juan María. *El régimen liberal, 1870-1930: sociedad, economía.* Asunción: Arandurã Editorial, 2004.

Lewis, Paul H. *Political Parties and Generations in Paraguay's Liberal Era, 1869-1940.* Chapel Hill: University of North Carolina Press, 1993.

THOMAS L. WHIGHAM

**GARAY, CARLOS** (1943–). Carlos Garay (*b.* 1 April 1943), Honduran impressionist painter. Born in Tegucigalpa, Garay studied at the Escuela Nacional de Bellas Artes in that city and from an early age became one of Honduras's few internationally recognized painters. In his formative period he often painted the human figure, but he eventually became known for his impressionist scenes of the Honduran countryside, which reflect an unusual mastery of light and color and a strong sensitivity to Honduran folk culture. In 1981 the Venezuelan government awarded him the Andrés Bello Prize. Garay's work has also been featured at the 2001 Chicago Art Fair and the "Honduras-Correa 2005" exhibit in Seoul, South Korea.

*See also* **Art: The Twentieth Century; Honduras.**

BIBLIOGRAPHY

J. Evaristo López R. and Longino Becerra, *Honduras: 40 pintores* (1989).

María Luisa Castellanos De Membreño, in *Aboard,* 16, no. 3 (May–June 1992): 61–66.

*Additional Bibliography*

López R., J. Evaristo, and Longino Becerra. *Honduras, visión panorámica de su pintura.* Tegucigalpa, Honduras: Baktun Editorial, 1994.

RALPH LEE WOODWARD JR.

**GARAY, EPIFANIO** (1849–1903). Epifanio Garay (*b.* 1849; *d.* 1903), Colombian artist. Born in Bogotá, Garay was the son of the portrait painter and cabinetmaker Narciso Garay. He studied first with his father and then with José Manuel Groot (1800–1878) while also training at the Academia de Música. He became an opera singer as well as the most important portrait painter in Colombian history. In

1865 he sang in a production of *La Traviata* and in Spanish musical comedies. His paintings during this period included genre, nudes, as well as religious subjects. In 1871 he received honorable mention for his painting *Dolor* at the Anniversary of the Independence show.

Thanks to his skill as a singer, Garay was able to travel extensively, giving him a sophistication noticeable in his paintings. From 1871 to 1880 he toured with the Compañía de Zarzuela, performing at the Musical Academy of New York. He returned to Bogotá in 1880 and was appointed director of the Academia Gutiérrez, but two years later he received a grant from the government to study in Paris with Bouguereau, Boulanger, Ferrier, and Bonnat. When civil war in Colombia led to the cancellation of his grant, he went on a singing tour through the capitals of Europe. He returned to Bogotá and, disappointed with the reception of his work, tried farming and cattle ranching before opening an art school in Cartagena. In 1894 he was named acting director of the School of Fine Arts in Bogotá, becoming director in 1898. With the onset of the revolution of 1899, the school closed. He died in Bogotá.

*See also* **Art: The Nineteenth Century; Groot, José Manuel.**

BIBLIOGRAPHY

Gabriel Giraldo Jaramillo, *La miniatura, la pintura y el grabado en Colombia* (1980).

Eduardo Serrano, *Cien años de arte colombiano, 1886 1986* (1986).

BÉLGICA RODRÍGUEZ

---

**GARAY, EUGENIO** (1874–1937). Eugenio Garay (*b.* 16 November 1874; *d.* April 1937), Paraguayan politician and military figure. Born in Asunción, Garay spent part of his early years in the interior town of Pirayú. He later attended the Colegio Nacional in Asunción, where he received a bachelor's degree. Shortly thereafter, he received a scholarship to attend the military academy in Chile, from which he graduated with honors in 1898.

Returning to Paraguay in 1902, Garay entered the army with the rank of captain. When the 1904 revolution removed him temporarily from military service, he entered the world of journalism, working as a reporter for *Los succesos*. In 1908 the government sent him to Europe as a diplomat, but within three years he was back in the country acting as a adviser to the war ministry.

The series of interparty conflicts in the 1910s and 1920s gave Garay the opportunity to rise rapidly through the ranks, but this process was frequently interrupted by reverses when the wrong party was in power. He served as commander at Barrero Grande, minister of war, and then ambassador to Bolivia.

When the Chaco War broke out in 1932, Garay was recalled to active service. He headed a regiment that opposed the Bolivian forces at Pampa Grande and then at Campo Vía. Suffering from overwork that bordered on combat fatigue, he was relieved from command at his own request in late 1933, only to be recalled once again by President Eusebio Ayala a few months later. Garay, now a full colonel, commanded the principal Paraguayan units at the battles of Carmen and Yrendagüe.

With the conclusion of the war, Garay was demobilized and returned to Asunción. His health now seriously deteriorated because of the intensity of the earlier fighting, he survived the end of hostilities by only two years. He died of a heart attack.

*See also* **Chaco War.**

BIBLIOGRAPHY

Leandro Aponte Benítez, *General Eugenio Garay: Héroe del Chaco,* 2d ed. (1956), esp. pp. 29–151.

Roque Vallejos, *Antología de la prosa paraguaya* (1973), pp. 85–86.

Carlos Zubizarreta, *Cien vidas paraguayas,* 2d ed. (1985), pp. 284–289.

*Additional Bibliography*

Carrón, Juan María. *El régimen liberal, 1870–1930: Sociedad, economía.* Asunción: Arandurã Editorial, 2004.

Lewis, Paul H. *Political Parties and Generations in Paraguay's Liberal Era, 1869–1940.* Chapel Hill: University of North Carolina Press, 1993.

Rodríguez Alcalá de González Oddone, Beatriz. *El íntimo universo de Eugenio Alejandrino Garay.* Asunción, Paraguay: Intercontinental Editora, 1991.

MARTA FERNÁNDEZ WHIGHAM

**GARAY, FRANCISCO DE** (?–1523). Francisco de Garay (*d.* 27 December 1523), governor of Jamaica (1515–1523) and rival of the conquistador Hernán Cortés. Garay arrived in the Americas in 1493 with the second voyage of Christopher Columbus. On Hispaniola, Garay combined government service, as notary and later chief constable, with economic venture. By the time he became governor of Jamaica in 1515, he was one of the richest men in the islands. In 1519 he sent four ships under the command of Alonso Álvarez De Pineda to search the Mexican coast north of Pánuco for a westward passage. Pineda and his men were the first Europeans to explore the Gulf coast west of Florida, but, badly damaged in conflicts with the indigenous peoples, the expedition limped back to Veracruz, where most of the men joined Cortés's army.

These mixed results notwithstanding, Garay obtained a royal decree making him *adelantado* (royal representative) and governor of this vast stretch of coastline. This created a conflict with Cortés, who also had claims to Pánuco. In 1523 Garay landed there with several hundred men to confront Cortés directly, but he was preempted shortly thereafter, when Cortés received royal recognition as conqueror of Mexico and governor of New Spain. His authority superseded, Garay quickly acknowledged his defeat and traveled to Mexico City, where he died three days after meeting with Cortés. It was rumored that Cortés had poisoned him, but this seems unlikely, since Garay no longer posed a threat to the conquistador.

*See also* **Cortés, Hernán; Jamaica.**

BIBLIOGRAPHY

Joaquín Meade, *El adelantado Francisco de Garay* (1947).

Robert S. Weddle, *Spanish Sea: The Gulf of Mexico in North American Discovery, 1500–1685* (1985).

Hernán Cortés, *Hernán Cortés: Letters from Mexico*, 2nd ed., translated and edited by Anthony Pagden (1986).

*Additional Bibliography*

Prescott, William Hickling. *History of the Conquest of Mexico.* New York: Modern Library, 2001.

R. DOUGLAS COPE

**GARAY, JUAN DE** (1528–1583). Juan de Garay (*b.* 1528; *d.* March 1583), conquistador, explorer, and governor of Río de la Plata (1578–1583). Born in Vizcaya, Garay arrived in Peru at the age of fourteen in the company of his uncle. He soon joined in the conquest of Tucumán (northern Argentina), settling first in Santa Cruz de la Sierra, where he served as one of the city's *regidores* (councilmen). In 1568 he moved to Asunción, where, awaiting the confirmation of his kinsman Ortiz de Zárate as governor, he was named *alguacil mayor* (chief constable). A dynamic, intrepid, and peripatetic leader, Garay founded the city of Santa Fé in 1573. During his lifetime he engaged in several military campaigns against the Charrúa along the lower Río de la Plata and against the Guaraní in Paraguay. He was also involved in putting down uprisings of discontented settlers in Santa Fé and Asunción.

After the death of Zárate in 1576, Garay, as his lieutenant, became acting governor and captain-general of the Río de la Plata. From Asunción, he organized an expedition of approximately sixty families who reestablished the city of Buenos Aires in 1580. He also headed an expeditionary force that explored south to the region of present-day Mar del Plata. Three years later, Garay was killed in a Querandí Indian attack while attempting to return to Buenos Aires to reinforce troops accompanying the newly arrived governor of Chile.

*See also* **Conquistadores.**

BIBLIOGRAPHY

Enrique Udaondo, *Diccionario biográfico colonial argentino* (1945), pp. 357–365.

*Additional Bibliography*

Di Tella, Torcuato S. *Historia argentina: Desde los orígenes hasta 1830.* Buenos Aires: Editorial Troquel, 1994.

SUSAN M. SOCOLOW

**GARCÉS, FRANCISCO TOMÁS HERMENEGILDO** (1738–1781). Francisco Tomás Hermenegildo Garcés (*b.* 12 April 1738; *d.* 19 July 1781), Franciscan missionary who traveled extensively in Sonora, Arizona, and California.

Born in Morata del Conde, Spain, Garcés entered the Franciscan order at age fifteen. In 1768 he joined the Franciscans in Sonora as a missionary to the Pima and Papago Indians. From his post at San Xavier del Bac, Garcés made several expeditions into the surrounding areas. In 1774 he joined Juan Bautista de Anza in opening a route from Sonora to Monterey, establishing a vital supply line to the Spanish settlements of California. In 1775 Garcés again joined Anza in a colonizing expedition to San Francisco. On his return from California, Garcés became the first to break a trail from the Pacific Coast to the Hopi pueblos of northeastern Arizona. In 1779 Garcés journeyed to Yuma to establish missions among the Indians on the Colorado River. Two years later, he was beaten to death in an uprising of Yuma Indians.

*See also* **Franciscans; Missions: Spanish America.**

BIBLIOGRAPHY

Elliott Coues, trans., *On the Trail of a Spanish Pioneer: The Diary of Francisco Garcés,* 2 vols. (1900).

Herbert Eugene Bolton, *Outpost of Empire* (1931).

John Galvin, trans., *A Record of Travels in Arizona and California 1775–1776,* by Fr. Francisco Garcés (1965).

John L. Kessell, "The Making of a Martyr: The Young Francisco Garcés," in *New Mexico Historical Review* 45, no. 3 (1970): 181–196.

*Additional Bibliography*

Wild, Peter. *True Tales of the Mojave Desert: From Talking Rocks to Yucca Man.* Santa Fe, NM: Center for American Places, 2004.

Garcés, Francisco Tomás Hermenegildo, John Galvin, and Alejandro Salafranca. *Diario de exploraciones en Arizona y California, 1775–1776.* Málaga: Algazara, 1996.

SUZANNE B. PASZTOR

**GARCÍA, ALEIXO** (?–1525). Aleixo García (*d.* 1525), Portuguese-born explorer, the first European in Paraguay. A minor member of the 1515–1516 Juan Díaz de Solís expedition to the Río de la Plata, García witnessed the murder of Solís at the hands of Charrúa Indians in Uruguay in mid-1516. Some months later, García and eighteen other Europeans were shipwrecked on the Brazilian island of Santa Catharina, where he remained several years, gaining a practical use of the local Guaraní language.

In 1524, he and several companions journeyed to the mainland. Traveling west, they discovered the massive Iguaçú Falls, crossed the Alto Paraná River, and made contact with the substantial Guaraní populations of Paraguay. Told of a fabulously wealthy "white king," who lived further west, García enlisted the aid of 2,000 warriors and immediately set off in that direction through the heavily forested Chaco region. Upon reaching the foothills of the Andes, the small army raided a score of Incan communities. García made off with considerable booty, including a quantity of silver, and returned to the area of the Paraguay River. He sent word of his adventures (along with a portion of the silver) to Santa Catharina. Before he himself could return to the coast, however, he was murdered by his Indian allies, evidently in late 1525. Some of the silver ornaments he had on his person at the time of his death were discovered a decade later by Spanish explorers entering Paraguay from the south.

*See also* **Paraguay: The Colonial Period.**

BIBLIOGRAPHY

Charles E. Nowell, "Aleixo García and the White King," in *Hispanic American Historical Review* 26 (November 1946): 450–466.

Carlos Zubizarreta, *Cien vidas paraguayas,* 2d ed. (1985), pp. 13–15.

*Additional Bibliography*

Bond, Rosana. *A saga de Aleixo Garcia: O descobridor do império inca.* Florianópolis, Santa Catarina, Brasil: Editora Insular: Fundação Franklin Cascaes, Prefeitura Municipal de Florianópolis, 1998.

THOMAS L. WHIGHAM

**GARCÍA, CALIXTO** (1839–1898). Calixto García (*b.* 4 August 1839; *d.* 11 December 1898), general during Cuba's wars for independence. García rose through the ranks of the liberating army during the first Cuban war of independence, the Ten Years' War (1868–1878). Captured by the Spaniards and set free at the end of the war, García attempted to reignite the rebellion by launching what came to be known as the Little War (1878–

1880). Once again taken prisoner, he was this time deported to Spain, where he lived until returning to Cuba to join the rebel uprising of 24 February 1895. García first became military chief of Oriente Province and was subsequently appointed second in command of the insurgent army. His troops rendered invaluable assistance to the U.S. expeditionary forces in the the Spanish–American War, but they were not allowed to march into Santiago de Cuba when the city was surrendered by the Spaniards in 1898. On this occasion García sent the U.S. military commander a letter of protest that is one of the high points of Cuban nationalism.

*See also* **Cuba: War of Independence.**

BIBLIOGRAPHY

There are no good studies of Calixto García available in English. See Gerardo Castellanos García, *Tierras y glorias de Oriente: Calixto García* (1927), and Juan J. E. Casasús, *Calixto García (el estratega)*, 4th ed. (1981).

*Additional Bibliography*

Escalante Beatón, Aníbal. *Calixto García Iñiguez, su campaña en el 95.* Ciudad de La Habana: Ediciones Verde Olivo, 2001.

Ferrer, Ada. *Insurgent Cuba: Race, Nation, and Revolution, 1868–1898.* Chapel Hill: University of North Carolina Press, 1998.

José M. Hernández

---

**GARCÍA, DIEGO** (c. 1471–c. 1535). Diego García (*b.* c. 1471; *d.* c. 1535), Portuguese navigator in Spanish service. After participating in Ferdinand Magellan's circumnavigation of the globe, García returned to Spain in 1522, organizing an expedition to the Río de la Plata in 1526. He explored Uruguay and established a shipyard near Colonia. During his expedition up the Paraná, he encountered and then joined forces with Sebastián Cabot in 1528. After returning to Spain in 1530, García and his caravel *Concepción* joined the expedition of Pedro de Mendoza, *adelantado* (royal provincial governor) of Río de la Plata, departing Spain in August 1535. While in the Canary Islands, García fell ill and died at Gomera.

*See also* **Explorers and Exploration: Spanish America.**

BIBLIOGRAPHY

Ione S. Wright and Lisa M. Nekhom, *Historical Dictionary of Argentina* (1978), p. 341.

J. H. Parry, *The Discovery of South America* (1979), pp. 249–252.

*Additional Bibliography*

Bergreen, Laurence. *Over the Edge of the World: Magellan's Terrifying Circumnavigation of the Globe.* New York: Morrow, 2003.

Thomas, Hugh. *Rivers of Gold: The Rise of the Spanish Empire, from Columbus to Magellan.* New York: Random House, 2003.

Christel K. Converse

---

**GARCÍA, GENARO** (1867–1920). Genaro García (*b.* 17 August 1867; *d.* 26 November 1920), Mexican politician, women's rights advocate, and historian. Born in Fresnillo, Zacatecas, García first attended school in San Luis Potosí but continued his studies in the capital, where he received a degree in law. He served as a congressional deputy for several terms; as governor of Zacatecas (1900–1904); as director of the National Museum of Archaeology, History, and Ethnology; and as director of the National Preparatory School.

García published many didactic works. From his *Desigualdad de la mujer* (1891) and *Apuntes sobre la condición de la mujer* (1891), arguing for greater rights for women, to his *Carácter de la conquista española en América y en México* (1901), presenting a pro-Indian perspective, García consistently was ahead of his time. However, he is best known as the editor of the thirty-six-volume *Documentos inéditos o muy raros para la historia de México* (1905–1911), and seven-volume *Documentos históricos mexicanos* (1901–1911), and *Documentos inéditos del siglo XVI para la historia de México* (1914). His library of twenty-five-thousand volumes and manuscripts forms the heart of the Mexican holdings of the Benson Latin American Collection at the University of Texas in Austin.

*See also* **Libraries in Latin America; Mexico: 1810–1910.**

BIBLIOGRAPHY

Roderic A. Camp, *Mexican Political Biographies, 1884–1935* (1991).

*Additional Bibliography*

Macías, Anna. *Against All Odds: The Feminist Movement in Mexico to 1940.* Westport, Ct: Greenwood Press, 1982.

CARMEN RAMOS-ESCANDÓN

## GARCÍA, JOSÉ MAURÍCIO NUNES

(1767–1830). José Maurício Nunes García (*b.* 20/22 September 1767; *d.* 18 April 1830), the most notable Brazilian composer of the early nineteenth century. Son of Lieutenant Apolinário Nunes García and Victoria Maria de Cruz, a black woman, José Maurício (as he is called in Brazil) learned to play the harpsichord and viola and studied *solfeggio* with Salvador José, a local teacher. Religious brotherhoods played a significant cultural role in nineteenth-century Brazilian society, and in 1784 José Maurício was one of the founders of the Brotherhood of St. Cecilia. Having entered the Brotherhood of São Pedro dos Clérigos in 1791, he was ordained a priest the following year on 3 March. In July 1798 José Maurício was appointed to the most important musical position in the city, *mestre de capela* of the cathedral of Rio de Janeiro, where his duties consisted of serving as organist, conductor, composer, and music teacher. For twenty-eight years he taught a music course that was open to the public free of charge, in which he trained some of the most important composers and musicians of the following generation, including Francisco Manuel da Silva, composer of the Brazilian national anthem.

The arrival of dom João VI in Rio de Janeiro in 1808 had a decisive influence on the professional career of Padre José Maurício. A member of the Bragança family, which had a remarkable history of musical patronage, dom João was soon informed of José Maurício's talents and appointed him on 15 June 1808 *mestre de capela* of the royal chapel, where his official duties included acting as organist, conductor, and professor of music. He also composed music for numerous official occasions, thirty-nine musical works in 1809, a year in which dom João decorated him with the Order of Christ.

In 1811 Marcos Portugal, the best-known Portuguese composer of his day, arrived in Rio and was appointed *mestre de capela* of the royal chapel, for practical purposes replacing José Maurício. Thereafter, José Maurício's standing in the royal musical establishment declined. However, his best-known and most significant work, a requiem mass, was written in 1816 after the death of Queen Maria. On 19 December 1819 José Maurício conducted the first performance of the Mozart *Requiem* in Brazil.

Accustomed to music composed and performed by Europe's best musicians, dom João was amazed at the abilities of the relatively unknown, native-born mulatto. In a period when musical excellence was judged by adherence to European styles, José Maurício, a devoted admirer of Haydn, made no attempt to deviate from European models.

After dom Pedro I returned to Portugal in 1831, many of his splendid musical reforms languished from lack of funds. José Maurício's lifelong pension was discontinued, leaving him in difficult financial circumstances until his death in 1830.

*See also* **Music: Art Music; Silva, Francisco Manuel de.**

BIBLIOGRAPHY

Cleofe Person De Mattos, *Catálogo temático das obras do Padre José Maurício Nunes Garcia* (1970).

Stanley Sadie, ed., *The New Grove Dictionary of Music and Musicians* (1980).

David P. Appleby, *The Music of Brazil* (1983).

Mauro Gama, *José Maurício, o padre compositor* (1983), Portuguese and English text.

*Additional Bibliography*

Mattos, Cleofe Person de. *José Maurício Nunes Garcia: biografia.* Rio de Janeiro: Ministério da Cultura, Fundação Biblioteca Nacional, Dept. Nacional do Livro, 1997.

DAVID P. APPLEBY

## GARCÍA, JUAN AGUSTÍN

(1862–1923). Juan Agustín García was an Argentine jurist, sociologist, historian, and writer. He earned his law degree in 1882 and taught at the Colegio Nacional in Buenos Aires, the University of Buenos Aires, and the National University of La Plata. During his celebrated career, he was also appointed to education-related and judicial posts in the federal government.

Born into a family with a long history in education (two relatives were rectors of the University of Buenos Aires), García published important books on subjects ranging from law to history, including the acclaimed *La ciudad indiana* (1900), a history of colonial Argentina, and *Introducción al estudio de las ciencias sociales argentinas* (1899). He founded and directed the renowned journal *Anales de la Facultad de Derecho y Ciencias Sociales* at the University of Buenos Aires and wrote literary fiction set in the colonial period, including the novel *Memorias de un Sacristán* (1906). García also became a playwright during the decade preceding his death. His plays include *El mundo de los snobs* (1920) and *Un episodio bajo el terror* (1923).

*See also* **Argentina: The Twentieth Century.**

BIBLIOGRAPHY

Levene, Ricardo. *La realidad histórica y social argentina vista por Juan Agustín García*. Buenos Aires: Imprenta de la Universidad, 1945.

PATRICK BARR-MELEJ

---

**GARCÍA, SARA** (1895–1980). Sara García (*b.* 8 September 1895; *d.* 21 November 1980), Mexican actress. García began her acting career on the stage in 1913. She made her cinematic debut in 1933 in the film *El pulpo humano* and went on to star in over 300 films. Noted for her work as a leading lady, in *Los tres García* (1936) she was cast in the role of the grandmother; from that moment on, García was the film world's perpetual *abuelita*. In 1970 she parodied her familiar screen role in Luis Alcoriza's *Mecánica nacional*. She is regarded as a national treasure and a leading member of the Mexican cinema.

*See also* **Ciniema: From the Silent Film to 1990.**

BIBLIOGRAPHY

Luis Reyes De La Maza, *El cine sonoro en México* (1973).

E. Bradford Burns, *Latin American Cinema: Film and History* (1975).

Carl J. Mora, *Mexican Cinema: Reflections of a Society: 1896–1980* (1982).

John King, *Magical Reels: A History of Cinema in Latin America* (1990).

*Additional Bibliography*

Hershfield, Joanne, and David Maciel. *Mexico's Cinema: A Century of Film and Filmmakers*. Wilmington: Scholarly Resources, 1999.

Muñoz Castillo, Fernando. *Sara García*. México: Clío, 1998.

DAVID MACIEL

---

**GARCÍA BERNAL, GAEL** (1978–). Mexican actor, director, and producer Gael García Bernal was born on 30 November 1978 in Guadalajara to actor parents. He acted in various theatrical productions before starring in the Mexican telenovela *El Abuelo y yo* (The Grandfathers and I) at the age of fourteen. He was invited to attend the Central School of Speech and Drama at the University of London to study acting formally. While still in the program, he auditioned for and won the part of Octavio in *Amores perros* (2000; *Love's a Bitch*, 2005), directed by Alejandro González Iñárritu.

*Amores perros* was shown at the Cannes Film Festival, and it was on the basis of his work in that film that director Alfonso Cuarón invited him to work on *Y tu mamá también* (2001; And Your Mother, Too) His next project, *El crimen de padre Amaro* (2002; *The Crime of Father Amaro*, 2002), was nominated for a Best Foreign Language Film Academy Award in 2003 and was followed by his portrayal of revolutionary leader Ernesto "Che" Guevara in the critically acclaimed *Diarios de motocicleta* (2004; *The Motorcycle Diaries*, 2004). He has since then worked with famous Spanish director Pedro Almodóvar on *Mala educación* (2004; *Bad Education*, 2004), and his most recent project, *Babel* (2006), reunited him with his *Amores perros* director, González Iñárritu. He recently established a documentary film festival, Ambulante, with his *Y tu mamá también*, co-star Diego Luna.

*See also* **Cinema: Since 1990; Cuaron, Alfonso.**

BIBLIOGRAPHY

Mena, Ennio. "Gael García: Es un imán de buena suerte." *Actual* 12, no. 139 (April 2005): 20–24.

STACY LUTSCH

## GARCÍA CALDERÓN, FRANCISCO

(1834–1905). Francisco García Calderón (*b.* 1834; *d.* 1905), a Peruvian lawyer and legal historian. Author of a compilation of nineteenth-century Peruvian law, he was forced to resign as minister of finance in the administration of José Balta when he could not end Peru's financial dependence on its guano consignees. He achieved prominence and notoriety during the War of the Pacific (1879–1883). A committee of wealthy Limeños elected him president in early 1881, when they anticipated high Chilean occupation taxes. He began the negotiations that eventually led to the Treaty of Ancón (1883) that ended the war. During the negotiations, García Calderón adamantly refused to cede the southern departments of Tacna and Arica to Chile. Yet he underwent severe criticism from former president Nicolás de Piérola, who resisted the Chileans from his position in Ayacucho, and from General Andrés A. Cáceres, who fought on in the central highlands. Fearing a rally of resistance among Peruvians and interference from the United States on the issue of cession of territory, the Chileans seized the president and imprisoned him in Santiago until the end of the war.

*See also* **Peru: Peru Since Independence; War of the Pacific.**

BIBLIOGRAPHY

David Werlich, *Peru: A Short History* (1978).

William F. Sater, *Chile and the War of the Pacific* (1986), esp. pp. 206–217.

*Additional Bibliography*

Guerra Martinière, Margarita. *La ocupación de Lima, 1881–1883.* Lima, Perú: Pontificia Universidad Católica del Perú, Dirección Académica de Investigación, Instituto Riva-Agüero, 1996.

VINCENT PELOSO

## GARCÍA CANCLINI, NÉSTOR

(1939–). Néstor García Canclini is a prominent author and researcher on Latin American culture. His work in the 1970s is a Marxist sociology of art, responding to innovative and radical art of the period. His later work, which has been translated into English, is part of an ongoing debate on postmodern culture and stresses the active role of users of media and culture. The key concept is cultural hybridity. García Canclini argues that culture in Latin America is both traditional and modern, boundaries between art and popular culture are eroded by mass media, and the concepts of hegemonic culture and resistance are no longer valid. In his widely read book *Hybrid Cultures*, he makes this case mainly using examples from art and literature rather than lived culture (agriculture, food, clothing, popular speech). His main intention is to argue for government policies for mass media and to make culture more widely available. His work is a response to developments in an increasingly urban continent and has been welcomed by some writers, but others see it as part of a conservative shift in Latin American intellectual life in the 1990s.

*See also* **Literature: Spanish America.**

BIBLIOGRAPHY

García Canclini, Néstor. *Transforming Modernity: Popular Culture in Mexico.* Translated by Lidia Lozano. Austin: University of Texas Press, 1993.

García Canclini, Néstor. *Hybrid Cultures: Strategies for Entering and Leaving Modernity.* Translated by Christopher L. Chiappari and Silvia L. López. Minneapolis: University of Minnesota Press, 1995.

García Canclini, Néstor. *Consumers and Citizens: Globalization and Multicultural Conflicts.* Translated by George Yúdice. Minneapolis: University of Minnesota Press, 2001.

ALAN O'CONNOR

## GARCÍA CATURLA, ALEJANDRO

(1906–1940). Alejandro García Caturla (*b.* 7 March 1906; *d.* 12 November 1940) Cuban composer, considered among the most talented musical artists of Cuba. Born in Remedios, Caturla was a lawyer by profession and became a judge. He studied music with Pedro Sanjuán in Havana (1926–1927) and attended Nadia Boulanger's classes in Paris (1928). He was founder and first conductor of the Orquesta de Conciertos Caibarién, a chamber ensemble. Together with composer Amadeo Roldán, Caturla became the leader of *Afrocubanismo,* a nationalist musical trend, which mixed elements of white and black culture, incorporating Afro-Cuban songs, rhythms, and dances. Later on he used advanced techniques and French Impressionist styles combined with primitive tunes; as a result, some of his works show surprising juxtapositions of chords and moods. He composed *Concierto de cámara, Obertura cubana, Danzas cubanas,* and a suite for orchestra (1938). Many vocal works were inspired by Cuban poets such as Alejo Carpentier and Nicolás Guillén; other works include one string quartet (1927), *Bembé,* for fourteen instruments, and *Primera suite cubana* (1930) among others. He produced numerous piano works, among them *Danza lucumí* (1928) and *Sonata* (1939). Murdered by a criminal tried in his court, he left unfinished one opera, a ballet, his *Primera sinfonía,* one concerto for piano and orchestra, and several piano and vocal works.

*See also* **Cuba: The Republic (1898–1959); Music: Art Music.**

BIBLIOGRAPHY

Alejandro García Caturla, "The Development of Cuban Music," in *American Composers on American Music,* edited by Henry Cowell, (1933).

A. Salazar, "La obra musical de Alejandro García Caturla," in *Revista Cubana* (January 1938): 5–43; *Composers of the Americas,* vol. 3 (1957).

Gérard Béhague, *Music in Latin America* (1979).

Stanley Sadie, ed., *The New Grove Dictionary of Music and Musicians,* vol. 4 (1980).

*Additional Bibliography*

Carpentier, Alejo. *Music in Cuba.* Minneapolis: University of Minnesota Press, 2001.

White, Charles W. *Alejandro García Caturla: A Cuban Composer in the Twentieth Century.* Lanham: Scarecrow Press, 2003.

SUSANA SALGADO

## GARCÍA CONDE, PEDRO (1806–1851).

Pedro García Conde (*b.* 8 February 1806; *d.* 19 December 1851), Mexican soldier. Born in Arizpe, Sonora, he began his military career as a cadet in the presidio company of Cerro Gordo and later served as director of the Military College from 1838 to 1844. In 1842 he was deputy to the national legislature and Secretary of War from 1844 to 1845 in the José Joaquín de Herrera (1792–1854) government. An ardent patriot, he helped plan and fought in the Battle of Sacramento (1847) against the invading U.S. forces.

An accomplished geographer, García participated in the first geographic survey of the state of Chihuahua in 1833 and in 1842 published *Ensayo estadístico sobre el estado de Chihuahua.* In 1848 he received appointment to the presidency of the Mexican Boundary Commission, which was charged with mapping the new border between Mexico and the United States. He held this position twice but died in Arizpe before finishing the survey.

*See also* **Herrera, José Joaquín Antonio Florencio.**

BIBLIOGRAPHY

Florence C. Lister and Robert H. Lister, *Chihuahua: Storehouse of Storms* (1966), pp. 126, 139.

*Additional Bibliography*

Hewitt, Harry P. "The Mexican Boundary Survey Team: Pedro Garcia Conde in California." *The Western Historical Quarterly* 21:2 (May 1990): 171–196.

Rebert, Paula. *La gran línea: Mapping the United States-Mexico Boundary, 1849–1857.* Austin: University of Texas Press, 2001.

AARON PAINE MAHR

## GARCÍA DE CASTRO, LOPE (?–c.1576).

Lope García de Castro (*d.* 1576), governor and captain-general of Peru (1564–1569). Born in the district of Astorga, in northwest Spain, García de Castro studied at the University of Salamanca (1534). He received the licenciate in law and taught at Salamanca until his appointment as *oidor* (justice) of the Audiencia of Valladolid (1541). In 1558, Philip II transferred him to the Council of the Indies.

In response to complaints against Viceroy Diego López de Zúñiga, conde de Nieva, the king sent García de Castro to Peru to investigate and replace the errant official. When García de Castro reached American shores, he learned the viceroy had been assassinated (20 February 1564).

In October 1564 he arrived in Lima, where he began five years of honest, effective, and dedicated administration. In 1565 he established the Casa de

Moneda (Mint Office) of Lima. (It was transferred to Potosí in 1572.) Ordered to increase royal revenues and cut expenses, he began the following year to collect the *almojarifazgo* (import duty) and undertook to organize effective exploitation of the mercury mines at Huancavelica. He divided Peru into provinces and established the *corregimiento* system for the local administration of Indians. In 1567 he founded an audiencia at Concepción, in Chile. (Suppressed in 1573, it was reestablished in 1609 at Santiago.)

García de Castro faced continued pressure from the Araucanians on the Chilean frontier and the Chiriguanos in lowland Bolivia, opposition from the neo-Inca state at Vilcabamba, northwest of Cuzco, and a bothersome uprising in the central Peruvian highlands associated with the Taki Onqoy movement. For more effective administration of Lima, he created El Cercado, an Indian town. During his rule the Tridentine reforms were announced in Lima (1565) and the Second Lima Church Council (1567–1568), which improved the administration of Indian *doctrinas,* was convened. At this time, also, the Jesuits began their work in Peru. García de Castro provided support for Captain Juan Álvarez Maldonado's exploration of the Mojos territory in the upper Amazon basin and, under his nephew Álvaro de Mendaña, also organized a voyage of exploration in the Pacific (1567–1568) that led to the discovery of the Solomon Islands. García de Castro returned to Spain in November 1569, shortly after welcoming the new viceroy, Francisco de Toledo y Figueroa.

*See also* **Peru: From the Conquest Through Independence.**

BIBLIOGRAPHY

Manuel De Mendiburu, *Diccionario histórico-biográfico del Perú,* vol. 5 (1933), pp. 345–350.

Rubén Vargas Ugarte, *Historia del Perú: Virreinato (1551–1600)* (1949), pp. 151–211; *Historia general del Perú,* vol. 2 (1966–1984).

### *Additional Bibliography*

Andrien, Kenneth J. *Andean Worlds: Indigenous History, Culture, and Consciousness under Spanish Rule, 1532–1825.* Albuquerque: University of New Mexico Press, 2001.

Lockhart, James. *Spanish Peru, 1532–1560: A Social History.* Madison: University of Wisconsin Press, 1994.

NOBLE DAVID COOK

## GARCÍA DEL RÍO, JUAN (1794–1856).

Born in Cartagena, Juan García del Río was a prominent nineteenth-century diplomat, government official, and writer. While receiving his education in Spain on the eve of Latin America's independence from Spain and Portugal, he befriended José de San Martín; this was his first link with an important leader. Later he would have ties with Simón Bolívar, Juan José Flores, and Bernardo O'Higgins, among others.

After the death of his royalist father in 1813, García del Río served as a diplomat in Great Britain representing the United Provinces of New Granada until it was reconquered by Spain in 1816. He remained in London until 1817, when he accepted an invitation to work in the newly independent Chile; there he wrote for and edited various newspapers. He accompanied San Martín's campaign to liberate Peru in 1820 and then represented that government in France. After San Martín's retirement in 1822, Garcia del Río resettled in London, where he concentrated on literary efforts, most notably collaborating with Andrés Bello on the serial *La Biblioteca Americana.* He returned to Gran Colombia in 1829 and published *Meditaciones Colombianas,* an argument for a constitutional monarchy under Bolívar. This earned him the enmity of those who came to power after the Liberator's exile in 1830, and he moved on. After serving the governments of Ecuador and Peru, he worked as a writer in Chile during the 1840s.

He yearned for a private life of letters, but spent his last years unsuccessfully pursuing the money that he had been promised when he was awarded La Orden del Sol by San Martín's Peruvian regime, as well as litigating over slander, arranging speculative ventures, and refuting accusations about monarchical plots. He died in Mexico, an elegant writer whose life exemplified the tumult, potential, and disappointments of Latin America's independence.

*See also* **Bolívar, Simón; Flores, Juan José; O'Higgins, Bernardo; San Martín, José Francisco de.**

BIBLIOGRAPHY

### *Primary Work*

*Meditaciones Colombianas,* 1829. Bogotá: Imprenta Nacional, 1945.

*Secondary Works*

Amunátegui Solar, Domingo. "Vida literaria, amorosa y política de don Juan García del Río." *Boletín de Historia y Antigüedades* 26, nos. 291–292 (1939): 1–47.

Kitchens, Lynne Brauer. "Juan García del Río, Spanish American Citizen: A Study of His Life and Works." Master's essay, Vanderbilt University, 1966.

JOSHUA M. ROSENTHAL

## GARCÍA DIEGO Y MORENO, FRANCISCO

**GARCÍA DIEGO Y MORENO, FRANCISCO** (1785–1846). Francisco García Diego y Moreno (*b.* 1785; *d.* 19 November 1846), bishop of California (1840–1846). The Mexican-born Franciscan was the first Catholic bishop of the Californias. Associated with the apostolic college of Guadalupe in Zacatecas, he arrived to serve in the Alta California missions in January 1833 with a contingent of Zacatecan Franciscans sent to replace their brethren from the college of San Fernando in the missions of southern Alta California.

The bishopric of the Californias was established by a Mexican law (19 September 1836) authorizing the president to negotiate with the papacy to establish the new bishopric. This initiative also allocated 6,000 pesos from public funds for the support of the new bishop and transferred the administration of the so-called Pious Fund, an endowment organized by the Jesuits to finance their activities in Baja California, to his jurisdiction, although the Mexican government later resumed control of the fund. The papacy approved the new bishopric on 27 April 1840.

President Antastasio Bustamante selected Diego y Moreno from a list of three candidates submitted by the papacy. After having sworn an oath of loyalty to the president of Mexico, Diego y Moreno was consecrated as bishop at the shrine of the Virgin of Guadalupe outside Mexico City on 4 October 1841. He served in Alta California for six years and died in Santa Barbara.

*See also* **Franciscans; Obras Pías.**

BIBLIOGRAPHY

Zephyrin Engelhardt, O.F.M., *Missions and Missionaries of California*, 4 vols. (1929–1930).

Maynard J. Geiger, O.F.M., *Franciscan Missionaries in Hispanic California, 1769–1848* (1968).

*Additional Bibliography*

Jackson, Robert H., and Edward D Castillo. *Indians, Franciscans, and Spanish Colonization: The Impact of the Mission System on California Indians.* Albuquerque: University of New Mexico Press, 1995.

ROBERT H. JACKSON

## GARCÍA GODOY, HÉCTOR

**GARCÍA GODOY, HÉCTOR** (1921–1970). Héctor García Godoy (*b.* 1921; *d.* 1970), Dominican provisional president (1965–1966). Born into one of the Dominican Republic's old elite families, García Godoy distinguished himself as a career diplomat whose skill, tact, and moderation prepared him for his role as provisional president after the overthrow of Juan Bosch (1963) and subsequent U.S. military invasion of his country (1965). Offered the position of president by U.S. ambassador Ellsworth Bunker, García faced the difficult task of reconciling opposing forces, the left-leaning Constitutionalists and the right-wing military elements, who had kept the country in a chaotic civil war since Bosch's fall. During his nine months in office, he faced pressures from both factions as well as the United States. He rose to the occasion by eliminating the most troublesome military leaders who had refused to negotiate. His presidency smoothed the way for elections in June 1966 and for the birth of a new Dominican government led by Joaquín Balaguer. Afterward, García served as Dominican ambassador to Washington. Many Dominicans hoped that, upon his return, he would run for president. In 1970, García founded the Movimiento de Conciliación Nacional (MCN) in preparation for the 1974 presidential campaign. Soon thereafter, however, he died of a heart attack.

*See also* **Bosch Gaviño, Juan; Dominican Republic.**

BIBLIOGRAPHY

Howard Wiarda, *The Dominican Republic: A Nation in Transition* (1969).

Ian Bell, *The Dominican Republic* (1981).

*Additional Bibliography*

Chester, Eric Thomas. *Rag-tags, Scum, Riff-raff, and Commies: The U.S. Intervention in the Dominican Republic, 1965–1966.* New York: Monthly Review Press, 2001.

Hartlyn, Jonathan. *The Struggle for Democratic Politics in the Dominican Republic.* Chapel Hill: University of North Carolina Press, 1998.

Palmer, Bruce. *Intervention in the Caribbean: The Dominican Crisis of 1965.* Lexington: University Press of Kentucky, 1989.

PAMELA MURRAY

**GARCÍA GRANADOS, MIGUEL** (1809–1878). Miguel García Granados (*b.* 29 September 1809; *d.* 8 September 1878), a leader in the Guatemalan liberal revolution of 1871. Born in Cádiz, Spain, García Granados went to Guatemala with his parents as an infant. While he was still a young man he became interested in military affairs and in liberal political philosophy, especially that of Voltaire and Rousseau. As Spaniards, his family was not involved in the independence movement, but they shared many of the new ideals. García Granados traveled to New York with his older brothers in 1823. He studied there and in Philadelphia and London before returning to Guatemala in 1826. When conflicts began developing with El Salvador, he followed his older brothers into military service.

García Granados participated in two invasions of El Salvador, where he was captured, held prisoner, and exiled to Mexico, not returning to Guatemala until 1840. During the following thirty years he became a leader in the movements for political change, a free press, public education, fiscal reform, and restrictions on the power of the church. He served as a leader of the liberal cause in the conservative-controlled National Assembly during the long dictatorship of Rafael Carrera. While in exile in Mexico he had met Justo Rufino Barrios. Together they planned the overthrow of the conservative government. They invaded Guatemala in May 1871 and, after a series of battles, entered Guatemala City victorious on June 30. García Granados became interim president and served until 1873, when Barrios succeeded him as the constitutionally elected president. The revolution of 1871 led to the expulsion of religious orders, to professionalization of the military, to expanded public education and public works throughout the country, and to a concept of the state as a positive force for introducing change in the society and the economy.

*See also* **Barrios, Justo Rufino.**

BIBLIOGRAPHY

Miguel García Granados, *Memorias* (1952).

José Santacruz Noriega, *Gobierno del Capitán General D. Miguel García Granados* (1979).

*Additional Bibliography*

Clegern, Wayne M. *Origins of Liberal Dictatorship in Central America: Guatemala, 1865–1873.* Niwot: University Press of Colorado, 1994.

DAVID L. JICKLING

**GARCÍA ICAZBALCETA, JOAQUÍN** (1825–1894). Joaquín García Icazbalceta (*b.* 21 August 1825; *d.* 26 November 1894), Mexican historian and bibliographer. One of the most recognized historians of Mexico, Joaquín García Icazbalceta dedicated a lifetime to collecting, editing, and publishing documents that centered on the Europeanization of Mexico in the sixteenth century. Born in Mexico City to a Spanish father and Mexican mother, he left with his family for exile in Spain, where they remained seven years (1829–1836). Though he received no formal education outside of tutoring in the home, early in life he showed a strong interest in literature. He joined the family business in Mexico City, where he successfully balanced a career in commerce with his literary interests.

In 1848, after participating in the war against the United States, García Icazbalceta began in earnest to collect original manuscripts of historical and linguistic value. He spent the remainder of his life compiling bibliographies, writing numerous books and articles, and publishing documents for use by future historians. Most notable among his works are the *Bibliografía mexicana del siglo XVI* (1954), the two-volume *Colección de documentos para la historia de México* (1971), and a four-volume biography of Juan de Zumárraga, first archbishop of Mexico. At the time of his death, García Icazbalceta served as director of the Mexican Academy of Language.

*See also* **Literature: Spanish America; Mexico: 1810–1910.**

BIBLIOGRAPHY

Henry R. Wagner, *Joaquín García Icazbalceta* (1935).

Manuel G. Martínez, "Don Joaquín García Icazbalceta: His Place in Mexican Historiography," in *Studies in Hispanic American History,* vol. 4 (1947).

Howard F. Cline, "Selected Nineteenth-Century Mexican Writers on Ethnohistory," in *Handbook of Middle American Indians,* vol. 13 (1973), pp. 370–427.

*Additional Bibliography*

Rivas Mata, Emma, editor. *Entretenimientos literarios: Epistolario entre los bibliógrafos Joaquín García Icazbalceta y Manuel Remón.* Mexico City: Instituto Nacional de Antropoligía y Historia, 2003.

Ruedas de la Serna, Jorge A., editor. *Historiografía de la literatura mexicana: Ensayos y comentarios.* México: Universidad Nacional Autónoma de México, Facultad de Filosofía y Letras, División de Estudios de Posgrado, 1996.

BRIAN C. BELANGER

**GARCÍA MÁRQUEZ, GABRIEL** (1927–). Gabriel García Márquez (born March 6, 1927) is Colombia's best-known novelist and short-story writer. The two most important years of García Márquez's career are 1967, when his masterpiece *Cien años de soledad* (1967; *One Hundred Years of Solitude*, 1970) brought him overnight fame, and 1982, when he was awarded the Nobel Prize in literature.

García Márquez was born in Aracataca, a town near the Atlantic coast, where he spent the first eight years of his life. His law studies at the National University in Bogotá were interrupted in 1948 by El Bogotazo, an outburst of violence triggered by the assassination of a popular politician. The university was closed, and García Márquez returned to the Atlantic coast, where he worked for several years as a journalist. The symbiotic relationship between his journalism and his fiction is one of the hallmarks of much of his work. An early example is the novella *Relato de un náufrago* (1970; *The Story of a Shipwrecked Sailor*, 1986), which is the result of interviews he held with a young Colombian sailor who spent ten days on a raft after being swept overboard in the Caribbean. The people, landscape, and atmosphere of the coast of Colombia are an important aspect of García Márquez's work. Many of his novels and short stories are set in the coastal towns of Colombia, portrayed either through the mythical town of Macondo or set in the colonial city of Cartagena.

In 1954 García Márquez published his first novel, *La hojarasca* (*Leaf Storm*, 1972), whose plot and style recall William Faulkner's *As I Lay Dying* (1930). Six years later, having lived as a journalist in Europe, Caracas, and New York, he published his novella *El coronel no tiene quien le escriba* (1961; *No One Writes to the Colonel*, 1968). It is the masterful portrait of an aging, poverty-stricken ex-military officer who waits for his pension while hoping that his fighting cock will win a fortune in an upcoming contest. This sparsely written volume (one detects Hemingway's influence) is enhanced by veiled allusions to a bloody civil conflict (La Violencia, a period of civil violence in Columbia) and by the good-humored but tenacious protagonist, who embodies the Colombian people's struggle against oppression.

García Márquez moved to Mexico in 1961 and the next year published *Los funerales de la Mamá Grande* (1962; *Big Mama's Funeral*, 1979), a collection of eight tales dramatizing the political and social realities of Colombia. In 1965, after several years of writer's block, the author was driving to Acapulco when he envisioned a fictional world he had endeavored to create for more than a decade. Eighteen months later he emerged from his study with the manuscript of *One Hundred Years of Solitude.* This novel, perhaps the second best (after *Don Quixote*) ever to be written in Spanish, tells the story of Macondo (the author's native Aracataca) from genesis to apocalypse. Seven generations of the Buendía family, the leading characters of the saga, find themselves caught up in the totality of human experience, ranging from the historical and the mythical to the everyday, the fantastic, the tragic, the comic, and the absurd. Major sections of the novel, which has been seen as a rewriting of history designed to refute official lies, deal with Colombia's nineteenth-century civil wars, the banana boom, and gringo imperialism.

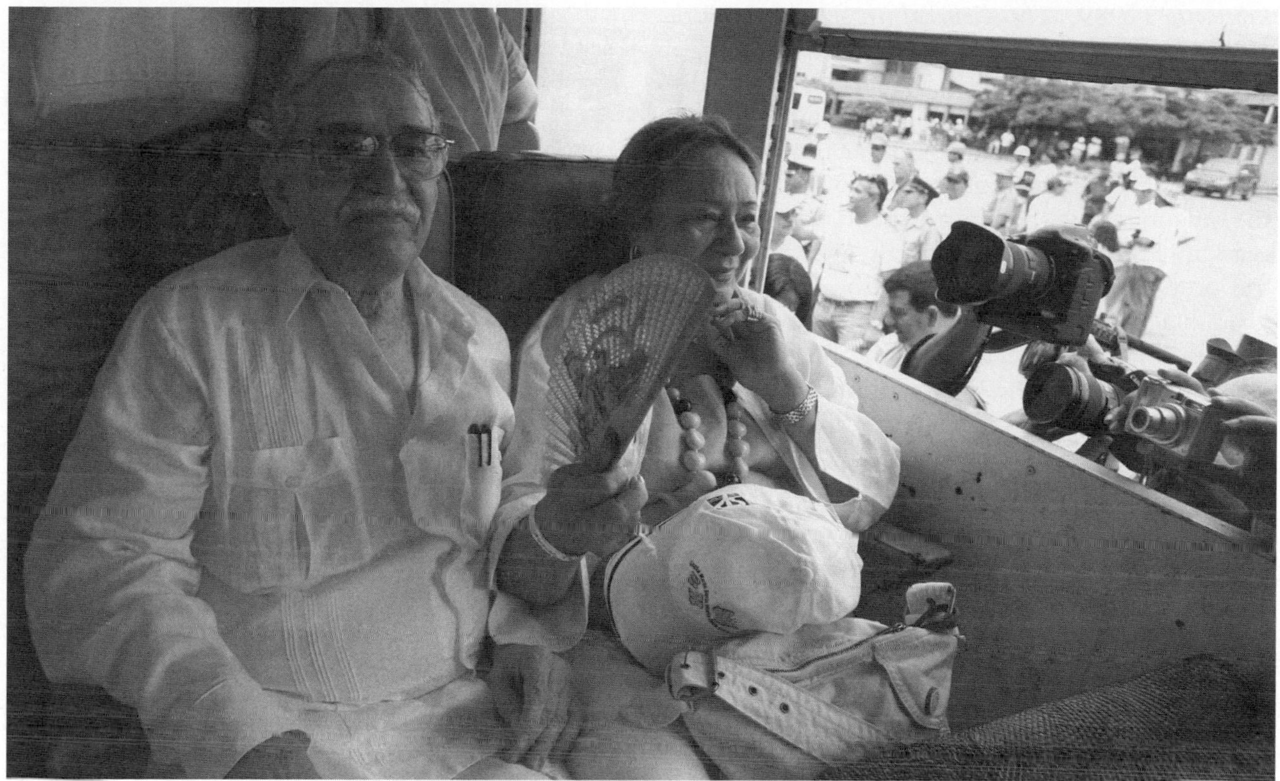

**The return home, 2007.** Gabriel García Márquez and his wife, Mercedes Barcha, return to his hometown, Aracataca, Colombia, for the first time in twenty-five years. AP IMAGES

Soon after the publication of *One Hundred Years of Solitude*, García Márquez moved to Barcelona to write *El otoño del patriarca* (1975; *The Autumn of the Patriarch*, 1976). This portrait of a prototypical Latin American dictator represents a daring experiment in the use of poetic language and literary technique, which explains in part why it is often considered the author's most significant achievement to date. The novel also is an example of the author's deep-seated interest in denouncing political and social injustice not only in Colombia but in all of Latin America. The protagonist embodies all the evils of despotism, but equally important is the solitude imposed on him by the absolute power he wields. Like its predecessor, *The Autumn of the Patriarch* is sprinkled with humor and fantasy, but its rambling style and shifting points of view make it far more demanding of the reader.

Continuing with Garcia Marquez's desire to analyze the roots of social injustice in Latin America, his next novel presents a study of irrational violence and unjust murder. *Crónica de una muerte anunciada* (1981; *Chronicle of a Death Foretold*, 1982) records the testimony of witnesses to the murder of Santiago Nasar, a youth accused of seducing Ángela Vicario prior to her marriage. When, on her wedding night, Ángela's husband discovers that she is not a virgin, he returns her to her parents. The following morning, her twin brothers kill Nasar on the doorstep of his home. A riveting mélange of journalism and detective story, the novel implicitly condemns not only the Catholic Church but also the primitive code of honor endorsed by the town citizens.

Two of García Márquez's subsequent novels rely on historical and geographical documentation to enrich setting and plot. *El amor en los tiempos del cólera* (1985; *Love in the Time of Cholera*, 1988) describes Cartagena between 1870 and 1930, a time when the decaying historic city was plagued by a series of epidemics. The action focuses on the aging process of the protagonists, two of whom, Fermina Daza and Florentino Ariza, are patterned after the author's parents. Reviewers have described this novel as one of the best love stories ever written. The protagonist of *El general en su laberinto* (1989; *The General in His Labyrinth*, 1990) is Simón Bolívar, the liberator of much of South America. In May 1830, mortally ill and disillusioned by his fruitless efforts to unite the continent under a single leader, Bolívar traveled down the Magdalena River from Santa Fe de Bogotá to the Atlantic coast, hoping to spend his remaining years in Europe. He died shortly after arriving in the port city of Santa Marta. Although the foreground action is a lineal account of Bolívar's arduous journey to his grave, numerous flashbacks evoke remnants of his life, molding an intricate labyrinth of memories, dreams, and hallucinations.

In 1992 Garcia Marquez published *Doce cuentos peregrinos* (*Strange Pilgrims*, 1993) and in 1994 *Del amor y otros demonios* (*Of Love and Other Demons*, 1995). The former is a collection of short stories about Latin Americans living in Europe; the latter, a novel, is set in a Colombian coastal city during the eighteenth century. Based on a legend, it narrates the strange tale of a young girl, Sierva María de Todos los Ángeles, who is bitten by a rabid dog, falls in love with a priest, and ultimately dies in a convent during the exorcism mandated by the Inquisition. This final episode, in addition to the vivid descriptions of decadence and poverty, dramatizes the negative impact of Spanish colonialism.

Garcia Marquez's *Memorias de mis putas tristes* (2004; *Memories of My Melancholy Whores*, 2005) was his first fictional work to appear in ten years. The novel tells the story of an eccentric, solitary old man who decides to celebrate his ninety years by giving himself the present of a night in a brothel with a young virgin. Once he meets her he finds himself close to dying, not of old age, but rather of love. The novel narrates his sexual adventures, for which he always paid, never imagining that this would be the way he would discover true love.

With his broad literary canvases laced with myths and fantasy, García Márquez rescued the contemporary novel from its rigid laws of logic. In its totality, his oeuvre depicts the stark reality of an underdeveloped, strife-torn continent universalized by the humanistic elements of unfettered imagination and aesthetic perception. García Márquez is one of the world's most widely admired writers of fiction. The end result of his prodigious enterprise is an original, comprehensive vision of human experience.

*See also* **Bolívar, Simón; Literature: Spanish America.**

BIBLIOGRAPHY

Bell-Villada, Gene H. *García Márquez: The Man and His Work*. Chapel Hill: University of North Carolina Press, 1990.

Luiselli, Alessandra. "Los demonios en torno a la cama del rey: Pederastia e incesto en *Memorias de mis putas tristes* de Gabriel García Márquez." *Espéculo: Revista de Estudios Literarios* 32 (2006). Available from http://www.ucm.es/info/especulo/numero32/camarey.html.

Martin, Gerald. "Translating García Márquez, or the Impossible Dream." In *Voice-Overs: Translation and Latin American Literature*, ed. Daniel Balderston and Marcy Schwartz. Albany: State University of New York Press, 2002.

McNerney, Kathleen. *Understanding Gabriel García Márquez*. Columbia: University of South Carolina Press, 1989.

Oberhelman, Harley D. *Gabriel García Márquez: A Study of the Short Fiction*. Boston: Twayne, 1991.

Olsen, Margaret M. "La patología de la africanía en *Del amor y otros demonios* de García Márquez." *Revista Iberoamericana* 68, no. 201 (2002): 1067–1080.

Palencia-Roth, Michael. "Gabriel García Márquez: Labyrinths of Love and History." *World Literature Today: A Literary Quarterly of the University of Oklahoma* 65, no. 1 (1991): 54–58. Reprinted in *Twayne Companion to Contemporary World Literature: From the Editors of World Literature Today*, ed. Pamela A. Genova. New York: Twayne Thomson/Gale, 2003.

Posada Carbó, Eduardo. "La historia y los falsos recuerdos (A propósito de las memorias de García Márquez)." *Revista de Occidente* 271 (2003): 101–114.

Rincón, Carlos. "*Del amor y otros demonios*, páginas 9 a 11; o, sobre la reescritura de las 'foundational fictions' norteamericanas." *Revista de Crítica Literaria Latinoamericana* 50 (1999): 199–224.

Rodríguez Vergara, Isabel. *El mundo satírico de Gabriel García Márquez*. Madrid: Pliegos, 1991.

Williams, Raymond L. *Gabriel García Márquez*. Boston: Twayne, 1984.

MAIDA WATSON

**GARCÍA MEZA, LUIS** (1932–). Luis García Meza is a Bolivian army officer who served briefly as head of government by military coup. García Meza was born in La Paz on August 8, 1932. Active in a series of military interventions between 1971 and 1979, he led a coup in July

1980 that deposed the civilian president, Lidia Gueiler. During his year-long rule, a bloody repression of political opponents was orchestrated by the Nazi fugitive Klaus Barbie and García Meza's comrade-in-arms, Colonel Luis Arce Gómez; the public treasury was opened to pillage, and cocaine trafficking benefited from thinly veiled government support. García Meza's downfall, in a countercoup, set the stage for a subsequent quarter-century of democratic rule in Bolivia. A succession of those governments prosecuted this former general and his chief henchmen. Convicted in absentia in 1993, García Meza was located in and extradited from Brazil in 1994. He is serving a thirty-year term in a maximum-security prison near La Paz for crimes against Bolivian individuals and against the state.

*See also* **Gueiler Tejada, Lidia; Nazis.**

BIBLIOGRAPHY

Kohl, Benjamin H., and Linda C. Farthing. *Impasse in Bolivia: Neoliberal Hegemony and Popular Resistance.* London and New York: Zed Books, 2006.

Navarro Miranda, César. *Luis García Meza, una pesadilla en nuestra historia.* Llallagua, Potosí Bolivia: Universidad Nacional Siglo XX, 2002.

DAVID BLOCK

## GARCÍA MORENO, GABRIEL (1821–1875).

Gabriel García Moreno (*b.* 24 December 1821; *d.* 6 August 1875), president of Ecuador (1861–1865, 1869–1875). Born in Guayaquil into a family of modest means, Gabriel García Moreno completed his early studies at home before going to Quito for his secondary and university studies. He received a doctorate in law at the University of Quito, and in 1846 married the aristocratic Rosa Ascásubi Matheu. In 1855–1856 he took courses in the natural sciences in France at the Sorbonne.

García Moreno entered politics as a liberal, an opponent of General Juan José Flores, and an admirer of the enlightened Vicente Rocafuerte. He gained notoriety as a publisher of three polemical newspapers: *El Zurriago* (1845), *El Vengador* (1846–1847), and *La Nación* (1853). His vehement opposition to the government forced him into exile three times between 1850 and 1856. Life abroad induced him to turn conservative, to become a francophile, and to champion the cause of the Catholic Church.

Upon completing scientific studies in Paris in 1856, he returned to Ecuador and was named rector of the University of Quito. Soon afterward he won a seat in the Senate. When the government became mired in a grave crisis with Peru, García Moreno took part in a campaign that toppled the government and precipitated a period of anarchy in Ecuador.

In May 1859 a *junta de notables* named García Moreno a member of a triumvirate. He quickly emerged as the dominant leader but soon suffered a military defeat that caused him to flee to Peru. After securing support from the Peruvian president, he managed in a few months to return to Quito and to take charge there. Desperate to pacify the nation, he secretly proposed to establish a French protectorate over Ecuador. France did not respond to the proposal.

By early 1861 the nation was sufficiently pacified for a national convention to elect García Moreno president for four years. He completed his term of office, bullied two successors for the next four years, and then seized power by force. He remained president until his violent death in 1875.

During his first administration García Moreno held power by ruthless repression of the opposition. He reformed the treasury, increased revenues, turned public schools over to the clergy, allowed the Jesuits to return to Ecuador, and defended his nation from the aggressive intentions of Colombia and Peru. His efforts to modernize the university and improve the transportation system gave the impression of continued liberalism, but his repression of criticism and his espousal of unabashed clericalism revealed a shift to authoritarian conservatism. Most revealing was the negotiation in 1862 of a controversial concordat with the Vatican that surrendered the *patronato* (government authority over clerical appointments and revenues), permitted church censorship of school texts, and called for reform of corrupt religious orders. A subsequent campaign to spiritualize the clergy helped turn the church into a strong pillar of the state.

The authoritarian Constitution of 1869 allowed García Moreno to become a legal dictator and to press his religious fervor to surprising extremes. Non-Catholics were denied civil rights, substantial sums of money were donated to the Vatican, and in 1873 the nation was dedicated to the Sacred Heart of Jesus. In secular affairs, García Moreno founded an astronomical observatory, a new military academy, and a polytechnical school. Public works included many new roads, especially a good cart road from Quito to Guayaquil, initiation of railroad lines, and a large prison in Quito.

While García Moreno was arranging his own reelection in 1875, copies of Juan Montalvo's *La dictadura perpetua,* an inflammatory indictment of the Ecuadorian dictator, arrived in Quito. Soon afterward a group of young liberals, probably incited by Montalvo's words, cut down the president with machete blows. This bloody act ended the dictatorship but turned García Moreno into a martyr of conservatism.

*See also* **Ecuador, Constitutions; Flores, Juan José; Jesuits.**

BIBLIOGRAPHY

George Howe, "García Moreno's Efforts to Unite Ecuador and France," in *Hispanic American Historical Review* 16, no. 2 (1936): 257–262.

Luis Robalino Dávila, *García Moreno* (1948).

Severo Gomezjurado, *Vida de García Moreno,* 10 vols. (1954–1971).

Benjamín Carrión, *García Moreno: El santo del patíbulo* (1959).

Richard Pattee, *Gabriel García Moreno y el Ecuador de su tiempo,* 3d ed. (1962).

### *Additional Bibliography*

Castillo, Ocarina. *Gabriel García Moreno, o, El orden de la piedad intolerante.* Caracas: Fundación CELARG: Ediciones FACES/UCV, 1998.

Ponce, Pilar. *Gabriel García Moreno.* Quito: Editorial El Conejo, 1990.

Ruiz Rivera, Julián Bautista. *Gabriel García Moreno, dictador ilustrado del Ecuador.* Madrid: Anaya, 1988.

Xavier, Adro. *García Moreno: siglo XIX, Hispanoamérica Ecuatorial* Barcelona: Editorial Casals, 1991.

MARK J. VAN AKEN

## GARCÍA MORILLO, ROBERTO

**GARCÍA MORILLO, ROBERTO** (1911–2003). Roberto García Morillo (*b.* 22 January 1911; *d.* 26 October 2003), Argentine composer and critic. He was born in Buenos Aires and studied at the National Conservatory of Music and Theater Arts under the guidance of Floro Ugarte, José Gil, José André, and Constantino Gaito. Garcia Morillo is noted for the absence of nationalistic elements in his music. His style evolved as atonal music, with modernistic, dissonant harmonies, and very contrapuntal lines but without harshly clashing sounds. Garcia Morillo evoked the Hispanic origins of his ancestors, using renovated archaic forms and textures in his works such as his cantata Marín (1948–1950). The municipality of Buenos Aires awarded a composition prize for his *Poema para orquestra* (1932) and for *Las pinturas negras de Goya* (1939). His ballets *Harrild* (1941) and *Usher* (1940–1941) were awarded distinctions from the National Commission on culture and the Wagnerian Society, as was his music for the film *Juvenilia,* which received the Municipal Prize for film music in 1943. In 1938 he began writing music criticism for the newspaper *La Nación* in Buenos Aires, and also wrote articles for *Modern Music, Musical Courier,* and the *Revista ARS.* He is the author of several books: *Mussorgsky* (1943), *Rimsky Korsakoff* (1945), *Estudios sobre la danza* (1948), with Dora Kriner, *Siete músicos europeos* (1949), and *Carlos Chávez* (1960).

Some of Garcia Morillo's earlier compositions contain traces of neoclassicism, like his Piano Sonata no. 3, op. 14 (1944–1945). Other works of the same period demonstrate his dexterity with rhythms and the use of engaging and intriguing melodies. Among his important works are *Tres pinturas de Paul Klee* (1944); *El tamarit* (1953), a chamber cantata for soprano, baritone, and orchestra; *Romances del amor y de la muerte* for bass (1959); *Música para oboe y orquestra* (1962); *Cantata de los caballeros* for soprano (1965); *Música para violin y cuerdas* (1967); Symphony no. 1 (1946–1948); *Obertura para un drama romántico* (1954); Symphony no. 2 (1954–1955); Symphony no. 3 (1961); *Divertimento sobre temas de Paul Klee* (1967); *Ciclo de Dante Alighieri* for chamber orchestra (1970); and *Variaciones apolíneas* for piano (1958–1959).

Garcia Morillo served as president of the Asociación Argentina de Compositores (1992–1998 and 2001–2002) and as president of the Academia Argentina de Música (1995).

*See also* **Buenos Aires; Music: Art Music.**

BIBLIOGRAPHY

*Cuarto Inter-American Music Festival* (1968), pp. 44, 47, 70; *Primer festival internacional de música contemporánea* (1970), p. 29.

Rodolfo Arizaga, *Enciclopedia de la música argentina* (1971), pp. 153–155.

Gérard Béhague, *Music in Latin America: An Introduction* (1979), pp. 276–277; *New Grove Dictionary of Music and Musicians* (1980).

ALCIDES LANZA

## GARCÍA ORTIZ, LAUREANO (1865–1945).

A writer and Colombian diplomat, García Ortiz was born in Rionegro, Antioquia Department, in 1865. In secondary school he was influenced by two German teachers, who introduced him to a new pedagogy, didactic elements, discipline, and values. He concluded his baccalaureate in Colegio Martínez Hernán, at Medellín City, where he had the benefit of instruction from intellectually recognized Antioquian teachers. He traveled to Bogota, where he received a degree in Ciencias Naturales y Agronomía of the Universidad National de Colombia and studied political and social sciences. Among his best friends were the poet José Asunción Silva and the essayist Baldomero Sanín Cano.

García Ortiz was elected to the Colombian senate. His diplomatic work was fruitful, helping to resolve, in a way favorable for Colombia, the issue of United States compensation for the loss of Panama and Colombia's border disputes with Peru and Brazil. He was a professor at the Universidad Nacional, belonged to several scientific and cultural associations, and was concurrently a member of the Consejo Nacional de Economía and the board of directors of the Banco de la Republica de Colombia during the period 1938–1940. He had a substantial library of classical and modern authors that included works on Colombian subjects and international diplomacy and relations. He published a good number of historical texts, chronicles, and literary works. Outstanding among his books is *Estudios históricos y Fisonomías colombianas* (1938). He bequeathed his library to the Banco de la República, which became part of the Biblioteca Luis Angel Arango.

*See also* **Silva, José Asunción.**

BIBLIOGRAPHY

*Works by García Ortiz*

*Estudios históricos y fisonomías colombianas.* Bogota: Editorial ABC, 1938.

"Santander, padre de la republica." *Vida: Revista de Arte y Literatura* 3, no. 31 (June 1940).

*Las ciudades confederadas del valle del cauca en 1811.* Bogota: Editorial Librería Voluntad, 1943.

*Algunos estudios sobre el general Santander.* Bogota: Imprenta nacional, 1946.

*Antioquia, Rionegro y Córdova.* Bogota: Kelly, 1979.

"Apuntamientos de un viaje a Bogota en 1880." *Estudios Sociales* nos. 8–9 (1995): 135–144.

*Other Works*

Mejía Robledo, Alfonso. *Vidas y empresas de Antioquia.* Medellín, Colombia: Imprenta Departamental de Antioquia, 1951. See p. 75.

Sánchez López, Luís Maria. *Diccionario de escritores colombianos.* Bogota: Plaza & Janes, 1985. See p. 291.

RODRIGO DE J. GARCÍA ESTRADA

## GARCIAPARRA, NOMAR (1973–).

Anthony Nomar Garciaparra is a major league baseball player who captivated Boston Red Sox fans with his stellar play and gained fame as one of the best-hitting shortstops of his era.

Of Mexican descent, Garciaparra was born in Whittier, California, on July 23, 1973. He attended Georgia Tech University, where he starred for that school's 1994 NCAA championship team. He was signed shortly afterward by the Red Sox and made his major league debut with the club in 1996. His 30 home runs, 98 runs batted in (RBIs), league-leading 209 hits, and .306 batting average earned him American League Rookie of the Year honors for 1997. At one point in that season he established an American League record for rookies when he hit in 30 straight games. The following year he ripped 35 home runs and accumulated 122 RBIs. In 1999 and 2000 he won consecutive batting crowns with averages of .357 and .372. Injuries dogged him thereafter, however, and in 2004 the Red Sox dealt him to the Chicago Cubs where, in the span of two seasons, he played slightly more than 100 games at shortstop and third base, and produced little for that club. Two years later he signed to play for the Los Angeles Dodgers, near his hometown. The Dodgers, as a means to protect the fragile infielder, assigned him to play largely first base, and in 2006 he responded by contributing a .303 batting average with 20 home runs and 93 RBIs. The following year his average declined slightly to .283. Garciaparra is married to Mia Hamm, the soccer star.

*See also* **Sports.**

BIBLIOGRAPHY

Wendel, Tim. *The New Face of Baseball: The One-Hundred-Year Rise and Triumph of Latinos in America's Favorite Sport.* New York: Rayo, 2003.

SAMUEL O. REGALADO

## GARCÍA PELÁEZ, FRANCISCO DE PAULA

**GARCÍA PELÁEZ, FRANCISCO DE PAULA** (1785–1867). Francisco De Paula García Peláez (*b.* 2 April 1785; *d.* 25 January 1867), archbishop of Guatemala, with jurisdiction over all of Central America (1846–1867). Born into a ladino family of modest means in San Juan Sacatepéquez, Guatemala, García Peláez studied law and theology at the University of San Carlos, where he received his doctorate in 1819. Although regarded as somewhat liberal in the late colonial period, as archbishop during the long, conservative dictatorship of José Rafael Carrera, he became known as an ultraconservative. He had offered the first course in political economy at the University of San Carlos in 1814.

In 1842 Pope Gregory XVI named García archbishop coadjutor, to succeed the archbishopric upon the death of Archbishop Ramón Casáus, after it was clear that Casáus would not return to Guatemala from his exile in Havana. Following Casáus's death in late 1845, García was formally installed as archbishop, although he had been acting archbishop since 1844. García's appointment was a setback for the Guatemalan elite and particularly for Juan José de Aycinena, who had expected to be named. Jorge Viteri y Ungo was especially influential in arranging García's appointment as part of a compromise to get papal approval of a separate diocese of El Salvador, of which Viteri was named bishop. In 1861 Pope Pius IX named García Peláez domestic prelate and attending bishop to the pontifical throne, essentially a step below cardinal.

García Peláez wrote a three-volume history of the colonial Kingdom of Guatemala, *Memorias para la historia del antiguo reino de Guatemala,* a work commissioned by Governor Mariano Gálvez.

*See also* **Carrera, José Rafael; Casáus y Torres, Ramón.**

BIBLIOGRAPHY

There is a detailed biographical sketch in *Gaceta de Guatemala* (27 June–25 August 1867). See also Francisco Fernández Hall, "Historiadores de Guatemala posteriores a la independencia nacional: El Doctor Don Francisco de Paula García Peláez," in *Anales de la Sociedad de Geografía e Historia* 15, no. 3 (1939): 261–278; and three articles in *Anales de la Sociedad de Geografía e Historia* 40, no. 1/2 (1967): 15–36, commemorating the centenary of the death of García Peláez: Francisco Gall, "En el centenario del fallecimiento de García Peláez"; Valentín Solórzano Fernández, "García Peláez: Cátedra prima de economía política en el Reino de Guatemala"; and Jorge Luis Arriola, "García Peláez, uno de los precursores del liberalismo económico en Guatemala."

*Additional Bibliography*

Sullivan-Gonzalez, Douglass. *Piety, Power, and Politics: Religion and Nation Formation in Guatemala, 1821–1871.* Pittsburgh: University of Pittsburgh Press, 1998.

RALPH LEE WOODWARD JR.

## GARCÍA PÉREZ, ALAN

**GARCÍA PÉREZ, ALAN** (1949–). Alan García Pérez was the president of Peru from 1985 to 1990 and again beginning in 2006. Born in Lima to middle-class parents active in the American Popular Revolutionary Alliance (APRA; or Partido Aprista Peruano [Peruvian Aprista Party], PAP) and seven when his father was released from political detention, García was active in APRA party politics from an early age. He earned a law degree from Peru's Universidad Nacional Mayor de San Marcos, a doctorate in political science from Universidad Complutense de Madrid, and a sociology degree from the Sorbonne. He won election to the Constituent Assembly in 1978, to the Chamber of Deputies in 1980, and the presidency in 1985, becoming, at thirty-six, Latin America's youngest chief executive.

Despite a promising start, by most accounts García's first presidency was a disaster. His economic reforms foundered after an ill-advised bank nationalization in 1987, and his efforts to stem the advance of the Shining Path insurgency met a similar fate following a prison massacre of some 270 guerrilla inmates by police and military in June 1986. Increased political violence, rapid economic deterioration, and hyperinflation marked his last three years in office. Forced into exile after his successor, Alberto Fujimori, staged a self-coup in April 1992, he spent almost nine years in Colombia and France before Peru's supreme court ruled that the statute of limitations for corruption charges brought against him in the early 1990s had run out.

Restored to the good graces of APRA, which had expelled him in 1994, García returned to Peru in 2001 after Fujimori's fall. He ran for president again but narrowly lost in the runoff. As head of APRA once more, he was selected as its presidential candidate for the April 2006 elections. In a field of twenty in the first round, García finished second—barely besting Lourdes Flores Nano of the National Union (UN) with 24.3 percent to her 23.8 percent—thus qualifying for the June runoff against the first-round winner, populist reformer Ollanta Humala of the Union for Peru (UPP), who received 30.6 percent of the vote. In a particularly vituperative campaign, García's more polished rhetoric and political acumen, combined with the public's fear of what they saw as Humala's radicalism as well as his open support by Venezuelan president Hugo Chávez, won the day (53% of the valid vote for García, 47% for Humala).

As of 2008 it remained to be seen whether García's second presidency will be able to overcome the dark legacy of his first. Without an APRA majority in the unicameral congress (36 of 120 seats, with UPP holding 45) and with the country sharply divided politically between the coast and the north, which supported García, and the central and southern highlands, which backed Humala, effective governance will be a major challenge.

*See also* **Peru, Political Parties: Peruvian Aprista Party (PAP/APRA); Peru, Revolutionary Movements: Shining Path.**

BIBLIOGRAPHY

Crabtree, John. *Peru under García: An Opportunity Lost.* Pittsburgh, PA: University of Pittsburgh Press, 1992.

Partida Aprista Peruano. Official Web site. Available from http://www.apra.org.pe.

DAVID SCOTT PALMER

## GARCÍA ROBLES, ALFONSO (1911–1991).

A Mexican foreign service officer and disarmament specialist, Alfonso García Robles was a native of Zamora, Michoacán. Born on March 20, 1911, García Robles completed his studies in law at the University of Paris, where he was one of two laureates at the Institute of International Studies in 1936. He also received a diploma from the International Law Academy at The Hague in 1938. García Robles joined the diplomatic corps in 1939, serving in a number of foreign assignments and posts within the secretariat of foreign relations. He is considered to have been largely responsible for the Nuclear Arms Treaty of Tlatelolco in 1967. Subsequently he served as Mexico's permanent representative to the United Nations Committee on Disarmament. For his efforts in regional disarmament, he was awarded the Nobel Peace Prize in 1982. He culminated his professional career as secretary of foreign relations (1975–1976), receiving the rank of ambassador emeritus in 1981. He died on September 2, 1991.

*See also* **Tlatelolco; United Nations.**

BIBLIOGRAPHY

*Alfonso García Robles, México, Nobel de la Paz.* Mexico: Secretaria de Educación Pública, 1984.

Marín Bosch, Miguel. *Armas nucleares, desarme y carrera armamentista: Homenaje a Alfonso García Robles.* Mexico: Ediciones Gernika, 1985.

RODERIC AI CAMP

## GARCÍA SALINAS, FRANCISCO (1786–1841).

Francisco García Salinas (*b.* 1786; *d.* 1841), Mexican cabinet minister and governor of the state of Zacatecas. García was born on a hacienda in the state of Zacatecas. As a young man he was involved in the mining business in Zacatecas. In 1821, he was the *regidor* (president) of the *ayuntamiento* (city council) of Zacatecas and was elected to represent the state in the First Constituent Congress of Mexico in 1822. García continued to serve in the Congress as deputy and then as senator from Zacatecas from 1823 to 1827, taking a special interest in financial matters and helping to reestablish Mexico's foreign credit. President Guadalupe Victoria selected García as his minister of the treasury, a post he held for only a few months (2 November 1827 to 15 February 1828) prior to his election as governor of the state of Zacatecas in 1828.

García's administration of Zacatecas was a model of liberal reform that made the state, with its strong militia, one of the bulwarks of the federal system. García attempted to use church property to create a bank for agricultural credit and to use state funds to redistribute agricultural land by dividing large properties for sale. His administration also sought to develop the mining industry and the manufacture of cotton, silk, and woolen textiles. The state of Zacatecas opened new schools under the Lancasterian system of "utilitarian" education and vaccinated thousands of children against smallpox. The defeat of the Zacatecas militia by conservative and centralist forces in 1832 and 1835 marked a turning point in the early republican history of Mexico. After stepping down as governor in 1834, García continued in command of the state's militia. He retired to his hacienda, where he died.

*See also* **Victoria, Guadalupe; Zacatecas.**

BIBLIOGRAPHY

Jesús Romero Flores, *Historia de los estados de la República mexicana* (1964).

Charles A. Hale, *Mexican Liberalism in the Age of Mora* (1968); *Diccionario Porrúa de historia, biografía y geografía de México,* 5th ed. (1986).

### *Additional Bibliography*

Delgado Wise, Raúl, and José Luis España Téllez. *El federalismo de Francisco García Salinas: Una visión no presidencialista.* Zacatecas: Universidad Autónoma de Zacatecas: Centro de Estudios para la Reforma del Estado, 1997.

Salinas Novoa, Carlos. *Francisco García Salinas: Gobernante modelo, modelo de gobernante: Zacatecas 1824–1835.* Zacatecas: Legislatura del Estado de Zacatecas, Gobierno del Estado de Zacatecas, 1991.

D. F. STEVENS

## GARCÍA Y GONZÁLEZ, VICENTE

(1833–1886). Vicente García y González (*b.* 23 January 1833; *d.* 4 March 1886), Cuban general. General García was one of the regional military caudillos who emerged in Cuba during the Ten Years' War (1868–1878). A native of the district of Las Tunas, Oriente Province, he was something of a feudal lord. He led his guerrilla troops to some brilliant victories over the Spanish army, but he was unruly and inconsistent, and his ambition prompted him to launch seditious movements against the insurgent provisional government, finally contributing to its collapse and the ultimate failure of the insurgent effort. García participated in some obscure way in the negotiations with the Spanish that culminated in the end of the war. Afterward he sought refuge in Venezuela, where he spent the rest of his life. He died in Río Chico, Venezuela.

*See also* **Ten Years' War.**

BIBLIOGRAPHY

There are no sources in English. His grandson wrote a book-length biography: Florencio García Cisneros, *El león de Santa Rita: El general Vicente García y la guerra de los diez años, Cuba, 1868–1878* (1988). García's military career is discussed in Fernando Figueredo, *La revolución de Yara* (1969).

### *Additional Bibliography*

Marrero, Victor Manuel, and Vicente García González. *Vicente García: Leyenda y realidad.* Havana: Editorial de Ciencias Sociales, 1992.

JOSÉ M. HERNÁNDEZ

## GARCILASO DE LA VEGA, EL INCA

(1539–1616). El Inca Garcilaso de la Vega (*b.* 12 April 1539; *d.* 22/23 April 1616), Peruvian author and historian. Born in Cuzco, son of Captain Sebastián Garcilaso de la Vega and Inca princess Chimpu Oello, his original name was Gómez Suárez de Figueroa. He studied, along with other mestizo children, under the cathedral canon Juan de Cuellar. About 1552 his father married a wealthy Spaniard, and Garcilaso's Inca mother and siblings were forced to leave the household. His father died in 1559, and the following year the young Garcilaso set sail for Spain, planning to live and study with the support of a small stipend provided by his father's will. He would never return to Peru.

After settling in Montilla, in southern Spain, under the patronage of his uncle, Alonso de Vargas, Garcilaso fought briefly (1570–1571) in Granada during the uprising of the Moriscos of Alpujarras. About 1591 he moved to nearby Córdoba and devoted much of the remainder of his life to writing. His first literary effort was the translation of the *Diálogos de amor* (Dialogues of Love) of Leon Hebreo (Madrid, 1590), which served as a model of stylistic accomplishment. His first history, *La Florida del Inca* (1605), tells the story of the famous Hernando de Soto expedition to what became the southeastern part of the United States. Based on published sources and the oral account of soldier Gonzalo Silvestre, Garcilaso was able to weave a detailed and compelling picture of the trials and tribulations of the Spanish exploration of Florida. When facts were lacking, he created with vivid ingenuity. His next history, the *First Part of the Royal Commentaries of the Incas,* appeared in Lisbon in 1609. Based on recollections of what he learned as a youth in Peru and on written sources, including the chronicle of Blas Valera, this is an articulate and compelling, if not always accurate, account of Inca civilization. With a brilliant prose style, and with the authority of speaking in the native American voice, he attempted to bring Inca institutions and history to the Europeans.

Continued reliance on Garcilaso as a primary source clouds and blurs an authentic vision of Tahuantinsuyu (The Land of the Four Quarters), even in the twentieth century. Indeed, Marcelino Menéndez y Pelayo, in his *Historia de la poesía hispano-americana,* wrote that the *Royal Commentaries* was not really history but might best be classified as a utopian novel. The second part of Garcilaso's commentaries, published one year after his death under the title of *Historia general del Perú* (1617), outlines the Spanish conquest of the Incas to the execution of Túpac Amaru I during the administration of Viceroy Francisco de Toledo (1567–1581). That Garcilaso was the first native American writer to be widely read in Europe, and continues to be read with pleasure and profit in spite of lapses into historical fantasy, is a lasting testament to his superb literary skills.

*See also* **Incas, The; Indigenous Peoples.**

BIBLIOGRAPHY

John Grier Varner, *El Inca: The Life and Times of Garcilaso de la Vega* (1968).

Donald G. Castanien, *El Inca Garcilaso de la Vega* (1969).

Margarita Zamora, *Language, Authority, and Indigenous History in the "Comentarios reales de los Incas"* (1988).

### *Additional Bibliography*

Fernández, Christian. *Inca Garcilaso, imaginación, memoria e identidad.* Lima: Fondo Editorial, Universidad Nacional Mayor de San Marcos, 2004.

Flores Quelopana, Gustavo. *La metafísica de la luz: Claves del primer filósofo mestizo Inca Garcilaso de la Vega.* Lima: Instituto de Investigación para la Paz Cultura e Integración de América Latina, Fondo Editorial, 2005.

Ortega, Esperanza. *Garcilaso de la Vega.* Barcelona: Ediciones Omega, 2003.

Valcárcel, Carlos Daniel. *Garcilaso: El inca humanista.* Lima: Universidad Nacional Mayor de San Marcos, 1995.

Noble David Cook

---

**GARDEL, CARLOS** (1890–1935). Carlos Gardel (*b.* 11 December 1890; *d.* 24 June 1935), arguably Latin America's greatest twentieth-century popular singer and the supreme figure in the story of the Argentine tango. Born in Toulouse, France, he was taken at the age of two by his unmarried mother to Buenos Aires, where he grew up in tenement rooms and on the streets. A naturally gifted baritone, he won local renown in the modest barrios of Buenos Aires before forming a celebrated folk duo with a Uruguayan friend, José Razzano (1887–1960), that lasted from 1913 to 1925.

In the early 1920s, with the development of the tango as a form of popular song, a movement Gardel himself strongly pioneered, he concentrated mostly on the new genre, making hundreds of recordings. Successful visits to Spain in 1925–1926 and 1927–1928 were followed by spectacular triumphs in the cabarets and music halls of Paris in 1928–1929. By now a superstar in Argentina and Uruguay, Gardel went on to gain unrivaled popularity all over Latin America by starring in seven movies, shot in Paris (1931–1932) and New York (1934–1935). These were mediocre, low-budget productions that nonetheless memorably projected Gardel's exceptional vocal talent and winning personality.

While undertaking a tour of countries around the Caribbean in 1935, the star was tragically killed in an airplane collision at Medellín, Colombia. His repatriated remains were accorded a solemn funeral attended by enormous crowds in Buenos Aires. Gardel's memory has been the focus of an assiduously cultivated popular cult. The centennial of his birth, December 1990, was extensively celebrated throughout Latin America.

*See also* **Cinema: From the Silent Film to 1990; Music: Popular Music and Dance.**

BIBLIOGRAPHY

Simon Collier, *The Life, Music, and Times of Carlos Gardel* (1986).

José Gobello, *Tres estudios gardelianos* (1991).

Miguel Ángel Morena, *Historia artística de Carlos Gardel: Estudio cronológico* (1991).

*Additional Bibliography*

Barsky, Julián, and Osvaldo Barsky. *Gardel: La biografía.* Buenos Aires: Taurus, 2004

Contreras, Marily. *Gardel: Es un soplo la vida: Biografía íntima de Carlos Gardel.* Buenos Aires: Libros del Zorzal, 2005.

Ruffinelli, Jorge. *La sonrisa de Gardel: Biografía, mito y ficción.* Montevideo: Ediciones Trilce, 2004.

SIMON COLLIER

**GARIBALDI, GIUSEPPE** (1807–1882). Giuseppe Garibaldi (*b.* 4 July 1807; *d.* 2 June 1882), Italian revolutionary and patriot. Garibaldi was born in Nice (then in Italy), son of Domenico Garibaldi, a sailor, and Rosa Ragiundo. A member of Giuseppe Mazzini's Young Italy, he was forced to flee the country because of his revolutionary activities. After arriving in Rio de Janeiro in 1836, he supported the revolutionary movement in Rio Grande do Sul as a privateer. Garibaldi was wounded during a naval engagement with Uruguayan lighters. After obtaining medical treatment at Gualeguay, Argentina, he returned to Rio Grande to fight alongside the rebels.

In 1841 Garibaldi and Ana María Ribeiro da Silva, a native of Santa Catarina, arrived in Montevideo, with their son Menotti. There they were married (16 June 1842) and had two more children, Riccioti and Teresita. For a few months Garibaldi was a business agent and a history and mathematics instructor; then he assumed command of President Fructuoso Rivera's small navy of five ships. His attempt to challenge Buenos Aires's control of the rivers failed when his ships were destroyed at Costa Bravo by Admiral William Brown on 15 August 1842, marking the end of Rivera's naval power. Garibaldi escaped overland to Montevideo.

During Manuel Oribe's siege of Montevideo, Garibaldi, who held the rank of colonel, organized the Italian Legion of 600 men and a small fleet to protect the port. He successfully kept the bay of Montevideo free of the enemy. In 1844 he commanded one of the three columns that General José María Paz led in an assault on Oribe's position in Cerrito. In 1845 he commanded a fleet of three ships with a landing force of 700 men of the Italian Legion, 200 Montevideo infantrymen under Colonel Lorenzo Batlle, and 100 cavalrymen. Escorted by an Anglo-French squadron, he took and sacked Gualeguaychú, Colonia, and Salto.

Upon returning to Montevideo, Garibaldi was promoted to general (16 February 1846), and briefly commanded the forces defending the city. In August 1847 he returned to Europe to resume his fight for Italian unification. After his defeat in Rome by French forces (1849), he lived in Tangier, New York, Sardinia, and finally Caprera. He resumed his struggle for Italian unification in 1856. Four years later, after the death of Ana María, he married the Marchioness Giuseppina Raimondi. That year, encouraged by the Sardinian minister Camillo Cavour, he went to the aid of the Sicilian revolutionaries. Garibaldi landed at Marsala, and from there went on to capture Palermo and Messina and to establish a provisional government. His dream finally was realized when Italian troops entered Rome in 1870. His *I Mille* (1874) is an account of his campaigns. Garibaldi and his sons fought for France in the Franco-Prussian War. After a brief term as national deputy, he returned to Caprera, where he wrote two novels and his *Memorie Autobiografiche* (*Garibaldi: An Autobiography,* 1860). He married Francisca Armorino in 1880 and died at Caprera.

*See also* **Paz, José María; Rivera, Fructuoso.**

BIBLIOGRAPHY

Jacinto R. Yaben, "Garibaldi, G." in *Biografiás argentinas y sudamericanas,* vol. 2 (1938), pp. 747–751.

Vicente O. Cutolo, "Garibaldi," in *Nuevo diccionario biográfico argentino, 1750–1930,* vol. 3 (1971), pp. 263–265.

Fernando Del Corro, *El Diario* (Paraná), 23 September 1980. In English see Theodore Dwight, *The Life of General Garibaldi, Translated from His Private Papers; with the History of His Splendid Exploits in Rome, Lombardy, Sicily, and Naples, to the Present Time.* (1877); *Autobiography of Giuseppe Garibaldi,* translated by A. Warner, with a supplement by Jessie White Mario, 3 vols. (1889); *The Memoirs of Garibaldi,* edited by Alexandre Dumas, translated with an introduction by R. S. Garnett, with contributions by George Sand and Victor Hugo. (1931).

Peter De Polnay, *Garibaldi: The Man and the Legend.* (1961).

David Glass Larg, *Giuseppe Garibaldi* (1934).

John Lynch, *Argentine Dictator: Juan Manuel de Rosas, 1829–1852* (1981), pp. 193, 275, 280.

Ysabel F. Rennie, *The Argentine Republic* (1945), p. 60.

*Additional Bibliography*

Arellano, Jorge Eduardo. *Giuseppe Garibaldi, héroe de dos mundos, en Nicaragua*. Managua: Ediciones del siglo/JEA, 1999.

Gradenigo, Gaio. *Italianos entre Rosas y Mitre*. Buenos Aires: Ediciones Ediliba, 1987.

Mello, Arnaldo Vieira de. *Os corsários nas guerras do Brasil e o dramático batismo de fogo de Garibaldi*. Rio de Janeiro: Sialul-Consultores Associados, 1992.

JOSEPH T. CRISCENTI

## GARIBAY, PEDRO

**GARIBAY, PEDRO** (1729–1815). Pedro Garibay (*b.* 1729; *d.* 1815), viceroy of Mexico (16 September 1808–19 July 1809). A Madrid-born military officer, Garibay arrived in New Spain after service in Europe and the Caribbean, eventually being promoted to the rank of field marshal before he retired. When Napoleon intervened in Spain in 1808, José de Iturrigaray, viceroy of Mexico, was overthrown because of his pro-Mexican sentiments in a coup led by Spanish merchants and supported by the Mexico City *audiencia* (royal court). As senior military figure in the colony, and thought by the conservatives to be easily manipulated, the elderly, infirm Garibay was appointed viceroy and eventually recognized by the caretaker government in Spain. Though his emasculated government lasted only ten months, he was honored in retirement and granted a large annual pension.

*See also* **Iturrigaray, José de; New Spain, Viceroyalty of.**

BIBLIOGRAPHY

Manuel Rivera Cambas, *Los gobernantes de México,* vol. 3 (1964), pp. 243–255.

Christon I. Archer, *The Army in Bourbon Mexico, 1760–1810* (1977).

Timothy E. Anna, *The Fall of the Royal Government in Mexico City* (1978).

ERIC VAN YOUNG

## GARIBAY KINTANA, ÁNGEL MARÍA

**GARIBAY KINTANA, ÁNGEL MARÍA** (1892–1967). Ángel María Garibay Kintana (*b.* 18 June 1892; *d.* 19 October 1967), Mexican scholar and priest who pioneered in the study and translation of the literary traditions of the ancient Mexicans. Garibay was born in Toluca. While at the Seminario Conciliar de México (1906–1917), he learned Latin and Greek (and later published works on Greek philosophers) and became interested in Nahuatl language and culture. In subsequent years Garibay added Hebrew, French, Italian, German, English, and Otomí, as well as Nahuatl, to his language repertoire. He was ordained in 1917; later (especially 1924–1941) he served as a missionary and became more and more focused on his Nahua and Otomí studies. In 1941 Garibay was named prebendary canon of the Basilica of Guadalupe. From 1956 he served as director of the Seminario de Cultura Nahuatl at the Universidad Nacional. In 1952 he was named extraordinary professor at the Faculty of Philosophy and Letters at the Universidad Nacional. Although he began publishing articles in 1913, his major works appeared from 1940 through 1965; they included *Poesía indígena de la altiplanicie, Llave del Nahuatl* (1940), *Historia de la literatura Nahuatl* (2 vols, 1940), and three important volumes on the songs and poetry of the ancient Mexicans. His numerous translations of Nahuatl prose, historical texts, epic hymns, religious and lyric poetry, *pláticas* (short lectures), and other texts opened new doors to understanding the pre-Hispanic cultures of Mexico, and stimulated intense scholarly and humanistic interest in these arenas. Garibay died in Mexico City.

*See also* **Mexico: Since 1910.**

BIBLIOGRAPHY

Miguel León-Portilla, "Ángel Ma. Garibay K. (1892–1992), en el centenario de su nacimiento," in *Estudios de cultura Nahuatl* 22 (1992):167–180.

*Additional Bibliography*

Herr Solé, Alberto. *Angel María Garibay Kintana, o, La confrontación de los orígenes.* Zinacantepec: El Colegio Mexiquense: Instituto Mexiquense de Cultura, 1992.

León-Portilla, Miguel, and Patrick Johansson. *Angel María Garibay: La rueda y el río.* México: Gobierno del Estado de México, Coordinación General de Communicación Social: Espejo de Obsidiana, 1993.

FRANCES F. BERDAN

## GARIFUNA. *See* Caribs.

## GARIMPO.

Garimpo, a small-scale, informal gold, diamond, and tin placer mining camp. *Garimpos* have been part of the penetration of the Brazilian interior since the first arrival of Europeans. *Garimpagem* (the mining activity itself) has involved primarily the poorer sectors of society, including escaped slaves who, during the colonial period, lived in runaway-slave communities (*quilombos*). *Garimpeiro* (miner) exploration led to major gold and diamond strikes at the beginning of the eighteenth century. Despite sporadic attempts by formal mining companies to mine gold in Brazil since that time, Brazilian gold mining remained dominated by *garimpos* until the 1960s.

In the 1970s, substantial gold deposits were discovered in the Amazon Basin, stimulating an extensive gold rush. Most of the *garimpos* that proliferated throughout the Amazon were run by independent operators; others were financed by wealthy entrepreneurs based in the mining areas or in Brazil's major cities. Though *garimpagem* remained largely within the informal economy, it maintained strong links to the formal economy through the market and purchase of manufactured items. In the late 1980s, *garimpos* contributed up to $1 billion annually to the Brazilian economy.

*Garimpo* technology has been rudimentary, involving the use of shovels, picks, carrying bags, sieves, and pans, and more recently small pump engines to control water. Mercury also has been employed to amalgamate with gold, causing severe ecological degradation of waterways and health problems for *garimpeiros.* Reflecting the widespread competition for resources in Brazil, *garimpos* have been in conflict at times with government and police authorities, large mining companies, native peoples, and the environment.

*See also* **Gold Rushes, Brazil; Mining: Colonial Brazil; Mining: Colonial Spanish America; Mining: Modern.**

BIBLIOGRAPHY

José Veríssimo Da Costa Pereira, "Faiscadores" and "Garimpeiros," in *Tipos e aspectos do Brasil,* 10th ed. (1975), pp. 163–168, 324–326.

G. Rocha, ed., *Em busca de ouro: Garimpos e garimpeiros no Brasil* (1984).

Marianne Schmink, "Social Change in the Garimpo," in *Change in the Amazon Basin: The Frontier After a Decade of Colonization,* edited by John Hemming, vol. 2 (1985), pp. 185–199; David Cleary, *Anatomy of the Amazon Gold Rush* (1990).

*Additional Bibliography*

Higgins, Kathleen J. *"Licentious Liberty" in a Brazilian Gold-mining Region: Slavery, Gender, and Social Control in Eighteenth-century Sabará, Minas Gerais.* University Park: Pennsylvania State University Press, 1999.

Mathis, Armin, and Regine Rehaag. *Conseqüências da garimpagem no âmbito social e ambiental da Amazônia.* Belém, Brazil: Buntstift e.V; FASE: Katalyse.

Santos, Márcio. *Estradas reais: Introdução ao estudo dos caminhos do ouro e do diamante no Brasil.* Belo Horizonte, Brazil: Editora Estrada Real, 2001.

ROBERT WILCOX

## GARMENDIA, FRANCISCO.

Francisco Garmendia, nineteenth-century capitalist and early industrialist, Peruvian born in Argentina. In 1861, Garmendia established one of the first factories in Latin America, a textile factory in Lucre; he imported industrial machines from France and, in an impressive feat of entrepreneurship, transported them by mule across the southern Andes of Peru to the town of Quispicanchis, near Cuzco. The factory replaced the old colonial textile mills (*obrajes*) of that region. The woolen textile it produced was of a coarse quality targeted for purchase by the Indian population. The factory had chronic financial and technical problems and faced increasing competition by export-import commercial firms based in Arequipa, but remained in business as the only factory in Cuzco Department up to 1898.

*See also* **Textile Industry: The Colonial Era.**

BIBLIOGRAPHY

Alberto Flores Galindo, *Arequipa y el sur andino: Ensayo de historia regional (siglos XVIII–XX)* (1977).

*Additional Bibliography*

Contreras, Carlos. *El aprendizaje del capitalismo: Estudios de historia económica y social del Perú republicano.* Lima: IEP Ediciones, 2004.

Escandell Tur, Neus. *Producción y comercio de tejidos coloniales: Los obrajes y chorrillos del Cusco, 1570-1820.* Cusco, Perú: Centro de Estudios Regionales Andinos, Bartolomé de Las Casas, 1997.

Alfonso W. Quiroz

## GARMENDIA, SALVADOR (1928–2001).

Salvador Garmendia (*b.* 1928; *d.* 13 May 2001), Venezuelan novelist and short-story writer. One of Venezuela's major fiction writers of the twentieth century, Garmendia published more than a dozen books. Although he is recognized by writers and critics alike, Garmendia has never been included among the writers of the Boom of Latin American literature in the 1960s and 1970s. Consequently, his fiction is far better known in the Hispanic world than in the United States, particularly his novels *Los pequeños seres* (1959), *Día de cenizas* (1963), *Los habitantes* (1968), and *El Capitán Kid* (1988).

The masterly use of a precise point of view makes Garmendia one of Latin America's best exponents of the narrative technique of the French *nouveau roman.* In his early novels, he portrays alienated characters in urban environments. The protagonist in *Los pequeños seres* becomes so desperate with his circumstances that he commits suicide. Protagonists in his other early fiction include such characters as an unemployed truck driver and a frustrated writer. In his later fiction, such as *El Capitán Kid* (1988), *Crónicas sádicas* (1990), and *Cuentos cómicos* (1991), Garmendia's tone is less anguished and often ironic and quite humorous. In 1989, he was awarded the Juan Rolfo Prize for his book *Tan desuda como una piedra.*

*See also* **Literature: Spanish America.**

BIBLIOGRAPHY

John S. Brushwood, *The Spanish American Novel: A Twentieth-Century Survey* (1975).

Giuseppe Bellini, *Historia de la literatura hispanoamericana* (1985).

George Mc Murray, *Spanish American Writing Since 1941* (1987).

*Additional Bibliography*

Rodriguez, Yesenia M. *La narrativa de Salvador Garmendia: Más allá de la razón.* Lewiston, NY. Edwin Mellen Press, 1997.

Vestrini, Miyó. *Salvador Garmendia.* Caracas: Grijalbo, 1994.

Raymond Leslie Williams

## GARRIDO CANABAL, TOMÁS (1891–1943).

Tomás Garrido Canabal (*b.* 20 September 1891; *d.* 1943), radical Mexican provincial politician who dominated political life in the Gulf state of Tabasco in the 1920s and early 1930s. He is most remembered for his fanatical persecution of Catholic priests during the church-state conflict in the 1920s.

Born in Catazajá, Chiapas, Garrido studied law in Campeche and Mérida before serving as interim governor in 1919. He was governor of Tabasco from 1923 to 1926, senator (1927–1930), and governor once again from 1931 to 1934. With the support of his own Red Shirt movement, he took such extreme steps against priests as to prompt an investigation by the English Roman Catholic novelist Graham Greene, which resulted in Greene's famous 1940 work *The Power and the Glory.*

Garrido joined General Lazaro Cárdenas's first cabinet as secretary of agriculture (1934–1935). He refused Cárdenas's offer of a continued post in the cabinet, shortly after which his mentor, General Plutarco Calles, was forced to leave Mexico. Garrido went into voluntary exile in Costa Rica, from which he returned to Mexico in 1940.

*See also* **Calles, Plutarco; Mexico: Since 1910.**

BIBLIOGRAPHY

Baltasar Dromundo, *Tomás Garrido, su vida y su leyenda* (1953).

Graham Greene, *The Lawless Roads* (1955, repr. 1992).

Alan M. Kirshner, "Tomás Garrido Canabal and the Mexican Red Shirt Movement" (Master's thesis, New York University, 1970).

Pepe Bulnes, *Gobernantes de Tabasco* (1979).

*Additional Bibliography*

Harper, Kristin A. "Revolutionary Tabasco in the time of Tomás Garrido Canabal, 1922–1935: A Mexican House Divided." Ph.D. diss., University of Massachusetts, Amherst, 2004.

Torres Vera, María Trinidad. *Mujeres y utopía: Tabasco garridista*. Villahermosa: Universidad Juárez Autónoma de Tabasco, 2001.

Tostado Gutiérrez, Marcela. *El intento de liberar a un pueblo: Educación y magisterio tabasqueño con Garrido Canabal, 1924–1935*. Mexico City: Instituto Nacional de Antropología e Historia, 1991.

RODERIC AI CAMP

## GARRIDO-LECCA SEMINARIO, CELSO

**GARRIDO-LECCA SEMINARIO, CELSO** (1926–). Celso Garrido-Lecca Seminario (*b.* 9 March 1926), Peruvian composer. Born in Piura, Peru, Garrido-Lecca was a student of Rodolfo Holzmann until moving to Chile, where he studied under Free Focke and Domingo Santa Cruz. He also studied orchestration with Aaron Copland in the United States. Later, at the Theater Institute of the University of Chile, he served as musical adviser, composition teacher, and composer. After the fall of the government of President Salvador Allende in 1973, he returned to Peru. He has taught at the National Conservatory in Lima and has represented Peru at various international events, including the Second Encuentros de Música Latinoamericana (Cuba, 1972) and the First International Rostrum of Latin American Music (TRIMALCA) International Music Council (IMC; Colombia, 1979). The music of Garrido-Lecca is often aleatoric, and utilizes modern signs and methods of notation. Garrido-Lecca has composed works for orchestra, string quartet, and piano, as well as chamber music and incidental music for theater and films. In October 2000 Garrido-Lecca receieved the Tomás Luis de Victoria award given to the best Ibero-American composer by the General Society of Authors and Publishers of Spain (SGAE).

*See also* **Music: Art Music; Musical Instruments.**

BIBLIOGRAPHY

John Vinton, ed., *Dictionary of Contemporary Music* (1971).

Samuel Claro Valdés, *Historia de la música en Chile* (1973).

Gérard Béhague, *Music in Latin America: An Introduction* (1979).

*Additional Bibliography*

Garrido-Lecca, Celso. "Rodolfo Holzmann habla de música peruana: Una conversación con Celso Garrido-Lecca." *Hueso Húmero* 43 (Dec. 2003): 67–76.

Véjar Pérez-Rubio, Carlos, Kaarina Véjar Amarillas, and Manuel de Elías. *Contrapuntos: Colegio de Compositores Latinoamericanos de Música de Arte, su nacimiento.* Mexico City: Archipiélago, 2000.

SERGIO BARROSO

## GARRINCHA

**GARRINCHA** (1933–1983). Garrincha led Brazil's national soccer team to World Cup victories in 1958 and 1962. Christened Manuel dos Santos in the rural factory town of Pau Grande, Rio de Janeiro, the nickname "Garrincha" derived from an ungainly songbird. The ultimate mestizo, Garrincha descended from Fulniô Indians as well as African and European ancestors. Despite being born in relative poverty and with contorted legs, he became a largely self-taught soccer genius in Pau Grande. Botafogo Soccer Club contracted Garrincha at age nineteen, and he became an instant sensation because of his ability to confound defenders with magical shimmies, feints, and dribbles that created unpredictable scoring opportunities. His inimitable style became legendary during the 1958 World Cup tournament when his wily moves left the world's best defenders reeling. He was voted the outstanding player of the 1962 World Cup when injury sidelined his now more remembered teammate Pelé. Garrincha's simple manners and artfully impish play earned him the popular epithets "the people's pride and joy" and the "Chaplin of soccer." His career reached its apogee in 1962, but he played professionally into the early 1970s. Debilitated by alcohol abuse and hounded by family scandal and financial problems off the field, Garrincha played past his prime, tarnishing the memory of his halcyon days. He died of pulmonary edema at age forty-nine.

*See also* **Pelé; Sports.**

BIBLIOGRAPHY

Castro, Ruy. *Estrela Solitária: Um brasileiro chamado Garrincha.* São Paulo: Companhia das Letras, 1995.

PETER M. BEATTIE

**GARRO, ELENA** (1920–1998). Elena Garro (*b.* 11 December 1920; *d.* 22 August 1998), Mexican novelist, short-story writer, and playwright. Although Garro spent much of her adult life in Spain and France, her writing reflects Mexican society, which she views pessimistically. Her coupling of detailed realistic descriptions and nightmarish fantasies places her among the magical realists. In her first book, *Los recuerdos del porvenir* (1963), she re-creates her hometown, Iguala, which she sees as a microcosm of Mexican society: desperate, defeated, and doomed. Garro actually wrote the book in the 1950s and published it later, with the encouragement of Octavio Paz, her husband from 1937 to 1959. Her first collection of stories, *La semana en colores* (1964), draws on Indian beliefs. Her second, *Andamos huyendo Lola* (1980), combines childhood memories with fantasy to create a kind of hell in which characters are constantly fleeing and scrounging for food. *Testimonios sobre Mariana* (1981) captures the anguish of modern society and parodies the bourgeois intellectual. *Reencuentro de personajes* (1982) examines the sober themes of violence, sexual manipulation, and psychological torture. In *La casa junto al río* (1983), Garro returns to her childhood village, still steeped in pettiness and mediocrity. *Y matarazo no llamó*, written in 1960 but published in 1991, is a kind of political thriller with existential undercurrents: the main character, an alienated loner, is lured into a political snare that drives him mad and leads him to an absurd end. Garro wrote a number of one-act as well as full-length plays featuring avant-garde techniques. *Felipe Angeles* (1979) is a three-act work that presents a negative view of the Mexican Revolution.

*See also* **Literature: Spanish America; Paz, Octavio.**

BIBLIOGRAPHY

Frank Dauster, "El teatro de Elena Garro: Evasión e ilusión," in *Ensayos sobre el teatro hispanoamericano* (1975), pp. 66–77.

Beth Miller and A. González, "Elena Garro," in *26 autoras del México actual* (1978), pp. 199–219.

Monique Lemaitre, "El deseo de la muerte y la muerte del deseo en la obra de Elena Garro: Hacia una definición de la escritura femenina en su obra," *Revista Iberoamericana* 55 (1989): 1005–1017.

Robert K. Anderson, "Recurrent Themes in Two Novels by Elena Garro," *Selecta* 11 (1990): 83–86.

Anita K. Stoll, ed., *A Different Reality: Studies on the Work of Elena Garro* (1990).

Anita K. Stoll, "The Old World vs. the New: Cultural Conflict in Four Works of Elena Garro," *Letras Peninsulares* 5 (1991): 95–106.

*Additional Bibliography*

León, Margarita. *La memoria del tiempo: La experiencia del tiempo y del espacio en Los recuerdos del porvenir de Elena Garro.* Mexico City: Universidad Nacional Autónoma de México, Instituto de Investigaciones Filológicas: Ediciones Coyoacán, S.A. de C.V., 2004.

Melgar-Palacios, Lucía, and Gabriela Mora, editors. *Elena Garro: Lectura múltiple de una personalidad complejas.* Puebla: Benemérita Universidad Autónoma de Puebla, Dirección General de Fomento Editorial, 2002.

Rosas Lopátegui, Patricia. *Testimonios sobre Elena Garro: Biografía exclusiva y autorizada de Elena Garro.* Monterrey: Ediciones Castillo, 2002.

Winkler, Julie A. *Light into Shadow: Marginality and Alienation in the Work of Elena Garro.* New York: P. Lang, 2001.

BARBARA MUJICA

**GARRO, JOSÉ DE** (1623–c. 1702). José de Garro (*b.* 1623; *d.* c. 1702), governor of Buenos Aires (1678–1682). Garro was born in Guipúzcoa, in the Basque country of northern Spain. He saw intense action in the wars in Portugal and Catalonia. In 1671 he came to America to govern Tucumán, where he was outstanding for his role in public works and in Indian fighting. As governor of Buenos Aires, Garro was responsible for confronting the advance of the Portuguese, who in 1680 had founded the colony of Sacramento in the eastern territory. Garro stormed the colony and took its founder, Manuel Lobo, prisoner. Later he served for ten years as governor of Chile (1682–1691), where his rule was particularly notable for the conversion of Indians. He went on to become military commander of Gibraltar (1693–1702) and finally of his homeland, Guipúzcoa (1702), where he died.

BIBLIOGRAPHY

Montaner y Simón, ed., *Diccionario enciclopédico hispano-americano* (1938).

Enrique Udaondo, *Diccionario biográfico colonial Argentino* (1945).

*Additional Bibliography*

Assunção, Fernando O. *Etopeya y tragedia de Manuel Lobo: Biografía del fundador de Colonia del Sacramento, 1635–1683.* Montevideo: Linardi y Risso, 2003.

Retamal Avila, Julio. *Testamentos de indios en Chile colonial, 1564–1801.* Santiago de Chile: Universidad Andrés Bello, Departamento de Derechos Intelectuales de Chile, 2000.

José de Torres Wilson

**GARVEY, MARCUS** (1887–1940). Marcus Garvey (*b.* 17 August 1887; *d.* 10 June 1940), Pan-African nationalist. Garvey was born in Saint Ann's Bay, Jamaica, to a comfortable family, possibly descendants of maroons. He attended school until the age of fourteen, when a financial crisis in his family obliged him to go to work as a printer's apprentice. By the age of nineteen, he had mastered the skills of this trade, which he was able to use later in his career as a publicist and propagandist in the cause of black nationalism. Between 1910 and 1914 he traveled in the Caribbean and Central America and resided in London. It was during this period that his political ideas took shape. In 1914 he returned to Jamaica and founded the Universal Negro Improvement Association (UNIA), which was received with little enthusiasm. In 1916, Garvey decided to travel to the United States, where his ideas gave rise to an important mass movement for the dignity and independence of blacks. In 1918 he formed a branch of UNIA in New York City and began the publication of the weekly *Negro World,* which quickly attained a large, international circulation. With the hope of aiding communication between African Americans and Africans, and to help further his "Back to Africa" vision, he founded the Black Star shipping line in 1919.

In 1920 UNIA reached its high point when it held its first international convention in New York. As the organization grew in size and importance, it faced increasing repression from U.S. authorities and from the European colonial powers that controlled Africa and the West Indies. Moreover, problems within UNIA derailed Garvey's plans. By 1921 the Black Star Line was a fiasco, as were efforts to colonize Africa and other projects begun in the United States. In 1923 the U.S. government accused Garvey of fraud, and he was sent to prison in 1925. In 1927 his sentence was commuted and he was deported to Jamaica. Although he continued his fight there and in London, where he relocated in 1935, he never regained the international influence he had had at the beginning of the 1920s. By the time of his death in London, he was forgotten.

The importance of Garveyism is that it was the first movement of the black masses based on black pride and dignity. Its international character also was significant. UNIA had branches in the countries of the Caribbean and Central America and was well received by the migrant plantation workers of the West Indies and Jamaica. Garvey is remembered as the forerunner of black nationalism in Africa and in the United States.

BIBLIOGRAPHY

David Cronon, *Black Moses: The Story of Marcus Garvey and the Universal Negro Improvement Association* (1955).

Theodore G. Vincent, *Black Power and the Garvey Movement* (1971).

Judith Stein, *The World of Marcus Garvey: Race and Class in Modern Society* (1986).

*Additional Bibliography*

Conyers, James L. *Reevaluating the Pan-Africanism of W. E. B. DuBois and Marcus Garvey: Escapist Fantasy or Relevant Reality.* Lewiston, NY: Edwin Mellen Press, 2005.

Giovannetti, Jorge L., and Reinaldo L. Román. "Special Issue: Garveyism and the Universal Negro Association in the Hispanic Caribbean." *Caribbean Studies* 31 (2004).

Stephens, Michelle Ann. *Black Empire: The Masculine Global Imaginary of Caribbean Intellectuals in the United States, 1914–1962.* Durham, NC: Duke University Press, 2005.

VÍCTOR ACUÑA

**GARZA SADA FAMILY.** Garza Sada Family, major Mexican entrepreneurial family. The original head of probably the single most influential and extensive capitalist family in Mexico was Isaac Garza Garza, the son of Juan de la Garza Martínez, mayor of Monterrey, and Manuela Garza, Jewish immigrants from Spain who had settled in the region of Monterrey, Nuevo León. After studying merchandizing in Santander, Spain, he went into the grocery business with José Calderón, who married his aunt. Isaac married Consuelo Sada Muguerza, daughter of Francisco Sada Gómez, and in 1899 founded with his father-in-law Fábrica de Vidrios y Cristales de Monterrey, of which he became president. With other partners, he established a number of major firms at the turn of the century, including Cervecería Cuauhtémoc (1890), whose partners, often related by marriage, included José A. Muguerza and Francisco Sada, and the Fundidora de Fierro y Acero, with Vicente Ferrara.

His union with Consuelo produced numerous children, among them Eugenio Garza Sada, Isaac Garza Sada, and Roberto Garza Sada. Eugenio, the oldest of this generation, took over the leadership of a major group of interlocking corporations, which became known popularly as the "Monterrey Group." These included the original brewery, Cervecería Cuauhtémoc; a bottling company, Hojalata y Lámina; and Empaques de Cartón Titán, a packaging firm. Another son, Isaac, took over another set of firms, and also developed his own businesses. These children, in turn, intermarried with other prominent Monterrey families, including the Laguera and Sepúlveda families.

The untimely death of Eugenio Garza Sada, who was murdered in September 1973, served as a catalyst in breaking up the beer, glass, and steel empire into four separate, but complementary, holding companies. All of these conglomerates rank among the top fifty companies in Mexico. The most famous of these groups, the ALFA industrial group, the largest in Latin America in the early 1980s, was founded by Bernardo Garza Sada, grandson of Isaac and son of Roberto. The other components are led by VITRO, VISA, controlled by the Garza Laguera family, and the CYDSA group, presided over by the Sada Zambrano family. The Garza Sadas continue to be a dominant force among Mexican capitalists, as shareholders and board members of leading industrial firms, as members of entrepreneurial interest groups, as leaders of business organizations, and as managers of major industrial holding groups.

BIBLIOGRAPHY

Isidro Vizcaya Canales, *Los orígenes de la industrialización de Monterrey* (1971).

Menno Vellinga, *Economic Development and the Dynamics of Class: Industrialization, Power and Control in Monterrey, Mexico* (1979).

Alex Saragoza, *The Monterrey Elite and the Mexican State, 1880–1940* (1988).

Roderic Ai Camp, *Entrepreneurs and Politics in Twentieth Century Mexico* (1989).

*Additional Bibliography*

Fernández Menéndez, Jorge. *Nadie supo nada: La verdadera historia del asesinato de Eugenio Garza Sada.* Mexico, D.F.: Grijalbo/Actualidad, 2006.

Franco Sáenz, Héctor. *Los beneméritos de Nuevo León.* Monterrey, Mexico: Comité de Archivo y Biblioteca, Congreso del Estado de Nuevo León, 2003.

Medina, Enriqueta, and Federico Arreola. *Don Roberto Garza Sada: La pasión por la excelencia.* Monterrey, México: Gobierno del Estado de Nuevo León, 1994.

RODERIC AI CAMP

**GASCA, PEDRO DE LA** (1493–1567). Pedro de la Gasca (*b.* August 1493; *d.* 10 November 1567), president of the Audiencia of Lima and bishop of Palencia and Sigüenza. Born in a hamlet in Ávila, Spain, Gasca briefly attended the University of Salamanca before leaving in 1508 to attend the recently founded University of Alcalá de Henares, where he received a master of theology. He continued in Alcalá as *colegial* in the Colegio Mayor of San Ildefonso. In 1522 he returned to

Salamanca to complete a study of law and in 1528 served briefly as rector of Salamanca.

In 1531, Gasca became affiliated with the Colegio Mayor de San Bartolomé, where he assumed the duties of rector for two terms. He received a prebend in Salamanca's cathedral (1531) and was named *maestrescuela* (teacher of divinity). Returning to Alcalá in 1537 as *vicario* (vicar), he was placed under the tutelage of Francisco de los Cobos, secretary of Holy Roman Emperor Charles V. Shortly thereafter he became general inspector of Valencia and, in 1540, justice of the Council of the Inquisition. Gasca served well in both capacities, impressing Cobos, who saw in him the qualities necessary to pacify Peru, then in the throes of rebellion. In late 1545 Gasca accepted the royal commission naming him president of the Audiencia of Lima and giving him power to offer pardons and make grants. He also was empowered to revoke the onerous chapter 30 of the New Laws, which prohibited inheritance of *encomiendas,* and to authorize new *entradas.* In addition he had general power to grant all types of office and to conduct any business in the name of the monarch.

Gasca left Spain in April 1546. When he reached Santa Marta, Colombia, on 10 July he learned of the execution of Viceroy Blasco Núñez Vela after the battle of Añaquito (18 January 1546). In Panama he entered into negotiations with Pizarrists, convincing many to abandon the rebels. By April 1547, when he headed south, he had gained the support of the Pacific fleet under Admiral Hinojosa. When they first landed, they discovered that several important cities in the north already had declared for the royalist cause. On 30 June Gasca reached Tumbes, on Peru's north coast, with a substantial force. During their one-and-a-half month's stay, Lima declared for the royalists, and the Pizarrists left for the highlands.

Gasca established military headquarters at Jauja, by which time he had collected 700 harquebusiers, 500 pikemen, and 400 horsemen. News of a stunning defeat of the royalist force (20 October 1547) under Diego de Centeno at Huarina, to the south, failed to discourage Gasca's forces. The final battle between Gonzalo Pizarro and Gasca (9 April 1548) on the plain of Jaquijahuana, not far west of Cuzco, ended in royalist triumph; most Pizarrists threw down their arms and surrendered. Gonzalo Pizarro and his leading commander Francisco de Carvajal, along with some 48 principal leaders, were executed; 350 rebels were sent to labor in the galleys; and 700 were exiled from Peru.

In July 1548, Gasca retired with his secretary and Archbishop Loaysa to the hamlet of Guaynarima to distribute the spoils (Indian *encomiendas*) to the victors. He then departed for Lima, leaving the archbishop to announce the awards in Cuzco. The results shocked most royalists, two-thirds of whom received no grants, while some rebels who returned to the crown at the last moment were well rewarded. In May 1548 Gasca ordered a general inspection and tribute assessment for the *encomiendas.* The first systematic census to be undertaken and largely completed, it began in March 1549, with two inspectors for each district. Gasca's purpose was to increase yet stabilize tribute collection and to protect the Native Americans as much as possible.

Gasca restored the administration of justice under firm royal authority. He licensed new expeditions, one of which led to the foundation of the city of La Paz, Bolivia. He also named Pedro de Valdivia governor and captain-general of Chile, thus recognizing him as conqueror of that land. Most important for the crown, he carried back an enormous treasure. Shipment of the king's fifth had long been delayed as a result of Peru's civil wars. Gasca left Lima in January 1550 and reached Seville in September. In November he reported to the Council of the Indies in Valladolid, where he was ordered to inform directly Charles V, who was then in Flanders. On 6 April, while he was in Barcelona preparing to travel to Germany, Gasca became bishop of Palencia. He sailed to Genoa, then north to Mantua, where he met Prince Philip in June. Passing through Trent, where the church council was in session, Gasca finally met Charles V (Charles I of Spain) at Augsburg on 2 July 1551. The emperor received him with gratitude, for Gasca had restored a rebellious colony and provided the treasure that would allow Charles V to continue his imperial religious and political policies in the heart of Europe.

Gasca returned to Spain early in 1553 and assumed his post at Palencia on 6 March. He was asked to report to the Council of the Indies several times in following years, and in 1556 he was called on by Charles V to escort his sisters, Queen Leonor of France and Queen Maria of Hungary, to interview the Infanta Maria of Portugal in Badajoz. Named Bishop of Sigüenza in 1561, he served there until his death at the age of seventy-four.

Pedro de la Gasca is buried in a beautiful stone coffin bearing his effigy in the center of the church of Santa María Magdalena, which he built in Valladolid.

*See also* **New Laws of 1542; Valdivia, Pedro de.**

BIBLIOGRAPHY

Juan Cristóbal Calvete De Estrella, *Rebelión de Pizarro en el Perú y vida de don Pedro Gasca* (1963–1965).

Teodoro Hampe Martínez, *Don Pedro de la Gasca (1493–1567), su obra política en España y América* (1989).

*Additional Bibliography*

Brunke, Jose de la Puente. *Encomienda y Encomenderos en el Perú: Estudio social y político de una institución colonial.* Seville: Publicaciones de la Excma. Diputación Provinical de Sevilla, 1992.

NOBLE DAVID COOK

**GASOHOL INDUSTRY.** *Gasohol* is the term for varying blends of gasoline and ethyl alcohol (ethanol) and can also describe any mixture of other petroleum fuels containing ethanol or methanol. In the United States, ethanol obtained from corn was used after the fuel shortage in the aftermath of the Arab oil embargo (1973–1974). The real story of gasohol as an industry, however, dates back to World War I in Brazil, with the production of ethanol from sugarcane for use in gasohol. Another spurt of mandated gasohol use occurred during the worldwide depression of the 1930s and again during World War II, because of uncertain oil supplies, but gasohol use evaporated in the 1950s with the availability of low-cost oil from the Middle East. It was not until the October 1973 oil price explosion coincidental with war in the Middle East that renewed attention was paid to renewable fuels. Brazil had to respond to balance-of-payments problems due to rising costs of oil imports, which significantly constrained economic development. In 1975 the country launched the largest initiative in the world to produce ethanol. The National Alcohol Program—Proálcool—had technical, economic, and social consequences. It created new technology in refining, agriculture, and transportation. It saved hard currency by reducing oil imports while creating new jobs, improving workers' incomes overall, and reducing pollution.

The oil crisis had been the catalyst for Proálcool, but developments in the sugar industry were also seminal. In that period, traditional cane sugar exports were declining with falling world prices. The replacement of sugar with ethanol production displaced imported oil and reduced world sugar supplies. Moreover, sugarcane has a highly favorable energy balance when ethanol is produced. Processing is self-sufficient because the caloric value of generated bagasse is sufficient to provide more than the fuel for refinery operations. The Brazilian Ethanol Producers' Special Committee reported that solar energy on one acre of sugarcane yields an average of 602 gallons of ethanol, while the same energy on one acre of corn yields only 375 gallons.

After the first decade, Proálcool, though remaining controversial, created over 2 million jobs directly and indirectly. Wages increased throughout Brazil; rural migration into urban centers was stemmed; higher-yield sugarcane varieties were developed; better management improved soil use and distillery processes and gave a higher yield of fermentation.

Gasohol in Brazil contains as much as 80% ethanol; undiluted ethanol is also used in vehicles with specially adapted engines. In its various forms in Brazil, where it is known as *álcool*, it is a national achievement. It has increased the domestic content of fuels, displaced imported oil (saving an estimated $8.5 billion on oil imports with subsequent annual savings exceeding $1 billion), and provided benefits for workers and industry. Ethanol is a renewable, but expensive fuel; government subsidies to offset high production costs were required to make gasohol competitive in established gasoline markets. The required subsidy depends on the price of petroleum. The oil price collapse in 1986 made the gasohol subsidy an economic catastrophe for the Brazilian government. In the late 1980s ethanol-fueled cars held 90 percent of the market, but demand fell sharply in the 1990s. After that, production costs fell and the investment paid off. Brazil is considered to be at the forefront of alternative energy. When oil prices rose in the twenty-first century, Brazilian consumers turned to the less expensive álcool and gás. Many converted their cars to run on mixed fuels. In addition to the cheaper conversion kits, "flex-fuel" cars that run on gas or ethanol have been available since 2003. As of 2007, 40 percent of the fuel used by cars in Brazil came from ethanol. High oil prices, war in the Middle East, and environmental distress have focused international attention on Brazil's forward-thinking energy policies, bolstered by an agreement between the United States and Brazil to expand global energy markets for ethanol-based fuel.

*See also* **Energy.**

BIBLIOGRAPHY

Dario Scuka, *The Economics of Gasohol* (1979).

Steven J. Winston, *Ethanol Fuels: Use, Production and Economics* (1981).

The Royal Society of Canada, *International Symposium on Ethanol from Biomass,* Winnipeg, Canada, 13–15 October 1982.

Harry Rothman, Rod Greenshields, and Francisco Rosillo Calle, *The Alcohol Economy: Fuel Ethanol and the Brazilian Experience* (1983).

World Bank, *Economic Aspects of the Alcohol Programme* (1984).

R. Serôa Da Motta, *A Social-Cost Benefit Study of Ethanol Production in Brazil,* Department of Economics, University College London, Discussion Paper No. 86.02 (1986).

Michael R. Leblanc, *Ethanol: Economic and Policy Tradeoffs* (1988).

Comissão Nacional De Energia, *Política de combustíveis líquidos automotivos* (1988).

Dario Scuka, *Ethanol Imports and the "Gasohol" Connection: Historical Background and Analysis in an International Perspective, 1978–1989* (1990).

*Additional Bibliography*

Audinet, Pierre. *L'état entrepreneur en Inde et au Brésil: Économie du sucre et de l'éthanol.* Montréal: l'Harmattan, 1998.

Barzelay, Michael. *The Politicized Market Economy: Alcohol in Brazil's Energy Strategy.* Berkeley: University of California Press, 1986.

Demetrius, F. Joseph. *Brazil's National Alcohol Program: Technology and Development in an Authoritarian Regime.* New York: Praeger, 1990.

Rotstein, Jaime. *Brasilesclerose.* Rio de Janeiro: Editora Nova Fronteira, 1993.

DARIO SCUKA

## GASTÃO D'ORLÉANS (1842–1922).

Gastão d'Orléans (Luís Filipe Maria Fernando, Conde d'Eu; *b.* 28 April 1842; *d.* 28 August 1922), husband to Isabel, heir to the Brazilian throne. A member of the French royal family, the Conde d'Eu spent his early years in exile, first in England and then in Spain, where he trained as an army officer, fighting in Morocco. Family connections—his uncle married Pedro II's sister—and personal qualities led to his marriage in 1864 to Isabel. Hard working, cultured, and liberal in political outlook, Conde d'Eu at first sought an active role in Brazilian affairs, which Pedro II denied him. In 1869 he was named commander in chief of Brazil's forces in the War of the Triple Alliance, and he secured total victory in 1870. His war experience left him psychologically insecure and subject to recurring depression, and he restricted himself thereafter to family affairs and to chairing a few army commissions. Despite his considerable talents, he did not shine in public life, in part owing to growing deafness. His lack of charisma and his erratic treatment of subordinates meant that he did not command support or sympathy. The Conde d'Eu never ceased to be an outsider in Brazil. After the empire's fall in 1889, he spent his final years in contented privacy in France.

*See also* **War of the Triple Alliance.**

BIBLIOGRAPHY

Alberto Rangel, *Gastão de Orléans (o ultimo conde d'Eu)* (São Paulo, 1935).

Alfredo D'escragnarolle Taunay, Visconde De Taunay, *Memórias* (Rio de Janeiro, 1960), pp. 308–314.

*Additional Bibliography*

Barman, Roderick J. *Citizen Emperor: Pedro II and the Making of Brazil, 1825–91.* Stanford, CA: Stanford University Press, 1999.

Costa, Revilio. *As Colônias italianas Dona Isabel e Conde d'Eu.* Porto Alegre: Escola Superior de Teologia, 1992.

Santos, Armando Alexandre dos. "Conselhos do conde d'Eu ao 'príncipe perfeito'." *Revista do Instituto Histórico e Geográfico Brasileiro* 159 (January–March 1998): 79–84.

RODERICK J. BARMAN

**GATÓN ARCE, FREDDY** (1920–1994). Freddy Gatón Arce (*b.* 27 March 1920; *d.* 22 July 1994), Dominican poet. Born in San Pedro de Macoris, Gatón was the longest surviving champion of La Poesía Sorprendida, a movement that in the 1940s set out to reform Dominican poetry by transcending the local reality and embracing new and regenerative influences from European and American literatures. His enigmatic prose poem *Vlía* (1944), a text credited with introducing to the country the poetic form of automatic writing, which makes no concessions to the reader's understanding, highlights the kinship of Gatón Arce to the poets of Dada and surrealism. Despite the hermetism of his early work, his subsequent texts are more accessible to the uninitiated reader, with themes that manifest a concern with love, the downtrodden, and the relationship between the matter and spirit. His poetry, partly collected in *Retiro hacia la luz: poesía 1944–1979* (1980), continued to evolve; a dozen volumes have appeared in print since 1980. A lawyer by profession, Gatón Arce was also a professor, an administrator at the Autonomous University of Santo Domingo, and the director of the newspaper *El Nacional.* He is acclaimed for having enriched journalistic prose in the Dominican Republic.

*See also* **Literature: Spanish America.**

BIBLIOGRAPHY

Alberto Baeza Flores, *La poesía dominicana en el siglo XX: 1943–1947* (1977).

José Alcántara Almánzar, *Estudios de poesía dominicana* (1979).

María Del C. Prosdocimi De Rivera, *La poesía de Freddy Gatón Arce: Una interpretación* (1983).

*Additional Bibliography*

Belliard, Basilio. *La espiral sonora: Antología del poema en prosa en Santo Domingo, 1900–2000.* Dominican Republic: Ediciones Librería La Trinitaria, 2003.

Gatón Arce, Freddy, and Andrés Blanco Díaz. *Opinión editorial, El Nacional, 1966–1974.* Santo Domingo: Ediciones de la Fundación Corripio, 2003.

SILVIO TORRES-SAILLANT

**GAUCHESCA LITERATURE.** Gauchesca Literature, a literary form invented by writers living in the city of Buenos Aires who recreated the speech characteristics of the gaucho and his octosyllabic verses, although with differences in rhymes and strophic distribution. It appeared toward the end of the eighteenth century in the littoral region of Argentina, in the province of Buenos Aires, and on the plains of Uruguay, and it is considered a literary genre within Argentine letters. Gauchesca literature was conceived, developed, and endured on the fringes of established Argentine literature; that is, it existed as a parallel literary genre. It was a dissident literature whose authors were considered rebels pitting the new, popular, and native against the established peninsular and cultured. It continued as marginal literature until its artistic worth was finally recognized in the first quarter of the twentieth century.

Gauchesca literature is composed of works written in verse by sophisticated, urban authors. The protagonist is the historical gaucho, from his appearance during the seventeenth century until his assimilation into sedentary life at the end of the nineteenth century, emphasizing his characteristic as an equestrian peasant without specific occupation. These works are set in the Pampas and reproduce the unique linguistic features of the gaucho, which include an archaic rural dialect rich in unique comparisons and metaphors. They are very graphic and humorous, and generally employ proverbial sentences, idiolects, and a lack of logical sequence in many parts of the discourse, with a resulting effect of intense laconism. The thematic repertoire is generally limited to injustice, poverty, the fight against the establishment (the local magistrate or justice of peace, the police, the military), life on the Estancia, the horse, and the mate (friendship), revealing the particular world and world view of the gaucho. Gauchesca works rely on the *cantar opinando* (singing, but giving an opinion) and usually adopt the form of dialogue and autobiographical narrative, and they are designed to attract the sympathy and the adherence of the reader to causes defended by the gaucho.

Although there were some timid expressions of gauchesca literature at the end of the eighteenth century, the genre formally begins with Bartolomé

Hidalgo (1788–1822) and his *Diálogos* (1820–1822) and *Relación* (1822). Hidalgo is credited with consciously selecting the socially marginal gaucho and building around him a literature with a sociopolitical message that the masses could understand. Although Hilario Ascasubi and Estanislao del Campo are other writers associated with gauchesca literature, the towering figure of the genre is José Hernández, author of the Argentine national poem, Martín Fierro (1872–1879), which represents the highest point of the genre. This poem, together with some of Hidalgo's texts, entered the folkloric oral tradition, which contributed to the idealization or mythicization of the figure of the gaucho. In this respect, the *folletines gauchescos* (gauchesco feuilletons) of Eduardo Gutiérrez, produced in the last quarter of the nineteenth century, should be cited, as well as the dramatization of one of them, *Juan Moreira,* which marks the beginnings of the Argentine theater. This process of mythicization reached its summit in 1926 with the novel of Ricardo Güiraldes, *Don Segundo Sombra.* From that time on, the gaucho is transfigured into an archetype, a symbol of the true Argentine and the Argentine nationality. As such, it can be found in poems, novels, short stories, the theater, and on the radio.

Gauchesca literature should be understood as one of the two specifically Spanish-American literary genres, the other being the Afro-Antillean poetry of Puerto Rico and Cuba. Gauchesca literature is unique in its semiconversational, semiliterary intonation obtained by using the octosyllabic verse and by adopting a careless syntax, which is almost always narrated by a person who either evokes old times (always arcadian) or is furiously propagandistic and critical of the present political times. Gauchesca is also original because of its nonliterary character, its introduction of rusticity into a cultured literary tradition. Confronted with a literature of illustrious men performing heroic deeds, gauchesca presented antiheroes, poor peasants who were scorned and hopeless. Finally, gauchesca literature is significant because it represents the first appearance of an indigenous Argentine literary art form.

*See also* **Hernández, José; Hidalgo, Bartolomé; Literature: Spanish America; Martín Fierro.**

BIBLIOGRAPHY

Jorge L. Borges, "La poesía gauchesca," in his *Discusión* (1964), pp. 11–38.

Ricardo Rodríguez Molas, *Historia social del gaucho* (1968).

Félix Weinberg, "Una etapa poco conocida de la poesía gauchesca: De Hidalgo a Ascasubi (1823–1851)," in *Revista Iberoamericana* 40, nos. 87–88 (1974): 353–391.

Horacio J. Becco et al., *Trayectoria de la poesía gauchesca* (1977).

Richard W. Slatta, "Man to Myth: Literary and Symbolic Images," in his *Gauchos and the Vanishing Frontier* (1983), pp. 180–192.

Josefina Ludmer, *El género gauchesco: Un tratado sobre la patria* (1988).

Rodolfo A. Borello, "El *Martín Fierro* y la poesía gauchesca," in *Boletín de la Academia Argentina de Letras* 54, nos. 211–212 (1989): 97–129.

*Additional Bibliography*

Carricaburo, Norma. *La literatura gauchesca: Una poética de la voz.* Buenos Aires: Editorial Dunken, 2004.

Heredia, Pablo, and Andrea Bocco. *Asperos clamores: La literatura gauchesca desde Mayo hacia Caseros.* Córdoba, Argentina: Alción Editora, 1996.

ANGELA B. DELLEPIANE

---

**GAUCHO.** Gaucho, the cowboy of Argentina and Uruguay. Gauchos played an important historical role in the Río de la Plata and remain important cultural and political symbols. Gauchos, first called *gauderios,* emerged as a distinct social group of wild-cattle hunters during the early eighteenth century.

Gauchos believed in common access to the pampa's resources: land, water, and livestock. During the colonial era the vast herds of wild cattle and horses on the plains seemed inexhaustible. Gauchos scorned or were ignorant of remote government officials who tried to monopolize the killing of cattle. They fled from or resisted official attempts to dominate, direct, and draft them.

The gaucho adopted much of his equestrian subculture from Indians of the pampas. He customarily wore a poncho, a Chiripá (baggy, diaper-like pants) held up by a stout leather belt (*tirador*), and on his feet homemade boots (Botas De Potro) and iron spurs. He armed himself with the Boleadoras and a swordlike knife (Facón).

**Competing for the title of best rider, Montevideo, Uruguay, 2005.** A Uruguayan gaucho displays his skill in riding a wild horse during a celebration of traditional cowboy culture. © ANDRES STAPFF/REUTERS/CORBIS

Colonial and early-national-period officials viewed the gaucho as an unlettered, uncivilized barbarian, not significantly superior to the Indians of the pampas. Only a shallow, superstitious acquaintance with the symbols of Catholicism separated the gaucho, in the official eye, from the "savages" of the plains. Gauchos became the targets of vagrancy and military conscription laws designed to end their free-riding lifestyle.

Conscripted gauchos fought against Indians on the frontier, the British who invaded Buenos Aires and Montevideo in 1806 and 1807, and the Spanish royalist forces during the independence wars. José Gervasio Artigas ably led his gaucho army in Uruguay. His military service somewhat improved the gaucho's image and gave him a reputation for valor and patriotism. The word "gaucho" became less an epithet than a description of the ranch worker who rode horses and tended cattle.

Gauchos worked seasonally on ranches (Estancias), rounding up and branding cattle. Some gauchos, such as the Domador (broncobuster) or Baquiano (scout), earned higher wages because of their special skills.

As the nineteenth century progressed, the landed elite and Europeanized politicians gradually subdued the gaucho and radically changed his life. More restrictive laws, new technology, and a diversified rural economy marginalized the gaucho.

Beginning in the late nineteenth century, the gaucho began a transition from the realm of history into folklore and literature. Many important writers of Argentina and Uruguay made the gaucho the focus of their work. Following the pioneering poetry of Bartolomé Hidalgo and Hilario Ascasubi, writers including José Hernández, Benito Lynch, Leopoldo Lugones, Ricardo Güiraldes, and Jorge Luis Borges honored the gaucho in poetry and prose. Today calling someone or something "very gaucho" remains a compliment.

*See also* **Artigas, José Gervasio; Ascasubi, Hilario; Borges, Jorge Luis; Güiraldes, Ricardo; Hernández, José; Hidalgo, Bartolomé; Livestock; Lugones, Leopoldo; Lynch, Benito.**

BIBLIOGRAPHY

Fernando Assunção, *El gaucho* (1963).

Ricardo Rodríguez Molas, *Historia social del gaucho* (1968).

Madaline Wallis Nichols, *The Gaucho* (1968).

Domingo F. Sarmiento, *Life in the Argentine Republic in the Days of the Tyrants,* translated by Mary Mann (1971).

Richard W. Slatta, *Gauchos and the Vanishing Frontier* (1983).

Richard W. Slatta, *Cowboys of the Americas* (1990).

*Additional Bibliography*

Assunção, Fernando O. *Historia del gaucho: El gaucho, ser y quehacer.* Buenos Aires: Editorial Claridad, 1999.

De la Fuente, Ariel. *Children of Facundo: Caudillo and Gaucho Insurgency During the Argentine State-Formation Process (La Rioja, 1853–1870).* Durham: Duke University Press, 2000.

Goldman, Noemí, and Ricardo Donato Salvatore. *Caudillismos rioplatenses: Nuevas miradas a un viejo problema.* Buenos Aires: Eudeba, Facultad de Filosofía y Letras, Universidad de Buenos Aires, 1998.

RICHARD W. SLATTA

**GAÚCHO.** During the nineteenth and early twentieth centuries, the Brazilian gaúcho, cousin of the Argentine and Uruguayan cowboy, was the cowboy of the Rio Grande Do Sul. The term also refers to a native of that region. Gaúchos roamed the open plain hunting semiferal cattle for their hides. They dressed in baggy *bombacha* pants and a poncho and wore a long knife. Gaúchos participated as cavalry soldiers in the nineteenth-century wars and rebellions of the border region. Twentieth-century modernization forced them into employment on newly fenced Estancias (ranches), ending their seminomadic way of life. Gaúcho life-style and customs have been preserved in music and dance, outdoor barbecues, and *chimarrão* (Yerba Maté).

*See also* **Vaqueiros.**

BIBLIOGRAPHY

Joseph Love, *Rio Grande do Sul and Brazilian Regionalism, 1882–1930* (1971).

Spencer L. Leitman, "Socio-Economic Roots of the Ragamuffin War: A Chapter in Early Brazilian History" (Ph.D. diss., Univ. of Texas, 1972).

Lindalvo Bezerra Dos Santos, "O Gaúcho," in *Tipos e aspectos do Brasil,* 10th ed. (1975), pp. 425–26.

Richard W. Slatta, *Cowboys of the Americas* (1990), pp. 56–57, 199.

*Additional Bibliography*

Bell, Stephen. *Campanha Gaúcha: A Brazilian Ranching System, 1850–1920.* Stanford: Stanford University Press, 1998.

Oliven, Ruben George. *Nación y modernidad: La reinvención de la identidad gaúcha en el Brasil.* Buenos Aires: Eudeba, 1999.

ROBERT WILCOX

## GAVIDIA, FRANCISCO ANTONIO

**(1864–1955).** Francisco Antonio Gavidia (*b.* 29 December 1864; *d.* 23 September 1955), Salvadoran romantic poet and writer, one of the originators of modernism in Spanish America. Gavidia was born in San Miguel. His *Versos* (1884) brought him great notice for their innovations in meter and imagery, and he is believed to have been an important influence on his friend Rubén Darío. A long career as leading literary figure in San Salvador followed, with perhaps his most significant poetic work being the epic and dramatic *Sóteer o tierra de preseas* (1920). Gavidia's classic ode *A Centroamérica* (1945) reflected his strong democratic conviction and belief in Central American union. His literary versatility was also reflected in dramatic works, critical essays, and historical works, among which his two-volume *Historia moderna de El Salvador* (1917–1918), focusing on the Salvadoran independence movements of 1811 and 1814, was the most important. Gavidia died in San Salvador.

*See also* **Darío, Rúben; Literature: Spanish America; San Salvador.**

BIBLIOGRAPHY

*Boletín de la Academi salvadoreña* 1, honoring Gavidia (August 1940).

Roberto Armijo and José Napoleon Rodríguez Ruiz, *Francisco Gavidia: La odisea de su genio,* 2 vols. (1965).

José Salvador Guadique, *Gavidia, el amigo de Darío,* 2 vols. (1965).

Mario Hernández-Aguirre, *Gavidia: Poesía, literatura, humanismo* (1968).

Cristóbal Humberto Ibarra, *Francisco Gavidia y Rubén Darío, semilla y floración del modernismo,* 2d ed. (1976).

Luis Gallegos Valdés, *Panorama de la literatura salvadoreña del período precolombino a 1980,* 3d ed. (1989).

John Beverley and Marc Zimmerman, *Literature and Politics in the Central American Revolutions* (1990), pp. 118–119.

*Additional Bibliography*

Chavarrià, Marià Gabriela. "El suenõ político de los primeros modernistas en Centroamerica a través de la imagen de sus ciudades: Ruben Darío, Juan Ramon Molina, Francisco Gavidia, y Enrique Gomez Carrillo." Ph.D. diss., University of Kansas, 2003.

Lara Martínez, Rafael. *Historia sagrada e historia profana: El sentido de la historia salvadoreña en la obra de Francisco Gavidia.* San Salvador: Dirección de Publicaciones e Impresos, Consejo Nacional para la Cultura y el Arte, Ministerio de Educación, 1992.

Rodríguez Díaz, Rafael Arturo. *Temas salvadoreños: Y unos pocos foráneos.* San Salvador: UCA Editores, 1992.

RALPH LEE WOODWARD JR.

## GAVIRIA TRUJILLO, CÉSAR AUGUSTO

**(1947–).** Born in Pereira, Colombia, on 31 March 1947, César Gaviria studied economics at the Universidad de los Andes, Bogota. At the age of twenty-three, he began his political career by winning election to the Pereira municipal council in 1970. He was appointed mayor of Pereira in 1974 and later served a term as vice-minister of development in the administration of President Julio César Turbay Ayala beginning in 1978. Gaviria combined political activities with the practice of journalism, first with the newspaper *La Tarde* in Pereira, of which he became editor in 1982, and then as political and economic correspondent for *El Tiempo* of Bogotá, from 1983 to 1986. He was appointed deputy director of the Liberal Party in 1986 and then served first as minister of the treasury and subsequently as minister of the interior in the administration of President Virgilio Barco. In 1989 he became the campaign director of presidential candidate Luis Carlos Galán Sarmiento. After Galán's assassination in August of that year, however, Gaviria was selected to be the presidential candidate of the Liberal Party. He was elected president of Colombia in 1990, with 47 percent of the vote.

Gaviria's election marked a generational and, to a lesser extent, ideological shift in Colombian politics. He was first of the post-Violencia generation to become president, elected with the support of a coalition of traditional Liberal Party bosses and the followers of the reform-minded Galán. Gaviria confronted the problems of narcotics-linked terrorism and a general lack of confidence in the political system with youthful energy and a neoliberal vision. He was the youngest elected president of Colombia in the twentieth century, and many of those who were appointed to serve in his government were younger than he. Continuing the process of reintegration of guerrilla groups into the political life of the country, which Gaviria had directed as a member of the Barco administration, he appointed M-19 leader Antonio Navarro Wolf, who had received 13 percent of the 1990 presidential vote, to his cabinet.

Perhaps the crowning achievement of the Gaviria presidency was adoption of a new constitution, the first since 1886, which modernized the state structure and the judicial system. The Constitution of 1991 sought to open the political system to more than the two traditional parties and to extend democratic participation. The Gaviria administration also promoted a more open economy, with an emphasis on privatization and deregulation. Trade barriers were lowered, regional economic integration (particularly with Venezuela) was supported, foreign investment was encouraged, labor legislation was modernized, and the role of private enterprise was emphasized. For these reasons and for Gaviria's general cooperation (despite some embarrassing lapses) in the effort to suppress the drug traffic, his administration was lauded by the U.S. government. By the end of his term, Gaviria was seen as an "efficiency-seeking technocrat" who had effectively initiated political and economic reforms that enabled Colombia to break out of the cycle of political and drug-related violence, slow economic growth, and political dissatisfaction that had characterized it in the 1980s.

In March 1994 Gaviria was elected to a five-year term as secretary-general of the Organization of American States (OAS), and after completion of his presidential term later in the year, he assumed that position. He was the second Colombian (after the first OAS head, Alberto Lleras Camargo) to hold the position, and his thirty-four to twenty victory over Costa Rican foreign minister Bernd Niehaus caused some resentment among the smaller Central American and Caribbean OAS members, which felt slighted by the larger states. But in 1999 he won a second term, aided by intense lobbying of the Colombian foreign ministry and once again with strong U.S. support. As head of the hemispheric organization, Gaviria sought to modernize the cumbersome OAS bureaucracy while strongly supporting efforts at trade liberalization, including the U.S. proposal for a free trade pact among the American nations. Under his leadership the OAS took an active role in support of political democracy in the hemisphere, monitoring elections and offering its good offices to help defuse conflicts, such as that between Venezuelan president Hugo Chávez and his opponents in late 2002 and early 2003.

After his tenure as head of the OAS, Gaviria worked for a time in New York, organizing a consultancy for firms doing business in Latin America. Before long he returned to Colombia, where he accepted sole leadership of the Liberal Party in opposition to the administration of Álvaro Uribe Vélez, even though the party had drifted away from the neoliberal economic policies that he himself had espoused as president. Despite Gaviria's best efforts, the party's candidate made an embarrassing third-place finish in opposition to Uribe's reelection in 2006, but under Gaviria's guidance, the Liberals did become a more cohesive force than it had recently been.

*See also* **Chávez, Hugo; Colombia, Constitutions: Overview; Colombia, Political Parties: Liberal Party; Lleras Camargo, Alberto; Navarro Wolff, Antonio; Organization of American States (OAS).**

BIBLIOGRAPHY

Gaviria, César. *Una década de transformaciones: Del fin de la guerra fría a la globalización de la OEA.* Bogotá: Planeta, 2004.

Palacios, Marco. *Between Legitimacy and Violence: A History of Colombia, 1875–2002.* Translated by Richard Stoller. Durham, NC: Duke University Press, 2006.

Vargas, Mauricio. *Memorias secretas del revolcón, la historia íntima del polémico gobierno de César Gaviria revelada por uno de sus protagonistas.* Bogotá: T-M Editores, 1993.

JAMES PATRICK KIEMAN

**GAY, CLAUDIO** (1800–1873). Claudio Gay (*b.* 1800, *d.* 1873), botanist, traveler, draftsman, whose research, drawings, and watercolors contributed to European knowledge of South America. Born in Draguignan, France, Gay lived for twelve years in Chile. Under the auspices of the Chilean government he traveled throughout the country between 1843 and 1851, studying and recording material for his *Historia física y politica de Chile.* The results of his research were published in twenty-four volumes, with two accompanying volumes of lithographs, in 1854. Of a total 289 lithographs, 103 describe plant life and 134 are devoted to fauna. Published under the general title of *History,* the remaining illustrations recorded various trades, costumes, pastimes, *tertulias* (social gatherings), views of cities, gauchos, and customs of the Araucanian Indians. The lithographs were based on Gay's own sketches and on drawings by various artists, such as the renowned German traveler and painter Johann Moritz Rugendas. The lithographic work was executed by Lehnert, Dupressoir, and Van Der Burch. Gay published several botanical studies of South America in European scientific journals. He died in France.

*See also* **Art: The Nineteenth Century.**

BIBLIOGRAPHY

Diego Barros Arana, *Don Claudio Gay: Su vida y sus obras* (1876).

Dawn Ades, *Art in Latin America: The Modern Era, 1820–1980* (1989), p. 68.

*Additional Bibliography*

Mizón, Luis. *Claudio Gay y la formación de la identidad cultural chilena.* Santiago de Chile: Editorial Universitaria: Centro de Investigaciones Diego Barros Arana, 2001.

Saldivia Maldonado, Zenobio. *La visión de la naturaleza en tres científicos del siglo XIX en Chile: Gay, Domeyko y Philippi.* Santiago de Chile: Universidad de Santiago de Chile, Facultad de Humanidades, Instituto de Estudios Avanzados, 2003.

MARTA GARSD

**GAZETA DE GUATEMALA.** *Gazeta de Guatemala,* Guatemalan periodical published 1729–1731 and 1797–1816. First published on 1 November 1729, *La Gazeta de Guatemala* (The Guatemala Gazette) arose from a dispute between civil and religious authorities over the best way to confront piracy. It was the second periodical published in Latin America and the third on the American continent. The first was the *Boston News-Letter* in 1704 (which followed the 1690 single edition of *Publick Occurrences* in Boston). The second was *La Gazeta de México* in 1722. The first edition of *La Gazeta de Guatemala* consisted of a calendar of religious feasts, notices of arrivals of ships and merchandise, items about tribute-paying Indians who belonged to religious orders, and other news. It continued as a monthly until 1731.

The periodical began its second life on 13 February 1797, when the Spanish Bourbons were attempting to implement reforms in America. This time it published the views of groups advocating the reform of the colonial system, through which it made known the profound problems in the captaincy general of Guatemala. Its writers were prominent members of the Economic Society of Friends of the Country, an organization whose members espoused the reformist ideas of the period. This time *La Gazeta de Guatemala* was published weekly. It was widely distributed throughout Central America and beyond.

The paper's publication was suspended in 1816. It was followed by Pedro Molina's *El Editor*

*Constitucional* and José Cecilio del Valle's *El Amigo de la Patria,* both in 1820. Thereafter a series of official newspapers were published under various titles, including *Gaceta del Gobierno, Boletín de Noticias, Boletín Oficial, El Tiempo, La Gaceta, Gaceta de Guatemala, El Guatemalteco,* and *Diario de Centroamérica.*

*See also* **Guatemala, Economic Society of; Journalism.**

BIBLIOGRAPHY

León De Gandarias, "Jornadas periodísticas," in *Etapas notables de la prensa guatemalteca* (1959).

Rigoberto Bran Azmitia, *Panorama del periodismo guatemalteco y centroamericano* (1967).

Carlos C. Haeussler Yela, *Diccionario general de Guatemala* (1983), vol. 3, pp. 1224–1231.

*Additional Bibliography*

Catalina Barrios y Barrios, *Estudio histórico del periodismo guatemalteco: (Período colonial y siglo XIX)* (1997).

OSCAR G. PELÁEZ ALMENGOR

**GAZETA DE LIMA.** *Gazeta de Lima,* Peruvian periodical of the mid-eighteenth century. The *Gazeta* (or *Gaceta*) *de Lima* was published on an irregular basis beginning in 1743 and continuing until the early nineteenth century. There were often about six issues a year. Initially the *Gazeta* contained reprints of material taken from European publications, especially the *Gazeta de Madrid,* but it also included some local news, such as appointments to office, the arrival and departure of ships at Callao, and deaths of local dignitaries. Beginning in 1793, it appeared as a government publication designed to present the official version of events in revolutionary France and Europe.

*See also* **Gazetas; Journalism.**

BIBLIOGRAPHY

Ella Dunbar Temple, *La Gaceta de Lima del siglo XVIII. Facsímiles de seis ejemplares raros de este periódico* (1965).

MARK A. BURKHOLDER

**GAZETAS.** Gazetas, newspapers published primarily from the 1760s on. Although the first *gazeta* appeared in New Spain in 1722 and a longer-lived successor lasted from 1728 to 1742, it was only in the late eighteenth century that these short newspapers, usually published on a biweekly or weekly basis, began to appear widely. Typically these later *gazetas* served as vehicles to present not only local news but also, and more important, enlightened thought and approaches to practical, everyday problems for the edification of their readers.

The best-known newspaper in Peru was the *Mercurio Peruano,* published from 1791 to 1795 as the expression of a group of self-styled "enlightened" intellectuals. Through the *Mercurio,* the supporters of progress tried to provide Peruvians with "useful knowledge" of their region and information relevant to their daily lives. Thus it published articles that, among other things, advocated burial outside churches for reasons of health, supported more efficient mining techniques, and analyzed the viceroyalty's commerce.

As in Peru, periodicals reached a broader audience in New Spain than did formal schooling. The foremost Mexican publicist was the cleric José Antonio Alzate y Ramírez (1729–1799), an enlightened advocate of scientific knowledge and its application to contemporary problems. His *Gaceta de literatura de México* (1788–1795) provided a stream of informative articles on medicine, applied science, agronomy, and a host of other scientific topics. A daily paper, *Diario de México,* originally edited by Carlos María Bustamante, appeared from 1805 to 1817.

In Guatemala the *Gazeta de Guatemala* (whose modern series began in 1797) reflected the curiosity of intellectuals in Guatemala City at the time. Published by Ignacio Beteta, the *Gazeta* sought to provide "useful knowledge" through articles on the economy, medicine, and commerce, and campaigned vigorously to end Latin's sway as the language of university instruction.

Newspapers also appeared in Havana, Bogotá, and Buenos Aires prior to 1808. After that date, the number of publications increased rapidly.

*See also* **Journalism.**

BIBLIOGRAPHY

Bailey W. Diffie, *Latin-American Civilization: Colonial Period* (1945; repr. 1967), pp. 553–561.

John Tate Lanning, *The Eighteenth-Century Enlightenment in the University of San Carlos de Guatemala* (1956), esp. pp. 83–91.

*Additional Bibliography*

Timoteo Álvarez, Jesús, Asención Martínez Riaza, and Enrique Ríos Vicente. *Historia de la prensa hispanoamericana* (1992).

MARK A. BURKHOLDER

**GÊ.** Gê (also Jê), the name of linguistically and culturally related Amerindian peoples located in what is now central and southern Brazil. Gê is one of the principal language families of native lowland South America. Based on linguistic affiliation, approximately 40,000 peoples are divided into northern, central, and southern branches, which are the three branches of the Gê linguistic family. Varying degrees of mutual intelligibility exist among speakers of the languages of any given branch; there is, however, little or no mutual intelligibility between speakers of different branches. The Northern Gê consist of the Eastern Timbira (Apaniekra, Ramkokamekra, Krĩkatí, and Krahó), Western Timbira (Apinayé), Kayapó (Gorotire, Xikrin, Kokraimôro, Kubenkrankegn, Kubenkrangnoti, Mekrangnoti, Txukamhamãe), and Suyá groups. The Shavante and Sherente peoples make up the central branch, and the Shokleng and Kaingang groups form the southern branch. Linguists also consider the Gê languages to be related to a wider network of lowland Amerindian languages and families known as Macro-Gê, which includes, among others, Maxacalí, Botocudo, Karajá, Fulniô, and possibly even Tupí. Today, the Gê groups span a large area stretching from the states of Maranhão and Pará in the north to the southern state of Santa Catarina.

Although reports of what appear to be Gê-speaking peoples date from the mid-seventeenth century, and eighteenth-century colonial records that document *aldeiamentos* (settlements) of Gê-speaking groups, little was known of the Gê until the middle of the twentieth century. The linguistic and cultural similarities of the various geographically dispersed Gê peoples were only formally recognized in 1867, when Karl von Martius named the family in his preliminary classification of the peoples and languages of central Brazil. The first descriptive accounts of Gê peoples did not, however, appear until the 1940s, when Curt Nimuendajú published his ethnographic accounts of the Apinayé (1939), the Sherente (1942), and the Eastern Timbira (1946). During this same period the Salesian missionaries Antonio Colbacchini and Caesar Albisetti published their monograph of the neighboring Bororo (1942). Their descriptions detail many aspects of a people who, despite significant differences, share many similarities with the Gê. The relationship between the Gê and Bororo continues to baffle specialists to the present day.

Although the Gê and Bororo had previously been classified by Julian Steward (1946) as marginal peoples, a category characterized by rudimentary technology and simple patterns of social organization (defined, in fact, in terms of traits they were reported to lack), both Nimuendajú's accounts and that of the Salesians depict societies possessing simple technologies yet characterized by extremely complex social systems. These descriptions presented social theorists with an apparent anomaly: How did peoples with such rudimentary technologies have such complex patterns of social organization?

Discarding speculations that attempt to explain the paradox by suggesting that the Gê and Bororo are the degenerate remnants of some higher civilization or that the reported complex social divisions are simply native mystifications, a group of scholars led by David Maybury-Lewis set out to unravel the puzzles of central Brazilian social organization through further ethnographic study within a comparative framework. This ambitious effort, known as the Harvard Central Brazil Project, has revised anthropological thinking concerning the basis of social organization among Gê and Bororo societies. Because a hypothesis pertaining to any one of the groups can be tested in other closely related societies, Gê peoples continue to be particularly appealing for the study of comparative social behavior. Subsequent studies have broadened the comparative picture along various dimensions, including material and expressive culture, and have contributed to knowledge of the Gê.

In the 1990s many Gê peoples were actively involved in struggles to preserve their lands and cultural traditions. For example, the Kayapó actively fought against a series of proposed dams that, if completed, would have inundated lands they traditionally inhabited. The Shavante and others sought to achieve economic independence from FUNAI. All the Gê are bent on preserving their heritage, thereby continuing a theme that has distinguished them since colonial times.

*See also* **Indigenous Peoples.**

BIBLIOGRAPHY

Irvine Davis, "Comparative Jê Phonology," *Estudos Lingüísticos* 1, no. 2 (1966): 10–24, and "Some Macro-Jê relationships," *International Journal of American Linguistics* 34 (1968): 42–47.

David Maybury-Lewis, *Dialectical Societies: The Gê and Bororo of Central Brazil* (1979), pp. ix–13.

LAURA GRAHAM

**GEFFRARD, FABRE NICOLAS** (1803–1878). Fabre Nicolas Geffrard (*b.* 1803; *d.* 31 December 1878), Haitian general and president (1859–1867). Geffrard rose to the rank of general under Emperor Faustin Soulouque (1785–1867). He was one of the few to emerge with credit from Soulouque's disastrous last invasion of the Dominican Republic (1856). As head of the army, Geffrard led a revolt against Soulouque in 1858 and restored the republican constitution. He became president the following year and sought to improve Haiti's international image, which had deteriorated under Soulouque's harsh and nationalistic regime. He signed a concordat with the Holy See in 1860, and he obtained U.S. recognition of the Haitian state in 1862. President Abraham Lincoln and Congress had proposed settling U.S. blacks in Haiti, but in spite of some cooperation from Geffrard, the scheme failed.

Internally, Geffrard favored the Catholic Church and attacked vodun, which had grown under Soulouque. He also favored the mulatto class, which had suffered under the regimes since 1844. Early in his term he attempted to install a more open and less authoritarian government, but assassination attempts against him and his family and a revolt led by Sylvain Salnave (1827–1870) at Cap Haïtien in 1865 pushed him to the familiar pattern of repression and executions. Geffrard was overthrown by Salnave in 1867, and he left for exile in Jamaica, where he died.

*See also* **Salnave, Sylvain; Soulouque, Faustin Élie.**

BIBLIOGRAPHY

Heinl, Robert Debs Jr., Nancy Heinl, and Michael Heinl. *Written in Blood: The Story of the Haitian People, 1492–1995*, 3rd edition. Lanham: University Press of America, 2005.

Largey, Michael. "Composing a Haitian Cultural Identity: Haitian Elites, African Ancestry, and Musical Discourse." *Black Music Research Journal* 14 (Autumn 1994): 99–117.

MURDO J. MACLEOD

**GEGO** (1912–1994). Gego (Gertrude Goldschmidt; *b.* 1 August 1912; *d.* 17 September 1994), Venezuelan artist. Trained as an architect, Gego immigrated to Venezuela from her native Germany in 1939. In the latter half of the 1950s, she began to create a geometric sculpture that explored perceptual aspects of planes and volumes. She taught at the Universidad Central de Venezuela from 1958 to 1967 and at the Instituto Nacional de Cooperación Educativa (INCE) from 1964 to 1977. Gego is best known for her innovative abstract works that extend a systematic approach to three-dimensional art into a poetic ineffability. Her *Reticuláreas* (1969), for example, comprise webs of wire segments that have been hooked together and hung from the ceiling; filling a room, the *Reticuláreas* confront the viewer with a quasi-geometric and semi-mobile linear articulation of space. Gego's architectural projects have included sculptures at the Banco Industrial de Venezuela, Caracas, in 1962 and (in collaboration with her husband, Gerd Leufert) on the facades of the Sede del INCE in 1969. Her one-woman exhibitions include those in Caracas at the Museo de Bellas Artes in 1961, 1964, 1968, 1969, and 1984; at the Museo de Arte Contemporáneo in 1977; and at the Galería de Arte Nacional in 1982. Gego died in Caracas.

*See also* **Art: The Twentieth Century.**

BIBLIOGRAPHY

Hanni Ossott, *Gego* (1977).

Marta Traba, *Gego* (1977).

Ruth Auerbach, *Gego: Entre la estructura y el objeto* (1988).

### *Additional Bibliography*

Gego. *Sabiduras and Other Texts: Writings by Gego*, edited by María Elena Huizi and Josefina Manrique. Houston: International Center for the Arts of the Americas; Caracas: Fundación Gego, 2005.

Peruga, Iris, and Josefina Núñez. *Gego: obra completa, 1955–1990.* Caracas: Fundación Cisneros, 2003.

Ramírez, Mari Carmen, and Héctor Olea, editors. *Inverted Utopias: Avant-Garde Art in Latin America.* New Haven: Yale University Press, 2004.

Ramírez, Mari Carmen, and Theresa Papanikolas. *Questioning the Line: Gego in Context.* Houston: Museum of Fine Arts; Austin: University of Texas Press, 2003.

JOSEPH R. WOLIN

---

**GEISEL, ERNESTO** (1908–1996). Ernesto Geisel (*b.* 3 August 1908; *d.* 1996), president of Brazil (1974–1979). A career army officer of German Protestant parentage from Rio Grande do Sul, Geisel entered the army on 31 March 1925. After graduating from the military college of Realengo in Rio de Janeiro, he served with the Brazilian Expeditionary Force (FEB) during World War II. He attended the U.S. Army Command and General Staff College at Fort Leavenworth, Kansas, and went on to fill various command and general staff positions. As a colonel he directed the Brazilian National Petroleum (Petrobrás) Refinery at Cubatão, São Paulo, in 1955–1956, and the next year he joined the National Petroleum Council. After his promotion to general on 25 March 1961, he served a series of military presidents as chief of military household (1964–1967), minister of the superior military tribunal (1967–1969), and president of Petrobrás (1969–1973).

Geisel's presidential candidacy was initiated by the military high command (his brother, Orlando, held the post of army minister from 1969 to 1974), confirmed by the National Renovating Alliance (Arena), the government party, and certified by 400 out of 503 members of the electoral college. Once inaugurated (March 1974), Geisel was confronted with the collapse of the "Economic Miracle," brought on by the oil crisis of 1973. His administration launched a series of petroleum-substitution plans, including hydroelectric projects such as Itaipú and gasohol refineries to convert sugar to fuel. His initial efforts to come to terms with socially active elements of the Catholic Church failed, but tentative attempts at relaxation (*distensão*) of the political process restricted after the 1964 coup were evident by the end of his term.

Also taking place during the Geisel years was the end of the "unwritten alliance" between the United States and Brazil that had endured for three quarters of a century. The U.S. defeat in Southeast Asia, Cuban military intervention in Angola, Communist involvement in Mozambique, U.S.–USSR détente, and U.S. economic decline were capped by U.S. allegations of human-rights abuses. Geisel responded by canceling the defense agreement with the United States and redirecting Brazilian foreign policy to encompass more productive partners who were also interested in containing Soviet expansion. These included Japan, West Germany, and, briefly, Iran, along with the outcast quartet of South Korea, Taiwan, Israel, and South Africa. Investments from these members of the New Inter-Oceanic Alliance were encouraged. Concurrently, Brazil launched a cultural and commercial campaign in Lusophone Africa—Angola, Mozambique, and Guinea-Bissau—then proceeded to initiate development (since canceled) of its own nuclear weapons under Project Solimões (1977–1991).

Geisel's efforts at a democratic opening domestically (*abertura*) and reorientation in foreign policy precipitated a crisis in the hard-line military that was not resolved by the closure of congress in April 1977. It resurfaced in October 1977, when Geisel fired army minister General Sélvio Frota and other officers who contested the new directions.

As his successor Geisel selected General João Baptista Figueiredo, who promised to proceed with the democratic opening up of the country. After retiring from public office on 15 March 1979, Geisel dedicated himself to private entrepreneurial activities. He also remained active in the petrochemical industry in Brazil. He died in Rio de Janeiro on 12 September 1996.

*See also* **Brazil: Since 1889.**

BIBLIOGRAPHY

William Perry, *Contemporary Brazilian Foreign Policy: The International Strategy of an Emerging Power* (1976).

Riordan Roett, ed., *Brazil in the Seventies* (1976).

Walder De Goes, *O Brasil do General Geisel* (1978).

Jan Knippers Black, "The Military and Political Decompression in Brazil," in *Armed Forces and Society* 6, no. 4 (1980): 625–637.

Robert Levine, "Brazil: Democracy Without Adjective," in *Current History* 78 (1980): 49–52.

*Additional Bibliography*

Gaspari, Elio. *A ditadura encurralada.* Sao Paulo: Companhia das Letras, 2004.

Guabiraba, Maria Celia de Araœja, and Celso Castro. *Dossie Geisel.* Rio de Janeiro: FGV Editora, 2002.

Mathias, Suzeley Kalil. *A distenso no Brasil: O projeto militar, 1973–1979.* Campinas: Papyrus Editora, 1995.

LEWIS A. TAMBS

## GELLY, JUAN ANDRÉS (1790–1856).

Juan Andrés Gelly (*b.* 1790; *d.* 1856), Paraguayan diplomat and author. Born in Asunción, Gelly left at an early age to complete his education at the Real Colegio de San Carlos in Buenos Aires. After the Platine states gained their independence, he became involved in the Argentine civil wars as a partisan of Manuel Dorrego and the Unitario Party. With the defeat of that party in the late 1820s, Gelly left Argentina. Instead of returning to Paraguay, where the dictator José Gaspar Rodríguez de Francia had already persecuted his family, Gelly went to Montevideo to continue his legal studies. He soon became a well-known figure in expatriate circles.

Gelly made his way back to Paraguay after Francia's death in 1840. Overcoming his initial suspicion of Gelly's intentions, President Carlos Antonio López decided to call him into government service. Gelly's considerable experience in Uruguayan journalism made him an obvious choice for editor of the new state newspaper *El Paraguayo Independiente.*

In 1846 Gelly was dispatched to Rio de Janeiro to negotiate a boundary and trade agreement with the Brazilian Empire. Though this agreement was stillborn, he remained in Brazil as agent and publicist for the Paraguayan government. During his stay, he wrote a laudatory account of Paraguay's progress under López, entitled *El Paraguay, lo que fue, lo que es, y lo que será* (1848). Acting as delegation secretary, he later accompanied the president's son, Francisco Solano López, on a mission to Europe (1853–1854). He died in Asunción two years later.

*See also* **Dorrego, Manuel; Francia, José Gaspar Rodríguez de; Unitario.**

BIBLIOGRAPHY

R. Antonio Ramos, *Juan Andrés Gelly* (1972).

Carlos Zubizarreta, *Cien vidas paraguayas,* 2d ed. (1985), pp. 139–140.

THOMAS L. WHIGHAM

## GELLY Y OBES, JUAN ANDRÉS

(1815–1904). Juan Andrés Gelly y Obes (*b.* 20 May 1815; *d.* 19 September 1904), Argentine general. Born in Buenos Aires, Gelly y Obes took exile in Montevideo with the rest of his family during the dictatorship of Juan Manuel de Rosas. In 1839 he joined the *unitario* forces fighting against Rosas. Returning to Argentina after the fall of Rosas, he held both military and political offices in the separatist government of Buenos Aires Province and in 1861 became minister of war for a united Argentina in the cabinet of Bartolomé Mitre. He became chief of staff of the Argentine army of operations during the War of the Triple Alliance as well as personally taking part in many of the battles.

After the war Gelly y Obes fought against rebellious *caudillos* of the interior, yet took part himself in Mitre's unsuccessful 1874 uprising and in the porteño rebellion of 1880 over the federalization of Buenos Aires. He continued to hold various political and military positions until his death.

*See also* **Argentina: Movements: Unitarists; Mitre Bartolomé; Juan Manuel de.**

BIBLIOGRAPHY

Arturo Capdevila, ed., *Vidas de grandes argentinos,* vol. 2 (1966), pp. 9–12.

José S. Campobassi, *Mitre y su época* (1980).

DAVID BUSHNELL

## GELVES, MARQUÉS DE (1500–1600).

Marqués de Gelves (Diego Carrillo de Mendoza y Pimentel; *b.* 1500s; *d.* 1600s), fourteenth viceroy of New Spain (1621–1624). The Gelves administration is an excellent example of the limitations of colonial reform in the seventeenth century. Gelves arrived in Mexico under orders to improve government efficiency, crack down on the widespread corruption in public administration, and increase tax revenue. He enjoyed some success, particularly in the last endeavor. But he also managed to offend nearly every important sector of colonial society, partly because of his high-handed and autocratic manner and partly because his reforms threatened the financial interests of merchants, the creole elite, and many government officials.

The viceroy's most serious feud, however, was with the equally proud and unbending archbishop of Mexico, Juan Pérez de la Serna. Their dispute quickly evolved into a contest between civil and ecclesiastical authority. Pérez de la Serna excommunicated Gelves; Gelves exiled the archbishop. En route to the coast, the archbishop placed Mexico City under interdict, which was to begin on the morning of 15 January 1624. The populace, already angry at the viceroy over high maize prices, sided with the archbishop. A riot broke out in the central plaza, and soon a crowd of some thirty thousand was shouting for the viceroy's blood. The rioters stormed the palace, but Gelves escaped, disguised in servant's clothing, and fled to the Monastery of San Francisco. The *audiencia,* claiming that Gelves had abandoned his post, assumed viceregal authority. Although the crown briefly reinstated Gelves before replacing him, the marqués was in effect the first Mexican viceroy overthrown in a popular revolt.

*See also* **Creole; New Spain, Viceroyalty of.**

BIBLIOGRAPHY

Chester L. Guthrie, "Riots in Seventeenth-Century Mexico City: A Study of Social and Economic Conditions," in *Greater America: Essays in Honor of Herbert Eugene Bolton* (1945), pp. 243–258.

Jonathan I. Israel, *Race, Class, and Politics in Colonial Mexico, 1610–1670* (1975).

Richard E. Boyer, "Mexico in the Seventeenth Century: Transition of a Colonial Society," in *Hispanic American History Review* 57, no. 3 (1977): 455–478.

*Additional Bibliography*

Bjork, Katharine. "The Link that Kept the Philippines Spanish: Mexican Merchant Interests and the Manila Trade, 1571–1815." *Journal of World History.* 9 (Spring 1998): 25–50.

Martínez Vega, María Elisa. *La crisis barroca en el virreinato de la Nueva España: El Marqués de Gelves, 1621–1625.* Madrid: Editorial de la Universidad Complutense de Madrid, 1990.

R. Douglas Cope

## GEMS AND GEMSTONES.

Gems and Gemstones have been important to both the early development and the present-day economy in several key areas of South America. Brazil now has the leading gemstone industry in Latin America, including mining, cutting, polishing, setting, marketing, and exporting.

### EMERALDS

Archaeological discoveries in Colombia have revealed the use of emeralds in pre-Columbian jewelry. Early accounts of the ceremonies that took place at Lake Guatavita, high in the Andes Mountains of Colombia, describe the use of both gold and emeralds as offerings thrown into the sacred lake. Soon after the arrival of the Spanish conquistadores, emeralds were being traded as far north as Mexico and as far south as Chile. Emeralds were soon discovered in the areas of Muzo and Chivor, located north and northeast of Bogotá. Chivor was particularly well known to the early Spaniards, who employed thousands of local Indians as slave labor. In the early seventeenth century, word of the brutal working conditions at Chivor resulted in both royal and papal decrees prohibiting the use of Indian slave labor, and the mines were forced to close. Both Muzo and Chivor have had a violent and checkered history since colonial times. Both mines are known to produce among the finest emeralds in the world, yet the mines have rarely been worked at a profit. In the 1970s, however, the government opened Muzo to private mining ventures, the operations of which have been relatively successful. Chivor remains less developed. Both areas retain an unfortunate reputation for violence because of anarchy among the independent miners. In 1976, an estimated 50,000 people were killed. Economic statistics are difficult to maintain, largely because of significant production from the independent miners, (*guaqueros*) of the area. It is certain, however, that emeralds are a very important part of the Colombian economy.

Today, Colombian emeralds can be seen in the crown jewels of the world as well as in the finest jewelry stores. Particularly important historic collections of Colombian emeralds are among the treasures of the Topkapi Museum in Istanbul, Turkey, and in the crown jewels of Iran. Many of these fine, historic emeralds made their way around the world. In the late sixteenth century, the Spanish brought back from the New World large quantities of emeralds, with which they reportedly flooded the emerald markets in Europe. Europeans, in turn, found a willing market with the Mogul rulers of India. The Moguls were particularly fond of carving large gems and attaching them to clothing. In 1739, however, invading Persian armies sacked the Mogul treasuries of Delhi and brought enormous quantities of emeralds back to the Middle East, where many remain today. Additional deposits of emeralds were discovered in Brazil in the 1960s, and are currently mined in Goiás and Bahia.

### DIAMONDS

Diamonds became an important part of the Brazilian economy in the mid-eighteenth century, after they were discovered in the river gravels around the town of Diamantina in the state of Minas Gerais in 1725. The world's production had previously come from the famous mines around Golconda in India. By the eighteenth century, however, these Indian mines were nearing depletion. The discovery of the Brazilian deposits shifted world attention on Brazil. The Portuguese explorer Sebastino Leme do Prado, who had previously lived in India, is credited with the first identification of diamonds in Brazil. It is reported that the diamonds were being used by local gold miners as chips in card games. These "chips" were sent off to Amsterdam for appraisal and the diamond-bearing area was immediately declared crown property. In its height of production in 1851, as many as 300,000 carats were mined annually from the Diamantina area as well as from a new find in the state of Bahia. The diamonds were recovered from the alluvial river gravels solely by panning. Gold commonly accompanied the diamonds. Several important diamonds were recovered from these river gravels, including the 726.6-carat Presidente Vargas Diamond, which was discovered in 1938.

By the 1880s, however, Brazil could not keep up with the world demand for diamonds. At the same time, the huge diamond deposits of southern Africa were discovered, and attention shifted away from Brazil. There is no doubt that diamonds had a significant impact on the Brazilian economy of the late eighteenth and early nineteenth centuries. Today, huge dredges still mine the gravels around Diamantina for gold and diamonds, although on a world scale, production is insignificant.

### OTHER GEMS

No other gem materials could be considered of importance until the outbreak of World War II. The great demand for "strategic" minerals such as quartz and tourmaline prompted a massive exploration program throughout South America. Success, however, was focused on the state of Minas Gerais in Brazil. Minas Gerais is rich in granite geologic formations known as pegmatites. These pegmatites are sometimes called "nature's jewel box" because of the vast array of gemstones that they may contain. In addition to the strategically important quartz and tourmaline, pegmatites are home to topaz, aquamarine and morganite beryl, kunzite, and many different species of garnet. While most of these gems were overlooked in favor of the relatively more important strategic minerals for the war effort, the end of the war brought on massive gem mining programs. Today, the majority of the world's supply of quartz, tourmaline, topaz, garnet, kunzite, and beryl come from Brazil.

Other areas of South America that can be considered of importance to today's gem market, but that have had little if any importance historically, include the great agate and amethyst deposits near Artigas, Uruguay, and bordering Rio Grande do Sul, Brazil. Huge quantities are mined from the basaltic lava flows to supply the gem markets around the world. Amethyst is also mined in Minas Gerais and Bahia. Opals that rival those from Australia come from Piauí, Brazil. Argentina is known for small quantities of "stalactitic" rhodochrosite, sometimes known as "Inca Rose." Venezuela is a minor producer of diamonds, and Chile of lapis lazuli.

Central America has produced a limited variety of gem materials historically, though some have been recovered in significant amounts. Most notable are the jade deposits near the Palmilla River in Guatemala, which were worked in pre-Columbian times. Artifacts made of jade from this region have surfaced throughout Mexico to the north and into Colombia to the south. In recent times, the Dominican Republic has supplied a good portion of the world's amber market.

Mexico has produced significant supplies of opal. This opal tends to have an orange body color with or without fire, or play of color. It can also be red and is sometimes called fire opal. Fire opals have been produced only since the late nineteenth century, although they may have been known to the Aztecs. Most of the opals come from the mines near Querétaro.

*See also* **Gold Rushes, Brazil; Mining: Colonial Brazil; Mining: Colonial Spanish America; Mining: Modern.**

BIBLIOGRAPHY

S. H. Ball, "Historical Notes on Gem Mining," in *Economic Geology* 26 (1931): 681–738.

Peter W. Rainier, *Green Fire* (1942).

R. Maillard, *Diamonds: Myth, Magic, and Reality* (1980).

Peter C. Keller, "Emeralds of Colombia," in *Gems and Gemology* 17 (1981): 80–92.

K. Proctor, "Gem Pegmatites of Minas Gerais, Brazil," in *Gems and Gemology* 20 (1984): 78–100.

*Additional Bibliography*

Carvalho, Fábio Lamachia. *Sonho verde: Aventura num garimpo de esmeraldas.* São Paulo: Geração, 2002.

Santos, Márcio. *Estradas reais: Introdução ao estudo dos caminhos do ouro e do diamante no Brasil.* Belo Horizonte: Editora Estrada Real, 2001.

PETER C. KELLER

**GENÍZARO.** *Genízaro* is a New Mexican term that appeared as early as 1610, given initially to Mexican Indians brought as servants to the Spanish. It continued to be used into the nineteenth-century to identify Plains Indian women and children (rarely adult men) captured in intertribal warfare and sold or ransomed to Spanish authorities who assigned them to Christian settlers for "civilizing" and service as domestics and herders. The term is most appropriately applied to the offspring of the captives. Intermarriage among the descendants of former members of different Plains tribes who had been reared in the Spanish milieu created a subpopulation that was biologically Indian, yet different from both Plains and Pueblo peoples, and culturally Hispanic (sometimes called "detribalized"). The *genízaro* population filled significant political, economic, and social niches as settlers of strategic frontier villages, as members of the militia (where their reputation as fearless combatants was recognized), as emissaries to Plains tribes, and as farmers and other types of workers.

*See also* **New Mexico.**

BIBLIOGRAPHY

Gilberto Benito Córdoba, *Abiquiu and Don Cacahuate: A Folk History of a New Mexican Village* (1973).

Frances Leon Swadesh, *Los Primeros Pobladores: Hispanic Americans of the Ute Frontier* (1974).

Angélico Chávez, "*Genízaros,*" in *Handbook of North American Indians,* vol. 9, edited by Alfonso Ortiz (1979).

Adrian Bustamante, "The Matter Was Never Resolved: The *Casta* System in Colonial New Mexico, 1693–1823," in *New Mexico Historical Review* 66, no. 2 (1991): 143–163.

*Additional Bibliography*

Ebright, Malcolm, and Rick Hendricks. *The Witches of Abiquiu: The Governor, the Priest, the Genízaro Indians, and the Devil.* Albuquerque: University of New Mexico Press, 2006.

ROBERT HIMMERICH Y VALENCIA

**GERCHUNOFF, ALBERTO** (1884–1950). Alberto Gerchunoff (*b.* 1 January 1884; *d.* 2 March 1950), writer and journalist, born in Proskuroff (Khmelnitski) Russia; he emigrated with his family to Argentina in 1889, settling in Moisés Ville, Santa Fe Province. After his father's murder, the family moved to Rajil in Entre Ríos Province. In his classic *Los gauchos judíos* (1910; *The Jewish Gauchos of the Pampas,* 1955), Gerchunoff envisioned the promised land based on the agricultural colonies founded by Baron Hirsch as a haven for Jews fleeing from pogroms in czarist Russia. He moved to Buenos Aires in 1895, where he met Enrique Dickmann and Alfredo L. Palacios—the major figures of the Socialist Party—and writer Leopoldo Lugones and Robert J. Payró. He began writing for the journal *Caras y Caretas,* where he developed a following for his sharp wit and satirical portrayals. Gerchunoff would later serve as a model for Abrahan Orloff in Manuel Gálvez's *El mal metafísico* (1916). In 1909 Gerchunoff joined the staff of *La Nacíon,* which for a young Jewish immigrant signaled acceptance into the literary establishment.

His most acclaimed work, *Los gauchos judíos,* was published during the centennial of Argentine independence. Gerchunoff considered Argentina a "new Zion" where Jews could become fully integrated and therefore forgo the notion of a return to Palestine. The impact of the Holocaust, however, about which he wrote in *El problema judío* (1945), persuaded him to advocate the establishment of the state of Israel. His faith in Argentina led him to dismiss as deviations anti-Semitic acts such as those that occurred during the *semana trágica* ("tragic week") in Buenos Aires in January 1919.

Gerchunoff achieved his own integration into Argentine culture through his assimilation of Spanish literary classics, such as *Don Quixote.* A superb prose fiction writer of twenty six books, he was also an acclaimed journalist and lecturer: *Retorno a Don Quijote* (1951), *Enrique Heine: El poeta de nuestra intimidad* (1927), *Las imágenes del país* (1931), and *El pino y la palmera* (1952) demonstrate the broad range of his literary production.

*See also* **Jews; Journalism; Literature: Spanish America.**

BIBLIOGRAPHY

Manuel Kantor, *Alberto Gerchunoff* (1969).

Myriam E. Grover De Nasatsky, *Bibliografía de Alberto Gerchunoff* (1976).

Leonardo Senkman, *La identidad judía en la literatura argentina* (1983).

Beatriz Marquis Stambler, *Vida y obra de Alberto Gerchunoff* (1985).

### *Additional Bibliography*

Berger, Silvia. *Cuatro textos autobiográficos latinoamericanos: Yo, historia e identidad nacional en A. Gerchunoff, M. Agosín, A. Bioy Casares y O. Soriano.* New York: P. Lang, 2004.

Degiovanni, Fernando. "Inmigración, nacionalismo cultural, campo intelectual: el proyecto creador de Alberto Gerchunoff." *Revista Iberoamericana* 66 (April–June 2000): 367–379.

Koremblit, Bernardo Ezequiel. *Gerchunoff, o, El vellocino de la literature.* Buenos Aires: Academia Nacional de Periodismo, 2003.

SAÚL SOSNOWSKI

**GERMAN-LATIN AMERICAN RELATIONS.** Although the Hansa cities and Prussia had earlier maintained consulates in independent Latin America, formal German–Latin American relations began only in 1871 with the founding of the German Empire. Diplomatic representation was accompanied by improved transatlantic communications, an upsurge in trade and investment, and modest increases in German immigration. By 1914, Germans held important mining concessions in Mexico, Peru, and Chile; Argentina was Germany's second most important trading partner outside Europe; German investments rivaled those of France and the United States, if not of Great Britain. German migration to South America, particularly to the temperate Southern Cone, increased, though it never equaled the massive movement to the United States. The emigrants included educators, scientists, and technicians; many made important contributions to the cultural and economic development of their new homelands. Germans went to Central America in smaller numbers, many becoming involved in the important coffee industry.

Following the lead of Chile, which welcomed a Prussian military training mission in the 1870s, several nations contracted with German military training missions before World War I; sales of German weapons also increased. Germany's colonial ambitions stimulated theorists of empire to dreams of expansion into South and Central America. Richard Tannenberg's 1914 plan, a publicist's vision of a reorganized South America under German tutelage, caused alarm in London, Paris, and Washington, but it is improbable that German strategists considered implementing it. It is, however, certain that those strategists did not consider the Monroe Doctrine a hindrance to German projects in the Western Hemisphere. From December 1902 to March 1903 a serious confrontation with the United States resulted when Venezuela defaulted on European debts. A German-led naval force threatened intervention, provoking President Theodore Roosevelt to threaten the Europeans with U.S. naval might (the dispute was adjudicated in 1904 by the Hague Court). Germany also fished in the troubled waters of the Mexican Revolution (1910–1917) and overreached itself in the Zimmermann Telegram affair of 1917, an immediate cause of U.S. entry into World War I.

Brazil and six small Central American and Caribbean nations also declared war on Germany and the other Central Powers; during the war German economic interests almost everywhere lost ground to competitors, especially the United States. With restored economic and diplomatic relations after 1918, German industrialists established branch plants in a number of countries; German-speaking immigrants—including noteworthy contingents from old areas of German settlement in Russia and Eastern Europe—resumed their move to the Southern Cone.

In the drive for economic self-sufficiency in the 1930s, Germany sought assured Latin American sources of foodstuffs and raw materials. The search culminated in 1934 in a trade policy of strict bilateralism, embodied in treaties with Brazil, Argentina, and other countries, which produced gains at British and North American expense. The economic offensive was accompanied after 1933 by strident propaganda and by strengthened relations between the Third Reich and the poorly assimilated German-speaking communities of the area; Nazis labored to organize these communities for purposes that were never clarified. The expansion of German-controlled airlines, particularly near the Panama Canal, worried the North American military. In the United States belief grew in a vast German strategic project to create—through subversion of undemocratic political elites and perhaps with the aid of German-speaking "fifth columns"—a congeries of Latin American client states of the Third Reich within the Western Hemisphere. Fears were aggravated in 1938 and 1939 by armed uprisings in Brazil and Chile that appeared to implicate German elements, by German negotiations for Mexican oil in the aftermath of the nationalization controversy of 1938, and by exposés of alleged German plots in Argentina and Uruguay.

In the late 1930s German rearmament reduced the amount of civilian goods available to trade for Latin American raw materials, and the economic offensive lost its impetus. Nevertheless, Hitler's military victories from 1939 to 1941 lent credibility to German promises to integrate Latin America into a reorganized European economy under German hegemony. Therefore, in 1940 the United States undertook a costly program of preemptive buying of Latin American commodities. (It should be noted that since 1945 historians have found no evidence of the widely believed-in "German master plan" for the Americas.)

German–Latin American communications and trade were interrupted by the outbreak of World War II in September 1939. At the foreign ministers' conference held in Rio de Janeiro early in 1942, the Latin American states, except Argentina and Chile, followed the United States in declaring war on the Axis powers (Germany, Italy, and Japan). Apart from Brazil and Mexico, Latin America's war effort was limited to increased production of raw materials for the Allies, closure of Axis embassies, seizures of Axis property, and expulsion of Axis nationals deemed dangerous. German espionage networks, continental in scope but centered in Argentina, were not suppressed until 1944. The threat of invasion—which proved ephemeral—caused Latin American governments to request and receive U.S. lend-lease arms; the result was increased military collaboration under U.S. leadership.

As the war ended, Washington, ostensibly out of concern that Axis war criminals would escape to Latin America, pressed Latin American governments to suppress German-language institutions and to close their doors to refugees. These pressures offended Latin American sovereignty and were unsuccessful: thousands of Axis nationals migrated to Latin America after 1945. Many were scientists and technicians; some were fugitives; some were both. The most notable was Adolf Eichmann, a high-ranking Nazi officer. The Israeli government eventually captured him in a Buenos Aires suburb in 1945. Normal relations were restored between the Federal Republic of Germany and the Latin American nations in the 1950s. With the growth of Germany's economic strength, in the postwar era it became one of the most important trading partners for the Latin American region. Germany is the top European exporter to Latin America, and Mexico is its largest market.

*See also* **Argentina: The Twentieth Century; Monroe Doctrine; Nazis; World War II; Zimmermann Telegram.**


BIBLIOGRAPHY

Barbara W. Tuchman, *The Zimmermann Telegram* (1966).

Jürgen Schaefer, *Deutsche Militärhilfe in Südamerika: Militär-und Rüstungsinteressen in Argentinien, Bolivien und Chile vor 1914* (1974).

Holger W. Herwig, *Politics of Frustration: The United States in German Naval Planning, 1889–1941* (1976).

Reiner Pommerin, *Das Dritte Reich und Lateinamerika* (1977).

Stanley E. Hilton, *Hitler's Secret War in South America, 1939–1945: German Military Espionage and Allied Counterespionage in Brazil* (1981).

Friedrich Katz, *The Secret War in Mexico: Europe, the United States, and the Mexican Revolution* (1981).

Leslie B. Rout, Jr., and John F. Bratzel, *The Shadow War: German Espionage and United States Counterespionage in Latin America During World War II* (1986).

Frederick C. Luebke, *Germans in Brazil: A Comparative History of Cultural Conflict During World War I* (1987).

Ronald C. Newton, *The "Nazi Menace" in Argentina, 1931–1947* (1991).

*Additional Bibliography*

Endries, Carrie Anne. "Exiled in the Tropics: Nazi Protesters and the Getúlio Vargas Regime in Brazil, 1933–1945." Ph.D. diss., Harvard University, 2005.

Friedman, Max Paul. *Nazis and Good Neighbors: The United States Campaign against the Germans of Latin America in World War II*. Cambridge, U.K., and New York: Cambridge University Press, 2003.

Goñi, Uki. *Perón y los alemanes: La verdad sobre el espionaje nazi y los fugitivos del Reich*. Buenos Aires: Editorial Sudamericana, 1998.

Mitchell, Nancy. *The Danger of Dreams: German and American Imperialism in Latin America*. Chapell Hill: University of North Carolina Press, 1999.

Schoonover, Thomas David. *Germany in Central America: Competitive Imperialism, 1821–1929*. Tuscaloosa: University of Alabama Press, 1998.


RONALD C. NEWTON

## GERMANS IN LATIN AMERICA.

German beginnings in Latin America were modest. In 1528 Emperor Charles V awarded a concession in present-day Venezuela to the Welser bank of Augsburg, from which he had borrowed heavily; in 1529 Germans settled at Coro. German governance of native peoples proved no more adept or humane than that of the Spanish; the colony failed to prosper, and the concession was revoked in 1548. From Coro, Nikolaus Federmann explored to the area of Bogotá in 1539 but found he had been preceded by Gonzalo Jiménez de Quesada. Ulrich Schmidl of Ulm, representing German bankers, chronicled the Mendoza expedition that in 1535–1536 founded Buenos Aires. In the seventeenth and eighteenth centuries German Jesuits—Martin Dobrizhoffer is the best known—were active in Paraguay and the Río de la Plata.

During the Wars of Independence Hansa traders provided rebels with arms and shipping. In the following years German merchants settled in Latin American port cities; not a few married local women, became landowners, and joined local oligarchies. German mercenary soldiers served in Brazil and fought elsewhere in the civil wars of the period. In the 1830s the Brazilian government brought German peasants to colonize the southern frontier in Santa Catarina, Rio Grande do Sul, and, later, Paraná. Ascending the rivers, Germans formed rural and small-town communities that retained a Germanic imprint for more than a century. Chile brought Hessian colonists to the southern frontier in the 1850s and 1860s. There, isolated from centers of Chilean population, they created a similar Germanic zone. Bernhard Forster (Friedrich Nietzsche's brother-in-law) headed a utopian colony in Paraguay in the 1880s. Well into the twentieth century, Germans continued to found or join agricultural colonies, particularly in southern Brazil, Chile, Argentina, Uruguay, and Paraguay. They played a major role, for example, in the opening of Argentina's Misiones Territory between the two world wars. In Guatemala they were prominent in the coffee industry.

However, North America remained the destination of the majority of German emigrants. As Germany rose to world power after 1871, German communities in Latin America remained small and typically comprised of well-to-do merchants;

bankers; managers and technicians of German electrical, chemical, metallurgical, and pharmaceutical firms; and educators and public service professionals under contract to Latin American governments. German military advisers were influential in Chile, Argentina, and Bolivia. Germans proved adaptable to Latin American business and social conditions, and—sheltered by insular, status-conscious, and largely Protestant communities—slow to assimilate.

In World War I, Allied blockades brought hardship; in Argentina and more notably Brazil (which declared war on Germany in 1917) nationalist riots destroyed property and terrorized individuals. German immigration resumed after 1918, now including war veterans and political irreconcilables, young people without prospects, businessmen ruined by inflation, and ethnic Germans driven from Russia and eastern Europe by war and Slavic nationalism. In the 1930s the Nazi government proselytized in German collectivities overseas, stimulating pan-German nationalism and creating the illusion of a resurgent worldwide German cultural community. Nazi publicists reckoned "racial" Germans to number 900,000 in Brazil, 240,000 in Argentina, and 50,000 to 80,000 in Chile. As war approached in Europe, Nazi activities provoked fear that German communities represented potential "fifth columns." Armed uprisings in Brazil and Chile in 1938 that appeared to implicate Nazis, and rumored plots in Argentina and Uruguay, caused Latin American governments, particularly Getúlio Vargas's dictatorship in Brazil, to restrict sharply the autonomy of German (and other ethnic) schools, churches, newspapers, and social institutions.

World War II brought further restrictions, as under U.S. urging all hemisphere governments except Argentina and Chile declared war on the Axis. Pressed by Allied blockades and blacklists, German businesses adopted local cover or closed. Intrigues involving clandestine German agents and Allied intelligence agencies kept alarm alive; Axis property was seized; "dangerous" individuals were deported. The U.S. State Department considered a program of forced assimilation of Germans and the dissolution of all German-language institutions in the Western Hemisphere; the program, however—impractical and violating Latin American sovereignty—was not implemented except (partly) in Argentina. After 1945 the United States also sought to prevent Germans from migrating to Latin America; nevertheless, many thousands of veterans, war criminals, political irreconcilables, and scientists and technicians valuable to Latin American industrialization succeeded in doing so. Since 1945, apart from remote Mennonite colonies in Paraguay and Uruguay, Colonia Libertad in Chile, areas of southern Brazil, and Central America, German-speaking collectivities have fragmented and declined. Many of German ancestry have assimilated. Still, German heritage continues to be celebrated throughout the region.

*See also* **Dobrizhoffer, Martín; Nazis; Vargas, Getúlio Dornelles; Wars of Independence, South America; World War I; World War II.**

BIBLIOGRAPHY

Emilio Willems, *A aculturação dos alemães no Brasil: Estudo antropológico dos imigrantes alemães e seus descendentes no Brasil* (1946).

Jean Roche, *La colonisation allemande et le Rio Grande do Sul* (1959).

Käthe Harms-Balzer, *Die Nationalisierung der deutschen Einwanderer und ihrer Nachkommen in Brasilien als Problem der deutsch-brasilianischer Beziehunger, 1930–1938* (1970).

Jean-Pierre Blancpain, *Les allemands au Chili, 1816–1945* (1974).

George F. W. Young, *Germans in Chile: Immigration and Colonization, 1849–1914* (1974).

Donald M. McKale, *The Swastika Outside Germany* (1977).

Ronald C. Newton, *German Buenos Aires, 1900–1933: Social Change and Cultural Conflict* (1977).

Hartmut Fröschle, ed., *Die Deutschen in Lateinamerika* (1979).

Alfredo M. Seiferheld, *Nazismo y fascismo en el Paraguay: Vísperas de la II guerra mundial, 1936–1939* (1983).

Frederick C. Luebke, *Germans in Brazil: A Comparative History of Cultural Conflict During World War I* (1987).

Ronald C. Newton, *The "Nazi Menace" in Argentina, 1931–1947* (1991).

*Additional Bibliography*

Brandariz, Gustavo A. *Alemania en la Argentina.* Buenos Aires: Manrique Zago Ediciones, 1997.

Fehleisen de Ibáñez, Elsa. *La colonización germana en el Río de las Conchas: Primera colonia agrícola del período de la Confederación.* Paraná: Tráfico de Arte, 2004.

Friedman, Max Paul. *Nazis and Good Neighbors: The United States Campaign against the Germans of Latin America in World War II.* New York: Cambridge University Press, 2003.

Hanffstengel, Renata von, and Cecilia Tercero Vasconcelos, eds. *México, el exilio bien temperado*. México, D.F.: Universidad Nacional Autónoma de México: Instituto de Investigaciones Interculturales Germano-Mexicanas: Insituto Goethe México; Puebla: Gobierno del Estado de Puebla, Secretaría de Cultura, 1995.

Krebs, Andrea, et al. *Los alemanes y la comunidad chileno-alemana en la historia de Chile*. Santiago de Chile: Liga Chileno-Alemana, 2001.

Magalhães, Marionilde Dias Brepohl de. *Pangermanismo e nazismo: A trajetória alemã rumo ao Brasil*. Campinas: Editora da Unicamp, 1998.

Siriani, Sílvia Cristina Lambert. *Uma São Paulo alemã: Vida quotidiana dos imigrantes germânicos na região da capital, 1827–1889*. São Paulo: Arquivo do Estado: Imprensa Oficial do Estado, 2003.

Wagner, Regina. *Los alemanes en Guatemala, 1828–1944*. Guatemala: Editorial IDEA, Universidad en Su Casa, Universidad Francisco Marroquín, 1991.

RONALD C. NEWTON

## GERZSO, GUNTHER (1915–2000).

Gunther Gerzso (*b*. 17 June 1915; *d*. 21 April 2000), Mexican painter. Born in Mexico City, Gerzso considered himself a self-taught artist. From 1941 to 1962, while painting, he designed sets for the Mexican cinema. In 1974 he studied lithography at the Tamarind Institute, University of New Mexico. His works have been shown since 1955 in exhibitions such as "Latin American Art Since Independence" at the Yale University Art Gallery (1966). He represented Mexico at the eighth biennial exhibition in São Paulo (1965). The University of Texas Art Museum in Austin in 1976 and the Museum of Modern Art in Mexico City in 1977 organized major retrospectives of his work. In 1978 he was awarded the national Fine Arts Prize by the Mexican government. He died in Mexico City on 21 April 2000. That same year, the New York gallery Mary-Anne Martin Fine Art mounted a retrospective of his work.

*See also* **Art: The Twentieth Century.**

BIBLIOGRAPHY

Du Pont, Diana C., et al. *Risking the Abstract: Mexican Modernism and the Art of Gunther Gerzso*. Santa Barbara, CA: Santa Barbara Museum of Art, 2003.

Eder, Rita, and Gunther Gerzso. *Gunther Gerzso: El esplendor de la muralla*. Mexico City: Consejo Nacional para la Cultura y las Artes, Dirección General de Publicaciones, 1994.

BÉLGICA RODRÍGUEZ

## GESTIDO, OSCAR DANIEL (1901–1967).

Oscar Daniel Gestido (*b*. 28 November 1901; *d*. 6 December 1967), Uruguayan military leader and president (1967). Gestido was born to a middle-class family in Montevideo. He began his military career in 1917 in the artillery. Beginning in 1923, he played an active role in organizing the Uruguayan Air Force. Between 1951 and 1955 he held the post of inspector general of the army. He later retired from the military, beginning his political career at a time of profound crisis in Uruguay. During the nationalist governments, Gestido had demonstrated skill in the administration of public bodies such as PLUNA, the state airline (1949–1951), and AFE, the state railroad (1957–1959). From 1963 to 1966 he was a member of the National Council of Government.

Gestido's image was one of honesty, which contrasted with the ever-more tarnished reputations of most politicians at the time. In 1966, the Colorado Front of Unity (List 515) was formed to support Gestido's successful presidential campaign. However, he died only nine months into his term, which was completed by his vice president, Jorge Pacheco Areco.

*See also* **Uruguay: The Twentieth Century; Railroads.**

BIBLIOGRAPHY

*Boletín del Estado Mayor del Ejército,* nos. 112–115.

Juan Carlos Pedemonte, *Los presidentes del Uruguay* (1984).

JOSÉ DE TORRES WILSON

## GHIOLDI, AMÉRICO (1899–1985).

Américo Ghioldi (*b*. 23 May 1899; *d*. March 1985), Argentine Socialist councilman, congressman, and party leader. Born in Buenos Aires, Ghioldi was a secondary school teacher, university professor, and prominent figure in Argentina's Socialist Party. He had joined the party by the early 1920s, and was elected, at the age of twenty-five, to the city council of Buenos Aires, where he served for five years. Following the course of a number of his council colleagues, he served three terms as national deputy from Buenos Aires (1932–1936, 1936–1940, 1940–1943). In Congress, Ghioldi was a leading member of the Socialist opposition to the conservative majority, noted especially for spearheading the struggle against what was considered undue concessions to foreign capital and interests in the 1930s.

Like most Socialist congressmen, Ghioldi concurrently held important positions in the party hierarchy, including editor of the Socialists' main newspaper, *La Vanguardia*, as well as of other publications. In the 1940s and thereafter, Ghioldi became one of the loudest Socialist voices in opposition to the regime of Juan Perón (1946–1955), publishing a number of books critical of Peronism. In the late 1970s, in a controversial decision, he accepted an appointment from the military government of General Jorge Videla (1976–1980) as Argentina's ambassador to Portugal.

*See also* **Argentina, Political Parties: Socialist Party.**

BIBLIOGRAPHY

Camarero, Hernán, and Carlos-Miguel Herrera. *El Partido Socialista en Argentina: Sociedad, política e ideas a través de un siglo.* Buenos Aires: Prometeo, 2005.

Consigli, Raquel E. *Breve historia del Partido Socialista Argentino, 1893–1943.* Córdoba, Argentina: Prosopis Editora, 2004.

RICHARD J. WALTER

**GHIOLDI, RODOLFO** (1897–1985). Rodolfo Ghioldi (*b.* 21 January 1897; *d.* 3 July 1985), Argentine political leader, born in Buenos Aires, brother of Américo Ghioldi. In 1918, he helped establish the Internationalist Socialist Party (PSI), which was renamed the Communist Party (PC) in 1920. Ghioldi traveled several times to the Soviet Union in the 1920s and 1930s and was one of only two Latin Americans to sit as an alternate delegate on the Comintern's executive committee. He served as the Argentine party's president in 1930–1931 and, along with Victorio Codovilla, dominated the Argentine Communists for most of their history. Ghioldi was his party's unsuccessful senatorial candidate in 1946 and a presidential candidate in the 1951 elections, but he never held public office.

As with most Argentine communists, he was a strict disciple of the party's often slavishly pro-Soviet line. Ideologically, Ghioldi adhered to orthodox positions on the role of the party and the necessity of passing through historical stages in the movement toward socialism.

*See also* **Argentina, Political Parties: Socialist Party; Communism.**

BIBLIOGRAPHY

Rollie Poppino, *International Communism in Latin America: A History of the Movement, 1917–1963* (1964).

Jorge Abelardo Ramos, *Historia del stalinismo en la Argentina* (1969).

Sheldon B. Liss, *Marxist Thought in Latin America* (1984).

*Additional Bibliography*

Azcoaga, Juan. *Rodolfo Ghioldi: Un luchador social.* Buenos Aires: Círculo de Legisladores de la Nación Argentina: Secretaría de Cultura de la Presidencia de la Nación, 1999.

Marín, Jaime. *Misión secreta en Brasil: El argentino Rodolfo Ghioldi en la insurrección nacional-liberadora de 1935 liderada por Prestes.* Buenos Aires: Ediciones Dialectica, 1988.

JAMES P. BRENNAN

**GIBBS AND SONS, ANTONY.** Antony Gibbs and Sons, a British merchant house that began operating in Peru shortly after independence in 1822. It was designated by the Peruvian state as the principal contractor or supplier of guano to Great Britain between 1842 and 1861. As such, Gibbs became a major financier to the Peruvian state during the so-called guano boom between 1840 and 1880. In a major economic and political shift, Gibbs was then deposed as consignee in 1862 by a group of native contractors, which included future president Manuel Pardo, who held the contract until 1869. Later, in a similar arrangement, Gibbs became the sole supplier of nitrates from southern Peru after the expropriation of the industry by the Pardo administration in 1875. The company continued to do business in Peru long after both the guano and nitrate booms ended in Peru in the late 1870s.

*See also* **Guano Industry; Nitrate Industry.**

BIBLIOGRAPHY

W. M. Mathew, *The House of Gibbs and the Peruvian Guano Monopoly* (1981).

*Additional Bibliography*

Gootenberg, Paul. *Imagining Development Economic Ideas in Peru's "Fictitious Prosperity" of Guano, 1840–1880.* Berkeley: University of California Press, 1993.

Raimondi, Antonio, and Luis Felipe Villacorta O. *Informes y polémicas sobre el guano y el salitre: Perú, 1854–1877.* Lima: Fondo Editorial, Universidad Nacional Mayor de San Marcos, 2003.

PETER F. KLARÉN

**GIBSON, CHARLES** (1920–1985). Charles Gibson, one of the leading historians of colonial Latin America, inspired a generation of scholars who went on to found the field of ethnohistory. Born in Buffalo, New York, Gibson received a bachelor of arts degree from Yale in 1941, a master's from the University of Texas, Austin, in 1947, and a doctorate from Yale in 1950. He served in the army during World War II and then from 1949 taught at the University of Iowa. In 1965 he accepted a position at the University of Michigan, where in 1977 he was named the Irving A. Leonard Distinguished University Professor.

Gibson's first major publication, with George Kubler, was a 1951 study of the sixteenth-century calendar by Juan de Tovar. In 1952 he published *Tlaxcala in the Sixteenth Century.* This work served as a prelude for his ground-breaking 1964 study of native peoples in the Valley of Mexico in the colonial period, *The Aztecs under Spanish Rule*, which became the touchstone for all further research on the general topic. He wrote scores of articles and several other books, including, in 1966, *Spain in America*, a synthesis of colonial Latin American history. Gibson served as the president of the American Historical Association in 1977 and was a member of the editorial boards of the *Hispanic American Historical Review*, the *American Historical Review*, and the *Handbook of Latin American Studies.*

*See also* **Handbook of Latin American Studies; Hispanic American Historical Review; Indigenous Peoples; Tlaxcala.**

BIBLIOGRAPHY

Gibson, Charles. *Tlaxcala in the Sixteenth Century.* New Haven, CT: Yale University Press, 1952. Reprint, Stanford, CA: Stanford University Press, 1967.

Gibson, Charles. *The Aztecs under Spanish Rule: A History of the Indians of the Valley of Mexico, 1519–1810.* Stanford, CA: Stanford University Press, 1964.

Gibson, Charles. *Spain in America.* New York: Harper and Row, 1966.

Gibson, Charles. *The Spanish Tradition in America.* New York: Harper & Row, 1968.

Gibson, Charles. *The Inca Concept of Sovereignty and the Spanish Administration in Peru.* New York: Greenwood, 1969.

Gibson, Charles. *The Black Legend: Anti-Spanish Attitudes in the Old World and the New.* New York: Knopf, 1971.

Gibson, Charles, and George Kubler. *The Tovar Calendar: An Illustrated Mexican Manuscript ca. 1585.* New Haven, CT: The Academy, 1951.

JOHN F. SCHWALLER

**GIL, GILBERTO** (1942–). Gilberto Gil (*b.* 3 March 1942), prominent and innovative Brazilian composer and musician. Gil, along with Caetano Veloso and others, was a major figure in the late-1960s cultural and musical movement known as *tropicalismo*, and continues to be one of the nation's most influential performers, especially as an articulator of a distinctly black idiom in popular music. Through the utilization in the 1960s of highly stylized versions of folk forms in compositions such as "Louvação" (1967; Homage) and "Procissão" (1965; Processional), the cinematographic construction of lyrics, and the original use of folk instruments in "Domingo no parque" (1967; Sunday in the Park), the introduction of electric instruments in "Questão de ordem" (1968; Question of Order), and the parodic use of advertising jargon in "Geléia geral" (1968; General Jelly), this last written with Torquato Neto. Gil was largely responsible for redefining the parameters of *música popular Brasileira* (Brazilian popular music).

Born and raised in the state of Bahia, like his contemporary Veloso, Gil was influenced by backlands *forro* singer Luís Gonzaga, *samba canção* composer Dorival Caymmi, and especially the major figure of Bossa Nova, João Gilberto. He also incorporated popular styles from Spanish America and consciously adapted the British rhythm-and-blues style of the Beatles to a Brazilian mode, most notably in "O sonho acabou" (1972; The Dream Is Over), released after his forced exile in England from 1969 to 1972 (presumably because he was a visible proponent of *tropicalismo*).

Two formal and thematic preoccupations that recur in Gil's numerous songs from the 1970s and 1980s are mysticism and the music and culture of the African diaspora. Of the latter type, the most significant work can perhaps be found on the albums *Refavela* (1977; an invented word meaning to "re-ghetto"), which prefigures the shift of primary identification among many young Brazilian blacks from being Brazilian to being of African descent, and *Raça humana* (1984; Human Race). This second album, which was partly recorded with the Wailers in Jamaica and popularized reggae as a style to be utilized in Brazilian popular music, simultaneously portrays the African diaspora as the epitome of a universal historical experience and implies that Gilberto Gil, as the logical heir to the legacy of Jamaican singer Bob Marley, is the bard of this diaspora. In 1998, his album *Quanta Live* won the Grammy award for Best World Music Album. In 2005, his *Eletracústico* won a Grammy for Best Contemporary World Music Album. In 2003, Brazil's newly elected president Ignacio Luiz da Silva named him Brazil's Minister of Culture.

*See also* **Caymmi, Dorival; Forró; Gilberto, João; Gonzaga, Luiz; Marley, Bob; Music: Popular Music and Dance; Tropicalismo.**

BIBLIOGRAPHY

Fred De Goes, ed., *Gilberto Gil: Literatura comentada* (1982).

Antônio Risério, ed., *Gilberto Gil: Expresso 2222* (1982).

Charles A. Perrone, *Masters of Contemporary Brazilian Song* (1989).

*Additional Bibliography*

Gil, Gilberto, Carlos Rennó, Marcelo Fróes, et. al. *Gilberto Gil: todas las letras: Incluindo letras comentadas pelo compositor.* São Paulo: Companhia Das Letras, 2003.

Lacerda, Francisco José Neiva. *Gilberto Gil: Partículas em suspensão.* Niterói: Editora da Universidade Federal Fluminense, 2002.

Velloso, Mabel. *Gilberto Gil.* São Paulo: Moderna, 2002.

ROBERT MYERS

## GIL, JERÓNIMO ANTONIO (1732–1798).

Jerónimo Antonio Gil (*b.* 1732; *d.* 18 April 1798), engraver. Trained in painting and engraving at the Academia de San Fernando in Madrid, Gil arrived in New Spain in 1778 to take charge of the Royal Mint in Mexico City and was entrusted with establishing a school of engraving there. His efforts in artistic education eventually resulted in the Academia de San Carlos, formally established in 1785, of which he was director until his death. His works include medals, coins, and illustrations. Especially noteworthy is the commemorative medal of Manuel Tolsá's equestrian statue of Charles IV.

*See also* **Art: The Colonial Era.**

BIBLIOGRAPHY

Jean Charlot, *Mexican Art and the Academy of San Carlos: 1785–1915* (1962).

Thomas A. Brown, *La Academia de San Carlos de la Nueva España* (1976).

*Additional Bibliography*

Báez Macías, Eduardo, Jerónimo Antonio Gil, and Gérard Audran. *Jerónimo Antonio Gil y su traducción de Gérard Audran.* México, D.F.: Universidad Nacional Autónoma de México, Instituto de Investigaciones Estéticas, 2001.

Fuentes Rojas, Elizabeth, et al. *La Academia de San Carlos y los constructores del Neoclásico: Primer catálogo de dibujo arquitectónico, 1779–1843.* México, D.F.: Universidad Nacional Autónoma de México, Escuela Nacional de Artes Plásticas, 2002.

CLARA BARGELLINI

## GILARDI, GILARDO (1889–1963).

Gilardo Gilardi (*b.* 25 May 1889; *d.* 16 January 1963) Argentine composer and teacher. Born in San Fernando, Gilardi began his musical studies with his father; later he studied with the composer Pablo Berutti. He was a founding member of the

Grupo Renovación (1929), an adviser to the Argentine National Orchestra and the National Cultural Commission, and a member of the Argentine Cinematography Academy. In his early works, Gilardi composed in the nationalist style, but as he matured he turned to more sophisticated compositional languages, as evidenced by the universalist style of his religious works, which include *Misa de requiem* (1914/ 1918), *Te Deum* (1936), *Misa de Gloria* (1936), and *Stabat Mater* (1952) all for organ, orchestra, and chorus. He composed two operas, as well as symphonic music, chamber works, music for children's chorus, vocal and piano works, and film and stage music. His opera *Ilse* (1919) premiered at the Teatro Colón in Buenos Aires, 13 July 1923, and *El gaucho con botas nuevas* (1936), a symphonic humorous piece, premiered in the United States under the baton of José Iturbi. Gilardi was a music critic and lecturer, and an excellent teacher. He was professor of harmony, counterpoint, and composition at the National Conservatory in Buenos Aires and at the School of Fine Arts of the National University of La Plata, and a juror in musical competitions. He died in Buenos Aires.

*See also* **Music: Art Music.**

BIBLIOGRAPHY

*Composers of the Americas,* vol. 12 (1966).

Jorge Oscar Pickenhayn, *Gilardo Gilardi* (1966); *New Grove Dictionary of Music and Musicians,* vol. 7 (1980).

*Additional Bibliography*

García Morillo, Roberto. *Estudios sobre música argentina.* Buenos Aires: Ediciones Culturales Argentinas, Secretaría de Cultura, Ministerio de Educación y Justicia, 1984.

SUSANA SALGADO

---

**GILBERTO, JOÃO** (1932–). João Gilberto (*b.* 1932), Brazilian singer and guitarist. Along with Antônio Carlos Jobim, Vinícius de Moraes, and Carlos Lyra, João Gilberto launched the bossa-nova musical movement in Brazil in the late 1950s. Born in Joazeiro, a small town in the interior of Bahia State, Gilberto moved in 1949 to Rio de Janeiro, where he performed initially with vocal groups such as Garotos da Lua. Gilberto's highly syncopated style of playing the acoustic guitar, which distilled complex samba rhythms into a simplified form while utilizing harmonically progressive chords, provided the basic beat of the emerging bossa-nova style. Meanwhile, he also mastered a low-key, precise, subtle, and highly rhythmic vocal style that would also mark the genre.

Gilberto's guitar playing was first heard on Elizeth Cardoso's 1958 album "Canção do amor demais"; his debut as a recording artist came later that year, when Odeon released his singles "Chega de saudade" and "Desafinado" (each cowritten by Antônio Carlos Jobim). In 1959, Gilberto launched his debut album, "Chega de saudade," considered the first bossa-nova album. He recorded several more bossa LPs in the next few years in Brazil and the United States, including the highly successful album "Getz-Gilberto," with American saxophonist Stan Getz in 1964. On it, João's then-wife Astrud dueted with him on "The Girl from Ipanema," one of the world's best-known songs of the late twentieth century.

Gilberto had a profound influence on the next generation of Brazilian musicians, but from the late 1960s on João has led a reclusive life, with only sporadic concert appearances and record releases. He recorded only a handful of records in the 1970s and 1980s, among them: "Brasil" (1981), "João Gilberto Interpreta Tom Jobim" (1985), "João Gilberto: Live in Montreux" (1987), and "João" (1991). His 1999 release, "João Voz e Violão" was produced by Caetano Veloso, but it did not receive critical acclaim. In 2000, his daughter, Bebel Gilberto, released her own album, "Tanto Tempo," which was nominated for two Latin Grammy awards. As of 2007, he lived a reclusive life in his Rio de Janeiro neighborhood, avoiding crowds when not performing.

*See also* **Bossa Nova; Jobim, Antônio Carlos "Tom"; Music: Popular Music and Dance; Samba.**

BIBLIOGRAPHY

José Eduardo Homem De Mello, *Música popular brasileira* (1976).

Augusto De Campos, *Balanço da bossa e outras bossas* (1978).

Ruy Castro, *Chega de saudade* (1991).

Chris Mc Gowan and Ricardo Pessanha, *The Brazilian Sound: Samba, Bossa Nova, and the Popular Music of Brazil* (1991).

*Additional Bibliography*

Garcia, Walter. *Bim bom: A contradiçao sem conflitos de João Gilberto.* São Paulo: Paz e Terra, 1999.

Mello, Zuza Homem de. *João Gilberto.* São Paulo: Publifolha, 2001.

CHRIS MCGOWAN

**GILDEMEISTER FAMILY.** Gildemeister Family, owners of sugar plantations in the Chicama Valley on the northern coast of Peru. In the early twentieth century they built a vast network of lands around Hacienda Casa Grande. Their successes led them to expand operations, and in the early 1920s they purchased Hacienda Roma, owned by the Larco family. The purchase signaled a trend toward centralization of land ownership that characterized the Peruvian sugar industry in the late nineteenth and early twentieth centuries. Centralization and heavy investment in technical improvements were accompanied by a search for cheap labor. Asian indenture had ended, and to expand the labor force with indigenous people, the Gildemeisters, Peruvians with strong German ties, sent labor agents to the highland villages, where they advanced money to young men. The highlanders became heavily indebted peons on the plantations. Later, this same labor force was set free through total conversion to wage labor. Proletarianization of the indebted workers signified that by World War I, Peruvian sugar had reached a period of major expansion. That is because the replacement of sharecroppers and tenants with a mobile labor force meant sugar agriculture was flexible enough to meet market fluctuations. Some scholars see the process as the beginning point in establishing links between anti-imperialism and anticapitalism in Peruvian politics. At this time the American Popular Revolutionary Alliance (APRA) emerged as a major political force in the sugar valleys of coastal Peru. Many of the party's earliest rank and file, formerly small sugar producers, were driven off the land and into artisanry and technical work for the big producers.

*See also* **Plantations.**

BIBLIOGRAPHY

Peter Klarén, *Modernization, Dislocation, and Aprismo: Origins of the Peruvian Aprista Party, 1870–1932* (1973).

Peter Blanchard, *The Origins of the Peruvian Labor Movement, 1883–1919* (1982).

*Additional Bibliography*

Klarén, Peter F. "The Sugar Industry in Peru." *Revista de Indias* LXV:233 (2005): 33–48.

Villanueva, Armando, and Guillermo Thorndike. *La gran persecución, 1932–1956.* Lima: s.n., 2004.

VINCENT PELOSO

**GIL DE TABOADA Y LEMOS, FRANCISCO** (1733–1810). Francisco Gil de Taboada y Lemos (*b.* 1733; *d.* 1810), viceroy of Peru (1790–1796). A native of Santa María de Sotolongo (Galicia), Gil pursued a naval career before serving briefly as viceroy, first, of New Granada (1789) and, soon thereafter, of Peru. Despite the increasing political confusion in Madrid in the early 1790s, Peru experienced considerable cultural development during his term of office: the progressive journal *Mercurio Peruano* appeared regularly, and the Society of Friends of the Country of Lima, which published the journal, sought, with viceregal support, to promote economic growth. Gil oversaw the production of a detailed census of the population in 1791, and a program of public works, and sought to restore the prestige of viceregal authority at the expense of the provincial intendants (first appointed in 1784).

On his return to Spain, Gil joined the Supreme Council of War, becoming commander of the navy in 1799, minister of marine in 1805, and a member of Ferdinand VII's Junta de Gobierno by means of which the latter forced his father to abdicate and assumed the throne in March 1808. Following Ferdinand's own abdication several months later, Gil refused to recognize Joseph Bonaparte as king of Spain and retired from office.

*See also* **Ferdinand VII.**

BIBLIOGRAPHY

Manuel A. Fuentes, ed., *Memorias de los virreyes que han gobernado el Perú*, vol. 6 (1859), pp. 1–353.

Carlos Deustúa Pimentel, *Las intendencias en el Perú, 1790–1796* (1965).

*Additional Bibliography*

Marks, Patricia H. "Confronting a Mercantile Elite: Bourbon Reformers and the Merchants of Lima, 1765–1796." *The Americas* 60 (April 2004): 519–558.

JOHN R. FISHER

## GIL FORTOUL, JOSÉ (1861–1943).

José Gil Fortoul (*b.* November 1861; *d.* 15 June 1943), Venezuelan historian, writer, and politician. Gil Fortoul obtained his early education in El Tocuyo. After his early training in philosophy at the Colegio La Concordia, he left for Caracas in 1880 to study law, but eventually earned a doctorate in political science from the Universidad Central de Venezuela in 1885. He came in contact with the intellectual elements of the city and quickly gravitated toward positivist circles. Gil Fortoul traveled to Europe to fill various diplomatic posts for the government and remained there for ten years, during which he was intensely active intellectually.

Returning to Venezuela in 1897, Gil Fortoul collaborated on *El Cojo Ilustrado,* an important cultural magazine of the era. By government order he was given the task of writing a history of Venezuela. In 1902 he was dispatched to Europe, again on a diplomatic mission, and there wrote *Historia constitucional de Venezuela* (2 vols., 1907–1909). Upon his return to Venezuela in 1910, he joined a circle of intellectuals close to General Juan Vicente Gómez, and subsequently became engaged in important public duties. Over the next several years, he served as senator, minister of public education, and chargé d'affaires for the presidency. As plenipotentiary minister of Venezuela (1917–1924), he was responsible for, among other things, negotiating the border conflicts between Venezuela and Colombia. In 1932 Gil Fortoul became director of *El Nuevo Diario,* a government publication. He also served as president of the Venezuelan Society of International Law.

Gil Fortoul is the author of a dense intellectual opus. Among his most outstanding books are *El hombre y la historia* (1890), *Filosofía constitucional* (1890), *Cartas a Pascual* (1894), *El humo de mi pipa* (1891), and *Historia constitucional de Venezuela* (2 vols., 1907–1909).

*See also* **Gómez, Juan Vicente; Positivism.**

BIBLIOGRAPHY

Juan Penzini Hernández, *Vida y obra de José Gil Fortoul (1861–1943)* (1972).

Tomás Polanco Alcántara, *Gil Fortoul: Una luz en la sombra* (1979).

Elena Plaza, *José Gil Fortoul: Los nuevos caminos de la razón, la historia como ciencia* (1985).

*Additional Bibliography*

Cappelletti, Angel J. *Positivismo y evolucionismo en Venezuela.* Caracas: Monte Avila Editores Latinoamericana, 1992.

Harwich Vallenilla, Natalie. "Venezuelan Positivism and Modernity." *The Hispanic American Historical Review* 70 (May 1990): 327–344.

Rivas Rojas, Raquel. "Del criollismo al regionalismo: Enunciación y representación en el siglo XIX venezolano." *Latin American Research Review* 37 (2002): 101–128.

INÉS QUINTERO

## GILL, JUAN BAUTISTA (1840–1877).

Juan Bautista Gill (*b.* 1840; *d.* 12 April 1877), president of Paraguay (1874–1877). Born into a well connected Asunción family, Gill spent his earliest years in the Paraguayan capital, where, for a time, he worked as apprentice to his father, a high official of the Carlos Antonio López government. In 1854 the younger Gill journeyed to Buenos Aires, where he spent several years studying medicine. He returned to Paraguay just before the beginning of the War of the Triple Alliance in 1864. During the fighting he distinguished himself as a medical orderly and participated in several battles before being captured at Angostura in 1868.

Upon his release one year later, Gill immediately involved himself in the turbulent politics of the postwar period. His vociferous support for Conservatives Cirilo Antonio Rivarola and Cándido Bareiro gave him some prominence on the Paraguayan scene, as did his friendly connections with the Brazilians, whose army occupied the country. These same connections, however, earned Gill many enemies in the liberal camp.

Between 1872 and 1874 Bareiro masterminded a series of revolts aimed at toppling the government of Salvador Jovellanos. Although Gill played only a minor part in these actions, he stood the most to gain when the Brazilians dropped their support of Jovellanos. With their help, he became president in 1874.

Gill has often been portrayed as a Brazilian puppet, but he sincerely wished to see foreign troops leave Paraguay and worked tirelessly to that end. In 1876 he signed the Machaín-Irigoyen treaty with Argentina, an agreement that provided for the arbitration of the border dispute involving the Gran Chaco territory and thereby hastened the evacuation of the remaining Brazilian troops.

Gill had little opportunity to enjoy his laurels. In April 1877, a band of assassins led by Juan Silvano Godoi murdered the president on his way to government house.

*See also* **Chaco Region; López, Carlos Antonio; War of the Triple Alliance.**

BIBLIOGRAPHY

Harris G. Warren, *Paraguay and the Triple Alliance: The Postwar Decade, 1869–1878* (1978), pp. 195–274 and *passim;* Carlos Zubizarreta, *Cien vidas paraguayas,* 2d ed. (1985), pp. 192–195.

THOMAS L. WHIGHAM

## GIMÉNEZ, SUSANA (1944–).

The actress and talk show host Susana Giménez is one of the most successful film, television, and stage personalities in Argentina. Born January 29, 1944, she began her career as an advertising model in 1969, when a soap commercial made her instantly famous. She became a star while alternating between a film and television career and theater revues. In 1974 she appeared in the film *La Mary* with world boxing champion Carlos Monzón, with whom she carried on a passionate romance until 1978. She then starred in several films with the comedian Alberto Olmedo and acted in musical comedies on stage. In 1987 she debuted a television entertainment program, *Hola Susana* (Hi, Susana), which gained great popularity.

*See also* **Argentina: The Twentieth Century; Radio and Television.**

BIBLIOGRAPHY

Internet Movie Database. "Susana Giménez." Available from www.imdb.com/name/nm0319880.

ELENA MOREIRA

## GINASTERA, ALBERTO EVARISTO (1916–1983).

Alberto Evaristo Ginastera (*b.* 11 April 1916; *d.* 25 June 1983), Argentine musician. Born in Buenos Aires, Ginastera began his studies at age twelve, at the Alberto Williams Conservatory, graduating in 1935 with a gold medal in composition. In 1936 he entered the National Conservatory of Music to study with Athos Palma (harmony), José Gil (counterpoint), and José André (composition). His career as a composer began in the early 1930s, while he was a student at the Conservatory. His first significant work in the Argentine national idiom was the ballet *Panambí* (1936), which premiered at the Teatro Colón, 12 July 1940; it later won both the Municipal and the National Prize for Music. The turning point of his career came with a commission from the American Ballet Caravan for which he wrote *Estancia* (1941), which earned him a place of distinction among young Argentine composers. That same year he was named professor of composition at the National Conservatory. In 1942 he received a Guggenheim fellowship, but he did not go to the United States until after World War II. He lived in New York from 1945 to 1947 and attended Aaron Copland's classes at Tanglewood.

In 1948 Ginastera returned to Buenos Aires, where he founded the Argentine chapter of the International Society for Contemporary Music (ISCM). He was appointed director of the Conservatory of the Province of Buenos Aires in La Plata. Over the years he attended concerts of his works in Frankfurt, Oslo, Rome, Stockholm, Paris, and London. He participated in the Latin American Music Festival of Caracas (1957), acting as juror for the composition competition. The following year he went to the United States to attend the premiere of his *Segundo Cuarteto* by the Juilliard Quartet at the First Inter-American Music Festival in Washington, D.C. During the Second Inter-American Music Festival (1961), Ginastera achieved world recognition with the premiere of the *Cantata para América Mágica* and the Piano Concerto No. 1, commissioned by the Fromm and Koussevitzky foundations, respectively. His opera *Don Rodrigo,* based on a libretto by Alejandro Casona, premiered at the Teatro Colón in July 1964. Soon there followed two additional operas, both commissioned by the Opera Society of Washington: *Bomarzo* (May 1967) and *Beatrix Cenci,* performed on 10

September 1971 during the inauguration of the Kennedy Center for the Performing Arts.

Ginastera was one of the most prominent Latin American composers of the twentieth century and much of his music has entered the international repertory. His works have an exuberant, dramatic quality, and they range in style from a subjective nationalism to a more objective, abstract mode, using advanced techniques: polytonality, microtonality, aleatory procedures, and twelve-tone writing. All of his compositions retain a lyrical, expressionistic aspect, involving the use of *Sprechstimme* (speech song) in the vocal works. He died in Geneva.

*See also* **Music: Art Music.**

BIBLIOGRAPHY

John Vinton, ed., *Dictionary of Contemporary Music* (1974); *New Grove Dictionary of Music and Musicians* (1980); *New Grove Dictionary of Opera,* vol. 7 (1992).

*Additional Bibliography*

Buch, Esteban. *The Bomarzo affair: Ópera, perversión y dictadura.* Buenos Aires: A. Hidalgo, 2003.

Scarabino, Guillermo. *Alberto Ginastera: Técnicas y estilo (1935–1950).* Buenos Aires: Facultad de Artes y Ciencias Musicales, Instituto de Investigación Musicológica "Carlos Vega," 1996.

Tabor, Michelle. "Alberto Ginastera's Late Instrumental Style." *Latin American Music Review/Revista de Música Latinoamericana* 15 (Spring 1994): 1–31.

Susana Salgado

**GINÓBILI, MANU** (1977–). One of the best-known Latin American athletes in the United States in 2007 is the Argentine basketball player Manu Ginóbili. Born Emanuel David on July 28, 1977, in Bahía Blanca, he, like his two older brothers, played for a hometown club coached by his father, then headed off to Italy (1998–2002), where he spent two years in Calabria, then with Kinder Bologna shared in four team titles and enjoyed eight individual All-Star or Most Valuable Player (MVP) awards. He also led the Argentine national team to second and fourth in the International Basketball Federation (FIBA) world championships in 2002 and 2006—he was named to both All-Tournament Teams—and to the Olympic gold medal in 2004, when he was named Olympic MVP. He joined the San Antonio Spurs of the National Basketball Association for the 2002–2003 season and shared in their NBA championships in 2003 and 2005. Labeled the team's "only flashy guy" and often filling his new role as sixth man, in 2007 Ginóbili helped the Spurs win their fourth NBA title in nine years; he was joined that season by Argentine national teammate Oberto Fabricio. The focus of "Manumania" in San Antonio, he has also achieved star status back home.

*See also* **Sports.**

BIBLIOGRAPHY

Beder, Germán and Andrés Pando. *Mundo Manu.* Buenos Aires: Ediciones Corregidor, 2006.

Frescó, Daniel. *Manu. El cielo con las manos.* Buenos Aires: Aguilar, 2005.

McCallum, Jack. "... Own Your Own Country." *Sports Illustrated,* October 27, 2003, p. 78.

Joseph L. Arbena

**GIRIBALDI, (VICENTE) TOMÁS E.** (1847–1930). (Vicente) Tomás E. Giribaldi (*b.* 18 October 1847; *d.* 11 April 1930), Uruguayan composer. Giribaldi was born in Montevideo, where he began his studies with Giuseppe Strigelli and the celebrated Italian bass player Giovanni Bottesini. Later, he studied with the Spaniard Carmelo Calvo and the Italian Giuseppe Giuffra, European composers who had settled in Montevideo. As a member of a family of musicians of Italian origin, Giribaldi became an active participant in the musical life of Montevideo at an early age. His first compositions were piano and vocal pieces; as he matured, he became attracted to the operatic forms. As the first opera written by a Uruguayan composer, *La Parisina,* which premiered at the Teatro Solís in Montevideo on 14 September 1878, earned for Giribaldi a place of honor in the music history of his country. The Italian libretto by Felice Romani was sung by the artists of the Italian Lyric Company Nazarino under the baton of maestro Leopoldo Montenegro. Giribaldi composed three additional operas: *Manfredi di Svevia, Inés de Castro,* and *Magda,* none of which achieved the success of *La Parisina.* In addition, he composed works for orchestra, band, and piano, as well as chamber music, including the symphonic poem *El*

*Athenaeum,* and the suite *Scènes militaires.* He died in Montevideo.

*See also* **Music: Art Music.**

BIBLIOGRAPHY

Susana Salgado, *Breve historia de la música culta en el Uruguay,* 2d ed. (1980); *New Grove Dictionary of Opera,* vol. 2 (1992).

Susana Salgado, *The Teatro Solís of Montevideo* (forthcoming).

*Additional Bibliography*

Salgado, Susana. *The Teatro Solís: 150 Years of Opera, Concert, and Ballet in Montevideo.* Middletown: Wesleyan University Press, 2003.

SUSANA SALGADO

## GIRÓN, FRANCISCO HERNÁNDEZ

**GIRÓN, FRANCISCO HERNÁNDEZ** (?–1554). Francisco Hernández Girón (*d.* 7 December 1554), leader of the last major uprising against royal authority during the Peruvian civil wars. Born in Cáceres, he probably participated in the conquest of Veragua in 1535, before continuing to Peru. A relative of Captain Lorenzo de Aldana, he marched under orders of Francisco Pizarro to remove Sebastián de Belalcázar from the north in 1538. Largely successful, he became a *vecino* of Pasto. He was a supporter of Viceroy Blasco Núñez Vela during the uprising of Gonzalo Pizarro, and was named a captain of a company of infantry pikemen. He served the viceroy as well, particularly in defense of the rear guard.

During the battle of Añaquito (January 1546), Girón was in charge of a group of harquebusiers but fell wounded and was captured by Gonzalo Pizarro. Pizarro forced the prisoner to negotiate with Belalcázar to gain his support. But with the arrival of Pedro de la Gasca (ca. 1547), both Belalcázar and Girón traveled to Andahuaylas to join the royal cause. Girón received substantial reward: la Gasca extended him the *encomienda* of Jaquijahuana. He was, nevertheless, dissatisfied. Realizing his disaffection, and hoping to rid himself of the malcontent, La Gasca appointed him leader of an expedition to conquer the fierce Chunchos Indians. At this juncture, however, Girón's disagreements with the *corregidor* of Cuzco got him charged and brought to the Audiencia of Lima for trial. Freed on bond, he returned to Cuzco, where on 12 November 1553 he organized another uprising, this time directed against authorities of the Audiencia of Lima, which had ordered a new tribute assessment and the end to personal service of the Indians. He and his forces left Cuzco on 4 January 1554.

Meanwhile, after learning of the uprising, Marshall Alonso de Alvarado amassed an army of 700 Spaniards and 7,000 native Americans in the name of the king. (In late December 1553 the *oidores* in Lima had revoked the order ending personal service and created a military force in Lima.) Both forces met and fought at Chuquinga on 21 May 1554. Victorious, Girón traveled to Cuzco; at the same time, royal forces were reorganized. The final battle took place 8 October 1554 at the Inca site of Pucará. There, Girón's fortunes ended. The majority of his soldiers deserted, but the rebel escaped capture and fled to Acarí, hoping to take flight to freedom. Unfortunately, the ship sailed out of the harbor as his weary soldiers arrived, so he marched northward to Chincha, then entered the highlands, taking refuge in Hatun-Jauja. It was there he was captured after a final skirmish. He was transported to Lima and beheaded as a traitor in the Plaza de Armas on 7 December 1554.

*See also* **Peru: From the Conquest Through Independence.**

BIBLIOGRAPHY

José Antonio Del Busto Duthurburu, *Historia general del Perú,* vol. 2, *Descubrimiento y conquista* (1978).

Alexandra Parma Cook and Noble David Cook, *Good Faith and Truthful Ignorance: A Case of Transatlantic Bigamy* (1992).

NOBLE DAVID COOK

## GIRÓN DE LEÓN, ANDRÉS DE JESÚS

**GIRÓN DE LEÓN, ANDRÉS DE JESÚS** (1946–). Andrés de Jesús Girón de León (*b.* 14 February 1946), Guatemalan priest and peasant leader. Girón was born in Santa Cruz del Quiché and was raised in the municipality of Tecpán in Chimaltenango. He received religious training at the seminary of Santiago de Guatemala and later in the United States.

Girón became an important national political figure when he founded the National Peasants' Association for Land (Asociación Nacional Campesina Pro-Tierra) in 1986. He received widespread media attention by leading 16,000 peasants on an 88-mile march from Escuintla to Guatemala City in May of 1986. His organization acquired several large landholdings for campesinos to farm cooperatively, but the movement lost membership and importance after 1989.

In 1990, Girón won a seat in Congress with support from the Christian Democrats. At the end of his four-year term, President Ramiro de Leon accused Girón of instigating a series of peasant land invasions. Girón denied these accusations and returned to his parish in Nueva Concepcíon, running for mayor in November 1995. In 2003, Girón was affiliated with the Partido Movimiento Social y Político Cambio Nacional.

*See also* **Catholic Church: The Modern Period; Guatemala.**

BIBLIOGRAPHY

Julio Castellanos Cambranes, *Agrarismo en Guatemala* (Guatemala and Madrid, 1986).

*Additional Bibliography*

Berryman, Phillip. *Stubborn Hope: Religion, Politics, and Revolution in Central America.* Maryknoll, NY: Orbis Books, 1994.

Perera, Victor. *Unfinished Conquest: The Guatemalan Tragedy.* Berkeley: University of California Press, 1993.

RACHEL A. MAY

## GIRONELLA, ALBERTO (1929–1999).

Alberto Gironella (*b.* 26 September 1929; *d.*2 August 1999), Mexican painter and illustrator. Born in Mexico City, Gironella considered himself a self-taught artist. He was a very talented draftsman and sensitive colorist. In 1959 he received a prize in the Paris Biennial of young painters. Since that time, his work has appeared in many individual and group exhibitions in the United States, Latin America, Europe, and Japan. His most noted individual shows have been at the Galería Prisse in Mexico City (1959), the offices of the Organization of American States in Washington, D.C. (1959), the Galería Juan Martín in Mexico City (1963, 1964, 1968, 1977, and 1979), the Sala Nacional of the Palacio de Bellas Artes in Mexico City (1972), and the Museo de Arte Moderno in Mexico City (1977). Gironella tempered crude naturalism with formal elements derived from Spanish painters, resulting in sarcastic reinterpretations of seventeenth-century court life. He also drew on familiar figures in Mexican folk art, such as the skeleton. The last exhibition of his career was held in Seville, Spain, in 1992.

*See also* **Art: The Twentieth Century; Mexico City.**

BIBLIOGRAPHY

Driben, Lelia; Alberto Gironella; and F. Calvo Serraller. *Alberto Gironella.* Mexico City: Consejo Nacional para la Cultura y las Artes, 2001.

BÉLGICA RODRÍGUEZ

## GIRRI, ALBERTO (1919–1991).

Alberto Girri (*b.* 1919; *d.* 1991), Argentine poet. Born in Buenos Aires, Girri may best be described as one of the last of the prominent male modernist poetic voices of the turbulent mid-twentieth century in Argentina. Girri wrote against the backdrop of some of the most violent and unstable times in his country's history, and his poetry evinces the firm conviction that a humanistic cultural tradition is the best refuge from and bulwark against the insecurities of life. Girri's modernist aesthetic put him outside the sphere of committed literature that was central at the time, and his poetry is marked by an emphasis on the solitude of the poetic voice and by extensive elaborations on the hermetic surrealism of the period, often with an impressive sense of the terror of existential anguish. Girri also published many translations of English-language poets.

*See also* **Literature: Spanish America.**

BIBLIOGRAPHY

Jorge A. Paita, "La poesía de Alberto Girri: Rigor de un intelecto exasperado," in *Sur,* no. 285 (1963): 92–99.

Santiago Kovadloff, "Alberto Girri: La poesía es el corazón de la literatura," in *Crisis* no. 40 (1976): 40–44.

Saúl Yurkievich, "Alberto Girri: Fases de su creciente," *Hispamérica* 10, no. 29 (1981): 99–105.

Alicia Borinsky, "Interlocución y aporia: Notas a propósito de Alberto Girri y Juan Gelman," in *Revista Iberoamericana* 49, no. 125 (1983): 879–887.

*Additional Bibliography*

Villanueva, Alberto. *Alberto Girri en el presente poético.* College Park, MD: Hispamérica, 2003.

Villanueva-Ghelfa, Celestino Alberto. "Alberto Girri, o de la poesía como razón hermenéutica." Ph.D. diss, Florida International University, 1999.

DAVID WILLIAM FOSTER

**GISMONTI, EGBERTO** (1944–). Egberto Gismonti, a Brazilian composer, guitarist, and pianist, was born December 5, 1944, in Carmo, Rio de Janeiro, into a family that included many professional musicians, including a grandfather and an uncle who were both band directors. He enrolled for his first music lessons in the musical conservatory of Nova Friburgo in the state of Rio de Janeiro at age five. After fifteen years of study with Jacques Klein and Aurelio Silveira, he was awarded a grant for study in Vienna. An arrangement of one of his compositions, *O Sonho*, written for an orchestra of one hundred performers, was performed in Rio in 1968. Shortly thereafter he went to France, where he continued his musical studies with Nadia Boulanger and Jean Barraqué, who had been a student of Anton Webern. He also worked as a professional accompanist.

Gismonti then moved beyond his conservatory roots to employ electronic instruments and a wide variety of percussion instruments, as well as to incorporate elements of the Amazonian Xingu people's sounds and sensibilities into his music. In the 1970s and 1980s his recordings for the European record label ECM gained an international following among those primarily interested in jazz or New Age music. He has been active as a composer of film music, scoring *A Penúltima Donzela* (1969), *Em Família* (1971), and *Confissões do Frei Abóbora* (1971). His compositions have also been performed by adventurous classical ensembles such as the Turtle Island String Quartet.

*See also* **Music: Art Music; Music: Popular Music and Dance.**

BIBLIOGRAPHY

Bahiana, Ana Maria. *Nada será como antes: MPB nos anos 70.* Rio de Janeiro: Civilização Brasileira, 1980.

Fregtman, Carlos D., and Egberto Gismonti. *Música transpersonal.* Barcelona: Kairós, 1990.

Marcondes, Marcos Antônio. *Enciclopédia da música Brasileira: Erudita, folclórica e popular.* São Paulo: Art Editora, 1977.

Souza, Tárik de, and Elifas Andreato. *Rostos e gostos da música popular Brasileira.* Porto Alegre: L&PM Editores, 1979.

DAVID P. APPLEBY
ANDREW KIRKENDALL

**GLANTZ, MARGO** (1930–). Margo Glantz (*b.* 28 January 1930), Mexican writer and critic. Professor emeritus of philosophy and letters at the National University of Mexico, Glantz was for a time director of the university's creative journal *Punto de Partida* and head of the department of literature at the National Institute of Fine Arts (1982–1986). Her work includes creative prose, literary and cultural criticism, and translations. Her memoir *Las genealogías* (1981), about her family of Ukrainian Jewish origin, won the Magda Donato Literary Prize in 1982. This was followed by the Xavier Villarrutia Prize for the prose poem *Síndrome de naufragios* in 1984. As a feminist, Glantz has defied the conventional "male" genres to render postmodern, innovative, and experimental texts in which a woman's perspective necessarily alters the traditional forms. As a critic, she is recognized for her controversial critique of "la generación de la Onda" (wave), a group of young writers influenced by the U.S. counterculture of the early 1970s. Glantz has also translated the works of Georges Bataille, Jerzy Grotowski, and Thomas Kyd.

Glantz was named a Council of the Humanities Fellow at Princeton University in 1994 and was inducted a year later into the Mexican Academy of Letters. In addition, she received a Rockefeller Fellowship (1996), a Guggenheim Fellowship (1998), and the Sor Juana Inés de la Cruz Award for her novel *El rastro* (2003). Other works include *Sor Juana Inés*

# TRADITION AND MODERNITY

**The anniversary of Evo Morales's election, Bolivia, January 2007.** An Aymara woman performs an indigenous rite in celebration of Evo Morales's first year in office as the president of Bolivia. Morales was the first indigenous Bolivian to be elected president; many of Bolivia's indigenous population saw him as a symbol of hope. © MARTIN ALIPAZ/EPA/CORBIS

LEFT: **A Brazilian rancher uses his laptop while on horseback.** The beef industry in Brazil has benefited from the use of new technologies. Management software has allowed large ranches and even some smaller farmers to multiply the number of cattle per acre and increase production. STEVE WINTER/NATIONAL GEOGRAPHIC IMAGE COLLECTION

OPPOSITE TOP: **Quechua women with llama, Cuzco, Peru.** Once crucial to Incan civilization, llamas are still used today as beasts of burden in remote areas of Peru. © MICHAEL FREEMAN/CORBIS

OPPOSITE BOTTOM: **Indigenous miner chewing and smoking coca leaves.** The government of Bolivia has found it difficult to develop practical ways of controlling coca production and drug trafficking, as demanded by the international community, while preserving ancient local customs, such as the chewing of coca leaves to combat the effects of altitude and to stave off hunger. AP IMAGES

BELOW: **Herding sheep on a newly paved road, Mataro Chico, Peru.** There are still more unpaved than paved roads in Peru. By improving and upgrading the road system, the government hopes to spur development. MARIA STENZEL/NATIONAL GEOGRAPHIC IMAGE COLLECTION

LEFT: **Blessing cars, Copacabana, Bolivia.** A man has his van, his modern steed, blessed by a priest in a ritual ceremony in front of the Basilica de Virgen de la Candelaria in Copacabana. Every weekend travelers come to have their vehicles consecrated, seeking protection from the Virgin for their ride home. PABLO CORRAL VAGE/ NATIONAL GEOGRAPHIC IMAGE COLLECTION

BELOW: **Members of the Kayapo tribe, Brazil, at a conference held by the Catholic Church, Brasília, 2002.** In 2002 the Catholic Church in Brazil's Campaign of Brotherhood, a national bishops' program intended to promote the social work of the church, focused on the needs of Brazil's indigenous peoples. AP IMAGES

**Good Friday procession, Rio de Janeiro, Brazil.** Archbishop Eugênio Sales passes in front of the Metropolitan Cathedral during Good Friday observances. The shape of the cathedral, designed by architect Edgar de Oliveira da Fonseca and built in the 1960s and 1970s, resembles a modern interpretation of the pre-Columbian Mayan pyramids of Mexico. AP IMAGES

INVESTIGORA RU MIA
TZUMPANCO.

ABOVE: **Day of the Dead skeleton figurines, Mexico.** This female skeleton figure, often dressed elaborately in nineteenth-century European clothing, is known as Santa Muerte, or Saint Death. She has gained a rapidly growing following among those at the margins of Mexican society. It is unclear whether her origins date back to pre-Columbian society or if she is the product of a more recent development. © DANNY LEHMAN/CORBIS

LEFT: **Day of the Dead commemorations, Sumpango, Guatemala.** This celebration revives an ancient Mayan custom of communicating to dead ancestors through giant paper kites. KENNETH GARRETT/NATIONAL GEOGRAPHIC IMAGE COLLECTION

RIGHT: **Vodou ceremony, Haiti.** In April 2003, Haitian president Jean-Bertrand Aristide declared vodou, which combines elements of Catholicism and traditional West African beliefs, a state-sanctioned religion. Vodou baptisms, weddings, and other rituals now have the same standing as Catholic ceremonies. THONY BELIZAIRE/AFP/GETTY IMAGES

LEFT: **Watching satellite TV, French Guiana.** Living in the midst of a rainforest, this Brazilian family is able to receive broadcasts from their native country. Satellite television and cellular telephones require much less infrastructure than fixed lines, making communication more accessible to those living in developing countries. © ALAIN NOGUES/CORBIS SYGMA

BELOW: **Musicians entertain diners at the historic Café Tacuba in Mexico City.** The restaurant, founded in 1912, is located in Mexico City's Centro Historico (historic center), which has been the focus of successful renewal efforts funded by the city and prominent business leaders. © JANET JARMAN/CORBIS

*de la Cruz: Hagiografía o autobiografía?* (2001), *Historia de una mujer que caminó por la vida con zapatos de diseñador* (2005), and *La desnudez como naufragio: Borrones y borradors* (2005). A prolific author, Glantz has also contributed chapters to numerous edited works.

*See also* **Feminism and Feminist Organizations; Literature: Spanish America.**

BIBLIOGRAPHY

Magdalena García-Pinto, "Margo Glantz" in *Women Writers of Latin America: Intimate Histories* (1988), pp. 105–122.

Nora Pasternac, "Margo Glantz: La escritura fragmentaria," in *Mujer y Literatura Mexicana y Chicana: Culturas en contacto,* vol. 1 (1988), pp. 205–210.

Magdalena García-Pinto, "La problemática de la sexualidad en la escritura de Margo Glantz," in *Coloquio internacional: Escritura y sexualidad en la literatura hispanoamericana,* edited by Alain Sicard and Fernando Moreno (1990), pp. 31–47.

Naomi Lindstrom, "*No pronunciarás* de Margo Glantz: Los nombres como señas de la imaginación cultural," *Revista Iberoamericana* 56, no. 150 (1990). 275–287.

### *Additional Bibliography*

Agosín, Marjorie, ed. *Memory, Oblivion, and Jewish Culture in Latin America.* Austin: University of Texas Press, 2005.

Bravo, María Dolores, and Blanca Estela Treviño, eds. *Margo Glantz: 45 años de docencia.* Mexico: Universidad Nacional Autónoma de México, Facultad de Filosofía y Letras, 2006.

Glantz, Margo. *Narraciones, ensayos y entrevista: Margo Glantz y la crítica.* Edited by Celina Manzoni. Valencia, Spain: Excultura, 2003.

NORMA KLAHN

**GLISSANT, ÉDOUARD** (1928–). Édouard Glissant (*b.* 21 September 1928), writer and teacher of Martinique. Aimé Césaire was Glissant's professor at the Lycée Schoelcher in Fort-de-France, Martinique. With the group Franc-Jeu, Glissant and Frantz Fanon worked for Aimé Césaire's election to the Constituent Assembly in 1945. Glissant went to France on a scholarship in 1946. Active in the Front Antillo-Guyanais pour l'Indépendance, Glissant was barred (1961) from returning to Martinique or traveling to Algeria. After the French government finally allowed Glissant to return to Martinique in 1965, he founded the Institut Martiniquais d'Études and the journal *Acoma* in an effort to develop cultural consciousness among young Martinicans. Glissant later accepted a chair in Francophone literature at Louisiana State University.

Édouard Glissant has become the major proponent of "creolization," a concept that underscores acceptance of a decentered position in the world, the willingness to encounter the other rather than take one's own standpoint as central, and the will to take cross-breeding (*métissage*) as normal rather than exceptional and reprehensible. Purists are shocked by the contagious mixing of cultures in the language of the young. "Alert to the intermingling of world cultures," poets, according to Glissant, "are delighted." Glissant wants to build the Tower of Babel "in all languages." The year 2007 saw the inauguration in Paris of L'Institut du Tout-Monde, founded by Glissant with the support of the Conseil Régional de l'île de France and the French Ministry of Overseas Affairs.

*See also* **Creole; Ethnic Studies.**

BIBLIOGRAPHY

Works by Édouard Glissant include: *Un champ d'îles* (poetry, 1953); *La lézarde* (novel, 1958); translated by J. Michael Dash as *The Ripening* (1985), *Monsieur Toussaint* (play, 1961), translated by Joseph G. Foster and Barbara Franklin (1981); *Le sang rivé* (poetry, 1961); *Le quatrième siècle* (novel, 1962), Prix Charles-Vallon; *Poèmes* ... (poetry, 1965); *Malemort* (novel, 1975); *La case du commandeur* (novel, 1981); *Le discours antillais* (essays, 1981), translated by J. Michael Dash as *Caribbean Discourse: Selected Essays* (1989); *Le sel noir* (rev. ed., 1983); *Les Indes; Un champ d'îles; La terre inquiète* (collected poems, 1985); *Pays rêvé, pays réel* (poems, 1985); *Mahagony* (novel, 1987); *Poétique de la relation* (essays, 1990); *Fastes* (poems, 1991).

Bernadette Cailler, *Conquérants de la nuit nue: Édouard Glissant et l'histoire antillaise* (1988). J. Michael Dash, *Caribbean Discourse: World Literature Today* 63, no. 4 (1989), special issue devoted to Glissant: bibliography, texts, critical articles; Patrick Chamoiseau and Raphaël Confiant, *Lettres créoles: Tracées antillaises et continentales de la littérature, 1635–1975* (1991), pp. 185–202.

### *Additional Bibliography*

Britton, Celia. *Edouard Glissant and Postcolonial Theory: Strategies of Language and Resistance.* Charlottesville: University Press of Virginia, 1999.

Dash, J. Michael. *Edouard Glissant.* Cambridge, U.K., and New York: Cambridge University Press, 1995.

Chancé, Dominique. *Edouard Glissant, un "traité du déparler": Essai sur l'œuvre romanesque d'Edouard Glissant.* Paris: Karthala, 2002.

Glissant, Édouard. *Poèmes complets.* Paris: Gallimard, 1994.

Glissant, Édouard. *Faulkner, Mississippi.* Paris: Stock, 1996.

Glissant, Édouard. *Introduction à une poétique du divers.* Paris: Gallimard, 1996.

Glissant, Édouard. *Traité du Tout-Monde.* Paris: Gallimard, 1997.

Glissant, Édouard. *Sartorius: Le roman des Batoutos.* Paris: Gallimard, 1999.

Glissant, Édouard. *Le mond incrée.* Paris: Gallimard, 2000.

Glissant, Édouard. *Ormerod.* Paris: Gallimard, 2003.

Glissant, Édouard. *La Cohée du Lamentin.* Paris: Gallimard, 2005.

CARROL F. COATES

---

**GLOBALIZATION.** Over the past century the world has seen two main phases of globalization. The first spanned the turn of the last century and is considered to have ended with the outbreak of World War I in 1914. The second wave of globalization took off in the 1980s and is still going strong in the early twenty-first century. Despite a basic consensus on these two historical periods, there remains some discord as to the actual definition of globalization and what this has, in fact, entailed. At a minimum, the phenomenon of globalization during both periods consisted of a burst of technological innovation, the liberalization of markets for investment and trade, and an explosion in the magnitude of cross-border exchange for goods, capital, and services.

The focus of this essay is the current phase of globalization, which despite the vagaries of fully defining this term, can be distinguished from the earlier phase in three main ways. First is the construction of a post–World War II institutional framework that promotes the continued liberalization of international trade and investment flows. Known as the Bretton Woods system, these institutions consist of such entities as the World Bank, the International Monetary Fund (IMF), and the General Agreement on Tariffs and Trade (GATT) / World Trade Organization (WTO). It was the widespread hardship caused by protectionist and mercantilist policies during the interwar years, and especially the Great Depression of the 1930s, that inspired the creation of these institutional champions of liberal economic policy in the late 1940s.

A second contrast between past and present forms of globalization is that the latter has been driven by the application of the Internet and other forms of high technology to trade, investment, and a multitude of production processes. The dynamism intrinsic to this trend was evident, for example, in the unprecedented boom in productivity and competitive upgrading that characterized the U.S. economy, in particular, during the 1990s. The spillover effects related to these technological breakthroughs are omnipresent and have vastly transformed politics, culture, and the media. But some of these global synergies have not been so benign, as in the case of the swift transmission of financial crises across Asia and Latin America in the 1990s, the ease with which environmental pollution has transcended state boundaries, and the tendency for new poles of economic activity to attract workers across borders regardless of their legal standing in a given labor market.

Together, these first and second attributes of the current wave of globalization have fostered a broadly shared view that this phenomenon has passed the point of no return. This gives rise to the third distinguishing feature of the present phase: a vibrant debate between those who applaud this inevitable process as a modernizing force in the international political economy, versus those who see it as a mechanism for externalizing a given state's problems (e.g., financial instability, pollution, undocumented migration) and perpetuating new sets of winners and losers within and among countries. In particular, some see these institutional structures and technological innovations that underpin contemporary globalization as having deepened the cleavages between the developed countries of the North and the developing countries of the South. As a group of middle-income developing countries, Latin America offers insights that both reinforce and challenge these divergent views during the current phase of globalization.

### LATIN AMERICAN GLOBALIZATION IN RETROSPECT

Whereas Latin America is most recently known for the generalized adoption of market reforms beginning in the late 1980s, its integration into world markets for trade and investment obviously has a much longer history. In fact, Latin America was one of the first regions of the world to be "globalized" and the inclusion of the Americas in buoyant patterns of international commercial exchange during the sixteenth century constituted the creation of the first truly global market. Thus, Latin America's colonial heritage, and the full implications of the region's economic dependence on the imperial powers, remains a powerful reference point for current discussions on globalization.

Turning to the more recent period in Latin America, in particular the second half of the twentieth century, three main periods can be identified. The first is the import-substitution-industrialization (ISI) era, which spanned the 1950s to the late 1970s—a period when the region doubled its participation in the world economy from 4 to 8 percent and per capita income grew at an unprecedented 2.75 percent annually. Second was the rapid entry of the region into international capital markets in the 1970s, as the buildup of excess liquidity resulting from the 1973–1974 oil price hikes prompted a recycling of commercial bank loans from North to South and a pattern of heavy borrowing by Latin American governments. Third was the adoption of market reforms based on privatization, liberalization, and deregulation in the late 1980s, under the banner of the so-called Washington Consensus. Driven largely by the liberal economic nostrums of the IMF and World Bank, market reforms were a response both to the debt crisis and hefty adjustment demands that beset the region in 1982 and to the obvious need for private sector participation in the restructuring of markets and restoration of economic growth. However, to entice private investors to come forward, Latin American governments found it necessary to secure the seal of approval from the Bretton Woods institutions, and hence the willingness to embrace liberal economic prescriptions that had been shunned since the 1950s.

Through the 1990s the region's growth did indeed rebound to an annual average rate of 3.3 percent (1.4 percent in per capita terms), outpacing the average growth rate of the rest of the world (2.4 percent annually) during this same decade. Yet Latin America's latest bout with globalization also ushered in high levels of volatility related to the abrupt and simultaneous opening of trade and capital flows. The liberalization and modernization of Latin American financial markets and the offering of high interest rates to compensate for increased risk also led to a new kind of capital inflow in the form of stocks, bonds, and equities, the mobility of which was further facilitated by the application of electronic technology to the financial sector. While buoyant and exciting at first glance, it was this "securitization" of capital flows, and the ease with which investors could flee the local economy, that triggered dramatic financial meltdowns in Mexico (1994–1995), Brazil (1999), and Argentina (2001).

It is the resulting economic fallout and political instability from these crises that has perhaps most fueled debates about globalization within Latin America. On one side is a highly vocal contingent of anti-globalization activists composed primarily of nongovernmental organizations (NGOs) with mass memberships, but also sprinkled with some old-fashioned protectionists and economic nationalists. This group has politicized the debate on the grounds that aggregate and per capita income in the region has failed to converge toward levels witnessed in the developed country bloc; Latin American labor markets have been exploited and besieged by unbridled competition, resulting in tenacious patterns of un- and underemployment; and poverty and inequality have been on the rise. From this viewpoint, the current wave of globalization in Latin America has meant a ratcheting down of democratic norms and a proverbial "race to the bottom" in the lowering of labor and environmental standards in these countries.

Conversely, the pro-globalization side argues that market reforms have not gone far enough, nor have they been properly implemented in most Latin American countries. The most commonly cited gap is the lack of transparency and failure to enforce property rights and the rule of law across the region. Composed mainly of policymakers, academic economists, and organized groups of producers and consumers that have most benefited from globalization in Latin America, this contingent has pushed for the deepening of international economic integration on the grounds that it would result in higher levels of productivity, growth, and competitiveness.

**Reform and reality**

| Years | Economic Reform Index[a] | Electoral Democracy Index | GDP per capita growth % | Poverty % | Indigence % | Gini coefficient[b] | Urban unemployment |
|---|---|---|---|---|---|---|---|
| **South American subregion (Argentina, Chile, Paraguay, Uruguay)** | | | | | | | |
| 1981–1990 | 0.66 | 0.44 | −0.8 | 25.6 | 7.1 | 0.509 | 8.8 |
| 1991–1997 | 0.82 | 0.88 | 1.3 | 20.3 | 5.5 | 0.527 | 8.7 |
| 1998–2003 | 0.84 | 0.91 | 1.0 | 26.0 | 8.7 | 0.519 | 12.1 |
| **Brazil** | | | | | | | |
| 1981–1990 | 0.52 | 0.70 | 1.8 | 48.0 | 23.4 | 0.603 | 5.2 |
| 1991–1997 | 0.75 | 1.00 | 0.6 | 40.6 | 17.1 | 0.638 | 5.3 |
| 1998–2003 | 0.79 | 1.00 | 1.2 | 37.0 | 12.7 | 0.640 | 7.1 |
| **Andean subregion (Bolivia, Colombia, Ecuador, Peru, Venezuela)** | | | | | | | |
| 1981–1990 | 0.53 | 0.83 | −0.5 | 52.3 | 22.1 | 0.497 | 8.8 |
| 1991–1997 | 0.76 | 0.86 | 0.9 | 50.4 | 18.2 | 0.538 | 8.3 |
| 1998–2003 | 0.82 | 0.83 | 0.0 | 53.1 | 25.5 | 0.545 | 12.0 |
| **Mexico** | | | | | | | |
| 1981–1990 | 0.61 | 0.31 | 1.7 | 47.8 | 18.8 | 0.521 | 4.2 |
| 1991–1997 | 0.78 | 0.70 | 0.4 | 48.6 | 19.1 | 0.539 | 4.0 |
| 1998–2003 | 0.81 | 1.00 | 2.1 | 43.1 | 16.7 | 0.542 | 2.6 |
| **Central American subregion (Costa Rica, Dominican Republic, El Salvador, Guatemala, Honduras, Nicaragua, Panama)** | | | | | | | |
| 1981–1990 | 0.55 | 0.59 | 4.0 | 45.2 | 31.1 | 0.551 | 9.1 |
| 1991–1997 | 0.80 | 0.89 | −3.7 | 52.1 | 27.9 | 0.526 | 9.1 |
| 1998–2003 | 0.85 | 0.97 | 2.6 | 52.5 | 28.9 | 0.554 | 8.7 |
| **Latin America** | | | | | | | |
| 1981–1990 | 0.58 | 0.64 | 0.7 | 46.0 | 20.4 | 0.554 | 8.4 |
| 1991–1997 | 0.79 | 0.87 | 0.7 | 41.9 | 17.9 | 0.557 | 8.8 |
| 1998–2003 | 0.83 | 0.92 | 1.2 | 41.8 | 17.4 | 0.566 | 10.4 |

[a]The Economic Reform Index is measured between 0 and 1 and is based on five sub–indices that form the core of the Washington Consensus policy reform agenda: "trade liberalization," "fiscal restructuring," "financial sector modernization," "privatization," and "capital account opening."
[b]The Gini coefficient is measured between 0 and 1, with 0 representing a perfectly equal distribution of income and 1 the least.

SOURCE: United Nations Development Programme (UNDP). *Democracy in Latin America* (NewYork UNDP, 2004)

**Table 1**

This is precisely the debate that encouraged Mexico's entry into the North American Free Trade Agreement (NAFTA) with Canada and the United States in 1994, as well as the finalization of a U.S–Central America Free Trade Agreement (CAFTA) in 2007. In essence, political and economic elites in these various Latin American countries bought into the notion of globalization as an inexorable force in the international economy, one from which developing countries simply could not insulate themselves. However, while this may be true, the track record since the 1980s suggests that there is still room for policy maneuver in the global era and that the more successful globalizers have also devised strategies that seek to make the market work in their favor.

### LATIN AMERICAN GLOBALIZATION: BETWEEN RHETORIC AND REALITY

Somewhere in between these two rhetorical stances on the effects of globalization on Latin America lie three separate realities: (1) the results of market reform and international economic integration have been highly variable across countries and subregions in Latin America; (2) the simultaneous pattern of economic liberalization and political democratization that has unfolded since the 1980s has proved surprisingly compatible, even if not all recently elected leaders (e.g., in Argentina, Bolivia, and Ecuador) fully support market reforms; and (3) political stability and economic growth have been most reinforcing under conditions of policy flexibility, institutional innovation, and a willingness on the part of policymakers to bolster market strategies with a complementary public policy framework.

With regard to the variable outcomes witnessed in Latin America during the current phase of globalization, Table 1 captures the extent to which country and region-specific structural characteristics can account for some of the diverse results seen in the early twenty-first century.

Of note in the table is the positive upward trend registered by the entire region on those indices that measure economic reform progress and the deepening of electoral democracy. In the aggregate, the region has also seen a favorable rise in per capita income, as well as a reduction in the percentage of the population living below the poverty line. Yet the rise in inequality (as registered by the Gini Co-efficient) and the spike in urban unemployment lend some credence to the claims of the anti-globalization camp. The picture is especially bleak for the Andean subregion, where the superimposition of market reforms on weak and ineffectual preexisting institutions has produced abysmal results in the way of per capita growth, poverty, inequality, and urban unemployment.

At the same time, underpinning this database are some concrete instances of policy success: Brazil's alternative fuels strategy, Argentina's processed food sector, Mexico's rapid diversification away from primary exports and into high-tech manufactured goods, and Chile's application of technology and competition-enhancing policies to the primary goods sector. Yet Chile is the only country within the region that has climbed into the ranks of the top 25 countries of the 104 included in the World Economic Forum's 2005–2006 Growth Competitiveness Index. As Chile's per capita income has risen three times faster than the average for Argentina, Brazil, and Mexico since the early 1990s, it is becoming increasingly common to compare Chile with the likes of countries such as New Zealand and Spain. Over time, Chilean policymakers have relied on institutional modernization and policy stealth or creativity in devising an export-led strategy proper, while at the same time improving per capita growth.

The qualitative difference between Chilean institutional reform and the rest of the region has been measured by the research arm of the World Bank in its Governance Matters Database, the most important variables being voice and accountability, regulatory quality, control of corruption, rule of law, and overall governmental effectiveness. It is worth noting that these variables bear remote resemblance to the more orthodox kinds of politico-institutional reforms advocated by the IMF, in particular, during the 1990s. Given the high ratio of political costs now associated with the completion of the IMF reform agenda, it is no wonder that political leaders in Latin America are now stepping more gingerly on the reform front. Unfortunately, some governments seem to have gone into repose on the pursuit of further reforms, including those more qualitative institutional measures that have served Chile so well.

### LATIN AMERICA AND GLOBALIZATION IN THE EARLY TWENTY-FIRST CENTURY

Almost unwittingly, Latin America has entered a fourth phase of globalization, but one which has more to do with rapid changes in the international context rather than any shared or explicit commitment to advance on the pending reform agenda. The most dramatic difference, of course, is the rise of China as a global trader and its rapid entry into Latin American markets in the early 2000s. China's performance on per capita and aggregate growth since the 1980s has towered over the Latin American record and in fact rendered it downright anemic. Moreover, China's gradualist heterodoxy has fundamentally challenged the kind of Washington Consensus orthodoxy that set the tone for Latin American reforms since the late 1980s. Given its advantages in sheer size and scale, as well as its massive supply of cheap semiskilled labor, China has made it all the more difficult for the Latin American countries to capture or retain international market niches for trade and investment.

Two main scenarios have come to life with regard to China–Latin American relations. The first invokes traditional images of comparative advantage, whereby China has displayed a voracious appetite for energy and raw material imports from the region. For example, Argentina, Brazil, and Chile have all experienced a vibrant growth cycle since 2003 based on the export of copper, nickel, soybeans, and other farm goods to China—all essential inputs for the continued expansion of the Chinese economy. In turn, China has exported mainly manufactured goods based on low and intermediate technology inputs to these South American markets. Despite the current aura of growth, complementarity, and brisk Chinese demand for these primary goods, this dependence of the South American countries on a primary export model riddled with adverse terms of trade possibilities and implicit comparative disadvantage suggests the need to tread carefully.

The second scenario involving China–Latin American relations in the early 2000s is a mirror image of the first: the stiff competition from China that the northern part of the region has experienced in these same low and intermediate technology-based industries, for example, textiles, electronics, and increasingly, auto parts. Especially since 2002, Mexico, and to a lesser extent Central America and the Caribbean, have felt the pinch from Chinese competition in their own domestic manufacturing markets, but also in the U.S. market. Given Mexico's and Central America's high levels of trade dependence on the United States, it is here where the battle for market share is being fought most fiercely with Chinese competitors. Be it cheaper costs for labor and utility inputs, a broader supplier base, or much lower corporate tax rates, both in terms of the dollar amount of exports to the United States and its percentage share, China is now outpacing Mexico in sectors once considered core to NAFTA (e.g., telecom, computer peripherals, sound and television equipment).

Both of these China–Latin American scenarios—comparative disadvantage or competitive edge-out—raise serious medium-run concerns regarding the prospects for competitive growth and political stability in most of the region. Only Chile has succeeded in formalizing its trade relationship with China, as the two countries implemented a bilateral free trade agreement in 2006. For the rest of the region, as China continues to ratchet up the competition, there seems to be no substitute for the hard work of further economic restructuring, institutional renewal, and policy innovation on the home front.

BIBLIOGRAPHY

Bhagwati, Jagdish. *In Defense of Globalization*. New York: Oxford University Press, 2004.

Bradford, S., and Robert Lawrence. *Has Globalization Gone Far Enough?* Washington, DC: Institute for International Economics, 2004.

Garrett, Geoffrey. "Globalization's Missing Middle." *Foreign Affairs* (November–December 2004): 84–96.

López-Claros, Augusto. "Chile: The Next Stage of Development." In *The Global Competitiveness Report 2004–2005*, ed. Michael Porter et al., pp.111–124. Geneva: World Economic Forum, 2004.

Milanovic, Branko. "The Two Faces of Globalization. *World Development* 31 (2003): 667–683.

Qian, Yingyi. "How Reform Worked in China." In *In Search of Prosperity: Analytic Narratives on Economic Growth*, ed. Dani Rodrik, pp. 297–333. Princeton, NJ: Princeton University Press, 2003.

Rodrik, Dani. "Understanding Economic Policy Reform." *Journal of Economic Literature* 34 (1996): 9–41.

Stallings, Barbara, ed. *Global Change, Regional Response: The New International Context of Development*. New York: Cambridge University Press, 1995.

Stiglitz, Joseph E. *Globalization and Its Discontents*. New York: Norton, 2003.

Wise, Carol, and Cintia Quiliconi. "China's Surge in Latin American Markets: Policy Challenges and Responses." *Politics and Policy* 35, no. 3 (2007): 410–438.

Wolf, Martin. *Why Globalization Works*. New Haven, CT: Yale University Press, 2005.

CAROL WISE

## GOA AND PORTUGUESE ASIA.

**GOA AND PORTUGUESE ASIA.** Goa, Daman, and Diu—all located in India—Malacca, the Moluccas, Macau, and Timor were the most im-portant Portuguese-controlled territories in Asia. Portugal was the major European commercial power east of the Cape of Good Hope during the sixteenth century. After 1650 Portugal maintained only a minor position in Asia as Brazil became the principal source of investments and profits.

### GOA

A Portuguese possession from 1510 to 1961, then a territory of India until 1987, Goa became an Indian state in the latter year. Located on the Arabian Sea about 250 miles (400 kilometers) south of Mumbai (formerly Bombay), Goa has two distinct areas: the Old Conquests, with a strong Catholic presence and including Ilhas, Bardez, and Salcette; and the New Conquests, with a predominantly Hindu majority, including the outlying districts taken from the Marathas between 1746 and 1782. Goa is about 60 miles (95 kilometers) in length and 40 miles (65 kilometers) in width at its widest point with a total area of some 1,400 square miles (3,600 square kilometers). The highest elevations, between 3,400 feet (1,035 meters) and 3,825 feet (1,165 meters) occur in the Western Ghats on the border with Karnataka.

Three distinct climates mark the seasons: hot in April and May at 90 to 95 degrees Fahrenheit (32 degrees to 35 degrees Centigrade); cooler and humid from June to September during the monsoon, with temperatures in the 80s Fahrenheit (26 to 31 degrees Centigrade); and cool and dry in the winter with temperatures ranging from 68 to 84 degrees Fahrenheit (20 to 29 degrees Centigrade). The soils, though below average for fertility, are well watered and receive between 110 and 130 inches (280 and 330 centimeters) of rain annually. The major crops are rice, cashews, areca, mangoes, and coconuts. In the twentieth century, iron ore and manganese were mined and exported on a large scale. Since the late 1980s, tourism has emerged as the primary industry, hosting between approximately 20 percent of all tourists to India in 2007.

Hindu Saraswat Brahmins, who were granted exclusive control of both internal and external state monopolies in the sixteenth century, have dominated Goan commercial life ever since. Catholic Saraswat Brahmins have been important landowners since the sixteenth century. Catholic Goans can be found living throughout the world; reportedly there are more Catholic Goans in Mumbai than in Goa itself. Konkani is the state's official language; other languages spoken in Goa include English, Portuguese, Marathi, Urdu, and Hindi.

The population of Goa totaled 266,000 in 1810, passed 1 million in the early 1990s, and reached 1.4 million in 2005 due to governmental barriers to non-Goan Indians entering Goa being diminished after 2000. Approximately 67 percent of Goans are Hindu, 30 percent are Catholics, and 3 percent are Islamic or Protestant. Goans enjoy the highest per capita income in India.

### DAMAN

Daman is a port city 28 square miles (72 square kilometers) in extent, located on the Gulf of Cambay in Gujarat State, approximately 100 miles (160 kilometers) north of Mumbai and 50 miles (80 kilometers) south of Surat (the major port of India in 1700). Daman was conquered by the Portuguese in 1559. The nearby districts of Dadra and Nagar Haveli were taken from the Marathas in 1780 and thereafter administered from Daman until 1954, when the Indians ousted the Portuguese from the inland areas. A flourishing port until Portuguese sea power declined in the seventeenth century, Daman nevertheless remained a major port within Portuguese Asia. Daman continued to be a major exporter of cotton textiles to an area extending from Goa to Hormuz and Mozambique until 1820. The port enjoyed a brief boom from 1815 to 1840 while exporting Malwa opium to the Far East. The city's population was 32,000 in 1810 and 65,000 in 1995.

### DIU

About 15 square miles (39 square kilometers) in total area, Diu consists of a fortified island, a larger island, and a narrow strip of land at the end of the Kathiawar Peninsula on the Saurashtra coast of Gujarat State, about 165 miles (265 kilometers) northwest of Mumbai. After seizing the area in 1534, the Portuguese constructed a fort at Diu, which thereafter served as a critical link in their control of the Indian Ocean. Diu's commercial ties extended from the Gulf of Cambay to the Red Sea area and East Africa. Cotton textiles were the major export in an economy dominated, like Daman, by Banyans. In the 1820s and 1830s, Diu shared in the export trade of Malwa opium to the Far East. Few Portuguese ever resided in Diu. The city's population was 9,500 in 1810 and 40,000 in 1995.

### MALACCA

A city in present-day Malaysia on the Strait of Malacca, the port is located about 120 miles (190 kilometers) northwest of Singapore. Prior to 1500, Chinese, Indian, and Arab merchants made Malacca the major commercial emporium for spices in the Far Eastern trade. Alfonso de Albuquerque conquered the city for Portugal in 1511, after which the Portuguese made huge profits in the spice trade. The Dutch expelled the Portuguese from Malacca in 1641.

### THE MOLUCCAS

The Moluccas are a group of approximately 1,000 islands comprising about 28,750 square miles (74,460 square kilometers) of land, located east of Celebes, west of New Guinea, north of Timor, and south of the Philippines. The Moluccas are a rich agricultural zone famous for abundant spices such as cloves, nutmeg, mace, and pepper. Christopher Columbus was seeking a quicker way to the Moluccas when he "discovered" the New World. The Portuguese established a presence in the islands in 1511 and thereafter fought almost continuously with the Spanish, English, and Dutch to maintain control of the area's spice wealth. The Dutch finally succeeded in expelling the Portuguese in 1612.

### MACAU

Macau consists of a small, narrow peninsula projecting from the Chinese mainland on the western side of the Pearl River estuary, about 40 miles (65 kilometers) southeast of Hong Kong, and the two islands of Taipa and Coloane. Macau has a total area of 10 square miles (26 square kilometers) and has expanded approximately 50 percent in land size from the 1970s to 2007 due to reclamation projects that continue at a steady pace. The southwest monsoon dominates the area's climate from April to September, and most of the annual rainfall of 80 inches (200 centimeters) falls during these summer months, which are also the warmest, with temperatures ranging from 84 to 93 degrees Fahrenheit (29 to 34 degrees Centigrade). The winter months of December to February enjoy cooler temperatures, from the upper 50s to the 70s Fahrenheit (about 14 to 26 degrees Centigrade).

Like Hong Kong, Macau owes its existence to its proximity to the key Chinese port of Guangzhou (formerly Canton). The Portuguese established Macau as an outpost for trade with China in 1557 and thereafter paid tribute to the Chinese emperor until 1849. From Macau, Portuguese merchants also developed links with Japan, the Philippines, Timor, Indonesia, and Southeast Asia. In 1784 the Portuguese built a new customhouse to handle increasing trade. From 1770 to 1840 Macau enjoyed an economic boom due to its middleman role in the opium trade from India (Calcutta and western India) to Guangzhou and other areas of China. As the opium trade declined in importance in Macau due to the rise of Hong Kong, Macau prospered anew from shipping Chinese coolies to Peru, Cuba, and elsewhere. During World War II Macau served as a refuge from the Japanese, who never attempted to seize the city (Portugal was a neutral state during the war). Casinos, tourism, manufacturing, and the re-export of Chinese products were the mainstays of the economy since the 1950s. This situation altered dramatically after 2000, and in 2006–2007, Macau passed Las Vegas as the most important gambling center in the world, catering annually to millions from the entire world, especially Asians, principally Chinese. On December 20, 1999, Macau reverted to China within the framework of a Special Administration Region (SAR) and will retain, in theory, considerable autonomy until 2049.

### EAST TIMOR

Timor is the easternmost island in the Lesser Sunda chain and is situated about 500 miles (800 kilometers) east of Bali and 400 miles (640 kilometers) northwest of Darwin, Australia. The entire island of Timor is 600 miles (960 kilometers) long with a maximum width of 60 miles (95 kilometers). The island is divided between Indonesia and East Timor, the latter occupying less than half of the island with 5,640 square miles (14,610 square kilometers). East Timor has a mountainous terrain, with its highest elevation slightly above 9,700 feet (2950 meters). Timor has a long dry season and an irregular monsoon season from December to April.

The Portuguese began to trade with Timor between 1513 and 1520, seeking sandalwood, honey, and beeswax. Missionaries arrived between 1562 and 1585, with permanent Portuguese settlers following in 1586. The Portuguese lost the western half of Timor to the Dutch in 1651. Thereafter, Macau dominated the Portuguese trade with Timor. Dili, the major port and capital of the Portuguese eastern half of Timor, sent sandalwood and slaves to Macau from 1769 to perhaps as late as the early 1900s. Opium, imported from Macau, was introduced into western Indonesia via Timor in exchange for agricultural products. Slavery, due to the gradual enforcement of the law, continued up to World War I. An insurrection just prior to World War I took the lives of approximately 14,000 Timorese and 500 Portuguese soldiers.

Coffee was the major export from the 1860s until the first decade of the twenty-first century. Oil exploration since the 1970s has resulted in significant discoveries of offshore oil and natural gas in the Timor Sea. Starting in 2006 oil by ship and liquefied natural gas have become the major sources of foreign exchange for East Timor. A liquefied natural gas pipeline operates 500 kilometers from the Timor sea to Darwin, Australia, where the liquefied natural gas is stored in two huge tanks prior to loading on ships bound to China and Europe. Hydrocarbons have replaced agriculture as the major exports since 2006.

The Japanese occupied Timor during World War II. Destruction was widespread, including the loss of the island's archives. The Portuguese Revolution of 1974 led to East Timor's unilateral declaration of independence from Portugal. Indonesia, with the tacit agreement of the United States of America, shortly thereafter invaded East Timor and annexed the entire island. From 1975 to 1999 East Timor encountered fierce guerrilla warfare and a campaign of genocide encouraged by the Indonesian government. These developments led to the "reported" mass killings (but these figures appear to be grossly exaggerated) 100,000 and 250,000 inhabitants. United Nations peacekeepers, numbering 5,000 to 8,000 soldiers, occupied East Timor from 1999 to 2002. East Timor gained full independence on May 20, 2002. The population of East Timor was slightly more than 900,000 in 1850, 550,000 in 1980, and was more than 1 million in 2005.

*See also* **Portuguese Empire.**

BIBLIOGRAPHY

Alden, Dauril. *The Making of an Enterprise: The Society of Jesus in Portugal, Its Empire and Beyond, 1540–1750.* Stanford, CA: Stanford University Press, 1996.

Bauss, Rudy. "Indian and Chinese Control of the Portuguese Eastern Empire." *Purabhilekh-Puratatva* 10, no. 1 (1992): 1–12.

Borges, Charles J. *The Economics of the Goa Jesuits 1542–1759: An Explanation of Their Rise and Fall.* Delhi: Concept, 1994.

Boxer, C. R. *Fidalgos in the Far East: 1550–1770.* London: Oxford University Press, 1968.

Boxer, C. R. *Portuguese India in the Mid-Seventeenth Century.* Delhi: Oxford University Press, 1980.

Clarence-Smith, Gervase. *The Third Portuguese Empire, 1825–1975.* Manchester, U.K.: Manchester University Press, 1985.

De Souza, Teotonio R. *Medieval Goa: A Socio-Economic History.* New Delhi: Concept, 1979.

Disney, Anthony R. *Twilight of the Pepper Empire: Portuguese Trade in Southwest India in the Early Seventeenth Century.* Cambridge, MA: Harvard University Press, 1978.

Greenlees, Donald. "In a Wave of Gambling Profits, an Undertow for Some." *New York Times*, October 10, 2007.

Matos, Artur Teodoro de. *Timor Português, 1515–1769: Contribuição para a sua história.* Lisbon: Faculdade de Letras da Universidade de Lisboa Instituto Histórico Infante Dom Henrique, 1974.

Pearson, M. N. *Coastal Western India.* New Delhi: Concept, 1981.

Pearson, M. N. *The Portuguese in India.* Cambridge, U.K.: Cambridge University Press, 1987.

Pinto, Celsa. *Situating Indo-Portuguese Trade History: A Commercial Resurgence, 1770–1830.* Tellicherry, India: Institute for Research in Social Sciences and Humanities, 2003.

Reid, Anthony. *Southeast Asia in the Age of Commerce, 1450–1680,* 2 vols. New Haven, CT: Yale University Press, 1988.

Subrahmanyam, Sanjay. *The Political Economy of Commerce: Southern India, 1500–1650.* Cambridge, U.K.: Cambridge University Press, 1990.

Subrahmanyam, Sanjay. *The Portuguese Empire in Asia, 1500–1700: A Political and Economic History.* London: Longman, 1993.

RUDY BAUSS

**GOBERNADOR.** In Spanish America the *gobernador* (governor) ranked behind the viceroy, captain-general, and president in the hierarchy of colonial administrators. Like so many colonial institutions, the governorship had its origins in medieval Spain when the monarchs of Castile and Aragon appointed *procuradores* to represent royal interests and enforce royal laws in areas where they could not rule personally. (Such officials became the viceroys in areas of Spain taken from the Moors.)

The first governor in the New World was Christopher Columbus, who received the title Governor of the Indies in the Capitulations of Santa Fe in April 1492. Soon after, however, Ferdinand and Isabella replaced him as governor of Española with two loyal subjects, first with Francisco de Bobadilla and then with Nicolás de Ovando, thus firmly establishing the governorship in the Indies. As the Spanish presence in the Caribbean increased, the crown appointed governors for the newly conquered islands, the best known of whom were Juan Ponce de León in Puerto Rico and Diego de Velásquez in Cuba.

Extension of the Spanish Conquest into Mexico and South America ultimately led Charles I to establish viceroys in New Spain (Mexico) and Peru and captain-generals in areas of the Spanish Indies far removed from the viceregal capitals such as Chile, Guatemala, and Venezuela. Governors served in less important areas such as Florida, Nicaragua, and Panama and in some of the key cities such as Cartagena, Huancavelica, and Veracruz. For most of these gubernatorial posts, the appointee had to have the military rank of colonel and to have been born in Spain, but the crown occasionally ignored one or both of these requirements if a would-be governor had demonstrated his fitness for office in other ways.

*See also* **Colonialism; Columbus, Christopher; Ponce de León, Juan.**

BIBLIOGRAPHY

*Recopilacíon de leyes de los Reynos de las Indias,* 4 vols. (1681; repr. 1973), libro V, título II.

John Jay TePaske, *The Governorship of Spanish Florida, 1700–1763* (1964).

*Additional Bibliography*

Barrios, Feliciano. *El gobierno de un mundo: Virreinatos y audiencias en la América hispánica.* Cuenca, Ecuador: Ediciones de la Universidad de Castilla-La Mancha: Fundación Rafael del Pino, 2004.

JOHN JAY TEPASKE

## GODOI, JUAN SILVANO (1850–1926).

Juan Silvano Godoi (*b.* 12 November 1850; *d.* 27 January 1926), Paraguayan historian, bibliophile, and political figure. Though born in Asunción, Godoi spent his early years in Buenos Aires, where he studied law. He interrupted his studies in 1869 to return to Paraguay to participate, at age nineteen, in the drafting of his country's first democratic constitution.

The defeat of Marshal Francisco Solano López a year later initiated a period of great political instability and foreign intervention in Paraguay; various factions vied for power. Godoi joined actively in a number of political intrigues, including the 1877 assassination of President Juan Bautista Gill, a Brazilian puppet. As a result of these activities, Godoi was forced into exile and went to Argentina, where he stayed eighteen years. While there, he remained active in emigré politics, however, and on several occasions helped to arm rebel groups who sought to invade Paraguay.

In the mid-1890s Godoi accepted a government compromise that permitted him to return to Asunción. While in exile, he had amassed a prize-winning library of 20,000 volumes, which he now used to form the nucleus of a new national library. From 1902 until his death, Godoi was director of the National Library, Museum, and Archive. He was also a historian of note, having written a dozen studies, including *Monografías históricas* (1893), *Últimas operaciones de guerra del General José Eduvigis Díaz* (1897), *Mi misión a Río de Janeiro* (1897), *La muerte del Mariscal López* (1905), *El baron de Río Branco* (1912), and *El Asalto a los acorazados* (1919). Godoi's personal diaries and manuscripts are now held in the Special Collections Library of the University of California, Riverside.

*See also* **Gill, Juan Bautista; Libraries in Latin America; López, Francisco Solano.**

BIBLIOGRAPHY

William Belmont Parker, *Paraguayans of To-Day* (repr. 1967), pp. 15–17.

Jack Ray Thomas, *Biographical Dictionary of Latin American Historians and Historiography* (1984).

Carlos Zubizarreta, *Cien vidas paraguayas,* 2d ed. (1985), pp. 218–222.

*Additional Bibliography*

Churukian, Araxie P. "The Juan Silvano Godoi Collection at the University of California, Riverside." *Latin American Research Review* 27 (1992): 121–124.

THOMAS L. WHIGHAM

## GODOY, MANUEL (1767–1851).

Manuel Godoy (*b.* 12 May 1767; *d.* 4 October 1851), first minister and favorite of Charles IV of Spain. Godoy was born into a modest hidalgo family in Estremadura. He obtained an adequate education in the liberal arts and, at the age of nineteen, entered the royal bodyguards. From this position he rose to power rapidly amid rumors that he was Queen María Luisa's lover. The titles he acquired included duke of

Alcudia, prime minister (1792), admiral general of Spain and the Indies, and Prince of the Peace (after negotiating the Peace of Basel with France in 1795). The unprecedented princely title set him above all other grandees in Spain.

Circumstances as well as favoritism played a role in Godoy's ascent. Previous ministers had failed to appease the revolutionaries in France, and Charles IV's change in policy toward France required someone not identified with the policies of the past.

In domestic policy, Godoy attempted to carry on the reforming spirit of the reign of Charles III, but his lack of experience led to a series of ad hoc policies and his most radical proposals were based on the royal need for revenue. His colonial policy, like those of his ministerial predecessors, also sought to increase revenue. Suspecting that he was treating with enemies of the Revolution, the Directory in France urged his dismissal and Godoy resigned his post on 28 March 1798.

Godoy returned to power in 1801 with the blessing of Charles IV and María Luisa. Although without formal office, Godoy enjoyed a powerful influence in policy making. Thereafter he became a pawn of Napoleon and, believing he had a future as the prince of the Algarve, was instrumental in allowing French troops to enter Spain.

Contemporaries despised Godoy as a young, inexperienced upstart, and although he tried to win the political support of moderate reformists, his foreign policy had disastrous results that fed his opponents' ire. Godoy was despised in the colonies as well as in Spain and the news of the riot at Aranjuez (1808) that led to his dismissal and Charles's abdication was joyously received in Spain and throughout the empire.

*See also* **Charles III of Spain; Charles IV of Spain.**

BIBLIOGRAPHY

Jacques Chastenet, *Godoy, Master of Spain, 1792–1808* (1953).

Richard Herr, *The Eighteenth-Century Revolution in Spain* (1958), esp. pp. 348–444.

Carlos Seco Serrano, *Godoy, el hombre y el político* (1978).

Douglas Hilt, *The Troubled Trinity* (1987).

*Additional Bibliography*

Belmonte Díaz, José, and Pilar Leseduarte. *Godoy: Historia documentada de un expolio.* Bilbao: Ediciones Beta III Milenio, 2004.

La Parra López, Emilio. *Manuel Godoy: La aventura del poder.* Barcelona: Tusquets, 2002.

SUZANNE HILES BURKHOLDER

---

**GODOY CRUZ, TOMÁS** (1791–1852). Tomás Godoy Cruz (*b.* 6 March 1791; *d.* 15 May 1852), Argentine businessman, educator, and politician. Born in Mendoza to a patrician family, Godoy Cruz earned degrees in philosophy and law from the University of San Felipe, Chile, in 1810 and 1813. When Facundo Quiroga invaded Mendoza in 1831, José Videla Castillo, de facto governor of the province, and his allies, of whom Godoy Cruz was one, were exiled to Chile. In exile during the 1830s, Godoy Cruz published a *Manual* (1838) on textiles, taught extensively in related fields, and invested in Argentine commerce, mining, and textiles. Aware of Godoy Cruz's expertise, Governor José Félix Aldao asked him back from exile and in 1846 appointed him to direct governmental policies regarding textile industries in the province. His most notable contribution, however, was in politics. A contemporary viewed him as someone "accustomed to the admiration and even respect of San Martín and O'Higgins, having a great appreciation for his own person and the conviction of his opinions." Godoy Cruz, a close collaborator of San Martín and a supporter of Platine independence who donated his homestead to the cause early in the conflict, displayed this self-confidence in the Congress of Tucumán (1816–1819) and as governor of Mendoza (1820–1822), where he died.

*See also* **Argentinas The Nineteenth Century.**

BIBLIOGRAPHY

Pedro Isidro Caraffa, *Hombres notables de Cuyo* (1912).

Enrique Udaondo, *Diccionario biográfico argentino* (1938), pp. 459–460.

Benito Marianetti, *Un mendocino en el Congreso de Tucumán* (1966).

*Additional Bibliography*

García-Godoy, Christián. *Tomás Godoy Cruz: Su tiempo, su vida, su drama; ensayo crítico.* Washington: Full Life/ Vida Plena; Impressions In Ink, 1991.

FIDEL IGLESIAS

**GOERITZ, MATHIAS** (1915–1990). Mathias Goeritz (*b.* 4 April 1915; *d.* 1990), Mexican painter, sculptor, and teacher. Born in Danzig, Goeritz studied medicine, art, art history, and philosophy in Berlin. He arrived in Mexico in 1949 and began an active life in the arts as a teacher, artist, and founder of four art galleries between 1950 and 1952 in Guadalajara, Jalisco. He is primarily known for his experimental museum El Eco, constructed in Mexico City in 1953, and his great Plaza of the Five Towers, constructed in 1957–1958 in Satellite City, a suburb of Mexico City. The monumental size of the towers and the spatial integration of a sculpture with the floor and walls of El Eco influenced primary structure and minimalist sculptors of the United States and Mexico in the 1960s and 1970s.

In 1960 Goeritz distributed "Please Stop," a printed leaflet, in front of the Museum of Modern Art in New York City to protest the exhibition of Jean Tinguely's *Homage to New York,* a self-destructing machine, because it exemplified the loss of spirituality in art. In 1961 a manifesto by Goeritz inspired Petro Friedeberg, José Luis Cuevas, and others to form a group in Mexico City called Los Hartos (Fed Up). Goertiz's other major works include Pyramid of Mixcose (1970) for a housing project in Mexico City; Centro del Espacio Escultorico (1979), sixty-four modules with sculpture near the ancient site of Cuicuilco; and Laberinto de Jerusalem (1973–1980), a community center in Jerusalem that is a wonderful example of sculpture combined with architecture.

*See also* **The Twentieth Century.**

BIBLIOGRAPHY

Gregory Battcock, *Minimal Art: A Critical Anthology* (1968).

Frederico Morais, *Mathias Goeritz* (1982).

*Additional Bibliography*

Carvajal, Rina, and Alma Ruiz. *The Experimental Exercise of Freedom: Lygia Clark, Gego, Mathias Goeritz, Hélio Octicica, Mira Schendel.* Los Angeles: Museum of Contemporary Art, 1999.

Kassner, Lily S. de, and Mathias Goeritz. *Mathias Goeritz.* México, D.F.: Instituto Nacional de Bellas Artes, 1998.

Museum of Contemporary Art (Los Angeles, CA), et al. *The Experimental Exercise of Freedom: Lygia Clark, Gego, Mathias Goeritz, Hélio Oiticica, Mira Schendel.* Los Angeles: Museum of Contemporary Art, 1999.

JACINTO QUIRARTE

**GOETHALS, GEORGE WASHINGTON** (1858–1928). George Washington Goethals (*b.* 29 June 1858; *d.* 21 January 1928), U.S. Army officer and engineer. After graduating from the United States Military Academy in 1880, Goethals studied engineering at Willetts Point, New York; taught for four years at West Point; and supervised improvement work on the Ohio and Tennessee rivers. He was chief of engineers with the First Army Corps during the Spanish-American War in 1898; supervised river and harbor works in New England from 1900 to 1903; and served on the U.S. Army's general staff from 1903 to 1907. Following the resignation of two civilian engineers, President Theodore Roosevelt in 1907 appointed Goethals chief of the army engineers supervising the construction of the Panama Canal. Goethals brought the project to completion in early 1914 after overcoming problems in engineering, supply, climate, disease, and living conditions. At that time President Woodrow Wilson appointed Goethals the first governor of the Canal Zone. During World War I, Goethals served as director of purchase, storage, and traffic for the War Department. He retired from the military after the war to establish his own engineering consulting firm.

*See also* **Panama Canal.**

BIBLIOGRAPHY

George W. Goethals, ed., *The Panama Canal: An Engineering Treatise,* 2 vols. (1916).

Joseph B. Bishop, *Goethals: Genius of the Panama Canal* (1930).

David Mc Cullough, *The Path Between the Seas: The Creation of the Panama Canal, 1870–1914* (1977).

*Additional Bibliography*

Griffin, Walt. "George W. Goethals and the Panama Canal." Ph.D. diss., University of Cincinnati, 1988.

THOMAS M. LEONARD

## GOIÁS.

**GOIÁS.** Goiás, a Brazilian state that had an area of 248,000 square miles until 1989, when the new state of Tocantins was created out of a portion of it. Goiás now covers 137,000 square miles and has a population of 4.8 million (2002 est.). The geographical center of Brazil, Goiás encompasses the Federal District and the new capital of Brasília. The name *Goiás* comes from one of the tribes of Indians who used to be very numerous throughout the territory. The first chronicler, Silva e Souza, counted seventeen tribes in existence at the beginning of the nineteenth century. Today they are nearly all extinct.

During the sixteenth and seventeenth centuries, Goiás was only occasionally reached by explorers and raiders who came from São Paulo to hunt Indians. It was officially discovered during the gold rush by Bartolomeu Bueno de Silva's ("The Anhanguera") expedition (1722–1725). The discovery of gold brought about the first colonization and the characteristics typical of a gold rush: violence, instability, a rapid boom, and a sudden decline. This period lasted about sixty years (1726–1785) and left behind a town and three dozen frontier settlements with a total population of about sixty thousand.

The gold gone, the population became sedentary, spreading out over the plains and sierras and dedicating themselves to subsistence farming and the raising of cattle. Throughout the entire nineteenth century and into the first decades of the twentieth, the export of livestock constituted the area's only commercial relationship with the rest of the country. The population grew slowly, aided by constant immigration from the neighboring states of São Paulo, Minas Gerais, Bahia, and Maranhão. The 1920 census registered 500,000 inhabitants living throughout the vast open spaces.

The third phase of colonization began with the Revolution of 1930 and the so-called "march to the west." This initiated a very dynamic period for the population of the Goiás area that was still going strong in the mid-1990s. In 1933 construction was begun on the new capital of Goiás, Goiânia, both symbolizing and stimulating the drive toward modernization and progress. Its establishment should have marked the fall of the old oligarchies and the beginning of economic progress. In both cases, however, the road proved longer than anticipated. The triumph of Goiânia was not the hoped for industrial modernization, but the great impulse given to the agricultural colonization of the east central region of the country.

By 1990, the population of Goiâna had reached over a million. The construction of Brasília begun in 1960 (as a political commitment to the development of Brazil's interior) and the completion of great nationalized railroads especially the one from Belém to Brasília—promoted the occupation of the last open spaces: the valleys of the Araguaia and the Tocantins rivers in the extreme north. In recent decades, government projects have aided the growth of the livestock industry and of exportable crops (soy, corn, and rice).

*See also* **Brazil, Geography; Gold Rushes, Brazil; Mining: Colonial Brazil.**

BIBLIOGRAPHY

Luis Palacin, *Goiás, 1722–1822: Estrutura e conjuntura numa Capitania de Minas* (1972).

F. Itami Campos, *Coronelismo em Goiás* (1983).

Luis Palacin and Maria Augusta De Sant'anna Moraes, *História de Goiás,* 4th ed. (1986).

Nasr N. Fayad Chaul, *A construção de Goiânia e a transferência da capital* (1988).

*Additional Bibliography*

Guy, Donna. *Contested Ground.* Tucson: University of Arizona Press, 1998.

McCreery, David. *Frontier Goiás.* Stanford, CA: Stanford University Press, 2006.

Toledo, Caio Navaro de. *Concepções e formacao do estado brasileiro.* São Paulo: Anita Garibaldi, 1999.

LUIS PALACÍN

## GOICURÍA Y CABRERA, DOMINGO

**GOICURÍA Y CABRERA, DOMINGO** (1804–1870). Domingo Goicuría y Cabrera (*b.* 23 June 1804; *d.* 6 May 1870), Cuban independence figure. Goicuría, a native of Havana, was a rich merchant who became even richer during the U.S. Civil War running supplies from Mexico to Texas. He favored slavery and the colonization of Cuba by whites. A tenacious opponent of Spanish colonial rule, at first he advocated the annexation of the island to the United States, and in 1855 he supported a U.S.-backed expedition to Cuba that failed. This led him to embrace the idea of independence, and a year later he joined forces with the American filibuster William Walker for the invasion of Nicaragua. He expected that after taking over Nicaragua, Walker would invade Cuba. But Walker wanted to conquer the rest of Central America rather than Cuba, and the two men quarreled. Afterward Goicuría intensified his anti-Spanish activities until he finally succeeded in invading Cuba after the 1868 outbreak of the Ten Years' War. He was captured in February 1870 by the Spaniards and three months later was publicly executed by garrote in Havana.

*See also* **Filibustering; Ten Years, War; Walker, William.**

BIBLIOGRAPHY

Gerald E. Poyo makes some references to Goicuría's activities in *"With All and for the Good of All"* (1989). See also Vidal Morales, *Iniciadores y primeros mártires de la revolución cubana* (1963), vol 3.

*Additional Bibliography*

May, Robert E. *Manifest Destiny's Underworld: Filibustering in Antebellum America.* Chapel Hill: University of North Carolina Press, 2002.

José M. Hernández

---

**GOLBERY DO COUTO E SILVA** (1911–1987). Golbery do Couto e Silva (*b.* 21 August 1911; *d.* 18 September 1987), Brazilian military officer and political figure. Born in Rio Grande do Sul, Golbery graduated from the military command college. He attended the U.S. Army Command and General Staff College at Fort Leavenworth in 1944 before serving in the Brazilian Expeditionary Force (FEB) in Italy in 1944–1945. In 1952 he began teaching at the recently formed Higher War College (Escola Superior de Guerra—ESG). Through his writings and work in the ESG, he exerted enormous influence on the formation of the National Security Doctrine. Golbery became the head of the National Security Council under Jânio Quadros in 1961 but resigned when João Goulart became president in the same year. Between 1961 and 1964 he headed the IPES (Instituto de Pesquisas e Estudos Sociais), a privately funded think tank and intelligence-gathering operation that played a notorious role in working for the overthrow of Goulart.

After the military coup of 1964, President Humberto Castello Branco created the SNI (Serviço Nacional de Informações) and named Golbery to head the agency with cabinet-level status. Along with other "moderates," Golbery lost influence with the "election" of Artur Costa E Silva (1967–1969) and then Emílio Médici (1969–1974) to the presidency. He served as the head of the civilian presidential staff during the administration of Ernesto Geisel (1974–1979) and in the first two years of the presidency of João Baptista Figueiredo (1979–1985).

Along with Geisel, Golbery was one of the principal figures in the shaky and tentative process of *abertura* (political opening). He resigned from the government in 1981 when he was unable to persuade the president to press an investigation of a political scandal implicating the hardliners in the government and the SNI.

*See also* **Brazil, National Security Doctrine; Military Dictatorships: Since 1945.**

BIBLIOGRAPHY

Golbery Do Couto E Silva, *Aspectos geopolíticos do Brasil* (1957), and *Geopolítica do Brasil* (1967).

Plínio De Abreu Ramos and Cid Benjamin, "Golberi do Couto e Silva," in *Dicionário histórico biográfico* (1983).

Maria Helena Moreira Alves, *State and Opposition in Military Brazil* (1985).

Thomas E. Skidmore, *The Politics of Military Rule in Brazil, 1964–85* (1988).

*Additional Bibliography*

Birkner, Walter Marcos Knaesel. *O realismo de Golbery: Segurança nacional e desenvolvimento global no pensamento de Golbery do Couto e Silva.* Itajaí: UNIVALI; Caçador: Universidade do Contestado, 2002.

Gaspari, Elio. *A ditadura encurralada.* São Paulo: Companhia das Letras, 2004.

Marshall C. Eakin

**GOLD.** *See* **Goldwork, Pre-Columbian; Gold Rushes, Brazil; Mining: Colonial Brazil; Mining: Colonial Spanish America; Mining: Modern.**

**GOLDEMBERG, ISAAC** (1945–). Isaac Goldemberg (*b.* 15 November 1945), Peruvian author. Goldemberg was born in the small town of Chepén. His father and his family, Russian Jews, had immigrated to Peru in the 1930s. His maternal grandmother, a mestiza medicine woman, was from Cajamarca. Goldemberg received a Catholic education under the supervision of the local parish priest and was unaware of his Jewish heritage for a number of years. Learning of his mixed religious background reinforced his sense of being different from both Catholics and Jews. It is not surprising that the question of identity and a sense of exile pervade his works.

Completely bilingual in Spanish and English, Goldemberg helped produce the English translation of *Hombre de paso,* which was published in a bilingual edition. Among authors and critics who have praised his work are José Miguel Oviedo, Severo Sarduy, Marco Martos, and Mario Vargas Llosa.

Since 1964 Goldemberg has lived in New York City, where he is Distinguished Professor of Humanities at Hostos Community College of the City University of New York and director of the Latin American Writers Institute/Instituto de Escritores Latinoamericanos, which organizes exhibitions of Latin American fiction and criticism, and editor of the *Hostos Review.* He is also on the staff of *Brújula/Compass,* a bimonthly magazine of bilingual Latino and Latin American literature written in the United States.

Goldemberg's published works include *Tiempo de silencio* (1969), poetry; *De Chepén a La Habana* (1973), poetry; *The Fragmented Life of Don Jacobo Lerner,* translated by Robert Picciotto (1976); *La vida a plazos de don Jacobo Lerner,* 2d ed. (1980); *Hombre de paso/Just Passing Through,* translated by David Unger and Isaac Goldemberg (1981); *Tiempo al tiempo* (1984); *Play by Play,* translated by Hardie St. Martin (1985); *La vida al contado* (1989), poetry, with a preface by Marco Martos and a sketchy and selective autobiographical account by Goldemberg; *El gran libro de América judía* (1998); *Cuerpo del amor* (2000), poetry; *El nombre del padre* (2002); *Crónicas del exilio* (2003), poetry; *Los cementerios reales* (2004), poetry. He is the recipient of numerous awards, including the Nuestro Award in Fiction (1977), the Luis Alberto Sánchez Award for Literary Essays (2002), and the Orden de Don Quijote (2005).

*See also* **Brazil, Organizations: Brazilian Institute of the Environment and Renewable Natural Resources (IBAMA); Literature: Spanish America; Mestizo.**

BIBLIOGRAPHY

Nouhaud, Dorita. *Isaac Goldemberg: El hombre del libro.* Lima: Ediciones El Santo Oficio, 2003.

Paredes Carbonell, Juan, ed. *Isaac Goldemberg ante la crítica. Una visión múltiple.* Lima: Ediciones del Instituto Luis Alberto Sánchez, 2003.

GUIDO A. PODESTÁ

**GOLDEMBERG, JOSÉ** (1928–). A Brazilian environmental and energy expert, José Goldemberg received a doctorate in nuclear physics at the University of São Paulo, where he rose to full professor and served as rector from 1986 to 1989. He has presided over national scientific societies and the State of São Paulo's energy company. Under the Collor government (1990–1992), he was secretary of the environment and helped plan the 1992 Earth Summit in Rio de Janeiro. As minister of education, he obtained autonomy for federally funded universities. In 2000 he and three other internationally known scientists won the Volvo Environmental Prize for their comprehensive study of future world energy needs. He is active in the study of climate change.

*See also* **Energy.**

BIBLIOGRAPHY

Goldemberg, José, et al. *Energy for a Sustainable World.* New York: Wiley, 1988.

JOSEPH LOVE

**GOLDEN LAW.** Golden Law, or Lei Áurea which was passed by the Brazilian Senate and sanctioned by Princess Isabel on 13 May 1888, freed all remaining slaves (approximately 600,000) and abolished the institution of slavery. Despite the desperate resistance of some planters (especially those whose properties were heavily mortgaged against the value of their slaves), the law recognized what had become fact. Slaves had fled plantations in increasing numbers, causing many planters to free their remaining slaves in hopes of retaining their services as wage workers or sharecroppers. Planters who had already begun to hire indentured immigrant laborers, notably in the São Paulo zone, found their economic position strengthened. In the cities slave populations had dwindled so dramatically that by 1888 in Rio de Janeiro only about 7,000 slaves remained of an estimated 100,000 slaves living there in the 1860s. Contemporary abolitionists—particularly Joaquim Nabuco and André Rebouças—were outspoken critics of what they regarded as only a partial abolition that had failed to include land reform, necessary in their view if Brazil was to realize its potential as a producing nation on a footing with the industrializing societies of Europe. Questions remain regarding the post-emancipation lives of former slaves and blacks as people seek to understand more precisely what changed and what persisted.

*See also* **Free Birth Law; Queirós Law; Sexagenarian Law.**

BIBLIOGRAPHY

Robert Conrad, *The Destruction of Brazilian Slavery, 1850–1888* (1972), esp. pp. 239–277.

Joaquim Nabuco, *Abolitionism: The Brazilian Antislavery Struggle,* translated and edited by Robert Conrad (1977).

*Additional Bibliography*

Azevedo, Celia Maria Marinho de. *Abolitionism in the United States and Brazil: A Comparative Perspective.* New York: Garland Publishing, 1995.

Baronov, David. *The Abolition of Slavery in Brazil: The "Liberation" of Africans through the Emancipation of Capital.* Westport, CT: Greenwood Press, 2000.

Machado, Maria Helena Pereira Toledo. *O plano e o pânico: Os movimentos sociais na década da abolição.* Rio de Janeiro: Editora UFRJ; São Paulo: EDUSP, 1994.

Needell, Jeffrey D. *The Party of Order: The Conservatives, the State, and Slavery in the Brazilian Monarchy, 1831–1871.* Stanford, CA: Stanford University Press, 2006.

SANDRA LAUDERDALE GRAHAM

**GOLD RUSHES, BRAZIL.** The quest for gold has been a significant part of Brazilian history, driving much of Portuguese and Brazilian penetration into the interior of the country. Large deposits of gold were discovered at the beginning of the eighteenth century in Minas Gerais, Mato Grosso, Goiás, and Bahia. The subsequent gold rush transformed the Portuguese colony, stimulating extensive immigration from Portugal, further exploration of the remote interior, and a substantial increase in African slave importations. Extracted primarily by slave labor, gold became the principal Brazilian export for more than half a century, supporting the Portuguese Empire worldwide and probably financing the foundations of the industrial revolution in Britain. Perhaps as much as one-half of production left the colony illegally. With the subsequent exhaustion of these deposits, gold's share of the Brazilian economy declined precipitously, even with the entry of foreign mining engineers and technology in the mid-nineteenth century. Gold mining came to be dominated by small-scale, informal placer operations (Garimpos).

The discovery of substantial gold deposits in the Amazon Basin in the 1960s and 1970s dynamized the mining sector, provoking the most extensive gold rush of the twentieth century in the Americas. Throughout the Amazon, hundreds of *garimpos* have competed with large mining companies for access to deposits. Gold mined in the late 1980s contributed more than $1 billion annually to the legal Brazilian economy, as well as fueling a lucrative black market. Nearly 90 percent was supplied by *garimpos.* At the same time, deforestation, burning, the use of mercury to amalgamate with gold, and the invasion of aboriginal lands have caused severe environmental and social disruption. Most notably the conflictive situation resulting from the miners' invasion of Yanomami lands in Roraima and Serra Pelada in Pará has provoked both international and Brazilian condemnation of the unregulated nature of the gold rush, an issue only partially addressed by Brazilian governments to date.

*See also* **Bahia; Goiás; Industrialization; Mato Grosso; Minas Gerais; Mining: Colonial Brazil.**

BIBLIOGRAPHY

Boxer, Charles *The Golden Age of Brazil, 1695–1750.* Berkeley: University of California Press, 1962.

Cleary, David. *Anatomy of the Amazon Gold Rush.* Iowa City: University of Iowa Perr, 1990.

Eakin, Marshall. "The Role of British Capital in the Development of Brazilian Gold Mining." In *Miners and Mining in the Americas,* ed. Thomas Greaves and William Culver, pp. 10–28. Dover, NH: Manchester University Press, 1985.

Higgins, Kathleen J. *"Licentious Liberty" in a Brazilian Gold-mining Region: Slavery, Gender, and Social Control in Eighteenth-Century Sabará, Minas Gerais.* University Park: Pennsylvania State University Press, 1999.

Rocha, G. A., ed. *Em busca do ouro: Garimpos e garimpeiros no Brasil.* São Paulo: Editora Marco Zero, 1984.

Santos, Márcio. *Estradas reais: Introdução ao estudo dos caminhos do ouro e do diamante no Brasil.* Belo Horizonte, Brazil: Editora Estrada Real, 2001.

ROBERT WILCOX

## GOLDSCHMIDT, GERTRUDE. *See* Gego.

## GOLDWORK, PRE-COLUMBIAN.

Gold and items made from it continue to fascinate now as they did 500 years ago when conquistadores first landed on the shores of the Americas. The metal was used by most cultures in the Americas, from Mexico south to Argentina. Although the level of craftsmanship varied considerably, techniques used in the New World were virtually the same as those utilized by craftsmen in the Old World, with the exception of vitreous enameling. The reasons for these parallels in cultural technologies are basic.

Gold, silver, and copper are easily worked with very simple technology. In fact, gold and silver are the two most malleable metals on earth. Pre-Hispanic goldsmiths utilized extremely dense, hard stone hammers (e.g. of magnetite) without handles; stone anvils; chisels; and chasing tools made of gold/copper alloys to cut and chase the gold. These tools no doubt were augmented by tools made of wood, bone, and leather.

With the addition of braziers to hold charcoal fires—and the use of long bamboo tubes, with ceramic tips, blown through to make the fires much hotter—metalworkers were able to make binary and ternary alloys, and to melt them into ingots from which they could forge sheet and wire—the raw stock necessary to manufacture some of the pieces that we see today in museums and that dazzled the conquistadores when they arrived.

Less important metals were platinum and lead. Platinum occurred in the southern Colombia/northern Ecuador borderland. Its extremely high melting point limited its use to what could be termed small experimental pieces. Lead was employed for ore extraction, probably of silver, in the southern half of Peru and northern Bolivia; other uses of lead have not been well documented.

The need to adorn the body with gold nuggets gathered from streams may well have been the earliest use of gold by Brazilian and other South American cultures, although much additional research remains to be done. It is certain that humankind's fascination with gold promotes its use as soon as it is introduced into a culture.

Sophisticated sheetmetal pieces were being made on the South American continent as early as 1500–1000 B.C. in the north coast culture known as Cupisnique. North coast Peru has also yielded evidence of gold fabricated into very complex pieces as early as 700–800 BCE. The La Tolita area of Ecuador/Colombia has yielded dates from 400 BCE–200 CE. It would seem likely from these dates that from about the time of Christ, gold working was moving northward in Colombia into Panama and thence Mexico, since reliable dating gets later as one moves north.

There were two loci of gold working in South America. One was the direct working characterized by Peruvian smiths. The other was indirect working of the gold characterized by the refined and intricate lost-wax cast designs of the goldsmiths in Colombia.

In Peru, the goldsmiths' industry tended to make mainly sheet and wire. The Peruvian cultures inclined toward large ceremonial or showy pieces (e.g., large ceremonial masks and very large raised gold vessels), with only small quantities of personal body adornment. Nowhere else on the continent were the technically more difficult direct metal-working techniques carried to such advanced extremes as in Peru.

Direct working of the metal involved forming by hammering and cutting individual parts that were then assembled with mechanical (e.g., strap and slot, tab and slot) or thermal joins. This is called fabrication. The major fabrication techniques used by pre-Hispanic goldsmiths were forging sheet and wire, raising vessels, chasing and repoussé, real filigree, granulation, proto-brazing, and depletion gilding. The cultures most associated with these techniques were on the north coast of Peru (e.g., Mochica and Sicán).

The Colombian smiths seemed to respond artistically to the indirect approach of fashioning the work in wax, to be cast in gold. It allowed them to fashion lovely small-scale cast pieces. Though the indirect approach certainly yielded some very large cast pieces, there was more preoccupation with personal, decorative body adornment such as necklaces, earrings, nose rings, and labrets. Many examples abound to show that Colombian goldsmiths knew direct metalworking techniques. However, their fascination with lost-wax casting, and the plenteous supply of beeswax available, certainly allowed them to master the indirect approach to metalwork; this skill was carried up into Mexico.

Indirect working of gold by lost-wax casting was done by making the piece in wax and then coating it with a liquid refractory material composed of caliche, powdered charcoal, and lime. When the refractory hardened, like plaster, the mold was placed in a heat source, the wax is eliminated; then molten metal could be poured in. After cooling, the refractory was broken away, revealing the casting piece. It could then be finished and polished. The cultures most associated with this technique are Costa Rica (Diquis), Panama (Coclé, Chiriqui'), and Colombia (Sinu', Muisca).

Studies of pre-Hispanic metalwork have been hampered by the conquistadores' massive looting, which virtually eliminated metalwork from Mexico, and grave robbing, which still occurs despite efforts to control it. This has affected efforts to locate workshop sites and undisturbed tombs so they may be scientifically excavated and the maximum information gleaned from their contents to aid in the understanding of the work and life of these ancient peoples.

*See also* **Art: Pre-Columbian Art of South America; Precontact History: Andean Region.**

BIBLIOGRAPHY

Surveys of ancient and modern techniques are in Oppi Untracht, *Jewelry Concepts and Technology* (1982). A more complete discussion of Peruvian goldsmithing techniques is in Heather Lechtman, "Traditions and Styles in Central Andean Metalworking," in *The Beginning of the Use of Metals and Alloys,* edited by Robert Madden (1988), pp. 344–378, and Izumi Shimada and Jo Ann Griffin, "Precious Metal Objects of the Middle Sican," in *Scientific American,* 270 (April 1994): 82–89. See also Julie Jones, ed., *The Art of Precolumbian Gold* (1985).

*Additional Bibliography*

Hearne, Pamela, and Robert J. Sharer, eds. *River of Gold—Precolumbian Treasures from Sitio Conte.* Philadelphia: University Museum, University of Pennsylvania, 1992.

Jones, Julie, and Heidi King. *Gold of the Americas.* New York: Metropolitan Museum of Art, 2002.

McEwan, Colin, ed. *Precolumbian Gold: Technology, Style, and Iconography.* Chicago: Fitzroy Dearborn Publishers, 2000.

Mayr, Juan, and Clara Isabel Botero. *The Art of Gold, the Legacy of Pre-Hispanic Colombia: Collection of the Gold Museum in Bogotá.* México, D.F.: Fondo de Cultura Económica; Bogotá: Banco de la República; Milano, 2007.

JO ANN GRIFFIN

**GÓLGOTAS.** Gólgotas, the younger, more radical wing of the Colombian Liberal Party in the first half of the 1850s. The label Gólgotas apparently came from a Conservative editorialist's criticism of José María Samper's positive comparison of socialism with the ideals of the martyr of Golgotha at a meeting of the Republican School. These men supported the separation of church and state, the elimination of clerical privilege, extreme federalism, the reduction of the power of the executive and military, universal manhood suffrage, the expulsion of the Jesuits, the abolition of slavery, absolute freedom of the press and of speech, and laissez-faire economics—principles that they helped incorporate into the Constitution of 1853. The more moderate, Santanderista wing of the Liberal Party, labeled Draconianos, so opposed the 1853 constitution that many assisted José María Melo's 1854 coup. Leading Gólgotas, including Manuel Murillo Toro, Rafael Núñez, Salvador Camacho Roldán, Francisco J. Zaldúa, and Aquileo Parra, dominated the 1863–1885 Liberal era.

*See also* **Colombia, Political Parties: Liberal Party.**

BIBLIOGRAPHY

Gerardo Molina, *Las ideas liberales en Colombia: 1849–1914* (1970).

Helen Delpar, *Red Against Blue: The Liberal Party in Colombian Politics, 1863–1899* (1981); *Los radicales del siglo XIX: Escritos políticos* (1984).

*Additional Bibliography*

Colmenares, Germán. *Partidos políticos y clases sociales.* Santafé de Bogotá: Universidad del Valle: Banco de la República: Colciencias: TM Editores, 1997.

Llano Isaza, Rodrigo. *Los draconianos: Origen popular del liberalismo colombiano.* Bogotá: Planeta, 2005.

DAVID SOWELL

## GOLPE DE ESTADO (COUP D'ÉTAT).

A *golpe de estado* (*coup d'état* in French, *Putsch* in German, often simply *coup* in English) refers to the unscheduled and illegal ousting of a government and its replacement by new authorities, whether civilian, military, or an alliance of civilians and military. Such ousters may be violent or peaceful, broadly supported by the population or against the desires of the citizenry. Sometimes the threat of a coup forces incumbent officials to resign—in a sense, a *golpe* without actual exercise of force. Golpes de estado may occur against incumbent regimes of all sorts—theocracies, traditional monarchies, constitutional monarchies, republics, and other political systems. They may oust constitutional governments, de facto regimes, authoritarian governments, and personalist dictatorships.

Most golpes involve the military or elements of the military in alliance with civilian political factions, movements, or political parties. In some instances, foreign nations encourage, support, or sponsor coups to bring into power governments more favorable to their interests. Typically, when military coups occur, they are followed by the organization of a military junta (small committee of officers) to replace the ousted government or at least the executive branch. In some instances self-coups (*auto-golpes*) occur, referring to unconstitutional usurpation of authority by incumbent governments with the concomitant closure or repression of legislative, judicial, and other agencies of the legally constituted government. In these cases the executive branch usually remains in place, supported by the military and national police, with "extraordinary powers" to govern until the political situation is "normalized."

Motivations for golpes de estado vary greatly: to prevent an election from occurring; to undo electoral results; to oust a government whose policies are opposed; to initiate new policies or impose fundamental change in the political system; or simply to take power away from some groups so that it can be assumed by others. Initially, most coup makers seek only to overthrow the extant authorities and replace them with new leadership. However, some coups may be motivated by a desire to carry out more profound political and socioeconomic change. In other cases, coups that begin with limited objectives may be transformed into more far-reaching political projects focused on institutional change and sweeping policy initiatives.

In Spain and Latin America, irregular changes in government through military and civilian coups were common in the nineteenth century and into the twentieth. From 1920 to 1960 successful military coups occurred in every Latin America country except Mexico and Uruguay; in Uruguay, irregular regime change with police and military participation occurred in 1933–1934, and in Mexico, unsuccessful military coups occurred at least four times before 1940.

In the 1960s military regimes came to power through coups in much of Central and South America. These regimes gradually gave way to elected civilian governments again in the 1980s and early 1990s, but successful or unsuccessful coups took place in almost half of Latin American countries between 1990 and 2006.

*See also* **Armed Forces; Military Dictatorships: Since 1945; Military Dictatorships: 1821–1945.**

BIBLIOGRAPHY

Fitch, Samuel. *The Military Coup as a Political Process: Ecuador, 1948–1966.* Baltimore, MD: Johns Hopkins University Press, 1977.

Loveman, Brian. *For la Patria: Politics and the Armed Forces in Latin America.* Wilmington, DE: Scholarly Resources, 1999.

Luttwak, Edward. *Coup d'État: A Practical Handbook.* Cambridge, MA: Harvard University Press, 1979.

Romero, Luis Alberto. *Los golpes militares, 1812–1955.* Buenos Aires: Carlos Pérez Editor, 1969.

Solaún, Mauricio, and Michael A. Quinn. *Sinners and Heretics: The Politics of Military Intervention in Latin America.* Urbana: University of Illinois Press, 1973.

BRIAN LOVEMAN

**GOMES, ANTÔNIO CARLOS** (1836–1896). Antônio Carlos Gomes (*b.* 11 July 1836; *d.* 16 September 1896), the first Brazilian musician to achieve considerable success in Italy as a composer of operas. Son of a bandmaster whose most notable achievement appears to have been fathering twenty-six children, Tonico (as Antônio Carlos was called as a boy) learned the fundamentals of music and an elementary knowledge of several instruments from his father at an early age. His *Hino acadêmico,* an early composition, was well received, and he went to Rio de Janeiro in order to enroll in the Imperial Conservatory of Music. His conservatory studies in composition with Joaquim Giannini reinforced his interest in opera, and two works, *A noite do castelo,* produced in 1861, and *Joana de Flandres,* in 1863, met considerable success, resulting in a government subsidy for study in Italy. The greatest success of Gomes's career was the performance of his opera *Il Guarany* at La Scala, in Milan, on 19 March 1870. *Il Guarany* was followed by *Fosca, Salvator Rosa, Maria Tudor, Lo schiavo,* and *Condor,* his last opera, but none of the later works achieved the success of *Il Guarany.*

Gomes chose Brazilian subjects for some of his operas, but his style of writing and approach was Italian at a time of rising musical nationalism in Brazil. Expecting unqualified and enthusiastic acceptance in his native country during a time of rising republican sentiments, he was instead considered an aristocrat out of touch with political realities. The fact that his family sought to forbid performances of his operas in the Portuguese language, insisting on Italian, did nothing to allay the suspicions of adherents of the new nationalist sentiments.

*See also* **Music: Art Music.**

BIBLIOGRAPHY

*Revista brasileira de música,* vol. 3 (1936).

Luis Heitor Correa De Azevedo, *150 anos de música no Brasil (1800–1950)* (1956).

*Additional Bibliography*

Béhague, Gerard. "Gomes, (António) Carlos." *New Grove Dictionary of Opera, vol. 2.* New York: Grove's Dictionaries of Music, 1992.

Volpe, Maria Alice. "Remaking the Brazilian Myth of National Foundation: Il Guarany." *Latin American Music Review* 23 (Fall/Winter 2002): 179–194.

DAVID P. APPLEBY

**GOMES, EDUARDO** (1896–1981). Eduardo Gomes (*b.* 20 September 1896; *d.* 13 June 1981), Brazilian Air Force officer and political leader. Born in Petrópolis, Rio de Janeiro, Gomes enlisted in the army in 1916. He was commissioned in 1919, and three years later he became a national hero as one of the *tenente* defenders and survivors of the Revolt of Fort Copacabana. Imprisoned for his role as an air observer during the revolt of 1924, he returned to active duty in 1927. His assignment to the army air corps included the task, in 1930, of establishing the Brazilian military air mail systems. With the creation of the Brazilian air force in 1941, Gomes served as commander of the First and Second Air Zones in the northeastern section of the country during World War II.

In 1945, Gomes helped to organize the anti-Vargas National Democratic Union (União Democrática Nacional—UDN) and ran unsuccessfully against General Eurico Dutra as its presidential candidate that year, and in 1950 against Getúlio Vargas. He was an official and elder statesman of the party until its dissolution in 1965. Appointed minister of the air force by President João Café Filho in 1954, Gomes retired from active service in 1961 with the rank of air marshal. President Humberto Castelo Branco recalled him to serve as air minister after the revolution of 1964. He died in Rio de Janeiro.

*See also* **Brazil, Political Parties: National Democratic Union of Brazil (UDN), Copacabana Fort, Revolt of.**

BIBLIOGRAPHY

Ronald M. Schneider, *Order and Progress: A Political History of Brazil* (1991).

E. Bradford Burns, *A History of Brazil* (1993).

*Additional Bibliography*

Bellintani, Adriana Iop. *Conspiração contra o Estado Novo.* Porto Alegre: EDIPUCRS, 2002.

MICHAEL L. JAMES

## GÓMEZ, BENIGNO

**GÓMEZ, BENIGNO** (1934–). Benigno Gómez (*b.* 1934), Honduran painter and sculptor. Gómez is a native of the department of Santa Barbara, Honduras. His woodcarvings of doves won him a scholarship in 1950 to study at the Escuela Nacional de Bellas Artes in Tegucigalpa, where he was strongly influenced by Max Euceda. In 1960 he won another scholarship to study in Rome, where he remained until 1966, when he returned to Tegucigalpa as a professor at the Escuela Nacional de Bellas Artes. By now his neorealist paintings of the human figure had won him much recognition, particularly for his innovative use of color, but later he became more noted for his surrealist paintings. A trademark of his work is the presence of doves in virtually all his paintings, symbols of Gómez's optimistic spirit.

*See also* **Art: The Twentieth Century.**

BIBLIOGRAPHY

J. Evaristo López R. and Longino Becerra, *Honduras: 40 pintores* (1989).

*Additional Bibliography*

Oyuela, Irma Leticia de. *La batalla pictórica: Sintesis de la historia de la pintura hondureña.* Tegucigalpa: Banco Atlántida, 1995.

RALPH LEE WOODWARD JR.

## GÓMEZ, EUGENIO

**GÓMEZ, EUGENIO** (1890–1963). Eugenio Gómez (*b.* 1890; *d.* 1963), leader of the Uruguayan Communist Party. As a barber in Montevideo he came into contact with the labor movement and joined the port workers' Federación Obrera Marítima (Maritime Workers Federation) and the Partido Socialista del Uruguay (Socialist Party—PSU), led by Emílio Frugoni. During the debate about PSU membership in the Third International and subscription to its twenty-one conditions (1920), Gómez, Celestino Mibelli, and Rodríguez Saraillé led the majority faction favoring acceptance. After a special party conference held on 16–18 April 1921, the PSU changed its name to Partido Comunista del Uruguay (PCU). Frugoni and his minority faction reestablished the PSU in 1923.

From 1921 to 1955 Gómez headed the party executive committee, serving as its general secretary from the time of party proscription during the dictatorship of Gabriel Terra (1937). Under his leadership the PCU became one of the most active promoters of Uruguayan solidarity with the Spanish Republic and the Anti-Nazi Action, and achieved its best election results in 1946.

Gómez was deputy from 1942 to 1946 and was a member of the parliamentary Special Commission on Working Conditions in Uruguay. After 1946 his leadership was characterized by an increasing loss of popularity due to personality cult and power abuse. In 1955 PCU membership stood at about 5,000.

*See also* **Terra, Gabriel; Uruguay, Political Parties: Socialist Party.**

BIBLIOGRAPHY

Eugenio Gómez, *Los intelectuales del Partido Comunista* (1945), *Historia del Partido Comunista del Uruguay hasta 1951* (1951), and *Historia de una traición* (1960).

Philip B. Taylor, *Government and Politics of Uruguay* (1966).

Rodney Arismendi, *Ocho corazones latiendo* (1987).

Rodney Arismendi et al. *El partido: 68 aniversario del PCU* (1955).

DIETER SCHONEBOHM

## GÓMEZ, INDALECIO

**GÓMEZ, INDALECIO** (1851–1920). Indalecio Gómez (*b.* 1851; *d.* 18 August 1920), Argentine statesman and author. Born in Salta and trained as a lawyer at the University of Buenos Aires, Gómez began his political career as a national deputy representing Salta Province. He gained national prominence as director of the National Bank of Argentina during the administration of Carlos Pellegrini (1890–1892). He remained active in national politics, serving as Argentina's ambassador to Germany under President Manuel

Quintana (1904–1906) and as the interior minister under President Roque Sáenz Peña (1910–1913). As interior minister, he orchestrated the passage of the Sáenz Peña Law (1911), which granted universal male suffrage and established a secret ballot for elections. Gómez supervised its implementation in the national congressional elections of April 1912. In numerous books and articles, including *El episcopado y la paz* (1895), he established his reputation as a political and social traditionalist who defended the elite values of Argentina's Generation of 1880 during an era of turmoil and reform.

*See also* **Quintana, Manuel; Sáenz Peña, Roque.**

BIBLIOGRAPHY

Natalio R. Botana, "La reforma política del 1912," in *El régimen oligárquico: Materiales para el estudio de la realidad argentina (hasta 1930)*, edited by G. Giménez Zapiola (1975), pp. 232–245; and *El orden conservador: La política argentina entre 1880 y 1916*, 2d ed. (1985), esp. pp. 217–291.

*Additional Bibliography*

Bertoni, Lilia Ana. *Patriotas, cosmopólitas y nacionalistas: La construcción de la nacionalidad argentina a fines del siglo XIX.* Buenos Aires: Fondo de Cultura Económica de la Argentina, 2001.

DANIEL LEWIS

## GÓMEZ, JOSÉ MIGUEL (c. 1720–1805).

José Miguel Gómez (*b.* c. 1720; *d.* 1805), best-known colonial painter of Honduras. Born in Tegucigalpa, Gómez painted mostly religious themes. He began his studies in Comayagua but later studied in Guatemala City. He returned to Comayagua, where his painting of San José de Calasanz for the Araque family brought him to the attention of Bishop Rodríguez de Rivera, who commissioned a series of works from him for the cathedral of Comayagua. Gómez's paintings were characterized by their natural realism. He later painted many religious canvases for churches in and around Tegucigalpa. His painting of Father José Simón Zelaya is especially notable, as was his final painting, in 1805, of *La Divina Pastora*, depicting the Virgin with Child and a lamb, a vivid painting that reflected the influence of his Spanish and Guatemalan teachers.

*See also* **Art: The Nineteenth Century; Honduras.**

BIBLIOGRAPHY

*Additional Bibliography*

López, R., J. Evaristo, and Longino Becerra. *Honduras, visión panorámica de su pintura.* Tegucigalpa, Honduras: Baktun Editorial, 1994.

Oyuela, Irma Leticia de. *La batalla pictórica: Síntesis de la historia de la pintura hondureña.* Tegucigalpa, Honduras: Banco Atlántida, 1995.

RALPH LEE WOODWARD JR.

## GÓMEZ, JOSÉ MIGUEL (1858–1921).

José Miguel Gómez (*b.* 1858; *d.* 1921), president of Cuba (1909–1913). General Gómez began his rise to prominence during the Ten Years' War and was governor of Santa Clara during the U.S. occupation under General Leonard Wood. An astute and clever politician, Gómez switched from the Conservative to the Liberal Party in 1906 when the former failed to support his bid for the presidency. He was also active in the insurrection against President Tomás Estrada Palma in 1906.

Running again on the Liberal Party ticket in 1908, Gómez won. During his presidency, the government was accused of corruption, patronage, and suspending duties on the exports of sugar and other products. The administration is perhaps better known for its expenditures that approached $140 million and for the 1912 military campaign against a black military force and its supporters, the Independent Party of Color.

Gómez was defeated in 1912 but remained in the political limelight. In 1920, opposed to Liberal policies and increasing internal strife, he plotted an unsuccessful revolution.

*See also* **Estrada Palma, Tomás; Ten Years' War.**

BIBLIOGRAPHY

William Fletcher Johnson, *The History of Cuba* (1920).

Louis A. Pérez, *Cuba: Between Reform and Revolution* (1988).

*Additional Bibliography*

Chomsky, Aviva. "'Barbados or Canada?' Race, Immigration, and Nation in Early-Twentieth-Century Cuba." *Hispanic American Historical Review* 80 (August 2000): 415–462.

Fuente, Alejandro de la. *A Nation for All: Race, Inequality and Politics in Twentieth Century Cuba*. Chapel Hill: University of North Carolina Press, 2001.

ALLAN S. R. SUMNALL

## GOMÉZ, JOSÉ VALENTÍN (1774–1833).

José Valentín Goméz (*b.* 8 November 1774; *d.* 20 September 1833), Argentine educator and diplomat. Born in Buenos Aires and educated as a cleric at the University of Córdoba, Goméz became an ardent supporter of the revolution and subsequently a diplomat of the new government. In 1813 he was elected to the National Assembly and thereafter was sent on several diplomatic missions. One of his most interesting illustrates the monarchist tendencies of the government he represented. Under Juan Martín de Pueyrredón in 1819 he went on a secret mission to France in order to persuade the French minister of foreign affairs, the Baron Dessolle, to establish a monarchy in La Plata under a European dynastic family. The duke of Lucca was the favored candidate, but Dessolle changed his mind and the scheme was abandoned. Gómez became the rector of the University of Buenos Aires in 1823 and was responsible for introducing the Lancastrian system of education and attempting other educational reforms. He died in Buenos Aires.

*See also* **Education: Overview; Pueyrredón, Juan Martin de.**

NICHOLAS P. CUSHNER

## GÓMEZ, JUAN CARLOS (1820–1884).

Juan Carlos Gómez (*b.* 1820; *d.* 1884), Uruguayan journalist and poet. The long siege of Montevideo by Blanco Party forces under Manuel Oribe, who was supported by Argentina's dictator, Juan Manuel de Rosas, provided Gómez with an incentive to move to Chile in 1843. While there he joined Argentines and fellow liberals Domingo Sarmiento and Bartolomé Mitre in the struggle against Rosas, and then in the task of implementing a liberal program of institutional renovation. His defense of freedom of the press in Valparaíso's *El Mercurio* in the 1840s and his promotion of liberal reforms in Buenos Aires's *El Orden, La Tribuna,* and *El Nacional* in the 1850s—and for a brief period in Montevideo's *El Nacional*—earned him wide respect.

Between 1852 and 1863 Gómez divided his time between Montevideo and Buenos Aires. In Montevideo he served as a representative in the national legislature and as minister of foreign relations. In Buenos Aires he supported Mitre's Nationalist Party. His principled opinions often sparked angry polemic: he stridently promoted the union of Uruguay and Argentina in a "United States of the Plata," and he was an outspoken critic, beginning in 1869, of Argentina's role in the War of the Triple Alliance. Following Juan Bautista Alberdi, he argued that the war "against the people" had weakened the Spanish-speaking countries of the Plata relative to their historical rival, Brazil. Gómez promoted the liberal ideas of the period, including the need to attract a European population to the regions of the Plata, to combat the retrograde rural society that joined despotic caudillos with illiterate gauchos, and to modernize at whatever cost. Gómez also wrote poetry. His "La libertad" is one of the finest in Uruguay's romantic canon.

*See also* **Mitre, Bartolomé; Rosas, Juan Manuel de; Uruguay: Before 1900; War of the Triple Alliance.**

BIBLIOGRAPHY

Julio María Isosa, *Juan Carlos Gómez* (1905).

*Additional Bibliography*

Montero Bustamante, Raúl. *Estampas: Fructuoso Rivera, Melchor Pacheco y Obes, Juan Carlos Gómez, Julio Herrera y Obes.* Montevideo: Ediciones Ceibo, 1942.

WILLIAM H. KATRA

## GÓMEZ, JUAN GUALBERTO (1854–1933).

Juan Gualberto Gómez (*b.* 12 July 1854; *d.* 5 March 1933), Cuban independence figure, journalist, and politician. Gómez was born in a sugar mill in Matanzas Province, the son of black slaves who managed to purchase his freedom upon his birth. When Cuba's struggle for independence began, his parents sent him in 1869 to study in Paris, where he became a journalist. Afterward he traveled through the Caribbean and Mexico, returning to Cuba in 1878 when the Ten Years' War ended. At this time he met José Martí, who would become his close friend and with whom he immediately began to conspire against Spain. Deported from Cuba on account of these activities, Gómez settled in Madrid, where he spent the next ten years working on various daily newspapers. He also became the secretary of the Madrid abolitionist society. When he finally was allowed to return to Cuba (1890), Gómez again worked as Martí's secret agent on the island, and when the 1895–1898 war of independence broke out, he was imprisoned and once more deported to Spain. Returning in 1898, he participated in the Cuban constituent assembly of 1900–1901, where he was one of the strongest opponents of the Platt Amendment. Afterward he became one of the editors of the daily *La Lucha,* and was elected to the Cuban Senate in the 1910s. Gómez died in Havana.

*See also* **Journalism; Martí y Pérez, José Julián; Slavery: Abolition; Ten Years' War.**

BIBLIOGRAPHY

There are no English sources on Gómez. See Octavio R. Costa, *Juan Gualberto Gómez: Una vida sin sombra* (1984); and Gustavo Duplessis, *Un hombre, sus ideas y un paraguas: Evocación de Juan Gualberto Gómez y su ideario* (1959).

*Additional Bibliography*

Aguirre, Sergio. *Un gran olvidado: Juan Gualberto Gómez.* Havana: Editorial de Ciencias Sociales, 1997.

Ferrer, Ada. *Insurgent Cuba: Race, Nation, and Revolution, 1868–1898.* Chapel Hill: University of North Carolina Press, 1999.

Helg, Aline. *Our Rightful Share: The Afro-Cuban Struggle for Equality, 1886–1912.* Chapel Hill: University of North Carolina Press, 1995.

Horrego Estuch, Leopoldo, and Olida Hevia Lanier. *Juan Gualberto Gómez, un gran inconforme.* Havana: Editorial de Ciencias Sociales, 2004.

José M. Hernández

**GÓMEZ, JUAN VICENTE** (1857–1935). Juan Vicente Gómez (*b.* 24 July 1857; *d.* 17 December 1935), president and dictator of Venezuela (1908–1935). During his twenty-seven-year dictatorship, Gómez created the modern Venezuelan nation-state. Like Porfirio Díaz of Mexico (1876–1911), Gómez brought an end to internecine struggles for power, established a strong central government, began the construction of a nationwide transportation and communication system, and put the economy on a stable basis through the judicious use of petroleum revenues. Along with Rómulo Betancourt, he is one of Venezuela's major twentieth-century political figures.

Gómez achieved power at midlife. A former butcher and cattle rancher from Táchira, he became involved in politics in 1892 when he joined Cipriano Castro in an abortive political movement. Forced into exile in Colombia following the failure of that struggle, Gómez returned in 1899 as an officer in Castro's small Army of the Liberal Restoration. At the age of forty-two, he entered Caracas for the first time. There he served Castro as a loyal and trusted associate, and played an instrumental role in defeating the many groups who rose up against Castro's regime. Gómez risked his life on numerous occasions to put down major revolts. In so doing, he won support from the Venezuelan military establishment, which considered him both brave and honest. He also gained allies among the civilian elites, who saw Gómez as an efficient, if ruthless, military leader. Like most caudillos, he also had a large following among the nation's campesinos, who revered him, in part because they believed he possessed supernatural powers.

In 1908, Castro named Gómez as acting president while he sought medical treatment in Europe. Gómez took advantage of his chief's absence to proclaim himself president of Venezuela. His pronouncement met with immediate success, both at home and abroad. Castro's enemies thought that Gómez was an individual they could control. Foreign powers, which had suffered through the Castro years, also believed they could trust Gómez. Within weeks of his coup, the United States recognized the new government, and European powers quickly followed suit. As a result, Gómez enjoyed good relations with the United States and European nations, all of whom played an important role in the development of Venezuela's oil resources.

At the turn of the twenty-first century, Venezuelan scholars began to revise part of the Gómez legacy. While continuing to condemn him for the torture and imprisonment of opponents; his monopolization of land and concessions for himself, his family, and his friends; his high-handed use of censorship and police violence to silence his critics; and his seeming surrender of Venezuelan petroleum to foreign economic interests, they started to recognize Gómez and his associates as important contributors to Venezuela's modernization. Without the Gómez administration, they argue, Venezuela would have continued as a wartorn nation, with a predominantly agricultural economy that depended on the vagaries of international demand for its chief export crops, coffee and cacao. Under Gómez, the nation enjoyed unprecedented economic stability and growth, as well as political calm. A close alliance with bankers, financiers, businessmen, and representatives of the United States assured the former. Constitutions of 1914, 1922, 1925, 1928, 1929, and 1931 guaranteed the latter.

From the outset of his administration, Gómez gave generous concessions to foreign interests. His oil policy followed a moderate course based on his desire to develop the industry rapidly, with the aid of foreign investment. Under the direction of Development Minister Gumersindo Torres (1918–1922), a mining law of 1918 and a petroleum code of 1920 limited the freedom of companies. But under pressure from the U.S. State Department, Gómez had Congress remove some of the most restrictive measures from the 1920 code. In 1922, a new law gave foreign oil companies what they wanted: low taxes and royalty payments to Venezuela, slow exploitation rates, and no restriction on the amount of land the companies held.

Gómez also made important changes in the organization of the national armed forces. In 1910, the first inspector general of the army, Félix Galavís, opened the Military Academy, which trained the next generation of professional officers. Military professionalization assured Gómez of an armed force that could defend the nation as well as put down domestic revolts. Since the officers often received higher salaries than their civilian counterparts, Gómez attracted candidates to the armed forces who had closer ties to the Caracas elites than did the older officers. Until his death, his brothers and fellow Táchiran officers comprised a separate and more powerful part of the officers, whereas the younger generation trained during his rule comprised the backbone of the post-Gómez generation of military leaders.

Perhaps as important as his reform of the military, his fiscal policies also had a long-term impact upon Venezuela. Gómez often showed his rancher background when it came to budgets. Like his minister of the Treasury, Román Cárdenas (1913–1922), he believed firmly in a balanced budget. Cárdenas's centralization of tax collection helped raise monies needed to run the government efficiently. Cuts in salaries and expenditures, along with amortization of foreign debts, turned Venezuela into a nation with no public debt by the mid-1920s. Vicente Lecuna [Salbach], who served as director of the Bank of Venezuela, also worked with Gómez on the national budget. His mastery of international monetary exchange placed Venezuela on a firm footing as the nation entered its oil boom. Gómez died in Maracay, Venezuela.

*See also* **Betancourt, Rómulo; Castro, Cipriano; Venezuela: Venezuela since 1830.**


BIBLIOGRAPHY

Daniel Joseph Clinton [writing as Thomas Rourke], *Gómez, Tyrant of the Andes* (1936).

Luis Cordero Velásquez, *Gómez y las fuerzas vivas* (1971).

Domingo Alberto Rangel, *Gomez, el amo del poder* (1975).

Elías Pino Iturrieta, *Positivismo y gomecismo* (1978).

Angel Ziems, *El gomecismo y la formación del ejército nacional* (1979).

Stephen G. Rabe, *The Road to OPEC: United States Relations with Venezuela, 1919–1979* (1982).

Brian Stuart Mc Beth, *Juan Vicente Gómez and the Oil Companies in Venezuela, 1908–1935* (1983).

*Additional Bibliography*

Pla, Alberto J. *La Internacional Comunista y América Latina: sidicatos y política en Venezuela (1924–1950).* Rosario, Argentina: Ediciones Homo Sapiens, 1999.

Rondón Nucete, Jesús. *Primeros años de gomecismo.* Mérida, Venezuela: Universidad de Los Andes, Ediciones del Vicerrectorado Académico, 2003.

Velásquez, Ramón J. *Confidencias imaginarias de Juan Vicente Gómez.* Caracas: Biblioteca Ayacucho, 1999.


WINTHROP R. WRIGHT

---

**GOMÉZ, MIGUEL MARIANO** (1890–1951). Miguel Mariano Goméz (*b.* 1890; *d.* 1951), Cuba's sixth constitutionally elected president (May–December 1936) and the son of José Miguel

Gómez, the second president. Gómez's term lasted for less than a year because he was the first president to be removed from office by Congress. A conservative member of Cuba's traditional ruling elite, he served in the House of Representatives for twelve years. Goméz was elected mayor of Havana during the Gerardo Machado y Morales administration. However, he attacked the repressive measures of the Machado regime. In January 1936, backed by the Liberal Party and army chief Fulgencio Batista y Zaldívar, he was elected president.

Goméz's biggest political shortcoming was his refusal to acknowledge the paramount position of General Batista. Inaugurated in May 1936, his first mistake was to choose his cabinet without consulting the general. His downfall came in December, when he vetoed a bill, supported by Batista, to set up a system of rural schools operated by the military. Goméz was adamant about reasserting civilian control over the government, and he believed that army control over rural education would erode constitutional and civilian power. Three days after the veto, General Batista had him impeached by the Senate.

*See also* **Batista y Zaldívar, Fulgencio; Cuba: The Republic (1898–1959).**

BIBLIOGRAPHY

Hugh Thomas, *Cuba; or, the Pursuit of Freedom* (1971).

Irwin F. Gellman, *Roosevelt and Batista: Good Neighbor Diplomacy in Cuba, 1933–1945* (1973).

Robert J. Alexander, ed., *Biographical Dictionary of Latin American and Caribbean Political Leaders* (1988).

*Additional Bibliography*

Argote-Freyre, Frank. *Fulgencio Batista.* New Brunswick, NJ: Rutgers University Press, 2006.

Valdéz-Sánchez, Servando. *Fulgencio Batista: El poder de las armas (1933–1940).* La Habana: Editora Historia, 1998.

Whitney, Robert. *State and Revolution in Cuba: Mass Mobilization and Political Change, 1920–1940.* Chapel Hill: University of North Carolina Press, 2001.

DAVID CAREY JR.

## GÓMEZ CARRILLO, ENRIQUE (1873–1927).

Enrique Gómez Carrillo (*b.* 27 February 1873; *d.* 29 November 1927), Guatemalan chronicler, novelist, and pioneer of modern journalistic reporting. As a child, Gómez Carrillo traveled with his parents to Spain, returning first to San Salvador and then to his birthplace of Guatemala City, where he studied. His mother taught him French at home. As a youth, he wrote for the local papers, praising modernism and severely criticizing the style of such revered Guatemalan writers as José Milla. Rubén Darío helped him travel to Spain, where he published his work in various literary magazines and edited the Madrid daily newspaper *El Liberal,* helping to modernize the Spanish press. In Paris, where he would reside until his death, he worked as a correspondent for several Latin American and Spanish periodicals. He befriended Paul Verlaine and was Mata Hari's lover. He published *Esquisses* (1892), *Sensaciones de arte* (1893), and *Del amor, del dolor y del vicio* (1898). Gómez Carrillo's legacy is his exquisite prose, the cosmopolitan vision which liberated him from provincialism, and especially the journalistic style of his literary stories.

*See also* **Journalism.**

BIBLIOGRAPHY

Juan Manuel Mendoza, *Enrique Gómez Carrillo, estudio crítico-biográfico: Su vida, su obra y su época,* 2 vols. (1946).

Alfonso E. Barrientos, *Enrique Gómez Carrillo* (1973).

Víctor Castillo López, *Bibliografía de Enrique Gómez Carrillo* (1984).

*Additional Bibliography*

Bauzá Echevarría, Nellie. *Las novellas decadentistas de Enrique Gómez Carrillo.* Madrid: Editorial Pliegos, 1999.

Preble-Niemi, Oralia, and Luis A, Jiménez, eds. *Ilustres autores guatemaltecos del siglo XIX y XX.* Guatemala: Artemis Edinter, 2004.

FERNANDO GONZÁLEZ DAVISON

## GÓMEZ CASTRO, LAUREANO (1889–1965).

Laureano Gómez Castro (*b.* 20 February 1889; *d.* 13 July 1965), president of Colombia (1950–1953). Born in Bogotá to middle-class parents from Ocaña, Norte de Santander, Gómez attended the Colegio de San Bartolomé and studied engineering at the Universidad Nacional (1905–1909). He was drawn, however, to politics. At twenty, he became editor of *La Unidad,* a

Conservative paper, and remained at its helm until its demise in 1916. In the same period, he was elected to Congress and to Cundinamarca's Chamber of Deputies (1911–1916). His oratory was usually vehement and often wounding. President Marco Fidel Suárez resigned in 1921 rather than suffer Gómez's taunts. After serving as minister plenipotentiary to Chile and Argentina (1923–1925), Gómez returned home in 1925 to become public works minister. His ambitious infrastructure program was rejected by the Congress, and he left public service until 1931, when he was appointed envoy to Germany. Some months later he was elected senator, remaining in office until removed—for calumny—in 1943.

A Liberal victory in 1930 left a power vacuum among Conservatives that Gómez, through his editorials in Bogotá's *El País* (1932–1934) and *El Siglo* (1936–1948), sought to fill. He unremittingly opposed the regimes of Enrique Olaya Herrera, Alfonso López Pumarejo, and Eduardo Santos. Gómez's enthusiasm for Franco's Spain reflected his authoritarianism. The collapse, in 1945–1946, of Liberal unity brought in Gómez's choice, Mariano Ospina Pérez, a Conservative, as president (1946). The increasing political violence led to Liberal withdrawal from the cabinet, and as a result Gómez became foreign minister in 1948. Nearly lynched in the Bogotazo of 9 April 1948, he fled to Spain. Gómez returned in 1949, ran unopposed (the Liberals abstained from voting), and won the presidency. His term was marked by repression, extreme partisanship, and violence. Some infrastructural improvements were achieved, however, including stadia in Bogotá and Medellín, roads, and oil pipelines. With no Congress to answer to, Gómez sent a Colombian battalion to join United Nations forces in Korea (1951–1953). On 13 June 1953, he was overthrown by General Gustavo Rojas Pinilla and exiled to Spain. In 1956, joined by Liberal politicians at Sitges, Spain, Gómez founded the National Front. He died in Bogotá.

*See also* **Bogotazo; Suárez, Marco Fidel; Violencia, La.**

BIBLIOGRAPHY

José Francisco Socorrás, *Laureano Gómez, psicoanálisis de un resentido* (1942).

Alberto Bermúdez, *El buen gobierno ... Laureano Gómez* (1974).

James D. Henderson, *Conservative Thought in Latin America: The Ideas of Laureano Gómez* (1988).

*Additional Bibliography*

Abella Rodríguez, Arturo. *Laureano Gómez.* Bogotá: Espasa, 2000.

Henderson, James D. *Modernization in Colombia: The Laureano Gómez Years, 1889–1965.* Gainesville: University Press of Florida, 2001.

Sáenz Rovner, Eduardo. *Colombia años 50: Industriales, política y diplomacia.* Bogotá: Universidad Nacional de Colombia, Sede Bogotá, 2002.

J. León Helguera

## GÓMEZ-CRUZ, ERNESTO (1933–).

Ernesto Gómez-Cruz (*b.* 7 November 1933), Mexican stage and screen actor. Born in Veracruz, Gómez-Cruz studied theater at his hometown university. In 1967 he debuted in the acclaimed film *Los caifanes,* and since then has starred or costarred in over eighty features. He has received more best actor or supporting actor awards than any other actor in Mexican cinema. Gómez-Cruz is known for his ability to play a wide range of roles. His noted films include *Actas de Marusia* (1975), *Cadena perpetua; La venida del Rey Olmos; La víspera; Auandar Anapu, El imperio de la fortuna* (1986), *El norte; Lo que importa es vivir* (1988), *Barroco* (1990), *The Mexican* (2001), *Pachito Rex, me voy pero no del todo* (2001), *El crimen del Padre Amaro* (2002), *Un mundo maravilloso* (2006), and *Luces artificiales* (2007). Gómez-Cruz has also had a successful television and stage career.

*See also* **Cinema: From the Silent Film to 1990; Cinema: Since 1990.**

BIBLIOGRAPHY

Luis Reyes De La Maza, *El cine sonoro en México* (1973).

E. Bradford Burns, *Latin American Cinema: Film and History* (1975).

Carl J. Mora, *Mexican Cinema: Reflections of a Society: 1896–1980* (1982).

John King, *Magical Reels: A History of Cinema in Latin America* (1990).

*Additional Bibliography*

Paranaguá, Paulo Antonio, ed. *Mexican Cinema*. Translated by Ana M. López. London: British Film Institute, 1995.

Solórzano-Thompson, Nohemy. "Vicarious Identities: Fantasies of Resistance and Language in Juan Ibáñez's *Los caifanes* (1966)." *Film & History* 34:2 (September 2004), 38–45.

DAVID MACIEL

**GÓMEZ DE AVELLANEDA Y ARTEAGA, GERTRUDIS** (1814–1873). Gertrudis Gómez de Avellaneda y Arteaga (*b.* 23 March 1814; *d.* 1 February 1873), Cuban poet, novelist and playwright. Gómez de Avellaneda has the rare distinction of being claimed by the literatures of two countries, Cuba and Spain. Born in the city of Puerto Príncipe (now Camagüey) to a Spanish father and a Cuban mother, she spent her childhood and youth in Cuba. In 1836 she left Cuba with her mother and stepfather and settled in Spain, where she embarked on a literary career and what was for the times a scandalous personal life: she had several love affairs and bore a child out of wedlock, who died a few months after birth.

Gómez de Avellaneda was a friend and peer of several of the most distinguished Spanish poets, writers, and politicians of the day. In June of 1845 she was the winner of the two top prizes given by the Liceo de Madrid (she submitted one of the entries using her brother's name). In 1846 she married but three months later was widowed. Afterward, she retired to a convent briefly, only to return with fervor to literary life. Between 1844 and 1858, several of her plays were staged in Madrid, some with great success. In 1852 she was denied membership in the Royal Spanish Academy because she was a woman.

In 1854 Gómez de Avellaneda married a powerful, well-known politician, Colonel Domingo Verdugo, who was later given an official post in Cuba. In 1859, she returned with him to her native land where she was warmly welcomed and awarded the highest official honors from the literary community, including coronation by Luisa Pérez de Zambrana, a renowned Cuban poet. She remained in Cuba until the death of her husband in 1863. In 1865 she left Cuba with her brother, and after touring the United States, London, and Paris, she settled in Madrid in 1864; she remaind there until her death.

Gómez de Avellaneda is regarded as one of the most important Cuban poets and a notable novelist. Many critics consider her a feminist, and her ideas about slavery, as depicted in her best-known novel, *Sab* (1841), were revolutionary at the time.

*See also* **Literature: Spanish America; Slavery: Abolition.**

BIBLIOGRAPHY

Many distinguished writers have written about the life and works of Gómez de Avellaneda: Gastón Baquero, Regino Eladio Boti y Barreivo, Belkis Cuza Malé, Marcelino Menéndez y Pelayo, Enrique José Varona, Pedro Henríquez Ureña, Dulce María Loynaz, José Lezama Lima among them. A compilation of her best works is *Sus mejores poesías* (1953). See also *Complete Works* (1961), which contains criticism and a bio-bibliography. Studies in English include Edwin Bucher Williams, *The Life and Dramatic Works of Gertrudis Gómez de Avellaneda* (1924).

*Additional Bibliography*

Albin, María C. *Género, poesía y esfera pública: Gertrudis Gómez de Avellaneda y la tradición romántica*. Madrid: Editorial Trotta, 2002.

Pastor, Brigida M. *Fashioning Feminism in Cuba and Beyond: The Prose of Gertrudis Gómez de Avellaneda*. New York: P. Lang, 2003.

ROBERTO VALERO

**GÓMEZ FARÍAS, VALENTÍN** (1781–1858). Valentín Gómez Farías, (*b.* 1781; *d.* 1858), liberal reformer, vice president and acting president of Mexico (1833–1834 and 1846–1847) during two of Antonio López de Santa Anna's presidencies. Born in Guadalajara, Gómez Farías received his degree in 1807 and practiced medicine in Aguascalientes. He began his political career as *regidor* (president) of the *ayuntamiento* (city council) of Aguascalientes and was later elected to the Spanish Cortes. After independence, the state of Zacatecas elected him to the First Constituent Congress (1822), and during the 1820s he served repeatedly in the national legislature. In early 1833 he was finance minister before serving as acting president during the absences of Santa Anna in 1833–1834.

During this period, Gómez Farías attempted to carry out radical changes in the social and political structure of Mexico. His government first advised the clergy to restrict themselves to religious matters when speaking from the pulpit. Prompted by Gómez Farías and his allies José María Luis Mora and Lorenzo de Zavala, Congress voted to end the monopoly of the Catholic Church over education and founded the Directorate of Public Instruction to organize public education in the Federal District and the national territories. Gómez Farías's government asserted its authority over the church hierarchy as well, claiming the right under the Patronato Real to name bishops and archbishops. Congress also abolished mandatory payment of the tithe and gave priests and members of religious orders the freedom to renounce their vows.

But these liberal reforms did not include toleration of other religions. Anticlerical legislation was combined with official "protection" for the Catholic Church. Although some church property was confiscated to pay for educational reforms, Gómez Farías supported Mora's plan to sell all nonessential church property and collect a 4 percent tax on the sales. The proceeds of the tax would be divided between the federal government and the states, and the proceeds of the sales would be used to pay the expenses of the church. Gómez Farías also sponsored reforms to limit the power of the national army by reducing its size and abolishing its *fuero,* thus requiring military officers to stand trial in civil courts. These reforms were aborted when the army, the church, and wealthy conservatives supported a rebellion for "Religion and Fueros," forcing Santa Anna to remove Gómez Farías from office in 1834.

Gómez Farías, his pregnant wife, and his three small children fled into exile with few resources, since Gómez Farías was unable to collect the pay due him. He returned to Mexico in 1838 and in 1840 supported an unsuccessful rebellion by General José de Urrea. Exiled again, he spent time in New York, Yucatán, and New Orleans before returning to Mexico in 1845.

Gómez Farías exercised presidential power as vice president under Santa Anna during the war with the United States in 1846–1847. When he sought to nationalize church property to pay for the war, the militia of Mexico City launched the "Rebellion of the Polkos" (1847), and Santa Anna reassumed the presidency. Gómez Farías was a member of the national legislature, where he opposed the Treaty of Guadalupe Hidalgo and supported the Revolution of Ayutla. He was elected to the Constitutional Congress of 1856–1857 and died in Mexico City.

*See also* **Anticlericalism; Santa Anna, Antonio López de.**

BIBLIOGRAPHY

Charles A. Hale, *Mexican Liberalism in the Age of Mora, 1821–1853* (1968), pp. 108–147, 165–175, 218–221.

Michael P. Costeloe, *La primera república federal en México (1824–1835): Un estudio de los partidos políticos en el México independiente* (1975), pp. 371–436.

Michael P. Costeloe, *Church and State in Independent Mexico—A Study of the Patronage Debate, 1821–1857* (1978).

Barbara A. Tenenbaum, *The Politics of Penury: Debt and Taxes in Mexico, 1821–1856* (1986), pp. 38–39, 80.

Michael P. Costeloe, "A Pronunciamiento in Nineteenth-Century Mexico: '15 de julio de 1840,'" in *Mexican Studies/Estudios Mexicanos* 4 (Summer 1988): 245–264.

*Additional Bibliography*

Fuentes Díaz, Vicente. *Valentín Gómez Farías: Santos Degollado.* México: Editorial Porrúa, 1997.

Villaneda González, Alicia. *Valentín Gómez Farías.* México: Planeta DeAgostini, 2002.

D. F. STEVENS

**GÓMEZ HURTADO, ÁLVARO** (1919–1995). Álvaro Gomez Hurtado, a Colombian attorney, journalist, and politician, was the son of the Conservative leader Laureano Gómez Castro. Born in Bogotá on May 8, 1919, Gómez Hurtado was a political activist from an early age, vigorously championing the Conservative Party and right-wing causes. He collaborated on *El Siglo* and other Conservative publications and during his father's presidency (1950–1953) led the pro-government bloc in the Colombian Senate. On the overthrow of Laureano Gómez in 1953, Álvaro, like his father, went into exile, but after the restoration of constitutional government in 1958 he played a leading role within the *laureanista* wing of the Conservative

Party. He opposed the 1961 agrarian reform; took a hard line against leftist insurgencies; occupied a number of important positions, including that of ambassador in Washington; and continued writing both in the press and in works analyzing national and international problems. He also became increasingly disillusioned with the traditional parties' preoccupation with factional and bureaucratic advantage. He ran for president, unsuccessfully, in 1974, 1986, and 1990, on the last occasion as candidate of the Movimiento de Salvación Nacional that he launched as an alternative to both traditional parties.

In 1988 Gómez Hurtado was kidnapped and held for six months by M-19 guerrillas, an experience that appears to have influenced the evolution of his ideas. As copresident of the 1991 Constituent Assembly he worked closely with former M-19 members in devising a new constitution notable for its democratic inclusiveness and ambitious social guarantees. While devoting himself to academic life, he continued to denounce his country's ills, with particularly harsh condemnation of the drug-tainted government of Ernesto Samper Pizano (1994–1998). In 1995 Gómez was assassinated, a crime that as of 2007 remained unsolved.

*See also* **Colombia, Constitutions: Overview; Colombia, Political Parties: Conservative Party; Colombia, Revolutionary Movements: M-19.**

BIBLIOGRAPHY

Cabrera, Gabriel. *Álvaro Gómez: Rasgos para un perfil.* Bogotá: Somos, 1996.

DAVID BUSHNELL

## GÓMEZ MORÍN, MANUEL (1897–1972).

A Mexican financial figure, intellectual, and opposition leader, Manuel Gómez Morín was born on February 27, 1897, in Batopilas, Chihuahua, the son of a miner. He completed a course of studies in Mexico City at the National Preparatory School (1913–1915) and legal studies at the National School of Law (1915–1918). He maintained close friendships with the "Seven Wise Men of Mexico," including Alfonso Caso, Vicente Lombardo Toledano, and Narciso Bassols. Appointed a professor in 1918, he went on to influence a generation of prominent political figures.

Gómez Morín quickly entered public life, serving as *oficial mayor* and undersecretary of the treasury (1919–1921). He was also a founder and first director (1925–1929) of the board of the Bank of Mexico, serving as a federal reserve. In 1923 he secretly gave financial support to the rebellion of Adolfo de la Huerta and later served as unofficial treasurer of José Vasconcelos's 1929 presidential campaign. After that he retired from public life, but two years later authored the first reform of credit institutions.

Meanwhile, Gómez Morín maintained his academic career as dean of the National Law School from 1922 to 1924. He subsequently went into private law practice and invested wisely in numerous major corporations at their founding. In 1939, disenchanted with the direction of the state, he and Efraín González Luna founded the National Action Party (PAN), which became Mexico's major opposition party until 1988. He spent his last thirty years as an investor and practitioner of law. Gómez Morín died on April 19, 1972.

*See also* **de la Huerta, Adolfo; Mexico, Political Parties: National Action Party (PAN).**

BIBLIOGRAPHY

Gómez Mont, María Teresa. *Manuel Gómez Morín: La lucha por la liberated de cátedra.* Mexico: UNAM, 1996.

Krauze, Enrique. *Caudillos culturales en la Revolución Mexicana.* Mexico: Siglo Veintiuno Editores, 1976.

Wilkie, James W. *Frente de la Revolución Mexicana.* Mexico: UAM, 1995.

RODERIC AI CAMP

## GÓMEZ PEDRAZA, MANUEL (1789?–1851).

Manuel Gómez Pedraza (*b.* 1789?; *d.* 14 May 1851), Mexican politician and general. Born in Querétaro to a prominent family, he fought for the royalist cause in the War of Independence and then supported the Iturbide empire. Gómez successfully managed the ideological switch to federalism in 1824 and held several government posts, civil and military, during the Guadalupe Victoria presidency (1824–1829). A Scottish Rite Mason, he was elected president of Mexico in 1828 but was prevented from taking office by the revolt of the Acordade. After returning from exile, he served the final three months of his presidential term in 1833.

He was elected to later congresses and held various ministerial posts. Known for his oratory and personal eccentricity—he forgot his own wedding day—he became a prominent member of the social elite in the capital. As one of the leaders of the moderate liberal federalists, Gómez was a presidential candidate on more than one occasion.

*See also* **Mexico, Wars and Revolutions: War of Independence.**

BIBLIOGRAPHY

Manuel Rivera Cambas, *Los gobernantes de México,* rev. ed. by Leonardo Pasquel, vol. 4 (1964), pp. 359–374.

Stanley C. Green, *The Mexican Republic: The First Decade* (1987), pp. 88, 156–160, 229.

*Additional Bibliography*

Gómez Pedraza, Manuel, and Ma Laura Solares Robles. *La obra política de Manuel Gómez Pedraza, 1813–1851.* México, D.F.: Instituto Mora, 1999.

Solares Robles, Ma Laura. *Una revolución pacífica. Biografía política de Manuel Gómez Pedraza, 1789–1851.* México, D.F.: Instituto de Investigaciones Dr. José María Luis Mora, 1996.

MICHAEL P. COSTELOE

## GÓMEZ ROJAS, JOSÉ DOMINGO

**GÓMEZ ROJAS, JOSÉ DOMINGO** (1896–1920). Born in Santiago, Chile, on August 4, 1896, José Domingo Gómez Rojas achieved literary fame at a young age. In 1913 he published *Rebeldías Líricas,* a collection of poems attacking class privilege and celebrating youthful rebellion that, by the decade's end, resonated with Santiago's middle-class youth and university students. As a law student at the University of Chile, he also worked with labor and anarchist movements in Santiago and Valparaiso and affiliated himself with the Chilean branch of the International Workers of the World. Taken into custody during a sweep of the offices of the Chilean Student Federation (FECH) in July 1920, he spent the next two months incarcerated. His condition deteriorated as a result of solitary confinements and physical abuse, and he was transferred in late September to an asylum, where he died on September 29. Gómez Rojas's death had a powerful impact on subsequent generations of Chilean intellectual and political leaders, and he has survived as a symbol of resistance to state repression: The Popular Front repeatedly eulogized him in the 1930s and 1940s, and nearly a half-century later in 1983 a student collective organized in opposition to Pinochet's dictatorship named itself "el grupo José Domingo Gómez Rojas."

*See also* **Literature: Spanish America.**

BIBLIOGRAPHY

*Primary Work*

*Rebeldías Líricas.* [1913]. Santiago: Ediciones Ercilla, 1940.

*Secondary Work*

Valle, Fabio Moraga, and Carlos Vega Delgado, eds. *José Domingo Gómez Rojas: Vida y Obra.* Punta Arenas, Chile: Editorial Atelí, 1997.

RAYMOND B. CRAIB

## GÓMEZ SEGURA, MARTE RODOLFO

**GÓMEZ SEGURA, MARTE RODOLFO** (1896–1973). Marte R. Gómez was a Mexican politician belonging to the Institutional Revolutionary Party from the northern border state of Tamaulipas. Born in Ciudad Reynosa on July 4, 1896, Gómez studied agricultural and hydraulic engineering at the Mexican national agricultural school at Chapingo. During his career he occupied many elected and appointed offices including deputy and senator in the Mexican Congress and governor of the State of Tamaulipas. Serving as secretary of agriculture during the presidency of Manuel Ávila Camacho, Gómez Segura was the only member of the cabinet to oppose the collaboration of the Mexican government in the infamous *bracero* program. He also wrote extensively about agriculture and agricultural reform.

*See also* **Ávila Camacho, Manuel; Mexico, Political Parties: Institutional Revolutionary Party (PRI).**

BIBLIOGRAPHY

Gómez, Marte R. *La reforma agraria de México: Su crisis durante el periodo 1928–1934.* Mexico: Miguel Porrúa, 1964.

Gómez, Marte R.. *La reforma agraria en las filas villistas, años 1913 a 1915 y 1920.* Mexico: Biblioteca del Instituto Nacional de Estudios Históricos de la Revolución Mexicana, 1966.

BARBARA DRISCOLL DE ALVARADO

**GÓMEZ Y BÁEZ, MÁXIMO** (1836–1905). Máximo Gómez y Báez (*b.* 18 November 1836; *d.* 17 June 1905), major military leader in the wars for Cuban independence (1868–1878, 1895–1898). Born in Baní, Santo Domingo, into a middle-class family, he attended a local elementary school and a religious seminary. He began his military career at age sixteen, in the war against the Haitians and later served as a lieutenant in the Dominican army. After the 1866 civil war in Santo Domingo resulted in the loss of all his property, Gómez fled to Cuba. Settling in Bayamó, he became a fervent advocate of independence. When Carlos Manuel de Céspedes's El Grito de Yara (The Shout of Yara) inaugurated the Ten Years' War (1868–1878), he joined Céspedes, quickly proving himself to be an invaluable military strategist and leader. With his promotion to the rank of general, he began a close association with the rebel leaders Antonio Maceo and Calixto García.

Gómez and Maceo came to believe that success in the war was unlikely without an expansion into the prosperous western provinces. They advocated the mass disruption of sugar production and the liberation of slaves, hoping that the damage to Cuba's economic base would bring a quick rebel victory. The revolution's civilian leaders opposed the plan, but in 1872 fear of defeat made them consent to a modified version of it. Gómez and Maceo marched west, burning sugar plantations and freeing slaves. After several months, heavy casualties and low provisions necessitated their return, but changes in the political climate made a renewal of the campaign impossible. Disillusioned and frustrated with the lack of progress, Gómez pressed for a truce with the Spanish. In 1878 the Pact of Zanjón ended the Ten Years' War, and the rebel leaders who were unwilling to accept the truce went into exile.

During his years in exile, Gómez joined Maceo and the poet José Martí and began preparations for a second revolution against Spain. Gómez and Martí had frequent disputes over strategy, resulting in a brief break in 1884; nevertheless, by 1893 their differences had been put aside and Martí named Gómez military commander of the Cuban Revolutionary Party. On 25 March 1895, he and Maceo issued the Manifesto of Monte Christi, renewing the Cuban Revolution.

When Martí died in a skirmish on 19 May 1895, Gómez assumed the mantle of leadership, becoming the commander in chief of the movement. Under his leadership, the war was immediately extended into the western provinces. He issued a moratorium on sugar production, promising death and destruction of property to anyone in violation of his decree. Although these tactics seriously endangered Cuba's economic future, they proved effective in the war. By 1897 the rebels had moved into Matanzas and Havana.

A year later, a Spanish counteroffensive left the rebels struggling to maintain their positions, but U.S. entry into the war (1898) put an end to Spanish resistance. Following a four-year occupation, during which time the rebel leaders were all but totally ignored, the United States withdrew. As the Republic of Cuba was being established (20 May 1902), Gómez was urged to run for president, but he declined to do so, saying, "Men of war for war, and those of peace for peace."

*See also* **Maceo, Antonio; Spanish-American War; Sugar Industry; Ten Years' War.**

BIBLIOGRAPHY

Charles E. Chapman, *A History of the Cuban Republic* (1969).

Hugh Thomas, *Cuba: The Pursuit of Freedom* (1971) and *Mayor General Máximo Gómez Báez: Sus campañas militares,* 2 vols. (1986).

Tomás Báez Díaz, *Máximo Gómez: El Libertador* (1986).

Juan Bosch, *Máximo Gómez: De Monte Christi a la Gloria, tres años de guerra en Cuba* (1986).

General Máximo Gómez y Báez, *Revoluciones...Cuba y hogar,*edited by Bernardo Gómez Toro (1986).

*Additional Bibliography*

Báez Díaz, Tómas. *Máximo Gómez: Episodios heroicos y sentimentales.* Santo Domingo, República Dominicana: Editora de Colores, 2001.

Helg, Aline. *Our Rightful Share: The Afro-Cuban Struggle for Equality, 1886–1912.* Chapel Hill, NC: University of North Carolina Press, 1995.

SARA FLEMING

**GONDRA, MANUEL** (1871–1927). Manuel Gondra (*b.* 1 January 1871; *d.* 8 March 1927), Paraguayan scholar, statesman, and president (1910–

1911, 1920–1921). Manuel E. Gondra's varied and distinguished career in education, the military, diplomacy, and politics established him as one of Paraguay's leading public figures of the twentieth century. Born of an Argentine father and Paraguayan mother, Gondra was educated in the schools of Asunción and the Colegio Nacional. It was at the Colegio Nacional that Gondra later built a reputation as a highly effective educational reformer. Entering public life in 1902, he served as Paraguay's minister to Brazil (1905–1908) before being elected president in 1920. Confronting escalating political violence, Gondra resigned within a year of assuming the presidency.

During the ensuing decade, Gondra served as minister of war, reorganizing Paraguay's army and clarifying his nation's legal claim to the disputed Chaco region. While serving as Paraguay's minister in Washington in 1920, Gondra was again elected to the presidency. He fell victim to civil strife once again, however, and resigned his office after only fifteen months. Achieving more as a statesman than as a politician, Gondra was awarded his greatest recognition for his sponsorship of a treaty to prevent war among the American states at the Fifth International Conference of American States at Santiago, Chile, in 1923. For this initiative, Gondra was lauded by the Pan-American Union soon after his death in 1927. An accomplished scholar, Gondra owned one of the finest libraries in South America. His collection, containing 7,283 books, 2,633 pamphlets, 20,000 pages of manuscripts, and 270 maps, is now housed in the Benson Collection at the University of Texas.

*See also* **Education: Overview; Gondra Treaty (1923); Paraguay: The Twentieth Century.**

BIBLIOGRAPHY

C. E. Castañeda and J. Autrey Dabbs, "The Manuel Gondra Collection," in *Handbook of Latin American Studies* 6 (1940): 505–517.

Arturo Bray, *Hombres y épocas del Paraguay* (1943), esp. pp. 152–159.

Harris Gaylord Warren, *Paraguay: An Informal History* (1949), esp. pp. 265–278.

Michael Grow, *The Good Neighbor Policy and Authoritarianism in Paraguay: United States Economic Expansion and Great-Power Rivalry in Latin America During World War II* (1981).

*Additional Bibliography*

Amaral, Raúl. *Los presidentes del Paraguay (1844-1954): Crónica política.* Asunción: Centro Paraguayo de Estudios Sociológicos, 1994.

DANIEL M. MASTERSON

---

**GONDRA TREATY (1923).** Gondra Treaty (1923), an agreement that is now viewed as the inspiration for the present-day peacekeeping mechanisms of the Organization of American States, it was named for the Paraguayan statesman Manuel Gondra, who sponsored the initiative at the Fifth International Conference of American States in Santiago, Chile, in May 1923. The treaty's seven articles detail procedures for the settlement of disputes between the American republics through an impartial investigation of the facts relating to the controversy. Disputes that could not be resolved through normal diplomatic means would be submitted to a commission of inquiry composed of five members, all nationals of American states, who would then render a final report within one year. The report would not have the force of arbitral awards and would be binding on the parties involved for only six months after its issuance. The treaty called for the establishment of permanent commissions in Washington, D.C., and Montevideo, Uruguay, to receive requests for inquiries and to notify the other parties involved. The Gondra Treaty mirrored the outlines of the February 1923 Washington Conference treaty between the United States and the Central American republics, which established similar procedures for commissions of inquiry to resolve disputes. Significantly, the Gondra Treaty called for disputes in the hemisphere to be resolved by the American republics themselves.

*See also* **Gondra, Manuel; Organization of American States (OAS); Washington Treaties of 1907 and 1923.**

BIBLIOGRAPHY

L. S. Rowe, "The Fifth International Conference of American States," in *Bulletin of the Pan American Union* 57, no. 2 (1923): 109–113, see also pp. 114–173.

Arthur P. Whitaker, *The Western Hemisphere Idea: Its Rise and Decline* (1954), esp. pp. 108–131.

Robert N. Burr and Roland D. Hussey, eds., *Documents on Inter-American Cooperation*, vol. 2 (1955), esp. pp. 87–89.

Samuel Guy Inman, *Inter-American Conferences, 1826–1954: History and Problems* (1965), esp. pp. 88–106.

DANIEL M. MASTERSON

## GONZAGA, FRANCISCA HEDWIGES

(1847–1935). Francisca Hedwiges Gonzaga (Chiquinha; *b.* 17 October 1847; *d.* 28 February 1935), a colorful key figure in the early history of Brazilian musical nationalism. Daughter of an imperial field marshall, José Basileu Neves Gonzaga, Francisca Gonzaga was married at the age of thirteen to an officer in the Merchant Marine at the insistence of her parents. She divorced her husband at the age of eighteen and left home with her children, whom she supported by giving music lessons. She was befriended by composer Joaquim Antônio da Silva Callado Junior, who, in spite of her basically classical training, introduced her to the *chorões,* popular musicians composing in an improvisational style. Gonzaga proved to be such an apt apprentice that she soon improvised a polka, "Atraente," at a party honoring composer Henrique Alves de Mesquita. This song achieved widespread popularity and was followed by a flood of popular pieces called *valsas,* polkas, tangos, *maxixes, lundus, quadrilhas, fados, gavotas,* mazurkas, *barcarolas, habaneras,* and *serenatas.* She is best known, however, as composer of seventy-seven pieces for theater, which consisted of comedies, operettas, and incidental music for plays that captured the imagination of the public and defined popular styles in a manner that influenced composers of art music. Her independent spirit and disregard for convention made her a sensation in her day. In addition to being the first woman in Brazil to conduct a theater orchestra and military band, Gonzaga also was extremely active in antislavery and republican causes, even selling manuscripts and using royalty funds to contribute to these causes.

*See also* **Brazil: Since 1889; Music: Popular Music and Dance.**

BIBLIOGRAPHY

Ary Vasconcelos, *Panorama da música popular brasileira* (1964).

David P. Appleby, *The Music of Brazil* (1983).

*Additional Bibliography*

Millan, Cleusa de Souza. *A memória social de Chiquinha Gonzaga.* Rio de Janeiro: s.n., 2000.

Mugnaini Jr., Ayrton. *A jovem Chiquinha Gonzaga.* São Paulo: Editora Nova Alexandria, 2005.

Vianna, Hermano. *The Mystery of Samba: Popular Music and National Identity in Brazil.* Translated by John Charles Chasteen. Chapel Hill, NC: University of North Carolina Press, 1999.

DAVID P. APPLEBY

## GONZAGA, LUIZ

(1912–1989). Luiz Gonzaga (*b.* 13 Dec. 1912; *d.* 2 Aug. 1989), Brazilian singer, composer, and accordionist. Gonzaga transformed the rural folk music of the Northeast into a national urban popular music in the late 1940s and early 1950s. Born in the state of Pernambuco, he learned the traditional music of the Northeastern backlands and distinguished himself as an accordionist. After a stint in the military he moved south to Rio de Janeiro in the late 1930s and began performing contemporary popular music in clubs and on radio shows. Success came in the mid-1940s, when he teamed up with Humberto Teixeira, a poet from the state of Ceará, and incorporated Northeastern music into his repertoire. Together they adapted syncopated rhythmic figures used by Northeastern folk guitarists to create a new song-and-dance genre they called *baião.* In 1946 the pair co-authored the song entitled "Baião," which became a commercial success and ushered in a Northeastern phase in the history of Brazilian popular music. During the late 1940s and early 1950s, Gonzaga and his co-writers, Teixeira and Zé Dantas, released a string of hit recordings based on the *baião* and other Northeastern genres, such as *chamego, xote, xaxado,* and *forró.* The songs spoke of the culture, history, and physical beauty of the Northeast, and Gonzaga became a spokesman for Northeastern culture. He was crowned "King of the Baião."

When the national *baião* craze waned in the late 1950s, Gonzaga returned to the Northeast to spend his time performing throughout the interior. In the late 1960s, Gonzaga's music found a new generation of Brazilian listeners when the contemporary popular musicians Caetano Veloso and

Gilberto Gil popularized new versions of his songs. During the 1970s and 1980s, Gonzaga performed with numerous Brazilian popular musicians, such as Gal Costa, Milton Nascimento, Fagner, Elba Ramalho, and his own son, Gonzaguinha. At the time of his death Gonzaga had made more than 200 recordings.

*See also* **Brazil, Geography; Music: Popular Music and Dance.**

BIBLIOGRAPHY

José Ramos Tinhorão, *Pequena história da música popular: Da modinha ao tropicalismo*, 5th ed. (1986).

Mundicarmo Maria Rocha Ferretti, *Baiaõ dos dois: Zedantas e Luiz Gonzaga* (1988).

Chris Mc Gowan and Ricardo Pessanha, *The Brazilian Sound: Samba, Bossa Nova, and the Popular Music of Brazil* (1991).

*Additional Bibliography*

Dreyfus, Dominique. *Vida do viajante: A saga do Luiz Gonzaga*. Sao Paulo: Editora 34, 1996.

Santos, José Farias dos. *Luiz Gonzaga, a música como expressão do Nordeste*. São Paulo: IBRASA, 2004.

Silva, Uéliton Mendes da. *Luiz Gonzaga: Discografia do rei do baião*. Bahia, Brasil: Editorial Memorial das Letras, 1997.

LARRY N. CROOK

**GONZAGA, TOMÁS ANTÔNIO** (1744–1810). Tomás Antônio Gonzaga (*b.* 1744; *d.* 1810), Brazilian poet. Born in Portugal to a Brazilian father from Rio de Janeiro and a mother of English background, Gonzaga went to Brazil as a child, where he studied in the Jesuit school in Bahia. After completing his law degree at Coimbra, Portugal, in 1768, he became a magistrate in Beja, Portugal, and later in gold-driven Vila Rica, in Minas Gerais province in Brazil. There, as both a *reinol* (that is, one born in Portugal and living in colonial Brazil) and a poet, he became involved in political and intellectual societies. Cláudio Manuel da Costa (1729–1789) and Inácio José de Alvarenga Peixoto (1744–1793) were among his closest friends and conspirators in the failed Inconfidência Mineira, the Mineiran Conspiracy of 1789. Gonzaga's judicial career in Brazil suffered because of a bitter political feud with the governor of Minas Gerais, Luís da Cunha e Meneses, who accused him of opportunism and corruption. Tried as a participant in the Mineiran Conspiracy, Gonzaga was sent into exile in Mozambique, where he married a rich widow, gradually regained his official position, and, at his death, was the Mozambican customs magistrate.

Gonzaga's poetry belongs to the Arcadian school, which flourished in late-eighteenth-century Minas Gerais. Using the name "Dirceu," he dedicated his lyrics to his beloved Marília, a sixteen-year-old girl he had intended to marry. He continued to write love poems throughout his exile in Mozambique, even when all hope of this marriage had already been dashed. Because his work was published on two continents and in several volumes (1792, 1799, 1812), the exact corpus of his poetry, published under the title *Marília de Dirceu*, has yet to be definitively established.

Perhaps more significant than his poems are the *Cartas chilenas* (1863), now attributed to Gonzaga. A veiled attack on Cunha e Meneses's government, these thirteen free-verse satirical letters offer a fascinating view of life in colonial Minas, in particular of the societal conflicts that surfaced among government officials, nobles, merchants, gold prospectors, and slaves.

Gonzaga's life and writings have inspired works by many other Brazilian writers down to the present, including Casimiro de Abreu, Castro Alves, and Drummond de Andrade.

*See also* **Inconfidência Mineira; Minas Gerais.**

BIBLIOGRAPHY

Wilson Martins, *História da inteligência brasileira* (1976–1983).

*Additional Bibliography*

Gonçalves, Adelto. *Gonzaga, um poeta do iluminismo*. Rio de Janeiro: Editora Nova Fronteira, 1999.

Polito, Ronald. *Um coração maior que o mundo: Tomás Antônio Gonzaga e o horizonte luso-colonial*. São Paulo: Editora Globo, 2003.

IRWIN STERN

**GONZÁLEZ, ABRAHAM** (1864–1913). Abraham González (*b.* 7 June 1864; *d.* 7 March 1913), governor of Chihuahua, Mexico (1911–

1913), minister of internal affairs (1911–1912). González was a gunrunner for the insurgency of Francisco I. Madero (1909–1910). As governor he instituted a number of political reforms, including the abolition of company towns and the hated office of *jefe político* (district boss). After an interlude in Madero's cabinet, González returned to Chihuahua to confront growing unrest that erupted in the rebellion of Pascual Orozco Jr., in 1912. He defeated the Orozquistas, only to die at the hands of the reactionary forces that overthrew Madero. González typified the Maderista, middle-class political reformers caught between the radical demands of their present and worker followers and the reactionary Porfirian oligarchy.

*See also* **Mexico: Since 1910; Weapons Industry.**

BIBLIOGRAPHY

There are two important biographies of González: Francisco R. Almada, *Vida, proceso y muerte de Abraham González* (1967), and William H. Beezley, *Insurgent Governor: Abraham González and the Mexican Revolution* (1973).

*Additional Bibliography*

Caraveo Estrada, Baudilio B. *Historias de mi odisea revolucionaria: La revolución en la sierra de Chihuahua y la Convención de Aguascalientes.* Chihuahua, México: Doble Hélice Ediciones, 1996.

McLynn, Frank. *Villa and Zapata: A History of the Mexican Revolution.* New York: Carroll & Graf Publishers, 2001.

Mark Wasserman

**GONZÁLEZ, BEATRIZ** (1938–). Beatriz González (*b.* 1938), Colombian artist, historian, and critic. González studied fine arts at the Universidad de los Andes in Bogotá (1959–1962) and printmaking at the Academia van Beeldende Kunsten in Rotterdam (1966). Her first individual exhibition was held at the Museo de Arte Moderno in Bogotá in 1964. González employs both popular imagery and well-known artworks as departure points, taking images from such European masterpieces as Leonardo da Vinci's *Mona Lisa* and Jan Vermeer's *The Lacemaker* and placing them within the context of Colombian daily life. She is also known for her satirical portraits of prominent Colombian figures. Her works of the 1960s and 1970s are generally characterized by strong colors and a sense of irony, thus bearing a relationship to pop art. González later explored social themes: questions of identity, the history of her culture, and the impact of these issues on the lives of contemporary Colombians. González was included in the Bienal de São Paulo (1971) and the Biennale di Venezia (1978). Retrospectives were held at the Museo de Arte Moderno La Tertulia in Cali (1976 and 1995), the Museo de Arte Moderno in Bogotá (1984), and the Museo de Bellas Artes in Caracas (1994). The retrospective *30 años en la obra gráfica de Beatriz González* was held at the Banco de República, Colombia, in 1996. In addition to painting, González has also written historical works on Colombian art, including *El arte colombiano en el siglo XX: Colección Bancafé* (2004).

*See also* **Art: The Twentieth Century.**

BIBLIOGRAPHY

*Additional Bibliography*

Botero, Fernando, et al. *Botero in the Museo Nacional de Colombia: New Donation, 2004.* Bogotá: Villegas Editores, Museo Nacional de Colombia, 2004.

Cobo Borda, J. G. *La mirada cómplice: 8 artistas colombianos.* Cali, Colombia: Ediciones Universidad del Valle, 1994.

Judith Gluck Steinberg

**GONZÁLEZ, CARLOS** (1905–1993). Carlos González (*b.* 1 December 1905; *d.* 1993), Uruguayan artist, who specialized in woodcut. Born in Melo, in the department of Cerro Largo, González studied with Andrés Etchebarne Bidart. In his youth, he traveled throughout the Uruguayan countryside selling his family's wheatmill products; later he devoted himself to forestry. It was not until 1938 that he began to make woodcuts. He received gold medals from the National Salon of Fine Arts in Montevideo in 1943 and 1944. His subjects were local legends, traditional countryside scenes, and socially concerned testimonies to the poverty-stricken rural areas. In a typical González woodcut, the central scene is surrounded by a printed border filled with written messages and symbols representing rural work, leisure, and culture. The figurative elements on the margins complement the central scene. Together, both marginal and central illustrations narrate events from

Latin American and Uruguayan history. His printing style was harsh and sketchy, often the result of carving wood with a common knife.

González wanted his art to have a didactic function, specifically, to tell the history and social reality of Uruguay as he interpreted it. This task, he believed, required a collective (or cooperative) effort. Feeling isolated, he abandoned artistic practice at the prime of his career, in 1944. In 1970 he was credited with the invention of Uruguayan printmaking at the Fourth American Biennial of Printmaking in Santiago, Chile.

*See also* **Art: The Twentieth Century.**

BIBLIOGRAPHY

Angel Kalenberg, *Carlos González o la invención del grabado uruguayo* (1970).

Alicia Haber, "Vernacular Culture in Uruguayan Art: An Analysis of the Documentary Function of the Works of Pedro Figari, Carlos González and Luis Solari," in *Latin American and Caribbean Center, Florida University, Occasional Paper Series* (Spring 1982): 9–15, and *Carlos González: El grabado como puente visual* (1988).

### *Additional Bibliography*

Museo Blanes. *Realismo social en el arte uruguayo: 1930–1950.* Montevideo: División Cultura IMM, Museo Municipal de Bellas Artes Juan Manuel Blanes, 1992.

MARTA GARSD

## GONZÁLEZ, ELIÁN

**GONZÁLEZ, ELIÁN** (1993–). In 1999 Elián González was a six-year-old Cuban exile who, when attempting to flee Cuba for Miami, became embroiled in an international tug of war between Cuba, the Cuban exile community in Florida, and the U.S. government. In November 1999 Elián, his mother, and twelve other Cubans left Cuba in a small aluminum boat. His mother and ten other passengers died en route to Miami; Elián survived by floating on an inner tube, and he was rescued by two fishermen off the coast of Miami on November 25. Local agents of the Immigration and Naturalization Service (INS) turned Elián over to his paternal great uncle, Lázaro González of Miami. Lázaro and Elián's other Miami relatives agreed that Elián should remain in the United States, even though his closest blood relative, his father, lived in Cuba. The ensuing struggle over where Elián would reside quickly became a flashpoint for the bitter conflict between pro-Castro Cubans and Miami's Cuban exile community, which traditionally has taken a strong stance against Castro and communism.

It was not until January 12, 2000 (more than five months after Elián's arrival in the United States), that Attorney General Janet Reno ordered that Elián be returned to his father in Cuba. Elián's Miami relatives made it clear that they would not cooperate with the order, and they were backed by hundreds of protestors from Miami's Cuban American community. Eventually, a family court judge revoked Lázaro's temporary custody of Elián, and on April 22 a fully armed SWAT team retrieved Elián from his relatives' home. Almost immediately after, crowds of protestors filled the streets of the Miami neighborhood of Little Havana. After being held at Andrews Air Force Base while his relatives appealed Reno's decision, Elián was finally returned to Cuba on June 28, 2000.

Throughout the entire episode, intense and highly polemical media coverage highlighted the troubled nature of the U.S.-Cuba relationship as well as the bitter divide between the Cuban community in exile in the United States and those faithful to Castro and the revolution who remained in Cuba. *Time* magazine celebrated Elián's reunion with his father; *Newsweek* focused on the INS raid as inappropriate. The day after Elián's reunion with his father at Andrews Air Force Base, the White House released a photograph of a happy Elián in his father's arms—the Miami relatives claimed the photo was a fake. The Cuban newspaper *Granma* ran photos of Elián in his communist youth league uniform. Fidel Castro personally attended Elián's seventh birthday party, and stood directly to his right as the boy blew out the candles on his birthday cake. In a September 2005 interview broadcast on the television program *60 Minutes*, Elián stated that Castro was his friend.

*See also* **Hispanics in the United States.**

BIBLIOGRAPHY

Bardach, Ann Louise. *Cuba Confidential: Love and Vengeance in Miami and Havana.* New York: Random House, 2002.

De La Torre, Miguel A. *La Lucha for Cuba: Religion and Politics on the Streets of Miami.* Berkeley: University of California Press, 2003.

Madan, Nora. *Batalla por la liberación de Elián González.* Havana: Editorial Política, 2000.

EMILY BERQUIST

## GONZÁLEZ, FLORENTINO (1805–1874).

Florentino González (*b.* 1805; *d.* 1874), Colombian political figure of the Liberal Party. Born in Cincelada, Santander, González studied at the College of San Bartolomé, obtaining the degree of doctor of jurisprudence in 1825. One of the participants in the attempt against Simón Bolívar's life in 1828, González barely escaped the firing squad. He went to Europe in 1841, remaining there until 1846.

González's claim to historical notoriety rests on his being widely credited as the foremost proponent of free trade, a position based on ideas he had picked up in Great Britain in the early 1840s. As minister of finance in the first administration of Tomás Cipriano de Mosquera (1845–1849), he implemented policies that reflected his ideas. In the ensuing Liberal Party split between an elite faction (the *gólgotas*) and a more popular faction (the *draconianos*), González attacked the *draconianos* as dangerous socialist levelers. As he became ideologically closer to the Conservatives and because he favored annexation to the United States to avoid political instability, he broke with his party and faded away from the political stage. In 1860 he left Colombia never to return. He died in Argentina in 1874 but his body was not returned to Colombia until 1934.

*See also* **Colombia, Political Parties: Liberal Party; Free Trade Act.**

BIBLIOGRAPHY

Gustavo Otero Muñoz, *Semblanzas Colombianas* (1938).

Gerardo Molina, *Las ideas liberales en Colombia, 1849–1914* (1970).

Jaime Duarte French, *Florentino González: Razón y sinrazón de una lucha política* (1982).

### *Additional Bibliography*

Jordán Flórez, Fernando, ed. *Antología del pensamiento y programas del Partido Liberal, 1820–2000.* 3 vols. Bogotaá: Partido Liberal Colombiano, 2000.

Llano Isaza, Rodrigo. *Los draconianos: Origen popular del Liberalismo Colombiano.* Bogotá: Planeta, 2005.

José Escorcia

## GONZÁLEZ, JOAQUÍN VÍCTOR (1863–1923).

Joaquín Víctor González (*b.* 6 March 1863; *d.* 21 December 1923), Argentine author, educator, diplomat, and statesman. Born in Chilecito, La Rioja Province, he received his law degree from the University of Córdoba in 1886. He began his political career in 1886, when he was elected as a deputy representing La Rioja. He then served as the province's governor (1889–1891) and senator (1907–1923). President Julio Roca (1898–1904) appointed him interior minister (1901) and later foreign relations minister (1903). He continued his service under President Manuel Quintana (1904–1906), heading the Ministry of Justice and Public Instruction. He concluded his public service by representing Argentina in the League of Nations.

An authority on law and politics as well as education, he is best known for his literary and historical works, including *La tradición nacional* (1888) and *Mis montañas* (1893). He taught law at the University of Córdoba (1894), served on the National Education Council (1896), and became the first rector of the National University of La Plata (1906).

BIBLIOGRAPHY

Joaquín V. González, *Obras completas de Joaquín V. González,* 25 vols. (1935–1937).

Arturo Marasso, *Joaquín V. González, el artista y el hombre* (1937).

### *Additional Bibliography*

Aguirre, Gisela. *Joaquín V. González.* Buenos Aires: Planeta, 1999.

Zimmermann, Eduardo A. *Los liberales reformistas: La cuestión social en Argentina, 1890–1916.* Buenos Aires: Editora Sudamericana, 1995.

Daniel Lewis

## GONZÁLEZ, JUAN NATALICIO (1897–1966).

Juan Natalicio González (*b.* 8 September 1897; *d.* 6 December 1966), Paraguayan poet, historian, journalist, statesman, and president (1948–1949). González was born in Villerrica and studied at the Colegio Nacional in Asunción. He began his literary career under the guidance of Juan O'Leary, with whom he shared many stylistic and thematic traits. González later became associated with many other Paraguayan apologists in the task of reconstructing the image of their country. In

1920, he founded the journal *Guaranía,* which went through several stages as a vital cultural vehicle and continued to be published into the 1940s. In 1925 González lived in Paris, where he was active in publishing. The dominant Colorado Party supported him in his bid for president and he assumed office on 15 August 1948. His own party quickly disagreed with some of his policies and had him removed in February 1949, after which he resided in Mexico.

Throughout his life he dedicated himself to national themes. His *Solano López y otros ensayos* (1926) is his best-known work, followed by *Proceso y formación de la cultura paraguaya* (1938).

*See also* **Argentina: The Twentieth Century; Literature: Spanish America.**

BIBLIOGRAPHY

J. Natalicio González, *Motivos de la tierra escarlata* (1952), and *Ideología guaraní* (1958).

Hugo Rodríguez Alcalá, *Historia de la literatura paraguaya* (1971), pp. 80–81; 98–99.

*Additional Bibliography*

Amaral, Raúl. *Los presidentes del Paraguay (1844–1954): Crónica política.* Asunción: Centro Paraguayo de Estudios Sociológicos, 1994.

Caeiro, Daniel. *Crónica de un matrimonio politico: La relación histórica entre peronistas y colorados.* Asunción: Intercontinental Editora, 2001.

Prieto Yegros, Leandro. *Natalicio y el "Guion Roja."* Asunción: Editorial Cuadernos Republicanos, 1997.

CATALINA SEGOVIA-CASE

**GONZÁLEZ, JUAN VICENTE** (1810–1866). Juan Vicente González (*b.* 28 May 1810; *d.* 1 October 1866), Venezuelan politician, writer, and journalist. Associated with the Liberals in 1840, González subsequently distanced himself from them to the extent that by 1845 he had become one of their most radical opponents, promulgating his politics through various newspapers: *Cicerón y Catilina, Diario de la Tarde,* and *La Prensa.*

González ceased political activity during the regime of José Tadeo Monagas, founded the El Salvador del Mundo school (The Savior of the World School) in 1849, and did an extensive and varied amount of literary and historiographic work. His *Biografía de José Felix Ribas* (1858) is representative of what is known in Venezuela as romantic historiography. Later on he opposed pro-federation propaganda and, together with defenders of civilian rule during the Federal War (1859–1863), opposed the dictatorship of José Antonio Páez. In 1863 González supported the regime of Juan Crisóstomo Falcón, and then left his public activities to dedicate himself primarily to literary work, founding the *Revista Literaria* in 1865.

*See also* **Federal War (Venezuela 1859–1863); Monagas, Josê Maria.**

BIBLIOGRAPHY

See Marco Antonio Saluzzo, *Juan Vicente González* (1901); Héctor Cuenca, *Juan Vicente González (1811–1866)* (1953); and Luis Correa, *Tres ensayos sobre Juan Vicente González, 1810–1866* (1987). A selection of his most important political and literary writings can be found in *Pensamiento político Venezolano del siglo XIX,* vols. 2 and 3 (1961).

*Additional Bibliography*

Caballero, Miguel and Sheila Salazar. *Diez grandes polémicas en la historia de Venezuela.* Caracas: Fondo Editorial 60 Años, 1999.

Machado Guzmán, Gustavo. *Historia gráfica de la Guerra Federal de Venezuela: Período de la federación.* Caracas: s.n., 2002.

INÉS QUINTERO

**GONZÁLEZ, MANUEL** (1833–1893). Manuel González (*b.* 18 June 1833; *d.* 8 May 1893), president of Mexico (1880–1884). Born in the state of Tamaulipas, González began his career as a professional soldier in 1847. During the War of the Reform (1857–1860), González fought on the losing Conservative side, but during the French Intervention (1862–1867), he served with Liberal general Porfirio Díaz and eventually became Díaz's chief of staff. Promoted to brigadier general in 1867, González served as governor of the National Palace and military commander of the Federal District (1871–1873).

After supporting Díaz's unsuccessful Plan of La Noria in 1871, González played a prominent military role in Díaz's triumph under the Plan of Tuxtepec in 1876. In March 1878 González was appointed minister of war by President Díaz. Ineligible for reelection in 1880, Díaz worked secretly for the election of González, who took office in December 1880.

As president, González adopted a policy of conciliation toward the national congress, the state governments, the Roman Catholic Church, and the military. In foreign relations, he eased long-standing border problems with the United States by agreeing to permit reciprocal crossing of troops and settled a lingering boundary dispute with Guatemala. Relations with Great Britain, broken in 1867, were renewed in 1884.

González accelerated government promotion of economic development, especially in the areas of transportation and communications. Federal lands were opened for settlement, and efforts were made to promote colonization and immigration. In 1884, the government issued a new mining code permitting private ownership of subsoil resources for the first time. Unfortunately for González, who had inherited an empty treasury, his spending for economic development only exacerbated the country's ongoing financial problems. The introduction of new nickel coinage in 1882 provoked inflation and devaluation. Negotiations aimed at settling the long-standing debt owed to British creditors also discredited González.

González completed his term of office amid mounting political crisis; he returned the presidency to Díaz in 1884. González later served three terms as governor of Guanajuato.

*See also* **Mexico: 1810–1910.**

BIBLIOGRAPHY

Daniel Cosío Villegas, *Historia moderna de México,* vol. 8 (1970), pp. 575–798.

Don M. Coerver, *The Porfirian Interregnum: The Presidency of Manuel González of Mexico, 1880–1884* (1979).

*Additional Bibliography*

González Montesinos, Carlos. *El general Manuel González: El manco de Tecoac.* México: C. González Montesinos, 2000.

Ponce Alcocer, María Eugenia. *La elección de Manuel González, 1878–1880: Preludio de un presidencialismo.* México, D.F.: Universidad Iberoamericana, 2000.

DON M. COERVER

**GONZÁLEZ, PABLO** (1879–1950). Pablo González (*b.* 5 May 1879; *d.* 4 March 1950), Mexican general and revolutionary. González is best known for his military exploits in the Constitutionalist army of revolutionary chief Venustiano Carranza and his role in the death of agrarian leader and revolutionary Emiliano Zapata.

González was born in Lampazos, Nuevo León, and orphaned at age five. He attended primary school in Nadadores, Coahuila, and then tried to enter the National Military College, but was turned down. He worked in a flour mill in Lampazos (1893), served as a laborer and later foreman on the Santa Fe Railroad (1902), and worked in California (1903). He joined the liberal political movement headed by Ricardo Flores Magón (1873–1922) and in 1907 edited the Mexican Liberal Party (PLM) newspaper *Revolución.* Later he joined the Anti-Reelectionist Party and supported Francisco I. Madero against long-time dictator Porfirio Díaz. He commanded Madero's forces in Coahuila, rising to the rank of colonel (1911). In 1912 he fought against the anti-Madero rebellion led by Pascual Orozco.

After joining the forces of Carranza in 1913, González rose to the rank of general and commander-in-chief of the armies of the Northeast and West. He participated in the Convention of Aguascalientes (1914–1915); became the zone commander of Morelos, Puebla, Oaxaca, and Tlaxcala; and served as the governor of Morelos (1916, 1919). While commander in Morelos he carried out an especially vicious military campaign against the Zapatistas and is considered to be the perpetrator of Emiliano Zapata's assassination (1919). In 1920 González ran unsuccessfully for the presidency and, upon Álvaro Obregón's overthrow of Carranza, rebelled against the new regime in July 1920. Captured and sentenced to death, González was allowed to seek asylum in San Antonio, Texas, where he remained until 1940. He died in Monterrey, Nuevo León.

*See also* **Díaz, Porfirio; Zapata, Emiliano.**

BIBLIOGRAPHY

José Morales Hesse, *El General Pablo González: Datos para la historia, 1910–1916* (1916).

John W. F. Dulles, *Yesterday in Mexico: A Chronicle of the Revolution, 1919–1936* (1961).

Charles C. Cumberland, *Mexico: The Constitutionalist Years* (1972).

Ramón Eduardo Ruíz, *The Great Rebellion: Mexico, 1905–1924* (1980).

Alan Knight, *The Mexican Revolution*, 2 vols. (1986), esp. vol. 2.

*Additional Bibliography*

Moguel, Josefina. *Venustiano Carranza, primer jefe y presidente.* Coahuila de Zaragoza, México: Gobierno del Estado de Coahuila, 1995.

DAVID LAFRANCE

## GONZÁLEZ, RODRIGO (1950–1985).

Rodrigo González, known as "Rockdrigo," was a Mexico City street musician who wrote and performed rock songs in Spanish with an acoustic guitar and harmonica in the early 1980s. He was born on December 25, 1950 in Tampico, Tamaulipas, and subsequently relocated to Mexico City, where he died on September 19 during the 1985 earthquake. He released the album *Hurbanhistorias* in 1985, and his friends subsequently compiled and released three others after his death. In 1984 Rockdrigo and friends founded the *rupestre* movement, a collective of soloist *trovadours* who produced semi-acoustic songs with social content to address daily trials and tribulations of life in Mexico City. Known as "el profeta del nopal" (the prophet of the nopal), a Bob Dylan type who employed Mexican humor, Rockdrigo composed songs that depicted the everyday reality of the lower socioeconomic classes and appealed to university-educated, middle-class audiences.

*See also* **Music: Popular Music and Dance.**

BIBLIOGRAPHY

*Discography and Videography*

González, Rodrigo. *Hurbanhistorias.* Mexico City: Pentagrama, 1985.

González, Rodrigo. *Rodrigo González: El profeta del nopal.* Mexico City: Pentagrama, 1986.

González, Rodrigo. *Aventuras en el DeFe.* Mexico City: Pentagrama, 1989.

González, Rodrigo. *No estoy loco.* Mexico City: Pentagrama, 1995.

Montero, Rafael. *No tuvo tiempo: La hurbanhistoria de Rockdrigo.* Mexico City: Pentagrama, 2005.

*Secondary Works*

Agustín, José. "Rockdrigo." In *El hotel de los corazones solitarios.* Mexico City: Nueva Imagen, 1999.

Hernández, Mark A. "Chronicles of Mexico City Life: The Music of Rockdrigo González." *Studies in Latin American Popular Culture* 26 (2007): 63–78.

López, Modesto, ed. *Rockdrigo González: El profeta del nopal.* Mexico City: Ediciones Pentagrama and Conaculta, 1999.

MARK A. HERNÁNDEZ

## GONZÁLEZ ÁVILA, JORGE (1925–1993).

Jorge González Ávila (*b.* 10 December 1925, *d.* 1993), Mexican composer. Born in Mérida, Yucatán, González Ávila was a pupil of the Spanish composer Rodolfo Halffter at the National Conservatory of Mexico. Like a number of Halffter's pupils, González Ávila became a true believer in the twelve-tone and avant-garde serial techniques that the Spanish master had been promoting in Mexico City's musical circles since his arrival in 1939. No dogmatist, González Ávila, who was predominately a composer of piano works, did not follow Halffter's style strictly but took an independent approach to the use of serial elements. Between 1961 and 1964 he wrote a collection of twenty-four inventions for piano; he was also the author of several collections of piano études, some of which demonstrate dodecaphonic writing.

*See also* **Music: Art Music.**

BIBLIOGRAPHY

Mario Kuri-Aldana, *Jóvenes compositores mexicanos* (1974).

Gérard Béhague, *Music in Latin America* (1979).

*Additional Bibliography*

Chroma Institute. *Chroma Report: The Chroma Institute's Report on Dodecaphonic Music Theory and on the Introduction of a Chromatic Music Notation.* Duncan, B.C.: Edition Chroma, 1997.

Vega, Alvaro. "Jorge González Ávila: Passion por el piano, el folklore y el dodecafonismo." *Camino Blanco. Arte y Cultura* 4 (2007).

SUSANA SALGADO

## GONZÁLEZ CAMARENA, JORGE (1908–1980).

Jorge González Camarena (*b.* 1908; *d.* 24 May 1980), Mexican artist. González Camarena is known for his murals and sculptures. He invented a system of geometric harmonies by fusing precise painting with subdued but vibrant color and textures. Among his public murals are *The Formation of Mexico* (1950), in the Instituto Mexicano del Seguro Social (in front of whose entrance stand his sculptures of *Man* and *Woman*); *Belisario Dominguez* (1956), in the Cámara de Senadores; and *Liberation* (1958), in the Palacio de Bellas Artes—all in Mexico City. Many of his other murals were commercial commissions.

*See also* **Art: The Twentieth Century.**

BIBLIOGRAPHY

Bernard S. Myers, *Mexican Painting in Our Time* (1956).

Antonio Rodríguez, *A History of Mexican Mural Painting*, translated by Marina Corby (1969).

*Additional Bibliography*

Luna Arroyo, Antonio. *González Camarena*. México, D.F.: Ciencia y Cultura Latinoamérica, 1995.

SHIFRA M. GOLDMAN

## GONZÁLEZ CASANOVA, PABLO

(1922–). Pablo González Casanova (*b.* 11 February 1922), Mexican social scientist and academic administrator. A rigorous scholar and theorist of internal colonialism, dependency, and other conceptual models of analysis of the Latin American historical and contemporary reality, González Casanova has authored and edited over 200 books and published nearly as many scholarly articles. His most important studies include the classic *La Democracía en México* (1965) and *El estado y los Partidos Políticos en México* (1981). He has also held important academic-administrative positions, including director of the Escuela de Ciencias Políticas y Sociales (1957–1965) and president of the National Autonomous University of Mexico (UNAM) (1970–1972). In 1984, González Casanova was awarded the National Prize in Mexico for Social Sciences and Humanities. UNESCO awarded him the José Martí International Prize in 2003 for his work on indigenous identity in Latin America. He contributes regularly to the Mexican periodical *La Jornada*. His recent works include *La universidad necesaria en el siglo XX* (2001) and *Las nuevas ciencias y las humanidades: De la Academia a la Política* (2004).

*See also* **National Autonomous University of Mexico (UNAM).**

BIBLIOGRAPHY

*Additional Bibliography*

*Pablo González Casanova, pensar la democracia y la sociedad: Una visión crítica desde Latinoamérica.* Barcelona: Anthropos, Editorial del Hombre, 1995.

Soto Rubio, Eduardo. *Diversidad y crisis de un proyecto de universidad: La reforma Académica de Pablo González Casanova.* Mexico City: Universidad Nacional Autónoma de México, Coordinación de Humanidades, Centro de Estudios sobre la Universidad, 1994.

DAVID MACIEL

## GONZÁLEZ DÁVILA, GIL

(1490–1550). Gil González Dávila (*b.* 1490; *d.* 1550), Spanish conqueror and explorer of Nicaragua. While still a young man, González achieved renown for his military exploits in Europe and won permission from the Spanish king to explore Central America. He left Spain in 1518, passed through Cuba, and reached Panama in 1519. Although holding a commission from the king himself, González fell afoul of the tyrannical governor of Panama, Pedro Arias de Ávila (Pedrarias), a circumstance that delayed his expedition for three years. These intervening years, however, enabled González to familiarize himself with New World conditions and gather information of use to his mission.

In 1522 González set out by sea with the fleet of the recently executed Vasco Núñez de Balboa and reached Costa Rica. Finding no easy riches there, González's interest in lands northward was aroused by a Costa Rican *cacique*. Abandoning his worm-eaten fleet, he continued inland on foot. Using his Costa Rican contacts, González obtained an introduction to Chief Nicarao, leader of a large settlement of Indians, and spent eight days with him in the area now known as Rivas. González subsequently claimed the entire region for the king of Spain and named it Nicaragua, a derivation of the chief's name. The Spaniards did not have much time to exploit their new acquisition, however; on

17 April 1522 a rival chief, Diriangen, attacked their group, forcing the would-be conquerors to withdraw.

Arriving in Panama, González recounted his accomplishments for the governor: the discovery of Lake Nicaragua, the addition of 224 leagues of land to the king's empire, the purported baptism of some 32,000 Indians, and the seizure of riches. González also claimed Nicaragua as his separate and independent authority, granted under the king's commission, something Pedrarias found unacceptable. A bitter competition for jurisdiction followed—a common occurrence among the Spanish conquerors—until Pedrarias stripped González of his right to primacy in the area and replaced him with Francisco Fernández De Córdoba. González managed to flee Panama with 112,524 gold pesos obtained during his Nicaraguan expedition. He remained in Santo Domingo for several years, all the while pressing his claims and plotting a military counterattack.

In 1525 González and his supporters defeated a detachment of Fernández's men and encouraged Fernández to rebel against Pedrarias. The three-way struggle for Nicaragua prompted a year-long civil war ending in 1526 and culminating in Fernández's execution when Pedrarias moved northward to assume the governorship himself

González remained in exile and returned to Panama in 1532, the year after the death of his arch rival, Pedrarias. He continued to fight for his claims and formed an alliance with Hernán Cortés against Cristóbal de Olid, who was attempting to set up his own authority in Honduras. González was found guilty of the assassination of Olid. But he had won the gratitude of Cortés, who permitted him to return to Spain, where he spent the remainder of his days enjoying his reputation and his riches.

*See also* **Nicarao; Nicaragua.**

BIBLIOGRAPHY

Harvey K. Meyer, *Historical Dictionary of Nicaragua* (1972).

Ernesto Chinchilla Aguilar, *Historia de Centroamérica,* 3 vols. (1974–1977).

Ralph Lee Woodward, Jr., *Central America: A Nation Divided* (1985).

*Additional Bibliography*

Montiel Argüello, Alejandro. *Nicaragua colonial.* Managua: Banco Central de Nicaragua, 2000.

KAREN RACINE

## GONZÁLEZ DE ESLAVA, FERNÁN

(c. 1534–c. 1601). Fernán González de Eslava, Spanish playwright in New Spain. González de Eslava wsas born in Spain, probably León, but his precise birthplace, along with many other details concerning his life, remain unknown. He arrived in Mexico around 1558, and within five years there were notices of his poetic activities. As a playwright he is known primarily for his *coloquios,* the first of which dates from about 1567. By 1572 he was preparing to be a cleric, but two years later he was jailed for seventeen days when his writing produced a conflict between the Viceroy Martín Enríquez De Almansa and Archbishop Pedro Moya De Contreras. He became a priest, probably by 1575 or 1576, and wrote his last *coloquio* in 1600.

As a playwright in the New World, González de Eslava was neither first (Juan Pérez Ramírez deserves that honor) nor American (having been born in Spain). His theater is religious with didactic aims. In the second half of the sixteenth century, theater was designed for the new, primarily creole, society being formed. His dramatic works consist of sixteen *coloquios,* four *entremeses,* and nine *loas.* The works tended to be light and facile, and to give a clear and honest vision of life in the colony. Without pretensions, they communicated a religious message (at least eleven of the *coloquios* are considered "sacramental") that was easily accessible to a wide public. González de Eslava had a gift for versification, and his plays are marked by a delightful use of language that incorporated New World structures. He is particularly known for an engaging sense of humor that pervades his language, his characters, and the situations. His *simple* is a likely precursor of the Siglo de Oro *gracioso.* On occasion González de Eslava revealed his disdain for the indigenous population, but for all his defects, he is still the major writer of Mexico who anticipated Sor Juana Inés De La Cruz by a full century.

*See also* **Theater.**

BIBLIOGRAPHY

Amado Alonso, "Biografía de Fernán González de Eslava," in *Revista de filología hispánica* 2, no. 3 (n.d.): 213–321.

Frida Weber Von Kurlat, "El teatro anterior de Lope de Vega y la novela picaresca (A propósito de los *Coloquios espirituales y sacramentales* de Hernán González de Eslava)," in *Filología* 6 (1960): 1–27, and *Lo cómico en el teatro de Fernán González de Esclava* (1963).

Julie Greer Johnson, "Three Celestina Figures of Colonial Spanish American Literature," in *Celestinesca,* 5, no. 1 (May 1981): 41–46.

### *Additional Bibliography*

Marrero-Fente, Raúl. *Perspectivas trasatlánticas: Estudios coloniales hispanoamericanos.* Madrid: Editorial Verbum, 2004.

Terán Elizondo, Ma. Isabel, and Alberto Ortiz. *Literatura y emblemática: Estudios sobre textos y personajes novohispanos.* Mexico: Universidad Autónoma de Zacatecas, Centro Interinstitucional de Investigaciones en Artes y Humanidades, 2004.

GEORGE WOODYARD

## GONZÁLEZ DE FANNING, TERESA

(1836–1918). Teresa González, one of the outstanding Peruvian writers of the late nineteenth century, was born on a family ranch in rural Peru, but educated in Lima. At seventeen she married a naval officer, Juan Fanning, who was killed in the War of the Pacific in 1881. Their two children died in infancy. A poet, essayist, fiction writer and acclaimed member of the prestigious El Ateneo (Atheneum) in Lima and a close friend of the major women writers of the time, such as Juana Manuela Gorriti, Clorinda Matto de Turner, and Mercedes Cabello de Carbonera, González published extensively in magazines and newspapers, first under pseudonyms (Maria de la Luz, Clara del Risco, Clara), and then under her own name. Her prizewinning novel *Regina* (1886) was followed by many others, in the collection *Lucecitas* (1893), *Indómita* (Untamed, 1904), and *Roque Moreno* (1904). Her speeches and essays about women's education were widely published, and some were collected in various editions of *Educación femenina* (1898, 1905). In 1881 she founded a girls' high school in Lima, and many other schools in Peru now bear her name.

*See also* **Gorriti, Juana Manuela; Matto de Turner, Clorinda; Nieves y Bustamante, María; War of the Pacific.**

BIBLIOGRAPHY

González de Fanning, Teresa. *Indómita.* Lima, Tipografía "El Lucero," 1904. Available from http://www.evergreen.loyola.edu/~tward/mujeres/Gonzalez/INDEX .HTM.

González de Fanning, Teresa. *Roque Moreno.* Lima: Tipografía "El Lucero," 1904. Available from http://www.evergreen.loyola.edu/~tward/mujeres/Gonzalez/INDEX.HTM.

González de Fanning, Teresa. *Educación femenina: Colección de artículos pedagógicos, morales y sociológicos.* Lima, Tipografía "El Lucero," 1905.

González de Fanning, Teresa. "Trabajo para la mugger/Work for Women." In *Madres del verbo/Women of the Word,* edited by Nina M. Scott. Albuquerque: University of New Mexico Press, 1999.

González de Fanning, Teresa. "Concerning the Education of Women." In *Confronting Change, Challenging Tradition: Women in Latin American History,* edited by Gertrude M. Yeager. Wilmington, DE: Scholarly Resources, 1994.

MARY G. BERG

## GONZÁLEZ DE SANTA CRUZ, ROQUE

(1576–1628). Roque González de Santa Cruz (*b.* 1576; *d.* 15 November 1628), Paraguayan Jesuit who founded many of the Jesuit missions (*reducciones*) in his native land, as well as in present-day Argentina and Uruguay. Born of Spanish parents in Asunción, he learned Guaraní as a child. He was ordained a priest around 1589 and worked among the Indians in the region of Jejuí, north of Asunción. In 1603 he was named rector of the cathedral in Asunción, and in 1609 he entered the Society of Jesus. As a Jesuit he returned to work with the Indians. He helped build the first of the *reducciones,* San Ignacio Guazú, south of Asunción. In 1614 he wrote a letter to his brother Francisco, the lieutenant governor of Asunción, in which he denounced the *encomenderos* for their mistreatment of the Indians. He went on to found many other *reducciones* in southern Paraguay, in the province of Misiones in present-day Argentina, and in Uruguay. In 1627 he was appointed superior of all of the *reducciones* in Uruguay. At Caaró, in modern Rio Grande do Sul, Brazil, he and two other Jesuits were killed by Indian shamans who were hostile to his efforts to Christianize the Indians in their region.

González was a skilled builder, leader, and organizer. Although he died at the hands of hostile Indians, he was greatly esteemed by the Indians in general, who appreciated his efforts to organize them in defense of their land and culture against Spanish exploiters. The first Paraguayan to be a missionary in his own land, he was also the first martyr born in the New World. He was canonized in 1988.

*See also* **Missions: Jesuit Missions (Reducciones).**

BIBLIOGRAPHY

Clement J. McNaspy, *Conquistador Without Sword: The Life of Roque González, S.J.* (1984).

Philip Caraman, *The Lost Paradise*, 2d ed. (1990).

Silvio Palacios and Ena Zoffoli, *Gloria y tragedia de las misiones guaraníes* (1991).

*Additional Bibliography*

Miglioranza, Contardo. *Los santos mártires rioplatenses: Roque González de Santa Cruz, Alonso Rodríguez y Juan del Castillo.* Buenos Aires: Comision Episcopal de Misiones: Misiones Franciscanas Conventuales, 1998.

Rojas, Antonio. *Un paraguayo fuera de serie: Roque González, visto y admirado por otro paraguayo.* Asunción: Distribuidora Montoya, 2000.

JEFFREY KLAIBER

**GONZÁLEZ FLORES, ALFREDO** (1877–1962). Alfredo González Flores (*b.* 15 June 1877; *d.* 28 December 1962), president of Costa Rica (1914–1917). Born in Heredia, González Flores received a law degree in 1902. The Costa Rican Congress chose him to be president of the Republic in 1914. Ironically, Costa Ricans were supposed to elect their president directly for the first time that year, but none of the three candidates received a majority, sending the matter to Congress, which selected González Flores, who had not even been on the original ballot.

González Flores became president at a time when Costa Rica's population was growing dramatically and the price for its principal export, coffee, was falling precipitously. Costa Rica was beginning to experience the effects of monoculture, wherin its "golden bean" was leaving a bitter taste. González Flores courageously proposed an income tax to try to alleviate the suffering of the poor, but he was too weak politically for such bold action.

The outbreak of World War I compounded his difficulties. With exports curtailed and imported goods scarce, Costa Rica experienced inflation and declining revenues. Though González Flores attempted progressive economic measures by imposing exchange regulations, levying export taxes, and cutting salaries of public employees, he had little support. The minister of defense, General Federico Tinoco Granados took advantage of the president's unpopularity to stage a coup on 27 January 1917, which established the second dictatorship in Costa Rican history.

González Flores persuaded President Woodrow Wilson not to recognize the Tinoco dictatorship. In recent years biographers have viewed him more favorably as a precursor of Costa Rican reform movements. He gave a lifetime of service to his native city, Heredia, and Costa Rica awarded him the Benemérito de la Patria in 1954.

*See also* **Coffee Industry; Costa Rica.**

BIBLIOGRAPHY

Eduardo Oconitrillo García, *Alfredo González Flores* (1980).

Charles D. Ameringer, *Democracy in Costa Rica* (1982).

Harold D. Nelson, ed., *Costa Rica: A Country Study*, 2d ed. (1983).

Marc Edelman and Joanne Kenen, eds., *The Costa Rica Reader* (1989).

*Additional Bibliography*

Lehoucq, Fabrice Edouard, and Iván Molina Jiménez. *Stuffing the Ballot Box: Fraud, Electoral Reform, and Democratization in Costa Rica.* New York: Cambridge University Press, 2002.

Salazar Mora, Jorge Mario. *Crisis liberal y estado reformista: Análisis político-electoral (1914–1949).* San José, Costa Rica: Editorial de la Universidad de Costa Rica, 1995.

CHARLES D. AMERINGER

**GONZÁLEZ GARZA, ROQUE** (1885–1962). The well-known Mexican revolutionary Roque González Garza was one of the principal intellectuals of Francisco "Pancho" Villa's movement and had an important role in the Convention of Aguascalientes. He was president of the convention and head of the executive branch of the Republic from January to June 1915. In his youth, González Garza studied commerce and worked in that field. He began his political career in 1908 when he joined Francisco Indalecio Madero's movement. During Madero's government González Garza was a federal deputy and, later, after the death of "the Apostle" (Madero), he joined Villa's movement. He participated in the biggest battles against Victoriano Huerta, including the battles of San Pedro de las Colonias, Torreón, and Zacatecas. His most notable revolutionary contribution, however, was at the Aguascalientes Convention, where he was one of most articulate ideologues. After the defeat of Villas's troops, González Garza went into exile in the United States until 1920. When he returned, he became a federal deputy and a member of the Legion of Honor, and he collaborated with the postrevolutionary governments until his death.

*See also* **Aguascalientes, Convention of; Madero, Francisco Indalecio; Mexico, Wars and Revolutions: Mexican Revolution; Villa, Francisco "Pancho."**

FELIPE AVILA

## GONZÁLEZ GOYRI, ROBERTO

(1924–). Roberto González Goyri (*b.* 1924), Guatemalan artist, inspired by pre-Conquest cultures. He studied with Rafael Yela Günther at the Academy of Fine Arts in Guatemala City, where he received academic training, and worked as a draftsman at the National Museum of Archeology. On a grant from the Guatemalan government, he studied in New York from 1948 to 1952. International recognition came in 1951, when he won a prize for a sculpture of the unknown political prisoner in a contest sponsored by the London Institute of Contemporary Arts. The Museum of Modern Art in New York acquired his semiabstract sculpture *The Wolf* (1951) in 1955. He was director of the National School of Plastic Arts in Guatemala City (1957–1958).

As a sculptor, González Goyri worked with terracotta, concrete, and metals combining an expressionist, symbolic style with abstract motifs. His mural and sculptural projects for public buildings, such as the Social Security Institute in Guatemala City (1959), and his monumental sculpture of the Guatemalan Indian hero Tecún-Umán (1963) symbolically depict Guatemalan history from the dawn of Maya civilization to independence. As a painter, he has worked primarily in a postcubist style, inspired by the strong colors found in Guatemalan crafts. His mural *Religion in Guatemala: Its Pre-Hispanic, Colonial, and Contemporary Roots* (1992) is a monumental interpretation of Guatemalan religious life, from the *Popol Vuh,* the sacred Maya book, to the present.

*See also* **Art: The Twentieth Century.**

BIBLIOGRAPHY

Gilbert Chase, *Contemporary Art in Latin America* (1970), pp. 46–48, 247–248.

José Gómez Sicre, *Roberto González Goyri* (1986).

Delia Quiñonez, *Mural "La religión en Guatemala, sus raíces prehispánicas, coloniales y sincréticas contemporáneas"* (1992).

*Additional Bibliography*

González Goyri, Roberto, Dennis Leder, and Luisa Fernanda González Pérez. *Roberto González Goyri.* Guatemala City, Guatemala: Editorial Antigua, 2003.

Méndez de la Vega, Luz, Roberto Cabrera, and Thelma Castillo Jurado. *Guatemala: Arte contemporáneo.* Guatemala: Fundación G & T, 1997.

MARTA GARSD

## GONZÁLEZ IÑÁRRITU, ALEJANDRO

(1963–). The Mexican filmmaker Alejandro González Iñárritu emerged on the international scene as a director, producer, and editor with his masterful *Amores Perros* (2000). Born in Mexico City on August 15, 1963, he studied filmmaking and directing in Maine and Los Angeles. At age twenty-seven he became one of the youngest producers for Televisa, Mexico's most important TV company. In 1991 he created Zeta Films, a production company for television commercials and programs and, later, films. By the mid-1990s he was directing short films including *El Timbre* (1996). Following the success of *Amores Perros* in 2000, he directed the "Mexico" segment of the film *11'09"01—September 11*; *The Hire: Powder Keg* (2001); and *21 Grams* (2003). His film *Babel* (2006) earned González Iñárritu the Best Director prize at the 2006 Cannes Film Festival and also won the Best

Motion Picture prize in the drama category at the 2007 Golden Globe Awards and seven Academy Award nominations.

*See also* **Cinema: Since 1990.**

BIBLIOGRAPHY

Elena, Alberto, and Marina Díaz López, eds. *The Cinema of Latin America.* London: Wallflower Press, 2006.

JUAN CARLOS GRIJALVA

## GONZÁLEZ LEÓN, ADRIANO (1931–).

Adriano González León (*b.* 1931), Venezuelan fiction writer. One of Venezuela's most innovative and demanding writers, González León is the author of one of the most accomplished Venezuelan novels of the century, *País portátil* (1969). He also published the novel *Asfalto-infierno* (1963) and several volumes of short fiction. His first set of stories, *Las hogueras más altas* (1957), portrays solitary and violent characters. González León used Faulknerian narrative techniques to construct his historical and political novel *País portátil,* which tells the story of the Barazarte family through the mind of one of its members, a young revolutionary. At the same time, *País portátil* also recounts Venezuelan history since the nineteenth century. The young revolutionary, Andrés, carries a bomb on a bus through the city of Caracas. The reader is bombarded with images of modern urban chaos in the city and the conscious and subconscious thoughts of Andrés. González León has published short fiction in the 1970s and 1980s, but no other novels.

*See also* **Literature: Spanish America.**

BIBLIOGRAPHY

John S. Brushwood, *The Spanish American Novel: A Twentieth-Century Survey* (1975).

Giuseppe Bellini, *Historia de la literatura hispanoamericana* (1985).

George Mc Murray, *Spanish American Writing Since 1941* (1987).

*Additional Bibliography*

Carrera, Liduvina. *Reflexiones de lozanía: Cinco ensayso de crítica literaria.* Venezuela: Fondo Editorial Toromaina, 1995.

Linares Angulo, Jorge. *País portatíl en la sociología de la novela.* Caracas: Ediciones Casa de Bello, 1994.

RAYMOND LESLIE WILLIAMS

## GONZÁLEZ MARTÍNEZ, ENRIQUE

(1871–1952). Enrique González Martínez (*b.* 13 April 1871; *d.* 19 February 1952), Mexican poet. A central figure in the literary life of the nation from the beginning of the Revolution until his death at mid-century, González Martínez was trained as a physician but spent most of his career in public service. His early poetry reflects the turn-of-the-century *modernista* techniques, and in the 1920s there are traces of *vanguardista* influences; he is noted, however, for his consistent, profound exploration of personal experience and metaphysical searching through his art. He is a master of traditional forms, especially of the sonnet; his language evolves toward simplicity; biblical and classical allusions are common, but never recondite. The condition of solitude, a certain pantheistic urging, a longing for lucidity and transcendent vision, the "resplendent moment," give shape to much of his work. An occasional trace of didacticism may also be found.

The early period culminates in the definition of his voice in *Siléntor* (1909) and *Los senderos ocultos* (1911). The latter collection includes the sonnet "Tuércele el cuello al cisne" ("Wring the Swan's Neck"), his most anthologized poem, often misread as marking the end of *modernismo.* González Martínez is best understood as one of the most important exponents of the symbolist strain in *modernismo* as it has subsequently evolved. *Parábolas y otros poemas* (1918), *El romero alucinado* (1923), and *Las señales furtivas* (1925) are major collections of his middle period. His later poetry is marked by the death of his wife and of his son, Enrique González Rojo (1899–1939), also a poet. These works include *Ausencia y canto* (1937), *El diluvio de fuego* (1938), *Bajo el signo mortal* (1942), and *El nuevo Narciso y otros poemas* (1952). The "Estancias," twenty-one octaves and a concluding sonnet that open this last collection, are an exceptionally beautiful summing up of his life and art. He wrote an autobiography published in two parts, *El hombre del buho* (1944) and *La apacible locura* (1951). He was a fine translator of French poetry. In 1911 he was elected to the Mexican Academy, and he was a member of the Ateneo de la Juventud and a founding member of the Colegio Nacional (1943).

*See also* **Literature: Spanish America; Mexico: Since 1910.**

BIBLIOGRAPHY

Antonio Castro Leal edited a fine edition of the *Obras completas* (1971). The fundamental study of the poet is John S. Brushwood, *Enrique González Martínez* (1969). Many important critical articles were collected by José Luis Martínez in *La obra de Enrique González Martínez* (1951). See also José Manuel Topete, *El mundo poético de Enrique González Martínez* (1967), and Harry L. Rosser, "Enrique González Martínez: 'Matacisnes' y concepción estética," in *Cuadernos Americanos* 243 (1982): 181–188.

*Additional Bibliography*

Rivera-Rodas, Oscar. *El pensar de la modernidad poética.* Guadalajara, Jal., México: Secretaría de Cultura, Gobierno de Jalisco, 1997.

MICHAEL J. DOUDOROFF

## GONZÁLEZ OBREGÓN, LUIS (1865–1938).

Luis González Obregón was a historian, author, and journalist whose aim, as he put it in the introduction to his collected newspaper columns, was to "rescue, demystify and restore the colonial past" of Mexico. Born in Guanajuato, Mexico, on August 25, 1865, he moved with his family to Mexico City two years later. During his childhood he received a bilingual education that cultivated his talents as a writer. In 1885 he became involved with the foundation El Liceo Mexicano. The foundation's mission to uncover Mexico's past and understand its present became his lifelong preoccupation. In 1890 he began his career as a journalist, working for the newspapers *Siglo XX* and *El Nacional.* His weekly columns for *El Nacional* were compiled in a collection, *México viejo*, in 1895. Notable among his subsequent works are *La vida en México en 1810* (1911) and *Los precursores de la Independencia Mexicana en el Siglo XVI* (1906). He also held public posts, including chief of publications of the National Museum, chief of publications at the National Library, and director and chief of historical investigation at the National Archives. He died in Mexico City, on June 17, 1938, on the street that the city named after him.

*See also* **Journalism.**

BIBLIOGRAPHY

De Morelos, Leonardo C. *Luis González Obregón (1865–1938): Chronicler of Mexico City.* New York: Hispanic Institute in the United States, 1956.

González Obregón, Luis. *México viejo (época colonial): Noticias históricas, tradiciones, leyendas y costumbres.* Mexico: Editorial Patria, 1991.

STACY LUTSCH

## GONZÁLEZ ORTEGA, JESÚS (1822–1881).

Jesús González Ortega (*b.* 1822; *d.* 1881), Mexican military officer and cabinet minister. Born on a hacienda near Teúl, Zacatecas, and educated in Guadalajara, Ortega held an office job in Teúl until the War of the Reform. Of liberal ideas, he was elected to the legislature of the state of Zacatecas in 1858 and soon after was designated the state's governor. Ortega began his military career by organizing and leading the Zacatecas militia. One of the most successful liberal generals, he was appointed by President Benito Juárez to succeed Santos Degollado. After a series of victories over the Conservatives, Ortega led the victorious liberal army into Mexico City on 1 January 1861, ending the War of the Reform.

After Juárez named him minister of war on 20 January, Ortega resigned three months later over political differences with the president. Under the Constitution of 1857, as the congressionally elected interim president of the Supreme Court, Ortega was first in line of succession to the presidency of the republic. During the French Intervention, President Juárez reluctantly turned to Ortega to take command of the Army of the East. After the siege of Puebla in 1863, Ortega was forced to surrender, but he escaped his captors and fled to the United States. Juárez decreed the extension of his own presidential term and announced that Ortega had renounced his claim to the presidency by remaining in a foreign country without permission. When Ortega returned to Mexico in 1866, he was arrested and held without trial. He was released in August 1868 with the stipulation that the government reserved the right to prosecute him. Ortega resigned as president of the Court and retired from politics.

*See also* **Juárez, Benito; Mexico, Constitutions: Constitutions Prior to 1917.**

BIBLIOGRAPHY

Ivie E. Cadenhead, Jr., *Jesús González Ortega and Mexican National Politics* (1972).

Laurens B. Perry, *Juárez and Díaz: Machine Politics in Mexico* (1978).

Richard N. Sinkin, *The Mexican Reform, 1855–1876: A Study in Liberal Nation-Building* (1979); *Diccionario Porrúa de historia, biografía y geografía de México*, 5th ed. (1986).

*Additional Bibliography*

Acevedo, Esther. *La definición del estado mexicano, 1857–1867.* México: Secretaría de Gobernación: Archivo General de la Nación-México, 1999.

D. F. STEVENS

**GONZÁLEZ PRADA, MANUEL** (1844–1918). Manuel González Prada was a noted Peruvian poet, essayist, and social reformer. Like José Martí and Rubén Darío, González Prada was a poetic innovator developing a style that would later be dubbed *modernismo.* Yet unlike the other two thinkers, who held important ambassadorial posts and worked as international correspondents for important North and South American newspapers, González Prada's literary influence was limited mostly to Peru, where his impact can be noted in the works of José Santos Chocano, César Vallejo, José Carlos Mariátegui, and José María Eguren. A poetic leading light, González Prada imported into Spanish forms from other European languages such as the French *trilet* and *rondel*. His prose style was electric and shocking, employing daring metaphors, neologisms derived from other languages, and a rejection of pure Spanish forms, which for him were a vestige of colonialism.

Born in Lima on January 5, 1844, Manuel G. Prada, as he often signed his name, came into his own after the War of the Pacific (1878–1883), which devastated Peru's economic and social structures. Gonzalez Prada's penetrating and biting essays did not mince words about the reasons for Peru's losses in the conflict. During the war many Peruvians of African and Asian descent—seeing an opportunity for liberty—rose up in a social revolt, whereas others, of the landowning elite, went over to the Chilean side in the hopes of preserving their property; still others, the mass of Quechua-speaking soldiers, did not understand the creole concept of Peru as a nation among Latin American nations and were not inspired to win the war on creole terms. Thus González Prada laid the blame for Peru's defeat squarely on the Peruvian people.

Responding to his inflammatory speeches against the ruling elite, the government censored his work, actually destroying some of the newspaper presses that published him. During those postwar years González Prada helped to establish a new political party, the Unión Nacional, which named him candidate for the presidential elections. Yet he was dismayed by the opportunistic switch by many of his party's members to the oligarchic parties. Disillusioned with this reality (and upset over his wife's two miscarriages), he went on a long journey to Europe (1891–1898). There he came into direct contact with anarchist thought, which prompted him to simplify his writing style and create an ideological system liberated from aristocratic panache and accessible to the working class. This new modernism was intimately related to the modernity resulting from and responding to industrial and monopolistic capitalism.

González Prada published two books of prose during his lifetime, *Páginas libres* (1894, 1915) and *Horas de lucha* (1908), as well as three books of poetry, *Minúsculas* (1901, 1909), *Presbitarianas* (1909), and *Exóticas* (1911). He died on July 22, 1918. The rest of his work remained forgotten in newspapers and magazines until his son Alfredo and the noted APRA politician and literary critic Luis Alberto Sánchez began collecting his poetry and prose, ultimately making possible the seven-volume *Obras* published during the 1980s. Since then scholars have engaged in a reassessment of González Prada's politics and poetics. Efraín Kristal has shown that his *civilismo* lasted longer than previously thought; Thomas Ward has shown that his anarchism can be documented earlier than had previously been accepted and that his anticlericalism did not imply atheism; and Isabelle Tauzin has traced his creative trajectory comparing different published versions of his published works. This new-found interest in González Prada is resulting in a new critical edition developed by Isabelle Tauzin in France, the first English translation of his essays edited by David Sobrevilla published by Oxford University Press, and the publication of some hitherto unknown works discovered by Isabelle Tauzin and released by Peru's National Library.

*See also* **Anarchism and Anarchosyndicalism; Chocano, José Santos; Darío, Rubén; Eguren, José María; Literature: Spanish America; Mariátegui, José Carlos; Martí y Pérez, José Julián; Matto de Turner, Clorinda; Palma, Ricardo; Positivism; Vallejo, César.**

BIBLIOGRAPHY


*Primary Works*

*Obras*, 7 vols. Edited by Luis Alberto Sánchez. Lima: PetroPerú, 1985–1989.

*Textos inéditos de Manuel González Prada*. Edited by Isabelle Tauzin Castellanos. Lima: Biblioteca Nacional, Fondo Editorial, 2001.

*Free Pages and Hard Times: Anarchist Musings*. Translated by Frederick H. Fornoff; edited by David Sobrevilla. New York: Oxford University Press, 2003.

*Secondary Works*

Chang-Rodríguez, Eugenio. *La literatura política: De González Prada, Mariátegui y Haya de la Torre*. Mexico: Andrea, 1957. See especially pp. 51–125.

Kristal, Efraín. *The Andes Viewed from the City: Literary and Political Discourse on the Indian in Peru, 1848–1930*. New York: Peter Lang, 1987. See esp. pp. 93–126.

Mead, Robert G. *Perspectivas interamericanas: Literatura y libertad*. New York: Las Américas, 1967. See especially pp. 103–184.

Sánchez, Luis Alberto. *Nuestras vidas son los ríos . . . : Historia y leyenda de los González Prada*. Lima: Universidad Nacional Mayor de San Marcos, 1977.

Tauzin, Isabelle, ed. *Manuel González Prada: Escritor de dos mundos*. Lima: Biblioteca Nacional, 2006.

Ward, Thomas. *La anarquía inmanentista de Manuel González Prada*. New York: Peter Lang, 1998.

Ward, Thomas. "González Prada: Soñador indigenista de la nación." In *La resistencia cultural: La nación en el ensayo de las Américas*, pp. 160–177. Lima: Universidad Ricardo Palma, 2004.

Velázquez Castro, Marcel. *Las máscaras de la representación: El sujeto esclavista y las rutas del racismo en el Perú, 1775–1895*. Lima: Universidad Nacional Mayor de San Marcos, 2005. See especially pp. 249–264.


THOMAS WARD

## GONZÁLEZ PRADA POPULAR UNIVERSITIES.

**GONZÁLEZ PRADA POPULAR UNIVERSITIES.** González Prada Popular Universities, politicized educational efforts in Peru during the early 1920s that were inspired by the student leader and politician Víctor Raúl Haya De La Torre. These popular universities offered free evening courses for workers while the Peruvian university under the regime of Augusto B. Leguía (1919–1930) was disrupted. Moreover, they were effective, practical means by which a growing populist movement, led by Haya de la Torre, won large sectors of labor away from earlier anarchist influences. Haya emphasized some of the anarchist elements of his own ideology among the universities' participants. The young Haya had been influenced in Lima by the eminent anarchist intellectual Manuel González Prada. Socialist leader José Carlos Mariátegui, besides offering a series of important lectures, collaborated with Haya until 1928 in the organization of the popular universities, which later were the basis of Aprista unions.

*See also* **González Prada, Manuel; Haya de la Torre, Víctor Raúl; Mariátegui, José Carlos.**

BIBLIOGRAPHY


Steve Stein, *Populism in Peru: The Emergence of the Masses and the Politics of Social Control* (1980).

*Additional Bibliography*

Alexander, Robert Jackson, Víctor Raúl Haya de la Torre, and Julia Elisa Alva Parodi. *Haya de la Torre, Man of the Millenium: His Life, Ideas and Continuing Relevance*. Lima: Víctor Raúl Haya de la Torre Institute, 2001.

Portocarrero, Ricardo. "José Carlos Mariátegui y las universidades populares 'González Prada'." *La aventura de Mariátegui: Nuevas perspectivas*. Ed. Portocarrero Maisch, Gonzalo, Eduardo Cáceres y Rafael Tapia, Rafael. Lima: Pontificia Universidad Católica del Perú, 1995

Soto Rivera, Roy. *Víctor Raúl, el hombre del siglo XX*. Lima: Instituto "Víctor Raúl Haya de la Torre," 2002.


ALFONSO W. QUIROZ

## GONZÁLEZ SUÁREZ, (MANUEL MARÍA) FEDERICO

**GONZÁLEZ SUÁREZ, (MANUEL MARÍA) FEDERICO** (1844–1917). (Manuel María) Federico González Suárez (*b.* 12 April 1844; *d.* 1 December 1917), noted Ecuadoran historian and archbishop of Quito (1906–1917). González Suárez, a native of Quito, is most remembered for his multivolume *Historia general de la República del Ecuador* (1890–1903), based on extensive research in local archives and in Spain. González Suárez's goal had been to write a general history of America, but he completed only the eight volumes that dealt with Ecuador's pre-Columbian and colonial eras. He devoted most of his attention to the ecclesiastical history of the city of Quito, giving scant notice to Guayaquil or to economic matters. González Suárez's mild criticism of the colonial Ecuadorian clergy evoked bitter attacks from the church and from conservatives. Other works by González Suárez are *Estudio histórico sobre las Canaris* (1878), *Historia eclesiástica del Ecuador* (1881), *Nueva miscelanea o colección de opusculos publicados* (1910), and *Defensa de mi criterio histórico* (1937).

During the terms of the Liberal president Eloy Alfaro y Arosemena (1895–1901, 1906–1911) and the drive to secularize Ecuadorian society (principally through measures for civil marriage and divorce), Archbishop González Suárez played a critical role in depoliticizing the clergy. A peacemaker, he provided a calm voice for moderation in the clergy. His publications inspired a group of young disciples, most notably Jacinto Jijón y Caamaño.

*See also* **Catholic Church: The Colonial Period.**

BIBLIOGRAPHY

For a discussion of González Suárez's contribution to Ecuadorian historical scholarship, see Adam Szászdi, "The Historiography of the Republic of Ecuador," in *Hispanic American Historical Review* 44, 4 (1964): 503–550.

George A. Brubaker, "Federico González Suárez, Historian of Ecuador," in *Journal of Inter-American Studies* 5, 2 (1963): 235–248. See also Nicolás Jiménez, *Biografía del ilustrísimo Federico González Suárez* (1936).

*Additional Bibliography*

González Suárez, Federico, and Carlos de la Torre Reyes. *González Suárez.* Quito: Banco Central del Ecuador, 1995.

Larrea, Carlos Manuel. *Tres historiadores: Velasco, González Suárez, Jijón, y Caamaño.* Quito: Casa de Cultura Ecuatoriana "Benjamin Carrión," 1998.

RONN F. PINEO

**GONZÁLEZ VIDELA, GABRIEL** (1898–1980). Gabriel González, born in La Serena, Chile, on November 22, 1898, was a politician and president of Chile. After serving in the legislature as a Radical Party representative, he became president in 1946, the candidate of an odd coalition of Radicals, Liberals, and Communists. Unfortunately for him, González confronted numerous problems: a postwar economic contraction, severe inflation, and increased worker militancy. Increasingly González came to feel that the Communists were fomenting labor unrest, particularly in the southern coalfield, as well as threatening to organize farm workers. Although elected with Communist support, he turned on them, expelling them from his cabinet. The Communists retaliated by organizing worker demonstrations that degenerated into riots. Fearing that he would lose the support of the Radical Party's right wing, which consisted of landowners, and the conservative Liberal Party, González's infamous "ley maldita" ("accursed law") outlawed the Communist Party in 1948. Some have argued that the promise of U.S. economic aid convinced González to turn on his former allies; others allege that he had done so out of fear of political unrest and the possibility of a military coup. Whatever the reason, González would complete his presidential term in 1952, supported by a new conservative alliance. His regime's passage marked the end of the Radical Party's control of the Chilean presidency that began with the 1938 election of Pedro Aguirre Cerda. Gonzalez's successors, Carlos Ibáñez and then Jorge Alessandri, did not represent an established political party.

González's government instituted other, less controversial reforms: enfranchising women, creating a technical university, and expanding the nation's economic infrastructure by building an oil refinery, various dams, and a steel mill. He enhanced Chile's sovereignty by claiming a 200-mile limit as well as establishing bases in the Antarctic. Continuing to be politically active, he broke with the Radical Party when it supported Salvador Allende. After the 1973 coup, González held a seat in General Augusto Pinochet's Council of State. González died in Santiago on August 22, 1980.

*See also* **Chile, Political Parties: Radical Party; Chile, Political Parties: Communist Party; Chile: The Twentieth Century.**

BIBLIOGRAPHY

Collier, Simon, and William Sater. *A History of Chile, 1808–2002*, 2nd edition. Cambridge, UK: Cambridge University Press, 2004.

WILLIAM SATER

## GONZÁLEZ VIGIL, FRANCISCO DE PAULA.

*See* **Vigil, Francisco de Paula González.**

## GONZÁLEZ VÍQUEZ, CLETO (1858–1937).

Cleto González Víquez (*b.* 13 October 1858; *d.* 23 September 1937), president of Costa Rica (1906–1910, 1928–1932). González Víquez was born in Barba de Heredia, Costa Rica, to an aristocratic family. He was an eminent attorney, distinguished politician, and one of the most illustrious historians of his country. With his colleague, friend, and adversary Ricardo Jiménez, he dominated national politics for four decades in an era characterized by *caudillismo.* He published numerous works on law and history, most notable of which are his investigations into historical geography and genealogy and his interesting studies of protocol, which reveal much about colonial life in Costa Rica. He studied law at the University of St. Thomas, where his performance was outstanding. He took part in the commission that drew up the civil, penal, and legal codes.

González Víquez had an important political career, in which he served twice as a representative to the national Congress and once as minister of Government. He defended liberal principles and opposed the reformist movements of the era. In 1906, after a controversial election in which his rivals were expelled from the country, he was elected president of Costa Rica, an office he held until 1910. In Congress he led the opposition to President Alfredo González Flores from 1916 to 1917 and supported the coup d'état that drove Flores from power. In the 1920s he maintained his liberal stance and continued to be influential in the National Republican Party. He was again elected president in 1928 in the last years of the liberal republic, and he was forced to face the effects of the economic crisis beginning in 1929.

*See also* **Costa Rica; González Flores, Alfredo.**

BIBLIOGRAPHY

Ralph Lee Woodward, Jr., *Central America: A Nation Divided,* 2d ed. (1985).

Carlos Araya Pochet, *Historia de los partidos politicos: Liberacíon nacional* (1968).

*Additional Bibliography*

Mahoney, James. *The Legacies of Liberalism: Path Dependence and Political Regimes in Central America.* Baltimore: Johns Hopkins University Press, 2001.

Palmer, Steven. *From Popular Medicine to Medical Populism: Doctors, Healers, and Public Power in Costa Rica, 1800–1940.* Durham, NC: Duke University Press, 2003.

JORGE MARIO SALAZAR

## GONZÁLEZ Y GONZÁLEZ, LUÍS (1925–2003).

Luís González y González, a Mexican historian, was born on October 11, 1925, in San José de Gracia, Michoacán. He studied history at the Colegio de México, Universidad Autónoma de México, and the Sorbonne in Paris and then taught history at some of Mexico's most prestigious institutions of higher education. He founded the Colegio de Michoacán (1978), an institution dedicated to the study of regional history as a reaction against the centrality of Mexico City in Mexican history. In his pathbreaking 1968 work, *Pueblo en vilo: Microhistoria de San José de Gracia* (published in English translation as *San José de Gracia: Mexican Village in Transition,* 1974), he applied the methodology of microhistory with total mastery. He also authored books about historical theory and methods in which he highlighted the importance of both local experiences and local social categories. Among his notable works are *La tierra donde estamos* (1971),

*Invitación a la microhistoria* (1972), *Michoacán y la querencia* (1982), *Nueva invitación a la microhistoria* (1982), and *El oficio de historiar* (1988). Recognized internationally for his work, he received numerous awards from Mexican, American, and French institutions (American Historical Association, 1971; Premio Nacional de Historia, Ciencias Sociales y Filosofia, 1983; Palmes Académiques, 1985; and Medalla Belisario Domínguez, 2003). He died on December 13, 2003, in Morelia, Michoacán.

*See also* **Colegio de México.**

BIBLIOGRAPHY

Ochoa Serrano, Alvaro, ed. *Pueblo en vilo: La fuerza de la costumbre: Homenaje a Luís González y González.* Guadalajara: El Colegio de Jalisco; Mexico: El

Colegio de México; Zamora: El Colegio de Michoacán, 1994.

CLAUDIA P. RIVAS JIMÉNEZ

**GOOD NEIGHBOR POLICY.** Good Neighbor Policy, a general description of the efforts of the United States to improve relations with Latin America in the 1930s and 1940s. The policy is most often associated with the administration of Franklin D. Roosevelt (1933–1945). The policy developed for several reasons. Some policymakers and politicians believed that the U.S. interventions in the early twentieth century provoked greater anti-Americanism; other critiques of U.S.–Latin American policy protested the high costs of interventions.

Because the Good Neighbor pledged nonintervention and noninterference in Latin America's domestic affairs, its most visible impact was political. In the Cuban crisis of 1933, Roosevelt intervened not with troops but with a special emissary, Assistant Secretary of State Sumner Welles, who ultimately negotiated the arrangement whereby Fulgencio Batista gained effective power. Roosevelt graciously received the new Panamanian president, Harmadio Arias, in 1933 and the following year dispatched Welles to thrash out a new canal treaty, which mollified Panamanian critics yet preserved U.S. interests. In the Mexican oil crisis of 1938, Roosevelt hesitated in joining the oil companies in their denunciation of Mexican President Lázaro Cárdenas's expropriation decree. Four years later, Mexico and the United States created a wartime economic alliance.

The Good Neighbor policy restored U.S. trade with Latin America and created a hemispheric bloc against the Axis powers. Neither was easily achieved, for German economic and cultural endeavors in Latin America in the 1930s appeared more compatible with the Latin corporatist political tradition. At the eighth inter-American conference at Lima (1938) and the special meetings of foreign ministers at Panama (1939), Havana (1940), and Rio de Janeiro (1942), Latin America's commitment to a united hemisphere steadily increased.

After Pearl Harbor, the efforts to create a united hemisphere intensified. The State Department created the post of coordinator of inter-American affairs to promote inter-American cultural understanding. As Latin American governments joined the war effort, the U.S. military, economic, and cultural presence expanded. By the end of the war, the Latin American economies were virtually intertwined with the U.S. economy. Regrettably, at war's end, much of the goodwill built through Good Neighbor cultural understanding dissipated under U.S. determination to fashion a solid anticommunist Latin American bloc. However, the Good Neighbor Policy is still cited as a plausible alternative to military action.

*See also* **United States-Latin American Relations.**

BIBLIOGRAPHY

Bryce Wood, *The Making of the Good Neighbor Policy* (1961).

David Green, *The Containment of Latin America* (1971).

Dick Steward, *Trade and Hemisphere. The Good Neighbor Policy and Reciprocal Trade* (1975).

Irwin F. Gellman, *Good Neighbor Diplomacy: United States Policies in Latin America, 1933–1945* (1979).

*Additional Bibliography*

Pike, Fredrick B. *FDR's Good Neighbor Policy: Sixty Years of Generally Gentle Chaos.* Austin: University of Texas Press, 1995.

Quintaneiro, Tania. "Cinema e guerra: Objetivos e estratégias da política estadunidense no Brasil." *Comunicação e Política* 23, no. 2 (May–August 2005): 41–69.

Roorda, Eric. *The Dictator Next Door: The Good Neighbor Policy and the Trujillo Regime in the Dominican Republic, 1930–1945.* Durham, NC: Duke University Press, 1998.

LESTER D. LANGLEY

**GORODISCHER, ANGÉLICA** (1928–). Angélica Gorodischer (*b.* 28 July 1928), Argentine writer. Born in Buenos Aires to an upper-middle-class Spanish family, Gorodischer began writing late in life in the port town of Rosario, where she settled with her husband and children. *Opus Dos* (1967), her first novel, the short stories contained in *Bajo las jubeas en flor* (1973; Under the Jubeas in Bloom) and in *Casta luna electrónica* (1977; Chaste Electronic Moon), and particularly her tales of the intergalactic trips of a traveling salesman from Rosario, *Trafalgar Medrano* (*Trafalgar*, 1979), would permit classifying her as a writer of speculative science fiction. However, these stories, together with some others, constitute what also could be labeled as "fantastic." Some could even be classed as thrillers, whodunits, and Gothic tales. She is interested in the absurd, monstrosities, dreams, myths; in the great themes that are a pretext for human beings to continue fighting to live; in the relationship between man and the universe, man and God, and power and death; in all that man does not know.

For Gorodischer, literature is a way of "unmasking" reality. In her works there is a counterpoint between the imaginary and the real worlds that gives transcendental meaning to her stories, so they end by being allegories, metaphors, or symbolic chronicles of the contemporary world and of the human condition, generally presented in a humorous vein.

Gorodischer's novel *Kalpa Imperial* (1983) was published in English in 2003 as *Kalpa Imperial: The Greatest Empire that Never Was.* Gorodischer organized two international conferences of women writers in Rosario in 1998 and 2000 and has won numerous awards for her work. In 2007 the city of Rosario awarded her the title of Illustrious Citizen.

*See also* **Buenos Aires; Literature: Spanish America.**

BIBLIOGRAPHY

M. Patricia Mosier, "Communicating Transcendence in Angélica Gorodischer's *Trafalgar,*" in *Chasqui* 12, no. 2–3 (1983): 63–71.

Angela B. Dellepiane, "Contar = mester de fantasía o la narrativa de Angélica Gorodischer," in *Revista Iberoamericana* 51, no. 132–133 (1985): 627–640, and "Narrativa fantástica y narrativa de ciencia-ficción," in *Plural* (Mexico), 188 (May 1987): 48–50.

### *Additional Bibliography*

Balboa Echeverría, Miriam and Ester Gimbernat González, eds. *Boca de dama: La narrativa de Angélica Gorodischer.* Buenos Aires: Feminaria Editora, 1995.

Corbalán, Rafael T., Gerardo Piña-Rosales, and Nicolás Toscano. *Acentos femeninos y Marco Estético del nuevo milenio.* New York: City University of New York, Graduate School and University Center, 2000.

ANGELA B. DELLEPIANE

## GOROSTIZA, MANUEL EDUARDO DE

**GOROSTIZA, MANUEL EDUARDO DE** (1789–1851). Manuel Eduardo de Gorostiza (*b.* 1789; *d.* 1851), Mexican military officer, diplomat, cabinet minister, and dramatist. Gorostiza was born in Veracruz, but his family returned to Spain after the death of his father, a colonial governor, when he was five. Because of his liberalism, Gorostiza was forced to flee from Spain to Mexico in 1822. He served as a Mexican representative in London, where he kept the British Parliament and public well informed about U.S. designs on Texas in the late 1820s. In 1830 he was named Mexico's minister plenipotentiary in London and minister to all the European countries. In 1933 Gorostiza was recalled to Mexico, where he served on Gómez Farías's commission on educational reform and was named the first director of the National Library and the National Theater.

After the fall of Gómez Farías, Gorostiza wrote and produced plays to support himself, reviving the theater in Mexico and becoming famous for his comedies in Spain as well. He later served as Mexican minister in Washington (1836), treasury minister (1838, 1842–1843, 1846), and foreign relations minister (1838–1839). During the U.S. invasion of Mexico in 1847, Gorostiza organized and paid for a battalion, which he led at the Battle of Churubusco.

*See also* **Gómez Farías, Valentin.**

BIBLIOGRAPHY

Carlos González Peña, *History of Mexican Literature,* translated by Gusta Barfield Nance and Florence Johnson Dunstan, 3d ed. (1968); *Diccionario Porrúa de historia, biografía y geografía de México,* 5th ed. (1986).

### *Additional Bibliography*

Gayón Córdoba, María. *La ocupación yanqui de la Ciudad de México, 1847–1848.* México, D.F.: INAH: Consejo Nacional para la Cultura y las Artes, 1997.

D. F. STEVENS

## GOROSTIZA ACALÁ, JOSÉ

**GOROSTIZA ACALÁ, JOSÉ** (1901–1973). José Gorostiza Acalá (*b.* 10 November 1901; *d.* 16 March 1973), Mexican poet and diplomat. He and his brother Celestino were major intellectual figures in Mexico and were members of the Contemporáneos intellectual circle with Jaime Torres Bodet. Octavio Paz considered Gorostiza to be a major Latin American poet.

A native of Villahermosa, Tabasco, Gorostiza began teaching at the National Preparatory School in 1921 and published his first book of poems in 1925. Joining the foreign service, he became first chancellor in London in 1927, after which he served as head of the fine arts department in public education. He returned to the foreign service where, in the 1930s and 1940s, he held a series of posts abroad, including ones in Italy, Guatemala, and Cuba. In 1950 he became ambassador to Greece and, a year later, permanent representative to the United Nations. He culminated his career as undersecretary of foreign relations (1953–1964), serving briefly as secretary in 1964. He won the National Literary Prize in 1968.

*See also* **Literature: Spanish America.**

BIBLIOGRAPHY

Merlin H. Forster, "The *Contemporáneos,* 1915–1932: A Study in Twentieth-Century Mexican Letters" (Ph.D. diss., University of Illinois, 1960).

Andrew P. Debicki, *La poesía de José Gorostiza* (1962).

José Gorostiza, *Death Without End,* translated by Laura Villaseñor (1969).

Juan Gelpí, *Enunciación y dependencia en José Gorostiza* (1984).

*Additional Bibliography*

Escalante, Evodio. *José Gorostiza: Entre la redención y la catástrofe.* México: Ediciones Casa Juan Pablos, 2001.

Gómez Montero, Vicente, and Miguel Angel Ruiz Magdonel. *José Gorostiza, la palabra infinita.* Chimalistac, Mexico, D.F.: CONACULTA, 2001.

Ruiz Abreu, Alvaro, and José Gorostiza. *Crítica sin fin: José Gorostiza y sus críticos.* México, D.F.: CONACULTA, 2004.

Roderic Ai Camp

## GORRITI, JUANA MANUELA (1816–1892).

Best known for her fiction and memoirs, the Argentine writer Juana Manuela Gorriti spent her life traveling among Argentina, Bolivia, and Peru and writing about these places and times. Born on July 16, 1816, and exiled from Argentina in 1831, Gorriti married Manuel Isidoro Belzú (later president of Bolivia) in 1833, but left him to live in Peru with their two daughters. She ran a girls' school and in 1845 published her first novel, *La quena*, set in colonial Peru and depicting conflicts among white, black, and indigenous races. She published major books of collected fiction in Buenos Aires—*Sueños y realidades* (1865), *Panoramas de la vida* (1876), *Misceláneas* (1878), and *El mundo de los recuerdos* (1886)—and many other texts, including a collection of recipes, *Cocina ecléctica* (1890), and autobiographical reflections, in *La tierra natal* (1889) and *Lo íntimo*, published after her death. During her years in Lima, Gorriti was renowned for her evening gatherings of the literary, artistic, and social elite. One volume of these proceedings was published as *Veladas literarias de Lima 1876–77* (1892). Gorriti's example inspired many of her Lima friends, including Mercedes Cabello de Carbonera and Clorinda Matto de Turner, to persevere in their writing of historical legends, stories, novels, essays, and poetry, often after reading them aloud at Gorriti's gatherings. In her own fiction, Gorriti wrote often of women characters who manage—sometimes to escape from social constraints and expectations. Gorriti often set her stories in the Peruvian or Argentine countryside, during times of the early conquest or, more often, during the tumultuous years of the nineteenth century wars of independence and their aftermath. In her 1864 novel, *Un viaje al país de oro*, two young Peruvians travel to California at the height of the gold rush. Her last novel, *Oasis en la vida* (1888), extols the merits of modernization. She died on November 6, 1892.

*See also* **Literature: Spanish America; Matto de Turner, Clorinda; Palma, Ricardo.**

BIBLIOGRAPHY

Batticuore, Graciela, ed. *El taller de la escritora: Veladas literarias de Juana Manuela Gorriti.* Rosario, Argentina: Beatriz Viterbo, 1999.

Gorriti, Juana Manuela. *Obras completas,* 6 vols. Salta, Argentina: Fundación del Banco del Noroeste, 1992–1999.

Gorriti, Juana Manuela. *Dreams and Realities: Selected Fiction of Juana Manuela Gorriti,* translated by Sergio Waisman; edited by Francine Masiello. New York: Oxford University Press, 2003.

Mary G. Berg

## GORRITI, JUAN IGNACIO DE (1766–1842).

Juan Ignacio de Gorriti (*b.* June 1766; *d.* 25 May 1842), Argentine priest and independence leader. Born in Los Horcones, Gorriti's early education in Latin and philosophy was directed by the Franciscans in Jujuy. From 1781 to 1789 he studied theology and literature at the Colegio Nusetra Señora de Monserrat in Córdoba, and he obtained a doctorate in sacred theology from the University in Charcas in 1791. He briefly worked as a parish priest in Cochinoca and Casabindo, small villages in the altiplano of Jujuy, earning distinction for his sermons. He participated in Argentina's independence movement, arguing that the authority of the viceroys and other Spanish officials had expired when the French deposed the legitimate king of Spain. In September 1810, he was named representative of Jujuy to the revolutionary Junta de Buenos Aires. He remained in politics as Salta's representative to the Congress in 1824 but was exiled to Bolivia by political enemies in 1831. There he wrote "Reflexiones sobre las causas morales de las convulsiones interiores de los nuevos estadoes americanos y examen de los medios eficaces para remediarlas" (Valparaíso, 1836), an early attempt to solve the problems facing the newly formed nations of South America. Gorriti died in Sucre, Bolivia.

*See also* **Franciscans; Jujuy.**

BIBLIOGRAPHY

Emilio A. Bidondo and Susan M. Ramírez, *Juan Ignacio de Gorriti: Sacerdote y patricio* (Buenos Aires, 1987).

Juan Ignacio De Gorriti, *Papeles* (Jujuy, 1936).

Abel Cháneton, *Historia de Vélez Sarsfield* (Buenos Aires, 1969).

*Additional Bibliography*

Calvo, Nancy, Roberto Di Stefano, Klaus Gallo, and Natalio R. Botana. *Los curas de la revolución: Vidas de eclesiásticos en los orígenes de la Nación*. Buenos Aires: Emecé, 2002.

J. DAVID DRESSING

## GOULART, JOÃO BELCHIOR MARQUES (1919–1976).

João Belchior Marques Goulart (*b.* 1 March 1919; *d.* 6 December 1976), Brazilian Labor Party (PTB) leader and president of Brazil (1961–1964), whose overthrow led to two decades of military rule.

João "Jango" Goulart was born in São Borja, Rio Grande do Sul. His family was allied politically and economically with that of Getúlio Vargas. Jango, the eldest boy of eight children, spent his early years on the family ranches that produced cattle, sheep, and horses. From the age of nine, he attended schools in larger cities, finally receiving a law degree in 1939. He soon took over the family businesses and became a millionaire.

Jango befriended Getúlio Vargas when the latter returned to São Borja in 1945. A popular figure, Jango formed district chapters of Vargas's PTB. Eventually he became a confidant, aide, and spokesman for Vargas during his 1950 campaign for president. At about that time his sister married Leonel Brizola, who would become his closest political ally.

After leading the PTB in Pôrto Alegre for a year, Jango transferred to Rio to help Vargas manage national labor politics, for which he was appointed labor minister in 1953. He showed great skill in handling workers, whom he favored with a 100-percent wage hike in 1954. The furor resulting from this decision forced Jango's resignation, but he continued to exercise great influence in labor matters through his leadership of the PTB.

In many ways Vargas's heir, Jango rode the PTB into the vice presidency in 1956 and again in 1961, allying with Juscelino Kubitschek and Jânio Quadros, respectively. He continued to use his position to help labor, and the PTB grew rapidly in Congress and the states—the only major party to do so.

Jango was in China when Quadros resigned in August 1961, creating a succession crisis. His many supporters—especially Brizola in Rio Grande—threatened civil war should the military attempt to deny the presidency to Jango. A compromise between Congress and the military chiefs allowed Jango to be titular president in a parliamentary system. The arrangement proved cumbersome, and when put to a plebiscite in early 1963, it was abandoned.

Goulart took the restored presidential powers as a vote of confidence, yet his tenure proved controversial and stormy. Although he continued to enjoy popularity among the working class, he never captured (as Vargas had) the support of the middle and upper classes. The U.S. government treated him with aloofness, especially after Brizola nationalized a subsidiary of International Telephone and

Telegraph. U.S. businessmen, abetted by increasingly cool diplomatic relations, worked to discredit Goulart, while Washington disallowed financial assistance. The country plunged into a depression, exacerbated by Goulart's erratic policies and mismanagement. Politics became dangerously polarized, and Goulart failed in several attempts to conciliate opposing groups. Finally, in March 1964 he decided to make a bold appeal to the workers, rural poor, and leftists by announcing a major reforms package, including redistribution of land near federal installations. This effort, as well as his mishandling of two military revolts, led the army to overthrow him on 1 April 1964 in order to rid the country of a leftist president and restore economic order. Goulart flew into exile and lived in Uruguay and Argentina until his death from a heart attack.

*See also* **Brizola, Leonel; Livestock; Vargas, Gétulio Dornelles.**

BIBLIOGRAPHY

Thomas E. Skidmore, *Politics in Brazil, 1930–1964* (1967).

John W. F. Dulles, *Unrest in Brazil* (1970).

Luís Alberto Moniz Bandeira, *O governo João Goulart* (1977).

Jan Knippers Black, *United States Penetration of Brazil* (1977).

Israel Beloch and Alzira Alves De Abreu, comps., *Dicionário histórico-biográfico brasileiro, 1930–1983* (1984).

Edgard Carone, *A república liberal* (1985).

*Additional Bibliography*

Fico, Carlos. *Além do golpe: versões e controvérsias sobre 1964 e a ditadura military.* Rio de Janeiro: Editora Record, 2004.

Francis, Paulo. *Trinta anos esta noita: 1964, o que vi e vivi.* São Paulo: Companhia das Letras, 1994.

Markun, Paulo, and Duda Hamilton. *1961: Que as armas não falem.* São Paulo: Editora SENAC São Paulo, 2001.

Otero, Jorge. *De Lula a Jango: João goulart, recuerdos en su exilio uruguayo.* Montevideo: Ediciones de la Plaza, 2003.

Villa, Marco Antonio. *Jango: Um perfil, 1945–1964.* São Paulo: Editora Globo, 2003.

MICHAEL L. CONNIFF

## GRAÇA ARANHA, JOSÉ PEREIRA DA (1868–1931).

José Pereira da Graça Aranha (*b.* 21 June 1868; *d.* 26 January 1931), Brazilian writer of the premodernist social novel. Graça Aranha was born to an aristocratic Maranhão family and graduated from law school in Recife. While municipal judge in the German settlement of Porto do Cachoeiro in 1890, his observations of the immigrants' struggle inspired the plot for his first and most famous novel, *Canaã* (1902; *Canaan,* 1920). Previous to its publication he was elected to a seat on the Brazilian Academy of Letters. From 1900 to 1920 he held diplomatic offices and traveled through many parts of Europe. Upon his return to Brazil he published *A estética da vida* (1920). Graça Aranha's thesis novels are sociological studies of the contemporary Brazilian problem of assimilation of races and cultures, and philosophical explorations of his theory of universalism and humanitarian evolutionism. His documentary prose contains brilliant descriptions and abstract characters.

Aside from a modest literary production, Graça Aranha's most important contribution is his role in initiating the modernist movement in Brazil. He organized Modern Art Week in 1922 to promote among Brazilian artists a reformation of national thought and sensibility, launching the modernist movement in the arts, which sought to rediscover Brazil in its native elements. He broke with the Academy of Letters in 1924, calling on its members to create a national literature.

*See also* **Brazilian Academy of Letters; Race and Ethnicity.**

BIBLIOGRAPHY

Graça Aranha, *Trechos escolhidos por Renato Almeida* (1958), esp. pp. 4–19.

João Cruz Costa, "Graça Aranha," in *A History of Ideas in Brazil* (1964).

Graça Aranha, *Obra completa,* edited by Afrânio Coutinho (1969), esp. pp. 17–36.

*Additional Bibliography*

Azevedo, Maria Helena Castro. *Um senhor modernista: Biografia de Graça Aranha.* Rio de Janeiro: Academia Brasileira de Letras, 2002.

LORI MADDEN

## GRACE, W. R., AND COMPANY.

W. R. Grace and Company, a major U.S. industrial company that played an influential role in the history of

Latin America from the 1850s to the 1950s. It was the first multinational in Latin America, and through its multifaceted commercial and industrial activities was long associated with the development and modernization of the region, but, by contrast, its critics linked it with the negative concomitants of imperialism and capitalism, such as exploitation of nonrenewable resources, creation of enclave economies, preferential treatment of foreigners, repatriation of profits, interference in host country politics, and numerous other activities they considered detrimental in the economic development of a region.

The company was founded in 1854 by a young Irish immigrant to Peru. William Russell Grace began working in the booming business of exporting guano from Peru to North America and Europe and then branched out into other aspects of the growing trade between the west coast of South America and the United States. He moved the headquarters of his fledgling company to New York City after the Civil War, but kept his connections with South America close and dependable by bringing in brothers, cousins, and other relatives to operate Grace trading houses in Valparaiso, Callao, and other South American ports and cities.

By the early twentieth century, W. R. Grace was the major presence in trade and commerce between North America and South America. The first steamship line between the Americas, the Grace Line, dominated shipping between New York City and South America, and the company diversified into activities as varied as owning and operating sugar plantations in Peru, buying and marketing tin from Bolivia, mining nitrates in Chile, financing railroads in Ecuador, and operating Panagra, the premier air carrier between the Americas from the 1930s to the 1950s. In the 1950s the company decided to focus its investments on the U.S. chemical industry and divested itself of its Latin American interests. By the 1970s the company that was known as Casa Grace along the west coast of South America no longer had any significant Latin American presence.

*See also* **Imperialism.**

BIBLIOGRAPHY

Jonathan V. Levin, *The Export Economies: Their Pattern of Development in Historical Perspective* (1960).

Mira Wilkins, *The Maturing of Multinational Enterprise: American Business Abroad from 1914 to 1970* (1974).

Lawrence A. Clayton, *Grace: W. R. Grace & Co.: The Formative Years, 1850–1930* (1985).

Marquis James, *Merchant Adventurer: The Story of W. R. Grace* (1993).

*Additional Bibliography*

O'Brien, Thomas F. *The Revolutionary Mission: American Enterprise in Latin America, 1900–1945.* New York: Cambridge University Press, 1996.

LAWRENCE A. CLAYTON

**GRACIAS.** Gracias, seat of Lempira Department in Honduras and first capital city in Central America. Founded, according to some accounts, in 1536 by Gonzalo de Arredondo y Alvarado, and on 14 January 1539 by Juan de Montejo, according to others, Gracias a Dios in western Honduras became the seat of the Audiencia De Los Confines as well as of the subsequent Audiencia of Guatemala. Its early economy was based upon gold and silver mining. However, the town began an economic decline by the end of the seventeenth century. In 1855 the forces of Guatemalan General Rafael Carrera defeated Honduran General Trinidad Cabañas there. In 1915 an earthquake devastated the town, which has since been rebuilt. Coffee, other agricultural crops, and more recently, tourism, are important to the local economy.

BIBLIOGRAPHY

Luis Mariñas Otero, *Honduras,* 2d ed. (1983).

Ralph Lee Woodward, Jr., *Central America: A Nation Divided,* 2d ed. (1985).

*Additional Bibliography*

Dym, Jordana. *From Sovereign Villages to National States: City, State, and Federation in Central America, 1759–1839.* Albuquerque: University of New Mexico Press, 2006.

Pearcy, Thomas L. *The History of Central America.* Westport, CT: Greenwood Press, 2005.

JEFFREY D. SAMUELS

**GRAEF FERNÁNDEZ, CARLOS** (1911–1988). Carlos Graef Fernández (*b.* 25 February 1911, *d.* 1988), Mexican mathematician and educator. A disciple of Manuel Sandoval Vallarta, Graef Fernández graduated from the National University with a degree in engineering before completing a Ph.D. at the Massachusetts Institute of Technology in 1940. He began teaching relativity at the National School of Science in Mexico in 1941 and then at Harvard from 1944 to 1945. He devoted many decades to teaching at the National University, serving as dean of the National School of Sciences (1957–1959) and director of the Institute of Physics. A leader in Mexico's efforts to harness nuclear energy, he coordinated its national commission in the 1960s and served as a governor of the International Organization of Atomic Energy (1960–1961). Mexico awarded him its National Prize in Sciences in 1970.

*See also* **Nuclear Industry.**

BIBLIOGRAPHY

*Enciclopedia de México,* vol. 5 (1976), pp. 493–494.

### *Additional Bibliography*

Graef Fernández, Carlos, José Luis Fernández Chapou, and Alfonso Mondragón Ballesteros. *Obra científica.* México: Universidad Autónoma Metropolitana, Azcapotzalco y Iztapalapa, 1993.

RODERIC AI CAMP

## GRAF SPEE.

**GRAF SPEE.** *Graf Spee,* German pocket battleship sunk in December 1939 off the coast of Uruguay. The *Graf Spee* had been sinking British merchant vessels almost from the outset of World War II. From 30 September to 7 December it sank nine merchant vessels. The *Graf Spee* was being hunted down by the British and French navies and on 13 December 1939, 250 miles east of Montevideo, the battleship was engaged in battle by the British cruisers *Achilles, Ajax,* and *Exeter.* At the end of the engagement, the damaged *Graf Spee* steered toward neutral Montevideo pursued by the British ships. The vessel was allowed to remain in Montevideo until 17 December. Captain Hans Langsdorff knew that his ship was not completely seaworthy, let alone battleworthy, and that the British were waiting to engage him again. So, on 17 December, he took the ship out of Montevideo and when it was a mile outside territorial waters, scuttled it.

*See also* **World War II.**

BIBLIOGRAPHY

Dudley Pope, "*Graf Spee*": *The Life and Death of a Raider* (1957).

Geoffrey Martin Bennett, *Battle of the River Plate* (1972).

Rony Almeida, *Historia del acorazado de bolsillo Almirante "Graf Spee"* (1977).

### *Additional Bibliography*

Grove, Eric. *The Price of Disobedience: The Battle of the River Plate Reconsidered.* Annapolis, MD: Naval Institute Press, 2001.

JUAN MANUEL PÉREZ

**GRANADA, NICARAGUA.** Granada, the earliest Spanish settlement in Nicaragua and the oldest continuously inhabited city in Central America. Located on the western end of Lake Nicaragua, Granada was founded in 1524 by Francisco Hernández de Córdoba. Built on the site of the ancient Indian town of Jaltepa, it became an important trading center and a major port for the new colony. Spanish seagoing ships sailed directly to Granada until an earthquake created shallows in the San Juan River, which connects Lake Nicaragua with the Atlantic coast. Access to the sea also made Granada a target for buccaneers in the seventeenth century. After independence it became the center of the Conservative Party. Followers of the opposition Liberal Party, led by the American filibuster William Walker, burned the city in 1856. Rebuilt, Granada has maintained its colonial appearance. It is the principal port on the lake and serves as the terminus for the railroad to Corinto. It is currently the third-largest city in the country, after Managua and León. Its estimated population is 105,171 (2005).

*See also* **Hernández (Fernández) de Córdoba, Francisco; Walker, William.**

BIBLIOGRAPHY

Alejandro Barbarena Pérez, *Granada, Nicaragua* (1971).

### *Additional Bibliography*

Arellano, Jorge Eduardo. *Granada: Aldea señorial en el tiempo.* Managua: Dirección General de Patrimonio y

Museos, Instituto Nicaragüense de Cultura: Organización de Estados Americanos, 1997.

Cruz S., Arturo J. *Nicaragua's Conservative Republic, 1858-1893.* New York: Palgrave, 2002.

Velázquez P, José Luis. *La formación del Estado en Nicaragua, 1860–1930.* Managua: Fondo Editorial, Banco Central de Nicaragua, 1992.

DAVID L. JICKLING

## GRANADA, SPAIN.

**GRANADA, SPAIN.** Granada, Spain, province in Andalusia and its capital city, with 240,661 inhabitants, (2001). Located at the foot of the Sierra Nevada mountains, Granada was historically known as a silk manufacturing center. The province included the city of Granada, one of the three largest cities in Castile in the fifteenth century, and a large concentration of Spain's Moorish population. The last refuge of the Moors during the Reconquest, Granada surrendered to Ferdinand and Isabella on 2 January 1492. In 1499, Cardinal Francisco Jiménez de Cisneros introduced forcible conversion of the Moors, an action that led to the revolt of the Alpujarras in 1500. After the revolt was crushed, the Moors were given the choice to convert or emigrate. After another revolt (1568–1570), the Moorish population was scattered and resettled throughout the rest of Spain.

### BIBLIOGRAPHY

Antonio Domínguez Ortiz and Bernard Vincent, *Historia de los Moriscos* (1978).

Henri Lapeyre, *Geografía de la España morisca* (1986).

### *Additional Bibliography*

Casey, James. *Family and Community in Early Modern Spain: The Citizens of Granada, 1570–1739.* Cambridge, U.K. Cambridge University Press, 2007.

Harris, A. Katie. *From Muslim to Christian Granada: Inventing a City's Past in Early Modern Spain.* Baltimore: Johns Hopkins University Press, 2007.

Peinado Santaella, Rafael Gerardo, Manuel Barrios Aguilera, and Francisco Andújar Castillo, eds. *Historia del Reino de Granada.* 3 vols. Granada: Universidad de Granada: Legado Andalusí, 2000.

SUZANNE HILES BURKHOLDER

## GRANADEROS A CABALLO.

**GRANADEROS A CABALLO.** The Granaderos a Caballo was an Argentine elite regiment created by José de San Martín. On his return to Argentina from Spain in 1812, San Martín obtained from the revolutionary government authorization to raise and command a regiment of mounted grenadiers (*granaderos a caballo*) who would be both carefully selected and rigorously trained. Moreover, San Martín hoped that this elite group would serve as a model of professionalism for the rest of the military. The unit first saw service under San Martín in early 1813 at the battle of San Lorenzo. It later fought in Chile and Peru (serving with the forces of Bolívar after San Martín's departure) and produced numerous officers who went on to command other units. It was dissolved in 1826 but restored in 1903 as a permanent unit whose duties include that of serving as ceremonial escort to the president of Argentina.

*See also* **Argentina: The Colonial Period; San Martín, José Francisco de.**

### BIBLIOGRAPHY

Ricardo Rojas, *San Martín; Knight of the Andes,* translated by Herschel Brickel (1967), pp. 28–33.

Luis Alberto Leoni, *Regimiento Granaderos a Caballo de los Andes: Historia de una epopeya* (1968).

### *Additional Bibliography*

Mendizábal, Francisco Javier de. *Guerra de la América del Sur, 1809–1824.* Buenos Aires: Academia Nacional de la Historia, 1997.

DAVID BUSHNELL

## GRAN COLOMBIA.

**GRAN COLOMBIA.** The union of all the Spanish Viceroyalty of New Granada—Venezuela, New Granada, and Quito (Ecuador)—in a single independent nation was proclaimed the Republic of Colombia by the Congress of Angostura in December 1819. It later came to be known as Gran Colombia, to distinguish it from the smaller Colombia of today. It received a formal constitution at the Congress of Cúcuta in 1821, when the liberation of Ecuador had only begun and no Ecuadorans were present. But Ecuador was successfully incorporated in 1822, after the forces of Simón Bolívar prevailed in its struggle for independence.

The creation of Gran Colombia was mainly a result of the personal influence of Bolívar and the manner in which independence was achieved: by armies composed of Venezuelans and New Granadans (and eventually Ecuadorans) that moved back and forth between sections under Bolívar's leadership. However, the union was fragile because of the great distances covered, the primitive state of transportation, and the lack of strong social, cultural, and economic ties among regions. Once the war was over, regionalist sentiments were expressed more forcefully, especially in Venezuela, which staged a first revolt in 1826. The union disintegrated completely in 1830, when Venezuela and Ecuador became separate republics, leaving the central core (present-day Colombia and Panama) to reconstitute itself as the Republic of New Granada. Even then, the separate nations continued to observe Gran Colombian legislation until it was repealed or revised; retained the same colors (yellow, blue, red) in their flags; and retained a common cult of Bolívar.

*See also* **Bolívar, Simón; New Granada, Viceroyalty of.**

BIBLIOGRAPHY

José Manuel Restrepo, *Historia de la revolución de la República de Colombia en la América meridional,* 3d ed., 8 vols. (1942–1951).

David Bushnell, *The Santander Regime in Gran Colombia* (1954; repr. 1970).

*Additional Bibliography*

León de Labarca, Alba Ivonne, and Juan Carlos Morales Manzur. *Algunos intentos de reconstrucción gran colombiana despueś de 1830.* Mérida, Colombia: Universidad de los Andes, Consejo de Publicaciones, 2001.

Riaño Cano, Germán. *El gran calumniado: Réplica a la leyenda negra de Santander.* Bogotá, Colombia: Planeta, 2001.

DAVID BUSHNELL

## GRANDE OTELO

**GRANDE OTELO** (1915–1993). Born Sebastião Bernardes de Souza Prata, Grande Otelo was one of the most important Brazilian actors of the twentieth century. He was born on October 18, 1915, in Uberabinha (now known as Uberlândia), Minas Gerais. His stage name derives from his experience as an aspiring operatic tenor whose African ancestry presumably destined him to play the part of Othello in Verde's opera and from an ironic reference to his diminutive stature. He joined the circus at the age of eight and began to perform in traveling shows. He later received an education after being adopted by a wealthy white family in São Paulo. In 1942 the North American director and actor Orson Welles, who saw him perform in nightclubs in Rio de Janeiro and became his friend, called him "the greatest comic actor of the twentieth century." From 1935 into the 1990s, he appeared in an estimated 100 films, most of which were comedies. Often the only black actor in any given movie, he frequently played the role of a *malandro,* living outside of the law and by his wits. From the 1940s on, he sought ways to affirm his Afro-Brazilian heritage in his roles. One of his greatest parts was that of the title character in the 1960 film adaptation of the Mário de Andrade literary classic, *Macunaíma* (1928). He also wrote songs and screenplays. He died in Paris on November 26, 1993.

*See also* **Cinema: From the Silent Film to 1990.**

BIBLIOGRAPHY

Moura, Roberto. *Grande Otelo: Um Artista Genial.* Rio de Janeiro: Relume Dumará, 1996.

Silva, Marília Trindade Barboza da. *Depoimentos de Grande Otelo, Haroldo Costa, Zezé Motta.* Rio de Janeiro: Museu da Imagem e do Som, 2003.

Stam, Robert. *Tropical Multiculturalism: A Comparative History of Race in Brazilian Cinema and Culture.* Durham, NC: Duke University Press, 1997.

ANDREW J. KIRKENDALL

## GRANDJEAN DE MONTIGNY, AUGUSTE HENRI VICTOR

**GRANDJEAN DE MONTIGNY, AUGUSTE HENRI VICTOR** (1776–1850). Auguste Henri Victor Grandjean de Montigny (*b.* 15 July 1776; *d.* 2 March 1850), French architect. Grandjean de Montigny studied at the École des Beaux-Arts in Paris. He arrived in Rio de Janeiro with the French Artistic Mission, which was organized by Joaquim Lebreton (1760–1819) at the invitation of the Portuguese crown. After his arrival on 26 March 1816, he was asked to design the future Academy of Fine Arts, and he was nominated professor of architecture and given two assistants. The construction of the academy began, but financial difficulties delayed its completion.

Meanwhile Grandjean de Montigny looked for other jobs, such as the Praça do Comércio (1820), a structure in which merchants conducted business. He was also responsible for the old market of Candelária (1836) and for several private houses. Grandjean de Montigny and other French artists were in charge of decorating Rio de Janeiro's Palace Square with ephemeral structures for the coronation of João VI (6 February 1818). Greek temples, Roman arches, and obelisks were the fashion for this kind of urban decoration in public festivities, after which they were destroyed. Montigny operated a private school of architecture until 1824, when Emperor Pedro I finally ordered that the construction of the Academy of Fine Arts, where Montigny held his lectures, be concluded.

*See also* **Architecture: Architecture to 1900; French Artistic Mission.**

BIBLIOGRAPHY

Adolfo Morales De Los Rios, Filho, *Grandjean de Montigny e a evolucão da arte brasileira* (1941).

Affonso De Escragnolle Taunay, *A missão artística de 1816* (1956).

*Additional Bibliography*

Schultz, Kirsten. *Tropical Versailles: Empire, Monarchy, and the Portuguese Royal Court in Rio de Janeiro, 1808–1821.* New York: Routledge, 2001.

MARIA BEATRIZ NIZZA DA SILVA

---

**GRAN MINERÍA.** Gran Minería, a massive Chilean copper complex encompassing three mines: El Teniente, Chuquicamata, and Potrerillos. Although Chile was a substantial copper producer in the mid-nineteenth century, its output began to flag in the late 1870s. Modernizing the mines, which would have increased their productivity, would have required massive infusions of expensive technology. Although Chilean capitalists had the funds, they preferred to invest either in the booming nitrate industry, which brought in a high rate of return, or in ventures abroad.

In 1904 the American capitalist William Braden purchased El Teniente, a mine located near Santiago, where he introduced techniques that permitted the exploitation of low-grade copper ore. Braden subsequently sold El Teniente to the Guggenheim mining interests, which in turn transferred it to the Kennecott Copper Company. Then in 1911 the Guggenheims acquired what became the world's largest open-pit mine, Chuquicamata, located in Chile's Norte Chico. With the infusion of large sums of money to upgrade it, this mine quickly matched El Teniente's production levels. After restructuring their holdings, in 1915, the Guggenheims turned over Chuquicamata to Kennecott. In 1923, Kennecott sold Chuquicamata to the Anaconda Copper Mining Company, which named it the Chile Exploration Company. This corporation also developed the third part of the Gran Minería, Los Andes, in Potrerillos, for which it is now named.

These mines became classic examples of company towns where the mines owned the housing, the store, and the social facilities. These isolated copper mines did not consume much in the way of locally produced goods, largely because Chile did not manufacture what the mining companies needed. The workforce, though well paid by Chilean standards, was never large. Consequently, the huge profits resulting from low labor costs and minimal taxation were remitted abroad.

In the twentieth century this situation slowly began to change. For one thing, improvements in working conditions and increased social benefits mandated by the 1925 Constitution increased the cost of labor. More significantly, during the Great Depression the Chilean government shifted the main tax burden from nitrates to copper. The Moneda, or executive branch, accomplished this in two ways: by imposing a direct levy on revenues and by setting up exchange controls, thus forcing those copper companies that wished to remit their profits to the United States to purchase the dollars from the Chilean state. The creation of CORFO (Corporación de Fomento, or Development Corporation) increased the burden on the copper companies, because the Moneda levied a special tax on the mines to finance the diversification of the Chilean economy. By 1939 the tax rate on American mining corporations had risen to 33 percent.

Copper sales boomed during World War II, when the U.S. government agreed to pay a special rate of 12 cents per pound and abolished the import tax on Chilean copper. The Moneda increased the tax on the copper industry, raising it to 65 percent of the companies' profits at the same time the mines were paying a premium of 60 percent to purchase dollars. Chileans would subsequently complain that since the world market price was higher than the 12 cents per pound the United States paid, Washington had cheated Santiago.

Prices did rise after the war, encouraging the owners of the Chuquicamata mine to expand its facilities, but the owners of the other two, because of sagging profits, did not. When the onset of the Korean War brought another surge in copper prices, the United States again negotiated a treaty with U.S.-owned copper companies, setting the price at 24.5 cents per pound. Vowing not to be cheated twice, the Chilean government nullified this agreement and reopened the negotiations. The result was the Washington Treaty of 1951, which fixed the price at 27.5 cents per pound. Not only would the Chilean government reap the extra 3 cents, but it would have the right to market directly 20 percent of the copper mined in Chile. The following year the Chilean government declared that it would purchase the mines' output and sell it directly, in order to benefit from the higher prices.

Taxes then became so prohibitive—in some cases 90 percent—that companies became reluctant to modernize their mines, particularly after 1953, when copper prices fell at the end of the Korean War. This failure to invest reduced Chile's share of the world market. Clearly, the government had to do something to increase production and raise its revenues.

In 1955, the Carlos Ibáñez administration instituted a new policy called *El nuevo trato,* the new deal, that set the tax rate on the copper companies at 50 percent. To encourage production the government also levied a 25 percent surcharge, which it offered to forgo if the mines increased their output. Most of the copper companies complied, but the results proved disappointing: mechanization reduced their work forces, and even though Anaconda opened a new mine, El Salvador, Chile's share of world copper declined. This dismal performance disappointed those who had expected more from *El nuevo trato.*

Eduardo Frei, a Christian Democrat, drastically altered the status of the Gran Minería companies. Frei wanted the state to purchase an interest in the copper corporations so that henceforth it would participate in all aspects of mining, from extraction to its ultimate sale. Under his direction, in 1965 the Chilean government purchased 51 percent of the El Teniente mine from Kennecott, which remained a junior partner.

Frei's "Chileanization" program failed to appease the nationalists, who argued that the copper companies had cheated the government. When, in 1969, the price of copper increased on the world market, Frei's critics demanded that he renegotiate his earlier agreement with the U.S.-owned copper companies. Anaconda subsequently agreed to sell 51 percent of its holdings in Chuquicamata and El Salvador.

After his 1970 election, President Salvador Allende announced that he would purchase the remaining 49 percent of Kennecott and Anaconda. Although he promised to pay compensation, he stipulated that he would deduct from that award all profits he considered excessive, meaning any amount over 12 percent. In September 1971 he declared that since Anaconda and Kennecott had made excess profits of approximately $770 million, these companies owed the Chilean government approximately $380 million. Clearly, politics, not international law, had motivated Allende's desire to end what he considered a cycle of dependency on the United States. Regrettably, politics often dictated the policies of the nationalized mines: worker discipline declined, and it became difficult to obtain spare parts. The mines, their workforces swollen, simply became less productive, and hence less profitable.

The Pinochet government (1973–1990), which returned stability to the mines, moved to seek an accommodation with Kennecott and Anaconda. In 1974 it agreed to pay them for their shares in their respective former holdings. Finally, after decades, the Gran Minería became completely Chilean.

*See also* **Chile, Organizations: Development Corporation (CORFO); Mining: Modern.**

BIBLIOGRAPHY

Clark Reynolds, "Development Problems of an Export Economy: The Case of Chile and Copper," in

Markos Mamalakis and Clark W. Reynolds, *Essays on the Chilean Economy* (1965) pp. 203–298.

Leland Pederson, *The Mining Industry of the Norte Chico, Chile* (1966).

Markos Mamalakis, "The Contribution of Copper to Chilean Economic Development, 1920–1967," in Raymond Frech Mikesell, *Foreign Investment in the Petroleum and Mineral Industries: Case Studies of Investor-Host Country Relations* (1971), pp. 387–420.

Eric N. Baklanoff, *Expropriation of U.S. Investments in Cuba, Mexico, and Chile* (1975).

Theodore H. Moran, *Multinational Corporations and the Politics of Dependence: Copper in Chile* (1975).

Joanne F. Przeworski, *The Decline of the Copper Industry in Chile and the Entrance of North American Capital, 1870 to 1916* (1980).

Paul E. Sigmund, *Multinationals in Latin America: The Politics of Nationalization* (1980).

Francisco Zapata, "Nationalization, Copper Miners and the Military Government in Chile," in Thomas C. Greaves and William Culver, *Miners and Mining in the Americas* (1985), pp. 256–276.

*Additional Bibliography*

Klubock, Thomas Miller. *Contested Communities: Class, Gender, and Politics in Chile's El Teniente Copper Mine, 1904–1951*. Durham, NC: Duke University Press, 1998.

WILLIAM F. SATER

**GRAU, ENRIQUE** (1920–2004). Enrique Grau (*b.* 18 December 1920, *d.* 1 April 2004), Colombian painter. Grau was born to a prominent family from Cartagena that encouraged his creative talents. His first exhibition, in 1940, preceded formal art studies, which he began at the Art Students League in New York City (1941–1942). Grau worked in many media, including set design, costumes, and films. However, his reputation as one of the most important Colombian artists—along with Fernando Botero, Alejandro Obregón, Edgar Negret, and Eduardo Ramírez Villamizar—was established in the early 1960s by his paintings. Although he was always a figurative artist, Grau's works of 1955–1962 show the influence of abstract geometry; his images—in painting, drawing, and sculpture from 1962—demonstrate the development of a style that combines refined mimetic skills with satire.

Retrospectives of Grau's work have been organized in Colombia by the Universidad Nacional, Bogotá (1963); the Museo de Arte Moderno, Bogotá (1973, 2002), and the Fundación Da Vinci, Manizales (graphic work, 1988). Grau's work also has been featured in international exhibitions focusing on contemporary Colombian and Latin American art: Latin American Art Since Independence (Yale University Art Gallery and University of Texas Art Museum, 1966); Lateinamerikanisch Kunstausstellung (Kunsthalle, Berlin, 1964); El Arte Colombiano a Través de los Siglos (Petit Palais, Paris, 1975); Perspective on the Present: Contemporary Latin America and the Caribbean (Nagoya City Art Museum, 1991). In 2004 the Enrique Grau Cultural Center opened in Cartagena.

*See also* **Art: The Twentieth Century.**

BIBLIOGRAPHY

Germán Rubiano Caballero, ed., *Enrique Grau* (1983).

Stanton L. Catlin, et al., *Enrique Grau, Colombian Artist* (1991).

*Additional Bibliography*

Fiorillo, Heriberto. *La Cueva: Crónica del Grupo de Barranquilla*. Bogotá: Planeta, 2002.

Grau, Enrique, et al. *Enrique Grau: Homage*. Bogotá: Villegas Editores, 2003.

FATIMA BERCHT

**GRAU, MIGUEL** (1834–1879). Miguel Grau (*b.* 1834; *d.* 1879), Peru's greatest naval hero, renowned for his prowess as admiral of the Peruvian navy in command of the ironclad *Huáscar* during the War of the Pacific (1879–1883). Born in Piura, Grau started his career as a sailor on whaling ships. In 1856 he obtained the rank of lieutenant. He participated in the caudillo struggles of the time in support of General Manuel Ignacio Vivanco against Ramón Castilla, a political decision that led to his ouster from the war navy in 1858. At the end of Castilla's second presidential term, however, Grau was back in the navy on a mission to Europe under Admiral Aurelio García y García to buy badly needed warships. In 1865, Grau supported Colonel Manuel Ignacio Prado's uprising against compliance with a forced treaty with Spain, and in 1866 he fought the bellicose Spanish fleet in the battle of Abtao.

In 1868, Grau was appointed commander of the *Huáscar.* He opposed the coup attempt by the Gutiérrez Brothers in 1872, after which he became commander in chief of the Peruvian navy as well as deputy for Paita (1876–1878). At the start of the War of the Pacific in 1879, Grau returned to the command of the *Huáscar,* one of two ironclads Peru sent against the far more numerous Chilean fleet. Grau performed legendary feats against Chilean vessels and ports trying to buy time for new warship purchases. He died in the naval battle of Angamos, which secured decisive naval superiority for Chile.

*See also* **War of the Pacific.**

BIBLIOGRAPHY

Jorge Basadre, *Historia de la República del Perú,* vol. 5 (1963).

*Additional Bibliography*

Moya Espinoza, Reynaldo. *Grau.* Cercado de Lima, Peru: Grupo Editorial Megabyte, 2003.

Ortíz Sotelo, Jorge. *Miguel Grau, el hombre y el mar.* Lima: Fondo Editorial del Congreso del Perú, 2003.

ALFONSO W. QUIROZ

---

**GRAU SAN MARTÍN, RAMÓN** (1887–1969). Ramón Grau San Martín (*b.* 13 September 1887; *d.* 28 July 1969), Cuban physician and politician, president of Cuba (1933–1934, 1944–1948). Born into a privileged and well-known family, Grau San Martín received a first-class education in both the sciences and the humanities. He earned a medical degree and began a lifetime involvement with the University of Havana, where he served on many committees. Beginning in 1927, Grau actively and consistently opposed the dictatorship of Gerardo Machado; indeed, he was the only faculty member who refused to sign the edict authorizing Machado's honorary doctorate from the university. For his efforts, Grau was jailed and exiled from Cuba in the late 1920s.

In the early 1930s, the tide of anti-Machado sentiment in Cuba was swelled by the Depression and growing anti-American feeling. Progressive elements of the military and civilian groups banded together to force out Machado, who resigned through the mediation of U.S. representative Sumner Welles. A provisional government, headed by Carlos Manuel de Céspedes, was itself quickly overthrown on 4 September 1933. This revolt brought to the forefront Sergeant Fulgencio Batista y Zaldívar as its chief and Grau as the most prominent member of a civilian pentarchy.

Events unfolded rapidly and, backed by his faithful students, Grau and Antonio Guiteras became the principals of a brief but extremely important political experiment. On 10 September, Grau abrogated the hated Platt Amendment, which had kept Cuba in a state of dependence on the United States. The revolutionary government effected other dramatic changes, including the requirement that at least 50 percent of a business's employees had to be Cuban, the granting of autonomy to the University of Havana and removal of restrictions for enrollment, the extension of the vote to women, compulsory trade unionization and the creation of professional associations, and an agrarian reform designed to benefit peasants. Not surprisingly, the government's activism spurred demonstrations for more radical reforms, earning it the enmity of the political Right and hostility from the United States. Furthermore, as the demands of the Left began to outpace the reforms, another potential support base for the Grau–Guiteras team was alienated. In January 1934 a military coup led by Batista, by then the army chief, toppled the government, although the legacy of the experiment lived on.

Grau remained active in politics and university life for the next decade. He founded the Authentic Party and won the presidential election in 1944. During his four-year term, Grau returned to many of his previous policies. This time, in the years of euphoria after World War II, Grau found a more fertile and sophisticated political climate for his ideas. Although he was an opportunist with a keen sense of symbolism and ceremony, Grau held to his basic principles of anti-imperialism, nationalism, and non-Marxist socialism throughout his life.

*See also* **Batista y Zaldívar, Fulgencio; Céspedes y Quesada, Carlos Manuel de.**

BIBLIOGRAPHY

Emma Pérez, *La política educacional del Dr. Grau San Martín* (1948).

Luis Aguilar, *Cuba 1933: Prologue to Revolution* (1972).

Samuel Farber, *Revolution and Reaction in Cuba, 1933–1960* (1976).

Antonio Lancís y Sánchez, *Grau, estadista y político* (1985).

Louis A. Pérez, Jr., *Cuba: Between Reform and Revolution* (1988).

*Additional Bibliography*

Valdéz-Sánchez, Servando. *Fulgencio Batista: El poder de las armas (1933-1940)*. La Habana: Editora Historia, 1998.

Vázquez García, Humberto. *El gobierno de la kubanidad.* Santiago de Cuba: Editorial Oriente, 2005.

Whitney, Robert. *State and Revolution in Cuba: Mass Mobilization and Political Change, 1920–1940.* Chapel Hill: University of North Carolina Press, 2001.

KAREN RACINE

**GREGORY XIII, POPE** (1502–1585). Born Ugo Buoncompagni, Gregory attained the papacy in his seventies, after a career largely in the Roman curia where he served as papal representative to the Council of Trent and on several diplomatic missions. In this he developed a relationship with Philip II of Spain. His papacy is noted for the calendrical reform that revised the older Julian calendar, causing ten days to be lost as October 5 became October 15, 1582. He issued two documents of particular importance to the New World. To address a shortage of priests in the Indies, the bull *Nuper ad nos* (1577) provided for the ordination of mestizos in spite of illegitimate birth. His brief *Universalis Christi Fideliter* (1585) curtailed the rights of religious orders by bringing them under the canon law of the church and authority of local bishops, especially with regard to the administration of parishes. Last, he attempted to develop a system of judicial appeals for cases from the New World that would bypass royal scrutiny, an action that Philip II felt was a violation of the royal patronage.

*See also* **Patronato Real; Philip II of Spain.**

BIBLIOGRAPHY

Shiels, W. Eugene. *King and Church: The Rise and Fall of the Patronato Real.* Chicago: Loyola University Press, 1961.

JOHN F. SCHWALLER

**GREMIOS.** *See* **Guilds (Gremios).**

**GRENADA.** Grenada is a Caribbean nation-state located in the southern part of the Windward Islands. Consisting of 133 square miles and an estimated 107,000 inhabitants (2006), Grenada is composed of three islands: Grenada proper and the smaller islands of Carriacou and Petit-Martinique. The islands were populated by Carib Indians who offered fierce resistance to European settlers until 1654, when the last Caribs committed suicide to avoid capture by the French colonizers.

French rule lasted for over a century and resulted in the importation of African slaves whose descendants make up the majority of Grenada's population today. The French introduced Roman Catholicism, which is still Grenada's predominant religion. The establishment of British control in 1783 brought an increase in the number of slaves, a worsening of their treatment, and the attempt to suppress the Roman Catholic faith. In 1795 a Grenadian mulatto, Julien Fedon, launched a revolt in order to restore French rule. His rebellion turned into a massive slave insurrection that took the British fifteen months to crush.

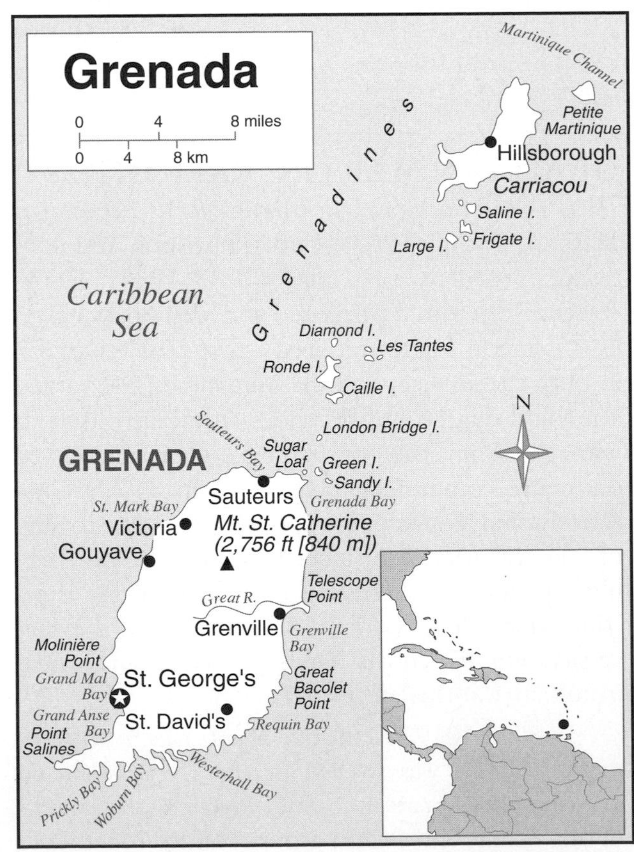

| **Grenada** | |
|---|---|
| **Population:** | 107,000 (2006 est.) |
| **Area:** | 133 sq. mi |
| **Official language:** | English |
| **Language:** | French patois |
| **National currency:** | East Caribbean dollar |
| **Principal religions:** | Roman Catholic 53%; Anglican 13.8%; other Protestant 33.2% |
| **Ethnicity:** | Black 82%; mixed black and European 13%; European and East Indian 5%; trace Arawak/Carib Amerindian |
| **Capital:** | Saint George's |
| **Annual rainfall:** | Varies from 60 in in the northern and southern coastal belts up to 150 in in the Central Highlands |
| **Economy:** | *GDP per capita:* US$3,900 (2005) |

Facing competition from larger sugar producers as well as the abolition of slavery (1838), Grenada's plantation owners switched from sugar to the production of cocoa and spices (particularly nutmeg and mace) by the second half of the nineteenth century. During the same period, the development of commerce produced a native bourgeoisie that resented the monopoly of power held by the British crown and the plantocracy, and demanded a voice in the political life of Grenada. Theophilus Albert Marryshow became the leader of this rising class, which he represented in Grenada's Legislative Council during the first half of the twentieth century. Also influential in Grenada's working-class politics was Tubal Uriah "Buzz" Butler.

Trade unions were legalized on Grenada in 1933, but they organized only the urban workers. The agricultural laborers continued to live in abject poverty until 1950, when they found a champion in Eric M. Gairy, who organized them in his Grenada Manual and Mental Workers' Union (GMMWU) and the Grenada United Labour Party (GULP). During 1951, Gairy was able to wring concessions from the landlords by violent strikes and demonstrations in the countryside. He dominated Grenadian politics until 1979.

It became apparent that Gairy was neglecting his constituents when he entered into questionable business ventures and tried to ingratiate himself with the British colonial authorities and Grenada's elite. Given that the only political opposition, Herbert A. Blaize's Grenadian National Party, championed the upper class, it is not surprising that the majority of Grenadians preferred the corrupt Gairy to the elitist Blaize. It was not until 1973 that Gairy met the real challenge of the New Jewel Movement (NJM), which appealed to the same social strata as he did. Gairy responded by dispatching his terrorist Mongoose Gang. With the granting of independence to Grenada on 7 February 1974, now Prime Minister Gairy cast off all restraints and established a quasi-dictatorship that was despised throughout the Caribbean. On 13 March 1979, the New Jewel Movement toppled Gairy, who was in New York City at the time, in a bloodless coup. Grenadians hailed his ouster.

It was soon evident, however, that Grenada had exchanged one dictator for another. While Maurice Bishop's party (the People's Revolutionary Government) introduced educational and health reforms and began construction of a needed international airport, the elections that the NJM had promised never materialized. Instead, all opposition newspapers and organizations were prohibited and critics of the new regime found themselves incarcerated. In the autumn of 1983, tensions within the revolutionary leadership led to fratricidal strife between Bishop and his deputy, Bernard Coard. Bishop and some of his closest advisers were executed on 19 October 1983. The subsequent Revolutionary Military Council was deposed on 25 October, when troops from the United States and various Caribbean islands invaded Grenada.

The first postinvasion national elections were held in December 1984. Herbert Blaize, representing the New National Party (NNP), became prime minister, an office he held until his death in December 1989. His tenure was marked by close friendship with the Reagan administration, large contributions of U.S. aid, the expansion of tourism as the country's major industry, and reprisals against former supporters of the Bishop regime. Since then, Grenada's Truth and Conciliation Commission and the Committee for Human Rights in Grenada (UK) (CHRGUK) have demanded new trials for members of the "Grenada 17," those charged with and imprisoned for the deaths of Bishop and other government supporters. New hearings, they maintain, will help close the deep fissures within Grenadian society produced by the era of Gairy and the subsequent Grenadian revolution.

The less conservative and more popular National Democratic Congress government of Nicholas Brathwaite was elected in 1990, though the center-right NNP returned and has remained in power since 1995. Keith Mitchell, a leader of the NNP, was elected prime minister in 1994, 1999, and 2003.

Hurricane Ivan in 2004 caused severe damage to homes, buildings, and the nutmeg crop, of which Grenada, the "isle of spice," is the world's second-largest producer. Hurricane Emily struck the northern islands in 2005. Although rebuilding proceeded quickly, the tourism and agricultural sectors struggled to return to pre-hurricane levels.

*See also* **Slavery: Abolition; Slave Trade; Windward Islands.**

BIBLIOGRAPHY

Raymund P. Devas, *The Island of Grenada, 1650–1950* (1964).

Patrick Emmanuel, *Crown Colony Politics in Grenada, 1917–1951* (1978).

Tony Thorndike, *Grenada* (1985).

Steve Clark, "The Second Assassination of Maurice Bishop," in *New International* 6 (1987): 11–96.

Kai P. Schoenhals, *Grenada* (1990).

*Additional Bibliography*

Crandall, Russell. *Gunboat Democracy: U.S. Interventions in the Dominican Republic, Grenada, and Panama.* Lanham, MD: Rowman and Littlefield, 2006.

McDaniel, Lorna. *The Big Drum Ritual of Carriacou: Praisesongs in Rememory of Flight.* Gainesville: University Press of Florida, 1998.

Noguera, Pedro A. *The Imperatives of Power: Political Change and the Social Basis of Regime Support in Grenada from 1951–1991.* New York: P. Lang, 1997.

Steele, Beverley A. *Grenada: A History of Its People.* Oxford, UK: Macmillan Caribbean, 2003.

Kai P. Schoenhals

**GRENADINES.** Grenadines, hundreds of islets, rocks, and reefs that comprise the top of a volcanic ridge between Saint Vincent and Grenada in the Windward Islands of the eastern Caribbean. Collectively they cover about 35 square miles. Ten are populated, having a population of about 12,000 in 1980. The Grenadines are dependencies of two independent nation-states: Saint Vincent and the Grenadines, and Grenada. Those between Grenada and Carriacou are dependencies of Grenada; the largest is Carriacou (pop. 7,000). The remainder are integral parts of Saint Vincent, the largest being Bequia (pop. 2,600).

Archaeologists surmise that the aboriginal Ciboney were followed and perhaps displaced by migrations of Arawak and Carib peoples from the South American mainland. Strong Carib resistance made European occupation a difficult process until late in the eighteenth century. The Caribs named these islands Begos; the Grenadines later were renamed by either the Spanish or the French, although Bequia and Canouan are linguistic corruptions of Carib names. The French claimed the Grenadines in 1664 as extensions of their holding of Grenada. In 1675 a slave ship sank in the Bequia–Saint Vincent channel. Surviving slaves swam to both islands, where Caribs took them in—the origins of the "Black Caribs," the descendants of the mixing of these two peoples.

These small islands changed hands often from the seventeenth through the nineteenth centuries as European conflicts spilled over into the West Indies, and the Caribs strenuously fought all comers. As a result of the Seven Years' War, Saint Vincent, Grenada, Dominica, and the Grenadines were ceded to Britain and formed into a Windward Islands Federation. For easier administration, the Grenadines were divided between Grenada and Saint Vincent. In 1770 the British made concerted efforts to colonize these islands by surveying and distributing land. The Windward Federation ended by 1776. Between 1779 and 1783 Saint Vincent and its Grenadines were under French rule, after which they returned to British control; colonists began to plant sugarcane, using African slave labor on large plantations. The Caribs rebelled one last time in 1795; their defeat led to their deportation to British Honduras.

The postemancipation period in the Grenadines was a difficult one. For all the efforts of British planters, final emancipation in 1838 effectively marked the steady decline of both cotton and sugar production, and the latter ultimately ended. The emigration of whites and blacks in the postslavery period was both a cause and a consequence of a decline of all cash crops for export. The resident population was left relatively free to develop its own Creole culture without many elite whites, and the small island economies were redirected to livestock raising for export, whaling, fishing, and subsistence agriculture. Somewhat isolated, Grenadine populations developed strong separate identities and customs that fueled suspicion of the larger, dominant islands of which they were political dependencies.

The first half of the twentieth century brought additional problems from a large eruption of Soufrière on Saint Vincent, trade disruptions from two world wars, and social unrest during the mid-1930s. During the post–World War II period, there was some economic development as a result of money sent home by those who had emigrated to look for work. Many Grenadine men found work as sailors as world trade recovered. In recent years, some of the Grenadines have become popular with tourists arriving by yacht, and the foreign exchange earned from tourism has increased, supplementing more traditional agriculture, fishing, whaling, and boat building.

In general, Grenadine inhabitants are descended from African slaves, from indentured European labor imported in the early period of European colonization, and from a mix of these two groups (ethnic proportions and economic activities vary depending on the island). Portuguese Madeirans and East Indian immigrants are also represented.

*See also* **Slave Trade; Windward Islands.**

BIBLIOGRAPHY

Michael G. Smith, *Kinship and Community in Carriacou* (1962).

Clive A. Frank, *History of Begos: The Grenadines from Columbus to Today* (1976).

Dana Jinkins and Jill Bobrow, *St. Vincent and the Grenadines: A Plural Country* (1985).

Robert B. Potter, comp., *St. Vincent and the Grenadines* (1992).

### *Additional Bibliography*

Gordon, Suzanne. *Searching for Sugar Mills: An Architectural Guide to the Caribbean.* Oxford: Macmillan Caribbean, 2005.

Grossman, Lawrence. *The Political Ecology of Bananas.* Chapel Hill: University of North Carolina Press, 1998.

Potter, Robert. *St. Vincent and the Grenadines.* Santa Barbara, CA: Clio Press, 1992.

ROSEMARY BRANA-SHUTE

---

**GREYTOWN (SAN JUAN DEL NORTE).** Greytown (San Juan del Norte), a small trading settlement in Nicaragua where the San Juan River enters the Caribbean. The port has served various nations—Spain, Nicaragua, Costa Rica, Great Britain, and the United States—for trade and transit since the sixteenth century. In the late colonial era, San Juan del Norte, as it originally was named, became an outlet for Costa Rican gold and other contraband goods that were exchanged for trade goods from Jamaica. The British and the Mosquito Indians claimed the port in 1841, but the British sent a naval force to drive away the Nicaraguan authorities in February 1848. They renamed the village Greytown, in honor of Charles Grey, governor of Jamaica.

Great competition for power made Greytown a place of considerable activity from 1848 until the 1880s. In 1848, the Royal West India Mail Steam Packet Company initiated monthly service between San Juan and Southampton, England. From 1849 to 1869, Cornelius Vanderbilt's Accessory Transit Company exercised transit rights up the San Juan River and across Lake Nicaragua with steamer connection to California. During the 1850s, Greytown served as a lifeline for reinforcements and supplies during U.S. filibustering. In mid-1854, the competition between Britain and the United States heated up to the point that the U.S.S. *Cyane* destroyed the town.

In 1860, Great Britain and Nicaragua signed a treaty that made San Juan del Norte a free port. In the 1860s, silting created sandbars in the estuary of the river that rendered the port of little use for ocean vessels. The British moved their commercial operations north to Bluefields, but U.S. promoters of a Nicaraguan canal attempted to keep the port as one terminal of the canal until bankruptcy ended the canal project during the depression of the 1890s. Since the 1890s, San Juan del Norte has shriveled into an isolated village of several hundred people, surrounded by decaying buildings and rusting equipment.

*See also* **Panama Canal.**

BIBLIOGRAPHY

Mario Rodríguez, *A Palmerstonian Diplomat in Central America, Frederick Chatfield, Esq.* (1964).

Murdo Mac Leod, *Spanish Central America: A Socioeconomic History, 1520–1720* (1973).

Craig L. Dozier, *Nicaragua's Mosquito Shore* (1985).

Ralph Lee Woodward, Jr., *Central America: A Nation Divided* (1985).

*Additional Bibliography*

Incer Barquero, Jaime. *Piratas y aventureros en las costas de Nicaragua: Crónicas de fuentes originales.* Managua: Fundación VIDA, 2003.

Romero Vargas, Germán. *Las sociedades del Atlántico de Nicaragua en los siglos XVII y XVIII.* Managua: Fondo de Promoción Cultural-Banic, 1995.

THOMAS SCHOONOVER

**GRIJALVA, JUAN DE** (c. 1489–1527). Juan de Grijalva (*b.* c. 1489; *d.* 1527), conquistador who first learned of the Aztec Empire and a nephew of Pánfilo de Narváez. Grijalva was born in Cuéllar and came to the Caribbean as a youth. He accompanied Diego Velázquez, and later his uncle, on their first expeditions to Cuba in 1511, and subsequently resided in prominence on the island. In 1518, Governor Velázquez dispatched him to expand upon the discoveries made by Francisco Fernández De Córdoba along the coast of Yucatán. His fleet discovered Cozumel, the Grijalva and Banderas rivers, and San Juan de Ulúa. After his force was attacked at the latter site by a number of natives in canoes, he decided not to attempt to colonize and returned to Cuba, an action that greatly displeased Velázquez. The first Spaniard to learn of the Aztec Empire, Grijalva reported its existence to Velázquez, but he did not accompany Cortés. He was killed in battle against natives near Villahermosa.

*See also* **Conquistadores.**

BIBLIOGRAPHY

Hugh Thomas, *Conquest of Mexico* (1993).

*Additional Bibliography*

Miranda, Leocésar. *Diego Velázquez, de Cuéllar, colonizador y primer gobernador de la isla de Cuba.* Santiago de Cuba: Ediciones Santiago, 2004.

JOHN E. KICZA

**GRILO, SARAH** (1919–). Sarah Grilo (*b.* 1919), Argentine painter. Born in Buenos Aires, Grilo lived in Madrid and Paris (1948–1950) and traveled throughout Europe and the United States (1957–1958). According to Damián Bayón, among the Buenos Aires group comprising José Fernández Muro, Clorindo Testa, Kasuya Sakai, and Miguel Ocampo, Grilo "always represented the extreme sensibility to color." From 1960 she showed this sensibility in compositions whose right-angled structures were permanently altered by the inclusion of circular forms. Her chromatic modulations are suggestive of the tonal values of Pierre Bonnard and his concept of color as a continuous state of exaltation in which form loses all importance. Later Grilo introduced tachiste effects (graphic signs). Her right-angled structures disappeared, giving way to a surface freely dotted with spots of paint and sprinkled with texts, words, letters, and numbers backed by radiant color, which created imaginary codices of great enchantment. Grilo has exhibited throughout North and South America as well as in Europe. She has received several awards, including the Wertheim Prize (Buenos Aires, 1961) and a Guggenheim Foundation Fellowship (New York, 1962).

*See also* **Art: The Twentieth Century; Buenos Aires.**

BIBLIOGRAPHY

*Museum of Modern Art of Latin America* (1985).

Lily Sosa De Newton, *Diccionario biográfico de mujeres argentinas,* 3d ed. (1986).

Vicente Gesualdo, Aldo Biglione, and Rodolfo Santos, *Diccionario de artistas plásticos en la Argentina* (1988).

*Additional Bibliography*

Barnitz, Jacqueline. *Twentieth-Century Art of Latin America.* Austin: University of Texas Press, 2001.

AMALIA CORTINA ARAVENA

**GRIMARD, LUC** (1886–1954). Luc Grimard (pseudonyms, Lin Dege; Marie Gérard; *b.* 30 January 1886; *d.* 24 October 1954), Haitian writer, educator, and diplomat. Luc Grimard finished a law degree at age nineteen. He taught classics, philosophy, and social science before serving as Haitian consul in Le

Havre (1922–1927). During his directorship of the Lycée Philippe Guerrier in Cap Haïtien (1927–1932), Grimard's resistance to the American occupation (1915–1934) was exemplary to his students. In 1932 he went to Port-au-Prince as inspector of the École Normale des Instituteurs. He was named director of *Le Temps* (1938) and later of the Catholic daily, *La Phalange* (1941–1950). President Elie Lescot appointed him conservator of the Musée Sténio Vincent (1941). Grimard also served as rector of the University of Haiti (1951–1954) and was a member of the Cuban Academy of Arts and Letters.

His first volumes of poetry were published in France in 1927. His early verse has been compared to that of Paul Verlaine. Later he turned to Haitian history, nature, and women for inspiration. From his early poetry through his stories there runs a thread of fascination with mystery and the supernatural.

*See also* **Haiti; Literature: Spanish America.**

BIBLIOGRAPHY

Among his other works are *Jours de gloire* (theater, with Dominique Hippolyte, 1917; *Ritournelles* (poetry, 1927); *Sur ma flûte de bambou* (poetry, 1927); *Du sable entre les doigts* (novellas, 1941); *Bakoulou* (novellas, with André F. Chevallier, 1950); and *L'offrande du laurier* (poetry, 1950). See also F. Raphaël Berrou and Pradel Pompilus, *Histoire de la littérature haïtienne illustrée par les textes*, vol. 2 (1975), pp. 437–452.

*Additional Bibliography*

Renda, Mary A. *Taking Haiti: Military Occupation and the Culture of U.S. Imperialism, 1915–1940.* Chapel Hill: University of North Carolina Press, 2001.

Shannon, Magdaline W. *Jean Price-Mars, the Haitian Elite and the American Occupation, 1915–1935.* New York: St. Martin's Press, 1996.

CARROL F. COATES

**GRINGO.** Gringo, a slang, usually derogatory term used in Mexico for Anglo-Americans or English speakers. Elsewhere in Latin America it can also refer to someone who speaks Spanish badly.

The origin of this term is veiled in mystery. According to folk legend, the term may have developed during the Mexican War, when the Mexican population heard U.S. soldiers singing a popular song, "Green Grow the Lilacs." Another possibility is that it is a corruption of the Spanish word *griego* (Greek), meaning strange or foreign words that are not understood.

BIBLIOGRAPHY

Don H. Radler, *El Gringo: The Yankee Image in Latin America* (1962); *Diccionario manual ilustrado de la lengua española,* 4th ed. (1989).

*Additional Bibliography*

Arriaga Weiss, Víctor Adolfo, and Ana Rosa Suárez Argüello. *Estados Unidos desde América Latina: Sociedad, política y cultura.* México, D.F.: Centro de Investigación y Docencia Económicas, 1995.

RICHARD GRISWOLD DEL CASTILLO

**GRIPPO, VÍCTOR** (1936–2002). Víctor Grippo (*b.* 10 May 1936), Argentine artist. Born in the town of Junín, in the province of Buenos Aires, Grippo studied chemistry and design at the University of La Plata. In 1971, he became a leading member of a group of thirteen artists (known as *Grupo de los Trece*). Named *Grupo de Cayc* (for the Centro de Arte y Comunicación where they met), these painters wanted to generate radical changes in the practice of art through the exploration of the relation of art to science and the use of massive communication techniques and inexpensive materials.

In his installation *Analogy 1* (1971), sprouting potatoes were strung together with zinc and copper electrodes and connected with a voltmeter. By means of written descriptions, Grippo drew parallels between the germinating tubers' energetic power and the awakening of human consciousness: the potato, a staple food native to South America, symbolizes the potential of autochthonous resources. Manual labor, in its most rudimentary forms, was the subject of his installation *Crafts* (1976). From the 1980s his work consisted of assemblages of quasi-geometric forms that resemble spheres, artificer's lead pencils, and *crusets.* Throughout his life, his work was shown in international venues such as the Ikon Gallery in Birmingham, England and the Palais des Beaux-Arts in Brussels. Grippo died in Buenos Aires in February 2002. His work was included in Documenta 11 (2002) in Kassel, Germany.

*See also* **La Plata.**

BIBLIOGRAPHY

Jorge Glusberg, *Del pop-art a la nueva imagen* (1985), pp. 167–176, and *Víctor Grippo: Obras de 1965 a 1987* (1988).

Waldo Rasmussen et al., *Latin American Artists of the Twentieth Century* (1993).

*Additional Bibliography*

Kalinovska, Milena, ed. *Beyond Preconceptions: The Sixties Experiment.* New York: Independent Curators International, 2000.

Ramírez, Mari Carmen, ed. *Cantos paralelos: La parodia plástica en el arte argentina contemporáneo.* Austin: Jack S. Blanton Museum of Art, University of Texas at Austin; Buenos Aires: Fondo Nacional de las Artes, 1999.

Zegher, M. Catherine de, and Elizabeth A. Macgregor, eds. *Victor Grippo.* Birmingham, U.K.: Ikon Gallery, 1995.

MARTA GARSD

## GRITO DE ASENCIO.

**GRITO DE ASENCIO.** Grito de Asencio, popular uprising in Uruguay that took place on 28 February 1811 on the banks of the Asencio River, near Mercedes, in the present-day department of Soriano. Inspired by José Artigas, who was in Entre Ríos, Argentina, at the time, two inhabitants of the area, Pedro Viera and Venancio Benavídez, led the revolt. Although the uprising was against the government in Montevideo and in support of the junta in Buenos Aires, with the problem of independence from Spain yet to be addressed, the Grito de Asencio is traditionally taken to signify the starting of the revolution in the Banda Oriental.

*See also* **Artigas, José Gervasio; Uruguay: Before 1900.**

BIBLIOGRAPHY

John Street, *Artigas and the Emancipation of Uruguay* (1959).

Washington Reyes Abadie and Andrés Vázquez Romero, *Crónica general del Uruguay,* vol. 2 (1984).

*Additional Bibliography*

Narancio, Edmundo M. *La independencia de Uruguay.* Madrid: Editorial MAPFRE, 1992.

JOSÉ DE TORRES WILSON

**GRITO DE BAIRE.** Grito de Baire, the declaration proclaimed at the village of Baire, near Santiago de Cuba, that began the Cuban War of Independence on 24 February 1895. Immediately, the Cuban forces in the western part of the island were defeated by the Spaniards. The main complaints against the Spanish crown were excessive taxation; a huge Cuban foreign debt; discrimination against Cubans for government positions; royal absolutism; and the lack of the basic freedoms of speech, press, and assembly. The Spanish crown was not singled out as the only enemy. Elite landowners were also recognized as an oppressive ruling class.

Led by José Martí and other veterans of the Ten Years' War, the insurrection appealed to oppressed groups such as poor blacks, whites, workers, and peasants as its main base of support. The goal was to create a truly sovereign nation and end the role played by Cuba as a bridgehead for further Spanish intervention in Latin America.

*See also* **Cuba, War of Independence.**

BIBLIOGRAPHY

Hugh Thomas, *Cuba; or, the Pursuit of Freedom* (1971).

James D. Rudolph, *Cuba: A Country Study* (1985).

Jaime Suchlicki, *Cuba from Columbus to Castro,* 3d ed. (1990).

*Additional Bibliography*

Elorza, Antonio. *La Guerra de Cuba, 1895–1898: Historia política de una derrota colonial.* Madrid: Alianza Editorial, 1998.

Ferrer, Ada. *Insurgent Cuba: Race, Nation, and Revolution, 1868–1898.* Chapel Hill: University of North Carolina Press, 1999.

Tone, John Lawrence. *War and Genocide in Cuba, 1868–1898.* Chapel Hill: University of North Carolina Press, 2006.

DAVID CAREY JR.

**GRITO DE DOLORES.** *See* **Mexico: 1810–1910.**

**GRITO DE LARES.** Grito de Lares (23–24 September 1868), Puerto Rico's first armed uprising against Spanish colonial rule. Organized by the physician Ramón Emeterio Betances, the lawyer Segundo Ruíz Belvis, and a dozen coffee planters from western Puerto Rico, the conspiracy sought to liberate the island from Spain, free the slaves, and end the peonage that kept free laborers in virtual servitude. Although parts of the plan were carried out the night of 23 September, following the rebels' occupation of Lares the movement was summarily crushed by the Spanish troops on the island. More than 500 of the suspected conspirators were sent to prison, where eighty of them died of disease. The rest were freed by an amnesty decree issued in January 1869 by a revolutionary government that had just deposed Queen Isabella II in Madrid. The revolt is believed to have pushed Spain to implement social and political reforms, among them the abolition of slavery and the creation of political parties in Puerto Rico.

*See also* **Betances y Alacán, Ramón Emeterio; Grito de Asencio; Grito de Baire; Grito de Yara; Puerto Rico.**

BIBLIOGRAPHY

A thorough account of the Grito de Lares is in Olga Jiménez De Wagenheim, *Puerto Rico's Revolt for Independence: El Grito de Lares* (1985, 1993). Brief accounts are also found in most general histories of Puerto Rico.

*Additional Bibliography*

Fernández Méndez, Antonio. *El significado histórico del Grito de Lares.* San Juan, Puerto Rico: s.n., 1998.

Frambes-Buxedoa, A., and Marisa Rosado. *Arte y carteles puertorriqueños sobre el grito de Lares.* San Juan, Puerto Rico: Universidad Interamericana de Puerto Rico, 2006.

Moscoso, Francisco. *Clase, revolución y libertad: Estudios sobre el Grito de Lares de 1868.* Rio Piedras, Puerto Rico: Editorial Edil, Inc.: 2006.

Olga Jiménez de Wagenheim

## GRITO DE YARA.

**GRITO DE YARA.** Grito de Yara, declaration of Cuban independence made in the eastern region of Yara (10 October 1868). Efforts at reform having failed, Carlos Manuel Céspedes led the organization of eastern Cuban planters in a conspiracy against continued Spanish rule in Cuba. On 10 October 1868, at his plantation of La Demajagua, near Bayamo, he proclaimed Cuban independence, universal suffrage, and an end to slavery. Freeing his thirty slaves, who then joined his rebel army, his "grito de Yara" thus launched the Ten Years' War (1868–1878). It became the rallying cry for the rapid expansion of the rebellion across eastern Cuba. The rebels enjoyed substantial early success, but the revolt eventually succumbed to internal divisions and Spanish repression. Although declaring his opposition to slavery, Céspedes called only for "the gradual, indemnified emancipation of the slaves." He later modified his position even more to reassure slaveholders of western Cuba whom he hoped to attract to the movement. This ambiguity contributed to the division within the independence movement among the Creoles.

*See also* **Creole; Cuba: The Colonial Era (1492-1898); Cuba, War of Independence.**

BIBLIOGRAPHY

Fernando Figueredo, *La revolución de Yara* (1902; repr. 1969).

Hugh Thomas, *Cuba, the Pursuit of Freedom* (1971).

Louis A. Pérez, *Cuba, Between Reform and Revolution* (1988).

*Additional Bibliography*

Abreu Cardet, José Miguel. *Introducción a las armas: La guerra de 1868 en Cuba.* Havana: Editorial de Ciencias Sociales, 2005.

Ferrer, Ada. *Insurgent Cuba: Race, Nation, and Revolution, 1868–1898.* Chapel Hill: University of North Carolina Press, 1999.

Pérez, Louis A. *Cuba and the United States: Ties of Singular Intimacy.* Athens: University of Georgia Press, 1990.

Prados-Torreira, Teresa. *Mambisas: Rebel Women in Nineteenth-century Cuba.* Gainesville: University Press of Florida, 2005.

Ralph Lee Woodward Jr.

**GRITO DE YPIRANGA.** *See* **Brazil, Independence Movements.**

## GROOT, JOSÉ MANUEL (1800–1878).

The Colombian educator, historian, artist, and Catholic polemicist José Manuel Groot (December 25, 1800–May 3, 1878) was born in late-colonial Bogotá. In 1819 he went to work in the commercial firm of an uncle under whose influence he joined a Masonic lodge and appeared to embrace the newest liberal intellectual currents. However, a few years later he experienced a religious conversion that made him for the rest of his life an outspoken defender of traditional Roman Catholicism.

Groot served briefly in the republican bureaucracy but in 1828 founded a school and from that point on was primarily an educator, directing his own school and giving classes in others. A largely self-taught painter, Groot also produced a body of portraits and *costumbrista* (folklore) scenes, and he is likewise remembered for prose and poetry writings in the *costumbrista* genre. But he wrote mainly to defend Catholic orthodoxy and political conservatism, in newspaper articles and pamphlets and in his *Historia eclesiástica y civil de Nueva Granada, escrita sobre documentos auténticos*, first published in 1869 and 1870, in three volumes, the last dealing with the Gran Colombian period. His style was unabashedly polemical, but his *Historia* reflected extensive research in published and unpublished materials and remains a significant source for Colombian history.

*See also* **Art: The Nineteenth Century; Masonic Orders.**

BIBLIOGRAPHY

Giraldo Jaramillo, Gabriel. *Don José Manuel Groot*. Bogota: Editorial ABC, 1957.

Méndez, Herminia. "La obra histórica de José Manuel Groot." *Boletín de la Academia Nacional de la Historia* (Venezuela) 72, no. 287 (1989): 259–274.

DAVID BUSHNELL

## GROUSSAC, PAUL

**GROUSSAC, PAUL** (1848–1929). Paul Groussac (*b.* 15 February 1848; *d.* 27 June 1929), Argentine essayist, philosopher, and historian. François Paul Groussac was born in Toulouse, France, and finished secondary school in Brest. He settled in Argentina in 1866, during the War of the Triple Alliance (Paraguayan War), and went on to become a leading intellectual in his adopted country. Groussac taught mathematics at the Colegio Nacional in Buenos Aires and spent many hours in the national library broadening his intellectual horizons. He lived in San Miguel de Tucumán in northwestern Argentina, taught at the Colegio Nacional in Tucumán (1871–1874), became superintendent of education in that province (1874–1878), and was appointed director of the Teachers' College in 1878.

Keenly interested in Argentine history and Latin American thought, Groussac wrote for Argentine newspapers and authored important books in the field. His works include: *Los jesuítas en Tucumán* (The Jesuits in Tucuman [1873]), *Les îles Malouines* (The Malvinas [1910]), *Viaje intelectual* (Intellectual Voyage [1904]), *El pensamiento de América* (American, i.e., Latin American, Thought [1989]), *El Congreso de Tucumán* (1916), *Los que pasaban* (Some Who Passed Through [1919]), and *Del Plata al Niágara* (1897). Combative in his newspaper articles, Groussac was befriended by such influential intellectuals and politicians as Nicolás Avellaneda, José Manuel Estrada, Eduardo Wilde, Lucio V. Mansilla, Aristóbulo Del Valle, and Carlos Pellegrini. Groussac's lasting contributions included the reorganization of the National Library, of which he became director in 1885; the publication of the scholarly journal *La Biblioteca* (1896), which became *Anales de la Biblioteca* in 1900 (it ceased publication in 1915); and participation in the founding of *El Sud Americano* and *La Nación*. He belonged to the influential group of educators and writers at the turn of the century who shaped modern Argentina. He died in Buenos Aires.

*See also* **Education: Overview; War of the Triple Alliance.**

BIBLIOGRAPHY

Alfonso De Laferrère, "Noticia preliminar," in *Páginas de Groussac* (1928), pp. 7–41.

Joaquín G. Martínez, *François Paul Groussac: Su vida, su obra* (1948).

Paul Groussac, *Jorge Luis Borges selecciona lo mejor de Paul Groussac* (1981).

*Additional Bibliography*

Bruno, Paula. *Paul Groussac: un estratega intelectual.* Victoria, Pcia. De Buenos Aires: Universidad de San Andrés, 2005.

Páez de la Torre, Carlos. *La cólera de la inteligencia: una vida de Paul Groussac.* Buenos Aires: Emecé, 2005.

GEORGETTE MAGASSY DORN

## GROVE VALLEJO, MARMADUKE

**GROVE VALLEJO, MARMADUKE** (1878–1954). Marmaduke Grove Vallejo (*b.* 6 July 1878; *d.* 15 May 1954), Chilean army officer and Socialist Party leader. Grove was born in

Copiapó. He enrolled at the Escuela Naval in 1892, was dismissed in 1894, but two years later entered the Escuela Militar. Upon graduation in 1898, Second Lieutenant Grove entered the artillery. In 1901 he became a first lieutenant and was assigned to the staff of the Escuela Militar. Four years later he was sent to Germany and spent time in an artillery regiment and at the Charlottenburg Artillery Training School, where he received a diploma. In 1910 he returned to Chile a captain. He studied at the Academia de Guerra (staff school) from 1912 to 1914. He married Rebeca Valenzuela in 1915.

As a young officer, Grove was known for his advanced social and political ideas. In 1918 he was promoted to major, served on the Division I staff, then on the general staff, and the next year was appointed subdirector of the Escuela Militar in Santiago. For his outspoken criticism of war ministry activities in 1920, Grove was transferred out of Santiago, but he moved back to the Escuela Militar in 1921. He was a key figure in the military-political activities of 1924–1925. Then after quarreling with army strongman Carlos Ibáñez Del Campo (president, 1927–1931), he was posted to Europe on a mission for Chile's fledgling air corps, which he had helped found. There he plotted against Ibáñez and tried unsuccessfully to overthrow him, for which he was exiled to Easter Island. He escaped and, following Ibáñez's ouster in 1931, was appointed air commodore. Grove became a key figure in the 1932 Socialist Republic, was exiled again, and was elected to the Senate (while in jail) soon after his return, serving from 1934 to 1949. He was an early leader of the Socialist Party, and the party's contender for the Popular Front presidential candidacy in 1938, before giving way to Radical Pedro Aguirre Cerda.

*See also* **Chile, Political Parties: Socialist Party; Ibáñez del Campo, Carlos.**

BIBLIOGRAPHY

Jorge Grove V., *Descorriendo el velo: Episodio de los doce días de la República Socialista* (1933).

Jack Ray Thomas, "The Evolution of a Chilean Socialist: Marmaduke Grove," in *Hispanic American Historical Review* (February 1967): 22–37.

William H. Beezley and Judith Ewell, *The Human Tradition in Latin America: The Twentieth Century* (1987), pp. 41–57.

*Additional Bibliography*

Brncic I., Moira. *Marmaduke Grove: Liderazgo ético.* Santiago, Chile: Ediciones Tierra Mía, 2003.

FREDERICK M. NUNN

**GRUPO DE CAYC.** Grupo de CAYC, a group of Argentine artists, based at the Centro de Arte y Comunicación (CAYC) in Buenos Aires, who pioneered the development of "systems art" in Argentina in the 1970s. The CAYC was founded in 1969 during the so-called Revolución Argentina of 1966–1973, which established General Juan Carlos Ongania's repressive military dictatorship. Its purpose is to unite artists and theorists from various disciplines—primarily art, architecture, and communications—and to encourage the integration of art, science, and social concerns through experimental projects in these fields. It has sponsored courses, exhibitions, symposia, and other events that have attracted intellectuals from throughout the world. The Grupo de CAYC, known occasionally as the Grupo de 13, was founded in 1971 by the art critic Jorge Glusberg. Inspired by a talk at the CAYC by the avant-garde Polish director Jerzy Grotowski, Glusberg invited twenty-five artists to establish a "laboratory" similar to Grotowski's Laboratory Theater in Warsaw. Twelve accepted. Jacques Bedel, Luis Benedit, Gregorio Dujovny, Carlos Ginzberg, Víctor Grippo, Jorge González Mir, Vicente Marotta, Luis Pazos, Alfredo Portillos, Juan Carlos Romero, Julio Teich, and Horacio Zabala.

These artists subsequently invited the English psychoanalyst David Cooper to analyze the group's internal dynamics. By 1975 it was formally constituted as the Grupo de CAYC with these members: Bedel, Benedit, Glusberg, Grippo, González Mir, Marotta, Pazos, and Portillos, as well as Leopoldo Maler and the architect Clorindo Testa. Since the early 1970s, these artists have pursued what Glusberg has called "systems art"—a nexus of nontraditional modes of art deriving from the tradition of Marcel Duchamp, including conceptual, ecological, body, and performance art. Their work is notable for its experimental quality, its commitment to affirming the inextricable relationship between art and society at large, and its ability to address simultaneously the Latin American condition and universal concerns. The Grupo de CAYC has exhibited widely in Latin America and Europe. In 1977 it received the Premio Itamaraty at the XIV Bienal de São Paulo.

*See also* **Buenos Aires; Onganía, Juan Carlos.**

BIBLIOGRAPHY

*The Group of Thirteen at the XIV Bienal de São Paulo,* exhibition catalog (1977); *CAYC Group at the Bank of Ireland, Dublin, in Association with ROSC '80,* exhibition catalog (1980).

Jorge Glusberg, *Art in Argentina* (1986).

Sally Baker, ed., *Art of the Americas: The Argentine Project* (1992).

*Additional Bibliography*

Ivelic, Milan, and Jorge Glusberg. *Grupo CAYC: 9 al 30 de agosto, Museo Nacional de Bellas Artes, Santiago-Chile.* Santiago: El Museo, 1994.

JOHN ALAN FARMER

**GRUPO MADÍ AND ASOCIACIÓN ARTE CONCRETO-INVENCIÓN.** Grupo Madí and Asociación Arte Concreto-Invención, Argentine abstract art movements. Both the Grupo Madí and the Asociación Arte Concreto-Invención emerged in Buenos Aires in the latter half of the 1940s. Each comprised a like-minded group of painters and sculptors working in more-or-less constructivist and geometric modes of nonrepresentational art. These artists came together for the purposes of exhibiting and supporting rival, although closely related, theoretical platforms, which were expressed in manifestos, publications, and "happenings." The art of both groups appeared radical by virtue of its experimentation with new and often industrial materials, and its break with conventional sculptural and pictorial formats; sculptures and reliefs often employed movable components that invited the spectator's participation.

Arte Concreto-Invención and Madí had a common point of origin in the magazine *Arturo,* published as a single issue in 1944, which had espoused the cause of abstract art in Argentina. Its contributors included Carmelo Arden Quin, Gyula Kosice, Tomás Maldonado, Lidy Prati, Rhod Rothfuss, and the poet Edgar Bayley. Maldonado, along with Prati, Alfredo Hlito, Manuel Espinosa, Enio Iommi, Claudio Girola, Raúl Lozza, Alberto Molenberg, and others officially inaugurated the Asociación Arte Concreto-Invención with a manifesto and an exhibition at the Salón Peuser in March 1946. That August, the Grupo Madí was launched with an exhibition at the Instituto Francés de Estudios Superiores that included Arden Quin, Kosice, Rothfuss, Diyi Laañ, and Martín Blaszko. The origin of the name "Madí" is contested; its meaning, depending on the source, is either nonexistent or an acronym, most convincingly of *"movimento arte de invención."* Madí, too, had its manifesto, but the group soon splintered when Arden Quin and Blaszko broke away in 1947 to found a parallel group with the same name.

That same year, Lozza, Molenberg, and Lozza's two brothers left the Asociación Arte Concreto-Invención and started yet another constructivism-based abstract group they called Perceptismo. The various factions of the Argentine avant-garde were invited to participate in the *Salon des réalités nouvelles* at the Palais des Beaux-Arts in Paris in the summer of 1948. In September, a similarly multilateral exhibition was held in Buenos Aires at the Van Riel Galería de Arte. Shortly thereafter, the Asociación Arte Concreto-Invención dissolved when Maldonado left for Europe at the end of the year. The Perceptismo group lasted until 1953, when its eponymous review ceased publication. Members of the Grupo Madí continued to exhibit together as a group until at least the early 1960s.

*See also* **Art: The Twentieth Century.**

BIBLIOGRAPHY

Nelly Perazzo, *El arte concreto en la Argentina en la década del 40* (1983).

Dawn Ades, "Arte Madí/Arte Concreto-Invención," in her *Art in Latin America: The Modern Era, 1820–1980* (1989); pp. 241–251.

Fatima Bercht and Joseph R. Wolin, "Asociación Arte Concreto-Invención, Arte Madí y Perceptisimo," and Aracy Amaral, "Abstract Constructivist Trends in Argentina, Brazil, Venezuela, and Colombia," in Waldo Rasmussen et al., eds., *Latin American Artists of the Twentieth Century* (1993), pp. 321–324, 86–99.

*Additional Bibliography*

Bois, Yve Alain. *Geometric Abstraction: Latin American Art from the Patricia Phelps De Cisneros Collection. Abstracción Geométrica Arte Latinoamericano En La Colección Patricia Phelps De Cisneros.* Cambridge, MA: Harvard University Art Museums, 2001.

Galerie von Bartha. *Arte Concreto Invención, Arte Madí.* Basel: Galerie von Bartha, 1994.

JOSEPH R. WOLIN

---

**GUADALAJARA.** Guadalajara is the commercial, industrial, and transportation center of western Mexico and with a population of approximately 6 million, the second largest city in the country. The capital of the state of Jalisco, Guadalajara lies about 325 miles (520 kilometers) west of Mexico City and at an altitude of 5,141 feet (1,569 meters). The city's rainy season lasts from midsummer to early fall, while the rest of the year is dry and the temperatures mild.

In pre-Columbian times, the Guadalajara area formed the northwestern frontier of the high civilizations of central Mexico against the hostile Chichimecs of the Mesa Central. In 1531 the brutal conquistador Nuño de Guzmán invaded the area, enslaved many Indians, and left a trail of death and destruction in his wake. The city of Guadalajara was founded in 1532 but was relocated a number of times to protect it from Indian attack. In 1542 it was finally situated in the valley of the Río Atemajac. The discovery of silver in Zacatecas in 1546 drew settlers to Guadalajara and its vicinity to provide food and supplies to the miners. In 1549 the bishop in the region moved his residence to Guadalajara, and the city was made the capital of the Audiencia of Nueva Galicia in 1560. Still, Guadalajara grew slowly but steadily. In 1600 it was inhabited by 500 Spaniards, but it had become a small city of 35,000 by 1803. In 1905 its population totaled more than 100,000. This growth during the nineteenth century was based largely on the production of foodstuffs, textiles, and animal products such as leather and soap, as well as the arrival of the railroad in the 1890s.

An almost explosive growth in population and demand for services characterized the city in the mid-twentieth century. For instance, its population doubled to about 750,000 during the decade of the 1950s alone. Guadalajara tried unsuccessfully to control the resultant sprawl of squatter settlements, and one major project related to this goal was the Plaza Tapatia, begun in 1960 and officially completed in 1982. Its primary intent was to preserve the city's downtown historic landscape and to blend it with modern architecture traditions by the placement of fountains, pools, and gardens on the open squares that formed the core of the project. Another component of the city is the quaint suburban neighborhood of Tlaquepaque. Located on the southeastern edge of Guadalajara, its streets and squares have been made into pedestrian walkways and its stores transformed into craft shops and boutiques. A recent addition to the suburban landscape in Latin America is the modern shopping mall, and one of the largest malls in all Latin America is the Plaza del Sol in Guadalajara (built in 1970 and renovated in 1996), with more than 250 commercial spaces. The *tapatíos,* or natives, of Guadalajara have been characterized as politically conservative and staunchly Catholic, a heritage that has frequently placed them at odds with the more liberal secularism of central Mexico. They also take pride in their regional culture for its mariachi music and Guadalajara's part in the origin of tequila.

*See also* **Cities and Urbanization; Guzmán, Nuño Beltrán de.**

BIBLIOGRAPHY

Gilbert, Alan. *The Latin American City*, 2nd edition. London: Latin American Bureau; New York: Monthly Review Press, 1998.

Greenow, Linda L. *Credit and Socioeconomic Change in Colonial Mexico: Loans and Mortgages in Guadalajara, 1720–1820.* Boulder, CO: Westview Press, 1983.

Lindley, Richard B. *Haciendas and Economic Development: Guadalajara, Mexico at Independence.* Austin: University of Texas, 1983.

Logan, Kathleen. *Hacienda Pueblo: The Development of a Guadalajaran Suburb.* University: University of Alabama Press, 1984.

Riding, Alan. *Distant Neighbors: A Portrait of the Mexicans.* New York: Knopf, 1984.

Van Young, Eric. *Hacienda and Market in Eighteenth-century Mexico: The Rural Economy of the Guadalajara Region, 1675–1820.* Berkeley: University of California Press, 1981.

JOHN J. WINBERRY

---

**GUADALUPE, BASILICA OF.** Basilica of Guadalupe, the church near Mexico City built to shelter the image of the Virgin of Guadalupe. Over the centuries several buildings have housed the famous image of the vision which is said to have appeared in 1531. The first sanctuary was modest, but a larger church was finished in 1622 when the cult had begun to acquire fame. A grander building in *tezontle* and limestone was erected between 1695 and 1709 by Pedro de Arrieta. However, an undated plan signed by José Durán may represent a first or an alternative project. In it the church has a central plan, as is appropriate for a sanctuary, and a tower at each corner. What was built by Arrieta and still exists is a Latin cross with a nave, side aisles, and a dome over the crossing—a building that was basically rectangular and retained the four towers. The considerable protrusion of the apse area, like the decoration of the interior, is due to extensive late-nineteenth-century restoration and remodeling. The facade portal with sober Corinthian columns, a narrative relief, and many angular elements is notable for its projection onto the plaza.

In 1904 the church was elevated to the rank of basilica. Despite repeated restorations, uneven settling of the ground under Arrieta's church provoked fears that it would collapse, and it was closed in 1976. Between 1974 and 1976, a new basilica with a tentlike silhouette was built by Pedro Ramírez Vázquez and his associates to house the image.

*See also* **Architecture: Architecture to 1900.**

BIBLIOGRAPHY

George Kubler, *Art and Architecture in Spain and Portugal and Their American Dominions, 1500 to 1800* (1959); *Álbum del 450 aniversario de las apariciones de Nuestra Señora de Guadalupe* (1981), pp. 284–289.

### *Additional Bibliography*

Cuadriello, Jaime, Carmen de Monserrat Robledo Galván, and Beatriz Berndt León Mariscal. *La Reina de las Américas: Works of Art from the Museum of the Basílica de Guadalupe.* Chicago: Mexican Fine Arts Center Museum, 1996.

CLARA BARGELLINI

## GUADALUPE, CONVENIO DE.

Convenio de Guadalupe (11 March 1844). Early in March 1844 José Rafael Carrera forced the resignation of a Guatemalan government dominated by the conservative elite of the capital. An army uprising followed, undoubtedly engineered by Carrera himself. Carrera and the army quickly agreed to the Convenio of Guadalupe, which barred the clergy from political office and dissolved the assembly, its authority to be replaced by a popularly elected council of state with one native representative from each department—a sharp break with earlier legislatures, which had been dominated by Guatemala City members. It also provided for clear executive authority over the legislative branch and expanded the authority of the military.

While the Convenio de Guadalupe immediately favored the liberals by checking the conservative elite of Guatemala City, its real significance was the increase of military power over civil government and the reduction of legislative and judicial power. The assembly obediently ratified the *convenio* on 13 March and dissolved itself on the next day, thus laying the foundation for Rafael Carrera to take over the presidency in December 1844 and reinforcing a pattern of military superiority over the civil government that has characterized Guatemalan government ever since.

*See also* **Guatemala.**

BIBLIOGRAPHY

*Gaceta oficial* (Guatemala City), 18 March 1844.

Ralph Lee Woodward, Jr., *Rafael Carrera and the Emergence of the Republic of Guatemala, 1821–1871* (1993).

### *Additional Bibliography*

Pompejano, Daniele. *La crisis del antiguo régimen en Guatemala (1839–1871).* Guatemala: Editorial Universitaria, Universidad de San Carlos de Guatemala, 1997.

RALPH LEE WOODWARD JR.

## GUADALUPE, VIRGIN OF.

Virgin of Guadalupe, preeminent devotion of Mexico, also popular throughout Latin America. The Virgin Mary is said to have appeared to Juan Diego, a Nahua peasant, in December 1531, at Tepeyac, a hill north of Mexico City. The Virgin commanded the building of a church on the site. When the bishop-elect of Mexico, Juan de Zumárraga, asked for a sign, she directed Juan Diego to gather roses from the top of the hill and take them in his mantle (*tilma*) to the bishop-elect. When Juan Diego opened the mantle before Zumárraga, the Virgin's image was imprinted on it. It is popularly believed to be the same image venerated today at the basilica of Guadalupe.

The historical substratum for the apparition account is weak. Although a chapel of ease (*ermita*), without a resident priest, existed at Tepeyac under the name Guadalupe as early as 1556, there is no incontrovertible evidence of the apparitions before 1648, when the story was first popularized by Miguel Sánchez. He made only the vaguest references to his sources. In 1649 Luis Lasso de la Vega published a Nahuatl account, now usually called the *Nican mopohua*. This is frequently accepted as the authentic account, in part because its authorship has been attributed to the noted native scholar Antonio Valeriano. This attribution is demonstrably mistaken. Most likely the story was a cult legend dating from the early seventeenth century, perhaps an offshoot of the story of the Virgin of Remedios, that was embellished and popularized by Sánchez. Other than the name, the Mexican Guadalupe has no connection with the Guadalupe of Estremadura. Similarly, the existence of a pre-Hispanic native devotion at Tepeyac is questionable, and there was no conscious substitution of the Virgin of Guadalupe for a native deity.

In addition to its religious significance, the image and cult of Guadalupe have had a profound social, cultural, and political impact on Mexico. In the period from 1648 until 1736, the devotion was confined to the criollos of New Spain, who viewed it as a sign of special divine favor. After the success attributed to the Virgin of Guadalupe in stopping an epidemic in 1736–1737, the cult spread to other parts of the Spanish Empire and was granted a proper feast by the papacy (1754). It also grew in popularity among the Indians, partly as the result of a deliberate evangelization by the church. Eventually, it became the only devotion that transcended regional boundaries and racial differences. Guadalupe has been viewed as a symbol of liberation (as in its use by Miguel Hidalgo y Costilla and Emiliano Zapata) and of submission (as by some preachers of the eighteenth and nineteenth centuries). It was also closely entwined with criollo consciousness in the colonial period and Mexican nationalism in the independence period. "Mexico was born at Tepeyac" is how it is often phrased. The Virgin of Guadalupe was proclaimed patroness of all Latin America in 1910 and of the Philippines in 1935. In 1945 Pope Pius XII called her the Queen of Mexico and Empress of the Americas.

*See also* **Catholic Church: The Colonial Period; O'Gorman, Edmundo.**

BIBLIOGRAPHY

Miguel Sánchez, *Imagen de la Virgen Maria, Madre de Dios de Guadalupe* (1648).

Jacques Lafaye, *Quetzalcoatl and Guadalupe: The Formation of Mexican National Consciousness 1531–1813,* translated by Benjamin Keen (1976).

Primo Feliciano Valázquez, *La aparición de Santa María de Guadalupe* (1931, 1981).

Ernesto De La Torre Villar and Ramiro Navarro De Anda, eds., *Testimonios históricos guadalupanos* (1982).

Ernest J. Burrus, S.J., *The Basic Bibliography of the Guadalupan Apparitions (1531–1723)* (1983).

William B. Taylor, "The Virgin of Guadalupe: An Inquiry into the Social History of Marian Devotion," *American Ethnologist* 14 (1987): 9–33.

Stafford Poole, C.M., *Our Lady of Guadalupe: The Origins and Sources of a Mexican National Symbol, 1531–1797* (1994).

*Additional Bibliography*

Brading, David A. *Mexican Phoenix: Our Lady of Guadalupe: Image and Tradition Across Five Centuries.* New York: Cambridge University Press, 2001.

Sousa, Lisa, Stafford Poole, and James Lockhart, eds. *The Story of Guadalupe: Luis Laso de la Vega's Huei tlamahuiçoltica of 1649.* Stanford: Stanford University Press; Los Angeles: UCLA Latin American Center Publications, 1998.

Poole, Stafford. *The Guadalupan Controversies in Mexico.* Stanford: Stanford University Press, 2006.

Zarebska, Carla, and Alejandro Gómez de Tuddo. *Guadalupe.* Oaxaca: J. Dalevuelta, 2002.

STAFFORD POOLE, C.M.

**GUADALUPE HIDALGO, TREATY OF (1848).** Treaty of Guadalupe Hidalgo (1848), the agreement that ended the war between the United States and Mexico. Signed on 2 February and entered into force on 30 May, it transferred to the United States more than half of Mexico's national territory, over 500,000 square miles, including the present states of California, Nevada, Arizona, New Mexico, and Colorado, in return for an indemnity payment of $15 million to compensate for losses inflicted on Mexicans by the Americans during the war. In Article V, the treaty established the Rio Grande as the boundary between the two countries. Articles VIII and IX promised protection of the civil and property rights of former Mexican citizens within the newly acquired territories. Article X, which specifically guaranteed the protection of land grants, was deleted by the U.S. Congress. Article XI provided guarantees that the U.S. government would police its side of the border to prevent Indian raids on Mexican settlements. Article XXI provided, for the first time in any treaty signed by the United States, for compulsory arbitration of future disputes between the two countries.

Mexican and Chicano scholars generally agree that the United States has violated most of the provisions dealing with civil rights and land. Some contemporary Southwestern American Indian tribes, such as the Hopis and Papagos, however, regard the treaty as a document that can be interpreted to protect them.

*See also* **Boundary Disputes: Overview; Mexico, Wars and Revolutions: Mexican-American War; Rio Grande; United States-Latin American Relations.**

BIBLIOGRAPHY

José María Roa Barcena, *Recuerdos de la invasión norteamericana, 1846–1848* (1883; repr. 1947).

David M. Pletcher, *The Diplomacy of Annexation: Texas, Oregon, and the Mexican War* (1973).

Richard Griswold Del Castillo, *The Treaty of Guadalupe Hidalgo: A Legacy of Conflict* (1990).

RICHARD GRISWOLD DEL CASTILLO

**GUADALUPES, LOS.** Los Guadalupes, one of the first secret political societies established in New Spain. (The other was the Sociedad De Caballeros Racionales.) Los Guadalupes was founded in Mexico City in 1811 by a group of autonomists and persons disaffected with the colonial regime who were convinced that aiding the insurgent movement by establishing an alternative organ of government was the best way to foster their interests. They were devoted to the Virgin of Guadalupe, whose image the insurgents placed on their banner. The society first aided the insurgents Ignacio Rayón and later José María Morelos, with whom they corresponded and to whom they sent information, arms, money, men, and a press. Based on a small group of leaders, and composed at the beginning of lawyers united by professional ties, friendship, and *Compadrazgo* (tie between a godfather and a father), the society expanded to include nobles, property owners, clergymen, merchants, several women, and even an Indian official. Besides aiding the insurgents, the Guadalupes took advantage of opportunities for political action within the system. Thus, they participated in the constitutional elections of 1812–1813, in which they joined forces with other autonomists to secure the victory of their candidates. The society's existence was discovered by the authorities in 1814, and several of its members were prosecuted and exiled. Shortly thereafter, the society ceased to function, but many of its former members continued their efforts to promote Mexican autonomy.

*See also* **Mexico City; New Spain, Colonization of the Northern Frontier.**

BIBLIOGRAPHY

Wilbert H. Timmons, "Los Guadalupes," in *Hispanic American Historical Review* 30 (Nov. 1950): 453–479.

Ernesto De La Torre Villar, *Los Guadalupes y la independencia, con una selección de documentos inéditos* (1985).

Virginia Guedea, *En busca de un gobierno alterno: Los Guadalupes de México* (1992).

*Additional Bibliography*

Archer, Christon I. *The Birth of Modern Mexico, 1780–1824.* Wilmington, DE: Scholarly Resources Inc., 2003.

VIRGINIA GUEDEA

**GUADELOUPE.** *See* **Martinique and Guadeloupe.**

**GUALE.** Guale, Spanish province in the state of Georgia. The Guales were a semiagricultural Muskogean people, organized politically into paired chiefdoms, who lived in southeastern North America. At the time of their first contact with Europeans, their territory stretched from Saint Andrews Sound to Edisto Island on the coast, and their language was understood for 200 leagues inland. Sapelo Sound, which may hold the site of Lucas Vásquez De Ayllón's 1526 settlement of San Miguel de Gualdape, was an area of dense Guale population.

Pedro Menéndez De Avilés visited the "Island of Guale" (Saint Catherines Island) in 1566 and was received as a rainmaker, but early Jesuit and Franciscan efforts at conversion were hindered by the demands of the Spanish garrison at Santa Elena on Parris Island and competition from French corsair traders. The Guale Rebellion of 1597, with its five Franciscan martyrs, was a civil war between Spanish and French factions that ended in the conquest by Spain of coastal Guale and its rebirth as a mission province.

In the seventeenth century the Christian towns of Guale served the presidio of Saint Augustine as buffer zone, breadbasket, and labor enclave. The extent of population loss in the province due to disease and fugitivism was concealed by an influx of Yamasees, whom the Guales sent to do their labor service. In the 1680s the trade rivalry of Charleston and assaults by pirates and by Indians with English firearms caused the province to shrink: the northern border retreated from Saint Catherines Island to Sapelo, then to Amelia. After Amelia Island was overrun by the forces of Colonel James Moore of Carolina in 1702, the last of the Guales fled to the presidio. Their few descendants were evacuated to Cuba in 1763, under the terms that ended the Seven Years' War.

*See also* **Seven Years' War.**


BIBLIOGRAPHY

John Tate Lanning, *The Spanish Missions of Georgia* (1935).

Maynard J. Geiger, *The Franciscan Conquest of Florida (1573–1618)* (1937).

Grant D. Jones, "The Ethnohistory of the Guale Coast Through 1684," *in* David H. Thomas et al., *The Anthropology of St. Catherines Island: (1) Natural and Cultural History, Anthropological Papers of the American Museum of Natural History,* vol. 55, pt. 2 (1978), pp. 178–210, 241–243.

Paul E. Hoffman, *A New Andalusia and a Way to the Orient: The American Southeast During the Sixteenth Century* (1990).

*Additional Bibliography*

McEwan, Bonnie. *Indians of the Greater Southeast: Historical Archaeology and Ethnohistory.* Gainesville: University Press of Florida, 2002.

Worth, John. *The Struggle for the Georgia Coast.* New York: American Museum of Natural History, 1995.


AMY TURNER BUSHNELL

## GUAMAN POMA DE AYALA, FELIPE

(c. 1535–c. 1615). Felipe Guaman Poma de Ayala (*b.* c. 1535; *d.* c. 1615), one of the most polemic and most admired native authors of the colonial period. Guaman Poma wrote *Primer nueva corónica y buen gobierno* (c. 1615), a long, illustrated history (1,188 pages with 398 pen-and-ink drawings) of ancient Andean times, Inca rule, and Spanish rule. The book was discovered in 1908 in the Royal Danish Library in Copenhagen and was first published in 1936. An abridged version, *Letter to a King,* translated by Christopher Dilke, appeared in 1978. Anthropologists consider the book a primary source of information on the pre-Columbian Andean world and on the first decades of Spanish colonization. Literary scholars, after ignoring the document for years, now regard it as a symbolic representation in which the author criticizes colonial rule while submitting a plan for "good government" to the Spanish king, Philip III, to whom the chronicle is addressed. Traditionally, historians have pointed out inaccuracies in Guaman Poma's work; however, recent research has explained how and why the author took advantage of information available from native and European sources to present an Andean version of history.

With the exception of what Guaman Poma says about himself in *Primer nueva corónica,* there is very little documentary evidence about his life. It is believed that he was born about 1535 in San Cristóbal de Suntunto (a small village in what is today the province of Ayacucho in Peru), lived for several years in Cuzco, and later moved (about 1562) to the city of Guamanga, now known as Ayacucho. According to Guaman Poma, his father was an ethnic lord of the Yarovilcas, a group conquered by the Incas and later incorporated into their empire; his mother was the daughter of the powerful Inca ruler Túpac Yupanqui. The historical evidence does not support Guaman Poma's claim to this distinguished lineage.

Educated in the Spanish language and culture, perhaps by missionaries, and well versed in Quechua, his native tongue, Guaman Poma became an interpreter in the campaigns against idol worship in the Andes (ca. 1568–1571). It is very probable that he also served as interpreter in the Third Council of Lima (1583–1584). In this regard, it has been speculated that it was through the library of the church inspector Cristóbal de Albornoz, as well as through books belonging to missionaries, that Guaman Poma became familiar with the writings of key religious, historical, and juridical authors and with engravings and illustrations of saints and biblical themes. These books and iconography, together with the Andean oral tradition and Guaman Poma's own experiences, became the sources of *Primer nueva corónica*.

Legal documents show that Guaman Poma served again as interpreter (1594) and, in addition, was the witness in a land claim presented by native Andeans (1595). He was later expelled from Guamanga (1600) and San Cristóbal de Suntunto (1611) for his defense of the native population and for claiming ancestral lands. Guaman Poma returned to Lima in 1601, to complain about the poor treatment that he and other Indians were receiving from colonial administrators, and in 1613, to present the manuscript of *Primer nueva corónica* to the viceroy. Even though he failed in this attempt, in a letter (Guamanga, 14 February 1615) to Philip III he states that his chronicle has been completed. After this date we lose all track of him.

Guaman Poma's encyclopedic work is the living and angry testimony of how a native Andean experienced and interpreted the cultural clash brought about by the Conquest and colonization. *Primer nueva corónica* exhibits the talents of an indigenous historian who took up the pen, thus bringing together European and Andean traditions, Spanish and Quechua, writing and painting, to praise the past, condemn colonial administrators, and demand a better society for his people.

BIBLIOGRAPHY

John V. Murra, "Guaman Poma de Ayala: A Seventeenth-Century Indian's Account of Andean Civilization," in *Natural History* 70 (1961): 25–63.

Franklin Pease, "Prólogo," in Felipe Guaman Poma De Ayala, *Nueva corónica y buen gobierno* (1980).

Raquel Chang-Rodríguez, *La apropiación del signo: Tres cronistas indígenas del Perú* (1988).

Mercedes López Baralt, *Icono y conquista: Guaman Poma de Ayala* (1988).

Roger A. Zapata, *Guaman Poma: Indigenismo y estética de la dependencia en la cultura peruana* (1989).

Rolena Adorno et al., *Guaman Poma de Ayala: The Colonial Art of an Andean Author* (1992).

### *Additional Bibliography*

Adorno, Rolena. *Guáman Poma: Writing and Resistance in Colonial Peru.* Austin: University of Texas Press, 2000.

González Vargas, Carlos A., Hugo Rosati, and Francisco Sánchez. *Guaman Poma: Testigo del mundo andino.* Santiago, Chile: LOM Ediciones, 2002.

Karttunen, Frances E. *Between Worlds: Interpreters, Guides, and Survivors.* New Brunswick, NJ: Rutgers University Press, 1994.

RAQUEL CHANG-RODRÍGUEZ

---

**GUANABARA BAY.** Guanabara Bay, Brazil's second-largest bay, located in the state of Rio de Janeiro. Its area is 165 square miles, and it measures 18 miles north to south. When the Portuguese navigator André Gonçalves first entered the bay on what is widely believed to be 1 January 1502, he thought he had discovered the outlet of an immense river, which he named the Rio de Janeiro, after the month of his arrival. The land on the bay's western shore adopted the name when the city of Rio de Janeiro was founded in 1567. Famous for its natural beauty, Guanabara Bay has one of the world's best locations for port facilities. Protection from wind and surf is insured by the small size of its entrance (1,650 yards), the depth of its water, and the surrounding mountains. Since the mid-nineteenth century the bay has held one of the busiest ports of Brazil's central-south coast. At the beginning of the 1990s it was a focal point for ecological campaigns to detoxify its polluted waters.

In January 2000 a pipeline run by the state oil giant Petrobras broke, spewing more than a million gallons of crude oil into the bay and coating scores of marine birds, fish, and other animals. This oil spill, which initially had been reported as minor, turned out to be the bay's second-biggest environmental disaster until 2001.

*See also* **Brazil, Geography; Rio de Janeiro (City).**

BIBLIOGRAPHY

*Additional Bibliography*

Hetzel, Bia, Silvia Negreiros, and Hugo Moss. *Guanabara Bay.* Río de Janeiro: Manati, 2000.

Negreiros, José A., and Jack Liebof. *Treze mil luas sobre a Guanabara.* Rio de Janeiro: Editora Record, 1995.

Sedrez, Lise Fernanda. *"The Bay of All Beauties": State and Environment in Guanabara Bay, Rio de Janeiro, Brazil, 1875–1975.* Stanford, CA: Stanford University, 2004.

SUEANN CAULFIELD

**GUANABARA STATE.** When Brazil's capital was transferred from the city of Rio de Janeiro to Brasília in 1960, the old municipal region that had included the capital of colonial Brazil (1763–1808), the seat of the Portuguese crown (1808–1822), the Brazilian Empire (1822–1889), and the capital of the Federal Republic (1889–1960) became the nation's smallest state and was given the name Guanabara. The creation of Guanabara State, and the transfer of the capital had been determined by the constitutions of 1891, 1934, and 1946.

Soon after these measures were implemented, however, it became clear that both Guanabara State and neighboring Rio de Janeiro were at a political and economic disadvantage compared with the bigger, more economically diverse Minas Gerais and São Paulo. Lack of capital and infrastructure in Rio de Janeiro and of natural resources in Guanabara, which depended upon its neighbor for water and electricity, together with the migration of urban industries from Guanabara to Rio de Janeiro, convinced most of the politicians of both states, including their two governors, that there should be a merger. In 1975 the national Congress decided that the two states would join, and named the new state Rio de Janeiro. The area that had been Guanabara State became the municipal district of Rio de Janeiro.

*See also* **Brasília; Brazil: Since 1889; Brazil, Constitutions; Brazil, Geography.**

BIBLIOGRAPHY

*Fatos e Fotos,* May 2, 1967, pp. 14–16; Feb. 12, 1970, pp. 4–7; June 10, 1974, pp. 14–17; *Grande enciclopedia Larousse* (1978).

*Additional Bibliography*

Dulles, John F. *Carlos Lacerda, Brazilian Crusader.* Austin: University of Texas Press, 1991–1996.

Motta, Marly Silva da. *Saudades da Guanabara.* Rio de Janeiro: Editora FGV, 2000.

SUEANN CAULFIELD

**GUANACASTE.** Guanacaste, the northwesternmost province of Costa Rica, bordering Nicaragua. Today it includes both the Nicoya Peninsula and the area from the volcanic mountain chain (Cordillera de Guanacaste) down to the Tempisque River basin. In colonial times Guanacaste referred only to the Tempisque plains or the settlement of Liberia, today the provincial capital but barely a collection of huts as late as the early nineteenth century.

Prior to independence both Nicoya and Costa Rica had been politically dependent upon Nicaragua, with the Costa Rican jurisdiction extending to just south of Liberia on the plain and the Partido de Nicoya controlling both the peninsula and the northern plains. During the Cortes of Cádiz era (1812–1814) all of Nicoya was added to Costa Rica for electoral purposes to reach the minimum figure of 60,000 inhabitants needed to elect one deputy. In a Cabildo Abierto of 25 July 1824, Nicoya allegedly chose to remain with Costa Rica rather than Nicaragua, a choice the Central American Federation provisionally approved on 9 December 1825. Nicaragua and Costa Rica argued repeatedly over this issue in a number of agreements signed during the nineteenth century, especially the Cañas-Jerez Treaty of 15 April 1858. This was upheld, from the Costa Rican point of view, by the arbitration of U.S. president Grover Cleveland in 1888. The entire province was briefly renamed Moracia (1854–1860), in honor of President Juan Rafael Mora's defeat of William Walker in Nicaragua.

Guanacaste was traditionally ruled by absentee landlords from Nicaragua and highland Costa Rica. Until the early twentieth century most settlement was in the Indian towns of Nicoya and Santa Cruz on the Nicoya Peninsula, with open-range cattle ranches on the plains. In the early twentieth century a substantial gold mining region opened up in the mountains at the southern end of the province, and by mid-century major improvements in cattle breeding and pasture were rapidly modernizing the plains areas. Some of the most violent and bitter agrarian conflicts in Costa Rican history came out of these processes.

Since the 1960s Guanacaste has developed a mechanized farming economy in rice, corn, and beans. It has also benefited from a large-scale tourist industry based on the province's beaches and national parks. However, much of the laboring population has been forced to migrate in search of better opportunities in the Central Valley region and farm work along the Atlantic and southern Pacific coasts.

*See also* **Costa Rica.**

BIBLIOGRAPHY

On Guanacaste, see Lowell Gudmundson, *Hacendados, precaristas y políticos: La ganadería y el latifundismo guanacasteco, 1800–1950* (1980).

Marc Edelman, *The Logic of the Latifundio* (1993). On boundaries, see Luis Fernando Sibaja Chacón, *Nuestro limite con nicaragua* (1974). For firsthand descriptions, see Carlos Meléndez Chaverri, ed., *Viajeros por Guanacaste* (1974).

*Additional Bibliography*

Cabrera, Roberto. *Santa Cruz, Guanacaste: Una aproximación a la historia y la cultura popular.* San José, Costa Rica: Ediciones Guayacán, 1989.

Monge-Nájera, Julián. *Historia natural de Guanacaste.* San José, Costa Rica: Editorial Universidad Estatal a Distancia, 2004.

LOWELL GUDMUNDSON

**GUANACO.** *See* **Llama.**

**GUANAJUATO.** Guanajuato, population 78,364 (2005), a city in Mexico best known as the leading producer of silver in New Spain and the world in the second half of the eighteenth century. Guanajuato was founded as a small mining camp in the northern Bajío about 1554. Alexander von Humboldt, a German traveler who visited the city in 1803, deemed the veins in Guanajuato (La Valenciana) to be the richest in the world. He also reported an estimated "5,000 miners and workmen" were occupied with mining operations there.

Guanajuato was not surrounded by primordial indigenous communities, but by only a few settler pueblos of Otomí and Tarascans. Nevertheless, it represented an attractive lure to Indians seeking work. Owing to both immigration and natural increase, its population jumped from 156,140 to 397,924 between 1742 and 1793. Compared to the central highlands, the region was much more urban and ethnically mixed, features that created a considerable internal market for the agricultural and manufactured goods of the Bajío.

Resistance to governmental controls and Jesuit expulsion prompted uprisings in Guanajuato in the 1760s. But it was the Hidalgo revolt of 1810 that endowed Guanajuato with even greater notoriety. Home to some three hundred peninsular-born Spaniards and the silver jewel in the crown, the city represented a prize conquest for the insurgents, who took it by storm in September of that year. Its capture was achieved largely through the defeat of the city's elite at the municipal granary, or *alhóndiga,* where many Spaniards sought refuge. The memory of bloody independence pursuits at Guanajuato stayed with Mexico's establishment for a long time afterward. Mining activity picked up again at the end of the nineteenth century and, along with agriculture and stockraising, sustains Guanajuato today. Investment and the designation of the city's colonial mines and historic center in 1988 by UNESCO as a World Heritage site has spurred tourism. Remittances from migrants in the United States are important to the state's economy.

Guanajuato is the administrative center for state government, and in recent years the National Action Party (PAN) has produced several governors, including former president Vicente Fox Quesada. The city is also the base for the University of Guanajuato.

*See also* **Mexico, Political Parties: National Action Party (PAN); Mining: Colonial Spanish America; New Spain, Colonization of the Northern Frontier.**

BIBLIOGRAPHY

Eric R. Wolf, "The Mexican Bajío in the Eighteenth Century," in *Synoptic Studies of Mexican Culture,* no. 17, edited by Robert Wauchope (1957), pp. 177–198.

Hugh M. Hamill, Jr., *The Hidalgo Revolt* (1966), pp. 51–52, 91–93, 124, 137–141, 149.

D. A. Brading, *Miners and Merchants in Bourbon Mexico, 1763–1810* (1971), pp. 223–339.

Alexander Von Humboldt, *Political Essay on the Kingdom of New Spain,* translated by John Black and edited by Mary Maples Dunn (1972), pp. 151–156.

*Additional Bibliography*

Blanco, Mónica, Alma Parra, and Ethelia Ruiz Medrano. *Breve historia de Guanajuato.* México, D.F.: Colegio de México, Fondo de Cultura Económica, 2000.

Chowning, Margaret. *Rebellious Nuns: The Troubled History of a Mexican Convent, 1752–1863.* New York: Oxford University Press, 2006.

Durand, Jorge, and Douglas S. Massey. *Crossing the Border: Research from the Mexican Migration Project.* New York: Russell Sage Foundation, 2004.

Meyer Cosío, Francisco Javier. *La minería en Guanajuato: Denuncios, minas y empresas (1892–1913).* Guanajuato, Mexico: Universidad de Guanajuato, 1998.

Serrano Espinoza, Luis Antonio, and Juan Carlos Cornejo Muñoz. *De la plata, fantasías: La arquitectura del siglo XVIII en la ciudad de Guanajuato.* México, D.F.: Instituto Nacional de Antropología e Historia, 1998.

Serrano Ortega, José Antonio. *Jerarquía territorial y transición política: Guanajuato, 1790 1836.* Zamora, Mexico: El Colegio de Michoacán, 2001.

STEPHANIE WOOD

**GUANGALA.** Guangala, an archaeological culture or ceramic phase defined for the southwest coast of Ecuador and dated from 100 BCE to 800 CE. First identified at the village of Guangala by G. H. S. Bushnell, Guangala cultural remains are distributed along the coast of Guayas Province from Puná Island north to southern Manabí Province; in the east the territorial limits of Guangala are unknown, but sites do not extend as far as the Guayas River. The Guangala way of life has been reconstructed from artifacts, human burials, and other remains excavated from a few sites on and near the Santa Elena Peninsula, a semiarid zone considered to have less agricultural potential than other portions of Ecuador.

Guangala ceramics are known primarily from artifacts without provenience. The style represents one of several regional variants that developed out of the preceding, geographically widespread Chorrera tradition. The Guangala style is characterized by innovative ceramic features which suggest that there was significant evolution also in other aspects of Guangala society and economy. Guangala society has been interpreted as less differentiated and hierarchical than some of the neighboring ethnic groups in the Regional Developmental period.

The earliest Guangala pottery is found in small sites scattered extensively along small rivers over the entire region—evidence of a large and expanding population. By middle Guangala times, people were numerous and lived in large and small permanent villages as well as in dispersed homesteads. One large site on the Bay of Santa Elena had "mounds" which, according to the excavator, may have supported houses. Some communities maintained water catchment structures. Many sites were located adjacent to beaches, river mouths, and mangrove estuaries, where people practiced a mixed economy of farming, fishing, gathering, hunting, craft production, and trade for exotic raw materials. Smaller, "rural" sites were often oriented to small parcels of fertile river bottom land, where farmers cultivated cotton, corn, squash, sweet potatoes, beans, peppers, and fruit. Some sites show domestic craft specialization such as the production of grinding stones or shell beads.

The Guangala people buried their dead, legs extended, in tombs beneath their habitation sites and accompanied by offerings, some of which were preserved: ceramic vessels, obsidian blades, lime containers made of shell (used during coca leaf chewing rituals), fishhooks, beads and ornaments, stone tools, sets of three stones, or three shark teeth, and copper artifacts.

The largest Guangala sites, presumably once occupied by the more powerful local shamans who used a variety of exotic and luxury goods, were located inland in the more well-watered valleys where the agricultural potential is high even today. These sites, several of which have been heavily looted, have produced the finest Guangala pottery and ceramic figurines. Artifacts such as clay seats, associated with shamanistic power, and elaborate figurines and musical instruments suggest that the people at these sites were socially complex and had elaborate rituals. Guangala material culture shows elegant pottery types, handsome figurines, whistles and ocarinas, and personal ornaments, all suggestive of the complexity of social life.

The Guangala people practiced local economic specialties such as fishing at coastal locations, agriculture at inland locations, manufacture of goods such as copper needles and fishhooks and shell artifacts. They no doubt engaged in both local and long-distance exchange, the latter perhaps involving sea voyaging by elites which brought into the region obsidian (volcanic glass for stone tool making), serpentine, rock crystal, and copper, possibly in exchange for export commodities like mother-of-pearl and *Spondylus*—much appreciated outside of the region. Exotic imports found their way into most Guangala sites, indicating that political leaders circulated rather than concentrated the wealth.

*See also* **Bahia; Chorrera; Jama-Coaque.**

BIBLIOGRAPHY

G. H. S. Bushnell, *The Archaeology of the Santa Elena Peninsula in South-West Ecuador* (1951).

Emilio Estrada, *Prehistoria de Manabí* (1957).

Betty J. Meggers, *Ecuador* (1966).

Allison C. Paulsen, "Patterns of Maritime Trade Between South Coastal Ecuador and Western Mesoamerica, 1500 B.C.–A.D. 600," in *The Sea in the Pre-Columbian World,* edited by Elizabeth B. Benson (1974), pp. 141–166.

Maria Ann Masucci, *Ceramic Change in the Guangala Phase, Southwest Ecuador: A Typology and Chronology* (Ph.D. diss., Southern Methodist University, 1992).

Karen E. Stothert, *Un sitio de Guangala Temprano en el suroeste del Ecuador* (Guayaquil, 1993).

*Additional Bibliography*

Cummins, Thomas B.F., Julio Burgos Cabrera, and Carlos Mora Hoyos. *Huellas del pasado: Los sellos de jama-coaque.* Quito: Museos del Banco Central del Ecuador, 1996.

Currie, Elizabeth J. *Prehistory of the Southern Manabí Coast, Ecuador: López Viejo.* Oxford: Tempvs Reparatvm, 1995.

Reitz, Elizabeth Jean, and Maria A. Masucci. *Guangala Fishers and Farmers: A Case Study of Animal Use at El Azúcar, Southwestern Ecuador.* Pittsburgh: University of Pittsburgh, Department of Anthropology; Quito: Libri Mundi, 2004.

KAREN E. STOTHERT

**GUANO INDUSTRY.** Guano, a superb natural fertilizer, was the dominant export of nineteenth-century Peru; the guano industry constitutes a classic example of a Latin American boom-and-bust export experience. Guano is the dried excrement of seabirds (from Quechua, *huanu,* "dung"). On small islands astride the southern Peruvian coast, favorable meteorological conditions of the Humboldt Current led, over the centuries, to unparalleled accumulations of unleached guano—sometimes hundreds of feet thick in the Chincha Islands. Rich in nitrogen and phosphates, guano was used extensively by pre-Columbian agriculturalists but sparingly by Spanish colonists. In the early 1840s, guano suddenly became an international export commodity, as Europe, undergoing an agricultural revolution, discovered its powerful chemical, productive, and economic properties.

Thus guano emerged, between 1841 and 1879, as Peru's critical export, in one of the busiest commodity trades of the nineteenth-century world. Peru entered its legendary Age of Guano. Over four decades, roughly 11.5 million tons of bird manure made its way to Britain, France, the southern United States, and a host of minor markets; at prices fluctuating between $25 and $50 a ton, the aggregate market value of the trade reached about $750 million. Peru's long-suffering state swiftly grasped the opportunity, declaring a national monopoly over the fertilizer in 1841, and deflecting over the years the inevitable foreign pressures to liberalize the guano trade. Innovatively led by General Ramón Castilla, Peru commercialized its deposits mainly through profit-sharing consignment sales, dominated during the initial two decades by the British firm of Antony Gibbs and Sons. By the 1860s, the state had turned to marketing contracts with emerging national merchants, Hijos del País (native sons) such as Manuel Pardo. In the 1870s this approach was replaced with a direct-sales policy linked to foreign-debt servicing and exemplified by the controversial Dreyfus Contract of 1869, signed by the government of Peru and the French company of Dreyfus Brothers. If its international marketing, finance, and politics proved complex, extraction of guano remained a primitive if oppressive affair. Modest numbers of convicts, coolies, and other hapless laborers funneled the unprocessed and toxic dung into the bowels of awaiting ships.

Abroad, guano use helped boost productivity of crops such as turnips, grains, and tobacco; within Peru, the staggering revenue injections revitalized national finance and a sagging postcolonial economy and polity in Lima. Overall, the Peruvian state deftly managed to capture an impressive 60 percent of final sales, or nearly $500 million. The boom, climaxing in the 1860s with annual sales of over $20 million, brought coastal Peru squarely into the world economy.

Guano, and the country's relatively easy access to London bond markets, activated a new commercial-entrepreneurial class, centered around the dramatic expansion of public finance and state activities (real estate spending grew fivefold between 1850 and 1870). In politics, such wealth allowed Peru finally to consolidate its shaky caudillo-style central state and smooth over political conflicts among the elite, eventually spawning the reformist politics of the Partido Civil, which superseded military rule in 1872. The social impact of guano was mixed; benefits were largely confined to connected *Limeño* families while popular groups (such as artisans) suffered the effects of intensified manufactured imports, inflation, and political neglect.

The singular economic fact is that Peru's guano industry led to little sustained, diversified, or nationwide development. In many respects, mounting dependence on bird dung heightened the vulnerability of the Peruvian economy. Apart from the urban commercial bonanza, a burgeoning banking system in the 1860s, and rising modern coastal sugar and cotton plantations in the 1870s, guano worked slowly on the private sector and on the economy and peoples of Peru's vast Andean interior. By the 1860s, official Peru, with its reduced tax base, resorted to ever larger issues on European capital markets. In part, this borrowing was to realize the schemes of visionary politicians who grasped the impending problems of guano exhaustion and the country's low level of national integration. For example, a mammoth railroad construction project, directed by the North American Henry Meiggs, absorbed fully one-fifth of all guano profits. After its frenetic start in the mid-1860s, Peru's national rail network lay largely uncompleted. Meanwhile, by 1875 Peru's foreign debt had soared to £35 million by far Latin America's largest on record.

As quickly as it appeared, the Age of Guano evaporated in the mid-1870s. The collapse struck all facets of a Peruvian economy and polity built upon the so-called fictitious prosperity. In a few short years, quality reserves dwindled, substitution and nitrates competition intensified, and European lenders retrenched. The result was Peru's world-shattering default on its foreign debt in 1876 and a broad political and social crisis. In the coup de grace of 1879, Peru and Chile went to war for control of the world's next natural fertilizer, the Atacama Desert nitrates. Peru's smashing defeat in the War of the Pacific, which exposed the frailty of her national development, ended in the loss of assets and accomplishments remaining from the export era. Through planning and conservation, the Peruvian government restarted the guano industry for domestic needs in the twentieth century. However, in the 1960s, the Peruvian government allowed fishing companies to remove the birds, which caused their population to fall again. Peru today retains a modest guano industry for local needs. Also, a small government agency cares for the remaining guano birds, which the state promotes as an ecotourism site.

Economic historians have long pondered the meaning of Peru's experience with guano. While all agree it was a lost opportunity for development, explanations widely differ. Traditionally, guano is seen as an adverse enclave economy. In this view, export-sector revenues and demand filtered abroad to foreign capitalists, merchants, and luxury imports, leaving little impulse for the backward domestic economy. The quantitative studies of Shane Hunt overturned this view by showing how guano produced significant demand effects for the Peruvian economy and a potential for competent public investment. However, cost-price pressures still led to a dangerously overspecialized and productively stagnant rentier economy. Some historians stress, in the absence of wide-ranging social reforms, the limited ability of guano to strengthen national markets and promote cogent national consciousness among national elites; guano exemplifies a tragic "dependency" experience. Other historians explore Peru's historical dynamics of integration with the world economy, which display a paradoxical blend of import liberalism and autocratic statism that stifled prospects for growth. Whatever the cause, the guano age left a legacy of superficial urban modernization and fragmented Andean society—persisting dilemmas for modern Peru.

*See also* **Agriculture; Foreign Trade.**

BIBLIOGRAPHY

Jonathan V. Levin, *The Export Economies: Their Patterns of Development in Historical Perspective* (1960), esp. ch. 2.

Heraclio Bonilla, *Guano y burguesía en el Perú* (1974).

W. M. Mathew, *The House of Gibbs and the Peruvian Guano Monopoly* (1981).

Shane J. Hunt, "Growth and Guano in Nineteenth-Century Peru," in *The Latin American Economies: Growth and the Export Sector, 1830–1930,* edited by Roberto Cortés and Shane J. Hunt (1985), pp. 255–319.

Alfonso W. Quiróz, *La deuda defraudada: Consolidación de 1850 y dominio económico en el Perú* (1987).

Paul Gootenberg, *Between Silver and Guano: Commercial Policy and the State in Postindependence Peru* (1989) and *Imagining Development: Economic Ideas in Peru's Fictitious Prosperity of Guano, 1840–1880* (1993).

*Additional Bibliography*

Cushman, Gregory Todd. "The Lords of Guano: Science and the Management of Peru's Marine Environment, 1800–1973." Ph.D. diss., University of Texas, 2003.

Raimondi, Antonio. *Informes y polémicas sobre el guano y el salitre (Perú, 1854–1877).* Edited by Luis Felipe Villacorta O. Lima: Fondo Editorial, Universidad Nacional Mayor de San Marcos, 2003.

PAUL GOOTENBERG

**GUANTÁNAMO BAY.** Guantánamo Bay is an inlet on the extreme southeast coast of Cuba. The bay makes an excellent harbor because it is sheltered from storms, has deep waters, and lies near the Windward Passage. After the U.S. Navy found it useful in the Spanish-American War (1898), the U.S. government decided to acquire the bay for a naval base. The right to do so was provided for in the Platt Amendment, which was appended to the Cuban constitution of 1901 and incorporated in a treaty between the United States and Cuba on 22 May 1903. On 2 July 1903, the United States leased the bay and its outer shoreline for $2,000 annually. Although the United States abrogated the Platt Amendment in 1934, it retained the right to the naval base in Guantánamo Bay. After coming to power in 1959, Fidel Castro unsuccessfully attempted to force the United States from the facility but continued to permit Cuban nationals to work for the U.S. Navy.

Guantánamo Bay has received considerable attention since 2002, when the U.S. government began to hold alleged terrorists there. Human rights groups and others have sharply criticized the Guantánamo detention camps because of the limited access to judicial review offered to detainees and because of poor conditions in the camp. Some groups have alleged that prisoners have been mistreated.

*See also* **Castro Ruz, Fidel; Cuba, Geography; Platt Amendment; Spanish-American War.**

BIBLIOGRAPHY

Emilio Roig De Leuchsenring, *Historia de la Enmienda Platt,* 2 vols. (1935).

David F. Healy, *The United States in Cuba, 1898–1902: Generals, Politicians, and the Search for Policy* (1963).

Gary L. Maris, "International Law and Guantánamo," *Journal of Politics* 29 (1967): 261–286.

Walter J. Raymond, "The Feasibility of Rapprochement Between the Republic of Cuba and the United States: The Case of the Guantánamo Naval Base," *Caribbean Quarterly* 21 (1975): 35–46.

*Additional Bibliography*

Butler, Clark. *Guantanamo Bay and the Judicial-Moral Treatment of the Other.* West Lafayette, IN: Purdue University Press, 2007.

Pérez, Louis A. *Cuba and the United States: Ties of Singular Intimacy,* 3rd edition. Athens: University of Georgia Press, 2003.

Reverter, Emma. *Guantánamo: Prisioneros en el limbo de la ilegalidad internacional.* Barcelona: Ediciones Península, 2004.

Saar, Erik, and Viveca Novak. *Inside the Wire: A Military Intelligence Soldier's Eyewitness Account of Life at Guantanamo.* New York: Penguin Press, 2005.

THOMAS M. LEONARD

**GUAPORE.** *See* **Rondônia.**

**GUARANÁ INDUSTRY.** Guaraná industry, the production of a range of products, including a popular Brazilian beverage, based on *guaraná* seeds.

*Guaraná* (hilea) seeds are found on small climbing plants (*Paullinia cupana*) that grow in the Maués Valley in the state of Pará or that grow wild in the tropical rain forest. Amazonian Indians invented the process of turning them into a drink. After removing the almond-like seeds from their black shell, Indians roasted and pounded them into powder. They pressed the powder into chocolate-colored disks or ten- to twelve-inch-long sticks, which they either traded or consumed in drinks. Before drinking it, Indians used the rasplike tongue bone of the *pirarucu* fish to file some of the pressed powder into a cup of hot or cold water.

*Guaraná* grew in popularity among Brazilians in the twentieth century. They believed it cured ailments such as fevers, headaches, and stomach cramps. Now sold in powdered or liquid extract form, it is the base for many other drinks. Maués Valley workers produce *guaraná* powder for bottlers in Rio and São Paulo, where they heavily sweeten and carbonate it before marketing it as a soft drink. Indians also work its paste into ornamental shapes, such as alligators, snakes, or birds, to sell in curio shops. By 1990, 300 tons a year were being produced for internal and external markets, but that was not nearly enough to keep up with the ever-increasing demand, especially from health-food stores in Brazil and abroad.

*See also* **Medicinal Plants.**

BIBLIOGRAPHY

Robert Southey, *History of Brazil* (1822).

John Hemming, *Amazon Frontier* (1987).

*Additional Bibliography*

Stasi, Luiz Claudio di, and Clélia Akiko Hiruma-Lima. *Plantas medicinais na Amazônia e na Mata Atlântica.* São Paulo: Editora UNESP, 2002.

Van Straten, Michael. *Guarana: The Energy Seeds and Herbs of the Amazon Rainforest.* Saffron Walden, England: C.W. Daniel Co., 1994.

CAROLYN JOSTOCK

**GUARANI INDIANS.** The Guarani Indians are a branch of the Tupi-Guarani linguistic family of east-central South America. A semi-sedentary people, they lived south of the Amazon between the Brazilian coast and the Río Paraná and Río Paraguay. Immediately before contact with Spaniards in the early 1500s, they were concentrated in the upper Platine region east of the Paraná and Paraguay rivers, when their population of perhaps 300,000 was divided into fourteen subgroups, or Guarás, of which the Carios of central Paraguay are best known. They moved frequently to find fertile land because they supported themselves by swidden agriculture, cultivating manioc, sweet potatoes, maize, and other crops, which they supplemented with hunting and fishing.

In the 1530s, Guaranis sought an alliance with Spanish expeditionaries to strengthen their efforts against their Payaguá enemies, who dominated the Río Paraguay. Guarani chiefs gave daughters and nieces to Spaniards as wives or concubines, which was their way of establishing a relationship of equals. Spaniards were supposed to reciprocate but looked down on Guaranis. Guaranis labored for Spaniards to obtain the iron tools that revolutionized aboriginal work habits.

Iron tools and new allies, Guaranis thought, would make their lives more secure. When they realized that Spaniards regarded them not as allies but as inferiors, some Guaranis in 1545 rose in revolt. Several other Indian rebellions followed but were unsuccessful, partly because many other Guaranis allied themselves with Spaniards. In 1556, to avoid uncontrolled exploitation of Guaranis, Govenor Domingo Martínez de Irala founded the Paraguayan encomienda, the dominant institution of Guarani labor in the early colony; declining numbers of Guaranis labored for elite colonists to the end of the colonial period.

Unions between Guarani women and Spanish men in the early years initiated a process of ethnogenesis. This fusion of Native Americans and Europeans continued to produce mestizo children and a distinctive Paraguayan culture based on nearly universal understanding of the Guarani language.

Guaranis at the margins of settler-controlled land along the Paranapanema in Guairá (now Parána in Brazil), Itaty (in northern Paraguay), and south of the Tebicuari River in Paraguay and Argentina joined Catholic missions staffed by Jesuits after 1610. Guaranis chose missions in order to obtain steady supplies of Spanish artifacts and food and to gain the security from Brazilian slave raiders that Jesuits promised. From such *encomienda* towns as Yaguarón and Tobatí, Guarani men and women throughout the colonial period escaped the degraded status of "Indian" and moved into Spanish society. Lesser members of Guaranis who left Jesuit missions did the same, but after the departure of Jesuits in 1767 and 1768, mission Guaranis also slowly dispersed into northern Argentina, Uruguay, and western Brazil and became ancestors of the popular classes of those republics. Their descendants in Paraguay form the Guarani-speaking rural population of today.

Guaranis in Paraguay numbered about 40,000 people, or a tenth of the population of the young republic in 1848, when the government of Carlos Antonio López liberated them from their discriminatory status. They officially became Paraguayans. They then were obligated to serve in the military, and their formerly protected lands were available for sale. In the twentieth century, isolated bands of Guaranis provided anthropologists with opportunities to explore their culture, but the lasting influence of the Guaranis lies in the everyday language of Paraguayans. Most of the people of the modern republic are descendants of Guaranis.

In April 2007, eight hundred Guarani from Brazil, Argentina, Paraguay, Uruguay, and Bolivia convened at the Continental Assembly II of the Guarani People in Porto Alegre, Brazil, to discuss proposals for self-determination and general improvements of Guarani living conditions. The overarching concerns of the assembly were the lack of land, non-Indian destruction of the environment, and education and health care that respects Guarani traditions.

*See also* **Guaraní (Language); Indigenous Peoples; Tupi-Guarani.**

BIBLIOGRAPHY

Alfred Métraux, "The Guaraní," in *Handbook of South American Indians,* vol. 3, edited by Julian H. Steward (1948).

Elman R. Service, "The *Encomienda* in Paraguay," in *Hispanic American Historical Review* 31, no. 2 (1951): 230–252, and *Spanish-Guarani Relations in Early Colonial Paraguay* (1954; repr. 1971).

Guillermo Fúrlong Cárdiff, *Misiones y sus pueblos Guaraníes* (1962).

John Hemming, *Red Gold: The Conquest of the Brazilian Indians* (1978).

James Schofield Saeger, "Survival and Abolition: The Eighteenth-Century Paraguayan Encomienda," in *The Americas: A Quarterly Review of Inter-American Cultural History* 38, no. 1 (1981): 59–85.

Branislava Susnik, *El rol de los indígenas en la formación y en la vivencia del Paraguay* (1982–1983).

JAMES SCHOFIELD SAEGER

## GUARANÍ (LANGUAGE).

Guaraní is a member of the Tupi-Guaraní language family, which was once widespread over most of lowland South America. Today Guaraní is spoken in parts of Brazil, Argentina, Paraguay, and Bolivia, with Paraguay being the geographic center of Guaraní speakers. The largest community of Guaraní speakers is the nonindigenous Paraguayans, some 90 percent of whom speak "Paraguayan" Guaraní.

Guarani was recognized as the national language of Paraguay in 1967. It was made an official second language, along with Spanish, in the 1992 constitution. Paraguay is one of the few bilingual nation-states in the world, and Guaraní has become the primary marker of Paraguayan ethnicity. Census figures over the last fifty years report approximately half the population as bilingual, between 30 and 40 percent of the population as monolingual in Guaraní, and the remaining population as either monolingual in Spanish or bilingual with another language.

### HISTORICAL BACKGROUND

Spaniards originally pushed inland by way of the Rio de la Plata seeking gold. In the area of present-day Asunción, the Spaniards found the Cario-Guaraní people, with whom they made alliances. To gain allies to fight their enemies in the Chaco on the right bank of the Paraguay River, the Cario-Guaran followed custom of forming reciprocal family bonds through intermarriage with the Spanish. In this manner, the Guaranies gained allies to fight their enemies in the Chaco on the right bank of the Paraguay river while the Spaniards gained allies to help them cross the Chaco safely. Although the Spaniards failed to cross the harsh Chaco territory, a colony was established at Asunción. The result was several generations of mixed Guaraní-Spanish offspring (mestizos) learning Guaraní from their mothers and Spanish from their fathers. The lack of gold, silver, or other forms of portable wealth guaranteed that there was little immigration to the Paraguayan colony, and mestizos were eventually permitted to inherit usufruct rights and *encomiendas* (rights to indigenous labor), given the dearth of pure Spanish offspring of the original settlers.

In 1575 Luis de Bolaños, a Franciscan missionary, became the first non-native speaker to study Guaraní and provide a written version. Antonio Ruíz de Montoya produced a standardized form of Guaraní from a multiplicity of dialects and published *Arte bocabulario de la lengua Guaraní* in 1640.

Guaraní served as an important means of resistance and conspiracy by Paraguayan mestizos against the Crown-appointed, Spanish-speaking governor. During the struggle for independence, it was instrumental in binding the Paraguayans together as a nation, both against Spain and Buenos Aires. By the time of independence from Spain in 1811, Guaraní was used extensively throughout Paraguay, not only in the home, but also during religious services, in business exchanges, and by government functionaries.

Throughout Paraguay's history, the popularity of Guaraní has waxed and waned depending on nationalistic exigencies. During the disastrous War of the Triple Alliance (1864–1870) against Brazil, Argentina, and Uruguay, nationalistic fervor caused a revival of the Guaraní language. *Cacique Lambaré*, a biweekly newspaper started during the war, was written in Guaraní and was meant to rally the troops and distinguish Paraguayans from their enemies.

During the Liberal Period following the war, the political elite discouraged the use of Guaraní because of the association of indigenousness with backwardness. The new government banned the speaking of Guaraní in all state schools. This situation continued until the 1920s, when there was a renewed sense of nationalism fostered by the Partido Colorado, one of the three major political parties at the time. The dramatic works of Julio Correa, the poetry of Narciso Ramón Colmán, and the establishment of an Academia de la Lengua Guaraní were all signs of this change in attitude toward the language. When hostilities with Bolivia erupted into the Chaco War (1932–1935), Guaraní reemerged as a symbol of national unity and as a means of confusing the non-Guaraní speaking enemy in the field. When Paraguay's contact with the international community increased during the 1950s, the government encouraged Guaraní as a symbol of ethnic and national identity that very clearly demarcated Paraguayans from other nations and knit the population together with a distinct ethnicity.

## BILINGUALISM AND DIGLOSSIA

The nationalist use of Guaraní has created a situation of bilingualism and diglossia within Guaraní. (Diglossia is a sociolinguistic situation where there are two forms of a language or two languages, usually designated as a high and low form by the language community; the high form is used for literature, business, and educated settings whereas the low form is used in the home and by the uneducated underclass.) This diglossia is formed by vernacular Guaraní and academic, or "technical," Guaraní. The academic form is respected but not actually spoken, limited instead to literary expression, primarily poetry and theater, and classrooms where it is taught as a second language along with English. The vernacular form is disparaged and referred to as *jopará*, or a mix of Spanish and Guaraní.

Since the mid-twentieth century academics in Paraguay have attempted to improve the original Guaraní grammars and to standardize its orthography. These efforts at improvement have resulted in the written grammars becoming more confusing and less like vernacular Guaraní. Modes and tenses have been added, attempts have been made to eliminate linguistic exceptions, and new words have been created to expand what some view as the deficient vocabulary.

## CURRENT GUARANÍ USE

Although there is no agreement on orthography, vocabulary, or the diglossic nature of the language, some cultural elites are aiming to have Guaraní named an official language of Mercosur, which would require all official documents to be written in Guaraní. This movement promotes the use of academic Guaraní, even coining a name for the language, Ñemby Ñemuha, that is undecipherable in vernacular Guaraní.

Most Paraguayans find the television shows, radio programs, books of poetry, plays, and newspaper supplements written in the literary form of Guaraní difficult to understand. In 2003 Carlos Martínez Gamba was awarded Paraguay's top literary prize, the Premio Nacional de Literatura, for his poetic novel *Ñorairõ ñemombe'u Guérra Guasúro guare*—the first time this award has gone to a work written entirely in Guaraní. However, as the text is largely inaccessible to the reading public, it quickly went out of print. Rural radio stations do broadcast in the vernacular, giving local news and weather. In the 1990s a bilingual education program was implemented in the first three grades of school to improve overall education by gradually teaching Spanish until all students are bilingual. The program has had mixed success, as teachers are still likely to use Spanish in instruction to teach the academic form of Guaraní, further confusing the young students.

In the 1990s the Catholic Church began offering services in vernacular Guaraní and in other indigenous languages of Paraguay. A widely disseminated Bible written in vernacular Guaraní, published in 1996, is helping the populace to read spoken Guaraní and possibly fueling a resurgence of interest in maintaining the language. Education reform and Church support of Guaraní may counteract, or at least lessen, the impact of forces that favor Spanish usage, such as an increasing urban population and the diffusion of television.

*See also* **Chaco War; Colmán, Narciso; Correa, Julio Myzkowsky; Indigenous Languages; Mercosur; Mestizo; War of the Triple Alliance.**

BIBLIOGRAPHY

Cadogan, León. "En torno al 'guaraní paraguayo' o 'coloquial.'" *Cahiers du Monde Hispanique et Luso-Brésilien/*Caravel*le* 14 (1970): 31–41.

Corvalán, Grazziella, and Germán de Granda, eds. *Sociedad y lengua: Bilingüismo en el Paraguay.* 2 vols. Asunción: Centro Paraguayo de Estudios Sociológicos, 1982.

Melià, Bartomeu. *La lengua Guaraní del Paraguay: Historia, sociedad y literature.* Madrid: Editorial MAPFRE, 1992.

Rubin, Joan. *National Bilingualism in Paraguay.* The Hague and Paris: Mouton, 1968.

Ruíz de Montoya, Antonio. *Arte de la lengua Guaraní.* Asunción: Centro de Estudios Paraguayos "Antonio Guasch" (CEPAG), 1993.

Villagra-Batoux, Sara Delicia. *El Guaraní Paraguayo: De la oralidad a la lengua literaria.* Asunción: Expolibro, 2002.

CHRISTINA TURNER

**GUARANI WAR.** The Guarani War (1753–1756) was a series of armed engagements between a joint Spanish-Portuguese force and a group of Guarani Indians who actively resisted Spanish cession of their lands to the Portuguese. In 1750 a treaty was signed in Madrid that transferred the Portuguese settlement of Colonia to Spain in exchange for a several-hundred-mile wedge of Spanish territory east of the Uruguay River. Within this territory, however, were several Guarani missions under the control of the Society of Jesus (Jesuits). The Indians of these missions adamantly rejected the idea of their lands being given to the Portuguese, their age-old enemies. Despite the orders of the Spanish governor, and of their Jesuit administrators, the Indians of the seven missions refused to evacuate their communities and instead organized a spirited military defense under a Guarani *corregidor* named Sepé Tiarayú.

Sepé met in February 1753 with Spanish and Portuguese commissioners but declined to make any concessions. The sixty-eight men under his command never constituted much of a threat, but the joint European force decided to withdraw anyway to avoid bloodshed. This act in fact made matters worse, for when news of the incident reached Madrid and Lisbon, it was made to look like cowardice in the face of Jesuit machinations. The Europeans thereafter began to fight in earnest and rarely offered quarter. For their part, the Guarani had prepared well for war, fashioning every piece of scrap metal into arrowheads and increasing the size of their rustic army to over a thousand.

In February 1754 the Indians besieged Santo Amaro, a small Portuguese fort they finally captured after a month's combat. In July an allied army of 3,000 men advanced from two directions to capture San Borja in order to cut off the flow of supplies from missions west of the Uruguay. Four months later several Guarani *caciques* surrendered after bloody resistance.

Switching tactics, Sepé forged an alliance with savage Charrúa Indians, a move that until that point had been unthinkable. Toward the end of 1755 a new European army began a merciless campaign. The Spanish and Portuguese faced a force of 1,600 Indians, armed mostly with bows and, according to one account, several rudimentary cannons fashioned from bamboo.

Sepé was killed at this time in a minor skirmish and his place taken by Nicolás Ñeenguirú, a minor *correquidor* who failed to inspire the same kind of loyalty as his predecessor. On 10 February 1756 a major battle took place at Caaybaté, in the hill country south of the Yacuí River. The Indians found themselves surrounded, and although Nicolás attempted to negotiate terms, the Indians ended up fighting hand-to-hand. The slaughter lasted more than an hour, with the trenches dug by the Guarani now serving as their burial pits.

Caaybaté broke the main Indian resistance, though guerrilla activities continued for a number of months afterwards. Some Indians fled into the jungles and swamps where they lived in isolation for decades. Ironically, in the 1760s, these same territories for which so many Indians had died were restored to the Spanish crown. The power and prestige of the Jesuits in that part of South America, however, was dramatically diminished.

*See also* **Portuguese Empire; Spanish Empire.**

BIBLIOGRAPHY

Magnus Mörner, *The Expulsion of the Jesuits from Latin America* (1965).

Philip Caraman, *The Lost Paradise: The Jesuit Republic in South America* (1990), pp. 235–255.

*Additional Bibliography*

Ganson, Barbara Anne. *The Guaraní Under Spanish Rule in the Río De La Plata.* Stanford: Stanford University Press, 2003.

Golin, Tau, and José Custódio de Sá e Faria. *A Guerra Guaranítica: Como os exércitos de Portugal e Espanha destruíram os Sete Povos dos jesuítas e índios guaranis no Rio Grande do Sul.* Passo Fundo, RS, Brasil: EDIUPF, Universidade de Passo Fundo, 1998.

THOMAS L. WHIGHAM

## GUARDIA, RICARDO ADOLFO DE LA

**GUARDIA, RICARDO ADOLFO DE LA** (1899–1970). Ricardo Adolfo de la Guardia (*b.* 14 June 1899; *d.* 29 December 1970), president of Panama (1941–1945). Minister of government and justice under president Arnulfo Arias Madrid, Guardia organized a movement to depose the dictator. He assumed the office of president with the support of the National Guard, the oligarchy, and much of the Panamanian populace. The attack on Pearl Harbor brought fear that the Panama Canal would become a target, and Guardia endorsed controversial plans for the construction of U.S. bases in Panama. In 1944 the National Assembly rebelled against Guardia's authority, insisting that he name a constitutional successor. In response, he dissolved the assembly and abrogated the 1941 constitution. He called elections in 1945 that established a new assembly and installed Enrique A. Jiménez as provisional president. Arias returned to power in 1949, forcing Guardia to flee to the Canal Zone, where he remained until 1951.

*See also* **Jiménez, Enrique A.; Panama Canal.**

BIBLIOGRAPHY

Manuel María Alba C., *Cronología de los gobernantes de Panamá, 1510–1967* (1967), pp. 329–333.

Ernesto J. Castillero R., *Historia de Panamá* (1982), pp. 253–255.

*Additional Bibliography*

Lindsay-Poland, John. *Emperors in the Jungle: The Hidden History of the U.S. in Panama.* Durham, NC: Duke University Press, 2003.

SARA FLEMING

## GUARDIA GUTIÉRREZ, TOMÁS

**GUARDIA GUTIÉRREZ, TOMÁS** (1831–1882). Tomás Guardia Gutiérrez (*b.* 16 December 1831; *d.* 6 July 1882), president and dictator of Costa Rica (1870–1882). Guardia is often seen as the expression of triumphant liberalism in Costa Rica with his dictatorial style, the rewriting of the Constitution of 1871, and the hegemony of an entire generation of elitist Liberals in the 1880s and 1890s. However, Guardia was not the first to champion liberal policies, and his reign was more a reflection of severe intra-elite tensions within a liberal framework than of liberalism's ascendancy for the first time. Indeed, the Constitution of 1871 proved to be a highly presidentialist document, with Guardia and his relatives rigidly controlling political power for some twenty years while pursuing liberal economic transformation of the country.

Guardia, born in Bagaces, was the son of leading ranching families in Guanacaste and Alajuela provinces. Nevertheless, his power transcended particular regions. His father's family was originally from Panama, and the family remained active in the politics of that nation as well. As a colonel in the Costa Rican army, Guardia led a revolt against the government, taking the artillery barracks in San José on 27 April 1870. He became general commandant of an interim government headed by Bruno Carranza Ramírez. He was elected president in 1872 under a system that centralized the election procedures in the executive branch. He engineered the election of an ally, Aniceto Esquivel Sáenz, in 1876, but soon thereafter (1877) he reassumed the presidency as virtual dictator. He convened yet another Constituent Assembly in 1880 and reestablished the Constitution of 1871 by decree in 1882. Guardia died of natural causes in 1882, prior to the scheduled presidential election.

Guardia was something of an outsider in mid-nineteenth-century Costa Rican politics. He was not a leading member of the coffee oligarchy, dominated by the Mora and Montealegre clans, which had ruled for over twenty years before his coup. Many of his policies can best be seen as designed to wrest political power from the family-based cliques of the coffee barons of the Central Valley. He exiled former President José María Montealegre Fernández to the United States for life in 1872, and, although his own family would benefit enormously, much of his regime's support came from non-oligarchic forces in the coffee economy. Coffee elite members who were more ideologically and institutionally than personally oriented, as well as liberals of more modest social origins, tended to support Guardia, while the "old money" families more often felt his wrath.

Guardia's regime was most highly identified with the long-lasting (until 1949) Constitution of 1871 and the building of the railroad to the Atlantic coast. The latter endeavor was contracted with Minor Keith and led to both the first serious foreign debt and to the United Fruit Company dominance of much of the Atlantic coast province of Limón. Other major achievements included the abolition of the death penalty in 1882, the beginning of a major effort at mass primary education, and, curiously for an avowedly presidentialist regime, the strengthening of both the legislative branch and legal norms in public affairs. A substantial group of ideologically committed liberal deputies and magistrates came to power during Guardia's reign, as is suggested by the reformulation of the Civil Code in 1886.

In foreign affairs Guardia was able to deter Central American unification efforts led by the Guatemalan strongman Justo Rufino Barrios, preserving local independence and a special commercial relationship with Great Britain. Perhaps the overzealous pursuit of British loan capital and investment, brokered by Keith, is today seen as the most negative aspect of Guardia's admittedly authoritarian form of liberalism.

*See also* **Costa Rica, Constitutions; Railroads; United Fruit Company.**

BIBLIOGRAPHY

For Guardia the most basic source is Donna Cotton, "Costa Rica and the Era of Tomás Guardia" (Ph.D. diss., George Washington University, 1972). See also Eugenio Rodríguez, *Don Tomás Guardia y el estado liberal* (1989); José Luis Vega Carballo, *Orden y progreso: La formacion del estado nacional en Costa Rica* (1981); Carlos Mélendez Chaverri, comp., *Documentos fundamentales del siglo xix* (1978); Eugenio Rodríguez, *El pensamiento liberal: Antología* (1979); and Rafael Obregón Loría, *Conflictos militares y políticos de Costa Rica* (1951).

*Additional Bibliography*

Mahoney, James. *The Legacies of Liberalism: Path Dependence and Political Regimes in Central America.* Baltimore: Johns Hopkins University Press, 2001.

Sáenz Carbonell, Jorge Francisco. *Los días del presidente Lizano: La muerte de don Tomás Guardia y la administración de don Saturnino Lizano Gutiérrez.* San José, Costa Rica: Editorial Universidad Estatal a Distancia, 1997.

LOWELL GUDMUNDSON

**GUARDIA NAVARRO, ERNESTO DE LA** (1904–1983). Ernesto De La Guardia Navarro (*b.* 30 May 1904; *d.* 2 May 1983), president of Panama (1956–1960). Born in Panama City, Guardia Navarro, a conservative businessman with a degree from Dartmouth, was the first Panamanian president since World War II to complete his term in office. Elected to the presidency in 1956 as a candidate of the National Patriotic Coalition, he furthered programs begun by President

José Antonio Remón Cantera (1952–1955). He created a minimum wage, sponsored housing projects, undertook minor educational reforms, and lowered unemployment levels. In 1958 he began negotiations with U.S. President Eisenhower over the fine points of the Eisenhower-Remón Treaty, seeking an equal status for the Spanish language and the Panamanian flag in the Canal Zone.

In April 1959 a group of Cubans intending to overthrow Guardia Navarro's government landed in Colón. The conflict was quickly resolved and the invaders deported. In November of the same year, violence erupted when protesters marched into the Canal Zone carrying Panamanian flags. Eisenhower conceded, and the Panamanian flag was raised in the zone. In 1960, Guardia Navarro's term ended peacefully with the election of a member of the opposition.

*See also* **Eisenhower–Remón Treaty (1955); Panama Canal, Flag Riots.**

BIBLIOGRAPHY

Manuel María Alba C., *Cronología de los gobernantes de Panamá, 1510–1967* (1967), pp. 360–364.

Ernesto J. Castillero R., *Historia de Panamá* (1982), pp. 267–270.

*Additional Bibliography*

Tack, Juan Antonio. *Ilusiones y realidades en las negociaciones con los Estados Unidos de América*. Panamá: Manfer, 1995.

SARA FLEMING

## GUARDIOLA, SANTOS (1812–1862).

Santos Guardiola (*b.* 1812; *d.* 11 January 1862), military figure and president of Honduras (1856–1862). Guardiola established himself as a prominent Conservative and military leader during the National War against William Walker's invasions. Known as "the butcher," Guardiola was considered a particularly ruthless and cruel commander. His forces defeated Walker and the latter's small force of fifty-five men at Rivas on 29 June 1855. Guatemalan Conservatives helped establish Guardiola as president of Honduras on 17 February 1856. He assumed a second term on 2 July 1860 and ruled until his assassination.

Guardiola's presidency had certain measurable successes at first but in the end was marred by violence and economic stagnation. After signing an alliance with Guatemala and El Salvador against Walker, Guardiola set out to assert Honduran sovereignty over the Bay Islands and Mosquito Coast, areas of permanent British incursions and long-standing dispute. British citizens were allowed to remain as inhabitants of the Bay Islands and were exempt from taxation. The Dallas-Clarendon Convention of 17 October 1856 removed the British protectorate over the Mosquito Coast but at the same time restricted Honduran sovereignty. Plans were made in January 1853 for an inter-oceanic railway with the founding of Ferrocarril Interoceánico de Honduras (Inter-oceanic Railway Company) on 28 April 1854, organized in Honduras with offices in New York and London. Walker's eventual capture and execution at Trujillo in 1860 represented the pinnacle of Guardiola's presidency.

Difficulties with Miguel del Cid, head of the diocese of Honduras, resulted in Guardiola's excommunication on 26 December 1860. Guardiola's rebuke and anticlericalism erupted in the *Guerra de los padres,* which pitted the church against its former Conservative ally in April 1861. The same month, Guardiola was forced by deteriorating economic conditions to authorize the issue of copper coins. The deteriorating economy, coupled with the violence of Guardiola's presidency, led to his assassination in early 1862 and, after several Conservative administrations, to the consolidation of power by the Liberal Party in 1876.

*See also* **Honduras; Walker, William.**

BIBLIOGRAPHY

Lorenzo Montúfar, *Reseña historica de Centro-América,* 7 vols. (1878–1888).

Luis Mariñas Otero, *Honduras,* 3d ed. (1983).

Pablo Yankelevich, *Honduras: una historia breve* (1988).

*Additional Bibliography*

Montúfar, Lorenzo, and Raúl Aguilar Piedra. *Walker en Centroamérica*. Alajuela, Costa Rica: Museo Histórico Cultural Juan Santamaría, 2000.

JEFFREY D. SAMUELS

## GUARNIERI, GIANFRANCESCO (1934–2006).

Gianfrancesco Guarnieri (*b.* 6 August 1934, *d.* 22 July 2006), Brazilian dramatist and actor. Guarnieri was a central figure in modern Brazilian theater and was particularly associated with the Arena Theater of São Paulo. His political orientation was Marxist, and his Brechtian theatrical technique requires the audience's direct emotional participation in the action to achieve a type of classical catharsis. *Eles não usam black-tie* (1958), his most celebrated play, presents the inevitable personal tragedy resulting from disunity in workers' struggles. Other dramas question the accepted truths of Brazilian history and the nation's contemporary reality. His *Ponto de partida* (1976) is an allegorical protest against the military regime's murder of journalist Vladimir Herzog. The last play he wrote, *A luta secreta de Maria da Encarnação*, was finished in 2001.

*See also* **Art: The Twentieth Century; Herzog, Vladimir; Theater.**

BIBLIOGRAPHY

Leslie Damasceno, "Theater History," in *Dictionary of Brazilian Literature* (1988).

Irwin Stern, "Guarnieri, Gianfrancesco," in *Dictionary of Brazilian Literature* (1988).

### *Additional Bibliography*

Anderson, Robert Nelson. *Realism, Allegory, and the Strangled Cry: Theatrical Semiosis in the Drama of Gianfrancesco Guarnieri.* Valencia, Spain: Albatros, 1998.

Roveri, Sérgio. *Gianfrancesco Guarnieri: Um grito solto no ar.* São Paulo: Cultura, Fundação Padre Anchieta, 2004.

Irwin Stern

## GUARNIERI, M[OZART] CAMARGO (1907–1993).

M[ozart] Camargo Guarnieri (*b.* 1 February 1907, *d.* 13 January 1993), Brazilian composer, conductor, teacher, and leader of the nationalist school of composers. Guarnieri was the son of a Sicilian immigrant remotely related to the Guarneri family of violin makers (the name was accidentally changed due to the mistake of an immigration official) and a Brazilian mother. His father, Miguel Guarnieri, an amateur musician, played the piano, flute, and string bass. He had a lifelong passion for opera and named his four sons Mozart, Rossini, Bellini, and Verdi. When Guarnieri became aware of the significance of the name Mozart, he dropped it and signed his name M. Camargo Guarnieri, feeling that it was presumptuous to be called by the name of the great master. Aware that his son had musical talent, and that educational opportunities were limited in the town of Tieté, Miguel Guarnieri moved to the city of São Paulo in 1922. In São Paulo, Camargo was placed under the tutelage of two teachers who exercised a decisive influence on his artistic and intellectual development: the Italian conductor and teacher Lamberto Baldi and Mário de Andrade, philosopher, teacher, and leader of the modernist movement in Brazil. Guarnieri studied with both teachers during the same period. Andrade undertook the direction of Guarnieri's studies in aesthetics and literature, and Baldi taught him counterpoint, fugue, and orchestration, while also gently guiding his efforts in composition. Guarnieri's first successful composition to exhibit obvious national characteristics was a sonatina for piano written in 1928. This work exhibited several characteristics of Guarnieri's mature style of composition: melodies that sounded folklike while avoiding direct quotations of folk melodies, use of typically Brazilian tempo and expression markings in Portuguese—*Molengamente* (indolently) and *Ponteado e bem dengoso* (with a plucked sound, coyly), contrapuntal writing, and use of layers of syncopated voices.

Guarnieri had a major influence on Brazilian music by his teaching of composition, by establishing a high level of craftsmanship in his own musical writing, and by providing a model of tonal and nontonal works with convincing national elements. Although Guarnieri did some writing in an atonal style, he soon came to the conviction that his style of writing was incompatible with what he regarded as the straitjacket of dodecaphony. He believed so strongly that atonality was incompatible with the development of national elements that he conducted a vigorous debate in Brazilian newspapers against what he regarded as the pernicious influence of atonality in the works of Brazilian composers.

Camargo Guarnieri wrote over six hundred musical works, many unpublished. The fifty *Ponteios* for piano are one of the most significant contributions to piano literature from any Brazilian composer and are a treasure of elements uniquely and distinctively Brazilian. Several orchestral works have won international acclaim, and his fourth and fifth sonatas for violin are masterpieces of the genre. He was also an important teacher of music, instructing students such as Vasconcellos Correa, Osvaldo Lacerda, and Aylton Escobar.

*See also* **Music: Art Music; Musical Instruments.**

BIBLIOGRAPHY

Marion Verhaalen, "The Solo Piano Music of Francisco Mignone and Camargo Guarnieri" (Ed.D. diss., Columbia Univ., 1971).

David P. Appleby, *The Music of Brazil* (1983).

*Additional Bibliography*

Grossi, Alex Sandra de Souza. "O idiomático de Camargo Guarnieri nos 10 improvisos para piano." M.A. thesis, Universidade de São Paulo, 2002.

Silva, Flávio. "Camargo Guarnieri e Mário de Andrade." *Latin American Music Review* 20, no. 2 (Fall–Winter 1999): 184–212.

DAVID P. APPLEBY

**GUATEMALA.** The modern republic of Guatemala occupies but a small part of what was the Spanish dominion of that name from the early sixteenth century to the beginning of the nineteenth. The colonial Kingdom of Guatemala included several diverse provinces that were often remote from and resentful toward the commercial and bureaucratic elites of the capital. The 1773 destruction by earthquake of the capital city, Antigua Guatemala, and the establishment of a new capital some twenty-five miles away coincided with the emergence of new economic and political forces that would characterize independent Guatemala.

The fragmentation that occurred with independence in 1821 left the state of Guatemala with boundaries approximating the present-day republic, bounded on the west by Mexico, on the south by the Pacific Ocean, on the east by El Salvador and Honduras, and on the north by Mexico, Belize, and the Caribbean Sea.

From a population of less than a million at the time of independence, Guatemala grew at the rate of about 1.3 percent annually during the nineteenth century, and then at rates between 2 and 3 percent annually during the twentieth century. By 2007 its population was more than 12.5 million. Guatemala has always been ethnically diverse, with a substantial indigenous majority, especially Mayas, who have generally been reported at about 60 percent of the total population during the second half of the twentieth century. Spanish is the first language for 56 percent of the population, an indigenous language is the first language for 44 percent. Careful demographic research has suggested that the indigenous population has been undercounted in modern Guatemalan censuses and that in the twentieth century the Indian population grew somewhat more rapidly than the mestizo (Ladino) population.

Guatemala is third in area (42,042 square miles) among the five Central American states, but it has always been the most populous. It has a population density of about 297 inhabitants per square mile with an annual population growth rate of 2.3 percent. In 2002 43 percent of the population was under age fifteen. The literacy rate was about 70 percent, urban population was 42 percent, and annual per capita gross national income was about $2,400.

## INDEPENDENCE TO 1850

Guatemala remained loyal to the Spanish crown throughout the difficult years of the Napoleonic wars and their aftermath. The Spanish Constitution of 1812, which allowed more political participation by the creoles of Guatemala City, paved the way for independence. The repressive ruler Captain General José de Bustamante y Guerra (1811–1818) sought to insulate the Kingdom of Guatemala from the war for independence in neighboring Mexico, but a pro-independence sentiment became more open after the restoration of the constitution in 1820. The fiery Pedro Molina led those favoring independence, and when news arrived of the Mexican Plan of Iguala (a plan engineered by Agustín Iturbide for the independence of New Spain), a council of notables in Guatemala City declared the independence of the kingdom on September 15, 1821. Guatemalan conservatives then succeeded in incorporating Guatemala and the other Central American states within Agustín de Iturbide's Mexican Empire in January 1822. When that empire fell little more than a year later, a Central American congress meeting in Guatemala declared its independence and established the United Provinces of Central America. In this turbulent period,

however, the province of El Salvador had separated itself from Guatemala, and the state of Chiapas decided to remain with Mexico, leaving the state of Guatemala with approximately its present territorial configuration. (There would be a number of subsequent minor adjustments to its boundaries, most notably the loss of Soconusco to Mexico.)

As the most populous province, Guatemala played a leading role in the Central American federation. It became embroiled in a bitter civil war (1827–1829) when the federal president, Manuel José Arce, a Salvadoran, intervened in the Guatemalan state government, removing its liberal governor, Juan Barrundia, and replacing him with the conservative Mariano Aycinena. When Aycinena usurped the power of the federal government in 1827, Arce resigned and was succeeded by vice president Mariano Beltranena, a Guatemalan and a kinsman of Aycinena. The civil war especially pitted Guatemala against El Salvador, but in the end liberal forces under Honduran General Francisco Morazán triumphed and dealt vindictively with the conservative Guatemalans, exiling most of the leading figures. Barrundia reclaimed the governorship of Guatemala. He was

**Guatemala**

| | |
|---|---|
| **Population:** | 12,728,111 (2007 est.) |
| **Area:** | 42,042 sq mi |
| **Official languages:** | Spanish and 23 different Amerindian languages |
| **National currency:** | quetzal (GTQ) |
| **Principal religions:** | Roman Catholic, approximately 50%; Protestant, approximately 40%; traditional Mayan beliefs influence Christian practice |
| **Ethnicity:** | mestizo (mixed Amerindian-Spanish) and European heritage, 59.4%; K'iche, 9.1%; Kaqchikel, 8.4%; Mam, 7.9%; Q'eqchi, 6.3%; other Mayan, 8.6%; indigenous non-Mayan, 0.2%; other 0.1% (2001 census) |
| **Capital:** | Guatemala City (est. pop. 951,000 in 2005) |
| **Other urban centers:** | Escuintla, Quezaltenango |
| **Principal geographical features:** | *Mountains:* Sierra de los Cuchumatanes; Sierra Madre, featuring Tajumulco (13,830 ft) and many other high peaks; many smaller ranges<br>*Rivers:* Motagua, Usumacinta<br>*Lakes:* Atitlan, Izabal, Petén Itza<br>*Other:* El Petén region in the north is a rolling limestone plateau largely covered by rainforest. |
| **Economy:** | *GDP per capita:* $5,000 (2006 est.) |
| **Principal products and exports:** | *Agricultural:* bananas, cardamom, coffee, cotton, sugar<br>*Manufacturing:* chemicals, food processing, furniture, pharmaceuticals, textiles<br>*Mining:* oil |
| **Government:** | Independence from Spain, 1821. Constitution, 1986; suspended for part of 1993, subsequently restored and amended that year. Constitutional parliamentary democracy. The president is popularly elected for a 4-year term, and is both chief of state and head of government. The legislature is a unicameral Congress of the Republic, whose 158 members are popularly elected for 4-year terms. Council of Ministers appointed by the president. 22 departments. |
| **Armed forces:** | *Army:* 27,000<br>*Navy:* 1,500<br>*Air force:* 700<br>*Paramilitary:* 19,000 National Police, 2,500 Treasury Police<br>*Reserves:* 35,200 |
| **Transportation:** | *Rail:* 550 mi<br>*Ports:* Champerico, Puerto Barrios, San José, Santo Tomas<br>*Roads:* 3,021 mi paved; 5,736 mi unpaved<br>*National airline:* Aviateca<br>*Airports:* 12 paved runway and 390 unpaved runway airports, international airport in Guatemala City |
| **Media:** | There are 3 major newspapers, *La Hora, Prensa Libre, Siglo Veintiuno.* 130 AM and 487 FM radio stations, and 26 television stations. |
| **Literacy and education:** | *Total literacy rate:* 69.1%<br>Nine years of education are compulsory and provided for free, but truancy is common. There are 6 universities, including Universidad de San Carlos. |

succeeded by Dr. Mariano Gálvez (1831–1838), who, more than any other individual, established the liberal agenda for nineteenth-century Guatemala.

Morazán moved the federal capital to San Salvador in 1834. Under Gálvez, the state of Guatemala launched major liberal reforms consistent with Morazán's policy against the conservative Creole elite of the Guatemalan capital that had inherited much of the economic and social power of the Spanish colony. Strong anticlerical measures reduced the power of the clergy, and the state auctioned off much of the church's land to encourage more rapid export-led economic development. Cochinea, a crimson dye produced mainly around Antigua and Amatitlán, was the leading export, as the British demand for imports for its growing textile industry tied the Guatemalan economy closely to Belize and England. Gálvez also encouraged immigration, and his friendly policy toward northern Europeans, including a massive land grant for an English colonization scheme, caused opponents to charge that he was more sympathetic to foreign than to national interests. Political and judicial reform, notably the adoption of the Livingston civil and penal codes in 1834, in a misguided attempt to replace the traditional Spanish legal system with a modern, English-based system, brought further opposition from lawyers and others. These reforms had created widespread opposition among both the Guatemala City elite and country people by 1836, when a serious cholera epidemic swept the country.

The government's well-intentioned efforts to control the cholera epidemic aroused the rural population, already aggrieved by the liberal reforms and encouraged by an irate clergy. Under the leadership of José Rafael Carrera, a Ladino from Guatemala City who had settled in Mataquescuintla after the civil war, isolated armed uprisings united into a powerful guerrilla insurgency that brought down the Gálvez government on February 1, 1838. Divisions between the liberals hastened the downfall of Gálvez, and when the successor government—strongly influenced by the more radical liberals José Francisco Barrundia and Pedro Molina—failed to meet the expectations of Carrera and his peasant guerrillas, it, too, fell. Carrera imposed a conservative government under Mariano Rivera Paz, who ruled most of the time between 1839 and 1844 and presided over a strong conservative reaction against the liberalism that had followed independence.

Carrera, meanwhile, supported by much of the conservative clergy, built a strong army. He was the real master of the country from 1839 until his death in 1865. While generally insisting on conservative policy, during the 1840s he trusted neither the liberal nor the conservative elites of the capital and tried to rule by using politicians from both factions. He became president of the State of Guatemala in December 1844, and in March 1847, strongly influenced by both conservative states' rights interests and British interests (represented by diplomat Frederick Chatfield), he established the Republic of Guatemala. The other states soon followed in declaring their absolute independence from the now defunct Central American federation.

Liberal ascendancy in the legislature, however, combined with growing popular resistance, forced Carrera from office and into exile in Chiapas in August 1848. Unable to provide effective government or to quell the rural insurgency, the liberals soon turned power over to the military under Colonel Mariano Paredes. Carrera then returned to highland Guatemala with a military force composed mainly of Indians. He quickly regained control of the country and on August 3, 1849, became commander in chief of the Guatemalan army. He consolidated his power in Guatemala with the unequivocal support of the conservatives while pursuing an aggressive policy against other Central American liberals, an effort that culminated in his stunning military victory over the National Army—composed of liberals from all of the states, but among whom José Francisco Barrundia was highly influential—at La Arada on February 2, 1851. On November 6, 1851, Carrera resumed the presidency and on October 21, 1854, formally became president for life, a virtual monarch with few restrictions on his power.

### 1850 TO 1900

Although strongly conservative and characterized by the active participation of the clergy in the government and legislature, after 1850 Guatemala adopted more liberal economic policies as it accelerated its dependence on agricultural exports and began to pay more attention to infrastructure development. Coffee replaced cochineal as the principal export, and by the end of the conservative era it amounted to 50 percent of all Guatemalan exports. Until his death in 1865, however, Carrera prevented large-scale alienation of Indian lands for the coffee expansion.

Carrera also had a heavy hand in the affairs of his Central American neighbors, intervening directly in Honduras and El Salvador to maintain governments friendly to Guatemalan interests. In 1856–1857 Guatemala sent the largest number of troops to the National War, a campaign in which Guatemala and the other Central American states combined forces to oust the North American freebooter William Walker from Nicaragua. In 1863, in Carrera's final military adventure, Guatemala put down the rising Gerardo Barrios and restored more conservative rule to El Salvador. By 1865 Guatemala had achieved considerable stability and prosperity, but military repression and dictatorial rule had become characteristic of its government.

General Vicente Cerna (1865–1871) succeeded Carrera. He continued Carrera's conservative rule but was less concerned about protecting Indian land and labor from exploitation by coffee and other producers. Thus, the Cerna administration was a transition—especially in economic and social terms—to the period known as la Reforma Liberal that began in 1871.

Liberal opposition to the conservative dictatorship had been largely driven into exile under Carrera except for the presence of Miguel García Granados in the weak Guatemalan legislature. García Granados came from a prominent capital family, so the government tolerated his eloquent liberal oratory, but he could not rally much support in the otherwise repressive environment of Carrera's Guatemala. After Carrera's death, however, more violent opposition began to emerge, especially from Serapio Cruz, who had expected to succeed Carrera, and from coffee planters and liberals in the populous highlands of western Guatemala. After the death of Cruz in 1870, Justo Rufino Barrios emerged as the military leader of the rebellion and Miguel García Granados finally joined it to form a provisional government in March 1871. The rebels defeated Cerna's army at San Lucas Sacatepéquez on 29 June 29, 1871, and marched into the capital on the following day. García Granados became president, but his close ties to the elite of the capital led to a break with Barrios and other highlanders who wanted more sweeping reforms. In the election of 1873 Barrios won the presidency and became the first of a series of strong liberal dictators.

**Guatemalan worker cutting sugar cane.** Guatemala is one of the largest sugar producers in Latin America and exports most of the sugar it produces. PHOTOGRAPH BY ANNE KALOSH. REPRODUCED BY PERMISSION

Barrios emphasized economic growth and courted foreign investment to begin the development of railroads and modern ports while greatly expanding the coffee industry. He began the modernization of Guatemala City and Quetzaltenango and represented the coming to power in Guatemala of the liberal-positivist philosophy that would remain dominant until at least 1944. Barrios promoted strongly anticlerical legislation, suppressed the tithe, abolished the regular orders, expropriated church property, and vastly reduced the number of priests in the country; he also established religious liberty, civil marriage and divorce, and state collection of vital statistics. He launched a public education system at all levels and took the University of San Carlos out of the control of the Church, making it the state university and establishing other secondary and normal schools. His educational reforms, however, benefited primarily the upper and middle sectors of Guatemala City and Quetzaltenango. Most rural Guatemalans continued to have little access to education and often now lost their village priests, who formerly had provided some education to parishioners. His restructuring of the university emphasized professional and technical education at the expense of the humanities and liberal arts, another reflection of positivist thinking.

Coffee exports soared as Barrios encouraged the encroachment of Ladino planters on Indian communal lands and made their labor more accessible to planters. He improved the transportation infrastructure for overseas trade and facilitated the formation of banks and other financial institutions to provide credit for economic development and modernization. New ministries of agriculture, development, and education reflected his emphasis on economic growth as well as the increased role of the state. He attracted foreign immigration and investment as German and U.S. influence increased significantly. His administration also codified the laws and promulgated a new constitution in 1879, under which he won reelection in 1880.

In foreign affairs Barrios played an important role in the neighboring states of El Salvador and Honduras, and he settled differences with Mexico at the cost of giving up Guatemalan claims to Soconusco and other parts of Chiapas. He renewed the

Guatemalan claim to Belize, however, repudiating the Wyke-Aycinena treaty of 1859 with Great Britain. He also tried to revive the unionist spirit of Francisco Morazán and to reestablish the Central American federation by means of Guatemalan military power. That effort, however, ended abruptly in 1885, when Salvadoran forces defeated the Guatemalan army at Chalchuapa, where Barrios died in battle.

Barrios established a new coffee elite, whose economic base was centered in the western highlands around Quetzaltenango, reducing the power of the Guatemala City merchant elite that had dominated the country since the late colonial period. At the same time, he greatly accelerated exploitation of the indigenous population and moved Guatemala more rapidly into an export-led economy dependent on foreign markets and investment. Although Barrios was celebrated in Guatemalan history as the reformer who ended the long conservative dictatorships of Rafael Carrera and Vicente Cerna, his own dictatorial rule and strengthening of the military established a pattern for subsequent liberal governments that made repression a characteristic of government in Guatemala extending into the twenty-first century. Barrios's personal wealth increased enormously during his rule, especially in comparison with earlier Guatemalan presidents. In this, too, he set a pattern that many of his successors would emulate.

General Manuel Lisandro Barillas (1885–1892), a political favorite from Quetzaltenango, succeeded Barrios and continued most of his development policies. Barrios's nephew, José María Reyna Barrios, succeeded to the presidency in 1892. When he was assassinated in 1898, another Quetzaltenango liberal, Manuel Estrada Cabrera, came to power and remained in office until 1920, his twenty-two-year rule being the longest uninterrupted presidency in Guatemalan history.

### 1900 TO 1950

Under Estrada Cabrera the liberal emphasis on economic development surged forward, while the political idealism of earlier liberals all but disappeared. Coffee exports continued to expand, but the most notable economic development was the rise of the United Fruit Company (UFCO), which developed the banana industry in Guatemala's lowlands. Its subsidiary, the International Railways of Central America, completed the railway from Guatemala City to the Caribbean, as well as other lines, and developed Puerto Barrios as Guatemala's leading port. UFCO, with its transport subsidiaries, thus achieved the dominant position not only in banana production but also in Guatemala's internal and external transportation systems. While UFCO gave Guatemala much of the material progress that liberals had advocated since the 1820s, its enormous economic strength, its abuses of its power, its virtual monopoly over Guatemalan overseas transport, and its obviously foreign character made many Guatemalans resentful throughout the first half of the twentieth century.

Despite great economic advancement, the harsh repression, uneven economic gains, and corrupt government under Estrada Cabrera exposed his regime to rising opposition. His mental deterioration after 1918 contributed to the success of a plot that forced him from office in April 1920. The new Unionist Party took power under the presidency of a leading businessman, Carlos Herrera, but in 1921 that government fell and Liberal Party generals José María Orellana (1921–1926) and Lázaro Chacón (1926–1930) ruled Guatemala for the remainder of the decade.

Despite their military appearance, the governments of the 1920s were more open and democratic than the Estrada Cabrera dictatorship that preceded them. For the most part, political participation was limited to rivalry among different segments of the elite, but labor unions and leftist parties, although not free from some repression, began to organize and gain some adherents. There was also continued economic growth, although most rural Guatemalans saw little of it, and as coffee and other agricultural exports expanded along with a more rapidly rising population, there began to be shortages of land for food production in some areas. The coffee elite retained strong control through alliance with the military, and fear of the major revolution taking place in adjacent Mexico kept them on guard against any genuine transfer of political power from the elite to the middle or working classes.

The Great Depression sharply arrested the modest progress of the 1920s. The value of coffee exports plummeted from $34 million in 1927 to $9.3 million in 1932. By 1931 there were serious economic and social problems arising from declining exports and

**Voter abstention in Guatemalan elections, 1944–2003**

| Year | Eligible Voters | Votes | Percent Abstention | Votes for Winning Candidate | % of Eligible Votes for Winning Candidate |
|---|---|---|---|---|---|
| 1944 | 310,000 | 296,200 | 4.5 | 255,700 | 82.5 |
| 1950 | 583,300 | 407,500 | 31.1 | 266,800 | 45.7 |
| 1958 | 736,400 | 492,300 | 33.1 | 191,000 | 25.9 |
| 1966 | 944,200 | 531,300 | 43.7 | 209,400 | 22.2 |
| 1970 | 1,190,500 | 640,700 | 46.2 | 251,100 | 21.1 |
| 1974 | 1,568,700 | 727,876 | 53.6 | 298,953 | 19.1 |
| 1985 | 2,753,572 | 1,907,771 | 30.7 | 648,681 | 23.6 |
| 1990 | 3,204,955 | 1,808,718 | 43.6 | 375,119 | 11.7 |
| 1995 | 3,710,681 | 1,737,033 | 53.2 | 565,393 | 15.2 |
| 1999 | 4,458,744 | 2,397,212 | 46.2 | 1,045,820 | 23.5 |
| 2003 | 5,073,282 | 2,937,169 | 42.1 | 921,233 | 18.2 |

SOURCE: Adapted from Julio Castellanos Cambranes, "Origins of the Crisis of the Established Order in Guatemala," trans. David O. Wise, in *Central America: Crisis and Adaptation,* ed. Steve C. Ropp and James A. Morris (Albuquerque: University of New Mexico Press, 1984), p. 136; *Centroamérica en Cifras* (San José, Costa Rica: FLASCO, 2002), pp. 190–191; Marco Fonseca, "The Guatemalan Elections and the Challenges of Peace and Human Development," *Focal Point* (Canadian Foundation for the Americas) 2, no. 11 (November–December 2003): 1–3.

**Table 1**

insufficient attention to subsistence agriculture. President Chacón became gravely ill, and upon his death in December 1930 the Assembly designated a civilian, Baudilio Palma, to succeed him. Palma served only four days, however, before a military coup replaced him with General Manuel Orellana on December 16. In an effort to restore at least a semblance of constitutional government, however, Orellana resigned on January 2, 1931, turning the office over to José María Reina Andrade, who had been one of Estrada Cabrera's ministers and was now serving as president of the Assembly. Reina Andrade served until a pro forma election could be held; the Liberal Party candidate General Jorge Ubico y Castañeda was overwhelmingly elected and took office on February 14, 1931.

Ubico built a strong political machine based not only on his military command but also on close alliance with the giant UFCO and with German coffee interests, at least until the outbreak of World War II, when he quickly abandoned his pro-German stance and made Guatemala the first Latin American country to join the United States in declaring war against Germany. He began this regime with a strong crackdown on communist and other leftist labor and political groups, assuring the elite that he was protecting them from the kind of revolution that was occurring in Mexico or the brief communist uprising that had occurred in El Salvador in January 1932. A ruthless purge of these opposition political parties rendered them impotent during Ubico's thirteen-year rule as their leaders suffered execution or exile. Ubico also strongly supported the system of ensuring the coffee planters an adequate supply of cheap Indian labor for their harvests. He abolished debt peonage in 1934, but replaced it with a system based on a vagrancy law that required the peasants to work on the coffee farms in a system resembling the colonial *repartimiento.* It also provided workers for Ubico's ambitious road-building program. He reduced Indian autonomy by a new system of municipal government that replaced the Indian mayors with presidential appointees.

### THE GUATEMALAN REVOLUTION

Opposition to the dictatorship began to surface during World War II. A strong anti-Fascist U.S. propaganda program attacking antidemocratic regimes, although directed against the Axis powers, had the effect of undermining the Ubico dictatorship in Guatemala. In addition, Ubico's expropriation of German-owned property in collaboration with the United States, although applauded by many Guatemalans who benefited by acquiring those properties and who had found the German "gringos" overbearing, nevertheless cost Ubico the support of a significant part of the coffee elite and resulted in a decline in Guatemalan coffee production. Moreover, wartime inflation hit the middle class hard. It was from this class, especially in the capital, that the most vocal opposition came, as university students began to stage demonstrations against the regime.

Opposition from students and intellectuals and other middle-class interests in the capital began to appear in 1942. After some street violence, Ubico, in ill health, stepped down on July 1, 1944, and turned power over to a loyal military junta. The Congress subsequently elected the head of the junta, General Federico Ponce Vaides, as provisional president. When Ponce could not check the rising opposition, a band of civilians and middle-grade military officers forced the downfall of the regime on October 20, 1944. Major Francisco Arana, Captain Jacobo Arbenz Guzmán, and a civilian, Jorge Toriello, formed a junta that presided over the country until the inauguration of the new president, elected in December 1944. In the meantime, a constituent assembly wrote a modern constitution that codified the ideals of the Guatemalan Revolution of 1944.

In the last years of Ubico's rule, in the more complex Guatemalan socioeconomic environment that the liberal economic growth had fostered, several new political parties representing disgruntled elite as well as middle-class and working-class interests formed underground. Most of these parties agreed on the candidacy of Juan José Arévalo, a young philosophy professor who had left Guatemala in protest against the Ubico dictatorship in 1934, soon after receiving his doctorate in Argentina. He had returned to Argentina and spent little of his adult life in Guatemala, but he had established a reputation as a learned man and one who had broken with Ubico. He won the 1944 presidential election in a landslide and began a six-year term dedicated to reforms that reflected both his Argentine experience and some obvious influence from the Mexican Revolution.

As had been the case in Mexico, the Guatemalan Revolution called for a return to the more idealistic liberalism of the early nineteenth century. It emphasized broader political participation, particularly of the middle and working classes, and was therefore friendly to renewed labor organization and a broad spectrum of political parties. It emphasized constitutional government, and the Constitution of 1945 was a twentieth-century charter that included many of the earlier liberal political guarantees while adding substantial social guarantees drawn from the Mexican Constitution of 1917. No reelection of the president and popular suffrage were important principles in reaction to the practice of *continuismo* under Estrada Cabrera and Ubico. Its strong support of labor required implementation of a modern labor code. There was also a hint of anticlericalism, bringing the opposition of the Roman Catholic hierarchy, which had begun to enjoy something of a rapprochement with the state under Ubico. The Church would become one of the most important opponents of the revolutionary governments of Arévalo and Arbenz.

Arévalo idealistically described his ideology as "spiritual socialism." Opponents railed against the revolutionary government as communist, but more accurately it was an attempt to encourage enlightened capitalism in Guatemala with adequate provision for social justice and a healthier distribution of wealth. Its duration under Arévalo (1945–1950) and his successor, Jacobo Arbenz (1951–1954), nevertheless represented a revolution in the sense of challenging the exclusive power of the coffee and military elites that had ruled since 1871. The phrase "Ten Years of Spring" has become common among those who have written on the period to reflect the emphasis on popular participation and social benefits in comparison with the periods both before and after.

Labor especially benefited from the revolution. The assembly abolished the vagrancy law of 1934. The new labor code provided a broad range of progressive rights to workers and their unions, but tangible benefits were much greater for urban than for rural workers. Marxists were in the vanguard of urban labor unions. Although Arévalo tolerated them, he made it clear that he was not their leader as he resisted Marxist attempts to establish a formal Communist Party. Arévalo, in fact, was one of a number of noncommunist social democratic leaders in the Caribbean region after World War II who represented what was often called the "democratic Left" in attempting to bring the emerging middle classes into more active participation in government and to provide a better distribution of wealth in their countries. Other notable members of this generation included José Figueres of Costa Rica, Juan Bosch of the Dominican Republic, and Rómulo Betancourt of Venezuela.

### THE ARBENZ PRESIDENCY

A struggle over succession in the election of 1950 moved Guatemala more sharply to the left and led ultimately to the downfall of the revolution. Rivals for the presidency were the two military leaders of the 1944 revolt, Francisco Arana and Jacobo Arbenz. The more conservative Arana commanded the army and had protected the revolution by putting down a score of attempted coups. Arbenz, more to the left, was minister of defense and closer to Arévalo. When Arévalo and Arbenz suspected Arana of plotting a coup of his own, the assassination of Arana at Amatitlán in July 1949 paved the way for Arbenz's easy victory in the 1950 election. But Arana's murder also triggered the most serious military coup attempt of Arévalo's administration. The growth of organized labor played a significant role here as a general strike in support of the government contributed to the coup's failure. In the election, Arbenz defeated General Miguel Ydígoras Fuentes, Ubico's minister of public works, who felt forced to flee the country in the face of rising violence during the election campaign.

Arbenz's election shifted the revolution markedly toward the left, especially with his strong rhetoric against UFCO and his talk of land reform. UFCO had responded to the threat with an active public relations campaign that marshaled U.S. public and government opposition to the Arbenz administration. Arbenz, much influenced by his wife, María Christina Vilanova de Arbenz, played into the hands of those opposing him by allowing communists openly to organize a party and by establishing a close relationship with the Marxist labor unions. The Guatemalan communist newspaper, *Octubre*, added fuel to the fire with its blatantly pro-Soviet and Marxist reporting. All this coincided with the election to the U.S. presidency of General Dwight D. Eisenhower, who appointed the zealous anticommunist John Foster Dulles as secretary of state.

Arbenz's agrarian reform act of June 27, 1952, Decree 900, laid the foundation for a program of expropriation of large landholdings that seemed to be aimed especially at UFCO, although it focused primarily on distributing public lands. Virtually no land in the highlands was touched by the act. Only 15 percent of the 650,000 acres owned by UFCO was marked for expropriation, but there was immediately a major dispute over Guatemalan compensation for this land, the government offering little more than $600,000 and the company claiming a value of almost $16 million.

The United States launched a diplomatic offensive against the Arbenz government in 1953, followed by a covert scheme of the Central Intelligence Agency to overthrow the regime in 1954 through its support of a small Guatemalan exile force commanded by Colonel Carlos Castillo Armas. Opposition to Arbenz within Guatemala was on the rise, although he still enjoyed wide popularity among urban labor and some elements of the middle class, despite his resort to widespread repression of opponents after 1953. Success of the CIA scheme, however, depended on the refusal of the Guatemalan army to defend the Arbenz regime. The army thus remained the arbiter of Guatemalan politics, as it had been since the 1840s, but in this case it was strongly supported by the agricultural and commercial elite and the Roman Catholic hierarchy.

### THE 1960S

The overthrow of Arbenz marked the beginning of one of the darkest periods in Guatemalan history, as a strong reaction against the revolutionary reforms under the presidency of Castillo Armas (1954–1957) resulted in the suppression of the labor movement and the repeal or non-enforcement of much of the social reform legislation, including agrarian reform. With strong U.S. backing, Castillo Armas and his National Democratic Movement (MDN) set the tone for the next thirty years of military rule. The communists and other leftists, to some degree united in the Guatemalan Labor Party (PGT), were outlawed and went underground. Divisions among the military, however, hindered the stability that might have been expected. After Castillo Armas was assassinated in July 1957, intense rivalry among the various military factions was accompanied by considerable corruption. Miguel Ydígoras Fuentes finally emerged triumphant with his National Redemption Party in the election of 1958. Ydígoras served until 1963.

Ydígoras attempted to restore the traditional Liberal Party oligarchy—greatly expanded with new agricultural and industrial enterprises resulting from large-scale U.S. investment encouraged by the Eisenhower and Kennedy administrations—while paying lip service to the middle-class and working-class interests stimulated by the Arévalo and Arbenz policies. He cooperated in the establishment of the Central American Common Market (CACM), which served the Guatemalan economy well. Less repressive than Castillo Armas, Ydígoras ran into difficulty when the Cuban Revolution alarmed right-wing Guatemalans. Ydígoras personally led the troops in putting down a Cuban-supported revolt in November 1960, but remnants of those insurgents escaped into the hills of eastern Guatemala, organized the Rebel Armed Forces (FAR), and launched a guerrilla war that continued into the 1990s. This activity, together with Ydígoras's apparent willingness to allow Arévalo's candidacy in the approaching 1963 presidential election, led to his overthrow by Colonel Enrique Peralta Azurdia, who ruled the country from 1963 to 1966.

Peralta attempted to create a broader base of support for his Democratic Institutional Party (PID), which he compared to the corporate Mexican Institutional Revolutionary Party (PRI). He also intensified the anticommunism campaign and became heavily involved in efforts to suppress the leftist guerrillas. Peralta's Constitution of 1965 provided a framework for cooperation between the PID and Mario Sandoval Alarcón's National Liberation Movement (MLN)—successor to Castillo Armas's MDN—on the right and the Revolutionary Party (PR)—successor to Arévalo's Revolutionary Action Party (PAR)—on the moderate left. Out of this arrangement came a relatively free election, although it was restricted to those three parties. Violence soared as right-wing death squads murdered labor and leftist leaders and the guerrillas stepped up their campaign against government forces.

Not long before the election, the PR candidate, Mario Méndez Montenegro, was probably assassinated (although his death appeared to be a suicide). His brother, Julio César Méndez Montenegro, succeeded him as the PR candidate and with strong reformist support won the election. Widespread popular demonstrations were expected if he were not allowed to take office. The PID accepted his presidency after Méndez gave secret assurance that the army leaders would retain their power, thereby precluding any real change. The repression thus continued, with strong U.S. counterinsurgency support in an effort to defeat the guerrillas, who were gaining adherents in the countryside although they controlled relatively little territory. A campaign of calculated terror led by Colonel Carlos Arana Osorio spread violence and lack of respect for human rights over the land as the army murdered thousands of people suspected of aiding the guerrillas. While Méndez enjoyed the distinction of completing his four-year term as the only civilian president of Guatemala between 1950 and 1985, he was unable to change the basic pattern of military rule and growing violations of human rights.

The FAR, led by Luis Turcios Lima until his death in a car accident in 1966, was the principal guerrilla group, but in 1965 it divided, with Marco Antonio Yon Sosa breaking away to form the November 13 Revolutionary Movement (MR-13). Yon Sosa died in a clash with Mexican troops in 1970, but both groups continued to harass the army. Some believed the army would not completely destroy the guerrillas because their presence justified continued high appropriations and other benefits for the military. In the 1970s two new guerrilla groups emerged: the Guerrilla Army of the Poor (EGP), which tended to replace the FAR, especially in the western highlands where it tried to mobilize the indigenous peoples, and the Organization of the People in Arms (OPRA).

### 1970–1985

Arana Osorio, the PID candidate in 1970, campaigned openly on an anticommunist platform that promised more repression. With the PR discredited, the Guatemalan Christian Democratic Democracy party (DCG) became the principal legal opposition to the military but was still too weak to have much of a chance; the PID easily won a controlled election in which fewer than half the registered voters participated. In the 1974 election General Kjell Laugerud continued PID domination of the country but faced a stiff challenge from a DCG-led coalition that nominated a conservative military officer, General Efraín Ríos Montt. Confronted with obvious and widespread electoral fraud, the DCG claimed to have won, but the official results gave Laugerud the victory. Laugerud, the son of a Norwegian immigrant, had

**Civilian defense force training, Guatemala, 1982.** The Guatemalan army trained individuals to become part of civil patrols aimed at weakening the strength of guerrilla groups in the countryside. ALAIN KELER/SYGMA/CORBIS

been Arana's chief of staff. He moderated the repressive appearance of the previous administration somewhat, although it remained a military dictatorship. There was some increase in labor union organization and opposition political activity, allowing the Christian Democrats in particular to gain ground. A devastating earthquake in February 1976 created special problems for his administration, but he met the opposition's political activities with new repressive tactics.

In 1978 General Romeo Lucas García of the PID succeeded to the presidency in another fraudulent election in which voter abstention reached new heights (see Table 1). Although by the early 1970s the expanding population and increased agricultural export production were contributing to rising poverty in Guatemala, the economy also made impressive gains owing to diversification of agricultural export production and industrial expansion. In Guatemala City business continued to expand and the growing middle class enjoyed affluence despite serious inflation. The petroleum crisis of the 1970s was less damaging to Guatemala than to many other Latin American states because of the exploitation of small but significant oil reserves in the Petén.

The military elite had begun to enter the economy in a major way. Not only did the generals receive enormous salaries when they served as president, but they used their position to acquire private companies, large landholdings, and monopolistic concessions. They established their own bank (Banco del Ejército) as another institutional base for their economic interests. The corruption associated with this economic expansion and the wealth of these military officers reached obscene proportions in a country beset with staggering poverty among the majority of its population. Combined with the earthquake, the general downturn in the international economy had by the early 1980s caused falling prices for Guatemalan coffee, cotton, and sugar exports, while domestic inflation

**Young boy in Guatemala making adobe bricks, late 20th century.** Guatemala is a young country, with almost half of the population under fifteen. BETTMANN/CORBIS

increased. Guatemala's trade deficit rose from $63 million in 1980 to $409 million in 1981.

Meanwhile, Lucas and the right-wing death squads launched a brutal policy of genocide against indigenous peoples suspected of supporting or joining the guerrillas, as Guatemala became notorious for its human rights violations. As the generals continued to seize large tracts of land, thousands of Indians fled to large refugee camps in Chiapas. All this focused unfavorable attention on Guatemala and damaged the important tourist trade. President Jimmy Carter sought to distance the United States from the Guatemalan military, ending official military aid altogether. Yet Carter's human rights policy only hardened the resolve of the Guatemalan officers to deal violently with the Left and even with moderate progressives such as the Christian Democrats. Guatemala simply made up for a partial cutoff of U.S. arms sales with arms and advisers from Israel. Terror and assassination took a horrifying toll among labor leaders and University of San Carlos students and faculty. Meanwhile, the general economic level of the population worsened. Following the 1982 rigged election of another PID general, Ángel Aníbal Guevara, several younger officers, supported by elements in both the extreme right-wing MLN and the DCG, engineered a coup that prevented him from taking office, ousting Lucas during the last days of his term and replacing him with a junta headed by General Ríos Montt. The elevation of Ríos Montt to the presidency reflected not only an end to the long domination by the PID but also the phenomenal rise of evangelical Protestantism in Guatemala, for General Ríos Montt was a minister of the California-based evangelical Church of the Word. Evangelical Protestantism had grown remarkably since about 1960, and an estimated 20 percent of Guatemala's population were Protestants by 1980. In contrast to the new Catholic evangelism in the country, often associated with "liberation theology" and the political Left, most of the Protestants were conservative and identified with pro-U.S. policies.

Ríos Montt's brief presidency served as a transition away from direct military rule. Superficially there was a noticeable effort to curb corruption and to encourage a higher degree of ethics in government. More impressive was the decline of death-squad activities and the restoration of security and peace in the central highlands. Political assassinations in the cities virtually ceased and the decline of tourism, to which the violence had contributed, was reversed for a time. Yet the economic and military strength of the powerful generals who had ruled the country since 1954 could not be easily turned back. Ríos Montt was in no sense sympathetic to leftist interests. He and the officers he represented were concerned with preserving the privileged position of the military and perceived that military abuses and corruption threatened the institution. In the countryside, Ríos Montt stepped up efforts to defeat the guerrillas. Massacres of Indian communities continued, as did the flow of refugees into Mexico. His government inaugurated a system of civil patrols, requiring Indians to serve, usually without firearms, as guardians against the guerrillas. Those who refused were killed. Ríos Montt also suspended the constitution, restricted labor unions, and prohibited the functioning of political parties in his effort to maintain order. In response, the leftists united in the Guatemalan National Revolutionary Unity (Unidad Revolucionaria Nacional Guatemalteca, URNG), an umbrella organization for the Guatemalan Labor Party (PGT), FAR, EGP, and OPRA.

Ríos Montt's challenge to the military oligarchy, his constant moralistic preaching, the excessively large role of North American Protestants in his advisory councils, the imposition of a sales tax, and his meddling with powerful economic interests ensured that his regime was short-lived. In August 1983 another coup replaced him with defense minister General Óscar Humberto Mejía Victores. Cynicism, corruption, and anticommunism were the most conspicuous characteristics of the Mejía government, with commitment to the same neoliberal policies on behalf of the elites that had characterized Guatemalan governments since 1954. However, concerned over their image and dismayed at their failure to manage the complex economic and social problems besetting the country, the military officers decided to turn the government over to civilians. International pressure from human rights activists, a sharp decline in tourism, falling coffee prices, and the military government's inability to solve Guatemala's severe economic problems all contributed to the army's decision to permit a free election and to turn over the presidency to a civilian.

Elections for a constitutional convention on July 1, 1984, again reflected widespread voter apathy, despite the participation of seventeen political parties. Under the resulting 1985 constitution, a free election was held and Guatemala was hailed for its "conversion" to civilian democracy after some three decades of military domination. A multitude of political parties ranging from extreme right to center vied for the presidency, while the left remained outside the legal political spectrum. A runoff between the top contenders resulted in the victory of a center-right and U.S.-backed Christian Democrat, Vinicio Cerezo. Popular participation in the election surged upward after years of declining voter turnout under the military regimes. A wave of optimism accompanied Cerezo's inauguration in January 1986, even though it was understood that he was strictly limited in his approach to the state's socioeconomic problems by the ultimate authority of the army.

### 1986–2007

Cerezo achieved some foreign policy successes as he established himself as a leader in the Central American peace process in alliance with Costa Rican president Óscar Arias. These efforts helped to end Nicaragua's civil war and bring about a free election there in 1990, opened talks between the governments and guerrillas in El Salvador and Guatemala, and laid the foundations for the Central American Parliament and a Central American summit conference to foster greater economic and political integration of the isthmus. Cerezo also moved toward resolution of Guatemala's long-smoldering dispute over sovereignty in neighboring Belize.

In domestic affairs, however, Cerezo ran into formidable obstacles. The new constitution emphasized open political dialogue and freedom of the press, yet the real power remained with the military. Furthermore, Cerezo not only failed to solve serious socioeconomic ills but saw them worsen considerably. During his administration labor and peasant participation in the political process remained weak. The deteriorating economy contributed to an increase in the level of violence, not only from the guerrillas but also from right-wing death squads, the military, personal vendettas, and rising common crime. Declining prices for Guatemalan exports, especially coffee, exacerbated the economic decline until a freeze in Brazil reversed the downward trend. The heavy foreign debt made balancing the budget impossible, especially when the government expanded the bureaucracy and appeared to tolerate widespread corruption and scandal.

Devaluation of the currency contributed to greater poverty during Cerezo's administration as inflation outran wages. Strikes and other work stoppages, especially in the public sector, seriously damaged government services. The Christian Democrats had appealed to middle-class and lower-class voters with promises of more social and economic benefits, but Cerezo's government carefully catered more to business interests, the military, and U.S. and international banking interests regarding the debt. Although it refused to turn over as much of the national resources to private ownership as U.S. advisers recommended, it privatized the national airline, Aviateca, and generally pursued conservative austerity programs in which the gap between rich and poor widened without reducing the debt significantly.

Ineligible for reelection (a legacy of the 1944 reaction to long dictatorships of the past), Cerezo left office in 1991. Popular rejection of his Christian Democratic administration was obvious when the DCG received but a small minority of the popular vote in the November 1990 election. In a runoff between two conservative candidates on January 6, 1991, Jorge Serrano Elías won in a landslide, defeating newspaper editor Jorge Carpio Nicolle by a two-to-one majority. Serrano, of the relatively unknown Solidarity Action Movement (MAS), gained many votes from those supporting Ríos Montt, who had been ruled ineligible because of the constitutional ban on candidates who had participated in a military revolt. A born-again Christian like Ríos Montt, Serrano became the first Protestant elected president in Latin American history. He promised to establish a social pact involving business, government, and labor. Voter apathy was again high, however, with 44 percent of the 3.2 million registered voters refusing to cast ballots in the November election and 54 percent abstaining in the runoff.

Serrano was careful not to antagonize the military, but as violence rose from both left and right, there was growing pessimism about his chances for success. In September 1991 a devastating earthquake, killing fifty-three and leaving thirty thousand homeless, aggravated the socioeconomic problems. Serrano, an industrial engineer, pursued neoliberal economic policies and was more acceptable to the conservative power structure than Cerezo, but was unable to cope with the rising opposition. In May 1993 he seized dictatorial power in what some called a "self-coup," disbanding the Congress and all political parties. Massive protests followed and the Congress refused to disband. When the army failed to back Serrano, he resigned on June 1. Congress chose Ramiro de León Carpio, the human rights ombudsman, as interim president. The military accepted this but insisted on their right to choose the minister of defense, making clear that the army still held ultimate authority in Guatemala. The military was suspected in the subsequent assassination of León Carpio's cousin, Jorge Carpio, the former presidential candidate.

Shifting political alliances brought new political coalitions in the 1990s that reduced the DCG and the Union of the National Center (UCN) to minor party status. Under the leadership of Álvaro Arzú, the neoliberal National Advancement Party (PAN) won the support of several center-right parties to form a congressional majority in 1995. Arzú had been popular as mayor of Guatemala City and was foreign minister under Serrano until he resigned in protest against Serrano's efforts to normalize relations with Belize. More extreme right-wing parties, meanwhile, joined with Ríos Montt and his Guatemalan Republican Front (FRG). Once again the courts denied Ríos Montt's eligibility to run for president, so Alfonso Portillo took his place as the FRG candidate in the November 1995 election. In a runoff the following January, Arzú narrowly defeated Portillo to become the new president. Voter abstention had again become serious as only about a third of the registered voters participated in this election.

Arzú's government followed strongly neoliberal policies with significant economic growth and the rejuvenation of the Central American Common Market, but his principal achievement was the conclusion of agreements with the guerrillas to end Guatemala's long civil war. The formal peace accord was signed in Guatemala City on December 29, 1996, although implementation of its provisions dragged on for years. The army accepted the accords along with dismissal of military officers accused of human rights violations. Yet the 1998 assassination of Bishop Juan Gerardi, who had published a detailed account of the atrocities committed during the thirty-six-year civil war and the failure of the government to

**Indigenous Guatemalans lining up to vote, Solola, Guatemala, November 9, 2003.** Over half of Guatemala's population consists of indigenous citizens, namely Mayan Indians. Throughout the mid 1970s and 1980s, thousands of Indians fled into neighboring Mexico as military dictators gained control of large amounts of land and executed anyone suspected of sympathizing with antigovernment guerrillas. © SUSANA GONZALEZ/REUTERS/CORBIS

stem the continued violence, highlighted the persistence of human rights abuses.

As Guatemala entered the twenty-first century violence and human rights abuses still haunted the country. Indigenous Guatemalans, however, had notably increased their representation in the government and had formed their own political party, the National Civic Political Forum of Mayan Unity and Fraternity (EPUM). It was the compassionate voice of an indigenous Quiché woman, Rigoberta Menchú, that brought the plight of the Guatemalan people to worldwide attention, increasing international pressure on the Guatemalan government to end the conflict by negotiating with the rebels. Menchú received the 1992 Nobel Peace Prize "in recognition of her work for social justice and ethno-cultural reconciliation." Menchú led efforts to prosecute those guilty of human-rights abuses and in 2007 she would declare her candidacy for the presidency of Guatemala.

In 1999 Portillo was again the candidate of the FRG and with Ríos Montt's backing defeated Guatemala City mayor Óscar Berger (PAN), winning 68 percent of the vote in the December 26 runoff and taking office in January 2000. Despite economic growth, the violence and widespread poverty in the country contributed to increased emigration to Mexico and the United States. Remittances to relatives remaining in Guatemala came to be a major source of foreign exchange for the country, second only to coffee export income. During Portillo's administration Guatemala also became a major clandestine exporter of illegal drugs to the United States. The U.S. Drug Enforcement Agency repeatedly claimed that Guatemala was a transfer point for Colombian heroin and cocaine, and Portillo agreed to allow U.S. military and other special agents to operate within Guatemala against the drug dealers.

Reports of corruption eroded support for Portillo, especially a legislative report in 2001 known as Guategate that resulted in twenty-four indictments, including one against Ríos Montt. Although the courts later exonerated Ríos Montt, there continued to be charges of government corruption and financial mismanagement. Attention to these problems as at least temporarily diverted by the visit of Pope John Paul II to Guatemala in July 2002, when he canonized the seventeenth-century friar, Pedro de San José Betancur, the only Central American ever to achieve sainthood in the Roman Catholic Church.

The FRG had little credibility left by the November 2003 election, but the Court of Constitutionality had finally ruled that Ríos Montt could be a candidate for the presidency. He was unable, however, to overcome the failing reputation of his FRG party and he finished well behind óscar Berger of the rightist coalition Grand National Alliance (GANA) and Álvaro Colom of the leftist coalition National Unity of Hope (UNE). In the December runoff, Berger won with 54 percent of the votes and took office on January 14, 2004. Berger continued the neoliberal agenda and promised greater productivity and a pledge to increase employment, emphasizing the need to improve the lot of Guatemala's indigenous majority. He recognized former governments' responsibility for much of the country's violence when he ordered compensation to peasants for lands and lives lost during the civil war, and he named Rigoberta Menchú to supervise implementation of the 1996 peace accords. He also reduced the size of the army, shifting some military personnel to the National Police in an effort to attack the continuing high rates of murder, violence against women, kidnappings, and violations of civil rights.

Rising coffee prices by 2005 and more diversification in manufacturing and agriculture created new jobs and more economic activity. There were improvements, too, in public health, thanks especially to considerable aid from the Cuban government, which equipped six new hospitals in Guatemala and sent physicians and other medical personnel to staff them. Cuba also provided scholarships for hundreds of Guatemalans to study medicine in Havana. The infant mortality rate in Guatemala dropped sharply and the occurrences of many epidemic diseases was significantly reduced. The neoliberal policies of the government, while controversial, moved Guatemala into a globalized economy, while the traditional dominance of the military in Guatemalan history appeared to be diminishing.

*See also* **Arana, Francisco J; Arana Osorio, Carlos; Arbenz Guzmán, Jacobo; Arce, Manuel José; Arévalo Bermejo, Juan José; Aycinena, Mariano de; Barrundia, José Francisco; Bustamante y Guerra, José; Carrera, José Rafael; Castillo Armas, Carlos; Central America; Central American Common Market (CACM); Central Intelligence Agency (CIA); Cerezo Arévalo, Marco Vinicio; Cerna, Vicente; Chacón, Lázaro; Cruz, Serapio; Estrada Cabrera, Manuel; Galván Rivera, Mariano; García Granados, Miguel; Guatemala, Audiencia of; Iturbide, Agustín de; Lucas García, Fernando Romeo; Mejía Victores, Oscar Humberto; Menchú Tum, Rigoberta; Méndez Montenegro, Julio César; Molina, Pedro; Morazán, Francisco; North American Free Trade Agreement (NAFTA); Orellana, José María; Paredes, Mariano; Peralta Azurdia, Enrique; Plan of Iguala; Reyna Barrios, José María; Ríos Montt, José Efraín; Serrano Elías, Jorge Antonio; Ubico y Castañeda, Jorge; United Fruit Company; Wyke-Aycinena Treaty (1859); Ydígoras Fuentes, Miguel; Yon Sosa, Marco Antonio.**

BIBLIOGRAPHY


Adams, Richard N. *Crucifixion by Power: Essays on Guatemalan Social Structure, 1944–1966.* Austin: University of Texas Press, 1970.

Bethell, Leslie, ed. *Central America since Independence.* Cambridge, U.K., and New York: Cambridge University Press, 1991.

Casaús Arzú, Marta. *Guatemala: Linaje y racismo.* San José, Costa Rica: FLACSO, 1992.

Casaús Arzú, Marta, and Óscar Guillermo Peláez Almengor, eds. *Historia intelectual de Guatemala.* Guatemala: Centro de Estudios Urbanos y Regionales, Universidad de San Carlos de Guatemala, 2001.

Cojti Cuxil, Demetrio. *El movimiento maya (en Guatemala).* Guatemala: CHOLSAMAJ, 1997.

Dosal, Paul. *Doing Business with the Dictators: A Political History of United Fruit in Guatemala, 1899–1944.* Wilmington, DE: Scholarly Resources, 1993.

Dosal, Paul. *Power in Transition: The Rise of Guatemala's Industrial Oligarchy, 1871–1994.* Westport, CT: Praeger, 1995.

Dunkerley, James. *Power in the Isthmus: A Political History of Modern Central America.* London: Verso, 1988.

García, Prudencio. *El genocidio de Guatemala: A la luz de la sociología militar.* Madrid: Sepha, 2005.

García Laguardia, Jorge M. *La reforma liberal en Guatemala: Vida política y orden constitucional,* 3rd edition. Guatemala: Editorial Universitaria, 1985.

Garrard-Burnett, Virginia. *Protestantism in Guatemala: Living in the New Jerusalem.* Austin: University of Texas Press, 1998.

Gleijeses, Piero. *Shattered Hope: The Guatemalan Revolution and the United States, 1944–1954.* Princeton, NJ: Princeton University Press, 1991.

González Davison, Fernando. *El régimen liberal en Guatemala, 1871–1944.* Guatemala: Editorial Universitaria, 1987.

Grandin, Greg. *The Blood of Guatemala: A History of Race and Nation.* Durham, NC: Duke University Press, 2000.

Grieb, Kenneth. *Guatemalan Caudillo, the Regime of Jorge Ubico: Guatemala, 1931–1944.* Athens: Ohio University Press, 1979.

Handy, Jim. *Gift of the Devil: A History of Guatemala.* Boston: South End Press, 1984.

Holden, Robert H. *Armies without Nations: Political Violence and State Formation in Central America, 1821–1960.* Oxford and New York: Oxford University Press, 2004.

Jonas, Susanne. *The Battle for Guatemala: Rebels, Death Squads, and U. S. Power.* Boulder, CO: Westview, 1991.

Luján Muñoz, Jorge, ed.*Historia general de Guatemala,* 6 vols. Guatemala: Asociación de Amigos del País, Fundación para la Cultura y Desarrollo, 1993–1999.

Macleod, Murdo J. *Spanish Central America: A Socioeconomic History, 1520–1720.* Berkeley: University of California Press, 1973.

May, Rachel. *Terror in the Countryside: Campesino Responses to Political Violence in Guatemala, 1954–1985.* Athens: Ohio University Press, 2001.

McCreery, David J. *Rural Guatemala, 1760–1940.* Stanford, CA: Stanford University Press, 1994.

Menchú, Rigoberta. *I, Rigoberta Menchú: An Indian Woman in Guatemala,* trans. Ann Wright; ed. Elizabeth Burgos-Debray. London: Verso, 1984.

Monteforte Toledo, Mario. *La revolución de Guatemala, 1944–1954.* Guatemala: Editorial Universitaria, 1975.

Pattridge, Blake. *Institution Building and State Formation in Nineteenth-Century Latin America: The University of San Carlos, Guatemala.* New York: P. Lang, 2004.

Reeves, René. *Ladinos with Ladinos, Indians with Indians: Land, Labor, and Regional Ethnic Conflict in the Making of Guatemala.* Stanford, CA: Stanford University Press, 2006.

Smith, Carol A., ed. *Guatemalan Indians and the State: 1540 to 1988.* Austin: University of Texas Press, 1990.

Taracena Arriola, Arturo, et al. *Etnicidad, estado y nación en Guatemala,* 2 vols. Antigua Guatemala: Centro de Investigaciones Regionales de Mesoamérica, 2002–2004.

Torres-Rivas, Edelberto. *Interpretación del desarrollo social centroamericano,* 12th edition. San José, Costa Rica: FLACSO, 1989.

Villagrán Kramer, Francisco. *Biografía política de Guatemala,* 2 vols. Guatemala: FLACSO-Editorial de Ciencias Sociales, 1993–2004.

Woodward Jr., Ralph Lee. *Rafael Carrera and the Emergence of the Republic of Guatemala.* Athens: University of Georgia Press, 1993.

Woodward Jr., Ralph Lee. *Central America: A Nation Divided,* 3rd edition. New York: Oxford University Press, 1999.

Woodward Jr., Ralph Lee. *A Short History of Guatemala.* Antigua Guatemala: Editorial Laura Lee, 2005.

Wortman, Miles. *Government and Society in Central America, 1680–1840.* New York: Columbia University Press, 1982.

RALPH LEE WOODWARD JR.

---

**GUATEMALA, AUDIENCIA OF.** Audiencia of Guatemala, an administrative unit of the Spanish colonial empire corresponding roughly to modern Central America. Properly, the term refers both to the territorial jurisdiction and to the highest royal tribunal located in it. The territorial unit was known also as the Kingdom of Guatemala, and for most of the colonial period it included what is today Guatemala, El Salvador, Honduras, Nicaragua, and Costa Rica as well as Belize and the Mexican state of Chiapas. Except for brief periods in the sixteenth century, it did not include Panama. The tribunal was known initially as the Audiencia of Los Confines (because its original seat was between the frontiers of Guatemala and Nicaragua), but it came later to be called simply the Audiencia of Guatemala.

### EARLY HISTORY

The earliest Spanish governors in Central America were powerful, personalistic dictators whose claims to rule were rooted in the Conquest or in the defeat of rival Spaniards. These men, who included Pedro de Alvarado in Guatemala and Pedro Arias de Ávila in Nicaragua and Panama, held royal commissions, but in practice they were only nominally subject to outside authority. The discovery of gold in Honduras and continuing abuses against the Indian population pointed to the need for a stronger royal presence in Central America proper.

In the New Laws of 1542, the Spanish crown created the *Audiencia de los Confines,* whose jurisdiction stretched from the Yucatán peninsula south to the isthmus of Panama. The new tribunal consisted of a president, Alonso de Maldonado (1542–1548), and three *oidores* (judges). In 1544, it established itself at Gracias a Dios, a gold-mining center in western Honduras. Gracias a Dios was isolated and a poor location for an administrative center. When its mines began to decline, it lost its early economic importance. In 1548, the crown ordered the transfer of the audiencia to Santiago De Los Caballeros (modern Antigua), in the more populous and accessible central valley of Guatemala. Maldonado's successor, Alonso López De Cerrato (1548–1555), supervised the move in 1549 and became known for his energetic enforcement of those parts of the New Laws designed to protect the Indians and restrict the *encomienda.*

The sixteenth century saw many adjustments and readjustments to the audiencia's jurisdiction. In 1550, the crown separated Panama from it and attached it to the Audiencia of Lima, which had also been created by the New Laws. In 1556, Guatemala gained jurisdiction over the Pacific Coast province of Soconusco, which had previously belonged to the Audiencia of Mexico, but four years later it lost the Yucatán peninsula to the same tribunal. The most radical change came in 1563, when the crown ordered the transfer of the audiencia seat from Santiago to Panama City. Although the audiencia regained jurisdiction over Panama, it lost Guatemala and part of Honduras, which were assigned to the Audiencia of Mexico. This arrangement proved unsatisfactory, however, and the crown soon reversed it. The audiencia returned to Santiago in 1570, with its previous jurisdiction restored. Panama's own audiencia, which the New Laws had dissolved, was reestablished, and this province thereafter remained independent of Guatemalan jurisdiction.

The Audiencia of Guatemala remained at Santiago for more than 200 years, until severe earthquakes in 1773 caused its relocation to newly founded Guatemala City, which would be its home until the region gained independence from Spain in 1821.

## POLITICAL INSTITUTIONS AND SUBDIVISIONS

Spanish colonial audiencias embodied powers and functions that we would today separate into the modern categories of executive, legislative, and judicial. The president and *oidores* sat both collectively and individually as legislators and as appellate and first-instance judges. In Guatemala, initially, they also functioned as a collegial executive, but in 1560, President Juan Núñez de Landecho (1559–1563) received a separate commission as governor general, with powers equivalent to those of the viceroy of New Spain. Although technically subordinate to the Viceroyalty of New Spain, the president-governors of Guatemala governed autonomously and reported directly to the Council of the Indies in Spain. The presidency itself evolved into a separate executive increasingly distinct from the audiencia, a development favored by the need for a centralized military command, which resulted from the growing foreign threat in the Caribbean. Early presidents were all *letrados* (university-trained lawyers), but in the seventeenth century the crown began to occasionally appoint military officers, with the additional title of captain-general. The first military president was the Conde de la Gómera (1611–1626). Especially after the mid-seventeenth century, most presidents came from military, rather than legal, backgrounds.

At the local level, the audiencia's jurisdiction was divided into district magistracies, governed by officials known variously as Corregidores, Alcaldes Mayores, and Gobernadores (governors, but not to be confused with the early post-Conquest governors or with the presidents in their function as governors-general). Although their titles differed, in accordance with perceived differences in the importance of their jurisdictions, these magistrates were identical in powers and responsibilities, if not in pay and prestige. They governed independently of each other and answered directly to the president and audiencia.

Salaries for all local magistrates were low, but opportunities to supplement one's income through corruption and abuse were great. Indeed, the crown expected its appointees to extract additional compensation from their Indian and mestizo charges. Such appointments provided a means of cultivating elite loyalty at minimal cost to the treasury.

## ECONOMICS AND SOCIETY

Central America was a poor colony. Honduran mines continued to produce after the early boom played out, but their output was negligible. Cacao became a major export in the second half of the sixteenth century, but export peaked by the beginning of the seventeenth. Indigo gained importance in the seventeenth and eighteenth centuries, and it transformed society and the landscape in what is today eastern Guatemala and El Salvador. Competition was stiff, however, and the most profitable world markets were closed to Central American producers because of mercantilist trade regulations.

Money was scarce in the colony, but Santiago, San Salvador, Granada, Cartago, and other cities and towns provided domestic markets for artisanries and foodstuffs. Much of this production was in the hands of Indian and mestizo communal and smallholders, but some prominent creole families built substantial fortunes and large landholdings based on wheat, sugar, and cattle production, especially in the central valley of Guatemala. Also, the colonial economy was able to support a small but powerful clique of peninsular merchants, who allied themselves by marriage with landed creole families, controlled strategic sectors of the economy, and dominated the influential *cabildo* (city council) of Santiago.

## WAR AND POLITICS

Despite the region's poverty, its strategic location between the Caribbean Sea and the Pacific Ocean made its security essential to the Spanish crown. Foreign incursions, which became more frequent throughout the seventeenth and eighteenth centuries, represented a chronic threat. Pirate raids were common on the Caribbean coasts, and buccaneers sacked Granada in 1665 and 1670. English interlopers established themselves in the Bay Islands (Islas de la Bahia) in the 1640s and at Belize in the 1660s; from these beachheads, they expanded their control to much of the Mosquito Coast during the following century. The colonial wars of the eighteenth century interfered with trade and placed a large financial burden on the colony as well.

The first priority of audiencia presidents throughout the colonial period was to maintain domestic order and to mobilize sufficient resources to pay for the fortifications, garrisons, and ships necessary to defend the province against foreign enemies. To this end, they made accommodations with local elites, who generally declined to be taxed, except on their own terms. The greatest financial burden fell upon the Indian population in the form of the tribute, or head tax. Indeed, the importance of Indian labor and production in general to the economic well-being of the colony was reflected in the fact that the attempts of the crown to prohibit exploitative and abusive practices by the colonial elite generally came to little. For example, the *repartimiento* (labor draft) for agriculture, which was abolished in New Spain in 1633, survived in the Audiencia of Guatemala until the end of the colonial period. Presidents found it expedient to wink at smuggling activities, both out of fear of provoking creole discontent and because illegal trade provided the needed specie to convert tribute payments in kind into cash, to pay other taxes, and to service the increasingly frequent "voluntary donations," *composiciones,* and other payments called for by the financially strapped crown.

Collusion with the entrenched colonial elite weakened Spanish government in Central America. Military presidents, such as Martín Carlos de Mencos (1659–1668) and Jacinto de Barrios Leal (1688–1695), frequently split with their lawyer colleagues on the audiencia and sided with local interests on questions that pitted them against royal policy. By the close of the seventeenth century, the colony had become factionalized and crisis-ridden. In an effort to maintain some control, the crown, between 1670 and 1702, commissioned no fewer than four general *visitas* of the province, none of which produced significant results, and at least two of which nearly provoked rebellions. The royal decision during the War of the Spanish Succession (1702–1713) to raise funds by selling audiencia positions further weakened Spanish authority in the region.

## BOURBON REFORMS

The energetic Bourbon monarchy attempted later in the eighteenth century to tighten its control over

Central America and to extract greater revenues from it. Some reform measures undertaken were long overdue. The crown created a mint in Guatemala in 1733 in an attempt to stimulate mining production and to increase the amount of money in circulation. Measures to liberalize the commercial system, especially the Free Trade Decree of 1778, opened up economic opportunities for colonial exports. In 1793, Guatemalan merchants finally received permission to organize their own guild, or Consulado, independent of that of Mexico. The Bourbons also sought to reform the complicated and corrupt system of colonial administration. Peninsulars were favored over creoles for bureaucratic appointments, and a new office (Regent of the Audiencia, introduced in 1776) was designed to counterbalance the power of the president. A major restructuring of local administration occurred with the intendancy reform of 1786, which consolidated several smaller jurisdictions into four larger ones: Chiapas, Honduras, Nicaragua, and El Salvador. Guatemala remained separate, but the loss of control over the indigo-rich Salvadoran jurisdiction was a blow to the power of its merchant elite and contributed significantly to the development of a separatist tradition in Central America.

Although admirable from the point of view of efficiency, honest administration, and economic development, the Bourbon Reforms undermined traditional accommodations and alienated established elites by closing them out of employment opportunities. Their economic benefits were largely undermined by the cost of ongoing warfare and by the earthquakes that devastated the capital city in 1773. Dissatisfaction with Spanish rule grew among the colonial elites, and although the strong-arm tactics of President José de Bustamante y Guerra (1811–1818) kept the colony quiet while wars of rebellion were raging elsewhere in the Americas, Central American creoles were receptive to independence when confronted with the collapse of royal authority in neighboring Mexico in 1821.

*See also* **Audiencia.**

BIBLIOGRAPHY

Two standard general works in English on colonial Central America are Murdo J. MacLeod, *Spanish Central America: A Socioeconomic History, 1520–1720* (1973), and Miles L. Wortman, *Government and Society in Central America, 1680–1840* (1982). A useful institutional study is Carlos Molina Argüello, "Gobernaciones, alcaldías mayores y corregimientos en el Reino de Guatemala," in *Anuario de estudios americanos* 17 (1960): 105–132. On the impact of war and international rivalry, see Troy S. Floyd, *The Anglo-Spanish Struggle for Mosquitia* (1967). Studies of political issues and conflicts in the sixteenth and seventeenth centuries include William L. Sherman, *Forced Native Labor in Sixteenth-Century Central America* (1979); Murdo J. MacLeod, "The Primitive Nation State, Delegation of Functions, and Results: Some Examples from Early Colonial Central America," in *Essays in the Political, Economic, and Social History of Colonial Latin America,* edited by Karen Spalding (1982); and Stephen Webre, "Política y comercio en la Guatemala del siglo XVII," in *Revista de historia* 15 (January–June 1987): 27–41, and "El trabajo forzoso de los indígenas en la política colonial guatemalteca, siglo XVII," in *Anuario de estudios centroamericanos* 13, no. 2 (1987): 49–61. On the Bourbon period, see Troy S. Floyd, "The Guatemalan Merchants, the Government, and the *Provincianos,* 1750–1800," in *Hispanic American Historical Review* 41, no. 1 (1961): 90–110; and Ralph Lee Woodward, Jr., "Economic and Social Origins of the Guatemalan Political Parties, 1773–1823," in *Hispanic American Historical Review* 45, no. 4 (1965): 544–566, and *Class Privilege and Economic Development: The Consulado de Comercio of Guatemala, 1793–1871* (1966).

### *Additional Bibliography*

Guatemala, Carlos Alfonso, Alvarez-Lobos Villatoro, and Ricardo Toledo Palomo. *Libro de los pareceres de la Real Audiencia de Guatemala, 1571–1655.* Guatemala: Academia de Geografía e Historia de Guatemala, 1996.

Hawkins, Timothy. *José De Bustamante and Central American Independence: Colonial Administration in an Age of Imperial Crisis.* Tuscaloosa: University of Alabama, 2004.

STEPHEN WEBRE

---

**GUATEMALA, ECONOMIC SOCIETY OF.** First established in 1795, the Sociedad Económica de Amigos del País de Guatemala was inspired by similar institutions in Europe and the New World that sought to spread the "new science" of the Enlightenment. Working in conjunction with the Gazeta De Guatemala, a liberal news daily, the society sought to improve the economy of colonial Guatemala by encouraging free trade, establishing trade and technical schools, improving agricultural techniques, and challenging established economic interests. After independence, some of Guatemala's most prominent citizens, including José Cecilio del Valle, played an active role in the society. With the failure of union in Central America, the society ceased to be an advocate of free-trade liberalism but continued to work to improve Guatemala's economy under the conservative guidelines established by Rafael Carrera and his successors. It continued in operation until 1881, when Liberal President Justo Rufino Barrios disbanded it.

The society was established by royal decree in 1795, with José Antonio de Liendo y Goicoechea, Alejandro Ramírez, Jacobo Villaurrutia, and Antonio Muró among the founding members. A school was established to teach arithmetic, hydraulics, optics, geography, and civil engineering. Through the *Gazeta,* articles were published by such Enlightenment writers as Buffon, Descartes, Locke, and Montesquieu. The society also presented scientific, historical, and social papers, one of which led to its suppression. In 1799, the society published a paper by Muró that argued that Indians be allowed to wear Spanish-style clothing, in essence defying a long-established practice in Spanish America. In 1800 the crown ordered the suppression of the society for this and other violations of the laws as recorded in the Recopilación, the Laws of the Indies.

The Society was reestablished in 1810, at least partly to appease the growing voices of liberalism in the colony. Captain-General José Bustamante y Guerra was openly hostile to the society, and in the confusion of independence and its aftermath, it ceased to operate in 1821. In 1829 the Legislative Assembly reestablished the society, and José Cecilio del Valle was named its director. After an initial period of activity, the society again declined, then revived in 1840, this time under control of the Conservatives.

Throughout the nineteenth century, the Society worked to promote literacy, especially among the Indians; training in marketable skills, such as weaving, horticulture, and engineering; and the cultivation of cash crops such as coffee and cochineal. But its efforts were poorly organized and haphazard, and the advancement of the economy and education likely would have continued even had the society not existed. Its inability to significantly improve the education and economy of Guatemala only underscored the backward nature of the country in the late colonial, independence, and postindependence periods. Guatemala today still suffers from many of the ills first identified in the 1790s: a low literacy rate, overdependence on a single cash crop, and an Indian population that has yet to be integrated into the national political, economic, and social structures.

*See also* **Enlightenment, The; Liberalism.**

BIBLIOGRAPHY

José Luis Reyes Monroy, *Apuntes para una monografía de la Sociedad Económia de Amigos del País* (1954).

Robert Jones Shafer, *The Economic Societies in the Spanish World, 1763–1821* (1958).

Elisa Luque-Alcalde, *La Sociedad Económica de Amigos del País de Guatemala* (1962).

Ralph Lee Woodward, Jr., *Class, Privilege, and Economic Development: The Consulado de Comercio of Guatemala, 1793–1871* (1966).

### *Additional Bibliography*

Casaús Arzú, Marta, and Oscar Guillermo Peláez Almengor. *Historia intelectual de Guatemala.* Ciudad Universitaria: Centro de Estudios Urbanos y Regionales, Universidad de San Carlos de Guatemala, 2001.

Meléndez Chaverri, Carlos. *La Ilustración en el antiguo reino de Guatemala.* San José: Editorial Universitaria Centroamericana, 1970.

Rubio Sánchez, Manuel. *Historia de la Sociedad Económica de Amigos del País.* Guatemala: Editorial Académica Centroamericana, 1981.

Michael Powelson

---

**GUATEMALA CITY.** Guatemala City, the capital of Guatemala, whose 2002 population was estimated at 2.5 million. The New Guatemala of the Assumption, better known as Guatemala City, was founded officially in Ermita Valley on 2 January 1776 as the seat of the Realm of Guatemala. The former capital city of Antigua (Old Guatemala), situated 25 miles from the present capital, was destroyed by a series of earthquakes in 1773. The cooperation of all levels of society was needed to move the capital. One notable aspect of the move was the forced relocation of seventeen Indian settlements to the new city in order to provide it with a labor force and essential products. The landless mestizos rapidly populated the new city, and as of 1778 the city had a population of 10,841. In order to assist the development of an adequate infrastructure, the Spanish crown halted the collection of taxes from the new city for ten years. One of the principal tasks was to provide drinking water.

The rebuilding of the Guatemalan capital during the last days of the colonial era was motivated not only by the earthquakes that devastated the original city but also by Bourbon political reforms of the last half of the eighteenth century. However, because of strong church as well as popular opposition to the relocation and the lack of resources, the new city did not achieve the physical stature or population size of Santiago until well after independence. In its physical as well as social structure it imitated the urban centers of Spain. Political independence in 1821 brought no significant improvement in living conditions for the city's population. On the contrary, in 1829 the wars of the United Provinces of Central America were waged in its streets, and in 1834 the president of the United Provinces, Francisco Morazán, moved the seat to the city of San Salvador.

With the triumph of Rafael Carrera in 1838–1840, the city experienced a second period of modest growth and stability as capital, first of the state of Guatemala, and after 1847, of the republic of Guatemala. The cultivation of kermes and the export of cochineal and coffee had a favorable impact on the city's economy. Projects begun in colonial days, such as the cathedral, were finally completed. The national theater (Teatro Carrera) was also inaugurated during this period.

With the arrival of the Liberals to power in 1871 and the impetus of a thriving coffee economy, the number of public projects grew as the functions of the state administration were expanded to meet the demands of the country's growing industry. New methods of transportation in the city were introduced, such as the horse-drawn tramway and the urban rail system. President José María Reyna Barrios backed efforts to beautify the city through the construction of new buildings and avenues.

During the dictatorship of Manuel Estrada Cabrera (1898–1920), Guatemala City experienced one of its worst disasters. In 1917–1918 it was almost totally destroyed by earthquakes. The poor were obliged to live in camps until the end of the 1920s. The ruin of the city was one of the factors contributing to the overthrow of Estrada Cabrera in April 1920. Subsequent governments applied themselves with little success to the task of rebuilding. The dictatorship of Jorge Ubico (1931–1944) initiated some of the most important infrastructural projects for the city, such as underground sewers. The present government palace was also built under Ubico.

The revolution of October 1944 brought about infrastructural development focused on athletic activities as well as new laws that encouraged people to rent houses in the city. Perhaps one of the most important urban reforms attempted in Guatemala in the twentieth century, the tenant law was stopped short by the counterrevolution of 1954. The earthquake of 4 February 1976, like the previous earthquakes, brought about changes and alterations in the city. Neighborhoods of low-cost housing grew due to the government's policy of selling inexpensive lots on which the victims of the disaster could build new homes. During Guatemala's thirty-six years of civil war, thousands of indigenous and peasant people fled to the city, constructing informal homes on the outskirts. Since then the growth of the city has been augmented by the concentration of industrial and state administrative centers. The original city occupied an area of approximately 3.5 square miles. As of the early 1990s it encompassed between 35 and 40 square miles. Besides its agreeable climate, one of the Guatemalan capital's strongest attractions is the natural beauty of the valley in which it is situated. Amid Guatemala's peace process (1994–1996), former mayor Álvaro Arzú Irigoyen won the presidency in 1996, owing to his constituents' decisive support. Following his term as president, Arzú returned to serve as the city's mayor from 2004 to 2007.

The city has a municipal development plan, "Guatemala 2020," that aims to improve transportation and revitalize the downtown, but it has experienced a recent crime wave, and, as is the case with many cities of Latin America, its deficiencies in public services are appreciable.

*See also* **Antigua; Carrera, José Rafael; Coffee Industry; Mestizo.**

BIBLIOGRAPHY

As of 2007 a comprehensive history of Guatemala City remains to be written, but Gisela Gellert and J. C. Pinto Soria, *Ciudad de Guatemala: Dos estudios sobre su evolución urbana (1524–1950)* (1992), is a useful beginning. On the movement of the city from Antigua to its present location, see Inge Langenberg, *Urbanisation und Bevölkerungsstruktur der Stadt Guatemala in der ausgehenden Kolonialzeit: Eine sozialhistorische Analyse der Stadtverlegung und ihrer Auswirkungen auf die demographische, berufliche, und soziale Gliederung der Bevölkerung (1773–1824)* (1981), and her briefer summary, "La estructura urbana y el cambio social en la ciudad de Guatemala a fines de la época colonial (1773–1824)," in Stephen A. Webre, ed., *La sociedad colonial en Guatemala: estudios regionales y locales* (1989), pp. 221–249. See also María Cristina Zilbermann De Luján, *Aspectos socioeconómicos del traslado de la Ciudad de Guatemala (1773–1783)* (1987); and Pedro Pérez Valenzuela, *La nueva Guatemala de la Asunción: Terremoto de Santa Marta, fundación en el Llano de la Virgen,* 2 vols. (1964).

*Additional Bibliography*

Bastos, Santiago. *Poderes y quereres: Historias de género y familia en los sectores populares de ciudad de Guatemala.* Guatemala: Facultad Latinoamericana de Ciencias Sociales (FLACSO), 2000.

Camus, Manuela. *Ser indígena en ciudad de Guatemala.* Guatemala: Facultad Latinoamericana de Ciencias Sociales (FLACSO), 2000.

Dym, Jordana, and Christophe Belaubre, eds. *Politics, Economy, and Society in Bourbon Central America, 1759–1821.* Boulder: University Press of Colorado, 2007.

Lida, Clara E., and Sonia Pérez Toledo. *Trabajo, ocio y coacción: Trabajadores urbanos en México y Guatemala en el siglo XIX.* México, D.F.: Universidad Autónoma Metropolitana, 2001.

Morán Mérida, Amanda. *Condiciones de vida y tenencia de la tierra en asentamientos precarios de la Ciudad de Guatemala.* Guatemala: Universidad de San Carlos de Guatemala, 1997.

Myers, David J., and Henry A. Dietz., eds. *Capital City Politics in Latin America: Democratization and Empowerment.* Boulder, CO: Lynne Rienner, 2002.

OSCAR PELÁEZ ALMENGOR
GISELA GELLERT

## GUATEMALA COMPANY.

**GUATEMALA COMPANY.** Guatemala Company, a trading company (sometimes known as the Pacific Company) formed in 1748 by a group of Guatemalan merchants in the wake of the Bourbon reform of the Sevilla–Cádiz monopoly over colonial trade. The reforms opened commerce to a wider number of Spaniards and colonists both to stimulate trade and to discourage smuggling. Inspired by the success of the Real Compañía Guizpuzcoana in the production and trade of cacao in Venezuela, the Guatemalans petitioned the crown in 1741 for the right to trade with Mexico, Peru, and Spain. The company was finally formed in 1748, and its merchants were especially interested in supplying the Honduran mining areas with Peruvian mercury and other goods, and in acting as the middlemen in the Pacific trade with Peru. Within a decade, however, the Peru trade had lost its importance for Central America, while the export of indigo to Spain, generally ignored by the Guatemalan merchants, had become lucrative. When the Guatemala Company finally turned its sights on the indigo trade, competition from Spanish merchants and Spanish capital prohibited the fledgling company from successfully entering this market. The company never got off the ground; Ramón de Lupategui exhausted the company's financial resources in Realejo, building only one of the two boats needed to launch the endeavor. This, combined with the decline of the Peruvian trade and competition from Spaniards, spelled the end of the Guatemala Company.

*See also* **Bourbon Reforms.**

BIBLIOGRAPHY

Roland Dennis Hussey, *The Caracas Company, 1728–1784: A Study in the History of Spanish Monopolistic Trade* (1977).

Miles L. Wortman, *Government and Society in Central America, 1680–1840* (1982).

Raquel Rico Linage, *Las reales compañías de comercio con América* (1983).

*Additional Bibliography*

Bustos Rodríguez, Manuel. *Los comerciantes de la carrera de Indias en el Cadiz del siglo XVIII (1713–1775).* Cádiz: Servico de Publicaciones, Universidad de Cádiz, 1995.

Dym, Irene, and Christophe Belaubre, eds. *Politics, Economy, and Society in Bourbon Central America, 1759–1821.* Boulder: University Press of Colorado, 2007.

J. DAVID DRESSING

**GUATEMALA, CONSTITUTIONS.** The 15 September 1821 Declaration of Independence for Central America led to the drafting of a Magna Carta by Central American delegates, including those from Chiapas. After a brief annexation of the isthmus by Mexico until 1823, the delegates convened again to reaffirm Central American independence. Chiapas, however, remained under Mexican authority. Influenced by the Spanish liberalism of the Cortes of Cádiz and the U.S. Constitution, the representatives drafted the Constitution of the United Provinces of Central America, promulgated 24 November 1824. Within the following year, each of the member states (Guatemala, Honduras, El Salvador, Nicaragua, and Costa Rica) drafted its own constitution, under the same terms. These constitutions, including the 1825 Constitution of the State of Guatemala, incorporated the three classic branches of legislative, executive, and judiciary. They provided the states with important powers, including those of tax collection and the creation of armed militias, which would lead to the eventual deterioration of federal power.

At the outset of a period dominated by conservatives, the Guatemalan authorities declared secession from the federation on 17 April 1839. May of that year saw the installation of a new constituent assembly, which drafted various temporary constitutional laws, including the Law of Guarantees, aimed at supporting the basic management of the Guatemalan state. There were various conflicts with the liberals, and other constituent assemblies convened in 1844 and 1845, but they were dissolved because the documents they drafted did not entirely reflect conservative thought. In 1847 the central government officially declared the Republic of Guatemala, but in 1848 another constituent assembly was dissolved after drafting a new constitution that failed to be ratified.

After the battle of La Arada in 1851, when President Rafael Carrera attained absolute power in the area, a new, conservative assembly convened. In October of that year, the group issued a Constitutional Act consisting of eighteen Articles. Afterward Carrera became President for Life, a dictatorship that was endorsed by both the Church and the elite.

In 1871 the so-called Liberal Revolution broke out. A constituent assembly was formed in 1872, but its sessions were suspended a year later. In 1876 the assembly met again, but only to ratify the dictatorship of Justo Rufino Barrios. Another constituent assembly met in 1879 and put into effect in December of that year the Constitution which, except for a few changes, remained in place until 1944. It contained the liberal principles of the Constitution of 1824, including an article that limited the term of office. However, the vote was reserved only for literates and conducted by voice under the supervision of an official delegate, whom no one would dare to go against. Thus the elected representatives met two or three months out of the year in order to ratify whatever the president had mandated. Except during the presidencies between 1885 and 1898, this formalism supported what was in fact a dictatorship. After that year it was routine for the Congress to modify the Constitutional Article that limited the term of office, in order to permit the president to remain in power. Manuel Estrada Cabrera made use of this practice, maintaining a dictatorship that lasted from 1898 to 1920.

After Estrada Cabrera's ouster and the brief conservative administration that lasted until 1921, some constitutional amendments were made. In that year the liberals returned to power, and despite some conflicts, continued to govern. Jorge Ubico made use of the same practice as Estrada Cabrera, ignoring the limit which the Constitution placed on his term of office. The Revolutionary Junta of November 1944 put an end to the "liberal" Constitution. The new Assembly ratified a new Constitution in March 1945 that assured democracy. It guaranteed the free organization of employers' groups, unions and political parties which was previously denied, and allowed for freedom of opinion and of the press. It created a Social Security program and workers' tribunals. Its articles also established the principle of the "social function of private property," which would be the focus of great conflict. Finally, members of the oligarchy, both liberal and conservative, met to confront social reform, especially when it affected landholdings.

With the Washington-assisted ouster of the reformist administration in 1954, the Constitution of 1945 was thrown out and a new one promulgated in 1956. Without changing the state administrative structure outlined in the previous constitution, this one restricted the participation of political parties and eliminated the concept of "the social function of private property." In 1963 the army took charge of the state and abolished the Constitution. Members of a new constituent assembly were chosen from among sympathizers with the authorities and from among the heirs of the liberals and conservatives. A new constitution, very much like the preceding one, was promulgated in September 1965. Authorized political parties remained subject to the State. The limit on the term of the presidency was respected, although military presidents predominated until the military coup in 1982.

Following the coup, differences among military leaders, and between the army and important landowners, were overwhelmed by a general insurgency that led to a violent civil war. Domestic and international opinion pressed for a new constitution that would expand democratic rights. A new constituent assembly, elected in a transparent manner, labored from 1984 to 1985, with little influence from the military. The new constitution and new electoral law contained important differences from their predecessors. Political parties are now free to operate and the rights of indigenous communities have been recognized. The Constitution calls for the creation of a Constitutional Court and a human rights prosecutor designated by the Congress—both founded to confront violations of individual rights. It strengthens the role of Congress. A constitutional reform to restrict the army's activities in civil life is being considered.

*See also* **Chiapas.**

BIBLIOGRAPHY

Luis Marinas Otero, *Las constituciones de Guatemala* (1958).

### *Additional Bibliography*

Azpuru de Cuestas, Dinorah, and Cynthia Arnson. *The Popular Referendum (Consulta Popular) and the Future of the Peace Process in Guatemala.* Washington, DC: Latin American Program, Woodrow Wilson International Center for Scholars, 1999.

FERNANDO GONZÁLEZ DAVISON

## GUATEMALA, POLITICAL PARTIES

*This entry includes the following articles:*



### GUATEMALAN LABOR PARTY (PGT)

The Guatemalan Labor Party (Partido Guatemalteco del Trabajo, or PGT) is a communist political party founded by José Manuel Fortuny. The party evolved from the secretive Democratic Vanguard created in 1947, which changed its name to the Guatemalan Communist Party and gained legal recognition from President Jacobo Arbenz in 1951. To avoid constitutional restrictions on political parties with international affiliations, the party dropped the word "communist" from its title and became the Partido Guatemalteco del Trabajo (PGT) in 1952. Attacked by opponents of the Guatemalan Revolution as a dangerous communist threat, in actuality the party had only modest political power. Party ranks never surpassed 1,000 members. PGT candidates failed to win more than four of the fifty-six seats in Congress. Party activists obtained subcabinet posts, but none achieved the level of cabinet minister. Party affiliates did, however, play important roles in agrarian reform and in labor organizations.

Banned after the fall of the Arbenz regime in 1954, the PGT went underground and operated clandestinely despite government persecution. The outlawed party sponsored guerrilla fronts in the early 1960s and in the 1970s. The PGT and three other rebel groups united to form the Guatemalan National Revolutionary Unity (URNG) in January 1982 to coordinate their antigovernment campaigns. The URNG remains active but only received 2.6% of the popular vote in the 2003 presidential election.

BIBLIOGRAPHY

Robert J. Alexander, *Communism in Latin America* (1957), esp. pp. 350–364.

Richard Gott, *Guerrilla Movements in Latin America* (1971), esp. pp. 31–90.

George Black, with Milton Jamail and Norma Stoltz Chinchilla, *Garrison Guatemala* (1984).

*Additional Bibliography*

Montenegro Ríos, Carlos Roberto. *Historia de los partidos políticos en Guatemala*. Guatemala: Mayaprin, 2002.

Soto Rosales, Carlos Rafael. *El sueño encadenado: El proceso político guatemalteco, 1944–1999*. Guatemala: Tipografía Nacional, 2002.

Streeter, Germán. *Managing the Counterrevolution: The United States and Guatemala, 1954–1961*. Athens: Ohio University Center for International Studies, 2000.

STEVEN S. GILLICK

## NATIONAL GUATEMALAN REVOLUTIONARY UNITY (URNG)

The National Guatemalan Revolutionary Unity was organized in January 1982 as a front for the four Guatemalan leftist guerrilla movements: the Guatemalan Labor Party—PGT (1949), the Rebel Armed Forces—FAR (1962), the Organization of the People in Arms—ORPA (1971), and the Guerrilla Army of the Poor—EGP (1972). It sought to stop repression and bring an end to the long Guatemalan civil war through negotiations with the governments of Marco Vinicio Cerezo (1986–1991), Jorge Serrano Elías (1991–1993), and Ramiro de León Carpio (1993–), but the government and the guerrillas failed to reach an accord. However, the group eventually laid down its arms after the United Nations negotiated peace accords in 1996. In 1998 it became a legal political party but only garnered 2.6 percent of the popular vote in the 2003 presidential elections.

*See also* **Guatemala, Political Parties: Guatemalan Labor Party (PGT).**

BIBLIOGRAPHY

James Dunkerley, *Power in the Isthmus: A Political History of Modern Central America* (1988).

Phil Gunson and Greg Chamberlain, *The Dictionary of Contemporary Politics of Central America and the Caribbean* (1991).

Victor Perera, *Unfinished Conquest: The Guatemalan Tragedy* (1993).

*Additional Bibliography*

Bornschein, Dirk. *Las izquierdas en Guatemala*. Guatemala: Fundación Friedrich Ebert, 2000.

McCleary, Rachel M. *Dictating Democracy: Guatemala and the End of Violent Revolution*. Gainesville: University Press of Florida, 1999.

Soto Rosales, Carlos Rafael. *El sueño encadenado: El proceso político guatemalteco, 1944–1999*. Guatemala: Tipografía Nacional, 2002.

RALPH LEE WOODWARD JR.

## REVOLUTIONARY ACTION PARTY (PAR)

The Revolutionary Action Party (Partido de Acción Revolucionaria, or PAR) the major electoral vehicle of both presidents Juan José Arévalo (1945–1951) and Jacobo Arbenz (1951–1954) during the revolutionary decade in Guatemala, was founded in 1945 by a merger of the two main parties of the October Revolution (1944), the Popular Liberation Front (Frente Popular Libertador—FPL) and the National Renovation Party (Renovación Nacional—RN). The party's ideological position was that of moderate socialism.

When the communist José Manuel Fortuny was chosen secretary general in November 1946, the more moderate wing of the party left to reconstitute the FPL. In late 1947 Fortuny and his followers secretly formed a communist party, the Vanguardia Democrática Guatemalteca, but continued to use the PAR to legitimize their political activities. However, a coalition of socialists and noncommunist Marxists led by Augusto Charnaud MacDonald recaptured the party leadership in March 1949.

PAR was the major party in the coalition backing Arbenz in the 1950 elections. Shortly thereafter the Fortuny faction split from the PAR, and the democratic socialist faction of Charnaud MacDonald formed the Socialist Party (PS) in 1951. The PAR then joined the FPL, RN, and PS in creating the Party of the Guatemalan Revolution (PRG) in 1952 to support Arbenz's agrarian reform program, but it later withdrew. The PAR was dissolved after the overthrow of Arbenz in 1954.

*See also* **Arbenz Guzmán, Jacobo.**

BIBLIOGRAPHY

Ronald M. Schneider, *Communism in Guatemala, 1944–1954* (1958).

Asies, *El rol de los partidos políticos en Guatemala* (1985).

*Additional Bibliography*

Bornschein, Dirk. *Las izquierdas en Guatemala*. Guatemala: Fundación Friedrich Ebert, 2000.

Montenegro Ríos, Carlos Roberto. *Historia de los partidos políticos en Guatemala*. Guatemala: Mayaprin, 2002.

Soto Rosales, Carlos Rafael. *El sueño encadenado: El proceso político guatemalteco, 1944–1999*. Guatemala: Tipografía Nacional, 2002.

ROLAND H. EBEL

## UNIONIST PARTY

On 25 December 1919, thirty-one prominent citizens of the republic of Guatemala gathered with eighteen representatives of the capital's organized laborers to found a new political party, the Unionist Party (Partido Unionista). Created under the banner of Central American unity, the party announced in a pamphlet that its primary concern was the creation of a Central American republic. Despite the denials of party founders, all Guatemalans soon realized that the real purpose of the organization was to oppose the outdated and repressive government of Manuel Estrada Cabrera (1898–1920). The active participation in the establishment of the Unionist Party by distinguished members of the Guatemalan business community and prominent labor activists indicated the deep sense of disillusionment almost a half decade of Liberal positivism—with its consolidation of power in the presidency, absence of political democracy, and emphasis on economic development—had fostered.

In the early weeks of 1920 support for the Unionist Party grew rapidly and soon became extremely widespread. Even Estrada Cabrera's close relationship with the United States was not sufficient to impede the development of a unified opposition of students, urban workers, military officers, and a large proportion of the disgruntled elite under the Unionist banner. In response to a number of government arrests, the Unionists, with the support of the Guatemalan legislative body, the National Assembly, chose to attempt the removal of Estrada Cabrera on 5 April. The Assembly responded decisively on 8 April 1920 by declaring President Estrada Cabrera insane and electing Carlos Herrera as the new president.

Unfortunately for Herrera and the Unionist Party, an economic crisis and the revival of traditional political animosities first weakened and ultimately destroyed the fragile Unionist government. Herrera's inability or unwillingness to heed the advice of his ministers and govern with authority and vigor when irresponsible journalism, labor unrest, or peasant discontent arose, was a major factor in his removal. However, most significant were the fears expressed by members of Guatemala's military and coffee elite, who accused the president and the Unionists of promoting unrest, failing to quell labor radicalism, and permitting outbreaks of peasant insurrections. By late 1921, it was obvious that Herrera had failed to satisfy the demands of the republic's coffee elite for stability and profitability. On the evening of 5 December 1921, three senior army officers led a successful military coup that forced Herrera to resign and effectively ended the Unionists' brief term in government.

*See also* **Estrada Cabrera, Manuel.**

BIBLIOGRAPHY

Rafael Arévalo Martinez, *¡Ecce Pericles! La tiranía de Manuel Estrada Cabrera en Guatemala* (1983), pp. 463–478.

Wade Kit, "Precursor of Change: Failed Reform and the Guatemalan Coffee Elite, 1918–1926" (Master's thesis, Univ. of Saskatchewan, 1989).

*Additional Bibliography*

Montenegro Ríos, Carlos Roberto. *Historia de los partidos políticos en Guatemala*. Guatemala: Mayaprin, 2002.

WADE A. KIT

# GUATEMALA, TERRORIST ORGANIZATIONS

*This entry includes the following articles:*

MANO BLANCA
OJO POR OJO

## MANO BLANCA

Formed in 1966 by landowners and politicians associated with the National Liberation Movement (MLN), this right-wing Guatemalan death squad justified its terrorist operations as a necessary part of the global struggle against communist subversion. Backed by the military and unrestrained by the police, Mano Blanca (White Hand) was one of several death squads that tortured, killed, and kidnapped reformists. The most notorious act of the vigilantes was the kidnapping of the reactionary Archbishop Mario Casariego in March 1968 in an effort to embarrass civilian president Julio César Méndez Montenegro (1966–1970). Its terrorist actions supplemented the military's brutal counterinsurgency against the guerrilla movements of eastern Guatemala. In the early 1970s, the Mano Blanca disappeared as the military severed its long-standing connections to the MLN. During the 1990s, however, there were reports that Mano Blanca had resurfaced.

*See also* **Méndez Montenegro, Julio César.**

BIBLIOGRAPHY

Susanne Jonas and David Tobis, eds., *Guatemala* (1974), esp. pp. 176–203.

James Dunkerley, *Power in the Isthmus* (1988), esp. pp. 456–461.

### *Additional Bibliography*

Grandin, Greg. *The Last Colonial Massacre: Latin America in the Cold War.* Chicago: University of Chicago Press, 2004.

Menjívar, Cecilia and Néstor Rodriguez. *When States Kill: Latin America, the U.S., and Technologies of Terror.* Austin: University of Texas Press, 2005.

Saavedra, Alfredo. *El color de la sangre: 40 años de represión y de resistencia en Guatemala.* Guatemala: Grupo de Apoyo Mutuo, 2001.

PAUL J. DOSAL

## OJO POR OJO

Ojo por Ojo (Eye for an Eye), a right-wing terrorist group in Guatemala, emerged from the escalating violence of the late 1960s. Although it formally initiated operations in April 1970, some of its members were linked to the Mano Blanca, a terrorist group that had been operating since 1966. Like the other paramilitary groups, it was formed to check the success of the guerrilla movement in eastern Guatemala. Organized and supported by wealthy landowners and the military, Ojo por Ojo likely received assistance and encouragement from high-ranking government officials. One of its alleged leaders, Mario Sandovál Alarcón, was a prominent right-wing politician involved in the 1954 "liberation" and the subsequent purging of alleged communists. Sandovál invoked the biblical injunction to take an eye for an eye to justify terrorist attacks on suspected leftist sympathizers. Ojo por Ojo targeted the "brains behind the guerrillas" at the University of San Carlos in Guatemala City.

*See also* **Guatemala, Terrorist Organizations: Mano Blanca.**

BIBLIOGRAPHY

Milton Henry Jamail, "Guatemala 1944–1972: The Politics of Aborted Revolution" (Ph.D. diss., University of Arizona, 1972).

Susanne Jonas and David Tobis, eds., *Guatemala* (1974), esp. pp. 176–203.

James Dunkerley, *Power in the Isthmus* (1988), esp. pp. 456–461.

### *Additional Bibliography*

Grandin, Greg. *The Last Colonial Massacre: Latin America in the Cold War.* Chicago: University of Chicago Press, 2004.

Menjívar, Cecilia and Néstor Rodriguez. *When States Kill: Latin America, the U.S., and Technologies of Terror.* Austin: University of Texas Press, 2005.

Saavedra, Alfredo. *El color de la sangre: 40 años de represión y de resistencia en Guatemala.* Guatemala: Grupo de Apoyo Mutuo, 2001.

PAUL J. DOSAL

---

**GUAYAQUIL.** Guayaquil is the largest city in Ecuador, with a population in 2003 of about two million and a greater metropolitan area with some three million people. Located 40 miles (64 kilometers) upriver from the Gulf of Guayaquil, Guayaquil is situated at one of the best natural harbors on the Pacific coast of the Americas. The city lies at the mouth of the Guayas River basin, a zone of approximately 25,000 square miles (65,000 square kilometers) of exceptionally fertile land with countless navigable rivers. These geographic advantages have helped make Guayaquil the commercial heart of Ecuador.

The date and founder of the city are not agreed upon, although Guayaquil is most commonly believed to have been established in 1531 by Spanish conquistador Sebastían de Belalcázar. During the colonial period the city enjoyed a modest prosperity as a contraband entrepôt and the principal shipbuilding and repair center on the Pacific. On October 9, 1820, Guayaquil, weary of the burden of Spanish war taxes and trade restrictions, declared its independence, becoming a free city. However, after Simón Bolívar's fateful meeting with José San Martín on July 26, 1822, in Guayaquil, the city was joined to Gran Colombia (subsequently the nations of Colombia, Venezuela, Ecuador, and Panama).

Agricultural exports have typically provided the mainstay of Guayaquil's economy. Cacao (chocolate beans), grown in the adjacent lowlands, became an increasingly important export from the late colonial era forward, and from the 1870s to the 1920s it dominated Ecuador's economy. During this period Ecuador emerged as the world's leading producer of cacao. Following the 1920s price collapse brought on by African competition, exports of cacao from the Guayaquil region lagged. In the 1950s, however, exports of bananas brought a new period of prosperity to the city and region, lasting until the early 1960s. Beginning in the 1970s Amazonian oil became the nation's chief export, eclipsing coastal products. Nevertheless, Guayaquil continues to serve as Ecuador's commercial center. The city is also home to such light industry, especially food processing, that the nation has.

Until the early twentieth century, Guayaquil had a special notoriety as a particularly disease-infested port. Beyond a high incidence of lethal endemic respiratory and digestive afflictions, epidemics—yellow fever, bubonic plague, cholera, typhoid, and smallpox—repeatedly haunted the city.

Culturally, Guayaquil is distinct from the highland city of Quito, the capital and the nation's second largest city. Indeed, the cities may be viewed as hostile competitors, two separate regional power bases in a nation profoundly divided by geography. Racism has informed this contentiousness. Historically, and sometimes even into the early twenty-first century, many white *quiteños* regarded Guayaquil as uncommonly ugly, irreligious, and crass, peopled by racially "inferior" and "illegitimate" mixed-blood *montuvios*. At the same time, many *guayaquileños* (people from Guayaquil) considered *quiteños* (people from Quito) to be prideful and sanctimonious, their ostentatious piety wrought with hypocrisy. *Guayaquileños* have tended to be more cosmopolitan, tolerant, and open than their sometimes reserved, provincial, and stern *serrano* (highland people) counterparts.

This contention between Guayaquil and Quito, coast and the sierra (highlands), has punctuated Ecuadorian politics. For Guayaquil, the principal difficulty has been that while taxes on its commerce nearly always provided the most important source of government revenue, these funds were controlled by the national government in Quito. This led to recurrent clashes between the cities. Because Quito and the sierra were more populous than Guayaquil and the coast, the capital prevailed in the struggles; Quito continually claimed the largest share of government outlays. Battles between regionally based caudillos, sometimes representing the elite in each region, have traditionally vexed Ecuador. During the cacao years, the prosperity of Guayaquil and the coast brought the two regions into closer balance, but following the collapse of cacao the advantage shifted back to Quito. After World War II the rise of mass urbanization in Guayaquil, coupled with the export boom in bananas, began a reconfiguration of regional political power, a development reflected in the emergence of coastal-based populist leader José María Velasco Ibarra (president in 1934–1935, 1944–1947, 1952–1956, 1960–1961, and 1968–1972). But by the late twentieth century the flood of tax revenues from the export of Oriente oil freed Quito from its fiscal dependence on Guayaquil.

The city has prospered in recent years since the late twentieth century, possibly due to its emerging role as a illegal drug money laundering center, a situation further stimulated by the Ecuadorian adoption of the dollar as the national currency in 2000. In that year the city completed a significant urban renewal project, opening a beautiful new river walk (the *malecón*) along the Guayas River.

*See also* **Diseases; Ecuador: Since 1830; Public Health; Velasco Ibarra, José María.**

BIBLIOGRAPHY

Clayton, Lawrence A. *Caulkers and Carpenters in a New World: The Shipyards of Colonial Guayaquil.* Athens: Ohio University, 1980.

Estrada Ycaza, Julio. *El hospital de Guayaquil.* 2nd ed. Guayaquil, Ecuador: 1974. Publicaciónes del Archivo Histórico del Guayas. One of Estrada Ycaza's innumerable books and articles in Spanish on Guayaquil.

Hamerly, Michael T. *Historia social y económica de la antigua provincia de Guayaquil, 1763–1842.* Guayaquil, Ecuador: Archivo Historico del Guayas, 1973. Provides socioeconomic data. Also available in English as "A Social and Economic History of the City and District of Guayaquil during the Late Colonial and Independence Periods" (PhD diss., University of Florida, 1970).

Pineo, Ronn F. "Misery and Death in the Pearl of the Pacific: Public Health Care in Guayaquil, Ecuador, 1870–1925." *Hispanic American Historical Review* 70, no. 4 (1990): 609–638.

Pineo, Ronn F. *Economy, Society, and the Politics of Urban Reform: Guayaquil, Ecuador, 1870–1925.* Gainesville: University Press of Florida, 1996. A profile of the city.

Roberts, Lois Crawford de. *El Ecuador en la época del cacaotera.* Quito: Editorial Universitaria, 1980. On the cacao era in Guayaquil and Ecuador. Also available in English as Lois Johnson Weinman, "Ecuador and Cacao: Domestic Responses to the Boom-Collapse Monoexport Cycle" (PhD diss., University of California, Los Angeles, 1970).

Townsend, Camilla. *Tales of Two Cities: Race and Economic Culture in Early Republican North and South America.* Austin: University of Texas Press, 2000. Compares the social realities in Guayaquil to those found in Baltimore, Maryland.

RONN PINEO

---

**GUAYAQUIL, GENERAL STRIKE OF 1922.** The collapse of international prices for Ecuador's monocultural export, cacao beans, led to deteriorating economic conditions. Popular frustration increased as the government proved unable to remedy the situation. Inspired by an earlier successful railroad workers' strike, Guayaquil trolley and power company workers walked out, soon followed by nearly all worker groups in the city. Growing in strength, workers called for aggressive government action to maintain the slipping value of the sucre (Ecuador's national currency). On 15 November 1922, workers and their families held a mass downtown rally. Police and the military opened fire, killing at least three hundred. Eyewitnesses agreed that the attack was unprovoked. For Ecuadorian labor, the victims stand as martyrs to the union movement. Historical interpretations of the general strike vary: standard accounts depict events as another example of anarchist-led protest; recent work sees the uprising as more spontaneous, and not effectively led by any single group.

*See also* **Labor Movements.**

BIBLIOGRAPHY

Ronn F. Pineo, "Reinterpreting Labor Militancy: The Collapse of the Cacao Economy and the General Strike of 1922 in Guayaquil, Ecuador," in *Hispanic American Historical Review* 68, no. 4 (1988): 707–736. For a concise overview of the evolution of the labor movement, see Richard Lee Milk, "Ecuador," in *Latin American Labor Organizations,* edited by Gerald Michael Greenfield and Sheldon L. Maram (1987), pp. 289–305. Also worthwhile is Patricio Ycaza, *Historia del movimiento obrero ecuatoriano,* 2d ed. (1984). For the broader political economic context, see Osvaldo Hurtado, *Political Power in Ecuador,* translated by Nick D. Mills, Jr. (1985).

*Additional Bibliography*

Alexander, Robert Jackson, and Eldon M Parker. *A History of Organized Labor in Peru and Ecuador.* Westport, CT: Praeger, 2007.

Gándara Enríquez, Marcos. *La semana trágica de Guayaquil, noviembre de 1922: Aproximación a la verdad.* Quito: Sociedad Ecuatoriana de Investigaciones Históricas y Geográficas, 1991.

Pineo, Ronn F. *Social and Economic Reform in Ecuador: Life and Work in Guayaquil.* Gainesville: University Press of Florida, 1996.

RONN F. PINEO

---

**GUAYAQUIL, GROUP OF.** Group Of Guayaquil, a circle of twentieth-century social protest authors. This literary movement began in 1930 with the publication of a collection of short stories, *Los que se van: Cuentos del cholo y del montuvio* (*Those Who Go Away: Stories of the Mestizos and Country People*), by Demetrio Aguilera Malta, Joaquín Gallegos Lara, and Enrique Gil Gilberto. The authors angrily denounced the racial and class inequities of modern Ecuador. The group, all young novelists from Guayaquil, sought in their work to offer a realistic depiction of life in Ecuador. As with others in the *indianista* tradition in Latin American literature, the Group of Guayaquil took the side of the exploited—the Indians, *montuvios,* blacks, mulattoes, Cholos, peasants, and workers—and attacked the exploiters—the elite, the overseers, the priests, and the local police. Two particularly influential novels focused on the government massacre of Guayaquil workers in 1922: Gallegos Lara's *Las cruces sobre el agua* (1946); and Alfredo Pareja y Diez Canseco's *Baldomera* (1938). Other Ecuadorian authors who followed in this tradition were José de la Cuadra, Ángel Felicisimo Rojas, Pablo Palacio, Pedro Jorge Vera, Humberto Salvador, and, most notably, Jorge Icaza Coronel, author of the classic *Huasipungo* (1934).

*See also* **Huasipungo.**

BIBLIOGRAPHY

For a discussion of Ecuadorian literature, see Angel F. Rojas, *La novela ecuatoriana* (1948). For the political context, consult David W. Schodt, *Ecuador: An Andean Enigma* (1987).

*Additional Bibliography*

Pérez Pimentel, Rodolfo. *Joaquín Gallegos Lara: En el cincuentenario de su fallecimiento, 1909–1947.* Guayaquil, Ecuador: Casa de la Cultura Ecuatoriana, Núcleo del Guayas, 1997.

RONN F. PINEO

**GUAYAQUIL, REPUBLIC OF.** Republic of Guayaquil (1820–1822). The city of Guayaquil moved toward independence in 1820 as a result of growing local dismay over ever more burdensome imperial war taxes and the weakening of Spanish sea power on the Pacific coast. Guayaquil city leaders declared independence on 9 October, followed by a *cabildo abierto* to ratify the action. José Joaquín Olmedo, poet, lawyer, *cabildo* member, and delegate at the Spanish Cortes in Cadiz, was the first governor of the republic. For Guayaquil several options but no clear consensus emerged: independence; joining Peru or Gran Colombia, or rejoining Spain. Given the continuing royalist military presence in the sierra, Olmedo sought the help of both José de San Martín and Simón Bolívar, hoping to avoid surrendering Guayaquil's independence to either. San Martín promised Guayaquil self-determination; Bolívar, however, saw Guayaquil as already comprising part of Gran Colombia. In May 1822 rebel general Antonio José de Sucre defeated the last royalist resistance in the sierra, forcing a decision on the disposition of Guayaquil. Quito quickly joined Gran Colombia and pressured Guayaquil to do likewise, fearing that the latter might become independent or, worse, might join Peru. Bolívar flatly rejected Olmedo's repeated assertions of a Guayaquileño right to self-determination. His liberation army entered Guayaquil in July 1822, and he placed the city under his authority. Three thousand troops surrounded the city. Given the uncertain loyalties of the greatly outnumbered city militia, Olmedo saw no choice but capitulation. San Martín met with Bolívar at Guayaquil in July 1822 and accepted Bolívar's deeds as a fait accompli. To some Guayaquileños, Bolívar's coup brought "the last day of despotism and the first day of the same." Guayaquil's brief experience as an independent state reflected a long-coveted autonomy and continues to inform the region's sense of separateness.

*See also* **Flores, Juan José.**

BIBLIOGRAPHY

Roger Davis's Ph.D. dissertation, "Ecuador Under Gran Colombia, 1820–1830: Regionalism, Localism, and Legitimacy in the Emergence of an Andean Republic" (University of Arizona, 1983), provides an excellent extended discussion. For an overview of the period, see Fredrick B. Pike, *The United States and the Andean Republics* (1977).

*Additional Bibliography*

Dobronski Ojeda, Fernando, ed. *El Ecuador: Los hechos más importantes de su historia.* Ecuador: s.n., 2003.

González Palacios, Tonny. *Fragmentos de nuestra historia.* Manta Manabi, Ecuador: Editorial Mar Abierto, 2004.

Núñez, Jorge. *El Ecuador en el siglo XIX: Ensayos históricos.* Quito: ADHILAC, 2002.

Sierra Castro, Enrique. *Ecuador, su pueblo: Raíces, drama y lucha: Síntesis.* Quito: EDARSI, 2001.

RONN F. PINEO

**GUAYAQUIL CONFERENCE (1822).** Guayaquil Conference (1822), a meeting between the two revolutionaries José de San Martín and Simón Bolívar. As an independent republic, the port city and province of Guayaquil in present-day Ecuador was of great interest both to San Martín in Peru and Bolívar in Colombia. After annexing Quito following the Battle of Pichincha (24 May 1822), Bolívar rushed down to Guayaquil with a large contingent of Colombian troops to ensure that the port also "joined" the Colombian republic. He entered the city on 11 July 1822. Two days later he abolished the government, annexing Guayaquil on 31 July.

General José de San Martín landed in Guayaquil on 26 July to discuss the status of the port and the province as well as the future of the struggle for independence. Although the province had not as yet been formally annexed to Colombia, it was totally in the control of that nation's troops. Thus, it was evident that the "question" of Guayaquil had been resolved in favor of Colombia. Although the two great liberators met several times during the next two days, the details of their conversations remain obscure. Apparently realizing that he could not complete the liberation of Peru without Colombian help,

San Martín suggested that the two leaders collaborate. That proved impossible. San Martín then returned to Lima and resigned, leaving the field open for Bolívar, to whom ultimately fell the honor of completing the liberation of South America.

Subsequently, the nature of the Guayaquil meeting has generated much heat and little light as historians of Venezuela and Argentina have taken up their pens in support of national paladins.

*See also* **Wars of Independence, South America.**

BIBLIOGRAPHY

William H. Gray, "Bolívar's Conquest of Guayaquil," in *Hispanic American Historical Review* 27, pt. 4 (November 1947): 603–622.

Gerhard Masur, "The Conference of Guayaquil," in *Hispanic American Historical Review* 31, pt. 2 (May 1951): 189–229.

Julio Estrada Ycaza, *La lucha de Guayaquil por el Estado de Quito,* vol. 2 (1984), esp. pp. 513–575.

### *Additional Bibliography*

Archer, Christon I., ed. *The Wars of Independence in Spanish America.* Wilmington, DE: Scholarly Resources, 2000.

Rodríguez O., Jaime E. *The Independence of Spanish America.* New York: Cambridge University Press, 1998.

Terán, Marta, and José Antonio Serrano Ortega. *Las guerras de independencia en la América española.* Zamora, Michoacán: Colegio de Michoacán, 2002.

JAIME E. RODRÍGUEZ O.

## GUAYAQUIL-QUITO RAILWAY.

Guayaquil-Quito Railway. During the late nineteenth century Ecuador sought to emulate the success of other nations that had used railroads to create commercial opportunities and to spread modernity. However, railroads are a technology poorly suited to Ecuador's rugged Andean topography. Under the initiative of President Gabriel García Moreno (1861–1865, 1869–1875), in the 1860s Ecuador began construction of a rail line from the port of Guayaquil to the mountain capital in Quito. Work went forward haltingly. The line, completed in 1908, proved an astonishing engineering feat, rising some 10,000 feet in but 50 miles, crossing the Chan Chan River some twenty-six times. The 281-mile line reduced travel time between the coast and the capital from two weeks to about twelve hours. Unfortunately, the railway proved as expensive to operate as it had been to build, and the enterprise almost never showed a profit. The high hopes for it proved unrealistic: The sierra remained economically isolated. Worse, servicing the foreign debt incurred in building the railroad became a bitterly contentious issue.

Ecuadorian railway workers, as was frequently the case elsewhere in Latin America, spearheaded the nation's small labor movement. In October 1922 the railwaymen of Durán (near Guayaquil) won a stunning victory over the U.S. company that operated the line. Support for the workers' position by President José Luis Tamayo (1920–1924) proved decisive. Guayaquil workers soon followed the railwaymen's lead, launching a general strike in November 1922. This popular movement, however, was not successful, ending in a government massacre of the strikers.

*See also* **Alfaro Delgado, José Eloy.**

BIBLIOGRAPHY

Dawn Ann Wiles, "Land Transportation Within Ecuador, 1822–1954" (Ph.D. diss., Louisiana State University, 1971), provides extended treatment of this topic. On financing, see the enormously valuable study by Linda Alexander Rodríguez, *The Search for Public Policy: Regional Politics and Government Finances in Ecuador, 1830–1940* (1985). On the labor movement, see Richard Lee Milk, "Growth and Development of Ecuador's Worker Organizations, 1895–1944" (Ph.D. diss., Indiana University, 1977). On events in 1922, see Ronn F. Pineo, "Reinterpreting Labor Militancy: The Collapse of the Cacao Economy and the General Strike of 1922 in Guayaquil, Ecuador," in *Hispanic American Historical Review* 68, no. 4 (1988): 707–736.

### *Additional Bibliography*

Brainard, Elizabeth Harman, and Katharine Robinson Brainard. *Railroad in the Sky: The Guayaquil and Quito Railway in Ecuador, 1897–1925.* Marion, MA: Atlantis LTD. Partnership, 2003.

Clark, A. Kim. *The Redemptive Work: Railway and Nation in Ecuador, 1895–1930.* Wilmington, DE: SR Books, 1998.

Maldonado Obregón, Alfredo. *Memorias del Ferrocarril del Sur y los hombres que lo realizaron, 1866–1958.* Quito, Ecuador: Talleres Gráficas de la Empresa de Ferrocarriles del Estado, 1977.

RONN F. PINEO

## GUAYAQUIL, SHIPBUILDING INDUSTRY.

**GUAYAQUIL, SHIPBUILDING INDUSTRY.** Shipbuilding in Guayaquil, Ecuador, during the colonial period became one of the leading maritime and naval enterprises in the Viceroyalty of Peru. Virtually isolated from the Atlantic world, the Pacific colonies of the Spanish Empire early on had to develop shipbuilding independently to meet the needs of an empire that grew to stretch along the Pacific coast from Mexico to Chile.

The small port city of Guayaquil, located along the lower reaches of the broad Guayas River in modern Ecuador, possessed excellent access to a hinterland rich in shipbuilding timbers, especially the resistant and durable wood from the *guachapeli* tree. As traffic continued to grow between the Viceroyalty of Peru and Spain via the Isthmus of Panama, especially after the discovery of silver at Potosí in modern Bolivia in 1545, the shipyards at Guayaquil expanded to meet the needs of transporting silver north and European merchandise south.

The creation and expansion of the Armada Del Mar Del Sur in the wake of English and Dutch attacks on the viceroyalty in the 1570s and 1580s further stimulated the industry. All of the large royal galleons built in the sixteenth and seventeenth centuries to transport silver and protect the viceroyalty were constructed at Guayaquil, endowing the port with a strategic importance of considerable value in the defense of the Spanish Empire in the Pacific.

Commercially, the ships built at Guayaquil supported the development of a lively inter- and intraviceregal trade that moved the colonies toward a greater self-sufficiency in the seventeenth century. Olive oil, wheat, sugar, cacao, tobacco, wine, textiles, wood, and myriad other products grown and produced along the west coast were carried on ship bottoms launched from the shipyards of Guayaquil. In 1590 there were about thirty-five to forty ships and barks in the merchant marine; a century later, at least seventy-two large seagoing vessels plied the waters of the Viceroyalty of Peru, most of them built in Guayaquil.

The earliest shipbuilders were Spaniards, caulkers and carpenters who brought their knowledge of shipbuilding to the New World. As time passed, increasingly larger numbers of blacks (slave and free) and mulattoes joined, and then supplanted, the original Spanish artisans and craftsmen. Native Andeans and mestizos rounded out the work force in a typical seventeenth-century shipyard. For a major royal job (two large galleons were occasionally built at the same time), it was not unusual for virtually all citizens to be involved in the shipbuilding, from the indigenous laborers felling trees in the interior to the master mulatto craftsmen overseeing the design.

By the eighteenth century, the industry was challenged by better ships from Europe, especially from France, which more and more frequently sailed into the Pacific to trade, navigate, and compete with ships built in the Viceroyalty of Peru. But the shipyards of Guayaquil proved the Spanish and colonials to have been an inventive and flexible lot, adapting to the necessities of trade and war at sea in a new environment with immense versatility and success. After independence, the shipbuilding industry declined, but still produced smaller boats for local traders.

*See also* **Armada del Mar del Sur; Mining: Colonial Spanish America; Mining: Modern.**

### BIBLIOGRAPHY

One book that deals directly with the subject is Lawrence A. Clayton, *Caulkers and Carpenters in a New World: The Shipyards of Colonial Guayaquil* (1980). A classic study of trade and navigation is Woodrow Wilson Borah, *Early Colonial Trade and Navigation Between Mexico and Peru* (1954). For an economic history of the seventeenth-century viceroyalty as a whole, see Kenneth J. Andrien, *Crisis and Decline: The Viceroyalty of Peru in the Seventeenth Century* (1985). On the defense of the viceroyalty, see Carla Rahn Phillips, *Six Galleons for the King of Spain: Imperial Defense in the Early Seventeenth Century* (1986); and Peter T. Bradley, *The Lure of Peru: Maritime Intrusion into the South Sea, 1598–1701* (1989).

### *Additional Bibliography*

Andrien, Kenneth J. *The Kingdom of Quito, 1690–1830: The State and Regional Development.* Cambridge, U.K.: Cambridge University Press, 1995.

Borchart de Moreno, Christiana Renate. *La Audiencia de Quito: Aspectos económicos y sociales (siglos XVI–XVIII).* Quito: Ediciones del Banco Central del Ecuador, 1998.

LAWRENCE A. CLAYTON

## GUAYASAMÍN, OSWALDO (1919–1999).

Oswaldo Guayasamín (*b.* July 1919, *d.* 10 March 1999), Ecuadoran painter. Born in Quito, to a humble Indian family, Guayasamín demonstrated his artistic talents at an early age. In 1932 he began studies at Quito's National School of Fine Arts, graduating with honors in 1941. In the following year he had his first solo exhibitions, in Quito and Guayaquil. In 1943, Guayasamín received an invitation through Nelson Rockefeller, who worked for the State Department, to visit the United States. This gave him the opportunity to study firsthand the works of masters like El Greco, Francisco Goya, and Pablo Picasso. The Mexican muralist José Clemente Orozco, whom Guayasamín met and worked with for a brief period in 1943, had a major impact on the development of his painting, especially on the expressive distortions of the human figure. In fact, throughout decades of prolific work—in painting, drawing, and printmaking—Guayasamín's main pictorial subject has been the human figure, rendered in isolation or as a part of epic scenes, a symbolic carrier of the artist's quest for social and political justice.

From the late 1940s, the ideological and humanitarian appeal of his images, inspired by past and current struggles in Latin America, won Guayasamín commissions for large murals, created for public spaces like the Casa de la Cultura Ecuatoriana, Quito (1948); Centro Bolívar, Caracas (1954); Palacio del Gobierno, Quito (1958); and Barajas Airport, Madrid (1982). Exhibitions of his work outside Ecuador include those at the Museo de Bellas Artes, Caracas (1954); Pan-American Union, Washington, D.C. (1955); IV Bienal de São Paulo (1957); Palacio de Bellas Artes, Mexico City (1968); Museo Español de Arte Contemporáneo, Madrid (1972); Musée d'Art Moderne de la Ville de Paris (1973); the Hermitage, Saint Petersburg, Russia (1982); Museo Nacional Palacio de Bellas Artes, Havana (1985).

*See also* **Art: The Twentieth Century.**

BIBLIOGRAPHY

Oswaldo Guayasamín, *De orbe novo decades* (1989).

Régis Debray, "Guayasamín et les hommes de maïs," in *Le Nouvel Observateur,* December 1973, reprinted in *Art d'Amérique Latine 1911–1968* (1992), 228–230.

Annick Sanjurjo, ed., *Contemporary Latin American Artists* (1993).

*Additional Bibliography*

Adoum, Jorge Enrique, and Oswaldo Guayasamín. *Guayasamín: el hombre–la obra–la crítica.* Nürnberg: Verlag Das Andere, 1998.

Blanco, Katiuska. *Un abrazo de Guayasamín para Fidel.* Melbourne, Vic: Ocean Press, 2006.

Flores Jaramillo, Renán. *Oswaldo Guayasamín.* Quito, Ecuador: Casa de la Cultura Ecuatoriana "Benjamín Carrión," 2002.

FATIMA BERCHT

## GUAYCURUANS.

*See* **Paraguay: The Colonial Period.**

## GUDIÑO KIEFFER, EDUARDO (1935–2002).

Eduardo Gudiño Kieffer (*b.* 2 November 1935, *d.* 20 September 2002), Argentine writer. Born in Esperanza, he was the son of Luis Gudiño Kramer, who wrote on the legendary gaucho Judíos in Entre Ríos at the turn of the century. Gudiño Kieffer never emerged as a major novelist in Argentina, but he attracted some attention in the 1960s and 1970s for his trenchant satiric characterizations of the mentalities and personalities that emerged from the cultural effervescence before the military coup of 1966 and the resistant countercultures it fueled. The effective destruction of this milieu by the Dirty War in the 1970s, the concomitant pessimism the latter engendered, and the sober (if not postmodern) attitudes that accompanied the return to constitutional democracy in 1983 appear to have left Gudiño Kieffer without much material. Yet his most significant work, *Guía de pecadores en la cual se contiene una larga y copiosa exhortación a la virtud y guarda de los mandamientos divinos* (1972), with all of its baroque counterreformation intertextualities, is both an acerbic denunciation of the moral righteousness of the Argentine neofascism of the period and a biting characterization of individuals more marked by libertinism than libertarianism. Published at the pivotal time of the brief and ultimately failed transition to a Peronista-led democracy (the 1973–1976 period between almost two decades of military rule), *Guía* can be read as a parable of the irresolvable ideological dilemmas of urban Argentine society at that time. Gudiño Kieffer's narrative style is also notable for the incorporation of multiple colloquial registers of urban, multimedia oriented life. *Carta abierta Buenos Aires violento* (1970) is an essay denouncing the violence in Argentine social life, a recurring emphasis in contemporary Argentine fiction. In honor of his contributions to the literary and cultural life of Buenos Aires, the city named him an Illustrious Citizen.

*See also* **Argentina: The Twentieth Century; Buenos Aires; Dirty War; Gauchesca Literature; Gaucho.**

BIBLIOGRAPHY

Raúl H. Castagnino, "*Para comerte mejor* y la crítica social," in *Nueva Narrativa Hispanoamericana* 3, no. 2 (1973): 121–130.

Augusto Tamayo Vargas, "Lo antiguo y lo novísimo en la picaresca de Eduardo Gudiño," in *Cuadernos Hispanoamericanos,* no. 295 (1975). 199 203.

Juan Epple, "Entrevista. Eduardo Gudiño Kieffer," in *Hispamérica* 6, no. 18 (1977): 47–61.

*Additional Bibliography*

Pueyrredón, Victoria. *Mis reportajes.* Buenos Aires: Lumen, 2003.

Vélez, Joseph F. *Escritores argentinos según ellos mismos.* Bogotá: Universidad INCCA de Colombia, 1994.

David William Foster

**GÜEGÜENCE.** Güegüence, central character in a famous Nicaraguan folk dance. Although it was performed until well into the twentieth century, the *Baile del Güegüence* (Güegüence's Dance) dates from the sixteenth century. Through their performance the dancers portray the clash of two peoples and the ability of indigenous cultures to survive such assault, through passive resistance and syncretism. The cast of characters includes Spanish and Creole officials who make demands on Güegüence, representing the Indians and Ladinos. The dance itself, though highly comical and entertaining, contains a clear message as Güegüence evades the authorities' orders by feigning deafness and ignorance. Although Güegüence is portrayed as the more clever and resilient of the combatants, the dance ends in accommodation when the son of Güegüence marries the governor's daughter. Symbolically, such a union implies the merging of the two to create a new people, but Güegüence continues to lament the new conditions. The persistence and continued popularity of the *Baile del Güegüence* indicates its relevance for the indigenous elements of Nicaraguan and Central American society that continue to struggle with authority and a foreign culture.

*See also* **Music: Popular Music and Dance.**

BIBLIOGRAPHY

Daniel G. Brinton, ed., *The Güegüence: A Comedy in the Nahuatl-Spanish Dialect of Nicaragua* (1883).

Enrique Peña Hernández, *Folklore de Nicaragua* (1968).

Francisco Pérez Hernández, *Estudios del folklore nicaragüense* (1968).

Emilio Álvarez Lejarza, *El Güegüence: Comedia-bailete de la época colonial* (1977).

*Additional Bibliography*

Silva, Fernando. *La historia natural de el Güegüence.* Managua: Academia Nicaraguüense de la Lengua, 2002.

Karen Racine

**GUEILER TEJADA, LIDIA** (1926–). Lidia Gueiler Tejada (*b.* 1926), president of Bolivia (16 November 1979–17 July 1980). Born in Cochabamba, Gueiler, a graduate of the American Institute in La Paz, was trained as an accountant. She served as a deputy in Congress on two separate occasions and as ambassador to the Federal Republic of Germany, Colombia, and Venezuela. Her *La mujer y la revolución* (1957) was about the role of women in the 1952 Bolivian national revolution. She joined the Nationalist Revolutionary Movement (MNR) in the 1940s but went on to join the leftist Revolutionary Workers Party (POR) in the 1950s. In November 1979, Gueiler emerged as the compromise candidate between Walter Guevara Arze and General Alberto Natusch Busch, who had ended the former's short-lived interim government on 2 November. On 16 November, she became the first woman ever to be elected president of Bolivia.

Gueiler presided over a particularly difficult time in Bolivian history when relations between the armed forces and civilians were at their lowest level. Her mission was mainly to hold power until a new round of elections on 29 June 1980 could determine the next constitutional president. The elections went off as scheduled, but Gueiler could do little to prevent disgruntled sectors of the armed forces tied to drug traffickers from launching a coup on 17 July 1980 that ended Bolivia's return to democracy. Gueiler spent the next two years in exile. When democracy returned to Bolivia in October 1982, Gueiler was named ambassador to Colombia and later served as ambassador to Venezuela. She published her autobiography, *Mi pasíon de lidereza,* (My Passion as a Leader) in 2000.

*See also* **Bolivia, Political Parties: Nationalist Revolutionary Movement (MNR).**

BIBLIOGRAPHY

James Dunkerley, *Rebellion in the Veins: Political Struggle in Bolivia, 1952–1982* (1984).

Raúl Rivadeneira Prada, *El laberinto politico de Bolivia* (1984).

*Additional Bibliography*

Crespo, Alfonso. *Lydia: una mujer en la historia.* La Paz, Bolivia: Plural Editores, 1999.

Gueiler Tejada, Lidia, and Luis Eduardo Siles. *Mi pasión de lidereza.* La Paz, Bolivia: Centro de Información y Desarrollo de la Mujer, 2000.

EDUARDO A. GAMARRA

**GÜEMES, MARTÍN** (1785–1821). Martín Gúemes (*b.* 7 February 1785; *d.* 17 June 1821), ruler of Argentina's northwestern province of Salta (1815–1821). Argentina's deep political divisions and Salta's peripheral location have combined to shroud Güemes in controversial, often erroneous images. No one, however, denies his forceful military leadership in ejecting Spanish royalists from the north. *Salteños* revere him as a patriot and defender of provincial autonomy against centralist political forces. Born and educated in Salta, Güemes joined the military as a cadet in 1799, at the age of fourteen. He first saw action during the English invasion of Buenos Aires in 1806. An aide to Santiago Liniers, he received a promotion to the rank of lieutenant and later to general.

Güemes joined the independence forces after the revolution of May 1810. He led a military unit into Upper Peru that gained intelligence on royalist movements and disrupted their communications. Güemes then served in Montevideo and Buenos Aires. In March 1814, General José de San Martín appointed him general commander of forces in Salta. The success of Güemes's gaucho cavalrymen in expelling the royalists from Salta created great popular support. Thanks to his kinship ties to the *salteño* landed elite, he was elected governor of the province in May 1815.

Like Juan Manuel de Rosas in Buenos Aires Province, Güemes drew support from both the gaucho masses and elements of the landed elite. But he aroused strong opposition from political rivals and from some wealthy *salteños* with his taxation and land-reform proposals. He died ten days after being wounded by a royalist supporter, possibly with the complicity of local opponents. The anti-Güemes Patria Nueva movement condemned him as a tyrant. Yet he effectively held royalist forces at bay and led his province through a period of brutal warfare and political conflict.

*See also* **Gaucho; Salta.**

BIBLIOGRAPHY

Atilio Cornejo, *Historia de Güemes* (1946).

Roger M. Haigh, *Martín Güemes: Tyrant or Tool?* (1968).

*Additional Bibliography*

Colmenares, Luis Oscar. *Martín Güemes: el héroe mártir.* Buenos Aires: Ediciones Ciudad Argentina, 1998.

Solá, Guillermo. *El gran bastion de la patria.* Salta: Maktub, 2005.

RICHARD W. SLATTA

**GÜEMES-PACHECO Y PADILLA, JUAN VICENTE DE.** *See* **Revillagigedo, Conde de.**

**GUERRA, RAMÓN** (1841–1922). Ramón Guerra (*b.* 1841; *d.* 1922), Venezuelan caudillo. Guerra began his political and military career during the Federal War (1859–1863), becoming a key figure in the Venezuelan political alliances of the era. He was an opponent of Juan Crisóstomo Falcón;

both an enemy and temporary ally of Antonio Guzmán Blanco; a successful military commander (1892) and later member of the Consejo Militar (1893) in the regime of General Joaquín Crespo; and a crucial figure behind the victory of Cipriano Castro, whom he later opposed in La Libertadora Revolution of 1901–1903. He supported the accession to power of Juan Vicente Gómez and was part of the Council of Government. When that body dissolved in 1914, Guerra retired permanently from public life.

*See also* **Federal War (Venezuela 1859–1863).**

BIBLIOGRAPHY

Ramón J. Velásquez, *La caída del liberalismo amarillo: Tiempo y drama de Antonio Paredes* (1977).

Inés Quintero, *El ocaso de una estirpe: La centralización restauradora y el fin de los caudillos histórico* (1989).

*Additional Bibliography*

*Cipriani Castro y su tiempo histórico.* Caracas: Fondo Editorial Nacional: José Agustín Catalá, 1999.

Machado Guzmán, Gustavo. *Historia gráfica de la Guerra Federal de Venezuela: Período de la federación.* Caracas: s.n., 2002.

Inés Quintero

---

**GUERRA, RUY** (1931–). Ruy Guerra is known as a pioneer in the Brazilian Cinema Novo movement of the 1960s and 1970s. Born on August 22, 1931, to Portuguese parents in what was then the Portuguese colony of Mozambique, he pursued his education in Portugal but then changed course to study filmmaking in Paris. He moved to Brazil in 1958 and directed two films that are characteristic of the Cinema Novo period: *Os Cafajestes* (The Delinquents, 1962), which was banned in Brazil and the United States for its violent content, and *Os Fuzis* (The guns, 1964), which won the Silver Bear at the Berlin Film Festival that year and gained him international recognition. The film is a treatise on violence and religious oppression in the rural backlands (*sertão*) of northeastern Brazil. His *Os Deuses E Os Mortos* (Gods and the Dead, 1970) was another Cinema Novo landmark.

In the late 1970s he returned to newly independent Mozambique and helped create the country's film institute. In the 1980s his films displayed higher production values and greater commercial appeal. He based two films on works by the Colombian novelist Gabriel García Marquez, *Eréndira* (1983) and *Fábula da Bela Palomera* (The Fable of the Beautiful Pigeon Fancier, 1988), both with magical realist elements. *ópera do Malandro* (The Opera of the Rascal, 1986) is a musical comedy on which he collaborated with the Brazilian composer Chico Buarque, and *Estorvo* (Turbulence, 2000) is an experimental work based on a novel by Buarque. Guerra has also worked as an actor, songwriter, producer, and director of photography.

*See also* **Cinema: From the Silent Film to 1990; Cinema: Since 1990; Cinema Novo.**

BIBLIOGRAPHY

Johnson, Randal. *Cinema Novo x 5: Masters of Contemporary Brazilian Film.* Austin: University of Texas Press, 1984.

Johnson, Randal, and Robert Stam, eds. *Brazilian Cinema,* expanded edition. New York: Columbia University Press, 1995.

Pick, Zuzana M. *The New Latin American Cinema: A Continental Project.* Austin: University of Texas Press, 1993.

*Films by Ruy Guerra*

*Quand le soleil dor.* (short) [When the Sun Sleeps]. 1954.

*Os Cafajestes.* [The Delinquents; also known as The Unscrupulous Ones]. 1962

*Os Fuzis.* [The Guns]. 1964.

*Ternos Caçadores.* [Sweet Hunters]. 1969.

*Os Deuses E Os Mortos* [Gods and the Dead]. (U.S. title: *Of Gods and the Undead*). 1970.

*A Queda.* [The Fall]. 1976.

*Mueda, Memoria e Massacre* [Mueda, Memory and Massacre]. 1980.

*Eréndira.* 1983.

*ópera do Malandro.* (U.S. title: *Malandro). 1986.*

*Fábula de la Bella Palomera* [The Fable of the Beautiful Pigeon Fancier]. 1988.

*Estorvo.* (U.S. title: *Turbulence*). 2000.

*Portugal S.A.* [Portugal Inc.] 2004.

*O Veneno da Madrugada.* [Poison at Dawn]. 2004.

Tamara L. Falicov

## GUERRA DOS FARRAPOS.

*See* **Farroupilha Revolt.**

## GUERRA GRANDE.

The Uruguayan civil war (1839–1851), the longest and hardest fought in the country's history, is known as the Guerra Grande, or "Great War." The struggle originated in the rivalry between the Colorado and Blanco parties and their respective leaders, Fructuoso Rivera and Manuel Oribe. On March 1, 1839, Rivera became president for a second time, after overthrowing Oribe with the help of Unitario exiles from Argentina. Ten days later, under pressure from the Unitarios, Rivera declared war on the Argentine dictator Juan Manuel de Rosas (himself allied to Oribe and the Blancos), an act that marked the beginning of the Guerra Grande.

Rivera defeated a first invasion from Argentina, but from 1842 to 1845 he suffered a series of defeats. With the help of Rosas, Oribe and the Blancos drove Rivera into exile in Brazil and confined the Colorado government to Montevideo, which for nine years remained under siege. Rivera returned to the struggle in the Uruguayan interior in 1846, but was removed from his command the following year. On each side, in fact, the war was marked by dissension among members of the respective Uruguayan parties and between those parties and their foreign allies.

Dissension was particularly severe on the Colorado side, pitting civilian party leaders against Rivera, and Colorados against foreign collaborators. The latter included not just the Unitarios, whose only interest was to overthrow Rosas, but the French and British, who in 1845 began a joint intervention in the Río De La Plata over questions of river navigation and the interests of their own subjects. Brazil also began to provide the Colorados with financial and naval support. The outsiders' interests coincided with those of the Colorados only in that both groups opposed the apparent intent of Rosas to convert Uruguay into an Argentine satellite. Tensions also arose simply from the crowding of thousands of foreigners—from Argentine enemies of Rosas to such European volunteers as the future champion of Italian unification, Giuseppe Garibaldi—into besieged Montevideo.

The stalemate ended when Governor Justo José de Urquiza of Entre Ríos Province, Argentina, broke with Rosas in May 1851. The Colorados quickly reached an agreement with Urquiza, whose subsequent advance into Uruguay caused Oribe and the Blancos to make peace in October of the same year. The siege of Montevideo was lifted, the Guerra Grande was over, and Rosas himself was overthrown in February 1852. Economically, the country was devastated. For instance, numbers of livestock fell from approximately 6.5 million to around 2 million at the end of the war. The country still remained under Brazilian and Argentine influence after the civil war. In 1865 Brazil helped the Colorados oust the Blancos from power. Because Paraguay saw this action as a threat to its national security, this coup sparked the War of the Triple Alliance, in which Argentina, Brazil, and Uruguay fought Paraguay for five years.

Uruguayan Blancos would later look back on Oribe as having bravely defended national values against foreign intruders, whereas the Colorado version of history extols the heroic defense of Montevideo against the dictator Rosas and his Uruguayan lackeys. Both versions ignore the lack of clear policy differences between the parties and the fact that their leaders were often engaged in negotiations in the very midst of the struggle. But the legacy of the war was an intensification of Uruguayan partisan alignments that lasted into the twentieth century.

*See also* **Uruguay, Political Parties: Blanco Party; Uruguay, Political Parties: Colorado Party.**

BIBLIOGRAPHY

John F. Cady, *Foreign Intervention in the Río de la Plata* (1929).

Juan E. Pivel Devoto and Alcira Ranieri De Pivel Devoto, *La Guerra Grande 1839–1851* (1971).

José Pedro Barrán, *Apogeo y crisis del Uruguay pastoral y caudillesco 1838–1875* (1974).

John Lynch, *Argentine Dictator: Juan Manuel de Rosas, 1829–1852* (1981).

### *Additional Bibliography*

Arocena Olivera, Enrique. *La rebeldía de los doctores: El Uruguay del fusionismo al militarismo, 1851–1886.* Montevideo, Uruguay: Librería Linardi y Risso, 1998.

McLean, David. *War, Diplomacy and Informal Empire: Britain and the Republics of La Plata, 1836–1853.* London and New York: British Academic Press, 1995.

Panizza, Francisco. "Late Institutionalisation and Early Modernization: The Emergence of Uruguay's Liberal Democratic Political Order." *Journal of Latin America Studies* 29, no. 3 (1997): 667–691.

DAVID BUSHNELL

## GUERRA Y SÁNCHEZ, RAMIRO

(1880–1970). Ramiro Guerra y Sánchez (*b.* 31 January 1880; *d.* 30 October 1970), Cuban historian. Because of the intrinsic value and influence of his writings, Guerra, a native of Batabanó, Havana Province, is arguably Cuba's foremost historian of the twentieth century. Starting as a teacher in a modest rural school, he rose to become professor and director of Havana's Normal School, school superintendent of Pinar del Río Province, and national school superintendent. In 1932–1933 he held the position of secretary to the president's cabinet. He also represented Cuba as technical adviser to numerous missions abroad. In his books Guerra severely criticized U.S. policies toward Cuba and Spanish America. Many of them are still classic studies, such as his *Guerra de los diez años, 1868–1878,* 2 vols. (1950). None, however, has had the impact of *Azúcar y población en las Antillas* (1927), originally a series of newspaper articles; many editions of it have appeared, including an abridged English translation as *Sugar and Society in the Caribbean* (1964). This volume, a sober indictment of the dangers of latifundism in Cuba, contributed greatly to shaping the views of the 1933 Cuban revolutionaries.

*See also* **Latifundia.**

BIBLIOGRAPHY

For a review in English of Guerra's work in the context of Cuban historiography, see Robert Freeman Smith, "Twentieth-Century Cuban Historiography," *Hispanic American Historical Review* 44 (February 1964): 44–73.

### *Additional Bibliography*

Whitney, Robert. *State and Revolution in Cuba: Mass Mobilization and Political Change, 1920–1940.* Chapel Hill: University of North Carolina Press, 2001.

JOSÉ M. HERNÁNDEZ

## GUERRERO.

Guerrero, state of southern Mexico (pop. 2,900,000 in 2001) formed in 1849 from portions of the states of México, Michoacán, and Puebla. Guerrero is perhaps best known as the site of violent social movements from Mexico's 1810–1821 War of Independence to the leftist guerrilla campaigns of the 1970s. The capital of the state is Chilpancingo; its largest city is Acapulco (pop. 409,335 in 1980). The state encompasses 24,631 square miles of extremely diverse topography and climate, from warm and humid coastal plains to rugged and arid mountain ranges.

In the colonial period mulatto sharecroppers cultivated cotton on the coast for Mexico's domestic textile industry, and Indian peasants and creole landowners produced food in the mountains and northern valleys for the silver mining center of Taxco. Beginning in 1810, these social groups joined forces in the War of Independence, first under José María Morelos y Pavón and then Vicente Guerrero. Fighting in the area ended when Guerrero and royalist commander Agustín de Iturbide issued the Plan of Iguala in 1821. After independence Guerrero was largely an economic backwater, although it benefited briefly from the demand for cotton generated by Mexico's first protectionist industrial experiments. Federalist movements based on alliances between peasants and local elites led to the creation of the state in 1849 and to the Revolution of Ayutla in 1854–1855. The latter, led by former insurgent Juan Álvarez, began the period of Mexican national history known as the reform.

Subsequently Guerrero faded from prominence. Although peasant rebellions continued, they no longer were strengthened by alliances with local elites. The rapid economic development of the Porfiriato largely bypassed the area. Railroad construction reached only northern Guerrero. However, population growth and the legal assault on peasant village landholdings increased agrarian tensions. During the Mexican Revolution local political activity was intense and confused. A rapidly successful movement against Porfirio Díaz later created a split along class lines, with most peasants eventually supporting Emiliano Zapata and his Plan of Ayala.

Guerrero has experienced little industrial development. Tourism in Acapulco and other coastal sites became the largest generator of income in the 1960s, followed by remittances from those who had migrated to Mexico City and the United States. The area's continuing poverty fueled 1970s guerrilla movements led by Lucio Cabanas and Genaro Vázquez. Although these movements were repressed, opposition to the ruling Revolutionary Institutional Party (PRI) remains strong.

*See also* **Mexico, Wars and Revolutions: War of Independence.**

BIBLIOGRAPHY

Moisés Ochoa Campos, *Breve historia del Estado de Guerrero* (1968).

Francisco Gomez-Jara, *Bonapartismo y lucha campesina en la Costa Grande de Guerrero* (1979).

Ian Jacobs, *Ranchero Revolt: The Mexican Revolution in Guerrero* (1982); *Ensayos para la historia del Estado de Guerrero* (1985); *Historia de la cuestión agraria mexicana: Estado de Guerrero 1867–1940* (1987).

Moisés Santos Carrera and Jesús Álvarez Hernández, *Historia de la cuestión agraria mexicana, Estado de Guerrero: Épocas prehispánica y colonial* (1988).

*Additional Bibliography*

Guardino, Peter. *Peasants, Politics, and the Formation of Mexico's National State.* Stanford, CA: Stanford University Press, 1996.

Jacobs, Ian. *Ranchero Revolt: The Mexican Revolution in Guerrero.* Austin: University of Texas Press, 1982.

PETER GUARDINO

## GUERRERO, VICENTE (1783–1831).

Vicente Guerrero (*b.* 10 August 1783; *d.* 14 February 1831), Mexican independence leader and politician. Born in Tixtla in the present state that bears his name, he joined the insurgent Hermenegildo Galeana in 1810 under José Maria Morelos. He continued the struggle after Morelos's defeat and death in 1815. In 1821 he joined Agustín de Iturbide's movement, emerging as one of the major military leaders after independence, but soon broke with Iturbide.

In the 1820s Guerrero, now a prominent populist, became the Grand Master of the Yorkinos (York rite Masons) in 1826. After losing the bitterly contested presidential election of 1828, he joined his supporters in the Revolt of Acordada, and became president in 1829. Guerrero attempted to introduce democratic programs as well as to address the nation's fiscal crisis. While dealing with the emotional issue of the expulsion of the Spaniards and mass politics, he also faced a Spanish attempt to reconquer Mexico in the summer of 1829. Although victorious against the invaders, the president faced a revolt by conservatives led by his own vice president, Anastasio Bustamante. He abandoned office in December 1830. But the Bustamante administration proved to be repressive and threatened the autonomy of the states. As a result, Guerrero was enticed to lead a revolt against the government that had driven him from office. Unable to defeat him on the field of battle, the Bustamante administration managed to capture him by treachery, then to court-martial and execute him.

*See also* **Acordada, Revolt of; Iturbide, Agustín de.**

BIBLIOGRAPHY

William F. Sprague, *Vicente Guerrero, Mexican Liberator: A Study in Patriotism* (1939).

Romeo R. Flores Caballero, *Counterrevolution: The Role of the Spaniards in the Independence of Mexico, 1804–38* (1974), pp. 47–142.

Michael P. Costeloe, *La Primera República Federal de México, 1824–1835* (1975), pp. 178–274.

Jaime E. Rodríguez O., *The Emergence of Spanish America: Vicente Rocafuerte and Spanish Americanism, 1808–1832* (1975), esp. pp. 210–228.

Stanley C. Green, *The Mexican Republic: The First Decade, 1823–1832* (1987), pp. 140–209.

*Additional Bibliography*

Martínez del Campo, Silvia. *Vicente Guerrero.* México, D.F.: Planeta Mexicana, 2005.

Vincent, Theodore G. *The Legacy of Vicente Guerrero: Mexico's First Black Indian President.* Gainesville: University Press of Florida, 2001.

JAIME E. RODRÍGUEZ O.

## GUERRERO, XAVIER (1896–1975).

Xavier Guerrero (*b.* 3 December 1896; *d.* 1975), Mexican artist. Xavier Guerrero learned painting from his house-decorator father. In 1921, he collaborated with Roberto Montenegro on murals in the old Colegio de San Pedro y San Pablo and with Diego Rivera in 1922–1923 on his mural in the Anfiteatro Bolívar in the National Preparatory School in Mexico City. Later he assisted Rivera with murals in the Secretaria de Educación, where he used a fresco technique. When David Alfaro Siqueiros was commissioned by the Mexican government to paint a mural for the Mexican-donated Escuela Mexicana in Chillán, Chile (1941), Guerrero joined him and painted murals in Chillán and Santiago. He also did murals in Chapingo, Cuernavaca, and Guadalajara.

*See also* **Art: The Twentieth Century.**

BIBLIOGRAPHY

Bernard S. Myers, *Mexican Painting in Our Time* (1956).

Antonio Rodríguez, *A History of Mexican Mural Painting*, translated by Marina Corby (1969).

### *Additional Bibliography*

Folgarait, Leonard. *Mural Painting and Social Revolution in Mexico, 1920 1940: Art of the New Order.* New York: Cambridge University Press, 1998.

SHIFRA M. GOLDMAN

## GUERRERO Y TORRES, FRANCISCO ANTONIO (1727–1792).

Francisco Antonio Guerrero y Torres (*b.* February 1727; *d.* 20 December 1792), Mexican architect. Guerrero y Torres, born in Guadalupe, is the most famous of the last architects of New Spain to achieve maturity and success before the establishment of the Academia de San Carlos and the subsequent adoption of academic neoclassicism. After he passed the examination for master architect in 1767, he designed buildings in a neoclassical style proper to New Spain (generally called *neostilo*), retaining the materials, taste for color, and many of the motifs of *estípite* baroque (or Churrigueresque). Favored by wealthy criollos of Mexico City, he designed and built palaces, notably those of Iturbide and of the counts of Santiago de Calimaya. Criticized by the Academia toward the end of his life, Guerrero y Torres nevertheless built, at his own expense and in his characteristic manner, the Chapel of the Pocito near the Basilica of Guadalupe, between 1777 and 1791. It is generally considered his masterpiece.

*See also* **Architecture: Architecture to 1900.**

BIBLIOGRAPHY

Heinrich Berlin, "Three Master Architects in New Spain," in *Hispanic American Historical Review* 27 (1947): 375–383. Ignacio F. González-polo, *El palacio de los condes de Santiago de Calimaya* (1983).

### *Additional Bibliography*

Fuentes Rojas, Elizabeth, Norma Vázquez García, Laura A. Corona Cabrera, and Bertha Alicia Arizpe Pita. *La Academia de San Carlos y los constructores del Neoclásico: Primer catálogo de dibujo arquitectónico, 1779–1843.* México, D.F.: Universidad nacional Autónoma de México, Escuela Nacional de Artes Plásticas, 2002.

CLARA BARGELLINI

## GUERRILLA ARMY OF THE POOR.

*See* **Guatemala, Political Parties: National Guatemalan Revolutionary Unity (URNG).**

## GUERRILLA MOVEMENTS.

In Latin America, guerrilla movements can be divided into several periods. The pre-Marxist period includes colonial resistance movements, early independence revolts, and revolutionary movements of the late nineteenth and early twentieth centuries, typified by the Cuban independence movement, the Mexican Revolution, and the movement led by Augusto C. Sandino in Nicaragua. They are the prelude to the *foco* guerrilla movements of the 1960s and 1970s, spawned by the victory of Fidel Castro's Cuban Revolution in 1959. By the 1980s, other tactics had superseded the guerrilla cadre, such as the Indian focus of Guatemala's National Guatemalan Revolutionary Union (URNG) and Peru's Sendero Luminoso. All Latin American guerrilla movements, although they borrow from other groups, are primarily products of local rebel traditions.

These traditions began in the resistance to European colonization. Renegade bands (Cimarrones, or Maroons) in inaccessible mountainous areas throughout Latin America offered sanctuaries for runaway slaves and Indians, who raided the

**Cuban revolutionaries atop a homemade armored vehicle, Sierra Maestra, 1959.** Though overwhelmingly national in origin and focus, guerrilla movements in Latin America affected global politics, especially during the Cold War. © EPA/CORBIS

European settlements. The Sierra Maestra in Cuba, the mountainous frontier areas of Nicaragua and El Salvador, the jungles of Petén and Yucatán, the Andes of Peru and Bolivia, the plains of Venezuela and Argentina, and coastal Brazil were all places that nurtured revolt.

In the eighteenth and nineteenth centuries, major guerrilla-style Indian revolts had temporary successes: those of José Túpac Amaru and Julián Túpac Catari in the Andes, and the Caste War of Yucatán. After independence, guerrilla-style armies were successful in Guatemala (José Rafael Carrera), Cuba (José Martí and Máximo Gómez y Báez), and Mexico (Benito Juárez, Pancho Villa, Emiliano Zapata); in the 1920s and 1930s the anti-imperialist struggles of Sandino in Nicaragua and Agustín Farabundo Martí in El Salvador inspired later guerrillas.

The modern guerrilla era began with Castro's successful revolution against Cuban dictator Fulgencio Batista, launched in late 1958. Castro's Twenty-sixth of July Movement was inspired by radical Christian Democracy, not the Communist Party. Purposely invoking nationalism, Castro made the headquarters of his army the Sierra Maestra, in Cuba's easternmost province. This had been the sanctuary of Martí and Gómez y Báez. There Castro, under the Marxist influence of his brother Raúl Castro and Argentine professional revolutionary Ernesto (Che) Guevara, developed the guerrilla tactics used later throughout Latin America. The main elements were a strong caudillist leader; revolutionary symbolism and myths utilizing movement leaders and past nationalist heroes; and a guerrilla nucleus (*foco*) inspiring national insurrection that was attached to, but not dependent on, local peasantry. After the Cuban triumph, Guevara proselytized this mixture (*focoismo*) as the winning revolutionary strategy for Latin America. He added the concept of the guerrilla as the revolutionary "new man," who, through the *foco* strategy, would make the "subjective" conditions necessary for revolutionary success. As articulated by Raúl Castro, "The *foco* is the little motor that sets in motion the big motor of the revolution."

With this formula, Guevara and Castro immediately started to urge other Latin revolutionaries to follow the example of the Cuban revolution, until then the only successful Marxist revolution in the hemisphere. Guevara's philosophy reached the masses through the articulate writings of the French intellectual Régis Debray. The heyday of *focoismo* was the 1960s and 1970s. Historian Donald Hodges sees Guevara's philosophy developing in four "insurrectionary waves." The first was against Caribbean-style dictators; the second, starting in 1962, expanded the struggle to "pseudo-democratic" regimes in Central and South America; the third, called "many Vietnams," was launched against U.S. neocolonialism; and the fourth, after Guevara's death in Bolivia, was the urban *foco* struggle in Uruguay and Argentina.

The first wave, immediately after Castro's triumph, was a series of abortive attempts to land *foco* units in Panama, Nicaragua, the Dominican Republic, and Haiti. The second was more serious: Guevara saw the Andes as the Sierra Maestra of Central and South America; this period featured struggles in Guatemala, Venezuela, and Colombia, and a rising competition with orthodox communism over the viability of *focoismo*.

Colombia had the earliest communist-backed guerrilla movement. The Colombian Communist Party (PCC) admitted in 1965 that it had undertaken guerrilla warfare as a secondary struggle in a prerevolutionary situation. This was necessitated by the 1964 government action to wipe out the independent peasant republics formed during La Violencia (1948–1957). The partisans regrouped as the Southern Guerrilla Bloc, and at the PCC's tenth congress (1965) they united with other units to become the Revolutionary Armed Forces of Colombia (FARC). In 1964, tired of the defensive strategy of the communist guerrillas (decried by Debray), the radical student Fabio Vásquez Castaño had formed an independent Guevarist guerrilla group, the Army of National Liberation (ELN). The radical priest Camilo Torres Restrepo joined it shortly before his death in 1965. Because the Communist Party always reverted to a noninsurrectionary strategy, the guerrilla movement in Colombia became just another player in the national anarchy.

As in Colombia, the Communist Party of Venezuela (PCV) gave ambivalent support to the guerrilla movement Armed Forces of National Liberation/National Liberation Front (FALN/FLN), led by a former army officer, Douglas Bravo. The PCV was originally pushed into supporting guerrilla action by the increasingly anticommunist stance of the populist president Rómulo Betancourt (1960–1962). However, legalization of the party in 1963 led to disavowal of guerrilla action and removal of Bravo and other guerrilla leaders from party leadership. This precipitated the major breach between *focoismo* and orthodox communism; Castro and Guevara (in absentia) supported Bravo and openly criticized the party. The conflict between young, revolution-prone New Leftists and older Communist Party functionaries had by then spread throughout Latin America.

At that stage, the third insurrectionary wave was in full swing. This consisted of a "Bolivarian/continental" strategy, using Bolivia as a central jumping-off point to encourage moribund guerrilla movements in Peru, Argentina, Chile, Uruguay, and Brazil. Guevara reasoned that the Cuban success had alerted the United States and its local bourgeois allies (thus rationalizing the lack of success for *foco* exports). Any revolutionary success would have to come through a prolonged "people's war." Vietnam, not Cuba, was the right model, and by 1967 Guevara hoped to spark "many Vietnams" in Latin America. The objective revolutionary conditions in Bolivia seemed perfect: peasant disillusion with a bourgeois land reform, low GNP, government reneging on mine labor reform, and increased encroachment by the United States into local politics. However, the preparations, strategy, and personnel were all faulty, and Guevara was captured and executed just months after establishing a guerrilla training camp in the Alto Beni area of southeastern Bolivia.

In Brazil, a variant of *focoismo* existed in Carlos Marighela's (also Marighella) Action for National Liberation (ALN), which criticized Guevarism for depending on one *foco* location (impractical for the continental dimension of Brazil). Instead, ALN opted to organize urban masses indirectly and from the rural areas. Due to failure to find satisfactory rural sanctuaries, ALN's urban organizing attempts were ended faster by the police than those of guerrilla groups in Argentina and Uruguay.

The death of Guevara ushered in Hodges's fourth insurrectionary period of urban struggle, which Debray, along with Hodges, saw as the future hope. The essential aspect of Uruguay's Tupamarus was a political-military *foco,* revolutionary nationalism easily identifiable by the urban masses. Raúl Sendic, a former student and union organizer, and Pedro Guillén were the founders. An escalating series of spectacular robberies, kidnappings of prominent individuals, and reprisals against mounting death squad activity ended in the brutal repression of September 1971; nearly 2,000 activists were captured and 29 were known dead.

Argentina's Montoneros, an independent urban guerrilla nucleus directed by Trotskyites, outlasted the Tupamarus by eight years. In 1959–1962, Cuban-style training camps were started by the Armed Forces of Liberation (FAL), a dissident Communist Party youth faction implementing Guevara's call to resist "pseudo-democratic" regimes. In 1969 the FAL evolved into the Montoneros, founded by Fernando Abal Medino and named after gaucho cavalry units in the 1810 War of Independence. The Montoneros were part of the radical Peronist wing, but after a series of urban disruptions (most famous the 1969 Corodobazo), kidnappings, and other urban actions, President Juan Perón officially broke with the Montoneros in May 1974. The military consequently cracked down on the Montoneros' rural *foco* in the city of Tucumán, and the Montoneros reciprocated by storming the army barracks at Monte Chingola. In 1977, the Treaty of Rome united the Montoneros and the Authentic Peronist Party (PPA) into the Montonero Peronist Movement. However, a month later the army effectively destroyed the People's Revolutionary Army (ERP), a Montonero army, and in 1979 a Montonero counteroffensive to the escalating dirty war of the military regime collapsed, ending the movement's effectiveness.

Mexico also had urban guerrillas in the 1970s. In 1974, the Fuerzas Revolucionarias Armadas del Pueblo (FRAP) kidnapped President Luis Echeverría's father-in-law, the governor of Jalisco. In the mountains of Guerrero, 10,000 army troops took over a year to eliminate former schoolteacher Lucio Cabañas and his guerrilla army, after they had kidnapped a gubernatorial candidate, Senator Rubén Figueroa, and assassinated the Acapulco chief of police. Later in the 1990s, a guerrilla movement calling itself the Zapatista Liberation Front emerged in Chiapas. Just before his assassination the presidential candidate of Mexico's Institutional Revolutionary Party, Luis Donaldo Colosio, made a spectacular peace accord with the Zapatistas. However, as of early 1995, the Zapatistas were still active, and several political assassinations were attributed to them.

In 1979, as the Montonero downfall signaled the end of South American *focoismo,* two Central American guerrilla movements took the spotlight. The Sandinista National Liberation Front (FSLN) was founded in 1961 by Carlos Fonseca Amador and others who had gone into exile after the abortive attempt to oust Luis Somoza Debayle during Guevara's Caribbean dictators stage of insurrection. Fonseca learned from the Cuban Revolution the need to fuse Marxism with local national and anti-imperialistic traditions. He thus studied the guerrilla campaign of Augusto César Sandino, who led the Army for Defense of the National Sovereignty (EDSN) against a combination of the U.S. Marines and Nicaraguan National Guard from 1927 through 1933.

In contrast with the Cuban scenario, it was a coalition of middle-class and working-class urban mass organizations that provided the impetus that overthrew Anastasio Somoza Debayle; the crucial battles were, therefore, fought by urban groups in Nicaragua's cities and towns, under guerrilla leadership. After triumph in 1979, the FSLN was attacked by a right-wing guerrilla force, the Contras. On the Honduran frontier, it was composed of former Somoza National Guard members and peasants disaffected with Sandinista Marxism, and was supplied and trained by the CIA. On the Costa Rican border, a guerrilla group independent of CIA control, and led by former Sandinista Captain Zero (Edén Pastora), fought a more modest campaign. The election in 1990 of Conservative president Violeta Barrios De Chamorro ended both the active contra conflict and the Sandinista attempt to build a hybrid socialist society. After that, various informal remnants of the contra movement, known as recontras, kept up hostilities against both the government and former Sandinista opponents.

The history of the El Salvador guerrilla movement is more complicated than that of Nicaragua.

The 1969 Soccer War with Honduras generated a crisis within the Salvadoran Communist Party (PCS), leading the party secretary, Salvador Cayetano Carpio, to found the guerrilla Popular Liberation Front-Farabundo Martí (FLP), named for Agustín Farabundo Martí, the popular communist and former aide to Sandino who led the disastrous 1932 revolt that culminated in the Matanza massacre of 10,000 to 30,000 Indian peasants. Carpio did not adhere to the *foco* theory, opting for the "prolonged people's war" concept of Vietnam and posited by Guevara in Bolivia. In 1972, however, a more middle-class group of Christian Democratic Party (PDC) deserters formed the *foco*-style Revolutionary Army of the People (ERP). Internal disputes in the guerrilla camps led to the assassination of the writer Roque Dalton and the suicide of Carpio. In 1980, the stalling of reforms by the new provisional government led to the formation of the umbrella opposition body, the Democratic Revolutionary Front (FDR), and to the establishment of a united guerrilla command (FMLN) as the military arm of the FDR in the same year brought on a decade-long civil war. In 1991, as a result of the collapse of Soviet support and U.S. impatience with the prolonged conflict, the FMLN and the government signed a demilitarization pact in exchange for political recognition of the Left.

In the 1980s and early 1990s, three other guerrilla groups took center stage, none of them *foco* oriented. They claimed to represent Indian interests in Guatemala, Peru, and Chiapas, Mexico.

Marxist guerrilla activity started in Guatemala in 1960, when two army refugees from a barracks uprising, Marco Antonio Yon Sosa and Luis Agusto Turcios Lima, formed the 13 November Revolutionary Movement (MR-13). As in Colombia and Venezuela, the Communist Guatemalan Workers Party (PGT) initially spoke for all guerrilla groups, which united in the communist-backed Rebel Armed Forces (FAR). The FAR broke up when the PGT dropped insurrection to back populist presidential candidate Julio César Méndez Montenegro, who, upon election, allowed the counterguerrilla offensive that by August 1967 reduced the FAR, with a rural support unequaled in Latin America, to a handful of survivors hiding in Guatemala City.

By the 1980s, Guatemala's guerrillas were making a comeback under the umbrella organization National Guatemalan Revolutionary Union (URNG). Major new leftist guerrilla groups included the Guerrilla Army of the Poor (EGP) and the Organization of People in Arms (OPRA). The government's scorched-earth policy, "frijoles y fusiles" (beans and bullets), plus URNG's refusal to cater to Mayan interests, led to a guerrilla decline. The rebels made a comeback starting in 1985, but despite an Indian–guerrilla fusion group, the failure of the white-led Marxist guerrillas to endorse specific Indian issues (such as an autonomous Indian state) left the movement's future uncertain.

In Peru, the effort to rouse the Indian majority to insurrection was temporarily successful. Peru's long history of rebellion goes back to the first known guerrilla campaign: the Inca pretender Manco Capac launched raids against the Spanish invaders from his Andes hideouts. The same tactic was repeated in the 1740s by Juan Santos Atahualpa. A century after the revolts of José Túpac Amaru and Julián Túpac Catari, Indian guerrillas in central Peru and Bolivia fought hacienda encroachment on lands of traditional Andean communities (Ayllus). In 1963, Trotskyite peasant organizer Hugo Blanco led an abortive uprising near the Inca capital of Cuzco, followed by *foco* guerrilla groups in south-central Peru. The most famous was the Movement of the Revolutionary Left (MIR), a radical APRA offshoot (APRA-Rebelde). These guerrilla groups of the 1960s and 1970s, although they spoke the Indian language and were integrated into Indian society, were co-opted by government agriculture reform, the basis of Indian discontent. However, by the 1980s reforms either did not work or were not implemented, creating a disillusionment receptive to the most extreme of all Latin American guerrilla groups, the Sendero Luminoso, named after the first nationalist Marxist philosopher José Carlos Mariátegui's allusion to a "shining path" (*sendero luminoso*) for Peruvian national aspirations.

Officially known as the Communist Party of Peru, a Maoist splinter of the Moscow-oriented Peruvian Communist Party, the Sendero was organized in the 1970s in Peru's most backward province, Ayacucho, where its claim that feudalism is the main obstacle still makes sense. Sendero has a hierarchical military structure topped by President Gonzalo (Abimael Guzmán); a strategy, opposite to the selectivity of *focoismo,* that has every party member also a soldier; and the prominence of women in intermediate leadership as well as the rank and file.

However, as in Guatemala, no serious integration of Indian programs appears in Sendero's strictly Marxist communiqués. The surprise capture of Guzmán, on 12 September 1992 at least temporarily disoriented the organization. In the wake of Guzmán's arrest, Óscar Ramírez assumed leadership of the group. In 1999 he too was arrested. In 2003 a militant splinter group known as *Proseguir*, or "onward," continued to be active, albeit on a small scale. The Peruvian government has accused the group of working with drug traffickers.

In 2003 a Shining Path group attacked Argentinean workers on a natural-gas pipeline project in Ayacucho. They held workers and police hostages and demanded ransom, which was purportedly paid by the Argentinean company, Techint. That same year, the Peruvian government launched another offensive against Sendero, capturing many leaders, but as of 2006, small-scale attacks and incidents continued.

*See also* **Caste War of Yucatán; Colombia, Revolutionary Movements: Army of National Liberation (ELN); Colombia, Revolutionary Movements: Army of Popular Liberation (EPL); Colombia, Revolutionary Movements: M-19; Colombia, Revolutionary Movements: Revolutionary Armed Forces of Colombia (FARC); Colombia, Revolutionary Movements: United Self-Defense Forces of Colombia (AUC); Communism; Cuba, Twenty-Sixth of July Movement; Paramilitaries in Latin America; Peru, Revolutionary Movements: Army of National Liberation (ELN); Peru, Revolutionary Movements: Shining Path; Terrorism.**

## BIBLIOGRAPHY

On pre-Marxist guerrilla movements, see Steve Stern, ed., *Resistance, Rebellion, and Consciousness in the Andean Peasant World, 18th to 20th Centuries* (1987), especially Florencio Mallon, "Nationalist and Anti-state Coalitions in the War of the Pacific: Junin and Cajamarca, 1879–1902" and pt. 1 of the book, "From Resistance to Insurrection: Crisis of the Colonial Order." Donald Hodges, *Intellectual Foundations of the Nicaraguan Revolution* (1986), provides detailed insights.

Works by guerrilla leaders or their theoreticians include Fidel Castro, *Revolutionary Struggle 1947–1958,* edited by Rolando E. Bonachea and Nelson P. Valdes, vol. 1 of his *Selected Works* (1972). Ernesto (Che) Guevara published selected works (1970). The most notorious is *Handbook of Revolution.* The most erudite defense of *focoismo* is offered by Régis Debray, *Revolution in the Revolution?,* translated by Bobbye Ortiz (1967). The tactics of Uruguay's Tupamarus are explained by that group's leading ideologue: Abraham Guillén, *Estrategia de la guerrilla urbana* (1965). Other works by guerrilla leaders include Hugo Blanco, *Land or Death: The Peasant Struggle in Peru* (1972); Carlos Marighela, *For the Liberation of Brazil,* translated by John Butt and Rosemary Sheed (1971); Camilo Torres, *Revolutionary Priest: The Complete Writings and Messages of Camilo Torres,* translated by June de Cipriano Alcantara (1971), and *Douglas Bravo Speaks: Interview with Venezuelan Guerrilla Leader* (1970). First-hand accounts of life in guerrilla camps include Charles Clements, *Witness to War* (1984); and Omar Cabezas, *Fire from the Mountain,* translated by Kathleen Weaver (1985).

Donald Hodges, *The Latin American Revolution: Politics and Strategy from Apro-Marxism to Guevarism* (1974), focuses on the fact that contemporary New Left movements sprang from earlier nationalism. His *Argentina, 1943–1987* (1988), is the main work on the Montoneros. Richard Gott, *Guerrilla Movements in Latin America* (1971), focuses on Guevarism up to Che's death.

Works presenting negative appraisals of guerrilla movements include Carlos Ivan Degregori, *Que difícil es ser Dios* (1989), a Marxist criticism of the Sendero Luminoso; Robert Moss, *Terrorism Versus Democracy* (1971), on the Tupamarus; Theodore Draper, *Castroism: Theory and Practice* (1965); and Tad Szulc, *Fidel* (1986).

Other analyses of guerrilla movements are John A. Booth, *The End and the Beginning: The Nicaraguan Revolution* (1982); James Dunkerley, *Power in the Isthmus* (1988); and Carol Smith, *Indians and the State in Guatemala* (1990).

### *Additional Bibliography*

Castro, Daniel. *Revolution and Revolutionaries: Guerilla Movements in Latin America.* Wilmington, DE: SR Books, 1999.

Finn, Devin. *Following the Shining Path of Peru to the Road Not Taken in Colombia.* Durham, NC: Duke University Press, 2003.

Gross, Liza. *Handbook of Leftist Guerilla Groups in Latin America and the Caribbean.* Boulder, CO: Westview Press, 1995.

Taylor, Lewis. *Shining Path: Guerilla War in Peru's Northern Highlands, 1980–1997.* Liverpool, U.K.: Liverpool University Press, 1997.

Wickham-Crowley, Timothy P. *Exploring Revolution: Essays on Latin American Insurgency and Revolutionary Theory.* Armonk, NY: M. E. Sharpe, 1991.

Wickham-Crowley, Timothy P. *Guerillas and Revolution in Latin America: A Comparative Study of Insurgents and Regimes since 1956.* Princeton, NJ: Princeton University Press, 1991.

Edmond Konrad

**GUEVARA, ERNESTO "CHE"** (1928–1967). Ernesto "Che" Guevara (*b.* 14 June 1928; *d.* 9 October 1967), Marxist revolutionary and guerrilla. Guevara was born into a middle-class family in Rosario, Argentina. He attended medical school in Buenos Aires and received a medical degree in 1953. Guevara traveled widely throughout Latin America and arrived in December 1953 in Guatemala, where he became active in the Guatemalan revolution and met exiled Cuban revolutionaries. When U.S.-backed forces toppled the Guatemalan government in 1954, Guevara fled to Mexico.

Guevara's Cuban friends introduced him to Raúl and Fidel Castro in Mexico City during the summer of 1955. Guevara joined Castro's rebel group as one of the eighty-two revolutionaries who landed on the coast of Cuba on 2 December 1956. When Castro created a second rebel column in 1957, he promoted Guevara to commander. Guevara and his troops were among the rebel forces that entered Havana on 2 January 1959.

Guevara championed insurrection against dictatorship and U.S. imperialism throughout Latin America. His book *Guerrilla Warfare,* published in 1960, offered a practical guide for aspiring revolutionaries. Guevara recommended the creation of guerrilla *focos* in the countryside to serve as bases of operations. From the *foco* guerrillas would serve as a vanguard and eventually create an invincible people's army. Guevara stressed that there was no need to wait for revolutionary conditions to develop; the insurrection itself would create such conditions. Guerrilla fronts, inspired by the Cuban model and Guevara's call to arms, emerged throughout Latin America in the 1960s, but these groups had limited impact.

Guevara played a central role in the early government of revolutionary Cuba. As director of the Industrial Department of the National Institute of

**Graffiti remembering Ernesto "Che" Guevara, Caracas, Venezuela, 2006.** A native Argentinean, Guevara joined Fidel Castro to overthrow the Cuban dictatorship of Fulgencio Batista. Many years after his death, Guevara continues to attract the devotion of anti-imperialists across the globe. MARIO TAMA/GETTY IMAGES

Agrarian Reform (INRA), president of the National Bank of Cuba, and Minister of Industry, Guevara shaped the early economic policy of the revolution. He favored extensive state ownership of productive enterprises and central economic planning. Guevara sought to create a "new socialist man" dedicated to the revolution and motivated by moral rather than material incentives. He hoped ultimately to abolish money altogether. Castro sided with Guevara against opponents who favored reliance on market forces within a socialist framework, and Guevara's economic policies enjoyed official sanction until the late 1960s. Guevara also carried out numerous diplomatic missions abroad.

Eventually Guevara's influence in Cuban government waned. In 1965 he resigned his post as minister of industry. The reasons are obscure. Some scholars suggest a falling out between Guevara and Castro, while others claim Guevara left to engage in guerrilla activity. Guevara planned to use Bolivia as a base for continental revolution, and he set up a guerrilla *foco* there in 1966. They launched their first military action in March 1967. The movement, however, suffered numerous difficulties, including failure to win the trust of local peasants, inhospitable terrain, internal divisions, and poor relations with the Bolivian Communist Party. Bolivian troops, assisted by U.S. military advisers, inflicted serious losses on Guevara's forces. A Bolivian army unit captured Guevara and his last followers on 8 October 1967. These same troops murdered Guevara the next day. His image and political theory, however, have remained an inspiration for Latin American leftists into the 1990s.

*See also* **Castro Ruz, Fidel; Cuba, Revolutions: Cuban Revolution.**

BIBLIOGRAPHY

Ernesto Guevara, *Guerrilla Warfare,* translated by J. P. Morray (1961).

Andrew Sinclair, *Che Guevara* (1970).

Michael Lowy, *The Marxism of Che Guevara: Philosophy, Economics, and Revolutionary Warfare,* translated by Brian Pearce (1973).

Ernesto Guevara, *Che Guevara and the Cuban Revolution: Writings and Speeches of Ernesto Che Guevara,* edited by David Deutschmann (1987).

Gary Prado Salmón, *The Defeat of Che Guevara: Military response to Guerrilla Challenge in Bolivia,* translated by John Deredita (1990).

### *Additional Bibliography*

Anderson, Jon Lee. *Che Guevara: A Revolutionary Life.* New York: Grove Press, 1997.

Cardona Castro, Francisco-Luis. *"Che" Guevara.* Madrid: Edimat Libros, 2003.

Castañeda, Jorge G. *Compañero: The Life and Death of Che Guevara.* New York: Knopf, 1997.

Dosal, Paul J. *Comandante Che: Guerilla Soldier, Commander, and Strategist, 1956–1967.* University Park: Pennsylvania State University Press, 2003.

Sweig, Julia. *Inside the Cuban Revolution: Fidel Castro and the Urban Underground.* Cambridge, MA: Harvard University Press, 2002.

STEVEN S. GILLICK

**GUEVARA ARZE, WALTER** (1911–1996). Walter Guevara Arze (*b.* 11 March 1911, *d.* 20 June 1996), interim president of Bolivia (August 1979–November 1979). As a young lawyer, Guevara formed part of the post–Chaco War generation that founded the Nationalist Revolutionary Movement (MNR) in 1941. Guevara was the author of the 1944 *Ayopaya Thesis,* a manifesto that advocated sociopolitical rights for Bolivia's indigenous masses. He joined Víctor Paz Estenssoro, Hernán Siles Zuazo, and others in leading the MNR revolution of 1952. In 1959, owing mainly to the MNR's refusal to recognize his claim to the presidency, Guevara split with the party and founded the Authentic Revolutionary Party (Partido Revolucionario Auténtico—PRA). Several years later, in 1964, Guevara joined General René Barrientos Ortuño to topple Paz Estenssoro and the MNR.

Guevara served several terms in Congress, was a cabinet officer for numerous governments between 1952 and 1974, and was Bolivia's ambassador to the Organization of American States, the United Nations, and France. The pinnacle of his career came in August 1979, when he was elected interim president of Bolivia following the failure of the nation's principal political parties to elect a head of state among the top three vote getters in the national elections.

Guevara was one of the principal opponents of military rule after the coup that toppled him on 2 November 1979. When democracy was reestablished in 1982, Guevara reclaimed his senatorship and played an important role as a frequent critic of the Siles Zuazo government. In the late 1980s, Guevara led a successful campaign to unite factions that had split away from the MNR. As a reward for his efforts, the MNR named him its vice-presidential candidate for the 1989 elections. His race was unsuccessful, however. In late 1993, he fell ill and ended most public appearances.

*See also* **Bolivia, Political Parties: Nationalist Revolutionary Movement (MNR).**

BIBLIOGRAPHY

James Dunkerley, *Rebellion in the Veins: Political Struggle in Bolivia, 1952–1982* (1984).

Horacio Trujillo, *Los partidos politicos en América Latina: Partidos politicos y sistema de partidos en Bolivia* (1991).

*Additional Bibliography*

Arze Cuadros, Eduardo. *Bolivia, el programa del MNR y la revolución nacional: Del movimiento de reforma universtaria al ocaso del modelo neoliberal (1928–2002).* La Paz, Bolivia: Plural Editores, 2002.

Burt, Jo Marie, and Philip Mauceri. *Politics in the Andes: Identity, Conflict, Reform.* Pittsburgh: University of Pittsburgh Press, 2004.

Guevara Arze, Walter, and Mariano Baptista Gumucio. *Fragmentos de memoria.* La Paz: [s.n.], 2002.

Zavaleta Mercado, René. *La caída del M.N.R. y la conjuración de noviembre: Historia del golpe militar del 4 de noviembre de 1964 en Bolivia.* Cochabamba, Bolivia: Editorial "Los Amigos del Libro," 1995.

EDUARDO A. GAMARRA

**GUEVARA ESPINOSA, ANA GABRIELA** (1977–). Ana Guevara is a Mexican track and field athlete. The future "Sonoran Arrow" or "Golden Lady" or "Aztec Queen" was born on March 4, 1977 in Nogales, Sonora, where she played basketball through high school. She then began seriously training for track after moving to Ciudad Juárez in 1997. Racing mainly the 400-meter and the 4x400 relay, she has since won gold at numerous international competitions and silver at the 2004 Olympics. She is part of a generation of female athletes who have raised Mexican national pride and appreciation of women's changing place in society. At its 2006 Youth Awards, Univision named her Most Electrifying Female Athlete.

*See also* **Sports.**

BIBLIOGRAPHY

Chusit, Jorge. "Ana Guevara rompe el molde." *American Airlines Nexos*, August–September 2004.

"Eres un Orgullo." Available from www.anagabrielaguevara.com.mx

Zamorán, Fabiola. "La medallista Ana Gabriela Guevara: El triunfo del coraje." *Proceso*, Agosto 8, 1999.

JOSEPH L. ARBENA

**GUGGIARI, JOSÉ PATRICIO** (1884–1957). José Patricio Guggiari (*b.* 17 March 1884; *d.* 1957), Paraguayan statesman and president (1928–1932). The son of Italian immigrants, Guggiari was born in Asunción, but as a young child moved to the interior town of Villarrica, where he received his early education. He returned to Paraguay to pursue legal studies and received a doctorate in law from the National University in 1910.

Guggiari began his political career by affiliating with the Liberal Party as early as 1903. At that time the Liberals were divided into various bickering factions unable to reach a consensus on overall policy for the country. Guggiari worked hard to reconcile these various groups. Though he was only partly successful, he gained a reputation as a level-headed and efficient democrat. He rose to the highest ranks within the party, as well as within the legislative branch of government. He was elected deputy in 1912, and in 1918 was chosen president of the Chamber of Deputies. Two years later, President Manuel Gondra chose him to become interior minister.

The 1928 presidential election in which Guggiari defeated Eduardo Fleitas was widely regarded as the most honest up to that time. As president, he dedicated himself to the consolidation of Paraguay's democratic institutions after years of instability. These efforts, however, were eclipsed by the worsening dispute with Bolivia over the Gran Chaco region. The ensuing tensions indirectly brought about Guggiari's downfall. On 23 October 1931, university students protested his government's cautious response to Bolivian incursions by staging a rally in front of the National Palace. The police fired upon the assemblage, killing eight and wounding thirty. Mortified by these events, Guggiari resigned the presidency two days later. He died in Buenos Aires after a long exile.

*See also* **Gondra, Manuel; Paraguay: The Twentieth Century.**

BIBLIOGRAPHY

William Belmont Parker, *Paraguayans of To-Day* (repr. 1967), pp. 199–200.

Efraím Cardozo, *Efermérides de la historia del Paraguay* (1967), pp. 401–402.

Charles J. Kolinski, *Historical Dictionary of Paraguay* (1973), p. 117.

*Additional Bibliography*

Amaral, Raúl, and Roberto Paredes. *Los presidentes del Paraguay.* Asunción: Servilibro, 2005.

Pesoa, Manuel. *José P. Guggiari, defensor civil del Chaco.* Asunción, Paraguay: Intercontinental Editora, 2005.

THOMAS L. WHIGHAM

---

**GUIANA HIGHLANDS.** Guiana highlands, the region in northern South America where Brazil, Guyana, and Venezuela meet at Mount Roraima at 9,094 feet. Most scholars mark the eastern boundary as the Essequibo River, but others extend the massif along northern Brazil and southern Guyana, Suriname, and French Guiana. The Highlands occupy almost half of Venezuela. Their waters drain into the Orinoco River on the west and north, into the Essequibo River on the east, and into the Negro and Branco rivers on the south. With elevations from 1,640 to 2,600 feet in most places but from 2,600 to 4,900 feet in others, the Highlands contain commercial amounts of manganese, nickel, bauxite, diamonds, gold, and iron. With some of the largest deposits of high-grade iron ore in the world, they explain Venezuela's development of its most underpopulated and underdeveloped state, Bolívar, and the location of Venezuela's hydroelectric power and iron and steel industries at Ciudad Guayana.

These resources are responsible for the ongoing boundary dispute between Venezuela and Guyana (British Guiana before its independence in 1966). The dispute, only over the easternmost part of the Highlands, but three-fifths of Guyana's territory, dates to the 1840s, when British agents pushed into the zone west of the Essequibo River. The Venezuelan claim rests on the string of missions that were planted in the eighteenth century along the major rivers and streams of the area but were destroyed as the result of the wars of independence and anticlerical measures of republican governments. Guyana's claim and current possession, not recognized by Venezuela, arise from a British presence there since the 1840s and an 1899 arbitration decision in its favor. In 1962 Venezuela presented historical documents with the "inside story" of why it would not abide by this decision.

In the 1990s conflict escalated and the United Nations appointed a Good Officer to mediate a solution. The former Dutch colony of Suriname joined the conflict in 2000 with claims to a potentially oil-rich area of Guyanaís territory. The conflict had not been resolved by the end of 2007, and the United Nations continued to act as a mediator.

The majority of inhabitants in the region are of indigenous and Afro-Guyanese heritage. Though Venezuela has tried to recruit these residents for their cause, many speak English and have been more integrated into Guyana.

BIBLIOGRAPHY

For the Venezuelan point of view, see the excellent survey by John V. Lombardi, *Venezuela: The Search for Order, the Dream for Progress* (1982). For Guyana's side, consult Chaitram Singh, *Guyana: Politics in a Plantation Society* (1988).

*Additional Bibliography*

Domínguez, Jorge, et al. *Conflictos territoriales y democracia en América Latina.* Buenos Aires: Siglo Veintiuno Editores Argentina, 2003.

Márquez, Oscar José. *La venezolanidad del Esequibo: Reclamación, desarrollo unilateral, nacionalidad de los esequibanos.* Caracas: Libreria Mundial, 2002.

Mondolfi, Edgardo. *El Águila y el León: El presidente Benjamin Harrison y la mediación de los Estados Unidos en la controversia de límites entre Venezuela y Gran Bretaña.* Caracas: Academia Nacional de la Historia, 2000.

Morales, Faustino. *Geografía física del territorio en reclamación: Guayana Esequiba.* Caracas: Fondo Editorial de la Facultad de Humanidades y Educación, Universidad Central de Venezuela, 1999.

Simancas, Francisco, and Elías R. Daniels H. *Conflicts and Controversies, Venezuela and Guyana.* Paramaribo, Suriname: Cátedra Libre Simón Bolívar, 2004.

MAURICE P. BRUNGARDT

**GUIDO, BEATRIZ** (1925–1988). Beatriz Guido (*b.* 1925; *d.* 4 March 1988), Argentine writer. Guido's fiction exemplifies the literary production of Argentina during the 1950s, which was deeply influenced by a postwar European sensibility of ethical despair and the imperative to manifest a social commitment, especially in the creation of fictional characters obliged to participate as fully conscious individuals in the dirty business of life. Many Argentine writers, including Guido, manifested their adherence to this imperative by addressing the historical upheaval produced in their country first by Peronism and then by the rabid reaction to it by the traditionalist oligarchy. A Rosario native, Guido was superbly skillful in portraying the alternately oblivious and cynical moral corruption at the core of the power elite (more the landed gentry than the nouveaux-riches capitalists who attracted the attention of a subsequent generation). Perhaps her two best works are her first, *La casa del ángel* (1954; *The House of the Angel,* 1957), of interest from a feminist perspective because of the dominant motif of the psychosexual abuse of the young female protagonist, Ana, and *El incendio y las vísperas* (1964; *End of a Day,* 1966), which centers on the torching in April 1953 by Peronista hoodlums of the Jockey Club, a legendary oligarchic bastion in Buenos Aires. The novel uses this event as an axis to portray the intersecting conflicts of two Peronista opponents: the decadent oligarchy and the emerging revolutionary left. Guido, whose novels provoked many outraged responses, saw several of her works filmed by her husband, Leopoldo Torre Nilsson, with whom she collaborated on numerous cinematographic projects.

*See also* **Cinema: From the Silent Film to 1990; Literature: Spanish America.**

BIBLIOGRAPHY

Arturo Jauretche, *El medio pelo en la sociedad argentina* (1966), pp. 193–216.

Fernando Pedro Alonso and Arturo Rezzano, *Novela y sociedad argentinas* (1971), pp. 184–193.

Beatriz Guido, *¿Quién le teme a mis temas?* (1977).

Nora De Marval De McNair, "Adolescencia y hechizo en el mundo literario de Beatriz Guido: Tres variaciones en torno a un mismo tema," in *Círculo* 10 (1981): 29–40.

José A. Mahieu, "Beatriz Guido: Las dos escrituras," in *Cuadernos Hispanoamericanos,* no. 437 (1986): 153–168.

*Additional Bibliography*

Flawiá de Fernández, Nilda María. *Voces y espacios de escritura: Argentina, 1950–1970.* San Miguel de Tucumán: Instituto Interdisciplinario de Literaturas Argentina y Comparadas, Facultad de Filosofía y Letras, 2001.

Mucci, Cristina. *Divina Beatrice: Una biografía de la escritora Beatriz Guido.* Buenos Aires: Grupo Editorial Norma, 2002.

DAVID WILLIAM FOSTER

**GUIDO, JOSÉ MARÍA** (1903–1975). José María Guido, born on August 29, 1903, was an Argentine politician who became interim president of Argentina when the armed forces deposed Arturo Frondizi in 1962. In 1954 Guido was named secretary of the national committee of the Radical Civic Union (Unión Cívica Radical, or UCR). In 1956 the UCR, incapable of coming up with a unified position on the restoration of Peronism to the political system, split into two factions: the Intransigent UCR (UCR Intransigente, or UCRI), led by Frondizi, and the People's UCR (UCR del Pueblo), led by Ricardo Balbín. Guido followed Frondizi, and in 1957 he was elected president of the UCRI. In the 1958 national elections, the UCRI came to power thanks to a semi-secret electoral alliance with the Peronists, who at the time were banned from political activities. Frondizi was elected president, and Guido became senator for the province of Río Negro. When Vice President Alejandro Gómez resigned because of internal struggles, Guido became interim president of the senate.

Frondizi allowed the Peronists to run in the 1962 elections, and they won ten of the fourteen provincial governorships. The military, already fed up with Frondizi and alarmed at the Peronist victory, removed the president from office. In accordance with the Vacancy Law (Ley de Acefalía), Guido moved up to the presidency. Backed into a corner by armed confrontations between the two opposing groups within the army, the "blues" (*azules*) and the "reds" (*colorados*), he oversaw passage during his term of a new law on political parties that explicitly outlawed Peronism. He also set a date for new elections in October 1963. He died on June 13, 1975.

*See also* **Argentina: The Twentieth Century; Argentina, Political Parties: Radical Party (UCR); Balbín, Ricardo; Frondizi, Arturo; Perón, Juan Domingo.**

BIBLIOGRAPHY

Potash, Robert A. *El ejército y la política en Argentina, 1962–1973: De la caída de Frondizi a la restauración peronista*, Vol. 1. Buenos Aires: Sudamericana, 1994.

Smulovitz, Catalina. *Oposición y gobierno: Los años de Frondizi*, 2. vols. Buenos Aires: Centro Editor de América Latina, 1988.

VICENTE PALERMO

**GUIDO Y SPANO, CARLOS** (1827–1918). For several generations of Argentineans, Carlos Guido y Spano was considered the country's national poet. His father, Tomás Guido (1788–1866), was an aristocratic military general who fought with José de San Martín for the independence of Spanish America, and later became a high-ranking minister during the *caudillo* regime of Juan Manuel de Rosas. As an elite young man, Guido y Spano spent his formative years abroad, living with the royal court of Brazilian monarch Dom Pedro II and participating in the 1848 antimonarchical revolts in France.

Guido y Spano began his writing career in Argentina as a journalist, and it was not until 1854 that his first poems were published in the *Revista de Paraná*. His first book of poetry, *Hojas al viento* (Leaves in the Wind) was published in Buenos Aires in 1871. In 1879 he published a two-volume work, *Ráfagas*, which included prose writing about politics and literature, as well as some of his journalistic writings. In this same year he published his *Autobiografía*, which is full of memories from his childhood, quotations from his travel notebooks, and excerpts from his letters.

Highly influenced by the literary style of the romantic era into which he was born, Guido y Spano's poetry reflects many of the main themes of this genre, such as unrequited love, nighttime journeys, and country ruins. At the same time, he is considered by many literary historians to have played a leading role in introducing the styles of American modernism into Argentina, specifically through his use of classical themes and his judicious use of language.

Guido y Spano's aristocratic background and political connections brought him to several political posts throughout his lifetime. He served as the subsecretary of foreign relations from 1854 to 1861, and in 1872 he was named secretary of agriculture. In 1874 he was designated director of the general archive of Buenos Aires province, and from 1881 to 1894 he served as the spokesperson for the National Council on Education. He died in Buenos Aires in 1918 after a long illness.

*See also* **Literature: Spanish America.**

BIBLIOGRAPHY

*Primary Works*

Guido y Spano, Carlos, and Angel Mazzei. *Carlos Guido y Spano: Autobiografía y selección de poesías.* Buenos Aires: Atlántida, 1975.

*Secondary Works*

Fortuny, Pablo. *Carlos Guido y Spano, poeta y "hombre de bien."* Buenos Aires: Ediciones Theoría, 1967.

Sarlos, Beatriz. *Carlos Guido y Spano.* Buenos Aires: Centro Editor de América Latina, 1968.

EMILY BERQUIST

**GUILDS (GREMIOS).** Guilds (gremios), self-governing organizations that established and enforced rules for the production and sale of specialized goods. Members were artisans such as shoemakers, silversmiths, carpenters, and harness makers. Guilds flourished chiefly in the colonial era.

At the time of European exploration and conquest of the New World, the artisan trades of Spain and Portugal were organized in guilds, which dealt with economic life, and Cofradías (lay brotherhoods), which supervised religious activities and social welfare for members. In the New World, migrant European craftsmen organized guilds initially to improve their social status and limit competition from indigenous producers. During the period 1545–1560, guilds were first established in the major cities of the viceroyalties of Mexico and Peru. Before the end of the century, guilds were sanctioned in secondary cities such as Guatemala City, Potosí, Guadalajara, and Puebla. Eventually, rudimentary craft organizations, if not recognized guilds, were formed in most Spanish colonial cities.

The self-interested initiatives of guild founders were supported by city governments, which sought to protect consumers from exorbitant prices and goods of shoddy quality. Municipal governments delegated a broad range of regulatory powers to guild authorities. Each guild maintained an effective monopoly of its market. It also determined membership and training criteria, the products that could be produced, prices, wages, and working conditions. From early times, religious, racial, and ethnic characteristics were used to limit access to guild membership.

Guilds were organized hierarchically in three ranks: masters, journeymen, and apprentices. Only masters could own shops and sell directly to the public. Masters also controlled all guild offices and the examination system that permitted younger craftsmen to achieve higher rank. In effect, these powers allowed masters to limit competition and favor the advancement of their own children and kinsmen.

Once guilds were in place, elected officers set prices and maintained quality control through inspections. They could assess fines, seize goods, and even close shops. Guild officers also served as judges and mediators when disputes arose among guild members or between guild members and customers.

There were fewer guilds organized in Brazilian cities. Those that were created lacked both the social status and independent economic power of the guilds in the Spanish colonies. In Brazil, the rapid development of slavery and the integration of large numbers of slaves in artisan trades proved to be a major obstacle to the delegation of self-governing powers.

Essential elements of the European craft tradition were common even where guilds were not formally organized. Nearly everywhere, apprenticeship was regulated by contract. Parents, guardians, or the state placed young boys with master artisans for set periods. Contracts stipulated living conditions in the master's house and the skills that would be taught, and explicitly sanctioned the master's authority to discipline his apprentice. Recognized masters were also granted the right to supervise the promotion of journeymen to the rank of master. Most commonly an aspiring journeyman was required to demonstrate theoretical and practical knowledge and then produce a master work selected at random from a book of designs sanctioned by a European guild.

Colonial guilds were weaker than those in Iberia because they reflected colonial social relations that were forged by the Conquest and the Atlantic slave trade. Although European artisans often recruited and trained apprentices among Amerindian, African, and mixed-race populations, efforts to exclude nonwhites from the rank of master or from guild offices led to racial divisions that undermined solidarity. Colonial authorities and powerful commercial interests also worked to limit the ability of artisans to restrict imports or eliminate competing production by indigenous groups.

By the eighteenth century, guilds were increasingly viewed as corrupt obstacles to economic progress. In Europe and Latin America, reformers associated with the ideas of economic liberalism sought to reform drastically or eliminate guilds. With the achievement of independence, the economic powers of guilds were nearly universally eliminated. Nevertheless, in many artisan trades a training regime based on apprenticeship was retained well into the modern period.


BIBLIOGRAPHY

Raul Carranco y Trujillo, *Las ordeñanzas de gremios de Nueva Espana* (1932).

Manuel Carrera Stampa, *Los gremios mexicanos* (1954).

Lyman L. Johnson, "The Artisans of Buenos Aires during the Viceroyalty, 1776–1810" (Ph.D. diss., University of Connecticut, 1974).

### *Additional Bibliography*

García-Bryce, Iñigo L. *Crafting the Republic: Lima's Artisans and Nation Building in Peru, 1821–1879.* Albuquerque: University of New Mexico Press, 2004.

Illades, Carlos. *Hacia la república del trabajo: La organización artesanal en la Ciudad de México, 1853–1876.* México, D.F.: Colegio de México, Centro de Estudios

Históricos: Universidad Autónoma Metropolitana-Iztapalapa, 1996.

Lida, Clara E., and Sonia Pérez Toledo. *Trabajo, ocio y coacción: Trabajadores urbanos en México y Guatemala en el siglo XIX.* México, D.F.: Universidad Autónoma Metropolitana, Unidad Iztapalapa, Casa Abierta al Tiempo, División de Ciencias Sociales y Humanidades, Departamento de Filosofía: Porrúa, 2001.

Paniagua Pérez, Jesús, and Gloria M. Garzón Montenegro. *Los gremios de plateros y batihojas en la ciudad de Quito, siglo XVIII.* México: Instituto de Investigaciones Estéticas, Universidad Nacional Autónoma de México, 2000.

Quiroz, Francisco. *Gremios, razas y libertad de industria: Lima colonial.* Lima: Universidad Nacional Mayor de San Marcos, 1995.

Ruiz Medrano, Carlos Rubén. *El gremio de plateros en Nueva Espanã.* San Luis Potosí: El Colegio de San Luis, 2001.

LYMAN L. JOHNSON

---

**GUILLÉN, NICOLÁS** (1902–1989). Nicolás Guillén (*b.* 10 July 1902; *d.* 16 July 1989), Cuban poet. A contender for the Nobel Prize for literature, Nicolás Guillén was Cuba's national poet. He developed an early interest in poetry and published his first poems in *Camagüey Gráfico* in 1920. That same year he enrolled in the University of Havana to pursue a degree in law. For lack of interest and for financial reasons, Guillén left the university a few weeks later and returned to his native city, where he earned a living as a printer, a trade he learned from his father. With Vicente Menéndez Roque he edited the literary section of the newspaper *Las Dos Repúblicas* and contributed to *Orto* and *Castalia,* both literary reviews.

Guillén made a second attempt to continue his studies in Havana in 1921 but, as before and for similar reasons, he returned to Camagüey. That same year he gathered his poems under the title "Cerebro y corazón," which remained unpublished as a book until 1965. He also published his sonnets in *Alma Mater,* published the magazine *Lis,* and edited *El Camagüeyano.*

In 1926 Guillén went to work as a typist for the Ministry of the Interior in Havana, but continued to write and publish poetry. It was through Gustavo E. Urrutia, who invited the poet to write for a section he edited, "Ideales de una raza," in the *Diario de la Marina,* that Guillén began to compose poems about Afro-Cubans, which resulted in the publication of *Motivos de son* in 1930. These poems, along with others by José Zacarías Tallet, Ramón Guirao, and Emilio Ballagas, became part of the Negrista movement of the 1920s and 1930s. In his poems Guillén explored the exoticism and rhythm of the other poets, but also added a social and cultural dimension about the lives of Cuban people of African descent.

After the *Diario de la Marina* ceased to publish Urrutia's column, Guillén continued to explore Afro-Cuban themes in Lino Dou's "La marcha de una raza," in the newspaper *El Mundo.* Subsequently, he published *Sóngoro cosongo* (1931) and *West Indies, Ltd.* (1934), which were more expressive about the subordinate conditions of blacks and their need to develop self pride not only in Cuba but throughout the Caribbean. During this period, Guillén was editor of the newspaper *Información* and the weekly *El Loco.*

Guillén's political life and literary activities began to merge. In 1935, as a result of his political activities, he was forced from his job at the Department of Culture. He became a member of the editorial boards of *Resumen,* a publication of the Communist Party, and *Mediodía,* which he edited when it was transformed into a politico-literary weekly. In 1937, with other Cuban and Latin American notables, he attended the Congress of Writers and Artists in Mexico and the Second International Congress of Writers for the Defense of Culture in Barcelona, Valencia, and Madrid. That same year he joined the Cuban Communist Party and the following year two of his poems were published in its newspaper *Hoy.* Guillén's *Cantos para soldados y sones para turistas* (1937) and *España: Poema en cuatro angustias y una esperanza* (1937), completed before his trip to Spain, address conditions mainly in Cuba and Spain, respectively, and belong to a period of ideological commitment.

For Guillén, the 1940s were characterized by an internationalist consciousness and extensive travel throughout the world. After an unsuccessful candidacy for mayor of Camagüey in 1940, he traveled to Haiti in 1942 and Venezuela in 1945, and later to Colombia, Peru, Chile, Argentina, Uruguay, and Brazil. *El son entero: Suma poética,*

*1929–1946,* published while he was in Buenos Aires in 1947, gathers poems written both prior to and following his travels. Following an unsuccessful run in 1948 as senatorial candidate for the Cuban Communist Party he returned to Havana. Other trips included attending the World Peace conference in New York City and meetings in Paris, Prague, and Mexico; he later traveled extensively throughout Eastern Europe and the Soviet Union. Between 1948 and 1958, he wrote and compiled his *Elegías.*

An active opponent of the Batista dictatorship, after 1953 Guillén lived in exile for six years and continued to travel in Latin America and Europe, where he received the Lenin International Peace Prize in 1954. Guillén lived in Paris from 1955 to 1958 and then moved to Buenos Aires, where he resided until Fidel Castro's revolutionary triumph. *La paloma del vuelo popular,* which contains six elegies, is a product of this period and was published in Buenos Aires in 1958. Guillén returned to Cuba on 23 January 1959 as a hero of sorts. In 1961 he became a member of the National Council of Education and was named president of the National Union of Writers and Artists of Cuba; he later joined the Central Committee of the Communist Party. *Tengo* (1964), *El gran zoo* (1967), *La rueda dentada* (1972), *El diario que a diario* (1972), and *Sol de domingo* (1982) draw upon Guillén's social and political concerns as well as his inventiveness and creativity in developing further his poetic talents, particularly so with *El diario que a diario,* but these later collections do not reach the levels of literary quality, innovation, or importance he attained in his early work. *Prosa de prisa, 1929–1972,* a three-volume collection of newspaper articles, was published in 1975–1976. Guillén is buried in the Colón Cemetery in Havana.

Nancy Morejón, Keith Ellis, Ángel Augier, and others have suggested that Guillén's poetry is limited to an ideological or revolutionary perspective. Other critics, however, such as Vera Kutzinski, Roberto González Echevarría, Antonio Benítez Rojo, and Gustavo Pérez Firmat place Guillén within a broader literary framework. For example, Pérez Firmat points to Guillén's interest in writing Italian sonnets and madrigals, González Echevarría to his fascination for Baroque poetry, and Benítez Rojo to the different stages in his career, shifting from Communist, to controversial, to subversive, and to philosophical positions. This more recent reading of Guillén confirms his greatness as a truly outstanding poet who appeals to a variety of readers.

*See also* **Cuba: Cuba Since 1959; Cuba: The Republic (1898–1959).**

BIBLIOGRAPHY

Nancy Morejón, ed., *Recopilación de textos sobre Nicolás Guillén* (1974) and *Nación y mestizaje en Nicolás Guillén* (1982).

Lorna Williams, *Self and Society in the Poetry of Nicolás Guillén* (1982).

Keith Ellis, *Cuba's Nicolás Guillén: Poetry and Ideology* (1983).

Ángel Augier, *Nicolás Guillén: Estudio biográfico-crítico* (1984).

Vera M. Kutzinski, *Against the American Grain* (1987), pp. 133–235.

Vera M. Kutzinski, ed., "Nicolás Guillén," in *Callaloo* 10 (1987).

Ian I. Smart, *Nicolás Guillén: Popular Poet of the Caribbean* (1990)

### *Additional Bibliography*

Augier, Angel I. *Lo que teníamos que tener: Raza y revolución en Nicolás Guillén.* Pittsburgh: Instituto Internacional de Literatura Iberoamericana, Universidad de Pittsburgh, 2003.

Barchino, Matías, and María Rubio Martín. *Nicolás Guillén: Hispanidad, vanguardia y compromiso social.* Cuenca: Ediciones de la Universidad de Castilla-La Mancha, 2004.

Branche, Jerome. *Vida y obra de Nicolás Guillén.* Ciudad de La Habana: Editorial Pueblo y Educación, 2002.

Brock, Lisa, and Digna Castañeda Fuertes. *Between Race and Empire: African-Americans and Cubans before the Cuban Revolution.* Philadelphia: Temple University Press, 1998.

William Luis

---

**GUILMAIN, OFELIA** (1921–2005). The Mexican actress Ofelia Guilmain, born on November 17, 1921, in Spain, starred in over 100 stage plays, 40 movies, and about 38 telenovelas (TV soap operas). A member of the "Guerrillas of Theater" troops during the Second Spanish Republic (1932–1939), she fled to Mexico after Franco took power in 1939. There, Guilmain began her career as a stage actress in *Mujeres* (Women) and went on to perform in radio shows, cinema, and television. In 1941 she married Lucilo Gutiérrez and took a decade off from acting to raise her four children. Two of her children, Lucía Guilmain and Juan Ferrara, followed in her footsteps and became actors. She is best remembered for her roles as a villainess and other strong female characters. She died of pneumonia on January 14, 2005. She was posthumously awarded the Medalla de Mérito (Medallion of Merit) at the Palacio de Bellas Artes during a ceremony held in homage of her sixty-five-year career.

*See also* **Cinema: From the Silent Film to 1990; Theater.**

BIBLIOGRAPHY

Pascual, Carlos. *Retablo rojo: El vida y obra y milagros de Ofelia Guilmain*. Mexico: Oceano, 2006.

SOPHIA KOUTSOYANNIS

## GUIMARÃES, ULYSSES SILVEIRA

**GUIMARÃES, ULYSSES SILVEIRA** (1916–1992). Ulysses Silveira Guimarães (*b.* 6 October 1916; *d.* 12 October 1992), Brazilian politician. Until his death in a helicopter crash off the coast of Rio de Janeiro, Ulysses Guimarães was one of Brazil's most prominent federal legislators. Although Guimarães suffered numerous setbacks during his lengthy career, including political repression, endemic legislative gridlock, and unsuccessful presidential bids in 1974 and 1989, his political persona symbolized a devout dedication to democratic principles in public service and national life.

As the long-standing president of the Brazilian Democratic Movement (MDB), which existed from 1966 to 1979, and its successor, the Brazilian Democratic Movement Party (PMDB), Guimarães led the party's legislative opposition to military rule and support of the restoration and extension of democracy. Guimarães played an instrumental role in the 1985 campaign for direct presidential elections, the 1987–1988 Constituent Assembly, and the 1992 impeachment proceedings against Fernando Collor De Mello. Toward the end of his political career, Guimarães's political influence faltered somewhat with the splintering of the PMDB into competing leftist and centrist parties.

A native of the state of São Paulo, Guimarães received a law degree from the University of São Paulo in 1940 and entered national politics in 1950 as a federal legislator for the Social Democratic Party (PSD). He served briefly as minister of industry and commerce (1961–1962) and represented the PSD in the Chamber of Deputies until 1966, when he joined the MDB. In 1974 Guimarães was the MDB "anticandidate" for president, running on a platform of opposition to repressive military rule. Although handily defeated by the military candidate, he remained a power broker throughout the 1970s and 1980s. Guimarães also represented Brazil in numerous international conventions.

*See also* **Brazil, Political Parties: Brazilian Democratic Movement (MDB).**

BIBLIOGRAPHY

"Ulisses Guimarães," in *Dicionário histórico-biográfico brasileiro* (1984), pp. 1,571–1,574.

Thomas Skidmore, *The Politics of Military Rule in Brazil, 1964–85* (1988); *Veja* (21 October 1992), pp. 16–31.

*Additional Bibliography*

Mattos, Marco Aurélio Vannucchi Leme de, and Walter Cruz Swensson. *Contra os inimigos da ordem: A repressão política do regime militar brasileiro (1964–1985)*. Rio de Janeiro: DP & A Editora, 2003.

Scartezini, A. C. *Dr. Ulysses: Uma biografia*. São Paulo: Marco Zero, 1993.

DARYLE WILLIAMS

## GUINÉ, GUINEA

**GUINÉ, GUINEA.** Guinea Guiné is an imprecise European term for western Africa in use since the fifteenth century. To the Portuguese, "Guiné" indicated a large part of coastal West Africa to the south of Cape Bojador. To other Europeans, "Guinea" defined all of western Africa from the Senegal River to the Orange River in South Africa, with a further division into Upper and Lower Guinea. Guinea-Bissau was the site of a Portuguese fort and trading factory, which supplied many enslaved Africans to Latin America. Guinea-Bissau and the former French colony of Guinea are now independent countries in West Africa. In 1958 the country gained independence from France, making it the first French African colony to gain independence and thus lose all French assistance. Guinea's population was an estimated 9,402,000 in 2005.

*See also* **Africa, Portuguese; Slave Trade.**

BIBLIOGRAPHY


Chaliand, Gérard. *Armed Struggle in Africa: With the Guerrillas in Portuguese Guinea*, Trans. David Rattray and Robert Leonhardt. New York: Monthly Review Press, 1969.

Curtin, Philip D. *The Atlantic Slave Trade.* Madison: University of Wisconsin, 1969.

Gifford, Prosser, and William Roger Louis, eds. *Decolonization and African Independence.* New Haven, CT: Yale University Press, 1998.

Klein, Martin A. *Slavery and Colonial Rule in French West Africa.* Cambridge, U.K.; New York: Cambridge University Press, 1998.

Miers, Suzanne, and Richard Roberts, eds. *The End of Slavery in Africa.* Madison: University of Wisconsin Press, 1988.

Serrão, Joel. "Guiné." In *Pequeno dicionário de história de Portugal.* Lisboa: Figueirinhas, 1987.


MARY KARASCH

**GÜIRALDES, RICARDO** (1886–1927). Ricardo Güiraldes (*b.* 13 February 1886, *d.* 8 October 1927), Argentine writer. Born in Buenos Aires into a patrician family of estancia owners, he spent the first three years of his life in Paris, speaking French before he learned his native language, an experience that permitted him to enrich his Spanish writings with bold transplants. His devotion to everything French and to his own land engendered a deep symbiosis of the European and Argentine heritages. A sophisticated European as well as a gaucho, skillful at tasks practiced by the cowboys of the Pampa, he was also a refined Argentine gentleman who helped to popularize the tango in Paris's café society. The First World War caused him to retreat into spiritualistic, existentialist, and oriental philosophies. In his yearly pilgrimages to Paris, he established deep friendships with the French writer Valéry Larbaud and the most important "decadent" poets of the time, who greatly influenced his literature. A man of authentic nationalistic feelings for Argentina, like many of his countrymen at the time, Güiraldes wanted to idealize his native roots while enriching them with the best European contributions. He had an ecumenical outlook and eagerness, although deeply rooted in his country and in his time. Güiraldes served as a board member of the influential literary magazines *Martín Fierro* and *Proa,* exercising a guiding role among younger writers. He published three volumes of poetry, two of short stories, and four novels; not a large body of work, but one of high quality and very avant-garde. In 1926, a few months before his death in Paris, he won the National Prize for Literature for his novel *Don Segundo Sombra,* a classic of Argentine literature. Güiraldes found his voice, at once "gaucha," full of peasant imagery, but also very French. The book was innovative in the very personal style of his narrative; in being a bildungsroman, in which Güiraldes proposed a model for the education of his people with its hyperbolized figure of the gaucho; and in its depiction of a free, stoic, lonely, and silent life.

*See also* **Gaucho; Literature: Spanish America.**

BIBLIOGRAPHY


P. R. Beardsell, "French Influences in Güiraldes's Early Experiments," in *Bulletin of Hispanic Studies* 16 (1969): 331–344.

William W. Megenney, ed., *Four Essays on Ricardo Güiraldes (1886–1927)* (1977).

Giovanni Previtali, *Ricardo Güiraldes and "Don Segundo Sombra": Life and Works* (1963).

Nina M. Scott, "Language, Humor, and Myth in the Frontier Novels of the Americas: Wister, Güiraldes, and Amado," in Program in Latin American Studies (Amherst, MA), *Occasional Papers,* no. 16 (1983): 1–34.

*Additional Bibliography*

Bordelois, Ivonne. *Un triángulo crucial: Borges, Güiraldes y Lugones.* Buenos Aires: Eudeba, 1999.

Peris Llorca, Jesús. *La construcción de un imaginario nacional: Don Segundo Sombra y la tradición gauchesca.* Valencia: Tirant lo Blanch Libros: Universidad de València, 1997.


ANGELA B. DELLEPIANE

**GUIRAO, RAMÓN** (1908–1949). Ramón Guirao (*b.* 1908; *d.* 17 March 1949), Cuban poet. A founding member of the *Sociedad de Estudios Afrocubanos,* Guirao first gained national attention with his poem "La bailadora de rumba," which appeared in the literary supplement of Havana's *Diario de la Marina* in 1928. From 1933 to 1940 he lived in Mexico, where he worked as a journalist. In 1937 he gained recognition for an essay on Cuba, which he presented to the secretary of education. He was the editor of the journal *Grafos*. Guirao played an instrumental role in the development of literature devoted to Afro-Cuban themes, as exemplified by such works as "Poetas negros y mestizos de la época esclavista," which appeared in *Bohemia* in 1934. He worked until the end of his life editing *Advance y Alerta*, and contributed to several other literary journals.

*See also* **Journalism; Literature: Spanish America.**

BIBLIOGRAPHY

Pedro Barreda, *The Black Protagonist in the Cuban Novel* (1979), pp. 15, 27, and 29; *Diccionario de la Literatura Cubana,* vol. 1, edited by Marina García (1980), p. 416.

William Luis, *Literary Bondage* (1990), pp. 7 and 178.

*Additional Bibliography*

González-Pérez, Armando. *Acercamiento a la literatura afrocubana: Ensayos de interpretación.* Miami: Ediciones Universal, 1994.

Mullen, Edward J. *Afro-Cuban Literature: Critical Junctures.* Westport: Greenwood Press, 1998.

MICHAEL A. POLUSHIN

**GUIRIOR, MANUEL** (1708–1788). Manuel Guirior (*b.* 23 March 1708; *d.* 25 November 1788), viceroy of Peru (1776–1780). Born into a noble family in Aoiz (Navarre), Guirior pursued a distinguished naval career, primarily in the Mediterranean, before taking up in 1772 his appointment as viceroy of New Granada. During this first period of office, which ended in 1776 with his transfer to Lima, he acquired a reputation for firmness in dealing with frontier Indians, for progressive economic policies, and for the expansion and reorganization of university education. His service in Peru, by contrast, was blighted by the loss of Upper Peru (present-day Bolivia), high defense costs occasioned by the outbreak of war between Spain and Great Britain, and a prolonged conflict with the *visitador general* (inspector general), José Antonio de Areche, who arrived in Lima in 1777 to undertake a radical program of administrative, judicial, and fiscal reform. Although recalled to Spain in disgrace in 1780, Guirior was rehabilitated by the Council of the Indies in 1785 and given the title Marqués de Guirior.

*See also* **Council of the Indies; New Granada, Viceroyalty of.**

BIBLIOGRAPHY

Eunice J. Gates, "Don José Antonio de Areche: His Own Defense," in *Hispanic American Historical Review* 8 (1928): 14–42.

Vicente Palacio Atard, *Areche y Guirior. Observaciones sobre el fracaso de una visita al Perú* (1946).

José Manuel Pérez Ayala, "Aspectos desconocidos de la vida del Virrey don Manuel de Guirior, co-Fundador de la Biblioteca Nacional de Bogotá," in *Boletín de Historia y Antigüedades* 43 (1956): 156–182.

*Additional Bibliography*

Fisher, John Robert. *Bourbon Peru, 1750–1824.* Liverpool: Liverpool University Press, 2003.

JOHN R. FISHER

**GUTIÉRREZ, EULALIO** (1880–1939). Eulalio Gutiérrez (*b.* 1880; *d.* 12 August 1939), Mexican revolutionary and convention president. Gutiérrez was born of a peasant family on the Hacienda Santo Domingo in the village of Ramos Arizpe, Coahuila, and was a shepherd in his youth. He later became a miner for the Mazapil Copper Company of Concepción del Oro, in Zacatecas.

Gutiérrez became a member of Ricardo Flores Magón's Liberal Party in 1906, and in 1909 he joined the group opposing the reelection of Porfirio Díaz to the presidency. With his brother Luis Gutiérrez, he supported Francisco Madero in 1910. In 1913 he joined the Constitutionalists, rising to military commander of San Luis Potosí in 1914. On November 3 of that year, at the Convention of Aguascalientes, he was selected by the representatives of the leading military commanders to serve as their president, a post he held until 16 January 1915.

The Convention failed, however, to obtain the support of all the victorious revolutionaries, and the Constitutionalists split their support between

Venustiano Carranza on the one hand and Francisco Villa and Emiliano Zapata on the other. Gutiérrez opposed both Carranza and Villa during 1915, and the following year went into exile. After returning to Mexico, he served as a senator from Coahuila in the 1920s, but left Mexico again after supporting the unsuccessful Escobar rebellion of 1929 by followers of the recently assassinated Álvaro Obregón. He retired permanently from politics thereafter.

*See also* **Díaz, Porfirio; Flores Magón, Ricardo.**

BIBLIOGRAPHY

Manuel García Purón, *México y su gobernantes, biografías* (1964).

Robert E. Quirk, *The Mexican Revolution, 1914–1915* (1981).

*Additional Bibliography*

Katz, Friedrich. *The Life and Times of Pancho Villa.* Stanford: Stanford University Press, 1998.

Turner, Ethel Duffy. *Ricardo Flores Magón y el Partido Liberal Mexicano.* México: Instituto Nacional de Estudios Históricos de la Revolución Mexicana, 2003.

RODERIC AI CAMP

**GUTIÉRREZ, GUSTAVO** (1928–). Gustavo Gutiérrez (*b.* 8 June 1928) is a Peruvian priest and founder of Liberation Theology. His attempt to interpret the meaning of Christianity within the context of the struggle for justice unleashed a revolution in Latin American theological inquiry. After training for the priesthood in Europe in the 1950s, Gutiérrez became part of a South and Central American network of Catholic Church reformers seeking to apply the teachings of the Second Vatican Council (1962–1965) to Latin American conditions. Influenced by radicalized students, the Peruvian Marxist José Carlos Mariátegui, the author José María Arguedas, and dependency theory, Gutiérrez came to champion the liberation of the Latin American poor. In 1968 he coauthored the central texts of the famous Medellín Latin American bishops' conference that denounced social and economic inequality. In his 1971 foundational text *Teología de la liberación: Perspectivas,* he proposed the new theological method of theology as reflection on the commitment of Christians to construct a just society.

The liberation theology movement that his ideas spawned committed some members of the Catholic Church to defend the rights of the marginalized. Because of his use of certain aspects of Marxist theory, Gutiérrez's theology has attracted Vatican and conservative criticism. Nevertheless, he has continued to refine his ideas through conferences, international theological networks, and contact with the poor. In later works Gutiérrez has developed a spirituality of suffering.

Gutiérrez is professor of theology at the University of Notre Dame and a member of the Peruvian Academy of Language. In 1993 the French government awarded him the Legion of Honor.

*See also* **Catholic Church: The Modern Period; Conference of Latin American Bishops (CELAM); Liberation Theology.**

BIBLIOGRAPHY

Gustavo Gutiérrez, *A Theology of Liberation,* rev. ed. (1988); *The Future of Liberation Theology,* edited by Marc H. Ellis and Otto Maduro (1989), esp. part II.

Penny Lernoux, *People of God* (1989).

Christian Smith, *The Emergence of Liberation Theology* (1991).

*Additional Bibliography*

Herndl, Carl G., and Danny A. Bauer. "Speaking Matters: Liberation Theology, Rhetorical Performance, and Social Action." *College Composition and Communication* 54, no. 4 (June 2003): 558–585.

Smith, Christian. "Las Casas as Theological Counteroffensive: An Interpretation of Gustavo Gutiérrez's *Las Casas: In Search of the Poor of Jesus Christ.*" *Journal for the Scientific Study of Religion* 41, no. 1 (2002): 69–73.

MATTHEW J. O'MEAGHER

**GUTIÉRREZ, JOSÉ MARÍA** (1831–1903). José María Gutiérrez (*b.* 20 June 1831; *d.* 26 December 1903), lawyer, journalist, and public figure deeply involved in issues concerning the character of Argentine nationhood, constitutionality, and administration. Gutiérrez served in numerous government positions, beginning in 1852 in the Ministry of Government of Buenos Aires Province, and as secretary of the Chamber of Representatives (1854–1857). He participated in the first Battle of Cepeda (1859) and in the Battle of Pavón, where the

Confederation of Provinces was defeated in 1861. From 1862, Gutiérrez founded and edited *La Nación,* a paper devoted to defending Bartolomé Mitre, who became the first constitutional president of Argentina in 1862; in 1878, Gutiérrez founded another paper, *La Patria Argentina.* He was minister of justice and public instruction in 1877, was minister of state from 1890 to 1892, and from 1895 until his death, served on the National Council of Education.

*See also* **Cepeda, Battle of; Pavón, Battle of.**

BIBLIOGRAPHY

Vicente Osvaldo Cutolo, ed., *Nuevo diccionario biográfico argentino,* vol. 3 (1971).

Tulio Halperín Donghi, ed., *Proyecto y construcción de una nación: Argentina, 1846–1880* (1980).

John Lynch, *Argentine Dictator: Juan Manuel de Rosas, 1829–1852* (1981).

*Additional Bibliography*

Adelman, Jeremy. *Republic of Capital: Buenos Aires and the Legal Transformation of the Atlantic World.* Stanford: Stanford University Press, 1999.

Rock, David. *State Building and Political Movements in Argentina, 1860–1916.* Stanford: Stanford University Press, 2002.

HILARY BURGER

**GUTIÉRREZ, JUAN MARÍA** (1809–1878). Juan María Gutiérrez (May 6, 1809–February 26, 1878), Argentina's first literary critic, studied at the University of Buenos Aires, where he obtained a degree *intopographical* engineering. Prominent in the New Argentine Generation movement of 1837, he was briefly arrested and then forced into exile by the régime of Juan Manuel de Rosas. In Montevideo from 1838 to 1843, he resided in Chile from 1844 to 1852. There, in addition to becoming the first director of Chile's Naval Academy (1846–1852), he published the first anthology of Latin American poetry, *La América poética* (1847), and Pedro de Oña's colonial epic of 1596, *El Arauco domado* (1848; The Tamed Araucan). In 1852 he became a member of the Constitutional Convention that drafted Argentina's 1853 Constitution, whose text he wrote (basing himself on J. B. Alberdi's blueprint, *Las Bases y puntos de partida para organizacion política de la República Argentina* [1852; *Bases and Starting Points for the Political Organization of the Argentine Republic*]). Minister of foreign affairs of the Argentine Confederation from 1854 to 1858, he abandoned active politics in 1861 after being appointed rector of Buenos Aires University (1861–1874).

This was the most active period of his career as critic and literary historian. His most important works, in addition to those mentioned, were: *Origen y desarrollo de la enseñanza pública superior en Buenos Aires* (1868; Origin and Development of Superior Public Education in Buenos Aires), *Juan Cruz Varela* (1874), the edition of Esteban Echeverría's *Obras completas* (1870–1874; Complete Works, 5 vols.), and the two posthumous compilations of newspaper articles, *Cartas de un porteño* (1926; Letter of a Buenosairean) and *Escritores coloniales americanos* (1957; American Colonial Writers). He was co-editor (with Andrés Lamas and Vicente Fidel López) of *La Revista del Río de la Plata* (1871–1877; Journal of the Río de la Plata), the most prestigious Argentine literary journal of the 1870s. As a critic, he sought to construct, in an anticolonialist vein, a genealogy of American literature exclusive of Spain and its literary tradition. Unlike most of his contemporaries, he considered indigenous literary works, such as Netzahualcóyotol's poetry, a legitimate part of Latin America's literary heritage.

*See also* **Literature: Spanish America; Netzahualcóyotl.**

BIBLIOGRAPHY

Morales, Ernesto. *Don Juan María Gutiérrez.* Buenos Aires: Editorial El Ateneo, 1937.

Myers, Jorge, "Una genealogía para el parricidio: Juan María Gutiérrez y la construcción de una tradición literaria." *Entrepasados* 3, no. 4–5 (October 1993): 65–88.

Sarlo, Beatriz. *Juan María Gutiérrez: Historiador y crítico de nuestra literatura.* Buenos Aires: Editorial Escuela, 1967.

JORGE MYERS

**GUTIÉRREZ ALEA, TOMÁS** (1928–1996). After achieving critical and commercial success in the 1960s with a series of films that skillfully combined humor, experimental techniques, and a critical analysis of Cuban politics, history, and culture, the Cuban director Tomás Gutiérrez Alea (December 11, 1928–April 16, 1996) came to be widely regarded as one of the most important filmmakers in Latin America. Gutiérrez Alea received a law degree from the Universidad de la Habana in 1951; then he studied cinema at the Centro Sperimentale di Cinematografia in Rome, graduating in 1953. After the triumph of the Cuban Revolution in 1959, Gutiérrez Alea contributed to the creation of the Instituto Cubano del Arte y la Industria Cinematográficos (ICAIC), a state-supported institute whose main vision was to use cinema to educate the people in revolutionary values. After contributing to several documentaries made by ICAIC, such as *Esta tierra Nuestra* (1959; This land of ours) (1959) and *Muerte al invasor* (1961; Death to the invader), and directing his first two feature films, *Las doce sillas* (1962; The twelve chairs) and *Cumbite* (1964; The communal gathering), Gutiérrez Alea directed his first truly important film, *Muerte de un burócrata* (Death of a bureaucrat), in 1966. The film includes several elements that would become trademarks of Gutiérrez Alea's films: a realistic, often somber portrayal of Cuban society that is counterbalanced by burlesque, albeit sometimes dark humor, and an honest, biting criticism of the limitations of the revolutionary regime (in this case, its official bureaucracy), to which Gutiérrez Alea remained nonetheless always loyal. In *Memorias del subdesarrollo* (1968; Memories of underdevelopment) (based on the novel of the same name by Edmundo Desnoes), those characteristics are joined by an experimental style in the form of a self-referential film in a documentary style that includes real footage of events such as the failed invasion of Bay of Pigs. In its episodic, fragmented plot, the film follows the life of a Cuban writer who is unable to join in the enthusiasm for the revolution and yet is also unwilling to leave Cuba; eventually, his life drifts into paralysis. The film is widely regarded as Gutiérrez Alea's masterpiece and as one of the most important films ever made in Latin America. Gutiérrez Alea's other films include: *Una pelea cubana contra los demonios* (1971; A Cuban fight against the demons) (based on the book of the same name by Fernando Ortiz) and *La última cena* (*The Last Supper*, 1976), which are explorations of nineteenth-century Cuban society; *Hasta cierto punto* (*Up to a Certain Point*, 1984), which deals with the position of women in revolutionary Cuba; *Cartas del parque* (*Letters from the Park*, 1989), a romantic comedy with a script by Gabriel García Márquez; *Fresa y chocolate* (1993; Strawberry and chocolate), about the prejudice against homosexuals in Cuba; and his last film, *Guantanamera* (1995), which combines his usual elements of humor and social criticism in the lighter form of a love story. Gutiérrez Alea won numerous national and international prizes, including an Oscar nomination for *Fresa y chocolate*. In addition to his work as a director, Gutiérrez Alea wrote several theoretical essays that address the relation between cinema and politics.

*See also* **Bay of Pigs Invasion; Cinema: From the Silent Film to 1990; Cinema: Since 1990; Cuba, Revolutions: Cuban Revolution; Cuba: Cuba Since 1959.**

BIBLIOGRAPHY

Evora, José Antonio. *Tomás Gutiérrez Alea*. Madrid: Cátedra, 1996.

Schroeder, Paul A. *Tomas Gutierrez Alea: The Dialectics of a Filmmaker*. London: Routledge, 2002.

Tomás Gutiérrez Alea. Official page. Fnac Espana. Available from http://www.clubcultura.com.

Víctor Figueroa

**GUTIÉRREZ BORBÚA, LUCIO** (1957–). Lucio Gutiérrez Borbúa emerged in Ecuadorian politics in January 2000 when, together with the leaders of the Confederation of Indigenous Nationalities of Ecuador, he led a failed uprising against President Jamil Mahuad, who had presided over a generalized economic crisis. After a brief incarceration Gutiérrez, a man of dark mestizo skin from working-class origins in the Amazonian region, won the 2002 elections with the support of the indigenous movement and the left. He appointed indigenous leaders to his cabinet but left the ministry of the economy in the hands of neoliberal technocrats. Following a brief honeymoon with the indigenous movement, he alienated his leftist supporters and divided the indigenous movement. To secure his grip on power, he formed a congressional alliance with the support of populist parties and reorganized the supreme court. The return of ex-president Abdalá Bucaram from exile in Panama, made possible by a supreme court appointment by Gutiérrez, ignited demonstrations in Quito. With the backing of the armed forces, the congress removed him from office in April 2005. After a brief exile in Brazil, Peru, and Colombia, Gutiérrez returned to Ecuador, where he was incarcerated. He was released from prison and is currently engaged in politics.

*See also* **Ecuador, Political Parties: Overview.**

BIBLIOGRAPHY

Gutiérrez, Lucio. *El golpe: Los rostros de la conspiración.* Quito: Edino, 2006.

Hernández, José, et al. *21 de enero: La vorágine que acabó con Mahuad.* Quito: El Comercio, 2000.

Hurtado, Edison. "Lo que pasó en CIESPAL. Apuntes etnográficos sobre el poder, los medios y los sin-sentidos de la violencia." *Íconos* 23 (September 2005): 63–82.

Ramírez Gallegos, Franklin. *La insurrección de abril no fue sólo una fiesta.* Quito: Ediciones Abya-Yala, 2005.

CARLOS DE LA TORRE

**GUTIÉRREZ BROTHERS.** Gutiérrez Brothers, Peruvian insurrectionists. Persistent military rule of Peru since 1821 had spawned widespread antimilitarism, especially in Lima, in the late nineteenth century. Popular sentiment in the election of 1872 therefore lay with Manuel Pardo, the wealthy merchant who promised a severely reduced military budget and weakening of the military's grip on public offices. Most of the military agreed to stay clear of the election, but the minister of war, Colonel Tomás Gutiérrez, considered the election a direct challenge to the rightful preeminence of the military in Peruvian politics. Gutiérrez organized his brothers, fellow military officers Silvestre, Marceliano, and Marcelino, to seize President José Balta and declared himself president of the republic on July 22, a week before the inauguration of Pardo. Local military garrisons received widespread public support to actively oppose the coup d'etat. The Gutiérrez brothers tried to organize a defense against the popular rejection of their actions, but armed civilians shot Silvestre in downtown Lima and beheaded him. When enraged mobs learned that the rebels had authorized the murder of Balta, they became uncontrollable. A mob killed Tomás and mutilated his body. The bodies of Tomás and Silvestre were then hung from the facade of the cathedral of Lima. Marceliano died fighting in Callao, and Marcelino escaped unharmed. The Gutiérrez uprising marked a nadir in the popular view of the military and may have undermined the confidence of the army and navy in preparing for the upcoming war with Chile.

*See also* **Military Dictatorships: 1821–1945.**

BIBLIOGRAPHY

David P. Werlich, *Peru: A Short History* (1978), esp. pp. 95–96.

Margarita Giesecke, *Masas urbanas y rebelión en la historia. Golpe de estado: Lima 1872* (1978).

*Additional Bibliography*

Valdizán Ayala, José. *José Balta Montero.* Lima, Perú: Editorial Brasa, 1995.

Velásquez Pérez-Salmón, Víctor. *El Ejército del Perú en el siglo XIX: su participación en la seguridad y en el desarrollo nacional.* Lima, Perú: CONCYTEC, Oficina de Subvenciones, 1998.

VINCENT PELOSO

**GUTIÉRREZ DE LARA, JOSÉ BERNARDO** (1774–1841). José Bernardo Gutiérrez de Lara (*b.* 20 August 1774; *d.* 13 May 1841), revolutionary during the Mexican War of Independence. Born in San Ignacio de Loyola, Tamaulipas, Gutiérrez de Lara was a blacksmith, merchant, and property owner, who participated in the independence struggle in Tamaulipas, served as an envoy from Miguel Hidalgo to the government of the United States, and led an invasion of Texas in 1812–1813. He later became involved in other military activities, including the expeditions of Francisco Javier Mina and James Long.

Following Mexican independence, Gutiérrez de Lara returned to Tamaulipas, where he was elected governor in 1824. He served until late 1825, when he became commandant general of the eastern Provincias Internas. Resigning the post in 1826, he did not again become involved in politics until 1839, when he opposed Antonio Canales's efforts to organize a Republic of the Río Grande.

*See also* **Mexico, Wars and Revolutions: War of Independence.**

BIBLIOGRAPHY

Julia Kathryn Garrett, *Green Flag over Texas* (1939).

Rie Jarratt, *Gutiérrez de Lara, Mexican-Texan* (1949).

*Additional Bibliography*

Ferrer Muñoz, Manuel. *La formación de un estado nacional en México: El Imperio y la República federal, 1821–1835.* México, D.F.: Universidad Nacional Autónoma de México, 1995.

Rodríguez O, Jaime E. *The Origins of Mexican National Politics, 1808–1847.* Wilmington: SR Books, 1997.

JESÚS F. DE LA TEJA

## GUTIÉRREZ DE PADILLA, JUAN

**GUTIÉRREZ DE PADILLA, JUAN** (c. 1590–1664). Juan Gutiérrez de Padilla (*b.* ca. 1590; *d.* April 1664), Spanish-born Mexican composer. Educated at the cathedral choir school in his native city of Málaga, Gutiérrez served as music director in Jérez de la Frontera and at the Cádiz cathedral in Spain before immigrating to New Spain around 1622. He was employed as a musician in the Puebla cathedral and in 1629 became its *maestro de capilla*. This post, held until his death, placed him in charge of all music activities, including instruction of the choirboys at the Colegio de San Pedro. The position was considerably enhanced by the support of the wealthy Bishop Palafox y Mendoza. His Latin sacred music bears the early baroque traits of chromaticism and double choir antiphony that prevailed in Europe, but he also wrote popular, dancelike *chanzonettas* and *villancicos* in the vernacular to be used on special feast days.

BIBLIOGRAPHY

Robert Stevenson, *Music in Mexico: A Historical Survey* (1952).

*Additional Bibliography*

Mauleón Rodríguez, Gustavo. *Música en el virreinato de la Nueva España: Recopilación y notas, siglos XVI y XVII.* Puebla, México: Universidad Iberoamericana, Golfo Centro: Lupus Inquisitor, 1995.

ROBERT L. PARKER

## GUTIÉRREZ DE PIÑERES, JUAN FRANCISCO

**GUTIÉRREZ DE PIÑERES, JUAN FRANCISCO** (1732–1802). Juan Francisco Gutiérrez de Piñeres (*b.* 25 August 1732; *d.* 7 October 1802), regent-visitor of New Granada (1776–1783). Born in Lebeña, León, Spain, Gutiérrez studied law in Seville, was appointed to the Audiencia of Valladolid in 1774, and two years later became oidor of the Casa de Contratación. In December 1776, José de Gálvez named him visitor-general of New Granada and regent of the Audiencia of Santa Fe, bearing instructions to improve the administration of royal revenues.

With the outbreak of war in 1779 came authorization to raise taxes and royal monopoly prices. A technocrat lacking political skills, Gutiérrez pursued his mission with such zeal that Viceroy Manuel Flores Maldonado Martínez y Bodquín urged caution, but to no avail. When Flores assumed military command on the coast, he relinquished his civil powers to Gutiérrez. The Comunero Revolt of 1781, protesting his measures, forced the regent-visitor to flee Santa Fe for Cartagena. Thereafter, Gutiérrez saw his effective powers diminished, although he returned to the viceregal capital in 1782. Recalled to Spain in 1783, he assumed a position on the Council of the Indies, where he remained until his death.

*See also* **Comunero Revolt (New Granada).**

BIBLIOGRAPHY

José María Restrepo Sáenz, *Biografías de los mandatarios y ministros de la Real Audiencia, 1671–1819* (1952), especially pp. 509–514.

Allan J. Kuethe, *Military Reform and Society in New Granada, 1773–1808* (1977).

John Leddy Phelan, *The People and the King: The Comunero Revolution in Colombia, 1781* (1978).

*Additional Bibliography*

Grahn, Lance Raymond. *The Political Economy of Smuggling: Regional Informal Economies in Early Bourbon New Granada.* Boulder, CO: Westview Press, 1997.

McFarlane, Anthony. *Colombia Before Independence: Economy, Society, and Politics Under Bourbon Rule.* Cambridge, UK: Cambridge University Press, 2002.

ALLAN J. KUETHE

## GUTIÉRREZ ESTRADA, JOSÉ MARÍA

**GUTIÉRREZ ESTRADA, JOSÉ MARÍA** (1800–1867). José María Gutiérrez Estrada (*b.* 1800; *d.* 1867), Mexican diplomat and politician.

Born in the city of Campeche, Gutiérrez Estrada moved to Mexico City with his family when he was young. He was appointed minister of foreign relations by President Antonio López de Santa Anna (1834–1835) and later served as Mexico's diplomatic representative in several European countries. Upon his return to Mexico in 1840, Gutiérrez Estrada published an open letter to the president in which he called for free discussion of a liberal constitutional monarchy in Mexico, arguing that the monarchical form of government was more consistent with the traditions, needs, and interests of the Mexican people. He warned of the need for a strong government to defend Mexico against U.S. aggression, saying "If we do not change our ways, perhaps twenty years will not pass before we see the flag of the United States waving above our National Palace."

The pamphlet caused a sensation, and Gutiérrez Estrada was denounced by both liberals and conservatives. Although he was forced to flee to Europe, he continued his campaign for a Mexican monarchy. His fears were realized in 1847, when the U.S. army conquered Mexico and raised the Stars and Stripes above the National Palace, after which his proposal gained greater support among Mexican conservatives. Gutiérrez Estrada received various diplomatic commissions and was president of the commission that offered the crown of Mexico to Maximilian at Miramar. Each of his three wives was from a noble family.

*See also* **Mexico: 1810–1910.**

BIBLIOGRAPHY

Alfred Jackson Hanna and Kathryn Abbey Hanna, *Napoleon III and Mexico: American Triumph over Monarchy* (1971); *Diccionario Porrúa de historia, biografía y geografía de México,* 5th ed. (1986).

### *Additional Bibliography*

Palti, Elías José. "La política del disenso: La "polémica en torno al monarquismo" (México, 1848–1850) ... y las aporías del liberalismo." México, D.F.: Fondo de Cultura Económica, 1998.

Ridley, Jasper Godwin. *Maximilian and Juárez.* London: Phoenix, 2001.

D. F. STEVENS

## GUTIÉRREZ GARBÍN, VÍCTOR MANUEL

**(1922–1966).** Víctor Manuel Gutiérrez Garbín (*b.* 10 January 1922; *d.* March 1966), Guatemalan educator and labor leader. Gutiérrez was born in the rural Guatemalan department of Santa Rosa. He was educated as a primary school teacher in Guatemala and taught at the National Boys' Institute in the western province of Chiquimula. After a short teaching stint in the capital, Gutiérrez was made the subdirector of the Industrial Institute for Boys in 1944.

During the revolutionary period (1944–1954), Gutiérrez became the most important and influential labor leader in the history of the country. His career as a labor leader began when he founded the Guatemalan Union of Educational Workers (Sindicato de Trabajadores en Educación de Guatemala, STEG) in 1944. After 1946, as president of the largest national workers' union, later the Confederation of Guatemalan Workers (Confederación de Trabajadores de Guatemala) and later the General Confederation of Guatemalan Workers (Confederación General de Trabajadores de Guatemala), he organized over 100,000 workers. He was known as a particularly honest and dedicated organizer who always maintained close ties to the rank-and-file of the labor movement. Gutiérrez was elected to Congress in 1950, and became first secretary of the Congress in 1954.

Because of his involvement with the Communist Party, Gutiérrez fled Guatemala in 1954. In March 1966, while attempting to return to Guatemala from Mexico, he disappeared, allegedly dropped from an airplane over the Pacific Ocean by Guatemalan security forces. His body was never found.

*See also* **Labor Movements.**

BIBLIOGRAPHY

Ronald Schneider, *Communism in Guatemala: 1944–1954* (1958).

Mario López Larrave, *Breve historia del movimiento sindical guatemalteco,* 2d ed. (1979).

Jim Handy, *Gift of the Devil* (1984).

### *Additional Bibliography*

Handy, Jim. *Revolution in the Countryside: Rural Conflict and Agrarian Reform in Guatemala, 1944-1954.* Chapel Hill: University of North Carolina Press, 1994.

Velásquez Carrera, Eduardo Antonio. *La Revolución de Octubre: Diez años de lucha por la democracia en Guatemala, 1944–1954.* Guatemala: Universidad de San Carlos de Guatemala, Centro de Estudios Urbanos y Regionales, Comisión de Conmemoración del Cincuentenario de la Revolución de Octubre de 1944 y de la Autonomía Universitaria, 1994.

RACHEL A. MAY

**GUTIÉRREZ GONZÁLEZ, GREGORIO** (1826–1872). Gregorio Gutiérrez González (*b.* 9 May 1826; *d.* 6 July 1872), Colombian poet considered the bard of his native Antioquia. After studying law in Bogotá, Gutiérrez held various judicial and legislative posts in Antioquia and represented the province in Congress. As a poet he is remembered partly for his romantic lyrics, such as the two poems entitled "A Julia" and the nostalgic and melancholy "Aures." His major literary achievement, however, is the *Memoria científica sobre el cultivo del maíz en Antioquia,* first published in 1866. A celebration of rural life in Antioquia, this long poem traces the cycle of corn cultivation from preparation of the field to the gathering of the crop. It also contrasts the delicious dishes made of corn with the "vile potato." The poem's bucolic imagery reveals the author's romantic roots yet its homely details impart a realistic flavor, as does the use of local dialect by Gutiérrez, who said that he wrote in *antioqueño,* not in Spanish.

*See also* **Antioquia.**

BIBLIOGRAPHY

Gregorio Gutiérrez González, *Obras completas,* edited by Rafael Montoya y Montoya (1958).

Javier Arango Ferrer, *Raíz y desarrollo de la literatura* (1965), pp. 255–263.

*Additional Bibliography*

Echavarría, Rogelio. *Quién es quién en la poesía colombiana.* Bogotá: Ministerio de Cultura: El Ancora Editores, 1998.

HELEN DELPAR

**GUTIÉRREZ GUERRA, JOSÉ** (1869–1929). José Gutiérrez Guerra (*b.* 5 September 1869; *d.* 3 February 1929), president of Bolivia (1917–1920). Born in Sucre, Gutiérrez Guerra was the last president of the period of Liberal Party domination (1899–1920). His administration was marked by rigged elections and government scandals. Gutiérrez Guerra initially included the main opposition party, the Republicans, in a cabinet of "national concentration" in an effort to sidestep a surge of nationalist fervor over recouping the Pacific coastal area lost during the War of the Pacific (1879–1884) with Chile. However, by 1919 party politics again turned acrimonious. The Liberal Party split over whether to fine Simón Iturri Patiño, the most important Bolivian tin-mine owner and important supporter of the party, who brought 80,000 cans of alcohol into the country after his contract to do so had expired. As a result, the Republican Party was able to organize an almost bloodless coup in July 1920 that toppled the government and ended twenty years of Liberal Party hegemony.

*See also* **Bolivia, Political Parties: Liberal Party; War of the Pacific.**

BIBLIOGRAPHY

The best treatment of the Gutiérrez Guerra government is contained in Herbert S. Klein, *Parties and Political Change in Bolivia: 1880–1952* (1969), pp. 53–61. For the position of an opposition politician, see David Alvéstegui, *Salamanca, su gravitación sobre el destino de Bolivia,* vol. 2 (1958), pp. 179–255.

*Additional Bibliography*

Irurozqui, Marta. *La armonía de las desigualdades: Elites y conflictos de poder en Bolivia, 1880-1920.* Madrid: Consejo Superior de Investigaciones Científicas; Cusco : Centro de Estudios Regionales Andinos Bartolomé de las Casas, 1994.

ERICK D. LANGER

**GUTIÉRREZ NÁJERA, MANUEL** (1859–1895). Manuel Gutiérrez Nájera (*b.* 22 December 1859; *d.* 3 February 1895), Mexican writer. Gutiérrez Nájera was born in Mexico City. His father was a journalist and writer and his mother a devout Catholic. The middle-class family privately educated him and he developed a strong interest in reading classic literature and contemporary French works. He worked as a journalist and in 1888 was appointed to a political post. Gutiérrez Nájera was one of the progenitors of Spanish American *modernista* writing in Mexico. Through his poetry, essays, short stories, and journalistic chronicles, he explored in Spanish the stylistic and linguistic potentials associated with the French Parnassian and Symbolist movements. He wrote under pseudonyms such as Mr. Can-Can, El Duque Job, Puck, and many others. Together with Carlos Díaz Dufoo, he founded *Revista Azul* (1894–1896; Blue Review), one of the principal *modernista* publications in Spanish America. He is frequently known only as a poet, but his prose writing in both the short story and chronicle genres is equally innovative and represents his aesthetic concerns and French cultural influences. His short stories include the collections *Cuentos frágiles* (1883; Fragile Stories) and *Cuentos color de humo* (1898; Smoke-Colored Stories). His chronicles appear in series such as *Crónicas color de rosa* (Rose-Colored Chronicles), *Crónicas color de lluvia* (Rain-Colored Chronicles), *Crónicas color de oro* (Gold-Colored Chronicles), and *Crónicas de mil colores* (Myriad-Colored Chronicles). Gutiérrez Nájera died in Mexico City at the height of his career.

*See also* **Journalism; Literature: Spanish America.**

BIBLIOGRAPHY

Marina Gálvez, "Manuel Gutiérrez Nájera," in *Historia de la Literatura Hispanoamericana*. Vol. 2, *Del neoclasicismo al modernismo,* edited by Luis Íñigo Madrigal (1987), pp. 583–590.

Ivan A. Schulman, "Manuel Gutiérrez Nájera," in *Latin American Writers,* edited by Carlos A. Solé and María Isabel Abreu, vol. 1 (1989), pp. 351–357.

*Additional Bibliography*

Clark de Lara, Belem. *Tradición y modernidad en Manuel Gutiérrez Nájera*. México, D.F.: Universidad Nacional Autónoma de México, Instituto de Investigaciones Filológicas, 1998.

Gutiérrez, José Ismael. *Manuel Gutiérrez Nájera y sus cuentos: de la crónica periodística al relato de ficción*. New York: Peter Lang, 1999.

Puga y Acal, Manuel, and Eugenia Revueltas. *Los poetas mexicanos contemporáneos: Ensayos críticos de Brummel: Salvador Díaz Mirón, Manuel Gutiérrez Nájera, Juan de Dios Peza*. Mexico, D.F.: Universidad Nacional Autónoma de México, Coordinación de Humanidades, 1999.

DANNY J. ANDERSON

## GUTIÉRREZ Y ESPINOSA, FELIPE

**(1825–1899).** Felipe Gutiérrez y Espinosa (*b.* 26 May 1825; *d.* 27 November 1899), Puerto Rican composer. Gutiérrez is considered the best Puerto Rican composer of the nineteenth century and the main figure of Puerto Rico's musical life during that period. Born in San Juan, Gutiérrez received music lessons from his father when very young; thereafter he was self-taught. Starting as a battalion musician, he won the position of maestro de capilla of the San Juan Cathedral in 1858. Later he conducted the orchestra of the Teatro Municipal (later the Teatro Tapia). Around 1873 he traveled to Europe, studying in Paris for one year. Gutiérrez composed sacred music: masses, one oratorio, eight Salve Reginas, and other minor religious works. Of his three operas, *Guarionex, El bearnés,* and *Macías,* the last is the only extant opera of the nineteenth century in Puerto Rico. It was awarded a gold medal in 1871, but went unperformed in the twentieth century until 19 August 1977 at the Teatro Tapia, because its manuscript had been lost. Gutiérrez also composed one zarzuela and other orchestral and chamber music.

*See also* **Music: Art Music.**

BIBLIOGRAPHY

Federico Asenjo, *Las fiestas de San Juan* (1868).

R. Stevenson, *A Guide to Caribbean Music History* (1975).

D. Thompson, "Musical Archaeology, Fine Talent Bring *Macías* to Life," *San Juan Star,* 7 June 1978; *New Grove Dictionary of Music and Musicians,* vol. 7 (1980); *New Grove Dictionary of Opera,* vols. 2 and 4 (1992).

*Additional Bibliography*

Thompson, Donald. *Music in Puerto Rico: A Reader's Anthology*. Lanham: Scarecrow Press, 2002.

SUSANA SALGADO

## GUYANA.

Guyana, the only English-speaking country in South America, independent since 1966. It is bordered by Venezuela, Suriname, Brazil, and the Atlantic Ocean. Two-thirds of Guyana's 83,000 square miles are covered with lush rain forests that yield valuable timber, especially greenheart. The country is also endowed with rich resources of gold, diamonds, and high-grade bauxite ore, as well as extensive areas of fertile coastland on which sugar and rice are grown. The Land of Many Waters, as it is called, boasts a plethora of rivers. The four major ones are the Demerara, on which Georgetown, the capital and chief port, is located; the Essequibo, the largest; the Berbice;

and the Corentyne. There are innumerable rapids and waterfalls along the rivers. Kaieteur Falls on the Potaro River thunders into a gorge at the height of 741 feet. Mount Roraima (9,094 feet), on the borders with Venezuela and Brazil, was the setting for Arthur Conan Doyle's fictional *The Lost World* (1912).

The population of this Land of Six Peoples was approximately 769,095 (2007) and was composed of Amerindians; Africans and East Indians, comprising the majority; and smaller groups of Europeans and Chinese, with varying mixtures. However, according to the 2002 national census, the Indians represented a significant nine percent of the total population. In fact, by the year 2002 there were nine distinctive tribal groups and 90 percent of indigenous communities were located in the rural areas. The culture and religion of the country thus reflect these ethnic groups. Hindu temples, Muslim mosques, and Christian churches of several denominations are located throughout. The Guyanese are bound together by a common language—English, a legacy of English colonialism—international foods, and a passion for cricket.

The Dutch were the first Europeans to colonize the Wild Coast of Guyana, which extended from the mouth of the Amazon to the Orinoco. The early colonies began in the late sixteenth century, establishing friendly relations with the indigenous peoples and carrying on trade in dyes and letterwood. By 1675 they had established sugar, coffee, tobacco, and cotton plantations worked by African slaves. In 1763 there was a massive slave revolt against the Dutch, which was quelled with the help of the indigenous peoples. At the end of the eighteenth century, there were short intervals of British and French control before Dutch rule was superseded by British control in 1803. The Dutch heritage remains in many place-names, such as Stabroek, Vlissengen, Beterverwagting, in the *kokers* or sluice gates, and in the famous Sea Wall.

The main developments in nineteenth-century British Guiana were the emancipation of nearly 83,000 slaves in 1834, the establishment of villages along the coastlands by former slaves, and the importation of indentured workers from Africa, Madeira, India, and China to meet the labor shortage. Two outstanding events marked the end of the nineteenth century: the promulgation of the new Constitution of 1891 and the 1899 Paris settlement, which awarded the Orinoco River to Venezuela, supposedly ending the fifty-five-year-old border dispute. The 1970 Protocol of Port-of-Spain, which established a twelve-year moratorium on the resuscitated boundary question, was not renewed in 1982.

In 1917 East Indian immigration to the colony was stopped, and in 1928 British Guiana became a crown colony. The Court of Policy and the Combined Court, legacies of Dutch government, were replaced by a Legislative and Executive Council. The 1940s, 1950s, and 1960s were years of much political agitation and many strikes as the leading political parties, the People's Progressive Party (PPP), the People's National Congress (PNC), and the United Force (UF) jockeyed for power. The PPP won the 1953 and 1957 elections with Dr. Cheddi Jagan at the forefront.

On 26 May 1966, Guyana gained its independence under a coalition government headed by the PNC leader, Forbes Burnham. On 23 February 1970, Guyana became the first Cooperative Republic within the Commonwealth to be governed by an elected president rather than a British-appointed governor-general. The dual control system of education (controlled by both church and state) was abolished in 1976, and free education from nursery school to university was initiated. The University of Guyana, established in 1963, was engaged on a cost recovery program in the early 1990s. The standard of education in Guyana, which once boasted the highest literacy rate in the Caribbean, has dropped considerably since the 1970s, exacerbated by the migration of many teachers to the Caribbean, North America, and the United Kingdom.

International funding, through the International Monetary Fund and the Inter-American Development Bank, among others, is supporting improvements and the rehabilitation of the country's infrastructure. The immense interior resources, especially gold, are attracting foreign and local investments. Eco-tourism is making marked strides and has much potential, but the country is sensitive to ecological exploitation. A large tract of forest—IWOKRAMA—has been dedicated to an experimental project for the study of rain-forest resources and their careful development. The building of roads is seen as a sine qua non for the development of the interior. The 220-mile road from Georgetown to Brazil has as of 2007 yet to be completed.

Timehri, Guyana's only international airport, 25 miles south of Georgetown, is served by a number of regional airlines with international connections to all major destinations. Guyana Airways Corporation (GAC) connects the country with North America and with a number of locations within the mining and interior areas of Guyana.

Guyana is a member of the United Nations, and in the mid-1990s maintained diplomatic relations with over ninety countries, of which fourteen had missions to the country. Its respected role in international affairs was illustrated by the election of its ambassador to the United Nations as the president of the General Assembly for 1993–1994.

| **Guyana** | |
|---|---|
| **Population:** | 769,095 (2007 est.) |
| **Area:** | 83,000 sq. mi |
| **Languages:** | English, Amerindian dialects, Creole, Caribbean Hindustani (a dialect of Hindi), Urdu |
| **National currency:** | Guyanese dollar |
| **Principal religions:** | Christian 50%; Hindu 35%; Muslim 10%; other 5% |
| **Ethnicity:** | East Indian 50%; black 36%; Amerindian 7%; white, Chinese, and mixed-race 7% |
| **Capital:** | Georgetown |
| **Annual rainfall:** | Averages 90 in along the coast and 65 in in the southwest |
| **Economy:** | *GDP per capita:* US$4,900 (2006) |

Despite a backdrop of rigid ethnic and racial divisions, two main political parties have dominated the Guayanese contemporary political scene through the 1990s. The governing People's Progressive Party-Civic (PPP-Civic), which is the coalition of President Bharrat Jagdeo, is primarily Indo-Guayanese. The opposition People's National Congress-Reform (PNC-R) is mostly Afro-Guyanese. The PNC dominated the political system for twenty-six-yeas. However, the PPP won the 1992 elections (the first free elections ever since) under Cheddi Jagan, who became president for a five-year term. Under Jagan, the economy began experiencing a more open investment climate in 1990; as a consequence, many private business enterprises have sprung up. In 1999, Bharrat Jagdeo from the PPP-Civic became the president of Guyana due to the sudden death of the previously elected Jagan and Jagan's wife resignation. Jagdeo's presidency was later reconfirmed by a general election held in March 2001 and he was re-elected again in August 2006. Despite a long-standing political stalemate that has a strong correlation between the specific ethnic and racial constituencies of both parties, this reelection has nonetheless forced both the PNC-R and the PPP-Civic to dialogue about municipal elections which have not been held since 1994. In May, 2007, a two-party local government reform task force met and in June, 2007 the current government agreed to sponsor a full voter registration exercise (the first since 1997) before local elections are held. This new plan was a direct result of the collaboration of both political parties, the Guyana Elections Commission, and diplomatic representatives of the United Kingdom, Canada and the United States. Internal divisions within each party became clearer as well. The most evident sign of schisms within the PNC-R included the rising rivalries to the party leader Robert Corbin.

*See also* **Bauxite Industry; Inter-American Development Bank (IDB); Jagan, Cheddi; Jagan, Janet; Plantations; Rice Industry; Sugar Industry.**

BIBLIOGRAPHY

For an understanding of early Dutch and British relationships with, and policy toward, the Amerindians, see M. Noel Menezes, *British Policy Towards the Amerindians in British Guiana, 1803–1873* (New Jersey: Biblio Distribution Centre, 1979). Major works on political and constitutional developments are Harold Alexander Lutchman, *From Colonialism to Co operative Republic: Aspects of Political Development in Guyana* (Puerto Rico: Institute of Caribbean Studies, University of Puerto Rico, 1974), and M. Shahabuddeen, *Constitutional Development in Guyana, 1621–1978* (Georgetown, 1978). Economic and social relationships among the Guyanese are discussed in Walter Rodney, *A History of the Guyanese Working People* (Baltimore, MD: Johns Hopkins University Press, 1981), as well as in Thomas J. Spinner, Jr., *A Political and Social History of Guyana, 1945–1983* (Boulder, CO: Westview Press, 1984). For the evolution of the Venezuela-Guyana border conflict since the 1960s, see Jacqueline Anne Braveboy-wagner, *The Venezuela-Guyana Border Dispute: Britain's Colonial Legacy in Latin America* (Boulder, CO: Westview Press, 1984). Later works in religious and cultural history are Dale Bisnauth, *History of Religions in the Caribbean,* 2d ed. (Trenton, NJ: Africa World Press, 1996), and Mary Noel Menezes, *The Portuguese of Guyana: A Study of Culture and Conflict* (London, 1994).

### *Additional Bibliography*

Bureau of Democracy, Human Rights, and Labor. *U.S. State Department Country Reports on Human Rights Practices 2006* (March 6, 2007).

SISTER M. NOEL MENEZES R.S.M.

## GUZMÁN, ABIMAEL

**GUZMÁN, ABIMAEL** (1934–). Abimael Guzmán Reynoso is the founder and head of the Shining Path guerrilla organization, which launched a people's war on May 17, 1980, that convulsed Peru for twelve years. The Shining Path declined dramatically after his capture on September 12, 1992. He earned degrees in philosophy and law (with theses on the philosopher Immanuel Kant and the bourgeois state) at the University of San Agustín de Arequipa, where he became a member of Peru's Communist Party. He then began teaching in 1962 at the University of San Cristóbal de Huamanga, in Ayacucho, which became his power base.

Once in Ayacucho, he revitalized the local party and developed a strong following among students, many of indigenous origins, as well as some faculty. There he met university student Augusta de la Torre, daughter of the local Communist Party leader, whom he married in 1964 and who was a member of Shining Path's Central Committee until her mysterious death in 1988. While at the university, he assumed positions as director of the teacher training school and general secretary, enabling him to influence a generation of students with his radical Marxist-Maoist perspective, reinforced by three trips to China during the Cultural Revolution. Separated from the university in 1975, he went underground to organize and conduct the people's war. By the early 1990s, the government was on the ropes and Guzmán became overconfident; a new counterterrorism approach led to his capture. Sentenced by a military court to life imprisonment, Guzmán came to advocate a political solution, a position he has repeated during retrials in civilian courts beginning in 2003 and culminating with his reconviction in late 2006.

*See also* **Peru, Revolutionary Movements: Shining Path; Peru: Truth Commissions.**

BIBLIOGRAPHY

Stern, Steve J., ed. *Shining and Other Paths: War and Society in Peru, 1980–1995.* Durham, NC: Duke University Press, 1998.

Bacca, Benedicto Jiménez. *Inicio, desarrollo, y ocaso del terrorismo en el Perú: El ABC de Sendero Luminoso y el MRTA ampliado y comentado.*Lima, Peru: Impr. Sanki, 2000.

DAVID SCOTT PALMER

## GUZMÁN, ANTONIO LEOCADIO

**GUZMÁN, ANTONIO LEOCADIO** (1801–1884). Antonio Leocadio Guzmán (*b.* 14 November 1801; *d.* 13 November 1884), Venezuelan politician and publicist. In 1825, Guzmán founded the newspaper *El Argos.* In 1830, he served as minister of interior, justice, and police. He helped organize the Liberal Party in 1840 and edited the party's newspaper, *El Venezolano,* which called for universal suffrage for males, emancipation of slaves, and the end of capital punishment. Guzmán served José Tadeo Monagas as minister of interior and justice and as vice president. In 1853, he went to Peru as ambassador. He joined the Junta Patriótica de Venezuela, led by Ezequiel Zamora, in 1858, and served as a propagandist. Guzmán's son Antonio Guzmán Blanco became president in 1870.

*See also* **Slavery: Abolition; Venezuela, Political Parties: Liberal Party.**

BIBLIOGRAPHY

Francisco González Guinán, *Historia contemporánea de Venezuela,* vols. 2–4 (1954).

John V. Lombardi, *Venezuela: The Search for Order, the Dream of Progress* (1982).

Hector Mujica, *La historia en una silla* (1982).

Antonio Leocadio Guzmán, *Antonio Leocadio Guzmán,* 2 vols. (1983).

*Additional Bibliography*

Caballero, Miguel, and Sheila Salazar. *Diez grandes polémicas en la historia de Venezuela.* Caracas: Fondo Editorial 60 Años, 1999.

Rodríguez Campos, Manuel, and Tomás Enrique Carrillo Batalla. *Antonio Leocadio Guzmán en la economía venezolana: Discurso de incorporación como individuo de número de la Academia Nacional de la Historia.* Caracas: Academia Nacional de la Historia, 1997.

WINTHROP R. WRIGHT

## GUZMÁN, AUGUSTO

**GUZMÁN, AUGUSTO** (1903–1994). Augusto Guzmán (*b.* 1 September 1903; *d.* 1994) Bolivian writer and historian. Guzmán was a prolific and diverse intellectual whose literary production includes novels, short stories, biographies, criticism, and literary history. He centered his historical work on the region of Cochabamba. His novel *Prisionero* *de guerra,* based on his own experience as a soldier, is an important testimony of the Chaco War (1932–1935). Another major theme in his work is the condition of Indians and mestizos (those of mixed blood) in the countryside of Bolivia. His most popular work, "La cruel Martina" (The Cruel Martina) is a short story that was made into a film in 1989. His literary criticism is a valuable source of information on Bolivian literature, while the biographies he wrote serve as a point of intersection between his literary and historical interests and are his best contribution to Bolivian studies. With the years, Guzmán became one of the most respected representatives of Bolivian intellectual life.

*See also* **Literature: Spanish America.**

BIBLIOGRAPHY

Baptista Gumucio, Mariano. *Mis hazañas son mis libros.* La Paz, Bolivia: Plural Editores, 2000.

LEONARDO GARCÍA PABÓN

**GUZMÁN, ENRIQUE** (1843–1911). Enrique Guzmán (*b.* 2 August 1843; *d.* 23 May 1911), Nicaraguan intellectual and politician. Guzmán is renowned throughout Central America as a writer and a politician. In 1862 he published his first satirical essays. As a youth he was a member of the Liberal Party, but from 1886 to 1911 he was affiliated with the Conservatives. Guzmán first became politically active during his father's run for the presidency in 1867. In 1879 he served as a deputy in Congress. Among his friends was President Joaquín Zavala (1879–1883; 1893). Guzmán encouraged Zavala to maintain good relations with neighboring states in order to preserve Nicaraguan neutrality and peace. Under Zavala, he served as minister to Chile and Peru. During the Zelaya dictatorship, he conspired against the government.

*See also* **Zavala, Joaquín.**

BIBLIOGRAPHY

Pedro Joaquín Chamorro Zelaya, *Enrique Guzmán y su tiempo* (1965).

Enrique Guzmán Selva, *Escritos biográficos de Enrique Guzmán* (1976).

*Additional Bibliography*

Cruz S, Arturo J. *Nicaragua's Conservative Republic, 1858–93.* New York: Palgrave, 2002.

Duque Estrada Sacasa, Esteban. *D. Enrique Guzmán: Tres facetas de su vida.* Managua: E. Duque Estrada Sacasa, 2001.

SHANNON BELLAMY

**GUZMÁN, MARTÍN LUÍS** (1887–1976). Martín Luís Guzmán (*b.* 6 October 1887; *d.* 22 December 1976), Mexican literary figure and cultural entrepreneur best remembered for his post-Revolutionary novels *El áquila y la serpiente* (1928) and *La sombra del caudillo* (1929). Based on personal experience, these works provide some of the best insights into the Revolution as well as a condemnation of the leading post-Revolutionary figures of the 1920s. Although he was part of the El Ateneo literary group in 1911, Guzmán largely abandoned his literary career in the 1930s, instead pursuing journalism and publishing.

The son of an army officer who died in combat during the Revolution, Guzmán joined the Constitutionalists. After founding many newspapers, he spent five years (1915–1920) of self-imposed exile in Spain and the United States. When his daily, *El Mundo,* was confiscated by the Obregón administration, he again exiled himself to Spain (ca. 1923–1936), where he directed several newspapers. In the 1940s he founded a number of publishing companies as well as the weekly magazine *El Tiempo* (modeled after *Time* magazine), which he directed until his death. He received the National Prize for Literature in 1958.

*See also* **Mexico, Wars and Revolutions: Mexican Revolution.**

BIBLIOGRAPHY

Ruth Stanton, "Martín Luís Guzmán's Place in Modern Mexican Literature," in *Hispania* 26 (1943): 136–138.

Martín Luís Guzmán, *Apunte sobre una personalidad* (1955); *Tiempo* (3 January 1977): 5–23.

William Megenney, ed., *Five Essays on Martín Luís Guzmán* (1978).

*Additional Bibliography*

Rosado, Juan Antonio. *El presidente y el caudillo: Mito y realidad en dos novelas de la dictadura: La sombra del caudillo, de Martín Luis Guzmán y El señor presidente, de Miguel Ángel Asturias.* México, D.F.: Ediciones Coyoacán, 2001.

Sánchez, Aideé. *La heterogeneidad en El águila y la serpiente de Martín Luis Guzmán.* Méxcio, D.F.: Plaza y Valdes Editores, 2002.

RODERIC AI CAMP

## GUZMÁN, NUÑO BELTRÁN DE

**GUZMÁN, NUÑO BELTRÁN DE** (c. 1485–1558). Nuño Beltrán de Guzmán (*b.* ca. 1485; *d.* 26 October 1558), governor of Pánuco (1527), president of New Spain's first *audiencia* (1528–1531), conqueror of Nueva Galicia (1529), and founder of Guadalajara (1531). Of the lower nobility of Guadalajara, Spain, Guzmán became noted for his corruption and brutality toward indigenous people. In Pánuco he earned the enmity of Hernán Cortés and other first conquerors by aggressively trying to expand his jurisdiction at their expense and, as *audiencia* president, by profiteering from the confiscation of their properties. Relations were not improved when in 1530 he tortured and then executed Cazonci, the Tarascan ruler of Michoacán, an ally of Cortés. In 1531, while Guzmán was still in Nueva Galicia, the first *audiencia* and its president were replaced, in part because of the complaints of such prominent figures as Bishop Juan de Zumárraga. Guzmán continued as governor of New Galicia until January 1537, when he was arrested. After languishing in jail for eighteen months, he left Mexico in mid-1538, arriving in Spain in December (or perhaps in early 1539). He remained with the royal court under a kind of house arrest until his death in Valladolid.

The overwhelmingly negative picture of Guzmán that has come down to us is partly the result of his conflict with Cortés; with the exception of Guzmán's own correspondence, most of the primary information comes from the pens and testimony of Cortés's adherents, such as Francisco López de Gómara, who wrote that if "Nuño de Guzmán had been as good a governor as he was a warrior, he would have had the best place in the Indies; but he behaved badly both to Indians and Spaniards" (*Life of the Conqueror,* p. 394).

*See also* **Cortés, Hernān.**

BIBLIOGRAPHY

The most complete biography of Guzmán remains Donald E. Chipman, *Nuño de Guzmán and the Province of Pánuco in New Spain, 1518–1533* (1967). J. Benedict Warren, *The Conquest of Michoacán* (1985), focuses on Guzmán's later career, especially his exploits among the Tarascans of Michoacán. See also Francisco López De Gómara, *Cortés: The Life of the Conqueror by His Secretary,* translated and edited by Lesley Byrd Simpson (1964).

*Additional Bibliography*

Blázquez, Adrián, and Thomas Calvo. *Guadalajara y el Nuevo Mundo: Nuño Beltrán de Guzmán, semblanza de un conquistador.* Lima: Editorial Milla Batres, 1992.

Marín, Fausto. *Nuño de Guzmán.* México: Siglo Veintiuno Editores; Sinaloa: Difocur, 1992.

ROBERT HASKETT

## GUZMÁN BLANCO, ANTONIO LEOCADIO

**GUZMÁN BLANCO, ANTONIO LEOCADIO** (1829–1899). After Simón Bolívar, Antonio Leocadio Guzmán Blanco (February 20, 1829—July 28, 1899) was Venezuela's most important nineteenth-century political leader, holding the presidency three times (1870–1877, 1879–1884, 1886–1888). The son of the founder of Venezuela's Liberal Party, Antonio Leocadio Guzmán, Guzmán earned a law degree and served in diplomatic and consular posts in New York, Philadelphia, and Washington, D.C., in the 1850s. In association with Liberal president Juan C. Falcón between 1859 and 1869, he became a successful military leader as well as a vice president, minister of foreign relations, and president of the Constituent Assembly that produced the federal constitution of 1864. Guzmán periodically represented Venezuela in Europe and negotiated a major loan from the British in 1863, from which he personally benefited. After taking the presidency by force in 1870, Guzmán dominated the nation until 1888. Local caudillos were persuaded that political control of their regions was more important than economic autonomy, and merchants and bankers surrendered political ambitions in exchange for influence over national finances. Guzmán reduced the power of the Catholic Church, instituted civil marriage and a civil registry, and promoted public education. New highways, railroads, telegraph, and port facilities encouraged the revival of the agricultural export economy. Modeled after Guzmán's beloved Paris, Caracas acquired new buildings, plazas, avenues, an aqueduct, and electricity to symbolize its dominant role in the nation. While he was in Venezuela, the country enjoyed relative tranquility, but Guzmán's frequent sojourns in Paris emboldened politicians to fight among themselves. Political disorder erupted after 1888 upon Guzmán's final residence in Paris, but his centralization, nationalism, and modernization had transformed the nation.

*See also* **Caudillismo, Caudillo; Venezuela: Venezuela since 1830.**

BIBLIOGRAPHY

González Deluca, María Elena. *Negocios y política en tiempos de Guzmán Blanco*, 2nd edition. Caracas: Universidad Central de Venezuela, 2001.

Wise, George. *Caudillo: A Portrait of Antonio Guzmán Blanco.* New York: Columbia University Press, 1951.

JUDITH EWELL

**HACIENDA.** In its most general sense, this word means "estate" or "all worldly possessions of an individual." In Latin America the word is used most commonly as a generic term for all types of large rural properties ranging in size from a few hundred hectares (1 hectare equals 2.47 acres) to hundreds of square kilometers (1 square kilometer equals 0.4 square miles). Large rural estates and the individuals and institutions who control them have dominated the peoples, politics, and economies of Latin America since the sixteenth century and still do in many places in the late twentieth century.

The origins of the great estate in Latin America can be traced back to two or three decades after the Conquest, when the first land grants (*mercedes*) were given to Spanish conquerors and to later immigrants. Other holdings were acquired less auspiciously by usurping unoccupied Indian land. These squatters' holdings were subsequently legalized and titled by payments to the crown (*composiciones*). Regardless of their legal or illegal origins, haciendas grew by later donations, sales, usurpations, and *composiciones*.

Most haciendas developed independently of the *encomienda*. Early *encomenderos*, using positions on the municipal councils in nearby Spanish towns, sometimes granted themselves one or more plots of land from among the parcels that had been used by their Indian charges. As more and more of the Indians died or moved away, however, their abandoned parcels were granted to other later-arriving Spanish immigrants in an effort to further colonization and settlement of the land, increase the quantity of needed foodstuffs and draft animals and reward individuals who had served the king. These *mercedes* far outnumbered those granted to *encomenderos*. Nevertheless, *mercedes* of both the *encomendero* and non-*encomendero* types became the nuclei of individual farms and stock raising enterprises that later grew into the large estates that dominated both countryside and city.

Large estates or haciendas can be grouped into three main types. One is the ranch, which developed from the *estancia* (*fazenda*, in Portuguese). The *estancia* was an early and popular type of enterprise because its establishment required relatively little capital and small numbers of laborers. Transportation costs were insignificant because cattle could be driven to market. Before the eighteenth century, however, an *estancia* was not the large ranch, in the legal sense, that we envision today. Typically, its owner (the *estanciero*) had legal title to only a few units of land, on which he usually built a house for himself or his steward (*mayordomo*), a storage shed or building, and one or more corrals. This became his operational headquarters. The *estancia,* in other words, was no more than a cattle station. Pastures were common domain. In the eighteenth century the crown, in need of money, sold the pastures to the highest bidder. It was only then that the *estanciero* consolidated control over a large area of pasturelands and the ranch was legally born.

A mixed farm was the second type of hacienda. Some *estancias* became haciendas when part of the land, usually that near the headquarters, was planted

**Hacienda la Vega, Caracas, Venezuela, 1966.** Property given to Spanish conquistadors and other immigrants acquired the name "hacienda" in Latin America. Ranching and farming generally took place on these large estates, using indigenous Indians, wage-earning Spaniards, or imported slaves as a labor force. JOSEPH FABRY/TIME LIFE PICTURES/GETTY IMAGES

in crops. The mixed farm required more capital and more labor than the *estancia* but less than a specialized farm.

The third type of hacienda was the specialized farm, usually dedicated to producing only one crop for a distant market. The typical crops grown—sugar cane, rice, cacao, and wheat—required processing. During colonial times these specialized farms, the forerunners of modern plantations, took their names from the type of mill or processing facilities installed on the premises. An *ingenio* referred to a water-powered mill. A *trapiche* was an animal-powered mill. Both of these terms usually referred to sugar estates. A *molino* could be either water- or animal-powered and usually referred to a wheat- or rice-producing enterprise.

All three types of estate relied on a dependent labor force: Indians who had left their communities and become personal retainers (*naborías* and *yanaconas*); community members working on a temporary basis to earn money to pay their tribute; and wage-earning or salaried Spaniards, creoles, mestizos, and mulattoes who worked on haciendas in various capacities from peon to *mayordomo,* or steward, over the years. In tropical areas, where haciendas produced sugar or cacao, owners sometimes purchased large numbers of black slaves to do much of the work. These laborers lived in huts or houses near the operational center of the estate, which, in some cases, grew to the size and complexity of small towns, complete with church and jail.

In contrast to earlier stereotypes of the self-sufficient hacienda, more recent studies have shown that most haciendas, however remote, produced for a market. The hacienda, while not always profitable, did generate revenues and, in some cases, became the basis of considerable fortunes. In the process it became the measure of a person's or a family's power and prestige.

Thus, land in Latin America became the hallmark of elite standing. It achieved this status because landowners, or *hacendados,* were wealthy. They controlled the means of production and as such provided employment for agricultural workers (plowing, herding, planting, harvesting, etc.), skilled craftsmen (carpenters, metal smiths, etc.), and urban professionals (scribes, lawyers, bankers). They also wielded political power, directly or indirectly, on the municipal council and often at higher levels of government as well.

The *hacendados* were, then, the epitome of success and as such were imitated. Mine owners, merchants, and professionals who achieved wealth bought land. Miners might acquire a hacienda to raise foodstuffs or mules needed in mining and thus vertically integrate their enterprises. But the prestige of owning vast tracks of land was also an incentive. Given the early prejudices against commerce, merchants too were attracted to landownership as a means of shedding their tainted image and validating their status. One reason nineteenth-century urban professionals were often politically liberal, and thus anticlerical, was their hope of wresting control of the church's vast landholdings. When the church lost hold of its properties, they were often sold, giving professionals and other monied segments of society the opportunity to acquire the one item that marked their ascension into, or established their permanent standing in, the elite.

In modern times, the issues of land concentration and land reform have become serious political matters, and increasing pressure for redistribution sometimes has erupted into revolts and guerrilla wars. Emiliano Zapata's demands for land reform and restitution during the Mexican Revolution brought the issue to world attention, since Mexico was not the only country where a small minority owned and controlled great proportions of arable land while the vast majority of rural inhabitants were landless and poor. President Lázaro Cárdenas (1934–1940) became an immortalized folk hero by redistributing land to Mexican peasants in the 1930s.

Bolivian peasants did not wait for governmental action. They began invading haciendas soon after the Bolivian Revolution of 1952. The Movimiento Nacionalista Revolucionario (Nationalist Revolutionary Movement), or MNR, subsequently issued a land reform law to legalize their seizures, thereby securing the peasants' allegiance and making this party of middle-class origins look more "revolutionary" than it in fact was.

Meanwhile, peasants everywhere were organizing. In the late 1950s in the southern Andes near Cuzco, Peru, Hugo Blanco, a young Trotskyist agronomist, organized a peasant federation, sparking a series of tenant strikes and land seizures. Peasant syndicates formed in northeastern Brazil, where "Land to the Tiller" became a rallying cry.

The Alliance for Progress (1961) challenged the governing elites throughout the hemisphere to redistribute property. Several countries passed land reform laws in the 1960s and 1970s, but few of them proved effective. Perhaps the greatest progress in redistributing land occurred during the short tenure of President Salvador Allende (1970–1973) in Chile while General Juan Velasco Alvarado (1968–1975) occupied the presidential palace in Peru, and under the Sandinistas in Nicaragua (1979–1990). After these regimes lost power, however, many of the expropriated properties were returned to their former owners. Thus, large estates and their owners still dominate the economy in many areas of Latin America. However, the efforts of peasants to protect the land they retain to recover those already lost promise continuing struggles over this issue.

*See also* **Alliance for Progress; Estancia; Finca; Fundo; Latifundia.**

BIBLIOGRAPHY

François Chevalier, *La formation des grands domaines au Mexique: Terre et société aux XVI^e^–XVII^e^ siècles* (1952).

Eric R. Wolf and Sidney W. Mintz, "Haciendas and Plantations in Middle America and the Antilles," in *Social and Economic Studies* 6, no. 3 (1957): 380–412.

James M. Lockhart, "*Encomienda* and *Hacienda:* The Evolution of the Great Estate in the Spanish Indies," in *Hispanic American Historical Review* 49, no. 3 (1969): 411–29.

Espinoza R. Gustavo and Carlos Malpica, *El problema de la tierra* (1970).

Robert G. Keith, *Conquest and Agrarian Change: The Emergence of the Hacienda System on the Peruvian Coast* (1976).

Henry Pease García et al., *Estado y política agraria: Cuatro ensayos* (1977).

Herman W. Konrad, *A Jesuit Hacienda in Colonial Mexico: Santa Lucía, 1576–1767* (1980).

### *Additional Bibliography*

Gómez Serrano, Jesús. *Haciendas y ranchos de Aguascalientes: Estudio regional sobre la tenencia de la tierra y el desarrollo agrícola en el siglo XIX.* Universidad Autónoma de Aguascalientes, 2000.

Lyons, Barry J. *Remembering the Hacienda: Religion, Authority, and Social Change in Highland Ecuador.* Austin: University of Texas Press, 2006.

Vegas de Cáceres, Ileana. *Economía rural y estructura social en las haciendas de Lima durante el siglo XVIII.* Lima: Pontificia Universidad Católica del Perú, Fondo Editorial, 1996.

Susan E. Ramírez

---

**HAITI.** Haiti occupies the western third of the island of Haiti, Quisqueya, or Bohio, the aboriginal names of the island that was, in the early twenty-first century, divided into two sovereign states: the Republic of Haiti and the Dominican Republic. Haiti has been the stage for some of history's most dynamic changes in terms of ethnicity, economy, politics, demography, and culture. Europeans completely displaced the island's aboriginal Amerindian populations and, in turn, they were pushed out by Africans and African descendants, all within the space of 300 years. The divisions between the colonies of French Saint-Domingue and Spanish Santo Domingo, and between the Republic of Haiti and the Dominican Republic, are relatively modern, and histories of the island as it was before the European invasions have tended to treat it as one whole.

## THE FRENCH COLONY OF SAINT-DOMINGUE

Beginning around 5000 BCE, successive waves of Amerindian migrations reached the island of Haiti via Central America or via the Caribbean island chain from South America. Sedentary horticulturists arrived in the Greater Antilles about 300 BCE or later. By 1000 CE complex chiefdoms headed by *Caciques* had developed, and the local peoples, of mainly Arrawak origins, called themselves *Tainos.* The chiefdoms of this island may have been fewer, larger, and more powerful than those in neighboring Puerto Rico, and they engaged in interisland, and possibly circum-Caribbean, trade.

The population of Haiti gradually increased, notably after about 600 CE. This growth was related to *conuco* agriculture—intensive cultivation of carefully prepared mounds that produced staggered, year-round supplies of starches of the manioc-cassava family. This system, while productive, required constant work, and was fragile and easily disrupted. There is some dispute about the size of the population supported by these *conucos* around 1490, with estimates ranging from 100,000 to 8 million.

In early December 1492, on his first voyage to America, Christopher Columbus's ships reached the northwest coast of the island at Môle Saint-Nicolas. Columbus took possession of the island on behalf of the Queen of Spain and therefore called it *Hispaniola*, or "little Spain." After a brief initial period of minimal intrusion, the Spanish invaders dramatically disrupted the ethnic and economic structures of the island. Disease, destruction of the fragile *conuco* system, massive forced and voluntary movements of slave and laboring populations, Spanish internecine strife, and an imposed tributary system based on gold reduced the aboriginal population to about 30,000 by 1514, and this remnant died out soon afterwards. The Spaniards attempted unsuccessfully to fill the demographic vacuum by importing Amerindian captives from the Bahamas and other Caribbean areas (causing severe losses in those places).

By 1550 or so Hispaniola had undergone a dramatic social and agricultural revolution. Its dense starch-consuming population had disappeared and had been replaced by a sparse meat-consuming group of Spaniards, a few other Europeans, and African slaves. The island had become a political dependency of distant power centers in Europe, having exported perhaps as much as 50 tons of gold to these centers in its first half century as a colony. Vast herds of semi-feral cattle, horses, and pigs roamed the abandoned *conucos* and the forests, and as alluvial gold in the rivers became exhausted, the Spanish population—much of it in the capital city of Santo Domingo—emigrated to Cuba or Mexico or turned their attention to transatlantic exports of hides. Hispaniola, originally

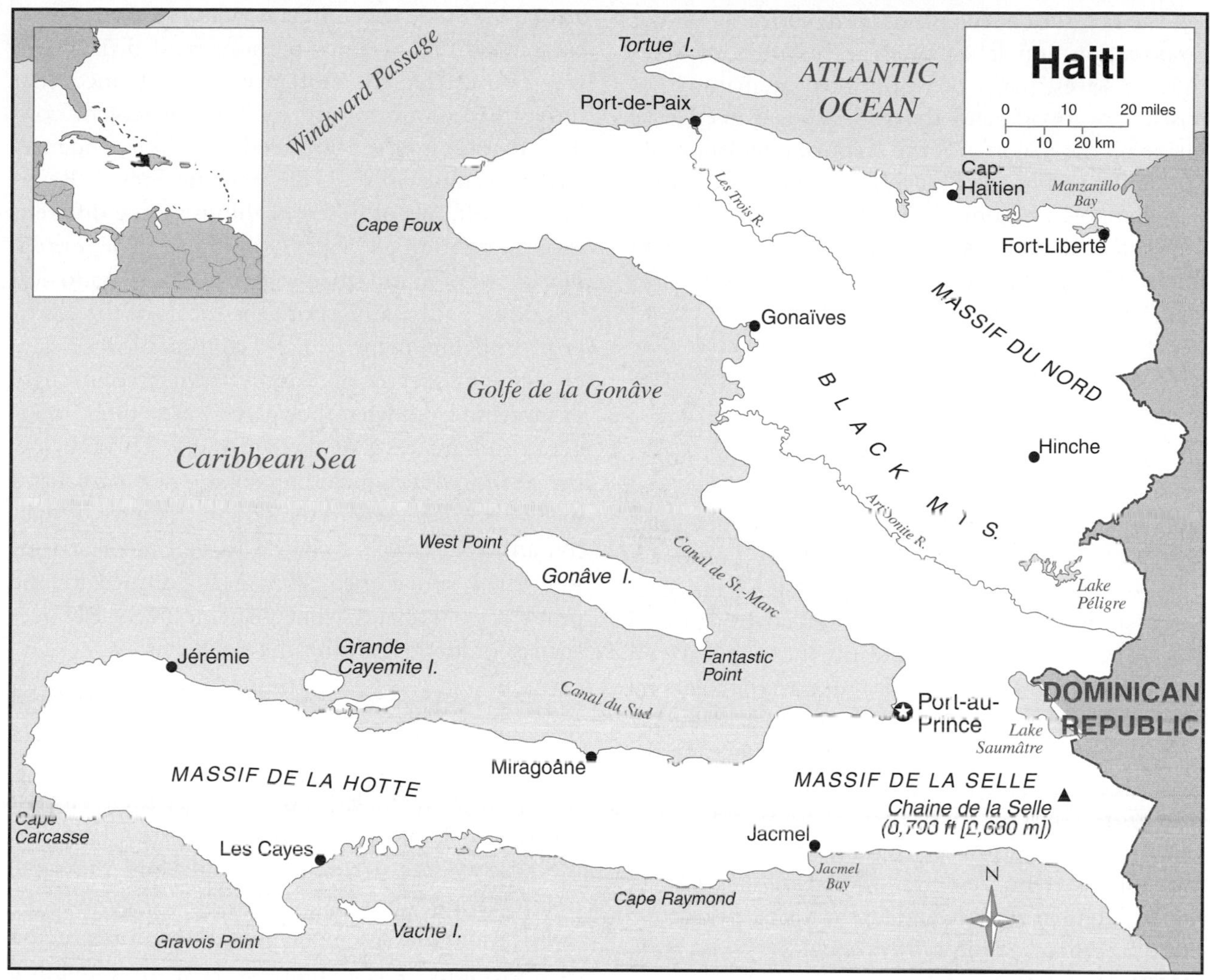


the center of Spain's American colonies, had become peripheral, and the Spanish part of the island remained throughout the colonial period.

French pirates began to infest the coasts in the 1550s. In 1553, for example, François Leclerc destroyed the small settlement of Yaguana, later the site of the Haitian capital of Port-au-Prince. For the rest of the century the countryside was left by the Spanish colonists to herds of grazing animals. Meanwhile French and English adventurers attempted, by intrusion, to establish themselves along the north coast of the island. By the 1620s French and English pirates and outlaws, some of them exiled French Huguenots, began to settle on La Tortue (Tortuga), an island off the north coast of the island. From this base they camped and hunted on the mainland. These buccaneers (from the French word *boucanier*) dried and smoked meat derived from the abundant cattle. As their settlements became more numerous and permanent settlers began to live on the north coast, the few remaining Spaniards withdrew to the eastern part of the island. The arrival in 1665 to La Tortue of a French governor, Bernard d'Ogeron, brought stability, and by the time of his death in 1675 an early planter society had emerged and the English pirates had been expelled. By the Treaty of Ryswick (1697), Spain ceded the western third of the island to France, and this became the official French colony of Saint-Domingue.

The new colony underwent important economic and ethnic transformations, becoming France's richest colony and the wealthiest in the Caribbean. By the late eighteenth century it was exporting great quantities of tropical produce, especially sugar, indigo, and coffee. This plantation agriculture depended on the rich soils of the plains, and, above all, on the importation and labor of large numbers of West African slaves, many of whom died prematurely of disease, overwork, and abuse. Slaves and free blacks made up the majority of the colonial population. By 1789, the year of the French Revolution, the colony was composed of some 450,000 black slaves, 30,000 *affranchis* (free blacks and mulattoes, many of them the result of sexual relations between white masters and black slaves, and other manumitted slaves and their offspring), and about 40,000 whites. The city of Cap-Français (present-day Cap-Haïtien) prospered.

The inherent exploitation and racial discrimination of chattel slavery by all created a divided society and an apparent caste system based on ethnic categories. The three principal social groups in the colony (which were based primarily on skin color) had their status confirmed and reinforced by colonial law. The whites held almost all the political and economical power, though the governor-general and the intendant were often at odds with the *grands blancs* (elite whites). In the middle of the social hierarchy, forming a sort of middle class, were the *petits blancs*, many of them artisans and tradesmen, mulatto landowners and merchants, and some free blacks, who resented the *grands blancs* yet aspired to their station, and feared the despised slave masses. Indeed, some *affranchis* had become prosperous landowners.

The slaves were the bottom rung, the possessions of their masters, and without any possessions of their own at all. Their resistance to the system and their conditions took many forms, from abortion, suicide, and infanticide to indolence at the plantations and marronage. Organized groups of fugitive slaves (Maroons) in the mountains, or across the border in Santo Domingo, harassed plantations. Riots in the cities and slave resistance on the plantations brought violent reactions from the authorities. Political movements everywhere and from all the social groups—from the "Grands Planteurs," who wanted the abolition of the French exclusive system; from the *affranchis*, who wanted greater civil and political liberties; and from the slaves, who agitated for general liberty—caused a generalized ebullition in the colony. The colonial power was incapable of responding satisfactorily to all the demands, and revolution was inevitable.

## THE HAITIAN REVOLUTION (1791–1804)

In spite of these claims, tensions, and divisions, it was a push from the mother country, France, that drove the colony toward its years of violent conflict, foreign intervention, and final independence. Events leading up to 1789, and the French Revolution itself, meant different things to the different groups fighting in Saint-Domingue. The *grands blancs*, who found themselves in the paradoxical position of advocating both the ideals of the European Enlightenment and the continuation of slavery, sought greater autonomy from revolutionary France and from what they perceived as their bondage to the interests of their markets. Those below the *grands blancs*, including some *petits blancs* and many *affranchis*, saw in the slogan "Liberty, Equality, and Fraternity" a chance to defeat, or at least join, the colonial aristocracy. Many argued for the principles of equality while glancing nervously over their shoulders, ignoring the slave masses.

The Société des Amis des Noirs et des Gens de couleur, founded in Paris in 1788 to advocate a gradual abolition of slavery, took up the cause of the *affranchis*, led by the mulattoes Vincent Ogé (c. 1755–1791) and Jean-Baptiste Chavannes (c. 1748–1791). Claiming equality and the same political and civil rights as the whites, they started a political and military movement in the north region of the colony. Their enterprise had some political success, but they were militarily defeated by the colonial power allied with the white forces. Ogé and Chavannes fled to Santo Domingo but were extradited, then condemned and broken on the wheel in February 1791. Mulattoes in the south continued to resist, and, led by André Rigaud (1761–1811), they obtained a provisional understanding from the region's whites that they would not oppose acts of the French National Assembly on behalf of freedmen. White masters and *affranchi* owners understood that their common enemy was the slaves; slaves understood that their enemy was the entire colonial slavery system and its direct beneficiaries, supporters, and the institutions.

On August 14, 1791, slave leaders of many plantations in the northern region of the colony secretly took part in a political congress and religious ceremony at Bois-Caiman, at Plaine du Nord. In that occasion, they made the solemn and supreme

| **Haiti** | |
|---|---|
| **Population:** | 8,706,497 (2007 est.) |
| **Area:** | 10,714 sq mi |
| **Official languages:** | French, Creole |
| **National currency:** | gourde (HTG) |
| **Principal religions:** | Roman Catholic, 80%; Baptist, 10%; Pentecostal, 4%; Adventist, 1%. Roughly half the population practices Voodoo in addition to other religious practices. |
| **Ethnicity:** | black, 95%; mulatto and white, 5% |
| **Capital:** | Port-au-Prince (est. pop. 1,961,000 in 2005) |
| **Other urban centers:** | Jacmel, Les Cayes |
| **Annual rainfall:** | 54 inches in Port-au-Prince |
| **Principal geographical features:** | *Mountains:* Massif du Nord; Sierra de Bahoruco, including La Selle (8,844 ft)<br>*Rivers:* Artibonite<br>*Lakes:* Saumâtre<br>*Islands:* Les Cayemites, Gonâve, Tortuga, Vache; also claims U.S.-held Navassa |
| **Economy:** | *GDP per capita:* $1,800 (2006 est.) |
| **Principal products and exports:** | *Agricultural:* coffee, mangoes<br>*Manufacturing:* assembly of imported parts, textiles |
| **Government:** | Independence from France, 1804. Constitution, 1987; suspended in 1988, partially reinstated 1989, suspended 1991, restored 1994, suspended 2004, restored 2006. Republic. The legislature is popularly elected and consists of a 30-seat Senate and a 99-seat Chamber of Deputies. Senators normally serve 6-year terms and deputies 4-year terms, some were serving shorter terms than usual in 2007 as part of an effort to reconstitute a government after the recent restoration of the constitution. A popularly elected president is chief of state. The head of government is the prime minister, who is appointed by the president and approved by the legislature. Cabinet chosen by the prime minister with input from the president.10 departments. |
| **Armed forces:** | 2,000 national police. There is no military. |
| **Transportation:** | *Ports:* Cap-Haïtien, Port-au-Prince<br>*Roads:* 628 mi paved; 1,957 mi unpaved<br>*Airports:* 4 paved runway and 10 unpaved runway airports, international airports at Cap-Haitien and Port-au-Prince. |
| **Media:** | Port-au-Prince newspapers include *Le Matin, Le Nouvelliste,* and *L'Union.* Roughly 400 radio stations and 3 television stations, Television Nationale d'Haiti is government-run. |
| **Literacy and education:** | *Total literacy rate:* 52.9% (2003 est.)<br>Children age 6 to 12 are required to attend school. There are roughly 12 institutes of higher education. |

resolution to fight against slavery and to gain freedom. One week later slaves on the northern plain revolted, burning plantations—the visible objects of their exploitation—and killing white owners of the plantations. This attack began what became known as the Haitian Revolution. Later the slaves' movement spread across the entire colony. Foreign powers whose ambition had been to capture Saint-Domingue took advantage of the situation, mobilizing their forces into the colony.

The English in Jamaica, fearful of slave revolts, began to help the whites. Spain, hoping to expel the French and regain their lost colony, sided with the rebels, denouncing the French as republican atheists. The United States feared the infection of revolution would cause slave uprisings in its southern states, but also wished to continue its lucrative trade with Saint-Domingue. The republicans in power in France sent a first civil commission to restore order, but it met with little success. A second commission was sent to the colony in 1792, led by Léger Félicité Sonthonax (1763–1813), a young lawyer and a Jacobin partisan, and two other members with full political powers, accompanied by military forces to renew peace negotiations. At first Sonthonax favored the political emancipation of the *affranchis* and made no concessions on slavery. The white planters were unwilling to concede anything to either the *affranchis* or the slaves in revolt, preferring to ally themselves with the rivals of France—England and Spain. By late August 1792, an invading Spanish army reached Le Cap, and the following month an English army disembarked in another strategic region as part of a plan by William Pitt the Younger to conquer the French colonies.

The French forces remained only in the center of the island, with little capacity to resist and to preserve Saint-Domingue for France. The *affranchis* were

**Christopher Columbus landing on Hispaniola,** etching, c. 18th century. CORBIS

powerless to defend the colony for France, so Sonthonax called on the slaves to help in exchange for their liberty. At the end of June 1793 the slaves rebelling in the northen region responded to Sonthonax's call and attacked white planters who were about to surrender the colony to the English forces. The mobilized black armies pushed them out of the colony definitively; they fled to the United States, to Cuba, and to other places in the Caribbean. The white domination of Saint-Domingue was over, and on August 29, 1793, in recognition of the blacks' support, Sonthonax proclaimed officially the abolition of slavery.

During the Anglo-Spanish invasion of Saint-Domingue in 1792, many black leaders joined either Spain or England, depending on the attractiveness of each side's political proposals. Among those who joined the Spanish army in the north was a former slave, Toussaint Louverture (1743–1803), who rose rapidly to a high rank and proved himself a skilled military and political leader. But by May 1794, in response to the French National Convention's abolition of slavery, Louverture had strategically abandoned the Spanish side. A series of problems, including disagreements with French planters and poor leadership in the face of Louverture's strong and skilled army, soon reduced both the Spanish and British expeditions to defensive remnants. In July 1795 Spain withdrew from the conflict and ceded Santo Domingo to France. England began to look for a diplomatic alliance with Louverture in order to end the conflict in a honorable manner.

Louverture proved to be a master of military tactics and political maneuverings. He gradually eliminated all internal and external opponents; in 1798 the English also withdrew. The French government, recognizing his talents and his political capacities, appointed him general of the armies of Saint-Domingue and then governor of the colony. Louverture then turned his attention to General André Rigaud, the mulatto leader in the south who refused to recognize his authority. Rigaud attacked Louverture's forces on June 16, 1799, and Louverture's forces responded vehemently in what is known in the historiography of the Haitian Revolution as the "War of South." Rigaud lost the war, and fled to France with some partisans. In the end, Louverture became the uncontested leader in Saint-Domingue, filling the vacuum left by the white planters after more than three centuries of complete dominance. Louverture established his political hegemony in the entire colony, and set out to reunify the island of Haiti.

After Louverture easily crossed the Spanish province of Santo Domingo, the Spanish governor, Don Garcia, gave him the keys of the city, and Louverture, still nominally loyal to France, was in fact the ruler of the whole island. In February 1801 he appointed a group of seven whites and three mulattoes to draw up a constitution for the island. As expected, the new constitution appointed Louverture governor for life, abolished slavery, and maintained the fiction of French rule. By the promulgation of this constitution, Louverture made the first steps toward independence for the colony.

Louverture's next projects were to rebuild the shattered economy. He encouraged all capitalists to own plantations in the colony, the former white planters to reconstruct the plantations, and persuaded by law and by force the former slaves to return to their plantations. This policy produced some results; the colony started exporting goods again in considerable proportions, but was halted by a strong Napoleonic military expedition in January 1802. After his defeat in Egypt, Napoleon Bonaparte turned his attention to the Caribbean and the Americas in general, where his attempt to restore French colonialism seemed to meet with the approval of England and the United States. But the French forces he sent in January 1802 miscalculated the skill and fervor of the black revolutionaries. The leader of the expedition, General Charles Leclerc, Napoleon's brother-in-law, shared Napoleon's optimism as well as his ignorance of the island. Leclerc had some early successes, seizing all the main ports, but Louverture, Jean-Jacques Dessalines (1758–1806), and Henri Christophe (1767–1820) continued to wage guerrilla war from the interior. Then, after a period of resistance, Louverture came to terms with Leclerc. Dessalines yielded to Leclerc soon after. Lesser guerrilla generals continued to resist, but Leclerc seemed to have won the island for Napoleon.

Three weeks after they had signed a peace treaty, Leclerc seized Louverture on suspicion of treason and sent him to France, where he died in prison on April 7, 1803. When Leclerc tried to disarm the black population, many former slaves, fearing that a return to plantation slavery was imminent, fled to the island's interior to join the guerrillas. Their decision was motivated by the restoration of slavery in the French colonies of Martinique and Guadeloupe.

By August and September 1802, the scope of the war broadened. By October the tide had turned, and Dessalines, Christophe, and Alexandre Pétion (1770–1818) abandoned the doomed Leclerc and rejoined the rebels to fight against the restoration of slavery. Leclerc died of yellow fever at Le Cap soon afterward. His command was taken up by General Donatien Rochambeau (1755–1813), a soldier experienced in the Caribbean, who added a new contingent of 10,000 troops. Rochambeau proved to be even more brutal than Leclerc—it seems that he believed that all the former black slaves should be exterminated and replaced by new slaves from Africa, and Napoleon apparently approved of these methods.

Rivalries among the colonial powers had a strong influence on the events in Saint-Domingue. England went to war against France in May 1803, and by June was attacking French port garrisons in Saint-Domingue. Meanwhile, Dessalines made alliances in his own ranks and consolidated his leadership. The *Armée Indigène* was formed to counter-attack French forces; it won two decisive battles against the French, at the Ravine de la Crête à Pierrot and at Vertières. The fate of France in Saint-Domingue was sealed. In November and December 1803 there was a mass exodus of local whites and French soldiers from Le Cap. After thirteen years of fighting between masters and slaves, colonizers against colonized, whites against *affranchis*, traditional *affranchis* against new *affranchis*, former slaves against new leaders, and France against Spain and England, a new independent state was proclaimed in America.

**Engraving of a runaway slave in Haiti, c. 1672.** To work their profitable sugar plantations, landowners began importing African slaves to Haiti in the seventeenth century. By the late eighteenth century, enslaved Africans comprised the majority of the French colony's population. HULTON ARCHIVE/ GETTY IMAGES

## AFTERMATH AND SIGNIFICANCE OF THE REVOLUTION

On January 1, 1804, in a popular convention held at Gonaives, the leaders of the *Armée Indigène* proclaimed the independence of the country and gave again the native name of Haiti to the independent state. Haiti thus became the first black independent nation in the Western Hemisphere and the first black republic in the world. The proclamation of this independence was significant for the subaltern classes throughout the world, and particularly for the slaves in colonies. General Dessalines became the first leader of the new independent nation.

In some respects, the Haitian Revolution has received little scholarly attention. Accounts have tended to emphasize the carnage and destruction and the inability of the leaders of this once wealthy colony to restore prosperity. Some historians have attempted rudimentary analyses of this failure; others have resorted to fatalistic or racist conclusions.

From the demographic point of view, the massive migration of the white population during the revolution and the elimination of some after the revolution was the culmination of the region's second great demographic shift. Whites had replaced Native Americans in the early sixteenth century. By the time fighting broke out in 1789, imported black slaves vastly outnumbered whites; rebel blacks completed the change by driving out the white population. These dramatic events and other hardships of the revolutionary years reduced the remaining population by as much as 50 percent, according to some estimates. (Of the half million inhabitants before the revolt began, only 250,000 or so remained.) Gender imbalance had always been pronounced among the slaves, especially in the bossal group, but by 1804 war casualties apparently had brought parity.

In 1804 the sugar plantation complex lay in ruins, and despite efforts to revive it, it failed to recover. Several factors were at play. One of them was the labor shortage arising from the disappearance of half of the population, a drop in numbers that was especially severe among black field workers. Another factor was the lack of capital. Sugar, far more than coffee, tobacco, or indigo, required large capital investments, but most local accumulations had been destroyed and, for obvious reasons, there were no foreign lenders. Former slaves, moreover, obviously loathed sugar plantations—attacks on them were a major feature of the war—and resisted all attempts to recruit them for sugar plantation labor. These factors, and above all the end of slavery, led to radical changes in land use during and after the revolution. But such changes did not necessarily mean a collapse of production, as many scholars have assumed. Agriculture had to become less labor- and capital-intensive, but the peasantry and export merchants adjusted, and foreign trade and domestic food supplies revived rapidly after 1804.

In the political arena, the Haitian Revolution brought to power a new elite of black and mulatto generals. Military prowess created the new legitimacy, and the foreign models that impressed the liberators were those that stressed the stability to be found in life presidencies, and even those that glorified Napoleonic imperial rule. This centralizing militarism was reinforced by the perception among the new elite that they and their infant nation were beleaguered. France had not yet relinquished its claims to Haiti, the white North Atlantic nations mocked the new leadership and deplored its existence, and because slavery was still the fate of most Caribbean people, Haitians dreaded its return.

Both England and Spain, though happy to see France defeated, were obsessed with the possible impact of Haiti's slave uprising on Cuba, Santo Domingo (which had reverted to Spain in 1809), and Jamaica. Haitians, in turn, feared Santo Domingo because of its potential use as a base for reconquest by European powers. In general, the success of the Haitian Revolution may have delayed political independence of other slave societies. In both Cuba and Brazil, the planter class reinforced its ties to the mother country. France declared an international boycott of the new state, and no power wanted to recognize the independence of Haiti. The United States declared an embargo against the country. England continued its lucrative trade with Haiti, but was reluctant to recognize its independence. In fact, most nations at that time considered Haiti's declaration of independence an anomaly, a threat, or a bad example.

## FROM INDEPENDENCE TO POLITICAL MODERNIZATION (1804–1888)

Jean-Jacques Dessalines governed Haiti, with difficulty, from 1804 to 1806. There were a lack of political cohesion and a common vision for the country, even in the sphere of power: Each group and social faction dreamt of a different Haiti. The former *affranchis* believed they were the most capable of leading Haiti now that the whites were gone, but the representatives of the new *affranchis*, who had led the revolution to victory, wanted to keep the political supremacy. For the majority of the people, the revolution meant, at the political level, abolition of slavery and political emancipation, and at the economic level, division of the plantations and self-ownership. Dessalines tried to maintain the exportation of agricultural products, but his success was relative: Nobody wanted to return to the plantations, either as owners or as laborers under the conditions that Louverture implemented.

In May 1805 Dessalines installed the imperial regime in Haiti and managed to defend the revolution and independence. He ordered the construction of a series of fortifications throughout the country to defend against a return by the French army. He made another attempt, without success, to reunify the island of Haiti. When he undertook a program to verify the titles of properties seized by former *affranchis* after the departure of the white planters, he was assassinated in 1806.

When Dessalines's empire ended, Haiti was divided into two states. In the west and the south of the country, Alexandre Pétion, a former partisan of André Rigaud, established a republican form of government; from the Artibonite to the north, Henri Christophe established a monarchy.

In the north, Christophe, following Louverture, attempted to restore the plantations by work, discipline, and obligatory labor. Although he established friendly relations with foreign powers, he was also aware of the threat of invasion, and so built numerous palaces and fortifications, including the famous mountaintop fortress of La Ferrière. Pétion in the south was more moderate, and many large estates were broken up and distributed to veterans of the wars. By prior arrangement, upon Pétion's death in 1818, his long-time ally Jean-Pierre Boyer (1776–1850) became president for life. He reunited the nation after Christophe died in 1820.

Boyer's long presidency (1818–1843) was a formative period for Haiti. He was successful in reunifying the island of Haiti in 1822, thus ending slavery throughout Santo Domingo, and opened negotiations with France. The French were adamant in their insistence that they were still the legal power in Haiti, and Boyer, worried about the precarious position of the small mulatto ruling class, appeared to be willing to accept some form of French allegiance. But popular hatred of the idea of French domination was so strong that Boyer finally secured French recognition in return for payment of an indemnity of 150 million francs/gold and favorable tariffs on French goods. The Boyer government received strong criticism for accepting that arrangement with France. Must critics believed that it put Haiti into an era of neo-colonialism by allowing foreign economic manipulation, which forced Haiti into foreign borrowing and internal taxation, and obviously lessened opportunities for local investment.

Boyer reversed Pétion's laissez-faire attitude toward the land question. Like Louverture and Christophe, he dreamed of a plantation economy geared to exports. His efforts to stop the alienation of public lands, and his infamous Code Rurale (1826) that attempted to restrict movement and force peasants to work, were clearly designed to create a stable labor force for the few large landowners. But his rural policies failed to reverse the trend toward small peasant subsistence holdings. Sugar production continued to fall, though small-holder crops such as coffee and cacao took up some of the slack. Unfortunately for the country's ecological future, timber, including valuable stands of hardwoods, became a valuable export. Commerce with the United States flourished.

Boyer's regime failed to halt the trend toward a small-holding peasantry, and his overthrow in 1843 showed that certain other characteristics of elite politics and Haitian life were becoming ingrained. Boyer's government had been dominated by mulattoes who enriched themselves through government office or favors. Excluded mulattoes and elite blacks, especially from the south, agitated for greater democracy, but they gave little thought to the inclusion of the rural black masses. The division between the tiny mulatto minority and small black elite became a major feature of elite politics in the nineteenth century, but in reality, this "ethnic politics" was more proclaimed than real.

After Boyer's exile in 1843, the government oscillated between long periods of dictatorial stability and unstable interregnums, with brief tenures in the presidency and turbulent politics. The quarter-century of Boyer's rule was followed by four brief

**Washing clothes, Haiti,** 1908–1909, by Harry Hamilton Johnston (1858–1927) (b/w photo). © ROYAL GEOGRAPHICAL SOCIETY, LONDON, UK/THE BRIDGEMAN ART LIBRARY

presidencies, none of which lasted for even one year. These interludes in office illustrate another feature of Haitian elite politics, the so-called *politique de doublure* ("understudy politics") by which elite politicians or merchants actually governed behind a black figurehead, often an army general with some peasant support. The four elderly generals who followed Boyer to the presidency showed little initiative, but the fifth general, a relative unknown from the presidential guard, Faustin Élie Soulouque (1788–1867), commenced another long reign.

Soulouque started his term in office by changing many facets of Haitian politics. He turned on his sponsors, setting up an urban terror squad, the *zinglins*, and used the southern *piquets* adroitly to frighten the merchants of Port-au-Prince. After a year or so in office, he arranged his elevation to emperor. His tenure in office lasted almost twelve years (1847–1859). Soulouque created a form of legitimacy for his rule among significant sectors of the population. He was preoccupied with national territorial integrity, and on two occasions tried to reunify parts of the island that had broken away after the fall of Boyer in 1843. For many Haitian authorities, the eastern part of the island, which had declared independence in 1844, represented a danger for the Haitian independence because it could be used as a base for foreign intrusion. Emperor Faustin I's insular policy was handicapped by internal difficulties and the hostility of the foreign powers that openly helped the Dominicans against the Haitian army. A short time later, the imperial regime collapsed.

General Fabre Nicolas Geffrard (1806–1878), a long-time ally of Faustin I, seized power after a military rebellion. Geffrard restored the republic and the presidency for life. His government started a vast program of education in urban areas and signed a concordat with the Holy See in 1860. Two years later, U.S. president Abraham Lincoln finally gave diplomatic recognition to Haiti, and Geffrard encouraged the immigration of black U.S. citizens, with little success. His government also played a prominent role aside Dominican patriots fighting against the reconquest of Santo Domingo by Spain. On May 6, 1867, Geffrard was overthrown by another general, Sylvain Salnave (1827–1870), and fled to Jamaica.

Salnave, who also declared himself president for life, was unusual in that he was a mulatto who had support from black factions. He seemed to have enjoyed some popularity among the poor of Port-au-Prince and elsewhere. But the *cacos* from the north opposed Salnave, and they played a large if intermittent role in politics until after the U.S. occupation of Haiti (1915–1934). They gave their support first to one general, then to another, on the basis of promises of short-term advantages. They seemed to be seeking benign neglect—promises that peasant land tenure or political arrangements in the rural areas would not be disturbed. Once their man was installed in the presidency, these rural groups usually disbanded, and thus failed to keep pressure on their leader; when a later generation saw new possibilities, they would rise again.

The period of Salnave's government (1867–1869) was characterized by political instability. Salnave had many political opponents, and the traditional power elite confronted him with determination; in turn, on many occasions, he mobilized his partisans against the economical interests of the elite. Traditional historiography presents this episode as a political confrontation between the mass of blacks, under the influence of a mulatto politician, and the mulatto elite. A new historiography characterizes Salnave's leadership as a historical attempt to change politics and social realities in the country. In the face of resistance, Salnave finally relinquished his office and went to the Dominican Republic, where he was captured by enemies and handed over to his political opponents in Haiti, who judged, condemned, and executed him publicly.

After Salnave's execution in January 1870, the political class seemed to have decided to modernize the political life of the nation. Two political parties were formed: the Liberal Party, made up in large part of preeminent mulattoes who advocated rule by the most able; and the National Party, composed principally of black figures who claimed power on behalf of the majority. As a result of this modernization, from 1870 to 1888 the political transitions were peaceful and constitutional, until the fall of General Salomon.

President Louis-Etienne Lysius Félicité Salomon, Jeune (1879–1888) was a well-known black who had served in Soulouque's cabinet. He found it expedient to support the concordat with the Holy See in spite of the anticlerical opinions of many of his followers. He negotiated with the United States for the lease of certain strategic points of Haitian territory to gain support both politically and economically. He founded the Banque Nationale de la République d'Haïti, backed by French capital; terminated payment of the French indemnity for recognition of Haitian independence; and accepted a French military mission to reform the Haitian army. He even permitted foreign companies to own Haitian land. Salomon's government published legislation to give access to land to some inhabitants, but unfortunately it lacked effective political determination and the capital investment to become a real policy. Once in power he survived the 1883 invasion by a faction of the Liberal Party backed by British merchants and activists. The government did not fall, but it was the beginning of its end. It survived in power until the middle of 1888.

### ATTEMPTS AT MODERNIZATION, AND FOREIGN INTERFERENCE

From Salomon's regime to the government of Tirésias Simon Sam (1896–1902), a movement toward modernization was afoot. Florvil Hyppolite (1889–1896), in particular, attempted to implement modernizing policies, but a lack of capital slowed him down. Haitian authorities looked principally to France for capital and foreign investment, and proposed to France an international alliance in the political arena. Unfortunately France did not respond adequately to their solicitation and offer: Haiti received only some loans, and those at exorbitant interest rates. Haiti did not participate in the flow of capital, international investment, human resources, and migration that characterized the Europeanization of the world at that time.

This was a period of European imperialism and confrontations. At the turn of the twentieth century, the independence of Haiti was difficult to maintain. To survive, in 1907 the Haitian authorities successively and separately signed treaties or conventions of good relations with France, Germany and the United States. All these powers—and their foreign merchants installed in the ports of Port-au-Prince, Jacmel, Cap-Haitian, and Gonaïves—were playing some role in the national politics of Haiti, pressuring authorities or supporting some Haitian politicians in exchange for favors and privileges. All these attitudes and policies were sources of turmoil and political instability.

The need for money, the relationship with the national bourgeoisie, and fear of foreign powers, were all issues that each president had to contend with, whatever his ethnic politics and proclamations. The welfare of the majority was forgotten, and several presidents found themselves appeasing foreign governments, negotiating new loans with them, or even negotiating leases of national territory. The rivalry for the presidency and the precariousness of tenure once in office was such that some Haitian leaders treacherously called in foreign military support against their compatriot opponents.

By the 1890s the United States gained some political influence in Haiti, but as an exporter of capital and an emergent international power, it regarded the sporadic unrest in Haiti as a threat to U.S. citizens and their interests. The United States found Haiti's nationalism to be an affront, and many of its policies, such as the constitutional provision against ownership of land by foreign whites, to be an obstacle to investment. Moreover, Haiti's geographical position at the entrance to the northern Caribbean (and its natural harbor at Môle St. Nicolas on the northeast coast) provoked interference from the United States and other powers.

Between 1911 and 1915 Haiti had six presidents. The last of them, Vilbrun Guillaume Sam, who ordered the execution of jailed opponents, was dragged out of the French embassy and killed. The U.S. Marines had been waiting for a reason to invade, and they landed that same day, July 28, 1915.

### FROM THE U.S. OCCUPATION TO THE DUVALIER REGIMES

The pretext for the U.S. occupation of Haiti was the rioting that preceded the murder of President Sam; the United States considered the unrest a threat to U.S. citizens and property in Haiti. They may also have wished to forestall the French, whose embassy had been violated, and certainly they were concerned about Germany, which, with World War I raging, had designs on Môle St. Nicolas on the northeast coast of Haiti. (Germany had at various times asserted its right to protect the sizable German merchant community in Port-au-Prince.) U.S. investors, moreover, had bought out the French interest in Haiti's Banque Nationale, but generally, U.S. business interests had been frustrated by difficulties in penetrating the Haitian economy. The British, for their part, often acted as protectors of the increasingly important Syrian-Lebanese merchant group that dominated much of Haiti's commercial life. The combination of these fears and frustrations, when added to the strategic hegemony that the United States was establishing in the Caribbean, was reason enough to justify the invasion and the occupation, which lasted nineteen years (1915–1934).

Those who defend the U.S. occupation refer to the political and financial stability it brought. They also point to material gains: Health conditions were improved; roads, hospitals, and schools were built; and finally more foreign investment flowed in. U.S. interests came first, however, and the Haitian public resented the reversal of the old policy prohibiting foreign ownership of land. Provoking even more resentment was the U.S. policy of favoring the mulatto elite, evidenced by the installation of a series of mulatto presidents. Rural anger at the imposition of the *corvée*, a system of obligatory labor drafts, sparked a *cacos* revolt in 1918 led by, among others, Charlemagne Péralte (1886–1919), who was killed after a violent campaign by the U.S. Marines. Nationalistic fervor increased after the revolt. In cultural terms, many of the Haitian elite constructed an ideology of an American as a subject materialist, with a lack of culture and good taste.

The U.S. occupation also gave birth to the indigenist movement in Haiti. A segment of the intellectual elite, inspired by Jean-Price Mars's book *Ainsi parla l'oncle* (1928), criticized the Haitian elite for looking only to Europe, particularly France, and neglecting Haiti's African roots, values, and culture. A vast sector in the Haitian community was mobilized. New theorists came and gave new interpretations and formulations of the nation's politics, economy, and social relations. Furthermore, they found the basis for a new aesthetics and finally formed a new vision of the world.

In this context, the United States was unwelcome in the country, and in 1934 President Franklin D. Roosevelt finally withdrew the U.S. troops.

Much has been made of the ethnological and nationalistic movement that began as a reaction to the foreign occupation. Now a group of intellectuals

**President-elect François Duvalier reads an acceptance speech at his swearing-in ceremony, 1957.** A former doctor and student of vodou religion, François Duvalier, nicknamed "Papa Doc," became dictator of Haiti, holding power for fourteen years until his death in 1971. Severe repression, abuse, and corruption characterize his regime. He named son Jean-Claude, "Baby Doc," his successor. © BETTMANN/CORBIS

strove to emphasize the African part of Haiti's heritage, moving from indigenism to négritude and to noirisme (black power). The griot movement was another movement, and the ethnologist Lorimer Denis and François Duvalier (1907–1971) were its principal exponents. In some of their writings they went so far as demanding a revolution that would throw off all European attachments in favor of the African values. They rewrote Haitian political history to emphasize the glorious black past and created a historical legend that favored the blacks.

From 1941 to 1942 the Catholic Church, with the support of President Elie Lescot, led an anti-superstition campaign in an attempt to eradicate vodou, the popular religion. This campaign divided the Haitian society, and fortunately it was stopped by the government before too much damage was done.

In 1946 a representative of the black elite, Dumarsais Estimé (1900–1953), became president. Estimé mobilized large subaltern social groups, and he made Haiti a tourist destination for the first time with the International Exhibition at the bicentenary celebration of the foundation of Port-au-Prince in 1947 to 1950. Considering the Haitian twentieth century as a whole, the four years of the Estimé government (1946–1950) were the most progressive. Estimé fell victim to a coup when he tried to change the constitution to allow his reelection by parliament. After his presidency, Haitian governments went from bad to worse.

At first, the ambition of General Paul-Eugène Magloire (1950–1956), the army chief who overthrew Estimé, was to continue the politics of his predecessor. He was welcomed by the Catholic Church, the Port-au-Prince business community,

**Reverend Sylvio Claude, a leading challenger of the Duvalier regime addressing supporters, Port-au-Prince, Haiti, 1979.** Opponents to the Duvalier family's rule (1957–1986) experienced repression and death for their dissidence, often at the hands of the Tontons Macoutes. LYNNE SLADKY/ BETTMANN/CORBIS

and the United States. There was a brief burst of prosperity, at least in the city, under Magloire, but his minority politics were dated. Magloire was forced to leave the country in 1956, when he, too, tried to remain in power. His departure brought another interregnum. Four preeminent figures, Clément Jumelle, Louis Déjoie, Daniel Fignolé, and François Duvalier, struggled for the power. Gradually, Duvalier, a physician and well-known ethnologist from the indigenist movement, gained the lukewarm support of the army and a majority among the electorate. He won the presidential election of 1957, presenting himself as the successor to Estimé.

Duvalier ruled Haiti as president for life for almost fourteen years (1957–1971). Once in power, he quickly threw off those who believed that he could be manipulated. He governed with the support of a praetorian guard, the Volontaires de la Sécurité Nationale (VSN), popularly known as the Tontons Macoutes. He never relaxed terrorist vigilance and authoritarian rule. By the mid-1960s, Duvalier reigned supreme: All his leading opponents were either dead or in exile.

Duvalier had elaborated his philosophy of government in many books and articles, but his rule failed to develop much of it. After the elimination of his rivals, his regime was fraught with revolutionary rhetoric and symbols, but his policies were conservative. He succeeded in replacing foreign priests with Haitian nationals. He also ferociously dismantled some sectors of the elites and thereby won the support of parts of the new black urban middle class, as well as political leaders of the villages. But under his presidency and that of his successor, his son Jean-Claude Duvalier (1971–1986), little was accomplished or even attempted to solve the sizeable economic and social problems of Haiti. A portion of the peasantry was coopted, another was punished for opposing his policies. Under the Duvalier regimes, the standard of living began to deteriorate more rapidly than before because of the growing population and the resultant division and subdivision of land holding. Many of the rural poor emigrated to the Dominican Republic, the Bahamas, and the United States. Haitians from the cities and educated professionals also went to foreign countries, particularly the United States, Canada, and France, to earn a living or to escape oppression.

The regime of the younger Duvalier was less violent than that of his father, but it became increasingly associated with the old elites and with spectacular corruption. In general, the economical situation of Haiti during the reign of the Duvaliers was disastrous. While other nations in the Caribbean region expanded through economic growth and development, Haiti entered more profoundly into poverty and a dictatorial political system. Finally, when Jean-Claude Duvalier's support disappeared in February 1986, he was flown to exile in France.

### TRANSITION AND DEMOCRACY

Since February 1986, Haiti has been in a long period of transition that is moving jaggedly, with both advances in establishing democratic institutions and attempts to restore dictatorships. During this long period, elections have been organized, others canceled; some presidencies have been ephemeral. The army has reasserted itself in national politics, directly governing the country and carrying out dramatic coups d'état.

Since 1986 Haiti has regressed at several levels. Poverty is striking and palpable. Haiti has lost a significant portion of its export capacity, and its imports, even of basic or essential products, remain substantial. From 1991 to 1994 an international embargo—a catastrophic one—was in force against Haiti, and the nation has not recovered its pre-embargo level of production and exchanges. Political instability does not permit a national plan of reconstruction or renovation for the long term.

One positive sign has been the more vigorous participation in decision making on the part of the peasants and the rapidly growing urban masses. The popular Catholic priest Jean-Bertrand Aristide (b. 1953) was elected to the presidency in December 1990 by a large popular vote, though that did not prevent his overthrow and exile soon afterward. In exile, Aristide has been unpopular among many leaders in the United States because of his radical rhetoric; nevertheless he received U.S. and UN help in his struggle to regain power. He was returned to the presidency of Haiti in October 1994. From 1994 to 1996 he managed (with help from international forces) to demobilize the army that committed the bloody coup d'état of 1991. In February 1996 he was succeeded in the presidency by René G. Préval (b. 1943).

Préval, who had been Aristide's prime minister (February–September 1991), ruled the country until the end of his constitutional mandate (1996–2001), largely with the support of Aristide and his political party, Fanmil Lavalas, though Aristide sometimes intervened unhelpfully, leaving the president little room to manoeuvre. President Préval instituted land reform in the rice-growing area of Artibonite and attempted to set up a real national road network, but both initiatives remained incomplete. Ultimately, at that time, Préval's government did not leave a great legacy; he merely waited, played for time, and prepared for Aristide's return to power, via fair or fraudulent elections.

Aristide did return to power, in February 2001 following presidential elections organized by a discredited interim electoral council with no mandate and no political legitimacy. Notwithstanding the opposition parties' boycott of the electoral process, the council prepared elections geared toward Aristide, proclaiming him president with decidedly suspicious results of over 95 percent. Thus Aristide returned to power in a political mêlée without the support of any organized political force. He ruled for three years, during which time he attempted to resolve the crisis in his own way. Although he gained a certain acceptance within the international community, at home his government was openly denounced and embattled. Aristide tried to rule by fear, intimidation, and political repression in a manner reminiscent of Duvalier, encouraging the formation of armed groups to terrorize opponents and intimidate the civilian population. The January 1, 2004, commemoration of national independence saw a political confrontation between Aristide's supporters and his political opponents. Two months

**Haiti, September 20, 1994.** Troubled by political and social unrest throughout its post-Columbian history, Haiti suffers from some of the Caribbean's most extreme poverty. After the democratically elected president Jean-Bertrand Aristide was overthrown in 1991, the international community aided his restoration of power in 1994. © LES STONE/SYGMA/CORBIS

later, the government was deposed and Aristide went into exile. Meanwhile, the United Nations sent a peace-keeping intervention force to Haiti to protect lives and property; it is expected that the UN force will remain for ten years to allow for the establishment of political institutions and consolidation of the sectors of the Haitian economy.

From February 2004 to May 2006 Haiti's fate was in the hands of an interim government headed by the Supreme Court judge Alexandre Boniface as president and Gérard Latortue as prime minister. The government's main mandate was the consolidation of the political institutions of the country, including the strengthening of political parties, and the organization of free and democratic elections with the participation of all political sectors. The government had great difficulty implementing its policy, partly because in July 2004 armed supporters of Aristide in the slums around Port-au-Prince launched "Operation Baghdad"—a program aimed at maintaining a state of terror among the population, making the country ungovernable. Nevertheless, parliamentary and presidential elections were held, and former president René Préval was once again successful at the polls. He took the oath in May 2006, and his term of office extends to February 2011. His government is implementing a calming policy, aimed at including all political sectors within the government. He has thus far been successful, yet the general socioeconomic conditions of the population still very bad.

Despite Haiti's many problems, one aspect has never failed—the artistic and intellectual production of the Haitian people. Haitian coffee remains a legend and a reference of good taste. Haitian paintings and craft are highly valued everywhere. Haiti has produced writers and thinkers of great value, including Anténor Firmin (1850–1911), Jean Price-Mars (1876–1969), Jacques Roumain (1907–1944),

Jacques-Stephen Alexis (1922–1961), Edwidge Danticat (b. 1969), and Frankétienne (b. 1936), to mention a few. Where there is the art of creation and strength of thought, change is always possible.

*See also* **Alexis, Jacques Stéphen; Aristide, Jean-Bertrand; Boyer, Jean-Pierre; Caste and Class Structure in Colonial Spanish America; Christophe, Henri; Columbus, Christopher; Danticat, Edwidge; Dessalines, Jean Jacques; Duvalier, François; Duvalier, Jean-Claude; Geffrard, Fabre Nicolas; Hyppolite, Louis Modestin Florville; Leclerc, Charles Victor Emmanuel; Louverture, Toussaint; Magloire, Paul Eugene; Maroons (Cimarrones); Napoleon I; Ogé, Jacques Vicente; Péralte, Charlemagne Masséna; Pétion, Alexandre Sabés; Rigaud, André; Rochambeau, Donatien Marie Joseph de Vimeur de; Roumain, Jacques; Salnave, Sylvain; Salomon, Louis Étienne Lysius Félicité; Sam, Jean Villbrun Guillaume; Sam, Tirésias Augustin Simon; Santo Domingo; Slave Revolts: Spanish America; Sonthonax, Léger Félicité; Soulouque, Faustin Élie; Tonton Macoutes.**

BIBLIOGRAPHY


Benoit, Joachim. "La bourgeoisie d'affaires haïtienne au 19ème siècle." *Nouvelle Optique* 1, no. 4 (1971): 50–70.

Berloquin Chassany, Pascale. *Haïti, une démocratie compromise, 1890–1911.* Paris: L'Harmattan, 2004.

Blancpain, François. *Un siècle de relations financières entre Haïti et la France (1825–1922).* Paris: L'Harmattan, 2001.

Butel, Paul. *Les Caraïbes au temps des flibustiers.* Paris: Aubier Montaigne, 1982.

Debien, Gabriel. *Plantations et esclaves à Saint-Domingue.* Dakar, Senegal: Université de Dakar, 1962.

Denis, Watson R. "L'éternelle question de la transition politique en Haïti." *Recherches haitiano-antillaises* 1, no. 2 (2005): 107–126.

Denis, Watson R. "Les 100 ans de Monsieur Roosevelt et Haïti. Comment Anténor Firmin posa les fondements des études et des relations haitiano-américaines." *Revue de la société haïtienne d'Histoire et de Géographie* 226 (July–September 2006): 1–41.

Denis, Watson R. "Origenes y manifestaciones de la francofilia haitiana: nacionalismo y política exterior en Haiti." *Secuencia* 67 (January–April 2007): 91–139.

Dominique, Max. "De l'ambiguité du nationalisme bourgeois en Haïti." *L'arme de la critique littéraire: Littérature et idéologie en Haïti.* Montréal: Centre international de documentation et d'information Haïtienne, 1988.

Dupuy, Alex. *Haiti in the World Economy: Class, Race, and Underdevelopment since 1700.* Boulder, CO: Westview Press, 1989.

Gaillard, Roger. *La République exterminatrice: La modernisation manquée.* Port-au-Prince, Haiti: Imprimerie Le Natal, 1984.

Geggus, David P. *Slavery, War, and Revolution: The British Occupation of Saint Domingue, 1793–1798.* Oxford, U.K.: Clarendon Press, 1982.

Girod, François. *La vie quotidienne de la société créole: Saint-Domingue au 18e siècle.* Paris: Hachette, 1972.

Hector, Michel, and Jean Casimir. "Le long XIXe siècle haïtien." *Itinéraires* (December 2004): 37–56.

Hurbon, Laennec. *Le barbare imaginaire.* Port-au-Prince, Haiti: Fardin, 1987.

James, C. L. R. *The Black Jacobins: Toussaint Louverture and the San Domingo Revolution.* New York: Random House, 1963.

Joachim, Benoît. *Les racines du sous-développement en Haïti.* Port-au-Prince, Haiti: Henri Deschamps, 1979.

Labat, Jean-Baptiste. *Voyage aux isles de l'Amérique (Antilles): 1693–1705.* 2 vols. Paris: Duchartre, 1931.

Manigat, Leslie. "La substitution de la prépondérance américaine à la prépondérance française au début du XXè siècle: La conjoncture de 1910–1911." *Revue d'Histoire Moderne et Contemporaine* (October December 1967): 321–355.

Moise, Claude. *Constitutions et luttes de pouvoir en Haïti.* 2 vols. Revised ed. Chicago: University of Chicago Press, 1997.

Moral, Paul. *Le paysan haïtien.* Paris: Larose et Maisonneuve, 1962.

Moreau De Saint-Méry, M. L. E. *Description topographique, physique, civile, politique et historique de la partie française de l'Isle Saint-Dominique*, 3rd edition, 3 vols. Paris: Société de l'histoire des Colonies Françaises, 1958.

Moya Pons, Frank. *La dominación haitiana, 1822–1844.* Santiago, Dominican Republic: Universidad Católica Madre y Maestra, 1972.

Nicholls, David. *From Dessalines to Duvalier: Race, Colour, and National Independence in Haiti.* Cambridge, U.K.: Cambridge University Press, 1979.

Ott, Thomas O. *The Haitian Revolution, 1789–1804.* Knoxville: University of Tennessee Press, 1973.

Plummer, Brenda Gayle. "The Metropolitan Connexion: Foreign and Semiforeign Elites in Haiti, 1900–1915." *Latin American Research Review* 19, no. 2 (1984): 119–142.

Plummer, Brenda Gayle. *Haiti and the Great Powers, 1902–1915.* Baton Rouge: Louisiana State University Press, 1988.

Price-Mars, Jean. *So Spoke the Uncle* [1928], trans. and introduction by Magdaline W. Shannon. Washington, DC: Three Continents Press, 1983.

Renda, Mary A. *Taking Haiti: Military Occupation and the Culture of U.S. Imperialism, 1915–1940.* Chapel Hill and London: University of North Carolina Press, 2001.

Schmidt, Hans R., Jr. *The United States Occupation of Haiti: 1915–1934.* New Brunswick, NJ: Rutgers University Press, 1971.

Trouillot, Michel-Rolph. *Haiti, State against Nation: The Origins and Legacy of Duvalierism.* New York: Monthly Review Press, 1990.

Trouillot, Michel-Rolph. *Silencing the Past: Power and Production of History.* Boston: Beacon Press, 1995.

Turnier, Alain. *Les Etats-Unis et le marché haïtien.* Montreal: Imprimerie Saint-Joseph, 1955.

Wilson, Samuel M. *Hispaniola: Caribbean Chiefdoms in the Age of Columbus.* Tuscaloosa: University of Alabama Press, 1990.

WATSON DENIS

**HAITI, CACO REVOLTS.** The armed fighters of Haiti known as the *Cacos* are perhaps most famous for their battles with U.S. Marines during the United States's occupation of their country between 1915 and 1934. Yet their history predates the U.S. intervention. The term *Caco*, which derives from the name of the feisty red-plumed bird found on the island (many Cacos wore patches of red cloth and hatbands), originally referred to the former slaves who joined up against the French during the Haitian Revolution (1791–1804). In the Cacos's revolt of 1867, armed bands from northern Haiti rose in opposition to President Sylvain Salnave (1867–1870). Throughout the nineteenth century, particularly in the northern region, the Cacos operated as hired armies for local chiefs and elite families. But they also worked nationally. Political contenders sometimes raised Caco armies to seize presidential power: between 1908 and 1915 seven presidents used these tactics.

The Cacos embodied Haiti's longstanding racialized tensions and regional and political divide. In the north, a darker-skinned black elite and poor were established, whereas in the south, lighter-skinned mulattoes held power. The Cacos were generally darker and came from humble origins, alternating their time fighting with cultivating small plots of land. Some had only old muskets and were more adept with rocks. Because the Cacos were compensated for fighting by looting and small amounts of cash, elites and the U.S. media often depicted the Cacos as bandits and pillagers. But for the protection they offered, the Cacos often won local mass support. In the Caco uprisings against U.S. intervention in 1915, 1916, 1918, 1919 and 1920, these rebels earned acclaim both locally and abroad as patriots and national heroes.

Indeed, the Cacos posed a problem for the U.S. Marines during the U.S. occupation of Haiti. In 1915 the Cacos objected to the presidential candidate, General Vilbrun Guillaume Sam (d. 1915), who had ordered the killing of 167 political prisoners. The murders sparked public outrage, and the Cacos came from the north to Port-au-Prince with Rosalvo Bobo (1873–1929) to seize power. Rather than support Bobo, the United States helped install President Phillipe Sudré Dartiguenave (1863–1926), who signed a treaty placing the Haitian government under U.S. control for the next twenty years. The Cacos rebelled. The Marines tried unsuccessfully to disarm the Cacos through arms buyouts. Although they had superior machinery and supplies, the U.S. Marines were handicapped by the Cacos's guerrilla tactics, and it took more than a year to defeat them. The Marines blew up the Cacos's eighteenth-century stronghold in the north, Fort Rivière, in 1916.

Despite this loss, in 1918 the Cacos launched a second revolt in the north under the leadership of Charlemagne Masséna Péralte (1886–1919) and Benoît Batraville (d. 1920). Aimed against U.S. imperialism generally, and specifically against the forced unpaid labor draft known as the *corvée*, the Cacos's rebellion had wide public support. The U.S. occupation and the Marines' racism generated broad anti-American sentiment throughout the country. Tough fighting lasted until November 1920, and only with additional troops and the unprecedented use of aircraft did the Marines suppress the Cacos. But the high death toll of Cacos and Haitians generated worldwide attention and outrage, and resulted in a U.S. Senate inquiry. Even with considerable resistance and criticism, U.S. troops only withdrew from Haiti in August 1934.

In the early twenty-first century, Cacos are regarded as national heroes of Haiti. Although originally associated specifically with the north, the Cacos came to represent anti-imperialist and national struggles. In 1994 their leader Péralte was depicted on Haiti's currency.

*See also* **Haiti.**

BIBLIOGRAPHY

Blancpain, François. *Haïti et les Etats-Unis, 1915–1934: Histoire d'une occupation.* Paris: L'Harmattan, 1999.

Gaillard, Roger. *La guérilla de Batraville: 1919–1934.* Port-au-Prince, Haiti: Le Natal, 1983.

Michel, George. *Charlemagne Peralte and the First American Occupation of Haiti*, trans. Douglas Henry Daniels. Dubuque, IA: Kendall and Hunt, 1996.

Renda, Mary A. *Taking Haiti: Military Occupation and the Culture of U.S. Imperialism, 1915–1940.* Chapel Hill: University of North Carolina Press, 2001.

Rogozinski, Jan. *A Brief History of the Caribbean: From the Arawak and the Carib to the Present.* New York: Plume, 2000.

MEREDITH GLUECK

**HAITI, CONSTITUTIONS.** Haiti has had about twenty constitutions, both real and nominal, many illustrating the apt creole proverb: "A constitution is paper; a bayonet is steel." A common characteristic of most of them has been a strong president and a weak legislature.

The first constitution, Autonomy and Independence (Toussaint, 1801), written ten years after independence from France, gave France suzerainty and provided for forced labor. The second (Dessalines, 1805) abolished slavery "forever," separated church and state, applied the word "black" to all Haitians, and prohibited foreign ownership of land. The third (Pétion's first, 1806) is modeled after that of the United States. The fourth (Christophe, 1811) created a nobility. The fifth (Pétion's second, 1816) granted the president his office for life. The sixth (Riché, 1846) empowered the joint chambers to elect the president. The seventh (Domingue, 1874) concentrated all power in the presidency. That of 1889 (Hyppolite) revised the previous constitution of 1879 (Salomon) and served as the basis of government until the U.S. occupation.

The Constitution of 1918, written during the U.S. occupation by Assistant Navy Secretary Franklin D. Roosevelt, cancelled the prohibition of foreign ownership of land and added individual democratic rights. The eleventh constitution (1927) increased the powers of the president, as did that of 1932 (Vincent).

The constitutions of the postoccupation and Duvalier era were the thirteenth (Magloire, 1950), a liberal one written by the scholar-diplomat Dantès Bellegarde that provided for female suffrage beginning in 1957, and the fourteenth (Duvalier, 1957), which increased the powers of the president and excluded foreigners from retail trade. Duvalier's second constitution (1961) reduced the legislature to one chamber and increased the powers of the president. Duvalier's third, which was the sixteenth constitution, made Duvalier president for life, authorized him to choose his successor, and changed the flag's colors.

"Baby Doc" Duvalier's first constitution, the seventeenth (1983), combined a set of progressive social goals with new presidential powers of appointment and new power over the legislature. Baby Doc's second (1985) provided the legislature with new powers, created the position of prime minister, and permitted political parties (a public-relations response to U.S. pressure, approved by a fraudulent referendum).

The first constitution of the post-Duvalier era, that of 1987, restored the two-chamber legislature, reduced the powers of the president by dividing the executive authority between president and prime minister, created a permanent electoral council, removed the new *force publique* from direct control of the president and minister of the interior, prohibited for ten years the participation in government of "any person well known for having been ... one of the architects of the dictatorship and of its maintenance during the last twenty-nine years," provided many basic human rights, recognized Creole (Kreyol) as the national language, legalized vodun, and recognized no state religion. It was approved by a free and popular referendum.

President Leslie François Manigat was removed by General Henri Namphy, who became president, dissolved the legislature, and abolished all constitutions. Namphy in turn was removed by General Prosper Avril, who restored the nineteenth constitution, except for thirty-eight articles.

General Avril was forced out in 1989 and he was replaced by supreme court judge Ertha Pascal-trouillot, who became provisional president in 1990 under article 149 of the constitution. (This article provides that if the office of president is vacant, the chief justice or a member will become acting president until elections are held.) In free elections, Jean-Bertrand Aristide, a leftist priest, was elected president; he was inaugurated in February 1991. While president, Aristide took advantage of article 295 of the constitution, which authorized him for a six-month period "to proceed to carry out any reforms deemed necessary in the Government Administration … and in the Judiciary." He gave some provocative speeches threatening the elite "bourgeoisie" and the military; the latter overthrew him in late September. The Organization of American States (OAS) responded by approving economic sanctions against the military government of General Raoul Cédras to bring about Aristide's restoration. The United Nations joined the OAS in 1993 and joint efforts were made to negotiate a settlement. An accord was reached in July, providing for the selection of a prime minister (Robert Malval), lifting of sanctions, political amnesty, and Aristide's return. The accord could not be implemented once the military reneged although sanctions were strengthened. In June 1994, the military government, acting under article 149, inaugurated Supreme Court Chief Justice Émile Jonassaint as provisional president. President Aristide was restored to power in late 1994.

*See also* **Aristide, Jean-Bertrand; Bellegarde, Luis Dantès; Duvalier, François; Duvalier, Jean-Claude.**

BIBLIOGRAPHY

James G. Leyburn, *The Haitian People* (1941), esp. chap. 13.

David Nicholls, *From Dessalines to Duvalier: Race, Colour, and National Independence in Haiti* (1979), esp. chap. 2.

Brian Weinstein and Aaron Segal, *Haiti: Political Failures, Cultural Successes* (1984), pp. 51–54.

James Ferguson, *Papa Doc, Baby Doc: Haiti and the Duvaliers* (1987), esp. pp. 80, 83–85, 156–158.

Patrick Bellegarde-Smith, *Haiti: The Breached Citadel* (1989), pp. 44–46, 123–126, 139–140.

*Additional Bibliography*

Samedy, Jean-Baptiste Mario. *De la démocratie en Haïti: culture, régime politique et idéologies contre le développement.* Ottawa; New York: Legas, 2002.

Stotzky, Irwin P. *Silencing the Guns in Haiti: The Promise of Deliberative Democracy.* Chicago: University of Chicago Press, 1997.

LARMAN C. WILSON

## HALFFTER, RODOLFO (1900–1987).

Rodolfo Halffter (*b.* 20 October 1900; *d.* 14 October 1987), Spanish composer. Mainly self-taught, Halffter in 1929 sought advice from the eminent composer Manuel de Falla with whose spare, neoclassic style his music is frequently compared. He gained recognition in Europe in the mid-1930s but moved to Mexico in 1939. A permanent resident and citizen of Mexico from 1940, he held posts as professor at the National Conservatory (from 1940) and director of the composers' cooperative publishing firm, Ediciones Mexicanas de Música (from 1946). In 1969 Halffter was inducted into the Mexican Academy of Arts. He wrote some twelve-tone serial music, the first in Mexico, but his style retained its characteristic clarity and melodiousness with tinges of dissonance and without any Mexican influences. His students include Héctor Quintanar and Eduardo Mata.

*See also* **Music: Art Music.**

BIBLIOGRAPHY

Dan Malmström, *Twentieth-Century Mexican Music* (1974).

Gérard Béhague, *Music in Latin America: An Introduction* (1979).

*Additional Bibliography*

Alvarez Coral, Juan. *Compositores mexicanos.* México: EDAMEX, 1993.

Ito, Misa. "The Piano Works of Rodolfo Halffter (1900–87)." Ph.D. diss., University of Cincinnati, 1999.

ROBERT L. PARKER

## HALLUCINOGENS.

*See* **Drugs and Drug Trade.**

## HALPERÍN-DONGHI, TULIO (1926–).

Tulio Halperín-Donghi (*b.* 27 October 1926), Argentine historian. Born and educated in Argentina,

Halperín-Donghi received his doctorate from the University of Buenos Aires in 1955. He taught at the universities of Rosario and Buenos Aires from 1955 until the military coup led by Juan Carlos Onganía in 1966. Since then, he taught at Harvard, Oxford, and the University of California at Berkeley. Halperín-Donghi's work covers a wide range of topics in political history, economic and fiscal history, and social and intellectual history. His contributions on the crisis of independence, the fledging efforts at national organization, and the social and economic continuities from the Bourbon to the post-Independence periods are particularly strong. His most important work is *Revolución y guerra: Formación de una elite dirigente en la Argentina criolla* (1972), which details the breakdown of the colonial order and the emergence of new elites in a context of social and political crisis. Other works include *Tradición política española e ideología revolucionaria de Mayo* (1961), *Guerra y finanzas en los orígenes del estado argentino* (1982), and *José Hernández y sus mundos* (1985). He has also written such comprehensive histories as *Historia contemporánea de América Latina* (1969), *Hispanoamérica después de la independencia* (1972), and *El espejo de la historia: Problemas argentinos y perspectivas latinoamericanas* (1987). This last volume places Argentina in a Latin American context and reveals how Halperín-Donghi's view of the region has been deepened by his years of life abroad. He retired from the University of California at Berkeley in 1994. Halperín-Donghi continues to write prolifically, exploring intellectual, political, and social movements in nineteenth- and twentieth-century Argentina, as in *Proyecto y construcción de una nación: 1846–1880* (1995) and *La República imposible (1930–1945)* (2004).

BIBLIOGRAPHY

John V. Lombardi, "Detail and the Grand Design in History," in *Latin American Research Review* 14, no. 2 (1979): 223–226.

Frank Safford, "History, 1750–1850," in *Latin America and the Caribbean: A Critical Guide to Research Sources,* edited by Paula H. Covington (1992).

*Additional Bibliography*

Halperín Donghi, Tulio, Roy Hora, and Javier Trimboli. *Pensar la Argentina: Los historiadores hablan de historia y política.* Buenos Aires: Ediciones El Cielo por Asalto, Imago Mundi, 1994.

Suasnabar, Claudio. *Universidad e intelectuales: Educación y política en la Argentina (1955–1976).* Buenos Aires: FLACSO Manantial, 2004.

IVÁN JAKSÍC

**HAMBURG-AMERICA LINE.** Hamburg-America Line, a shipping company founded in 1847 by Hamburg shipowners to provide a "regular connection between Hamburg and North America by means of sailing ships under Hamburg flags." Originally the Hamburg-Amerikanische-Packetfahrt-Actien Gesellschaft, it was called HAPAG even after the line changed its name in 1893 to Hamburg-Amerika Line. The company slogan was "Mein Feld ist die Welt" (My field is the world). It began operations in Latin America in the 1850s, but entered that region most seriously when it reached an agreement with the Kosmos Line in 1901 and purchased the Atlas line. These two steps conceded HAPAG major European influence in freight service with Latin America.

About 1905, a serious conflict between HAPAG and the United Fruit Company arose when one of HAPAG's acquisitions, Atlas Steamship Company, entered into a profitable relationship with American Fruit and other banana exporters that competed with United Fruit. In 1913 United Fruit opposition and poor reception of the bananas in Europe persuaded HAPAG to sell Atlas to United Fruit and to terminate its ties to American Fruit.

HAPAG service to Latin America was disrupted in World War I and reestablished through a shared steamer service, the Deutsche Westküsten-Dienst (Germany West Coast Service). This service was disrupted again in 1939 and resumed its functions in 1953.

*See also* **United Fruit Company.**

BIBLIOGRAPHY

Otto Mathies, *Hamburgs Reederei 1814–1914* (1924).

Peter Franz Stubmann, *Mein Feld ist die Welt: Albert Ballin: Sein Leben* (repr. 1926; 1960).

Warren Armstrong, *Atlantic Highway* (1962).

Lamar Cecil, *Albert Ballin: Business and Politics in Imperial Germany, 1888–1918* (1967).

*Additional Bibliography*

Cooper, James, Arnold Kludas, and Joachim Pein. *The Hamburg South America Line.* Kendal, Cumbria: World Ship Society, 1989.

Kludas, Arnold. *Record Breakers of the North Atlantic: Blue Riband Liners, 1838–1952.* Washington, DC: Brassey's, 2000.

THOMAS SCHOONOVER

**HAMMOCK.** Hammock, a woven portable bed hung from posts or hooks, originally produced by indigenous peoples from crude cotton or palm fibers, also known as *hamaca* in Spanish and *rede* in Portuguese. The use of the hammock in Latin America was first recorded by Pero Vaz da Caminha in 1500 in his description of a Tupiniquin home. He used the word *rede,* or fishing net, for its similarity in appearance. Christopher Columbus also appropriated the term after noting its use among the Taíno-Arawakian peoples in the early 1500s. Europeans soon adopted the design after discovering the advantages of a portable, washable, ventilated bed that elevated the user above the rodents, insects, and floodwaters of the tropics.

Hammocks flourished throughout most of Mexico, the Caribbean, and Central and South America (especially within the Amazon Basin), with the exception of Chile and Argentina (where their use was limited) and Bolivia. They were not documented elsewhere in the world by the earliest explorers. Scholars are still undecided as to the place of origin of the hammock. The foremost Brazilian authority, Luís da Câmara Cascudo, believes that they were invented by the Arawaks (though many scholars favor the Caribs), who passed them on to the Tupi.

Particularly in colonial Brazil, beautifully woven linen or silk hammocks with floor-sweeping overhangs became symbols of wealth and prestige. The Portuguese employed hammocks of many sizes as delivery tables and cradles, nuptial and trysting beds, porch rockers, offices, and coffins for the dead. Hammocks called *taboca* or *palanquins* carried by two slaves were also used as transportation. They are now used principally by the poor of the North and Northeast, where they are produced manually and industrially.

*See also* **Caribs; Tupi.**

BIBLIOGRAPHY

Luís Da Câmara Cascudo, *Rêde-de-dormir: Uma pesquisa etnográfica* (1959), and *Dicionário do folclore brasileiro,* 3d ed. (1972).

*Additional Bibliography*

Dantas, Cristina, Antonio Carlos Werneck, and Pedro Ariel Santana. *Artesãos do Brasil.* São Paulo: Editora Abril, 2002.

Schmitz, Hubert. *Manufacturing in the Backyard: Case Studies on Accumulation and Employment in Small-Scale Brazilian Industry.* Totowa, NJ: Allanheld, Osmun, 1982.

GAYLE WAGGONER LOPES

**HANDBOOK OF LATIN AMERICAN STUDIES.** In 1935 fifteen scholars from many of the disciplines that then comprised Latin American studies met in the New York offices of the Social Science Research Council to discuss the future of their respective fields. The participants in that conference, eager to promote crossdisciplinary collaboration and the sharing of research and resources, created the *Handbook of Latin American Studies,* an annotated multilingual bibliography and reference work for Latin American studies. The American Council of Learned Societies agreed to support the publication of the first two volumes of the new compilation, and the historian Lewis Hanke, then at Harvard, took charge of its content.

Hanke approached some of the true pioneers of the field for essays, with the understanding that they would look on their work as an unpaid service to the profession, requiring the highest level of commitment and scholarship. He also insisted on including Brazil along with Spanish-speaking countries. At that time, few academics in the United States thought Latin America worthy of analytical study, but with the inclusion of work by major scholars, the *Handbook* elevated the stature of the field. Since its inception the *Handbook* has served as a guide to the articulation of major subjects, with trends, ideologies, and tropes evolving or disappearing through its pages. As such, the *Handbook* has become the historical record for Latin American studies from 1935 onward.

Since 1939, with the inception of its Hispanic Division, the Library of Congress has been responsible for editorial direction and, since number eleven, for financing; the *Handbook* has been published by Harvard University Press, the University of Florida Press, and, since 1979, the University of Texas Press. The *Handbook* was divided into separate humanities and social sciences volumes in 1964, with each published in alternating years. In 1990 the *Handbook* was entered into its own database at the Library of Congress, and its own Spanish- and Portuguese-language interfaces soon became available on the Web, together with the original English. The *Handbook* continues to survey notable works in the field, providing free access to its online database (updated weekly), and publishing an annual print volume.

*See also* **Library of Congress, Hispanic Division.**

BIBLIOGRAPHY

*Handbook of Latin American Studies.* Available from www.loc.gov/hlas.

BARBARA A. TENENBAUM

**HANDELMANN, GOTTFRIED HEINRICH** (1827–1891). Gottfried Heinrich Handelmann (*b.* 9 August 1827; *d.* 26 April 1891), German historian of Hispaniola and Brazil. Son of a prosperous saddle maker of Altona, Hamburg, Handelmann studied history at the universities of Heidelberg, Berlin, Göttingen, and Kiel under some distinguished scholars, including Leopold von Ranke. As a student in Kiel, Handelmann was active in the German population's struggle against Danish authority in Schleswig-Holstein. In 1854 the University of Kiel accepted his doctoral dissertation on relations between the German Hanseatic League and the Scandinavian powers. In 1866, after Schleswig-Holstein's incorporation into Prussia, Handelmann was named curator of Schleswig-Holstein antiquities and professor of history at the University of Kiel, positions he held until his death.

Concerned by the rising tide of German immigration to the Western Hemisphere, Handelmann in the 1850s turned to the study of the history of colonization in the Americas. In short order he produced *Geschichte der Vereinigten Staaten* (History of the United States, 1856), *Geschichte der insel Hayti* (History of the Island of Hispaniola, 1856), and *Geschichte von Brasilien* (History of Brazil, 1860). The last is by far the most important and, with nearly a thousand pages, longer than the other two combined. The first history of Brazil by an academically trained historian, it takes a regional approach to the colonization of Portuguese America and lacks a unifying theme. The final section of the book, dealing with the 1808–1844 period, is most useful for its coverage of Brazilian immigration policy, which is compared unfavorably with that of the United States.

*See also* **Brazil: The Colonial Era, 1500–1808; Brazil: 1808–1889.**

BIBLIOGRAPHY

John Hyslop, "Heinrich Handelmann and Brazilian History," in *Teaching Latin American History,* edited by E. Bradford Burns et al. (1977), pp. 40–50.

NEILL MACAULAY

**HANKE, LEWIS ULYSSES** (1905–1993). Lewis Ulysses Hanke (*b.* 2 January 1905; *d.* 26 March 1993), pioneering historian and educator. In 1935, as a Harvard instructor, Hanke became the first editor of the multidisciplinary annotated bibliography, *Handbook of Latin American Studies,* which was begun following a meeting of Latin American historians who decided that such a bibliography would play a pivotal role in advancing the field. Still appearing yearly, the *Handbook* is now also available on the Internet.

Born in Oregon City, Oregon, Hanke graduated from Northwestern University. He then became an instructor at the University of Hawaii (1926–1927), taught at the American University of Beirut, Lebanon (1927–1930), and in 1936 received a doctorate in history from Harvard, where he remained teaching until 1939. From 1939 to 1951 he was the first director of the Hispanic Foundation (later Hispanic Division) of the Library of Congress. Hanke brought the *Handbook* to the Library, where he edited it and where it remained after he left. In his books *The Spanish Struggle for Justice in the Conquest of America* (1949) and *Aristotle and the American Indians: A Study in Race Prejudice in the Modern World* (1959), Hanke ushered in a new era in examining human-rights issues in Latin American history. After leaving the Library of Congress he taught at the University of Texas (1951–1961), Columbia University (1961–1967), the University of California at Irvine (1967–1969), and the University of Massachusetts (1969–1975).

Hanke also strove to preserve Latin American and Caribbean archives and initiated many guides to archival holdings. He was editor of the *Hispanic American Historical Review* from 1954 to 1960, edited the *History of Latin American Civilization* (2d ed.; 1973), and coedited *Historia de la Villa Imperial de Potosí por Bartolomé Arzáns de Orsúa y Vela* (3 vols.; 1965) and *Los virreyes españoles en América durante el gobierno de la casa de Austria* (12 vols.; 1976–1980). Another remarkable publication coedited by Hanke is the *Guide to the Study of United States History Outside the U.S.* (5 vols.; 1945–1980). Hanke's wife, Kate, collaborated on most of his books. In 1974 Hanke became the first Latin Americanist to be elected president of the American Historical Association. Other high honors bestowed on him include membership in the Hispanic Society of America; the Gulbenkian, Rosenbach, and numerous other fellowships; and in 1992 Spain's prestigious Antonio Nebrija Prize.

*See also* **Handbook of Latin American Studies.**

BIBLIOGRAPHY

Richard Graham and Peter H. Smith, eds., *New Approaches to Latin American History* (1974).

Dan Hazen, "The *Handbook of Latin American Studies* at (Volume) Fifty: Area Studies Bibliography in a Context of Change," in *Inter-American Review of Bibliography* 41, no. 2 (1991): 195–202.

GEORGETTE MAGASSY DORN

**HARO BARRAZA, GUILLERMO** (1913–1988). Guillermo Haro Barraza (*b.* 21 March 1913; *d.* 23 April 1988), Mexican astronomer and physicist. Born in Mexico City, the son of José Haro and Leonor Barraza, Haro graduated from the National University and did postgraduate work at the Harvard University Observatory (1943–1944). A full-time researcher at the National University, he initiated an extensive fellowship program to train future Mexican scientists. He directed the National Astronomical Observatory for two decades (1948–1968) as well as the Tonantzintla Astrophysics Observatory. Among them were the detection of a large number of planetary nebulae in the direction of the galactic center and the discovery (also independently done by George Herbig) of the nonstellar condensations in high density clouds near regions of recent star formation (now called Herbig-Haro objects). Haro and coworkers discovered flare stars in the Orion nebula region, and later on in stellar aggregates of different ages. His intense activity detecting flare stars continued until the end of his life.

Other major research projects carried out by Haro included the list of 8746 blue stars in the direction of the north galactic pole published jointly with W. J. Luyten in 1961. Work made with the 48-inch Palomar Schmidt using the three-color image technique developed at Tonantzintla. At least 50 of these objects turned out to be quasars (which had not yet been discovered in 1961). Haro's list of 44 blue galaxies, compiled in 1956, was a precursor to the work of Markarian and others in searching for such galaxies. Haro also discovered a number of T Tauri stars, one supernova, more than 10 novae, and one comet.

With Samuel Ramos and Elí de Gortari, he cofounded the Seminar of Scientific and Philosophical Problems, which published dozens of works. His own work has appeared in English, and he has edited several scientific journals. He became a member of the National College in 1953, and Mexico awarded him its National Prize in Sciences (1963) and the Lomonosow prize for pedagogical achievement (1987).

*See also* **Astronomy; Ramos y Magaña, Samuel; Science.**

BIBLIOGRAPHY

*Enciclopedia de México,* vol. 6 (1977), p. 365.

*Additional Bibliography*

Cantó, Jorge, and Eugenio E. Mendoza. *Proceedings of the Symposium on Herbig-Haro Objects, T Tauri Stars and Related Phenomena, to Honor Guillermo Haro.* Mexico City: Instituto de Astronomía, Universidad Nacional Autónoma de México, 1983.

Haro, Guillermo. "Obituary." *Sky and Telescope* 60 (1980): 11.

Haro, Guillermo. "The Possible Connexion between T Tauri Stars and UV Ceti Stars." *Symposium* 3 (1955): 26.

Mújica, Raúl, and Roberto Maiolino, eds. *Multiwavelength Agn Surveys: Proceedings of the Guillermo Haro Conference 2003, Cozumel, Mexico 8–12 December 2003.* Hackensack, NJ: World Scientific, 2003.

RODERIC AI CAMP

## HARO Y TAMARIZ, ANTONIO DE

(1811–1869). Antonio de Haro y Tamariz (*b.* 1811; *d.* 1869), Mexican politician. Born in the city of Puebla, Haro y Tamariz studied law in Rome. He served as finance minister in 1844, 1846, and 1853 and was elected to the Senate in 1850 and 1852. During the war with the United States in 1846, Haro y Tamariz proposed that church property be sold and that the government collect taxes on the sales. Prices would be set on the assumption that annual rents represented 5 percent of the value of the property. Renters would have first preference in purchasing their homes. The church delayed implementation of the plan, and the government's desperate need for funds forced it to drop the disentailment plan, but it later served as a model for the Liberal reforms of 1856.

A lifelong associate of Antonio López de Santa Anna, Haro y Tamariz himself became more conservative, collaborating with Lucas Alamán and serving in Santa Anna's cabinet in 1853. Unable to convince the church to make any further loans to the government and unwilling to borrow from *agiotistas* (moneylenders), Haro y Tamariz resigned only three months later. After the liberal Revolution of Ayutla overthrew Santa Anna, Haro y Tamariz launched a conservative rebellion in Puebla in December 1855 with the support of the army and the clergy. His Plan of Zacapoaxtla (1855) called for a restoration of the privileges of the church and the army and a return to the conservative Constitution of 1842. After a ferocious battle for the streets of Puebla, Haro y Tamariz was forced to surrender but managed to escape his captors. He supported the Conservative cause during the War of the Reform and the empire of Maximilian.

*See also* **Mexico: 1810–1910; Santa Anna, Antonio López de.**

BIBLIOGRAPHY

Jan Bazant, *Antonio Haro y Tamariz y sus aventuras políticas, 1811–1869* (1985).

Barbara A. Tenenbaum, *The Politics of Penury: Debt and Taxes in Mexico, 1821–1856* (1986), pp. 78–79, 121–126, 150–153; *Diccionario Porrúa de historia, biografía y geografía de México,* 5th ed. (1986).

### *Additional Bibliography*

Di Tella, Torcuato S. *National Popular Politics in Early Independent Mexico, 1820–1847.* Albuquerque: University of New Mexico Press, 1996.

D. F. STEVENS

## HAVANA.

Havana, Cuba's capital and principal seaport, with 2.3 million inhabitants in the city and 3 million in the metropolitan area (2005 estimate). Founded by Diego de Velázquez in 1514 on the island's southern coast, San Cristóbal de la Habana was transplanted in 1519 to its present location because of both the magnificent natural harbor and the proximity to the Gulf Stream. Becoming the colonial capital in 1553, the city lay on the western side of the bay, which bottlenecked into an easily defended passage at its mouth. Eventually, the massive Morro castle was erected at the entrance's eastern shore.

Known as the "Key to the New World," Havana commanded the exit from the Caribbean Sea and the route to and from Veracruz, Mexico. As the imperial commercial system evolved during the sixteenth century, Havana's bay harbored the Mexican treasure fleet returning to Seville and the southern fleet on its return voyage from Cartagena. Service industries enriched the city, and its immediate hinterland enjoyed a periodic market for foodstuffs, although the economy generally remained underdeveloped until the eighteenth century.

When Spanish mercantilist strategy broadened to emphasize tropical agricultural products as well as precious metals, Havana's hinterland responded, and the city assumed the role of exporter. In 1717 the royal tobacco monopoly began its century-long existence, emphasizing the importance of the Cuban leaf. The Havana Company, established in 1740, promoted the marketing of sugar in Spain. The 1765 Regulation of Free Trade for the Caribbean Islands permitted Havana access to nine Spanish ports and enhanced marketing flexibility. The Free Trade Act of 1778, especially when broadened to include Veracruz in 1788, afforded Havana the additional role of entrepôt for important portions of the Mexican and Caribbean trade. Although the Havana Company quickly faded from importance after 1765, local entrepreneurs plunged Havana's hinterland into the sugar revolution of the late eighteenth century. Thus, as deregulation dismantled the historic convoy system that had assigned Havana central importance, it simultaneously provided the port with new, larger opportunities.

During the early nineteenth century, after revolution had destroyed the sugar economy of Saint-Domingue, Cuban production assumed world leadership. Although the collapse of Spain's continental empire diminished Havana's function as entrepôt, the city, now permitted international free trade, emerged as a major commercial center owing to continuing demand for its sugar and tobacco, a role set to endure into modern times. The population of Havana, counted at 41,000 in 1778, had climbed to 94,000 by 1827, and some 240,000 at century's end.

Heavily fortified and stoutly garrisoned, strategic Havana ranked as the most important strongpoint of the Spanish Empire. A major naval base, Havana also developed into a primary shipbuilding center during the eighteenth century. Following Havana's capture in 1762 and the subsequent eleven-month British occupation, Spain invested huge quantities of Mexican silver to enhance its military. Defense waned as a major industry following Spain's loss of its continental colonies, but Havana regained its historic role as a strategic military base after Cuban independence, during the United States' protectorate. Although this role diminished following World War II, it reappeared forcefully when Cuba fell under Soviet influence during the Castro dictatorship, again earning its capital from massive outside subsidies.

The government devoted funds in the 1980s to restore *La Habana Vieja*, the colonial historic center UNESCO designated as a World Heritage Site in 1982. Further measures to attract international tourists to Havana followed the Soviet Union's collapse in the 1990s and Cuba's ensuing economic crisis known as the "special period." In response, the government eased restrictions on foreign investment, and since the late 1990s tourism in Havana has grown significantly, and the city continues to expand westward.

Nevertheless, Havana, once one of the world's most beautiful, vibrant cities, experienced hard times under the Castro regime and its commercial isolation from its American economic base.

*See also* **Cuba: The Colonial Era (1492-1898); Cuba: The Republic (1898-1959); Cuba: Cuba Since 1959.**

BIBLIOGRAPHY

Hugh Thomas, *Cuba: The Pursuit of Freedom* (1971).

Leví Marrero, *Cuba: Economía y sociedad,* 15 vols. (1972–1992), especially vols. 1–2, 7–10, and 12.

John Robert McNeill, *Atlantic Empires of France and Spain: Louisbourg and Havana, 1700–1763* (1985).

Jaime Suchlicki, *Cuba: From Columbus to Castro,* 3d ed. (1990).

Allan J. Kuethe, "Havana in the Eighteenth Century," in *Atlantic Port Cities: Economy, Culture, and Society in the Atlantic World, 1650–1850,* edited by Franklin W. Knight and Peggy K. Liss (1991).

### *Additional Bibliography*

Colantonio, Andrea, and Robert B. Potter. *Urban Tourism and Development in the Socialist State: Havana during the "Special Period."* Burlington, VT: Ashgate, 2006.

Estrada, Alfredo José. *Havana: Autobiography of a City.* New York: Palgrave Macmillan, 2007.

Kapcia, Antoni. *Havana: The Making of Cuban Culture.* New York: Berg, 2005.

Segre, Roberto, Mario Coyula, and Joseph L. Scarpaci. *Havana: Two Faces of the Antillean Metropolis.* Chichester, U.K.: Wiley, 1997.

Tapia-Ruano, Osvaldo de. *La Habana en el siglo XXI: Urbanismo actual.* Miami, FL: Ediciones Universal, 2006.

Allan J. Kuethe

---

**HAVANA COMPANY.** Havana Company (La Real Compañía de Comercio de la Habana), established by the Cédula of 18 December 1740, was intended to guarantee its royal, metropolitan, and (majority) Cuban investors a monopoly of the trade between Spain and Cuba, as well as to stimulate ship construction in Havana, supply troops stationed there, and provide coast-guarding services against smugglers and pirates. Over the next twenty years, the company introduced approximately 5,000 slaves into the island, while dominating the exportation of tobacco and sugar and the importation and sale of provisions and European goods. The Havana Company was reorganized in 1760 and suffered severe losses with the fall of Havana to the British two years later, although it continued in existence until the end of the century.

*See also* **Spanish Empire.**

BIBLIOGRAPHY

Julio Le Riverend, *Economic History of Cuba* (1967).

Vicente Báez, ed., *La enciclopedia de Cuba: Historia,* vol. 5 (1974), pp. 170–171.

Leví Marrero, *Cuba: Economía y sociedad,* vol. 7 (1978), pp. 102–165.

*Additional Bibliography*

Tornero Tinajero, Pablo. *Crecimiento ecónomico y transformaciones sociales: Esclavos, hacendados y comerciantes en la Cuba colonial (1760–1840).* Madrid: Ministerio de Trabajo y Seguridad Social, 1996.

Linda K. Salvucci

## HAVANA CONFERENCES (1928, 1940).

*See* **Pan-American Conferences: Havana Conference (1928); Pan-American Conferences: Havana Meeting (1940).**

## HAWKINS, JOHN

(1532–1595). John Hawkins (*b.* 1532; *d.* 12 November 1595), an Englishman active in the West Indies from 1562 to 1600 who was primarily interested in trading. In the early 1560s, a new group of interlopers, the English, were led by the ingenious John Hawkins of Plymouth, who organized four trading voyages to the Indies from 1562 to 1568, personally leading three of them. His purpose was trade: to exchange cloth and merchandise from England and slaves from Africa with the Spanish in return for sugar, hides, and silver. Hawkins wanted to legitimize his activities with the Spanish government by securing a license to trade freely. Even though he vowed to fight privateers if the Spanish would grant him the license he desired, the Spanish refused to do so, wishing to avoid setting a precedent.

Hawkins's earliest venture was successful in business terms, although his overall plan failed. The first voyage embarked in October 1562 and prospered greatly, as he traveled among the Caribbean islands trading English goods and African slaves for hides and sugar, returning to England in September 1563. Hawkins's first effort succeeded in the midst of relative peace between the English and Spanish. Relations between the two nations soured quickly, however, as the peace between England and Spain that was based on common opposition to France broke down when France weakened from internal religious wars.

Thus, Hawkins's second and third voyages faced greater difficulties as Spain clamped down on its colonies and fervently attempted to prohibit foreign trade. Meanwhile, by the time of the second voyage (October 1564–September 1565), Hawkins had received more direct support from the English government. Nevertheless, the second and third voyages proved relatively unsuccessful in terms of trade, though each had its own accomplishments.

On his third and final voyage (October 1567–January 1569), Hawkins was bound for home in September 1568 when bad weather forced his fleet to dock at San Juan de Ulúa, the port of Veracruz. Later that month, a Spanish *flota* encountered his fleet there and destroyed most of it. In early 1569, after great hardships, he and fifteen remaining companions reached England. The Spanish, in fact, had proved unwilling to allow open trading, treating foreigners like Hawkins as pirates.

After aiding in the English defeat of the Spanish Armada in 1588, Hawkins and Francis Drake returned to the Caribbean in 1595 with a large fleet, attempting an Indies Voyage, a plan intended to break the territorial power of the Spanish in the New World. The well-prepared Spanish defeated this ill-fated effort at San Juan, Puerto Rico, and at Cartagena, Colombia. They also defeated the English on the Isthmus of Panama at Porto Bello. John Hawkins's career thus came to an ignominious end.

*See also* **Piracy.**

BIBLIOGRAPHY

Kenneth R. Andrews, *The Last Voyage of Drake and Hawkins* (1972).

Sir Julian S. Corbett, *Drake and the Tudor Navy,* 2 vols. (1898, repr. 1988).

C. H. Haring, *The Buccaneers in the West Indies in the XVII Century* (1910).

J. H. Parry et al., *A Short History of the West Indies,* 4th ed. (1987).

J. A. Williamson, *Sir John Hawkins: The Time and the Man* (1927) and *Hawkins of Plymouth* (1949).

*Additional Bibliography*

Hazlewood, Nick. *The Queen's Slave Trader: John Hawkyns, Elizabeth I, and The Trafficking in Human Souls.* New York : William Morrow, 2004.

Kelsey, Harry. *Sir John Hawkins: Queen Elizabeth's Slave Trader.* New Haven, CT: Yale University Press, 2003.

BLAKE D. PATTRIDGE

## HAYA DE LA TORRE, VÍCTOR RAÚL

(1895–1979). Víctor Raúl Haya de la Torre (*b.* 22 February 1895; *d.* 2 August 1979), pivotal politician in Peruvian politics of the twentieth century, founder in 1924 of the Popular Revolutionary Alliance of America (APRA), a movement with continental ambitions, and in 1931 the local Peruvian Aprista Party (PAP). Haya developed an ideology that was initially anti-imperialist but gradually turned conciliatory. He was supported mainly by the lower middle classes of Peru, who were attracted by his charisma, his populist-nationalist views, and his syncretic-Indianist appeal.

Haya was born in Trujillo to a family of provincial distinction. However, his father, Raúl Edmundo, had to rely on his professional income as a journalist to support his family. Peter Klarén proposes that Haya's initial ideological positions were possibly minted in reaction to the expansion of land property by foreign companies in La Libertad at the turn of the century. Haya studied law in Trujillo (1915) and Lima (1917). After meeting the intellectual Manuel González Prada in the Peruvian capital, Haya added anarchistic elements to his provincial bohemian stance.

In 1919, Peruvian workers were fighting for the eight-hour workday. Haya's policy of solidarity with the workers allowed him to surface as student leader. He was president of the Student Federation in 1919 and 1920, leading a student congress in Cuzco, fighting for the reform of the university, and establishing the "popular universities" that constituted the bases of the future PAP. Haya was initially a fellow traveler of the rising socialist movement and collaborated in journalistic activities with socialist intellectual José Carlos Mariátegui.

By 1924, Haya had developed a strong opposition to President Augusto B. Leguía and was imprisoned and exiled. Haya was invited by Mexican indigenist and minister of education José Vasconcelos to Mexico, where he started his continental ideological movement. He broke politically with Mariátegui and became a stern opponent of communism.

After extensive travel and study in Europe he returned to Peru when Leguía fell in 1930. In the 1931 elections, Haya lost to the nationalist colonel Luis Sánchez Cerro. Apristas claimed fraud and organized an uprising in Trujillo in 1932 which was brutally repressed by the army. Haya was imprisoned but then freed after Sánchez Cerro's death in 1933. Thereafter he engaged in clandestine politics, and did not return to open campaigning until 1945, with the election of APRA-supported Luis José Bustamante y Rivero. In 1948, however, another Aprista uprising, this time in Callao, led to repression by General Manuel Odría and Haya's political asylum in the Colombian embassy in Lima (1949–1954).

By 1956 a more subdued Haya established with President Manuel Prado a pact whose objective was an Aprista victory in the 1962 elections. However, once again Haya's presidential ambitions were thwarted by a military coup against Prado. Elections in 1963 resulted in the defeat of Haya by Fernando Belaúnde. During Belaúnde's regime, Haya's party formed a coalition of opposition with his former enemy Odría. The military coup of 1968 against Belaúnde further delayed Haya's ambitions. Only in 1978–1979 was Haya able to occupy the largely honorary post of president of the Constituent Assembly.

*See also* **Prado y Ugarteche, Manuel; Peru, Political Parties: Peruvian Apristá Party (PAP/APRA).**

BIBLIOGRAPHY

Harry Kantor, *The Ideology and Program of the Peruvian Aprista Movement* (1966).

Víctor Raúl Haya De La Torre, *Obras completas,* 7 vols. (1976–1977).

Fredrick Pike, *The Politics of the Miraculous in Peru: Haya de la Torre and the Spiritualist Tradition* (1986).

Steve Stein, *Populism in Peru* (1980).

*Additional Bibliography*

Alexander, Robert Jackson, Víctor Raúl Haya de la Torre, and Julia Elisa Alva Parodi. *Haya de la Torre, Man of the Millennium: His Life, Ideas and Continuing Relevance.* Lima: Víctor Raúl Haya de la Torre Institute, 2001.

Chinguel, Miguel Facundo. *El pensamiento hayista.* Lima, Perú: Universidad Inca Garcilaso de la Vega, 2004.

Graham, Carol. *Peru's APRA: Parties, Politics, and the Elusive Quest for Democracy.* Boulder: L. Rienner Publishers, 1992.

Reveco del Villar, Juan Manue. *Vida y obra de Victor Raul Haya de la Torre.* Lima: Cambio y Desarrollo, Instituto de Investigaciones, 1992.

ALFONSO W. QUIROZ

## HAY–BUNAU-VARILLA TREATY (1903).

Hay–Bunau-Varilla Treaty (1903), an agreement between Panama and the United States providing the legal basis for U.S. construction of the Panama Canal and the creation of the Canal Zone. It was signed on 18 November by U.S. Secretary of State John Hay and Philippe Bunau-Varilla two weeks after the Panamanian revolution against Colombia. Early in 1903, the United States had negotiated a canal treaty with Colombia, but opposition within the Colombian National Assembly to concessions made by the Colombian negotiator (Tomás Herrán) and concerns that Colombia would not receive sufficient economic benefits from the sale of the French canal company's properties to the U.S. led to its defeat. In the U.S. Senate, those who favored a Nicaraguan canal were heartened. As a French national with a strong commitment to a canal in Panama, Bunau-Varilla lobbied for the Panama route and served as intermediary between dissident Panamanians, French canal interests, and important U.S. officials who favored the Panama route. Through his contacts, Bunau-Varilla knew that the U.S. government would guarantee the revolution's success once the Panamanians had acted. As Panama's first representative to the United States, Bunau-Varilla granted virtually every right and privilege the United States had asked for in the earlier Hay–Herrán Treaty with Colombia. These included the right to construct a canal, fortify it, and to "act as if it were sovereign" in the Canal Zone, for $10 million and a $250,000 annual rental. The treaty expired in 1979.

*See also* **Good Neighbor Policy; Panama Canal; Roosevelt, Theodore; Taft Agreement (1904); United States-Latin American Relations.**

BIBLIOGRAPHY

Walter La Feber, *The Panama Canal: The Crisis in Historical Perspective* (1978).

Richard H. Collin, *Theodore Roosevelt's Caribbean: The Panama Canal, the Monroe Doctrine, and the Latin American Context* (1990).

Michael Conniff, *Panama and the United States: The Forced Alliance* (1991).

LESTER D. LANGLEY

## HAYEK, SALMA

**HAYEK, SALMA** (1966–). Actress and television producer Salma Hayek was born on September 2, 1966, in Coatzacoalcos, Mexico. Her portrayal of the title character on the telenovela *Teresa* in 1989 brought her fame in her native Mexico. In 1991 she moved to Los Angeles to study acting. While continuing her studies in the United States, she starred in the Mexican feature *El callejón de los milagros* (1994; Miracle Alley), for which she was nominated for an Ariel, the Mexican equivalent of the Oscars. In 1995 director Robert Rodriguez cast her in his U.S. feature film *Desperado*, and her performance garnered the attention of other Hollywood directors. She then won parts in films such as *From Dusk till Dawn* (1996), *Fools Rush In* (1997), *Dogma* (1999), and *Wild Wild West* (1999); she also starred in the television adaptation of the Julia Alvarez novel *In the Time of the Butterflies* (2001). She was nominated for a 2003 Best Actress Oscar for her portrayal of Mexican artist Frida Kahlo in the film *Frida* (2002), becoming one of only three Mexican actresses to be so nominated. Hayek's own production company, Ventanarosa, was a co-producer of the film. She worked with Robert Rodriguez again for 2003's *Once upon a Time in Mexico.* She is executive producer of the popular American sitcom *Ugly Betty* (which debuted in 2006), an adaptation of the popular Colombian telenovela *Yo Soy Betty la Fea.*

*See also* **Cinema: Since 1990; Kahlo, Frida; Telenovelas.**

BIBLIOGRAPHY

De la Concha, Emilio. "Salma Hayek exporta 'churros' hollywoodenses." *Contenido* 515, no. 4 (May 2006): 60.

Fernández, Melina. "Salma Hayek: Continúa conquistando a Hollywood." *El Mensajero* 17, no. 19 (September 14, 2003): 8–9.

STACY LUTSCH

## HAY-HERRÁN TREATY (1903).

Hay–Herrán Treaty (1903), the agreement of 22 January which, had it been ratified, would have authorized the United States to build a canal through Colombia's province of Panama. The agreement, negotiated by John Hay, U.S. secretary of state, and Tomás Herrán, Colombian chargé d'affaires in Washington, was rejected by the Colombian Senate. That prompted President Theodore Roosevelt and other canal promoters to endorse Panama's separation from Colombia. After independence, the treaty served as a draft for rights ceded by the new republic to the United States.

The treaty empowered the United States to purchase the machinery and works of the French Compagnie Nouvelle in Panama and to build a canal along the route worked by the French. Colombia would grant to the U.S. government a zone six miles wide (excluding the terminal cities of Panamá and Colón) for construction, operation, maintenance, and defense of the canal. Colombia, in exchange, would retain sovereignty over the zone. The United States would pay $10 million upon ratification and $25,000 per year upon completion of the canal. The treaty would remain in effect for one hundred years and was renewable at the sole discretion of the United States. Finally, the United States would operate all administrative services in the zone except the police.

On 12 August 1903 the Colombian Senate unanimously rejected the treaty, which had become hugely unpopular in Bogotá. The main reasons were insufficient compensation, threat to sovereignty, and perpetuity. At this point, agents of the Compagnie Nouvelle and Panamanian conservatives conspired to declare Panama independent, with the blessing of the U.S. government.

*See also* **Colombia: Since Independence; Panama Canal; United States-Latin American Relations.**

BIBLIOGRAPHY

E. Taylor Parks, *Colombia and the United States, 1765–1934* (1935).

Eduardo Lemaitre Román, *Panamá y su separación de Colombia,* 2d ed. (1972).

James M. Skinner, *France and Panama: The Unknown Years, 1894–1908* (1989).

John Major, *Prize Possession: The United States and the Panama Canal, 1903–1977* (1993).

MICHAEL L. CONNIFF

## HAY–PAUNCEFOTE TREATIES (1901).

The Hay–Pauncefote Treaties (1901), were agreements between the United States and Great Britain that permitted the former to build a canal in Central America, thereby clearing the way for U.S. construction of the Panama Canal. The first version, signed on February 5, 1901, envisioned a waterway like the Suez Canal, without fortifications. When U.S. public opinion disputed the neutrality clauses and the Senate amended the treaty to include military protection, U.S. secretary of state John Hay was obliged to renegotiate it with British ambassador Julian Pauncefote. The second treaty, signed on November 18, 1901, did not mention fortifications, implicitly allowing the United States to defend the canal with military installations. It was approved by the newly inaugurated president, Theodore Roosevelt (who aspired to build a canal in Central America), and won easy ratification in the Senate.

Roosevelt and congressional leaders believed that the canal had to be wholly owned and operated by the United States. Simultaneously with the Hay–Pauncefote treaties, the U.S. State Department negotiated a treaty with Nicaragua permitting construction of the canal there. Later events, however, led to selection of the present site in Panama.

These treaties nullified portions of the controversial Clayton–Bulwer Treaty of 1850, which committed the United States and Britain to a jointly run canal with no fortifications. This treaty had elicited severe criticism ever since its approval and was a definite irritant in Anglo-American relations. British acquiescence to its modification signaled recognition of a U.S. sphere of influence in the Caribbean basin and foreshadowed the country's rise to world power status.

*See also* **Clayton-Bulwer Treaty (1850); Panama Canal; Roosevelt, Theodore.**

BIBLIOGRAPHY

Mack, Gerstle. *The Land Divided: A History of the Panama Canal and Other Isthmian Canal Projects.* New York: Octagon Books, 1974.

McCullough, David. *The Path between the Seas: The Creation of the Panama Canal, 1870–1914.* New York: Simon and Schuster, 1977.

Naylor, Robert A. *Penny Ante Imperialism: The Mosquito Shore and the Bay of Honduras, 1600–1914.* London: Associated University Presses, 1989.

Williams, Mary Wilhelmine. *Anglo-American Isthmian Diplomacy, 1815–1915,* 2nd edition. New York: Russell & Russell, 1965.

MICHAEL L. CONNIFF

**HAYWORTH, RITA** (1918–1987). The actress known as Rita Hayworth was born Margarita Carmen Dolores Cansino in Brooklyn on October 18, 1918, to dancer Eduardo Cansino of Seville, Spain, and Volga Hayworth, a showgirl of English-Irish descent. Eduardo and his sister Elisa performed as the Dancing Cansinos. Eduardo trained Margarita in dance from a young age, and some years later, after the family had moved to California and Elisa returned to Spain, he replaced his sister in the act with his daughter. They performed at hotels and clubs in the Southern California-Tijuana area, and it was in one of these venues that Margarita was spotted by a Fox executive and invited to do a screen test. Her dark hair and eyes led to her being typecast as a Latina in her first films in the 1930s, and throughout her career, even after the studios lightened her hair, moved her hairline back and changed her name, she played "exotic" types. In fact, she shot to fame with her performance as Doña Sol in *Blood and Sand* (1941), a story set in Spain based on a novel by Spanish writer Vicente Blasco Ibañez.

Hayworth's photograph in the August 11, 1941 issue of *Life* magazine was one of the most requested pinups during World War II; her sex symbol image earned her the nickname of "The Love Goddess." But Hayworth was not only stunningly beautiful and a talented dancer, she was able to perform in a variety of genres, from musical comedies to noir dramas. She costarred in a number of films with Glenn Ford, including *Gilda* (1946), in which she played the title character, a role recognized by critics and viewers alike as *the* classic Hayworth role. This film brought together her talents as a dramatic actress, dancer and singer, and one of its most famous moments is the "striptease" number (she took off only her gloves), "Put the Blame on Mame."

Hayworth's short-lived marriages included one to Orson Welles (their daughter Rebecca was born in 1944), with whom she stared in *The Lady from Shanghai* (1947), and another to Prince Aly Khan (their daughter Yasmin was born in 1949). Unfortunately, she suffered from early-onset Alzheimer's disease and made few films after the 1950s, mainly minor roles in foreign or independent productions. She was nominated for a Golden Globe Award for Best Motion Picture Actress in 1965 for the film *Circus World* (1964). She died in New York from complications related to Alzheimer's on May 14, 1987.

*See also* **Cinema: From the Silent Film to 1990.**

BIBLIOGRAPHY

Chow, Lesley. "Mish-Mash Planet: The Cult of Rita Hayworth in *You Were Never Lovelier.*" *Bright Lights Film Journal* 53 (August 2006). Available from http://www.brightlightsfilm.com/53/rita.htm.

Dyer, Richard. "Resistance through Charisma: Rita Hayworth and Gilda." In *Women in Film Noir*, new (3rd) edition, ed. E. Ann Kaplan. London: British Film Institute, 1998.

Evans, Peter William. "Putting the Blame on Carmen: The Rita Hayworth Version." In *Carmen: From Silent Film to MTV*, ed. Chris Perriam and Ann Davies. Amsterdam and New York: Rodopi, 2005.

McLean, Adrienne L. *Being Rita Hayworth: Labor, Identity, and Hollywood Stardom.* New Brunswick, NJ: Rutgers University Press, 2004.

Swift, William J., and Graham Cody. "Gilda: Fear and Loathing of the Exquisite Object of Relentless Desire." *Gender and Psychoanalysis* 3:3 (1998): 301–330.

CARYN C. CONNELLY

**HEIREMANS, LUIS ALBERTO** (1928–1964). Luis Alberto Heiremans (*b.* 14 July 1928; *d.* 25 October 1964), Chilean dramatist and writer. With the Chileans Egon Wolff and Jorge Díaz, Heiremans shared international renown as a dramatist. He was an outstanding writer of his country's Generation of '50. He was an active member of the movement that began in the 1940s to reform drama in the university, which has had a great effect on the Latin American stage.

Aside from his highly praised brief narratives, collected in *Los mejores cuentos de Luis Alberto Heiremans* (1966), the critical world has identified three phases of his work. Outstanding in the initial phase is *Moscas sobre el mármol* (1958). The transitional phase includes *Los güenos versos* (1958), *Sigue la estrella* (1958), and *La ronda de la buena nueva* (1961), and the mature phase includes *Buenaventura* (1961), and his exceptional trilogy *Versos de ciego* (1961), *El abanderado* (1962), and *El Tony chico* (1964). His sensibility tended toward the existentialist, and he went beyond traditional literary realism. His works developed a poetic theater that symbolically codifies, sometimes through certain biblical correlations, the elements of custom and folklore in Chile, with the effect of making them universal.

*See also* **Theater.**

BIBLIOGRAPHY

Grinor Rojo, "Luis Alberto Heiremans," in *Latin American Writers,* edited by Carlos A. Solé and Maria Isabel Abreu, (1989).

*Additional Bibliography*

Hurtado, María de la Luz. *Teatro chileno y modernidad: identidad y crisis social.* Irvine: Ediciones de Gestos, 1997.

Thomas Dublé, Eduardo. *La poética teatral de Luis Alberto Heiremans.* Chile: Red Internacional del Libro, 1986.

LUIS CORREA-DÍAZ

---

**HEMISPHERIC AFFAIRS.** Understanding Latin America is not an easy task, particularly given the vast heterogeneity of the region. But despite divergences, many issues are common to the countries in the region and can provide guidance in the endeavor. Latin America can be seen from two perspectives: as a region with its own intra-regional dynamics, and also as it interacts with the United States. The countries of Latin America can be compared in the ways the different countries relate to each other, how their domestic politics compare, how those politics come into play when acting in the international arena, and how these interests help create differing coalitions when dealing with various issues. The disproportionate power of the United States—both political and economic—defines its role in the hemisphere, and also influences both the individual countries of Latin America and their varying alliances.

Excluding either of these dimensions would provide an incomplete picture of the complex forces at work in the hemisphere. The distinction is more apparent in some issues than others. Population migration and drug trafficking are broadly defined issues that create similar problems for most Latin American countries in their relations with the United States, although global issues such as human rights and democracy create overlaps that make the distinctions less neat. Trade, development, and economic growth are less easily categorized because the priorities of the United States do not always align with those of Latin America, and even within Latin America priorities diverge depending on political leanings. An awareness of these interrelationships is essential to fully understand Latin America, its affairs, and its dynamics.

### U.S.–LATIN AMERICAN RELATIONS

Relations between Latin America and the United States are among the most studied and scrutinized issues in any review of the hemisphere's past, present, and future, and also among the most controversial. There has never been a consensual vision of this relationship, either in the United States or in Latin America. From the time of the Monroe Doctrine in 1823, when the United States declared that it would not countenance any intervention by a foreign (meaning European) power in the hemisphere, through the Texan secession in 1836 and the subsequent Mexican-American War (1846–1848), extending to the so-called Spanish–American War in 1898 and all the way to George W. Bush's 2001 attempt to truly elevate the hemisphere's priority on Washington's agenda, the relationship has been a difficult one, to say the least.

U.S.–Latin American relations have encompassed a variety of issues over the years: territorial expansion and U.S. claims against Latin American states; trade and investment; geopolitical and ideological questions during the cold war; human rights and democracy (sporadically); security (cooperation to keep communism out of the continent during the

**A Mexican army officer burns confiscated marijuana plants, 1977.** Crop eradication in the late twentieth century failed to control the cultivation of marijuana and other drugs and has since been abandoned. The issue of Latin American supply and U.S. consumption of illegal drugs remains a contentious issue on both sides of the border. © TOM NEBBIA/CORBIS

cold war or to counter terrorism in the early twenty-first century). In the latter twentieth century the particularly sensitive and problematic issues of immigration and drugs arose, though some nations, such as Chile and Argentina, rarely find either issue raised in their conversations with Washington, and Uruguay, Costa Rica, and Venezuela have few disputes with the United States over immigration. For most other countries in Latin America, these are among the most salient questions in their dealings with the United States. There is no link between the two issues, although many people often associate them, on occasion even tying them to terrorism and security. But these issues are nonetheless complex, long-standing, and defiant of any simple solutions or answers.

***Hemispheric Drug Issues.*** The traditional view of the hemispheric drug issue has been, on the part of the United States, that Latin American nations are the producers of most of the illicit substances consumed in the United States—cocaine, heroin, marijuana, and meta-amphetamines—and that because of corruption and negligence, their governments fail to carry out a proper job of drug enforcement. The traditional Latin American perspective has always been that the United States is the world's largest consumer of drugs, and that as long as its insatiable demand is not curbed, it will remain almost impossible to control the supply side of the equation. Both sides have a point. On one hand, Washington asked Mexico during World War II to cultivate poppies in the mountains of Sinaloa to make morphine for the military, because the traditional Asian sources were unavailable. On the other hand, the complicity between some Latin American states, including Mexico, Guatemala, Cuba, Colombia, Bolivia, and Peru, and the drug trade has never really been rebutted by the states themselves. What is in dispute is where the responsibility lies.

In the early twenty-first century the drug issue between the northern and southern halves of the hemisphere is more convoluted than ever. Most drug-enforcement efforts in the past have largely failed. Crop eradication through spraying and weeding, for example, became too noxious or expensive, environmentally, socially, and economically, and most such projects have been abandoned. Alternative crop support programs have failed because the price differential between what coca leaf, marijuana, or poppies and conventional crops will fetch on the market is just too wide. In some cases cultivation is simply shifted from one country to another, as occurred with the spread of coca leaf cultivation from the Chapare region in Bolivia to the Upper Huallaga Valley in Peru, then to Colombia and more recently to the Brazilian Amazon. The same happens with transshipment routes. In the mid-1980s the south Florida route to the United States from Colombia was largely shut down; the drug cartels moved to Mexico, where they have remained ever since. To compound the problem, even when progress is made in reducing the demand for certain substances, cocaine and crack, for example, the use of other drugs, such as meta-amphetamines, increases to take their place. Even if by some standards overall drug consumption is dropping in the United States, it appears to be rising in other wealthy nations, such as those of western Europe.

A further complication stems from the fact that the while most Latin American nations were once primarily involved in drug production and transshipment, many have ultimately become major consumers as well. In countries such as Colombia, Brazil, and Mexico, the notion of Latin America as the source of supply and the United States as the source of demand has become increasingly obsolete. Moreover, the money for drugs and the traffic in arms and precursor chemicals for producing cocaine and meta-amphetamines flows in a north-south direction, not the other way around. Consequently, the violence and criminality generally associated with drug trafficking and consumption is more frequently appearing everywhere, in the major cities of Latin America as well as in the larger U.S. cities. The distinction between producer and consumer societies is more and more blurred, and the problems facing both the United States and Latin America are increasingly similar. This has begun to lead to greater cooperation, and also to a broader debate about what the best response may be to the challenges drugs represent for everyone.

Legalization does not seem to be a viable approach anywhere: not in Latin America, because unless the United States followed suit it would provoke a major crisis in hemispheric relations; not in Europe (with a few urban exceptions) because drug users would flock to the continent if it were to legalize unilaterally as was exemplified in the Zurich needle park experiment in the 1990s; not in the United States, because the political environment does not seem to be conducive to it. So what can be done? Not very much. Each country can be more or less effective in attempting to fend off the scourge of drug trafficking and consumption, but paradoxically, as a larger number of Latin American countries experience economic success and broaden their middle classes, they also, inevitably, expand their market for drugs. Some, such as Mexico, can perform much more effectively, for example, in sealing off its southern border and stop drug traffic through its territory but that will only drive the flows going northward to other areas; a win for Mexico, but a loss for others, and a draw for the United States. Ultimately the best solution is either that the consumption of illicit substances be freed of the stigma, enormous profits, and criminality wrought by its illegal character, or that through education, jobs, and publicity, demand be driven down so dramatically that prices fall, and drug trafficking is no longer a profitable trade.

***Immigration.*** Immigration is an even more delicate affair, full of twists and turns. It has become one of the most important items on the U.S.–Latin American agenda for countries ranging from Mexico to Ecuador, and including almost all of Central America and the Caribbean. It involves more than ten million undocumented citizens of these nations in the United States, with an influx of probably above half a million yearly. Immigrants are responsible for more than $40 billion in remittances every year and account for an average of more than a death per day at the Mexican border, as well as uncounted other deaths on the trip north from countries as far away as Brazil and Bolivia. While migration is not a new issue—the first emigrants from Mexico to the United States traveled in the late nineteenth century—it has always been a

**Migrant farm workers in rural North Carolina, 2005.** U.S. agriculture relies heavily on undocumented migrant workers, mostly from Latin America. Some estimates put the number of undocumented immigrants in the United States at eleven million. © ANDREW LICHTENSTEIN/CORBIS

contentious one (witness Operation Wetback in the early 1950s, when hundreds of thousands of Mexicans were forcibly deported). Immigration issues have attained greater prominence in the twenty-first century than ever before, and the related problems have no easy solution.

By its very nature, immigration reflects a dual perspective. Americans acknowledge that their economy needs workers from abroad, and that theirs is a country of immigrants. But, they insist, those immigrants must enter and reside in the country legally. Latin Americans point out that U.S. law is constantly changing, that it is hypocritical—Washington has been letting people in without authorization since the early twentieth century—and that immigrants' contributions to U.S. society and well-being are not appreciated or recognized. Americans are deeply divided about immigration questions—some favoring legalization and a guest worker program, others supporting deportation and a fence on the border—and many Latin Americans wonder whether at the end of the day out-migration is good for their countries or not.

Public opinion is inflamed in Latin America when children die in trucks or railroad cars on their way north, or when the U.S. Congress votes to build a wall in the Arizona Sonoran Desert; U.S. citizens are shocked when the extent of unauthorized immigration becomes apparent in communities across the United States heretofore unaccustomed to a foreign presence. Latin Americans want and need the remittances sent home by emigrants, but not the loss their departure entails for their society; Americans want the quality of life, competitiveness, and low prices for many goods that unauthorized immigration provides, but not the violation of the rule of law it implies, nor the diffusion of immigration to areas of the country unfamiliar with the phenomenon.

**Utah Army National Guard soldiers build a wall at the U.S./Mexican border, 2006.** The question of immigration from Latin America to the United States has become one of the most prominent issues in the early twenty-first century, with no easy solutions. © JACK KURTZ/ZUMA/CORBIS

In the long term, several converging trends may provide at least a partial solution to this controversial and sensitive issue. At some point, the enormous wage differential between the main sending countries—Mexico, Central America, the Caribbean, and increasingly Peru and Ecuador in South America—and the United States will diminish, making the costs and perils of out-migration too high in relation to its benefits for migrants. And at some point—no one knows for certain when—the American economy's appetite for low-wage, low-skill labor will slake, and unauthorized migrants, or legal ones for that matter, will no longer find employment almost immediately on arrival in the United States. In addition, as population growth in most sending countries continues to drop precipitously, the population will age, and the pool of potential emigrants will shrink. But all of this will take years.

In the meantime, the best way to address the issue is cooperatively, that is, not as an exclusively domestic U.S. concern but as a hemispheric problem. Moreover, reaching even temporary solutions will require compromises both within the United States and also by the originating countries' governments. Washington could legalize those who have already crossed the border; the Latin American nations could make greater efforts to control outflows. The United States could accept a temporary worker program that avoids and corrects abuses and mistakes of the past; the Latin American countries could share responsibility with Washington in managing these programs and ensuring that their citizens are not exploited or mistreated. It will not be easy.

There have never been simple answers to the riddles and conundrums of U.S.–Latin American relations. Some, such as questions of trade and investment, have been settled partly through lengthy negotiations. Others have been largely laid to rest thanks to history: The end of the cold war eliminated the main geopolitical component that had poisoned hemispheric relations since 1947. New issues have emerged, and on occasion greater accord than ever before has been achieved, on human rights, democracy, and the fight against corruption. But some issues, such as drugs or immigration, will just not go away. They will continue to be present and to plague north-south relations in the hemisphere for years to come. Impatience, over-simplification, and extreme points of view, however understandable on occasion, cannot be a substitute for wisdom, tolerance, and statesmanship. Only thanks to virtues of this nature will these immensely difficult matters be addressed appropriately.

## HUMAN RIGHTS AND DEMOCRACY

Democracy and human rights should have been present on Latin America's agenda in the past, although neither the hemisphere's elites nor the general population have typically recognized this fact. That is perhaps the best way to sum up the hemisphere's attitude toward these fundamental matters in the past; it also illustrates how far Latin America has traveled since the early 1990s: In the early twenty-first century these are perhaps the central questions facing its societies and future.

As the nineteenth century wore on and the twentieth century approached, some Latin American countries began to construct a very basic structure of democratic rule, usually of a highly elitist nature. Chile, Argentina, Uruguay, and Brazil (after the end of the Empire) all established electoral procedures. In general they all restricted suffrage rather severely, tolerated labor unions (relatively), and accepted at least a partial separation of powers, in most cases featuring a powerful legislative branch, an overwhelming executive branch, and, almost always, a submissive judiciary. This was in the best of cases; in others, the chaos of insurrections, foreign invasions, coups d'état, assassinations, and revolutions was met with the emergence of perennial dictatorships such as that of Porfirio Díaz in Mexico and Juan Vicente Gómez in Venezuela, with numerous shorter-lived variations across Central America and the Caribbean.

Unfortunately, even the best of the post-colonial governments ultimately collapsed. With the coming of the Great Depression, highly fragile democracies, erected on excessively unequal social foundations that excluded and disenfranchised the bulk of the population, were rapidly replaced by military or semi-military regimes. Takeovers by the armed forces or other authoritarian sectors occurred in Argentina and Brazil in 1930, and in Colombia, Peru, and even to some extent in Chile during the first half of the twentieth century.

The chasm between theory and practice present in the early Latin American democracies extended to the realm of human rights. Basic rights such as freedom of expression, association, and religion, due process, and habeas corpus were largely absent from the real life of practically every Latin American nation, with the possible exceptions of Uruguay and Costa Rica. Certain regimes were more repressive than others; some governments were every now and then democratically elected, but were soon overthrown; some political systems achieved lasting stability and regularity through pro forma rigged elections; but by and large democratic rule and respect for human rights continued be sorely lacking in the region as a whole until the early 1960s.

Then two events precipitated a short-lived but promising change that was a harbinger of things to come. The Cuban Revolution of 1959 showed that even if broad sectors of sophisticated though unequal societies were not hungry for democracy and human rights, they certainly were desperate for social justice and economic progress. The route sketched out by Fidel Castro and Che Guevara was appealing in many nations eager for equality and prosperity, or in their absence, at least the trappings of democracy. In Washington, the Kennedy administration decided that any response to the perceived threat from Havana had to include a restoration, or in some cases the beginning, of democratic rule and a minimum respect for human rights. The Alliance for Progress, an economic aid and development plan launched by John F. Kennedy in 1961, never really got off the ground, but it laid the groundwork for what would happen later. In Colombia, Venezuela, Peru, Chile, Uruguay, Argentina, and Brazil, mainly for domestic reasons, but also very clearly in response to actions in Havana and Washington, democratic rule and human rights flourished during a brief but significant interlude in the early 1960s.

It could not last. The menace of the Cuban Revolution led elites throughout the region to retrench behind bloody dictatorships, and Kennedy's death together with the Vietnam quagmire quickly dissipated any interest on Washington's part in what was occurring south of the Rio Grande. One country after another lapsed into authoritarian rule, increasingly managed by the armed forces directly, and taking repression and human-rights violations to extremes unknown until then. Beginning with the 1964 coup in Brazil and extending into the early 1980s, even countries previously distinguished by their democratic traditions, such as Chile and Uruguay, were engulfed by the authoritarian tide.

Despite these setbacks, the seed of change had been sown. From the early 1980s onward, Latin America began to move firmly in the direction of representative democracy and respect for human rights. The military began to withdraw from power, either because of its utter humiliation, as in Argentina's defeat by Britain in the Falkland Islands (Malvinas); through sheer exhaustion and internal divisions (Brazil after 1985); or through miscalculation, as when Chilean dictator Augusto Pinochet lost a 1988 referendum to extend his presidency. For whatever reason, elections began to be held almost everywhere. In addition, they were increasingly free and fair, thanks to civil watchdog groups, international observers from various organizations, better electoral laws and independent authorities, and because outgoing rulers were reluctant to step in and blatantly rig the vote. Even Mexico, known both for the stability and fraudulent nature of its electoral processes, began to change.

The political situation in Latin America in the early twenty-first century is remarkably different from what it had been during the first two centuries of independence. With the exception of Cuba, power is contended for, and obtained only at, the ballot box. State repression, at a national or federal level, has been largely eradicated; due process has started to prevail in most cases; freedom to create political parties, unions, and associations is widely guaranteed; the media are largely free from direct censorship; vibrant groups in civil society fight for women's rights, indigenous people's rights, reproductive health, and choice (or the opposite); and the armed forces have gone back to their barracks, if not for good, at least for a considerable period of time. What's more, this progress has been partly locked in by a series of international and regional treaties that most Latin American governments have signed and ratified. These covenants are not iron-clad, and can of course be broken, but instruments such as the Inter-American Democratic Charter, and the now better-funded and more accredited Inter-American Commission on Human Rights (in Washington) and the Inter-American Court of Human Rights (in Costa Rica) constitute significant obstacles to backsliding.

Furthermore, in poll after poll, year after year, country after country, Latin American public opinion shows itself increasingly convinced of the virtues of democracy in comparison to any other type of government. Ratings of well over 70 percent prevail in most countries, and the lowest ones are never below 50 percent. The notion that people are becoming disenchanted with democracy because it has not delivered prosperity or eliminated poverty and inequality is simply not born out by continent-wide surveys carried out over several years. This does not mean that Latin Americans are satisfied with how democracy functions in their societies, but simply that they prefer it to the alternative: the authoritarian regimes they previously suffered under.

Despite this undeniable progress, very real problems in the realms of democracy and human rights still plague Latin America. Although electoral systems are in place that generally guarantee free and fair elections, they do not insure against other excesses. Losing candidates in various countries, including Mexico, Venezuela, and Brazil, have complained that reelection procedures or their equivalent have allowed incumbents to use the power and resources of the state in favor of their candidates and against the opposition. Media coverage is unregulated, and in some countries, outrageous. National elections generally work well, but local elections are often beset by tampering and cheating. Representation mechanisms in congress are still deficient—congressional representation is still deficient as members of congress typically do not respond to their constituencies, but to other political interests—and the prevailing political systems in place at least nominally since independence, modeled on the U.S. system of checks and balances, have led (now that the laws are respected in their letter and spirit) to gridlock or outright paralysis and endless bickering between the legislative and executive branches.

Democracy and respect for human rights are not limited to electoral matters and basic freedoms, as essential as these may be. If the state no longer directly engages in repression or violence against its citizens, other individuals, and sometimes local and regional authorities, do. Indeed, the violence and criminality suffered by millions of Latin Americans is largely inflicted upon them by gangs, drug cartels, paramilitary groups, and other criminals tolerated or even encouraged by governments at the local level. There is scant recourse against them: The judicial system is often in the hands of the very perpetrators of the crimes it should be judging and punishing. Democracy starts with elections, but does not end there. Protection from abuse and violence is one of the main responsibilities of a democratic government, and most Latin American states fail miserably at this.

Transparency and accountability is another weak area. While many countries have transparency laws and strong sanctions against corruption, the scandals that continue to emerge in practically every Latin American nation show that the problem has not gone away. Transparent, honest, and accountable governance is a requirement of democratic rule, even if it can never be totally and permanently achieved. In this respect, Latin America still has a long road to travel. The rule of law is also problematic. Due process, property rights, and legal security for people, property, and transactions are woefully inadequate in most of the region. Judicial procedures are slow, opaque, often corrupt, and seriously skewed in favor of those with money. Enormous numbers of crimes go unreported; large tracts of slums around and within the great cities of the hemisphere lack deeds or land titles; the size of the underground or informal economy can sometimes reach that of the formal one; bureaucracies are still notoriously slow, inefficient, corrupt, and expensive. In these complex and subtle aspects of democracy and human rights, the region has its work cut out for it.

Despite the advances democracy has made in Latin America, a new and troubling trend seems to be emerging in many countries. Since 1998, in nations including Argentina, Venezuela, Bolivia, and Ecuador, leaders have been elected in an unquestionably democratic fashion but have subsequently begun to change constitutions, stack legislative and judicial branches, control the media, govern from the streets, harass and intimidate the opposition, and manipulate elections brazenly. Leaders come to power in democratic elections, but govern less and less democratically. They rarely broach the limits of democracy and respect for human rights, but they stretch those limits as far as they can. They seek to transform the constitutional framework in which they operate in a direction that clearly is aiming toward a concentration, and perpetuation, of power. It is too soon to know whether this represents a lasting trend or a brief and partial interruption in the progress toward democratic governance. Despite these problems, however, Latin Americans have much to celebrate. The region appears to have made its peace with representative democracy and the respect for human rights that so many of its founders sought, and never achieved.

## THE SURGE OF THE LEFT

One of the most significant political developments in Latin America is the marked trend since the 1990s for parties self-identified with the ideological left to be elected, one after another, in various countries. Leftist governments have taken power in Argentina, Bolivia, Brazil, Chile, Ecuador, Nicaragua, Peru, Uruguay, and Venezuela. Together, these countries represent more than half of the Latin American nations, and account for about 60 percent of the population in the hemisphere. Few of these leaders will face presidential elections again until the end of 2010 and those who do are highly unlikely to lose power, so this phenomenon will most likely last at least until 2010. Aside from the symbolic importance of having parties from the left in power, or the possibility of a policy shift derived from their ideological orientation, the redefinition of political alliances in the hemisphere represents a significant trend. In political terms, it is hard to understand Latin America without acknowledging these developments and their effects both on relations among Latin American countries and between Latin America and the United States.

***Precedents and Historical Background.*** With very few exceptions, the ideological left in Latin America has been a constant political presence in the hemisphere since the 1950s, assuming different forms in a variety of countries. Communists, socialists, social democrats, populists, or left-leaning political-military groups emerged either as ideological currents, as political parties or, especially during the 1960s to 1980s, as armed groups seeking to change the political landscape. Yet with the exception of Cuba, and briefly in Chile in the 1970s and Nicaragua in the 1980s, the left was never able to assume power and enact its agenda, let alone be competitive in the polls. Until, that is, the 1990s.

The most celebrated benchmark for the left in Latin America was the Cuban Revolution and Fidel Castro's entry into Havana on January 8, 1959. As a result of this feat, advocates of a revolutionary approach to power gained prominence and the influence of Cuba was ubiquitous among the Latin American left. The 1960s and 1970s were thus characterized by a politically active but later marginal left in some countries (including Brazil, Chile, and Uruguay) or by an actively revolutionary left in others (including Uruguay, Brazil, and Argentina, Venezuela, and Bolivia), usually supported by Cuba and usually with little success. The exceptions were the Socialist Party of Chile (PS) that took Salvador Allende to the presidency from 1970 to 1973, when he was overthrown by a military coup, and the Sandinista National Liberation Front (FSLN) that defeated Nicaragua's Anastasio Somoza on July 19, 1979 and remained in power until they were defeated in elections on February 25, 1990.

The 1980s followed a different pattern, both in the intensity of political activity on the left and in rapidly changing economic and political conditions. On the one hand, Cuban-backed guerrilla movements were much more active than in the previous decade in countries including El Salvador, Grenada, Guatemala, and Nicaragua, although without much success. On the other hand, the end of the cold war, prompted by the implementation of perestroika in the USSR and culminating with fall of the Berlin Wall in 1989, as well as a 1980s shift in economic paradigms toward neoliberalism, changed the political landscape in which the Latin American left would operate, and forced it to adapt to these new conditions. By the end of the decade, almost all Communist parties had virtually disappeared (except for El Salvador and Uruguay), and the prevalent view on the left had evolved to advocating legal elections as the preferred means to achieve power.

On the opposite end of the spectrum, by the beginning of the 1990s a new type of radical leftist guerrillas emerged in various Latin American countries: Peru's Shining Path, Colombia's Revolutionary Armed Forces of Colombia (FARC), El Salvador's Farabundo Martí National Liberation Front (FMLN), and Guatemala's Guerrilla Army of the Poor (EGP). Unlike their predecessors, their relative success was based on creating a base of supporters among peasants and advocating change through long-term struggle. None of them became powerful enough to change their countries' government, as had occurred in Cuba, or to force radical changes in the political landscape.

***Political Characteristics.*** At the beginning of the 1990s only Cuba, Nicaragua, and Chile had governments linked to the left. Cuba and Nicaragua had gained theirs by means of armed revolution, and Nicaragua's Sandinistas were defeated in the polls in February of 1990. Chile, through an alliance of parties that included the Chilean left, elected Patricio Aylwin president on December 14, 1989. Aside from the Chilean socialists, no other parties from the left were elected into office between the 1970s and the 1980s, although some of its candidates were able to amass significant amounts of votes during this period, including Cuauhtémoc Cárdenas in Mexico and Luiz Inácio Lula da Silva in Brazil. Prior to the election of Salvador Allende (1970–1973) in Chile, there had been some brief experiments with governments that advanced a leftist agenda in Guatemala with Jacobo Arbenz (1951–1954), the Dominican Republic with Juan Bosch (1963), and Brazil with João Goulart (1961–1964).

The left became more adept at playing by democratic rules in the 1990s, presenting candidates in regular elections and seeing encouraging results. The left has been in power in Chile since 2000, Venezuela since 1999, Brazil since 2003, Argentina since 2003, Panama since 2004, Uruguay since 2005, Bolivia since 2006, Nicaragua since 2007, Peru since 2006, and Ecuador since 2007. The winning candidates in these countries all portrayed themselves as leftists. An interesting question is whether all of these governments have enough common traits to share that single category.

A closer assessment of the various parties suggests that there are clear differences between them. At the very least, there are two clearly distinguishable groups, one a moderate and modern left identifiable in Chile, Brazil, and Uruguay, and another a populist version seen in Venezuela, Nicaragua, Bolivia, Ecuador, and Peru, and to an extent in Argentina and Mexico. The leftist parties have varying origins: Some are the natural descents of the traditional left, others appeared with appealing new candidates and discourse. Some aim for long-term results that derive from sustainable policies, others look for more immediate results as means to remain in power. Some play by the rules, while others simply ignore institutions that stand in the way of their goals.

Many reasons have been advanced to explain the recent surge of the left. The failure of previous economic models to cope with poverty and reduce inequality is frequently cited. The left advocates redistribution of wealth and elimination of poverty as a matter of principle, so it seems reasonable that it should be supported by those who would benefit the most from these policies, namely the poor in Latin America, who constitute the majority of the population. The argument would carry more weight if it could also explain why it was not until the 1990s that the left began to win elections. Poverty and inequality have been constants in Latin America that have not particularly worsened during those years. In fact, the new leftist governments have not implemented many radical or self-sustaining programs to reduce poverty. Those countries most successful at reducing poverty, namely Chile and Brazil, have done so by implementing programs inspired by principles more in accordance with the right, as is the case of the Brazilian Bolsa Família program or the Mexican Progresa program, designed and implemented by the orthodox government of Ernesto Zedillo.

A much better explanation for the rise of the left in Latin America and the policies it implements can be found in the confluence of two factors: better candidates and change in voters' tastes. There is little doubt that the leftist parties have been able to nominate superior candidates since the 1990s, whether they are evaluated in terms of discourse, charisma, effectiveness, or credibility. And these candidates have been able to appeal to enough voters to win elections. At the same time, assessments of ideological values among Latin Americans show that the candidates from the left have broadened their appeal and acquired votes from the center and the right of the ideological spectrum. As their constituencies have broadened, governments from the left have less leeway to enact radical policies if they want to remain in office. And this explains why many governments from the left typically enact centrists policies. These seemingly contradictory trends help explain why most of the leftist candidates are not more radical: The voters would not re-elect them.

***U.S. Relations.*** The surge of the left since the 1990s has had an important impact on relationships both within Latin America and between Latin American countries and the United States. On the international front, ties between the United States and Latin America have become strained. This began with a shift in U.S. priorities following the terrorist attacks of September 11, 2001, and worsened as a result of the strengthening position of Venezuelan president Hugo Chávez Frías (1999– ), who undertook the task of preserving Cuban ideals in the hemisphere. This translated into a new political landscape in the region for the United States. As a political offspring of Cuban socialism, President Chávez has assumed the hemispheric role of critic of American policies. His administration supports a closely knit offensive to free trade alternatives ranging from proposing alternative treaties to organizing protests against U.S. presidents. Venezuela finances missions of Cuban doctors in various countries in the hemisphere and has formed commercial and diplomatic ties with countries on the U.S. blacklist. As a result of these tactics, Venezuela has gained the support of Bolivia, Argentina, Ecuador, and Nicaragua.

Chávez's activism has resulted in a de facto division of the Latin American countries into two camps: one that actively opposes the United States, and one that passively resists Chávez's influence. While the populist left engages constantly in confrontations over American policies and initiatives, the moderate left has not aligned itself directly with the United States but does not oppose Chávez directly either, in an effort to maintain a semblance of balance in the hemisphere.

## REGIONAL TRADE AND ECONOMIC INTEGRATION

The case for Latin American unification has arisen time and again as an echo of the Bolivarian dream of a unified hemisphere. Attempts to integrate

Latin America have been made in the political arena through alliances such as the Organization of American States (OAS) and in the economic realm through common or enhanced trade policies. In the twenty-first century the trend is to economic unity and is mostly based on free trade and investment theories that believe that economies operating without the distortions generated by tariffs and with investment allocated efficiently should grow more quickly, specialize, and engage in virtuous cycles of growth.

Ideologically, the processes and policies that represent sound economic policy have undergone a paradigm shift since the 1980s. The economic and trade policies of import substitution industrialization (ISI) advocated by the United Nations Economic Commission for Latin America and the Caribbean (ECLAC) since the 1950s led to a period of excessive growth without integration and ended with the economic crises of the early 1980s. They were replaced with a new paradigm, the so-called Washington Consensus, a form of market economics or neoliberalism that advocated self-sustained growth by reducing the size of government, keeping regulation to a minimum, and reducing distortions in domestic markets. Crucial in this mix was the reduction of tariffs and subsidies to allow the free flow of goods and capital across borders. The resulting efficient allocation of resources was expected to contribute to lower production costs, increase employment, and foster long-lasting and sustainable periods of economic growth.

A variety of attempts to achieve economic integration have been undertaken since the beginning of the 1990s and were based on regional trade. They included the Southern Common Market (Mercosur; 1991), the Central American Common Market (CACM; since its reinstatement in 1991), the Andean Community of Nations (CAN; since its trade reorientation in 1993), the North American Free Trade Agreement (NAFTA; 1992), and the Dominican Republic-Central America-United States Free Trade Agreement (CAFTA-DR, 2004). Parallel attempts at a comprehensive reduction of trade barriers were negotiated in Free Trade Area of the Americas (FTAA) discussions beginning in 1994 and from 2001 in the Doha Round of the World Trade Organization (WTO), which was not specific to the Americas but would have a strong impact on lowering trade barriers worldwide.

Trade liberalization has been implemented through two main modes. The first is a hybrid in which a group of countries lower or eliminate barriers among themselves while maintaining them for outside countries. In this scheme, countries can agree to protect a given industry during its developing stages, strengthen its exporting potential, and eventually integrate it into an open market. This is the premise underlying Mercosur. The second model is much more ambitious and attempts the regional integration of blocks and regions where the asymmetries between members can be utilized to exploit competitive advantages. For instance, a member might produce and freely export labor-intensive products at a lower price than the same good produced in a capital-intensive economy. This is the premise of CAFTA–DR and was the original aim of the FTAA.

***Mercosur.*** The Southern Common Market (Mercosur) was created by the Treaty of Asunción on March 26, 1991. Mercosur brought together Argentina, Brazil, Paraguay, and Uruguay in the common task of lowering trade barriers, coordinating economic policies, and establishing a common external tariff that would shape its customs-union character. Unlike previous domestic-market approaches, Mercosur explicitly sought to take advantage of the free flow of goods among members by lowering trade barriers while maintaining a degree of protection from nonmember countries using a common external tariff.

Early on in the implementation of Mercosur, there were clear signs of success in coordinating tariff reductions, increasing intra-regional trade, and fostering investment in the region. But the economic crises of the 1990s highlighted the ideological differences among its members, especially Brazil and Argentina, who were particularly affected. The shared objectives of Mercosur played a secondary role to individual country's needs to deal with their own economic imperatives. By the second half of the 1990s, Argentina and Brazil had engaged in a series of measures ranging from unilateral increases in tariffs for nonmember countries to using antidumping measures against other members. The stability of the agreement was further complicated as the time came

**Protestors demonstrate against globalization and NAFTA at the third World Social Forum in Porto Alegre, Brazil, 2003.** AP IMAGES

to enact the agreed-upon reductions in tariffs on sensible areas for all members, chiefly the automotive and sugar sectors. This, in turn, highlights the difficulties of enforcing trade agreements when no supranational body exists, as is often the case in international relations. There are obviously mechanisms to resolve controversies, but the enforcement of resolutions is based on members' compliance or on the threat of retaliation in the trade arena, which might not be effective when a country is willing to pay the cost in order to protect a politically sensitive sector. Despite these problems, Venezuela became the fifth member of Mercosur on December 8, 2005. Bolivia, Chile, Colombia, Ecuador, and Peru participate as associate members, and Mexico as an observer.

***NAFTA and CAFTA-DR.*** An alternative economic paradigm takes advantage of asymmetries between economies, mainly centered on providing members preferential access to the U.S. market while opening borders to new markets for U.S. exports. This strategy was formally inaugurated with the entry into force of the North American Free Trade Agreement (NAFTA) between Canada, the United States, and Mexico in 1994, with mixed results. The three countries' economies have definitely integrated, to the extent that some believe NAFTA helped Mexico rebound from the 1994–1995 peso crisis, which could have spread throughout the region.

NAFTA is not the only agreement to follow this path. Ever since president George W. Bush obtained trade promotion authority (also called fast-track authority) from Congress in August 2002, the United States formally began to negotiate the Central America Free Trade Agreement (CAFTA), based on the same economic premises as NAFTA. Negotiations between Costa Rica, El Salvador, Guatemala, Honduras, Nicaragua, and the United States were initiated. The Dominican Republic joined in 2004, and the agreement was renamed the Dominican Republic-Central America-United States Free Trade Agreement (CAFTA-DR).

CAFTA-DR's main purpose was to create a free-trade zone between these countries and the

United States, but one interesting feature of CAFTA-DR was that some of its members' trade privileges were widened by virtue of membership in other free trade agreements. Members of CAFTA-DR could benefit from rules of origin exemptions from other agreements where the United States is a member, such as NAFTA, when exporting to the United States using materials originating in Canada or Mexico, and by virtue of NAFTA and bilateral free-trade agreements with other countries in CAFTA-DR, Mexico could also benefit from preferential treatment in this area. This is especially important in the case of textiles, because one of the aims of CAFTA-DR is to enhance competitiveness with Asian markets. As a result, a de facto integrated area was created (although a more efficient way of achieving this outcome would be by engaging in comprehensive regional agreements, such as the stalled FTAA).

***The Free Trade Area of the Americas.*** The first Summit of the Americas, held in Miami in December 1994, saw the launching of an initiative aimed at eliminating trade barriers, unfair practices, and subsidies among all countries in the hemisphere. The initiative came to be known as the Free Trade Area of the Americas (FTAA). In theory, by enhancing free trade, it would contribute to economic integration in the region, which in turn would spur investment, fostering a virtuous cycle of growth. By linking the sustainability of democratic regimes to economic well-being, the FTAA would become a de facto discursive instrument of democratic stability and poverty alleviation in the region that would be in place no later than 2005.

The FTAA, built upon existing bilateral and multilateral trade agreements, would become the largest block of countries (in terms of territorial expansion) to integrate through free trade. The natural asymmetries within such a varied group of countries were bound to create difficulties and complicate the alignment of interests. The United States and Canada were the only two fully industrialized democracies in the Americas, which meant that their priorities diverged from those of the Latin American countries, especially when dealing with agricultural subsidies. The two largest Latin American economies were already engaged in their own unique trade strategies: Mexico actively opened its economy to the world through free trade and reciprocal investment agreements; Brazil engaged in export-oriented trade strategies coupled with tight protection of its own domestic markets. Further complications resulted because members of Mercosur, the South American tariff union, were reluctant to lose their preferential status relative to nonmembers, which would be a necessary condition if they were to become FTAA partners.

The United States engaged early on in a negotiation strategy that used preferential access to its own market to gain leverage in convincing reluctant countries to join the union. The FTAA would give preferential access to the largest market in the world, namely the U.S. market, so few countries wanted to be excluded from gaining or improving their access to it. By 2002 the United States had engaged in a parallel strategy of bilateral and subregional negotiations with Chile, Central America, and the Dominican Republic, and announced negotiations with Panama, Bolivia, Colombia, Ecuador, and Peru. This strategy was something of a two-edged sword: It had the potential to undermine the efforts for a unified agreement, but it could also advance bilaterally on issues that were hard to deal with multilaterally.

The negotiations were further complicated by an overlap of deadlines: The Doha Round of the World Trade Organization (WTO) was also scheduled to be completed by 2005. The fate of the FTAA was inevitably linked to that of the Doha Round. Both negotiations had the common objective of eliminating trade barriers. Unfortunately, progress in the FTAA could translate into disadvantages in the WTO negotiations, and vice versa. Concessions granted by Latin American countries in the WTO negotiations had to be automatically granted in the FTAA negotiations, as the former included a larger number of countries. But concessions made at the FTAA table could reduce leverage in WTO negotiations, as Latin American countries would be losing bargaining chips. The conflicts proved fatal. The Doha Round negotiations collapsed in the fifth WTO ministerial meeting on September of 2003 in Cancún and the FTAA negotiations did the same during the eighth FTAA ministerial meeting in Miami in 2005.

A further effort to revive the WTO negotiations was attempted at the sixth ministerial meeting in Hong Kong on December of 2005, without much success. The FTAA has not progressed since 2005. Neither of these initiatives has been cancelled, but they have stalled despite various efforts to revive them.

***ALBA.*** Regional integration via trade is clearly not a purely technical issue, but one in which political considerations play a major role; consequently, regional trade initiatives can become controversial. Cuba, of course, and subsequently Venezuela under the leadership of president Hugo Chávez, spearheaded the opposition to regional trade-based initiatives. Chavez portrayed them as imperialist instruments of the United States to consolidate and deepen its economic and political control over the region. To counter the U.S. influence, Venezuela and Cuba signed an agreement that would become the foundation of the Bolivarian Alternative for the Americas (ALBA) on December 14, 2004. Bolivia and Nicaragua joined ALBA in 2006 and 2007. With this platform in place, they called for an international alliance to counter the FTAA, especially among the governments of the left in the region. Brazil and Argentina, however, while sympathetic to alternative efforts, have maintained their distance both from ALBA and the FTAA. It is too early to tell what the economic effects of ALBA might be. But it is clear that it has had political effects, by breaking down the consensus that is required for general trade rules to work properly, and by generating a clearly defined opposition to trade-based integration in the region. These effects will undoubtedly last at least until 2010, when some of the governments from the left face elections again.

## ECONOMIC DEVELOPMENT

Economic development is a comprehensive concept that encompasses not only economic growth, but also issues of poverty and inequality, which are among the most pressing and resilient problems facing Latin Americans. The traditional approach to economic development presupposes growth, in the belief that the more economic growth a country can achieve, the more wealth will be available to be redistributed. So long as wealth continues to be distributed unequally, however, economic growth will have scant impact on poverty and inequality, so countries in the region generally utilize specialized social-spending programs to target poverty and reduce inequality. A growth-based economic development strategy also faces shortcomings when the global economy is sluggish or when closely interconnected economies rapidly transmit economic problems from one country to another.

Latin America was severely affected by the economic crises of the 1970s and 1980s, which resulted in increased economic inequality in every Latin American country. According to World Bank estimates, Latin America is by far the most inequitable region in the world, a situation that dates back to colonial times, when a small minority of the population owned the majority of the resources, a pattern reinforced over time through inheritance. When the ownership of assets is so concentrated, an inequitable distribution of wealth and income is difficult to overcome. In a modern economic setting, where income from labor provides an alternative to income from capital, lack of access to education makes it difficult for large portions of the population to get the training they need to command increased wages and overcome poverty. The strata of society with a very low income faces a tradeoff between working for survival in the present or investing in education in hopes of a higher income in the future. Under these conditions, it is not surprising that those in extreme poverty remain in poverty for generations, with very little chance of improving their situation.

During the 1990s, most Latin American governments instituted deep reforms in their economic structures. Countries began opening their borders to trade and reducing tariffs on imported goods, in a reversal of previous inward-looking development strategies. The introduction of new markets and the benefits of specializing in goods that a country can produce more efficiently were expected to generate higher growth rates resulting from enhanced aggregate demand for goods. These reforms were accompanied by greater liberalization in financial markets, under the belief that capital mobility across borders was an essential feature for investment in industries and for financing trade deficits. Neither of these reforms came alone; they were accompanied by a significant rescaling of the size of government. Previously state-owned industries were sold in an effort to induce more efficient management, but also to reduce the size of the budget and deficits, all extremely high in many Latin American countries. With these reforms in place, a call for the sustained implementation of sound economic policies also appeared. As a result, countries emphasized controlling inflation, the role of independent central banks, reduction of government deficits, and balanced budgets as standards that would reduce the likelihood of economic contagion as crises arose elsewhere in the world.

As a result of the peso crisis in 1994–1995 and the Asian crises of the late 1990s that reverberated across Latin America (and especially in Brazil and Argentina), the region did not show the vigorous growth economists expected. Consequently, there was little room during this time to effectively cope with poverty and inequality. According to United Nations estimates corresponding to 2004, 19 percent of the population in Latin America is rated as extremely poor, and 43 percent as poor. Extreme poverty in Latin America did decline by about 4 percent during the 1990s. But it is important to note that extreme poverty rates vary widely across countries. Honduras ranks highest with approximately 54 percent of its population under the poverty line, Mexico and Brazil are at about 13 percent, and Uruguay about 2 percent according to United Nations' projections for 2002. Despite the overall decline in extreme poverty levels, inequality did not change much during the decade, as the ratio between the richest and the poorest quintiles of society remained nearly unchanged.

***Domestic Efforts.*** Recognizing that robust growth rates do not necessarily translate into a reduction of poverty, governments in Latin America have engaged in programs that aim instead at breaking the cycle. These programs are considered an investment in human capital, designed to encourage poor families to keep their children healthy and in school for longer periods of time. If new generations are healthy, well nourished, and well educated, they will be likely to achieve higher incomes than the previous generation. If this pattern is reproduced in the following generation, poverty could be drastically reduced over time, with the appealing feature that the effect would be sustainable, being the result of human capital, which cannot be taken away from the individual once it has been obtained.

Most programs aim to generate incentives for parents to keep their children in school and obtain regular medical attention. Some offer cash incentives to families as long as their children attend the local public school and receive medical attention at local public clinics. If the money offsets the income children could provide by working, parents can afford to keep their children in school, and the resulting potential for higher earnings should allow future generations to break free of the intergenerational cycle of poverty. Perhaps the best known among these programs are Progresa-Oportunidades in Mexico and Bolsa Família in Brazil. Progresa, started in 1997 by the Zedillo administration, targeted children in families below the poverty line in rural areas. Five years later, its scope was broadened to include some urban areas as well; its name was changed to Oportunidades under the Fox administration. In Brazil, Bolsa Família, launched in 2003, targets families using a similar approach.

Despite these efforts, the only country in Latin America that has come close to eliminating extreme poverty is Chile. This occurred as a result of a two-pronged strategy. On the one hand, Chile achieved what has been dubbed growth with equity, a program of trade-based growth with a commitment to a permanent budget surplus as protection against potential shocks to the economy that would require cutting back assistance to the poor. On the other hand, it implemented a comprehensive poverty-reduction program that included raising minimum wages, instituting subsidies for poor families, and expanding social expenditures in health, housing, and education. The sustained implementation of this strategy over three administrations and eighteen years was successful enough to eliminate extreme poverty. This was supplemented in 2002 by a new program, Chile Solidario, which specifically targets families and provides temporary aid in the form of a guaranteed minimum income, access to social services, schooling for children, and training for the adults in the family to obtain stable jobs.

Venezuela has used a different approach to reducing poverty, based on social missions (*misiones*) that bring services such as health care, schools, and roads to the poor in an ad hoc scheme financed by oil revenues. The program has produced short term results, but the long-term effects and sustainability of these policies are still questionable.

***International Efforts.*** Eradicating poverty and inequality in Latin America is an ambitious goal that requires the commitment of both the governments in the region and international agencies. A variety of programs have been attempted, with varying degrees of success. A trade-based approach was proposed in the World Trade Organization's Doha Round negotiations, which stalled over issues including access to agricultural and textile markets in the developed countries, an issue of particular importance for the developing world. Implementation would require a coordinated reduction of subsidies, tariffs, and other trade barriers that would permit developing countries, including those in Latin America, to export more agricultural goods, which would eventually translate into increased growth.

A more comprehensive approach has been advocated by the United Nations as part of its Millennium Development Goals. Proposed programs include debt forgiveness for heavily indebted poor countries (HIPCs), which in Latin America include Bolivia, Guyana, Honduras, and Nicaragua, and increased official development assistance (ODA). These efforts underscore the importance of poverty relief, reduction of inequality, and economic development on the main agendas of international organizations.

None of the issues facing Latin America can be adequately defined in isolation. Developments in one area are likely to have an influence on other issues, directly or indirectly, throughout the region. The ideological orientations of governments, the domestic programmatic priorities in each country, the ad hoc coalitions generated among countries, previous historical developments and current agendas, all contribute to the constantly changing landscape in a complex and diverse hemisphere.

*See also* **Democracy; Drugs and Drug Trade; Economic Development; Free Trade Area of the Americas (FTAA); Human Rights; Mercosur; Migration and Migrations; North American Free Trade Agreement; United States-Latin American Relations.**

BIBLIOGRAPHY

Bulmer-Thomas, Victor. *The Economic History of Latin America since Independence*, 2nd edition. New York: Cambridge University Press, 2003.

Carr, Barry, and Steve Ellner, eds. *The Latin American Left: From the Fall of Allende to Perestroika*. Boulder, CO: Westview Press, 1993.

Castañeda, Jorge G. *Utopia Unarmed: The Latin American Left after the Cold War*. New York: Knopf, 1993.

Castañeda, Jorge G. "Latin America's Left Turn." *Foreign Affairs* 85, no. 3 (2006): 28–43.

Cerdas Cruz, Rodolfo. "United States Foreign Relations and the Promotion of Democracy in Latin America." In *The United States and Latin America: The New Agenda*, edited by Victor Bulmer-Thomas and James Dunkerley. Cambridge, MA: Harvard University Press, 1999.

Domínguez, Jorge I., and Michael Shifter. *Constructing Democratic Governance in Latin America*. Baltimore, MD: Johns Hopkins University Press, 2003.

Fernández-Armesto, Felipe. *The Americas: A Hemispheric History*. New York: Modern Library, 2003.

Franko, Patrice. *The Puzzle of Latin American Economic Development*. Lanham, MD: Rowman & Littlefield, 2003.

Grindle, Merilee S. *Audacious Reforms: Institutional Invention and Democracy in Latin America*. Baltimore, MD: Johns Hopkins University Press, 2000.

Hartlyn, Jonathan, and Arturo Valenzuela. "Democracy in Latin America Since 1930." In *Latin America: Politics and Society since 1930*, edited by Leslie Bethell. New York: Cambridge University Press, 1998.

Kryzanek, Michael. *U.S.–Latin American Relations*, 2nd edition. New York: Praeger, 1990.

Latinobarómtero. *Informe Latinobarómtero 2005*. Santiago de Chile: Author, 2005.

Machinea, José Luis, Alicia Bárcena, and Arturo León. *The Millennium Development Goals: A Latin American and Caribbean Perspective*. Santiago, Chile: ECLAC, 2005.

O'Donnell, Guillermo. "Poverty and Inequality in Latin America: Some Political Reflections." In *Poverty and Inequality in Latin America: Issues and New Challenges*, edited by Victor Tokman and Guillermo O'Donnell. Notre Dame, IN: University of Notre Dame Press, 1998.

Perry, Guillermo E., et al. *Poverty Reduction and Growth: Virtuous and Vicious Circles*. Washington, DC: World Bank, 2006.

Smith, Peter H. *Democracy in Latin America: Political Change in Comparative Perspective*. New York: Oxford University Press, 2005.

Stallings, Barbara, and Wilson Peres. *Growth, Employment, and Equity: The Impact of the Economic Reforms in Latin America and the Caribbean*. Washington, DC: Brookings Institution Press, 2000.

Thorp, Rosemary. *Progress, Poverty, and Exclusion: An Economic History of Latin America in the Twentieth Century*. Washington, DC: Johns Hopkins University Press, 1998.

Winn, Peter. *Americas: The Changing Face of Latin America and the Caribbean.* Berkeley, CA: University of California Press, 1999.

JORGE G. CASTAÑEDA
MARCO A. MORALES

## HENEQUEN INDUSTRY.

**HENEQUEN INDUSTRY.** Located primarily in Yucatán, the extraction of raw fiber from the henequen agave and the production of rope and twine therefrom was at one time a thriving industry. Henequen rope was used by the ancient Maya and then by the Spaniards as rigging. Extraction of the fiber was so labor-intensive that production was limited. In the 1850s, however, when the Yucatecan invention of the steam-powered decorticator to remove the fiber made mass production possible, the hacienda owners of northwestern Yucatán began planting large quantities of henequen. Demand abroad was stimulated by the invention in 1878 of the McCormick reaper, which required large quantities of binder twine.

The economy of Yucatán came to be based on henequen exports, especially to the United States, and the state became the wealthiest and most opulent in Porfirian Mexico. Profits at first went mostly to the landowning elite; the workers—Maya Indians, many of whom were debt peons—received few benefits. Labor relations reflected cultural values. While labor shortages existed, landowners would not hire women because this would have created tension with male indigenous workers. However, with the creation in 1902 of the International Harvester Corporation—a U.S. trust that established almost complete control over the purchase of henequen on the world market—a large part of the profits went to the United States. This situation continued until the breakup of the trust in 1915.

The Mexican Revolution brought about the abolition of peonage and the emergence of free labor on the haciendas, while competition from other producers changed the world market for twine and led to declining prices. Agrarian reforms in the 1930s resulted ultimately in the destruction of the landowning class, but mismanagement and corruption in the state-run economy led to the impoverishment of the peasants. Foreign competition also cut into profitability, and by 1990 henequen production was no longer a significant segment of the economy of Yucatán. The state also privatized the industry in 1990. The Cordemex factory, which employed 5,000 people in the 1980s, had only 500 workers in 1998.

*See also* **Debt Peonage; Maya, the; Yucatán.**

BIBLIOGRAPHY

Narcisa Trujillo, "Las primeras máquinas desfibradoras de henequén," *Enciclopedia yucatanese,* vol. 3 (1947), pp. 627–656.

Gonzalo Camara Zavala, "Historia de la industria henequenera hasta 1919," *Enciclopedia yucatanese,* vol. 3 (1947), pp. 657–725.

Enrique Aznar Mendoza, "Historia de la industria henequenera desde 1919 hasta nuestros días," *Enciclopedia yucatanese,* vol. 3 (1947), pp. 727–787.

Moisés González Navarro, *Raza y tierra: La Guerra de Castas y el henequén* (1970).

Allen Wells, *Yucatán's Gilded Age: Haciendas, Henequen, and International Harvester, 1860–1915* (1985).

Jeffrey Brannon and Eric N. Baklanoff, *Agrarian Reform and Public Enterprise in Mexico: The Political Economy of Yucatán's Henequen Industry* (1987).

*Additional Bibliography*

Baños Ramírez, Othón. *Neoliberalismo, reorganización y subsistencia rural: El caso de la zona henequenera de Yucatán, 1980–1992.* Mérida, Mexico: Universidad Autónoma de Yucatán, 1996.

Sabido Méndez, Arcadio. *Los hombres del poder: Monopolios, oligarquía y riqueza Yucatán, 1880–1990.* Mérida, Mexico: Universidad Autónoma de Yucatán, 1995.

ROBERT W. PATCH

## HENRÍQUEZ, CAMILO (1769–1825).

Camilo Henríquez (*b.* 20 July 1769; *d.* 16 May 1825), Chilean patriot, revolutionary, and propagandist, "the father of Chilean journalism." Henríquez was born in Valdivia, but in 1784 he was sent for his education to Lima, where he lived for the next quarter century, entering a minor religious order in 1787. He was three times investigated by the Inquisition because of his interest in prohibited books, such as those of Jean-Jacques Rousseau (1712–1778), Guillaume-Thomas-François de Raynal (1713–1796), and Louis-Sébastien Mercier (1740–1814).

Henríquez returned to his native Chile at the end of 1810 and threw himself into politics with enthusiasm. When the patriot government acquired its first printing press (from the United States), he was given the task of editing the first Chilean newspaper, *La Aurora de Chile* (13 February 1812 to 1 April 1813). The prospectus he issued prior to the first issue made a resonant claim: "After the sad and intolerable silence of three centuries—centuries of infamy and lamentation!—the voice of reason and truth will be heard amongst us." The newspaper contained many articles by its editor. On 6 April 1813 *La Aurora* was replaced by a second newspaper, *El Monitor Araucano,* which ran until the eve of the battle of Rancagua (1–2 October 1814) and the downfall of patriot Chile. Henríquez used these newssheets to spread his own revolutionary ideas. Between 1814 and 1822 he lived in exile in Buenos Aires, once again publishing newspapers for a time. In 1822 he returned to Chile at the invitation of Bernardo O'Higgins and played a minor role in public affairs for what remained of his life.

Henríquez's place as a publicist of patriot and revolutionary ideas during the Patria Vieja in Chile was unrivaled. His writing is always clear and direct. A brief flirtation with monarchism during his Argentine exile was no more than a temporary aberration from his liberal, democratic, and republican ideas.

*See also* **Journalism; Rancagua, Battle of.**

BIBLIOGRAPHY

Raúl Silva Castro, ed., *Escritos políticos de Camilo Henríquez* (1960), Simon Collier, *Ideas and Politics of Chilean Independence, 1808–1833* (1967), chap. 3.

*Additional Bibliography*

Wood, James Alderfer. "Building a Society of Equals: The Popular Republican Movement in Santiago de Chile, 1818–1851." Ph.D. diss., University of North Carolina at Chapel Hill, 2000.

SIMON COLLIER

## HENRÍQUEZ UREÑA, MAX (1885–1968).

Max Henríquez Ureña (*b.* 16 November 1885; *d.* 23 January 1968), Dominican educator, writer, and diplomat. Henríquez Ureña, born in Santo Domingo, was the son of Francisco Henríquez y Carvajal, president of the Dominican Republic (1916), and the Dominican poetess and educator Salomé Ureña De Henríquez. After receiving a law doctorate in 1913, he began his public career in 1916, as secretary to his father. This appointment was followed by twenty years of diplomatic service as his country's representative in various European capitals, the League of Nations, and the United Nations. During the first year of Rafael L. Trujillo's reign (1930–1931), Henríquez Ureña was in charge of Dominican public education. Along with other Dominican intellectuals, he established the Dominican Academy of History. In Cuba, he founded the journals *Cuba Literaria* and *Archipiélago.* Henríquez Ureña contributed to important Hispanic magazines, such as *El Cojo Ilustrado* (Venezuela), *Cuba Contemporánea* and *El Fígaro* (Cuba), and *Caras y Caretas* (Argentina). He taught at various universities in the Dominican Republic and abroad, including the Universidad Nacional Pedro Henríquez Ureña (UNPHU). Henríquez Ureña's most famous literary work is *Los Estados Unidos y la República Dominicana* (published in Cuba in 1919), in which he denounced the armed intervention by the United States in the Dominican Republic during 1916. Another well-known work is *Panorama histórico de la literatura dominicana,* a survey of Dominican literature published in Rio de Janeiro in 1945. Henríquez Ureña died in Santo Domingo.

*See also* **League of Nations; United Nations.**

BIBLIOGRAPHY

Henríquez Ureña's writings include *Cuentos insulares* (1947); *Breve historia del modernismo* (1954); *Garra de luz* (1958); *De Rimbaud a Pasternak y Quasimodo* (1960); *El retorno de los galeones,* 2d ed., rev. and enlarged (1963); *La independencia efímera,* 3d ed. (1967); *"Mi padre": Perfil biográfico de Francisco Henríquez y Carvajal* (1988). See also *Enciclopedia dominicana,* vol. 3 (1978), p. 264.

*Additional Bibliography*

Fernández Pequeño, José M. *En el espíritu de las islas: los tiempos posibles de Max Henríquez Ureña.* Santo Domingo: Grupo Santillana, 2003.

KAI P. SCHOENHALS

## HENRÍQUEZ UREÑA, PEDRO (1884–1946).

Pedro Henríquez Ureña (*b.* 29 June 1884; *d.* 11 May 1946), Dominican and Spanish American intellectual, educator, philologist, and literary critic. Born in Santo Domingo of a prominent family, he spent most of his lifetime outside his native country. His early schooling was in the Dominican Republic and in the United States (1902–1904), and he began his literary activities during a first residence in Cuba (1904–1905). He lived in Mexico from 1906 through 1914, where he completed a law degree, taught at the Preparatory School of the University of Mexico, and together with Alfonso Reyes, Antonio Caso, and other young intellectuals took part in the founding of the Ateneo de la Juventud. He traveled to the United States again in 1914, and between 1916 and 1921 he both taught and did postgraduate work in Spanish literature at the University of Minnesota (his doctoral thesis, defended in 1918, was on versification in Hispanic poetry). In a second and shorter Mexican residence (1921–1924) he undertook a number of teaching and administrative responsibilities. In mid-1924 he left Mexico for Argentina, and for more than twenty years held secondary and university teaching positions in both Buenos Aires and nearby La Plata. He also carried on wide-ranging intellectual activities: a steady stream of books and articles on linguistics and literature, lectures, and consultations with journals and publishing houses. In 1931–1933 he served for a short time as General Superintendent of Education in the Dominican Republic, and in 1940–1941 he was invited to deliver the Charles Eliot Norton lectures at Harvard University.

Henríquez Ureña's influence was evident in several generations of well-trained students, but clearly his most significant contribution as a thinker and scholar has come in the expansiveness and persuasive clarity of his own writings. His publications are voluminous and contribute brilliantly to the study of language, literature, and culture in the Spanish-speaking world. As a linguist, Henríquez Ureña's best contributions are probably his *Gramática castellana* (1938–1939), his much reprinted grammar done with Amado Alonso, and his dialectal studies on American Spanish: *El español en México, los Estados Unidos y la América Central* (1938) and *El español en Santo Domingo* (1940). His most influential literary studies are the published doctoral thesis on versification, *La versificación irregular en la poesía castellana* (1920), and the Norton lectures from Harvard, *Literary Currents in Hispanic America* (1945; translated by Joaquín Díez Canedo and published in 1949 as *Las corrientes literarias en la América Hispánica*). As a cultural observer, his best-known work is *Seis ensayos en busca de nuestra expresión* (1928), a series of six persuasive essays on the possibilities of expressing an authentic American culture in Spanish.

*See also* **Ateneo de la Juventud (Athenaeum of Youth); Ureña de Henríquez, Salomé.**

BIBLIOGRAPHY

Juan Jacobo De Lara, *Pedro Henríquez Ureña: Su vida y su obra* (1975).

Enrique Anderson Imbert, "Pedro Henríquez Ureña," in *Latin American Writers,* edited by Carlos A. Solé and Maria Isabel Abreu, vol. 2 (1989).

Juan Jacobo De Lara, ed., *Obras completas,* 10 vols. (1976–1980).

Emma Susana Speratti Piñero, *Obra crítica* (1960)

José Alcántara Almánzar, *Ensayos* (1976)

Angel Rama and Rafael Gutiérrez Girardot, *La utopía de América* (1978).

Emma Susana Speratti Piñero, "Crono-bibliografía de Pedro Henríquez Ureña," in *Obra crítica,* pp. 751–793.

Alfredo A. Roggiano, ed., *Pedro Henríquez Ureña en los Estados Unidos* (1961), *Pedro Henríquez Ureña en México* (1989).

*Additional Bibliography*

González Tapia, Carlisle. *El pensamiento lingüístico de Pedro Henríquez Ureña.* Santo Domingo: Editora Universitaria, 1998.

Inoa, Orlando. *Pedro Henríquez Ureña en Santo Domingo.* Santo Domingo: Comisión Permanente de la Feria del Libro, 2002.

Zuleta Alvarez, Enrique. *Literatura y sociedad: Estudios sobre Pedro Henríquez Ureña.* Buenos Aires: Ediciones Atril, 1999.

MERLIN H. FORSTER

---

**HENRÍQUEZ Y CARVAJAL, FRANCISCO** (1859–1935). Francisco Henríquez y Carvajal (*b.* 14 January 1859; *d.* 1935), provisional president of the Dominican Republic (1916). After the U.S. Marines invaded the Dominican Republic in 1916, Washington was unwilling to allow direct rule. The Dominican Congress reacted by meeting in secrecy and selecting Francisco Henríquez y Carvajal as provisional president. The United States was willing to allow Henríquez y Carvajal to take power under the conditions it determined. Unwilling to become a puppet of the United States, Henríquez y Carvajal resigned and left the country in November 1916. The Dominican Congress was dissolved and the United States imposed martial law by the occupying marines. These conditions prevailed until the marines were withdrawn in 1924.

*See also* **Dominican Republic.**


BIBLIOGRAPHY

Ian Bell, *The Dominican Republic* (1981).

Selden Rodman, *Quisqueya: A History of the Dominican Republic* (1964).

Howard J. Wiarda, *The Dominican Republic: Nation in Transition* (1969).

Howard J. Wiarda and M. J. Kryzanek, *The Dominican Republic: A Caribbean Crucible* (1982).

*Additional Bibliography*

Martínez Vergne, Teresita. *Nation & Citizen in the Dominican Republic, 1880–1916.* Chapel Hill: University of North Carolina Press, 2005.


HEATHER K. THIESSEN

**HENRY THE NAVIGATOR** (1394–1460). Henry the Navigator (*b.* 4 March 1394; *d.* 13 November 1460), Portuguese prince noted for promoting the voyages of discovery that led to Portugal's creation of an overseas empire. Third son of King John I and Philippa of Lancaster, daughter of John of Gaunt of England, Prince Henry (Infante Dom Henrique) was duke of Viseu, governor of the city of Ceuta (captured in 1415 by the Portuguese from the Moroccans in an expedition in which Henry played a key role), the governor of the Algarve, Portugal's southernmost province, where Henry established his own court at Sagres in 1419.

Prince Henry is one of the most controversial figures in Portuguese historiography, for historians differ widely in their assessments of the extent and motives of his leadership role in Portugal's voyages of discovery. In the *Crónica da Guiné,* Gomes Eanes de Azurara, a contemporary chronicler of the discoveries, portrays Prince Henry as a model crusader: a tireless fighter, a pious man, and a chaste saint who never married. Azurara's portrait does not, however, match other evidence concerning Henry's character, which suggests that he was a skilled politician with an acute sense of *raison d'état,* that he was a crafty courtier who knew how to employ court intrigue for his own advantage; or that he was a practical man of affairs whose preoccupation with overseas expansion reflected his purpose of serving both God and Mammon.

On several occasions Henry's actions put the lives of his own brothers or half brothers in peril. For example, his unsuccessful expedition to Tangiers in 1437 resulted in the capture of his younger brother, Dom Fernando, by the Moors. The Moors demanded the return of Ceuta as the price of Fernando's release. Hardliners in the Portuguese court, including Henry, opposed giving up Ceuta, and as a result Fernando died in captivity in Fez in 1443. Henry also supported the war against Dom Afonso, duke of Bragança, and his half brother, who was involved in a power struggle with Dom Pedro, his older brother. At the battle of Alfarrobeira in 1449 Dom Pedro was killed. Many Portuguese historians blame Dom Pedro's death on Henry's intrigues.

Concerning his role in overseas expansion, Azurar notes that Joâo de Alenquer, the *vedor da fazenda,* had convinced Prince Henry of the economic advantages of capturing Ceuta, then believed to be a bridgehead to the gold-producing lands south of the Sahara. Similarly, Diogo Gomes, one of the sea captains Henry supported, confided to Martin Behaim of Nürnburg that Prince Henry had been told about Saharan gold by the Moors of Ceuta and that he had vowed to find it by land or sea. This view of Henry's thirst for gold has been developed by a school of Portuguese historians led by Alexandre Herculano and presently is reflected in the writings of Vitorino Magalhães Godinho and others, who contend that the economic motive and maintaining the security of Portugal were the main reasons for the overseas expansion.

Nevertheless, in 1960 the Portuguese marked the five-hundred-year anniversary of Prince Henry's death by honoring him as the "saint of the Promontory of Sagres," a heroic visionary who initiated Portugal's overseas discoveries and was the fountainhead of its empire.

*See also* **Explorers and Exploration: Brazil; Portuguese Empire.**

BIBLIOGRAPHY

C. R. Boxer, *The Portuguese Seaborne Empire* (1969).

Gervase Clarence-Smith, *The Third Portuguese Empire, 1825–1975* (1985).

A. H. De Carvalho E Araujo Herculano, "Cogitações soltas de um homem obscuro," in *Opusculos,* vol. 6 (1897).

A. H. De Oliveira Marques, *História de Portugal,* 3 vols. (1981–1983).

Joaquim Pedro De Oliveira Martins, *Os filhos de D. João I* (1936).

Bailey W. Diffie and George D. Winius, *Foundations of the Portuguese Empire: Europe and the World in the Age of Expansion* (1972).

Duarte Leite, *História dos descobrimentos,* edited by Vitorino Magalhães Godinho (1960).

Vitorino Magalhães Godinho, *Os descobrimentos e a economia mundial,* 2 vols. (1965–1968).

Joaquim Veríssimo Serrão, *História de Portugal,* 12 vols. (1978–1990).

*Additional Bibliography*

Russell, P. E. *Prince Henry the Navigator: A Life.* New Haven, CT: Yale University Press, 2000.

Tomé N. Mbuia João

**HERBS.** *See* **Spices and Herbs.**

**HEREDIA.** Heredia, one of the four provinces in the Central Valley of Costa Rica. Heredia was settled in the eighteenth century by Spanish and Creole farmers. Although it had rich volcanic soil, like the rest of Costa Rica, it had a minuscule indigenous labor force, and thus remained only sparsely settled. By 1824, the town of Heredia had still fewer than four thousand inhabitants. It became the provincial capital of Heredia Province in 1848, when the boundaries of the region were extended northward to include the Sarapiquí Valley.

During the twentieth century, Heredia became more closely tied to metropolitan San José, although the provincial capital still retains its legal identity. In 1972, Costa Rica established its second national university in Heredia.

*See also* **Costa Rica.**

BIBLIOGRAPHY

Carolyn Hall, *Costa Rica: A Geographical Interpretation in Historical Perspective* (1985).

Héctor Pérez-Brignoli, *Las variables demográficas en las economías de exportación: El ejemplo del Valle Central de Costa Rica* (1978).

Ralph Lee Woodward, Jr., *Central America: A Nation Divided* (1985).

*Additional Bibliography*

Ossa, A. de la. *Sociedad civil y Resistencia pacífica en Centroamérica.* San José: Facultad Latinoamericana de Ciencias Sociales, 1998.

Meléndez Chavarri, Carlos. *Heredia—historia, tradiciones y vivencias.* Heredia: EUNA, 1997.

Virginia Garrard-Burnett

**HEREDIA ACOSTA, ALEJANDRO** (1788–1838). This Argentine military man and politician was born in Tucumán and educated in Córdoba. For his performance in the war for independence he was promoted to colonel and became one of the most distinguished leaders in the Argentine northeast. He reached the cusp of his power when Juan Manuel de Rosas became governor of the province of Buenos Aires but fell victim to Rosas's plots and corruption.

In July 1816 the Tucumán Congress, which had just declared the independence of the United Provinces of the Río de la Plata, entrusted Heredia with the responsibility of reestablishing order in the neighboring province of La Rioja. Because of his success, subsequent central governments looked to him to control upheaval in the neighboring region. In 1820 he played a significant role in what was known as the Mutiny of Arequito, which blocked the federal government's attempt to use the army to pursue the northern centralists. This was to earn him enemies among the federalist group. Nevertheless, in 1829 he faced off against the centralists and allied himself with Rosas, by then governor of Buenos Aires. As a result Heredia was appointed governor of Tucumán and Salta two years later. His leadership was strengthened in 1834 following the assassination of the Rioja leader Facundo Quiroga, his only rival of standing in these provinces.

This power aroused distrust in Buenos Aires. Rosas put him in charge of the Northern Army in 1837, when war broke out with the Peru-Bolivia Confederation over control of Tarija, Jujuy, and Salta. But Rosas did not send the necessary reinforcements, alleging that there were other urgent needs on the coast and in Uruguay. Despite achieving some partial successes, Heredia's troops were ill equipped and poorly trained and were finally defeated. In the retreat, Heredia was overthrown in an ambush and murdered by troops of his own nation. It is not known who was responsible for the attack.

*See also* **Rosas, Juan Manuel de; Tucumán Congress.**

BIBLIOGRAPHY

Bulgheroni, Raúl. *Argentina: Imagen de un país: Summa andina.* 5 vols. Buenos Aires: Bridas, 1986–1997

Halperín Donghi, Tulio. *De la revolución de independencia a la Confederación rosista.* Buenos Aires: Paidós, 2000.

Pavoni, Norma L. *El Noroeste Argentino en la época de Alejandro Heredia.* Vol. 1: *La Política.* Tucumán, Argentina: Ediciones Fundación Banco Comercial del Norte, Colección Historia, 1981

MARCOS NOVARO

## HEREDIA Y HEREDIA, JOSÉ M.

(1803–1839). José M. Heredia y Heredia (*b.* 31 December 1803; *d.* 7 May 1839), Cuban Romantic poet. Heredia, born in Santiago de Cuba, was the most important literary figure of Latin American romanticism. His early education was directed by his father, José Francisco Heredia y Mieses, an important politician who traveled extensively in the colonies. Heredia graduated from the University of Havana Law School in 1823 and became an important member of the anti-Spanish movement on the island.

The Spanish authorities transferred Heredia's father to the Audiencia of Mexico in 1819. That year José followed him there and published his first book of poems, *Ensayos poéticos,* in Mexico. In 1821 he returned to Cuba, married, and published three books: *La inconstancia, Misantropía,* and *El desamor.* Also in 1822 Heredia was appointed rector of the Pontífica Universidad de la Habana. The following year he embarked for the United States, where in Boston he met Felix Varela and José Saco, Cuban liberals and advocates of independence. In 1824, he visited Niagara Falls, which inspired one of this best-known poems, "El Niágara." In December 1824 the Cuban government condemned him to perpetual exile for his involvement in revolutionary activities. Heredia died in Toluca, Mexico.

*See also* **Cuba, War of Independence; Cuba: The Colonial Era (1492–1898).**

BIBLIOGRAPHY

For the complete works of Heredia, see *Poesías completas* (1970); *Diccionario de la literatura cubana,* vol. 1 (1980), pp. 430–438; Emilio Díaz Echani and José María Roca Franquesa, *Historia de la literatura española e hispanoamericana,* 3d ed., vol. 1 (1982), pp. 741–746.

### *Additional Bibliography*

Altenberg, Tilmann. *Melancolía en la poesía de José María Heredia.* Frankfurt am Main: Vervuert; Madrid: Iberoamericana, 2001

Cairo Ballester, Ana. *Heredia, entre cubanos y españoles.* Santiago de Cuba: Editorial Oriente, 2003.

Méndez, Roberto. *José María Heredia: la utopía restituida.* Santiago de Cuba: Editorial Oriente, 2003.

DARIÉN DAVIS

## HERMOSILLO, JAIME-HUMBERTO

(1942–). Jaime-Humberto Hermosillo (*b.* 1942), Mexican film director. Born in Aguascalientes, Hermosillo studied film direction at the Center of Film Studies of the National Autonomous University of Mexico (UNAM). He began his career by producing short narrative films and documentaries. His first full-length film was *La verdadera vocación de Magdalena* (1971). Since that debut, Hermosillo has been one of the most consistent and dedicated directors of contemporary Mexican cinema. His main themes are the changing middle-class family, sexuality and alternative life-styles, and the demise of tradition and values. Many of his leading characters are women or gay men. Among his most critically praised films are *La pasión según Berenice* (1976), *Matine* (1977), *Naufragio* (1977), *Amor libre* (1979), *María de mi corazón* (1979), and *La tarea* (1991). Hermosillo was awarded the Ariel for best direction by the Mexican film academy for *La pasión según Berenice* and *Naufragio.*

Hermosillo's films present a fresh look at Mexican society. He prefers comedy, something not often found in Mexican cinema. His films respond, in an original way, to the Mexico behind the *charro* (horseman), the *bandido*, the *margarita*, and the *burrito*. His recent works include *El Malogrado amor de Sebastián* (2006), *Amor* (2006), *Dos auroras* (2005), and *Rencor* (2005), among others.

*See also* **Cinema: Since 1990; National Autonomous University of Mexico (UNAM).**

BIBLIOGRAPHY

Luis Reyes De La Maza, *El cine sonoro en México* (1973).

E. Bradford Burns, *Latin American Cinema: Film and History* (1975).

Carl J. Mora, *Mexican Cinema: Reflections of a Society: 1896–1980* (1982).

John King, *Magical Reels: A History of Cinema in Latin America* (1990).

*Additional Bibliography*

D'Lugo, Marvin. "Cinema of Solitude: A Critical Study of Mexican Film, 1967–1983." *Film Quarterly* 48, no.1 (Autumn 1994): 41–42.

Hermosillo, Jaime Humberto. *La pasión según Berenice.* Mexico: Katún, 1981.

Hermosillo, Jaime Humberto. *La tarea, o, De cómo la pornografía salvó del tedio y mejoró la economía de la familia Partida: Guión cinematográfico original de Jaime Humberto Hermosillo.* Mexico: Sistema, Sistemas Técnicos de Edición, 1991.

Hermosillo, Jaime Humberto, and Arturo Villaseñor. *Intimidades en un cuarto de baño: Guión cinematográfico.* Xalapa, Mexico: Universidad Veracruzana, 1992.

DAVID MACIEL

## HERNÁNDEZ, AMALIA (1917–2000).

Mexican dancer and choreographer Amalia Hernández was born September 19, 1917. She was the founder and artistic director of the renowned Ballet Folklórico de México, one of the largest and most widely respected international folkloric ballet companies. Founded in 1952, the company presents theatricalized and recontextualized interpretations of Mexico's Hispanic and pre-Columbian ritual, folklore, history, and culture. During an illustrious career that spanned half a century, Hernández developed the original company of eight dancers into a 600-member organization, including a school, a resident company housed at the Mexico City Palace of Fine Arts, and a touring company. Her signature works include *La Danza del Venado* and *Navidad en Jalisco.* She died on November 4, 2000.

*See also* **Music: Popular Music and Dance.**

BIBLIOGRAPHY

Aguirre Cristiani, Gabriela, and Felipe Segura Escalona. *El Ballet Folklórico de México de Amalia Hernández.* Mexico City: Fomento Cultural Banamex, 1994.

Shay, Anthony. *Choreographic Politics: State Folk Dance Companies, Representation, and Power.* Middletown, CT: Wesleyan University Press, 2002.

ANDREA MANTELL-SEIDEL

## HERNÁNDEZ, FELISBERTO (1902–1964).

Felisberto Hernández (*b.* 20 October 1902; *d.* 1964), Uruguayan writer. During his adolescence he studied music and performed as a concert pianist. Along with the Argentine Jorge Luis Borges, he is considered one of the foremost writers of fantasy literature in the Río de la Plata countries. Hernández's lifelong commitment to music can be seen in his work. In the short story "El balcón" ("The Balcony," 1947), the narrator is a concert pianist. The narrative exemplifies the author's deceptively simple but ingenuous prose style, which he uses to analyze sensations, turning them into metaphors.

Early works such as *Libro sin tapas* (1929), *La cara de Ana* (1930), and *La envenenada* (1931) are characterized by humor, the writer's power of observation, and an exuberance in the construction of fantasies. His most acclaimed works begin with *Por los tiempos de Clemente Colling* (1942) and *Nadie encendía las lámparas* (1947), novels of "evocation" in which the anecdotal takes second place to poetic reconstruction of reality and real people, on the basis of memory. *Las hortensias* (1949), *La casa inundada* (1960), and *El cocodrilo* (1962) mark the culmination of his fictional narrative, in which memory and fantasy constitute the dual pillars of narrative discourse.

Additional works by Hernández include *El caballo perdido* (1943); *Tierras de memoria* (1965); and *Obras completas,* 3 vols. (1983).

*See also* **Borges, Jorge Luis; Rió de la Plata.**

BIBLIOGRAPHY

Rosario Ferré, *El acomodador* (1986).

Norah Giraldi De Dei Cas, *Felisberto Hernández: Del creator al hombre* (1975).

Ricardo Pallares and Reina Reyes, *¿Otro Felisberto?* (1983).

Walter Rela, *Felisberto Hernández: Bibliografía anotada* (1979).

Roberto Echavarren Welker, *El espacio de la verdad: Práctica del texto en Felisberto Hernández* (1981).

*Additional Bibliography*

Graziano, Frank. *The Lust of Seeing: Themes of the Gaze and Sexual Rituals in the Fiction of Felisberto Hernández.* Lewisburg, PA: Bucknell University Press, 1997.

Rocca, Pablo. *Felisberto Hernández 1902-2002.* Florianópolis: Editora DA UFSC, 2002.

Rosario-Andújar, Julio A. *Felisberto Hernández y el pensamiento filosófico.* New York: Peter Lang, 1999.

WILLIAM H. KATRA

**HERNÁNDEZ, FRANCISCO** (c. 1517–1587). Francisco Hernández (*b.* ca. 1517; *d.* 1587), medical doctor and botanist from Puebla de Montalbán, Toledo, Spain. While studying at Alcalá de Henares, Hernández learned of Erasmus of Rotterdam's doctrines and those of the most outstanding humanists of his time. He practiced medicine in Toledo and Seville and was King Philip II's court physician. Upon his appointment as *Protomédico de Indias* in 1570, he went to New Spain, where he became deeply interested in Nahuatl medicine, the therapeutic uses of American flora and fauna, and the Nahuatl cultural approaches to diseases.

Antagonized by the Mexican viceroy, Hernández returned to Spain in 1577. He was then dismissed as court physician and replaced by Nardo Antonio Recco, who severely abbreviated Hernández's written works, many of which were destroyed by fire in 1671. Nevertheless, a large number of Hernández's botanical and medical writings are extant. They include *Rerum medicarum Novae Hispaniae* (Rome, 1628), *Quatro libros de la naturaleza y virtudes medicinales de las plantas y animales de la Nueva España* (Mexico, 1615), and *De antiquitatibus Novae Hispaniae* (Mexico, 1926).

*See also* **Medicine: Colonial Spanish America.**

BIBLIOGRAPHY

Germán Somolinos D'ardois, *Vida y obra de Francisco Hernández* (1960).

Bernard Ortiz De Montellano, *Aztec Medicine, Health, and Nutrition* (1990).

Guenter B. Risse, "Medicine in New Spain," in *Medicine in the New World: New Spain, New France, and New England,* edited by Ronald L. Numbers (1987).

*Additional Bibliography*

López Piñero, José María, and José Pardo Tomás. *La influencia de Francisco Hernández, 1515–1587, en la constitución de la botánica y la materia médica modernas.* Valencia: Instituto de Estudios Documentales e Históricos sobre la Ciencia, Universitat de València, 1996.

Varey, Simon, Rafael Chabrán, and Dora B Weiner. *Searching for the Secrets of Nature: The Life and Works of Dr. Francisco Hernández.* Stanford, CA: Stanford University Press, 2000.

CARMEN BENITO-VESSELS

**HERNÁNDEZ, JOSÉ** (1834–1886). José Hernández (*b.* 10 November 1834; *d.* 21 October 1886), Argentine poet, legislator, journalist, politician, soldier, and author of *Martín Fierro.* He exemplified the dual personality typical of the Argentine writer of the nineteenth century: a man of action and of thought. Paradoxically, although he created the most celebrated piece of Argentine literature, he was mostly a man of action. Endowed with great physical dexterity and well acquainted with the life-style of gauchos, Hernández enrolled in the army at age nineteen, fighting in the internecine wars between the central government and the provinces. He retired as assistant captain and in 1858 emigrated to the province of Entre Ríos, where he participated in the revolutions in that part of the country. There, Hernández began his journalistic career, but in 1859 he was back in the army as assistant to General Justo José de Urquiza, taking part in the battles of Cepeda (1859) and Pavón (1861). An opponent of General Bartolomé Mitre and of President Domingo F.

Sarmiento, Hernández returned to Buenos Aires to found the newspaper *El Río de la Plata,* where he defended the gauchos and attacked Sarmiento. After participating in the Ricardo López Jordán rebellion, Hernández escaped to Brazil.

In 1872, back in Buenos Aires, he published the first part of *Martín Fierro;* the second appeared in 1879. He became a legislator (representative and senator) and was instrumental in founding the city of La Plata. His very active life illustrates his commitment to serve his country politically and militarily. It explains also the ideology of the heroic poem he created. Hernández wrote *Instrucción del estanciero* (1881; Education of the Rancher), and political and journalistic pieces that reflected his views as a public persona, citizen, and politician. In his ideology and language, Hernández epitomized the "interior" (provinces) of Argentina. His major work, the poem *Martín Fierro,* is a combative denunciation of social injustice and the virtual genocide of a social strata of the population, that of the gaucho. He adhered to the Argentine Confederation, a political alliance that confronted the Buenos Aires *estancieros* (ranchers) and defended the right of the provinces to share power with the domineering city. He defended the rights of the gauchos, unjustly and cruelly repressed by a government that reduced them to pariahs, without rights to possess land, real freedom, or a hopeful future.

*See also* **Gaucho; Literature: Spanish America.**

BIBLIOGRAPHY

Rodolfo A. Borello, *Hernández: Poesía y política* (1973).

Olga Fernández Latour De Botas, *José Hernández* (1973).

Juan Carlos Ghiano, "Hernández, en el centenario de su muerte," in *Boletín de la Academia Argentina de Letras* 51, no. 201–202 (1986): 293–301.

Antonio Pagés Larraya, "José Hernández," in *Latin American Writers,* edited by Carlos A. Solé and Maria Isabel Abreu, vol. 1 (1989) pp. 235–245.

Horacio Zorraquín Becú, *Tiempo y vida de José Hernández* (1972).

*Additional Bibliography*

Feinmann, José Pablo. *Filosofía y nación: Estudios sobre el pensamiento argentino.* Buenos Aires: Seix Barral, 2004.

Salaverría, José María. *Vida de Martín Fierro: Y otros ensayos.* Buenos Aires: Ediciones El Elefante Blanco, 2002.

Shumway, Nicolas. *The Invention of Argentina.* Berkeley: University of California Press, 1991.

Angela B. Dellepiane

## HERNÁNDEZ, JOSÉ MANUEL (c. 1853–1919).

José Manuel Hernández (*b.* ca. 1853; *d.* 1919), Venezuelan caudillo and politician. A native of Caracas and a perennial revolutionary, Hernández was injured in battle in 1870. After extensive travel in the West Indies and throughout Venezuela, and engaging in various business ventures, "El Mocho" (the maimed) became the president of Bolívar State, where he opposed attempts at centralization by the authorities in Caracas, and also served in Congress. One of three candidates in the 1887 presidential election, Hernández gained enormous popularity by waging Venezuela's first modern political campaign through appealing directly to the masses and campaigning throughout the country under the banner of the Liberal Nationalist Party. Losing in a grossly fraudulent election, the idealistic populist then led an unsuccessful rebellion against the new government of the official candidate, Ignacio Andrade. Hernández was imprisoned and later exiled, but returned to Venezuela in 1908 to accept a high post in the regime of Juan Vicente Gómez.

*See also* **Caudillismo, Caudillo; Venezuela: Venezuela Since 1830.**

BIBLIOGRAPHY

Judith Ewell, *Venezuela: A Century of Change* (1984).

Robert L. Gilmore, *Caudillism and Militarism in Venezuela, 1810–1910* (1964).

Ramón J. Velásquez, *La caída del liberalismo amarillo* (1972).

*Additional Bibliography*

Carvallo, Gastón. *Próceres, caudillos y rebeldes: Crisis del sistema de dominación en Venezuela, 1830–1908.* Caracas: Grijalbo, 1994.

Winfield J. Burggraaff

## HERNÁNDEZ, LUISA JOSEFINA (1928–).

Luisa Josefina Hernández is one of the most important and innovative playwrights of the 1950s in Mexico, alongside Emilio Carballido and

Sergio Magaña. Hernández. She was born in Mexico City on November 2, 1928, and has distinguished herself not only as a dramatist but as a novelist, translator, critic, and essayist. She studied theory and dramatic composition under Rodolfo Usigli at the National Autonomous University of Mexico, and received a master's degree in theater in 1955. She earned her doctorate with a study of the religious iconography of the colonial period and eventually became the first woman to be awarded emeritus status by the same university.

Hernández began to write when she was twenty-two and has published approximately forty plays and twenty novels. Her fictional works are noted for the range of their subject matter, their stylistic and structural variety, and their ironic tone and assiduous avoidance of sentimentality. Her literary production is known for her feminist critique of the macho figure and the themes of the transcendence of anger through mysticism, and the self-realization of women, among others. In addition, she has translated German, English, French, Latin, and Greek authors, ranging from Shakespeare to Euripides to Arthur Miller to Brecht. Hernández has taught in Mexico, the United States, and several other countries.

A recipient of several major prestigious prizes for literature in Mexico, including the Xavier Villaurrutia and Juan Ruíz de Alarcón National Prizes, Hernández's more recent works are the novel *Almeida* (1989), and a dramatic adaptation of this novel by the same name.

*See also* **Carballido, Emilio; Magaña, Sergio; Theater; Usigli, Rodolfo.**

BIBLIOGRAPHY

*Dramatic works by Hernández*

*Aguardiente de Caña* (1950).

*Los Sordomudos* (1951).

*Agonía* (1951).

*La corona del Angel* (1951).

*Botica Modelo* (1954); El Nacional Prize.

*Afuera llueve* (1952).

*Los duendes* (1952).

*La llave del cielo* (1957).

*Los frutos caídos* (1957); Bellas Artes Prize.

*Los Huéspedes Reales* (1958).

*Arpas Blancas . . . conejos dorados* (1959).

*La paz ficticia* (1960).

*Historia de un anillo* (1961).

*La calle de la gran ocasión* (1962).

*Escándalo en Puerto Santo* (1962).

*Novels by Hernández*

*El lugar donde crece la hierba* (1959).

*La plaza de Puerto Santo* (1961).

*Los palacios desiertos* (1963).

*La cólera secreta* (1964).

*La noche exquisita* (1965).

*El valle que elegimos* (1965).

*Los trovadores* (1973).

*Las fuentes ocultas* (1979).

*Nostalgia de Troya* (1986); Magda Donato Prize.

*La cabalgata* (1988).

*Secondary Sources*

Gutiérrez Estupiñán, Raquel. *La realidad subterránea: Ensayo sobre la narrativa de Luisa Josefina Hernández.* Tijuana: Fondo Regional para la Cultura y las Artes del Noroeste, 2000.

JUAN CARLOS GRIJALVA

## HERNÁNDEZ COLÓN, RAFAEL

**HERNÁNDEZ COLÓN, RAFAEL** (1936–). Rafael Hernández Colón (*b.* 24 October 1936), president of Puerto Rico's Popular Democratic Party and twice governor of Puerto Rico. As the son of Rafael Hernández Matos, associate justice of the supreme court of Puerto Rico, Hernández Colón began his education in local schools in Ponce and continued at the Valley Forge Military Academy in Pennsylvania. He graduated from Johns Hopkins University and received his law degree from the University of Puerto Rico, where he taught law from 1961 until 1966.

Hernández Colón entered politics in 1965 by appointment to the post of secretary of justice, where he wrote the Political Code, the Mortgage Code, and the Plebiscite Act of 1967. In 1968 Hernández Colón was elected senator-at-large and served as president of the Senate from 1969 to 1972.

At age thirty-six he was the youngest person to fill the post of governor when first elected in 1972.

His inability to deal with growing economic problems led to his defeat in a 1978 reelection bid, but he won the office again in 1984.

*See also* **Puerto Rico, Political Parties: Popular Democratic Party (PPD).**

BIBLIOGRAPHY

Kenneth R. Farr, *Historical Dictionary of Puerto Rico and the U.S. Virgin Islands* (1973); *Personalities Caribbean,* 7th ed. (1983).

Robert J. Alexander, ed., *Biographical Dictionary of Latin American and Caribbean Political Leaders* (1988).

*Additional Bibliography*

Hernández Colón, Rafael. *Derecho Procesal Civil.* San Juan, P.R.: Michie de Puerto Rico, 1997.

Hernández Colón, Rafael. *La nueva tesis.* Río Piedras: Editorial Edil, 1986.

Hernández Colón, Rafael. *Retos y luchas: 24 años de historia política puertorriqueña en los discursos de Rafael Hernández Colón.* San Juan, P.R.: Hernández Colón, 1991.

Hernández Colón, Rafael. *San Juan de Puerto Rico y su Barrio Ballaja.* San Juan, P.R.: The Officina Estatal, 1992.

Hernández Colón, Rafael. *Vientos de cambio, 1964 a 1972.* San Juan, P.R.: R. Hernández Colón, 2004.

Muriá, José María. *Reflexiones sobre Puerto Rico.* Zapopan, Jalisco: El Colegio de Jalisco, 1999.

David Carey Jr.

## HERNÁNDEZ (FERNÁNDEZ) DE CÓRDOBA, FRANCISCO (?–1526).

Francisco Hernández (Fernández) de Córdoba (*d.* 1518), Spanish navigator and conquistador from the province of Córdoba. (He is not to be confused with Francisco Fernández de Córdoba [*d.* 1526], the conqueror of Nicaragua.) A leading settler of Cuba under Governor Diego Velásquez, Hernández agreed to lead the first major effort to conquer the Maya on the Yucatán Peninsula (1517). The Maya defeated him, however, killing more than half his expedition. Hernández suffered thirty-three wounds, from which he died soon after his return to his home at Villa de Sancti-Spiritus. Although it failed, this expedition stimulated new interest in Mexico, which led eventually to the expedition of Cortés in 1519. News of the expedition also reached and worried the Aztec emperor, Motecuhzoma II.

*See also* **Explorers and Exploration: Spanish America.**

BIBLIOGRAPHY

Bernal Díaz Del Castillo, *The True History of the Conquest of New Spain,* translated by Alfred P. Maudslay, vol. 1, (1908–1916), pp. 14–26.

John H. Parry and Robert G. Keith, *New Iberian World: A Documentary History of the Discovery and Settlement of Latin America to the Early Seventeenth Century,* vol. 3, (1984), pp. 131–143.

*Additional Bibliography*

Benavente, Fray Toribio de ("Motolinía"). *Colección Crónicas de América.* Madrid: Dastin, 2000.

Kirkpatrick, Frederick Alex. *Los conquistadores españoles.* 3rd edition. Madrid: Rialp, 2004.

Thompson, I.A.A., and Bartolomé Yun Casalilla. *The Castilian Crisis of the Seventeenth Century: New Perspectives on the Economic and Social History of Seventeenth-Century Spain.* Cambridge: Cambridge University Press, 1994.

Wagner, Henry Raup. *The Discovery of Yucatan by Francisco Hernández de Córdoba.* Berkeley, CA: The Cortes Society, 1942.

Ralph Lee Woodward Jr.

## HERNÁNDEZ MARTÍNEZ, MAXIMILIANO (1882–1966).

Maximiliano Hernández Martínez (*b.* 1882; *d.* May 1966), career army officer and politician, president of El Salvador (1931–1934 and 1935–1944).

Born in San Salvador and educated at the Guatemalan military academy, Martínez entered the army in 1899. Rising rapidly during the 1906 border war with Guatemala, he reached the rank of major three years after receiving his commission. By 1919 he held the rank of brigadier general. Highly regarded by his colleagues for his ability as a planner and strategist, Martínez spent most of his army career as a professor at the Salvadoran Military Academy and in the office of the chief of staff. His features were both Indian and boyish, and he always appeared considerably younger than his age. Despite a calm exterior, he was regarded as a stern commander and a strong-willed, ambitious man.

Martínez's political rise began in 1930. One of six candidates for the presidency, Martínez withdrew to become the vice-presidential candidate of Arturo Araújo, a wealthy landowner who enjoyed labor movement support. Receiving only a plurality of the votes in the January 1931 election, the pair was elected by the National Assembly. General Martínez was appointed minister of war in addition to his vice presidency. The regime proved controversial and was confronted with the economic and financial crises caused by the global depression.

The maneuvering resulting from a military coup on 2 December 1931 brought Martínez to power. Although Martínez was not directly involved in the coup and was apparently held prisoner by the junior officers who led the revolt during its initial stages, he was suspected of complicity. After several days of confusion, Martínez was released by the military directorate and installed as provisional president (5 December) in accordance with the constitutional provisions. While the junior officers apparently intended that he be a figurehead, he eventually outmaneuvered them to take full control.

Martínez's consolidation of power was facilitated by a leftist-led peasant uprising during January 1932. The bloody rebellion, which reflected peasant discontent, numbered Communists among its leadership. Attacks on landowners and towns in many areas of the country greatly alarmed the elite, which turned to the army for protection. The army put down the revolt after incurring extensive casualties, variously numbered from 10,000 to 30,000, in what became known as the matanza (massacre). The result changed the nation's political climate, solidifying the power of General Martínez, creating support for a military regime, and leaving the entire isthmus frightened of communism.

Initially other Central American governments, in particular that of General Jorge Ubico in Guatemala, supported the United States in opposing Martínez. Contending that the Washington Treaties of 1923 precluded recognition of anyone who came to power as the result of a coup, the United States insisted on Martínez's resignation. Martínez and Ubico became rivals in a diplomatic contest for support throughout the isthmus. When nonrecognition failed to topple Martínez because of his control of the internal government security apparatus and U.S. reluctance to intervene militarily, the United States recognized the Martínez regime in January 1934. The general arranged his own reelection in violation of the Salvadoran constitution in 1934, beginning his second term in March 1935. After a prolonged stalemate, the Central American Conference of 1934 was convened to modify the Washington Treaties of 1923.

Martínez held the nation in the tight grip of a harsh dictatorship until 1944. A theosophist and spiritualist who believed in the transmigration of human souls into other persons, he was rumored to be involved in rituals and was often regarded as a witch doctor. The security apparatus controlled all aspects of Salvadoran life, including the press, ruthlessly suppressing dissent.

The general did stamp out corruption, cease foreign borrowing, and stabilize the currency. His regime was best known for its public works program, which though not as extensive as that of his Guatemalan contemporary, changed the face of the nation. His efforts included extensive road building as well as the construction of many government buildings. He was periodically reelected, save for a brief interim regime.

After a few years of continued rivalry, Martínez and Ubico joined the leaders of Honduras and Nicaragua in a détente in which each agreed to prevent rebel movements against his neighbors, thereby acknowledging that none could gain ascendancy. This agreement gave rise to the myth of a Central American Dictators League, which seemed to gain further credence when both Guatemala and El Salvador became the first governments to recognize the new Spanish regime of Generalíssimo Francisco Franco in Spain. In fact, however, there was no formal agreement and certainly no linkage to the Axis powers. Rather, the respective Central American military presidents merely adopted a mutual nonintervention policy.

Martínez was forced from office on 8 May 1944 by a general strike protesting a new effort to extend his tenure yet again. The revolution proved short-lived, but though the military regained control, Martínez's hour had passed, and he remained in exile in Honduras until his death.

*See also* **Military Dictatorships: 1821–1945; Washington Treaties of 1907 and 1923.**

BIBLIOGRAPHY

Thomas P. Anderson, *Matanza: El Salvador's Communist Revolt of 1932* (1971).

Kenneth J. Grieb, "The United States and the Rise of General Maximiliano Hernández Martínez," in *Journal of Latin American Studies* 3, no. 2 (1971): 151–172.

Patricia Parkman, *Nonviolent Insurrection in El Salvador* (1988).

*Additional Bibliography*

Ching, Erik Kristofer. "From Clientelism to Militarism: The State, Politics and Authoritarianism in El Salvador, 1840–1940." Ph.D. diss., University of California, Santa Barbara, 1997.

Martínez Peñate, Óscar. *El Salvador: Historia general.* San Salvador: Editorial Nuevo Enfoque, 2002.

KENNETH J. GRIEB

**HERNÁNDEZ MONCADA, EDUARDO** (1899–1995). Eduardo Hernández Moncada (*b.* 24 September 1899; *d.* 1995), Mexican composer and conductor trained in the National Conservatory under Rafael Tello. He was Carlos Chávez's assistant conductor with the Mexican Symphony Orchestra from 1929 to 1935 and was named director of the new National Symphony Orchestra of the Conservatory, formed in 1947. He assisted Carlos Chávez's composition workshop briefly in 1960 and was well-known for his work as choirmaster of the National Opera Chorus. Mexican folk elements moderately imbue his music, such as the ballet *Ixtepec* and his only opera, *Elena*. In 1992, he received the Medalla Candelario Huízar in honor of his work. He died in 1995.

*See also* **Music: Art Music.**

BIBLIOGRAPHY

Dan Malmström, *Twentieth-Century Mexican Music* (1974).

*Additional Bibliography*

Contreras Soto, Eduardo, and Eduardo Hernández Moncada. *Eduardo Hernández Moncada: Ensayo biográfico, catálogo de obras y antología de textos.* México, D.F.: Centro Nacional de Investigación, Documentación e Información Musical "Carlos Chávez," 1993.

ROBERT L. PARKER

**HERRÁN, PEDRO ALCÁNTARA** (1800–1872). Pedro Alcántara Herrán (*b.* 19 October 1800; *d.* 26 April 1872), president of New Granada (1841–1845). Born to gentry in Bogotá, Herrán served with the patriots from 1814 to 1816 and the royalists from 1816 to 1820, rising from private to captain. In the service of New Granada from 1821, he became a general by 1828. A partisan of Bolívar, he left Colombia in mid-1830 for Europe, where he lived until 1834. During that sojourn, he forged ties to generals Francisco de Paula Santander and Tomás Cipriano de Mosquera, and he married the latter's daughter in 1842. Back in Colombia, Herrán served as minister of interior and foreign affairs (1838–1839), and commanded the army during the War of the Supremes (1839–1842). During his presidency, the regime sponsored education, recalled the Jesuits (1842), and centralized government via the 1843 Constitution. Herrán was minister to the United States from 1846 to 1848. He later worked for Mosquera and Company (1851–1854) in New York, then returned to Colombia to lead the constitutionalist army against General José María Melo (1954). He was Colombian envoy in Washington from 1855 to 1859. The following year he returned home; he was fired by Mosquera (1862). Again in Washington, he was Guatemalan minister to Peru (1863) and Salvadoran minister to Peru (1865). After being restored to Colombian military service (1866–1867) by Mosquera, Herrán returned to Colombia, where he was elected senator from Antioquia (1870–1872). He died in Bogotá.

*See also* **New Granada, United Provinces.**

BIBLIOGRAPHY

Robert H. Davis, "Apuntes biográficos e interpretativos sobre el General Pedro Alcántara Herrán," in *Archivo epistolar del General Mosquera ...Correspondencia con ... Herrán,* vol. 1, edited by J. León Helguera and Robert H. Davis (1972).

Eduardo Posada and Pedro María Ibáñez, *Vida de Herrán* (1903).

*Additional Bibliography*

Arizmendi Posada, Ignacio. *Manual de historia presidencial: Colombia, 1819–2004.* Bogotá, D.C.: Planeta, 2004.

Sanders, James E. *Contentious Republicans: Popular Politics, Race, and Class in Nineteenth-century Colombia.* Durham, NC: Duke University Press, 2004.

Tirado Mejía, Alvaro. *El estado y la política en el siglo XIX.* Bogotá: El Ancora Editores, 2001.

J. León Helguera

**HERRÁN, SATURNINO** (1887–1918). Saturnino Herrán (*b.* 9 July 1887; *d.* 8 October 1918), Mexican artist. Born in Aguascalientes, Herrán was one of the pioneers of the modern Mexican movement and is known primarily for a mural project for the National Theater, *Our Gods,* for which he did numerous studies from 1914 to 1918. It was never completed, but his focus on issues of Mexican identity have assured him a place in the history of Mexican art. He emphasized the dual nature of Mexican identity by using the Aztec earth goddess Coatlicue as the central motif, on which he superimposed an image of the crucified Christ. The Aztec deity symbolizes the indigenous character of Mexico and the Christ figure its European aspect. Figures making offerings are shown on each side of the central motif, Indians on the left and Spaniards on the right. Easel paintings by Herrán on Mexican subjects (people at work, fiestas, traditions, and history) inspired the artists of the Mexican School of the 1920s through 1940s. In portraits and a series of paintings he called "the creoles," he used distinctive colonial churches in the background to identify the sitters as Mexican and the location as Mexico. Each of the criollas portrays a beautiful woman as a symbol of Mexico. In his early paintings of 1912 and 1914, Herrán placed elderly figures in thematic contexts that emphasized their hopeless condition, exhausted by a life of toil and suffering. In his later works of 1917, the elderly figures have a serenity and peace that reflects a spirituality or intense religiosity.

*See also* **Art: The Twentieth Century; Creole; Theater.**

BIBLIOGRAPHY

Saturnino Herrán, *Saturnino Herrán,* edited by Felipe Garrido, with texts by Ramon Lopez Velarde (1988).

Jacinto Quirarte, *Mexico: Splendors of Thirty Centuries* (1990), pp. 579–584.

Fausto Ramírez, "Notas para una nueva lectura de la obra de Saturnino Herrán," in *Saturnino Herrán, 1887–1987,* of Museo de Aguascalientes (Mexico, 1987).

*Additional Bibliography*

Muñoz, Victor. *Herrán: La pasión y el principio.* México: Bital Grupo Financiero, 1994.

Jacinto Quirarte

**HERRÁN Y ZALDÚA, ANTONIO SATURNINO** (1797–1868). Antonio Saturnino Herrán y Zaldúa (*b.* 11 February 1797; *d.* 7 February 1868), Colombian prelate. Born in Honda, Tolima, Herrán studied in Bogotá, where he received his doctorate in law. He was ordained in 1821, then served in various parishes around and in Bogotá until 1830, when he became a canon of the Bogotá cathedral. In 1833 he assisted in the escape of General José Sardá, a conspirator against President Francisco de Paula Santander. By 1840 Herrán was vicar general of Bogotá and a close associate of Archbishop Manuel José Mosquera. As second in command of the archdiocese, he became enmeshed in the church–state conflict during the presidency of José Hilario López (1849–1853). In October 1852 he was imprisoned by the government. The exile of Mosquera left him in charge of the archdiocese from 1853 to 1854, and he was elected its archbishop in January 1856. Herrán devoted his time (unsuccessfully) to re-creating his predecessor's reforms and to forming groups to aid the needy. The virulence of Tomás Cipriano de Mosquera's anticlericalism (1861–1863) brought rupture with the church. Herrán was exiled to Cartagena (1861–1864), was back in favor (1864–1866) during Manuel Murillo Toro's presidency, then had to deal again with Mosquera's ill will (1866–1867). He died in Villeta, about forty miles from Bogotá.

*See also* **Santander, Francisco de Paula; Sardá, José.**

BIBLIOGRAPHY

José María Samper, *Galería nacional de hombres ilustres o notables, o sea colección de bocetos biográficos* (1879), pp. 227–240.

José Restrepo Posada, "Illmo. Señor Don Antonio Herrán y Zaldúa ...," in *Arquidiócesis de Bogotá: Datos biográficos de sus prelados,* vol. 2 (1963), pp. 325–525.

Gonzalo Uribe Villegas, *Los arzobispos y obispos colombianos desde la colonia hasta nuestros días* (1918), pp. 266–289.

*Additional Bibliography*

Guevara Cobos, Eduardo. *Resistencia eclesiástica al proyecto liberal en el estado soberano de Santander 1860–1886.* Santander, Colombia: Escuela de Historia, Universidad Industrial de Santander, 2004.

López Rodríguez, Marta Helena, and Patricia Pinto Quintero. *La iglesia católica y el estado en Colombia.*Bogotá, D.E.: Pontificia Universidad Javeriana, Facultad de Ciencias Jurídicas y Socioeconómicas, 1991.

Tirado Mejía, Alvaro. *El estado y la política en el siglo XIX.*Bogotá: El Ancora Editores, 2001.

J. León Helguera

## HERRERA, BARTOLOMÉ (1808–1864).

Bartolomé Herrera (*b.* 1808; *d.* 10 August 1864), one of a group of Roman Catholic Church leaders at the time of independence in Peru who sought to retain for the church the same privileged position it had held in colonial society. He was the leading advocate of the continuation of Rome's dominance over the Peruvian church. A man of humble origins who became an orphan at the age of five, Herrera later studied and taught philosophy. But he did his best work as a priest, among people in poor parishes. Basically he believed in leadership of republics by intelligent, moral elites, be they Inca or Spanish, and respect for faith and legitimate authority. He served the government of José Rufino Echenique (1851–1855) at the head of two ministries, and later he acted as Peru's ambassador to Rome. In 1860 he presided over a constitutional convention and was disappointed that the delegates did not restore to the church the privileges it had lost in 1855. He then served as bishop of Arequipa until his death.

*See also* **Anticlericalism; Catholic Church: The Modern Period; Echenique, José Rufino.**

BIBLIOGRAPHY

Jeffrey L. Klaiber, *Religion and Revolution in Peru, 1824–1976* (1977) and *The Catholic Church in Peru, 1821–1985: A Social History* (1992), esp. pp. 64–70.

*Additional Bibliography*

García Jordán, Pilar. *Iglesia y poder en el Perú contemporaneo, 1821–1919.* Cusco: Centro de Estudios Regionales Andinos "Bartolomé de Las Casas," 1993.

Pérez Quiroz, Tito. *Iglesia y Estado: 180 años de discriminación religiosa en el Perú.* Lima: Fondo Editorial del Pedagógico San Marcos, 2004.

Vincent Peloso

## HERRERA, BENJAMÍN (1850–1924).

Benjamín Herrera (*b.* 1850, *d.* 29 February 1924), Colombian Liberal Party leader. Herrera was born in Cali of northern Colombian parents. He fought for the Liberal government in the revolution of 1876–1877 and was an officer in the Colombian army until the Liberals lost power in the mid-1880s. During the War of the Thousand Days (1899–1902), Herrera emerged along with Rafael Uribe Uribe as a top Liberal military leader. By late 1902 Herrera controlled most of Panama, but he was urged to make peace by Uribe, who himself took this step in October. When U.S. officials warned that they would not permit fighting near Panama City or Colón, Herrera signed a treaty with the Colombian government on 21 November 1902 that virtually ended the war.

In the postwar period Herrera often differed with Uribe regarding Liberal policy in the face of Conservative hegemony in government, but he remained a proponent of peaceful opposition. In 1922 he was the Liberal presidential candidate but was defeated by Conservative Pedro Nel Ospina by a vote of 413,619 to 256,231 in what Liberals claimed was a fraudulent election.

*See also* **Colombia, Political Parties: Liberal Party; Ospina, Pedro Nel.**

BIBLIOGRAPHY

Charles W. Bergquist, *Coffee and Conflict in Colombia, 1886–1910* (1978).

Lucas Caballero, *Memorias de la guerra de los mil días* (1939).

J. A. Osorio Lizarazo, "Biografía de un caudillo: Benjamín Herrera," in *Revista de América* 10 (April 1947): 36–63.

*Additional Bibliography*

Galindo H, Julio Roberto. *Benjamín Herrera, Jorge Eliécer Gaitán: Grandes caudillos liberales, gestores de la Universidad Libre.* Santafé de Bogotá: Corporación Universidad Libre, 1998.

Helen Delpar

## HERRERA, CARLOS (1856–1930).

Carlos Herrera (*b.* 1856; *d.* 6 July 1930), interim president of Guatemala. Herrera assumed the Guatemalan presidency as leader of the Guatemalan Unionist Party on 8 April 1920 after the removal of the nation's longest reigning dictator, Manuel Estrada Cabrera. A member of one of Guatemala's premier families, and the owner of large sugar and coffee plantations, Herrera supposedly possessed no strong political ambitions. But in the wake of Estrada Cabrera's ouster, he acknowledged the nation's need for a fair and competent interim leader. Herrera was considered by his peers to be a cultured and learned gentleman. Of distinguished seventeenth-century Spanish heritage, he was widely respected for his qualities of honesty, incorruptibility, and administrative prowess.

After only twenty months in office, however, political instability and a severe economic crisis had overwhelmed Herrera's ill-prepared Unionist government. On the evening of 5 December 1921 a group of senior army officers headed by generals José María Orellana, José María Lima, and Miguel Larrave entered the residence of the president and demanded his resignation. He promptly complied with their request.

Although a member of the coffee elite himself, Herrera chose to govern in a manner that often disregarded the concerns of the dominant political and economic sector of the country. Although willing to suppress peasant unrest as severely as previous Liberal regimes, he occasionally permitted the lower classes to voice their concerns. Because of this, coffee growers, merchants, army officers, and some urban professionals were convinced that his administration jeopardized their interests and so they acted to undermine his authority.

*See also* **Coffee Industry; Guatemala, Political Parties: Unionist Party.**

BIBLIOGRAPHY

Joseph A. Pitti, "Jorge Ubico and Guatemalan Politics in the 1920's" (Ph.D. diss., University of New Mexico, 1975).

Wade Kit, "The Unionist Experiment in Guatemala, 1920–1921: Conciliation, Disintegration, and the Liberal Junta," in *Americas* (July 1993).

### *Additional Bibliography*

Valle Pérez, Hernán del. *Carlos Herrera: Primer presidente democrático del siglo XX.* Nueva Guatemala de la Asunción: Fundación Pantaleón, 2003.

Yashar, Deborah J. *Demanding Democracy: Reform and Reaction in Costa Rica and Guatemala, 1870s–1950s.* Stanford: Stanford University Press, 1997.

WADE A. KIT

## HERRERA, DIONISIO DE (1781–1850).

Dionisio de Herrera (*b.* 9 October 1781; *d.* 13 June 1850), chief of state of Honduras (1823–1827) and Nicaragua (1830–1833). Born to a wealthy creole family in Choluteca, Honduras, Herrera obtained a law degree in 1820. After serving as secretary to the municipal council of Tegucigalpa, Honduras, he became representative to the Cortes from Comayagua Province. He wrote the 28 September 1821 Declaration of Independence of Tegucigalpa and later represented Honduras in the Imperial Congress of Mexico (1822). After Central America separated from Mexico and formed the United Provinces of Central America in 1824, he became chief of state of Honduras and defended the country unsuccessfully against Federal president Manuel Arce. Herrera was imprisoned in Guatemala until 1829, when the Liberal forces under Francisco Morazán overthrew the Arce regime after a three-year civil war.

Herrera returned to politics and was elected president of the assembly of Honduras while also representing Choluteca. Later the government sent him as an envoy to Nicaragua, where he became chief of state from 1830 to 1833. He was elected by the Salvadoran assembly in 1834 to serve as chief of state in El Salvador, but he abandoned politics, except for a brief term as vice president of the Constituent Assembly of Honduras in 1839. He died in San Salvador.

*See also* **Honduras.**

BIBLIOGRAPHY

Rómulo Durón y Gamero, *Historia de Honduras* (1956).

Rafael Heliodoro Valle, "Dionisio de Herrera, 1783–1850: A Centennial Tribute," in *Hispanic American Historical Review* 30 (November 1950): 554–558.

José Reina Valenzuela, *El prócer Dionisio de Herrera* (1965).

### *Additional Bibliography*

Argueta, Mario. *La primera generación liberal: Fallas y aciertos (1829–1842).* Tegucigalpa: Banco Central de Honduras, 1999.

Gudmundson, Lowell, and Héctor Lindo-Fuentes. *Central America, 1821–1871: Liberalism before Liberal Reform.* Tuscaloosa: University of Alabama Press, 1995.

Zúñiga Huerta, Angel. *Presidentes de Honduras.* Lima: Tegucigalpa: Graficentro Editores, 1992.

JEFFREY D. SAMUELS

## HERRERA, FLAVIO (1895–1968).

**HERRERA, FLAVIO** (1895–1968). Flavio Herrera (*b.* 19 February 1895; *d.* 31 January 1968), noted Guatemalan romantic author and poet. Born in Guatemala City, Herrera graduated in law from the national university. He traveled widely in Europe, Asia, Africa, and America. His first major collection of stories, *La lente opaca,* was published in Germany in 1921 while he lived there. Herrera served as ambassador for his country to Uruguay, Brazil, and Argentina. He established the first school of journalism in Guatemala at San Carlos University, where he also was a professor of law. His novels include *El tigre* (1934), *La tempestad* (1935), and *Caos* (1949). His poems were published in *Solera* (1962). An owner of coffee farms, he lived the last years of his life in Guatemala City with an elderly uncle.

*See also* **Coffee Industry; Journalism.**

BIBLIOGRAPHY

Enrique Anderson-Imbert, *Spanish-American Literature: A History,* 2d ed. (1969).

Epaminondas Quintana, ed., *La generación de 1920* (1971).

### *Additional Bibliography*

Arias, Arturo. *La identidad de la palabra: Narrativa guatemalteca del siglo veinte.* Guatemala: Artemis & Edinte, 1998.

Toledo, Aída. *Vocación de herejes: Reflexiones sobre literatura guatemalteca contemporánea.* Guatemala: Academia Editora: Editorial Cultura, 2002.

DAVID L. JICKLING

**HERRERA, JOSÉ JOAQUÍN ANTONIO FLORENCIO** (1792–1854). José Joaquín Antonio Florencio Herrera (*b.* 23 February 1792; *d.* 10 February 1854), Mexican general and politician. Born at Jalapa, Herrera was twice president of Mexico (1844–1845 and 1848–1851) and had a distinguished career in both the army and in political life. He fought for the royalists in the War of Independence, retiring in 1820 with the rank of lieutenant-colonel to Perote, where he opened a drugstore. After the publication of the Plan of Iguala, he joined the insurgency and was promoted to brigadier-general. A member of the first independent congress, he opposed Agustín de Iturbide and was jailed. His subsequent career alternated between senior military commands and political posts as minister of war, member of congress, and governor of the Federal District. Known as a moderate liberal federalist, he was elected interim president in 1844 and president in 1845. Forced to resign as the result of a military revolt, he was accused of being willing to negotiate the surrender of Texas to the United States. He was elected to congress in 1846–1847 and was military commander of Mexico City during the U.S. invasion. In 1848, he was again elected president, and served until the completion of his term in 1851, only the second Mexican head of state up to that time to do so. Herrera was director of the national pawn shop (Monte de Piedad) after he left the presidency, and retired in 1853.

*See also* **Mexico: 1810–1910; Plan of Iguala.**

BIBLIOGRAPHY

Thomas Ewing Cotner, *The Military and Political Career of José Joaquín de Herrera (1792–1854)* (1969).

### *Additional Bibliography*

García Icazbalceta, Joaquín, and Martínez, Manuel Guillermo. *Biografías, estudios.* México: Porrúa, 1998.

González Avelar, Miguel. *México en el umbral de la reforma.* México: Federación Editorial Mexicana, 1971.

Infante Padilla, Ricardo. *Semblanza del General José Joaquín de Herrera y Ricardos.* México: Ediciones Diaro de Guerrero, 1998.

Rivera Cambas, Manuel, and Pasquel, Leonardo. *José Joaquín de Herrera.* México: Editorial Citlaltépetl, 1972.

Trueba, Alfonso. *Presidente sin mancha.* México: Editorial Jus, 1959.

MICHAEL P. COSTELOE

**HERRERA, LUIS ALBERTO DE** (1873–1959). The Uruguayan lawyer and Blanco (National Party) politician Luis Alberto de Herrera Quevedo (he did not publicly use Quevedo) represented a current of political thought that came to be known as *Herrerismo*, still followed by some Blanco politicians in the early twenty-first century, and became recognized as a twentieth-century caudillo. Born in Montevideo on July 22, 1873, into a family with a strong presence in Uruguayan politics, he graduated from the Facultad de Derecho in Montevideo and practiced law before beginning his long political career. His first contacts with the Blanco Party came as a contributor to the paper *El Nacional* and as a soldier in the revolutionary army led by the Blanco caudillo Aparicio Saravia in 1897. Along with those of Eduardo Acevedo Díaz, Herrera's writings in this paper played an important role in the outbreak of this revolution against the Colorado president Juan Idiarte Borda. Herrera chronicled this experience in the book *Por la patria*. From 1902 to 1904 he held diplomatic posts in the United States and Canada, but he returned to Uruguay to take part in the 1904 revolution led again by Saravia, this time against the Colorado president José Batlle y Ordóñez. He served twice as a national representative, integrated the committee that reformed the national constitution in 1918, and later served as senator (1934–1942). He ran six times unsuccessfully for president. From 1943 to 1958 Herrera headed the largest sector of the Blanco Party.

A strong critic of Colorado domestic economic policies and international relations, during World War II he supported neutrality and nonintervention and advocated for national sovereignty. These positions contributed to his polemical reputation as a nationalist and fueled accusations that he was sympathetic to fascism. In the 1958 presidential elections he led his party to victory for the first time in ninety-three years. In addition to articles in newspapers, Herrera authored numerous studies of Uruguayan and regional political history and wrote essays on international relations and diplomacy. He died in Montevideo on April 8, 1959.

*See also* **Uruguay: The Twentieth Century; Uruguay, Political Parties: Blanco Party; Acevedo Díaz, Eduardo Inés; Batlle y Ordóñez, José; Caudillismo, Caudillo.**

BIBLIOGRAPHY

Castellanos, Alfredo R. *Nomenclatura de Montevideo*. Montevideo: Intendencia Municipal de Montevideo, 1977.

Haedo, Eduardo Víctor. *Herrera: Caudillo Oriental*. Montevideo: Cámara de Representantes, 1990.

Scarone, Arturo. *Uruguayos contemporáneos: Nuevo diccionario de datos biográficos*. Montevideo: A. Barreiro y Ramos, 1937.

Zubillaga, Carlos. *Herrera: La encrucijada nacionalista*. Montevideo: Arca, 1976.

WILLIAM G. ACREE JR.

**HERRERA, TOMÁS** (1804–1854). Tomás Herrera (*b*. 21 December 1804; *d*. 5 December 1854), army officer and governor of Panama (1831–1840; 1845–1849). Born in Panama City, Herrera participated in the Wars of Independence, serving under Simón Bolívar. After rising to the rank of colonel in the armed forces of New Granada, he was named governor of Panama in 1831.

In the midst of the political chaos created by the liberal revolt in New Granada in 1839–1840, a Panamanian popular assembly declared its independence on 18 November 1840 and persuaded Herrera to assume the presidency. In 1841, however, discussions with negotiators from New Granada convinced Herrera to denounce Panamanian autonomy, and in December he signed an agreement that provided for the reintegration of Panama.

As a result of his participation in the act of secession, Herrera was forced into exile in 1841. But by 1845, Herrera was rehabilitated and that year was appointed as governor of Panama by the president of New Granada, Tomás Mosquera. After Herrera's term ended in 1849, he became minister of war in the cabinet of New Granada's liberal president José Hilario López. In 1854 Herrera took a leading role in the defense of New Granada against the dictator José María Melo (1854) and was mortally wounded in battle near Bogotá on 4 December.

*See also* **Bolívar, Simón; Panama.**

BIBLIOGRAPHY

Concha Peña, *Tomás Herrera* (1954).

Juan Cristóbal Zúñiga, *El General Tomás Herrera, Hoy* (1986).

*Additional Bibliography*

Araúz, Celestino Andrés, and Patricia Pizzurno Gelós. *El Panamá colombiano (1821–1903)*. Panamá: Primer Banco de Ahorros y Diario La Prensa de Panamá, 1993.

Gaviria Liévano, Enrique. *Historia de Panamá y su separación de Colombia*. Santa Fe de Bogotá, Colombia: Editorial Temis, 1996.

WADE A. KIT

## HERRERABARRÍA, ADRIANO (1928–).

Adriano Herrerabarría (*b.* 28 Dec. 1928), Panamanian painter. After completing a master of fine arts at the San Carlos Academy in Mexico City (1955), Herrerabarría returned to Panama, where he was an art professor and later director of the Escuela Nacional de Artes Plásticas.

Herrerabarría's early work reflected the influence of social realism and Mexican muralism. In his mature style, which can be described as a surrealism of organic forms, he combined sociopolitical and racial issues with a visionary mysticism, as in *Posesión* (1981). Unorthodox and rebellious, he published his radical views in numerous articles. In addition to his easel paintings, he created numerous murals.

*See also* **Art: The Twentieth Century.**

BIBLIOGRAPHY

Rodrigo Miró, *4 artistas panameños contemporáneos* (1981).

Erik Wolfschoon, *Las manifestaciones artísticas en Panamá* (1983).

### *Additional Bibliography*

Paniza, Nayubel, and Adriano Herrerabarría. *Faena y legado: Adriano Herrerabarría*. Panamá: Pixartprint, 2005.

MONICA E. KUPFER

## HERRERA CAMPINS, LUIS (1925–).

Luis Herrera Campins (*b.* 1925), Venezuelan president (1979–1984). A long-time leader of the Social Christian COPEI (Comité de Organización Política Electoral Independiente) Party of Venezuela, Herrera Campins began his political career as president of the (Catholic) National Union of Students in the 1940s and later became the head of COPEI's youth organization. While in exile during the military dictatorship (1948–1958), he received a law degree in Spain. In 1958 Herrera Campins returned to Venezuela and was elected first to the Chamber of Deputies and subsequently to the Senate on the COPEI ticket. During the 1960s and 1970s he served as president of COPEI, president of the party's congressional delegation, and secretary-general of the Latin American Congress of Christian Democratic Organizations. After a bitter primary battle Herrera Campins won COPEI's nomination for president in 1978 and was victorious in the general election. His presidency was marked by falling oil prices, rising foreign debt, and economic crisis. His leadership was regarded by many as weak and ineffective.

*See also* **Venezuela, Political Parties: Social Christian COPEI Party.**

BIBLIOGRAPHY

Alfredo Peña, *Conversaciones con Luis Herrera Campins* (1978).

Donald L. Herman, *Christian Democracy in Venezuela* (1980).

David E. Blank, *Venezuela: Politics in a Petroleum Republic* (1984).

### *Additional Bibliography*

COPEI (Political Party). *Gestión 89: fracción parlamentaria del Partico Social Cristiano, COPEI.* Caracas, Venezuela: COPEI, 1989.

Herrera Campins, Luis. *Second Message to Congress, March 12, 1981.* Caracas, Venezuela: Ediciones de la Presidencia de la República, 1981.

Herrera Campins, Luis. *Sobre la reforma del Estado: Ponencia.* Caracas, Venezuela: Fracción Parlamentaria de COPEI, 1985.

Herrera Campins, Luis. *Voz y Caminos: 24 editoriales de oposición (mayo 1984–1986).* Caracas, Venezuela, 1986.

Herrera Campins, Luis, and Peña Alfredo. *Acusa Luis Herrera, Lusinchi fracasó.* Caracas, Venezuela: Editorial Ateneo de Caracas, 1987.

Little, Walter, and Eduardo Posada Carbó. *Political Corruption in Europe and Latin America.* Houndmills: Macmillan Press, 1996.

Mainwaring, Scott, and Timothy Scully. *Christian Democracy in Latin America: Electoral Competition and Regime Conflicts.* Stanford, CA: Stanford University Press, 2003.

WINFIELD J. BURGGRAAFF

## HERRERA LANE, FELIPE (1922–1996).

Felipe Herrera Lane (*b.* 17 June 1922; *d.* 17 September 1996), Chilean economist, lawyer, author, and leader of international organizations. Born in Valparaiso, Herrera studied law and philosophy at the University of Chile and then economics at the London School of Economics. He returned to teach economics and political economy at the University of Chile from 1947 to 1958, spending 1950–1951 teaching at the London School of Economics. At the same time, he served in various Chilean ministries, acted as a general director of the Chilean Central Bank from 1953 to 1958, and was a member of the boards of governors of the World Bank and the International Monetary Fund, where he acted as executive director from 1958 to 1960. Herrera's most important achievement was his involvement as one of the principal figures in the conception and establishment of the Inter-American Development Bank in 1959. He was elected first president of the new institution in 1960 and continued in that position until 1971. As one in charge of implementing the high ideals conceived for the bank, Herrera played the instrumental role in determining the initial thrust of development programs for Latin America. After his resignation, he returned to Chile to pursue his academic career. He briefly became involved in the Socialist politics of his past (he was defeated in a bid to become rector of the University of Chile in 1972), but ultimately rejected a cabinet position in the Salvador Allende government in 1973. During much of the 1970s and 1980s, Herrera acted as executive of various international organizations, promoted international and Latin American development programs, and authored numerous books. In 1997 the Inter-American Development Bank in Washington, D.C., held a ceremony to unveil a statue of Herrera at its world headquarters. In Santiago a cultural foundation was established in his honor.

*See also* **Economic Development; Inter-American Development Bank (IDB); International Monetary Fund (IMF).**

BIBLIOGRAPHY

Felipe Herrera Lane, *Vigencia del Banco Interamericano de Desarrollo: Antecedentes y perspectivas* (1982) and *El Banco Interamericano de Desarrollo: Experiencias y reflexiones* (1989).

*Additional Bibliography*

**Major Works**

*Seminario cultura y desarrollo: Homenaje a Felipe Herrera.* Santiago: La Fundación, 1998.

*Pluralismo, sociedad, y democracia: La riqueza de la diversidad.* Santiago: La Fundación, 2002.

**Secondary Works**

Castedo, Leopoldo. *Fundamentos culturales de la integración latinoamericana.* Caracas: Dolmen Ediciones, 1999.

J. David Dressing

## HERRERA Y OBES, JULIO (1841–1912).

Julio Herrera y Obes (*b.* 9 January 1841; *d.* 6 August 1912), Uruguayan politician and journalist, president of Uruguay (1890–1894). Herrera y Obes came from a prestigious family of professionals affiliated with the Colorado Party. He served as secretary to General Venancio Flores in the War of the Triple Alliance in 1865. He was minister of foreign affairs in 1872, representative to the national Parliament (*diputado*) from 1873 to 1875, and minister of government from 1886 to 1887 in the constitutional government of General Máximo Tajes. He was the principal inspiration behind the transition to civilian democracy from the militarism of Colonel Lorenzo Latorre and General Máximo Santos. Elected president in 1890, Herrera y Obes immediately faced a serious financial crisis during which various banks failed, including the National Bank. He overcame the crisis by a consolidation of debts arranged in Great Britain and by maintaining the gold standard in Uruguay. These moves later brought enormous advantages for Urugayan public finance. A man of refined culture and from a wealthy landowning family, he represented an era of civil elitism in which little faith was placed in the idea of people governing themselves. He brought before the Parliament the notion of "directive influence," in which the president would be involved in all the actions of his administration.

Herrera y Obes was a romantic personality, for decades the beau of Elvira Reyes. He began visiting her by carriage in his days of splendor and ended as an old man taking the tramway to see her in her Prado villa. He retained his prestige among elite members of his party until the end of his days, but when he died, President José Batlle y Ordóñez denied him funerary honors. The term "oligarchic democracy" is used when referring to this period because the idea of "directive influence" implied the involvement of the president in the designation of his own successor.

*See also* **Uruguay, Political Parties: Colorado Party.**

BIBLIOGRAPHY

Enrique Méndez Vives, *El Uruguay de la modernización* (1975).

Luis Melián Lafinor, *Apuntes para la biografía del doctor Julio Herrera y Obes* (1920).

Raúl Montero Bustamante, *Estampas* (1942).

Washington Reyes Abadie, *Julio Herrera y Obes, el primer jefe civil* (1977).

*Additional Bibliography*

Altesor, Homero. *Cronología filosófica del Uruguay*. Montevideo: Indice, 1993.

José de Torres Wilson

**HERRERA Y REISSIG, JULIO** (1875–1910). Julio Herrera y Reissig (*b.* 9 January 1875; *d.* 18 March 1910), poet and essayist who belonged to the Uruguayan Generation of 1900. Herrera was born in Montevideo into a prominent family; he was the nephew of Julio Herrera y Obes, president of Uruguay (1890–1894). Because he suffered from a heart condition, his education was sporadic in private schools and from relatives. He resigned for health reasons from his job as clerk in the Customs Office and later from his position as assistant inspector-general of the National Board of Elementary Schools. Herrera flirted briefly with politics, but grew disenchanted. For the most part financially dependent on his family, after 1897 he devoted his life to literature and in 1899–1900 published the literary journal *La Revista*. A follower of modernism, Herrera stressed ideals of beauty and harmony and opposed the prevailing materialism of his age. Herrera was an important part of a brilliant decade in Uruguayan literature—the first decade of the twentieth century. After his worst heart attack in 1900, he wrote "La vida," first published in 1906, and "Las pascuas del tiempo," written in 1900 but not published until 1913. There followed *Los peregrinos de piedra* (1909), *Ópalos: Poemas en prosa* (1919), *Los parques abandonados* (1919), and *Las lunas de oro* (1924). Herrera's poetry was imbued with aestheticism, imagination, inventiveness, and irony. He also wrote essays and newspaper articles. His prose writings include *Epílogo wagneriano a la "política de fusión"* (1902) and *Prosas: Críticas, cuentos, comentarios* (1918). Important editions of his collected works are *Poesías completas* (1942), *Obras poéticas* (1966), with a prologue by Alberto Zum Felde, and *Poesía completa y prosa selecta* (1978), with an introduction by Idea Vilariño.

*See also* **Literature: Spanish America.**

BIBLIOGRAPHY

Gwen Kirkpatrick, *The Dissonant Legacy of Modernismo: Lugones, Herrera y Reissig, and the Voices of Modern Spanish American Poetry* (1989).

Antonio Seluja, *Julio Herrera y Reissig: vida y obra* (1984).

*Additional Bibliography*

Alvarez, Mario. *Ensueño y delirio: Vida y obra de Julio Herrera y Reissig*. Montevideo: Academia Nacional de Letras, 1995.

Benítez Pezzolano, Hebert. *Interpretación y eclipse: Ensayos sobre literatura uruguaya (Lautrémont, Julio Herrera y Reissig, Felisberto Hernández, Juan Carlos Onetti y Marosa dei Giorgio)*. Montevideo: Linardi y Risso, 2000.

Espina, Eduardo. *El disfraz de la modernidad*. Toluca: Universidad Autónoma del Estado de México, 1992.

Malabia, Santiago. *El enigma desvelado: Sentido y descodificación de La torre de las esfinges de Julio Herrera y Reissig*. Montevideo: Ediciones del C.E.H.U., 2003.

Georgette Magassy Dorn

**HERRERA Y TORDESILLAS, ANTONIO DE** (1549–1625). Antonio de Herrera y Tordesillas (*b.* 1549; *d.* 1625), Spanish colonial historian and official chronicler of the Indies. Antonio de Herrera had a long and distinguished career in which he wrote one of the most encyclopedic accounts of Spanish activities in the New World. In his early years, he was appointed as secretary to Vespasiano Gonzaga, viceroy of Naples, where he began his history of the reign of Philip II. Herrera's loyalty to the cause of the crown attracted the attention of the court, and in 1596 he was appointed the official historian of the Indies, with the task of providing a favorable account of the Conquest and settlement of the New World to combat the negative versions being written by Black Legend partisans in England and northern Europe.

Herrera's most famous work, the eight-volume *Historia general de los hechos de los castellanos en las islas y tierra firme del mar océano,* was published in Madrid from 1601 to 1615. As official historian, Herrera had access to persons and documents not available to other contemporary writers. He had never set foot in the New World and therefore relied upon information contained in the *relaciones geográficas* and other state-sponsored informational surveys and reports, the writings of Bartolomé de las Casas, Diego de Landa, Gonzalo Fernández Oviedo, and Francisco López de Gómara. Like others of his time, Herrera was obsessed with chronology and inclusiveness; his synthesis is remarkable, but the wealth of information renders his *Historia general* difficult for the modern reader.

Herrera's mission was to glorify the work of Ferdinand and Isabella by emphasizing their Christianizing mission and true concern for the Indians. As an imperialist historian, he sought to justify the empire as a unit and accordingly deemphasized the accomplishments of individual conquerors. Nevertheless, unlike Gómara and Oviedo, Herrera gave Columbus credit for his unique achievement. The chronicle is told from a clearly European perspective; it opens with a description of the Spanish Empire and continues with a discussion of official activities in the New World from 1492 to 1546. Herrera was intellectually honest enough to admit to some of the abuses that had occurred, but he refused to condemn the process of the Conquest in general. He did incorporate many of Las Casas's ideas and did much to restore his good name, but on the question of official policy toward Indians, Herrera took the side of Oviedo and Sepúlveda. Herrera's *Historia general* is a substantial and informative work, and it is a major example of the sophistication of the late imperialist school of colonial historiography.

*See also* **Ferdinand II of Aragon; Isabella I of Castile; Spain.**

BIBLIOGRAPHY

David A. Brading, *The First America: The Spanish Monarchy, Creole Patriots, and the Liberal State, 1492–1867* (1991).

C. Pérez Bustamente, "El cronista Antonio de Herrera y la historia de Alejandro Farnesio," in *Boletín de la Universidad de Santiago de Compostela* 6, no. 21 (1934): 35–76.

Manuel Ballesteros Gaibrois, "Antonio de Herrera, 1549–1625," in *Handbook of Middle American Indians.* Vol 13, *Guide to Ethnohistorical Sources,* edited by Howard F. Cline (1973), pp. 240–255.

*Additional Bibliography*

Murray, James C. *Spanish Chronicles of the Indies: Sixteenth Century.* New York: Twayne Publishers, 1994.

KAREN RACINE

**HERRERISMO.** Herrerismo, a political movement of Uruguay's Blanco (National) Party, organized around the figure of Luis Alberto de Herrera (1873–1959). The movement was distinguished by conservative and populist paternalism, devotion to its hero, and nationalism. It was the most important political force in the Blanco Party between 1920 and 1960.

Herrera fought in the country's civil wars in 1897 and 1904. With Aparicio Saravia's defeat in 1904, the Blanco Party made its definitive entrance into electoral politics. Herrera was the architect of this transition, in which the old party exchanged "swords for votes." Herrerismo played a key role in the plebiscite that defeated Batllismo in 1916 and was the principal force opposing the ruling Colorado Party in 1922, 1926, 1930, 1942, 1946, and 1950.

In 1933 the movement supported Gabriel Terra's coup and was a principal ally of his regime. Herrerismo symbolized the existence of a popular conservative party and the system of Coparticipación between Blancos and Colorados. Allied with the Ruralista leader Benito Nardone, the movement triumphed in the general elections of 1958. The following year Herrera died while openly opposing his former ally Nardone. Not until 1989 did Herrerismo regroup under Herrera's grandnephew Alberto Lacalle De Herrera, whose neoconservative/neoliberal views won over the majority of his party and triumphed in the national elections.

*See also* **Batllismo; Herrera, Luis Alberto de; Uruguay, Political Parties: Blanco Party; Uruguay, Political Parties: Colorado Party.**

BIBLIOGRAPHY

Carlos Real De Azúa, "Herrera: El colegiado en el Uruguay," in *Historia de América en el siglo XX* (1972).

Washington Reyes Abadie, *Breve historia del Partido Nacional* (1989).

Ricardo Rocha Imaz, *Los Blancos: De Oribe a Lacalle, 1836–1990* (1990).

*Additional Bibliography*

Nahum, Benjamín. *El Uruguay del siglo XX*. Montevideo, Uruguay: Ediciones de la Banda Oriental, 2001.

FERNANDO FILGUEIRA

## HERTZOG GARAIZABAL, ENRIQUE

(1897–1981). Enrique Hertzog Garaizabal (*b.* 10 November 1897; *d.* 31 July 1981), Bolivian physician and politician, president of Bolivia (March 1947–October 1949). Hertzog, a native of La Paz, served as cabinet minister three times during the presidency of Daniel Salamanca. In the 1947 election Hertzog and his vice president, Mamerto Urriolagoitía, served as standard-bearers of the reconstituted Partido Unión Republicana Socialista. From the beginning of his administration, Hertzog faced severe labor unrest and a vocal political opposition. Concluding that his astute and tough-minded vice president was more adept in achieving results, Hertzog voluntarily left the office to Urriolagoitía, who completed the term in May 1951. Yet during Hertzog's two years in office, his government achieved improvements in education, social services, and communications. Hertzog returned to private life with the reputation of a dedicated citizen. He died in Buenos Aires.

*See also* **Bolivia: Bolivia Since 1825.**

BIBLIOGRAPHY

Herbert S. Klein, *Parties and Political Change in Bolivia 1880–1952* (1969).

Carlos D. Mesa Gisbert, *Presidentes de Bolivia: Entre urnas y fusiles,* 2d ed. (1990).

*Additional Bibliography*

Alexander, Robert J. *The Bolivarian Presidents: Conversations and Correspondence with Presidents of Bolivia, Peru, Ecuador, Colombia, and Venezuela*. Westport CT: Praeger Publishers, 1994.

Heenan, Patrick. *The South America Handbook*. Oxford: Routledge, 2002.

Mesa, José, Teresa Gisbert, and Carlos D. Mesa. *Historia de Bolivia*. La Paz, Bolivia: Editorial Gisbert y Cia, 2001.

CHARLES W. ARNADE

## HERZOG, VLADIMIR (1937–1975).

Vladimir Herzog (*b.* 1937; *d.* 24 October 1975), a prominent victim of torture under Brazil's repressive military regime. Herzog was a widely respected São Paulo journalist who had worked for the newspaper *O Estado de São Paulo,* for the British Broadcasting Company, and in films. Herzog earned his degree from the University of São Paulo and later taught in its School of Communications. At the time of his death he was the news director of São Paulo's television station TV Cultura.

Brazilian security forces considered Herzog, a Yugoslavian Jew who had emigrated with his family to Brazil, a communist. In September 1975 he voluntarily presented himself for questioning to the local Center for Internal Defense–Department of Internal Order at the headquarters of the Second Army. The following day Herzog's body was returned to his wife with the explanation that he had hanged himself in his cell. Herzog's wife received the body in a sealed coffin and was warned not to open it. Military guards kept a watchful eye over the burial services to ensure that the coffin remained closed.

Herzog's death caused a swift, angry public reaction and became a symbol for supporters of the human rights movement to end state-sanctioned violence in Brazil. Despite government efforts to cover up the incident, Herzog's murder created a national and international scandal for the administration of Ernesto Geisel because of its brutality and anti-Semitic undertones. Geisel, who was already in the process of moving the state apparatus away from brutal repression (*distensão*), took advantage of the scandal prompted by Herzog's death to neutralize the most repressive elements in São Paulo who were resisting *distensão.*

*See also* **Geisel, Ernesto; Human Rights.**

BIBLIOGRAPHY

Maria Helena Moreira Alves, *State and Opposition in Military Brazil* (1985).

Fernando Jordão, *Dossie Herzog-Prisão: Tortura e morte no Brasíl* (1979).

Report of the Archdiocese of São Paulo, *Torture in Brazil* (1986).

Lawrence Weschler, *A Miracle, a Universe: Settling Accounts with Torturers* (1991).

### *Additional Bibliography*

Markun, Paulo. *Meu querido Vlado.* Rio de Janeiro: Objetiva, 2005.

Perosa, Lilian Maria Farias de Lima. *Cidadania proibida: o caso Herzog através da imprensa.* São Paulo: Sindicato dos Jornalistas Profissionais no Estado de São Paulo: Imprensa Oficial do Estado, 2001.

SONNY B. DAVIS

---

**HEUREAUX, ULISES** (1845–1899). Ulises Heureaux (*b.* 21 October 1845; *d.* 26 July 1899), Dominican military officer and dictator (1882–1899). Known as Lilís, Heureaux was born at Puerto Plata to a Haitian father and a mother from the Lesser Antilles. Although raised in poverty, Heureaux acquired a good knowledge of economics, public finance, French, and English. He distinguished himself in the War of Restoration (1863–1865), during which he became the close friend of the leader of the insurrection against Spain, General Gregorio Luperón.

After the restoration of Dominican independence, Heureaux became one of the outstanding leaders of the Partido Azul (Blue Party), on whose behalf he fought the Partido Rojo (Red Party) of the Dominican caudillo Buenaventura Báez. During Báez's notorious Regime of the Six Years (1868–1874), Heureaux successfully opposed the caudillo's forces in the south of the country. In 1876 he defended militarily the presidency of Ulises Espaillat. On orders of Luperón, Heureaux terminated the presidency of Cesareo Guillermo in 1879. He became minister of the interior and the police during the presidency of Archbishop Fernando Arturo de Meriño (1880–1882), whom he succeeded as president (1882–1884).

Heureaux became president again in 1887 and ruled the Dominican Republic as an iron-fisted dictator until his assassination on 26 July 1899 at Moca. The establishment of his dictatorship led to his complete break with Luperón, who was driven into exile in Puerto Rico. After decades of chaotic political strife, civil war, and fiscal irresponsibility, Heureaux's dictatorship provided the necessary climate for a great influx of foreign (especially U.S.) capital to the Dominican Republic and for the rapid development of the sugar industry. Heureaux's dictatorship served as a model for that of Rafael Leónidas Trujillo.

*See also* **Báez, Buenaventura; Sugar Industry; Trujillo Molina, Rafael Leónidas.**

BIBLIOGRAPHY

Jaime De Jesús Domínguez, *La dictadura de Heureaux* (1986).

Mu-Kien A. Sang, *Ulises Heureaux* (1987).

### *Additional Bibliography*

Cassá, Roberto. *Ulises Heureaux: el tirano perfecto.* Santo Domingo: Tobogan, 2001.

Novas, José C. *Lilís y los agentes del Tío Sam.* Santo Domingo: Cocolo Editorial, 1999.

KAI P. SCHOENHALS

---

**HICKENLOOPER AMENDMENT.** The Hickenlooper Amendment was an amendment to the Foreign Assistance Act of 1962. Named after its sponsor, Senator Bourke B. Hickenlooper (Republican of Iowa), the amendment provided for a cutoff of economic assistance from the United States to any government that failed to take adequate steps for the compensation of expropriated U.S. companies. Following a military coup in 1968, the Peruvian government sought to reduce its economic dependency on the United States by nationalizing the International Petroleum Company. In an effort to secure adequate compensation for IPC, the Nixon administration threatened to terminate Peru's economic assistance and its access to international credit institutions. By the mid-1970s, Congress had dropped the amendment from its foreign assistance legislation.

BIBLIOGRAPHY

Eric N. Baklanoff, "The Expropriation of United States Investments in Latin America, 1959–1974," *SECOLAS Annals* 8 (1977): 48–60.

Frank Church, "Toward a New Policy for Latin America," in *Latin America and the United States in the 1970s,* edited by Richard B. Gray (1971).

Adelberto J. Pinelo, *The Multinational Corporation as a Force in Latin American Politics: A Case Study of the International Petroleum Company in Peru* (1973).

*Additional Bibliography*

Jochamowitz, Luis. *Crónicas del petróleo en el Perú.* Lima: Grupo REPSOL YPF, 2001.

O'Brien, Thomas F. *The Century of U.S. Capitalism in Latin America.* Albuquerque: University of New Mexico Press, 1999.

THOMAS M. LEONARD

## HIDALGO.

**HIDALGO.** Hidalgo, a Spanish term that originally meant "son of some means" (*hijo d'algo*) and over time became shortened to "hidalgo." As its origin suggests, the term indicated a person of some means, but not an heir to a great fortune or nobility. The term applied to some of the leaders of expeditions of the Conquest who were members of the lesser nobility seeking their fortune in the Americas.

In the sixteenth century, Spanish hidalgos were identified by the title "Don," as in Don Hernán Cortés, and women were identified by the feminine "Doña." Spanish leaders also flattered native elites who collaborated with them by addressing them as "Don." In the conquest of Mexico, the lord of Tetzcoco, who provided critical support against the Nahuas, was called Don Fernando de Alva Ixtlilxóchitl. Cortés's female companion and interpreter was called "Doña Marina." After the Conquest, Spaniards continued to use "Don" in addressing native political leaders.

Over the course of the colonial era, the European identification of "Don" or "Doña" with the lesser Spanish nobility ended, and it became a general term of respect used for an older person, a master craftsman, an employer, or someone in a position of authority.

*See also* **Caste and Class Structure in Colonial Spanish America.**

BIBLIOGRAPHY

Lyle McAlister, "Social Structure and Social Change in New Spain," *Hispanic American Historical Review* 43, no. 3 (1963): 349–370.

*Additional Bibliography*

Hamnett, Brian R. *Social Structure and Regional Elites in Late Colonial Mexico, 1750–1824.* Glasgow: University of Glasgow, 1984.

Henríquez Ayin, Narda. *El hechizo de las imágenes: Estatus social, género y etnicidad en la historia peruana.* Lima: Pontificia Universidad Católica del Perú, 2001.

Pérez Toledo, Sonia, and Herbert S Klein. *Población y estructura social de la Ciudad de México, 1790–1842.* Mexico City: Universidad Autónoma Metropolitana, Unidad Iztapalapa, 2004.

Ruiz, Teofilo F. *Spanish Society, 1400–1600.* New York: Longman, 2001.

Silverblatt, Irene Marsha. *Moon, Sun, and Witches: Gender Ideologies and Class in Inca and Colonial Peru.* Princeton, NJ: Princeton University Press, 1987.

PATRICIA SEED

## HIDALGO, BARTOLOMÉ (1788–1822).

**HIDALGO, BARTOLOMÉ** (1788–1822). Bartolomé Hidalgo (*b.* 24 August 1788; *d.* 28 November 1822), Uruguayan gauchesco poet, fervent defender of the independence of his native country, and a close friend of its liberator, José Artigas. Hidalgo attended a Friars Franciscan school. He became a bookkeeper in the ministry of the royal public treasury in 1806 and then joined the militia. Hidalgo fought the English and the Portuguese and was declared *Benemérito de la Patria* (National Hero) for his *Himno oriental* (Oriental [Uruguayan] Anthem). He carried out a series of political functions in the newly liberated Uruguay, including administrator of the general post office, interim finance minister, and censor at the Casa de Comedias. In 1818 he went to live in Argentina, where he died in the village of Morón. He wrote "militant" poetry (*Cielitos y Diálogos patrióticos,* 1820–1822), inspired by his fervid participation in the civil movement for independence.

Hidalgo was the initiator of gauchesca literature, poetic compositions written from the point of view of the gauchos, recreating also their speech, an archaic form of Spanish (see the *Diálogos* as well as *Relación de las fiestas mayas de 1822*). A neoclassic poet, Hidalgo nevertheless was very successful in creating this form of *rioplatense* (Argentine and Uruguayan) popular poetry, which attracted the mass of the citizenry at a moment when it was necessary to impress on them the need for independence. His passion for freedom and concern for subjects that inspired the people ensured the success of this new kind of authentically American sociopolitical poetry.

*See also* **Artigas, Josó Gervasio; Gaucho.**

BIBLIOGRAPHY

Rodolfo Borello, "Hidalgo, iniciador de la poesía gauchesca," in *Cuadernos Hispanoamericanos* 204 (December 1966): 619–646.

Nicolás Fusco Sansone, ed., *Vida y obras de Bartolomé Hidalgo, primer poeta uruguayo* (1952).

Martiniano Leguizamón, *El primer poeta criollo del Río de la Plata,* 2d ed. (1944).

*Additional Bibliography*

Benavides de Abanto, Flora. *El lenguaje dialectal en un texto de la poesía gauchesca: Nuevo diálogo de Bartolomé Hidalgo; análisis fonético, morfológico y sintáctico.* Lima: Universidad de Lima, Facultad de Ciencias Humanas, 1993.

Orgambide, Pedro G., editor. *Gauchos y soldados.* Buenos Aires: Instituto Movilizador de Fondos Cooperativos, 1994.

Zárate, Armando, comp. *Literatura hispanoamericana de protesta social: una poética de la libertad.* Córdoba: Lerner Editor, 1990.

ANGELA B. DELLEPIANE

## HIDALGO, ENRIQUE AGUSTÍN

(1876–1915). Enrique Agustín Hidalgo (*b.* 28 August 1876; *d.* 27 September 1915), Guatemalan satirical writer. Born in Guatemala City, Hidalgo did not finish secondary school owing to family financial problems. He worked as a newspaper writer, businessman, and teacher. As a writer he used the pseudonym "Felipillo," the name of an Indian interpreter who had accompanied the Spanish conquistadores. His most famous work of humor, the poem *Latas y latones,* was published posthumously in 1916.

*See also* **Literature: Spanish America.**

BIBLIOGRAPHY

Enrique A. Hidalgo, *Latas y latones,* 2d ed. (1961).

Humberto Porta Mencos, *Parnaso Guatemalteco,* new ed. (1977).

DAVID L. JICKLING

## HIDALGO DE CISNEROS, BALTASAR.

*See* **Cisneros, Baltasar Hidalgo de.**

## HIDALGO Y COSTILLA, MIGUEL

(1753–1811). Miguel Hidalgo y Costilla (*b.* 8 May 1753; *d.* 30 July 1811), leader of the Mexican Independence movement (1810–1811). Born near Pénjamo, Guanajuato, the son of a hacienda administrator, Hidalgo distinguished himself as a philosophy and theology student at the Colegio de San Nicolás Obispo in Valladolid, Morelia, and at the Royal and Pontifical University in Mexico City. In 1778 he was ordained a priest. He gained recognition for his innovative thought and in 1791 became rector of the Colegio de San Nicolás. In 1792, however, his fortunes changed and he was appointed curate of the distant provincial town of Colima. Although the causes of Hidalgo's removal are not known, historians speculate that financial mismanagement, gambling, heterodox thinking, or his well-known affairs with women were responsible. He is known to have fathered several children.

Hidalgo was transferred to San Felipe near Guanajuato, and in 1803 to the prosperous town of Dolores. A landowner, educator, and restless reformer, Hidalgo devoted much of his time to stimulating industrial development at Dolores, introducing a pottery works, a brick factory, mulberry trees for silkworms, a tannery, an olive grove, apiaries, and vineyards. He knew the French language, which was unusual for a Mexican cleric, read modern philosophy, learned Indian languages, and loved music. He spent much of his time in the nearby city of Guanajuato, where he was highly respected in intellectual circles. Some of Hidalgo's activities brought him into conflict with colonial administrators, and he was investigated on several occasions by the Inquisition.

Although it is not known exactly where Hidalgo began to support the idea of independence, he knew Ignacio Allende before 1810, had many contacts with the 1809 conspirators of Valladolid, and probably attended secret meetings of disgruntled creoles at Guanajuato and Querétaro. Many creoles in the Bajío region would not forgive the Spaniards for the 1808 overthrow of Viceroy José de Iturrigaray. As with the 1809 conspiracy in Valladolid and other plots, the creole leaders planned to achieve their goals by mobilizing the Indian and mestizo populations. The denunciation of the Querétaro conspiracy by some of its participants caught Hidalgo, Allende, and the other leaders by surprise. Although Hidalgo had manufactured some lances at Dolores and developed ties with members of the local provincial militia units, the exposure of the plot forced him to initiate the revolt prematurely.

The revolt commenced on 16 September 1810 with Hidalgo leading his brother Mariano, Ignacio Allende, Juan Aldama, and a few others to free prisoners held at the local jail and to arrest the district subdelegate and seventeen Spanish residents. After gathering some militiamen and others who possessed arms, Hidalgo marched on San Miguel el Grande and Celaya, arresting European Spaniards and threatening to execute them if there was armed resistance. Under the banner of the Virgin of Guadalupe, the rebellion recruited large numbers of Indian and mestizo villagers and residents of haciendas armed with lances, machetes, slings, bows, agricultural implements, sticks, or stones. They joined what became a triumphant if anarchic progress from town to town.

Hidalgo's revolutionary program remained unclear, but he sanctioned the confiscation of Spanish wealth at the same time he claimed to support King Ferdinand VII. The *ayuntamiento* of Celaya and the rebel chiefs named Hidalgo supreme commander. At Guanajuato on 28 September 1810, armed resistance by Intendant Juan Antonio Riaño at the fortified Alhóndiga led to the massacre of royalists and looting of the city by Hidalgo's followers and local plebeian elements. After taking some preliminary steps toward creating a new government, an organized army, a cannon foundry, and a mint, Hidalgo and his enormous force—estimated to be 60,000 strong—moved to the city of Valladolid, Morelia, which was occupied without resistance.

Declared generalíssimo, Hidalgo marched toward Mexico City by way of Toluca. On 30 October 1810, the inchoate rebel masses confronted a fairly well-disciplined royalist force commanded by Torcuato Trujillo. Following the battle of Monte de las Cruces, the royalists withdrew, granting a theoretical victory to the insurgents, but the green rebel troops had suffered such heavy casualties that many deserted. Hidalgo hesitated until 2 November before abandoning his plan to occupy the capital, realizing that his forces needed better military discipline, munitions, and weaponry. From this point, Hidalgo and Allende led a peripatetic march to disastrous rebel defeats by the royalist Army of the Center, commanded by Félix Calleja, at Aculco (7 November), Guanajuato (25 November), and Puente de Calderón, near Guadalajara (17 January 1811). After each battlefield defeat, the rebel forces dispersed, abandoning artillery, equipment, and transport.

Hidalgo did not fully formulate his ideas about independence or the form of government that was to replace the colonial regime, and he failed to develop a strategic plan to fight the war. At Guadalajara, however, he appointed ministers of justice and state, and he named a plenipotentiary to the United States. He abolished slavery, ended the unpopular tribute tax for Indians, and suspended the state monopolies of paper and gunpowder. The availability of a press at Guadalajara permitted the insurgents to publish a paper, *El Despertador Americano,* in which they disseminated their ideas and responded to royalist propaganda. Despite these advances, Hidalgo's dependence upon the lower classes and willingness to condone the cold-blooded slaughter of Spanish prisoners polarized the population and compelled the great majority of creoles to espouse the royalist cause.

Notwithstanding the continued popularity of Hidalgo and the rebellion, by the beginning of 1811 it was obvious that the military advantage rested with the royalist armies of Calleja and José de la Cruz. At Guadalajara, Allende opposed a definitive battlefield confrontation and proposed the division of the poorly armed and inexperienced rebel forces into several groups. This proposal was quite logical, but Hidalgo believed that the enormous numbers in the rebel force at Guadalajara—estimated by some historians at over 100,000 men—would overrun the royalists. However, in the six-hour battle at Puente de Calderón, the royalists annihilated the main force of the rebel army, freeing Calleja and other royalist commanders to pursue remaining rebel concentrations.

The senior insurgent leaders fled north with Hidalgo to Zacatecas. Differences between Hidalgo and the more moderate Allende had broken out previously, but even stronger denunciations followed in the wake of the disastrous military defeats. At the hacienda of Pabellón, near Aguascalientes, Allende replaced Hidalgo as the senior political and military chief of the rebellion. In the march across Coahuila to seek assistance in the United States, Hidalgo and his senior commanders were surprised and captured. Sent to Chihuahua for trial, Hidalgo was defrocked and executed by firing squad. His head was sent with those of Allende, Aldama, and Mariano Jiménez to be displayed in iron cages at the four corners of the Alhóndiga of Guanajuato. Following independence, Hidalgo's remains were reinterred in Mexico City.

*See also* **Indigenous Peoples; Mexico: The Colonial Period.**

BIBLIOGRAPHY

Lucas Alamán, *Historia de México desde los primeros movimientos que prepararon su independencia en el año de 1808 hasta la época presente,* 5 vols. (1849–1852; repr. 1942).

David A Brading, *Haciendas and Ranchos in the Mexican Bajío: León, 1700–1860* (1978).

Carlos María De Bustamante, *Cuadro histórico de la Revolución Mexicana,* 3 vols. (1961).

Nancy M. Farriss, *Crown and Clergy in Colonial Mexico, 1759–1821: The Crisis of Ecclesiastical Privilege* (1968).

Hugh M. Hamill, *The Hidalgo Revolt: Prelude to Mexican Independence* (1966).

Brian R. Hamnett, *Roots of Insurgency: Mexican Regions, 1750–1824* (1986).

José María Luis Mora, *Mexico y sus revoluciones,* 2d ed., 3 vols. (1965).

John Tutino, *From Insurrection to Revolution in Mexico: Social Bases of Agrarian Violence, 1750–1940* (1986).

Eric Van Young, "Moving Toward Revolt: Agrarian Origins of the Hidalgo Rebellion in the Guadalajara Region," in *Riot, Rebellion, and Revolution: Rural Social Conflict in Mexico,* edited by Friedrich Katz (1988).

*Additional Bibliography*

Guzmán Pérez, Moisés. *Miguel Hidalgo y el gobierno insurgente en Valladolid.* Morelia: Universidad Michoacana de San Nicolás de Hidalgo, 1996.

Ibarra Palafox, Francisco A. *Miguel Hidalgo: Entre la libertad y la tradición.* Mexico City: Porrúa: Facultad de Derecho, U.N.A.M., 2003.

CHRISTON I. ARCHER

**HIDES INDUSTRY.** The hides industry was a major economic activity of colonial Latin America. Livestock accompanied the early Spanish explorers to the Río de la Plata. During the seventeenth century, rapidly growing herds of wild cattle and horses grazed the fertile pampas. Enterprising Indians developed a significant livestock trade through Andean passes with Araucanians (Aucas) in Chile.

Conflict among Spaniards, mestizos, and Indians over plains resources worsened during the eighteenth century. Municipal officials in Buenos Aires and elsewhere tried to regulate the rapidly expanding traffic in hides. On a month-long Vaquería (wild-cattle hunt), gauchos might harvest thousands of hides. Legally, wild-cattle hunters had to obtain a special permit (*acción*). Many gauchos, however, engaged in illegal, freelance wild-cattle hunts and sold the animals they killed to unscrupulous merchants.

The early colonial hides trade was crude but profitable. Gauchos used hocking blades attached to long lances to hamstring and thus disable the animals. The riders then returned to kill and flay them. The hides were then staked out on the pampa to dry in the sun.

Hides were sold in both internal and external markets, but exports to Europe boomed during the eighteenth century. Buenos Aires exported about 185,000 hides from 1726 to 1738. City officials, concerned over the diminishing herds, took sterner measures to limit unsanctioned hunting by Indians and gauchos. By the mid-1700s, *estancieros* began laying claim to well-watered sections of the pampas and to the animals that grazed there. *Mataderos* (slaughterhouses) appeared on some *estancias.*

Buenos Aires exported more than 500,000 cattle hides during the 1810s; the figure rose to 2.3 million during the 1840s. Hides accounted for 65 percent of total exports in 1822. By the 1890s, however, they accounted for 26 percent. Other products, notably refrigerated beef, wool, and grains, marginalized the hides industry. Nevertheless, Argentina remains a leading producer of leather clothing and shoes.

*See also* **Meat Industry.**

BIBLIOGRAPHY

Jonathan Brown, *A Socioeconomic History of Argentina, 1776–1860* (1979).

Bailey W. Diffie, *History of Colonial Brazil, 1500–1792* (1987).

*Additional Bibliography*

Amaral, Samuel. *The Rise of Capitalism on the Pampas: The Estancias of Buenos Aires, 1785–1870.* Cambridge: Cambridge University Press, 1998.

Gelman, Jorge. *Campesinos y estancieros.* Buenos Aires: Editorial Los Libros del Riel, 1998.

Gelman, Jorge. *Rosas, estanciero: Gobierno y expansión ganadera.* Buenos Aires: Capital Intelectual, 2005.

RICHARD W. SLATTA

**HIGHWAYS.** Geography and culture have made highways important in Latin America since the earliest civilizations. Vast spaces and lack of navigable rivers put a premium on good roads in much of Latin America, yet until the twentieth century highway networks expanded very little. Throughout most of their history, many Latin American highways could hardly be called roads—they were defined more by the traffic that used them than by any physical features. Yet highways have always served as vital links between otherwise isolated and distinct regions, connecting centers of power with the periphery and producers with their markets, communicating information and ideas, acting as axes of change and growth, and, in the twentieth century especially, promoting the development of previously unexploited areas.

Both the Aztec and the Inca empires expanded along roads necessary for the movement of their armies. Rugged mountain territories made such passage difficult, however, and each state devised appropriate strategies for moving its forces. In Aztec Mexico, cross-country roads were merely unsurfaced trails, wide enough only for single-file traffic. Heavy *tameme* traffic linked principal towns in the Valley of Mexico with the tributary towns outside it via many complementary routes that ran both north-south and east-west. A primary east-west route linked the gulf coastal trading villages with the Valley of Mexico—the route followed by Cortés—and then down the western slopes of the sierra to the Pacific at the village of Huatalco near Acapulco. North-south routes went in many directions from the valley, funneling tribute into the center and Aztec armies outward on marches of conquest. In Mexico's rough terrain the armies were limited to established roads, but because of their size they often had to use more than one route to deliver their forces efficiently. Control of roads was critical and proved one of the first objectives of conquest and warfare. At the height of Aztec power their highways reached as far south as Central America and north into the lands of the Chichimecs, and were to be used by the Spaniards during their own marches.

Cuzco was the center of the Inca empire and hub of its sophisticated highway network, described in glowing terms by the Spanish chronicler Pedro de Cieza de León:

> This road which passes over deep valleys and lofty mountains, by snowy heights and waterfalls, through living rock and along the edges of torturous currents. In all these places, the road is well constructed, on the inclining mountains well terraced, . . . in the snowy heights well built with steps and resting places, and along its entire length swept cleanly and kept clear of debris—with post stations and storehouses and Temples of the Sun at appointed intervals along its length.

Inca administration of their roads was strict and efficient, enforcing local maintenance of road beds as well as *tambos,* or rest houses. In the Andes, importantly, roads were traveled by packs of llamas hauling goods.

The Inca network consisted of four primary trunks radiating from Cuzco. The northern route, the Camino de Chinchasuyu, ran into what is today Ecuador, linking the towns of Vilcas, Cajamarca, Quito, and, at the far north, Huaca. The main southern route, the Camino de Collasuyu, ran to Lake Titicaca and into modern Bolivia. Two branches took the Camino de Collasuyu farther south; one went down out of the Andes into modern Argentina, and the other continued south from Bolivia into Chile as far south as Santiago. The Camino de Cuntisuyu led west from Cuzco, providing access to Pacific coastal regions, and a fourth, less significant route, the Camino de Antisuyu, led east from Cuzco.

During the colonial period, indigenous highway networks changed little or fell into disrepair. Roads were still defined more by the traffic that used them than by actual tracks that marked their route. Lyle N. McAlister notes that while Spaniards may have extended and supplemented some existing roads, efforts concentrated on easing access to new mining areas. Most colonial roads were nothing more than trails, especially in the highlands, and were vulnerable to slides, erosion, and flooding. The development of livestock breeding, however, began to change the face of highways. Beasts replaced human bearers in Mexico and augmented llamas in the Andes. A carting industry developed on Iberian tradition developed in suitable regions such as northern Mexico and in Argentina.

In colonial Mexico, the main routes included the Veracruz–Mexico City–Acapulco road, linking the Atlantic with the Pacific and Europe with Asia. Another main trade route led north from Mexico City to Santa Fe de Nuevo México, passing through the mining towns of Querétaro, Guanajuato, Zacatecas, Durango, and Chihuahua to Santa Fe and Taos. A similar southern route to Guatemala, through Oaxaca, linked the cities of Puebla, Tepeaca, and Tuxtla with Guatemala City and passed through many distinct ethnic regions. Secondary routes, still of some significance, linked Mexico City with San Luis Potosí and Monterrey, with Toluca and Valladolid (Morelia), and with León and Guadalajara. These roads not only served the silver economies and regional trade of New Spain, but they also brought Iberian culture to the farthest and most isolated outposts of the empire. The European institutions represented by such settlements hastened the acculturation of many native peoples.

There was no primary land route running the length of Central America, but the transisthmian route across Panama was among the most important in the Indies. The difficult mountain trail channeled Peruvian silver from Panama City to Nombre de Dios and later Portobelo, then on to Europe. A much longer, equally important silver road traversed a large part of the Andes in South America, serving the mines of Upper Peru.

Peruvian roads were built on the Inca system linking the capital of Lima with the mines of Potosí and then through the South American interior to the Atlantic ports of Buenos Aires and Montevideo. The dominant trade and communication route in South America, it connected all the major cities. From Potosí, the northern route passed through La Plata (or La Paz), Cuzco, Huamanga (Ayacucho), Huancavelica and its mercury mines, and finally Lima and its port of Callao. South from Potosí, the route ran down out of the Andes through the Argentine settlements of Jujuy, Salta, San Miguel de Tucumán, and Córdoba before reaching the Río de la Plata. Spaniards also developed some important secondary routes in South America, such as one connecting Potosí with the closer port of Arica and another crossing the pampas from Buenos Aires to Mendoza, then over the Andes into Santiago, Chile. As in New Spain, South American roads hastened the consolidation of empire.

There was little change in the highway systems of Latin America through the colonial period, except for the volume of traffic dictated by economic prosperity. Several late-eighteenth-century efforts to improve the main routes, mainly through bridge construction and some paving, proved costly and difficult, and most fell through with the advent of the independence wars.

An exception, however, was Brazil. By 1800 coffee was a major export crop from the area of Rio de Janeiro and São Paulo, and ever-increasing production was being successfully hauled from plantation to port via a dynamic, adaptive transport sector that included mule trains, slave labor, and new roads. Brazil's first railroads replaced this complex, which had shown that it could support sustained economic growth.

The damage and crisis occasioned by war and its aftermath stifled road development in most of Latin America in the early nineteenth century, and railroads precluded their development in the second half. Roads certainly would have encouraged economic progress in many areas, but patterns of development favored export-oriented economies and the primacy of export-oriented infrastructures. Modern, efficient railroads serving producing regions and ports expanded at the expense of internal highway development. Significant highway construction awaited the appearance of automobiles and trucks.

Motor transportation made possible the exploitation of previously unsettled lands. Most Latin American nations began comprehensive highway construction programs in the first decades of the twentieth century, with varying degrees of success. Argentina, riding a wave of prosperity through the 1920s, improved its system significantly. In Mexico, despite the widespread destruction of the Revolution, highway construction increased dramatically after 1925. From 1925 to 1950, with the first phases of a national program, some

**The circular highways of the planned city of Brasília, c. late 20th century.** In the twentieth century, many Latin American nations undertook extensive highway construction. Linking different regions, these road systems were also seen as a devolopment tool, distributing industrialization and population from traditional centers. © JAMES DAVIS; EYE UBIQUITOUS/CORBIS

13,600 miles of paved road were completed; in the next ten years this number doubled. By 1975 Mexico had completed 115,000 miles of paved highway reaching into all regions of the country. In general, most Latin American nations saw important expansion in the years after World War II with the emergence of nationalist governments and import-substitution development strategies. By the 1970s and 1980s, however, difficulties in financing slowed many programs and brought others to a virtual standstill.

The Pan-American Highway system is an international project linking the Northern and Southern Hemispheres. Sponsored by the Organization of American States (OAS) and largely funded by the United States, the Pan-American system was first proposed in 1925 with the purpose of establishing a physical link among the capital cities of the American states. This concept was soon replaced by a more extensive highway system that included other routes between countries. The Pan-American system is generally regarded as a success, often serving as a major route in the areas through which it passes, and it is also recognized as a unifying link between American countries. In 2006 the Pan-American highway between Alaska and Chile was the site of a conceptual art project, the "School of Panamerican Unrest," that included performances, discussions, and screenings.

Perhaps the most ambitious road construction program has occurred in Brazil, with the Transamazon Highway. Part of a long-term plan to populate and develop Brazil's "backlands," it has been constructed in several phases. The first route completed was the Belém-Brasília highway, built between 1957 and 1967, linking the capital with the eastern edge of the Amazon Basin and much of Goiás Province. The second route, the Cuiabá-Santarém highway, was started several years after the first. This road leads from the state of Mato Grosso into the northwest and the state of Rondônia, and it too triggered significant internal migration and an economic boom based on the extraction of forest resources. The third major link, the Transamazonica, links the Northeast with the far west, through the provinces of Pará and Amazonas. This major stretch was intended to integrate these isolated regions with the rest of the country, free the Amazon Basin from dependence on the river for transport, provide an emigration route for land poor Northeasterners, facilitate the discovery of mineral wealth, and promote the economic growth of unexploited regions. All the aims, it is argued, were intended to strengthen the hand of the military governments that planned and began the network. However, in 1989 travel was still extremely difficult in many regions; it sometimes took three days to travel the 1,000 kilometers (621 miles) from Belém to Altamira. Similar projects, although on a much smaller scale, in Colombia, Ecuador, Peru, and Bolivia have also attempted to penetrate parts of the Amazon, often with similar social and economic results.

*See also* **Cuzco; Pan-American Highway; Transamazon Highway.**

BIBLIOGRAPHY

Alberto Regal, *Los caminos del Inca en el antiguo Perú* (1936).

Pedro De Cieza De León, *The Incas,* translated by Harriet de Onís, edited by Victor Wolfgang von Hagen (1959).

José Joaquín Real Díaz and Manuel Carrera Stampa, *Las ferias comerciales de Nueva España* (1959).

Concolorcorvo, *El Lazarillo: A Guide for Inexperienced Travelers Between Buenos Aires and Lima, 1773,* translated by Walter D. Kline (1965).

David Ringrose, "Carting in the Hispanic World: An Example of Divergent Development," in *Hispanic American Historical Review* 50, no. 1 (1970): 30–51.

Secretaria De Obras Públicas, *Caminos y desarrollo: México, 1925–1975* (1975).

Kenneth Lederman, *Modern Frontier Expansion in Brazil and Adjacent Amazonian Lands* (1981).

Lyle N. McAlister, *Spain and Portugal in the New World, 1492–1700* (1984).

Ross Hassig, *Aztec Warfare: Imperial Expansion and Political Control* (1988).

*Additional Bibliography*

Engel, Eduardo; Ronald D. Fischer; and Alexander P. Galetovic. *Privatizing Highways in Latin America: Is It Possible to Fix What Went Wrong?* New Haven, CT: Economic Growth Center, Yale University, 2003.

Zeitlow, Gunter. "Road Funds: Sustainable Financing and Management of Latin America's Roads." *Transport and Communication Bulletins for Asia and the Pacific* 75 (2005): 1–23.

JEREMY STAHL

## HILDEBRANDT PEREZ TREVIÑO, CÉSAR (1948–).

César Hildebrandt, born in Lima, September 7, 1948, is a Peruvian journalist who started writing for tabloids in the late 1960s. Known for his acid style, he became an avatar of accuracy in investigative journalism in the 1980s. In his print journalism career Hildebrandt has been an interviewer for *Caretas* magazine and the editor of *Sí* and *Testimonio* magazines and the *Liberación* newspaper. He served as anchor and director of political television programs on all Peruvian channels (except for state TV), including *En Persona, Enlace con Hildebrandt*, and *Hoy con Hildebrandt*, tending to quit programs after disagreements with station owners.

*See also* **Journalism.**

BIBLIOGRAPHY

Hildebrandt, César. *Cambio de palabras: 26 entrevistas.* Lima: Mosca Azul Editores, 1981.

JACQUELINE FOWKS

## HINOJOSA-SMITH, ROLANDO (1929–).

Rolando Hinojosa-Smith is a novelist and short-story writer whose works deal primarily with the everyday life of Chicanos along the U.S.-Mexico border in south Texas. Born January 21, 1929, he is the Ellen Clayton Garwood Professor of Creative Writing in the Department of English at the University of Texas at Austin. He has played a pivotal role in establishing Chicano literature as an academic discipline and shown the connections between Chicana-Chicano literature and Latin American literature. The son of a Hispanic father and a mother of English background, he is fully bilingual and bicultural and writes novels in English and Spanish, including English versions of his own Spanish-language novels. He has been instrumental in facilitating a dialogue among Chicano and Chicana authors and writers from Latin America, the Caribbean, and Spain. His best-known work is the Klail City series, novels based in or around a mythical city in south Texas.

*See also* **Hispanics in the United States; Literature: Spanish America; United States-Mexico Border.**

BIBLIOGRAPHY

*Primary Works*

*Estampas del valle y otras obras: Sketches of the Valley and Other Works.* Berkeley, CA: Quinto Sol, 1973.

*The Valley.* Ypsilanti, MI: Bilingual Press, 1973.

*Klail City y sus alrededores.* Havana: Casa de las Américas, 1976.

*Korean Love Songs from Klail City Death Trip.* Berkeley, CA: Editorial Justa, 1980.

*Mi querido Rafa.* Houston, TX: Arte Público Press, 1981.

*Rites and Witnesses: A Comedy.* Houston, TX: Arte Público Press, 1982.

*Dear Rafe.* Houston, TX: Arte Público Press, 1985.

*Partners in Crime: A Rafe Buenrostro Mystery.* Houston, TX: Arte Público Press, 1985.

*Claros varones de Belken/Fair Gentlemen of Belken County.* Tempe, AZ: Editorial Bilingüe, 1986.

*Klail City: A Novel.* Houston, TX: Arte Público Press, 1987.

*Becky and Her Friends.* Houston, TX: Arte Público Press, 1990.

*Los amigos de Becky.* Houston, TX: Arte Público Press, 1991.

*The Useless Servants.* Houston, TX: Arte Público Press, 1993.

*Ask a Policeman.* Houston, TX: Arte Público Press, 1998.

*Secondary Works*

Calderón, Héctor. "'Mexicanos al grito de guerra': Rolando Hinojosa's *Cronicón del condado de Belken.*" In *Narratives of Greater Mexico: Essays on Chicano Literary History, Genre, and Borders.* Austin: University of Texas Press, 2004.

Saldívar, José David, ed. *The Rolando Hinojosa Reader: Essays Historical and Critical.* Houston, TX: Arte Público Press, 1985.

MARK A. HERNÁNDEZ

## HIPPOLYTE, DOMINIQUE (1889–1967).

Dominique Hippolyte, (pseudonym, Pierre Breville; *b.* 4 August 1889; *d.* 8 April 1967), Haitian writer and lawyer. Hippolyte anticipated the themes of the Indigenist School. Besides nature and love, he demonstrated close knowledge of peasant beliefs. As a student, he acted in a play by Massillon Coicou and was deeply affected by the execution of the Coicou brothers in 1908. Patriotic disapproval of the U.S. occupation of Haiti (1915–1934) is to be found both in his poetry and in the drama *Le forçat* (1933). Hippolyte early introduced the poetry of the black American Countee Cullen in *La revue indigène,* helping to make the Harlem Renaissance known among Haitian intellectuals. He is the outstanding Haitian playwright of the first half of the twentieth century.

Hippolyte was trained in law and eventually was named *bâtonnier* of the attorneys in Port-au-Prince. He served at one time as a *commissaire* in the civil court. He headed the Haitian Commission of Intellectual Cooperation and the Alliance Française of Port-au-Prince. Laval University awarded him an honorary doctorate.

*See also* **Haiti.**

BIBLIOGRAPHY

F. Raphaël Berrou and Pradel Pompilus, *Histoire de la littérature haïtienne illustrée par les textes,* vol. 2 (1975), pp. 460–469, and vol. 3 (1977), pp. 424–441.

Robert Cornevin, *Le théâtre haïtien des origines à nos jours* (1973), pp. 132–135.

Naomi M. Garret, *The Renaissance of Haitian Poetry* (1963), pp. 47–48.

Dominique Hippolyte, *Jours de gloire* (theater; with Luc Grimard, 1917).

Dominique Hippolyte, *Quand elle aime* (theater, 1918).

Dominique Hippolyte, *Le baiser de l'aïeul* (theater, 1924).

Dominique Hippolyte, *La route ensoleillée* (poetry, 1927).

Dominique Hippolyte, *Tocaye* (theater, 1940).

Dominique Hippolyte, *Anacaona* (theater, with Frédéric Burr-Reynaud, 1941)

Dominique Hippolyte, *Le torrent* (theater, with Placide David, 1965).

CARROL F. COATES

## HIRSCH, MAURICE VON (1831–1896).

Maurice Von Hirsch (*b.* 9 December 1831; *d.* 21 April 1896), European-born philanthropist and founder of the Jewish Colonization Association. Baron Maurice von Hirsch established himself as a generous benefactor in Jewish affairs in Europe and as an important leader in efforts to resettle European Jews in Latin America.

Born in Munich to a wealthy and influential banking family, Hirsch likewise pursued a banking career, first in his family's business, than later with the firm of Bischoffsheim and Goldschmidt. Hirsch further increased his personal fortune by investing in the railroad and sugar industries.

The Hirsch family had long been involved in assisting persecuted Jews in Europe, a tradition Hirsch continued with efforts to provide relief in Russia. Pessimistic about the future in Europe, Hirsch looked to colonization in the Americas as a new beginning for persecuted Jews. He founded the Jewish Colonization Association in London in 1891 with precisely this goal in mind.

During the late nineteenth century, Argentina welcomed the prospect of immigration from Europe, particularly to its rural agricultural areas. Thus, in 1892 the Jewish Colonization Association chose Buenos Aires as the location for its headquarters in Latin America and established colonies throughout Argentina. These colonies organized around agricultural development and livestock, provided homes for nearly thirty thousand Jews by the start of World War II, by which time the majority of new settlers had emigrated, to escape the rise of Nazism in Germany.

As his legacy, Maurice von Hirsch left not only a tremendous personal fortune but also an association which after his death became one of the world's largest charitable organizations.

*See also* **Argentina: The Twentieth Century; Jews; Livestock.**

BIBLIOGRAPHY

Theodore Norman, *An Outstretched Arm: A History of the Jewish Colonization Association* (1985).

### *Additional Bibliography*

Sheinin, David, and Lois Baer Barr. *The Jewish Diaspora in Latin America: New Studies on History and Literature.* New York: Garland Publishers, 1996.

Zablotsky, Edgardo Enrique. *Filantropía no asistencialista: El caso del Baron Maurice de Hirsch.* Buenos Aires: Universidad del CEMA, 2004.

JOHN DUDLEY

## HISE–SELVA TREATY (1849).

Hise–Selva Treaty (1849), an agreement between the United States and Nicaragua that was signed on 21 June 1849 but never presented to the U.S. Senate. It was negotiated by U.S. chargé Elijah Hise and Buenaventura Selva, a Nicaraguan special agent sent to Guatemala to collaborate with Hise. Although he had not been given specific instructions, Hise was aware that he was to advance U.S. transit possibilities and stop British encroachments, which undermined U.S. transit options. The U.S. government supported the Nicaraguan claim to Greytown (San Juan del Norte) and the whole Mosquito coast.

The Hise–Selva Treaty granted the U.S. government and its citizens the right of transit and fortification of transit routes. In return, the United States pledged to protect Nicaraguan soil from foreign incursions. U.S. Secretary of State John Clayton used this and a treaty by Ephraim George Squier with Honduras to persuade the British to negotiate the Clayton–Bulwer Treaty in 1850.

*See also* **Clayton-Bulwer Treaty (1850).**

BIBLIOGRAPHY

Mario Rodríquez, *A Palmerstonian Diplomat in Central America: Frederick Chatfield, Esq.* (1964).

Wilbur Devereau Jones, *The American Problem in British Diplomacy, 1841–1861* (1974).

Karl Berman, *Under the Big Stick: Nicaragua and the United States Since 1848* (1986).

THOMAS SCHOONOVER

**HISPANIC AMERICAN HISTORICAL REVIEW.** The *Hispanic American Historical Review* (*HAHR*), published quarterly by Duke University Press in cooperation with the Conference on Latin American History of the American Historical Association (AHA), pioneered the study of Latin American history in the United States. *HAHR* publishes articles of original research, a comprehensive book review section, and special features such as forums, commentaries, and archival reports. Senior editors serve a five-year term; this post had been held by many of the most important scholars in the field.

The 1915 meeting of the American Historical Association, held in Berkeley and Palo Alto, California, in connection with the Pacific Panama Exposition, showcased the growing interest in and depth of scholarship on Latin America. Two attendees, William Spence Robertson and Charles Edward Chapman, met again the next year at a conference of historians and bibliographers held in conjunction with the centennial of Argentine independence, where they discussed the need for a scholarly journal in the field. At the AHA meetings in 1916, a dinner session to explore its development attracted some thirty supporters. The name Hispanic American Historical Review was selected from several variants; it was decided that *HAHR* should publish "social, economic, and political (including diplomatic) history" and not just "the mere external narration of events" (Chapman 1918, p. 9). The geographic scope was to include not only Central and South America but "the entire Caribbean area and those parts of the United States formerly under Spain and Mexico" (Chapman 1918, p. 9). The journal would consider articles in English, Spanish, Portuguese, and French. The spirit of these editorial policies has remained remarkably constant as *HAHR* approaches its tenth decade. When the first issue appeared in January 1918, it was hailed by no less than President Woodrow Wilson, who felt it "ought to lead to very important results both for scholarship and for the increase of cordial feeling throughout the Americas" (Wilson 1918, p. 1).

The founding editors struggled to secure funding; donations and subscriptions felt short of what they had hoped for, and publication ceased in 1922 when the largest private donor withdrew support. The journal was resuscitated in 1926 by rapidly expanding Duke University. *HAHR* weathered another difficult period during the years of World War II, facing this time a shortage not of funds, but of submissions. However, the expansion of American universities and their scholarly endeavors in the postwar years ensured the continued success of the *Review*. By the 1950s the journal was receiving upwards of sixty manuscript submissions a year, a rate that would hold steady through the first years of the twenty-first century.

BIBLIOGRAPHY

Butler, Ruth Lapham, ed. *Guide to the Hispanic American Historical Review, 1918–1945.* Durham, NC: Duke University Press, 1950.

Chapman, Charles E. "The Founding of the Journal." *Hispanic American Historical Review* 1, no. 1 (January 1918): 8–23.

Gibson, Charles, ed. *Guide to the Hispanic American Historical Review, 1946–1955.* Durham, NC: Duke University Press, 1958.

Meyer, Michael C. "Reflections on the *Hispanic American Historical Review.*" *Hispanic American Historical Review* 60, no. 4 (November 1980): 672–675.

Ross, Stanley R., and Wilber A. Chaffee, eds. *Guide to the Hispanic American Historical Review, 1956–1975.* Durham, NC: Duke University Press, 1980.

Simpson, Lesley Byrd. "Thirty Years of the *Hispanic American Historical Review.*" *Hispanic American Historical Review* 29, no. 2 (May 1949): 188–204.

Wilson, Woodrow. "A Letter from President Wilson." *Hispanic American Historical Review* 1, no. 1 (January 1918): 1.

KATHRYN J. LITHERLAND

**HISPANICS IN THE UNITED STATES.** "Hispanics" or "Latinos" in the United States trace their ancestry to one of twenty-two Spanish-speaking countries, including Spain, Mexico, Puerto Rico, and Cuba. In 2006, the U.S. Census Bureau estimated the Latino population at 42.7 million people, or 14 percent of the general population—up from 14.5 million in 1980—making it the fastest-growing population in the United States. These figures do not include the 3.9 million residents of the commonwealth, or *estado libre asociado* (free associated state), of Puerto Rico, who are U.S. citizens and can travel freely to the United States; nor does it include the ten to fifteen million people from Latin America estimated to be working in the United States undocumented. Immigration accounts for the rapid population growth of the Latino population (53 percent were born outside the United States), and the Census Bureau projects that with continued immigration and natural increase, the Latino population will reach 102.6 million by 2050.

The term "Hispanic" was first used by the Census Bureau in the 1970s and has become a common term of reference in U.S. popular culture. The term is used regularly by writers and journalists, by governmental and educational bureaucracies, as well as in day-to-day conversation. The terms "Latino"/ "Latina" have also become increasingly popular in reaction to the term "Hispanic," which some feel privileges the Spanish ancestry of this population at the expense of its African and indigenous origins. However, studies show that most Hispanics/ Latinos prefer to identify themselves according to their national ancestry or ethnic or regional identification (e.g. those who trace their ancestry to Mexico usually identify as Mexican-American or Chicano/ Chicana while those from Puerto Rico might identify as Boricua, *puertorriqueño*, or Puerto Rican).

Whereas the terms "Hispanic" and "Latino" are convenient when referring to this large population as a whole, they mask the very real differences that exist within and across these various groups, not all due to national ancestry. Some Latinos are first-generation immigrants to the United States, while others trace their families' presence in the U.S. back several generations, some as far back as the seventeenth and eighteenth centuries. Some have come to the United States as immigrants, others as refugees or temporary workers. Racially they identify as white, black, Asian, Indian, or multiracial. The majority are at least nominally Roman Catholic, but they are also mainline and evangelical Protestant, Jew, Buddhist, and believers in syncretic religions such as *santería*. The experiences of Latinos and Latinas in the United States vary, shaped by factors such as citizenship and political status, race and indigeneity, class and employment, gender and sexuality, religion, and the region of the country in which they settle. In sum, they reflect the diversity of the Latin American countries from which they trace their ancestry, as well as the diversity of the societies to which they migrate in the United States. Even the ways they speak Spanish and English are different, reflecting the national and regional variations of the Spanish and English languages. Some 31 million Latinos five years of age and older speak Spanish at home, making the United States the third-largest Spanish-speaking nation in the Americas, but with each generation in the United States, acculturating Latino families prioritize English at the expense of Spanish. Consequently, it is not unusual for many self-identified Latinos to speak only English. Similarly, thousands of the immigrants categorized as "Latino" by the U.S. government do not speak Spanish at all because they are indigenous peoples, speaking a wide range of indigenous languages.

### DEMOGRAPHIC PROFILE OF LATINOS

Latinos are a young population. The median age is 27.2, compared to 36.2 for the U.S. population as a whole. Socioeconomic levels of the Latino population tend to lag behind that of the general population. In 2006, 58 percent of Latinos age twenty-five and older had at least a high school education (86 percent for the general population), and 12 percent at least a bachelor's degree (28 percent for the general population). According to census figures, the Latino median income was less than $36,000 per year ($46,326 for the general population) and close to 22 percent lived below the official government poverty line (12.6 percent for the general population). Income and poverty rates are correlated with youth, limited educational opportunities, and the first-generation status of more than half the population. But figures vary from one group to the next, and by generation: second-generation Cuban Americans, for example, have among the highest rates of postgraduate education, exceeding that of the general population; whereas Puerto Ricans in the U.S. and Mexican Americans have among the highest high school dropout rates. Socioeconomic indicators reflect upward mobility the longer Latino families remain

**On the set of *Nuestro Barrio* (Our Neighborhood), a telenovela filmed and set in the United States.** No longer exclusively the province of Latin America, U.S. telenovelas reflect the issues facing the Hispanic population in the United States. AP IMAGES

in the United States. However, due to the changes in the U.S. economy since the mid-1970s, from an industrialized to a more service-oriented economy, Latinos face challenges that immigrants who arrived earlier in the century did not: that is, limited opportunities for the higher wages and economic mobility open to skilled labor. Most Latino immigrants realize that if they are to stay and make a life for their families in the United States, then education and/or self-employment is key to this mobility. The number of Latino-owned businesses grew 31 percent between 1997 and 2002, compared to the national average of 10 percent. In 2002 there were 1.6 million Latino-owned businesses that generated $222 billion in revenues.

Aspiring politicians often speak of—and pander to—the "Hispanic vote," but Latinos do not consistently identify with one specific political party. Mexican Americans and Puerto Ricans have historically voted Democratic because of that party's greater commitment to civil rights and the rights of the working poor, whereas Cuban and Nicaraguan Americans, many of whom are refugees, have tended to vote Republican because of that party's perceived stronger stance against left-wing regimes. But as Latinos assimilate culturally and structurally, they are more likely to identify with class or localized interests than ethnic interests. Journalists frequently refer to the Latino population as the "sleeping giant," especially during election years, because of the potential influence its votes may have on local, state, and national contests, but in reality this influence is tempered by the youth of the population and the low naturalization and voting participation rates. Only 38 percent of immigrants had naturalized by the year 2000, compared to 60 percent of other immigrants. And in 2004, only 7.6 million Latinos, or 47 percent of registered Latino voters, reported voting. However, history has demonstrated that when mobilized, Latino voters can serve as a formidable voting bloc.

As of 2007 there are 24 Latinos serving in the U.S. Congress, including Puerto Rico's resident commissioner (a nonvoting member).

At 64 percent, Mexican Americans are the largest Latino population, followed by Puerto Ricans (10 percent) and Cubans, Salvadorans, and Dominicans (each 3 percent). The remaining 17 percent trace their ancestry to other countries. Some Latino groups are associated with particular regions of the United States. Mexican Americans, for example, are historically associated with the southwestern states, the territory that was "acquired" from Mexico as a result of the Texas revolution (1836), the Mexican War (1846–1848), and the Gadsden Purchase (1854). Puerto Ricans are associated with the New York metropolitan area because of the "Great Migration" of the post-World War II period, which brought more than a million people to work in the factories and shipyards of the New York City boroughs. Similarly, Cuban Americans are associated with southern Florida, and especially its largest city, Miami, where more than half of the post 1959 migration settled. But these and other groups have moved beyond these traditional strongholds and reside in towns and cities across the country. In the early twenty-first century, Mexican immigrants are the largest Latino population in Washington Heights in Manhattan, a New York City neighborhood once associated with Puerto Ricans and Dominicans. Central Americans outnumber Cubans in Miami's Little Havana.

Forty-nine percent of Latinos are concentrated in just two states: California and Texas; 35 percent of the population of each is Latino (12.4 million and 7.8 million respectively). Thirteen states have Latino populations of half a million or larger, and in nineteen states they constitute the largest minority group. In the last census, the southern state of North Carolina registered the largest growth in Latino population, mostly from Mexico and Central America.

## THE SPANISH PRESENCE IN NORTH AMERICA

The United States as a nation emerged out of the thirteen predominantly English colonies on the Eastern Seaboard. But decades before the English established their first colonial settlements at Jamestown and Plymouth, the Spanish had explored parts of North America, and settled in the territories that are now Florida and New Mexico. Francisco de Garay, Juan Rodríguez Cabrillo, Juan Ponce de León, Pánfilo de Narváez, Hernando de Soto, Francisco Vázquez de Coronado, and Alvar Nuñez Cabeza de Vaca are among the many men who explored these northernmost reaches of the empire before they became American territories. The first Spanish settlement, consisting of 600 colonists, was founded in present-day Georgia in 1526 by Lucas Vázquez de Ayllón of Toledo and called San Miguel de Guadalpe but within months the settlement was abandoned, the colonists decimated by the harsh weather and by disease. In 1565, Admiral Pedro Menéndez de Avilés founded the first successful Spanish settlement at Saint Augustine, Florida, as a means of protecting the territory against French encroachment. It remains the oldest continually inhabited city in the United States. In 1598, Juan de Oñate established the first Spanish capital of New Mexico at the site of a Tewa village he renamed San Juan; in 1609, Governor Pedro de Peralta moved the capital to Santa Fe. By the time the Declaration of Independence was signed in 1776, a network of Spanish missions, presidios, and settlements extended from the Florida peninsula to California.

Spain's control over this southern section of the United States ended during the period 1819 to 1821. In 1819 Spain ceded Florida to the United States as part of the Adams-Onís Treaty, which established a clear boundary between Spanish lands and the Louisiana Territory. Florida remained a U.S. territory until 1845, when it officially became a state of the union. In 1822 Joseph Marion Hernández of Florida became the first Hispanic to serve in the U.S. Congress, as a representative of the territorial government. The first territorial census in 1825 counted 15,000 residents, including slaves, and the majority were descendants of Spanish colonists; but Anglo-American immigration to Florida increased, and by statehood the Spanish population was only a fraction of the estimated 85,000 people living in Florida. Nevertheless, the Spanish heritage of this region continues to be evident in the names of cities and geographic landmarks, and in the cultural pageants, food, folkways, and lexicon of the state's residents.

In 1821 Mexico won its independence from Spain, and the southwestern settlements were automatically incorporated into states and provinces of Mexico's republic. Over the next two decades, various U.S. administrations tried to acquire the southwestern territories as part of a national campaign to expand its boundaries to the Pacific coast, and thus expand the nation's commerce, trade, and political influence. To thwart U.S. expansionism, as Mexico granted the first of its *empresario* (land agent) grants in 1821 as a means of populating and establishing greater control over its northern boundaries, especially Texas. Disagreements between the American settlers who settled in increasingly larger numbers in this area and the Mexican government that tried to control their allegiances and activities culminated in the Texas Revolution of 1835–1836. When the United States annexed the republic of Texas nine years later, and claimed the Rio Grande as its southern boundary, the stage was set for a military confrontation between the two countries that would result in even greater territorial losses for Mexico.

The descendants of the Spanish colonists of North America, many of whom also claimed African and/or Indian heritage, identified themselves in many different ways according to their race, sex, class, and station in life. After Spanish settlements became American or Mexican territories, a distinct Spanish identification became less and less common. In the southwestern territories, for example, most increasingly identified as *mexicanos* rather than *criollos*, *gente de razón*, or any of the other social and political designations typical of Spanish colonial life.

However, despite Spain's loss of influence in North America, over the next two centuries Spaniards continued to settle in the urban and rural areas of the United States. From 1820 to 1900, an estimated 42,000 Spaniards migrated to the United States; and from 1900 to 1924, 174,000 migrated to the United States (although some 70,000 returned by the 1930s). By the mid-twentieth century, Spanish immigrants had a wide geographic distribution. Galicians worked as shopkeepers and factory workers in New York City and as steelworkers in Pennsylvania and Ohio; Andalusians were recruited to work in Hawaii's sugar plantations; Asturians worked as cigar makers in Ybor City and Tampa, Florida, and as coalminers in West Virginia; Basque sheepherders settled in rural areas of Nevada, Oregon, and Idaho. Wherever they settled they established cultural institutions, and newspapers and other publications, some of which continue to operate. In the early twenty-first century, the U.S. Census counts fewer than 400,000 self-identified Spaniards in the United States, most of them located in large metropolitan areas such as Miami, New York, and Los Angeles. Although they are popularly regarded as "Hispanics," they are more likely to identify with other European immigrants than with the immigrants from Latin America.

### MEXICAN AMERICANS/CHICANOS

The close to 30 million Latinos of Mexican ancestry represent several models of migration and accommodation to U.S. society: The first became Americans by conquest; since 1848, Mexicans have migrated to the United States as refugees, immigrants, and as *braceros* (temporary workers).

The Treaty of Guadalupe Hidalgo that ended the U.S.–Mexican War of 1846–1848 ceded to the United States close to half of Mexico's territory, out of which were carved the present-day states of California, New Mexico, Arizona, and parts of Utah and Colorado. (Texas became an independent republic in 1836 and was annexed by the United States in 1845.) The Treaty of Guadalupe Hidalgo and the Protocol of Queretaro guaranteed the rights and privileges of Mexicans in the conquered territories, but during the second half of the nineteenth century, the approximately 80,000 *tejanos*, *californios*, *hispanos*, and others of Mexican descent living in those territories in 1850 struggled to defend and assert those rights.

There was no one typical "Mexican American experience" in the postwar Southwest, but certain general patterns can be distinguished. As American settlers moved into the southwestern territories to reinvent their lives and establish economic and political control over the new territories, they clashed with the original inhabitants, especially over property rights. Because the Spanish-Mexican land grants had no fixed boundaries, and in some cases had not been officially registered (or the titles and registries had been destroyed), the boundaries and claims were easily challenged by squatters. In each state and territory, land commissions were appointed to adjudicate existing titles. Some cases took years to decide, and in the meantime landholders could not dispose of their land; had to pay for legal representation, interpreters, and other assorted court costs; and had to defend their lives and property from those who lay claim to their land. Even when the land commissions ruled in their favor, the high cost of litigation forced families to sell part or all of their land. Exemplifying this process was the Californio General Mariano Vallejo, one of the eight Californios who participated in the state's constitutional assembly. In 1846, his estate stood at an estimated 175,000 acres; by the time of his death in 1890, his homestead was only 200 acres.

In some communities, merchants, bankers, lawyers, and politicians conspired to raise taxes, increase foreclosures, and bar access to goods, resources, and services, all in an effort to drive Mexican Americans from their farms, ranches, and businesses, and from political office. In California, for example, the Foreign Miners' Tax of 1850, a $20 monthly fee for the right to mine, was applied to Mexicans born in California, even though they were U.S. citizens; and the state antivagrancy law (the so-called "Greaser Law") restricted their movement in towns. Violence and intimidation were also commonly used to drive people from their homes. In Texas, for example, the Texas Rangers became the agents of American cattle barons such as Richard King and Mifflin Kenedy and helped them expand their economic interests by intimidating Mexican families into selling or abandoning their properties. Vigilante groups used lynching as a form of social control: There are 282 documented cases of lynching of tejanos alone between 1848 and 1928, although the number of casualties was probably higher due to the press's tendency not to report such events. State and territorial governments also played a role in the disenfranchisement of Mexican Americans, seizing communal lands, most notably in New Mexico and Arizona, to establish state or federal park lands, or as entitlements for railroad companies and other private interests.

Mexican elites were sometimes able to protect their economic and political interests by aligning themselves through marriage with the new American order, most commonly by marrying their daughters to influential members of the Anglo community. Elite hispanos used such connections and were appointed to political office and other influential positions well into the twentieth century. In New Mexico, for example, Octaviano Larrazola was elected governor in 1918 and served as U.S. senator in 1928 and 1929, and Soledad Chacon, the first woman elected to public office, was elected secretary of state in 1922. But in most areas of the Southwest the odds were against Mexican Americans. Even those who were able to retain their property into the twentieth century found it increasingly difficult to compete in the changing capitalist economy of the Southwest that relied on large-scale commercial agriculture and ranching, and on the restrictive enclosure of large tracts of land. Spanish-Mexican inheritance practices that distributed land equally among family members made it difficult for families on increasingly smaller homesteads to engage in anything other than subsistence farming.

With the loss of land came a further loss of influence, respect, and prestige in a society that already devalued all things Mexican. Historians such as David Weber, Rodolfo Acuña, Arnoldo De León, and others have examined the ways the "Black Legend" about Spanish character shaped American experiences of borderland peoples during the early nineteenth century. The Texas Revolution and the Mexican War only exacerbated anti-Mexican sentiment. In newspapers, journals, travel diaries, and fiction, white settlers justified their political and economic domination by portraying Mexicans and Mexican Americans as the descendants of two inferior cultures that produced a lazy, apathetic, conniving, amoral, and intellectually deficient population that could not be trusted to understand or participate in democratic institutions.

Legal historians have noted that the Treaty of Guadalupe Hidalgo rendered the Mexicans of the Southwest "white" by virtue of the fact that only whites could be citizens in 1848, but nineteenth-century social attitudes and state policies relegated them to a second-class citizenship. Discriminatory hiring practices limited opportunities, which resulted in Mexican Americans' becoming concentrated in unskilled labor and excluded from managerial positions and membership in trade unions. "White primaries," literacy tests, poll taxes, and gerrymandering prevented the majority of Mexican Americans (and other Latinos) from exercising an effective political voice until well into the twentieth century when the 1960s civil rights legislation finally abolished many of these practices. From 1900 to 1953, only two Tejanos were elected to the Texas state legislature, both from the border city of Brownsville, which had a majority Mexican American population. Likewise, in California no Mexican Americans were elected to the state assembly from the 1880s to 1962. Segregation in housing, education, and public areas such as theaters, restaurants, pools, and even churches and cemeteries was enforced by custom if not by law. The 1876 Texas Constitution, for example, provided for separate schools only for white and black students, but by the 1940s segregated "Mexican schools" were established in 122 districts in fifty-nine counties throughout the state.

Mexican American history, then, chronicles this loss but also the many ways that Mexican Americans empowered themselves in a society that limited their opportunities. The legal histories of the nineteenth century borderlands document how Mexican Americans used the courts to assert their political and economic rights in a changing society. And when the vehicles for legal redress were limited or failed them, Mexican Americans did not hesitate to forcefully defend their families and communities. During the period 1850 to 1920, "social bandits" such as Juan Nepomucena Cortina, Catarino Garza, Tiburcio Vazquez, Gregorio Cortez, and groups such as *las Gorras Blancas* (the White Caps) physically challenged the individuals and institutions responsible for their people's displacement. Their "lawlessness" is celebrated in folklore and *corridos.* Rebellions such as the 1857 Cart War, the Salt Wars of the 1870s, and the Plan de San Diego (1915–1917), as well as the labor strikes in factories, agricultural fields, mines, and other industries during this period further challenged the stereotypes of a docile and apathetic population.

During the *Porfiriato* and the Mexican Revolution, more than a million Mexicans migrated to the Southwest, facilitated by the expansion of the railroads and the reality of a poorly patrolled border. By 1930, an estimated one million displaced Mexicans had migrated to the United States. The Mexican populations of Texas and New Mexico doubled. Towns such as San Antonio, Los Angeles, and El Paso tripled in size. Many of the Mexican exiles did not come to stay in the United States permanently; they hoped to return once political conditions in their country stabilized. They published a number of Spanish-language newspapers, including *La Prensa* in San Antonio and *La Opinion* in Los Angeles, to keep their people informed of the latest events in Mexico, and to interpret social realities in their host country. It is impossible to ascertain how many actually returned voluntarily once political conditions stabilized in Mexico. Many of those who did return to Mexico in the 1930s were forcefully "repatriated" by the U.S. government as part of a campaign to rid the country of "foreigners" who they claimed competed with Americans for jobs and relief in the Depression-era economy. The United States government, working with settlement houses, churches, and other institutions, as well as with Mexican consulates in the United States, pressured Mexican nationals to return to their country with the promise of land and jobs in northern Mexico that in many cases never materialized. Thousands of others were forcefully rounded up and deported, sometimes without regard for citizenship. As much as 40 percent of the population (estimated at 1.5 million in 1930) may have been repatriated or deported during the 1930s, many of them U.S. citizens and the American-born children and spouses of Mexican nationals.

By 1930, then, the Southwest had a diverse population of Mexican Americans. Some had been "Americans" for several generations; others were recent arrivals, immigrants and refugees with strong political and cultural ties to Mexico. Others were transnational workers who moved back and forth across the border with ease, spending part of their working lives in each country.

In communities across the country, from San Antonio and Los Angeles to Chicago and Detroit, Mexican Americans created numerous forums for political expression in the first half of the twentieth century: the *mutualistas* and benevolent associations that educated them about, and instilled pride in, their Mexican heritage; the *congresos* that brought people together to address common issues and concerns; labor unions such as the *Confederación de Uniones de Campesinos y Obreros Mexicanos* (CUCOM), representing more than 5,000 workers; the civil rights organizations such as the League of United Latin American Citizens (LULAC), which provided legal counsel for some of the most important civil rights cases of the twentieth century; and the veterans groups such as the American G.I. Forum, which represented the hundreds of thousands of Mexican Americans who have served their country in the armed forces since the Spanish-American War.

World War II marked a turning point in the history of the Mexican American population. As Americans of all races and ethnicities went to fight overseas, high-paying skilled jobs in factories and war industries suddenly became available to men and women who remained on the home front.

**Felix Longoria's funeral at Arlington National Cemetery, 1949.** The refusal of the funeral home in Three Rivers, Texas, to bury GI Felix Longoria's body in the local "whites-only" cemetery was a striking example of the intractable prejudice faced even by Hispanic soldiers returning from World War II. © BETTMANN/CORBIS

Thousands of Mexican Americans relocated to the industrial centers of the country to take advantage of these higher-paying jobs. With higher salaries came a higher standard of living: the opportunity to buy better homes, automobiles, and consumer goods; and the opportunity to be trained in skills that might be used after the war. It also produced a large-scale migration outside the southwestern border states, especially to the Midwest and Great Lakes region.

Over 300,000 Mexican Americans (500,000 Latinos in all) enlisted or were drafted to serve in the armed forces during World War II. They distinguished themselves in battle: Twelve soldiers received the Medal of Honor, the country's highest military distinction, and many more received the Bronze Star, Distinguished Service Cross, the Purple Heart, and other military distinctions. Mexican Americans who served overseas were especially affected by their experience. For many, military service provided the first opportunity to leave their segregated communities. Wherever they were stationed, local townspeople regarded them as just another group of American GIs and not second-class citizens. When on furlough they did not have to enter restaurants through back doors or sit at segregated lunch counters, nor were they forced to sit in theater balconies reserved for people of color. When they used public transportation, they could sit in any section. When they returned to the United States, the GI Bill allowed many to attend college for the first time or have access to loans for homes and businesses. These opportunities gave them a glimpse of what full citizenship could actually mean.

However, as veterans of other wars discovered, military service did not always guarantee respect and appreciation once they returned home. One of the saddest episodes of this period involved Private Felix Longoria of Three Rivers, Texas, who died in the Philippines. When Longoria's body was sent back to his home town for burial, the only funeral parlor in town refused to allow his family to use its premises for a memorial service or to bury his body in the local cemetery, both of which were reserved for "whites." The American G.I. Forum, the leading Mexican American veterans' association, was unable to persuade the owners of the funeral parlor. In the end, Congressman Lyndon Baines Johnson intervened and arranged Longoria's burial in Arlington National Cemetery. Even Medal of Honor winners, such as Macario García, of Sugar Land, Texas, soon learned that service to one's country did not change the circumstances of day-to-day living. Despite his many honors, one local diner refused to serve García a meal.

The labor shortages created by World War II led to the creation of the Mexican Farm Labor Program Agreement, popularly known as the bracero program. Over the next two decades, various such agreements were negotiated with the Mexican government. By the time the program was terminated in 1964, approximately 4.6 million Mexican workers had been brought in to work throughout the United States, primarily in agriculture. However, in the 1950s, Mexican workers were once again deported in large numbers, some as part of Operation Wetback (1954), a campaign to crack down on illegal immigration. Estimates of the number of deportees range from half a million to 1.3 million. One of the great ironies of the 1950s, then, was that as the bracero program imported hundreds of thousands of workers from Mexico, the INS was actively deporting hundreds of thousands of those who were undocumented. Since 1990, the H-2A visa program established by that year's Immigration Act has served as a type of bracero program, allowing growers to bring in agricultural workers if they can prove that a labor shortage exists and that these workers will not lower wages for American workers.

Not surprisingly, it was the World War II generation that was at the forefront of the decisive civil rights battles of the 1950s and 1960s. In the years following the war, legal cases such as *Mendez* v. *Westminster* (1946) and *Delgado* v. *Bastrop* (1948) successfully challenged the segregation of Latino children in public schools in California and Texas; in cases decided by the Supreme Court, *Hernández* v. *the State of Texas* (1954) challenged the exclusion of Mexican Americans from juries and *Escobedo* v. *Illinois* (1964) addressed criminal procedure and affirmed the right to counsel. Mexican Americans created a host of new political organizations in the post-war years such as the Viva Kennedy clubs, the Mexican American Political Association (MAPA), and the Political Association of Spanish-Speaking Organizations (PASSO), among many others, to encourage voter registration and voting. By 1964, five Mexican Americans had been elected to the U.S. Congress (four to the House of Representatives and one to the Senate), at the time the largest electoral representation of Mexican Americans in national politics in the twentieth century.

Some of the most important accomplishments in civil rights came in the late 1960s and the 1970s, through a series of events collectively known as *El Movimiento* or the Chicano Movement. Inspired by the Black Civil Rights Movement and especially the Black Power Movement, young activists held rallies, sit-ins, walkouts, and other mass demonstrations to call national attention to the poverty, high school dropout rates, and discrimination faced by Mexican Americans and other racial and ethnic minorities. This generation of activists reappropriated the terms "Chicano" (which had once been a pejorative) and *la raza*, and drew on Mexican and indigenous symbols and mythology to signify their new cultural identity and political consciousness. To call oneself "Chicano" or "Chicana" meant that one was culturally aware and committed to social justice. Among the most popular symbols of this cultural and political movement was the myth of Aztlán, the belief that the U.S. Southwest was the geographic area from which the first Mexicas originated. Chicanos, it was argued, were thus the true heirs of the Southwest.

A number of individuals and organizations were at the forefront of the civil rights struggles of this period. Cesar Chavez, Gil Padilla, and Dolores

**Luis Valdez and César Chávez outside the theater where Valdez's play *Zoot Suit* was playing, 1979.** The Chicano Movement of the 1960s and 1970s saw the collaboration of artists with community activists, such as playwright and director Valdez and Chávez, organizer and president of the United Farmworkers Union. © BETTMANN/CORBIS

Huerta organized the National Farmworkers Association in California (later renamed the United Farmworkers) to strike for better wages and working conditions for the agricultural workers of California and other parts of the Southwest. Reies López Tijerina and the *Alianza Federal de Mercedes Libres* occupied the Kit Carson National Forest and the county courthouse at Tierra Amarilla, both in New Mexico, to call attention to the intense poverty that resulted from land loss. Rodolfo "Corky" González and the Denver-based Crusade for Justice organized a national conference for Chicano youths in 1969 where they drafted the "*Plan Espiritual de Aztlán*" to articulate the goals of Chicano activism in the next decade. Chicano college students founded organizations such as the Mexican American Youth Organization (MAYO) and the *Movimiento Estudiantil Chicano de Aztlán* (MEChA) to call for educational reforms including a new curriculum that would incorporate the histories of racial and ethnic minorities; the creation of Chicano Studies programs in colleges and universities; and the hiring of Chicano teachers and administrators. José Ángel Gutiérrez and Mario Compean founded a political party, La Raza Unida Party, in 1970 to make the political system more responsive to Chicano needs and concerns. Its first national convention drew over 1,500 participants; and in the 1972 Texas gubernatorial election, the LRUP candidate received 6 percent of the popular vote, a notable accomplishment for a recently-formed third party.

The Chicano Movement saw a corresponding renaissance in the arts and letters. Luis Valdez's *Teatro Campesino* inspired the creation of community theater groups across the southwest to educate and entertain through productions of original works as well as classic Spanish and Latin American works. Alurista (Alberto Urista), Tomás Rivera, Rolando Hinojosa-Smith, Cherrie Morraga, Evangelina Vigil

Piñón, Rosemary Catacalos, Sandra Cisneros, Gloria Anzaldua, and Carlos Morton are just a few of the many writers and poets who received international attention for their work during this period. Chicano artists, inspired by the works of Mexican muralists Rivera, Orozco, and Siqueiros, used posters and painted on the walls of public buildings to make their art accessible to a broad audience and to celebrate family, community, history, and tradition. Others, such as Santa Barraza, Carmen Lomas Garza, Amado Peña, and Luis Jimenez used more conventional media such as canvas and sculpture. Because "mainstream" institutions rarely published or exhibited the work of Latinos, writers and artists created their own literary journals, newspapers, publishing houses, theaters, and art galleries to showcase their work. Their critical and commercial success eventually forced institutions to take interest. In the early twenty-first century, the works of Chicano and Chicana writers are published by the largest publishing houses and are translated into more than a dozen languages, and their art is exhibited in the leading museums and cultural institutions around the world.

The conservative political shift of the 1980s and 1990s made it difficult to sustain the political activism of the previous two decades. Many of the organizations at the forefront of the Chicano Movement disbanded and their members dispersed, some in disillusionment and frustration, others to take advantage of the new opportunities generated by their activism. Acuña and others have referred to the 1980s as the "Hispanic decade," a reactionary period when Chicanos became more complacent, satisfied by reform rather than revolution, and lost the cultural nationalism they had regarded as essential to addressing the social and economic problems that continued to challenge their communities. However, Chicano activism did result in significant opportunities for a new generation and a growing Latino presence in education, the news media, government, and business. At the same time, there were many signs that each succeeding generation would need to recommit itself to the struggle for equal opportunity: in 2000, one generation after El Movimiento, 44 percent of Latino young adults born outside of the United States (and 27.8 percent of U.S.-born Latinos) had dropped out of school, and Latinos remained overrepresented on the nation's poverty rolls. A new generation of activists continues to address these challenges.

### PUERTO RICANS IN THE UNITED STATES

Puerto Ricans, the second-largest Latino group in the United States, are the only Latin American population that migrates to the country as U.S. citizens. As residents of a dependency, or "commonwealth," of the United States, they are exempt from visa requirements and immigration quotas. Given the long American political and cultural presence on the island, some Puerto Rican migrants are also at least nominally exposed to the English language and U.S. political culture before they migrate to the continental United States.

Long before Puerto Rico became a U.S. territory, a small Puerto Rican population lived in the United States, predominantly in the Northeast, consisting of a few thousand merchants, students, and agricultural and factory workers. During the nineteenth century, some of Puerto Rico's leading intellectuals and revolutionary leaders spent part of their adult lives in self-imposed or forced exile in the United States, including Ramón Emeterio Betances, Eugenio María de Hostos, Lola Rodríguez de Tío, and Sotero Figueroa. Many joined forces with Cubans and other Caribbean immigrants to work toward the independence of their countries. Puerto Ricans played a prominent role, for example, in José Martí's *Partido Revolucionario Cubano.* The poet and exile Lola Rodríguez de Tío described Puerto Rican and Cuban revolutionary causes as "two wings of the same bird."

Even though Spain had granted Puerto Rico autonomy the previous year, the United States acquired it in the 1898 Treaty of Paris that concluded the four-month-long Spanish-American War. The United States established a military government on the island and rejected all appeals for self-rule or for statehood. In 1900, the Foraker Act allowed Puerto Ricans to elect representatives to a House of Delegates, but the president appointed the governor and all top administrators. For the next seventeen years Puerto Ricans were neither citizens of the United States nor citizens of an independent sovereign nation. The Jones-Shafroth Act of 1917 finally gave the Puerto Ricans U.S. citizenship and established a locally elected bicameral legislature. However, the governor continued to be appointed by the president of the United States until 1948, and Congress continued to exercise veto power over all legislation passed by the Puerto Rican legislature. The Jones Act also made Puerto Ricans eligible for the military draft, and Puerto Ricans have served in the U.S. armed forces since World War I. It was not until 1948, under pressure from the United Nation's decolonization campaign, that the United States finally permitted Puerto Ricans to elect their own governor. Luis Muñoz Marín, the head of the *Partido Democrático Popular* (PDP), was elected that year. Four years later, Puerto Ricans drafted their commonwealth constitution.

With the American presence on the island came a radical restructuring of Puerto Rican agricultural production and a transformation of the economy in general. U.S. sugar companies established plantation-style agriculture, displacing small farmers from their lands, and making coffee and tobacco production less important. Sugar production offered employment, at best, for a few months of the year. Many of those who could not find employment in the fields and sugar mills migrated to San Juan and other coastal towns in search of employment in service industries or in the island's small manufacturing sector, where they joined the large unemployed and underemployed population in these cities; others migrated to Cuba, El Salvador, the Dominican Republic, and the continental United States. More than 6,000 went to Hawaii (then a U.S. territory) during the first decades of the twentieth century as contract labor on sugar cane plantations, but the largest number of migrants went to the continental United States. By the 1920 census, forty-five states reported residents of Puerto Rican heritage. In the continental United States, Puerto Rican men and women established economic niches working in garment and cigar factories, docks and shipyards, and building the infrastructure of American cities.

Migration continued and increased as a result of World War I. The Department of Labor authorized the hiring of some 10,000 temporary contract workers from Puerto Rico to offset labor shortages causes by the war, and at the conclusion of their contracts many stayed in the United States. Until the Jones Act of 1917, Puerto Ricans were subject to the immigration laws, but after they received U.S. citizenship their migration was greatly facilitated. Puerto Rican labor became all the more desirable after Congress passed a series of restrictive immigration laws from 1917 to 1927, which essentially barred the migration of Asians and southern and eastern Europeans, and forced American industrialists and employers to look for alternative sources of cheap labor.

While many Puerto Ricans returned to the island during the 1930s, the Great Depression and the drop in world sugar prices only encouraged outmigration because it exacerbated the many problems on the island. By the end of the decade an estimated 36 percent of the population on the island was unemployed. Seven out of ten persons were illiterate and only half of Puerto Rican children attended schools. Life expectancy was forty-six years. Puerto Rican migration to the continental United States increased, especially to New York City. There they settled in the Lower East Side, Chelsea, and Brooklyn, but also established a foothold in East and south central Harlem, henceforth referred to as Spanish Harlem or *El Barrio* (the District). This largely working class population created dozens of organizations: *mutualistas* (mutual aid societies), trade unions, cultural and political organizations. Ironically, as residents of the island, they had no right to vote for president or congressional representatives, but once they established residency in the United States they were eligible to do so. Puerto Rican political clubs—both Democratic and Republican—sponsored and endorsed candidates for office, organized voter registration drives, and campaigned for issues important to the community. In 1937, Puerto Ricans elected their first representative to the New York State Legislature, Oscar García Rivera, a Republican from East Harlem. At the same time, Puerto Rican residents of New York continued to maintain an active interest in the politics of their homeland, and actively discussed issues at social and political gatherings, and in press editorials.

Eighteen thousand Puerto Ricans served as members of the American armed forces during World War I, mostly in racially segregated units in Europe or stationed at the Panama Canal. They have served in every war since then. From 1940 to 1946, more than 65,000 Puerto Ricans served in the armed forces, most notably as part of the 295th and 296th Infantry Regiments of the Puerto Rican National Guard, which served in the Pacific Theater. Some 200 Puerto Rican women served in the Women's Army Corps (WAC), where some served as linguists

**Dancers in New York's Puerto Rican Day Parade, 2007.** The parade celebrating Puerto Rican culture, one of the best attended in New York City, marked its fiftieth anniversary in 2007. AP IMAGES

and cryptologists. Later, 43,434 Puerto Ricans served in Korea. The 65th Infantry Regiment distinguished itself in battle, receiving a Presidential Unit Citation, a Meritorious Unit Commendation, and two Republic of Korea Unit Citations. Individual members of the unit received one Medal of Honor, four Distinguished Service crosses and 124 Silver Stars.

The so-called "Great Migration" of Puerto Ricans began in the wake of World War II and continued for two decades, facilitated by the rise of affordable air transportation and installment credit, and encouraged by the economic developments on the island. Under the guidance of the four-term governor Luis Muñoz Marín, Puerto Rico experienced a radical economic transformation—popularly known as Operation Bootstrap—that benefited some sectors of society but compelled others to leave for the United States. During this period, the Puerto Rican government lured hundreds of U.S. companies to the island through Section 936 of the federal tax code, which offered tax exemptions to Puerto Rican subsidiaries of U.S. companies. The island's ports, transportation and communication networks were developed in preparation for the projected increase in production and trade. By the 1970s Puerto Rico had became one of the top revenue-producers for American companies in Latin America, but Muñoz Marín's goal of diminishing poverty on the island had less spectacular results. For those fortunate enough to find employment in one of the new factories that dotted the landscape, incomes and living standards improved. But a large number of those who migrated to the towns and cities in search of steady employment never found the opportunities they sought, and instead capitalized on the new transportation networks to facilitate their travel to the continent.

By 1960, more than one million Puerto Ricans lived in the continental United States. Once again, New York City was the most popular destination (inspiring the popular term "Nuyorican"), followed by Chicago, Philadelphia, Camden, and other northeastern cities. By the 1950s the migration to the Northeast was so institutionalized that the Migration Division of the commonwealth's Department of Labor established offices in New York City and Camden, New Jersey, to provide referral services to Puerto Rican migrants, as well as to provide information on the island and its population to potential employers, business investors, and labor unions. The Migration Division published a number of reports and brochures for these various constituencies, including the eighty-page illustrated booklet "New York and You" that was distributed to migrants traveling to the city, providing basic information about housing, employment, transportation, medical services, taxes, military service, and legal assistance. The 1960 brochure "How to Hire Agricultural Workers from Puerto Rico" was distributed to growers throughout the United States.

The growth and concentration of this population in New York City in a relatively short period of time generated controversy, and citizens groups unsuccessfully lobbied to restrict further migration into the city. As early as 1949, the mayor's office established an advisory committee on "Puerto Rican affairs" to assist in addressing perceived problems created by this population, and to improve community relations. Puerto Ricans inspired the popular Broadway musical *West Side Story* (made into a Hollywood film in 1961), which even in the early 2000s, despite its one dimensional portrayals, continues to be the dramatic work most associated with the Puerto Rican community in the continental United States.

However, a more accurate representation of the experiences of Puerto Rican migrants can be found in the works of the writers and musicians who settled in New York City, Chicago, and other American cities before or as part of the Great Migration. These writers and musicians spoke to an experience that drew on and yet was distinct from the experiences of Puerto Ricans on the island. While many of Puerto Rico's best-known authors used the United States as a setting for some of their novels and short stories, it was not the central setting for all of their work. But for essayists such as Bernardo Vega and Jesus Colón, and later, the writers and poets who came of age during the 1960s and 1970s, such as Piri Thomas, Pedro Pietri, Tato Laviera, Miguel Piñeiro, and others, it was their experience as (im)migrants and ethnic minorities that preoccupied them. Race, class, inequality, language, and *puertorriqueñidad* acquired new meaning for them as Nuyoricans living in the center of the country that colonized them. Likewise, musicians such as Rafael Hernández composed traditional folk music—the *danzas, bombas,* and *plenas* that were popular on the island—but adapted these forms to the unique challenges of life in the United States. Others, such as Tito and Johnny Rodríguez, Tito Puente, Ray Barretto, Eddie Palmieri, and Johnny Pacheco were among the many Puerto Rican musicians who contributed to the Afro-Cuban rhythms and jazz styles that were popular in New York in the 1940s, 1950s, and 1960s, and which inspired a distinct musical style that became known as *salsa*.

For most Americans during the first half of the twentieth century, it was music and sport that first exposed them to Puerto Ricans on and off the island. This was especially true of baseball. Baseball was introduced on the island by Puerto Ricans who had learned the game in the United States. By 1897 Puerto Rico had established its first professional team (Cuba had teams by 1872), and over the next decades, Puerto Rican and Cuban teams competed regularly against American teams. By 1905, baseball players from Puerto Rico were hired to play in the Negro Leagues in the United States. In 1942 Hiram Bithorn became the first Puerto Rican to play major league baseball. Since 1942 approximately 220 players from Puerto Rico have played professional baseball in the United States (one hundred are currently active). Among the early players who distinguished themselves in the sport were Roberto Clemente, who became the first Latino to have 3000 hits and the first to be elected to the Baseball Hall of Fame; Rubén Gómez, the first Puerto Rican player to pitch in a World Series game and win a championship; and Willie Hernandez, the first Puerto Rican to win both the Cy Young award and the American League's Most Valuable Player Award. Many major league players return to Puerto Rico after their regular season to play in Puerto Rico's winter leagues.

Despite their U.S. citizenship, Puerto Ricans faced as many challenges as other immigrants—and perhaps even more, because of the changing economy of New York in the final decades of the twentieth century. By the 1950s there was a grassroots leadership tackling a host of problems that confronted the

**Roberto Clemente sliding into home base, 1971.** Pittsburgh Pirates' player Roberto Clemente became the first Latino elected to the Baseball Hall of Fame. © BETTMANN/CORBIS

Puerto Rican population in the United States, from the exceptionally high dropout rates among school students (estimated at 80 percent in 1960) to the high poverty rates to the need for vocational and language training for the changing U.S. labor market. Scores of young, idealistic, and bilingual graduates of universities and professional schools returned to their communities and created organizations to advocate on their behalf, among them the Puerto Rican Association for Community Affairs (PRACA); the Puerto Rican Forum; ASPIRA; the Puerto Rican Family Institute; and the Puerto Rican Legal Defense and Education Fund. The educator Antonia Pantoja played a key role in the creation of most of these organizations.

By the late 1960s, organizations with a more radical agenda emerged in New York City and Chicago, inspired by the national liberation movements around the world and the civil rights struggles of other racial and ethnic communities at home. According to Andrés Torres, et al. (1998), the core of the new Puerto Rican Movement consisted of eight organizations: the Young Lords, the Puerto Rican Socialist Party U.S. branch, El Comité–Puerto Rican Nationalist Left Movement (MINP), the Puerto Rican Student Union, the Movement for National Liberation, the Armed Forces for National Liberation (FALN), the Nationalist Party, and the Puerto Rican Independence Party. Most of these organizations focused on both U.S. and island politics, but their goals and strategies varied according to their self-identification. For some groups, it was their nationality as *puertorriqueños* that was most important, and thus they dedicated their energies to working for Puerto Rican independence. For others it was their status as members of an ethnic/racial minority in the continental United States that was most important, and such organizations concentrated on issues such as discrimination and poverty in their local communities.

The Young Lords was perhaps the best example of an organization that fused both causes. This political organization was founded in Chicago in the 1960s, drawing on the membership of a well-known street gang by the same name that had operated in the city for many years. Most of its members were second-generation children of Puerto Rican agricultural workers who had eventually settled in the immigrant enclaves of Chicago. Inspired by Fred Hampton of the Black Panthers, José "Cha Cha" Jimenez took on the political education of the youths associated with the Young Lords. Among their first activities were protests and demonstrations against the proposed destruction of traditional Puerto Rican neighborhoods in Chicago in the name of urban renewal (which some nicknamed "urban removal"). Over the next decade, chapters of the Young Lords were opened in New York and other major cities to raise the political consciousness of Puerto Rican youth. Working with the Black Panthers and various Chicano organizations, the Young Lords called attention to issues ranging from police brutality to the lack of affordable housing and health care. The organization also provided a number of services to its communities including street cleanup campaigns, legal aid and health clinics, and public information sessions. At the same time, it worked with pro-independence groups on the island, such as the Nationalist Party, to demand an end to Puerto Rico's colonial relationship with the United States, which they argued contributed to the poverty of Puerto Ricans on and off the island.

The most controversial group by far, however, was the FALN, which operated most actively during the period 1974 to 1983. FALN members placed bombs at sites they associated with the oppressors of the Puerto Rican people: the military, the government, and the U.S. capitalist economy. Most of the eighty bombings attributed to the FALN during this period occurred in New York City. The FALN was not the first of the pro-independence organizations to use violence to call attention to its cause, but the fact that the FALN's targets were in the United States rather than on the island drew unusual media coverage. Not since the 1950 attack on Blair House and the 1954 attack in the gallery of the U.S. House of Representatives by Puerto Rican nationalists had the U.S. press shown any interest in the Puerto Rican independence movement. Dozens of FALN members were eventually arrested and convicted for conspiracy.

As happened with the Chicano Movement, by the mid-1980s, the Puerto Rican Movement was essentially over. The idealism and energy required of activism was hard to sustain over an extended period of time, especially when organizations came under government surveillance. Activists grew weary, fearful, and disillusioned. Infighting was common when members disagreed about goals and strategies. In the early twenty-first century some organizations such as the Young Lords continue to have a visible presence in many communities, but by the 1990s they had lost the media attention or following they had once commanded. Their legacy endures, however. Many community activists were trained in one of these organizations. The emergence of bilingual education programs to help children stay in school, the hiring of Latino faculty and administrators, the growing political clout of Puerto Rican constituencies, the election of Puerto Ricans to public office, the rise of new political and cultural institutions, and the emergence of Puerto Rican and Caribbean studies programs by colleges across the Northeast are all testimony to the social activism of the period.

The literature, music, and popular culture created by Puerto Ricans in the continental United States continues to generate international attention, as voices and forms distinct from those on the island. The list of writers who are read and taught around the world has grown to include Nicholasa Mohr, Judith Ortiz Cofer, Tato Laviera, Sandra María Esteves, Esmeralda Santiago, and Edward Rivera, among many others. Likewise, Puerto Rican jazz, pop, hip-hop, and reggaetón have crossed borders and influenced musical styles around the world.

## CUBAN AMERICANS

The majority of the 1.4 million Cuban Americans currently in the United States arrived after 1959, when revolutionaries led by Fidel Castro assumed control of the Cuban government. Over the next forty years, more than one tenth of Cuba's present-day population migrated to the United States, and thousands more to other countries in the Caribbean, Latin America, and Europe.

The pattern of Cuban migration to the United States was established several centuries earlier, however, the product of commercial ties and geographical proximity. During the eighteenth and nineteenth centuries, Cuban merchants and businessmen conducted business and established homes in cities as diverse as Boston, New York, Philadelphia, Wilmington, and Baltimore. *Criollo* elites sent their children to boarding schools and colleges and universities in the United States rather than to Europe. Over time these expatriates established local ties, assumed U.S. citizenship, and even advocated for Cuba's annexation to the United States.

As a result of the Ten Years' War (1868–1878) and *La Guerra Chiquita* (1879–1880) a larger and more diverse migration from Cuba occurred during the final decades of the nineteenth century. The wars caused massive destruction of property and life, and the drop in world sugar prices in the years after the wars further devastated Cuba's colonial economy. While the Spanish Crown offered some political and economic concessions in the aftermath of these revolutionary wars, including the emancipation of Cuba's slaves, the political and economic turmoil pushed thousands of Cubans of all races and social classes to the United States.

The expanding cigar industry in the U.S. provided employment to thousands of these displaced Cuban workers. Florida, Louisiana, and New York, in particular, became important production centers in the American tobacco and cigar industry and attracted large numbers of Cuban workers. By 1895 distinct Cuban communities existed in Key West, Tampa, Martí City (in Ocala, Florida), Jacksonville, New Orleans, and New York City. Tampa and its cigar factory district, Ybor City, had the largest concentration and became the heart of the Cuban expatriate community. Interestingly, the first Cuban elected to public office in the United States was elected in the nineteenth century, not in the twentieth as is generally believed: Carlos Manuel de Céspedes y Castillo, the son of the Cuban insurgent leader, was elected mayor of Key West in 1876. All in all, more than 100,000 Cuban expatriates are believed to have settled outside of Cuba by 1900, the majority of them in the United States by the end of the nineteenth century.

Migration continued even after Cuba achieved independence. Because of the close proximity between the two countries, and the higher wages across the Florida straits, it was not uncommon for some Cuban workers to spend at least part of their adult working lives working in the United States. Records show that from 1920 to the eve of the Cuban revolution, an estimated 130,000 Cubans migrated to the United States, although these figures are probably an undercount. They came from all different classes, motivated by a variety of political and economic concerns, and most migrated with the intention of one day returning to their homeland to enjoy the hard-earned fruits of their labor in the United States. Joining these transnational workers were thousands more who came temporarily to the United States to vacation, to study, to invest or transact business, all contributing to the Cuban presence. By the eve of Castro's revolution, there were dozens of daily flights linking Havana and Miami alone. Just one airline, Pan American, scheduled twenty-eight daily flights between the two cities, and during peak travel periods, flights left every twenty minutes.

Cubans influenced American popular culture as much as Americans influenced theirs—in food, music, sports, and dance. From the music and dance rhythms of the mambo and cha cha crazes in the 1940s and 1950s to the baseball and boxing greats who inspired young boys around the country, Cubans left their mark on American popular culture. Entertainers such as Frank "Machito" Grillo and his Afro-Cuban band, Beny Moré, Desi Arnaz, and Chano Pozo found welcoming fans in the United States. The roster of Cubans who distinguished themselves in American sports during this period was equally impressive, from Minnie Minoso and Camilo Pascual in baseball to Kid Chocolate and Kid Gavilán in boxing.

After 1959 Cuba's historic ties to the United States once again made it logical that Cuban exiles would turn to the United States for political and economic refuge. Cuban migration to the United States occurred in distinct waves. The first wave occurred between January 1, 1959, to the Cuban Missile Crisis of October 1962 and brought a quarter million Cubans to the United States. Whereas the first to leave were those who were in some way connected to the old regime, the majority of the exiles were members of the disaffected middle class who became increasingly alienated by the social upheaval and the political and economic transformation that followed

Castro's rise to power. Agrarian and urban reform laws changed the character of ownership and production and placed most properties under the control of the state. Basic civil liberties such as freedom of speech, religion, and assembly were restricted, and the monitoring of the population became common under the watchful eyes of neighborhood committees called CDRs (Committees for the Defense of the Revolution). Shortages in basic food staples and consumer goods, brought on by the restructuring of the Cuban economy and later by the trade embargo imposed by the United States and several other nations, also affected Cubans across society. These and other factors proved to be decisive in forcing many people to leave their country. For those who left Cuba, the general feeling was that their popular nationalist revolution had been betrayed in favor of a communist one.

The migration out of Cuba followed a logical socioeconomic progression. The elites were the first to leave, followed by members of the middle and working classes. By 1962 the majority of émigrés were office and factory employees, artisans, and skilled and semi-skilled laborers. Arriving in the midst of the Cold War, the Cubans became powerful symbols for Americans of the clash between democracy and authoritarianism, between free enterprise and communism. Laws were bent or broken to facilitate the Cubans' entrance into the United States and to accommodate them once they had arrived.

Most Cubans who traveled to the United States did so under the assumption that they were exiles and not immigrants in the traditional sense of the term, and that they would soon return to their homeland. Because of the United States' long history of involvement in Cuban affairs, and in other parts of Latin America, they believed that it was only a matter of time before the United States intervened to depose Castro. They were correct: In 1960 the CIA began planning an invasion to overthrow the revolutionary government, an effort that culminated in the Bay of Pigs invasion of 1961. Until they could return home, the majority of exiles settled in South Florida because of its geographic proximity, its familiarity, and the existence of a resident Cuban population of some 30,000. South Florida's similarity to Cuba in topography and climate was an added bonus.

Under the Kennedy administration the federal government assumed a more assertive role in refugee relief efforts. President Kennedy established a Cuban Refugee Program within the Department of Health, Education, and Welfare that provided Cubans with monthly relief checks, health services, job retraining, adult educational opportunities, surplus food distribution, and resettlement to other parts of the country where jobs were more plentiful than in South Florida's tourism-based economy. The program also oversaw foster care for the more than 14,000 Cuban children who arrived in the United States unaccompanied as part of operation Peter Pan. By the time the program was phased out in 1975, it had spent $957 million for resettlement, relief, and other services.

Air traffic between the two countries ceased after the missile crisis, but during the next three years approximately 60,000 Cubans still found a way to reach the United States. The majority came via third countries, particularly Spain and Mexico, arriving with immigrant visas acquired at the U.S. embassies in those countries, or they sailed clandestinely from Cuba on small boats, rafts, and even inner tubes.

A second wave of Cuban migration began in September 1965 when Fidel Castro announced that Cubans with relatives in the United States who wished to leave the island would be permitted to do so. He designated the small fishing port of Camarioca as the port of departure for would-be emigrants and urged Cubans in the United States to return to the island by their own means to transport their families out of Cuba. The Johnson administration reacted quickly to exert control over the migration. Castro's announcement coincided with the passage of the 1965 Immigration Act, and President Johnson announced that the United States was willing to accept more refugees from Cuba but wanted greater say in determining who migrated and in what numbers. Representatives from the two countries met and negotiated a "memorandum of understanding": The United States agreed to send chartered planes to the seaport town of Varadero each day, transporting between three and four thousand Cubans each month. The flights continued until April 1975 when the Castro government once again halted emigration to the United States. By then 3,048

**The Mariel boatlift, 1980.** Negative publicity surrounded Cubans who arrived in the United States through the Mariel wave of migration, once it became known that the Cuban government had used the boatlift as an opportunity to rid the country of some of its prisoners and mentally ill. © BETTMANN/CORBIS

"freedom flights" had carried three hundred thousand refugees to the United States.

The end of the freedom flights did not stall Cuban migration to the United States. Several thousand more Cubans emigrated to the United States. over the next few years via third countries or by sailing illegally to the Florida shore. By September 1977 the total number of Cubans to arrive in the United States since January 1, 1959, through legal and illegal channels reached 665,043. Unlike undocumented immigrants from other countries, Cubans who arrived illegally were allowed to stay in the United States.

The third and most controversial wave of migration of the Castro era occurred during a five-month period in 1980. Echoing his actions fifteen years earlier, Castro announced in April of 1980 that all who desired to leave Cuba would be permitted to do so, and once again he invited Cuban exiles to sail to Cuba—this time to the port of Mariel—to pick up their relatives. Hundreds of exiles took him up on his offer and sailed across the Florida straits to pick up their relatives and any other compatriots who wished to leave the island. 124,776 Cubans arrived in the U.S. from April to October 1980 in what became known as the "Mariel boatlift."

However, in contrast to the previous two waves of migration, the Castro government dictated the terms. As the migration was underway, it became clear that the Castro government was using the boatlift to rid the country of people it considered undesirables. Cuban police removed citizens from hospitals, jails, and other institutions and forced them to board boats against their will. Cubans navigating the vessels were forced to take extra passengers whether they wanted to or not. As they sailed back to Key West, many sailboats and yachts sank from the additional weight, and passengers had to be rescued by the U.S. Coast Guard.

An estimated 1,500 of those who arrived in South Florida suffered from various mental and physical disabilities. Some 26,000 reported criminal records. Estimates varied, but of these 26,000, approximately 2,000 had committed serious felonies in Cuba, and once identified, most of these were sent directly to prisons in the United States to await deportation. The majority of the offenders had served time either for lesser crimes or for activities not criminalized in the United States. Under Cuba's *ley de peligrosidad* (law of dangerousness) Cubans could be incarcerated for gambling, drug addiction, homosexuality, prostitution, buying or selling on the black market, and promoting "subversive" ideas. The news media in the United States concentrated on the sensational news that the Castro government had "unloaded its undesirables" on the American people. The Cubans of Mariel were branded and stigmatized.

In the United States, the Federal Emergency Management Agency (FEMA) assumed responsibility for coordinating refugee relief efforts. Finding sponsors became an especially difficult task because close to half of the Cubans had no friends or family in the United States, and the negative publicity scared away many potential sponsors. The federal government opened up three military camps to house the refugees: Fort Chaffee, Arkansas; Fort Indiantown Gap, Pennsylvania; and Fort McCoy, Wisconsin. Almost half the Mariel immigrants, 65,541 people, waited for sponsorship in one of these camps; some stayed a few days, others remained for more than a year.

Demographically, the Cubans of Mariel were different from the Cubans who had arrived during the 1960s. The Mariel population was disproportionately male, younger by about ten years (averaging thirty years of age), contained a higher percentage of Blacks (roughly 20 percent), and reflected a wider geographic distribution. Despite these differences, the Cubans of Mariel had much in common with the working-class Cubans who emigrated during the freedom flights, especially in their occupational history. In education, they rated slightly higher, having completed more years of schooling than their earlier working-class compatriots.

The Mariel migration was most distinctive, however, in how it was perceived by the federal government and the larger society. Unlike the Cubans who immigrated from 1959 to 1973, the Cubans of Mariel were not considered legitimate refugees. The Justice Department determined that under the terms of the 1980 U.S. Refugee Act (which came into effect a month before the boatlift), the Cubans did not qualify for refugee status nor for the special assistance offered to those who held that status. This marked the first time since the Cold War began that the government denied refugee status to individuals leaving a communist state. For the next four years they held the ambiguous status of "entrant: status pending." It was not until 1984 that the Cubans of Mariel were able to regularize their status.

During the 1990s, the number of Cubans who sailed clandestinely to the United States increased dramatically as a result of the worsening economic conditions after the fall of the Soviet bloc. Soviet subsidies—estimated at $6 billion per year—evaporated; and a series of agricultural crises caused even greater shortages in basic consumer goods. Cubans, desperate to improve their economic situation, took to the seas on homemade rafts. During 1990 alone, the U.S. Coast Guard rescued 467 *balseros* (rafters), but their numbers increased steadily over the next few years. In 1993, the Coast Guard picked up 3,656 balseros, prompting Cuban American pilots to form an organization called Hermanos al Rescate (Brothers to the Rescue) to patrol the Florida straits by helicopter and small plane, to alert the Coast Guard and assist with the rescue missions.

The balsero crisis peaked during the summer of 1994. Despite warnings from the Clinton administration that balseros would henceforth be redirected to Guantanamo Bay, the U.S. naval base on Cuban soil, the balseros kept leaving the island. During the last two weeks of August 1994, the U.S. Coast Guard picked up an average of 1,500 each day. With no end to the migration in sight, the Clinton administration was forced to negotiate another migration accord with the Castro government. Under the terms of the 1994 agreement, the United States committed itself to accept a minimum of 20,000 per year, and the Castro government finally agreed to intercept any balseros, and to accept the Cubans detained at Guantanamo without reprisals. However, the 1994 accord has not stopped illegal boat traffic to the United States or to other countries.

Cuban Americans are often portrayed as one of the most successful immigrant groups in recent history. In the course of just one generation they came to occupy important positions in key institutions of South Florida society: colleges and universities, labor unions, political parties, the news media, and city government. Beyond South Florida, they are well-represented in the Florida state capital at Tallahassee; in Washington, D.C.; Wall Street; Hollywood; and even Cooperstown, New York, home of the Baseball Hall of Fame. The roster of Cuban Americans who are immediately recognizable in American popular culture include actors Andy García and Cameron Díaz, singers Gloria Estefan and the late Celia Cruz, athletes Orlando "El Duque" Hernández and José Canseco, Pulitzer-Prize winning author Oscar Hijuelos, the late Academy Award-winning cinematographer Nestor Almendros, fashion designer Narciso Rodriguez, and television personalities Bob Vila and Cristina Saralegui. Cubans have created the wealthiest Latino business community in the nation and are credited with the "Miami Miracle"—turning a sleepy resort town into a bustling metropolis, the so-called "Gateway to the Americas," the "capital of Latin America."

Cubans did especially well in Florida, and particularly the immigrant enclave of Miami. As early as 1980, they exhibited the highest income and educational levels of the three largest Latino groups, levels that were only slightly below the national average. The Cubans' success was attributed to several factors. On the individual or family level, the structure of the Cuban family ensured success because it was built around economic cooperation. Women had a high rate of participation in the labor force. As early as 1970, they constituted the largest proportionate group of working women in the United States. Many Cuban households also contained three generations, and the elderly contributed to the families' economic well-being directly, by salaries or Social Security benefits, or indirectly, by raising children and assuming household responsibilities. These factors, along with the Cubans' low fertility rates and high levels of school enrollment, facilitated their families' comparatively quick economic integration. The U.S. government's initial investment in their financial future through the job retraining programs of the Cuban Refugee Program also contributed to their success.

On the broader community level, the Cubans created prosperous businesses, built with the skills and capital of the middle-to-upper-class exiles that comprised the first wave of immigrants. Some of the wealthier Cubans were fortunate to have had money invested in U.S. banks at the time of the revolution, and when they settled in Miami or other cities they invested that capital in new business ventures. The middle classes did not have that type of capital, but they did have the kinds of skills and business know-how that transferred across borders. They identified the needs of the growing exile community and built businesses catering to those needs. When the major banks would not lend start-up money to Cuban entrepreneurs without collateral—which only the wealthier emigrés had—the smaller banks in the area (some Cuban or Latin American-owned) lent applicants money on the basis of their reputations back in Cuba. By the late 1960s, Cuban entrepreneurs also had access to loans from the federal Small Business Administration (SBA). Over time South Florida became home to a thriving entrepreneurial community, which provided job opportunities for the new immigrants arriving each year from Cuba and all over Latin America, assisting their assimilation into the economic mainstream.

The Cuban presence attracted domestic and international investments and helped convert Miami into a major production, trade and commercial center linking North and South America. Many U.S. industries, particularly the garment and textile industries, relocated to South Florida to take advantage of the large, initially non-union, labor pool. By 1980, more than a hundred multinational corporations had established regional offices in the Miami area, eager to take advantage of a large bilingual Cuban middle class adept at doing business in the Americas. The Port of Miami replaced New Orleans as the chief port of trade with Latin America, and Miami International Airport became one of the busiest airports in the world.

U.S.-born Cuban Americans fare better than their Cuban-born elders, and better than the non-Hispanic white population: By 2000 26.1 percent of second-generation Cuban Americans were educated beyond the high school level, as compared to 20.6 percent of non-Hispanic whites; and 36.9 percent of U.S.-born Cuban Americans had incomes above $50,000, as compared to 18.1 percent of

**Cuban Americans protest the return of six-year-old Elián González to his father in Cuba, 2000.** Despite the media's portrayal of Cuban Americans as politically homogenous, the community has become increasingly divided since 2000 over the role the United States should play toward Cuba. MIAMI HERALD/GETTY IMAGES

non-Hispanic whites. U.S.-born Cubans, however, are less likely to vote than their elders. Although turnout in presidential elections has reached more than 90 percent in some years, only 50 to 60 percent of Cuban Americans between the ages of twenty-five and thirty four vote, and fewer than 30 percent of those between the ages of eighteen and twenty-five turn out.

The political activism of the first generation of Cuban immigrants generates even more media attention than their economic success, since they are believed to exert an influence that far exceeds their numbers. Those who arrived in the 1960s immediately became entangled in the politics of U.S. foreign policy decisions. The Bay of Pigs invasion, the commando raids of Operation Mongoose, and the CIA's secret war against Castro are just a few examples of how the refugees were employed in military actions against their homeland. Elsewhere around the world, Cuban exiles played supporting roles in East-West struggles in the Congo, in Vietnam, and in Nicaragua. Not surprisingly, by the 1980s, Cuban Americans had tired of their role assisting other liberation efforts as well as their inability to bring about democratic change in their homeland. They abandoned paramilitary activities and turned to more traditional political strategies, namely, voting, advocacy, and lobbying. Because Cuban naturalization and voting participation rates exceeded those of other immigrants from Latin America, they positioned themselves to play an important role in the domestic affairs of the United States. Literally hundreds of political organizations have emerged in the Cuban exile/Cuban American communities, from the left *Brigada Antonio Maceo* to the rightist Cuban Liberty Council, to influence U.S. policy according to their vision of what Cuban society should look like. While the news media portrays the Cuban immigrant community as politically monolithic, the population has always been extremely heterogeneous.

Since 2000, Cuban Americans have become increasingly conflicted over the proper course of action for the United States to take in regard to Cuba. A 2000 poll conducted by Florida International University, for example, revealed that Cuban Americans acknowledged that the U.S. trade embargo on Cuba was a failed policy, but more than 60 percent favored enforcing it anyway. However, the poll also revealed that more than half of the Cuban Americans also favored selling medicine and food to Cuba, establishing dialogue and permitting unrestricted air travel to the island, which calls into question their understanding and commitment to the political concept of an embargo. Other public opinion polls also suggest that there is a cleavage between first and second generations, and between those who arrived before and after 1980. In a 2003 poll, 72 percent of Cuban American respondents between the ages of eighteen and forty-five said that spending time and money to improve their quality of life in the United States was more important than working for a regime change on the island, and 68 percent believed that Cubans on the island should be the ones to decide when and if their political system should change. Similarly, immigrants who arrived after 1980 are more likely to favor more open relations between the two countries because they still have relatives on the island. According to sociologists Susan Eckstein and Lorena Barbería, those who arrived after 1980 are more likely to admit migrating for economic as well as political reasons, and the more Cubans emigrate for income-earning purposes, the less likely they are to let politics stand in the way of transnational family ties. However, because these Cuban Americans are more recent arrivals, they are less likely to be naturalized and registered to vote and thus to play a role in shaping U.S.-Cuba relations. Like the second-generation Cuban Americans, their views on Cuba are less well-represented in political races and elections.

It is unclear how many Cubans would actually return to their homeland if the democratic changes that they insist upon were actually implemented. It is probable that those who have raised families in the United States would stay because over the course of a generation they have established ties in the United States, in spite of their original intentions. Those most likely to return are those who are disaffected or have lived in the United States a comparatively shorter period of time. Regardless of how many people return, the shared history and the geographical proximity between the two nations will guarantee the reemergence of a transnational working class that will migrate back and forth across the Florida straits, and play an active role in both economies and political systems.

### DOMINICAN MIGRATION

Migration from the Dominican Republic is largely a late-twentieth century phenomenon. For much of its history, the country was an importer of workers rather than an exporter. There is no tradition of Dominican contract agricultural labor in the United States, as there is for the Puerto Ricans and Mexicans. However, since 1961, political and economic developments on the island have encouraged large-scale migration to the United States (and to Puerto Rico), and in the early twenty-first century Dominicans are one of the fastest growing Latino populations.

Like many other immigrants from the Caribbean, they migrate to the United States because of the historic ties between both countries. U.S. efforts to annex the Dominican Republic were blocked by the Senate in 1869, but the American presence on the island expanded nonetheless. Over the next century, the United States maintained an active interest in the Dominican Republic, not only because of American investments and the growing American population on the island, but because of the island's strategic location in the Caribbean, along the approaches to the Panama Canal. During the late nineteenth and early twentieth centuries, the United States blocked European intervention in Dominican affairs; restructured and oversaw the repayment of the Dominican Republic's foreign debt; and in 1905, created the General Customs Receivership to administer the finances of the government. After President Ramon Cáceres was assassinated in 1905 and warring factions threatened the stability of the country, President Taft sent a commission to broker a peace, accompanied by a 750-man unit of marines. The Marines were sent in once more, in 1916, to restore the peace, and remained on the island until 1924. During this period a U.S. military government oversaw all aspects of Dominican society, from law enforcement to the national budget. By the 1920s Americans also controlled almost all aspects of Dominican sugar production.

When the U.S. Marines finally left the island, one of the American institutions that remained was the *Guardia Nacional.* Rafael Trujillo rose through the ranks of the Guardia, and used his connections and influence to become the country's president in 1928. He ruled directly or through puppet presidents for the next three decades, ruthlessly eliminating his most vocal critics at home or in exile. In 1937 he ordered the massacre of more than 20,000 Haitians living in the country. Thousands of his countrymen were tortured and/or "disappeared" for speaking against him. Even foreign presidents became his targets: In 1960, he tried to have Venezuelan President Rómulo Betancourt assassinated. This event, more than any other, provoked the ire of the U.S. government, and in 1961, Trujillo was assassinated (with weapons reportedly provided by the CIA). By the time of his assassination, he had amassed an enormous fortune, controlling two-thirds of the country's sugar production and 35 percent of all arable land.

Trujillo's government had restricted the number of passports given to Dominican citizens, and consequently his assassination opened the door to a large-scale migration out of the country. During the 1950s only 990 Dominicans were permitted to emigrate, but between 1961 and 1986, 372,817, or five percent of the population in 1986, emigrated legally to the United States. Migration was especially heavy during the first three terms of Joaquin Balaguer's presidency (1966–1978) because of the economic changes on the island. On the surface, many of these changes were good: Industry expanded creating new jobs and opportunities, especially in the new industrial export zones; the gross domestic product increased; and there was a substantial growth in the number of students going on to vocational schools and colleges. However, the new industrial zones on the island failed to offer sufficient high-paying jobs to accommodate internal migration. Economic conditions deteriorated during the administration of Antonio Guzmán, which coincided with the world economic crisis of the 1970s. The stage for a large migration was set.

Those who emigrated to the United States did so in search of jobs or higher incomes, to continue their educations, or to join family members. By the 1980s most emigrants were from urban areas and were relatively better educated and more highly skilled than the Dominican population as a whole. Currently 77 percent of all Dominican emigrants live and work in the New York metropolitan area, which is home to the largest concentration of Dominicans outside the Dominican Republic (prompting one sociologist to coin the term *Dominicanyorks* for them). There they are concentrated in manufacturing and in the retail trades. In New York City, they settled in Washington Heights, in upper Manhattan, which is regarded as the heart of the Dominican community in the U.S. Over a third of Dominicans in the U.S. live in Washington Heights (nicknamed "Quisqueya Heights"). Other large concentrations were established in New Jersey, Florida, Massachusetts, Rhode Island, Pennsylvania, and Connecticut. An estimated 200,000 Dominicans live in Puerto Rico, many of them without documentation. One common and dangerous way to enter the country is to travel on a *yola* (a small boat) across the Mona Channel to Puerto Rico, sometimes with the assistance of a paid smuggler. Once in Puerto Rico, it is easier to acquire the documents and mannerisms that will help them "pass" as Puerto Rican if they choose to continue on to the United States.

By 2000, the Dominican population in the United States had grown to 1.4 million, making it the fourth-largest Latino population in just one generation. Because of its concentration in New York, most Americans outside the Northeast are unfamiliar with this Latino population. Their principal exposure to it is through the sport of baseball. More Dominicans have played professional baseball than any other Latin American group: Since 1956, 448 Dominican-born players have played major league baseball in the United States, and several U.S. teams openly scout (and run highly controversial training camps) for very young prospective players in the Dominican Republic. Among the contemporary players who have attracted extraordinary media attention are Alex Rodriguez and Sammy Sosa. For non-sports lovers, however, the works of author Julia Alvarez, which have been adapted to film, have provided some introduction to the Dominican population.

Unemployment rates among U.S. Dominicans are high: The mean annual per capita household income of the Dominican population in the United States was $11,065 in 1999, or half of the national average. Female-headed households in New York City were among the most likely to live in poverty.

However, the socioeconomic data shows that the U.S.-born population is making significant strides. In 2000, close to 60 percent of all Dominicans born in the United States who were 25 years of age or older had received some college education, with 21.9 percent completing a college education. In New York City, Dominican high school retention rates exceeds that of other Latinos.

Despite the poverty of the first generation, cash remittances from Dominicans living abroad have become an integral part of the Dominican national economy. Remittances are sent to support family members, finance higher education, buy land, or establish family businesses. An estimated 71 percent of Dominicans in the United States send remittances on a regular basis, amounting to $1.6 billion per year (with an additional $1.1 billion coming from emigrants in Europe and other parts of the Americas). Much of the new construction in the country has been financed by the remittances sent by family members abroad.

## CENTRAL AMERICANS

Like the Dominicans, the majority of Central Americans arrived in the late twentieth century. By 1970, tens of thousands of Central Americans lived in Los Angeles, San Francisco, New York, Miami, and Washington D.C. and its suburbs, and a few other cities. As the wars in Central America escalated and affected neighboring countries, these smaller northern populations served as magnets. The 1980 U.S. census, for example, counted 94,447 Salvadorans and 63,073 Guatemalans, and close to half had arrived in the previous five years. Their numbers increased dramatically after 1980, especially from Nicaragua, El Salvador, and Guatemala.

Only a small percentage of the Central Americans who arrived in the United States in the 1980s and 1990s came with immigrant visas. Some entered with some type of temporary visa such as a student or tourist visa and simply stayed once it expired, but the majority arrived illegally across the U.S.-Mexico border. The Central Americans who came to the United States were a cross-section of their societies: urban and rural dwellers, factory and agricultural workers, students and professionals, young and old. Some traveled alone; others came as part of family units. All were trying to escape the generalized climate of violence in their countries.

Those who arrived in the United States after 1980 encountered a society that was less than enthusiastic about their arrival. Since the passage of the 1965 Immigration Act, the United States had accommodated millions of immigrants and refugees from a variety of countries, but the welcome had worn thin. The influx of so many people from so many parts of the world in a relatively short period of time contributed to an anti-immigrant backlash that led to the passage of four new pieces of legislation during the 1980s and 1990s to control their numbers.

The majority of Central Americans did not qualify for asylum in the United States under the terms of the recently passed 1980 Refugee Act. The 1980 act adopted the United Nations' definition of refugee expanded by the 1967 Protocol, in an attempt to standardize the process by which people were officially recognized as refugees and asylees. Prior to 1980, U.S. Cold War policies rewarded those fleeing communist nations. But after 1980 a petitioner for asylum had to prove certain conditions: a refugee was a person who "owing to a well-founded fear of persecution for reasons of race, religion, nationality, membership of a particular social group or political opinion, is outside the country of his nationality and is unable, or owing to such fear, unwilling to avail himself to the protection of that country." The challenge, then, was to provide evidence of a well-founded fear of persecution, and in practice the evaluation of that evidence continued to be politicized. By 1990 more than 90 percent of the refugee admissions from abroad came from communist countries. For the next decade, then, refugees from Central America and their advocates faced an uphill legal battle.

A vocal segment of the U.S. population challenged U.S. refugee policy as a means of protesting U.S. foreign policy in Central America. These Americans argued that the United States had a legal obligation to protect the refugees based on domestic precedent and the international conventions to which it was a signatory, and a moral obligation to do so based on its long history of economic exploitation of the region as well as the role it was then playing in supporting corrupt military regimes and death squads. Much of their energy focused on the campaign to win Eventual

Voluntary Departure (EVD) status for Central Americans, especially for the Salvadorans who were believed to be in the most desperate situation. EVD, popularly known as "safe haven," would allow Salvadorans to remain legally in the United States until conditions improved in their homeland. In 1983 Senator Dennis DeConcini (D-Arizona) and Representative Joseph Moakley (D-Massachusetts) introduced the first safe haven legislation for Salvadorans, which was debated on and off for the next seven years.

Community groups along the U.S.-Mexico border mobilized to provide Central American refugees with shelter, medical attention, and legal and psychological counseling. The Border Association for Refugees from Central America (BARCA), for example, provided food, shelter, and clothing to the refugees; raised funds to pay the bail bonds of detainees at Port Isabel and other detention centers; and located sponsor families for refugee children alone in this country. Groups such as *Proyecto Libertad*, *El Rescate*, the Central American Refugee Center (CARECEN), the Rio Grande Defense Committee, Texas Rural Legal Aid, and the Immigrant and Refugee Rights Project provided free legal counseling and representation. Shelters for the refugees sprang up throughout the Southwest, including *Casa Oscar Romero*, in the border town of San Benito, Texas, just outside the Brownsville city limits. By the mid-1980s thousands of Americans were engaged in one of the most important acts of civil disobedience of the late twentieth century: the sanctuary movement, a grass-roots resistance movement that protested U.S. foreign policy through the harboring and transporting of refugees, in violation of immigration law.

In 1986 Congress passed the Immigration Reform and Control Act (IRCA) that tried to reduce illegal immigration by expanding the border patrol and penalizing employers who knowingly hired undocumented workers. A key provision in the law was an amnesty program that allowed undocumented workers to regularize their status if they could prove that they had entered the country prior to January 1, 1982. Under IRCA's amnesty program 277,642 Central Americans were able to legalize their status (60 percent Salvadorans, 25.4 percent Guatemalans, and 6 percent Nicaraguans, and the remainder from other countries). However, the majority of Central American refugees arrived after January 1982, making them ineligible.

As the Border Patrol increased its surveillance of the U.S.-Mexico border, detention centers along the border filled to capacity with the people the Border Patrol called "OTMs" (Other than Mexicans). Abuses at detention centers in Texas and California, especially Port Isabel (popularly known as *el corralón*, or "the yard"), Los Fresnos, and El Centro, prompted numerous lawsuits, including *Noe Castillo Núñez, et al.* v. *Hal Boldin, et al.*; *Orantes-Hernández, et al.* v. *Smith, et al.*; *El Rescate Legal Services, Inc., et al.* v. *Executive Office for Immigration Review, et al.*; and *INS* v. *Cardoza-Fonseca*. U.S. judges hearing these cases ruled in favor of the plaintiffs and ordered the INS to inform detainees of their right to petition for asylum, to meet with legal counsel, and to have their legal rights explained in Spanish and English. According to the courts, no one could be deported or coerced to sign voluntary departure forms without being informed of these rights. But over the next few years, these injunctions were repeatedly violated. None of the lawsuits halted the deportation of Central Americans.

The decisions handed down in the various lawsuits against the INS did serve to buttress a larger class-action lawsuit against the government filed by eighty religious and refugee assistance groups, with the goal of securing asylum for Salvadoran and Guatemalan refugees. The 1991 settlement of *American Baptist Churches in the USA, et al.* v. *Edwin Meese III and Alan Nelson* (popularly known as the ABC lawsuit) assisted Salvadorans and Guatemalans to remain in the United States. Among the requirements of the settlement were the following: a) Salvadorans and Guatemalans still in the United States, whether previous petitioners for asylum or not, were entitled to a new adjudication process to be overseen by a newly trained corps of asylum officers; b) petitioners were entitled to work authorization while they awaited decisions in their cases; and c) asylum officers were not allowed to consider prior denials of asylum in their deliberations, nor the petitioners' countries of origin, nor the State Department's opinions and recommendations, but were allowed to consider human rights reports from nongovernmental agencies such as Amnesty International. The settlement agreement stipulated that "the fact that an individual is from a country whose government the United States supports or with which it has favorable relations is not relevant to the determination of whether an applicant for asylum had a well-founded fear of persecution."

The ABC settlement overturned more than 150,000 cases, granting new hearings to Salvadorans who had entered the United States before September 19, 1990, and all Guatemalans who had entered before October 1, 1990. In a parallel development, Congress passed the omnibus Immigration Act of 1990, which included the statutory basis for safe haven by creating a category called Temporary Protected Status (TPS). More than 200,000 Salvadorans living in the United States registered for TPS. On the expiration of their TPS status, Salvadorans became eligible for a new category, Deferred Enforced Departure (DED), which delayed deportation for one year.

Through TPS, DED, and the new asylum adjudication process, Salvadorans now had more vehicles through which to negotiate their legal stay in the United States. For sanctuary workers, legal counsel, and all those involved in the protests of the 1980s, these developments were a significant victory. Nicaraguan immigrants, in turn, won a major victory in 1997 when Congress passed the Nicaraguan Adjustment and Central American Relief Act (NACARA) which offered suspension of deportation to Nicaraguans who could prove that they had been continuously present in the United States as of December 1, 1995. Salvadorans and Guatemalans benefited from this law as well: They too qualified if they could prove seven years of continual residence in the United States, good moral character, and that deportation would cause extreme hardship to themselves, their spouses or their legally resident children.

One of the legacies of the Central American refugee crisis was the increased surveillance of the U.S.-Mexico border. By 2000 more 10,000 agents served in the Border Patrol, most of them along the Mexican border. Miles of new fences were erected with remote video surveillance systems. As a result, apprehensions of undocumented immigrants from Mexico, Central America, and other parts of the Americas increased to 1.64 million in 2000.

While there was some return migration after the 1990 Nicaraguan elections and after peace accords were signed in El Salvador in 1992 and Guatemala in 1996, the migration of undocumented Central Americans continued as a result of ongoing criminal and political violence, as well as natural disasters that have caused economic disruption and exacerbated poverty. Migration from Honduras and Nicaragua increased exponentially as a result of Hurricane Mitch in 1998, and from El Salvador after the earthquakes of 2001. By 2004 Salvadoran officials estimated that nearly one fourth of Salvadorans lived in the United States. These communities send billions of dollars in remittances to their homelands each year.

### SOUTH AMERICANS

South Americans are among the most understudied of the Latino populations, perhaps because of their fairly recent arrival. Close to half of the 1.9 million South American immigrants in the United States today (46.7 percent) have arrived since 1990, mostly from Brazil, Venezuela, Paraguay, and Colombia. The four largest populations overall are the Colombians, Ecuadorans, Peruvians, and Brazilians, with Colombians comprising the largest South American group (26.4 percent in 2000). Socioeconomic status varies from group to group: those from Venezuela, Argentina, and Brazil are among the most likely to have a college degree or higher, while those born in Ecuador, Guyana, and Colombia are the least likely; Argentines and Venezuelans have the highest median incomes, while Colombians and Ecuadorans have the lowest. But overall, as a group, the rates of education, employment, and income are comparable to that of other foreign-born populations in the United States.

South Americans reflect a variety of migration experiences. Some have migrated as political refugees from rightist or leftist regimes; others are more traditional immigrants and sojourners, migrating alone or as part of family units, trying to improve their economic prospects.

During the 1970s thousands of Brazilians, Uruguayans, Argentines, and Chileans sought refuge in other countries to escape the authoritarian military governments in their homelands. Most of them did not fit the general U.S. profile of refugees because they were not fleeing communist governments;

rather they were fleeing governments regarded as strong allies of the United States, which did not attract the sympathy of Cold War-minded politicians in Congress. Consequently, the numbers of refugees from South America admitted to the U.S. during the 1970s were comparatively small. Other countries, most notably Canada, had a better record of accommodating those fleeing rightist regimes. Such was the case with the Chileans who fled their homeland after September 11, 1973, when General Augusto Pinochet overthrew the democratically elected Socialist government of Salvador Allende.

In order to buttress Pinochet's pro-U.S. military government, U.S. aid to Chile increased from $10.1 million in 1973 to $177.3 million in 1975 despite overwhelming evidence of human rights abuses. Much of that aid was used to equip the military, which played a key role in controlling the population and silencing dissidents. Thousands were imprisoned, raped, and tortured. More than 3,000 were executed or made to "disappear." Thousands more took refuge in foreign embassies in the capital city of Santiago or crossed the border into neighboring countries. But even exile could not offer total protection; there were cases of Chilean refugees who were kidnapped in the countries where they had taken refuge and returned to Chile for "interrogation." One of the most notorious cases involved former Chilean foreign minister Orlando Letelier, who was assassinated in Washington, D.C., in 1976 by agents of Pinochet's secret police, DINA. A bomb exploded under his car, killing Letelier and his personal assistant Ronni Karpen Moffitt, an American, and wounding her husband.

The United Nations High Commissioner for Refugees (UNHCR) and other international nongovernmental organizations (NGOs) tried to rescue those detained in Chile's prisons, negotiating with the Pinochet government to relocate them to other countries. Hoping to improve its international reputation, in 1975 the Pinochet government announced that sentences could be commuted if the prisoners agreed to emigrate. Dozens of countries assisted the UNHCR's efforts to find new homes for the political prisoners and dissidents, and by 1979 some 30,000 Chilean refugees had been resettled throughout Europe and Latin America. The United States delayed participating in the resettlement program because congressional leaders expressed concern that the pro-Allende refugees might pose a security threat. Congressional bills introduced by Representative Robert Drinan and Senator Edward Kennedy (both D-Massachusetts) to support the Chilean refugees failed to gain support in either house.

However, the news media kept the human rights abuses in Chile on the front pages of U.S. newspapers, and this public pressure, as well as the pressure exerted by international organizations, forced the State and Justice departments to act. In 1976 the United States enacted a limited parole program for the Chilean refugees. The United States agreed to accept Chile's political prisoners as long as they did not claim membership in the Communist Party. The Inter-Governmental Committee on European Migration (ICEM) acted as liaison between the prisoners and the U.S. government, assisting them to fill out the necessary paperwork. It took months and sometimes years to navigate the bureaucracy: Applicants were subjected to rigorous security screenings by U.S. Embassy personnel and the Chilean government; and the INS had to locate a sponsor for each refugee and his or her family. Once approved, the Chileans received "parolee" status, allowing them to legally enter the United States, but they received no assistance comparable to that offered to Cuban refugees a decade earlier. Instead, they had to sign a declaration of nonintervention in the political affairs of the United States, and had to agree to reimburse the U.S. government for travel expenses once they became economically self-supporting. By 1977, only 1,100 Chileans had resettled in the United States.

Similarly, the Argentine military junta that removed Isabel Perón from the presidency in 1976 maintained its grip on power by silencing dissents. During the period known as the "Dirty War" (1976–1983), those suspected of working against the government "disappeared," that is, were taken to secret government detention centers where they were tortured and eventually killed. Between fifteen and thirty thousand people are believed to have become *desaparecidos*, including members of minority groups and Chilean and Uruguayan refugees who had fled to Argentina to escape their own countries' rightist regimes. Thousands of Argentines fled their country during this period, mostly to neighboring countries, but others as far away as Europe and North America, to await a change in the political climate.

**Celeste Vila dances with her father during her quinceañera, 1999.** The quinceañera is a rite of passage among a number of Latin American groups in the United States, marking a girl's passage into womanhood on her fifteenth birthday. JOE RAEDLE/ GETTY IMAGES

The majority of those who have emigrated from Argentina, however, have done so for economic rather than political reasons. The first significant wave of economic migration from Argentina occurred during the 1960s and 1970s when close to 400,000 high-skilled workers emigrated, mostly to the United States and Spain. Since then, chronic unemployment and underemployment have continued to compel Argentines to emigrate. After the collapse of the Argentine economy in 2001 and 2002 an estimated 300,000 people left the country. By 2005, an estimated 1.05 million Argentines lived abroad, mostly in the United States (60 percent live in California, Florida, and New York), and remittances to Argentina reached close to a billion dollars per year.

The largest group of South Americans in the United States are the Colombians, who have come fleeing political and criminal violence as well as an unstable economy. During the period known as "La Violencia" (1948–1966), an estimated 200,000 Colombians were killed and another 200,000 internally displaced. Thousands chose to emigrate to other countries during this period. However, the majority of Colombians who have emigrated have done so since the 1970s, when the political violence between government forces, guerrillas, paramilitary squads, and narco-traffickers escalated. According to human rights agencies, over three million Colombians have become internally displaced since 1985. More than a million have emigrated, half a million of them to the United States. Although Colombians have among the highest asylum approval rates in the United States (roughly 60 percent), few actually request asylum for fear that they will be rejected and then deported back to their country. Thus, official figures for the Colombian population in the United States are most likely an undercount, failing to include those who have overstayed their visas or entered illegally by other means.

**CONCLUSION**

In the wake of the terrorist attacks of September 11, 2001, the United States rapidly revamped its immigration bureaucracy, increased security personnel at airports and border checkpoints, installed new physical barriers and high-tech monitoring equipment along the U.S.-Mexico border, expanded the number of detention centers, and enacted new deportation procedures. The USA Patriot Act, passed just forty-five days after the 9/11 attacks in 2001, expanded the powers of law enforcement agencies to search, monitor, and detain; allowed the indefinite detention of noncitizens suspected of a crime; and expanded the grounds under which a person could be deported from the United States. The new Department of Homeland Security, and its agencies, the bureaus of Customs and Border Protection (CBP) and Immigration and Customs Enforcement (ICE, which replaced the old Immigration and Naturalization Service [INS]), were created in an attempt to convey a greater sense of security to the general public. The U.S. government made it more difficult for students, tourists, and immigrants from certain nations to receive visas to come to the United States. Under the US-VISIT program, the United States began collecting biometric data on all visitors, including digital fingerprints and photographs, at all ports of entry. And the Real ID Act of 2005 set the stage for a national identity card by establishing national standards for state-issued drivers' licenses.

Immigrants and refugees have become victims of these new security measures. In 2002 and 2003, for example, refugee admissions sank to fewer than 29,000. Vigilante groups such as the Minutemen Project patrolled the U.S.-Mexico border to assist the Border Patrol in their detection work and committed egregious violations of civil liberties in the process. In 2006 and 2007, public pressure forced Congress to introduce new immigration control legislation. Congressional compromisers tried to reconcile immigration control with the ongoing need for labor, introducing provisions for a guest worker program similar to the bracero program of the mid-twentieth century as well as a limited legalization program for some of the millions of undocumented workers already in the United States. The bill also included provisions for an expanded Border Patrol and new physical barriers along the 2,000-mile border with Mexico, among other control procedures. It ultimately failed, however, because the differences among the supporters of its various, contradictory proposed provisions were irreconcilable.

The United States urges other countries in the Americas to assist in border control efforts, and the pressure is particularly felt by Mexico. As a result, Mexico's *Instituto Nacional de Migración* has expanded its presence in the southern border zone, and begun denying visas to nationals of countries the United States has identified as supporting terrorism, in order to prevent their using Mexican territory to gain access to, or stage actions against, the United States. Would-be immigrants trying to escape poverty or violence in their homelands have become the victims of Mexican and U.S. obsessions with border control. By end of 2002, for example, Mexico deported 3,000 Central Americans each week.

The political and economic realities in the Americas continue to produce a large migration of workers who seek opportunities in the United States, either as immigrants or temporary workers. In 2001 alone, for example, the U.S. Embassy in Mexico City processed more than 2.6 million nonimmigrant visa applications, mostly from nationals who work in the United States. The waiting list for an immigrant visa is long, and sometimes it is easier to overstay a visitor's visa and work illegally in the underground economy. Immigrant workers from Latin America generate billions of dollars in remittances each year. These remittances—$10 billion annually to Mexico alone—constitute one of the principal sources of income for many countries in the Americas, and their total far exceeds the development aid provided by the United States, Canada, and other industrial economies.

Ironically, as the United States seeks to control the movement of labor, it has negotiated a record number of free trade agreements providing for the unrestricted movement of goods and capital, which have generated billions of dollars in corporate revenues. According to the Migration Policy Institute, the U.S. borders with Mexico and Canada, its two largest trading partners, are among the most active in the world: an average of $1.2 billion is traded every day with Canada, and $733 million with Mexico. However, decades of ineffective immigration restriction measures have demonstrated the difficulties of controlling the migration that is a byproduct of such free trade policies. Restrictions on visas, fines on airlines and shipping companies, increased border security, criminal penalties on smugglers, streamlined detention and deportation procedures, and multinational crackdowns on undocumented labor may temporarily reduce the number of immigrants and refugees in a given year, but only until new entry points, transportation networks, and legal loopholes are created or identified.

In the meantime, migration from Latin America continues, whether legal or not, and Latinos have become the largest minority group in the United States. In some ways they are changing the cultural landscape of the United States. Journalists euphemistically refer to this process as *la reconquista* or "the browning of America," prompting xenophobes with access to media outlets to issue national calls for deportations and for closing the border. No longer are there areas of the United States unaffected by Latino immigration. Distinct Latino communities are found from Oregon to Georgia. Businesses cater to this multibillion dollar market, while politicians try either to engage them or curtail their potential influence.

At the same time, Latinos continue to exert significant influence on their countries of origin through remittances and even direct political participation. Several Latin American countries have come to allow immigrants in the United States to participate in their electoral processes, and Latin American presidential candidates today campaign in Miami, New York, and Los Angeles as readily as they do in Managua, Santo Domingo, or Mexico City. The Mexican state of Michoacán even designates one seat in its legislature as the "migrant seat," to represent Mexicans abroad.

Even though studies show that over the course of generations Latinos adapt and acculturate in ways similar to other immigrants, the first generation—which comprises half the present-day Latino population—exemplifies the transnational processes that so intrigue social scientists. In the United States, they are redefining and expanding what it means to be American.

*See also* **Aztlán; Black Legend; Corrido; Cuba, Revolutions: Cuban Revolution; Cuban Missile Crisis; Dirty War; Gadsden Purchase; Guadalupe Hidalgo, Treaty of (1848); Mexico, Wars and Revolutions: Mexican-American War; Mexico, Wars and Revolutions: Mexican Revolution; Migration and Migrations; Neoliberalism; Porfiriato; Santería; Ten Years' War; United Farm Workers Union; Violencia, La.**

BIBLIOGRAPHY

Acuña, Rodolfo. *Occupied America: A History of Chicanos*, 6th edition. New York: Harper & Row, 2007.

Aguayo, Sergio, and Patricia Weiss Fagen. *Central Americans in Mexico and the United States: Unilateral, Bilateral, and Regional Perspectives.* Washington, DC: Hemispheric Migration Project, Center for Immigration Policy and Refugee Assistance, Georgetown University, 1988.

Alonzo, Armando C. *Tejano Legacy: Rancheros and Settlers in South Texas, 1734–1900.* Albuquerque: University of New Mexico Press, 1998.

Bendixen and Associates. *Remittances and the Dominican Republic: Survey of Recipients in the Dominican Republic, Survey of Senders in the United States.* New York: Columbia University, November 23, 2004. Available from http://www.earthinstitute.columbia.edu/cgsd/remittances/documents/bendixen_NYN ov04.pdf.

Camarillo, Albert. *Chicanos in a Changing Society: From Mexican Pueblos to American Barrios in Santa Barbara and Southern California, 1848–1930.* Cambridge, MA: Harvard University Press, 1979.

Carrigan, William D., and Clive Webb. "The Lynching of Persons of Mexican Origin or Descent in the United States, 1848 to 1928." *Journal of Social History* 37 (2003): 411–438.

Clark, Juan. "The Exodus from Revolutionary Cuba (1959–1974): A Sociological Analysis." Ph.D. diss., University of Florida, 1975.

Davis, Mike. *Magical Urbanism: Latinos Reinvent the American City.* London and New York: Verso, 2000.

De León, Arnoldo, with a contribution by Kenneth L. Stewart. *The Tejano Community, 1836–1900.* Albuquerque: University of New Mexico Press, 1982.

De León, Arnoldo. *They Called Them Greasers: Anglo Attitudes toward Mexicans in Texas, 1821–1900.* Austin: University of Texas Press, 1983.

Deutsch, Sarah. *No Separate Refuge: Culture, Class, and Gender on an Anglo-Hispanic Frontier in the American Southwest, 1880–1940.* New York: Oxford University Press, 1987.

Dixon, David, and Julia Gelatt. "Detailed Characteristics of the South American Born in the United States." Migration Policy Institute, *Migration Information Source.* Available from http://www.migrationinformation.org/USFocus/display.cfm?ID=400.

Duany, Jorge. *The Puerto Rican Nation on the Move: Identities on the Island and in the United States.* Chapel Hill: University of North Carolina Press, 2002.

Dysart, Jane. "Mexican Women in San Antonio, 1830–1860: The Assimilation Process." *Western Historical Quarterly* 7:4 (October 1976): 365–375.

Eckstein, Susan, and Lorena Barbería. "Grounding Immigrant Generations in History: Cuban Americans and their Transnational Ties." *International Migration Review* 36:3 (Fall 2002): 799–837.

"Facts on the Hispanic or Latin Population." U.S. Census Bureau, *Minority Links.* Available from http://www.census.gov/pubinfo/www/NEWhispML1.html.

Fagen, Richard R., Richard A. Brody, and Thomas J. O'Leary. *Cubans in Exile: Disaffection and the Revolution.* Stanford, CA: Stanford University Press, 1968.

Gamboa, Erasmo. *Mexican Labor and World War II: Braceros in the Pacific Northwest, 1942–1947.* Austin: University of Texas Press, 1990.

García, Ignacio M. *Chicanismo: The Forging of a Militant Ethos among Mexican Americans.* Tucson: University of Arizona Press, 1997.

García, María Cristina. *Havana USA: Cuban Exiles and Cuban Americans in South Florida, 1959–1994.* Berkeley: University of California Press, 1996.

García, María Cristina. *Seeking Refuge: Central American Migration to Mexico, the United States, and Canada.* Berkeley: University of California Press, 2006.

Garcia, Mario T. *Desert Immigrants: The Mexicans of El Paso, 1880–1920.* New Haven, CT: Yale University Press, 1981.

Grasmuck, Sherri, and Patricia R. Pessar. *Between Two Islands: Dominican International Migration.* Berkeley: University of California Press, 1991.

Griswold del Castillo, Richard. *The Treaty of Guadalupe Hidalgo: A Legacy of Conflict.* Norman: University of Oklahoma Press, 1990.

Gutiérrez, David G. *Walls and Mirrors: Mexican Americans, Mexican Immigrants, and the Politics of Ethnicity.* Berkeley: University of California Press, 1995.

Gutiérrez, David G., ed. *The Columbia History of Latinos in the United States since 1960.* New York: Columbia University Press, 2004.

Hagan, Jacqueline María. *Deciding to be Legal: A Maya Community in Houston.* Philadelphia: Temple University Press, 1994.

Haney-López, Ian. *White by Law: The Legal Construction of Race.* Revised and updated edition. New York: New York University Press, 2006.

Hernández, Ramona, and Francisco L. Rivera-Batiz. "Dominicans in the United States: A Socioeconomic Profile, 2000." Dominican Research Monographs, The CUNY Dominican Studies Institute, October 6, 2003. Available from http://www.earthinstitute.columbia.edu/cgsd/advising/documents/rivera_batiz.pdf.

Hill, Kevin A., and Dario Moreno. "Second-Generation Cubans." *Hispanic Journal of Behavioral Sciences* 18 (May 1996).

Jachimowicz, Maia. "Argentina: A New Era of Migration and Migration Policy." Migration Policy Institute, *Migration Information Source.* Available from http://www.migrationinformation.org/Profiles/display.cfm?ID=374.

LaFeber, Walter. *Inevitable Revolutions: The United States in Central America*, 2nd edition. New York: W. W. Norton, 1993.

Masud-Piloto, Felix Roberto. *From Welcomed Exiles to Illegal Immigrants: Cuban Migration to the U.S., 1959–1995.* Lanham, MD: Rowman & Littlefield, 1996.

McWilliams, Carey. *North from Mexico: The Spanish-Speaking People of the United States*, new edition updated by Matt S. Meier. New York: Praeger, 1990.

Menjívar, Cecilia. *Fragmented Ties: Salvadoran Immigrant Networks in America.* Berkeley: University of California Press, 2000.

Montejano, David. *Anglos and Mexicans in the Making of Texas, 1836–1986.* Austin: University of Texas Press, 1987.

Nostrand, Richard L. "Mexican Americans Circa 1850." *Annals of the Association of American Geographers* 65:3 (September 1975): 378–390.

Oboler, Suzanne. *Ethnic Labels, Latino Lives: Identity and the Politics of (Re)presentation in the United States.* Minneapolis: University of Minnesota Press, 1995.

Paredes, Américo. *"With His Pistol in His Hand": A Border Ballad and Its Hero.* Austin: University of Texas Press, 1958.

Paredes, Américo. *George Washington Gómez: A Mexicotexan Novel.* Houston, TX: Arte Publico Press, 1990.

Passel, Jeffrey S. "The Latino and Asian Vote." Urban Institute, *Election 2004*, July 27, 2004. Available from http://www.urban.org/publications/900723.html.

Pérez, Lisandro. "Immigrant Economic Adjustment and Family Organization: The Cuban Success Story Re-Examined." *International Migration Review* 20 (Spring 1986), 4–20.

Pérez, Louis A., Jr. *On Becoming Cuban: Identity, Nationality, and Culture.* Chapel Hill: University of North Carolina Press, 1999.

Pérez, Louis A., Jr. *Cuba and the United States: Ties of Singular Intimacy*, 3rd edition. Athens: University of Georgia Press, 2003.

Pitt, Leonard. *The Decline of the Californios: A Social History of the Spanish-Speaking Californians, 1846–1890*, updated with a new foreword by Ramón A. Gutiérrez. Berkeley: University of California Press, 1998.

Portes, Alejandro, and Rubén G. Rumbaut. *Immigrant America: A Portrait*, 3rd edition. Berkeley: University of California Press, 2006.

Portes, Alejandro, and Alex Stepick. *City on the Edge: The Transformation of Miami.* Berkeley: University of California Press, 1993.

Rodriguez, Clara E. *Puerto Ricans: Born in the U.S.A.*. Boston: Unwin Hyman, 1989.

Rodriguez, Clara E. *Changing Race: Latinos, the Census, and the History of Ethnicity in the United States.* New York: New York University Press, 2000.

Rosenbaum, Robert J. *Mexicano Resistance in the Southwest: The Sacred Right of Self-Preservation.* Austin: University of Texas Press, 1986.

Ruiz, Vicki L. *Cannery Women, Cannery Lives: Mexican Women, Unionization, and the California Food Processing Industry, 1930–1950.* Albuquerque: University of New Mexico Press, 1987.

Ruiz, Vicki. *From Out of the Shadows: Mexican Women in Twentieth-Century America.* New York: Oxford University Press, 1998.

San Miguel, Guadalupe, Jr. *"Let All of Them Take Heed": Mexican Americans and the Campaign for Educational Equality in Texas, 1910–1981.* Austin: University of Texas Press, 1987.

Sánchez Korroll, Virginia E. *From Colonia to Community: The History of Puerto Ricans in New York City.* Berkeley: University of California Press, 1994.

Torres, Andrés, and José E. Velázquez, eds. *The Puerto Rican Movement: Voices from the Diaspora.* Philadelphia: Temple University Press, 1998.

Vargas, Zaragosa. *Proletarians of the North: A History of Mexican Industrial Workers in Detroit and the Midwest, 1917–1933.* Berkeley: University of California Press, 1993.

Weber, David J., ed. *Foreigners in their Native Land: Historical Roots of the Mexican Americans.* Albuquerque: University of New Mexico Press, 1973.

Weber, David J. *The Mexican Frontier, 1821–1846: The American Southwest under Mexico.* Albuquerque: University of New Mexico Press, 1982.

Weber, David J. *The Spanish Frontier in North America.* New Haven, CT: Yale University Press, 1992.

Weintraub, Sidney, and Sergio Díaz-Briquets. *The Use of Foreign Aid to Reduce Incentives to Emigrate from Central America.* Geneva: International Labour Organisation, 1992.

MARIA CRISTINA GARCIA

---

**HISPANIOLA.** Hispaniola (also Española), the island, named by Christopher Columbus, between Cuba and Puerto Rico; its western half became Haiti and eastern half the Dominican Republic. The island may have been called Bohío by its native Taino inhabitants, the same name the exploring Spaniards attributed to house compounds occupied by extended families throughout the West Indies. After his first voyage, Columbus left behind on Hispaniola a group of men who settled a garrison town known as Navidad. Upon returning to Hispaniola, late in November 1493, Columbus found the settlers dead and Navidad in ruins. So ended the first recorded colonization by Europeans of the Americas.

Undeterred, Columbus sailed back eastward along the coast of Hispaniola, and on 1 January 1494 laid out the town of Isabela, named in honor of his patron queen. Other settlements, for the most part as ephemeral if not as unfortunate as Navidad, were established throughout the island, but it was not until the founding of Santo Domingo, in August 1496, that the Spaniards secured a permanent, functional base of operation. For the next two decades Santo Domingo served as a strategic port from which to explore, conquer, and colonize the surrounding islands and mainland. It was from Santo Domingo that Ponce de León set out for Puerto Rico, Velásquez and del Campo for Cuba, Esquivel for Jamaica, Balboa for Panama and the Pacific, and Pizarro for Peru.

If Santo Domingo was successful as a point of embarkation, it had a far less distinguished role in putting its own house in order. Hispaniola's woes began early. The relatively peaceful Tainos, unlike their Carib neighbors, at first offered no great resistance to Spanish intrusion. They were so abused and exploited, however, that an uprising took place in 1494. Mismanagement by Columbus in his fever for gold set a crippling trend no reforms could reverse. Within scarcely a generation Hispaniola was gutted. The native population, which numbered between 200,000 and 300,000 before contact, was depopulated to extinction in a tragedy that would be enacted again and again elsewhere, if not always to the same fatal degree. Spanish interest in Hispaniola dwindled as fast as its native groups perished, to such an extent that a rival

European power (France) was able to establish a colony on its western perimeter, while other imperial nations (the British and Dutch foremost among them) filled in the surrounding islands' vacuum.

*See also* **Explorers and Exploration: Spanish America.**

BIBLIOGRAPHY


Sherburne F. Cook and Woodrow Borah, in "The Aboriginal Population of Hispaniola," *Essays in Population History* 1 (1971): 376–410.

David Henige, "On the Contact Population of Hispaniola: History as Higher Mathematics," in *Hispanic American Historical Review* 58:2 (1978): 217–237.

Robert D. Heinl and Nancy G. Heinl, *Written in Blood: The Story of the Haitian People, 1492–1971* (1978).

Irving Rouse, *The Tainos: Rise and Decline of the People Who Greeted Columbus* (1992).

Carl O. Sauer, *The Early Spanish Main* (1966; 2d ed. 1992).


*Additional Bibliography*


Bray, Warwick. *The Meeting of Two Worlds: Europe and the Americas, 1492–1650.* Oxford: Published for the British Academy by Oxford University Press, 1993.

Deagan, Kathleen A. and José María Cruxent. *Columbus's Outpost among the Taínos: Spain and America at La Isabela, 1493–1498.* New Haven, CT: Yale University Press, 2002.

Deive, Carlos Esteban. *La Española y la esclavitud del indio.* Santo Domingo: Fundación García Arévalo, 1995.

Errasti, Mariano. *Los primeros franciscanos en América: Isla Española, 1493–1520.* Santo Domingo: Fundación García Arévalo, 1998.

Livi-Bacci, Massimo. "Return to Hispaniola: Reassessing a Demographic Catastrophe." *Hispanic American Historical Review* 83:1 (February 2003): 3–51.


W. George Lovell

## HOCHSCHILD, MAURICIO (1881–1965).

Mauricio Hochschild (*b.* 17 February 1881; *d.* 1965), Bolivian tin magnate. A naturalized Argentine citizen of Jewish ancestry who was born in Biblis, Germany, Hochschild emigrated to Chile in 1911. Twenty years later he was one of three tin barons of the Bolivian oligarchy (the Rosca) whose economic, social, and political privilege dominated the country until 1952. His mines, the second-largest tin producers, averaged 25 percent of Bolivia's total tin output after World War II and provided most of the ore sold to the United States. Hochschild influenced public opinion through his La Paz newspaper, *Última Hora.*

A mining engineer educated at Freiburg University, Hochschild was a metals broker until depressed tin prices after World War I enabled him to buy up bankrupt mines. By 1911 he had acquired the Minera Unificada del Cerro de Potosí; subsequently he consolidated the Compañía Minera de Oruro and the San José, Itos, Colquiri, and Matilde mines into the Hochschild Group. He narrowly escaped the animosity of the military socialist governments of Germán Busch, who ordered him shot for opposing the 1939 mining law, and of Gualberto Villarroel, who had him kidnapped. The 1952 revolution nationalized his mining properties.

*See also* **Aramayo Family; Tin Industry.**

BIBLIOGRAPHY


Víctor Andrade, *My Missions for Revolutionary Bolivia, 1944–1962,* edited by Cole Blasier (1976) pp. 69–70, 114–121, 123–124.

Alfonso Crespo, *Los Aramayo de Chichas, tres generaciones de mineros bolivianos* (1981), pp. 249–250, 311–316, 325–335.

Eduardo Arze Cuadros, *La economía de Bolivia* (1979), pp. 259–261.


*Additional Bibliography*


Bieber, Leon E. "La Sociedad de Proteccion a los Inmigrantes Israelitas: Su aporte a la integracion economica de judios en Bolivia, 1939–1945." *Latin American Research Review* 34 (1999): 152–178.

Hillman, John. "Bolivia and the International Tin Cartel, 1931–1941." *Journal of Latin American Studies* 20 (May 1988): 83–110.

Waszkis, Helmut. *Dr. Moritz (Don Mauricio) Hochschild, 1881–1965: The Man and His Companies: A German Jewish Mining Entrepreneur in South America.* Frankfurt am Main: Vervuert; Madrid: Iberoamericana, 2001.


Waltraud Queiser Morales

## HOLANDA, SÉRGIO BUARQUE DE (1902–1982).

Sérgio Buarque de Holanda (*b.* 11 July 1902; *d.* 24 April 1982), Brazilian historian. Born in São Paulo, Holanda was the son of a civil servant who had migrated there from the former

Dutch colony of Pernambuco, a fact reflected by his surname. After completing his secondary education in São Paulo, Holanda left for Rio de Janeiro in 1921 to attend law school. In Rio he abandoned his legal studies for a precarious career as an essayist, literary critic, and free-lance journalist. He became part of the "modernist" movement, which rejected Portuguese formalism and exalted Brazilian popular culture. Holanda's writings attracted the attention of São Paulo press lord Assis Chateaubriand, who sent him to Germany as correspondent for his newspaper *O Jornal*. In Berlin in 1929–1930 Holanda familiarized himself with the main trends of German historiography and social science and developed a taste for the works of Max Weber. In Germany, Holanda felt the call to write a history of Brazil, to explain his country to the world. The result was *Raízes do Brasil* (Roots of Brazil) published in Brazil in 1936, after his return from Europe.

In *Raízes do Brasil* Holanda introduces the concept of the "cordial man"—the predominant Brazilian political type, the leader who prefers conciliation to confrontation. The cordial interaction of its leaders, according to Holanda, enabled Brazil to survive and expand on a fragmented continent, but thwarted necessary social change. The book launched Holanda on an academic career that culminated with his tenure as professor of the history of Brazilian civilization at the University of São Paulo from 1957 to 1969. His other major works include *Monções* (Monsoons [1945]), a study of westward movement from São Paulo; *Caminhos e Fronteiras* (Roads and Frontiers [1957]), a cultural interpretation of Brazilian colonial expansion; and *Visão do paraíso* (Vision of Paradise [1959]), an analysis of the images that drew colonists to the frontiers of Brazil. Holanda is the general editor of the first six volumes of the *História geral da civilização brasileira* (General History of Brazilian Civilization [1960–1971]) and the sole author of volume seven, *Do império à república* (From the Empire to the Republic [1972]).

*See also* **Brazil: Literature.**

BIBLIOGRAPHY

Richard Graham, "An Interview with Sérgio Buarque de Holanda," in *Hispanic American Historical Review* 62, no. 1 (1982):3–17.

Richard M. Morse, "Sérgio Buarque de Holanda (1902–82)," in *Hispanic American Historical Review* 63, no. 1 (1983):147–150.

*Additional Bibliography*

Cândido, Antônio, and Antônio Arnoni Prado. *Sérgio Buarque de Holanda e o Brasil.* São Paulo: Editora Fundação Perseu Abramo, 1998.

Pesavento, Sandra Jatahy. *Um historiador nas fronteiras: O Brasil de Sérgio Buarque de Holanda.* Belo Horizonte: Editora UFMG, 2005.

Piva, Luiz Guilherme. *Ladrilhadores e semeadores: A modernização brasileira no pensamento político de Oliveira Vianna, Sérgio Buarque de Holanda, Azevedo Amaral e Nestor Duarte (1920–1940).* São Paulo: Departamento de Ciência Política da USP: Editora 34, 2000.

Wegner, Robert. *A conquista do oeste: A fronteira na obra de Sérgio Buarque de Holanda.* Belo Horizonte: Editora UFMG, 2000.

NEILL MACAULAY

**HOLGUÍN, JORGE** (1848–1928). Jorge Holguín (*b.* 30 October 1848; *d.* 2 March 1928), Colombian statesman who twice served as acting president (1909 and 1921–1922). Born in Cali, Holguín was well connected socially and politically. He was a nephew of Manuel María Mallarino (1808–1872), who was president from 1855 to 1857, and the younger brother of Carlos Holguín, who served as chief executive from 1888 to 1892. His wife, Cecilia, was the daughter of Conservative paladin Julio Arboleda.

Like his kinsmen, Jorge became involved in Conservative politics, fighting in the revolution of 1876–1877 and serving as a party director in the 1880s. During the Conservative-dominated regeneration, he served in the senate and in the cabinets of Miguel Antonio Caro and Manuel A. Sanclemente. A long-time supporter of Rafael Reyes, Holguín was a member of the commission headed by Reyes that unsuccessfully sought redress from the United States after the secession of Panama in 1903. During Reyes's presidency, Holguín negotiated an agreement with foreign bondholders (1905) that revived Colombia's international credit. When Reyes was forced from power in mid-1909, he designated Holguín to serve as president until a successor was chosen. Holguín again served as chief executive upon the resignation of Marco Fidel Suárez in 1921.

*See also* **Panama; Reyes, Rafael.**

BIBLIOGRAPHY

Jorge Holguín, *Desde cerca: Asuntos colombianos* (1908).

Julio Holguín Arboleda, *Mucho en serio y algo en broma* (1959).

### *Additional Bibliography*

Holguín Pardo, Arturo. "Un presidente caleño en medio de las guerras civiles: Don Jorge Holguín." *Boletín de Historia y Antigüedades* 73 (January–March 1986): 239–276.

Morales de Gómez, Teresa. "Recuerdos de don Jorge Holguín." *Boletín de Historia y Antigüedades* 86 (January–March 1999): 119–150.

HELEN DELPAR

## HOLY ALLIANCE.

**HOLY ALLIANCE.** Holy Alliance, an agreement among the monarchs of Russia, Austria, and Prussia made in Paris on 26 September 1815 after the Congress of Vienna tried to rearrange Europe in the aftermath of the Napoleonic Wars. The alliance consisted of a philosophical pledge to carry out foreign relations on the basis of Christian morals. Eventually it was signed by all European rulers except the king of Britain and the pope. The United States feared that the European powers would use the alliance as a pretext to attempt to restore Spanish dominion over South America by force. Seeing the agreement as a threat to liberal regimes, the United States announced the Monroe Doctrine on 2 December 1823, arguing that any attempt by the European monarchies to impose absolutism in the Western Hemisphere would be interpreted as a threat to the security of the United States.

*See also* **Monroe Doctrine.**

BIBLIOGRAPHY

Arthur Preston Whitaker, *The United States and the Independence of Latin America, 1800–1830* (1941).

Dana Gardner Munro, *The Latin American Republics: A History,* 3d ed. (1960).

Donald Marquand Dozer, *Latin America: An Interpretive History* (1962).

### *Additional Bibliography*

Lewis, James E. *The American Union and the Problem of Neighborhood: The United States and the Collapse of the Spanish Empire, 1783-1829.* Chapel Hill: University of North Carolina Press, 1998.

HILARY BURGER

## HOLZMANN, RODOLFO (1910–1992).

**HOLZMANN, RODOLFO** (1910–1992). Rodolfo Holzmann (*b.* 27 November 1910; *d.* 4 April 1992), Peruvian composer and ethnomusicologist. Born in Breslau, Germany, Holzmann began his music studies at age six and moved to Berlin in 1931 to study with Wladimir Vogel (composition), Winfried Wolf (piano), and Robert Robitschek (conducting). In 1933 he participated in the Session of Musical Studies organized by Hermann Scherchen in Strasbourg, taking conducting lessons with Scherchen. He later moved to Paris to study with Karol Rathaus (1934) and attended the twelfth festival of the International Society of Contemporary Music in Florence, Italy. He also studied oboe at the Zurich Conservatory. In 1938 Holzmann moved to Lima, where he was professor of oboe at the Alzedo Academy of Music as well as the violinist for the National Symphony. In 1945 he became professor of composition at the National Conservatory of Music in Lima, later becoming professor of orchestral conducting. He also taught at the University of Texas at Austin (1957–1958). His ethnomusicological studies of Peruvian music are among the most important in the twentieth century and have received worldwide praise. Among his compositions are orchestral works, choral music, chamber music, and an extensive collection of songs based on Spanish and Peruvian melodies. He died in Lima.

*See also* **Music: Art Music; Music: Popular Music and Dance.**

BIBLIOGRAPHY

*Composers of the Americas,* vol. 4 (1958), pp. 96–104.

Enrique Pinilla, "Rodolfo Holzmann y su panorama de la música tradicional del Perú," in *Revista peruana de cultura* 7–8 (1966): 274; *New Grove Dictionary of Music and Musicians,* vol. 8 (1980).

### *Additional Bibliography*

Romero Cevallos, Raúl R. "Nacionalismos y anti-indigenismos: Rodolfo Holzmann y su aporte a una música 'peruana'." *Hueso Húmero* 43 (December 2003): 77–95.

Romero, Raúl R. "Development and Balance of Peruvian Ethnomusicology." *Yearbook for Traditional Music* 20 (1988): 146–157.

SUSANA SALGADO

**HOMAR, LORENZO** (1913–2004). Lorenzo Homar (*b.* 1913; *d.* 16 February 2004), Puerto Rican graphic artist. Homar, a native of San Juan, migrated to New York with his family in 1928. His early training was in design; he worked for Cartier from 1937 until 1950. He took courses at the Art Students' League (1931) and Pratt Institute (1940). In 1946, after military service, Homar attended the Brooklyn Museum Art School, where he studied with Rufino Tamayo and Arthur Osver and came into contact with Ben Shahn. Returning to Puerto Rico in 1950, Homar founded the Center for Puerto Rican Art (CAP) with Rafael Tufiño and José A. Torres Martinó. CAP was part of a movement to create a national art that was both accessible and contemporary.

In 1951 Homar began working with the Division of Community Education, which produced educational materials, including silk-screen posters, books, and films for Puerto Rico's rural population. He became the director of its graphics workshop in 1952. Awarded a Guggenheim fellowship in 1956, Homar returned to New York. From 1957 to 1973, he headed the graphic arts workshop at the Institute for Puerto Rican Culture and trained many of the island's most prominent printmakers in xylography, silk screen, and other techniques. In 1970 Homar was one of the organizers of the first Bienal de San Juan del Grabado Latinoamericano. He established his own workshop in 1973. He has been awarded numerous prizes, and his work has been shown internationally.

*See also* **Art: The Twentieth Century; Hispanics in the United States.**

BIBLIOGRAPHY

Museo De Arte De Ponce, *Exposición retrospectiva de la obra de Lorenzo Homar* (1978).

The Squibb Gallery (Princeton, NJ), *Puerto Rican Painting: Between Past and Present* (1987).

Bronx Museum Of The Arts (Bronx, NY), *The Latin American Spirit: Art and Artists in the United States, 1920–1970* (1988).

*Additional Bibliography*

Alegría, Ricardo E., and Lorenzo Homar. *The Three Wishes: a Collection of Puerto Rican Folktales.* New York: Harcourt, 1969.

Homar, Lorenzo. *Lorenzo Homar a los 80 años.* San Juan: Galeria Palomas, 1993.

Homar, Lorenzo. *Maestros de verdad.* Hato Rey, P.R.: Galerías Prinardi, 2005.

Homar, Lorenzo, and Flavia Marichal Lugo. *Lorenzo Homar: Abrapalabra: la letra mágica: carteles, 1951–1999.* Río Piedras: Universidad de Puerto Rico, 1999.

Homar, Lorenzo Antonio Martorell, and Arcadio Díaz Quiñones. *Carteles de Lorenzo Homar.* Turabo, P.R.: Universidad del Turabo, 1994.

Lloréns Torres, Luis, and Lorenzo Homar. *Luis Lloréns Torres.* San Juan de Puerto Rico: Instituto de Cultura Puertorriqueña, 1975.

MIRIAM BASILIO

**HOMOSEXUALITY AND BISEXUALITY IN LITERATURE.** Literary representations of the experience of sexual minorities have been an important strand of Latin American literature since the publication in Brazil of Adolfo Caminha's *Bom-Crioulo* (1895; English trans., *The Black Man and the Cabin Boy*, 1982), a path-breaking novel about a romance between an ex-slave and a cabin boy. Other early texts in this vein include the short story "El hombre que parecía un caballo" (1914; English trans., "The Man Who Looked Like a Horse"), about the Colombian poet Porfirio Barba Jacob, by the Guatemalan Rafael Arévalo Martínez; a novel about a priest in love with an altar boy, *Pasión y muerte del cura Deusto* (1924; Passion and death of Father Deusto), by the Chilean Augusto D'Halmar; several texts from Cuba, Hernández Catá's *El ángel de Sodoma* (1928; The angel of sodom), Ofelia Rodríguez Acosta's *La vida manda* (1929; Life commands), and Carlos Montenegro's *Hombres sin mujer* (1935; Men without women); and the writings of members of the Mexican Contemporáneos group, especially Salvador Novo, Xavier Villaurrutia, and Elías Nandino. Major novels of the 1950s and 1960s that focus on same-sex desire are João Guimarães Rosa's *Grande Sertão: Veredas* (Brazil, 1956; English trans., *The Devil to Pay in the Backlands*, 1963); José Donoso's *El lugar sin límites* (Chile, 1966; English trans., *Hell Has No Limits*, 1995); and José Lezama Lima's *Paradiso* (Cuba, 1966; English trans., 1974). Two key texts in the contemporary tradition on these topics come from Argentina: Manuel Puig's *El beso de la mujer* *araña* (1976; English trans., *Kiss of the Spider Woman*, 1979), and Sylvia Molloy's *En breve cárcel* (1981; English trans., *Certificate of Absence*, 1989). Since the 1980s there has been an explosion of writing on this topic; key figures include Luis Zapata and Carlos Monsiváis (Mexico); Senel Paz, Ena Lucía Portela, Norge Espinosa, and Pedro de Jesús (Cuba); Fernando Vallejo, Albalucía Angel, and Alonso Sánchez Baute (Colombia); Armando Rojas Guardia (Venezuela); Jaime Bayly (Peru); Caio Fernando Abreu and Márcia Denser (Brazil); Juan Pablo Sutherland and Pedro Lemebel (Chile); and Néstor Perlongher, Diana Bellessi, Osvaldo Bazán, and María Moreno (Argentina). Critical attention has also been devoted to recovering homoerotic elements in a variety of canonical writers from Sor Juana Inés de la Cruz, the colonial Mexican nun, to Gabriela Mistral, the Chilean poet who won the Nobel Prize for Literature in 1945.

*See also* **Literature: Brazil; Literature: Spanish America; Sexuality: Same-sex Behavior in Latin America, Modern Period; Sexuality: Same-sex Behavior in Latin America, Pre-Conquest to Independence.**

BIBLIOGRAPHY

Balderston, Daniel. *El deseo, enorme cicatriz luminosa: Ensayos sobre homosexualidades latinoamericanas.* Rosario, Argentina: Beatriz Viterbo, 2004.

Balderston, Daniel, and José Maristany. "The Lesbian and Gay Novel in Latin America." In *The Cambridge Companion to the Latin American Novel*, edited by Efraín Kristal, pp. 200–216. Cambridge: Cambridge University Press, 2005.

Balderston, Daniel, and José Quiroga. *Sexualidades en disputa.* Buenos Aires: Libros del Rojas, 2005.

Foster, David William, ed. *Latin American Writers on Gay and Lesbian Themes: A Bio-Critical Sourcebook.* Westport, CT: Greenwood Press, 1994.

Quiroga, José. *Tropics of Desire: Interventions from Queer Latino America.* New York: New York University Press, 2000.

DANIEL BALDERSTON

**HOMOSEXUALITY AND LESBIANISM.** *See* **Sexuality: Same-sex Behavior in Latin America, Pre-Conquest to Independence; Sexuality: Same-sex Behavior in Latin America, Modern Period.**

**HONDURAS.** In 1823 the short-lived Mexican Empire, which had incorporated Central America after the rupture with Spain, collapsed. The failure of the Spanish and Mexican empires in rapid succession prompted Honduras, in many ways the poorest of Spain's former American provinces, to join the United Provinces of Central America. With fewer than 150,000 inhabitants widely dispersed in small villages tucked away in isolated mountain valleys, Honduras seemed more an administrative designation than a nation in gestation. Cattlemen running large herds on the savannas of Olancho in the east and on the coastal plains of Choluteca in the south had little in common, or contact with the indigenous and mestizo peasant smallholders in the western borderlands with El Salvador and Guatemala, or with the gangs of mahogany cutters on the North Coast. Treacherous mule tracks winding over mountains and through rivers comprised the only links among these diverse communities. Municipal rivalry between Comayagua, the run-down seat of provincial government during the colonial era, and Tegucigalpa, an insurgent mining and commercial town thirty miles to the south, further divided the province. Nevertheless, a sufficient sense of national identity had taken root; in time the province became the nation of Honduras.

As Spanish, Mexican, and, somewhat later, Central American dominions successively fell away due to circumstances largely beyond their control, the prospect of national independence, ready or not, reverberated across Honduras. These events inflamed the long-standing rivalry between Comayagua and Tegucigalpa. Men of means in both these dusty towns and throughout Honduras—generally government bureaucrats, soldiers, lawyers, church officials, mine operators, retail merchants linked to mercantile houses in Guatemala and Belize, and cattle ranchers and exporters—tried to discern the implications of this devolution of power to the province and took whatever steps they deemed expedient to protect their interests. Elites in Tegucigalpa briefly tried to end their subordination to Comayagua by becoming a separate province within the Central American confederation.

Soon, however, events in the neighboring provinces of Guatemala, El Salvador, and Nicaragua began to dictate the Honduran political agenda.

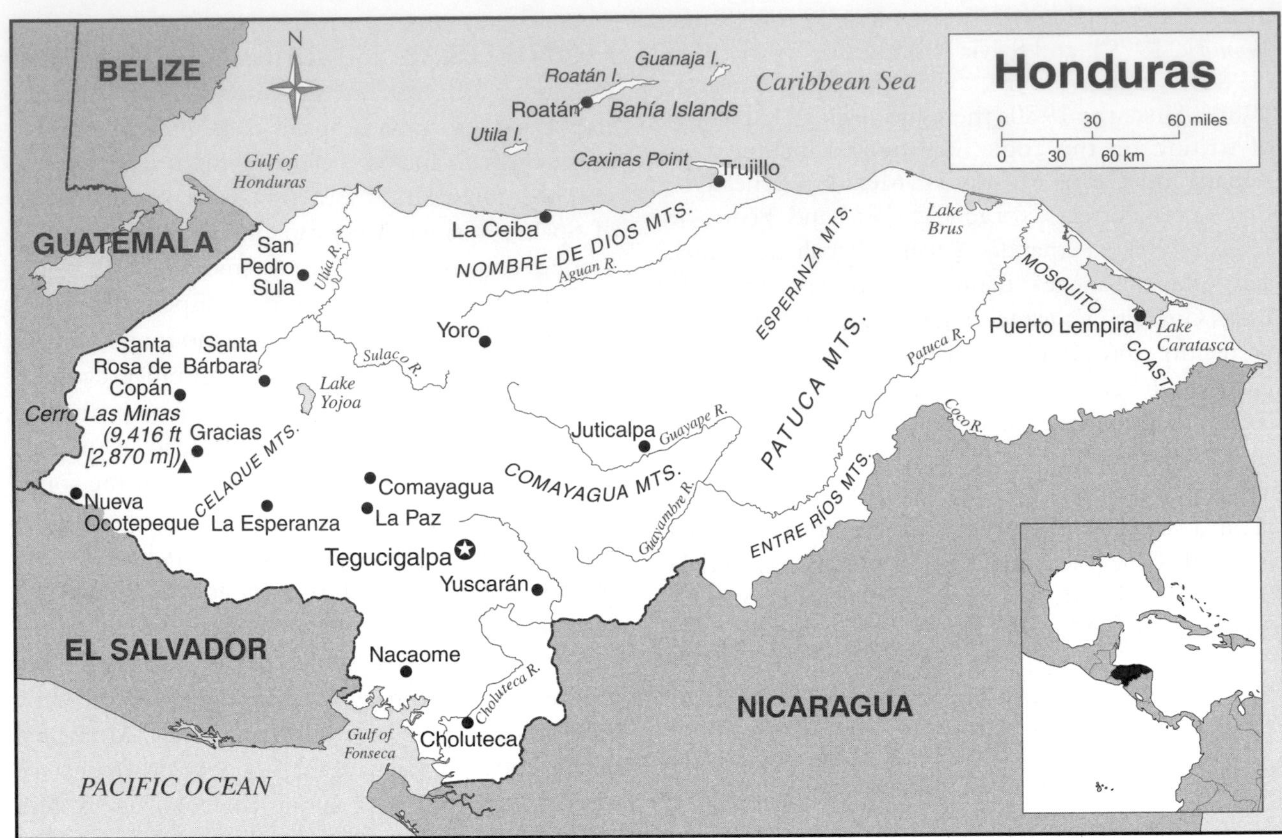


Two native sons, José Cecilio del Valle, a poor but ambitious lawyer and self-taught philosopher originally from Choluteca, and Francisco Morazán, an equally ambitious military and political man of humble Tegucigalpa origins, quickly emerged as leaders, respectively, of the Conservatives and Liberals in the confederation. Both were elected president of Central America: Morazán in 1830 and again in 1834 after del Valle, elected earlier that same year, died before taking office.

These early struggles between Liberals and Conservatives kept the provincial government at Comayagua in a constant uproar as one provisional head of state succeeded another, but the rest of Honduras was generally spared serious upheaval. Morazán's supporters in Comayagua sought to impose on Honduras the variant of liberalism then in vogue in Guatemala and El Salvador, which advocated the disestablishment of the Roman Catholic Church. Such enlightened iconoclasm goaded Conservatives to revolt. As Morazán's impending defeat became evident in 1838, Conservatives took control and helped dismantle the Federation by declaring Honduras an independent republic on October 26, 1838.

**CONSERVATIVE HEGEMONY (1838–1875)**

During the subsequent forty years, Conservatives, such as Francisco Ferrera (1840–1847), Juan Lindo Zelaya (1847–1852), Santos Guardiola (1885–1862), and José María Medina (1864–1871), elaborated a republican facsimile of the colonial regime. The resurrected and renovated colonial institutions were familiar to, and aptly suited, the mestizo and indigenous peasant majority in Honduras. Nonetheless, unreconstructed Liberals, such as Trinidad Cabañas (1852–1855) intransigently refused to abandon the liberal agenda. All too often, the ideological struggles degenerated into personal feuds between rival *caudillos* (warlords) and their small, poorly armed bands of retainers. As a result, endemic civil anarchy and widespread social banditry persisted year after year.

That these conflicts were often succored by partisans in Guatemala, El Salvador, and Nicaragua certainly helped to perpetuate them; and diplomats from beyond the isthmus meddled as well as exacerbated them. Frederick Chatfield, the first British consul to Central America (1834–1852), made a career of gunboat diplomacy to advance what he deemed to be Britain's interests. The British repeatedly took and abandoned the Bay Islands until 1859, and they bombarded and occupied North Coast ports in 1849 and again in 1873 to compel loan repayments. At mid-century, the United States, in the person of amateur archaeologist Ephraim George Squier, briefly challenged Chatfield over, among other things, coaling rights to Tigre Island in the Gulf of Fonseca. Even private filibusters contributed to the domestic turmoil in Honduras: most notably the Tennessee soldier of fortune William Walker, who in the aftermath of his astonishing saga in Nicaragua, tried to recoup his dream of empire in Honduras but ended up before a firing squad instead.

Meanwhile, Forty-Niners seeking passage to California inspired Squier to promote an interoceanic railway across Honduras from Puerto Cortés to the Gulf of Fonseca. Conflicting survey reports, wildly varying estimates of costs, and a soft financial market led Squier to abandon the project. Alternate routes across Panama and the continental United States soon made a Honduran interoceanic railway virtually irrelevant to the needs of world trade. Honduran elites, however, had been beguiled by the dream of opening up their nation's undeveloped hinterland by means of an interoceanic railroad. In the 1860s, President José María Medina borrowed enough money from London bankers to construct a sixty-mile section of narrow-gauge track from Puerto Cortés through and beyond San Pedro Sula. This short spur of track did little to alter the primary means of transportation for most Hondurans from what it had been since the earliest colonial days—feet, horses, and mules; but the enormous foreign debt Honduras incurred hovered over the country for almost a century and thwarted almost every bid to coax foreign capital there.

Despite the impediments of political turmoil, rural isolation, and the lack of modern means of transportation, the ordinary Honduran campesino, though poor, may actually have fared better than his counterparts elsewhere in Central America. The Honduran elites, on the other hand, were much poorer than their Central American peers. Because the peasants lived in widely scattered villages isolated by rugged mountain ranges and had ample land to cultivate, the elites found it impossible to mobilize them for export agricultural production. Moreover, widespread folk participation in diversified exports—livestock, hides and pelts, precious metals, logwood, indigo, sarsaparilla, rum, and tobacco—supplemented peasants' subsistence but never provided a large surplus for the elite.

## THE NEW LIBERALISM (1875–1903)

In the early 1870s, a new kind of liberalism dedicated to order and material progress had replaced conservative doctrines in Guatemala and El Salvador. The new Guatemalan strongman, Justo Rufino Barrios, in order to secure his eastern flank against cross-border raids from sanctuaries in Honduras, masterminded the overthrow of Conservative President Medina and his replacement by a handpicked fellow Liberal. Barrios initially chose Céleo Arias (1872–1874), but when Arias was unable to maintain order, he backed Ponciano Leiva. When Leiva (1874–1876) also failed to quell dissent, Barrios replaced him too.

The third replacement, Marco Aurelio Soto (1876–1883), although a Honduran, had risen to high office in Guatemala under Barrios. As Barrios's disciple, Soto espoused the new liberal gospel of rapid economic progress and absolute social and political obedience. Soto and his chief adviser, Ramón Rosa, quickly restored order, wrote a new constitution, and drafted numerous legal codes. With order restored, they turned their attention to progress. By 1880, Soto had tied all the important towns and many small villages into a telegraph grid and connected it to international cable networks in the United States and Europe. He also began construction of the Southern Highway, a cart road designed to link Tegucigalpa, the newly designated capital, to the port of San Lorenzo on the Gulf of Fonseca.

In 1880, Soto and a New York export-import merchant established the New York and Honduras Rosario Mining Company to work an abandoned silver mine the president owned. The merchant's son, Washington S. Valentine, took charge of the company's operation at San Juancito, a few miles northeast of Tegucigalpa. The Rosario turned out to be the richest silver mine between Mexico and

| **Honduras** | |
|---|---|
| **Population:** | 7,483,763 (2007 est.) |
| **Area:** | 43,278 sq mi |
| **Official language:** | Spanish |
| **Languages:** | Spanish, English, Amerindian languages |
| **National currency:** | lempira (HNL) |
| **Principal religions:** | Roman Catholic, 97%; Protestant, 3% |
| **Ethnicity:** | mestizo (mixed Amerindian and European), 90%; Amerindian, 7%; black, 2%; white, 1% |
| **Capital:** | Tegucigalpa (est. pop. 1,007,000 in 2005) |
| **Other urban centers:** | El Progresso, La Ceiba, San Pedro Sula |
| **Annual rainfall:** | 95 inches in the north, 33 inches in Tegucigalpa |
| **Principal geographical features:** | *Mountains:* Central American Cordillera; Volcanic Highlands include the peak Las Minas (9,417 ft)<br>*Rivers:* Choluteca, Goascorán, Nacaome, Patuca, Ulúa<br>*Lakes:* Yojoa<br>*Islands:* Islas de la Bahía |
| **Economy:** | *GDP per capita:* $3,100 (2006 est.) |
| **Principal products and exports:** | *Agricultural:* bananas, coffee, shrimp<br>*Manufacturing:* assembly plants, paper, textiles, wood products |
| **Government:** | Independence from Spain, 1821. Constitution, 1982; frequently amended. and is governed as a democratic constitutional republic. The president is popularly elected to a 4-year term, and is both chief of state and head of government. The 128-seat National Congress is the legislature, its members are elected in proportion to the votes their party's presidential candidate receives and serve 4-year terms. Cabinet appointed by the president. 18 departments. |
| **Armed forces:** | *Army:* 8,300<br>*Navy:* 1,400<br>*Air force:* 2,300<br>*Paramilitary:* 8,000 Public Security officers<br>*Reserves:* 60,000 |
| **Transportation:** | *Rail:* 434 mi<br>*Ports:* Puerto Castilla, Puerto Cortes, San Lorenzo, Tela<br>*Roads:* 1,724 mi paved; 6,728 mi unpaved<br>*Airports:* 12 paved runway and 100 unpaved runways airports; international airports at Tegucigalpa and San Pedro Sula. |
| **Media:** | Major newspapers include *El Heraldo, La Prensa, La Tribuna,* and *Tiempo.* There are 241 AM, 53 FM, and 11 television stations. |
| **Literacy and education:** | *Total literacy rate:* 80% (2001)<br>Public education is free, and required for children ages 6 to 12. The National Autonomous University of Honduras is the most prominent of several universities in Honduras. |

Bolivia, and a mining boom soon gripped the Honduran Pacific Slope. Foreign capitalists, primarily North American, formed more than one hundred companies to rework abandoned colonial silver and gold mines using modern techniques and imported machinery. Despite staunch support from Soto and his successor, Luis Bográn (1883–1891), almost all of the concerns failed before they produced any bullion—Rosario being a singular exception. Anemic capitalization, incompetent management, inappropriate technology, and steadily falling silver prices conspired to snuff the boom. Although mining failed to realize the Hondurans' high expectations, it did stimulate highway construction, wholesale and retail commerce, and a range of small-scale industries.

Much of what was accomplished during the decade and a half of sustained peace under Soto and Bográn was undone during a bloody civil war that erupted soon after Bográn left office. Near the end of his first term in 1887, Bográn had organized the Progressive Party to withstand former president Céleo Arias's challenge to his re-election later that year. In the next election, former president Ponciano Leiva, the Progressive Party's candidate, was challenged by Dr. Policarpo Bonilla, leader of the Liberal Party since Céleo Arias's death. Leiva won the openly rigged election, but after a little more than a year (1891–1893), he was edged out of office and eventually replaced by his minister of war, Domingo Vásquez (1893–1894).

Vásquez's heavy-handed tyranny soon provoked rebellion by Liberal exiles in Nicaragua headed by Policarpo Bonilla, General Manuel Bonilla (no relation to Policarpo), and General Terencio Sierra—all future presidents of Honduras. Although Vásquez destroyed the initial invasion force, a second assault, generously supported by fellow Nicaraguan Liberal, José Santos Zelaya, dislodged Vásquez.

The victorious invaders, at Policarpo Bonilla's insistence, immediately convened a constituent assembly to rewrite the Honduran constitution according to liberal precepts. With his personal prestige at an all-time high, Bonilla easily won election as president. During his term (1895–1899), he relentlessly centralized power in the executive branch, embedded his surprisingly advanced ideas of public administration and jurisprudence in revisions of the country's legal codes, did what he could to heal the ravages of the civil war, and tried to put the country's economy on a sound footing. Bonilla was a fanatical proponent of disciplined political parties that offered voters clearly distinct choices. He also believed that regularly held democratic elections for single-term presidents would solve the bulk of Honduras's political problems. In keeping with his convictions, Bonilla refused to run for a second term. Unfortunately, his popularly elected successor, Terencio Sierra (1899–1903), shared little of Bonilla's vision for Honduras. Instead, he spent the bulk of his administration laying the groundwork for perpetuating his power.

### THE BANANA REPUBLIC (1903–1956)

By 1900, bananas had already emerged as the nation's most important export product. Schooner and tramp steamer captains had begun to visit North Coast ports to purchase bananas for sale in New Orleans and other Gulf Coast cities. Although exports gradually rose during the late nineteenth century, large-scale commercial banana production lagged until a complex set of technological innovations were developed. After 1900 North American banana pioneers—the most prominent in Honduras being the Vacarro Brothers of New Orleans, founders of Standard Fruit Company at La Ceiba, and Samuel "the Banana Man" Zemurray, founder of Cuyamel Fruit Company and a later director of United Fruit Company—parlayed their entrepreneurial skills and access to investment capital into banana empires featuring vast plantations, fleets of cargo ships, precision marketing networks, and state-of-the-art radio communication systems. By 1930 United Fruit and Standard Fruit had made Honduras the leading banana exporter in the world, at 30 million bunches a year. Large numbers of Hondurans left their highland villages to work on the plantations, thus shifting the population center from the Pacific Slope to the North Coast. By 1940, however, the Great Depression, World War II, and Sigatoka and Panama banana plant diseases pushed Honduras behind Ecuador in production.

This dynamic banana economy further destabilized an already precarious political system. Because the banana companies needed land grants, favorable labor laws, and permission to build railroads and other facilities from the government, they increasingly meddled in Honduran political affairs. At first, however, they received spontaneous support from the government. The 1903 electoral contest, which ended with Manuel Bonilla getting the largest number of votes but not a majority, was thrown into the National Congress. When the Congress gave the election to a rival, General Bonilla revolted and took power. During his first term (1903–1907), he awarded generous concessions of every stripe to the fledgling banana companies, but his repression of opposition politicians and closure of the National Congress in 1904 ultimately led to his ouster by militant Liberals led by General Miguel R. Dávila.

President Dávila (1907–1911), despite the protection of the 1907 Central American Peace Treaties and the attendant Court of Justice, was plagued by repeated cross-border raids by political foes. His downfall, however, came when Samuel Zemurray financed an invasion by former president Manuel Bonilla in order to prevent Dávila from adopting a debt settlement plan that would have given vast power to mining magnate Washington S. Valentine and financier J. P. Morgan. Bonilla's term (1911–1913) was cut short by his death; he was succeeded by his vice president, Francisco Bertrand (1913–1919).

Bertrand was acceptable to both his fellow countrymen and the banana companies until he tried to engineer the election of his brother-in-law as president in 1919. The most popular opposition leader, General Rafael López Gutiérrez, led the resistance and ultimately won the presidency (1920–1924).

The seventeen uprisings that occurred during López Gutiérrez's term were a prelude to the civil war that erupted when General Tiburcio Carías Andino won the 1923 election without a majority. Despite the presence of U.S. ships on both coasts and marines in North Coast towns and in the capital, much blood flowed before U.S. State Department special envoy Sumner Welles finally persuaded the rival factions to meet aboard the USS *Milwaukee* anchored off Amapala in the Gulf of Fonseca.

New elections were held, and Dr. Miguel Paz Baraona, Carías's running mate in 1923, was voted in. President Paz Baraona (1925–1929) temporarily reduced political tensions, managed to reschedule the massive Honduran foreign debt by negotiating the Lyall Plan with Great Britain, and held free elections at the end of his term in 1928, in which the opposition Liberal candidate Dr. Vincent Mejia Colindres (1928–1932) won. Mejia Colindres, in turn, also held free elections, in which the National Party leader, General Carías, emerged victorious, retaining power by various stratagems until 1948.

By 1924, the year of the last major political upheaval before mid-century, the United Fruit and Standard Fruit Companies had absorbed their lesser competition and had acquired virtually every concession they might need for the foreseeable future. Moreover, because of large profits, they were able to substitute economic pressure for strong-arm tactics. Still, the sharp plunge in employment and revenues that accompanied the Great Depression, the ravages of banana diseases, and World War II produced severe strains that would have automatically led to political disorder in earlier times. Carías (1933–1948), however, was able to surmount these difficulties (while meticulously repaying British bondholders on schedule). He even brought a modicum of prosperity to his country, put the national budget in the black, built many new roads in rural areas, and inaugurated air transport service to many otherwise isolated towns and villages. The cost, however, was high. The Carías dictatorship shelved democratic practices for the duration, reduced the National Congress to a rubber stamp, and harshly repressed labor organizations on behalf of the banana and mining companies.

In the mid-1940s, university students, taking their cue from successful student-led coups in neighboring dictatorships, began agitating for a return to democracy, and women protested outside the presidential palace seeking the release of political prisoners. Carías, finally bowing to these demands and to pressures from the United States, announced that he would not run again in 1948. He did, however, handpick his successor, Juan Manuel Gálvez Durán (1949–1954).

Despite his long association with the Carías dictatorship, Gálvez granted opposition parties and labor unions considerable latitude to organize and mobilize support. On the eve of the 1954 elections, U.S. Central Intelligence Agency agents in Honduras launched a covert operation against the leftist government of Guatemala, and more than fifty thousand North Coast workers went on strike against the United Fruit and Standard Fruit Companies. In these unsettled conditions, none of the three candidates—General Carías for the National Party, Abraham William Calderón for the National Reformist Movement, and physician Ramón Villeda Morales for the Liberal Party—received a majority. Gálvez, meanwhile, had suffered a heart attack and turned the government over to his vice president, Julio Lozano Díaz. Lozano declared himself chief of state and cobbled together an interim government with initial support from all three candidates in the 1954 election. But when it later became clear that Lozano intended to prolong his stay indefinitely, the small professional military founded by Carías acted on its own for the first time and ejected Lozano in October 1956.

## MILITARY DOMINANCE (1956–1990)

The military junta, increasingly dominated by the head of the air force, Colonel Oswaldo López Arellano, negotiated a peace accord between the Liberals and Nationals in preparation for calling a constituent assembly to elect a civilian president for a six-year term. The junta also demanded that the new constitution guarantee the armed forces' political autonomy. The assembly elected the Liberal Villeda Morales, the candidate with the largest vote total in 1954. During his term (1957–1962), Villeda Morales worked to implement the Alliance for Progress, the Kennedy administration's plan to aid modernization and economic growth in Latin America. Labor unions prospered, and peasants began to acquire land through a small, government-sponsored agrarian reform which made the banana

**Outdoor market in Honduras.** Markets such as these are an example of the informal sector, which flourishes throughout much of Latin America. Unregulated by the government, vendors are able to make a livelihood in areas where other work may not be available to them. PHOTOGRAPH BY CORY LANGLEY. REPRODUCED BY PERMISSION

companies and the traditional landed elite nervous. Rapid population growth and the expansion of export agriculture (cotton, sugar, beef) since the 1940s had created a large landless population to which Villeda Morales promised further relief. When the Liberal Party chose as its candidate for the next elections Modesto Rodas Alvarado, a firebrand who pledged to restore civilian control over the armed forces, López seized power in October 1963, sending Villeda into exile. The Honduran military, in one guise or another, would remain the country's hegemonic political actor for the next thirty years.

In 1960 the Central American nations had formed a common market to circumvent the obstacles to economic development inherent in their small, separate domestic markets. Many Hondurans, however, later resented the fact that more aggressive Salvadoran entrepreneurs took advantage of new cross-border investment and trade opportunities to become a powerful force in the Honduran economy, the least developed in the region. In addition, shortly after López had himself named to a six-year term as president (1965–1971), acute economic problems were blamed on 300,000 Salvadoran peasants who had moved into rural Honduras because of extreme land scarcity in their own country. The continuing economic crisis and rising tensions with El Salvador over Honduran mistreatment of its citizens began to erode López's support within the armed forces and the National Party. His fall from power was postponed, however, when the so-called Soccer War erupted in mid-1969. The Honduran air force acquitted itself with distinction, but the Organization of American States intervened before the superior Salvadoran ground forces could make serious inroads into Honduras. The war stimulated popular support for the armed forces, but aggravated already poor economic conditions.

In 1971, López stood aside briefly to allow an elected bipartisan civilian government under National Party politician Ramón Ernesto Cruz to take office. When his government soon proved ineffective at controlling increasing social unrest, the military removed it in late 1972. The formerly conservative López returned to power at the head of a populist coalition composed of peasant organizations, labor unions, and progressive North Coast business groups. His government redistributed land to thousands of peasant families and increased the role of the state in the economy. However, after López was ousted in 1975 over an alleged United Brands bribe for slashing the export tax on bananas, right-wing military factions allied with the National Party and conservative economic interests regained influence under Colonel Juan Melgar Castro (1975–1978) and later General Policarpo Paz García (1978–1982).

The collapse of the Nicaraguan Somoza regime in 1979 helped the United States to persuade the Honduran military to return to the barracks and allow democratic elections. The Liberal Party won both the subsequent constitutional assembly elections (1980) and the presidential contest (1981), but the armed forces remained politically dominant. The new civilian president, Dr. Roberto Suazo Córdoba (1982–1986), formed a political alliance with armed forces chief General Gustavo Álvarez Martínez, a fanatical anticommunist trained in Argentina. Vastly increased U.S. military aid expanded and modernized the armed forces while the Contras, the anti-Sandinista rebels organized and armed by the United States, took up residence on the border with revolutionary Nicaragua. Until his ouster in an internal military dispute in 1984, Álvarez presided over a brutal "dirty war" against anyone suspected of radical political sympathies in Honduras. The military employed torture, secret prisons, and political assassinations without any protest from Suazo or the United States.

Suazo's democratically-elected successor, Liberal José Azcona del Hoyo (1986–1990), was less closely tied to the military, but he was too weak to challenge its political hegemony or address widespread corruption within the officer corps as Honduras became a major transhipment point for Colombian cocaine. The military left economic policymaking to the civilian authorities, but neither Suazo nor Azcona proved able to halt the economy's deterioration despite heavy financial assistance from the United States. Fiscal and trade deficits mounted, although military spending continued to rise.

### THE MILITARY IN POLITICAL DECLINE (1990–1999)

Rafael Callejas (1990–1994) was the first National Party candidate to win the presidency since elections were resumed in the early 1980s. His victory represented the first time one of the nation's two principal competing political parties had replaced the other democratically and without violence in almost sixty years. Nevertheless, the conservative Callejas was a close friend of the armed forces, which had no plan to reduce its prerogatives. Instead, he concentrated on an ambitious economic reform program demanded by the International Monetary Fund (IMF) and the United States Embassy. Callejas reduced the nation's chronic fiscal deficit, liberalized trade, and convinced foreign entrepreneurs to invest in new *maquiladora* assembly industries on the North Coast. The Honduran economy improved although corruption allegations and politically-motivated overspending late in Callejas's term tarnished his economic record.

The challenge to the military was launched not by Callejas but by United States ambassador Cresencio Arcos. The end of the Cold War and the winding down of the armed conflicts in Central America reduced the Honduran military's importance to the United States. What had once been seen in Washington as a valuable anticommunist ally was now perceived as an expensive obstacle to democracy. American military aid fell dramatically, and Ambassador Arcos became one of the armed forces' fiercest critics. This abrupt, unexpected reversal of United States policy encouraged a wide range of Hondurans to mobilize against the military's power and prerogatives. Human rights organizations, unions, and students joined with the Roman Catholic Church and much of the private sector to demand an end to the armed forces' privileges. Honduran journalists added fuel to the fire by publishing a steady stream of articles implicating high-ranking military officers in corruption and other serious crimes.

Increasing political pressure ultimately forced a reluctant Callejas to appoint an independent human rights commissioner to investigate the military's 1980s suppression of opposition and an Ad

Hoc Commission for Institutional Reform to examine allegations of corruption and abuse of power within the military's police branch. When these investigations concluded, the human rights commissioner's report provided evidence of the armed forces involvement in 184 specific cases of torture and political assassination, and the Ad Hoc Commission recommended that the notorious police investigative service be disbanded.

The Honduran military's decline accelerated rapidly under the two Liberal Party presidents who followed Callejas in office. Carlos Roberto Reina (1994–1998), former president of the Inter-American Court of Human Rights, was a politician from the left of the Liberal Party whose appointment to head the foreign ministry had been blocked by the military high command some years before. After he was inaugurated, Reina immediately implemented the Ad Hoc Commission's recommendations. In spite of strong military objections, he then persuaded the National Congress to pass amendments to the constitution that abolished entirely the military's control over the national police and ended obligatory military service. No longer able to force young Honduran men into the armed forces, the military shrank to about one-third its former size by the time Reina left office. In addition, with United States support, Reina reduced the military budget and removed the nation's telecommunications system and other lucrative public institutions from armed forces control.

Reina's administration continued the program of economic reform begun under Callejas. After a series of disruptive strikes, Reina was forced to make concessions to organized labor, but the Liberal government still met most IMF fiscal targets. Bouyed by surging maquiladora exports and increasing coffee prices, the Honduran economy was growing respectably by the end of Reina's term.

Liberal Carlos Flores Facussé (1998–2002) completed the subordination of the armed forces to civilian authority. The wealthy North Coast engineer and newspaper publisher passed a landmark constitutional reform that rescinded the formal political autonomy first granted the military in the 1957 Constitution. He appointed a civilian defense minister over military opposition and abolished the independent position of armed forces chief as well as the Superior Council of the Armed Forces, the military's collegial decision-making body. When resentment against these measures surfaced within the armed forces, Flores dismissed the armed forces chief of staff and a number of other high-ranking individuals and replaced them with officers willing to accept civilian control without question.

### A TROUBLED DEMOCRACY (1999–)

The subordination of the once all-powerful Honduran military to civilian democratic control by 1999 was a major achievement. Hondurans could also be proud of the institutionalization of a system of free national elections during the 1980s and 1990s. Nevertheless, Honduras's new democracy was marred by poverty, corruption, and rising crime.

International financial institutions generally praised the economic management skills of Liberal presidents Reina and Flores as well as their National Party successor, former Central Bank head Ricardo Maduro (2002–2006). Flores spent most of his term rebuilding the country after Hurricane Mitch in 1998 destroyed the entire banana crop and most of the nation's roads and bridges The Honduran economy recovered under Stanford-educated economist Ricardo Maduro on the strength of rising agricultural export prices, the success of the maquiladora sector, and mounting remittances (US$2.4 billion by 2006) from Hondurans living in the United States. The benefits of renewed economic growth, however, were distributed very unevenly, leaving most Hondurans mired in poverty. Per capita income remained under US$900 in 2006, and almost two thirds of the Honduran population of 7.3 million continued to live on less than two dollars a day. Taxes on elite and middle-class Honduras were too light to fund robust social programs to aid the poor urban majority or to restart the rural agrarian reform halted by Callejas.

Although corruption allegations against the Reina, Flores, and Maduro administrations were less serious than those that had been directed at the Callejas government, global monitoring organizations such as Transparency International judged Honduras to be one of the most corrupt countries in Latin America. Bribery and embezzlement scandals were common, as most Honduran politicians at all levels still viewed political office more as a prize to be exploited for personal gain than an opportunity to serve the public. Few corruption cases ever came to trial.

By the mid-1990s, many Hondurans began to view violent crime as the nation's number-one problem. Rates of robbery, assault, extortion, kidnapping, car theft, and homicide all exploded during the 1990s, especially in Tegucigalpa and San Pedro Sula. Many of these trends were associated with the arrival in Central America of the Los Angeles-based MS-13 (*Mara Salvatrucha*) and 18th Street youth gangs. These rival organizations took root after the United States deported thousands of Central American-born gang members to the region. Both gangs recruited aggressively in Honduras; by 2005, youth gangs encompassed an estimated 35,000 to 70,000 members. These new gangs also distributed narcotics for more established criminal organizations in the region. With only 7,500 poorly equipped, poorly trained, and often corrupt police officers, Honduran authorities were overwhelmed by rising crime.

President Maduro, who lost his own son in a kidnap attempt, instituted a hard-line zero-tolerance program that made gang membership a felony, increased resources for public security, and committed the army to the battle against crime. His policy resulted in the imprisonment of hundreds of gang members and led thousands of others to remove their tattoos and alter their style of dress. Analysts disagreed about the impact of Maduro's approach on crime rates, and the public security issue dominated the next presidential campaign. Liberal rancher Manuel "Mel" Zelaya (2006–), who narrowly won that contest, launched a new assault on crime early in his term that mobilized the country's large corps of private security guards to assist the police and army. He also promised social reforms to address the causes of crime as he developed closer relations with left-leaning governments in Latin America. Nonetheless, crime rates appeared to increase during Zelaya's first year in office.

*See also* **Alliance for Progress; Álvarez Martínez, Gustavo; Azcona Hoyo, José Simón; Bertrand, Francisco; Bonilla, Policarpo; Bonilla Chirinos, Manuel; Cabañas, José Trinidad; Callejas Romero, Rafael Leonardo; Carías Andino, Tiburcio; Chatfield, Frederick; Comayagua; Contras; Cruz Ucles, Ramón Ernesto; Dávila, Miguel R; Drugs and Drug Trade; Ferrera, Francisco; Gálvez, Juan Manuel; Guardiola, Santos; López Arellano, Oswaldo; Lozano Díaz, Julio; Maquiladoras; Morazán, Francisco; Paz Baraona, Miguel; Paz García, Policarpo; Rodas Alvarado, Modesto; Rosa, Ramón; Soto, Marco Aurelio; Squier, Ephraim George; Standard Fruit and Steamship Company; Suazo Córdova, Roberto; Tegucigalpa; United Fruit Company; Vaccaro Brothers; Valle, José Cecilio del; Villeda Morales, Ramón; Walker, William; Welles, Sumner; Zelaya, José Santos; Zemurray, Samuel.**

BIBLIOGRAPHY

Argueta, Mario. *Tiburcio Carías: Anatomía de una época, 1923–1948.* Tegucigalpa: Editorial Guaymuras, 1989.

Bowman, Kirk S. *Militarization, Democracy, and Development: The Perils of Praetorianism in Latin America.* University Park: Pennsylvania State University Press, 2002.

Bulmer-Thomas, Victor.*The Political Economy of Central America Since 1920.* Cambridge and New York: Cambridge University Press, 1987.

Dunkerley, James. *Power in the Isthmus: A Political History of Modern Central America.* London and New York: Verso, 1988.

Euraque, Darío. *Reinterpreting the "Banana Republic": Region and State in Honduras, 1870–1972.* Chapel Hill: University of North Carolina Press, 1996.

Finney, Kenneth V. *In Quest of El Dorado: Precious Metal Mining and the Modernization of Honduras, 1880–1900.* New York: Garland, 1987.

Funes, Matías H. *Los deliberantes: El poder militar en Honduras.* Tegucigalpa: Editorial Guaymuras, 1995.

Karnes, Thomas L. *Tropical Enterprise: The Standard Fruit and Steamship Company in Latin America.* Baton Rouge: Louisiana State University Press, 1978.

Meza, Victor. *História del movimiento obrero Hondureño.* Tegucigalpa: Editorial Guaymuras, 1980.

Morris, James A. *Honduras: Caudillo Politics and Military Rulers.* Boulder, CO: Westview Press, 1984.

Paredes, Lucas. *Drama político de Honduras.* Mexico City: Editorial Latinoamericano, 1958.

Posas, Mario, and Rafael del Cid. *Construcción del sector público y del Estado Nacional en Honduras, 1876–1979.* 2nd ed. San José: Editorial Universitaria Centroamericana, 1983.

Mahoney, James. *The Legacies of Liberalism: Path Dependence and Political Regimes in Central America.* Baltimore, MD: Johns Hopkins University Press, 2001.

Merrill, Tim L., ed. *Honduras: A Country Study.* Washington, DC: Federal Research Division, Library of Congress; U.S. Government Printing Office, 1995.

Ruhl, J. Mark. *Ejércitos y democracia en Centroamérica: Una reforma incompleta.* Managua: LEA Grupo Editorial, 2004.

Salomón, Leticia. *Militarismo y reformismo en Honduras.* Tegucigalpa: Editorial Guaymuras, 1982.

Salomón, Leticia. *Democratización y sociedad civil en Honduras.* Tegucigalpa: Centro de Documentación de Honduras, 1994.

Schulz, Donald E., and Deborah Sundloff Schulz. *The United States, Honduras, and the Crisis in Central America.* Boulder, CO: Westview Press, 1994.

Stokes, William S. *Honduras: An Area Study in Government.* Madison: University of Wisconsin Press, 1950.

Woodward, Ralph Lee, Jr. *Central America: A Nation Divided.* New York: Oxford University Press, 1976; 3rd ed., 1999.

KENNETH V. FINNEY
J. MARK RUHL

**HONDURAS COMPANY.** Honduras Company, a trading enterprise established by the Spanish monarchy. The Honduras Company (La Compañía de Comercio de Honduras) was chartered by the Spanish king, Philip V on 25 January 1714, as one of the earliest of the Bourbon Reforms. It granted the marquis of Montesacro an exclusive license to trade with Honduras; but only one trading expedition, from Cádiz, was ever made, and the Honduras Company ceased to exist after its return to Spain in 1717. It launched, however, a pattern of more liberal trade policies to follow, notably with the establishment of the Caracas Company in 1728, the Havana Company in 1740, two Guatemalan companies in 1750–1756, and the passage of the Free Trade Act of 1778. Such trading companies were established to engage in officially regulated commerce with limited geographic regions, thus beginning the breakdown of the Seville-Cádiz merchant monopoly.

*See also* **Havana Company.**

BIBLIOGRAPHY

Roland Hussey, *The Caracas Company, 1728–1784: A Study in the History of Spanish Monopolistic Trade* (1934).

Carmelo Sáenz De Santamaría, "La Compañía de Comercio de Honduras, 1714–1717," *Revista de Indias* 40 (1980): 129–157.

Luis Mariñas Otero, *Honduras,* 2d ed. (1983).

*Additional Bibliography*

Arazola Corvera, Ma Jesús. *Hombres, barcos y comercio de la ruta Cádiz-Buenos Aires, 1737–1757.* Sevilla: Diputación de Sevilla, 1998.

Cavieres Figueroa, Eduardo. *Servir al soberano sin detrimento del vasallo: El comercio hispano colonial y el sector mercantil de Santiago de Chile en el siglo XVIII.* Valparaíso: Ediciones Universitarias de Valparaíso de la Universidad Católica de Valparaíso, 2003.

Fisher, John Robert. *The Economic Aspects of Spanish Imperialism in America, 1492–1810.* Liverpool: Liverpool University Press, 1997.

Martínez Shaw, Carlos, and José María Oliva Melgar. *Sistema atlántico español: Siglos XVII–XIX.* Madrid: Marcial Pons Historia, 2005.

Romano, Ruggiero. *Mecanismo y elementos del sistema económico colonial americano, siglos XVI–XVIII.* México: El Colegio de México, Fideicomiso Historia de las Américas: Fondo de Cultura Económica, 2003.

Vila Vilar, Enriqueta, and Allan J. Kuethe. *Relaciones de poder y comercio colonial: Nuevas perspectivas.* Sevilla: Escuela de Estudios Hispano-Americanos: Texas Tech University, 1999.

JEFFREY D. SAMUELS

**HONDURAS, CONSTITUTIONS.** Honduras has been governed under many constitutions, beginning with the Spanish Constitution of Cádiz (1812). Other constitutions were promulgated in 1825, 1839, 1848, 1852, 1865, 1873, 1874 (putting the Constitution of 1865 back in force), 1880, 1894, 1936, 1957, 1965, and 1982. In general, these constitutions produced in the nineteenth century alternated between reflecting the tenets of the Liberal and the Conservative parties. Of the myriad documents, those which have impacted Honduran political development more thoroughly include the constitutions of 1812, 1824, and 1965.

The Constitution of Cádiz was produced by the Cortes of Cádiz during the Napoleonic occupation of Spain (1808–1814) by Spanish and American representatives. The Kingdom of Guatemala was allotted twelve deputies to the parliament in Spain and regional *diputaciones provinciales* were set up in

León, Nicaragua; Ciudad Real, Spain; and Guatemala City. Although this constitution was nullified by King Ferdinand VII upon his return to the Spanish throne in 1814, it was restored in 1820 and served as the basis for subsequent constitutions. It provided a division of powers among legislative, judicial, and executive branches, as well as constitutional restrictions on royal (executive) powers vis-à-vis legislative powers.

The Constitution of 1824 was promulgated throughout Central America upon the dissolution of the Mexican Empire and Central American secession. The five states of Honduras, Guatemala, El Salvador, Nicaragua, and Costa Rica formed the United Provinces of Central America, a federal system that ultimately failed to hold together the five states. Yet, this same constitution set the framework for unification sentiments that have permeated the histories of all five, especially during the remainder of the nineteenth century. The Constitution of 1824 drew heavily on the Constitution of Cádiz and on the U.S. Constitution of 1789, as well as on the French legal tradition. The chamber of deputies held most of the political power and was elected by proportional representation of the eligible electorate. The electorate was limited by gender, literacy, and property qualifications. The legislative branch controlled the judicial and executive branches, and executive functions were divided between the executive and a senate. Provisions granting the "freedom and independence" of the states led to a struggle between the advocates of centralism and federalism and correlated directly with Liberal-Conservative divisions. After the dissolution of the United Provinces in 1839, Honduras was governed under a series of constitutions that alternated between Liberal ideals of free education, foreign investment, free trade, religious tolerance, and Conservative ideals of trade restrictions and protection of the church and indigenous peoples. The structure and balance of power did not alter as greatly on paper as it did in practice.

A Constituent Assembly, elected in 1963 following the overthrow of President José Ramón Villeda Morales, promulgated the Constitution of 1965. The Constitution of 1957 had already made significant changes in social policies, education, the family, electoral procedures, the role of the armed forces, and labor. Human rights had also been guaranteed under the Villeda administration. Dominated by National Party members (more a Liberal splinter group than a successor to the Conservative Party), the Constituent Assembly of 1965 designated Colonel Oswaldo López Arellano as the new president, to serve for six years. The assembly also declared itself the first Congress under the new constitution. The document divided the government into the same three branches and specified that the president be the commander of the armed forces. The legislature was unicameral and proportionally representative. The Supreme Court of Honduras consisted of seven justices serving limited terms.

The constitution is divided into fourteen "titles," which, despite hinting at the restoration of union, produce a very centralized government with a strong executive and a relatively weaker legislative branch. Over time, Honduran constitutions showed a political evolution from colony to state to republic, and from a strong legislative branch to a strong military and executive branch. However, the Constitution of 1965 reminded Hondurans that they were still part of "the Federal Republic of Central America" and, while assuring Honduran sovereignty, left open the possibility of Central American reunification in the future.

*See also* **Cortes of Cádiz; López Arellano, Oswaldo; Villeda Morales, Ramón.**

BIBLIOGRAPHY

Ramón Rosa, "Social Constitution of Honduras," in Ralph Lee Woodward, Jr., ed., *Positivism in Latin America, 1850–1900: Are Order and Progress Reconcilable?* (1971).

Harvey K. Meyer, *Historical Dictionary of Honduras* (1976).

Mario Rodríguez, *The Cádiz Experiment* (1978).

Luis Mariñas Otero, *Las constituciones de Honduras* (1982); and *Honduras,* 2d ed. (1983).

James A. Morris, *Honduras: Caudillo Politics and Military Rulers* (1984).

*Additional Bibliography*

García Laguardia, Jorge Mario. *Honduras: evolución político constitucional, 1824–1936.* México: Universidad Nacional Autónoma de México, 1999.

Rojas Carón, León. *La constitución Hondureña analizada.* Tegucigalpa: Litografía López, 2006.

JEFFREY D. SAMUELS

## HONDURAS, NATIONAL PARTY (PNH).

**HONDURAS, NATIONAL PARTY (PNH).** The National Party of Honduras emerged in the early twentieth century as the principal opposition to the Liberal Party, which had dominated the country since the 1870s. Made up of both disgruntled Liberals and former Conservative Party members, it formally organized in 1916 under the leadership of Francisco Bertrand, although it did not become a cohesive organization until Tiburcio Carías Andino took over its leadership in the 1920s. Despite lip service to nationalism, the party became closely allied to the U.S.-owned United Fruit Company. Carías failed in efforts to unseat the Liberals in 1923 and 1928. However, he finally won the election of 1932 and ruled Honduras from 1933 to 1948, firmly establishing the National Party in Honduran politics.

Ideologically, the party was much influenced in its formative years by Dr. Paulino Valladares and has tended to be somewhat to the right of the Liberal Party. Personalism, however, has always been more important than ideology in the party. In the post-Carías period, the party developed close ties with the Honduran army, although not to the exclusion of the Liberal influence there. The Liberals ended the long National Party rule in 1957. Beginning in 1956, however, the army established itself as the principal political power in the country, and in 1963 it restored the National Party to power. Since then the National and Liberal parties have often joined in unity pacts to share power.

Civilian government was restored in 1981. The National Party, led by Rafael Leonardo Callejas, lost to the Liberals that year and again in 1985. But in 1990 Callejas returned to power on a strongly neo-liberal economic platform. Deteriorating economic conditions, however, led to another Liberal victory in the 1993 presidential election. The party has continued to be a strong presence in Honduras winning the presidency in 2001 and coming in a close second in the 2005 presidential elections.

*See also* **Bertrand, Francisco; Callejas Romero, Rafael Leonardo; Carías Andino, Tiburcio.**

BIBLIOGRAPHY

James D. Rudolph, ed., *Honduras, a Country Study,* 2d ed. (1983).

Alison Acker, *Honduras: The Making of a Banana Republic* (1988).

James Dunkerley, *Power in the Isthmus: A Political History of Modern Central America* (1988).

Tom Barry and Kent Norsworthy, *Honduras: A Country Guide* (1990).

*Additional Bibliography*

Dodd, Thomas J. *Tiburcio Carías: Portrait of a Honduran Political Leader.* Baton Rouge: Louisiana State University Press, 2005.

Meza, Víctor, Leticia Salomón, and Mirna Flores. *Democracia y partidos políticos en Honduras.* Tegucigalpa: Centro de Documentación de Honduras, 2004.

Sierra Fonseca, Rolando. *Colonia, independencia y reforma: Introducción a la historiografía hondureña (1876–2000).* Tegucigalpa: Universidad Pedagógica Nacional Francisco Morazán, Fondo Editorial, 2001.

Ralph Lee Woodward Jr.

## HOPKINS, EDWARD AUGUSTUS

(1822–1891). Edward Augustus Hopkins (*b.* 1822; *d.* 10 June 1891), U.S. diplomat and entrepreneur active in Paraguay and Argentina. The son of an Episcopalian bishop in Vermont, Hopkins was twenty-two years old when he decided to abandon a faltering career in the U.S. Navy and try his luck as an entrepreneur in South America. He obtained a commission as U.S. agent to Paraguay in 1845.

President Carlos Antonio Lopéz welcomed the young man as though he were a full-fledged ambassador. Hopkins actually encouraged this attitude by exaggerating his own authority, claiming that he was empowered to mediate between the Paraguayan government and the *porteño* dictator Juan Manuel de Rosas. Eventually, the U.S. State Department had to repudiate the grandiose claims of its agent and order his return to Washington.

Hopkins refused to give up. Over the next few years, he returned to Paraguay five times. He explored its rivers and gained a comprehensive knowledge of its commercial potential. Though somewhat chastened by his earlier experience, López agreed to extend a series of trade privileges to Hopkins if the United States were to recognize Paraguayan independence.

In 1853, when the United States recognized Paraguay, Hopkins returned to Asunción as consul and quickly moved to take advantage of López's offer. He had already organized a corporation—the United States and Paraguay Navigation Company—and with the capital it provided, set up a half-dozen enterprises in Paraguay. These included a cigar factory, a brick factory, a sawmill, and a distillery, all of which operated under license from López. The Paraguayan president even extended loans to Hopkins as well as the labor of state prisoners for the various projects.

Things did not go as planned. Hopkins's blustering personal style had always irked the punctilious López, but the North American's open-ended promises had always caused him to ignore his instincts. López, however, revoked the concessions granted Hopkins and, in 1854, expelled him from the republic.

By this time, the bad feelings between the two men had grown into a diplomatic incident that ultimately resulted in an abortive U.S. naval intervention. López reluctantly agreed to mediation to settle the dispute.

After his Paraguayan fiasco, Hopkins stayed on in the Platine region. He lived for another thirty-seven years in and around Buenos Aires, where he made a name for himself promoting telegraph companies, steamships, and railroads. Throughout this time he maintained a quasi-official position within the Argentine government and was a personal friend of many highly placed Argentine politicians. In the early 1890s, he returned to the United States as secretary of the Argentine delegation to an international railway conference. He died in Washington, D.C.

*See also* **Paraguay: The Nineteenth Century; Rosas, Juan Manuel de; Water Witch Incident.**

BIBLIOGRAPHY

Harold F. Peterson, "Edward A. Hopkins: A Pioneer Promoter in Paraguay," in *Hispanic American Historical Review* 22, no. 2 (1942): 245–261.

Thomas L. Whigham, *The Politics of River Trade: Tradition and Development in the Upper Plata, 1780–1870* (1991), pp. 145–147.

Robert D. Wood, *The Voyage of* Water Witch (1985).

THOMAS L. WHIGHAM

---

**HORN, CAPE.** The Cabo de Hornos is a promontory located on the Isla Hornos in Chile at 55 degrees south and 67 degrees west latitudes, considered the southernmost tip of the continent. Discovered by the Dutch corsairs W. C. Schouten and J. Le Maire on 29 January 1611, it was named Hoorn, for the birthplace of Schouten. The discovery dispelled the belief that Tierra Del Fuego was the northern margin of a large southern continent, Terra Australis, and established a second passage from the Atlantic Ocean to the Pacific Ocean. Sailing ships preferred the open oceanic passage to the narrow and treacherous Strait of Magellan, although heavy storms and the strong westerlies would sometimes paralyze vessels for weeks. Steam navigation dealt a blow to the Cape Horn route by making navigation along the Strait of Magellan safer.

*See also* **Magellan, Strait of; Tierra del Fuego.**

BIBLIOGRAPHY

Webb Chiles, *Storm Passage: Alone Around Cape Horn* (1977).

Erroll Bruce, *Cape Horn to Port* (1978).

Hal Roth, *Two Against Cape Horn* (1978).

*Additional Bibliography*

Catalán Labarías, Rodrigo. *Bosques y comunidades del sur de Chile.* Santiago de Chile: Editorial Universitaria, 2006.

Coloane, Francisco. *Cabo de Hornos.* Santiago de Chile: Editorial Andrés Bello, 1998.

Davis, Charles G. *Around Cape Horn: A Maritime Artist/Historian's Account of His 1982 Voyage,* edited by Captain Neal Parker. Camden, ME: Down East Books, 2004.

Inda, Enrique S. *El náufrago del Cabo de Hornos.* Buenos Aires: Cefomar Editora, 2005.

Riesenberg, Felix and Briesemeister, William. *Cape Horn: The Story of the Cape Horn Region.* Woodbridge, CT: Ox Bow Press, 1994.

CÉSAR N. CAVIEDES

---

**HORNERO BIRD.** The hornero bird is a songbird species native to the flat eastern pampas of Argentina. It is known for its ovenlike mud nests, which it builds on fence posts and other likely spots on the flat, treeless grasslands. Its sweet songs and blithe spirit are mythologized in popular gaucho poetry and song.

BIBLIOGRAPHY

Durrell, Gerald M. *The Drunken Forest.* New York: Viking Press, 1956.

Hudson, William H. *Far Away and Long Ago: A History of My Early Life.* New York: E. P. Dutton, 1918.

KRISTINE L. JONES

**HORSES.** *See* **Livestock.**

**HOSTOS Y BONILLA, EUGENIO MARÍA DE** (1839–1903). Eugenio María de Hostos y Bonilla (*b.* 11 January 1839; *d.* 11 August 1903), Puerto Rican philosopher, sociologist, educator, patriot, and man of letters. Born in Río Cañas, Hostos attended elementary school in San Juan, secondary school at the Institute of Balboa in Spain, and enrolled in law school in Madrid. He joined the Spanish republican movement and gained their promise of independence for Puerto Rico and Cuba. When the republicans abandoned that promise, Hostos moved to the United States in 1869.

In New York, he joined the Cuban Revolutionary Junta and became managing editor of its official periodical. Realizing that Cuban independence could not be fought from New York, he began a four-year journey in 1870 that would take him throughout South America to win support for the independence cause. Long an advocate of abolition of slavery and of Antillean federation after independence, Hostos involved himself during his travels with various social injustices. In Lima, his writings proved instrumental in turning public opinion against the mistreatment of Chinese laborers and against the Oroya railway project, despite the fact that its builders offered to donate $200,000 to the movement. In 1872, he taught at the University of Chile in Santiago, where his writings helped gain women the right of admission to professional programs. While in Argentina in 1873, he became a spokesman for a transandean railroad to Chile. In honor of his efforts, the first locomotive to complete the journey was named the *Eugenio María de Hostos.*

In 1875, he settled in Santo Domingo, where he founded a newspaper that echoed one of his strongest dreams, a federation of the Hispanic West Indies. After a brief trip to Venezuela where he married, he returned to Santo Domingo and revamped the education system, introducing the scientific method to the curriculum. He stated that the only revolution that had not taken place in Latin America was in education and he added the reformation of educational systems to his political agenda. After a disagreement with the Dominican dictator, Ulises Heureaux in 1888, he accepted an invitation from officials to return to Chile and reform its educational system.

Hostos returned to New York in 1898 and for two years unsuccessfully agitated for a plebiscite to determine the future status of Puerto Rico, even participating in a delegation that presented demands to President William McKinley. After the assassination of Heureaux, he returned to the Dominican Republic as inspector general of schools.

Hostos wrote fifty books and numerous essays. The impact of his novel, *La peregrinación de Bayoán,* is said to be as profound for Cuban independence as *Uncle Tom's Cabin* was for the abolitionist movement in the United States. His treatise on the scientific education of women made him a precursor of later feminist causes and his political writings made him a forerunner of the doctrine of self-determination in his homeland. It is said that no national literature evolved in the Dominican Republic until after his service to that country. His educational endeavors included founding schools, writing textbooks, and authoring the laws governing education. He wrote best of his own beliefs when he said in *La peregrinación,* "I wish that they will say: In that Island [Puerto Rico] a man was born who loved truth, desired justice, and worked for the good of men."

*See also* **Chinese Labor (Peru); Liberalism; Puerto Rico.**

BIBLIOGRAPHY

Juan Bosch, *Hostos, el sembrador* (1976).

Eugenio Carlos De Hostos, ed., *Eugenio María de Hostos: Promoter of Pan-Americanism* (1954).

Loida Figueroa, *Hostos, el angustiado* (1988).

Adelaida Lugo Guernelli, *Eugenio María de Hostos, ensayista y crítico literario* (1970).

Eugenio María de Hostos y Bonilla *Obras Completas.*

Arturo Morales Carrión, *Puerto Rico: A Political and Cultural History* (1983).

Emilio Rodríguez Demorizi, *Luperón y Hostos* (1975).

Emilio Roig De Leuchsenring, *Hostos y Cuba,* 2d ed. (1974).

*Additional Bibliography*

Arpini, Adriana. *Eugenio María de Hostos, un hacedor de libertad.* Mendoza: Editorial de la Universidad Nacional de Cuyo, 2002.

Méndez, José Luis. *Hostos y las ciencias sociales.* San Juan: Editorial de la Universidad de Puerto Rico, 2003.

Rivera, Angel A. *Eugenio María de Hostos y Alejandro Tapia y Rivera: avatares de una modernidad caribeña.* New York: P. Lang, 2001.

Rosa, Richard. *Los fantasmas de la razón: Una lectura material de Hostos.* San Juan: Isla Negra, 2003.

JACQUELYN BRIGGS KENT

---

**HOUSSAY, BERNARDO A.** (1887–1971). Bernardo A. Houssay (*b.* 10 April 1887; *d.* 21 September 1971), Argentine physiologist, teacher, and researcher, Latin America's first Nobel laureate in science. Born to a French family in Buenos Aires, Houssay studied and, beginning in 1910, taught medicine at the University of Buenos Aires. In 1919 he was named professor of physiology and director of the Institute of Physiology. In 1933, at the initiative of the "Houssay group," the Asociación Argentina para el Progreso de las Ciencias was founded; it played a commanding role in obtaining and disbursing funding for Argentine scientific research. With his associates and hundreds of other intellectuals, Houssay was dismissed by the military government in 1943; he later clashed with President Juan Perón. Out of official favor, he continued his research under private auspices. By the late 1940s his writings on endocrinology, nutrition, physiology, pharmacology, diabetes, and medical education gained him an international reputation. Honors and awards culminated in 1947 in the Nobel Prize in physiology or medicine (shared with Carl F. and Gerty T. Cori), awarded to him in recognition of his research on the role of the pituitary gland in carbohydrate metabolism—research that pointed the way toward alternatives to insulin. Houssay served as president of the National Council for Scientific and Technical Research and remained professionally active until his death. His works include *Concepto de la universidad* (1940), *La crisis actual y bases para el adelanto de la universidad* (1943), *Human Physiology* (1965), and *La emigración de cientificos, profesionales, y technicos de la Argentina* (1966).

*See also* **Perón, Juan Domingo; Science.**

BIBLIOGRAPHY

Marcelino Cereijido, *La nuca de Houssay: Las ciencia argentina entre Billiken y el exilio* (1990).

Carl F. Cori et al., eds., *Perspectives in Biology* (1963).

Guenter B. Risse, "Houssay, Bernardo A.," in *Dictionary of Scientific Biography,* vol. 15 (1978), pp. 228–229.

Sir Frank Young and V. G. Foglia, "Bernard A. Houssay," in *Biographical Memoirs of Fellows of the Royal Society,* vol. 20 (1974), pp. 247–270.

*Additional Bibliography*

Cueto, Marcos. "Laboratory Styles in Argentine Physiology." *Isis* 85 (June 1994): 228–246.

Marco, Miguel Angel de. *Houssay: La Argentina de los sabios.* Rosario: Fundación Libertad, 1997.

RONALD C. NEWTON

---

**HOUSTON, SAM** (1793–1863). Sam Houston (*b.* 2 March 1793; *d.* 26 July 1863), president of the Republic of Texas (1836–1838, 1841–1844). Born near Timber Ridge Church, Rockbridge County, Virginia, Houston received little formal schooling and spent three years among the Cherokee Indians. In 1813, he enlisted in the U.S. Army and was wounded in an engagement with the Creek Indians at Horseshoe Bend. He left the army in 1818 to study law in Nashville. His popularity led to a variety of elected and appointed offices, including two terms in Congress (1823, 1825) and election as governor of Tennessee (1827). He resigned the governorship in 1829 and spent the next six years establishing diplomatic and trade relations with the Indians.

Houston moved to Texas in 1832 and was caught up in the turmoil between the Mexican government and the Anglo-American population. He was elected a delegate to the Consultation of all Texas communities in 1835, and the revolutionary government awarded him a commission as major general. He signed the Declaration of Independence on 2 March 1836, and two days later he was selected to command the Texas Army, which he led to victory at the battle of San Jacinto on 21 April of that year. On 5 September 1836, Houston was elected president of the Republic of Texas, an office he held twice during that nation's nine-year history. When Texas joined the United States, Houston was sent to the U.S. Senate, where he served for fourteen years. On 21 December 1859 he was inaugurated governor of Texas, but his opposition to secession and his refusal to swear allegiance to the Confederate government forced him to relinquish the office in 1861. He spent the last years of his life at his home in Huntsville, Texas.

*See also* **Texas Revolution.**

BIBLIOGRAPHY

Llerena Friend, *Sam Houston, the Great Designer* (1969).

Sam Houston, *The Autobiography of Sam Houston,* edited by Donald Day and Harry Herbert Ullom (1954).

Amelia W. Williams and Eugene. C. Barker, *The Writings of Sam Houston,* 8 vols. (1938–1943).

Marion Karl Wisehart, *Sam Houston, American Giant* (1962).

*Additional Bibliography*

Campbell, Randolph B., and Mark C. Carnes. *Sam Houston and the American Southwest.* New York: Pearson Longman, 2007.

Haley, James L. *Sam Houston.* Norman: University of Oklahoma Press, 2002.

MICHAEL R. GREEN

**HOWARD, JENNIE ELIZA** (1845–1931). Jennie Eliza Howard (*b.* 24 July 1845; *d.* 29 July 1931), North American schoolteacher and educator. Born in Coldbrook Springs, Massachusetts, Howard studied at the Framingham Normal School and taught in Boston and Worcester, where she became an assistant principal in a boys' school. Howard was an experienced teacher by 1883, when she joined Domingo Faustino Sarmiento's program that brought North American teachers to Argentina. She is the best remembered of the more than eighty-eight teachers who worked in Argentina from 1867 to the turn of the century because she wrote a book about her experiences: *In Distant Climes and Other Years* (1931). Howard taught or ran schools in Paraná; in Corrientes, where she established a normal school; and in San Nicolás de los Arroyos, at the eastern limit of the pampa. There she was assistant principal of the normal school and head of the model grade school, both of which she established.

Howard retired in 1903, when she lost her voice, but she remained in Argentina where she became the mainstay of the English-speaking community in Buenos Aires. When the government cut all pensions, more than one hundred of Howard's former students organized to get hers restored, and they feted her on her eighty-fifth birthday in a public hall. Her portrait still hangs in the public school she founded in San Nicolás. Howard died in Buenos Aires.

*See also* **Education: Overview; Pampa.**

BIBLIOGRAPHY

Alice Houston Luiggi, *65 Valiants* (1965).

*Additional Bibliography*

Szurmuk, Mónica, editor. *Mujeres en viaje: Escritos y testimonios.* Buenos Aires: Aguilar, Altea, Taurus, Alfaguara, 2000.

GEORGETTE MAGASSY DORN

**HUACA.** *Huaca* has a meaning that is widespread throughout the pre-Hispanic world. According to the Quechua dictionary by Fray Domingo de Santo Tomás, it means "temple of idols or the idol itself." In other words, *huacas* were ceremonial centers where pilgrimages, rituals, and festivals of various magnitudes and purposes were held. For example, Pariacaca is an immense mountain range that was worshiped by the inhabitants of the Lima foothills. Titicaca is a great lake on the high plateau of the Andes in the Collao area and was venerated as a *huaca mayor* (greater huaca). Pachacamac, near Lima, is a huge ceremonial temple where pilgrims arrived from all parts of Tahuantinsuyo, the Inca empire. There were also *huacas menores* (lesser huacas), which were places or objects of smaller magnitude or religious importance, such as the *apachetas* (stone mounds left by travelers to avoid hazards along the road) or *cántaros de chicha* (jugs of corn liquor), whose drink was a symbol of fertility. Overall, *huacas* played a key role in 1565 in the Taki Onqoy movement, when the Indians led a violent attack against Spanish rule with the understanding that the *huacas* were the force behind the rebellion and that they possessed the spirit of the rebels to expel the Spaniards and defeat the power of the Catholic gods.

*See also* **Incas, The; Quechua.**

BIBLIOGRAPHY

Chapdelaine, Claude, Victor Pimentel, and Helene Bernier. "A Glimpse at Moche Phase II Occupation at the

Huacas of Moche Site, Northern Peru." *Antiquity* 75, no. 288 (June 2001): 361–372.

"Feats of Clay: Ancient Peruvian Pottery Factory Yields Clues to Production of Ceramics." *National Geographic* 201, no. 6 (June 2002): xxii.

D. WILFREDO KAPSOLI-ESCUDERO

**HUANCAVELICA.** Huancavelica, city and department of Peru made famous by colonial mercury mines. Located 150 miles southeast of Lima, the city lies in a steep mountain valley along the Icho River, 11,895 feet above sea level with a population of approximately 40,000. The famous Santa Bárbara mine of colonial times lay atop cliffs south of the city at an altitude of 14,300 feet.

Indians worked the quicksilver deposits during pre-Hispanic times, but the district became economically important only when the Spaniards began to refine silver through amalgamation. In 1563 Amador Cabrera, an *encomendero* (agent) from Huamanga, learned about the site from the *kuraka* (Indian headman) Gonzalo Ñavincopa. Miners and operators founded the Villa Rica de Oropesa, named for Viceroy Francisco de Toledo's home in Spain, on 4 August 1571. (After Toledo's departure the city gradually reverted to the name of Huancavelica.) Toledo expropriated the district for the crown in 1572. He then contracted with mine operators to produce mercury at a set price and agreed to provide them with cheap, forced Indian labor known as the Mita.

The Huancavelica mine quickly became a deathtrap for the Indian laborers. In its greed and inexperience the mining guild neglected to dig a ventilation shaft, and the mercury dust poisoned many. Indian villages subject to the *mita* looked upon the labor draft as a death sentence and were encouraged in their opposition by governors, priests, *hacendados,* and *kurakas* who wanted to exploit the workers themselves. As Indians died or fled, population in the *mita* provinces declined dramatically. Conditions improved in 1642 with completion of the Our Lady of Belén adit, which ventilated the mine. Thereafter more Indians were willing to work as wage laborers at the mine.

Huancavelica was the only American mercury mine of any significance, and until the 1770s it provided nearly all the quicksilver used by Peruvian silver refiners. It also made occasional shipments to Mexico, but the crown generally supplied the northern viceroyalty from its mines at Almadén, Spain. With the Peruvian mining expansion of the eighteenth century, Huancavelica struggled to meet mercury demand, its richest ores exhausted. Production costs were five times higher than at Almadén.

Blaming Huancavelica's problems on corruption and primitive technology, the royal inspector (*visitador*) José Antonio de Areche abolished the guild in 1779 and turned the Santa Bárbara mine over to Nicolás de Saravia, who agreed to produce greater quantities at a much lower price. When Saravia died unexpectedly the following year, Areche decided to turn the mine over to government administration, which had been very successful at Almadén. In 1784, because of the mercury mine, Huancavelica became a small intendancy, independent of the intendant of Huamanga's jurisdiction.

Nevertheless, Fernando Márquez de la Plata, the intendant, knew little about mining and allowed his unscrupulous mine director to extract the ore-laden natural supports of the mine to increase mercury output. On 25 September 1786 the top half of the mine collapsed. As head of a royal technological mission to Peru, Baron Thaddeus von Nordenflicht made comprehensive recommendations to renovate the mine in 1792, but his proposal died from lack of money and xenophobic resistance. Perhaps as important, Spanish authorities decided to halt Huancavelica production and supply Peru from Almadén in order to make the colonists dependent upon Spain for mercury.

Despite those imperial intentions, Almadén was unable to provide secure and adequate supplies, and Huancavelica intendants permitted private interests to work deposits outside the Santa Bárbara mine, where huge quantities of low-grade ore were available. Some production at Huancavelica continued after Peruvian independence, along with periodic attempts to reopen the great mine itself. The low price for mercury on the world market crippled those attempts, however, and Huancavelica stagnated in modern times, a colonial city dependent on grazing and wool for its scant existence.

*See also* **Mining: Colonial Spanish America.**

BIBLIOGRAPHY

Arthur P. Whitaker, *The Huancavelica Mercury Mine: A Contribution to the History of the Bourbon Renaissance in the Spanish Empire* (1941).

Guillermo Lohmann Villena, *Las minas de Huancavelica en los siglos XVI y XVII* (1949).

Robert G. Yates, Dean F. Kent, and Jaime Fernández Concha, *Geology of the Huancavelica Quicksilver District, Peru* (1951).

Henri Favre, "Caracteres sociales fundamentales de la aglomeración urbana de Huancavelica," in *Cuadernos de antropología* 8 (1965): 25–30.

Gwendolin Cobb, *Potosí y Huancavelica: Bases económicas del Peru, 1545–1640* (1977).

Carlos Contreras, *La ciudad del mercurio: Huancavelica, 1570–1700* (1982).

Mervyn Lang, "El derrumbe de Huancavelica en 1786: Fracaso de una reforma borbónica," in *Histórica* 10, no. 2 (1986): 213–226.

Kendall W. Brown, "La crisis financiera peruana al comienzo del siglo XVIII, la minería de plata y la mina de azogues de Huancavelica," in *Revista de Indias* 10, no. 182–183 (1988): 349–383.

*Additional Bibliography*

Contreras, Carlos. *Estado y Mercado en la historia del Perú.* Perú: Pontificia Universidad Católica del Perú, 2002.

Patino Paúl, Mariano. *Huancavelica colonial: Apuntes históricos de la ciudad minera más importante del Vierraynato peruano.* Huancavelica: El Autor, 2001.

KENDALL W. BROWN

**HUANCAYO.** Huancayo, province in the central highlands of Peru encompassing primarily the area of the fertile Mantaro Valley. Its capital city, also named Huancayo (1990 population 252,000), developed into an important commercial center in the mid-nineteenth century. Prior to the arrival of the Spanish colonizers, the Huancas, an ethnic group initially hostile to Incan expansion, inhabited the area. Just north of today's Huancayo province, Francisco Pizarro founded the town of Jauja as the initial center of his Peruvian conquests, but later opted for the city of Lima on the coast for defensive purposes. The city of Huancayo was founded in the eighteenth century. In the nineteenth century the city hosted the Constitutional Congress of 1839 and the declaration of the abolition of slavery. During the War of the Pacific it was a center of the resistance led by General Andrés Avelino Cáceres against the Chilean occupation.

The major productive activities of the region are agriculture (potatoes, cereals), livestock, and light manufacturing (in the city). A variety of produce is sold in the city of Huancayo in picturesque weekly fairs, which were originally a way of exchanging regional rural products for manufactures and cash. A branch of the central highland railway system arrived in Huancayo in 1908 to enhance the city's commercial character. The main communication route with Lima today is the Central Highway, which displaced the railway in importance in the 1930s and 1940s.

*See also* **Cáceres, Andrés Avelino.**

BIBLIOGRAPHY

Florencia Mallon, *The Defense of Community in Peru's Central Highlands* (1983).

Fiona Wilson, "The Conflict Between Indigenous and Immigrant Commercial Systems in the Peruvian Central Sierra, 1900–1940," in *Region and Class in Modern Peruvian History*, edited by Rory Miller (1987).

*Additional Bibliography*

Peñaloza J., José. *Huancayo: Historia, familia y región.* Lima: Instituto Riva-Agüero, 1995.

ALFONSO W. QUIROZ

**HUÁNUCO.** Huánuco, department in the north-central highlands of Peru. At an altitude of 6,273 feet, its capital city of Huánuco (1999 population 170,588) is a commercial center and traditionally the gateway to the colonization of the jungle region to the east. The canyons and valleys of the Huallaga and Pachitea rivers, tributaries of the Marañón and Ucayali, which eventually form the Amazon River, provide two of the few access routes to the jungle, connecting with the easternmost towns of Tingo María and Pucallpa.

Prior to the founding of Huánuco Viejo, the first Spanish settlement and missionary post not far from contemporary Huánuco, the Inca state controlled the administrative center of Huánuco Pampa, just north of the city of Huánuco. Recent archaeological studies have determined that Huánuco Pampa was part of an infrastructural system that facilitated ritual reciprocities between the state and the local ethnic groups. Prior to the Incas, a Chavín-influenced culture built what are today known as the ruins of Kotosh. In 1742–1753 the region and the city were the scene of the Indian messianic rebellion led by Juan Santos Atahualpa.

*See also* **Atahualpa (Juan Santos); Pampa.**

BIBLIOGRAPHY

Craig Morris, "The Infrastructure of Inka Control in the Peruvian Central Highlands," in *The Inca and Aztec States, 1400–1800,* edited by George Collier et al. (1982).

*Additional Bibliography*

LeVine, Terry. *Inka Storage Systems.* Norman: University of Oklahoma Press, 1992.

León Gómez, Miguel. *Paños e hidalquía encomenderos y sociedad colonial en Huánuco.* Lima: Instituto de Estudios Peruanos, 2002.

ALFONSO W. QUIROZ

**HUARAZ.** Huaraz, the capital city of the province of the same name in the highland department of Ancash, Peru has an estimated population of 90,000 (2007). Created by decree on 25 July 1857, the department is bounded on the north by the province of Huaylas, on the south by Cajatambo province, on the east by Pomabamba and Huari provinces at the top of the Cordillera Nevada mountain range, and on the west by Santa province. Its origins can be traced back to a community of Indians that was given in *encomienda* to Sebastián de Torres. During the next two centuries, the town became an increasingly important economic and religious center. In 1788 its citizens were granted the right to elect a municipal council (*cabildo*), and the settlement was officially given the title of *villa*.

During the next century, military leaders such as Simón Bolívar and Agustín Gamarra used Huaraz as a base, as much for its rich agricultural hinterland, which produced wheat, barley, potatoes, corn, and cotton for cloth, as for its strategic position *vis à vis* Lima to its southwest. In the twentieth century, Huaraz was the scene of an Aprist uprising against the government of Luis Sánchez Cerro in 1932. In 1970 Huaraz was 90 percent destroyed as a result of an earthquake that was labeled the worst natural disaster recorded in the Western Hemisphere.

*See also* **Earthquakes.**

BIBLIOGRAPHY

Mariano Felipe Paz Soldán, *Diccionario geográfico estadístico del Perú* (1877).

Ruben Vargas Ugarte, *Historia general del Perú,* 10 vols. (1971).

David P. Werlich, *Peru: A Short History* (1978).

*Additional Bibliography*

Alba Herrera, C. Augusto. *La revolución aprista de 1932: Huaraz-Ancash.* Lima: Ediciones de Desarrollo Gerencial, 2006.

SUSAN E. RAMÍREZ

**HUARI.** Huari (Wari), the earliest recognized pre-Columbian empire in Peru and the name assigned to a large Middle Horizon (ca. 650–1000 CE ) city located in the eastern Ayacucho Valley that is recognized as its capital. The size and complexity of Huari remained unrecognized because it was overshadowed by early colonial descriptions of the Bolivian site of Tiwanaku in the Lake Titicaca Basin, to which the Incas refer in their origin myths. However, recent research indicates that the Incas most likely inherited an imperial tradition that was first developed by the Huari during the Middle Horizon. In the absence of any known form of writing, quipus (colored, knotted strings) were developed and used to record state transactions, an information system also later adopted by the Incas. A road system was built to connect the capital of Huari with its hinterland, some parts of which now lie below the Inca highway system.

Several construction phases are evident in the city. Within the urban center, a Huari building plan consisting of a pattern of regularly arranged rooms of standardized shapes can be detected. One of the dominant architectural components in this style is the repetition of square (sometimes trapezoidal) ground plans with a central courtyard or patio surrounded by narrow two- or three-story galleries or corridors. The provincial Huari towns share similarities in architectural layout, which suggests a central decision-making body was responsible for their plan, while construction efforts probably relied on local masons and workers.

Huari officials gained control of distant territories to the north, south, and west through religious proselytization and military force. These expansion efforts are inferred from changes in regional Middle Horizon settlement patterns that coincide with the appearance of Huari architectural compounds and pottery. Ceramic styles and votive offerings of oversized vessels with Huari figural iconography occur at the capital and within provincial centers and smaller communities as part of the religious images that were propagated throughout the empire. The city of Huari as the seat of imperial power reached its demise in the mid-ninth century. Pachacamac, on the central coast, was a principal Huari oracle and pilgrimage center.

*See also* **Andes; Art: Pre-Columbian Art of South America; Huarpa; Indigenous Peoples; Precontact History: Andean Region.**


BIBLIOGRAPHY

Luis Lumbreras, "La cultura Wari," in *Etnología y arqueología* 1, no. 1 (1960): 130–227, *Las fundaciones de Huamanga* (1974), and *The Peoples and Cultures of Ancient Peru* (1974).

William Isbell and Katharina Schreiber, "Was Huari a State?" in *American Antiquity* 43, no. 3 (1978): 372–389.

Anita G. Cook, "The Middle Horizon Ceramic Offerings from Conchopata," in *Ñawpa Pacha* 22–23 (1984–1985): 49–90.

William Isbell and Gordon Mc Ewan, eds., *Huari Administrative Structure: Prehistoric Monumental Architecture and State Government* (1991).

Katherina Schreiber, *Wari Imperialism in Middle Horizon Peru,* Anthropological Papers, no. 87 (Museum of Anthropology, University of Michigan, 1992).

Craig Morris and Adriana Von Hagen, *The Inca Empire and Its Andean Origins* (1993).

*Additional Bibliography*

Covey, R. Alan. *How the Incas Built Their Heartland: State Formation and the Innovation of Imperial Strategies in the Sacred Valley, Peru.* Ann Arbor: University of Michigan Press, 2006.


Anita Cook

## HUARPA.

**HUARPA.** Huarpa was an ancient culture that flourished during the Early Intermediate period (circa 1–550) in the Peruvian central highland valley of Ayacucho. The culture is distinguished for its black-and-white ceramics, which are found scattered on the surface of many archaeological sites throughout the valley. Huarpa settlement patterns strongly indicate that this was an agricultural society. Most of the known Huarpa settlements are found below the elevation of 3,300 meters, often on hillsides, overlooking irrigable land, but rarely on agriculturally fertile land. This evidence indicates that agricultural fields, which are scarce in the region, were carefully managed. Furthermore, the earliest terraces and irrigation canals were built by the Huarpa. The absence of fortified sites indicates that warfare or other kinds of conflict were not predominant in the region during this period. The occurrence of the same kind of bichrome pottery in all known Huarpa sites indicates that the inhabitants of the several settlements of the valley intermarried. Pottery appears to have been manufactured at each household level.

Huarpa established the economic foundation for the later development of the Huari state that emerged in the Ayacucho Valley and expanded throughout much of what is now Peru during the Middle Horizon period (circa 550–1000). Many Huari sites in the region grew out of Huarpa settlements. Despite the critical role played by Huarpa in the emergence of Huari, Huarpa remains little studied. Few Huarpa sites have been investigated; an exception is Ñawinpukyo, regarded as the main Huarpa settlement. Archaeological excavations at Ñawinpukyo indicate that one of the critical aspects of Huarpa society was the worship of sacred mountains, a tradition that continues in the region to the present. Other Huarpa sites deserve to be investigated toward the goal of fully comprehending the cultural dynamics in the region prior to the emergence of the Huari state.

*See also* **Andes; Archaeology; Huari.**


BIBLIOGRAPHY

Leoni, Juan B. "La Veneración de montañas en los Andes preincaicos: El caso de Ñawinpukyo (Ayacucho, Perú) en el período Intermedio Temprano." *Chungara* 37, no. 2 (2005): 151–164.

Lumbreras, Luis Guillermo. *Las fundaciones de Huamanga: Hacia una prehistoria de Ayacucho.* Lima: Club Huamanga, 1975.

Schreiber, Katharina J. *Wari Imperialism in Middle Horizon Peru.* Anthropological Papers 87. Ann Arbor: Museum of Anthropology, University of Michigan, 1992.

Valdez, Lidio M. "The Early Intermediate Period beyond the Ayacucho Valley, Peru." In *Debating Complexity: Proceedings of the Twenty-sixth Annual Chacmool Conference,* edited by D. A. Meyer, P. C. Dawson, and D. T. Hanna, pp. 600–606. Calgary, Alberta: Archaeological Association of the University of Calgary, 1996.

Valdez, Lidio M. "Ecology and Ceramic Production in an Andean Community: A Reconsideration of the Evidence." *Journal of Anthropological Research* 53, no. 1 (1997): 65–85.

LIDIO M. VALDEZ

**HUASCAR** (c. 1495–1532). Huascar (*b.* ca. 1495; *d.* 1532), son of Inca Huayna Capac. Huascar, born near Cuzco, had one of the most legitimate claims to leadership of Tahuantinsuyu at the time of the death (1525) of his father, for his mother was the primary wife Ragua Ocllo. In accordance with their customs, the Inca elite in Cuzco quickly performed the religious ceremonies acknowledging the assumption of power of the new ruler.

Half brother Atahualpa, who according to some had been named as one of the successors during the fevered last days of Huayna Capac, refused to come to Cuzco for the celebrations, preferring instead to remain in the Quito district with the large military force that had helped subjugate the area. The ill-treatment accorded the emissaries Atahualpa sent to Huascar led to open hostilities between the two factions. Atahualpa's army, under capable leaders Quizquiz and Chalicuchima, moved southward, and finally Chalicuchima succeeded in capturing Huascar outside Cuzco. By then the Cañaris, a northern ethnic group who strongly supported the Huascar faction, had been thoroughly beaten. General Quizquiz went on to march into the capital of Cuzco and attempt to destroy completely Huascar's supporters.

It was at this juncture that the Europeans under Francisco Pizarro entered the Andean highlands and captured Atahualpa at Cajamarca on 16 November 1532. Atahualpa, fearing that the Spaniards might attempt to supplant him and rule through Huascar, ordered the execution of his half brother. The escort that was accompanying Huascar from Cuzco to Cajamarca carried out the orders at Andamarca, between Huamachuco and Huaylas. Huascar's demise was followed within months by the Spanish execution of Atahualpa on 26 July 1533, thus bringing to an end the effective independence of Tahuantinsuyu.

*See also* **Atahualpa; Huayna Capac; Tahuantinsuyu.**

BIBLIOGRAPHY

John Hemming, *The Conquest of the Incas* (1970).

Franklin Pease, *Los últimos Incas del Perú* (1972).

*Additional Bibliography*

Betanzos, Juan de. *Narrative of the Incas,* translated and edited by Roland Hamilton and Dana Buchanan. Austin: University of Texas Press, 1996.

Gose, Peter. "Oracles, Divine Kingship, and Political Representation in the Inka State." *Ethnohistory* 43 (Winter 1996): 1–32.

Vega, Juan José. *Los incas frente a España: Las guerras de la resistencia, 1531–1544.* Lima: Peisa, 1992.

NOBLE DAVID COOK

**HUASIPUNGO.** Huasipungo, a forced labor system of the Ecuadorian sierra. The word was derived from the Quechua language (*huasi,* "house," and *pungo/pungu,* "door"). Most Indians submitted to variations of this system from the colonial period until recently. In order to obtain access to a small parcel of land (a *huasipungo*), Indian families would consent to provide agricultural labor and to serve as domestic servants for a hacienda owner. The Indians had the right to collect wood and straw from the owner's land or to graze animals upon it. The owner paid wages for labor and typically supplied Indians with food, clothing, animals, and cash.

Most Indian families quickly lapsed into debt, losing their freedom of movement until they retired their obligations. This seldom happened. Thus restricted, the Indians suffered various abuses, either at the hands of the hacienda owner or, more commonly, from foremen, police, or the local clergy. Legislative decrees designed to end this system of debt peonage, such as the ban on *concertaje* in 1918, did little to halt the practice.

However, the Agrarian Reform Law of 1964 finally turned the *huasipungos* over to the Indian families that worked them. Jorge Icaza's Indianist novel *Huasipungo* (1934) provided a vivid depiction of the oppression of Indians under this forced labor arrangement and increased the attention given to the problem.

*See also* **Guayaquil, Group of; Mita; Slavery: Indian Slavery and Forced Labor.**

BIBLIOGRAPHY

On sierra relations of production, consult Magnus Mörner, *The Andean Past: Land, Societies, and Conflicts* (1985); Osvaldo Hurtado, *Political Power in Ecuador,* translated by Nick D. Mills, Jr. (1985); and Enrique Ayala Mora, ed., *Nueva historia del Ecuador: Época republicana I,* vol. 7 (1983).

*Additional Bibliography*

Icaza, Jorge. *Huasipungo.* Buenos Aires: Editorial Losada, 1953.

Lyons, Barry J. *Remembering the Hacienda: Religion, Authority, and Social Change in Highland Ecuador.* Austin: University of Texas Press, 2006.

Trujillo León, Jorge. *La hacienda serrana, 1900–1930.* Quito: Instituto de Estudios Ecuatorianos: Abya Yala, 1986.

RONN F. PINEO

## HUASTECA, THE.

**HUASTECA, THE.** The Huasteca, a huge and historically important region of northeastern Mexico once inhabited by the Huastec Indians. Today this topographically and climatically diverse area is divided among the states of Veracruz, San Luis Potosí, Hidalgo, Querétaro, and Tamaulipas. Beginning in the arid eastern reaches of the elevated central plateau and stretching through the abrupt Sierra Madre Oriental, the Huasteca expands in the humid, tropical lowlands of the Gulf of Mexico. Soils, rainfall, and vegetation vary widely in this broad expanse and have fostered many forms of adaptation by both the ancient Huastec inhabitants and the largely mestizo population that has extensively replaced them since Spanish contact.

Archaeological evidence suggests that the Huasteca had fluctuating borders that once extended far southward down the Gulf coastal plain in the direction of the Maya Indians, who are linguistically and culturally related to the Huastecs. The conflictive migrations of other pre-Hispanic groups, as well as Aztec conquests, produced enclaves at some points and a strong regional tradition of warfare.

Spanish seaborne expeditions to the Huasteca began from Cuba in 1518 and Jamaica in 1519 and were followed by a difficult overland conquest by Hernán Cortés in 1522. Between 1526 and 1533 Nuño de Guzmán brutally crushed numerous revolts when the province, then called Pánuco, was governed separately from New Spain. In modern times much of the once forested coastal zone has become man-made savannah for cattle ranching. The discovery of major oil deposits at the turn of the century has brought roads and industrial concentration at the port of Tampico.

*See also* **Cortés, Hernán; Guzmán, Nuño Beltrán de.**

BIBLIOGRAPHY

Long-term ethnographic studies have been undertaken by Guy Stresser-Pean, "Les indiens Huastèques" in *Huastecos, Totonacos y sus vecinos* (1953). Recent archaeological and historical interpretations are in S. Jeffrey K. Wilkerson, *Ethnogenesis of the Huastecs and Totonacs* (1973); and "Presencia huasteca y cronología cultural en el norte de Veracruz Central," in *Huaxtecos y Totonacos,* edited by Lorenzo Ochoa (1989), pp. 257–279. Two major studies of early colonial history are Manuel Toussaint, *La conquista de Pánuco* (1948); and Donald E. Chipman, *Nuño de Guzmán and the Province of Pánuco in New Spain, 1518–1533* (1967). The principal study of regional flora is Henri Puig, *Végétation de la Huasteca, Mexique* (1976).

*Additional Bibliography*

Ducey, Michael. *A Nation of Villages: Riot and Rebellion in the Mexican Huasteca.* Tucson: University of Arizona Press, 2004.

Montoya Briones, José de Jesús. *Etnografía de la domination en México.* México: Instituto Nacional de Antropología e Historia, 1996.

Robles Gil, Patricio. *The Great Tamaulipan Natural Province.* Ciudad Victoria: Tamaulipas Sate Government, 2004.

S. JEFFREY K. WILKERSON

## HUASTECOS.

**HUASTECOS.** Two Native American ethnic groups, the Huastec and Nahua, populate the Huasteca, an area in present-day Mexico that includes the states of San Luis Potosí, Hidalgo, and Veracruz. Descended from the Mayan population in southern Mexico, the Huastecos moved to central eastern Mexico between 1500 BCE and 900 BCE, but continued to maintain their own Mayan dialect. The peak of Huastec society occurred before the rise of the Nahuatl-speaking Aztecs, who defeated the Huastecos in 1450. After the Spanish conquest and the introduction of new diseases from Europe, the Huastec and Nahuatl populations dramatically declined, but both maintained their ethnic identities. Between 1845 and 1850 indigenous communities and peasants in the Huasteca warred with the national elite, who wanted to abolish indigenous land and cultural rights; scholars continue to debate the relative importance of cultural identity and class issues in this conflict. In the early twenty-first century approximately 100,000 Huastecos and 179,000 Nahuas live in the region. Both groups continue to defend land sacred to their past.

*See also* **Huasteca, the; Nahuas.**

BIBLIOGRAPHY

Ducey, Michael Thomas. *A Nation of Villages: Riot and Rebellion in the Mexican Huasteca, 1750–1850.* Tucson: University of Arizona Press, 2004.

Ochoa, Lorenzo. *Historia prehispánica de la Huaxteca.* México: Universidad Nacional Autónoma de México, Instituto de Investigaciones Antropológicas, 1979.

BYRON CRITES

**HUAYNA CAPAC** (c. 1488–c. 1527). Huayna Capac (*b.* ca. 1488; *d.* ca. 1527), Inca emperor (ca. 1493–1527), the last undisputed ruler of the Inca empire. The son of the emperor Topa Inca and the grandson of the great Pachacuti, he ruled during the time of the first Spanish contact with Andean South America. During his reign the empire was extended northward to the Ancasmayo River, the present boundary between modern Colombia and Ecuador. Although the extent of Huayna Capac's conquests were substantially less than those of his father and grandfather, they took much longer; he was absent from the capital at Cuzco for nearly twenty years. His prolonged absence and his preference for maintaining his royal court in the city of Quito, far to the north of the imperial capital, eventually generated a schism within the Inca state.

Huayna Capac died suddenly during one of the great plagues brought to the New World by the Europeans. His presumptive heir, Ninan Cuyochi, also died about the same time, leaving the succession unclear. As a result, two of Huayna Capac's sons, Huascar, who was in Cuzco, and Atahualpa, who had been with his father in the north, initiated the civil war that greatly weakened the empire just prior to its conquest by Francisco Pizarro.

*See also* **Incas, The.**

BIBLIOGRAPHY

Principal sources on Huayna Capac include John H. Rowe, "Inca Culture at the Time of the Spanish Conquest," in *Handbook of South American Indians,* vol. 2 (1946), pp. 183–330; Burr Cartwright Brundage, *The Empire of the Inca* (1963) and *The Lords of Cuzco: A History and Description of the Inca People in Their Final Days* (1967); *The Incas of Pedro de Cieza de León,* translated by Harriet de Onis (1959); and Bernabe Cobo, *History of the Inca Empire,* translated by Roland Hamilton (1979).

*Additional Bibliography*

Assadourian, Carlos Sempat. *Transiciones hacia el sistema colonial andino* México, D.F. Colegio de México; Lima: Instituto de Estudios, 1994.

Cook, Noble David. *Born to Die: Disease and New World Conquest, 1492–1650.* Cambridge: Cambridge University Press, 1998.

Guillén Guillén, Edmundo. *La guerra de reconquista Inka.* Lima, Perú: E. Guillén Guillén, 1994.

León, Luis A. "La enfermedad y muerte de Huayna Capac: Historia y trascendencia en la epidemiología Ecuatoriana." *Revista Ecuatoriana de Medicina y ciencias biológicas* 21, no. 2 (July–Dec. 1985): 99–123.

Maldonado Aguilar, Aurelio. *Huayna-Cápac: Su corazón en Tumipamba.* Cuenca, Ecuador: Ediciones Grafisum, 2003.

Niles, Susan A. *The Shape of Inca History: Narratives and Architecture in an Andean Empire.* Iowa City: University of Iowa Press, 1999.

Ravines, Rogger. *Huayna Cápac.* Lima, Perú: Editorial Brasa.

Zarzar, Alonso. *"Apo Capac Huayna, Jesús Sacramentado": Mito utopía y milenarismo en el pensamiento de Juan Santos Atahualpa.* Lima: Centro Amazónico de Antropología y Aplicación Práctica, 1989.

GORDON F. MCEWAN

**HUAYNO.** The most common and popular genre of Andean traditional music, the *huayno* (*wayno, wayñu*) is heard with many variations from

Ecuador to northern Argentina. It is most prominent among highland indigenous and mestizo communities in Bolivia and Peru. Often described as originating in the Inca epoch, the first concrete references to the genre do not appear until the colonial era, when it gained popularity as a secular couples' dance. Musically *huaynos* are strophic songs in duple meter, with highly syncopated melodies in contrasting phrases (e.g., *aabb*), accompanied by a variety of string and wind instruments. In mestizo forms of the genre, it often concludes with a faster section known as a *fuga*. In the mid-twentieth century the huayno took on a new popularity among highland migrants to Lima, Peru, leading to significant changes in its presentational style and its dissemination via recordings and radio. While still popular in rural areas, its urban form continues to evolve in the early twenty-first century, particularly through fusion with other popular music styles.

*See also* **Music: Popular Music and Dance; Music: Pre-Columbian Music of South America.**

BIBLIOGRAPHY

Roel Pineda, Josefat. "El wayno del Cusco." *Folklore Americano* 6–7 (1959): 129–245.

Romero, Raul. *Sonidos Andinos: Una antología de la música campesina del Perú.* Lima: Pontificia Universidad Católica del Perú/Centro de Ethnomusicologia Andina, 2002.

Turino, Thomas. "The Music of Andean Migrants in Lima, Peru: Demographics, Social Power, and Style." *Latin American Music Review* 9, no. 2 (1988): 127–150.

JONATHAN RITTER

## HUDSON, WILLIAM HENRY (1841–1922).

**HUDSON, WILLIAM HENRY** (1841–1922). William Henry Hudson (*b.* 4 August 1841; *d.* 18 August 1922), British naturalist and writer. Born on a farm near Buenos Aires to American parents, William Henry Hudson spent the majority of his youth on the Argentine pampas before emigrating to England in the late 1860s. He lived a good part of his life in poverty and obscurity until the publication in 1885 of his first novel, *The Purple Land that England Lost*. This book, characteristic of his early work, was a romantic fiction set in Latin America, filled with detailed descriptions of the natural beauty of the region. Hudson's ideas were apparently shaped largely by his reading of Darwin and a belief in the ultimate authority of nature.

Although Hudson's writing had not gained a wide audience, he established friendships with several influential literary figures of the late nineteenth and early twentieth centuries, including Joseph Conrad and Ford Madox Ford. He followed his early romances with several works of fiction as well collections of essays and studies of the natural sciences. Among Hudson's most acclaimed works are *A Hind in Richmond Park* (1922), *Green Mansions* (1904), *Birds of La Plata* (1920), and his autobiographical writings, *Idle Days in Patagonia* (1893) and *Far Away and Long Ago* (1918).

Commercial success eluded Hudson until late in life, when, in the years before and after World War I, he wrote stories of English rural life expressing his philosophy of acquiescence to nature, a philosophy which would gain influence as the naturalistic movements of the twentieth century progressed.

*See also* **Foreign Travelers in Latin America; Literature: Spanish America.**

BIBLIOGRAPHY

David Miller, *W. H. Hudson and the Elusive Paradise* (1990).

Amy D. Ronner, *W. H. Hudson: The Man, the Novelist, the Naturalist* (1986).

*Additional Bibliography*

Martínez Estrada, Ezequiel. *El mundo maravilloso de Guillermo Enrique Hudson.* Rosario: Beatriz Viterbo Editora, 2001.

JOHN DUDLEY

## HUERTA, DAVID (1949–).

**HUERTA, DAVID** (1949–). The son of one of Mexico's most renowned poets, Efraín Huerta (1914–1982), poet David Huerta was born in Mexico City. He graduated from the College of Philosophy and Letters at the National Autonomous University of Mexico (UNAM). He has defined his own work as traditional, incorporating images, metaphors, similes, and unusual linguistic vocabulary. He has written essays and worked as a translator, and has served as the editorial secretary of the Fondo de Cultura Económica's *Gaceta*, as well as coordinator of the UNAM Casa del Lago literary workshops. Huerta has authored numerous books of poetry, beginning with his first published work *El jardín de* *la luz* (1972). Guillermo Sheridan, in his review of a later book, *Cuaderno de noviembre* (1978), describes Huerta's poems as extraordinary and complex, even difficult to read. Like his father, Huerta has been politically active. His poetry has received numerous awards, including the Carlos Pellicer Prize in 1990 and the prestigious Xavier Villaurrutia Prize in 2006.

*See also* **Literature: Spanish America.**

BIBLIOGRAPHY

Haladyna, Ronald. *La contextualización de la poesía postmoderna mexicana: Pedro Salvador Ale, David Huerta, y Coral Bracho.* Toluca, Mexico: CICSH, 1999.

RODERIC AI CAMP

---

**HUERTA, VICTORIANO** (1854–1916). Victoriano Huerta was a Mexican general who became president of the Republic after heading the coup d'état that overthrew Francisco Madero in February 1913. He stepped down in July 15, 1914, following the revolutionary surge that forced him to resign and go into exile.

José Victoriano Huerta Márquez was born March 23, 1854, in Colotlán, Jalisco, and had a brilliant career in the military academy. He distinguished himself by his military skills and his strength of character. He won prestige by successfully putting down rebellions led by Canuto Neri in Guerrero in 1893, and by the Mayan Indians of the Yucatán and Quintana Roo in 1901–1902. These campaigns brought him recognition and promotions. In 1905 he was a close associate of Bernardo Reyes, the most prestigious and powerful officer of Porfirio Díaz's army, and became one of his staunch supporters. When Reyes was disgraced, Huerta continued serving in the army but with a much lower profile.

Huerta's well-known association with Reyes, his military skill, and his prestige within the army put him in an ambivalent relationship with Francisco Madero once the latter took power. Madero distrusted him, but at the same time needed him, both to reach out to Reyes supporters and to win the support of the armed forces. He therefore ordered him to lead campaigns against the three largest anti-Madero rebellions: one led by Pascual Orozco in the north, in which Huerta won a distinguished victory; one led by Emiliano Zapata in Morelos, whom he was unable to vanquish; and finally, the rebellion that cost the life of Madero, led by Bernardo Reyes and Félix Díaz in Mexico City.

With this rebellion, Huerta heeded the pressure coming from the army and the nation's economic, religious, and political elites, who had decided to put an end to the political instability generated by Madero's rule and overthrow him. Huerta headed up the betrayal and maneuvered deftly to get rid of Félix Díaz and become president, using a legal ploy that culminated in the resignation and assassination of Madero and vice-president Pino Suárez: According to the Mexican legislation in the absence of the president, the minister of foreign affairs would occupy the position; Huerta forced the congress to appoint him, so when Madero resigned, and his substitute Pedro Lascurain resigned the same day he assumed the presidency, Huerta became president legally.

The legal but illegitimate methods that Huerta used to gain power, together with general outrage at the assassination of the former president and vice-president, cost him popular support. The government soon became isolated and had to resort to repression to stay in power in the face of rising opposition movements led by the Constitutionalist faction and Emiliano Zapata and Pancho Villa. Huerta dissolved the congress and wielded dictatorial powers that were still insufficient to contain the revolution, which defeated and cornered the federal army. Huerta was forced to resign and leave the country in July 1914. Huerta's behavior triggered the culmination of the revolutionary process that Madero had left unfinished. The revolution became more radical in those years, and ended in the elimination of the federal army and the dissolution of the regime created by Porfirio Díaz, of whom Huerta was the last representative.

In March 1915 Huerta entered the United States, where he became involved in counterrevolutionary activities. The U.S. authorities arrested him and imprisoned him at Fort Bliss. Because of his sickness, he was set free for two weeks November 1915, but returned to jail by mid December. He died in his house of cirrhosis January 13, 1916, in El Paso, Texas.

*See also* **Díaz, Félix, Jr.; Madero, Francisco Indalecio; Mexico, Wars and Revolutions: Mexican Revolution; Reyes Ogazón, Bernardo; Villa, Francisco "Pancho"; Zapata, Emiliano.**

BIBLIOGRAPHY

Langle Ramírez, Arturo. *El militarismo de Victoriano Huerta.* México, D. F.: Universidad Nacional Autónoma de México, 1976.

Meyer, Michael C. *A Political Portrait.* Lincoln: University of Nebraska Press, 1972.

Rausche, George, J. Jr. "The Exile and Death of Victoriano Huerta." *Hispanic American Historical Review* 42, no. 2 (1962): 133–151.

FELIPE AVILA

**HUERTAS, ESTEBAN** (1876–1943). Esteban Huertas (*b.* 1876; *d.* 1943), Panamanian general and a key figure in the independence of Panama. He was born in Umbita, Boyacá, Colombia, and went into the army at an early age. He was sent to Panama and participated in the War of the Thousand Days, fighting in the province of Coclé. In October 1903 the Colombian government, nervous about the revolutionary activities in Panama, sent the Tiradores battalion, under the command of Generals Juan B. Tobar and Ramón G. Amaya, to relieve Huertas as military commander because they believed that he was conspiring with the revolutionaries. When General Tobar arrived in Panama City with his officers on 3 November, Huertas had them arrested. Once the news of the arrests reached the revolutionaries, they declared for independence. When the army was abolished after independence, Huertas was given the title of Hero of the Fatherland.

*See also* **War of the Thousand Days.**

BIBLIOGRAPHY

Ernesto De Jesús Castillero Reyes, *Historia de Panamá,* 7th ed. (1962).

Jorge Conte Porras, *Diccionario biográfico ilustrado de Panamá,* 2d ed. (1986).

*Additional Bibliography*

Beluche, Olmedo. *La verdadera historia de la separación de 1903: Reflexiones en torno al centenario.* Panama: ARTICSA, 2003.

Santos Molano, Enrique. *1903, adiós Panamá: Colombia ante el Destino Manifiesto.* Bogotá: Villegas Editores, 2004.

JUAN MANUEL PÉREZ

**HUGUENOTS.** *See* **French Colonization in Brazil.**

**HUICHOLS.** The Huichols are a Mexican Indian group largely concentrated in the rugged mountains of the Sierra Madre Occidental, mainly in the states of Jalisco and Nayarit. They are by far the largest Indian group in Mexico to have maintained relatively intact its indigenous religion and ritual, without significant Catholic modification.

The Huichols bear a stronger resemblance to other northwestern Mexican Indians than to those of central Mexico. Their language has a close relationship to Cora, both of which belong to the Aztecoidan branch of the Greater Nahua (Uto-Aztecan) language family. Their own name for themselves is Wixárika, or Wixarite; "Huichol" is a Spanish corruption, perhaps of Guisole or Guachichil, a now-extinct population of desert hunter gatherers.

The Huichol settlement pattern is one of scattered extended-family farmsteads, most with their own *xiriki* ("god-house"). There are no villages as such, and until recently the ceremonial and governmental centers in the five indigenous communities were virtually deserted except during community-wide celebrations of Spanish colonial origin. Large circular temples (*tuki*), with adjacent god houses, are located in the ceremonial centers and in a few other sacred places in the mountains; the *tuki* and its ceremonies are in the charge of graded religious functionaries with fixed terms of office. There are also many shrines within and outside the Huichol territory.

The Huichols have a long and well-developed tradition of sacred art and, more recently, of folk art for sale, especially colorful wool yarn "paintings" of mythological subjects. The native deities are mainly those of nature: fire, sun, earth and growth, deer, maize, rain, terrestrial water, and mountains. All are addressed by kinship terms. Among the most important are Tatewarí (Our Grandfather), the old fire god; Tayaupá (Our Father Sun); Takutsi Nakawé, the old earth and creator goddess; and Great-grandfather Maxa Kwaxi (Deer Tail). The culture hero-cum-trickster and Deer Person Kauyumari is the intermediary between mortals and gods and the principal assistant to the *mara'akáte* (sing. *mara'a-káme*), the numerous shaman-priests who conduct the many ceremonies, some community-wide, others pertaining to the family. Deer, maize, and the sacred hallucinogenic peyote cactus, which is collected on annual pilgrimages to the north-central desert in San Luis Potosí, are conceptually merged.

Precise population figures for the Huichols are hard to come by; a 1959 estimate gives the total as just over 7,000, but this was probably low. The 2000 census gives them a population of 30,304 over the age of five, of whom about half reside within the five indigenous communities in the Sierra. There is a sizable colony on the lower Río Lerma, in Nayarit, dating from the 1920s and 1930s, when some communities were virtually depopulated during the so-called Cristero Rebellion (1926–1929). Huichols have also settled in or near such cities as Tepic, Guadalajara, Durango, and Zacatecas, and even as far away as Mexico City. Most, easily recognizable by their distinctive native costume, continue to maintain ties to their old homeland and religion.

*See also* **Art: Pre-Columbian Art of Mesoamerica; Cristero Rebellion; Indigenous Peoples.**

BIBLIOGRAPHY

Carl Lumholtz, *Symbolism of the Huichol Indians* (1900).

Barbara G. Myerhoff, *Peyote Hunt: The Sacred Journey of the Huichol Indians* (1974).

Kathleen Berrin, *Art of the Huichol Indians* (1978).

### *Additional Bibliography*

Comisión Nacional para el Desarrollo de los Pueblos Indígenas, Programa de las Naciones Unidas para el Desarrollo. "Sistema Nacional de Indicadores sobre la Población Indígena de México." 2002. Based on *XII Censo General de Población y Vivienda*. Mexico: Instituto Nacional de Estadística, Geografía e Informática, 2000.

Rojas, Beatriz. *Los huicholes en la historia*. Mexico: Centro de Estudios Mexicanos y Centroamericanos, Colegio de Michoacán, Instituto Nacional Indigenista, 1993.

PETER T. FURST

## HUIDOBRO FERNÁNDEZ, VICENTE

**(1893–1948).** Vicente Huidobro Fernández (*b.* 10 January 1893; *d.* 2 January 1948), Chilean poet. The principal figure of the avant-garde movement in Latin American literature, Huidobro was born in Santiago to an aristocratic family; his privileged upbringing included education in Chilean private schools. In 1916 Huidobro moved to Paris, where he started publishing the most innovative poetry in the Spanish language. He was a cofounder, with the French poets Guillaume Apollinaire and Pierre Reverdy, of the literary review *Nord-Sud* (1917–1918), and along with Max Jacob, Paul Dermée, and the cubist painters Juan Gris and Pablo Picasso, helped design a new spatial poetry that used calligrammatic and ideogrammatic forms. His personal poetic style, which he called creationism, was a modality that emphasized the autonomy of poetic expression, a result of the transformation of external referents and of laws of grammar and "sense," and created its own images, descriptions, and concepts. In 1918 he brought fresh air to Spanish poetry with four volumes published in Madrid, *Poemas árticos, Ecuatorial, Tour Eiffel,* and *Hallali.*

The Spanish poets Gerardo Diego and Juan Larrea were his most faithful and direct disciples, but many other young poets imitated his creationist poetry. As a consequence of his influence, the literary movement Ultra was developed by Rafael Cansinos-Asséns and Guillermo de Torre. Ultraism was developed also in Buenos Aires by Jorge Luis Borges, and Imagism arose in Chile, Simplicism in Peru, and Estridentism in Mexico. During the 1920s, Huidobro published three books in French: *Saisons choisies* (1921), *Tout à coup* (1925), and *Automne régulier* (1924). The most genial poetic expression of Huidobro is *Altazor; o, El viaje en paracaídas* (1931), a poem in seven cantos, which narrates a simultaneous flight and fall through seven regions, equating death with mystical experience. The work constitutes a poetic Babel, employing a variety of poetic languages that intimates both a plenitude of meaning and the gradual destruction of language. *Altazor* stands as an extraordinary example of the poetic avant garde. *Temblor de cielo* (1931), a prose poem written simultaneously with *Altazor,* deals with the meaning of life under the Nietzschean concept of the death of God. Huidobro's later poetic works include *Ver y palpar* (1941) and *El ciudadano del olvido* (1941). In these books his creative ingenuity manifests itself in whimsical as well as tragic visions of life and world. His last poems were collected in *Últimos poemas* (1948), published posthumously.

Huidobro's life in Paris, Madrid, and Santiago touched in various ways the literary cultures of these cities. Contacts with cubist poets and painters and with dadaists in Paris, with ultraists in Madrid, with the younger groups of Runrunists and Mandrágora in Santiago, all speak of his wide-ranging ability to disseminate the forms and concepts of the new poetry. The general content of *Nord-Sud, Índice de poesía americana nueva* (1926), and *Antología de poesía chilena nueva* (1935) marks the breadth and significance of his influence. In 1925 he published *Manifestes,* a collection of essays on creationism and poetic theory. Huidobro also contributed significantly to the renewal of narrative forms with his *hazaña* (heroic feat) *Mio Cid Campeador* (1929), his film-novel *Cagliostro* (1934), *Papá; o, El diario de Alicia Mir* (1934), *La próxima: Historia que pasó en un tiempo más* (1934), *Sátiro; o, El poder de las palabras* (1938) (*Satyr; or, the Power of Words,* [1939]), and *Tres inmensas novelas* (1935) in collaboration with the German poet Hans Arp. His collections of essays include *Pasando y pasando* (1914), *Finis Britannia!* (1923), and *Vientos contrarios* (1926). Huidobro also wrote two plays, *Gilles de Raíz* (1932), in French, and *En la luna* (1934).

*See also* **Art: The Twentieth Century; Literature: Spanish America.**

BIBLIOGRAPHY

René De Costa, *Vicente Huidobro: The Careers of a Poet* (1984).

Merlin H. Forster, "Vicente Huidobro," in *Latin American Writers,* edited by Carlos A. Solé and Maria Isabel Abreu, vol. 2 (1989), pp. 755–764.

Cedomil Goic, *La poesía de Vicente Huidobro,* 2d ed. (1974).

George Yúdice, *Vicente Huidobro y la motivación del lenguaje* (1978).

*Additional Bibliography*

Ellis, Keith. *Nueve escritores hispanoamericanos ante la opción de construir.* Havana: Ediciones Unión, 2004.

Fernández, Jesse. *El poema en prosa en Hispanoamérica: Del modernismo a la vanguardia: estudio crítico y antología.* Madrid: Hiperión, 1994.

Fernández Pedemonte, Damián. *La Producción del sentido en el discurso poético: Análisis de "Altazor" de Vicente Huidobro.* Buenos Aires: Edicial, 1996.

CEDOMIL GOIC

**HUINCAS.** Huincas, Araucanian/mapuche word used to refer to non-Mapuche (also said to mean "thief"). Mapuche oral tradition and the construction of the word (*pu,* from, and *Inca*) suggest that the term for "outsider" came into use during the decades of Mapuche resistance to the expansion of the Inca Empire in the fifteenth century. The word came into common usage among Spanish speakers in Chile and Argentina in the eighteenth and nineteenth centuries, when Creole settlement in the southern frontier zones intensified intercultural contact.

*See also* **Araucanians; Mapuche.**

BIBLIOGRAPHY

Rodolfo Lenz, *Diccionario etimológico* (1910).

*Additional Bibliography*

Nacuzzi, Lidia Rosa, ed. *Funcionarios, diplomáticos, guerreros: Miradas hacia el otro en las fronteras de Pampa y Patagonia, siglos XVIII y XIX.* Buenos Aires: Sociedad Argentina de Antropología, 2002.

Zapater, Horacio. *Huincas y mapuches (1550–1662).* Santiago: Eds. Historia, 1997.

KRISTINE L. JONES

**HUITZILOPOCHTLI.** Huitzilopochtli, Aztec deity of war, patron of the Mexica. According to native histories, the Mexica brought Huitzilopochtli from their original home at Aztlan to the site of Tenochtitlán, the center of their future empire. The deity guided their journey and their subsequent rise to military power. His cult was a major focus of Aztec state ritual, especially the heart sacrifice of prisoners of war. He was one of the four Tezcatlipocas, gods responsible for cosmic creation and destruction; he was also associated with the sun of the winter dry season. He shared the Great Temple of Tenochtitlán with the rain god Tlaloc, patron of the rainy season. The name Huitzilopochtli, "Hummingbird-Left," alludes to the winter sun's passage through the southern sky (seen as being on the sun's left hand); hummingbirds were also associated with the sun and with the souls of those who died in war and in sacrifice. Huitzilopochtli's birthplace was the mythical Coatepec,

"Serpent Mountain," where his mother, the earth goddess Coatlicue, was magically impregnated while sweeping the mountaintop temple. Huitzilopochtli foiled a plot by his elder sister and brothers by emerging from the womb fully grown and armed with the Fire Serpent that encircles the Mesoamerican cosmos.

*See also* **Aztecs; Indigenous Peoples; Nahuas; Precontact History: Mesoamerica.**

BIBLIOGRAPHY

Diego Durán, *Book of the Gods and Rites and the Ancient Calendar,* translated and edited by Fernando Horcasitas and Doris Heyden (1971).

Eva Hunt, *The Transformation of the Hummingbird* (1977).

Elizabeth H. Boone, "Incarnations of the Aztec Supernatural: The Image of Huitzilopochtli in Mexico and Europe," in *Transactions of the American Philosophical Society* 79, pt. 2 (1989).

*Additional Bibliography*

León Portilla, Miguel. *La filosofía náhuatl.* México: Universidad Nacional Autónoma de México, 1983.

LOUISE M. BURKHART

---

**HULL, CORDELL** (1871–1955). Cordell Hull (*b.* 2 October 1871; *d.* 23 July 1955), U.S. secretary of state (1933–1944) during the administration of Franklin D. Roosevelt. Although Roosevelt bypassed his secretary of state on many matters, Hull played an active role in Latin American affairs. Along with Roosevelt and Assistant Secretary of State Sumner Welles, Hull formulated the Good Neighbor Policy, which sought to improve relations between the United States and the nations of Latin America. Hull's principal contributions to the Good Neighbor Policy were threefold. First, in 1933, at the Pan-american Conference in Montevideo, he surprised and pleased fellow delegates by endorsing the principle of nonintervention in the affairs of Latin American nations. Second, Hull was the principal architect of the reciprocal trade agreements that increased commerce between the United States and its hemispheric neighbors. Finally, as World War II approached, he helped negotiate mutual defense agreements among nations of the Western Hemisphere.

*See also* **Good Neighbor Policy; United States-Latin American Relations.**

BIBLIOGRAPHY

*The Memoirs of Cordell Hull,* 2 vols. (1948).

Julius W. Pratt, *Cordell Hull, 1933–1944,* 2 vols. (1964).

Irwin F. Gellman, *Good Neighbor Diplomacy: United States Policies in Latin America, 1933–1945* (1979).

*Additional Bibliography*

Butler, Michael A. *Cautious Visionary: Cordell Hull and Trade Reform, 1933–1937.* Kent, OH: Kent State University Press, 1998.

Schoultz, Lars. *Beneath the United States: A History of U.S. Policy toward Latin America.* Cambridge: Harvard University Press, 1999.

PATRICK J. MANEY

---

**HULL–ALFARO TREATY (1936).** Hull–Alfaro Treaty (1936), an agreement signed on 2 March by the United States and Panama that made certain concessions regarding the operation of the Panama Canal in keeping with Franklin Roosevelt's Good Neighbor Policy. It did not, however, alter the relationship of great power–client state established in the Hay–Bunau-Varilla Treaty of 1903. The treaty, ratified reluctantly by the U.S. Senate only in 1939, did not mollify Panamanian nationalists for long.

Initiative for reforming canal operating policies came in 1933, when Panama's president, Harmodio Arias, visited Washington to explain his country's economic problems stemming from the Depression. Between 1933 and 1936, Roosevelt's secretary of state, Cordell Hull, and Arias's foreign minister, Ricardo Alfaro, labored to produce several treaties and agreements that would make good neighbors of the two countries. The United States gave up its protectorate role and powers of territorial acquisition, and it raised the annuity payment to $436,000 to compensate for the devaluation of the dollar. Hull also agreed to curtail commissary sales to those not employed by the canal, to curb contraband, to give Panamanian merchants access to passing ships, and to allow Panamanians free transit across the Canal Zone. Finally, an ancillary note promised equal employment treatment of Panamanian and U.S. nationals.

The armed services opposed most of these measures and fought ratification by the Senate. The main elements were approved only upon a special appeal by Roosevelt to set the stage for an inter-American defense conference in Panama. The outbreak of World War II, meanwhile, made the canal a major security concern and postponed effective implementation of many parts of the treaty.

*See also* **Good Neighbor Policy; Hay-Bunau-Varilla Treaty (1903); Roosevelt, Franklin Delano.**

BIBLIOGRAPHY

William D. Mc Cain, *The United States and the Republic of Panama* (1937, repr. 1966).

John Major, *Prize Possession: The United States and the Panama Canal, 1903–1977* (1993).

MICHAEL L. CONNIFF

---

**HUMAITÁ.** Humaitá, a strategic point on the left bank of the Paraguay River some 20 miles north of its confluence with the Paraná. At this spot the Paraguayans constructed a fortress that prevented the advance of the Brazilians and Argentines during the War of the Triple Alliance (1864–1870). A guardpost had been established near Humaitá in the late colonial era to discourage smuggling. Yet, it was only during the 1850s, when Brazilian vessels began to freely transit the river to Mato Grosso, that the government of Carlos Antonio López decided to build a solid structure with the help of British military engineers. This "Sevastopol of South America" eventually grew to massive size and boasted some 380 cannons of various calibers.

During the war, Humaitá provided Paraguay with its principal defensive bastion; it warded off a thirteen-month Allied siege that started in June 1867. During this period a series of bloody engagements was fought along the periphery of the fort, leaving perhaps as many as 100,000 dead. The Allied navies regularly pounded the earthworks, leaving the defenders with little hope of relief. They, nonetheless, held on until July 1868, when the last starving remnants of the garrison evacuated the fort. This capitulation left open the way to the Paraguayan capital of Asunción, enabling the Allies to move in that direction a few months later. Today, the ruins of Humaitá, especially those of the small church at its center, have been partially restored as a national monument.

*See also* **War of the Triple Alliance.**

BIBLIOGRAPHY

George Thompson, *The War in Paraguay* (1869).

Charles J. Kolinski, *Independence or Death! The Story of the Paraguayan War* (1965).

*Additional Bibliography*

Bethell, Leslie. *The Paraguayan War (1864-1870).* London: Institute of Latin American Studies, 1996.

Leuchars, Chris. *To the Bitter End: Paraguay and the War of the Triple Alliance.* Westport, CT: Greenwood Press, 2002.

Marco, Miguel Angel de. *La guerra del Paraguay.* Buenos Aires: Planeta, 1995.

Whigham, Thomas. *The Paraguayan War.* Lincoln: University of Nebraska Press, 2002.

THOMAS L. WHIGHAM

---

**HUMAN RIGHTS.** Human rights became a major framework for organizing resistance to state-sponsored political violence and other injustices in Latin America during the second half of the past century. Nongovernmental human-rights groups emerged as major political actors during the authoritarian military regimes of the 1960s and 1970s. Although these organizations used international norms as the basis for their claims and relied on important international allies, their work was deeply rooted in local political cultures and histories. Critics of the human-rights movements have charged that their focus on legal issues and the courts is excessive and risks depoliticizing grassroots efforts for social change, and that they have been more responsive to international funders than to authentic local concerns. New kinds of human-rights institutions, including state agencies and military programs, further complicate the political terrain of activism in the early twenty-first century.

### LEGAL AND PHILOSOPHICAL ROOTS OF RIGHTS IN THE AMERICAS

Latin American rights debates encompass the European and North American philosophical and legal rights debates, but also incorporate the older traditions of Catholic scholasticism as well as original contributions from Latin American thinkers. Much early debate was devoted to the rights of Latin American indigenous people, most notably in the works of the sixteenth-century Dominican friar Bartolomé de Las Casas, who defended their rights in the face of Spanish exploitation and military conquest. Enlightenment ideals and the works of French and North American revolutionaries were widely discussed in the colonies and profoundly influenced a generation of proindependence Creoles, who nevertheless remained suspicious of popular sovereignty, mass democracy and anticlerical views. The adoption of republican forms of government and constitutions guaranteeing rights did not overcome the colonial legacy of authoritarianism, paternalism, personalism, and unequal application of the law, which resulted in significant barriers to full political participation, as well as widespread poverty and inequality.

The twentieth century saw the development of new rights charters. The Mexican Constitution of 1917 was the first in the world to significantly incorporate social and economic rights by, for example, making property rights subordinate to the public interest, restricting foreign control of resources, and regulating working conditions. It served as a model for subsequent constitutional reforms in Latin America and Europe. The American Declaration of the Rights and Duties of Man was the first general international human-rights instrument, adopted at the Ninth International Conference of American States in Bogotá in April 1948; Latin American leaders used this experience when helping to draft the Universal Declaration of Human Rights six months later.

These international legal instruments were not the only influences shaping human-rights debates; other important factors included the Catholic Church (particularly Catholic Social Action and, later, Liberation Theology) and revolutionary and progressive political movements. Nongovernmental activists produced the 1976 Universal Declaration of the Rights of Peoples, known as the Algiers Declaration, which stressed collective rights and autonomy. "People's tribunals" were organized outside the formal legal system; the Russell Tribunal II focused on human-rights abuses in Latin America during two sessions, in 1974 to 1976 and in 1989 to 1991.

### RESPONDING TO AUTHORITARIAN MILITARISM

A comprehensive history of human-rights activism in Latin America, and the relationship among national groups, has yet to be written. Prior to 1960 there was only one organization in the Southern Cone explicitly concerned with human rights. The military regimes that took power in Brazil (1964–1985), Uruguay (1973–1985), Chile (1973–1990), and Argentina (1976–1983) employed significant political violence against their real and perceived opponents; resistance to them included the creation of nongovernmental human-rights organizations and solidarity groups.

In Brazil the Justice and Peace Commission of the Archdiocese of São Paulo and other church-based groups played a critical role, documenting violations and providing legal and other assistance; growing repression led to increased cooperation with secular organizations. As state terror declined in the mid-1970s, these and other groups refocused their attention on ongoing problems such as urban and rural working conditions, particularly of landless peasants, slum dwellers, and indigenous peoples.

Chilean activists formed numerous human-rights groups immediately after the 1973 coup. Over the course of the Pinochet regime, several generations of human-rights groups emerged: The first were supported directly by the Catholic Church, the next were made up of family members of victims, and finally were the groups organized by political parties. The best known of these groups was the Vicaría de la Solidaridad, created in 1976. Important factors in the creation of Chilean groups were the support of the Catholic Church, and preexisting transnational and national social and political networks linking religious leaders, progressive students, academics, and other professionals.

Despite sharing Chile's democratic political culture and institutions, Uruguay developed Latin America's fewest and smallest human-rights organizations, in part because of the limited role of the Catholic Church, and was unable to marshal moral authority and devise a way to channel resources to victims of repression in a largely secular society. Greater militarization at the time of the coup in 1973 and the existence of prior legal restrictions meant that much of the repression occurred with a legal framework; Uruguay had fewer disappearances than other nations, but the highest concentration of political prisoners anywhere in the world. Even following the defeat of the generals' constitutional amendment in 1980, the efforts of Servicio Paz y Justicia (SERPAJ) in Uruguay were severely limited by the lack of an institutional funnel through which international funds could be received.

In Argentina, the Catholic Church displayed an ambivalent attitude toward the military government, and the country lacked the embedded activists networks found in Chile. Because of abuses and the erosion of legal rights following pre-coup counter-insurgency efforts, three human-rights groups were established before the 1976 coup, with ecumenical church leaders playing critical roles in all three. The one with the highest profile was SERPAJ, founded in 1974, which focused on local aid and popular education; its founder, Adolfo Pérez Esquivel (b. 1931) won the 1980 Nobel Peace Prize. Immediately following the coup in 1976, family members of the disappeared created three new human-rights groups: the Madres (mothers), the Abuelas (grandmothers), and the Familiares (relatives) of the disappeared. Similar associations began appearing in other countries, eventually forming in 1981 a network known as the Latin American Federation of Associations of Relatives of the Detained-Disappeared. Argentine exiles played a critical role in assisting human rights groups throughout the continent, in part because of Argentina's earlier transition to democracy in 1983.

Human-rights groups have played complicated roles in transitions to democracy. In many cases, pressure from these organizations helped to hasten the return to elections and greater political freedoms. During the dictatorship of Alfredo Stroessner (1945–1989) the Paraguayan human-rights community remained relatively small and focused on particular cases, but his government's loss of legitimacy was in large part due to elite awareness of chronic rights violations. In many countries, groups were accused of being excessively focused on accountability for past abuses and the limitations of newly formed democratic governments. Many countries (including El Salvador, Guatemala, Uruguay, Brazil, Chile, Argentina, and Peru) established commissions with varying mandates to clarify events and responsibilities during military governments, but groups were largely unsuccessful in bringing to trial the military and civilian officials responsible for atrocities. These issues remain controversial, however, and amnesty laws and the issue of impunity continue to be debated and to be the subjects of legal cases in Argentina, Chile, and other countries.

Cuba is an exception to these trends: an authoritarian government that has focused on promoting socioeconomic rights despite significant economic limitations. Although the Castro government has not resorted to widespread political violence, civil and political rights, including freedom of religion, association, and expression, have been severely restricted, generating significant numbers of political prisoners. In addition, human-rights groups have been the target of repression.

## FRAGILE DEMOCRACIES AND INSURGENCIES

The Central American civil wars of the 1980s led to the creation of a number of human-rights groups, particularly in El Salvador and Guatemala. Although documentation of these conflicts has demonstrated that the great majority of human rights abuses were generated by repressive governments and security forces, human-rights groups also turned their attention to violations by nonstate actors for the first time. In the case of Nicaragua, although the Sandinista government did commit some abuses, extensive abuses by the U.S.–backed Contra forces were documented by rights groups. Agreements to establish human-rights monitoring institutions sponsored by the United Nations (UN) and the Organization of American States (OAS) played a critical role in the peace agreements that settled these conflicts.

Both Peru and Colombia suffered from long-running, serious insurgencies, with massive violence and displacement. The drug trade in both nations has exacerbated political violence by providing financing for illegal armed groups, and complicated human-rights efforts to promote accountability. The most powerful guerrilla group in Peru was the neo-Maoist Shining Path, which viewed civil society (including human-rights leaders) as competition and subjected them to violent attacks, causing Peruvian rights groups to categorically reject revolutionary violence. After the Shining Path was largely defeated with the capture of its leader in 1992, Peru experienced a crisis of democracy. In 1992 Alberto Fujimori staged an *autogolpe* (self-coup), dissolving Congress and severely weakening the judiciary and other democratic institutions; he used antiterrorism legislation to imprison more than 20,000 people. During this period human-rights groups played a central role in galvanizing civil society support for democracy and pushing for accountability. In Colombia, the largest guerrilla group, the Revolutionary Armed Forces of Colombia, has committed an increasing number of abuses while expanding their military power; human-rights groups have continued to focus on illegal paramilitary forces supported by members of the military and civilian elite, which commit the majority of abuses.

In Mexico, Haiti, and other countries throughout the region, corruption, poverty, and limits on political participation continue to be problems. Abuses of state power, together with violations of socioeconomic rights, contributed to a peasant uprising in Chiapas, Mexico, in January 1994. Haitian human-rights organizations both on the island and abroad have fought for democratic government and socioeconomic justice, but their work has been complicated by the violent struggles for power by Jean-Bertrand Aristide and the intervention of a UN and OAS mission.

### INTERNATIONAL ALLIES AND NEW MANDATES

International nongovernmental organizations (NGOs) have provided training, support, and public awareness for human-rights groups throughout the continent. The most important NGOs include Amnesty International, founded in 1961, which campaigned on behalf of prisoners of conscience and fair trials and against torture; their role during the dictatorships of the 1970s and 1980s was particularly important. The Washington Office on Latin America was founded in 1974, and was a critical link for groups interested in influencing U.S. policy and needing training in international advocacy. Human Rights Watch established their Americas program in the 1980s, with a focus on documenting abuses and political lobbying. None of this work could have been accomplished without the financial support of individuals, European governments, and private foundations, particularly the Ford Foundation, which was instrumental in funding the best-known human-rights institutions throughout the continent. Solidarity and exile groups in the United States and Europe also played a critical role.

In addition, activists have employed the United Nations system, including the Human Rights Commission and the High Commissioner for Human Rights, for remedies and support. The OAS and the Inter-American system also played a growing role by the end of the last century; its American Convention on Human Rights (also known as the Pact of San José) was adopted in 1969 and entered in force in 1978, with compliance overseen by the Inter-American Commission on Human Rights and the Inter-American Court of Human Rights. In 1988 the Court issued its first ruling, finding the government of Honduras responsible in a case of forced disappearance. Since then, the Commission and the Court have played an important and expanding role in addressing human-rights issues. The OAS has adopted a number of measures focused on protecting human-rights work in the region.

State human-rights organizations, including ombudsman offices, national human-rights commissions, thematic human-rights commissions (which address particular issues or vulnerable populations), and national bodies devoted to international humanitarian law, have become increasingly important. Their numbers multiplied throughout Latin America in the 1990s, some as part of the democratization efforts, and most funded by outside sources. Their missions often have been to provide human-rights education programs, documentation of abuses, and support for NGOs, but often they do not have the political power and funding to implement significant reforms or bring cases to trial. In some countries, such as Colombia, the military has developed its own human-rights programs, publishing human-rights reports, hosting conferences, and establishing a network of battalion-level human-rights offices. They claim that military officers are the victims of due-process violations by NGOs, and they incorporate human rights—understood as nonabusive treatment of local populations—into the traditional military doctrine dealing with civic-military relations, psychological operations, and civic action.

Human-rights groups throughout the region continue to struggle with the most effective ways to ensure that rights are respected. New issues include high crime rates that generate public rejection of rights claims, ongoing economic inequality, and new modalities of violence. Constitutional reform in some countries during the 1990s presented new opportunities by creating new legal rights; rights groups have expanded their work to include the rights of women, children, indigenous and Afro-descendent populations, and gays and lesbians.

*See also* **Asylum; Catholic Action; Las Casas, Bartolomé de; Liberation Theology; Mexico, Constitutions: Constitution of 1917; Military Dictatorships: Since 1945; Organization of American States (OAS); Pérez Esquivel, Adolfo; Stroessner, Alfredo; Truth Commissions; United Nations.**

BIBLIOGRAPHY

Cleary, Edward. *The Struggle for Human Rights in Latin America.* New York: Praeger, 1997.

Hayner, Priscilla. *Unspeakable Truths: Confronting State Terror and Atrocity.* New York: Routledge, 2001.

Hillman, Richard, John Peeler, and Elsa Cardozo da Silva, eds. *Democracy and Human Rights in Latin America.* New York: Praeger, 2001.

Jelin, Elizabeth, and Eric Hershberg, eds. *Constructing Democracy: Human Rights, Citizenship, and Society in Latin America.* Boulder, CO: Westview Press, 1996.

Melish, Tara. *Protecting Economic, Social, and Cultural Rights in the Inter-American System: A Manual for Presenting Claims.* New Haven, CT: Orville H. Schell Jr. Center for International Human Rights, Yale Law School, and Centro de Derechos Economicos y Sociales de Ecuador, 2002.

Stern, Steve. *Remembering Pinochet's Chile.* Durham, NC: Duke University Press, 2004.

Tate, Winifred. *Counting the Dead: The Culture and Politics of Human Rights in Colombia.* Berkeley: University of California Press, 2007.

WINIFRED TATE

## HUMBOLDT, ALEXANDER VON

(1769–1859). Alexander von Humboldt (*b.* 14 September 1769; *d.* 6 May 1859), German scientist and traveler to the New World. Humboldt was born in Berlin into a wealthy family. He attended several German universities and by 1790 had developed a keen interest in botany and obtained a solid introduction to physics and chemistry. A trip to England that year confirmed his interest in nature and a love for foreign travel. Named assistant inspector in the Department of Mines in 1792, Humboldt embarked upon a short-lived bureaucratic career that led him through eastern Europe. The death of his mother in 1796, however, freed him from the necessity of working for a living and allowed him to travel as he chose.

Humboldt was the most illustrious of a number of foreigners who went to the New World in the closing decades of the colonial era. With the permission and recommendation of the Spanish crown, in 1799 he and his traveling companion, the French botanist Aimé Bonpland, reached Venezuela and began their five-year voyage through Spanish America. Laden with scientific instruments, they were able, in good Enlightenment fashion, to measure such things as latitude, longitude, temperature, and air pressure, and to illustrate their findings. The volume of data collected was enormous and established Humboldt as a major scholar of international reputation.

Humboldt's journey took him into the interior of Venezuela, to New Granada, Quito, Lima, Cuba, and finally, to New Spain. A keen observer of the landscape and the political, economic, and social conditions of its inhabitants, Humboldt also mingled with the elites in the cities and gained access from royal officials to numerous government documents containing demographic and economic information. Because he was well educated and familiar with current intellectual trends, Humboldt was able to share modern ideas and techniques from Europe with colonial intellectuals and bureaucrats, and thus helped disseminate European knowledge and the belief in material progress throughout the New World. He also commented on hindrances to progress resulting from Spanish fiscal and commercial policy and stimulated creoles to believe that improvement in government was necessary. At the same time, Humboldt accurately observed the state of science in the New World at the end of the colonial period. His conclusions emphasized that modern scientific thought was more widespread in New Spain than in Peru and other parts of South America—and, not surprisingly, that it was more widespread in urban centers than in the provinces.

After returning to Europe, Humboldt wrote about his voyage in major works treasured by both contemporaries and historians. His writings include the *Voyage aux régions équinoxiales du nouveau continent*... (34 vols., 1805–1834); *Essai politique sur le royaume de la Nouvelle-Espagne* (3 vols., 1811–1812; a part of the *Voyage*); *Essai politique sur l'île de Cuba* (2 vols., 1826); and publications devoted to scientific topics.

The *Essai politique ... Nouvelle-Espagne* included considerable official data made available as a result of Humboldt's royal introduction to colonial officials in New Spain. More important, it had profound political implications because the creole elite believed its descriptions of Mexican wealth and progress meant that Mexico had the resources necessary for an existence independent from Spain.

*See also* **Foreign Travelers in Latin America; Science.**

BIBLIOGRAPHY

D. A. Brading, *The First America: The Spanish Monarchy, Creole Patriots, and the Liberal State 1492–1867* (1991), chap. 23.

Peggy K. Liss, *Atlantic Empires* (1983), esp. pp. 182–183.

Alexander Von Humboldt, *Political Essay on the Kingdom of New Spain,* (abridged), translated by John Black, edited by Mary Maples Dunn (1972; repr. 1988).

*Additional Bibliography*

Fernández Pérez, Joaquín. *El descubrimiento de la naturaleza: Humboldt.* Madrid: Nivola Libros Ediciones, 2002.

Helferich, Gerard. *Humboldt's Cosmos: Alexander von Humboldt and the Latin American Journey that Changed the Way We See the World.* New York: Gotham Books, 2004.

Pérez Mejía, Angela. *La geografía de los tiempos difíciles: Escritura de viajes a Sur América durante los procesos de independencia, 1780–1849.* Medellín: Editorial Universidad de Antioquia, 2002.

Zea, Leopoldo, and Hernán Taboada. *Humboldt y la modernidad.* México: Instituto Panamericano de Geografía e Historia: Fondo de Cultura Económica, 2001.

MARK A. BURKHOLDER

**HUMBOLDT CURRENT.** The Humboldt Current (or Peru Current) is a system of sea flows along the western coast of South America, from latitude 42 degrees south to 45 degrees south. Cold surface waters—57 degrees Fahrenheit (14 degrees Centigrade) in Talcahuano, Chile; 63 degrees Fahrenheit (17 degrees Centigrade) in Valparaiso, Chile; 64 degrees Fahrenheit (18 degrees Centigrade) in Arica, Chile; 63 degrees (17 degrees Centigrade) in San Juan; Puerto Rico; 64 degrees Fahrenheit (18 degrees Centigrade) in Callao, Peru; 66 degrees Fahrenheit (19 degrees Centigrade) in Puerto Etén, Peru; and 68 degrees Fahrenheit (20 degrees Centigrade) at Punta Pariñas, Peru—sustain a marine ecosystem characterized by high primary productivity (>300 gC/m2-yr), and one of the largest biomasses on Earth (400 million metric tons per year). About 20 percent of the world's catches are extracted from the Humboldt Current.

The surfacing of cold water and its equatorward flow (at an average speed of 10 knots [11.5 miles, 18.5 kilometers) per hour is caused by wind shear against the coast. In addition, several upwelling centers caused by rises of the ocean floor and coastal inflections at Lachay and San Gallán-San Juanin Peru, and at Iquique, Caldera, Punta Lavapié, in Chile, reinforce the cold conditions of the sea. Under the surface water, a north-south directed flow of high salinity and nutrient content, the Gunther Current, maintains the ocean mass balance of the eastern Pacific basin. At Punta Pariñas (4.5 degrees south latitude), the Humboldt Current veers westward in the direction of the Galapagos Islands. Cooler than normal sea surface temperatures allow the existence of penguins and seals on these equatorial islands. The Humboldt Cuttent reaches as far as 120 degrees west longitude, where the surface water temperatures begin to rise above 75 degrees Fahrenheit (24 degrees Centigrade). This warmer westward flow is called the South Equatorial Current.

During particular years, when the winds in the eastern Pacific are weak and the upwelling centers lose strength, warm equatorial waters seep—by means of Kelvin waves—from the western Pacific into the eastern Pacific and temporarily overlap the cooler waters of the Humboldt Current. These warm water invasions, known as El Niño events, usually develop during the southern summer (which occurs during the change of calendar years). El Niños occurred in 2006–2007, 1997–1999, 1992–1994, 1982–1983, 1972–1973, and 1957–1958. The larger of these events are accompanied by worldwide climate anomalies, as happened in 1940–1941, 1925–1926, 1911–1912, and 1891. El Niño events dating back to 12,000 years before the present have been detected with the help of geological and archaeological techniques. Some geophysicists postulate that El Niño may have started 50,000 years ago.

After a warm El Niño episode, the return to normal conditions in the eastern Pacific basin occurs frequently through a brisk change to abnormal cold ocean conditions known as La Niña (or Anti-Niño in Spanish). At that time, the biosystems of the Humboldt Current, which are severely stressed during El Niño events, slowly return to normality. This applies particularly to the swarms of anchovies, pilchard, and jack mackerel that are reduced considerably during the warm waters of El Niño and to the sea lions, seals, and coastal birds (cormorants, pelicans, and penguins) that feed on them.

*See also* **El Niño; Fishing Industry.**

BIBLIOGRAPHY

Arntz, Wolf, and Eberhard Fahrbach. *El Niño: Experimento Climático de la Naturaleza*. Mexico: Fondo de Cultura Económica, 1996.

Caviedes, César N. *El Niño in History: Storming through the Ages*. Gainesville, FL: University Presses of Florida, 2001.

Pauly, Daniel, P. Muck, J. Mendo, and I. Tsukayama, eds. *The Peruvian Upwelling Ecosystem: Dynamics and Interactions*. Manila, Philippines: International Center for Living Aquatic Resources Management, 1989.

CÉSAR N. CAVIEDES

**HUNDRED HOUR WAR.** *See* **Football War.**

**HURRICANES.** With considerable luck Columbus explored portions of the Caribbean in the late summer and fall of 1492 without encountering the characteristic storms of those latitudes in that season—the hurricanes. The Spaniards probably experienced their first hurricane when a storm struck the settlement at Isabela on Hispaniola and two ships were lost. Thereafter, Spaniards and other Europeans who sailed or settled on Caribbean coasts and islands came to know and fear the hurricanes. A colonial official in Puerto Rico complained in 1765 that the local people counted time by the coming and going of governors and fleets, visits of the bishops, and the hurricanes.

Of course, the indigenous peoples of the Caribbean region had known the great storms. There is considerable debate over the etymology of the word "hurricane," some believing it is a Maya term that was somehow introduced into the Caribbean prior to 1492 and others seeing its origins in the Taino word *hurakán*. Peter martyr used the term *furacanes* in his *Decadas* (1511). The Arawaks of the Bahamas counted hurricanes, along with fire, sickness, and enemy raids, as a chief danger. The Taino seem to have recognized the circulatory nature of these storms; their curved, legged symbol for a hurricane is much like that used by modern meteorologists, a rather remarkable fact because not until William Reid's *Law of Storms* (1838) were the rotary circulation and progressive motion of hurricanes generally recognized.

Modern meteorology defines a hurricane as a tropical cyclone with winds exceeding 65 knots (73 miles) per hour, although winds exceeding 175 knots (200 mph) have been recorded. The storms usually include heavy rainfall and are accompanied in coastal regions by high tides or storm waves that often are their most destructive features. Hurricanes usually originate in the Caribbean or in the eastern Atlantic. The latter, "Cape Verdean" hurricanes have been among the most destructive. Although hurricanes can occur throughout the year, the traditional season is June to November, with highest incidence in August and September. The force of hurricanes has been felt from Central America (Belize was badly damaged in 1787 and again in 1931) to New England, but the islands of the Lesser and Greater Antilles from Barbados to Cuba and the Gulf coasts of Mexico and the North American mainland have suffered the most in terms of numbers of hurricanes and levels of damage.

Hurricanes have been a constant threat to populations, property, and commerce in the region. In the colonial era, the Spanish fleet was organized around the hurricane season, with departure of the homeward-bound fleet from Havana scheduled to precede the beginning of the hurricane season in June. Delays and mishaps, however, often resulted in shipwrecks and other disasters following hurricanes. The sinking of silver-bearing galleons in 1622, 1624, and 1630 contributed to a financial crisis in Spain. In the Caribbean, hurricanes brought severe destruction of property and crops. The town of Santo Domingo was virtually destroyed in 1508 and again in 1509. Havana lost over 1,000 people and thousands of homes in the hurricane of 1768. The "Great Hurricane" of 1780 killed some 9,000 in Martinique and 4,000 in Barbados, and wreaked havoc on British, French, and Spanish fleets. The Cuban town of Santa Cruz del Sur was devastated by a 1932 hurricane.

Agricultural losses also result from the storms. In Puerto Rico (where hurricanes are named for the saint on whose feast day they occur) San Narciso (1867) resulted in major agricultural losses, San Ciriaco (1899) wreaked havoc on the coffee areas in the center of the island, and San Felipe (1928) essentially ended Puerto Rico's coffee exports. Cuban sugar production declined by half after devastating hurricanes from 1844 to 1846. The production of bananas in Cuba was wrecked by a hurricane in 1898. Hurricanes Gilbert (1988) in Jamaica and Hugo (1989) in Puerto Rico have demonstrated the continued vulnerability of societies and economies to hurricanes. In more recent times, Hurricanes Mitch (1998), Ivan (2004), and Wilma (2005) have been responsible for thousands of fatalities, injuries, and displacements, millions of dollars of damage, and major disruption and destruction of agriculture and tourist industries.

Given the impact of the hurricanes on the economy and lifestyle of the Greater Antilles, it is not surprising that Spanish and Caribbean scientists have been important in the study of these storms. Andrés Poëy y Aguirre published a chronology of 400 Caribbean hurricanes, accompanied by an extensive bibliography, in 1855. He became the first director of the Observatorio Fisico-meterológico of Havana in 1860. The Spanish meteorologist Father Benito Viñes, director of the College of Belén observatory in Havana (1870–1893), concentrated on meteorological observations of hurricane formation and tracks. He made the first successful hurricane forecast in 1875. He later published important scientific works on hurricane structure and behavior.

Although scientific and communication advances such as the barometer in the seventeenth century, the telegraph in the nineteenth century, and satellite observation in the twentieth century have enabled better prediction and preparation for hurricanes, human and property losses have intensified with the growth of population and the settlement of areas of higher risk. These losses are often suffered disproportionately by poorer nations and by poorer segments of the population. Recently, some scholars have suggested that global warming has provoked an increase in the intensity and number of hurricanes.

*See also* **Caribbean Sea; Environment and Climate; Mexico, Gulf of; Viñes y Martorell, Benito.**

BIBLIOGRAPHY

Luis A. Salivia, *Historia de los temporales de Puerto Rico* (1950).

David M. Ludlum, *Early American Hurricanes, 1492–1870* (1963).

José Carlos Millás, *Hurricanes of the Caribbean and Adjacent Regions* (1968).

Fernando Ortiz, *El huracán: Su mitología y sus símbolos,* 2d ed. (1984).

*Additional Bibliography*

Pérez, Louis A., Jr. *Winds of Change: Hurricanes and the Transformation of Nineteenth Century Cuba.* Chapel Hill: University of North Carolina Press, 2001.

STUART B. SCHWARTZ

---

**HURTADO DE MENDOZA, ANDRÉS** (c. 1500–1561). Andrés Hurtado de Mendoza (marquis of Cañete), viceroy of Peru (ca. 1556–1561). The marquis of Cañete arrived in Peru with the express purpose of strengthening royal authority, which had been lessened by four years of rule by the *audiencia*, the high court of Lima that held executive power within the colony in the absence of a viceroy. As part of this effort, a rival *audiencia* and administrative network for Upper Peru were established in Charcas in 1559. Committed to solidifying the crown's power over Peru's Indian population, Cañete sought to claim lands and reclaim labor service that had been granted to local elites through *encomiendas* (grants of Indian labor). The opening of the mercury mines of Huancavelica in 1560 increased the demand for Indian labor, and Cañete became the first viceroy responsible for the production and transportation of Huancavelica mercury to the colony's silver mines, particularly Potosí.

*See also* **Encomienda.**

BIBLIOGRAPHY

For an account of the establishment of royal authority in Peru see Henry F. Dobyns and Paul L. Doughty, *Peru: A Cultural History* (1976), esp. pp. 59–87. For information on Huancavelica see Arthur P. Whitaker, *The Huancavelica Mercury Mine* (1941).

Steve J. Stern, *Peru's Indian Peoples and the Challenge of Spanish Conquest: Huamanga to 1640* (1982).

*Additional Bibliography*

Davies, Nigel. *The Ancient Kingdoms of Perú.* New York: Penguin, 1998.

Hickling Prescott, William. *History of the Conquest of Peru.* Lenox, MA: Hard Press, 2006.

Vallejo y Guijarro, Maria Luisa. *Don Andrés Hurtado de Mendoza y Cuenca Ecuatoriana: Recuerdo y ofrenda en el IV Centenario de su fundación.* Madrid: Editorial Bullon, 1982.

ANN M. WIGHTMAN

## HURTADO DE MENDOZA, GARCÍA

(1535–1609). García Hurtado de Mendoza (*b.* 1535; *d.* 1609), Spanish conquistador, governor of Chile, and viceroy of Peru. Hurtado de Mendoza was the second son of the marqués de Cañete (a title he eventually inherited). His father, then viceroy of Peru, appointed him governor of Chile. He arrived there in 1557 and almost immediately launched offensives against the Araucanians of the south, whom he defeated in the battles of Lagunillas (Bío-bío) and Millarapue. After founding the new settlement of Cañete, he ventured further south, where he discovered the archipelago of Chiloé and founded Osorno (1558). In December 1558 he won another victory over the Araucanians at Quiapo. The governor also sent ships to explore the Strait of Magellan and an expedition across the Andes to conquer Cuyo: the Argentine city of Mendoza (founded in 1561) is named after him.

Dismissed from the governorship by King Philip II (1527–1528) (his father was concurrently stripped of office), Hurtado de Mendoza left Chile in February 1561. The king later restored him to favor and made him viceroy of Peru (1588–1596). Hurtado de Mendoza was a celebrated figure in his own time. two plays were written to eulogize his exploits, one of them, *El Arauco domado,* by Lope de Vega.

*See also* **Conquistadores.**

BIBLIOGRAPHY

Fernando Campos Harriet, *Don García Hurtado de Mendoza en la historia americana* (1969).

### *Additional Bibliography*

Calderón Ruiz de Gamboa, Carlos. *Don García Hurtado de Mendoza y los fundadores de Osorno.* Santiago, Chile: Editorial La Noria, 1996.

SIMON COLLIER

## HURTADO LARREA, OSVALDO

(1939–). Osvaldo Hurtado Larrea was president of Ecuador from 1981 to 1983. He studied at the Catholic University in Quito, where he emerged as a leader of the Christian Democratic Party (PDC). He taught political sociology at the university and published widely on the need for structural and social reforms. In 1978 the military government appointed Hurtado chair of the commission charged with revising electoral legislation in preparation for a return to civilian rule.

In the 1978–1979 presidential election, Hurtado ran successfully as the vice presidential candidate on the Concentration of Popular Forces (CFP) ticket with Jaime Roldós Aguilera. They represented a new generation of political leaders, whose desire to expand the electorate, strengthen democratic institutions, and implement planned national development, threatened traditional political and economic elites. When Roldós died in a plane crash on May 24, 1981, Hurtado became president. He inherited a severe budgetary crisis precipitated by the decline of the world price of petroleum and by growing opposition from organized labor—who opposed the government's commitment to fiscal restraint—and from business groups—who opposed the expansion of the state and its growing autonomy in economic policy making. He became the first president in almost thirty years to complete his term and peacefully transfer power to a democratically elected successor.

Hurtado served as president of the 1998 constituent assembly, which drafted Ecuador's new constitution. He ran in the 2002 presidential elections but came in tenth (out of eleven candidates) with barely 1 percent of the vote. Hurtado heads the nonprofit Corporation for Development Studies (CORDES) in Quito.

*See also* **Ecuador, Political Parties: Concentration of Popular Forces (CFP); Roldós Aguilera, Jaime.**

BIBLIOGRAPHY

Corkill, David, and David Cubitt. *Ecuador: Fragile Democracy.* London: Latin American Bureau, 1988.

Hurtado, Osvaldo. *Political Power in Ecuador.* Translated by Nick D. Mills Jr. Boulder, CO: Westview Press, 1985.

Schodt, David W. *Ecuador: An Andean Enigma.* Boulder, CO: Westview Press, 1987.

LINDA ALEXANDER RODRÍGUEZ
MARC BECKER

**HYPPOLITE, HECTOR** (1894–1948). Hector Hyppolite (*b.* 16 September 1894; *d.* 1948), Haitian painter and vodun priest. Hyppolite led a simple, hard life in rural Haiti until he was discovered in 1944 by the European surrealist poet and art connoisseur André Breton and the Haitian art patron DeWitt Peters. Hyppolite's primitive paintings brought him immediate international attention and introduced the world to Haitian folk culture. His works were exhibited at a UNESCO show in Paris in 1947 and have spawned many imitators. The paintings of Hector Hyppolite are noted for their free, bold colors, their technical naïvete, and themes drawn from Haiti's unique, syncretic religion and vodun customs. Today his work hangs in many of the world's finest galleries.

*See also* **Art: The Twentieth Century.**

BIBLIOGRAPHY

Eleanor Ingalls Christensen, *The Art of Haiti* (1975).

Selden Rodman, *The Miracle of Haitian Art* (1974).

Ute Stebich, ed., *Haitian Art* (1978).

*Additional Bibliography*

Bourguignon, Erika. "Haiti and the Art of Paul-Henri Bourguignon." *Research in African Literatures* 35 (Summer 2004): 173–188.

Congdon, Kristin G., and Kara Kelley Hallmark. *Artists from Latin American Cultures: A Biographical Dictionary.* Westport: Greenwood Press, 2002.

Lerebours, Michel-Philippe. "The Indigenist Revolt: Haitian Art, 1927–1944." *Callaloo* 15 *Haitian Literature and Culture,* Part 2 (Summer 1992): 711–725.

KAREN RACINE

**HYPPOLITE, LOUIS MODESTIN FLORVILLE** (1827–1896). Louis Modestin Florville Hyppolite (*b.* ca. 1827; *d.* 24 March 1896), president of Haiti (1889–1896). On 9 October 1889 the Haitian Constituent Assembly elected Florville Hyppolite to the Haitian presidency following his successful revolt against the government of François Denys Légitime. The United States had supplied weapons in support of Hyppolite against his French-backed opponent and expected the new president to reward its generosity with a naval station in Haiti. But Haitian national pride more than the resistance of Hyppolite blocked U.S. acquisition of the harbor at Môle Saint-Nicholas. Many U.S. newspapers of the time blamed U.S. ambassador to Haiti Frederick Douglass rather than recognize this fact.

Hyppolite, though a black and from the north, had leanings toward the mulatto-dominated Liberal Party. On the domestic scene, his greatest achievements were public-works projects, especially those involving communication and transportation. Hyppolite's biggest domestic problems, however, were heavy internal debt and French infringements on Haitian sovereignty. He found no solutions. He forced the French embassy to cease its practices of granting French citizenship to Haitians of proven Gallic ancestry. This had been a mulatto ploy to dodge Haitian law, but it became a Pyrrhic victory when Hyppolite borrowed 50 million francs from France to redeem his internal debt.

In 1893 Hyppolite scored a diplomatic triumph by appointing Frederick Douglass to represent Haiti at the World's Columbian Exposition of 1893 in Chicago. The old abolitionist had frequently expressed pride in Haiti but never to the extent that it confused his ambassadorial duties (1889–1891). Three years later Hyppolite died during a coup against his government.

*See also* **Haiti.**

BIBLIOGRAPHY

Jacques N. Leger, *Haiti: Her History and Her Detractors* (1907).

James Leyburn, *The Haitian People* (1941).

Rayford W. Logan, *The Diplomatic Relations of the United States with Haiti, 1776–1891* (1941).

David Nicholls, *From Dessalines to Duvalier: Race, Colour, and National Independence in Haiti* (1979).

### *Additional Bibliography*

Dayan, Joan. "A Few Stories about Haiti, or, Stigma Revisited." *Research in African Literatures* 35 (Summer 2004): 157–172.

Gaillard, Roger. *Une modernisation manquée (1880–1896).* Port-au-Prince: R. Gaillard, 1984.

THOMAS O. OTT

## IANNI, OCTAVIO

**IANNI, OCTAVIO** (1926–2004). Octavio Ianni (*b.* 13 October 1926; *d.* 2004), Brazilian sociologist. Ianni, a native of Itu, São Paulo, taught at the university of São Paulo. In 1950 he worked with Florestan Fernandes and Fernando Henrique Cardoso, doing research on race relations sponsored by UNESCO. After teaching in the United States (1967), England (1969), and Mexico (1968–1973), Ianni returned to Brazil in 1977. He then taught at the Pontifical Catholic University of São Paulo and the State University of Campinas.

Ianni's writings include *Estado e capitalismo no Brasil* (1965), *Raças e classes sociais no Brasil* (1966), *Sociologia da sociologia latino-americana* (1971), *Sociologia e sociedade no Brasil* (1975), *Escravidão e racismo* (1978), *O ABC da classe operária* (1980), *A ditadura do grande capital* (1981), and *Origens agrárias do estado brasileiro* (1984). His final publication was *A sociedade global* in 1992. He died of cancer in São Paulo in April, 2004.

*See also* **Sociology.**

BIBLIOGRAPHY

Thomas E. Skidmore, *Politics in Brazil, 1930–1964; An Experiment in Democracy* (1968).

John Kenneth Galbraith, *The New Industrial State* (1967).

*Additional Bibliography*

Faleiros, Maria Isabel Leme, and Regina Aída Crespo. *Humanismo e compromisso: Ensaios sobre Octávio Ianni.* São Paulo, SP: Editora Unesp, Fundação, 1996.

Lima, Marcos Costa, Filho Zaidan, et al. *A sociología crítica de Octavio Ianni: Uma homenagem.* Recife: Editora Universitaria, 2005.

ELIANA MARIA REA GOLDSCHMIDT

## IBÁÑEZ, ROBERTO

**IBÁÑEZ, ROBERTO** (1902–1978). Roberto Ibáñez (*b.* 1902; *d.* 1978), Uruguayan poet, writer, literary critic, politician, educator, and husband of Sara de Ibáñez. Among his important positions were director of the National Institute of Literary Investigations and Archives and editor of *Anden.* Although his poetry was published as early as 1925, in the work *Olas,* it is his 1939 collection, *Mitología de la sangre,* that is the most memorable, with its controlled technical virtuosity and vivid representation of psychological suffering, nostalgia for infancy, and horror of existence. In other collections Ibáñez treats the creative process and the sense of his own totality: "La poesía es el testimonio de mi ser" (Poetry is the testimony of my being). *La frontera* (1966) won the prestigious prize of Cuba's Casa de las Américas.

Other major works by Ibáñez are *La danza de los horizontes* (1927), *La leyenda patria y su contorno histórico* (1959), and *Americanismo y modernismo* (1968). With Esther de Cáceres and Fernando de Pereda, Ibáñez is a major representative of the Ultraist school of literature.

*See also* **Literature: Spanish America.**

BIBLIOGRAPHY

Francisco Aguilera and Georgette Magassy Dorn, *The Archive of Hispanic Literature on Tape: A Descriptive Guide* (1974); *Diccionario de autores iberoamericanos* (1982).

### *Additional Bibliography*

Fitts, Dudley, ed. *An Anthology of Contemporary Latin American Poetry.* New York: New Directions, 1947.

Ibáñez, Roberto. *Introducción. Canto póstumo: Diario de la muerte, Baladas y Canciones, Gavilla. De Sara de Ibáñez.* Buenos Aires: Losada, 1973.

Ibáñez, Roberto. *La frontera y otras moradas.* México: Universidad Nacional Autónoma de México, 1966.

San Román, Gustavo F. "Emir Rodríguez Monegal versus Roberto Ibáñez: Las rivalidades de la crítica y las andanzas del Diario de viaje a París de Horacio Quiroga." *Boletín de la Academia Nacional de Letras* 3a. Epoca, No. 5 (January-June 1999), 15–42.

WILLIAM H. KATRA

## IBÁÑEZ, SARA DE (1905–1971).

**IBÁÑEZ, SARA DE** (1905–1971). Sara de Ibáñez (*b.* 1905; *d.* 1971), Uruguayan poet, literary critic, and educator. Born Sara Iglesias Casadei in Tacuarembó, she married Roberto Ibáñez in 1928. In 1940 she produced her most important collection of poetry, *Canto.* With a prologue by Pablo Neruda, it won the top prize in a Montevideo poetry competition in 1941 because of its wide range of vocabulary and its classical purity of form. Most distinguished among Ibáñez's eight other poetry publications is the epic poem *Canto a Artigas* (1952), which won a prestigious prize from Uruguay's National Academy of Letters.

Some of Ibáñez's poems reveal nature and the inner soul as sources of inspiration. A poet's poet, Ibáñez in much of her work allows often dark symbolism, ornate expression, and attention to lyrical technique to predominate over human issues. A key theme of her verses is the anguished rift between physical and spiritual love. Additional sources of inspiration are historical themes and nature.

Ibáñez's major works include *Canto a Montevideo* (1941), *La batalla* (1967), and *Canto póstumo* (1973). She was acclaimed as a major poet by Gabriela Mistral, Carlos Drummond de Andrade, Manuel Bandeira, and Cecilia Meireles.

*See also* **Literature: Spanish America; Neruda, Pablo.**

BIBLIOGRAPHY

Francisco Aguilera and Georgette Magassy Dorn, *The Archive of Hispanic Literature on Tape: A Descriptive Guide* (1974).

Lidice Gómez Mango, *Homenaje a Sara de Ibáñez* (1971); A. Geysse, *Diccionario universal de las letras* (1973).

### *Additional Bibliography*

Mantaras Loedel, Graciela, and Jorge Arbeleche. *Sara de Ibáñez: Estudio crítico y antología.* Montevideo: Editorial Signos, Instituto Nacional del Libro, 1991.

Scott, Renée Sum. *Escritoras uruguayas: Una antología crítica.* Montevideo: Ediciones Trilce, 2002.

WILLIAM H. KATRA

## IBÁÑEZ DEL CAMPO, CARLOS (1877–1960).

**IBÁÑEZ DEL CAMPO, CARLOS** (1877–1960). Carlos Ibáñez del Campo (*b.* 3 November 1877; *d.* 28 April 1960), Chilean army officer and president (1927–1931 and 1952–1958). Born in Linares, Ibáñez entered the Escuela Militar in Santiago in 1896. Two years later he was commissioned a second lieutenant and in 1900 he was promoted to first lieutenant. While a student at the Academia de Guerra, he was selected for the first El Salvador mission (1903) directed by Captain Juan Pablo Bennett. There he took charge of the new military school and formed the tiny nation's cavalry corps. Ibáñez won acclaim in the Central American country for his horsemanship and for taking part (against orders) in a minor battle between Salvadoran and Guatemalan forces in 1906, an adventure that made him the only Chilean officer to participate in a real war after 1883. He held the rank of colonel in El Salvador and made an advantageous marriage there to a young Salvadoran woman, Doña Rosa Quiroz Avila, with whom he returned to Chile in 1909.

Ibáñez served with the Cazadores cavalry regiment and then returned to the Academia de Guerra to complete his staff training. In 1914 he was on the staff of Division I, Tacna, and in 1919, now a major, was named police prefect in Iquique.

In 1921 President Arturo Alessandri Palma named Ibáñez director of the Cavalry School, where he came to know a number of political figures in the capital professionally and socially. He became involved with political affairs culminating in the military movements of 1924–1925 that resulted first in Alessandri's resignation and then his return. In 1925 Ibáñez became war minister, rising quickly from colonel to general. He quarreled frequently with Alessandri. In 1927, after brief stints as interior minister and vice president, he was elected president under the new 1925 Constitution. Then a widower, he married his second wife, Graciela Letellier, during his presidency.

Ibáñez's authoritarian administration (1927–1931) borrowed heavily from abroad to finance public works projects. He manipulated a spuriously elected Congress, brooked no political opposition, and applied the new constitution selectively, thus enhancing the powers of the executive branch. He involved the state in public health, communications, education, economic development, welfare, social security, and transportation more than ever before. His administration's economic policies made Chile vulnerable to the worldwide economic collapse, thus weakening his position and undermining his popularity by 1930.

Ibáñez resigned the presidency in 1931 during a general strike. He lived for a time in Argentina, returned to Chile, and was a contender for the Popular Front presidential candidacy of 1938 until his association with Chilean fascists became an embarrassment. He remained politically active in the 1940s and served as senator before being elected to a second term as president (1952–1958), as the candidate of a broad coalition of independent groups, small parties, and the corporativist Agrarian Labor Party. His repeated attempts to manipulate the army did not help him in any way and restored democratic processes precluded any return to the "good old days" of strong executive leadership. He died two years after turning the presidency over to Jorge Alessandri Rodríguez, son of his old nemesis.

*See also* **Chile, Political Parties: Popular Front.**

BIBLIOGRAPHY

Luis Correa Prieto, *El presidente Ibáñez, la política, y los políticos: Apuntes para la historia* (1962).

René Montero Moreno, *La verdad sobre Ibáñez* (1952).

Frederick M. Nunn, *Chilean Politics, 1920–1931: The Honorable Mission of the Armed Forces* (1970), and *The Military in Chilean History: Essays on Civil-Military Relations, 1810–1973* (1976).

Ernesto Würth Rojas, *Ibáñez: Caudillo enigmático* (1958).

*Additional Bibliography*

Fowler, Will. *Authoritarianism in Latin America since Independence.* Westport: Greenwood Press, 1996.

Rojas Flores, Jorge. *La Dictadura de Ibáñez y los sindicatos (1927-1931).* Santiago: Dirección de Bibliotecas, Archivos y Museos, Centro de Investigaciones Diego Barros Arana, 1993.

San Francisco, Alejandro, and Angél Soto. *Camino a La Moneda: Las elecciones presidenciales en la historia de Chile, 1920-2000.* Santiago: Instituto de Historia: Centro de Estudios Bicentenario, 2005.

Tuozzo, Celina. *El Estado Policial en Chile, 1924-1931.* Buenos Aires: Proyecto Actores y Coaliciones en la Integración Latinoamericana: La Crujía: Instituto Torcuato de Tella/Programa de Naciones Unidas para el Desarrollo, 2004.

FREDERICK M. NUNN

**IBARBOUROU, JUANA DE** (1892–1979). Juana de Ibarbourou (Juana Fernández Morales; *b.* 8 March 1892; *d.* 1979), Uruguayan poet and fiction writer. Born in Melo, she was educated in a convent and later in the public school system. In 1914 she married Captain Lucas Ibarbourou, with whom she had a child. In 1918 they moved to Montevideo, where she began to publish her poems in the literary section of *La Razón.* Her poems were so well received that the prestigious Argentine magazine *Caras y Caretas* dedicated an issue to her. *Las lenguas de diamante* was published in 1919 by the Argentine writer Manuel Gálvez, then director of Editorial Buenos Aires.

Her poetry was first conceived within the modernist aesthetic, but with less ornamental language. *Raíz salvaje* (Wild Root, 1922) and *El cántaro fresco* (Fresh Pitcher, 1920) offer a more intimate tone, with themes of love, life, and the sensual pleasure of being alive. In 1929 the title of "Juana de America" was officially bestowed upon her by the Uruguayan public in a ceremony presided over by Juan Zorrilla De San Martín, José Santos Chocano, and Alfonso Reyes and attended by delegations from twenty Spanish American countries.

In *La rosa de los vientos* (Compass, 1930) Ibarbourou experiments with the language of earlier avant-garde writers. In 1934, two years after her father died, she published a volume of lyric prose with religious themes, *Loores de Nuestra Señora* (Praise to Our Lady), and another volume of works with similar concerns, *Estampas de la biblia* (Scenes from the Bible). She continued to be hailed throughout the continent. In 1944 she published *Chico Carlo,* a book of "memoirs" of her childhood, and in 1945 she wrote a children's play (*Los sueños de Natacha*). In 1947, Ibarbourou became a member of the Uruguayan Academy of Letters. *Perdida,* whose title came from D'Annunzio's chosen name for dancer Eleonore Duse, appeared in 1950. In this book, she renewed her seemingly diminished interest in poetry, and from then on she did not cease to write.

When her mother died, Ibarbourou became ill and depressed, a condition that lasted for some years and was a theme reflected in her poetry. At the same time, as Angel Rama has pointed out, she also continued to insist on frozen imagery, enabling the poetic voice to retain the past in an idealized construction, as shown in *Azor* (1953), *Romances del destino* (1955), *Oro y tormenta* (Gold and Storm, 1956), and *Elegía* (1967).

In 1957 a plenary session of UNESCO was organized in Montevideo to honor Ibarbourou. Attending as a representative of the poetry of Uruguay and of America, she presented her *Autobiografía lírica,* a recollection of some thirty-five years as a poet. Her *Obras completas* were first published in Spain in 1953 by Editorial Aguilar. Her other works are *La pasajera* (The Passenger, 1967) and *Juan Soldado* (Johnny Soldier, 1971).

Ibarbourou, who had enjoyed fame and a comfortable life, experienced considerable hardship in her later years. She died in Montevideo, poor and mostly forgotten by the very public that acclaimed her.

*See also* **Gálvez, Manuel.**

BIBLIOGRAPHY

Jorge Arbeleche, *Juana de Ibarbourou* (1978).

Ethel Dutra Vieyto, *Aproximación a Juana de Ibarbourou* (1979).

Esther Feliciano Mendoza, *Juana de Ibarbourou* (1981).

Jorge Oscar Pickenhayn, *Vida y obra de Juana de Ibarbourou* (1980).

Sylvia Puentes De Oyenard, *Juana de Ibarbourou: Bibliografía* (1988).

Isabel Sesto Gilardoni, *Juana de Ibarbourou* (1981).

*Additional Bibliography*

Caballé, Anna. *La pluma como espada.* Barcelona: Lumen, 2004.

Larre Borges, Ana Inés. *Mujeres uruguayas: El lado femenino de nuestra historia.* Montevideo: Alfaguara: Fundación Banco de Boston: Ediciones Santillana, 1997.

Scott, Renée Sum. *Escritoras uruguayas: Una antología crítica.* Montevideo: Ediciones Trilce, 2002.

MAGDALENA GARCÍA PINTO

---

**IBARGÜENGOITIA, JORGE** (1928–1983). Jorge Ibargüengoitia (*b.* 22 February 1928; *d.* 27 November 1983), Mexican novelist, playwright, and journalist. Ibargüengoitia was born in Guanajuato, studied engineering and drama at the National Autonomous University of Mexico (UNAM), and won scholarships from the Sociedad Mexicana de Escritors (1954, 1955) and the Rockefeller (1955) and Gusseheim (1969) foundations. Among his works are the imaginative novels *Los relámpagos de agosto* (1964), *La ley de Herodes* (1967), and *Maten al león* (1969). His farcical comedies resemble those by Samuel Beckett and Harold Pinter: *Susana y los jóvenes* (1954), *Clotilde en su casa* (1955), and *Llegó Margo* and *Ante varias esfinges,* both in 1956. Later a disagreement with his mentor Rodolfo Usigli and some unfortunate stage productions alienated Ibargüengoitia from the theater. His last play, *El atentado* (1962), a historical farce about a presidential assassination, received the Casa de las Américas Prize in 1963. Two of his books are available in English translation: *Muertas* (*The Dead Girls,* 1983) and *Dos crímenes* (*Two Crimes,* 1984).

His sardonic sense of humor and imaginative techniques made him one of the best writers of his generation. He died in a plane crash in Spain.

*See also* **Theater.**

BIBLIOGRAPHY

Willis Knapp Jones, *Behind Spanish American Footlights* (1966).

Walter M. Langford, *The Mexican Novel Comes of Age* (1971).

Vicente Leñero, *Los pasos de Jorge* (1989).

### Additional Bibliography

Batis, Huberto. *Crítica bajo presión: Prosa mexicana, 1964-1985.* Mexico City: Universidad Nacional Autónoma de México, Coordinación de Humanidades, Programa Editorial, 2004

González, Alfonso. *Voces de la posmodernidad: Seis narradores mexicanos contemporaneous.* Mexico City: Coordinación de Difusión Cultural, Dirección de Literatura/UNAM, 1998.

Reyes Fragoso, Arturo. *Dos artistas en pantalón corto: Ibargüengoitia y Felguérez, scouts.* Mexico City: Editorial Praxis, 2003.

Von Son, Carlos. *Deconstructing Myths: Parody and Irony in Mexican Literature.* New Orleans: University Press of the South, 2002


GUILLERMO SCHMIDHUBER

**IBARGUREN, CARLOS** (1877–1956). Carlos Ibarguren (*b.* 18 April 1877; *d.* 3 April 1956), Argentine statesman and nationalist intellectual. A distinguished lawyer, Ibarguren served as under secretary of finance and under secretary of agriculture during President Julio Argentino Roca's second administration (1898–1904). He subsequently became secretary of the Federal Supreme Court (1906–1912) and minister of justice and education, under President Roque Sáenz Peña (1912–1913). One of the founders of the Democratic Progressive Party in 1914, he was a candidate for the presidency in 1922. As a historian, he was awarded a national prize for his work *Juan Manuel de Rosas: Su vida, su tiempo, su drama* (1930). He supported General José Félix Uriburu's 1930 military coup and that same year was appointed *interventor* (delegate of the federal government) in the province of Córdoba, where he made it clear he shared Uriburu's belief in the need for a corporatist reorganization of the country's economic and political institutions. The corporatist leanings of the "nationalist revolution" were made even more explicit in Ibarguren's *La inquietud de esta hora* (1934), clearly inspired by the corporatist experiments of Italy, Germany, Austria, and Portugal, and by Pope Pius XI's encyclical *Quadragesimo anno* (1934). Although plans for a constitutional reform along those lines did not prosper, Ibarguren became one of the leading intellectuals of the nationalist reaction against the classical model of liberal democracy.

*See also* **Sáenz Peña, Roque.**


BIBLIOGRAPHY

Sandra Mc Gee Deutsch, *Counterrevolution in Argentina, 1900–1932: The Argentine Patriotic League* (1986).

Carlos Ibarguren, *La historia que he vivido,* 2d ed. (1969)

David Rock, "Intellectual Precursors of Conservative Nationalism in Argentina, 1900–1927," in *Hispanic American Historical Review* 67, no. 2 (1987): 271–300.

### Additional Bibliography

Chávez, Fermín. *El pensamiento nacional: Breviario e itinerario.* Buenos Aires: Nueva Generación: Distribuye Editorial Galerna, 1999.

Huertas, Marta María Magdalena. *Carlos Ibarguren: Su producción historiográfica.* Mendoza: Universidad Nacional de Cuyo, Facultad de Filosofía y Letras, 1996.


EDUARDO A. ZIMMERMANN

**IBARRA, DIEGO** (c. 1510–1600). Diego Ibarra (*b.* ca. 1510; *d.* 1600), Mexican miner. A hidalgo from Guipúzcoa and a knight of Santiago, Ibarra came to New Spain in 1540 during the time of Viceroy Antonio de Mendoza and participated in the wars against the Chichimec tribes and the Caxcanes in Jalisco. Ibarra, Juan de Tolosa, Cristóbal de Oñate (1504/1505–*c.* 1570), and Baltazar de Temiño de Bañuelos (1530–1600) are credited with discovering and opening the great silver mines of Zacatecas and founding that city on 1 January 1548. After amassing a great fortune in the mines, Ibarra married Ana de Valasco y Castilla, a daughter of Viceroy Luis de Velasco. In 1561 he loaned his nephew Francisco Ibarra 200,000 pesos to explore Nueva Galicia and Nueva Vizcaya. In 1576, Ibarra succeeded Francisco (*d.* 1575) as governor of Nueva Vizcaya. Ibarra organized an expedition of conquest into Sinaloa in 1583. He dedicated some of his fortune to constructing parish churches, the most notable of which being the parochial church at Pánuco. Ibarra moved to Mexico City later in life and finally to Tultitlán, where he died in 1600.

*See also* **Mixtón War.**


BIBLIOGRAPHY

Peter Bakewell, *Silver Mining and Society in Colonial Mexico: Zacatecas, 1546–1700* (1971), pp. 11–12.

Phillip Wayne Powell, *Soldiers, Indians, and Silver: The Northward Advance of New Spain, 1550–1600* (1952), pp. 11–14.

*Additional Bibliography*

Bakewell, Peter, editor. *Mines of Silver and Gold in the Americas.* Aldershot and Brookfield: Variorum, 1997.

AARON PAINE MAHR

## IBARRA, JOSÉ DE PINEDA (1629–1680).

José de Pineda Ibarra (*b.* 1629; *d.* 1680), first master printer of Guatemala. Ibarra was born in Mexico City to Diego de Ibarra and Juana Muñiz de Pineda. After a period of collaboration with noted printers of the metropolis, Ibarra moved to Puebla, where he married María Montez Ramírez. With the financial assistance of Payo Enríquez de Rivera, Bishop of Guatemala, he purchased a printing press and related equipment. Under contract with Enríquez, Ibarra set out for the Kingdom of Guatemala, arriving in the capital, Santiago de los Caballeros, in July 1660. In Santiago (present-day Antigua) he established a printing shop, the first of its kind in the country. Ibarra's only son, Antonio, who took over the business after his father's death, was born in 1661. Though granted a monopoly by Captain General Martín Carlos Mencos on the printing of religious and school materials, he was forced to engage in a variety of business ventures in order to supplement his meager earnings as a printer. He died, debt ridden, in Antigua.

*See also* **Antigua.**

BIBLIOGRAPHY

Víctor Miguel Díaz, *Historia de imprenta en Guatemala desde los tiempos de la colonia hasta la época actual* (1930).

Alexander A. M. Stols, *La introducción de la imprenta en Guatemala* (1960).

Lawrence S. Thompson, *Printing in Colonial Spanish America* (1962; rev. ed. 1976).

José Toribio Medina, *La imprenta en Guatemala (1660–1821)* (1910; rep. 1964).

David Vela, *La imprenta en Guatemala colonial* (1960).

*Additional Bibliography*

Lujan Muñoz, Luis. *Semblanza de José de Pineda Ibarra.* Guatemala: Editorial José de Pineda Ibarra, 1980.

JORGE H. GONZÁLEZ

## IBARRA, JUAN FELIPE (1787–1851).

Juan Felipe Ibarra (*b.* 1 May 1787; *d.* 15 July 1851), Argentine military leader and Federalist governor of the province of Santiago del Estero (1831–1851). A native of Santiago del Estero, Argentina, Ibarra studied briefly for the priesthood before he began his military career in 1810. During the Wars of Independence, he served with distinction on the staffs of San Martín and Belgrano, rising to the high rank of graduate sergeant major in 1817. In 1820, in response to an appeal by the local autonomists, he used the urban Abipone garrison to expel from the province of Santiago del Estero the occupying forces of Governor Bernabé Aráoz of Mendoza and subsequently was elected political and military governor by a *cabildo abierto* (open town council). He encouraged economic development by protecting local industries from competition with imports and by authorizing the minting of real and half-real coins. A Federalist, Ibarra admired the state system and the internal economic organization of the United States. He survived a plot by the Unitaristos to have the poet Hilario Ascasubi assassinate him, but the Unitarists finally overthrew him. Other Federalists restored him to power, and in 1831 the legislature elected him governor and brigadier general, a post he held until his death.

A paternalistic ruler, Ibarra encouraged education, built churches, exercised the *patronato real*, banned imports that threatened the local economy, and condemned gambling, alcoholism, and other vices. Some see him as a barbarian, ignorant and cruel; others, as a popular caudillo and Federalist.

*See also* **Argentina, Movements: Federalists.**

BIBLIOGRAPHY

Joseph T. Criscenti, ed., *Sarmiento and His Argentina* (1993), pp. 105, 156.

Tulio Halperín-Donghi, *Politics, Economics, and Society in Argentina in the Revolutionary Period,* translated by Richard Southern (1975).

John Lynch, *Argentine Dictator: Juan Manuel de Rosas, 1829–1852* (1981), pp. 67, 226.

*Additional Bibliography*

Alén Lascano, Luis C. *Ibarra, un caudillo norteño.* Buenos Aires: Crisis, 1976.

Newton, Jorge. *Juan Felipe Ibarra: El caudillo de la selva.* Buenos Aires: Plus Ultra, 1973.

JOSEPH T. CRISCENTI

**IBARRA DE PIEDRA, ROSARIO** (1927–). Rosario Ibarra de Piedra, born in Saltillo, Coahuila, is a Mexican social activist famous for her slogan, "They were taken alive—we want them alive." She began her activism in 1975, during the Luis Echeverría administration, when federal police arrested and disappeared her son, Jesús Ibarra. (In Latin America the term "disappeared" describes a situation in which a member of the political opposition is kidnapped by security forces or death squads and never seen again.) In 1979, together with the family members of other people who were disappeared for political reasons, she founded the National Front for Struggle against Repression. Known in the twenty-first century as Eureka, the organization continues its efforts for justice and truth. Through protests and hunger strikes, she has been pressuring the federal government to provide information on the whereabouts of the disappeared and to give amnesty to political prisoners and targets of political repression. On the political scene, she has twice been a presidential candidate, in 1982 and 1988, making her the first woman to run for that office. As a member of the PRD political party, she is a "plurinominal" senator—one of the three senators representing the Federal District for the 2006–2012 period.

*See also* **Echeverría Álvarez, Luis; Mexico: Since 1910; Mexico, Political Parties: Democratic Revolutionary Party (PRD); Truth Commissions.**

BIBLIOGRAPHY

DePalma, Anthony. "Among the Ruins of the Left, a Pillar Stands." *New York Times*, October 5, 1994, International Section. Profile of Rosario Ibarra de Piedra.

ELENA AZUCENA CEJA CAMARGO

**ICA.** Ica, central coastal Peruvian department and city. Located approximately 170 miles southeast of the capital of Lima, the department has a surface area of 8,205 square miles and a population of 695,489 (2005 census). The city of Ica has over 200,000 residents (2005). The Ica River, flowing into the Pacific from January to April, when rainfall is sufficient on the upper western slopes of the Andes, provides water for irrigation of fertile coastal fields. The valley is extremely dry, with less than one-half inch of rainfall yearly. In the winter (May through August) there are dense mists (*garúa*). Cacti will grow on slopes above 2,300 feet, but it is only by irrigation that the coastal desert bears crops.

Under the Incas, numerous agricultural crops were cultivated in the region, and various marine resources were exploited. With European contact following the 1530s, the native population fell sharply, by over 90 percent, the consequence of disease, the breakdown of hydraulic systems, exploitation, and the introduction of Old World crops and animals that changed the ecological balance. Wheat and vegetables were grown and transported to the Lima market. Grapes were quickly introduced, as the soil and climate seemed perfect for viticulture. By the 1590s wine and subsequently brandy (Pisco) supplied growing urban markets in Lima and highland mining centers. In the sixteenth century, African slaves were imported to replace the declining number of indigenous *iqueños* and *mitayos* (transplanted Andeans), and by the mid-nineteenth century Chinese workers or coolies came to play an important role in the local labor market. During the twentieth century, cotton replaced grapes as the primary agricultural commodity, although Pisco is still a prized commodity in Lima. Ica continues to be a major supplier of fresh vegetables to the capital.

*See also* **Alcoholic Beverages; Pisco.**

BIBLIOGRAPHY

Alberto Rossel Castro, *Historia regional de Ica* (1964).

Eugene A. Hammel, *Power in Ica: The Structural History of a Peruvian Community* (1969).

Robert G. Keith, *Conquest and Agrarian Change: The Emergence of the Hacienda System on the Peruvian Coast* (1976).

*Additional Bibliography*

Angeles Caballero, César A. *Peruanidad del pisco.* 4th ed. Lima: Banco Latino, 1995.

Menzel, Dorothy. *Pottery Style and Society in Ancient Peru: Art as a Mirror of History in the Ica Valley, 1350–1570.* Berkeley: University of California Press, 1976.

Schreiber, Katharina Jeanne, and Josue Lancho Rojas. *Irrigation and Society in the Peruvian Desert: The Puquios of Nasca.* Lanham, MD: Lexington Books, 2003.

NOBLE DAVID COOK

---

**ICA, PRE-COLUMBIAN.** Pre-Columbian Ica. The Ica Valley of the Peruvian south coast has been continuously inhabited for more than four thousand years. The Ica pottery-making tradition, which began about 2500 BCE, has been studied more intensively than that of any other part of the Andes. It provides a chronological yardstick, divided into three periods and three horizons, against which other local pottery-style sequences can be measured in a system of relative chronology. From earliest to latest are the Initial Period, Early Horizon, Early Intermediate Period, Middle Horizon, Late Intermediate Period, and Late Horizon.

Ica was occasionally subjected to outside influence: from Chavín in the Early Horizon, from Moche near the end of the Early Intermediate Period, from Huari in the Middle Horizon, and finally as a result of the Inca conquest in the Late Horizon. Such influence is reflected in pottery form and decoration as well as other aspects of culture. Changes in the pottery of Ica are used to mark the beginnings of the periods and horizons.

New religious elements from Chavín reached Ica around 1500 BCE, perhaps brought by missionaries. Moche influence, arriving around CE 100, was weaker but also involved religious elements. The Huari state, which conquered Ica around CE 600, also brought religious changes, which are reflected in the art; but after the fall of Huari, around CE 800, Ica potters abandoned these foreign symbols, creating geometric decoration executed in red, black, and white on an unpolished surface.

The Ica style of pottery began some hundred years later when Ica artists revived some of the colors and designs from Huari art, including mythical birds and animals. The interpretation of these designs suggests that they were copied from older objects with no understanding of their earlier meanings. Such archaism, or copying from earlier art styles, was not uncommon in pre-Columbian Peru. From this archaized base, then, the Ica style developed and changed throughout the Late Intermediate Period and beyond. The animal figures were soon dropped, as were the additional colors, but the bird figures changed and multiplied, and to them were added fishes, indicating the importance of the sea to these people. Combined with geometric designs, these figures were applied to elegantly shaped and highly polished vessels, which acquired considerable prestige outside the valley. The wide distribution of Ica-style pottery indicates far-flung contacts and the possibility of a growing influence of the Ica Valley polities in the Late Intermediate Period, an influence cut short by the Inca conquest of Ica and the rest of the south coast about 1476.

The Incas involved some of the Ica nobility in the local administrative organization, and Inca shapes and designs were mingled with those of the local art style. Nevertheless, when the Inca Empire fell, Ica artists again rejected the foreign elements and returned to their own pre-Conquest trends. Their persistence in abolishing the symbols of conquest provides us with a key to the nature of the proud and independent people of Ica before their culture was destroyed by the Europeans.

*See also* **Art: Pre-Columbian Art of South America.**

BIBLIOGRAPHY

Dorothy Menzel et al., *The Paracas Pottery of Ica: A Study in Style and Time,* University of California Publications in American Archaeology and Ethnology, 50 (1964).

Patricia J. Lyon, "Innovation Through Archaism: The Origins of the Ica Pottery Style," in *Nawpa Pacha* 4 (1966): 31–62.

Donald A. Proulx, *Local Differences and Time Differences in Nasca Pottery,* University of California Publications in Anthropology, 5 (1968).

Dorothy Menzel, *Pottery Style and Society in Ancient Peru: Art as a Mirror of History in the Ica Valley, 1350–1570* (1976) and *The Archaeology of Ancient Peru and the Work of Max Uhle* (1977).

*Additional Bibliography*

Tiballi, Anne E. *Castoffs and Snippets: The Textile Evidence from Casa Vieja, Ica Valley, Peru.* Thesis (M.A.,) State University of New York at Binghamton, Department of Anthropology, 2005.

PATRICIA J. LYON

## ICAZA CORONEL, JORGE (1906–1979).

Jorge Icaza Coronel (*b.* 10 July 1906; *d.* 26 May 1979), Ecuadorian novelist, playwright, and short-story writer. In general, Icaza's fiction has become linked to the regionalist movement of social protest of the 1930s; his best-known novel, *Huasipungo* (1934), attacks the exploitation of Indians in Ecuador. Written from the point of view of the dominant urban class in Ecuador, the novel highlights the ethnic and class gulf between Indians and whites by following, on the one hand, an idyllic love relationship between two young Indians and, on the other, the encroachment of foreign capitalism on an Indian community that is eventually destroyed. Grotesque, sordid descriptions of harsh living conditions and exploitation are meant to create a better awareness of the plight of the Ecuadorian Indians, most of whom lack the bare necessities of life in the novel.

In similar fashion, *En las calles* (1935) narrates a historical event in which an Indian soldier, assigned to quell a battle between rival political factions, ends up firing upon his own community. Icaza's next novels, *Cholos* (1937) and *Huairapamushcas* (1948), take a more complicated view of the struggle between Indians and whites. The *cholo*, or half-breed, works for the exploiter against the Indians until he realizes that his people are being oppressed. While no one survives the massacre in *Huasipungo,* in *Huairapamushcas,* an allusion to the survival of the *cholo* suggests the creation of a symbiotic relationship between Indians and whites. While not as well known as Icaza's first novel, by far his best is *El chulla Romero y Flores* (1958), a masterly recreation of the trials and tribulations of a marginalized *cholo* as he moves from a rural to an urban environment, thus complicating his life even more as he comes to grips with his mixed racial heritage. Icaza's last novel, *Atrapados* (1972), is more artistically rendered and contains autobiographical elements that portray the concerns of a writer whose creativity is vastly limited to the confines of the sociopolitical world in which he lives.

*See also* **Indigenous Peoples; Race and Ethnicity.**

### BIBLIOGRAPHY

Manuel Corrales Pascual, *Jorge Icaza: Frontera del relato indigenista* (1974).

Enrique Ojeda Castillo, *Cuatro obras de Jorge Icaza* (1961).

Theodore A. Sackett, *El arte en la novelística de Jorge Icaza* (1974).

Anthony J. Vetrano, *La problemática psico-social y su correlación lingüística en las novelas de Jorge Icaza* (1974).

### *Additional Bibliography*

Fabre-Maldonado, Niza. *Americanismos, indigenismos, neologismos y creación literaria en la obra de Jorge Icaza.* Ecuador: Abrapalabra Editores, 1993.

Lavou, Victorien. *El indio malanga: écrire la domination en Amérique latine: Rosario Castellanos, Balun Canan, 1957; José Maria Arguedas, Los ríos profundos, 1958; Jorge Icaza, El chulla romero y flores, 1958.* Perpignan: CRI-LAUP, Presses Universitaires de Perpignan, 2004.

Sacoto, Antonio. *Indianismo, indigenismo y neoindigenismo en la novela ecuatoriana.* Quito: Augusto Zuniga Yanez Gemagrafic, 2006.

DICK GERDES

## IGLESIAS, JOSÉ MARÍA (1823–1891).

José María Iglesias (*b.* 1823; *d.* 1891), Mexican jurist and politician. Born in Mexico City and educated at El Colegio de San Gregorio, Iglesias began his political career in 1846 as a Mexico City councilman. As editor of *El Siglo XX* (1847–1850), he opposed the administration of Santa Anna and the Treaty of Guadalupe Hidalgo (1848). After the triumph of the Liberal Revolution of Ayutla in 1854, Iglesias served in the ministries of treasury and justice and was later elected to the Supreme Court. The War of the Reform (1857–1860) forced his return to private life, but he filled a variety of positions between 1863 and 1871 during the Benito Juárez presidency: minister of justice (twice), minister of the treasury (twice), and minister of government. He was elected president of the Supreme Court in 1873.

As head of the Supreme Court, Iglesias fought against presidential-gubernational control of elections. He became part of a three-way contest for power in 1876, when President Sebastián Lerdo De Tejada (1827–1889) ran for reelection. Iglesias maintained that the 1876 elections were fraudulent and that presidential power had devolved upon him as the constitutional successor to the president. Earlier, Porfirio Díaz had pronounced against Lerdo de Tejada in the Plan of Tuxtepec (1876). Repeated efforts to bring Díaz and Iglesias together failed. After Díaz dealt Lerdo's troops a major defeat at the battle of Tecoac on 16 November 1876, he turned on Iglesias.

As a professional soldier, Díaz's ability to attract military support proved crucial. Although supporters of Iglesias controlled over one-half of the country in December 1876, defections and military defeats forced Iglesias into exile in the United States in January 1877. He returned to Mexico in October 1877, but he did not resume his public career.

*See also* **Judiciary in Latin America; Mexico, Wars and Revolutions: The Reform.**

BIBLIOGRAPHY

Laurens Ballard Perry, *Juárez and Díaz: Machine Politics in Mexico* (1978).

Frank A. Knapp, Jr., *The Life of Sebastián Lerdo de Tejada, 1823–1889* (1951).

José María Iglesias, *Autobiografía* (1893).

*Additional Bibliography*

Guzmán López, Miguel Angel. *La participación del gobierno del estado de Guanajuato en el movimiento decembrista de 1876.* Guanajuato: Ediciones La Rana, 1999.

Moctezuma Barragán, Javier. *José María Iglesias y la justicia electoral.* Mexico City: Universidad Nacional Autónoma de México, Instituto de Investigaciones Jurídicas, 1994.

DON M. COERVER

---

**IGLESIAS, MIGUEL** (1830–1909). Miguel Iglesias (*b.* 11 June 1830; *d.* 7 November 1909), provisional president of Peru (1884–1885). A wealthy landowner from the northern Peruvian department of Cajamarca, Iglesias was commander of Peruvian forces in the War of the Pacific (1879–1883). In August 1882, with Peru occupied by the Chilean army and beset by internal political divisions, Iglesias issued the Cry of Montán, in which he advocated pursuing peace with Chile even if it meant the loss of some Peruvian territory. In October 1882, he convened an assembly of northern Peruvian departments that proclaimed him supreme leader of the country.

Recognized as president of Peru by the Chilean government, Iglesias signed the Treaty of Ancón (October 1883), which ended the war between the two nations. Iglesias convened a constituent assembly in Lima that ratified the treaty and designated him provisional president of Peru (1 March 1884). General Andrés Avelino Cáceres immediately opposed the Iglesias government, and after a long and bloody civil war, his forces occupied Lima in December 1885. Iglesias renounced his claims to the presidency and left the country. He died in Lima.

*See also* **Ancón, Treaty of (1883); War of the Pacific.**

BIBLIOGRAPHY

Jorge Basadre, *Historia de la República del Perú* (1964), vol. 6, pp. 2619–2620.

Fredrick B. Pike, *The Modern History of Peru* (1967), esp. pp. 146–152.

*Additional Bibliography*

Leciñana Falconí, Carolina. *La Guerra del Pacífico, 120 años después: diplomacia y negociación.* Lima: Tarea Asociación Gráfica Educativa, 2004.

Stein, William W. *El levantamiento de Atusparia.* Lima: Mosca Azul Editores, 1988.

WILLIAM E. SKUBAN

---

**IGLESIAS CASTRO, RAFAEL** (1861–1924). Rafael Iglesias Castro (*b.* 18 April 1861; *d.* 11 April 1924), president of Costa Rica (1894–1898, 1898–1902). After graduating from the Colegio de Cartago, Iglesias studied law at the University of Santo Tomás but left before obtaining his law degree. His first significant political experience came in 1889 when he supported the presidential candidacy of José Joaquín Rodríguez. When Rodríguez assumed the presidency in 1890, he named Iglesias minister of war. In 1893 Iglesias became minister of finance and commerce, and also married the president's daughter. As a presidential candidate in 1894 he enjoyed the support of the incumbent administration and took power after the government had suppressed his political opposition. In 1897 Iglesias secured congressional passage of a constitutional amendment that permitted his reelection and subsequently won a second presidential term when his opponents withdrew from the electoral process. During his two terms Iglesias placed the nation on the gold standard; inaugurated the National Theater; promoted railroads, highways, and port facilities; and oversaw the construction of a number of schools and hospitals. An authoritarian figure who often abused the political rights of the opposition, Iglesias nonetheless allowed freedom of the press. He stepped down from power in 1902 and ran unsuccessfully for the presidency in 1910 and again in 1914.

*See also* **Costa Rica, Constitutions; Theater.**

BIBLIOGRAPHY


Harold H. Bonilla, *Nuestros presidentes* (1942).

James L. Busey, "The Presidents of Costa Rica," in *Americas* 18 (1961): 55–70.

Theodore S. Creedman, *Historical Dictionary of Costa Rica* (1977).


RICHARD V. SALISBURY

## IGLESIAS PANTIN, SANTIAGO (1872 1939).

Santiago Iglesias Pantin (*b.* 22 February 1872; *d.* 5 December 1939), Puerto Rican labor leader. Born in La Coruña, Spain, Iglesias Pantin arrived in Cuba in 1886 as a stowaway and remained there until sailing for Puerto Rico in 1896. He began his political activities in 1898, being arrested for attempting to raise the "cost of labor." In 1900, he traveled to New York because of ill-health. While in New York, he became acquainted with members of the American Federation of Labor. The following year he was appointed union organizer for Puerto Rico and Cuba. In 1918, Iglesias Pantin organized the Pan American Federation of Labor and continued to participate and promote labor concerns until his death from malaria in 1939.

*See also* **Labor Movements.**

BIBLIOGRAPHY


Gonzalo F. Cordova, *Santiago Iglesias: Creador del Movimiento Obrero de Puerto Rico* (1980).

Clarence Ollson Senior, *Santiago Iglesias: Labor Crusader* (1972).


### *Additional Bibliography*


Cordova, Gonzalo F. *Resident Commissioner, Santiago Iglesias and His Times.* Río Piedras: Editorial de la Universidad de Puerto Rico, 1993.


ALLAN S. R. SUMNALL

## IGUAÇÚ.

Formerly a part of the states of Amazonas and Mato Grosso in Brazil, the Federal Territory of Iguaçú was formed at the meeting point of Brazil, Argentina, and Paraguay as a result of the Constitution of 1946. This constitution allowed the military government to establish new states in the interior in order to improve its position in the Senate and to minimize the influence of larger, more populated states such as São Paulo and Minas Gerais. In the early seventeenth century this area was central to the struggle between the frontier slave raiders and European missionaries. Not until the middle of that century were the Jesuits able to maintain some security against Paulista resistance to Indian protection.

*See also* **Brazil, Constitutions.**

BIBLIOGRAPHY


Rollie E. Poppino, *Brazil: The Land and People* (1968).

Robert Wesson and David V. Fleisher, *Fleisher, Brazil in Transition* (1983).


### *Additional Bibliography*


Costa, Emilia Viotti da. *The Brazilian Empire: Myths and Histories.* Chapel Hill: University of North Carolina Press, 2000.

MacLachlan, Colin M. *A History of Modern Brazil: The Past against the Future.* Wilmington, DE: Scholarly Resources, 2003.

Meade, Theresa A. *A Brief History of Brazil.* New York: Facts on File, 2003.

Vincent, John S. *Culture and Customs of Brazil.* Westport, CT: Greenwood Press, 2003.


CAROLYN E. VIEIRA

## IGUAÇU FALLS.

The Iguaçu Falls (in Portuguese, Iguaçu; in Spanish, Iguazú) are situated on the Iguazú River, along the border between the Argentine province of Misiones and the Brazilian state of Paraná, and lie chiefly within the Iguazú National Park of Argentina. Discovered in 1541 by the Spanish governor, Álvar Núñez Cabeza de Vaca, the falls are made up of 275 waterfalls that range from 130 to 230 feet in height. The Iguazú National Park (Argentina) and the Iguaçu National Park (Brazil) were declared World Heritage Centers by UNESCO in 1984 and 1986, respectively. The two parks work together to conserve the habitat.

The name Iguazú (as well as Iguaçu) comes from the Guaraní indigenous language and means "great water." The climate is humid subtropical, with the average temperature in the area 60 degrees F in winter and 85 degrees F in summer. Flora are rich and abundant (laurel, ceibo, cedar, lapacho, silk floss tree, ombu, bamboo, tacuara cane), as are fauna (grey foxes, pumas, coatis, tapirs, and coral snakes). The ecosystem is similar to that of the Amazonian rainforest. Insects, toucans, and lizards can also be found. The Iguaçu area was transformed by the construction nearby of the Itaipú hydroelectric dam, on the border between Brazil and Paraguay, which began operations in 1984 and has become another tourist attraction.

The waterfalls in Argentina's Iguazú National Park can be approached on foot via two paths, the lower and the upper. There is also a tour available by train and another by boat, which takes visitors to within 165 feet of the largest fall (in terms of its height and volume), the Devil's Throat (Garganta del Diablo). Brazil's Iguaçu National Park has extraordinarily beautiful panoramic views. The infrastructure at the waterfalls, visited by thousands each year, is adequate to handle tourism. Nearby cities are Foz do Iguaçu (Brazil, 300,000 inhabitants) and Puerto Iguazú (Argentina, 35,000 inhabitants). The Jesuit ruins of San Ignacio, of exceptional cultural interest, are located 37 miles from Posadas, in the Argentine province of Misiones.

*See also* **Argentina, Geography; Brazil, Geography; Cabeza de Vaca, Alvar Núñez; Guarani Indians.**

BIBLIOGRAPHY

Comamala, Martín, and Ariel Mendieta. *Cataratas del Iguazú; Argentina*. Buenos Aires, Edifel Libros, 2006.

Petraglia de Bolzón, María Luisa, and Bolzón Norberto Domingo. *Gazú: Guía de Flora y Fauna*. Series Vida y color. Buenos Aires, Autores Editores, 2006

VICENTE PALERMO

**IGUANA.** The iguana is a warm-climate lizard that has a long body covered with scales, a crest along its back, and short limbs ending in five digits. The common iguana (*Iguana iguana*), found in tropical America, is green. It may reach six and a half feet in length, including its tail. Extensively hunted for its chickenlike meat, it is very popular in Central American markets. An excellent swimmer, it drops into water if threatened by danger. The Rhinoceros iguana (*Cyclura cornuta*), extremely rare, inhabits the island of Hispaniola. It is so named for the three horns on its snout.

The Galápagos marine iguana (*Amblyrhynchus cristatus*) is black. The Hood Island iguana, which has reddish spots, is the only lizard known to feed in the surf, mainly on seaweed. During the mating season, each iguana has a carefully marked territory. If one male invades the territory of another, a long, nonfatal fight ensues. If a female iguana trespasses on the territory of another female, there is a bloody battle. An excellent swimmer, the Galápagos marine iguana spends time underwater and basking in the sun.

The Galápagos land iguana (*Conolophus subcristatus*) is a brown, quiet, inoffensive leaf eater that lives in dry, sparsely vegetated areas. It has a heavy body and strong limbs. The total length averages 43 inches, including a 24-inch tail. During the mating season, males fight ritual battles. This species is threatened with extinction due to hunting by humans, birds of prey, and introduced wild animals. It is strictly protected in the Galápagos National Park; eggs are collected and iguanas are raised at the Charles Darwin Research Station on Santa Cruz Island in the Galápagos.

*See also* **Galápagos Islands.**

BIBLIOGRAPHY

Baschieri Salvadori, Francesco B. *Rare Animals of the World*. New York: Mallard Press, 1990.

Bates, Marston. *The Land and Wildlife of South America*. New York: Time, 1964.

Patzelt, Erwin. *Fauna del Ecuador*. Quito: Banco Central del Ecuador, 1989.

RAÚL CUCALÓN

**ILLAPA.** Illapa, the Inca thunder god, was believed to control the weather. The Incas prayed to Illapa for rain and protection from drought. He was envisioned as a warrior in the sky who held a sling and was dressed in shining garments. The lightning was believed to be the flashing of his clothing, and the thunder was the crack of his sling. His sling stone was the lightning bolt that broke his sister's water jug, causing the rain to fall. In a land of frequent drought, where the people depended on agriculture to sustain them, the god of rain was of paramount importance.

*See also* **Incas, The.**

BIBLIOGRAPHY

John H. Rowe, "Inca Culture at the Time of the Spanish Conquest," in *Handbook of South American Indians,* vol. 2 (1946), pp. 183–330. Additional sources include Burr Cartwright Brundage, *The Empire of the Inca* (1963) and *The Lords of Cuzco: A History and Description of the Inca People in Their Final Days* (1967).

### *Additional Bibliography*

Barham Ode, Walid. *Apu pitusiray = Realismo mítico.* Calca: Asociación Cultural Pumaruna, 2005.

Jones, David M. *Mythology of the Incas: Myths and Legends of the Ancient Andes, Western Valleys, Deserts, and Amazonia.* London: Southwater, 2007.

Rosa, Greg. *Incan Mythology and Other Myths of the Andes.* New York: Rosen Group, 2007.

Sullivan, William. *The Secret of the Incas: Myth, Astronomy, and the War against Time.* New York: Crown Publishers, 1996.

Urton, Gary. *Inca Myths.* Austin: University of Texas, 1999.

GORDON F. MCEWAN

## ILLESCAS, CARLOS (1918–1998).

Carlos Illescas (*b.* 19 May 1918; *d.* 1998), Guatemalan poet, considered one of the best in the "Generation of the 1940s" and the *Acento* literary circle. During the presidency of Jacobo Arbenz Guzmán (1951–1954), he was the president's personal secretary. As a result, Illescas was forced into exile after the 1954 invasion of the country that led to the overthrow of the Arbenz government. He has lived in Mexico City ever since. Illescas is renowned not only as a poet but also as a radio and television scriptwriter, and as a distinguished professor of creative writing. His poetry is characterized by its mixture of classical Castilian language and powerful surrealist metaphor and imagery. His books are *Friso de otoño* (1958); *Ejercicios* (1960); *Réquiem del obsceno* (1963); *Los cuentos de Marsias* (1973); *Manual de simios y otros poemas* (1977); *El mar es una llaga* (1980); and *Usted es la culpable* (1983).

*See also* **Arbenz Guzmán, Jacobo.**

BIBLIOGRAPHY

Francisco Albizúrez Palma and Catalina Barrios y Barrios, *Historia de la literatura guatemalteca,* vol. 3 (1987), p. 136.

ARTURO ARIAS

## ILLIA, ARTURO UMBERTO (1900–1983).

Arturo Umberto Illia was an Argentine politician who served as president from 1963 to 1966. Born on August 4, 1900, he became a member of the Radical Civic Union (Unión Cívica Radical; UCR) during his youth; he graduated with a degree in medicine in 1927 and was elected provincial senator from Córdoba in 1936. In 1940 he became vice-governor of the province but was forced to resign following the coup d'état of 1943. He was a national deputy in 1948 and was elected governor of that province in 1962. However, the military that overthrew President Arturo Frondizi (1958–1962) annulled those elections.

In the 1963 presidential elections, the People's UCRP, whose main leader, Ricardo Balbín, had little hopes of seeing his party win, ran Illia as its candidate. With the Peronists outlawed, he won the election with 25.1 percent of the vote; but the blank ballots (Peronists) accounted for 20 percent. Illia began his term in office suffering from a low degree of electoral legitimacy and growing military hostility toward the democratic system.

During his term in office he oriented the economy in a nationalist-populist direction: he annulled the petroleum contracts that had been renewed by Frondizi, promoted industrialization, reduced the foreign debt, increased spending on education and health, and set price controls on medicines. His macroeconomic policy was expansive, with a strong tendency toward redistribution of wealth. The Gross Domestic Product grew at a rate of 10 percent from 1964 to 1965, but not in any sustainable fashion. In 1965 he opposed sending troops to the Dominican Republic during the Organization of American

States invasion advocated by the United States. This further irritated the Argentine military.

His deep democratic beliefs prevented him from allowing the ban on Peronism to continue, and he refused to renew it in 1965. But conflicts with the powerful Peronist trade unions, along with discontent among national and foreign businesses and opposition from the local press, created an environment conducive to renewed military intervention. In June 1966 there was a military coup under the banner of the "doctrine of national security." Illia died on January 18, 1983 in the city of Córdoba.

*See also* **Argentina: The Twentieth Century; Argentina, Political Parties: Radical Party (UCR); Balbín, Ricardo; Frondizi, Arturo; Perón, Juan Domingo.**

BIBLIOGRAPHY

Cavarozzi, Marcelo. *Autoritarismo y democracia, 1955–1996: La transición del Estado al mercado en la Argentina.* Buenos Aires: Ariel, 1997.

Terán, Oscar. *Nuestros años sesentas: La formación de la nueva izquierda intelectual en la Argentina, 1956–1966.* Buenos Aires: AR Puntosur, 1991.

VICENTE PALERMO

---

**IMPERIALISM.** The various senses of *imperialism* require definition and an outline of their historical and theoretical components. According to *The Oxford Universal Dictionary* the word "imperial" comes from the Latin *imperium,* meaning "pertaining to an empire or emperor"; it defines imperialism as "the rule of an emperor, especially when despotic" or "the principle or spirit of empire." Other dictionaries define imperialism as "the policy of extending a nation's authority by territorial acquisition or by the establishment of economic and political hegemony over other nations," or "the policy of seeking to extend the power, dominion, or territories of a nation." The historian Tony Smith defines imperialism as "the effective domination by a relatively strong state over a weaker people whom it does not control as it does its home population, or the effort to secure such domination" (*The Pattern of Imperialism,* p. 6). He notes that the imperial power commonly permits the local population some areas of control. Any of these definitions allows for formal and informal imperialism.

The term *imperialism* has at heart subordination and the clash of sovereignty. In formal imperialism, the dominant power assumes sovereignty over the subject people in the form of annexation, colonialism, or an avowed protectorate. In informal imperialism, the dominant power asserts control over the sovereignty of subject peoples through various forms of domination (all of which carry the implied threat of force or other forms of harm). For example, the Monroe Doctrine was a policy that restricted the sovereignty of the Latin American nations because it denied them (without their consent) sovereignty over their territory (they could not alienate it) and over their political systems (they could not choose a form unacceptable to the United States). Imperialism was the product of the quest for glory, a higher purpose (God, the nation, civilization, or destiny), gold and wealth, and the strategic need for ports, outposts, and resources to achieve the first three objectives (or to protect early successes in achieving them).

### RELATIONSHIPS OF STATES

World systems theory, associated with American sociologist Immanuel Wallerstein but based upon the work of the great French historian Fernand Braudel, defines the relationships of states within the world economy as metropole (core), semiperiphery, and periphery. A metropole power is defined, in part, by its urge to incorporate areas beyond its sovereignty into its political economy in order to enlarge the pool of land, labor, and capital from which its entrepreneurs accumulate profit. A metropole state not only controls the factors of domestic production and distribution, but also acquires the political power and technology to control foreign factors of production and distribution in the periphery and semiperiphery. Metropoles are constantly in a state of competition with each other as they strain to obtain hegemony within the world economy. A semiperiphery state functions both as exploited and exploiter in the world economy. Metropoles and semiperiphery states exploit areas of the periphery (such as Central America), which lack some factors of production or are unable to control them. Metropole states preserve their political stability and improve the lifestyle and capital accumulation of their working and entrepreneurial classes in part by manipulating the periphery. Mexico, Brazil, and Argentina are three countries that acquired semi-peripheral status in the late nineteenth or twentieth centuries. They acquired considerable control over land and labor, and some capacity to distribute the imports and exports necessary for their economies. But they are still dependent upon foreign capital to a considerable extent and also rely upon foreign communications and transportation to an appreciable degree.

The explorers were the first foreign intruders into New World society. While the Viking raiding parties and the French and British fishermen were transitory, the adventurers and captains in the service of the Spanish, British, Portuguese, French, Dutch, Swedish, Danish crowns, and Italian states marked the New World societies permanently with maps, ports, and settlements. The outward thrust of Europe was a response to its commercial expansion and its desire to reach the East more directly. Spanish experience with several centuries of reconquest of its peninsula from the Moors influenced its conquistadors; the mental and physical activity of many Spanish noble families had been directed toward conquest for generations. The Portuguese and the Dutch stressed trade more than settlement; the Spanish did a bit of both, while the British were heavily involved in both. Latin America was exploited for land, labor, and communication routes. The chief products of export under the Spanish and Portuguese were gold, silver, sugar, tobacco, chocolate, cotton, hides, dyes and dyewoods, and fruit.

The European mercantilists of the fifteenth through the eighteenth centuries overran the whole New World. In addition to the Spanish Empire, which stretched from the Great Plains to Cape Horn, the Portuguese, Dutch, French, British, Russian, Danish, and Swedish nations established colonies in the New World. Centuries of competitive European expansion contributed to the formation of modern Latin America.

The European states used ship-building and navigational technology for exploration, and they employed military technology for domination and acquisition of territory. The elements of Western expansion in Latin America were the missionaries, settlers, and adventurers, the latter of which was reemphasized in new forms (filibusterers and economic adventurers) in the nineteenth century in the greed unleashed by the philosophy of liberalism and material progress. Western expansion (based on written records and maps and the transatlantic ties to settlers and colonists) attempted to alter empty or lightly settled regions or regions occupied by peoples without advanced technology and sociopolitical organizations. Europe's technology, economic power, and advanced political and social organization developed from the geographical closeness of its states and the internecine and feudal wars fought to reestablish a centralized authority after the decline of the Roman Empire. The Renaissance enthusiasm for knowledge, new things, and new experiences of the mind also encouraged expansion. The European interaction with the indigenous peoples of Latin America in the sixteenth and seventeenth centuries was very one-sided: Europe borrowed some crops, but little else. Spanish, British, French, and Portuguese ideas, diseases, technology, and power carried the day.

Spanish and Portuguese institutions, the world economy, and the pre-Columbian societies shaped the agrarian structures in modern Latin America. The first two are part of the imperial order. The Incas, Aztecs, and Mayas had communal property (*capulli* for Aztecs and *ayllu* for Incas) but little private property. The Hispanics instituted private property and land grants to reward the soldiers and their leaders. The Spanish used *encomiendas* and the Portuguese *sesmarias* to distribute land and coerced labor for the production or extraction of wealth. Scholarship of the late twentieth century has indicated that institutions such as the *encomiendas* were less exploitative than originally thought. Indigenous groups, for example, entered Mexico's *encomiendas* voluntarily. In subsequent centuries, foreigners continued to assume a right to the land and labor needed to amass wealth. The church lands were also private, but held in *mano muerto* (dead hand or inalienable), hence outside the marketplace. Thus church property became a target of laissez-faire liberals and the ambitious nineteenth-century bourgeoisie.

Missionaries were important in the dissemination of European imperial rule because they penetrated the backlands and rain forests that were without the gold or silver, which attracted adventurers in the colonial period.

Except for the United States and Canada, the New World nations quickly became mixed racial and ethnic societies—mulattoes, Mestizos, and Zambos. Anthropologist Marvin Harris has argued that the various racial and cultural components in Latin

America were "in large measure the consequence of the attempt to harness the aboriginal population on behalf of European profit-making enterprises." Admittedly the Repartimiento was the cheapest form of labor in the New World because it required no capital investment as slavery did. Still, if one adds land and resources to the harnessing of New World factors for European profit, the thought is more accurate.

### ONE ECONOMIC SYSTEM

The age of exploration and discovery (fifteenth to eighteenth centuries) and of imperialism (nineteenth and twentieth centuries) completed the bonding of the world into one economic system. The "new imperialism" of the 1870–1931 period was more emotional and nationalistic and also tied closely to industry and cultural consciousness. Nationalism, liberalism, and the industrial revolution influenced and shaped European and U.S. imperialism in the late eighteenth and the nineteenth centuries. The imperialism and nationalism of the sixteenth through the early twentieth centuries left much of Africa, Latin America, Asia, and the Middle East with political boundaries and populations that suited the objectives of European imperial divisions of authority and economic power rather than local and indigenous factors of language, kinship, culture, or geography.

The imperial rivalry occurred within the world system which integrated all political units that controlled land, labor, capital, and distribution into a world economy. The Old World came to the New World quite consistently, although once the ties were made and the nature of the European and U.S. offerings became clear and evident, the indigenous peoples and the ethnically mixed authorities and businessmen of the New World states often solicited aid or programs. Desmond C. M. Platt argues that only after 1860 did U.S. and European economic ties with Latin America grow important and industrial markets more focused, drawing upon non-European labor and land (for raw materials and food) to foster material progress.

The shock waves of the world economic crisis of 1873–1898 persuaded political, business, and military leaders in metropole nations to expand through formal colonialism and informal imperialism in the years between 1870 and 1929. Around 1910, various European thinkers (Vladimir I. Lenin, John Hobson, and Joseph Schumpeter) advanced theories to explain the European expansion of the late nineteenth century. The time period strongly influenced these thoughtful and provocative explanations, which are linked to the question of power and to the economic, social, and strategic consequences of the liberal and Social Darwinian competition of industrial states. This focus upon the economic and strategic aspects of imperialism, however, overlooks an unusually enduring quality of imperialism: It restricted the sovereignty of the subject peoples. While European thinkers and politicians debated the merits of Marxist-Leninist and leftist critiques of European expansion, inhabitants of Latin America were more likely to debate the merits of pursuing European liberalism (most often in a positivist form) or condemning such a course through appeals to cultural nationalism (rooted in either Hispanic or indigenous cultures) or some variation of socialism.

U.S. efforts to plant and nurture the idea of a Western hemisphere became intense in the 1880s, but followed a vacillating course thereafter. U.S. officials cited a special relationship or shared Pan-Americanism, but they have continually encountered significant resistance among parts of all classes of Latin America. The special relationship was less cultural and emotional than fixed to a need for raw materials, markets for production, and investment opportunities. U.S. investment in Latin America rose dramatically from $308 million in 1897 to almost $5.5 billion in 1929. Trade rose almost as spectacularly from about $63 million in the late 1870s to $986 million in 1929. This era saw the rise of the *hispanismo* movement (Spanish efforts to rekindle cultural ties and then economic bonds with Latin America) and anti-Americanism, perhaps best evident in the APRa (Alianza Popular Revolucionaria Americana movement of Peru to redeem "Indo-America" and to resist "Yankee imperialism").

By the early twentieth century much of the world had become colonies of metropole states, and multinational corporations became important actors in local politics. Metropole firms frequently controlled the production and distribution systems (often in enclaves) that drove the political economies in the periphery (those societies lacking most factors of production or unable to control them). Large transnational firms dominated the shipping, transoceanic telegraph cables, maritime services, and marketing operations that serviced Latin America. Other international organizations (dealing in labor, health, legal, cultural, and other matters) developed the capacity to interact with the gigantic firms at the level of the world economy. Through these large transnational institutions, metropole states dominated the political, judicial, social, cultural, labor, and professional organizations of the periphery. Yet eventually Latin American countries began to regulate foreign companies and side with foreign workers, limiting the power of international businesses. Moreover, countries seeking greater autonomy, like Mexico, became adept at playing imperial powers off one another.

### SOCIAL IMPERIALISM

Social imperialism and dependency theory are useful tools for analyzing the international history of Latin America. Social imperialism (defined as metropole policies that ameliorated domestic problems such as labor dissatisfaction, social disorder, and unemployment by transferring them abroad to peripheral states) sheds light on the impulses operating within many metropoles, and dependency theory (which focuses on political sovereignty and economic and social autonomy) illuminates the consequences of metropole intrusions in the periphery.

The historians Bernard Semmel, Hans-Ulrich Wehler, and Thomas McCormick have described social imperialism as a policy through which the metropole hoped to ameliorate domestic social woes and preserve its well-being and security through exploitation of opportunities in the periphery. McCormick has described policies that aimed "to export the social problem" and "to export the unemployment." Policy makers commonly discussed the impact of their foreign relations on their own domestic economy, but they rarely examined the consequences of their policies upon the host peripheral and semiperipheral states.

Social imperialism frequently brought dependent status to the societies on the periphery. Fernando H. Cardoso, Enzo Faletto, André Gunder Frank, and Samir Amin have described *dependencia* well. They have pointed out that metropole development in the competitive world economy required the underdevelopment of the periphery: if the periphery ever became developed, the option to exploit and extract accumulation would dissipate. Dependency theory focuses on the international structure as a means to restrict weaker participants rather than as a system to distribute bilateral justice in the metropole-periphery relationship.

The world economy, of course, is not a static structure, but a dynamic, changing system. Since ancient times, some producers and distributors have recognized that the exchange of commodities over large distances generates a large accumulation of value. The variety of products received from distant interchange by raising popular expectations, redefining the notion of well-being, and expanding the possibilities for accumulation became the motor for economic growth. As some European states applied technology to mass-produce goods and to develop new products, their need for raw materials and food expanded. Pressure grew to incorporate more areas into Europe's accumulation system—its production and distribution network. The European and North American states men, entrepreneurs, and military leaders contemplated the narrow land strip at the Central American isthmus as a key spot in a distribution system encompassing the whole world. This interest in world trade routes explains much of the urgency, intensity, and determination shown by metropole and Latin American geopoliticians, entrepreneurs, and intellectuals in the nineteenth and early twentieth centuries.

In the nineteenth century, informal means did not entirely replace formal imperial control in Latin America. Even after the formal Spanish (ca. 1820s) and Portuguese (1822) rule ended, the European states and the United States pursued political and economic authority in the New World, using formal colonialism or acquisition upon occasion. The British control of the Falkland Islands (1833); the Spanish in Santo Domingo (1862) and the Chincha Islands (1864–1866); the British in the Bay Islands, Belize, and the Mosquito Coast (ca. 1860s); the French in Mexico (1861–1867); and the United States in Puerto Rico (1898), the Virgin Islands (1917), Guantánamo Bay (1898), and the Panama Canal zone (1903–1999) are some examples of formal imperial authority, in an age when power was more commonly exercised through informal means.

By the late nineteenth century, the leaders in the metropoles needed to implement policies of social imperialism and simultaneously to mediate the internal discord arising from the bitter domestic competition during the crisis of comparatively unrestricted laissez-faire industrial capitalism. The mediating order they created was organized (or corporate) capitalism, which developed into a varied body of economic, political, social, and cultural organizations (as well as ideas and common wisdom), many of which formed symbiotic relations to government regulatory agencies (often at the wish of the giant entrepreneurs and financiers). Organized capitalism sought to preserve the image and the rhetoric of a laissez-faire system in order to justify privatization of profit and at the same time institutionalize cartel, oligopolistic, monopolistic, or holding-company arrangements that initially joined government and leaders of the economic sectors, but soon attempted to incorporate leaders of labor and social and cultural movements into cooperative situations.

Abroad, the United States and other metropoles implemented social imperialism through a variety of forms, but the most common forms were multinational corporations, nonbusiness transnational organizations, governmental or quasi-governmental agencies, and private social and cultural bodies. The metropoles provided social overhead capital abroad in the form of diplomatic and consular services, military forces to maintain order, special commissions, experts, subsidies, and tariff and tax advantages, all of which were indirect aid to corporations. These actions could be obscured abroad, and, according to some scholars, the greatly reduced standards of living and lower expectations in the periphery allowed organized capitalism to pursue policies there with smaller sums of money. The corporations and cartels struggled and competed to acquire use of the factors of production in the periphery which would ameliorate their own domestic problems. Scholarship of the late twentieth century, however, has shown a more complicated picture, including the limitations of corporate power. For instance, the Argentine government often sided with Argentine labor unions against the British-owned railroad companies. Also, foreign companies, such as the oil industry in Mexico, paid much higher wages. The interest of foreign powers did not completely align with business goals. As a case in point, the U.S. government never backed the demands of U.S. oil companies for invasion in the 1920s.

Imperialism flourished in an era of intense competition between metropole states. It meant that the Latin American nations—which had limited resource bases, smaller and less educated populations, and less development of capital, communications, and technology—bore some of the burden of metropole unemployment and social disorder in addition to their own problems. Not surprisingly, some of the internal disorder in the Latin American societies derived from their ties to the metropole states. Social imperialism relied upon the power of the informal authority of metropole financial, business, political, and military groups in alliance with compradors—usually members of the bourgeoisie or military on the periphery. The metropole states and the multinational corporations established comprador relations with individuals and groups in Latin America. The compradors had two chief functions: they facilitated the entrance of foreign corporations and political influence, and they managed the domestic order to favor foreign business enterprises.

Compradors normally collaborated with metropole wishes for stability and order to stifle the discontent generated by the loss of sovereignty and the protest of exploited workers. But political repression generated violent and nonviolent resistance, and the ensuing spectacle alienated supporters of democratic and human rights in the metropoles. Metropole officials—under siege because of the outcry against inhumane and undemocratic conduct by the compradors—sought rescue in the quick restoration of order, at times through military intervention, because disorder in the periphery was perceived as a threat to the home country. At times, however, domestic leaders sided with locals. Scholarship on Porfirian Mexico has shown that President Porfirio Díaz promoted domestic industries and labor rights.

Metropole entrepreneurs engaged corrupted laissez-faire ideology—evident in free-trade rhetoric covering government-supported multinational business ventures—to support their competition for land, labor, markets, and communication routes. This competition was clothed in strategic, political, social, and cultural language to reinforce the home countries' determination to assure maximum access to the capacity of Latin America and isthmian transit to generate wealth and security by linking the Atlantic and Pacific half-worlds.

The evidence for Western world extraction of value from Latin America changed in character over time, but it is overwhelming. There was capital in flight from Latin America's elite, extracted as profit or controlled by European-U.S.-Japanese investors when left in Latin America; labor was exploited but scarcely educated or trained; land and resources were exhausted, used, or controlled; communications (both domestic and international) were dominated; technology and research were stifled or located abroad. These forms of economic exploitation continue after five hundred years of European and North American contact with Latin America. In addition, the sovereignty of these states is still subject to foreign interference, as has been evident in U.S. activity in Guatemala (1954), Cuba (since 1961), the Dominican Republic (1964), Chile (1973–1974), Grenada (1983), Nicaragua (1981–1990), Panama (1991), and Haiti (1992–1994).

*See also* **Encomienda; Monroe Doctrine; Repartimiento.**


BIBLIOGRAPHY

Marvin Harris, *Patterns of Race in the Americas* (1964).

Stanley J. Stein and Barbara H. Stein, *The Colonial Heritage of Latin America: Essays on Economic Dependence in Perspective* (1970).

Fernando Henrique Cardoso and Enzo Faletto, *Dependency and Development in Latin America*, translated by Marjory Mattingly (1979).

James D. Cockcroft, André Gunder Frank, and Dale L. Johnson, *Dependence and Underdevelopment: Latin America's Political Economy* (1972).

Ariel Dorfman and Armand Mattelart, *Para leer al pato donald: comunicación de masa y colonialismo* (1972).

Desmond C. M. Platt, *Latin America and British Trade, 1806–1914* (1972).

Immanuel Wallerstein, *The Modern World System* (3 vols; 1974–1988).

Ciro F. S. Cardoso and Héctor Pérez Brignoli, *Centro América y la economía occidental (1520–1930)* (1977).

Fernand Braudel, *Civilisation matérielle, économie et capitalisme, xv^e–xviii^e siècle* (3 vols.; 1979), translated as *The Structures of Everyday Life, the Wheels of Commerce,* and *The Perspective of the World* (1984).

Tony Smith, *The Pattern of Imperialism: The United States, Great Britain, and the Late-Industrializing World Since 1815* (1981).

Ronald H. Chilcote and Joel C. Edelstein, eds., *Latin America: Capitalist and Socialist Perspectives of Development and Underdevelopment* (1986).

Peter Klarén and Thomas J. Bossert, eds., *Promise of Development: Theories of Change in Latin America* (1986).

E. Bradford Burns, *Latin America: A Concise Interpretive History,* 5th ed. (1990).

*Additional Bibliography*

Baskes, Jeremy. *Indians, Merchants, and Markets: A Reinterpretation of the Repartimiento and Spanish-Indian Economic Relations in Colonial Oaxaca, 1750–1821.* Stanford, CA: Stanford University Press, 2000.

Castro, Daniel. *Another Face of Empire: Bartolomé De Las Casas, Indigenous Rights, and Ecclesiastical Imperialism.* Durham, NC: Duke University Press, 2007.

Daniels, Christine, and Michael V. Kennedy. *Negotiated Empires: Centers and Peripheries in the Americas, 1500–1820.* New York: Routledge, 2002.

Grandin, Greg. *Empire's Workshop: Latin America, the United States, and the Rise of the New Imperialism.* New York: Metropolitan Books, 2006.

Joseph, G. M., Catherine LeGrand, and Ricardo Donato Salvatore. *Close Encounters of Empire. Writing the Cultural History of U.S.-Latin American Relations.* Durham, NC: Duke University Press, 1998.

Mitchell, Nancy. *The Danger of Dreams: German and American Imperialism in Latin America.* Chapel Hill: University of North Carolina Press, 1999.

Petras, James F., and Víctor Hugo Porto Carrero, et al. *América Latina: Imperialismo, recolonialización y resistencia.* Quito, Ecuador: Ediciones Abya Yala, 2004.

Schoonover, Thomas David. *Germany in Central America: Competitive Imperialism, 1821–1929.* Tuscaloosa: University of Alabama Press, 1998.


THOMAS SCHOONOVER

---

**INCAS, THE.** When the Spanish conquistadores arrived in Peru in 1532, they found the major part of Andean South America under control of the empire of Tahuantinsuyu. The ethnic group that ruled this empire was known as the Incas, and their emperor was the Sapa Inca. Between 1438 and 1532 the Incas expanded their domain throughout the Andean region of modern Ecuador, Peru, Bolivia, northern Chile, and northwestern Argentina. They transformed the terrain through massive public works of engineering and architecture, and restructured society through social engineering. In the process, the Incas accumulated great wealth that eventually filled the coffers of the Spanish Empire. Inca domination of the Andes was brought to an end by the Spanish conquest led by Francisco Pizarro in 1532.

## HISTORY

Inca history during the reigns of the emperors who preceded the Inca Pachacuti had been known largely from myths and legends. More recently archeologists have suggested that the Incas grew out of and on top of the Huari civilization. But it is the mythology and colonial chronicles that are best known. These accounts tell that around 1200 a small band of highlanders migrated into the valley of Cuzco in the southern Peruvian sierra. Over the next few centuries, the huge empire of the Inca was to spring from this small group. According to Inca legends, their place of origin was the town of Pacaritambo, a few miles southwest of Cuzco, where their ancestors had come forth into the world from three caves. This original group was led by the first Inca or ruler, Manco Capac, and was comprised of his three brothers and four sisters. After many adventures, Manco led his small band into the valley of Cuzco, where they established themselves by force of arms and brought order and civilization. Other stories held the place of origin to be an island in Lake Titicaca, south of Cuzco, from which the Incas were led by Manco north to the valley of Cuzco. Yet other accounts combined these two legends into one, having the Incas migrating underground from Lake Titicaca to Pacaritambo, where they emerged from the caves of origin.

Following their arrival in Cuzco, the Incas slowly increased their influence through intermarriage and by military raids against their neighbors during the reigns of the second through seventh Incas (Sinchi Roca, Lloque Yupanqui, Mayta Capac, Capac Yupanqui, Inca Roca, and Yahuar Huacac). The city of Cuzco probably grew from a preexisting settlement, but through the reign of the eighth Inca, it was little more than an ordinary Andean highland town. The turning point in the history of the city and the Incas themselves was the great Chanca war near the end of the reign of Inca Viracocha (1438). By this time, the Incas had increased their domain to include the whole of the valley of Cuzco, including the Oropesa and Lucre basins, and a large part of the neighboring Yucay valley. A powerful warlike confederation known as the Chanca began to expand to the south, probably from the Ayacucho basin, the earlier Huari imperial seat. Cuzco was threatened and the Inca forces very nearly defeated. The Inca Viracocha abandoned the city and fled to the neighboring valley, but at the last moment one of the royal sons, Inca Yupanqui, rallied the Inca armies and, in a heroic effort, defeated the Chanca forces. Following this victory he deposed his father, whose failure to defend Cuzco was viewed as a disgrace. Inca Yupanqui took the name Pachacuti and assumed the throne to become the first of the great Inca emperors and the first to be considered a true historical personage.

### PACHACUTI INCA

The name Pachacuti (or Pachacutec, as it is sometimes given in the chronicles) means "he who shakes the earth" or "cataclysm" in Quechua, the language of the Incas. It was an appropriate name for a man who literally reorganized the Inca world. His first acts as emperor included subduing the neighboring peoples in the Cuzco region. Whereas they had previously been associated rather loosely with the Incas, mostly by persuasion and family ties, they were now firmly brought under control as vassals of the lords of Cuzco. Pachacuti then launched a series of conquests that rapidly transformed what had been the tiny Inca domain into an expanding empire. He conquered large areas of the sierra, moving north into the central Peruvian highlands and south to the shores of Lake Titicaca. He also turned his attention to reorganizing and rebuilding the city of Cuzco and designing the empire.

Pachacuti set himself the task of reconstructing Cuzco as a suitable capital for the empire he envisioned. The city was constructed in the form of a puma, incorporating the fortress–temple of Sacsayhuaman as its head. The body was comprised of residential buildings and palaces laid out in a grid between the Tullumayo and Saphi rivers. Like so many New World peoples, the Incas held felines, especially the puma or mountain lion, to be sacred. The basic building unit of the city plan was an architectural form called the *cancha,* which was comprised of a series of small houses arranged within a rectangular enclosure. The *cancha* form and the grid plan of the city may have been derived from the old Huari imperial administrative center of Pikillacta, located in the lower end of the valley of Cuzco. Other architectural features, such as the double-jamb doorway, are seen earlier in the imperial style of Tiahuanaco. However, the distinctive style of stone working for which Inca architecture is justly famous, was purely a creation of the Incas. So skilled were their masons that walls laid without mortar achieved a near perfect fit between stones.

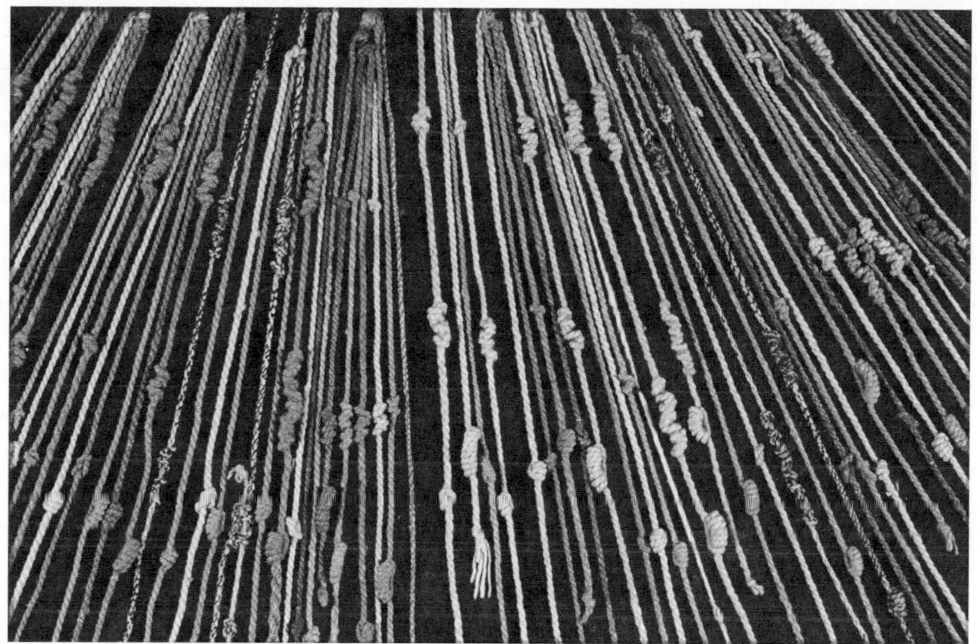

**Quipu.** These knotted cords were used as accounting devices by Incan officials. Although quipu originated in pre-Incan societies, the Inca perfected the system; Incan quipu specialists were known as *quipukamayuq*. THE ART ARCHIVE/ARCHAEOLOGICAL MUSEUM LIMA/MIREILLE VAUTIER. REPRODUCED BY PERMISSION OF THE PICTURE DESK INC.

The city of Cuzco was conceived as the center of the empire where the four quarters into which it was divided came symbolically and physically together. Four highways, one coming from each of the four quarters (*suyus*) converged in the great central plaza of the city. From this four-part division the empire took its name of Tahuantinsuyu, meaning "the land of four quarters."

In addition to rebuilding Cuzco, Pachacuti initiated building projects in the environs of Cuzco and on his royal estates in the Urubamba valley. The most famous of these is the "lost city" of Macchu Picchu; he also built royal estates at Ollantaytambo, Patallacta, and many smaller sites in the valley.

Other building projects initiated by Pachacuti included the famous royal highway of the Inca. It provided for communication within the expanding empire and supplied a means of rapidly moving the army wherever it was needed. Following and expanding the routes of the old highways of the earlier Huari empire, standardized highways, often walled and paved, linked the various regions of the growing empire to Cuzco. Storehouses (*qolqa*) and rest stops (*tambos*) were built to provision and serve the army as it marched. A system of relay runners (*chasqui*) formed an effective postal system for the transmission of verbal messages and instructions. Towns and provincial administrative centers were built by Pachacuti and his successors in the various conquered territories as the empire expanded.

### TOPA INCA

Pachacuti's son, Topa Inca, succeeded him as emperor in 1471 and continued to expand the empire. Topa Inca moved the imperial frontier north into what is now Ecuador and south into what is now Bolivia, northern Chile, and northwestern Argentina. By 1476 he had achieved the conquest of the Chimú, the last serious rivals for total control of the Andean area. The absorption of the Chimú had an important impact on Inca art, especially on goldwork. Chimú artisans were brought to the capital at Cuzco to create golden vessels for the royalty. On the north coast, a hybrid Chimú-Inca art style developed with stylistic elements from both cultures. Topa Inca reigned until 1493 and was succeeded by his son Huayna Capac.

### HUAYNA CAPAC

Huayna Capac continued to expand the boundaries of the empire to the north and east, incorporating much of what is modern Ecuador and the northeastern Peruvian Andes. Compared with his father, however, his conquests were modest. Huayna Capac spent so much time on his difficult northern campaign that severe strains began to grow in the social fabric of the empire. He was absent for many years at a time. Surrogates had to stand in for him at important festivals and ceremonies, and the people of Cuzco began to feel out of touch with their emperor. A new and potentially rival court grew up around him at his northern headquarters at Tomebamba in Ecuador. Administratively the empire had become difficult to govern. Decisions from the emperor took a long time to reach Cuzco and even longer to be disseminated to the rest of the empire. Controlling the far-flung outposts of empire became increasingly difficult.

A severe crisis finally came when Huayna Capac suddenly died of what may have been smallpox in 1527. The disease, introduced by Europeans, preceded the Spanish conquistadores as they journeyed across South America. Thousands died in a very short space of time, including Huayna Capac's appointed heir, who survived his father by only a few days. The confusion about the succession created even more strain on Inca society, and finally a civil war broke out between two brothers who were rival claimants for the throne.

### HUASCAR AND ATAHUALPA

Huascar, one of the two rival brothers, had succeeded to the throne in Cuzco in 1527. He was challenged by Atahualpa, who had been with his father and the imperial army in Ecuador at the time of Huayna Capac's death. A large part of the army rallied behind Atahualpa, and a bloody war ensued. The forces of Atahualpa, which took the city of Cuzco in 1532, eventually prevailed. Huascar was captured and imprisoned.

As Atahualpa moved south to Cuzco with a large army, he was met by the Spanish forces led by Francisco Pizarro at the town of Cajamarca in the northern highlands. In a stunning surprise move, Pizarro and his small band of 168 men attacked and captured Atahualpa in the midst of his huge army (November 1532). Pizarro held the emperor captive for nearly eight months, waiting for the ransom that would secure Atahualpa's release. The emperor had offered to fill a room once with golden objects and twice with silver. This treasure chamber measured twenty-two feet by seventeen feet and was filled to a height of over eight feet. In all, almost eleven tons of treasure was collected throughout the empire and sent to Cajamarca. While he was in captivity, Atahualpa had secretly sent orders to have the Inca Huascar killed. He eliminated his rival, but to no avail, since he himself was killed by the Spaniards shortly thereafter, in July 1533. With the death of Atahualpa, the last of the independent Inca rulers had fallen. The Incas continued to resist the Spanish for many years thereafter, but the Inca Empire ceased to exist.

### INCA SOCIETY

Most of what is known of Inca society is based on the Spanish chronicles, some of which were eyewitness accounts. Inca history viewed the great emperor Pachacuti as the founding genius of the Inca state. His reconstruction of the Inca capital coincided with a complete reorganization of Inca society. At the apex was the emperor himself, called the Sapa Inca, and the noble families of pure Inca blood. This lineage or extended family owned the empire. All of the important governmental posts, the governors of each of the four quarters of the empire, the army, and the religious institutions were held by pure-blooded Incas. There were never more than about 500 adult males, and perhaps 1,800 people in all who carried pure Inca blood. Below them were the Incas by adoption, or Hahua Incas, comprised of neighboring peoples held in high enough esteem by the pure-blood Incas to be trusted with important positions when there were not enough royal Incas to fill these posts.

Below these were provincial nobility, who were local ethnic lords confirmed by the Inca administration. At the bottom of the social pyramid were the *hatun runa* (big men), the common heads of households (the family being the basic taxpaying unit). *Hatun runa* were organized in groups of 10, 50, 100, 500, 1,000, 5,000, and 10,000 families for administrative purposes. Each decimal division had an official responsible for its administration. This organization was the key to the success of the empire. Each family provided a set amount of labor or service to the state rather than wealth in the form of material goods. The state, in turn, used this labor to generate wealth through

**Planting corn.** Incan agriculture, as portrayed by Felipe Guaman Poma de Ayala, late 16th century. THE GRANGER COLLECTION, NEW YORK

the production of goods, cultivation of lands, construction projects, or military conquest of new territory.

The social organization of the empire was based on a complex series of reciprocal obligations between the rulers and the ruled. Taxes were paid to the imperial government in labor service by the *hatun runa*. In return, the government provided social services to protect the population in times of want and natural disaster. Food and other goods were collected and stored to form a surplus for use during times of drought or famine. Some income from government lands was set aside for widows and orphans. Maize beer and food were provided for ritual feasting on holidays. The imperial government ensured that every citizen was fed and clothed.

## INCA RELIGION

Pachacuti organized Inca religion into an imperial institution. The major gods of the various peoples incorporated into the empire were included in the Inca pantheon, and appropriate temples and shrines for them were built and maintained. In addition to the Inca patron, Inti the sun god, there were Illapa, the god of thunder; Pachamama, the earth-mother goddess; Mamacocha, the sea goddess; and Mamaquilla, the moon goddess. Above all was Viracocha, the great creator deity of the Andean peoples. In a separate category were deities called Huacas, animistic spirits that inhabited everything in nature. Their specific manifestations occurred in mountain peaks, unusual natural phenomena, odd-shaped stone outcrops, mummies, and stone idols.

Inca religion emphasized ritual and organization rather than mysticism or spirituality. Religious rites focused chiefly on ensuring the food supply and curing disease. Divination was also of considerable importance. The Incas maintained an elaborate ritual calendar of public ceremonies and festivals, most associated with stages in the agricultural cycle such as plowing, planting, and harvesting. Others were related to solstice observations, puberty rites, and new year celebrations.

Inca society was highly stratified, and upward mobility was very limited. The only way in which a person could improve his position was through success as a warrior or by being attached as a servant to an important noble household or being selected as an *aclla* (chosen woman). The state controlled most aspects of the lives of its citizens, and a strict code of law applied more harshly to the nobility than to the commoners. Travel and dress were strictly regulated; no one could move about the empire or change from his native costume without the state's permission. The basic social unit beyond the immediate biological family was called the Ayllu. Land was held communally by the members of the *ayllu*, and decisions were often taken collectively.

Inca culture was the culmination of thousands of years of Andean civilization. From their predecessors they had inherited a body of statecraft and much of the physical infrastructure for the empire. This does not in any way diminish their achievement, however. It was the peculiar Inca genius for organization that allowed them to make profitable use of their cultural inheritance. They alone of the late Andean societies were able to weave together the disparate elements of the many Andean cultures through military prowess and extraordinary statecraft, and through drawing on thousands of years of cultural inheritance. In terms of geographical extension, military power, and political organization, the Inca created the greatest of the pre-Columbian empires.

*See also* **Archaeology; Ayllu; Cuzco; Indigenous Peoples; Inti; Machu Picchu; Mamaquilla; Precontact History: Andean Region.**

BIBLIOGRAPHY

The best single source for Inca culture and history is in the classic article by John H. Rowe, "Inca Culture at the Time of the Spanish Conquest," in *Handbook of South American Indians,* vol. 2 (1946), pp. 183–330. Additional sources include Burr Cartwright Brundage, *The Empire of the Inca* (1963) and *The Lords of Cuzco: A History and Description of the Inca People in Their Final Days* (1967). The definitive study of the Inca economy is John Victor Murra, *The Economic Organization of the Inca State* (1980). On the Spanish conquest, see John Hemming, *The Conquest of the Incas* (1970). For a discussion of Inca origin myths, see Gary Urton, *The History of a Myth: Pacariqtambo and the Origin of the Incas* (1990). The two most important and accessible Spanish chronicles are *The Incas of Pedro de Cieza de León,* translated by Harriet de Onís (1959); Bernabé Cobo, *History of the Inca Empire,* translated by Roland Hamilton (1979). One chronicle written from an Incan perspective is Garcilaso de la Vega, el Inca's *Royal Commentaries of the Incas and General History of Peru* (2006) and another, from a Quechuan but non-Inca perspective is Felipe Guamán Poma de Ayala's *Nueva corónica y buen gobierno* (2005).

### *Additional Bibliography*

Bauer, Brian S. *Ancient Cuzco: Heartland of the Inca.* Joe R. and Teresa Lozano Long series in Latin American and Latino art and culture. Austin: University of Texas Press, 2004.

Covey, R. Alan. *How the Incas Built Their Heartland: State Formation and the Innovation of Imperial Strategies in the Sacred Valley, Peru. History, Languages, and Cultures of the Spanish and Portuguese Worlds.* Ann Arbor: University of Michigan Press, 2006.

Ramirez, Susan Elizabeth *To Feed and Be Fed: The Cosmological Bases of Authority and Identity in the Andes.* Stanford, CA: Stanford University Press, 2005.

Rostworowski de Diez Canseco, María. *Historia del Tahuantinsuyu.* Lima: IEP, Instituto de Estudios Peruanos, 1999.

GORDON F. MCEWAN

## INCHÁUSTEGUI CABRAL, HÉCTOR

(1912–1979). Héctor Incháustegui Cabral (*b.* 25 July 1912; *d.* 5 September 1979), Dominican poet. Born in Baní, Incháustegui Cabral wrote a sort of social poetry that ranges from raw identification with the disinherited to meditations on love, death, and mankind's relationship to God. He is best known for *Poemas de una sola angustia* (1940). His poetic texts appear in *Obra poética completa: 1940–1976* (1978), published by the Universidad Católica Madre y Maestra, where he taught literature for many years. The verse novel *Muerte en el Edén* (1951); the autobiography *El pozo muerto* (1960); two collections of essays on Dominican writers; three plays in verse based on ancient Athenian themes; and the novel *La sombra del tamarindo* (1984), which appeared posthumously, complete his vast production. A diplomat and public official during the dictatorship of his friend, Rafael Trujillo, Incháustegui Cabral held prestigious government positions throughout his life. Despite his association with the Trujillo regime, his literary legacy has been highly regarded by subsequent generations of Dominican writers.

*See also* **Trujillo Molina, Rafael Leónidas.**

BIBLIOGRAPHY

José Alcántara Almánzar, *Estudios de poesía dominicana* and *Imágenes de Héctor Incháustegui Cabral,* in Contemporáneos 2 (1980).

Angel Flores, "Héctor Incháustegui Cabral," in *Spanish American Authors: The Twentieth Century* (1992).

### *Additional Bibliography*

Espina, Eduardo. "Entre la isla y el cielo: la poesía socio-religiosa de Incháustegui Cabral." *Revista Iberoamericana* 54 (January-March 1988): 187–197.

SILVIO TORRES- SAILLANT

## INCOME DISTRIBUTION.

The term *income distribution* is normally used to describe the process that directly determines the division of income and indirectly provides an indication of the division of consumption, saving, and welfare. The two-way relationship between income distribution and development in Latin America has been complex and ever-changing. An examination of the

**Relative distribution of per capita household income in Latin America and the Caribbean**

| Country | Year | Lowest 20 percent | Second quintile | Third quintile | Fourth quintile | Highest 20 percent | Highest 10 percent |
|---|---|---|---|---|---|---|---|
| Argentina | 1989 | 4.1 | 8.6 | 13.3 | 21.3 | 52.6 | 35.9 |
| Bolivia | 1989 | 3.5 | 7.7 | 12.0 | 19.3 | 57.5 | 41.2 |
| Brazil | 1989 | 2.1 | 4.9 | 8.9 | 16.8 | 67.5 | 51.3 |
| Chile | 1989 | 3.7 | 6.8 | 10.3 | 16.2 | 62.9 | 48.9 |
| Colombia | 1989 | 3.4 | 7.3 | 11.7 | 19.2 | 58.3 | 41.8 |
| Costa Rica | 1989 | 4.0 | 9.1 | 14.3 | 21.9 | 40.8 | 34.1 |
| Dominican Republic | 1989 | 4.2 | 7.9 | 12.5 | 19.7 | 55.6 | 39.6 |
| Ecuador | 1987 | 5.4 | 9.4 | 13.7 | 21.0 | 50.5 | 34.6 |
| El Salvador | 1990 | 4.5 | 9.4 | 14.5 | 21.7 | 50.0 | 33.6 |
| Guatemala | 1989 | 2.2 | 6.0 | 10.7 | 18.7 | 62.4 | 45.9 |
| Honduras | 1989 | 2.7 | 6.0 | 10.2 | 17.4 | 63.5 | 47.9 |
| Jamaica | 1989 | 5.1 | 9.5 | 14.4 | 22.0 | 49.2 | 32.5 |
| Mexico | 1989 | 3.9 | 7.7 | 12.1 | 19.3 | 57.0 | 41.3 |
| Panama | 1989 | 2.0 | 6.3 | 11.6 | 20.3 | 59.8 | 42.2 |
| Paraguay | 1990 | 5.9 | 10.5 | 14.9 | 22.6 | 46.1 | 29.5 |
| Peru | 1990 | 5.6 | 9.8 | 14.0 | 20.2 | 50.4 | 35.1 |
| Uruguay | 1989 | 5.4 | 10.0 | 14.7 | 21.5 | 48.3 | 32.6 |
| Venezuela | 1989 | 4.8 | 9.5 | 14.4 | 21.9 | 49.5 | 33.2 |

SOURCE: Calculated from statistics in Annex 3 of George Psacharopoulos et al., *Poverty and Income Distribution in Latin America: The Story of the 1980s* (Washington, D.C.: World Bank, Latin America, and the Caribbean, Technical Department, Regional Studies Program, Report No. 27, Revised June 1993).

**Table 1**

relative, factoral, sectoral, and other aspects of the distribution of income and the issue of poverty yields a multitude of information on the absolute and relative welfare of Latin Americans and of the forces behind it.

*Relative income distribution* (referring to personal or household income) represents purchasing power over commodities (goods and services) and thus provides an indirect measure of relative consumption, saving, welfare, and well-being of people in Latin America. *Factoral distribution of income* (class or functional income) focuses on the welfare of persons as determined by the prices of the labor, land, and capital services—wages, rent, and interest-profit—they offer in the market. It also focuses on the relationship between the price of these factor services and their supply, especially skilled labor and capital, which ultimately determine total output and welfare. Until the 1960s most research focused on the forces determining the distribution of income between the labor and capitalist classes and their respective wage and profit income shares. Since the 1970s research has focused almost exclusively on the nature and determinants of the relative distribution of income and poverty. *Sectoral distribution of income* focuses on the welfare of people as determined, in a derived way, by the output value of the sectors (agriculture, mining, industry, finance, education, trade, transport, government, and other services) in which their incomes are generated.

## RELATIVE DISTRIBUTION OF TOTAL INCOME

Have a few families received most of the income in Latin America or has there actually been little inequality? Has the distribution of income been more or less unequal in Latin America than in other regions? The relative distribution of income (wealth or consumption)—the terms *size, personal,* and *household* distribution have also been widely used—deals with the distribution of a mass of income (wealth, consumption) among the members of a set of economic units (families, households, individuals) considering either the total income (wealth, consumption) of each economic unit or its disaggregation by source of income, such as wages and salaries, property income, self-employment income (or by type of consumption, such as individual, semipublic, or collective; or wealth, such as land, home equity, financial assets).

The relative distribution of income typically presents percentage income shares of *deciles* (tenths) or *quintiles* (fifths) of the total population of households, families, or individuals. Table 1 presents, in quintiles, the relative distribution of per capita household income in Latin America and the Caribbean, primarily in 1989. The distribution of income can be considered as being highly unequal if the income share of the poorest 20 percent is less than 3.0 percent or if the income share of the lowest 40 percent is less than 12 percent. According to the first criterion, relative income distribution was highly unequal in Brazil, Guatemala, Honduras, and Panama. If the second criterion is used, the distribution of income was also highly unequal in Chile, Colombia, and Mexico. The lowest degree of inequality is found in Paraguay and Uruguay. (All tables in this entry provide snapshot pictures, not lifetime reels, of inequality and absolute poverty. Lifetime mobility between income groups is ignored. For a detailed examination of limitations of these household-survey-based statistics, see Markos Mamalakis' 1999 paper, "Distributional Mobility and Justice in Latin America: Macro, Meso and Micro Issues.")

The relative distribution of income is, most frequently, visually illustrated by the so-called Lorenz curve and numerically measured by the related Gini coefficient of income concentration. The Lorenz curve, devised by the statistician Max Lorenz, is an ingenious device most widely used to graphically demonstrate and analyze the relative distribution of income (wealth, consumption). The Lorenz curve is a graph of the cumulative percentage of income (wealth, consumption) received (owned) by the cumulative percentage of population (families, households, individuals) arranged from the poorest to the richest. The difference between this graph and the line of perfect equality (the diagonal between the two corners of the square in which the Lorenz curve is graphed) is a visual illustration of the degree of inequality of an income (wealth, consumption) distribution.

In their 1993 study, George Psacharopoulos and colleagues present Lorenz curves of the income distribution in most Latin American and Caribbean (LAC) countries, primarily in 1989 but also in a few preceding years. (The most comprehensive study of relative distribution and poverty in Latin America in the 1980s, this study, and consequently also the materials in this entry, has the same limitations as the household surveys on which it is based.) Figure 1 presents the Lorenz curve of the per capita household income distribution in Brazil during the fourth quarter of 1989, along with the underlying statistics. These statistics show that the lowest 10 percent of the population received 0.7 percent of per capita household income, the lowest 20 percent received 2.1 percent, the lowest 40 percent received 7.0 percent, the lowest 60 percent received 15.9 percent, and so on, until the lowest 100 percent received 100 percent of income. These points are then plotted on figure 1 to show the Lorenz curve of income distribution. The Psacharopoulos study contains a comprehensive analysis and bibliography of the vast number of studies of the relative distribution of income and consumption in Latin America in the pre-1990

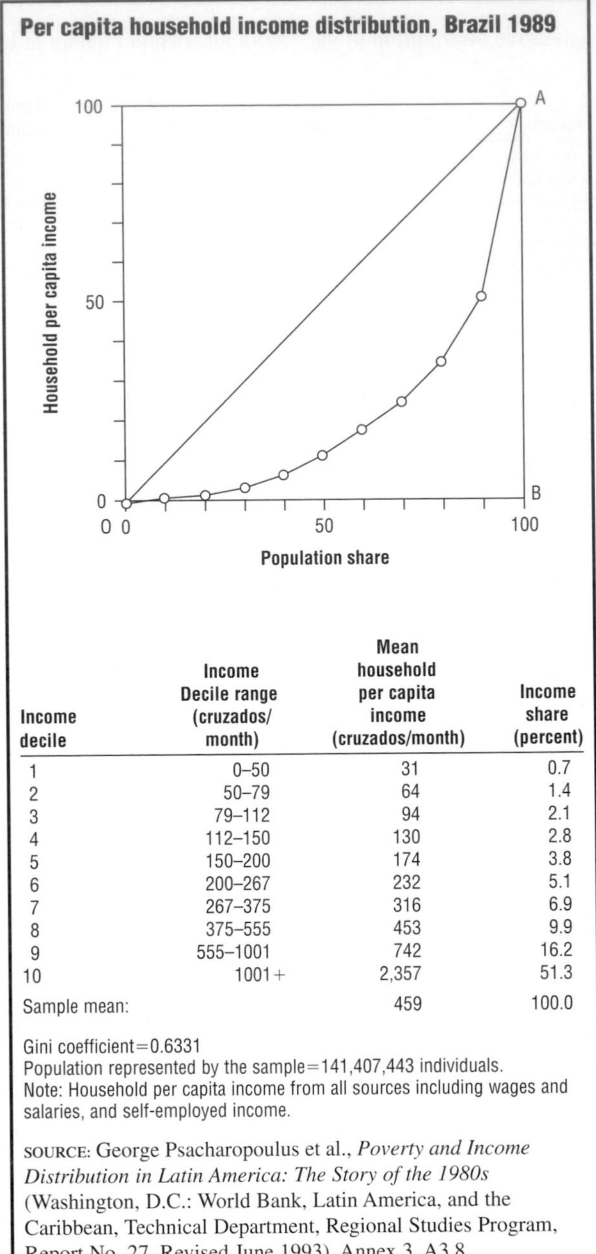


| Income decile | Income Decile range (cruzados/ month) | Mean household per capita income (cruzados/month) | Income share (percent) |
|---|---|---|---|
| 1 | 0–50 | 31 | 0.7 |
| 2 | 50–79 | 64 | 1.4 |
| 3 | 79–112 | 94 | 2.1 |
| 4 | 112–150 | 130 | 2.8 |
| 5 | 150–200 | 174 | 3.8 |
| 6 | 200–267 | 232 | 5.1 |
| 7 | 267–375 | 316 | 6.9 |
| 8 | 375–555 | 453 | 9.9 |
| 9 | 555–1001 | 742 | 16.2 |
| 10 | 1001+ | 2,357 | 51.3 |
| Sample mean: | | 459 | 100.0 |

Gini coefficient=0.6331
Population represented by the sample=141,407,443 individuals.
Note: Household per capita income from all sources including wages and salaries, and self-employed income.

SOURCE: George Psacharopoulus et al., *Poverty and Income Distribution in Latin America: The Story of the 1980s* (Washington, D.C.: World Bank, Latin America, and the Caribbean, Technical Department, Regional Studies Program, Report No. 27, Revised June 1993), Annex 3, A3.8.

**Figure 1**

**Gini coefficient and bottom 20 percent share of income at the individual level, Latin America and the Caribbean, 1980, 1989**

| Country | Year of survey | | Gini coefficient | | % share of income of bottom 20% of population | |
|---|---|---|---|---|---|---|
| | | | Circa 1980 (or earliest) | Circa 1989 (or latest) | Circa 1980 (or earliest) | Circa 1989 (or latest) |
| Argentina (Buenos Aires) | 1980 | 1989 | 0.408 | 0.476 | 5.3 | 4.2 |
| Bolivia (urban) | 1986 | 1989 | 0.516 | 0.525 | 3.9 | 3.5 |
| Brazil | 1979 | 1989 | 0.594 | 0.633 | 2.6 | 2.1 |
| Chile | N/A | 1989 | N/A | 0.573 | N/A | 3.7 |
| Colombia (urban) | 1980 | 1989 | 0.585 | 0.532 | 2.5 | 3.4 |
| Costa Rica | 1981 | 1989 | 0.475 | 0.460 | 3.3 | 4.0 |
| Dom. Republic | N/A | 1989 | N/A | 0.503 | N/A | 4.2 |
| Ecuador (urban) | N/A | 1987 | N/A | 0.445 | N/A | 5.4 |
| El Salvador (urban) | N/A | 1990 | N/A | 0.448 | N/A | 4.5 |
| Guatemala | 1986–1987 | 1989 | 0.579 | 0.587 | 2.7 | 2.2 |
| Honduras[a] | 1986 | 1989 | 0.549 | 0.501 | 3.2 | 2.8 |
| Jamaica[b] | N/A | 1989 | N/A | 0.435 | N/A | 5.1 |
| Mexico | 1984 | 1989 | 0.506 | 0.519 | 4.1 | 3.9 |
| Panama | 1979 | 1989 | 0.488 | 0.565 | 3.9 | 2.0 |
| Paraguay (Asunción) | 1983 | 1990 | 0.451 | 0.398 | 4.9 | 5.9 |
| Peru (Lima)[b] | 1985–1986 | 1990 | 0.428 | 0.438 | 6.2 | 5.7 |
| Uruguay (urban) | 1981 | 1989 | 0.436 | 0.424 | 4.9 | 5.4 |
| Venezuela | 1981 | 1989 | 0.428 | 0.441 | 5.0 | 4.8 |

Note: Individual income has been calculated by dividing household income by the number of individuals in the household.
[a]Results are not strictly comparable due to differences in geographical coverage between the 1986 and 1989 surveys. The Gini coefficient based on urban households only for Honduras 1989 is 0.556 while the bottom 20 percent income share is 3.5 percent.
[b]Based on consumption data.

SOURCE: George Psacharopoulos et al., *Poverty and Income Distribution in Latin America: The Story of the 1980s* (Washington, D.C.: World Bank, Latin America, and the Caribbean, Technical Department, Regional Studies Program, Report No. 27, Revised June 1993), p. 18.

**Table 2**

decades. It also describes and uses other, less common, measures of the relative distribution of total as well as workers' income.

The straight line between $O$ and $A$ is called the line of perfect equality, or the egalitarian line. If the Lorenz curve coincides with the egalitarian line, it means that each unit receives the same income (wealth, consumption), which is the case of perfect equality of incomes (wealth, consumption). In the case of perfect inequality of incomes (wealth, consumption), the Lorenz curve coincides with $OA$ and $AB$, which implies that all income (wealth, consumption) is received (owned) by only one unit. Because the Lorenz curve displays the deviation of each individual income (wealth, consumption) from perfect equality, it graphically captures, in a sense, the essence of inequality. The closer the Lorenz curve is to the line of perfect equality, the more equal the distribution of income (wealth, consumption) will be. The further the Lorenz curve is from the line of perfect equality, the more unequal the distribution of income (wealth, consumption) will be.

The Lorenz curve presented in Figure 1 is far below the diagonal $OA$ line of perfect equality, thus revealing a highly unequal relative distribution of income in Brazil. The richest 20 percent of households received 67.5 percent of total income, while the poorest 60 percent of households received only 15.9 percent of total income.

The most commonly used summary measure of distributional inequality is the Gini coefficient, which is defined as the ratio of the area enclosed between the 45-degree line of perfect equality and the Lorenz curve to the area of the entire triangle enclosed by the 45-degree line. The closer the Lorenz curve is to the diagonal, the closer the ratio of this area to the area below the diagonal would be to zero. At the same time, the farther the Lorenz curve dips away from the line of perfect equality, the greater the area between the two and the closer the ratio of this area and all the area enclosed by the 45-degree line will be to 1. Hence, a Gini coefficient closer to zero indicates greater equality in a distribution, whereas one closer to 1 represents greater inequality in a distribution.

According to many scholars and studies, Latin America has historically exhibited a high degree of inequality in the relative distribution of income and consumption in comparison with the rest of the world. For example, according to a joint study by the World Bank and the International Labor Office (ILO) (cited by Psacharopoulos et al., p. 19), for years during the 1970s, and in some cases the 1960s, twenty non-Latin American and Caribbean countries had a mean Gini coefficient of 0.39 and a mean bottom 20 percent income share of 6.5 percent of total income. In comparison, the three LAC countries in the World Bank/ILO study had a mean Gini coefficient of 0.52 and a mean bottom 20 percent income share of 3.1 percent of total income. Furthermore, the LAC countries in the Psacharopoulos study had a mean 1989 Gini coefficient of 0.50 and a mean bottom 20 percent income share of 4.0 percent of total income. Thus, although the World Bank/ILO study was based on data from the 1960s and the 1970s, the disparities that they find between LAC countries and non-LAC countries continued to hold true and may even have increased in the 1980s. During that decade, according to the Psacharopoulos study, and the statistics presented in Table 2, the relative distribution of income, as measured by the Gini coefficient, became more unequal in Argentina (Buenos Aires), Bolivia (urban), Brazil, Guatemala, Honduras, Mexico, Panama, Peru (Lima), and Venezuela; it improved, however, in Colombia (urban), Costa Rica, Paraguay (Asunción), and Uruguay (urban). In 1989 the degree of inequality was highest in Brazil and lowest in Paraguay.

No consensus exists, however, that the relative distribution of income in Latin America has been unusually high in the 1960s and 1970s. According to Miguel Urrutia's 1993 study, Brazil, Colombia, Mexico, and Peru appear to have had high degrees of concentration of relative distribution of income in the 1970s, but these rates were not too different from those found after the first phase of industrialization in England and Wales or Denmark. Because the explanations of the high inequality in relative income distribution are similar to those offered about poverty, they are discussed together in subsequent sections.

### RELATIVE DISTRIBUTION OF LABOR INCOME

Few characteristics of Latin American economies stand out as much as the pervasive inequality in the relative (size, personal) distribution of labor income—that is, compensation of employees. Ever since the end of the colonial era, the high inequality in the relative distribution of total income has coincided with an equally pronounced high inequality in the relative distribution of labor income, that is, wages and salaries.

There have been poor, middle, and rich workers, and the income differences among them have been vast. The average income of the richest workers (top decile) was 89 times the average income of the poorest workers (bottom decile) in Colombia in 1980 but only 29 times in 1989; it was 46 (1986) and 44 (1989) times in Guatemala; 46 (1979) and 68 times (1989) in Brazil; 12 (1980) and 22 times (1989) in Argentina; 30 (1981) and 20 (1989) times in Costa Rica; and 24 (1981) and 15 (1989) times in Uruguay (calculated from data presented in the Psacharopoulos study). Mamalakis' 1965 study found sharp inequalities in the distribution of workers' income in Chile between 1940 and 1963. Indeed, during much of the modern history of Latin America, the differences in income within the working class have been as great as, or even greater than, between the labor and capitalist classes. These differences have been so pronounced that they cast doubt about the existence of a homogeneous labor class, or proletariat, with common features—that is, in conflict with a homogeneous capitalist class. To many, the Latin American problem of an unfair and unequal distribution of income has been primarily a problem of a highly unequal and unfair distribution of labor income, of income within the working class.

The high inequality in the relative distribution of workers' income was evident in the 1980s. According to chapter 3 of the Psacharopoulos study, the distribution of workers' income continued to be highly unequal in the 1980s in Argentina (Buenos Aires), Bolivia (urban), Brazil, Colombia (urban), Costa Rica, Guatemala, Honduras, Panama, Uruguay (urban), and Venezuela.

The concentration of labor income in the hands of the richest 20 percent of workers was extremely high both in earlier years and in 1989. The following are selected statistics for 1989: The richest 20 percent of workers received 42.1 percent of total workers' income in Argentina, 46.9 percent in Bolivia, 67.2 percent in Brazil, 57.0 percent in Colombia, 47.1 percent in Costa Rica, 57.0 percent in Guatemala, 57.7 percent in Honduras, 49.6 percent in Panama,

**Inequality in workers' income**

| Country | Gini index | |
|---|---|---|
| | Early | Late |
| Argentina (Buenos Aires) | 0.389 | 0.461 |
| Bolivia (urban) | 0.479 | 0.515 |
| Brazil | 0.574 | 0.625 |
| Colombia (urban) | 0.578 | 0.515 |
| Costa Rica | 0.451 | 0.410 |
| Guatemala | 0.532 | 0.528 |
| Honduras[a] | 0.528 | 0.533 |
| Panama | 0.376 | 0.446 |
| Uruguay (urban) | 0.452 | 0.420 |
| Venezuela | 0.512 | 0.498 |

Note: Most early Gini coefficients are for years around 1980. All later ones are for 1989.
[a]Early and late values are not strictly comparable due to differential survey coverage.

SOURCE. George Psacharopoulos et al., *Poverty and Income Distribution in Latin America: The Story of the 1980s* (Washington, D.C.: World Bank, Latin America, and the Caribbean, Technical Department, Regional Studies Program, Report No. 27, Revised June 1993), p. 36.

**Table 3**

47.7 percent in Uruguay, and 52.2 percent in Venezuela. In contrast, the poorest 20 percent of workers received only 1.6 percent of total workers' income in Argentina, 1.4 percent in Bolivia, 0.8 percent in Brazil, 1.1 percent in Colombia, 1.6 percent in Costa Rica, 0.9 percent in Guatemala, 1.1 percent in Honduras, 1.5 percent in Panama, 1.6 percent in Uruguay, and 1.1 percent in Venezuela. Furthermore, even the poorest 40 percent of workers received extremely small fractions of total workers' income. This share was 14.2 percent in Argentina, 12.1 percent in Bolivia, only 7.8 percent in Brazil, 12.3 percent in Colombia, 16.0 percent in Costa Rica, 10.9 percent in Guatemala, 10.7 percent in Honduras, 14.1 percent in Panama, 15.5 percent in Uruguay, and 9.4 percent in Venezuela. The remaining, intermediate ("middle") 40 percent of workers (5th–8th deciles) received 33.7 percent of total workers' income in Argentina, 30.9 percent in Bolivia, 25.1 percent in Brazil, 30.7 percent in Colombia, 37.0 percent in Costa Rica, 32.2 percent in Guatemala, 31.0 percent in Honduras, 36.2 percent in Panama, 36.9 percent in Uruguay, and 38.4 percent in Venezuela.

The Gini coefficients for these countries (Table 3) confirm the presence of high inequality in the distribution of workers' income. The highest degree of inequality in the distribution of income in 1989 was found in Brazil and Honduras; the lowest in Costa Rica and Uruguay.

Many factors have contributed to the differences in workers' incomes. Unequal endowments of human capital—for example, education—explains a significant part of these differences. Other factors include employment status (being an employee, self-employed, or an employer), age, gender, sector of employment, or belonging to indigenous populations.

## FACTORAL DISTRIBUTION OF INCOME

The factoral distribution of income (the terms *class* and *functional* distribution of income are also widely used) describes the levels of payments to the services provided by the trinity of land, labor, and capital factors of production—rents, wage rates, and rates of profits—and by extension the shares of these factors in the total income.

According to the classical school (as exemplified by the economists Adam Smith and David Ricardo) and its followers, the class distribution critically affects income and welfare growth because landowners—the recipients of rents—and workers—the recipients of wages—largely consume their incomes, whereas capitalists—the recipients of profits—largely save them. Because the supply of capital in the long run is the supply of saving, a higher return (profit rate) on capital is expected to increase saving, investment, and income growth.

Since 1820 saving and investment have been low in most of Latin America, in spite of a favorable distribution of income, that is, a high profit share of capitalists. Saving and investment have been less than 20, or even 10, percent of gross domestic product (GDP), whereas the share of profits (operating surplus) has fluctuated between 40 and 60 percent of GDP. During the so-called golden age of free trade and exports, which lasted from 1860 to 1930, vast operating surpluses and profit shares did not increase saving and investment enough to transform the underdeveloped Latin American countries into developed ones. Similarly, during the era of protectionism from 1930 to 1980, government intervention, promotion of industry, and saving and investment never reached the levels needed to transform Latin America into a developed region, in spite of high profit shares. Even during the years 1980 to 2006, with the exception of Chile, high and rising profit shares did not give rise to the investment levels needed to achieve sustained development. Since 1820 the often fabulous resources of Latin America were used primarily for consumption rather than saving and investment.

## SECTORAL DISTRIBUTION OF INCOME

The sectoral distribution of income examines the welfare of people in Latin America as determined by the creation and redistribution of sectoral incomes. Mamalakis' "Theory of Sectoral Clashes and Coalitions" (1971) attempts to offer an explanation of both inequality and poverty. He argues that, before 1930, the relative distribution of income was unequal because the fabulous riches created by agriculture and mining were appropriated primarily by the richest 40 percent of households. Even semipublic services funded by sectoral, export-generated surpluses were provided largely to the privileged upper classes. These sectoral, or mesoeconomic, constitutions failed to generate either the demand for or the supply of skilled labor that could sustain rapid growth and eradicate poverty and extreme inequality. Use of sectoral surpluses primarily for consumption by the rich rather than for tangible and intangible human capital for all, but especially the poor, largely contributed to the failure of export "miracles" in Argentina, Brazil, Bolivia, Chile, Colombia, Cuba, Ecuador, Guatemala, Honduras, Mexico, Peru, Uruguay, Venezuela, and other countries.

Public policies shaping the sectoral distribution of income also slowed down growth and perpetuated inequality and poverty between 1930 and 1990. Redistribution of sectoral income from agriculture and exports to industry and selected services led to agricultural, export, and, ultimately, overall stagnation. Furthermore, systematic discrimination, that is, an unfair, artificially low share of income in financial services, led to hyperinflation and chaos in much of the continent, but especially in Argentina, Chile (before 1973), Brazil, Nicaragua, and Peru. In Venezuela and Ecuador from 1973 till 2000, it was once again the use of fabulous oil

**Percentage of individuals in poverty and extreme poverty in Latin America and the Caribbean**

| | | | Poverty headcount index (% below $60 poverty line) | | Extreme poverty headcount index (% below $30 poverty line) | |
|---|---|---|---|---|---|---|
| Country | Survey | Year | 1980 or earliest | 1989 or latest | 1980 or earliest | 1989 or latest |
| Argentina (Buenos Aires) | 1980 | 1989 | 3.0 | 6.4 | 0.2 | 1.6 |
| Bolivia (urban) | 1986 | 1989 | 51.1 | 54.0 | 22.5 | 23.2 |
| Brazil | 1979 | 1989 | 34.1 | 40.9 | 12.2 | 18.7 |
| Chile | N/A | 1989 | N/A | 10.0 | N/A | 1.5 |
| Colombia (urban) | 1980 | 1989 | 13.0 | 8.0 | 6.0 | 2.9 |
| Costa Rica | 1981 | 1989 | 13.4 | 3.4 | 5.4 | 1.1 |
| Dominican Republic | N/A | 1989 | N/A | 24.1 | N/A | 4.9 |
| Ecuador (urban) | N/A | 1987 | N/A | 24.2 | N/A | 4.0 |
| El Salvador (urban) | N/A | 1990 | N/A | 41.5 | N/A | 14.9 |
| Guatemala | 1986–1987 | 1989 | 66.4 | 70.4 | 36.6 | 42.1 |
| Honduras (urban) | 1986 | 1989 | 48.7 | 54.4 | 21.6 | 22.7 |
| Jamaica[a] | N/A | 1989 | N/A | 12.1 | N/A | 1.1 |
| Mexico | 1984 | 1989 | 16.6 | 17.7 | 2.5 | 4.5 |
| Panama | 1979 | 1989 | 27.9 | 31.8 | 8.4 | 13.2 |
| Paraguay (Asunción) | 1983 | 1990 | 13.1 | 7.6 | 3.2 | 0.6 |
| Peru (Lima)[a] | 1985–1986 | 1990 | 31.1 | 40.5[b] | 3.3 | 10.1[b] |
| Uruguay (urban) | 1981 | 1989 | 6.2 | 5.3 | 1.1 | 0.7 |
| Venezuela | 1981 | 1989 | 4.0 | 12.9 | 0.7 | 3.1 |

Note: "Poverty" is defined as having an income of $60 per person per month or less. "Extreme poverty" is defined as having an income of $30 per person per month or less.
[a]Based on consumption data.
[b]Estimate based on extrapolation from 1985–1986 Peru poverty figure, adjusted for changes in poverty due to a fall in per capita income according to national accounts. This adjustment assumes an elasticity of poverty with respect to per capita income of −1.60, as determined by regression analysis.

SOURCE: George Psacharopoulos et al., *Poverty and Income Distribution in Latin America: The Story of the 1980s* (Washington, D.C.: World Bank, Latin America, and the Caribbean, Technical Department, Regional Studies Program, Report No. 27, Revised June 1993), p. 62.

**Table 4**

surpluses for consumption and entitlements by the privileged social groups that caused developmental "failure."

The policy implications are clear: Unless all forms of discrimination in the sectoral distribution of income are eliminated, and sectoral surpluses are used for both tangible and intangible (human) capital, stagnation, inequality, and poverty will persist. Only nondiscriminatory sectoral (mesoeconomic) and microeconomic policies can guide resources to their most efficient uses—which is the function of income distribution—and accelerate growth. Such policies were adopted in the 1980s in Chile, and to a lesser extent in Mexico, Peru, Uruguay, and elsewhere.

## ABSOLUTE POVERTY

Absolute poverty, a measure of those members of the population who have a welfare that is below some absolute standard, is closely related to the various facets of income distribution. Latin America and the Caribbean have experienced high degrees of poverty throughout the period from 1800 to 2006. Absolute poverty has declined over time, even though it has increased during periods of severe crisis and unemployment. Table 4 presents statistics of the percentage of individuals in poverty and extreme poverty in selected years between 1979 and 1990.

The ideal approach for making poverty assessments is to formulate a constant basket of commodities (goods and services) that satisfies a set of minimum basic needs with respect to nutrition, housing, clothing, education, and health, that is, a minimum level of composite consumption. The poor are then defined as those individuals whose consumption, or equivalent level of income, is less than the value of the poverty line. A uniform $60 income per person per month in 1985 purchasing power parity (PPP) dollars, that is, having the same purchasing power in all countries, was chosen as the national poverty line for the entire Latin American and Caribbean region. To assess levels of extreme poverty, economists chose an additional extreme poverty line at $30 per month in 1985 PPP dollars. Psacharopoulos developed a regional absolute poverty standard that represents a uniform welfare level across all countries and presents the most comprehensive assessment of poverty in Latin America in the 1980s. Poverty was defined in terms of per capita household income because this is the single most identifiable factor for assessing welfare levels across the Latin American and Caribbean region through available household surveys.

The poverty lines for each Latin American country were assessed as two times the cost of a basic food basket for metropolitan/urban areas, and 1.75 times the cost of a basic food basket in rural areas. The relative income distribution and poverty estimates of the Psacharopoulos study were based on thirty-one household surveys. These surveys covered eighteen countries for various years in the 1980s. Some countries counted only labor income, while less than half of the surveys included in-kind income or the value of owner-occupied housing. None of these surveys included estimates of the welfare benefits derived from the distribution of free educational, health, and other social services to households.

The simplest and most commonly used index of poverty is the headcount ratio, defined as the fraction of the population with income that is below the poverty line. Table 4 presents the headcount ratios for poverty and extreme poverty. The highest degree of absolute poverty in 1989 was encountered in Guatemala, where the headcount index was 70.4 percent. High degrees of absolute poverty, as measured by a poverty headcount that was about 50 percent of the population, were also found in the urban regions of Bolivia and Honduras. The lowest poverty rates of 3.4 percent and 5.3 percent were observed in Costa Rica and Uruguay (urban), respectively.

A similar picture emerges when the headcount indices of extreme poverty are considered. Again, Bolivia (urban), Guatemala, and Honduras (urban) reveal headcounts of above 20 percent of the population living in extreme poverty. In contrast, the incidence of extreme poverty was the lowest in Argentina (Buenos Aires), Chile, Costa Rica, Jamaica, Paraguay (Asunción), and Uruguay (urban), with less than 2 percent of the population in each of these countries having an income below $30 per month in 1985 PPP dollars in the 1980s.

Table 5 presents estimates of the size and distribution of the total population in Latin America with income that was below the $60-per-month poverty reference in 1980 and 1989. In absolute terms, 131 million people in Latin America had a per capita income that was less than the $60-per-month

**Changes in rural and urban poverty, 1980–1989**

[population in millions]

| Year | LAC region | Total population | Population in poverty | Headcount index (% points) |
|---|---|---|---|---|
| 1980 | All | 345.4 | 91.4 | 26.5 |
| | Urban | 227.4 | 38.2 | 16.8 |
| | Rural | 118.0 | 53.2 | 45.1 |
| 1989 | All | 421.4 | 130.9 | 31.0 |
| | Urban | 300.1 | 66.0 | 22.0 |
| | Rural | 121.3 | 64.8 | 53.4 |
| Change 1980–1989 | All | 76.0 | 39.5 | +17.0 |
| | Urban | 72.7 | 27.8 | +31.0 |
| | Rural | 3.3 | 11.6 | +18.4 |

SOURCE: George Psacharopoulos et al., *Poverty and Income Distribution in Latin America: The Story of the 1980s* (Washington, DC: World Bank, Latin America, and the Caribbean, Technical Department, Regional Studies Program, Report No. 27, Revised June 1993), p. 71.

**Table 5**

poverty reference defined in the Psacharopoulos study. Poverty, which in 1989 was probably near its highest level for the entire decade, subsequently declined in countries experiencing rapid economic growth. A disproportionately large share (more than 70 percent) of the poverty in the region, as compared to their population share (48 percent), was concentrated in Brazil, Peru, and the small, relatively impoverished, countries of Bolivia, El Salvador, Guatemala, Haiti, Honduras, and Nicaragua. More than 45 percent of the poor lived in Brazil, even though it had only one-third of the population in the region. Brazil's high degree of poverty reflected the extreme inequality that has historically characterized its income distribution. More than 9 percent of the poor were concentrated in Peru, and 19 percent in the aforementioned small countries.

The statistics of Table 5 also reveal large, but changing, inequalities in regional and intraregional poverty and income distribution. In 1989 the percentage of people living in poverty was more than double in rural regions (53.4 percent), which were generally neglected by government, than in urban regions (22.0 percent). However, because Latin America has become increasingly urbanized, the absolute number of people living in 1989 in poverty in the cities (66.0 million) has exceeded those in the rural areas (64.8 million). Inadequate provision of social and public services by the state, that is, discriminatory mesoeconomics of government, has thus contributed not only to rural but also urban inequalities and poverty.

Economists have offered numerous explanations of the high inequality in the distribution of income, and of persistent absolute poverty, in major parts of Latin America. Although a complete consensus is absent, many emphasize the following explanatory factors: Inequality has been more extreme and poverty more concentrated in Brazil, Peru, Guatemala, and Honduras because of vast differences in the quality of labor among socioeconomic groups. These differences in the quality of labor, which constitute a supply-side problem, have been attributed, in turn, to public policies that have failed to provide minimum levels of social services to the poor, often indigenous, populations. Inequality in labor skills contributed to inequality in income, welfare, and to absolute poverty. In turn, unequal incomes, and unequal consumption of the semipublic services of education, health, and welfare (that is, unequal and unequitable mesoeconomic constitutions) perpetuated inequalities in labor quality. Inequality has persisted, and poverty has been aggravated also, however, by low, even declining income growth rates that barely have exceeded the growth of population. Low saving and investment levels, as a consequence of domestic policy failures and external factors, have been widely advanced as demand factors preventing the synchronous achievement of growth and equality.

## INEQUALITY-RELATIVE DISTRIBUTION OF INCOME, 1990–2006

Inequality, as measured by relative distribution of per capita household income or consumption, remains high during the period from 1990 to 2006. Although the data presented in Table 6 is only for selected years between 1992 and 2003, it can be considered as representative of the whole period. The poorest (lowest) 20 percent of households receives between 1.5 percent (Bolivia, 2002) and 6.7 percent (Jamaica, 2000) of income or consumption. The richest (highest) 20 percent of households receives between 45.9 percent (Trinidad and Tobago, 1992) and 64.1 percent (Guatemala, 2000). The richest 20 percent receives more than 60 percent of income in Bolivia (63.0, 2002), Brazil (63.2, 2001; 62.1, 2003), Chile (62.2, 2000),

**Relative distribution (percentage share) of per capita household income in Latin America and the Caribbean, selected years, 1992–2003**

| Country | Survey year | Lowest 20 percent | Second quintile | Third quintile | Fourth quintile | Highest 20 percent | Highest 10 percent |
|---|---|---|---|---|---|---|---|
| Argentina | 2001 | 3.1 | 7.2 | 12.3 | 21.0 | 56.4 | 38.9 |
| | 2003 | 3.2 | 7.0 | 12.1 | 20.7 | 56.8 | 39.6 |
| Bolivia | 1999 | 4.0 | 9.2 | 14.8 | 22.9 | 49.1 | 32.0 |
| | 2002 | 1.5 | 5.9 | 10.9 | 18.7 | 63.0 | 47.2 |
| Brazil | 2001 | 2.4 | 5.9 | 10.4 | 18.1 | 63.2 | 46.9 |
| | 2003 | 2.6 | 6.2 | 10.7 | 18.4 | 62.1 | 45.8 |
| Chile | 2000 | 3.3 | 6.6 | 10.5 | 17.4 | 62.2 | 47.0 |
| Colombia | 1999 | 2.7 | 6.6 | 10.8 | 18.0 | 61.8 | 46.5 |
| | 2003 | 2.5 | 6.2 | 10.6 | 18.0 | 62.7 | 46.9 |
| Costa Rica | 2000 | 4.2 | 8.9 | 13.7 | 21.7 | 51.5 | 34.8 |
| | 2001 | 3.9 | 8.1 | 12.8 | 20.4 | 54.8 | 38.4 |
| Dominican Republic | 1998 | 5.1 | 8.6 | 13.0 | 20.0 | 53.3 | 37.9 |
| | 2003 | 3.9 | 7.8 | 12.1 | 19.4 | 56.8 | 41.3 |
| Ecuador | 1998 | 3.3 | 7.5 | 11.7 | 19.4 | 58.0 | 41.6 |
| El Salvador | 2000 | 2.9 | 7.4 | 12.4 | 20.2 | 57.1 | 40.0 |
| | 2002 | 2.7 | 7.5 | 12.8 | 21.2 | 55.9 | 38.8 |
| Guatemala | 2000 | 2.6 | 5.9 | 9.8 | 17.6 | 64.1 | 48.3 |
| | 2002 | 2.9 | 7.0 | 11.6 | 19.0 | 59.5 | 43.4 |
| Honduras | 1999 | 2.7 | 6.7 | 11.8 | 19.9 | 58.9 | 42.2 |
| | 2003 | 3.4 | 7.1 | 11.6 | 19.6 | 58.3 | 42.2 |
| Jamaica | 2000 | 6.7 | 10.7 | 15.0 | 21.7 | 46.0 | 30.3 |
| Mexico | 2000 | 3.1 | 7.2 | 11.7 | 19.0 | 59.1 | 43.1 |
| | 2002 | 4.3 | 8.3 | 12.6 | 19.7 | 55.1 | 39.4 |
| Nicaragua | 2001 | 5.6 | 9.8 | 14.2 | 21.1 | 49.3 | 33.8 |
| Panama | 2000 | 2.4 | 6.5 | 11.2 | 19.6 | 60.3 | 43.3 |
| | 2002 | 2.5 | 6.4 | 11.2 | 19.6 | 60.3 | 43.6 |
| Paraguay | 2002 | 2.2 | 6.3 | 11.3 | 18.8 | 61.3 | 45.4 |
| Peru | 2000 | 2.9 | 8.3 | 14.1 | 21.5 | 53.2 | 37.2 |
| | 2002 | 3.2 | 7.1 | 11.8 | 19.3 | 58.7 | 43.2 |
| Trinidad and Tobago | 1992 | 5.5 | 10.3 | 15.5 | 22.7 | 45.9 | 29.9 |
| Uruguay | 2000 | 4.8 | 9.3 | 14.2 | 21.6 | 50.1 | 33.5 |
| | 2003 | 5.0 | 9.1 | 14.0 | 21.5 | 50.5 | 34.0 |
| Venezuela | 1998 | 3.0 | 8.4 | 13.7 | 21.6 | 53.4 | 36.3 |
| | 2000 | 4.7 | 9.4 | 14.5 | 22.1 | 49.3 | 32.8 |

SOURCE: USAID (United States Agency for International Development), Bureau for Latin America and the Caribbean, *Latin America and the Caribbean: Selected Economic and Social Data* (2005, 2006), Table 2.2. The primary sources for these statistics are the United Nations Economic Commission for Latin America and the Caribbean and the World Bank.

**Table 6**

Colombia (61.8, 1999; 62.7, 2003), Guatemala (64.1, 2000), Panama (60.3, 2000, 2002) and Paraguay (61.3, 2002).

Income/consumption inequality, as measured by the Gini coefficient—the relevant statistics presented in Table 7—also is high during the period from 1992 to 2003. The value of the Gini coefficient ranges between a low of 37.9 percent (Jamaica, 2000) and a high of 60.1 percent (Bolivia, 2002). It is above 55.0 percent in Brazil (59.3, 2001; 58.0, 2003), Chile (57.1, 2000), Colombia (57.6, 1999; 58.6, 2003), Guatemala (59.9, 2000; 55.1, 2002), Honduras (55.0, 1999), Panama (56.4, 2000, 2002) and Paraguay (57.8, 2002). It is below 45.0 percent in Bolivia (44.7, 1999), Ecuador (43.7, 1998), Jamaica (37.9, 2000), Nicaragua (43.1, 2001), Trinidad and Tobago (40.3, 1992), Uruguay (44.6, 2000; 44.9, 2003), and Venezuela (44.1, 2000). Furthermore, as also presented in Table 7, the percentage share of income of the poorest 10 percent of population is less than 1 percent in Bolivia (0.3, 2002), Brazil (0.7, 2001; 0.8, 2003), Colombia (0.8, 1999; 0.7, 2003), Ecuador (0.9, 1998), El Salvador (0.9, 2000; 0.7, 2002), Guatemala (0.9, 2000, 2002), Honduras (0.9, 1999), Panama (0.7, 2000; 0.8, 2002), Paraguay (0.6, 2002), and Peru (0.7, 2002).

Latin America and the Caribbean also have experienced, not only from 1990 to 2006, but throughout their history, high degrees of inequality in the satisfaction of individual final needs (food, clothing,

**Gini coefficient and bottom 10 percent share of income at the individual level, Latin America and the Caribbean, selected years, 1992–2003**

| Country | Survey year | Gini coefficient | % share of income of bottom 10% of population |
|---|---|---|---|
| Argentina | 2001 | 52.2 | 1.0 |
| | 2003 | 52.8 | 1.1 |
| Bolivia | 1999 | 44.7 | 1.3 |
| | 2002 | 60.1 | 0.3 |
| Brazil | 2001 | 59.3 | 0.7 |
| | 2003 | 58.0 | 0.8 |
| Chile | 2000 | 57.1 | 1.2 |
| Colombia | 1999 | 57.6 | 0.8 |
| | 2003 | 58.6 | 0.7 |
| Costa Rica | 2000 | 46.5 | 1.4 |
| | 2001 | 49.9 | 1.3 |
| Dominican Republic | 1998 | 47.4 | 2.1 |
| | 2003 | 51.7 | 1.4 |
| Ecuador | 1998 | 43.7 | 0.9 |
| El Salvador | 2000 | 53.2 | 0.9 |
| | 2002 | 52.4 | 0.7 |
| Guatemala | 2000 | 59.9 | 0.9 |
| | 2002 | 55.1 | 0.9 |
| Honduras | 1999 | 55.0 | 0.9 |
| | 2003 | 53.8 | 1.2 |
| Jamaica | 2000 | 37.9 | 2.7 |
| Mexico | 2000 | 54.6 | 1.0 |
| | 2002 | 49.5 | 1.6 |
| Nicaragua | 2001 | 43.1 | 2.2 |
| Panama | 2000 | 56.4 | 0.7 |
| | 2002 | 56.4 | 0.8 |
| Paraguay | 2002 | 57.8 | 0.6 |
| Peru | 2000 | 49.8 | 0.7 |
| | 2002 | 54.6 | 1.1 |
| Trinidad and Tobago | 1992 | 40.3 | 2.1 |
| Uruguay | 2000 | 44.6 | 1.8 |
| | 2003 | 44.9 | 1.9 |
| Venezuela | 1998 | 49.1 | 1.8 |
| | 2000 | 44.1 | 1.6 |

SOURCE: USAID (United States Agency for International Development), Bureau for Latin America and the Caribbean, *Latin America and the Caribbean: Selected Economic and Social Data* (2005, 2006), Table 2.2. The primary source of these statistics is the United Nations Economic Commission for Latin America and the Caribbean.

**Table 7**

and shelter consumption inequality), semipublic final needs (education, health, and welfare consumption inequality) and collective final needs (political freedom consumption-satisfaction-inequality), where political freedom is the pillar of procedural democracy. As Mamalakis has observed (2005a, 2005b), the region has also experienced high degrees of consumption-satisfaction inequalities in terms of the five moral collective needs that provide the foundation of civil society: 1) economic freedom(s), (2) safety, security, and protection of life and private property, (3) equal treatment by government, (4) social harmony, and (5) environmental protection.

Latin America and the Caribbean also display throughout their history high parallel degrees of inequality in the satisfaction of "means" needs of all institutional units (households, corporations, nonprofit institutions [NPI] and government units) and sectors (financial and nonfinancial corporations, nonprofit institutions serving households [NPISH], general government and households). There is inequality in the satisfaction of their needs for such means as final individual, semipublic, and collective commodities, (agricultural, industrial and service value-added) components thereof, factor services, labor and property incomes (compensation of respective services), and labor (skilled) and property (land and other) endowments that are required to satisfy their final needs. These production or income means inequalities, as Mamalakis (2005a, 2005b) notes, are found across groups classified by gender, age, ethnicity, employment status, and so forth.

### ABSOLUTE POVERTY, 1990–2006

Absolute poverty, as measured by the headcount index (percentage of population below $60 poverty line), also differs significantly among countries. As revealed by the statistics presented in Table 8, it is highest in Nicaragua (79.9, 2001) and lowest in Uruguay (4.56, 1998). It exceeds 40 percent in Bolivia (42.2, 2002), Ecuador (52.3, 1995; 40.8, 1998), El Salvador (45, 1998; 40.6, 2002), Honduras (44.4, 1998; 44, 1999), Nicaragua (79, 1998; 79.9, 2001), and St. Lucia (59.8, 1995). Poverty is below 10 percent in Chile (8.64, 1998; 9.58, 2000), Costa Rica (7.52, 2001), and Uruguay (4.56, 1998; 5.73, 2003).

Extreme absolute poverty, as measured by the extreme poverty headcount index (percentage of population below $30 poverty line), is highest in Nicaragua (45.1, 2001) and lowest in Chile (<2.0, 1998, 2000), Jamaica (<2.0, 1999, 2000) and Uruguay (<2.0, 1998, 2003). It exceeds 20 percent in Bolivia (20.4, 1997; 23.2, 2002), Ecuador (20.2, 1995), El Salvador (21.4, 1998), Honduras (23.8, 1998; 20.7, 1999), Nicaragua (44.7, 1998; 45.1, 2001), and St. Lucia (25.4, 1995).

Furthermore, Latin American and Caribbean countries have experienced different degrees of individual (food, clothing, shelter), semipublic (health,

**Percentage of individuals in poverty and extreme poverty in Latin America and the Caribbean, selected years, 1992–2003**

| Country | Survey year | Poverty headcount index (% below $60 poverty line) | Extreme poverty headcount index (% below $30 poverty line) |
|---|---|---|---|
| Argentina | 1998 | 15.9 | 7.69 |
| | 2003 | 23 | 7.04 |
| Bolivia | 1997 | 39.1 | 20.4 |
| | 2002 | 42.2 | 23.2 |
| Brazil | 1998 | 23.7 | 9.94 |
| | 2003 | 21.2 | 7.54 |
| Chile | 1998 | 8.64 | <2.0 |
| | 2000 | 9.58 | <2.0 |
| Colombia | 1000 | 26.8 | 14.5 |
| | 2003 | 17.8 | 7.03 |
| Costa Rica | 1998 | 14.3 | 6.94 |
| | 2001 | 7.52 | 2.22 |
| Dominican Republic | 1996 | 11.7 | <2.0 |
| | 2003 | 11 | 2.52 |
| Ecuador | 1995 | 52.3 | 20.2 |
| | 1998 | 40.8 | 17.7 |
| El Salvador | 1998 | 45 | 21.4 |
| | 2002 | 40.6 | 19 |
| Guatemala | 1998 | 29.6 | 7.89 |
| | 2002 | 31.9 | 13.5 |
| Guyana | 1992 | 27 | 8.14 |
| | 1998 | 11.2 | 2.98 |
| Honduras | 1998 | 44.4 | 23.8 |
| | 1999 | 44 | 20.7 |
| Jamaica | 1999 | 14 | <2.0 |
| | 2000 | 13.3 | <2.0 |
| Mexico | 1998 | 24.4 | 7.98 |
| | 2002 | 20.4 | 4.45 |
| Nicaragua | 1998 | 79 | 44.7 |
| | 2001 | 79.9 | 45.1 |
| Panama | 1997 | 12.9 | 3.2 |
| | 2002 | 17.1 | 6.52 |
| Paraguay | 1999 | 30.3 | 14.9 |
| | 2002 | 33.2 | 16.4 |
| Peru | 1996 | 28.4 | 8.88 |
| | 2002 | 31.8 | 12.5 |
| St. Lucia | 1995 | 59.8 | 25.4 |
| Trinidad and Tobago | 1988 | 15.3 | 2.25 |
| | 1992 | 20 | 3.95 |
| Uruguay | 1998 | 4.56 | <2.0 |
| | 2003 | 6.73 | <2.0 |
| Venezuela | 1997 | 28.6 | 9.65 |
| | 2000 | 27.6 | 8.29 |

SOURCE: USAID (United States Agency for International Development), Bureau for Latin America and the Caribbean, *Latin America and the Caribbean: Selected Economic and Social Data* (2005, 2006), Table 2.1. The primary source of these statistics is the World Bank.

**Table 8**

education, welfare) and collective (freedoms, protection of life and private property, equal treatment by government, social harmony, and environment protection) output-consumption poverty, depending on such factors as ethnicity, gender, age, employment status, and so forth. People in these countries also have experienced means absolute poverty, that is, final individual, semipublic, and collective commodities (shortfall in production), value-added components, labor and property factor services, income and endowments poverty.

As Mamalakis (2004, 2005a, 2005b) has argued, final output and means poverty resulted from an excessive emphasis on (re)distribution, rather than on accumulation and increased production, of means, that is, from neglect of the two golden rules. Collective markets have been inefficient and production has suffered because the first golden rule of recognition of the complementarity (complementary nature of) between procedural democracy and civil society has not been recognized and satisfied. Furthermore, collective markets have been inefficient and output growth has suffered because the second golden rule of recognition of the complementarity of the five moral collective needs has also not been recognized and satisfied. Ultimately, persistent inequality and absolute poverty are attributed, and explained by, the neglect and inadequate satisfaction of the moral collective needs for political freedom (absence of procedural democracy), as well as for economic freedom, safety of life and private property, equal treatment by government, social harmony (absence of civil society), and environmental protection. All existing indices and measures of inequality, absolute poverty, income, and consumption, while including the basket of minimum basic needs, exclude any reference to the usefulness and costliness of the satisfaction of these eternal, indestructible, moral collective needs.

Yet satisfaction of these needs determines, on the one hand, who has the power of the state (the degree of satisfaction of the political freedom need) and, on the other hand, how and whether the power of the state is used to create a civil society (satisfaction of the other four moral collective needs).

Inequality and absolute poverty have persisted in those countries where collective markets have failed to establish sustainable electoral democracy and civil society (Argentina, Brazil, Peru, Bolivia, Venezuela, Mexico, Guatemala, Ecuador, El Salvador, Ecuador, and others). Inequality and absolute poverty have, however, been reduced in those countries where collective markets have succeeded in establishing both procedural democracy—that is, where the power of the state is in the hands of politically free people—and civil society—that is, where the power of the state has been used to satisfy all five complementary moral collective needs, as in Chile since 1990

It can be argued that the proximate explanation of the enduring, widespread, absolute poverty and income/consumption inequality in Latin America and the Caribbean is the low rate of growth of labor productivity and per capita output/income. However, a better explanation, according to the Mamalakis political economy approach of collective markets, is the failure of collective markets to satisfy the two golden rules of sustainable democracy and growth: to obtain both procedural democracy and civil society.

*See also* **Economic Development.**

BIBLIOGRAPHY


Altimir, Oscar. "Income Distribution and Poverty through Crisis and Adjustment." In *Latin America's Economic Future*, ed. Graham Bird and Ann Helwege, pp. 265–302. London and San Diego: Academic Press, 1994.

Commission of the European Communities-Eurostat, International Monetary Fund, Organisation for Economic Co-Operation and Development, United Nations, and World Bank. *System of National Accounts 1993.* Brussels/Luxembourg, New York, Paris, Washington, DC: Commission of the European Communities-Eurostat, 1993. Also available from United Nations Statistics Division, National Accounts, at http://unstats.un.org/unsd/sna1993/toctop. asp.

Mamalakis, Markos J. "Public Policy and Sectoral Development: A Case Study of Chile 1940–1958." In *Essays on the Chilean Economy*, by Markos J. Mamalakis and Clark Winton Reynolds, pp. 1–200. Homewood, IL: R. D. Irwin, 1965.

Mamalakis, Markos J. "The Theory of Sectoral Clashes." *Latin American Research Review* 4, no. 3 (1969): 3–46.

Mamalakis, Markos J. "The Theory of Sectoral Clashes and Coalitions Revisited." *Latin American Research Review* 6, no. 3 (1971): 89–126.

Mamalakis, Markos J. "Urbanization and Sectoral Transformation in Latin America, 1950–1965." 29th Congresso Internacional de Americanistas Lima. *Actas y Memorias*, Vol. 2: *El Proceso de Urbanizacion en America desde sus Origenes Hasta Nuestros Dias*, pp. 193–345. Lima: Instituto de Estudios Peruanos, 1972.

Mamalakis, Markos J. *The Growth and Structure of the Chilean Economy: From Independence to Allende.* New Haven, CT: Yale University Press, 1976. See especially chapters 3 and 10.

Mamalakis, Markos J. "Sectoral Clashes, Basic Economic Rights and Redemocratization in Chile: A Mesoeconomic Approach." *Ibero-Americana, Nordic Journal of Latin American Studies* 22, no. 1 (1992).

Mamalakis, Markos J. "Sectoral Conflicts in the U.S. and the Soviet Union: A Mesoeconomic Analysis." *Eastern Economic Journal* 18, no. 4 (1992): 421–428.

Mamalakis, Markos J. "Distributional Mobility and Justice in Latin America: Macro, Meso and Micro Issues." In *Distributional Mobility in Latin America: Evidence and Implications for Public Policy.* Latin American Program Working Paper 242, pp. 7–121. Washington, DC: Woodrow Wilson International Center for Scholars, November 1999.

Mamalakis, Markos J. "Las reglas doradas" [The golden rules]. In *Supplemento Anniversario 16 años of Diario Financiero* (Santiago, Chile), November 29, 2004, p. 133. Published in English as "Sustainable Democracy and the Golden Rules." Center for International Education, University of Wisconsin-Milwaukee, *Global Currents* 1, no. 2 (2005a): 18–19.

Mamalakis, Markos J. "Social Justice in a Global Environment: A Theory of Natural Law and Social Justice." In *The Quest for Social Justice III: The Morris Fromkin Memorial Lectures, 1992–2002*, ed. Peter G. Watson-Boone, pp. 227–304. Milwaukee: UWM Libraries, University of Wisconsin-Milwaukee, 2005b.

Psacharopoulos, George, et al. *Poverty and Income Distribution in Latin America: The Story of the 1980s.* World Bank, Regional Studies Program, Report No. 27. Washington, DC: World Bank, 1993.

Urrutia, Miguel, ed. *Long-Term Trends in Latin American Economic Development.* Washington, DC: Inter-American Development Bank, 1991. See especially chapter 1 by Angus Maddison and chapter 2 by Miguel Urrutia.

World Bank. *World Development Report 1990: Poverty.* Oxford: Oxford University Press, 1991.


MARKOS J. MAMALAKIS

## INCONFIDÊNCIA DOS ALFAIATES.

Inconfidência dos Alfaiates (Conspiracy of the Tailors), an unsuccessful plot for independence in Salvador, Bahia, in 1798. The conspiracy was a two-stage response to changing economic and social conditions in Bahia as sugar growing experienced a resurgence within the context of increasing despair among Salvador's poor. Initially, Bahian elites, strongly influenced by French physiocratic thought and the ideas of the French Revolution disseminated by a newly formed Masonic society, the Knights of the Light, sought to lead a movement whose objectives were independence and free trade. As the plot developed, however, it became radicalized as a large number of working-class artisans (especially tailors), enlisted men, slaves, and ex-slaves became involved. The goals of this latter group constituted a radical agenda: an end to racism, equality of opportunity, equality before the law, abolition of slavery, and the establishment of an independent Catholic Church. The political goals of the plotters included establishing a republic with leadership open to all, based on ability. Where the initial plot had been socially conservative, the second was a plan for social revolution.

The royal authorities discovered the plot because of the indiscreet actions of some of the participants and through informers. As with the Inconfidência Mineira, punishment fell disproportionately on the poorest of the plotters—four of whom were executed. The initial, elite plotters were punished either lightly or not at all. In some cases they were not even questioned.

The plot demonstrated the dichotomy between Brazilian elites, for whom independence did not imply social transformations, and the colony's poor, for whom independence was part of a process of radical social change.

*See also* **Masonic Orders.**

BIBLIOGRAPHY

Luis Henrique Dias Tavares, *História da sedição intentada na Bahia em 1798 ("A Conspiração dos Alfaiates")* (1975).

Donald Ramos, "Social Revolution Frustrated: The Conspiracy of the Tailors in Bahia, 1798," in *Luso-Brazilian Review* 13 (Summer 1976): 74–90.

### *Additional Bibliography*

Barman, Roderick J. *Brazil: The Forging of a Nation, 1798-1852.* Stanford, CA: Stanford University Press, 1988.

Donato, Hernani. *O cotidiano Brasileiro no século XVIII.* Sao Paulo: Melhoramentos, 1998.

Garcia, Paulo. *Cipriano Barata, ou A liberdade acima de tudo.* Rio de Janeiro: Topbooks, 1997.

Souza, Iara Lis Carvalho. *Pátria coroado: O Brasil como corpo político autonomo, 1780-1831.* São Paulo: Editora UNESP Fundaçao, 1999.

DONALD RAMOS

---

**INCONFIDÊNCIA MINEIRA.** Inconfidência Mineira, a plot for independence involving significant members of the elite of Minas Gerais, Brazil, in 1788–1789. Key plotters included Tomás Antô nio Gonzaga, the royal judge of Vila Rica, poet, and satirist; Cláudio Manuel da Costa, a local town councillor, poet, and the first historian of the mining zone; José Álvares Maciel, son of a local tax farmer and a recent graduate of Coimbra; Inácio José de Alvarenga Peixoto, a gold miner and poet; Francisco de Paula Freire de Andrade, the commander of dragoons; Father José da Silva de Oliveira Rolim, a priest, slave trader, and dealer in diamonds; and Joaquim José da Silva Xavier (Tiradentes), an ensign (*alferes*) in the dragoons. The plot was never implemented because the governor was informed and was able to arrest most of those involved.

Since the revolt was frustrated, the Inconfidência Mineira is less significant for its effects than for its symbolism and its implications for the end of Portuguese control over Brazil. It is important because key sectors of the elite of Minas Gerais, both lay and ecclesiastical, were involved in a plot to end Portuguese domination. The plot emerged from the alienation of a key segment of the Mineiro elite, which was bound by close familial ties. This alienation grew out of the economic impact of diminishing gold production. Several of the participants in the plot were heavily in debt.

Because of the failure to implement the plot, its objectives are known only through the investigation and questioning conducted by royal authorities. The objectives of the plotters included independence, although the extent of the plans for the new republic is not clear. The plotters sought to extend their efforts beyond Minas Gerais to include Rio de Janeiro and São Paulo. Recognizing the shift in the economic center of Minas Gerais, the plotters sought to move the capital from Vila Rica to São João del Rei and to create Brazil's first university in Vila Rica. The republic would be governed by a written constitution implemented by a parliament in the capital and smaller legislative bodies in each urban center. The plotters planned to establish industries—especially for gunpowder and iron, necessary for defense, and cheap agricultural and mining implements—thereby reviving the economy. There would also be free trade. On social issues the plotters were divided. Some supported the emancipation of slaves born in Brazil as a means of making them supporters of the new republic. Others favored maintaining slavery as an economic necessity. There was agreement on providing incentives for an increase in population. Finally, of great interest to many of the plotters, a pardon of debts owed to the treasury was proposed.

The Portuguese response to the plot reflects the nature of colonial rule. The activists and ideologues of the Inconfidência were brought to trial, but only Silva Xavier was executed. Key backers of the conspiracy were not tried, no doubt out of deference to their high social status. The plot demonstrated that there was substantial dissatisfaction with the colonial status of Minas Gerais, the most powerful captaincy in Brazil. Although a failure, the Inconfidência Mineira demonstrated the existence of republican and nationalist values in a key part of colonial Brazil.

*See also* **Minas Gerais.**

BIBLIOGRAPHY

Kenneth R. Maxwell, *Conflicts and Conspiracies: Brazil and Portugal, 1750–1808* (1973).

*Additional Bibliography*

Fiúza, Rubens. *Tiradentes: Cronicas da vida colonial brasileira.* Belo Horizonte: Rita Soares de Faria, 2006.

Focas, Junía Diniz. *Inconfidencia mineira: A história dos sentidos de uma historia.* Belo Horizonte: Faculdade de Letras/UFMG, 2002.

Furtado, Jaci Pereira. *Inconfidencia mineira: Um espetáculo no escuro (1788-1792.)* São Paulo: Moderno, 1998.

Furtado, João Pinto. *O manto de Pénelope: História, mito, e memória da Inconfidencia Mineira de 1788-9.* São Paolo: Companhia das Letras, 2002.

Oliveira, Dilce Alves de. *O papél da defensoría pública na Inconfidencia Mineira: Um sonho da cidadania.* Belo Horizonte: Ephata Produçoes, 2002.

Perrin, Dimas. *Inconfidencia mineira, causas e conseqüencias.* Brasília: Coordenada, 1969.

Donald Ramos

**INDEPENDENCE.** *See* **Wars of Independence, South America.**

**INDEPENDENT REPUBLICS (COLOMBIA).** Independent Republics (Colombia), the regions of Sumapaz, Marquetalia, Río Chiquito, El Pato, Guayabero, and Viotá in central Colombia, which were "independent" of state control during the Violencia of the 1950s. These mountainous frontier zones were the sites of widespread land conflicts in the 1920s and 1930s, intensive mobilization efforts by Gaitán Liberals and Communists in the 1930s and 1940s, and brutal Conservative repression in the late 1940s and early 1950s. After the Rojas Pinilla amnesty of 1953, men such as Juan Cruz Varela, Fermín Charry Rincón ("Charro Negro"), and Manuel Maralunda Vélez ("Tirofijo") helped organize peasant organizations to defend their agricultural and political autonomy. Although Cruz Varela entered the political mainstream in the 1960s, winning election to the House of Representatives, others faced military repression. Under the Plan Lazo, formulated with the assistance of the Central Intelligence Agency, the Colombian military brutally subdued the regions in the mid-1960s, prompting Tirofijo and others to form the Revolutionary Armed Forces of Colombia (FARC) in April 1966. During the 1970s the group maintained a low profile, but by the 1980s, the FARC had become heavily involved with the illegal drug trade. After repeated bombings and other attacks, including a large-scale attack on a military base in Guaiviare in 1996, in which at least 130 people were killed, the Colombian president, Andrés Pastrana Arango, tried unsuccessfully to negotiate a peace settlement. Under President Alvaro Uribe, in 2004 and 2005 attacks abated, but on June 28, 2007, the group kidnapped and murdered at least eleven provincial deputies from the Valle de Cauca department in the western mid-coastal region of the country.

*See also* **Colombia, Revolutionary Movements: Revolutionary Armed Forces of Colombia (FARC); Rojas Pinilla, Gustavo; Varela, Juan Cruz; Violencia, La.**

BIBLIOGRAPHY

Germán Guzmán Campos, *La violencia en Colombia: Parte descriptiva* (1962).

Richard Gott, *Rural Guerrillas in Latin America,* rev. ed. (1973).

*Additional Bibliography*

Appelbaum, Nancy P. *Muddied Waters: Race, Religion, and Local History in Colombia, 1846–1948.* Durham, NC: Duke University Press, 2003.

Hylton, Forrest. *Evil Hour in Colombia*. London: Verso, 2006.

Palacios, Marco. *Between Legitimacy and Violence: A History of Colombia, 1875–2002*. Durham, NC: Duke University Press, 2006.

Safford, Frank, and Marco Palacios. *Colombia: Fragmented Land, Divided Society*. New York: Oxford University Press, 2002.

DAVID SOWELL

## INDIANISMO.

**INDIANISMO.** Indianismo, a term used in studies of Brazilian literature to refer to the use of Indian characters and themes. In this type of literature, writers have combined aesthetic and ideological goals. In chronological order, the most significant examples are found in the mid-1800s with José de Alencar's romantic representation of an idealized inhabitant of the New World (e.g., *Iracema,* 1865); in the 1920s with the modernist Mário de Andrade's humorous fictional view of Brazilian national identity (e.g., *Macunaíma,* 1928; Eng. trans. 1976); and in the late twentieth century with Darcy Ribeiro, whose novels incorporate an anthropological approach (e.g, *Maíra,* 1976). Subsequent critiques have emphasized the theme of *indianismo* within Brazilian music during the Romantic period as an important element in the process of national identity formation.

*See also* **Literature: Brazil.**

BIBLIOGRAPHY

An all-encompassing study is David Brookshaw, *Paradise Betrayed: Brazilian Literature of the Indian* (1988).

*Additional Bibliography*

Cuccagna, Claudio. "Utupismo modernista o índio no ser-não-ser da brasilidade (1920–1930)." Ph.D. diss. São Paulo, 2005.

Volpe, Maria Alice. "Indianismo and Landscape in the Brazilian Age of Progress Art Music from Carlos Gomes to Villa-Lobos, 1870s–1930s." Ph.D. diss. University of Texas at Austin, 2001.

PEDRO MALIGO

## INDIANISMO, SPANISH AMERICA.

*Indianismo*, as used in the Spanish-speaking countries of Latin America, refers to a literary movement that predates the more overtly political *indigenismo.* This primarily nineteenth-century phenomenon represents a first pass at wiping out colonialist tendencies in literature. Some of its strongest adherents were the Argentine Juana Manuela Gorriti (1818–1892), the Cubans Gertrudis Gómez de la Avellaneda (1814–1873) and José Fornaris (1827–1890), the Ecuadorian Juan León Mera (1832–1894), the Puerto Rican Eugenio María de Hostos (1839–1903), the Dominicans Manuel de Jesús Galván (1834–1910) and José Joaquín Pérez (1854–1900), and the Uruguayan Juan Zorrilla de San Martín (1855–1931). Although some of these authors would have seen themselves as defenders of indigenous peoples in their fictional endeavors—Hostos, for example, closely following in his narrative *Brevisima relacion de la destruccion de las Indias* written by Bartolomé de Las Casas, the sixteenth century Spanish priest and earliest defender of indigenous peoples—their idealism and romanticism prohibited them from taking a more engaged stance. Their writing can be characterized as a nostalgic evocation of the indigenous past, as in the case of novels by Gómez de Avellaneda and Hostos modeled on historical figures. Oftentimes their works oversimplify indigenous realities by filtering out negative, innate human characteristics, as in Zorrilla's *Tabaré,* and exemplify the nineteenth-century trend toward creolization, as with León Mera's *jíbaro,* an indigenous person who turns out to be white. Notwithstanding these authors' good intentions, most of the indigenous characters they created tend to be one-dimensional and lacking real-life complexities.

*See also* **Galván, Manuel de Jesús; Gómez de Avellaneda y Arteaga, Gertrudis; Gorriti, Juana Manuela; Hostos y Bonilla, Eugenio María de; Indigenismo; Las Casas, Bartolomé de; Mera, Juan León; Zorrilla de San Martín, Juan.**

BIBLIOGRAPHY

Meléndez, Concha. "La novela indianista en Hispanoamérica (1832–1889)." In vol. 1 of *Obras completas,* pp. 77–300. San Juan: Instituto de Cultura Puertorriqueña, 1970.

Sommer, Doris. *Foundational Fictions: The National Romances of Latin America.* Berkeley: University of California Press, 1991.

Young, Richard A. "Juan León Mera y el discurso indianista de *Cumandá,* o un drama entre salvajes." In *El indio, nacimiento y evolución de una instancia discursiva,* edited by Edmond Cros, pp. 185–204. Montpellier,

France: Université Montpellier, Centre d'études et de recherches sociocritiques, 1994.

THOMAS WARD

**INDIAN POLICY, BRAZIL.** Brazil Indian Policy. The Indian Protection Service (Serviço de Proteçao dos Indios—SPI) was founded in 1910 as a government institution specifically dedicated to the tutelage of Brazil's native peoples. In accordance with the positivist philosophy of its founder, Colonel Cândido Mariano da Silva Rondon, its mission was to bring the descendants of Brazil's original inhabitants into contact with civilization by peaceful means, protect their lands and lives, and gradually, by education and example, assist their development as farmers and cattle raisers who, as Brazilians, would help to integrate the frontier regions with the rest of the country.

As a young army officer, Rondon had become acquainted with unacculturated indigenous peoples when he led expeditions to lay telegraph lines in remote regions of northwest Brazil. With a perspective common to many intellectuals of the time, he saw "Indian" societies as arrested at an early stage of cultural development, but capable of progressing when aided. At that time tribes were resisting the advance of German farmers who were opening up new lands for settlement in the south, and reports of these hostilities placed in jeopardy the government's plan to attract European immigrants. Many argued that any means necessary, including force, should be used to prevent the indigenous from standing in the way of this process. However, the legislation that established the SPI embodied Rondon's liberal ideas for acculturation and, while self-determination for tribal groups was not a consideration, Brazil's Indian policy was perhaps the most enlightened of that of any nation in the early twentieth century.

Over the years, the SPI gained prestige for its success in attracting, pacifying, and eventually settling resistant groups. Typically, a camp would be set up near the territory of the hostile group and "gifts" left along trails; these offerings consisted of knives, steel tools, aluminum pots, and other articles designated to impress the Indians with white technology. At the same time, the members of the expedition would attempt to assure the indigenous of their friendly intentions. Even when their advances were met with arrows, the men of the Indian Protection Service were not to retaliate but to follow their motto, "Die if need be, but never kill." Eventually the Indians' curiosity would overcome their fears, and unarmed groups would venture out of the forest and accept face to face the gifts offered.

Once the acculturating peoples had become dependent on manufactured goods, they tended to settle near the government Indian post. Unfortunately, these new relations with the outside world were often fatal. Commonly 50 to 80 percent of the members of a newly contacted tribe succumbed within the first year to introduced infectious diseases. According to a 1970 text by Darcy Ribeiro, eighty-eight Indian groups disappeared in the Brazilian Amazon between 1900 and 1957.

Although in principle one aim of the SPI was to preserve for the natives the lands they occupied, in practice much of it was claimed by settlers once hostilities were no longer a threat. Government resources, which were freely expended for pacification, tended to dry up after resettlement. As a result, the government agent assigned to an Indian post had little power to assist the people he had been assigned to protect.

As Rondon aged, the influence of his humanistic philosophy on the SPI grew weaker. The dedicated workers that Rondon had trained were replaced by military administrators for whom economic rather than humanitarian considerations were primary. The agency became increasingly corrupt and demoralized. In 1967 the Brazilian minister of the interior ordered an investigation of SPI practices, which resulted in a 20-volume report detailing crimes committed against native people by SPI personnel at all levels, and painting a shocking picture of corruption, greed, and sadism. When the results of the investigation were made public, they were widely reported in both the foreign and Brazilian press. After the scandal broke, the SPI was disbanded and replaced by the National Indian Foundation (FUNAI). However, the policy in defense of indigenous rights initiated by the first governing board of FUNAI lasted only two years.

In 1970 the civilian president of FUNAI was succeeded by General Oscar Jerônimo Bandeira de Melo, a military man dedicated to carrying out the aggressive development policies of the authoritarian military regime headed by President Emílio Garrastazú Medici. The policy instituted at this time was directed toward the rapid integration of native groups into the national economy and class structure of Brazil. The government saw FUNAI's mission as that of a buffer organization, providing limited assistance and protection to Indians, while at the same time making sure they did not impede the government's development plans.

The legal status of tribal peoples in Brazil is that of minors under tutelage. Reservations are not communal tribal property but federal lands held in trust for the Indians, with FUNAI acting as administrator. During the last decades of the twentieth century, a network of roads opened up the interior of Brazil to settlement and economic development, putting great pressure on Indian lands whose owners have resisted these incursions, which has sometimes led to violent confrontations. The weak and ambiguous role of FUNAI made it distrusted by the Indians and probably led directly to increased indigenous efforts, assisted by nongovernmental organizations, to organize in defense of their own interests.

By the early 1980s some indigenous groups were growing in political sophistication as well as determination to preserve their distinct identity and traditions. As international concern about deforestation and environmental destruction in the Amazon increased, the indigenous found allies in organizations supporting conservation and the rights of tribal peoples. FUNAI came under pressure to expedite the official demarcation of the reservations, even as some powerful groups within the country, including the military, contended that setting aside large territories undermined Brazil's need to develop its resources and constituted a threat to national security. The 1988 constitution stated that indigenous groups had rights to land and their own unique culture. As of 2006 the federal government had designated 12.5 percent of national land as indigenous territory. However, mining companies and large landowners still argue that this is too high a percentage of land, considering the size of the indigenous population.

FUNAI has neither the resources nor prestige to arbitrate these positions. Indeed, in 2006 the president of FUNAI stated that Indians had too much land. When Sydney Possuelo, a prestigious anthropologist in the agency, criticized these statements, FUNAI promptly dismissed him. FUNAI, moreover, organized the first National Conference of Indigenous Peoples in 2006 but many native groups complained it did little to push for pro-indigenous policies. Essentially the question is whether Brazil as a society is willing to accept the rights of its Indians, which make up less than 1 percent of the population, to maintain their cultural distinctiveness and to determine the course of their development.

*See also* **Brazil, Organizations: Indian Protection Service (IPS); Brazil, Organizations: National Indian Foundation (FUNAI); Positivism; Rondon, Cândido Mariano de Silva.**

BIBLIOGRAPHY

David Stauffer, "The Origin and Establishment of Brazil's Indian Service: 1889–1910 (Ph.D. diss., University of Texas at Austin, 1955).

Darcy Ribeiro, *A política indigenista brasileira* (1962), and *Os Índios e a civilização* (1970).

Shelton H. Davis, *Victims of the Miracle: Development and the Indians of Brazil* (1977).

Roberto Cardozo De Oliveira, "'Plural Society' and Cultural Pluralism in Brazil," in *The Prospects for Plural Societies,* edited by David Maybury-Lewis (1982).

David Price, "Overtures to the Nambiquara," in *Natural History* 93 (October 1984), and *Before the Bulldozer: The Nambiquara Indians and the World Bank* (1989).

David Maybury-Lewis, "Brazil's Significant Minority," in *The Wilson Quarterly* 14 (Summer 1990): 33–42.

Antônio Carlos De Sousa Lima, "On Indigenism and Nationality in Brazil," and David Maybury-Lewis, "Becoming Indian in Lowland South America," in *Nation States and Indians in Latin America,* edited by Greg Urban and Joel Sherzer (1991).

### *Additional Bibliography*

Almeida, Rita Heloísa de. *O diretório dos índios: Um projeto de "civilização" no Brasil do século XVIII.* Brasília, D.F.: Editora UnB, 1997.

Garfield, Seth. *Indigenous Struggle at the Heart of Brazil: State Policy, Frontier Expansion, and the Xavante Indians, 1937–1988.* Durham, NC: Duke University Press, 2001.

Rocha, Leandro. *A política indigenista no Brasil, 1930–1967.* Goiânia: Editora UFG, 2003.

Nancy M. Flowers

---

**INDIANS.** *See* **Indigenous Peoples.**

**INDIAN SLAVERY AND FORCED LABOR.** *See* **Slavery: Indian Slavery and Forced Labor.**

**INDIGENISMO.** *Indigenismo* is a multifaceted cultural and social phenomenon. From the colonial period to the present, there have been different views on the situation the indigenous populations of Latin America confronted and still confront in its struggles for recognition. From the political perspective, the tension between ethnic identity and class identity has been a constant presence in the history of Latin American *indigenismo.* During the colonial era, ethnic identity was part of a social stratification by caste; after the region's independence from Spain, social stratification, and hence the concept of social class, tended to subsume ethnic identities. The modernizing projects implemented in the first half of the twentieth century attempted to create a homogeneous national identity as the political-cultural complement to the process of capitalist integration and to the development of the modern nation-state.

In the early twentieth century, political *indigenismo* attempted to create class awareness among the indigenous peasants through unions and alliances between political parties and indigenous movements. In the second half of the twentieth century, many constituent social groups of the national identity demanded separate rights along with their own identity and history, prompting the breakdown of the modernizing movement and the revaluation of ethnicity as an element of political participation. The recognition of territory and local issues became the fundamental axis of the indigenous movement and its relationship to the state. With the adoption of the neoliberal socioeconomic model in the 1980s, state policy began to promote multiculturalism—hence shaping the political-cultural dynamic of the indigenous movement.

### PERU

In the late nineteenth and early twentieth centuries, Peruvian *indigenismo* abandoned its focus on local customs and manners, known as *costumbrismo.* Instead, *indigenista* intellectuals produced a series of works on the marginalization and exploitation of the peasant and indigenous population. When the railroad reached Cuzco, intellectuals and businessmen of that Andean city, seeking to remove what they saw as a significant obstacle to modernization, began to reconceive the role of the indigenous population and the large landowner class within the new economic situation. The objective of this early-twentieth-century *indigenismo* was to transform the indigenous peasant into a modern worker and citizen, a consumer of the products of incipient industry. To counter the national discourse, which devalued the Andean region and considered Lima the cradle of the modern nation, Cuzco intellectuals, through the university and the press, promoted Inca culture and the indigenous population.

Peasant movements were a constant presence in the Andean region of Peru in the early twentieth century. A strong official *indigenismo* developed during the second presidential term of Augusto B. Leguía (1919–1930) and indigenous rights organizations, Patronato de la Raza Indígena and Comité Pro-derecho Indígena Tahuantinsuyo, were created. These organizations convened several indigenous congresses attended by such national intellectuals as José Carlos Mariátegui and Pedro Zulen. Between 1918 and 1923, the press reported extensively on peasant mobilizations, bringing to light problems such as border disputes between haciendas and indigenous communities, the appropriation of land and livestock, and serf-like labor relations—all problems that were exacerbated by the expansion of business capital in the Peruvian Andes in the late nineteenth century. Within this context, the majority of the Cuzco indigenists believed the solution to the indigenous problem was to promote small farm ownership and to liquidate the large estates. For their part, the indigenous movements developed their own organizations and resistance strategies, including sit-down strikes on the haciendas, and the development of cooperatives to finance their activities. Movement leaders had either to cooperate or compete with the official *indigenismo* of the government and of the regional intellectuals, which produced a struggle on several fronts to control the peasant mobilizations. Despite this history of indigenous unrest, a strong contemporary indigenous movement did not arise in Peru, largely because of the strong centralism of Lima. At first the state and then the Shining Path guerrilla movement took over representation of indigenous peoples. The emergence in 2000 of the nationalist/indigenist *etnocacerista* political movement has not changed the isolation of the Peruvian indigenous movement.

## ECUADOR

After Ecuador's independence, internal colonialism and the socioeconomic system of the haciendas continued to determine the relationship between the indigenous communities and the state. These phenomena promoted a paternalistic integration of the peasant-indigenous sectors through an asymmetrical reciprocity and a patronage system. The "pact" between the landowner class and the communities became the model by which the state and society viewed and treated the indigenous people. Early on the state also promoted a process of racial mixing, characterized by the subordinate assimilation of the indigenous people into the dominant culture. This paternalism allowed some reforms under liberal regimes, such as payment of debts contracted through the labor relationship and redistribution of Church lands. Liberals on the Ecuadorian coast supported reforms, linked to an expanding global economy, that promoted remaking the serf-like peasant into a "free" worker. The state proclaimed itself the "protector" and "modernizer" of indigenous people. Despite these reforming intentions, the state did not confront the hegemony of the landowner class until the hacienda system began to decline around the mid-twentieth century. Only with the indigenous rebellion of 1990 has the state's representation of indigenous people—which has been characterized as "ventriloquism"—begun to break down. A key factor in this process of change has been the move from a peasant identity based on a class scheme to one based on ethnicity.

In 1930 the Communist Party founded an indigenous union organization that reinstated communal land ownership. Subsequently there was an alliance between the Left and the indigenous movements, and legislation was passed that allowed indigenous communities legally to register themselves and receive certain rights. Although this legislation took into account the cultural particularities of the indigenous people, ultimately it conceived of community political structure simply as a transitional stage toward other, more "modern" forms of political participation; thus it reproduced a colonialist outlook that assumes indigenous people are backward and lack initiative. In reality, the modernizing notion anticipated the cultural disappearance of indigenous people. Nevertheless, modernization in the countryside produced massive migration to the cities, where newly created ways of "being Indian" contributed fundamentally to the creation of ethnically based political movements. The dialogue between indigenous activists of the Andes and the Amazon basin produced a common ideology. This ethnic identity developed in parallel with the formation of alliances between worker and peasant unions, although these unions frequently labeled the ethnic philosophy as racist or divisive. During the reformist military regime of Rodríguez Lara (1972–1977) and the reformist constitutional administration of Jaime Roldós and Osvaldo Hurtado (1980–1984), opportunities arose for indigenous organizations along with an acknowledgment of Ecuador's ethnic and cultural pluralism. The rhetoric of multiculturalism that arose with neoliberalism encouraged the process, leading to the creation of the Confederación de Nacionalidades Indígenas del Ecuador (Confederation of Indigenous Nationalities of Ecuador; CONAIE), an entity uniting the country's diverse indigenous nationalities. The idea of a plurinational state would become central to this organization's ideology, with a more heterogeneous ethnic discourse less oriented toward the state.

## BOLIVIA

In Bolivia the corporatist state was for many years the main enemy of the indigenous movement, which was aligned with the revolutionary ideology of the Left. In contrast to Ecuador, in Bolivia the hacienda system was not dominant until the turn of the twentieth century. However, the republican state promoted agrarian reforms that increased serf-like labor relationships on the haciendas. At the same time, the state could not do without the indigenous tax and so established a pact with peasant communities that created opportunities for political autonomy on the local level. In 1899 the indigenous Aymara were vital to the liberals' triumph in their civil war with the conservatives, but this did not lead to a state policy of inclusion.

Struggles over land produced an indigenous movement that, between 1910 and 1930, restored the colonial titles to communal lands. After Bolivia's defeat by Paraguay in the Chaco War in 1935, new political parties were formed and an "Indianist" ideology developed among indigenous leaders and elite intellectuals. Several indigenous congresses in the 1940s proposed alliances between indigenous peasants and the workers' movement in the cities. In the countryside, indigenous organizations promoted sit-down strikes and indigenous activist-intellectual groups promoted an ethnically based political ideology. This mobilization was violently repressed between 1946 and 1952. The Movimiento Nacionalista Revolucionario (Revolutionary Nationalist Movement; MNR) united the sectors opposed to the oligarchy and led the April Rebellion of 1952 that installed a nationalist administration.

The new government adopted a model of development that took for granted the colonial outlook, in which everything European or Western was the model and everything mixed-race and indigenous was to be integrated. State reforms and the creation of state peasant organizations produced a process of de-ethnicization and promoted the label of peasant (*campesino*) instead of "Indian." During the right-wing dictatorship of General Hugo Bánzer (1971–1978), an indigenous movement arose that sought to free itself of state sponsorship and to form alliances based on ethnic identity. The massive peasant-indigenous migration to the cities (as to El Alto in La Paz) produced a group of indigenist activists and intellectuals, thanks in part to access to university education.

The period 1970–1986 was also pivotal in the formation of the ethnic identity of rural workers. The creation of Bolivia's confederation of peasant workers (Confederación Sindical de Trabajadores Campesinos de Bolivia; CSUTCB) broke the state's monopoly on unionism, and Katarista ideology arose. Making use of the legend of eighteenth-century Aymara rebel Tupaj Katari, indigenous intellectuals constructed an ideology that blended discourses of race/ethnicity, nation, and class but gave priority to the racial-ethnic aspect. With the return to liberal democracy in 1982 and the establishment of neoliberalism, multicultural discourse gained supremacy on the political stage. Lowland indigenous organizations began to emerge in 1990. Bolivia's western indigenous council, Central de Indígenas del Oriente de Bolivia, found allies in nongovernmental organizations; their main adversaries were mining and agro-industrial businesspeople rather than the state itself. Evo Morales Ayma, an indigenous leader of coca farmers, entered union leadership during the same period and, using an eclectic political discourse, was elected president of the republic in 2005.

### MEXICO

For Mexican social scientist Francisco Pimentel in 1864, the segregation of the Indian race was mainly due to the Indian's spiritual distance from society, and he proposed an ideal of national unity. For many intellectuals, the origins of the segregation of Indians lay in the Spanish conquest of the New World. In the opinion of the historian and politician Francisco Bulnes in 1899, independence was a struggle by the oppressed indigenous people against the European exploiter. It is only one step from this notion of race to that of social class. For Andrés Molina Enríquez in 1909, notions of race and class were mutually implicating, proposing a social classification for the country that mixed the ethnic components and the inherently economic and social elements. Bulnes blamed the conservative parties for the situation of indigenous people and believed they had held on to power by isolating the Indians. In this view liberalism, which represented the small, nascent bourgeoisie and championed industrialization and democratic revolution, was in a struggle against the reactionary landowner classes.

Liberalism's championing of indigenous communities was not purely philanthropic or ideological but in part pragmatic: liberals wanted the indigenous peasant as a political ally. Molina Enríquez is very open about this political interest. Between the national, landowner, or capitalist classes and the indigenous peasant class is a group that Molina called *mestizo*, which fought to gain the power of the state. Allied to a national party, mestizos entered government with the presidency of Benito Juárez, himself an indigenous national, in 1858, and have maintained a nominal leadership role in state bureaucracy ever since. However, it is a new national group, formed by elites linked to British and U.S. capital, that actually holds economic and political power. That elite group supported the regime of Porfirio Díaz, while the mestizo group allied itself with the indigenous peasants to take on the Porfirio Diaz regime in the Revolution of 1910.

Pimentel suggested that the Indian should abandon his system of communal ownership and acquire the habit of private ownership, becoming a small rural landowner without attacking the landowner interests. Molina Enríquez shared this opinion, but instead of protecting the interests of landowners, he proposed an agrarianism that supported peasant farmers. Despite the differences between Pimentel and Molina, both argued that Indians must recognize the mestizos through their labor. But this recognition is not reciprocal, because the Indian race is only the means for the realization of racial blending known as *mestizaje*, and also for establishing the concept of "cosmic race" (a homogeneous mixed race in which every racial trait conflates) as the official indigenist ideology of the state. In the 1950s, Manuel Gamio, a sociologist working for indigenista state institutions, proposed an indigenism with social leanings that is, in fact, only accidentally indigenism because it has to do with the liberation of the oppressed of any race. In the 1980s, particularly with the Zapatista rebellion in Chiapas, studies appeared emphasizing the cultural diversity of the Mexican national territory and exploring the ethnic dimension of sociopolitical identities.

*See also* **Bulnes, Francisco; Díaz, Porfirio; Gamio Martínez, Manuel; Indianismo; Indianismo, Spanish America; Indian Policy, Brazil; Indigenous Languages, Indigenous Organizations; Instituto Nacional Indigenista; Juárez, Benito; Leguía, Augusto Bernardino; Literature: Spanish America; Mariátegui, José Carlos; Molina Enríquez, Andrés; Zulen, Pedro S., [and] Dora Mayer de Zulen.**

BIBLIOGRAPHY

Andolina, Robert J. *Colonial Legacies and Plurinational Imaginaries. Indigenous Movement Politics in Ecuador and Bolivia*. Ph.D. diss., University of Minnesota, 1999.

Ari, Waskar T. *Race and Subaltern Nationalism: The AMP Activist-Intellectuals in Bolivia, 1921–1964.* Ph.D. diss., Georgetown University, 2004.

Calla, Ricardo. "Identificación étnica y procesos políticos en Bolivia (1973–1991)." In *Democracia, etnicidad y violencia política en los países andinos*, edited by Alberto Andrianzén et al. Lima: IEP, 1993.

Cornejo Polar, Antonio. "El *indigenismo* andino." In *América Latina: Palavra, literatura e cultura*, edited by Ana Pizarro. 3 vols. São Paulo: Universidade Estadual de Campinas, 1994.

Deustua, José, and José Luis Rénique. *Intelectuales, indigenismo y descentralismo en el Perú, 1897–1931.* Cusco: Centro Bartolomé de Las Casas, 1984.

Díaz-Polanco, Héctor. *La cuestión étnico-nacional.* México: Editorial Línea, 1985.

Guerrero, Andrés. "De sujetos indios a ciudadanos étnicos: De la manifestación de 1961 al levantamiento indígena de 1990." In *Democracia, etnicidad y violencia política en los países andinos*, edited by Alberto Andrianzén et al. Lima: IEP, 1993.

Hurtado, Javier. *El katarismo.* La Paz: HISBOL, 1986.

Knight, Alan. "Racism, Revolution, and Indigenism: Mexico, 1910–1940." In *The Idea of Race in Latin America, 1870–1940*, edited by Richard Graham. Austin: University of Texas Press, 1990.

Larson, Brooke. *Trials of Nation Making: Liberalism, Race, and Ethnicity in the Andes, 1810–1910.* Cambridge, U.K., and New York: Cambridge University Press, 2004.

Lomnitz-Adler, Claudio. *Exits from the Labyrinth: Culture and Ideology in the Mexican National Space.* Berkeley: University of California Press, 1992.

Manrique, Nelson. *Yawar Mayu: Sociedades terratenientes serranas, 1879–1910.* Lima: Instituto Francés de Estudios Andinos, DESCO, 1988.

Méndez, Cecilia. "Incas Si, Indios No: Notes on Peruvian Creole Nationalism and Its Contemporary Crisis." *Journal of Latin American Studies* 28, no. 1 (1996): 197–225.

Rivera Cusicanqui, Silvia. *Oprimidos pero no vencidos: Luchas del campesinado aymara y qhechwa de Bolivia, 1900–1980.* (English translation: *Oppressed but not Defeated: Peasant Struggles among the Aymara and Qhechwa in Bolivia, 1900–1980.*) Geneva: United Nations Research Institute for Social Development, 1986.

Salmón, Josefa. *El espejo indígena: El discurso indigenista en Bolivia, 1900–1956.* La Paz, Bolivia: Plural Editores: Facultad de Humanidades y Ciencias de la Educación, Universidad Mayor de San Andrés, 1997.

Sanjinés C., Javier. *Mestizaje Upside-Down: Aesthetic Politics in Modern Bolivia.* Pittsburgh, PA: University of Pittsburgh Press, 2004.

Stabb S., Martin. "Indigenism and Racism in Mexican Thought: 1857–1911." *Journal of Inter-American Studies* 1, no. 4 (1959): 405–423.

Stavenhagen, Rodolfo. "Challenging the Nation-State in Latin America." *Journal of International Affairs* 45, no. 2 (1992): 421–440.

Stefanoni, Pablo, and Hervé Do Alto. *Evo Morales, de la coca al palacio: Una oportunidad para la izquierda indígena.* La Paz: Malatesta, 2006.

Van Cott, Donna Lee. *From Movements to Parties in Latin America: The Evolution of Ethnic Politics.* Cambridge, U.K., and New York: Cambridge University Press, 2005.

Villoro, Luis. *Los grandes momentos del indigenismo en México.* México: CIESAS/SEP, 1987. Original edition, 1950.

ROBERTO PAREJA

**INDIGENOUS LANGUAGES.** In discussing the indigenous languages of Latin America, it is necessary to begin by qualifying the geolinguistic zones of relevance. For North America, linguists prefer to speak of languages north of Mexico. For Central America, however, linguists allude either to the geographic area otherwise known as Middle America, including Mexico and Central America, or to Mesoamerica, a region extending from northern Mexico, south of the Pánuco River, to El Salvador, but also including Pacific coast of southwestern Nicaragua and northwestern Costa Rica, and excluding most of Honduras, Nicaragua, and Costa Rica. The latter region—eastern Honduras, Nicaragua, Costa Rica, and Panama—is referred to as lower Central America, and is more properly included in the treatment of the indigenous languages of South America, along with continental South America and the Antilles. South America includes the following geographic regions: "continental South America, lower Central America, and the Antilles: i.e., Latin America without MesoAmerica" (Kaufman, p. 13). It can be further subdivided into several geolinguistic subregions (Kaufman, pp. 32–35): Northwest, Amazonia (western, central, and northern), Foothills (northern and southern), Southern Cone, Chaco, and Brazil (eastern and northeastern).

## DIVERSITY, HISTORICAL RELATIONSHIPS, AND LINGUISTIC AREAS

A conservative estimate of the number of language families and isolates for North America stands at fifty-eight, and at about fifteen for Mexico and Central America. The total number of extant languages is approximately 200 in the United States and Canada, and 350 for Mexico and Central America. In the United States and Canada, at least twice as many languages may have existed at the time of European contact. A few ethnolinguistic groups from the United States migrated south after 1500 (e.g., Apachean, an Athapaskan language, and Kickapoo, a Central Algonquian language), and at least one, Carib, a member of the Arawakan family from South America, arrived after 1797, when its speakers were relocated from Saint Vincent and became the so-called "Black Carib" of Central America, that is, the Garífuna (Belize, Guatemala, Honduras, Nicaragua). Excluding these late arrivals, North America and Central America contain about seventy-three conventionally accepted language families. Opinions on the number of language families and isolates in South America (by Morris Swadesh, Jorge Suárez, Joseph Greenberg, Terrence Kaufman, Alden Mason, and Čestmír Loukotka, among others) differ in important ways. Lyle Campbell (1997) follows Kaufman's classification into 118 phylogenetic units, 48 of which consist of language families, and 70 of isolates. Campbell notes that it is likely to be a conservative, and in some cases merely tentative, estimate that can serve as a starting point for further refinement.

In terms of total number of languages, in the early twenty-first century between about 350 and 422 languages are spoken; this may be about one-fifth of the total number of languages that were spoken in South America at the time of contact with the Europeans. It is likely that throughout the Americas, more than 2,000 languages may have been spoken prior to the arrival of the Europeans, of which fewer than half have survived to the present. The majority of speakers of indigenous languages are found in Mexico, Guatemala, Perú, Bolivia, Ecuador, and Paraguay, where they number in the hundreds of thousands or millions, at least for a few languages: Nahuatl, Yucatec Maya, K'iche', Kaqchikel, Q'eqchi', Aymara, Quechua, and Guaraní. After these languages, most of the indigenous languages of the Americas are spoken by 100,000 to a few thousand to a handful of speakers, depending on the language. In South America, Manuel Lizarralde (1988, pp. 10–11) reports that out of a maximum of 472 ethnolinguistic groups, 141 have fewer than 100 speakers, 241 fewer than 300, and 346 fewer than 1,000; at the same time, all these 472 groups constitute about 3.71 percent of the total population of South America, based on estimates for 1976 to 1987.

## LONG-DISTANCE RELATIONSHIPS AND SOCIOLINGUISTIC SITUATIONS

A number of scholars have proposed long-distance phylolinguistic relationships among some or many of these language families, most notoriously Edward

Sapir, with his Penutian stock, and Joseph Greenberg (1987), who classified all of the languages of the Americas into three families: Eskimo-Aleut, Na Dene, and Amerind. Amerind would include all of the languages of North America, Central America, and South America not included within Eskimo-Aleut or Na Dene. These and other proposals so far lack support from most specialists, and in some respects, as in the case of Greenberg's Amerind, are known to exhibit serious methodological flaws. Some proposals exist for broader groupings of language families and isolates in South America. Some such proposals have been rejected through more detailed analysis (e.g., Maya-Chipaya, Maya-Chipaya-Yunga), whereas for others the jury is still out (e.g., Quechumaran, or Quechua-Aymara).

In terms of linguistic typology, there is also considerable diversity in North America and Central America. The works by Joel Sherzer (1976) and Yoshiho Yasugi (1995) document the major areal and typological traits for North America and Middle America, respectively. There is also great diversity among South American languages; however, there is no synthesis of South American languages comparable to those by Sherzer and Yasugi. Comprehensive surveys exist (Pottier 1983; Tovar and Larrucea de Tovar 1984; Fabre 1998), but these tend to catalog nonlinguistic data for the languages, such as population estimates and geographic location, in addition to proposed genetic groupings, with the exception of the 1961 work of Antonio Tovar, which covers some typological traits, but not as many, and not as systematically, as in the approaches by Sherzer and Yasugi.

There are approximately twenty-three linguistic areas, areas that show persistent—lexical, phonological, morphological, syntactic—linguistic traits that have diffused geographically, even among nonrelated languages, after long periods of contact, which can be properly considered as part of North America and Mesoamerica. Of the twenty-two defined for the United States and Canada, two in particular have experienced contact with Spanish: the Southern California–Western Arizona Area (compare Chumash Indians) and the Pueblo Area (compare Pueblo Indians). The remaining linguistic area is the Mesoamerican Linguistic Area. In South America the following seven linguistic areas have been defined: the Colombia–Central American Area, the Venezuelan-Antillean Area, the Andean Area, the Ecuadoran-Colombian Area, the Orinoco-Amazon Linguistic Area, the Amazon Linguistic Area or Lowland South America, and the Southern Cone Area. Some of these are regarded as preliminary definitions, requiring further research to confirm and refine, as well as to incorporate into future considerations of genetic linguistic relationships.

Regarding linguistic contacts, aside from the linguistic area phenomenon, it is of course evident that Spanish has exerted a major influence in the form of hispanisms, which include not only lexical items, but also grammatical particles. Hispanisms of both types are found in a considerable number of terms from Nahuatl, the language of the Aztec Empire, which was diffused throughout the North and Central America into Spanish, English, and Portuguese, and from other indigenous languages, through Spanish. The same process is evident throughout South America with regard to terms from Quechua (also Quichua or Kichwa), the language of the Inca Empire, adopted by and diffused through Spanish, and in a more limited fashion, in Paraguay, with regard to terms from Guaraní, although this time as the result of the unusual acceptability of Guaraní as a national language, compared to other situations in Latin America. Prior to the arrival of the Europeans, linguistic diffusion of both types was already extensive in numerous instances among indigenous languages. In fact, this phenomenon has been key to the reconstruction of culture histories in different parts of Latin America, as with the case of the ancient prestigious status of Mixe-Zoquean in Mesoamerica, which suggests a very influential role by its speakers, who may have been the bearers of Olmec civilization.

## LINGUISTIC ENDANGERMENT, DOCUMENTATION, AND MAINTENANCE

Linguistic diffusion, sometimes resulting in long-term linguistic convergence, which can lead to the formation of linguistic areas, is often the result of social forces such as economic and political interactions. Since the arrival of the Spanish, and continuing through the colonial and postcolonial periods, socio-economic and political marginalization, and outright genocide, have generally resulted from intensive modernization, nation-building, and globalization policies, and have led to more extreme forms of short-term linguistic change, such as language shift and language loss—two stages in the process of language endangerment. Many ethnolinguistic groups have experienced (and in some cases, continue to experience) marginalization and discrimination, even violence. Language shift and loss have been all too common in such cases, and many groups have shifted to English, Spanish, or Portuguese as a result. Particularly as a result of increasing numbers of illegal migrants from Mesoamerica to the United States, many indigenous people from that region are now engaged in contact with English, and thus it is possible that a new model of language shift and loss will soon emerge within immigrant communities in the United States—a shift to English, as in the case of the Yucatec Mayans in San Francisco, and the Awakatek Mayans in Morganton, North Carolina.

There have been positive responses to language endangerment in Canada, the United States, Mexico, Guatemala, Central America, Colombia, Bolivia, Ecuador, Paraguay, and Peru; some of these efforts, as well as their successes and persisting problems, are discussed by contributors to Nancy Hornberger's *Indigenous Literacies in the Americas* (1997). In the last three countries, for example, several indigenous languages have national, co-official status (e.g., Quechua and Aymara in Peru and Bolivia, Guaraní in Paraguay). Indigenous-language–education programs have been implemented in Mexico, as with the case of Yucatec Maya in the Yucatan peninsula, and have become official policy in Guatemala, where implementation is only in its initial stages. In Colombia the indigenous communities have achieved semiautonomy from the government, a factor that could lead to successful indigenous-education programs.

The major problem remains the pervasive negative perception of indigenous languages as obstacles to economic opportunity, not only by the mainstream, nonindigenous populations of these countries, but also by the marginalized, indigenous populations themselves. Save for the few indigenous languages that are spoken by hundreds of thousands or even millions of people, it remains entirely possible that most of the indigenous languages of the Americas will become extinct by the end of the present century (Krauss 1992). The languages can survive only by the sincere efforts on the parts of governments and nongovernmental organizations—that is, efforts including adequate funding and continuing support, not just policy writing, and especially efforts sanctioned and spear-headed by indigenous communities, focusing both on indigenous language education and on culturally prestigious and economically advantageous social uses of the languages. In other words, such efforts must focus on the role of linguistic and ethnic identity, the very factor that modernization and nation-building enterprises have tried to erase. This method has been implemented successfully in Latin America by indigenous organizations during the past few decades, and shows promise for the future. Evo Morales, the current president of Bolivia and himself an Aymara Indian, may be particularly helpful in promoting such efforts.

*See also* **Indigenous Peoples.**

BIBLIOGRAPHY

Campbell, Lyle. *American Indian Languages: The Historical Linguistics of Native America.* New York: Oxford University Press, 1997.

Fabre, Alain. *Manual de las lenguas indígenas sudamericanas,* 3 vols. Munich: Lincom Europa, 1998.

Greenberg, Joseph. *Language in the Americas.* Stanford, CA: Stanford University Press, 1987.

Hornberger, Nancy H., ed. *Indigenous Literacies in the Americas: Language Planning from the Bottom Up.* Berlin and New York: Mouton de Gruyter, 1997.

Kaufman, Terrence. "Language History in South America: What We Know and How to Know More." In *Amazonian Linguistics: Studies in Lowland South American Languages,* ed. Doris L. Payne. Austin: University of Texas Press, 1990.

Krauss, Michael E. "The World's Languages in Crisis." *Language* 68 (1992): 4–10.

Lizarralde, Manuel. *Índice y mapa de grupos etnolingüísticos autóctonos de América del Sur.* Caracas: Fundación La Salle, Instituto Caribe de Antropología y Sociología, 1988.

Pottier, Bernard, ed. *América Latina en sus lenguas indígenas.* Caracas: Monte Avila Editores, 1983.

Sherzer, Joel. *An Areal-Typological Study of American Indian Languages North of Mexico.* Amsterdam, Oxford, and New York: North-Holland, 1976.

Tovar, Antonio. *Catálogo de las lenguas de América del Sur: Enumeración, con indicaciones tipológicas, bibliografía y mapas.* Buenos Aires: Editorial Sudamericana, 1961.

Tovar, Antonio, and Consuelo Larrucea de Tovar. *Catálogo de las lenguas de América del Sur.* Madrid: Editorial Gredos, 1984.

Yasugi, Yoshiho. *Native Middle American Languages: An Areal-Typological Perspective.* Osaka, Japan: National Museum of Ethnology, 1995.

DAVID MORA-MARÍN

## INDIGENOUS ORGANIZATIONS.

Indigenous organizations in Latin America emerged as key political players during the last quarter of the twentieth century. The rise of these organizations both fueled and resulted from the politics of identity that have become increasingly prevalent in Latin America. These organizations represent a population that has suffered a history of exclusion and that is generally poorer than the average in Latin America. Indigenous grassroots organizations have mobilized to gain political recognition for cultural rights and access to land and economic resources.

The constitutions of many major Latin American countries, including Bolivia, Brazil, Peru, and Colombia, were rewritten in the early 1990s to include indigenous cultural rights, reflecting indigenous organizations' varying degrees of success in political mobilization. The political strength and impact of these organizations in each Latin American country was not necessarily related to the indigenous group's relative demographic presence. In Peru, where the indigenous population represents 40 percent of the total population, indigenous organizations have had a minimal impact in gaining political recognition and greater access to economic wealth for their people. In contrast, in Colombia, where the indigenous population represents only 2 percent of the total population, indigenous organizations such as the Consejo Regional Indígena del Cauca (CRIC; Regional Indigenous Council of the Cauca) were instrumental in pressuring the national government to grant close to 25 percent of the national territory to indigenous communities.

For the most part, Latin American indigenous organizations emerged from a class-based mobilization in the 1970s. In a second stage, indigenous communities mobilized either according to geographical and ecological origin (lowland areas versus highland) or by political region. For instance, in Bolivia, the lowland Confederation of Indigenous People of Bolivia (CIDOB) organized indigenous communities from the lowlands in the early 1980s. A third stage usually consisted of indigenous organizations acquiring national clout by joining other indigenous organizations and morphing into a national organization. International organizations such as the United Nations and various nongovernmental organizations (NGOs) also played a crucial role in giving indigenous organizations greater political legitimacy in recent decades. Undoubtedly indigenous organizations will evolve, reflecting the changing demands of indigenous communities, but they are now an integral part of the Latin American political landscape.

*See also* **Indigenous Languages; Indigenous Peoples.**

BIBLIOGRAPHY

Garcia, Maria Elena. *Making Indigenous Citizens: Identities, Education, and Multicultural Development in Peru.* Stanford, CA: Stanford University Press, 2005.

Lucero, José Antonio. "Representing 'Real Indians': The Challenges of Indigenous Authenticity and Strategic Constructivism in Ecuador and Bolivia." *Latin American Research Review* 41, no. 2 (2006): 31–56.

Rappaport, Joanne. *Intercultural Utopias: Public Intellectuals, Cultural Experimentation, and Ethnic Pluralism in Colombia.* Durham, NC: Duke University Press, 2005.

Rivera Cusicanqui, Silvia. *Oppressed but Not Defeated: Peasant Struggles amongst the Aymara and the Qhechwa in Bolivia, 1900–1980.* Geneva: United Nations Institute Research for Social Development, 1987.

Van Cott, Donna. *The Friendly Liquidation of the Past: The Politics of Diversity in Latin America.* Pittsburgh, PA: Pittsburgh University Press, 2000.

BRETT TROYAN

## INDIGENOUS PEOPLES.

The term *indigenous peoples* generally refers to those ethnic groups descended from populations that were present in a geographic region prior to the colonial era. In Latin America it has come to replace the term *Indians,* which was a misnomer applied by Columbus that is also generally taken as a pejorative term. Although most Latin Americans could claim some pre-European ancestral link, those who are identified and self-identify as indigenous also share a set of distinguishing traits. These often include close and long historical connection to place and distinct language and culture practices; however, it is difficult to create a single set of markers. Many indigenous populations have moved over time, and there are some widely accepted indigenous groups with distinct language and culture who did not exist as distinct ethnic groups prior to colonialism.

Because of such complexities in categorization, one of the key indicators is self-identification.

### PRE-COLUMBIAN POPULATIONS

The ancestors of present-day indigenous peoples came to the Americas from Asia in several waves over the Bering land bridge beginning 15,000 to 20,000 years ago, and perhaps as long as 30,000 to 40,000 years ago. Like all humans of the time, these first settlers were late stone-age hunter-gatherers with small and highly mobile populations. They expanded throughout the Americas, developing a wide range of adaptations to local environments. The majority moved with the seasons or to follow game, whereas some encountered abundant resources in coastal areas that enabled larger and more sedentary populations.

The domestication of a wide range of plants (such as corn, beans, squash, potatoes, and manioc) and a small handful of animals (such as turkey, llama, and guinea pig), beginning around 8,000 BCE, set the stage for the evolution of larger populations and more complex societies. Only in areas where the environment significantly hindered the development or diffusion of agriculture did nomadic hunting and gathering lifestyles remain common, such as in parts of Patagonia, the Chilean Archipelago, Tierra del Fuego, and the pampas of Argentina. Elsewhere, populations became agricultural experts, and sedentary villages became common between 3,000 and 1,000 BCE. In some cases ethnic groups maintained small villages, political decentralization, little specialization, and a high degree of egalitarianism, as was the case in the Gran Chaco region and much of Amazonia. In other cases population pressures on resources, competition with neighbors, and the demands of managing trade networks, earthworks, and irrigation led societies to grow increasingly complex sociopolitical organization. Where conditions permitted, chiefdoms with a centralized authority and control over multiple communities developed, as well as states with centralized authority and formal bureaucracies.

In both the Antilles and the Amazon basin, chiefdoms were the most complex form of sociopolitical organization to evolve. In the Antilles, hunter-gatherers who had arrived from the Yucatán and/or Central America around 5,000 BCE were displaced between 1 and 500 CE by a migration of pottery-making horticulturalists from the Orinoco River Valley. By 1000 CE, these evolved into Arawak chiefdoms, and by 1492 there were villages of up to five thousand people with ball courts and ceremonial plazas. In the Amazon basin, chiefdoms are indicated by large mounds and extensive pottery remains on Marajó Island, and by expansive networks of raised fields and canals in the Llanos de Mojos of Bolivia. Evidence that has come to light since the early 1990s, including large villages with defensive moats and linked by roads, has also challenged the long-held assumption that such complexity could not develop in the central Amazon. A number of other large ethnic groups also developed chiefdoms by the time of contact, such as the Tupinambá and Guaraní of the Atlantic Coast of Brazil, the Mapuche of central Chile, and the Muiscas of Colombia, whose integrated village system of perhaps one million persons was one of the last to be conquered by the Spanish.

Only in Mesoamerica and the Central Andes is there undisputed evidence of the rise of states. In Mesoamerica the Olmec, who many believe were ancestral to all later states in the region, appeared about 1500 BCE and lasted until 1 CE. During the "Classic" period, 250–900 CE, there were several city-states in Mexico. These included the Maya, who built impressive cities such as Tikal in Guatemala and Chichén Itzá in the Yucatán. In 1325 the Aztec used causeways and raised farm plots to establish their capital of Tenochtitlán on an island in Lake Texcoco in central Mexico. Within a century, through conquest and alliances, they built the largest civilization ever seen on the continent. By the time the Spanish arrived, the capital had grown to about 300,000 persons. As with the Maya, they developed extensive trading networks, metalwork, math, writing, and a calendar. Religion and ritual were central to the state, and priests were part of the noble class in a rigid hierarchy. Human sacrifice was believed necessary to ensure the survival of the world and was practiced on a large scale. The Aztec centralized rule and united the region through taxation and tribute; however, their heavy exploitation of commoners and lack of redistribution to conquered groups created hostility against them.

In the Andes the first regional states, such as the Moche group on the northern coast of Peru, began to appear after 200 BCE and demonstrated both pyramidal construction and metalworking. By the thirteenth century there were a number of competing military powers in the Central Andes. Within a century the Inca emerged through conquest to become the largest empire of the Americas, stretching from northern Ecuador to central Chile. Agriculture was expanded through complex terracing and irrigation systems, and surplus production was controlled and redistributed by the empire. The Inca's exceptional organization included an expansive road system and warehouse network that enabled trade and communication. These, as well as monumental architecture, were built and maintained through collective labor recruited by tax (the *mitá*) on local allyus (kin-based local political and economic units). Religion, focusing on ancestor worship, played an important role in the empire but less so than for the Aztec.

## COLONIALISM AND INDIGENOUS PEOPLES

Perhaps fifty to sixty million indigenous peoples and a great diversity of cultures occupied the Americas in 1492. By the end of the sixteenth century, most were conquered by much smaller European forces. Indigenous spear throwers in cotton armor were no match for mounted cavalry, steel weapons and armor, and artillery. For example, in one battle 168 Spanish conquistadors were able to defeat an army of 80,000 Inca warriors. The Spanish also took advantage of opposition to the Aztec and an Inca civil war to build temporary alliances. The most important weapon in the conquest was introduced disease, such as smallpox and influenza. The indigenous populations had little or no immunity, and their populations were decimated. Smallpox killed as many as one-quarter of the Aztec shortly after the arrival of Cortez, and preceded Pizarro to the Andes, inducing the civil war. Soon after contact, populations plummeted by more than 90 percent in some places. The Arawak population of the Antilles, for example, dropped from around one million to virtually disappear by the mid-sixteenth century. Numerous ethnic groups were completely eliminated, which is reflected by the estimate that only one-third of the linguistic diversity that existed at contact survives in the early twenty-first century.

A primary goal of the new rulers was to extract mineral resources and surplus production. Those indigenous populations that survived the epidemics became subject to intense exploitation, which, combined with the impact of disease, significantly disrupted their traditional economic and political systems. Initially, indigenous peoples were taken as slaves or subjected to the *encomienda* system, in which the rights over an indigenous cacique and his people were given to a conquistador. In many areas these systems were replaced by a compulsory labor draft, such as *repartamiento*, which was largely supplanted by the middle of the seventeenth century by free wage labor, in which indigenous peoples without land or wishing to avoid compulsory labor demands could live and work on haciendas. Where they existed, royal indigenous families were pushed aside, and colonists married royal women to obtain claims on resources. The outcome of this combination of practices was that indigenous peoples were displaced from lands, moved to work in mines, their exchange relationships were broken, specialization was eliminated, and accumulated wealth was destroyed. The new lords extracted surplus but did not redistribute goods or reinvest in the colonial economy. In addition, offspring of mixed marriages were often recognized as legitimate heirs and aided in entrenching the nonindigenous rulers.

Evangelical efforts exerted another kind of pressure. Indigenous inhabitants were frequently open to this, as they perceived the great power of the Europeans to reflect the power of the Christian God. Franciscans, Dominicans, Augustinians, Jesuits, and other orders joined in the conversion effort, which in part involved destroying indigenous religions. Native priests were persecuted and religious sites were replaced with churches. There was also an effort by the Church to concentrate the indigenous into villages and missions where they could be protected from the physical and moral pressures of colonists, provided with social services, and instructed in religion and European culture. Friars learned and promoted Nahuatl in Mexico, Quechua in Peru, and Tupi in Brazil. These efforts together with the social and economic policies of the colonial rulers served to socially segregate the native populations from the European immigrants, while at the same time diminishing the significance of ethnic and class distinctions among the indigenous groups.

Indigenous populations responded in a number of ways to the pressures of colonialism. Whereas some chose to remain in their communities and bear the weight of new demands, some physically resisted. In Mesoamerica, Maya groups were among the most resistant. The Yucatec Maya, largely because of their political decentralization, held off the Spanish until the end of the seventeenth century. In 1712 Maya in Chiapas rebelled when the church denied a young Maya woman's sighting of the Virgin Mary. In the Andean region there were dozens of uprisings in the second half of the eighteenth century. Among the most significant were those of Túpac Amaru and the Kataris, who demanded better treatment and reductions in tributes. They were defeated by a combination of royal troops and *allyu* (leaders loyal to the crown) at the cost of 100,000 lives. Another strategy of indigenous groups was isolation. The lowland forests of South America, for example, provided haven for a number of groups until the twentieth century. Resistance was also shown in indigenous peoples' ability to maintain key traditions, such as communal landholdings. And despite the evangelical efforts to eliminate "false idols," indigenous peoples developed religious syncretisms that incorporated traditional beliefs. Yet, under the intense pressures of colonialism, many also accepted varying degrees of assimilation. They left their communities for work on Spanish farms and ranches, or they moved to urban areas to join the working class.

## THE POSTCOLONIAL PERIOD

By 1826 Latin America had secured its independence from Spain and Portugal, and constitutions established equality and ended forced labor and tribute. The status for indigenous peoples did not improve, however, as those seeking to modernize the new nation states and participate in export economies often saw indigenous traditions as an obstacle. There was an "Indian problem." A primary concern was traditional community lands, and numerous states passed laws or otherwise sought to divide up and privatize these. Many indigenous peoples were forced into exploitative and coercive labor arrangements such as debt peonage (the use of indebted laborers under conditions of servitude) or sharecropping. Other policies sought to acculturate indigenous populations to the national ideal through strategies such as forbidding the use of indigenous languages in schools and discouraging traditional dress. In some areas, state-sponsored violence against the indigenous was common. In parts of Central America, for example, indigenous communities supporting land reform in the twentieth century were frequently labeled as leftist and suffered military crackdowns.

The pressures on indigenous economy and culture and growing inequalities in landholding and wealth led to rebellions in a number of Latin American countries. One of the most successful of these occurred in Panama, where Kuna of the east coast rebelled in 1925, and eventually received legal recognition and semi-autonomy over a region now known as the Comarca de Kuna Yala. In Mexico, Indian communities under Emiliano Zapata in the southern state of Morelos played a key role in the revolution, which led to the distribution of communal lands (*ejidos*), including about one million acres to twelve thousand villages under Lázaro Cárdenas. In many cases, indigenous interests in land redistribution coincided with liberals' views that existing semifeudal relations were depressing economic growth. Peru, Bolivia, and Ecuador underwent reforms in the mid-twentieth century that were quite successful in eliminating semifeudal systems and reducing the relevance of the latifundio (landed estates). Yet most indigenous peoples who benefited gained only small amounts of poor-quality land and no additional support. In addition, Brazil, Ecuador, Bolivia, and Peru all looked to Amazon lowlands as a source of unoccupied lands that could relieve population pressures and spur the economy, and many indigenous groups that had remained largely isolated came under intense pressure.

## INDIGENOUS PEOPLES TODAY

In the early twenty-first century, indigenous peoples make up between 7.5 and 10 percent of the population, or about 34 million to 55 million people. Of these, 90 percent are concentrated in Mexico, Peru, Bolivia, Guatemala, and Ecuador. Although there was certainly no sense of shared identity in 1492, their social segregation and treatment since that time have resulted in an intense shared experience and common challenges. The "indigenous" identity forged by this experience is evident in the rapid rise since the 1980s of a large number of ethnic-based movements with common goals that have linked at national and transnational scales and often taken the national and international center stage. In Brazil this was seen in the alliances between indigenous groups and environmentalists to fight large-scale development in the Amazon. In Chiapas, Mexico, it was seen

**Guatemalan indigenous leader and Nobel Prize winner Rigoberta Menchú (center) and Evo Morales (left), Bolivia's first indigenous president, at a ceremony to celebrate the UN Declaration on the Rights of Indigenous Peoples, 2007.** AP IMAGES

with the Zapatista rebellion, which commenced the day that the North American Free Trade Agreement (NAFTA) went into effect in 1994. In Ecuador and Bolivia it has been seen in the alliances between highland and lowland groups that have forced presidents from office and major legislative reforms.

One of the key concerns of these movements has been access to and control over territories and natural resources. Most indigenous cultures are integrally connected to their local environments through their economy and a range of cultural practices, such as those tied to health and religion, thus making threats on these resources threats to cultural survival. Indigenous movements have pushed for a new wave of land reforms to include the demarcation and delineation of indigenous territories. They have often received support from environmental groups, who view indigenous practices as alternatives to large-scale development projects. Such land-titling programs have been initiated in a number of states, including Bolivia, Brazil, Colombia, Ecuador, Peru, and Venezuela, and are often also associated with varying degrees of increased regional autonomy.

A second major set of issues concerns social and economic development. Despite increased attention over the last decade by the United Nations and the World Bank, indigenous populations tend to be the poorest, with the lowest levels of education and literacy, the poorest schools, the least income per year of schooling, and the worst access to healthcare. Most indigenous communities depend on national and global economies and want to benefit from and participate in social and economic development, though in ways that are appropriate to their cultures and needs. They are aware of their relative status and are becoming increasingly impatient with states' evident failures to recognize their needs and with the unfulfilled promises that neoliberal economic policy will benefit all. Increasingly, communities have looked to their own organizations or partnered with nongovernment organizations (NGOs) to provide projects that both serve basic needs and strengthen community and culture. Although there has been much enthusiasm for these efforts, grassroots organizations are often unprepared to meet the combined demands of their constituents and funding agencies, and NGOs are often criticized for fostering dependence.

A final major issue is the legal recognition and political participation of indigenous peoples. Policies of the postcolonial states generally did not recognize ethnic diversity. The rights and protections for indigenous peoples were ambiguous, and the effort was to assimilate them. Modern movements are seeking full citizenship rights for indigenous peoples and the recognition of the multiethnic nature of states. In response, a number of states have redrafted their constitutions to recognize themselves as pluricultural nations. In some countries this has included education reforms that enable schooling in native languages. A number of indigenous groups have also chosen to enter politics as a means to address their broader agenda. For example, the 2005 election of Evo Morales, an indigenous Aymara, as president of Bolivia is a testament to the political power that indigenous organizations were able to amass.

The shared history and challenges of indigenous groups throughout Latin America should not obscure the great diversity that still exists. This diversity is well reflected by the distinct languages, estimated to number between four hundred and seven hundred, still spoken in Latin America, each of which attests to distinct cultural practices and differing sets of knowledge and beliefs concerning the natural and supernatural world. Some groups inhabit tropical forests, others highland plateaus. Some subsist primarily on hunting and gathering, some by slash-and-burn horticulture, some by agropastoralism, some by intensive agriculture, and some through trade of manufactured goods. Many have extensive knowledge of their distinct local environments. Although most practice some degree of Christianity, this is frequently combined with a great variety of practices and beliefs, such as witchcraft, shamanism, and ancestor worship. Across Latin America there is a great assortment of ritual practices, mythologies, dress, and craftsmanship. Family and kinship are powerful organizing devices, but there is diversity in how these are reckoned and the roles that they play in individual lives. Finally, even within ethnic communities there is diversity. Like communities elsewhere in the world, indigenous communities are complex social and political entities. "Traditional" knowledge is not shared equally, community and regional politics can be contentious, and there can be considerable disagreement over the desired future and the ways to achieve it.

*See also* **Indigenous Languages; Guarani Indians; Incas, The; Indianismo; Indianismo, Spanish America; Indian Policy, Brazil; Indigenismo; Indigenous Organizations; Katarismo; Kuna (Cuna); Maya, the; Morales, Evo; Nahuatl; Neoliberalism; Quechua; Slavery: Indian Slavery and Forced Labor; Túpac Amaru; Tupi.**

BIBLIOGRAPHY

*Edited Works: Ethnographic and Historical Studies of Regions*

Adams, Richard E. W., and Murdo J. MacLeod, eds. *The Cambridge History of the Native Peoples of the Americas.* Vol. 2: *Mesoamerica.* Cambridge, U.K., and New York: Cambridge University Press, 2000.

Kicza, John E., ed. *The Indian in Latin American History: Resistance, Resilience, and Acculturation.* Wilmington, DE: SR Books, 2000.

Roosevelt, Anna, ed. *Amazonian Indians from Prehistory to the Present: Anthropological Perspectives.* Tuscon: University of Arizona Press, 1994.

Salomon, Frank, and Stuart B. Schwartz, eds. *The Cambridge History of the Native Peoples of the Americas.* Vol. 3: *South America.* Cambridge, U.K., and New York: Cambridge University Press, 1999.

Steward, Julian H., ed. *Handbook of South American Indians* L, 7 vols. Washington, DC: U.S. Government Printing Office, 1946–1959.

Wauchope, Robert, ed. *Handbook of Middle American Indians,* 16 vols. Austin: University of Texas Press, 1964–1976. *Supplement,* 5 vols., 1981–1986.

Wilson, Samuel, ed. *The Indigenous People of the Caribbean.* Gainesville: University Press of Florida, 1997.

*Contemporary Indigenous Issues*

Hall, Gillette, and Harry Anthony Patrinos, eds. *Indigenous Peoples, Poverty, and Human Development in Latin America.* New York: Palgrave Macmillan, 2006.

Maybury-Lewis, David, ed. *The Politics of Ethnicity: Indigenous Peoples in Latin American States.* Cambridge, MA: Harvard University Press, 2002.

Menchú, Rigoberta. *I, Rigoberta Menchú: An Indian Woman in Guatemala,* edited by Elisabeth Burgos-Debray; translated by Ann Wright. London: Verso, 1987. Famous but controversial account of indigenous life and state repression in an indigenous testimonial style.

Urban, Greg, and Joel Sherzer, eds. *Nation-States and Indians in Latin America.* Austin: University of Texas Press, 1991.

*Single-Author Syntheses of Major Regions*

Mayer, Enrique. *The Articulated Peasant: Household Economies in the Andes.* Boulder, CO: Westview Press, 2002. Andean ethnology from Incas to present.

Olson, James S. *The Indians of Central and South America: An Ethnohistorical Dictionary.* New York: Greenwood Press, 1991. Concise but uncritical survey of indigenous groups.

Rouse, Irving. *The Tainos : Rise and Decline of the People Who Greeted Columbus.* New Haven, CT: Yale University Press, 1992.

Wolf, Eric. *Sons of the Shaking Earth.* Chicago: University of Chicago Press, 1959.

J. MONTGOMERY ROPER

---

**INDIGO.** The cultivation of indigo (*tinta añil*) in the New World dates to pre-Hispanic times. The Indians of northern Central America harvested wild indigo plants, called *xiquilite,* which they traded extensively and used as a rich blue dye for textiles.

During the late sixteenth century, the Spaniards domesticated the cultivation of indigo in Central America and established indigo plantations in Yucatán and along the fertile Pacific coasts of present-day El Salvador, Guatemala, and Nicaragua. Spaniards exported their first indigo in 1576, when a shipload was sent from Nicaragua to New Spain, where it was used in Mexico's nascent textile industry. By 1600, indigo had replaced cacao—until that time Central America's most profitable commodity—as the leading export. In the early seventeenth century, indigo also became the leading source of hard currency for the isthmus.

Indigo was highly valued in the Old World, where it supplanted more expensive blue dyes from the Far East and inferior dyes produced from woad in northern Europe. From 1580 to 1620 the Central American indigo industry thrived. *Añileros* (indigo planters) employed Indians for harvesting and processing the plant. Because the work was difficult and dangerous (extended contact with the toxins present in the indigo plant often proved fatal, as did constant exposure to the swamp waters used to extract dye from the plants), the industry was limited by the size of the indigenous labor supply. Although the work was dangerous, labor scarcity gave the indigenous workers some power in the colonial order, according to recent research. The *repartimiento* (distribution or assessment) system, traditionally explained as a way of forcing indigenous communities to buy unwanted goods, may have provided an incentive to keep the laborers producing indigo. This interpretation suggests that the repartimiento was a form of forced credit that intended to keep the labor force motivated. By the mid-seventeenth century, the indigo industry had stagnated. In the late seventeenth century, however, a resurgence in the size of the Indian population allowed the industry to expand again, at which time African slaves were imported to augment the labor force.

By 1635, San Vicente, El Salvador, had become the hub of the indigo trade, although other important centers were located in Guatemala and Nicaragua. The locus of the trade later shifted to Sonsonate, El Salvador, once the center of the colonial cacao trade, and to Guatemala. In addition to the European trade, Central American indigo also made its way to Mexico and Peru.

Indigo remained the most important export of the Kingdom of Guatemala throughout the colonial period. The industry reached its peak during the second half of the eighteenth century, when the expanding textile industry in northern Europe created a significant demand for the rich blue hue. The "free trade" economic policies of the Spanish Bourbons in the eighteenth century also enhanced the indigo trade, and in 1782 *añileros* formed an Indigo Growers Society based in Guatemala City. By the last years of the colonial period, indigo generated more than 2 million pesos worth of profits per year.

By the last decades of the eighteenth century, however, indigo exports from Central America began to decline, although the dye continued to bring heavy profits for planters in South Carolina, Venezuela, and the East Indies. In the mid-eighteenth century, Brazil's reformer, the Marquis de Pombal, introduced indigo production to Rio de Janeiro and Maranhão, where the dye's high price helped compensate for the decline of sugar production in that country.

Indigo's importance as a commodity diminished worldwide during the nineteenth century, as cheaper synthetic dyes became available. El Salvador continued to export some indigo into the late nineteenth century.

*See also* **Free Trade Act; Slavery: Spanish America.**

BIBLIOGRAPHY

Ralph Lee Woodward, Jr., *Class Privilege and Economic Development: The Consulado de Comercio of Guatemala, 1793–1871* (1966).

Murdo J. Mac Leod, *Spanish Central America: A Socioeconomic History, 1520–1720* (1973).

William L. Sherman, *Forced Native Labor in Sixteenth Century Central America* (1979).

Woodward, *Central America: A Nation Divided* (1985).

*Additional Bibliography*

Fernández M., José Antonio. *Pintando el mundo de azul: El auge añilero y el mercado centroamericano, 1750–1810.* San Salvador: Dirección de Publicaciones e Impresos, Consejo Nacional para la Cultura y el Arte, 2003.

VIRGINIA GARRARD- BURNETT

**INDUSTRIALIZATION.** Industrialization, an increase in the proportion of total gross domestic product (GDP) resulting from the manufacture of goods in mechanized factories. This process began relatively late in Latin America and has, partly as a consequence, developed slowly and unevenly. Since the conquest and colonization of Latin America by European powers, the economies of the area have been oriented toward the production of agricultural commodities and mineral resources for export. While Latin America possesses the natural and mineral resources required for industrial growth, the international division of labor has not favored the creation of manufacturing enterprises. The export orientation of Latin America, fashioned during three hundred years of colonial rule, retarded the growth of a domestic market, limited the purchasing power of domestic consumers, and either obstructed or concentrated capital formation. Some development theorists explain the relative weakness of the industrial sector as a reflection of the natural comparative advantage enjoyed by Latin American countries in the production of tropical commodities such as coffee, sugarcane, and bananas. Others argue that agro-export specialization was forced on Latin America by imperial powers whose industrial growth required a steady supply of primary materials and captive markets for their manufactured products. Whatever the cause of industry's belated appearance, the fact remains that industrial production did not surpass agricultural output in any of the Latin American republics until the mid-twentieth century.

**Average annual industrial growth rates, 1950–1978**

| | 1950–1965 | 1965–1978 | 1973–1978 |
|---|---|---|---|
| Argentina | 4.8 | 5.9 | -1.0 |
| Brazil | 7.3 | 12.0 | 6.3 |
| Chile | 5.5 | 3.4 | -1.4 |
| Colombia | 6.2 | 7.7 | 5.4 |
| Guatemala | 5.4 | 7.7 | 6.2 |
| Mexico | 7.2 | 8.1 | 6.3 |
| Latin America | 6.3 | 8.2 | 4.5 |

SOURCE: Robert N. Gwynne, *Industrialization and Urbanization in Latin America* (1986), p. 36.

**Table 1**

Industrialization resulted from deliberate government efforts to break out of an international division of labor in which Latin America specialized in agricultural exports. Government policies have been influenced by a bitter initial experience with free-trade policies in the early independence period. Spanish and Portuguese colonial policies permitted a degree of growth in small cottage industries. In colonial Mexico a primitive textile industry developed in the eighteenth century. While English textile plants mechanized the production process, the Mexican plants (*obrajes*) mass-produced cotton textiles by using cheap manual labor working inefficient looms, yet satisfied a substantial portion of Mexican demand for cotton textiles. As less expensive and higher-quality English textiles flooded the market after the lifting of trade restrictions in the early independence period, these native industries were wiped out by the competition. Subsequent efforts to revive the textile manufacturers failed, but the political leadership in Mexico and elsewhere learned that weak native industries could not modernize and grow stronger without substantial government protection.

With the spread of liberalism in the nineteenth century, governments adopted policies that encouraged the development of mechanized factories. The first stage of industrial development occurred between 1850 and 1914, when a dramatic increase in export production, combined with indirect government incentives for industry, established the foundations for the region's first manufacturing plants. Railroad construction, designed primarily to facilitate agricultural exports, also stimulated industrial growth by reducing transportation costs and uniting the domestic market. New banking laws and the confiscation of communal and church lands fostered capital accumulation, while educational reforms and immigration incentives helped to produce a skilled labor force. Capital surpluses generated in the industrializing countries also made some capital available for investment in Latin America.

Yet the major impetus for industrialization came from the dramatic expansion of agricultural exports. In São Paulo, Brazilian entrepreneurs diverted some of the proceeds from the coffee boom (roughly 1830–1910) to the establishment of factories producing the bags in which they exported a majority of the world's coffee. In and around Buenos Aires, a few meat-packing plants developed with the expansion of the cattle industry. While the early industries in Latin America were often tied to the export sector, the increase in agricultural productivity also expanded the domestic market for consumer goods. A few consumer-goods industries developed to supply domestic demand for processed foods, beer, cigarettes, shoes, and textiles.

Hence the first stage of industrialization is often referred to as an era of export-led industrial growth, characterized by the establishment of small, low-technology industries processing agricultural products or manufacturing light consumer goods for local consumers. The total contribution of industry to the GDP paled in comparison to the leading economic sector—exports of primary products—yet the foundations of Latin America's consumer-goods industry were laid in the late nineteenth century. The emergence of the manufacturing sector is reflected in the establishment of industrial organizations such as the Society of Manufacturing Development in Chile (1883), the Industrial Union of Argentina (1887), and the National Society of Industries of Peru (1897). Industry made its most significant advances in the largest countries, Argentina, Brazil, and Mexico, where natural and mineral resources, a relatively large domestic market, and a measure of capital accumulation favored the development of a manufacturing base. Mexico began producing steel in 1901, Argentina's industries employed 323,000 workers by 1915, and the Rio de Janeiro–São Paulo axis was a hub of industrial activity around the turn of the twentieth century. Even in the smaller countries of Central America a few consumer-goods industries had developed by 1900.

The onset of World War I disrupted international trading patterns and ushered in a second stage of industrial development, which lasted from 1914 to 1945. With war reducing demand for Latin American exports and cutting off imports, Latin Americans were faced with the choice of forgoing consumption of some manufactured goods or producing them in domestic plants. Governments chose to foster industrial development through import-substitution industrialization (ISI) strategies, a set of policies designed to promote the manufacture of products previously imported from foreign plants. While ISI is a development strategy associated with the post–World War II era, Latin American governments established the broad framework of ISI between 1914 and 1945. In their ad hoc responses to emergency situations, such as revenue shortages and scarcity, governments found that by increasing tariffs, a common practice for revenue-starved governments, and offering fiscal incentives, they could stimulate growth in the industrial sector. Protective tariffs and fiscal incentives made investment in industry more attractive to domestic entrepreneurs, who had always feared competition with British and American industries. Some foreign capitalists invested in South American industry, but the stimulus for industrial expansion was generated locally. Governments gave greater incentives to industry because the new factories provided employment for a growing urban population, reduced the total cost of the country's imports, and improved the national balance of payments.

From 1914 to 1945, through two world wars and one Great Depression, import-substitution policies accelerated the rate of Latin American industrialization. Between 1915 and 1947, the number of industrial plants increased from 40,200 to 83,900 in Argentina and from 13,000 to 78,400 in Brazil. During the same period, industrial employment increased from 45,000 to 176,000 in Chile and from 323,000 to 1,921,000 in Argentina. Most of the industrial expansion occurred in the primary or consumer-goods sector, but a few intermediate and heavy industries were established.

Chilean factories manufactured paper, glass, and cement; Brazil produced iron and steel; and Argentina manufactured farm machinery. By 1950, the industrial output of Latin America exceeded agricultural production. Import-substitution industrialization policies, while they were not popularly labeled as such at the time, had transformed the economic structure of Latin America.

Industrialization also contributed to significant changes in politics and society. With the emergence of industries came an industrial bourgeoisie, a proletariat, and a larger middle class, most of them resident in increasingly more populous urban centers. Urbanization reflected the growth of industry and also promoted it, for with a larger domestic market came greater incentive to increase manufacturing capacity. Moreover, the industrial bourgeoisie and the proletariat, occasionally united in populist political parties by a charismatic leader, penetrated the political structure and pushed forward development programs that accelerated industrial development. This was especially true during the populist regimes of Getúlio Vargas in Brazil (1930–1945 and 1951–1954), Juan Domingo Perón in Argentina (1946–1955 and 1973–1974), and Lázaro Cárdenas in Mexico (1934–1940).

**Volkswagen factory in São Paulo, Brazil, 1975.** Brazil's automobile industry, while largely owned by multinational firms, contributed to the country's industrialization goals. © DIEGO GOLDBERG/SYGMA/CORBIS

Populist politics of the post-1945 era ushered in the third stage of industrial development, an era one might label "dependent industrial growth" or "advanced import-substitution industrialization." Development issues took center stage in national politics, and reformists advocated more ambitious development projects to combat unemployment, raise the standard of living, and "catch up" with the more advanced industrial economies. Beginning in the late 1940s under the forceful leadership of Raúl Prebisch, an Argentine economist, the United Nations Economic Commission for Latin America (ECLA) urged the republics to promote industrialization in order to escape increasingly unfavorable world-market conditions for raw-material exporters. In the minds of policymakers in Latin America and the United States, industrialization became a panacea for a whole range of economic, social, and political problems that plagued the region. By the end of the 1950s, virtually every nation of Latin America was committed to rapid industrial growth.

Political factors at the national level coincided with and were perhaps strengthened by conditions that favored the growth of multinational industries. Industries based in Europe and North America, looking for new markets and new outlets for their capital, began to invest more heavily in Latin American industry. Prior to 1945, foreign investment was concentrated in agriculture, transportation, and mining. In the postwar period, foreign capital flowed in ever larger amounts to the manufacturing sector. In 1949, the German multinational company Volkswagen set up a plant in Brazil, and it was followed by Ford, General Motors, and Mercedes Benz in the 1950s. In the third stage of industrial development, governments attempted to harness and coordinate the domestic and foreign factors that propelled industrial growth to its highest levels in the 1970s.

While a manufacturing base existed in 1945, plants were generally small, inefficient, and incapable of competing directly with foreign enterprises. Moreover, with some exceptions in the larger countries, few plants existed in the intermediate and capital-goods sectors, the industries that generate self-sustaining growth by producing tools, machines, and equipment that are subsequently utilized in other productive enterprises. Consequently, ISI in the post-1945 period has involved a higher degree of state intervention to expand manufacturing into the so-called heavy industries. States erected tariff barriers, subsidized and occasionally nationalized industries, funded industrial development banks, constructed hydroelectric plants and other power facilities, and loosened restrictions on foreign investment.

Government policies stimulated even higher levels of foreign investment, as multinational corporations were eager to get behind tariff barriers and take advantage of government incentives. Although foreign capital contributed less than 10 percent of total investment per year, it helped establish key industries like steel, petrochemicals, pharmaceuticals, automobiles, and other capital-goods industries. While ECLa economists and some political leaders would have preferred to industrialize with only national capital, others argued that foreign capital was a necessary ingredient in the total development program. Without it, few countries could have developed intermediate and heavy industries.

International political factors also contributed to an increase in industrial productivity. In an effort to correct the conditions that bred revolutionary movements in Latin America, the United States committed itself to finance the Alliance for Progress in 1961. Over the next ten years, the U.S. government made available billions of dollars in low-interest, long-term loans to finance economic diversification, infrastructural development, and other projects that governments could not have financed otherwise on such flexible terms. A significant part of the development effort involved regional economic integration. Recognizing that the growth of industry required the expansion of markets, governments in Central and South America attempted to form common markets in which tariffs on manufactured goods would be gradually eliminated. While these integration measures failed to achieve all that had been intended, they helped to stimulate industrial exports and attract foreign investment.

**Level of industrialization (manufacturing GDP as % of GDP)**

| | 1950 | 1978 | 1990 | 2005–2006 |
|---|---|---|---|---|
| Argentina | 26 | 33 | 22 | 36 |
| Brazil | 22 | 30 | 27 | 38 |
| Chile | 23 | 24 | 21 | 49 |
| Colombia | 13 | 18 | 22 | 35 |
| Guatemala | 12 | 16 | 15 | 19 |
| Mexico | 19 | 26 | 28 | 26 |
| Latin America | 20 | 26 | 25 | — |

SOURCE: Robert N. Gwynne, *Industrialization and Urbanization in Latin America* (1986), pp. 37–38; Inter-American Development Bank, *Economic and Social Progress in Latin America: 1992 Report* (1992), pp. 286–291; Central Intelligence Agency, *The World Factbook 2007.*

**Table 2**

A combination of domestic incentives, increased levels of foreign development assistance, direct foreign investment, and economic integration produced spectacular increases in industrial productivity. Between 1950 and 1978, Latin America's manufacturing sector grew at an average annual rate of 6.5 percent. The value of the industrial product increased more than five times, from $13 billion in 1950 to $77.2 billion in 1978. As shown in the accompanying table, the growth in industrial productivity was greatest in Brazil, which recorded a remarkable 12 percent annual growth rate between 1965 and 1973, during the so-called Brazilian miracle.

As a result of these high growth rates, the industrial sector replaced agriculture as the leading economic sector. In 1950 the agricultural sector accounted for 25 percent of the GDP, while industrial output represented 19.6 percent of the GDP. By 1978 industry was the leading economic sector in Latin America, accounting for 26 percent of the GDP. Brazil led all Latin American countries in the value added by the manufacturing sector, producing a record $97.7 billion in 1987. Mexico's industrial sector, however, contributed a greater percentage of the country's gross domestic product, as shown in the associated table.

High industrial growth rates were accompanied by significant changes within the manufacturing sector. The contribution of the consumer-goods sector to total GDP declined from almost 66 percent in 1950 to 40 percent in 1980. During the same period, the contribution of intermediate industries increased from 25 percent to 33 percent, and consumer durables increased from 11 percent to 25 percent. The development of heavy industries was most successful in Argentina, Brazil, and Mexico, which even began to export industrial products in significant quantities during the third stage of industrial development.

The world recession of 1979–1984 slowed the rate of industrial growth throughout the region, and Latin American industry has still not recovered the high growth rates of the previous decades. Burdened by foreign debt and shortages of foreign exchange, the most industrialized countries were still registering negative growth rates in the mid-1980s. The decline in industrial productivity forced policymakers to reconsider the strategies that had been so successful since World War II. In the 1980s and 1990s particularly, many countries embarked on neoliberal development strategies, eliminating tariff protection for industries, privatizing state corporations, and offering incentives to foreign manufacturers. International firms established export-manufacturing facilities throughout the region. Liberalization policies brought Latin American industries into global competition in more profound ways. In spite of macroeconomic instability, some industries survived and also succeeded. The manufacturing sector showed signs of recovery in the 1990s, but the adoption of neoliberal policies will not likely reduce industry's dependence on foreign capital and the state. Some of the most productive Brazilian industries (automobiles, tires, cement, and pharmaceuticals) are controlled by multinational firms. As these firms are free to repatriate profits, critics are openly questioning the contribution of foreign enterprises to Brazilian development. At the same time, business leaders have called for an industrial policy that will enhance national firms' competitiveness, encourage efficiency, and regulate unfair trading practices. Moreover, in the twenty-first century, several countries have derived sizable export revenues from traditional and new commodities. Thus, despite high growth rates in Brazil and elsewhere, industrialization has not been the panacea for the many social and economic problems faced by Latin America.

*See also* **Economic Development; Technology.**

BIBLIOGRAPHY

Werner Baer, *Industrialization and Economic Development in Brazil* (1965).

Albert O. Hirschman, "The Political Economy of Import-Substituting Industrialization in Latin America," in *Quarterly Journal of Economics* 82, no. 1 (1968): 1–32.

Warren Dean, *The Industrialization of São Paulo, 1880–1945* (1969).

Celso Furtado, *Economic Development of Latin America,* 2d ed. (1976).

Fernando Henrique Cardoso and Enzo Faletto, *Dependency and Development in Latin America* (1979).

Frederick Stirton Weaver, *Class, State, and Industrial Structure: The Historical Process of South American Industrial Growth* (1980).

Robert N. Gwynne, *Industrialization and Urbanization in Latin America* (1986).

Stephen H. Haber, *Industry and Underdevelopment: The Industrialization of Mexico, 1890–1940* (1989).

Fernando Fajnzylber, *Industrialization in Latin America: From the "Black Box" to the "Empty Box"* (1990).

### *Additional Bibliography*

Altenburg, Tilman, and Dirk Messner, eds. *América Latina competitiva: Desafíos para la economía, la sociedad y el estado.* Caracas: Nueva Sociedad: Instituto Alemán de Desarrollo (IAD); Deutsche Gesellschaft für Technische Zusammenarbeit (GTZ), 2002.

Cárdenas, Enrique, José Antonio Ocampo, and Rosemary Thorp, eds. *Industrialización y Estado en la América Latina: La leyenda negra de la posguerra.* México, D.F.: Fondo de Cultura Económica, El Trimestre Económico, 2003.

Davis, Diane E. *Discipline and Development: Middle Classes and Prosperity in East Asia and Latin America.* Cambridge, U.K.: Cambridge University Press, 2004.

Dijkstra, A. Geske. *Trade Liberalization and Industrial Development: Theory and Evidence from Latin America.* The Hague: Institute of Social Studies, 1997.

Durand, Francisco, and Eduardo Silva, eds. *Organized Business, Economic Change, and Democracy in Latin America.* Coral Gables, FL: North-South Center Press, 1998.

Katz, Jorge M., and Ricardo Bielschowsky, eds. *Estabilización macroeconómica, reforma estructural y comportamiento industrial: Estructura y funcionamiento del sector manufacturero latinoamericano en los años 90.* Buenos Aires: Alianza Editorial, 1996.

Murga Frassinetti, Antonio. *Industrialización y capital extranjero en Honduras.* Tegucigalpa: Centro de Documentación de Honduras, 1999.

Olmedo Carranza, Bernardo. *Apuntes sobre industrialización y sector externo en América Latina: El caso de México.* México: Universidad Nacional Autónoma de México,

Instituto de Investigaciones Económicas: Miguel Ángel Porrúa, 2006.

Schneider, Ben Ross. *Business Politics and the State in Twentieth-Century Latin America.* New York: Cambridge University Press, 2004.

Shadlen, Kenneth C. *Small Industry in Postwar Latin America: Economic Internationalization and the Institutional Bases of Business Activism in Argentina, Brazil, and Mexico.* Storrs: Center for Latin American & Caribbean Studies, University of Connecticut, 1999.

Ugarteche, Oscar. *El falso dilema: América Latina en la economía global.* Lima: Fundación Friedrich Ebert-FES (Perú); Caracas, Venezuela: Editorial Nueva Sociedad, 1997.

PAUL J. DOSAL

---

**INFANTE, JOSÉ MIGUEL** (1778–1844). José Miguel Infante (*b.* 1778; *d.* 9 April 1844), Chilean patriot and politician. Infante played a number of important roles in the Chilean struggle for independence and in its aftermath. As *procurador* (attorney) of the *cabildo* (municipal government) of Santiago in 1810, he was active in putting forth the creole case for a national government. At the *cabildo abierto* (open town meeting) of 18 September 1810, he was given the task of making the keynote speech in favor of this change. He was a member of the first national congress (1811) and of the governing junta (1813–1814). He happened to be in Argentina at the time of the battle of Rancagua (1–2 October 1814), and remained there until 1817. Under Bernardo O'Higgins (1778–1842), Infante was briefly minister of finance (1818). He played one of the more important roles in the events of 28 January 1823, when O'Higgins relinquished power. As a senator in 1823 he was responsible for the law abolishing slavery in Chile.

Infante's moments of greatest influence came in the years 1824–1826, when his now strongly held "federalist" views dominated discussion in the Chilean congress. A federalist constitution, however, was never introduced, and Infante's influence quickly waned. Between 1827 and 1844 he published 206 issues of his own newspaper, *El Valdiviano Federal*, in which he continued to expound his increasingly dogmatic (and totally unfashionable) federalist views. He was widely respected as a man of great integrity. His death in 1844 made a deep impression on a new generation of Chilean liberals.

*See also* **Federalism; Journalism.**

BIBLIOGRAPHY

Simon Collier, *Ideas and Politics of Chilean Independence, 1808–1833* (1967), chap. 8.

*Additional Bibliography*

Heise González, Julio. *Anos de formacion y aprendizaje politicos, 1810–1833.* Santiago: Editorial Universitaria, 1978.

SIMON COLLIER

---

**INFANTE, PEDRO** (1917–1957). Pedro Infante (*b.* 18 November 1917; *d.* 15 April 1957), Mexican actor and singer. Born in Mazatlán, Sinaloa, Infante learned the trade of carpentry, then made a guitar and taught himself music. In 1939, while in Mexico City, he began his singing career on the radio. He was "discovered" by the director Ismael Rodríguez and cast in the film *La feria de las flores* (1942). One year later he became a major star in *¡Viva mi desgracia!* He starred in a total of forty-five films, including *Nosotros los pobres* (1947), *Ustedes los ricos* (1948), *Escuela de vagabundos* (1954), *Dicen que soy mujeriego* (1948), *Las Islas Marías* (1950), *Ahí viene Martín Corona* (1951), and *Dos tipos de cuidado* (1952). A versatile actor who performed comedy and drama with equal distinction, Infante has attained the status of a cultural icon in Mexico.

*See also* **Cinema: From the Silent Film to 1990.**

BIBLIOGRAPHY

E. Bradford Burns, *Latin American Cinema: Film and History* (1975).

John King, *Magical Reels: A History of Cinema in Latin America* (1990).

Carl J. Mora, *Mexican Cinema: Reflections of a Society: 1896–1980* (1982).

Luis Reyes De La Maza, *El cine sonoro en México* (1973).

*Additional Bibliography*

García, Gustavo. *No me parezco a nadie: La vida de Pedro Infante.* Mexico City: Clío: Espejo de Obsidiana, 1994.

Rubenstein, Ann. "Bodies, Cities, Cinema: Pedro Infante's Death as Political Spectacle." In *Fragments of a Golden Age: The Politics of Culture in Mexico since 1940.* Joseph, Gil, Anne Rubenstein, and Eric Zolov, editors. Durham: Duke University Press, 2001.

DAVID MACIEL

**INFLATION.** High inflation not only paralyzes economic growth, but also wreaks personal devastation on those with fixed incomes or frozen wages, whose lifetime savings can be wiped out literally overnight. These factors have contributed to middle-class unrest leading to the overthrow of governments in Brazil in 1964 and 1992, Argentina in 1966 and 1975, Uruguay in 1971, and Chile in 1973.

Since 1950 Latin America has experienced several inflationary crises followed by the introduction of numerous innovative governmental plans and reforms designed to combat the threat. The period spanning 1950 to 1960 was marked by import substitution, a policy of encouraging domestic industrial growth through a combination of import tariffs, quotas, price controls, and government subsidies. The following decade saw the exhaustion of that growth strategy and the beginning of an outward-looking (export-promoting) developmental model. From 1971 to 1981 the region pursued a debt-led development plan as nations continued to mix import-substitution and export-promotion strategies financed primarily by foreign borrowing. This policy brought Mexico and Brazil to the brink of defaulting on their foreign debts in the early 1980s, followed by large negative resource transfers from Latin America to the industrialized world to service the debts. Throughout the 1980s and into the early 1990s, Latin America experienced an upward trend in inflation rates, and even traditionally low-inflation countries such as Nicaragua and Peru experienced crippling bouts of hyperinflation (monthly rates exceeding 50 percent).

### MONETARISM

Monetarist theory dictates that growth in the money supply and fiscal deficits cause inflation. Most Latin American countries went through the import-substitution period without a central bank, leaving monetary issues directly in the hands of the treasury or of a central bank subservient to financing the needs of the treasury. Given the weak markets for government bonds, budget deficits became the primary source of monetary expansion and cause of inflation. Monetarists believe that inflation interferes with economic growth by diverting investment to unproductive assets as a hedge; shifting resources away from projects with long gestation periods in favor of those that promise lower returns in the shorter term; increasing real exchange rates; and prompting government intervention in the foreign-exchange markets and trade flows. Inflation also leads to higher government deficits by decreasing the real income of public utilities, while provoking shortages and underinvestment in wholly or partially privatized companies.

Latin American countries signed policy packages with the International Monetary Fund (IMF) to receive balance-of-payments assistance and agreed to prescribed commitments including real currency depreciation, fiscal austerity coupled with increased prices for public transportation and basic commodities, monetary austerity, and wage freezes. The political and economic impacts of such prescriptions were enormous in that they usually provoked long and deep recessions with a corresponding increase in unemployment. Many think the IMF inflation stabilizations fell too heavily on the working class, which responded with demonstrations and strikes.

### STRUCTURALISTS

Raúl Prebisch, Hans W. Singer, and their successors at the U.N. Economic Commission for Latin America and the Caribbean (ECLAC or CEPAL) postulated that inflation was caused by an inelastic food supply, chronic lack of foreign exchange, and structural government deficits arising from the necessary expansion of social overhead infrastructure. Structuralists believed that inflation (at reasonable levels) benefited economic growth by leading to the transfer of savings into productive investment rather than into financial markets. However, they also noted the inflationary pressure of chronic balance-of-payments deficits that arose from periods when rising demand for imported, manufactured goods from industrialized nations surpassed primary goods exports. More specifically, foreign exchange deficits pressured governments to engage in inflationary-related activities such as imposing trade restrictions, devaluing currency, and increasing social spending.

### RATIONAL EXPECTATIONS AND EXPECTATIONS MANAGEMENT APPROACHES

The rational expectations school agreed that inflation came from the money supply, but was rooted in present and future expected government deficits. In the view of such economists, governments could end inflation by undertaking credible reforms. In Latin America, this approach was generally associated with the Chicago Boys in Argentina and Chile, who believed that a credible fiscal reform coupled with trade liberalization and slowing in the rate of devaluation of the currency would simultaneously stabilize the inflation rate at low levels and improve the balance of payments. Over time, the currency devaluation would fall to zero and the domestic inflation rate would come to equal that of the average for the country's trading partners. This framework propelled the so-called tablita (tablet) and the corresponding liberalization policies imposed on Argentina, Chile, and Uruguay in the late 1970s.

Unfortunately, the slowing of the depreciation rate led to overvalued exchange rates, large trade deficits, and increased foreign debts. Because domestic inflation did not converge to foreign inflation, the "credibility" of the exchange-rate policy declined, producing devaluation expectations and a predictable run on the Central Bank's reserves followed by a large devaluation and a repudiation of the stabilization policy. A similar policy was undertaken in Mexico in 1988 at the end of the Miguel de la Madrid administration, with its Economic Solidarity Pact, and continued into the Carlos Salinas de Gortari administration with the Pact for Economic Stability and Growth. In any event, Mexico's plan collapsed in late 1994 in a fashion similar to the collapses in the Southern Cone. But what distinguished Mexico's pacts is the incorporation of wage and price guidelines similar to those recommended by the new structuralists.

## NEW STRUCTURALISM

The new structuralists, or neostructuralists, articulated the theory of "inertial" inflation that concentrated on the role of formal and informal indexation of incomes, and asserted that competing income sectors made claims on domestic product in excess of its capacity. Inflation brought the claims into alignment with gross domestic product. Inertial inflation resulted from the fact that indexing reflected the last period's inflation as automatic inflation correction occurred on an economy-wide scale, making it difficult to shift. A policy of inflation stabilization based on incomes policy (wage and price freezes) that removed the inertial aspects of inflation was supposed to reduce inflation at a lower cost to society. The heterodox stabilization measures of the Austral Plan (1985–1987) in Argentina and the Cruzado Plan (1986–1987) in Brazil presumably combined the policies of eradicating inertial inflation using incomes policies and monetary reform with the more orthodox policies of austere monetary and fiscal policy. Although these policies failed because of their reliance on wage, price, and exchange-rate pegging, stabilization attempts in Brazil (1964–1972) and in Mexico (1988–1994) were more successful.

## SUPER-MONETARIST-FISCALISM

The new monetarist-fiscalists shifted the focus away from the usual aspects of fiscal reform and onto the growth in the internal government debt. Faced with the need to repay foreign loans, governments that increased public debt levels accelerated the growth of the monetary base. Brazil and Argentina responded with successive plans that effectively repudiated parts of the internal debt by pegging their currencies to the dollar. The plans succeeded in "confiscating" a large portion of real liquidity of the economies and temporarily reducing inflation rates from hyperinflationary ones to high ones. But in early 1991, in response to deteriorating macroeconomic situations and a fall in investor confidence, both plans collapsed and hyperinflation resumed.

Argentina boldly introduced a currency regime board in 1991 that strictly pegged the peso to the dollar. Brazil followed in 1994 with its Real Plan, which initially floated its currency, but introduced stronger controls to defend against the collateral fallout of the 1994 Mexican peso crisis. Although both plans successfully reduced inflation to moderate levels, efforts to sustain the monetary pegs proved too costly for either country to sustain. Beginning in 1998 Brazil gradually released its peg in response to the successive Asian and Russian economic crises, which pushed hedge fund and emerging market managers to pull "hot money" investments from Brazilian markets to cover their losses. The recession that ensued was exacerbated by doubts about Brazil's ability to continue servicing its foreign and internal debts, which had risen dramatically in response to years of maintaining foreign reserves through higher interest rates. Faced with a similar dilemma, Argentina was forced to release its hard peg in the midst of a debt default in 2002. A severe recession and high employment immediately followed.

## THE END OF HYPERINFLATION

Since the turn of the twenty-first century, inflation has largely dissipated in Latin America owing to several factors. First, an international economic boom has increased the demand for natural resources and emerging market bonds, which has contributed to economic growth, decreased pressure on interest rates, and given governments more leverage to institute sound macroeconomic policies throughout the region. Second, the increasingly independent central banks of Brazil, Mexico, Colombia, Peru, and Argentina have inspired international and domestic confidence in their currencies by following Chile's model of setting inflation targets with phased-out exchange bands. Third, Ecuador and El Salvador have each successfully adopted the U.S. dollar as their national currency, forcing those countries to adhere to rigid macroeconomic standards.

Unfortunately, the economic cost of instituting these policies has hampered economic growth through much of the region. In elections in 2006, Brazil, Peru, Colombia, and Mexico narrowly succeeded in combating political reversals in the midst of a rising surge of "reform fatigue"—as occurred in Venezuela, Argentina, and Bolivia between1998 and 2005. If Latin American countries continue to decrease debt levels, global demand for natural resources remains strong, political and social reform initiatives continue to progress, and lower interest rates lead to greater domestic-led economic growth, inflation levels will likely remain low for the foreseeable future.

*See also* **Chicago Boys; Economic Development.**

BIBLIOGRAPHY

Alesina, Alberto. "Political Models of Macroeconomic Policy and Fiscal Reforms." In *Voting for Reform: Democracy, Political Liberalization, and Economic Adjustment*, edited by Stephan Haggard and Steven B. Webb. New York: Oxford University Press, 1994.

Baer, Werner, and Isaac Kerstenetzky, eds. *Inflation and Growth in Latin America*. Homewood, IL: R. D. Irwin, 1964. Repr., New Haven, CT: Yale University Press, 1970.

Baer, Werner, and John H. Welch, eds. "The Resurgence of Inflation in Latin America." *World Development* 15, no. 8 (1987): 989–990.

Bernanke, Ben S. "Inflation in Latin America: A New Era?" Presentation at Stanford Institute for Economic Policy Research Economic Summit. Stanford, CA, February 11, 2005. Available from http://www.federalreserve.gov/boarddocs/speeches/2005/20050211/default.htm.

Bruno, Michael, et al., eds. *Inflation Stabilization: The Experience of Israel, Argentina, Brazil, Bolivia, and Mexico*. Cambridge, MA: MIT Press, 1988.

Calderón Villarreal, Cuauhtémoc, and Thomas M. Fullerton, Jr., eds. *Inflationary Studies for Latin America*. Ciudad Juárez, Chihuahua: Texas Western Press, 2000.

Drake, Paul W. *Money Doctors, Foreign Debts, and Economic Reforms in Latin America from the 1890s to the Present*. Wilmington, DE: SR Books, 1994.

Fernández, Roque B. "The Expectations Management Approach to Stabilization in Argentina during 1976–1982." *World Development* 13, no. 8 (1985): 871–892.

Heyman, David, and Fernando Navajas. "Conflicto distributivo y deficit fiscal: Notas sobre la experiencia Argentina, 1970–1987." Working Paper, Oficina de la CEPAL, Buenos Aires, 1989.

Kirkpatrick, Colin, and Frederick Nixson. "Inflation and Stabilization Policy in LDCs." In *Surveys in Development Economics*, edited by Norman Gemmell. Oxford and New York: B. Blackwell, 1987.

Salvatore, Dominick, James W. Dean, and Thomas Willett, eds. *The Dollarization Debate*. Oxford and New York: Oxford University Press, 2003.

Sargent, Thomas J. *Rational Expectations and Inflation*, 2nd edition. New York: HarperCollins College Publishers, 1993.

Taylor, Lance. *Structuralist Macroeconomics: Applicable Models for the Third World*. New York: Basic Books, 1983.

JOHN H. WELCH
CHRISTOPHER L. MURCHISON

## INFORMAL ECONOMY.

*See* **Economic Development.**

## INGAPIRCA.

Ingapirca, "Inca wall" in Quechua, a name loosely applied to archaeological ruins throughout the former Inca Empire. In Ecuador, Ingapirca is the name given to the best preserved of Inca sites. Located in the Cañari region of the southern highlands, the site of Ingapirca contains both monumental architecture and high-quality stonework. The site is best known for a large oval structure of fine Cuzco masonry called the Castillo. The oval form is rare in Inca architecture. Other Inca constructions at the site include rectangular buildings, storage units, waterworks, and agricultural terraces.

Archaeological evidence indicates that many of the Inca structures at Ingapirca were erected over preexisting architectural features. Radiocarbon dates and associated Cashaloma pottery indicate that the site was occupied by the local Cañari population prior to the Inca invasion of the region. The sector of the site referred to as Pilaloma is believed to have been the original Cañari precinct. Excavations in this area revealed a walled enclosure containing a series of rectangular rooms organized around a central patio. A monolith in the center of the patio marked the location of a shallow sepulchre containing the remains of eleven individuals and a wealth of funerary offerings, including Cashaloma pottery vessels, copper objects, and *Spondylus* shell.

The Cañaris were conquered by Topa Inca Yupanqui the latter half of the fifteenth century. Ethnohistoric and archaeological data suggest that Ingapirca, known originally as Hatun Cañar, was the principal settlement and sacred origin place of the ancient Cañari nation. A well-known strategy of Inca imperial expansion was to symbolically subordinate local deities and sacred places to the state religion. The superimposition of Inca structures over the Cañari capital likely reflects a conscious effort on the part of the Inca lords to dominate and co-opt the sacred significance of this site.

*See also* **Archaeology; Incas, The.**


BIBLIOGRAPHY

On the archaeology of Ingapirca, see Antonio Fresco, *La arqueología de Ingapirca (Ecuador): Costumbres funerarias, cerámica y otros materiales* (1984), or José Alcina Franch, "Ingapirca: Arquitectura y áreas de asentamiento," in *Revista Española de Antropología Americana* 8 (1978): 127–146. On the protohistoric Cañari ethnic group, see Niels Fock and Eva Krener, "Los Cañaris del Ecuador y sus conceptos ethnohistóricos sobre los Incas," in *Estudios Americanistas,* edited by R. Hartmann and U. Oberem, vol. 1 (1975), pp. 170–181. For a general discussion of the regional archaeology, see Donald Collier and John Murra, "Survey and Excavations in Southern Ecuador," *Field Museum of Natural History, Anthropological Series no. 35* (1943).

*Additional Bibliography*

Bray, Tamara L. "Inka Pottery as Culinary Equipment: Food, Feasting, and Gender in Imperial State Design." *Latin American Antiquity* Vol. 14, No. 1. (Mar., 2003): 3-28.

Hemming, John, and Edward Ranney. *Monuments of the Inca*. Albuquerque: New Mexico Press, 1982.

Jamieson, Ross W. *Domestic Architecture and Power: The Historical Archaeology of Colonial Ecuador*. New York: Kluwer Academic/Plenum Publishers, 2000.

Molina, Manuel J. *Arqueología ecuatoriana: Los canaries.* Roma: LAS; Quito: Ediciones Abya-Yala, 1992.

Rojas C., J. Heriberto. *El complejo arqueológico de Ingapirca.* Azogues: J.H. Rojas C., 2006.


Tamara L. Bray

---

**INGENIEROS, JOSÉ** (1877–1925). José Ingenieros (*b.* 24 April 1877; *d.* 31 October 1925), Argentine intellectual. Born in Buenos Aires, Ingenieros was one of early twentieth-century Argentina's most prolific and influential intellectual figures. A graduate of the medical school of the University of Buenos Aires, he was particularly interested in and wrote extensively on psychology, psychiatry, and criminology. Ingenieros was an early adherent of socialism, which he later abandoned, and was also active in the formation of the Unión Latino Americana, an organization of Latin American intellectuals and political leaders advocating continental solidarity against the growing influence of the United States in the region. In 1915, he took a teaching position in the school of philosophy and letters of the University of Buenos Aires and founded and edited two journals (the *Revista de Filosofía* and *La Cultura Argentina*), dedicated to literary and philosophical issues.

Ingenieros was the author of scores of articles and many books, his best-known publications being *El hombre mediocre* (1913), a discussion of the spiritually deadening effects of modern society, and *Evolución de las ideas argentinas* (1918–1920), a two-volume examination of Argentine history. Ingenieros was also a strong supporter of and inspiration for the university reform movement that began in 1918.

*See also* **Argentina: The Twentieth Century.**


BIBLIOGRAPHY

Aníbal Ponce, *José Ingenieros: Su vida y su obra* (1977).

Jane Van Der Karr, *José Ingenieros: The Story of a Scientist-Humanist* (1977).

*Additional Bibliography*

Aguirre, Gisela. *José Ingenieros.* Buenos Aires: Planeta, 1999.

Barrientos, Justo Ramón. *Líderes e intelectuales de la Argentina moderna (1880-1930).* La Plata: Fondo Editorial "Esto es Historia," 2005.

Díaz Araujo, Enrique. *José Ingenieros.* Buenos Aires: Ciudad Argentina, 1998.

Genovesi, Alfredo. *Perfiles latinoamericanos: Mariátegui, Ingenieros, Palacios.* Lanús: Ediciones Mariátegui, 2005.


RICHARD J. WALTER

**INGENIOS.** Ingenios (Port., *engenhos*), water-driven sugar mills established throughout Spanish and Portuguese America in the early sixteenth century. The *ingenios* became a major commercial enterprise for the colonies in Cuba and Brazil. Sugar production in the New World was the most intensively organized agro-industry in the Indies. Mill ownership was often more important than land ownership as it meant the control of the actual production process. The *ingenios,* along with the animal-driven mills (*trapiches*) ground the sugar cane and processed sugar for export and local consumption. The *ingenio* was also a central social institution that fostered the development of permanent settlements. Frequently, slaves provided labor in the *ingenio* until the abolition of slavery, which was late in both Brazil and Cuba. Modernization of the industry in the late nineteenth century led to their replacement with steam-drive mills, and the term *"ingenio"* fell out of common usage. In Cuba, for example, larger steam-powered *"centrales"* replaced the older *ingenios.* A romantic depiction of a sugar *ingenio*—not completely uncritical of the slave system that was its backbone—can be found in Gertrudis Gómez de Avellaneda's 1841 novel *Sab.*

*See also* **Engenho; Slavery: Brazil; Sugar Industry.**


BIBLIOGRAPHY

Lyle McAlister, *Spain and Portugal in the New World 1492–1700* (1984).

James Lockhart and Stuart B. Schwartz, *Early Latin America: A History of Colonial Spanish America and Brazil* (1983).

*Additional Bibliography*

Araújo, Tatiana Brito de. *Os engenhos centrais e a produção açucareira no Recôncavo Baiano, 1875–1909.* Salvador: FIEB, 2002.

Gaytán Ruelas, J. G., and R. González. "Mecanización del campo cañero ingenio 'San Sebastián,' Michoacán." *Revista Chapingo: Serie Ingeniería Agropecuaria* 2, no. 2 (1999): 147–151.

Knight, Franklin W. "Origins of Wealth and the Sugar Revolution in Cuba, 1750–1850." *Hispanic American Historical Review* 57, no. 2 (1977): 231–253.

Knight, Franklin W. "The Caribbean Sugar Industry and Slavery." *Latin American Research Review* 18, no. 2 (1983): 219–229.


HEATHER K. THIESSEN

**INQUILINAJE.** Inquilinaje, a rural labor system similar to peonage that is peculiar to Chile. In the colonial period, *inquilinos* were often ex-soldiers who resided on the fringes of large estates called *fundos* to protect them from incursion by squatters. When Chile's farms were converted from pastoral activities to cereal raising, landlords moved the *inquilinos* closer to the main house to facilitate closer supervision of their labor. Housed in wretched hovels, paid in scrip, and deprived of their political rights through vote fraud and intimidation, the *inquilinos* seemed virtually defenseless, especially because the landlords often controlled the instruments of state power: the judiciary, the police, and the militia. As Chile's rural population grew, landlords increased the duties extracted from the *inquilinos,* who had to devote increasingly large amounts of their labor to maintaining the patron's fund.

Happily, the system began to collapse in the 1950s, and with the creation of the Corporation for Agrarian Reform (CORA), the state began to enforce labor laws in the countryside. The Christian Democratic agrarian reform program of the late 1960s eradicated the last vestiges of the *inquilino* system.

*See also* **Chile, Organizations: Corporation of Agrarian Reform (CORA).**


BIBLIOGRAPHY

George M. McBride, *Chile: Land and Society* (1936).

Brian Loveman, *Struggle in the Countryside: Politics and Rural Labor in Chile, 1919–1973* (1976), p. 49.

*Additional Bibliography*

Academia Chilena de la Historia. *Vida rural en Chile durante el siglo XIX.* Santiago: Academia Chilena de la Historia, 2001.

Gómez Leyton, Juan Carlos. *La frontera de la democracia: El derecho de propiedad en Chile, 1925-1973.* Santiago: LOM Ediciones, 2004.

Góngora, Mario. *Origen de los "inquilinos" de Chile central.* Santiago: Universidad de Chile, Seminario de Historia Colonial, 1960.

Orellana Muermann, Marcela, and Juan Guillermo Muñoz Correa. *El Agro colonial.* Santiago: Universidad de Santiago de Chile, Departamento de Historia, Instituto de Investigaciones del Patrimonio Territorial de Chile, 1992.

Tinsman, Heidi. *Partners in Conflict: The Politics of Gender, Sexuality, and Labor in the Chilean Agrarian Reform, 1950-1973.* Durham, NC: Duke University Press, 2002.

WILLIAM F. SATER

## INQUISITION, THE

*This entry includes the following articles:*
BRAZIL
SPANISH AMERICA

### BRAZIL

The Portuguese Inquisition was founded under King João III in 1536 and abolished in 1821, but no permanent tribunal of the Holy Office sat in Brazil. Inquisition business in the captaincies of Portuguese America was directly administered by the Lisbon Inquisition. The Inquisition was always most active in the states of Bahia, Rio de Janeiro, and Pernambuco, where there was the highest concentration of voluntary lay auxiliaries, the "familiars" (often Portuguese immigrant merchants not of New Christian descent). As a result of distance and its less effective system of repression, Brazil became a haven for New Christians, the descendants of converted Jews, who were particularly suspected of apostasy to Judaism. Denounced individuals were shipped to Lisbon if there seemed sufficient grounds for a trial. If found guilty, they could be punished by confiscation of their property, imprisonment, whippings, and even execution in Portugal. The number of individuals put to death after sentencing by the Inquisition for Judaizing in Brazil did not exceed 500. Arrests and confiscations at the behest of the Inquisition damaged the economic life of Portugal and its colonies by disrupting the system of personal credit drawn on rich New Christian merchants. Reforms carried out from 1768 to 1773 under the Marquês de Pombal forbade the use of the term "New Christian" and ended Inquisitorial activity against them in Brazil for accusations of Jewish ritual practices.

Lisbon ordered a series of Inquisitorial visitations to Brazil in response to reports of moral and doctrinal laxity there. Father Heitor Furtado de Mendonça collected confessions and denunciations in Bahia from 1591 to 1593, then in Pernambuco from 1593 to 1595. Father Marcos Teixeira investigated in Bahia from 1618 through 1620. Father Giraldo de Abranches was active in Grão-Para from 1763 to 1769. The number of Inquisitorial investigations fluctuated from year to year in response to instructions sent from Lisbon and the zeal of the agents in Brazil. Much documentation of these visitations has been published during the twentieth century and has provided historians with information about colonial social conditions and religious beliefs. Outside of the visitation periods, denunciations were forwarded to Lisbon, which then instructed clerical commissaries resident in Brazil to investigate, and to arrest, if necessary, the accused, who were to stand trial in Portugal. Catholics were reminded annually by the Edict of the Faith of their duty to denounce a list of offenses, including the practice of Jewish rituals, bigamy, witchcraft, sodomy, clerical solicitation of penitents, and blasphemy. Those accused of these offenses in Brazil were usually white males. The proportion of white women, Native Americans, African-born slaves, and free blacks investigated was lower than their proportions of the total population. Article 9 of the 1810 Anglo-Portuguese Treaty of Alliance and Friendship signed in Rio specified that no tribunal would be set up in Portuguese America. In 1821 the Inquisition was abolished throughout Portuguese territories by the liberal Cortes that sat in Lisbon.

*See also* **Catholic Church: The Colonial Period.**

BIBLIOGRAPHY

Arnold Wiznitzer, *Jews in Colonial Brazil* (1960).

Anita Novinsky, *Cristãos Novos na Bahia* (1972).

Sonia A. Siqueira, *A Inquisição portuguesa e a sociedade colonial* (1978).

Laura De Mello E Souza, *O diabo e a terra de Santa Cruz* (1986).

Ronaldo Vainfas, *Trópico dos pecados: Moral, sexualidade e Inquisição no Brasil* (1989).

Elias Lipiner, *Izaque de Castro: O mancebo que veio preso do Brasil* (1992).

Luiz Mott, *Rosa Egipcíaca: Una santa africana no Brasil* (1993).

### *Additional Bibliography*

Cohen, Thomas M. *The Fire of Tongues: António Vieira and the Missionary Church in Brazil and Portugal.* Stanford, CA: Stanford University Press, 1998.

Grinberg, Keila. *Os judeus no Brasil: Inquisição, imigração e identidade.* Rio de Janeiro: Civilização Brasileira, 2005.

Novinsky, Anita. *Inquisicão: Prisioneiros do Brasil, séculos XVI-XIX.* Rio de Janeiro: Editora Expressão e Cultura, 2002.

Pieroni, Geraldo. *Banidos: A Inquisição e a lista dos cristãos-novos condenados a viver no Brasil.* Rio de Janeiro: Bertrand Brasil, 2003.

Silva, Lina Gorenstein Ferreira da. *A Inquisição contra as mulheres: Rio de Janeiro, séculos XVII e XVIII.* São Paulo: Associação Editorial Humanitas: FAPESP: LEI, 2005.

Vainfas, Ronaldo. *Confissões da Bahia: Santo Ofício da Inquisição de Lisboa.* São Paulo: Companhia das Letras, 1997.

Wadsworth, James E. *Agents of Orthodoxy: Honor, Status, and the Inquisition in Colonial Pernambuco, Brazil.* Lanham: Rowman & Littlefield Publishers, 2007.

DAVID HIGGS

## SPANISH AMERICA

The Inquisition was a special tribunal for trying and punishing heresy. In its most basic form, it was one of several powers which the local bishop, as ordinary ecclesiastical justice, exercised.

Pope Sixtus IV approved the creation of the Spanish Inquisition in Seville in 1478. Four years later the pope allowed the Spanish kings to extend the Inquisition to all of their realms. The king governed the Holy Office in Spain and the colonies, in conjunction with the Supreme Council of the Inquisition, called the Suprema, one of several councils of state which functioned in the Spanish imperial system. The monarch appointed local inquisitors. The inquisitors did not necessarily have to be members of the clergy, although nearly all were. Secular authorities meted out the punishments decreed by the Inquisition in a public display, called an auto-da-fé.

In Spanish America, local bishops and prelates of religious orders, or their appointees, conducted inquisitions prior to 1569. In that year King Philip II created two jurisdictions of the Holy Office of the Inquisition in the New World: Mexico and Peru. With the creation of the Holy Office, direction of the Inquisition passed from the local ecclesiastical authorities to a bureaucracy developed under the king of Spain. In 1610 a third seat of the Holy Office was created in Cartagena with jurisdiction over New Granada.

Some of the most famous cases concerned Indians who had reverted to their traditional worship. In Mexico, in 1539, Don Carlos, the *cacique* of Texcoco, was exonerated from idolatry but found guilty of heretical dogmatizing and burned at the stake by Fray Juan de Zumárraga, first bishop of Mexico, who had been given the authority of Apostolic Inquisitor by the Holy Office of Seville in 1535. Similarly in Yucatán, Fray Diego de Landa, prelate of the Franciscan Order, conducted inquisitions against the local Indians on charges of idolatry. Eventually, the crown and Inquisition officials concluded that the Indians, as neophytes to the faith, could not be held to the same standard as Europeans. Under these circumstances, Indians were removed from the jurisdiction of the Holy Office, and local clergy undertook the extirpation of idolatry among the Indians.

The Inquisition customarily handled cases dealing with heresy and in general sought to maintain religious orthodoxy. Usually this involved cases against Protestants, Jews, and Muslims, as well as Catholics with a faulty comprehension of true doctrine. The Inquisition also raised suits against priests who broke their vows or who violated the sanctity of the sacraments. Common among these cases were priests who solicited sexual favors in the confessional. The Inquisition exercised censorship over books and maintained the Index of prohibited books. Simple issues among the faithful, such as fornication, homosexual acts, and the like, were not normally pursued by the Inquisition but rather by the office of the vicar-general and the diocesan courts. The bulk of the cases handled by the Inquisition then concerned heresy against religious orthodoxy; blasphemy, normally involving the swearing of oaths and other curses that got out of hand; sorcery, often involving local medical practitioners and diviners; and bigamy and other violations of the sanctity of the sacraments.

Each office of the Inquisition usually had four officials: two inquisitors; a *fiscal*, or prosecuting attorney; and a secretary or notary. These officials could then appoint others to assist them. Because the territories administered by the inquisitors were so large, initially there were Holy Offices only in Mexico and Lima, and the inquisitors appointed assistants in the major Spanish cities of the realm. These assistants, called *comisarios* (commissaries), normally came from among the ranks of the local clergy. Additionally, the Inquisition maintained a network of lay agents who were granted special status as familiars. In return for serving the Inquisition, these individuals enjoyed high social status and received the *fuero inquisitorial*. The inquisitorial fuero was the privilege of having legal suits heard by the Inquisition rather than the royal courts.

Proceedings of the Inquisition were kept secret. The legal process could begin in any of several ways, but often a wrongdoer was denounced to an inquisitorial official. The Inquisition would then investigate the denunciation to weigh the merits of the case. If the Inquisitors felt that there was sufficient evidence to warrant a fuller investigation, they would take sworn testimony from witnesses, and eventually from the accused. During the investigation the accused was kept in the secret jail of the Inquisition and out of contact with family and friends.

Questioning of an accused followed a standard form. The accused was first asked to identify himself or herself. The Inquisitors asked if the accused or any relatives had ever been investigated or condemned by the Holy Office. Next the accused was asked to tell about his life. Only after these preliminary data had been collected did the Inquisitors ask the accused if he knew why he had been arrested. At this point the accused might confess the details of the case that interested the Inquisitors. It was also possible that the accused might incriminate himself on other charges, unknowingly. Often people had no idea why they had been arrested. If no testimony were forthcoming, the accused would be admonished to conduct a personal soul search for anything that might be against Christian doctrine in order to confess it at a later occasion. All witnesses, as noted, were sworn to secrecy. If the inquisitors were unable to secure a confession from the accused on the original grounds after several sessions of questioning, the accused could be subjected to judicial torture. This was an extremely serious step, and safeguards were included in the operating procedures of the Inquisition to avoid unnecessary torture. Furthermore, certain groups, such as clerics, could not be subjected to torture, except under very extreme circumstances.

Because the inquisitorial proceedings were so thorough, they could easily last several years. This meant that some defendants were imprisoned for long periods of time without any normal contact with family or friends. However, only a very small percentage of all cases initially considered by the Inquisition actually came to trial.

People found guilty by the Inquisition were subject to both penance and punishment. The penance was administered by the Inquisition, while punishment was meted out by secular authorities. Normal penance included wearing distinctive garb, such as the *sanbenito,* a small cape or scapulary worn around the shoulders; the saying of prayers and other devotions; and public humiliation in the auto-da fé. Punishments ran the gamut from whipping and other corporal punishment to execution. Many of those convicted were exiled, either from their place of residence, the immediate territory, or from the Americas. In some situations, persons convicted by the Holy Office in the New World, once exiled, found themselves arrested by the Inquisition in Seville upon arrival there. The property of those convicted could also be confiscated by the Holy Office and sold, the proceeds used to pay court costs. The principle behind sentencing was the eventual reconciliation of the sinner with the body of the church. Consequently, punishments and penances were meant to provide not only a public ceremony where society could see the wages of sin but also occasions for private repentance. Executions were, therefore, to be used only against the most obdurate sinners who refused reconciliation or whose crimes had significantly destroyed the local social fabric.

Over the course of the 250-year history of the Inquisition in Spanish America, the main targets were foreigners, members of the clergy, and suspected Jews. Executions and large public autos-da-fé were far more frequent early in the history of the Holy Office than later on. The last formal execution in Mexico, prior to the upheavals of the Wars of Independence, occurred in 1781, and only fourteen people were executed in the 100 years prior to that. The Holy Office of the Inquisition was first suppressed by the Cortes of Cádiz in 1813, only to be restored by Ferdinand VII in 1814, when he gained the throne. Consequently, the Inquisition was used against some of the leaders of the Independence movements in Spanish America. Eventually, with the triumph of liberal forces in Spain, the Holy Office came to its final end in 1820.

Although the Holy Office was staffed by clerics, and had the charge to maintain the purity of Christian doctrine, in effect it was a secular institution, under the control of the monarch. The high officials were appointed by the monarch, and policies established by the Suprema were subject to the monarch's approval. Making no distinction between religious and political philosophy because it assumed that the former determined the latter, the Inquisition sought to maintain the homogeneity of the body politic by assuring the existence of only one religious philosophy. On the other hand, because the Inquisition fell beyond the normal authority of local officials, either royal or ecclesiastical, it had a relatively high degree of independence from immediate oversight. By and large, however, the Spanish population of the Indies supported the actions of the Inquisition and did not themselves feel threatened by it.

*See also* **Catholic Church: The Colonial Period.**

BIBLIOGRAPHY

Henry C. Lea, *The Inquisition in the Spanish Dependencies: Sicily, Naples, Sardinia, Milan, the Canaries, Mexico, Peru, New Granada* (1908).

José T. Medina, *Historia del Tribunal del Santo Oficio de la Inquisición en México,* 2d ed. (1952), and *Historia del Tribunal de la Inquisición de Lima,* 2d ed., 2 vols. (1956).

Richard E. Greenleaf, *Zumárraga and the Mexican Inquisition* (1961) and *The Mexican Inquisition of the Sixteenth Century* (1969).

*Additional Bibliography*

Baudot, George, and María Águeda Méndez, eds. *Amores prohibidos: La palabra condenada en el México de los virreyes: Antología de coplas y versos censurados por la Inquisición de México.* México, D.F.: Siglo Veintiuno, 1997.

Duviols, Pierre, ed. *Procesos y visitas de idolatrías: Cajatambo, siglo XVII: con documentos anexos.* Lima: Instituto Francés de Estudios Andinos: Pontificia Universidad Católica del Perú, 2003.

Giles, Mary E. *Women in the Inquisition: Spain and the New World.* Baltimore: Johns Hopkins University Press, 1999.

Lewis, Laura. *Hall of Mirrors: Power, Witchcraft and Caste in Colonial Mexico.* Durham, NC: Duke University Press, 2003.

Medina, José Toribio. *Historia del Tribunal del Santo Oficio de la inquisición en Chile.* 2nd ed. Santiago: Fondo Histórico y Bibliográfico J.T. Medina, 1952.

Palma, Ricardo. *Anales de la Inquisición de Lima.* 3rd. ed. Madrid: Ediciones del Congreso de la República, 1997.

Perry, Mary Elizabeth, and Anne J. Cruz, eds. *Cultural Encounters: The Impact of the Inquisition in Spain and the New World.* Berkeley: University of California Press, 1991.

Silverblatt, Irene M. *Modern Inquisitions: Peru and the Colonial Origins of the Civilized World.* Durham, NC: Duke University Press, 2004.

DAVID JICKLING

**INSTITUTE OF NUTRITION OF CENTRAL AMERICA AND PANAMA (INCAP).** Institute of Nutrition of Central America and Panama (INCAP), a regional nutritional research and development agency located in Guatemala City. Representatives of the five Central American countries plus Panama met in 1946 under the auspices of the Pan-American Health Organization to consider regional health problems. They decided to create a cooperative organization to work on common nutritional problems. The government of Guatemala agreed to erect the building to house the institute, the W. K. Kellogg Foundation provided funds for staff-development scholarships and for initial equipment, and the Pan-American Health Organization gave administrative support. Money for continuing operating costs was provided by member countries and by supporting international agencies.

INCAP was inaugurated on 15 September 1949. Its program has included the study of nutritional problems in the region, the search for solutions to those problems, and assistance to the member countries in implementing those solutions. One of INCAP's major successes has been the introduction of iodized salt to counter a widespread incidence of goiter. A high-protein, child-feeding supplement called Incaparina was developed with private manufacturers. Other programs have focused on vitamin A deficiencies and on child survival techniques. INCAP has been a leader in studying the nutritional status of specific populations and the relationship between prenatal and postnatal malnutrition and the development of children, including learning and behavior.

*See also* **Nutrition.**

BIBLIOGRAPHY

Nevin S. Scrimshaw and Moisés Behar, eds., *Symposium on Nutrition and Agricultural and Economic Development in the Tropics* (1976).

Incap, *Desarrollo del proceso de planificación multisectorial de la alimentación y nutrición en Centro America y Panama* (1979).

*Additional Bibliography*

Cueto, Marcus. *El valor de la salud: historia de la Organización Panamericana de la Salud.* Washington, DC: OPS, 2004.

Institute of Nutrition of Central America and Panama. *How INCAP Supports Maternal and Child Health in Central America.* Washington, DC: World Bank, 2005.

LaForgia, Gerard M. *Health System Innovations in Central America: Lessons and Impact of New Approaches.* Washington, DC: USAID, 2005.

León, Arturo. *Pobreza, hambre y seguridad alimentaria en Centroamérica y Panamá.* Santiago: CEPAL, División de Desarrollo Social, 2004.

National Center for Chronic Disease Prevention and Health Promotion. *Reproductive, Maternal and Child Health in Central America: Trends and Challenges facing Women and Children: El Salvador, Guatemala, Honduras, Nicaragua.* Guatemala City: The Institute, 1992.

DAVID L. JICKLING

**INSTITUTIONAL ACTS.** Institutional Acts, decrees issued by Brazil's military regime during the 1960s to provide legal justification for its assumption of greater power. Designed to restructure the political system, the seventeen Institutional Acts, of which the first and fifth are most significant, enabled the regime to establish an authoritarian government.

The first Institutional Act was announced on 9 April 1964, eight days after a military coup had left the office of the presidency vacant. Under this act, the chief executive could cancel electoral mandates, suppress individual political rights, and suspend constitutional liberties. The act limited the power of Congress by forbidding it to increase the amount of any expenditure measures submitted by the president and giving it only thirty days to consider executive-proposed amendments to the constitution. Another provision of the act established an electoral college that chose General Humberto Castelo Branco to lead the new government.

The military regime hoped to maintain popular support while using the first Institutional Act to create a national security state capable of eliminating subversion. When the government's party fared poorly in the October 1965 elections, however, hard-liners convinced Castelo Branco to issue a second Institutional Act. This act's strictures, viewed as temporary measures needed to ensure the regime's control over government, abolished the existing political parties, provided for the indirect election of the president, restricted the amount of time Congress could consider legislation before it automatically became law, and stipulated that persons accused of crimes against national security were to be subject to military justice.

Brazil's next president, General Artur Costa E Silva, was aligned with the less moderate military faction. On 13 December 1968, in response to student protests, labor strikes, and congressional noncompliance, he issued his first Institutional Act, the fifth overall. This notorious act suspended constitutional and individual liberties and signaled an attempt by hard-liners to increase the military regime's control over Brazil. In the following year, the government issued twelve Institutional Acts of lesser significance but accompanied by Supplementary Acts and other decrees that canceled upcoming elections, suspended Congress indefinitely, and further expanded the powers of the executive.

*See also* **Brazil: Since 1889; Castello Branco, Humberto de Alencar.**

BIBLIOGRAPHY

Maria Helena Moreira Alves, *State and Opposition in Military Brazil* (1985).

Thomas Skidmore, *The Politics of Military Rule in Brazil, 1964–85* (1988).

Alfred Stepan, *Rethinking Military Politics* (1988).

*Additional Bibliography*

Gaspari, Elio. *A ditadura envergonhada.* São Paulo: Companhia das Letras, 2002.

Gaspari, Elio. *A ditadura escancarada.* São Paulo: Companhia das Letras, 2002.

MICHAEL POLL

## INSTITUTO HISTÓRICO E GEOGRÁFICO BRASILEIRO.

**INSTITUTO HISTÓRICO E GEOGRÁFICO BRASILEIRO.** Instituto Histórico e Geográfico Brasileiro (IHGB), Brazilian research center characterized by its patriotic historiography and amateur scholarship. Its origins date to 1838 and are associated with the beginnings of Brazilian romantic nationalism, a milieu heavily indebted to contemporary French ideas and institutions. The institute was founded under the official protection of the emperor Pedro II, who often presided over its meetings. Founders included celebrated literati, imperial statesmen, and associates of the French Institut Historique. Establishment backgrounds remained the rule through the monarchy and the Old Republic (1889–1930). The IHGB continues to include members of traditional elite families, including the former dynasty, and to enjoy an official link to the national government.

The mission of the institution was to strengthen the new empire by identifying it with, and defining, the national past. To that end, the IHGB has collected, organized, and published historical and geographical documents and has established relations with similar foreign organizations. It has also published the *Revista do Instituto Histórico e Geográfico Brasileiro,* which since 1839 has been fundamental to Brazilian studies. The IHGB library has more than 100,000 volumes; its archives hold 50,000 documents and 5,000 maps. Among its great strengths, perhaps foremost, is its material on the monarchy and its personal archives for statesmen of that era and the Old Republic.

*See also* **Varnhagen, Francisco Adolfo de.**

BIBLIOGRAPHY

Rollie E. Poppino, "A Century of the *Revista do Instituto Histórico e Geográfico Brasileiro,*" in *Hispanic American Historical Review* 33, no. 2 (1953): 307–23.

Manoel Luís Salgado Guimarães, "Nação e civilização nos trópicos," in *Estudos Históricos* 1 (1988): 5–27.

*Additional Bibliography*

Adonias, Isa. *Instituto Histórico e Geográfico Brasileiro: 150 anos.* Rio de Janeiro: Studio HMF, 1990.

Losada, Janaina Zito. *Desejos e melancolias: Uma história da idéia de natureza no Brasil, 1839-1870.* Curitiba: Aos Quatro Ventos, 2000.

JEFFREY D. NEEDELL

## INSTITUTO NACIONAL DE LAS MUJERES.

**INSTITUTO NACIONAL DE LAS MUJERES.** Instituto Nacional de las Mujeres (INMUJERES; National Institute for Women) was formed in Mexico in March 8, 2001, in conjunction with the Comisión Nacional de Derechos Humanos (CNDH; National Commission of Human Rights) to prevent violations of the human rights of women. It is a public institution independent from the federal government. The institute's primary goal is to create and develop a culture of equality, nondiscrimination, and nonviolence and to help women exercise their rights.

The institute paired with the Mexican government, private organizations, academic institutions, and civic associations to establish Foros Nacionales de Consulta (National Forums of Consultation) to create the Programa Nacional de Igualdad de Oportunidades y no Discriminación contra las Mujeres (PROEQUIDAD; National Program for the Equality of Opportunity and Nondiscrimination against Women). The primary goal of PROEQUIDAD is to promote social conscience and gender equality among men and women. INMUJERES works with Coordinación de Relaciones Públicas y Comunicación Social (Coordination of Public Relations and Social Communication) through campaigns, publications, press conferences, newspapers, and events to promote the institution's goals, objectives, image, and principles of equality. Other Latin American countries have created similar institutions to protect and promote women's rights, such as the Instituto Nacional de las Mujeres

(INAMU) in Costa Rica, the Instituto Nacional de la Mujer(INAM) in Honduras, Instituto Nacional de la Mujer (INAMUJER) in Venezuela, and Instituto Nicaragüense de la Mujer (INIM).

*See also* **Comisión Nacional de Derechos Humanos; Women.**

BIBLIOGRAPHY

Instituto Nacional de la Mujer (Honduras). Available from http://www.inam.gob.hn.

Instituto Nacional de la Mujer (Venezuela). Available from http://www.inamujer.gov.ve.

Instituto Nacional de las Mujeres (Costa Rica). Available at http://www.inamu.go.cr.

Instituto Nacional de las Mujeres (Mexico). Available from http://www.inmujeres.gob.mx.

CLAUDIA CARBALLAL BENAGLIO

**INSTITUTO NACIONAL INDIGENISTA.** The Instituto Nacional Indigenista (INI) was formed on December 4, 1948, by the Mexican government to design culturally sensitive policy regarding the indigenous people of Mexico. The institute coordinated projects, programs, and services for indigenous people and compiled resources pertaining to the indigenous groups of Mexico, including national media, statistics, and census information. Further, the Institute supported cultural programming and indigenous languages through radio, television, and film that served Native audiences. Mexico is home to approximately twelve million indigenous people with diverse cultural backgrounds and languages. Throughout Mexico's history, many indigenous communities have faced economic underdevelopment and suffered from a lack of political recognition. By the 1980s and 1990s, the assimilatory INI had evolved to a participatory model, allowing indigenous groups the space to organize. The institute headed up campaigns to train community promoters who enabled indigenous communities to better represent themselves in the justice system. The Mexican government has since made legislative changes to promote the development of indigenous communities and preserve Native languages. In 2003 the Instituto Nacional Indigenista was replaced by the Comisión Nacional para el Desarrollo de los Pueblos Indígenas (CDI, translated as National commission for the development of native towns).

*See also* **Indigenous Languages; Indigenous Organizations.**

BIBLIOGRAPHY

Armendáriz, Lorenzo. *Instituto Nacional Indigenista, 1948–1998.* Mexico, D. F.: Instituto Nacional Indigenista, 1998.

Comisión Nacional para el Desarrollo de los Pueblos Indígenas. Available from http://www.cdi.gob.mx/ini/. The Internet site of the CDI.

ALISON FIELDS

**INSTITUTO POLITÉCNICO NACIONAL.** The National Polytechnic Institute is a Mexican public university system with a presence in fourteen states. It focuses on undergraduate and graduate technical degrees. The institute was founded in 1936 during the administration of President Lázaro Cárdenas del Rio with the goal of providing free technical education to workers and peasants in order to advance the economic, social, and political development of Mexico. In addition to its college and postgraduate programs and research centers, the university system incorporates a number of high schools. The university operates independently with regard to the administration of its patrimony and its self-generated income. It operates a TV station based in Mexico City that offers cultural and scientific programming as well as foreign films and TV shows. In 2006 the university's name was inscribed in gold letters on the Wall of Honor of the Plenary Sessions Hall of the Chamber of Deputies in Mexico City.

*See also* **Cárdenas del Río, Lázaro; Universities: The Modern Era.**

BIBLIOGRAPHY

Instituto Politécnico Nacional. Available from http://www.ipn.mx.

CLAUDIA CARBALLAL BENAGLIO

**INSTITUTO TECNOLÓGICO AUTÓNOMO DE MEXICO.** The Autonomous Technological Institute of Mexico is a private university located in Mexico City. Originally called Instituto

Tecnológico de Mexico, it was founded in 1946 by the Asociación Mexicana de Cultura (Association of Mexican Culture), led by a group of wealthy individuals presided over by Raúl Baillères. Considered one of the top business schools in Mexico and one of the nation's preeminent institutions of higher learning, the institute was established with the goal of educating professionals who would be able to facilitate economic change. In 1947 the undergraduate school of business was founded. With the opening of the accounting school the institute grew from fifty-two students to five hundred students in 1951.

In 1963 the president of the Republic, Adolfo López Mateos, recognized the institute as autonomous. However, it was not until 1985 that the Secretaría de Educación Pública (Secretariat of Public Education) recognized the institute's autonomy and allowed the institution to adopt its current name. In the 1970s various degrees were added, such as applied mathematics, social sciences, administration, and master's in administration. In the 1980s the law school was opened, and degrees were established in computer science, political science, international relations, and industrial engineering, as well as joint degrees. In 1991 the Centro de Investigación y Estudios de Posgrado (Center for Investigation and Postgraduate Studies) was founded.

*See also* **López Mateos, Adolfo; Universities: The Modern Era.**

BIBLIOGRAPHY

Instituto Tecnológico Autónomo de Mexico. Available from http://www.itam.mx.

CLAUDIA CARBALLAL BENAGLIO

**INSTITUTO TECNOLÓGICO DE ESTUDIOS SUPERIORES DE MONTERREY.** The Institute of Technology and Higher Education of Monterrey, known as Tecnológico de Monterrey, or simply the "Tec," is a multi-campus university system founded in 1943 by a group of Monterrey industrialists and businessmen led by Eugenio Garza Sada. The primary goal of the institute, which was modeled on the Massachusetts Institute of Technology, was to create a culture of entrepreneurship and provide professionals for local enterprises. It is considered among the most prestigious Latin American institutions of higher technical education. It is a private, independent, nonprofit institution, not related to any political party or religious group, and operates under the statute of a free university.

The work of the institute and of all of its campuses throughout Mexico is supported by civil associations made up of leaders from all parts of the country who are committed to quality in higher education. It offers a Virtual University system that has been in operation since 1989 and has consolidated itself as a pioneering institution in distance education. The institute offers programs of study at the upper secondary, undergraduate, and graduate levels and in research and development. It has thirty-three campuses and international offices in North America, Europe, and Asia. Tecnológico de Monterrey is considered one of the first serious users of the Internet in Mexico and also a pioneer in the use of wireless technologies among Mexican enterprises. These technologies have been extensively used to facilitate online education throughout the campuses. In 1950 the institute was accredited by the Southern Association of Colleges and Schools of the United States.

*See also* **Internet; Universities: The Modern Era.**

BIBLIOGRAPHY

Instituto Tecnológico de Estudios Superiores de Monterrey. Available from http://www.itesm.mx.

Rudolf, James D., ed. *Mexico: A Country Study.* Foreign Area Studies, the American University. 3rd edition. Washington, DC: Headquarters, Department of the Army, 1985.

CLAUDIA CARBALLAL BENAGLIO

**INTENDANCY SYSTEM.** Intendancy system, administrative and territorial subdivisions of viceroyalties, headed by an intendant or superintendent, and implemented in Latin America in the last half of the eighteenth century. The Bourbon dynasty assumed the Spanish throne in 1700 and began a series of reforms to centralize its power, reduce creole influence, increase its revenues, and eliminate corruption both on the Peninsula and throughout the empire. Philip V ordered intendancies created in Spain in 1718 but full implementation of the decree was delayed until 1749. A study of the economic conditions of the empire written by José del Campillo y Cossío in 1743 recommended that a series of investigations be conducted throughout the empire to identify the problems of each region and suggested utilization of the intendancy system to correct them. With the return of Havana to Spanish control in 1762, Charles III adopted Campillo's recommendations and sent José de Gálvez to examine New Spain and Alejandro O'Reilly to study the Caribbean colonies. Cuba, changed by its exposure to international trade during the British occupation, received first attention, and in 1764 Charles created an intendancy for the island. José de Gálvez submitted the reports of his investigation in New Spain to the crown in 1768, recommending solutions to the problems of that colony and calling for implementation of the intendancy system throughout the empire. Resistance from New Spain's viceroy, Antonio María de Bucareli, delayed application of this recommendation until 1782.

In that year, the king issued the Ordinance for Intendants, creating a position in Buenos Aires for a superintendent with nominal control over the remaining seven intendancies in the viceroyalty of Río de la Plata, including Upper Peru. The following year, the plan was applied to Venezuela and in 1784 to Peru and the Philippines. By 1786, a revision of the initial ordinance appeared called the New Code for Intendants, issuing instructions to create twelve intendancies for New Spain, and its provisions were applied to the remainder of the empire. In 1812 the intendancy of Cuba was divided into three jurisdictions, with a superintendent in Havana and separate intendancies in Santiago and Puerto Principe. In some cases, as in Spain, the governor of a region also served as intendant, although Gálvez recognized this as a source of corruption and inefficiency. The last intendancy filled in 1814 separated the positions on the island of Puerto Rico.

Older studies of the intendancies tended to suggest that all were alike, created for the same reasons, and existing under the same rules and regulations. There were, however, functional and territorial distinctions that made them different. The theoretical role of all intendants, nevertheless, was the same. Their instructions asked them to streamline the bureaucracy, promote efficiency, eliminate corruption and contraband, increase the tax yields, develop new raw materials for export to Spain, widen the colonial markets for Spanish goods, improve colonial facilities, promote education and technology, foster immigration to colonize agricultural areas, stimulate activities of the *cabildos,* and reorganize the militia. In order to achieve these ends, they took powers from all officials from the top down. In the viceregal centers of New Spain and Peru, and in Central America, they replaced the *alcaldes mayores* and *corregidores* in Indian regions, jurisdictions long plagued by low salaries and massive corruption. For example, the twelve intendancies created in New Spain replaced 200 of these officials. However, the provinces created in that colony were so large that the intendancies were divided into districts (*partidos*) and the intendants appointed subdelegates in each to serve in their stead. Because of continuing low salaries and a lack of qualified individuals, many of the former officials became subdelegates and continued the corruption and exploitation of Indian populations.

In practice, all intendants had jurisdiction over taxation and financial aspects of the military. The Caribbean colonies, limited to these two areas, suffered constant jurisdictional disputes with the captains-general and other officials. Their situation was different from that on the mainland since the Caribbean colonies had no major Indian populations and had a disproportionate concern with trade and international interests because of their locations. Caribbean intendants had limited jurisdictions until the end of the system in 1853. The intendants on the mainland colonies enjoyed expanded powers that included administrative and judicial functions and stronger control over the military. They were given powers to examine and correct deficiencies in administration, and they became the first court of appeal in matters regarding trade and commerce, controlling function, composition, and movement of the military.

To further wrest colonial power and control from the creole elites, the crown generally appointed peninsular Spaniards to these positions. The intendants generally had good educations and approached their positions with the zeal evident in the late Bourbon period. They often received the appointment based on experience. For example, those named in Nicaragua and Honduras required prowess in martial skills to counter contraband and foreign colonization efforts. Those in Chiapas and El Salvador, regions with serious economic and legal problems, required men with fiscal and judicial expertise.

In general, the intendants increased revenues appreciably through commercial and agricultural diversification and a more efficient tax collection system, though they seem to have been more successful in peripheral areas than in the viceregal centers. Abuses of Indian populations did not cease because of the subdelegados, and in fact Indian tribute declined in New Spain because of the greater subdivision of territory. The bureaucracy created by the system increased the costs of administration, but the increased revenues, channeled into development of each region, did tend to benefit its residents. Immigration programs brought Spaniards into commercial centers and they, not the creole merchants, derived the benefits of the reforms. The appointment of peninsular Spaniards to most of the positions and the effects of their reforms further exacerbated creole frustration and animosity against Spain. In some areas, like Chile, the immigration program changed the face of the colony by whitening the population. The geographic divisions created regional autonomy and its creoles developed a regional loyalty rather than the hoped-for loyalty to Spain. During the wars for independence, the emerging states took on physical boundaries similar to those created under the system.

Differences in regions governed and in individual personalities determined the success or failure of a particular intendant. Early historians praised the system for achieving Bourbon goals. Some condemn the system altogether and say it caused more problems than it solved. Others believe some were successful while others were not. Studies of the careers of individual intendants are few, so an accurate conclusion on the effectiveness of the system is impossible. The available evidence shows that the force of the intendant and the cooperation of creoles in the Caribbean and Central America allowed progress, but that an entrenched system of creole elite power and uncooperative officials thwarted chances of success in Chile.

*See also* **Viceroyalty, Viceroy.**

BIBLIOGRAPHY

The basic study is Lillian Fisher, *The Intendant System in Spanish America* (1929). Various regions are discussed in John R. Fisher, *Government and Society in Colonial Peru: The Intendant System 1784–1814* (1970).

John Lynch, *Spanish Colonial Administration, 1782–1818: The Intendant System in the Viceroyalty of the Río de la Plata* (1958).

Hector Humberto Samayoa Guevara, *El régimen de intendencias en el Reino de Guatemala* (1978). Most individual studies are doctoral dissertations, but two are published, M. Isidro Méndez, *El Intendente Ramírez* (1944), and Jacques Barbier, *Reform and Politics in Bourbon Chile, 1755–1796* (1980).

Altagracia Ortiz, *Eighteenth Century Reforms in the Caribbean* (1983).

### *Additional Bibliography*

Franco Cáceres, Iván. *La intendencia de Valladolid de Michoacán, 1786-1809: Reforma administrativa y exacción fiscal en una región de la Nueva España.* México: Instituto Michoacano de Cultura, 2001.

Pietschmann, Horst. *Las reformas borbónicas y el sistema de intendencias en Nueva España: Un estudio político administrativo.* México, D.F.: Fondo de Cultura Económica, 1996.

JACQUELYN BRIGGS KENT

---

**INTER-AMERICAN CONGRESS OF WOMEN.** Inter-American Congress of Women, an international conference held in Guatemala City, Guatemala, 21–27 August 1947. Sponsored by the Committee of the Americas of the Women's International League for Peace and Freedom and hosted by the Guatemalan Union of Democratic Women, the meeting was comprised of representatives of women's groups from nineteen western hemisphere nations who convened to "denounce the hemispheric armament plan under discussion at the Rio Conference" and demand that "the cost of the arms program be used to support industry, agriculture, health, and education for our people."

The belief that "women of our continent" have a particular right to speak out on "inter-American political problems," as stated in the minutes of the congress, had a long precedent, as did the delegates' concern with international peace and issues of social and economic justice. The women sent cablegrams to the Rio Conference asking that the delegates respect the peaceful intent of the Charter of the United Nations and urging that "the expansion of communism will not be contained by force of arms." Their efforts were unrequited.

The Primero Congreso Interamericano de Mujeres (to give the official title) was not the "first" inter-American congress of women; rather, the title underscored the discontinuity of the historical record of women's activities at the international level. Convening the congress demonstrated the women's conviction that a separatist strategy continued to be necessary for women to make their voices heard on political issues in the post-World War II world. The legacy of the congress is clear in the 1949 mandate to the Inter-American Commission of Women in the charter of the Organization of American States.

The Congress illustrates an important moment in the first wave of the international women's movement. Although the cold war largely stifled this initial phase of women's internationalism, the global activism of women since the 1970s and into the twenty-first century is built on these foundations.

*See also* **Feminism and Feminist Organizations; Pan-American Conferences: Rio Conference (1947); Rio Treaty (1947).**

BIBLIOGRAPHY


The papers of the Primero Congreso Interamericano de Mujeres, 1947, are in the Collection of Alicia Moreau de Justo, Montevideo, Uruguay. See also Francesca Miller, "Latin American Feminism and the Transnational Arena," in *Women, Culture, and Politics in Latin America* (1990) and *Latin American Women and the Search for Social Justice* (1991).

### *Additional Bibliography*

Molyneux, Maxine. *Women's Movements in International Perspective: Latin America and Beyond.* New York: Palgrave, 2001.

Potthast, Barbara, and Eugenia Scarzanella, eds. *Mujeres y naciones en América Latina: Problemas de inclusion y exclusion.* Princeton, NJ: M. Wiener, 2003.

Rock, David. *Latin America in the 1940s: War and Postwar Transitions.* Berkeley: University of California Press, 1994.

Rupp, Leila J. *Worlds of Women: The Making of an International Women's Movement.* Princeton, NJ: Princeton University Press, 1997.

Sheinin, David, ed. *Beyond the Ideal: Pan Americanism in Inter-American Affairs.* Westport, CT: Greenwood Press, 2000.


FRANCESCA MILLER

**INTER-AMERICAN DEMOCRATIC CHARTER, 2001.** The thirty-four members of the Organization of American States (OAS) unanimously adopted the Inter-American Democratic Charter on, by coincidence, September 11, 2001. Designed to reinforce the collective defense and promotion of democracy in the Western Hemisphere, the charter builds on Resolution 1080, adopted in 1991. Peruvian prime minister Javier Pérez de Cuéllar proposed the charter in 2000 to address threats to democracy falling short of the forceful overthrow of an elected government. Negotiations were convened by a declaration of leaders of the Western Hemisphere at the end of the Quebec City Summit of the Americas in April 2001.

The charter offers a broad definition of democracy and holds that "the peoples of the Americas have a right to democracy and their governments have an obligation to promote and defend it" (article 1). As a legally nonbinding document, it cannot be enforced without the political will of member states. Chapter IV of the charter adumbrates steps to be taken in the event of an unconstitutional alteration or interruption of a democratic regime. It does not specify what constitutes such an event, but a member state can, in principle, be suspended from the OAS if the General Assembly determines that democracy, and all diplomatic efforts to restore it, have failed.

*See also* **Organization of American States (OAS); Pérez de Cuéllar, Javier.**

BIBLIOGRAPHY


Axworthy, Lloyd, et al. Special issue on Inter-American Democratic Charter. *Canadian Foreign Policy* 10, no. 3 (2003): 1–116.

Organization of American States. Inter-American Democratic Charter. September 2001. Available from http://www.oas.org/charter/docs/resolution1_en_p4.htm.


MAXWELL A. CAMERON

**INTER-AMERICAN DEVELOPMENT BANK (IDB).** The Inter-American Development Bank (IDB) is the world's oldest and largest regional development bank. Since its founding in 1959, the IDB has become the single greatest source of multilateral support for social and economic development in Latin America and the Caribbean. Each year the IDB provides $9 billion of financial and technical assistance to nations throughout the region. The bank plays an important role in promoting social equity, private sector development, state modernization, and environmental preservation.

### MEMBERSHIP AND STRUCTURE

The IDB is headquartered in Washington, D.C., and has forty-seven member nations. Twenty-six of these nations are from Latin America and the Caribbean and are eligible to borrow from the bank. The remaining countries are non-borrowing members from North America, Europe, and East Asia. The highest policy-making body of the IDB is its Board of Governors. The governors establish broad institutional policies and oversee the bank's lending programs. Each member nation is permitted to appoint one governor. The IDB also has a fourteen-member Board of Executive Directors. The executive directors serve three-year terms and are responsible for approving project proposals and setting the administrative budget. The bank's president, who is elected by the Board of Governors and serves for a renewable five-year term, chairs meetings of the executive directors and manages a staff of eighteen hundred.

IDB operations are divided into three subregional departments. The first department oversees bank-supported projects in Mexico, Central America, and the Caribbean; the second department is responsible for the northern part of South America (Colombia, Ecuador, Guyana, Peru, Suriname, and Venezuela); and the third department covers the southern part of the continent (Argentina, Bolivia, Brazil, Chile, Paraguay, and Uruguay). The IDB also has offices in each of its borrowing member countries. These country offices are directly involved in the design, implementation, and supervision of bank-supported projects and programs. They also provide advisory services to local government authorities.

**Road construction in Yungas, Bolivia, 2006.** The Inter-American Development Bank (IDB) provides funding throughout Latin America and the Caribbean for social and economic improvements to education, health care, and infrastructure, in accordance with its mandate to improve the living conditions for impoverished citizens. © BRUNO FERT/CORBIS

### RESOURCES AND PROGRAMS

The IDB obtains its resources from a number of different sources. Member countries are assessed an annual subscription that is calculated to reflect the relative size of each nation's economy. Member countries are required to pay only a small fraction (4.3 percent in 2007) of the subscription. The remainder is considered "callable capital" in which governments agree to contribute as needed. Each country's voting power within the bank is based on its capital subscriptions. Unlike other multilateral financial institutions, such as the World Bank and the International Monetary Fund, borrowing member countries of the IDB have always held a majority of the voting shares.

The IDB's largest source of revenue is private capital markets. The bank is able to use its callable capital as collateral to borrow resources at competitive rates from international capital markets. The IDB also receives repayment of principal on previously extended loans and generates earnings through various investments. Lastly, the bank participates in cofinancing arrangements with other multilateral institutions, including the World Bank, Caribbean Development Bank, Central American Bank for Economic Integration, and Andean Development Corporation.

The IDB provides assistance in the form of loans, grants, and technical advice. Most lending programs come from the bank's Ordinary Capital account. Loans from this account are extended at near-market interest rates and are allocated for projects that are expected to become profitable within a reasonable period of time. The IDB established an Intermediary Financial Facility (IFF) in 1983 to reduce interest rates on loans from its Ordinary Capital account to a number of low-income countries including the Dominican Republic, Ecuador, El Salvador, Guatemala, Jamaica, Paraguay, and Suriname. In addition, the IDB administers more than fifty separate Trust Funds that have been established by a single country or group of countries and provide grants in specific sectoral or technical areas.

The IDB also has a concessional or soft loan window. The Fund for Special Operations (FSO), which was established in 1960, extends loans at low interest rates with forty-year maturities and ten-year grace periods. Use of FSO resources is limited in 2007 to Bolivia, Guyana, Haiti, Honduras, and Nicaragua. The FSO can also extend loans to the Caribbean Development Bank for use in countries that are not members of the IDB.

### SOCIAL DEVELOPMENT

Accelerating the social development of Latin America is the preeminent objective of the IDB's lending strategy. The bank has long worked to meet the basic needs of poor communities throughout the region. Under the bank's mandate, lending for poverty reduction and social equity must reach at least 40 percent of total resource allocations and at least 50 percent of total operations. These benchmarks are considerably larger than those of most other multilateral institutions.

Expanding basic health coverage for the poor is an important part of the IDB's social development work. The bank has funded mobile teams to provide integrated health care in remote areas of Peru, trained community health agents in Brazil, and initiated programs to improve maternal and child health in Guatemala, Honduras, Nicaragua, and Panama. The IDB has also supported immunization campaigns in Colombia and Guatemala and helped modernize the national epidemiological surveillance system in Bolivia. The bank has also worked to further health care policy reform. Programs in Argentina, Belize, El Salvador, Guyana, and Uruguay have helped modernize public health systems and ensure more equitable access to clinics and hospitals.

The IDB has also funded a wide range of educational initiatives in Latin America. Bank loans have been used for the construction and renovation of schools in El Salvador, Haiti, and Venezuela and for the installation of information technologies in Argentina, Barbados, El Salvador, Jamaica, and Uruguay. The IDB also supported the creation of distance learning centers in Nicaragua that are designed to reach secondary students in rural areas. In Brazil and Jamaica the bank supported curriculum development, and in the Dominican Republic, Ecuador, Guatemala, and Haiti the bank helped develop new instructional methodologies for primary and secondary school teachers.

The IDB's social development projects have frequently targeted those groups that have been historically excluded from the benefits of economic growth. The bank has placed special emphasis on meeting the needs of women. This includes strengthening its institutional capacity to mainstream gender issues into all bank activities. The subregional departments use gender experts to assist project teams in designing bank-supported programs. The IDB has also funded projects to improve the lives of ethnic minorities. In 2001 the bank adopted an Action Plan for Combating Social Exclusion Based on Race and Ethnicity, which includes institutional procedures to incorporate underprivileged minority groups into the daily activities of the bank. Support for community development projects in Central America and the Andean region has been contingent on specific measures to ensure access by indigenous groups. Additionally, the bank funded projects to enhance educational and economic opportunities for people of African descent in Brazil, parts of Central America, and the Caribbean.

### PRIVATE SECTOR DEVELOPMENT

Private sector development has also been a long-standing objective of the IDB. A number of bank projects and programs have been designed to create an enabling environment for private businesses. This, it is argued, helps generate economic growth, higher living standards, and the ability to compete in the global economy. The bank's Private Sector Department, established in 1994, is largely responsible for the coordination and oversight of private sector activities.

Investments in physical infrastructure have been a key component of the IDB's private sector strategy. Bank officials frequently link the region's poor infrastructure to an inability to attract sufficient investment. The IDB has invested heavily in transportation systems. This includes highway construction in Belize, Brazil, Guyana, Jamaica, and Nicaragua; repairs to bridges and roads in the Dominican Republic, El Salvador, and Peru; improved air transportation in Ecuador; and the creation of integrated mass transit systems in Colombia. Loans from the IDB have also helped improve the quality of passenger train service in Argentina and port operations in Chile. The bank has also funded improvements in the energy sector. This includes electrical power projects in Argentina, Brazil, the Dominican Republic, Paraguay, and Uruguay, a rural electrification project in Bolivia, the construction of a geothermal facility in Costa Rica, and the building of hydroelectric power plants in Colombia.

The IDB extends a small number of loans directly to private businesses without government guarantees. These loans are frequently channeled through the Inter-American Investment Corporation (IIC), the bank's private sector affiliate. The IIC, which began operations in 1989, provides long-term loans to help modernize small- and medium-size enterprises. The corporation also provides financing in the form of direct equity investments. The IIC can finance up to 30 percent of the cost of a new enterprise and up to 50 percent of the cost of an expansion project. The Multilateral Investment Fund (MIF), which was established in 1992, also provides loans, grants, and technical assistance to micro and small enterprises in the region.

## POLICY-BASED LENDING

Since the 1990s the IDB has become much more directly engaged in the promotion of macroeconomic policy reforms in member countries. This is a response to the continued economic difficulties that many of these countries have experienced, including chronic budget deficits, deteriorating foreign reserves, and debilitating external debts. The bank has introduced policy-based loans that support institutional changes on the sector and sub-sector levels. Loans are granted after recipient nations agree to alter sectoral policies that are deemed inimical to growth and create an environment that is more private-sector friendly. Particular emphasis is placed on the privatization of state-owned industries. Nations are also encouraged to further integrate their economies in global markets through the promotion of exports and reduction of barriers to foreign goods. Lastly, governments are called upon to create incentives for foreign direct investment, such as legal protections for investors, more efficient financial markets, the removal of entry restrictions on capital markets, and liberalizing credit and interest rates.

The introduction of policy-based lending has been a source of considerable controversy for the IDB. Critics charge that the sectoral reforms advocated by the bank intensify social and economic inequalities. Poor communities, it is argued, are most adversely affected by these reforms. The IDB has responded by creating Social Investment Funds, which help mitigate the social costs of adjustment. Job-training programs, for example, have been expanded in response to loss of public sector employment. The IDB has placed a limit on the size of its policy-based lending programs: Work in this area cannot exceed 25 percent of total bank lending.

## STATE MODERNIZATION

Since the mid-1990s, the IDB has become engaged in the promotion of public sector reform in Latin America. This also represents a departure from past practices. The bank traditionally focused on supporting social and economic projects and avoided interference in the internal political affairs of member countries. In the early twenty-first century, however, bank officials argue that "state modernization" is necessary for the success of its social and economic work. A new division on State, Governance, and Civil Society was established to coordinate political reform programs, and State and Civil Society divisions were set up within each of its three subregional departments.

The IDB has heavily invested in public administration reform. A bank project in Uruguay helped improve the management of public resources by modernizing the administration of state revenues and enhancing the transparency of public sector procurement. The IDB has provided technical assistance to the governments of Bolivia, Colombia, Honduras, Nicaragua, and Peru to establish performance-based administrative systems, restructure the organization and functioning of central government agencies, and introduce integrated financial management, procurement, and accountability systems. In Argentina, Brazil, the Dominican Republic, El Salvador, and Guatemala, IDB projects have helped streamline administrative procedures and improve the supervisory capacity of the executive branch.

The IDB has worked to strengthen legislatures and judiciaries throughout Latin America. The bank has provided advisory services to ensure that oversight and control functions are properly administered and has established training programs for legislative and judicial leaders. In Colombia and El Salvador the IDB helped make national assemblies more independent and transparent and introduced ethics codes for lawmakers. In Brazil, Chile, Paraguay, and Peru the IDB provided support to modernize federal, state, and municipal legislatures. In Bolivia, Honduras, Nicaragua, and Panama the bank helped strengthen oversight mechanisms, upgrade information systems, and improve communication between legislators and their constituents. IDB projects have helped modernize judicial administration in Costa Rica, Ecuador, and Venezuela, reform court procedures in the Dominican Republic, and improve the organization and operation of judicial offices in Nicaragua and Panama. In Guatemala, Honduras, and Uruguay the IDB worked to strengthen the managerial, technical, and administrative capacities of court systems.

## ENVIRONMENTAL PRESERVATION

The IDB is placing greater emphasis on the preservation of natural environments in Latin America. New projects and programs have been formulated to ensure sustainable resource management and conservation. The bank established an Environmental Protection Division to oversee its work in this area and has incorporated environmental impact assessments as part of its evaluation of all project proposals.

Reforestation programs and community-based forestry management plans have been supported by the IDB in Brazil, Ecuador, and Peru. It has supported biodiversity conservation projects to preserve fragile ecosystems such as the Galapagos Islands of Ecuador and Pantanal wetlands of Brazil. The IDB has supported a regional biodiversity strategy to conserve ecosystems in the Andean region. It has fortified management of water resources, especially coastal and marine resources. In El Salvador, Guatemala, Honduras, and Panama, bank projects have strengthened the management of watershed areas.

The IDB has worked to develop capacity of national environmental regulatory bodies. This includes the establishment of legal and institutional frameworks for environmental management in Panama, training and logistical support for the principal environmental agency of Suriname, and the development of a national environmental management system in Ecuador. The IDB has also worked with governments throughout the region to rationalize environmental policy and strengthen environmental laws.

## CONCLUSION

The Inter-American Development Bank plays an important role in the social and economic progress of Latin America and the Caribbean. The bank has consistently supported public sector projects and programs to help meet the basic needs of the region's poor. The IDB channels a large share of its resources to the poorest communities in the poorest countries. IDB support has been especially critical in the provision of primary healthcare and basic education. The bank has also worked to accelerate private sector development, modernize public administration, and preserve natural environments.

The IDB has a strong record of success in Latin America and the Caribbean. The vast majority of the development projects it has funded have achieved their intended objectives and many became self-sustaining after support from the bank ended. The IDB has been successful for a number of reasons. It has accumulated considerable experience and expertise since its founding in 1959 and has forged close working relationships with governments in the region. The bank is careful to tailor its projects to the specific requirements of each member country while retaining the capacity to respond rapidly to changing conditions. Lastly, the IDB ensures that the intended beneficiaries of its lending programs actively participate in the planning, design, and implementation of development projects. This is a crucial component of the bank's lending philosophy. Poor communities are not simply viewed as the recipients of assistance but as active participants in improving their own conditions. This helps create more self-reliant communities which have the resources and skills necessary to meet their own needs on a long-term basis. Given the IDB's past achievements and continued expansion, it will certainly play a critical role in the social and economic progress of Latin America and the Caribbean in the years to come.

*See also* **Banking: Overview; Economic Development; Pan-American Conferences: Montevideo Conference (1933); Pan-American Conferences: Washington Conference (1889); World Bank.**

BIBLIOGRAPHY

Bruggman, Hugo. *El Banco Interamericano de Desarrollo Renovado para los años 90.* Bogotá: Fondo Editorial CEREC, 1991.

Culpeper, Roy. *Crossroads or Cross-Purposes: The IDB at 31.* Ottawa, ON: North-South Institute, 1990.

Dell, Sidney. *The Inter-American Development Bank: A Study in Development Financing.* New York: Praeger, 1972.

Griffith-Jones, Stephany, et al. *An Assessment of the IDB Lending Programme.* Sussex: Institute of Development Studies, 1994.

Max-Neef, Norbert. *El Banco Interamericano de Desarrollo: Su origen, sus objectivos.* Tegucigalpa: Graficentro Editores, 1992.

Scheman, L. Ronald. "Banking on Growth: The Role of the Inter-American Development Bank" *Journal of Inter-american Studies and World Affairs* 39, no. 1 (1997): 85–100.

Tussie, Diana. *The Inter-American Development Bank.* Boulder, CO: Lynne Rienner, 1995.

FRANCIS ADAMS

## INTER-AMERICAN FOUNDATION (IAF).

The Inter-American Foundation (IAF) is an autonomous U.S. government corporation created in December 1969 as the Inter-American Social Development Institute. It arose from concern among key congressional members and executive branch officials in the development community that the efforts of the Alliance for Progress during the 1960s had failed to produce a noticeable effect on the social conditions of the poor in Latin America and the Caribbean, in spite of the advances shown by macroeconomic indicators. This lack of significant social progress was partly attributed to an undue emphasis on basic infrastructural projects as opposed to social policy and human resource development. However, it was also felt that the customary linkage of U.S. development assistance to short-term foreign policy interests related to host-country governments unnecessarily constrained what ought to be a long-term process of support related to host-country people.

Thus, under the congressional leadership of Representative Dante Fascell, the new agency was given considerable autonomy from the executive branch, particularly the State Department and the U.S. Agency for International Development, and a mandate to take its development assistance directly to the beneficiaries, bypassing government institutions in the host countries. To emphasize this autonomy, the new agency was to be governed by a nine-member board of directors appointed by the White House; six of its members were to come from the private sector. Most unusual, perhaps, the legislation emphasized the experimental nature of the initiatives to be undertaken by the new agency, granting it the privilege to take risks—and thus sometimes to fail—and the responsibility to document the lessons learned. It was to be funded by direct congressional appropriations and—after subsequent negotiations—from the U.S.-funded Social Progress Trust Fund in the Inter-American Development Bank. After selection of board members and president, negotiations about its modus operandi, and debate about its location and even its name, the IAF opened for business in 1971.

Operationally, the IAF functions much like a private foundation. Its programs of direct grants, organized by country and region rather than by topic, are directed by appointed foundation representatives with administrative support. All its staff members are U.S. civil servants. Prior to 2007 the IAF has distributed more than $600 million in grants in 26 countries to more than 4,500 organizations. Grants typically range in size from several thousand to several hundred thousand dollars, and durations range from several months to (rarely) more than three years, although continuation of projects for longer periods through amendments is common. For fiscal year 2006 the IAF had an authorized staff of forty-six and a total budget of $25 million, 68 percent of which was devoted to programs. It accepts proposals on an ongoing basis and has no set format or schedule for these presentations.

By design, and to emphasize its autonomy from U.S. foreign policy interests, the IAF bases all of its staff in its U.S. headquarters in Arlington, Virginia. To compensate for the lack of a permanent country presence, it has relied on a very experienced staff, frequent visits, and an intensely hands-on style of relating to grantees and other country nationals. In the early 1980s the IAF began experimenting with a supplemental system of contracted in-country support services for administration, information clearinghouse, logistics, and evaluation of projects. By the 1990s the system had expanded to a network of support centers in all countries, some with a capacity to handle disbursements for small projects.

In line with its mandate to experiment and document, the IAF maintains an active learning and dissemination effort based on its quarterly journal, *Grassroots Development*, and frequent publication of books and occasional papers by staff and outside experts.

*See also* **Inter-American Development Bank (IDB).**

BIBLIOGRAPHY

Breslin, Patrick. *La Fundación Interamericana y el desarrollo de base.* Rosslyn, VA: Fundación Interamericana, 1990.

Glade, William P., Charles A. Reilly, and Diane B. Bendahmane, eds. *Inquiry at the Grassroots: An Inter-American Foundation Fellowship Reader.* Arlington, VA: Inter-American Foundation, 1993.

Mashek, Robert W. *The Inter-American Foundation in the Making.* Rosslyn, VA: Inter-American Foundation, 1981.

RAMON E. DAUBON

## INTER-AMERICAN ORGANIZATIONS.

Inter-American Organizations, the constituent organizational, institutional, and legal-constitutional elements of the Inter-American System. From 1889 to the present there has been a gradual evolution of the Inter-American System, the successive creation of Inter-American organizations, first through the Pan-American Union and then through the Organization of American States (OAS).

### ORGANIZATION OF AMERICAN STATES

The OAS is the central inter-American institution. The principal components of the OAS include the following:

***General Secretariat.*** The central, permanent institution of the Inter-American System that implements the programs and policies as directed by the General Assembly and the various decision-making councils. The General Secretariat is headquartered in Washington, D.C., with national offices and specialized institutes located in member countries.

***General Assembly.*** The supreme decision-making organ of the OAS. The Assembly, which meets at annual sessions in one of the member states or at OAS headquarters in Washington, D.C., sets the policy and budget for the OAS and its agencies.

***Meetings of Consultation and Ministers of Foreign Relations.*** Conferences may be convened (by the OAS Permanent Council at the request of a member state) "to consider problems of an urgent nature and of common interest" (OAS Charter) or in cases of attack or threats to peace and security.

***Permanent Council.*** Body that guides and monitors the daily business of the OAS. It is comprised of permanent representatives (holding ambassadorial rank) from each of the thirty-four active member states. The Council meets more than twice a month at OAS Headquarters in Washington, D.C.

***Inter-American Council for Integral Development (CIDI).*** The "Protocol of Managua," approved at the June 1993 OAS General Assembly and now subject to ratification, merges the Inter-American Social and Economic Council (CIES) and Inter-American Council for Education, Science and Culture (CIECC) into a single Inter-American Council for Integral Development, which will provide greater coordination and efficiency of technical cooperation programs.

### INTER-AMERICAN SPECIALIZED AGENCIES

The other inter-American organizations which, together with the councils of the OAS comprise the Inter-American System, include the Inter-american Development Bank, the Inter-American Defense Board, and the following specialized institutions and agencies:

***Inter-American Institute for Cooperation on Agriculture (IICA).*** Founded in 1942 and based in Costa Rica, the Institute initiates projects to help member states plan and evaluate agriculture policies, develop and share technology, promote rural development, improve animal health, and generate trade.

***Pan-American Health Organization (PAHO).*** Based in Washington, D.C., this agency cooperates closely with governments of the hemisphere to promote health care. Founded as the Pan-American Sanitary Bureau in 1902, it is both an OAS specialized organization and a regional arm of the World Health Organization.

***Inter-American Commission of Human Rights (IACHR).*** Created in 1969, it is governed by the American Convention on Human Rights, which was signed in 1969 and put into force in 1978. The Commission, based in Washington, D.C., has seven members, who are proposed by member states and elected, in their own right, by the OAS General Assembly. The IACHR represents the thirty-five member states of the OAS.

***Inter-American Court of Human Rights.*** Created by the Pact of San José in 1969, the court is an autonomous judicial institution whose purpose is to apply and interpret the American Convention of Human Rights. It is composed of seven jurists from OAS member countries and is located in San José, Costa Rica.

***Inter-American Drug Abuse Control Commission (CICAD).*** Established by the General Assembly of the OAS in 1986, it has a current membership of twenty-four states, which will increase to twenty-nine by 1995. CICAD's mandate is to promote and facilitate close cooperation among the member countries in the control of drug trafficking, production, and use in accordance with the Inter-American Program of Action of Rio de Janeiro (1986).

***Inter-American Commission of Women (CIM).*** A specialized agency of the OAS, which was established in 1928 at the Sixth International Conference of American States in Havana, Cuba. It is the first official intergovernmental agency created expressly to ensure recognition of the civil and political rights of women in the Americas—the first not only in the region, but in the world.

***Inter-American Children's Institute (IACI).*** Founded in 1927 and located in Montevideo, Uruguay, the IACI strives to achieve better health and living conditions for children and the family. The Institute serves as a center of social action, carrying out programs in the fields of health, education, social legislation, social service, and statistics.

***Pan-American Institute of Geography and History (PAIGH).*** Founded in 1928 and located in Mexico City, the Pan-American Institute of Geography and History seeks to encourage, coordinate, and publicize geographic, historical, cartographic, and geophysical studies in the Americas.

***Inter-American Indian Institute (IAII).*** Created in 1940 and located in Mexico City, the IAII is concerned primarily with initiating, coordinating, and directing research for better understanding of Indian groups in the hemisphere and for the solution of their health, educational, economic, and social problems. It provides technical assistance in establishing programs of Indian community development.

*See also* **Pan-Americanism.**

BIBLIOGRAPHY

Charles G. Fenwick, *The Organization of American States: The Inter-American Regional System* (1963).

Henry H. Ham, *Problems and Prospects of the Organization of American States* (1987).

Organization of American States, *The OAS and the Evolution of the Inter-American System* (1988).

L. Ronald Scheman, *The Inter-American Dilemma: The Search for Inter-American Cooperation at the Centennial of the Inter-American System* (1988).

G. Pope Atkins, *Latin America in the International Political System*, 2d. rev. ed. (1989).

### *Additional Bibliography*

Cooper, Andrew Fenton, and Thomas F. Legler. *Intervention without Intervening?: The OAS Defense and*

*Promotion of Democracy in the Americas.* New York: Palgrave Macmillan, 2006.

Marichal, Carlos. *México y las conferencias panamericanas, 1889-1938: Antecedentes de la globalización.* México: Secretaría de Relaciones Exteriores, 2002.

Sheinin, David. *Beyond the Ideal: Pan Americanism in Inter-American Affairs.* Westport, CT: Greenwood Press, 2000.

Shaw, Carolyn M. *Cooperation, Conflict, and Consensus in the Organization of American States.* New York: Palgrave Macmillan, 2004.

MICHAEL GOLD-BISS

**INTER-AMERICAN SYSTEM.** The Inter-American System originated with the First International Conference of American States (Washington, D.C., 1889), which established the International Union of American Republics and the Commercial Bureau of the American Republics in Washington, D.C. This effort built on the unsuccessful series of international "Americanismo" and Pan-Americanism–driven congresses, which tried to form a Spanish American union, beginning with the Panama Congress of 1826 and ending with the Second Lima Congress of 1865. Parallel endeavors for regional cooperation were the international law conferences held from 1887 to 1889. Such attempts were unsuccessful until, with encouragement of the United States, the American republics managed to place their hopes for political cooperation in a union governed by the rule of international law. The principal missions of the Inter-American System have included the maintenance and guarantee of peaceful relations and the nonviolent resolution of conflicts, security, and development. Its initial mandate was the establishment of the rule of international law to replace the rule of force in inter-American relations.

Representatives of American nations attended a series of conferences that created the treaties, conventions, and legal instruments upon which the multilateral cooperation between those nations is based. The conferences included eleven International Conferences of American States, thirteen Meetings of Consultation of Ministers of Foreign Affairs, eight Special Inter-American Conferences, and dozens of specialized conferences that focused on particular areas of concern from agriculture to public health.

The first International Conference of American States, held in Washington, D.C., from 1889 to 1890 bore fruit in 1910 in the form of the Pan-American Union, which served as the permanent secretariat for the Pan-American conferences and, after 1948, for the Organization of American States (OAS). After 1890 the International Conferences of American States met every five years except during the two world wars. The Second International Conference of American States (Mexico City, 1901) adopted a protocol of adherence to the conventions framed by the First Hague Peace Conference in 1899. The Third International Conference (Rio de Janeiro, 1906) set conventions regarding copyright law, commercial arbitration, and international law, a process continued by the Fourth (Buenos Aires, 1910), which established conventions related to patents, artistic property, and commercial statistics, and set standards for the Pan-American railroad. The Fifth Conference (Santiago, 1923) adopted the Gondra Treaty to avoid conflicts between American states and approved the formation of the Pan-American Highway system. The Sixth Conference (Havana, 1928) approved conventions on political asylum, maritime neutrality, private international law (the Bustamante Code), extradition, and the duties of states in the event of civil strife.

The three conferences in the 1930s as well as the first three Meetings of Consultation of Ministers of Foreign Affairs (1939, 1940, 1942) responded to U.S. concerns about the increasing likelihood of war in Europe, the need to guarantee inter-American cooperation in that event, and U.S. and Latin American participation in the war effort. In 1933, the Seventh International Conference of American States (Montevideo) adopted the Convention of the Rights and Duties of States. Article VII of the Convention established that "no state has the right to intervene in the internal affairs of another." This Convention drew on the Calvo and Drago doctrines of nonintervention. The 1936 Special Conference for the Maintenance of Peace (also known as the Buenos Aires Conference) established procedures for the peaceful settlement of disputes in the event of an international war outside the hemisphere, and the Eighth International Conference (Lima, 1938) created the mechanism for meetings of consultation of ministers of foreign affairs.

The Special Inter-American Conference on the Problems of War and Peace (Mexico City, 1945) created the Inter-American Economic and Social Council and adopted the Act of Chapultepec, which declared that an act of aggression against any of the American states would be considered aggression against them all. The Special Inter-American Conference for the Maintenance of Continental Peace and Security (Rio de Janeiro, 1947) established principles for collective defense in the form of the Inter-American Treaty of Reciprocal Assistance, or Rio Treaty, that served as the basis for security arrangements in the Americas for the next forty years. The Ninth Conference (Bogotá, 1948) approved the Charter of the Organization of American States (OAS), the American Declaration of the Rights and Duties of Man, and conventions granting civil and political rights to women. The Tenth Inter-American Conference (Caracas, 1954) approved the creation of the economic, social, and cultural development programs of the OAS and adopted conventions on territorial and diplomatic asylum. In 1959, the Inter-American Development Bank (IDB) was established to promote economic development, following suggestions offered by the United Nations Economic Commission for Latin America and its executive secretary, Raúl Prebisch. At the Fifth Meeting of Consultation (Santiago, 1959) the Inter-American Commission on Human Rights was created. During the meeting of American chiefs of state (Punta del Este, Uruguay, 1961), the Declaration to the Peoples of the Americas and the Charter of Punta del Este, creating the Alliance for Progress, were adopted.

Economic cooperation was soon overshadowed by the tension caused by the cold war, which climaxed with the 1962 expulsion of the government of Cuba from the OAS. Cuba's ouster was based on the understanding that "the adherence by any member of the Organization of American States to marxism-leninism is incompatible with the Inter-American System." Following the 1964 intervention by the United States in the Dominican Republic, the OAS created the Inter-American Peace Force, which helped end the fighting in that country and allowed elections in order to reestablish a constitutional government.

After 1970, in accordance with the 1967 revision of the OAS Charter, the International Conferences of American States were replaced by annual meetings of the General Assembly of the OAS. In the ensuing years, the OAS met to condemn and respond to various security-related incidents, including Cuban aggression against Venezuela, Bolivia, and other American states; the armed conflict between El Salvador and Honduras; the clash between Nicaragua and Costa Rica in 1978; the Nicaraguan crisis that ended with the triumph of the Sandinistas in 1979; the Peruvian-Ecuadorian clashes of 1981; and the Falklands/Malvinas War between Argentina and Great Britain in 1982. This last event threatened to undermine the Inter-American System because the United States supported the British venture to regain the islands, despite the Latin American perception that Great Britain was an extracontinental aggressor as defined by the Rio Treaty. The U.S. invasions of Grenada in 1983 and Panama in 1989 further weakened the cohesion of the Inter-American System, but the return to democratic rule in every American republic except Peru revived the OAS.

The future of the Inter-American System in the post–cold war era of economic integration and competition is contingent on the continued cooperation of all the hemisphere's nations. The integration efforts of the United States, Canada, Mexico, and Chile are being followed with great interest by the rest of the hemisphere, given the lack of success of such subregional efforts as the Central American Common Market and the Andean Pact. In 1994 the OAS proposed the Free Trade Area of the Americas (FTAA) to be implemented by 2005. Because of political pressures in Latin America and in the United States, FTAA as of 2007 still remains an unfinished policy. Cooperation continues on other matters, including health issues (for example, AIDS and cholera), resource development and management, energy security, environmental protection, narcotrafficking and violence, and nuclear proliferation. Democracy has become a central policy of the OAS. In 2001 the OAS approved the Inter-American Democratic Charter, which aimed to develop democratic institutions in the region. The charter was invoked in 2002 to condemn the temporary removal of Venezuelan president Hugo Chávez.

The most important Pan-American conferences are treated in individual articles elsewhere in this encyclopedia, under the title "Pan-American Conferences."

*See also* **Pan-American Conferences; United Nations.**

BIBLIOGRAPHY

Pan American Union, *The Pan American Union and the Pan American Conferences* (1940).

Francisco Cuevas Cancino, *Del Congreso de Panamá a la Conference de Caracas, 1826–1954* (1955).

John D. Martz and Lars Schoultz, eds., *Latin America, the United States, and the Inter-American System* (1980).

L. Ronald Scheman, *The Inter-American Dilemma: The Search for Inter-American Cooperation at the Centennial of the Inter-American System* (1988); and, especially, G. Pope Atkins, *Latin America in the International Political System,* 2d rev. ed. (1989).

### *Additional Bibliography*

Bouvier, Virginia Marie. *The Globalization of U.S.-Latin American Relations: Democracy, Intervention, and Human Rights.* Westport, CT: Praeger, 2002.

Cooper, Andrew Fenton, and Thomas Legler. *Intervention without Intervening? The OAS Defense and Promotion of Democracy in the Americas.* New York: Palgrave Macmillan, 2006.

Marichal, Carlos, ed. *México y las conferencias panamericanas, 1889–1938: Antecedentes de la globalización.* Mexico: Secretaría de Relaciones Exteriores, 2002.

Shaw, Carolyn M. *Cooperation, Conflict, and Consensus in the Organization of American States.* New York: Palgrave Macmillan, 2004.

Sheinin, David. *Beyond the Ideal: Pan Americanism in Inter-American Affairs.* Westport, CT: Greenwood Press, 2000.

MICHAEL GOLD-BISS
JAMES PATRICK KIERNAN

## INTER-AMERICAN TREATY OF RECIPROCAL ASSISTANCE.

*See* **Rio Treaty (1947).**

## INTERNATIONAL COFFEE AGREEMENT.

International Coffee Agreement, the 1962 and 1983 accords reached by the coffee-producing and consuming nations of the world to stabilize the international coffee market and to alleviate the difficulties related to excessive fluctuations in the levels of world supplies, stocks, and prices of coffee. The agreements sought to establish a balance between supply and demand and to maintain prices at equitable levels. The principal mechanism of the agreements was the apportionment of export quotas, adjusted to world demand, among the producing nations.

The first international agreement to protect the coffee industry was the 1940 Inter-American Coffee Marketing Agreement, which expired in 1948. Aimed at providing a market for fourteen Latin American coffee-producing countries who were affected by the closing of European markets during World War II, the agreement established U.S. import quotas at reasonable prices. Surplus production and falling prices in the late 1950s led Portugal and Latin American producers to create the International Coffee Organization (ICO) to promote international consumption of coffee and to research ways of improving the quality of coffee and the reduction of production costs.

The short supply of coffee and changing production conditions after 1970 led to disagreement between producing and consuming nations that might have jeopardized the continuation of the 1962 treaty. In 1983, a new agreement endorsed the same principles outlined in the 1962 treaty and highlighted, in addition, the promotion and maintenance of employment and income in member countries to help bring about fair wages, higher living standards, and better working conditions.

Three additional agreements were negotiated after 1983. The 1994 agreement established that the focus of the ICO would be production and diffusion of knowledge on sustainable management of the coffee industry and trade, as well as the effects of coffee on health. In 2001 the parties agreed to encourage the development of a sustainable coffee economy and promote the consumption of the product while raising its standards for quality. The agreement of 2007 encouraged members to adopt safety standards and develop strategies to help local communities in coffee producing areas, while recognizing their responsibility to the achievement of international development goals.

*See also* **Coffee Industry.**

BIBLIOGRAPHY

Helen Delpar, ed., *Encyclopedia of Latin America* (1974).

Department of State, *International Coffee Agreement, 1983, Between the United States of America and Other Governments* (1983).

### *Additional Bibliography*

Frederick, Kenneth D. "Production Controls under the International Coffee Agreements: An Evaluation of Brazil's Programs." *Journal of Inter-American Studies and World Affairs,* 12:2 (Apr 1970), 255-270.

Mueller, Charles Curt. "O impacto do acôrdo internacional do café sôbre o preço do café/The Impact of the International Coffee Agreement on the Price of Coffee." *Revista Brasileira de Economia*, 25:3 (July-Sept 1971), 131-166.

NANCY PRISCILLA S. NARO

**INTERNATIONAL CONGRESS OF AMERICANISTS.** The International Congress of Americanists is a traditional event that has been held since 1875 for the purpose of advancing the historical and scientific knowledge of the American continent and its inhabitants. The first such congress, organized by the Société Américaine de France, was chaired by Baron Guerrier de Dumast and held in the city of Nancy, France, with the aim of fostering knowledge of the history and ethnography of precolonial America. With the clear goal of minimizing Spain's influence on the American continent, the first congress focused on the theme of the origins and discovery of the Americas. Subsequent conferences in Luxemburg (1877), Brussels (1879), and Madrid (1881) maintained this focus. These congresses were followed by those in Copenhagen (1883), Turin (1886), Berlin (1888), Paris (1890), Huelva (1892), and Stockholm (1894).

A congress was convened on American territory for the first time in 1895, in Mexico City. Since then the event has been held in other important American cities (Buenos Aires, New York, Rio de Janeiro, and Santiago de Chile), alternating with European cities. In 1900 it was again held in France. At that time it was decided to adopt Spanish and English as official languages, in addition to French. Portuguese (in 1908) and German and Italian (both in 1964) were later accepted.

Since the late twentieth century, the studies presented at the conferences have not been limited to Americanism, but also include contemporary issues facing the continent. Scientific and other activities held at the congress cover various fields, such as anthropology, archaeology, art, literature, environmental studies, economics, and society in general. Among the congress's most renowned speakers was the French anthropologist Claude Lévi-Strauss, at the 1947 conference held in Paris. Turning away from the Eurocentrism of the first meetings, the present-day congresses, held every three years, assemble thousands of lecturers, the majority of them Hispanic Americans.

*See also* **Hemispheric Affairs.**

BIBLIOGRAPHY

Comas, Juan. *Cien años de Congresos Internacionales de Americanistas.* Mexico City: UNAM, 1974.

VICENTE PALERMO

**INTERNATIONAL MONETARY FUND (IMF).** The International Monetary Fund (IMF) is a multilateral financial institution that has supervised the global financial system since the end of World War II. Headquartered in Washington, D.C., it acts as a lender of last resort for member governments who face problems in meeting their external financial obligations. The relationship between the IMF and Latin American governments has been a contentious one, as the latter have faced chronic payments difficulties since the 1950s.

The IMF and the World Bank, its sister organization, institutionalized the international cooperation that their architects hoped would prevent a recurrence of the economic instability that had led to political upheaval and, ultimately, world war. Soon after the Japanese attack on Pearl Harbor, Harry Dexter White and his colleagues in the U.S. Treasury Department developed a blueprint for a multilateral fund to stabilize exchange rates and control private capital flows. White and his colleagues believed that foreign lending and speculative movements of capital by Wall Street banks constituted a major cause of the Great Depression. In their view, the establishment of such a fund, anchored by the dollar, would "drive the usurious money lenders from the temple of international finance," as Treasury Secretary Henry Morgenthau put it.

The IMF gave member governments more flexibility over their domestic policies than they had enjoyed under the gold standard, which had collapsed under the weight of World War I and the Great Depression. Its designers intended it to provide liquidity that governments needed to replenish foreign exchange reserves while their policy changes took effect. Governments would not have to engineer sharp recessions to stem outflows of capital that depleted reserves, as the gold standard had required.

Members paid in subscriptions to both the IMF and the World Bank based on the size of their economies. These subscriptions, or quotas, formed the basis of both voting and drawing rights. As the member with the largest economy, the United States enjoyed the largest vote and wielded an effective veto over IMF policy; this power was an acute source of controversy during the Cold War. Members could draw automatically only on the 25 percent of the subscription that they paid in gold. Access to the balance of the quota (and beyond, as credits) required consultation with and surveillance from the IMF. Under procedures formalized in 1952, the IMF divided drawings into units of 25 percent of the quota, known as *tranches*, and used financial incentives to encourage short-term borrowing (three to five years) of small amounts. The IMF facilitated access to these resources by means of stand-by agreements, whereby governments agreed to change their monetary and fiscal policies to alleviate their balance-of-payments problems.

The IMF and the World Bank lacked the resources to address the reconstruction of postwar Europe and Asia. Instead, U.S. bilateral assistance met these needs, principally through the Marshall Plan. Once it emerged from its institutional dormancy in the 1950s, the IMF operated more conservatively than its designers intended. Indeed, critics routinely charged the IMF with abetting U.S. political hegemony and derailing development programs on behalf of liberal economic orthodoxy.

## LATIN AMERICAN DEVELOPMENT STRATEGIES

During the 1930s Latin American countries adopted import substitution industrialization (ISI) as a development strategy. The value of their commodity exports had plummeted, and the United States and Europe had erected barriers to trade. ISI involved state-directed investment in manufacturing and infrastructure at the expense of agriculture. It aimed to reduce the dependence of national income on commodities, whose value relative to manufactured goods many experts expected to fall over time, and trade with industrialized countries. ISI also involved the heavily subsidized redistribution of population and income from rural to urban areas. For two decades Latin Americans enjoyed relatively high growth rates, owing to increased consumption and the U.S. demand for strategic minerals during World War II and the Korean conflict. By the 1950s expanded government bureaucracies, state control of the "commanding heights" of the economy, fiscal deficits, inflation, overvalued exchange rates, and inefficient industry characterized the political economy of many Latin American countries.

The fall of commodity prices at the end of the Korean conflict precipitated balance-of-payments crises across the region. ISI was not autarkical: governments accumulated foreign debt because the strategy required large imports of capital equipment. Now they were unable to sell their manufactured goods overseas and their investment-starved agricultural sectors were too weak to generate the foreign exchange needed for debt service. At the same time, governments sustained imports of capital equipment to maintain the industrial production that provided jobs and growth. By the 1960s almost all the governments of the region were turning to the IMF for financial assistance.

For IMF economists, the solution to balance-of-payments difficulties broadly entailed reducing the role of the state in economic decision making. To access IMF funds, borrowers agreed to balance budgets by cutting spending and subsidies and raising taxes; control inflation by limiting credit and suppressing wages; and remove price distortions by reducing tariffs, removing ceilings, eliminating exchange rate discrimination, and devaluing their currencies. By adopting these changes, the IMF believed, borrowers would alleviate their payments problems and improve the performance of their economies.

IMF austerity programs alleviated balance-of-payments problems, to be sure, but delivered little of the economic growth or stability that they promised. They failed to balance budgets, quell inflation, or reduce state direction of the economy. At the same time, they redistributed income from labor to capital, even as economies overall suffered recession. One reason was that a stand-by agreement was politically risky for the borrower. It represented capitulation to foreign interests and the interference of Washington in a country's domestic affairs. Needing to show that they had driven a hard bargain, governments often won concessions that reduced the effectiveness of the program. Moreover, the IMF favored the political elites and capitalists whose approval of any agreement was required. Thus, for instance, taxes were invariably regressive, imposed on consumption rather than income. The IMF also paid scant attention to structural rigidities that characterized many Latin American societies, such as concentrated land and corporate ownership. With the IMF's seal of approval came foreign loans and direct investments that enabled governments to delay structural reforms. As a result, payments problems recurred and external debts accumulated, culminating in the Latin American debt crisis of the 1980s.

The IMF now became responsible for coordinating the actions of both creditors—mainly U.S. commercial banks—and debtors to prevent a collapse of the international financial system, which widespread defaults might have precipitated. Its lending rose to unprecedented levels in the late 1980s and early 1990s, even though the economic conditions of the borrowers were poor by historical standards. As a result, IMF put greater emphasis on institutional reform as a condition for borrowing, recommending a set of market-oriented policies that the economist John Williamson dubbed the Washington Consensus. Nevertheless, subsequent Latin American growth rates were below their post–World War II averages and poverty remained widespread.

*See also* **Economic Development; Foreign Debt; Foreign Investment.**

BIBLIOGRAPHY

James, Harold. *International Monetary Cooperation since Bretton Woods.* Washington, DC: International Monetary Fund, and New York: Oxford University Press, 1996.

Kofas, Jon V. *The Sword of Damocles: U.S. Financial Hegemony in Colombia and Chile, 1950–1970.* Westport, CT: Praeger, 2002.

Manzetti, Luigi. *The International Monetary Fund and Economic Stabilization: The Argentine Case.* New York: Praeger, 1991.

Pastor, Manuel, Jr. *The International Monetary Fund and Latin America: Economic Stabilization and Class Conflict.* Boulder, CO: Westview, 1987.

Woods, Ngaire. *The Globalizers: The IMF, the World Bank and Their Borrowers.* Ithaca, NY: Cornell University Press, 2006.

Michael Adamson

**INTERNATIONAL PETROLEUM COMPANY (IPC).** The International Petroleum Company (IPC) is a foreign oil concern active in Peru. Breaking Latin American legal precedent, Simón Bolívar granted to one of his followers outright ownership of the subsoil of the oil fields on the haciendas La Brea and Pariñas in the department of Piura in 1824. They were later developed by the London and Pacific Petroleum Company, which was sold to the Standard Oil Company—which became the International Petroleum Company (IPC) in 1913. While the legal ownership of the La Brea and Pariñas fields became a long-standing matter of dispute between the government of Peru and IPC, the company expanded its holdings and profits over the years. Because of the enclave nature of the industry, among other things, those profits amounted to around 70 percent of gross income from oil exports. The government consented to such high profit rates largely because of the company's repeated willingness to provide for its short-term financial support, particularly at times of severe deficit crises. Continued high-profit repatriation and charges of company intervention in Peru's internal and external affairs, as well as corruption and the legal dispute over ownership, all combined to intensify public resentment against IPC, which became a focal point of nationalist sentiment. The government's complicity in the company's abuses became the pretext for the military overthrow of the Belaúnde Terry regime in 1968 and the subsequent nationalization of the company that same year.

The expropriation of IPC, among other things, roiled the relationship between the United States and the revolutionary government of General Juan Velasco Alvarado (1968–1975). The company demanded $120 million in compensation; Peru claimed IPC owed $690 million in back taxes for the petroleum that it had extracted illegally over the years. As a result, U.S. foreign aid effectively dried up, as did loans from international agencies such as the World Bank. Negotiations continued as both the Peruvian and the U.S. governments pragmatically sought to defuse the issue. Peru needed outside aid, and the Nixon administration was concerned about a looming worldwide shortage of oil and other minerals abundant in Peru in real and potential supplies.

The issue was creatively resolved in February 1974 when Peru agreed to compensate a list of U.S. companies that had lost assets through nationalization. Although IPC was not on the list, it received compensation funds from the U.S. government, thus providing political cover for the Velasco government in such a long festering and explosive nationalist issue.

*See also* **Bolívar, Simón; Petroleum Industry.**

BIBLIOGRAPHY

McClintock, Cynthia, and Fabian Vallas. *The United States and Peru: Cooperation at a Cost.* New York: Routledge, 2003.

Thorp, Rosemary, and Geoffrey Bertram. *Peru 1890–1977: Growth and Policy in an Open Economy.* New York: Columbia University Press, 1978.

PETER F. KLARÉN

## INTERNATIONAL RAILWAYS OF CENTRAL AMERICA (IRCA, FICA).

International Railways of Central America (IRCA, United States–based company that controlled key railroads in Guatemala and El Salvador. In 1912 IRCA assumed ownership of nearly all Guatemalan railways, including Guatemala's only link with the Caribbean, and purchased a major Salvadoran Railroad. The company connected the Guatemalan and Salvadoran lines in 1929 to provide El Salvador with access to the Caribbean. The United Fruit Company of Boston purchased controlling interest in IRCA in 1936. IRCA and its parent company became targets of economic nationalism and labor activists during the Guatemalan Revolution (1944–1954). Critics attacked IRCA's monopoly on freight transportation and its inequitable rate structures. United Fruit sold much of its IRCA holdings after the revolution. The government purchased IRCA in December 1968 and placed rail transportation under the auspices of a state-owned agency, Ferrocarriles de Guatemala (FEGUA).

*See also* **United Fruit Company.**

BIBLIOGRAPHY

Charles D. Kepner and J. W. Soothill, *The Banana Empire: A Case Study of Economic Imperialism* (1935; repr. 1967).

Stacy May and Galo Plaza, *The United Fruit Company in Latin America* (1958; repr. 1976).

Richard H. Immerman, *The CIA in Guatemala: The Foreign Policy of Intervention* (1982).

Stephen C. Schlesinger and Stephen Kinzer, *Bitter Fruit: The Untold Story of the American Coup in Guatemala* (1983).

Ralph Lee Woodward, Jr., *Central America: A Nation Divided,* 2d ed. (1985), esp. pp. 179–182.

### *Additional Bibliography*

Piedra-Santa Arandi, Rafael. *La construcción de ferrocariles en Guatemala y los problemas financieros de la IRCA.* Guatemala: Instituto de Investigaciones Económicas y Sociales, 1967.

Ross, Delmer G. *Development of Railroads in Guatemala and El Salvador, 1849–1929.* Lewiston, NY: Edwin Mellen Press, 2001.

STEVEN S. GILLICK

## INTERNATIONAL REPUBLICAN INSTITUTE.

The International Republican Institute (IRI) is a nonprofit organization funded by the U.S. Congress through the National Endowment for Democracy and the U.S. Agency for International Development. Founded in 1983 and with close ties to the Republican Party, the IRI works worldwide to strengthen democratic institutions and practices. In Latin America, the IRI has carried out programs in up to ten countries (Argentina, Bolivia, Cuba, El Salvador, Guatemala, Haiti, Mexico, Nicaragua, Peru, and Venezuela) that include party strengthening and leadership training, election monitoring, ministry coordination, civic education, and promotion of ethics in government. The IRI, like its democratic party counterpart NDI, was established as a non-partisan organization. In the Latin American countries where it works, like NDI, partisan political criteria are not applied. Country selection is allocated to ensure roughly equal representation by either IRI or NDI.

*See also* **National Endowment for Democracy (NED).**

BIBLIOGRAPHY

International Republican Institute. Information available from http://www.iri.org.

DAVID SCOTT PALMER

## INTERNET.

Latin America's public Internet usage grew after 1993, when an easy-to-use Web browser, Mosaic, integrating text and graphics, went public. High infrastructure costs and low demand have generally kept Latin America's online growth below the world average. Nevertheless, e-commerce continues to grow steadily, consumers increasingly post their own blogs and personal videos onto Web sites, and social movements with the help of the Internet have brought greater attention to their causes in the public sphere.

Brazil and Mexico in 1989 became the first two countries in Latin America to set up computer systems at universities using the standard Internet protocols. During the early 1990s, Latin American universities led the Internet's development, followed by businesses and home users. In 1993 the University of Chile launched the first Web server in Latin America. Mexico and Brazil have had the largest number of Internet users. However, a higher percentage of the population in Chile and Argentine regularly browse the Web. Although many in the region cannot afford private home connections, public access sites, such as Internet cafes, have allowed for greater numbers to go online. Public Internet connections in Mexico accounted for only 2 percent of online connections in 1999, but that figure rose to 32 percent in 2003. Indeed, Latin American countries in the early twenty-first century have some of the fastest adoption rates in the world. In 2006 broadband Internet services grew by 54 percent. The determinants of cyberspace adoption in Latin America appear to be related to market liberalization in the telecommunications sector and government policy. To promote a broad base of World Wide Web access, Argentina and Chile, for example, set Internet pricing at reasonable rates in the late 1990s, which caused a noticeable expansion of Web users.

Even with tremendous growth, a sizable digital divide persists in Spanish America and Brazil, limiting online business. Overall, online broadband access for Latin America remains low at approximately 2.5 percent of the population as of 2007. A 2003 study indicated a strong correlation between wealth and Internet usage. In Venezuela, 70 percent of e-commerce consumers were men, and a high proportion of those men had high incomes. Consequently, the general lack of digital access has limited the development of e-business. Furthermore, most people in the region do not have credit cards or bank cards and cannot purchase consumer goods over the Internet. Because many Latin American countries have underfunded postal services, basic delivery also remains an obstacle to the growth of online consumer purchases. For these reasons, the number of business-to-consumer purchases over the Internet remains very small. Instead, business-to-business transactions dominate Internet purchases: In 2000 such purchases made up roughly 94 percent of Chilean e-commerce.

The digital divide limits the social and economic impact of the World Wide Web, but clear cultural changes have occurred. Many Latin Americans blog about issues ranging from their personal lives to politics using Orkut or MySpace accounts. Demand for blogs in Mexico proved great enough to prompt MySpace to open a local site. On YouTube, the popular video hosting site, everything from Spanish telenovela snippets to political debates from Latin American elections can be found. Traditional media companies, such as Mexico's Televisa, are beginning to set up interactive sites to allow consumers to comment, participate, and create their own content, rather than simply watching mainstream entertainment. Slowly, the Internet has begun to shape Latin American government and politics. The Mexican government during the administration of Vicente Fox Quesada (2000–2006) began to post government expenditures online, thereby increasing public sector transparency. Ironically, this policy led to sharp criticism of Fox for the excessive amount of government funds spent on his household.

Marginalized groups clearly have less access to the Internet, yet they have managed to use the Web to influence public debates. Protesting widespread poverty and injustice, an indigenous group located in Chiapas, called the Zapatistas, rose up in 1994 against the government. These rebels could not win militarily; however, news of their actions spread quickly via the Internet. International organizations quickly came to their aid, and many observers believe this support helped prevent the Mexican government from simply crushing the uprising. Indigenous peoples throughout Latin America have taken advantage of the Internet to make their problems known and to connect with international nongovernmental organizations.

The impact of the Internet has been uneven in Latin America. E-commerce has yet to bring substantial benefits to the average consumer and small business. Yet even with this limited online participation, consumers and social movements alike have already used the Web's services and information in substantial ways. The high growth rates in the early twenty-first century indicate that the Internet will lead to shifts in society, business, and government.

*See also* **Computer Industry; Fox Quesada, Vicente; Mexico, Zapatista Army of National Liberation; Telenovelas.**

BIBLIOGRAPHY

Caetano, Gerardo, and Rubén M. Perina, eds. *Informática, internet & política.* Montevideo: Centro Latinoamericano de Economía Humana, and Washington, DC: Organization of American States, 2003.

Chahin, Ali, Maria A. Cunha, Peter T. Knight, and Solon L. Pinto. *E-gov.br: A próxima revolução brasileira.* São Paulo: Pearson Prentice Hall, 2004.

Ronfeldt, David F., John Arquilla, Graham Fuller, and Melissa Fuller. *The Zapatista "Social Netwar" in Mexico.* Santa Monica, CA: Rand, 1998.

BYRON CRITES

**INTI.** Inti, special patron deity of the Incas. The most important servant of the creator was the sun god Inti, who was believed to be the divine ancestor of the Inca dynasty. The Incas referred to themselves as Intip Churin, which means in Quechua "children of the sun." The sun was conceived of as male and was represented by an idol in the form of a golden disk with rays and a human face. The sun idol was kept in the temples of the sun throughout the empire along with the other members of the Inca pantheon. The sun was believed to protect and mature crops, a function of vital importance to a farming-based economy.

*See also* **Incas, The.**

BIBLIOGRAPHY

John H. Rowe, "Inca Culture at the Time of the Spanish Conquest," in *Handbook of South American Indians,* vol. 2 (1946), pp. 183–330. Additional sources include Burr Cartwright Brundage, *The Empire of the Inca* (1963) and *The Lords of Cuzco: A History and Description of the Inca People in Their Final Days* (1967).

*Additional Bibliography*

Rubio, María del Carmen Martín. "'Inti Raymi' La fiesta del solsticio Inca" in *BOLETÍN: Museo de Arqueología y Antropología* (2005) 6 (1): 31–36.

GORDON F. MCEWAN

**IQUITOS.** Iquitos, the only major city in the Peruvian jungle and the capital of Loreto Department, Peru's largest in area. Its 2005 population of 350,000 places it among the ten largest cities in the country. Founded in 1863, it is located on the west bank of the Amazon River about 2,000 miles from its mouth and some 500 miles downriver from Pucallpa, the only other sizable city in the jungle of Peru. Iquitos can be reached only by air or by water; there are no roads connecting it to the rest of the country. The city more than tripled in size between 1961 and 1981, largely as the result of commercial activity associated with oil exploration and production in the Peruvian Amazon region.

Iquitos grew from a fishing village to a major commercial base of operations during the rubber boom of 1890–1920. While the economic impact of the rubber bonanza was felt primarily in Iquitos and the lower Amazon Basin of eastern Peru, the oil boom affected the country's western coastal region much more, due to the construction in the mid-1970s of an oil pipeline over the Andes to the Pacific. Currently the major administrative center of the government and military in the northeastern region of Peru, and home to the Universidad Nacional de la Amazonía Peruana (1961), Iquitos contains impressive architecture dating from its heyday in the nineteenth century.

*See also* **Petroleum Industry; Rubber Industry.**

BIBLIOGRAPHY

Rosemary Thorp and Geoffrey Bertram, *Peru 1890–1977: Growth and Policy in an Open Economy* (1978).

Richard F. Nyrop, ed., *Peru: A Country Study,* 3d ed. (1981).

*Additional Bibliography*

Casement, Sir Roger, and Angus Mitchell. *The Amazon Journal of Roger Casement.* Dublin: Lilliput Press, 1997.

Rodríguez, Isacio R., and Jesús Alvarez Fernández. *Monumenta histórico-augustiniana de Iquitos.* Valladolid: Centro de Estudios Teológicos de la Amazonía, 2001.

Vílchez Vela, Percy. *El linaje de los orígenes: La historia desconocida de los Iquitos.* Iquitos: Editora Regional, Fondo Editorial, 2001.

DAVID SCOTT PALMER

## IRALA, DOMINGO MARTÍNEZ DE

**(1509–1556).** Domingo Martínez de Irala (Captain Vergara; *b.* 1509; *d.* 3 October 1556), Spanish explorer and conquistador. The youngest of six children, Irala was born in Vergara, Guipúzcoa, Spain, to a family of hidalgos. His father, Martín Pérez de Irala, was a royal office holder.

In 1534, Irala went on an expedition to the Río de la Plata, with the *adelantado* Pedro de Mendoza. In 1535 he participated in the founding of Buenos Aires. The following year, he went on an expedition to the Paraná River with his friend Juan de Ayolas. On 2 February 1537, Ayolas founded the port of Candelaria on the Paraguay River, and then continued north, leaving Irala in command.

In 1537 the *veedor* (colonial inspector) of the Río de la Plata, Alonso Cabrera, appointed Irala lieutenant governor. Soon after this appointment, Irala went to Asunción and founded several new settlements.

Irala participated in many other expeditions, such as an exploration of the Paraguay River and a region near Peru. In 1543 he participated in an Indian campaign under the second *adelantado* of the Río de la Plata, Alvar Núñez Cabeza De Vaca. He was also the main force behind the arrest of Cabeza de Vaca on 26 April 1544. When Irala sent him back to Spain one year later, he became the undisputed master of Paraguay.

In late 1547 and early 1548, Irala faced a rebellion in Asunción by some of Cabeza de Vaca's followers. He quelled the rebellion, and in order to ensure peace in the region, he gave his four daughters in marriage to four of the leaders. In 1555, the crown appointed him governor. He died the following year.

*See also* **Conquistadores; Río de la Plata.**

BIBLIOGRAPHY

Ricardo De La Fuente Machain, *El gobernador Domingo Martínez de Irala* (1939).

Enrique De Gándia, *Historia de la conquista del Río de la Plata y del Paraguay; los gobiernos de don Pedro de Mendoza, Alvar Núñez y Domingo de Irala, 1535–1556* (1931).

Jorge Roberto Payro, *El capitán Vergara* (*Domingo Martínez de Irala*) (1932).

*Additional Bibliography*

Levillier, Roberto. *El Paititi, El Dorado y las Amazonas.* Buenos Aires: Emecé Editores, 1976.

Juan Manuel Pérez

## IRIGOYEN, BERNARDO DE

**(1822–1906).** Bernardo de Irigoyen (*b.* 18 December 1822; *d.* 27 December 1906), cattle baron and politician in Buenos Aires province and Argentina. Born in Buenos Aires, Irigoyen received his law degree from the University of Buenos Aires in 1843. He obtained his first important political position in 1844, when Federalist dictator Juan Manuel de Rosas appointed him intervenor in Mendoza Province.

As a member of the National Autonomist Party, he was elected to the Buenos Aires Province Chamber of Deputies in 1873 and advanced to the provincial Senate two years later.

In the 1880s, he returned to national politics. Under presidents Nicolás Avellaneda (1874–1880) and Julio Roca (1880–1886) he held various cabinet-level positions. Although he broke from the National Autonomist Party, helping form the Civic Union Party and the Radical Civic Union Party, he remained influential. In the final decades of his life he served as governor and national senator of Buenos Aires Province.

*See also* **Argentina, Political Parties: Personalist Radical Civic Union; Argentina, Political Parties: National Autonomist Party.**

BIBLIOGRAPHY

Natalio R. Botana, *El orden conservador: La política argentina entre 1880 y 1916,* 2d ed. (1985).

Oscar Cornblit Et Al., "La generación del ochenta y su proyecto—antecedentes y consecuencias," in *Argentina, sociedad de masas,* edited by Torcuato S. di Tella, et al. (1956), pp. 18–59.

*Additional Bibliography*

Alonso, Paula. *Between Revolution and the Ballot Box: The Origins of the Argentine Radical Party in the 1890s.* New York: Cambridge University Press, 2000.

Mallo, Susana, Rafael Paternain, and Miguel Angel Serna. *Modernidad y poder en el Río de la Plata: Colorados y Radicales.* Montevideo: Editorial Trazas, 1995.

Rock, David. *State Building and Political Movements in Argentina, 1860–1916*. Stanford, CA: Stanford University Press, 2002.

DANIEL LEWIS

**IRIGOYEN, HIPÓLITO** (1852–1933). Hipólito Irigoyen (or Yrigoyen) was the president of Argentina (1916–1922 and 1928–1930), the first to assume office through free elections. Controversial and charismatic, Irigoyen was Argentina's most popular president before Juan Domingo Perón. As leader of the Unión Cívica Radical (UCR), he built a democratic, populist, and nationalistic organization comprising an efficient urban-based political machine and a national party sharing many features with the U.S. Democratic Party (i.e., a federally organized, catch-all coalition based on strong local parties). In 1930, in the context of a deteriorating economy, profound disenchantment of the conservative political elites with democracy (having been unable to win any free election within full constitutional rule of law), and a loss of support by a military minority allured by the "time of the sword," a coup removed Irigoyen from power.

Born on July 12, 1852, into an middle-class family in provincial Buenos Aires, Irigoyen developed a personality that defies easy explanation. Virtually every author who has assumed the task has resorted to the term *enigmatic*. Over the masses he exercised an extraordinary fascination and displayed a quiet charisma, with a strong power of conviction in person-to-person campaigning; indeed, he never made a public speech. His political mission was buried in the moralistic rhetoric of his manifestos, and his eclectic philosophy, derived partly from the works of the German philosopher Karl Krause, was equally somewhat obscure, stressing a mystical belief in God-given harmony, moral living, and a principled political behavior that, when projected toward the international arena, resulted in an autonomous and idiosyncratic foreign policy that was at the same time rather effective. Even in later life, he continued to wear suits of somber shades, lived in modest dwellings in the poorer districts of Buenos Aires, and shunned photographers.

Irigoyen's public career began in 1872. His uncle, Leandro Alem, secured for him the position of police superintendent in the district of Balvanera, Buenos Aires. In 1877 Irigoyen, together with Alem and Artistóbulo del Valle, formed the short-lived Republican Party, which supported provincial rights and attacked corrupt politics. In 1879 he successfully ran for a seat in Congress and in 1880 was chosen for a high position on the National Council for Education. When his term of office ended in 1882 he bought land and entered the cattle-raising business, which helped him fund successive revolutions to attain constitutional rule.

In 1890 Irigoyen joined the Unión Cívica and participated in "El Noventa," an armed insurrection that sought respect for fundamental rights and toppled the government of Miguel Juárez Celman. Following a struggle over the extent of reforms and leadership, the party split in 1891 into two factions. The Unión Cívica Nacional was led by Bartolomé Mitre, a reformist within the oligarchical elite. The Unión Cívica Radical was initially guided by Leandro Alem, who thought of free elections and public liberties, politics as an ethical creation, and federalism as the Argentine way of life—as nonnegotiable values that the UCR needed to sustain against the oligarchic regime. Irigoyen, advocating intransigence and civil resistance, worked successfully to wrest control of the UCR from Alem (who committed suicide in 1896). By 1898 Irigoyen was the acknowledged leader of radicalism. Irigoyen's leadership meant a distancing from the radical liberalism of Alem and a partial mutation of the UCR's idea of political representation. From the UCR's perspective, illegitimate government legitimized insurrection. In the words of Irigoyen (1905): "Revolutions are an integral part of the moral law of society." The UCR refused to run as an electoral party for fifteen years, pursuing a strategy of abstention from polls until 1912, and became an all-encompassing reform crusade. According to Manuel Gálvez, Irigoyen realized that he had a mission and destiny that called for the moral and political regeneration of the nation. In this respect, he thought of the UCR not as a party but as a *movement*, as the incarnation of the growing nation, and he believed that the only UCR program was the Constitución Nacional. At any rate, after 1900 he cultivated an air of

**Crowd drags statue of deposed president Hipólito Irigoyen, Buenos Aires, 1930.** Voters twice brought the popular Hipólito Irigoyen to the presidency in Argentina (in 1916 and again in 1928). His reform-minded and nationalistic administration expanded health and education, though the economic crisis and unpopular military policies in his second term contributed to his overthrow in a 1930 coup. © BETTMANN/CORBIS

mystery that he effectively combined with a remarkable behind-the-scenes personal persuasiveness. Electoral abstention slowly eroded the old regime. Argentina's political scene shifted fundamentally in 1912, when an electoral reform law that provided for universal male suffrage and obligatory and secret voting took effect. Offered a long-awaited political opening, the UCR ran candidates for elected office. In 1916 Irigoyen won the presidency of Argentina.

Irigoyen's first term (1916–1922) was marked by contradiction. Whereas the UCR purported to stand for open and honest politics, Irigoyen did not hesitate to use his executive powers for political ends associated with the fulfillment of the political program of moral regeneration. He intervened in provincial elections to assure Radical victories because most of the districts were not holding free local elections as Roque Sáenz Peña (president of Argentina 1910-1914, responsible for reforming the Argentine electoral system) had assured. The Senate was appointed by state legislatures mainly controlled by the fraudulent conservative opposition, so Irigoyen used (and abused) his decree powers to mitigate legislative impasses, including congressional refusal to approve any kind of federal budget.

Irigoyen was popular among middle- and lower-class voters, and with the end of World War I—during which Irigoyen stubbornly stuck to a neutrality policy in the face of international and domestic pressure—the Argentinean economy prospered. Social security benefits were extended and education was a top priority of the government, which built a record number of schools and initiated a thorough restructuring of universities to make improvements in teaching quality, democratic policies, and universal access. Irigoyen's noisy economic nationalism targeted foreign capital investment and was particularly strident at election time. Resisting strong pressures from Royal Dutch Shell and Standard Oil, he devised a new model of public corporation to exploit national oil fields and distribute fuel at lower prices than those of its private competitors. The UCR attempted to forge an alliance with organized labor, and eventually the strong unions with anarchistic roots turned into steadfast supporters. But the violence of the times and the impact of the Russian Revolution led to the use of government-authorized violence against strikers in some cases, particularly during the meat-packing plants strikes and riots of 1921.

Ostensibly a party of the middle class but reaching out to all sectors of society, the UCR under Irigoyen's personalist rule, according to Susan and Peter Calvert, "failed to build up a middle-class political philosophy or establish viable institutions for the continued political involvement of newly mobilised groups" (p. 97). Lacking programmatic unity, the UCR acted pragmatically as it played to the wide-ranging interests and coalitions that had to be rewarded for their political support. Importantly, the focus of the party's unity became its leader, Irigoyen. Personalism, patronage, and political loyalty rather than open participation came to typify the years of Radical control. (Although it must be noted that his power of patronage was much less than his opponent would have: An ECLAC study shows that the rise of public expenditure was chiefly due to investments, not pork-barrel politics.) In his second term, he stood up to U.S. President Herbert Hoover's expansionist policies in Central America and the Caribbean.

Irigoyen's most problematic policy was his so-called politicization of the Argentine military. He offended their sense of professionalism when he promoted officers dropped from military service for their participation in the 1905 uprising in defense of the Constitution. He challenged their perceived sense of mission when he used troops to break strikes or to monitor federal interventions in elections; he became deeply involved in the army's inner institutional life. After Irigoyen won a second term as president in 1928, his meddling in military matters became intolerable, helping to lay the groundwork for the military coup of 1930 that removed him from power.

To military unrest must be added spreading economic dislocation occasioned by the Great Depression (though some measures taken by decree after congressional refusal, such as abandonment of the gold standard, prevented Argentina from suffering the worst extremes of the depression). The depression destroyed the ability of the state to grant patronage and undermined the UCR's popular base of support. As the party disintegrated and economic conditions worsened, Irigoyen lost prestige. But the main issue at stake was that, in what was regarded as a serious challenge to the whole economic system, the ruling elite could not permit the state apparatus—a key player since the 1880s—to remain in the hands of an outsider such as Irigoyen. On September 6, Irigoyen was deposed by retired General José Félix Uriburu, an open admirer of Fascist doctrines and procedures. Irigoyen died on July 3, 1933, and, in the words of the Calverts, "was accorded the spontaneous tribute of a splendid funeral and became a myth, a symbol of the aspirations of the middle class"

*See also* **Alem, Leandro; Argentina, Political Parties: Radical Party (UCR); Juárez Celman, Miguel; Mitre, Bartolomé; Sáenz Peña, Roque; Uriburu, José Félix.**

BIBLIOGRAPHY

Aboy Carlés, Gerardo. *Las dos fronteras de la democracia argentina: La reformulacion de las identidades políticas de Alfonsín a Menem.* Rosario, Argentina: Homo Sapiens, 2001.

Alonso, Paula. *Entre la revolución y las urnas.* Buenos Aires: Sudamericana, 2000.

Calvert, Susan, and Peter Calvert. *Argentina: Political Culture and Instability.* Pittsburgh: University of Pittsburgh, 1989. See especially pp. 91–107.

Del Mazo, Gabriel. *El Radicalismo: Ensayo sobre su historia y doctrina*, vol. 2. Buenos Aires: Ediciones Gure, 1957.

Gálvez, Manuel. *Vida de Hipólito Yrigoyen: El hombre del misterio*, 2nd edition. Buenos Aires: G. Kraft, 1939.

Passalacqua, Eduardo H. "El Yrigoyenismo." *Todo es Historia* 100 (1983).

Potash, Robert A. *The Army and Politics in Argentina, 1928–1945: Yrigoyen to Perón*. Stanford, CA: Stanford University Press, 1969. See chapter 2.

Rock, David. *Politics in Argentina, 1890–1930: The Rise and Fall of Radicalism*. Cambridge, U.K.: Cambridge University Press, 1975.

Romero, José Luis. *A History of Argentine Political Thought*. Stanford, CA: Stanford University Press, 1963. See chapter 8.

Smith, Peter H. *Argentina and the Failure of Democracy: Conflict among Political Elites, 1904–1955*. Madison: University of Wisconsin Press, 1974. See Chapter 1.

Solbert, Carl. *Oil and Nationalism in Argentina: A History*. Chaps. 2, 3, and 5. Stanford, CA: Stanford University Press, 1979. See especially chapters 2, 3, and 5.

PAUL B. GOODWIN
VICENTE PALERMO

## IRISARRI, ANTONIO JOSÉ DE (1786–1868).

Antonio José de Irisarri (*b.* 7 February 1786; *d.* 10 June 1868), Spanish-American patriot, diplomat, historian, and journalist. Born in Guatemala, Irisarri settled in 1809 in Chile, where he played a prominent part in patriot politics during the *Patria Vieja*, among other things as editor of *El Semanario Republicano* from 1813 to 1814. His pen rarely idle, he also wrote many political works. Obliged to leave Chile in August 1814 because of his opposition to José Miguel Carrera, he went to England, where, together with Andres Bello, he published the pro-independence *El Censor Americano*. Upon his return to Chile in 1818, he was appointed a diplomatic agent by Bernardo O'Higgins and sent back to Europe, where he contracted the £1 million Chilean loan of 1822. In 1826 he moved back to his native Guatemala, but in 1830 resettled in Chile. He was appointed Intendant of Colchagua in November 1835. He accompanied the first Chilean expedition to Peru in 1837, during the war against the Peru-Bolivia Confederation, and negotiated the Treaty of Paucarpata (17 November 1837) with Andrés de Santa Cruz. Seen as ignominious in Chile, the treaty was repudiated.

Finding it inadvisable to return to Chile, Irisarri spent the remainder of his life in Ecuador, Colombia, Venezuela, and the United States, finally settling in New York in November 1849. In 1855 he became ambassador of Guatemala and El Salvador to the United States, and was named as plenipotentiary for Nicaragua at the time of William Walker's filibustering incursions. Irisarri died in Brooklyn.

*See also* **Walker, William.**

BIBLIOGRAPHY

John D. Browning, *Vida e ideología de Antonio José de Irisarri* (1986).

Ricardo Donoso, *Antonio José de Irisarri*, 2d ed. (1966).

### *Additional Bibliography*

García Bauer, Carlos. *Antonio José Irisarri: Insigne escritor y polifacético prócer de la independencia americana*. Guatemala: Tipografía Nacional de Guatemala, 2002.

Perdomo Interiano, Claudio Roberto. *Pensamiento positivista y liberal de Ramón Rosa*. Tegucigalpa: "Mejores Ideas," 1994.

SIMON COLLIER

## IRISARRI Y LARRAÍN, JUAN BAUTISTA (c. 1740–1805).

Juan Bautista Irisarri y Larraín (*b.* ca. 15 February 1740; *d.* 4 May 1805), Guatemalan merchant, banker, and planter. Irisarri was born in Aranaz, Spain. After coming to Guatemala he was successful in finance, commerce, and indigo production. By 1805 he was regarded as the wealthiest man in the kingdom. An active member of the Sociedad Económica de Amigos del País de Guatemala, he especially promoted the development of a Pacific coast port in the late colonial period. His second marriage linked him to the prominent creole Arrivillaga family. He also had family ties in Chile, where his illustrious son, Antonio José (1786–1868), migrated after independence.

*See also* **Irisarri, Antonio José de.**

BIBLIOGRAPHY

Edgar Juan Aparicio y Aparicio, "La familia de Irisarri," in *Revista de la Academia guatemalteca de estudios genealógicos, heráldicos e históricos* 1 (1967): 17–25.

Ralph Lee Woodward, Jr., *Class Privilege and Economic Development: The Consulado de Comercio of Guatemala, 1793–1871* (1966).

*Additional Bibliography*

García Bauer, Carlos. *Antonio José Irisarri: Insigne escritor y polifacético prócer de la independencia americana.* Guatemala: Tipografía Nacional de Guatemala, 2002.

RALPH LEE WOODWARD JR.

---

**IRMANDADES.** *See* **Brotherhoods.**

---

**IRON AND STEEL INDUSTRY.** Historically, iron and steel have been the backbone of industrialization. Throughout the 1990s world steel production remained flat: at the lowest, 720 million metric tons in 1992, and at the highest, 789 million tons in 1999. In 2000 worldwide production reached 845 million tons, steadily climbing to 1 billion tons by 2004. In 2005 the total production of steel reached 1,132 million metric tons. According to industry projections, worldwide production will continue to increase now that China and India have effectively entered the expansion phase of their consumption patterns.

Latin America's overall production of steel has increased, but its share of total world output has decreased. In 1992 Latin America's output was 27.5 million tons of steel, or roughly 6 percent of the total world output; in 2006 its output was 45.4 million tons (Brazil alone produced 31.6 million tons), or about 4 percent of world output. This loss in terms of proportion of world output is due to the rapid expansion in production in Asia. Moreover, steel output is often a reflection of the growth trajectory of gross domestic product (GDP), and Latin America has been growing more slowly than Asia in general. Brazil's economy, long the largest in the region, has been growing at a faster rate than that of other Latin American economies, which helps to explain its rank as number one among Latin American steel producers, accounting for 70 percent (up from 57 percent in 1992) of all steel in Latin America. The continent's oldest producer is Brazil's Companhia Siderúrgica Nacional (CSN), which reached 6 million metric tons in 2006. Aside from Brazil, only Mexico, Argentina, Venezuela, and Chile, in descending rank order, have the capacity to produce 1.5 to 2 million tons per year. These four countries are also the most advanced of the industrialized Latin American economies.

## LATIN AMERICAN PRODUCTION IN A GLOBAL ECONOMY

The iron and steel industries in Latin America have had a checkered history, marked by alternate periods of foreign domination, nationalization, global competition, and privatization of the sector. All of Brazil's major steelworks were state-owned enterprises (SOEs) until the early 1990s, when the Brazilian government began to privatize. The country's largest integrated steel mill is in the early 2000s privately owned and managed by CSN. In Argentina, Mexico, and Chile, the mills are all in private hands. Venezuela is the sole Latin American country to retain state control over its steel company, the Corporación Venezolana de Guayana (CVG).

The major iron ore deposits in Latin America are found in Brazil, Venezuela, Chile, Peru, and Mexico. The quality of the ore mined in Brazil, Venezuela, and Peru is equal to that of the best in the world. Latin America produced 1 billion tons of ore in 2005; it exported 488 million tons and used the rest for domestic still production. Brazil's Companhia Vale do Rio Doce (CVRD) alone accounted for a third of Latin American production, with its 2008 production projected to reach 330 million tons. CVRD, which operates in sixteen countries worldwide in addition to fourteen Brazilian states, is a private firm, with the state retaining a minority share. It has diversified into steel mills, seeking to become a fully integrated company—from iron-ore production in upstream to steel-making downstream. This integration is vital for the success of the firm in the highly competitive environment of the global steel market.

Mergers and acquisitions were common among the world's steel makers and iron ore producers around the turn of the century. The trend is to build a globally integrated system. Rather than focus on a segment of the production process at home, CVRD, for instance, acquired coal deposits in Indonesia, Australia, and Mozambique and nickel mines in Canada; its strategy is to add more value to its massive iron ore deposits in Carajás and other mines in Brazil by obtaining uninterrupted access to processing materials for steel making.

Another strategy Latin American iron and steel firms are pursuing is forming supply networks with the world's major consumers. Japan and Korea have been ongoing buyers of Latin American iron ore; joining this Asian clientele is China, and India is not far behind. It may be cheaper for India's Tata and Mittal to feed their European mills with iron ore hauled from Latin America than with ore hauled from India. Other Latin American countries have taken steps to adapt to the globalization of the steel industry. In the mid-1990s Peru sold its iron-ore mining monopoly to Shougang of China, now Shougang Hierro Peru. Mexico has allowed foreign mining companies to operate in the country by granting them 100 percent economic rights of exploitation through a system of long-term leasing to circumvent the constitutional restrictions imposed on foreign ownership of Mexican land.

Iron and steel production is no longer considered the key sign of industrial prowess and the road to economic prosperity. Singapore, Hong Kong, Taiwan, and other political economies deficient in resources have achieved high levels of economic development by other means. Although Latin America remains overwhelmingly dependent on the export of nonrenewable natural resources for economic growth and development, its superior endowment in iron and steel cannot alone guarantee future prosperity for the region. Moreover, because there are many substitutes for steel, such as aluminum, plastics, ceramics, polymer, concrete, and other manufactured materials, the growth of steel consumption in Europe, the United States, and Japan may not expand as quickly as it did in the late twentieth century. Nevertheless, steel retains its primacy for construction, automobiles, and ship building, and China and India, at least for a period of some years, will import more iron and keep Latin American miners busy.

## A CHANGING INDUSTRY

At one time, the production of steel and iron had considerable military and security implications. In many Latin American countries during the cold war, the desire for national security and fear of communist insurgencies convinced the military and civilian industrialists that self-sufficiency in arms production must become the national objective. From the 1960s to the 1980s, national security exigencies called for state-owned companies to provide steelworks with subsidized low-cost energy that enabled them to expand. With privatization, this is no longer an option. Often, the managers of state-owned enterprise (SOE) iron mines and steel mills came from the ranks of retired military officers. Decades of security-conscious military rule throughout Latin America reinforced this national security approach to economic development; at one time, Brazil, Argentina, Peru, and even Mexico considered the steel SOEs national security concerns. Also, a boom in civil construction, auto manufacturing, and infrastructure, as well as ship building in Brazil, increased demand for steel and stimulated the expansion of iron and steel industries. But globalization and the digital age have changed the old economic thinking and patterns of trade and development. The iron and steel industries in Latin America in the early twenty-first century are more export-driven and globally linked; their survival rides high on the demand coming from external markets in Europe and the United States, where smoke stack industries are dying, and in Asia, where steel consumption has been increasing and importing steel is cheaper than building new mill complexes.

New technologies, including the use of new alloys, that produce stronger and lighter steel have made steel making both more complicated and more expensive. The oil price crises in the 1970s and early 1980s forced automobile industries around the world to switch to aluminum, plastics, and other substitutes for steel to make cars lighter and therefore more fuel efficient. Steel does not require as much energy as aluminum or titanium (wherein energy accounts for 80 percent of production cost), but the energy cost becomes the critical factor in newer methods of steel production and marketing. Conservation, recycling, and environmental measures play a major role in determining the cost of steel making. There are reasons to anticipate a further structural change in the steel industry the world over. Given the high cost of energy, countries will be forced to abandon energy-intensive industrial projects.

*See also* **Companhia Vale do Rio Doce; Economic Development; Energy; Industrialization.**

BIBLIOGRAPHY

Baer, Werner. *The Development of the Brazilian Steel Industry.* Nashville, TN: Vanderbilt University Press, 1969.

Companhia Siderúrgica Nacional. Available from http://www.csn.com.br.

Companhia Vale do Rio Doce. Available from http://www.cvrd.com.br.

Escobar, Janet Kelly. "Comparing State Enterprises across International Boundaries: The Corporacion Venezolana de Guayana and the Companhia Vale do Rio Doce." In *Public Enterprise in Less-Developed Countries*, ed. Leroy P. Jones. Cambridge, U.K., and New York: Cambridge University Press, 1982.

International Iron and Steel Institute. Available from http://www.worldsteel.org.

Marshall Lagarrigue, Isabel. *Restructuring and Protectionism in the U.S. Steel Industry: The Impact on Brazil.* 1987.

Martino, Orlando, Jerome Machamer, and Ivette Torres. *The Mineral Economy of Mexico.* Washington, DC: U.S. Department of the Interior, Bureau of Mines, 1992.

*Mineral Commodity Summaries.* Washington, DC: U.S. Department of the Interior, Bureau of Mines, 1978–.

Rakowski, Cathy A. *Production and Reproduction in a Planned, Industrial City: The Working- and Lower-Class Households of Ciudad Guayana, Venezuela.* East Lansing: Women in International Development, Michigan State University, 1984.

Weintraub, Sidney, ed. *Industrial Strategy and Planning in Mexico and the United States.* Boulder, CO: Westview Press, 1986.

EUL-SOO PANG

**Farmer inspecting irrigation system, Delicias, Mexico, 2006.** Examples of Latin American farmers developing irrigation systems began in Mexico as early as 900 BCE. Modern farmers must continue to search for new ways to stretch the limited amount of water available in the semi-arid regions of Latin America. ALFREDO ESTRELLA/AFP/GETTY IMAGES

**IRRIGATION.** Irrigation, the artificial watering of crops. Much of Latin America receives insufficient precipitation for farming. To expand and improve arable land, pre-Hispanic horticulturalists had developed water management systems by the first millennium BCE in both Mesoamerica and the Andes. The simplest method, pot irrigation, is familiar to all gardeners and leaves few, if any, archaeological traces. Water is carried by hand and applied to individual plants. Very effective use is made of limited amounts of water, but labor demands are high, so early farmers began to devise other methods of redirecting water's natural flow.

In central Mexico, rubble or earthen storage dams may have been built across natural channels to collect ephemeral surface runoff at the site of Teopantecuanitlán, in northern Guerrero State between 1200 and 1000 B.C., and in the Tehuacán Valley, between 750 and 600 B.C. However, the earliest undisputed remains of a Mexican irrigation system are at Santa Clara Coatitlán, now within metropolitan Mexico City. Here unlined canals branched off a channelized gully and took water to fields from about 900 B.C. Near the present city of Puebla, canal networks carried water from ephemeral stream channels by the middle of the first millennium B.C. In Tlaxcala State, there is evidence that terraced fields were watered by a dam, reservoir, and canal system around the same time.

A canal fed from a dammed reservoir is found just below the archaeological site of Monte Albán, Oaxaca. Part of this canal is cut into bedrock, demonstrating that its builders had the theoretical knowledge to plan water flow without trial and error. The Monte Albán canal carried water from about 550 to 250 B.C. By A.D. 200, mortared masonry storage dams and aqueducts were functioning near Monte Albán.

By 1519, when Hernán Cortés arrived in the Valley of Mexico, hydraulic works had reached monumental proportions. Tenochtitlán, the Mexica (Aztec) capital, occupied an island in Lake Tetzcoco. The Mexica redirected rivers and constructed aqueducts, dams, dikes, and open canals. Mortared aqueducts carried sweet water from springs at Chapultepec (later a park in Mexico City) and Coyoacán across the lake to Tenochtitlán, where it was used for drinking, bathing, and watering gardens.

The Peruvian and north Chilean coasts receive little or no precipitation, so agriculture is dependent upon irrigation. Dozens of small rivers and streams, many seasonally dry, flow down the western slopes of the Andes, through the coastal deserts, and into the Pacific. Pre-Hispanic farmers drew water directly off these rivers; directed water in long-distance canals from higher, moister elevations; diverted spring flow; and dug wells and trenches down to the water table. The early prehistory of Andean irrigation is unclear, but simple canals were probably built as early as the second millennium B.C. to extend floodwater farming of coastal valleys.

On Peru's north and central coasts, attempts were made in the mid-first millennium A.D. to build open canal irrigation networks supplied by two or more rivers. However, some of the long-distance linkages, including a 71-mile canal joining the Chicama and Moche drainages, may never have functioned. In the Chilca Valley, and elsewhere on Peru's central coast, ancient farmers dug a few meters to the water table, creating moist sunken fields called *mahames* or *hoyas.* This practice extended agriculture into areas without surface water.

The Andean Central Highlands receive unreliable precipitation during a wet season from November to April. To extend the growing time, or to produce two crops per year, agriculturalists made extensive use of open canals combined with terraces. These techniques were well established by the mid-first millennium A.D., the apogee of the Wari state. By 1500 the Incas had brought basic irrigation to near perfection. Water was so important to the lords of Cuzco that they conceptualized their whole social structure in terms of its natural and artificial flow.

In parts of Latin America, waterlogged or flooded fields are a major problem for farmers. Both in lowland Mesoamerica and the Lake Titicaca basin, indigenous cultivators built extensive systems of ridges and furrows for planting and water containment. Some Maya cities and the early Andean state of Tiwanaku depended heavily upon such raised fields. However, construction of some Andean raised fields predated the rise of the Tiwanaku state by more than one thousand years. Remnants of chinampas, or "floating gardens," can still be observed in the Valley of Mexico. These are artificial planting platforms constructed and maintained in shallow lakes.

The aridity of Spain and Portugal stimulated the development of Iberian irrigation and made the conquistadores appreciative of the sophisticated indigenous hydraulic systems they encountered in the New World. Native waterworks and concomitant social structure were often retained. However, the requirements of sugarcane, water mills, and horses meant that Iberians needed more water than the pre-Conquest Indians. The most remote branches of canals were often abandoned to provide greater volume and flow elsewhere. This has preserved remnants of ancient systems, especially in the valleys of Peru's north coast. The Spanish introduced many Old World hydraulic devices, including the arched aqueducts that were a hallmark of ancient Roman technology. Examples can still be seen in Mexico near Zempoala and Hidalgo and at the city of Querétaro; in Peru at Cuzco; and in Brazil at Rio de Janeiro.

Another Iberian introduction may have been filtration galleries, also called *minas, ganats, foggaras,* or *puquois.* Such galleries are lines of vertical wells linked at their bottoms by slightly sloping tunnels with the main water outlet at the tunnel's mouth. The largest and best-studied Spanish water *mina* is in Madrid. It was begun in the early thirteenth century under Christian control. Spanish engineers built several filtration gallery systems in Mexico, including those at Tehuacán and Puebla. Dozens of others were constructed in the Andes during the viceregal period, but many scholars believe that the systems in the Nasca drainage were built in the first millennium A.D. by people of the indigenous Nasca culture.

Latin American agriculture remains dependent upon irrigation. Ambitious, high-tech projects have become almost impossible to finance in the wake of the 1980s debt crisis. However, in remote areas farmers continue to employ the agricultural technology of their pre-Columbian and Spanish ancestors.

A major change since the late 1980s has been the privatization of water resource management. The World Bank and other critics have accused Latin American governments of mismanaging water resources. Yet, many groups in Ecuador, Peru, and Bolivia have successfully protested water privatization schemes, as exacerbating social and economic inequality. A vigorous debate in the early twenty-first century continues over whether water and irrigation projects should be public or private or if a third, moderate, approach can be achieved.

*See also* **Agriculture; Potato.**


BIBLIOGRAPHY

For an excellent survey of ancient Mexican hydraulic technology see William E. Doolittle, *Canal Irrigation in Prehistoric Mexico* (1990). A study of the important prehistoric, colonial, and modern Tehuacán system can be found in Kjell I. Enge and Scott Whiteford, *The Keepers of Water and Earth: Mexican Rural Social Organization and Irrigation* (1989). A good general work on the central Andes is Michael E. Moseley, *The Incas and Their Ancestors: The Archaeology of Peru* (1992). A beautifully illustrated pioneering study of ancient Andean waterworks is Paul Kosok, *Life, Land, and Water in Ancient Peru* (1965). An influential article on the social organization governing canals is Patricia J. Netherly, "The Management of Late Andean Irrigation Systems on the North Coast of Peru," in *American Antiquity* 49, no. 2 (1984): 227–254. Sunken fields have been described in Ana María Soldi, *Chacras excavadas en el desierto* (1979). A general discussion of raised fields can be found in Clark L. Erickson, "Prehistoric Landscape Management in the Andean Highlands: Raised Field Agriculture and Its Environmental Impact," in *Population and Environment* 13, no. 4 (1992): 285–300. For a controversial study of Andean filtration galleries see Monica Barnes and David Fleming, "Filtration-Gallery Irrigation in the Spanish New World," in *Latin American Antiquity* 2, no. 1 (1991) : 48–68; an opposing point of view is Ronald I. Dorn et al., "New Approach to the Radiocarbon Dating of Rock Varnish, with Examples from Drylands," in *Annals of the Association of American Geographers* 82 (1992): 136–151. A solid book on highland irrigation, with emphasis on present practice, is William P. Mitchell and David Guillet, *Irrigation at High Altitudes: The Social Organization of Water Control Systems in the Andes* (1994).

*Additional Bibliography*

Aboites, Luis. *El agua de la nación: Una historia política de México (1888–1946)*. Mexico City: Centro de Investigaciones y Estudios Superiores en Antropología Social, 1998.

Bennett, Vivienne, Sonia Dávila-Poblete, and Nieves Rico. *Opposing Currents: The Politics of Water and Gender in Latin America*. Pittsburgh, PA: University of Pittsburgh Press, 2005.

Eakin, Hallie Catherine. *Weathering Risk in Rural Mexico: Climatic, Institutional, and Economic Change*. Tucson: University of Arizona Press, 2006.

Gelles, Paul H. *Water and Power in Highland Peru: The Cultural Politics of Irrigation and Development*. New Brunswick, NJ: Rutgers University Press, 2000.


MONICA BARNES

---

**ISAACS, JORGE** (1837–1895). Jorge Isaacs (*b.* 1 April 1837; *d.* 17 April 1895), Colombian poet, politician, and ethnologist. Born in Cali, to an English father—a Christian convert from Judaism—and a Catholic Spanish mother, Isaacs was also Indian, Catalan, and Italian. He epitomized the Spanish American quest for personal and cultural identity in his life and his works. Educated in Cali and Bogotá, he soon showed his strong, varied, and captivating personality. At seventeen he enlisted in a revolutionary army; he later fought in several civil wars and summarized the history of one failed revolution in *La revolución radical en Antioquia* (1880). Although he entered politics as a Conservative, his rebellious nature pushed him to the Liberal Party, whereupon he declared, "I have moved from shadow to light." Once involved in politics, he applied either democratic or authoritarian means to make good on his party's programs.

Isaacs traveled through La Guajira as secretary of a scientific commission for the study of natural resources. Lacking even experienced guides, the daring Isaacs began the exploration on his own and succeeded in finding coal mines and oil fields.

More than as a poet, explorer, politician, or ethnologist, Isaacs is known as a novelist for his only and unique novel. *María* (1867; *Maria,* 1890) won him a place in history and in the hearts of millions around the world. Published in every Spanish-speaking country and translated into many languages, *María* caused critics to proclaim it the "most exquisite sentimental novel" and "one of the most beautiful creations and . . . closest to perfection" for its "clear aesthetic conscience." Latin America, in its postindependence search for identity, found itself in *María*'s landscape and humane romantic soul. After a life dedicated to his country and in the midst of economic hardships, Isaacs died of a disease contracted during his exploratory treks.

BIBLIOGRAPHY

*Additional Bibliography*

Cortés, Aura Rosa. *Facetas desconocidas de Jorge Isaacs, el humanista polémico.* Cali, Colombia: República de Colombia, Ministerio de Gobierno, 2005.

López Cano, Luis Francisco. *La tumba de María Isaacs: genesis y desarrollo de una leyenda vallecaucana.* Bogotá: Ministerio de Cultura, 2002.

J. DAVID SUÁREZ-TORRES

## ISABEL, PRINCESS OF BRAZIL

**ISABEL, PRINCESS OF BRAZIL** (1846–1921). Isabel, Princess of Brazil (*b.* 29 July 1846; *d.* 14 November 1921), heiress to the Brazilian throne. Isabel was the daughter of Pedro II and Empress Teresa Cristina Maria of Bourbon. Married to Gastão of Orléans, count d'Eu, on 15 October 1864, she assumed the regency in her father's absence in 1871, 1876, and 1887. Strong-willed, she displayed an uncommon ability to govern during her first regency. In Brazilian history her name is associated with emancipation and the abolition of slavery. In 1871 she signed the Law of the Free Womb (Free Birth Law), which freed newborn slaves. Her major achievement was the *Lei Aurea* of 13 May 1888, which abolished slavery. Her experience in government, combined with her abolitionist views, led Princess Isabel to evaluate correctly the chaotic political climate created by the abolitionist movement in the first months of 1888 and to decide that the crown had to intervene directly to end slavery. She disregarded some of the unwritten rules followed by her father for decades when she forced the resignation of the Cotegipe cabinet, selected the head of the cabinet that was to abolish slavery, and did not seek the advice of the plenary Council of State, the emperor's advisory body.

Despite her achievements, Princess Isabel was plagued by a degree of unpopularity caused by several factors. Her marriage to a Frenchman led to suspicion of foreign influence and dominance, and her husband's unpopularity had a ripple effect of its own. Her Catholicism was equally unpopular, for fear of papal influence in the affairs of state. Above all, the fact that she was a woman made her in the view of many unsuitable to govern. The adulation that surrounded her after she abolished slavery was ephemeral. With the fall of the monarchy on 15 November 1889, she was exiled with her family and spent the last part of her life in France.

*See also* **Slavery: Abolition.**

BIBLIOGRAPHY

Hermes Vieira, *Princesa Isabel, uma vida de luzes e sombras* (1990).

*Additional Bibliography*

Barman, Roderick J. *Princess Isabel of Brazil: Gender and Power in the Nineteenth Century.* Wilmington, DE: SR Books, 2002.

Daibert Junior, Robert. *Isabel, a "redentora" dos escravos: Uma historia da princesa entre olhares negros e broncos, 1846-1988.* Bauru, SP, Brasil: FAPESP, Editora da Universidade do Sagrado Coração, 2004.

LYDIA M. GARNER

## ISABELLA I OF CASTILE

**ISABELLA I OF CASTILE** (1451–1504). Isabella I of Castile (*b.* 22 April 1451; *d.* 26 November 1504), called "la Católica," Spanish queen of Castile and León (1474–1504). The daughter of John II of Castile, and his second wife, Isabella of Portugal, Isabella faced a rival claimant to the throne, Juana La Beltraneja, the daughter of her half-brother, Henry IV of Castile. Although Juana's paternity was in doubt, Henry IV and the powerful Mendoza family supported her claim. In 1468 Henry IV acknowledged Isabella's claim on the condition that she marry Alfonso V, king of Portugal. Isabella chose to ignore this arrangement and secured the approval of her noble supporters, led by the archbishop of Toledo, to marry Ferdinand II of Aragon in 1469. Her assertion of independence prompted Henry IV to disown her, and his death in 1474 initiated a civil war of succession between Isabella and Juana's noble supporters and Isabella's husband, Ferdinand, and Juana's suitor, Alfonso of Portugal. Isabella and Ferdinand's titles were secured by a peace treaty (1479) and Juana retired to a convent, although she asserted her claims until her death in 1530.

The primary task of Ferdinand and Isabella was to bring peace and order to their realms through the exercise of direct personal authority. Isabella traveled throughout Castile, covering as much as 1,200 miles in a single year. She also revived the medieval brotherhoods (*hermandades*) to restore law and order in the towns. Isabella governed with a Royal Council (*Consejo Real*) staffed by university-trained legists (Letrados) and dispensed justice (after 1489) through *audiencias* established in major cities.

Isabella was determined to assert royal authority over the powerful Castilian nobility and recover territories and rights alienated by her ancestors. During her reign, the crown reclaimed the most recently alienated parcels and took three strategic cities—Cádiz, Gibraltar, and Cartagena—from their respective lords. She also brought the wealthy and powerful military orders under royal control when Ferdinand became their grand master.

Un-Christian and heretical influences in Spain disturbed the devoutly Catholic queen and in 1480 she commissioned a newly established Inquisition to root out heresy. In 1492 Isabella expelled the Jews who, because they were not baptized Christians, could not be classified as heretics. The monarchs also launched a crusade against the Moorish kingdom of Granada in 1482 and triumphantly claimed the capital city in 1492. Initial religious tolerance ended with the advent of the archbishop of Toledo and queen's confessor, Francisco Jiménez de Cisneros who, with Isabella's support, forced conversion through mass baptism (1499). Similarly, Isabella offered the choice of conversion or exile to the Moors elsewhere in Castile (1502) and thus limited Islamic and Jewish influence in her realm. Isabella's concern with Christian conversion extended to the native populations in the New World.

In addition to eliminating religious plurality in Spain, Isabella increased crown control over the Catholic Church. During her reign, Pope Alexander VI granted the crown patronage over all ecclesiastical appointments in Granada, the Canaries, and the New World. The monarchs also acquired greater control over the nomination of bishops in Castile.

When Christopher Columbus was rebuffed by the king of Portugal, he sought backing from the Castilian monarch; after much bargaining, he received Isabella's support in 1492. However, she opposed his enslavement of Indians and encouraged the formation of *encomiendas* and payment for wage labor. Her propitious decision to finance the first voyage was soon followed by the Treaty of Tordesillas (1494), which legitimated present and future Spanish claims in the New World.

*See also* **Ferdinand II of Aragon; Tordesillas, Treaty of (1494).**

BIBLIOGRAPHY

Tarsicio De Azcona, *Isabel la Católica* (1964).

L. Suárez Fernández and M. Fernández, *La España de los reyes Católicos* (*1474–1516*) (1969).

J. N. Hillgarth, *The Spanish Kingdoms,* vol. 2, *1410–1516: Castilian Hegemony* (1978).

William H. Prescott, *History of the Reign of Ferdinand and Isabella* (1838).

*Additional Bibliography*

Alvar Ezquerra, Alfredo. *Isabel la Católica: Un reina vencedora, una mujer derrotada.* Madrid: Temas de Hoy, 2002.

Boruchoff, David A., ed. *Isabel la Católica, Queen of Castile: Critical Essays.* New York: Palgrave Macmillan, 2003.

Liss, Peggy K. *Isabel the Queen: Life and Times.* Philadelphia: University of Pennsylvania Press, 2004.

SUZANNE HILES BURKHOLDER

**ISAMITT ALARCÓN, CARLOS** (1887–1974). Carlos Isamitt Alarcón (*b.* 13 March 1887; *d.* 2 July 1974), Chilean composer and painter. Along with Carlos Lavín and Pedro Humberto Allende, Isamitt, who was born in Rengo, Chile, is noted for his extensive research on the native music of the Araucanian Indians. In 1932, he published a seminal classification of the Araucanian musical repertoire according to performance medium and function. In 1936, Isamitt became one of the founding members of the Asociación Nacional de Compositores de Chile. His early music could be described as nationalistic, expressed through the spirit and techniques of musical impressionism. Later, however, his work became more abstract through use of the twelve-tone technique, of which he was one of the first exponents in Chile. Isamitt is a major figure in the trend called "musical Indianism" in Chile, although he also explored creole folklore. For his use of indigenous folklore in his own compositions, he was awarded Chile's Premio Nacional de Arte in 1965. He held the posts of director of the Santiago School of Fine Arts and artistic director of the primary schools in Santiago. His large musical output includes music for orchestra, chamber groups, voice, piano, and ballet.

*See also* **Music: The Twentieth Century; Theater.**

BIBLIOGRAPHY

Paul H. Apel, *Music of the Americas, North and South* (1958).

Raquel Barros and Manuel Dannemann, "Carlos Isamitt: Folklore e indigenismo," in *Revista musical chilena* 20, no. 97 (1961): 37–42.

Gérard Béhague, *Music in Latin America: An Introduction* (1979).

Samuel Claro Valdés and Jorge Urrutia, *Historia de la música en Chile* (1973).

Samuel Claros Valdés, *Oyendo a Chile* (1979).

Samuel Claros Valdés et al., *Iconografía musical chilena*, vols. 1 and 2 (1989).

Magdalena Vicuña, "Carlos Isamitt," in *Revista musical chilena* 20, no. 97 (1961): 5–13.

John Vinton, ed., *Dictionary of Contemporary Music* (1971).

### *Additional Bibliography*

Varas, José Miguel, and Juan Pablo González Rodríguez. *En busca de la música chilena: Crónica y antología de una historia sonora*. Santiago, Chile: Publicaciones del Bicentenario, 2005.

SERGIO BARROSO

---

**ISLAM.** Muslims arrived in Latin America several centuries before immigrants from the Middle East arrived in the region, and mostly hailed from non-Arabic-speaking parts of the Islamic world. In fact, of the three historical strands of Muslim arrivals in Latin America, only the most recent one was part of the major migration from Lebanon, Syria, and Palestine.

The first strand was composed of large numbers of Islamized West Africans, especially from Ghana, Dahomey (now Benin), Mali, and Nigeria, who were among the millions of Africans enslaved and shipped to work in Brazilian and Caribbean plantations until the second half of the nineteenth century. Most became Christian, at least in name, while others were reported to have held secretly to their Islamic faith, which appears to have been the case in the Brazilian cities of Salvador and Rio de Janeiro. Although little survives of this first strand, some have traced elements of Afro-Brazilian religions such as Umbanda, Candomblé, and Xango to Islam.

The second strand is intimately linked to the abolition of slavery in the colonial possessions of Great Britain and the Netherlands in the Indian subcontinent and Southeast Asia. Indeed, while the British introduced indentured labor to India, the Dutch did the same in Indonesia. By 1917 the British had encouraged some 250,000 Indians to settle in Guyana, where legislation dating back to 1871 exempted their children from attending Christian schools. Nearly one-sixth of these East Indians were Muslim. By 1940, the Dutch had succeeded in settling 33,000 Javanese Muslims in today's Suriname. Some 34,000 Indians, less than a fifth of them Muslim, were also introduced in that country. Although their work contracts included the provision of return fares at the end of a five-year stint, few indentured laborers managed to accumulate the wealth they had originally envisaged; therefore, they settled for land in lieu of passage to their home countries. Against this backdrop, Panama is the only Latin American state where the Islamic presence is partly due to the more recent arrival of Indian Muslim businesspeople, attracted by the country's role as a regional trade entrepôt.

The Middle Eastern strand of Muslim arrivals in Latin America dates back to the end of the nineteenth century and, unlike the two previous influxes, was not a result of recruitment, but rather a move to improve their economic circumstances and to avoid conscription into the Ottoman army. Most Arab Muslims sought to go to the United States but, because of strict health screenings and tightened immigration quotas, landed instead in Argentina and Brazil, whence they moved to neighboring countries. Reliable figures are hard to come by, but various estimates suggest that most settled in Argentina and Brazil. The Institute of Muslim Minority Affairs estimated in 1980 that nearly 94 percent of the region's Muslims of all origins live in Brazil (500,000), Argentina (370,000), Trinidad and Tobago (115,000), Suriname (104,500), and Guyana (74,500).

East Asian Muslims have long achieved recognition for openly practicing and furthering Islam among their offspring. Not surprisingly, the largest network of Muslim institutions in Latin America is in Britain's former colonies in the region. This includes more than two hundred mosques, as well as Koranic and other schools. In Guyana, the Muslim school system enjoys state subsidies, and Muslim religious festivals are recognized as national holidays. The same is the case in Suriname, where Muslims are said to make up 22 percent of the population. On the other hand, conflict between the African-descended majority and the Asian Muslim minorities has been more the rule than the exception in the Caribbean.

Muslims in the Catholic countries of Luso–Spanish America have not enjoyed the same degree of legitimacy as in Suriname and Guyana. Unpropitious circumstances at the receiving end—such as the erroneous assumption that all Muslims, including the penniless migrants, were polygamous, and intolerance of religious pluralism—pushed Muslim newcomers into a self-effacing posture. Some adopted Hispanic identities, and many more abandoned their faith while retaining their original names. Whereas Argentina's Syrian 'Alawite-descended president Carlos Saúl Menem and Druze-descended military leader Muhammad Alí Seineldín are among the latter, Zulema Yoma was Latin America's first Muslim first lady before becoming estranged from Menem.

Those who held to their faith established social and mutual-help institutions, but generally refrained from building mosques, in a reluctance to call attention to themselves in these Catholic countries. Not surprisingly, therefore, most purpose-built prayer houses and Islamic centers in Brazil and the Spanish-speaking countries date back to the 1973 rise of the Gulf States, as well as to Iranian activism among the Muslims since the ouster of Shah Muhammad Reza Pahlavi in 1979. In Argentina and Mexico, for instance, mosques went up in the 1980s with Tehran's help, a fact suggesting that a proportion of the Muslim immigrants are Shiite. Saudi- and Iranian-backed proselytism is not unknown in Latin America, as intimated by the mid-1980s revelation by an Iranian diplomat that the number of conversions in Argentina was on the increase. It is possible that a sizable proportion of these are none other than the descendants of earlier Muslim immigrants now becoming more assertive of their identity.

*See also* **Arab-Latin American Relations.**

BIBLIOGRAPHY

R. Guevara Bazán, "Muslim Immigration to Spanish America," in *Muslim World* 56 (1966); "Les musulmans dans le monde," la documentation française (August 1952).

Rolf Riechert, "Muslims in the Guyanas: A Socio-Economic Overview," in *Journal Institute of Muslim Minority Affairs* (Winter 1981): 120–126.

S. A. H. Ahsani and Omar Kasule, "Muslims in Latin America: A Survey," in *Journal Institute of Muslim Minority Affairs* (July 1984): 454–457.

Clayton G. Mackenzie, "Muslim Primary Schools in Trinidad and Tobago," in *Islamic Quarterly* (First Quarter 1989): 5–16.

Estela Biondi Assali, "L'insertion des groupes de langue arabe dans la société argentine," in *Revue Européenne des Migrations Internationales* 7, no. 2 (1991): 139–153.

Ignacio Klich, "Argentine-Ottoman Relations and Their Impact on Immigrants from the Middle East," in *Americas* (October 1993).

### *Additional Bibliography*

Batista, Vera Malaguti. *O medo na cidade do Rio de Janeiro: Dois tempos de uma história.* Rio de Janeiro: Editora Revan, 2003.

Jozami, Gladys. "The Manifestation of Islam in Argentina." *The Americas* Vol. 53, No. 1 (July, 1996): 67-85.

Khan, Aisha. *Callaloo Nation: Metaphors of Race and Religious Identity among South Asians in Trinidad.* Durham: Duke University Press, 2004.

Lesser, Jeffrey, and Ignacio Klich, eds. *Arab and Jewish Immigrants in Latin America: Images and Realities.* London: Frank Cass, 1998.

Reis, João José. *Slave Rebellion in Brazil: The Muslim Uprising of 1835 in Bahia.* Baltimore: Johns Hopkins University Press, 1993.

Truzzi, Oswaldo. *Patrícios: Sírios e libaneses em São Paulo.* São Paulo: Editora Hucitec, 1997.

IGNACIO KLICH

**ISRAELI–LATIN AMERICAN RELATIONS.** During the first United Nations debates on Palestine in 1947, democratic and liberal Latin American regimes generally supported the creation of a Jewish state in parts of that territory, while conservative Catholic governments took a reserved attitude. Thus, Guatemala and Uruguay followed a marked pro-Zionist line in the United Nations Special Committee on Palestine (UNSCOP), which prepared the Partition of Palestine proposal. Eventually, thirteen out of twenty Latin American countries voted in favor of the Partition Plan in November 1947, and eighteen Latin American countries supported Israel's admission to the UN in May 1949.

Guatemala recognized Israel three days after its establishment in May 1948, and the other Latin American countries followed suit in 1948 and 1949. Peronist Argentina, which had abstained in the partition vote, was the first to open an embassy in Tel Aviv, then Israel's capital. It was followed by Brazil and Uruguay. In 1955 Guatemala set up the first Latin American representation in Jerusalem. Israel established its first diplomatic missions in Uruguay, Argentina, Brazil, and Mexico from 1949 to 1953.

In the 1960s relations between Israel and most Latin American states flourished, due partly to Israeli agricultural aid programs. There were by then fourteen Latin American embassies in Israel (of which ten were located in Jerusalem), while the number of Israeli embassies in Latin America had risen to sixteen. The closer relations manifested themselves within international organizations. One notable setback in the relationship occurred in 1960, when Israel captured Adolf Eichmann, the Nazi officer directly responsible for implementing the genocide against European Jews, who had fled to Argentina in 1950; Israeli secret service agents smuggled him out of the country to put him on trial in Israel. Argentina protested this action to the UN, which agreed that Israel's action was illegal, but the countries ended their dispute later in the year. In the UN General Assembly in 1967, after the Six-Day War between Israel and Arab nations, the Soviet Union and nonaligned countries demanded Israel's unconditional withdrawal from the occupied territories. Twenty Latin American states then sponsored a resolution based on withdrawal, an end of belligerency, and "coexistence based on good neighborliness." The Latin American draft was defeated, but its presentation was a decisive factor in the rejection of the Soviet-nonaligned proposals and later in the formulation of Security Council Resolution 242.

In the 1970s Israeli–Latin American relations deteriorated in the wake of political changes in Latin America, such as left-wing military rule in Peru (1968–1980), the Allende government in Chile (1970–1973), the reestablishment of a Peronist regime in Argentina (1973–1976), and the Sandinista regime in Nicaragua (1979–1990). These states adhered to the nonaligned movement, of which Fidel Castro's Cuba was already a member. They were gradually followed by other left-leaning Latin American countries. From the 1960s to the 1980s, fifteen new Caribbean states emerged which, because of ethnic ties, felt close to Africa and to Third World ideologies. The result was significant Latin American participation in international political and economic alignments that pursued anti-Israeli policies. By contrast, because of Central American governments' support for the creation of a Jewish state in the 1930s and 1940s, Israel maintained a strong relationship with these countries. During the 1980s the United States used Israel as a conduit to provide money to military governments in Central America faced with insurgencies and the Contras in Nicaragua.

The oil crises of 1973–1974 and 1979, which severely affected the Latin American economies, created a dependence on the cartel known as the Organization of Petroleum Exporting Countries (OPEC) and its Arab members. Brazil turned pro-Arab, while oil-producing Latin American states like Venezuela, Ecuador, and Mexico strengthened their relationships with Arab OPEC countries.

In several Latin American states there was also an awakening of political consciousness among the population of Arab origin (about 3 million persons, as compared to fewer than half a million Jews). All this led to the growth of diplomatic relations between Latin American and Arab states and the opening of Palestine Liberation Organization embassies and offices in Cuba, Nicaragua, Peru, Mexico, Brazil, and Bolivia. In the UN in 1975, five Latin American and Caribbean states (Brazil, Cuba, Guyana, Grenada, and Mexico) supported Resolution 3379, which equated Zionism with racism and questioned the moral ground for Israel's existence. Ten Latin American countries voted against the resolution and eleven abstained. By the 1980s some countries such as Mexico, and to a lesser extent Argentina, Brazil, and Peru, routinely supported anti-Israeli resolutions.

The change in the UN also affected bilateral relations. In 1980, after Israel had adopted a law declaring Jerusalem as its capital, the Security Council called on all states whose diplomatic missions were located in Jerusalem to "withdraw them from the Holy City." In consequence all twelve Latin American embassies in Jerusalem were transferred to Tel Aviv. (Costa Rica returned its embassy to Jerusalem in 1982, and El Salvador did the same in 1984.) Three Latin American states broke diplomatic relations with Israel: Cuba in 1973, Guyana in 1974, and Nicaragua in 1982. Nevertheless, the Israeli diplomatic network in Latin America continued to grow, and in the early 1990s Israel had eighteen embassies in Latin America and hosted seventeen Latin American missions. Significant developments included the visits of President Chaim Herzog to Argentina in 1990 and of President Carlos Menem to Israel in 1991. In 1990 Israel maintained technical assistance missions in several Central American and Caribbean countries and hosted about 600 trainees each year from Latin America. In 1992 Islamic Jihad, which had established a cell in Argentina, bombed the Israeli embassy in Buenos Aires, killing 29 and injuring 242. This bombing remains the deadliest attack on an Israeli diplomatic mission.

Israeli-Latin American trade relations were always of secondary importance. In 1990 Israeli exports to Latin America reached $98 million (not including classified military exports and oil supplies), and Israeli imports from there amounted to $43 million.

*See also* **Allende Gossens, Salvador; Arab-Latin American Relations; Perón, Juan Domingo; United Nations.**

BIBLIOGRAPHY

Edy Kaufman, Yoram Shapira, and Joel Barromi, *Israel-Latin American Relations* (1979).

*Additional Bibliography*

Bahbah, Bishara, and Linda Butler. "Israel and Latin America: The Military Connection." London: Macmillan, 1986.

Klich, Ignacio, and Jeff Lesser, eds. *Arab and Jewish Immigrants in Latin America: Images and Realities.* London and Portland, OR: F. Cass, 1998.

Metz, Allan. "Israeli Military Assistance to Latin America." *Latin American Research Review* 28, no. 2 (1993): 257–263.

JOEL BARROMI

---

**ITABORAÍ, VISCONDE DE** (1802–1873). Visconde de Itaboraí (Joaquim José Rodrigues Tôrres; *b.* 1802; *d.* 1873). Born into a landowning family of Rio province, Itaboraí graduated from Coimbra University in 1825 and became an instructor at the Rio Military Academy. A doctrinaire Liberal, he served as a minister in 1831 and 1833. Converted to Conservative views, he was prominent in the Regresso movement (1835–1839) in favor of central authority and law and order. He was elected a deputy in 1834 and was named a senator in 1844. After Pedro II's majority, Itaboraí served as minister in the Conservative cabinet of 1843–1844. On the Liberals' fall from office in 1848, he became minister of finance and, over the next five years, reorganized the fiscal system. He was prime minister from May 1852 to September 1853. Appointed president of the Bank of Brazil, he exerted considerable influence on monetary questions. In July 1868, Itaboraí formed a cabinet that, despite financial and political difficulties, brought the War of the Triple Alliance to a successful end. A *fazendeiro* (plantation owner) and opposed to any meddling with slavery, Itaboraí voted but did not speak against the Free Birth Law of 1871. Very much the intellectual in politics, Itaboraí was perhaps the most capable and is certainly the most understudied leader of Pedro II's reign (1840–1889).

*See also* **War of the Triple Alliance.**

BIBLIOGRAPHY

João Lyra Filho, *Visconde de Itaboraí, a luneta do império* (Rio de Janeiro, 1986).

*Additional Bibliography*

Barman, Roderick J. *Citizen Emperor: Pedro II and the Making of Brazil, 1825–1891.* Stanford, CA: Stanford University Press, 1999.

Needell, Jeffrey D. *The Party of Order: The Conservatives, the State, and Slavery in the Brazilian Monarchy, 1831–1871.* Stanford, CA: Stanford University Press, 2006.

RODERICK J. BARMAN

## ITAIPÚ HYDROELECTRIC PROJECT.

**ITAIPÚ HYDROELECTRIC PROJECT.** Itaipú Hydroelectric Project, power station and reservoir located on the Paraná River on the border between Brazil and Paraguay. Itaipú has an installed capacity of 12,600 megawatts and an annual output of 77,000 gigawatt-hours, making it the largest and one of the most productive hydroelectric projects in the world. The dam complex is 4.6 miles long, reaches a maximum height of 216 yards, and houses eighteen 715-megawatt Francis turbines. Technologically distinctive features of the Itaipú project include the most powerful hydrogenerators and turbines, the highest direct-current transmission voltages and power ever used (+600 kilovolts and 6,300 megawatts), and some of the longest transmission lines in the world (about 600 miles of 765-kilovolts alternating current transmission). Both 50-hertz and 60-hertz generators were required in order to meet each country's national frequency standard.

The energy potential of the Paraná River has been known since at least the mid-1950s and has been previously exploited in a series of smaller dams within Brazil. The Acta Final (Acta de Iguaçú), signed in June 1966, ended a border dispute between Brazil and Paraguay and provided that the energy potential of the river between the site of the border dispute and the mouth of the Iguaçú River would be shared in condominium. Feasibility studies were undertaken and in April 1973, the Itaipú Treaty was signed, establishing a binational entity owned by the two state-owned electric utilities, the Administración Nacional de Electricidad (ANDE) in Paraguay and the Centrais Elétricas Brasileiras S.A. (Eletrobras) in Brazil. With an initial capital of $100 million, the binational entity secured financing from Brazilian agencies and international commercial banks (with the guarantee of the government of Brazil) to finance construction of the project. The Itaipú Dam created a 540-square-mile reservoir, which flooded the disputed area in October 1982. The first generator began commercial operation in 1984 and the project was completed in 1991 at an estimated total cost of $18 billion. Itaipú Binacional operates the facility, selling electric power to the two owners.

*See also* **Boundary Disputes: Brazil.**

BIBLIOGRAPHY

Gerd Kohlhepp, *Itaipú: Socio-economic and Ecological Consequences of the Itaipú Dam* (1987) provides a good overview of the Itaipú project, especially in the Brazilian context. The text of the Itaipú Treaty and definitive coverage of the debate surrounding it is found in E. E. Gamon, *Itaipú: Aguas que valen oro* (1975). Ricardo Canese, *Itaipú y la cuestión energética en el Paraguay,* Biblioteca de Estudios Paraguayos, vol. 7 (1983), provides an excellent discussion of the project, the pricing of its electric power, and the potential uses of its energy in Paraguay. The impact of the Itaipú project on the Paraguayan economy may be found in Werner Baer and Melissa H. Birch, "Expansion of the Economic Frontier: Paraguayan Growth in the 1970s," in *World Development* 12, no. 8 (1984): 783–798. For technical information, see Julival De Moraes and Victor F. Salatko, "Coming: 12,600 Megawatts at Itaipú Island," in *IEEE Spectrum* (August 1983): 46–52.

### *Additional Bibliography*

Davidson, Frank Paul, and Kathleen Lusk-Brooke. *Building the World: An Encyclopedia of the Great Engineering Projects in History.* Westport, CT: Greenwood Press, 2006.

Debernardi, Enzo. *Apuntes para la historia política de Itaipú.* Paraguay: s.n., 1996.

Mazzarollo, Juvencio. *A taipa da injustiçia: Esbanjamento economico, drama social e holocausto ecológico em Itaipú.* Curitiba, PR: CPT-PR, Comissão Pastoral da Terra do Paraná; São Paulo: Edições Loyola, 2003.

MELISSA H. BIRCH

## ITU, CONVENTION OF.

**ITU, CONVENTION OF.** Convention of Itu (18 April 1873), a meeting of the newly formed Paulista Republican Party in the São Paulo town of Itu to discuss the future of republicanism in that province. The convention was attended by 133 individuals, 76 of whom were planters. The Paulista Republicans, having attracted more wealthy planters than had Republican parties elsewhere in Brazil, staunchly supported slavery and resented the relative exclusion of São Paulo planters from politics at the national level. The party thus favored a federalist republic but opposed the abolition of slavery. During the last years of the empire, Republicans gained their greatest strength in the province of São Paulo, where they came to control 25 percent of the electorate.

*See also* **Brazil, Political Parties: Republican Party (PR).**

BIBLIOGRAPHY

Heitor Lyra, *História da queda do império,* 2 vols. (1964), esp. vol. 1, pp. 22–26.

Emilia Viotti Da Costa, *The Brazilian Empire* (1985), esp. pp. 226–228.

*Additional Bibliography*

Mendonça, Joseli Maria Nunes. *Entre a mão e os anéis: A lei dos sexagenários e os caminhos da abolição no Brasil.* Campinas: Editora da UNICAMP: CECULT, 1999.

Nabuco, Joaquim, ed. *A abolição e a República.* Recife: Editora Universitária UFPE, 1999.

JOAN MEZNAR

**ITURBIDE, AGUSTÍN DE** (1783–1824). Agustín de Iturbide (*b.* 27 September 1783; *d.* 19 July 1824), military figure and emperor of Mexico. Born in Valladolid, Morelia, Iturbide entered the militia at age sixteen. Although vaguely involved with the Valladolid Conspiracy of 1809, he refused to join the revolt of Miguel Hidalgo y Costilla in 1810. Instead, he served the royal government, distinguishing himself as an able officer and an implacable foe of the insurgents. In 1816 Colonel Iturbide was relieved of command because of charges of corruption. He spent the next years in Madrid defending himself. There he came into contact with important members of the elite who favored autonomy within the Spanish Empire. While New Spain's elite had reached a consensus regarding autonomy, only Iturbide acted decisively.

Restored to command, Iturbide negotiated in 1821 with the leading royalist officers as well as with the principal insurgents, convincing them to accept autonomy under the Plan of Iguala, which called for a constitutional monarchy with the Spanish king as sovereign, recognized the Constitution of 1812, and established equality among all groups. Independence was assured when Juan O'Donojú, the newly appointed Spanish *Jefe Político Superior* (Superior Political Chief) ratified the plan by signing the Treaty of Córdoba (24 August 1821). Thereafter, the autonomists, New Spain's elite who had sought home rule since 1808, rapidly came into conflict with Iturbide. While they believed that the legislature should be dominant, he insisted on exercising his personal power resulting from the immense popularity that he had gained when he proclaimed independence. When Spain refused to ratify Mexican autonomy, Iturbide crowned himself emperor on 19 May 1822 with the backing of the army and strong popular support.

The new nation faced immense problems, among them the near bankruptcy of the government. Although there was a widespread national desire to form a strong and unified nation, the empire failed primarily because Iturbide proved unwilling to accept the figurehead role that the new Spanish-Mexican parliamentary tradition required. As a result, he and Congress were continually at odds. On 26 August 1822 he ordered the arrest of sixty-six persons, including twenty congressmen, for conspiracy, and on 31 October he dissolved congress. Discontent emerged in the provinces, but the military finally undermined him. The Plan of Casa Mata, which provided the provinces the opportunity to gain home rule, ultimately forced him to abdicate on 19 March 1823. He and his family were exiled to Italy, but supporters convinced him to return in July 1824 in an effort to regain the throne. He was captured, court-martialed, and executed. Although he succeeded in emancipating his country, he failed, like his contemporaries throughout the region, to establish a stable regime and, thus, became an ambiguous figure in Mexican history.

*See also* **Valladolid Conspiracy.**

BIBLIOGRAPHY

Timothy E. Anna, *The Mexican Empire of Iturbide* (1990).

Christon I. Archer, "'La Causa Buena': The Counterinsurgency Army of New Spain and the Ten Years' War."

William S. Robertson, *Iturbide of Mexico* (1952).

Jaime E. Rodríguez O., "From Royal Subject to Republican Citizen: The Role of the Autonomists in the Independence of Mexico."

Jaime E. Rodríguez O., "The Struggle for the Nation: The First Centralist-Federalist Conflict in Mexico," in *The Americas* 49 (July 1992): 1–22.

Barbara A. Tenenbaum, "Taxation and Tyranny: Public Finance During the Iturbide Regime, 1821–1823," in *The Independence of Mexico and the Creation of the New Nation*, edited by Jaime E. Rodríguez O. (1989).

### *Additional Bibliography*

Archer, Christon I. *The Birth of Modern Mexico, 1780–1824.* Wilmington, DE: SR Books, 2003.

Caudet Yarza, Francisco. *Agustín de Iturbide.* Las Rozas, Madrid: Dastin, 2003.

JAIME E. RODRÍGUEZ O.

**ITURBIDE, GRACIELA** (1942–). Using black and white film as her medium of choice, the Mexican photographer Graciela Iturbide captures images that interpret the daily affairs and rituals of indigenous peoples and the lives of women throughout Mexico. Born in Mexico City on May 16, 1942, Iturbide initially studied filmmaking at the Center for Cinematographic studies of the National Autonomous University from 1969 to 1972 and later trained under Mexican photographer Manuel Álvarez Bravo. Her most renowned body of work, executed in the late 1970s, centers on the matriarchal culture of the Zapotecs of Juchitán, a town near the Isthmus of Tehuantepec on Mexico's southern Pacific coast in the state of Oaxaca.

Among other projects, Iturbide has documented the singular manner in which the Mexican people approach death, and, in East Los Angeles, California, the daily lives of *cholos*, young Mexican American street gang members. Her recent works include subjects from India and Argentina, as well as the southwestern United States. Although her images are photojournalistic, they are characterized by a level of intimacy and candor not necessarily associated with the documentary tradition. Exhibitions of her work have been mounted internationally, and her photographs are included in the permanent collections of many major museums. Iturbide lives and works in Coyoacán, Mexico.

*See also* **Álvarez Bravo, Manuel; Photography: 1900-1990; Zapotecs.**

BIBLIOGRAPHY

Ferrer, Elizabeth. "Manos Poderosas: The Photography of Graciela Iturbide." *Latin American Literature and Arts* 47 (1993): 69–78.

Gili, Marta. *Graciela Iturbide.* London and New York: Phaidon, 2006.

Hopkinson, Amanda. "Meditated Worlds: Latin American Photography." *Bulletin of Latin American Research* 20, no. 4 (October 2001): 520–527.

Iturbide, Graciela. *Sueños de papel.* Mexico City: Fondo de Cultura Económica, 1985.

Iturbide, Graciela, and Elena Poniatowska. *Juchitán de las mujeres.* Mexico City: Ediciones Toledo, 1989.

Iturbide, Graciela. "Mexican Street Gangs of Los Angeles and Tijuana." In *Desires and Disguises: Five Latin American Photographers*, ed. and trans. Amanda Hopkinson. New York: Serpent's Tail, 1992.

Iturbide, Graciela. *Images of the Spirit.* New York: Aperture, 1996.

Iturbide, Graciela. *La forma y la memoria.* Monterrey, Mexico: Museo de Arte Contemporáneo de Monterrey, 1996.

Iturbide, Graciela. *Pájaros.* Santa Fe, NM: Twin Palms Publishers, 2002.

Iturbide, Graciela. *Naturata: Graciela Iturbide, 1996–2004.* Mexico City: Galería López Quiroga; Paris: Toluca Editions, 2004.

Iturbide, Graciela. *Eyes to Fly With.* Austin: University of Texas Press, 2006.

Martín, Eduardo Vázquez. "Graciela Iturbide: La forma y la memoria." *Artes de México* 33 (1996): 88–89.

Medina, Cuauhtémoc. *Graciela Iturbide.* London and New York: Phaidon, 2001.

Snow, K. Mitchell. "Lens of Ritual and Revelation." *Américas* 51, no. 1 (January–February 1999): 22–29.

CHARLENE VAN DIJK

**ITURRIGARAY, JOSÉ DE** (1742–1815). José De Iturrigaray (*b.* 27 June 1742; *d.* 1815), fifty-sixth viceroy of New Spain (1803–1808). A military man, he obtained the post of viceroy as a protégé of Spanish Prime Minister Manuel Godoy (1767–1851). He won the sympathies of New Spaniards with programs such as smallpox vaccinations. He organized the defense of the viceroyalty and stationed troops to protect the road to Mexico City. He took every opportunity to amass wealth, as evidenced by his implemention of the Royal Law of Consolidation (26 December 1804), from which he received a percentage of the amount collected.

When news arrived that King Charles IV (1748–1819) had abdicated in favor of Napoleon I (1769–1821), the Ayuntamiento (city council) of Mexico City proposed the establishment of a junta of authorities while an assembly of cities was convened. The Audiencia of Mexico, fearful that such action might lead to independence, proposed, instead, the recognition of one of the juntas formed in Spain. Backing the Ayuntamiento, Iturrigaray held several meetings, to which the Audiencia responded by encouraging a coup d'état. On the night of 15 September 1808, Gabriel de Yermo (1757–1813), at the head of 300 Spaniards, imprisoned the viceroy and detained several members of the Ayuntamiento as well as Fray Melchor de Talamantes (1765–1809). Thereafter, the conflict between *criollos* and *peninsulares* became acute. Removed from command, Iturrigaray was sent to Spain, where he was prosecuted for disloyalty, but his case was stayed. He underwent a *juicio de residencia,* which posthumously found him guilty of peculation. He died in Madrid in 1815.

*See also* **New Spain, Viceroyalty of; Yermo, Gabriel de.**

BIBLIOGRAPHY

Enrique Lafuente Ferrari, *El virrey Iturrigaray y los orígenes de la independencia de Méjico* (1941).

José M. De Salaverría, "Relación o historia," in *Documentos históricos mexicanos,* edited by Genaro García, vol. 2 (1985), pp. 296–469.

### *Additional Bibliography*

La Parra López, Emilio. *Manuel Godoy: La aventura del poder.* Barcelona: Tusquets, 2002.

VIRGINIA GUEDEA

---

**ITUZAINGÓ, BATTLE OF.** Battle of Ituzaingó, the most important contest in the war between the Brazilian Empire and the United Provinces of the Río De La Plata (1825–1828) over the territory referred to by some as the Provincia Oriental and by others as Cisplatine Province. In Brazil this battle is often known as the Passo do Rosário. Ituzaingó is located in present-day Argentina. The battle took place 20 February 1827 and ended in a decisive victory for the troops of Río de la Plata. The number of combatants is estimated at approximately 16,000. The Brazilian forces were slightly superior in numbers and more so in arms and supplies. General Carlos de Alvear commanded the troops of Río de la Plata, among whom figured 3,000 men from the Provincia Oriental, led by General Juan Antonio Lavalleja. The victory of the forces of Río de la Plata at Ituzaingó dealt a strong blow to Brazilian hopes of extending its territory to Río de la Plata. Brazil was further frustrated in this effort by the Preliminary Peace Pact of 1828, out of which was born the independent nation of Uruguay.

*See also* **Brazil: 1808-1889.**

BIBLIOGRAPHY

Alfredo Castellanos, *La Cisplatina: La independencia y la república caudillesca, 1820–1838* (1974).

Washington Reyes Abadie and Andrés Vázquez Romero, *Crónica general del Uruguay,* vol. 2 (1984).

### *Additional Bibliography*

Golletti Wilkinson, Augusto. *Guerra contra el imperio del Brasil: A la luz de sus protagonistas.* Buenos Aires: Editorial Dunken, 2003.

Vale, Brian. *A War betwixt Englishmen: Brazil against Argentina on the River Plate, 1825-1830.* New York: I.B. Tauris, 2000.

JOSÉ DE TORRES WILSON

---

**ITZCOATL** (c. 1380–1440). Itzcoatl (*b.* ca. 1380; *d.* 1440), Aztec ruler from 1426 to 1440. Itzcoatl ("Obsidian Serpent"), fourth Mexica ruler or *tlatoani* ("speaker"), was the son of Acamapichtli, the first *tlatoani,* and a slave woman. Itzcoatl led the rebellion against the Tepanac polity centered at Azcapotzalco, to which the Mexica had been tributaries. Itzcoatl's nephew (half-brother in some sources) and predecessor, Chimalpopoca (r. 1415–1426), died under mysterious circumstances. The accession of Itzcoatl, a mature man with a low-ranking mother, may have been engineered by Mexica leaders desiring to fight the Tepanecs. A skilled warrior and strategist, Itzcoatl joined forces with the Acolhua under Nezahualcoyotl and the dissident Tepanecs of Tlacopan (Tacuba), forging the "Triple Alliance" that defeated Azcapotzalco's ruler, Maxtla, in 1428. According to native tradition,

Itzcoatl then destroyed the manuscript records of Mexica history, thus obscuring the humble origins of the now-triumphant Mexica. To the nascent Aztec Empire, Itzcoatl added Coyoacan, Xochimilco, and Cuitlahuac. He was succeeded by his nephew, Motecuhzoma I.

*See also* **Aztecs.**

BIBLIOGRAPHY

Burr Cartwright Brundage, *A Rain of Darts: The Mexica Aztecs* (1972).

Nigel Davies, *The Aztecs: A History* (1980).

Diego Durán, *The Aztecs: The History of the Indies of New Spain,* translated by Doris Heyden and Fernando Horcasitas (1964).

*Additional Bibliography*

Borboa, Martín. *Itzcóatl, emperador mexica.* México, D.F.: Plaza y Valdes, 1997.

LOUISE M. BURKHART

## IVALDI, HUMBERTO (1909–1947).

Humberto Ivaldi (*b.* 1909; *d.* 1947), Panamanian painter. He trained initially under Roberto Lewis and later at the San Fernando Academy in Madrid (1930–1935). In Panama, he became an art teacher and later director of the Escuela Nacional de Pintura, where he influenced a generation of Panamanian artists. A frustrated man, he left many unfinished works and his early death is presumed to have been a suicide.

Ivaldi's academic background stands out in his traditional still lifes and numerous portraits. However, his more "modern" genre paintings and landscapes, for example, *Viento en la Loma* (1945), are characterized by expressive brush strokes, dynamic compositions, and the rich atmospheric quality of his colors.

*See also* **Art: The Twentieth Century.**

BIBLIOGRAPHY

H. Calamari, "Breves apuntaciones sobre la obra de Humberto Ivaldi," in *El Panamá América, Suplemento Literario* (23 March 1947).

Rodrigo Miró, "Lewis, Amador, Ivaldi," in *Revista Lotería,* no. 219 (May 1974): 72–80.

*Additional Bibliography*

Rajer, Anton. *París en Panamá: Roberto Lewis y la historia de sus obras restauradas en el Teatro Nacional de Panamá.* Madison, WI: Banta Book Publishing Corp., 2005.

MONICA E. KUPFER

## IXIMCHÉ.

Iximché (Ee-sheem-cháy), capital city of the Kaqchikel (Cakchiquel) Maya from around 1470/1480 to 1524. In return for Kaqchikel support during the Conquest, the Spaniards made Iximché the first Spanish capital (Santiago) in the kingdom of Guatemala. However, Spanish abuses soon led the Kaqchikel to revolt, and the Spaniards abandoned Iximché in 1526.

According to Kaqchikel history, Iximché was founded by Huntoh and Vukubatz after the Kaqchikel broke with the neighboring K'iche'. This marked the end of K'iche' subjugation and the beginning of Kaqchikel expansion, during which they subjugated former K'iche' territory.

The site of Iximché is located near modern Tecpan, Guatemala, a town settled in the sixteenth century by former residents of Iximché. Iximché occupies a naturally defensible position, atop a plateau that is surrounded on three sides by deep ravines. The site is divided into a residential precinct and a civic precinct that consists of temples, palaces, ball courts, altars, and plazas. Some buildings in the civic zone were painted with murals. Archaeological investigations have been conducted periodically at Iximché since the early 1950s, and today portions of the civic precinct have been reconstructed.

*See also* **Kaqchikel.**

BIBLIOGRAPHY

George F. Guillemin, "Urbanism and Hierarchy at Iximché," in *Social Process in Maya Prehistory,* edited by Norman Hammond (1977).

John W. Fox, *Quiché Conquest* (1978), esp. pp. 176–187.

*Additional Bibliography*

Contreras R., J. Daniel, and Jorge Luján Muñoz. *El "Memorial de Sololá" y los inicios de la colonización española en Guatemala.* Guatemala: Academia de Geografía e Historia de Guatemala, 2004.

Nance, Charles Roger, Stephen L. Whittington, and Barbara E Jones-Borg. *Archaeology and Ethnohistory of Iximche*. Gainesville: University Press of Florida, 2003.

JANINE GASCO

---

**IZABAL.** Izabal (Puerto Izabal, Puerto del Golfo), the main port for commerce entering Guatemala from the Caribbean after its establishment in 1804 until the completion of the railroad, Ferrocarril del Norte, in 1908. The port was located on the south shore of Lake Izabal, the largest lake in Guatemala, known during the nineteenth century as the Golfo Dulce. The Río Dulce connects the lake to the Caribbean. Goods and passengers traveled up the river and lake by steamship and then were carried from Izabal to Guatemala City overland by mule train, crossing the Sierra de las Minas and following the Motagua River valley to the city.

Spanish authorities established Izabal after publicly declaring the necessity of relocation because of unhealthy conditions at the old port of Bodegas, about 4 miles to the east. Archival records indicate, however, that the shift was made in order to control customs taxes then collected by the Dominican order of the Roman Catholic Church, which had dominated Bodegas from its founding in 1567.

Great Britain became the main international trade partner of Guatemala after the country gained independence from Spain in 1821. Commerce came to Izabal by steamship via Belize, then a British colony. Nearly all imported goods entered Guatemala by this route until the early 1850s. At that time a railway across Panama made the Pacific port of Iztapa, nearer and more accessible to Guatemala City, the major port of entry for the country. After that time the route was used mainly by travelers to Guatemala on the Atlantic route, and Izabal was a transshipment point for coffee and bananas from the eastern part of the country.

With the arrival of the railroad at Puerto Barrios on the Caribbean, Izabal was abandoned as a port. Today it is a small fishing and farming village. Ruins of the church and army garrison remain as evidence of its earlier role.

*See also* **Railroads.**

BIBLIOGRAPHY

For a nineteenth-century view of Izabal, see John L. Stephens, *Incidents of Travel in Central America, Chiapas and the Yucatán*, 2 vols. edited by Richard L. Predmore (repr. 1969), esp. pp. 34–41. Great Britain's role in Guatemala's economic history is examined in Robert A. Naylor, *Influenica británica en el comercio centroamericano durante las primeras décadas de la independencia* (*1821–1851*), translated by J. C. Cambranes (1988).

*Additional Bibliography*

Pompejano, Daniele. *La crisis del antiguo régimen en Guatemala (1839-1871)*. Guatemala: Editorial Universitaria, Universidad de San Carlos de Guatemala, 1997.

Woodward, Ralph Lee. *Rafael Carrera and the Emergence of the Republic of Guatemala, 1821-1871*. Athens: University of Georgia Press, 1993.

REBECCA J. OROZCO

---

**IZAPA.** Izapa, an archaeological site located on the Pacific coast of the Isthmus of Tehuantépec in the Soconusco district of the state of Chiapas, Mexico. It is a regional center famous for its hundreds of Late Formative Guillen (300–50 B.C.) sculptures. The Izapan style, temporally and stylistically intermediate between the Olmec and the Maya, is distributed along the Pacific coast and in the highlands of Guatemala.

Izapa is a large ceremonial center of 1.5 square miles. Boulder-faced platforms define eight large plazas. Structures are oriented to astronomical events and the Tacaná Volcano. Distributed throughout the plazas are stone monuments, including stelae, altars, and thrones, just over fifty of which are carved.

The Izapan sculptures are important for their unique style. Stelae are decorated with low relief narratives. Unlike later Maya sculptures of deified humans, they show scenes of ritual confrontation involving human figures with feline, serpentine, or crocodilian characteristics or of communication with serpentine deities. The art depicts rituals of sacrifice and death, water and fertility, worldview and creation, and astronomy. Such scenes are usually framed top and bottom by stylized zoomorphic beings and terrestrial bands, respectively.

Izapa has been interpreted as having been a residence for religious rulers and a pilgrimage center. The ceremonial and symbolic stone art, evidence of incense burning, and large ritual deposits of valuable materials are evidence of its importance as a religious center.

*See also* **Maya, the; Mesoamerica; Olmecs.**

BIBLIOGRAPHY

V. Garth Norman, *Izapa Sculpture,* 2 vols., New World Archaeological Foundation Paper 30 (1973–1976).

Jacinto Quirarte, *Izapan-Style Art: A Study of Its Form and Meaning,* in *Studies in Pre-Columbian Art and Archaeology,* no. 10 (1973).

Gareth Lowe, Thomas A. Lee, Jr., and Eduardo Martínez Espinosa, *Izapa: An Introduction to the Ruins and Monuments,* New World Archaeological Foundation Paper 31 (1982).

*Additional Bibliography*

Barba de Piña Chan, Beatriz. *Buscando raíces de mitos mayas en Izapa.* Campeche: Ediciones de la Universidad Autónoma del Sudeste, 1988.

Guernsey, Julia. *Ritual & Power in Stone: The Performance of Rulership in Mesoamerican Izapan Style Art.* Austin: University of Texas Press, 2006.

Malmström, Vincent Herschel. *Cycles of the Sun, Mysteries of the Moon: The Calendar in Mesoamerican Civilization.* Austin: University of Texas Press, 1997.

EUGENIA J. ROBINSON

**IZQUIERDO, MARÍA** (1902–1955). María Izquierdo (*b.* 1902; *d.* 2 December 1955), Mexican artist. María Izquierdo was largely self-taught. In the early 1930s she was the companion of Rufino Tamayo, with whom she shared stylistic affinities. Izquierdo's works include self-portraits, in which her Indian features are proudly evident, still lifes, and landscapes. "My greatest strength," she said about her work, "is that my painting reflects the Mexico that I know and love.... In the world of art, a painting is an open window to the human imagination." Along with her populism, she celebrated her passion for color, texture, and careful composition while maintaining a delight in spontaneity. Her palette changed over time from more obscure tones to contrasting and rich ones close to those of textiles, ceramics, and lacquered folk ware. Despite her often brilliant use of color, there is a tragic or melancholy undertone to many works along with a wry humor.

*See also* **Tamayo, Rufino.**

BIBLIOGRAPHY

Miguel Cervantes, ed., *María Izquierdo* (1986): Raquel Tibol, "María Izquierdo," in *Latin American Art* 1 (Spring 1989): 23–25.

*Additional Bibliography*

Poniatowska, Elena. *Las siete cabritas.* México, D.F.: Ediciones Era, 2000.

Vaughan, Mary K., and Stephen E. Lewis, eds. *The Eagle and the Virgin: Nation and Cultural Revolution in Mexico, 1920–1940.* Durham, NC: Duke University Press, 2006.

SHIFRA M. GOLDMAN

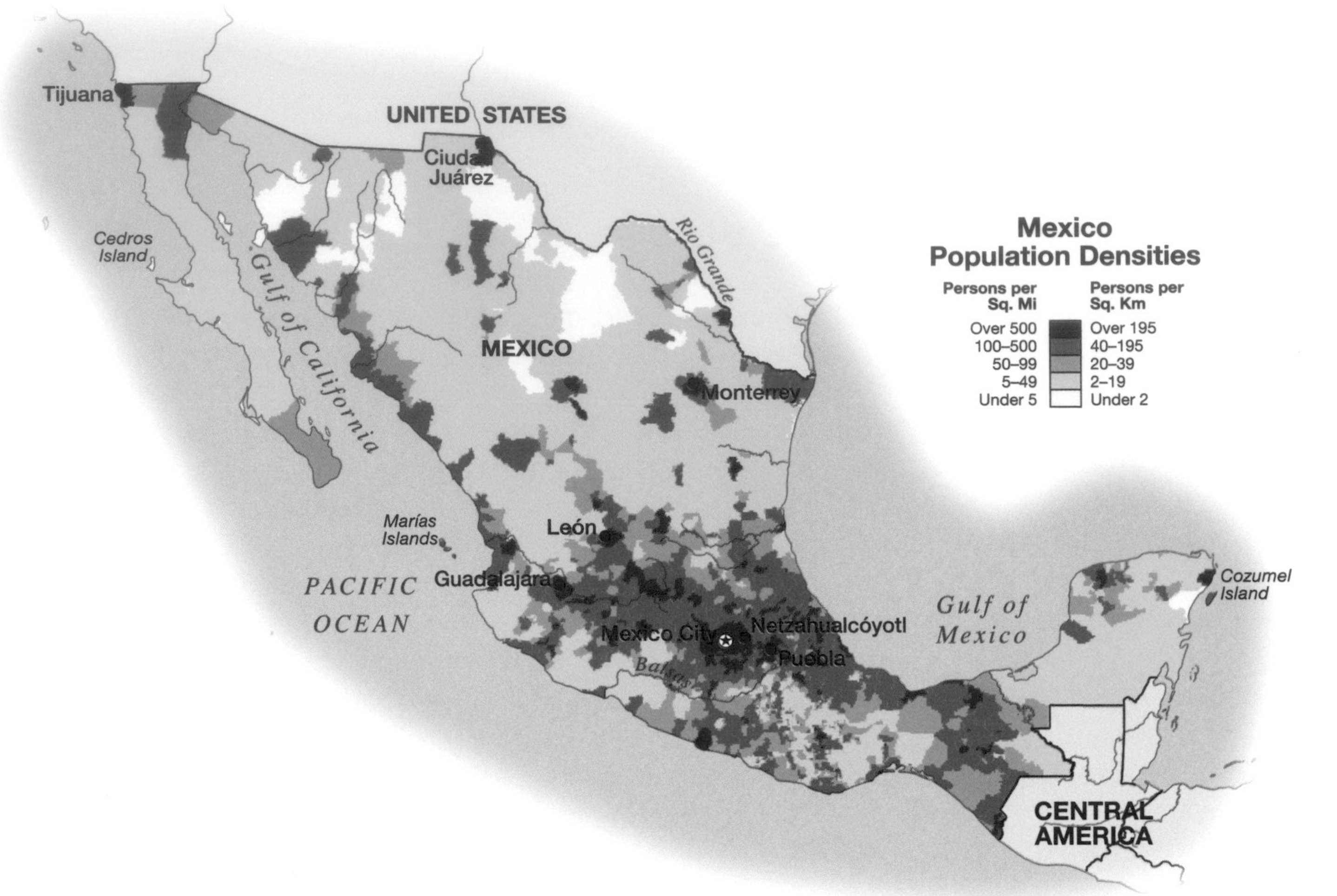

## Mexico Population Densities

| Persons per Sq. Mi | Persons per Sq. Km |
|---|---|
| Over 500 | Over 195 |
| 100–500 | 40–195 |
| 50–99 | 20–39 |
| 5–49 | 2–19 |
| Under 5 | Under 2 |

Tijuana
UNITED STATES
Ciudad Juárez
Cedros Island
Gulf of California
Rio Grande
MEXICO
Monterrey
Marías Islands
León
Guadalajara
PACIFIC OCEAN
Mexico City
Netzahualcóyotl
Puebla
Balsas
Gulf of Mexico
Cozumel Island
CENTRAL AMERICA

## Central America and the Caribbean Population Densities

| Persons per Sq. Mi | Persons per Sq. Km |
|---|---|
| Over 500 | Over 195 |
| 100–500 | 40–195 |
| 50–99 | 20–39 |
| 5–49 | 2–19 |
| Under 5 | Under 2 |

Grand Bahama
UNITED STATES
BAHAMAS
Gulf of Mexico
Nassau
Andros
ATLANTIC OCEAN
Havana
CUBA
Isla de la Juventud
Turks and Caicos Islands (U.K.)
Cayman Islands (U.K.)
Virgin Islands (U.S.)
Virgin Islands (U.K.)
Anguilla (U.K.)
ANTIGUA AND BARBUDA
HAITI
DOMINICAN REPUBLIC
Puerto Rico (U.S.)
Port-au-Prince
Santo Domingo
San Juan
Basseterre
St. John's
MEXICO
JAMAICA
Kingston
Hispaniola
ST. KITTS AND NEVIS
Montserrat (U.K.)
Belmopan
BELIZE
Guadeloupe (Fr.)
DOMINICA
Roseau
Martinique (Fr.)
GUATEMALA
Caribbean Sea
Guatemala City
HONDURAS
Tegucigalpa
Castries
ST. LUCIA
San Salvador
Kingstown
Bridgetown
EL SALVADOR
Grande
Aruba (Neth.)
Netherlands Antilles (Neth.)
ST. VINCENT AND THE GRENADINES
BARBADOS
NICARAGUA
St. George's
GRENADA
Managua
TRINIDAD AND TOBAGO
Port-of-Spain
San José
COSTA RICA
Panama City
PANAMA
SOUTH AMERICA
Coiba Island